ISBN 978-0-483-12370-0
PIBN 10784229

THE INDEPENDENT

Index for Volume LXXXV (January to March, 1916)

(Ed., Editorial; Week, The Story of the Week; Rev., Book Review; M. P., The Market Place; Pic., Picture)

The Independent

FOR SIXTY-SIX YEARS THE
FORWARD-LOOKING WEEKLY OF AMERICA

THE CHAUTAUQUAN

Merged with The Independent June 1, 1914

JANUARY 3, 1916

OWNED AND PUBLISHED BY
THE INDEPENDENT CORPORATION, AT
119 WEST FORTIETH STREET, NEW YORK
WILLIAM B. HOWLAND, PRESIDENT
FREDERIC E. DICKINSON, TREASURER

WILLIAM HAYES WARD
HONORARY EDITOR

EDITOR: HAMILTON HOLT
ASSOCIATE EDITOR: HAROLD J. HOWLAND
LITERARY EDITOR: EDWIN E. SLOSSON

PUBLISHER: KARL V. S. HOWLAND

ONE YEAR, THREE DOLLARS

SINGLE COPIES, TEN CENTS

Postage to foreign countries in Universal Postal
Union, $1.75 a year extra; to Canada, $1 extra.
Instructions for renewal, discontinuance or
change of address should be sent two weeks
before the date they are to go into effect. Both
the old and the new address must be given.

We welcome contributions, but writers who
wish their articles returned, if not accepted,
should send a stamped and address envelope. No responsibility is assumed by The
Independent for the loss or non-return of
manuscripts, tho all due care will be exercised.

Entered at New York Post Office as Second
Class Matter

Copyright, 1915, by The Independent

Address all Communications to
THE INDEPENDENT
119 West Fortieth Street, New York

CONTENTS

ALWAYS MISTAKES

An eye-witness's vivid story of the
brief drive of the Allies on the Western front, which by some chance escaped the censor's pencil, and which
reached this country in the form of a
personal letter from M. Bert Noble,
formerly of Hamilton, Bermuda, a
sharpshooter in the Bermudian contingent, fighting with the British army
in France, is interesting reading in
view of the growing charges of incompetency brought against the British. We quote fragmentarily from the
New York Evening Sun.

SOMEWHERE IN FRANCE—Oct. 2, 1915

Dear Al:
You've read, of course, of the big strike
all along the line! We did most of the
"getting ready" for that and a deuce of a
job it was too. . . . However, we got
it done at the cost of two lives and several
wounded men, for we were under fire all
the time, and a week before the show was
to come off we moved up to the firing line
to finish up there.
Then the fun began. The fact that we
were working was soon spotted by the
Huns. Hence one Sunday afternoon we
were way out working peacefully when
without any warning Fritz's artillery
opened full on us. Laddie, you should have
seen the scatter-action. . . .
We dropt the shovels, made grabs at
our rifles, and beat it to the trench. Having arrived there, all hands lay down until
it subsided. But it wasn't doing any sub-
siding—it grew worse. . . . It is estimated that they put a thousand shells into that
acre of ground in two hours, so you can imagine it was pretty lively! And they
treated us to this exhibition every day for
six days. Every time we came out they let
us get started, and then—bang, crash, over
they came again. But by dint of working
nights we got it done in spite of them.
Then we shifted over to a reserve trench.
We were to go up to hold them and stave
off the counter-attacks. Well they got the
trenches O. K., but they didn't hold them.
There were mistakes made—there always
are mistakes with this man's army—and
the attacking regiments got cut to blazes.
So we didn't get our show after all. But
oh, Lord, spare me that experience again.
The trench we were in was little more
than a ditch—no parapet, nor bottom
boards, few dug-outs. It rained solid for
two days, you couldn't hear yourself speak
for shells, didn't dare show your head for
machine guns, not only the German's but
our own were sweeping across us. No cooking, very little food, and waiting, waiting,
waiting, for the orders that never came.

From 3 a. m. to 10 p. m. the bombardment went on. Just picture us, will you,
one of the biggest battles of the war raging
all around us, front, back and sides, and
we in the middle of the maelstrom—
waiting.
Then came the news that the attack had
failed and we crawled out wet, dispirited,
into the soaking, muddy wood to try to
clear up some of the mess. Here we found
a gorgeous confusion. Communication
trenches jammed with wounded, reliefs,
working parties and all manner of people.
Fellows who'd got lost, wounded, who'd
been dumped down anywhere; fragments
and remnants of companies, all struggling
to get along, and raining all thru it and
underfoot mud, mud, and slimy, slippery,
slushy mud so that you could hardly keep
your feet!
However, we got thru and finally got
back to our ditch and in due course started
for camp.

REMARKABLE REMARKS

JESS WILLARD—Wear loose clothing.
THE POPE—Our sorrow increases day
by day.
HILAIRE BELLOC—All that cats think
is evil.
GEN. JOFFRE—Oh, our women! They are
sublime.
ENRICO CARUSO—St. Patrick was an
Italian.
LILLIAN RUSSELL—I am not afraid of
getting fat.
SENATOR TOWNSEND—Mr. Wilson is not
a Democrat.
LAURA JEAN LIBBEY—He will return if
he loves you.
ARTHUR BRISBANE—Don't try to write
"effectively."
WOODROW WILSON—Talk is a very dan-
gerous thing.
JOHN R. MOTT—Conscience is the alarm
clock of the soul.
JAY E. HOUSE—Life is on the streets,
not on the stage.
LINCOLN STEFFENS—Her face looked
like an old hatchet.
FIELD MARSHAL VON HINDENBURG—I
do not like to be fêted.
BART HOWARD—Roosevelt is our cham-
pion hammer thrower.
PROF. M. JOHNSON—The best children
are the fourth and fifth.
SIR HERBERT BEERBOHM TREE—Humor
is the onion of the human salad.
ED HOWE—The greatest bonehead I ever
knew accused me of being one.
BILLY SUNDAY—England will not con-
cede a shilling or a mutton chop.
EUGENE V. DEBS—I'd rather be a molly
coddle than be Theodore Roosevelt.
REV. HUGH BLACK—All the problems
of America are religious problems.
GEORGE ADE—Let us go back to Chicago.
I hope I am not asking too much.
GIFFORD PINCHOT—I know positively
that a food trust is being organized.
NICHOLAS VACHEL LINDSAY, POET—I
want permanent readers or else enemies.
PRINCIPAL EDWIN FARLEY—The study
of formal grammar is almost valueless.
VICE-PRESIDENT MARSHALL—I never
was a candidate for any office in my life.
THE INFANTA EULALIA—The rule of
money is no better than the rule of rank.
KING CONSTANTINE—What is happening in Greece today may happen in America tomorrow.
YUAN SHIH-KAI—Firm refusal unavailing I have been forced to submit to the
people's will.
JUDGE G. A. WILLIAMS—Women ought
to be ashamed of themselves to wear such
short skirts.
CONGRESSMAN MANN—The President
cannot call me to the White House and
give me orders.

The Independent

| VOLUME 85 | JANUARY 3, 1916 | NUMBER 3500 |

A RIDICULOUS CHRISTMAS DREAM

IT was the morning of Christmas Day, and the Editor had read in the morning paper the day's report how fire and brimstone had dropt down from Hell upon the field of carnage, for Hell has invaded Heaven, God, it would seem, has retired far beyond the starry spheres, and we ask if God is dead. Then the Editor went to church and heard the Gospel song and vision of peace on earth, goodwill to men. In the evening he read aloud, as he reads every Christmas night, the Hymn to the Nativity:

No war or battle sound
Was heard the world around;
The idle spear and shield were high up hung.

And the promise:

Yea, Truth and Justice then
Shall down return to men
Orbed in a rainbow, and like glories weaving
Mercy shall sit between
Clothed in celestial sheen.
With radiant feet the tissued clouds down steering,
And Heaven as at some festival
Shall open wide the gates of her high palace hall.

But where was Heaven now?

Then the Editor slept and dreamed. He dreamed the war had ended. He dreamed that the Allies had conquered and had driven the Teutons back within their own borders. Their armies were crushed and could no longer resist the overwhelming force against them. They were forced to submit, and their foes were prepared to require in Berlin hard conditions of peace; loss of provinces and huge indemnity to Belgium, and for the cost of the war. Then he dreamed that in France the Socialists and the allied workmen met and protested. The German workmen, the German People, said they, are our brothers; they did not wish this war, it was forced upon them. They have already suffered all they can bear. Five million of their strong young men have been disabled or have died in this horrible war. We, too, have suffered and we must bear our misfortunes, but we will add nothing more than we can help to the burdens of those across the Rhine. The provinces in question shall be French or German as the people choose. The indemnity to be paid to Belgium shall be as moderate as possible, and the world must help.

Very strange, quite absurd and ridiculous, was this decision. But dreams are absurd, and in dream the French Government accepted the folly, and England and Italy and Russia agreed to spare Germany the humiliation of a treaty of peace signed in Berlin and the peace was concluded at The Hague.

Meanwhile, Father Clark, of the Christian Endeavor, called a great congress of his Young People in Chicago. With them came the delegates of the Young Men's Christian Association and the young women also, and the Epworth League, and the Federation of Catholic Societies, and the Hebrew Charities, all of one mind, and they voted that the neutral nations, of which the United States is the chief, must save the impoverished peoples from any added burdens of war. They sent a monster delegation to Washington to see the President and Congress. The President shared their enthusiasm and he sent a message to Congress urging generous appropriations from the public treasury. The House took the matter immediately in hand and voted, the Senate concurring, to expend two hundred million dollars to Germany to pay her indemnity to Belgium, then another hundred million direct to Belgium, and two hundred million more for Serbia and Poland and the new buffer Armenian state. Oh! it was absurd, incredible, impossible, but the President, in a grand address to the people, declared that it had saved the country more than half a billion dollars which would otherwise have had to be expended on formidable additions to the army and navy, for defense.

Then, strange to relate, but it was only in dream, Henry Ford and J. P. Morgan and Jacob H. Schiff called a meeting in the Morgan library of the great masters of finance in the country. They were told that, while Europe had been deluged in blood and had piled up billions of debts, this country, and this country only, had been vastly enriched by the war, and that it was only decent that they personally should give their hundred, or hundreds, of millions to relieve the losses that have enriched us. Strange to say, they did it. They were glad to follow where the boys and girls had led; for a little child shall lead them.

IT was all a foolish dream. Once our nation gave a few hundred thousand dollars to China to help her educate her young men, but that was an altruism, not to be repeated. Our business is, have we not been told? to take care of ourselves, and let other nations take care of themselves; not to meddle; not to help—not to get entangled; to leave charity to individuals, to preach and practice thrift and wisdom, and wealth. America is for Americans, and America must be the greatest, strongest, richest country in the world. That should be our national ambition and glory; the biggest guns, the heaviest ships of war; New York the money center of the world; gold, gold pouring in upon us thru every port, and every bank of every village bursting with credit. That is the true political economy, and let it shower down upon us from the same sky from which fire and brimstone dropt down upon the sodden fields of war.

It was a foolish dream. We will dream no more till Christmas comes round again.

W. H. W.

A TRIAL BALANCE OF THE WAR

O N December 31 it is customary to take an inventory of stock and balance accounts. Let us then look over the battlefields and see where the belligerents stand at the end of seventeen months of war. Altho a dozen nations are engaged in the fighting and the greater part of the world is involved, the military situation in its main outlines is remarkably simple.

It is essentially the siege of a big fortress. A region about the area of our Mississippi Valley states, stretching from France to Mesopotamia and from the Adriatic Sea to the Gulf of Riga, is besieged on every side, by sea or land. The garrison has tried many sorties by land, but has never broken thru the investing lines at any point, altho it has pushed forward its entrenchments in many directions. It has not yet tried a sortie by sea. The besiegers have so far failed to make a breach in the walls and they have never been able to capture and hold any important outworks of-the defenses.

Now there are four ways of reducing a besieged fortress: by assault, by failure of its ammunition, by the killing of its defenders, or by starvation of the whole population. All these methods are being tried together, and no man living is wise enough to say for certain when or whether they will succeed. But without attempting to forecast the future we may profitably consider the possibilities involved. All attempts to break thru the defenses of the Central Powers have, as we have said, practically failed. But the total population of the Allied countries is nearly six times that of the Central Powers, their area about twenty times as great. In wealth and natural resources and especially the ability to draw upon the whole outside world for munitions and supplies, the Allies have an overwhelming advantage. If the war were to be determined by matching pennies or matching men, we could count them victors from the start. The line of circumvallation of the four besieged countries, extending as it does over thousands of miles of sea and desert, mountains and rivers, cannot all be fortified or strongly defended, so if the Allied forces keep pounding away at it long enough, the chances are of course that they will break thru somewhere sometime.

So far, however, there are no signs of weakening at any point in the Teutonic line. The defenses are stronger than a year ago and apparently as well manned. It is commonly assumed that the Germans by advancing two hundred and fifty miles into Russia have dangerously extended their line. A glance at the map will dispel that illusion. The Austro-German line on this side is at least thirty-five per cent shorter than it was when the war began, because now it is nearly straight north and south from Dvinsk to Tarnopol, while before the war it bent about the menacing salient of Poland. But on the other hand their present line, tho shorter, is not so easy to defend as their national boundaries, because they have here no permanent fortifications and no railroad lines paralleling the front. As the situation stands now the Austro-German forces in the east seem to be able to hold their lines indefinitely against Russians outnumbering them four to one, the Austrians against the Italians three to one, and the Germans against French and British two to one.

Leaving now unsettled the question of the defeating of the Central Powers by breaking thru or shoving back their lines, let us consider the possibility of wearing them down by attrition, starvation or exhaustion of material. Here the difference between a besieged city and a besieged country appears. The four countries of Germany, Austria-Hungary, Bulgaria and Turkey altogether cover such a range of climate and such varied resources that if a Chinese wall of unsurmountable hight were erected around them, there is no reason why they should not live and prosper till Doomsday. Any shortage of South-Sea products or Yankee notions might be remedied by German science, and thus thrown upon their own resources, it might happen that when the last trump brought the walls down the imprisoned peoples would make as good a showing as the outside world, which would be mostly yellow, brown and black.

The only question then is whether the natural resources of the four Central Powers are sufficiently available for the immediate purposes of the war, and this of course cannot be ascertained. It may be that some indispensable metal or organic substance for munitions will soon run short and cripple the defense, but there is no evidence of this. Cotton is undeniably needed. Wood pulp is a possible but probably not a satisfactory substitute. The sunny fields of Asia Minor may eventually supply all the cotton desired for the mills and munition works of Germany, but not for several years yet. Rubber is also lacking, but here synthetic chemistry may come to the rescue. Several years ago a German chemist exhibited in New York a couple of automobile tires which had been made in the laboratory and had done their thousand miles. The only reason why the caoutchouc tree has not been put out of business like the indigo plant is that the process of manufacture has been too expensive. The conquest of Serbia has helped out the copper shortage, and by the utilization of the low grade ores of Mansfeld in the Harz mountains, Germany is or can be made permanently independent of copper importation. The lack of gasoline, which threatened for a time to be fatal, has been relieved by the recovery of the Galician fields. In the matter of coal and iron, Germany is better off than ever thru the possession of the mineral region of Belgium, Luxemburg and northern France.

The breaking of a pathway thru the Balkans brings to Germany and Austria-Hungary the harvests of Bulgaria and Asia Minor. No doubt there will be much suffering among the people this winter. There have been bread riots or rather "fat riots" in German cities, but taken as a whole the beleaguered empires can eventually raise enough food for their needs and with their efficiently organized system of distribution, they are probably in no immediate danger of starvation.

But most important of all is the supply of men. How long will this hold out? We need not consider the Allied side in this matter. Russia alone, with her birthrate of seven million a year, would alone suffice to keep the armies full. The Central Powers, on the other hand, have no such exhaustless human reservoirs to draw upon. But there are 840,000 young men coming of military age every year in Germany and this is more than the number of Germans killed during the first year of the war. Since we do not know how many of the wounded are able to return to the ranks, it is impossible to tell how much, if at all, the Central Powers have actually lost in military manhood so far. The acquisition of the Bulgarian and Turkish forces will probably come near balancing the accession of Italy on the other side.

If we should attempt to decide the game on points as it stands, that is, on territory gained since the war began, we must declare England the winning nation, with Germany second. The British have obtained possession of more than two million square miles in Africa, Asia and the Pacific. These acquisitions comprise an area about forty times the size of England. The German and Austrian armies have conquered about 150,000 square miles of new territory in Belgium, Luxemburg, France, Serbia and Russia, an area larger than Prussia itself. Russia has a slight compensation in the bit of eastern Galicia which she still holds and in the rapidly increasing area of northern Persia and eastern Turkey which is coming under her control. France clings to a strip of Alsace some ten miles wide and thirty miles long.

The war has come to be primarily a contest between Great Britain and Germany. But this means a fight between a whale and an elephant, or, as the Germans put it, between Mahanism and Moltkeism. Each has won on its own element and failed on the other. "Britannia rules the wave" in the most literal sense of the words. That is to say, over eighty per cent of the earth's surface the British flag is supreme, for seventy-two per cent of the surface is oceanic and a quarter of the land belongs to the British Empire. The unchallenged supremacy of England on the seas has enabled her to sweep away absolutely the shipping of her enemies and to exert a control over the shipping of neutral nations admittedly unauthorized by existing international law. She is frankly determined to prohibit all commerce with her enemies even in goods non-contraband, such as food conveyed by neutral vessels to neutral ports, and she will not allow the German ships to be purchased by other nations. In carrying out this policy she has not scrupled to seize American vessels engaged in the coastwise trade between American ports and to stop in transit the American registered mail.

The attempts of the German submarines to destroy British commerce have had little effect except to arouse against Germany the abhorrence of the outside world. Both the British and German fleets have been kept mostly in home harbors, and there has been no decisive battle between them. We may suppose that the Kaiser will never give up without making some use of the navy which he has taken such pride in building up. If it should happen that the German fleet was victorious, then the whole situation would be reversed, for the British Isles might be starved out in a few months with Germany in command of the sea. Such an event, tho conceivable, is most improbable, for the British navy is twice the strength of the German, and there are the French and Italian navies to count upon besides.

Supreme on the sea, the British have not distinguished themselves on land. The French, the Belgians, the Serbs and the Russians have exprest their dissatisfaction in plain language, and recently similar sentiments have found utterance in England itself. It is sufficient on this point to quote the opinion of the military expert of the London *Times*.

Never did any government possess such great means of action as ours; never was public support more complete; never were greater mistakes made in the organization and conduct of war.

The expeditions to Antwerp, to Gallipoli, to Salonica and to Bagdad were ill advised and ill managed, and altogether failed of their purpose. The raising of an army of three or four million men without resorting to a draft is an unprecedented triumph of patriotism in which the British may well take pride, but this after all is a promise rather than an achievement.

Such are some of the visible and in part calculable factors of the problem. But it would not be safe to base a solution on them, because there are too many unknown quantities, and at any moment some unforeseen chance may determine the issue. A supreme military genius may appear; or a great inventor with a new weapon of unprecedented power. So far the surprize weapons, such as the forty-two centimeter guns, the asphyxiating bombs, the jets of blazing oil, the novel airships and big submarines, have not materially altered the balance of power. But other inventions may appear or these be multiplied. What, for instance, if the Zeppelins rained bombs every night on London or if the fleet of five thousand aeroplanes, which England is said to have secretly prepared, flies in a continuous swarm over Essen?

Most incalculable and most important of all is the human will. The making of peace, as the making of war, is in the hands of a few men. Who can read their minds? What, for instance, if the Kaiser should die? His successor is supposed to be more belligerent and less able than he. What would be the effect of the change? This is essentially a contest of endurance. Which people can or will stand the strain longest? What is the breaking point of human nature? That, after all, is the determining factor.

CAN WAR BE PREVENTED?

WE are not asking whether the present war can be stopped by any intervention, personal, moral or economic. War once begun may or may not have to run its course, like a fever; we do not undertake to say. But the world has learned that some fevers, at least, can be prevented.

The inquiry is imperative, and is imperative now. Of all the kinds of preparedness in relation to war that should interest mankind, none is so basic and none so obligatory as preparation to prevent war if war is, in fact, preventable.

In fact: there is the crux; and how are we to know? How did typhoid and yellow fever become preventable? Not by *a priori* theorizing; not by exhortation, nor even by diligence in general well doing. They became preventable when their respective causes were discovered. War, in like manner, will not be prevented by good intentions nor by preaching; by prudence nor by hocus pocus. It will be prevented, if ever, when its causes become known. There is no more serious business confronting the human race at this hour than to discover, if possible, the causes of war.

It is nonsense, it is incredible folly, to pretend that the causes of war are known now. Are they moral? Perhaps Mr. Ford believes so, but if they are, we might as well make our plans in practical certainty of plenty of war ahead for generations, for the overwhelming majority of mankind is not yet too good or too proud to fight. Are. they economic? The great bankers of America and Europe were as sure of it as Karl Marx was; and until a year and a half ago they confidently believed that an international syndicate of bankers could hold kings in leash. Are they racial and national? So believed the socialists, who expected by international proletarian organization, cross-cutting nationalistic lines, to make military mobilization impossible. Are they diplomatic? The question provokes no answer but the cynic's smile. Are they structural in society, as faults in rock strata are the cause of earthquakes? When war begins has something merely slipt, without will of man?

Dr. Frederick Adams Woods in his painstaking attempt to answer the question "Is War Diminishing?" gives us a statistical table showing that since 1450 the European nations have spent approximately half their time in waging war. Have they sacrificed half of their populations, and destroyed half or more of their wealth? Who knows? We do not even know whether by systematic research it would be possible now to learn even roughly what the sacrifice has been.

But it is time to begin research, determined, costly, scientific, exhaustive, to ascertain, in the scientific man's sense of the word, what is the cause, or what are the causes of war. Until this research has brought forth a positive, unimpeachable result, our efforts to prevent war are likely to be but sentimental and visionary.

A KILOWATT MEAL

THE people of Kansas City, Kansas, are raising their own electric currents from their own plant. The new municipal power station costing a million dollars is already paying operating expenses and interest on the investment and the sinking fund. A thousand housewives have abandoned gas and are now using electricity, which puts the heat just where it is wanted and nowhere else. If the housewife is rich enough to own an electric range costing $40, she gets her electricity at the rate of three cents per kilowatt hour; if she is content with a grill costing $5.95 (marked down from $6), she pays six cents. But even the higher rate is not ruinous. A six-cent kilowatt hour will cook five lamb chops, five cups of coffee, twenty biscuits, a pound of potatoes and two pumpkin pies, which is as much as even a Kansas man can consume at a meal.

Three cent electricity is the equivalent of fifty cent gas. We wish that the Kansas City plant would extend its lines to New York, where people have to pay eight cents for electricity and eighty cents for gas.

ARMS—OR NOTHING

ANY hint of a peace movement from neutral nations meets with furious resentment in England. The Spectator in its leading editorial of November 20 declares that if the United States shuts off the shipment of munitions to the Allies will certainly retaliate by cutting off all commercial intercourse with the United States. This would undeniably be a serious blow to American commerce, for it would destroy our export trade with the whole British empire, with Russia,

France, Italy and Japan, with all of Africa except Liberia, with all the Pacific Islands except our own possessions, with all of Asia except perhaps the southern part of China. The only openings left to our products would be the republics south of us and such neutral countries of Europe as could not be persuaded or coerced into joining in the boycott. It certainly looks as tho the Allies had the whip hand of us.

But The Spectator need not brandish the whip. We have no intention of prohibiting the export of munitions, not because they want us to continue, but because our duty as a neutral nation requires us not to discriminate against either side in the conflict.

WHO SHALL HAVE THE HORN?

IT is proposed in some quarters to abolish automobile horns on the ground that they cause more accidents than they prevent, as the chauffeur relies upon the harsh blast to scatter the people in front of him and so does not slow down. The argument is good, but the conclusion is wrong. The horns should not be prohibited, but given to the pedestrian. He has the right of way, for he was on the ground first, and even tho he be a Populist and insist upon walking in the middle of the road, it is the business of the chauffeur to look out for him. The automobilist takes pride in his swiftness and quickness. Has he not shown us how he cracks a watch crystal without injuring the watch? Now if those unfortunate people who on account of the uneven distribution of wealth are still obliged to go on foot would wear acetylene lights in their hats like miners and would carry a bellows under their arms like bagpipe players by which they could squawk, toot or whistle whenever they crost the danger zone, it would throw the responsibility upon the machine. If under such circumstances they still got run over and killed it would be a consolation to them in the next world to know that the chauffeur was quite in the wrong.

OUT OF OIL IN 1937

OWNERS of automobiles are warned by the Secretary of the Interior that it is not enough to get their machines insured; it is more important to insure their gasoline supply. For he figures that if we go on using up petroleum at the present rate of 250,000,000 barrels a year, our subterranean storage tanks will run dry in about twenty-two years. Then the American automobilist will be as badly off as when he gets stuck between two towns for lack of fuel. He may find that there is no more oil to be had nearer than Persia or China. In his desperation he will be apt to take to alcohol—as a fuel for his motor, we mean of course.

This is the most serious of our conservation problems. Timber used up will grow again in the course of time. The conservation of water-power means "Use it now, otherwise it is lost forever." But the petroleum supply is strictly limited and irreplaceable and yet we are using it with increasing lavishness. It is well that our government, like others, has awakened to the necessity of keeping a bit in reserve for the time of need which is surely and quickly coming. Since preparedness is being preached from Ezekiel let oil conservation be preached from Matthew 25:1-13.

THE STORY OF THE WEEK

Gallipoli Campaign Abandoned

The British have abandoned their attempt to take the Dardanelles and have withdrawn their troops from all parts of Gallipoli except the tip of the peninsula. According to the statement of Premier Asquith in the House of Commons the withdrawal was effected so secretly and with such skill that not a man was killed and only three wounded. A relatively small proportion of the stores and a few guns were left behind but were destroyed by the troops on leaving. The Constantinople statement on the contrary asserts that the British suffered heavy losses from the Turkish artillery fire during the retirement, that they left sick and wounded behind and that the booty abandoned included eight heavy guns, two field guns and a great quantity of ammunition, tents and provisions.

The British and French troops have been mostly shipped away from the Aegean Islands of Tenedos, Imbros and Lemnos, which have served as a base of operations during the Dardanelles campaign. It is not so stated, but presumably they have gone to Salonica to defend that port against the attack of the Germans and Bulgars or to Alexandria to defend Egypt against the attack of the Germans and Turks.

Thus ends ignominiously an expedition which has long been recognized and is now acknowledged to have been unwise and mismanaged. Ten months ago the combined fleets undertook the forcing of the Dardanelles, but the British lost here five battleships and the French one without being able to get thru the strait or reduce the forts guarding it on either side. Contrary to the reports at first sent out the bombardment of the Turkish fortifications suffered comparatively little from the bombardment by big guns of the dreadnoughts. But the Turks did run short of ammunition, and it appears that the Allies were nearer success at one time than they dreamed. The officers in charge of the Chanak fort, on the right of the narrows, are reported to have said that they had only seventeen big shells left on the night of March 18 and these would have been used up in a few minutes if the naval attack had been renewed in the morning. The court and German Embassy were already packing up to leave Constantinople.

But the Allies considered it hopeless and too risky to attempt to gain Constantinople by the fleet alone so they waited for the coöperation of land forces. This delay gave the Turks under German engineers opportunity for the construction of entrenchments so when on April 25 troops were landed at Sedd-el-Bahr on the southern extremity of Gallipoli, they were not able to force their way up the peninsula. In June another attempt was

made about ten miles further up the coast. The Australian and New Zealand Army Corps established themselves on a shore named from the initials of the force "Anzac Cove." But they also were unable to make their way inland so in August another landing was made

at Suvla Bay, five miles beyond. The reports coming to us thru London of their success in gaining the crest of the ridge overlooking the Dardanelles proved fallacious. At no point have the Allies been able to get more than two or three miles from the shore, altho they have had the heavy artillery of the fleet to back them and have made the most persistent and daring assaults on the Ottoman entrenchments. Altogether the British, up to December 9, had lost 114,555 at Gallipoli, of whom 26,172 are dead. The French loss is not stated, but is much smaller, as fewer troops were engaged. There has been a good deal of illness in this army, apparently because sanitary matters were not as well managed as in other fields. On account of blunders in carrying out the operations or other evidences of incompetency several officers have been removed, among them, it is said, Sir Ian Hamilton, the commander in chief. Lieutenant General Sir Archibald Murray will have charge of the troops left at Sedd-el-Bahr to guard the entrance to the Dardanelles.

The Defense of Salonica

The city of Salonica, the ancient Thessalonica to which the Pauline epistles were directed, is now the chief objective in the Great War. It has long been a bone of contention among the Balkan states and the cause of more than one war. Greece, Serbia, Bulgaria and Austria intrigued and struggled for its possession when Turkey should relinquish it because it is the most important port on the Aegean and the natural outlet of the rich agricultural region in the vicinity and of the countries to the north. When the Balkan coalition of Greece, Serbia, Bulgaria and Montenegro attacked Turkey, the Bulgars and the Greeks raced for Salonica, but the Greeks got there first and obtained possession. Then the disappointed Bulgars attacked the Greeks in the hope of gaining either Salonica or the port of Kavala to the east of it, but in this second Balkan war Bulgaria was defeated by her late allies, the Greeks and Serbs. But the Serbs were by no means satisfied with the result, for they had failed to obtain by their two wars their great desire, a port on either the Aegean or the Adriatic.

The policy of the Austro-Hungarian empire has for more than fifty years been directed toward securing a trade route thru Serbia to the sea at Salonica. It was this ambition which brought about the conflict between Austria-Hungary and Serbia and so precipitated the Great War a year ago last July. Twice the Austro-Hungarian troops tried to force their way down thru Serbia and failed. The third time they succeeded with the help of the Germans and Bulgars and the armies of these four nations now stand on the Greek frontier, only thirty-five miles north of Salonica. But between them and the desired haven are the lines now being fortified by the French and British. The first line of defense is established on the hills close about the port; the second front a larger semi-circle of about twenty-five miles radius. The Greek troops have been withdrawn from the prospective battlefield between Salonica and the Serbian frontier. They are said to have been transported to Kavala. The inhabitants of the towns of this region were forced by the Allies to leave their homes on forty-eight hours notice in order to clear the ground for the military operations.

The delay of the Central Powers in crossing the Greek frontier, whether due to the necessity of gathering a larger force or to the fear of offending the Greeks, is at any rate giving the Allies the time they needed to prepare for the defense of Salonica. The French and British troops already there are said to number 200,000, which is about twice the population of the city, and more are arriving every day. The British hold the right wing and the French the left.

The positions of the attacking party are reported to be as follows: The Bulgarian troops, said to number 120,000, but soon to be raised to 180,000, occupy the center in the Vardar Valley, about Strumnitza and Lake Doiran. On their left to the east is a strong force of Turkish troops, now coöperating with their late foes, the Bulgars, in a land which only three years ago the Bulgars took from the Turks. At Monastir,

sixty miles to the west, an army of 60,-000 Germans is stationed, ready to march down this railroad and attack Salonica from the west, while the Bulgars come down the railroad along the Vardar from the north.

The Dilemma of Greece Germany is said to have notified the Greek Government of her intention of following the British, French and Serbian troops who have retreated into Greek territory unless they are, in accordance and with international law, disarmed and interned. Since the Allies are determined to stay in Salonica any attempt on the part of the Greeks to enforce such a measure would bring them into the war on the German side which they would dislike even more than going in on the side of the Allies. Premier Skouloudis has stated the dilemma in an affecting appeal he has made thru the press to the English people:

Greece's friendship has been repaid in a singular way. An embargo has been laid on our commerce and our ships held up. A people friendly to the Entente has been within an ace of being starved for want of bread. Our cable communication, too, has been supprest.

Our aid was spurned, nevertheless we have given freely. We have done our utmost for you and your cause; that is to say, the utmost you in your own blundering, high-handed, haughty way would permit us do. Now we are faced by a still more terrible problem. How are we to stop our land from being deluged with blood? One set of the belligerents already is there and a second set is soon to come. Strictly, they have a perfect right to do so since the Allies have been allowed to enter. The Austro-Germans may bring their allies, the Bulgars—what can we do? How can we prevent the ingress of an enemy who, already

THE GREAT WAR

December 20—British evacuate Anzac and Suvla positions on Gallipoli. Russian warships bombard Bulgarian port of Varna.

December 21—French take trenches on Hartmannsweilerkopf, in Vosges mountains. Japanese liner, "Yasaka Maru," sunk in Mediterranean by Austrian submarine. No lives lost. One American on board.

December 22—Rebellion against Monarchy in Yunnan province, China. Russians take Kum, Persia.

December 23—British repulse Turkish attacks at Kut-el-Amara on Tigris. Germans regain trenches on Hartmannsweilerkopf.

December 24—Montenegrins repulse Austrian attacks. British losses to December 9 reported to be 528,227.

December 25—French and British at Salonica prepare for attack of Germans and Bulgars. Austrians taking offensive on the Isonzo river.

December 26—Heavy artillery fire in Artois and Champagne. British Cabinet consider conscription.

successful in Macedonia, has an eye on Kavala and Seres?

How can we make war on Germany and Austria and two Balkan powers all to oppose the passage of the Bulgars? We stand every chance of being overwhelmed. Our enemies will be on top of us, because, while our determination to resist invasion by the Bulgars remains unaltered, our power of offensive has been weakened thru our army at the request of the Allies having modified its hold on certain strategic positions essential to the successful conduct of a campaign.

So, as I see it, Greece is to be ravaged by a cruel, relentless war because the Allies badly blundered in a diplomatic as well as a military sense.

There appears to be no way by which Greece can avoid being made a battlefield during the next few weeks. To add to her anxieties an Italian army is advancing toward Salonica thru that part of Albania which the Greeks desire to possess. Italian troops have been landed at the two Albanian ports of Durazzo and Avlona. Roads are rare in this region, but from Durazzo an ancient Roman military road led to Elbasan and Lake Ochrida, and these, tho now in a ruinous state, may serve the modern Romans as it did their ancestors as a route to Salonica. The remnants of the Serbian army which defended Monastir retired into Albania and are said to have met the Italian expedition at Elbasan, which is half way across Albania. The Bulgars are reported to be in close pursuit and will try to intercept the Italian expedition in Albania and so prevent it from making a junction with the French and British. William of Wied, the Prussian officer who was selected by the Powers at the close of the Balkan war to become Mpret or Prince of Albania, but who fled from the country at the outbreak of the present war, is now back again and said to be spending money freely to win over the tribesmen to the German cause.

Russian warships have again bombarded the Bulgarian port of Varna, on the Black Sea, but the report that Russian troops have been landed here seems to have been unfounded.

THE BALKAN STORM CENTER

The armies of nine nations are now hastening toward Macedonia. British and French troops are being landed at Salonica to defend this port against the Austro-Hungarian, German and Turkish troops assembling on the Serbian frontier. That part of the Serbian army which escaped into Albania is being reorganized to renew the conflict and Italian troops have been landed at Avlona and Durazzo. The Russians have shelled the Bulgarian port of Varna and are expected to land troops here or to send them across Rumania. Greece and Rumania are still technically neutral, but likely at any moment to be drawn into the maelstrom. Austrian troops are slowly spreading over Montenegro. The Serbian government has made Scutari its headquarters. The shaded area is that dominated by the arms of the Central Powers.

The Russian Invasion of Persia — The ill-fated expedition of the British into Mesopotamia is not yet out of its troubles. A month ago they were within ten miles of Bagdad, the goal toward which they had been working for a year. Now they are having a hard time to defend themselves at Kut-el-Amara, a hundred miles down the Tigris. They lost 4567 at Ctesiphon and during the retreat down stream and 1127 since reaching Kut-el-Amara. This is very heavy, considering the size of the force, which was at first said to consist of only one division, that is about 20,000 men, altho the Marquis of Crewe states that it is "considerably larger."

It is at any rate considerably outnumbered by the Turks and Arabs under the command of Field Marshal von der Goltz, the famous German strategist. So far the British seem to have been able to keep open their line of communications down the river to the Persian Gulf, but the agitation among the Mohammedans in Turkey and Persia makes it harder to maintain freedom of operations in this region. Bagdad is regarded as a holy city by both the Shiite and Sunnite sects and the Mohammedan world regarded with dislike the advance of the British toward it. Doubtless their sudden retreat when it was almost within their grasp is being heralded as a miracle by the priests who are now preaching the Jehad or Holy War in Africa and Asia. This propaganda is evidently having more effect than has been hitherto supposed by the British. It is rumored that the Mohammedan troops from India, who at first formed part of the expedition into Mesopotamia, manifested so much aversion to fighting under a Christian flag against their coreligionists for the capture of one of the sacred places of Islam that they had to be sent back.

The propaganda among the Persian Mohammedans resulted in an uprising of tribesmen reinforced by part of the troops trained under Swedish officers in the Persian gendarmerie. These left Teheran with the German Minister at the court of the Shah, Prince Henry of Reuss, and established themselves at Hamadan and Kum. But the Russians came down from the north and have captured both places after some hard fighting. It is expected that Teheran, the capital, will soon be occupied by the Russian forces who are now fighting the Turks and Persians only twelve miles away. The capture of Hamadan brings them within about 220 miles of Kut-el-Amara, where the British are besieged. If the Russians can reach the Tigris and join in with the British they will have a chain stretching from the Caucasus to the Persian Gulf, and "the German road to India," of which there has been so much talk recently, will be barred. Prince Firman Firma, who has been foremost among the Persians favoring the Russian side, has now been made premier and virtual ruler of the country, since the Shah is only seventeen years old. This shows that Russian influence is now dominant in Te-

heran and that the effort of Prince Henry to win over the Shah has failed.

The German Plotters — Paul Koenig, the Hamburg-American Steamship Company's chief of police, and believed to be the head of Germany's secret service in this coun-

try, who was arrested a few days ago, has now been indicted in New York for plotting the destruction of the Welland Canal in Canada. If found guilty on all the counts he may be imprisoned for thirty years. Richard E. Leyendecker, a New York merchant, and Edmund Justice, both of whom were

A Petition from the Moros to the American People

[Arabic script petition text]

WE, THE UNDERSIGNED, HAVE FAITH IN THE EFFORTS OF BISHOP BRENT AND HIS FELLOW-WORKERS TO HELP THE SUG PEOPLE.

WE WANT HIM TO CARRY OUT THE PLANS HE HAS LAID BEFORE US. WE NEED THE SCHOOLS AND MEDICAL WORK HE DESCRIBES, AND WE APPRECIATE WHAT HAS ALREADY BEEN DONE BY HIS GROUP OF VOLUNTEER WORKERS AND THEIR ASSOCIATES NOW WITH US.

WE HOPE THE AMERICAN PEOPLE WILL GIVE BISHOP BRENT THE SUPPORT NEEDED.

WE WILL GIVE HIM ALL THE HELP WE CAN.　　　(TRANSLATION)

MOROS TO AMERICANS

A petition asking this country to support the work of the Rt. Rev. Charles H. Brent, Episcopal Bishop of the Philippines, who described his efforts to educate and Christianize the Moros in The Independent for April 26, 1915

THE RUSH TO AVOID CONSCRIPTION IN ENGLAND—A BATCH OF LORD DERBY'S VOLUNTEERS

associated with Koenig, were also indicted. A full confession has been made by Frederick Metzler, who was Koenig's private secretary for five years, and because of his disclosures several trunks full of incriminating papers have been seized. It is said that these affect men prominent in the diplomatic service at Washington. Otto F. Mottola, an officer of the New York police force, received $3 a day from Koenig. The arrest of Frederick Schleindl, an audit clerk in the foreign department of the National City Bank, of New York, for stealing messages about the shipment of arms and selling these to Koenig, has been followed by the dismissal of several other German employees of the bank. A man, name not published, who had intended to blow up the power houses on the Canadian side at Niagara Falls, and to destroy railroad bridges there, discovered that he was pursued and for that reason threw his explosives into the lake at Erie, Pennsylvania.

The grand jury's inquiry at New York concerning Labor's National Peace Council, an organization which received money from Franz von Rintelen to be used in causing strikes, will soon be followed by indictments. One of the witnesses was President Gompers, of the Federation of Labor, who testified, he says, about the failures of the plotters to corrupt labor union officers. A notable example was the futile attempt to cause a strike of longshoremen on both coasts. For this plot $1,-250,000 was available. This money was to be paid to the men during the strike. It appears that Von Rintelen, now in the Tower of London, is a captain in the German navy and an intimate friend of Admiral Von Tirpitz. He was interested, it is said, in an attempt to buy control of the Union Metallic Cartridge Company, at Bridgeport, Conn. He and those whom he represented offered $17,000,000, or more than twice the value of the company and its property. Their purpose was to cause strikes there and elsewhere, and thus to prevent shipment of ammunition to the Allies. They failed, owing to the action of a banker who thus sacrificed a very large commission.

Plans for the shipment of considerable quantities of rubber from New York to Germany, where it is needed for auto truck tires, came to nothing last week when the personal baggage of Miss Anna Dekker was seized. In four trunks and eight packing cases, were 3500 pounds of rubber. She had taken passage for Rotterdam, and other women, with similar baggage, were to follow her. The project was in the hands of Max Jaeger, a naturalized German who has lived in this country thirteen years. Additional arrests in San Francisco are expected, as the result of an inquiry as to the expenditure of $400,000 or $500,000 for supplies forwarded some time ago to German warships by means of false clearance papers. It is asserted that the Department of Justice has evidence, with photographs of checks, that about $1,-000,000 was expended by German agents in Washington to promote legislation designed to prevent exportation of war supplies. The project included a series of lectures, and the supervising agent was paid $1000 a week. The de-

struction of the Du Pont powder works in Wisconsin was prevented a few days ago by the work of detectives. Captain Franz von Papen, the German military attaché recalled at the request of our Government, sailed for Holland last week, Great Britain having undertaken not to interfere with his passage.

Defense and the Navy Reports
Current discussion concerning the Administration's plans for enlarging the army and the navy, and the questions of national policy involved, had for a prominent subject last week the exports of the General Board of the Navy, of which Admiral Dewey is chairman. Secretary Daniels published a report, prepared in October, in which the Board, at his request, gave its views as to the best plan for expending an average of $100,000,000 a year for five years for new ships. Afterward he published the Board's annual report, dated November 9, relating to the condition and needs of the

MORE COPPER!
One of the many collections of miscellaneous household copper utensils which serve to reinforce the German supply for the making of ammunition

SERBS, REFUGEES FROM THEIR CONQUERED COUNTRY, SEEKING FOOD AT A RUMANIAN SOUP KITCHEN

navy, the lessons of the Great War, etc. But there was an earlier report, prepared and submitted in July, in response to a request from President Wilson. Representative Gardner and others asserted that the Secetary was suppressing this report. In the November annual report, however, the Board referred to this earlier statement, saying that in it the following opinion had been exprest:

The Navy of the United States should ultimately be equal to the most powerful maintained by any other nation of the world. It should be gradually increased to this point by such a rate of development year by year as may be permitted by the facilities of the country, but the limit above.defined should be attained not later than 1925.

On the 22nd, Henry A. Wise Wood, a member of the new Naval Advisory Board, of which Mr. Edison is chairman, resigned, saying in his letter of resignation, addrest to Secretary Daniels, that he desired to be "free to attack the thoroly inadequate, and therefore dangerously weak, naval and military policy of the President," as exprest in the recommendations of Secretary Daniels and Secretary Garrison. The Secretary of the Navy, he added, had withheld the Board's July report. In his long letter there was much emphatic criticism of the plans of the Administration. Mr. Wood is president of the American Society of Aeronautic Engineers.

Secretary Daniels on the 24th gave to the public the General Board's July report. It recommends an expenditure of $265,521,000, instead of $100,000,000, for new construction in 1917, saying this would be an adequate program of the expenditure and should be "continued in subsequent years on a similar scale." The present session of Congress, in the opinion of the Board, should provide for eight dreadnoughts, and this rate should be increased hereafter, in order that at least 48 dreadnoughts may be begun in the next six years and completed by 1925. This program would require an expenditure of $1,593,126,-000 for new construction alone in the next six years, or about $1,000,000,000 more than the sum needed in five years for the Administration's plans. The list for one year, besides the eight battleships, includes 37 submarines, 28

destroyers, 6 gunboats, 6 scout cruisers and a dozen ships of other kinds. The President of the National Security League, Mr. Menken, after making inquiries and attending conferences in Washington, says the prospect is uncertain because of a lack of agreement in Congress about the legislation relating to the defense plans. There is said to be little support for the proposed Continental Army of 400,000 volunteers.

Prices and War Orders Owing to the demand for war supplies, and also to embargoes on the exportation of certain products to this country, remarkable advances in prices are reported. Bromides, used in the treatment of nervous diseases, are $5.50 a pound, altho the price before the war was only 25 cents. Permanganate of potash has risen from 7 or 8 cents to $1.75. The effect of the advances in drugs and acids has been, it is said, to multiply the cost of a considerable number of druggists' prescriptions by twenty. The price of platinum, $41 an ounce a few months ago, is now $100. Copper was 13 cents a pound one year ago. Recently the price has been rising, and last week it was 21½ cents, the highest figures reached in nine years. The price was affected by a contract, signed by the British Government, for 135,000,000 pounds, to be supplied by three or four mining companies. This is the largest single order ever known, and the price was about 21 cents. Large quantities of this metal are used here in the manufacture of ammunition. An advance in the price of crude petroleum has been accompanied by higher prices for gasoline. Oklahoma crude has risen in a year and a half from 40 cents to $1.20, and Pennsylvania crude from $1.35 to $2.15. For gasoline, selling at 13 cents a gallon when the present year began, 21 cents must now be paid. Great quantities are used here in automobiles, farm engines and motor boats. There is also a demand from abroad, for use in the many millions of dollars worth of auto trucks we have exported to the Allies.

Among the new war orders is one given to Pennsylvania foundries by the French Government for 100,000,000

hand grenades, and the British Government is in the market for such munitions. Orders for suits of woolen underwear and sweaters are taxing the capacity of many mills. A recent law-suit for a commission relates to a Russian order for $6,000,000 worth of motor trucks, and another similar suit asks for a commission of $282,000 on a sale of 3,000,000 pairs of boots to Russia. There were reports that from France the Midvale Steel Company had received a $28,000,000 order for shells and one of $45,000,000 for guns of large caliber. In Canada, where the industry has been developed by the British Government, 320 companies or firms are now at work on war orders.

Labor Movements There are indications that the first part of the new year will see a widespread movement by organized labor for a reduction of hours and an increase of wages. Prominent in this movement will be the demand of the four railroad unions, the brotherhoods of engineers, firemen, conductors and trainmen, for an eight-hour day, with time and a half for overtime. The demand has been formulated by the four executive councils, and members of the union, about 400,000 in number, will have sixty days to vote on it. Almost unanimous approval is expected. Present contracts or agreements will expire in May. One of them, the result of an arbitrators' award, will end on May 16. This award was quite unsatisfactory to the employees, and prominent union officers say that there will be no arbitration this time. Every railroad in the country will be involved. It is said that eight hours will be demanded by 700,000 coal miners. A strike of 70,000 makers of shirtwaists is predicted. In New York last week 6000 umbrella makers decided to ask for a week of forty-eight hours and a wage increase of ten per cent, and 15,000 girls in the millinery trade voted to demand a week of fifty hours. Four-fifths of the 4000 waiters on strike at East Side restaurants in that city have been successful, and 10,-000 on the West Side are now to be called out. The demand is for a week of sixty-four hours, an increase of ten per cent, and recognition of the union.

The Texas and Pacific Railroad Com-

CANADA'S THIRD TRANSCONTINENTAL SYSTEM, THE CANADIAN NORTHERN
To the east is a short line from Capreol to Ottawa and Montreal, on which the track is laid but operation has not commenced, another from Toronto to Ottawa and from Montreal to Quebec, beside the Halifax and South Western Railway in Nova Scotia. The dotted lines are routes proposed or under construction. The short-haul low-grade line from Alberta to Vancouver will take much of the traffic now moving eastward to the lakes. Transcontinental service from Toronto to Vancouver commenced in November, 1915. See the article on page 18

pany has added $14,000 a year to the wages of its telegraphers, and increases ordered by the Brooklyn Rapid Transit Company affect the pay of 7000 men. A company in Providence that makes machinery used in the manufacture of shells has added an increase of five per cent to one of the same value granted in August

Announcement is made by the American Federation of Labor that its program of legislation to be sought in Congress includes the following: restriction of immigration; old age pensions and retirements; an industrial education act; eight hours for interstate railroad telegraphers; a compensation act for interstate railroad employees and workers in the District of Columbia; additional safety laws; prohibition of goods made in whole or in part by convicts in foreign countries; prohibition of the interstate transportation of goods in the manufacture of which the labor of children is employed. The Federation's executive council has instructed subsidiary organizations to begin a campaign for legislation against the use of armed guards, supplied by detective bureaus, by corporations when a strike is in progress. These "private armies," it says, "must be legislated out of existence." In New Jersey the Federation is exerting its influence against the proposed bill for a state constabulary.

The Change in Mexico Altho Villa's generals signed the peace agreement with representatives of Carranza, Villa himself denounced them and remained in the field with a few hundred men. The agreement provided for amnesty to all of his soldiers, 4000 of whom surrendered, the reception of Villa in the United States as a political refugee; a transfer of the local governments in Villa's territory, and the addition of his men to Carranza's army. The governments at Juarez and in the State of Chihuahua were transferred, but Villa, after his small force had been whipped by General Trevino, disappeared, and at the end of last week had not been found. Altho assurance had been given that his extradition from this country for any political offense would not be permitted, he feared arrest for his crimes. His brother, Hippolito, had crost the line and been placed in jail at El Paso

for stealing cattle and getting money on worthless checks. It was reported that Villa would go to Cuba, and then to Argentina, where he has bought a large tract of land. Before the peace agreement was signed he confiscated the great Babicora ranch of 1,000,000 acres, owned by William R. Hearst and his mother and situated in the State of Chihuahua, and took the cattle from it. Nearly all of the employees were made prisoners, but one escaped to tell the story in El Paso; after a journey of nine days. Some weeks earlier, Villa had looted silver and copper mines in which Congressman Sherwood, of Ohio, has an interest, and had killed several of the miners. It is estimated that the losses suffered by foreign interests in Villa territory exceed $50,000,000. After the peace agreement a party of Villa's soldiers, returning hungry and destitute to Juarez, looted the shops there, and in the course of the ensuing riot an American railroad brakeman on Texas soil was shot and killed.

In the Mexican capital there are not less than 30,000 cases of typhus fever, and there are also thousands of cases in Puebla and Pachuca. On the 23d

BOOKER T. WASHINGTON'S SUCCESSOR
Major Robert R. Moton, twenty-five years commandant at Hampton Institute, and a close friend of Mr. Washington's, has been elected principal of Tuskegee

three cases were found in Laredo, Texas, the infection having come up on the railroad. Some months ago the American Red Cross withdrew from Mexico at the request of Carranza, who said that its services were no longer needed. The Red Cross is now willing to return and with the aid of the Rockefeller Foundation, to stamp out this typhus epidemic, as the similar epidemic of more than 40,000 cases was stamped out by the same agencies in Serbia. Our Government some weeks ago sought the consent of Carranza for such an attack upon the disease. At the end of last week his response had not been received.

The Catholic Archbishop of Oaxaca sends word to Cardinal Gibbons that confessions and the taking of collections in churches there are prohibited. Carranza, asking his Governors for reports concerning church property, asserts that all of it is owned by the national Government. Zapata has put to death publicly in Cuautla General Rafael Liz, the leading artillery expert in Mexico, and his staff. General Liz had been assisting Zapata, but the latter learned that he was about to accept Carranza's offer of amnesty.

The Danish West Indies Reports from Denmark say that Councillor of State Hageman recently made the following remark about a suggestion that the Danish islands in the West Indies should be sold to the United States: "If the question of selling the Danish West Indies should arise again I am sure that it would receive favorable consideration, as it is useless to continue spending large sums without gaining any benefit." It is not known whether any proposition from Denmark has been received at Washington.

A treaty for the cession of the islands to the United States was approved by our Senate thirteen years ago, and by the lower branch of the Danish Congress, but the upper house rejected it. Such a transfer of the islands has since been a subject of consideration. An article on the question appeared in The Independent last week, December 27.

12

FROM STATE TO STATE

ARKANSAS: Federal Judge Trieber has decided that the Arkansas Railroad Commission's distance freight tariff No. 5 is confiscatory as it applies to the St. Louis & San Francisco and the Kansas City Southern railroads. He declined to grant an immediate injunction against the commission because a similar case is soon to be decided by the United States Supreme Court on appeal taken by the state, but in the meantime the roads will continue to operate under the tariff they are now using—a tariff approved by the Federal Court. The decision applies only to the two roads named.

IDAHO: Senator Borah will ask the present Congress to set apart 145,000 acres in the heart of Idaho to be known as Sawtooth National Park. These acres include one of the wildest and most rugged mountain regions in this country. Last March the Idaho Legislature adopted a memorial asking Congress to take this action. The territory in the proposed park adjoins a state game preserve of 220,000 acres, which, it is contended, would add greatly to the interest of tourists to this park.

IOWA: Muscatine is to be headquarters of an important barge line to operate between St. Paul and New Orleans. Its present purpose is to handle only such freight as is too bulky for transportation by rail, but it is expected ultimately to develop a general freight service for all Mississippi River points. Mr. B. Layton, the contractor in charge of the Muscatine levee improvement work, is the moving spirit in the enterprise.

MAINE: It is believed that this is to be a record winter for Maine trappers, professional and amateur. Last winter the European war had so upset the fur market that very little trapping was done, with the result that fur-bearing animals are now greatly increased in number. Also the styles this winter, calling for extraordinary use of fur trimming, and the largely increased number of automobilists desiring for coats and gloves have extended the demand and raised the price of pelts. The Oneida Community, which makes 95 per cent of all the game traps used in the world, reports that its sales there indicate that nearly everybody in the game sections of Maine is going into trapping.

MISSOURI: A steam railway in this state recently made application to the Missouri Public Service Commission for an increase of its passenger and freight rates. The commission, deeming the increase just, but doubting its right to grant a rate higher than the statutory one, went to the Supreme Court of the state and got a favorable decision. Thereupon it granted the application, with the result that this railway is now charging higher rates than those prescribed by the Legislature which created the commission. Since most of the railroads cen-

tering in St. Louis have gone into the hands of receivers, the people and press of the state are generally applauding the commission's act.

MONTANA: What is described as the tallest and largest chimney in the world was recently completed at Great Falls for a smelting company. It was built for the very practical purpose of carrying gases off to a great hight, but it serves also the purpose of a show place, attracting many persons long distances to see it. The chimney proper rises 506 feet above its foundation, and altho it tapers 8 per cent in the first forty-six feet, seven per cent in the next 180 feet, four per cent in the next 100 and two per cent in the remaining 180 feet, its internal diameter at the top is just fifty feet. These variations in taper, adopted to obtain the desired bearing pressures, due to both weight-and wind loads, give the chimney a very graceful appearance despite its enormous size.

NEBRASKA: The people of Kearney and Buffalo counties have adopted a new way to get good roads. They recently held a six-day fair at Kearney to which nearly everybody in the two counties contributed either money or some article which was sold by auction. Merchants donated goods from their stores and farmers contributed grain, live pigs, chickens and all sorts of farm products, and much fun, to say nothing of money, was realized at the sales. Also each of the farmers living along the twenty miles of road to be improved gave two days' work upon it. It is said that not one farmer refused to do his share either in the matter of work or in making contributions.

NEW HAMPSHIRE: As a result of a movement started at the recent Merrimack County Family Gathering in Concord that city expects soon to have a public cold storage plant, the first in the state. A committee then appointed is said to favor the project, as giving to merchants and farmers as well as to citizens in general a means of storing products at times when the prices are low and drawing on them when the prices are high. Another argument advanced is that such a plant would give the people 'a place for storing their furs during the summer.

NEW JERSEY: The ship canal across New Jersey is believed to be a part of the plan for national defense in the minds of many members of Congress. Its strategic value as an inland protected water course between the bases of Philadelphia and New York has been recognized by military and naval experts, it is said. As the case now stands the enterprise will not become a Government project until New Jersey purchases the right of way and pledges itself to liquidate any damages due to the taking over of water power. But it is believed the Legislature will take the necessary steps early in its next session to accomplish this.

NEW MEXICO: One of the most noticeable features of the recent state fair in New Mexico was the surprise exprest by people of different sections of the state at the variety, excellence and cheapness of products of other sections. Never before, it seemed, had the several parts of the state come so close together. Each section had subsisted on its own products and those imported from other states. As a result of this new knowledge a state commercial body is forming, having for its chief purpose the bringing about of closer trade relations and interchange of products among the different parts of the commonwealth.

NORTH DAKOTA: Beavers, which are protected by law in this state, have become so numerous as to be a menace to timber lands and a nuisance to farmers in many parts. Old settlers who remember when the trapping of these animals was the principal industry of a large portion of the state say there are as many beavers now as there were then. Along the shores of creeks, where timber is most abundant, beaver dams are only a few feet apart, ranging from three to thirty feet in length and from two to four feet in hight. These require large contributions of trees, the result being that most of the groves are thickly dotted with stumps.

OHIO: Credit is given to state and local boards of health by the Ohio Registrar of Statistics for the decreasing mortality in the cities of this state. His figures show a steady decrease in those cities which during recent years have given the most active support to these boards. While Cleveland during these years has shown the lowest death rate among the larger cities of the state, the decrease from year to year has been about the same in Cincinnati, Columbus and Toledo. Cleveland's rate for the last year was 12.7, while for the year before it was 14.1. In the same period Cincinnati's rate dropt from 17.2 to 16.1; Columbus's from 15.3 to 14.7, and Toledo's from 16.4 to 15.9.

OKLAHOMA: A sale of segregated coal lands and unallotted lands in Eastern Oklahoma is to be made by the Government this month. One person may purchase 160 acres of the agricultural land and 640 acres of the coal land, suitable only for grazing. Minimum prices range from $1 to $25 an acre. 25 per cent to be paid in cash. Bids may be placed in person or by authorized agents. The lands lie in the reserves of the Choctaw and Chickasaw nations, and information concerning them may be obtained from the superintendent of the Five Civilized Tribes at Muskogee.

OREGON: A committee of the Portland Chamber of Commerce appointed to consider methods of relieving conditions of unemployment recommends that an effort be made to prevent the suspension of construction work on state, county,

municipal and individual enterprises at the beginning of winter. The committee says this suspension is a result of habit rather than of necessity, since in the mild climate of the Pacific coast more than 75 per cent of the work which is now discontinued at the approach of winter could be carried on the year round, thus stabilizing the employment situation. The report refers specifically to many public and private operations which are unnecessarily and uneconomically suspended at the beginning of winter merely because the habit of doing so, formed in more rigorous climates, has been brought here without reason.

PENNSYLVANIA: Work has begun on the survey, provided for by the last Legislature, to extend the park system of Philadelphia and make it, so Pennsylvanians say, the finest in the United States. In Fairmount the city already possesses the largest park of the kind in the world, and now a chain of surrounding parks is to be connected by broad boulevards with this great pleasure ground. The work now in hand is an extension along the banks of the Wissahickon to Fort Washington. Under the new law the commission may acquire the necessary land by gift, purchase or condemnation, but since the route lies thru many wealthy estates which will be benefited by the extension, it is believed a large part will be donated. The extension includes those two historic spots, Fort Hill and Militia Hill, which constituted old Fort Washington.

VERMONT: Interest in apple growing in Vermont is steadily increasing. The state has now four of the largest apple orchards in New England and many other extensive ones are in prospect. This awakened interest is largely due to the efforts of the Vermont State Horticultural Society and the State Publicity Bureau. A great deal of favorable attention was attracted to this industry by the campaign made at the time of the recent fruit show in Boston, when large advertisements of the Vermont apple exhibit appeared in the Boston newspapers and more than 5000 of the apples were given away in a single day to as many visitors at the show.

WISCONSIN: The hydroelectric operation which the Wisconsin-Minnesota Light and Power Company is undertaking on the Chippewa River at Paint Creek is one of the largest pieces of construction for the development of electric energy ever attempted in the Middle West. The dam is to be sixty feet high, with a spillway 900 feet long and will impound water over 6000 acres. Six turbines of 7500 horse power each, and six electric generators with rated capacity of 6600 kilowatts each will be installed, and seventy-four miles of high-tension line will carry the current to St. Paul and Minneapolis.

O. F. Browning

A WALKING DELEGATE OF AMERICAN DIPLOMACY

COLONEL E. M. HOUSE, INTIMATE FRIEND AND ADVISER OF PRESIDENT WILSON, WHO IS LEAVING FOR
EUROPE TO ADVISE WITH OUR DIPLOMATIC REPRESENTATIVES IN THE BELLIGERENT NATIONS,
BOTH AS TO WASHINGTON'S ATTITUDE AND AS TO CONDITIONS ABROAD

TRAINING OUR YOUTH FOR DEFENSE

BY GEORGE E. CHAMBERLAIN

UNITED STATES SENATOR FROM OREGON AND CHAIRMAN OF THE COMMITTEE ON MILITARY AFFAIRS

MILITARY efficiency — by means of compulsory training for American young men between the ages of twelve and twenty-three years—is the object of the bill which I have introduced and which has been referred to the Senate Committee on Military Affairs. This bill is a modification of the Swiss military training plan, and would provide an army and navy reserve of young men who complete active training for a prescribed period.

Briefly, the bill provides for a citizens' cadet corps of boys from twelve to seventeen years of age. From eighteen to twenty-three years of age the cadets would become members of the citizens' army or the citizens' navy, as they might elect. The citizen force thus organized would be subject to call by the President of the United States in time of war, threatened war, insurrection, rebellion or when the public safety requires. When thus mobilized and called into the service of the United States, the individuals shall receive the same pay and allowances as may be authorized by law for corresponding grades in the regular army or navy, and those who might incur disabilities in line of duty while in active service or while actually undergoing training, and while proceeding to or returning from training centers and camps of instruction, shall be entitled to pen-

sions as provided under existing laws.

For the first two years ninety hours of drilling without arms would be required, and this instruction could be given in public or private schools. The third year requires ninety hours and at least ten continuous days in camp. The training during this period shall include field exercizes and target practice, in ad dition to other training that may be prescribed. The training for members of the citizens' army shall be not less than 120 hours, or twenty whole days each year, and shall continue for six years.

All able-bodied male inhabitants of the United States who have resided within the continental limits for twelve months who are citizens of the United States or who have declared their intention to become citizens, shall be liable to be trained between the ages of twelve and twenty-three years.

I am convinced that this military instruction serves the double purpose of being useful in a national way and of being useful to each individual in a physical and moral way. To make it attractive to boys and, at the same time, to keep this military instruction from interfering with their school attendance, the bill provides that the necessary training for the Citizen Cadet Corps and for the Citizen Army and Citizen Navy may

be given in public and private schools, academies, colleges and universities, in the organized militia or naval militia of the several states, in organizations of Boy Scouts or similar organizations, provided that it conforms to the prescribed training for the corresponding years, is of equal annual duration, and is so certified by the district commandant of the district in which such instruction is imparted.

Penalties are prescribed for persons who, without lawful excuse, fail to register or who evade or fail to render the personal service required by the act, and they become ineligible for employment in any position of trust and profit created and authorized by the Congress of the United States. Employers who prevent, or attempt to prevent any employee who is serving or is liable to serve from registering or rendering the personal service required of him, or who penalize such employees in the way of reduction of wages or dismissal, are subject to fines of from $50 to $500.

This bill is strictly one in favor of efficiency in any and every respect. Every young man is to join the branch of the service which he prefers. The military training given each individual under its provisions will, at the very outset, be of great physical and moral advantage.

Washington, D. C.

BUYING THE ULTIMATE CAR

BY BRONSON BATCHELOR

BUYING a motor car ten years ago was something of an adventure. Sometimes one got a car; more generally it was likely to be a fine assortment of trouble under a highly finished, beautifully upholstered body. A man bought an automobile to satisfy a child-like longing for the toy; or because his wife had social ambitions. He delivered himself eagerly at the nearest salesroom, and a blind, deaf and dumb agent could have done the rest.

Selling an automobile today is a much more difficult thing. The evolution of buyers has been as great as that of motor cars. A decade's experience has shown that there are gold-bricks in cars as in real estate and mining stock; and now, when

the public invests $500 or $3000 in four wheels, it does so not with infantile trustfulness, but with a Missourian "show me" attitude.

The reason is that the automobile has lost much of its novelty, much of its glamor of romance. Instead, like electric lights, sanitary plumbing, or a furnace in the basement, it has become a necessity in more than two million American homes. People plan today to have motor cars just as they plan to send their children to college; in fact, cases have been known where the cars were preferred to the children. Last year more than 600,000 persons found that they could not do without them any longer.

Yet in this state of things is another fact, equally significant. For

those 600,000 cars the public paid only the same half billion dollars it had spent on 500,000 machines the previous year. It gained in quality, in quantity, and got a fifth more for its money. People are learning to discriminate in automobile values as in other necessities, and merit brings its own reward.

But the task of pointing out the merits among so many contenders for the honors, makes the manufacturer a sharer in the problem of salesmanship. For it is not enough that the public must think merely in terms of automobiles; the maker must see to it, by constant advertising and unremitting efforts, that they think in terms of his own particular product.

It is difficult to recall, from the

modern sophisticated point of view, what a simple, trusting soul the automobile buyer was a dozen years ago. With the perfected motor of to-day, it is so easy to forget man's helplessness before its prototype, the terror that attended its operation, the constant dread that the mysterious mechanism would refuse to perform its functions. Yet to appreciate the modern sales-problem one needs to contrast that era with this.

The garageman of that day, as he is remembered now for the repairs he was called on to make, seemed a first cousin to the burglar. Always extracting something for gasoline, oil, prestolite, tires, and a thousand what-nots, he presented bills each month that were as long as Tammany ballots.

Those were the days, too, of the "tours," by which one was expected to prove his membership in the motorists' fraternity. The departure was something of a ceremony: the family, begoggled and bedustered, squeezing itself thru a narrow back entrance into the sardine-tin the French had christened for us the "tonneau"; the luggage strapped on the running boards, or bestowed in baskets above the back-fenders; and then the asthmatic gasps from the straining car as the bumpity-bump journey began.

It is as a veteran of those early, amateurish, pioneering days that the automobile buyer has come into his own. And if today he is a worry to the manufacturer it is because he has had his fling of motor madness: bought cars for speed, for horse-power, for style, and for comfort. Nearly thirty per cent of sales are to previous owners. In the models they buy today, they are interested largely in one thing—efficiency.

Thus the automobile sells best which is simplest and "service proven," which has fewest parts to get out of order, which can stand knocks and wear, and still do the essential thing—go. Company after company, and car after car, have gone into the discard, because those behind them failed to perceive that the public, tired of makeshifts, wanted a car that would last—the ultimate car.

For those manufacturers who have seen the public mandate it has set a new problem and a new opportunity. They have had first to simplify their product, lop off every non-essential and at the same time give it the durability and reliability of a finely attuned watch. This the public insisted on to insure freedom from chauffeurs it could not afford, and repair-shops that never repaired.

And the resultant dependability and efficiency of the medium, and even the low-priced, car is as much an American engineering triumph as the building of the Panama Canal. No manufacturers in the world can compete with ours in quality, quantity, or price. As a result, even before the war, the American car was fast becoming the standard the earth over.

The standardization that came with simplification has given the manufacturer his chance. It has enabled him to embark on large-scale production, and by lowering costs and his margin of profit, make new economic groups of the community potential purchasers. Thus in five years the average price of automobiles has fallen from $1500 to less than $600.

Never has there been a trade romance like the Aladdin-like growth of the automobile industry in the past decade. From a mere 25,000 cars in 1905 to 703,000 in 1915, is but the first chapter of the story; there remain whole cities like Detroit, Toledo, and Flint to be put on the map; huge factories, rivaling the steel mills, to be developed; and the habits and customs of a people to be changed.

To learn how all this has been brought about, one needs only to enter a salesroom, or pick up a popular magazine. The gospel of both as preached by young and enthusiastic salesmen and ad-writers is that of the ultimate car. They no longer tell you of all the fancy stunts their cars have performed, their horse-power, or the express speed they are capable of. Instead the watchword of motor salesmanship today is economy.

Manufacturers talk now of miles per gallon rather than miles per hour; of cheapness of operation rather than initial cost. They are not only willing but anxious to prove the bona fide value of their product. Witness this sentence from a recent advertisement of one of the largest makers:

"Despite the lower price, we guarantee the ——— car to contain more drop forging, better upholstery, better paint and finish, greater quality than previous models." And that guarantee is more than empty talk, for the periodical in which it appeared rigorously censors and insists on the truth in its advertisements.

Instead of climbing hills and running two, three or four miles an hour on high gear, low cost records of operation are among the most popular selling arguments today. Like watches that run frozen in ice,

motor engines are kept going for days in closed rooms without cooling, to prove the quality of their metal; while others, under sealed hoods, negotiate the perils of desert and mountain roads to demonstrate the worthiness of their pedigree.

Still more convincing are the statistics of customers, showing the cost of up-keep, repairs, and supplies, compiled in the belief that Mr. Average Man's testimony is "best in the long run."

How reasonably a car can be operated today can be seen from a glance at this table, issued by the maker of one of the most popular of the low-priced cars

	Per Mile.
Gasoline, 25 miles per gal. at .20	.008
Oil, 800 miles per gal. at .60	.0075
Tires, one set at $12 each	.0032
Repairs, at $50 a year	.0033
Insurance, theft, fire, etc	.00066
Depreciation, 25% yearly	.00066
Interest, 6%	.0016
Total cost per mile	.02417

Similar schedules, reams on reams of them, can be produced from the files of every agency, and their cumulative effect is to prove that the cost of operation, like the cost of cars, has declined from nearly ten cents a mile ten years ago to less than three cents today. Machines representing a greater capital investment than that above can show similar economies.

This brings us to another feature peculiar to the automobile industry —the motor service department. There is scarcely a business today where the maker assumes such care of his product after it has passed from his control. Not merely does he make good defective parts—which has long been the practice of most reputable manufacturers in all lines—but he pledges himself as part of his duty to his customer to a general looking after of the car. Every conceivable kind of a device, from a year's free supervision to coupon books good for so many hours' work, has been adopted to prove that the manufacturer is interested not merely in making a sale, but in seeing that the customer gets service from his car.

One reason for this service of the manufacturer is that the average buyer, even tho he has operated a car, is generally ignorant of the mechanical principles underlying the automobile. To acquaint its customers with these fundamental things one company has adopted the plan of giving seven thoro inspections within six months after a sale.

A complete record is made of the mechanical condition of the car, and the owner is asked to review this record with the Service Manager, who points out to him how he should handle the car to avoid the repetition of whatever faults have been found. Within the six months, any man, whether mechanically inclined or not, is thus enabled to know how to handle his car intelligently and wisely.

Or, again, in the matter of accessories, how a decade has revolutionized the customs of a trade! It used to be that when a man paid $1500 or $4000 for a car, he promptly had to spend another $100 or $400 in fitting it out with lights, a top, extra seats, a horn, and on some models, even its first set of tires! Today all these essentials, and scores of other little refinements, are furnished with practically all cars. Turn to the specifications of any one of two dozen or more popular makes, and you will see items like these:

"Double lubrication; full semi-elliptic or cantilever springs; special floating axles, running on special ball bearings; double ignition system; self-starter; electric horn and head-lights, wind shield built in body; speedometer; demountable rims, and tire-carriers in rear; adjustable footrests; robe-rail"; even down to the license bracket.

Each one of these features represents the product of some highly specialized side-line of the industry, perfected thru years of study, yet now made a part of the car, and the cost assumed by the motor company.

For all this—the perfection of the car and its accessories—despite what trust economists may say to the contrary, competition has been largely responsible. Under the stimulus of a free market, open on equal terms to all, the automobile busi-ness has developed, and over-developed, until each year the selling of the output becomes more of a problem.

Only by adding to the comfort and convenience of the public could makers win an outlet for their wares. And the public, jealous of its new-found independence, condemned for all past sins and commended for new joys. It picked its favorites here and there, and as it did so, unconsciously it performed one of nature's old functions—that of selection—and brought nearer the ultimate car.

And today the ultimate car is practically here. Different makers have their different selling points, of course; but stripped to essentials, they aim at the same result, which is—to give the buyer the least possible worry for his money.

New York City

© *Paul Thompson*

TO SPOIL THE EGYPTIANS

The Arabs and Turks of Palestine are being called to the colors at Jerusalem to form an army under German officers for the invasion of Egypt. It remains to be seen whether this new and reversed exodus will get thru the wilderness of Sinai in less than forty years

THE TEN-MILLION BUSHEL WHEAT ELEVATOR OF THE CANADIAN NORTH⸫

A NEW GATEWA

BY GEDI

W ESTWARD the course of empire takes its way. But, in Canada, at least, the freight moves eastward. As the great West has been built out of the wilderness into the world's granary, the east-bound water-route to the Atlantic thru the Great Lakes, and the land routes to the north and south of the Lakes that are called into play when navigation closes, have been developed to carry the grain to Liverpool. Over 225,000,000 bushels of wheat are available for export from this year's great crop. The elevator pictured here, with the tremendous capacity of 10,000,000 bushels, suggests the scale of the traffic.

Now that picture is not as inappropriate in an article on a gateway to the Pacific as it looks, and for two reasons. First, there probably never would have been this particular gateway—the Canadian Northern Railway, 0.7 (we're coming to that later)—if the grain traffic from the prairie provinces passing thru this and similar elevators had not laid the foundation for the further extension of the road east and west. The Canadian Northern was a tangle of tracks in central Canada years ago; its transcontinental service is brand new. The system may be likened—see the map on page 12 showing most of the lines—to a substantial and active dog with a

18

new-grown tail in each direction. Just now the dog does all the wagging.

The other reason is that the big elevator stands for a condition of things which the new lines are going to change—and in that change lies the chief significance of the road to Canadian trade. But we're coming to that later.

William Mackenzie and Donald Mann, one a school teacher to begin with, the other a railroad navvy, are the great railroad adventurers of present day Canada. Sir William, as he is now, president of the Canadian Northern, is the wizard whose prowess in getting capital is the talk of the country. Sir Donald is the construction expert. There wasn't much capital when the road began, in 1896, with a line of tracks north from Gladstone, in central Manitoba. The road was built cheaply, piece by piece, "build a mile and mortgage it to build the next." Light rails were laid; improvements would have to come

TO THE PACIFIC

SMITH

ut of earnings. They have come, too, tho there are pieces of track still eloquent of pioneer days. Like all Canadian railroads, the Canadian Northern leaned heavily on Government aid. Tho the later comers have had nothing like the sweeping land grants given to the Canadian Pacific, they have been generously treated. The road was built, so a genial Liberal bureau chief in one of the provincial governments remarked, by a policy of taking by way of subsidy "everything that wasn't hot or tied down." But as I said, he was a Liberal, and it was the Conservatives who decided in 1914, after the road had already enjoyed Government credit to the extent of $280,-09,705, to guarantee bonds for $45,000,000 more to complete transcontinental construction. The Government olds $40,000,000 of the road's hundred millions of stock.

But to get back to the elevator. It was put up in 1901, the year before service was started across Manitoba to Port Arthur, with a capacity of 1,500,000 bush-els. Three years later it was increased to five times that size. In 1912 it was again enlarged to its present capacity. Meanwhile the system was growing, too. Lines were bought and built in Quebec and Nova Scotia, and the rails crept north from Toronto along Georgian Bay. Westward, the main line reached Edmonton in 1905, the first railroad to enter that surprizing city that grew 848 per cent from 1901 to 1911, and then jumped in two years from 25,000 to sixty or seventy thousand.

One link was forged quickly. The Canadian Pacific had leased the Qu'appelle, Long Lake and Saskatchewan Valley Railroad and Steamboat Company's line from Prince Albert thru Saskatoon to Regina. The lease expired; the big system felt secure in its control and offered to renew on terms the owners did not like. It was thought to be pretty poor country, anyway. At five o'clock one day in 1906 the road was offered to the Canadian Northern. By midnight the deal was closed. The next year that road carried ten million bushels of grain. In the East the last spike was driven in the Montreal-Port Arthur line on January 1, 1914, where the link thru the New Ontario forests was the last to be completed. A year later the line to the coast was spiked thru, making it possible to operate approximately 10,000 miles by the end of 1915.

,nsequently there was a new
. on the train which I boarded
Toronto on November 19, 1915. It
.d, for the first time—
Vinnipeg—Edmonton—Vancouver
ne train was as new as the sign.
he Pullman showed here and there
. convenience one had never noticed
before. The inside of the baggage
car shone like a bride's kitchen.

A night's run takes us to Capreol,
and from there we cut thru the
New Ontario wilderness, where
there is yet little but trees, Ojib-
ways, big game, and mining prospects. At Winnipeg the service
breaks, and a new train pulls out for
Vancouver at night. Between Winnipeg and Edmonton we are on a long
traveled route, thru country rougher
and more wooded than the bona fide
prairie to the south, tho with some
great stretches of flat country.

But beyond Edmonton lie the
Rockies. Here is the newest part of
the road; here it begins to be unique.
Three or four hours beyond the city
the mountains can be seen—a blue
jagged line far over the purple distances of the roughened prairie. We
climb easily over an excellent road-
bed. At Entrance, where we pass
into Jasper Park, a Dominion game
and forest preserve, we are fairly in
the superb country that makes the
Canadian Rockies dear to the "See
America First" traveler.

Yellowhead Pass, like Tête Jaune
Cache and all the Jaspers, is named
for a Scotch fur trader, Jasper
Hawes, who was here in 1811 or
1812 for the old Northwest Company.
It is the key to the new railroad's
usefulness. Not only does it allow the
road to cross the mountains at a
maximum hight of 3706 feet (the
Canadian Pacific goes 5321, the
Santa Fé 7421, and the Union Pacific
8200), but it made possible the astonishing feat of building a road over
the Rockies with maximum grades of
0.5 per cent westward (six inches in
a hundred feet) and 0.7 per cent
eastward (eight and a half inches
per hundred feet). Like the Grand
Trunk Pacific, which has practically
the same advantages, the road follows in general the route first located
by the Dominion Government in the
seventies. It was intended for the
Canadian Pacific, but it was then
pretty far north to seem feasible,
and the more southerly route was
chosen, tho it led at first to grades of
4.4 per cent and even now, after new
engineering exploits, is burdened
with a maximum of 2.2 per cent, and
the better pass was left to this century for utilization.

Once over the Continental divide,
we begin to follow down the Fraser
River. Mt. Robson, whose 13,067-foot

peak, the highest in Canada, is pictured on the cover of this number, is
in view for nine miles of the journey, and if well-intentioned meddlers
in Eastern Canada do not succeed in
getting its name changed to Edith
Cavell Mountain, Mt. Robson will remain the glory of the railroad.

The most difficult construction
work came not in the Rockies, but
down thru the Thompson and Fraser
River Canyons, which carry the line
southwest into Vancouver. The milky
green streams rush along between
precipitous and wejrdly configured
rock walls for many miles. There are
numerous tunnels, and the cliffs that
are not tunneled are sufficiently
threatening. One tunnel stood serenely for eight months and then
simply slid off—roof and side—into
the river below! The construction
gangs tackled what was left, leveled
it off, and now there is open track.
Twelve miles from Vancouver the
track joins that of the Great Northern, and for the present trains enter
Vancouver by the borrowed route.

But Canada has already two transcontinental lines, the old Canadian
Pacific and the new Grand Trunk
Pacific - National Transcontinental
Railway system. Does it need another? To the bald question the answer is probably, "No—not yet." But
it is worth noting just what the new
line offers Canada. In two sections
new country is being opened.

One is in the great waste of New
Ontario. For 150 miles west of Sudbury the road runs thru mineral
country with nickel, copper and iron.
(chiefly magnetite ore). The nickel
deposits in the Sudbury district are
the greatest known in the world.
There is enough iron along the line
between Sudbury and Winnipeg, it
is estimated, to make 53,000,000 tons
of steel. In the form of 80-pound rails
that would build over one hundred
four-track railroads between New
York and Chicago. For 250 miles beyond the mineral belt the road runs
thru the "clay belt," where the deep
clay soil produces phenomenal berries, fruits and vegetables and will
support a large farming population
when it is cleared. Meanwhile there
is a tremendous store of timber.
There are said to be 10,000,000 cords
of pulpwood tributary to the line—
enough to make 7,500,000 tons of
news print—which would keep the
New York *Times* going, at its present circulation, for 205 years.

On the other part of the system,
in British Columbia, the promise of
development is similar—but the figures are larger. For instance, the
stand of commercial timber in the
province is estimated at 400,000,-
000,000 feet! There are great min-

eral values, and along the river valleys one finds good farm and fruit
lands.

But the important thing about this
British Columbia line is that it provides a new outlet for the prairie.
While the new line swings far to the
north of the Canadian Pacific, its
mileage between Winnipeg and Vancouver is only 116 miles greater than
the old, and as we have said, the
grades are incomparably better. The
Parliamentary Special, which ran
from Quebec to Vancouver in October to celebrate the completion of the
route, was a fifteen-car train, weighing, including the engine, 1200 tons.
One locomotive—and that not of the
most powerful classification—took
the train over the mountains at
thirty or forty miles per hour.

Canadian Northern men are very
proud of that, and travelers who remember the two engines puffing
away with a shorter train over the
Canadian Pacific will appreciate
their satisfaction. The Canadian
Northern can haul thru the mountains freight trains that are long
enough to pay, and can therefore
offer shippers of the Western prairie provinces rates that will make it
desirable to send their produce to
Vancouver instead of Port Arthur or
Duluth. Of course the route for grain
from Vancouver is via the Panama
Canal to Liverpool. Vancouver is
never closed to navigation; the lake
elevators are stuffed full of storage
wheat all winter. Edmonton is 773
miles from Vancouver, 1261 miles
from Fort William—the rail haul is
cut by a third. Vancouver, which
has rather too hopeful visions of
being a 200,000,000-bushel wheat
port and already has a 1,350,000-
bushel government elevator, expects
to receive shipments from points as
far east as Moose Jaw in southern
Saskatchewan. That is probably too
much to expect, but the crops of Alberta alone were worth nearly $70,-
000,000 this year, and all of Alberta,
once the mountain barrier is discounted, is naturally tributary to
Puget Sound.

The Canadian Northern, in a word,
is the natural route for the exchange
of lumber, grain and manufactured
imports between the Western and
particularly the Northwestern prairie country and Europe and the East.
Its grades give it a tremendous advantage over the Canadian Pacific;
its choice of an established port,
Vancouver, gives it an advantage
over the Grand Trunk Pacific route
to Prince Rupert. Something is bound
to happen to the monopoly enjoyed
by the eastern route. The newest
transcontinental is going to serve
Canada both ways.

An African Elephant Hunt

The honor of obtaining the record pair of elephant tusks in the Mount Kenya region of British East Africa, a "land of promise to the elephant hunter," belongs to a woman. It was Mrs. Carl E. Akeley who braved the dangerous country of the Wakikuyu and followed the hunt thru the jungles, "up and down the slippery trails worn in places by the passing of generations of elephants into giant stairways" and in the dismal bamboo forests, until thru the mist the hunters finally spotted "the indistinct outline of the great, rounded back of a 'big un.'"

"We crept carefully forward," says Mr. Carl Akeley in his description of the hunt in the *American Museum Journal*, "to within forty feet of where the giant stood. Breathlessly we waited until, as he moved slowly forward, there came into view a splendid pair of tusks, followed by the massive head and great, flapping ears of the best elephant we had seen. Bibi, as the na-

tives called Mrs. Akeley, raised her rifle and with steady aim placed a bullet in just the right place.

"The news of a kill spreads rapidly among the native Wandorobo hunters, and in a short time they had gathered from all quarters. Little camps of men, women, and children were scattered all about the place, while over each fire festoons of elephant 'biltong' were being cured for the future. The killing of an elephant is a blessing to these poor wretches.

"Finally six days had past, six days of exhausting, disagreeable work; but the skin, reduced by shaving to half its original weight, and thoroly salted, had been made into three oblong packages and firmly lashed to long poles, ready for the porters, four or more for each load, to begin their heart-breaking journey out of the forest."

But meantime the gun-bearers had been scouting for more elephants and brought the news that they had found a herd only two miles from camp. Luck was with the hunters again here, for they succeeded in tracking the game and Mrs. Akeley surpassed her previous shot by bringing down the biggest prize of all—with tusks nineteen and a half inches in circumference, and eight feet ten inches long, right and left weighing, respectively, one hundred and fifteen, and one hundred and twelve pounds—the record elephant for a woman.

Courtesy *American Museum of Natural History*
THE PRIZE WINNER

A Railroad on End

The rack road up Mt. Pilatus, one of the loftiest peaks of the Bernese Alps, in Switzerland, is said to have the steepest grade of any road in the world not operated by cables. Rising from the western shore of Lake Lucerne, it ascends 6998 feet up the mountainside to the summit.

The railroad starts from an elevation of 1450 feet above sea level and climbs 5400 feet in a distance of 15,150 feet to the top. The grade at the station of Alpnachstad is 36°. At no place is it less than 19°, and in some

Feature News Service
THE STEEPEST GRADE IN THE WORLD

it is as much as 48°, or more than half a right angle.

The roadbed is built thruout of solid masonry, capped with granite flagstones. The ties are steel channel bars, anchored to the masonry with U shaped bolts every three feet. The rails merely support the weight of the train. The rack bars are set on edge, so that the cogs are vertical—an arrangement made necessary by the fact that on the steepest grades cog-wheels would have a tendency to climb out of any horizontal rack.

Engine and car are built on a single frame. The boiler, six feet long, is placed crosswise of the track, so that the water level in it will not be disturbed on the grades. The speed is a little more than three feet a second, or about two miles an hour. Thirty-two passengers is the maximum capacity.

Easy Electroplating

An almost absurdly simple and easy method of electroplating, in which not only the plating-bath but all external sources of electricity are dispensed with, was devised by an English investigator, A. Rosenberg.

The plating is carried out simply by rubbing on the article to be plated a powder moistened with water. The Rosenberg process is a refinement of the old contact method in which the metal to be coated was immersed in an electrolyte, containing, for example, a silver solution In contact with this metal a more electropositive one was placed, also dipping into the electrolyte. This metal, usually zinc, past into solution, and an electric current was generated which deposited the silver on the less electropositive metal.

In the English process the electropositive metal is employed in the form of a fine powder, and generally mag-

Courtesy *American Museum of Natural History*
THE FIRST BIG TUSKER—NOW IN THE FIELD MUSEUM IN CHICAGO

SCHOOLWORK THAT PAYS

nesium is used. This is mixed with a metallic salt or with the powdered metal it is, desired to plate-out, and ammonium sulphate or some other ammonium salt. In order to plate a piece of metal the powder is moistened with water and rubbed over its surface by means of a piece of cloth or a brush. By this means adherent and bright deposits are obtained in about one minute, the thickness of the deposit depending upon the time employed and the quantity of powder used.

The magnesium, being strongly electropositive, reacts with the moist electrolyte, and goes into solution, causing the metal to be plated-out upon the metallic surface which is being rubbed. In other words, each particle of the powdered magnesium may be said to function as a minute anode. One of the difficulties in electroplating is to plate a substance upon itself. It is claimed that in the English process this difficulty does not occur.

The process is certainly ingenious, and will no doubt be found useful for small work, but it is hardly likely to enter into competition with ordinary electroplating for large work or for irregular articles. Nor is it likely to be employed in cases where heavy coatings of metal are required, because it would not be an easy matter to rub the powder on evenly enough to obtain uniform and thick deposits.

Building a Schoolhouse

The boys of the Manual Training Department of the Central Grade School at Klamath Falls, Oregon, are busy erecting their own building. This novel innovation in the curriculum has been recently instigated, but it is working out very successfully and incidentally proving a substantial economy in the department's expense budget.

The new building, made necessary by this year's increased enrollment, is being erected adjacent to the main building. It is a frame structure, 25 by 45 feet ground measure, and 16 feet high.

Most of the work was marked and laid out by the instructor; but the as-

sembling has all been done by the youngsters, about twenty in number. Scorning the use of scaffold or platform, they wriggle up the studding and over the rafters like so many monkeys, presenting a most unique and amusing spectacle.

The interest of these juvenile carpenters in their work is decidedly marked. Instead of going off to play at the hour of dismissal, they stay "on the job" with a strong disregard of union hours, until sent home by the instructor at supper time.

Other Cities Please Copy

St. Louis is going to try a new experiment. Music rolls are to be circulated free to the public at the public library. It is estimated that there are several thousand of player-pianos in St. Louis, and anyone who knows anything about musical human nature knows that every one of their owners is tired of playing some of his pieces and these he would gladly exchange for new ones. As the library has no appropriation to establish such a department, the music rolls must be supplied at first by the player-piano owners themselves. But it is morally certain that when the experiment proves a success the city will feel justified in financing the whole plan, keeping its own stock of rolls on hand for circulation.

Librarian Bostwick has also signified his willingness to accept phonograph records to be cataloged and distributed

in the same way, provided these are given as gifts.

Rolled and canned music is such a comparative novelty that the people have not as yet realized that it is in all essentials as worthy of public support and distribution as a book. For anything that diffuses popular education or elevates public taste is primarily within the jurisdiction of the community.

And when the time comes—as it surely will—when no home will be complete without its own moving picture outfit, then the art that is destined to rank with printing in its educational and inspirational value, must likewise be furnished free to the individual by the community.

Won't those be the great days, tho, when you can go around the corner after supper to the public library and bring home to the expectant family the latest volumes by Bergson, Wells and Harold Bell Wright (perhaps), together with a couple of Caruso records, a Paderewski Minuet roll, and a six-reel complete life of Theodore Roosevelt acted by himself?

Uncle Sam's Signature

Imagine one man devoting all his time to signing checks! That is what Frank J. F. Thiel, the Assistant Treasurer of the United States, was called upon to do in his official capacity. For with the stint of 500,000 checks a year before him he found time for practically nothing else.

Recently, however, a check-signing machine has been installed in the Treasury and Mr. Thiel's efficiency at that particular task increased more than 3000 per cent. One hundred checks in fifty-four seconds is his present rate. That means 6666 signatures in an hour, and 64,662 in a seven-hour working day. Signed by hand a good day's work would be about 2000.

Harris & Ewing

THE MAN WHO SIGNS 500,000 CHECKS A YEAR

WAS THE DOCTOR RIGHT?

SOME INDEPENDENT OPINIONS

IN our issue of November 29, we asked our readers to give their opinions on the propriety of the conduct of the Chicago physician, who, with the consent of the parents, decided not to operate upon a baby who was born in the hospital badly malformed in body and presumably defective in mind. An operation might have prolonged its life, but the baby, being unable to assimilate food, died six days after birth.

The grand jury of Independent readers to whom we submitted the case return a verdict of "not guilty" by an overwhelming majority. The letters commending the doctor's course in letting the crippled baby die are four times as many as those that condemn him and hold that every effort should have been made to prolong the life of the unfortunate child as long as possible. The doctors, who are regarded by some as hard-hearted scientists, are divided in opinion, but the clergymen, who are accused of being rigid moralists or soft-hearted sentimentalists, are almost unanimous. Every letter except one bearing a minister's name answers our question, "Was the doctor right?" by a "Yes." It is interesting to note that the Ethical Relations Committee of the Chicago Medical Society recommends the expulsion of the doctor, not, as might have been imagined, for his action in this doubtful case, but for "advertising himself", by permitting his name to be used in a newspaper account and being photographed for a motion picture weekly, which at the worst is not a question of ethics at all, but merely a violation of trade union rules.

We can only quote from a small proportion of the letters received and of these only a few sentences to bring out the many different arguments and points of view. The quotations do not, therefore, give an adequate idea of the character of the whole letters, which are often long and thoro discussions of the questions. Most of those who think the doctor did right in this case are careful to point out the danger of abuses and recommend some sort of a commission of experts to pass on doubtful cases. Almost all who mention it, repudiate with abhorrence the suggestion that the aged and incurable adults should be relieved of life by euthanasia.

We quote first from the head of the Department of Political Economy at Yale, the author of *National Vitality* and chairman of the Committee of One Hundred on Public Health:

So far as I have been able to get at the facts, I may say that I emphatically approve of the attitude of the mother and the physician. Of the many questions involved, the important one is the eugenic question. In fact the chief significance of this event lies in the recognition that the vitality of the human race must be duly considered. The fact that the incident has attracted so much attention thruout the country shows that this eugenic idea is a new one. Only new ideas are startling. I hope the time may come when it will be a commonplace that the interests of the race are paramount. When that time comes, not only will defective babies be allowed to die a natural death, but they will, for the most part, cease being born. IRVING FISHER
New Haven, Connecticut

From the Biologist in Charge of Maine Agricultural Experiment Station and one of our foremost authorities on heredity we have:

In my judgment, it was not only biologically wise, but normally right from the highest ethical standards, to make no effort to preserve the life of the Chicago baby referred to in your editorial "Was the Doctor Right?" According to the detailed reports in the newspapers the congenital malformations in this case were of so extreme a character as to make it certain to any person of competent biological training that this infant could never develop into anything even approaching a normal human being, even granting that its life could have been saved by operation, which appears to have been very doubtful. This and like cases, however, should be regarded each on its own individual merits and not be made the basis of far-reaching generalizations. RAYMOND PEARL
Orono, Maine

The head of the Department of Sociology at Columbia and professor of the History of Civilization draws this distinction between mental and physical incapacity:

MENTAL CAPACITY THE TEST

Since Richard III, as Shakespeare portrays him, became a malcontent and enemy of the human race because he had
"Been sent into this breathing world scarce half made up,"
the question of letting the defective baby live or die has been debated but not acted on in the modern world. In the ancient world it was acted on without debate. Each plan has been incomplete and ineffective. There should be a legal and careful determination of the kind and degree of incapacity. The idiotic child should mercifully be allowed to die. The child with a good brain, however crippled otherwise, should be saved. FRANKLIN H. GIDDINGS
New York City

The Director of the Carnegie Station for Experimental Evolution and of the Eugenics Records Office speaks with the authority of one who has for years devoted himself to the investigation of the laws of heredity and the influence of defectives on society:

Man is a social species; in successful social species the functions of the individual must be subordinated to the best interests of the race. If, with the best knowledge available, a wise and conscientious surgeon is forced to conclude that surgical interference in a case will be to the determent of society, such interference on his part would be anti-social. If the progress of surgery is to be used to the detriment of the race (and incidentally, as in this case, to the artificial preservation of those whom the operation of natural agencies tends to eliminate) it may conceivably destroy the race. Shortsighted they who would unduly restrict the operation of what is one of Nature's greatest racial blessings—death. C. B. DAVENPORT
Cold Spring Harbor, N. Y.

The letter from which we quote below the closing sentence brings out a point which many others refer to:

Is it not strange that the whole country should be so shaken, almost hysterical, over the death of a babe never consciously alive, and so callous to the degradation and abortening of life in conditions that might be remedied; to the thousands of needless deaths and tens of thousands of preventable accidents; to the millions of victims of war to which we give only a languid interest. H. E. WARNER
Washington, D. C.

As to the one-eyed, one-eared babies born, that Nature would not permit to live but for medical intervention, how can anyone possest of a drop of the milk of human kindness desire that such should survive? Handicapped from birth to death, what but pain, shame, humiliation and distress awaits them.

To cant about the sacredness of human life in the present cataclysmic waste of the most fit in Europe, and talk of "preparedness" for the same result here, is too hypocritical and ridiculous. EDWARD BERWICK
Pacific Grove, California

Will Providence be inexorably offended if we do not make frantic efforts to save the life of a hopeless idiot? Is it true that the wrath of God will overtake us if we attempt, for instance, to limit the multiplication of the Juke family? When men finally got up their courage sufficiently to make a decided effort to control the workings of natural law, they found that the earth did not open and swallow them. The creation of modern civilization was the result.

We are breaking away from the mediaeval conception of God as a stern and arbitrary despot. We are growing into the larger conception of God as the Father, whose love is infinite toward his children, which is simply Jesus' view. We believe that our intelligent, honest, sincere attempts at improvement, instead of being contrary to, are fundamentally in harmony with God's purposes. WALTER B. BROCK
Auburn, New York

Why shall not humanity, of which the child is a minute part, be permitted to say thru its medical representatives, "This little creature is a step backward in the progress of the race. Not only will it be unable to bear its own burden, but it will ever be a load on its parents, and after them, should it live, on a community which already is burdened with the unfortunate who are always with us. A natural death is its natural right." EDWARD G. CLAPHAM
Fulton, New York

THE EFFECT ON CIVILIZATION

The Professor of History in Texas Christian University sends us a long and well considered analysis of the case from which, however, we can only quote the final sentences:

In the long run, the issue is: Which civilization would be the most efficient, the one with or the one without the distorted lives which are in the balance? Sentiments are not to be despised—they are to be evaluated and cultivated, so that they may help in conquering the world and subduing it. As to the general effect on men of society's preservation of idiots in order to avoid the act of killing them, or the contributory negligence of allowing them to die, this is an appeal to our experience. I always think of a great, sixteen-year-old product of this deluded moral scruple, in a family across the street from my boarding place in a Colorado town. Until I die, I shall not forget the effect it always had upon my spirits to see this great, overgrown idiot go thru his horrible contortions, mouth open, palate gone, as he leaned over the yard fence and stared into the sun. M. M. KNIGHT
Fort Worth, Texas

Mr. Klein, who as assistant Secretary of the Prison Association of New York, has had large experience with the defective classes, writes us as follows:

I ask further: is it right or wrong to execute people for crime, to incarcerate for life "the habitual criminal," to sterilize the feeble-minded and insane, or permanently segregate them, etc. And I presume that by right is meant that which makes for the bettering of the life of man. I do not think it is a choice between two principles, one right, the other wrong. It is rather a question of the *order of importance* among a number of principles, all of them valid. Such principles are, for example: 1. The recognition of the supreme value of human life as an absolute essential for the progress of society. 2. The recognition of the value of sympathy and love as the great factors in the life of the community. 3. The recognition of the competence of science to appraise facts and make just inferences; and the duty of society to profit by the advice of science as it profits by sympathy and self-love.

What shall be the order in which these principles shall be applied? This must be determined by the particular facts in the case, as interpreted by competent opinion, and above all it must be determined by the general sentiment of the age.

PHILIP KLEIN
New York City

The human body, we are told, is the temple of the living God. Such a body as that of the babe in question would be a poor receptacle for the indwelling Holy Spirit. Holy Writ teaches that we should eat our bread by the sweat of our brow. As a Christian and a Socialist I believe most sincerely in that doctrine, and hope the day of the parasite, who eats his bread without earning it, will soon pass, whether he be mentally or physically incompetent or not.

DR. J. C. HOWELL
Orlando, Florida

WHY PROLONG SUFFERING?

The pastor of a Congregational church in Wisconsin holds that the course adopted was dictated by mercy:

One can but marvel at that civilization that is merciful to a suffering animal, but prolongs as far as possible the agony of those who are hopelessly ill or injured. If we love our friends or relatives, why should we wish them to suffer needlessly? Such a principle could have originated only in the mind of him who had no life but the present, and to whom physical death was the end of all things.

These questions are largely a matter of the age in which they present themselves. What is wrong today by the weight of universal opinion, will be right in the conception of our descendants. If this case had come up a hundred years ago, as it undoubtedly did come up many, many times, death would have followed birth because there was no known way of preventing such an outcome.

Science has divinely-given rights, but these rights are only for good and merciful ends, and cannot rightly be exercised to prolong human misery needlessly, or to cause unnecessary suffering.

BENJAMIN WALKER SAUNDERS
Prairie du Chien, Wisconsin

Several of the letters can hardly be read without tears, for they come from some who wish for themselves or their dependents that their doctor had acted as the Chicago doctor did. A minister, whose name it would not be proper to reveal, writes of a "backward" child of his who at the age of ten was taken with a dangerous contagious disease from which only surgery could save it. The father and mother decided against an operation, but the physicians overruled them and they consented to their lifelong regret.

The child lived. The "backwardness" has not mended. We accepted the care. We are now facing that care multiplied. Shall we give up that calling to which I once thought I was called that we may care for the child while we live? Or shall we put the child in an institution, where good doctors tell us, the last ray of hope will vanish for the child, and where, knowing the child as we do, we believe it would die in a month or less of utter loneliness and fear?

I love children. There is nothing in this world that appeals to me anywhere as a child does. "Suffer the children to come unto Me, and forbid them not!" Do I need to tell you whose the quotation is? Did it never occur to you that that might have a meaning rarely if ever given to it?

I make this solemn statement, knowing its meaning as I write it. I believe that the Father was calling for my child thru the open door of pain. I believe that Heaven is *Heaven*, where there is no more sickness, nor sighing, nor pain, nor death, nor "backwardness" any more. And I believe that a lot of surgical operations not on children only, but on those older, are no more nor less than forbidding the children to go to Him when He calls.

A CRIPPLED CHILD'S OPINION

Here is another letter of the same sort which was sent directly to the physician:

Dear Doctor Haiselden—Just a line of praise from a little crippled girl for your not letting that baby live. I know God will be good to you, for I know how it is. My experience and that of other crippled children is that our hearts always ache. We can't dance nor play like other children. We are in every one's way but mother's, and her poor heart aches with ours. We are just a curiosity for people to look at.

Why don't those ladies who are attacking you adopt a crippled child? I am tired of life at fifteen. What will become of me when mother dies?

Those of our readers who have read that inspiring book, *The House on Henry Street*, will need no introduction to Miss Wald. In establishing the nurses settlement in the congested district of New York she has been a pioneer in a most useful field of philanthropy:

The controversy concerning the Chicago doctor is not new. Informally this has been discussed for many years, and in the early days of my own experience in the hospital, when vivid impressions were being made, I was perplexed and unable to understand whether the physician's oath or pride in the case moved the doctors to extraordinary measures for prolonging the suffering of "hopeless cases."

However, the inevitable conclusion that, I think, almost everybody has come to is that the right to decide upon life or death cannot be left to fallible human judgment; every doctor must, at some time in his practise, ponder upon the responsibility in this. The most conscientious may at times decide from high ethical reasoning that *extraordinary* measures are not justified in prolonging life in a being who is destined to misery and suffering and who may be a positive menace to society.

It does not seem impossible to some time define the boundaries within which decision may be made according to high moral convictions. To be sure that they are upholding the sanctity and traditions of this priestly profession, the doctors ought to take it up frankly, if necessary boldly, and confer with serious social thinkers.

LILLIAN D. WALD
Henry Street Settlement, New York

The Professor of History in Des Moines College, like many other corre-

The music that brings back the dreams

HOW the memory thrills at the music of the Steinway! It stirs thoughts of the long-ago years when, even as now, the songs of the heart were enriched by its exquisite tones.

Three-score years ago, even as now, the Steinway was the ideal piano. In many a family, the Steinway which grandmother played is today a cherished possession—its durability a tribute to superior craftsmanship.

Consider the Steinway as a gift to wife or daughter or sister—an enduring evidence of the noblest sentiment. Nothing could be more appropriate. Consider, too, that this marvelous piano can be conveniently purchased at a moderate price.

Illustrated literature, describing the various styles of Steinway pianos, will be sent free, with prices and name of the Steinway dealer nearest you.

STEINWAY

STEINWAY & SONS, STEINWAY HALL
107-109 EAST FOURTEENTH STREET, NEW YORK

spondents, cites the example of the ancients:

The old Greek and Roman "paterfamilias" inspected the new born babe and decided whether it was fit to live. If not, the babe was destroyed. The result was a strong and vigorous race as long as the old custom was observed. While we in the twentieth century would hardly advise a return to the old custom "in toto," we believe the general principle is right.
S. P. FOGDALL
Des Moines, Iowa

The publicity for which the President of New Mexico Normal University blames the physician was due primarily to a reporter with an abnormally keen "scent for news" who got wind of the case. After it has been made a public sensation in this way the discussion of it was unavoidable.

I think all monstrosities should be permitted to die, but I do condemn the physician for making such a public ado about the matter. He has done nothing more than many physicians have done, but done more wisely; and this publicity will prompt others less wise to go farther in this matter than they should.
FRANK H. H. ROBERTS
Las Vegas, New Mexico

It is interesting to see by what different routes our readers arrive at the same conclusion. Some view the question from the sociological standpoint, others from the personal; some argue from theological grounds; others from scientific.

"HE MADE THEM WHOLE"

Morally, was the doctor wrong? Would you, my reader, wish to assume the responsibility of a fellow being's embarkation upon such a life? Christ went about "Doing good," and in this case Christ could and might have caused the little one to live by the exercise of his miraculous power, but it is inconceivable that He would have merely worked a miracle in order simply to preserve life. He would at the same time have removed the entire physical disability, which is impossible for man to do. To confer life with the maximum chance to enjoy it is God-like. To confer life with preponderating chances of its being denied of enjoyment is—shall we not justly call that fiendish?
E. E. LUSK, M.D.
Baraboo, Wisconsin

Mr. Alexander Johnson, Field Secretary on Provision for the Feeble Minded, returns a non-committal answer:

A cardinal principle of our civilization, as opposed to that of ancient Sparta, is that of the preservation as long as possible of every human life, no matter how defective nor in what agony. There is a present tendency towards some reversion from this principle, as shown by the popular leaning toward the sterilization of the unfit. Between extinction and sterilization the difference seems rather of degree than of kind. Those who advocate sterilization must surely approve of the course taken in this extreme case.

I believe, however, that a matter of such vital importance should not be left to the decision of one man, but that some form of collective or legalized action should be required.
ALEXANDER JOHNSON
Philadelphia, Pennsylvania

The answers in the negative are, as we have said, fewer, and they are also less varied, being for the most part absolute condemnation of the action on dogmatic grounds as contrary to the commandment, "Thou shalt not kill," or arguments as to the possible benefit of such a life to the world. The following quotations will indicate their general character·

NO! NO!! NO!!! God gives life. God alone can say when he will take it. That was first degree murder. The doctor *should have done everything in his power to save the child.* Even tho the mother did give her consent, it must have been obtained under duress, for she was weakened, nervous, sick. She could not think properly for herself. She was in dire need of some one to think for her; to think right and properly. She had chosen this doctor and HE FAILED HER! Had she been allowed to keep her child, to nurse it, care for it, and lavish the love of her heart upon it, her life would have been broadened, bettered, purified, for with such suffering comes the purification of character.

     WILLIE MAY REDDIN
Janesville, Wisconsin

"THOU SHALT NOT KILL"

I believe that the fifth commandment needs no amending. I believe that the Constitution of the United States was right in guaranteeing that *no* person shall be deprived of life, liberty, or property without due process of law. And I believe that the criminal code of Illinois should be enforced against persons who have no regard for moral and statute law.

     PAUL KAYSER
Milwaukee, Wisconsin

If, according to Emerson's law of compensation, for everything we have missed we have gained something else, who knows but what this babe—deformed and malformed as it is said to have been—might have possessed some gift that would have added a little mite to the world's spiritual or intellectual heritage? We cannot help congratulating ourselves and the world at large that in the past so utilitarian a standpoint as regards defective lives was not taken. For we would then never have had the songs of Fanny Crosby, or read of the wonderful transformation in the life of Helen Keller.   P. SMITH
Detroit, Michigan

Professor McElroy, of Ohio Wesleyan, urges that to endorse the deed would be "to Australianize our ethics":

The ethics of the doctor's position represent the ethics of Australia and the savage world. His act can only be regarded as a survival. The Australians stand· at the bottom of the human ladder. On their lean island starvation ever looks them in the face. Hence their peculiar restrictions on marriage and their shrewd adjustment of population to food supply. When a child is born among them, the question of its life is settled by a council. If permitted to live the child is treated kindly. By the growth of knowledge, the advance of civilization, and the influence of religion, the world has for ages been moving away from the ethics of savagery.   B. L. McELROY.
Delaware, Ohio

Dr. Walsh, a Catholic physician well known to the public as the author of *The Thirteenth Greatest of Centuries* and other works on the history of science, condemns the act of the Chicago physician on the following grounds:

The physician has assumed the exercize of a power that is not his. Doctors have the care of life, not death. Physicians are educated to care for the health of their patients, but so far at least as I know we have no courses in our medical colleges as yet which teach how to judge when a patient's life may be of no service to the community so as to let him or her die properly. Some of us physicians may thank God that we are not yet the licensed executioners of the unfit for the community, and some of us know how fallacious our judgments are even with regard to the few things we know.   JAS. J. WALSH
New York City

" Don't be discouraged!

Resinol Soap
will improve your skin "

Many and many a girl has a clear, healthy complexion today because some friend came to her with this sound advice, based on her own experience.

Resinol Soap nöt only is delightfully cleansing and refreshing, but its daily use reduces the tendency to pimples, offsets many ill-effects of cosmetics, and gives nature the

chance she needs to make red, rough skins white and soft.

Hands protected by Resinol Soap rarely chap or roughen in winter. Used for the shampoo, Resinol Soap helps to keep the hair rich, glossy and free from dandruff.

If the skin or scalp is in bad shape, through neglect or improper treatment, a little Resinol Ointment should at first be used with the Resinol Soap, to hasten the return to normal conditions.

Resinol Shaving Stick also contains the Resinol medications. The discriminating man appreciates the way it soothes his face and prevents most shaving discomforts. Trial on request.

Resinol Soap and Resinol Ointment are sold by druggists and dealers in toilet goods everywhere. For a sample of each, free, write to Dept. 12-B, Resinol, Baltimore, Md.

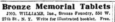

THE NEW BOOKS

PRECIOUS STONES

The Magic of Jewels and Charms is by George F. Kunz, whose long connection with the Tiffany establishment has made him the leading American authority on precious and semi-precious stones, as well as on cut gems. It is he who has prepared for a number of years the United States Government's annual report on gems and minerals found in this country. This magnificent volume contains chapters on magic stones, meteorites, stones popularly used medically, the virtues of fabulous stones, concretions and fossils, snakestones, the religious use of various stones, amulets, ancient, medieval, oriental or primitive, with various facts and fancies about precious stones. This makes a remarkable collection in a very curious and interesting line, having much to do with the history of human superstition and imagination gathered from many recondite sources. Not least in value to the reader are the many striking and unfamiliar illustrations.

The Magic of Jewels and Charms, by George F. Kunz. Philadelphia: Lippincott. $5.

YOUTH AND OLD AGE

It is characteristic of living things that they change with time in such manner that they finally reach a state in which the life processes can no longer continue. The metaphysical and poetical speculations on this theme may have brought resignation and consolation, but they have not brought understanding. Now it is the scientist's turn. In a dignified and attractive volume entitled *Senescence and Rejuvenescence,* Professor Charles Manning Child of the University of Chicago has brought together the results of years of experimental study, of which his own researches form a considerable part.

Professor Child defines the aging phenomena in general terms, as a decrease in the rate of the dynamic processes of the organism, conditioned by the accumulation of substances, differentiation, and other changes in the material substratum. He has little patience with the biological theories that assume the perpetual youth of some portion of the organism—as "the germ plasm," for example. All living involves differentiation, and differentiation involves senescence. To account for the cyclic reappearance of youth, Dr. Child points to the phenomena of dedifferentiation, which may not be a reversal of the aging process in the chemical sense, but which is a regression that results in the reëstablishment of the undifferentiated condition of protoplasm. Thus is rejuvenescence brought about—an increase in the rate of dynamic processes. The young organism arises from the old, and the young becomes old again.

Various theories of senescence are discussed, as the accumulation of poisonous excretions, made familiar chiefly thru the work of Metchnikoff; the exhaustion of some essential ferments; the mathematical theory of the changing ratio of surface and volume; the differentiation of the protoplasmic structure, and others; and the inadequacy of each theory is pointed out. A consideration of the facts gathered in developing these various theories, however, leads the author to question whether the live substance returns with each regression or rejuvenation to exactly the same condition as that in which it existed in the previous cycle. In other words, he suggests that there is a gradual, progressive senescence of protoplasm in the course of evolution. Such a senescence would account for the extinction of whole races of organism, without reference to the usual Darwinian factors of "struggle" and "survival of the fittest." On the other hand, it may be the basis for progressive mutations, in the sense of DeVries, or for the kind of orthogenesis described by Osborn. While only some three or four of the chapters in this book are of direct interest to the general reader, the work is a valuable contribution to the analysis of fundamental biological problems.

Senescence and Rejuvenescence, by Charles Manning Child. University of Chicago Press. $4.

IRISH RECITATIONS

Captious indeed would be that entertainer who, seeking to regale his audiences with selections of the choicest Hibernian flavor, could not find something to his taste in the five hundred odd pages of *The Reciter's Treasury of Irish Verse and Prose,* which has recently made its appearance here. Rarely in books of this sort is the level of literary excellence so high, or selections made with a shrewder eye for the reciter's demand for material of a kind that will make a hit with the average audience. The popular note, comic, tragic, pathetic, is sounded again and again, nor are the editors above including a good bit of stirring melodrama, wit with a forceful "punch," or boisterous, rollicking fun. There are readyreference indices and an admirable critical introduction, which tells the reciter many things he should be happy to know about the selections and their authors.

The Reciter's Treasury of Irish Verse and Prose, comp. 2nd ed. by Alfred Percival Graves and Ernest Fertwee. Dutton. $1.50.

OUR FRIENDS IN NEED

An unusual and illuminating picture of life in America during and just after the Revolution is that drawn by Charles H. Sherrill in *French Memories of Eighteenth Century America.* The officers and other gentlemen of France who fought in our battles or came later on official business left many and full records of their visits and in these surprizingly understanding as well as friendly records and criticisms we see ourselves as we appeared to our benefactors. The description of the American army is of especial interest and of some moment in connection with our present discussion of preparedness. It illustrates Washington's statement of the piteous and needless waste entailed by untrained troops. The French government in sending aid to the rebel colonies was probably as disinterested as governments are apt to be, but the soldiers and officers who risked and lost their lives in our behalf deserve everlasting gratitude. Tho the book is a history, riot in the least an appeal, one closes it with the feeling that since money and goods are all the return we may make today to suffering France, it is to our shame if this return be not without stint.

French Memories of Eighteenth Century America, by C. H. Sherrill. Scribner. $2.

RECORDS OF CIVILIZATION

The publication of the first volume in a series of researches and studies planned to illustrate the total process of the evolution of the civilization of Western Europe from the early Greeks down to modern times, calls for more than a passing notice. The series, Records of Civilization, is edited by Prof. James T. Shotwell, of Columbia University, in collaboration with eight colleagues from Columbia and the Union Theological Seminary, including Prof. Franklin H. Giddings of the department of sociology and Prof. Munroe Smith of the department of law, and the seventeen or more volumes are on such varied topics as The History of History, The Records of the Jews, Persian and Hindu Documents, Early Medieval Law, The Papacy, The Expansion of Europe, The Social History of Modern England, and Reprisals in the History of International Law.

These volumes are designed to be more than simple translations of interesting documents, such as we have in various "source-books." In addition to the translation of extended sources, they will contain scientific introductions and commentaries, with full bibliographical guides. If the introductory essay of Professor Botsford, covering the first sixty-two pages of *Hellenic Civilization,* is a fair sample of the quality of the epexegetical material that is to appear in this series, we may at once say that the series will take rank with the *recueils* and *corpora* of European scholars. It seems hardly like overpraise to hail this project of American scholars as the beginning of our *Monumenta Historica.*

Aside from their great value as works of reference to which both teachers and students will go for material on politics, philosophy, literature, religion, science, social customs, and a hundred and one other subjects of interest in ancient and medieval times, the series will help to supply a want which is being more and more keenly felt as the study of the Greek and Latin languages ceases to be the inevitable basis of our education. The Loeb Classics, with their parallel pages of classical text and English translation have already made a score or more of the important works of Greek and Roman antiquity and the early middle ages accessible to English readers. Prof. Shotwell's series will greatly extend this material, incorporating many hitherto untranslated texts and preserving for the general educated public rich treasures of the ancient and the medieval mind which are in danger of becoming the exclusive possession of the comparatively small number of classical experts in these days of pragmatic and scientific education. It is this happy combination of respectable popularization and critical scholarship which seems to us to constitute the chief value of the series.

In the volume before us, *Hellenic Civilization*, we are confronted by an embarrassment of riches. From the Minoan Age to the late Roman Republic, every stage of Hellenic and Hellenistic culture is presented. Such common things as business contracts, popular festivals, domestic relations, medical superstitions, farming, trading, the duties of wives and housekeepers take their place with the more formal, but far less "typical," extracts on politics, philosophy, and stately literature that usually fill the pages of a source-book on ancient history, and the range of authors cited is no less remarkable than the variety of topics.

Chapter VIII is devoted to the private and criminal law of the fifth century, B. C.—the private law represented by the Gortysian code of Crete, and the criminal law represented by the Draconian decrees. The editors, assisted by Prof. Munroe Smith and other scholars, have given us a masterly presentation of these laws, with critical notes, introduction and bibliography, making a chapter not only intensely interesting for its information on the laws of slavery, divorce, widows and children, inheritance, adoption, but also most gratifying to American scholars as an essay worthy to stand with the work of Bücheler, Darest, Reinach and other continental scholars.

Another remarkable chapter is that on Administration, Industry, and Education in the Hellenistic Kingdoms, 337-330 B. C., contributed by Prof. W. L. Westermann of the University of Wisconsin. This gives a new light on a period singularly neglected in our histories. Most of the material is from papyri lately discovered. The last two chapters of the book (Science and Invention, and Social Conditions) deserve "honorable mention" for the new and interesting material in them—especially the delightful anthology of epigrams at the end, translated by Prof. William C. Lawton of Hobart.

Hellenic Civilization, ed. by G. W. Botsford and E. G. Sihler Columbia University Press. $3.75

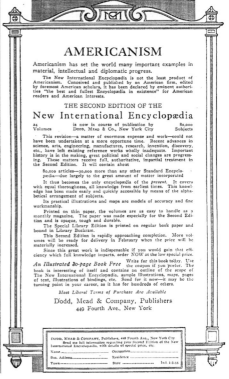

INSURANCE

CONDUCTED BY W. E. UNDERWOOD

MUTUALITY IN LIFE INSURANCE

Looking over a list of more than two hundred life insurance companies which have been organized in the United States during the past ten years, one acquainted with the nature and practicabilities of the business is astonished at the paucity of mutuals among them. I don't think that there are as many as ten. The condition should be reversed. As I have observed on several occasions in this place, the system of insuring lives is one that should not be subordinated to the purpose of making dividends for invested capital. Its objects are too closely bound up with human misery, sorrow and affection, to permit of its exploitation for profit by the owners of money which, to a successful, going company, is a superfluous encumbrance.

The greater number of these new stock companies are the creations of professional promoters outside the insurance business, who took advantage of the excitement caused by the New York investigation of 1905 to provide comparatively small communities with "home" institutions, thus to save them from the evils attendant upon sending their money away. Their schemes were fostered by the existence, in almost every state, of laws which render it very difficult, if not impossible, to organize mutual companies. Millions of dollars were made by promoters organizing new stock life companies which, when ready for business, were turned over to local men to operate and manage, the promoters, like a circus, moving on to another locality—a new field of conquest—selected in advance.

The people were exploited. The country was supplied with innumerable superfluous companies, most of them of the wrong kind. A fourth of the number have already failed or retired. Many more will do so within the next decade. By that time there will again be room for twenty or thirty properly organized new companies and, if in the meantime the laws are altered so that encouragement and help will be extended by the state to new mutual companies, they should all be of that class. Among insurers and insured, the tendency is strongly toward pure mutuality in life insurance, unburdened by stockholders' dividends and—what is more objectionable—stockholders' control.

J. B. S., Franklin, Ind.—You have had an unfortunate experience with one of the new and unnecessary companies which I occasionally caution the public against. You have lost your money and several years. Your endowment policy in the Presbyterian Ministers' Fund is a solid security. Yes, I think you should have more life insurance; in fact, as much more as the whole sum invested at five per cent will yield at least at your present annual earnings. The ac-

celerative endowment policy of the New York Life about which you inquire is a splendid contract. You might also look into that and other companies' thirty-five-year endowments.

A. G. C., Ottawa, Kans.—Money put into the stock of new life insurance companies is a speculation, not an investment. There are now 250 life insurance companies in the United States. Sixty-five life companies have failed or retired in the past ten years, involving their stockholders in losses aggregating about $15,000,000. Life insurance is a beneficence, and there is a growing prejudice against its being used as a dividend earner for capital. In time the pure mutual will have the field—and it should.

R. F., Mount Vernon, N. Y.—Observation of the matter inclines me to the conclusion that the insurance laws of Pennsylvania provide as effective protection to policyholders as do those of Massachusetts or Wisconsin; but that they are not as efficiently administered in Pennsylvania as they are in the other two states. The Massachusetts Insurance Department is particularly efficient. If the representatives of the John Hancock Mutual and the Northwestern Mutual have recommended a convertible-term policy, it is because, having knowledge of all the conditions, they have concluded you could prudently carry it. Generally, the use of term insurance is injudicious. The saving in premium is not invested faithfully and too often conversion to a higher form of contract is not made. Why don't you secure a 40- or 45-years endowment? I don't clearly understand the figures you send and, under the circumstances, am unable to explain the differences you mention. In conclusion, you may rely on getting exact facts from the two companies mentioned above, both of which render the best of service. The other is not their equal in character.

O. C. L., Columbus, O.—I can answer your question respecting the conversion of the term policy only in a general way in the absence of the contract itself, the terms of which I do not know. I presume you have a ten-year term policy and will suppose that the conversion will be to a whole life. I will also assume that the difference in premium at the initial age is $8.88 per $1000 a year. Now assuming that the company will charge you interest at three and one-half per cent on this difference, you will have to pay $107.82 for your new whole life policy, plus $20.60, the new premium rate. The immediate cash value of the new policy is $101; the paid-up value, $242. At your present age, the premium on a whole life policy is $27.20, which is $6.60 a year for life greater than the policy you can get by converting the term policy. If you lapse the term policy and take a whole life at your present age, you will retain the $107.82, difference in back premiums, pay $27.20 for the new policy and at five per cent the remainder ($80.62) will be worth in twenty years $213.88. But at the same interest rate, in the same time, the $6.60 difference per year between the premiums at your initial and your present age will be worth $229.14. In ten years from now the cash value of the converted policy (then twenty years old) will be $239; while the cash value of the other (then but ten years old), will be $147. I would convert the term policy. As between the Mutual Benefit, Equitable of Iowa and Union Central, all the advantages, from a policyholder's viewpoint, are with the Mutual Benefit. The special $5000 policy of the Metropolitan cuts as close to net cost as can be, and now that the company is a mutual, if there are any savings to lower it, policyholders will get the benefit.

PEBBLES

Something tells us that the King of Greece doesn't even carry a latch key.—*Chicago Tribune.*

THE "ANCONA" NOTE

Well, there's nothing left but an antepenultimatum!—*New York Tribune.*

'Blessed are the peacemakers," but they are overbearing a lot of unflattering remarks just now.—*Sunshine.*

No doubt the ablest peace advocate in the world would fail as a maker of automobiles.—*New York Herald.*

Italian soldiers get a little wine each day. But we seem to miss the old-time Roman punch.—*Columbia State.*

The reason for Woodrow Wilson's success is now disclosed. He was once a Managing Editor. — *Philadelphia Evening Ledger.*

Adv.—"Quick, Watson, the needle," chuckled Sherlock Holmes, as he slowly wound up the Victrola again.—*Dartmouth Jack-o-Lantern.*

Glimpsed by G. B. M., from a New Haven church bulletin: "Morning service 10:30. 'Prepare for the Worst.' Quartet will sing."—*N. Y. Tribune.*

The San Francisco Fair closed with a surplus, which is more than some of those who visited it had when they got back home.—*Philadelphia Evening Ledger.*

The *Fatherland* says that the accidents in American munitions factories were the acts of God. At any rate, there has been a growing suspicion that some of the Kaiser's adherents were responsible for them.—*Nashville Southern Lumberman.*

First Mother—Mrs. Clancy, yer child is badly spoiled.
Second Mother—Gawan wid yez.
First Mother—Well, if you don't believe it, come and see what the steam roller did to it.—*Harvard Lampoon.*

"My son," said the father impressively, "suppose I should be taken away suddenly, what would become of you?"
"Why," said the son, irreverently, "I'd stay here. The question is, what would become of you?"—*The Boy Builder.*

A Scotch minister in need of funds thus conveyed his intentions to his congregation:
"Weel, friends, the kirk is urgently in need of siller, and as we have failed to get money honestly we will have to see what a bazaar can do for us."—*Tit-Bits.*

"I wish a doormat," announced Mrs. De Style.
"Here is a very nice pattern," said the salesman, "with the word 'Welcome' woven into the fiber."
"I see. I suppose that will do if you can add the words 'Tuesdays and Fridays.'"—*Kansas City Journal.*

"So my daughter has consented to become your wife. Have you fixt the day of the wedding?"
"I will leave that to her."
"Will you have a church or a private wedding?"
"Her mother can decide that."
"What have you to live on?"
"I will leave that entirely to you, sir."—*Yale Record.*

A lot of people hate the war because it has upset their routine and the running of their apparatus.
Some of them think the best way is to ignore it, and go right on as if there were no war.
These are the kind of people who, when they hear the last trump, will say: "Oh, bother this day of judgment. It will be bad for business, and besides, it will make me late to dinner."—*Life.*

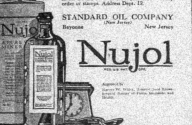

MOBILIZING AMERICAN SECURITIES

BY HAROLD J. HOWLAND

THE proposal of the British Government for "a mobilization of American securities" is a gratifying one to American pride. But it is a puzzling one to any but the trained financier. Its announced purpose is to "stabilize exchange." But what is exchange and how will this procedure give it stability? Let us see if it can be made clear.

There are owned in Great Britain about three billion dollars' worth of stocks and bonds in American corporations. But capital has been invested to that extent in American enterprises. As we recently pointed out, when the war began there was great anxiety lest there should be a rush to sell those securities over here with disastrous results to our security market. The Stock Exchange was closed to avoid this threatening danger and kept closed until the sterling exchange market had righted itself and it was seen that the necessities of Europe would create such a demand for American merchandise that we could pay for our securities in bills of exchange offered against our sales of commodities instead of in gold, which would otherwise have been demanded. Apparently the British investor realized the sound value of American stocks and bonds as investments in these topsy turvy days and was loth to let them go. The American market absorbed without a ripple all that were offered and proceeded to ask for more.

Now the British Chancellor of the Exchequer proposes a plan for bringing these American securities out of their British hiding places and using them for the benefit of the Empire. In the pursuit of his great task of financing England's share—the lion's share among the Allies—in the war he has come to realize that here England has a great asset which is not being put to use. He has been authorized by Parliament to invite the holders of the American stocks and bonds either to sell or to lend their holdings to the Government. They will be paid for if sold outright in Government bonds bearing five per cent interest. If the securities are merely lent, the Government will turn over to the owner all dividends or interest as they accrue and pay in addition one-half of one per cent on the face value of the securities.

The process is simple and will presumably not put too great a burden on the patriotism of the British owner of the stocks or bonds. But what will the Government do with them once it has them?

The securities, as has been said, are to be used primarily for the purpose of stabilizing exchange. Some will be sold in the American market; others, including those which are only lent to the Government, will be used as collateral for loans. How will this affect the question of exchange? To know this we must clearly understand what this question is.

32

PROGRESS OF THE UNITED STATES TOWARD FINANCIAL SUPREMACY

From a table published in the New York Times, based on figures compiled by L. F. Loree, president of the Delaware and Hudson Company.

AMERICAN SECURITIES OWNED IN EUROPE JULY 31, 1915

	Par Value.	Approximate Average Price.	Market Value.
Railroads..	$2,223,510,228	78	$1,751,437,908
Industrials, etc.	$18,300,000	90	466,400,000
Total	**$2,741,810,228**	**81**	**$2,217,837,908**
Held here for foreign account ..	123,000,000	81	99,630,000
Gr'd total.	**$2,864,810,228**	**81**	**$2,317,467,908**

BOUGHT BACK IN SIX MONTHS

Owned in Europe Jan. 31, 1915 ...	$3,486,100,000	71	$2,475,060,000
Owned in Europe July 31, 1915 ...	2,864,810,228	81	2,317,467,908
Decrease..	*$621,289,772		$157,592,092

*During the six months from January 31 to July 31 the average price of the foreign-held securities increased from about 71 to about 81, which accounts for the fact that the decrease in market value, $157,592,092, is so much less than the decrease in par value. It is the latter which shows the volume of securities which we bought back from Europe.

When an exporter in the United States sells goods to an English importer, it is desirable that he should receive payment for them without the actual shipment of gold across the Atlantic. For the shipping of gold is an expensive and to a degree a hazardous process. He receives therefor, instead of the actual money called for by his bill, a bill of exchange or a draft on London. The seller's problem is then to get his money in place of this instrument, which is a certificate of his right to the payment of so much money. The way in which he can get this money without its actual transportation across the ocean may be shown by a simple example.

Let us suppose that Smith of New York has sold goods worth $100 to Brown of London, Brown then owes him $100. Let us suppose that at the same time Jones of London has sold to Robinson of New York goods worth $100. Robinson then owes him $100. Smith receives from Brown in place of his goods a bill of exchange worth $100. Now if Robinson will buy from Smith his bill of exchange he can send it to Jones in payment of his debt to him. Jones can then take this instrument to Brown, who will give him its value in place of it. Smith and Jones then have their money, while Brown and Robinson has their money, and everybody is satisfied. The two original transactions taking place across the ocean have been completed by two transfers of money, each taking place not across the broad Atlantic, but within the narrow limits of a single city. Smith has

shipped goods across the ocean and received his payment in money handed to him in New York; while Jones has also shipped goods across the ocean and received his payment in money handed to him in London. All the expense of shipping gold both ways across the Atlantic has been eliminated, to the profit of all concerned.

Multiply this group of transactions by thousands and we have the elaborate structure of foreign exchange. Obviously, however, the great mass of transactions that result cannot be carried on by each buyer in New York dealing directly with a seller in the same city; and each seller in London dealing similarly with a single buyer in London.

It would take too much trouble for each to find the other; and when he had found him, there would be little probability that the needs of one would exactly correspond with what the other had to offer. Smith might have a bill of exchange for $90 which he wished to sell, while Robinson might need a bill for $110 with which to satisfy his foreign creditor.

Middlemen are therefore essential, and they are provided by the banks and bill brokers. These agencies buy bills of exchange from thousands of Smiths and sell them in turn to thousands of Robinsons. They deal in exchange bills as a jobber deals in dry goods or groceries or hardware. Exchange bills become an article of commerce, a commodity.

Like any other commodity, the price of exchange bills is immediately subject to the law of supply and demand. If many Smiths are offering bills to the New York banks, and few Robinsons are ready to buy them, the price goes down. Smith becomes willing to sell his bill of exchange for £100—normally worth $485.66—for $480; while Robinson is unwilling to pay more than $480 for a bill for £100 because if Smith No. 1 will not let him have it for that, Smith No. 2 or 3 or 4 will. So the price of exchange goes down and the exchange value of the sovereign falls.

During the war it has fallen as low as $4.50—from the normal of $4.87—and is now hovering about $4.73. There comes, however, a point below which the exchange will not go; for as soon as it becomes cheaper to ship gold than to buy exchange, gold will be shipped in payment of debts. Then the demand for exchange bills will decrease, and the price will naturally go up.

Now, the supply of exchange bills and the demand for them depends upon one thing—the quantity of goods that are being shipped in each direction between the two countries. If the United States were selling large quantities of goods to England, and absolutely none were being sold in the opposite direction, there would be no possibility of exchange at all. All England's debts to us would have to be paid in gold. If the opposite were true, we should have to pay in gold everything we owed to England for the commodities we were buying. If we were selling England exactly the same value of commodities that she was selling us, exchange would do the whole thing, and not an ounce of gold would need to be shipped either way.

But none of these conditions ever exists. So the supply of exchange on London in the New York market depends on the quantity of goods New York is shipping to London, and the demand for it depends on the quantity of goods New York is buying from London. The rate of exchange, therefore, goes up and down in harmony with the fluctuating balance of trade.

Exchange on London has been and continues to be phenomenally low in New York precisely because we have been and are selling such gigantic quantities of goods—food, munitions, clothing, equipment, to say nothing of all the usual exports—to England, and because England is not selling more than, if as much as, usual to us. The balance of trade between the two countries has swung widely to the other end of the arc.

The problem before British financiers, therefore, and before the British Government, is to restore the rate of exchange on London to something like its normal position. They must find a way of paying their debts in America without the reckless shipping of gold, which is a serious menace to a nation's credit, and without creating a tremendous supply of exchange bills in New York for which there is no demand.

There are several ways in which these debts can be paid.

By shipping gold; that soon becomes dangerous.

By shipping goods; but England has not enough goods to ship that we want, and her need for our goods shows no probability of decrease.

By sending over her own Government securities, as she does when she borrows money here; but England, in partnership with France, has just borrowed $500,000,000 here and the effect upon the exchange rate, while it has been encouraging, has been by no means sufficient to solve the problem.

Meanwhile the balance of trade stays firmly at the American end of its swing. England owes us more and more every day, and the debts which we are incurring with her are by no means commensurate with those she is piling up here.

The plan which the British Government is now entering upon to solve this troublesome problem of exchange is a combination of two of the methods mentioned above. The people of England have certain assets which have a readily realizable value in this country. They hold $2,864,810,228 worth of American stocks and bonds. If they can get these securities together, or any considerable part of them they can either sell them in our markets or use them as collateral in borrowing money from us.

In either case the effect upon the exchange value of the sovereign will be salutary. If they sell them here, they will immediately cause the creation of exchange bills to pay for them; and the resulting increase in the supply of exchange in London will send the value of the sovereign up. If they borrow money here on them as security, by sending their own government bonds or notes over as evidences of the loans, they will equally create a supply of exchange, with the same favorable effect upon the value of the sovereign as in the first case.

It will be of just as much efficacy in its effect upon exchange to send American securities 'from London to New York, or to send British Treasury notes, as to send Sheffield steel, or Manchester cottons.

But what will be the effect upon our own security markets? Will not this mean the unloosing of that flood of foreign selling, the fear of which closed the New York Stock Exchange for over four months? Can our market absorb the possible offerings without disaster?

The answer must be a matter of probability, not of certainty. But there is good reason to believe the United States to be in such a strong financial and commercial position that nothing that is likely to happen can bring serious harm to us.

In the first place, the flood cannot overwhelm us unless it comes. In the early months of the war its coming seemed probable and the Stock Exchange was closed to avoid the danger. But the flood did not come. The market absorbed all the American securities that were offered from abroad, and seemed to thrive on the diet. In spite of the foreign selling stocks have gone up and not down. The British investor evidently realized the value of his investments in the one great Western country that is not at war, and preferred to hold on to them. It is a question, then, whether even the urge of the British Government's appeal will be sufficient to draw these securities from the strong boxes in sufficient numbers to disturb the American market's equilibrium. In addition the British Government has declared that the securities collected will not be used in any way that will disturb the American financial world.

In the second place, there is a considerable reserve of absorptive power in this country which is not being called upon at the present time. In normal years the American public invests in from one and a half to two billion dollars' worth of new securities a year. Since the war began the issues of new securities have been nothing like these figures. A vast amount of buying power, which in ordinary times is taken up in new enterprises, under the strained and abnormal conditions of war time is to a large extent available for other purposes. It is probable that we should hardly have to make a wry face at swallowing a big dose of our own securities, provided they were not thrust down our throats too brutally.

LIGHTING THE HOUSE

The actual selection of lighting fixtures is a matter which may well be left to the architect who has planned the lighting system of the house, since the fixtures largely affect the method of distributing the light as well as the decoration of the rooms.

The character of the wall coverings has much to do with the selection. Dark colors and such fabrics as velvet require vastly more illumination than wood painted white, cream or gray, or hangings which reflect rather than absorb the light. The light of the ceilings must be considered, too.

Chandeliers, when they may be appropriately used in large or somewhat formal rooms, are extremely decorative. For the ordinary home, however, wall lights or reading lamps are usually in better taste. Should it be necessary to light a room from the top and yet avoid the use of a chandelier there are various forms of lighting which keep the bulbs close to the ceiling.

The most satisfying fixtures are those which are based upon antique motifs, but developed by the skill of present day designers. Our American homes are being built, to a great extent, in what is popularly known as the Colonial style, which is, of course, our American adaptation of the Georgian style in England. The designers of this picturesque period were particularly fortunate in the fashioning of their lighting fixtures and their beautiful designs are available for use today.

Especially successful are their wall lights, often designed as sconces and holding electric candles, or sometimes having the light bulb concealed by a cut glass shade hung about with glass prisms or pendants. To brighten the decorative effect of these candle lights the tips of the candles may be cleverly concealed beneath tiny shades made in a great variety of forms and fabrics.

The "Craftsman" and "Mission" styles, while frequently misused, are both appropriate and beautiful in their proper place. For use in such surroundings there are attractive and highly distinctive fixtures of wrought copper, bronze, brass or iron.

For dining rooms there is hardly anything more serviceable than a broad domed shade of metal, glass, or porcelain hung directly over the dining table. It casts the light upon the table, where it belongs, instead of in the eyes of those there assembled.

Just at present the system of illumination known as "indirect lighting" is having increasing popularity. The fixtures consist of inverted metal, glass or alabaster bowls hung from the ceiling by several chains. Within the bowls are placed groups of lighting bulbs casting their light upward, where it is reflected by the ceiling, usually white, and diffused about the room.

WHEN IT'S COLD AT CHAUTAUQUA

BY E. H. BLICHFELDT

THE TOWN ON THE COAST

WHAT Chautauqua, New York, can do in January or February can be done by any one of a hundred little communities in the zero belt. It is only during July and August tht Chautauqua has unique advantages for a scheme of outdoor enjoyment and indoor entertainment and instruction. During the winter it may boast only such favoring conditions as are found elsewhere. Population shrinks to a minimum of about 500 before Christmas. Diversities of interest akin to those of "town and gown" naturally exist among institution employees, cottages and more or less permanent residents. There is a union church, a consolidated township high school, and the usual quota of local societies, Chautauqua Circle, W. C. T. U., fire department, Young People's Society and the like. But the birth of a new community spirit, which many a small town craves, yet somehow fails to obtain, began here with a winter week of indoor lectures and entertainments, plus provision for outdoor coasting and skating. It was a voluntary home application of the Chautauqua idea to winter small-town conditions. It began timidly with a question on somebody's part as to whether an indoor winter program of lectures and entertainments on a very modest scale, accompanied by some livelier activities for those whose blood runs warm within, would be given support. It "caught on" so imperceptibly but grippingly that about $400 was subscribed for tickets at $1.50 to assure another carnival the next winter.

Again in 1915 the program and the sports were inaugurated. Money was spent out of the fund to scrape and flood a skating rink on the green in the center of the town. This rink was lighted by a big electric bulb over the middle and at the corners by two quite marvelous towers of ice with electric bulbs encased within. Volunteer labor supplemented the little expenditure for this innovation. Lecture fees were, of course, paid; but the ticket sellers and ushers gave their time. The Institution, whose offices are at Chautauqua thruout the year, regarded it not as a philanthropy but as a good piece of business to give every employee three hours during the week and encourage its officers to give their services as fully as possible, on the platform or on the snow scraper. The people, not by companies or cliques, but as individuals, gathered to help the various efforts, here in force, there a little weakly, but on the whole with increasing unanimity, and before many days everybody knew that something had happened to the town. The thing that had happened was good, and there was no longer any vagueness about the idea of its merit of continuance. The Chautauqua annual carnival would seem to be established if everybody is discreet enough to remember that it isn't his affair or the affair of his group, or the affair of any other group of whom his might be mildly jealous. It is *everybody's* affair and is possible only as everybody claims part in it, and lends it his good will. This has been so apparent that probably nobody will overlook or forget it. It is the carnival spirit that deserves emphasis as creative of all that rescued Chautauqua from monotony for ten days in February, and seems to have unified its elements in a new way.

An inventory of the products of the enterprise would be made up first of intangible things, tho they are sure to bring tangible consequences after them. Men and women fifty years of age, who had not skated in years, brought out their wooden-bodied, hand-forged skates of the model of 1879 and zigzagged over the ice, exchanging partners. Reserved or shy grownups who had been suspected of being a little crusty became pals with the neighbors' children. Glove fingered gentlemen heaved on a five-man snowshovel. Half-grown barbarians of both sexes found legitimate vent for their energies. Overnice young ladies fell down and lost their precious airs without any damage to proper reserve. Boys of eighteen discovered that lectures need not be a deadly affliction if the lecturer is a normal member of the human race and if the fellow on the bench is sportsman enough to reciprocate the good fellowship that older folk have shown him out on the ice. In short, the greatest accomplishment of the affair was in making better friends of those who thought they had nothing in common, who will still differ very much in their daily interests, but who have discovered unsuspected fine qualities in each other and learned that they can unite in enthusiasm for what benefits all.

It has been demonstrated that some counterpart of the Chautauqua week may become a local institution in a thousand villages of America.
Chautauqua, New York

ICE-BOATING FOR THE MORE VENTURESOME FEW

The Independent

FOR SIXTY-SEVEN YEARS THE
FORWARD-LOOKING WEEKLY OF AMERICA

THE CHAUTAUQUAN
Merged with The Independent June 1, 1914

JANUARY 10, 1916

OWNED AND PUBLISHED BY
THE INDEPENDENT CORPORATION, AT
119 WEST FORTIETH STREET, NEW YORK
WILLIAM B. HOWLAND, PRESIDENT
FREDERIC E. DICKINSON, TREASURER

WILLIAM HAYES WARD
HONORARY EDITOR

EDITOR: HAMILTON HOLT
ASSOCIATE EDITOR: HAROLD J. HOWLAND
LITERARY EDITOR: EDWIN E. SLOSSON

PUBLISHER: KARL V. S. HOWLAND

ONE YEAR, THREE DOLLARS

SINGLE COPIES, TEN CENTS

Postage to foreign countries in Universal Postal
Union, $1.75 a year extra; to Canada, $1 extra.
Instructions for renewal, discontinuance or
change of address should be sent two weeks
before the date they are to go into effect. Both
the old and the new address must be given

We welcome contributions, but writers who
wish their articles returned, if not accepted,
should send a stamped and addressed envelope. No responsibility is assumed by The
Independent for the loss or non-return of
manuscripts, tho all due care will be exercised.

Entered at New York Post Office as Second
Class Matter

Copyright, 1916, by The Independent

Address all Communications to
THE INDEPENDENT
119 West Fortieth Street, New York

CONTENTS

PEBBLES

Germany's peace terms are evidently put
forth for domestic consumption.—*New
York World.*

"Do you blay chess?"
"Chess?"
"Chess."
"Chess."—*Sun Dial.*

"Ladies—30 pounds washed and dried,
$1; excess, 4 cents per pound. Denver Wet
Wash. Phone Gallup 1234."—*Rocky Mountain News.*

Visitor—"Do you give your dog any
exercise?"
Owner—"Yes, he goes for a tramp every
day."—*Burr.*

One way to obtain an adequate navy
would be to establish Government shipyards in every Congressional district.—
St. Paul Pioneer Press.

First Officer—I hear Bangs is taking
life easy nowadays.
Second Officer—I should say he is; he's
running a rapid fire gun.—*Yale Record.*

G. B. Shaw says that the Allies must
not crush Germany. Latest advices from
the front indicate that the Allies are taking his suggestion very seriously.—*Macon
Evening News.*

Ted—Last night a mouse jumped out
of my stove, and altho I had a gun in my
hand I didn't shoot it.
Ned—Why didn't you shoot it?
Ted—Well, you see, it was out of my
range.—*Pelican.*

"Germany has such immense stores of
copper as to suffice for years to come." said
the Chancellor in the Reichstag, and the
cheers that greeted this statement almost
drowned the sound of the workmen's hammers stripping off the copper roof.—*Wall
Street Journal.*

Kind Old Lady—I'm sure you won't
mind my asking you, but are you a relative
of Captain Jones of Mudford?
The Officer—Madam, I am Captain
Jones of Mudford.
Kind Old Lady—Ah, then that accounts
for the extraordinary resemblance!—*London Opinion.*

"I hope your constituents appreciate the
value of your patriotic services," said the
prominent citizen.
"I don't know that I care to make it a
question of actual value," replied Senator
Sorghum. "The market for patriotic service is terribly fluctuating."—*Washington
Star.*

REMARKABLE REMARKS

GEN. JOFFRE—The French Army will
never crack.

JOHN HAYS HAMMOND—The Republican
Party is reunited.

BLISS CARMAN—Heaven is no larger
than Connecticut.

EMPEROR YUAN SHIH-KAI—My heart is
full of love for the people.

WOODROW WILSON—After all the most
vitalizing thing in life is Christianity.

CONGRESSMAN "CYCLONE" DAVIS—I
haven't worn a collar in twenty years.

ELLA WHEELER WILCOX—On a few occasions I have received messages from the
beyond.

PROF. CHARLES McCARTHY—The day of
the "boo-hoo" and "eat-'em-alive" freak is
passing.

REV. CHARLES B. MITCHELL—About the
meanest skunk on the footstool is the
snobbish minister.

WILLIAM ALLEN WHITE—Kansas is the
sole legatee and custodian of the New England conscience.

SENATOR TOWNSEND—True democracy
demands that wheelbarrows be taxed, if
automobiles are to be.

INEZ MILHOLLAND BOISSEVAIN—Certainly women should have the right to
propose. I did it myself.

SECRETARY LANE—The Bureau of Education should either be abolished or put
to serious high purpose.

SENATOR J. HAMILTON LEWIS—The Republican masters are bent on picking another Mark Hanna for 1916.

DR. HEINZ BOTHOFF—If necessary we
must kill hundreds of thousands of prisoners who are consuming our food.

ELIHU ROOT—If the nomination were
offered to me, I should feel it my duty to
accept it, even if it should kill me.

MRS. HENRY FORD—I'd rather give up
my own life than send my son into battle
to seek the life of another mother's boy.

ROBERT E. PEARY—The 40th parallel of
North Latitude is the most fateful and
suggestive line upon the earth's surface.

SIR FREDERICK TREVES, M.D.—As soon
as King George's health is entirely restored he will resume total abstinence.

ALEXANDER GRAHAM BELL—I can imagine men with coils of wire about their
heads and communicating thought by induction.

MARY PICKFORD—Today I had fifteen
letters asking me if my hair is naturally
curly. Just to be saucy, I won't answer
one of them.

BOURKE COCKRAN—Roman Catholic
schools are the real non-sectarian schools,
while the so-called public school system
based on agnosticism is sectarian.

SIR WILLIAM OSLER—In time our civilization is but a thin fringe like the layer
of living polyps on the coral reef, capping
the dead generations on which it rests.

PETER FINLEY DUNNE—"Is th' Prisi-
dent a good goluf player, d'ye know, at
all?" asked Mr. Hennessy. "As a goluf
player he cud give Lincoln a shroke a
hole," said Mr. Dooley.

HELEN KELLER—Let us start a world-
encircling revolt which shall make a junk
heap out of civilization, of Kaisers and
Kings and all the things that make of man
a brute and of God a monster.

PUBLISHER ERMAN J. RIDGWAY—We
covenant with you, and solemnly, to edit
without malice, without self-interest, not
even for your self-interest, but for the good
of all, as God, the Father, gives us to see
what is good for all.

H. J. CALLAHAN—I always carried a
supply of dead cockroaches with me. When
I had finished eating I would throw one
on the plate. Then I would call the restaurant proprietor, point disgustedly at it,
and walk indignantly from the place without settling the bill. It never failed.

© Modern Photo Service

THE LOOKOUT
A FRENCH ARMY OFFICIAL PHOTOGRAPH
SHOWING MEN WITH GAS MASKS
AT A TRENCH OPENING

The Independent

VOLUME 85.   JANUARY 10, 1916   NUMBER 3501

TWENTY-ONE AMERICAN REPUBLICS

THAT the twenty-one American republics should all be represented in the Scientific Congress in Washington by a thousand of their most distinguished citizens is a notable event, but far more notable is the fact that the twenty-one independent American nations are all republics. Besides these, Canada is to all intents and purposes a republic, tho nominally governed by an appointed representative of an European nation. Apart from British America, only a few insignificant fringes along the Atlantic coast have an exotic color; the continent is self-governed and republican.

That this is the great fact is to the credit of our own nation. Ours was the first of these republics, and is stronger and richer than all the rest put together. It was our example that made them republics. And when independent, it became our privilege to protect them. Hence, nearly a century ago, came the Monroe Doctrine. Under the shadow of that Doctrine they have grown, some of them to a fine maturity. It is not strange that our Secretary of State in welcoming the delegates to this Pan-American Congress and the delegates in their responses should have recognized what the Monroe Doctrine has done, and should have anticipated a more intimate sentiment of Pan-American good-will.

The Monroe Doctrine had no purpose to control or patronize the infant republics. It simply said, and wholly for the protection of our own nation, that no European Power should obtain a new foothold on our Continent. The camel should not put its nose into our tent. The Doctrine has been efficient. During the century no European Power has gained one inch of American territory. When one threatened it has been resisted. Meanwhile

Africa has been portioned out among the nations of Europe, but not America. When some European creditor nation has threatened to enforce payment of some little republic's extravagant debts we have peacefully intervened at the request of the endangered state. We have taken no advantage to ourselves beyond the advantage of keeping the Eastern Continents out of the Western.

Nor have we interfered in the differences between the twenty republics, unless our own Mexican War is an exception, when we recognized the independence of Texas and were thereby involved in war. Chile and Peru had their war and we did not interfere. Chile and Argentina divided Patagonia between them with no objection from us. We have also added one to the number of independent American republics, Cuba, by our war with Spain, and relieved Porto Rico from European domination.

It is not strange that the other republics should at times have feared that our purpose was selfish. Such it is not, and the twenty republics are coming to recognize our friendly purpose. This is what is implied in Pan-Americanism, each for all. It means peace, it means prosperity and wealth. While the three continents of the Eastern hemisphere are drenched in blood, slaughtering and impoverishing each other and themselves, the American policy brings peace and wealth and added population. To the Monroe Doctrine it adds the Pan-American Doctrine of good-will, mutual and trustful helpfulness. We are twenty-one sister nations, and when this fearful war is ended the nations of the old world will be quick to learn our lesson and we are confident will follow our example. Then the league of peace shall encircle the earth.

MORAL PREPAREDNESS

WE have already discussed at length the President's preparedness program from the military and financial standpoint. Is there not an aspect of the problem, however, more fundamental than either?

Here we are in the midst of the direst calamity known to history. Europe is bleeding to death. Asia is straining every nerve to hold our friendship. We would seem to be safer from invasion than at any time during our history. We are not only safe, but we are prosperous. Our prosperity, however, is not the result of our own planning. It is coined out of Europe's agony. And yet at the very time when our hearts should open as never before to the piteous cries from across the water, when all our thoughts and all our substance should be freely given to binding up the broken wounds, when the hour calls for a supreme and glorious unselfishness, we are proposing

to retire within our little world and proclaim as our national policy, "safety first."

Instead of considering how to embark on a course that would bring us the gratitude and love of every nation—such for instance as taxing ourselves to lend them a billion dollars to repair their losses after the war—we propose a plan that will inevitably make each one of them hate us a little more.

Some years ago we returned to China $10,000,000, which was an overpayment on the Boxer indemnity. That was not a present to China, but only a refusal to keep what did not rightfully belong to us. Yet the return of that sum—half the cost of a modern dreadnaught—has made the United States the most beloved nation on earth in the hearts of that great Asiatic people now so sincerely groping for light and liberty. Is there not a lesson here for a nation that would plan preparedness for peace?

Let us then make haste slowly in increasing our armaments. By the time the war is over we shall most likely find the nations ready to organize the world for peace and some sort of disarmament. If that is the case, any great burden of taxation now imposed on the American people for armament purposes will be wasted.

If the nations, however, instead of making a durable peace, only declare a truce in order to continue the mad scramble for greater and ever greater armaments, then the United States, having lost neither in treasure nor in men, will be in a better position than any other nation to enter the inevitable and crushing race whose end is death to all but the most powerful.

PANAMA AND SUEZ

THE inclusion of the Suez Canal within the zone of war seems likely to effect a decided change in the status of the Panama Canal. The Hay-Pauncefote treaty upon which the neutralization of the Panama Canal depends states in Article III that

The canal shall be free and open to the vessels of commerce and of war of all nations observing these Rules, on terms of entire equality.
The canal shall never be blockaded nor shall any right of war be exercised nor any act of hostility be committed within it.

The words "observing these rules" refer, as stated in the preceding paragraph of the treaty, to "the Convention of Constantinople, signed the 28th of October, 1888, for the free navigation of the Suez Canal" and which "the United States adopts as the basis of the neutralization of such ship canal."

Let us see then what this "basis of neutralization" stipulates. The chief clauses of the Convention of Constantinople bearing on this point are:

Article I. The Suez Maritime Canal shall always be free and open in time of war as in time of peace, to every vessel of commerce or of war, without distinction of flag. Consequently, the high contracting parties agree not in any way to interfere with the free use of the canal, in time of war as in time of peace. The canal shall never be subjected to the exercise of the right of blockade.

The high contracting parties agree that no right of war, no act of hostility, nor any act having for its object to obstruct the free navigation of the canal, shall be committed in the canal and its ports of access, as well as within a radius of three marine miles from those ports, even tho the Ottoman Empire should be one of the belligerent powers.

In time of war belligerent powers shall not disembark nor embark within the canal and its ports of access either troops, munitions, or materials of war.

This Convention was signed by the representatives of Great Britain, Germany, Austria-Hungary, France, Italy, Russia, Turkey, Spain, and Netherlands. Their agents in Egypt are charged to watch over the execution of the Convention. The Sultan of Turkey and the Khedive of Egypt are permitted to take such measures for the defense of Egypt "by their own forces" as may be necessary, but Article I, the first paragraph of the above quotation, is not so waived.

The Great War has left little or nothing remaining of the Convention of Constantinople. All of the signatories are involved except Spain and the Netherlands. The Suez Canal has been the scene of one conflict and is likely to become the center of another and fiercer struggle. The British Government has deposed the

Khedive, set up a Sultan independent of Turkey and declared a protectorate over Egypt. Since even neutral lines like the Dutch are now going around by the Cape of Good Hope instead of thru the canal we may imagine what would happen if a vessel flying the German or Austrian flag should try to go thru.

On August 5, 1914, the day after Great Britain declared war on Germany, the Government seized all German ships of over 5000 tons displacement and fourteen knots speed in Egyptian ports. German and Austrian men anywhere in Egypt were arrested and deported. All these acts took place, it should be understood, while Great Britain was still legally at peace with Turkey and while the Sultan was still nominally sovereign of Egypt and the canal zone.

During the autumn and winter of 1914 the Suez Canal was fortified on both sides and 12,000 men brought from Australia, New Zealand and India to defend it. In February and March Suez was attacked by the Turks, but they were repelled by the artillery of the forts and the warships which patroled the canal.

We are not here questioning the propriety of any of these acts, but merely considering their bearing upon our rights at Panama. Referring back to the quotation from the Hay-Pauncefote treaty at the beginning of this article we see that it specifies that only nations "observing these rules" are entitled to equality of treatment in regard to tolls and the passage of vessels of commerce and war. These words "observing these rules" were not in the first draft of the treaty, which was amended by the Senate and never ratified, but were inserted in the final draft which was ratified. The clause "no fortifications shall be erected commanding the canal or the waters adjacent" and the phrase "in time of peace as in time of war" following the words "the canal shall be free and open" which were originally in the treaty were struck out of its final form. This has permitted us to fortify the canal, but by a curious inconsistency the treaty debars us from "any act of hostility" in Panama.

This inconsistency has now, it seems to us, been recently removed. It cannot be said that Great Britain has recently been "observing these rules" in Suez and she is the only nation who possesses any treaty rights in Panama, for the United States refused to agree with her proposal that the same guarantees be extended to "all nations which shall agree to observe these rules." Whether her violation of the Convention of Constantinople invalidates *per se* the Hay-Pauncefote Convention is a question for constitutional lawyers to decide. But anyhow, the acts of Great Britain in Suez during the present war have established a precedent which would debar her from objecting if in a similar emergency we used the Panama Canal Zone as freely for belligerent purposes as we would use any part of our own territory.

WHAT GOOD WAS YOUR SCHOOLING ?

CRITICIZING schools is a very popular pastime. It amuses the public and the teachers don't seem to mind. Besides—who knows?—perhaps the criticism may some time take effect and then we shall see radical changes in our educational system. Meantime we can at least continue to talk about it.

As soon as we leave school or college and plunge into active life, we make two discoveries. We find out that our education has in some ways given us valuable preparation for our new duties and we also feel the lack of certain other forms of training which our schooling might have given us but did not. Now the studies or discipline which have proved beneficial to one person may turn out to be quite useless for another, and we must have the experience of many if we are to draw any safe conclusion as to the sins of omission and commission in our educational system.

So we are going to hold an experience meeting on this subject. We wish every reader of The Independent would answer two questions:

1. Of all you were taught at school what has proved most useful to you in after life?

2. What have you had to learn since leaving school which you might have been taught there?

Make your answer definite, brief and sincere. Give your reason why that particular study was or might have been valuable to you, but do not write over a hundred words about it. If you use fifty words it is much more apt to be published. These questions might well be put to clubs and teachers' meetings, for they would bring out an interesting discussion and we should like to have the results of such collective questioning. Of course we do not necessarily limit the word "useful" to its narrow or vocational sense. You may think that what has helped you most was some special form of training, a new viewpoint or an inspiring ideal, but in that case to avoid vagueness you should point just why that particular study and not some other had such an effect upon your mind and character. All replies should be in by February 20. A postal card will do.

TOM OSBORNE

THE indictment of Thomas Mott Osborne, warden of Sing Sing prison, is but another example of the ingratitude of democracies.

Here is a man who has dared to substitute the law of love for the law of force in the community which he governs, a man who before our very eyes and in a few months has turned a cage of wild beasts into a self-respecting community of law and order, a man who in any other country would be decorated for his great public services, and yet now the victim of a foul conspiracy to ruin his character and drive him from public life. It seems incredible!

When he is acquitted—for it is inconceivable that he should not be acquitted—he should be reappointed to the wardenship of Sing Sing. We sincerely hope that Governor Whitman will take no uncertain attitude on this question. If he goes back on Tom Osborne, his own political death knell will have been sounded. There is not a shadow of a doubt that the whole people are with Osborne.

To Professor Kirchwey, who unselfishly stepped into the breach and assumed the wardenship of Sing Sing until the trial is over, the citizens of the state of New York and the country owe a debt of gratitude. Without his willingness to come forward to see that the Osborne policies are continued, the powers of evil might have conquered and Sing Sing would have been thrown back into the jungle.

As for State Superintendent of Prisons Riley, who has been fighting Osborne from the beginning, the sooner he goes the better. What is the Governor thinking of in keeping him in office?

THE MAN OF THE HOUR

THE latest speech of Lloyd George in the House of Commons has produced a more powerful effect than any oratorical effort of recent times. His warning that the delay in military operations and the obstructive rules of the trades unions might prove fatal to the cause of the Allies has startled and thrilled the nation:

We have been too late in this, too late in that, too late in arriving at decisions, too late in starting this enterprise or that adventure. The footsteps of the Allies have been dogged by the mocking specter of too late. Let not "Too Late" be inscribed on the portals of our workshops.

It is a curious fate that has made this poor and despised Welsh lawyer the leading man in England. A few years ago he was execrated by the ruling classes, the aristocracy, the clergy and the capitalists, who now look to him as the savior of the country. Yet he is imposing taxes ten times greater than those then thought intolerable and controlling the industries of the nation in a way that would once have been denounced as rank socialism. In appearing before the trades union congress a few months ago he introduced himself, quite correctly, as "the most extensive employer of labor in the world." He has brought the manufactories of army supplies up to an unprecedented state of efficiency and the British workman finds himself, much to his surprize, getting more money than he ever saw before.

Lloyd George is now the dominant figure in a cabinet composed of the ablest men of all parties, and in case of Asquith's fall he is likely to become Prime Minister.

"AMERICAN BARONS"

THAT is what the newspapers call them, these men who were born American citizens but have become British noblemen, William Waldorf Astor and Thomas Shaughnessy. But it is an obvious misnomer, a contradiction in terms. For those who accept a title, especially an hereditary title, are thereby repudiating the fundamental principle of this republic. Columbia disowns such degenerate sons, for what they esteem an honor is an insult to her. As old Ben Franklin puts it:

'Tis neither manliness, sense nor grace
For a man to spit in his mother's face.

We do not mind it when an American goes to live in England and becomes naturalized there because he likes the climate or the society better than ours, or finds there better business, professional or marital opportunities. Such freedom of migration is altogether desirable. We have the highest respect and admiration for the hundreds of young Americans who have taken service under the British flag in this crisis, for we realize that, altho they have had to swear allegiance to King George, they are really fighting in large part for the political principles which the two countries share.

But to join the peerage which England is trying to shake off, to accept titles which are admittedly purchasable and treated as party graft, to seek a fictitious ennoblement which is tainted with historic tyranny and which the noblest of Englishmen, such as Bright and Gladstone, have declined, proves that they are not merely aliens to America but enemies of Americanism. It seems strange that King George, now at a time when American sympathy and aid are desired, should needlessly offend American sentiment by making two ^merican barons."

WHICH DO YOU PREFER ?

BY FRANKLIN H. GIDDINGS

PROFESSOR OF SOCIOLOGY AND THE HISTORY OF CIVILIZATION, COLUMBIA UNIVERSITY

O N June 18, 1888, William II of Germany in an address "To My People" said:

Called to the throne of my fathers, I have taken over the government, looking to the King of all kings, and have vowed to God, following the example of my father, to be a righteous and gentle prince, to foster piety and the fear of God, to maintain peace, to further the welfare of the country, to be a help to the poor and opprest, and to be to the righteous man a true protector.

On July 27, 1900, this "righteous and gentle prince," addressing German soldiers departing for Pekin to avenge the death of the German Minister, Baron von Ketteler, instructed them:

You know very well that you are to fight against a cunning, brave, well-armed, and terrible enemy. If you come to grips with him, be assured quarter will not be given, no prisoners will be taken. Use your weapons in such a way that for a thousand years no Chinese shall dare to look upon a German askance. Show your manliness. The blessing of God be with you! The prayers of an entire people and my wishes accompany you, every one. Open the way for culture once for all!

On March 22, 1905, the same peace-loving potentate addrest the burgomaster and citizens of Bremen on the occasion of the dedication of a monument to Frederick III. Picturing the glorious destiny of his empire, he said:

For what has become of the so-called world-empires? Alexander the Great, Napoleon I, all the great warriors, have swum in blood and have left subjugated peoples behind them, who, at the first opportunity, have risen up again and brought the empire to ruin. The world-empire of which I have dreamed shall consist in this, that the newly-created German Empire shall first of all enjoy on all sides the most absolute confidence as a quiet, honorable, and peaceful neighbor; and that if in the future they shall read in history of a German world-empire or of a Hohenzollern world-ruler, it shall not be founded upon acquisitions won with the sword, but upon the mutual trust of the nations who are striving for the same goals.

On August 4, 1914, the German army attacked Liège. On August 20 it entered Brussels, and on August 27 it burned Louvain, all in violation of "a scrap of paper," wherein the Prussian Government had promised to respect and guarantee the neutrality of Belgium. On May 12, 1915, a commission headed by the Right Honorable Viscount Bryce, reported upon the atrocities, forever infamous, committed in the devastation of Belgium by an empire in which that helpless kingdom had placed confidence as a "quiet, honorable and peaceful neighbor."

On May 7, 1915, an Atlantic passenger steamer, the "Lusitania," was torpedoed by a submarine in the service of the "righteous and gentle prince." Of the nearly 1200 lives destroyed more than 100, including many women and children, were American citizens. On May 13 the Government of the United States sent a "firm" note to the German Government, setting forth that the destruction of the "Lusitania" was in violation of international law and of humanity. On May 31, Germany replied, justifying the act as proper under her conception of war. On June 9 our Government sent a second "firm" note, and on July 16 a third one. Whereupon, on September 1, Germany ostensibly accepted the American view of the lawful conduct of submarine warfare.

On November 1, the "Lusitania" case being still open, an Austrian submarine torpedoed, in the Mediterranean, after she had stopped, as the Austro-Hungarian Government has officially admitted, the Italian passenger steamer "Ancona," thereby sending to death defenseless non-combatants, including American citizens, among whom were women and children. On December 6 our Government dispatched a note to Vienna demanding that the "wanton slaughter of defenseless non-combatants" be denounced, that the responsible submarine officer who had destroyed the "Ancona" be punished, and that

reparation be made for the killing and injury of American citizens. On December 15 the Austro-Hungarian Government asked for "particulars" and an "exchange of views." On December 19 our Government sent to Vienna a second "firm" note. On December 29 the Austro-Hungarian Government replied to the second "Ancona" note, repudiating the sinking of the "Ancona," stating that the commander of the offending submarine had been punished, offering indemnity, and pledging the safety of neutrals and non-combatants at sea.

On December 30, simultaneously with the publication of this Austrian reply, the passenger steamer "Persia," from London for Bombay, was torpedoed and sunk in the Mediterranean. Among the hundreds of lives destroyed was that of a consul of the United States on his way to his post at Aden.

Washington, it was reported, was "shocked." Certain newspapers intimated that Washington was "amazed."

Self-respecting reader: Which would you rather be, a subject of a "righteous and gentle prince" who, fostering "piety and the fear of God," opens "the way for culture once for all" by ravaging a kingdom that has trusted him "as a quiet, honorable and peaceful neighbor," and by drowning non-combatant women and children; or a citizen of a republic whose President, having ignored or failed to perceive the greatest opportunity ever offered in human history for a firm exhibition of moral courage in defense of civilization and liberty, deals, month after month, in high-sounding periods with governments doubly and trebly forsworn, on the assumption that they may still be believed, under oath or otherwise, and who advises his masters, the American people, to suppress their indignation and hold their tongues in neutrality of thought and speech as of technically illegal acts? Think it over.

New York City

42

THE STORY OF THE WEEK

The Sinking of the "Persia" The British steamer "Persia," of the Peninsular and Oriental Line, on her way to Alexandria, was sunk about three hundred miles northwest of that port at five minutes past one on the afternoon of December 30. No torpedo was seen, but the second officer reports seeing the track of one. The vessel went down five minutes after the explosion and only four boats got away. Of the 182 passengers only 59 were saved; of the 154 in the crew, 94 were saved, according to the latest reports. This gives a total loss of 247 lives, of whom 70 were women and 30 were children, a death list second only to that of the "Lusitania." That a larger proportion of the crew escaped than of the passengers is surprising but may be due to the suddenness of the sinking as it is said there was no panic. The crew mostly consisted of Lascars. Two Americans were on board. One of them was drowned, Robert Ney McNeely, of North Carolina, who was on his way to Aden, at the entrance to the Red Sea, where he was to be Consul. The nationality of the submarine attacking the "Persia" is not known and there is a possibility that it was sunk by a mine instead of a torpedo. Altho the disaster occurred on Thursday no detailed news of it was made known to the United States until Monday morning. The "Persia" carried 4.7 inch guns but this is permissible to a merchant vessel under the rules of the United States. It is not known certainly whether troops or munitions were carried.

British Near Conscription The House of Commons passed without opposition the Government bill extending the life of the present Parliament for eight months and increasing the army to 4,000,000 men. According to a recent statement of Premier Asquith there are now about a million and a quarter British troops in the various theaters of war. But since their losses average over a thousand a day it is necessary to secure a continuous supply of men in greater numbers than hitherto. The opposition to conscription is so strong that the Government tried to avoid it by adopting the recruiting scheme of Lord Derby by which all the men of the United Kingdom, but not Ireland, were registered and classified and then personally interviewed by Government agents to ascertain what excuse, if any, they had for not volunteering. The nine weeks campaign of Lord Derby brought out an immense number, estimated to be over two million, but still not enough. The recruits under the Derby scheme are to be regarded as reserves and called out by classes according to age and condition. Classes 2, 3, 4 and 5, comprising unmarried men from nineteen to twenty-two, have already been summoned to the colors.

The Premier promised in November that "if the young men did not, under stress of national duty, come forward voluntarily other and compulsory means would be taken before married men were called upon to fulfill their engagement to serve." The Cabinet seems to have agreed to this altho there were some dissidents among the Ministers and several resignations are expected in consequence. That of Sir John

AUSTRIA'S PAPER COMPLIANCE WITH AMERICA'S DEMANDS

The reply of the Austro-Hungarian Government to the second American note on the sinking of the Italian steamer "Ancona" as handed to the American Ambassador at Vienna on December 29 is given in large part below:

The Imperial and Royal American Cabinet that the sacred commandments of humanity must be observed also in war. . . .

The Imperial and Royal Government can also substantially concur in the principle, exprest in the very esteemed note, that private ships, in so far as they do not flee or offer resistance, may not be destroyed without the persons aboard being brought into safety.

Guided by the same spirit of frankness as the Government of the Union, the Imperial and Royal Government, altho it does not find in the note, frequently legitimate questions submitted by it, is willing to communicate to the Federal Government the result of the investigation which, in accordance with existing departmental regulations, was begun immediately after the receipt of the first report on the sinking of the "Ancona," and which was just recently received. [Here follows the detailed report.]

The weather at the time of the incident was good and the sea calm, so that the lifeboats could have reached the nearest coast without danger, as indeed the lifeboats actually were damaged only by the unskilled lowering, but not after they had struck the water.

The loss of human lives is in the first instance by no means ascribable to the sinking of the ship, but (and in all probability in a much higher measure) to the rapid lowering (hinunter werfen) of the boats during full speed, as well as to the fact that the crew, concerned only for itself, did not rescue the passengers of the capsized boats.

It is also probably ascribable to shots which hit the fleeing vessel, but the death of persons who sank with the steamer is also, above all, ascribable to the disloyal conduct of the crew.

As appears from the above-adduced state of affairs, the very esteemed note of December 9 is based in many points on incorrect premises. Information reaching the United States Government that solid shot was immediately fired toward the steamer is incorrect; it is incorrect that the submarine overhauled the steamer during the chase; it is incorrect that only a brief period was given for getting the people into the boats. On the contrary, an unusually long period was granted to the "Ancona" for getting passengers into the boats. Finally, it is incorrect that a number of shells were still fired at the steamer after it had stopped.

The facts of the case demonstrate further that the commander of the submarine granted the steamer a full forty-five minutes' time, that is, more than an adequate period to give the persons aboard an opportunity to take to the boats. Then, since the people were not all saved, he carried out the torpedoing in such a manner that the ship would remain above water the longest possible time, doing this with the purpose of making possible the abandonment of the vessel on boats still in hand.

Since the ship remained a further forty-five minutes above water, he would have accomplished his purpose if the crew of the "Ancona" had not abandoned the passengers in a manner contrary to duty.

With full consideration, however, of this conduct of the commander, aimed at accomplishing the rescue of the crew and passengers, the Imperial and Royal Marine authorities reached the conclusion that he had omitted to take adequately into consideration the panic that had broken out among the passengers, which rendered difficult the taking to the boats, and the spirit of the regulation that Imperial and Royal Marine officers shall fail in giving help to nobody in need, not even to an enemy.

Therefore the officer was punished in accordance with the existing rules, for exceeding his instructions. . . .

The investigation into the sinking of the "Ancona" could naturally furnish no essential point to show is how far a right to an indemnity is to be granted American citizens. The Imperial and Royal Government cannot, indeed, even according to the view of the Washington Cabinet, be held liable for damages which resulted from the undoubtedly justified bombardment of the fleeing ship.

It should just as little have to answer for the damages which came to pass before the torpedoing of the ship thru the faulty lowering of lifeboats or the capsizing of lowered boats.

If, however, because of possible lack of material proofs, the particular circumstances under which American citizens suffered damage should not have become known to the Union Government, the Royal Government, in consideration for the humanely deeply regrettable incident, and by a desire to proclaim once again its friendly feelings toward the Federal Government, would be gladly willing to disregard this gap in the evidence and to extend indemnities also to those damaged whose cause cannot be established.

While the Imperial and Royal Government may probably consider the affair of the "Ancona" as settled with to itself at this time the right to bring up for discussion at a later period the difficult questions of international law connected with submarine warfare.

BURIAN

WAITING FOR THE CHARGE

A French advance trench just before the attack on the German lines, over which a shell is bursting. As soon as the bombardment has done its work the crouching men will leap into action and rush the enemy's position

A. Simon, the Home Secretary, is already announced.

It is argued by those opposed to conscription of any form or degree that the national register shows that there are only 600,000 unmarried men who have not attested and of these more than half are ineligible for military service on account of physical deficiency and of the rest a large proportion are either working in essential trades or are supporting families. Would it then be good policy to introduce a measure so repugnant to national traditions and popular sentiment as conscription in order to bring the comparatively small number of real "slackers?"

Most of the radicals and labor men and many of the old fashioned Liberals are constitutionally opposed to compulsory military service, so an opposition party to the Coalition Cabinet may be formed. A national congress of labor has been called for January 5 to determine whether the trades unions will consent to conscription.

The Irish party is also opposed to any form of compulsion and no attempt will be made to extend it to Ireland at present. John Redmond, the Nationalist leader, is still supporting the Government, the critical of the conduct of the war. John Dillon, who represents another Irish faction, attacked the Government in the following language:

Before we sanction the fourth million of men we ought to be told what is the basis of the Government's demand. In no case have the failures of the war been due to lack of men, and before the Government enforces conscription the men responsible for these failures must be removed. What is the use of sending more troops to be led by men like those responsible for the Suvla Bay and Anzac failures?

Lloyd George, who has thrown the weight of his influence on the side of conscription, is trying at the same time to bring the munition factories up to a state of efficiency. In a very impressive speech he warned the House of Commons that "unless we quicken our movements damnation will befall the great cause for which so much blood has been shed." He told how it took four months to accumulate the stock of shells which were expended in a few days in the vain attempt to break the German line in September. Now, he said, a month and soon, he hoped, a week would produce such a supply. In May, when the Germans were manufacturing 250,000 high explosive shells a day, the British works were only turning out 2500. The manufacturers were then delivering only 16 per cent of what they had promised. But the supply of machine guns is still short and 92 per cent of the casualties are due to these. For such work there are needed 80,000 skilled and 300,000 unskilled workers. Unless the unions can be induced to suspend the rules preventing the employment of unskilled labor, Mr. George fears for the outcome of the war.

The Defense of Salonica

After the conquest of Serbia the Anglo-French troops retreated southward into Greece and the Serbs westward into Albania. It was the expectation of the Allies at Salonica that the Austro-German and Bulgarian troops would follow them into Greece and accordingly they began to entrench themselves with feverish haste and to rush in all available reinforcements. Since Salonica was at first unfortified and the French and British around Salonica did not number more than a third of what could have been brought against them, it seems likely that they could have been overcome if the Austro-German and Bulgarian troops had continued their advance. But they stopped instead at the Greek border. Whether for the purpose of preparation, or because their real interests lie elsewhere remains to be seen. At any rate, their delay has given the Allies time to encircle Salonica with fortifications, to bring up 1200 guns and to accumulate troops to the number of some 250,000.

General Castelnau, the French Chief of Staff, who has visited Salonica, pronounces it impregnable and says his only fear is lest the enemy should decide not to attack but to stay where they are, which, "in view of our preparations to receive them fittingly, would be a pity." The only sign of hostility against Salonica manifested so far is the appearance of several German aeroplanes flying high over the city. One of the Taubes, apparently mistaking a flock of sheep for the British army, dropt a bomb which killed the shepherd and four of his sheep.

On the suspicion that they were giving information about the defenses, the Austrian, German and Turkish consuls at Salonica have been arrested and transported by order of General Sarvail, the French commander. The papers of the consulates were seized and the consuls with their families and servants, sixty-two altogether, put on board a French vessel for transportation to parts unknown. The Bulgarian consul escaped. The Greek Government has protested against this new violation of Greek neutrality by the Allies.

The War in Albania

On the western side of Serbia there is more activity. The Austrians, who invaded Montenegro from the Sanjak of Novibazar, have been driven back over the frontier into Serbia with a loss of over 2000 in killed and wounded. The Austrian attack upon the other side of Montenegro, tho supported by a vigorous fire from the artillery of the forts and fleet, was also ineffective. The Austrian official reports are non-

44

committal in regard to the fighting in this field.

It seems that the Austrians are trying to gain entrance into northern Albania by way of Dalmatia to the west of Montenegro. The Austrian territory extends down along the Adriatic coast nearly to Antivari, the sole Montenegrin port, and this is only fifty miles from Scutari, the chief town of northern Albania, now the headquarters of the Serbian Government and the rallying point of its scattered troops.

It is said that the Serbian soldiers which have been collected and reorganized in Albania number about 80,000. They are being supplied with food and ammunition by the Italians, who hold the ports of Durazzo and Avlona on the Albanian coast. A squadron of five Austrian destroyers from Cattaro entered the harbor of Durazzo and sunk two vessels there but one of the destroyers struck a mine and another was sunk by shell fire. The Italian authorities have expelled from Durazzo William W. Howard, of New York, secretary of the Albanian Relief Fund, and other Americans who were engaged in the succor of the starving Albanians and Serbian refugees. The 30,000 Austrian prisoners which the Serbian troops managed to take with them into Albania when they were driven out of Serbia, have been turned over to Italy and are now interned in Sardinia.

The Bulgars who pursued the Serbs into Albania overtook and defeated them at Elbasan, in the middle of Albania and about forty miles east of Durazzo. The Bulgars are said to be still moving westward, seemingly with the intention of attacking the Italians at Durazzo, perhaps with the aid of the Austrians by land or sea. The Albanians, hereditary enemies of the Serbs, are taking advantage of the opportunity to rob and slay the helpless Serbian refugees out of revenge for the devastation of Albania by the Serbs three years ago.

The peak of Hartmanns-Weilerkopf The peak of Hartmanns-Weilerkopf which figures so prominently in the despatches from time to time stands on the southeastern verge of the Vosges mountains, overlooking the Rhine valley. From its name one would presume it to be German, but whether it is now in German hands or French cannot yet be told, for Paris and Berlin during the past fortnight have been claiming alternate or simultaneous victories. The crest of the peak, over 3000 feet above sea-level, was captured by the French last April, or at least they gained a lodgement there, for the Germans still held part of the summit. The opposing trenches were in fact only a few yards apart and sharp-shooting has been incessant between them.

On December 21 the French took the offensive and drove the Germans from their trenches on the summit and the southeastern slope. The Germans came back on the following day and regained most of their lost positions. This seesaw conflict continued all thru Christmas week, but on the whole it appears that the French are gaining ground and are now in possession of the slope of Hartmann's Weilerkopf as well as the valley lying between this peak and the lesser elevation of Hirzenstein, a mile to the southeast. Whether this attack portends another attempt of the French at the conquest of Alsace remains to be seen.

Fighting continues at various points along the western front, especially in the Champagne, Artois and Ypres sectors where the Allies tried to break thru last summer. Artillery duels, aeroplane raids and mine explosions are reported every day, but there are as yet no definite signs of a serious offensive on either side.

More Plotters Indicted The long inquiry of a Federal grand jury in New York concerning the conduct of Labor's National Peace Council, an organization formed in June last, but not regarded with favor by the labor unions, ended last week with the indictment of eight men. These are Congressman Frank Buchanan, of the Seventh Illinois District, who was president of the Council for a time; ex-Congressman H. Robert Fowler, of the Twenty-fourth Illinois District, a lawyer, who was the organization's chief counsel; Captain Franz von Rintelen, of the German navy, an intimate friend of the Kaiser and of Admiral von Tirpitz, who came to this country in April last to instigate strikes at munition factories and to force intervention in Mexico by means of a movement under the leadership of Huerta, and who fled by means of a fraudulent passport and is now a prisoner in the Tower of London; David Lamar, the "Wolf of Wall Street," who was recently found guilty of impersonating Congressman A. Mitchell Palmer in a financial transaction; Frank S. Monnett, formerly Attorney General of Ohio, a member of the organization's executive council; Jacob C. Taylor, Buchanan's successor in the presidency, vice-president of the cigar-makers' union; Henry B. Martin, the Council's secretary, and Herman Schulteis, an associate of Lamar. The indictment was found under the Sherman Anti-Trust law. It accuses the men of conspiring to restrain foreign trade and commerce by instigating strikes in munition factories, inducing employees to quit work, bribing officers of labor unions to prevent manufacture and shipment, and using other means as occasion might arise. The penalty is one year in prison, or a fine of $5000, or both. It is the first indictment of its kind in the movement against plotters here. The jury had been at work since the first week in September. Another jury will now make similar investigations. The District Attorney says this is only a beginning.

Congressman Buchanan at first said he was immune, because of his office, but after a time he consented to plead, and with others gave bonds. It is alleged that von Rintelen expended about $400,000 upon the work of the Peace Council before he ran away. Buchanan says the prosecution is a conspiracy to check his fight against militarism. He has introduced in the House a resolution designed to cause the impeachment of District Attorney Marshall, who conducted the inquiry. Fowler says the prosecution is the Government's answer to his suit (in which Monnett is interested) for damages because of injuries suffered by a woman passenger on the "Lusitania." The Government, it is asserted in this suit, should have excluded munitions from the ship. Monnett says the shipment of munitions is illegal and criminal. Fowler declares that the prosecution is the work of the Trusts.

Anton E. Mente, the Austro-Hungarian whose room in New York was found to be full of bombs and bomb material, has been sent to prison for one year because he had explosives in a tenement house. He had threatened to blow up a factory in New Jersey. Additional explosions on ships have been reported. In the hold of the British steamship "Inchmoor," loaded with sugar and nearly ready to sail from Brooklyn, fire suddenly broke out in a dozen places, and $100,000 worth of the cargo was destroyed. The "Barksdale," which has returned to New York from Bordeaux, reports that on her recent eastward voyage a bomb exploded in her hold and that the fire destroyed 200 bales of cotton. There have been bomb explosions or fires on 23 ships or barges in the last few months. The American Truth Society has issued a report, signed by Bernard H. Ridder and Jeremiah O'Leary, about the work of its Bank Depositors' Committee against the Anglo-French loan. This report contains a blacklist of fifty-six banks and trust companies and two life insurance companies that favored the loan. It says these "should not be forgotten or forgiven."

Underwood & Underwood

SHE DRIVES LLOYD GEORGE
The Minister of Munitions could not consistently employ a man chauffeur, and Miss Marsh is an efficient substitute

Pan-American Union The Pan-American Scientific Congress at Washington is one of the most notable meetings ever held in this or any other country. In it are sitting eminent representative men from twenty-one republics. From the very beginning the purely scientific purpose of the meeting has been in the background, and the keynote of nearly all the addresses has been Pan-American unity and brotherhood. (See page 68.)

It became known that our Government was proposing a convention or agreement for the arbitration of boundary disputes and to prevent shipment of arms to revolutionist factions. John Barrett, Director General of the Pan-American Union, said that the American nations should form an alliance before the end of the great war to meet the possible aggression of the victors. He would have a new Doctrine requiring South America to come to the defense of the United States, if necessary, as quickly as the United States would oppose unjust attack upon the southern republics. Several delegates spoke for arbitration. A representative of Salvador would have it compulsory and in a Pan-American court. Uruguay's delegates asked for a permanent commission.

An Institute of International Law was formed, with 105 members, five from each republic. Elihu Root is honorary president, and the president is James Brown Scott. This institute hopes to rehabilitate and improve the international code after the war. A Pan-American Union of women was organized at a meeting over which Mrs. Lansing presided, and it voted to erect a building in Washington. Ernesto Quesada, of the Argentine delegation, proposed a confederation of all the

© American Press
PREPAREDNESS IN JAPAN—WHERE THE BOY SCOUTS HANDLE RIFLES

American universities, with an interchange of professors and students. A hymn, the music and words by Chileans, was sung. It had been made for the Congress and it was adopted as the official hymn of Pan-America.

The New Prohibition States In seven states, at midnight on the last day of the old year, the sale or manufacture of intoxicating liquors was prohibited by statute or by laws enforcing constitutional amendments. These states are Iowa, Colorado, Oregon, Washington, Idaho, Arkansas and South Carolina.

In each of them several counties had been enforcing prohibition under local option laws, but they are now to have state-wide prohibition for the first time. More than 3000 saloons, breweries, wholesale liquor houses and distilleries went out of business in the seven states at the end of the year. The number of prohibition states is now eighteen.

There were only 150 saloons left in Idaho, as there had been prohibition in a considerable part of the state. The law there is a drastic one, making the possession of spirituous or malt liquors a crime, the exceptions being wine for sacramental uses and pure alcohol for use in medicine or scientific work. But for these there must be a court order. In South Carolina the dispensary system, used in fifteen of the forty-four counties, is to be known no more. Individuals are permitted to obtain by shipment one gallon of spirituous liquor every month. It is reported that between $2,000,000 and $3,000,000 was expended by residents of Colorado for liquors in the last week of the saloons. There were bargain sales in Iowa in the 502 saloons that were about to be closed. The Washington law permits residents to buy from dealers outside of the state two quarts of spirituous liquor or twelve quarts of beer every twenty days. In Arkansas, agents of the Anti-Saloon League will be on duty to see that the new law is enforced. In Oregon drug stores are not permitted to sell liquor with or without a doctor's prescription, but in any period of four weeks a family may import two quarts of spirituous liquor or twenty-four quarts of malt liquor for personal use.

Underwood & Underwood
SHIVERING AT SALONICA
A British outpost at an exposed point on the fifty-mile defensive line which the Allies have thrown about the Greek port where they are now awaiting the Teuton attacks. It is said that the German schedule calls for the occupation of Salonica on January 15

Higher Wages At the end of the year there were many announcements of increases of wages, and these may fairly be regarded as proofs of prosperity. While several of the additions were due to profitable work on war orders, others were not associated directly with such a cause. The Amoskeag and Stark cotton goods manufacturing companies, in Manchester, New Hampshire, gave 5 per cent to 20,000 employees. Similar action was taken at Nashua, Lowell and Lawrence, and in all the number of cotton mill employees thus benefited was 65,000. It was predicted that eventually the increase would be granted to about 200,000 in this industry. The American Woolen Company gave notice of an increase of not less than 5 per cent for the 35,000 persons employed in its forty-four mills. Following the Brooklyn Rapid Transit Company's additions to the pay of 7000 men, the Interborough Railway Company and two other street railway companies in New York ordered increases for motormen and conductors which affect 14,500 men and amount to $470,000 a year. To the longshoremen at Boston was given an increase of from 2 to 5 cents an hour.

The Calumet and Hecla Copper Company, to which the high price of copper is giving large profits, informed the 14,000 men employed in its mines and on its railroads that they were to have a bonus of 10 per cent every month until July next. An increase of 10 per cent was given by the New Jersey Zinc Company to its employees as a New Year's present. From 5 to 10 per cent was granted to the 3500 men of the Reading Iron Company, and $50,000 in additions was paid by the Thomas B. Jeffrey Company in Wisconsin. To 9000 conductors and porters the Pullman Car Company gave about 10 per cent, or $600,000 a year. Employees of the Allis-Chalmers Iron Company whose salaries were reduced a year ago received checks for the sums that had been taken. The United States Steel Corporation offered 35,000 shares of its common stock to employees at $85, the market price being now about $89. There was no offer last year, but in 1914 the employees took 47,680 shares of the common stock at $57, and 42,826 preferred shares at $105. This year's offer is regarded as foreshadowing resumption of dividend payments on the common stock.

Advances ordered by the Navy Department, in some instances about 10 per cent, affect a considerable number in the navy yards, but there is complaint from the sheet metal workers that both their minimum and their maximum wages have been reduced by nearly 14 per cent.

For the Los Angeles Crime The dynamite explosion by which the building of the Los Angeles *Times* was wrecked in 1910, and twenty-one employees were killed, is recalled by the conviction in Los Angeles, last week, of Matthew A. Schmidt, as an accomplice of the McNamara brothers in that crime. Four years ago James B. McNamara, who confest that he placed the bomb, was found guilty and sent to prison for life. For a long time Schmidt could not be found, but he was arrested in New York City in February last thru the efforts of William J. Burns. He now goes to prison for life, this punishment having been fixed by the jury that found him guilty of murder in the first degree.

It will be remembered that the Los Angeles *Times* was owned and edited by General Harrison Gray Otis, who had incurred the enmity of certain labor unions and their officers. David Caplan, another man accused of being an accomplice of the McNamaras, was arrested near Seattle in February last. He is in jail, awaiting trial.

The Situation in Mexico Nearly all of Villa's soldiers, and all of his leading officers except General Rodriguez, have surrendered and taken amnesty. To each soldier the Carranza Government gave $10 and a railroad pass to his home, but a considerable number joined Carranza's army. Villa himself, with about 400 men, remained in the mountains, west of Chihuahua City. His family has arrived in Havana. There are seventeen in the party. One report says that Villa is going south to join Zapata. But he holds General Obregon's brother, Francisco, as a hostage for amnesty to himself. In a proclamation brought to El Paso by cowboys he says that he intended to leave Mexico and join his family, but that after he resigned his command he was informed that the promises and agreements upon which he had relied had already been broken. "Because of that," he adds, "and because I believe that my people will never accomplish peace, liberty and justice under the present controlling elements, I will devote my time and energies to opposing those unfair elements to the end that the objects of the revolution may be realized." The thirty men of the Pearson plant whom he held for ransom have been released and are in Texas.

Carranza has ordered by decree that his successor, if he should "default," shall be the head of his Cabinet, or Minister of Foreign Affairs, and not a military leader. This excludes Obregon. He has not yet said that he will permit the Red Cross and the Rockefeller Foundation to take up the work of stamping out the epidemic of typhus fever. It is said that our consul at Juarez, Mr. Edwards, recently called him "a bull-headed old fool." Our State Department will inquire about this. At Washington the appointment of Henry P. Fletcher, a Republican, now Ambassador to Chile, to be Ambassador to Mexico, is said to be opposed by influential Democrats. Republicans also, it is asserted, may oppose confirmation on the ground that there is no real Government in Mexico to which an ambassador can be accredited. It is also said that they may use the appointment as the text for an attack upon the President's Mexican policy. Henry Lane Wilson, who was Minister to Mexico when President Madero was assassinated, declares that Carranza's Government must fall, because Carranza is incompetent, arrogant, bombastic and conceited. He repeatedly warned Madero, he also says, and urged him to seek safety in flight. With the consent of Huerta he procured for him a special train which was ready to take him to Vera Cruz, when Huerta intercepted a telegram in which Madero's wife urged the Governor of Vera Cruz to organize a revolt to support her husband upon his arrival. This changed the attitude of Huerta. But he promised that Madero's life should not be taken. Mr. Wilson adds that he has never been able to ascertain in what manner and by whom Madero was assassinated.

PACIFISTS AT PLAY
The Reverend Doctor Charles Frederic Aked of San Francisco leaping over the Reverend Doctor Jenkin Lloyd Jones of Chicago, on board the Ford peace ship, *Oscar II*, outbound

FROM STATE TO STATE

CALIFORNIA: The California Art Club, of Los Angeles, has begun work upon a plan to popularize art thruout this state. Representative collections of the works of Western painters will be sent to cities and towns, accompanied by lecturers qualified to explain the purposes of the artists and to awaken interest in the art. The working side of the artists' craft will be described, colored slides of details being shown not only of the collections, but also of other notable works of art. The general purpose of the movement is to show that art is not for high days and holidays, nor for the intellectual appreciation of the few, but is for the daily life of every one.

COLORADO: The children of Colorado Springs, aided and directed by a local chapter of the Daughters of the American Revolution, gave the birds of the Pike's Peak region a merry Christmas by loading down the branches of a large tree in Monument Valley Park with dainties especially pleasing to the feathered flocks. The supply was sufficient to last for several days, and the children and their elders were so much interested in seeing the birds' enjoyment that it has been determined to serve the banquet regularly thruout the winter season.

CONNECTICUT: Other cities in this state are watching with interest the movement started by the New Haven Civic Federation for a complete survey of that city's various departments with a view to ascertaining just how much overlapping of duties there is and how the municipality may be managed with more efficiency. At the instance of the federation the city manager plan is to be carefully considered. City managers from other parts of the country are to be invited to address public meetings. The federation is planning to establish a window in a central location where the work of its several committees may be displayed for the enlightenment of the public as to what is being done under the present city government.

DELAWARE: Never before have the people of this state been so busy as they are now, nor have they ever before handled so much money. Most of this prosperity is due, of course, to the Great War, but it is not confined to the business of making munitions. In Wilmington alone there are no less than 200 industrial establishments producing other things, and nearly every one of them is running to capacity. The three shipyards in the old Swede settlement, the fifteen leather factories, the huge fiber industries, the four car shops and twenty-one foundries and machine shops are all either employing full forces of workmen or trying to get them. A year ago it was estimated that there were 6000 unemployed in the city. Since that time more

than 15.000 are said to have been put to work.

FLORIDA: The Florida First Commission, the permanent organization of which was recently effected, has started upon a nation-wide campaign of advertising in which it purposes to show the advantages of Florida not only as a winter resort, but as an all-year place of residence and of business. Altho the commission was formed too late to give the founders an opportunity for canvassing the entire state and too late to expect much return this winter, it has deemed it advisable to begin the advertising campaign at once. More than thirty Florida cities, thru their chambers of commerce or boards of trade, are giving aid to the commission. All the money contributed is to go for advertising, since the members of the commission serve without pay and there are to be no headquarters expenses.

GEORGIA: The State Board of Entomology has issued charts showing the exact progress made by the boll weevil in Georgia and fixing the bounds of present infested territory. The boundary line begins at Newsville on the Alabama state line and runs eastwardly thru Tallapoosa, Bremen, Billarp and Chapel Hill to a point just north of Red Oak, where it turns to the south, passing thru or near Brooks, Molena, Thunder, Junction City and Americus. Here it veers toward the southeast and, passing thru Philema, Shingler and Doaia and slightly east of Valdosta, ends at the Florida state line. The infested territory is all in the western and southwestern part of the state. Together with the twenty mile safety zone along its border it comprises almost a quarter of the state.

KANSAS: Altho the demand for new Kansas corn is so great that in many counties the farmers cannot husk it fast enough to keep up with the demand, the crop is so abundant that the cribs and warehouses of the state are inadequate and thousands of bushels are piled upon the ground. The yield has run all the way from fifty to 100 or more bushels to the acre, and the price ranges from 55 to 65 cents a bushel right from the field, before any shrinkage has taken place.

KENTUCKY: The Cumberland Telephone and Telegraph Company is removing its system of cables in the business section of Louisville, installing a complete new and improved equipment and making a net profit of about $10,000 on the change. The explanation is that the company bought the new equipment before the European war began, and the total cost of the new system, including purchase price, transportation to Louisville, storage and installation, amounts to about $10,000 less than the old copper in the worn out system is worth as junk at the present prices.

MICHIGAN: The "I Will" club, a Detroit organization which started with a membership of more than 1000 motorists, is making an energetic campaign against reckless driving. Not only are the members pledged to careful driving themselves, but they are to report all cases of careless driving that they see. Moreover they are enlisting the aid of all the public school children and of every citizen who can be reached thru public mass meetings and lavish advertising. Their purpose is to interest everybody in the city in careful driving and then to keep the interest permanently alive.

RHODE ISLAND: At the instance of Secretary Dunn of the State Board of Agriculture and Professor R. B. Cooley of the Rhode Island State College, dairy farmers thruout the state are organizing cow testing associations. each having a membership of from twenty-four to twenty-six farmers. Members pay a small fee for each cow owned, thus enabling the association to hire an expert who spends a day a month on each farm. His work is to keep an exact account of what each cow produces in milk and butter fat and what her maintenance costs. By this means members are learning which of their cows are profitable and which are merely "boarders." Also the associations, thru coöperative buying, are saving much on food and supply bills.

SOUTH CAROLINA: The Columbia Chamber of Commerce is reorganizing upon a wholly new plan. The membership is to be divided into five main bureaus and a trade group, the chairman of each to be a member of a central board of directors. Each bureau is to be a separate entity, with secretaries and special committees, and is to have charge, under the board of directors, of all matters pertaining to its particular department. There is also to be a members' council, made up of representatives of the trade and professional subdivisions, whose duty it shall be to provide for a public forum where short talks by representative men may stimulate an intelligent public interest in matters affecting the trade and welfare of Columbia. The council is to have no power of action, but is to recommend action by the directory.

SOUTH DAKOTA: The United States Supreme Court has decided against South Dakota in its long contested express tax cases. In 1909 the state assessed the Wells-Fargo and the American express companies on their gross earnings instead of on their property within the state. Judge Willard of the United States District Court decided against the state. The state took no appeal, but in the next year assessed the companies in the same way, and Judge Elliott of the United States District Court sustained it. The companies appealed, and now the Supreme Court has reversed Judge Elliott.

TEXAS: The Texas Economic League is a new organization formed by leading business men of all parts of the state. It will endeavor, thru the enlightment of the public, to promote the interests of those engaged in productive pursuits and allied industries and seek a more equitable distribution of the fruits of labor among those employed in producing, manufacturing and distributing the products of the farm, forest and mine. The slogan of the league will be "Citizenship First," and those applying for membership will be asked to place Federal, state and community citizenship, in the order named, above class or partisan interests.

UTAH: By installing fourteen portable schoolhouses. Salt Lake City has solved the problem of housing its surplus school children without straining its finances to the breaking point. These buildings, set up on the grounds of the most congested schools, cost about $1500 apiece and accommodate, all told, about 1100 pupils. Each building consists of two large rooms with a hallway between. which is used as a cloak room. The heating, ventilating and lighting are said to be even better than in some of the large, expensive buildings.

VIRGINIA: The Virginia press and public are showering praise upon the militia, and especially upon Major E. W. Bowles of the Richmond Light Infantry Blues, for the skilful manner in which the difficult situation at Hopewell following the fire was handled. On the night of the fire Governor Stuart ordered the Richmond Blues and the Richmond Grays there. As senior officer Major Bowles took command and at once made martial law effective by confiscating all the liquor in the town and disarming all the citizens and visitors. This immediate and thoro action prevented drunkenness, rioting and looting. It is said that 5000 gallons of whiskey and many hundred weapons were captured before the rough element had time to make use of them.

WASHINGTON: A statewide game of hide and seek has been going on ever since the Supreme Court of Washington decided, early in December, that the state prohibition law was constitutional and must go into effect on January 1. The law provides that for personal use twelve quarts of beer or two quarts of other liquor may be imported every twenty days, but many persons who feared this might not be enough for them and others who shrank from the public manner in which these importations must be made are said to have devoted the last days of open selling to laying in large stocks and hiding them away. The fact, however, that any citizen may make complaint without waiting for officers of the law to move, gives hope to the prohibitionists that the law will be fairly effective.

48

THE WEST AND PREPAREDNESS

BY ARTHUR CAPPER

GOVERNOR OF KANSAS

THE people of Kansas, and I believe the people of the entire West, are strongly opposed to a reversal of the country-old policy of the United States—to adopting a policy of militarism, under the specious name and the false pretense of "preparedness."

In Kansas, we believe the clamor for the immediate beginning of a hurried program of warship-building, to extend over a series of years, is the result of popular hysteria, deliberately engendered in the minds of the hyper-impressionable and the timid by a systematic propaganda conducted by interests having ulterior motives.

It is not against preparedness in the true meaning of the word that we protest, but against the evident attempt to stampede the American people into a hasty and ill-considered adoption of that policy of militarism which has demonstrated so tragically its futility and wickedness in Europe.

As the army and navy may not be directly responsible for the appalling waste which for years has attended their maintenance — the wretched pork-barrel and log-rolling system of Congress rendering any well-planned expenditures impossible —the people of the West would look upon this clamor for more millions with equanimity if they had some assurance that the money to be poured out, should the program be adopted, would be expended wisely, honestly and efficiently, and not go to fatten favored contractors or be frittered away in favored communities. And if our present state of defense, on which we are spending so much, is so wretchedly poor and inadequate that it amounts to no defense, shall we throw away twice as much money on it instead of first investigating and checking the waste and extravagance of our present mismanagement?

It is interesting to note that Kansas, the "emotional state" where vagaries are supposed to grow wild and hair-brained cranks to abound, has been singularly sane in its determination not to join the stampede to militarism. Our people are not "seeing things" at night. Neither the popular magazines, the more popular movies, the war news, nor the wild talk of invasion, have created panic among them. And yet, should the unspeakable calamity of war ever befall our country, Kansas, the state which sent a larger percentage of its

Paul Thompson

GOVERNOR CAPPER

sons into the Civil War than any other state, could be depended on to contribute its full share of treasure and men to the nation's defense.

Here is a list of organizations that have formally gone on record against so-called "preparedness" in Kansas:

The Kansas State Teachers' Association, in a convention of 6,000; the Kansas State Grange, with 24,000 members; the Kansas State Farmers' Union, with 21,000 members; the Kansas State Federation of Labor, with 30,000 members; the Kansas State Mutual Insurance Association, with 60,000 members; the Kansas Association of Machinists, with 7200 members; more than 100 churches, 150 fraternal organizations and 40 women's clubs.

Up to this time not one organization of any description has declared for the "preparedness" program in the State of Kansas.

Our people are convinced this clamor for increased armament comes from two easily traced sources.

On the one hand, we have emotional, excitable persons who become alarmists, who see a spook in every shadow and a murderer in every stranger. They are easily played upon by the demagog. A sensational article in a magazine; a subsidized picture at a movie show; a melodramatic grouping of waxworks in a window display—for which some financially interested person pays—is sufficient to upset them. They are given to violent action and re-action. They are temperamentally hyster-

ical, unsafe, a constant menace to their community and the nation. Their alarm is genuine; their fears frightful to them; but it is the duty of sane and better balanced citizens to quiet their fears, allay their alarms and help them regain poise.

On the other hand, we have quite apparently a well-organized propaganda systematically and cruelly promoting this war hysteria in the United States. Manufacturers who see fat contracts looming ahead of them are deliberately playing upon the imaginations of the excitable and the fears of the timid, in order to stampede the nation into a campaign of extravagant expenditures, regardless of all other consequences.

Back of the manufacturers are the professional fighting men of the nation whose trade is war—men whose training and environment have made them military above everything else and warped them to the narrow point of view of the military specialist. They are schooled to glory in war. Their life-long ambition is to practise actual warfare in a great campaign conducted on a modern scale. They believe might makes right. In bloodshed they see the regeneration of the race, the development of the stern and manly virtues and a panacea for all ills.

The manufacturers, with their heads turned by the prospect of easy profits and the men of war aroused by the prospect of a real fight, or by greater professional opportunities, fully realize that they must strike now if they are to gain their ends. They must take advantage of the scare. Hence the adroitly worked-up panic and the insistent demand that war preparations begin *now*—without waiting the outcome of the European war or to see what lessons may be learned from that conflict.

We can see, therefore, only unending misfortune in this preparedness step. Let the United States arm itself to the teeth and straightaway the rapidly growing republics of South America, with their enormous natural resources and teeming populations, will take up arms in self-protection. They never have trusted us, never have understood us. If we begin arming now, history will see the old-world blunder repeated in this hemisphere. We are human. We shall soon be carrying a chip on our shoulders; the bully in us will assuredly assert itself and will be the means of turning these western nations into armed camps, just as occurred in

Europe. Then a coalition against the feared and misunderstood United States by these South American Latins will bring about the inevitable conflagration we now see as a result of this policy in Europe, But long before this we shall lose their trade. They will fear to build up a dreaded rival by buying goods of him.

But more than the commercial loss, a greater calamity even than the loss of human lives which attends warfare, is the deterioration of national character which follows the policy of militarism. We now are a peaceful people, loving the ways of peace. Given over to the rule of jingoes we shall become a swaggering, aggressive, bullying nation that puts its trust in might rather than right. The reign of peace on earth may, as the alarmists tell us, be a long way off, but surely it cannot be hastened by transforming this great nation into a military camp.

I have great faith in the efficacy of economic pressure as a defensive measure. I do not think that the idea embodied in the proposal of a "League to Enforce Peace" is at all visionary. An international court is as possible among civilized nations as are courts for the adjustment of disputes between individuals, The combined forces of the powers, economic and military, against any one of their number who fails to take its case before an international court, could hardly fail to keep the peace. A cycle of preparedness in Europe and of the very sort now demanded with such clamor for the United States, has resulted in the greatest cataclysm of history. Are we prepared to pay that price?

I think not. I do not believe that the sober-minded people of this country will be frightened by any bogeyman into so wicked a program. Unless we go mad in the heat of a political campaign, the wave of hysteria will recede and the United States will again put her trust in open dealing in diplomacy; in common honesty between nations; in right rather than in might.

Topeka, Kansas

I RESOLVE TO BE RESTLESS

BY ELINOR BYRNS

I AM a restless woman. Almost all my chosen companions are restless women. When physicians, essayists, and timid gentlemen whose place is the home, rail at the modern spirit of unrest and at the women who are a menace to society, they are thinking of us. Their attacks haven't troubled us, however. We have been too much absorbed in the activities induced by mental and moral unrest to analyze ourselves or to weigh the words of our critics.

From the accounts in the daily press I judge that my friends are as restless as ever. As for myself, I decided on November the third (the day after election) to enjoy a period of rest. Since that time I have done nothing but keep house, earn my living outside the home, acquire some new clothes and some made-overs, and rest between-whiles.

I was not lured to Paterson by free speech and Gurley Flynn. I have not been to Washington to lobby congressmen with the Union or to gnash my teeth over the Union with the National Suffrage Association. I have not been cruising on the Oscar II. I have not been to a single committee meeting or protest dinner. I have no notion what Margaret Sanger is doing, and I have not made a speech on any subject. Result? My temper is improved, my nerves are rested, I look five years younger, I am enjoying life, my family and friends are enjoying me? Not at all. I have been low in my mind. I have felt for two weeks as tho I were going to have grippe. I have been unduly critical of my family, my friends, and even our household treasure; and I realize they have all been bored with me. Worst of all I have had again that horribly letdown, passive feeling to which I said farewell ten years ago, when I stopped thinking whether I was a lady or not. So, these last few days I have been searching a cause for my disquieting symptoms. My search has forced me to a few conclusions on the subject of unrest. I give them to you for what they are worth.

Consider, first, the daily routine of a restless woman. I'll be personal because it is easier, but I understand that the days of other restless women are like mine only more so. Well, when I am in the full tide of unrestful activity I never have to force myself to get up. I am forced out of bed by the ringing of the telephone. At once, my brain has to begin working at full speed; otherwise I find myself committed to a speech or a committee for which I have no desire, or refusing to participate in a stunt which I might enjoy.

After this telephone stimulus— usually repeated several times between bed and breakfast—I dress quickly because I am eager to start my day. I have no time to sit sadly in front of my mirror counting my gray hairs and wrinkles or wondering whether I shall have a double chin after I am forty. At breakfast I give treasure her directions for the day. She receives them graciously, knowing I shall be too tired at night to consider anything but results. If she wants to fly around in the morning and go to the movies in the afternoon, she may. If she wants to dawdle all day over four hours' work, she may. The dinner is always good, she is happy, and so am I. The menus for the day I have made out on the way home to dinner the evening before. It is much easier, you know, to plan good meals before dinner, when you are hungry, than after breakfast, when food seems absolutely uninteresting. Moreover, after breakfast I haven't time.

One frequently hears of women who each morning sadly leave their homes for their dreary toil. They are undoubtedly women who are doing work they don't like, work which offers them no opportunities, work which is in no sense creative. But I always start out happily, being just as glad to leave the home in the morning as I am to get back at night —which is saying a good deal. And I actually look forward to the moment when I settle myself on the train and open my newspaper. It's a poor paper, indeed, which doesn't in each edition give a revolutionist like me new cause for anger, increased desire for activity. If by any chance the news of the day fails to furnish a burning issue—socialistic, feministic, or what not—I can always find one in the editorials. Second in interest to the finding of a burning issue is reading what my friends have done by way of making news in the last twenty-four hours. Those of us whose unrestful activity is a bit limited by the necessity for earning a living, take, you see a real and stimulating pride in the reported doings of our more conspicuous friends who are able to give all their time to unrest.

After I get to town I begin at once to work as hard as I can, because my mind is already alert. My experience is that anyone who gets up reluctantly, dreams over her toilette, and regards commuting as a dreary means to an end, instead of an interesting preface to a day, is not thoroly awake for an hour after she begins to work.

Lunch—well, lunch may mean malted milk with an egg in it, if I want the hour free to distribute leaflets on something or other, or to help in a suffrage publicity stunt. It may mean conspiring with a few trusted friends at a woman's club or a quiet restaurant. It may mean talking while we eat with some one who wants me to do some work for money. At any rate, there is always something to look forward to in the middle of the day.

Then there is tea. As many days in the week as I can find time for it, I tea and talk things over—don't ask me what things; I am always amazed to realize how many things there are—or combine a committee meeting with tea. Before tea is well over it is of course dinner time. Sometimes I dine with a friend at her house, or apartment, or flat, or studio (following the unrestful life means friends who are far apart financially), so that we can conveniently go together to some meeting; sometimes at a club, so that we can 'work on something connected with a Cause; sometimes at a gay restaurant, if we want a complete change before beginning an evening of uplift. And all these evenings make me enjoy the other evenings, when I have nothing to do but go home, sew in fresh neck things, write notes and telephone—always with the vision before me of going to bed early and reading foolish magazine stories till I fall asleep.

There is a great deal of hard work as well as talk and food involved in unrest. Numerous electors of the State of New York said to me, while I was watching at the polls on Election day, "Now that I see you care enough about the vote to stay here all day and work, I think you ought to have it." Apparently those gentlemen had no notion that November 2 was the most restful day any of us suffrage campaigners had known for months. I thought of the evening when I went to Bayonne after an exhausting day's work in Manhattan, and made seven speeches, talking almost continuously—tho probably not intelligently—from eight till eleven-thirty, and reaching home at one. I thought of last parade day—the climax of weeks of parade work—when I was out on the cold, windy streets from noon till nine in the evening, without food (or drink) and with my only peaceful moments those when I was marching up Fifth avenue. And I thought of suffrage conventions when for a week we work from seven in the morning till three the next morning, doing more business (so the newspaper men say) than any body of men in convention.

Perhaps it was thinking of these things—and many more—which made me decide next day to take a rest. But now that I have suffered the evil effects of restfulness, I have come to a realization of the blessings of unrest. In the first place, unrest keeps us well. We have no time to imagine ourselves ill, and we lead lives of healthful activity. If you are looking for frail, worn-out women, will you find them speaking on a street corner, or managing a mass meeting? No, you must look in houses, shops, and hotels for women who have plenty of money and no work. You must look for women who do uncongenial work in factories, shops, or offices, and never have any fun. Or you must look for women whose lives are so full of household drudgery they have no time and no strength to uplift themselves or to give inspiration to their children. We restless women have work we like plus more work plus stimulating comradeship plus absorbing interest in something bigger and more important than ourselves.

In the second place, unrest saves time for us. Everybody knows we are busy, we restless women, so our neighbors don't drop in for a moment and spend hours telling us scandal; our out of town relatives aren't insulted when we give them the name of a professional shopper instead of doing their errands ourselves; and we no longer feel obliged to look for bargains for our own wardrobes; we go to a good place, buy one expensive garment, and wear it on all occasions, our friends tactfully assuming that we haven't time to change. But our greatest time-saver is the fact that we soon lose all desire for popularity, as evidenced by many social engagements—which are not really social—and week-ends which tire us rather than rest us. We say we are too busy to go, and then that hostess never invites us again, or invites us to something worth while. And then perhaps we find that, between waves of unrest, we actually have a little time for gardening, for reading, or for visiting the friends who are restless in spirit, but temporarily kept in a rut by poverty or babies.

Lastly, unrest makes us happy. If you can't guess why from what I have said before, any explanation of mine won't convince you. Seriously, the more I think of the many women I know, and the many women I've read about—good women, bad women, passive women, intriguing women, selfish women, charitable women —the more firmly I believe that we restless women here in New York this minute (for I am restless again from now on) are having a better time than any women in the world ever had before. And there is just a chance, you know, that we may be doing the world some good.

New York City

I SHALL GROW OLD

BY MARGUERITE O. B. WILKINSON

I shall grow old; when the wild earth is calling
  I shall sit quietly, at last, nor go
To race the quickened winds where rain is falling
  In woods I used to know.

Tho I still feel the lure of wings that flutter
  Across the bayou on the edge of day, .
And of the silver stream where quick fish scutter,
  I shall not go, but stay.

Yet I shall smile, and smiling shall remember
  The streams I forded and the trout I caught,
Or the leaf-kindled fires of mild November
  And the strange peace they brought, .

Glory of earth in her midsummer madness,
  Glory of great, grave trees and sunny sea,
The swimmer's lithe dominion won in gladness,
  In youth and health set free. !

I shall be glad of sunburn and rough going,
  Of weariness that found a perfect rest
Where our firm mother earth made ready, showing
  Her rough and rugged breast.

I shall grow old—but memories strong and tender
  · Shall give me joy while earth's wild song is sung;
The great, glad earth I know, in all her splendor—
  With her I have been young!

Macmillan

JOHN MASEFIELD, POET

THE MAN WHOM MANY READERS REGARD AS THE OUTSTANDING FIGURE OF PRESENT DAY ENGLISH POETRY CAME TO THIS
COUNTRY ON JANUARY 5 FOR AN EIGHT-WEEK LECTURE TOUR THRU THE EAST AND MIDDLE
WEST. HE HAS BEEN SHOWERED WITH INVITATIONS

FOUR OF JOHN MASEFIELD'S POEMS

A man whose most significant work lies in his long narrative poems is not to be lightly anthologized in a page. But here is one poem that expresses Masefield's purpose, and three others which the editors of The Independent happen to like particularly. They are reprinted from "Salt Water Ballads" by courtesy of the publishers, the Macmillan Company.

A CONSECRATION

Not of the princes and prelates with periwigged charioteers
Riding triumphantly laurelled to lap the fat of the years—
Rather the scorned—the rejected—the men hemmed in with the spears;

The men of the tattered battalion which fights till it dies,
Dazed with the dust of battle, the din and the cries,
The men with the broken heads and the blood running into their eyes.

Not the be-medalled commander, beloved of the throne,
Riding cock-horse to parade when the bugles are blown,
But the lads who carried the koppie and cannot be known.

Not the ruler for me, but the ranker, the tramp of the road,
The slave with the sack on his shoulders pricked on with the goad,
The man with too weighty a burden, too weary a load.

The sailor, the stoker of the steamers, the man with the clout,
The chantyman bent at the halliards pulling a tune to the shout,
The drowsy man at the wheel and the tired look-out.

Others may sing of the wine and the wealth and the mirth,
The portly presence of potentates goodly in girth;—
Mine be the dirt and the dross, the dust and scum of the earth!

Theirs be the music, the color, the glory, the gold;
Mine be a handful of aches, a mouthful of mold.
Of the maimed, of the halt and the blind in the rain and the cold—

Of these shall my song be fashioned, my tales be told.
AMEN.

C. L. M.

In the dark womb where I began
My mother's life made me a man.
Thru all the months of human birth
Her beauty fed my common earth.
I cannot see, nor breathe, nor stir,
But thru the death of some of her.

Down in the darkness of the grave
She cannot see the life she gave.
For all her love, she cannot tell
Whether I use it ill or well,
Nor knock at dusty doors to find
Her beauty dusty in the mind.

If the grave's gates could be undone,
She would not know her little son,
I am so grown. If we should meet
She would pass by me in the street,
Unless my soul's face let her see
My sense of what she did for me.

What have I done to keep in mind
My debt to her and womankind?
What woman's happier life repays
Her for those months of wretched days?
For all my mouthless body leeched
Ere birth's releasing hell was reached?

What have I done, or tried, or said
In thanks to that dear woman dead?
Men triumph over women still,
Men trample women's rights at will,
And man's lust roves the world untamed.

* * * * *

O grave, keep shut lest I be shamed.

PRAYER

When the last sea is sailed, when the last shallow's charted,
When the last field is reaped and the last harvest stored,
When the last fire is out and the last guest departed,
Grant the last prayer that I shall pray, be good to me, O Lord.

And let me pass in a night at sea, a night of storm and thunder,
In the loud crying of the wind thru sail and rope and spar,
Send me a ninth great peaceful wave to drown and roll me under
To the cold tunny-fish's home, where the drowned galleons are.

And in the dim green quiet place, far out of sight and hearing,
Grant I may hear at whiles the wash and thresh of the sea foam
About the fine, keen bows of the stately clippers steering
Towards the lone northern star and the fair ports of home.

TEWKESBURY ROAD

It is good to be out on the road, and going one knows not where,
Going thru meadow and village, one knows not whither nor why;
Thru the gray light drift of the dust, in the keen, cool rush of the air,
Under the flying white clouds, and the broad blue lift of the sky.

And to halt at the chattering brook, in the tall green fern at the brink
Where the harebell grows, and the gorse, and the fox-gloves purple and white;
Where the shy-eyed, delicate deer troop down to the brook to drink
When the stars are mellow and large at the coming on of the night.

O, to feel the beat of the rain, and the homely smell of the earth,
Is a tune for the blood to jig to, a joy past power of words;
And the blessed green comely meadows are all a-ripple with mirth
Of the noise of the lambs at play and the dear wild cry of the birds.

Copyright, 1914, by John Masefield

EXPLORING THE ROSE

BY· FANNY BULLOCK WORKMAN, F. R. G. S.

THE Rose Glacier, "Siachur" on the Indian survey maps, altho spoken of vaguely by early British travelers, appears until quite recently to have escaped any investigation. The reason for this is doubtless its great inaccessibility. Its tongue or snout lies at the end of the long, wild, sparsely inhabited Nubra valley, in the Eastern Karakoram mountains of Kashmir, the northernmost state of India. The small villages offer almost nothing in the way of supplies to the explorer. Indeed, the last habitation, some seven miles below the glacier tongue, is only a monastery inhabited by Buddhist Lamas.

A still more formidable obstacle is the Nubra River, which issues from the tongue, a seething flood which has to be forded five times. Because of the depth of the water and numerous quicksands in the river bottom, it is dangerous to man or beast between May and September 15th. The three summer months being the only ones in which such a great glacier can be investigated, it can readily be seen that nature has placed formidable barriers to the proper approach to the Rose Glacier by its tongue.

The Nubra valley natives, as an earlier explorer learned, call the glacier "Siachen." Sia means rose and chen, a collection of thorns. The pink wild rose bush bristling with thorns grows luxuriantly both in Baltistan and Nubra far up the high valleys, even on the banks above the glaciers as far as vegetation exists; hence the name means rose bush, or as I have called it, Rose Glacier.

In 1913, after completing some exploration in Baltistan, Dr. Workman and I went to the Saltoro valley, and ·in August ascended the Bilaphon Glacier, crost the Bilaphon Pass, 18,400 feet, and descended to the Rose. We remained nearly three weeks in the region, camping always at hights greater than Mont Blanc, enduring great cold and snow storms lasting two or three days at a time. Still, we managed to explore two of its most im-

Mrs. Fanny Bullock Workman, whose story of her "Recent First Ascents in the Himalaya" was published in The Independent of June 2, 1910, has made many important geographical discoveries in her twenty-five years of mountain climbing and exploration among the peaks and glaciers of the Himalaya. By making the first ascent of one of the Nun Kun peaks (23,300 feet) Mrs. Workman won in 1906 the world mountaineering record for women. She has made nearly twenty pioneer ascents. At the request of President Loubet in 1904 Mrs. Workman was made Officier de l'Instruction Publique, France. She is a member of the American Geographical Society and also a gold medalist of the Club Alpin Français.—THE EDITOR.

portant affluent glaciers and climb a peak of 21,000 feet which showed the importance of the great unexplored ice stream and afforded a glimpse of its distant snowy sources, probably overlooking the Turkestan mountains.

THE ROUGH APPROACH TO TARIM SHEHR
In the background is Junction Peak, 20,856 feet. This was first climbed by Dr. and Mrs. Workman

ON THE GREAT ROSE GLACIER
The upper part of the forty-eight-mile ice river, which Dr. and Mrs. Workman explored. Tarim Shehr peninsula juts into the foreground

But by September 16 a return over the high pass had to be made at the risk of starvation to our caravan and perishing in winter storms. Meantime I had become Rose mad, being imbued with the single desire to return the next summer and with a thoroly organized caravan, including alpine guides and topographer, to visit the sources and have the glacier mapped in detail.

While passing the winter in India I prepared for the coming snow campaign. Two caravans were to work on the glacier, our own, which would include an Italian guide, three porters and native servants, and that of our English surveyor, who traveled with one Italian porter and a native plane-tabler. Besides these I brought with me two Sepoy reservists from the Royal Indian Army, who were to take charge of coolies going to and from the base village to the Rose Glacier with supplies. Then last, but not least, as he proved a thorogoing rascal, was the Srinagar Baba, who was to act as agent and interpreter at the glacier base camps, keep accounts, distribute grain and forward coolies and supplies to us at higher camps.

Altogether a fair sized regiment of us left Srinagar early in June. At Goma village, which was the last valley base, the better part of twenty-four hours was taken up in hearing what had and had not been accomplished in the way of advance preparation by the agent. To my relief I found the topographers, who had preceded us from Kashmir, had already crost the high pass and arrived· on the Rose, ˙so that their work was progressing. Also fifty loads of wood had been carried up to a point below the pass to await further expediting to the Rose. Everything, from a box of matches to a stick of wood, had now to be carried over twenty-four miles of glaciers, which included the Bilaphon Pass, on the backs of men, and of men none too desirous of venturing on such a rough route, and who might desert at any minute. The task was her-

54

culean, but it had to be accomplished. My idea had been to start with 100 coolies and get over as much food as possible at first.

The valley was alive with men and the Parsee said 100 would be ready to start on the day set. The night before he had his coolies ready and present, but when we struck tents in the morning only sixty turned up for loads. The only way was to leave, taking the most necessary things, for it never does to wait on such occasions, so off we tramped, the agent promising to send forty more loaded coolies the next day.

From the Saltoro valley we turned north and ascended the five-mile Ghyari Nala to the foot of the Bilaphon Glacier. Our last grass camp was at 12,000 feet at the base of the boulder-strewn snout of the Bilaphon Glacier. Henceforth all work was strictly mountaineering, moraine clambering for hours on end, followed by difficult marching thru belts of snow pinnacles, or over greatly crevassed ice areas. A mile an hour was not a bad stint for coolies loaded to fifty pounds and over, in such a region.

After two days' hard march camp was pitched on a moraine ridge at 17,000 feet, near the base of the great snow-fields leading up to the pass. Here were found the fifty loads of wood which had been forwarded by the agent. We reached this cold, elevated bivouac in a blinding snow storm which kept us up most of the night beating the snow off the tent roofs from within to prevent their caving in on our heads. This storm lasted sixteen hours, but that was a detail, for one has to exist thru many such, often of longer duration, in high Himalaya.

The usual thing happened afterward. The weather turned gloriously fine, and we had to wait two days to allow the mass of new snow to settle before the pass could be attempted. This storm also prevented the arrival of the second caravan of necessary supplies from Goma.

On a perfect morning, as the caravan was ascending to the pass, I with the porter Chenoz went aside a thousand feet to be photographed near some ice pinnacles. When the snapshot was finished, he and I went on over the snow, intending to join the others at a higher point. Of a sudden, without uttering a word, the porter disappeared a step in front

OUT OF THE DEPTHS
Mrs. Workman resting at the mouth of a deep crevasse from which she had been lifted by the guides' ropes

OVER A GLACIER RIVER
These icy streams, sometimes ten or twelve feet across, had to be crost frequently in the course of a day's march

of me into the glacier. Luckily for me I stopped short and thus did not share his fate. It was not possible to extricate him from the crevasse, eighty feet deep, into which he had fallen, for an hour and a half, and altho he was brought out alive and carefully cared for, he died that night from shock and long exposure under the ice. We waited here two more dreary days, while the guide and porters took the body of their confrère down to the grass region for burial. During this gruesome time, news was brought from the surveyors' camp on the Rose Glacier that a coolie had died of the results of falling into a deep glacier river. This caused a serious panic in that camp.

After ten days, when we had finally crost the Bilaphon Pass, the skies remaining clear, I succeeded in making the first ascent of a beautiful snow peak of 21,000 feet lying west of the pass, which commanded an illuminating view of the Rose Glacier region. Then we went on to the Rose, where base camps were arranged, and the exploration of the upper Rose and its source was at once begun. Even the base camps, where boxes, bags and wood were stacked, were on ice sparsely covered by rock debris, and our own bivouacs beyond these were on snow or glacier ice with one notable exception. This one we were fortunate enough to make on a small mountain spur at the altitude of 18,400 feet in the snow wilderness of the upper Rose plateau en route to the north water-parting, or as I have named it, the Indira Col.

There is just one place on this desert glacier where grass grows from July 15 to September and here burtsa, a woody shrub, the roots of which can be used for fuel, is found. Here the sheep and goats that crost the snowy Bilaphon Pass with us were pastured in charge of a goatherd. It is a large shale promontory, descending from the peaks which form the barrier wall between the Rose and its largest east affluent, which we have named the Tarim Shehr Glacier.

This promontory, ice-bound on three sides by the Rose and its great tributary, lies opposite the point where the expedition first arrived on the glacier, and about it hangs the romance of the Rose. On it several acres of grass hillocks are found at hights varying from 15,700 to 17,000 feet. It is watered by glacial torrents and at a hight of 16,000 feet are two large, limpid blue lakes.

When I was sitting in my tent on the Rose Glacier during our first reconnaissance visit, I looked out after a snow squall just as the sun peered thru a rift in the clouds, transforming the grass on the distant peninsula into patches of golden green. Everywhere else ice, rock and storm reigned. The next day we struck across the three miles of intervening ice to visit this apparent oasis.

It took hours to reach. Distance counted not at all, what with fording ten or more glacier rivers often twelve feet wide, and climbing over stretches of huge corrugated séracs, such as are seen in the illustration. In the afternoon, after a very hard march, the lower grass area, bordering the Rose, was reached. It was certainly most difficult of access. No one, so far as I could learn, had ever been there, not a coolie of ours had ever stepped foot on the promontory, yet —most unfathomable of native mysteries—our coolies said they knew it was a good camping place and called it by the name Tarim Shehr.

The mystery deepened on the discovery not far from camp of a stone circle twelve feet in diameter. The stones of it had lain untouched for years and were covered with lichens. Inside the circle large ibex horns attached to the skulls were piled up certainly by human hands, and these were decayed, falling apart in shreds when touched.

At a higher camp on the same peninsula huge ibex appeared on the scene and grazed calmly within 300 feet of the tents. Large snow partridges flew out from the rocks when disturbed by footsteps. Foxes also made their home here, and we saw footprints of wolves. Coy little tailless mouse-hares ran in and out of the tents, eyeing us shyly; in fact, all the animal life of the region seemed to be concentrated upon Tarim Shehr, the only oasis of the Rose. Saxafraga, gentians, small orchids and edelweiss added life and color to the coarse grass tapis about the tents.

There is a story of this promontory. When I inquired among the learned men of the Saltoro valley as to whether they had any previous knowledge of the Rose, they told me this legend. The old time Baltis, inhabiting the Ghyari Nala, crost the Bilaphon Pass and met the Garkandis of Tarim Shehr, with whom they played polo. The "learned men" did not say how the Garkandis came to the isolated ice region of Tarim Shehr; they only reported that a large Garkandi city was supposed to exist there. The Baltis feared the Garkandis, who are said to have crost to the Ghyari Nala to steal cattle and destroy property in the Balti villages. On one occasion, so runs the legend, they kidnapped one of the best looking Balti women who was working in the fields.

A Balti high priest, Hazret Ameer, happened to be in the village at the time, and he gave the enraged Baltis a "Tawiz," or magic amulet, telling them to put it on the top of the Bilaphon Pass and ordered them to return, not the same way, but via Garkand to their village. The Baltis, having placed the Tawiz on the pass, disobeyed the priest's order and returned the same way from the pass. Soon after a great storm visited Tarim Shehr "and the snow from the mountains slipped and fell upon the

city," destroying it and its people, including those who had stolen the woman. The Balti priests of today say the calamity would have been even greater had the avengers of the woman gone around by Garkand home as ordered by Hazret Ameer, and that had they done so, the Rose Glacier would not now possess even its one fine grass oasis of Tarim Shehr.

The word Tarim in Chinese Turkestan is used for oasis, and the word Shehr in Persian means city. I have given on my map this name to the unique spot, in the heart of the Rose, surrounded by miles of glaciers and ice-girt peaks. As I have several times said, it was very difficult of access. Thus even as a base-camp we were unable to avail ourselves of its sheltering hillocks, and the work of exploration had to be carried on from camps pitched on the glacier ice.

It was on the site of the fabled city of Tarim Shehr that I became fully persuaded that Rose was the most suitable name for this glacier. We were camped there on September 15 of our first visit, in wild weather, waiting to recross the pass to Baltistan.

I had been kept awake late by great gusts of wind rocking my tent and more especially by the loud chanting of the coolies in their camp, which rose above the howling of the wind. Exasperated at last, I threw on a coat and went out into the frigid air to call the guides and have them stop the coolie noise. It was still snowing and blowing on the glacier, but above Tarim Shehr the clouds had broken and a full moon shone with silver splendor on an exquisite scene. As I walked I saw all about me the rolling hillocks covered with large feathery full blown snow roses. It was not an hallucination; they appeared completely formed, altho the snow-covered grass-blades aided no doubt in their composition. I buried my hands in their silvery, cold beauty. A tall snow peak, silvered from base to apex, looked down upon the Rose hills, the chant of the coolies rose stridently, yet in harmony with the now distant roar of the wind, and the moon, hung in a black sky, cast its resplendent light over all. The weird glory of the scene and the discovery of the roses of my Rose Glacier so impressed me that I returned to the tent without stopping the dirge of the coolies, feeling for the first time in years that their voices mingled fittingly with those of nature. I had quite forgotten that the rural Balti always chants prayers to the gods at the full moon, and doubtless on this evening our Baltis

were vigorously exhorting their favorite gods to take them safely back over the dangerous snow pass the next day.

Details of our numerous ice hikes cannot be given. They were in the main carried thru with much success, altho in a summer's Himalayan work it is never possible to do all one plans, particularly when most of one's goals lie from 17,000 to 22,000 feet. To reach a coveted important point of, say, 20,000 feet separated from one's glacier base by twenty miles of ice, may take two or three weeks. Coolie vagaries, non-arrival of supplies, weather conditions come in to interfere.

Of all interesting months I have past in Himalayan work the two seasons spent on the Rose Glacier were perhaps the most stimulating and satisfying. There was just so much time for activity at such hights, six weeks for us and perhaps seven for the surveying party, with forty-eight miles of Rose Glacier and its affluents to map.

It was a race between the weather on the one hand and between one's mental and physical energies on the other, and the prime stimulant of all was uncertainty. We might plan, organize and calculate the number of days and supplies needed for reaching a given objective, yet we seldom turned into our sleeping sacks at night with any certainty that the morrow's work would be accomplished as laid out. But when weather favored us for a week and a watershed, a new group of high peaks, or a snow pass which would lead home by an unknown route was discovered, all hardships and obstacles disappeared from memory in the supreme satisfaction of accomplishment of the tasks before laid out and so necessary to a successful exploration of the Rose. We reached the three most important geographical points on the Rose and had the satisfaction of discovering the water-parting ridge between the Indus River and Chinese Turkestan at this part of the Karakoram and the relation it bears to the Turkestan glaciers.

On reaching the valleys later on by a new route it was the privilege of this expedition to discover, I felt as if nothing ahead were worth the candle. Of what interest was the path seen leading away from the small outpost village arrived at? It would only wind on and on over passes and thru larger villages to the final vitiated air and commonplace environment of railways, motor cars and city civilization. Paths made by others had played no role on the vast snow expanses just left behind.

Paris

WHY I WEAR A SMOCK

By BOUCK WHITE

I REFUSE to dress in the fashion of a world that permits war. A refusal to wear the garment of civilization is an affront to civilization, the most energetic that could be devised, and, exactly because it is an energetic protest, I have adopted it. The hour demands an energetic protest. The murder madness that is upon the world is of unusual violence. And unusual measures are going to be necessary to combat it.

Nowhere in history, not in Babylon in its prime, not in the Rome of magnificent decadence, can I find another era when the money-lust was so unrestrained and universal as now. And this orgy of militarism is the result. War is a combination of the money-makers in one country to tread down and exploit the money-makers in another country.

And this dirty hunger for dollars is going from more to more. So that war, which is the money lust come to its red ripe fruitage, is maturing into grand and fatal fruition. Chemistry and all applied sciences are equipping men with the means of warfare on a scale ever more gigantic, ever more slaughterous. In the five decades since grandfather fell asleep, war, thanks to improvements in transportation, in man's conquest of nature, and his organizing intelligence, has grown fortyfold in frightfulness. I have on my mantelpiece the time fuse of a shrapnel shell which I got this summer at the firing line in Flanders. It is an infernal machine made with a nicety of craftmanship that stamps it as the work of a highly intelligent monster. It gives me an uncanny feeling, as tho I were in the presence of a lunatic of highest education and of diabolic cleverness.

From five months as war reporter in Europe I came back to America this fall; back from a Europe that is passing away in darkness and in blood. I returned to America. And what did I find? An America sobered by the spectacle, and repenting of her own mad dollar mania, whereby she, too, is inviting the curse?

I found an America emptier of head and shallower of heart than when I went away. I found God driven further off, and Mammon more securely in the ascendant.

And among the rulers? In not one man in the seats of the mighty found I a statesmanly realization of the problem. Not one of them could I see pointing to Mammon as the seed and the infallible root of militarism, not one voice calling upon America to pause in her money madness and re-

Bouck White was a radical author and preacher, best known for his book, "The Call of the Carpenter," when he attempted to interrupt the services at the Calvary Baptist Church in New York and was imprisoned for disturbing the peace. He presented his side of this widely discussed case in an article, "Why I Am in Prison," in The Independent for October 26, 1914. He is now serving as the pastor of the Church of the Social Revolution in New York.—THE EDITOR.

turn to a life of fellowship. To the contrary, their only thought was to steer our nation into the same evil torrent, and, by a billion dollar preparedness, make America the next menace to the peace of the world. Oh, yes, I found the peace-peace-peace people and they were a more depressing spectacle than the preparedness crowd. The latter were criminal, but the former were stupid; and stupidity is more harmful to the world than crime. The peace-peace-peace people are very tender toward Mammon, and rage only against Mars. But Mars is the prog-

THE "AFFRONT TO CIVILIZATION"

eny of Mammon—its legitimate and inevitable offspring; by a demonstrated consanguinity, money-worship goes over into musket-worship.

Set thus in the midst of a people that was making great mirth at the moment when war's conflagration is spreading to envelop the earth, what was I to do? This is what I did: I stepped aside from that people. I have separated myself unto the task of telling the awfulness of modern war and its trend toward still more awfulness, unless society can be revolutionized into a scheme of things held together by heart ties instead of cash nexus. To these stupid glorifiers of the Golden Calf, I refuse recognition, even to the extent of wearing the clothes they wear.

Today, leisure class ideas are dominant; and leisure class clothing is, therefore, the fashion. I have thrown in my lot with the toiler class. And I give notice of that fact by wearing a garb that has been consecrated to toil by many thousand years of association therewith. Only by an overturn that will put labor at the top and leisure at the bottom can the world be saved from the red Niagara toward which it is at present swinging. Mammonism, the messenger of militarism, comes up only when men cease to be laborers and seek to exploit other men who are laborers.

To cure the sickness wherewith the present world is sick will not be easy. There is a remedy, but it is neither cheap nor pleasant. The remedy is an overturn—a revaluation of the values of life, whereby we shall find our joy in works of public aggrandizement instead of, as now, in works of private aggrandizement. They who are the pioneers in that work of overturn will have a bitter price to pay.

In an age of blatant materialism with its luxuriousness of raimenting, the churches at least should have been a sanctuary of lofty thinking and lowly living. But they have capitulated, yes have become the sanctuaries of dress and pomp and the prides of life. Judgment must begin at the house of God. I rejoice to be the preacher of a church in New York City where people dare to worship in the uniform of poverty. In assembling ourselves in divine service, we don sacredly the smock that by immemorial ages has been consecrated to toil. We exalt clothing into a religious principle. By every other means, and by this means also, we publish an insurgency against Mammon and the red hell of homicide it has let loose.

New York City

KING AND PEOPLE FLEE FROM SERBIA

OLD KING PETER ON HIS WAY TO ITALY

The aged and troubled monarch consented to leave the army in his son's command and took refuge in Italy after a hard ride thru Albania to Durazzo. Here he is just changing from motor car to horse

REFUGEES STREAMING SOUTHWARD THRU THE TOWN OF TABARI

The negative of this photograph was carried by aeroplane from Scutari in Albania to Durazzo. It was taken by a correspondent attached to King Peter's suite

The New Books

TWO KINDS OF SATIRE

There is an interesting contrast in the viewpoints of the two men who have recently satirized with unusual skill the follies of everyday life. They both write of the same subject—the foibles of humanity—and they both "show them up" without prejudice or favor. But in their methods and their attitudes they differ widely. John Galsworthy is first, last and always a philosopher—and somewhat of a cynic, too. Stephen Leacock is ever the good-natured humorist, offering his readers a word for a laugh, and almost never failing to make the trade. In *Moonbeams from the Larger Lunacy* he has brought together a peddler's pack assortment of fun-making. Spoof, a Sample of a Thousand Guinea Novel is a delicious satire on up-to-date fiction, in which for once "the eternal triangle" finds a brand new solution. Under the head of Afternoon Adventures at My Club are grouped some particularly clever character sketches of the bores that every man must know. Ram Spudd, the New World Singer and Passionate Paragraphs reduce to a delightful absurdity some of the present-day tendencies in literature. But perhaps the best of all is the ingenious suggestion of Education Made Agreeable, in which Mr. Leacock re-writes the romance of Calculus and plays up the journalistic features of Euclid, such as

AWFUL CATASTROPHE
PERPENDICULAR FALLS HEAD-
LONG ON A GIVEN POINT

The Line at C Said to Be Completely Bisected

President of the Line Makes Statement Etc.

In Mr. Galsworthy's *The Little Man and Other Satires* there is none of this jolly trifling. Humor is subordinated to analysis and a moral frequently allowed to make itself evident. The character studies take on the dignity of types—in The Plain Man, the Critic, or the Housewife a whole class is keenly portrayed and subtly ridiculed. Each essay exposes, with the deft sureness of a master of words, some sham or flaw in people. The Latest Thing shows Mr. Galsworthy's irony at its best—a poignant description of the restlessly modern woman who "had flung open all the doors of life, and was so continually going out and coming in, that life had some considerable difficulty in catching a glimpse of her at all." The Voice of ——? is a dramatic description of the popular love of the spectacular. All of the sketches are well worth reading—that goes without saying. But it is rather unfortunate that The Little Man is marred by such a trite caricature of the American, whose dialect and ideas are by no means representative and whose every other word is "vurry."

Moonbeams from the Larger Lunacy, by Stephen Leacock. Scribner. $1.30. *The Little Man and Other Satires,* by John Galsworthy. Lane. $1.25.

HUMAN RUSSIA

Russian Silhouettes, a collection of short stories, will add much to the fame of Anton Tchekoff as an interpreter of Russian life and thought. The simplicity of his style is refreshing and the people he describes delightfully human, with none of the introspective morbidity that characterizes so much of Russian literature. The Stories of Childhood are particularly enjoyable. In *The Steppe and Other Stories* are some longer, but rather less interesting stories of Russia—vivid descriptions packed with detail, and illustrations of the peasant philosophy, patient, naive, idealistic.

Russian Silhouettes, by Anton Tchekoff. Scribner. $1.35. *The Steppe and Other Stories,* by Anton Tchekoff. Stokes. $1.25.

MORE LOEB CLASSICS

There are five new volumes issued in the Loeb Classics, that fine series of small books giving the original text and the translation side by side. These include *Hesiod* and *Pindar,* and those who have never read Hesiod's "Works and Days" will be surprized to learn how much its gnomic sayings parallel the wisdom of Solomon's Proverbs. *Pliny's Letters* the reader will like to compare with Cicero's Letters already issued; and Apuleius story, ridiculous and extravagant, of the *Golden Ass,* is an early romance of adventure and witchcraft.

In *Greek Genius and Other Essays,* with papers on Shakespeare, Balzac and Parisian Life, John Jay Chapman gives seven essays to Euripides. The emphatic point in these is that the English genius and culture are so utterly different from the Greek, that the reader or translator inevitably spoils the original. He cannot feel it, he cannot understand it properly. And in particular the author falls afoul of Gilbert Murray, and at considerable length he delights to show how Sir Gilbert in his "Notes and Translations of the Bacchantes" has misrepresented the Greek dramatist by putting into his language religious and moral sentiments which Euripides had never meant to express. He says that "Shakespeare may come to his end and lie down among the Egyptians, but Homer will endure forever." We might wish that the author's style were somewhat more restrained. It overflows with similes and daring metaphors and emphasis.

A History of Latin Literature, by Marcus Dimsdale, is a volume of the Literature of the World Series, edited by Edmund Gosse. The early Latin poetry was accentual, and changed in imitation of the Greek to quantitative. This early Saturnian meter pays no regard to regular feet any more than does Hebrew poetry, which it much resembles. A line is divided into two parts with three accents in the first part and two in the second. Of these rude beginnings but few fragments remain. The true Latin literature begins with Ennius and Plautus. The author shows the conquest of the Hellenic influence in comedy and tragedy; and then follow chapters on Lucretius and Catullus, Cicero, Cæsar and Sallust, till we come to the Augustan Age of Virgil and Horace and Livy. Succeeding chapters explain the decadence of literary art till the time of Trajan and the African Latinity and the end of the national literature with Boethius. The history is given as completely as is feasible in a manual. The series is meant for the ordinary reader, and the quotations are translated into English.

Hesiod, the Homeric Hymns and Homerica, ed. by H. G. Evelyn White. *Pindar,* ed. by Sir J. E. Sandys. *Pliny's Letters,* ed. by William Melmoth. 2 vols. *Apuleius' The Golden Ass,* ed. by S. Gaselee, Loeb Classics. Macmillan. Each $1.50. *Greek Genius and Other Essays,* by John Jay Chapman. Moffat, Yard. $1.75. *A History of Latin Literature,* by M. S. Dimsdale. Appleton. $2.

SOCIOLOGY FOR STUDENTS

The study of sociology is now sufficiently far advanced to warrant its systematic treatment in colleges without the assumption that every student of the subject will become a specialist in it. The *Introduction to the Study of Sociology,* by Professor Edward Cary Hayes of the University of Illinois, is therefore a welcome addition to the textbooks in this field, in that it presents a comprehensive outline of the subject, instead of an intensive analysis of some special aspect; and assumes a practical, every day application of the study, instead of an academic pursuit of abstractions. The author does not take for granted too much preliminary training in special sciences on the part of the reader, and introduces such references to biological and psychological data as are essential to an understanding of the problems discussed. The chapters on social control bring the reader directly into contact with the current problems of the day.

Introduction to the Study of Sociology, by E. C. Hayes. Appleton. $2.50.

RUNNING DOWN A DREAM

How Mrs. Piper and her "spirit control," the fictitious "Dr. Phinuit," proved to be mistaken, is told in *The Quest for Dean Bridgman Conner,* by A. J. Philpott, the newspaper man who followed the trance trail into Mexico.

Boston: Luce. $1.25.

LIVES DISTINGUISHED BY SERVICE

A dozen and a half short, racy sketches of noted Christian workers are found in the little volume by Mr. John T. Faris, *Reapers of His Harvest.* Men as far apart in time and character of service as John Wesley and Professor Steiner are included.

Philadelphia: Westminster Press. 60 cents.

AMERICAN MASTER WORKMEN

In *Early American Craftsmen* Walter A. Dyer sketches all too briefly the lives of the more important personalities in the early development of the industrial arts in America—such men as Duncan Phyfe, maker of beautiful furniture; Samuel McIntyre, master carpenter; Baron Stiegel, ironmaster and creator of exquisite glassware; Paul Revere, silver.

"Instruction by correspondence is the cheapest and best way for the poor man"

Thos. A. Edison

Edison is Right !!!

You admit the International Correspondence Schools are a good thing. You'd take a course right now "if"—"except"—

"If" what? If you weren't so "overworked," with such "long hours," or had more strength and energy?

Wasn't it Edison who stayed up half the night to educate himself in spite of every handicap you could ever have?

All big men who have made their mark in the world had the *ambition*—the *determination*—to improve their spare time, to train themselves for big work. You, too, can possess power, money and happiness if you'll only make the effort. The reward is great—it's worth it.

Here's all we ask : Merely mail this coupon. Put it up to us without paying or promising. Let us send you the details of others' success through the I. C. S., and then decide. Mark and mail this coupon now.

smith, engraver and bell-founder. The book is a good introduction to a subject worthy, on the biographical side particularly, of more extended treatment.
Century. $2.40.

UNORGANIZED UNITY
Dr. William H. Cobb finds *The Meaning of Christian Unity* and its present actual existence in the spiritual bonds of the true Christian life. He holds that no forms are necessary or helpful. The leaven of Christian love is all-sufficient. No program of organization is needed beyond that of establishing the Kingdom of God.
Crowell. $1.25.

WHAT THE STATE STANDS FOR
In this time of international upheaval, when national ideals are pitted against each other, it is fitting to examine anew what it is after all that constitutes a state. This, in *The People's Government*, a series of essays on the relations of force and law to government, Dr. David Jayne Hill attempts to do. Particularly illuminating is his discussion of the contributions of the American and French Revolutions to popular enfranchisement.
Appleton. $1.25.

DAYS THAT ARE GONE
Reminiscent of days that seem gone never to return are William Winter's *Vagrant Memories* of the time when acting was a great art and great artists made it so. By intimate accounts of the personal conceits and vanities of actors as well as of their ideals of their calling, Mr. Winter reconstructs the days of Edwin Booth, Henry Irving, Ada Rehan, Clara Morris, and Laura Keene, to whom and to many more he was friend, comrade and critic.
Doran. $3.

A NEW TYPE OF SCHOOLING
In *Prevocational Education in the Public Schools*, Frank M. Leavitt and Edith Brown explain the rise of the special schools for preadolescents, in which the usual work of the seventh and eighth school years is combined with practical handwork, and modified to make use of the concrete interests of the children. Here is much of significance to parents as well as to teachers. Most of the technical material has been tried out in some of the Chicago schools.
Houghton, Mifflin. $1.10.

THE SYNOPTIC PROBLEM
Carl S. Patton's résumé of critical theories concerning the *Sources of the Synoptic Gospels* fills the real need among Bible students for a concise yet detailed account of recent investigations into the literary relationship of the first three gospels, clear enough for lay readers. Part 2 attempts to analyse the common non-Markan source of Matthew and Luke into two recensions. This more original effort is highly technical and the hypothesis exceedingly uncertain.
Macmillan. $1.50.

FOR PIANO TEACHERS AND STUDENTS
In *Piano Mastery* Harriette Brower, herself a musician and teacher, prints a series of personal interviews with some thirty eminent pianists and teachers on how they obtained piano mastery ; gives an account of a von Buelow class, records some hints on interpretation by Dr. William Mason and William H. Sherwood, and summarizes therefrom the vital points in piano playing ; all of which makes up a volume of real worth and helpfulness for piano teachers and students.
Stokes. $1.50.

UNSEEN SOURCES OF SUCCESS
Professor Arthur S. Hoyt has added to his previous practical volumes of instruction to young clergymen, a new book on the *Vital Elements of Preaching*, in which he takes into consideration the spiritual qualities of the pastor and the flock as contributing elements to the successful work of the ministry. He gives an analysis of the more intimate and less obvious qualities that give power and effectiveness to the preacher's work.
Macmillan. $1.50.

EFFICIENCY QUESTION BOX

CONDUCTED BY
EDWARD EARLE PURINTON
DIRECTOR OF THE
INDEPENDENT EFFICIENCY SERVICE

192. Mr. N. M.., Peking, China. "I have read your answer to Question 188 in The Independent for September 6, 1915, regarding application of Efficiency methods to the farm. I agree with you that Prof. Bailey and the Farmers' Bureau are experts. By a curious coincidence, the same mail that brought your paper brought me a letter from a friend in which I learn that Mr. Geoffrey Burlingame, of Cazenovia, New York, is not only a successful farmer, but also an agricultural engineer, and that in a number of recent cases he has overhauled farms for other people to their satisfaction. Your correspondent will probably be grateful for this additional knowledge."

He will be, and we are. While the Service aims to cover the United States, new developments, constantly under way, temporarily may escape us. But to readers of The Independent the world is so small that a friend in China tells us in New York City what an Efficiency expert is doing a few miles up state. We call this efficient coöperation!

193. Mr. P. H. M., Wisconsin. "A lady well versed in ornithology wishes to take some kind of correspondence course that will enable her to write available articles on her specialty. Can you suggest any school or institution where she can get the help desired."

What to write is more important than *how* to write. The first step is to find what has been written, where published, how made "available." Any current literature on the subject would be valuable. Particulars should be requested of the work of The National Association of Audubon Societies, 1974 Broadway, New York; *Journal of Outdoor Life*, 289 Fourth avenue, New York; *Field and Stream*, 456 Fourth avenue; *Outing Magazine*, 141 West Thirty-sixth street; *Suburban Life*, 334 Fourth avenue, New York; *Nature Study Review*, edited by E. R. Downing, University of Chicago; American Ornithologists' Union, Secretary John H. Sage, Portland, Connecticut. From these varied sources ideas should be gained as to what the publishers want. Suggestions on form of presentation might be had from *The Editor*, Ridgewood, New Jersey; *The Writer's Magazine*, "Writing English," published by Funk and Wagnalls, 360 Fourth avenue, New York.

194. Miss S. C., Ohio. "Will you put a teacher in the way of finding out how she may develop efficiency systems in regard to personal belongings, buying and saving, and advancement in her profession?"

Obtain copies of *Woman's Magazine*, Spring street, New York; *Housewives' League Magazine*, 450 Fourth avenue, New York; *System*, Wabash and Madison, Chicago; *American Club Woman*, 35 West Thirty-ninth street, New York. Study the advertising pages for suggestions. Look thru back files of Efficiency Question Box for ideas of possible value. A correspondence course in Efficiency. Accounting or Finance would be likely to help you. Other items worth investigating : "Family Purse" envelope system. Seaver-Howland Press, 273 Franklin street, Boston; "Economy Expense Book," George C. Woolson & Co., 120 West Thirty-second street, New York; "Household Expense Book," Noble Cutshaw, Salem, Indiana; topical index of published articles from *Engineering Magazine*, 140 Nassau street, New York. Write Secretary of Teachers College, 525 West One Hundred and Twentieth street, New York, for suggestions on ways to advance in your profession.

Anticipating Telephone Needs

When a new subscriber is handed his telephone, there is given over to his use a share in the pole lines, underground conduits and cables, switchboards, exchange buildings, and in every other part of the complex mechanism of the telephone plant.

It is obvious that this equipment could not be installed for each new connection. It would mean constantly rebuilding the plant, with enormous expense and delay. Therefore, practically everything but the telephone instrument must be in place at the time service is demanded.

Consider what this involves. The telephone company must forecast the needs of the public. It must calculate increases in population in city and country. It must figure

the growth of business districts. It must estimate the number of possible telephone users and their approximate location everywhere.

The plant must be so designed that it may be added to in order to meet the estimated requirements of five, ten and even twenty years. And these additions must be ready in advance of the demand for them—as far in advance as it is economical to make them.

Thus, by constantly planning for the future and making expenditures for far-ahead requirements when they can be most advantageously made, the Bell System conserves the economic interest of the whole country while furnishing a telephone service which in its perfection is the model for all the world.

AMERICAN TELEPHONE AND TELEGRAPH COMPANY
AND ASSOCIATED COMPANIES

One Policy   **One System**   *Universal Service*

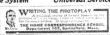

PLACING JANUARY FUNDS

AT this period of the year when large sums are usually seeking a proper investment channel, discriminating people make selections which are not apt to cause them any worry in the distant future. There are bonds suitable for trustees, savings banks, widows, insurance companies, corporations, business men, private investors, etc. Savings bank bonds, commonly called legal investments, can form a part of the holdings of any class of investors, but the sort of a bond that a business man could purchase with a part of his surplus might not be suitable, or even safe, for a widow, a trustee or a savings bank.

Savings banks and trustees are guided in the purchase of investments by the laws of the states in which they are located, tho trustees are often given discretionary powers. State laws with respect to the investments of savings banks and trustees vary in conservatism; in New York, Connecticut and Massachusetts, for example, the laws are very strict tho not perfect, and the standing of a bond declared legal under their laws is not likely to be injured excepting in extraordinary cases. In other states, Maine for instance, the laws are so lax that the bonds of very weak corporations have been technically legal altho such bonds would not be purchased for a trust fund by any trustee with the average degree of intelligence. Trustees who invest funds according to the laws of states like New York can be reasonably sure that the moneys intrusted to them are safely placed.

In many states a trustee is liable for any loss that may result from the investment of funds in other than strictly legal issues. Trust funds that are honestly and efficiently managed should show no losses excepting the ordinary decreases in market value of bonds which occur during the periodical depressions. Such losses, however, are only book losses unless it is necessary for some reason or other to liquidate the holdings in order to secure cash. On the other hand, trust fund investments purchased in times of stress, for example in the twelvemonth ended June 30, 1915, should show a great appreciation in time. Bonds purchased last year on from a 4.50 per cent to a 5 per cent basis are now selling on from a 4.25 per cent to a 4.75 per cent basis, and we do not yet seem to have reached the top of the movement. As a matter of general opinion, it appears as tho, with the continuance of easy money rates, the standard bonds will reach their high level around a 4 per cent to a 4.25 per cent basis without much difficulty.

While trustees are usually confined to legal investments, diversification of holdings is desirable, particularly in large estates. Only geographical diversification is warranted in states like New York, where investments can only be in municipal bonds, railroad bonds or mortgages on real property in the state. In other states, where public utility bonds are included in the eligible list, a greater diversification can be effected. Geographical diversification is quite important and should receive more than passing notice.

Trustees and widows, particularly widows entirely dependent for a livelihood upon their income from securities, should not only purchase legal investments, but arrange their holdings to include securities of strong municipalities and railroads located in various

Bonds suitable for Trustees and Investors who especially require safety				Yield about Per cent.
Atchison, Topeka & Santa Fe Railway..	General	4s	1995	N-C-M	4.25
Baltimore & Ohio Railroad............	Gold	4s	1948	C-M	4.50
Chicago, Milwaukee & St. Paul Railway	General	4½s	1989	N-C-M	4.40
Nashville, Chatt. & St. Louis Ry......	Consol.	5s	1928	N-C-M	4.30
Cleveland Short Line Railway.........	First	4½s	1961	N-C-M	4.50
Lake Shore & Mich. Sou. Railway....	Mortgage	4s	1931	N-C-M	4.50
Norfolk & Western Railway...........	Consol.	4s	1996	N-C-M	4.25
Southern Pac. San Francisco Term....	First	4s	1950	C	4.95
Mohawk & Malone (N. Y. Central)....	First	4s	1991	N-C-M	4.30
United N. J. R. R. & Canal Co. (Penn. R. R.)	Consol.	4s	1944	N-C-M	4.05
Chicago, Burlington & Quincy Railroad.	General	4s	1958	N-C-M	4.35
Atlantic Coast Line Railroad.........	Consol.	4s	1952	N-C	4.35
Pennsylvania Railroad	Consol.	4½s	1960	N-C-M	4.20
Southern Pacific Railroad	Refund.	4s	1955	N-C	4.50
Union Pacific Railroad	Refund.	4s	2008	N-C-M	4.45
Northern Pacific Railway............	Prior	4s	1997	N-C-M	4.20

N, Legal in New York; C, in Connecticut; M, in Massachusetts.

Bonds suitable for Trustees having discretionary powers, or as a part of a widow's investment holdings, or for business men in general					Per cent.
Baltimore & Ohio Railroad...........	Mtge. Conv. 4½s	1933	N-C-M		4.75
Canada Southern Railroad	Consol.	5s	1962		4.80
Central of Georgia Railroad..........	Consol.	5s	1945		4.90
Cleveland, Cin., Chicago & St. Louis Ry.	General	5s	1993		4.90
Colorado & Southern Railway........	First	4s	1929		4.82
Kansas City Southern Railway........	First	3s	1950		4.78
Carolina, Clinchfield & Ohio Railway..	First	5s	1938		5.20
New York Central Railroad...........	Refund.	4s	2013	N-C-M	4.85
Chicago, Milwaukee & St. Paul Railway.	Refund.	4½s	2014	N-C-M	4.80
Baltimore & Ohio Railroad...........	Refund.	5s	1995	N-C-M	4.95
American Telephone & Telegraph Co...	Collat.	4s	1929	M	4.90
Chicago Great Western Railroad......	First	4s	1959		5.50
Southern Pacific Company...........	Convertible	4s	1929		5.10
Southern Railway	Consol.	5s	1994		4.85
New York Central Railroad..........	Debent.	4s	1934	C-M	4.62
Brooklyn Union Elevated Railroad....	First	4s	1950		4.95

Public Utility Bonds suitable for general investment purposes				Per cent.
Brooklyn Rapid Transit Co...........	First	5s	1945	4.80
California Gas & Electric............	Unif.	5s	1937	5.20
Cumberland Tel. & Tel. Co...........	First	5s	1937	5.00
Detroit Edison	First	5s	1933	4.70
Interborough Rapid Transit Co........	Refund.	5s	1966	5.00
Joliet Economy Light & Power Co.....	First	5s	1956	5.00
Laclede Gas Light Co. (St. Louis)....	First	5s	1934	4.95
New York Telephone Co.............	First	4½s	1939	4.60
Pacific Telephone & Telegraph Co.....	First	5s	1937	5.00
Omaha & Council Bluff St. Ry. Co....	First	5s	1928	4.90
Syracuse Lighting Co...............	First	5s	1951	5.00
Third Avenue Railway Co............	Refund.	4s	1960	4.90
Westchester Lighting Co............	First	5s	1950	4.80
Southern Bell Telephone & Tel. Co....	First	5s	1941	5.00

64

parts of the country. There are grain roads, coal roads, cotton roads, lumber roads, ore roads and roads carrying a widely diversified tonnage. There are cities located in sections where one or two industries predominate. Bonds of such cities or such railroads should not form a large part of the holdings of any trust fund or widow, but only small blocks of each should be bought after the intrinsic value was found to be satisfactory. Trustees and widows are not always able to judge investments but investment bankers of established reputation are always willing to give freely impartial and valuable advice, based on years of experience.

Only passing notice need be made here of the desirability of American municipal bonds, since it is generally known that they stand among the premier securities. Defaults in either principal or interest have been practically unknown in years. Municipal bonds are direct credit obligations of states or their political subdivisions and interest is unconditionally guaranteed by the taxing power of the community issuing them. Such bonds have become very much in demand during the past few years due to the fact that they are exempt from the operations of the Federal Income Tax Law; no certificate of ownership need be filed with coupons to be collected and no mention of the income from municipal or United States Government bonds is necessary on income tax returns. There seems to be every indication that the demand will continue, as the supply is small and competition has been very keen among investment houses. Good municipal bonds are now selling at prices to yield from 3.50 per cent to 5 per cent and better, all depending upon the standing of the municipality, and a ready market is maintained for them in financial centers.

First mortgage bonds of public utility corporations which serve large cities and have been in operation for many years should form a part of the holdings of conservative investors. In some states such bonds can be purchased by savings banks and trustees but in states where trustees are confined strictly to municipal and railroad issues such bonds are desirable for private investors and even widows can purchase well-secured public utility bonds to advantage. Public utility corporations that serve growing centers with electric power, railway lines, gas mains, etc., usually have enough demand for two or more commodities to enable them even in times of stress to pay interest and even dividends with regularity. While in the period of depression experienced in 1914-1915 some public service corporations had to defer dividend payments and public utility bonds declined in market value along with railroad bonds, this was an extraordinary period and the setback was only temporary. It was further accentuated by the "jitney" competition which was more or less of a bugaboo and has been so stringently regulated that it has begun to die out. Public utility bonds yield from 4.75

per cent to 6 per cent and are quite readily marketable, altho they do not enjoy the same marketability as a bond in the class of Pennsylvania Consolidated 4s. Underlying bonds of well-known tractions and electric light or gas corporations operating in large cities like New York are particularly attractive investments for such trustees and widows as can purchase them.

From the list of railroad bonds that are legal investments in New York and other states, shown herewith as an aid to the reader, it will be seen that the yield ranges from about 4.05 per cent to 4.95 per cent. The yield is necessarily lower than that obtainable on public utility bonds, as the supply on legal investments is somewhat limited and due to the fact that we are dealing with the highest grade of securities, for which there is always a demand. Banks, institutions, trustees, corporations and business men create a healthy demand for legal investments.

In the case of a trustee of a fund from which a larger income than that obtainable from legal issues is required, it is permissible to invest in sound bonds not classified as legal if such trustee has discretionary powers and is a good judge of investments or deals with a firm of investment bankers which is known to be reliable. There are such bonds which yield considerably in excess of 5 per cent and if such bonds are purchased only with a view to increasing the average income, they are desirable additions to a trust fund, particularly when the fund is invested in bonds yielding as low as 4.25 per cent. In the list of bonds showing a higher yield than the legal investments only the better known issues have been selected with a view to meeting the requirements of investors who desire to own bonds which have a ready market.

The ordinary private investor or business man is allowed much more latitude in the selection of securities than the trustee of an estate. He should, of course, insist that his list include some legal investments, high grade short-term notes, general mortgage railroad bonds yielding around 5 per cent, industrial bonds not affected by war business to a great extent, public utility bonds yielding 5.50 per cent or better, and even preferred and common stocks of reputable corporations. Some business men make it a practise to watch railroads in the hands of receivers and study their bonds which appear to be intrinsically good. In a period of depression such bonds can be purchased at bargain prices and investors who purchased such bonds as St. Louis & San Francisco Railroad refunding 4s, Chicago & Eastern Illinois general 5s and bonds in that class have been rewarded with a substantial profit after it was generally realized that the bonds had a fundamentally good lien. We are still in a period of reorganization in so far as railroads are concerned and there are undoubtedly many railroad bonds which today are considered highly speculative which in years to come may have a sound position.

Insurance

Conducted by

W. E. UNDERWOOD

A. A. M., Pastaskala, Ohio—The Great Western Accident of Des Moines is a good little company, well managed. Total incomes of those you name were, in 1914: Great Western, $347,617; Continental Casualty, $3,057,588; Great Eastern, $1,-$1,143,486.

B. R. L., Washington, D. C.—Figures quoted are for the Western Travelers Accident Association of Omaha, Neb. as of December 31, 1914: total admitted assets, $56,514; total liabilities, $13,384; total income, 1914, $72,196; claims paid, $48,986; expenses paid, $21,293; total disbursements, $70,279. None of the reference books I have list the Commercial Travelers Health Association.

C. P. W., Los Angeles, Calif.—Your accident policy in the Pacific Mutual, considering its unrestricted character and the multiple benefits it grants, is worth the price. That company also writes a combined life and disability policy which you should investigate. All the companies you name are first class. You have shown good judgment in your selections. No, I do not think you are spending too much on your family's protection.

G. K. E., Selah, Wash.—The United Insurance Company of Arizona, New York and Illinois was a promoters' scheme which only succeeded in victimizing a number of people thruout the country who subscribed for its stock. The organization was never completed, and practically all the money .aid in by subscribers was used for expenses. The assets of the New York office of the ncern were valued by the Insurance Department at $6,500 in March, 911. There i no probability that holders of its stock will ever receive anything.

J. C. B., Eagleville, Mo.—If the advantages claimed for total abstinence are completely set forth in the statement you send me, then I conclude that they are not sufficient, substantial to merit special consideration. The company has instituted a comparison between results attained in its abstainers' and its general classes, using an accumulative dividend policy for the purpose. In arriving at its periodical cash values that company includes *estimated* dividends. Let us compare its total abstinence results with those attained by a company which does not segregate abstainers from non-abstainers. I find in the statement you send that the illustration uses a $1000 policy at age thirty, the annual premium for which is $28.29, and that the cash value (including *estimated* dividends) at the end of thirty years is $1006. I find that a thirty-year endowment in the Provident Life and Trust Company of Philadelphia, $1000, costs $29.58 a year ($1.29 a year more than the other), and that, of course, being an endowment contract, the *guaranteed* cash value at the end of thirty years is $1000. To this must be added the value of the dividends at that time. I think we can safely estimate them at 15 per cent of the premiums in that company. Compounding them at 3 per cent we have $217, bringing the total estimated and guaranteed cash value at the end of thirty years to $1217. Now we will allow the value of the $1.29 a year in premium, which in thirty years amounts to $63. Deducting the latter, we have a cash value in the Provident Life of $1154 as against $1006 in the total abstinence class of the other company. We can at least say that the case made by the latter is inconclusive —that it proves nothing in favor of total abstainers.

All out-doors
invites your Kodak.

No trip too long, no conditions too rough for a Kodak outfit.

You can take, title and finish the negatives on the spot by the Kodak system. You can make sure.

Kodak catalog free at your dealer's, or by mail

EASTMAN KODAK CO., ROCHESTER, N. Y., *The Kodak City.*

CONVENTION WEEK AT THE CAPITAL

SPECIAL CORRESPONDENCE FROM WASHINGTON

A CITY filled with the best brains of the two Americas. That describes Washington this week and will be a fitting description of the national capital during each of the thirteen days that the Second Pan-American Congress is in session.

Never before, perhaps, has such a comprehensive group of organizations of national and international importance been assembled in an American city as that which met in Washington the beginning of the week. To the hundreds of distinguished scientists, educators, civic workers and jurists who came as delegates to the Second Pan-American Scientific Congress from all the countries of the two Americas, were added an even greater number of men and women of prominence who attended the sessions of nearly a dozen societies and associations, meeting in the city on invitation of the congress. The combined attendance of delegates as well as men and women not officially connected with the organizations, who were attracted by their interest in the unusually comprehensive programs of discussions, numbered several thousands; and to the meetings of the numerous groups was added a brilliant array of social gatherings at which private citizens as well as government officials were hosts and hostesses to the visitors.

The Second Pan-American Scientific Congress opened its sessions Monday morning in the auditorium of the stately Continental Memorial Hall of the Daughters of the American Revolution, where a larger gathering could be accommodated than in the adjoining Pan-American Union building. With the entwined flags of the twenty-one republics of the Americas forming a background, the Vice-President of the United States, the Secretary of State, the Ambassador of Chile, president of the congress, and leaders of delegations from the other countries represented, delivered addresses which struck a warmer note of friendliness and union for the nations of the New World than has ever before been struck in even the most enthusiastic gatherings of Pan-Americans.

The outstanding fact at this initial session of the scientists was that for the time all thought of science was thrust aside while the speakers talked with earnest enthusiasm of the growing solidarity, political and economic, that is emerging in the feelings and thoughts of all the American republics as a reflex from

the great struggle that is taking place among the countries of the Old World.

To the impression of magnitude that the congress created by its initial session, with its assemblage of distinguished participants, was added on the second day an impression of diversity, for the congress then resolved itself into its nine component sections devoted to special fields of science and knowledge. The formal opening session of each of the sections was addrest by cabinet members and other high officials and again the note of Pan-Americanism in politics, economics and science was sounded. It was not until the third day of the congress, when the division of labor was carried further with each section dividing itself into several sub-sections, that the delegates began to consider in earnest the specific scientific problems which had drawn them together.

Another phase of the diversity of interests under the banner of science came with the second day of the con-

---

PAN-AMERICANISM

From an address by Secretary Lansing, who heads the governing board of the Pan-American Union, before the second Pan-American Scientific Congress in Washington:

Pan-Americanism is an expression of the idea of internationalism.

America will become the guardian of that idea, which will in the end rule the world.

The policy of Pan-Americanism is practical.

The Pan-American spirit is ideal. It is the offspring of the best, the noblest conception of international obligation.

The American family of nations might well take for its motto "One for all; all for one."

We must not only be neighbors, but friends; not only friends, but intimates.

The Republics of America are no longer children in the great family of nations. They have attained maturity.

The Pan-American spirit is a policy which this Government has unhesitatingly adopted and which it will do all in its power to foster and promote.

Whatever is of common interest, whatever makes for the common good, whatever demands united effort is a fit subject for applied Pan-Americanism. Fraternal helpfulness is the keystone to the arch. Its pillars are faith and justice.

---

gress when most of the invited associations opened their sessions. Joint meetings between these associations and sections and sub-sections of the congress began on the following day. Organizations devoted to history, economics, education, health, civic advance, anthropology and the various technical professions and industries added their proceedings to the already diversified activities of the week.

Among these the American Civic Association met for its annual convention and proved by the greetings that came to it on the opening day from civic workers at home and abroad that it has won a place of international importance. The Marquis of Aberdeen, recently governor general of Ireland, testified especially to the spread of the influence of the association to Ireland. Last year, he said, because of the association's inspiration and thru the assistance of its officers, the pioneer civic exhibition of the island was held in Dublin.

What was in many ways the culmination of a week of unusual activities in the Capital was marked on Wednesday by a special session of the American Civic Association, presided over by Miss Margaret Wilson, for consideration of "The School as a Social Center." Delegates to many of the other associations, who happened to be possest of dominant civic interests, left their special sessions for the time to attend the school center meeting and to join their enthusiasm with that of Miss Wilson in the movement for a wider and better use of the school plant.

The speakers at this meeting are leaders in some of the most vital movements before the country. Following Miss Wilson's introductory address, in which she urged the general adoption of the school social center plan for its value in developing democracy, Prof. E. J. Ward of the University of Wisconsin drew attention to the needs for individual development and culture to give strength to the nation and to the valuable aid toward this development that the great country-wide school organization, properly used, can contribute. The theme was developed further by Raymond F. Crist, deputy federal commissioner of naturalization, who described the work of the federal bureau of naturalization, in coöperation with schools and community centers, in the production of better citizens from the raw materials that immigration brings to our shores.

68

The Independent

FOR SIXTY-SEVEN YEARS THE
FORWARD-LOOKING WEEKLY OF AMERICA

THE   CHAUTAUQUAN
Merged with The Independent June 1, 1914

JANUARY 17, 1916

OWNED AND PUBLISHED BY
THE INDEPENDENT CORPORATION, AT
119 WEST FORTIETH STREET, NEW YORK
WILLIAM B. HOWLAND, PRESIDENT
FREDERIC E. DICKINSON, TREASURER

WILLIAM HAYES WARD
HONORARY EDITOR

EDITOR: HAMILTON HOLT
ASSOCIATE EDITOR: HAROLD J. HOWLAND
LITERARY EDITOR: EDWIN E. SLOSSON
PUBLISHER: KARL V. S. HOWLAND

ONE YEAR, THREE DOLLARS

SINGLE COPIES, TEN CENTS

Postage to foreign countries in Universal Postal
Union, $1.75 a year extra; to Canada, $1 extra.
Instructions for renewal, discontinuance or
change of address should be sent two weeks
before the date they are to go into effect. Both
the old and the new address must be given.

We welcome contributions, but writers who
wish their articles returned, if not accepted,
should send a stamped and addrest envelope. No responsibility is assumed by The
Independent for the loss or non-return of
manuscripts, tho all due care will be exercised.

Entered at New York Post Office as Second
Class Matter

Copyright, 1916, by The Independent

Address all Communications to
THE INDEPENDENT
119 West Fortieth Street, New York

CONTENTS

JUST A WORD

"I have already built several air castles with that $100 prize" writes one of our contributors to our contest on "What Is the Best Thing in Your Town?" Perhaps all the other contestants—a thousand or more—have done likewise, and are wondering how long a lease those air castles will require.

For when we first announced this contest we did not promise the decision for definite date—and when we saw the manuscripts come pouring in—over a hundred in a single mail—we were very glad that we hadn't. A careful consideration of a thousand able presentations of "the best thing in your town," differing widely in subject and in treatment, is a task as long as it is pleasant.

However the contributions are being judged with as much speed as is compatible with the consideration they deserve, and the prize-winner will be announced in an early issue. So many of the articles are well worthy of publication that we plan to quote a great deal and to use as many of the excellent illustrations as possible, too. In case the contributions that we want to use prove to be too numerous for one issue, we may continue to publish them at intervals as a sort of informal department.

With a brilliant article called "Government of the People, By the People, For the People," William Allen White will inaugurate in an early issue of The Independent a forward-looking series of striking and significant articles on "The Next Generation in American Life."

In these articles, to be published at regular intervals during 1916, men and women who have studied long and accomplished much in dealing with important phases of American life today will project their knowledge of the trend of our national development into the future and tell what, in their judgment, the next phases of American evolution will be. Among contributors to this series are Gutzon Borglum: "The New Birth of Art in Ame-

rica"; George E. Vincent: "The Expansion of Popular Education"; Liberty H. Bailey: "Country Living in the Next Generation"; Melvil Dewey: "What the Next Generation Will Read and How"; Margaret Deland: "Women in the World and at Home"; Shailer Mathews: "Religion, the Church and the People."

REMARKABLE REMARKS

PRESIDENT POINCARÉ—1916 will be our year of victory.

LAURA JEAN LIBBEY—I do not approve of indiscriminate kissing.

GUGLIELMO MARCONI—The plain fact is that Germany is sick of the war.

FIELD MARSHAL VON HINDENBURG—The Russian soup is getting ever thinner.

DR. KARL MUCK—I do not in the least believe in popular music for the masses.

WILLIAM A. BRADY—It does not pay to be decent. I know what I am talking about.

REV. F. L. STREETER—It makes a fellow feel he is in the suburbs of heaven to be in love.

SECRETARY LANSING—The ambitions of this country do not lie in the path of conquest.

CROWN PRINCE FREDERICK WILLIAM—Forward with God, for the Emperor and Germany.

JAY E. HOUSE—Do not fall into the common error of mistaking flapdoodle for patriotism.

ANTONIO GHISLANZONI—In case of fire the cellist will save his cello first and then his wife.

MARION HARLAND—Patchwork has charms those who have never made it cannot understand.

REV. GEO. W. SHELDON—Every old goat in Pittsburgh is trying to hide behind some old "burry" sheep.

FRANK A. VANDERLIP—There ought not to be an idle man in the United States for years to come.

SENATOR L. Y. SHERMAN—I shall hereafter endeavor to change my shirts every time the moon quarters.

SUPERINTENDENT ELLA FLAGG YOUNG—There is one objection I have to San Diego. It is always windy there.

LINA CAVALIERI—A lovely woman in an evening gown always reminds me of a beautiful bouquet rising out of a vase.

WOODROW WILSON—For seventeen years I taught my classes that the initiative and referendum would not work. The trouble is they do.

BILLY SUNDAY—It is radically wrong when a prize fighter in fifteen minutes can make more than a country parson does in fifteen years.

PROF. SCOTT NEARING—When the church advocates armament it should pull down the cross from the steeple and replace it with the torpedo.

ED. HOWE—When I go to a hotel if I am treated well I turn out the lights on leaving my room. But if the clerk is snippy I let them burn.

W. J. BRYAN—A thousand years from now the name of Woodrow Wilson and my name will be linked together in the capitals of the world.

LILLIAN RUSSELL—Hold a pencil at arm's length. Draw it slowly up to the bridge of the nose. looking closely at it all the time. Do this ten times.

MRS. S. B. FIELD—I know of certain women in our suffrage states who have denied themselves the privilege of motherhood until they receive their vote.

FRANCIS L. GARSIDE—When the oldest daughter reaches sixteen her parents, without going thru the formality of a vote, make her the head of the family.

The Independent

VOLUME 85   JANUARY 17, 1916   NUMBER 3502

© International Film Service

THE MOST TERRIBLE FORM OF MODERN WAR

THE BEGINNING OF AN ACTUAL GAS ATTACK MADE BY THE GERMANS ON THE RUSSIAN LINES. THE PHOTOGRAPH WAS TAKEN FROM A RUSSIAN AEROPLANE. THE SUN IS LOW IN THE SKY, AND THE GERMAN INFANTRYMEN STANDING IN LONG LINES AT THE RIGHT OF THE PICTURE CAST LONG SHADOWS BEFORE THEM. CLOUDS OF GAS ARE ROLLING TOWARD THE RUSSIAN LINES, AND WHEN THE CHLORINE HAS DONE ITS WORK THE GERMANS WILL CHARGE

NO DISUNITED STATES

SOME of our foreign critics, disappointed that the United States has not openly and officially espoused the cause of the Allies, have of late been describing us satirically as "the Disunited States," and the term has been caught up here and there by our own citizens, deeply troubled by the disloyalty of the hyphenated element in our population. The satire is harmless and alarm is baseless. There will be no Disunited States. That matter was attended to fifty years ago.

Nevertheless, the conditions that have provoked the jeer and the fear are interesting enough to deserve attention. When the European war began American reaction to the situation was instantaneous and tremendous. On every hand the remark was heard that American feeling had never been so nearly unanimous as it was in holding Germany blameworthy for the appalling catastrophe. It is not to be wondered at that France and Belgium expected that such unity of conviction, with so much apparent moral heat to give it driving force, would carry our people and our Government into active cooperation with the defenders of liberty.

Soon, however, interest in responsibility for the war diminished, and more specific issues began to engross attention. The rights of neutrals on the high seas, the right to export munitions, the possibility that this nation might any hour find itself actually at war, and the question of preparedness, became instant and vital topics. From that moment differences of attitude and conflicts of opinion multiplied. Today it is obvious to everybody that public opinion in the United States verges upon a state of intellectual and moral anarchy. Yet no greater mistake of judgment could be made than to conclude that our condition is one of disunity. Under the storm-lashed surface are the unsounded depths of our political ocean.

In political thinking nothing is easier than to see clearly every one of a hundred facts and a dozen big tendencies, and yet go all wrong. The facts and the tendencies must be seen quantitatively as well as qualitatively. Ratios count in the realm of human affairs as in mechanics. The American people do not get together on every question. There are some questions upon which they are a unit and always will be; and there are some issues upon which they get together more or less, and with a good deal of shifting of pluralities from time to time.

It is because we fall into forgetfulness of these more and less relations that we waste time in debating the questions: What is an American? What is Americanism? The true answer to them is the simplest and most obvious fact in American life, and upon it the entire American people is a unit. An American is a man, born here or elsewhere, who wholeheartedly and unreservedly accepts and shares the good or the bad fortune of this nation. To it he gives his allegiance. He has renounced all other governments and every conflicting loyalty. We venture the assertion that there is no other issue upon which human beings might unite or divide that would bring together in feeling, opinion and relentless action so nearly one hundred per cent of the entire population of the United States as that of the single allegiance. If there are misguided residents here who are with us, but not of us, they will realize this truth in a bitter awakening before American public opinion gets thru with them.

There are other things upon which we are nearly united, for which the majority vote would be overwhelming. One of these is the supremacy of the nation and of the national government over all sectionalism, localism, racial differences, and class differences. Nobody wants to see any coercing of states or of interests if it can be avoided. But it is as certain as the rotation of the earth that if any state or any interest by cantankerous behavior endangers our relations with foreign powers or our internal peace and quiet, that state or that interest will get hurt.

We could add to the list, but these two items are enough. We shall differ, no doubt, over the extent and the method of desirable preparedness. We shall have pacifists and militarists. We shall have citizens exporting munitions and others demanding an embargo upon such traffic. Upon a thousand other things we shall differ; but upon the fundamental issues of Americanism and nationality we shall be, as we have been for fifty years, a united people. There will be no Disunited States.

AT LAST

A COMPLETE victory is all but won in our submarine controversy with Germany.

In the "Lusitania" case Germany consents to pay an indemnity for the American lives destroyed.

In the matter of German submarines operating in the Mediterranean Germany declares that merchant ships—except in case of flight or resistance—will not be sunk by German submarines until passengers and crew have been put in safety.

If any submarine commander should violate this principle and kill or injure American citizens in destroying a merchant ship, Germany will punish him and make reparation for the death or injury.

In the case of the "Persia"—the cause of whose sinking is still undetermined—Germany intimates that if it should prove to have been sunk by a German submarine, the foregoing procedure will be followed.

There is only one thing lacking in all this. Germany seems still unwilling to admit that the "Lusitania" was wrongfully sunk. It still apparently clings to the doctrine that its submarine warfare in the war zone about the British Isles was justified as an act of retaliation for the British blockade of Germany.

This the United States cannot admit. It is a contention unknown to international law. It is an unjustifiable contravention of the universally recognized rights of non-combatants upon the high seas. We could not accept as final a settlement of the "Lusitania" case involving even a tacit acceptance on our part of such a doctrine. It might involve us in the creation of a false precedent dangerous in the future to the vital principle of the inviolability of the lives of non-combatants at sea. But Germany has come far since the "Lusitania" was sunk; it ought not to prove an impossible task to induce her to take this last inconsiderable step and end the matter. The people of the United States may well congratulate themselves upon a peaceful victory of great proportions. It is not only a vindication of the rights of American citizens; it is a triumph for principles of humanity and the rights of mankind. To contend that the victory might have been won more quickly and more lives and suffering saved if we had gone about the matter in a different way from the beginning is beside the point. That no man can tell.

That the victory has been won and won in more complete measure than many have believed possible is the outstanding fact. The whole world will be the gainer.

MONROE AND WILSON

NEARLY a century ago James Monroe proclaimed a doctrine that, probably more than any other single act of statesmanship, has brought peace and prosperity to the nations of this hemisphere. Tho never accepted as a principle of international law, the Monroe Doctrine as an American policy has been sufficient until today to maintain the independence of every nation in the New World.

The Monroe Doctrine, however, goes no farther than guaranteeing the nations of the New World from the interference of the Old. It does not guarantee them from the interference of the United States or of each other.

Last week Woodrow Wilson proclaimed a new Pan-American policy. In his address before the Pan-American Scientific Congress on January 6 he outlined his policy in these words:

It will be accomplished in the first place by the States of America uniting in guaranteeing to each other absolute political independence and territorial integrity. In the second place, and as a necessary corollary to that, guaranteeing the agreement to settle all pending boundary disputes as soon as possible and by amicable process; by agreeing that all disputes among themselves, should they unhappily arise, will be handled by patient, impartial investigation and settled by arbitration; and the agreement necessary to the peace of the Americas, that no state or either continent will permit revolutionary expeditions against another state to be fitted out on its territory, and that they will prohibit the exportation of the munitions of war for the purpose of supplying revolutionists against neighboring Governments.

These proposals if carried out will eventually bring into being nothing less than a Pan-American Confederation or League of Peace. They establish a defensive alliance against any nation within or without the league which attacks a member of the league. They create a method of settling controversies within the league by judicial process. They propose to remove some of the chief causes that now lead to civil or international war in the New World.

There is, however, one defect, in that they seem to maintain the status quo in all nations, even the backward ones. They would prohibit a liberty loving people from extending aid and comfort to a revolutionary minority in another country fighting for the cause of freedom against a tyrannical oligarchy. A league which guarantees the permanence of the existing régime and prevents any outside control over any of the backward republics or any outside aid to revolutionists may actually retard progress. Some plan must be devised for the growth of civilization in the dark spots of the world as well as in the light spots. Nations cannot and ought not to be kept to bounds they happen to possess at present. A failure to recognize the possibility of such changes is one of the chief causes of war.

President Wilson has apparently provided no way for the progressive expansion of New World civilization. In the Pan-American Conferences we already have the germ of the idea that will bring this about. Let the president propose a legislative power for his Pan-American League in addition to the judicial and executive powers that he advocates, and then he will have provided a well-rounded plan for the development of peace, prosperity and progress of this hemisphere.

But, in any event, President Wilson's proposals are the most significant yet uttered by any New World statesman, not only for what they will accomplish if put into execution, but for what they logically lead to. As Mr. Taft well says, "A League of Nations in the Western Hemisphere would be a definite, and, I think, a long step toward a League of Nations in both hemispheres."

RUSSIA'S SETBACK

IT has often been hinted that the British were not so much grieved as they might be by Russia's failure to run the steam-roller over all Germany within the first few months of the war. Too strong a Russia might have been hard to handle afterward. The Sydney, Australia, Bulletin, which is the enfant terrible of British journalism, gives frank expression to this feeling:

The enemy of the civilized world is destroying itself in the effort to destroy Russia, which is indestructible; and meanwhile the Britisher, who is able to regard the progress of the war with the cold and far-seeing eye of the business person, may console himself permissibly with at least one reflection. If Russia had been as strong as the blitherers averred and hoped, if it had been capable of routing the land forces of what everybody regarded as the world's greatest military power, it might have been well for the Allies' cause, but it would probably have been ill, in the long run, for the British Empire. National aspirations live longer than the most firmly welded alliances. At the end of the war Britain's hold on India and British interests in Persia would have been in no wise strengthened by the circumstance that Russia, in addition to its natural resources and its strength on a population basis, was efficient enough in the military sense to overrun western Europe. These are natural and obvious sentiments which need not conflict in any way with sympathy and warm admiration for a brave ally.

But probably now when Germany is grasping at Persia and the road to India, the British wish that Russia had been a little stronger than she proved to be. A good strong army from the Caucasus would be heartily welcomed on the Tigris, where General Townshend's division is besieged by Turk and Arab at Kut-el-Amara.

THE THREE SACRED TONGUES

IN the beginning of the sixteenth century there lived three great scholars versed in the three sacred tongues, Hebrew, Greek and Latin, the three languages of religion and literature, John Reuchlin, Erasmus Desiderius and Martin Luther. It was Reuchlin who gave again to the world of scholarship the forgotten Hebrew Bible; Erasmus was the first to print the Greek New Testament, while out of the two original languages Luther translated the two Testaments into the language of the people.

There is hardly a more notable production in literature than that in which Erasmus in one of his Colloquies beatifies Reuchlin on the news of the latter's death.

There are in it lessons that do not grow old. One of the interlocutors in the dialog tells how he had visited the University of Louvain, where he had heard a sermon by one Camelus, who had abused the new learning as impious. "A stupid camel, indeed," says his friend, "as if a thing was good because old, and bad because new." Then he went to Tübingen, where Reuchlin had just died; and there he met a Franciscan friar famed for his sanctity who related the wonderful vision he had seen in his sleep. He beheld beyond a bridge a marvelously beautiful meadow bespangled with flowers of all colors. As he was ravished with its beauty he saw Reuchlin approaching the bridge, gray haired, and clad in a single garment. There followed him at a little distance great obscene birds, as it were harpies, which sputtered and screamed after him, but did not dare to attack him. As he crost the bridge Reuchlin turned and said, "Depart, you can reach me no more with your detractions." With a foul odor, they flew away.

As Reuchlin crost the bridge there met him Saint Jerome, who embraced him and clad him in shining garments, like his own; for Jerome was the holy scholar, traduced and abused while alive, as was Reuchlin, who was master of the three sacred tongues, and had translated the Bible out of Hebrew and Greek into Latin. Jerome was not as the painters feign, squalid and infirm, nor did he need a lion to accompany him, but with all his years he was fresh and full of dignity. His garments, which reached to his ankles, were lucent like crystal, and embroidered to the fringes in colors of ruby, emerald and sapphire with texts of the three sacred tongues; and such were the garments he gave to Reuchlin. Then the whole heaven was thronged with welcoming spirits, so many that they would have obscured the sky had they not been themselves translucent. Jerome led his companion to the top of the hill where again he kissed him. The heavens opened and they past up from view. Such was the Franciscan's vision, and the next day he learned that at that hour John Reuchlin died.

"Shall we not call him a saint?" the Colloquy continues. "But Rome has not made him a saint." "True, but who proclaimed Jerome a saint, or James, or John, or Mary? To us he shall ever be a saint." And so in memory of him they salute him in words like these: "O holy soul, do thou foster the sacred tongues, do thou foster those who study them. Let the sacred tongues prosper, but let the evil tongues perish infused with the poison of hell." And then follows a collect:

"O thou God who lovest the race of man and who thru thy chosen servant has restored to the world the gift of tongues thru which in olden time Thou didst from heaven teach thy holy Apostles by thy Holy Spirit to preach thy holy Gospel, grant that in all languages all men may preach everywhere the glory of thy Son Jesus, and that Thou mayest confound the tongues of false apostles who are conspired together to rebuild the impious tower of Babel that they may obscure Thy glory by striving to raise their own, for Thine only shall be all the glory with Jesus Christ, Thy Son our Lord, and the Holy Spirit, forever and ever. Amen."

When that collect is repeated we would add the name of Erasmus, who framed the prayer, to that of Reuchlin.

Do we live in evil days? We would not say it lest we be like the Camel of Louvain. The new is not worse but better than the old. And yet in our American Louvains and Tübingens we find the sacred tongues dishonored, so that the utterance of the collect might be a prayer for their confounding. Learning is something vastly greater than it was in the sixteenth century, and room must be made for it, but may the time never come when our students of theology shall cease to foster the three sacred tongues, and our universities and colleges as well shall fail to send out graduates who have a knowledge of at least two of the languages that have given us our religion and our civilization.

AMERICAN NEUTRALITY

WHAT we Americans mean by national neutrality is generally misconceived by Europeans, even those inclined to be sympathetic. The United States is variously accused or suspected of being cowardly, mercenary, hardhearted, indifferent, inconsistent or torn by internal dissensions. But no matter what motives are ascribed to us it should be made plain to Europe that neutrality is no new thing with us, but the established policy of our country enjoined upon us by George Washington and followed persistently thruout our national life in spite of all inducements and incitements to depart from it. Daniel Webster has given a definition of it which might well be stamped at the head of the White House note-paper:

Our neutrality is not a predetermined abstinence, either from remonstrances, or from force. Our neutral policy is a policy that protects neutrality, that defends neutrality, that takes up arms, if need be, for neutrality.

American neutrality is not based on indifference, and it does not necessarily mean pacifism.

THE HOPE OF CHURCH UNION

NEXT to the work of making the world better, the Church's first task is to unify itself. The divided condition of the Protestant churches is nothing less than a disgrace. A multitude of its members of the elder generation know it and mourn it, but they do not seem to know how to go to work to correct it by actually getting together. Federation is about the best thing that they seem able to understand.

The task and duty awaits the accomplishment of the coming generation, and most fortunately they are getting accustomed to the idea and trained to the work.

Take the three organizations, the Young Men's Christian Association, the Young Women's Christian Association and the Young People's Society of Christian Endeavor—their members are members of all the sects, but their labors and interests are not for the sect but for the Church Universal. Of this the Christian Endeavor is an extraordinary example. Its societies are now found in every Protestant denomination, with one or two insignificant exceptions—something over a hundred denominations in all. It is a pity that there are so many, but the young people are not responsible for their formation or their continued existence, and it is a good sign of the times that they are ready to come together on a common platform and that their churches do not object to this union. There are something like ten thousand or more C. E. conventions, or union meetings, held every year thruout the world, which bring together the young people of all these denominations. Sometimes there are only a few denominations represented in one locality and sometimes many. In the Pennsylvania state union, among five thousand societies there are no less than forty-seven different denominations. These meetings of these 80,000 societies thruout the world, with their four million members—and their number ever growing—are a fruitful promise of Church union not to be indefinitely delayed.

The Independent has a special interest in the history of the Christian Endeavor. It was Edward Eggleston, editor of The Independent, who organized in Brooklyn the church to which he gave the name of the Church of the Christian Endeavor. That name the Rev. Francis E. Clark chose as the name of the young people's society organized in his church, and Father Endeavor Clark has lived to see it cover the Protestant Christian world. He is now on a tour of visitation to direct and encourage his young people of both hemispheres.

===

THROWING THE BLAME UPON OXFORD

THE French in 1871 frankly acknowledged that they had been beaten "by the Prussian schoolmaster," and accordingly they set themselves to reform their educational system. The English, altho still confident of victory, are beginning to recognize that their educational system is in large part responsible for their inability to cope with the crisis. Professor Henry E. Armstrong, one of the foremost chemists of England, uses strong language on this point:

This country is governed primarily by and from Oxford. If the lessons of the war do not cause Oxford to reform, we shall be forced to confess that there is no health in us and, like the snark, our industry will "softly and silently steal away."

Since war has become a branch of applied chemistry the British are now paying the penalty for permitting Germany to oust England from that leadership in the chemical industries which she held a half century ago. Professor Armstrong calls the Oxford degree in chemistry "worthless for practical purposes," and urges that Greek and Latin have no right to monopolize the field as they have done hitherto.

It will be remembered that five years ago the necessity of reforming Oxford was generally recognized by those in charge of the university as well as outsiders. The resident staff favored the abolition of compulsory Greek, but the alumni of the university, especially the country clergy, voted repeatedly against any modification of the ancient régime.

===

THE FREEDOM OF THE SEAS

IN our present struggle with Great Britain and France to maintain the rights of neutral shipping on high seas it is well for us to remember that one of the Allies is, or should be, on our side of the controversy. Russia has always supported us in our former endeavors to establish the American principle of "Free ships make free goods," and this has at times drawn the two countries together by a bond of common policy. John Randolph of Roanoke, our Ambassador to Russia in 1830, did not put it too strongly when he declared that "From the reign of the illustrious Catherine the Great Russia and the United States have been identified in regard to maritime rights and principles." His successor at St. Petersburg, James Buchanan, wrote to Count Nesselrode:

The maintenance of the principle has contributed much to the glory of Russia and constitutes one of the brightest pages in her history. . . . All those who can justly appreciate the vexations and outrages which neutral commerce has suffered from the practise adopted by one or two belligerents of capturing neutral vessels upon the high seas, merely because the property of enemies might be found on board, will ever award to her exertions the fame which she so justly deserves.

By the following year treaties had been made with Prussia, Spain, the Netherlands and South American states to maintain the "free ships, free goods" idea against British and French encroachments.

The "line-up" in the present controversy is the same as it used to be except that the three Scandinavian countries are added to our side and Russia is seemingly identified with the other. But it is not probable that Russia, in spite of her present alliance with France and Great Britain, has repudiated her historic principles on this point. At any rate her prepossessions in favor of free shipping might incline her to lend a more sympathetic ear to our protests than Great Britain and France, whose policy has always been opposed. It might be well for our Ambassador at Petrograd to sound the Russian Government on this point and see if Russia would use her influence with her allies to mitigate the unjust and injurious restrictions upon neutral commerce against which our Government protests in vain.

===

THE BACHELOR AND THE MARRIED MAN

THE report of the Derby recruiting scheme showing that 53 per cent of the unmarried men and 59 per cent of the married men have volunteered for the army, will give obvious opportunity for the wit of the misogynist humorist—and somehow most professional humorists are constitutional misogynists. But there is another and more probable interpretation of these figures than that which ascribes them to the desire of husbands to seek the comparative peace of the firing line. We find this in Kipling's familiar lines:

The bachelor 'e fights for one
   As joyful as can be;
But the married man don't call it fun.
For 'Im an' 'Er an' It
   (An' Two an' One makes Three)
'E wants to finish 'is little bit,
   An 'e wants to go 'ome to 'is tea!

The bachelor will miss you clear
   To fight another day;
But the married man, 'e says, "No fear!"
   'E wants you out of the way
Of 'Im an' 'Er an' It
   (An' 'is road to 'is farm or the sea).
'E wants to finish 'is little bit,
   An' 'e wants to go 'ome to 'is tea.

It is indeed the most serious defect of the volunteer system that the appeal to the patriotism of the people brings out the good citizen and leaves the slacker. It exposes the conscientious to danger and preserves the coward. Such a reversal of the law of natural selection by which courage and patriotism have been developed would prove disastrous to a nation if practised on a large scale and for long. In this regard universal military service has the advantage, for it takes in all except the physically incompetent and so does not tend to favor the selfish at the expense of the unselfish.

THE STORY OF THE WEEK

GERMAN RULES FOR MEDITERRANEAN SUBMARINES

On January 7 the German Ambassador at Washington informed our Government that the German submarines in the Mediterranean were under the following instructions. It is understood that the same rules apply to the Austrian and Turkish submarines.

1. German submarines in the Mediterranean had from the beginning orders to conduct cruiser warfare against enemy merchant vessels only in accordance with general principles of international law, and in particular measures of reprisal, as applied in the war zone around the British Isles, were to be excluded.

2. German submarines are therefore permitted to destroy enemy merchant vessels in the Mediterranean—that is, passenger as well as freight ships so far as they do not try to escape or offer resistance—only after passengers and crews have been accorded safety.

3. All cases of destruction of enemy merchant ships in the Mediterranean in which German submarines are concerned are made the subject of official investigation and besides submitted to regular prize court proceedings. In so far as American interests are concerned, the German Government will communicate the result to the American Government. Thus also in the "Persia" case if the circumstances should call for it. If commanders of German submarines should not have obeyed the orders given to them they will be punished; furthermore, the German Government will make reparation for damage caused by death of or injury to American citizens.

Three Hundred Miles of Battle It was thought by some that there would be a cessation of activity on the eastern front during the winter, especially since the weather is unusually severe even for Russia. But during Christmas week the Russians undertook a new offensive along the southern section of the line between the Pripet and the Dniester rivers. These rivers run eastwardly about three hundred miles apart, but they come near being connected by water, for two of their tributaries, the Styr and the Strypa, both have their origin near the Galician frontier. It was on or near these two rivers that the Austro-German advance halted last fall, and since this formed a good line of defense, no serious attempt has been made at a further drive eastward. The later efforts of the Germans were directed toward the capture of Riga and Dvinsk, in the extreme north, but in this they failed.

During the last four months the Russian army has been reorganized and obtained a new supply of guns and ammunition, largely, it appears, of Japanese manufacture. They are said to have 1,500,000 on this southern section between Pinsk and Czernowitz. Pinsk, the northern end of this section, is in the swampy valley of the Pripet River. Czernowitz is situated on the slope of the Carpathian Mountains and some twenty miles south of the Dniester River. On the northern side of the Dniester there are also high lands of over a thousand feet altitude, in the midst of which stands Tarnopol, on the Sereth River. North of Tarnopol, are the three fortresses of Lutsk, Dubno and Rovno, designed to be the chief defenses of southern Russia. Two of these are in the hands of the Germans. The third, Rovno, they have not been able to take.

This, then, is the lay of the land in the new battlefield. The Russians seem to be concentrating their efforts on the southern part in the attempt to make

another drive up the Dniester to recapture Czernowitz and Lemberg as

they did in the first months of the war. On the north side of the Dniester they are attacking Buczacz on the road to Lemberg. On the south side of this river they have occupied the hights which overlook Czernowitz. The Russian army which is attempting to invade Bukovina is under the command of General Ivanoff and it is rumored that Field Marshal Mackensen, the conqueror of Serbia, has been brought back from the Balkans to oppose him. The Russians are said to have massed here 60,000 men on a front of less than a mile. After a bombardment of fifty hours, in which 400 guns took part, they began the attack and charged the German trenches fourteen times in one day, in spite of appalling losses. The Austrian War Office estimates the Russian losses in the recent operations at 50,000.

Further north the fighting is no less severe. The Austrians under General Pflanzer are trying to capture Tarnopol

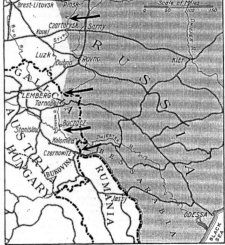

THE NEW RUSSIAN OFFENSIVE

The three-hundred mile line between Pinsk and Czernowitz which the Germans have held ever since last September is now being subjected to energetic attacks from the Russians at various points. The line follows roughly the course of two rivers, the Styr running north and the Strypa running south. Both these have been crost by the Russians, who are also directing an attack upon Czernowitz, the capital of Bukovina. If the Russians should regain Bukovina, Rumania would be likely to take the side of the Allies or at least permit the Russian armies to cross Rumania and invade Bulgaria from the north while the English and French at Salonica attacked Bulgaria from the south

76

Paul Thompson

THE BUILDERS

Germany moves promptly to restore to their normal condition the territories her armies have seized. Here is a bridge being rebuilt in Poland. Railway engineers have been known to repair a bridge destroyed by the enemy, and needed for immediate advance, in six hours' time

and the Russians have taken the town of Czartorysk, which gives them a chance to advance along the railroad toward the important junction of Kovel.

The Submarine Question — Both Germany and Austria-Hungary now seem anxious to satisfy the American Government on all points at issue. The voluntary assurance given by Count von Bernstorff, which we quote in another column, concedes the main points for which our Government has contended, and if these rules are faithfully followed there may be no further cause of complaint, at least so far as the Mediterranean is concerned. It is also promised in advance that if it turns out that the "Persia" was sunk by a German or Austrian submarine without warning or when it was not resisting or trying to escape, the commander will be punished and reparation made. It is said also that Germany has exprest a willingness to pay an indemnity for the loss of American lives on the "Lusitania" tho the wording of the disavowal demanded by the United States has not yet been agreed upon.

The "Frye" case was virtually settled by a note dated November 29, which has just been made public. In this the German Government agrees to leave the amount of the indemnity to be paid by Germany to be settled by two experts, one named by each of the Governments. The German Government has named Dr. Greve, of Bremen, director of the North German Lloyd. The German Government expresses regret that Dr. Greve cannot go to Washington in compliance with the desire of the American Government, owing to "the danger of capture during the voyage in consequence of the conduct of the war by England contrary to international law." The German Government regards the appointment of a neutral umpire as a third arbiter as unnecessary if it is merely a matter of appraising the damages.

As to the arbitration of the questions of maritime warfare involved the German Government wishes to have the Prussian-American treaty of 1899 made the basis of procedure rather than the Hague rules. Until these questions are settled by arbitration the German navals will sink only such American vessels as are loaded with absolute contraband. when the pre-conditions provided by the Declaration of London are present. In this the German Government quite shares the view of the American Government that all possible care must be taken for the security of the crew and passengers of a vessel to be sunk. Consequently, the persons found on board of a vessel may not be ordered into her lifeboats except when the general conditions, that is to say, the weather, the condition of the sea. and the neighborhood of the coasts afford absolute certainty that the boats will reach the nearest port. For the rest the German Government begs to point out that in cases where German naval forces have sunk neutral vessels for carrying contraband, no loss of life has yet occurred.

The "Persia" case is still a mystery and, like the "Maine," may never be cleared up. The affidavits of the survivors throw no light on the cause of the explosion which blew up the steamer, for nobody saw a submarine and the only direct evidence to show that the "Persia" was sunk by a submarine is the statement of the second officer that he saw the wake of a torpedo. The number of missing is 336, of whom 119 were passengers and 217 crew. Of those saved 65 were passengers and 214 crew. Besides Consul McNeeley it seems there was another American drowned, for among the missing is the Rev. Dr. Homer R. Salisbury, a Seventh Day Adventist missionary, who came on board at Marseilles to go to India. He came from Battle Creek, Michigan, and is supposed to be an American. If the Austrian or German government has any information as to how the "Persia" was sunk it has not been made public.

Parliament Votes Conscription — The amazing change which has come over Great Britain is shown by the passage of a conscription act in the House of Commons by a vote of 403 to 105. Counting out the Irish members, since Ireland is not included, there were only forty votes against it by the representatives of the country covered by the bill. Even the Labor party was divided, for ten out of the twenty-three representatives of that party voted for it. Among them was Arthur Henderson, leader of the Labor party, who had just resigned his cabinet position of President of the Board of Education, because the Labor caucus had decided that no Labor members should remain in the Government. The two other Labor men in the Coalition Ministry resigned for the same reason,

Press Illustrating Co.

AN OLD CEREMONY IN TODAY'S WAR

The Austrians here have decorated their cattle with festive garlands in celebration of a victory quite as if they were living in the palmy days of the classics

William Bruce who was Parliamentary Under Secretary for Home Affairs and George H. Roberts, Lord Commissioner of the Treasury. The Cabinet also lost on this issue Sir John Simon, Secretary of State for Home Affairs, who made a speech against the conscription bill and criticized Lord Derby's figures.

According to Lord Derby's report the recruiting campaign of the six weeks ending December 15 induced 1,150,000 out of 2,179,231 single men and 1,672,-261 out of 2,832,210 married men to volunteer. Many of the single men who have not come forward are ineligible or needed for the Government service for manufacture of munitions, but there are about 600,000 single men who are available and these the bill aims to get. Quakers and others who have "conscientious objections to undertaking combatant service" are exempt. The penalties of attempting to evade military service may be six months imprisonment and $250 fine.

The Unionists and Conservatives all supported the bill and the most influential speech in its favor was made by A. J. Balfour, formerly leader of the Opposition, but now First Lord of the Admiralty in the Asquith Ministry. He said:

I have never favored conscription in any form, but it is no longer an abstract question. We are dealing with a stern reality. First, the Prime Minister has given a pledge for this bill which it would be dishonorable to ignore, and, second, the safety and success of the country are at stake. Let me say with the greatest emphasis that those of us who know the conditions in the field know that this bill is absolutely essential to the proper carrying on of the war.

If this house refuses this bill to the Government, it refuses what the Government considers an absolute military necessity. This is not a precedent for universal conscription. It is not the thin edge of the wedge, or the first drop of poison to corrupt our whole system. In truth, this bill is a tribute to voluntarism, for we have raised 6,000,000 volunteers, and now this bill merely brings in those few shirkers who have failed to respond to the volunteer system.

No future Prime Minister can ever use this bill as a precedent for permanently fixing on the country the taint of Prussian militarism.

Militarism is an affair of the heart, and it is in the hearts of the German people to have militarism, while it is in the hearts of Englishmen not to have it.

But for the moment we are dealing with a stern necessity, and our greatest danger is not that traditions will be abandoned, but that we are lulling ourselves with a great illusion of false security.

In spite of the large majority which the bill drafting single men into the army received in the House of Commons it is doubtful whether it can be put into effect without a general election, for the trades-unions are strongly opposed even to this partial measure of conscription. The National Labor Congress held its session at the same time as Parliament protested unanimously against any form of compulsory military service. On the specific question of Asquith's bill the votes in favor represented 783,000 workingmen and those against 1,998,000.

THE GREAT WAR

January 3—British complete conquest of Kamerun, Africa. Turks claim victory over Russians in Persia.

January 4—Italy has spent $561,000,-000 on war to January 1. Turks attacking British at Kut-el-Amara on Tigris.

January 5—Four members of British ministry resign on account of conscription bill. Russians attacking Czernovitz, capital of Bukovina.

January 6—Conscription bill for unmarried men passes House of Commons. Russians capture Czartorysk.

January 7—Germany agrees to settle "Frye" and "Lusitania" cases and ameliorate submarine warfare. Nancy bombarded by Germans.

January 8—Russian warships bombard Varna, on Black Sea. Trenches on Hartmanns-Weilerkopf, Vosges, changing hands.

January 9—British abandon Gallipoli altogether. British battleship "King Edward VII" sunk by mine.

The Balkan Campaign   In spite of repeated rumors of a Teutonic attack upon the Allied base at Salonica there have been no evidences of such a movement. It is in-

Underwood & Underwood
THE "VALERIE" BRINGS CABARACHE
A big Norwegian bark which put into port at New York the other day with a cargo of dyewood from Buenos Ayres. There is a faint echo of the old clipper days in New York's shipping now that sailing vessels, which were thought to have gone forever, have been called back to replace steamers destroyed or interned in the war

deed doubtful whether it would prove a profitable enterprise, for the French and British troops at Salonica are said to number over 200,000 and are strongly entrenched in the hills about the city. Having the command of the sea the Allies can land reinforcements and munitions to any amount directly on the docks at Salonica while supplies for the German and Austrian troops would have to be brought down on the single track railroad from Belgrade. If the Bulgars and Turks should join them in the invasion of Greece the Greeks would be quite likely to take up arms in defense of Salonica, which within the last four years they fought the Turks to gain and then the Bulgars to retain. If the Germans and Austrians try to take Salonica by themselves they will doubtless require more troops than the defenders and must expect heavy losses which they can ill afford, since they are already greatly outnumbered both in France and Russia and are extending the field of operations into Asia. Even if they should succeed in driving the Allies out of Salonica they could not hope to hold that city, since it can be bombarded at any time by the Allied fleet. But by letting things stay as they are a large body of Allied troops is virtually kept interned at Salonica and the Bulgars may be trusted to guard the border if they should attempt again to advance into Serbia.

What acts perhaps as a greater deterrent still is the energetic attack of the Russians on the Austro-German lines north of Rumania. If the Russians should again occupy Bukovina and Galicia, Rumania would be very apt to join with them and this would open the way for an invasion of Bulgaria from the northern side. It is reported that General Mackensen and many of his troops have been recalled from Serbia to meet this new danger.

The second Bulgarian army is said to have been brought back to Sofia. The first Bulgarian army is driving the Serbs thru Albania to the sea. The Montenegrins are stoutly resisting the Austrian invasion of their country.

Greece has protested to Washington and the other neutral governments against the violation of her neutrality thru the occupation of Salonica by the French and British and their arrest of the German, Austrian, Bulgarian and Turkish consuls at that port. Additional offense has been given to Greece by the Allies in the arrest of the Austrian and German consuls at Mitylene, and by the occupation of the Greek islands of Melos, in the Aegean, and Corfu, in the Adriatic. In retaliation for this the Bulgars arrested the French consul at Sofia and tried to arrest the British vice-consul, but he took refuge in the American embassy.

The Near East   The withdrawal of the Allied troops from the Anzac and Suvla shores of Gallipoli left only Sedd-el-Bahr, the tip of the peninsula, in the hands of the British. This apparently they intended to hold as a sort of second Gibraltar, for it commands the en-

THE "FILIPINO CARNEGIE"

Sr. Teodoro R. Yangco, a leading business man and philanthropist of the Philippines, who is visiting this country to study business conditions, the Y. M. C. A., and charitable institutions. He is president of the Philippine Chamber of Commerce and of the Manila Y. M. C. A.

trance to the Dardanelles and its possession would enable them to control the only entrance to the Black Sea, as they control the only entrance to the Mediterranean, Gibraltar and Suez. But even this foothold proves to be untenable. Heavy artillery, transported from Germany by the Orient railroad thru Serbia and Bulgaria, was brought to bear upon the British entrenchments and upon the French and British warships defending them. So the British and French troops have been withdrawn from Sedd-el-Bahr, without losses, according to the British report, with heavy losses, according to the Turkish report. All guns were taken away except seventeen, which were worn out and were blown up before being abandoned.

Whether the Germans have any serious intention of undertaking an invasion of Egypt is still questionable, for the hints of which are allowed to leak out may be intended merely to divert British troops to the Suez and so prevent the concentration of Kitchener's army in France. We hear, however, that Field Marshal von der Goltz has established his headquarters at Aleppo, from which point he can send troops by rail part way to Bagdad or nearly all the way to the Egyptian frontier. Since there is no knowing which way he intends to strike, the British are obliged to keep a sufficient force to meet an attack both on the Tigris River and the Suez Canal. Von der Goltz is one of the leading authorities on strategy in the world, his textbooks being used at West Point. For many years before the war he had

been engaged in reorganizing the Turkish army and planning their system of fortifications. For the training of the navy the Ottoman Government employed British officers. The troops under General von der Goltz are estimated at 300,000 to 500,000.

The Dutch and the Japanese lines running to the Far East have abandoned the Suez route and are sending their steamers around by the Cape of Good Hope. The insurance rate on all cargoes going thru the Suez has been trebled, which will make the expense practically prohibitive for most traffic. The activity of the Austrian submarines in the Mediterranean may account for this diversion of traffic, but it confirms the expectation of a conflict on the canal within a short time.

In northern Persia the Russians have had several engagements with the Persian insurgents in which both sides claim victories. The British at Kut-el-Amara, on the Tigris, are still holding their own against the repeated attacks of the Turks and Arabs.

War and the Industries

Owing partly to the war demand, the price of gasoline continues to rise, and is now 22 cents a gallon. At the beginning of last year it was only 13 cents. In the House at Washington two resolutions were adopted, last week, one asking the Attorney General to report as to the existence of an unlawful combination in the industry, and the other providing for an inquiry by a House committee. The Attorney General replied that thus far there was no evidence to justify a prosecution for violation of the law against restraint of trade by combinations, and that the Federal Trade Commission had undertaken an investigation of the oil trade. It is now known that the commission has decided to inquire at once about the price of gasoline. The rapidly growing number of automobiles in use here, the demand from abroad, especially in and near the battle fields, and the decreased output of certain oil fields in this country, appears to account for the high price. Some predict that it will rise to 40 cents.

Reviews of the zinc industry for the past year show how it has been affected by the war demand. While the output of spelter increased by 38 per cent. the value of the product was $139,000,000 against only $36,000,000 in 1914. The demand for ammunition accounts for this change. We have imported large quantities of tin, nearly all of it from Malaysia. The effect of the war upon prices and transportation, together with our more intimate trade relations with South America, has promoted the establishment here of a new industry, the smelting and refining of tin ore from Bolivia. The work will be done in New Jersey, and on a large scale.

Few additional war orders have recently been reported. There have been negotiations for large quantities of shrapnel. The Canadian Car and Foundry Company, whose first order from Russia was for $83,000,000 worth of shrapnel, was looking for $10,000,000

GERMANY'S SCIENTIFIC CHIEF OF STAFF

The success of the Germans in the field and their still more remarkable success in maintaining the nation when all commerce was cut off are due to the organization of industry under scientific direction. Dr. Walther Rathenau, the head of the General Electric Company, was called upon at the outbreak of the war by the Minister of War to take charge of manufacture of war material. His greatest achievement is the development of the process of making nitric acid from the nitrogen and oxygen of the air by means of the electric spark. This provides the nitrates necessary for ammunition and agriculture and frees Germany, probably permanently, from her previous dependence upon the British nitrate beds of Chile

last week, to be used in the business, and the company's stock declined sharply in the market because the money was not promptly obtained. But $4,000,000 was supplied by Russia, and the remainder was expected from the same source in a few days. Russia's original advance had been $20,000,000, but a large part of this was distributed among the many manufacturers to whom the company gave sub-contracts.

Defense Plans in Congress

It is admitted that the Washington that the Government's plans for enlarging the army and the navy are in some danger of being rejected by Congress. The army plans are regarded with less favor than those relating to the navy, and there is pronounced opposition to the Continental force proposed by Secretary Garrison. In the House the Administration is in need of leadership for its policy, which is opposed by the appointed Democratic floor leader, Mr. Kitchin. Only with the aid of Republican votes can the new plans gain approval there.

In recent speeches opposition has been more prominent than support, even on the Democratic side. In some cases the opposition has been manifested in relation to side issues rather than to the plans. In the Senate Mr. O'Gorman and Mr. Hitchcock, Democrats, have favored an embargo, or prohibition of the shipment of munitions. Mr. O'Gorman and Mr. Owen would have the Government prevent American citizens from taking passage on the liners of the belligerents. Several Republicans were in agreement with them on this. In the House Mr. Sherwood, of Ohio, a Democrat, in a long speech ridiculed and denounced the Administration's plans. To tax the people for them, he said, would be a crime. Mr. Bryan sent him a letter of congratulation, saying he hoped the speech would cause the defeat of the plans.

On the other hand, Senator Williams uttered a warning as to hostile action against this country after the war by the victorious side, saying that we should be bullied at least, and that we ought to enlarge both the army and the navy. Senator Chamberlain, chairman of the Senate's military committee, is in favor of compulsory military education, with a short term of service. Before the House Committee, Secretary Garrison has made an elaborate argument in support of his plans. Representative Gardner, of Massachusetts, whose advocacy of preparedness is well known, provoked a warm debate in the House by attacks upon pro-German plotters. His denunciation was so comprehensive that several Republicans who have many German-American constituents defended them and sharply criticized what he had said.

Strike Riots in Ohio Riots causing loss of life and the destruction of much property have accompanied a strike of 3600 employees of the Republic Iron and Steel Company and the Sheet and Tube Company at East Youngstown, Ohio. The men went on strike about three weeks ago for an increase of pay from 19½ to 25 cents an hour. After the United States Steel Corporation, on the 6th, announced an increase of ten per cent for more than 150,000 men, the Youngstown companies offered an increase from 19¼ to 22½ cents. This was rejected. The riots began on the 7th in the evening. A mob of strikers gathered at the end of a guarded bridge which workmen who had not gone on strike must cross; and hooted at them, also throwing stones. A pistol shot was followed by several warning shots in the air from the guards. The return fire wounded several persons, among them two women. Immediately the mob began to set fire to buildings and to loot saloons and stores.

Before morning ten blocks of buildings, practically the entire business section of East Youngstown, had been destroyed by fire, with a loss of about $2,000,000; nearly one hundred persons had been wounded, and eighteen of the town's twenty saloons had been looted and burned. The bottled liquors had been taken, and in the streets were seen barrels of whisky, with the heads knocked in, while drink-crazed strikers were around them. The small police

Paul Thompson

HATE IN WOOD AND HATE IN COAL
Gott strafe England, stamped on the briquets furnished as fuel for the soldiers at the front, may be expected to make the fire hotter. A Dutch customer who received this sort of fuel from a German dealer, however, refused to use it

force could do nothing. When the firemen came, the mob cut their hose and drove them away. One of the burned buildings was the post office. After some delay a party of policemen and citizens from the neighboring city of Youngstown dispersed and drove away the rioters. More than 100 were placed in jail. At daybreak three regiments of militia, 2400 men, arrived and they have since been on guard. It does not appear that more than three persons were killed, altho others may die of their wounds.

For a New Pan-American Agreement Until the close of the session of the Pan-American Scientific Congress, at the end of last week, the dominant topics were those relating to political association and coöperation. There were addresses in which business credits were considered, with plans for facilitating commercial interchanges. Two or three speakers drew attention to South America as an inviting field for investments which would promote trade with

© *International News*

HE IS AN ENGLISHMAN
The new warfare on the trench-fronts has become a grotesque masquerade since gas became a weapon. The picture on page 71 shows why it is necessary to clothe the men thus

the United States. Mr. Bryan said our Government might well underwrite loans to South American countries for development of their resources. He hoped the pending treaty, which provides for the payment of a large sum to Colombia, would be ratified. But political coöperation was the leading subject in the minds of delegates, and new prominence was given to it on the 5th by the news that what some have called an extension of the Monroe Doctrine had been proposed by our Government to the twenty American republics.

At the direction of the President, Secretary Lansing has formally laid before the Latin-American Ambassadors and Ministers, to be submitted to their Governments, the plan of a general treaty or series of treaties in which the United States and all the other nations of this hemisphere shall agree to guarantee the territorial integrity of the several countries; to maintain the republican form of government; to submit to settlement by diplomacy, arbitration, or investigating commissions disputes of all kinds, boundary disagreements included, but controversies affecting national independence excepted; to prohibit exportation of arms to any but the legally constituted governments, and to enact neutrality laws that will prevent filibustering expeditions from fomenting or carrying on revolutions in neighboring republics. There has not been time for a reception of answers from the nations to which the proposition was submitted.

In an address to the members of the Congress and their friends, on the 6th, President Wilson referred to this movement. A conference was recently held in Washington, he said, to consider the financial relations of the two American continents and to ascertain the practical means by which commercial intercourse could be facilitated. Those who took part in the conference realized that back of the community of material interest there must be a community of political interest. If nations are politically suspicious of one another, all their intercourse is embarrassed. The Monroe Doctrine, which this country always will maintain upon its own responsibility, did not, the President said, disclose the use which the United States intended to make of her power, with the implied and partial protectorate which she was trying to set up, and therefore fears and suspicions prevented complete confidence and trust between the Americas. There has been doubt, and it must be removed. He believed it would be removed by such an agreement as the one outlined above. Speaking of its requirements, he said he was confident that they would lead to something long prayed for by America. They were based upon self-restraint, respect for the rights of all, absolute political equality among the nations, and the eternal foundations of justice and humanity. The next session of the Congress will be held at Lima, Peru, in 1921.

SHOULD THE UNITED STATES FIGHT ?

AND WHAT IS THE NATURE OF A PRUSSIAN?

BY G. K. CHESTERTON

HOW long will the war last? That's a difficult matter to determine. I may say, however, that I rather look for a *sudden* ending. Endings *are* sudden when you come to think of it, aren't they? We get into the habit of regarding most happenings as gradual. We watch the details of this stupendous conflict daily and our minds move slowly toward the contemplation of its definite end. Beginnings and endings are never gradual. Death itself is always a very definite happening and so I rather think Germany's end of this war may be as sudden as a volcano.

The Battle of the Marne dashed forever her hopes of conquest in the West. She then turned her face to the East in the hope of a definite decision. After many ups and downs, successes, failures, hopes and despairs, I do not believe she can now look for a definitely final decision there after her repulse in Russia. The likelihood of German conquest no longer exists. The only question for the Allies now is how long will it take for Germany to be worn out, exhausted. It is now only a question of *when*. When Russia sufficiently recovers herself to assume the offensive at the same time that the Allies push forward, the end will not be far off. Of course any conjectures of mine of this character must not be taken too seriously, for when you are dealing with self-respecting maniacs you can't be sure of anything. Self-respecting maniacs, because they really believe they're engaged in some kind of holy, uplifting work, which, sad to say, has to be forced on the rest of the world. They remind me of the Zealots during the fall of Jerusalem.

They have all the bumptiousness of a gas balloon. They're far too stupid for any likelihood of an internal revolution, and even if there were any chance of it, Prussianism would nip it in the bud. And by the way, the Prussian hypnotism of the whole of Germany is one of the most amazing things I've ever heard of. Do you know that as recently as the taking of Schleswig-Holstein, Prussians

---

Mr. Chesterton, unlike most authors, is equally interesting whether he writes or talks. In both cases he is merely thinking openly and all the reader or listener has to do is to follow his train of thought thru all its nimble windings. The listener in this case is Percy Waxman, who went to Mr. Chesterton at his home and asked him to talk about the war. The following interview was the result.—THE EDITOR.

were regarded as *aliens* in Germany? It was not until after the intoxicating success of the Franco-Prussian War that the Prussian was able to make himself the symbol of Germany. He made the rest of Germany believe that he was divinely ordained to boss them.

BISMARCK typified Prussianism at its acme. Prussianism never consisted of a desire for leadership unless secured by conquest. And that idea holds good in Germany today. At one time the King of Prussia was actually offered the crown of United Germany, but he refused it on the

G. K. CHESTERTON

---

ground that he had no desire to gain a throne at the behest of the people. He must win it by conquest or not at all.

It is hard to say today where Prussia ends and the rest of Germany begins. All Germany is absolutely hypnotized. Why, an ordinary German is incapable of governing himself, and if you suggested that he could do it, you would offend *his* sense of state rule. That's Prussianism for you—an entire squelching of the individual and individual right. The German character, with its strange inability to see anything true about humanity, is wonderfully well exemplified by those curious creatures known as German governesses whom we see in so many English families; or rather did see, with their monstrously serious and monstrously sensitive temperaments.

They are just as likely to burn down your house for some imagined grievance as they are to perform some marvelous act of self-sacrifice which a normal person could see was entirely unnecessary. Germans are nearly all of this hysterical governess type. When they find themselves in the wrong, they explode temperamentally, deliberately behaving as devils, while honestly believing themselves to be angels. They are nationally afflicted with an egregious form of self-love which in a large measure has been pandered to and fostered by their mythology.

Germans dignify their mythology with the name of history. Fancy calling that spurious Treitschke-Bernhardi rubbish about waking up the whole world to Teutonism, history. Germans keep on judging the historic by the pre-historic, which is to say the least, a curious habit. All this undefined twaddle about Celts and Teutons is largely German pedantry, and we were almost catching the ghastly complaint in England. Learning *real* history is a far more difficult task than to talk rot about the prehistoric. You can always detect the sham student of history by his love of indefinite terms. For instance, you hear a lot about Celts, Teutons and

81

Anglo-Saxons, whoever they are. Now if I say I'm an Englishman, it means something definite. You conjure up a picture of a man who likes tea and toast for breakfast, makes a fuss over his morning tub, is rather aggressively individual and that sort of thing. But if I say I'm a Teuton, it is really meaningless. Who knows any definite characteristics about Teutons? And yet it is just this vague kind of stuff that Germany has been yelling and screaming about for ages. She has told us time and again that we should love her more than we do, because the Germans and English all belong to the one great Anglo-Saxon-Teutonic family. Think of it. She has tried to prove to us by some mathematical formula that we are all one family. Utter nonsense. Who has more miserably and totally failed to understand us than the Germans?

Their colossal failure to understand anything about us almost proves that we must be related, for the failure of families to understand each other is proverbial. German "frightfulness," as exemplified by Zeppelin raids and submarine murders, not only shows an absolute misunderstanding of England, but is direct proof of German fear at home. Only the fearsome becomes desperate.

Germans regard the English joking habit as evidence of a ghastly shallowness and abandoned debauchery. With their own troops singing *Deutschland über Alles* in perfect time and perfect tune as they march into action, they look upon English light-hearted irony under such circumstances as approaching blasphemy. The newest battle-cry for our troops as they dash for enemy trenches is "Front seats two-and-sixpence." No self-respecting German would ever dream of using irony as a relaxation. This lack of humor is what produces Germany's somber egotism. Germany's idea, too, of a gentleman is what most other people regard as a cad. They seem to have a genius for thinking exactly the opposite things about humanity from what any one else in the world thinks.

Shortly after the war broke out, a typical Englishman of what is known as the old school, said: "If Germany should prove to be successful, Europe would be no place for a gentleman." That sums the matter up very adequately, I think.

There's been a veritable wave of the democratic idea all over England. The great difficulty just now is its lack of coherence. The idea is growing here, there and everywhere, but it hasn't concentrated its forces yet, and the grievances it wishes to combat are not neatly labeled and ready to be destroyed. It is not a clean-cut task to instil the really democratic idea into English people. The issues are very complicated and entangled. Our evils are not labeled. Everything seems vague. When the French idea came about, there was King Louis pleasantly concrete as the foe of the democratic idea. So they cut off his head and the crown with it. With us we are mistily sensible of great grievances needing to be destroyed, but as yet we only feel is that them. Our tyrants aren't visible. They exist mostly as impersonal groups, not as individuals. What we seem to need is a sort of detective-democracy that will seek out what needs to be destroyed and then destroy it. We'll see daylight no doubt when the war gives us more time to look for it.

A S for America, I am sorry to confess that whenever the average Englishman talks about America, his viewpoint becomes tainted by the same sort of German folly that makes Germans talk of us and themselves as one big family. We are likely to think of America as Anglo-Saxon, one of ourselves, chip off the old block, one blood and such like nonsense. It is true, of course, that America and England do speak the same language—almost, but when it comes to race there must be veritable cataracts of blood running thru American veins by now that can't by any stretch of imagination be called Anglo-Saxon. I'm afraid many of us in England will never rightly understand America until we begin by regarding her as a great nation,—entirely dissociated from ourselves. Let us regard America as we might any other great nation speaking English, and we'll understand her better.

It is very idiotic to adopt any maternal attitude toward the United States. We make much of "one blood, one tongue," and other accidental incidents whenever American policy dictates a course of action that appears favorable to the English mind. When, on the other hand, America, in pursuit of her own individual nationalism, commits some act we don't agree with, or does not commit some act we think she should have, we play the role of maternal scold. Too many Englishmen regard America as being in some mysterious way still bound up with ourselves by ties other than national friendship.

Whether America should do this or that in regard to Belgium, I don't know. I don't know enough of what her obligations were to pass an opinion. This much I do know, and that is that your President would have been foolish to bundle the American people into the hateful furnace of war just because many of my countrymen considered her bound to assist Belgium. England herself was in a very different position. She was in honor bound to help Belgium, and even if we hadn't gone to her assistance, we would have eventually been compelled to take a hand in the war for our own protection.

America is not in any such position, and why anyone should expect her to adopt the role of world-savior, I don't know. I have a great sympathy with America's difficulties in a most trying situation. I admire President Wilson very much, and I regret that both here, and at home in his own country, there has been a great deal of most unfair criticism, mostly due to cloudy vision.

He is paid by the people to protect the interests and welfare of the United States. He can't dip his country into Hell just to show the world he has a keen sense of being an individual savior. Why do people expect him to be a celestial person? There has been too much of this indignant rushing to protect the honor of others.

We know that America, like all other detached democracies, favors the Allies, but without cause why should they enter the bloody arena? I'm aware that there are many, many American citizens who think their country should take a hand, including your famous American citizen Roosevelt (altho perhaps he may consider that term an insufficient description for him). It's for Americans to decide what they should or should not do, isn't it?

Beaconsfield, England

Photograph by Capt. F. E. Kleinschmidt
WHERE A SHELL BURST INTO KING PETER'S THRONE ROOM IN THE PALACE AT BELGRADE

Photograph by Capt. F. E. Kleinschmidt
THE CITY AND FORTRESS OF BELGRADE FROM 3000 FEET IN THE AIR. NOTE THE SHELL CRATERS

FOR a period of four years I have been the chief executive of an enterprise which ranks among the oldest in the United States and is now owned by nearly 2,000,000 shareholders. A purely physical valuation of its entire plant amounts, at a notoriously moderate estimate, to $2,700,000,000, of which some $200,000,000 is represented by assets directly owned, backed by $1,800,000,000 in assessed real and $600,000,000 in personal erty. It would be difficult to name many other corporations, however inflated their capitalization, which approach it in magnitude. And over against those real and tangible assets there exists only $100,000,000 of liabilities, in the form of a bonded debt. Evidently here is an enterprise which is not merely solvent; it is positively rolling in wealth. Yet it stands in need today, most urgently, of an efficient administration of its affairs—not, I hope, quite so urgently as it did four years ago; but surely with a pressure of need that should enlist the active interest and coöperation of every one among its many shareholders, children by no means excepted. Oh, yes; those shareholders include children, by hundreds of thousands; and not only do they own a vital interest in the welfare of the enterprise, but their small voices are capable of exerting a powerful influence for its successful conduct.

In the past, it has suffered grievously from lack of interest on the part of many of its shareholders as well as from a chronic misconception of its purposes on the part of many others; in the same way it can suffer as much, or more, in the future. And because it is representative of very many other such corporations in this country—among them two of even greater magnitude, the majority much smaller—the essentials of its efficient management constitute the essentials of the class, with the nation as a whole as vitally concerned as are the millions of individual shareholders.

For the City of Philadelphia, like other cities, is in reality nothing but a coöperative corporation, the type of the oldest form of coöperative enterprise organized. Happily removed

MAYOR BLANKENBURG

as they do—and nothing ell. For its aim it has the production of ... safety, health, comfort and ... opportunities, to be supplied to its citizen shareholders at a ... reasonable cost. It has proved no political service to sell and ... have

izen shareholders in the corporation must keep up an organizat'o of disinterested, public-spirited r n and women which shall be ')nstant menace to would-be pli derers, which shall hold them in chck and, if necessary, take them i 'tra court of justice as has been d-n in San Francisco and New Yorl.

A permanent basis o. ficiency can be attained only by t le.limination of politics as a factc in the conduct of the city's aff: ir and by the inculcation of such a ci c spirit as will make all citizens illing to serve the municipality. Toay most cities are served by a less esirable class than could readily beobtained if genuine public spirit pre iled and induced men of merit to ive their time, their probity and the brains.

Such fundamental chanes, however, can be accomplishec only by educating the shareholde in the protection of their own nterests, and by fixing upon a few ublic officials the responsibility 'or honest and economical admi stration. When I appointed my d ectors I said to each of them:

"You have absolute cont l of your department. The responsibility must be yours. Come and consult me whenever you wish; but for results I look to you."

That is what executive responsibility should amount to. In councils, in Philadelphia, there are 132 men of no responsibility except the responsibility which many of them think they owe to the bosses who made possible their election. We cannot expect anything in particular from individuals who, their individuality lost in a servile majority, have become nobody in particular. But if there were a small council, the citizen shareholders could get at every one of them. A council of nine, every one paid $10,000 a year for his services, and a city manager paid an attractive salary, would produce best results, I think, in a city as large as Philadelphia. But even so small a council could be as dangerous as the present unwieldly number if the highly paid few were amenable to partizan influences. Men in such a position must think and act solely for the welfare of the corporation, just as directors think and act for a great railroad, when they have been wisely chosen.

It all resolves itself into this: that the citizens shall take an intelligently selfish view of their individual interest in the welfare of the municipality. They must expect to know its business as they do their own private ventures and they must endeavor to conduct it at least as well.

Under conditions existing almost everywhere in the United States, as well as in Philadelphia, the hope of making such an ideal citizenship must begin with education of the very children. The results may not be immediately apparent; but they will be felt as the children grow. Some effect would follow speedily, for children really have an influence in the home; and child questions, the outcome of simple yet wise instruction in the schools, have made many fathers think who have not thought before. It is reasonable to expect that appreciable consequences would appear within a decade of the time when such instruction was begun.

There is hope for the suggestion, because the present generation of political bosses may decide that the full consequences of such a course in education will fall upon their successors, rather than themselves.

Philadelphia

AS USUAL

BY BURTON KLINE

WHAT IS A CITY?

BY RUDOLPH BLANKENBURG

FOR a period of four years I have been the chief executive of an enterprise which ranks among the oldest in the United States and is now owned by nearly 2,000,000 shareholders. A purely physical valuation of its entire plant amounts, at a notoriously moderate estimate, to $2,700,000,000, of which some $300,000,000 is represented by assets directly owned, backed by $1,800,000,000 in assessed real estate and $600,000,000 in personal property. It would be difficult to name many other corporations, however inflated their capitalization, which approach it in magnitude. And over against those real and tangible assets there exists only $100,000,000 of liabilities, in the form of a bonded debt. Evidently here is an enterprise which is not merely solvent; it is positively rolling in wealth. Yet it stands in need to-day, most urgently, of an efficient administration of its affairs—not, I hope, quite so urgently as it did four years ago; but surely with a pressure of need that should enlist the active interest and coöperation of every one among its many shareholders, children by no means excepted. Oh, yes; those shareholders include children, by hundreds of thousands; and not only do they own a vital interest in the welfare of the enterprise, but their small voices are capable of exerting a powerful influence for its successful conduct.

In the past, it has suffered grievously from lack of interest on the part of many of its shareholders as well as from a chronic misconception of its purposes on the part of many others; in the same way it can suffer as much, or more, in the future. And because it is representative of very many other such corporations in this country—among them two of even greater magnitude, the majority much smaller—the essentials of its efficient management constitute the essentials of its class, with the nation as a whole as vitally concerned as are the millions of individual shareholders.

For the City of Philadelphia, like other cities, is in reality nothing but a coöperative corporation, the type of the oldest form of coöperative enterprise organized. Happily removed

Mayor Blankenburg completed his four-year term in Philadelphia at the close of the year. He was by charter ineligible for reëlection, and the reform candidate to succeed him was badly beaten by the organization Republican, Thomas B. Smith. But Mr. Blankenburg retains the distinction of having given to boss-ridden Philadelphia four years of clean and business-like administration.—THE EDITOR.

MAYOR BLANKENBURG

from the necessity of coöperative defense, both by its era and its situation, this association of owning residents has developed into precisely such a business enterprise as is any other great corporation, requiring for its prosperous conduct precisely such business honesty and acumen as they do—and nothing else. For its aim it has the production of domestic safety, health, comfort and trade opportunities, to be supplied to its citizen shareholders at a minimum reasonable cost. It has properly no political service to sell and should have no political bias—less, indeed, than an industrial corporation like the United States Steel Corporation or a transportation corporation like the Pennsylvania Railroad. So purely non-partizan and so exclusively business are its functions that every smallest interjection of politics necessarily acts like the traditional monkey wrench thrown in among the cogs of a piece of machinery.

The round of its functions is simplicity itself. It assesses its shareholders, directly and indirectly, for the sums required to provide them with the protection, comforts, facilities and necessaries they desire. That is all. It has, inherently, no province or duty to meddle with the tariff, to support any party, to favor any political candidate. Its sole reason for existence is that it shall serve its shareholders effectively and economically. True, there are various political parties represented among its citizens; but what public service corporation, like the United Gas Improvement Company, would tolerate the impairment of its efficiency or the waste of its income by reason of political conflicts among its stockholders? Yet in the municipal corporation of Philadelphia contractors allied with political bosses have been a chronic handicap; under the old Gas Trust, it lost $400,000 a year for coal alone, paid for at extravagant prices or never so much as delivered when paid for.

It has been my main effort to eliminate the contractors and political bosses who, between them, controlled city councils, the body holding the purse strings of this enterprise. They have thwarted me as much as they dared; but withal we have laid the foundation, during these four years, of the greatest development Philadelphia will have ever experienced. There will be available $140,000,000 for my successors to utilize in the building of a system of subways and elevated railways, for the abolition of grade crossings, for the opening of 4000 acres of hitherto undeveloped land within two miles of the City Hall, for a sewage disposal plant, for the finishing of the Parkway, for the building of an art museum and for the construction of a dozen piers in the Delaware River that will equal the best to be found anywhere in the world.

This municipal business enterprise has $140,000,000 to expend, if it choose, within the next four years. I fear itching palms will grasp again for the public funds, altho the people, the shareholders, having had a taste of honest administration of their affairs, will never return to the old, slovenly, dishonest way of carrying on city business.

Under existing conditions, the citizen shareholders in the corporation must keep up an organization of disinterested, public-spirited men and women which shall be a constant menace to would-be plunderers, which shall hold them in check and, if necessary, take them into a court of justice as has been done in San Francisco and New York.

A permanent basis of efficiency can be attained only by the elimination of politics as a factor in the conduct of the city's affairs and by the inculcation of such a civic spirit as will make all citizens willing to serve the municipality. Today most cities are served by a less desirable class than could readily be obtained if genuine public spirit prevailed and induced men of merit to give their time, their probity and their brains.

Such fundamental changes, however, can be accomplished only by educating the shareholders in the protection of their own interests, and by fixing upon a few public officials the responsibility for honest and economical administration. When I appointed my directors I said to each of them:

"You have absolute control of your department. The responsibility must be yours. Come and consult me whenever you wish; but for results I look to you."

That is what executive responsibility should amount to. In councils, in Philadelphia, there are 132 men of no responsibility except the responsibility which many of them think they owe to the bosses who made possible their election. We cannot expect anything in particular from individuals who, their individuality lost in a servile majority, have become nobody in particular. But if there were a small council, the citizen shareholders could get at every one of them. A council of nine, every one paid $10,000 a year for his services, and a city manager paid an attractive salary, would produce best results, I think, in a city as large as Philadelphia. But even so small a council could be as dangerous as the present unwieldy number if the highly-paid few were amenable to partizan influences. Men in such a position must think and act solely for the welfare of the corporation, just as directors think and act for a great railroad, when they have been wisely chosen.

It all resolves itself into this: that the citizens shall take an intelligently selfish view of their individual interest in the welfare of the municipality. They must expect to know its business as they do their own private ventures and they must endeavor to conduct it at least as well.

Under conditions existing almost everywhere in the United States, as well as in Philadelphia, the hope of making such an ideal citizenship must begin with education of the very children. The results may not be immediately apparent; but they will be felt as the children grow. Some effect would follow speedily, for children really have an influence in the home; and child questions, the outcome of simple yet wise instruction in the schools, have made many fathers think who have not thought before. It is reasonable to expect that appreciable consequences would appear within a decade of the time when such instruction was begun.

There is hope for the suggestion, because the present generation of political bosses may decide that the full consequences of such a course in education will fall upon their successors, rather than than themselves.

Philadelphia

AS USUAL

BY BURTON KLINE

I'M not thinking of Ezry. Whatever Ezry needs, it isn't money, certainly. He has plenty of that —and keeps it, too. For forty years he's been deaf as a hemlock post, and scarcely hears a word that his wife says. Hence it isn't sympathy he needs, either!

I'm thinking, instead, of Ezry's wife.

Ezry is seventy now. That makes her sixty-five. Spry, both of them, too. How Ezry does clamber down the rocks and into his dory!

That's life, for Ezry—a day's fishin' in his dory. God knows what he does with the rest of his time. For fifty years Ezry has had that cottage by the Maine shore. Nine months of the year it isn't enough for him. Even during the other three months when winter obliges him to live ten miles inland, it takes the devil of a storm to keep Ezry from his reg'lar Sunday visit to the cottage.

He likes the sea.

But I'm thinking of Ezry's wife. I asked her once if she too liked the sea.

She said, "I have no use for water, except to wash in."

Yet every summer for forty years she has gone to that cottage by the sea, with Ezry.

It's a lonely place, far out on a ragged spit. Once a day the postman comes—at the urgence of duty. Otherwise nobody's there but Ezry. The Portland boat comes up. The Portland boat goes down. So does the sun. That's all.

But no, I'm forgetting. Ezry has still two other loves. To learn what they are, get a scratch on his dory, or pick one of his poppies. He grows all kinds of them—wonderful poppies.

But I'm thinking of Mrs. Ezry.

She, too, has money. At any time she could carry out her threats. And every spring for forty years she has threatened to cut the cottage and see life. Her nearest neighbor has seen California. The next nearest has done Europe.

I know what Mrs. Ezry does with her time. I see her knitting on the piazza of the cottage every afternoon. That's what she does with her fingers. But I know what she does with her mind. She thinks of Europe and California.

This spring Mrs. Ezry grew desperate—as usual. After sixty-five years, there isn't much left of life. And with Europe and California still to see.

Her guilty heart beat high when she went "up" to Boston and bought a new spring dress, as usual. And had three fittings "into" it. And pored over a dozen schedules and illustrated folders when she got home —with Ezry snoring away, as usual.

That was February the first.

Promptly on the 25th Ezry packed up for the shore, as usual.

On the 27th he said, "Well! Are you ready?" And with that Ezry's wife looked at Ezry.

They were young when they were married, forty-eight years before. And oh, Ezry could hear then, and wanted to hear! Sweet things he had heard, sweet things he had said. They all came back to her. . . .

"Well, are you ready?" says Ezry. And then what followed?

Ezry's wife put her lips to Ezry's ear and shouted, till Ezry must, and California may, have heard.

"Yes," she said. "I'm ready."

Boston

AFTER A WEARY DAY OF WAR

THE RETURN OF THE POETIC DRAMA

BY JOYCE KILMER

AUTHOR OF "SUMMER OF LOVE," "TREES AND OTHER POEMS"

A LYRIC was something about Love and Death which just fitted in between the bottom of the page and the end of this month's instalment of the serial. Editors of magazines welcomed it if its rimes were correct, and if there was a little surprize in the last two lines. And if they had on hand a vacant painting or drawing by some well-known artist, they were glad to receive an interesting ballad to print on the page opposite it. But a play in rime, a poetic drama . . . !

What could one do with a poetic drama? To have it produced was out of the question, unless the poet hired a theater and a company. To have it published in a magazine was impossible, unless the poet were Dr. Henry Van Dyke or Mr. Theodore Roosevelt or some other public character. All that the poet could do with a poetic drama was to read it to his friends and to give an encouraging Boston publisher three hundred dollars to print it in a pretty little blue-backed volume with a neat pasted label.

But *nous*, it may be said, *avons changé tout cela! Nous* are all sorts of people—Stephen Phillips, Thomas Walsh, Alfred Noyes, John Masefield, Condé Pallen, Ridgely Torrence, Hermann Hagedorn, Josephine Preston Peabody, Edith Thomas, Lord Dunsany, about eighty-five other English and American poets, and the General Public.

Of course the General Public deserves most of the credit. The General Public has very recently shown its willingness to pay money to see poetic drama on the stage—even in vaudeville. And the General Public is now showing its willingness to buy books containing poetic drama, and to regard with cheerful enthusiasm magazines which give to this hitherto most unpopular form of artistic expression space which might have been filled with stories about young married couples living in the suburbs, or the personal narratives of Arctic explorers.

For the magazine editors to print poetic drama is even more surprizing than for the publishers to bring them out. What changed the hearts of the magazine editors I do not know, but I am inclined to think that the activities of Mr. Thomas Walsh had something to do with it. For several years this poet has been putting into spirited verse romantic or amusing incidents in the lives of El Greco and Goya and Velasquez, and other painters of his beloved Spain. His poetic dramas are so skilfully made, so colorful, so human, that they have appealed to editors as strongly as the best short stories would appeal, and they have been important features of *Scribner's* and the *Century*. Other English and American magazines, monthly and weekly, have followed the distinguished precedent set by the *Century* and *Scribner's*, and Thomas Walsh, Hermann Hagedorn, Ridgely Torrence and the rest now see, to their amazement, that poetic drama, the sort of writing which for years has been done only for its own sake, is now a thing which editors desire, a thing for which one receives money!

This is, the publishers tell us, the worst season for the sale of novels and the best season for the sale of books of verse the world has seen for many a year. And among the tales of verse of the chief publishers, the poetic dramas are conspicuous. Here is, for example, Mr. John Masefield. He has given up the long narrative poem which made him famous, no longer does he write pseudo-epics like "The Widow in the Bye Street" and "The Everlasting Mercy." His newest book, *The Faithful*, is a play, the scene of which is not modern England but ancient Japan. Not all of it is in verse, but so rhythmical and imaginative is his prose that the play can only be classified as poetic drama. Mr. Stephen Phillips's new book, *Armageddon* (alas, that it is the last book that we shall have from this true poet!), is called a modern epic drama; it is a savagely realistic and savagely romantic play dealing (of course from an intensely British standpoint) with the great war. In connection with its publication in book form it is interesting to note that this poetic drama was one of the most successful of the wartime offerings on the London stage.

The Macmillan Company has published Mr. Thomas Walsh's *The Pilgrim Kings*. It contains many beautiful lyrics, but its chief reason for existence is found in "Greco's Last Judgment," "The Maids of Honor," "Goya in the Cupola" and the other brief plays in which the men who were Spain's pride utter their souls in English verse instead of in Castilian prose. The title poem of Miss Edith M. Thomas's *The White Messenger and Other War Poems* is a play; one of the strongest pieces of pacifist propaganda that has been published since August, 1914.

Mr. Alfred Noyes's *Rada*, a dramatic poem, was more popular than his narrative poem *Drake;* he has revised it in the light of recent events, and it has many new readers under its new title, *A Belgian Christmas Eve*. In Dr. Condé Pallen's *Collected Poems*, the two most conspicuous poems are dramatic in form—"Ablâë" and that interesting reply to Tennyson's "St. Simeon Stylites," "A Feast of Thaliarchus."

These are only a few of the books which illustrate the popularity and commercial practicability of the poetic drama. The return of the epic, confidently prophesied by admirers of Mr. Masefield's "The Everlasting Mercy," has failed to come about. But the poetic drama has returned; it has returned largely and triumphantly; a proof of this is to be found not in the work of one poet but in the pages of our greatest magazines and the lists of our greatest publishers.

It is possible that this may be traced back to the recent popularity of the printed drama. During the last three or four years, numerous publishers, among them Mr. Henry Holt, Mr. Mitchell Kennerley and the University of Chicago Press, have issued numerous series of plays. People have been buying and reading plays; being led to do so largely by the Little Theater movement and various amateur theatrical enterprises. Now, it is a fact that a play, even one that it is delightful to watch on the stage, is likely to be dull reading—unless the author be a wit like Bernard Shaw or Sir James Matthew Barrie. But a play which has, in addition to the exciting quality inherent in the dramatic form, the charm of high imagination, lovely rhetoric, and the forceful condensation which is the essence of poetry—this sort of play may be read with delight.

This fact the reading public has discovered; people have been taught to find pleasure in reading plays, and their reading of the prose play has prepared them for what is certainly the highest form of the play and perhaps the highest form of the poem—the poetic drama. And this shows that the public is prepared for the writer who shall combine at their best the art of the dramatist and the art of the poet; that the public is prepared, indeed, for its new Shakespeare.

New York City

88

THE TRIUMPH OF THE MAN WHO ACTS

BY EDWARD EARLE PURINTON

THIS is the day of the man who acts.

The world wants him, well knowing that he is bound to forge ahead and achieve what compels rightful admiration.

We respect a man because he has taken what we had, or acquired what we haven't. We respect the man who acts because he displays *control over crises*. This spells opportunity, this makes history, this creates destiny. For to see what should be done—then do it on the instant, caring nothing for appearance, precedent or preachment, is the common mark of the great of all time.

The man who acts possesses courage, promptness, faith, quickwittedness, farsightedness, a huge will, a holy zeal, and the power to mass his forces on a set point at a set time for a set purpose. Such traits are rare, worth money, and deserving of praise. They command the rewards of the world, they summon the gifts of the gods. If any boon to you be lacking, see why it goes to the man who acts.

Health attends the man who acts, Wisdom guides him, Hope frees him, Joy helps him, Power moves him, Progress makes him, Fame follows him, Wealth rewards him, Love chooses him, Fate obeys him, God blesses him, Immortality crowns him.

*H*EALTH attends the man who acts. Loss of health is, first, loss of initiative. Disease attacks inert bodies. Germs feed on dead tissue. Every sick man has begun to die; and conversely, no man thoroly alive can be sick. To be energized from head to foot—body, brain, heart and soul—is to be radio-active and hence immune. Never blame or fear a germ—typhoid, rheumatic, catarrhal or tubercular—blame your own negligence, fear your own ignorance, and make friends with the germs so they will do their work more eagerly. If a householder left a pile of garbage in his dining-room, then were driven to despair by rats and flies, who would pity him? We should say to him, "You are lazy, shameless and careless—clean up or go to jail!" Yet we pity the invalid —who also has garbage in his dining-room or elsewhere in his body— and we say to him, "The way to be well is to fill up on more poison from the drug store!" when pills are used for pillars, health is bound to topple.

The finest remedy in the world is for a sick man to realize that he

himself must do something. He must eat less and exercize more; learn to breathe to the bottom of his lungs; find what water will do for him inside and out; smash the fripperies and follies of custom and expediency; understand what life means and get a real object for living; cultivate faith in himself and his fellows; work and play all over; study the birds and the trees and the stars, and be as frank and free as they—in short, get down to first principles, back to Nature, on to Destiny, up to God. Nothing is "incurable" save lack of courage. Many a man doomed to die has outlived his doctor, first by *willing* to have health, then by *working* to secure it. For perfect health is only a by-product of efficiency; whoever does things and delights in the doing thereby unconsciously grows deep chested, lithe limbed, red blooded, stout hearted, clear eyed, strong nerved, calm visaged, clean souled.

*W*ISDOM guides the man who acts. No book contains wisdom. A book merely echoes what a man learned by doing things. Hence most of our pedagogs are busily engaged telling the young how to follow echoes. The crime in popular education lies in regarding the mind as a memory box instead of as a motor. The only hopeless fool is a highly educated fool. Many a "fool" who knew nothing but dared all became the world's idol. You see, we begin to have real education only as we long and dare to plan and execute our own adventures in life. What if we err? We have been bold. What if we suffer? We have been honest. What if we come to disaster? We have chosen the path of our heart, and tho our possessions vanish, our principles rise immortal.

No man has mounted the first step to achievement who has not learned

to make mistakes nobly and retrieve them gracefully. The child walks by trusting his muscles despite his falls. The man wins by trusting his aspirations, desires and hopes despite his failures. Civilization throttles instinct, doubts intuition, denies inspiration, attempting to substitute logic or policy or mob rule for the deeper, higher, finer voices of the soul. Not by heeding the warnings of timid friends or the mutterings of rabid enemies, but by forgetting, and if need be defying, the words and habits of others, choosing to heed the inner voices and follow to the end, do we grow apace in wisdom.

*H*OPE frees the man who acts. The chick is a timorous bird, the eagle a valiant. Why? Because the eagle knows the strength of his wings, by his action he overcomes his fear; whereas the chick, feeling his wings helpless, merely squawks and flutters at the approach of danger. Most men, and the vast majority of women, have had their wings clipped. Freedom in action they know not, hence they fear. What do they fear? Poverty, illness, enmity, old age, solitude, night, sorrow, unpopularity— countless things that lie in the shadows of ignorance and indolence. Fear is but chronic inability to act. And what we fear, we invite. If the business of being a desperado were as moral as it is hygienic, we might all profit by a course in brigandage. No man fears himself; hence the way to rout fear is to be one's self so thoroly and constantly that no outer shadow may intrude. Fears are the centipedes and lizards of the mind, hopes are the butterflies and larks. Hopes lead when we do as impulse or inspiration prompts; fears haunt as we lie prone. When a man despairs call him a drone. At least that will anger him—and ire gets action!

*J*OY helps the man who acts. The pessimist is always a theorist— never a practical man. From the nagging housewife, lacking system, love and tact, to the magazine "muckraker," lacking a job and envious of men with good ones, the preacher of wo is always a person with an unsolved problem. But to the earnest and the energetic, life is a splendid game; and he who knows the game and "plays fair" is always expecting a victory. Men and women need to limber up; they are too dignified, too conventional, too timid, too expressionless, too unreal—and too rheumatic. A little boy in mischief is always contented. We may not like the mischief, but the action of him is ideal, also the courage that defies a rule-of-thumb. And in mature life, the youngest, cheeriest, soundest man is he who always delves in something new. A destiny, like a diamond, is a matter of digging. Happiness lies at the heart of some herculean task. And the mere act of stretching our mental and spiritual muscles creates a physical buoyancy, to thrill and impel and renew us. Wo is merely a blind wish of a weakling. The lion, fettered and bound in his cage, presents a sorry countenance; the lion, speeding from his lair to the open, grapples with his foe and mightily exults in life.

*P*OWER *moves the man who acts.* From the new science of experimental psychology we learn that the average man uses only a small fraction—a third to a tenth—of his inherent brain power. The rest lies dormant. Why? Because *original* thought is lacking, and that is the only kind that really builds the cells of the brain. Now, original thought and independent action are closely related. All discoveries and inventions, all great commercial undertakings, all humane projects and philanthropic institutions were the outcome of the brain of a man who had a new idea, recognized its value, became absorbed in it, worked it out for himself, and by proving it challenged the world's attention. The human brain is an electric battery, Universal Spirit the power house, and personal ambition the set of wires on which the current runs. Seldom is the battery connected aright, with the source of power above, or with the channels of power in human life. Great deeds are the products of great desires. And most human beings are so trivial, so unattractive, so commonplace, because whatever desires they had in childhood have been crushed in the world's routine of repression, monotony and apathy. Try this experiment: The next time you feel a conviction, inspiration or desire that seems unusual or even untenable—*act* on it, fully, promptly and implicitly. If the result seems a mistake, never mind—a new channel of power will have been opened in your brain, and as you grow familiar with this, you will be astonished at the increase in efficiency.

*P*ROGRESS *marks the man who acts.* One of the popular fallacies of the day is that we can grow healthy, wealthy, happy or great by merely thinking ourselves so. Does an artist need only a frame? The artist of character or achievement may well choose the right frame of mind—but to create the picture he must toil hard and long. The worst cases of failure, mental, moral and financial, that the writer has ever seen were those of habitual, professional thinkers and dreamers who scorned the busy life of the world, imagining themselves beyond the need of exertion. A definite plan of action, and a determined execution of that plan, must underlie all 'permanent advancement. History is peace where prophecy was action. The whole aviation art and industry is based on the unremitting efforts of two plain men—the Wright brothers, who kept trying while others merely talked. Ask such a captain of the world's progress as Frank A. Vanderlip or Elbert H. Gary what brought him where he is—he will say, "I did more than was expected of me."

*F*AME *follows the man who acts.* Not that fame is desirable—it is rather most uncomfortable. But to those who have not outgrown the small boy habit of wanting to carve their name on the scenery, this is an argument for action. Study the lives of famous men of the present time—Edison, Marconi, Burbank, Peary, Caruso, Wanamaker, Belasco, Roosevelt. Each of these can do, has done, some one thing better than anybody else. They were not content to be idle while things could be improved. They are great because they kept going in spite of great discouragements. Fame is but the echo of a man's determination. Only those remain obscure who did not take a strong enough vow.

*W*EALTH *rewards the man who acts.* The fortunes of the plutocratic families—the Astors, Goulds, Vanderbilts, Rothschilds and Rockefellers—were founded on the action of a man who first saw and filled a great public need. Money is the measure of what people want; but they have to be shown before they know what they want. They did not know they wanted the telephone, telegraph, sewing machine or automobile—until somebody foresaw the demand and prepared to meet it while his neighbors slept. Somewhere, in the acquiring of every great fortune, a man took his future in his hands and stepped off into space. Somewhere, also, he came back to earth so completely that his method, his machinery, his regularity, surpassed that of his rivals no less than his dream outshone theirs. Both in imagination and in execution the builder of riches displays a lordly stride.

*L*OVE *chooses the man who acts.* When woman suffrage has become universal, the science of eugenics a part of the college curriculum, and sex instruction a feature of sound home training, the present standards of marriage will be standards no longer. Then the question will be, not, "Is the girl a beauty, a social queen, and a deft caterer to man's conceit?" but rather "Is the man a worthy specimen, physically, mentally and morally; will he make a true husband and a good father?" The right marriage dower is not coin for the woman—it is character for the man. So, when women legislate, the dower customs will be changed. Such a revolution will be hard for the ousted lords of creation to accept. The way to prepare for it is to do things, morally and spiritually, as eagerly and effectively as they have always done with brute strength. For the woman always yields to strength in the man. Even the poet—man, soft thing—has a power of imagery that the millionaire must acquire if he keeps all of his lady's heart. The matinee idol and the soldier on parade maintain a semblance of action. This is what endears them to feminine worshipers. Would you win your lady's adoration? Do something, anything, that no other man she knows could or would do. For every woman's king must be a conqueror. . . . . . .

*F*ATE *obeys the man who acts.* Luck is a myth, Chance plays no part in success. Whoever looks on a leader with envy merely looks at him with ignorance. For every man who attains supremacy of any kind has done something to earn it. Paderewski was born musical—yet so were thousands of others. What made Paderewski the world's greatest pianist was the habit he had of playing a note or phrase until he got it right—often three hundred times at a stretch. Edison was born with a gift for mechanics; but his matchless wizardry is only his capacity for work; he can go for weeks on half the food and sleep that his helpers demand. Beethoven, meeting deafness, went on writing music in his mind. Milton, stricken with blindness, learned to see with his soul. Napoleon, weak and sickly, grew healthy by growing lion hearted. All these men did things, either using a good heritage or overcoming a poor one, to an extent beyond the zeal or courage of the many. Each act, each word, each thought of our life today becomes a mosaic in the mansion of our destiny. Thus we decree our fate to ourselves.

GOD blesses the man who acts. God is Light and Light is energy. God is Love and Love is power. Thus vitality is the backbone of virtue, and no man can be good who is lazy. The great religious leaders have called themselves most blest of God, and they were all men of action—Luther, Calvin, Savonarola, Spurgeon, Moody, Mott. God even prospers "bad" men who use their brains and bodies to effect. Their sins are punished, but equally their talents are rewarded. Why are the churches losing ground, why are false sects springing up? Because the churches have as a rule wasted their finest energies and opportunities in talking. You can't build a kingdom by splitting hairs. If clergymen had waked up fifty years ago, as they are now doing in the glorious effort called the Men and Religion Forward Movement, they would not now be apprehensive of Christian Science, New Thought, Mysticism, Socialism, or any other cult that really aims to supply what the Church failed to consider. In theology, the doctrines are dying, because bereft of deeds. A zealous Buddhist is a better Christian than a lukewarm Baptist. And there comes a time, in the growth of every soul, when he regards weakness as more unpardonable than wickedness. For sin is generally blind, while indifference knows well its own guilt. Honest effort, just that and nothing more, builds our estate in heaven. So the ignorant, the poor, the afflicted, the oppressed, have a better chance to be exalted hereafter, because they are forced by harsh necessity to exert themselves.

IMMORTALITY crowns the man who acts. John Jacob Astor thought to make his name undying by willing his fortune to his male heir. But the real immortality of John Jacob Astor was to come in a far different way; in the heart of the world he found his place when he gave up his right to live, that the weaker souls on the doomed "Titanic" might be saved. He followed an impulse greater than himself; and he will be remembered for that one smile in the face of death, that radiant moment when the god in him rose to the need and took command. Who before that night had known the name of Mrs. Isidor Straus? Who since that night has failed to honor her? In every home her likeness, and her choice of death with the man she loved, should be enshrined as a tribute to the power of the soul, the loyalty of love, and the

Encyclopaedia

Do you want to get ahead ?

Have you an ambition?

Are you really in earnest about it?

If you say to yourself "I would like more money to spend and less work to to" and call *that* ambition, you don't mean what we do by being ambitious.

Have you planned how you're to get ahead?

Are you working on your plans and ambitions?

If you *do* think and plan, you've got this far:

You've decided that the principal thing you need to get ahead is not brute strength or bigger muscles but a better trained mind and more "know how."

You cannot become a good porter, handling boxes of specie in a bank, or loading freight in a railway yard, if your wrist-bones are small or your lungs none too strong.

But weak lungs and puny wrists won't prevent your becoming a bank president or a railway manager.

The Help You Need

What you need is something that other people have learned and something that you can learn from other people. You'll have to *work* to get it, but not anywhere near as hard as if you were the first ambitious person in a bank or a railway or any other business. Those who "have been there before" started where you did, got where you want to get, and can share with you their laboriously learned "know how."

You can't expect to get much help from people in your office or bank, no matter how friendly they may be. You don't like to ask for help or hints or suggestions. And you soon learn that many who know the job best and can tell you right away whether you are right or wrong, *cannot explain why*, so that you never get the reason for what you're to do.

The new Encyclopaedia Britannica

contains careful summaries of what is known about electricity and its practical uses, about groceries, about banking, about railroads, about photography, about cotton and woolen goods, about engineering, about the manufacture of alkali or of coal-tar products, or any other business or manufacture—and in each instance the summary is written by one *who knows the subject* thoroughly at first hand and can convey knowledge to others. The Britannica is a work you can use for the narrowest, most technical part of the job you want to make good in.

And the Britannica will give another sort of help that you need constantly—*general information* on subjects connected with your work, written by men just as expert and accurate and trustworthy as those who write on your more particular specialty. In the railroad office the man who is successful is the one who knows a great deal about crops and ores and manufactures in the whole region that his railroad serves, and the latest decisions of the state public service commission.

divine import of supreme disaster. The world is full of heroes, of whom perhaps only the angels sing. But of all those whom the world forever honors, each one has taken a super-human risk, and so achieved a super-human task. This alone repays for the ills and hurts and heartbreaks of life; and this alone makes one immortal.

SUPPOSE now that a man wished more of the health, wisdom, joy, power and progress of action, how might we suggest that he energize himself for greater efficiency? By starting right now to put a few simple things into operation, letting their cumulative force renew and reconstruct his life. So our answer would be this:

Stop talking—learn to speak only in such a way that you and your friends will somehow profit thereby.

Stop worrying—when you can handle the present as well as God will handle the future, you will laugh at your worries.

Stop wishing—a wish is confession of weakness. Want what you want hard enough to get it, or else feel superior to the need.

Stop criticizing—only an ass wastes energy in braying.

Stop hesitating—it is the plunger who goes to the bottom of things. And whether gold or mud is at the bottom, the man who has found it rests.

Stop imitating—a real ruby is worth more than an artificial diamond.

Stop idling—either work, or play, or sleep, or travel; in short, make even your rest period a thing of ambition, volition, system.

Stop hurrying—when you teach your brain to outrun your body your body will stay quiet.

Sit up straight, walk with your chest out, look every man in the eye, and declare yourself as good as the best. Humility is not hump-shoulderness.

Go to the open window and take a dozen huge breaths, deeply and slowly, stretching your legs and arms at the same time, and feeling the purified blood leap thru your veins and arteries. Do this whenever you have a headache or a grouch.

Read books that build—not the mush in the six "best sellers." Goethe, Shelley, Browning, Emerson, Whitman, Darwin, Epictetus, Kant—these men produced food for the minds of real men. And of all literature of action, biography is best—you can judge the progress of your neighbor on the achievement path by the heroes whose lives he studies.

Eliminate idlers from your acquaintance. This includes all who enjoy play more than work.

Lose yourself in your work. Come early and stay late. Use every spare moment in developing methods first to work better and then faster. If there is a man higher up in the same business, devote an evening a week to studying how he got there.

Analyze your average day and find how many hours a week you waste. Then consider that your time outside of working hours is worth twice as much—because that belongs to you, while the other is only your employer's. Thus, if you earn ten dollars a day, every hour outside the office routine is worth at least three dollars —too much to squander.

Line your walls with portraits of the world's conquerors, starting with Napoleon and Lincoln, finishing with the greatest man in your own special field. Traits of character map themselves on the face. The countenance of a winning pioneer is of itself a heaven-born stimulus.

Picture yourself in absolute command of the place you aspire to, in permanent possession of the thing you want, with every ambition satisfied and every aspiration met. Failure is a fool's name for lack of grit; not being a fool, you will not talk of failure.

Face to the front, unceasingly and unqualifiedly. Consider that the past never was, excepting in the lessons it has brought. No man regrets while still he marches on.

Attack the hardest job in sight. Do this first. A little reflection will show what it is—probably a slip-shod habit or ugly propensity or chronic weakness that needs handling without gloves. The man of might is he who was merciless to himself.

If you have done all these things, and whatever else occurs in the doing, then look for a chance to help somebody who is down, lift a burden that has grown too heavy, whisper a word of love and sympathy to the lonely, the forlorn, the misunderstood. For the sad and poor and helpless can most appreciate, and will most bless, the prompt and generous nature of The Man Who Acts.

New York City

The Wonders of Today

A thousand prominent scientists in both America and Europe were recently asked to vote on the Seven Wonders of the Modern World. Their answers are an interesting indication of the change in ideals and values that has taken place since the days of the Pyramids and the Hanging Gardens of Babylon. Wireless telegraphy comes first with 244 votes; the telephone next with '85.' Whether the aeroplane or radium should be third is somewhat disputed, but the aeroplane has 167 to 165 for radium. The spectrum analysis and the X-ray have the next two places, and the Panama Canal, which of all these seven wonders is perhaps most like those of the Ancient World, comes last.

Only one ballot, made out by a distinguished chemist in Munich, named all seven of these wonders which won the final vote. Ninety-four scientists gave a place to anesthesia, but their votes were not enough to include it in the first seven.

The New Books

IRISH PROSE AND VERSE

The Library of Irish Literature, the
first six volumes of which have recently made their appearance, has a
two-fold distinction. In the first place
there is new and valuable material embodied in the volume entitled *Legends
of Saints and Sinners*, a collection of
folk tales which Douglas Hyde himself
took down from the lips of peasants who
still use Gaelic speech. Dr. Hyde trans-
lates them and so adds one more to the
long list of services which he has rendered to Irish literature. The material
in this volume has never before found
its way into print, Gaelic or English.
The excellence of the editorial equipment is the second distinction of this
series. A reader who comes to Irish
literature as a stranger will find the
critical introductions and interpretations accompanying these volumes a
present help to a right understanding
and enjoyment of what he reads. For
such aid thanks are due in the last
analysis to the Irish Literary Revival,
a movement of which we do not hear
as much today as we did a decade ago,
but which has had a lasting and tonic
effect upon Irish literary criticism,
leading Irish men of letters to bring the
precise knowledge of the scholar and
the spirit of culture to bear upon the
task of appraising and expounding
works of Irish talent and genius.

Dr. Hyde's volume is the only one
that contains hitherto unpublished material. The remaining five are reprints,
and of these but one is the reprint of a
complete work, William Hamilton Maxwell's racy *Wild Sports of the West*, a
book popular in its day, and even now
fresher and more invigorating than
many a book of the hour. It is the
chronicle of a sporting summer in the
Wild West of Ireland, interspersed with
stories and legends. An introduction by
the present Earl of Dunraven dwells
upon its interest for sportsmen, and
comments upon it as a picture of the
sporting life of the reckless, devil-
may-care Irish squirearchy, whose picturesque ways are now a thing of the
past. The opening volume of the Library is a selection made by T. W.
Rolleston of prose and verse from the
writings of Thomas Davis. It is thoroly representative as regards the prose,
and includes all Davis's poems that
have any value as poetry. The most
popular of this series will certainly
be *Humours of Irish Life*, composed of
humorous short stories and selected
passages from Irish novels from the
time of William Maginn to the present
day of the latest recruit to the ranks
of the story-tellers of the Literary Re-

vival. On the whole the short stories are of prime quality. Indeed the book would have been the better for the inclusion of more of these to the exclusion of the passages from novels. In *Irish Orators and Oratory*, Prof. T. M. Kettle has brought together representative speeches, or parts of speeches, beginning with Edmund Burke's "American Taxation" and including John Redmond's speech in the House of Commons on England's declaration of war in August, 1914. No one who has read this book will willingly omit the mead of praise that belongs to Prof. Kettle on the score of his introduction—a brilliant and illuminating piece of criticism.

Library of Irish Literature, ed. by Alfred Percival Graves, William Magennis and Douglas Hyde. 6 vols. Stokes. Each $1.

THE CAUSE OF WORRY

Dr. William Lee Howard in his *Sex Problems in Worry and Work* puts in popular language some of the recent results of physiology and psycho-analysis, but avoids the extravagances of the ultra-Freudian school.

New York: E. J. Clode. $1.

AN EXPOSE OF BAHAISM

Dr. Samuel G. Wilson, in *Bahaism and Its Claims*, subjects this latest of oriental religions seeking hospitality in America to scathing criticism. From personal observation in Persia and study of the literature he charges the sect with dissimulation, quarrelsomeness, assassination and polygamy.

Revell. $1.50.

THE "MEN OF THIRTY"

For an instant one wonders what more can be said about *The Barbizon Painters*, but Arthur Hoeber's biographical and critical essays prove delightful and informing. Not technical, they are however the more worth while in that they are written with the understanding and assurance of the fellow craftsman. The illustrations are many and include specimens of the early, less known work of these masters.

Stokes. $1.75.

THE CHRISTIAN WAY

Professor Francis G. Peabody's books on practical Christian problems have always a grip in them that causes the reader to stop and think of his own relation to such questions. His *Christian Life in the Modern World* contains sane, clear, practical and deeply moving chapters on the social teachings and demands of Christianity, probing the defects in social life and raising the noblest ideals of service.

Macmillan. $1.25.

A SOUTH CAROLINA STATESMAN

Full of entertaining anecdotes and vivid pictures of the times, D. D. Wallace's *Life of Henry Laurens* is none the less a valuable study of the Revolutionary period. Of French Huguenot blood, reared in the finest traditions of the South, Henry Laurens' services as President of the Continental Congress were great, and his imprisonment in the Tower one of the romantic stories of our heroic period.

Putnam. $3.50.

FOR OLDER YOUNG MEN

The second series of admirable *Essays for College Men* chosen by Norman Foerster, Frederick A. Manchester, and Karl Young, of the University of Wisconsin, contains with the exception of Academic Leadership, by Paul Elmer More, selections which have stood the test of time and criticism. The first essay is What Is a College For? by Woodrow Wilson, Emerson's War and The Modern Equivalent of War, by William James, are timely reprints.

Holt. $1.25.

"Sweets to the Sweet"—and what confection could better complement smiling eyes and ruby lips? The crisp, fragile wafers—the rich creamy centers of Nabisco Sugar Wafers make these dessert sweets beloved by all. In ten-cent and twenty-five-cent tins.

FESTINO—An almond-shaped dessert confection with a sweetened-cream filling of almond flavor.

NATIONAL BISCUIT COMPANY

Independent Opinions

Whatever may be our several opinions on how large an army we should have, we all agree that it should be as efficient and economical as possible. Here is an interesting suggestion on this point:

The great lesson from all our own wars and the present Great War is that every regiment must have a depot battalion in which recruits and remounts are trained and from which the combat strength of the regiment is maintained by sending up trained men as casualties occur. The strength of the depot battalion varies from 25 per cent to 100 per cent of that of the combatant regiment. Consider the case of a French company—It went into an engagement on the 20th with 250 men and lost 135 men. By the 23d it had received from the depot battalion 185 trained men. It was engaged again on the 25th and lost 160 men. What would have become of an American fighting unit, with no feeder battalions to draw from? It would have been annihilated, as were the British regiments in the first months of the war.

Economy and efficiency require that provision be made for maintaining the strength of combat units, not the ruinous policy of our Civil War of letting the veteran regiments be shot to pieces and new green ones be raised and sacrificed to the better policy of the enemy.

Every captain in the Regular Army is capable of training three or four times more men than he is allowed now and in half the time. The Regular Army is the best school in this country for preparing men for war and it is training only one-sixth of its capacity working, with only one-sixth efficient. The strength of the Regular Army can be increased three times without adding one cent to the overhead cost and a thousandfold in efficiency, if in addition to increasing the number of enlisted men, regiments are trained in brigades, brigades in divisions, and divisions in field armies.

Bristol, Virginia JAMES SANFORD

———

The Independent has received letters from officers of Howard and Atlanta Universities complaining that we have not properly recognized the standard of these two institutions. That they seek and claim equality of scholarly rank with leading institutions in the North is to their credit, and that their educational standard has risen we are glad to admit and are willing to be corrected. When students from these institutions and from Fisk University transfer to our better Northern colleges, if not received *ad eundem*, we are informed that they may expect to be put back only a single year. The three institutions we have mentioned are in the front rank of negro colleges in the South. We quote from the letter of the Dean of the College of Arts and Letters of Howard University:

In your interesting editorial of December 13th under the head "Three College Presidencies" you state: "We suppose that the training given at Fisk or Howard ranks hardly higher than two years at Harvard or Yale." This statement does palpable injustice to the curriculum at Howard, as I presume it does to that of

Fisk also. The College Department of Howard University requires fifteen units of secondary work as approved by the Carnegie Foundation for college admission. Our courses of instruction cover the usual range of four years of college work. Our faculty consists of twenty-seven professors and instructors, who by scholastic training and teaching experience are qualified for the work assigned to them. Many of these instructors are graduates of such colleges as Harvard, Yale, Dartmouth and Columbia, a number of whom have gained their master's degree and doctorate from these institutions. Our students frequently transfer to the colleges of the North and West and are usually admitted *ad eundem gradum*. The College of Arts and Sciences is recognized by the Regents' Board of New York as fulfilling the requirements of collegiate work in that state.

KELLY MILLER

Washington, D. C.

Miss Jane Addams' article on "The Food of War" in the issue of December 13 excites the indignation of Dr. Guillet of the Massachusetts State Normal School:

To this distrest woman all the combatants in this great controversy—alike the aggressive Germans and the defenders of liberty and nationality and international law and comity—are on the same plane. In what a cool, supercilious manner this writer refers even to the "Lusitania" outrage, finding it really impossible, don't you know, to reach any just conclusion about it, so extreme and irreconcilable are the views held by London and Berlin, upon whose "extravagance" this lofty critic lingers as the gloating over the frailties of poor mortals demented by war!

No one can read this mass of the most sordid details culled from hasty glances at newspapers and flying visits to garrulous soldiers, without reflecting that peace-at-any-price-ism leads inevitably to cynicism and misanthropy. And for the simple reason that so few people are for peace at any price. Many of the incidents she quotes are far more susceptible of a noble than of an ignoble setting and interpretation. But she seeks everywhere to produce the latter. How she was able to write her last paragraph and then publish the rest is more than I can understand.

CEPHAS GUILLET

Westfield, Massachusetts

The editorial of December 13 on "The Falsification of the News," in which we specified certain instances where the newspaper reader would get a wrong idea of what actually occurred, evidently exprest what many of our readers have felt and wanted to say. We quote from the letter of a New York banker:

An old friend of mine was wont to say: "That's what he said; what did he think?" If he is sincere we can respect the antagonist quite as much as the contagonist, but one who holds to anything in which he does *not* believe, that man is a hypocrite. The man who went to scoff and remained to pray we respect. The man who goes to church presumably to praise, and carps continually at the sermon, should remain away. The man who on Sunday fervently says "Amen" to the prayer "beseeching our heavenly Father with His favor to behold and bless this servant, the President of the United States," and on Monday holds him up to ridicule or scorn, ought to stay away from both church and the polls; for he is neither a good churchman nor a good citizen. If we had less "Falsification of News" we would have less falsification of statement, less false opinion, and party politics would be inclined to yield more readily to patriotism.

Tycos Thermometers

"NONE BETTER" YOUR DEALER WILL TELL YOU

Tycos

Taylor Instrument Companies
ROCHESTER N.Y.
There's a *Tycos* or Taylor Thermometer for Every Purpose

DIVIDENDS

American Telephone and Telegraph Company

A dividend of Two Dollars per share will be paid on Saturday, January 15, 1916, to stockholders of record at the close of business on Friday, December 31, 1915.

G. D. MILNE, Treasurer.

American Telephone and Telegraph Company

Four Per Cent. Collateral Trust Bonds

Coupons from these bonds, payable by their terms on January 1, 1916, at the office of the Treasurer in New York will be paid by the Bankers Trust Company, 16 Wall Street.

G. D. MILNE, Treasurer.

AMERICAN LIGHT & TRACTION COMPANY

DIVIDEND NOTICE.

The Board of Directors of the above Company at a meeting held January 4, 1916, declared a cash dividend of one and one-half per cent. (1½%) on the Preferred Stock; a cash dividend of two and one-half per cent. (2½%) on the Common Stock, and a dividend at the rate of two and one-half (2½) shares of Common Stock on every One Hundred (100) shares of Common Stock outstanding, all payable February 1, 1916.

The Transfer Books will close at 12 o'clock noon on January 16, 1916, and will reopen at 10 a. m. on February 1, 1916.

C. N. JELLIFFE, Secretary.

WESTINGHOUSE ELECTRIC & MANUFACTURING COMPANY.

A dividend of one and one-half per cent. on the COMMON stock of this Company for the quarter ending December 31, 1915, will be paid January 31, 1916, to stockholders of record as of December 31, 1915.

H. D. SHUTE, Treasurer.
New York, December 22, 1915.

The Annual Meeting of the Stockholders of the Corporation known as Henry Romeike, Inc., for the purpose of electing directors and transacting such other business as may properly come before the meeting, will be held on the 20th day of January, 1916, at 2 p. m. at the office of the Corporation, 106-110 Seventh avenue, New York City.

HENRY ROMEIKE, INC.
Per Albert Romeike, Secretary.

LIGGETT & MYERS TOBACCO COMPANY. St. Louis, Mo., December 31, 1915. The Transfer Books of the Registered 5 per cent. Bonds of Liggett & Myers Tobacco Company will close at 3 o'clock p. m., January 17, 1916, for the payment of interest on said bonds, due February 1, 1916, and will reopen at 12 o'clock a. m., February 2, 1916.

T. T. ANDERSON, Treasurer.

The Market Place

STEEL AND PROSPERITY

At the beginning of the year, our iron and steel industry is in a highly favorable condition. New records of production have been made at the mills, which are overwhelmed with orders. The output of many of them is sold ahead as far as September. Never before since the Steel Corporation was formed have prices for future delivery been so high, and with respect to many products the prices at which sales have recently been made are above the highest figures of the last fifteen years. When comparison with the prices of one year ago is made, it is seen that advances have been as follows: pig iron, about 40 per cent, with Bessemer selling at $21 a ton; billets, 60 per cent; bars, 75; beams, 80; wire nails, 40; plates, 100. Manufacturing plants have been, or soon will be, enlarged to meet the pressing demand, about 75 per cent of which is for domestic consumption. Plans have been prepared for 91 open-hearth furnaces, whose annual capacity would be 4,265,000 tons of ingots. Production at present is at the rate of 41,000,000 tons a year, against 16,000,000 tons one year ago and 35,000,000 in the year (1912) of largest output before this time.

At the base of the industry the pig iron furnaces have surpassed all previous records. In the last two months of 1914 and the first two of 1915, the average monthly output was a little more than 1,500,000 tons. But the product grew until last October, with 3,125,491 made a new high total. Those who thought this would not be exceeded were surprised by the figures shown for December. In that month 3,206,322 tons were made. At the present time the output is at the rate of more than 38,000,000 tons a year, which is nearly 5,000,000 more than the best previous annual total.

Those who are qualified to speak of this great and important industry agree in saying that there is fair promise of continued prosperity thruout the coming twelve months. But Judge Gary, chairman of the Steel Corporation, in a published statement, has given a few words of caution. It is true, he says, that demand for prompt delivery cannot be supplied, and that prices could easily be increased, altho he thinks some of them are high enough. Pointing to evidence of prosperity thruout the land, he fears inflation and severe jolts when normal conditions are restored. It is quite plain that he expects

---

an earlier end of the war than many others can foresee. This is his view because, as he says, the war can yield little, if any, benefit to any one of the belligerents, or to the world at large, unless it be "the firm establishment of an international tribunal for the settlement of all international differences"; and also because every one of the warring nations "is starving for both men and money." After the close of the war our business men, he adds, will be confronted by new conditions. The belligerents will stop buying from us, and will seek to sell abroad the products of cheap labor. Therefore we must meet most difficult competition, unless we are then protected by an adequate tariff law. He also sees danger of overproduction and of undue expansion of credit, and says we should proceed with caution.

These opinions have been the subject of much comment. Men prominent in finance assert that there is no unsound expansion in banking. Others oppose his plea for tariff protection, saying that such competition as he predicts, if it should come, should be met by greater efficiency here and new economies of production. His great company, on account of its prosperity, has decided to increase by 10 per cent on February 1 the wages of more than 150,000 of its employees, at a cost of about $12,000,000 a year.

Since the recent sale of 135,000,000 pounds of copper to the British Government, at a little over 21 cents, the price of this metal has risen to 24 cents a pound. At the beginning of last year it was between 13 and 14 cents. Even higher prices are expected. The price of lead is advancing.

PROMOTING INTERNATIONAL TRADE

Some months ago the Pacific Mail Steamship Company, owing to the requirements of the new Seamen's Act, withdrew from the trans-Pacific trade and decided to go out of business. To the International Mercantile Marine Company it sold five large ships, for $5,250,000. These are to be used on the Atlantic. One of them, the "Siberia," recently arrived at New York from San Francisco, having gone around South America. This ship will enter the freight service between New York and London.

There remained in the company's possession seven smaller ships which have been engaged in trade between our West coast and Central America. These have now been purchased, for $1,250,000, by the American International Corporation, the company recently formed in New York, with a capital of $50,000,000, to promote the trade and commercial interests of the United States in foreign lands. The Corporation made this investment with the coöperation of W. R. Grace & Co., a house for a long time prominent in our trade with South America. The ships will be operated under the direction of this firm. In April last the

"Instruction by correspondence is the cheapest and best way for the poor man"

Thos. A. Edison

Edison is Right ! ! !

You admit the International Correspondence Schools are a good thing. You'd take a course right now "if"—"except"—

"If" what? If you weren't so "over-worked," with such "long hours," or had more strength and energy?

Wasn't it Edison who stayed up half the night to educate himself in spite of every handicap you could ever have?

All big men who have made their mark in the world had the *ambition*—the *determination*—to improve their spare time, to train themselves for big work. You, too, can possess power, money and happiness if you'll only make the effort. The reward is great—it's worth it.

Here's all we ask : Merely mail this coupon. Put it up to us without paying or promising. Let us send you the details of others' success through the I. C. S., and then decide. Mark and mail this coupon now.

twelve ships which have since been sold for $6,500,000 were valued by the Pacific Mail Company at $11,299,000.

The seven steamships will continue to be employed as they have been in the past, and will remain under the American flag. If they had been sold for service elsewhere and withdrawn from our Pacific coastwise trade, Central American ports would have lost shipping facilities of much value to them, and the trade connections of our Western States with the Central American countries would have been severed. This would have been unfortunate in its effect upon our commercial interests and might have checked a growth of friendly international relations which is much to be desired. The transaction is one of considerable importance, and it is a good beginning for the new American International Corporation.

INVESTING SMALL AMOUNTS

We have inquiries from those who desire to invest small sums from time to time, safely, in stocks or bonds, and who ask for an opinion as to the instalment plan. There are several trustworthy houses that sell bonds and stocks in this way, taking partial payments. We see no reason why the small investor should not use this method, provided that he selects a good house and marketable securities of recognized soundness, with an agreement as to a settlement if something unforeseen should prevent completion of the instalments. The investor of small amounts should also know that bonds of several prominent railway companies, the St. Paul and Burlington, for example, and of other great corporations, are now sold in denominations of $100, instead of $1000, and are offered by banking and brokerage firms.

The following dividends are announced :

American Telephone and Telegraph Company, $2 per share, payable January 15.

American Telephone and Telegraph Company, coupons from 4 per cent Collateral Trust Bonds, payable January 1.

The Bank of America, semi-annual, 14 per cent, payable January 3.

Bank of New York, semi-annual, 8 per cent, payable on and after January 3.

German Savings Bank, 4 per cent per annum, payable on and after January 21.

Importers and Traders National Bank, 12 per cent, payable January 3.

Niagara Falls Power Company, $2 per share, payable on and after January 15.

Otis Elevator Company, quarterly, preferred, $1.50 per share; common, $1.25 per share; both payable January 15.

Atlantic National Bank, semi-annual, 3 per cent, payable on and after January 1.

Westinghouse Electric and Manufacturing Company, preferred, quarterly, 1¾ per cent; common, quarterly, 1½ per cent, payable January 15.

Union Dime Savings Bank, 3½ per cent per annum, payable on and after January 20.

Franklin Savings Bank, 3½ per cent per annum, payable on and after January 17.

Wells, Fargo & Co., 3 per cent, payable January 15.

United States Realty and Improvement Company, Coupons on 20-year Debenture 5 per cent bonds, payable January 3.

Westinghouse Electric and Manufacturing Company, common, quarterly, 1½ per cent, payable January 31.

American Light and Traction Company, preferred, 1½ per cent; common, 3½ per cent, and 2½ shares of common stock on every 100 shares of common stock outstanding; all payable February 1.

Insurance

Conducted by

W. E. UNDERWOOD

FOR A YOUNG MAN

There lies before me a letter from a young man in Idaho who tells me he is twenty-three years old and would like to know what form of life insurance he should take. That inquiry is representative of scores received from young men during the past year, and I marvel that they have missed the innumerable army of expert life insurance solicitors who are canvassing this country daily.

A young man should endeavor to carry a twenty-year endowment policy. That form combines life insurance with savings. If, perchance, he requires a greater amount of protection for the money, he can make it an endowment for a longer term—thirty-five or forty years. In one of the standard companies the annual rate per $1000 for a twenty-year endowment is $44.55; a thirty-five-year endowment costs $23.85; a forty-year endowment, $21.25. An ordinary life policy is rated at $18 a year in the same company.

Now, the ordinary life would serve almost as well if its holder would permit the savings made out of his premiums, inaccurately called dividends, to accumulate. Compound interest, a most potent factor, would perform wonders in creating a small capital for him. But that's the weak spot in the scheme. He will not persistently permit his dividends to remain. It is easier to pay $15 premium than $18, and the accumulative power of $3 during, say, forty years is lost and the principal is dissipated. A dividend of 16⅔ per cent is common in good companies, and 16⅔ per cent of $18 a year is worth in forty years, at 3½ per cent, $296.48. Add the cash surrender value of $520 to that, and we have an endowment of $816.48. Charging the premiums paid with no interest, we have $816 ultimate cash on a total expenditure of $720.

A. H. A., Morgan Hill, Calif.—I am inclined to the opinion that the Inter-State Business Men's Accident Association of Des Moines Ranks well among the assessment accident associations of its class. They are numerous. The Illinois Commercial Men's Association of Chicago, and the Iowa State Traveling Men's Association of Des Moines are prominent. Their premiums are lower than those of the stock companies for two principal reasons: they don't employ an agency staff, each member acting in that capacity, the principal expense being for a secretary and clerical force at headquarters; and as compared with the contracts issued by stock companies, the benefits are quite restricted. Every man earning a salary, having a family to support, should protect himself and them by carrying both life and accident insurance.

The Independent's
Shakespeare Contest
For American Schools

THE year 1916 marks the three-hundredth anniversary of the death of William Shakespeare, the man who "was not of an age, but for all time." To celebrate his greatness, and to encourage appreciation of his art, various institutions in all parts of the United States will hold civic celebrations. The New York City Shakespeare Tercentenary Celebration Committee says that "colleges, social settlements, churches, recreation centers, playgrounds, clubs, public schools, parochial schools, private schools, dancing schools, art schools, Public School Athletic League, gardens, Y. W. C. A.'s, Y. M. C. A.'s, Masonic lodges, and continuation classes in department stores" are among the institutions planning to take part.

To aid in this nation-wide celebration in memory of the great poet, The Independent will publish a series of eight articles concerning Shakespeare, his times, his works, and his relation to present-day thought, to appear weekly beginning with the February 14th number.

Every article will be accompanied by a list of books for further reading, and by carefully selected illustrations.

Every article will be designed to awaken interest in the reading of Shakespeare's plays.

The author of the series is Frederick Houk Law, Ph.D., Lecturer in English in New York University, and Head of the Department of English in the Stuyvesant High School, New York City. His close study of Shakespeare and the Elizabethan period, and his practical experience as lecturer and teacher, have enabled him to write a highly interesting and instructive series of articles equally suitable for schools, for clubs and for private reading.

The titles of the eight articles are as follows:

Number 1. Shakespeare the Man: A résumé of the important facts in Shakespeare's biography; and an analysis of Shakespeare's attitude toward life.

Number 2. Shakespeare's England: The conditions of life in Shakespeare's times, with especial reference to life in Stratford and in London, and with particular reference to Shakespeare's plays.

Number 3. Shakespeare's Comedies: Plays of Fun and Fancy: The leading characteristics of the group of plays including The Comedy of Errors, The Taming of the Shrew, Henry IV, I and II, The Merry Wives of Windsor, Love's Labour's Lost, The Two Gentlemen of Verona, and A Midsummer Night's Dream.

Number 4. Shakespeare's Comedies: Plays of Joy and Contemplation: The leading characteristics of the group of plays including The Merchant of Venice, Much Ado About Nothing, As You Like It, Twelfth Night, Henry V, All's Well that Ends Well, Measure for Measure, Troilus and Cressida, Pericles, Cymbeline, The Tempest, and A Winter's Tale.

Number 5. Shakespeare's Tragedies: Plays of Romance and War: The leading characteristics of the group of plays including Romeo and Juliet, Titus Andronicus, Henry VI, Richard II, Richard III, King John and Henry VIII.

Number 6. Shakespeare's Tragedies: Plays of Character and Deepest Pathos: The leading characteristics of the group of plays including Julius Caesar, Hamlet, Othello, Macbeth, King Lear, Antony and Cleopatra, Coriolanus, and Timon of Athens.

Number 7. Shakespeare's Relation to Present-Day Thought: The effect of Shakespeare upon the drama of to-day, upon literature in general, and upon daily thought and action.

Number 8. Why One Should Read Shakespeare: a summary of the chief points of value to be gained from a reading of Shakespeare's plays.

The Independent Offers a Shakespeare Anniversary Medal

The Independent offers a Shakespeare Anniversary Medal for the best essay from any school in the United States on the life and works of William Shakespeare. Any American school, private or public, elementary or secondary, may take part in the contest, but the medal cannot be awarded unless ten pupils at least compete from that school. Each competitor must complete an original essay of from 500 to 2500 words and hand it in to the judges by May 5.

In case of elementary schools the school authorities shall select three judges from among the faculty, pupils or outsiders (including no contestants). In case of secondary schools the contestants themselves may get together and select any three judges they may choose except a contestant.

This contest is open free to all schools and a subscription to The Independent is not obligatory. If 1000 schools take part in this contest, 1000 medals will be awarded. Your school does not have to compete with any other school.

THE INDEPENDENT SHAKESPEARE CONTEST DEPARTMENT, 119 West 40th Street, New York:
We wish to enter The Independent Shakespeare Contest for American Schools. Please send full details.

Signed...

School...

City and State...

The Independent

FOR SIXTY-SEVEN YEARS THE
FORWARD-LOOKING WEEKLY OF AMERICA

THE   CHAUTAUQUAN
Merged with The Independent June 1, 1914

JANUARY   24,   1916

OWNED   AND   PUBLISHED   BY
THE INDEPENDENT CORPORATION, AT
119 WEST FORTIETH STREET, NEW YORK
WILLIAM   B.   HOWLAND,   PRESIDENT
FREDERIC E. DICKINSON, TREASURER
WILLIAM   HAYES   WARD
HONORARY EDITOR

EDITOR: HAMILTON   HOLT
ASSOCIATE EDITOR: HAROLD J. HOWLAND
LITERARY EDITOR: EDWIN E. SLOSSON

PUBLISHER: KARL   V.   S.   HOWLAND

ONE   YEAR,   THREE   DOLLARS

SINGLE   COPIES,   TEN   CENTS

Postage to foreign countries in Universal Postal
Union, $1.75 a year extra; to Canada, $1 extra.
Instructions for renewal, discontinuance or
change of address should be sent two weeks
before the date they are to go into effect. Both
the old and the new address must be given.

We welcome contributions, but writers who
wish their articles returned, if not accepted,
should send a stamped and addrest envelope. No responsibility is assumed by The
Independent for the loss or non-return of
manuscripts, tho all due care will be exercised.

Entered at New York Post Office as Second
Class Matter

Copyright,   1916,   by   The   Independent

Address   all   Communications   to
THE   INDEPENDENT
119   West   Fortieth   Street,   New   York

CONTENTS

A CORRECTION

In the issue for November 22, 1915,
The Independent published an interview with Yuan Shih-kai, then President of China and now Chinese Em-
peror-elect. We have since been informed by the Chinese Minister at
Washington that the interview never
took place. Dr. Koo transmits to us a
cablegram from the Department of
Ceremonies of the Chinese Government
in which the following statement is
made:

Independent published on November 22
copyright article purporting to be statement made by Yuan Shih-kai at interview
alleged to have been given to one Carl
von Resslinger at which interview President is represented to have given categorical replies to series of questions submitted
on behalf of Independent by his personal
secretaries Honorable Li-Chi-Tung and
Lieutenant-Colonel Semplee. You will state
on authority of President Yuan Shih-kai
that no such interview was ever given, that
no such person as Resslinger is known in
Peking, that no questions were ever submitted on behalf of Independent, that no
such persons as Li-Chi-Tung and Semplee
are known in Peking; whole article is malevolent fabrication.

The interview came to the office of
The Independent thru a channel in this
country which we have had no reason
in the past to regard as unreliable; and
came with every appearance of authenticity. It is the same channel thru
which was secured the first interview
with Yuan Shih-kai, published in The

Independent for July 26, 1915. The
genuineness of that interview has
never, to our knowledge, been questioned.

In view, however, of the categorical
denial on the part of the Chinese Government, The Independent can only express its deep and sincere regret that
the alleged interview should have been
made public thru its pages.—THE ED-
ITOR.

From the picture entitled "Pacifists
at Play," on page 47 of The Independent for January 10, 1916, the credit
line was accidentally omitted. The picture is copyrighted by Underwood &
Underwood, New York.

THE NEW PLAYS

The Weavers. Wonderfully effective
presentation of Hauptmann's grim, gray
drama of capitalistic oppression and industrial revolution. Unrelieved tragedy infused with power of conviction that stirs
and stimulates. (Garden.)

Bunny. Melodramatic farce and romantic fantasy, wistful charm and robust humor, brisk action and quiet pathos, combined with rare dramatic skill. No more
delightful entertainment will you find in a
twelvemonth. (Hudson.)

Ruggles of Red Gap. Adaptation of one
of Harry Leon Wilson's stories. English
butler and two noble lords in Far-western
"high society." Fair to middling farce—
foolish, funny. (Fulton.)

Major Barbara, one of our "only living
Shakespeare's" poorest plays, which is in
no sense saying that anything that Bernard
Shaw writes is inferior to the products of
other playwrights. Grace George and company render it most effectively. (Playhouse.)

Cock o' the Walk gives Henry Arthur
Jones a chance to use the coming Shakespeare Tercentenary as the theme and to
provide a suitable rôle for Otis Skinner's
sympathetic voice and irresistible swagger.
(Cohan.)

The Devil's Garden—a book dramatized.
Badly constructed and over-emotional, but
well staged and at times very well acted.
On the whole the play drags. (Harris.)

The Washington Square Players present
four one-act plays: pantomime, farce, war
play—of a new sort—and delightful whimsicality. "The Roadhouse in Arden." Original acting and artistic stage settings.
(Bandbox.)

The Pride of Race, starring Robert Hil-
liard. A harrowing negro problem play, full
of melodramatic situations, admirably acted. (Maxine Elliott.)

Sadie Love is one of those matrimonial
farces in which clever lines, funny situations and some very good acting are spoiled
by the vulgarity of the whole idea.
(Gaiety.)

Hip! Hip! Hooray! There is nothing to
be seen in the United States like the Hippodrome, and this year's show beats all
previous successes in variety and magnificence. A skating ballet is a novel attraction. (Hippodrome.)

E. H. Sothern, in his revival of *Lord
Dundreary,* which made his former famous
presents a wonderful characterization of a
caricature. This generation will enjoy it as
much as the last. He has followed it with
an able revival of that sentimental antiquity *David Garrick.* (Booth.)

EVERY SUPERIORITY

of the PACKARD T'WIN-SIX *has been*
Verified at the Hands of Owners

WITH the production schedule now fully met, new cars
each day are shattering all automobile traditions. ¶On
road, boulevard, track and mountain trail the twelve-cylinder
motor has shown itself to be the eventual power for every
particular service. ¶It throttles down to the lowest pace or
swings away to racing speed with such amazing ease that
passengers are unaware of change. ¶A new thrill awaits
you, a new experience in luxurious travel, in your first
Packard Twin-Six demonstration. *Arrange for it now.*

PACKARD MOTOR CAR COMPANY, DETROIT

Builders, also, of PACKARD *Chainless Motor Trucks*

TWIN-SIX

Ask the man who owns one

The Independent

VOLUME 85 JANUARY 24, 1916 NUMBER 3503

SHALL THE UNITED STATES PROTECT ITS CITIZENS?

SIXTEEN American citizens, traveling peaceably upon their legitimate business in Northern Mexico, have been murdered. It is reported by the United States Department of State that they were killed because they were Americans.

What will the United States do about it?

The President promptly sent a demand to General Carranza for the "immediate and efficient pursuit, capture and punishment of the perpetrators of the dastardly crime." This is well, but what reason is there to suppose that it will be effective? What reason to believe that Carranza can accomplish what we demand?

Mr. Lansing declares that these law-abiding Americans were killed by bands operating under the orders of General Villa and in accordance with the general policy publicly announced recently by him. Señor Carranza is the de facto ruler of Mexico; the United States has formally recognized him as such. Villa and his lawless supporters offer the chief challenge to the completeness of his rule. Obviously Carranza would not permit Villa to flout his authority and terrorize Northern Mexico if he could help it. If Carranza cannot suppress Villa for his own sake, what likelihood that he can do so for ours?

General Carranza has already exprest his purpose to punish the murderers. The method he proposes to adopt is that of declaring the offenders, when he can ascertain who they are, to be outlaws and authorizing any citizen to arrest them without warrant and execute them without formality. This is not a civilized method of procedure. It may possibly secure the death of the guilty persons, but it is quite as likely to result in the death of innocent persons. It is not the application of governmental authority; it is a confession of governmental impotence and an invitation to anarchy. It furnishes a significant commentary on the inability of General Carranza's administration to execute the primary function of government.

It is not merely a question of punishing the murderers. The future must be secured and safety guaranteed to American citizens who have good and legitimate reasons for living and traveling in Mexico. The President's keen regret that the murdered Americans did not heed the Administration's specific warnings to stay out of the disturbed parts of Mexico is an unsatisfactory comment on the existing situation. It implies an evasion of our national duty to protect American citizens in their unquestioned rights parallel to the proposal of Mr. Bryan and other Democratic leaders, which we discuss elsewhere in these pages, that Americans shall be prohibited from traveling upon belligerent-owned merchant ships. It puts the issue squarely before the American people: Shall the United States protect its citizens?

This is a primary duty of governments. The citizen of a nation is entitled to the protection of his government unless he is engaged in some unneutral or other act that by its very nature relieves his government from the responsibility of protecting him. The responsibility is one which the government may not ignore without dishonor.

The United States must protect its citizens in Mexico. If it can do so effectively by requiring the Mexican Government to afford the necessary protection, well and good. If the Mexican Government cannot afford the protection, the Government of the United States must do it itself. An example of the way in which protection can be given is provided by the Allied march to Peking. In 1900 the lives of foreigners in the Chinese capital were in grave danger from the Boxer revolutionaries. The Chinese Government was impotent. Great Britain, Japan, Germany, Russia and the United States sent armed forces to Peking and rescued their imperiled nationals. Subsequently the allied forces withdrew and left Chinese sovereignty unimpaired.

The march to Peking suggests the course we ought to follow now. But in the present instance we should act alone; it is American citizens that have been killed, American citizens primarily whose future security must be assured.

UNLESS within a very brief time Carranza shows himself able to comply with our demand to punish the murderers and to provide guarantees for the future, the President should send armed forces into Northern Mexico. Those forces should demand and secure the full punishment of the murderers of Chihuahua. They should establish conditions of peace and order under which Americans may live and travel and pursue their occupations in safety and tranquillity.

At the same time the President should inform the de facto ruler of Mexico that we have absolutely no purpose of aggression against the Government and the people of Mexico. He should assure Señor Carranza that when the guilty have been punished and the security of Americans in Northern Mexico has been assured, the American forces will be withdrawn and the Mexican Government left in complete and peaceful possession of the pacified region.

Our course in returning to China the indemnity received for the killing of American citizens during the Boxer rebellion is an example of the spirit of unselfishness and international friendliness in which the United States can carry out a project of this kind. In that spirit we should act again. But we should act with a full determination that the rights of Americans shall be respected and a sincere purpose to invoke the power of the United States to protect those rights whenever and wherever they are violated.

PREPAREDNESS BETTER THAN PREPARATION

NOW that we are being urged to increase our military efficiency it is time to examine closely what is the basis of such efficiency as is shown in this war. Germany is most frequently referred to as an example of what can be accomplished by preparedness, but it is commonly assumed that this preparedness consists in putting down concrete foundations secretly in the neighborhood of a fortress to be bombarded some years later, in laying up a stock of shells enough to last thru the war, and in having an envelope containing plans for all emergencies in the right-hand pigeonhole of von Moltke's desk. The concrete gun-bed legend was exploded long ago, and, while the Germans undoubtedly gained an advantage in the first days of the war by having abundant supplies of munitions ready for instant use and their campaign plans well worked out in advance, yet these advantages were quickly lost and do not account for the continued success of the Germans, which is more remarkable than their initial gains.

What we need to understand is not how the Germans got within sight of Paris within a month after the war began, but how they are able to get within sight of Riga and Salonica and Bagdad eighteen months after. The expenditure of shells has been vastly greater than even the Germans calculated, but their supply has not been exhausted because, as Lloyd George says, they were turning out last May nearly 250,000 high explosive shells a day, while the British were able to turn out only 2500. This was accomplished by converting all sorts of factories to provide for the army. Russia could not do this because she did not have the factories. England was slow in doing it because of the inflexibility of her industrial system and her national temperament.

The war now is being fought largely with new weapons of offense and defense and according to new tactics. In the introduction of innovations Germany has led and her enemies have imitated. We may explain the failure of the French and English to make first use of novel weapons like streams of fire and asphyxiating gases as due to moral scruples, but that does not account for the fact that the Germans were ahead of them in realizing the full value of such things as high explosives, machine guns and entrenchments.

It is quite likely that the German plans have gone agley as often as those of the Allies, but the Germans have been quicker at devising new ones to meet the changed conditions. Baffled on one front, they have turned to another and struck first, too. The gold stored in the war chest of Spandau castle for use in a future war was a drop in the bucket compared to the enormous expenditure required, but the reorganization of the financial and industrial system of the country has enabled Germany to stand the unanticipated strain with surprizing equanimity. The food supply of Germany was known to be inadequate to such a long siege, but by carefully regulated distribution famine has been avoided.

In short, the resources of the Allies are vastly greater, but in resourcefulness the Germans have shown themselves superior. No preparations can be adequate to a war like this; the chief security is a high state of preparedness.

The lesson for America is obvious and encouraging. Our wealth and our workshops are our greatest defense. A million men in arms would not alone suffice to protect our country. Russia had six million and she was defeated. Doubtless we should have an army and navy strong enough to meet a first attack of any probable force. Our coast batteries should, we admit, have enough shells on hand to last them longer than fifteen minutes. But the important thing is to have back of this a well educated and adaptable people, with men in authority who can organize and direct the resources of the nation according to the needs of the hour.

A PAN-PACIFIC CONFERENCE

WAR will cease when the causes of war are apprehended and removed. The chief way of apprehending and removing the causes of war are first to agrée on what they are and then to apply the remedy. Agreement results from deliberation based on the exchange of views. The exchange of views can best be carried on in a conference where representatives of the parties meet in personal contact.

These truths are elementary. But they show why conferences in the long run have the precedence over courts in maintaining the peace, for legislative bodies tend to prevent the issue from arising, whereas courts can only remedy the issue after it has already arisen and the bad feeling has been engendered. Arbitration, therefore, is neither the only nor usually the best way of preserving the peace.

Take the present war, for instance. Serbia appealed to The Hague court, but the proposition was not even considered in the various chancellories of the great powers. Will not the verdict of history, however, in apportioning the blame, almost absolve Europe in her refusal to resort to arbitration after the crisis arose, and rather find all nations guilty for not making a determined attempt in times of peace to assemble together and thresh out their differences and thus lay the foundations for a durable peace?

Accordingly we give hearty welcome to the suggestion that has come from several quarters of late that a Pan-Pacific conference be held in the near future where the great nations with vital interests on the Pacific can assemble for the purpose of discussing and settling if possible the common problems that confront them. These nations would certainly include Japan, China, England, Russia, France and the United States. Whether Siam, Holland, Germany and the Pacific Coast Latin-American republics should be included is a detail of not supreme importance. Ex-President Eliot suggests that the conference be held in Honolulu early this summer, but probably that will be found to be too soon, for the nations will doubtless find it impossible to come until the war in Europe ends.

Next to Europe, the Far East furnishes the greatest issues now confronting world statesmanship. The issues of Pan-America are nothing to compare with them. The sooner, therefore, the nations seriously and jointly enter upon a discussion of the whole Asiatic question, the more likelihood is there that it will be settled by law rather than by war.

It is vital, however, that any Pan-Pacific congress that expects to bring about large results must be strictly official in character. Pacific problems can of course be discussed—and with profit—by all sorts and conditions of private gatherings—but if any solution of them is wanted, they must be taken up by the governments themselves, who alone can act in the premises.

Let President Wilson, therefore, initiate the movement for a Pan-Pacific conference. Within a few days he has proposed a Pan-American policy that if carried out will prove the most important act of New World statesmanship since the promulgation of the Monroe Doctrine. He has now the opportunity to do an even greater service for the world.

THE PROGRESSIVES PROPOSE AMALGA-MATION

UNLESS all signs fail or some one makes a blunder later, the Republicans and the Progressives will enter the Presidential campaign shoulder to shoulder. The Progressives have made the first move toward union. They have arranged their national convention for the same date and place as that of the Republicans—Chicago, June 7.

This step has been taken with the frankly exprest hope that the two conventions will nominate the same candidate and write the same principles into their platforms. Nothing but a possible short-sighted unwillingness on the part of the Republicans to meet these overtures in ungrudging spirit could now seem to stand in the way of a complete and harmonious readjustment of the relations of the two groups. It is possible, of course, that the Progressives may yet do something themselves to make the amalgamation difficult; but they have begun well. If they go on in the same spirit the Republicans must meet them or bear the responsibility for the continued lack of harmony.

The Progressive committee announced the continued allegiance of their party to the following principles:

A broader nationalism;
Regulation rather than disruption of efficient business organizations, behavior and not size being the test;
A permanent, non-partisan, scientific tariff commission;
Revision of the tariff to fit war conditions and for the protection of new industries introduced as a result of the war;
Equal suffrage;
Dethronement of the invisible government;
An adequate merchant marine.

To these old planks, with their slight modification to fit the times, the Progressives add two new ones growing out of present conditions:

Complete preparedness, not only military, but economic; a preparedness that will unify American citizenship and create a renewed loyalty;
"The faith of our forefathers which made the American flag the sufficient protection of an American citizen around the world."

The declaration of the committee closed with the statement: "In this turning point in world history we will not stick on details; we will lay aside partisanship and prejudice. But we will never surrender those principles for which we stand and have stood. We will follow only a leader who we know stands for them and is able to put them through."

This was interpreted by some of the leaders, notably Mr. Perkins, as not necessarily meaning an insistence upon Mr. Roosevelt as the nominee, tho it is becoming increasingly evident that the thought of many, not only among Progressives but among Republicans, is turning in his direction.

The impulse toward amalgamation evidenced by this action of the Progressives is a good thing. The Ameri-can people do not want or know what to do with more than two great political parties.

PRESIDENTIAL TERMS AND PRESIDENTIAL NOMINATIONS

IT is a very interesting letter from the pen of President Wilson written a month before his inauguration that the New York *World* has just made public. It raises several important questions.

In the letter Mr. Wilson declares his opposition to the proposal for a constitutional limitation of the President to a single term of office. It was written to the vice-chairman of the Democratic National Committee and probably put a quietus upon the movement then going on in Congress for a constitutional amendment upon the subject. Mr. Wilson's arguments against the proposal are convincing. He first declares his cheerful readiness to abide by the judgment of his party and the public as to his candidacy for a second term, and pledges himself "to resort to nothing but public opinion to decide that question." He then proceeds:

The President ought to be absolutely deprived of every other means of deciding it.

And yet, if he is deprived of every other means of deciding the question, what becomes of the argument for a constitutional limitation to a single term? The argument is not that it is clearly known now just how long each President should remain in office. Four years is too long a term for a President who is not the true spokesman of the people, who is imposed upon and does not lead. It is too short a term for a President who is doing or attempting a great work of reform and who has not had time to finish it.

To change the term to six years would be to increase the likelihood of its being too long, without any assurance that it would, in happy cases, be long enough. A fixed constitutional limitation to a single term of office is highly arbitrary and unsatisfactory from every point of view.

Put the present constitutional limitation of two terms into the Constitution, if you do not trust the people to take care of themselves, but make it two terms (not one, because four years is often too long), and give the President a chance to win the full service by proving himself fit for it.

As things stand now the people might more likely be cheated than served by further limitations of the President's eligibility.

We singularly belie our own principles by seeking to determine by fixed constitutional provision what the people shall determine for themselves and are perfectly competent to determine for themselves. We cast a doubt upon the whole theory of popular government.

I believe that we should fatally embarrass ourselves if we made the constitutional change proposed. If we want our Presidents to fight our battles for us, we should give them the means, the legitimate means, the means their opponents will always have. Strip them of everything else but the right to appeal to the people, but leave them that; suffer them to be leaders; absolutely prevent them from being bosses.

With this statement of the case The Independent is in hearty accord. The people are to be trusted. They can be trusted just as well to decide whether they want to reëlect a President as to determine whether they want to elect him in the first place. The people in this matter do not need to be protected against themselves.

But Mr. Wilson's statement does not agree with the platform of his party upon which he ran for office. That document declared:

We favor a single Presidential term, and to that end urge the adoption of an amendment to the Constitution making the President of the United States ineligible for reëlection, and *we pledge the candidate of this convention to this principle.*

Can a party convention pledge the candidate it nominates to any policy or principle? Obviously President Wilson does not believe that it can. For he refused to hold himself bound by the categorical pledge of his party associates. He took a position diametrically opposed to the one to which they sought to bind him, and induced Congress to accept his view rather than theirs. It is unfortunate, in view of his complete disagreement with this plank in the platform of his party, that President Wilson did not either make a protest while the convention was still in session or announce his dissent publicly when the matter came up in Congress. The President ought to be frank with the people on a matter of such fundamental importance.

On the question of his right to dissent from the view of the convention, however, we agree with Mr. Wilson. A nominating convention should have no power to bind its nominee to every last pronouncement of the platform it has drawn up. As a matter of actuality it has no such power, and most candidates are wont to recognize, without any particular blowing of trumpets, the fact that it has not.

But the matter goes deeper than that. There ought to be no such thing as a nominating convention. Again Mr. Wilson is right, for in his letter he said:

There ought never be another Presidential nominating convention and there need never be another. Several of the states have successfully solved that difficulty with regard to the choice of their Governors, and Federal law can solve it in the same way with regard to the choice of Presidents. The nominations should be made directly by the people at the polls.

He further declared that "conventions should determine nothing but party platforms and should be made up of the men who would be expected, if elected, to carry those platforms into effect."

This is all perfectly sound doctrine. But why has not Mr. Wilson urged upon Congress action along these lines? Three years ago he was confident that the change would surely come. For he said, "I think it may safely be assumed that that will be done within the next four years." But what has he done to bring about the change he advocates?

This is one of the important reforms in our political machinery that ought to be carried out in the name of popular government. President Wilson ought to have included the Presidential primary among the measures behind which he put the effective weight of his power and influence.

RELIGIOUS LIBERTY ACHIEVED

FOR over fifteen years a campaign for religious liberty has been going on in three of the South American republics.

In Ecuador, Bolivia and Peru no public worship was allowed except in the established Catholic Church, and no marriages could be contracted except under Catholic forms. Several years ago these restrictions were removed in Ecuador and Bolivia and full religious liberty was permitted; but in Peru liberty of worship was still forbidden, and any other than Catholic religious service had to be behind closed doors in private houses to which admission was by card. Altho petitions and protests had been directed over and over again from citizens of this country to the Peruvian Government seeking full liberty

of worship, it seemed as if the Congress of Peru would never yield.

We are glad to learn thru our State Department that with the beginning of this year that section of the Peruvian constitution which prohibited any public worship except after the Catholic manner has been annulled and legislation adopted granting full religious liberty.

This does not mean that Catholicism ceases to be the established religion of Peru, but only that other forms of religion may be freely and publicly exercised. But it is a great victory that at last, thruout the entire Western Hemisphere, religious liberty has been achieved. This marks an epoch in the religious history of the continent. No longer anywhere will those who would worship God in their own way be compelled to hide themselves behind locked doors. The Dark Ages have past away. No longer will those who are not of the established Church be compelled to live without the sanctions of legal marriage.

The next religious campaign will be over the question of an established church. At a period in the history of our older states it was thought the business of the government to care for and support religion. In New England the town meeting made contracts with the minister and paid his salary. In Maryland the Roman Catholic Church was established, as also in Louisiana and other states; in New York the Dutch Reformed; in Virginia the Church of England; but long ago the country learned that everybody should pay for his own religion, and that way the whole world moves. The example of the United States and Canada will before long be followed in South America.

OUR ELDEST BROTHER

THO The Independent has got along in years so far that we can brag a bit about its age and cast aspersions on the "mushroom periodicals" of the day, we have to take off our hat to the Congregationalist and Christian World, which announces its one hundredth birthday. The Boston Recorder, of which the Congregationalist is the lineal descendant, was the first religious weekly newspaper in this or any other country. The hundredth anniversary number of January 6, 1916, contains contributions from some fifty well-known names, leaders of modern thought in various fields of religion, politics, philanthropy and literature. The record of its first century is a splendid one and we trust that its second century will prove to be no less prosperous and useful than its first.

A PEN PICTURE

CAN the reader guess what American statesman is characterized in the following pen picture?

Parliamentary government is government by speaking. In such a government the power of speaking is the most highly prized of all the qualities which a politician can possess; and that power may exist, in the highest degree, without judgment, without fortitude, without skill in reading the characters of men or the signs of the times, without any knowledge of the principles of government or political economy, and without any skill in diplomacy or in the administration of war.

No American statesman whatever. It is from Macaulay's Essay on William Pitt.

THE STORY OF THE WEEK

The Capture of Mount Lovcen

The Austrian occupation of the Montenegrin mountains behind Cattaro is, as we explain on page 129, a serious blow to both Montenegro and Italy. The aged King Nicholas has sent to Rome the Crown Prince Danilo Alexander and Crown Princess Jutta with a piteous appeal for help. What the Austrian victory means to him may be inferred from the following:

Lovcen is the Olympus of our race, the cradle of the dynasty, the stronghold which resisted the invasion of the Turks, even when they reached the walls of Vienna. Lovcen is more precious than if it were a colossal diamond.

His daughter, Queen Helena of Italy, is naturally supporting the appeal with all her influence and since Italy has always considered that the possession of Mount Lovcen by Austria would be inimical to her interests in the Adriatic, doubtless every effort will be made to recover it, but the chances are not hopeful, judging by the ease with which the Austrians have defended the mountains of the Trentino and the Karst ledges along the Isonzo River against the entire Italian army.

The Austrians had in the Gulf of Cattaro and in the outer bight three battleships, four cruisers and a number of torpedo boats and submarines. The heavy guns of some of the warships were brought to bear upon the mountains of the Montenegrin frontier by careening the vessels, and with this support the assault on the Karst barrier began on December 29.

The Montenegrin and Serbian troops defending the Cattaro frontier are said to number 3000, while the attacking force of Austrians was more than five times as great. Nevertheless they put up a stout resistance and it took the Austrians four days to capture the frontier entrenchments tho they used asphyxiating gases in the assault. This position was defended by twenty-two guns and four large mortars, most of which were taken intact by the Austrians and used against their fleeing foes.

The loss of Mount Lovcen soon followed this defeat and no attempt was made to defend the capital, Cettinje (variously spelled Cetinjé or Cettigne and pronounced Chet-teen-yay). King Nicholas has removed his headquarters to Niksic (pronounced Neetshitch), about thirty miles from the coast—and is said to be negotiating a permanent truce.

Montenegro Yields

The capture of the capital of Montenegro by the Austrians virtually removes the third of the three buffer states first involved in the war. The Belgians in France and the Serbians in Albania are continuing the fight, but the Montenegrins are cut off from retreat and their king is said to have succumbed to the inevitable. Montenegro

THE GREAT WAR

January 10. — Austrians capture Mount Lovcen, Montenegro. German attacks in Champagne make slight gains at great sacrifices.

January 11—French occupy Greek island of Corfu. British expedition to relieve besieged army at Kut-el-Amara is cut off by Turks twenty miles away.

January 12—Allies blow up Greek bridges above Salonica. Four British aeroplanes brought down by Germans.

January 13—French submarine sinks Austrian cruiser near Cattaro. Conscription bill passes second reading in Parliament by 431 to 39.

January 14—Austrians enter Cettinje, Montenegrin capital. Heavy Russian offensive against Bukovina continues.

January 15—Germany threatens reprisals for act of British warship Baralong. First thru train for Constantinople leaves Berlin.

January 16 — Russians advancing toward Kermanshah, Persia. British bombard Lille.

has not yet been overrun by hostile armies like Belgium and Serbia, but it

Underwood & Underwood
CLOCKS THAT RUN BY STONES—BECAUSE OF THE WAR
Two ancient timepieces in the Black Forest that have lost their copper weights to the bulletmakers

is surrounded on three sides by the Austrians and on the fourth side are the Albanians, hardly less hostile to the Montenegrins.

The conquest of Montenegro is an important victory for Austria, not because it adds much to her territory or relieves her of a dangerous foe, for Montenegro is both small and weak; but because it put Austria in secure possession of the bay of Cattaro, "the Gibraltar of the Adriatic." So long as this port was dominated by the guns on Mount Lovcen the Austrian warships were not safe here. In fact they were in October, 1914, driven out of the inner basin, the Gulf of Cattaro, as well as the middle basin, Teodo Bay, by the four guns of 4½ inch caliber which the French marines stationed on Mount Lovcen. If the French had carried out their plan of mounting 6-inch guns on the summit, the Austrian shipping would have been swept from the outer harbor and the forts about the bay reduced. The concrete foundations for these guns had already been laid when in May, 1915, Italy entered the war and undertook the defense of the Adriatic.

But the Italian navy failed to guard the Mouths of Cattaro as closely as the French and British had done previously, so the Austrian submarines have got out and have been raiding Mediterranean commerce with impunity. The Italians also failed to keep their promises to send troops and heavy guns to defend Mount Lovcen, altho they had been free to cross the Adriatic any time during the last seven months. So it seems as if Nicholas had lost his kingdom thru the neglect of his son-in-law, the King of Italy. In reality the fatal delay was doubtless due to a difference of opinion among the Italian authorities as to the conduct of the war, some of them being strongly opposed to any participation in the Balkans. Recently, however, it was decided to enter upon a campaign in Albania and troops have been transported across the Adriatic to Durazzo and Avlona, altho apparently too late to prevent the Bulgars and Austrians from overrunning Albania as well as Montenegro.

The Occupation of Corfu

The French have landed troops upon the Greek island of Corfu, which lies off the coast of southern Albania, and the Serbian soldiers are being brought here from Albania for recuperation. The wounded have been lodged in Achillelon Castle, the Mediterranean villa of the German Emperor, which was built for the Princess Elizabeth of Austria in 1890.

The German papers denounce the raising of the French flag over Achillelon as a personal insult to the Kaiser as well as a violation of Greek neutrality, worse even than the occupation of

111

Paul Thompson

HE KEEPS THE COW IN THE PARLOR—BECAUSE OF THE WAR

A Flemish farmer who has lost his outhouses and who dares not take the risk of letting his cow graze takes it indoors at night

Salonica since Corfu is, like Belgium, under a guarantee of perpetual neutrality by England, Russia, Austria, Prussia and France in the treaties of November 14, 1863, and March 29, 1864. Corfu was up to that time under the protection of Great Britain,. but the inhabitants longed for union with their Hellenic brethren and manifestations of disaffection were frequent. Finally Bulwer Lytton, when Secretary of State for the Colonies, took the unconventional step of sending Gladstone, because of his interest in Greek literature, to the Ionian Isles as a commissioner to learn the desires of the people, and as a consequence the seven islands were transferred to Greece, which was then placed under a Danish prince. George, father of the reigning King Constantine.

The Greek Government has protested to the Allied Powers against this new violation of her neutrality, but is not likely to take any further action since the Allied troops already on Greek territory outnumber the Greek army. The Allied Powers have informed Greece that their occupation of the island is only temporary "in order to save the heroic Serbian soldiers from famine and destruction." It is claimed that the German and Austrian submarines have been using the sheltered inlets of Corfu for repairing, and replenishing their fuel.

The German Attack in Champagne It appears that the German assault of the French lines last week was a more serious affair than was at first reported. According to the French account the Germans bombarded their entrenchments along a front of five miles near the butte of Le Mesnil for four days, firing 400,000 shells in the last twelve hours. Then they charged, not in solid column as they used to but in four successive waves. Three waves were stopped by the curtain of fire from batteries of the French 75's, but the fourth wave gained the first line of trenches for a distance of three or four hundred yards. Most of this was recovered later by the counter-attacks of the French. The Germans used asphyxiating gases but to little effect, for the wind changed and blew the fumes back over their own ranks. The French unofficial estimates give the enemy's losses as over 25,000.

The "Baralong" Case The threat of Germany to resort to reprisals if the British Government refuses to punish the officers of the "Baralong" may make this case one of the pivotal points of maritime warfare. According to the German note the British steamer "Nicosian" was overtaken by a German submarine on August 19, 1915, as she was carrying a cargo of mules for the British army. After the crew had been sent off in boats, and, while the "Nicosian" was being shelled by the submarine, the British patrol boat "Baralong" came up and signalled that she wanted to rescue the "Nicosian's" crew in the boats. Since the "Baralong" was flying the American flag and carried on her sides large shields of the American colors, she was allowed to approach, but when she came within range she opened fire with her concealed cannon and displayed her true colors. As the submarine sank under the fire the commander and most of the crew jumped overboard and some climbed up the ropes into the "Nicosian." The commander of the "Baralong,", it is alleged, ordered his men to fire upon the Germans clinging to the ropes and swimming in the water. Then the "Nicosian" was boarded and the Germans found there, were shot. The commander of the submarine who jumped overboard from the "Nicosian" and swam toward the "Baralong" was killed by a rifle shot as he held up his hands in surrender. This is supported by the evidence of six American muleteers, who have returned to this country. Their affidavits were presented by Count Bernstorff to our Government last October with the request that they be forwarded to England.

In his reply Sir Edward Grey expresses doubt of the correctness of the German version and offers to have the case referred to a neutral court of inquiry, say one composed of American naval officers, together with three cases of German atrocities committed within the same forty-eight hours; namely, the sinking of the "Arabic," destruction of a British submarine in Danish waters by a German destroyer and the attack on the "Ruel."

The German note in answer to this explains the "Arabic" case by saying that the commander of the submarine believed that the "Arabic" was about to ram his craft, that in the second case the submarine was defending itself by gun fire and that the "Ruel" was sunk as a reprisal for the British violations of international law. The German Government expected that when the evidence in the "Baralong" case was presented, based upon the affidavits of neutral witnesses, the British authorities would investigate the case for themselves, "not doubting for a moment that a court-martial composed of British naval officers would inflict suitable punishment for the cowardly and perfidious murder." The note concludes:

The German government, therefore, takes the ground, as the final result of the negotiations, that the British government, under empty pretexts,. has left unfulfilled the justified demands for an investigation of the "Baralong" case, and thereby has made itself responsible for the crime of defying international law and humanity, showing that it desires no longer to observe, in respect to German submarines, one of the first rules of war—namely, to spare enemies incapacitated for further action—in order to prevent them from conducting warfare at sea in accordance with established international law.

Inasmuch as the British government has declined to make amends for this outrageous incident, the German government feels itself compelled to take into its own hands punishment for this unatoned crime and to adopt measures of reprisal corresponding with the provocation.

A new phase of the war on commerce is expected to come by the declaration of a blockade of Germany by the British Government. Hitherto the Government has endeavored to attain the object by Orders in Council, but these failed to prevent food from getting into Germany and yet exasperated the United States and other neutral nations because of their violation of international law. Even England has been exporting food to Germany by way of Holland and the Scandinavian countries. For instance, the exports of cocoa to these countries are over a thousand tons a month more than they were before the war and cocoa is a very nutritious substance. With a formal and effective blockade the commercial isolation of Germany may be made more legal and complete.

Yuan to Become Emperor

It is announced from Peking that President Yuan Shih-kai will be formally made Emperor of China on February 12. He anticipated the honor by seating himself upon the Yellow Chair on New Year's Day. On December 11 the members of the State Council notified the President that the 1993 national citizens' representatives who had been consulted on the question had voted unanimously in favor of a constitutional monarchy and requested him to ascend the throne. Yuan replied, according to Chinese custom, with a modest refusal:

I, the President, find that the sovereignty of the republic resides with the people. Since the Citizens' Representative Convention has unanimously decided in favor of the constitutional monarchy there is left no more for me to say, but the fact of requesting me to ascend the throne is indeed astonishing. At the beginning of the republic, I made an oath to develop the republic to the best of my ability. Now, if I made myself Emperor I would break my oath, and there is no excuse on the point of faith.

My primary object, however, is to save the country and to save the people, and I do not care to sacrifice myself for the attainment of this object. But, in self-examination, I find there is nothing to justify me to cast aside the great principles of morality and faith. I hope the Citizens' Representatives who love me will not bear to force upon me the task which would be difficult for me to execute. I further hope that the General Representatives of the Citizens' Representative Convention will take careful and mature deliberation to request somebody else to ascend the throne.

But on the following day the State Council renewed its petition and Yuan Shih-kai accepted.

As was anticipated the news of the overthrow of the republic was the signal for an insurrection in the south, where the republican feeling is strongest. The Province of Yunnan is in active revolt under the leadership of its Governor, General Tang Chi-wao, and the movement is obviously spreading altho the censorship prevents anything from being accurately known. The Chinese Government has warned travelers and missionaries to stay out of the provinces of Yunnan, Kwang-si, Sze-chuen, and Kwei-chow. Yuan has announced that a system of compulsory military service will be put into effect at first in the provinces of Chili and Shang-tung and later thruout the empire. This plan, if carried out in the population of over 300,000,000, will produce the biggest army that the world has ever known.

Americans Murdered in Mexico

The murder of nineteen Americans in the Mexican State of Chihuahua has caused sharp debates in the Senate at Washington, where resolutions authorizing armed intervention have been introduced and supported in speeches attacking the policy of the Administration. On the 11th, a small force of soldiers who were formerly in Villa's army, commanded by General Lopez and General Reyna, stopped a train near Santa Ysobel, about fifty miles west of the city of Chihuahua, took from it nineteen Americans who were on their way to the Cusi mines (owned by the estate of the late Potter Palmer, of Chicago), robbed them, tore off their clothing, and put them to death. The condition of their bodies, which have been recovered and brought to El Paso shows that they were mutilated after the fatal wounds had been received. One of the men, Charles R. Watson, was general manager of the mines and chairman of the Chihuahua Miners' and Smelters' Association. Another, W. J. Wallace, was the general superintendent of the mining property. In the group were also the company's chief chemist, the foreman and the bookkeeper. A majority of the victims were graduates of our colleges or technical schools, and one, C. A. Pringle, had been a noted athlete at the University of California. The first news of the murders was brought by Thomas H. Holmes, the only member of the mining party who escaped. Accidentally falling into some bushes, he was concealed by them until night, when he began to make his way to a place of safety.

It is said that these men were invited by General Obregon, the Carranza commander, to return to the mines. General Trevino now says that at Chihuahua City they refused a military escort. Mr. Edwards, our Consul at Juarez, asserts that he was asked by Secretary Lansing to procure a protecting force from the Carranza leaders, and that General Trevino and General Gavira assured him that a military guard had been sent with the train. At Washington, however, it is said that Secretary Lansing's instructions related not to this party but to the protection of all Americans in the state. His warning that Americans should come out of Mexico had not been revoked. There is evidence that Villa, resenting the recognition of Carranza's Government, had threatened to kill Americans. It is thought that in this way he planned to embarrass Carranza and to force intervention.

In response to a demand from Secretary Lansing, Carranza undertook to pursue, capture and punish the murderers. He declined the aid of Americans, offered from Texas. On the 13th, a small force of Americans and Mexicans, who were guarding property at Madera, captured General Almeida and General Rodriguez, of the Villa army. Almeida was at once shot, and Rodriguez was put to death a day or two later. Forty of their followers had been killed. It became known that two more Americans, George F. Pearson and Bert Kramer, had been murdered. At the request of our Government, American mining companies ordered their employees to leave the country. Several hundred refugees arrived at El Paso last week on special trains. General Huerta, for seventeen months President of Mexico, died last week at El Paso, where he had recently been subjected to four surgical operations. He was under arrest and was to have been tried this month.

The Question in Congress

Before the nineteen men were killed near Santa Ysobel, our Senate had taken up the Mexican problem, and had adopted without opposition a resolution introduced by Mr. Fall, Republican, of New Mexico. This resolution, suggested by the pending nomination of Henry P. Fletcher to be Ambassador to Mexico, asked the President for information. mainly in answer to ten questions, relating to the recognized Government, its character and history, its assurances of protection for the lives and property of Americans, its ability to pay claims for

Paul Thompson

AT HARD LABOR—BECAUSE OF THE WAR
An English woman worker standing at the rolling mill to catch the red hot plates as they come thru and return them. It is severe work for a man

Underwood & Underwood

HAVING THEIR PICTURES TAKEN—BECAUSE OF THE WAR
The Germans are photographing the women and children of Northern France, identifying each by a number, and those who wish to move or travel must identify themselves before they can get passports

damages, etc. Mr. Wilson was requested to send all the reports of the Brazilian Minister who has been representing our Government, the reports of all our consuls for four years past, and a history of the occupation of Vera Cruz, with an explanation of the evacuation of that port. Speeches were made in which Republicans criticized the President's policy.

The news of the murders was followed by demands for intervention. On the first day, Senator Sherman, Republican, introduced a resolution (with a long preamble), providing that we should invite the six Latin-American nations that were members of the recent Mexican conference to join us in demanding action by Carranza, and, if he should fail, to stand with us in intervention, with the understanding that after the restoration of order we should withdraw. Mr. Borah and Mr. Gallinger, Republicans, made speeches in which it was said that the time had come for laying aside the policy of "watchful waiting." Mr. Stone, Democrat and chairman of the Foreign Relations Committee, said he had supported the President's policy and that of Mr. Taft for five years against his own convictions, for he had thought that armed force should be sent into Mexico. But he asked for delay now, in order that the President might pursue his chosen course. Senator Thomas, of Colorado, blamed the oil companies for the trouble.

On the second day there was a resolution in the Senate from Mr. Lewis, Democrat, authorizing the President to order the army into Mexico, to pursue the murderers and protect American property. In the House there was one authorizing such use of the army and the navy. The third day was marked by a bitter debate in the Senate, where the attitude of some Democrats had

undergone a change. Mr. Stone had been talking with the President. With Mr. Lewis he accused the Republicans of acting in the interest of politics. Mr. Lewis said they sought to make the Mexican question an issue because they had no other. Intervention would turn South America and Central America against us. Mr. Stone asserted that it would be monstrous to go to war after recognizing Carranza and without giving him an opportunity to do what is required. Mr. Fall attacked the President's policy, and Mr. Works, Republican, of California, put in a resolution empowering him to use the army in Mexico. In the House, Mr. Slayden, of Texas, Democrat, uttered a warning about danger along the border, where the patience of Americans was nearly exhausted. But Governor Ferguson, of the same state, had just published a statement in which he said that those opposing the President should remember that the United States was wholly unprepared for armed intervention. Mr. Roosevelt said that we should send the regular army at once, and that General Wood was the man to lead it.

There was no indication that the President would change his policy. He will continue, it is said, to look to Carranza for the capture and punishment of the guilty. If Carranza fails, other aspects of the question will be considered.

National Politics At a meeting of the national committee of the Progressive party in Chicago last week a declaration of principles was adopted, and it was decided that the national convention should be held in that city on June 7, the date of the Republican convention there. "We take this action," said the committee, referring to the date and place, "believing that the surest way to secure for our

country the required leadership will be by having, if possible, both the Progressive and the Republican parties choose the same standard bearer and the same principles. We are confident that the rank and file of the Republican party and the very large independent vote of this country will support such an effort. If the Republican convention meets this crisis in the spirit of broad patriotism that rises above partisanship, the effort for a common leadership will be successful." George W. Perkins, the committee's chairman, said all the members hoped for agreement upon a candidate, who would "not necessarily have to be Colonel Roosevelt." There were indications that Justice Hughes was regarded with much favor.

The declaration of principles, after reaffirming the old platform, severely criticized the Wilson Administration, saying it had failed to deal adequately with national honor and industrial welfare, had suffered Americans to be slaughtered in Mexico and on the high seas, permitted American liberty to travel and trade to be subject to the arbitrary and lawless coercion of foreign belligerents, had made no adequate protest when the law of nations disappeared, and had shown a supine spirit, "whose sure consequence is the contempt of the world." Our people, it asserted, had become impatient of "leaders who hold that comfort, prosperity and material welfare are above honor, self-sacrifice and patriotism." Complete preparedness was demanded, not merely in military armament, but preparedness that would mobilize resources and create a spirit unalterably opposed to militarism while it would view the doctrine of peace at any price as futile, cowardly and unrighteous. In a letter to the committee, Mr. Roosevelt said we must insist on the most thoro-going preparedness to protect our rights against all possible attacks by any aggressors, and that this would be the best guarantee of any honorable peace.

President Wilson has not objected to the publication of a very long letter, relating to the proposed limitation of the presidential term, sent by him in February, 1913, after his election but before his inauguration, to Congressman A. Mitchell Palmer. This has been read with interest because of its bearing upon his candidacy for a second term and the Baltimore platform's utterance in favor of a single term. In the letter, most of which is an argument against constitutional limitation of the term of service, he pledged himself to resort to nothing but public opinion to decide whether he would be a candidate again in 1916. Constitutional limitation, he said, would be unsatisfactory from every point of view. We should fatally embarrass ourselves by it. One term of four years might be too short for a President engaged in a great but unfinished work of reform. The people might be cheated, rather than served, by limitation. In his opinion there ought to be no more nominating conventions, but nominations should be made directly by the people at the polls.

It is generally understood that Mr. Wilson is a candidate for renomination. Ex-Senator Elihu Root has asked that his name be not permitted to appear on the primary ballots in Minnesota, saying that he is not a candidate. It is said that the New York delegates will go to the Republican convention without instructions in favor of any one.

The New Haven Trust Case In the suit of the Government against eleven former directors of the New York, New Haven and Hartford Railroad Company, under the criminal provisions of the Sherman Anti-Trust law, the jury, after being out for fifty-one hours, brought in a verdict, on the 9th, acquitting six of the defendants and disagreeing as to the remaining five. Those acquitted are A. Heaton Robertson, New Haven, a lawyer and formerly a judge; Robert W. Taft, Providence, banker and manufacturer; D. Newton Barney, Farmington, Conn., prominent in electric lighting companies; James S. Hemingway, president of a bank in New Haven; Frederick F. Brewster, New Haven, a prominent merchant and yachtsman; Henry K. McHarg, Stamford, Connecticut, formerly one of the governors of the New York Stock Exchange. The most widely known of the five as to whom there was disagreement is William Rockefeller, brother of John D. Rockefeller, the Standard Oil multimillionaire. With him are Charles M. Pratt, associated with Standard Oil interests; Lewis Cass Ledyard, formerly

© International Film Service

LAWSON PURDY

The newly elected president of the National Municipal League has been president of the New York Department of Taxes and Assessments since 1906. He knows taxation thoroly and believes in the city manager idea. It is a new thing for a city official—and a New York city official at that—to have contributed so much to the cause of good city government that he deserves and receives such an honor as this

Underwood & Underwood

HOMELESS AND BITTER COLD—BECAUSE OF THE WAR
But this time it's industrial war—and the refugees are in East Youngstown, Ohio, where they were burned out in the fires that followed strike riots

counsel for the late J. Pierpont Morgan; Edward D. Robbins, formerly general counsel of the New Haven Company; and Charles F. Brooker, a brass manufacturer, and formerly the Connecticut member of the Republican National Committee. The number of those originally indicted was twenty-one, but immunity was granted to three, and six were permitted to have separate trials.

For seventeen ballots the vote was eight for acquittal to four for conviction of all of the defendants. Then, the judge having said that there could be a divided verdict, the jury by unanimous vote acquitted six. The defendants were accused of conspiring to monopolize the common carrier transportation of New England by acquiring and combining steam railroads, trolley lines and steamship companies. The trial consumed nearly three months, and there were more than 2,000,000 words in the record. It is said that the cost of the trial was $200,000 to the Government, and $575,000 to the defendants.

The Government has decided to try again the five men as to whom there was disagreement, and to proceed no further against those who were permitted to have separate trials. Two of these are George F. Baker, a prominent New York banker, and Theodore N. Vail, president of the American Telephone and Telegraph Company.

Higher Wages At the present time about 400,000 members of the four great railroad unions are voting to decide whether a demand for an eight-hour day, with time and a half for overtime, shall be made in April. Railroad officers held a conference last week about this movement. One of them afterward said that the demand would not be

granted, because the proposed change would mean great loss and might even drive some roads to bankruptcy. He estimated the increase of pay at more than 30 per cent and said the change might require the employment of 80,000 more men.

The Steel Corporation's grant of 10 per cent to between 150,000 and 175,000 men will add at least $12,000,000 a year to the payroll. It is said that the number of the company's employees now exceeds 240,000. By the terms of the new agreement with its men, the Colorado Fuel and Iron Company is required to increase wages when advances are made in a kindred industry. Therefore an increase promptly followed the announcement made by the Steel Corporation. Other similar increases have since been announced. The Pennsylvania Steel Company has given 10 per cent to 6000 men, and the Harrisburg Pipe Company an equal advance to 2000.

Order has been restored at East Youngstown, Ohio, where twenty-six of the strikers have been indicted for rioting, burglary and the destruction of property. Work has been resumed in the mills, the strikers accepting an increase of 10 per cent. Thomas H. Flynn, general organizer of the Federation of Labor, publicly asserted that the riots had been caused by capitalists who desired to depress the price of the companies' stock, in order that they might buy it at low figures for a projected steel combination. As he connected the Colorado Fuel and Iron Company with the project, John D. Rockefeller, Jr., says that those who control that company have no interest in or knowledge of such a combination. In Meriden, Connecticut, two companies manufacturing silver goods have sued local unions for damages due to a recent strike.

FROM STATE TO STATE

ALABAMA: Boys' pig clubs are becoming important institutions in this state. Demonstration agents, aided by teachers in rural schools, are organizing them everywhere, and the success of those boys who have been induced to keep up their interest in the work has attracted others to it. A report from one county gives a fair idea of what is being done in many others. Of 130 members enrolled last February fifty-one sent in the September report called for, tho only ten of these answered all the questions. These ten, however, with one pig apiece, showed a net profit of $90. This, together with the valuable prizes awarded to the ten boys at an exhibition in October and the local fame achieved by their success, aroused the interest of many more boys, and this year's enrollment embraces nearly every eligible boy in the county.

ARKANSAS: What is known as the Newberry statewide prohibition law went into effect at the beginning of this year. This law and the Woods nuisance act form a combination which, it is believed, will make the manufacture, sale or gift of liquor in Arkansas too dangerous for anybody to undertake. Under the law as it now stands no person may plead guilty and no court may suspend sentence for a first offense. No second chance is to be given. All persons convicted must go to the penitentiary for at least one year.

IOWA: A recent survey of the farming situation showed that Iowa is no longer the grain-selling state that it was a few years ago. Of all the sales now made by its farmers 75 per cent represent live animals and animal products, 22 per cent crops and 3 per cent miscellaneous produce. In other words, the Iowa farmer has learned that there is more profit in feeding grain to animals than in selling it.

LOUISIANA: A large delegation of prominent Louisianans has been sent to Washington to induce Congress to open the port of New Orleans to Central and South American cattle. It was the ticky condition of these cattle that caused the Government to close this port to them, but since the port of Galveston is open to Mexican cattle, which are said to be no less ticky, the Louisianans hold that they are discriminated against. They say they have all the facilities for dipping cattle that Galveston has, and they want the same privilege of bringing them in. They also say that in addition to needing these cattle for their farms they can produce a large packing plant for New Orleans if the restrictions on importation are removed.

MAINE: High class municipal music on a self-supporting basis has been thoroly established by the City of Portland. It is now in the midst of its fourth successful season since Cyrus H. K. Curtis gave a great organ to the city as a memorial to

116

the former local musical leader, Kotzschmar. Will C. Macfarlane, the municipal organist, receives a salary from the city, but the balance remaining after the winter subscription concerts and the summer pay concerts has more than offset this every year. So, while the city does the business, the cost to the city government is nothing; and some of the best musical talent in the world is heard at its concerts.

MASSACHUSETTS: The rivers and harbors committees of Congress are going to hear much about Massachusetts this winter. The people of the Merrimac Valley are going to tell them that this valley handles in value of raw material and finished product 7.5 per cent of the foreign trade of the United States; that this trade represents $1,000,000 for every working day in the year; that it exceeds the foreign trade of Boston by more than $97,000,000 a year and that, therefore, the improvement of the Merrimac River to Lowell, against which a United States engineer has twice reported, should be made. Also the people of Holyoke are going to show that they pay exorbitant freight rates because the one railroad reaching there has no competition, a condition of things which might be remedied if the Connecticut River were made navigable from Hartford to Holyoke.

MINNESOTA: At the recent largely attended convention of the Equity Coöperative Exchange in St. Paul farmers of Minnesota, Wisconsin, North Dakota, South Dakota and Montana organized what is to be known as the National Buying and Marketing Association. Its purpose is to cut out middlemen by buying supplies for its members directly and in quantity. It is not to interfere with the Equity Exchange, but is rather to work with it. Another incident of the convention was the breaking of ground for what is said to be the first terminal elevator to be erected by farmers in the United States. When the first shovelful of earth had been turned President Anderson of the Equity Exchange said: "This is the beginning of a day when justice will prevail in the grain markets of the country."

MISSOURI: The new Coliseum in St. Louis was one of the weightiest arguments used in favor of that city for the Democratic national convention of this year. The building is of concrete, steel and glass, and is said to be one of the best ventilated and lighted convention halls in the United States. Its acoustic qualities are so excellent that grand opera has been successfully given in it. The actual seating capacity is 14,000 persons, and there are many and ample committee rooms. All balconies and galleries have separate entrances. The Coliseum is within easy walking distance of the downtown hotels and two street car lines pass its doors, with transfer privileges to all parts of the city for one fare.

MONTANA: The successful completion of the first electrical unit of the Chicago, Milwaukee & St. Paul Railroad was celebrated at Butte after the electric locomotives had shown their superiority over steam engines on an up grade in the Rocky Mountains. In the test one train, weighing 2200 tons, was drawn with difficulty by three steam locomotives. Another train, weighing 3000 tons, was drawn by two electric motors which swept up the grade with no apparent effort. President Earling of the St. Paul road, after witnessing the test, predicted that steam will be supplanted by electricity on all the railroads of the country.

NEVADA: The "Jolly Good Fellows" of Reno to the number of about 100, combined charity with sport a few days before Christmas by spending a day in the mountains shooting rabbits for the poor of the city. As a result of what they called a day of delightful sport they marched into town that evening with more than 1200 rabbits, all of which were turned over to the Salvation Army and other philanthropic organizations. It is said that not less than 500 families who otherwise would have had no meat for their Christmas dinners were bountifully supplied.

NEW HAMPSHIRE: The United States Government has purchased, under the Weeks forestry act, a tract of 5500 acres in the White Mountains. This will be added to the lands already acquired and set aside as a public reservation. The new tract is situated on the slopes of the Presidential range and includes the summits of Mt. Webster, Mt. Jackson and Mt. Clinton. It contains one of the finest growths of virgin spruce remaining in the White Mountains region. This purchase gives the Government control of practically all the peaks of the Presidential range and brings its holdings in New Hampshire up to more than 270,000 acres.

NEW YORK: The special export course established a few weeks ago in connection with the College of the City of New York has proved so interesting to exporters that it has been necessary to prepare a waiting list. The course includes such branches as sales organization and sales methods in the foreign field, transportation problems and government regulations affecting international trade, special problems arising from war conditions and decrees and regulations of foreign governments. The direction of the course is in the hands of an advisory committee composed of recognized experts in marketing, financing, shipping and in legal and commercial education matters, representing the college, the Merchants' Association, the National Association of Manufacturers and the Board of Trade and Transportation.

NORTH CAROLINA: Colonel Benehan Cameron of this state, vice-president of the Southern National Highway, reports that

the completion of that transcontinental route is in sight. Colonel Cameron and President D. M. Potter of Clifton, Arizona, have been the moving spirits of this enterprise since its inception more than three years ago. With only a few gaps to fill, the highway is practically completed from Morehead, North Carolina, on the Atlantic, to San Diego, California, on the Pacific. It is intended especially as a winter route, lying sufficiently far south to avoid the snow and ice which in winter may block the Lincoln and other more northerly highways.

TENNESSEE: The experiment of working Negro convicts on the roads of Tennessee has convinced the State Board of Control that this plan is a great improvement upon the old contract system. Of fifty-five state prisoners, all Negroes and unshackled, who worked on the roads of Williamson County nearly all summer, twenty-five were made trusties and only three attempted escape. The health and tractability of the prisoners were said to be much better than under the old system. President Denton of the Board of Control says the experiment has been successful and that a number of contracts with counties will probably be made for next season's road work.

WEST VIRGINIA: Forty years ago the salt industry in the Kanawha Valley and Pomeroy Bend was one of the most profitable in West Virginia. Many thriving towns were built up about factories which produced salt by evaporation of water pumped from wells. Bromine was a by-product barely worth with marketing. When the Michigan and other rock salt beds were developed and salt was dug from the ground the West Virginia factories could not compete and the towns were deserted, save for a few factories that struggled on in a very small way. These relied mainly on bromine, while the rock salt beds did not produce. Now the European war has sent the price of bromine from 25 cents to $5 a pound, and the deserted towns are again becoming prosperous. One factory recently sold twenty tons to the Germans for $200,000 cash. Bromine is used in the manufacture of munitions, especially asphyxiating bombs.

WYOMING: A land case of exceptional interest is going thru the Wyoming courts. Early in November a court commissioner issued an injunction restraining H. F. Ketchum and others from entering upon valuable oil lands in the Elk basin which they claim by right of location. The same land is claimed by C. L. Woods and others by right of discovery of oil thereon. Judge C. E. Raymond, sitting at Cody, has sustained the injunction, holding that the locators had done nothing to develop the land, while the discoverers of oil had given it the greater part of its value. The case will go to the higher courts.

THE WRONG WAR

BY PRESTON W. SLOSSON

Because of a war that came not
  The world bleeds in a trench,
And mothers and wives are molding shot
  For the German lad or the French;
For league on league the corpses lie
Looking to heaven and asking why.

The evil war is upon all lands,
  The war that the great kings made,
Because the peasants had held their hands,
  Because the workers had stood afraid;
The mercy shown to the lords and the crown
Is wringing blood from the field and the town.

Men die for the high lords' fancied gain
  Who would not die for their own;
They sin for another the sin of Cain,
  For another's guilt they atone;
Obedient servants to Kaiser and Tsar,
They are paying the price in shame and scar.

Oh, better had perished the Kaiser's name
  In a clamorous forest of pikes and blades,
And the Tsar's tall palaces all aflame
  In a bloody battle of barricades;
That Cromwell's ax or the guillotine
Had swept off the rubbish and left all clean!

L'Envoi

Prince, you are making a war today
  Which is turning God's footstool Hell's own hue;
You are teaching your subjects how to slay,—
  Why *didn't* they turn their swords on you!

WHY WE SHOULD READ BOOKS

BY CORRA HARRIS

AUTHOR OF "A CIRCUIT RIDER'S WIFE," "IN SEARCH OF A HUSBAND," "THE CO-CITIZENS"

WE cannot always choose the people with whom we associate in real life. And we cannot always escape such associations. One's own family may be of a different class. A woman may marry a brute, a man may marry a fool. Our children may be far removed from us in mind and sympathy. Poverty may force a man or a woman of refinement and the highest aspirations into the lowest strata of society where his or her companions are stupid or perverted by their condition into a poisoned sense of things and values which are abhorrent and destructive. Certain professions remove people from normal and healthy relations with their kind. Crime, or any other form of illness, may do the same thing.

These conditions exist because we exist. But whatever one's condition in life, there is a great society from which we may choose our companions, our thoughts and our scenes. The poorest laborer, the drudge, the man in the factory, or the woman in the sweat shop may choose companions from among the greatest men and women who have ever lived in poetry, history or fiction. Nothing else is so easy to accomplish. He may do it without changing his clothes, without toadying to his superiors in authority, without enduring those humiliations which often overwhelm him when he seeks to better his social relations. There is no society so good, so varied and so surely in reach of every man as that to be had from an intimate knowledge of books. Any man, however lonely, or friendless,

or removed from the currents of modern life, may, if he will, surround himself with philosophers, poets, the most interesting women in the world, and the wittiest companions, at a cost far less than the price he pays for saloon privileges, moving pictures, vaudeville shows or more doubtful forms of amusement.

The trouble is that the people, the great body of the people, have not yet discovered that life and character are finished in time and recorded in books, and that the life and character of living men are only phases, the illuminated script of passing conditions, not altogether worth the absorbing attention which they receive, and that these still transitory people are not nearly so helpful nor so refreshing as companions because they are swayed by all the uncertainties and errors of standard by which they live.

The only men who live forever are the dead men, or those great characters conceived by poets and other faithful interpreters of human nature.

Therefore it is better to balance the influence of one's transient mortal associations by acquiring a peaceful intimacy with these ever living men and women whose deeds, aspirations, loves and courage are recorded in books, who are never against us, who never despise us, nor fail us, nor betray us, being stripped now of that mortal part which renders all men uncertain, liable to hypocrisies, conceits and a sort of human heinousness which life in the flesh never quite escapes.

There is no braver, wiser, more Christian counselor for any man than Socrates, no nearer brother than Jesus, no more faulty or endearing character to be found in life or literature than that of King David. If one reads it simply, without prejudice and without the merely theological interpretations of preachers and commentaries, there is no book which compares with the Bible in charm, dignity and wisdom, and in the immediate companionship of great souls and little souls and just common souls. The men and women, the angels and even the God of this book are all co-temporary with us. This is the Book of all books for every man and every woman of whatever condition.

It is necessary to read histories in order to learn the facts, the forces which evolved and established such and such a civilization. But no history, however carefully compiled, is so veracious as interpretative fiction of the same period. Novels are to history what illustrations are to any text. They portray the lights and shades of character, draw the lineaments of life itself, as well as facts. They dramatize manners, customs, tempers, petty emotions, virtues and vices where history chiefly records the effects of these human elements upon society. The novels of Dumas, Balzac and Hugo are an essential part of the history of the French people. No man can know England without reading Dickens' novels. They contain the drama as well as the record of those reforms which completely revolutionized certain

117

English institutions. We cannot know our own country, even if we read every history, if we do not also read certain novels covering the same periods. In times to come, the historian himself must turn to the socialistic and suffrage fiction now being produced here in order to visualize to himself the changes in economics and forms of government which are now upon us. Fiction is the flesh and blood of literature, as history is its bones and sinews, and as poetry and religion and art show the wings and spirit of it. Nothing is so lasting, or so important to know as what is written in books. You may see all the moving pictures and only learn in the most casual way what is already preserved in the lasting forms of literature. And the moving pictures are reels which fail. They pass like the leaves on the trees, and you must turn again to the history or the novel to recall those scenes, however vivid. The retina of the eye does not retain the images of natural scenery through which you pass so swiftly during an automobile tour. At the end it is all blurred, one memory upon another memory. But there is scarcely a mountain, or plain or valley or desert in this country which is not perfectly visualized in some novel or poem, or history with an art and sympathy which approaches the vividness of that first scene in Genesis when the light was divided from the dark and the waters gathered together in one place, and when the dry land appeared, virgin clean from the depths of virgin seas,—all of life and the nature of life that is worth having, and that we *know* we have, is finished and recorded in books.

Even this is not enough to claim for the value of books. For the most inspiring and helpful men and women we can meet in them have no part in history. They have never lived at all in the flesh. They are, and will ever remain, immortal creations which sum up and portray in themselves more than any one living character can portray. They are the kindred of every man, and the mirror souls of all men, and of all women. The heroine of Hawthorne's "Scarlet Letter" is the eternal plea for all the women of her class, known or unknown—the secret companion of their sufferings, the very truth of their sad hearts. It is the fashion now to pass over the knights of King Arthur's round table. But it is a bad fashion, and has no basis in the truth of life. These men are still among us, still making lonely pilgrimages for the Holy Grail, and they find it. This is the good of reading poetry and of believing it. The

man who does that believes good of himself, which is a needful faith.

Thus one may learn what is best and that which is worst in himself and even in his generation by making the acquaintance of people, in fiction no less than in life. John Barclay, the hero of "A Certain Rich Man," is a typical American financier. To read this novel and follow this man thru the various phases of his development is to know and understand the methods by which wealth is acquired and markets controlled as the average reader never would learn from a treatise upon finances and industrial conditions, because this story dramatizes the power of wealth, and the frenzy of greed in a generous man's heart.

If you wish to understand racial distinctions, books compile these differences as you could never find them in the separate individual. Read Du Bois and comprehend the "Heart of the Black Folk," and read Booker Washington's autobiography in order to discover the way of their salvation, which cannot be found in Du Bois' lament.

If you would know the Jews, who are both spiritual and decadent, read Isaiah first, and then read the novels of a certain Jewish author in this country, who spent years in prison and whose only companions were characters chosen from books in the prison library.

If you desire to know the most genial and companionable side of England, mirus war and hate, choose those of Joseph Conrad, a Polish Jew, who never saw or pronounced an English word until after he was nineteen years of age. He is today a master of that tongue, the gentlest, wisest and most whimsical interpreter of the English character. This was achieved by a study of English literature as well as of the English people. No foreigner has the time in his own lifetime to understand the people of his adoption without learning more of them from their books than he can from actual association with them.

This is a plea for reading books, not merely good books. For every thoughtful person has observed that the person who reads only "good books," "useful books" and "profitable books" is invariably afflicted with a certain invincible conceit, intolerance, hypocrisy and a meanness of the mind which is incurable. To read only good books is like associating with only the "best people"—very debilitating to the mind and character. It results in snobbishness and in a lack of knowledge and sympathy with other kinds of people—who are fortunately in the majority.

Therefore read books, good, bad and indifferent, as you would hearken to a good man, love something sadly kin to you in a bad one, and as you would bear with the frailties of just the common fellow. Thus only is it possible to attain a broader understanding, which is something mere wisdom often fails to impart. The point is to keep your balance and go ahead into books as you would make your way into any other mixed crowd. Bear in mind that the immoral man who preaches morality is a liar and a thief tho he speak with the tongue of men and of angels. Likewise the book which portrays vice even while affecting to condemn it, is really written to feed the reader upon offal, however masterly its style. But read it, in order that you may familiarize yourself with this commonest form of deceit in men and literature—not, however, for the purpose of condemnation, which is also one of the subtlest forms of self-congratulation, but that you may avoid this ignoble quality in your own character, which, if you are as observant of it as you are of other men's characters, you will find needs constant shriving.

Finally, but not least important, one should read books for the pleasure, the relaxation which comes from associating with other men's thoughts. If one seeks this same refreshment in society, he must furbish himself, go somewhere, and play his part, give as much as he receives or more, take his chances with fools or dangerous friends, while in a book the author lays the scene and plays all the fools, friends and women for his benefit. All that is required is that he shall read and understand. One of the most distinguished and one of the bravest and best men this country ever produced always kept one of Laura Jean Libbey's books upon his desk. It was easy going after a hard day's work, reading this simplest syntax of love and adventure. Such books cannot injure any man unless he is a maudlin sentimentalist, and in that case nothing can preserve him. So he may as well, and better, take his foamy romance instead of the literally frothing society he would choose if he went abroad for the evening.

Books are not better comrades than people, but they are often safer and kinder, always less expensive and less exacting. And no one can know people without knowing the books into which they have been laid for generations, and out of which they all come, elegant or dingy replicas of other men and women who live and move in those pages.

The Valley

BRITISH BISCUITS IN THE BALKANS
THIS SMALL MOUNTAIN OF HARD TACK IS BEING
PILED UP FOR THE USE OF TOMMY
ATKINS AT SALONICA

THE MOTHERS

WHEN WAR HAS PASSED BY

THE GHASTLINESS OF WAR

ADD to the revulsion and horror which all neutral nations have felt at the dreadful war—and which our own cartoonists express vigorously—the more intimate sympathy with war suffering which Holland has had ever since Belgian refugees began pouring over her boundary, and express it all thru the pencil of an able craftsman, and you have the war cartoons of Louis Raemaekers, of *De Telegraaf* of Amsterdam. They have stirred all Europe. In

CARTOONS BY LOUIS RAEMAEKERS

spite of Dutch neutrality M. Raemaekers is not hesitant in speaking freely even when the outrages he attacks are distinctly partizan. He was born the year before the Franco-Prussian War; studied art in Amsterdam, Brussels and Paris, and has exhibited both portraits and landscapes. For eight years he has been busy with newspaper and magazine work, and the war has given him all his themes for the past year.

KREUZLAND, KREUZLAND, UBER ALLES
"Where are our fathers lying?"

CHRISTMAS DAY!
Hypocrisy, manslaughter and despotism at the manger

DOING THEIR BIT IN CANADA

BY GEDDES SMITH

SUPPOSE Congress should call for a volunteer army of six and a quarter million men. Can you imagine the mighty gasp that would go up from a hundred million throats? Yet, in proportion to her population, that is what Canada has actually decided to do—and is well on her way toward accomplishing.

If you took every man, woman and child in Canada, including the babies who couldn't stand up for themselves, and called every sixteenth person to step out and be measured for khaki, and then bought him a soldier's outfit, fed, housed and trained him for six months, and paid him $1.10 a day from his enlistment until he was killed or retired, you would be doing no more than the Dominion is doing for the British Empire. And that takes no account of separation allowances, gifts of supplies and money, the Red Cross, or the Patriotic Fund. It is no slight thing for Canada to undertake to raise half a million troops from her population of eight millions—a population peace-minded like our own. It could not be done unless the country was united in support of the war.

We in the United States are living next door to a nation in arms, a training camp three thousand miles long. Enter it, as I did, by the familiar Niagara Falls gateway. On the American side, on Mediation Island in the little lake in the State Reservation, the A B C flag flies serenely in commemoration of the international peace making that was done at Niagara. But the bridge that you cross to the other side is guarded by sentries in khaki, rifles over their shoulders, bayonets fixed. Before the Clifton House, where the mediators sat, paces another guard. Queen Victoria Park is a military post. If you have business at the administration building you are received by a sentry who whistles shrilly for an orderly to conduct you into the soldier-filled offices.

Go further; the man in khaki is everywhere. Walk down Yonge street, the Broadway of Toronto, in the evening, when the ten thousand soldiers quartered about the town are released from the barracks. They swarm over the sidewalks, in the poolrooms, the restaurants, the movie theaters, even in the jewelry auction rooms, where wrist-watches and trinkets for stay-at-homes can be bought. Highlanders with the rakish bonnet; fresh-faced young lads in swinging "British warms"; soldiers with girls, soldiers with their pals—the men in uniform that you marvel at the improvement army rations and army garb can make—soldiers with more soldiers. You almost catch the habit of saluting, yourself. The

STIMULATING NATIONAL PRIDE TO GAIN RECRUITS

This poster, widely circulated in Canada, not only combines the Union Jack and the Maple Leaf, but bases its plea on the heroic conduct of the first Canadian contingent. Thirty thousand men were landed in England ten weeks after the war began and made Canada famous by their heroic conduct at the front. At Ypres they held a thin line against a bitter German attack

hard-skinned ruddy cheeks, the bristly yellow mustache, the swagger stick—these are omnipresent.

Or walk down quaint, tortuous St. Paul street in St. Catherine's, type of the smaller Ontario city; recruiting streamers flung across the road urge you to enlist, and all roads lead to the armory. Listen to the smoking room talk on the Pullman; here is a man on his way home, still husky from the chlorine gas that drove him from the trenches; here are two old army men whose boys are at the front in the old regiments; here is a farmer whose crops are in and who is on his way to enlist at the old home. In Prince Edward Island the best of the young fellows are missing this winter, so the girls tell you. Away across the continent on Vancouver Island an adventurous squad of clean-cut lads is learning that hazardous business of scouting by aeroplane. On Winnipeg's main street three or four battalions jostle each other with their recruiting stations, gaudy with posters. In Peace River Crossing, away off at the end of the railroad in the north, the walls of the primitive hotel display the call to the colors. Edmonton of a Sunday flocks to greet returned soldier-invalids at special church services. Even the Yukon has sent its contingent.

Last summer men were in training at field camps scattered over the Dominion, one in each militia division. When cold weather came they "hiked" in to the cities, where in several cases they found admirable quarters at the fair grounds. Those who had spent the summer at Niagara-on-the-Lake marched to Toronto and took possession of Exhibition Park, where the biggest fair of all Canada is held every autumn.

Here I visited them one rainy morning when only occasional squads were marching over the soggy lawns. They had made a drill hall out of the largest building, and were filling it with a babel of vibrating khaki, as squad by squad they went thru the manual of arms or stabbed imaginary foes

James, Toronto
RECRUITING MEN AND CIGARETS
There are hundreds of schemes on foot thruout Canada for adding to the comfort of men at the front—newspaper tobacco funds, bargain bake-shop offers, and the like. Here is a basket to catch gift cigarets

with the bayonet. The overseas force is recruited both from the established militia regiments and from untrained civilians, so that men of all grades and no grade of military proficiency will be found in a single battalion. The seven thousand men then in camp were housed, a battalion to a building (1157 men of all ranks), in the exhibition halls. Long lines of wooden bunks in two tiers had been put up, and in one building the men were sprawling over them—bedding and equipment shoved to one side—while their platoon commanders lectured them; a fine display of Canadian manhood where prize pumpkins and potatoes had been shown a few months before. The refreshment pavilion had been brevetted mess hall, with army cooks in charge who were eager to explain how little they wasted and how good was the food. In the A. S. C. (Army Supply Corps) storehouse they were checking incoming edibles, and showed me tins of powdered milk on which—when transmogrified—they assured me cream would rise! Outside there were trenches for bomb practise and sham fights. The men would have more of that sort of training when their work in Canada was done and they were transferred to the Shorncliffe camps near London, to wait the call to France.

Down in the armory courtyard the rookies who had not yet been uniformed were flinging out their chests and shouting numbers in their first drill. Up at the University boys in khaki punctuated the strolling crowds in the corridors between lec-

tures. At Toronto, as at a dozen other universities and colleges, there is an Officers' Training Corps which prepares men to accept commissions. There is no obligation on its members to enlist for overseas service, but they form the majority of the eight hundred undergraduates which this university alone has already sent. Naturally most of the officers thruout the Canadian Expeditionary Force are university men and four Universities Companies, with college men in all the ranks, have gone. At the University of Manitoba this year only 67 out of 800 men students have failed to join either the O. T. C. or the overseas forces. St. Chad's, a little theological school in Regina, lost its whole student body and closed its doors.

At the end of 1915, when the Government announced that Canada's force was to be 500,000 instead of 250,000, there had actually been enlisted 220,000 men of all ranks, and nearly 120,000 of these had been sent overseas. Recruits had been coming in at the rate of nearly a thousand a day. Naturally the western provinces, where the proportion of footloose men of military age is large, have done better than the east. Alberta, with about a twentieth of the population, has raised over a tenth of the army. But for that matter Ontario, too, has done somewhat more than her share, and only Quebec has fallen far behind.

The French-Canadian situation has caused much discussion. Henri Bourassa,

leader of the Nationalists, has openly opposed recruiting, and the French-Canadian enlistments all told have been under 9000, from a total population of over two million. The devout Quebec Catholic is little moved by the plight of anti-clerical France, and has always been out of sympathy with the English-speaking majority in Canada. Yet Oliver Asselin, prominent in Bourassa's party, has offered to raise a regiment and has himself taken service, and the province is by no means wholly apathetic.

More than half the men already recruited from the Dominion are of British birth. The famous and unfortunate "Princess Pats" were mostly old British army men, with only a sprinkling of native Canadians. The percentage of native-born recruits has been climbing, but recent figures show that it had not yet touched fifty per cent—far below the ratio of native to foreign-born citizens. This is not surprizing, for the home ties and the kin in the trenches must be the strongest motives for enlistment. The Toronto *Globe* asserts that the great mass of the native-born between twenty and thirty years old are still available for service.

England's difficulty with backward bachelors is not duplicated in Canada, where married recruits are now in the minority. Consequently, while the pinch is beginning to be felt in clerical offices, where trained young men can ill be spared, the effect in the shops so far has been chiefly to transfer jobs held by bachelor recruits to unemployed married men. But the Royal Northwest Mounted Police, equally notable for their efficiency and their gaudy uniforms (even the Canadian postman, in blue and red, outshines the sol-

© American Press
ROOKIES DRILLING IN A VANCOUVER STREET
Tho pay commences with enlistment it is naturally impossible to outfit men immediately and drill often begins before the men are put into khaki. Six months' training is given them before they leave Canada

dier), have lost so many men, in spite of stringent restrictions, that the officers are forced to do prisoners' guard duty, and are in high dudgeon. In Leith, Alberta, there are already a handful of woman car conductors, but that is still a novelty.

Canada does more than send her men to fight. There is no space to enumerate the gifts that the Dominion, the provinces, and the people poured into Britain's storehouses in the early days of the war. "If you can't fight, you can pay," is the slogan for stay-at-homes. The women of Canada divide their energies between the Red Cross and the Patriotic Fund. It is a bad year for other philanthropies. Ontario alone has given $1,875,000 to the British Red Cross. The Patriotic Fund, which supplements the separation allowances made to the wives and dependents of soldiers, has passed the six million mark. And if every man, woman and child in the Dominion has not bought something to eat, smoke, chew or wear and sent it off to some homesick Tommy in the trenches, it is not the fault of some thousands of shopkeepers who litter their windows with suggestive offers. As to the war loan of $50,000,000, it is only necessary to say that ten hours after it was thrown open Ottawa had been assured of an oversubscription, and that after the subscriptions had reached $106,000,000 the Government decided to keep an extra fifty millions and loan it to Britain to pay for war purchases in Canada.

Meanwhile it is not a pleasant year for Germans and Austrians in Canada. They are distrusted everywhere. A number have been interned. Rumors of German plots in the early days of the war filled Canada. The Welland Canal revelations and actual attempts to destroy bridges justify the guards which have been placed at danger points all across the continent. But it is hard for the delicatessen dealers and their like—men and women who have lost their little circle of patrons and cannot collect their accounts from those who still do buy, because they're Germans, you know.

Canada has no such rigorous and muddleheaded censorship to fetter her newspapers as England has, but the telegraph news furnished by the press agencies is inspected before it goes out, and editors are warned not to print unauthorized matter. The Government has officially requested the press, moreover, to make no unfriendly editorial comment on the course of the United States.

This does not prevent a good deal of badinage and a pretty definite popular feeling that the United States has played a shabby rôle. "We don't want you to fight," the Canadian says. "Your navy isn't needed, you couldn't raise an army in time to count, and we want your munitions ourselves. But in the name of democracy and the small nations you ought to have protested at the Belgian and Armenian outrages. And you should have made it perfectly clear to the world that the safety of noncombatants on the high seas was of all-surpassing importance, instead of complaining in your mercenary way about your shipping." This feeling of disappointment at America's attitude is well voiced by the Winnipeg *Free Press:*

Perhaps the official attitude of the United States will best be described as one of the tragedies of the war. For the spectacle of a great nation, which bled itself white for freedom, which has done vast things for democracy, and which has produced heroes and martyrs, now adopting an official attitude of unconcern while the bloodiest struggle of the ages against autocracy is in full swing, is depressing and uninspiring.

Canada feels so strongly that the Allies are fighting America's battle as well as their own that it seems entirely natural that Americans should enlist. Just how many have already done so is uncertain. There have been estimates, probably exaggerated, running as high as six thousand. A few adventuresome lads slip into Canada over the border, and there have been many enlistments from the western provinces, where the proportion of American immigrants is high. But at least there is an American Legion now being formed in Toronto, the Ninety-seventh Battalion, Canadian Expeditionary Force. At its head is Lieut.-Col. A. B. Clark, formerly of the Twenty-third N. G. N. Y., a Brooklyn regiment. Recruiting for this battalion, already two-thirds full, is going on all over Canada, the men who join being required to take the oath of allegiance only for the duration of the war. There are special physical restrictions, and it promises to be a

James, Toronto

RECRUITING BY TRAMCAR

The work of getting enlistments is entrusted to the various battalion officers and such novel methods as this sometimes result. Mass meetings, "recruiting concerts," handbill and poster publicity, and personal solicitation are all bringing in new men

James, Toronto

DRILLING ON THE FAIR GROUNDS AT TORONTO

Recruits are gathered at the little villages and larger towns and first drilled in the local armories. Then they are concentrated at the divisional mobilization points in the larger cities. A recruiting train has done good service in Ontario

fine body of men. An ingeniously international device has been adopted: Canada's maple leaf in combination with the Washington coat of arms, which introduces the Stars and Stripes in an unimpeachable British-American version.

After all, a Canadian enlists in this war for much the same reasons as an American. I heard a young engineer who had just finished his job —a piece of railway construction— talking of his plans. "There's no more construction work," he said. "Hell, I don't want to go into the operating department. And I figure it this way: after the war I'll meet fellows I know on Yonge street and they'll say 'Were you over there?' and I'd feel pretty cheap to say 'No.' It's a shame not to back up men who need help." Here were three of the most powerful motives for enlistment: the desire for action, the pull of friends, the pressure of pride. At the other end of the scale were a crowd of applicants whom I saw in the Toronto recruiting station, forlorn ineffective men who were probably moved largely by the announcement, "Pay starts at once."

Certainly the king does not count for much in the matter, altho he fits well into stereotyped phrases like "Your king and country need you— now," which even that staunch liberal sheet, the Toronto *Globe*, prints every day. A genial Scotch railroad man put it this way: "George is a verra good fellow, but he don't bother me and I don't bother him." And it is doubtful, too, whether the idea of the Empire is responsible for Canada's devotion, except with the extreme Conservatives. Rather it seems to be a personal adherence to the old country and the old country friends on the part of those closely bound to

© *American Press*

MAJOR-GENERAL THE HONORABLE SIR
SAM HUGHES, MINISTER OF MILITIA.
IN CHARGE OF RECRUITING

England; and then a firm conviction that Britain's cause is worth fighting for on its merits—a conviction that does not necessarily involve loyalty to the Empire or even patriotism. And to some extent there seems to be a national pride in Canada's own achievements. You hear the boast that Canada won the South African War for England; you can buy little books about *The Battle Glory of Canada;* the "heroes of St. Julien and Festubert" are invoked on recruiting posters.

It will be considerably harder to raise the second quarter-million than it has been to find the first. Canada began briskly, mobilizing a division within six weeks of the beginning of the war and putting 30,000 men into Great Britain before the middle of the first October, and has continued steadily, but she may well pause before going on to complete a levy that amounts almost to half the men of military age in the Dominion.

But she is absolutely confident of victory. And, curiously enough in so independent a member of the British family, she is quite content to furnish men and money and to let Britain run the war. "We're only amateur soldiers," a leading newspaperman said to me. "We would hesitate to think we knew as much about fighting as Kitchener." So there is little criticism of British blunders, and a cool, matter-of-fact way of talking and thinking about the war (always excepting that rather florid expectation of humiliating Germany), and, in a word, considerably more self-possession than might be expected from a nation which, long confident of her political vigor, has just begun to feel her economic strength, and yet chooses to remain British.

PEACE AT ANY PRICE
BY DAVID STARR JORDAN
Chancellor of Leland Stanford, Jr., University

Are we "For Peace at any Price?" Let us face the issue squarely. When we do this, the phrase has no meaning. For when the question really comes up, there is no peace to be had at any price. If any price will bring peace, real peace, let us pay it. In this war, no peace was offered at any price to Serbia, to Belgium, to France. Some sort of peace was offered at a price to Austria, Russia, Germany, and Great Britain. Should these nations have taken it at the price? This question each may answer for himself. And paying the price, would they have had peace, real peace, well worth the cost? And when real peace is offered, whatever the price, there is no need to talk of war.

What could not Europe have afforded to pay to prevent the great catastrophe? What has war cost Europe and when will it be able to repay?

And for us, we would see the price lists first. With Lincoln, we would count the cost. If we do not, it may stagger us. And will we get peace when we pay for it? Not the armed peace of fear and hate, for that is war scarcely half disguised, but the peace of mutual trust and international confidence. Sooner or later that must come, for as sure as the day follows night, the principle of federation must succeed unbalanced nationalism in the development of the civilized world.

IS THE CHURCH GOING BACKWARD?

BY REV. CHARLES STELZLE

W HEN the Federal Council of Churches — representing thirty Protestant denominations and seventeen million members —adopted its social service platform seven years ago, it was regarded as a great step forward. Various denominational agencies had been carrying on a social service propaganda, but it was felt that what was needed was an expression of opinion and a concrete program which should represent the entire Protestant forces of the United States. Included in this document were the statements that "the churches must stand for equal rights and complete justice for all men in all stations in life; for the right of all men to the opportunity of self-maintenance; for the right of workers to some protection against the hardships often resulting from the swift crises of industrial change; for the protection of the worker from dangerous machinery, occupational disease, injuries and mortality; for the abolition of child labor; for the suppression of the sweating system; for the release from employment one day in seven; for a living wage as a minimum in every industry; for the highest wage that each industry can afford; for the most equitable division of the products of industry that can be ultimately devised; for the abatement of poverty."

Then came the statement which more than any other, perhaps, brought joy to the hearts of many social workers and workingmen in general: "To the toilers of America and to those who by organized effort are seeking to lift the crushing burdens of the poor, and to reduce the hardships and uphold the dignity of labor, this Council sends the greeting of human brotherhood and the pledge of sympathy and of help in a cause which belongs to all who follow Christ."

The immediate response from both church and labor to the Federal Council's statement on the social question was most gratifying. Many of the leading denominations adopted the statement as their own social ideal; and leading labor papers gratefully printed the document.

But the long hoped-for revival of social justice has failed to materialize. Indeed, among most ecclesiastical bodies there is not even the same enthusiasm that was so apparent when the social

*Charles Stelzle has devoted his life to the study of industrial problems; particularly the relations between the church and labor. He was for ten years superintendent of the Department of Church and Labor of the Presbyterian Church. He is on the staff of the Newark (New Jersey) "News" and is the author of numerous books on Christian problems—most recently "Church and Labor," "American Social and Religious Conditions" and "The Gospel of Labor."—*THE EDITOR.

service platform of the Federal Council was adopted seven years ago. Within the past two or three years there has been a decided reaction in this respect, which has resulted in the dominance of the conservatives in practically every evangelical denomination in this country. At any rate, this is the impression that one gets from the discussion and the legislation which develops in ecclesiastical conferences and conventions.

At the Columbus meeting of the executive committee of the Federal Council of Churches, held recently, the hopelessness of securing action on any social or economic matter which involved legislation of any sort became quite apparent. And what great social reform *can* be put thru without legislation?

It was amusing to hear it reported that the Washington office of the Federal Council was carried on merely to seek national legislation on "spiritual matters"! Even the delegates representing the Southern Presbyterian Church—one of the chief objectors to political action—were compelled to smile!

The chief reason for this attitude on the part of the Federal Council lies in the fact that it is unwilling to alienate those ecclesiastical bodies which object to the church having anything to do with questions which involve the state, even tho these organizations are few in number and comparatively small in their membership.

The decision of the Federal Council's executive committee is contrary to the well-understood attitude of the stronger denominations in their fight against the saloon. These denominations have long believed in taking direct political action when engaged in putting the saloon out of business. Precisely the same principle is involved in "one day's rest in seven" campaigns, in which, by the way, even the Federal Council has participated. It seems as tho the Federal Council were determined to take a backward step in its social program, for the sole purpose of retaining within its organization the denominational groups which for various reasons cannot coöperate in helping to secure social justice thru legislation.

But meanwhile—does the Federal Council's apparent desire to keep out of all legislative affairs, no matter how imperative, for the safeguarding of health and the conservation of human life, meet with the approval of the men and women of the churches who have been stirred by appeals for economic justice and social service? Furthermore, if the Federal Council declines to speak in the name of the churches in this regard, where is the religious body to which legislators and statesmen may look for guidance in social matters which are fundamentally ethical in character? If it is true that the great social problems now confronting us are deeply religious, is it not reasonable to suppose that an organization which makes a specialty of religion should have something definite and official to say about these problems—even to legislative bodies?

It is not a question of having the church interfere in purely political affairs, nor of attempting to control the state for its own benefit. It is entirely a matter of making a fight in behalf of helpless men and women by securing the enactment of such laws as will give them more of the blessings of life here and now.

New York City

A WINTER PICTURE

BY BLISS CARMAN

When winter comes, along the Silvermine,
And earth has put away her green attire,
With all the pomp of her autumnal pride,
The world is made a sanctuary old,
Where Gothic trees uphold the arch of gray,
And gaunt stone fences on the ridge's crest
Stand like carved screens before a crimson shrine,
Showing the sunset glory thru the chinks.
There, like a nun with frosty breath, the soul,
Uplift in adoration, sees the world
Transfigured as a temple of her Lord;
While down the soft blue-shadowed aisles of snow
Night, like a sacristan with silent step,
Passes to light the tapers of the stars.

THE WORLD OVER

Frictionless America

There is more than one way to reduce friction in the world. And tho the United States may not be entirely successful in bringing peace out of the Great War, we can at least claim that we smooth the way of the world in one respect.

For the United States produces more talc and soapstone than all the rest of the world combined. Moreover our production has nearly doubled in the last decade, so that we now produce about 170,000 short tons a year, valued at about $1,860,000.

Talc is a simple mineral of which soapstone is a massive impure form. Because of its softness it has a wide and varied use: talcum powder can be used for putting a tire on an automobile or (we can't resist it) attire on a lady. In the schoolroom it takes the form of chalk, and in the factory it bleaches cotton cloth or becomes one of the ingredients of paint. One of its chief uses is as a filler for many kinds of paper.

There are nine states in our country that produce talc. Fifty-seven per cent of it comes from New York and about forty per cent—mostly in the form of soapstone—from Vermont.

Y. M. C. A. and the War

There was a time when the Y. M. C. A. did not stand very high in the opinion of the English people, when it was regarded as a rather flabby, colorless institution, by no means occupying the place in the life of the community that it fills on this side of the Atlantic.

But with the coming of the war the Britisher's opinion altered. Of all the work done for the British Army and Navy none stands so high in public estimation as that of the Y. M. C. A.

Within a few days of the outbreak of war it had two hundred and fifty centers, and today there are over a thousand such centers within the Empire—one as far afield as Mesopotamia. France has nearly a hundred, India forty, Egypt thirty, and so on.

The "huts," as the Y. M. C. A. calls its tents or buildings, are by far the most popular places in the great camps, whether at the bases or in England. Thousands of the troops use the huts for recreation, and as reading or writing-rooms — the Association gives away about 11,000,000 pieces of stationery a month, which are chiefly used by the men for writing home. The organization of athletics at the base camps is largely in the hands of the Y. M. C. A. too.

The huts are also used for religious services, the

126

OPERATING THE NEW STREET CLEANER

INSPECTORS APPROVE ITS WORK

only condition being that no one shall interfere with another's religion. The religious side is, indeed, placed in the forefront of the Association's endeavors to help the soldiers—tho there is none of the "button-hole" method; the men are influenced by what is done, not by talk.

Munition works have sprung up all over England in the recent months and the Y. M. C. A. is doing highly useful work in providing huts near the great centers, where the workers, who come in such crowds that the localities cannot deal with them immediately, can obtain food and find sleeping accommodation. Another excellent piece of work is the establishment of open-all-day-and-night refreshment bars and rest-rooms near the great railway stations in London where men going to and returning from the front often arrive in the middle of the night, tired out and with nowhere to go.

AN ENGLISH ARMY "HUT"
Tommy Atkins writes home—and has his picture taken

Cleaning Streets by Suction

A new method of street cleaning which will do for the streets what the vacuum carpet sweeper is doing in the home in the way of better sanitation has been tried out in Sandusky, Ohio. This suction street cleaner was sent over the streets the day after they had been cleaned by the old broom machine method, and four cubic yards of dirt were swept up from 27,280 square yards.

The revolving broom is especially made so that it will dislodge even the finest particles of dust. The dust is carried by the broom into an air current created by a large suction fan and from there it goes thru a conduit to a dust box in the rear of the machine.

There are two compartments to this large dust box (which is in the form of a trailer and can be detached), one receives the heavier particles of dirt and the other the powdery dust.

A test of the machine was made on an asphalt block of pavement which contained the accumulated dirt of the entire winter with the result that the amount of dirt swept up by the machine averaged eighteen cubic yards to the mile of thirty-foot pavement.

The trailer can be detached and the broom can be removed and a squeegee attached to scrub the streets. The squeegee developed for this machine is composed of adjustable shovels each having a flexible shoe, which will enable the shovels to adjust themselves to the irregularity of the pavement.

More Nerve

Crossing a river on a rope bridge to test the condition of one's nerves is the latest method advocated by physical culture instructors. The idea originated with W. Ward Beam, of the Philadelphia College of Pharmacy, who has made it a part of the regular course of physical culture for both men and women students.

One advantage of the method is that the outfit required is both cheap and easily portable, as it consists simply of two stout ropes, one of which is fastened between two trees on the opposite banks of a river, and serves as a support for the feet, while the other is stretched overhead and used as a balance by the person crossing the stream.

The whole object of Mr. Beam's plan is to harden the nerves of the students. We lack nerve, he says, chiefly because we never do anything to cultivate strength in this direction. Crossing a stream on a rope

THE PRESENTATION OF "THE SEVEN GIFTS"—AN OUTDOOR CHRISTMAS PLAY IN NEW YORK

he considers one of the very best exercizes to correct this fault. It isn't such a nervy thing to do, but it simply shows a lack of nerve to be afraid to do it.

New York's Christmas Fantasy

New York City has had a community celebration of Christmas often, but the climax of its entertainment has always been a tree. This year the committee in charge decided to give a play.

Of course the difficulties in the way were many. It must be out of doors, to insure room enough for all who would share in the celebration. It must suit people of all ages. It must be something different—not the wise men and the manger, not Santa Claus with fairies and brownies, but something to include all these, the real holiday spirit, the very essence of Christmas.

And Mr. Stuart Walker, playwright, producer, and the creator of the Portmanteau Theater, met all these conditions, and more. On Christmas night in Madison Square his company gave, for the community tree committee, a fantasy called "The Seven Gifts."

It was the story of the seven who came with their presents to the court of the Emerald Queen. Not a word was spoken, from the appearance of the Wanderer, asking what the theater was and why the great audience was assembled, till the lights dimmed, leaving the Dear Child and her doll sitting on the throne. Yet not a guest had the least difficulty in following the pantomime, for occasionally a sentence on the screen told who was coming next, or just what was to happen, to make absolutely sure that no one was puzzled; a device borrowed from the movies, but used at either side of the stage, so that the action of the fantasy was never interrupted.

The Lowly Man, who thought to better his gift by imitation; the Haughty Lady who learned from the Humble Woman consideration for others; the Richest Man in the World, finding that a mere bauble interested the Queen more than his rare gifts; the Strolling Player, whose gift, a playlet telling the adventure of Pierrot and the Moon-

lady, was filled with imagination and beauty; the Bravest Man who presented a tiger skin, introducing a delicious comedy touch in his contest with the tiger, impersonated by Jack-in-the-box; and last of all the Dear Child, whose gift of a battered doll was the only one worthy of the name, for it alone came from the heart and represented some sacrifice.

At the climax of the fantasy, the community Christmas tree suddenly burst into light, its decorations becoming an integral part of the play.

But the remarkable thing about this performance was not the success of the committee's plans, nor even the success of the Portmanteau Theater folk, but the fact that this fantasy, given in a portable playhouse, in the people's park, is a step toward a civic theater. It suggests wonderful possibilities of what may be done, all during pleasant weather, by presenting in any of the parks performances free to all the city.

A Census Curiosity

Tucked away in the huge census volumes are many interesting facts. Perhaps one of the most remarkable concerns the ages of our population. In the accompanying chart is shown the age

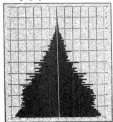

THE AGES OF OUR POPULATION

The vertical line thru the center divides the males (on the left) from the females (on the right). The horizontal distance from this line shows the number (by hundreds of thousands) of males or females at each year of age

distribution by single years of the total population of the United States in 1910. The vertical line thru the center divides the males from the females. The horizontal distance from the vertical line shows the number (by hundreds of thousands) of males or females at each year of age. Thus there were in 1910 about 950,000 males at the age of ten.

The fact that this country receives annually a large immigration, tends to broaden the age pyramid or triangle from about the twentieth year. This gives the triangle a somewhat smaller base than if the numbers were recruited entirely by births.

The peculiarity about the shape of the age pyramid lies in the fact that at certain ages the lines project over those directly underneath. This would imply that there must be an extremely large number of persons at these particular ages. But there is a strange regularity noticeable with regard to these projecting lines, for beginning at about the twenty-fifth year we find that at the ages ending in 5 and 0 there is an extraordinarily large number of survivors. This is probably due to the fact that those who are in doubt about their exact age report themselves as "about forty-five" or "about fifty."

In one respect the women of this country have been great sinners in reporting their ages. It is evident that the native born women who were from fifteen to twenty-four years of age in 1910 must have been the survivors of the group who were five to fourteen years of age in 1900. Since death had been continually reducing their numbers during the ten years elapsed, we should expect to find a much smaller number from fifteen to twenty-four in 1910 than from five to fourteen in 1900. On the contrary, we find that this group of women had apparently increased in numbers by 40,513 during the decade from 1900 to 1910! The obvious explanation is that a large number of women who should have reported their ages as twenty-five or over in 1910 preferred to be considered from twenty to twenty-four. It seems to take more than ten years for a large number of our native women to pass from their fifteenth to their twenty-fifth year.

THE CONQUEST OF THE BLACK MOUNTAIN

THE MEANING AND IMPORTANCE OF THE AUSTRIAN INVASION OF MONTENEGRO

THE capture of Mount Lovcen by the Austrians as a military operation is insignificant compared with the constant conflicts between the millions of soldiers who confront one another in France and Poland, for Montenegro is the least of the twelve nations involved in the Great War and the casualties of the assault will not appreciably swell the daily death list. Yet on some accounts it is an event of tremendous significance and far-reaching influence. It means for one thing that another of the smaller countries is likely soon to lose, at least for a time, its freedom and independence; the seventh of such to be overrun by hostile or alien armies, Luxemburg, Belgium, Serbia, Greece, Albania, Persia and Montenegro.

When King Nicholas of Montenegro celebrated his seventy-first birthday on October 8, 1912, by declaring war on the Sultan, he little realized—tho there were many who did and warned him—that he was thereby precipitating a general European war which would be likely to engulf his kingdom. How should he realize it? It was the custom of his country to fight the Turks on any favorable opportunity. Every boy babe is pledged at birth to avenge Kassovo, the battle in which the Serbs and Montenegrins were defeated by the Turks 526 years ago as they were again defeated a month ago by the Austrians and Bulgars on the same field. Ever since then the men of Serbia and Montenegro have worn a band of crape on their crimson caps, to be removed only when all their race shall be free. There is no question of volunteering or conscription. Every man is a soldier and his wife is his commissary department, cooking his meals and carrying them to him at the front. The law requires there what the law here forbids, that every man carry a revolver whenever he steps out of doors. And every bride goes out into the desert alone to practice the widow's keen, that she may be ready suitably to lament the death of her husband in battle whenever his time shall come. The history of Montenegro, said Gladstone, "excels in glory all the war annals of the world."

But native courage of this primitive kind is of no avail against modern scientific warfare. From the concrete emplacements of their hidden forts about the Mouths of Cattaro the Austrian howitzers shelled the rocky hights above and the Montenegrins were almost as helpless as the Aztecs against the Spanish matchlocks.

Tourists have often wondered why these forts, constructed twenty years ago, were so placed that their heaviest guns pointed inward and landward toward insignificant little Montenegro instead of outward and seaward whence some foemen more worthy of their steel might be expected to come. Now we know why. We see that the Austrians were right in suspecting that when the time came it would not be Montenegrins they would have to fight but more powerful nations behind them. It is then not surprizing that when French and Russian cannon which replied to them from Mount Lovcen and that Italian troops are hastening to its defense. What is surprizing is the Allies did not send such aid before. It seems that the fatal words "too late!" which, as Lloyd George says, have dogged all the operations of the Allies, must here again be used. If the hundreds of thousands of Italian lives which have been wasted in vain attempts to break the Austrian lines to the north had been spent in the Balkans it may be that Serbia, Montenegro and Albania might have been saved and the Kaiser kept from Constantinople. Italian interests are here almost as closely concerned as in Trentino

or Triest. The Queen of Italy is the daughter of the King of Montenegro. The Albanian and Dalmatian coast has long been coveted by Italy. And if Italy is to become again "Queen of the Adriatic" she must possess the Bocche di Cattaro, for it is one of the strongest as well as most beautiful of the harbors of the world, and has played an important rôle in the history of many nations. Teuta, the pirate queen of Illyria, made here her haven, over two thousand years ago, and Rome had to resort to bribery to accomplish her overthrow. Greeks, Romans, Goths, Byzantines, Venetians, Turks, Spanish, Russians, Austrians, Hungarians, Bosnians, Serbs and French have at one time and another held possession of this landlocked bay.

The reason of its strategic value may be seen by a glance at the map. The Bocche di Cattaro or the "Cattaro Mouths" form a triple harbor, a veritable naval cerberus. It would be foolish for any warship to try to penetrate such a labyrinth. The entrance to the inner harbor is still called Le Catene, from the chains that used to be stretched across it to keep out pirates, but doubtless mines take their place nowadays. Here probably have been hidden the Austrian submarines which have recently been raiding the shipping of the Mediterranean.

Cattaro looks like a Norwegian fiord which somehow has got misplaced on the Dalmatian coast. It is a jagged channel cleft into the limestone ridge known as the Karst or Carso which stretches along the eastern shore of the Adriatic and forms the boundary between Italy and Austria further north. Against this rocky barrier about Görz the Italian armies have been beating in vain for many months. The culmination of the Karst is Montenegro, a disorderly heap of mountains, and b a r r e n ledges, cuplike sinks and deep crevasses, blistering hot in summertime and freezing cold in winter. Let geologists explain it how they will, the natives have their own theory, which other people may prefer because it is easier to imagine. When, according to the legend, God Almighty was putting the finishing touches to crea-

THE GULF OF CATTARO

By the capture of Mount Lovcen the Austrians have made secure their naval base at Cattaro, called "the Gibraltar of the Adriatic" because of its impregnability. The narrow inlets of the bays are flanked with cliffs over a thousand feet high beneath which the Austrian dreadnoughts were sheltered even from Montenegrin guns. The carriage road which zigzags up the mountain side to the eyre of the Montenegrins is esteemed by tourists one of the most picturesque drives in the world. Just beyond Mount Lovcen is Cettinje, the capital of Montenegro, where the Austrian flag now waves

128

tion by sowing the stones evenly over the land, the bag burst as he past over Montenegro and all the stones ':e had left were spilled there.

Montenegro is about the size of Connecticut and Rhode Island taken together, and has about the population of Rhode Island alone. The Black Mountain it has been called in all ages and all languages; Kara Dagh is the Turkish name for it and in the Serbian tongue, which is also the Montenegrin, it is known as Crngora, not so impossible to pronounce as it appears, for the Slavs have discovered that if you roll an r you can make a vowel of it. The initial C is pronounced Ch or Tch.

The Montenegrin people are among the most warlike in the world, but in numbers they are insignificant, for even before the war their war strength only amounted to 30,-000 or 40,000 men, that is, about the same as the mobile troops of the United States army.

Right at the head of the inner gulf of Cattaro, and less than three miles from salt water, is the Sacred Mountain of Lovcen (pronounce it Lovtchen and you will get it as near correct as can be expected). This is 5770 feet high and overlooks on one side the Bocche di Cattaro, where Herzegovina, Dalmatia and Montenegro meet, and on the other the valley which conceals Cettinje, the village capital of Montenegro. Here Ivan the Black made his stronghold when the Turks drove him out of the lowlands of Scutari over four centuries ago. Gathering his little band of mountaineers about him he pledged his people to perpetual warfare until the Turk should be driven back into Asia and the assemblage then and there decreed that any Montenegrin who left the field of battle without orders when fighting the Moslems should be drest in woman's clothes and driven out of the country by the women with blows of their spindles.

One of the first undertakings of the Allies after the declaration of war was an attempt to capture the Bocche di Cattaro. On August 12, 1914, the French and British warships in the Adriatic bombarded the Austrian forts at the mouth of the bay while the Montenegrins attacked them from the land side. But their efforts then and since were in vain.

Ivan the Black is not dead but sleeping, say the Montenegrins. Hidden in a cave in the heart of Mount Lovcen, he sleeps, like the Emperor Barbarossa, waiting for the day of his triumph when all Europe has been free from the Turk. Three years ago when his successor, King Nicholas, threw down his gauntlet to the Turk, Black John must have felt that the time had come for him to awake, for it seemed that with Serbia, Bulgaria, Greece and Montenegro fighting shoulder to shoulder the Cross must surely drive out the Crescent. But the Allies fell out over the parting of the spoils, leaving their task unfinished, and now at the invitation of three Christian Powers the Moslem armies are being brought back into Europe. Surely the sleeping hero must have groaned as he heard over his head the march of Austrian boots and the rumble of the cannon wheels.

But this is not the end of it. History does not so reverse itself. Let us reread for our encouragement the poem Chesterton wrote three years ago on "The March of the Black Mountain":

But men shall remember the Mountain
　Tho it fall down like a tree,
They shall see the sign of the Mountain
　Faith cast into the sea;
Tho the crooked swords overcome it
　And the Crooked Moon ride free,
When the Mountain comes to Mahomet
　It has more life than he.

A WAY TO HELP THE ARMENIANS

BY WILLIAM T. ELLIS

AUTHOR OF "MAN AND MISSIONS," EDITOR AFIELD OF "THE CONTINENT"

THE apparent hopelessness of the case of the Armenians now suffering "deportation" has been the last touch of horror to a situation perhaps without equal in the world's history. There has seemed almost nothing that could be done to aid them. Civilization has stood helpless. The Turkish Government has turned a deaf ear to all appeals. It shuts the doors of the land against all relief expeditions. Missionaries are not allowed to assist the suffering with food and raiment, except in the most limited and local way. What can be done?

There occurs to me one plan that should be practicable. Since Red Cross and missionary relief work is interdicted, why should not the United States Government do in this case what it did in Europe immediately after the outbreak of the war —so enlarge its consular and diplomatic staffs that the exceptional needs of the sufferers could be met? The splendid company of tactful, efficient, resourceful young men who have passed the examination for the consular and diplomatic service are uniquely qualified to meet this condition. By drawing upon consulates and embassies which are not especially crowded, and by utilizing the waiting list, the State Department can at once marshal a force adequate to administer relief within the respective zones of the consulates and embassies.

Prompt action would save tens of thousands of lives. Great-hearted America has already given, or will quickly give, to these national representatives, all the relief supplies that can be administered. Turkey will doubtless extend the privileges which she has already granted Ambassador Morgenthau; Persia and Russia would not think of objecting to the enlargement of America's representation in the regions of distress. Even now at several consular cities there are camps of Armenian refugees numbering many thousands, with no one to administer relief. Does not this seem to be clearly one of the higher obligations of humanity devolving upon American diplomacy?

The possible centers for this service are familiar to the State Department and to all who have followed closely the Armenian tragedy. Aside from additional help at Constantinople and Teheran, the most obvious points, now maintaining consulates, where immediate and important relief work can be done are Aleppo, Alexandretta, Harput, Urfa, Brusa, Mersina, Trebizond, Samsun, Smyrna, Bagdad, Bassorah, Damascus, Jerusalem, Beirut, Tripoli, Haifa, and Jaffa and Tabriz. In addition Konia, Afion Kara Hissar, Van, Aintab, Mosul, Bitlis, Diarbekir, Urumiah and Hamadan at present call for the oversight and assistance of accredited representatives of the United States Government.

Even if there were no precedent for this special service, the situation is unprecedented and calls for red blood rather than for red tape.

Swarthmore, Pennsylvania

THE BEST REASON
IN THE WORLD FOR
BUYING A CADILLAC
IS WHAT EVERYONE
THINKS, AND SAYS,
AND <u>KNOWS</u> ABOUT
THE CADILLAC ╱ ╱

THE NEW BOOKS

A PROPHET OF THE MOVING PICTURE

To Vachel Lindsay, twentieth century troubadour, author of General Booth's "Himmelfahrt" and similar poems of fantasy and feeling, belongs the honor of being the first to bring out a book of serious criticism of *The Art of the Moving Picture*. He has seen widely and he criticizes frankly, praising and condemning actors, producers and technique. As a subtitle to the volume he suggests "How to Classify and Judge the Current Films," then in accordance with the custom of estheticians from Aristotle to Ruskin he proceeds to arrange his categorical pigeonholes and fit the films into them. His first category is Action Pictures which are "sculpture-in-motion"; his second is Intimate Pictures which are "paintings-in-motion," and his third is Splendor pictures which are "architecture-in-motion.".

But fortunately, he, like the other art critics, soon forgets his rigid classification and rather ill-fitting analogies and gives us some of his personal impressions and eloquent imaginings. His comparison of the technique of D'Annunzio as shown in "Cabiria" with the art of Griffith as shown in "Judith of Bethulia" is well considered, altho in our opinion he hardly does justice to the Carthaginian drama. But the motion picture which most rouses his enthusiasm is "The Battle Hymn of the Republic," produced by the Vitagraph Company four years ago. "This film should be studied in the high schools and universities till the canons of art for which it stands are established in America." Of the Intimate Pictures he prefers Cabanne's "Enoch Arden." Of the Action Pictures he distinguishes "The Spoilers," of Rex Beach and "Man's Genesis," an old Griffith Biograph, which, after being shelved for awhile, has recently entered upon a new season of popularity.

But the best part of the book is the latter half, in which Mr. Lindsay lets his imagination go as to the possibilities of the future film and its influence upon our ideals and morals.

"Author-producer-photographer, who would prophesy, read the last book in the Bible, not to copy it in form and color, but that its power and grace and terror may enter into you. Delineate in your own way, as you are led on your own Patmos, the picture of our land redeemed. After fasting and praying, let the Spirit conduct you till you see in definite line and form the throngs of the brotherhood of man, the colonnades where the arts are expounded, the gardens where the children dance.

"That which man desires, that will man become. He largely fulfils his own prediction and vision. Let him therefore have a care how he prophesies and prays. We shall have a tin heaven and

132

a tin earth, if the scientists are allowed exclusive command of our highest hours."

The producer who wants to get ahead of the times should attach Vachel Lindsay to his staff—if indeed such a rolling stone can be attached by any salary. His is the sort of inspiration which the motion picture business needs.

The Art of the Moving Picture, by Vachel Lindsay. Macmillan. $1.25.

THE ANTICHRIST

Since Nietzsche, the Slav and fierce hater of everything German, is nowadays regarded as the chief inspirer of Germanic egotism and militarism, it is necessary to become acquainted with him and there is no better introduction to his personality than Halévy's *Life*, which now appears in cheaper edition. It is a sympathetic study of this strange and contradictory character, but only incidentally explains his views. For that one should turn to some of Nietzsche's own works, preferably

---

FOR THE SUNDAY SCHOOL TEACHER

The Good Samaritan, by Edna Earle, puts eleven Bible stories into dialog form for youngsters to act.
Boston: Badger. $1.

Josephus' History of the Jews, a book to which every Bible student is constantly referred, is out in the handy Everyman's Library form.
Dutton. Cloth 35 cents; leather 70 cents.

On Nazareth Hill, by Edward Bailey, describes northern Palestine, as doubtless it looked to the carpenter Joseph and the lad Jesus. The clear pictures and explanatory notes make the handy book of real value to the Sunday school worker.
Boston: Pilgrim, Press. $1.

Tales with a moral, of course are *Stories of Thrift for Young Americans*, by M. T. Prichard, and G. A. Turkington, but they are direct, interesting, unforced, and will be helpful in making plain the value of economy in effort, strength and time, as well as money.
Scribner. 60 cents.

How to Become an Efficient Sunday School Teacher, by Wm. A. McKeever, is not a guide to lesson teaching, but a study of the problems confronting boys and girls, which, after all, is probably what the Sunday School teacher most needs to understand.
Cincinnati, Ohio: Standard Pub. Co. $1.

The Boy Scout Movement Applied to the Church, by N. S. Richardson and O. E. Loomis, is introduced by the chief scout executive, James E. West, and is a valuable handbook for Boy Scout workers, and a suggestive study of boy needs and how to treat them for all who have to do with growing boys. It gives the history of the organization, plans for all sorts of activities and a broad minded discussion of the aim of all these efforts, and the methods and qualities necessary to success.
Scribner. $1.50.

"Thus Spake Zarathustra," or if one prefers a compendium, an excellent volume of selections is provided by Willard Huntington Wright in *What Nietzsche Taught*. This gives abundant quotations from each of Nietzsche's works, prefaced with an explanation of the leading thought and of the circumstances under which it was written; in short, just what the beginner needs.

Nietzsche and the Ideals of Modern Germany, by Professor Stewart of Dalhousie University, Halifax, is one of those books which explain why American universities are always trying to entice Canadian professors over the borders. In scholarship, style and temper it is admirable, and remarkably free from partizan exaggeration and misconstruction, considering the time, place and purpose of the lectures here published. As an analysis of Nietzsche and a contribution to the history of modern thought the book would doubtless have been better if it had been written five years before the war or ten years after—but it would have found fewer readers than now.

The author would then probably have also considered Nietzsche's influence over other countries than Germany. He devotes a footnote to France but omits mention of Russia and Italy, where, to judge from recent literature, Nietzscheism has been rampant. But we long ago resolved never to find fault with an author for not writing on some other subject than he did and Professor Stewart has debarred us from criticism on this point by the limitation of his title. His analysis and refutation of Nietzsche's attack and Christianity is excellent and we agree with him that Nietzsche has had a bad influence over German ideals and character. But we question whether the Great War as a whole can be summarized, even "very roughly" as a conflict of "Nietzschean immoralism against Christian restraint," considering that many of the races involved are followers neither of Christ nor Nietzsche. Judging by its literary manifestations German ruthlessness in war draws its sanction more from the Old Testament than from Nietzsche.

Life of Friedrich Nietzsche, by Daniel Halévy. Macmillan. $1.25. *What Nietzsche Taught*, by W. H. Wright. Huebsch. $2. *Nietzsche and the Ideals of Modern Germany*, by H. L. Stewart. Longmans, Green. $2.10.

BABYLON

Professor Jastrow, of the University of Pennsylvania, is as well known abroad as in this country as an authority on Assyriology. He has devoted himself especially to the study of the religion of Babylonia. *The Civilization of Babylonia and Assyria* is a comprehensive work covering the excavations, the decipherment of the cuneiform script; the history of Babylonia and Assyria, their gods, temples and cults, their commerce and art, followed by seventy pages of specimens of their literature. This splendid volume gives the results of the latest discoveries, and a very complete knowledge of the general subject. The illustrations present not only the older and familiar work of Botta Layard, George Smith and others, but the results of the latest diggings in both Assyria and Babylonia.

Civilization of Babylonia and Assyria, by Morris Jastrow. Philadelphia: Lippincott. $6.

CARD PUZZLES

Twenty mystifying *Card Tricks* so clearly explained by L. Widdop that anyone can quickly learn to do them. None of them demand proficiency in sleight of hand.

Philadelphia: Lippincott. 35 cents.

BOWNE'S PHILOSOPHY

Ralph Tyler Flewelling in *Personalism and the Problems of Philosophy* gives a discursive exposition of the Christian philosophy of the late Borden P. Bowne in its relation to other systems. Professor Rudolf Eucken, of Jena, in his introduction, speaks highly of Bowne's work.

Methodist Book Concern. $1.

OPERAS

One hundred and ten operas, classics and recent productions, are described in *The Opera Book*, by Edith Ordway. She gives the name of composer and librettist, the date of the first performance, the singing parts of the different characters, and the plot in scenes. The book is illustrated by pictures of noted singers in their roles.

Sully & Kleinteich. $2.50.

A GENTLE CHRONICLE

Hempfield, by David Grayson, is the story of a little group of people who foregathered in the office of a weekly newspaper, *The Hempfield Star*. From editor to office boy the staff of the *Star* is attractive. Hempfield is no Spoon River, and the reader of the quiet annals of a pleasant town is glad to live there and share the village stories full of friendly but very human goodness.

Doubleday, Page. $1.35.

SHAKESPEARE

An excellent student's edition of Shakespeare's plays, each in a separate volume of convenient size and attractive print and binding—*The New Hudson Shakespeare* fills an ever-present need. An explanatory introduction gives the sources, date of composition and editions of each play, considers the dramatic structure, the diction and versification, presents a brief sketch of each of the characters and a general criticism of the whole play.

Boston: Ginn. 30 cents each.

INDIANS OF THE PLAINS

Dr. Grinnell's *The Fighting Cheyennes* is a contribution to American history of the greatest value, a record of the red men of the plains who, with their pitiful yet glorious story, are fast disappearing. Much of this story the writer has gathered from their own lips; and it reveals what sturdy manhood has been wasted. The history is one of thrilling adventures, but, related in the colorless manner of a court record, it is a book for reference rather than for reading.

Scribner. $3.50.

ROLLAND'S MUSICAL STUDIES

A book to be welcomed by all students of musical history is Mary Blaiklock's translation of Romain Rolland's *Some Musicians of Former Days*. This has past thru four French editions and become one of the classics of musical criticism in France. In it the author of "Jean-Christophe" treats of the Place of Music in General History, the Beginnings of Opera, the First Opera Play in Paris: Rossi's "Orfeo," and of many musicians.

Holt. $1.50.

PEBBLES

The trouble with the belligerents is that each side is unbeaten and knows it.—*Buffalo Enquirer.*

The proposition that cemeteries be turned into bird sanctuaries is one of grave importance.—*Trenton State Gazette.*

"The choir of the Memorial church was full Sunday and the music was excellent." "Some do sing better in that condition.—*Federal Record.*

Lady—And you say you are an educated man?
Wearied Will—Yes, mum, I'm a roads scholar.—*Michigan Gargoyle.*

"I assure you, madam, my ancestors came over with the first settlers."
"Very likely. We had no immigration laws then."—*Baltimore American.*

Student (writing home)—"How do you spell 'financially'?"
Other—"F-i-n-a-n-c-i-a-l-l-y, and there are two r's in 'embarrassed.'"—*Harpers.*

First American Citizen—Just back from Eu-rope?
Second American Citizen—Yes.
"What steamer were you rescued from?"—*Life.*

Villain—"Where are those papers?"
First Assistant Villain—"In the blacksmith shop!"
Villain—"Ha, ha—I suppose being forged?"
First Assistant—"No, being filed!"—*Michigan Gargoyle.*

"Pa," inquired a seven-year-old seeker after the truth, "is it true that schoolteachers get paid?"
"Certainly it is," said the father.
"Well, then," said the youth indignantly, "that ain't right. Why should the teachers get paid when us kids do all the work?"—*Ladies' Home Journal.*

An impecunious actor was approached by a friend, who said:
"Hello, Jones! I hear your watch has been stolen."
"Yes," said Jones, "but the crook that got it has already been arrested. Just imagine! the fool took it to the pawn-shop. There it was at once recognized as mine, and the thief was locked up."—*Harpers.*

One day a keeper was out walking with a number of harmless lunatics, and the party met a pedestrian not far from the railway tracks. With a nod toward the tracks, the traveler asked one of the lunatics:
"Where does this railway go to?"
The lunatic surveyed him scornfully for a moment, and then replied:
"Nowhere. We keep it here to run trains on."—*New Idea.*

The special-article writer had been sent for by the magazine editor. "We want a piece," said the magazine editor, "about the high cost of gasoline. The wholesale price this morning is twenty-two cents a gallon. Jump on the oil trust, for about five thousand words. How much do you want?" "Twenty cents a word," said the special-article writer. "Is my price." "Gosh!" said the m. e., "that's a lot." "I know," the writer admitted, "but I can get it; and I have to charge all I can get."—*New York Tribune.*

The train stopped in a Prohibition town. A man thrust his head out of a window and excitedly called out: "A woman has fainted in here! Has any one any whisky?" A man in the crowd reluctantly put his hand to his hip pocket and drew forth a bottle about half full, and handed it up to the man at the open window. To the astonishment of all, the man put the bottle to his lips and drained the contents. Then, as the train pulled out, he called back to the bewildered onlookers:
"It always did make me nervous to see a woman faint!"—*Everybody's.*

The Market Place

OUR SECURITIES ABROAD

In response to the British Government's invitation or request, address to owners of American securities, in accordance with the mobilization plan, so many have been sent in that the Bank of England has found it necessary to extend the hours assigned for the receipt of them. The Government has published a list of the prices it will pay for about fifty issues of American bonds, and to this list additions are to be made.

There have been large holdings of United States Steel Corporation stock on the other side of the Atlantic. It has recently been ascertained that since the beginning of the war the number of shares of the common stock so held has been reduced by sales from 1,285,636 to 696,631, or by about 46 per cent. The 589,005 shares thus sold back to buyers here are worth at present prices about $51,000,000. Sales of the preferred stock were only 37,723 shares, or 12 per cent of the 312,311 shares held abroad. Continued payment of the 7 per cent dividend prevented many from selling, but suspension of the dividend on the common shares made them less desirable. Less than 3000 shares were owned in Germany. The greatest quantities were held in England and Holland, the first of these countries having 801,497 shares of the common stock four months before the beginning of the war, and the second 357,293.

MORE LOANS

Norway has negotiated here a loan of $5,000,000, represented by notes or bonds at 6 per cent, with a term of seven years. Nearly a year ago there was another loan of $3,000,000, on notes for two and three years. A banking syndicate in New York recently bought from Argentina 6 per cent notes for $6,000,000. This makes a total of $46,-000,000 borrowed here by Argentina since the beginning of the war. There were two loans of $15,000,000 and $25,-000,000, also at 6 per cent. A few days ago the President of Peru asked his Congress to authorize the negotiation of a loan of $15,000,000 in New York.

At the end of the year it was reported that Russia was seeking a loan of $60,000,000, and that a prominent trust company in New York had the matter in charge. It does not appear that progress has been made in the negotiations. The supplementary loan of $50,-000,000 to Great Britain, arranged by groups of banks in London and New

DIVIDENDS

American Telephone and Telegraph Company

A dividend of Two Dollars per share will be
paid on Saturday, January 15, 1916, to stockholders of record at the close of business on
Friday, December 31, 1915.

G. D. MILNE, Treasurer.

American Telephone and Telegraph Company

Four Per Cent. Collateral Trust Bonds

Coupons from these bonds, payable by their
terms on January 1, 1916, at the office of the
Treasurer in New York will be paid by the
Bankers Trust Company, 16 Wall Street.

G. D. MILNE, Treasurer.

York, and based upon collateral deposited in the Bank of England, became
effective a few days before the close of
the year. Bonds of the $500,000,000
Anglo-French loan, a few of which
were sold at a little less than 94½ in
the last days of December, have now
risen to 95½.

INTERLOCKING DIRECTORATES

At the annual meetings of the stockholders of national banks, last week,
there were many changes in the boards
of directors, owing to the requirements
of the Clayton Anti-Trust law. This
law says that after October 15 next "no
person shall, at the same time, be a
director or other officer or employee of
more than one bank, banking association, or trust company organized or
operating under the laws of the United
States," if the entire resources of either
institution exceed $5,000,000, and that
"no private banker or person who is a
director in any bank or trust company
organized and operating under the laws
of a state," if the institution's resources are more than $5,000,000, "shall
be eligible to be a director in any bank
or banking association organized or
operating under" the Federal laws. The
purpose of this prohibition was to prevent what have been called interlocking
directorates. Some of the directors affected by it will wait until October, but
a majority decided to comply with the
statute at the present time.

As an example, the effect upon the
board of the National Bank of Commerce, in New York, may be shown.
Four directors resigned. These are
Frank A. Vanderlip, president of the
great National City Bank; Albert H.
Wiggin, president of the Chase National Bank; F. L. Hine, president of
the First National Bank, and W. A.
Simonson, vice-president of the National City Bank. Mr. Vanderlip also retired from the boards of the Farmers'
Loan and Trust Company, the American Security and Trust Company, in
Washington, and the Riggs National
Bank, in the same city. James J. Hill,
the well known railroad man of the
Northwest, withdrew from the board
of the Chase National Bank, and was
succeeded there by his son, James N.
Hill. The elder Mr. Hill has been a director of national banks in St. Paul and
Chicago. A. Barton Hepburn, chairman of the Chase National's board
is no longer a director of the First National, in New York, and he also resigned from the board of the Fidelity
Trust Company, in New Jersey. Many
changes are to be made in trust companies and state banks.

THE COUNTRY'S RAILROADS

In the last four months of the old
year the railroads of this country
handled more freight than in any preceding period of the same length. The
number of their cars was insufficient,
and the shortage was increased by congestion at or near Eastern ports, where
for a long time there have been more
than 40,000 cars on sidings or in terminal yards, waiting to be unloaded.
The New Haven Company recently

asked several other roads for loans of locomotives, but got only three. Congestion has now been slightly relieved by the many embargoes upon freight. The protests of commercial associations against the reduction of the time allowance for free storage from 30 to 15 days have had no weight with the Interstate Commerce Commission. It was reported last week that the Boston and Albany Company was clearing away the accumulation of cars at Albany at the rate of 1100 per day.

Earnings have been very perceptibly affected by the great increase of traffic. This is shown by the reports of several companies. The latest report of the Interstate Commerce Commission relates to November. In that month returns from 89,295 miles of road showed an increase of net earnings from $26,000,000 to $48,000,000. While the increase of operating expenses was about 11 per cent, there was an addition of 31 per cent, or $30,000,000, to the gross revenue. The largest gains were in the East, where the net revenue per mile rose from $351 to $713. These profits have caused orders to be given for considerable quantities of new equipment.

Such advances as might reasonably be expected as a result of this improvement have not yet been seen in the prices of shares, altho there were considerable net gains in the past year. The continued selling of our railroad stocks by foreign owners has had some effect, but the stability of railroad stocks at times when the entire list was subjected to depressing influences has been shown by the record.

During more than half of the past year the condition of the railroads was unfavorable, and promise of betterment was not seen. There is evidence of this in the record of construction and bankruptcies. Only 933 miles of new track were built—the smallest addition in any year since 1864. The new mileage had declined from 3071 in 1913 to 1532 in 1914. The mileage held by receivers in October last, 41,000, was the greatest ever known, but at the end of the year it had been reduced to 38,661. This, however, is nearly one-sixth of the entire mileage. The prospect at the present time is quite encouraging, with no cause of trouble in sight except a possible controversy with the four great unions of employees this spring.

A billion units are believed to be beyond the capacity of any human mind to grasp. But we are becoming accustomed to speaking of money in terms of the billion, with billion-dollar Congresses, exports of a billion and the immensity of war finance.

A French newspaper, the better to impress its readers with the magnitude of the "loan of victory," exceeding $4,000,000,000 francs—in our money $2,800,000,000—reminds them that "only 1,907,212,000 minutes have elapsed since the death of Christ." That is certainly a striking allusion. Even counted in our money, the aggregate of dollars poured out of the "swollen stocking" of France is more than twice the number of minutes in the centuries since the dawn of the Christian era. . . . With all the belligerents the debt is piling up so that it is counted in billions while a billion itself cannot be counted or scarcely comprehended.—*Providence Journal.*

Insurance
Conducted by
W. E. UNDERWOOD

BE CAUTIOUS ABOUT CHANGING

There is no business in the world that is worked more assiduously than that of life insurance. The companies are numerous; their field representatives aggressive; and competition is keen. The struggle for applications long ago bred two evils which legislation has endeavored to eradicate—one called "twisting," which consists in persuading an insured to lapse a policy he has for the purpose of replacing it with one issued by the company the agent represents; the other, "rebating," is a division of the agent's first commission with his customer. Nearly, if not quite, all the states prohibit these practises. But the laws are not implicitly obeyed thruout the country.

On general principles, and in the vast majority of cases, "twisting" is unprofitable to policyholders, and always profitable to the agent who does the "twisting," for he makes a commission on the new policy he places. Policyholders should regard a "twisting" proposition with suspicion. There are exceptional cases where a policyholder, having made a bad choice, either because the system under which he is insured is faulty, or the financial condition of the company is or becomes unsatisfactory, is warranted in changing a poor equipment for a good one. But these situations are comparatively rare. Time is an invaluable element in life insurance, and he who has invested even but a few years under a policy will find difficulty in securing compensation for the time past if he abandons that particular venture.

The injustice of "rebating" is obvious. Nearly all policyholders must pay their first premiums in full. Those who secure a discount on them by accepting a portion of the agent's wage, are receiving the service rendered by the insurers at a price lower than that paid by their associates, and the essential principle of equity is violated. Aside from this, the practise abridges the fair reward the agent should receive for his labor; for I am of those who hold that the man who can persuade his neighbors to protect his family and himself properly thru life insurance has conferred a favor, compared with which the agent's compensation is but a trifle.

Not infrequently readers seeking information and advice thru this department, after describing the line of insurance they are carrying, certain faults in which they have discovered, ask if they would not do better by surrendering it and securing new policies in its place. It is for that reason I have

briefly discussed "twisting" and its disadvantages on this occasion. In most cases, such changes are as risky as "swapping horses when crossing a stream."

WAR LOSSES OF AMERICAN LIFE COMPANIES

As previously reported in this department on several occasions, the general effect of the war in Europe on the mortality experience of the American life insurance companies transacting a foreign business may be set down as negligible up to the end of 1915, after seventeen months of perhaps the most sanguinary fighting in the history of the world. In a statement just issued by President Kingsley, of the New York Life, the American company with the largest European business, we find that the total deaths amongst its members, due to the war, number but 534 from August 1, 1914, to December 31, 1915; and that for the twelve months of 1915 the toll was 409.

By way of illustrating the matter, Mr. Kingsley contrasts this record with the company's mortality due to common causes. For example: we find that during 1915, deaths of members due to accidents numbered 448; to cancer, 707; to pneumonia, 772; to tuberculosis, 950.

In further demonstration of the claim previously made by the management that the war would have no material effect on the company, Mr. Kingsley furnishes us with the percentages of "actual" to "expected" mortality for the years 1912, 1913, 1914 (five months of war) and 1915 (twelve months of war). The "expected" mortality is that for which the premium rates provide; the "actual" is that which, at the end of the year, is found to have occurred. In 1912 the "actual" was 76 per cent. of the expected; in 1913 it was 73 per cent.; in 1914 it was 73 per cent.; and in 1915 it was 73 per cent.

These figures leave no room for apprehension on the part of American policyholders of companies transacting a foreign business. As has been shown, there are greater hazards than war to be encountered by those who constitute the largest companies. As Mr. Kingsley has pertinently observed: "In the grim battle of life with its inevitable mortality and its unnecessary slaughter, the mortality of a world war, even while it is being prosecuted, amongst a membership that is also world wide, is about 91 per cent. of that caused by accident in the same membership; 58 per cent. of that caused by cancer; 53 per cent. of that caused by pneumonia; and 43 per cent. of that caused by tuberculosis."

E. G. S., Ames, Ia.—Young men, because the probability of survivorship during many years is very strong and also because their producing powers are constantly growing, should, if they can, take some of the endowment forms of life insurance. At twenty-two with an income and without immediate family responsibilities should be able to maintain a twenty-year endowment. If more protection is desired for the premium, take a thirty-five-year endowment.

Hartford Policies Buried in a Keg at Midnight

After the conflagration that swept Charleston, S. C., during the Civil War in 1861, the policy holders in the Hartford Fire Insurance Company despaired of collecting their claims against an "enemy" corporation. Proofs of loss could not be forwarded through the battle lines, and the Company was under no legal obligation to pay.

"Give me your papers," said the Hartford's local agent. "I will take care of them and you will get your money." The documents, together with other valuables, were placed in a keg and buried at midnight in the middle of a large field which was afterwards ploughed over. There they remained until the end of the war, when they were forwarded to Hartford and the claims promptly paid. This is the motive back of the

INSURANCE SERVICE
OF THE
TWO HARTFORDS

For over a century the Hartford Fire Insurance Company, through war, panic and disaster, has met every honest obligation fully and fairly. As a result it writes today more fire insurance than any other company in the United States.

The Hartford Accident & Indemnity Company in the field of casualty and bonding insurance is noted for the same prompt, fair treatment of its policy holders for which the parent company is famous.

The two companies, between them, write practically every form of insurance but life insurance.

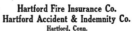

BOTH SIDES A DEBATE

PUBLIC DEFENDER

RESOLVED: That the office of
Public Defender should be created
thruout the United States.

THE idea of a Public Defender, who, in the name of the state, shall defend persons accused of crime, just as the Prosecuting Attorney prosecutes them for the state, was first considered by the states about twenty years ago. The first state to establish the office was Oklahoma, in 1911. The model for other localities, however, is usually the work begun in Los Angeles County, California, in January, 1914, described in The Independent of October 18, 1915. Brief prepared by Mary Prescott Parsons.

ARGUMENT FOR THE AFFIRMATIVE

I. Some change is needed in our method of administering criminal justice.
  A. Innocent persons are convicted.
    1. Courts are overcrowded.
    2. The innocent often plead guilty. (a) They are ignorant of the safeguards allowed them by the law. (b) They prefer accepting a minimum penalty to the delay of trial. (c) Unscrupulous lawyers advise them to plead guilty.
    3. Some convictions are due to lack of proper counsel.
    4. Fees or political advancement of Prosecuting Attorneys sometimes depend on the number of convictions secured.
  B. It discriminates unjustly against the poor.
    1. They cannot afford expert counsel.
    2. Assigned counsel serving for nothing or for nominal fees from the state, are rarely satisfactory, being often (a) young lawyers lacking experience, (b) older men who have been failures, or (c) competent lawyers who are too busy to give the necessary time.
    3. They cannot meet the necessary expenses of defense.
II. Needed reforms can best be accomplished thru the creation of the office of Public Defender.
  A. Such work is properly a function of the state.
    1. The state admits the right of the accused to defense and should provide means to make the defense adequate.
    2. The Public Defender's work provides such means. (a) It insures able and just defense to the poor. (b) It makes appeals possible. (c) Respect of the public and the courts for the Public Defender prevents the following evils: 1. Convictions because of popular clamor. 2. Overpunishment. 3. Unnecessary and damaging indictments. (d) It secures equal justice for all classes.
  B. The work of the Public Defender is economical for the state.
    1. More cases are dismissed without trial.
    2. Money is saved by coöperation between the Prosecutor and Defender.
    3. Costly delays are eliminated.
    4. Unnecessary imprisonments are prevented.
  C. The need cannot be met by the following proposed substitutes:
    1. Legal aid societies. (a) Their income, from private funds, is inadequate and uncertain. (b) It is wrong to make citizens depend upon charity to secure their rights.
    2. Payment of counsel and other expenses of defense by the state. (a) Being unsystematized, this would cost more than the Public Defender. (b) It would lead to favoritism and graft.

III. Aside from criminal cases, the Public Defender directly benefits the state.
  A. Economically.
    1. Small debts are collected at a minimum expense.
    2. Many persons are thus prevented from becoming public charges.
  B. Socially.
    1. It raises the standards of criminal courts and criminal lawyers.
    2. It tends to prevent anarchy by assuring security and justice.
    3. It tends to increase the number of just convictions.
    4. It diminishes crime.
IV. The success of the Public Defender has been established in Los Angeles.

ARGUMENT FOR THE NEGATIVE

I. Office of Public Defender is unnecessary.
  A. The assertion that innocent 'persons are convicted is unfounded.
    1. It is not supported by facts.
    2. It loses sight of the many safeguards now provided by the law. (a) Assumption of innocence. (b) Duty of the Prosecuting Attorney to prevent unjust indictments. (c) Necessity of indictment before prosecution. (d) Requirement of unanimous verdict for conviction.
    3. Protection against "shyster" lawyers can be accomplished by better administration of law.
    4. Assigned counsel give good service. (a) Reputation depends on it. (b) No lawyer who neglects his duty is allowed to continue with a case.
  B. Present methods with some changes will insure justice to rich and poor.
    1. Laws should be amended to prevent the escape of wealthy criminals, not to enable poor criminals to escape also.
    2. Where Prosecuting Attorneys' fees depend upon convictions the remedy should be a change in the laws.
    3. Payment of necessary expenses of defense by the state would be preferable to the creation of Public Defenders. (a) It involves less radical changes in the laws. (b) It is less expensive. (c) It is satisfactory.
  C. Much of the work of the Public Defender is now done by other agencies—Prosecuting Attorneys, probation officers, legal aid societies.
II. Public Defender not practically useful.
  A. Its seeming success in Los Angeles is of too short duration to be a criterion.
  B. The Public Defender could not try to acquit the guilty as well as the innocent.
    1. This would merely block the work of the Prosecuting Attorney.
    2. A legal battle between two public officials would destroy respect for law.
    3. It would double the work and expense of the courts.
    4. Public funds would be misspent.
  C. The office would not be justified if the Public Defender should defend only those whom he believed to be innocent.
    1. He would usurp the functions of the judge and jury. (a) He would be obliged to give up a case if he found evidence of guilt. (b) The fact that he undertook the defense would prejudice the court in favor of the accused.
    2. There would be no one to defend the prisoner who refused to plead guilty on the advice of the Public Defender.
    3. His services would be sought only by the few who were innocent.
    4. We should not establish the office for these few. (a) The work of the Public Defender would coincide with that of the Prosecuting Attorney. (b) Adequate safeguards now exist.

  D. The Public Defender could not always undertake the collection of debts.
    1. The office would be swamped by the number of unjust claims.
    2. Expensive investigations would be necessary to distinguish genuine from false.
III. It would be unwise for the country.
  A. It would be expensive at first.
  B. Ultimately the state would have to defend in all criminal cases.
    1. It would be hard to draw the line.
    2. It would be the only way to prevent injustice to persons of moderate means. (a) The Public Defender and his assistants would be able lawyers for the poor. (b) The rich could employ experts.
  C. It would be dangerous.
    1. More criminals would escape.
    2. Crime would increase.
    3. It would endanger the liberty of citizens. (a) It would give one man too much power. (b) Citizens would be defended by a paid servant of the prosecution. (c) It would lead to the denial of their right to employ private counsel.
    4. Once created, the office would be difficult to abolish.
    5. Free administration of justice is socialistic.

REFERENCES

Code of Criminal Procedure of the state in which the question is under discussion. Globe (N. Y.), Public Defender: a series of seven articles, January 12-19, 1915. Journal of Criminal Law and Criminology, 5:601-3, November, 1914; 6:370-84, September, 1915. Legal Aid Society of Chicago, Annual Reports. Legal Aid Society, New York City, Annual Reports. Milwaukee Bureau of Economy and Efficiency, Bulletin 7, October 20, 1911. National Municipal Review, 3: 391-2, April, 1914. Oklahoma, Commissioner of Charities and Corrections, Annual Report, 1911-12. Review of Reviews, 50:741-2, December, 1914. World's Work, 28:15, May, 1914.

Affirmative

American Academy of Political and Social Science, Annals, 52:177-80, March, 1914. Bench and Bar, 9:138-40, July, 1914. Case and Comment, 19:207-15, October, 1912; 582-5, February, 1913; 21:468-73, November, 1914. Commonwealth Club of California, Transactions, 10:115-114, March, 1915. Everybody's, 31:246-9, August, 1914. International Socialist Review, 6:228-33, October, 1905. Journal of Criminal Law and Criminology, 1:725-47, January; 2:398-9, September, 1911; 704-15, January, 1912; 4:650-4, January; 5:97-9, May; 283-90, July; 441-4, September; 494-7, November, 1914; 660-5, January; 925-3, March; 6:18-27, May, 1915. Independent, 84:86, 94-5, October 18, 1915. Law Notes, 17:223, March, 1914. Nation, 99:124, July 30, 1914. New Republic, 4:47-8, August 14, 1915. New York Times, June 7, 1914. 1:6-11. Outlook, 106:157-8, January 24; 660-1, March 28; 107:828-9, August 8, 1914. Parmelee, Maurice, Principles of Anthropology and Sociology in Their Relations to Criminal Procedure, 1908, chapter 8. Public Forum Weekly, 1:1-8, June 12, 1915. Wood, W. J., The Office of Public Defender: Letters from W. J. Wood, Public Defender, to the Bar Associations of New York and Milwaukee; comments of the District Attorney, Judges and press of Los Angeles; Los Angeles County charter provisions, 3d ed., June 1914. Wood, W. J., Place of the Public Defender in the Administration of Justice; address before California Bar Association. 5th annual convention, November 19-21, 1914.

Negative

Association of the Bar of the City of New York: Necessity and Advisability of Creating the Office of Public Defender; being the 8th report of the Law Reform Committee, January 12, 1915. Bench and Bar, 9:32-4, June; 100, July; 309-19, November, 1914. Commonwealth Club of California, Transactions, 10:129-39, March, 1915. Evening Post (N. Y.), October 23, 1915, II:10:3-5. New York County Lawyers' Association, Majority Report of a Sub-committee on Courts of Criminal Procedure, 1914, typewritten. New York Times, June 14, 1914, II: 14:6. North American Review, 201:823-5, June, 1915. World (N. Y.), October 25, 1914, IV: 1:1-2; May 28, 1915, 12:4-5.

The Independent

FOR SIXTY-SEVEN YEARS THE
FORWARD-LOOKING WEEKLY OF AMERICA

THE CHAUTAUQUAN
Merged with The Independent June 1, 1914

JANUARY 31, 1916

OWNED AND PUBLISHED BY
THE INDEPENDENT CORPORATION, AT
119 WEST FORTIETH STREET, NEW YORK
WILLIAM B. HOWLAND, PRESIDENT
FREDERIC E. DICKINSON, TREASURER

WILLIAM HAYES WARD
HONORARY EDITOR

EDITOR: HAMILTON HOLT
ASSOCIATE EDITOR: HAROLD J. HOWLAND
LITERARY EDITOR: EDWIN E. SLOSSON

PUBLISHER: KARL V. S. HOWLAND

ONE YEAR, THREE DOLLARS

SINGLE COPIES, TEN CENTS

Postage to foreign countries in Universal Postal
Union, $1.75 a year extra; to Canada, $1 extra.
Instructions for renewal, discontinuance or
change of address should be sent two weeks
before the date they are to go into effect. Both
the old and the new address must be given.

We welcome contributions, but writers who
wish their articles returned, if not accepted,
should send a stamped and addrest envelope. No responsibility is assumed by The
Independent for the loss or non-return of
manuscripts, tho all due care will be exercised.

Entered at New York Post Office as Second
Class Matter

Copyright, 1916, by The Independent

Address all Communications to
THE INDEPENDENT
119 West Fortieth Street, New York

CONTENTS

A LA CARTE

The New York, New Haven and
Hartford Railroad Company, which
our readers have possibly seen references to in the papers during the last
year or so, runs a de luxe, excess fare,
pan-parlor car train every day from
New York to Boston yclept the Merchants Limited.

The Editor of The Independent, as
befits his dignity and position in the
community, is accustomed to grace this
train with his presence, whenever the
search for some mute inglorious Emerson, or some impulse to improve his
Harvard accent—he was but educated
at Yale—or some other imperious demand calls him to the Athens of
America.

Last Friday it was his fortune to be
aboard this aristocratic conveyance.
On hearing the proclamation of the
third call for dinner about 7 p. m., he
started to go forward when he learned,
much to his surprise, that in addition
to a dusky lady's maid and other
lucullan appendages too numerous to
enumerate, the Merchants Limited now
boasts of two dining cars—one forward
providing a table d'hote dinner, the
other rearward furnishing an à-la-
carte service.

The Editor before making the momentous decision confronting him
visited both cars. He found that the
table d'hote car was half empty, but
the à-la-carte car was packed to the
limit. There was even a waiting line in
the alley next the galley.

Without imposing on the valuable
space of The Independent, or on the
more valuable time of its readers to the
extent of telling in which car the
Editor dined (or was it in both?), or
on what delicacies he made his repast,
suffice it to say that having eaten his
money's worth, he surreptitiously
seized a menu from each car, while the
steward was not looking, and then
went back to his coach, the "Eurydice"
—for such was its name—and sitting
down in his green upholstered revolving chair (it stuck fast and
wouldn't revolve as every parlor car
traveler knows) he critically compared
the purloined menus before him.

And what, pray do you think was
the result? You can hardly guess. He

found that the two menus were alike
with the exception of Buttered Beets,
Banana Fritters and Saltines on the
table d'hote bill of fare and Gher-
kins and Fried Haddock with Alle-
mande Sauce on the à-la-carte bill
of fare. The Editor then made
a brief calculation with his fountain pen on the back of a discarded
paper sanitary drinking cup that he
found under the ice cooler. He discovered—mirabile dictu—that the precise
dinner that cost $1.25 in the table
d'hote car, if ordered in the à-la-carte
car would cost exactly $6.25, or five
times as much.

Now you can't stump the Editor of
The Independent, if you ask him when
the Great War will end or who is going
to win it. He knows to a certainty
whether he of the gleaming teeth or he
of the envisaged whiskers will be the
Republican nominee next June, or
whether some darker horse like President James, of the University of Illinois, will be chosen (the James boom is
now and hereby launched. The Editor
would prefer the court of St. James's).
He can even fathom the reason why
"and jetsam" invariably follow when
the word "flotsam" is used. But what
for the life of him he cannot understand is why five times as many presumably human beings deliberately
choose the à-la-carte service when they
have to pay five times as much for it
as they would for the same fare in the
table d'hote car with second and third
helps thrown in to boot. The mystery
becomes more insoluble when it is remembered that the patrons of the à-la-
carte car frequently pay considerably
more than $1.25 for their meal.

JUST A WORD

The Ice Ballet at the Hippodrome
has set the example for the latest fad
of New York fashion—ice skating. Toe
dancing on skates, with all the whirls,
glides, spirals, jumps, and pirouettes
conceivable, is the principal feature of
the exhibition, in which Miss Katie
Schmidt, whose picture appears on the
cover of The Independent for this issue, takes a leading part. This is the
first appearance of the Ice Ballet in
America, altho Berlin has found it a
popular entertainment for some years.

About the war?—yes. You've read
scores of articles. But here is a fragment from one in the war—a Frenchman with a seeing eye and a touch of
philosophy. Captain Paul Vignon, he is,
and Dr. Charles Peabody, of Cambridge, has translated, under the title
The Meeting, his vivid reflections on a
phase or two of the horror he lives in
day by day.

"Good or bad government must go
back to good or bad citizenship," writes
Thomas R. Marshall, Vice-President of
the United States, in a paper on The
Essence of Democratic Government
which he will contribute to an early
issue. The Vice-President makes a ringing defense of "Jeffersonian democracy."

Useful Books for Everybody

SOME books are designed for entertainment, others for information. This series combines both features. The information is not only complete and reliable, it is condensed and readable. These volumes are replete with valuable material, compact in form and unequaled in point of merit and cheapness. They are the latest as well as the best books on the subjects of which they treat. No one who wishes to have a fund of general information or who has the desire for self-improvement can afford to be without them. They are 6 x 4½ inches in size, well printed on good paper, handsomely bound in green cloth, with a heavy paper wrapper to match.

EACH 50 CENTS

THE FAMILY FOOD. By T. C. O'Donnell. How to get the most efficient food for little money, with food-values, menus, and a balanced diet.

THE FAMILY HEALTH. By Myer Solis-Cohen. To keep well, read this book. It treats problems of ventilation, heating, lighting, drainage, clothing, and food.

THE FAMILY HOUSE. By C. F. Osborne, Architect. Helpful hints as to what to look for in the location of a house, amount of rent, exposure, and fixtures.

CANDY-MAKING AT HOME. By Mary M. Wright. Two hundred kinds of candy-fondant, fruit and nut candies, cream candies, fudges and caramels, bonbons and little cakes.

THE CARE OF THE CHILD. By Mrs. Burton Chance. A new treatment of an ever new problem, in its mental, moral and physical aspects.

HOME DECORATION. By Dorothy T. Priestman. You may learn here what is good taste in the treatment of walls, furniture, ornaments, etc.

RECEIPTS AND REMEDIES. By Louis A. Fleming. A thousand and one "best ways" to preserve health, comfort and appearance.

FIRST AID TO THE INJURED. By F. J. Warwick. What to do in all kinds of accidents and the first stages of illness. Illustrated.

NURSING. By S. Virginia Levis. The fullest particulars given for the care of the sick in all of the simple and serious ailments of life.

DEATH DEFERRED. By Hereward Carrington. Read this and live to be a hundred. A practical discussion of human life and how to prolong it.

ELECTRICITY. By George L. Fowler. If you wish to install a door-bell, construct a telephone, or wire a house, the information is here.

THE HORSE. By C. T. Davies. Are you choosing a horse, raising or keeping one? You need this handy little compendium of the latest veterinary science.

THE DOG. By John Maxtee. All the essentials of dog-keeping are given, from kennel to show bench, from biscuit to flea-bane.

GOLF. By Horace Hutchinson. This standard book gives a complete history of the game, instructions for the selection of implements, and directions for playing.

DAIRY-FARMING. By D. S. Burch, State Dairy Commissioner of Kansas. A practical book telling what cows to buy and how to make dairying pay.

CHICKENS. By A. T. Johnson. A book that tells all about chickens, how to raise them, combat disease, and otherwise care for the growing brood.

FLOWERS; HOW TO GROW THEM. By Eben E. Rexford. With the help so clearly given in this book no one need fail to raise flowers.

HOME GAMES. By George Hapgood, Esq. A collection of the newest and best ways of amusing people who have come together for a good time.

PARLOR GAMES. By Helen E. Hollister. With this volume at hand no one need ever be at a loss for games of amusement, entertainment and instruction.

SOLITAIRE AND PATIENCE. By George Hapgood, Esq. Fifty games; here are fifty friends for as many moods and able to make a lonely hour pass quickly.

WHIST. By Cavendish. The beginner's best friend and the experienced player's constant companion.

DANCING. By Marguerite Wilson. A complete instructor, beginning with the first positions and steps and leading up to the square and round dances.

DANCES OF TO-DAY. By A. L. Newman. An up-to-date manual of the latest dances with clear diagrams and photographs.

CONVERSATION. By J. P. Mahaffy. What to say, just when and how to say it, is the aim of this work.

STORIES WORTH TELLING. By Herbert Leonard Coggins. The cream of all the funny stories. Illustrated by 100 pictures by Claire Victor Dwiggins.

READING AS A FINE ART. By Earnest Legouvé. The suggestions contained in this work of standard authority will go far toward the attainment of this accomplishment.

CLASSICAL DICTIONARY. By Edward S. Ellis, A.M. All the classical allusions worth knowing, so arranged as to lose no time in looking them up.

BUSINESS LETTERS. By Calvin C. Althouse. An expert here shows by numerous examples from real business how to write letters.

SHAKESPEAREAN QUOTATIONS. By C. S. Rex. Here are more than one thousand subjects, arranged alphabetically; under each apt quotations are given.

BIBLICAL QUOTATIONS. By John H. Bechtel. Thousands of quotations, arranged alphabetically by subjects, providing quotations for each one.

CIVICS; WHAT EVERY CITIZEN SHOULD KNOW. By George Lewis. Information on such topics as the Monroe Doctrine, Behring Sea Controversy, Extradition, Treaties, etc.

SLIPS OF SPEECH. By John H. Bechtel. No necessity for studying rules of rhetoric or grammar; this book teaches both. It is counselor, critic, and guide.

ETIQUETTE. By Agnes H. Morton. Success in life is often marred by bad manners. Social blunders may be prevented by the knowledge of the right thing to do.

QUOTATIONS. By Agnes H. Morton. A clever compilation of pithy quotations, alphabetically arranged according to the sentiment.

EPITAPHS. By Frederick W. Unger. Full of quaint bits of obituary fancy, with a touch of the gruesome here and there for a relish.

PROVERBS. By John H. Bechtel. This volume contains a collection of proverbs, old and new, indexed to enable one to find readily just what is wanted.

THINGS WORTH KNOWING. By John H. Bechtel. Information for everybody, about health, household affairs, business, domestic and foreign countries; all indexed.

A DICTIONARY OF MYTHOLOGY. By John H. Bechtel. The convenient arrangement here makes knowledge of mythological subjects easily acquired.

PRONUNCIATION. By John H. Bechtel. Over 5,000 words, pronounced in the clearest manner, according to the best authority.

PRACTICAL SYNONYMS. By John H. Bechtel. Invaluable for enlarging your vocabulary and cultivating a more precise manner of speech.

THE DEBATER'S TREASURY. By William Pittenger. Directions for organizing and conducting debating societies, with a list of over 200 questions.

PUNCTUATION. By Paul Allardyce. Few persons can punctuate correctly. Keep this book on your desk to remove difficulties and make all points clear.

ORATORY. By Henry Ward Beecher. A unique and masterly treatise on the fundamentals of true oratory.

ENGLISH WRITERS. By R. V. Gilbert. For those who wish to know the main facts about our great writers.

STORIES OF THE OPERAS. By Ethel Shubert. This gives the complete story of every opera ordinarily produced in America and many less frequently heard.

JOURNALISM. By Charles H. Olin. What is news, how is it obtained, how handled, and how to become a journalist? These questions and others are answered.

ASTRONOMY; THE SUN AND HIS FAMILY. By Julia MacNair Wright. Can you tell what causes day and night, seasons and years, tides and eclipses? Here is your information.

BOTANY; THE STORY OF PLANT LIFE. By Julia MacNair Wright. The scientific study of Botany made as interesting as a fairy tale.

LAW, AND HOW TO KEEP OUT OF IT. By Paschal H. Coggins, Esq. Every busy man and woman will find here information on just such points as are likely to arise in everyday affairs.

PARLIAMENTARY LAW. By Paschal H. Coggins, Esq. This is parliamentary law in a nutshell, for people who need plain rules, and the reasons for them.

SOCIALISM. By Charles H. Olin. Here is given, in a clear and interesting manner, a complete idea of the economic doctrines taught by the leading socialists.

PLUTARCH'S LIVES. By Edward S. Ellis, A.M. The lives of the leading Greeks and Romans of ancient times, in concise form.

READY-MADE SPEECHES. By George Hapgood. A collection of carefully planned model speeches to aid those who, without some slight help, must remain silent.

AFTER-DINNER STORIES. By John Harrison. Nothing adds so much zest to a dinner as a good story well told. There are hundreds of them, short and pithy.

TOASTS. By William Pittenger. What would you not give for the ability to respond to them? This little book will tell you how to do it.

LETTER WRITING. By Agnes H. Morton. This admirable book shows, by numerous examples, just what kind of letters to write for all occasions.

ASTROLOGY. By M. M. Macgregor. If you wish to know in what business you will best succeed, or whom you will marry, here is the solution.

DREAM BOOK. By Madame Xanto. The old traditions proved by time and the experience of famous Oriental, Celtic and early English observers.

CURIOUS FACTS. By Clifford Howard. Why do you raise your hat to a lady? and why do you offer the right hand? The answers are here.

PRACTICAL PALMISTRY. By Henry Firth. Follow the directions here and every hand will tell you its story like a printed page.

VENTRILOQUISM. By Charles H. Olin. This book exposes the secrets of the art completely, shows how anyone may learn to "throw the voice." Fully illustrated.

CONUNDRUMS. By Dean Rivers. This book contains an excellent collection of over a thousand of the latest and most up-to-date conundrums.

MAGIC. By Ellis Stanyon. Full descriptions of all the well-known tricks with coins, handkerchiefs, hats, flowers and cards. Fully illustrated.

FORTUNE TELLING. By Madame Xanto. All the approved ways of piercing the future by cards, dominoes, dice, palmistry or coffee grounds.

PHYSIOGNOMY. By Leila Lomax. How can we judge of character? Physiognomy as here explained shows clearly how to read character in every face.

PHRENOLOGY. By C. H. Olin. How to examine the head and learn how its shape influences character.

HYPNOTISM. By Edward H. Eldridge, A.M. By following this simple and concise instructions contained in this complete manual, anyone may readily learn how to exercise this unique and strange power.

GRAPHOLOGY. By Clifford Howard. Anyone who understands Graphology can tell by your handwriting what sort of person you are.

The following titles are published in full red morocco leather, flexible, with the title in gold, and each book in a box. In this form they make very handsome gift books. Price, $1.00 each.

After-Dinner Stories	Stories of the Operas	Letter Writing	Quotations
Bridge, and How to play It	Conundrums	Toasts	Solitaire and Patience
Business Letters	Etiquette	Parlor Games	Dances of Today

For sale at all bookstores or will be sent to any part of the world upon receipt of price

THE PENN PUBLISHING COMPANY,   931 FILBERT STREET, PHILADELPHIA

The Independent

| VOLUME 85 | JANUARY 31, 1916 | NUMBER 3504 |

PRACTISE WHAT YOU PREACH, MR. PRESIDENT

WHY all this fuss about the Postmastership of New York?

If one may believe the reports, the question which the president is trying to decide is whether he shall appoint a certain Tammany politician or some other politician. But why a politician at all?

The one thing a postmaster ought to know is how to run a post-office. What do politicians know about that? There is just one logical, sensible appointment to be made. The present postmaster, Edward Morgan, does know how to run a post-office. He has been at work in the New York post-office for forty-three years. He was assistant postmaster for ten years and postmaster for the same length of time. There is no breath of criticism of his efficiency. How could New York hope to have better postal service by putting a politician in his place?

Here is a sharp and clean cut issue between efficient public service and selfish spoils politics. Here, Mr. President, is a splendid opportunity to make good in practise the high political morality you have so earnestly preached.

PUBLIC RIGHTS AND INDIVIDUAL OPPORTUNITIES

AMONG American public men Mr. Justice Hughes is hardly surpassed in the sanity of his judgment, the clearness of his intellectual perceptions, the breadth and sincerity of his devotion to human rights. Time and again in his career upon the bench of the Supreme Court his voice has been heard with unmistakable force upon the side of the public welfare as opposed to the technical rights of special interests and the privileges of property.

In a recent address before the New York Bar Association, Justice Hughes made illuminating comment upon a subject of vital importance to our national progress, a subject apparently purely legal, but in reality intensely human. It is concerned with the "due process of law" section of the Fourteenth Amendment to the Federal Constitution. That section provides, among other things, that no state shall deprive any person of property without due process of law.

It is one of the historic clauses of our national Bill of Rights securing life, liberty and property. It was enacted by the Fathers as a defense of individual opportunity against possible governmental tyranny. As such it was and is an indispensable part of the fundamental law of the nation. But with new times and new conditions of industry and of life it has come to be invoked with greater or less success as an instrument of industrial aggression against the general welfare.

Within the past few years it has been appealed to with success in the single state of New York to prevent the Legislature from prohibiting the manufacture of cigars in tenement houses—although every student of the subject knew that such manufacture was attended with grave dangers to the public health—and to make impossible the enactment of a Workman's Compensation Act. In other states it has been appealed to, happily without success, to prevent a legislative restriction of hours of labor for women.

The success of the appeals to this constitutional provision for the purpose of estopping legislation in the public interest has arisen largely from three causes: A misconception on the part of judges as to their proper function in such cases; a misinterpretation on their part of the real purpose of this provision; and a judicial ignorance of or unwillingness to take proper account of the real facts of life involved.

Justice Hughes puts an unerring finger upon these three causes and in relation to them sets the judicial function in its proper perspective. On the first point he says: "It is manifest that the prohibition was not intended to override legislative action by the views of judges as to its wisdom." This is perfectly true. It is the business of the Legislature to decide whether a given piece of legislation is wise or not. It is only the business of the judiciary to determine whether the Legislature has the Constitutional right to enact the legislation and whether in so doing it has violated any fundamental individual right.

In regard to the second point he says:

What was thus sought was not a privilege to deny the legislative authority to enact reasonable measures for the protection of the safety, health, morals and welfare of the people, not to make improvement or rational experimentation impossible, but to preserve and enforce the primary and fundamental conceptions of justice which demand proper notice and opportunity to be heard before a competent tribunal in advance of condemnation, immunity from the confiscation of property, and, with respect to every department of government, freedom from the exercise of purely arbitrary power.

This aspect of the case could hardly be better stated.

On the third point Mr. Hughes declares that the judicial function of scrutinizing legislation in order to conserve what have been deemed to be the essentials of liberty is not likely to be disturbed "so long as judges in the discharge of their delicate and difficult duty exhibit a profound knowledge and accurate appreciation of the facts of commercial and industrial activity. . . ."

This undeniable fact has been stated by another

prominent American in the succinct phrase, "Judges should know life."

This keen and forceful presentation of an important aspect of the judicial function affords new, convincing proof of Mr. Hughes's eminence among the members of America's judicial system. It is an admirable illustration of the qualities of mind and spirit which have given rise to the strong and growing demand, with which The Independent strongly sympathizes, for the nomination of Mr. Hughes for the Presidency. It also suggests the reason why the nomination of Mr. Hughes would not be an unmixed benefit. We need just such qualities upon the bench. They are not so common there that their loss even in the person of a single judge would be lightly felt.

Mr. Hughes would make a splendid President; but he is already a splendid judge.

THE PARAMOUNT ISSUE

THIS country at the present moment is quite literally in the grip of an epidemic of influenza. Indeed the disease is so widely diffused that it is easy to understand why the term pandemic should be used because it affects practically the whole people. It has considerably raised the death-rates in every important city of the country and New York City during the past three weeks has had double as many deaths from pneumonia and related diseases as during the corresponding weeks of last year, and of preceding years. The affection carries off particularly the old and the young, but also those of all ages who are in delicate health. It is one of the most insidiously dangerous diseases that we have, and will undoubtedly have been the direct or indirect cause of many thousands of deaths before the present epidemic has exhausted itself.

Grip is due to a bacillus which was discovered by Pfeifer in Germany nearly twenty-five years ago, shortly after the first great modern epidemic of the disease which began in Turkestan or Southern Russia in the spring of 1889. Within a year the disease had spread to nearly all parts of the earth. Ever since then it has become endemic in most of the countries of the West and every winter sees a number of cases of it. Whenever the season is very damp, the sky much overcast and the temperature not low, the atmospheric conditions seem to favor the growth of the bacillus of influenza. Dry cold weather with cloudless skies greatly lessens the danger. After all our best germicide is sunlight. The bacillus of influenza seems to be particularly susceptible to its germicidal influence and to thrive on dark damp days. The present rather mild damp winter has fostered its virulence and by tempting people to be out more than usual has aided in the diffusion of the disease.

While influenza is an air-borne disease, it is not due to a miasm, that is, to some active element in the air, but to the presence in the atmosphere surrounding the people who have the disease of the germs of the affection. Because of this no one who has influenza should ever cough or sneeze without having a handkerchief before his mouth or nose. The disease constantly runs thru families. It is contagious; that is, it is spread by contact and not by an infection of the air or the water or food. Boards of health have taken up the crusade to lessen expectoration on the street and in cars and public buildings. All the oral and nasal secretions should be disinfected. This seems an over-meticulous precaution to take, but any one who wants to spare members of his household will find it well worth while to adopt it.

The disease, like diphtheria, does not protect against subsequent attacks except perhaps for a few weeks immediately after recovery. On the contrary influenza at the beginning of winter often seems to make people particularly susceptible to the disease later in the season and the danger of pneumonia as a complication rises with each succeeding attack. There is always danger of contracting the disease in crowds. Many people would escape attacks if after working all day in close, dry, overheated offices, when the mucous membrane has become incapable of protecting them thoroly, they did not have to ride home in crowded cars. A walk in the free open air at that time for fifteen or twenty minutes would probably arouse the vitality of their mucous membrane and make it better able to protect them. Quinine and whisky are still taken as prophylactics, tho they are not only useless, but probably predispose to the affection. The one all-important prophylactic is fresh air both day and night. Even in rainy weather and when the temperature is low the disease is practically never caught overnight, as many people think, but has an incubation period of three or four days. Thus when people tell their physicians that they caught the grip sitting in a draft yesterday morning or last night they are usually quite wrong. When we have reached a stage of civilization in which the present barbarous crowding of cars during rush hours will be looked upon as a relic of savagery, influenza will probably cease to be the danger that it has been at nearly all times during the wintry weather in the last twenty-five years.

CRUMBLING REPUTATIONS

IT is an old saying that those who begin a war are not the ones who carry it thru. The military organization like any other gets rusty in disuse, and when the stress and strain of actual combat puts it to the proof it is found that the men who have come to the head of it in time of peace are not always the best fitted to lead it in war. The McClellans have to be retired and the Grants promoted.

The present war is not the same war as that which started in August, 1914. It is being fought mostly on new battlefields with new weapons by new men under new leaders. The changes in the staff have been proportionally as numerous as the changes in the rank and file. When we look over the back numbers of illustrated periodicals or the early issues of some current "History of the War" we find that few of the names and faces which figured there are now prominent in the despatches.

On the Russian side the Grand Duke Nicholas, who was then hailed as a supreme strategist—of the Fabian type—has been banished to the Caucasus. Ruszky, Rennenkampf and Sievers have been removed from commands. Radko Dmitrieff, the "Bulgar Napoleon," is in retirement, but professes himself ready to head a Bulgarian rising against King Ferdinand.

On the German side von Moltke as chief of staff soon proved not to have the genius of his name. Von Kluck, von Deimling and von Hausen, who led the German armies in their first onslaught against the French, are hardly heard of nowadays. The Prussian Crown Prince, the "Victor of Longwy," is doubtless still alive in spite of having been reported killed at various times and places, but since his failure either to keep up with the march on Paris or to capture Verdun he is no longer "featured" in the official communications. The redoubtable von Hindenburg, who knew his way blindfolded thru the swamps of East Prussia, seems to have got stuck in the swamps of Courland and von Mackensen has taken his place in the limelight. In the Austrian army those who were in command at the start have been largely replaced by German generals or by the promotion of other Austrian officers.

In France before the war recurrent scandals had disclosed a deplorable condition in the army, where political, racial, sectarian and secret society influences were shown to control the appointments. The fatal month of August revealed cases of incompetency if not of cowardice or treachery in the higher commands. But Joffre had the courage to remove generals by the score without fear or favor and replace them by able men, whatever their previous rank or their political pull. So the French army is now practically under new management and Joffre himself has been raised to a position of more extensive scope, but perhaps less personal power.

In the British army, where it has long been alleged that court favor and social position counted for more than military proficiency, the weeding out process was less prompt and drastic than elsewhere, but the changes quietly and gradually made have revolutionized the command. When the summer past without the expected advance Field Marshal French was withdrawn. When the Gallipoli campaign failed Sir Ian Hamilton was removed. And now General Nixon, who commanded the ill-fated expedition up the rivers of Mesopotamia, has been sent home.

These removals do not, of course, necessarily mean incompetence. In some cases illness is alleged as the reason for the resignation, and we may well believe it. Never before in the history of the world has the fate of so many millions been placed in the hands of a single man and the only wonder is how human nature can stand the strain of such terrible responsibility without breaking down.

LET US HAVE CLEAR THINKING

SENATOR WORKS of California and Senator O'Gorman of New York gave expression in the Senate the other day to a view of the submarine problem that seems to have considerable popular approval among the unthinking. They seem to assert that American citizens sail the waters infested by submarines at their peril. They seem to deny the right and the responsibility of the United States Government to assure them of protection against deliberate attacks by war-vessels of belligerent nations. Mr. Bryan in the *Commoner* categorically asserts that American citizens should be prohibited by law from sailing on belligerent ships.

This is mere confusion of thought.

It may well be that it would be the part of wisdom and prudence for Americans to travel in war zone waters only when the most pressing occasion demands, and then, wherever possible, on neutral ships.

So it would be wise and prudent for a citizen of a great city to keep out of a thug-infested neighborhood after dark. But this obligation of personal precaution on the part of the individual does not relieve the city police of their duty of protecting him from thug attack or absolve the courts of the state from their obligation to punish the thug if caught.

Nor is the National Government relieved of any of its responsibility for protecting American citizens in life and property wherever they are proceeding upon their lawful occasions. It is lawful for non-combatants to sail the high seas so long as the vessels on which they sail do not violate certain well understood rules. Except in the case of resistance or flight, a merchant ship may not be sunk until the safety of the non-combatants on board has been assured.

This principle is unquestioned by the German and Austrian Governments. The first has said in the "Arabic" case:

Liners will not be sunk by our submarines without warning and without safety of the lives of the passengers, provided the liners do not try to escape or offer resistance.

The second has declared even more explicitly in the "Ancona" case:

The Imperial and Royal Government can also substantially concur in the principle . . . that private ships, in so far as they do not flee or offer resistance, may not be destroyed without the persons aboard being brought into safety.

Since the offenders in these two cases do not question this principle, why should any Senator of the United States or Mr. Bryan, even by loose implication?

The rights of American citizens upon the high seas are beyond question. It is the duty of the United States Government to maintain them against encroachment by any nation. It cannot release itself from this obligation by any attempt to throw the responsibility upon individual Americans to travel the seas only in American or neutral vessels.

It is of vital importance that the issue should not be confused. On this subject everyone, even United States Senators and editors, ought to strive after clear thinking.

A COUNSEL OF WISDOM

IT may be a counsel of perfection, it is at least a counsel of wisdom, that Mr. Gutzon Borglum has offered in his plan for permanent peace. The creative imagination which he puts into sculpture he has brought to bear upon constructive statecraft.

In letters to the *Evening Post*, Mr. Borglum singles out, as a factor in the European war, which, after the conflict is over, will be recognized as one of the keys of final peace, the right of free and unrestricted trade with the world, and freedom upon the high seas and thru the great waterways of world commerce.

A dozen great nations have been growing with mighty strides. They will continue to grow; in wealth, population and power. They must have opportunity, outlet for energy, room. The opportunity is the world, but the world is a finite area. The nations cannot each and all expand territorially without limit. The alternative is economic expansion through trade. Monopolization of trade, or of ports, or of trade routes by one or more nations is a highly dangerous repression of the expansive energies of the nations that are shut in or out. It is the old-time Mississippi River steamboat device of sitting on the safety valve. The "sooner or later" result is not doubtful.

This bit of sociology is not new, but Mr. Borglum's further proposition we think is. He proposes that the United States take the initiative in creating a great merger of the international highways and commercially strategic points. We should put into the pool the Panama Canal Zone and certain Pacific islands, or ports, in the Hawaiian group, in the Philippines, at Guam and at Samoa. The European Powers, on their part, should put in the Straits of Gibraltar, the Dardanelles and the Sea of Marmora, the Suez Canal, the Kiel Canal and Heligoland, and various minor places. All of these routes and places should be put under an International Board of Governors, to fortify, govern and administer.

That the scheme is theoretically sound, that practically it would be, as Mr. Borglum says, "good business," we suppose will not be denied. It is the sort of thing that "big business" has evolved to prevent those industrial conflicts that were threatening to become of warlike destructiveness, and it is a step in the direction of that League of nations which already is clearly indicated as the next stage in political integration, upon which all hope of worldwide and enduring peace necessarily rests.

Unhappily it is because it is practical and business-like that we do not dare to expect that Mr. Borglum's plan will easily be put into realization. It is concrete and specific, and there's the rub. It is easy and reputable to subscribe to a world peace program until we are asked to make over a definite right or other valuable consideration. We are glad to bless and help mankind until we are urged to put a certain sum into the contribution box. Yet, only by putting it in, shall we get on.

UNDERSTANDING WAR NEWS

IF, as Disraeli said, war is useful because it teaches us geography, we fear that many people are not learning their lessons.

The following list of questions designed to discover the amount of knowledge possest on the Great War has been used in New York University, Bowdoin and Barnard Colleges and elsewhere.

Where is Gallipoli?
What is the capital of Bulgaria?
What countries bound Serbia?
In what country is Salonica?
On what sea is Montenegro?
Who is in command of the French army?
Who is the Prime Minister of England?
Who is Von Bethmann-Hollwex? Poincaré? Venizelos? Briand? Von Hindenburg? General French? Sir Edward Grey? Viviani?
Name, with proper title, the ruler of Germany, Greece, England, Italy, Bulgaria, Russia, Turkey.

The results show a general neglect of current events in our institutions of higher education. No one gets every question right, and the averages of the various classes are usually between fifty-two and sixty-three per cent. Some cases show a surprizing degree of ignorance of the fundamental facts in the Great War, even among students of maturity, and in some cases teachers. The King of England was variously named as Edward V, Edward VIII, George II, III, IV, and VI. Gallipoli was located in Italy, Austria, Greece and Buda-

pest. Viviani was commonly supposed to be an Italian, but one student thought him a "Mexican general," and another a "poem by Tennyson." Montenegro was quite naturally placed upon the Black Sea, Salonica was supposed to be in Poland, Italy, Serbia and Turkey. Poincaré, it appears, is a "French artist."

The questions are not altogether well selected. It is, for instance, of little importance to know the name of the Sultan of Turkey, for he is less of a "ruler" than Enver Pasha, and those who persist in speaking of Albert as "King of Belgium" are not necessarily ignorant of what has happened there. But most of the questions ask for no more knowledge than is essential for the comprehension of what one reads in the daily newspaper.

The lamentable ignorance of this necessary minimum has been generally interpreted as indicating that our college students do not read the war news, and they have been scolded in many a chapel talk and editorial for neglect of the papers. To us the results of the quiz seem to show that they are guilty of something far less excusable. We fear that they *have* been reading the war news, but have made no effort to understand it. Such diligence and complete absorption in the required studies as to prevent a student from looking at a daily or even a weekly would indeed be unwise, but not discouraging. But to think that students of all people should read day by day the narrative of the epoch-making events now occurring in Europe without knowing or caring what it meant, is most appalling, for it shows that they have not yet learned how to read. It is better not to read at all than to read without any effort at understanding, for this habit is not only a waste of time but destructive to the intellect.

These students may, indeed must, know how to read books, but reading newspapers is a different art. The first thing to learn about it is to skip the headlines except as a guide to what the topic is. The headlines of the dailies are often unreliable and sometimes intentionally misleading as to the nature of the news beneath. To compare the history of the war as written in the headlines of certain American papers with the actual course of events would be an amusing tho profitless occupation. Second, it is impossible to understand the progress of a campaign without a map of the field of operations. Third, it must be remembered that the date and place at the head of the despatches are often put on in the office and so cannot be relied upon to indicate the source. Fourth, nearly all the cablegrams coming to us from any part of the world are subjected to British censorship, and the wireless messages from Berlin are subjected to German censorship. Fifth, the various belligerents differ widely in the authenticity of their reports, but none of them is as prompt and candid in admitting its defeats as it is in announcing its victories. Sixth, sending out false rumors of intentions and even false news of events is the custom of warfare.

But making due allowance for these things, it is quite possible for anyone to gain from the news a tolerably correct idea of the course of the war. For those who cannot give the time necessary for reading critically the full despatches day by day, the weekly periodicals provide a means for keeping well informed. There is no excuse for contemporary ignorance of one of the most tremendous periods in the world's history.

THE STORY OF THE WEEK

The Montenegrin Mystery — Last week our narrative closed with the capture of Mount Lovcen and the occupation of the Montenegrin capital by the Austrians. The next chapter, which would be still more exciting, cannot yet be written because the dispatches, triply censored in most cases, throw little light on the actions of the defeated King and leave his motives altogether in the dark. At the beginning of the week it was reported that King Nicholas had surrendered to the Austrians. In the middle of the week it was officially announced by the Montenegrin consuls that the King had never consented to surrender, but would stay and fight to the last. At the end of the week we learn that he has fled to France.

According to the first report the King of Montenegro, after the loss of Mount Lovcen had made his capital, Cettinje, thirty miles west, untenable, had retired into the interior. At Grahovo, thirty miles west, he is reported to have surrendered his sword to General Herlees of the Austrian army and issued a proclamation declaring that the country could only be saved from ruin by surrender and calling upon his people to receive the Austrian troops with rejoicing. All of the Montenegrin cabinet are said to have signed the agreement of unconditional surrender.

The Austro-Hungarian terms stipulated that the men in each district should be required to bring all of their arms to some designated place for surrender. This requirement, tho obviously necessary, was particularly objectionable to the Montenegrins since to them, as to Americans, "the right to keep and bear arms," is regarded as essential to a free people. The army, or part of it, refused compliance with these terms and under the leadership of General Martinovitch retired into Albania and established themselves at Scutari. This city, it is said, they propose to defend with the aid of the Albanian

THE GREAT WAR

January 17—British relief column within six miles of Kut-el-Amara. King Nicholas of Montenegro surrenders to Austrians.

January 18—Allies bombard Bulgarian port of Dedeagatch. Kaiser Wilhelm and Czar Ferdinand of Bulgaria meet at Nish.

January 19—Austrians attacking Italian positions on hights opposite Görz. Sweden resents British interference with her mails and commerce.

January 20—England calls to the colors 100,000 unmarried recruits between nineteen and twenty-two years of age. Montenegrin army will oppose Austria at Scutari, Albania.

January 21—Russians continue attacks north of Czernovitz. Yuan Shih-kai informs Japan that reestablishment of the monarchy is postponed.

January 22—Russians from Caucasus approach Erzerum. Austrians take Montenegrin ports of Antivari and Dulcigno.

January 23—King Nicholas of Montenegro flees to Italy. England raided by German aeroplanes.

troops of Essad Pasha, a curious instance of the whirligig of time, for it was Essad Pasha who three years ago defended Scutari for many months against the attacks of the Montenegrins and when King Nicholas finally got possession of the city, April 27, 1912, the British took it away from him and gave it to the Prussian Prince, William of Wied, who is now fighting Serbia to regain it.

King Nicholas blamed Italy for the loss of his kingdom. The French, he said, had given him guns and kept him supplied with food until Italy entered the war and assumed responsibility for the defense of the Adriatic. Since then Montenegro has been neglected and at the time of the surrender of Mount Lovcen his troops were fighting against odds of ten to one, altho they had not received rations for five days.

These reproaches aroused counter recriminations in Italy. Altho the Queen of Italy is the daughter of King Nicholas, the censor allowed the press to indulge in a furious tirade against him and even to cable abroad their accusations of treachery. He was charged with having made a secret compact with Austria some months ago by which he was to be given the Albanian town of Scutari and Serbian town of Mitrovitza in exchange for the surrender of Mount Lovcen to the Austrians. According to the alleged agreement the Montenegrins were to refrain from any active assistance to the Serbs and to offer only formal resistance to the Austrian invasion.

The indignation of the Montenegrin King and Queen at these accusations of bad faith and cowardice are surmised to be the reason why they refused to accept the hospitality of their son-in-law, the King of Italy, but past thru Rome on their way to Lyons without staying overnight. But King Victor Emmanuel and Queen Helena came down to the station at Rome to see Queen Milena of Montenegro and brought with them their children, Prince Humbert and Princesses Yolanda and Mafalda, whom their grandmother had never seen. With Queen Milena were two of her daughters, the Princesses Xenia and Vera. King Nicholas, who also had escaped thru Scutari, arrived at the Italian port of Brindisi, four days later. The Montenegrin Crown Prince, Danilo Alexander, has been for some time in Italy and Prince Mirko, who arrived there recently, will go back to the army at Scutari.

The Balkans — Another week has past and still the Teutonic and Bulgarian armies show no signs of moving on Salonica. On the contrary, it is reported that the 16,000 Austro-German troops who had occupied Monastir on the Serbian side of the Greek frontier have been withdrawn because of the difficulty of keep-

Underwood & Underwood

THE CROSSES

This photograph of a Russian military graveyard near Sokal is startlingly suggestive of the Raemaekers cartoon, "Kreuzland, Kreuzland, über Alles," which we reprinted last week

THE WAR IN ASIA

The British relief expedition going up the Tigris River has nearly reached Kut-el-Amara, where the army which tried to reach Bagdad has been besieged by an overwhelming force of Turks. The Russian expedition, which is advancing thru Persia in that direction, is between Hamadan and Kermanshah. Another Russian force is fighting the Turks west of Lake Urmia and a third has advanced half way to Erzerum. The object of these movements is to gain possession of the valleys of the Tigris and Euphrates, once the seat of rich and powerful empires and capable of being restored to their pristine prosperity thru irrigation. One of the main causes of the war was the conflict of interests between the Germans who were trying to enter this region by railroad from the west and the British who were working their way up by the rivers from the east

ing up communications, since the only railroad from Monastir runs to Salonica. The French and British at Salonica are therefore able to continue their work of fortifying the hills about Salonica without interruption except from the flying visits of the aeroplanes.

There are all sorts of unauthenticated rumors of further aggression by the Allies on the neutrality of Greece, such as demands for the expulsion of the German, Austrian and Bulgarian representatives, landings of Allied troops at Piraeus, the seaport of Athens, etc. The King of the Greeks has given out another interview to an American correspondent because he says he cannot get a hearing in the French or British press. In it King Constantine says:

It is the merest cant for Great Britain and France to talk about the violation of the neutrality of Belgium and Luxemburg after what they themselves have done and are doing here.

Just look at the list of Greek territory already occupied by the Allied troops—Lemnos, Imbros, Mitylene, Castelloriza, Corfu, Salonica, including the Chalcidice Peninsula, and a large part of Macedonia. In proportion to all Greece it is as if that part of the United States which was won from Mexico after the Mexican War were occupied by foreign troops—and not so much as by your leave.

What matters that they promise to pay for the damage done when the war is over? They cannot pay for the sufferings of my people, driven out of their homes. They plead military necessity. It was under the constraint of military necessity that Germany invaded Belgium and occupied Luxemburg.

It is no good claiming that the neutrality of Greece was not guaranteed by the Powers now violating it, as was the case in Belgium, for the neutrality of Corfu is guaranteed by Great Britain, France, Russia, Austria, and Prussia. And yet that has not made any difference in their action.

And what about that plea of military necessity? Where is the military necessity of destroying the Demir-Hissar bridge, which cost a million and a half drachme

and which was the only practicable route by which we can revictual my troops in Eastern Macedonia?

They say that they are occupying Castelloriza, Corfu, and other points in search for submarine bases. The British Legation at Athens has a standing offer of £2000, a great fortune to any Greek fisherman, for information leading to the detection of a submarine base, but never yet received any news about a submarine base in Greece, and never yet have any submarines been seen supplied from Greece.

In reply the Allies claim that they are not "occupying" Greek territories but only making temporary use of them with the tacit consent under the formal disapproval of the Greek Government, and that the population welcome their advent instead of opposing them as the Belgians did the Germans. "It was from the coasts of these islands or peninsulas that the pirates who sank the 'Ancona' and the 'Persia' set out." As for the bridges destroyed, they will be paid for later.

The German Emperor and the King of Bulgaria met at Nish, the former capital of Serbia, and exchanged compliments and honors. King Ferdinand was made a German Field Marshal and Emperor William honorary commander of the Twelfth Balkan Infantry Regiment. This is the first time that a German Emperor has visited Serbia since Frederick Barbarossa.

The Tigris Relief Expedition   One of the most remarkable campaigns in the war is that of which the outside world has heard the least, the British invasion of Mesopotamia. General Sir John Eccles Nixon, who was in command first, secured the head of the Persian Gulf and the oil fields to the north and then dispatched two expeditions into Turkey, one up the Tigris and the other up the Euphrates. The former under General Townshend had got to the ancient Persian capital of Ctesiphon last

November and London was expecting to hear that it had reached Bagdad, only twenty-five miles away, when it was met and defeated by an overwhelming force of Turks. The British beat a retreat downstream a hundred miles to Kut-el-Amara, a position on the northern side of the Tigris which the Turks had entrenched, but had failed to hold, as the British advanced up the river. Here General Townshend was compelled to stop and wait for reinforcements to come up the river, for he was enveloped on all sides by a force of Turks said to number 60,000 and commanded by German officers. The British troops are probably less than 40,000. Two British gunboats which tried to reach the besieged garrison were stopped by the shallow water. The Turks were well provided with artillery under cover of which they made repeated attacks upon the British trenches. On Christmas Day they managed to effect an entrance on the northern side, but were driven out with heavy losses.

The relief expedition under General Aylmer came up the Tigris to Shelk Said, an Arab village about twenty miles below Kut. Here they found the Turks entrenched on both sides of the river, but dislodged them on January 11, and pushed on to within seven miles of Kut. Here a battle took place last week in a heavy rainstorm. The losses were heavy on both sides and victory is uncertain. If the relief expedition can break thru the Turkish ring and the two forces united, the advance upon Bagdad may be resumed, for it should be easier for the British to get supplies up the rivers from the Persian Gulf than for the Turks to get them from Constantinople, for the German railroad probably lacks at least three hundred miles of reaching Bagdad. It is said that the Germans have brought from Constantinople 3000 automobiles to bridge this gap across the desert.

General Nixon, whose Mesopotamian campaign came to such an unfortunate ending, has been relieved of his command and recalled on the ground of ill health. Lieutenant General Sir Percy Lake, chief of the Indian staff, has been appointed to his place.

The Caucasian Campaign   In the effort to relieve the dangerous plight of the British on the Tigris, the Russians are sending two expeditions south from the Caucasus. One is advancing from the Caspian Sea toward Kermanshah, the headquarters of the Nationalists, as the Persians opposing Russian and British control of their country call themselves. They have received the support of Turks and Germans and have possession of many of the cities of central Persia. The Russian expedition has taken Hamadan and gone about fifty miles beyond toward Kermanshah. But even when they have reached that city there will still be 150 miles of mountain and desert between them and the beleaguered British garrison at Kut-el-Amara.

The other Russian offensive is directed toward Erzerum, which is about sixty miles southwest from the boundary line of the Russian province of Transcaucasia. The Russians undertook an invasion of Turkey in this quarter more than a year ago, but met with such stout resistance a few miles from the frontier that the effort was abandoned. The Armenians of this region welcomed the Russian invasion and in some places rose against the Turks because they had reason to believe that the Allies intended to set up an autonomous Armenia. But the failure of the Russians to occupy the country left the Armenians exposed to the vengeance of the Turks and more than a million have been massacred or driven into the desert to perish.

The new Russian invasion of Armenia began early in January with an advance across the frontier at various points on either side of Mount Ararat along a front of a hundred miles. Their chief point of attack seems to be the ancient city of Erzerum and in this direction they have got as far as Koprikoi, about twenty-five miles from their goal. The Russians took Erzerum in 1829 and again in 1878, but each time it was by the insistence of England restored to the Turks.

Restrictions on Commerce It is expected that Great Britain will soon declare a real blockade since it has become evident that the system of search and seizure is not preventing Germany from getting goods from neutral countries or even from the United Kingdom itself. France and Italy, which have hitherto been reluctant to sanction a blockade, are now said to be consenting. The United States, which has protested vigorously that the stoppage of shipping thru the British Orders in Council was unwarranted by law, could not object to a legal blockade. But according to international law a blockade must be effective, must be impartial and must not apply to neutral ports. Here is likely to arise the difficulty with the United States and other neutral powers, for the British fleet has so far not been able to control the Baltic Sea and the German imports which it is now desired to prevent come in thru Holland and the three Scandinavian countries.

These nations are already incensed by British interference with their commerce and any further restrictions are likely to alienate their sympathies from the Allies. Especially do they resent the action of the British authorities in searching their mail for contraband and subjecting their letters to British censorship. In retaliation for this the Swedish Government is holding up the English mail passing thru Sweden to Russia and has prohibited the export of chemically prepared wood pulp to England. This will increase the embarrassment of English periodicals, many of which have had to suspend publication on account of increased expense and less advertising. The British Foreign Office has assured Mr. Page, our Ambassador at London, that mail from American to neutral ports which has

been found on opening by the British censor to be "innocent" will be allowed to go forward without delay.

On the opening of the Riksdag the King of Sweden spoke strongly of the interference with neutral commerce. He said:

The belligerents have neglected in ever increasing degree the written international laws for the protection of neutrals and limiting violence in war. The Swedish Government has more than once been obliged to intervene against attempts to put Sweden's industrial and commercial life under the usurped control of another Power.

The seizure of the Swedish steamer "Stockholm" by the British fleet while on her way from New York to Gothenburg has caused intense feeling against England and some are urging that Sweden should enter the war on the German side not only for the protection of her commerce but to free Finland from Russia. The "Stockholm" when taken to Kirkwall was found to contain 1500 tons of oleo, pork and beef, which in the opinion of the British was more than was needed by the Swedes.

The Situation in Mexico Following Carranza's promise, given in response to Secretary Lansing's demand, that the murderers of nineteen Americans at Santa Ysobel should be pursued, captured and pun-

ished, three parties of troops were sent to look for Villa and his men. Villa they did not find. He was hiding in the mountain fastnesses with which he became familiar when he was a brigand. But Colonel Baca-Valles, who had been called Villa's executioner, was taken and brought to Juarez, where he was publicly put to death. His body was exhibited there by the side of the body of General José Rodriguez, one of Villa's commanders, who was recently at the head of 4000 soldiers. Colonel Ayana, also one of Villa's officers, had been captured and shot. Carranza, at Queretaro, published a decree declaring that Villa, General Costa, Colonel Lopez and certain other "reactionary leaders" were "outside the pale of the law," and authorizing any citizen to capture them and put them to death.

Hundreds of American refugees arriving at El Paso said that Villa's men were looting ranches and mines. In the vicinity of Torreon a considerable force composed of followers of Villa and Zapata, with men who had been in Huerta's army, had recently defeated a part of Carranza's army. The commander of this force is General Argumedo, who proclaimed his hatred of all foreigners. It is said that his men were shouting for Felix Diaz, and there has been published a story about a new revolutionary project in his interest which was

Underwood & Underwood

COULD THE SON-IN-LAW SAVE THE OLD KING?
Nicholas of Montenegro, driven almost to the last extremity, is father-in-law to Victor Emmanuel, king of Italy. The Italians have so far failed to strike any decisive blow on behalf of their Allies, small or great, in the Balkans

Underwood & Underwood
GERMAN SOLDIERS AS FRENCH JOURNALISTS
Mailing the 108,000 copies of the *Gazette des Ardennes* which the German military authorities publish three times a week for the people of the French territory which they occupy

recently the subject of inquiry by our Government. It was said that a loan was to be obtained in New Orleans, that 5000 men were to cross the boundary from Guatemala, that 5000 were to be added by the Governor of Oaxaca, and that Salina Cruz was to be attacked. Arms and ammunition were to be shipped to the soldiers by way of Guatemala. But Felix Diaz is in New York, and he says that, so far as he knows, the tale is all nonsense. He adds that Carranza should have a chance to restore order, but he does not believe Carranza can do it.

At the end of the week it became known that an American ranchman, James B. Akers, had been killed by two Mexicans while he was trying to recover stolen cattle, not far from Juarez. The Mexicans were captured by Carranza's soldiers and are to be put to death. Reports from Oaxaca said that the bodies of eight Americans were hanging from trees in that state. There was no truth in the published report that seven United States cavalrymen had been captured, on the Texas border, by Mexican bandits. Investigation concerning the murders at Santa Ysobel shows that at the request of Watson, one of the victims, Carranza had sent nearly 1000 soldiers to the mining settlement. Neither the Carranza authorities at Chihuahua City, nor the Wason party, thought that an armed escort was needed. Some say, however, that Watson had at first suggested that there should be one. The party had passports from Carranza officers.

Dispatches from Queretaro, Carranza's headquarters, say that he and his followers have decided to abandon Mexico City as a capital, and to build a new capital at Dolores Hidalgo, in the state of Guahajuato. They intend to sell nearly all of the Government buildings in the present capital, and think these can be sold for $50,000,000. Foreign Governments and foreign investors will suffer considerable loss by the proposed change. Dolores Hidalgo is a town of 6000 people.

The Question in Congress — In our Congress no action concerning Mexico was taken last week, but there were many speeches and a few additional resolutions. One introduced by Senator Gore provides for a neutral zone in northern Mexico, to be policed jointly by our army and Carranza's. When, as a part of the remarks of Senator Lippitt, the clerk began to read a newspaper editorial attacking President Wilson, objection was made, and the reading was stopped by vote of the Senate. Mr. Borah spoke in favor of immediate action upon a pending resolution, authorizing the President to use the army in Mexico. He was unwilling to wait for a report from the Committee on Foreign Resolutions. Mr. Lippitt referred to a published story to the effect that our Government had privately agreed with the six Latin-American nations represented in the Mexican Conference that it would not intervene without their approval. Mr. Stone said the story was not true. Mr. Lippitt remarked that if he had been in the President's place when the news of the Santa Ysobel murders came he would have sent the army into Mexico immediately and would have kept it there until every American resident was as safe as he could be in Washington.

In reply, Mr. Stone said he did not believe that many of the Republican Senators really thirsted for war. Those who had spoken indiscreetly and unwisely were speaking only for themselves. A declaration of war would break the hearts of the conservative and sensible men in the party. Mr. Newlands said it would not be difficult to push the nation into war with Mexico or Europe. He urged the Senate to leave the matter in President Wilson's hands.

At a meeting of the Foreign Relations Committee, Mr. Lodge and Mr. Borah argued for a favorable report authorizing the President to use the army in Mexico, saying that such a report would have weight with the Carranza Government and might assist Mr. Wilson. This was not the view of the Democratic members of the committee. They asserted that a favorable report would embarrass the President. Nothing was done. It is predicted that a motion to take the resolution from the committee and act upon it in the Senate would surely be defeated. The great mass of information called for by Senator Fall's resolution has not yet been sent to the committee, and therefore there has been no action upon the nomination of Mr. Fletcher, to be Ambassador. Senator Sherman introduced a resolution asking the Government about the story concerning an agreement with the six Latin-American nations.

In the House, Mr. Mondell, of Wyoming, made a speech in which he criticized the President's course with some bitterness. Mr. Wilson's policy, he said, had been not one of "watchful waiting," but one of "mischievous meddling, impertinent interference, base betrayal, and callous indifference to the welfare of Americans." The logical fruit of it was the murders at Santa Ysobel.

At the close of a ten Trust Suits weeks' trial in Philadelphia the jury brought in a verdict for the defendant in the suit of the Bluefields Steamship Company against the United Fruit Company, a corporation of large capital which has many steamships in the fruit trade with Central America and the West Indies. This was known as the Banana Trust suit, was brought under the Sherman act, the Bluefields company asking triple damages of $15,000,000, alleging that the defendant corporation, exerting influence partly by means of stock interest, had ruined its business.

By the Supreme Court at Washington the suit of the Government against twelve prominent transatlantic steamship companies—among them the Cunard, Canadian Pacific, White Star and Hamburg-American — has been dismissed. The defendants were accused of violating the Anti-Trust law because by agreement they had apportioned the steerage traffic. In the lower courts, four judges concurring, it was held that this was a "reasonable restraint of trade," but the use of what were called "fighting ships" against competitors who were not parties to the agreement was found to be unlawful. The suit is dropped because the agreement has become "void of actualities on account of the war."

In the Senate, Mr. Norris has introduced a bill making it unlawful for an interstate railroad company to purchase the stock of any other railroad company or corporation without first securing the consent of the Interstate Commerce Commission. This was suggested to him, he said, by the recent failure of the Government, in the suit under the Anti-Trust law, to convict any of the former directors of the New Haven Railroad Company. The minority stockholders of that company, who have sued those directors for $102,000,000, on account of losses alleged to have been caused by improper purchases of railroads and steamship lines, ask the Federal Court in Boston to permit them to amend their suit and to authorize them to proceed in the name of the company. They say the present directors will not proceed against their predecessors in any movement to compel restitution.

The suit for dissolution of the Corn Products Refining Company, which is accused of monopolizing the trade in glucose, is now on trial. Answering an inquiry, the Department of Justice says that the recent agreement of the National, American and Federal Baseball Leagues is not in violation of the Anti-Trust law.

Labor and Wages　Ten years of litigation in the Danbury hatters boycott case now ends with an order from the Federal court in New Haven for foreclosure proceedings affecting the real estate of 140 defendants. In nearly every instance the home of a union workman is involved. D. E. Loewe & Co., of Danbury, manufacturers of hats, sued more than 200 members of the hatters' union for boycotting them, and got a judgment of $252,000. To satisfy it, the property is to be sold. The defendants expect that other union men thruout the country will save them from loss, as the boycott was ordered or approved and supported by national unions. Both the American Federation of Labor and the national Hatters' Union have promised to aid the men in Danbury. The Federation has asked all of its members to make a contribution on January 27, equal to the pay for one hour's work.

It appears to be a foregone conclusion that the result of the balloting in the four great unions of railroad employees will be practically a unanimous vote of the engineers, conductors, firemen and trainmen of all the railroads in favor of the proposed demand for an eight hour day (instead of ten hours) with time and a half for overtime. The demand will be presented in the first week of March, and at one of the meetings of executive officers when the movement was started resolutions were passed saying that the unions would not again submit to arbitration.

In a strike riot at the works of the Edward Valve Company, in East Chicago, Indiana, on the 19th, one man was killed and five were wounded. A party of strike guards met a party of strike-breakers, whom they were to escort to the factory. Each party believed the other to be composed of strikers, and began to use their revolvers. In a short time the police and a considerable number of strikers were in the fight. The man killed was a guard. In New York the waiters' union, which recently won in a strike on the East Side, is about to call out 6000 men on the West Side. About 20,000 garment workers are on strike, and there are in-

dications that the number will be increased to 60,000 if certain demands are rejected. These demands are for a forty-eight hour week, a wage increase of 25 per cent, and improved conditions. In sixteen states the miners' agreements expire this year. The union has been holding a convention at Indianapolis. It is said that an increase of 10 cents a ton will be sought by the bituminous miners, and that those in the anthracite field will ask for an addition of 20 per cent.

To 25,000 men employed in the mines and smelting works at Butte, Anaconda and Great Falls, Montana, an addition of 25 cents a day has been voluntarily granted. An increase of 10

per cent, from February 1, has been given to 30,000 employees in the Michigan and Minnesota iron ranges. In New Bedford, 32,000 in the cotton mills are to have 5 per cent more pay. In a glass factory at Washington, Pennsylvania, 1000 will receive an addition of 8 per cent. At Syracuse, the Solvay Process Company is distributing among 8250 men special bonuses amounting to $414,000. By agreement with employers, the wages of the plasterers in New York City will hereafter be $6 a day. The Utah Copper Company gives notice of an increase of 25 cents a day, to be paid as long as the price of copper exceeds 20 cents a pound. The price is now 25 cents.

© *Underwood & Underwood*

AT NEW YORK—A ROPE-SKIPPING CLASS ON A HOTEL ROOF

© *International Film Service*

AT SALONICA—A BRITISH WAR NURSE MAKING CAMP
OUT-DOOR EXERCISE FOR WOMEN

FROM STATE TO STATE

ARIZONA: Many Arizona people are interested in the experiment being made by the Federal forestry service on 50,000 acres of the old Santa Rita range. Twelve years ago this range was withdrawn because it was "broken down," but now it is so far restored as to make it suitable for these experiments. The plan is to fence the range into four divisions, two being used for summer range and two for winter. Eight hundred cattle are to be turned in, this number to be increased or decreased as experience suggests, the object being to determine just how many the 50,000 acres will support throuout the year. Two distinct types of land are included in the range, one growing mesquite with scanty grass among the brush, the other growing grama grass, which ripens in the fall and makes excellent winter feed. Information gained here is to be applied to similar tracts in other states.

CALIFORNIA: Paul Shoup, president of all the electric railroads of the Southern Pacific Company in this state, says that, owing to the competition of automobile omnibuses and freight carriers, his railroads are not earning money enough to pay operating expenses, taxes and street paying; that they even have to borrow money to pay interest on their bonded indebtedness. He is campaigning the state in an endeavor to secure the passage of ordinances putting automobiles used for commercial purposes in competition with electric lines on an equal footing so far as taxes and franchise costs are concerned. Several of the cities and towns which his lines serve have promised him this relief.

COLORADO: In November, 1914, the electors of Colorado adopted statewide prohibition, to become effective January 1, 1916. In 1914 state liquor licenses were held by 1430 saloons, 345 drugstores, 69 clubs, 63 rooming houses, 31 cafes and 14 breweries. Most of these took out licenses for 1915 and did business up to the last hour. Authentic information as to the number of persons in the state employed in the liquor traffic on December 31 last is lacking, but in Denver, where there were 520 saloons, the Labor Council now says 5000 men were deprived of employment; and the council demands that Governor Carlson call a special session of the Legislature to provide work for them. Mass meetings of the unemployed and demonstrations on the grounds of the State Capitol are of frequent occurrence. Meanwhile other states, notably Pennsylvania, are crying aloud for men to help in their farm and manufacturing industries.

CONNECTICUT: The Boardman Apprentice Shops' have now been an established part of the New Haven public school system for more than two years, and the claim is made that they constitute the most

complete trade school of its character, and the first of its kind in America. The school is a business proposition and an educational institution combined. Contracts are taken for outside work and the pupil workmen are paid at regular union rates for these jobs. They are now building a handsome $8000 bungalow for a private citizen, the classes doing all the work to prepare it for occupancy. All the printing for the Board of Education and the renovating, plumbing, wiring, painting and decorating of the school buildings is done by these boys, while the girls cook for and conduct the school restaurants and carry on a large dressmaking department, filling orders for everything from a baby's dress to a wedding outfit.

IDAHO: Southern Idaho bids fair next year to be one vast seed farm. The success last year of the many farmers who raised great crops of clover, alfalfa, timothy and other products for seed has induced many others to specialize next season in these crops. In the Twin Falls country one farmer on fifteen acres raised $3000 worth of white cloverseed; another, near Buhl, put 320 acres to clover and alsike and received more than $15,000 for his seed crop; a third received upward of $10,000 for seed from eighty acres. In the seed bean section, near Wendell, twenty-two bushels were threshed to the acre, while near St. Anthony the seed pea crop brought more than $1,000,000, and in the Long Valley timothy seed threshed twenty-two bushels to the acre. Buyers from large seed houses took most of these crops at good prices.

NEBRASKA: The Omaha Bureau of Publicity has begun a campaign for the advertising of its city and state thru the medium of motion pictures of their principal industries and attractions. The plan is to show the pictures, accompanied by lectures, during thirty-minute daily periods, covering several weeks, in the public schools, the purpose being not only to inform the pupils, but also to make them "boosters" for their state. The pictures will also be shown to the general public of Nebraska before being sent on their advertising journey to other states.

NEW HAMPSHIRE: The question whether military instruction shall be given in the high schools of this state is provoking wide discussion. A plan which was some time ago laid before Henry C. Morrison, State Superintendent of Public Instruction, by the New Hampshire branch of the League for National Defense, met his approval in some respects, but he said he was not in favor of having our higher educational institutions become the chief medium of preparation for the national defense. "Military drill in the high schools," he said, "should be the smallest part of any con-

tribution which the young men might make to the national preparedness."

NEW JERSEY: For some time the physical supervision of children in Newark up to one year of age has been exercised by the Bureau of Child Hygiene. Now it is said the Board of Health intends to exercise similar supervision of children above one year old up to school age. Dr. Elmer G. Wherry, chairman of the Board of Health committee on child hygiene, says that children frequently retrograde after their first year and before they come under the supervision of the Board of Education. "Part of the economy inherent in extended supervision," says Dr. Wherry, "lies in the fact that if the child entered school in perfect health there would be little lost time in the school career and less backwardness in school work."

NEW MEXICO: A California syndicate is reported to have bought 21,000 acres fifteen miles north of Santa Fe, the purpose being to cut it into ten and twenty acre tracts, plant trees and crops and build a modern house on each tract, with a view to selling to colonists, who will be permitted to pay for the land and improvements out of the crops. The houses are to be built at once and the crops planted early in the spring.

NORTH DAKOTA: Under the constitution of this 'state school lands bearing lignite coal must be withheld from sale. A year ago the Board of University and School Lands with a view to selling lands in Burke, Divide, Dunn, Mercer, Stark and Williams counties, ordered an examination of them. State Engineer Bliss has just completed the task of examining 468,822.12 acres, of which he recommends the withholding of 265,068.35 acres as being coal lands under the constitutional definition. This is a much larger proportion of coal lands than was counted on when the constitutional provision was made. Now it is believed an amendment will be adopted under which surface rights may be sold while reserving 'title to the coal and all necessary rights of entry for the mining of it.

OKLAHOMA: The Oklahoma Federation of Women's Clubs is centering its efforts on the eradication of illiteracy in this state. For several years it has given prizes for literary productions and has advanced money to young women to enable them to secure college education and become self-supporting. Now the federation is establishing moonlight schools throuot the state and offering special prizes to volunteer teachers of them.

OREGON: Manager J. G. Camp, of the Klamath Falls branch of the Reclamation Service, is making the final test of a novel plan for reclaiming 80,000 acres of the finest agricultural land in Klamath County. Tule Lake is a broad, shallow body of water covering a

rich deposit of soil which rests upon a bed of lava. Not far away is a large fissure in the lava bed known as the "Big Crack." Manager Camp's plan is to bore a tunnel from the fissure to a point under the lowest part of the lake bed, then sink a shaft to meet it and let the lake drain into the Big Crack.

PENNSYLVANIA: The dairy farmers of this state are experiencing the greatest difficulty in obtaining help enough for the feeding and milking of their cows. The high wages paid by the manufacturing plants, especially by those producing munitions, have attracted not only country boys and regular farm hands, but also the "Boaters," who have been relied on in the past to furnish needed extra help. Then, too, immigration has been greatly reduced. Farm wages in this state have doubled in the last year, yet it is impossible, even with the aid of the state and Federal employment bureaus, to get men enough for the comparatively little work necessary upon farms in winter. Thinking forward to the planting season, some say prosperity may yet starve the state.

VERMONT: Of the 1816 accidents reported to the Vermont Industrial Accident Board in the first five and one-half months of its existence, 1327 were finally settled in that time either by agreement of the parties, approved by the board after investigation, or by order of the board after hearing. Of the remaining 489 more than half had been practically closed, but were not so classed because the final papers, showing that the medical expenses and compensation due had been paid, had not been filed. In no case had either side appealed from the decision of the board, and in only one case had either employer or employee been represented before the board by an attorney. Everybody concerned —and that includes nearly everybody in the state—seems highly satisfied with the working of the new law, which has saved so much time, litigation and money to both employers and employees.

WISCONSIN: The prohibitionists of Wisconsin hope to drive liquor out of the northern part of this state without the necessity of submitting the question to vote of the people. In 1854 large portions of northern Wisconsin, northern Minnesota and the upper peninsula of Michigan were set apart by the United States as Indian reservations, the treaties stipulating that no spirituous liquors should be sold or used in that territory. Minnesota temperance workers recently succeeded, after a long fight, in convincing the Federal authorities that the prohibiting clause in the treaty was not abrogated when the Indians ceded the lands back to the United States. Now Wisconsin temperance people claim that the Federal Government must enforce the prohibition in their state as it is enforcing it in Minnesota.

152

THE WORLD'S FUNDAMENTAL ERROR

BY DARWIN P. KINGSLEY

INTO the terror and chaos which today misrule the greater part of the world certain questions are increasingly thrusting themselves:

First, What was the fundamental error in the civilization of the world on August 1, 1914?

Second, What fundamental change must be made in order to correct that error?

Of written and spoken answers to the first question there is no end. Answers to the second question are naturally fewer, because the facts necessary to coherent thinking cannot be arrived at until the first question has been answered.

All the peoples of all the warring countries believe their cause is just, that they are fighting defensively for their existence. And the paradox of it is that all these beliefs are true. They are all fighting for existence and for fatherland.

I heard Dr. Bernhard Dernburg say in the early days of the conflict, defending Germany for her invasion of Belgium, that the act was a necessity, that a nation could not be expected to consent to its own destruction.

Commenting on our last and formal protest to Great Britain, against what we deem her violation of international law, and her disregard of the rights of neutrals, one of the great London dailies, justifying England's determination to retain control of the seas at all hazards, said "A nation cannot be expected to commit suicide."

These expressions from either side, almost identical in phraseology and absolutely identical in philosophy, reflect the existence of a cause of war not often referred to, under the compulsion of which, however, the whole world rests today.

THE flames which burst into a world conflagration fifteen months ago were not only already burning under cover fiercely everywhere in Europe, but unquestionably were lighted, unquenchably lighted when world civilization based on the doctrine of sovereignty began to take form centuries ago.

The civilization of 1914 rested on that doctrine. And what is sovereignty? Sovereignty is final authority, the thing greater than the law, that indeed protects the law. Sovereignty is the highest expression of authority in a civilized state, not inferior, however, to the authority of any other sovereignty, be that sovereignty physically greater or smaller, and not qualified in its completeness by any other power.

The president of the New York Life Insurance Company attacks the problem of international relations freely and directly in this address, which made a profound impression upon Mr. Kingsley's hearers at the recent annual dinner of the Chamber of Commerce of the State of New York.—THE EDITOR.

Pirie Macdonald
DARWIN P. KINGSLEY

This is the language of sheer authority, and sovereignty is the doctrine of authority. Democracy can no more live in its atmosphere than Jefferson's theory of inalienable rights can live in a world ruled by 42-centimeter guns and superdreadnoughts. Its demands are such that peace is now only a period of preparation for war. If any branch of human endeavor is anywhere developed along purely commercial lines, it is almost certain ultimately to be held an error. Highways should be built for military purposes; railroads should primarily be planned to transport armies; ships of commerce should be so constructed that they can be converted quickly into cruisers or transports. In obedience to the demands of sovereignty, the shadow of war rests over us at all times.

At the very outset sovereignty assumes that it must ultimately fight, that war is its true explanation, and, therefore, it reserves the right to take the last dollar of its citizens or subjects, and, if necessary, to demand the sacrifice of their lives as well. The favorite phrase of sovereignty runs this wise: "In defense of our liberties and our soil we will fight to the last man."

Whatever the form of government, the sentiment is the same. Behind that sentiment and in obedience to its necessities the prejudices, the provincialisms, the misconceptions, the hates, the fears, and the ambitions that so bitterly divide nations, were born. On the first of August, 1914, they had grown to uncontrollable proportions.

Add to these conditions the fact that we were living in the age of electricity, when the impalpable and imponderable ether had become not a dead wall, but a shining highway thru infinite space, when the spoken word was seized by a messenger whose speed and orbit far outreached the imagination of the people who kept and guarded for uncounted centuries that glorious word picture finally exprest in the first chapter of Genesis, and the conclusion is inevitable—in such an age, and in a world so small, a civilization based on eight great aggressive unyielding unconditioned sovereignties was no more possible without war than that two solid bodies should occupy the same space at the same time under the laws of physics.

Unconditioned sovereignty was the fundamental error in the civilization of 1914.

A STRIKING feature of this war is that its divisions do not follow the usual lines of cleavage. Neither race nor color nor religion is primarily responsible for the conditions in Europe, nor for the cataclysm which has occurred. Christians are fighting Christians; Jews are killing Jews; Moslems are against Moslems; whites are murdering whites; men of color are fighting their kind; Saxons are fighting their own breed; Slavs are against Slavs. The special favor of the God of the Christians is blasphemously claimed by both sides.

The ordinary causes of war had unquestionably decreased on August 1, 1914, but the hope which that fact held out to many of us proved finally to be a false hope. In the impact of unyielding sovereignties, in the fear which created a race in armaments, in the belief that national preservation was the supreme duty and sovereignty the supreme good, there was abundant fuel for the fires already lighted. The conflagration was certain. Every new invention by which time and space were annihilated, presumably bringing humanity

153

increased comfort and safety and happiness and efficiency, served even more markedly to increase international friction. Sovereignties were jammed together; they met everywhere; they jostled each other on every sea; they crowded each other even in desert places. They had no law by which they could live together. They could have none. Each was itself the law. When, therefore, thru the elimination of individual prejudices and provincialisms on the one hand, and the conquest of time and distance on the other, the world had reached a point where human brotherhood was conceivably attainable, humanity found itself in the clutch of this monster called sovereignty. Then came the tragedy! Not alone in squandered life and property, but in missing the great moment prepared thru centuries of human fidelity and suffering, the moment when humanity was prepared to see itself thru eyes suffused with sympathy and understanding rather than as now thru eyes blinded by hate and blood-lust.

THE people of the various great powers of the world in 1914 in fundamentals were not dissimilar. Never in the story of man's evolution had he been so nearly homogeneous. Everywhere he had approached common standards. His dress was much the same over most of the Christian world, and this uniformity had even made headway against the ancient prejudices of the Orient. He thought much the same everywhere. His standards of justice were strikingly alike. He was kindly and merciful. His vision reached far beyond the borders of his own land, and he was beginning to understand that all men are brave and should be brothers. The various instrumentalities that brought all peoples severely face to face, that promised still further to increase understanding and sympathy and therefore the prospect of peace, unhappily and finally had just the opposite effect. Men grew in international sympathy; sovereignties did not. Men dropt their prejudices; governments did not. The rigid barriers which geographically delimit nations became more rigid and more unyielding as individual knowledge grew and common sympathy spread. The light that penetrated to the individual and banished his bigotry could not penetrate national barriers as such. Its effect indeed was not to banish the darkness, but to cast deeper shadows. The condition that made men gentle made nations harsh; the impulse that drew the peoples of the world together drove sovereignties apart. The movement which foreshadowed a demo-

cratic world, the brotherhood of man, meant the end of the existing international order, and sovereignty instinctively knew and feared that.

So far as governments would permit, men made world-wide rules of action. They traded together internationally when tariffs allowed. They joined in great coöperative movements where race and creed and all the usual distinctions that separate men were ignored—ignored because men found when they came face to face that the old hates and prejudices were based on lies. The units of humanity became homogeneous; the units of civilization, the great sovereignties, did not. Here were two irreconcilable conditions. Sovereignties were in desperate straits. Each, menaced by every other, assumed that its integrity must be preserved at any cost. None was able to change its point of view; none was permitted to qualify its attitude toward other sovereignties, because each feared, as Shakespeare puts it, that

To show less sovereignty than they,
Must need appear less King-like.

No sovereignty except that of Germany saw it long ago. Sovereignty from the beginning meant ultimate world-dominion by some nation. It could mean nothing less.

THIS explains why the splendidly efficient machines of modern civilization, moving, from the standpoint of the individual, coöperatively, happily and helpfully under the guidance of powerfully advancing human sympathy, were on the first of August, 1914, suddenly swerved by the savagery of unregulated internationality and sent crashing into each other. How complete the ruin of that collision no one can yet tell! What was destroyed, or is to be destroyed, is not yet clear. Was it democracy? Or was it sovereignty? The ultimate destruction of one or the other is probable. World peace is possible under either, but not under both.

Out of this hideous ruin will sovereignty ultimately arise rehabilitated and increasingly aggressive? Will a group of powers finally emerge substantially victorious and will the controlling power of that group by perfectly logical processes gradually make its civilization dominant over the whole world? That is the only process by which sovereignty can ever bring permanent peace. So long as there are even two unconditioned sovereignties in the world, there can be no lasting peace.

Or is it possible that out of the ruin will come the revolt of humanity? Will a real Demos appear? A

democracy that has no frontiers, the Democracy of Humanity? Remembering not only the slaughter of 1914 and 1915, but the program of slaughter followed all thru the Christian era, will the people say with young Clifford in Henry VI:

Oh War, thou Son of Hell.

Is it conceivable that they may say to sovereignty—

You have in some things served us well in ages past. You have awakened in us heroic aspirations and led us to noble achievements; but now, alas! your hands drip with innocent blood, you are guilty of deeds which the beasts of the jungle would not commit—deeds that show you to be inherently and necessarily, in the present condition of the world, the arch enemy of the human race, and therefore we must now fundamentally modify your demands.

Milton, in the Sixth Book of "Paradise Lost," tells how Satan, rebellious, and all his hosts, after a terrific struggle, threw themselves headlong

Down from the verge of Heaven.

He tells us, too, how the Almighty stayed his own hand because

. . . . he meant
Not to destroy, but root them out of Heaven.

Flanders and Poland tell a tale of horror, record the use of machines and instruments of destruction, register a story of cruelty and hate, such as even the Miltonic imagination did not compass. The Satanic crew now busy in Europe, whether their blood guilt is the result of dynastic and race ambitions or, as I believe, the product of forces beyond their control, must in like fashion be cast out if we are ever to have peace in this world.

That process will raise profound issues here. The Transatlantic problem includes more than lies on the surface. What indeed of democracy? Will it again be strangled as it was at the Congress of Vienna a century ago, under the leadership of Austria and Prince Metternich? We are involved because if democracy has a future in Europe, it will largely be the result of its triumph here—a condition that Metternich and his fellow reactionaries did not have to face.

For a hundred and thirty-five years of organized life, and indeed thru all the years since the settlement of Jamestown and the landing at Plymouth, America has been the beneficiary of the human race. Wrapt in her all but impenetrable isolation, beyond the reach of dynastic ambition, and until recently substantially beyond the impact of other sovereignties, and therefore measurably unaffected by internationality and its savagery, she has taken to her bosom the restless, the wronged, the adventurous, the bold, the brave —of all lands, indeed she has gathered into her fertile soil seed sifted from all the world.

Our country has not been unworthy of the opportunity. With all her blundering, she has done well; and whether she is now to be branded as selfish after all depends on what she clearly stands for when this war closes. One great thing she has done —perhaps the greatest democratic thing that men have ever done. She has shown how so-called sovereign states can be merged into a larger state without losing their individuality and without parting with democratic principles. She has shown how local citizenships can coalesce into a master citizenship and yet remain vital. But, unless we misread the signs of Fate, she is now nearing the period when she must do more than that, or prove herself recreant and an unworthy beneficiary.

BEFORE considering what we should do in the interest of humanity, what we should do to discharge our obligation and our duty, let us consider what we should do at once, not as a measure of philanthropy, but as a measure of safety.

First, we should arm, and arm adequately; not because we believe in that theory of government; we do not, we hate it; nor because we believe in that method of settling international difficulties, but because we must at all hazards protect this home of democracy from the Satanic brood which, driven from Heaven, apparently fell in Flanders and Poland.

Second, we must at the same time try at least to show that we are as great as Fate has decreed that we may be.

"But specifically," you ask, "what should we do?"

We should signify our willingness to meet representatives of all the considerable powers of the world in an international congress, the purpose of which shall be similar to that of the convention which met in Philadelphia in 1787. That convention met in the historic mansion where the Declaration of Independence was signed. Those two great assemblages, the second no less than the first, have made the words "Independence Hall," in the imagination of the plain people of all the world, to shine like the Divine Presence over the Mercy Seat.

We should in that congress stand for the civilizing and humanizing of international relations by whatever steps may be necessary. If to do that the present doctrine of unconditioned

sovereignty must be abandoned, if as a nation we must surrender what each colony seemed to surrender in 1789, we should stand for that. We should find when the time came—as our fathers did—that we had actually surrendered only a little false pride, a little hate, a little prejudice and a little fear, and had entered, as the colonies did, upon the only order that leads to peace and true greatness.

If such a program were presented to the stricken people of Europe at this war's close, it probably would not raise any larger problem than Washington and Franklin and Madison and Hamilton faced in 1787. The whole civilized world is no larger nor more obsessed by prejudice than the colonies were then. You remember how bitterly they hated each other. Perhaps you recall what Mr. James Bryce says in his "American Commonwealth," that if the people of the colonies had voted directly on the adoption or rejection of the Federal Constitution, it would not have been adopted.

You certainly recall that New York State was against it, and the convention called to vote on it was hostile until Alexander Hamilton compelled acceptance by the force of his logic and eloquence. We narrowly missed reverting to political chaos.

John Fiske calls the years between the Peace of Paris and the adoption of the Federal Constitution the critical period of American history. So indeed it was. During that period prejudice was put aside, jealousies were overcome, hatreds were forgotten, and the common aims of the people, their natural sympathy, their homogeneity, were gathered up into a triumphant democracy.

No exact figures are available, but the population of the European states now at war—excluding Japan, Turkey, Asiatic Russia, and the Balkans—was at the beginning of the nineteenth century approximately the same as the population of the United States now. Our territory, geographically, is about equal to that of the countries I have included.

At the close of the Napoleonic Wars the people of Europe expected a new order and the end of war. They looked for the United States of Europe. Metternich and his associates denied that hope and so readjusted continental Europe as to strangle democracy. But the dream of the people was borne over seas and the United States of America in 1915 is the colossal fact which damns the continental sovereignties of 1815, and points the way to a regenerated Europe.

Emerging from this hopeless, senseless, and desperate struggle, the people of Europe will desire democracy as never before. They first brought democracy to us. Shall we now take it back to them?

We shall not, of course, reach the ultimate goal at one bound. A world state modeled after our Federal Constitution may be a long way off, but a real beginning would be a transcendent achievement. Ex-President Taft's League to Enforce Peace, with its modest suggestion of a modified sovereignty, if achieved would be worth centuries of European diplomacy.

We did not ourselves achieve peace immediately after 1789, nor a national citizenship, but after our feet were once fairly set in the way of the Constitution, the people would not be denied. Once the people of Europe feel their feet firmly set upon a road that leads away from the savagery which now commands them, away from the slaughter which periodically claims their sons, from the shame that claims their daughters, no dynastic or degamogic ambition can indefinitely deny them the achievement of the civic brotherhood which is the glory of America.

The people of Europe are not essentially different from us. They are bone of our bone and flesh of our flesh. The difference lies in this: We have been the darlings of fortune. We have realized the noble vision of democracy which Europe glimpsed and lost a century ago. After a hundred years of agony, the Fates bring again to those stricken peoples conditions not dissimilar to those of 1815.

IF now we arm—as we should—and do only that, we shall show ourselves a nation of ingrates. If we arm and say to Europe that we are ready at any time to disarm, ready with them to create an international state, a state in which the central authority shall act directly on the people as our Federal Government does—a state democratically controlled as our Union is—a state in which international questions shall be settled as our interstate questions are—a state in which war would ultimately become as impossible, as unthinkable as it now is between Massachusetts and New York—if we do that, aye, if we try to do that—we shall show ourselves morally at least to be worthy descendants of the intrepid men who signed the Declaration of 1776, worthy successors of the great democrats who fashioned the charter of our liberties in 1787.

New York City

THE CALL OF FLORIDA

BY E. P. POWELL

Mr. Powell, long a neighbor of Elihu Root at Clinton, New York, spent his winters on the shores of Lake Lucy, at Sorrento, Florida, and for several years before his death spent all his time there. The possibilities of Florida fascinated him and he wrote much of agricultural development there and elsewhere. This is the last article from his pen which The Independent has in its files.—THE EDITOR.

ONE of the most astonishing sights in the traveling world is the annual flow and flux of tourists in Florida. It starts when the snow begins to bluster in Maine and Minnesota; and the tide turns back when the winds grow mild in Massachusetts. It is exactly like the passage of birds, and for the most part it ends in a sort of robinade. Robins and bluebirds come South to feed and flutter in our bayheads, and pass away the shortest and coldest days. They gather in huge flocks to reach us, and they go North in the same flocks in March. Tourists differ only in that they are picked up by railroads, stop at notable stations, herd in costly hotels; and when they go North know little and have seen little of the real South.

Florida is almost the same size as New England, and one would know very little of New England if he confined his tours to Boston and Providence. I have seen tourists of a dozen years who did not know that the backbone of Florida, for seventy-five miles north and south, was a ridge of hills; and who had never seen the hundreds of lakes which gem the whole of the center of the state. Florida in reality is a vast tropical garden thrust out into the ocean; but at the same time it is becoming a stock farm for the whole of the United States. The palms are mainly along the coast, and with them are the swamps and alligators. The orange country and home-building land lies more inland. It is here that our Northerners should find their way, not only to escape the cold and find the best of all climate, but to discover the real values of the peninsula. I was fortunate enough to be dumped in the very heart of the state, and here I found the conditions so admirable that I have constructed my old-age home on Lake Lucy, among the orange groves and loquats.

A neighbor of mine, a Pittsburgh millionaire, tells me that after searching the world for a wholesome climate, he found nothing better than central Florida. If you want to find his home, you will get off at a little station, in no way associated with wealth, and trek it down thru the pine woods, until you come to a ninety-thousand-dollar ranch; but you will see at a glance why he came here; the lake on the borders of which he has built is one of the deepest and sweetest bodies of water you ever saw. It is just big enough for one man to hold as his private possession. All around here you will note his Jersey cows, his velvet-bean fields and his cow-pea gardens, and groves of oranges and grape fruit.

Five miles away we come upon another sort of ranch, that of a Chicago merchant. Here you find stock raising carried on extensively, pointing the way to what Florida must do in the immediate future. It is going to breed cattle to rival Argentine, and to replace the lost ranges of Texas. Home-building will go on in Florida in spots, but a vast part of this Southern New England will be given over to herding cattle, with goats and sheep. It looks now as if the Jersey and Guernsey would rival each other, but the Swiss-belted are going to have something to say about it. All this will end in a Florida cow, a cross of the tough little native with the best and most successful hybrid. You should see the effect on the better stock, having full pasture range for nine months of the year or ten; and ultimately to be fed bought rations only for two or three months. We have new grasses that will serve all the purposes of timothy and bluegrass, and there will be plenty to export. Natal gives us fine crops for mowing on high pine lands, and Rhodes grass does full as well on low lands. Velvet beans are just as good as cottonseed meal or a little better, for protein, and cow pea hay cannot be surpassed. My Jerseys play like kittens, and act more as the Ayrshires do in the North, frisky and frolicsome.

The effect of the climate on folk is no more enervating. There are more hot noons; but we get in the tropical habit of staying indoors from eleven until three. We get quite as much work done, taking advantage of the cool mornings and the cool evenings. Beside this habit of working early and late, we have the whole year to work in. One does not get accustomed to a winterless year, a year when the plow can be put into the soil every day, and winter gardens are planted as regularly as summer gardens. We plant potatoes in January, and then again in September; lettuce, cabbage, and green peas coming almost every month in the year. I cannot say that we do not get a little more tired of some of these delicious foods than if we had to wait for them till midsummer. Mosquitoes we have; but in the lake region they are kept well under by the fish in the lakes, that swallow the larvæ. Malaria we leave to the marshy sections, and these are not one whit worse than in New Jersey and Michigan.

The passion of Florida just now is good roads. County after county is voting to bond itself for improvements of this sort. The main lines are being constructed, in some cases paved brick; in other cases with clay, which, spread over the sand a few inches thick, dries into a solid roadway not likely to be broken up. Where the strain is not so heavy, pine needles, which can be raked up anywhere under the pines, make a very good driveway. It will be a good many years, however, before the bulk of the driving follows any other lines than the cattle trails under the trees. The state where the razor-back lorded it, and wild cattle had their own way up to within five years, is rapidly coming under the control of stock laws. The automobile has to be credited with much of this change, and with more ahead.

By all means the tourist or the homeseeker, going to Florida for the winter, should hire a cottage. Chasing about in rail cars gives him, at the very best, a narrow vision and false opinion of the territory. Let your cottage be somewhere in the central part of the state, but near enough a town to hire a motor; provided you do not own one yourself. It is possible to get such a cottage for about $25 per month, nestling on the banks of a small lake and in easy reach of the post office, depot and stores.

Make sure that the cottage is free from infection; is not already the property of mosquitoes; and that the water supply is perfect. These are vital points, and they are exactly where you are liable to discover neglect. It is a curious suggestion, but important, that you demand a cellar under the house. For an unknown reason central Florida has imitated the coast sections, and left out the cellar. This is utterly without excuse, for a good cellar I know to be possible and wonderfully enjoyable. Without it you have no place to store your vegetables, and, during a hot summer day, a really good sub-

A LAKESIDE IN FLORIDA

THE BACKBONE OF THE STATE IS A
RIDGE OF HILLS GEMMED WITH
HUNDREDS OF LAKES

apartment makes a cool room for your rocking chair.

Now from this "pou sto" start out, as you get the inspiration, and hunt up the state. Three or four of these excursions, in your own automobile, will show you more than you would get in a month of railroad traveling.

Be sure not to locate near a swamp, and listen not at all to land sharks. Look for yourself, and observe for yourself, even where the towns are of good size, and the land fairly well settled. It will take at least half a century to make a large part of this state comfortably inhabitable. Old traditions are also as thick as mosquitoes. I found at Sorrento that commercial fertilizers were so much in demand that the value of crops was about used up before getting them. The art of making soil, and the use of lime; especially the value of legumes and of all sorts of weeds was a part of agriculture not yet apprehended. Even barnyard manure remains unused, to breed flies.

Another peculiarity of these frontier counties is the passion for getting rich quick. The majority of settlers exhaust their surplus money rapidly, in speculative crops—with the possibility of coming out at the end of the first year or the second, bankrupt. Melons are a fascinating crop, grand to look at, when paving forty or fifty acres with forty-pound fruit; but this crop invariably runs a gauntlet of ravenous middlemen. Citrus fruits turn in a fortune occasionally; but it is by no means certain that the annual crop will be profitable.

The settlers first conviction will be that Florida soil is worthless; tho he sees that it has been able to grow great forests of pine and oak, eighty feet tall. He has to learn in the first place that the soil is very sour, and needs a heavy annual dose of lime; and, if he has not a supply of barnyard manure, he will need to supply commercial fertilizers until he can grow legumes and plow them under, but no longer. He will wonder at the provision of Nature to secure fertility. Hardly anything else is growing wild but legumes; and if he will make the conditions such that he can plow them under, as well as feed himself and cattle from them, he will soon have the fattest soil that was ever cultivated.

The Northern farmer will not know anything about what to do with a climate that is divided into a dry season and a wet season. It rains every day in haying time, and it very seldom rains thru the winter, that is, during the six months beginning with November. A home in Florida needs a a good well and a big cistern to tide over dry spells.

The one thing I have missed above all others in Florida is brooks. I would immensely like to see a brook here and there, gurgling, laughing, tumbling, and playing as only a brook can. The best substitute is a small lake, half a mile to a mile across; full of fish, while the herons and egrets surround it, doing their own fishing, and flocks of ducks play over the surface; while during the winter robins and bluebirds crowd the bayheads that pour into the lakes by the thousands.

As to what crops you should plant, you need to decide nothing at all till you get here. Nine settlers out of ten begin at once with speculative crops, such as the citrus fruits and melons. If the object be to create a home, begin with such fruits, cereals, and so forth, as can be consumed by the family. All our Northern vegetables, potatoes, tomatoes, beans, cabbage, thrive as well here as in Ohio. I am growing apples, pears, plums, quinces; and should have plenty of cherries, only that they forget the calendar—blossoming out whenever it happens. Peaches and pears frequently do the same thing; yet we have new sorts of peaches and of pears, from China, that do remarkably well; and they have crossed with the older sorts. We are in sight of something superb.

Yet you cannot possibly find in Florida a duplicate of New York or New England. You have not only to work all the year round, but you must learn some features of farming entirely novel. As for the ordinary tourists, whether they come for a short season or for a home, in the bulk no more whimpering set can be discovered on the globe. Homesick from the outset; uneasy, restless, on the go, hunting for a place that will demand nothing of them, as to their brains; and little as to their hands. The Florida home builder must be content to be a pioneer, and build from the bottom up, with as much self-denial and persistence as characterized the New Englanders when they went westward. With such settlers Florida is destined to lead the states in agricultural industry.

STONEHENGE

BY BATTELL LOOMIS

(Stonehenge was recently bought from the estate of Sir Edmond Antrobus by a Mr. Chubb)

O Lean, long lain! O Lean, long lain!
Where are thy graves, O Neolithians?
Where are thy tombs that ye burst not from them?
Lean men—lank of hair, thin of shank and belly-spare—
Hurlers of bronze at dinosaurians,
Masters of mammoths, foes of the bear,
Wild in thy worship—who built to the Sun
Or the Serpent a temple ere God had begun—
Where are thy graves, O fierce Neolithians!

Strong tho thy tombs, ye should burst them asunder,
Raising the wail of thy war-cry like thunder,
Warriors, quarriers, keen in revenge,
Time's obese insult is on thy Stonehenge!

O Lean, long lain! O Lean, long lain!
Is the callous clean gone that once crackt at thy labors?
Do ye forget how at midnight and morning
Ye toiled at the ways?

Do ye forget how thy stern Druids charg'd thee?
Delay not to fortify praise.

How grew yon trilithons? Dost not remember
The heating with fire, the hissing, the Ember
Enthusiasm!
Living past flame and the waters that choke it,
The heave of thy back and the heft that nigh broke it,
The craft of the shirker who hit on the lever
(Ere Archimedes)
And his who twined vines that by tribal endeavor
The vast bars should rise in their circle of wonder
To rest on the up-stones thy great will thrust under?

Wake, Masons of Stonehenge, unearth the fell club
That beat back the she-wolf and finished the cub,
Warriors, quarriers, keen in revenge,
Time's obese insult is on thy Stonehenge—
Thy world-marvel's sold to none other than Chubb!

THE FINE ART OF SKATING

BY GEORGE H. BROWNE

AUTHOR OF "A HANDBOOK OF FIGURE SKATING," "THE NEW SKATING"

LIFE is short, art is long; and few arts are longer than the beautiful modern art of skating. All praise, therefore, to the deft performers on the New York Hippodrome stage and other metropolitan ice-surfaces, if they succeed in rousing Americans to a real appreciation of the possibilities of this wonderful art of physical self-expression. But expensive skating equipment and professional instruction will not alone, or very quickly, make artistic skaters, no matter how ardent the "craze" for dancing on the ice. Any couple may have great fun in waltzing and in two-stepping with the sprawl and the clatter of the old American "locomotive" figures, instead of in quiet, rhythmic, gliding form; and in the sunny winter out of doors, this vigorous exertion on skates may be as exhilarating and health-giving as any sport on the calendar; but it is not "skating," according to the standards of the latest developments of the art. These require patience, persistence, and esthetic sensibilities—not so much exceptional strength, as skill in the expenditure of moderate force—not so much expensive skates and costumes, as the intelligent appreciation of the problems to be solved. The solution is within the power of nearly everybody, old and young; but it is not to be bought; it is to be won only by intelligent study, consistent practise, and some hard work; yet the struggle with the difficulties is the most fascinating in the whole realm of combined physical and intellectual effort, and the accomplishment is worth all the effort it costs. For of one thing, at least, we may be sure: all that is claimed for physical self-expression in its most artistic form, esthetic dancing, may be claimed with greater force for artistic skating, for the simple reason that in skating, the gliding motion is continuous—there are not the unavoidable pauses that turn the graceful poise, even for a moment, into a rigid pose. This superiority of skating as a means of physical self-expression is ample justification for the effort needed to overcome the technical handicap of skates; a handicap, however, which in these days of improved tools and instruction is reduced to a minimum. Balance on the skate-edge once acquired, however, the freedom of action in skating, quite as complete as in swimming, is nearer than in dancing to the perfect freedom of flying; which, alas, is not yet attainable by man. The possibility of physical self-expression, therefore, thru the freedom of skating, is practically unlimited.

The recent revelation of these possibilities by the European professionals, expatriated by the war, strikes the American public as something new. There is, however, nothing new about the skating they represent except its simple system. The elements of all figure-skating have been reduced to two, the curve and the turn (on one foot). Combinations of these outside and inside edges and turns, forward and back-

AN INSIDE FORWARD AND OUTSIDE BACKWARD HAND-IN-HAND SPIRAL.
The skaters are Miss Edith Ritch and F. F. Munroe of the Skating Club of Boston

ward, together with loops, pirouettes and jumps, make up all the figures skatable. The fine art of the new skating in the International Style, however, is chiefly in the manner of execution, or in good form—arms and legs slightly bent, and all members of the body contributing to an artistically beautiful performance on the ice, which by the grace and charm of its harmonious movements, may satisfy the esthetic sense of both performers and spectators. Experience has proved that for the execution of every figure, there is usually one position and movement that is easiest and most conducive to success. These positions often strike the beginner as unnatural; but the finer balance required by the more difficult figures makes it economical for the beginner to learn the correct positions at the start, even if they seem at first like artificial poses. To make these positions and movements easy and natural is the challenge and the charm of the art. Grace is the perfect, responsive obedience of a moving person's body to his will, the perfectly adequate expression of that will in his positions and movements. Not, however, until the positions and movements required by the new skating can be assumed unconsciously and automatically, can the skater be graceful. No physical attribute is more to be desired than rhythmic grace. Some can never acquire it. None can acquire it more quickly or more effectively than in modern artistic skating. Modern artistic skating, therefore, is the finest of physical arts.

Some of the beauties of this fine art are being daily revealed to theater goers by professional skaters, chiefly from Berlin. Their evolutions, however, savor too much of the very kind of skating that fifty years ago Jackson Haines revolted from in the New York Skating Club. He carried to Europe in 1865 no great repertory of figures—rocking turns had hardly been discovered—and he died (1875) before the first bracket was skated; but he was a dancing master by profession, and tho he "always skated alone," he introduced into Vienna long.

159

graceful, sweeping curves and dance steps to music —a style which the dance-loving Viennese soon developed into pair-skating. The Jackson Haines American style and the Jackson Haines two-stanchion, round-toed skate immediately spread all over Europe.

The British, meanwhile, had brought their big, flat curved, stiff, combined skating to a high state of perfection. During the '80's the Continental Style, as expounded by the Viennese School, was modified by the addition of the new rocking turns on big (English) circles; so that when the International Skating Union was formed in the early '90's, a new style of skating was ripe for standardization in the annual European and World's Championship competitions that the Union began to hold. The holding of the World's Championship for 1898 in London opened the eyes of the British to the resources of the Continental Style, and the National Skating Association adopted it in 1900. In that year I published, in my *Handbook of Figure Skating*, an exposition of the Continental Style, from the official documents and from correspondence with European skaters; and in the winter of 1902-3 I saw it for the first time. On my return, I published a full exposition of the International Style (1904) and began to demonstrate it on a pair of Jackson Haines skates which Salchow, the world's champion, sent me from Stockholm. My crude efforts undoubtedly deserved the ridicule I endured (I was forty-five years old!); but I stuck to it, and now the laugh is on my side. Irving Brokaw, who won the United States championship in 1906, took up the International Style the next year, and in February, 1908, with Karl Zenger (Champion of Germany in 1905), gave on Greater Boston rinks the first exhibition of pair-skating in the International Style in this country. He is today our most accomplished skater in this style.

A PAIR-SKATING FIGURE
George Müller and Fräulein Elsbeth Müller, instructors at the Boston Arena, skating thru a long spiral

Boston skaters had long been practising English combined skating in a compromise style; so that when the Arena was built in 1909-10, there was an appreciable number of accomplished skaters ready to profit by the professional instruction which

THE NATIONAL CHAMPION PAIR-SKATERS
Miss Theresa Weld skating with Nat W. Niles on Hammond's Pond, Brookline, Massachusetts. Niles is a ranking tennis player

the Boston Club has since enjoyed for six consecutive years. It is not surprizing, therefore, that Greater Boston has had for several years the best skaters in the United States in the International Style.

The Skating Club of Boston has exchanged friendly visits with the Minto Club of Ottawa (1904), and the Winter Club of Montreal (1908), and their competitions have brought out the best International skating in America. No European or world's champion has ever come to the United States; but, thanks to the generous efforts of Mr. Brokaw, the Skating Union of America held the first competition in the International Style at New Haven in March, 1914, in which Norman Scott, of the Winter Club of Montreal, won the Men's Championship. Miss Theresa Weld of the Skating Club of Boston, the Ladies' Championship, Mr. Scott and Miss Chevalier, of Montreal, the Pair-Skating championship, and Mr. Nat W. Niles and Miss Weld, of Boston, the Waltzing Championship. Last year there was no International competition either here or abroad; but the New England Association held a competition in Boston, in which the Men's Championship was won by William P. Chase.

The illustrations printed herewith tell better than words of the charm of this style. The sensations of these exhilarating big curves and spirals in graceful form, the accurate striking and gliding, partners coming together and separating in perfect rhythm with each other and with the beat of the music, the limitless combination of figures, control of which challenges the intellectual and physical skill and ingenuity of young and old alike—provide a variety of physical and esthetic pleasure and a free opportunity for self-expression, such as no other out-of-door sport provides; for skating of this kind is sport and art in one, and can be acquired earlier and pursued later in life than any other.

Cambridge, Massachusetts

HOT SOUP

FRENCH SOLDIERS REST WARMLY BY A

THE GREATER ENGLISH NOVELISTS

BY EDWARD EVERETT HALE, JR.

THE last few months have seen a good many novels of note in England. Probably most people would agree that the most eminent English novelists of our day are Arnold Bennett, H. G. Wells, John Galsworthy, and Joseph Conrad. Of these the first three have produced works which may be reckoned among their best. Next to them in current interest at least come the younger group, Hugh Walpole, D. H. Laurence, J. D. Beresford, Compton Mackenzie, Oliver Onions, and George Cannan. These have not written so much, but Mr. Walpole and Mr. Mackenzie have published books which, if not so large in scope as the work by which we have come to know them, are excellent in their kind. To them should be added Mr. W. Somerset Maugham, hitherto best known as a dramatist, whose *Of Human Bondage* was lately republished in this country. But best worth reading are the books of the three who would count as England's most distinguished novelists. Mr. Conrad rests on the laurels of his *Victory*, which by this time is well known.

Mr. Arnold Bennett's *These Twain* has long been looked for with interest, and now that it has appeared it has probably answered all expectations. A trilogy would seem to be a dangerous thing; it is said that continuations are dangerous, but to go on continuing! Perhaps such books are not continuations; it may be that all three are implicit in the very beginning. One cannot say. Even in these days of literary gossip and confession nothing that you want to know about authors can be found out. The real secrets of authors are well kept. At the end of *Clayhanger* the author indicated *Hilda Lessways* and *These Twain*; perhaps he had it all in mind from the start, beginning with Clayhanger on the bridge looking forward to life he ends with Clayhanger on the bridge looking back over experience. Between the two have passed many years and with the years the boy has grown into a man. But it is the same Edwin just as it is the same Hilda, as real and living at the end as at the beginning, and just the same however different, like the people around them. Not pleasant people to live with, one may think, but people it is good to read about nevertheless. For—as is the way with Arnold Bennett—one sees that life, even the life of such obviously dull and disagreeable people (not all of course, but a good many of them) has in it something fine and, if not noble, at

*Readers will be interested in comparing this study of the recent work of the older English novelists with the article on several of the younger men, "The New Realists," contributed to The Independent for August 30, 1915, by Dr. Hale, who is professor of English in Union College.—*THE EDITOR.

least distinguished. (And if this be so with such as Edwin and Hilda, Clara and Auntie Hamps, how much more with nicer people like ourselves.) The three books make for Arnold Bennett sufficient title to fame. He can almost vie with Richardson in the matter of length, and he can certainly vie with that great master of the secrets of the human heart in the largeness of his appreciation of life.

Mr. Wells is, of course, a very different sort of person, whether greater or less is a matter of little immediate importance. His *Research Magnificent* is not (I feel) one of his greatest works, but it is very characteristic. It is not exactly one of the autobiographies which he foretold in *The World Set Free*, of which he there gave a specimen in his extracts from Frederick Barnet's *Wanderjahre*, but it is of much the same kind. A little of the irregularity of real life is given by the fiction that Benham's papers have been turned over to White to make a book of, and that the novelist turns about and about in his material as Carlyle was distracted in the largeness of his work with Wells. Benham is the successor of George Ponderevo in *Tono-Bungay*, of Remington in *The New Macchiavelli*, of Stratton in *The Passionate Friends*. The man sets out to live a fine life, or at least to determine (for posterity?) what is most of a limitation. He sees particularly fear, sex, jealousy, prejudice—the last enemy to be conquered —one feels that he might have generalized as was done centuries ago and say, once for all, *Self*. It is wonderful that a man can go on and on, talking of his ideas for the regeneration of the world, and make us think that he is telling of men and women, of Benham and Amanda—but Mr. Wells can do it.

Mr. Galsworthy's *The Freelands* belongs not so much with *The Dark Flower*, which preceded it, as with the earlier books by which he became known. Those five books presented Mr. Galsworthy's indictment,

we may call it, of the complacent conventionality of the upper half of society. *The Patrician, The Country House* and *The Island Pharisee, Fraternity*, and *The Man of Property* gave us a view of the nobility, the landed gentry, the "intellectual," the middle class of business people, and showed how in all of them life meant the crushing of the original man or woman, the idealist, the adventurer, the wanderer, anybody whose own life was more important to him than the way other people chose to live and look on life; they were in a way an incentive to revolt, if not a textbook of revolution. After that demonstration Mr. Galsworthy seemed rather to settle back and view life with less of definite criticism, tho still ironically as always. In his next novel, *The Dark Flower*, he had in mind no especial element of our present civilization, but one of the necessary limitations of life in general as we know it. In *The Freelands* he has in mind something particular, the dominance exercised by the landowning class, and the extension of that influence over the lines and affairs of other people.

It is worthy of mention that in none of these books nor in any other of the best English fiction of the year do we get an echo of the war nor anything that seems a direct influence of it. Mr. Walpole, it is true, pauses in his study of the spirit of our century of which *The Duchess of Wreze* was a beginning, to give us a fanciful view of childhood in *The Golden Scarecrow*. Mr. Compton Mackenzie's *Plashers Mead* is a tragic episode in a life something like that of Michael Fane. Mrs. Ward's *Eltham House* is based on a suggestion of nineteenth century history transferred to the earlier years of the twentieth. Sir Gilbert Parker's *The Money Master*, tho perhaps suggested by thoughts and feelings aroused by his own work for England, yet bears no obvious mark of connection with the great events now stirring the world.

England is said to be powerfully moved by spiritual forces, and it would be astonishing if it were otherwise. But it would be hard to find in the best English novels much that we might not have expected had England been at peace. It is not strange. Our own great civil struggle, which is the thing most like the present war that we know anything about, produced little in fiction till many years after. It may well be so in England today.

Schenectady, New York

162

THE SILHOUETTES OF CAPRI

BY EULALIE OSGOOD GROVER

WEARING a loose gray robe, and with sandaled feet, Karl Wilhelm Diefenbach presents a striking figure as he moves thru the narrow streets of the quaint old town of Capri, that delightful place whose people, from the happy, dark-eyed peasants to the owners of beautiful villas, appear to have drunk from the fountains of joy and peace.

Many years ago Herr Diefenbach was exiled from his northern home because his ideas concerning life and religion were too radical to be tolerated in his home autocracy. He believed that all men should be free and equal, and should live at peace with each other. He believed that it is not God's will for man to feed upon the weaker animals, but that men and animals are essentially alike, differing only in the degree of their development. Because of this belief he was considered demented and, as a dangerous citizen, was compelled to leave his Fatherland.

He found his Paradise, as he calls it, on the lovely island of Capri, and there he is living his quiet life in undisturbed happiness. Many young artists seek him there to study the mystery of his palette and the delicacy and charm of his drawing.

He attempts to make no proselytes for his philosophy of life, tho he enjoys talking of it with those who care to listen.

On the hights of Anacapri Herr Diefenbach has an exhibition studio, to which these artists and art lovers find their way. But Diefenbach's drawings are known to thousands who have never visited Capri, and especially to the children, whose naïve outlook on life he has never ceased to share.

His most unique and strikingly beautiful work is the frieze painted in black silhouette upon the stuccoed walls surrounding his tropical garden. It is a series of running, leaping, dancing figures of children and animals, the very incarnation of

Illustrations © and Published by the Prang Co., New York

A GAY FRAGMENT FROM "PER ASPERA AD ASTRA"

grace and gaiety. Single figures, also in silhouette, are painted above doors and windows, and all are equally charming.

Thirty-four of these pictures are reproduced in panel form to illustrate a long poem by the artist, which he entitled: "Meines Lebens Traum und Bild; auf Rauher Bahn zu den Sternen hinan," or "Per Aspera ad Astra."

The picture and poem together make a masterly plea for

Frieden auf Erden,
Für Menschen und Tiere,
Heiligen Frieden der ganzen Natur!

Indeed, we have in this combination poem-picture a noble peace epic.

Tho well along in years, Herr Diefenbach, in his quiet corner of the world, is doing original work without thought of reward. Much of this work deserves to be ranked with the best of modern European art. His color is vibrant and realistic; his drawing is true and full of grace; his subjects and design reveal the poet and philosopher.

But to the world and the world's children he stands as the sympathetic creator of those rippling, elfish processions of light-hearted youngsters who skip thru the silhouettes of Capri.

Oberlin, Ohio

163

The New Books

THE MONROE DOCTRINE

Our most disputed public policy could have had no better interpreter than Professor Albert Bushnell Hart, of Harvard University, whose study of *The Monroe Doctrine* is a storehouse of information and intelligent comment, not only upon the relation of the United States to Latin America, but also upon its position in the world at large. The book is careful and scholarly but at the same time racily written; a perpetual quiet chuckle at the irony of events runs thru the volume to the delight of the reader. For example, after severely criticizing Secretary Olney's aggressive attitude towards Great Britain in the Venezuela boundary dispute of 1895, Professor Hart continues:

All the suavity of Seward, the courtesy of Evarts, and the fineness of Blaine, had not availed to break up the notion that the British Empire was a great power in America, as well as in Europe, Asia, Africa, and Australia. The rough and inconsiderate despatches of Olney and the undiplomatic firmness of Cleveland accomplished that miracle.

Professor Hart narrates the chief political events in the history of the Doctrine and its various interpretations given in "the formal statements of ten presidents and twenty secretaries of state." The narrative is, in general, well presented, altho the author seems to have confused (on page 151) the two attempts made under Grant and under Roosevelt to purchase the Danish West Indies. But the history of the Doctrine has been written more than once and the chief importance of the new study lies in the author's own interpretation. He rejects the idea that the Americas are any longer to be regarded as apart from the international polity of Europe and Asia: "The fiction of the Two Spheres may be dismissed for it is neither a social fact nor an international need." He is skeptical as to the possibility of any Pan-American federation, even in the form of a customs union, and is somewhat excessively alarmed at the financial protectorates established under Roosevelt, Taft and Wilson over the Central American and Caribbean republics. He fears that in time these may become dependencies and eventually colonies which cannot be assimilated into our system of self-governing states.

Rejecting what he terms the "Monrovoid" doctrines of Pan-Americanism and imperialist expansion, the author bases his own conception of the Doctrine upon the "permanent interest" of the United States in the political status of parts of the world liable to become a menace to our peace and safety. "If the

---

Doctrine is not a bulwark to the United States," he writes, "it never ought to have been born, and it will certainly die out." He urges the defense of the Monroe Doctrine by a very considerable extension of our army and navy, for policies do not enforce themselves and "without a different kind and degree of military preparation on our part, the time may come when Brazil will pronounce a new doctrine forbidding European nations to meddle with the feeble United States."

The Monroe Doctrine, by Albert Bushnell Hart. Boston: Little, Brown. $1.75.

BEHIND THE SCREENS

Ernest A. Dench endeavors to satisfy the curiosity of the public as to "how they do it all" in his little volume *Making the Movies.* The adventures, the tricks, the methods and the accidents of motion photography in the studio and on the battlefield are told in a lively manner.

Macmillan. $1.25.

BATTLES AND BYSTANDERS

The Black Fiddler, the Hired Man, the Refugee, the Planter, and a Man from the Ranks are some of the many authors of *Battleground Adventures in the Civil War,* a picturesque and very human record of the war's effect on communities and on individuals. How property was destroyed and industry disrupted, and how much those not directly concerned in the fighting suffered is shown by these graphic impressions, collected and edited by Clifton Johnston.

Houghton, Mifflin. $2.

A LIFE OF JESUS

Mary Austin, in *The Man Jesus,* seeks to bring home to present day readers the sense of Jesus' towering humanity projected on the background of His natural and social surroundings. She writes her brief but brilliant story in the light of Gospel criticism and interprets Jesus' life entirely from the naturalistic point of view. Her book is reverent and suggestive, but destructive of dogmatic and traditional notions.

Harper. $1.20.

MORE WAR POEMS

Even if Amy Lowell and Sara Teasdale had never written, Edith M. Thomas would have to do much better than she has done in *The White Messenger and Other War Poems* to justify her publisher's claim, that she is "the foremost woman poet in America." The volume is full of serious, sincere verse; but one must be more than earnest to be effective. In most of the poems, Miss Thomas is far too didactic to be poetic; it is only when she paints a strong picture like "Spilt Wine" that the artist emerges.

Boston: Badger. 50 cents.

HEALTH THRU EDUCATION

No movement in recent times gives a better practical demonstration of Humboldt's maxim—What you would have in society place first in your schools—than that for improved community health. An excellent compendium on this topic is found in *Educational Hygiene,* edited by Professor Louis W. Rapeer. The tables, diagrams, etc., make this a valuable reference book for every school and health administrator.

Scribner. $2.50.

SYSTEMATIZING WELFARE WORK

An attempt to point out the methods and principles applicable to child-helping agencies is made in *Elements of Record Keeping for Child-Helping Organizations,* by Georgia G. Ralph, of the Russell Sage Foundation. The various relations in which records are needed, and the advantages of adequate records are fully set forth. Miss Ralph makes no fetich of red tape and system, and expects records, after being standardized, to give way to new forms adapted to changing conditions.

Survey Associates. $1.50.

show value of work you have done. General ideas and information to assist you might be obtained from the literature of the Hull House, Chicago; of the Bureau of Child Hygiene (Dr. S. Josephine Baker, Director) in the New York City Department of Health; of the Child Welfare Committee, No. 30 East Forty-second street, New York; of the Children's Aid Society, 105 East Twenty-second street, New York; of the American Institute of Social Service, Bible House, New York; of the Juvenile Court, Denver, Colorado; and of the International Sunday School Association, 1416 Mallers Building, Chicago.

199. Miss N. S., Pennsylvania. "In a recent number of The Independent you referred to Barrett's 'Modern Banking Methods.' Kindly tell me the publisher, and price, of this book."

For your benefit, and that of many readers who inquire about the titles of books, names of publishers, prices and other details of literature on Efficiency, we have arranged a plan to save you time and money. The Efficiency Press Syndicate, Woolworth Building, 233 Broadway, New York City, is a clearing-house for Efficiency publications of all kinds. We have secured from this Syndicate a promise to furnish readers of The Independent with details of books and other literature, on various modern Efficiency lines. Mail to the Syndicate a list of books, or subjects, in which you are interested, ask for particulars, enclose self-address stamped envelope for reply.

200. Mr. H. J. C., New York City. "I have read your articles with interest, but will you tell me how to protect myself against the efficient man who meets me at every turn in the road? For example, the present day salesman has been educated up to such perfection that he sells me things I don't want. He is so efficient that he makes me do things I don't want to do, which are not altogether beneficial. I know of many others like myself."

You poor man, yours is a sad, sad case. Why don't you study Efficiency yourself, and learn how not to buy things you don't want? Efficiency is defense as well as offense. We advise you to join a temperance society, and take the pledge to say "No" to financial dissipation.

But the salesman you refer to is not efficient. He is not even a salesman—merely an itinerant peddler. A good salesman looks for "repeat" orders, based on the satisfaction of the customer. In creating dissatisfaction, your alleged salesman violates the first principle of real salesmanship.

The next time a huckster violently assails you, read to him the gist of the foregoing paragraph, then ask him whether he is a salesman or a peddler. This should give you time to catch your breath, and extricate yourself.

201. Mr. R. S. R., Pennsylvania. "I have read your article on 'The Orderly Life' in The Independent of September 27, in which you suggest a standard system which will enable a person to get full control of his nerves in a half hour after rising in the morning; also a standard breakfast menu with the least amount of food. Kindly advise me further."

You might obtain exercises for nerve control from Alois P. Swoboda, Aeolian Hall, Forty-second street, New York; or Paul von Boeckmann, 110 West Fortieth street, New York; or Robert Duncan, United States Express Building, New York. No set rule for any meal can be given here. Personal study and experiment is required, based on conditions of health, age, work, taste and temperament. In general, a standardized breakfast might specify one to three of such dishes as the following: Poached or soft-boiled eggs; toast well done; wheat or corn flakes; a wholesome hot drink; baked apple, stewed fruit or orange marmalade. The ideal breakfast is the smallest amount of easily digested, properly combined food that will "stay in the stomach" during the morning's work. I know of many people who have reduced their breakfast to a hot drink or a glass of fruit juice, and they declare both health and work much improved.

The Market Place

THE BETHLEHEM DIVIDEND

At last the common stock of the Bethlehem Steel Company has a dividend. The directors voted, on the 20th, to pay $30 a share, or 30 per cent, out of the earnings of last year, and also to increase the wages of 10,000 workmen by 10 per cent. But this dividend is to be paid in quarterly instalments hereafter, and the fourth payment will be made on January 3, 1917. The most sensational advances in the group of war order stocks on the New York Exchange last year were those which marked the rise of these Bethlehem Steel common shares from 46 in January to 600 on October 22. In the preceding year the price had fallen to 29¾, and sales were made a few years ago at 8. Samuel Untermyer bought 15,000 shares at less than 30, because, he said, he had confidence in Charles M. Schwab, the company's president. Of these shares, 8800 were standing on September 27 of last year, in the names of his sons, and the new dividend exceeds the purchase price by 60 per cent. It is understood that Mr. Schwab holds about one-third of the entire issue of 150,000 shares.

While the price was rising, last year, there was no promise of a dividend. Mr. Schwab said that it was the policy of the company to use a large part of its earnings for additions and improvements. It is said that $12,000,000 was expended in this way last year. But it was known that the company was making great profits on extensive contracts for ammunition and guns, procured by Mr. Schwab himself in London, and buyers of shares were confident that eventually there would be a distribution among the stockholders. The first of these contracts was obtained about two months after the beginning of the war. After rising to 600, the price of shares declined. During the week which preceded the announcement of the dividend it advanced from 415 to 479, but on sales of only 2500 shares.

Those who were confidently looking for a dividend expected a larger one, and therefore the market price declined again after the news had come, falling from 485 to 460. But there was recovery, and on the 21st there were sales at 484.

Several other companies holding profitable war contracts have declared special dividends or increased their former dividend rates. A special dividend of 28¾ per cent gave nearly $18,000,000 to stockholders of the Du Pont Powder Company. The General Motors Company, whose stock advanced in 1915 from 82 to 558 and is now about 480, declared a special cash dividend of $50 a share and has made a regular 20 per cent rate. Dividends have been resumed by the Cast Iron Pipe Company; the American Brass Company gives 3½ per cent extra; the American Window Glass Company 7 per cent; the E. W. Bliss Company 11¼ per cent, and the Reo Motor Company a stock dividend of 100 per cent. Among the extra allowances announced last week were 16 per cent by the National Screw and Tack Company, and a stock dividend of 50 per cent by the Standard Oil Company of California.

THE STOCK MARKET

For some time past the war order stocks have lacked the support in the share market that was given to them last year, and the tendency of a majority of them has been downward. This was seen on the New York Stock Exchange last week until Friday, when there was an upward reaction. This movement also affected railroad shares, which had suffered some loss, altho they exhibited firmness. Copper mining shares had also declined a little, altho the price of copper is very high, under pressure of great demand from Europe and from our own manufacturers.

Our stock market has felt the pressure of continuous selling of American securities by foreign holders. The arrivals of such securities by steamship during the last two months are estimated to have been from $10,000,000 to $15,000,000 a week. This European liquidation has not seriously affected first-class bonds, the prices of which are several points higher than they were when the Stock Exchange reopened, fourteen months ago, and are not far from the highest prices in 1914, before the war. Investment by our own people has been opposed to the sales from abroad.

An exception in the war order group has been United States Industrial Alcohol, which advanced from 15 to 131 last year and from 136 to 169 last week. The stock has never had a dividend. There is a demand for alcohol in the manufacture of powder, and it is said that the company's output for more than a year to come has been sold.

United States Steel shares declined from 86 to 83%, with recovery to 84. The quarterly meeting was near at hand, and some expected that the dividend would be restored, because the recent quarter's net earnings might exceed $50,000,000. They rose from $12,500,000 in the first quarter of last year to $28,000,000 in the second and $38,700,000 in the third. Steel prices were still rising, last week, and mills, full of work, were refusing orders.

The following dividends are announced:

Federal Sugar Refining Company, preferred, quarterly, 1¾ per cent, payable January 31.

Pacific Gas and Electric Company, quarterly, first preferred and original preferred, $1.50 per share, payable February 15.

REMARKABLE REMARKS

AUGUST RODIN—Sorrow ripens the soul.

W. H. TAFT—Call me anything but Colonel.

HENRY HOLT—American literature is going to the dogs.

WOODROW WILSON—My reputation will take care of itself.

JOSEPH H. CHOATE—For Heaven's sake let Congress do something.

SENATOR CHAMBERLAIN—Now let us bring Great Britain to book.

ELLA WHEELER WILCOX—Abraham Lincoln had spiritualistic leanings.

KING CONSTANTINE—I am no more Pro-German than President Wilson.

MARGARET WILSON—There can be no such thing as non-partizan views.

DR. J. B. QUACKENBOS—The surest cure for the drink habit is hypnotism.

PROF. EMILY G. BALCH—After the war women will be a drug on the market.

JOHN KENDRICK BANGS—Will George the Sixth be better known as Lloyd George?

PROF. J. W. SEARSON—Few of the better class periodicals are sold in a purely college town.

CONGRESSMAN LONDON—I promise the House at some future time to be a great deal better.

WILLIAM J. BRYAN—American citizens should not be permitted to travel on belligerent ships.

GERTRUDE ATHERTON—Germany is essentially a plebeian race and as such is grossly carnal.

CARDINAL GIBBONS—I would be sorry to see an immense standing army organized in this country.

DON MARQUIS—Always try to have a grandparent about the place for the baby to cut his teeth on.

JANE ADDAMS—This war began in secret diplomacy. It will end in secret conferences by diplomatists.

JUDGE JOHN STELK—I have been married fifteen years and have learned to keep quiet on women's wear.

ED. HOWE—There is something unnatural about any one who has spent all his life as a student or teacher.

HELEN KELLER—Be not dumb driven slaves in the army of destruction, be heroes in the army of reconstruction.

HETTY GREEN—I don't believe in Woman Suffrage and I haven't any respect for women who dabble in such trash.

JOHN GALSWORTHY—Doping soldiers with ether, rum or other spirits before the attack has been largely resorted to.

THEODORE ROOSEVELT—If we have war you'll see that young fighting officers of the army want to be in my command.

ENVER PASHA. TURKISH MINISTER OF WAR—I am thankful to the English and French for the Dardanelles expedition.

BILLY SUNDAY—Some people are so tight that, if you asked them to sing "Old Hundred," they would sing "Ninety and Nine."

PROF. GEORGE P. BAKER—No greater material for a drama can be found than in the twenty-second Chapter of the book of Genesis.

WILLIAM ALLEN WHITE—There she stands—this Kansas of ours—a robust, hard working, wholesome old girl, in her middle fifties.

CONGRESSMAN SHERWOOD—Instead of increasing our standing army, already costing the taxpayers $100,000,000 a year, I favor reducing it one-half to 50,000 men.

Insurance

Conducted by

W. E. UNDERWOOD

FOR THE AVERAGE MAN

What is the best thing in life insurance for the average man? In effect, this is the question propounded by readers hundreds of times a year. Define the average man. He would be in early middle age—not beyond 45. He would be a wage-earner, say from $15 a week to $2,000 a year. He would have family responsibilities heavy enough to absorb nearly all his income. Now, what is the answer to the question? The most serviceable form of life insurance for that man is the one commonly called the Ordinary Life plan, because it affords him the greatest amount of protection under a full reserve policy for the smallest amount of premium. To make it complete the annual dividends should be left with the company to increase the amount payable at death. If in the course of twenty or thirty years the need for the protection has ceased, the policy may be surrendered for its cash value; or it may be continued to accumulate additional reserves which, later, can be converted into an annuity in old age. Helpless old age is worse than death.

J. R. H., Columbia City, Ind.—The twenty-year endowment policy alluded to is probably non-participating at $42.25 per $1000, a figure slightly higher than the same policy in the Travelers, Metropolitan and other old companies. The company you mention is sound and well managed. As the coupon policy grants more protection for the money and has endowment features I regard it as better than the endowment.

C. E. C., Boulder, Colo.—Until I see the annual financial report of December 31 last, I cannot form a judgment of the Southern Surety. That company was merged with the Southwestern Surety of Denison, Oklahoma, several months ago. In 1914 the business of the Southern yielded fair results, but during the four years previous to that time its underwriting was very unprofitable.

Mrs. J. L. L., Harvey, N. D.—The Brotherhood of American Yeomen is a fraternal order writing life insurance on the assessment plan. It accumulates a reserve, but, as the latter is not scientifically calculated, it is more than probable that there will be trouble when the membership ages. I cannot recommend it. The National Casualty is eleven years old as a stock company. Most of its business is on the "industrial" plan. The company is of average merit.

H. Z. B., Berkeley, Calif.—The only information I have on the Wabash American Fire Insurance Company dates back to the middle of last year and is to the effect that a number of reputable business men of Wabash, Ind., are engaged in organizing it with a capital of $200,000 and a like amount of surplus. This indicates a sale price for the stock of not less than two for one. The fire insurance business is perilous for small new companies. I should regard an investment in their stocks as injudicious.

The Qualifications of a Competent Trustee

INTEGRITY, responsibility, good judgment regarding investments, knowledge of the law respecting trusteeship, executive ability—and all of these sustained without interruption—are necessary under modern conditions before a trustee can be considered wholly competent.

No individual can possess all of these essential qualifications. He may have integrity, responsibility, good judgment, knowledge and executive ability, yet he lacks the continuous existence which assures that uninterrupted management so necessary to the welfare of an estate.

The Bankers Trust Company possesses all of the essential qualifications of a competent trustee, including assured existence throughout generations of beneficiaries. The Company will afford complete protection to your estate, if appointed executor and trustee under your will.

A fact not generally understood is that the highly specialized and competent service rendered by this Company costs no more than the uncertain service of an individual trustee.

The officers of the Company will be glad to confer with you, or to send you information in regard to this very important matter or in regard to any trust or banking matters you may have in mind.

Bankers Trust Company's Building

BANKERS TRUST COMPANY

16 Wall Street　　　　New York

Resources over $250,000,000

1916

ATLANTIC MUTUAL INSURANCE CO.

ATLANTIC BUILDING, 51 WALL STREET, NEW YORK

Insures Against Marine and Inland Transportation Risk and Will Issue Policies Making Loss Payable in Europe and Oriental Countries.

Chartered by the State of New York in 1842, was preceded by a stock company of a similar name. The latter company was liquidated and part of its capital, to the extent of $100,000, was used with consent of the stockholders, by the Atlantic Mutual Insurance Company and repaid with a bonus and interest at the expiration of two years.

During its existence the company has insured property to the value of	$27,964,578,109.00
Received premiums thereon to the extent of	287,324,800.99
Paid losses during that period	143,820,874.99
Issued certificates of profits to dealers	90,801,110.00
Of which there have been redeemed	83,811,450.00
Leaving outstanding at present time	6,985,660.00
Interest paid on certificates amounts to	23,000,223.85
On December 31, 1914, the assets of the company amounted to	14,101,674.46

The profits of the company revert to the assured and are divided annually upon the premiums terminated during the year, thereby reducing the cost of insurance.

For such dividends, certificates are issued subject to dividends of interest until ordered to be redeemed, in accordance with the charter.

A. A. RAVEN, Chairman of the Board

CORNELIUS ELDERT, Pres.　　　　　　　　　　　　CHARLES E. FAY, 2d Vice-Pres.
WALTER WOOD PARSONS, Vice-Pres.　　　　　　　G. STANTON FLOYD-JONES, Sec.

A Number of Things

by
Edwin E. Slosson

THERE seems now some prospect that all parties may get together upon the Ezekiel platform next election. Roosevelt, Wilson and Bryan, tho holding opinions on the question of preparedness which, without exaggeration, might be called antagonistic, have nevertheless recently exprest their approval of the view of the matter given by Ezekiel in Chapter xxxiii, verses 2 to 6, of his well known, tho too little read, work on political economy and international relations

Son of man, speak to the children of thy people, and say unto them, When I bring the sword upon a land, if the people of the land take a man of their coasts, and set him for their watchman;

If when he seeth the sword come upon the land, he blow the trumpet, and warn the people;

Then whosoever heareth the sound of the trumpet, and taketh not warning; if the sword come, and take him away, his blood shall be upon his own head.

He heard the sound of the trumpet, and took not warning; his blood shall be upon him. But he that taketh warning shall deliver his soul.

But if the watchman see the sword come, and blow not the trumpet, and the people be not warned; if the sword come, and take any person from among them, he is taken away in his iniquity; but his blood will I require at the watchman's hand.

First, Mr. Roosevelt quoted this passage with approval in the *Metropolitan Magazine* for August. Next by a curious coincidence or a natural post incidence, Mr. Wilson put it into a published letter as his own view. Then Mr. Bryan, not to be left behind in any moral movement, added his endorsement to the passage, but called attention to the point that the people were not to take up the sword until the enemy hove in sight.

And then *The New Republic*, representing a more radical viewpoint than any of those named above, spoke up for Ezekiel commending especially:

Son of man, prophesy against the shepherds of Israel, prophesy, and say unto them, Thus saith the Lord God unto the shepherds: Woe be to the shepherds of Israel that do feed themselves; Should not the shepherds feed the flocks?

Ye eat the fat, and ye clothe you with the wool, ye kill them that are fed: but ye feed not the flock.

The diseased have ye not strengthened, neither have ye healed that which was sick, neither have ye bound up that which was broken, neither have ye brought again that which was driven away, neither have ye sought that which was lost; but with force and with cruelty have ye ruled them.

And they have scattered, because there is no shepherd: and they became meat to

all the beasts of the field, when they were scattered.

My sheep wandered thru all the mountains, and upon every high hill: yea, my flock was scattered upon all the face of the earth, and none did search or seek after them.

This surprizing unanimity of diverse minds suggests that the campaign of 1916 might be simplified by all parties adopting the book of Ezekiel as a platform, tho each of course would be free to pick from it such passages as it chose to emphasize and ignore the rest.

Certainly it would be hard to find a document more timely, more comprehensive or more outspoken in its denunciation of current abuses in our political, financial and social system. In fact, its language would probably have to be toned down a bit to avoid interference by the postal authorities and police. For instance, a soap-box orator in New Jersey would be apt to get into trouble with the authorities if he uttered such revolutionary sentiments as "Exalt him that is low and abase him that is high (xxi, 27). I will overturn, overturn, overturn." The Society of Moral and Social Prophylaxis, while it would heartily approve of Ezekiel's stand on this question, would hardly venture to discuss it so frankly. In fact, even the socialists would be shocked at some of the things he says about the luxury of the capitalist class and the oppression of the poor.

It must be confest that Ezekiel is an extremist and altogether too radical in some of his reforms. Nobody but the Mennonites and Dukhobors could approve of his absolute condemnation of taking interest on money loans, and even they would hesitate to make capital punishment the penalty for the crime, as he does. For, mind you, when he says "he that hath not given forth upon usury neither taken any increase" (xviii, 8), he means not merely those wicked people who get twelve per cent on their investments, but those of us who are content with four per cent in the savings bank. Blessed are they who have their money in the New Haven & Hartford, for they are living in obedience to the Bible.

But, as I say, such objectionable passages can be eliminated or quietly ignored in the ordinary way. All platforms as well as all creeds contain some things which have to be subordinated at times. Ezekiel contains so much that each one of us can approve that we can afford to overlook, such passages as we do not quite understand or do not wish to. The militarists can quote vi, 25, "They shall seek peace and there shall be none," or xi, 8, "Ye have feared the sword and I will bring the sword upon you, saith the Lord God." The pacifists can retort with other passages from the same chapter: "Ye shall fall by the sword . . . . for ye have not walked in my statutes . . . . but done after the manner of the heathen that are round about you." The opposition to La Follette on account of the seamen's act is voiced in:

All that handle the oar, the mariners, and all the pilots of the sea, shall come down from their ships, they shall stand upon the land, and shall cause their voice

to be heard against thee and shall cry bitterly.

The impression produced by our policy in the Philippines is referred to in: "All the inhabitants of the isles shall be astonished at thee." The immigration question is touched upon in many passages, such as "I will take you from among the heathen and gather you out of all countries," and:

As they gather silver and brass and iron and lead and tin into the midst of the furnace to blow the fire upon it, to melt it; so will I gather you in mine anger and in my fury and I will leave you there and melt you.

Ezekiel would be the first political platform to give proper attention to the problems of the great West. The Bible is a product of the arid region and only those who have lived in the arid region can appreciate either its symbolism or its doctrine. Ezekiel understood as our eastern politicians do not, the importance of irrigation to national prosperity. Comparing the Assyrian to a cedar of Lebanon he says:

The waters made him great, the deep set him up on high with her rivers running round about his plants, and sent her little rivers unto all the trees of the field.

On forest conservation Ezekiel comes out strong: "So they shall take no wood out of the field, neither cut down any out of the forests."

The question of the open range, which has cost this country millions of dollars and many lives, is yet unsettled and no party has dared tackle it. But Ezekiel points out the only way of stopping the cattle and sheep wars that are ruining our public lands:

Behold, I judge between cattle and cattle, between the rams and the he goats. Seemeth it a small thing unto you to have eaten up the good pasture, but ye must tread down with your feet the residue of your pastures? and to have drunk of the deep waters, but ye must foul the residue with your feet?

It does "seem a small thing" to the statesmen at Washington but not to the people of the West.

I fail to find in Ezekiel any reference to the tariff, the short ballot, woman suffrage and some other questions of the day, but doubtless a more thoro student or one familiar with the Hebrew could do so. I am not familiar enough with feminine fashions of the day to know what effect the following clause in the platform would have upon its changes in the suffrage states:

Wo to the women that sew pillows to all armholes and make kerchiefs on the head of every stature to hunt souls.

Of course Mr. Wilson could not run upon a platform which contained, xliv, 22, "Neither shall they take for their wives a widow."

It is expected that every platform should contain some spread-eagleism, but here again Ezekiel is adequate, for his "riddle" in Chapter xvii would be easily guessed by any true American. I have space to quote only the opening:

A great eagle with great wings, longwinged, full of feathers, which had divers colors, came unto Lebanon, and took the highest branch of the cedar; he cropped off the top of his young twigs and carried it into a land of traffic; he set it in a city of merchants.

The Independent

FOR SIXTY-SEVEN YEARS THE
FORWARD-LOOKING WEEKLY OF AMERICA

THE   CHAUTAUQUAN
Merged with The Independent June 1, 1914

FEBRUARY   7,   1916

OWNED AND PUBLISHED BY
THE INDEPENDENT CORPORATION, AT
119 WEST FORTIETH STREET, NEW YORK
WILLIAM   B.   HOWLAND,   PRESIDENT
FREDERIC E. DICKINSON, TREASURER

WILLIAM   HAYES   WARD
HONORARY EDITOR

EDITOR: HAMILTON HOLT
ASSOCIATE EDITOR: HAROLD J. HOWLAND
LITERARY EDITOR: EDWIN E. SLOSSON

PUBLISHER: KARL V. S. HOWLAND

ONE YEAR, THREE DOLLARS

SINGLE   COPIES,   TEN   CENTS

Postage to foreign countries in Universal Postal
Union, $1.75 a year extra; to Canada, $1 extra.
Instructions for renewal, discontinuance or
change of address should be sent two weeks
before the date they are to go into effect. Both
the old and the new address must be given.

We welcome contributions, but writers who
wish their articles returned, if not accepted,
should send a stamped and addrest envelope. No responsibility is assumed by The
Independent for the loss or non-return of
manuscripts, tho all due care will be exercised.

Entered at New York Post Office as Second
Class Matter

Copyright, 1916, by The Independent

Address all Communications to
THE   INDEPENDENT
119 West Fortieth Street, New York

CONTENTS

AN OPEN FIRE

These logs with drama and with dreams
are rife.
For all their golden Summers and green
Springs
Thru leaf and root they suck'd the forest's
life,
Drank in its secret, deep, essential things.
Its midwood moods, its mystic runes.
Its breathing bushes stirred of faery
wings,
Its August nights and April noons:
The garnered fervors of forgotten Junes
Flare forth again and waste away;
And in the sap that leaps and sings
We hear again the chant the cricket
flings
Across the hawthorn-scented dusks of May.
—From *Dreams and Dust*, by Don Mar-
quis, Harpers.

THE WEST

Out where the handclasp's a little stronger,
Out where the smile dwells a little longer,
That's where the West begins.
Out where the sun is a little brighter,
Where the snows that fall are a trifle
whiter,
Where the bonds of home are a wee bit
tighter,
That's where the West begins.

Out where the skies are a trifle bluer,
Out where friendship's a little truer,
That's where the West begins.
Out where a fresher breeze is blowing,
Where there's laughter in every streamlet
flowing,
Where there's more of reaping and less of
sowing,
That's where the West begins.

Out where the world is in the making.
Where newer hearts in despair are aching,
That's where the West begins.
Where there's more of singing and less of
sighing,
Where there's more of giving and less of
buying,
And a man makes friends without half
trying—
That's where the West begins.
—From the *American Bar Association
Journal*.

REMARKABLE REMARKS

JOHN KENDRICK BANGS—War is shell.
JEROME K. JEROME—"Never again" is
fools' talk.
GUGLIELMO MARCONI—The Zeppelins
are of no military value.
THE CROWN PRINCE OF BAVARIA—Every
day the English push decreases.
JACOB H. SCHIFF—Wars will never
cease as long as custom houses exist.
JOSEPH H. CHOATE—This is the best
year I have ever known for raising money.
HARRY KEMP, POET—The Government
should institute honeymoon colonies.
YUAN SHI-KAI—My patriotism is not
a whit less than any other man's.
GEN. LEONARD WOOD—The volunteer
system has absolutely failed us in every
war.
SENATOR JOHN SHARP WILLIAMS—The
gentlest woman when aroused is a fiendish
thing.
WINIFRED S. STONER—My children
are taught that a cow is a cow and not a
"moo-moo."
THEODORE ROOSEVELT—The poltroon and
professional pacifist are out of place in a
democracy.
ELLA WHEELER WILCOX — Methinks
there is no greater work in life than making beauty.
J. D. ROCKEFELLER, JR.—Combinations
of capital are sometimes conducted in an
unworthy manner.
FLORENZ ZIEGFELD, JR.—Of the fifty
girls who marry from my chorus each year
thirty have dimples.
THE INFANTA EULALIA—King Haakon
is the only ruler in Europe at present secure in his people's affections.
WOODROW WILSON—I don't know anything about what is going to happen when
the war is over and neither do you.
PREMIER OKUMA—There will be no more
free space left on the earth after about
300 years for human beings to settle
ED. HOWE—Sometimes I wonder that
the people do not form a great mob and
burn Washington, D. C.
BOOTH TARKINGTON—Seventeen needs
only some paper lanterns, a fiddle, and a
pretty girl—and Versailles is all there.
CONGRESSMAN LONDON—There was a
time when the saloon was the only university and inspiration of the Democratic
party.
VICE-CONSUL BABBITT—There were exported from Shanghai during the past
three months of last year 410,760 dozen
Chinese eggs.
CORNELIUS VANDERBILT—The holding of
New York City for ransom would pay
many times over the cost of any war
against us.
ANSON PHELPS STOKES—The permanent
defeat of American jingoism would be a
surer guarantee of peace than the victory
of Preparedness.
CONGRESSMAN CYCLONE DAVIS—This
week I pulled off a silken muffler that cost
me $1.50 and put on a 15 cent collar and
became a national sensation.
SENATOR NORRIS—This elaborate plan
for preparedness will not only make many
millionaires, but it will make billionaires
of many present millionaires.
SENATOR CUMMINGS—Somewhere between the armed camp of William of Germany and the open dovecote of William of
Nebraska there must be an honorable abiding place for a great nation which is prepared to head the world toward peace.
HENRY JAMES—Strange withal some of
the turns of the whirligig of time: the
priceless structure came down to the sound
of lamentation, not to say of execration
and of the gnashing of teeth, and went up
again before cold and disbelieving, quite
despairing eyes; in spite of which history
appears to have decided once more to cherish it and give a new consecration.

The Independent

VOLUME 85   FEBRUARY 7, 1916   NUMBER 3505

A GREAT AND COURAGEOUS APPOINTMENT

PRESIDENT WILSON has done a great and courageous thing in sending to the Senate the nomination of Louis D. Brandeis, of Massachusetts, to be a member of the Supreme Court.

It is a great thing, because Mr. Brandeis is ideally equipt in learning, statesmanship and character to discharge the functions of that exalted office.

It is a courageous thing because Mr. Brandeis has incurred powerful enemies while defending the people's rights, and a political storm is bound to brew at a time when the President needs every atom of support he can get from both friend and foe.

Let the Senate not hesitate to confirm the appointment of this able great-hearted and just Jew. He will add strength to the court, especially when those momentous questions of social justice come before it that from now on seem destined to challenge with increasing insistence its august arbitrament.

WHAT SHALL WE DO ABOUT ENGLAND?

THE question of the British blockade of Germany—which is not a blockade—is a puzzling one. It puzzles the British Government, it puzzles the German Government, it puzzles the American Government. No wonder it puzzles the rest of us. The question seems to be, When is a blockade not a blockade? With the further complication, When it isn't, can it behave as if it were?

The House of Commons, following the counsel of Sir Edward Grey, has refused to declare a formal blockade of German ports. But the actual difference that such an action would make in the operations of British naval vessels against shipments of goods from the United States seems negligible. England could hardly do more under a formal blockade than it is actually doing under the famous Orders in Council. So the proposal to change the form without increasing the substance does not seem to be as important as it has been represented to be.

What are the merits of the British endeavor to stifle trade with Germany? Let us look at both sides of the case.

The British plan, which has been in operation for nearly a year, is to prevent any goods whatever from reaching Germany from the outside world, and equally to prevent any German goods from going to the outside world. This plan is carried out not only by stopping all ships bound into and out of German ports, and taking possession of their cargoes, but also by stopping upon the seas all shipments of goods thru neutral countries believed to have originated in Germany or to be destined to Germany.

Let us make the plan concrete. If a ship from New York carrying any kind of a cargo whatever enters the English Channel bound for a German port, it is captured by a British vessel, taken into port, and its cargo seized. Similarly, if a ship were destined for a Dutch, a Danish, a Swedish or a Norwegian port, it would be halted and taken into port. If then, upon investigation, the British authorities had reason to believe that the goods in the ship's cargo were destined for Germany, they would be seized just as tho they were actually going to a German port.

The same procedure is followed in the case of the cargo of a ship bound to New York either from a German port or from the port of a neutral country adjacent to Germany.

In one respect this is like the usual blockade; in one respect it is unlike it. If England had established a formal blockade, its procedure in regard to ships actually bound into or out of German ports would be perfectly regular. Tho even then, in order to make the procedure exactly in order, England would be obliged to establish an efficient blockade in the Baltic, to prevent intercourse between Germany and Scandinavia, for a blockade to be binding must apply equally to all neutral countries.

This procedure is unlike the usual blockade in that England assumes the right to stop shipments to and from neutral countries which it believes to be intended for Germany, or to have originated in Germany. This involves an extension of the doctrines of "continuous voyage" maintained by the United States during the Civil War. But this extension is in direct contradiction of the interpretation of this doctrine made by the United States Supreme Court in the much-quoted "Matamoras" cases.

Great Britain naturally denies the validity of the "Matamoras" decision, for it is the time-honored custom of belligerents to interpret the matter of neutral rights to suit their own purposes. In this denial the British have a good deal of reason upon their side, tho it would take more space than is now available to discuss the matter in all its bearings.

Great Britain, however, has definitely refused to declare a formal blockade. What, then, is the British case? It has two branches.

England has claimed and exercized the right to cut off food shipments to Germany because in January last the German Government issued a decree confiscating all the grain and flour in the empire. These articles thereupon, according to the British view, became legitimate subjects of seizure by the British navy, since conditional contraband, which includes foodstuffs by the law of nations, is seizable when destined for the government or the armed forces of the enemy. It matters nothing, say the British, that Germany promptly altered its decree so that imported foodstuffs were exempted from confiscation, for, as a matter of fact, this pretended exemption was not made in good faith nor actually carried out. It is further urged that under the conditions of modern warfare, in a country like Germany, which put an entire people under arms, it is impossible to maintain the distinction between food intended for the armed forces of a nation and food intended for its civil population. Under such conditions foodstuffs tend by the very logic of events to assume the status of absolute contraband. So much, then, for the British right to cut off food supplies from Germany.

As to other goods, the matter stands on a different basis. The British order in council decreeing the stoppage of all goods going into or coming out from Germany was adopted in retaliation for the famous German war zone proclamation of February, 1915. This proclamation, as it has been interpreted by the subsequent actual practise of German submarines, was a deliberate violation of the rules of international law and the British had no alternative save that of opposing it by any means in their power. They resorted to retaliation or reprisal, under the recognized procedure of nations, best described in the opinion of Sir W. Scott in the Santa Cruz case quoted with approval by Wheaton in his "Elements of International Law." Nations at war have the right to rely upon receiving reciprocal justice. What if this reliance should be disappointed? "Redress must then be sought from retaliation, which, in the disputes of independent states, is not to be considered as vindictive retaliation, but as the just and equal measure of civil retribution. This will be their ultimate security, and it is a security sufficient to warrant the trust."

The only difficulty with accepting this British justification of its program of stifling German trade is that Germany contends that its war zone decree was in fact a measure of reprisal for previous illegal acts of the enemy, especially for the determination of Great Britain to starve the German people.

The whole matter is as puzzling as it can be. Diplomats, experts, international lawyers find it hard to get the matter straight in their own minds. It is no wonder that the American people have not found the way to apportion the right and wrong with unerring judgment.

One thing, however, is clear. The majority of the American people will not view with an equal mind the act of cutting off the outside supplies of a nation and the act of killing non-combatant men, women and children in cold blood. Murder is murder, while blockade, however irregular and however unjustified in its severity, is quite another thing.

What, in the face of such a puzzling situation, should the United States do? Three courses are open to us:

We could no nothing. But that, unless we are prepared definitely to throw in our lot with the Allies, would be supinely to accept a view of the respective rights of belligerents and neutrals that is by no means established in international law and that cavalierly subjects neutral property rights to the arbitrary will of the dominant maritime power.

We could resent the British program with a definite-

ness and a peremptoriness that might find its logical outcome in participation in the war on the side of the Central Powers. But in the present temper of the American people it is inconceivable that the United States should go to war for a mere depredation upon property rights. It would be fantastic if the United States were to be satisfied with a money payment for American lives wantonly taken upon the sea and appeal to the arbitrament of war on behalf of American property. In addition, the predominant sentiment of the people of the United States is so clearly in favor of the Allied cause that a junction with the enemies of that cause is unthinkable.

We can protest strongly and with weighty logic against the invasion by Great Britain of the rights of American shippers upon the high seas, we can hold England to a strict accountability for every damage done to American property rights thru the arbitrary acts of its naval forces, and when the war is over we can press for the satisfaction of our demands and claims in a court of the nations.

From the puzzling situation in which our country finds itself because of the unusual conditions of the war upon the sea, there is no thoroly good way out. The third alternative which we have considered seems to have fewer disadvantages and to be on the whole in better accord with the spirit and convictions of the American people than any other.

═══

THE PANAMA CONGRESS

WHAT is called the Congress on Christian Work in Latin America holds this month a ten days' session in Panama and will then continue in a series of sectional meetings in the principal cities of South America and in Cuba and Porto Rico. It was first entitled the Latin-America Missionary Conference, and under this name, which fairly gave its purpose, great preparations were made for it by a strong committee of twenty or more missionary societies engaged in the work from the Rio Grande to Patagonia; but opposition from Catholic and High Church Episcopalian sources led to the change of the title, dropping the word "Missionary," but the thing remains the same, for a missionary conference it is, whatever it may be called. It will be attended and conducted by delegates and missionaries of all Protestant missionary societies at work in the Catholic countries of America.

Those who are responsible for this Congress wish to make it clear that it is not intended as an attack on the Roman Catholic Church. They show that there is room for evangelical work among the millions of Latin America who have no religion whatever. They tell us, and doubtless truly, that the bulk of the intelligent and educated people of those countries are not believers in Christianity as they know it. This is true of the forty thousand young men in the universities of South America. In nearly every one of its countries the ecclesiastical authorities regard themselves as persecuted by the government. The condition religiously is worse than it is in any country in Europe and the mass of ignorance is appalling. While the rich are traveled and educated, there is not one country in which half the people can read and write.

Modern missions mean education as well as religion,

and there is deplorable need for both in Latin America. South America is really the great undiscovered country. There is room for all the Christian work which both Protestants and Catholics can do. We rejoice when in our predominantly Protestant States or in Protestant Scotland Catholics do active mission work. The field is the world, and the purest truth will win in the end, and it is to be hoped that the zeal of the thousand delegates who will visit Panama and then spread over all Latin America will spur the older church to better work.

There is need of rivalry in doing good. We give all welcome to Christians of whatever name who are casting out the devils of ignorance, superstition, and immorality; and even if they do not follow with us, we say with the Master, Forbid them not.

JOURNALISM IN THE TRENCHES

THO this be a machine-made war the frolic spirit of the soldier cannot be altogether extinguished, but manifests itself in new forms. One of the most interesting of these is the appearance of a novel kind of journalism, the leaflets published, or, rather, prepared, by the men at the front. The curio collectors are already after sample copies of these very limited editions. The Bibliothèque Nationale of Paris has specimens of more than sixty different "periodicals" of this kind, and a bibliography of them has been published, *Tous les Journaux du Front*, by Pierre Albin.

Many of them are merely handwritten or typewritten broadsheets, in purple ink, appearing wherever a group of irrepressible writers and artists happen to find themselves together. The gelatine pad or mimeograph gives a better chance for pictorial embellishment and strange typography than the printing press, so there is great variety and not a little artistic skill. In contents they run largely to verse, personalities and local "gags," often unintelligible to one not familiar with the soldier slang of that particular corps, and not always suitable for translation. Those who know the comic papers of the boulevards may imagine what they would become when translated to the trenches. But among the editors and contributors appear the names of academicians and others well known in art and letters, and probably more than one piece of permanent literature will be found in these ephemerides.

Their names alone are interesting as characteristic of their spirit. *La Woëvre joyeuse* and *Le Sourire de de l'Argonne* show that even those who have stood the brunt of the German attack on the eastern front in the Woëvre and Argonne forests may still be joyful and smile. *A mon Sac* (My Knapsack), *La Fusillade*, *Le Troglodyte*, *Le Cri de Guerre* (The War-Cry), *Le Clarion territorial*, *L'Indiscret*, *Le Marcheur du 88ᵉ* (The Hiker of the 88th), *L'Imberbe grognard* (The Grumbling Tenderfoot); so the list runs. The *Periscope* is such a good name that some permanent periodical is likely to adopt it. The *Autobus* refers not so much to the commissary conveyance as to the tough meat which it brings. For *Poilu*, French slang for an experienced soldier, we have by rare good luck an English equivalent in our "roughneck." There are half a dozen *Poilus* coming from the front; such as *Le Poilu grognard* (The Grumbling Roughneck), *Le Terrible poilu-torial*, and *Le Canard poilu* (The Roughneck Hoax), *Le Poilu enchaîné*,

the last from Clemenceau's journal, which used to be *L'Homme libre* (Free Man) until the censor supprest it and since has appeared as *L'Homme enchaîné* (The Manacled Man).

THE COLLEGES IN CONGRESS

IN England the leading universities are represented directly in Parliament by members elected by the alumni. In the United States we have no such system, but, nevertheless, our colleges—and our astonishingly large number of them—get represented in Congress. By the 380 members of the present Senate and House who report collegiate education, 173 different institutions are named. No college would have more than two if they were equally distributed, but they are not. The University of Michigan, with twenty-seven of its graduates in Congress, still holds the Washington pennant which it wrested from Yale some years ago. The University of Virginia, as we should expect under a Democratic régime, follows next with twenty. Then come Harvard 19, Yale 13, Wisconsin 10, Alabama 7, Mississippi 7, Missouri 7, Minnesota 6, Iowa 6 and Georgia 6. The fact that of the eleven institutions which have more than five representatives in Congress, all but two are state universities, shows what an important factor in political life these institutions have become. It is equally interesting to observe that such large and important universities as Columbia, Pennsylvania, Cornell and Princeton have only three of their men in Congress and Johns Hopkins and Stanford none at all. Twenty-eight per cent of the members mention no institution of higher education and presumably attended none.

CONSCRIPTION AND EUGENICS

A MAJOR part of the discussion which has been going on in England over conscription, and which, less strenuously, is developing in this country, has been a thrashing over of considerations not new and not relatively significant, certainly not fundamental. The emphasis of the immediately expedient is doubtless one of the inevitable shortcomings of popular government. Human beings are prone to put off the evil day, in thought as in action; and they therefore rarely get beyond the urgent, which they mistakenly identify with the vital or the profound.

The nearest approach that has hitherto been made to a more searching examination of the relative demerits of conscription and a volunteer system, has been offered by those who have insisted upon the democratic quality of the universal service plan. It treats all citizens alike; it eliminates from the beginning the possibility of such charges of injustice as were freely made when the national Government in our Civil War resorted to the draft, and poor men said that they and their sons were without escape, while the rich man and his sons could pay for substitutes. That the superb solidarity of France at the present hour, contrasting dramatically with the factional struggle in Great Britain, is largely a product of the fundamental equality and justice of the universal service system, is contended by not a few thoughtful students of the problem.

Yet more fundamental, and going deeper down into the scientific realities of the whole matter, is a consideration which has almost been overlooked, but which has just now been brought to public attention with startling clearness by President Charles Alexander Richmond of Union College, in connection with the proposed policy of offering military instruction to college students. In the Civil War the small undergraduate body of Union College students sent one hundred and eighty-one men into the army. If the United States were now to be attacked by a foreign power and our young college men should be as patriotic as they were half a century ago, at least seventy-five per cent of them would instantly offer their services. At the present moment over nine thousand Oxford men and more than ten thousand Cambridge men are actively in service under the British colors. More than ten per cent of those who have gone forth from these universities since the war began already have fallen.

Leaving out of account, for the moment, the question whether college and university men include a higher percentage of superior ability than can be found in other social groups, it is not denied that on the whole they include a far higher percentage of highly trained men. Not speaking of the so-called literary professions, they include the physicists and chemists, the civil, mechanical and electrical engineers, the biologists, the surgeons and sanitarians, upon whose intellectual power and skill the whole structure of our material civilization depends.

If, now, to the college and university men we add the volunteers who can certainly be counted upon to step forward promptly from other social groups—business and professional men, farmers, and skilled mechanics,—it is beyond doubt that they collectively represent the relatively high moral qualities, the relatively high intelligence, the relatively high physique, of a nation's population. And these are the men that are cheerfully sent forth to the initial slaughter, to bear the brunt of the fighting while strategists and corps commanders are experimentally learning their job, making the tragical mistakes that mark the earlier stages of every war. Meanwhile, the rejected for physical unfitness, the slackers, the unskilled in vast numbers, are safe at home. If at any time during the progress of a serious war twenty-five per cent of the unskilled workers of the population should volunteer, the fact would be hailed as an extraordinary manifestation of profound patriotism. What a showing! Seventy-five per cent of the selected intellectuals, twenty-five per cent of the unskilled! This is the bed-rock meaning of a volunteer system, as over against universal military service, which makes its demand upon all grades of ability, upon all social ranks and classes, impartially. The idea of conscription is so repugnant to the Anglo-Saxon mind that it is only in such vital emergencies as our Civil War or the Great War in Europe that the United States and Great Britain resort to it. But this serious defect of the volunteer system must be frankly recognized and, if possible, obviated.

Surely in this day of awakened scientific intelligence, when even great bodies of our citizens who make no claim to technical knowledge or judgment are beginning to understand the true meaning of the eugenics problem, it would be unpardonable to decide upon our future policy in military matters without full recognition and weighing of the considerations which Dr. Richmond has thrust upon our attention.

A CONTAGIOUS SOCIAL DISEASE

THE recent lynching in Georgia of five men, who were taken from jail and killed with much the same evidence of deliberation and cold-blooded purpose that marked the Leo Frank case, gives point to the diagnosis by an important Southern organization of lynching as "a contagious social disease."

The movement to put an end to lynching comes from the right source. It comes from the leading universities of the Southern states. The University Commission on Southern Race Questions has been holding its sessions at Durham, North Carolina, and it has issued an address on the subject of lynching, directed primarily to the college men of the South. The commission consists of eleven college professors representing as many Southern states.

It is true that lynching is not confined to the Southern states, nor is it wholly a race evil. Whites lynch whites and negroes lynch negroes, but this only proves it to be a contagious social disease and the danger is in the contagiousness. The address does not attempt to convince any one that lynching is a crime. The colleges to which it speaks know it well enough, but it is lukewarmness and timidity on the part of educated "good citizens" which makes it spread.

One of the bad features of lynching, says this address, is that it quickly becomes a habit and like all bad habits deepens and widens rapidly. Formerly lynchings were mainly incited by rape and murder, but the habit has spread until now such outrages are committed for much less serious crimes, and even those are lynched who have been falsely accused and finally proved innocent.

We have received again from Tuskegee Institute the record of the lynchings which during the past year have disgraced the country. During the year just closed there have been sixty-nine. Of those lynched fifty-five were negroes and fourteen whites. Last year we were pleased to note a diminution of lynchings, but this year six more negroes and eleven more whites were put to death by mobs than in 1914, showing that this evil recourse to lawless violence manifests less discrimination of race as time goes on.

Three women were among the victims last year. In four cases it was later proved that the persons lynched were innocent. Georgia maintains its bad preëminence, as more than one-fourth of the lynchings occurred in that state. Of the sixty-nine lynchings only fifteen persons were charged with offenses against women. Three men, all white, were charged with stealing hogs, and two white men for disregarding warnings of night-riders. Obviously lynching cannot maintain even the poor justification that it is the revolt of outraged masculine chivalry in defense of womankind.

These Southern scholars ask whether there is not sufficient legal intelligence and machinery to take care of every case of crime committed. Why fall back on the methods of the jungle?

This protest is properly addressed to the educated men of the South. They have wide vision. They know the contagiousness of the disease. They have the power if they will only exercize it to put a stop to the evil which more than any other disgraces the country, and particularly the South. We look to the colleges and the universities of the South to regenerate public sentiment and remove a stain on the whole nation.

The President's Speeches

President Wilson began at New York, on the 27th, his series of public addresses relating to plans for national defense. They were suggested in part by the condition of the defense program in Congress, where action upon it has been delayed and the Administration's projects for new taxes have encountered formidable opposition. Before leaving Washington, Mr. Wilson urged the chairmen of committees to work for progress with respect to all the pending and proposed legislation. In his first address, in New York, at the dinner of the Railway Business Men's Association, he said that the question of national defense had been clouded by passion and prejudice. Partizan feeling should be excluded and in dealing with it all should draw together, like the peoples of the nations now at war. He paid a tribute of respect and obligation to Congressman Mann, the Republican leader in the House, who had forgotten party lines in his recent speech for the defense plans. The passion of our people was for peace, and he had sought to maintain peace against very great and sometimes very unfair odds. Americans would not seek a contest or cravenly avoid one. They would fight for the vindication of their honor and character, for liberty and their free institutions. We must maintain our own sovereignty, and we had become the champions of free government thruout the western hemisphere. We must stand as the strong brother of others. If we should intervene with arms in Mexico, the other countries south of us would look across the water and not to us.

We must be ready to defend the things we love. This country would never endure militarism, the preparation of a great machine whose only use would be for war, but we should develop a system of industrial and vocational education under Federal guidance, and to this might well be added training in the use of arms, camp sanitation and military discipline, to make men serviceable for national defense. Such an educational system could not be made in a short time. Training should be given to a sufficient body of citizens without delay. He admired and respected the National Guard. Congress should do more for it. But it was under the control of the states, and the President could call upon it only in case of actual invasion. There should be a citizens' reserve of at least half a million trained men, immediately available in time of necessity.

Mr. Wilson also made an address at a meeting of the Moving Picture Board

of Trade, and another before 700 clergymen at the Clerical Conference of the Federation of Churches. In the course of the latter speech he said that we believed in peace, but also in justice and righteousness and liberty, and we could not have peace without these. From Cardinal Farley there came to this meeting a message in which he warmly commended the President and promised the support of the Catholic Church for all the efforts he should make to restore peace.

In the Middle West

Two days later, the President spoke in Pittsburgh. Back of our army, he said, should be a trained reserve of half a million men accustomed to handle arms and to live in camps. This would not point to militarism. He was confident that men would volunteer to join such a force (here he had in mind the proposed Continental Army) and he had no anxiety about the action Congress would take. The world was on fire and sparks were liable to drop anywhere. There were dangers due to our lack of a merchant marine and our dependence upon others for ocean transportation. New conditions made it absolutely necessary that this country should prepare itself, not for war or for anything like aggression, but for adequate national defense. "When you know that there are combustible materials everywhere in the life of the world and in your own

@ O. F. Browning

PRESIDENT WILSON, PREPARATIONIST
The hearty smile was in evidence when the President began his preparedness campaign with a speech in New York

national life, and that the sky is full of floating sparks from a conflagration, are you going to sit down and say it will be time enough when the fire begins, to do something about it?" He was asked to keep the country out of the war, and to maintain the country's honor. The time might come when he could not do both. It was his duty to counsel his fellow-citizens that preparation for national defense could no longer be postponed.

In an address at Cleveland he said it had not been easy at Washington to avoid the entanglements which seemed to beset the Government. One side or the other had repeatedly urged us to protest or intervene with our moral influence, if not with force. He regretted that this was a political campaign year, and he urged all to forget politics when considering national defense. There were not enough coast defenses, the navy should be enlarged, and the army should be supplemented by the trained reserve, ready to go out at the call of the Government upon the shortest possible notice. "Let me tell you very solemnly that you cannot afford to postpone this thing. I do not know what a single day may bring forth." He was not thinking of some particular danger, but he knew that we were treading daily amid the most intricate dangers, not of our own making and not under our control. "No man in the United States knows what a single week or a single day or a single hour may bring forth."

Mr. Bryan, who says he intends to remain in Florida until the end of February, has published a statement about the President's tour. The people have heard, he says, from the manufacturers of munitions, the big corporations that want a large army to overawe their employees, and the army and navy experts who magnify their calling, and should now hear Mr. Wilson.

Philippine Independence

It is expected at Washington that the pending bill concerning the Philippine Islands will soon be passed in the Senate, where it has been the subject of debate. Much interest was shown in an amendment offered by Senator Clarke. This in its original form provided that independence should be granted to the Filipinos in not less than two years. It was afterward so modified that the proposed grant is to be made in not less than two years nor more than four years. Reports in Washington say that the change was suggested by President Wilson, who pointed out that successful negotiations with the great Powers for a maintenance of independent Filipino sovereignty (negotiations required by the bill and the amendment) might be prevented or delayed by the war.

After the amendment had been in the Senate for two or three days, Mr.

179

Hitchcock, chairman of the committee having charge of the subject, reported a substitute bill which virtually repeats the amendment's provisions as to two years and four years, but allows delay beyond the expiration of four years, if conditions, in the opinion of the President, call for it. Independence, having been granted, is to be guaranteed for five years by the United States. The bill as it stands has the approval of Manuel Quezon, the resident Philippine Commissioner, and the Philippine Assembly passed a resolution last week asking Congress to make it a law.

In the course of the debate Mr. Borah, Progressive Republican, supported the Clarke amendment. While half a century might elapse, he said, before the people were ready for self-government, it was advisable that our control should be given up as soon as practicable. "If we stay it must be for the benefit of the Filipinos themselves, and not for any material benefit for the United States." The bill's preamble virtually told the Filipinos they were prepared for independence and promised it to them. Not to keep the promise within a few years would cause discontent and disturbance. Mr. Sutherland, Republican, predicted that a Republican President succeeding Mr. Wilson would decline to grant independence because the people needed education for another generation to qualify them for self-government. This delay, if the pending provisions as to time should be enacted, would probably cause insurrection and bloodshed.

Tests for Immigrants A favorable report has been ordered by the House Immigration Committee on the Burnett Immigration bill, which provides for a literacy test that has excited much opposition in the past and caused the bill to be vetoed by two Presidents. This provision is, in brief, that no alien over sixteen years of age who cannot read English or some other language shall be admitted. There had been hearings on the bill before the committee. Among those who spoke in favor of the test were Mr. Fitzpatrick, vice-president of the Railway Trainmen's Union, and Frank Morrison, secretary of the Federation of Labor. They asserted that those excluded by the test would, if admitted, work for low wages and tend to prevent maintenance of good standards of living. This was the opinion exprest by Mr. Burnett, author of the bill and chairman of the committee. John H. Kimball, representing the Farmer's National Grange, supported the test. Those whom it would exclude, he said, could not be induced to work on the farms.

Louis Marshall, of New York, a lawyer, opposed the test, saying it was unjust and un-American. His foreignborn father was a railroad trackwalker, and the father of Mr. Fitzpatrick (the latter was formerly a railroad section hand) was also foreignborn. "Mr. Fitzpatrick," said Mr. Marshall, "would close the door that was left open for his father, and I would leave it open for the others. Are we to bar these people for the protection of the old Americans of our generation?"

The committee practically agreed some time ago that there should be a paragraph distinctly excluding "Hindus and all persons of the Mongolian or yellow race and the Malay or brown race." Final action on this was deferred to await the result of a conference with the Secretary of State, because of its relation to Japan. As reported, however, the bill excludes Hindus, in response to the demands of Pacific Coast Representatives, and also excludes all Asiatics, altho really the Japanese are excepted on account of a provision that the bill shall not apply to a country with which we have immigration treaties or agreements. The head tax is increased from $4 to $8. At the beginning of the hearings the bill exempted Canadians, Cubans and Mexicans from the literacy test, but afterward this exemption was stricken out.

CANADIAN VOLUNTEERS DRILLING IN SNOW-TRENCHES IN QUEBEC

GETTING THE BEST OUT OF WINTER IN QUEBEC

For the Supreme Court The President's nomination of Louis D. Brandeis, of Boston, to be an associate justice of the Supreme Court, filling the vacancy caused by the death of Justice Joseph R. Lamar, of Georgia, was unexpected, because Mr. Brandeis had not been mentioned in connection with the office. It has been the subject of much comment, owing mainly to the prominence of Mr. Brandeis in recent years as an advocate of advanced social legislation, as counsel for workingmen and women in contests over legislation relating to work hours and wages, as counsel in the Ballinger conservation inquiry and in proceedings before the Interstate Commerce Commission concerning railroad rates, as the successful promoter of legislation for savings bank insurance, as an adviser concerning legislation against Trusts, and as a leader of the Zionist movement. He is the first Jew to be named for the Supreme Court.

At first it was reported that there might be a majority in the Senate against confirmation. One newspaper found only forty-six favorable votes, or three less than the number required, but another counted fifty-one. Later reports point to confirmation when the vote is taken, altho there will be some delay, as the Judiciary Committee, it is said, will make an inquiry. Party lines will not be strictly drawn. Several Democrats, it is understood, will vote against Mr. Brandeis, while a larger number of Republicans will support him.

The New Taxes It is expected now that the additional revenue needed for the expenditures of the defense program will not be procured by the special taxes which President Wilson has suggested, but will be obtained by higher income tax rates, with notable increases for large incomes. Many Democrats protested against the proposed new taxes on gasoline, automobiles, iron, steel and bank checks. Mr. Kitchin, chairman of the Ways and Means Committee and floor leader of the Democratic majority, says it will be "impossible to pass any revenue bill that does not place all appropriations for the increase of the army and the navy on the income tax," and that the income tax exemption limit "will not be lowered." He adds that all the stamp taxes of the present war revenue act must be repealed. Speaker Clark goes further and gives notice that he will oppose the re-enactment of any part of this law. Mr. Kitchin also says that "undoubtedly there will be a tax on war munitions." A bill introduced in the Senate provides for a tax of 2 cents a pound on high explosives and one of 10 per cent on "implements of war." It is well known that Mr. Kitchin opposes the defense plans.

President Wilson, in letters to him, recommends that a permanent nonpartizan tariff commission be created, and the committee will probably report a bill for one, with provisions relating to the "dumping" of foreign goods on our market at low prices after the war. The committee will be empowered to investigate as to rates and the working of the law, and to report to Congress. Mr. Wilson has changed his mind about such a commission, he says, because conditions have changed, but his views about the protective policy have not been modified.

Mexico It appears that the Carranza forces are doing what they can in accordance with his promises concerning the punishment of those who have killed Americans in northern Mexico, but the pursuit of Villa has not been marked by earnestness and vigor. It was reported last week that he was on the Babricora ranch (which is owned by the Hearst estate) with 1000 men, and that he was laying up a supply of provisions by killing 250 cattle a day. There were also reports that safe deposit vaults in our cities held several million dollars which he had placed in them. Before leaving Chihuahua City he looted the shops there. To a party of mining officers and workmen going to mines not far from Santa Ysobel, where Watson and his eighteen associates were murdered, Carranza, last week, gave a military escort. The two Mexicans who killed James B. Akers, the American ranchman, while he was looking for stolen cattle not far from Juarez, were publicly put to death last week in that city. They admitted their guilt, and died cursing Americans. Francisco Perez, who had been associated with them and was also accused of killing Akers, was captured by an American customs officer on the Texas side of the boundary and taken to jail in Isleta. Because he attempted to kill his captors, he was shot to death. As about half of the inhabitants of Isleta are Mexicans, this affair caused resentment there.

Near Brownsville, two of our soldiers swam across the river and were made prisoners by the Mexican troops. The two men asserted that they had crost in response to invitations from the Mexicans. Three American lieutenants, at the head of a small party of soldiers, crost to rescue the prisoners. They were not successful, and four of the soldiers were drowned while attempting to return. The lieutenants are under arrest for crossing the boundary, and the two prisoners have been released.

Carranza's Minister of War has prepared an elaborate plan for compulsory military service, affecting all able-bodied men between the ages of twenty-one and forty-five. His Governor in Sonora has ordered the confiscation of the large landed estates there owned by wealthy supporters of Diaz or Huerta, intending to distribute the land among the common people.

The Conquest of Albania The Austrian army is sweeping down the Adriatic coast from Cattaro without encountering any serious resistance and at this rate it will not be long before Albania is practically in their hands. The Italians were

Press Illustrating Co.

WHITE-CLAD GUNNERS OF THE GERMAN SNOW-BATTALION

Paul Thompson

THE WAR AMONG THE PEAKS

depended upon to defend Albania with the aid of the Serbian soldiers there, since they have always regarded Albania as within their sphere of influence and they were already in possession of its chief harbors, Durazzo and Avlona. General Giovanni Ameglio, who had charge of the Italian conquest of Libya, is in command of the Italian army in Albania, which includes some of the veterans of his African campaign. He was said to have at his disposal 175,000 Italian troops besides the remnants of the Serbian army which retreated into Albania, perhaps a hundred thousand more. Then there was also an Albanian force of unknown number under Essad Pasha, who might be expected to defend Scutari against the Austrians as stoutly as he did against the Montenegrins three years ago. All these together with such Montenegrins as refused to surrender to the Austrians would certainly have been able to hold the Albanian mountains against the invaders for some time, especially since Italy has command of the Adriatic and would supply the armies from the coast while the Austrians and Bulgars must come a long distance overland without railroads or even highways back of their line.

It is no wonder then that England and France were shocked to hear that Italy was withdrawing her troops from Durazzo as rapidly as possible and had apparently no intention of trying to hold any part of Albania except the port of Avlona. The munitions and provisions which had been stored at Durazzo for the campaign are being taken back to Italy; not to Avlona as might have been expected.

By the Rivers of Babylon   The British forces on the Tigris and Euphrates are in a very critical situation. A heavy and long continued rainstorm, unusual in this region, has raised the Tigris four feet

© Underwood & Underwood
WHERE THE BRITISH ARE BESIEGED
General Townshend's expedition, having failed to reach Bagdad, fell back to Kut-el-Amara, where it was enveloped by a large Turkish force. The relief expedition has been checked twenty-three miles down the Tigris River

and flooded the low banks on each side where the English and Indian soldiers are encamped. The level and barren plain affords no natural protection and elaborate entrenchments like those in Belgium are impossible.

Last week we said that the relief expedition under General Aylmer had arrived at Essain, within six miles of the beleaguered force under General Townshend at Kut-el-Amara. This was the statement made to Parliament by Austen Chamberlain, Secretary of State for India, but it seems that he was muddled in his geography, for a few days later it was acknowledged that a mistake had been made in the location of Alymer's army, which was

twenty-three miles away instead of six. Apparently the relieving army has been held in check by strong force of Turks near Sheik Said. The Turkish War Office reports that the British have been driven back several miles with a loss of three thousand. If this is true it puts off indefinitely the rescue of General Townshend's army, which is entrenched at Kut-el-Amara and surrounded by the enemy; and since this force, variously surmised to number between ten and thirty thousand men, is altogether cut off from the base of supplies at the mouth of the Tigris it cannot be expected to hold out very long unless it gets food and ammunition. The Turks report the capture of a thousand of the camels used in bringing up supplies.

Perhaps the pressure upon the British along the Tigris may be relieved by the necessity of diverting Turkish troops to the Caucasian frontier where the Russians have taken the offensive. The Grand Duke Nicholas was placed in command of the Caucasus when he was superseded by the Czar as head of the Russian armies in Europe after the loss of Poland and Galicia. His winter campaign in this new field opens out most promisingly by a westward drive that has brought him within gun-shot of Erzerum. The Turks, dislodged by a sudden attack from the position they have held for the past year in the mountains near the border, were driven back toward Erzerum by the Cossacks who took four thousand prisoners as well. According to the Russian account the Turks were completely routed and abandoned tents, guns and ammunition in enormous quantities. Erzerum is the strongest fortified city in eastern Turkey and has formerly stood long sieges by the Russians. Modern artillery may have made it more vulnerable.

© American Press
A HUGE SHOVEL CLEARING THE CHANNEL AT PANAMA

The Austrian Advance

Altho King Nicholas of Montenegro fled to France without concluding the peace negotiations which he had initiated, the Austrians found in Montenegro two members of the Montenegrin cabinet, General Becèr and Major Lampar, with whom their delegates, Field Marshal von Höfer and Major Schuppich, arranged the terms of surrender. The conditions imposed do not appear to be onerous. All arms are to be given up except those of the Montenegrins, who are to assist in policing the country. The people are to lend all possible assistance to the Austro-Hungarian forces by furnishing them food and water, means of transportation and housing, but they will not be required to enter the army of their conquerors. The 2900 Austro-Hungarians taken by the Montenegrins were released.

After having occupied Cettinje, the capital, and Antivari and Dulcigno, the sole seaports of Montenegro, the Austrian forces crossed over the southern border into Albania and entered Scutari without opposition. Scutari, with its 30,000 inhabitants, is the most important town of northern Albania and occupies a position of great strategic strength on the steep hills at the foot of the lake of the same name. Its sieges have been famous in history. In the fifteenth century Scutari stood out against the Turks for eight months and in the twentieth against the Montenegrins for six months. But Essad Pasha, who had held it in the latter case, thought it more prudent this time to retreat southward toward Avlona and join forces with the Italians there.

So the Austrians moved on down to the coast and took possession of the port of San Giovanni di Medua, where the Allies had stored hundreds of tons of food and munitions for the use of the Montenegrins. Now the Austrian vanguard is reported to have reached Kroya, only twenty-four miles from the port of Durazzo, which Prince William of Wied made his capital while he was nominal ruler of Albania. He is now reported to be at Prizrend, just over the border in conquered Serbia, waiting to reenter in triumph the capital from which he fled.

The tribesmen of this part of Albania are mostly Catholics and have been sedulously cultivated by the Austrians for many years. They hate the Serbs and Montenegrins worse than they do the Turks and many of the refugees from these two conquered kingdoms have been murdered by the Albanians.

South of Avlona or Valona Greek influence predominates. This part of Albania was occupied by the Greeks in the Balkan war of 1912, but they were forced to give it up by the combined efforts of Italy and Austria. But the Greeks have never given up their ambition to annex this territory, as is proved by the recent admission to the Greek Chamber of sixteen deputies from the Epirus, altho this is nominally a part of Albania.

British Conscription

The session of the British Parliament which opened on November 11, 1914, and closed on January 27, 1916, has broke more precedents than any other in history. Money in unparalleled amount has been appropriated in lump sums for the use of the Government without restrictions or criticism. The largest volunteer army the world has ever seen has been organized and finally compulsory military service has been introduced for the first time since Cromwell.

This last measure was carried thru the House of Commons on its third reading by a majority of more than ten to one, an astonishing triumph for the Government considering the heated opposition which the proposal at first aroused. The act makes liable to conscription the unmarried men of military age in Great Britain (not Ireland) with the exception of those who are needed in essential industries like the munitions plants, or who are the sole support of parents or who, like the Quakers, have conscientious scruples against bearing arms. When it was perceived that the Government was determined to resort to conscription many of the single men who had declined to volunteer under the enlistment scheme of Lord Derby were moved to come forward and the reopening of the recruiting offices brought out 114.000 more within a few weeks. Even under the new law the British army will consist of 93 per cent of volunteers.

While the bill was pending in Parliament a conference of trade unionists was called at Bristol to decide upon the attitude of labor in regard to it. The conference declared itself, by a vote of 1,746,000 to 219.000 of the members represented, emphatically opposed to the adoption of conscription in any form "as it is against the spirit of British democracy and full of danger to the liberties of the people." The conference specifically opposed the pending conscription bill but voted against agitating for its repeal. The three members of the Labor party now in the coalition ministry were authorized to remain. In view of the support given by the labor conference to the Government it is believed that there is no dan-

By arrangement with the London Sphere. © N. Y. H.

THE NEW BATTLEFIELD OF THE GREAT WAR

Albania is now being invaded from all sides by hostile or alien armies. The Bulgars from Serbia on the east have penetrated as far as Elbasan, the Greeks have occupied the southern provinces, and the Italians have occupied the ports of Avlona and Durazzo on the western coast. The Austrians, having conquered Montenegro, are overrunning the country from the north. They have already taken Scutari and San Giovanni di Medua

ger of the extreme anti-militarists carrying out their plans for a strike which would tie up the coal mines, railroads and shipping.

Two other bills, almost equally momentous, were passed last week. One of them is intended to root out all German capital and influence in British industries and commerce by empowering the Board of Trade to discontinue any businesses, either within Great Britain or abroad, judged to be inimical to the interests of the Allies or in favor of their enemies. The other bill authorizes the employment of unskilled labor in the less difficult tasks of the manufacture of war supplies. Hitherto the union rules have prevented this and the production of munitions has been seriously retarded on this account.

The War in the Air In the first year of the war aeroplanes were used almost entirely for scouting purposes, and the defense against them was entrusted to guns on the ground. Since then, however, the aeroplanes have been developed into veritable fighting machines which have duels with one another and raid distant parts of the enemy's country. The Serbian and Montenegrin soldiers, painfully toiling thru the Albanian mountains toward the sea and safety, were pursued by Austrian aeroplanes sailing easily overhead. The swamps which protect Dvinsk and Riga are passed over by the aviator as readily as dry land.

But the greatest activity is manifested on the western front. Nineteen air battles in a single day were reported from France and Belgium. When a couple of German aeroplanes bombarded Nancy by night, the French retaliated at once by sending a squadron of twenty-four machines, which dropt 130 bombs on the railroad station and barracks and then returned in safety except for one aviator who was obliged to descend near Metz. A Zeppelin night raid on Paris caused the destruction of several tenements and the death of twenty-three persons, mostly women and children. The airship passed over

the city at a hight of 14,000 feet in a fog.

The supremacy of the air which the British and French have hitherto held is now seriously threatened by the new and more powerful machines which the Germans have introduced. Most prominent among these is the Fokker monoplane, which is equipt with two rotary engines of 150 horse power. The Fokker can travel at a speed of over a hundred miles an hour and can turn and mount with surprizing quickness. The machine gun is mounted so as to shoot forward thru the propeller; the small number of bullets which hit the propeller blades are harmlessly deflected. The Fokker attacks like a hawk by rising above its enemy and then striking head down toward it, firing as it dives. By a slight spiral motion in the descent the stream of bullets envelopes the opposing aeroplane in a cone of fire.

New German Drive That sector of the line in front of Lens where the French and British attempted to break thru last summer is again the scene of activity. This time it is the Germans who have taken the offensive. They struck at the position near Neuville-St. Vaast, on the road from Arras to Lens, where the French occupy the old German trenches of Valkyrie, Odin and Nietzsche. By running tunnels toward the French lines seven mines were planted within twenty yards of the first trenches. When these were exploded immense craters were formed eighty feet wide and thirty feet deep. The scene that

followed is described by a *Times* correspondent.

Before the smoke was cleared away the Germans charged, wearing masks to protect themselves against the gas fumes. They occupied the craters and flowed over the rims upon the trenches beyond. A French counter-attack repulsed them, except at a few points where the trenches were practically destroyed.

Then came a terrible battle in the craters. Men reeled as they grappled down the steep sides and fought, stamping on the heaps of dead and dying.

One Breton sergeant killed three Bavarians with a beak-shaped broken pick. He was then stabbed through the throat by a young German, who in turn was killed by a grenade. The artillerymen were unable to use their quick-fire guns lest they shoot their own men.

As each side alternately gained the mastery and tried to surmount the edges of the craters, they were beaten back by the terrific cannonade. Finally the struggle ceased from mutual exhaustion. Except where the Germans clung desperately to the ruins of the French trenches, honors were even. Most of the craters were divided by a barrier of sandbags, across which came an occasional grenade.

According to the Berlin report the Germans gained over 1800 yards of trenches and captured 237 men and nine machine guns. This gives them possession of Hill 140 and Hill 70, taken by the French and British in September.

Twelve miles south of this on the Somme the Germans have started a new offensive which seems to have taken the French by surprize. One of their outposts here, the village of Frise, was stormed and 1287 unwounded prisoners were captured as well as thirteen machine guns and four mine-throwers. The Germans claim an advance on a front of two miles.

Underwood & Underwood

SYDNEY, AUSTRALIA, TURNS OUT TO HELP THE SOLDIERS

Allies' Day, when the street was filled with booths and an open-handed crowd that swelled the funds for war relief

JUST THE MAN FOR JUDGE

BY HAMILTON HOLT

IN The Independent for July 27, 1914, appears an article entitled "Up From Aristocracy." I especially liked the title, partly, no doubt, because it was my invention and not the author's, but largely because it seemed exactly to characterize the career of the one sketched.

Our readers, by referring back to that article, will learn of a man who was born in Louisville, Kentucky, in 1856 of Jewish parents lately emigrated from Prague, who received most of his schooling in Germany, who was graduated at the head of his class in the Harvard Law School, at twenty, and who ever since has practised law and served the public.

This man has now risen to the very hight of his profession, and is perhaps today the most admired and the most hated practitioner at the bar in America. He is an authority on corporation law. His knowledge of industrial relations is probably unsurpassed by any man in the country. He is an efficiency expert. He is a religious leader. And, above all, he is in his intellectual prime.

Among his achievements — and many more could be cited—are the introduction of industrial insurance into the savings banks of Massachusetts, the adoption of the doctrine of the preferential union shop in the garment industry of New York City which is a solution of the open versus closed shop controversy, the introduction in Boston of profit-sharing between corporations and consumers, the establishment of an eight-hour law for women factory workers first in Oregon, then in Illinois, the battle with Ballinger, the victory over the New Haven Railroad, and the recent argument for a minimum wage law before the Supreme Court.

Thus the public knows Louis D. Brandeis, who was nominated last week by President Wilson as a member of the Supreme Court of the United States. Everybody—friend and foe alike—concedes his extraordinary legal attainments, his intimate knowledge of the great economic and social problems confronting the American people, and his energy, resourcefulness, experience and capacity.

What some are not certain of is whether he has the judicial temperament and whether there is any truth in the charges against his sincerity, whether, in fact, it is himself or the public that he serves.

In respect to these two queries perhaps my testimony may be not without value.

In the summer of 1910 a great strike took place in the garment trade of New York City. Mr. Brandeis was called in to settle it, and, largely owing to his conciliatory efforts, the strike was called off and an agreement made by the Manufacturers' Association and the union, by which their mutual enterprise should be carried on in the future without strike or lockout. This agreement, known as the "Peace Protocol," is in my judgment the farthest step yet taken in the United States toward the goal of industrial peace. Under the protocol there is established, among other novel devices, a board of arbitration to which all disputes must eventually come if appealed. This board consists of three members—one appointed by the manufacturers, one by the union, and one —the chairman—by both. From the beginning Mr. Brandeis has been chairman of the board and I have been one of his two associates.

In the past five years the board has been called together frequently, our sessions have been protracted, lasting usually two or three days at a stretch.

It is the custom of the judges between the sessions to take luncheon together and discuss the case as it proceeds. And if sessions are held at night, as is not infrequently the case, we dine together as well. Then, after the hearing is over, we retire for final deliberation, which often takes several hours or even days. As the board in every instance has come to a unanimous decision, it is evident that in many instances much discussion was required to fuse opinions.

I mention these details merely to show that if ever a man had an opportunity to see another man's mind work and to judge his intellectual caliber, I had that opportunity in the case of Mr. Brandeis.

I therefore say—and I weigh my words—that Mr. Brandeis' mind is the clearest, the keenest and the justest I have ever known. His unerring sense of justice and ability to get at the truth quickly have been a never failing source of wonder.

He is at his very best when delivering an oral judgment. Time and again I have sat amazed at hearing him, fresh from our judicial conference and without having taken even a second aside to collect and arrange his thoughts, begin in polished, modulated and measured voice and continue for half an hour or more without hesitation or reiteration in delivering the opinion of the court. The case may have involved the wages of over 100,000 workers or the yearly profits of the whole industry. It may have required the utmost precision of thought and balance of language so as not to give unnecessary offense to either side or to offer loopholes out of which the lawyers could subsequently wriggle. And yet when we came to read it scarcely a comma had to be changed.

I am therefore in a position to say positively that Mr. Brandeis is not the type of man that his enemies declare. For in the perplexing cases that have come before us—cases that involve pretty nearly all the human passions, good and bad—a man with an insincere mind would have been sure to betray himself sooner or later. If ever, then, I have met an honest man, it is Louis Brandeis. I would as soon trust him as my own father.

In conclusion let me recall an hour we spent together before the great fire in the Harvard Club not many months ago when he told me something of the story of his life. He started his career, it seems, having only the ambition to be an honored member of his profession and to become prosperous. He was a thoro aristocrat, something of an art critic and esthete, and he found little difficulty in entering the charmed circle of the Back Bay elect. Indeed, he became a sort of darling of the rich. But the change came—it was the reading of Henry D. Lloyd's "Wealth Against Commonwealth," and he resolved from that time on to rise from aristocracy to democracy. He then arranged his work so as to give up half his time to public service. So long as he confined his activities to serving as counsel for charities or as mediator in industrial disputes, he received practically unanimous praise from Boston's "best citizens." But when he began to attack privilege in high places and to show up corporate mismanagement, then praise turned to blame and friends to foes.

I shall not soon forget how his dark eyes wistfully rested on the embers, as he concluded, without a shred of bitterness: "And now, if my wife had social ambitions, or if I wanted to join a club, or if I needed to borrow money at the bank, or if I should run for office, they would get me. Fortunately, we don't care for society; I am already a member of the clubs I like, I seem to be able to earn more money than I need. and I shall never seek public office."

Will "they" now prevent his confirmation to the Supreme Court of the United States?

WILLIAM ALLEN WHITE
AUTHOR OF "WHAT'S THE MATTER WITH KANSAS?"
"A CERTAIN RICH MAN," "THE OLD
ORDER CHANGETH"

THE NEXT GENERATION
IN AMERICAN LIFE
A SERIES OF EIGHT FORWARD LOOKING ARTICLES BY

WILLIAM ALLEN WHITE   ELBERT H. GARY
MARGARET DELAND   LIBERTY H. BAILEY
MELVIL DEWEY   GUTZON BORGLUM
GEORGE E. VINCENT   SHAILER MATTHEWS

GOVERNMENT OF THE PEOPLE, BY THE PEOPLE, FOR THE PEOPLE

BY WILLIAM ALLEN WHITE

IT is unfortunate that prophecy, as yet, is rather an inexact science. And the chief losers by reason of the inexactitude of prophecy are those brave spirits who go pioneering. If the pioneers of any generation of our modern times—pioneers in any field of human activity—could only see how well the following generations have come up to the outposts set by the pioneers, instead of being rather sadly dubious at the end of their day's work, the pioneers would be so cocky there would be no living with them.

Consider the political reformers of the generation of the late eighties and early nineties in the last century—the men and women leading the reform movements of twenty-five years ago: George William Curtis, E. L. Godkin, Carl Schurz, Susan B. Anthony, John P. St. John, James B. Weaver, Henry George. From the politics of their day—at least from the vastly impractical politics of their day, the politics that held the offices, administered government, crowded legislative halls, and ran the courts—these reformers of the last generation were outcasts. Popularly these men and women striving for the common good were esteemed as mugwumps or cranks. But in the sanhedrin of officialdom they were lumped as cranks, yet today the work of the hands of the mugwumps and cranks of the last generation is an enduring edifice in our government. Who remembers, or what does it matter, what Blocks-of-five Dudley stood for, what Gorman stood for, what

With this article by one of America's sturdiest veterans of the daily press, The Independent inaugurates its series on "The Next Generation in American Life," presenting the hopes and expectations of some of the wisest men and women in America. Mr. White, as everybody knows, is the owner and editor of the Emporia Daily and Weekly Gazette, author of "A Certain Rich Man" and "The Old Order Changeth" and other books, and long an interpreter of American life.—THE EDITOR.

Philetus Sawyer stood for, what Clarkson advocated, what Alger maintained, what David B. Hill, or Croker and Kelly, or Quay and Dave Martin contended for? Or what banner any of those blind dreamers carried to glorious but inconsequential victory in the days of the Force bill and the McKinley tariff and the Dependent Pension bill? Only this is important—that the winners lost, and the losers won.

OUR HERITAGE FROM THE MUGWUMPS

THE issues and institutions vital in our politics today, the ideals and aspirations most vigorous today do not hark back to the men and parties dominant twenty-five years ago; but rather our political tendencies find their ancestors in the humble and unadvertised meetings of the Civil Service Association, the Ballot Reform League, the Prohibition Phalanx, the Populist platform, and the Equal Suffrage Society. The secret ballot, corrupt practices acts, publicity for campaign contributions, the direct primary, the so-called "short ballot," the nonpartisan nomination, the initiative and referendum, the recall—what a procession of political changes have sallied forth from the old protest of the mugwump against the partizan domination of politics! The party henchman laughed and lost; the mugwump smiled and won!

DREAMS COME TRUE

THE saloon banished from half the people of America and from more than half of the geographical area of the land; a majority in Congress against the saloon, the courts against it, the churches all militantly against it, and a body of public opinion so strongly against the saloon that time-serving politicians are afraid of it; and woman suffrage in twelve states, more or less restricted woman suffrage in half a dozen others—that is the dream come true of the long-haired men and short-haired women of the palmy days of Belva Lockwood. But these changes —representing not the completed work of those who saw definite visions of righteousness a generation ago, but representing instead only certain tendencies of American public opinion that have not been checked as yet, mark only the changes in our political life.

Contemporary changes in our social and economic life are manifest as plainly as our political evolution is manifest. Strongest among the social and economic changes that have risen during the quarter of a century last past, is that which may be called the federalization of industry. The railroad commission, a national arbitration law, the industrial commission, the Pure Food law, the Reserve Banking act, the postal savings bank, and the parcels post have brought or are bringing under Federal control or government ownerships the whole industrial system of the country. Moreover the

187

differences between Federal control and government ownership — at least according to those coming newly under control—are hardly worth discussing. The Civil War did not so drastically revolutionize economic America as the acts of Congress during the last fifteen years have changed it.

Nor has the economic revolution stopt with the Federal Government. State after state is going thru a parallel revolution. As the people have secured for their use the secret ballot, the primary, party campaign publicity, in something like a score of states the initiative and referendum, and in half a score the recall and the headless ballot, they have in less than a decade changed the attitude of the state to the citizen. Compulsory education is now almost universal; child labor is being rapidly abolished. The eight-hour day for women, with sanitary shop conditions, is found in the more civilized of the commonwealths and is coming into the other states as fast as legislatures can enact the laws.

THIS MUCH HAVE WE DONE

THE most radical legislatures we have ever had have been in session during these most recent dark days of reaction in several of our states. Twenty-six states have working-men's compensation laws, breaking down the old common law defenses of capital against labor in personal injury cases. Twenty states have adopted mothers' pension laws. The minimum wage for women is only a few laps behind the mothers' pension law in our American legislatures. Eight hours is the standard day's work on state and city contract work in so many states that labor unions have no trouble in establishing the eight-hour standard day in most of the continuous industries that are unionized. State bank guarantee laws have been approved by the United States Supreme Court, and state insurance is slowly coming into American life. State labor bureaus, acting as employment agencies, are vaguely feeling out the great unexplored problem of chronic or seasonal unemployment.

The state government in America is readily becoming socialistic. And the Federal Government already has become so strongly paternalistic that dear old General Weaver twenty years ago on the hustings running for President—whether as a Greenbacker or a Populist or what not—asked for nothing so radical as the order that exists today in Washington. And Eugene Debs languishing in an Illinois county jail after the strike of '94 could not have hoped in his most sanguine moments that a bloody revolution would have turned things over so completely as they are turning in the states today.

A NEW SPIRIT IN CONTROL

NOW these changes in our political institutions, and in our social and economic status, are merely laws and administrative acts. The real changes that have come into our life, the changes upon which these laws and executive orders have been founded, are much subtler, but vastly stronger than their legal and institutional expressions. It is hard to put this impalpable spirit of the times into the confines of definition. Yet these who feel its power, feel something ruthless, something terrible in the new attitude of America toward them. Former Senator Elihu Root, speaking before the Union League Club of Philadelphia, March 23, 1915, said:

I recall how, eighteen years ago, I came here upon a telegram to meet him (McKinley), and that lead to reflections, not upon the specific differences between President McKinley and his administration, between the legislation or the policies of that time and this, but to reflection upon what, in the retrospect, can be seen to have been a great nation-wide movement along the path of the nation's unconscious purpose. When we elected McKinley in 1896, and again in 1900, it was the business men of the United States who controlled the election . . . how great has been the change. The scepter has passed from the business man. The distinguishing characteristic of recent years has been the conduct of the government of the country by men who have but little concern with the business of the country, by men who distrust the man of business, who suspect the man of business. .

Now former Senator Root, in the course of his Union League address, put his finger upon the change that has come into our government, and he pointed out the meaning of the change to American business. But he does not seem to have diagnosed intelligently the cause of the change. Yet in that cause will be found the only basis for prophecy about changes imminent in the coming quarter of a century.

JUSTICE FIRST, PROSPERITY SECOND

THE difference between the men in office now in city, in state and in Federal government, and those men in office twenty years ago, in those rather narrow but controlling areas of our politics where there are actually marked differences, lies not in matters of honesty, not in matters of capacity, not in matters of party faith. The real difference is found in their philosophy of life. The political leaders of majorities in the eighties and nineties of the last century believed in business for itself, that prosperity was an end of itself. To-day our governments, city, state and national, are more or less under the control of men who all profess, and who in the main believe, that justice is more important than prosperity. And the politicians are only taking their cue from the people. A sense of justice—with here a back-set, and there a reaction—is growing steadily and overwhelmingly in the American heart.

Upon the awakened sense of justice in the hearts of the people prophecy may be safely based. For only a war with its brutalizing influences can stop the awakening of the popular mind.

During twenty years this movement toward justice and away from materialism in politics resistlessly has been gaining strength. The movement has been blind at times; foolish often, frequently (and properly) defeated. But always it has broken the dams of defeat. The movement has appeared dominant in one great party, then in the other and back again in the first party; thus it was a "barbaric yawp" in the Democratic party under Mr. Bryan's leadership in the late nineties; then after Bryan's defeat in 1904, in his own party, the movement appeared under the leadership of stronger, clearer sighted men in the Republican party, men like Senator LaFollette and former President Roosevelt. The "Insurgent" protest directed against the reactionary shock of the Taft administration was the feeling of justice as opposed to the desire for mere prosperity, moving strongly in the American people. The spirit of the people had its voice in the terrific punishment in November, 1912, that fell upon the conservative group then and now controlling the Republican party. The election of President Wilson was a by-product of that punishment. His response, even in a small measure, and under the handicap of a stupid party, to the spirit of the times is the basis of his personal strength before the people.

The feeling for justice first and prosperity afterward in our politics is as strong as ever among the American people. There has been no serious check in the movement; yet it does stand confused. It is unsure of its leadership. It is uncertain how best to proceed. And the confusion and uncertainty of course mean the reaction of the moment, but not a change of conviction. The issues of a war may rise above the issues of humanity. But only a war will prevent the forces that have been dominating politics for ten years—the forces that took the scepter from Mr. Root's good Union League Club friends — from reassembling and moving forward with intelligence and power.

Naturally, the leaders of reaction may win elections. It is not difficult to fool the people before an election, but after an election, when a public servant begins to perform, then he must be unequivocal; then the power that he seemed to have, fails him. For in the face of public wrath the reactionary quails. Often when he has the gun he dares not shoot. Political "buck ager" often is the salvation of the Republic. For no matter how grounded in reaction a majority may appear, no matter how brave its leaders may seem, the backward step is not taken! Conservatives who toil their heads off for victory at the polls often find their victory empty. For when it comes to elections, the people are tolerant; but in judging action, the people are ruthless; they will "suffer not the old kings under any name."

A MIDDLE-CLASS EXPERIMENT

NOW then, in order to see where we are going, it is necessary to see in what direction we have gone for twenty-five years; to ask, not for a list of the laws we have past, but for a glimpse at the kind of institutions we are building. The federalization of industry under the Interstate Commerce Commission, under the new commerce board, under the various new cabinet officers and bureaus at Washington—what does it all mean? And the enlargement of the powers of the states over local intra-state corporations and enterprises; the broadening of the powers of the state in its control over the citizen; from the child hygiene bureau to the licensing of undertakers—does this also mean what the federalization of industry means? Are not all guns pointing at the same target? And is not the aim of all our recent legislation and of "the great nation-wide movement along the path of the nation's unconscious purpose" a readjustment of our economic order to avoid its wreck? Looking back at the whole movement, one finds evidence to warrant the conclusion that "the nation's unconscious purpose" is a middle-class try at mending the present capitalistic profit system, by reducing and equalizing profits, under strong social control, to prevent the wreck of the whole profit system by the rise of socialism.

We are a middle-class people. We have a strong feeling for justice. This sense of justice has turned its attention to economic problems in this generation. And the middle class masses seem to have reached the conviction that many who reap large profits—brokers and middlemen, venders of intangible property of various sorts—are operating in a market made by our common civilization; and that these brokers, venders and middlemen are not using exceptional trading skill, nor rare vision in their business on the one hand, while on the other hand they are taking exorbitant profits, profits that are due only to men who have unusual skill and rare vision. "So," says the middle class oracle of justice, "down come unearned profits —and we shall share them.

"We shall share them in taxes—inheritance taxes, income taxes, land taxes—that shall build public institutions, roads, and schools; provide public hygiene; buy books and pictures; make parks and playgrounds; pay for bands and orchestras. And we shall share the unearned profits of today by cutting these profits down tomorrow, thru workingmen's compensation acts, mothers' pension acts, improved shop conditions, shorter hours, insurance against unemployment, and old age. At any rate," says the middle class oracle of justice, "unearned profits must come down, and we shall share them."

Reform is defined by the late Professor Sumner as "A conferring with B, as to what C should do for D." Of course the obvious answer to that jibe, is that in a complex civilization, the affairs of C and D may easily be of vastly more consequence to A and B than to C and D. As slaveholder and slave, the C and D of seventy years ago justified the final conference between A and B at Appomatox. Indeed C and D have no rights in this world which A and B are bound to respect, if those rights interfere with the progress of the race, with what is seen in a small way by Mr. Root as "the Nation's unconscious purpose"— the folkways, founded on folk-justice, well considered and well tried.

In this "great nation-wide movement" we are considering and trying things; considering what profits are just; trying to find out what wealth is equitably held for private uses.

The adoption of the amendment to the Federal Constitution providing for the direct election of United States Senators took great power from the holders of centralized wealth. By legislative action—state and Federal—half a score of other strong political weapons had been taken from the hands of organized wealth before the Federal Constitutional amendment came. "I say that the scepter has passed," repeats Mr. Root, and in the next paragraph of his speech asks his embattled friends in the Union League: "Now what is going to be done about it?"

OUR RADICAL SUPREME COURT

HIS question is belated. It already has been done. It was done with the passage of the income tax amendment. Those two amendments to the constitution of the United States—the one stripping great power from the organized wealth-holding minority—the other legalizing what Mr. Jerome once called "the moral yearnings of rural communities," make Mr. Root's question futile. The decisions of our Supreme Court during the past fifteen years in cases hinging upon public welfare—as, for instance, the hours and service of women and children, the state bank guarantee laws, powers of the Federal commissions and a multitude of cases wherein the people have sought to improve life and inexorably reduce unearned profits—have been almost uniformly with the public conscience, and rather consistently out of sympathy with the viewpoint of Mr. Root's friends of the Union League. Compared with varying tempers of congresses and of presidents in a decade and a half, our Supreme Court, judged by its decisions, well may be deemed the most unflinchingly radical branch of our government.

So the brakes against reaction are firmly set. The constitution has been amended; the Supreme Court decisions have been rendered. A return to those good old days "when we elected McKinley in 1896 and again in 1900," and when "the business of the United States controlled the election," seems to be, on the whole, a forlorn hope.

WHAT WILL COME OF IT?

SO now let's to our prophecies with a will! First of all, let's eliminate the millenium. In its place, suppose we substitute for the world of the coming generation a rather hard cruel world. But from its hardship and cruelty, let's subtract at least as many hardships and cruelties as our fathers took away for us during the generation that is all but past. Housing for the poor must improve; the economic status of the poor must be better than it is today. For a better status must follow when capital, not labor, bears the expenses of trade-accidents and diseases; when the state, by increasing taxes, pensions the unsupported mother holding her brood together under a home influence; when the child is schooled well into its teens and the mother who works, works at a living wage for only a short day, and when the father works on an eight-hour shift. These things will help a little; but not much. A sturdier, keener, more independent, less contented laboring class will make more intelligent demands on all the Josiah Bounderbys of all the Coketowns of that blessed day. Labor will demand more "golden spoons," more "turtle soup and venison," more "carriages and six"—and will come slightly nearer getting these baubles than Mr. Bounderby could have dreamed labor would come. But still we shall have a hard and cruel world. We still shall have "many inventions," material and legal, over which to struggle for just control; even as today we are struggling to bring justice out of the world of steam and electricity.

> *T*HE *second article in this series,* COUNTRY LIVING IN THE NEXT GENERA-TION, *by Liberty H. Bailey, author of "The Country Life Movement," will be published in the issue of March 6.*

It is a long and tedious, yet always for the man of faith, a joyful job—this business of saving his country. For always, just as he gets his Indians whipped, or his Boston tea party over, or his immortal Declaration written, or his Constitution adopted, or his bill of rights accepted, or his slaves freed, or his Union cemented, or his specie payments resumed, or his railroads con-trolled, or his social and industrial justice in the hearts of the people, and his country all baled up tightly in its perfection—bang! comes a new calamity (and a very real one it always is), hitting the precious country between the aurora borealis and the Gatun dam, breaking the bales and leaving a man's-sized job for the youth of the next "jocund day" that "stands tiptoe on the misty mountain-tops."

And you, oh youth, who shall see the vision, who shall follow it thru long marches, and hard bivouacs, over the hill that rises black beyond the trenches of today, we, who only hear old bugles call, who only dream old dreams, we who are about to die —salute you!

Emporia, Kansas

THE BEST THING IN OUR TOWN

IF any one doubted the existence of community spirit and local patriotism in the United States he would be reassured by the answers we received when in our issue of October 4 we asked our readers, "What is the best thing in your town?" Not only has every city and village in the country some institution, object or person of its own which it regards with a proper pride, but its citizens know how to tell about it in a way to make all other towns envious of the distinction. When the replies began to come in we selected a large drawer to put them in until they could be looked over. But that was soon too full to shut so we commandeered our biggest waste basket, then another and finally as you see they were both full prest down, heaped up and running over. When we came to count them there were nearly a thousand.

But there was not one too many. The object of the contest, as we may now confess, was not so much to get one article worth $100 and several others worth $25, as it was to get an idea of what our readers considered the most valuable features of community life. For this purpose the many which get no prize are, one and all, as valuable as the prize winners.

From every state we received· contributions and from Hawaii, Porto Rico, Canada, Panama and Brazil, besides. Ohio and Pennsylvania with seventy each tied for first place in this competitive display of local spirit. Iowa comes next with sixty-three, then New York with fifty-two, California with forty-four, and Michigan with forty-three.

In determining the prize-winners all of the manuscripts were read and sorted and sifted until we got them down to four, which were of so nearly equal interest, that it was hard to choose between them. By the application of the. preferential ballot system by five members of the editorial staff the first prize was awarded to D. R. Piper, of La Grange, Missouri, for a eulogy of his town paper which we shall soon print. The other prizes go to William O. Stevens, of Annapolis, Maryland; E. W. Beimfohr, of Aberdeen, Washington, and James C. Alvord, of Littleton, Massachusetts. Mr. Stevens writes of "The Oasis." What the oasis and what the desert we leave our readers to puzzle over for the present. Mr. Beimfohr tells of a "Coöperative Merchants' Delivery" and Mr. Alvord of "A Glori-

THE THOUSAND BEST THINGS

fied Millpond." These will be published in the near future.

In variety of topic and distribution of locality these four are representative of the whole. It so happens that the prize winners are all men, tho we received twice as many replies from women as from men. But since we made the selection without regard to this we are sure that the most fervid feminist among the disappointed contributors would not wish us to change our choice on that account.

But as we said before the most interesting feature of this contest is the number and diversity of replies received. We had no idea that there were so many different things which could make a town famous or that there were so many interesting things to be found in places we never heard of. It makes us long to start out on a tramping tour to see these thousand towns and others which perhaps have equal reason to be proud of themselves if they did but know it. How many different topics are brought forward we cannot say until our arithmetician has completed the classification of our census returns. Then we shall publish the full report with extracts from as many of the letters as we can find space for. It will constitute a unique ·exhibit of the ideals and achievements of American towns and will, as we hope, set all other towns not represented to thinking how they can make life better worth living.

TURKISH TRANSPORTS ON THE TIGRIS

ALL SUPPLIES FOR THE BRITISH EXPEDITION INTO MESOPOTAMIA HAVE TO BE BROUGHT UP THE TIGRIS FROM THE PERSIAN GULF.
THE NATIVE RAFTS, AS MAY BE SEEN, ARE QUITE INADEQUATE, AND STEAMERS HAVE HARD
WORK GETTING UP THE RIVER ON ACCOUNT OF THE FLOODS

AT THE EDUCATION COUNTER
A pupil in a department store continuation class making a sale to the teacher while the rest of the class criticizes

THE CASH GIRL'S ALMA MATER

BY CAROLINE SLATER

MORE than 40,000 children in Greater New York leave school every year to go to work. Between the ages of fourteen and sixteen they are required by law to combine school work with their wage earning. Before that "no wages" is the law; after that "no studies" is the general rule—or has been until recently, when the organization of continuation classes in department stores, in hotels, and in factories has given the boy or girl who must earn a living, but who wants more education, a chance to get it.

The continuation classes are held during the daytime in schoolrooms provided by the employer, who also pays all the expenses of equipment and teaching. They are under the jurisdiction of the Board of Education. In general their curriculum follows that of the ordinary grammar school, wisely adapted to the interests and ambitions of the boy or girl with a job.

The course of study for department stores is arranged to cover the common branches—arithmetic, English, spelling, geography, penmanship, and hygiene.

Arithmetic takes up concrete problems involving materials, and subjects used in the business—measuring lengths in yards with tape and yardstick; computing fractions of a dollar; making change; practising with actual sales-checks, bills, receipts, business forms and letters. Geography includes the study of New York and its environs, with special reference to distributing centers and parcel post zones.

In spelling, the words are selected from the store's catalog and from the geographical directory used in the shipping department, and the drill is thoro. Penmanship aims first of all at legibility. Simple composition work, social and business letter writing, discussions of subjects vital to the business and personal life of the pupil, and technical oral lessons in textiles and salesmanship make up the course in English. Every effort is made to develop ease and correctness in impromptu talking.

In all the class work emphasis is laid on the development of the "store spirit," a feeling of coöperation among the workers and of loyalty to the work and the employer. The traditional thrill of pride in Harvard or Smith is no more impelling than the loyalty of these pupils to the Wanamaker school or to the Looking Forward Club. They have their songs and their cheers and they form their alumni organizations to carry on the good work when they graduate.

Continuation classes were established primarily for the benefit of the juniors, but a large part of the older workers are potentially juniors in their lack of knowledge of the English language, American customs, laws of the country, and ordinances of the city. Consequently classes have been organized to meet their demand for learning English.

The men who come into these classes are chiefly night-workers, bakers, porters, night watchmen, and moving picture men, who find the day a convenient time to study. Many of the women receive here their first lessons in reading and writing. The mothers, having children in school, are themselves ambitious to learn, realizing that if they fail to keep up, they lose caste in the eyes of their family.

The progress made by some of these pupils is marvelous. One man in this country only four weeks, and in the class only three weeks, was able to give a twenty minute address in his own words.

This new impulse toward practical education is felt everywhere. The training nowadays must be of the sort that can be put on and worn to business.

Results thus far show what? One distinct effect is the almost entire elimination of the annoying tendency on the part of the worker who has just accepted a position to look for a change as soon as the edge of interest is dulled. Altho there have been some dismissals and removals, not one member of the classes has resigned from the business house thru discontent or for any other voluntary reason. There has been, on the contrary, a marked increase in steadfastness, in holding and continuing in a job for which definite training has been provided.

A second tangible result of this work, closer coöperation with the firm, has been secured thru the teacher's giving a careful personal study of the individual workers under her supervision. Progress is noted and special cases are reported to the employer. From a class of fifteen messenger girls at McCreery's last year, thirteen have been "raised" to more responsible work, or to office positions, with increased wages.

New York City

New Plants and Seeds

Five hundred and thirty different plants were imported and listed in the three spring months of 1915 by our Government Office of Foreign Seed and Plant Introduction, which searches the whole world for plants and seeds that can be transplanted to this country and made useful here.

Among them were a melocoton from South and Central America, an edible fruit of the melon variety, so fragrant that it is used for perfuming clothing; a honey-carob from Spain; a Manchurian wild pear, which will grow in spite of intense cold; a red currant from the Altai Mountains; a large-fruited variety of Chinese haw of great hardiness, and a yellow potato from the Andes.

Our agricultural explorers are conducting their search particularly in the remoter regions of the earth. Probably few of their discoveries will be of direct usefulness, but many of them are valuable for experiments in hybridization and may give an entirely new characteristic to some of our familiar varieties.

As yet there has been no organized plan to exchange the information gained with other countries. An international bureau which would file all the data collected and answer inquiries or suggest experiments might well find a wide field of permanent usefulness.

Another "Safety First" Device

A new electric automobile horn switch has just been invented by W. P. Seng, of Chicago. On account of the method of construction and operation this switch has been termed "The Safety First Switch." Its principal feature is embodied in the fact that without removing either of the hands from the wheel, as is the general practice of automobile drivers, the operator may sound the warning signal. It takes a simple pressure of one of the fingers against any part of the ring to "trip" this switch and the chauffeur loses no time in feeling around for the button before he sounds the horn.

The value of this feature will be realized by the person who has ever done any driving in congested traffic of cities, in mountain climbing, and in fact anywhere where both hands are needed upon the wheel. The exact benefit derived from the use of this device is shown by the fact that over seventy per cent of the controlling power is lost the instant one hand leaves the wheel.

This device is operated by the same dry cell that runs the horn. Instead of

FIRST AID TO THE CHAUFFEUR
A horn that can be sounded from any part of the wheel

being run to some other point of the machine, the wires are run from the battery and the horn up the steering post, both wires in one covering, but separately insulated. One wire is fastened to the "wheel" section, while the other is connected to the "spokes." A simple pressure forces the rim contact point against the contact point on the spoke and in this way a connection is made and the electrical circuit is completed. Just as soon as this takes place over the electric button is due to the fact that the button is located at one particular point and cannot be reached except at that point, while this device may be "tripped" from any side of the wheel.

Mercenary Music

A dry-cleaning establishment in Cincinnati, employing some 300 persons, has come to the conclusion that if these people hear music at frequent intervals while they work it will not only make them happier, more contented workers, but that they will do more work than if they were without the music.

So, following this theory, the enterprising firm has installed thruout the big establishment enough phono-

Paul Thompson
RAGTIME
Lively music makes the laundry work easier, and quicker, too

graphs to keep lively music playing almost all day long. It is like one big entertainment.

This new use of the phonograph is a pleasant way of saying "speed up." The lively music does it. There are no lagging moments, and no one gets a drowsy feeling over the work. They have lively dance records and popular songs. The workers hum and sing, and the speed of the music puts the speed into their work.

The manager of the firm says that music-while-they-work is an idea that prevails in South American factories. Nearly every South American establishment has its musicians to play for its employees during business hours. The phonograph is the Yankee version of the idea and it has been found to work as well in North America as the factory musician in South America.

The phonograph has been found capable of solving better than any shop foreman or superintendent the problem of promoting voluntary "speeding up" among employees.

Saved! A Dialect

In many of the Yorkshire districts of England the dialect, which has long been famous for its richness and variety, is fast dying out, Philologists, after giving much serious consideration to the problem of preserving as full and accurate records as possible, have finally hit upon the dictaphone as a solution.

On a recent visit to the Keighley Museum, Prof. F. W. Moorman, of Leeds University, used a dictaphone to "take down" several specimens of the Yorkshire dialect in its purest form. Among them were the "shepherd's numerals," dictated by one Tattersall Wilkinson, of Roggersham, who recalled their use in his boyhood days when the old Celtic superstition prevailed among the farmers that the sheep must always be counted by these numerals and that ill luck would surely follow the use of the common one, two, three, four.

The Growth of Our Universities

The universities of the United States have grown so rapidly in recent years that few people keep track of them. The statistics of attendance as annually published in *Science* always contain some surprizes for every one, altho the order of the leading institutions does not alter much from year to year. The registration figures up to November 1, 1915, are given in the accompanying diagram. These include students of all sorts enrolled for regular work, including

193

HE BELONGS IN THE AFRICAN JUNGLE

the summer session. Omitting the summer session the leading universities of the list are Columbia (7042), Pennsylvania (6655), California (5977), New York (5853), Michigan (5821), Illinois (5511), Harvard (5435).

THE SIZE OF AMERICAN UNIVERSITIES

Columbia	11,888
California	10,555
Chicago	7,968
Pennsylvania	7,404
Wisconsin	6,810
Michigan	6,684
New York	6,656
Harvard	6,251
Cornell	6,251
Illinois	6,150
Ohio State	5,451
Minnesota	5,376
Northwestern	4,408
Syracuse	4,012
Missouri	3,868
Texas	3,572
Pittsburgh	3,569
Nebraska	3,356
Yale	3,303
Iowa	3,138
Kansas	2,806
Cincinnati	2,624
Indiana	2,347
Tulane	2,160
Stanford	2,061
Western Reserve	1,825
Princeton	1,615
Johns Hopkins	1,586
Washington	1,284
Virginia	1,068

The greatest gain during the past year has been in California (2375), which is in large part due to the number of teachers who were drawn to the Pacific coast by the combined attractions of the summer session, the exposi-

tion and the conventions. Other considerable gains are those of Pennsylvania (900), Minnesota (892), Chicago (837) and Columbia (594). Four institutions, Tulane, Washington University, Harvard and Princeton report a decrease in total attendance.

In college undergraduates California leads with 1294 women and 2023 men, followed by Harvard with 2516 men and 653 women (Radcliffe).

Introducing the Okapi

Much has been written about the okapi, discovered in the wilds of Africa, and first reported by Sir Harry Johnston, of England, in 1903. The okapi looks somewhat like an antelope and is considered one of the rarest animals in the world. It has seldom been seen by a white man.

Herbert Lang, who recently returned from Africa, after spending six years in the jungle, had the good fortune to secure a baby okapi alive. The explorer took a picture of the young okapi in the forest of Ituri, which is herewith reproduced for the first time. It was one of the principal objects of Mr. Lang's expedition in the Congo, to secure specimens of the prized okapi for the American Museum, and the members of the exploration party returned with enough to form a striking habitat group.

A stampede of okapis in the Ituri forest led to the capture of this young one, by the native hunters, who are noted for tracking these animals in the dense woodland of the interior.

The habitat group of okapis will prove of unusual interest, and doubtless will attract widespread attention when placed on view at the American Museum in New York City. Brussels also has an okapi group in one of the institutions of that city.

The Shadow of the Snowflake

Comparatively few people have really looked at snow. For to do this carefully and scientifically requires a compound microscope and certain favorable weather conditions.

According to Professor Huxley more than a thousand differing snow crystals have been described. Every one of these various crystals has six sides or angles.

Wilson A. Bentley, of Jericho, Vermont, has specialized on snow crystals for some years, and by means of microphotography has been able to visualize the beautiful forms of snow crystallography. Some photographs of the recent work in this field by Mr. Bent-

ley show a crystal like a conventionalized flower. Another of the new Bentley group of snow crystals shows a triple form of crystallization that is broken by a second triple manifestation of the crystalline formation. Such combinations lend themselves admirably to design forms and might easily be adapted to textile and decorative use in many fields.

A State Prison Honor System

For several years the idea has been growing that the criminal should be treated not like a brute but as a man, to be reformed, not simply punished for his crime. One of the most successful applications of this idea has been made by Warden Edmund M. Allen, at the State Prison of Illinois, located at Joliet.

The Legislature of Illinois recently put its stamp of approval on two of his reform plans. A bill was past by the Legislature giving convicts sentenced to a life term a chance to be paroled after spending twenty years in prison.

The other bill concerned the warden's "road camp" scheme, by which prisoners are privileged to work at the building of roads, with no restrictions except that they shall not leave the camp, and that they shall not partake of intoxicating liquors. This privilege of road building has previously been accorded only to those convicts who have less than five years of their term yet to serve. Now the State Legislature has past a bill which will extend the privilege to other prisoners.

At the Illinois State Prison at Joliet, 2200 fertile acres, purchased by the State a few years ago, are being worked profitably, both to the state treasury and to the character of the prisoners. Last year, when work on the honor farm began, about sixty convicts were housed and employed there. This season for some months there have been 136 men living in the farmhouses and doing the work of the farm.

Under the direction of the farm superintendent, 2100 acres have been put into crops. Many of the houses and outbuildings have been repaired and rebuilt, by prison labor. Two hundred acres were laid out this year and planted as a truck garden. The vegetables raised here are supplied to the inmates of the penitentiary. A start has been made also in the direction of stocking the farm with milch cows.

The results of this experiment, as regards the men themselves, who have been thus trusted, are very satisfying.

This honor farm is still considered an experiment, but it looks like a long step forward.

IF WE WERE EUROPE

BY PRESTON W. SLOSSON

IN 1914-15, after more than a century of disastrous wars and unstable periods of peace, America was swept from end to end by the conflagration of a general war, and the folly of a generation which had failed to federate the Disunited States into a single republic became apparent to the world. The Governor of Arkansas had been assassinated by a cowboy from the little peasant community of Central Texas, which had but recently won its independence from the Mexican Empire. Central Texas offered to submit the case in all its bearings to the Supreme Court (a well-meant unofficial institution quite devoid of power to enforce its decisions). But behind the murdered man lay the power of the Confederation of South Central States and of its ally, the Confederation of North Central States, and their answer was a declaration of war.

These two rich, populous, heavily armed and centrally located nations filling the Mississippi Valley had by their aggressive policies frightened and leagued against them most of the other nations on the continent. Hence, the war in Texas once begun, it proved impossible to localize it. The western half of the American continent, united under the autocratic rule of Governor Nicholas Romanoff and his machine, could not tolerate the new move on the part of the Central States, and so mobilized the western army to overawe them. Governor William Hohenzollern, of the North Central States, replied by a declaration of war against the Western Empire and its ally, the Southeastern Republic. The latter nation, with a three years' term for military service for all its able-bodied men, an excellent railroad system, and an unequaled series of forts in the Appalachians, was regarded by the Central States as their most dangerous foe. The general staff of the North Central States did not dare risk a prolonged campaign in the difficult Appalachian country, so the Central armies kept to the level plains north of the Ohio River. In so doing they violated the neutrality of two tiny independent nations formed of counties in southern Ohio and made inevitable the hostile intervention of the United Kingdom of New England, New York and New Jersey. This nation had long feared and hated the Central States, but its temper was pacific and it was much distracted by internal problems, notably the question of home rule for the state of Maine. This new ally brought with it all the advantages of its excellent harbors on the Atlantic seaboard, its densely settled industrial population, its vast overseas empire (including the Philippines, Hawaii, the West Indies, the Panama Canal, and many parts of Latin-America), and, above all, its unrivaled fleet. The only formal ally of the Central States (the nation of Louississippi) deserted them and joined the coalition against them.

But after the initial diplomatic failure the Central States did very well. To be sure, the great fleets of the coalition succeeded in establishing an absolute blockade both on the Great Lakes and in the Gulf of Mexico. But the Mexican Empire threw in its lot with the Central States, the naval expedition to the Rio Grande proved a failure, and such of the petty Texan states as were not already involved in the war began to cool toward the coalition and one joined the Central States. The armies of the latter drove out the invading hordes of the Western Empire, overran the rich grain states of Kansas and Nebraska, maintained their hold in the east by throwing up trenches along the Ohio River, utilized the coal, iron and oil regions of Ohio, West Virginia and the Pittsburgh district, and at last effected a junction with the Mexican Empire.

And none can tell what the end may be or when it will be. Airship raids compel New York to darken the "great white way" every night. Innocent Ohio, whose only fault was its geographical position, is starving and dependent on the bounty of Europe. Merchant ships have been torpedoed in Chesapeake Bay and oft the New England coasts. The war in the Eastern States has developed into a hideous contest of endurance waged with shrapnel, poison gas, and squirts of burning oil. The plains of Kansas, torn by invasion and counter-invasion, are no longer able to support their own population, and are far from the aid of Europe. We hear with hardly a pause of wonder the news of the extermination of more than half a million people across the Mexican border. Chicago and Wisconsin universities are devoting the talents of their scientists and scholars to prove that the people of the Mississippi Valley are the only civilized folk in the world, and Harvard and Yale to prove that they are Huns and barbarians. Multimillionaires are gladly surrendering half their income to the extortionate tax gatherer. The Independent is supprest for printing news not approved by the censor. Our only imports from Europe are munitions and our only exports are money. American soil is drenched with the blood of millions of young men, sectional hatred is intensifying, and every part of the continent is struggling under a load of debt that will spell bankruptcy in another year or two of war. No one, however, dares suggest that the present system of the "balance of power among the states" should be replaced by some form of federal organization which might reconcile the autonomy of the state with the peace of the nation. That, of course, would be Utopian!

New York City

WAR MAP OF THE DISUNITED STATES
Fold over a map of the world along a north and south line in mid-Atlantic so that Europe falls on the United States and this is what you get

HE BELONGS IN THE AFRICAN JUNGLE

the summer session. Omitting the summer session the leading universities of the list are Columbia (7042), Pennsylvania (6655), California (5977), New York (5853), Michigan (5821), Illinois (5511), Harvard (5435).

THE SIZE OF AMERICAN UNIVERSITIES

Columbia	11,868
California	10,555
Chicago	7,968
Pennsylvania	7,404
Wisconsin	6,810
Michigan	6,684
New York	6,656
Harvard	6,351
Cornell	6,351
Illinois	6,159
Ohio State	6,451
Minnesota	5,976
Northwestern	4,408
Syracuse	4,012
Missouri	3,868
Texas	3,572
Pittsburgh	3,569
Nebraska	3,356
Yale	3,138
Iowa	3,103
Kansas	2,806
Cincinnati	2,524
Indiana	2,347
Tulane	2,180
Stanford	2,061
Western Reserve	1,825
Princeton	1,615
Johns Hopkins	1,586
Washington	1,254
Virginia	1,008

The greatest gain during the past year has been in California (2375), which is in large part due to the number of teachers who were drawn to the Pacific coast by the combined attractions of the summer session, the exposi-

tion and the conventions. Other considerable gains are those of Pennsylvania (900), Minnesota (892), Chicago (837) and Columbia (594). Four institutions, Tulane, Washington University, Harvard and Princeton report a decrease in total attendance.

In college undergraduates California leads with 1294 women and 2023 men, followed by Harvard with 2516 men and 653 women (Radcliffe).

Introducing the Okapi

Much has been written about the okapi, discovered in the wilds of Africa, and first reported by Sir Harry Johnston, of England, in 1903. The okapi looks somewhat like an antelope and is considered one of the rarest animals in the world. It has seldom been seen by a white man.

Herbert Lang, who recently returned from Africa, after spending six years in the jungle, had the good fortune to secure a baby okapi alive. The explorer took a picture of the young okapi in the forest of Ituri, which is here-with reproduced for the first time. It was one of the principal objects of Mr. Lang's expedition in the Congo, to secure specimens of the prized okapi for the American Museum, and the members of the exploration party returned with enough to form a striking habitat group.

A stampede of okapis in the Ituri forest led to the capture of this young one, by the native hunters, who are noted for tracking these animals in the dense woodland of the interior.

The habitat group of okapis will prove of unusual interest, and doubtless will attract widespread attention when placed on view at the American Museum in New York City. Brussels also has an okapi group in one of the institutions of that city.

The Shadow of the Snowflake

Comparatively few people have really looked at snow. For to do this carefully and scientifically requires a compound microscope and certain favorable weather conditions.

According to Professor Huxley more than a thousand differing snow crystals have been described. Every one of these various crystals has six sides or angles.

Wilson A. Bentley, of Jericho, Vermont, has specialized on snow crystals for some years, and by means of microphotography has been able to visualize the beautiful forms of snow crystallography. Some photographs of the recent work in this field by Mr. Bent-

ley show a crystal like a conventionalized flower. Another of the new Bentley group of snow crystals shows a triple form of crystallization that is broken by a second triple manifestation of the crystalline formation. Such combinations lend themselves admir-ably to design forms and might easily be adapted to textile and decorative use in many fields.

A State Prison Honor System

For several years the idea has been growing that the criminal should be treated not like a brute but as a man, to be reformed, not simply punished for his crime. One of the most successful applications of this idea has been made by Warden Edmund M. Allen, at the State Prison of Illinois, located at Joliet.

The Legislature of Illinois recently put its stamp of approval on two of his reform plans. A bill was past by the Legislature giving convicts sentenced to a life term a chance to be paroled after spending twenty years in prison.

The other bill concerned the warden's "road camp" scheme, by which prisoners are privileged to work at the building of roads, with no restrictions except that they shall not leave the camp, and that they shall not partake of intoxicating liquors. This privilege of road building has previously been accorded only to those convicts who have less than five years of their term yet to serve. Now the State Legislature has past a bill which will extend the privilege to other prisoners.

At the Illinois State Prison at Joliet, 2200 fertile acres, purchased by the State a few years ago, are being worked profitably, both to the state treasury and to the character of the prisoners. Last year, when work on the honor farm began, about sixty convicts were housed and employed there. This season for some months there have been 136 men living in the farmhouses and doing the work of the farm.

Under the direction of the farm superintendent, 2100 acres have been put into crops. Many of the houses and outbuildings have been repaired and rebuilt, by prison labor. Two hundred acres were laid out this year and planted as a truck garden. The vegetables raised here are supplied to the inmates of the penitentiary. A start has been made also in the direction of stocking the farm with milch cows.

The results of this experiment, as regards the men themselves, who have been thus trusted, are very satisfying.

This honor farm is still considered an experiment, but it looks like a long step forward.

IF WE WERE EUROPE

BY PRESTON W. SLOSSON

IN 1914-15, after more than a century of disastrous wars and unstable periods of peace, America was swept from end to end by the conflagration of a general war, and the folly of a generation which had failed to federate the Disunited States into a single republic became apparent to the world. The Governor of Arkansas had been assassinated by a cowboy from the little peasant community of Central Texas, which had but recently won its independence from the Mexican Empire. Central Texas offered to submit the case in all its bearings to the Supreme Court (a well-meant unofficial institution quite devoid of power to enforce its decisions). But behind the murdered man lay the power of the Confederation of South Central States and of its ally, the Confederation of North Central States, and their answer was a declaration of war.

These two rich, populous, heavily armed and centrally located nations filling the Mississippi Valley had by their aggressive policies frightened and leagued against them most of the other nations on the continent. Hence, the war in Texas once begun, it proved impossible to localize it. The western half of the American continent, united under the autocratic rule of Governor Nicholas Romanoff and his machine, could not tolerate the new move on the part of the Central States, and so mobilized the western army to overawe them. Governor William Hohenzollern, of the North Central States, replied by a declaration of war against the Western Empire and its ally, the Southeastern Republic. The latter nation, with a three years' term for military service for all its able-bodied men, an excellent railroad system, and an unequaled series of forts in the Appalachians, was regarded by the Central States as their most dangerous foe. The general staff of the North Central States did not dare risk a prolonged campaign in the difficult Appalachian country, so the Central armies kept to the level plains north of the Ohio River. In so doing they violated the neutrality of two tiny independent nations formed of counties in southern Ohio and made inevitable the hostile intervention of the United Kingdom of New England, New York and New Jersey. This nation had long feared and hated the Central States, but its temper was pacific and it was much distracted by internal problems, notably the question of home rule for the state of Maine. This new ally brought with it all the advantages of

its excellent harbors on the Atlantic seaboard, its densely settled industrial population, its vast overseas empire (including the Philippines, Hawaii, the West Indies, the Panama Canal, and many parts of Latin America), and, above all, its unrivaled fleet. The only formal ally of the Central States (the nation of Louississippi) deserted them and joined the coalition against them.

But after the initial diplomatic failure the Central States did very well. To be sure, the great fleets of the coalition succeeded in establishing an absolute blockade both on the Great Lakes and in the Gulf of Mexico. But the Mexican Empire threw in its lot with the Central States, the naval expedition to the Rio Grande proved a failure, and such of the petty Texan states as were not already involved in the war began to cool toward the coalition and one joined the Central States. The armies of the latter drove out the invading hordes of the Western Empire, overran the rich grain states of Kansas and Nebraska, maintained their hold in the east by throwing up trenches along the Ohio River, utilized the coal, iron and oil regions of Ohio, West Virginia and the Pittsburgh district, and at last effected a junction with the Mexican Empire.

And none can tell what the end may be or when it will be. Airship raids compel New York to darken the "great white way" every night. Innocent Ohio, whose only fault was its geographical position, is starving and dependent on the bounty of Europe. Merchant ships have been

torpedoed in Chesapeake Bay and off the New England coasts. The war in the Eastern States has developed into a hideous contest of endurance waged with shrapnel, poison gas, and squirts of burning oil. The plains of Kansas, torn by invasion and counter-invasion, are no longer able to support their own population, and are far from the aid of Europe. We hear with hardly a pause of wonder the news of the extermination of more than half a million people across the Mexican border. Chicago and Wisconsin universities are devoting the talents of their scientists and scholars to prove that the people of the Mississippi Valley are the only civilized folk in the world, and Harvard and Yale to prove that they are Huns and barbarians. Multimillionaires are gladly surrendering half their income to the extortionate tax gatherer. The Independent is supprest for printing news not approved by the censor. Our only imports from Europe are munitions and our only exports are money. American soil is drenched with the blood of millions of young men, sectional hatred is intensifying, and every part of the continent is struggling under a load of debt that will spell bankruptcy in another year or two of war. No one, however, dares suggest that the present system of the "balance of power among the states" should be replaced by some form of federal organization which might reconcile the autonomy of the state with the peace of the nation. That, of course, would be Utopian!

New York City

WAR MAP OF THE DISUNITED STATES
Fold over a map of the world along a north and south line in mid-Atlantic so that Europe falls on the United States and this is what you get

195

A DON QUIXOTE OF THE BATON

BY JAMES HUNEKER

AUTHOR OF "IVORY, APES AND PEACOCKS"

IN the twilight atmosphere of the orchestra at the Metropolitan Opera House, an atmosphere of smothered fire and gloom, stood a tall, thin figure, thin to meagerness, whose long, delicate hands played upon an invisible instrument which sang and thundered; a river which became a cataract of jewelled sounds at the relentless call of those outstretched fingers of the left hand and the electric wand in the right. It was Artur Bodanzky conducting a Wagner music-drama, and when I caught sight of his profile, a mere silhouette in the dimmed light, I thought of the Knight of the Rueful Visage, of Don Quixote, the idealist and dreamer of La Mancha. Clap a helmet and a pair of moustachios on him and he would need no armor to complete the illusion. Doré might have drawn him. He has lofty ideals. And with his baton he too, tilts at windmills? Are not Wagner's singers windmills? Alert, vivacious are his movements, and his orchestral army responds to every gesture. The simile of the river is not a fanciful one; a stream of tones, caressing, liquid and euphonious, flows beneath this magician from Vienna. Yet how melancholy is that mobile face of his when in repose. The sharply modeled features, firm, thin lips, indicative of self-control, are contradicted by the large black-brown eyes with dancing golden flecks in them, and the broad, sloping forehead, the emotional front of the musician born. Add to these a bold, jutting nose, the rudder of the face, as George Meredith would say. Perhaps the expression I noted may be the result of a racial crasis; in the veins of Bodanzky are mixed bloods: Austrian, Hungarian and Eastern. His name is Slavic-Bohemian, tho his origin is partly Magyar. He was born in Vienna, and is still under forty; a youthful age for one to have achieved such a reputation as a Wagner conductor.

But if Artur Bodanzky may seem, because of his physique and bearing, a typical Don Quixote, he is far from such by temperament. He may look like a pessimist, but he is the reverse. He is as fiery as a Hungarian and as elastic in his moods as a Viennese. He is as gay as a boy at times. It is his delight to conduct Italian operas, to lead Mozart and—Johann Strauss. He conducted "The Bat" in Vienna and Paris. A Don Quixote of the boulevard and the Prater! He

ARTUR BODANZKY

has officiated in Petrograd and London. In Vienna, after a thoro musical training at the Imperial Conservatory, and violin with Grün, he graduated from operetta to the Opera House under the famous composer and conductor, the late Gustav Mahler. Bodanzky then received the appointment at Prague as conductor of opera and symphony. In 1910 he went to Mannheim as director of an important operatic post, and he now controls the German forces at our Metropolitan Opera House. His musical pedigree is sound, his personality a strong, yet ingratiating one; and I may add, few conductors have so quickly won their way. Orchestral players are susceptible beings. Like high-bred and well-drilled steeds they respond to the slightest pressure of the bridle. Whip them and they rebel, or run away. They immediately know their rider and instinctively obey him. But by the same token they may refuse to budge if a leader lacking in magnetism or in authority, attempts to guide them. The orchestra at our opera is an admirable organization. Successive generations of conductors have made it both sen-

sitive and plastic. Under Arturo Toscanini it was so, and now under this "Viennese Toscanini" it is still sensitive and plastic; these qualities are marked in the art of Bodanzky. His men were his friends from the first moment he lifted his baton.

He made his début here with Wagner's "Twilight of the Gods," and nobly stood the tremendous test. And a test it was for a new conductor to interpret the eloquent message of that epical work. There were few slips, the cast was not impeccable—how could it have been, as the great Wagner singers of yester-year have vanished!—but the hero of the evening was the conductor. For the first time in a blue moon we heard the singers. The sympathetic musician at the helm did not drown them with the turbulent waves of the score. There was power, potential and exprest. There was poetry. And there was a rhythmic vitality that swept us along on the wings of the mighty song of Wagner's. Naturally, comparisons were made; without comparisons, invidious or otherwise, there would be no musical criticism. Judicious cuts appreciably shortened the performance. The emotional surge was unmistakable. A sagacious intellect controlled the work; cerebral as well as temperamental. Now, I am no believer in such an impossible thing as an "authorized version" of Wagner. I have heard all the Wagner conductors from the Pope of the Wagnerian Church, Hans Richter, to son Siegfried Wagner, weakest of acolytes at the holy altar. And no two were alike. (No two grains of sand are alike, say scientists.) There were giants in the old days, and there are among the younger conductors of today several suffering with the growing pains of genius. But not many. We shall never see again a Seidl or a Levi; yet we have Nikisch —the savior of the three Arthurs— and Weingartner, R. Strauss, Mengelberg, Toscanini, Muck, Bodanzky (for he belongs to this inner brotherhood of the baton); as we once had Von Bülow, Mottl, Sucher, Von Schuch, Mahler. There are as good fish in the sea as ever came out of it,

"Cadillac—Standard of the World"
—a phrase or a fact?

IS THE Cadillac, in fact, the Standard of the World?

Is it the one car which is accepted as a pattern of excellence and efficiency?

Look back over the past twelve years and ask yourself what other car has wielded so wide an influence over the industry.

Ask yourself if motor cars, as a whole, are not better cars today because of Cadillac progressiveness and Cadillac initiative.

You recall that the first Cadillac was also the first practical, enduring motor car.

You remember the period in which the Cadillac inaugurated the thorough standardization of parts.

You remember that the Cadillac accomplished also the first production in large quantities of a really high grade car at a moderate price.

The introduction by the Cadillac of electric starting and lighting is still fresh in your memory.

And you know finally, that the Cadillac as a climax to its other constructive contributions to the industry, brought forth the high-speed, high-efficiency V-type engine.

Around the world that V-type multi-cylinder engine is admittedly at the zenith of design and of efficiency.

And the Cadillac has pushed the process of perfecting the V-type engine to the highest point yet attained.

Upon its first appearance, the Cadillac Eight received the unique tribute of a larger purchase on the part of other makers than any other car has probably ever known.

Its scientific design and superb workmanship compelled their most intense admiration—its performance was pronounced nothing short of marvelous.

If the Cadillac had not been the standard of the world before, the V-type multi-cylinder Cadillac would have made it so.

It has become the standard of the world in smoothness and in swift acceleration, in flexibility and in hill climbing power.

It is the world's standard in its incomparable roadability, its luxury, its ease of operation and control, and in absence of fatigue after long journeys.

These characteristics, added to its world-wide reputation for dependable and enduring service, have furnished for the industry, *new inspirations— new incentives—new goals for ambitions.*

Is not the Cadillac deserving of the title it has so long and so honorably held?

Is not the Cadillac, in fact, the Standard of the World?

Styles and Prices

Standard Seven passenger car, Five passenger Salon and Roadster, $2080, Three passenger Victoria, $2400, Four passenger Coupe, $2800, Five passenger Brougham, $2950, Seven passenger Limousine, $3450, Berlin, $3600. Prices include standard equipment. F. O. B. Detroit.

Cadillac Motor Car Co., Detroit, Mich.

and we should not lose sight of the fact that conductors come and conductors go, but Wagner lasts forever—at least, lasts till the abbreviated eternity we call fame ends. This man reads a scene slower, the other man takes it faster, yet what do these variations spell? Bodanzky differs from his predecessors, Hertz and Toscanini; nevertheless in the chiefest matter he is on the side of the angels. He is a versatile, brilliant and subtle conductor, and it is a bold dissenter who takes exception to his broad musical conception, tho one may demur here and there as to details.

When I first heard the delightful "Rose Cavalier" of Richard Strauss, conducted by the composer at Stuttgart in 1912, I missed the champagne in that sparkling score, compounded as it is of Wagner and Johann Strauss—Weimar and Vienna. But I tasted it to the full when Bodanzky decanted the magic musical bottle for us. His early training in light opera told. His touch was feathery light, the music bubbled over the edge of the "mystic abyss" of the orchestra, and we left the Metropolitan elated. Nor were the finer nuances missing. Bodanzky is a master of nuances. His orchestra is ever transparent. It vibrates. It glows. But it always reveals the musical structure. One can hear the inner voices, while the larger tonal balance and ensemble are in evidence. For the singers the conductor has a peculiar care; every entrance is signaled, every variation in tempo or rhythm indicated. "Parsifal," for example, lost something of that droning, psalm-singing quality which makes this sacrosanct religious festival play such a bore to genuine musical people. It was conducted as if it had red blood in it, which, in spots, it has, and the second act was as exotic and sensuous as it should be. I admired the "Tristan and Isolde" interpretation because of its fine blending of imagination and emotion. The orchestra moved like a richly-wrought, richly-colored tapestry. The climaxes were stirring, the mystic ecstasy present, and the love episodes intense.

Artur Bodanzky is never nervous during a performance; afterward he is sometimes unstrung, for he dispenses an incredible amount of energy, and he becomes discouraged over such trifles as a false entrance by a singer or a player, or because of the vagaries of the electric switch. At the first "Tristan" the light failed at his desk during a crucial moment. It made no difference in his conducting—he could conduct the entire work without score —but it annoyed him, and later I saw his features grow melancholy as his eyes stared at imaginary windmills—the Wagner singers—and he straightway became the dreamer of dreams, who waved long, thin hands across a river of multicolored music; a veritable Don Quixote of the baton.

New York City

Seemingly they think a canal is like the millinery trade—two grand openings a year and the rest of the time business is dead.—*Montague Glass, New York Tribune.*

The New Books

NEW POETRY

Six poets, who are all working along the same lines, have published *Some Imagist Poets*, an anthology, for which each individual has selected a certain number of his, or her, own poems with no restriction other than that none of them should have appeared before in book form. In an introduction the poets explain to the public what the new school which they represent aims to do. This is: "to create new rhythms as the expression of new moods"; "to allow absolute freedom in the choice of subject"; to present images, particular images, definite, clear and vivid. Vivid is the word which best characterizes the poems in this anthology. You may like this poetry, or you may detest it; but you can not escape it. It impresses you whether you will or not. Richard Aldington's "Round Pond," H. D.'s "Sea Iris," F. S. Flint's "Lunch," D. H. Lawrence's "A Woman and Her Dead Husband" recur persistently to one's mind after they have been once read. Or take these lines from Amy Lowell's Letter:

"I am tired, Beloved, of chafing my heart
    Against the want of you;
Of squeezing it into little inkdrops,
    And posting it."

Or John Gould Fletcher's struggle against the hard, unyielding city:

"Yet I revolt: I bend, I twist myself,
. . . .
Anything to be soft and woolly,
Anything to escape."

A better example of Mr. Fletcher's work, however, is contained in the swift, intense, infinitely varied impressions in *Irradiations*, and the wet, salt, windy music of *Sand and Spray*.

These writers of *vers libre* are doing for poetry what the futurists are doing for art. They are revolting against a monotonous, slavish following of tradition. They are taking poetry on a spree; but it is only a one night spree, and he will come back in the morning refreshed and rejuvenated.

Some Imagist Poets. An Anthology, Houghton, Mifflin. 75 cents, *Irradiations; Sand and Spray*, by John Gould Fletcher. Houghton, Mifflin. 75 cents.

PREPAREDNESS

The three addresses contained in General Wood's little volume, *The Military Obligation of Citizenship*, were delivered, one at Princeton, one at Mohonk, and one at St. Paul's school. From three somewhat different standpoints he stresses the points that we are not equipped for defense; we should be; the citizen has a military duty; the army a civil duty. President Hibben introduces the collection. General Wood in turn introduces Frederick L. Huide-

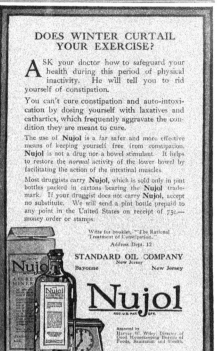

koper, who is probably our greatest tactical writer since General Upton. Mr. Huidekoper has written an elaborate history of *The Military Unpreparedness of the United States*. It is an octavo of about seven hundred pages and it traces from the standpoint of the military expert or board of strategy every important military movement of each of our wars save the minor Indian outbreaks. Generous citations from contemporary and later authorities of the first rank enforce the judgments exprest. One is breathless and baffled by the multitude of examples shown here of delay, bad judgment, careless neglect, rejection of advice and refusal to profit by sad experience. We note a few instances, of scores, of the sort that caused the continual prayers of Washington for real preparation and discipline. His repeated warnings have not been disputed and his principles are sound today. But the errors he fought have created protest and appeal from his day to ours. They even caused Jefferson's conversion to seeking disciplined soldiers as against militia and hasty armies of bounty bought men. Such instances are the fluke by which Louisburg was taken; Arnold's doleful disaster at Quebec due to foolish enlistment methods; Jackson's lack of equipment to pursue and extend his victory at New Orleans; the mad tho successful operation of Scott in leaving his base for Mexico City, where Santa Anna, having six times his force, could have overwhelmed him had Santa Anna been half alive to his chance. Then came the Civil War with its Antietam and even Gettysburg when Lee was allowed to get away; the Spanish War, where the Cuban expedition might have been annihilated on landing, by a regiment with Mausers; and the Philippine War which was marred by long delays and where finally the bounty method of getting volunteers, a pitfall censured by all authorities, was proposed.

Delay, waste of money and of men, lack of disciplined men and of coördination, meager and unfit equipment and imperfect campaign plans—these are noted on nearly every page of the book. High credit is often given to courage and resource and skill. But the volume cites chapter and verse to prove its charge that the nation has in military matters trifled with its own life. From the history our author draws his lessons and tells in sufficient detail what in his judgment our land forces should be, how organized and how governed and trained. He would have 250,000 regular army, and reserves, together numbering in seven years 670,000 men, this result to be reached by enforced intensive drill from six weeks in the first year to two weeks in the last, of all capable men within service age, thus taking a leaf from the Swiss system and another from the Australian. He cordially approves the volunteer summer camps.

Military education in the schools and colleges has been widely advocated and vigorously opposed. A bird's-eye view

of this burning topic will be found in the Debaters Handbook on *Military Training*, which arrays extracts from the utterances of leading educators and editors, of military authorities and peace advocates.

The *ABC of National Defense*, a reprint of already published articles by J. W. Muller, is for the layman, since it goes, in the fashion of the Chautauqua text book, to the root of the subject without technicality, likening an army to a fighting man, with aeroplanes and scouts for eyes, the infantry for the hard body, artillery for fists, cavalry for quick footing, and so on. The illustration is clumsy and incomplete, yet good, in that it emphasizes all that the author says on efficient and prompt coördination. "The army that needs time is already half defeated. Time is the one thing that a capable enemy does not mean to give his opponent."

Dr. George H. Maxwell, in *Our National Defense*, has developed a theory of conservation applicable to peace as well as to war, one that should go far to preserve the first and prevent the second. He calls for "a reserve of enlisted men under civil control, doing the work of peace in time of peace and ready for the work of war in time of war." It would be a "National Construction Reserve, organized primarily to fight nature's forces instead of to fight the people of another nation." The reserves should be Homecrofters, owning their homes and living rural lives with a practical school system and with work under enlistment for five years. Irrigation and forestry, fruit culture and poultry culture and marketing along with military drill, all under experts, would occupy this citizen soldiery. This might be called an attempt to fit the Swiss system to our needs.

Statistics showing the number of years in which the leading nations have engaged in wars during the past odd three centuries show that there has been large decrease in the time spent in war. These figures, hopeful as they might seem, relate to time only, not to causes, severity or extent. Yet the authors of *Is War Diminishing?* raise some puzzling but illuminating questions on causes and purposes.

Sixty-six important war documents on *The Protection of Neutral Rights at Sea* have been collected by Professor W. R. Shepherd; they include the pertinent articles in the Declaration of London, Orders in Council and the diplomatic notes between our country and the countries at war as to neutral rights generally and as to such notable cases as the "Lusitania," "Dacia," and "William P. Frye."

It is a collection serviceable to prevent the loose talking and writing on so delicate and technical a subject. The introduction outlines the whole situation and urges the United States to call a Congress of Neutrals to unite in defining and claiming their rights. In view of that, the pamphlet would have been more useful had it contained

some of the Swedish, Norwegian and Danish notes of protest.

The Military Obligation of Citizenship, by Leonard Wood. Princeton University Press. 75 cents. *The Military Unpreparedness of the United States*, by F. L. Huidekoper. Macmillan. $4. *Selected Articles on Military Training*, comp. by Corinne Bacon. White Plains, N. Y.: Wilson. 25 cents. *The A B C of National Defense*, by J. W. Muller. Dutton. $1. *Our National Defense, The Patriotism of Peace*, by G. H. Maxwell. New Orleans: Rural Settlements Ass'n. $1.25. *Is War Diminishing?* by F. A. Wood and A. Baltzly. Houghton, Mifflin. $1. *The Protection of Neutral Rights at Sea*, by W. R. Shepherd. Sturgis & Walton. 25 cents.

DISMEMBERED POLAND

The Second Partition of Poland, by Dr. Robert Howard Lord, of Harvard University, is an admirably careful unwinding of the most tortuous and intricate tangle of intrigue in the entire eighteenth century. This second partition which sealed the fate of the Polish commonwealth showed all the powers of Europe at their worst; Russia, pursuing the tactics lately copied in the partition of Persia, choosing the moment of attempted national regeneration to strike the death blow; Prussia deceiving the unhappy country by promises of aid till the last, when she treacherously turned on her ally and joined Russia to dismember her; Austria, France and Great Britain pretending infinite sympathy, but secretly consenting to all that was done, and, last of all, Poland herself "an anarchy tempered by civil war." The author bases his study largely upon personal research in the Russian archives.

The Second Partition of Poland, by Robert Howard Lord. Harvard University Press. $2.25.

THE CHURCH'S BUSINESS

Christian people are just awaking to their responsibilities and opportunities in the matter of recreational activities. The old ascetic attitude of self-repression in religion is being replaced by the joyous duty and privilege of self-expression. Sports and games are no longer regarded as concessions to evil to uncontrollable desires, but rather as a divinely appointed means of cultivating a vigorous body, a nimble mind and a cheery, robust character. In Mr. Henry Atkinson's new book on *The Church and the People's Play*, he points out the causes which have operated in earlier times to create on the part of Christian leaders a feeling of suspicion, aloofness and opposition in regard to sports, amusements and recreation in general. In the most progressive sections of the Christian church a change in theological conceptions has removed the occasion for such opposition and placed upon the conscience of the church the task of leadership and reconstruction in the people's play. The utilization of these universal and sacred social instincts opens great opportunities for the moral development of the individual and the purification of the social life. The author of this valuable book does not advise that the church in every case should carry on the work of organizing and developing the play life of the community, but rather that this should become a subject of Christian interest as a part of

man's normal life. If other agencies, however, fail to provide proper and wholesale recreation it is the duty of the church to fill the gap. Mr. Atkinson would include not only the sports and games approved by the Y. M. C. A., but theatricals, card games and dancing. All these activities should be carried on under proper supervision and the best moral leadership. What will the church do in response to this high call to service in a field which has always been neglected and often spurned as incompatible with its ideals? Many Christians will evade the responsibility on the plea that this is not the proper sphere of religion. But already in isolated cases much is being done, and those who are moved by the new impulses in religion and are in touch with the life and needs of the common people will heed this call to service.

The Church and the People's Play, by Henry A. Atkinson. Boston: Pilgrim Press. $1.25.

EDUCATION FOR COUNTRY LIFE

Very systematic and full of pertinent information is *Means and Methods of Agricultural Education* by Albert H. Leake, another prize essay in the Hart, Schaffner and Marx series. The problem of increasing farm products to keep pace with the growth of population is dependent upon having plenty of farmers, and upon having the farmers efficient producers. Both factors are closely related to education; the school must not only teach people how to do their work, but also how to conduct their lives, their community as well as their personal affairs. Mr. Leake would put into the educational program all the latest devices for making life more attractive in rural districts. The needed reforms and reorganization in rural education are well presented, and the example of Denmark is pointed out to show that practical results may really be attained.

Means and Methods of Agricultural Education, by A. T. Leake. Houghton, Mifflin. $2.

THE SHIFTING SCIENCE

From the "time of the Physiocrats" to the present day the science of economics has undergone quite as radical changes as has the industrial life of society; and a *History of Economic Doctrines* by Charles Gide and Charles Rist is a worthy footnote to a history of the industrial and intellectual revolutions of the past hundred and fifty years. Professor Gide's texts in economics have been almost as well known in this country as those of any English or American author, and they owe their popularity as much to his scientific and scholarly treatment of the subject as to his lively and human method of presentation. Too much of our economic doctrine is colored by political association and class interest; a study of history is the best countervailing influence one can have. Individualist and socialist, banker and syndicalist, could all profit from getting this wider outlook. The translation is excellent. Unfortunately the well selected references are not as serviceable as they might be if the translator and editors had taken

Resinol Soap

a friend to tender skins

The soothing, healing medication in Resinol Soap which is so helpful in clearing poor complexions, is equally dependable for protecting delicate skins from the havoc of wintry wind and cold.

To use Resinol Soap for the toilet is usually to make sure that one's complexion will come through the cold weather unharmed, and that the hands will be kept free from redness, roughness and chapping.

If lack of proper care *should* result in painful and unsightly chapping, a little Resinol Ointment will generally afford complete relief.

Resinol Soap is not artificially colored, its rich brown being entirely due to the Resinol medication it contains. Sold by all druggists and dealers in toilet goods. For a trial size cake, with a sample box of Resinol Ointment, free, write to Dept. 8-E, Resinol, Baltimore, Md.

Resinol Shaving Stick also contains the Resinol medication so that it soothes and refreshes the face, while supplying a rich, creamy, non-drying lather. The best druggists carry it.

the trouble to introduce English translations in place of the many foreign titles, since such editions are available for the most valuable sources.

A History of Economic Doctrines, by Charles Gide and Charles Rist. Boston: Heath. $3.

THE SUBLIME PORTE

Sir Edwin Pears resided forty two years in Constantinople, employed as advocate in the consular courts and correspondent for British papers. During this time he has witnessed three revolutions, three Sultans deposed, the establishment of the Young Turk Party and has known most of the great public men connected with the Near East. In *Forty Years in Constantinople* he gives, in autobiographical fashion, an account of all the principal events in which he was interested, and of the Turkish statesmen and British and other ambassadors with whom he was in intimate relation.

Constantinople is the center of international intrigue, and European nations send to the Porte their ablest diplomats. An account of the doings of these forty years cannot fail to be intensely interesting and instructive. The author of this work speaks frankly, unveils many secrets of state, and explains many facts that have puzzled historians, such as, for example, the reason why the Russians did not occupy Constantinople after the Russo-Turkish war. The American reader will be especially interested in the admiration exprest for the work of Robert College; for the succession of American ministers and ambassadors; and especially for the indefatigable labors of Ambassador Morgenthau for the protection of Christians. One will gain from the volume a fresh sense of the atrocities inflicted by the Turks in the succession of Bulgarian and Armenian massacres.

Forty Years in Constantinople, the Recollections of Sir Edward Pears, 1873-1915. Appleton. $5.

OPERAS

The new edition of J. W. MacSpadden's excellent handbook of *Opera Synopses* has added twenty-four numbers to its old list, being those given in America in the past four years and some of the novelties of this season.

Crowell. $1.

FERDINAND AND ISABELLA

Isabel of Castile and the Making of the Spanish Nation, by Irene L. Plunkett, is an interesting study of the disputed character of the Spanish Queen and of the reign that saw the Inquisition, the expulsion of the Jews, and the discoveries of Columbus.

Putnam. $2.50.

FOR ALL MEN

Mrs. Katrina Trask allows the imperative necessity of social and economic betterment, but finds the world's greatest need in an inward solvent of spiritual and moral power. *The Mighty and the Lowly* are as one in this realm where the life and work of Jesus were consummated, and neither the rich nor poor may claim Him as their special champion.

Macmillan. $1.

BLINDNESS

The parts of *Hitting the Dark Trail*, the touching story of Clarence Hawkes's courageous life that will be most enlightening to us with eyes, are the analysis of his mental suffering in the first years after the loss of his sight, the chapter on the psychology of sightlessness and the description of how he watches a baseball

sweet with the breath of gardens, bright with the glinting wings of scarlet tanagers. The subjects range from Rheims Cathedral —1914 to A Breath of Mint, but the workmanship, tho exquisite, has a certain sameness. The mint arouses emotions too similar to those stirred by the cathedral.

Houghton, Mifflin. 75 cents.

HISTORY OF PAINTING

A good short guide to the development of that art is *Masterpieces of Painting*, by Louise Rogers Jewett, of Holyoke. There are chapters on mural decoration, on tempera, on oils, and on the ideals of the different schools and periods with a helpful bibliography.

Boston: Badger. $1.

ARTHURIAN ENGLAND

What a relief it is to escape from this prosy, scientific world and its sophisticated fiction and slip back into the Greenwood that the author of "The Broad Highway," Jeffery Farnol, has again unrolled enticingly in *Beltane the Smith!* Romance, love, adventure, told in the fascinating style of Old England, fill the 500 pages that recount the quest of Beltane for Lady Helen.

Boston: Little, Brown. $1.50.

A CHILD'S BIBLE

William Canton has succeeded where many have failed in telling *The Bible Story, Old and New Testament*, so that children may understand its teachings and at the same time appreciate its beauty and reverence its power. A simple map of the Holy Land and eighteen particularly good illustrations in color increase the value of the book, which deserves first rank among those stories that every child should know.

Doran. $2.

ASPECTS OF ART

The function and meaning of each of the four great types of art: sculpture, painting, music and poetry, and their relations to one another, are set forth by Edward Howard Griggs with his usual skill and facility in *The Philosophy of Art*. His interpretations and applications to life are everywhere enlivened and made impressive by his quotations and illustrations from a wide range of literature and history.

Huebsch. $1.50.

TO THE MIDDLE CLASS

Whether you mean well and have your doubts, or whether you are quite confident that Providence must carry all the responsibility for prevailing social and economic conditions, you should read Seymour Deming's little book, *A Message to the Middle Class*. It may disturb your complacence, it may challenge your Americanism, it may clear up some uncertainties, it may strengthen your resolution. It will take but an hour or two, and is worth while.

Boston: Small, Maynard. 75 cents.

A PHYSICIAN'S VIEWS ON EUGENICS

From a wide experience as physician, as instructor and as social investigator, and from wide reading, Dr. Frederick A. Rhodes writes *The Next Generation*. The discussions of crime, vice, heredity, charity, immigration, insanity and other social problems show an acquaintance with actual conditions as well as with "authorities." The personal touch and the direct simplicity of the style adapt the book to the needs of the ordinary reader.

Boston: Badger. $1.50.

THE SPIRIT OF RUSSIA

Stephen Graham's new work on Russia, *Mary and Martha*, is more than a study of Russian life and thought. It is a comparison of Eastern and Western Christianity, and as such takes in a visit to the Coptic monastery in the Sahara and a discussion of many matters far from Russia itself. Loving the Russians, he yet does not gloss over characteristics unpleasant and more, to western eyes, so that one feels this an uncommonly true picture of this Slavic people, of their strength and their weakness.

Macmillan. $2.

PEBBLES

United we stand for a whole lot.—*Columbia State.*

We have seen many a skating-beginner this season temporarily lose his amateur standing.—*New York Tribune.*

Looks as if England realizes that if she avoids a draft she will lose her grip.—*Philadelphia North American.*

It begins to look as tho the ultimate fate of little nations is to be fed by the United States.—*Washington Post.*

"Let's go out to Central Park and look at the animals."
"I can't—I've got to study my zoology."
—*The Masses.*

The principal mistake Greece made, like Belgium and Poland, seems to have been in her selection of a place on the map.—*Kansas City Star.*

"Seven U. S. Troopers Captured by Mexican Bandit Raiders."—Headline.
A serious depiction of our available forces.—*New York Tribune.*

Spain is placing $20,000,000 munition-contracts in this country. She knows something about the effectiveness of American guns.—*Philadelphia North American.*

By reversing all the protests that Great Britain made to the United States during the Civil War it is possible to obtain a fairly correct notion of contemporary British theory of international law.—*New York World.*

"Pop Merlin," Earl S. discovers, "was the original War-lord. 'But look ye, all barons',"—it is from "Morte d'Arthur" I, 4—"'be before King Uther to-morn, and God and I shall make him to speak.'"—*New York Tribune.*

"What is an amateur?" is still one of the raging queries of the hour. But, in spite of all the recent discussion, we haven't changed the answer we evolved four years ago, viz., "Any one who can get away with it."—*New York Tribune.*

This is the famous Wilson Limerick which is making the rounds:
As a beauty I am not a star,
There are others more handsome by far;
    But my face, I don't mind it,
    For I am behind it—
The people in front get the jar.—*Woodrow Wilson, Bruno's Weekly.*

Three times had King Canute ordered the waves to recede.
And three times had the waves paid no attention whatever to his commands.
"The only thing to be done in a case like this," said the King, "is to break off diplomatic relations with Father Neptune."
And it was so ordered.—*New York World.*

One bit of humor came to the soldiers from home when the pages of a copy of the London *Chronicle* were eagerly unfolded in the trenches. There the headline stood:
KING GEORGE SHAKES HANDS WITH V. C.
GALLANT FEAT THAT COST A LEG.
—*New York Globe.*

Senator Gallinger—Of jewelry Germany is a great producer, and Germany cannot send any kind of jewelry out into the markets of the world today, so that for the time being New Jersey is finding a market for jewelry, but it will not last.
Senator Martine, of New Jersey—If there were no prosperity in this country, the people of this country would not be able to buy jewelry.
Senator Gallinger—I think they probably could afford to buy the kind of jewelry made in New Jersey under any circumstances. (Laughter on the floor and in the galleries.)—*Congressional Record.*

MARK ANTONY DELIVERING THE ORATION OVER CAESAR

CÆSAR'S name has stood through all the ages as the embodiment of imperial power. His intimely end after reaching the pinnacle of earthly glory is one of the great tragedies of history. The greatest tragedy in all human history is now being enacted on the bristle fields of Europe. All the underlying causes of this conflict, the racial antipathies, the commercial rivalries, the sting of past defeats, the undying ambitions of every Empire and Kingdom may be discerned from the pages of history. The one great history of every Empire, Kingdom, Principality and Power from the beginning of civilization to the present, is

Ridpath's History of the World

Dr. Ridpath is universally recognized as America's greatest historian. Other men have written histories of one nation or period; Gibbon of Rome, Macaulay of England, Guizot of France, but it remained for Dr. Ridpath to write a history of the entire World from the earliest civilization down to the present. We offer the remaining sets of the last edition, brand new, down to date, beautifully bound in half morocco.

At a Great Sacrifice in Price

We will name our special low price and easy terms of payment only in direct letters. A coupon for your convenience is printed on the lower corner of this advertisement. Tear off the coupon, write your name and address plainly and mail now. Our plan of sale enables us to ship direct from factory to customer on approval and guarantee satisfaction. We employ no agents, nor do we sell through book stores, so there is no agents' commission to pay. Mail this coupon now before you forget it. The sample pages are free.

46 Page Booklet Free

We will mail you 46 free sample pages without obligation on your part to buy. These will give you some idea of the splendid illustrations and the wonderfully beautiful style in which the work is written. You can purchase this great work at the lowest price ever offered and pay for it in small sums monthly if you prefer.

Six Thousand Years of History

Ridpath takes you back to the dawn of history long before the Pyramids of Egypt were built, down through the romantic troubled times of Chaldea's grandeur and Assyria's magnificence; of Babylonia's wealth and luxury; of Greek and Roman splendor; of Mohammedan culture and refinement; up to the dawn of yesterday. He covers every race, every nation, every time and holds you spellbound by his wonderful eloquence. Mail the coupon.

Western Newspaper Asso. Chicago

FREE COUPON
Western Newspaper Association
H. E. SEVER, President
CHICAGO, ILL.
Please mail 46 free sample pages of Ridpath's History of the World, containing photogravures of Napoleon and Queen Elizabeth, and diagram of Panama canal and write me full particulars of your special offer to The Independent readers.

Name..
Address..
Independent

THE MARKET PLACE
A REVIEW OF FINANCE AND TRADE

BABY BONDS FOR SMALL SAVINGS

WE have been called a nation of spenders. That this is not far from true is demonstrated from a compilation of savings bank depositors of various countries showing that Switzerland headed the list with 554 depositors to the thousand of population, while the United States had only ninety-nine. This compilation is not of very recent date, but it proves that up to a comparatively short time ago, saving was not one of our popular virtues.

Since the war broke out, however, savings banks and postal savings agencies have reported enormously increasing deposits with the result that a steady demand has been produced for high grade investments and a consequential increase in bond prices in spite of continued liquidation from abroad.

Everybody has money to invest in something—automobiles, sealskin coats, diamonds, and, of course, the war stocks. During the boom, young men and women employees in New York did not center their attention on the sporting page or the women's page of a newspaper, but on the financial section, where they looked eagerly for the latest news on Bethlehem, Crucible, Submarine, etc. But the war stocks have had their day, much to the sorrow of many people who bought at the top and are either expecting advances which do not come or sold at a loss.

The investment of the future for the small investor lies in the *sound* bond of small denomination—$100 and $500. In France and Holland, widely known as countries where the working people are exceedingly thrifty, bonds of this class have been sold for years. When bonds of American railroads could only be purchased in this country in denominations of $1000 or more, they were available in France in pieces of 100 francs (normally $20) and every peasant had his wad of *rentes* or our railroad bonds of some sort stowed away in a corner of his cottage. That is why we hear so much about the thrift of the French.

Almost everybody one meets today has at least a hundred dollars lying idle or in the savings bank drawing interest at from 3½% to 4%. We do not wish to minimize the usefulness of the savings bank, but many of these people do not know that they can invest so small an amount as $100 in a coupon bond of a government, municipality, railroad, industrial or public service corporation. They feel that bonds are investments for men of wealth and therefore are content to carry their hoard with them or place it in a savings bank. It is surprising how many people have never heard of $100 and $500 bonds in spite of the great publicity given them by specialists. Those people who want their money to earn more than four per cent should be told that it can be done with almost as much safety as tho the funds were entrusted to a bank.

For instance, there can be purchased in $100 pieces the joint five per cent bonds of Great Britain and France due 1920 at about $95.50; or, if preference is in local securities, New York City 4½s of 1962 can be bought at 106¼, Chicago Harbor Construction 4s of 1917 at 96, Vancouver 4½s of 1923 at 93¼, etc. Among the railroad bonds we have Baltimore & Ohio Convertible Mortgage 4½s due 1933, legal investments for savings banks in New York, Connecticut and Massachusetts, selling at 98½. These bonds are secured on the entire system and are followed by over $210,000,000 dividend-paying stocks. Southern Pacific Company-San Francisco Terminal 4s due 1950, selling at 85, are secured by a first mortgage on the extensive terminals of the Southern Pacific at San Francisco; these bonds are legal for Connecticut savings banks. Other "legal" issues include Chicago, Burlington and Quincy-Denver Extension 4s due 1922, at 99, and Chicago, Milwaukee & St. Paul General and Refunding Convertible 5s, due 2014, at 109. A carefully diversified list has been compiled for the benefit of the reader, showing prices and return on each issue.

Many young people who have money to invest find more satisfaction in buying a $100 bond every little while than

BONDS OF $100 DENOMINATION

		Price about	Yield about Per cent.
Government and Municipal			
Anglo-French Loan 5s	1920	96	6.00
Baltimore, Md. 4s	1962 n	97	4.15
Chicago, Ill., Harbor Const. 4s	1917 n	100	4.00
New Orleans, La., Improvement 5s	1929	101	5.00
New York City 4½s	1960 n	102	4.15
New York City 4½s	1963 n	107	3.95
Vancouver 4½s	1923	93¼	5.60
Railroad Bonds			
Prime Issues:			
†Baltimore & Ohio—Mortgage Conv......4½s	1933 n	98½	4.60
Chicago, Burl. & Quincy-Denv. Ext......4s	1922 n	99	4.12
Chicago, Mil. & St. Paul, Conv. Gen. Ref..5s	2014 n	109	4.55
Norfolk & Western First Consolidated....4s	1996 n	94	4.25
Secondary Issues:			
Colorado & Southern, Ref. & Ext........4½s	1935	87	5.50
Erie-N. Y. & Greenwood Lake, Prior Lien..5s	1946	99	5.00
New York Central, Conv. Deb...........6s	1935	116	4.70
New Haven Railroad, Conv. Deb........6s	1948	115	5.00
Seaboard Ail Line, First & Consol.......6s	1945	100	6.00
Virginian Railway, First 5s	1962	99	5.00
Southern Pac.-San Francisco Terminal...4s	1950 c	85	4.95
Miscellaneous Corporation Issues			
American Telephone & Telegraph, Coll....4s	1929 c-m	91	4.90
Bethlehem Steel, First & Ref...........5s	1942	103	4.80
Central Leather Co., First..............5s	1925	100	5.00
Denver Gas & Electric, First............5s	1949	96	5.25
General Electric Co., Debenture........3½s	1942	80	4.85
Lackawanna Steel, First Cons...........5s	1950	96	5.25
Laclede Gas Light Co., First............5s	1919	100	5.00
Liggett & Myers, Debenture...........5s	1951	101 ·	4.95
P. Lorillard, Debenture................5s	1951	102	4.90
Pocahontas Consol., Collieries First.....5s	1957	90	5.60

†$500 Pieces.
n-Legal investment for New York savings banks.
c-Legal for Connecticut.
m-Legal for Massachusetts.

in placing that sum in the savings bank. The hundred dollar bond has been the foundation of many a modest fortune; it does not require very much of a sacrifice for a moderately salaried young man or woman to set aside enough each week to provide for a purchase of a few $100 bonds yearly. It is quite easy to save ten dollars a month, once one gets started, for eight or ten months, and then purchase a well secured bond with the proceeds.

This method can be continued for years until five or ten $100 bonds have been acquired when in many cases they may be exchanged for a $500 or $1000 piece. Ten dollars a month for five years means a fund of $600, not including interest. This plan of saving starts the non-investor on the road to economic independence in the best manner known, provided investments are selected with care, with more attention to safety of principal than high yield.

Bonds may be purchased on the "partial payment" plan, as are books or furniture, and the investor must never forget that until the bond is paid for in full, he is not actually its owner or even in possession of it as in the case of books. So unless he deals with an investment firm of recognized standing, he is very likely to find himself called upon to furnish more margin to his investment in case of a sharp decline in the market; unless, of course, his margin is large enough to protect his banker. In all cases, whether buying $1000 bonds or $100 ones, the selection of the banker is an all-important step.

There are several reputable firms which specialize in bonds of small denominations and sell them for cash or on the partial payment plan. This usually involves a payment of 10% or 20% of the face value of the investment and $5 per month until the entire purchase price has been paid. A minimum commission of $6 per $100 is charged, but this includes interest, taxes, etc. As interest is received on the bond it is either sent to the owner or credited to his account. Between the cash and the partial payment plan, preference should be given to the cash plan as in that case the bond is held by the owner.

In conclusion, there are several points which the investor should bear in mind, viz:—

1—Select a conservative banker.
2—Buy bonds that yield under 5½% except in extraordinary cases.
3—Buy only mortgage bonds having a large equity in stock or bonds.
4—Ask for a description of the bond and read it.
5—Do not purchase any more bonds than you can pay for.
6—Never become frightened if the market value of your bonds drops five points. Ask your banker's advice when this happens.
7—If you have money to invest do not wait for a "bear market." You are losing interest meanwhile.
8—Do not buy securities of mining companies, construction companies, munitions concerns, etc., unless you have other means to rely upon. If you buy such securities, remember the risk.
9—Read all the literature on securities that is available.

Insurance
Conducted by
W. E. UNDERWOOD

RESERVELESS LIFE INSURANCE

A heavy proportion of my mail from correspondents contains inquiries relating to insurances carried in assessment, coöperative, or fraternal associations and orders. Most of the inquiries have their origin in an attained or a growing conviction that their premium payments have increased unreasonably, or are about to do so. Some of my correspondents inform me that they have met every demand made in these rate advances, that they are now 65, 70 and 75 years old and that the assessments called exceed their ability to pay.

To be just, no one is censurable for these conditions, unless we may condemn people wholesale for what they do not know and cannot learn except at first hand thru bitter experience. The promoters of life insurance schemes which are devoid of the reserve element are the most sanguine lot of people I ever knew in any business. They can all "figger"; they are so adept in the art of plausibility as to successfully deceive themselves. They, innocently and unwittingly, have hundreds of thousands of victims in this country whom they "convinced." These victims have spent millions of dollars on so-called life insurance; they are from twenty to forty years older than they were when they commenced; and they possess not one dollar's worth of equity of any character for their money.

What is saddest of all, the vast majority of them are physically impaired, or too old to secure old line insurance. I have before me now a letter from a man 72, who holds a \$500 certificate in an association on which he paid last year in monthly instalments \$59. And the rate is steadily advancing—of course. Twenty years ago that man could have bought \$2000 of real life insurance for \$98 a year which now would have been worth \$1304 in fully paid-up insurance or \$1038 in cash. But he carried the association policy more than thirty years. At age 42 a policy for \$3000 life insurance would have cost \$99, and been worth today in paid-up, \$1770; or \$1218 in cash.

Some of the assessment associations and fraternal orders have, as far as their limitations would permit, reformed their mathematics; and on the newer business are accumulating a reserve, so-called. Very few of them, if any, are providing for an adequate reserve. This is a stop-gap only; the sole effect is to defer the evil day.

Paradoxically, the lucky persons in

an unscientifically constructed life insurance scheme are those who die early, for they have secured the proverbial something for nothing. Those who stayed, paid and grew old, are victims for whom there is no relief.

A. Y. D., Asheville, N. C.—The Penn Mutual is a sound, well managed life insurance company, providing excellent service for its policyholders.

R. P. A., Mocksville, N. C.—On the principle that a going concern, however weak, is better than one which has failed and for the further reason that your father is too old to secure other insurance, I would advise him to accept the offer made by the Order of Puritans. On January 1, 1915, the assets of the latter were $158,169, and the liabilities $29,186.

E. S., Twin Falls, Idaho.—Take your insurance in an old line company, preferably one which maintains what is called a *full* reserve. There are so many it would be impossible to list them here. Write to your State Insurance Department at Boise City for a pamphlet listing them and giving their statistics. The United States Casualty is first class in every way.

B. T., Onawa, Iowa.—You do not state how long you have been carrying the endowment policy. However your age and circumstances warrant the maintenance of that policy. If you desire to protect the indebtedness mentioned against your death, add $1,500 or $2,000 ordinary life insurance in the same company. You will doubtless live to reap wider benefits from it as the years pass.

F. W. C., Denver, Colo.—A number of stock life insurance companies (barring the small dividends paid stockholders) operate on a purely mutual basis. The argument against them lies not so much in the fact that the business yields an income to the owners of the capital stock, as that the company is controlled by them. In a few instances this control has been injurious to the interests of policyholders.

N. F. D., Chicago, Ill.—The company is financially solvent, but not strong. It is one of the small and young institutions which possess no distinctive merits and which have to pay large commissions to secure business. To be entirely candid, I am of the opinion that the balance of chance is against the company's lasting to the maturity of your policy. But it may. If there is any doubt respecting the assured's physical condition, he should not give up the policy until after he has passed a satisfactory examination and secured a policy from another company. Nothing is to be gained by using the loan value of a life insurance policy as payment in reduction of a mortgage on the home. In the event of death the result would be the same. But that mortgage should be protected by life insurance of the first grade.

J. A., Lafayette, La.—A résumé of the financial condition of the Pan-American Life Insurance Company as of December 31, 1914 (later figures unavailable), shows total assets of $2,416,370. Liabilities total $1,775,460 and include capital stock, $1,000,000 and policy reserve, $747,976. The net surplus is $640,910. The premium income was $532,120; total income, $685,960. As nearly as my facilities permit I find the management expenses to be $265,819, which seems to be about 39 per cent of the income. The company made gains on its assumptions for interest, mortality and lapses aggregating $138,824, while its actual expenses exceeded its "loading" by $108,365. I know of no way of appraising the book value of the stock. In 1912 the new business written was $4,522,000, bringing the total in force to $8,425,000; in 1913, new business, $6,223,000, with a total in force at end of year of $12,624,000; in 1914, new business written $5,681,000, with $15,670,000 in force at end of year. The company seems to be conducted with good business judgment and its first years indicate a successful future.

Journalism As An Aid To History Teaching

By Edwin E. Slosson, Ph. D.
Literary Editor of The Independent
Associate in the School of Journalism, Columbia University

This address, which was given before the History Section of the New York State Teachers' Association at Rochester, November 23, 1915, has been published in pamphlet form and will be furnished free to teachers—Write to W. W. Ferrin, 119 West 40th Street, New York.

HE Next Issue of The Independent will be a Shakespeare Number. It will contain a double-page reproduction on fine paper of Leopold Flameng's etching of the famous Chandos portrait of Shakespeare, and also the first of the series of Eight Articles which are the basis of The Independent's Shakespeare Contest for American Schools. Concerning this Contest many expressions of approval have been received from men high in position and influence in the educational world. A few of these expressions are printed below. The author of the series is Frederick Houk Law, Ph.D., Lecturer in English in New York University, and Head of the Department of English in the Stuyvesant High School, New York City. His close study of Shakespeare and the Elizabethan period, and his practical experience as lecturer and teacher, have enabled him to write a highly interesting and instructive series of articles equally suitable for schools, for clubs and for private reading.

HON. PHILANDER P. CLAXTON, Superintendent of Education of the United States: "I sincerely hope that The Independent's Shakespeare Contest and the medal offered in connection with it may serve to increase interest in the celebration of the tercentenary of the death of the great dramatist. Anything that may be done this year for the purpose of emphasizing this anniversary and of promoting the study of Shakespeare in the schools of the United States should be encouraged."

C. P. CARY, State Superintendent of Public Instruction, Wisconsin: "We are making brief announcement in our Educational News Bulletin of The Independent's Shakespeare Contest for American Schools. This will bring the contest to the attention of most of the prominent school people in the state of Wisconsin and may do something to encourage entry in the contest."

J. Y. JOYNER, State Superintendent of Public Instruction, North Carolina: "Believing that it will stimulate the study of Shakespeare in the schools, I approve most heartily of The Independent's Shakespeare Contest for American Schools."

H. A. DAVEE, Superintendent of Public Instruction, Montana: "I am very glad to endorse The Independent's Shakespeare Contest for American Schools. I hope no less than one hundred Montana schools will take part in this contest."

C. O. CASE, State Superintendent of Public Instruction, Arizona: "In reply to your favor of recent date I wish to commend your efforts toward stimulating an interest in the Great Bard, William Shakespeare. Your plan of holding contests in the schools meets with my approval and I shall be glad to cooperate with you in any way that I can."

HON. JOHN H. FINLEY, Commissioner of Education for the State of New York: "I heartily applaud your effort to interest the teachers and students in the schools of the state in the reading of Shakespeare, and I hope that you will find yourself under the compulsion of awarding a thousand medals. But I wish, when all this is done, that there might be a rating of all the first papers in the various schools receiving the medals, and the bestowal of another medal for the best essay written in the state."

PAYSON SMITH, State Superintendent of Public Schools, Maine: "I can heartily commend the Shakespeare Contest for American Schools inaugurated by The Independent."

M. L. BRITTAIN, State Superintendent of Schools, Georgia: "In reply to your letter of recent date I take pleasure in commending your Shakespeare Contest for American Schools."

HOWARD A. GASS, State Superintendent of Public Instruction, Missouri: "A person cannot claim to be well educated without a more or less thorough knowledge of Shakespeare. I approve of any movement that will lead to a greater familiarity with Shakespeare and his works. It seems to me that a Shakespeare contest would be one of the most satisfactory ways of arousing the interest of teachers in the study of the greatest English author."

R. C. STEARNES, State Superintendent of Public Instruction, Virginia: "I thank you very much for your letter of January 6, calling my attention to the Shakespeare Contest for American Schools inaugurated by The Independent. This seems to me to be a very happy thought on the part of the management of The Independent, and I hope the result will be a renewed and greater interest in the study of the works of the great English dramatist by our high school pupils."

The Independent Offers a Shakespeare Anniversary Medal

for the best essay from any school in the United States on the life and works of William Shakespeare. Any American school, private or public, elementary or secondary, may take part in the contest, but the medal cannot be awarded unless ten pupils at least compete from that school. Each competitor must complete an original essay of from 500 to 2500 words and hand it in to the judges by May 5. In case of elementary schools the school authorities shall select three judges from among the faculty, pupils or outsiders (including no contestants). In case of secondary schools the contestants themselves may get together and select any three judges they may choose except a contestant. The contest is open free to all schools and a subscription to The Independent is not obligatory. If 1000 schools take part in this contest, 1000 medals will be awarded. Your school does not have to compete with any other school.

Feb. 7, 1916

THE INDEPENDENT SHAKESPEARE CONTEST DEPARTMENT, 119 West 40th Street, New York: We wish to enter The Independent Shakespeare Contest for American Schools. Please send full details.

Signed...

School...

City and State...

The Independent

FOR SIXTY-SEVEN YEARS THE
FORWARD-LOOKING WEEKLY OF AMERICA

THE CHAUTAUQUAN
Merged with The Independent June 1, 1914

FEBRUARY 14, 1916

OWNED AND PUBLISHED BY
THE INDEPENDENT CORPORATION, AT
119 WEST FORTIETH STREET, NEW YORK
WILLIAM R. HOWLAND, PRESIDENT
FREDERIC E. DICKINSON, TREASURER

WILLIAM HAYES WARD
HONORARY EDITOR

EDITOR: HAMILTON HOLT
ASSOCIATE EDITOR: HAROLD J. HOWLAND
LITERARY EDITOR: EDWIN E. SLOSSON
PUBLISHER: KARL V. S. HOWLAND

ONE YEAR, THREE DOLLARS

SINGLE COPIES, TEN CENTS

Postage to foreign countries in Universal Postal
Union, $1.75 a year extra; to Canada, $1 extra.
Instructions for renewal, discontinuance or
change of address should be sent two weeks
before the date they are to go into effect. Both
the old and the new address must be given.

We welcome contributions, but writers who
wish their articles returned, if not accepted,
should send a stamped and addrest envelope. No responsibility is assumed by The
Independent for the loss or non-return of
manuscripts, tho all due care will be exercised.

Entered at New York Post Office as Second
Class Matter

Copyright, 1916, by The Independent

Address all Communications to
THE INDEPENDENT
119 West Fortieth Street, New York

CONTENTS

THE CANADIAN OVERSEAS

England, to a Canadian soldier freshly arrived from Canada, is like a new
pair of boots on a school boy; he is
proud of the boots but uncomfortable.
The Canadian Tommy, to the appreciative eyes of England, is like a miracle,
a geyser, or a water spout, or a river
in flood; something to be admired,
treated with infinite kindness and respect yet somehow dangerous, liable to
do unexpected things or smash sacred
conventions. Having seen England
calls the English "sir" and damns their
climate. He takes off his hat in the presence of the great monuments and he
fumes at the mud. He likes their beer
and he works himself into a rage over
the drizzle of rain. Rain in his boots, in
his great coat, on his hat. If they would
let him fight, how he would fight! But
they won't, so he schemes to get leave
or prays for a Zepp raid to liven things
up, and if he is very, very temperamental, writes home a grouchy letter. On
leave his spirits improve. On London
leave he is elated. He hires taxis and
buys refreshment like any other gentleman, tips commissionaires, and takes
rooms "with bath" so long as his funds
hold out. He is abashed only when he is
"broke." He is subservient only in letter, not in spirit. He delights and as-
tounds the grave people of England
every day of their lives. And all unconsciously. . . . Money! Phst! That
for it, says the Canadian Tommy
after sending his wife's share home.
Decorum! Eh? Spell it!
Subservience!—What? He romps like
an Airedale and looks as solemnly innocent and hurt as a three-year-old when
he is caught at it. Discipline? General
Alderson told me in France that you
could tell a Canadian by the smart cut
of his salute! But in England he salutes
only up till seven o'clock. After seven
on leave he does not see you, and if you
are a wise officer you don't see him
either.—Edmonton Journal.

REMARKABLE REMARKS

GEN. LEONARD WOOD—We are menaced
on all sides.

SENATOR JAMES HAMILTON LEWIS—
What is preparedness?

SECRETARY REDFIELD—Economy is not
the absence of spending.

WINIFRED BLACK—To most women nowadays love is a side issue.

AMBASSADOR CHINDA—How little is
known here in America of Japan.

LAURA JEAN LIBBEY—Positively do not
allow kisses if you desire to wed.

PREMIER OKUMA—The average Japanese
has lost the dignity of human stature.

OTIS SKINNER—Your real New Yorker
goes to the theatre, but from a sense of
duty.

ED. HOWE—Plenty of boarding houses
are pleasanter places of residence than
plenty of homes.

JAMES SEXTON, OF THE DOCK WORKERS'
UNION—If Germany wins, nothing else on
God's earth matters.

WALT MASON—All girls should marry
when they can. There's naught more useful than a man.

SENATOR JOHN SHARP WILLIAMS—The
Confederate soldier was the most quixotic
human being in the world.

BERTRAM GOODHUE, ARCHITECT—You
can't get comfort and beauty in a house
that costs $6000 or $7000.

THEODORE ROOSEVELT—There can be no
greater waste of time than to debate about
non-debatable things.

CHARLES RANN KENNEDY—I wrote my
"The Terrible Meek" by direct inspiration
from Heaven

LOUIS D. BRANDEIS—What we must do
in America is not to attack our judges, but
to educate them.

EMPEROR WILLIAM—All hostile assaults
will break to pieces upon the power of a
clean conscience.

JANE ADDAMS—This war began in secret diplomacy. It will end in secret conferences by diplomatists.

NORMAN HAPGOOD—I do not pretend to
guess exactly what rôle religion will play
in the future.

WOODROW WILSON—There ought never
to be another presidential nominating convention.

BILLY SUNDAY—The Holy Spirit don't
want to take a bath of beer and swim
around in booze. Not on your tintype.

SIR WILLIAM OSLER—Up to fifteen a
boy can be appealed to thru his stomach
and then thru his heart, but not thru his
head.

HENRY HOLT—The Government carries
the Police Gazette at a cent a pound and
charges eight times as much to carry a
spelling book or a Bible.

SENATOR HOLLIS—We should abandon
foolish talk about there being any "quarrel" between President Wilson and Mr.
Bryan.

THOMAS EWING, COMMISSIONER OF PAT-
ENTS—The new rules, while elaborate and
technical, make for brevity, simplification,
speed and efficiency.

BISHOP LAWRENCE OF MASSACHUSETTS
—I personally would as lief have this country overrun by every nation of the earth
as to have it under the bondage of militarism.

HENRY BRIGHAM—Fricky Hancock took
his bass fiddle to the Gander Creek bottoms
yesterday and played several selections
under hickory trees, but had little success,
as the hickory nuts are nearly all gone.

HENRY J. PIERCE—Were it not for the
discovery of processes whereby it is now
possible, with the aid of electric energy, to
obtain supplies of fixt nitrogen from the
atmosphere, the perpetuation of the human
race would be endangered.

The Independent

| VOLUME 85 | FEBRUARY 14, 1916 | NUMBER 3506 |

THREE HUNDRED YEARS AFTER

WILLIAM SHAKESPEARE, of Stratford on Avon, died three hundred years ago next April. During the next three months millions of school children in the whole English speaking world will study his life, his writings, and his influence. There will be plays and pageants, lectures and readings, essays and books, meetings and dinners, all in memory of Shakespeare.

Why?

Every one must find out the reason for himself. Nobody can tell him why Shakespeare is worth while. All that the professor of literature can do for us is to say: "Here is good poetry. Read it." They have been, all of them, saying this about Shakespeare's works for the last three hundred years, but because this is a busy world and we are apt to forget the best things in it, advantage is taken of this anniversary to remind us of Shakespeare and what we may get from him if we would.

We celebrate this memorial not for the benefit of Shakespeare's memory, but for our own memory. He does not need to be remembered, but we need to remember him. Not because he died three hundred years ago but because he still lives. His bones lie buried in the chancel of the Stratford church underneath a slab which calls down a curse on whoever shall disturb them. But nobody needs to disturb them. Nor does anybody need to dig up his private life.

How Shakespeare looked and lived and what he ate and wore are not important. For in his person and habits Shakespeare was very much like other men of his time. Wherein he differed was in what he wrote and this we have today. Among those who lived in London in 1600 there were doubtless many who were taller and handsomer than he and who wore finer clothes, but there was nobody who wrote such good poetry. By grubbing over the musty piles of legal documents in the London vaults scholars may unearth another signature of Shakespeare's, but that would merely serve to show perhaps another way of spelling his name. They are not going to discover another "Hamlet" there.

It is fortunate on the whole that we do not know so much about Shakespeare's life and personality as we do, for instance, about Queen Elizabeth, for then we might make the mistake of thinking that we knew Shakespeare when we had read his biography. But since all that is actually known about Shakespeare's life can be put in half a dozen pages, there is nothing to distract our attention from his dramas. "The play's the thing."

A poet's influence is to be measured in three dimensions:

Length—How long is he remembered?

Breadth—How widely is he read?

Depth—How deeply is he felt?

It is when Shakespeare is thus estimated by cubic measurement that his greatness can be appreciated. With faults that any schoolboy may detect, he combined merits that no author can surpass. "Next to God," said Alexander Dumas, "Shakespeare has created most." He has filled the world for us with fictitious personages more real than most of the living. He calls them from all ages and countries, Greeks, Romans, Moors, Italians, Danes, Englishmen. He interests us in all classes and degrees of intelligence: Jack Cade and Caesar, Hamlet and Caliban, Portia and Audrey. They are not types but human beings, the heroes with failings, and the villains with virtues. Comedy and tragedy are mingled together as they are in real life.

Shakespeare lived close to his times. He was a successful theatrical manager with all that that implies. He was quick to adapt his themes to changes of taste in people or patron. He gave the public what it wanted, and by so doing he came nearer giving what the public wants today than any other dramatist of his time. He put in something to catch the ears of the groundlings of the Globe Theater and something to hold the attention of the philosophers of the twentieth century.

It may be, our reader, that you have not got as much out of Shakespeare as you might. If so this year is a good time to find out what it is and to get it. If you are "tired of hearing of Shakespeare" it means that you do not know him well enough yet. So we advise you, however well read you may be, to take the time to go thru the eight articles on Shakespeare's life and work which we begin to publish in this issue.

Why is it that some familiarity with Shakespeare's writings is regarded in every country as an essential part of education? The Germans, who are now angrily repudiating most things English, lay claim to Shakespeare on the ground that they study him more and play him oftener than his countrymen. The plans which have for years been in preparation for a great national celebration of the Shakespeare Tercentenary in England will have to be abandoned on account of the war. It devolves then upon us Americans, as majority stockholders in the English language, to show that we are not behind in our appreciation of the greatest poet of that language.

THE PRESIDENT'S PREPAREDNESS TOUR

OPINIONS will differ as to what effect the President's tour will have on the furtherance of his preparedness program. But of this we may be certain: The throngs that came within the spell of his personality have been undeniably moved, and all, whether those who were privileged to hear him or those who have been obliged to read his speeches the next day in cold type, have been imprest anew with the dignity, the responsibility, the moderation and the rectitude of the man. Woodrow Wilson knows how to make a speech. He has something to say, and he says it as befits the Chief Magistrate of a great and free people.

What is then the burden of the President's plea? He repeatedly denies that there is any special war cloud on the horizon. "There is no sudden crisis," he said at Milwaukee. "Nothing new has happened. I am not on this errand because of any unexpected situation."

"I believe in peace. I love peace," he said in Pittsburgh. "I am ready at any time," he declared at New York, "to use every power that is in me to prevent such a catastrophe as war coming upon this country."

There can be no doubt that these are sincere statements. The American people could not have a more tried and true friend of peace at the White House in these dark hours.

The President, however, calls for a large increase of our army and navy. "We have not," he said in Chicago, "enough men in the army now for times of peace." "Such coast defenses as we have," he said at Cleveland, "are both strong and ample, but we have not got enough coast defenses in enough places." "What I am for," he said in New York, "is a body of at least half a million trained citizens who will serve under conditions of danger as an immediately available National Reserve."

The President avers that the navy ranks fourth instead of second on paper. This is so if tonnage is the measurement, tho we remember that the naval officers who testified before the House Committee on Naval Affairs last spring declared that our navy ranked third in fighting power, being a trifle behind Germany and a little ahead of France. But whether it be third or fourth our navy is a competent one. "I do believe," said the President at Cleveland, "that from the standpoint of efficiency our navy is among the finest in the world and second to none." Nevertheless he declared at St. Louis "that our navy ought, in my judgment, to be incomparably the greatest navy in the world." This is an astounding statement and must be a rhetorical exaggeration. We cannot conceive that the President would have the United States embark on a program to outdistance Great Britain, which insists upon maintaining a navy equal to any two other powers.

Now what arguments did the President marshal to convince the people that it is necessary to increase our annual military expenditures by over $100,000,000 a year. We have searched his speeches thoroly and are able to discover only three.

These are:

First. To maintain the honor of the United States.

Second. To maintain the Monroe Doctrine.

Third. To be ready in case we are forced into the war.

1. "You have laid upon me," said the President at Chicago, "the double obligation of maintaining the honor of the United States and maintaining the peace of the United States. Is it not conceivable that the two might become incompatible?" "You have bidden me," he said in Milwaukee, "see that nothing stains the honor of the United States, and that is matter not within my control. That depends on what others do."

This is a somewhat indefinite argument. A nation's honor, like a man's honor, is, after all, in its own keeping. No one can dishonor another. All honor's wounds are self-inflicted, as Mr. Carnegie has well said. Nevertheless, we are living in an age with no international court to which the nations are compelled to take their affairs of honor. Hence each nation is now the sole guardian of its honor. The question, then, is whether our honor and vital interests are more likely to be violated now than a year ago, before the President changed his mind on the preparedness issue. There is much argument to be made on both sides of this question. The President has submitted nothing concrete to prove his point.

2. The President touched upon the Monroe Doctrine in both his New York and Chicago speeches. At Chicago he said: "We are not asking ourselves, Shall we be prepared to defend our own shores and our own homes? Is that all that we stand for? To keep the door securely shut against enemies? Certainly not. What about the great principles we have stood for, for the liberty of government and national independence in the whole Western Hemisphere?" In New York he referred to our "obligation to stand as the strong brother of all those in this hemisphere who will maintain the same principles and follow the same ideals of liberty [as the United States]. . . . . What America has to fear, if she has to fear anything, are indirect, roundabout flank movements upon her regnant position in the Western Hemisphere."

What "flank movements" the President contemplates "on our regnant position in the Western Hemisphere" he does not state. We cannot ourselves surmise what they may be. Suffice it to say that never since the Monroe Doctrine was promulgated has it been questioned by any nation on earth. The United States, moreover, is better prepared to defend it today than it has ever been in its history, while the South American nations would probably come now almost unitedly to our support, as they might not have done in the past. Moreover, if the Monroe Doctrine was seriously threatened, the British fleet would almost certainly come to its defense. England has nearly as much at stake in maintaining the New World free from the curse of European politics as we have. On the whole, it looks as tho the Monroe Doctrine is in the "most regnant position" it has ever occupied during its entire existence.

3. The President fears that we may be drawn into the present war. No man's opinion in the United States is entitled to greater weight on this question than his. "I cannot tell," he said in New York, "what the international relations will be tomorrow. America does not control the circumstances of the world." At Cleveland he said: "The dangers are infinite and constant. The world is on fire and there is tinder everywhere." At Chicago he said: "No man can completely say whether we will be drawn into the struggle or not." At Milwaukee he said: "The thoughts of men who are engaged in this struggle

are concentrated upon the struggle itself, and there is daily and hourly danger that they will feel themselves constrained to do things which are absolutely inconsistent with the rights of the United States." At Des Moines he said: "Do you want the situation to be such that all the President can do is to write messages, to utter words of protest?"

But the only speech where the President, specified what some of the belligerents "might feel constrained to do" was in the one delivered at St. Louis. "One reckless commander of a submarine," he remarked, "choosing to put his private interpretation upon what his government wishes him to do, might set the world on fire. . . . . There are cargoes of cotton on the high seas, cargoes of wheat on the seas, there are cargoes of manufactured articles on the seas, and every one of these cargoes may be the point of ignition."

The United States might have to fight to save American life. It ought never to fight simply to avenge lives already taken. Nor should the United States fight simply to save property. American lives have been taken by belligerents in this war. But in each instance the offending nation has offered reparation and has exprest itself as willing to give guarantees that similar acts would not recur. There is no evidence that these protestations are insincere. When the "Alabama" was fitted out in England as a privateer for the Confederacy and was committing her depredations on Northern commerce, President Lincoln did not immediately declare war on England, but notified her that at a suitable time he would demand reparation. After the Civil War was over and passions had cooled the matter was taken to arbitration, and, altho England declared the question affected her honor, damages were duly awarded the United States.

The President is right therefore in holding that we are more in danger of having our citizens killed and our property and other rights under international law invaded than before the war. But if the President takes the course he has unswervingly maintained hitherto we are more than likely to find that there will be no deliberate assaults on our honor, and all other questions that cannot be settled during the heat of hostilities can well be postponed till the war is over and the nations are ready to consider more equitably the rights of neutrals.

The President may be right in his demands. In order that there may be no misunderstanding let us repeat, as we have frequently said before, that The Independent is on the whole in favor of his military program as suggested in his message to Congress. It is moderate and in no sense a militaristic departure. But the President's speech-making tour has not thrown sufficient light upon the question of special and immediate need for an increase of naval and military strength as he desires. The country is entitled to know before taking his advice.

<hr/>

FIFTY YEARS OF Y. W. C. A.

IN February, 1866, in Boston an inconspicuous organization for the welfare of working-girls was founded. In February, 1916—after fifty years of growing usefulness, working always toward its early ideal, "not a charity, not a creed, not a club, but a comradeship based on the democracy of a common faith"—the Young Women's Christian Association of America is planning to celebrate its anniversary by a great jubilee, a month long and a nation wide.

Reminiscences and prophecies are both in order; the achievements of the Y. W. C. A. in the past offer a broad basis of hope for the future. But 'the organization is planning to make the most of its opportunities to remind the people of the United States during its anniversary celebration of all that it is doing and hopes to do.

Pageants showing the various steps in its history and suggesting its future plans are being given in nearly every city of the United States. Probably the most spectacular of these is the one in New York City, where over a thousand girls are to take part in a dramatic presentation of "Girls of Yesterday and Today."

In connection with these anniversary celebrations the campaign for a half million endowment fund for the Y. W. C. A. all over the country is being carried along vigorously. Contributions have already come in in large quantities and the prospect of a satisfactory total at the end of the month seems to justify the theory that the people are glad to pay for an institution that has proved adequate to meet their needs.

The growth of the Y. W. C. A. has kept pace with the revolution of woman's work in the world, which is just another way of saying that its progress has been swift as well as sure. Its international relationships have grown and strengthened. The scope of its work has come to include all classes of women and girls, and to offer them nearly every kind of advice or training. Fifty year's good work well done! May the next fifty be equally successful!

<hr/>

INDEPENDENCE OR SELF-GOVERNMENT

THE Democrats in Congress are resolved to set a definite date for our abandonment of the Filipinos. The Senate has passed the Philippine Government bill with an amendment directing the President to give the islands independence in four years unless when the four years have passed he thinks Congress ought to take another year to reconsider the matter.

This provision is better than the vague preamble which was urged last year, promising independence some time. For it brings two questions uncompromisingly before the people of the United States: What is our duty to the Philippines? Can we discharge that duty by going away and leaving them now?

On this question The Independent has perfectly clear convictions. When the United States took over the Philippines from Spain it assumed complete responsibility for their future. It became then our appointed task to protect the islands from outside aggression, to promote their industrial and commercial welfare, to educate the people of the islands, and to prepare them for self-government.

What profit and advantage this country could get from the islands was, from the point of view of right and duty, a purely secondary consideration. Our own action in accepting the islands from Spain imposed on us the solemn duty of putting their interests first in every action we took in relation to them.

How can the United States best discharge that duty? The Democratic party evidently believes it can be best done by making the islands independent forthwith. From this view The Independent—in spite of its name and the earnest convictions that the name symbolizes—strongly dissents.

The proponents of immediate independence are in confusion of mind over two things—independence and self-government.

Self-government is the inalienable right of every civilized people. As soon as a people are fitted for self-government, they are entitled to it as a matter of fundamental justice. The existence of autocracy is always wrong; the fact of democracy is always right.

But democracy and independence are not synonymous; they are not even inseparable. Without self-government a people that is fit for it is oppressed; without independence they may be as free from oppression as any people on the earth.

The peoples of Canada and Australia have self-government without independence. The peoples of Hayti and Mexico have independence without self-government. Which are the happier?

The American Revolution had its origin in the intense conviction of the inhabitants of the Colonies that they must have self-government. It became the War for Independence only because it was impossible to get self-government without independence.

It is self-government that we owe to the Filipinos. We must see that they have it just as fast as they are fitted for it, or be false to our trust. But we cannot be sure that they will get it best and most quickly by being made independent. Indeed the chances are all the other way.

The majority of the people of the Philippines are not yet fit for self-government. A people thus largely unfit is the ripe prey of selfish aggression from without and selfish exploitation from within. It is to the duty of the United States is plain. It is to bend its best energies to the task of fitting the Filipinos for self-government; to extend the measure of their control over the affairs of the islands just as rapidly as they are fitted to exercize it; and to leave the question of independence until that future time when the Filipinos shall be in fact a self-governing people, and as such competent to decide intelligently and wisely the question of their own future.

The Democratic proposal, speciously attractive in appearance, is in reality a plan for spurning this duty and violating the trust we assumed when we took over the islands from Spain.

THE NON-JEWISH SABBATH

IT has been a debated question among scholars whether the Sabbath was a purely Jewish institution or whether it was known also to the surrounding nations. There is no evidence of an Egyptian Sabbath, for the Egyptians had a week of ten days; nor have we any proof of a Phenician Sabbath and the evidence of a Babylonian Sabbath has been meagre; but in a volume just published by the Yale University Press Professor A. T. Clay has made important addition to the proof that in Babylonia a seventh day of worship was recognized.

Up to this time there had only two inscriptions been found which could be interpreted as referring to the Sabbath. One of these was a list of words which were defined and it read *um nuh libbishabattum*, which was at first translated, "The day of the rest of the heart is the Sabbath." But this translation must be explained, for by the "rest of the heart" is meant the appeasement of the gods and by *shabbattum* is meant the full moon, that is, the time of the full moon is the time for appeasing the gods. There appears to be here no mention of the Sabbath, altho the passage may be of value in a discussion of the origin of the word Sabbath. The other inscription would seem more definitely to refer to a seventh day. It is a list of the days of the month with the duties of each, and on the 7th, 14th, 19th, 21st, and 28th certain acts were forbidden. It is thus translated by Professor Clay:

An evil day. The shepherd of great peoples shall not eat flesh cooked over coals of an oven; he shall not change the garment of his body; he shall not put on clean (clothes); a sacrifice he shall not offer; the king shall not ride in his chariot; he shall not speak as a king; the diviner shall not give a decision in a secret place; the physician shall not lay his hands upon the sick; it is not suitable to pronounce a curse. At night the king shall bring his gift before Marduk and Ishtar; he shall offer a sacrifice. The lifting up his hands is pleasing to the god.

It will be seen that this "evil day" is like the Jewish Sabbath a day of taboo, a day on which certain things were forbidden. The king was not even to sacrifice, but when the day was over he could sacrifice. This seems to imply that the day was supposed to begin in the evening, and it was at the evening that the new moon would first be seen, indicating that the day and month had begun. No explanation is given why the 19th day was included, but the other days clearly indicate the recognition of a seven-day week except that the weeks begin with the new moon, and as the month has a little over twenty-nine days, one week has eight days. This "evil day" Sabbath rests on the four quarters of the moon.

We now come to Professor Clay's new evidence. In the Yale collection Professor Clay has found a group of twenty-three tablets containing a report of monthly receipts of sheep intended for temple service at Erech, a very ancient city in southern Babylonia. They are dated from the fifth year of Cyrus, 534 B. C., to the sixth year of Cambyses, 523 B. C. inclusive. The tablets are all of the same nature, and after stating that the sheep have been received for sacrifice, a report is made in four columns for each day. Now the important thing is that a note is added to the record for the 7th, 14th, 21st and 28th days stating that an additional sacrifice of a lamb was offered on that day. Here is a definite recognition of a special religious observance celebrated at the temple on those days. The evidence is indubitable that four days which we may call Sabbaths were observed each lunar month seven days apart, and this evidence is of great value for religious history.

To be sure, these tablets come from a comparatively late period, towards the end of the Jewish Babylonian captivity; but taken with the other evidence it is clear that no Jewish influence is here to be discovered. And the Babylonian Sabbath was of very little account as compared with that of the Hebrews. It did not enter into the daily life of the people. We have thousands of contract tablets all dated and they prove conclusively that there was no interference with ordinary business and work. This discovery is of much importance, but much more needs to be learned as to the origin of the observance of the Sabbath, a point on which the text of the Fourth Commandment in Deuteronomy gives a different reason from that in Exodus.

The Arrival of the "Appam" The steamer "Appam" of the Elder Dempster Line, bound from Africa to England, had not been heard from for more than two weeks and had been given up as lost when to the amazement of everybody she appeared at Norfolk, Virginia, in charge of a German prize crew. She had left Dakar on the Senegal coast and had passed the Canary Islands on her northward voyage when on January 15 she was overhauled by a German raider. The strange vessel looked like a disreputable tramp, but as she came close to the "Appam" she hoisted the German flag and at the same moment the sides of her forecastle fell away, disclosing a battery of six-inch guns. A shot from a small gun fired across the bow and the "Appam" brought about her prompt surrender. A prize crew of twenty-two in command of Lieutenant Hans Berg took charge of her and the crews of other captured vessels were put aboard. All of the naval and military men on the "Appam," about fifty in number, were transferred to the raider. So also was the 36,000 pounds of gold bullion carried by the "Appam."

On the following day the raider fell in with the Australian freighter "Clan MacTavish," carrying 10,000 tons of meat to England. Altho she carried only small guns and her crew was Hindu, the "MacTavish" showed fight and only after losing fifteen men did she surrender. Four of her wounded crew were taken on the "Appam" which then set sail for America.

On February 2 she arrived at Newport News flying a German naval flag and giving the name of "His Majesty's Ship Buffalo." There were on board 452 persons, comprizing 116 of the passengers and 155 of the crew of the "Appam," 138 seamen from the other vessels captured, twenty German civilians who were being taken to England for internment and the prize crew. The German civilians assisted the prize crew in keeping guard and the crew of the "Appam" did the work. All arms and possible weapons even to penknives were taken away from the English and they were put on parole not to mutiny. There was some talk among them of overpowering their guards or seizing Captain Berg, as he went about freely, but the plan was abandoned on account of the danger to the women and the probability that the ship would be blown up. Explosives had been placed in various parts of the ship and wires run so that they could be fired by an electric key from the bridge in case the vessel was in danger of being captured.

All the passengers agree that the Germans treated them with courtesy and kindness and did all that they could to make them comfortable. Food ran very short toward the end of the voyage across the Atlantic, but the Germans

THE GREAT WAR

January 31—Zeppelins bombard England, killing fifty-nine. Food riots in Lisbon.

February 1—British steamer "Appam" brought to Norfolk as a German prize. Turkish heir-apparent commits suicide.

February 2—French blow up German tunnels in Argonne. Russians advance north and south of Erzerum.

February 3—Germans attack British near Loos. Stürmer succeeds Goremykin as Russian premier.

February 4—Austrians within fourteen miles of Durazzo, Albania. British relief expedition held up on Tigris.

February 5—Germans bombard allied fortifications north of Salonica. Germans abandon African Kamerun.

February 6—England refuses Americans permission to send food to Polish sufferers. Austrians and Bulgars join forces at Elbasan, Albania.

shared the same fare as their captives. The steward continued to print menu cards even when they got down to little but bread and rice.

The Mysterious Raider What the vessel was which captured the "Appam" and where she hailed from is still a mystery. According to Lieutenant Berg she was the "Möwe" (Seagull) and this name was on some of the caps of the prize crew, but the only "Möwe" known was a small surveying vessel which was reported sunk by the British when they bombarded Dar-es-Salaam in German East Africa early in the war. This German sea-rover is reported to be a swift vessel of some 6000 tons and is supposed by some to be the German fruit steamer "Ponga" converted into a disguised cruiser. Lieutenant Count Dohna, of the German navy, is in command.

Carter in New York Evening Sun
"HERE, UNCLE SAM, SAVE THIS FOR ME"

If she was fitted out in a German port she must have made her way unsuspected thru the British fleet which guards the mouth of the North Sea. She seemed, at any rate, to have no difficulty in eluding the British cruisers which are patrolling the American coast outside the three mile limit for the express purpose of catching German vessels. She could hear them talking together by wireless and since they did not use a code she was able to find their position and dodge them.

It is disconcerting to the British Government to find that in spite of their vigilance there is one and perhaps more German cruisers at sea and infesting the route around Africa, which liners have been taking of late to escape the submarines in the Mediterranean. It appears that the "Möwe" or whatever she is picked up seven British vessels within a week between the Canaries and Madeira. Her first prize was the steamer "Farringford," carrying 5000 tons of copper ore. This she sank, on January 10. The same day she encountered the "Corbridge," with 600 tons of coal. She was taken along as a collier. Next the "Möwe" captured and sank the Admiralty transport "Dromonby," with 6000 tons of coal, the "Author," with 8000 tons of general cargo, the Admiralty "Trader," with 6000 tons of sugar, then the "Ariadne," with 5000 tons of wheat. The crews of all these with their effects were carefully transferred to the "Appam" and so sent to the United States. The frozen beef and mutton on the "MacTavish" was used to provision the "Möwe."

The "Appam" Case The proper disposal of the "Appam" is one of the most perplexing questions which has been brought before our Government in the present war. Is she a prize or a German cruiser? What are the rights and status of her passengers, who include British officials, gunners and seamen, American citizens, East Indians and Germans who were prisoners of the British when the "Appam" was captured?

Lieutenant Berg, on the assumption that he was in command of a German naval vessel, paid an official call upon the commandant of Fort Monroe as soon as he had cast anchor off Old Point Comfort. Then he went with the German Vice Consul to the Collector of the port of Norfolk and asked permission to purchase food and to send the four wounded men to the hospital.

All of those on board except the German prize crew and those who served as such on the "Appam" were released by orders from Washington after two days of lively discussion between the British and German embassies and our Government. Among the passengers thus released the most distinguished are Sir Edward Merewether, Governor of Sierra Leone, and Lady Merewether, Lieutenant Frederick James, Secretary

ENGLISH CAPTIVES TAKEN ON THE HIGH SEAS

Passengers on the "Appam," brought into port at Norfolk, Virginia, by a German prize crew from the "Möwe," which had seized her after sinking five other English vessels. All were released within a few days

Administrator of Nigeria; F. C. Fuller, Commissioner-General of Ashanti, and the captains of the six captured vessels.

This action of our Government implies that the "Appam" is to be regarded as a prize of war, instead of an auxiliary cruiser, but the question of her disposition remains to be settled and may form the subject of long controversy or litigation with either the German or British Governments. The British will doubtless contend that according to Article 21 of the Hague Convention of 1907 a prize brought into a neutral port must be ordered to leave at once and if the order is not obeyed the ship is to be released and turned over to her original owners and the prize crew interned during the rest of the war. In this case, of course, the "Appam" leaving Hampton Roads would at once fall into the hands of the British cruisers waiting outside and would be captured or sunk. But Great Britain has refused to consider herself bound by the Hague Convention since it was not signed by two of the belligerents, Serbia and Turkey. Moreover, neither the United States nor Great Britain subscribed to Article 21.

It is thought likely that the American Government will base its ruling not on the Hague Convention but on the treaty between the United States and Prussia concluded in 1799 and modified in 1828. According to this a prize ship may come and go freely.

More Zeppelin Raids The most serious of the air attacks on England took place on Monday night, January 31. A squadron of six or seven Zeppelins passed over the midland counties and dropt over 300 explosive and incendiary bombs. Most of these fell harmlessly in the fields and canals. Those that exploded in the towns destroyed scores of working-class homes, but, according to the English reports, doing no harm to the munition works or military buildings. The counties mentioned as suffering from the visitation are Norfolk, Lincolnshire, Staffordshire, Suffolk, Leicestershire and Derbyshire. The casualties reported amount to 160, of which fifty-nine were killed and 101 wounded. These comprise eighty-six men, sixty-eight women and one girl child.

The Zeppelins passed over some places twice or hovered for several

220

hours over a particular spot, trying with their searchlights to discover where they were. Upon one farmhouse which they apparently mistook for an important building they wasted thirty bombs with no other result than the maiming of some sheep and the killing of a lot of sparrows.

Fourteen towns are said to have been attacked, but their names are concealed by the censor. At one place a Congregational chapel was struck, where a religious service was being conducted by a woman. A bomb falling close to the building killed her and two women in the audience. At another point a family consisting of an elderly couple, their married daughter, her husband and their children were sitting around the fire when a bomb exploded in the garden path outside the door and they were all torn to pieces. Hardly had their bodies been removed from the ruins of their home when the Zeppelin came back and dropt two more bombs in the vicinity.

The Germans justify the raid on the ground that it was a blow struck at the heart of industrial England, the center of the munition manufacture, and they claim that the Zeppelins went as far as Liverpool on the western coast and demolished factories and docks. The German War Office denies the statement recently made in Parliament that the Allies held the supremacy of the air. In proof of the contrary they assert that from October to February they lost fifteen aeroplanes on the western front while the Allies lost at least sixty-three.

Altho the British anti-aircraft guns fired upon the aerial fleet whenever they could sight them, none of the Zeppelins were brought down on the land. A British trawler, however, reports having sighted a wrecked Zeppelin floating in the North Sea. The Germans who were on the platform of the airship begged for rescue, but the British skipper refused to take any of them on board, for he said he could not trust the Germans, and since they numbered more than twenty and his crew only nine he left them in the water and went away to report to the authorities.

Lord Rosebery's demand for reprisals on Germany is echoed generally from the British press and pulpit. But the *Manchester Guardian* on one side and the German Socialist pa-

per *Vorwärts* on the other argue that airship raids are futile for military purposes and serve only to exasperate the enemy and stir them to fiercer resistance. The coroner's jury, which held the inquest on the thirteen Zeppelin victims in Staffordshire, returned a verdict of "wilful murder against the Kaiser and the Crown Prince as being accessories to and after the facts of the death."

Paris was visited by a Zeppelin on the night of January 29. It flew at a height of over two miles and was concealed from view by the fog. Thirty aeroplanes took to the air in search of it, but it escaped safely and returned to Paris on the following evening. Fourteen men, nine women and one baby were killed and twenty-nine other persons injured. The bombs mostly fell in the tenement district. In one of the demolished houses a Zouave, who had returned from the front on a furlough, was seated at the table telling war stories to welcome him, his wife and daughter, his father-in-law, and his sister with her two little boys. The bomb, which tore off the front of the house, killed all seven of them instantly.

The Zeppelin attacks on Paris are stated by the Germans to be in reprisal for the bombardment of Freiburg and other German unfortified towns by the French aeroplanes.

The War in Asia There are three distinct but interrelated campaigns in the region between the Caucasian mountains and the Persian Gulf. On the north the Russians are fighting the Turks about Erzerum. On the south the British are trying to advance up the Tigris River. On the east the Russians are invading Persia from the Caspian Sea.

In the first campaign the Russians are progressing famously, if we may credit the Petrograd reports, which are, indeed, but faintly contradicted from Constantinople. They claim that the Turks were driven back from the Caucasian border with such slaughter and confusion that they failed even to rally behind the line of fortifications which had been prepared for the defense of Erzerum and which extend for more than a dozen miles to the north of that city. It is rumored that the Turks have evacuated Erzerum. This, however, is too incredible to be accepted without confirmation, for Erzerum occupies a strong and easily defensible position among the mountains and should be capable of standing a long siege. In 1878 an English officer who happened to be in the city at the time it was attacked assumed command and held it against the Russians till the end of the war. The Turks are renowned for stubborn resistance when besieged and their defense of Gallipoli shows that they have not lost their former ability. The Russians launched their first attack at Erzerum a year ago last October, so the Turks and their German allies have had abundant time to put the city in a state of defense. If then Erzerum surrenders shortly it will mean a very complete collapse of Ottoman courage. It is much more probable that the Russians will be content with investing the city and then pass on as they did in the case of Przemysl in their Galician campaign. The reports of their advance to the north and the south of Erzerum indicates that this is what they are doing.

Of the British on the Tigris we hear little, but General Townshend's force at Kut-el-Amara is still holding out and General Aylmer's relief expedition is reported to be making progress up the rivers. The "rivers of Babylon" came to the aid of the English in their distress. The flooding of the Tigris filled the Turkish entrenchments at Kut and drove out their defenders. When the British came to examine the works they found twenty-two rows of immensely deep trenches with miles of communicating trenches.

In Persia the Russians have taken Sultanabad, but this is southeast of Hamadan. whereas they must go southwest if they are to give any aid to the English on the Tigris. Their advance in this direction appears to be barred by a force of Persian tribesmen, said to number 16,000, under German officers, between them and Kermanshah.

Prince Yussuf Izzedin, the heir apparent to the Turkish throne, is reported to have committed suicide. Rumor has it that he was assassinated or forced to kill himself by Enver Pasha, the virtual ruler of Turkey, against whom the Prince was conspiring.

The President's Speeches President Wilson returned to Washington on the 4th, believing that he had been successful in arousing public sentiment for the support of the Administration's defense plans. He had made ten speeches in large public halls, and as many short addresses from the platform of his train. His reception in those parts of the Middle West where there are many German-Americans, and in places where the defense program was said to be regarded with hostility, had been enthusiastic. On the 31st, in Milwaukee, he said the danger of any division of domestic sentiment on account of race affiliations had been exaggerated. He knew that when the test should come every man's heart would be for America first. But there were dangers which we could not control. Our vital interests might be touched to the quick at any moment. He was determined to keep out of the war, if possible, but the time might come when it would be impossible to preserve both peace and honor. He repeated his arguments in favor of creating a trained reserve of volunteers, men who would not be mere targets, but would know something about arms, discipline and camp sanitation. The impulse behind the movement for preparation had not come from the manufacturers of arms and ammunition. He had urged Congress to provide for a Government armor plate factory and for plants at which munitions could be made. The Government could take care of itself. This was not a dupe. "I am not so innocent as I look," said he. The navy had not been neglected, but it had been built slowly. It was of fine quality, a splendid navy, but it was lacking in quantity. The proposed five years' program would make it adequate for defense.

In Chicago he said that no one could tell whether the United States would be drawn into the war or not. We were continually called upon to assert and uphold the international law standards of times of peace, and had been cruelly misjudged abroad, where many held that we remained neutral merely to make money. It was a terrible thing to have the honor of the United States placed in one's keeping. We might have to assert the principles of right and humanity. What force was available? He was confident that Congress would approve the defense plans. If they should fail, "I may have to suffer the mortification and you the disappointment of having the combination of peace with honor proved impossible."

In Iowa, Kansas and Missouri Addressing a great audience in Des Moines, the President said some were preaching war and asserting it was the duty of the United States to seek entanglements abroad and deliberately to enter the war. Others were preaching peace at any price and in any circumstances. There was a price which was too high for peace, and that price was the loss of self-respect. He had found it an anxious and difficult task to keep out of the war. There was no danger arising in our own country, but the danger lay in what other nations might do. Was the President to do nothing but write messages? Was he to do nothing when our vital interests and honor were attacked by violations of international law? Was there to be peace at the expense of honor? There should be men behind the President so trained that they would not be sacrificed. As for the profits of manufacturers, the Government plants which he had suggested would be enough to control prices.

At Topeka he said there was no new or special crisis, but the situation was combustible material in this country, and at Washington they were trying to cover up the exposed tinder. He was asking not for a great armament, but for a slight increase of the regular army, which was not large enough now to patrol the Mexican border. The force was not to be used for aggression or invasion. But if this country should be invaded, what would Kansas do? It might be necessary to vindicate the rights of American citizens on the seas and in foreign trade. Only on a most solemn occasion would he make such an appeal. The final test of the validity and strength of American ideals had come.

© *International Film Service*

WHERE THE UNITED STATES ARMY IS BUSY

A supply pack train crossing sixty miles of Texas wilderness on the way from Marfa to an army patrol post. The trip is dangerous on account of Mexican bandits. President Wilson declares that he has been embarrassed by the want of men to protect the American frontier

© International Film Service

WELCOMING THE PRESIDENT ON HIS PREPAREDNESS PILGRIMAGE
Great crowds greeted him and heard him enthusiastically wherever he went on his Middle Western tour. This is the way Waukegan, Illinois, turned out to see and hear him

The rest of the world must be made to realize just what America stands for.

There were 18,000 people in his audience at Kansas City. "I may have to ask," said he, "who stands back of me. Where is the force?" Editorial sneers at his "notes" in papers that opposed preparation did not show the real temper of the people. He pointed out again the need of a trained reserve of volunteers. Our great sweep of coast called for an adequate navy, but ours was fourth in size. At St. Louis he said he had found no indifference in the Middle West. No other navy had to cover so great a coast area for defense and ours ought to be incomparably the greatest navy in the world.

Philippine Independence By a vote of more than two to one the Senate last week passed the Philippine bill, with the Clarke amendment, which provides that the islands shall be made independent in not less than two nor more than four years, altho the President is permitted, if in his judgment it is expedient and proper, at the end of four years to delay independence during one session of our Congress. This makes the final date not later than March 4, 1921, but the action may be taken before the end of 1918. The vote was 52 to 24. All the Democrats present were counted in the affirmative, and with them six Republicans—Senators Borah, of Idaho; Clapp, of Minnesota; Kenyon, of Iowa; La Follette, of Wisconsin; Norris, of Nebraska, and Works, of California. Two days earlier the Clarke amendment had been adopted by a tie vote of 41 to 41, the Vice-President breaking the tie.

All provisions requiring the President to negotiate with other nations for the neutrality of the islands, and another binding the United States to guarantee their independence for five years if neutrality agreements should not be obtained, were excluded from the bill by a vote of 53 to 31. The retention of naval and coaling stations for our use was made permissive, instead of mandatory, but a motion to exclude all reference to such stations was lost by a large majority.

Many amendments designed to modify the Clarke amendment were proposed. Mr. Hitchcock, chairman of the committee, offered one providing for some additional delay and conditioning independence upon the adoption of a Filipino constitution. This was rejected. Another rejected amendment was Mr. Cummins's providing for an American commission to work with the Filipinos for a constitution, the adoption of which should precede independence. It is said that the bill, as passed, has the support of President Wilson. It now goes to the House, where it was passed in the preceding Congress, but with no date for independence, altho ultimate independence was promised in the preamble. The Philippine Assembly and Commission passed last week a bill for the purchase of the Manila railroad by the payment of $4,000,000.

Treaties Favorably Reported The treaties with Colombia and Nicaragua, which have been awaiting action for two years, are soon to be considered by the Senate. Favorable reports on both of them have been ordered by the Senate Committee on Foreign Relations. It will be recalled that the treaty with Colombia provided for the payment of $25,-000,000 by the United States, with an expression of regret that anything had occurred to disturb the relations between the two countries. Some in the Senate held that $25,000,000 was too much; others objected to the provision that Colombia's war vessels and merchant ships in the coastwise trade should not be required to pay tolls for

passing thru the Panama Canal, and some complained that the expression of regret was equivalent to an apology and an admission that we had done wrong in connection with the secession of Panama. Before the favorable report was ordered, the sum to be paid was reduced to $15,000,000, and the expression of regret was made a mutual one, in the following words:

The Governments of the United States and the Republic of Colombia, in their own names and in the names of their respective peoples, wishing to put at rest all controversies and differences between them arising out of the events from which the present situation on the Isthmus of Panama resulted, express sincere regret that anything should have occurred to interrupt or to mar the relations of cordial friendship that had so long subsisted between the two countries.

The vote in committee was 8 to 7, all the Republicans opposing a favorable report, while all the Democrats, except Mr. Clarke, of Arkansas, were for it. A motion made by Mr. Borah, for open discussion of the report in the Senate, is pending. Predictions are made that the two-thirds required for ratification cannot be obtained, as nearly all of the Republicans and several Democrats are in opposition. The Minister from Colombia has publicly exprest his disapproval of the changes made by the committee.

The treaty with Nicaragua was reported by a vote of 10 to 3. It provides that we shall pay $3,000,000, receiving in return the exclusive right to make a canal on the Nicaragua route, three small islands, and a naval base in the Bay of Fonseca. Salvador and Honduras have objected to such a use of the bay, which touches their coasts. Probably the committee will soon order a favorable report on the treaty with Hayti, under which we are already exercising the powers of a financial protectorate in that country. There is said to be no serious opposition.

The Situation in Mexico Villa, with a few followers, has thus far defied the Carranza bands that have been pursuing him. At the beginning of last week there were reports that he had been surrounded. Two days later it became known that he had destroyed railroad bridges between Juarez and Chihuahua City, intercepted a train, robbed the passengers and killed one of them. This was General Oruelas, formerly for two or three years in command of the Villa garrison at Juarez. Not long ago he accepted amnesty from Carranza, and he was on his way to join Carranza's army in the south. Having taken him from the train, Villa denounced him as a traitor, and put him to death with his own hand. On the following day it was said that Villa was approaching the boundary at Ojinaga, with several mules carrying stolen gold and silver bullion. The American troops were watching for him, and had been instructed to put him under arrest. But instead of trying to cross the line, he attacked the Carranza garrison at Montezuma, 100 miles south of Juarez. It is said that General Argumedo, another rebel who was successful recently in the vicinity of Torreon, has been defeated and made a prisoner. But on the east coast, in the oil district, between Tuxpam and Tampico, the Carranza forces have suffered reverses, and the oil camps have been looted. Bandits are in possession of the country between Vera Cruz and the capital, and brigandage prevails thruout southern Mexico. The people are fleeing to the towns for safety.

Carranza's Minister of Justice explains that the acquisition of real estate by foreigners has been forbidden because Mexican owners, being in distress, are driven to sell at very low prices, and also for the reason that speculators have been using the country's depreciated currency to their disadvantage in making purchases. Carranza desires to keep the land in Mexican hands. It is understood that bankers in New York are not willing to make loans to the Carranza Government, which is sorely in need of money, unless they receive both from Carranza and from our Government assurances which neither is expected to give. Some have suggested such a financial protectorate as has been established in Santo Domingo. There is in Mexico a movement for woman suffrage, originating in Yucatan, where a Woman's Congress was recently held. In the Mexican capital a thousand clerks employed in the retail stores are on strike for a wage increase of twenty-five per cent, to be paid in gold.

The Canadian Capitol Burned   A fire, which originated in an explosion, destroyed a large part of the Canadian Parliament Building at Ottawa on the night of the 3d inst. The House of Commons was in session when the fire started in the reading room, and there were many persons in the great building, one of the finest examples of Gothic architecture, which was erected at a cost of $6,000,000. The Speaker's wife, Mme. Sevigny, escaped with her children by

Underwood & Underwood

WHEN THE MOUNTAIN STRIKES AT THE RAILROAD

An avalanche hurled two cars of a Great Northern train from the track near Corea Station, Washington, in the Cascade Mountains, on January 22. This steel day coach was carried seventy feet down the mountain side

leaping from a window into a life net, but two of her guests, Mme. Bray and Mme. Morin, of Quebec, lost their lives. Other victims were the assistant clerk of the House of Commons; B. B. Law, a member from Nova Scotia; a policeman and two employees. Martin Burrell, Minister of Agriculture, was severely burned. The legislators had great difficulty in reaching places of safety, as the rooms and corridors were quickly filled with smoke. Sir Robert Borden, the premier, was rescued by the Minister of Public Works. Firemen saved the Library of Parliament and the two wings in which were ministerial offices, but the main part of the structure, containing the House and Senate chambers, was almost wholly destroyed.

Fire Chief Graham, of Ottawa, says that the fire was the work of an in-

cendiary. The initial explosion burst open the doors of the reading room. Hand extinguishers that were used only added fuel to the flames, for they had been filled with gasoline, probably by those who caused the fire. In the following two days there were explosions and fires in four neighboring factories where munitions or clothing for soldiers are made. One factory was destroyed. Soldiers on guard drove away with rifle shots a man who, it is believed, was planning to wreck the great Victoria bridge at Montreal. One man arrested because it was thought that he started the fire in the Parliament Building has been released, his innocence having been shown. It is asserted that warning was given to an officer of our Government three weeks ago that attempts to destroy the Parliament Building, two or three other prominent buildings and several Canadian munition factories, would soon be made.

Woman Suffrage in Manitoba   By a unanimous vote the legislature of Manitoba, Canada, has passed an act giving women the right to vote. Only one member, Joseph Hamelin, Conservative, even spoke against the measure and his argument that "votes for women might cause domestic troubles at election time" did not prevent his voting for it. As soon as the royal assent is given the women of Manitoba will have the right to vote at all except Federal elections, and to sit in the legislature.

The fight for suffrage in Canada is being carried on by women of all classes thru their various societies and organizations. Most of their work has been a direct appeal to the legislators —a method similar to that being used by the suffragists at Washington now— and there has been little or no popular agitation thru a general campaign.

© *Underwood & Underwood*

CANADA'S PARLIAMENT BUILDING IN FLAMES

Fire destroyed the Dominion Parliament Building in Ottawa on February 3 and 4, causing a loss of seven lives and about five million dollars. All Canada suspects a German plot, but incendiarism had not been proved

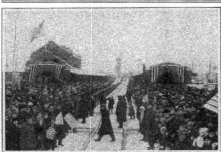

WELCOMING THE PRESIDENT ON HIS PREPAREDNESS PILGRIMAGE
Great crowds greeted him and heard him enthusiastically wherever he went on his Middle Western
tour. This is the way Waukegan, Illinois, turned out to see and hear him

The rest of the world must be made to realize just what America stands for.

There were 18,000 people in his audience at Kansas City. "I may have to ask," said he, "who stands back of me. Where is the force?" Editorial sneers at his "notes" in papers that opposed preparation did not show the real temper of the people. He pointed out again the need of a trained reserve of volunteers. Our great sweep of coast called for an adequate navy, but ours was fourth in size. At St. Louis he said he had found no indifference in the Middle West. No other navy had to cover so great a coast area for defense and ours ought to be incomparably the greatest navy in the world.

Philippine Independence By a vote of more than two to one the Senate last week passed the Philippine bill, with the Clarke amendment, which provides that the islands shall be independent in not less than two nor more than four years, altho the President is permitted, if in his judgment it is expedient and proper, at the end of four years to delay independence during one session of our Congress. This makes the final date not later than March 4, 1921, but the action may be taken before the end of 1918. The vote was 52 to 24. All the Democrats present were counted in the affirmative, and with them six Republicans—Senators Borah, of Idaho; Clapp, of Minnesota; Kenyon, of Iowa; La Follette, of Wisconsin; Norris, of Nebraska, and Works, of California. Two days earlier the Clarke amendment had been adopted by a tie vote of 41 to 41, the Vice-President breaking the tie.

All provisions requiring the President to negotiate with other nations for the neutrality of the islands, and another binding the United States to guarantee their independence for five years if neutrality agreements should not be obtained, were excluded from the bill by a vote of 58 to 31. The retention of naval and coaling stations for our use was made permissive, instead of mandatory, but a motion to exclude all reference to such stations was lost by a large majority.

Many amendments designed to modify the Clarke amendment were proposed. Mr. Hitchcock, chairman of the committee, offered one providing for some additional delay and conditioning independence upon the adoption of a Filipino constitution. This was rejected. Another rejected amendment was Mr. Cummins's providing for an American commission to work with the Filipinos for a constitution, the adoption of which should precede independence. It is said that the bill, as passed, has the support of President Wilson. It now goes to the House, where it was passed in the preceding Congress, but with no date for independence, altho ultimate independence was promised in the preamble. The Philippine Assembly and Commission passed last week a bill for the purchase of the Manila railroad by the payment of $4,000,000.

Treaties Favorably Reported The treaties with Colombia and Nicaragua, which have been awaiting action for two years, are soon to be considered by the Senate. Favorable reports on both of them have been ordered by the Senate Committee on Foreign Relations. It will be recalled that the treaty with Colombia provided for the payment of $25,000,000 by the United States, with an expression of regret that anything had occurred to disturb the relations between the two countries. Some in the Senate held that $25,000,000 was too much; others objected to the provision that Colombia's war vessels and merchant ships in the coastwise trade should not be required to pay tolls for passing thru the Panama Canal, and some complained that the expression of regret was equivalent to an apology and an admission that we had done wrong in connection with the secession of Panama. Before the favorable report was ordered, the sum to be paid was reduced to $15,000,000, and the expression of regret was made a mutual one, in the following words:

The Governments of the United States and the Republic of Colombia, in their own names and in the names of their respective peoples, wishing to put at rest all controversies and differences between them arising out of the events from which the present situation on the Isthmus of Panama resulted, express sincere regret that anything should have occurred to interrupt or to mar the relations of cordial friendship that had so long subsisted between the two countries.

The vote in committee was 8 to 7, all the Republicans opposing a favorable report, while all the Democrats, except Mr. Clarke, of Arkansas, were for it. A motion made by Mr. Borah, for open discussion of the report in the Senate, is pending. Predictions are made that the two-thirds required for ratification cannot be obtained, as nearly all of the Republicans are in opposition. The Minister from Colombia has publicly exprest his disapproval of the changes made by the committee.

The treaty with Nicaragua was reported by a vote of 10 to 3. It provides that we shall pay $3,000,000, receiving in return the exclusive right to make a canal on the Nicaragua route, three small islands, and a naval base in the Bay of Fonseca. Salvador and Honduras have objected to such a use of the bay, which touches their coasts. Probably the committee will soon order a favorable report on the treaty with Hayti, under which we are already exercising the powers of a financial protectorate in that country. There is said to be no serious opposition.

The Situation in Mexico Villa, with a few followers, has thus far defied the Carranza bands that have been pursuing him. At the beginning of last week there were reports that he had been surrounded. Two days later it became known that he had destroyed railroad bridges between Juarez and Chihuahua City, intercepted a train, robbed the passengers and killed one of them. This was General Oruelas, formerly for two or three years in command of the Villa garrison at Juarez. Not long ago he accepted amnesty from Carranza, and he was on his way to join Carranza's army in the south. Having taken him from the train, Villa denounced him as a traitor, and put him to death with his own hand. On the following day it was said that Villa was approaching the boundary at Ojinaga, with several mules carrying stolen gold and silver bullion. The American troops were watching for Him, and had been instructed to put him under arrest. But instead of trying to cross the line, he attacked the Carranza garrison at Montezuma, 100 miles south of Juarez. It is said that General Argumedo, another rebel who was successful recently in the vicinity of Torreon, has been defeated and made a prisoner. But on the east coast, in the oil district, between Tuxpam and Tampico, the Carranza forces have suffered reverses, and the oil camps have been looted. Bandits are in possession of the country between Vera Cruz and the capital, and brigandage prevails thruout southern Mexico. The people are fleeing to the towns for safety.

Carranza's Minister of Justice explains that the acquisition of real estate by foreigners has been forbidden because Mexican owners, being in distress, are driven to sell at very low prices, and also for the reason that speculators have been using the country's depreciated currency to their disadvantage in making purchases. Carranza desires to keep the land in Mexican hands. It is understood that bankers in New York are not willing to make loans to the Carranza Government, which is sorely in need of money, unless they receive both from Carranza and from our Government assurances which neither is expected to give. Some have suggested such a financial protectorate as has been established in Santo Domingo. There is in Mexico a movement for woman suffrage, originating in Yucatan, where a Woman's Congress was recently held. In the Mexican capital a thousand clerks employed in the retail stores are on strike for a wage increase of twenty-five per cent, to be paid in gold.

The Canadian Capitol Burned A fire, which originated in an explosion, destroyed a large part of the Canadian Parliament Building at Ottawa on the night of the 3d inst. The House of Commons was in session when the fire started in the reading room, and there were many persons in the great building, one of the finest examples of Gothic architecture, which was erected at a cost of $6,000,000. The Speaker's wife, Mme. Sevigny, escaped with her children by

WHEN THE MOUNTAIN STRIKES AT THE RAILROAD
An avalanche hurled two cars of a Great Northern train from the track near Corea Station, Washington, in the Cascade Mountains, on January 22. This steel day coach was carried seventy feet down the mountain side

leaping from a window into a life net, but two of her guests, Mme. Bray and Mme. Morin, of Quebec, lost their lives. Other victims were the assistant clerk of the House of Commons; B. B. Law, a member from Nova Scotia; a policeman and two employees. Martin Burrell, Minister of Agriculture, was severely burned. The legislators had great difficulty in reaching places of safety, as the rooms and corridors were quickly filled with smoke. Sir Robert Borden, the premier, was rescued by the Minister of Public Works. Firemen saved the Library of Parliament and the two wings in which were ministerial offices, but the main part of the structure, containing the House and Senate chambers, was almost wholly destroyed.

Fire Chief Graham, of Ottawa, says that the fire was the work of an in-

cendiary. The initial explosion burst open the doors of the reading room. Hand extinguishers that were used only added fuel to the flames, for they had been filled with gasoline, probably by those who caused the fire. In the following two days there were explosions and fires in four neighboring factories where munitions or clothing for soldiers are made. One factory was destroyed. Soldiers on guard drove away with rifle shots a man who, it is believed, was planning to wreck the great Victoria bridge at Montreal. One man arrested because it was thought that he started the fire in the Parliament Building has been released, his innocence having been shown. It is asserted that warning was given to an officer of our Government three weeks ago that attempts to destroy the Parliament Building, two or three other prominent buildings and several Canadian munition factories, would soon be made.

Woman Suffrage in Manitoba By a unanimous vote the legislature of Manitoba, Canada, has passed an act giving women the right to vote. Only one member, Joseph Hamelin, Conservative, even spoke against the measure and his argument that "votes for women might cause domestic troubles at election time" did not prevent his voting for it. As soon as the royal assent is given the women of Manitoba will have the right to vote at all except Federal elections, and to sit in the legislature.

The fight for suffrage in Canada is being carried on by women of all classes thru their various societies and organizations. Most of their work has been a direct appeal to the legislators—a method similar to that being used by the suffragists at Washington now— and there has been little or no popular agitation thru a general campaign.

CANADA'S PARLIAMENT BUILDING IN FLAMES
Fire destroyed the Dominion Parliament Building in Ottawa on February 3 and 4, causing a loss of seven lives and about five million dollars. All Canada suspects a German plot, but incendiarism had not been proved

FROM STATE TO STATE

DELAWARE: Citizens interested in the civic welfare of Wilmington, working in concert with the United States Bureau of Education, have inaugurated a movement to make Wilmington an English-speaking city. The large number of foreigners attracted to that city and vicinity by the great munition plants and by the enlarged operations of its many other industrial institutions has well-nigh overwhelmed the English-speaking population. But it is believed that the day and evening schools which are being opened for the study of English will soon bring about the desired change, since the foreigners generally are eager, and therefore quick, to learn the language of the country.

DISTRICT OF COLUMBIA: The committee appointed by Congress to investigate the relations between the Federal Government and the District of Columbia has just presented a unanimous report. The half-and-half plan is to be abolished; a fair system of taxation of residents is to be devised; the proceeds of this taxation are to be covered into a special fund to be applied to the expenses of the District; any supplementary needs are to be met by Congressional appropriation from the Federal Treasury. There seems to be a general conviction that the report will be adopted, thereby eliminating one great source of delay in Congress and providing a system of government for the city far better adapted to its needs. The half-and-half plan was a source of endless bickerings, and gave occasion for any amount of petty politics. It will now rest with Congress alone to make the city a truly National Capital.

ILLINOIS: After four and a half years of careful investigation, costing upward of $500,-000, a committee of the Chicago Association of Commerce has reported that it is utterly impractical to electrify the steam railroad terminals in that city. Technically it could be done, but financially it is out of the question. The investigation was probably, the most exhaustive ever made in this country for a similar purpose, which was to ascertain how far due to railroad locomotives and what it would cost to electrify the terminals. The committee finds that electrification would subtract only 1,291,282 tons of coal from the total of 21,208,-886 now consumed annually in the city and that the cost of the change would probably be nearly $275,000,000. Dean Goss, of the college of engineering at the University of Illinois, signs the report as chief engineer.

INDIANA: The committee appointed by Governor Ralston some time ago to study the problem of mental defectiveness in Indiana, has done its preliminary organization work and is now beginning a survey of mental defectives in the state. The Rev. Francis H. Gavisk, chairman of the committee, says: "As a state we do not know our problem and have not been able to solve it intelligently. We need a program that will be accepted by those among us who are informed and that can be presented by us to the people as a practicable plan for the next fifty years. We realize that the mentally disturbed are sick persons and should not be incarcerated in jails and poor asylums. We shall strive to agree on what can be done to prevent insanity, how knowledge as to prevention can be diffused and what is best to be done with the problem of the feeble minded."

KENTUCKY: The fiction, so pleasing to humorists, that Kentucky is the home and headquarters of the moonshiner is officially denied by Internal Revenue Commissioner Osborn's recent report, which gives that distinction Georgia. In the last year a total of 3832 illicit distilleries were seized by revenue agents. Of these seizures 1212 were in Georgia, 786 in North Carolina, 530 in Alabama, 402 in Virginia, 320 in Tennessee and 232 in Kentucky, leaving only 350 for all the rest of the United States and territories. As an indication either that moonshining is increasing or that revenue officers are becoming more active, the fact may be cited that as against the 3832 seizures in 1915 there were only 2677 in 1914.

MARYLAND: After three years of investigation the vice commission appointed by Governor Goldsborough in January, 1913, has made its report. The most striking feature of the altogether distressing report is an allegation that there are several institutions in Baltimore which traffic in new-born babes, eighty or ninety per cent of whom die soon after birth. The commission avers that no less than 5000 of these babies have been buried since 1886 in a certain plot of ground approximately fifty-five feet square. Now the Baltimore Grand Jury is demanding from the commission all books and papers on which it bases its report, but it is said n.embers of the commission have declared they will go to jail before giving up the names and dates which they omitted from their report.

MICHIGAN: Official Michigan, led by State Veterinarian Dunphy, with the approval of Governor Ferris, is making a bitter fight on the United States Department of Agriculture. In his latest annual report to Congress Secretary Houston placed the blame for the recent nation-wide spread of foot-and-mouth disease on the Michigan state officials in charge of live stock sanitation. Dr. Dunphy now comes back with an open letter, approved by Governor Ferris, in which he asserts that after the Michigan authorities reported several cases as showing symptoms of this disease, the Federal authorities investigated the cases and declared them to be another and non-contagious disease. The letter concludes with the assertion that had not the Department of Agriculture made this error the foot-and-mouth disease might easily have been confined to one county in Michigan and one in Indiana.

OHIO: At the recent convention of the Ohio National Guard in Cincinnati a movement was begun toward the establishment of a state constabulary in Ohio similar to that of Pennsylvania. Colonel Charles Hake, of the First Regiment, and other leaders urged this as the only means of allaying the antagonism of organized labor to the militia. They would have the National Guard removed from the possibility of service as strike breakers, since such service results in ill feeling on the part of labor unionists and keeps many desirable men from cooperating with the state militia.

RHODE ISLAND: The City Plan Commission of Providence has proposed a new eighty-foot highway along the water front from the city's center to South Providence, with many attractive improvements between this boulevard and the harbor, such as the regrading of a large territory and the establishment of spacious playgrounds. Since much of the space to the east of the proposed highway is waste land, it is argued that its reclamation would be an investment instead of an expense. The total cost of the improvement is estimated at $1,258,900, but it is claimed that enlarged valuation of adjoining properties and the greatly increased assessable value of the improved territory would much more than offset this.

SOUTH CAROLINA: One of the most noticeable effects of the European war so far as this state is concerned is the large increase in production of sulphuric acid by the many fertilizer plants located here. While the sale of fertilizers has fallen off considerably, this loss has been far more than offset by the sales of sulphuric acid to the munition plants. Another feature of this business is the revival of trade in American sulphur. For many years those fertilizer plants which manufacture their own acid have been using iron pyrites from Spain, but the difficulty of procuring this material has turned them to purchasing cake sulphur from the western Gulf states, where it is now produced in abundance by a new process.

SOUTH DAKOTA: The Attorney General of this state has decided to appeal from the recent decision of Judge James D. Elliott, of the United States District Court, which declared the South Dakota "blue sky" law unconstitutional. The case was instituted by William and Harry Morley, father and son, who were arrested at Parker, in this state, on a charge of selling stock of a Sioux Falls stockyard company without having first secured authority to do so from the state officers. Similar laws in other states have been declared unconstitutional, but this is the first case to be appealed to the United States Supreme Court.

TEXAS: Experts and sight-seers from all parts of the country are thronging to the White Point gas field, seven miles from Corpus Christi, to see what is described as the most wonderful gas well in the world. This well was "brought in" on the last day of 1915, when gas gushed from it with such force that its roar could be heard for fifteen miles. Within the next few days it had been visited by hundreds of experts, and all agreed that it was the greatest "gasser" ever known. At last accounts all attempts to control it had failed. Heavy casing set in 2500-feet of cement with a 5000-pound valve at the top proved insufficient and resulted in an explosion which caused the earth to cave in for a hundred feet around the well. Indeed, with gas, water and rocks bursting from it, the basin has become practically the crater of a small but very active volcano.

VIRGINIA: Friends of higher education for women in this state believe that this year they are going to win the battle which has been repeatedly lost in the General Assembly. A bill, approved by the rector and board of visitors of the University of Virginia, and practically approved by Governor Stuart in a message to the General Assembly, has been introduced in the House of Delegates, where seventeen leading members stand as sponsors for it. The bill provides for the establishment "near the University of Virginia of a co-ordinate college for women, which shall be affiliated with the university and form an integral part thereof," but in which there shall be no co-education of the sexes in the collegiate, master of arts, law, engineering and medical departments.

WASHINGTON: These are busy days for officers charged with the duty of enforcing the new prohibition law. It is said that very little of the large quantity of liquor which was known to be in the state just before this law went into effect has been shipped away. In Seattle, which is now one of the largest "dry" cities in the world, it is estimated that in the last two weeks of open selling not less than $1,000,000 worth of strong drink was bought and hidden away in private houses. A large number of saloons throuut the state continue to do business, pretending to stock only soft drinks, tho strongly suspected of hardening them for known customers. Yet the law must be to a considerable extent effective, since hospitals everywhere are said to be filled with patients suffering from the sudden stoppage of their liquor supplies.

CONFESSIONS OF A PEACE PILGRIM

BY HELEN RING ROBINSON

SOME of the members of the Henry Ford Peace Expedition that sailed to Europe last December believed the "miracle" might happen. I was one of them. The miracle—that somehow, thru God's providence, we might hasten the establishment of a righteous peace for blood-soaked Europe. There might be only one chance in a million, but with a world aflame I was even willing to gamble on miracles.

Moreover, there were those documents in the keeping of Mme. Rosika Schwimmer! Documents duly authenticated, we were assured, which showed that the belligerents were all eagerly awaiting the "miracle," too. And the fact that most of us on the Peace Ship were people of no importance could count as nothing against the expedition, whose strength must lie in the compelling power of a big, unselfish, courageous idea—not on "Who's Who in America."

But the "miracle" did not happen.

MME. SCHWIMMER, a brilliant Hungarian woman, was from the beginning of the adventure to its close the controlling force of the expedition. By the time we reached Norway every member of the party who was not absorbed into her remarkable personality realized that this was a heavy handicap.

Mme. Schwimmer was on fire with zeal for the success of the expedition. But the very fact of her race, in a certain sense the fact of her sex, also, with the years of her life set against a background of suspicion and intrigue and autocracy, made her peculiarly unfitted for the leadership of some 170 Americans, many of them given to large language on the subject of "democracy."

And yet, as her devotees would indignantly protest, if ever a daring soul questioned the infallibility of her leadership or her right to dictate the very thoughts of the Peace Pilgrims, "there never would have been a Henry Ford Peace Expedition if it had not been for Rosika Schwimmer."

That is quite true.

So much the finer, then, would have been her renunciation if she had been great enough to renounce it, after formulating the big idea, after enlisting Henry Ford for the adventure, by the force of her vibrant earnestness, after placing her knowledge and her documents at the disposal of the expedition, she had shown the still greater devotion of effacing herself from it, who knows but the "miracle" might have waited on the renunciation?

The first woman senator in the United States is already known to the readers of The Independent thru the story of her experiences in the State Senate of Colorado, published in The Independent of April 20, 1914, Mrs. Robinson also wrote a strong plea for industrial peace among the Colorado miners, which appeared in The Independent for May 11, 1914.—THE EDITOR.

AS these are my confessions, I am willing to admit that I do not carry my pacifism to the point of belligerency. But a super-pacifist is different. It was the super-pacifists who gave the Peace Pilgrims the "third degree" on a stormy December night in mid-ocean.

There were, of course, some self-seekers and grafters in the expedition. It could hardly be otherwise with a company of nearly two hundred Americans, gathered together in great haste, to travel what was, after all, a rainbow route—with a multimillionaire and unlimited pots of gold at the end of it.

Most of the Peace Pilgrims, however, were devoted lovers of humanity, so moved by the horrors of the war which is making a desert of civ-

Donahey in Cleveland Plain Dealer
THE ACE OF CHIVALRY

New York Evening Mail. © S. S. McClure
WELL, DAVID DID IT

ilization that they had left their homes and their business, had endured inconvenience and ridicule and financial loss, had dared the wintry gales of the North Atlantic and the perils of mine-strewn waters to follow a vision of peace and good will.

It would seem that they could read their titles clear to honorable standing on the Peace Ship.

But some of the self-elected elect among the super-pacifists thought otherwise. They believed the time had come for a sifting of souls.

Somebody-Or-Other appointed a committee and this committee, in collaboration with Mme. Schwimmer, prepared a platform with three planks. The first two planks dealt, in placid, platonic terms, with world peace and international disarmament. Then came the third plank, better known as the "third degree" which pledged the unyielding opposition of all members of the Ford Peace Expedition to any increase whatever, under any circumstances whatever, of the naval or military forces of the United States, and called upon all good Americans everywhere to oppose the recommendations of President Wilson's message on preparedness, lately delivered to Congress.

Now only one member of the company, Mr. S. S. McClure, had read the President's message. There were some, therefore, who felt incompetent to pass judgment upon it. There were others who thought themselves unequal to fixing the policy of America amid whatever flux of circumstances in a war-tossed world. There were those whose indignation at the manner of presenting the platform left them little concern with its matter.

"If we must sign such a document in order to be welcome guests at this 'house party,' surely, in common courtesy, a copy of it should have been sent us with the invitation," protested one of these, a woman from the West who had sacrificed much to join the expedition.

But there was no escaping the "third degree." The platform committee were determined. There could be no discussion. No comma in the document could be altered. The oracle had spoken. The tripod was unshaken. Only those who were willing to sign the platform could remain "full members" of the Henry Ford Peace Expedition. The souls of the expedition must be sifted.

They were.

It is an interesting fact that the name of every self-seeker in the party is written large after that famous platform, with the names, I gladly grant, of many sincere and earnest men and women who believed in the declaration and lost sight of the other issues involved.

It was about this time that, for all my knack of hoping, I lost hope of the "miracle."

But my belief in the good to be accomplished by the expedition never faded. And even assuming, as I am willing to, that the "Unofficial Neutral Conference" which we left behind us may accomplish little or nothing, the results of the expedition justify that belief.

It is unfortunate that our Eastern press has created so different and so false an impression. But here again I blame the incompetency of the Peace Party administration for much of the cynicism of the newspaper people attached to the expedition. Most of the newspaper men and women came with open minds. That was their business. Some of them thrilled to the same hope that inspired Henry Ford. One of them, the representative of a great news-gathering agency, a hater of war and injustice, an incurable idealist, told me on the first day of our outward journey that he also believed in the possibility of the "miracle." Yet before we reached Christiania his wireless reports bit like acid, and others of the press people grew increasingly antagonistic.

Much of this was mere contagiousness. But for some of it Mme. Schwimmer and her subordinates were plainly responsible. Newspaper men mistrust the oracle and the tripod. And even a reporter is human, after all. You rarely melt him to tenderness and praise by calling him a liar and a brute—even if he is one. Doubtless it is all very different in Hungary.

THERE are "war millionaires" in Norway as in America, twenty-five newly made ones in the small city of Bergen alone. Perhaps that was one reason why, when we reached the capital of Norway, we found the press not apathetic but hostile. Moreover our expedition had been tagged as "pro-German"—and Christiania sympathizes with the Allies.

Yet in Christiania, from the beginning of our stay there, the big idea of the Peace Ship justified itself.

Bartholomew in the Minneapolis Daily News
ON THE PEACE SHIP

Remember that this "big idea" was not the "miracle" of which a few of us mild-minded voyagers dreamed. While Jenkin Lloyd Jones was swathing the idea in metaphors and things like that, Henry Ford stripped it of all its trappings and observed casually, "It pays to advertise."

To advertise; to mobilize the forces of peace as the forces of war have been advertised for ten thousand years—that was the true purpose of the Henry Ford Peace Expedition.

Ours was the first great peace advertising expedition in history. And the peace we advertised was not a mere negation, a cessation of strife. It was a deep, abiding constructive force. It was the soul of an individual, the soul of a nation. We advertised that the soul of America was peace. And Norway answered that her soul was peace also. The science and the scholarship of Norway as represented in the famous organization rather ineptly styled "The Student Body" welcomed us and joined in our campaign. The ministerial alliance arranged a great mass meeting for us. The Social Democrats arranged another. And when we left Norway a representative group of men and women accompanied us as members of the party.

In Stockholm the story was repeated with emphasis. The waves of war are breaking very close to those Scandinavian countries, cruel waves and high. And only war was talked of when we reached Stockholm; when we left the city a week later everyone was talking peace.

The orators of our party feared our mission might prove fruitless in Denmark, for that little nation, in the grip of a monstrous fear, passed some months ago a law forbidding all public meetings to discuss public questions. Yet a score of private receptions a n d club meetings gave ample opportunity for explaining the purposes of the expedition, while at a banquet given by *The Politiken*, the greatest newspaper of all Scandinavia, the speakers were assured an audience of a million readers.

The last stopping place before the disbanding of our party was at The Hague.

Now The Hague is a little blasé about peace, tho she thinks she invented it. Yet it was in that city I had my most inspiring experience.

I was riding with two other members of the expedition in an open taxi. Our car stopped for a moment just as a middle aged Hollander, an artizan, plainly, was passing. He looked at us, then stopped, and lifting his hat said just two words. "America! Peace!" while his voice had a tone and his eyes had a light as if he were before a shrine.

WE had all, no doubt, fallen far short of what we meant, we Peace Pilgrims who had left our own country with the gibes of newspaper paragraphists ringing in our ears. But for all our failures we had at least done this for our native land: People had reproached us with being a buzzard nation when first we landed. They accused us of feeding too noisily on war profits.

From the beginning we had told them another story, of the millions on millions of plain Americans like ourselves who shared in Europe's agony and ardently longed for peace.

They had listened to us. Sometimes we could feel that our words carried conviction. And here was a man who had learned the truth—that the real soul of America is peace.

I recalled how various militant Americans, including a former President of the United States, had been distrest . last December lest our expedition should make America appear ridiculous. I am glad to record now how the expedition helped to make the name of the United States once more respectable.

S. S. Rotterdam

LOWER CALIFORNIA

WHY WE NEED IT AND IT NEEDS US

BY EDWIN E. SLOSSON

ONE of the important questions coming before the present Congress is that of the rectification of our Mexican frontier. Two bills have been introduced, one providing for the purchase of Lower California and the other for the purchase of that strip of it which bars us from the Gulf of California. It is an exceptionally favorable time to secure these much needed accessions of our territory, now when the presidency of Mexico is held by a man who owes his position to American support and when the Powers whose ambitions such action would thwart are occupied elsewhere. Lower California is of little value to Mexico, the population is sparse, less than one to the square mile, and its resources are undeveloped. The money we would pay for it would be very welcome to Mexico, now impoverished by five years of anarchy.

The need for at least a rectification of the boundary line will be apparent to any one by a glance at a map of the territorial expansion of our country. He will see that the line between Mexico and the United States, established by the treaty of Guadalupe Hidalgo in 1848, starts out along the southern side of New Mexico, the thirty-two-degree parallel, as tho it were going straight west to the Gulf, but as it approaches Arizona it seems to change its mind suddenly and turns north to the Gila River, which brings it out on the Colorado River some seventy miles above the head of the Gulf.

While puzzling over the erratic course of this boundary line he will see that an attempt was made later to rectify it by what is marked on the map as the "Gadsden Purchase, 1853." Here a line starts straight westward, about forty miles south of the former line, but it, too, gets somehow switched off the track and makes a dive to the north instead of going on to the Gulf of California.

The impression one gets from the map is that both boundary lines were intended to be drawn straight west to the Gulf,

but were intentionally deviated just enough to miss it. This impression is historically correct. The map reveals two unfortunate episodes in American diplomacy. Whenever the physicist sees a line like these, which starts out straight in one direction and suddenly turns off at an angle he knows that the change of direction is due to the conflict of two forces. Now the conflict in this case is that between the North and the South which culminated a little later in the Civil War, the desire of the Southerners for more territory, the determination of the Northerners to prevent their getting any. Sometimes how between the two the nation got cheated out of the territory it thought it was buying.

Exactly how it happened is a mystery that historians have never been able to clear up. According to Mexican tradition the Yankees for all their shrewdness were outwitted; the commissioners, with their heads muddled by mescal, were fooled with false maps. We know at least that the treaty of Guadalupe Hidalgo was negotiated by a man, N. P. Trist, who had been recalled and disavowed four months before. How creditable a representative of the United States

AN ERRATIC BOUNDARY

When Western school children study geography they wonder why our south-western boundary runs so as to give to Mexico the mouth of the Colorado River, and the more they find out why the less they like it. In 1848 and 1853 the American Government tried to purchase land which would give us access to the Gulf of California and both times it was foiled—not by Mexico but by the jealousy of the Northeastern States. Now another effort is being made and we shall see what comes of it

he was will be understood from what President Polk says of him in his diary:

A very base man. . . . An impudent and unqualified scoundrel. . . . Destitute of honor or principle. . . . He admits he is acting without authority and in violation of a positive order recalling him. . . . If there is any legal provision for his punishment he ought to be severely handled.

No wonder the President was dissappointed at Trist's bargain with Mexico. The instructions given to Trist stated that it was of the "utmost importance" to get Lower as well as Upper California and New Mexico. If he could not induce the Mexicans to cede Lower California he was to insist upon the thirty-two-degree line south of the Gila River. He was authorized to offer up to $20,000,000 for Upper California and New Mexico, $5,000,000 more for Lower California and $5,000,000 more for the right of way across the Isthmus of Tehuantepec. The treaty Trist signed at Gaudalupe Hidalgo gave us only half of the Gila and no access to the Gulf. Lower California was left out. So was Tehuantepec, for the Mexican commissioners stated that they had just sold out the Isthmian rights to English capitalists, whence it comes that it is a British and not an American railroad which rivals the Panama Canal at Tehuantepec.

As might have been expected the Mexican President was surprised, relieved and pleased and the Mexican people "in a great state of exultation" over so favorable a treaty granted to a defeated nation. What our President thought about it may be inferred from what he said about Trist. Nevertheless he recommended it to the Senate, for he knew that he would be lucky even to get so much in the face of the opposition of New England. As it was the treaty would have been lost if there had been three more votes cast against it.

Daniel Webster, who led the opposition, said:

I hope it will be remembered, in all future time, that on this question of the accession of these new

227

territories of almost boundless extent, I voted against them and against the treaty which contained them.

Webster need not have worried. He is remembered all right—and with execration by the millions who live in the "almost boundless" territories which he would have consigned to Mexican rule forever. The school children of Texas, Oklahoma, Kansas, Wyoming, Colorado, Arizona, New Mexico, Utah and California as they learn history come to regard Webster as the New Yorkers do Benedict Arnold.

When it was realized that the treaty of Guadalupe Hidalgo cut us off from the Gulf of California and prevented us from running a railroad on the southern side of the Gila River an effort was made to rectify the blunder by buying another strip of Mexican territory. General Gadsden found President Santa Anna willing to sell, and he arranged for the purchase of 39,000,000 acres in Chihuahua and Sonora for $20,000,000, the new line to run along parallel thirty-one degrees to the Gulf of California. But the Senate apparently did not consider the land worth fifty cents an acre so the price and the area acquired were both cut down by half and again the boundary line was run so as to shut us off from the Gulf.

That did not matter much when the country was unsettled, but now there are 250,000 acres of farms and homes on the American side of the boundary and twice as much more of American land which might be brought under irrigation if we were not debarred from the control of the river on the southern side of the imaginary line which forms the boundary. As it is the people of the Imperial Valley, one of the most prosperous parts of California, are dependent upon the good will and efficiency of the Mexican Government and their farms and homes may be swept away unless the United States obtains the mouth of the Colorado River.

The acquisition of the whole of *Baja California* is a matter of greater importance and greater urgency. It is needed both for its agricultural and mineral value and as a protection to our western coast and the Panama Canal. The peninsula extends southward about seven hundred miles. It is therefore as long as Italy, the only half as wide.

That the control of the peninsula of Lower California is necessary for national safety is evidenced by the Lodge resolution of 1912, which extends or interprets the Monroe doctrine to prohibit the acquisition by a foreign power of any harbor which "might threaten the communications or safety of the United States." This was past by the Senate at the time when it was supposed that Japan was trying to acquire Magdalena Bay in Lower California. That the significance of this action was well understood by the Germans is shown by the discussion of the *Magdalena-Bay-Fall* in Dr. Kraus's comprehensive work on *Die Monroedoktrin in ihren Beziehungen zur amerikanischen Diplomatie und zum Völkerrecht.* Back in the nineties the Kaiser tried to purchase from Mexico two of the harbors of Lower California "for his own personal use," but Secretary Hay was on the watch for him and put a stop to it.

During the present war Turtle Bay in Lower California has been used as a coaling station by Japan and Great Britain. Mexico was in no condition to prevent the violation of its neutrality and our Government was under the circumstances not disposed to interfere. The warships may be there yet for aught we know.

These three incidents of many simply illustrate the difficulties which arise inevitably from the present situation. So long as Mexico holds the peninsula there is danger that we may be involved in trouble over it either with Mexico or some other power. The best kind of preparedness is the exercize of foresight in the removal of the causes of possible quarrels. A few million dollars spent in the purchase of Lower California would be better insurance against war than a billion spent on army and navy. The severance of the Californias in 1848 has been injurious to *Alta California* and ruinous to *Baja California* and their reunion now would be of benefit to both.

THE CHARGE

BY GERTRUDE HUNTINGTON McGIFFERT

Dread thunderbolts of Thought! Truth's bugle calls!
Lo! upon echoing worlds of dull contentment falls
The blare and shock of battle! Everywhere
The dust of doomèd faiths and grim despair
Of frenzied cults—the wrath and gore
Of War!
On—on over ditchen of mangled dead Truth thundered.
Hell's torches of scorn flamed high then blackened.
Creation wondered
At trampled traditions and reeling creeds.
Sin whined and hissed beneath the charging steeds—
Beneath the grinding chariot wheels that cut
Their murderous ruthless rut
Thru the weakness and woes and hates of blinded men.
And then
Upon God's chosen pinnacle Truth hurled

Her ensign to the world—
"Hope, Beauty, Love."
It fluttered—a whirlwind—far above
The huddling, sickening carnage. Circles of glory flashed
Thru toil's barbaric gloom. Sin's rafters crashed
As stricken ignorance passed. Eternity
Leaned down to see.
Hells kneeled. The strongholds of the ages rocked.
A silence fell. Not a universe sneered, not a star mocked.
And then, triumphant, Truth again
Flung out her ensign before men.

They felt the stir beyond their ken and lifting curious eyes
Felt a breathlessness of spirit—a dim surprize—
And as a sleeping child
They dreamed of Truth—and smiled.

M. William Shak-ſpeare:

EIGHT PAPERS BY FREDERICK HOUK LAW
IN OBSERVANCE OF THE THREE HUNDREDTH
ANNIVERSARY OF SHAKESPEARE'S DEATH

Shakespeare the Man

HREE hundred years ago this April William Shakespeare died in his native Stratford-on-Avon, whither he had retired after a successful dramatic career in London. His plays bring us into personal touch with the man, and from all sources together we know more concerning him than concerning most of his contemporaries.

A man of remarkable energy, he wrote thirty-seven plays and several poems in about twenty-two years, writing about two new plays a year besides revising old plays, acting, and directing his company.

Born in Stratford about April 23, 1564, he certainly spent a vigorous boyhood, for his plays show high spirit, love of the countryside, and a daredevil zest for fun. If his father, John Shakespeare, the glover or agricultural dealer and once Bailiff of Stratford, sent him to the Stratford school Shakespeare probably sympathized little with its Latin teaching. His education was to be by experience. When his father's fortunes declined he may have become a butcher's apprentice, a lawyer's clerk, or a country school teacher. At nineteen he married Anne Hathaway, and about four years later, possibly because he and some wild companions shot deer in Sir Thomas Lucy's estate at Charlecote, he left home and went up to London to seek fortune, going perhaps with the actors known as "Leicester's Men," who were in Stratford in 1587.

In London, living at first as horseholder or call-boy, he became a reviser of old plays, then a full-fledged dramatic writer, and a shareholder in the Blackfriars and Globe theaters. His company won royal approval and brought him such sums that he bought property in Stratford and became "William Shakespeare, Gentleman."

His energetic career drawing to a close, he spent five or six quiet years in beautiful Stratford and there died April 23, 1616. His life story is one of well-applied practical energy—a vigorous, productive, highly successful life.

It is not difficult to estimate the mind and character of this greatest of English writers, for his plays unite with tradition to tell us much.

His quickness of wit, for example, is evident to all who read "As You Like It" and similar comedies; and Thomas Fuller, telling in 1662 of wit-combats between Shakespeare and Ben Jonson, says Shakespeare "could turn with all tides, tack about, and take advantage of all winds, by the quickness of his wit and invention."

Shakespeare was surely a man among men. His Prince Hal in "Henry IV" skylarks with Falstaff and yet rises to greatness, and his Henry V jests with soldiers and never loses royalty. Traditions of his early life show a happy-hearted, lively companion. John Aubrey, writing in 1680, says Shakespeare was a mimic and fun-maker, and Nicholas Rowe, in 1709, says he was "A good-natur'd man, of great sweetness in his manners and a most agreeable companion."

His vocabulary of fifteen thousand words and the wide scope of his plays show an open eye, an attentive ear, and a wide and varied reading. He shows his belief in the school of the world in "Love's Labour Lost," where he says:

"Small have continual plodders ever won,
Save base authority from others' books."

And again in "The Two Gentlemen of Verona," saying:

"He cannot be a perfect man,
Not being tried and tutor'd in the world:
Experience is by industry achiev'd
And perfected by the swift course of time."

Legends of deer-stealing and other escapades, his early marriage and romantic departure for London,

and stories of gay meeting with Ben Jonson, Burbage, and Davenant, fellow-dramatists, testify to a romantic temperament. He may have traveled over much of England, and perhaps in Italy and other lands.

That Shakespeare was a lover of music seems certain from Lorenzo's speech in "The Merchant of Venice":

"The man that hath no music in himself,
Nor is not moved with concord of sweet sounds,
Is fit for treasons, stratagems and spoils. . . .
Let no such man be trusted."

In play after play he makes room for exquisite songs, rollicking as in "As You Like It":

"In the springtime, the only pretty ring time,
When birds do sing, hey ding a ding, ding:
Sweet lovers love the spring";

sweet lullabies as in "A Midsummer Night's Dream":

"Philomel, with melody,
Sing now your sweet lullaby:
Lulla, lulla, lullaby; lulla, lulla, lullaby.
Never harm,
Nor spell nor charm,
Come our lovely lady nigh;
So good-night, with lullaby";

and sometimes sad songs, as in "Cymbeline":

"Golden lads and lassies must,
As chimney-sweepers, come to dust."

Shakespeare loved the music and beauty of language, making his characters express themselves in wonderful poetry, as in "Romeo and Juliet":

"What envious streaks
Do lace the severing clouds in yonder east:
Night's candles are burnt out, and jocund day
Stands tip-toe on the misty mountain tops."

Always a lover of the picturesque, he made his scenes marvelously suggestive. What pictures arise when we think of the balcony scene in "Romeo and Juliet!" of the sleepwalking scene in "Macbeth"! and of the grave-digging scene in "Hamlet"! What a picture when we think of Othello telling his story to the listening and enraptured Desdemona! When we think of Lear in the madness of the tempest!

Himself a father, Shakespeare's heart went to childhood. The kindly-pathetic figure of Prince Arthur in "King John"; Lady Macduff's heroic little son in "Macbeth," and the boy-ish Princes in "Richard III" show loving and sympathetic touches. Constance's lament for Arthur in "King John" may be Shakespeare's own sorrow at the death of Hamnet, his twelve-year-old son:

"Grief fills the room up of my absent
   child,
Lies in his bed, walks up and down
   with me,
Puts on his pretty looks, repeats his
   words,
Remembers me of all his gracious parts,
Stuffs out his vacant garments with
   his form. . . .
My life, my joy, my food, my all the
   world!"

Stratford-on-Avon is a place of green fields, limpid streams, flowers and country peace. Shakespeare could not have courted Anne Hathaway without walking a mile along sweet country ways, nor have gone to Charlecote without noting the beauty of the landscape. He loved his country home so much that he returned to it from the gay London life and made it the home of his prosperity. In most of his plays he extols the loveliness of such natural beauty as that around Stratford. It may be a real experience lovingly remembered when he says in "A Midsummer Night's Dream":

"I know a bank where the wild thyme
   blows,
Where oxlips and the nodding violet
   grows;
Quite over-canopied with luscious wood-
   bine,
With sweet musk-roses, and with eg-
   lantine."

It is a lover of the outdoor world who speaks in "Twelfth Night" of

"The sweet south
That breathes upon a bank of violets,
Stealing, and giving odour."

It is a lover of the country who speaks in "The Two Gentlemen of Verona" of the brook that

"Makes sweet music with the enamell'd
   stones,
Giving a gentle kiss to every sedge."

It is one who himself had rejoiced in the coming of the flowers, who sings in "Love's Labour's Lost" of the time

"When daisies pied and violets blue
And lady-smocks all silver white
And cuckoo-buds of yellow hue
Do paint the meadows with delight."

England has never had a more patriotic poet than Shakespeare. In many of his plays he speaks lovingly and proudly of England. In "King John," for example, he says:

"This England never did, nor never
   shall,

Lie at the proud foot of a conqueror,
But when it first did help to wound
   itself."

There is more passionate patriotism in "Richard II" where he calls England:

"This royal throne of kings, this scep-
   ter'd isle,
This earth of majesty, this seat of
   Mars,
This other Eden, demi-paradise;
This fortress built by Nature for her-
   self . . .
This blessed plot, this earth, this realm,
   this England, . . .
This land of such dear souls, this dear,
   dear land!"

Like Lincoln, Shakespeare could never resist the impulse of the humorous. An inveterate punster, he plays upon words at all times, and in "Romeo and Juliet" makes Mercutio die with a jest. He was so fond of humor of the rougher sort, as in "The Comedy of Errors" and "The Merry Wives of Windsor," that we feel sure he must have taken part in many a wild prank. Sometimes his humor is farcical; sometimes, as in his romantic plays, it is quiet and delicate; sometimes, as in "Macbeth" and "Hamlet," it exists side by side with the tragic. His nature was not narrow but had room for both laughter and tears.

If Shakespeare had not been a man of deeply sympathetic heart he could not have written plays that "purge by pity and fear." He is thinking of the humble in "Henry VI" when he says:

"Thus are poor servitors,
When others sleep upon their quiet
   beds,
Constrain'd to watch in darkness, rain
   and cold."

On the other hand, it is the very sympathy with which he has treated his great characters like Macbeth and Othello that makes their tragedies so appealing.

We believe that he must have had a rugged and lovable manhood. His active and successful career; his contrast in "Henry IV," between Hotspur, the rough man of action, and the gentleman "perfumed like a milliner"; and the soul-dignity that he gave to characters like Richard III

BOOKS RECOMMENDED FOR FURTHER
   READING

Encyclopedia Britannica, Shakespeare; The Facts About Shakespeare, by W. A. Neilson and A. H. Thorndike; *Shakespeare,* by Walter Raleigh; *The Life of Shakespeare,* by W. J. Rolfe; *The Life of William Shakespeare,* by Sidney Lee; *Shakespeare the Man,* by Goldwin Smith; *The Man Shakespeare and His Tragic Life Story,* by Frank Harris; *Shakespeare the Boy,* by W. J. Rolfe; *Shakespeare, His Mind and Art,* by Edward Dowden; *William Shakespeare Portrayed by Himself,* by R. Waters; *Shakespeare's Inner Life as Intimated in His Works,* by J. A. Heraud.

---

and Macbeth because he made them so preëminently men of action, make us think that his own manhood was stalwart. Certainly Ben Jonson, his chief rival, called him the

"Soul of the age!
The applause, delight, the wonder of
   our stage!"

and said: "I loved the man, and do honor his memory (on this side idolatry) as much as any." And Ben Jonson was not the man to love a weakling.

In an age when the drama had much license· Shakespeare wrote without the extreme coarseness that characterized many of his contemporaries. Without ever writing for moral effect he so centered his plays around truth that all his work is intensely moral. Behind the joy-in-life of the comedies, and behind the truths of the tragedies we feel an intense nature that saw

"Some soul of goodness in things evil,
Would men observingly distil it out."

In fact, his plays show such an understanding of the laws of life that we call Shakespeare a philosopher. All his plays proclaim a man who meditated on life and its mysteries. He is an idealist, saying:

"What is man,
If his chief good, his market of his time,
Be but to sleep and feed?"

He looks upon the transitoriness of life and says:

"We are such stuff as dreams are made
   on."

He sees that nothing purely physical is eternal:

"The cloud-capt towers, the gorgeous
   palaces,
The solemn temples, the great globe
   itself,
Yea, all which it inherit, shall dissolve,
And like this insubstantial pageant
   faded
Leave not a wrack behind!"

He does not pretend to know

"What dreams may come
When we have shuffled off this mortal
   coil,"

And yet the heart of all his philosophy, the sum and substance of all his plays is that life is beautiful and noble, and only the highest manhood can lead to the greatest happiness:

"Give me that man
That is not passion's slave, and I will
   wear him
In my heart's core, ay, in my heart of
   hearts."

On the whole, we know a great deal concerning Shakespeare and his inner life. The result is that, in spite of certain faults characteristic of his age, we may say of him as Antony said of Brutus:

"His life was gentle, and the elements
So mix'd in him that Nature might
   stand up
And say to all the world 'This was a
   man!'"

AT THE THEATER IN SHAKESPEARE'S DAY—"HENRY IV" AT THE GLOBE

Around the unroofed yard (the "pit"), square or roughly circular, where common folk stood, ran galleries for those who could afford them. The stage, with a curtained recess and a gallery at the back, thrust itself far into the pit and on this open platform most of the action took place. It was "smart" to have a seat on the rush-strewn stage. The use of tobacco, newly introduced from America, had already become fashionable

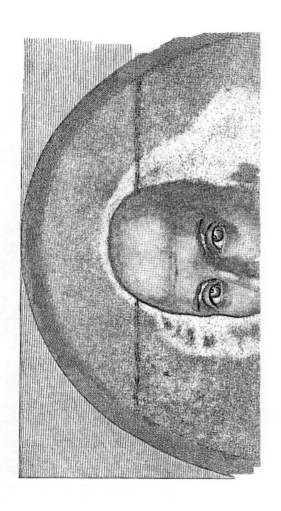

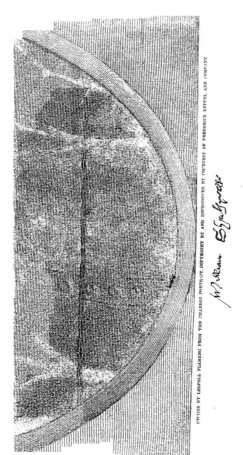

ETCHED BY LEOPOLD FLAMENG FROM THE CHANDOS PORTRAIT. COPYRIGHT BY AND REPRODUCED BY COURTESY OF FREDERICK KEPPEL AND COMPANY

William Shakespeare

THE MARQUIS AND MARCHIONESS OF ABERDEEN AND TEMAIR

They are visiting this country in the interest of the Women's National Health Association of Ireland, of which Lady Aberdeen is president. Lord Aberdeen has been Lord Lieutenant of Ireland and Governor-General of Canada. Lady Aberdeen is president of the International Council of Women

WHAT YOUNG IRELAND NEEDS

THE MISSION OF THE MARQUIS AND MARCHIONESS OF ABERDEEN

TWO hundred little girls, with hair-ribbons of blue or green or white or yellow, each squad after its kind, every one from alien stock, happy to the last pair of flying feet, danced a Highland Fling and an Irish Lilt and a Nigarapolska and raced with an absurd and beautiful intensity of endeavor thru all sorts of relay games in the big covered playground of an East Side school in New York City the other day. When they had finished, a slender man, gray-bearded, his cheeks furrowed in a kindly fashion, unmistakably Scotch, rose and thanked them. Then he introduced his wife. Her face—with the fresh color of a young girl—broke into reminiscent smiles as she told how the sight of a similar exhibition three years ago had delighted her so much that, going home to Dublin, she borrowed a teacher from Public School 188, taught the same sort of play-exercize to the school children there, and had all young Dublin dancing thru the hard winter of the great strike, dancing in the schools and playgrounds and streets, up the stairs and down, she said, and thus adding a neat bit of cheer to the hard-prest city. On this new visit to the city she had asked that the white-bloused youngsters might go thru their drill again so that her husband, too, could see school folk-dancing as it should be done.

For it happens that Sir John Campbell Gordon, Marquis of Aberdeen and Temair, formerly Governor-General of Canada and lately Lord Lieutenant of Ireland, and the Marchioness of Aberdeen, president of the International Council of Women, have no interest greater than their devotion to child welfare and the health of Ireland. And never were two people more completely one in their enthusiasm for a single cause.

Lady Aberdeen is president of the Women's National Health Association, which is working along many lines for the betterment of Irish life. It centers in Dublin, but serves the whole island. It commands the support and seeks the welfare of Protestant and Catholic alike. It carries on full two dozen kinds—two bakers' dozens, indeed—of work for the benefit of women and children. Beginning with visiting nurses and health lectures for expectant mothers, babies' clubs and milk stations, it helps the youngsters to grow up healthy and good-natured by providing playgrounds and school gardens, folk dancing, cheap meals, dental clinics, and boot clubs, and then branches out into the wider field of public health, with sanatoriums and preventoriums, health lectures and pamphlets, a health legislation committee, a caravan that carries hygiene-help thru the country lanes, traveling exhibits. Due largely to its anti-tuberculosis campaign, on which special emphasis has been thrown, the deaths from consumption in Ireland are 2500 per year fewer now than when it opened fire in 1907.

Into the midst of all this burst the war.

"It was like a blow from a sledgehammer," Lord Aberdeen says. "It threatens the very existence of the work."

He speaks with nervous vigor,

The City of the Future

BY MAYO FESLER

Secretary of the Civic League of Cleveland, Ohio

A city, sanitary, convenient, substantial; where the houses of the rich and the poor are alike comfortable and beautiful; where the streets are clean and the sky line is clear as country air; where the architectural excellence of its buildings adds beauty and dignity to its streets; where parks and playgrounds are within the reach of every child; where living is pleasant, toil honorable and recreation plentiful; where capital is respected but not worshipped; where commerce in goods is great but not greater than the interchange of ideas; where industry thrives and brings prosperity alike to employer and employed; where education and art have a place in every home; where worth and not wealth give standing to men; where the power of character lifts men to leadership; where interest in public affairs is a test of citizenship and devotion to the public weal is a badge of honor; where government is always honest and efficient, and the principles of democracy find their fullest and truest expression; where the people of all the earth can come and be blended into one community life; and where each generation will vie with the past to transmit to the next a city greater, better and more beautiful than the last.

---

throwing out his hands and stressing heavily the words that count.

"That was the reason we came to America, to save this noble enterprize. If an orphanage stood on the mountain-side and you saw an avalanche approaching it, you know what you would do. There is no other country that can do it. And your sympathies are quickened by the war."

There is no money on the other side for such philanthropies today. War economies and war taxation—Lord Aberdeen tells of one landowner, for instance, whose taxes have been increased by $40,000 this year—have dried up the sources of income. Not only do the times bring new necessities, which the Association is meeting by distress workrooms, clothing and comforts depots, and nursing classes, but projects begun before the war cannot be finished and must be abandoned at a loss unless help comes quickly.

"The child welfare work is everything now," says Lady Aberdeen. "We must build for the future. And it is particularly necessary for the women of the world to be organized and unified now so that they will be ready for their work of moral reconstruction after the war."

After the two hundred little girls had finished their dancing and had received thru Lady Aberdeen greetings from Dublin children—Irish youngsters who were doing Irish folk-dancing because immigrant children in New York showed them the way—their leader, a dark-haired girl with all the moral frenzy of the college cheer-leader, called for a cheer for the children of Dublin. The cordial response, ringing stridently thru the big paved courtyard, was deafeningly convincing.

Lord and Lady Aberdeen will carry back to Dublin the vociferous love of Public School 188, but they will take also other evidence, no less hearty and somewhat more substantial, that folks on this side of the water have a friendly interest in those children of Dublin.

Harris & Ewing

THE MARQUIS AND MARCHIONESS OF ABERDEEN AND TEMAIR

They are visiting this country in the interest of the Women's National Health Association of Ireland, of which Lady Aberdeen is president. Lord Aberdeen has been Lord Lieutenant of Ireland and Governor-General of Canada. Lady Aberdeen is president of the International Council of Women

WHAT YOUNG IRELAND NEEDS

THE MISSION OF THE MARQUIS AND MARCHIONESS OF ABERDEEN

TWO hundred little girls, with hair-ribbons of blue or green or white or yellow, each squad after its kind, every one from alien stock, happy to the last pair of flying feet, danced a Highland Fling and an Irish Lilt and a Nigarapolska and raced with an absurd and beautiful intensity of endeavor thru all sorts of relay games in the big covered playground of an East Side school in New York City the other day. When they had finished, a slender man, gray-bearded, his cheeks furrowed in a kindly fashion, unmistakably Scotch, rose and thanked them. Then he introduced his wife. Her face—with the fresh color of a young girl—broke into reminiscent smiles as she told how the sight of a similar exhibition three years ago had delighted her so much that, going home to Dublin, she borrowed a teacher from Public School 188, taught the same sort of play-exercise to the school children there, and had all young Dublin dancing thru the hard winter of the great strike, dancing in the schools and playgrounds and streets, up the stairs and down, she said, and thus adding a needed bit of cheer to the hard-prest city. On this new visit to the city she had asked that the white-bloused youngsters m i g h t go thru their drill again so that her husband, too, could see school folk-dancing as it should be done.

For it happens that Sir John Campbell Gordon, Marquis of Aberdeen and Temair, formerly Governor-General of Canada and lately Lord Lieutenant of Ireland, and the Marchioness of Aberdeen, president of the International Council of Women, have no interest greater than their devotion to child welfare and the health of Ireland. And never were two people more completely one in their enthusiasm for a single cause.

Lady A b e r d e e n is president of the Women's National Health Association, which is working along many lines for the betterment of Irish life. It centers in Dublin, but serves the whole island. It commands the support and seeks the welfare of Protestant and Catholic alike. It carries on full two dozen kinds—two bakers' dozens, indeed—of work for the benefit of women and children. Beginning with visiting nurses and health lectures for expectant mothers, babies' clubs and milk stations, it helps the youngsters to grow up healthy and good-natured by providing playgrounds and school gardens, folk dancing, cheap meals, dental clinics, and boot clubs, and then branches out into the wider field of public health, with sanatoriums and preventoriums, health lectures and pamphlets, a health legislation committee, a caravan that carries hygiene-help thru the country lanes, traveling exhibits. Due largely to its anti-tuberculosis campaign, on which special emphasis has been thrown, the deaths from consumption in Ireland are 2500 per year fewer now than when it opened fire in 1907.

Into the midst of all this burst the war.

"It was like a blow from a sledge-hammer," Lord Aberdeen says. "It threatens the very existence of the work."

He speaks with nervous vigor,

throwing out his hands and stressing heavily the words that count.

"That was the reason we came to America, to save this noble enterprise. If an orphanage stood on the mountain-side and you saw an avalanche approaching it, you know what you would do. There is no other country that can do it. And your sympathies are quickened by the war."

There is no money on the other side for such philanthropies today. War economies and war taxation—Lord Aberdeen tells of one landowner, for instance, whose taxes have been increased by $40,000 this year—have dried up the sources of income. Not only do the times bring new necessities, which the Association is meeting by distress workrooms, clothing and comforts depots, and nursing classes, but projects begun before the war cannot be finished and must be abandoned at a loss unless help comes quickly.

"The child welfare work is everything now," says Lady Aberdeen. "We must build for the future. And it is particularly necessary for the women of the world to be organized and unified now so that they will be ready for their work of moral reconstruction after the war."

After the two hundred little girls had finished their dancing and had received thru Lady Aberdeen greetings from Dublin children—Irish youngsters who were doing Irish folk-dancing because immigrant children in New York showed them the way—their leader, a dark-haired girl with all the moral frenzy of the c o l l e g e cheer-leader, called for a cheer for the children of Dublin. The cordial response, ringing stridently thru the big p a v e d c o u r t y a r d, was deafeningly convincing.

Lord and Lady Aberdeen will carry back to Dublin the vociferous love of Public School 188, but they will take also other evidence, no less hearty and somewhat more substantial, that folks on this side of the water have a friendly interest in those children of Dublin.

OLD WINTER IN HIS HOME

BY HAROLD J. HOWLAND

WINTER is like trouble. There are two ways of meeting it. The one way is not to meet it at all, but quietly steal away. This plan has its merits. There is a peculiar satisfaction in loafing under laughing skies, basking in balmy airs, draining a "beaker full of the warm South"—when you know that your own proper home is vext and tormented with the conscienceless vagaries of a climate that can never make up its mind for two minutes on end whether it is frigid or torrid, wet or dry. So you can easily do worse, when winter shrills its shrewish challenge in your ears, than to temper your valor with discretion and go South.

But there is a better way, if you are a robust soul, liking to meet trouble face to face and by defeating it make it your slave. If such you are, go North and conquer winter on its own chosen ground. It only needs a stout heart and a bold front to make the blustering giant give up his best and pour his treasures into your lap.

A night's ride from the shivering feverishness of the Great White Way will take you to his lair. There you will find a warm welcome; indeed that "warmest welcome" of the poet's inn with still a little added to it. If there is one thing better than an inn, it is the right kind of a club.

On a six hundred acre tract in the heart of the Adirondack Mountains stands a unique institution. In all your travels you will find nothing just like the Lake Placid Club. You may find many single things like parts of it; nothing quite like it in the "altogether."

GRAVE MEN CURL

Christmas week in the year of grace just passed found four hundred odd of us indulging at the Club in that sensible custom better known till recent years in Europe than with us busy Americans, a winter holiday.

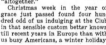

MAYOR MITCHEL SNOWSHOES

232

The mercury in the thermometer swung thru a regular arc from ten below at night to ten above by day, with a single excursion to twenty below just as a sample and another to twenty above just to prove to us that we did not really like such heat. It was cold, but we were not. The long rambling clubhouse and the twenty-five cottages that were open —there are seventy-five scattered thru the Club's square mile of wooded grounds—were warm as toast. Nor were we cold outdoors. Eighteen hundred feet above the sea the air is pure and rare and dry. In air like that the cold comes as a tonic not a torment; it stimulates but does not stab. It snowed, too, how many days I cannot possibly remember. For snow up there is quite a different thing. It falls as naturally as sunshine in the South. In the city snow is an impertinence, a nuisance to be loathed and cleared away. In a suburb it is a beauty while it falls, a bother when it has fallen, a menace as it thaws and slops away. But in the mountains it is logical, as welcome as the day, as harmless as the air itself, a constant beauty, an unobtrusive natural happening. There is always snow upon the ground, a foot, two feet, who knows how many? At home we sweep or shovel our paths to get the snow away; up there we roll them with a huge wooden roller to pack it down. It is all so different; here Old Winter is at home.

TWO GO SKIJORING

At home we dress for looks, and shiver if the style demands. Up there we dress for warmth and comfort and efficiency, and do not shiver if we lose good looks thereby. We men, that is; for the feminine is just as eternal among the everlasting hills as down among the haunts of men. The styles are different from the home styles, it is true; but the style is there none the less. The fact that it is mixt with common sense does not detract a bit. That woman there, her skirt up to her knees, looks neither bold nor scant in modesty; just sensible—and chic. Those

two girls starting off on ski, in trig blue suits of coat and knickerbockers, strong boots, puttees and rakish cap administer no shock, unless it be a shock to find the unconventional

EVERYBODY SKIS

can seem so natural. Up there we dress for use first, and only then for charm; and find ourselves no losers either way.

Well, being dressed thus warm and sensibly, what shall we do this morning? Bright, snapping, white, and gold, the day allures us out, and who would stay indoors? What will you have? A little indolent, today, perhaps. Here is a cutter, or a double sleigh, or even, if a party wants to go, a big wood sled, stuffed warm with straw and rugs and furs. The roads lead off among the woods, thru avenues of stately forest trees, their rich green half hidden now by heavy feathery coats of driven snow. The roads are solitary. Not a sound but the cheerful chatter of the bells; no company, but the looming hills, the marching trees, the river murmuring underneath the ice until a sudden rapid breaks the icy spell and lets it tumbling out. This is the sleigh ride in its perfectest estate. Some day we will take food and drive far off and build a fire, broil ham, make coffee, and enjoy a feast with appetites that have a razor edge given by this tingling air. But not today.

Now for a skate before dinner; we have still an hour to spare. The rink is close at hand, not ten steps from the clubhouse door. Warm within doors we change our boots for skate-shod ones and step upon the ice. The rink is popular already. In a central box a hockey match waxes fast and furious as the rival fortunes rise and fall. In another fenced off space eight men of weight and gravity—their weight perhaps explains why it is not hockey they are playing at—are curling, sending the big gray granite "stanes" sailing across the ice and "sooping" with their "besoms" craftily to speed them or retard them as they near their goal. In still another space the artist skaters, on the inner and the outer edge, with grape vines, figure threes

THE MOUNTAINS GROW HOARY

and eights, turns, jumps and pirouettes, exemplify, with more or less success, the fine art of skating. While round and round outside the boxes skate the rest of us who find just skating a joyous, exhilarating, red blooded sport.

What next? Luncheon of course; this splendid air permits no laggard appetite. But after that? Why not the *ski*—pronounce it *she* if you would be correct. A quarter of a mile thru the sweet smelling woods we shuffle—we have yet to learn the free running stroke that takes the Finnish postman a good eight miles an hour on his rounds—to the quondam golf course. There we halt a moment, our senses captured by the sudden view. The course drops down before us to the valley and on its farther edge stand ranged the everlasting hills, Gothic—the Elephant its more descriptive name, Tahawus, or Marcy, the Adirondack's highest peak; Colden—or Avalanche—called so for the sharp angled scar upon its steepest side; and McIntyre, broad shouldered and immense. Purple and blue and violet their snowy sides refract the wintry light.

Our homage paid, we turn to *skiing*. Dozens of figures dot the slope below us, some sliding swiftly down, more toiling slowly up. It does not look so hard; it does look fun. We hesitate a moment on the brink, try to absorb the counsel of a volunteer friend, and take the plunge. We start, the motion quickens, down we go, knees bent, arms balancing, blood racing, nerves a-tingle. What sport this is; it's flying like the birds. Why have we never *skied* before? This is the sport for us. Must we ever stop?

Ah, now we know. What happened to those *ski?* Well, anyhow, the snow is soft; it did not hurt a bit to fall. But getting up's another story. How long the things are; how slippery the snow. But easy, crafty does it. Now for the climb. That's good hard work, but the prospect of another swoop, once we have reached the summit, lightens it. Well, here we are again; this time we'll keep the old things parallel, so they won't trip us up. All ready? Now we're off again; that's splendid. We've got it now. What speed! What thrilling rush! Let's top that little ridge and turn into that little gully there beyond. It's easy now. Why do those others fall; they haven't caught the knack. There, here's the ridge; now for the other side. Oof! Down again! Well, up again, wary and slow; we'll get it next time.

So goes the sport. Now a little encouragement, now dire disaster. But the result is always the same. Have we done well this time; it's so splendid we must do it again forthwith. Has ignominy caught us by the leg? Better luck — or better skill — next time; let's up and at it once again.

FOURTEEN PLAY HOCKEY

What? Time for supper? Impossible. Still we're hungry enough; but tomorrow bright and early will find us out again.

Skating and *skiing* are not the only sports. As we *ski* and *ski* and *ski* again, the warning cries, the triumphant shouts, and the giggling shrieks of the toboganers drift across the snow. The slide begins on a structure high above the golf house roof and runs a mile down into the valley. Toboggans, Flexible Flyers and an occasional venturesome spirit on *ski* keep the pot a-boiling. Over by the lake another slide, built of great blocks of ice, provides a runway for the plunging bob-sleds that hurl their breathless crews across the lake a mile a minute gait. Snow shoeing is a less strenuous sport; but the tramps across the drifted fields and thru the sparkling woods fill the lungs with ozone, the muscles with delicious weariness and the mind with pleasant pictures of Nature in a tranquil mood. *Skijoring*, behind a

horse of mettle, combines the joys of speed, of horsemanship, of muscular control. The sports are endless, but alas the time is not. You cannot pursue them all, but each you try seems better, for the moment, than the rest.

But sport, splendid as it is, is not the whole. Better than all is the spirit of the Club, its atmosphere. For instance, children first is a maxim honored faithfully in the observance. They are welcomed, provided for, made much of; and the best of all is, they are not in the way. Which might suggest to a philosopher the thought that children only become a nuisance when we do not welcome them and try to make them happy.

The spirit of the Club is shown, too, in the celebrations that are held to mark the holiday season. One night during the week fifty of us pile into sleighs and ride over to the village church. There with fifty other of the villagers we don long Druid robes, horned helmets, breastplates and sheepskins and, armed with spears and torches, march to an open space beside the lake. There, while hundreds of other villagers and Club folk watch from above, we enact a pageant of "The First Christmas Tree," after Van Dyke's beautiful story. It is a striking scene, a reverently acted play. We stand ankle deep in snow, the wind blows shrill and drives a young snow storm into our faces. But we do not care.

Another night we hunt the mistletoe with ancient rites, red torches, quaint costumes, mirth and merriment. It is a lark, but it is more than that. No one who has taken part in that symbolic march thru the winter woods will be likely to forget the story of the slaying of Baldur the Beautiful by the mistletoe arrow sped by the jealous hate of Loki.

These are some of the things that make the Club more than an inn and a visit to Old Winter under the Club's fostering direction an experience to be repeated.

THE FORESTS DRESS UP

THE YOUNGSTERS TOBOGGAN

BOTH SIDES A DEBATE

LITERACY TEST FOR IMMIGRANTS

RESOLVED: That immigration into the United States should be further restricted by a literacy test.

THE Lodge literacy bill was the first attempt to restrict immigration on the ground of illiteracy. President Cleveland vetoed this bill in 1897 after it had been passed by both houses. Bills providing for the literacy test were vetoed by Presidents Taft and Wilson in 1912 and 1915. The House Immigration Committee has just reported favorably on the Burnett bill. This brief was prepared by R. S. Fulton.

AFFIRMATIVE

I. Further restriction of immigration is desirable.
  A. There is little need for more unskilled labor.
    1. About three million unemployed wage earners in this country now.
    2. Army of unemployed wage earners due to displacement of older laborers by newer immigrants.
  C. Restriction necessary for the protection of American unskilled laborers.
    1. Americans cannot compete with unskilled immigrants. (a) Standard of living is lower for immigrants. (b) Immigrants are willing to work for less. (1) In many industries they have lowered wages. (2) In some industries they have prevented wage increase. (c) Immigrants will work under poorer conditions.
    2. Unskilled immigrants are hostile to labor organizations.
II. Illiterate immigrants are undesirable.
  A. Industrially.
    1. Ninety per cent of illiterate immigrants are unskilled.
    2. Their ignorance makes them detrimental to American labor. (a) Willing to reduce wages. (b) Unable to comprehend instructions, they cause deterioration of working conditions. (1) Mining inspectors agree that employment of illiterate aliens is one cause of increase in mining accidents.
    3. Few illiterate immigrants go on farms.
    4. Illiterate immigrants not wanted on farms. (a) Land companies strongly oppose illiterate Southern and Eastern Europeans.
  B. Socially undesirable.
    1. They tend to congest the city slums. Forty out of every hundred in the Baltimore slums and fifty-nine out of every one hundred in the New York slums are illiterate foreigners.
    2. They cannot understand health ordinances and sanitation.
    3. They furnish a disproportionate share of the foreign born criminal, insane, and pauper class; eighteen per cent of foreign born insane; thirty per cent of foreign born paupers; forty two per cent of foreign born murderers.
    4. Difficult to assimilate. (a) They come without any permanent interest in our country. (b) They have no common language. (c) Mentally unable to adopt our customs. (d) Majority of illiterate immigrant laborers are single or have left their wives at home.
  C. Politically undesirable.
    1. About forty per cent return home.
    2. An easy prey to corruptionists.
    3. They come to America without political experience.
    4. They are slower in securing accurate information on political questions than those who can read.
III. The literacy test is the most feasible

method of dealing with the immigration problem.
  A. It will reduce the number of illiterates.
    1. Fifty per cent of the present immigrants are illiterate.
    2. Admits only the necessary number. (a) A commission could fix a flexible test to be raised or lowered as the supply of needed unskilled labor exceeds or falls below the demand.
  B. Promotes assimilation.
    1. Lessens the difficulty of providing a common language. (a) Literate can more easily master a new tongue.
    2. Makes adequate distribution of the immigrant less difficult. (a) Education fosters self-reliance.
    3. Immigrant who attains literacy in order to enter the United States would probably become a citizen.
  C. Admits a better quality of immigrants.
    1. Literates have more good qualities than illiterates.
    2. It would exclude the undesirable classes.
    3. Struggle for an education would make the literate a better American.
    4. Mental training an advantage.
  D. A simple means of exclusion.

NEGATIVE

I. Further restriction of immigration is undesirable.
  A. No oversupply of unskilled immigrant labor.
    1. Immigrant labor comes in response to economic demand.
  B. Immigration does not lower wages and cause unemployment.
    1. No causal relation. The Twelfth United States Census Report shows wages relatively higher and unemployment less prevalent where immigrants are most numerous. (a) In such Northern states as Indiana, Kansas, and Missouri, where the foreigners are less than ten per cent of the population, there are from forty-seven to fifty per cent of the laborers unemployed at some time during the year. (b) Where sixty-five per cent of the laborers are foreign born, as in Massachusetts, Rhode Island, New York, and Connecticut, there are but forty per cent of the workers unemployed. (c) New York, Illinois and Massachusetts, having a large immigrant population, show a higher scale of wages.
    2. The same report shows that in trades where immigrants are most numerous wages are above average and unemployment less.
    3. Unemployment due to deeper causes than immigration. All trades suffer a seasonal shifting in activity.
  C. Immigrant is a producer.
    1. An economic factor in reducing the cost of living.
II. Illiterate immigrants not undesirable.
  A. No causal relationship between illiteracy and undesirability.
    1. No relation between illiteracy and pauperism. (a) Our laws require immigrants to have sufficient funds to maintain themselves until a position is obtained. (b) Statistics show pauperism no more prevalent among illiterates.
    2. No relation between illiteracy and crime. (a) Opinion of Immigration Commission. (b) Comparative statistics show 87 per cent of criminals in jails and penitentiaries can read and write.
    3. No relation between illiteracy and insanity. The Immigration Commission says our present laws adequate to exclude insane.

    4. No relationship between illiteracy and strong character, healthy body, and honest intention. As ex-President Eliot says, inability to read is due to lack of opportunity.
  B. Illiterate immigrants are sturdy farming class of Europe.
    1. Literate immigrants come from cities of southeastern Europe.
  C. Desirable characteristics as prevalent among the rural classes as in city.
III. Literacy test not the most feasible method of dealing with the problem.
  A. The literacy test ignores the problem still unsolved.
    1. Strikes at the social and political phase already provided for by laws.
    2. Disregards laboring conditions. (a) Demand for labor fluctuates. (b) Class of immigrants desired varies.
  B. Literacy not a test of immigrant's mental qualities.
    1. Illiteracy represents the lack of educational facilities and bad government.
  C. Additional industrial legislation will give us desirable Americans.
    1. Present immigration laws provide for social and political status.
    2. Present restrictions exclude undesirable aliens.
    3. Evils of immigration due to industrial conditions. (a) An oversupply of laborers in a particular locality.
  D. Literacy test will not solve problem of congestion.
    1. No relation between congestion and literacy.
    2. Tends to increase problem of congestion. (a) The literate immigrant prefers large cities.
  E. Not practical in application.
    1. Admits foreigners from cities and excludes those from country.

REFERENCES

Balch, E. G., Our Slavic Fellow Citizens. Clark, F. E., Old Home of New Immigrants. Commons, Races and Immigrants in America. Dinglow, European Immigrants. Fairchild, H. F., Immigration. Hall, P. F., Immigration and Its Effects upon the United States. Haskins, F. J., God's Melting Pot. Hourwich, Immigration and Labor. Jenks, J. W., and Lauck, W. J., The Immigration Problem. Roberts, The New Immigration. Sanderson, J. P., Republican Landmarks; the Views and Opinions of American Statesmen on Foreign Immigration. Smith, R. M., Emigration and Immigration.

Affirmative

American Journal of Sociology, 17:687-46, Clark, F. E., Old Home of New Immigrants, March, 1912. Atlantic Monthly, 110:888-95, September, 1912. Century, 67:466-73, January, 1904. Forum, 14:805-14, February, 1912. Fortnightly Review, 96:166-69, July, 1911. Harper's Weekly, 52:23, December 19, 1908; 56:9, October 19, 1912; 56:18, December 23, 1912; 57:10, July 26, 1913. Independent, 50:77, January, 1898; 72:659, February 29, 1912. Literary Digest, 44:195-6, February 3; 923-4, May 4; 1085-9, May 25, 1912. Nation, 96:481, November 21; 96:626-7, December 26, 1912. North American Review, 192:66-67, July, 1910; 195:94-102, January; 201-11, February, 1912. Outlook, 101:882-4, June 22; 102:91, September 14, 1912. Survey, 25:817-19, January 7; 605-4, January 7; 789-92, February 4, 1911; 28:801-2, May 18; 724-30, September 7, 1912. World's Work, 19:12815-5, April, 1910; 26:287-8, July, 1913. Report 7, Labor Commission.

Negative

American Journal of Sociology, 17:478-90, March, 1912. Arena, 3:415-20, March, 1891; 27:234-66, March, 1902; 35:804-6, May, 1906. Independent, 72:266-6, February 1; 304-7, February 8, 1912. Literary Digest, 45:725-4, October 26, 1912; 46:442-4, March 1; 156-8, June 21, 1913. Outlook, 97:857-60, February 18, 1911; 99:988, December 23, 1911; 103:377-8, February 22, 1913. Political Science Quarterly, 26:615-42, December, 1911. Survey, 24:386-92, June 4, 1910; 25:627-9, January 7, 1911; 28:347-9, May 25, 1912; 29:419-20, January 4; 497-9, January 18, 1913; 30:270-1, June 14, 1913.

234

THE NEW BOOKS

THE NEW GENERATION

How to Know Your Child satisfies unusually well the exacting conditions of a really helpful book for mothers. There is also a good chapter for fathers. Miriam Finn Scott applies the case method to child training and shows concretely how the best of the so-called new systems, as the Montessori, is within the reach of the ordinary family. The entire work is a tribute to Dr. Dewey, whom the author seems to have first appreciated fully when she found the Tolstoy School in Moscow exemplifying the principles of America's leading educator.

The first edition of Dr. Berle's *The School in the Home* brought him 10,000 letters, many from as far away as Siam, Japan and Persia. The answer to them is this second edition and a second book, *Teaching in the Home.* His principles of "fertilization of the child mind" and "negotiable knowledge" are needed protests against the underestimates commonly placed upon the ability of children in learning, health and happiness. The best elements of the old, aristocratic education are restated for use in the modern, complex homes of democracy. There is an evident trace of inability on the part of the author to see the classic in the making.

The editor of the Childhood and Youth series recommends *Backward Children* for use by parent, teacher, medical inspector or clinician as a botanist would use a key in identifying and classifying flowers. Dean Holmes states very sensibly that "backwardness is not wholly or always bad and that it needs to be studied in each individual case to determine its exact nature." In this work as in those discussed above the most valuable part results from the use of the case method.

The Health Care of the Growing Child, by Louis A. Fischer, is a most valuable "first aid" for mothers and nurses in diet, emergencies, accidents, development of the body, gymnastics, and all kinds of diseases. Particularly good are the diagnoses of nutrition difficulties and the instructions concerning food with recipes and dietaries.

In order to determine the relation existing between moral and religious instruction and actual every-day conduct, 600 children of each sex were carefully studied for a period of five years. As a result in *Moral Education* a relationship is shown "scientifically" between deportment and scholarship and between deportment and religious training. An idea of the method is gained from the measurement of the latter in terms of church membership of parents and attendance upon Sunday School, etc., of the children, and the decision is that "the school is doing more than its part. The home is not handling. its problem as well as it did fifteen years ago." It "no longer provides moral

training. Parents are no longer assuming their obligation," etc., etc.

How to Know Your Child, by M. F. Scott. Boston: Little, Brown. $1.25. *The School in the Home and Teaching in the Home,* by A. A. Berle. Moffat, Yard. $1.25 each. *Backward Children,* by Arthur Holmes. Indianapolis: Bobbs-Merrill. $1. *The Health Care of the Growing Child,* by L. Fischer, M.D. Funk & Wagnalls. $1.25. *Moral Education,* by William T. Whitney. Boston: Leroy Phillips.

RECENT WAR BOOKS

It is certainly not an exaggeration to pronounce Mrs. Wharton's *Fighting France* a profoundly impressive and dramatic picture of the rebirth of a nation. On every face she perceives the in-

vincible flame of an heroic resolve, beneath each calmly steadfast countenance the determination to obliterate all personality in the united purpose of driving an invader from a sacred soil. At times she strikes, with apparent unconsciousness, a note which rings thru many pages, for example, when she was given the password of the night at Chalons—*Jéna.* To the French soldier that touch alone should make her book forever memorable, as recalling in the hour of darkest need the figure of the Great Commander who led the French armies to victory.

Mr. Long's *Colours of War* follows by way of contrast. In Berlin the supreme conflict brought to spiritual awakening. The long anticipated day dawned swiftly to reveal a nervous patriotism. The people sang, but Mr. Long found there was "no sporting war spirit." A glimpse of the Emperor delivering a public appeal suggests Pilate's distrest vindication of himself. Mr. Long quotes the Emperor as saying: "They have thrust a sword into my hand." It is as if he were performing a symbolical ablution before the shedding of innocent blood. He gives us graphic Russian war scenes, and with clear insight analyzes the psychology of the Russian military spirit. Tho the Russian will fight doggedly, it is with little enthusiasm. Apparently within him is something which does not joy in indiscriminate slaughter. His thoughts turn backward to the soil he cherishes, while between officers and men there exist unique fraternal relations. Mr. Long's impartial reckoning of the strength of his country's enemy, his plea for truth and emphatic warning, set his book apart from others of the kind written by Englishmen.

In *Kings, Queens and Pawns,* Mrs. Rinehart writes in a chatty, interesting way of her "escape from England" to France, and her wanderings thereafter as a member of the American Red Cross. While vividly describing the many and varied places visited, and recounting exciting, pathetic and tragic incidents, she also gives timely advice to those moved to aid in the work of rescue and mercy. In this latter respect Mrs. Rinehart is to be congratulated in bringing forth from bewildering and often hopeless surroundings a clear view to strengthen her appeal.

Personally conducted trips of war correspondents begin to wear a curious resemblance on both sides of the fighting line. Mr. Powell, however, has been able to see a great deal more than wayside glimpses from an automobile dash, and the peep thru a leafy spy hole upon an enemy nowhere visible. In his *Vire la France* the chapter on the Battle of Champagne is most powerful, impressive and frightful writing of what scientific warfare has achieved. He fears disbelief, but it is a tribute to Mr. Powell's veracity to state that no human

| Operator | Installer | Lineman | Clerk |

The Picked Army of the Telephone

The whole telephone-using public is interested in the army of telephone employees—what kind of people are they, how are they selected and trained, how are they housed and equipped, and are they well paid and loyal.

Ten billion messages a year are handled by the organization of the Bell System, and the task is entrusted to an army of 160,000 loyal men and women.

No one of these messages can be put through by an individual employee. In every case there must be the complete telephone machine or system in working order, with every manager, engineer, clerk, operator, lineman and installer cooperating with one another and with the public.

The Bell System has attracted the brightest, most capable people for each branch of work. The training is thorough and the worker must be specially fitted for his position.

Workrooms are healthful and attractive, every possible mechanical device being provided to promote efficiency, speed and comfort.

Good wages, an opportunity for advancement and prompt recognition of merit are the rule throughout the Bell System.

An ample reserve fund is set aside for pensions, accident and sick benefits and insurance for employees, both men and women. "Few if any industries," reports the Department of Commerce and Labor, "present so much or such widely distributed, intelligent care for the health and welfare of their women workers as is found among the telephone companies."

These are some of the reasons why Bell telephone service is the best in the world.

AMERICAN TELEPHONE AND TELEGRAPH COMPANY
AND ASSOCIATED COMPANIES

One Policy   *One System*   *Universal Service*

brain could conjure forth such a cataclysm of horror. If his partisanship for the Allies be pronounced, he is not thereby deterred from a frank criticism of the British military organization. He joins with the French officers in resenting the superior attitude of their British comrades, asserts this is "not a sporting war," and that packs of hounds are entirely out of place. But it is with the finger of an otherwise admiring friend that he points to the vulnerable joints in British armor. Both from a military and civilian estimate, Mr. Powell's book should hold a permanent place in this "greatest war" literature.

Twenty years ago Mr. Kipling wrote soldier stories which gave him a wide popularity. It is with much the same distinctively Kiplingesque attitude he mingles with the officers and men of the French army. His little volume, *France at War*, therefore, will not disappoint those who still delight in his famous soldier models.

Military science is indebted to Mr. Talbot's *Aeroplanes and Dirigibles* for a well written and comprehensively informing book. While professional in tone, with no attempt made to "play up" unduly exciting incidents in the airman's career, such parts as the struggle of Count Zeppelin for success should interest every reader.

Previous to the publication of General Baden-Powell's *My Adventures as a Spy*, one confesses to a vague impression that a spy is no better than the term seems to imply—a despicable fellow who, when detected, is hardly worth praise or regret. General Powell, however, not only defends and classifies the spy, but gives us his psychology. The result is to kindle a better feeling for the villain—or hero—of devious ways, ready resource and ample courage. For one who is tired of life, General Powell recommends the trade of a spy as a bracing occupation.

Fighting France, by Edith Wharton. Scribner. $1. *Colours of War*, by R. C. Long. Scribner. $1.50. *Kings, Queens and Pawns*, by Mary Roberts Rinehart. Doran. $1.50. *Vive la France*, by E. Alexander Powell. Scribner. $1. *France at War*, by Rudyard Kipling. Doubleday, Page. 50 cents. *Aeroplanes and Dirigibles*, by F. A. Talbot. Philadelphia: Lippincott. $1.25. *My Adventures as a Spy*, by Sir Robert Baden-Powell. Philadelphia: Lippincott. $1.

MODERN HEROES OF FAITH

That the world is still rich in men who are willing and able to sacrifice for their faith, and so extend the influence of their religion, is clearly shown in Dr. John T. Faris' *The Book of Faith in God.* These short chapters recounting each an instance of high devotion and service are encouraging as well as interesting.   Doran. $1.

A BOOK FOR A RAINY AFTERNOON

Most of the sonnets, particularly the three called Idolatry, in Brian Hooker's *Poems,* have true originality and distinction. The songs are real songs, full of lilt and music. The other poems, tho not particularly new in matter and form, have charm, imagination, sincerity of purpose and an idealism all too rare in modern poetry.

Yale University Press. $1.

COMEDY FOR THE EYE

A good example of the play to be seen rather than read, is Thompson Buchanan's *A Woman's Way,* produced in 1909 by Grace George and now included in the Drama League Series. Lacking epigramatic force or literary polish in dialog, its blunt, slangy speech, so characteristic of American life, breaks harshly from the page. It is perhaps the nearest approach to the English high comedy and Sir Henry Arthur Jones that has yet been made on the American stage.

Doubleday, Page. 75 cents.

LIGHT ON THE DARK AGES

Medieval Italy, by H. B. Cotterill, covers more than a thousand years of Italian history in very condensed narrative. The book contains a great deal of interesting material on medieval coins and mosaics and the development of architecture.

Stokes. $2.50.

INDIANS AND REGULARS

A Baby of the Frontier is a breathless story of the plains in the days of frontier army posts, roving bands of Cheyennes and Sioux, and heroic cavalry squads fighting against fearful odds. This is a familiar field to the author, Cyrus Townsend Brady, who narrates a well-unfolded tale with genuine enthusiasm and realism.

Revell. $1.25.

HEBREW LEGEND AND HISTORY

A useful volume of the handy Lake English Classics is a collection of *Old Testament Narratives* edited by Charles Elbert Rhodes. Arranged in short stories, without chapter or verse, the book will be interesting to those who already know their Bible as a sacred book, as well as to those, and the college examinations say they are legion, who have to be introduced to it along with Chaucer and Ben Johnson.

Scott, Foresham. 40 cents.

A NEW COUNTERBLAST TO TOBACCO

Bruce Fink opens his essay on *Tobacco* by declaring it a physical poison and closes by denouncing it as a moral evil. Strictly speaking, the book disqualifies itself from consideration as a scientific treatise by its admission of hearsay evidence and exhibits of dubious evidential value. But Prof. Fink, after all is said, makes out a strong case concerning the effect of tobacco on boys and college men, and the waste of money entailed in its use.

Abingdon Press. 50 cents.

TROUT VS. BULLS AND BEARS

By whimsical tradition the real interest of the ordinary financier is not his office, but his cabin in the woods. *Wall Street and the Wilds* is, however, an autobiography which realizes this conceit. Anthony Weston Dimock, a powerful "operator" in his younger days, is one of the foremost exponents of the joy of cabin life, and his book will be intensely interesting both to the Wall Street men of today and to those who care more for fishing than for finance.

Outing Co. $3.

LITTLE MOHAMMEDANS

Dr. S. M. Zwemer is an authority on life in Moslem lands. The photographs of pretty, merry children illustrating his *Children of the Moslem World* are a startling commentary on the text, reminding one that these might be, should be just like other children. We see the Mohammedan at his best in the efforts of Young Turks, in the courage and endurance of the Turkish soldier. The children of Persia, India, Egypt, Southern Africa are the other side of the picture.

Revell. $2.

KIPLING

Uncommon and charming are the photographs illustrating Dr. Arley Munson's account of *Kipling's India*, while her text is warranted to send one back to the old stories even tho one agree with the conclusions of John Palmer's striking critical study *Rudyard Kipling*, in the Writer's of the Day series. As he puts it, the critic is "mainly concerned with looking for tl. inspired author under a mass of skilful journalism." The Simla and soldier tales are the latter; the stories of Kim, Puck of Pook's Hill and the Jungle are art.

Kipling's India, by Arley Munson, Doubleday, Page. $1.50. *Rudyard Kipling*, by John Palmer. Holt. 60 cents.

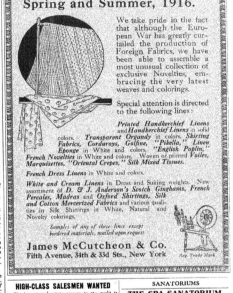

PEBBLES

Voice—"Is this the Weather Bureau? How about a shower tonight?"
Prophet—"Don't ask me. If you need one, take it."—*Chaparral.*

"Put your car up for the winter?"
"No. I'd like to, but none of the pawnbrokers are willing to lend me any money on it."—*New York World.*

Prosecutor (to talesman): "Do you object to capital punishment?"
Talesman: "Wal, no. Not if it ain't too severe."—*Harpers.*

Willis—How did Christmas go off at your place?
Gillis—As usual. Christmas Eve we wrapped all the presents we gave and Christmas Day we rapped all the presents we received.—*Life.*

Jim—What is Bill doing now?
James—He's a post impressionist.
Jim—You're stringing me.
James—No; he's got a job with the Western Union branding numbers on the telegraph poles.—*Dartmouth Jack-o'-Lantern.*

There is a little railroad down in south Georgia bearing the impressive title of "L. K. & W." Just what the initials originally stood for no one recalls, and the road is known locally as the "Look, Kuss & Wait" and the "Lord Knows When."—*Harpers.*

"All Things Come to He Who Waits—and Hustles."—*Oral Hygiene.*
"Father Arrests Son Whom, He Says, Looted Home."—*Bronx Home News.*
Headline writers, too, seem to have a fear of losing their amateur standing.—*New York Tribune.*

Curate: "Mai dead children, in accordance with Scriptural behest, Ai want you to regard me as the shep-ard, and Ai shall look on you as mai sheep. Of course you all know what the shep-ard does to the sheep?"
Dear Kid: "Yes, please sir, 'e shears 'em."—*Sydney Bulletin.*

The Wells family, who resided in an interior city, had one of those maids of the invariably heavy hand. Not long ago the town experienced a slight shock of earthquake. Pictures were thrown down, furniture and crockery rattled about. During the tumult the mistress went to the head of the basement stairs and called out in a patient, forbearing tone:
"Well, Lizzie, what are you doing now?"—*Harpers.*

Two Englishmen crossing from Europe were both of a serious and conservative turn of mind. Altho they shared the same stateroom, had seats at the same table, and sat side by side in their deck chairs they did not speak to each other, for they had not been introduced.
On the last day, however, one of them decided to wave conventionality.
They were standing side by side on the rail and he ventured an introductory remark:
"Goin' over?"
"Yas," replied the other Englishman, "I rather thought I would."—*Everybody's.*

"Henry," a Jersey commuter's wife began, thoughtfully, "I've been thinking a lot about you lately."
"What's up?"
"Since we moved here to Jersey and you've gone back and forth every day to the city you have seen absolutely nothing of the children."
"I don't see how that can be helped," said Henry. "When I leave in the morning they are not up, and when I come back in the evening they're in bed."
"Yes," said the wife, "that is so, but you might at least send them a souvenir postcard now and then."—*New York Times.*

Independent Opinions

It is startling to open an envelope postmarked "Oklahoma City" and find in it an old and faded letter dated nearly fifty years ago and long before Oklahoma had been heard of. Mrs. K. S. Carlisle, of that city, had been looking over some old letters of her mother's and found one which she thinks—as do we—will interest The Independent readers of today.

WAR DEPARTMENT
Paymaster General's Office
Washington, Dec. 23d, 1868.

My Dear Sister:
I have just subscribed for The Independent, one of the finest weekly papers in the world, devoted to Religion, Politics, Literature and News, and have made you a present of it for one year from January 1st. It will be your New Year's gift from me. It is published in New York City, and the postage will be about twenty cents a year, payable at your post office quarterly in advance. I enclose you twenty-five cents to pay the postage on it, so it will be of no expense whatever to you. Mary takes The Independent and would not be without it.

Last night I attended the lecture of "Petroleum V. Nasby" (D. R. Locke, Editor "Toledo Blade") and was never more amused and interested. Nasby is one of the smartest men of the times. The enormous ball was packed full. General Grant and many other distinguished persons were present.

Tell Tully I would like to spend a few days with him hunting deer and turkey and prairie chickens.

Give my best respects. Write to us,
Your brother,
"HENDERSON."

In our editorial of November 29, "What Are You Fighting For?" we urged the belligerents to put into concrete terms what they considered necessary for their national safety, satisfaction and honor. Then we enumerated the terms of peace which had been mentioned in discussions of the question, such as indemnities, reduction of the enemies' armaments and territorial cessions. The Professor of Philosophy in Washington and Jefferson College thinks we laid too much stress on the territorial side of it.

No doubt the phrase so current in the discussions of diplomats of southern Europe—"the realization of our national aspirations"—refers usually to territorial expansion. No doubt territorial changes will come about as result of the conflict, but after all these will be in the nature of byproducts of the sacrifices. Germany indeed sought more space as a necessity in view of her increasing population. England indeed laid her hand on certain undefendable outlying German territory. France fought to protect her own borders, else for her there would be scarcely ground for a fight at all. At the same time, to suppose that this superb demonstration of human emotions is caused by a desire on the part of any citizen of Europe for a strip of territory in Africa or Asia, not as his own but as a national possession, is to view the struggle as a business affair carried out for the realization of values too vague to believe in.

The real motives of the war are certain

Stop Eating Poisonous Food Combinations!

Noted Scientist Shows How Certain Combinations of Good Foods Are Responsible for Over 90% of All Sickness, While Others Produce Sparkling Health and Greatly Increased Efficiency

Twenty years ago Eugene Christian was at death's door. For years he had suffered the agonies of acute stomach and intestinal trouble. His doctors—among them the most noted specialists in the country—gave him up to die. He was educated for a doctor, but got no relief from his brother physicians, so as a last resort he commenced to study the food question in its relation to the human system, and as a result of what he learned he succeeded in *literally eating his way back to perfect health* without drugs or medicines of any kind—and in a remarkably short space of time.

Today Eugene Christian is a man 55 years young. He has more stamina, vitality and physical endurance than most youngsters in their 'teens. He literally radiates mental energy and physical power.

23,000 People Benefited

So remarkable was his recovery that Christian knew he had discovered a great truth which, fully developed, would result in a new science—the Science of Correct Eating.

Without special foods, drugs or medicines, he has up to this time *successfully* treated over 23,000 people for almost every kind of non-organic ailment known and has greatly increased the physical energy and mental power of as many more who were not suffering from specific troubles.

After his twenty years of study and practice Eugene Christian has come to the definite conclusion that 90% of all sickness is due to wrong eating. He says we are poisoning ourselves through our ignorance of food values. Many good foods when eaten in combination with other good foods form a chemical reaction in the digestive tract and are converted into the most dangerous poisons, from whence come most ills. Many scientists have long recognized this, but until now all their efforts have been directed toward removing the poisons *after* they had formed, while Christian removed the *cause by preventing* the poisons from forming.

Little Lessons in Correct Eating

24 Pocket-Size Booklets in Leatherette Container

Send No Money—Only $3.00 if You Keep Them

Christian's Course of 24 lessons is written expressly for the layman in easy-to-understand language. It does not, however, merely tell you why you should practice correct eating and what the results will be. It gives actual menus, curative as well as corrective, covering every condition of health and sickness from infancy to old age, and covering all occupations, climates and seasons. To follow these menus you do not have to upset your table—nor eat things you don't enjoy—in fact you will enjoy your meals as you never have before.

Vigorous Health— Increased Efficiency

It has been the almost invariable experience of those who follow Christian's simple suggestions that they enjoy a new type of health—a health so perfect that it can only be described as a kind of super-health. Christian's ideal of health is to be literally stamping at the bit with vital physical energy and mental power—not once in a while—but every moment of the day and every day of the year from youth to deferred old age—and that is what he gives you through these little lessons. There can be no doubt of the increased personal efficiency that this will develop. The better you feel, the better work you can do. And greater material prosperity naturally follows.

No Money in Advance

The price of the Christian Course of 24 lessons — containing rules, methods and actual menus which are literally priceless—is only $3.00. We will gladly send you the course without deposit for five days' free inspection. Merely mail the coupon or write a letter and the complete course will be mailed you at once, all charges prepaid. Then if you decide to keep the course, you can send the money. If not, mail the books back to us; no obligation will have been incurred.

If the more than 300 pages contained in Christian's Course yield but one single suggestion that will bring you greater health, you will get many times the cost of the course back in personal benefit—yet hundreds write us that they find vital help on every page. Tear out and mail the coupon now, before you forget, as this announcement may not appear here again.

Corrective Eating Society, Inc.
42 Hunter Ave., Maywood, N. J.

imponderables, making for power and security. Has Mr. Asquith not exprest the sentiment of the British people? Do they not know what they are fighting for? Germany just now has a multitude of counsellors, but there are many who do not advocate the retention of the conquered territories. In her own way she desires to crush the militarism of France and Russia and the sea power of England. Dimly the war seems to be resolving into a struggle for and against certain lingering traces of mediaevalism and an assertion of principles of societal independence.

EDWARD M. WEYER
Washington, Pennsylvania

Why is it that the latest super-dreadnaught of the United States, the "Nevada," is able to make only some twenty knots per hour, when the latest that Great Britain is building, the "Queen Mary," is required to make 34.4 knots per hour?

Is it not a fact that the two naval engagements in this war, thus far, have demonstrated two things regarding success: first, that it depends on speed, and, second, gun carrying power.

If, then, this is true, how can the United States be satisfied to meet these requirements with only a twenty-knot speed, at least twelve knots per hour below the requirements of other nations?

E. C. VOSE
Concord, New Hampshire

(1) When the "Nevada" was authorized, twenty-one knots per hour was the standard speed for battleships, and theoretically is so yet, but England has built and is building battleships of much higher speed—tho not thirty-four knots as our correspondent suggests. That speed is only proposed for battlecruisers. Probably our battleships Nos. 43 and 44, not yet named, will be given much higher speed than that of the "Nevada."

(2) Every naval engagement depends on speed and gun power.

(3) The United States is *not* satisfied with twenty knots speed.

We are glad to hear again from an old correspondent, Mr. or Mrs. P. B. Publico, who used to write a great deal for the papers, but has not appeared often in print in recent years:

Why all this fuss with Austria and Germany over their submarine warfare? Why not apply the same principles followed here at home and let the various governments take out a license and pay a certain sum into the treasury in consideration of which we will shut our eyes and ears and lips and permit them to do anything they like with our men and women and children. That is what we are doing here and in every town where saloons are licensed. Certainly the number killed every day by these destructive forces which we legalize is immensely greater than will be killed by submarines during the whole course of the war. Such a solution of the problem confronting the State Department ought to be acceptable to the foreign governments and would be altogether in harmony with our policy in home affairs.

PRO BONO PUBLICO

From General Anderson we receive the following courteous criticism of our attitude on military training in the schools:

I regret to find that you disapprove of military training in High Schools. As I understand it, this method of training is not in the line of vocational instruction. It is not supposed by its advocates that the boys who are given this training should become soldiers or officers of the army. The object sought is not a preparation for offensive war or conquest, which nobody favors, as far as I know; but for defensive war or security if unfortunately war should be forced upon us. It is only favored as the best and least expensive method of elementary military instruction.

It is opposed, as far as I can see, from a sentimental prejudice against what is termed militarism. Military organization is not an ism, like despotism, socialism, or any form of autocracy. It is only a method—a means to an end. It may be perverted to a bad end, but it is as often used against a bad ism. Has there ever been or can there ever be a dangerous militarism in this country? Who has ever proposed it or used it? It cannot exist without appropriation and that, of course, is under civil control. The Presidents of the country and the Secretary of War are always civilians.

T. M. ANDERSON
Vancouver, Washington

In an editorial of January 24 on the initiative shown by Germany in methods of warfare we ventured to suggest that the failure of the French and English to make first use of novel weapons like streams of fire and asphyxiating gases was due to moral scruples. This strikes fire as follows:

Moral Scruples? of England! What about her moral scruples of 1863? It has been shown that England in her yearning to see the Union destroyed violated every honorable obligation to our country. She knew that the cruisers "Alabama," "Shenandoah" and "Florida," built in her shipyards, went to sea and inflicted great injury on our commerce, and when she saw no other way out of the trouble she settled the "Alabama" claims as they were called by paying $15,500,000 to be distributed among our citizens whose ships and property had been destroyed. But we need not go back to 1863. What about her *Moral Scruples?* when the British made seizure of the American ship "Wilhelmina," carrying a cargo of wheat to Germany. Here she violated international law for the sake of producing famine, not to the German soldier, but to his wife and children. And what about her *Moral Scruples?* when she made use of the American flag to protect her ships against submarines? Old England may be a great country, but in our estimation she does some very small things.

ADAM HIRN
Spenceville, Ohio

A Catholic priest writes in approval of the plan of the Audubon Society to convert all of the cemeteries of the country into sanctuaries for birds.

What a move for the better if birds were allowed to roam unmolested among the harmless dead. Visitors to the graveyard would be cheered by their singing, their chirping would replace the voices now stilled of those under the sod. May the press do its utmost to make this new move a reality. If New York succeeds in humanizing bird killers, other cities will attempt to do the same. Honor to New York for its proposed protection of God's songsters. RAYMOND VERNIMONT
Denton, Texas

When you think as I think, then you think wisely. When you think the President should appoint a professional post office man, not a professional politician, to manage the New York post office, then you think as I think. When enough of us think wisely, then politicians will not choose Presidents. Then Presidents will not choose politicians. WILLIS BROOKS
Brooklyn

When all our correspondents write letters as succinct as this, then more of them will get published.

er, make fine candy or home-cooked dishes, or take up designing or decorating. See announcements of Woman's Business Bureau, 37 East Twenty-eighth Street; Woman's Guild, 200 West Fifty-second Street; Woman's Work Magazine, 156 Fifth Avenue; Women's Exchange, 334 Madison Avenue; all of New York.

206. Mr. M. H. T., Iowa. "Have you any statistics showing the effects on efficiency in a business office of an eight-hour day and a half holiday a week? I am interested from the employer's standpoint."

Efficiency is generally increased by such a reduction in working hours, provided also the employees are taught scientific working methods. Consult back files of *System* magazine for information of value; also the National Civic Federation, Metropolitan Tower, New York; also the Business Bourse, 260 Broadway, New York; also the United States Department of Labor, Washington, D. C. Books on scientific management, as those of Taylor and Gilbreth, contain references of importance.

207. Mr. P. E. N., Connecticut. "Your articles in The Independent have been both a revelation and an inspiration to me. May I ask for some more personal advice? I am just beginning a three-year term in a theological seminary, with the ultimate object of going into missionary work in Turkey. Can you recommend a filing system suitable for ministers? I want to adopt some plan now that I can gradually build up while I am studying."

Congratulations on your idea. If you can learn business method while studying theology, you will be twice as effective in the missionary field. Various good filing systems are adapted to various purposes. Your choice depends on the material to be filed—whether clippings, memoranda, names and addresses, newspaper and magazine articles, etc. Write the following New York City concerns for details of their methods and appliances: Yawman and Erbe, 360 Broadway; Library Bureau, 316 Broadway; Weis Manufacturing Company, 75 John Street; Charles C. Dilts Company, 377 Broadway; Shaw-Walker Company, 60 Franklin Street; Meilink Manufacturing Company, 399 Broadway; Amberg File Company 75 Duane Street; Safe-Cabinet Sales Company, 15 East Twenty-sixth Street; Permanent Educational Exhibit Company, 70 Fifth Avenue.

208. A Reader in Missouri. "For a number of years I have held the position of church organist, and am considered by many an efficient organist. Yet sometimes I become so afflicted with fear that I actually tremble, and I feel pretty much like a shipwrecked sailor clinging to the top of a mast. I seem to lack the nerve that many less competent organists possess. How can I overcome timidity and gain self-confidence?"

You are in good company—so great an orator as Beecher had trembling of the knees and fluttering of the heart before he got into his sermon far enough to forget himself. Nerve and merit have no relation to each other necessarily. We would suggest that you obtain a few such books as Horace Fletcher's "Forethought Minus Fearthought," Frank Channing Haddock's "Culture of Courage," and one or more of the inspirational works by Orison Swett Marden. A standard volume on mental suggestion or autosuggestion, would probably help you. A course in vigorous gymnastic training should set you up. Could you not arrange a group of potted palms or other large plants between you and the audience? Your timidity may lie chiefly in the consciousness of being seen. Your success is to be heard, and not seen.

209. Miss F. C. M., Massachusetts. "In my reading I often find articles that I wish to keep on file for my work as a teacher of English. Will you kindly suggest the best filing system?"

The frequency and method of use determines. A pocket envelope file, a scrap-book file, a topical card index file, a safe cabinet file, are among the good ones. Procure a copy of *System* Magazine, Chicago; then study the advertising pages for suggestions. Also note Question Box reply to Mr. P. E. N., Connecticut, No. 207.

Could You Fill His Shoes?

The Market Place

OUR GREAT FOREIGN TRADE

Official figures concerning our foreign trade during the calendar year 1915 have now been published by the Government. They show that the extraordinary growth of exports continued to the very end, for the value of shipments in December, $359,301,274, made a new high monthly record, with another new record for the excess of exports over imports. Our exports rose from $2,114,257,000 in 1914 to $3,550,915,000 last year, and it is noticeable that this increase of sixty-eight per cent was accompanied by only a very slight decrease of imports, for the total, $1,778,655,000, was only about half of one per cent, or $10,400,000, below the imports in 1914, and only three-quarters of one per cent, or $14,000,000, less than those of 1913. An impression has prevailed that our receipts of goods from abroad have been much reduced by the war. It is corrected by these figures.

Not only the great and unprecedented volume of exports, but also the very large excess of exports over imports, especially command attention. This excess, so beneficial to the United States, was $1,772,309,000 for the twelve months, with which may be compared $325,000,000 in 1914, and an average of about $450,000,000 for a series of years before the war. December's excess, $187,459,000, surpassed that of October, which had been at the head of the list. It will be seen that December's favorable balance was at the rate of more than $2,250,000,000 (instead of $1,772,309,000) for a full year. While the official figures for January have not been published, it is known that the excess for twenty-eight days of the month, at ports doing ninety per cent of the export business, was $164,500,000. The month's total, therefore, may have been $190,000,000, or even $195,000,000.

Shipments of arms and munitions are steadily increasing, as the gain in December over November was $10,-000,000. And on many large orders there have been no exports. This is true of those given to our manufacturers by the Canadian Car and Foundry Company, which has contracts with Russia for about $150,000,000 worth of ammunition. As an example of war supply cargoes, that of the White Star liner "Adriatic," when she sailed from New York on January 12, may be cited. The steamship carried 18,000 tons of munitions, metals and

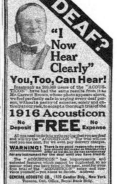

other products ultimately to be used in the war. This cargo's value was $10,-000,000, and the freight charges were nearly $400,000.

Exports of food have been nearly equal in value to those of munitions. In December, from the port of New York alone, they amounted to $34,500,000. Our shipments of breadstuffs, meat and dairy products have risen from $330,-000,000 in 1913, a year not affected by the war, to $760,000,000 in 1915. The exports of last year included $125,-000,000 worth of horses and mules.

The gold movement should not be overlooked. In 1914 we were losing gold, exports having exceeded imports by $165,228,000. Last year, on the contrary, gold was pouring in, and the net gain was $420,528,000.

Owing to the war, our trade with South America has been growing. Our exports to that part of the world in October, for example, were twice as large as those of the corresponding month in 1914. But the balance is in South America's favor. For the ten months that ended with October the exports advanced from $80,000,000 to $116,000,000, and imports from $193,-000,000 to $259,000,000. Many are asking whether this increased trade can be retained after the close of the war. For some time the European nations that have had, and still have, large interests in the South American countries may be unable to do anything there. Eventually, however, the retention of our enlarged trade will depend upon our interest in South American enterprises, our willingness to satisfy local preferences in goods, our acceptance of the prevailing credit practices, and the investment of our people's money in railways and other South American undertakings.

THE STOCK MARKET

It has been difficult at times in the last two or three weeks to account for the course of the stock market, because it has been at variance with the current news relating to industrial and transportation interests. The week ending on January 29 saw a general decline. Resumption of the dividend on Steel common shares, highly favorable reports of the Steel Corporation's net earnings, an increase of the St. Paul road's dividend rate from four to five per cent, a very satisfactory sale of four per cent bonds (at 103.27) by the state of New York, the rising price of copper, and good reports of railroad earnings, failed to stimulate the market, and there were net losses of from two to four points in railroad shares, with a downward movement in the industrials. The Steel Corporation's net earnings had advanced to $51,232,788 in the year's last quarter, from $12,-457,000 in the first, $27,950,000 in the second, and $38,710,000 in the third. In the corresponding quarter of 1914 they had been only $10,933,000. But the price of shares fell from 86 to 82¼.

The decline appears to have been due to apprehension excited by President Wilson's speeches, the movement for a

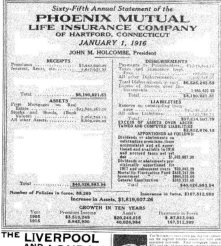

general increase of railroad wages, the demand of the coal miners for higher pay, reports of a coming sharp disagreement with Germany concerning the "Lusitania," the continued selling of American securities by British holders in connection with the mobilization plan, and a withdrawal of "the public" from speculation in war order shares.

At the beginning of last week the decline continued, and on Monday there was a sharp break, with only slight recovery, Steel common shares going below 80. On the following day, however, prices advanced, and the upward movement was not checked until Friday. There were additional reports of good railroad earnings in December, those of the New Haven and Pennsylvania companies being notably encouraging. January's output of pig iron had been 3,188,344 tons, or almost equal to the record-breaking output of December. In January of last year only 1,601,000 tons were made. The price of copper had risen to 26 cents a pound, and the annual reports of several war order companies showed large profits. But on Friday prices fell again, owing partly to disquieting reports about our relations with Germany. The result of the five days' trading was slight net gains for nearly all the war order shares, with fractional changes for the railroad stocks. During the week there had been some increase of activity, for the daily average had risen to 755,000 shares. The course of the market in the immediate future promises to be determined. by our international relations and the' movement for higher wages. It may be affected by the plans for taxing munitions.

CANADA'S GRAIN

It has been well known that Canada's grain crops last year were exceptionally large, but official figures were lacking until a few days ago, when the Government published them. The great increases for wheat and oats are especially noticeable, the wheat yield rising from 161,280,000 bushels in 1914 to 376,303,600 in 1915, while the gain in the crop of oats was from 313,078,000 bushels to 520,103,000. The grain was of better quality than in the preceding year, and the value of the country's field crops rose from $568,161,900 to about $800,000,000.

Of course, the gains were made in the new northwestern provinces of Manitoba, Alberta and Saskatchewan, where the wheat crop was more than doubled, rising from 141,000,000 to 343,000,000 bushels, while the yield of oats advanced from 150,143,000 bushels to 384,840,000. The crop of barley there also was increased from 19,500,000 to 35,317,000 bushels.

The following dividends are announced: Pacific Gas and Electric Company, first preferred and original preferred, quarterly, $1.50 per share, payable February 15.
American Cotton Oil Company, common, quarterly, 1 per cent, payable March 1.
General Development Company, $1.25 per share, payable March 1.

Insurance

Conducted by
W. E. UNDERWOOD

CONCENTRATION IN FIRE INSURANCE

There is a decided tendency in fire insurance toward concentration of resources and expansion of undertakings. Within the past two years several of the largest companies have made heavy additions to their capital funds. The Home increased its capital from $3,-000,000 to $6,000,000. The Continental multiplied its $2,000,000 by five, making it $10,000,000. This company's stockholders also own the Fidelity-Phenix with assets of $18,000,000 and the American Eagle, assets $2,500,000. The Aetna increased its capital to $5,-000,000 several years ago. A number of companies are operating auxiliaries of respectable financial proportions; a greater number are running "feeders" known as underwriters' agencies. Within a year three millionaire companies of Philadelphia passed to the control of more powerful companies in this vicinity. The trend is toward concentration of interests controlling big capital.

H. H. S., Washington, D. C.—You are only postponing the day of reckoning in carrying the assessment insurance. Nine years ago you could have secured $1000 in one of the leading mutual old line companies at about $18 a year; your dividends since would have reduced that cost to about $14; and your cash value now would be about $65 or paid-up value $175. Your Continental Casualty policy is all right.

A. B., Le Mars, Iowa—The Register Life of Davenport is a good company, with about $1,500,000 assets and a small surplus. The Continental Life of Salt Lake City is controlled by reputable business men and is progressing satisfactorily. Its assets are about $1,500,000. Most of its business, however, is on the deferred dividend plan, which I regard as disadvantageous to policyholders.

E. T. R., Argenta, Ark.—In my judgment, your company has in reasonable measure everything but a future. It may survive the competition it must face for years before winning a place. There is a surfeit of young small life companies in the South and West, and I can see nothing in store for most of them better than reinsurance in some stronger companies. A due proportion of them will fail.

L. P. N., Anaheim, Calif.—Life insurance companies generally will convert an ordinary life into a limited payment life policy for the same amount without reexamination of insured. Dividend distribution methods vary in details with different companies, but the results are not material. In mutual companies all savings go to policyholders. There are two kinds of stock companies: (1) Those in which stockholders' dividends are restricted to a specific percentage on the capital, all other surplus going to the policyholders; (2) those which distribute such surplus as they see fit among policyholders, dividends to stockholders being unrestricted as to amount. Of course such stock companies, all transact a non-participating business pay no dividends to policyholders. The net cost of insurance in the Postal is not as low as it is in some of the leading mutual companies.

66th Annual Statement
OF THE

Ætna Life Insurance Company
HARTFORD, CONNECTICUT
MORGAN G. BULKELEY, President

LIFE, ACCIDENT, HEALTH, LIABILITY AND WORKMEN'S COMPENSATION INSURANCE

JANUARY 1, 1916

ASSETS		LIABILITIES	
Home Office Building.....	$1,000,000.00		
Real Estate:		Reserve on Life, Endowment and Term Policies........	$92,123,089.00
Acquired by Foreclosure $26,759.86			
Supply Depart- ment 75,000.00	101,759.86	Additional Reserve, not included above	1,061,444.00
Cash on hand and in banks	5,687,509.78	Premiums paid in advance, and other Liabilities......	1,045,740.25
Stocks and Bonds..........	38,792,077.47	Unearned interest on Policy Loans	313,891.07
Mortgages secured by Real Estate	58,361,612.03	Taxes falling due in 1916..	825,830.37
Loans on Collateral........	825,910.00	Reserve for special class of Policies and Dividends to Policyholders payable in 1916	3,416,204.96
Loans secured by Policies of this Company...........	12,042,326.83		
Interest due and accrued December 31, 1915.......	2,466,090.49		
Due from Re-Insurance Companies and others......	82,731.16	Losses and Claims awaiting proof and not yet due....	878,129.09
Premiums in course of collection and deferred premiums	2,734,256.33	Unearned Premiums on Accident, Health and Liability Insurance	3,483,739.08
Amortized value of Bonds and Market Value, December 31, 1915, of Stocks, over Book Value, less Assets not admitted........	2,144,078.98	Reserve for Liability claims.	3,113,266.29
		Surplus to Policyholders amortized basis for Bonds.	17,077,212.82
TOTAL ASSETS $124,238,552.93		TOTAL LIABILITIES...$124,238,552.93	

GAINS DURING 1915

Increase in Surplus to Policyholders .... $	2,476,383.45
Increase in Income	3,211,173.24
Increase in Assets	4,721,816.50
Increase in Life Insurance in Force	27,160,694.19
New Life Insurance Issued in 1915........	84,516,726.97
Life Insurance Paid for in 1915	72,494,448.97
Life Insurance in Force, Jan. 1, 1916 ...	407,959,099.22
Payments to Policyholders during 1915..... $	17,145,573.79
Payments for Taxes during 1915..........	768,702.51
Paid Policyholders since organization in 1850	280,863,477.79

1916

ATLANTIC MUTUAL INSURANCE CO.
ATLANTIC BUILDING, 51 WALL STREET, NEW YORK

Insures Against Marine and Inland Transportation Risk and Will Issue Policies Making Loss Payable in Europe and Oriental Countries.

Chartered by the State of New York in 1842, was preceded by a stock company of a similar name. The latter company was liquidated and part of its capital, to the extent of $100,000, was used with consent of the stockholders, by the Atlantic Mutual Insurance Company and repaid with a bonus and interest at the expiration of two years.

During its existence the company has insured property to the value of....	$27,964,378,109.00
Received premiums thereon to the extent of...................	287,324,309.99
Paid losses during that period...........................	147,859,574.91
Issued certificates of profits to dealers...................	90,881,110.00
Of which there have been redeemed.......................	83,811,450.00
Leaving outstanding at present time......................	6,989,663.00
Interest paid on certificates amounts to...................	25,075,417.00
On December 31, 1914, the assets of the company amounted to.......	14,101,674.46

The profits of the company revert to the assured and are divided annually upon the premiums terminated during the year, thereby reducing the cost of insurance.

For such dividends, certificates are issued subject to dividends of interest until ordered to be redeemed, in accordance with the charter.

A. A. RAVEN, Chairman of the Board

CORNELIUS ELDERT, Pres.   CHARLES E. FAY, 2d Vice-Pres
WALTER WOOD PARSONS, Vice-Pres.   G. STANTON FLOYD-JONES, Sec.

CHAUTAUQUA HOME READING CIRCLES

At the famous Tuskegee Institute, Alabama, the literary club has adopted the Chautauqua Reading Course.

There is a Chautauqua Reading Circle of about twenty-five girls at Irving College, Mechanicsburg, Pennsylvania.

Monongahela, Pennsylvania, has four Chautauqua Circles, a Society of Hall in the Grove, and the Friday Conversational Club, which is also Chautauquan.

The Superintendent of Schools, Mr. Herbert Blair, is secretary of the new Chautauqua Reading Circle at Hibbing, Minnesota, composed chiefly of teachers.

Four hundred graduates of the Chautauqua Reading Circle attended the annual alumni banquet in the Hotel Atheneum, Chautauqua. Every class from 1882 to 1915 was represented.

Winter residents from many states make up the Chautauqua Circle at St. Petersburg, Florida. This Meddie O. Hamilton Circle of over forty members is now in its third year of reading.

Among women's clubs which this year have adopted the Chautauqua Course for their literary departments are the Ebell Club of Long Beach, California, the Woman's Club of Albany, Georgia, and the Woman's Club of Paris, Tennessee.

Mrs. Ida B. Cole, Field Secretary of the Chautauqua Reading Circles, is lecturing and meeting circles in Florida during the month of February. Meddie O. Hamilton, field secretary, is similarly engaged in New York, Pennsylvania and New Jersey.

Each class of Chautauqua graduates has headquarters at Chautauqua. Three or four have separate class buildings which they own and maintain, but the majority share the Alumni Hall. Every class from 1887 to 1919 is represented by a trustee in the management of the building, where class banners and many class memorials are housed.

The Study Circle of the Woman's Club at Albany, Georgia, twenty-eight members, finished the four-year Chautauqua Course and graduated this year. Their report in the Albany *Herald* says that The Independent "with its liberal and interesting treatment of current topics, is one of the best features of this year's course. At every meeting, roll call is answered by current events and followed by general discussion, giving vital, human interest to the work."

The Lakewood, New York, Chautauqua Circle has been given charge of the High School Library and is using it as a public library, open to all residents free. The library room is used two evenings and one afternoon as a public reading room, some member of the Circle being responsible. Chautauqua graduates of Falconer, New York, have started a library in that town and are giving a series of lectures and entertainments to buy the needed books. The Circle at Parkhill, Ontario, has placed the Chautauqua books in the public library.

The Independent

FOR SIXTY-SEVEN YEARS THE FORWARD-LOOKING WEEKLY OF AMERICA

THE   CHAUTAUQUAN
Merged with The Independent June 1, 1914

FEBRUARY 21, 1916

OWNED AND PUBLISHED BY
THE INDEPENDENT CORPORATION, AT
119 WEST FORTIETH STREET, NEW YORK
WILLIAM B. HOWLAND, PRESIDENT
FREDERIC E. DICKINSON, TREASURER

WILLIAM   HAYES   WARD
HONORARY EDITOR

EDITOR: HAMILTON HOLT
ASSOCIATE EDITOR: HAROLD J. HOWLAND
LITERARY EDITOR: EDWIN E. SLOSSON

PUBLISHER: KARL V. S. HOWLAND

ONE YEAR, THREE DOLLARS

SINGLE   COPIES,   TEN   CENTS

Postage to foreign countries in Universal Postal Union, $1.75 a year extra; to Canada, $1 extra. Instructions for renewal, discontinuance or change of address should be sent two weeks before the date they are to go into effect. Both the old and the new address must be given.

We welcome contributions, but writers who wish their articles returned, if not accepted, should send a stamped and addrest envelope. No responsibility is assumed by The Independent for the loss or non-return of manuscripts, tho all due care will be exercised.

Entered at New York Post Office as Second Class Matter

Copyright, 1916, by The Independent

Address all Communications to
THE   INDEPENDENT
119 West Fortieth Street, New York

CONTENTS

THE SHAKESPEARE CONTEST

The Independent's Shakespeare Contest for American Schools is meeting with wonderful success. We have already received word from over two hundred English instructors to the effect that their schools will enter ten or more contestants. One school used more than two thousand copies of The Independent containing the first of the eight consecutive articles on the life and works of Shakespeare, even tho it is not obligatory to purchase The Independent to compete for a medal. We have published in previous issues of The Independent the hearty approval of Hon. Philander P. Claxton, Superintendent of Education of the United States, as well as nineteen endorsements from the following State Superintendents: Hon. John H. Finley, New York; C. P. Cary, Wisconsin; J. Y. Joyner, North Carolina; H. A. Davee, Montana; C. O. Case, Arizona; Payson Smith, Maine; M. L. Brittain, Georgia; Howard A. Gass, Missouri; R. C. Stearnes, Virginia; William F. Feagin, Wisconsin; George B. Cook, Arkansas; Edward Hyatt, California; W. N. Sheats, Florida; Edith K. O. Clark, Wyoming; W. H. Smith, Mississippi; Alvan N. White, New Mexico; R. H. Wilson, Oklahoma; E. J. Taylor, North Dakota; C. G. Schulz, Minnesota. We have since received the following endorsements of the contest:

FRANCIS G. BLAIR, Superintendent, Illinois: "I have your letter with enclosure relating to The Independent's Shakespeare Contest for American Schools. Your proposal to give a medal for the best essay from any school in the United States on the life and works of William Shakespeare is a worthy plan and cannot fail to stimulate a new study into the life and works of this incomparable writer."

A. M. DEYOE, Superintendent of Public Instruction, Iowa: "Your proposed Shakespearean Contest for American Schools meets with our hearty approval. It is our hope that such an interest may be created thru the medium of these contests that there will be an increased activity among our High School students, in the right attitude toward the great dramatist, by the intense study of his masterpieces. True it is that we do not have time to

read good things in literature—only the best should have our attention—and there is enough of that type to occupy the time and talent of any student. May the success of your plan be fully realized."

CHARLES A. GREATHOUSE, Superintendent, Indiana: "Your letter of January 5th enclosing an announcement of The Independent's Shakespeare Contest for American Schools has been received in this department. I desire to state that I am very much interested in this contest. Being a lover of Shakespeare's writings, I think it is well to interest the young people of this country in these valuable works."

BERNICE McCOY, Superintendent of Public Instruction, Idaho: "It certainly gives me great pleasure to indorse The Independent's Shakespeare Contest and your effort to arouse an interest in the celebration of the tercentenary of the death of this great dramatist. It seems to be a psychological time for creating an interest in the study of Shakespeare in the schools of the United States, as well as in those other organizations having for their aim the education and improvement of the individual. I shall be most happy to cooperate with you to the end that an enthusiastic interest in Shakespeare may be aroused in this state."

V. O. GILBERT, State Superintendent, Kentucky: "I feel sure that The Independent's Shakespearean Contest and the medal offered in connection with it will serve to increase interest in the celebration of the tercentenary of the death of this great writer. I shall certainly encourage and promote the study of Shakespeare in the schools of Kentucky."

C. N. KENDALL, Commissioner of Education, New Jersey: "In this, the year of the three hundredth anniversary of the death of Shakespeare, there is sure to be a renewed public interest in his great contribution to the permanent literature of the world. I am glad to commend any movement to encourage the reading and study of this literature in the schools. I hope there may be a generous response to the plan of The Independent."

J. E. SWEARINGEN, State Superintendent of Education, South Carolina: "The plan of The Independent to celebrate the 300th anniversary of the death of Shakespeare deserves the support of teachers, students and lovers of English literature everywhere. Our boys and girls cannot learn too much about this great dramatist and his writings."

C. H. LUGG, Superintendent, South Dakota: "I note your plan for offering 'a Shakespeare Anniversary Medal' for the best essay from any school in the United States on the life and works of William Shakespeare. Your plan is deserving of hearty commendation, and I hope that many of our schools will avail themselves of this opportunity to arouse an interest in Shakespeare and his writings on the part of their pupils. You may use this statement in any way that you desire to further the success of your Anniversary Plan."

W. F. DOUGHTY, State Superintendent, Texas: "I hope that this contest and the medal offered in connection with it may serve to increase interest in Shakespeare and his great works. If I can be of any assistance to you in this matter I shall be glad for you to advise me further."

E. G. GOWANS, State Superintendent of Public Instruction, Utah: "I am very much interested in your contest and I am sure that it will be very valuable to those who may participate."

If you wish to enter your school in The Shakespeare Contest write for full details to Shakespeare Contest Department, The Independent, 119 West Fortieth Street, New York City.

The Independent

| VOLUME 85 | FEBRUARY 21, 1916 | NUMBER 3507 |

THE SECOND BREAK IN THE CABINET

IT is exceedingly regrettable that Mr. Garrison has felt constrained to resign as Secretary of War. The country has felt, and with justice, that he was one of the strongest men in President Wilson's Cabinet. His departure takes away from the Administration a keen mind, a forceful personality, and a spirit marked by high devotion to the national good.

But the break was apparently inevitable. On two important subjects with which Congress is just now deeply engaged Mr. Garrison has definite and strong convictions. They are matters with which the Department of War is primarily concerned; the question of Philippine independence and of the national defense. He felt that on these subjects he did not see eye to eye with the President. For that reason he did not believe it right for him longer to retain his place in the circle of the President's immediate advisers.

On neither of these matters did Mr. Wilson directly disagree with the position which Mr. Garrison believed to be the only sound one. On each of them the President has an open mind.

The difference between the two men is best shown by extracts from the correspondence that has passed between them. On February 9, Secretary Garrison said in a letter to his chief:

Two matters within the jurisdiction of this department are now of immediate and pressing importance, and I am constrained to declare my position definitely and unmistakably thereon. I refer, of course, to the Philippine question and the matter of national defense.

You know my convictions with respect to each of them. I consider the principle embodied in the Clarke amendment an abandonment of the duty of this nation and a breach of trust toward the Filipinos; so believing, I cannot accept it or acquiesce in its acceptance.

I consider the reliance upon the militia for national defense an unjustifiable imperilling of the nation's safety. It would not only be a sham in itself, but its enactment into law would prevent if not destroy the opportunity to procure measures of real, genuine national defense. I could not accept it or acquiesce in its acceptance.

The President in his reply wrote as follows:

First, that it is my own judgment that the action embodied in the Clarke amendment to the bill extending further self-government to the Philippines is useless at this time, but it would clearly be most inadvisable for me to take the position that I must dissent from that action, should both Houses of Congress concur in a bill embodying that amendment. That is a matter upon which I must of course withhold judgment until the point of action of the two Houses reaches me in definite form. What the final action of the Houses will be no one can at this time certainly forecast. I am now of course engaged in conference with Mr. Jones and others with regard to the probable action of the House of Representatives in this matter, and do not yet know what it is likely to be. The one obvious thing, it seems to me, is the necessity for calm and deliberate action on our part at this time, when matters of such gravity are to be determined, and not only calm and deliberate action, but action which takes into very serious consideration views differing from our own.

Second, as I have had occasion to say to you, I am not yet convinced that the measure of preparation for national defense which we deem necessary can be obtained thru the instrumentality of the National Guard under Federal control and training, but I feel in duty bound to keep my mind open to conviction on that side and think it would be most unwise and most unfair to the Committee of the House, which has such a plan in mind, to say that it cannot be done. The bill in which it will be embodied has not yet been drawn, as I learned today from Mr. Hay. I should deem it a very serious mistake to shut the door against this attempt on the part of the committee in perfect good faith to meet the essentials of the program set forth in my message, but in a way of their own choosing.

It is apparent that the difference is not of that clean cut kind in which one man is convinced of the soundness of a proposed plan and the other man is equally certain of the soundness of a plan diametrically opposed to the first, while each is resolutely opposed to the other's plan. In such a condition there would be no question that the Cabinet officer thus differing with his chief should withdraw from the Cabinet. But in the present case the situation is different, and the logical course of action not quite so clear.

Mr. Garrison is convinced of the truth of two "fundamental principles," as he describes them in a later letter. The first is, that the United States ought not at this time to decree that the Philippines shall be given their independence in four years. The other is, that the military force upon which the United States is to rely as its second line of defense upon the land must be a national force and not an aggregation of state forces. He believes in them so strongly that unless the Administration is to adopt them as a definite part of its program he is unwilling longer to be a part of it.

On both of these principles President Wilson seems to be inclined to agree with Mr. Garrison. But he evidently does not consider them "fundamental." In any event he is unwilling at this time to use the prestige and influence of his position in the Government and in his party to force his associates in Congress to accept them as "fundamental."

The rupture seems largely explicable in terms of differences of mind and temperament. Given the personalities of the two men it was as inevitable as it is regrettable.

Mr. Garrison is justified in resigning because of what he feels to be a matter of principle. Mr. Wilson is right in keeping an open mind when dealing with a coordinate and equally sovereign branch of the Government. But if Mr. Garrison was a bit too hasty in leaving the ship when it was by no means certain he could not have steered into the harbor of his choice, so Mr. Wilson was a bit too indecisive in not perceiving that it is his duty to lead in the formulation and adoption of national policies. The President of the United States should make his influence felt on great questions during the process of legislation, and not merely by means of his power of approval or veto when the process is completed.

THE VALUE OF THE TROPICS

THE story of the struggle for the possession of Africa which is told on another page of this issue has its lesson for America just now when a certain faction in Congress is urging contraction instead of expansion as our national policy. Africa affords the striking illustration of the rise in the value of tropical real estate in recent years. England needs all her men to hold her lines in France and Flanders, in Egypt, Mesopotamia and Greece, yet she is preparing a new army for the conquest of German East Africa. But this same territory which she is now making such sacrifices to get was once offered to her by the Sultan of Zanzibar, and Mr. Gladstone declined the gift! He tried his best to keep England out of Egypt, but fate was fortunately too strong for him. In 1877 Gladstone said

Our first site in Egypt, be it by larceny or be it by emption, will be the almost certain egg of a North African empire that will grow and grow . . . till we finally join hands across the equator with Natal and Cape Colony.

And this he dreaded! His foresight was better than his judgment. His scuttling policy led to the sacrifice of Gordon and Khartum in the north and to the Boer War in the south. The honor that might have been his has gone to Disraeli, who bought the majority stock in the Suez Canal, and Cecil Rhodes, who projected the Cape to Cairo railroad. What Gladstone threw away has had to be bought back with blood.

The same blindness to the possibilities of tropical colonies then prevailed in Germany. Bismarck when he took Alsace-Lorraine ironically recommended the French to seek compensation on the southern side of the Mediterranean. They did and now Algeria is a prosperous French province which is sending its men freely to the defense of the mother country against the Germans. Bismarck's successor as German Chancellor, General Caprivi, said: "No greater misfortune could befall us than to be presented with the whole of Africa." But now Germany is pouring out men and money by the million to get a part of what she then might easily have had. The British White Paper shows that in July, 1914, the German Government was willing to promise to leave Belgium and France intact if England would remain neutral, but was unwilling to agree to let their African possessions alone.

In the latter part of the nineteenth century, when it was realized that a country without the resources of the tropics to draw upon was permanently crippled, the Grand Scramble began. The seven Powers grabbed any territory they could lay their hands on, whatever it was or wherever it lay. Flags were raised over mission stations, stray islands and casual trading posts. Miasmic swamps and barren deserts that had remained unpeopled since man had been on earth became prizes worth fighting for.

When the Grand Scramble was over in 1912—unless we call the present war a continuation of it—the map of Africa looked like another Europe. Here were the same names repeated, France, Great Britain, Italy, Belgium, Germany, Spain and Portugal, and in similar juxtaposition; a chance arrangement, a geographical crazy-quilt, in which no regard had been paid to commercial convenience, strategic boundaries, ethnic divisions, historic claims or mutual advantage. Less than four per cent of the continent remained independent; little Liberia, which was founded as a colony for American negroes

and which the United States has protected from conquest, and Abyssinia, where the aged Menelik, with a wisdom which is the sole evidence of his alleged descent from Solomon, maintained a quasi-independence by playing off one power against another and putting up a hard fight when he had to.

The present war will probably remake the map of Africa, but it will not unmake it. It will never again become a Dark Continent where the blank spaces on the map have to be filled up with pictures of elephants, giraffes and dog-headed men. Civilization moves onward somehow, and if one nation shirks the duty of carrying it forward, another takes it up and reaps the reward. Those who falter and draw back will fall behind—and deserve to. The work that Americans are doing for the regeneration of the Philippines is, we believe, as efficient and useful as that done by the British in Egypt, and better in many respects than that done by the French in Algeria and by the Germans in East Africa. It is certainly free from the cruelty and corruption of the administration of the Belgian Congo or the German Southwest Africa or the Portuguese possessions. We have, therefore, good reason for our belief that the United States is as competent as any other power to administer the affairs of the Philippines.

WHY NOT PERMANENT?

THE London *Spectator* is urging forward a popular movement under the slogan, "Down Glasses during the War." Its purpose is obviously what might be described as Temporary Total Abstinence.

The *Spectator* states the case for the reform with effectiveness: "We must fight the Germans with both hands and not with one hand grasping a glass of beer or spirits."

In the midst of one's admiration for the proposed self-denying ordinance, another thought persists in intruding. If a man needs two hands to fight with successfully, how can he get along effectively with fewer to work with? If a nation at war cannot spare a hand to hold the liquor glass, how can a people at peace?

Some one should move to amend the "Down Glasses" program by striking out the word "Temporary."

DISARMAMENT OR REPUDIATION

THE great world war is now half thru its second year, and it is necessary that financiers as well as statesmen should begin to think very seriously how long the expenditure of men and money can be carried on. "The courage never to submit or yield" may seem boundless, but the end must come. And what then?

President Van Hise, of the University of Wisconsin, sums up the national debts of Great Britain, France, and Germany at the end of 1915. That of Great Britain he estimates as $10,419,000,000; that of France $10,314,000,000, and that of Germany $7,275,000,000; and the war has lasted only a year and a half.

We can hardly expect peace in less than a year, at which time these national debts will have amounted to half as much more. How will they ever be paid? How will even the interest be paid?

Of course it is assumed that the interest will be paid. At four per cent it would amount to $400,000,000 a year for either Great Britain or France, and for Germany to about $300,000,000, and half as much more if the war continues another year. Meanwhile the people have been fearfully impoverished. The whole principal of these loans has been destroyed. Many millions of wealth-producers have been killed or disabled. Business has been disorganized. There will be poverty everywhere, and taxation will be intolerable.

Already the question is asked by far-seeing men: Will it be possible for these countries to pay even the interest on these enormous debts? Repudiation is a very evil word, but we cannot avoid thinking of it. Great Britain and France are very wealthy nations and they have great recuperative power, and yet there is a limit to what can be squeezed out of a people. Germany is also a rich nation and unlike Great Britain and France her national debt is almost wholly held by her own citizens. She could scale it down or reduce interest and other nations could not complain, while the debt of the allied nations is largely foreign, and can in no way be repudiated without national dishonor.

We have said nothing about the likelihood of billions of indemnity being imposed by the victors on the conquered. It seems to be assumed that indemnity will be demanded, and if so, while some burdens will be lightened, others will be made more intolerable. It is difficult to see how the fearful burden of taxation on all these nations, and on Austria and Italy as well, can be borne and these national obligations met except by a general concerted disarmament. The nations will not be able while paying for the old wars to add unlimited and interminable taxation to prepare for new wars, so we shall come to what all good citizens must desire as the one happy effect of this disastrous war, compulsory disarmament. But disarmament can hardly take place without an agreement of the nations to establish the international machinery for the doing of the international business that must be done and which is now done in the last analysis by the cruel and stupid resort to armaments. The nations must also feel that their integrity and vital interests are as fully conserved and guaranteed after the reduction of armaments as they were when each nation was the sole guardian of its liberty and sovereignty. The requirements can only be brought about by substituting for our present system of competitive armaments a system of collective armaments under a League to Enforce Peace. Then and then only will a plan be devised for the creation, adjudication and execution of international law and the universal limitation of armaments. This we may hope for and even expect whether with or without revolution.

ARMOR PLATE PATRIOTISM

LAST week the Senate Naval Committee reported out a bill authorizing the establishment of an armor plate factory to be owned and operated by the Government.

Senator Penrose said to the committee that the armor plate makers had told him that if the Government went into the business they would raise the price $200 a ton, which would cost the United States about $20,000,000 more if it bought armor for the contemplated five year building program.

The President of one of the companies also told the committee that if the Government manufactured armor plate he would recommend to his board of directors that they go out of that branch of the steel business.

While the Government should never attempt to monopolize the production of war supplies, lest in times of emergency it could not manufacture fast enough, this action of the armor plate makers absolutely demonstrates the need of Government competition in the business to keep down prices.

If the manufacturers do not adopt a more patriotic spirit, the Government, as Senator Tillman suggests, will not hesitate to "seize their plants and operate them by the right of eminent domain."

Congress can hardly afford to ignore this exhibition of corporate greed and disloyalty. As an example of arrogance, naked and unashamed, its like is hard to match.

NO MILITARY TRAINING IN PUBLIC SCHOOLS

DO the advocates of military training in the public schools know what they are talking about? A few of them do; most of them evidently do not. The few who do will not dissent from a remark or two that we have to make to the many who do not.

A newspaper canvass of New York City parents of public school children shows a large majority in favor of military training in the schools. Statistically the showing is of little or no value. Data so collected always comes chiefly from persons on one side of the question raised. Persons on the other side do not in equal numbers take the trouble to reply. The interviews, in like manner, with which the vote is followed up, are prevailingly indorsements of the military training plan. There is no evidence here of conscious selection in support of a foregone conclusion, but a glance over the reasons offered discovers the intellectual unpreparedness of the prominent gentlemen who so readily vote with the recorded majority.

The precise betrayal of mental non-equipment is this: The advocates of military training in the schools obviously have never thought whether this plan fits into a larger plan of reliance on a volunteer army in time of danger, or fits into a wholly different larger plan to require universal military training, and, when the need arises, universal military service. It is evident on the face of their remarks that seventy-five or eighty per cent of the interviewed could not, without further "preparation," tell which scheme the proposed school training belongs with.

As a matter of logic, psychology, and experience, it belongs, of course, with the volunteer army scheme. A nation that exacts universal training and service, as Germany, France, Switzerland and Australia do, does not fool with drilling its school children. When the time comes it takes its young men in hand, in a businesslike way, and puts them thru a discipline that earlier years could not endure.

The military drilling of children is not the real thing, it never can be made the real thing. It is a characteristically American piece of hocus-pocus. Nevertheless, it could have a certain place in a nation which depends on a volunteer army. It can not prepare boys technically to be soldiers, but it can fill their heads with militaristic ideas. In the impressionable school years war has a look that can not be conjured up in the mind of the young man forced by the strong arm of the state to endure the hardships of barracks and drill grounds and forced marches. School militarism has just one rational purpose, to wit, to prepare not bodies and minds, but impulses and emotions for military service.

When the American people has thought this thing thru, if it ever does, it will not vote eighty to twenty in favor of military training in the public schools. The compulsory training and service of all fit adults may or may not be militaristic. The compulsory military training of children in the public schools of the country is militarism or it is humbug.

WELDING THE HAMMER

DO you believe that children under fourteen years of age ought to work in factories or mills or canneries? Do you believe that boys and girls under sixteen ought to work more than eight hours a day or more than six days a week?

Of course you do not. But there are actually people who do. Some of them—men of prominence, too, in their communities—have appeared before congressional committees and argued against the Federal Child Labor bill. Perhaps the most cynical of the arguments which they had the effrontery to present was this:

A roll of cotton cloth made by child labor is just as long, just as wide, just as white, and just as good as if made by adults.

In spite of this and other equally attractive pleas the bill has passed the House by a tremendous majority. But the Senate is often a harder nut to crack. There is only one hammer infallibly heavy enough—public opinion. If you want to be sure that the cotton goods you wear, the canned goods you eat, the glassware on your table, the flowers on your hat, are not the product of the slavery of little children, make your own contribution to the welding of that hammer.

Write today to the United States Senators from your own state urging the passage of the Keating-Owen bill.

IRONING OUT THE YEAR

IN the good old days when our forefathers lived the simple life near to Nature's heart, one could tell what time of year it was by the looks of the dinner table. The four seasons and even the twelve months were marked by the appropriate products of field and orchard. In the spring radishes, peas, beans and corn followed one another in orderly procession, and in the fall tomatoes, squash, pumpkin and rutabagas brought the year to a fitting close.

Certain combinations of meats and vegetables which have come to seem as inevitable and eternal as the preestablished harmonies of Leibnitz owe their conjunction to the chance coincidence of their time of appearance. When the spring lambs reached table size the green peas came in and the mint was ready to sauce it. This triplex dish still figures on our menu cards, altho its seasonal significance has vanished.

The good old rule "Eat oysters when the month has an *r* in it and drink whisky when it has a *k* in it" has long ago lost its validity. Canned or cove oysters are independent of the season and whisky can either be obtained at all times or not at all depending upon what state you are in. Canning and cold storage have obliterated the climatic zones and reduced the months to a common denominator. Almost any kind of fruit or veg-

etable can now be had anywhere any day in a more or less palatable state by those who are willing to pay for it, and even the price curve is being leveled down thruout the year. It is no longer the mark of a millionaire to eat strawberries in December or grapes in May. We can have a more varied diet than when we were restricted by the seasons; but it is questionable if we do.

With the culinary calendar have vanished most of the other characteristics of the year. The violets of spring are sold in the fall and the chrysanthemums of autumn appear in the spring. Summer roses bloom in midwinter and holly may be had in midsummer. There are few boys nowadays who can tell marble time from kite time or when top time comes in. Fireworks have been banished from the Fourth of July in many parts of the land, but appear in other parts at Christmas. Thanksgiving is no longer a harvest festival. Our fasts and feasts have all been smudged together into one dull common gray. All Fools' Day and All Saints' Day have disappeared. A man can be a fool or a saint on any of the 365 or 366 days. The attraction of gravitation tends to bring all things to a dead level of monotony.

THE NOSE OF THE CAMEL

ONE need no longer look to Germany to see what havoc may be wrought by a pernicious theory. Only open the *Poetry Journal*, and read the heart-breaking lines of Robert Carlton Brown to learn what thrusting cookery in among the Arts and Sciences has done not only to women, but to literature.

I know a nice, affectionate girl
Who goes about
Patting beefsteaks on the back,
Running her fingers fondly through the beards of oysters,
Holding hands for hours with breaded veal cutlets,
Rubbing noses with pork chops,
And having affairs with boiled onions.
Her emotional eyes light with amorous interest
In the presence of food;
They fill with great glistening tears
When the plates are taken out
And she sits despondent
Weeping gently into her coffee.

Now a pet theory, ready to play with as one sits decorously before a dull speaker, or recovers from the grippe, is an innocent comfort so long as one does not share it. But there is nothing more dangerous than generosity with a theory. The next fellow may take it in earnest, may even try to act on it, will surely repeat it, and then Pandora's box is open.

No one foresaw any danger to poetry, for instance, when Professor James took the public into his confidence as to what he had been thinking as he waited daily on Boston corners for the street cars. But the advertising value of Pragmatism was not missed by practical folk. They inscribed the word on their banners and went on, more triumphant than ever, pushing the classics from the seats of learning, and setting in their places, carpentry, magazine verse, millinery and cooking. The saucepans won the day.

Mr. Brown shows us whither we are hurrying. We have been too bewildered to read the same message in the art galleries, but the few who know assure us that at last painters are truthfully depicting what is as it is. Shortly our plays will be constructed out of random conversations copied down for the playwright by a pocket phonograph, and we shall have symphonies built on themes sung by the wheels of the Chicago Limited.

THE STORY OF THE WEEK

Secretary Garrison Resigns

Lindley M. Garrison, Secretary of War, resigned on the 10th, and his resignation was immediately accepted by the President, who exprest warm appreciation of his services. The Secretary withdrew from the Cabinet because he was in disagreement with the President concerning the attitude of the Administration toward the proposed Continental Army reserve of 400,000 men, and the Senate's bill granting independence to the Filipinos in not less than two nor more than four years. Henry Breckenridge, Assistant Secretary, also resigned because he agreed with his chief, and his resignation was promptly accepted. Major General Scott, Chief of Staff, will be Secretary of War until Mr. Garrison's successor is appointed. Those most prominently mentioned in connection with the coming appointment are Secretary Lane, of the Interior Department; Secretary Houston, of the Department of Agriculture, and General Goethals. The letters which passed between Secretary Garrison and the President were promptly published. They fill three newspaper columns of fine print.

Beginning on January 12, the Secretary, in a long letter, argued in support of his plan for the Continental Army and urged Mr. Wilson to exert his influence for it in Congress, where it was in a critical condition. There could be, he said, no honest or worthy solution of the problem except one that should give national forces, under exclusive control of the national Government. Chairman Hay, of the House Military Committee, had openly rejected the Continental Army, turning from Federal volunteers to a project for federalizing the militia of the states. Acceptance of this plan would set back the whole cause of legitimate national defense and would be a betrayal of trust. Among members of the House there was very little knowledge of or intense interest in military affairs, and

THE GREAT WAR

February 7—Germans gain 800 yards of trenches west of Vimy. Germans retire from Kamerun into Spanish colony of Rio Muni.

February 8—German guns bombard Belfort. British repel Turks at Kut-el-Amara with heavy losses on both sides.

February 9—German sea planes raid coast of Kent. Russians gain dominant position near Czernovitz.

February 10—Premier Briand of France visits Italy. German Government issues warning that after March 1 armed merchantmen will be treated as warships.

February 11—Greek Chamber votes neutrality. Austrians encounter Italians ten miles from Durazzo.

February 12—French gain 300 yards near Butte de Mesnil, Champagne.

February 13—Germans renew attack on Dvinsk, Russia. Chinese rebels take Chung-king.

the proposed payment of Federal money to militia men and officers appealed to the personal and political interests of members. He urged the President to use his influence without delay. Writing again two days later he referred to Mr. Wilson's remark that he had been assured by Chairman Hay that the same end could be reached by utilizing the militia, and that he (the President) had said he would accept that plan if it would be effective. The Secretary insisted that there was no room for compromise, and offered to leave the Cabinet if this would serve the President's purpose.

The President's Reply

Mr. Wilson, replying on the 17th, said that while he believed the chief thing needed was a trained citizen reserve under Federal direction, he was not irrevocably committed to any one plan and was willing to consider all propositions. It would not be proper for him to say to Congress that it must take his plan or none. He did not share

the Secretary's opinion that members charged with the duty of dealing with military affairs were ignorant of them or of the nation's military necessities. On the contrary, he had found them well informed and actuated by a most intelligent appreciation of the grave responsibilities imposed upon them. If a bill by which the essential things could not be accomplished should come to him, he would veto it. He had told Mr. Hay that he would consider any plan that would give a national reserve under unmistakable national control.

Mr. Garrison, on February 9, said he was expected to make an address before the Chamber of Commerce on the following day. As to the Philippines, he regarded the Senate bill as an abandonment of the duty of this nation and a breach of trust toward the Filipinos, and he exprest again his disapproval of the militia project. If he was in disagreement with the President, he could not set forth his views in the address and remain the President's seeming representative. In reply, Mr. Wilson said he regarded the independence provision of the Philippine bill as unwise at this time, but must await the action of Congress. And it was his duty to keep his mind open about the militia. and not to try to shut the door against the committee's plans. The Secretary should express his own views without hesitation, but should draw very carefully the distinction between them and those of the Administration. Responding at once, Mr. Garrison resigned, saying: "It is evident that we hopelessly disagree upon what I conceive to be fundamental principles."

Effect in Congress

The effect of the resignation in Congress appears to have been more support for the President and the defense plans. the Continental Army excepted. The House already has passed a bill appropriating $600,000 for improvements that will make it possible to build battleships of the most powerful class at

COSSACKS ON THE SNOW PLAINS

Modern Photo Service

THE INDEFATIGABLE SARAH BERNHARDT

"Les Cathedrales" is a dramatic poem in which six French and Flemish cathedrals tell their tragic story. Mme. Bernhardt, third from the left, is the Cathedral of Strasbourg, which has waited forty years for deliverance. Her passionate voice dominated the recent performance of the play in London, whither the great actress was determined to go in spite of her age and the amputation of her leg

the New York and Mare Island navy yards, and another providing for an increase of the number of midshipmen at the Annapolis school by 540. In the debate on these measures—which were passed without an opposition measured by recorded votes—many prominent members spoke for the preparedness policy. Speaker Clark earnestly supported projects for enlarging the navy and creating a military reserve. Mr. Mann, the Republican floor leader, urged the House to support the President's program. Mr. Wilson's commendation of the members of the Military Committee, in his letter to Secretary Garrison, was quite satisfactory to that committee, which sent him a resolution expressing appreciation of his confidence. There was a movement on the Democratic side for action that would possibly cause the retirement of Mr. Kitchin from the office of floor leader, with a suggestion that his place should be taken, as far as possible, by Speaker Clark. Mr. Kitchin opposes all the defense plans.

It was generally admitted that the project for a Continental Army was dead. It was opposed by every member of the House Committee. That committee, it is expected, will prepare a bill designed to make service in the militia so attractive that the number of enlisted men will be increased from 125,-000 to 400,000. There may be provisions for dual service, or for enlistments subjecting the men to the call of the national Government without the restrictions now existing. The committee's aim will be to make the militia a Federal or national force, if this can be done. In the Senate, on the other hand, the tendency at present is in favor of creating a trained reserve by modifying requirements for the regular army—increasing the number of soldiers, and shortening the term to two years, or even to one, with the provision that the men so enlisting shall go into a reserve for four or six years.

The Question of the Submarine

The long and bitter controversy over the rights of merchant vessels and the regulation of submarines seems to have reached a highly critical stage. Our Government has come to the conclusion that the only way to hold the submarines to accountability for their attacks upon the merchant vessels of belligerents is to draw a strict line of demarkation between them and warships by prohibiting the armament of merchant vessels. Secretary Lansing has addrest a note to the Powers in the hope that some acceptable formula may be agreed upon by which the lives of non-combatants may be safeguarded without depriving the submarines of all power. The rules he proposes are quoted in another column.

The Secretary of State argues that the privilege of carrying guns hitherto accorded by international law to merchant vessels was not with the idea that they should offer resistance to a cruiser which overhauled them but merely for the purpose of defense against pirates and privateers. But the submarine tho powerful in the offensive is so weak in the defensive that even a small caliber gun would suffice to sink it if it approached above water to warn and search the merchant vessel as international law requires. He continues:

Moreover, pirates and sea rovers have been swept from the main trade channels of the sea and privateering has been abolished. Consequently the placing of guns on merchantmen at the present date of submarine warfare can be explained only on the ground of a purpose to render merchantmen superior in force to submarines and to prevent warning and visit and search by them. Any armament, therefore, on a merchant vessel would seem to have the character of an offensive armament.

If a submarine is required to stop and search a merchant vessel on the high seas, and in case it is found that she is of an enemy character and that conditions necessitate her destruction and removal to a place of safety of persons on board, it would not seem just nor reasonable that the submarine should be compelled, while complying with these requirements, to expose itself to almost certain destruction by the guns on board the merchant vessel.

It would therefore appear to be a reasonable and reciprocally just arrangement if it could be agreed by the opposing belligerents that submarines should be caused to adhere strictly to the rules of international law in the matter of stopping and searching merchant vessels, determining their belligerent nationality and removing the crews and passengers to places of safety before sinking the vessels as prizes of war, and that merchant vessels of belligerent nationality should be prohibited from carrying any armament whatsoever.

It is anticipated that the British and French will regard this as a concession to the German point of view and will refuse to take the guns from their merchant vessels. If so our Government would be obliged to treat them as auxiliary cruisers and forbid them the use of our harbors except for brief and occasional visits. Probably also our Government would issue a warning to American citizens not to travel upon such armed merchantmen.

The German Submarine Note

The German Government has issued a memorandum announcing its intention in a short time of treating the armed merchantmen of the enemy as warships, and neutral nations are warned not to entrust their persons or property to such vessels. In defense of this policy a list is given of nineteen cases in which British merchantmen have fired upon German submarines and in many cases sunk them. Pages of the secret book of instructions issued by the British Government to the captains and gunners of the merchant marine are reproduced by photography in the appendix. These show that the ship is expected to open fire on an enemy submarine approaching within 800 yards even when the submarine has not opened fire first. "Armaments should be concealed as far as possible" by a canvas cover in neutral ports. The "Drill Book for 12-Pounder Quick Firing Guns" found on British merchant ships was issued by the Admiralty on May 7, 1915. The note calls attention to the facts that the British Ambassador at Washington had stated to the American Government on August 29, 1914, that British merchantmen were never armed for offensive purposes but purely for defense and that they, therefore, would never fire unless fired upon first. But on the other hand the British Government in its first Order in Council had ruled that any armed vessel was a warship.

The Pending Treaties By the Senate Committee on Foreign Relations a report in favor of the pending treaty with Hayti has been ordered. The treaty with Nicaragua, which was reported favorably by a vote of 10 to 3, was considered last week in executive session, the'question being Mr. Borah's motion for a discussion of the treaty in open session. Mr. Stone, chairman of the committee, opposed this motion in a speech two hours long. Others took part in the debate. The motion was lost by a vote of 19 to 42. But the treaty requires an appropriation of $3,000,000, the sum to be paid to Nicaragua, and it will be the subject of debate in open session when the appropriation bill is taken up. In the secret session an addition was proposed which is designed to assure Central American republics that there is no disposition on the part of the United States to disregard their rights and sovereignty. It is said that the Colombian Minister, who does not like the pending treaty with his country, called upon Secretary Lansing and was told that President Wilson had not exprest approval of it. Before reporting this treaty (by a vote of 8 to 7) the committee amended it by reducing the sum to be paid from $25,000,000 to $15,000,-000, and by making the expression of regret concerning the Panama incident a mutual one.

The treaty with Hayti provides for control of that country by our Government. There is to be a receiver of customs, appointed by Hayti's President on nomination by our President, and with this officer there will be a financial adviser, appointed in the same way. The constabulary, composed of native Haytians, is to be officered and organised by Americans. There are to be both urban and rural forces. Eventually the officers will be replaced by Haytians whose fitness has been shown by examinations. The constabulary is to have control of "arms and ammunition, military supplies and traffic therein thruout the country." Hayti agrees not to increase its public debt except by previous agreement with the President of the United States, or to contract any financial obligation unless the ordinary revenues, after the payment of current expenses, are sufficient to pay the interest and provide a sinking fund for final settlement. Hayti also agrees not to surrender any territory by sale, lease, or otherwise to any foreign government. Engineers are to be appointed, on our President's nomination, to have sanitation and public improvements in charge, and there is provision for inter-

vention in a paragraph which says that "should the necessity occur, the United States will lend efficient aid for the preservation of Haytian independence and the maintenance of a government adequate for the protection of life, property and individual liberty." By agreement with Hayti, parts of this treaty are already in force.

The Plotters In San Francisco seventy-six persons have been indicted for plotting to destroy property and to defraud the United States in the interest of Germany. There is a long list of offenses named in the forms[1] accusations, and in these proceedings our Federal Government has for the first time attacked official representatives of Germany. Among those who must go to trial are Franz Bopp, the German Consul General; Baron von Shack, vice-Consul General; Baron von Brincken, military attaché of the consulate; Henry Kauffmann, chancellor of the consulate, and Maurice Hall, consul of Turkey. The long list also includes Dr. Reimer, said to be a German naval officer; Robert Capelle, agent of the North German Lloyd Steamship Company; Johannes von Koolbergen, who confessed that he had been hired to blow up railroad tunnels and bridges in Canada; Charles C. Crowley, a detective employed by Bopp; Captain Fred Jebsen, and several ship owners. A considerable number of the defendants are charged with having caused the destruction of cargoes of munitions in our Pacific ports and of powder factories in California and other states. Several are indicted for using false clearance papers in sending out the steamship "Sacramento" and three other ships with supplies for German warships. The indictments cover violations of our neutrality laws and the Sherman act.

Published facsimiles of checks and other papers taken from Captain von Papen, the recalled German military attaché, by the British authorities show

SALONICA—WAITING

The French and British at Salonica, however, depend on far stronger defences than these crumbling walls. Their double line is so strong that General Castlonau remarked that it would be a pity if the Germans and Austrians did not attack it

that while he was in Washington he paid $700 to Werner Horn, on January 18, 1915. Two week later, on February 2, Horn attempted to blow up the international railroad bridge across the St. Croix River at Vanceboro, Maine. He is now in jail. It has been asserted by Von Papen's friends that the payment was made after Horn had been arrested for this crime.

In Canada, since the fire at the Parliament Buildings, the number of guards at all the bridges, public buildings and munition factories has been doubled. In Parliament attention has been directed to several Germans holding prominent places in the civil service, one of them being the confidential secretary of the Minister of Naval Affairs. Another, the superintendent of Government dredging, has been asked to resign. He refused and will be dismissed. Owing to attacks in the Ottawa press upon the New York Symphony Orchestra, of which Walter Damrosch is the head and which contains musicians of foreign birth, a concert which was to have been given there this week has been indefinitely postponed.

The Situation in Mexico Carranza's forces have not been able to capture Villa or to prevent his followers from looting mines and ranches in the state of Chihuahua. Villa has only a few men with him, one of these being Colonel Lopez, who caused the murder of Watson and his companions at Santa Ysobel. But there are several hundred in small independent bands. Several of these are within thirty miles of Chihuahua City, where the Carranza garrison has been guilty of many excesses. These soldiers, whose pay is said to be only eight cents a day, have looted the shops and killed many civilians. One or two hundred miles south, parties of bandits who formerly were in Villa's army, have killed not less than 300 civilians in the last ten days. Nearly all of the victims were Mexicans. At Belleza, west of Parral,

BOSTON TO NEW ORLEANS
The City Council of Boston has voted to return to the city of New Orleans this Confederate flag, which was seised by General Benjamin F. Butler in the Civil War. Mayor Curley in front

they sacked the town, burned the houses and took twenty young women to the mountains. In another town an aged German physician was tortured to compel him to disclose the place where his money was hidden. His house was burned. In a village near this one, all the men were locked up in a building, the young women were captured, and then the building where the men were imprisoned was burned. An American ranchman, Guy Johnson, was attacked while he was making his way to the boundary. Before he gave up his life he killed five of his assailants. The bodies of the five have been found near his own.

In the state of Oaxaca, Zapata's men hold the capital, and several other towns are occupied by forces of the old Federal army. The Federals are bitter enemies of the Zapatistas, and both are foes of Carranza, who has sent troops to subdue them. These troops have taken possession of several towns. In Minititlau, by order of their commander, the parish Catholic priest was put to death for having associated with the rebels and conferred with them in his house. The Carranza Government's official statement was that this was "a severe but necessary lesson" which should "teach ministers of the Catholic Church not to meddle with matters foreign to their mission, or to disturb public order by their hypocritical and obstructionist labors."

It is expected that a general election will be held on July 3, and that Congress will assemble on September 16, to make a new constitution. At the request of our Government, Villa's brother, Hipolito, has been arrested in Havana and is held for extradition. At El Paso he has been indicted for sending men to wreck a train in Texas that was carrying Carranza soldiers to the relief of Agua Prieta, some months ago. The capital is still suffering from the typhus epidemic, and in Tampico hundreds are dying of smallpox. There is still no in-

dication that the Carranza Government will be able to negotiate a loan in New York.

Fighting in France

There is a decided renewal of activity on the western front, but with no decisive results so far as can be learned. We are yet in the dark as to whether this portends a serious offensive on either side, and if so, in what quarter. So far as the operations have developed they seem to be merely intended to gain more defensible positions in readiness for a supreme effort in the spring. The battlefields are the same as last fall; namely, the hills that lie to the west of Lille in the Artois region and to the east of Rheims in the Champagne.

While the Germans were making their spectacular drive toward Paris in August, 1914, these hills were being entrenched for use in case the drive failed. When the French defeated them on the Marne early in September they retired as rapidly as possible to the positions which had been prepared for them and here they have so far successfully resisted all attempts to dislodge them. In the spring and fall the British and French made desperate efforts to break the line at these two points, but only gained a mile or two. But, altho these gains were insignificant and disappointing considering the terrible sacrifices made, yet they gave the Allies certain strategic advantages. On the Artois front the Germans were left with a precarious hold upon the last ridge which protects the lower and more level ground on which stand Lens and Lille. On the Champagne front a further advance of a couple of miles on the part of the French would put them in possession of the railroad which runs just behind the German lines. If, then, the Germans are forced out of these positions they may have to retire a considerable distance before finding as strong a line of defense as that they now hold. But a great setback at either of these points would involve the withdrawal from the apex of the triangle which the Germans have driven into the heart of France. That is why the Allies have kept pounding away at these two points on the two sides of the angle which has been pointed at Paris for the last year and a half.

The lay of the land in both battlefields is much the same, limestone bluffs or buttes, as they are called in France and our Western states. These are honeycombed with caves and quarries, the caverns in the Champagne region being used for the storage of the wine which takes its name from the district. The chalky rock is easily cut so that veritable labyrinths of trenches, tunnels and dugouts have been constructed. Never before has underground warfare been conducted on such a gigantic scale.

In the news of the week from the Artois sector we hear first that the Germans have gained over 800 yards of trenches on the hill near Vimy, about five miles southwest of Lens. The

French in following days succeeded in recovering the greater part of their lost positions. On the Navarin farm in the Champagne the French gained about 300 yards of German trenches and held them against the counter-attack. Here the French shells smashed the German tanks containing suffocating gases under pressure and the wind carried the fumes back over the German lines.

The only novelty in the week's news is that the Germans have trained their long-range guns upon Belfort, one of the strongest fortresses on the eastern frontier of France. From three to ten big shells were dropped within the city's fortifications for several days.

The Albanian Puzzle

It is difficult to understand the news, or rather the lack of news, from the Balkans. Last week Albania was being rapidly overrun by Austrians from the north and Bulgars from the east and the Italians and Serbs were reported to have been withdrawn from Durazzo, the capital. But this week the invaders appear to have made little or no progress and the garrison of Durazzo is said to have been strengthened. The apparent inactivity of the Austrians may be plausibly explained by the difficulty of carrying forward a campaign in mid-winter in a mountainous country devoid of roads, yet on the other hand there is reason for believing the rumors that the check is due more to diplomatic than military causes. Certainly the Austrians met with no serious resistance until they came within ten miles of Durazzo, where they encountered and apparently defeated a small force of Italians sent out from that city.

That part of northern Albania thru which the Austrians are now passing is mostly inhabited by the Mirdite tribesmen, who are Roman Catholics and hostile to both the Serbs and Mon-

Harris & Ewing
A LEADER OF AMERICAN BUSINESS
R. S. Rhett, a banker of Charleston, South Carolina, elected president of the Chamber of Commerce of the United States at its recent annual meeting in Washington

tenegrins, who are Slavic and Orthodox. It is said that the Austrians are inciting the Mirdites to massacre the Serbian and Montenegrin refugees, but that is an unnecessary supposition. Their native hatred of their Slavic neighbors and the memory of the wrongs they suffered during the Serbian invasion only four years ago are quite sufficient to arouse the spirit of revenge which is being manifested in their attacks on the fugitives. The Austrians have for many years been conducting an active propaganda by means of school and church in the hope of winning them over and now they are reaping the reward of their efforts in the friendliness of their reception by the Albanians.

It is said that the Albanian immigrants in the United States have sent home considerable sums which are being spent for arming the Albanian bands now aiding the Austrians. In 1912, when the Albanians were brought to the verge of starvation by the Serbian conquest, 'American citizens of all races contributed generously to the relief of their distress, especially by sending them seed corn.

Those of the Serbian soldiery who, when they were driven out of their own country, succeeded in making their way to the coast, have been carried by Italian ships to the Greek island of Corfu, of which the Allies have taken possession. Since Corfu lies close to the coast of southern Albania they will be ready for service in the conquest of Albania whenever they are recuperated and reorganized. They are said to number about eighty thousand.

One theory to account for the cessation of the advance in Albania is that the Bulgars and Austrians have fallen out over the division of the spoils just as the Balkan States did four years ago. It is even rumored that the Bulgars, having obtained all the territory they are likely to get, refuse to take any further part in the war and are negotiating a separate peace with the Allies. To conclude this bundle of Balkan rumors we should mention that Rumania is again alleged to be on the eve of casting in her lot with the Allies.

Losses of the War   As the observant reader has discovered for himself the estimates appearing in print of the casualties and the number of available men in the belligerent countries have a wide range of variation. This is because the data necessary for accurate calculation are altogether lacking. Naturally no country has revealed the number of men it has in its armies or the number it has still to draw on. The estimates of military strength which are published in the newspapers now and then are mostly made by assuming that a certain proportion of the population, usually between ten and thirteen per cent, is eligible for military service. For instance, it is customary to figure out in this way that Germany has some nine million potential soldiers. But how many of these must be kept at home to run the necessary industries is pure guesswork.

The calculation of losses is still more

uncertain. In the first place Germany and Great Britain are the only countries publishing casualty lists. These are presumably truthful tho sometimes belated. But adding them up does not give the net loss, for the "missing" are not always dead or captured. Many of them turn up later. And a considerable proportion of the wounded eventually return to the ranks perhaps to figure once or twice more among the wounded. Owing to the advance of surgical science and the efficiency of the hospital service the number recovering is much greater than ever before. The percentage of the wounded returned to the ranks is variously estimated at 60, 70 or 80 per cent in the different armies, but the Germans make the astonishing claim that out of every 100 wounded 89.5 were again fit for service, 8.8 were discharged or given indefinite leave of absence, and only 1.7 died.

The estimates of enemy losses in battle are naturally exaggerated and usually quite worthless. If all the losses reported in the papers had been genuine the armies engaged would long ago have been wiped out. Under the circumstances the best thing we can do is to consider such figures as appear to have some authority and avoid making rash speculations as to the rest.

We have, for instance, the statement of Premier Asquith that the total British casualties up to January 9 amounted to 549,457, distributed as follows:

Underwood & Underwood

ST. PAUL TAKES WINTER JOVIALLY

Tepees and a toboggan slide for the use of thousands who have been celebrating the Outdoor Sports Carnival which has been revived after a lapse of twenty years. The State Capitol in the background

FRANCE AND FLANDERS

	Officers.	Other Ranks.
Killed	5,138	82,130
Wounded	10,217	248,090
Missing	1,691	52,844
Total officers and men, 400,510.		

DARDANELLES

	Officers.	Other Ranks.
Killed	1,745	26,455
Wounded	3,143	84,952
Missing	353	10,901
Total officers and men, 117,549.		

OTHER FRONTS

	Officers.	Other Ranks.
Killed	918	11,752
Wounded	816	15,165
Missing	101	2,656

As for the German losses the sum of her casualty lists has been stated to be from 3,500,000 to 4,000,000 up to January 1, 1916, but Harold J. Tennant, Parliamentary Under Secretary of the British Foreign Office, gives much lower figures, namely a total for all Germany of 2,535,768, of whom 588,-986 were killed, 1,566,549 wounded and missing, 356,153 prisoners and 24,-080 died of disease.

Of the wounded and missing an undetermined number have, as we noted above, returned to the front. The military expert of the London *Times* calculates that Germany has now about one million men in France and Flanders, two million on the Russian front and from one to two and a half million on other fields and in the interior. She has some two million prisoners who can be set to work. He calculates that since Germany has lost an average of nearly two hundred thousand men a month since the war began her military strength will begin to fail some time between May and October. A French statistician is more definite and sets August 1 as the date of Germany's collapse for lack of men. On the other hand the pro-German calculators, figuring that in Germany 850,000 boys arrive at military age every year and 550,000 in Austria-Hungary and that Bulgaria and Turkey can be drawn upon, are convinced that the Central Powers can hold out indefinitely.

No official figures are available for France, but a French Socialist Deputy speaking at the Bristol Labor Conference said that 800,000 soldiers had been killed, 1,400,000 had been wounded, and 300,000 had been taken prisoners.

The Russians are said to estimate their own casualties at three million.

WINTER LIGHTS AND SHADOWS

THE SCENE HAPPENS TO BE MT. KOSCIUSKO, NEW SOUTH WALES, BUT
THE SHARP TINGLING SUNLIT DAY IS EVIDENTLY NOT

WANTED: A COLUMBUS

BY THOMAS R. MARSHALL

VICE-PRESIDENT OF THE UNITED STATES

AMERICA has no right to be unless she stands for man and for the rights of men. Evils are abroad in the land, now as always. Notwithstanding our boast, our government is not of and by and for the people. Yet I make bold to say that it is still a representative democracy. Our coördinate system of government was formulated by Thomas Jefferson, and many a man wholly ignorant of Jefferson's theory of government is now proclaiming himself a Jeffersonian Democrat. Public speakers and the public press have been giving voice for twenty years to the fact that this is not a people's government. It has been shouted that the bosses are in control from ocean to ocean; that their machines have taken over the politics and legislation of the country; that they have prevented the people from crystallizing our ideals into enforceable laws. To be sure, we have had bosses and we have had machine politics in America. We have had legislation which, in enactment and construction, has not tended to promote the ideal of equality and the opportunity for honest success. But it has also been loudly proclaimed that the people, if they could only get a chance to express themselves, would declare in unmistakable terms their belief that this system was vicious; that they would smash the machines, banish the bosses and select officials who would always stand four-square with the theories of the fathers of the republic.

As a matter of fact, opportunity has been given us during the last three or four years to agonize over conditions and correct them; revealing to us what we should have known all along, what, indeed, we had known, but had been allowed to forget: This is a government not of stocks and bonds and mortgages, not of factories and mines, but a government of men—men who will neglect the common good in looking after their own welfare, unless they are touched with the weight of that responsibility which rests upon them as individual citizens.

We have adopted in many of the states and many of the cities the direct primary as a means of giving the citizen a chance to insure for himself office-holders who are honest and who believe in the high ideals of the republic and will stand for them. What has been the result? Has the average elector been deeply impressed with the weight of responsibility which rests upon his shoulders? He has cried out bitterly at conditions; he has charged the office-holder with being corrupt and controlled by corrupt bosses, but he fails to vote at the primary as he failed to attend his party caucus; he does nothing to prevent the renomination of the office-holder he has been railing against.

EQUITABLE enforcement of the laws can never be made to rest upon the office-holders of the land. It must rest upon the individual. You may abolish the caucus and adopt in its stead the primary; you may go further and have a second primary to determine who shall run in the primary for the nomination to be voted for at the election; you may keep on adding machinery and machinery to the system of nominating and electing officials, and your effort will come to naught until a public sentiment, which puts upon the conscience of every man his great responsibility for good government in this country, is aroused.

The direct primary has disclosed that the citizen is not deeply concerned about public affairs, and that conditions will have to grow far worse before we can hope for them to get much better. The primary has failed to bring out the vote. It has aroused suspicion. Many are inquiring whether the new system is not the result of a scheme to syndicate candidates and fool the people.

The people's rule does not depend necessarily upon the system of government under which they vote. Good or bad government must go back to good or bad citizenship, to intelligent or ignorant, to honest or dishonest electors. American democracy was intended to mean, and, I believe, does mean, something more than voting, something more than selecting officers. It does not depend upon caste or creed or condition, upon race or color, upon wealth or poverty, upon success or failure; it does depend upon the inner life of the individual citizen. It is an inspiration and an aspiration. It does not always depend upon the ticket which a man votes. It does depend always upon the motive back of the ballot.

Political events have disclosed, especially during the last few years, that we have been mistaken in some of our popular conclusions touching government in America. We have yielded a quiet assent to the proposition that a majority is all-powerful and that a minority has no rights which a majority is bound to respect. But now we know that the theory of the historic Democratic party that it is the right of a majority to rule, but only within constitutional limitations and without usurpation of a single inalienable right of a single individual, is correct.

It cannot be said that it is the system of government which is wrong. It is the unjust use of the system. It has not been the use but the misuse of the powers of government which has produced this discontent in the minds of men.

THE individualism of Thomas Jefferson is not dead. It has not moldered back to dust in the grave at Monticello. It walks the earth this day knocking at the door of rich and poor, of wise and ignorant alike, calling upon all men to make this age the millennium of statecraft, wherein no one shall claim to be the master and all shall be glad to be the servants of the Republic.

This is the land of the pioneer and the pathfinder. It has been suggested that his work is done, that he rests from his labors, and that men now know where and how to go. If there were an end to pathfinding, this would be a time of great sorrow rather than of unbounded exultation. But it is not so. The pioneer and the pathfinder will be as needful for the future as they have been to the past. Men walk ofttimes when they stand still, and they go farther in dreams than in thoughts or deeds. The mission of the Republic is vain if it be not to bring the blind by a way they know not, to lead them in paths that they have not known, to make darkness light before them, and crooked things straight. And none of these things can be done without vision and thought.

Old things have passed away. No one can convince me that the awful cataclysm in Europe has not swept aside all that we have known as safe and sure charts on the sea of life. I think it is necessary for some new Columbus to discover again a new America, and I do believe that there must exist today some new Columbus who will discover a new America not bound by the selfish interests of the past, but bound by the commonwealth of the Americas.

Washington, D. C.

THE MEETING

BY CAPTAIN PAUL VIGNON

TRANSLATED FROM THE FRENCH BY CHARLES PEABODY

LIFE is made up of nothing but contrasts; life is nothing but a series of stirring paradoxes; ever since this war has been piling one astonishment on another, each day is marked by something astounding, which, while it too often overwhelms, yet sometimes calls forth the tenderest feeling.

I have seen suffering and strength meet and pass by in the person of two soldiers, and I shall always remember it.

I have seen—at the moment when the combat begins to relax because night and fatigue are too much for the fighters, when anxiety rules the weary soldiers who yet watch——

I have seen, by the light of the sparkling rockets, in the trench all green and dirty, full of corpses, full of slops, redolent of noxious smells, in this melting pot of death and transfiguration, blood and tears, of hero and of madman, of the most sublime of spirits and of the most repulsive decay——

I have seen suffering and force meet and pass by, and I shall always remember it.

In that setting of opposites fixed tremendously face to face—there, where we talk low while the cannons roar furious and loud; there, where we scold and where we pray—there where we think it over of the having killed; killed so as not to be killed—so as to save France—there, where we laugh after we have wept; there, where we forget all—family, self-pride, egotism and all the ordinary motives that one so clings to otherwise—there, where we snap our fingers at prejudice, custom and foolish habit—there, where usage faces usage.

I have seen the kindly contrast, suffering and force meet and pass by. This war, like all that calls forth madness, ecstasy, fury, dash, often places side by side insanity and coolness, indomitable will and pity, ugliness and beauty—it opposes the extravagances of the body to the emotions of the soul.

Yes, I have seen the frightful onslaught of battalions charging to the front; I have seen whole columns dissolve, nearer and nearer to the ground, and disappear then in the mud, their only burial, the sticky, chalky clay.

I have seen all these soldiers, so many that they made a great big blue spot reflected in the sky marching happily, gaily into battle—into mud and their own blood.

Let us follow this march to the front—first it is the passing thru the villages all full of ambulances—then a slow procession by unnumbered paths in field and wood.

Sometimes they stop to wait for the night; then the men spattered with mud, soused with the rain which always falls, halt and sup.

But as soon as the dark seems black enough they start on again with the long, slow train thru endless ditches till they reach the trench.

Shells burst and bullets whistle; what of it? Onward anyhow; that's the way to conquer. Perhaps this instant there'll be the charge and we'll go with a good heart, full of heart, all of us, singing victory, singing the "Marseillaise."

There will be wooden crosses tomorrow, but what matter? Afterwards there will be the *Croix de Guerre.*

What's a man worth when he goes to the charge? All and nothing.

All, for one single one may save the situation; nothing, for France goes first and self-love follows after.

The soldier knows it and he says it then, when all the guns go off, the bayonets flash under the lightning of the rockets showing up the trenches, the labyrinth, and all the works—then, when the crazy raging, pitiless charge is imminent.

I have seen this march to triumph and to death; I have seen at the same time the procession of stillness, that of suffering which pity walks beside.

Just now there passed by singing men by hundreds; a few hours, and there are but rags and tatters that they bring back to the village where there are so many ambulances.

How well I can see these hospitals of passage that I would not look at just now when I was running with the mob of soldiers.

They have fixed them up the best they could, they have cleared out the mud round about, chocked up the roofs smashed by the shrapnel, and even set up beds in the chilly, gloomy church.

The village is full of them and everywhere you see the little lantern with its red cross shining near another one all white.

It is the refuge of pain, some kilometers from the tourney-field of might.

All along the road that's all you meet—these two figures tragic and poignant, varying according as might is the more brutal, or suffering the more worthy of pity.

A hundred times I have seen these scenes that make me weep, but never have I been so moved as one evening when the cannon raged and the general assault had been ordered.

I was waiting near a rest-shelter until all the reinforcing and attacking columns should have come out of the ditches.

The going and coming was incessant, wearisome, crushing, even for the looker-on; for in the darkness the ground never stopped groaning under the tramp of men, nor the air resounding with whistling shells and rattling arms.

Suddenly they cried near me, "Look out!" It was the bearers who were carrying a wounded man on a litter: a piece of shell had pierced his breast; he was all pale and the hospital men had hard work to avoid knocks and bounces—not easy in this crooked, hollow path, full of ruts. They stopped.

The rockets blazed up the sky and each time the white face of the wounded man could be seen in the night.

Suddenly I felt some one touch me; a commanding officer had taken me by the arm and whispered low: "Pardon, Lieutenant, but it seems to me that this wounded man is not unknown to me."

Another rocket went up into the sky among the black bellying clouds; the face of the dying man appeared again wan and white as the chalk of the road.

"My son!" cried the officer, coming near to him and bending over as if to speak to him.

He remained thus motionless for some minutes while the flashes in the sky came quicker and the columns continued their solemn, tragic march.

Each soldier who passed cast his shadow on the white spot, the wounded man; it was a reflection of life and force resting like a dare on the prey of Destiny and Death.

"Can we go on now that the way is clear?" asked the hospital corporal of the officer. "The road is long and hard and we have no time to lose."

"Go," said the superior officer.

I was going to ask him if I could help, but he had already kissed his son and I heard him say very quietly, without a sob, "Thus suffering and strength come face to face." He disappeared at top speed to regain the head of his regiment.

Somewhere in France

ARNOLD BENNETT'S PROVINCIALISM

By J. W. CUNLIFFE

ASSOCIATE DIRECTOR OF THE SCHOOL OF JOURNALISM IN COLUMBIA UNIVERSITY

PROVINCIALISM is not confined to any particular locality; it is (like Boston) "a state of mind." One may be provincial in a big city or metropolitan in a small one, for size is obviously no guarantee of superiority. Life in many a city of 25,000 is, on the average, cleaner and happier and more wholesome than life in New York. There is nothing ideal about the subway or a railroad apartment or the glare of Broadway.

The difference lies in the point of view: the metropolitan New Yorker knows that the Great White Way is a horror; the provincial thinks his brilliantly lighted Main Street a model for the world. Provincialism consists chiefly in this self-satisfaction, encouraged by lack of artistic opportunity and of contact with the great currents of thought. It is the presence of these elements that makes the metropolitan attitude critical.

If we compare Arnold Bennett with the writers of his time with whom he naturally groups himself —Shaw, Wells, Galsworthy—we see that he is, in this sense, provincial, and they are metropolitan. They voice the latest heresies—humanitarianism, socialism, feminism, and so on —each with his particular note—Mr. Shaw with rhetorical exaggeration and ingenious paradox, Mr. Wells with passionate vehemence, Mr. Galsworthy with a superficially cold detachment which only half conceals a white heat of indignation. Mr. Bennett disregards these great issues, or presents them merely as incidents in the intellectual and emotional life of his characters. In *These Twain*, recently reviewed in these columns as completing the *Clayhanger* trilogy, Edwin Clayhanger does concern himself (to the extent of one paragraph) with the low wages of his work people:

Those greasy, slatternly girls, for instance, with their coarse charm and their sexuality,—they were underpaid. They received as much as other girls, on pot-banks, perhaps more, but they were underpaid. What chance had they? But he dismisses the evil from his mind forthwith as beyond remedy. In the same fashion (also to the extent of one paragraph) Hilda reasons about her economic dependence on her husband:

No, they were not equals. The fundamental unuttered assumption upon which the household life rested was that they were not equals. She might cross him, she might momentarily defy him,

she might torture him, she might drive him to fury, and still be safe from any effective reprisals, because his love for her made her necessary to his being; but in spite of all that his will remained the seat of government, and she and George were only the Opposition. In the end, she had to incline. She was the complement of his existence, but he was not the complement of hers. She was just a parasite, tho an essential parasite. Why? . . . The reason, she judged, was economic, and solely economic. She rebelled. Was she not as individual, as original, as he? Had she not a powerful mind of her own, experience of her own, ideals of her own? Was she not of a nature profoundly and exceptionally independent? . . .

But her meditations do not lead her any further. She wants a dog cart and a house in the country and she cajoles her husband into indulging her in both. They get on in the world by the old-fashioned plan of pulling down their barns and building greater; they get on together thru the traditional force of sex-attraction, which Shaw, Wells and Galsworthy, following the lead of Hardy, make out to be "evanescent as steam." Yet both characters are presented to us as noble and elevated, worthy of our admiration and sympathy. Mr. Bennett's point of view is their point of view—the point of view of the Five Towns.

It is one of the oddest of popular fallacies that Mr. Bennett should be generally regarded as the mordant critic of provincial life in a small district of the English Midlands. He is really the sympathetic interpreter of provincial life as it exists all over the English-speaking world. The eye of the ordinary reader is caught by Mr. Bennett's skill in making fun of externals—the houses the Five Towns people live in, their trains and street cars, the food they eat and the clothes they wear. But these things, tho amusing because of the mastercraft by which they are realized, are secondary, and in a sense indifferent, mere background. What really interests Mr. Bennett is not what his characters eat and wear, but how they think and feel. It is their essential right-mindedness, their honesty and endurance, their courage and faithfulness to their standards of clean and straight living—such as they are. These are the qualities that attract us to the stay-at-home Constance, the original heroine of *The Old Wives' Tale;* the more enterprising Sophia was an afterthought. In this novel and in the *Clayhanger* series—upon which Mr. Bennett's fame

will rest secure, despite his too numerous pot-boilers—it is not the material ugliness of life in the Five Towns which is the permanent impression, but its spiritual beauty. In these novels Mr. Bennett is faithful to the literary principle he has laid down in *The Author's Craft:*

No man's instinct can draw him towards material which repels him— the fact is obvious. Obviously, whatever kind of life the novelist writes about, he has been charmed and seduced by it, he is under its spell—that is, he has seen beauty in it. He could have no other reason for writing about it. He may see a strange sort of beauty; he may—indeed he does—see a sort of beauty that nobody has quite seen before; he may see a sort of beauty that none save a few odd spirits ever will or can be made to see. But he does see beauty.

The spiritual beauty, it should be noted, is not associated by Mr. Bennett with organized religion, which finds its place merely among the grotesque material conditions of life in the Five Towns as a dead convention, affording comic relief, as in the incidents of the penknife sent in answer to prayer in *These Twain*, and the attempt to make Edwin Clayhanger treasurer of the Macclesfield District Additional Chapels Fund. The people in Mr. Bennett's novels live without religion, and die without it, in spite of their church activities and the parsons at their funerals. What counts for them as religious feeling —quite dissociated from the religious organization to which they may happen to belong—is the stedfast courage with which they meet the ordinary trials of life. They are, as he says of the Five Towns characters in *What the Public Wants* fundamentally "decent" and sagacious people, and it is their standards that are upheld in the great novels and in this play, in which the metropolitan newspaper proprietor, so far as he has departed from Five Towns standards, is condemned. Mr. Bennett has fled from the Five Towns to London, to Rottingdean, to Fontainebleau. He is no longer in the Five Towns, but he is still of them, and if he chose to return it is to be hoped (and believed) that the Five Towns would have common sense enough to give him as warm a welcome as Warwickshire gave to Shakespeare, in spite of Justice Shallow and Silence, and as Tarascon gave (after the first impulse of resentment had evaporated) to Daudet.

New York City

263

CARRYING THE WAR INTO AFRICA

WHERE THE BIGGEST PRIZE IS AT STAKE AND THE
BIGGEST GAINS HAVE BEEN MADE

THE biggest prize in the Great War is Africa. However the conflict may come out, there will be but comparatively slight changes in the map of Europe. In Asia the chief issue at stake is which shall control Turkish and Persian territory. But the fate of practically the whole continent of Africa depends upon which side wins. If the Allies are victorious they are not likely to restore to Germany any of her African colonies. If Germany is victorious she can take her pick of the British, French, Belgian, Italian and Portuguese possessions. If the war is a drawn game and settled by bargaining, the peace terms will be some compromise between these extremes, but probably involving a shift of territory larger than any of the belligerent countries of Europe.

The struggle for the possession of Africa, which had occupied the European Powers for twenty-five years, seemed to have come to a close in 1912, when France declared a protectorate over Morocco and Italy conquered Libya. The partition of Africa was complete except for the tiny state of Liberia under the protection of the United States and Abyssinia, which was still in dispute. The map of Africa as it appeared to have been definitely drawn two years before the outbreak of the war is given on the adjoining page. In figures it was as follows:

THE PARTITION OF AFRICA

	Square Miles
French	4,100,000
British	2,100,000
Egypt and Sudan	1,600,000
Total British	**3,700,000**
German	900,000
Belgian	900,000
Portuguese	800,000
Italian	600,000
Spanish	80,000
Abyssinia	350,000
Liberia	40,000

The world breathed more freely when the long process of partitioning came to an end, for more than once it had brought Europe to the verge of war. One such critical occasion came in 1898 when a dashing French captain encountered a square-jawed young Englishman at Fashoda in the heart of Africa. Captain Marchand had come overland from the French Congo. Sir Herbert Kitchener had steamed up the White Nile from Khartum. Neither man would give way, so two flags, the French and the Egyptian, were hoisted side by side over the mud-

264

flat in the midst of the swamp. In France and England there was clamor for war, but cooler counsel prevailed. France swallowed her pride and withdrew from Fashoda, leaving England in undisputed possession of the Nile valley.

The same sensible system of compromise was later adopted in the division of the territory along the Mediterranean. By mutual agreement it was arranged that France should be free to take Morocco and England Egypt at any time they chose, and that Spain should have the strip of Moroccan territory opposite Gibraltar and Italy should be allowed to conquer Tripoli for herself. The Anglo-French treaty was. signed in 1904, but the secret clauses which provided for the ultimate disposition of Egypt and Morocco were not disclosed until 1911, when Germany, suspecting that she was being shut 'out in the cold, sent a cruiser to the Moroccan port of Agadir and demanded "a place in the sun." Within the last few months we have heard from English sources that war was then thought to be imminent and inevitable. The British fleet was ready for instant action when Germany backed down and consented to accept a bit of Congo land from France in compensation for refraining from interference with French designs on Morocco. According to the treaty signed at Algeciras in 1906 by the European Powers and the United States, the independence and sovereignty of the Sultan of Morocco was to be respected and his territory maintained intact. But when within six years thereafter Morocco was invaded by the French and the country divided between France and Spain nobody in America seems to have suggested that it was the duty of our Government to intervene in behalf of the sanctity of treaty obligations. Perhaps this is because it was generally recognized that it was not possible for the French or anybody else to rule Morocco worse than she has been ruled for many centuries by her own sovereigns. Some people would say that shutting Germany out from the final partition of Africa was not fair and many people would say that it was not good politics, but they would agree that Morocco, like all the other waste places of the world, must be taken in hand and cleaned up by somebody.

In accordance with the secret clauses of the Anglo-French treaty of ten years before Egypt has now been incorporated into the British

empire. On December 18, 1914, the Khedive Abbas Hilmi was deposed by the British and Hussein Kamil, his uncle, made Sultan of Egypt, thus definitely separating Egypt and the Sudan from the Ottoman empire. This is, of course, merely a paper change since Egypt has ever since 1883 been governed from London and greatly to her advantage. It is questionable if the pyramids, during the "forty centuries" that they have seen it so peaceful and prosperous as it has been under British rule. Everybody except her envious rivals is glad now that England has never kept her promise to evacuate Egypt.

The Suez Canal has been strongly fortified in anticipation of an attack from Turkish and German forces now rumored to be preparing in Palestine. A year ago the Turks attempted the conquest of Egypt, but by the time they had crossed the desert of Sinai they had not the strength left to capture the Canal.

On the other side of Egypt, the western frontier, the British outposts have had to meet some sharp attacks from the Senussi, a militant Moslem sect. Their activities in Tripoli have driven the Italians out of the hinterland and now they have only a precarious hold on the coast cities.

At the outbreak of the Great War efforts were made by both the Belgian and German governments to prevent central Africa from becoming involved in the conflict. The conference of the Powers called by Bismarck at Berlin in 1885 to establish the Congo Free State decided that free trade in time of peace and neutrality in time of war should prevail thruout the region watered by the Congo and its tributaries including Lake Tanganyika, an area of a million and a half square miles. On August 7, 1914, the Belgian Government asked France and Great Britain to declare their Congo colonies neutral in accordance with the Berlin convention. France was willing, but Great Britain refused on the ground that it was impractical and that hostilities had already begun in Africa. The German Government on its part solicited the United States, as one of the signatories of the Berlin convention, to arrange an agreement among the belligerents to exclude the Congo basin from war. Such an appeal to us was natural. since the United States had taken an active part in launching the Congo Free State and was the first to recognize its flag.

Germany was the second. But our Government excused itself from undertaking the negotiation of such an agreement on the ground that the Senate had never ratified the Berlin convention.

In Africa, as in Europe, each side accuses the other with having "begun it first." Obviously the temptation to pounce upon interior stations, still unaware of the war, was too strong to be resisted, and there were raids over the border on several frontiers early in August.

But it was by an ironical coincidence in the "Harbor of Peace,"

Dar-es-Salaam, that hostilities definitely opened. On August 8, 1914, the British cruiser "Pegasus" appeared before Dar-es-Salaam, which is the chief port of German East Africa, and bombarded the city and shipping. On November 28 and January 13 the bombardment was repeated in spite of the protests of Germany that such attacks upon an unfortified city were in violation of international law. In one of these raids the surveying vessel "Möwe" was sunk. The name reappeared recently attached to the much larger vessel which captured the "Appam."

German East Africa is not an island, yet there have been "naval engagements" on all four sides of it, that is, on lakes Nyanza, Nyassa and Tanganyika as well as the sea. Tanganyika, which separates the German colony from the Belgian Congo to the west is the longest lake in the world. A railroad 780 miles long has recently been completed which connects it with the coast at Dar-es-Salaam. On this railroad and in the heart of the country is Tabora, which has now been strongly fortified to resist the British attack. Big guns have been brought

THE PARTITION OF AFRICA

At the outbreak of the war the African continent had been divided up among the European Powers in this fashion. Abyssinia and Liberia were nominally independent. B stands for British possessions; F for French, G for German, P for Portuguese, S for Spanish, I for Italian. Since the war began Great Britain has formally declared a protectorate over Egypt and the Sudan. The South Africans have conquered German Southwest Africa. The French and British together have conquered Togoland and Kamerun. The British are now undertaking the conquest of German East Africa. If we count in all these the new acquisitions of the Allies will amount to over 2,500,000 square miles

from the cruiser "Königsberg," which the British fleet ran to earth, and rifles have been obtained thru Portuguese territory. In this way 4000 white soldiers and 30,000 natives have been armed to meet the British invasion. That the British Government is aware of the difficulty of the conquest of a territory nearly twice the size of Germany is shown by the fact that Sir Horace Smith-Dorrien was ordered from France to take charge of the expedition, but on account of his illness General Smuts will replace him.

All of the other German possessions in Africa have now been conquered. The Kamerun colony, which was attacked on three sides in August, 1914, held out till February, 1916, altho there were probably not two thousand Germans in the colony. The early invasions of Kamerun from British Nigeria on the west and from French and Belgian Congo on the east did not do much, and the conquest was accomplished by a joint British and French force which followed up the two railroad lines from the coast. On the first of January they took Yaunde, the last tenable post in the interior. The Governor and his soldiers escaped into the Spanish enclave of Rio Muni.

Togoland was the first of the German colonies to capitulate, which is not surprizing when we know that the German army in this colony consisted of only sixty Europeans and four hundred natives. The joint French and British force which was sent in against them lost seventeen per cent of its men before the Germans surrendered, August 26, 1914.

German Southwest Africa was conquered by General Botha, Premier of the Union of South Africa,

with a force of 50,000 men, half Boer and half British. This was more than ten times the number of German troops defending the colony, nevertheless it was a considerable achievement to conquer a territory about the size of all of our Atlantic states put together, especially since he also had a rebellion on his hands at the same time. General De Wet with a small number of irreconcilable Boers tried to take advantage of the opportunity to reëstablish the Boer republics. It was understood that the Kaiser had promised to guarantee their independence if they would rebel. Colonel Maritz, who commanded the Union forces on the northwestern frontier, at once joined with the Germans from over the border. But General Botha and General Smuts actéd with promptness and energy. The rebellion was soon crushed and De Wet captured. He was tried for high treason, convicted —and released. The South Africans practise mutual forgiveness more than any other people, and somehow it seems to work.

The conquest of German Southwest Africa was a motor car campaign, just the thing for an open arid country. When the Germans took possession of the territory in 1884—it was the first fruit of their expansion policy—the British held possession of Walfish Bay, the only good harbor on the coast. But the Germans put in expensive harbor works at Swakopmund and so made of it a far better port than Walfish Bay. In January Swakopmund was taken by the aid of the British fleet. The South African forces then advanced into the interior along the railroad lines and on May 12, 1915, captured Windhuk, the capital, 129

miles from the coast. Here they found a wireless station, completed just before the war, of such power that it could with one relay communicate directly with Berlin.

The campaign in German Southwest Africa cost the Union $80,000,-000, but it is worth it. The Germans have spent more than that on public works in the colony. They were just beginning to get their money back when they lost it. In the casualties of the campaign the two races by chance shared almost equally; 126 British killed, 126 Boers killed, 273 British wounded, 275 Boers wounded.

When Portugal at the beginning of the war declared her sympathies with the Allies the Germans invaded from German Southwest Africa and captured the border fort of Naulila in December, 1914.

To sum up the situation as it stands after a year and a half of war: Germany has lost all her African possession except one; Great Britain and France acquired at comparatively small cost in life and money over two million square miles of territory, that is, an area equal to two-thirds of the United States. The rich and fertile lowlands of the tropics are capable of producing wealth incalculable and there are immense tracts of healthful plateaus, where communities of the highest civilization may flourish. No wonder that the long struggle for African territory has become fierce as it nears the end. We know what a wild rush there was in Oklahoma when the last of the public lands was opened for settlement. The present war is the last chance at the last of the continents on which the Powers may stake out their claims.

MY BATTLE-PRAYER

BY F. F. V.

I do not ask for peace,
Nor yet that on my path
The sounds of war shall shrill no more,
The way be clear of wrath.
But this I beg Thee, Lord,
Steel Thou my will with might,
And in the Strife that men call "Life,"
Grant me the strength to fight.

I do not pray for arms,
Nor shield to cover me.
What tho I stand with empty hand,
So it be valiantly!
Spare me the coward's fear—
Questioning wrong or right:
Lord, among these mine enemies,
Grant me the strength to fight.

I do not pray that Thou
Keep me from any wound,
Tho I fall low from thrust and blow,
Forced fighting to the ground;
But give me wit to hide
My hurt from all men's sight,
And for my need, the while I bleed,
Lord, grant me strength to fight.

I do not pray that Thou
Shouldst grant me victory;
Enough to know that from my foe
I have no will to flee.
Beaten and bruised and banned,
Flung like a broken sword,
Grant me this thing for conquering—
Let me die fighting, Lord!

A FIREMEN'S AERIAL PARADE IN TOKYO

ON NEW YEAR'S DAY IN JAPAN THE FIREMEN ARE INSPECTED—SHOW OFF, IN OTHER WORDS—
ALL OVER THE COUNTRY. THIS SCALING LADDER CONTEST, WITH MEN COMING DOWN
"HANDS ONLY" IS A SIGHT WORTH GOING FAR TO SEE

Royal Master Model 10
Price $100

The Royal cuts the cost and betters the quality of your letters

NO matter how quick, how intelligent, how efficient, how prompt your stenographers are—their ability is worth just as much to you as is shown by the quality of their *typewritten work*.

With the Royal Typewriter your stenographers can do more work, better work, and with less effort. And the Royal stands up under the most strenuous usage, day in and day out, because it is accurately designed for just that purpose, and built by master-workmen who know the value of *quality* in materials and workmanship.

Compare the Work

The Royal proves itself not only in the quality of typewritten work done on it, but in the actual saving in the cost of that work.

It saves *day by day*, because its users are enabled to turn their work out better and faster.

It *cuts the cost* of producing every letter written on it—the saving being almost enough to pay the postage bills.

It saves *in the long run* because it ends the necessity of "*trading-out*" after two or three years, and because it does away with excessive repairs.

Get the facts. Know the Royal.

Write or telephone us or any of our branches or agencies, and a representative will call and demonstrate the Royal without the least obligation on your part.

Write today for these free booklets

'Better Service'' and "One Problem Solved" tell how to cut the cost of typewritten letters—save operators' time—give your correspondence "class." A postal brings them now.

ROYAL TYPEWRITER COMPANY, INC.
104 Royal Typewriter Building, 364 Broadway, New York City
Branches and Agencies the World Over

"Compare the Work"

Royal Master Model 10
Price $100

The typewriter you will not have to "trade-out"—and why

THE Royal Typewriter does not have to be "traded-out"—because it is built for long life and finest work

The very *looks* of the Royal convince you that the masterworkmen who make it, build endurance into it, build the capability for best work into it, build into it that superiority which ends the necessity for "trading-out."

Only the most exact, correct scientific design and construction could insure the unfailing responsiveness, the precise harmony of all moving parts which result in the perfect presswork for which the Royal is famous.

Compare the Work

Compare the *work* done on the Royal. Note the clean, clearcut typewriting; the exact, properly-spaced lines; the smooth even presswork which carries with it the undoubted impression of class.

Compare the *convenience* of the Royal. It typewrites letters, cards and does billing and charging—all on the one machine and without a single extra attachment.

Compare the *ease* with which the work is done. Nothing but master-workmanship could build a machine which takes the "grind" out of typewriting, and always turns out work of super-class.

Investigate the Royal. Study it from all angles. You will quickly appreciate why the demand for it is testing every resource of the model Royal factory.

Write for "Facts About the 'Trade-Out'"

—a little book which doesn't mince words in telling the story of the typewriter. Every typewriter owner or user should have it. We want to place a copy in your hands. A postal will bring it to you free.

ROYAL TYPEWRITER COMPANY, INC.

104 Royal Typewriter Building, 364 Broadway, New York City

Branches and Agencies the World Over

"Compare the Work"

M. William Shak-ſpeare:

EIGHT PAPERS BY FREDERICK HOUK LAW
IN OBSERVANCE OF THE THREE HUNDREDTH
ANNIVERSARY OF SHAKESPEARE'S DEATH

Shakespeare's England

SHAKESPEARE when he went to London, about 1587, might have heard "The shrill trump, the spirit - stirring drum, the ear-piercing fife," or heard the shout along the street:

The trumpets sound: stand close, the Queen is coming,

and hurried with a picturesque crowd to see a wonderful procession sweep by—company after company in linked armor or glittering steel, with fantastic pikes; strangely-costumed dancers with tinkling bells; rumbling cannon; carts with caged animals; and then—proud, self-reliant, magnificently drest — the great Queen Elizabeth, for whom hats went into the air and the populace yelled itself hoarse. All England in those days saw the superb sweeping by of the wonderful queen who had lifted England into prosperity and developed the spirit that now lives in Elizabethan literature, and especially in the plays of Shakespeare.

A great spirit filled little England then—for little England it was, with scarcely five million inhabitants, fewer people than now live in Greater New York alone; and the London of those days with about 200,000 people, was smaller than today's Denver or Rochester. But

Like little body with a mighty heart

England was thrilling with a national life that made her great in war, in wealth and in literature.

The fall of Constantinople in 1453, by spreading Greek learning, had stimulated new thought; Caxton's printing-press, set up in Westminster in 1476, had opened the gates of literature; Luther's daring theses in 1517 had declared religious freedom; and Columbus' discovery of America in 1492 had encouraged voyages to lands of wonder

To try the fair adventure of tomorrow.

When Shakespeare was thirteen Francis Drake made a voyage around the world

Full of peril and adventurous spirit.

When Shakespeare was twenty-one Drake plundered the Spanish possessions in America and returned with incredible wealth. Three years later thirty-four royal English vessels and a few seaport sailing boats surprizingly defeated Philip of Spain's Great Armada of one hundred and thirty-two magnificently outfitted ships of war. After such events it is small wonder that all England quivered with national life.

The whole spirit of the times was full of interest, romance and greatness. The romantic story of Mary Queen of Scots was moving toward its end—with her execution—in 1587, when Shakespeare was twenty-three. Elizabeth's femininity, her love of dress, of flattery, of ostentation, and her romance with Leicester, made the Queen a romantic influence. When Shakespeare was twenty-seven he must have heard how Sir Richard Grenville, with one little ship and a hundred men, fought with fifty great Spanish vessels of war. Such deeds made it a gallant thing to be an Englishman, for they

Did all the chivalry of England move
To do brave acts.

Elizabeth had found England poor in money and men, her trade and commerce small, and her unity threatened by religious differences. The present vast commercial life of England is largely due to Elizabeth, who strengthened English

LONDON ABOUT THE TIME OF SHAKESPEARE'S DEATH

Looking from the south bank of the Thames toward the city. London Bridge in the center, with "Traitor's Gate" at its near end, where the heads of decapitated traitors were exposed. St. Paul's is the large church in the background. No public theaters were allowed within the city limits; they were built either to the north or on the Bankside in Southwark (foreground). Three of them, octagonal buildings with a flag flying, are seen to the left, the "Swan," the "Hope," and the "Globe." From an old print

Every Moment
A Pleasanter
Moment ⁓ Every
Mile a Smoother
Steadier Mile ⁓
Every Hour an Hour
of Greater Ease

commerce and wealth when the rest of Europe plunged into war. She developed a vast export trade, especially in woolen goods sent to the low countries.

With the resulting wealth the great lords made castles into palaces, where they held

Nightly revels and new jollity.

Beautiful buildings in brick and stone took the place of wooden dwellings, Shakespeare bought in 1597 New Place, the most substantial house in Stratford.

Glass windows took the place of lattice, of which Lafeu says in "All's Well that Ends Well":

My good window of lattice, fare thee
  well: thy casement
I need not open, for I look through
  thee.

Well-constructed chimneys added much to comfort. Rushes still covered the floors, but rich furniture and costly tapestry gave a magnificence that delighted the eye. Shakespeare often speaks of rich houses, as in "Cymbeline," where Iachimo says:

Her bedchamber . . .
    . . . was hang'd
With tapestry of silk and silver . . .
    . . . a piece of work
So bravely done, so rich, that it did
  strive
In workmanship and value . . .
    . . . The roof o' the chamber
With golden cherubims is fretted: her
  andirons
    . . . were two winking Cupids
Of silver.

In "The Taming of the Shrew" Gremio gives us some idea of the prevailing delight in luxury when he says:

My house within the city
Is richly furnished with plate and gold;
Basins and ewers to lave her dainty
  hands;
My hangings all of Tyrian tapestry;
In ivory coffers I have stuff'd my
  crowns;
In cypress chests my arras, counter-
  points,
Costly apparel, tents, and canopies,
Fine linen, Turkey cushions boss'd with
  pearl,
Valance of Venice gold in needlework,
Pewter and brass, and all things that
  belong
To house or housekeeping: then, at my
  farm
I have a hundred milch-kine to the pail,
Sixscore fat oxen standing in my
  stalls.

Table-knives, forks, silver spoons and china dishes were just coming into use in Shakespeare's time, and the plays have contemptuous references to lead, pewter and wood, Marcius, in "Coriolanus," saying:

Cushions, leaden spoons,
Irons of a doit, doublets that hangmen
  would
Bury with those that wore them, these
  base slaves
Ere yet the fight be done, pack up.

And Pompey, in "Measure for Measure," says apologetically:

A fruit-dish, a dish of some three-pence; your honours have seen such dishes; they are not China dishes, but very good dishes.

The humbler people in Stratford and elsewhere ate at one and seven without ceremony, the very poor using wooden dishes and helping themselves with their fingers, a custom that the First Stranger, in "Timon of Athens," refers to when he says satirically:

Why, this is the world's soul;
And just of the same piece is every
  flatterer's spirit.
Who can call him his friend that dips
  in the same dish?

The very rich dined in state at eleven and five, having many meat-courses and a great number of wines, the more important guests being at an elevated table and seated according to rank, a custom referred to by Macbeth when he says to his guests:

You know your own degrees: sit
  down: at first
And last the hearty welcome.

Then, if ever, was England "Merrie England," filled with

Revels, dances, masks and merry
  hours.

At Christmas time the wassail-bowl, the boar's head, the mistletoe and the holly delighted gay companies: men in doublet and hose, with white ruffs, laces, gems and sometimes earrings; ladies in gowns of rich material, with ruffs, jewels, and most elaborate coiffeurs. In "Much Ado About Nothing" Margaret says:

THE SWAN THEATER IN LONDON
This drawing, made by a Dutchman, John de Witt, probably in 1596, is the earliest picture known of the interior of a playhouse. Note the broad open stage, with an inner stage under a balcony, and the encircling galleries in whose "rooms" or boxes spectators sat. Others stood in the pit. After 1620 the Swan was used for prize-fights

Cloth o' gold, and cuts, and laced with silver, set with pearls, down sleeves, side sleeves, and skirts, round underborne with a bluish tinsel: but . . . yours is worth ten on't.

And in "The Taming of the Shrew" Petruchio promises his bride she shall

Revel it as bravely as the best,
With silken coats and caps and golden
  rings,
With ruffs and cuffs and fardingales
  and things;
With scarfs and fans and double-
  change of bravery,
With amber bracelets, beads and all
  this knavery.

In this love of display the Queen set the fashion, having no less than three thousand dresses! New Year's Day, Twelfth Night, Candlemas, May Day and other holidays gladdened the people, and what with Elizabeth's royal progresses, court splendors, weddings, masquerades, morris-dancing, archery contests, fairs and village sports, life was full of pageant and frolic.

In Shakespeare's youth school-boys and university students frequently acted Latin plays, and sometimes plays in English, but the first regular English theater was not built until Shakespeare was a boy of twelve. Under the influence of prosperity the drama developed rapidly, so that in a period of eighty-four years fifteen hundred new plays were produced! When Shakespeare reached middle age there were seven regular London theaters and many other places where plays were given at times. The old religious plays gave way to plays for mere amusement. Shakespeare's rivals were many in number and included Peele, Lyly, Marlowe, Nash, Kyd, Ben Jonson, Chapman, Marston, Middleton, Dekker, Tourneur, Webster, Massinger, Beaumont and Fletcher, and dozens of others, but Shakespeare's works alone have survived for common reading.

A penny or two admitted to the wooden theater, but the floor was bare ground, and there were no seats and no roof except for those who paid a shilling: such people could sit in protected galleries or on the stage. Sometimes there was crude scenery, but more often the foreground represented any open place; a permanent balcony might be an upper chamber or a tower; and a curtained recess below served as an inner room. Shakespeare felt the restrictions of the stage and theater of his day, and, in the prolog to "Henry V," says:

But pardon, gentles all,
The flat unraised spirits that have
  dared
On this unworthy scaffold to bring
  forth

So great an object; can this cockpit hold
The vasty fields of France? or may we cram
Within this wooden O the very casques
That did affright the air at Agincourt?

The companies sometimes consisted entirely of boys, and, as there were no actresses, boys always took the parts of women, a custom referred to in "Antony and Cleopatra" when Cleopatra says:

I shall see
Some squeaking Cleopatra boy my greatness.

When we think of the inimitable women of Shakespeare, Rosalind, Viola, Portia, we wonder how Shakespeare could have endured seeing the parts enacted by boys. And yet, in spite of all difficulties, the plays were well presented, with gorgeous costuming and excellent acting. Richard Tarlton, John Heming, Edward Alleyn, Richard Burbage and other actors of the day gained great fame.

Many companies were licensed, but less than half a dozen were maintained for a long time. The Earl of Leicester's men, at various times known as Strange's, Derby's, Hunsdon's, The Lord Chamberlain's, and The King's, were among the best known and gave their plays in The Theater, The Globe, and The Blackfriars. With this company Shakespeare was closely associated as actor, playwriter and shareholder.

In the England thus throbbing with national life, and under the crude conditions of the theater of his time, Shakespeare, sublimely careless concerning the preservation of his great work, and writing quickly for a changing public, wrote always for the stage and never for publication. He based his work on material ready at hand—old plays, histories, poems, Italian romances—whatever seemed best, but adding to bare plot effective arrangement,

---

BOOKS FOR FURTHER READING

The Age of Elizabeth, by M. Creighton; *The Age of Shakespeare*, by J. W. Allen; *Shakespeare, His Times and Contemporaries*, by G. M. Tweddell; *Shakespeare and His Times*, by N. Drake; *Shakespeare's London*, by H. J. Stephenson; *Shakespeare's London*, by T. F. Ordish; *Stratford-on-Avon*, by Sidney Lee; *Shakespeare's England*, by William Winter; *In Shakespeare's England*, by Mrs. F. S. Boas; *History of the London Stage and Its Famous Players*, by H. B. Baker. At Columbia University there is a *Dramatic Museum* containing very interesting models of an inn-yard theater and the Fortune Theater, which was built in Shakespeare's time.

---

beautiful poetry and wonderfully searching and realistic character portrayal. In spite of his apparent failure to seek renown and hand down a name to posterity we can say of him as he wrote concerning Coriolanus:

His fame folds in
The orb o' the earth.

In the dim old London streets, in the cramped circle of the wooden theaters, or in the smoke of the Mermaid Inn, Shakespeare moved with the world of London life. We know from his works that his thoughts ran frequently to the thatched roofs, green lanes and spreading meadows of Stratford, where one might see

In emerald tufts, flowers purple, blue, and white;
Like sapphire, pearl, and rich embroidery.

And yet the world of Shakespeare was only in part this wonderful Elizabethan world of city and country life. It is as tho his own Henry V said to him:

You and I cannot be confined within the weak list of a country's fashion.

His world was more than London, more than England—he saw so clearly into the heart of life that he lived in the abiding world of humanity.

BÁRÁNY AND NYSTAGMUS REACTIONS

THE NOBEL PRIZE WINNER IN MEDICINE AND HIS WORK

ALL of us are familiar as children with what happens when we have "turned round and round" a number of times and then find that we are dizzy or "drunk" and have to stagger for a moment and can scarcely stand, or may actually fall. It is practically this phenomenon that Dr. Robert Bárány, of the University of Vienna, has investigated to such good advantage that he has been awarded the Nobel Prize in Medicine for 1914 for his work in the physiology and pathology of certain structures connected with the ear, the vestibule and semi-circular canals. The award was delayed by the war and has been but recently announced, while no prize is given for 1915.

While clinical assistant in the great ear clinic of Professor Politzer at Vienna, Dr. Bárány was able to employ the results of his study in the diagnosis of pathological disturbances of the middle ear and also in the differential diagnosis of various pathological conditions of the cerebellum or posterior part of the brain.

That such a childish bit of play should prove to be so significant

seems almost impossible, but in medicine a number of very simple and apparently trivial bits of technic have proved invaluable. Auenbrugger "drummed on the chest" and his colleagues made fun of him for doing so; Galvani played, as envious contemporaries said, "the dancing master to frogs"; Laennec introduced what was contemptuously called "a toy hearing tube," but their contributions to medical practise are now indispensable.

So it has proved with Bárány's studies of the consequences of revolving patients on specially constructed stools, noting the subsequent movements of the individual and particularly of his eyes, which give a characteristic nystagmus or oscillatory movement for the different conditions immediately afterwards, or noting the effect on the individual's feeling and his nystagmus reaction after the injection of warm and cold water into the ear, or after the increase or decrease of the air pressure in the auditory canal.

As Dr. Bárány himself notes in his lectures on the subject, which

have attracted specialists to his courses from all over the world, the study of the various forms of nystagmus or oscillation of the eyes is also valuable for the investigation of vision itself as regards the visual field and color and spark vision. Such phenomena as blushing, spontaneous perspiration, palpitation of the heart, or distinct slowing of the pulse, tremor, and slowing and deepening of the breathing may be noted in nervous persons in connection with rotary and vertical nystagmus. Dr. Bárány's work has come to be of special service in the study of those extremely puzzling cases of accidental injury followed by nervous conditions of various kinds which occupy so much attention in our courts. In a word the faithful development by experimental research of the hint given by childish playfulness has resulted in a series of diagnostic developments that are of invaluable service.

Dr. Bárány was captured by the Russians last year and is now serving as physician to the Austrian prisoners in Russia.

THE EQUITABLE

LIFE ASSURANCE SOCIETY OF THE U. S.

120 BROADWAY, NEW YORK

The 56th Annual Report of the Society, which will be sent to any address on application, shows:

NEW INSURANCE PAID FOR IN 1915	$	158,456,612
(The maximum which the Society was permitted to write in that year under the Insurance Law of the State of New York.)		
OUTSTANDING INSURANCE DEC. 31, 1915		$1,529,886,053
ADMITTED ASSETS, DEC. 31, 1915	$	546,961,912
GENERAL INSURANCE RESERVE $448,826,331		
OTHER LIABILITIES 10,079,766	$	458,906,097
SURPLUS RESERVES:		
For Distribution to Policyholders in 1916 .. $ 13,573,499		
Held awaiting apportionment upon deferred dividend policies 63,910,551		
For Contingencies 10,571,765	$	88,055,815
RECEIPTS FROM PREMIUMS IN 1915	$	56,015,862
RECEIPTS FROM INVESTMENTS	$	24,899,405
TOTAL INCOME FROM ALL SOURCES	$	83,290,810
PAYMENTS TO POLICYHOLDERS	$	58,371,388

During the year the Society invested $27,888,067 at an average yield of 5.06%.

The Annual Report contains the Financial Statement, verified by Certified Public Accountants, schedules of investments, and full details regarding the substantial advances made during the year.

It also describes a variety of new policies including one under which the Equitable will pay an income for life to the person insured if he should become totally and permanently disabled, as well as an income for life to the beneficiary after his death.

Of the death claims paid in the United States and Canada, over 98% were settled within twenty-four hours after receipt of due proof of death.

President.

OFFICE EFFICIENCY

BY EDWARD EARLE PURINTON

DIRECTOR OF THE INDEPENDENT EFFICIENCY SERVICE

EVERY business, like every wheel, has a hub. The office is the hub.

A spoke of a wheel may be damaged and repaired, without much loss. But when the hub is smashed, the wheel is gone, with the cargo it conveys.

If the enterprise you carry seems shaky, or the road to your goal eternally hard and long, the fault is not with the load or the road, but with the hub of your conveyance. Look for all your business troubles in the office. You may say you have enough and don't need to "look" for more! You are wrong—a man never has enough trouble till he stops making it.

We may carry the analogy further. We may name the four wheels of every business, calling them the *Product* wheel, the *Employer* wheel, the *Employee* wheel, and the *Consumer* wheel. The hub, in each case, is the office. By means of the office the Product must be measured and delivered; the plans of the Employer carried forth and his dynamics gaged; the skill and service of the Employee extended; the satisfaction and profitable patronage of the Consumer quickly and easily attained.

By the word "business" I mean every human service for which pay is received. The teacher, the preacher, the doctor, the poet, the sage, all are business men. Or if they are not, they should be. A man without a business side to him is an unfinished product. He is no more complete than a wagon-bed off its wheels.

GOING IT BLIND

Industrial experts tell us that in the United States about 90 per cent of all business undertakings end in the ditch. The explanation is quite simple—about 90 per cent of the business offices are improperly managed and equipt. Success is a compound of shrewd thought, good work, and kindly feeling. But, alas, only about 10 per cent of the office managers in this country are awake to their opportunities. The other 90 per cent are headed for destruction —going it blind.

A brief survey of the modern science of office management would include the following items, which may be held of first importance, among others of lesser utility.

An office needs an architectural plan;—to choose and occupy one bereft of this plan would be as unscientific as to build a factory on a guess,

or open a store in a barn. The basic feature of this floor plan is the *time value* of the respective workers, from the manager to the errand boy. Large offices occupy an entire floor, the circuit of which means a walk of perhaps 100 to 300 feet. Suppose the manager travels this route a dozen times a day, to execute or supervise a task or group of tasks. He walks perhaps 3000 feet, wastes probably a half hour, and expends at least 150,000 foot-pounds of nervous energy, simply on a mechanical operation of walking a certain distance without rime or reason. This largely explains the "tired business man," who frequents the low-brow comedy on the homœopathic principle—to relieve his own absurdity. By a sane "routing" system the desks and departments requiring his personal attendance may be grouped near his private office; while the work needing his general supervision may be carried to him by the office boy. Suppose the time of the manager is worth $2 an hour, that of the office boy 10 cents an hour; by transferring a half-hour of daily promenading from the manager to the boy, we save approximately 95 cents a day, and put the physical fatigue where it belongs, on the worker whose strength is least valuable to the company. The constantly recurring interviews between executives, managers and department heads may be disposed of in a shorter order than before if a properly arranged system of automatic or inter-communicating telephones has been established.

We referred to the manager's "private office." We assume that he has one. If he hasn't, he should get one. That word *Private* on a glass door exerts a magic power. It raises the inmate of the secret room far above common mortals, in the opinion of his clerks, his clients, and himself. The chief executive in any business requires a certain amount of silence and seclusion. Should space or funds be limited, a temporary partition of opaque glass, or even a set of plain, substantial screens, would give the psychological effect of a private office.

The nervous and muscular effort required in the day's work of any high-salaried man should be reduced to a minimum. All his routine duties may be handled by trained employees, or by special devices and machines. Roughly, a $10 man should do four times as much physical toil

as a $40 man, the latter being paid for mental efficiency, not muscular force. The mind can expend in one hour as much nervous energy as the body would in five hours.

Let S represent the salary of an office worker, UT the useless time he spends, UF the useless fatigue he carries around with him, and P the profit to the company that hires him. Then here we have an efficiency formula, by which to measure his value:

$$S-(UT+UF)=P$$

The problem of first importance in any office is to make UT and UF as near zero as possible. A good way to start would be for somebody to count the steps taken by a "good business man" in his office during one whole day—without his awareness —then figure how a little head-work would save most of the foot-work, and present him with the tabulation. A general rule for subordinate employees holds to this effect: A good stenographer, a good office boy, and a set of mechanical devices will do the work of three ordinary stenographers, and do it better. I have applied this rule to my own office, where one $15 typist and a $5 boy have turned out as much work as three $10 typists formerly handled; the $10 weekly saving soon paid for the machines we bought, and one $15 clerk is usually a better investment than three $10 ones.

SPECIALISTS AND MACHINES

A pertinent example of the growing use of machines may be found in the art of bookkeeping, which is now performed chiefly by a moderate-priced man operating a few keys on a mechanical invention that will add, subtract, multiply and divide, compute interest, and do other interesting and necessary things more quickly and accurately than the human brain could. Also more cheaply, in the long run. The time is coming when all the work of an office will be divided between highly-skilled, highly-paid, specialists who plan, order and supervise, and a few low-priced workers who manipulate a large number of marvelous tools and instruments. Adding machines may now be had from $2.50 up. Mimeographs and multigraphs not only produce letters, blank forms, and other typewritten documents in ten-thousand lots, but also print your letter-heads, bill-heads, and advertising booklets. For a small business, a small duplicator guaranteed to re-

276

produce 1000 copies of a letter or other one-sheet manuscript may be purchased for little. Every growing business has a mailing list of customers or clients, actual and prospective; for the regular communications that should be sent these individuals a high-quality addressing machine will be found worthy of a trial—it should surpass the typewriter in speed, accuracy and economy, for the recurrent mailing of bills or announcements to the same list of names.

EFFICIENT TYPING

The typewriter of today is 300 per cent more efficient than the machine of fifteen years ago. It will be news to many office managers to learn that fifty special varieties of typewriter, each designed for a special use or line of business, are now manufactured; and to buy one without looking up the other forty-nine is to run the risk of losing a time-saver and money-saver. In both dictation and transcription, many short-cuts have been found. The dictating machine, properly worked, will save perhaps 20 per cent of the manager's time usually spent on dictation, and perhaps 30 per cent of the stenographer's time. A new method of fingering the typewriter is said to reduce the fatigue and double the daily output of the typist. One of the most revolutionary changes abolishes the whole scheme of shorthand hieroglyphics, prints on a small device the dictation notes in phonetic English characters, preserves the notes in legible form, and enables a lower-priced clerk to complete the transcription while the higher-priced one takes more dictation.

What is your corps of typists doing every day? What should they do? What can they do? Are they given a scientific daily schedule, to complete or surpass? These questions, applying also to every other clerk or official, seldom find the proper answer in an office. A leading typewriter company has evolved a system of cutting stenographic costs by measuring, facilitating and improving the daily output of the typewriter; some book on this line should be read and studied by every stenographer and every office manager; the probable saving would be 30 cents in every dollar spent for stenography and typewriting.

Regarding his equipment, schedule, training, methods and supplies, every office worker—manager as well as clerk—should ask himself these questions: "Have I borrowed my alleged system from my neighbor? Have I inherited it from my predecessor? Have I hit upon it by guess-

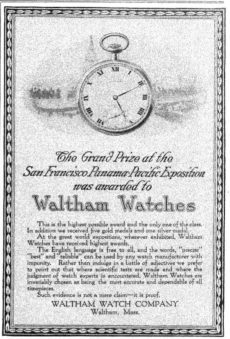

ing out of my own ignorant head?" If the honest reply to any of these queries is "Yes"—now is the time to wake up, look around, and get in line with progress. First rule in business: Remember that the biggest grows out of the best. The quantity of a man's work is fixt by the quality, hence every man may determine the size of his own future.

The difference between the president and the manager of a concern is that the president works a telescope and the manager a microscope. A few examples of managerial, microscopic, mastery of detail: Carbon paper that gives twenty clear copies; typewriter ribbon guaranteed for 75,000 clean impressions; typewriter cabinet with special drawers, files and racks, to hold all records and supplies needed by the operator; cushion pads to silence noise of typewriter; self-closing inkstand to prevent waste of ink, smearing and spilling; bottle for liquid paste with patent device to save daubing the fingers; waste paper baling machine, reducing fire risk and turning loss into profit; envelope opener and sealer; parcel sealer and labeler; stamp perforator; detacher and affixer; paper clips of diverse forms and sizes, to suit the best work of each, with clipping machine for permanent binding of loose sheets; rubber bands guaranteed not to break for five years; waste-basket solid, rustless, fire-resisting.

Under the heading *Safety and Sanitation* come various implements, inventions and precautions; such as the fire-proof filing cabinet, at least one being essential in every office; the check writer and protector, that makes forgery and check "raising" impossible; an economy expense book for each department, serving as an automatic guard against waste; patent ventilators in' all windows, permitting free access of pure air at all times without draught or discomfort; sanitary mouthpiece for telephone; sanitary moistener for stamps and envelopes; fit-the-back chairs for all sedentary workers; overhead electric lights carefully shaded, with a brilliant, hooded, portable and turnable drop light for each desk or table where close work, hard on the eyesight, is demanded; liquid soap; individual towels or paper towels; abundance of pure, soft, drinking water in a closed, sanitary container; individual glasses or paper drinking cups; teaching of health habits to employees, with assurance of regular and reliable examination by a physician.

LIGHT AND AIR—YOU NEED THEM

A primary factor in good office work is a large number of large windows, and the location of each desk so that a constant flood of light pours over the left shoulder of the worker. To avoid the glare of direct reflection, some office managers prefer window-shades hung at the bottom, which are raised to meet the angle of the sun. The color of walls and ceilings makes a pronounced difference in the illumination—the superior brands of white paint are said to increase daylight about twenty-five per cent, and of course the bills for artificial lighting are reduced, together with the costs of spoilage and accident, while more

<hr>

OFFICE EFFICIENCY TEST

FOR APPRAISING ANY OFFICE IN ITS USE OF MODERN METHODS

DIRECTIONS. If answer is Yes, write 4 in blank space at end of dotted line. If answer is No, or indeterminate, leave space blank. To find your percentage, add column of figures. Most of these questions, to be answered properly, demand supervision by an expert. Even then, the resulting grade will be only partial and approximate. If any point is not understood, consultation may be arranged with Mr. Purinton, care of Independent Efficiency Service, 119 West 40th Street, New York.

1. Is every operation standardized and recorded?..................................... ......
2. Are all desks, supplies, departments, arranged on a scientific "routing" plan? ....
3. Is all your buying done wholesale, on a comparative, competitive basis? ....
4. Have you adopted the best cost-finding, cost-keeping, and cost-cutting systems?..................... ......
5. Was each employee obtained, and assigned, according to reliable vocational tests?.................. ......
6. Has the formula S—(UT+UF)=P been applied to every employee? ....
7. Have you installed approved charting, filing and recording systems? ....
8. Are salaries and wages governed solely by quality and quantity of work done?....................... ......
9. Have you reduced stenographic and typewriting costs 30 per cent, relatively, from what they were a year ago? ....
10. Are machines, mechanical aids and electrical devices used wherever possible? ....
11. Are the heat, light, ventilation, drinking water, etc., approved by sanitation experts?............... ......
12. Have you answered pertinent advertisements in the best trade journals and business magazines—then studied the results? ....
13. Has every employee a daily schedule and memorandum pad to work by?............................ ......
14. Is the talk in your office the least and best possible?... ......
15. Can you yourself do as much in one hour as you formerly could in 3 hours?........................ ......
16. Is it your invariable rule to "satisfy the customer" at any cost? ....
17. Have your credit losses been reduced to zero?.. ......,
18. Do you maintain a business library of books and magazines chosen by experts, and do you instruct employees how to use it?... ......
19. Have you changed the "time-clock" penalty system to the time-stamp reward system? ....
20. Do you somehow make every employee a partner in the business? ....
21. Is the "continuation school" a part of your efficiency scheme? ....
22. Would every employee rather work for you on three-quarters pay than for any other concern on full pay? ....
23. Do you belong to a national efficiency organization? ....
24. Have you had your whole business analyzed by an efficiency engineer? ....
25. Are your net profits increasing every year?.. ......

Total equals your approximate grade in Office Efficiency.

work and better work is accomplished.

Health statistics recently compiled show that mental capacity and endurance relate not only to the supply of pure, fresh air in a room, but also to its circulation. If air partially breathed is kept moving, the minds and fingers of the workers act more swiftly and forcefully. A good custom is to ventilate the office completely at the noon hour, every day; and a wise experiment would be to use an electric fan at low speed, during the afternoon hours, even in the winter time. Currents of air generate currents of thought. Speaking of "currents" reminds us of electricity —one of the growing aids to office management. The old - fashioned "buzzer" is being replaced by an electric sign-system; when the manager wants a certain document or assistant, he presses a button and flashes a light of a certain color— presto, the paper or the person is beside him. And instead of giving roundabout orders to a particular department on a particular job, he gets the man directly on the wire from his own desk by the new inter-phone system of communication.

THINK

A good habit in an office—one to be highly recommended—is the habit of thinking. While unusual, this habit may be cultivated. For instance, have we compared in our work the economy and utility of wood pencils, paper pencils, and those of the metallic "propel" variety? Do we sharpen away 30 per cent of the lead without thinking? Do we pay ten cents for one pencil beautifully varnished and engraved —or three cents for one just as good if not so pretty, bought in gross lots? Have we figured the cost of producing our letter-heads by the four different methods—printing, lithographing, embossing, engraving? Lithographing, in large orders, may be cheaper than printing; while embossing is cheaper than engraving, and often serves as well. A glass desk pad is clean, attractive, expeditious; but if a man writes much, or signs his name to hundreds of letters and checks, a large blotter pad, with a dozen blotter sheets inserted, will save the man the usual fatigue of writing on a hard surface. A steel pen, a fountain pen or a glass pen— which is better for us? Every pen point should be temperamental, chosen to fit the user, according to the slant, curve and force of his handwriting. Much pen work in the average office will be found superfluous, and may be saved by a complete set of rubber stamps for routine records and labels, with a

Is Your Organization Running You?

Are your department heads and foremen continually at your elbow? Are you besieged by your subordinates with a thousand interruptions? Or, are you realizing full efficiency by an Inter-phone system? The best way to keep your organization on the job and save your time for your own executive work is with

Western Electric Inter-phones

Then you can get your man when YOU want him—without taking him away from his desk. In the Inter-phone system any station can talk direct to any other station. Any reliable electrician can put in the system. Built by the makers of all "Bell" telephones, and fully guaranteed.

Drop us a post card for booklet No. 42-BJ, "When Minutes Mean Money," and let us demonstrate what Inter-phones will save you in *your* business.

WESTERN ELECTRIC COMPANY
463 West Street, New York
Houses in All Principal Cities of the U. S. and Canada

rack for the stamps and the name of each lettered above its place. Another little thing of large effect is the proper use of the end-flap, open-seal envelope, with or without the "window" feature; in some lines of trade this envelope, carrying one-cent postage, has brought results that mean a saving of hundreds of dollars a year in postage alone.

Office management deserves a volume in itself; we can here but suggest a few points of recent development. The most vital principle we consider to be this: Change your "time-clock" for a time-stamp! The old idea of good workmanship was that a man should spend nine or ten or twelve hours on the job—then a "time-clock" was needed, to threaten the man with loss of pay if he didn't stick around. The new idea of good workmanship is that a man shall do the most and best possible, in the least time possible, with the least annoyance and fatigue possible—and now the time-stamp merely records what the man *does*, this alone being the reckoning of his pay. The value of a worker is not how much he is "on the job," but how much he is in the job. Certain things that formerly took me three days to accomplish I can now finish in three hours—I have learned to focus mind, body and soul on the thing I am doing.

STANDARDIZE YOUR OFFICE

We mentioned the time-stamp. Every act, order, and operation in a business office should be standardized, whether it be wrapping a bundle, typing a letter, posting an account, or entertaining a visitor. Each employee, from the manager down, should know in how short a time his work can be done effectively, and should keep a daily record until he forms the habit of equalling the standard of possible output. Here the machine called a "time recorder" will be found essential, to compute amount and cost of work. I have had a typist who could write with a flourish five letters on her machine while the girl next her barely had two letters finished. Why should they get the same salary? Promotions and rewards should follow not only a maximum record-breaking feat, but also a steady improvement over one's daily habit.

Here a caution should be noted. Often the most faithful clerk is the least rapid in his mental processes, and should not be reprimanded for lack of interest. When employees are chosen by the new vocation tests for physical, mental and temperamental fitness, both employer and employees gain immensely. To make a typist of a born executive, or a salesman of a born mechanic, is a fatal business blunder—and a frequent money loss. By alternating the positions of slow and fast workers, a total net gain is often reached, as the rapid clerks by spirit and example hasten the sluggards. Two girls who naturally gossip and chew gum should not be located alongside each other—granted that they belong in a business at all. When a worker has fully mastered his job, it may be well to segregate him, by a partition or otherwise, in order that lazy and foolish employees may not disturb him, and that he may have

a little time and space in which to prepare himself for greater advancement.

Many offices unwittingly employ a hidden corps of peculiar but highly efficient specialists. These persons are specialists in small talk and imitation conversation, and they begin to specialize whenever the "boss" goes out. Small talk is the kind that makes you feel small when somebody says you said it. Imitation conversation includes slang, bluff, boast, roast, raillery and gossip. A low and loose kind of talk in a business ends in a low profit and a loose credit. What about the speech in *your* office?

MAKE EVERY EMPLOYEE A PARTNER

The best way to eliminate friction and ensure satisfaction among the workers in any trade or profession is to adopt this rule: *Make every employee a partner in the business.* Whoever is not worth becoming a partner is not worth being an employee. How to engineer this radical move would require a long, technical discussion, and the yielding of certain adjustments and concessions on both sides, which are seldom granted without a full explanation of the principle and method of profit-sharing. We commend the subject to every business official, as worthy of deep study. The force in an "office force" is the force of attraction—not compulsion. To make the work attractive is to make the worker effective.

We pause, for lack of space. A thousand other items belong to good office management. We have not here presented the facts about filing systems; cost-finding, cost-keeping, and cost-reducing methods; advertising and salesmanship; office furniture and furnishings; books and magazines for an office library; health habits of all workers; training, education and promotion of employees; treatment of clients or customers; principles and policies of the management, with qualitative and quantitative measure of the product. These matters belong in the realm of the business counsel, or efficiency engineer, who should be consulted personally. A number of firms and institutions recommending or supplying efficiency engineers may be found in almost any large city, about seventy of these being located in New York. Some are very good—and very expensive. Others are quite good—and reasonable in price. A few are poor—and as costly as poor things always are. It is wise, before entering into contract with an efficiency engineer, to consult an impartial authority.

Next to ability and effort, the greatest thing in a man's vocation is Opportunity. Every office means concentrated opportunity. Here alone may every worker have direct touch with his fellow employees, with the heads of the business, with their patrons, and with their associates and friends in the entire commercial world. A man who does good work will be discovered sooner in an office than anywhere else. And Destiny waits for the man who is found quietly doing his best.

The New Books

CHINA AND JAPAN

While all eyes have been fixt upon
Europe little attention has been paid
to events in another part of the world
which will very likely affect the course
of history even more. In the opinion of Mr. Jefferson Jones, May 9,
1915, is a date of stupendous importance, for it marks "Japan's deathblow
to China and the passing of the oldest
nation in the world." In *The Fall of
Tsing-tau* he describes the siege of the
German city, of which he was the only
American civilian eye-witness, and discusses the demands subsequently made
upon China by Japan. He praises the
courtesy of the Japanese in their treatment of the Germans, but condemns
their conduct toward the Chinese as
treacherous and brutal. The crossing
of the Shantung peninsula by the Japanese troops to get at Tsing-tau was,
he says, a violation of territorial neutrality as much as that of the Germans
in Belgium, yet England did not utter
a word of protest against the conduct
of her ally. The Germans had made of
Tsing-tau "the finest, the prettiest, the
most modern and sanitary city in the
Orient" and it was becoming the most
popular part of China for residence
and business.

The Fall of Tsing-tau, by Jefferson Jones.
Houghton, Mifflin. $2.

THE NATION

The first issue of *The Nation*, projected by Mr. Godkin, with Wendell
Phillips Garrison as his associate,
marked an epoch in American journalism. Godkin was a young Englishman
with an ambition to create an American weekly equal to the British *Spectator,* and Mr. Garrison was a youth of
twenty-five, literary editor of The Independent, and son of the Abolitionist.
The time was ripe for such a venture,
for it was their aim to provide a weekly which should be utterly free from
partizan bias, absolutely fearless,
thoroly scholarly and represent the
highest idealism in politics and sociology. The third issue secured five thousand subscribers and for years it set
the standard of criticism for the country. In the historical volume, *Fifty
Years of American Idealism,* Mr. Pollak's account of this journal's career is
followed by selected editorials and book
reviews, every year being represented
by one or more. As we run them over
we recall the critical questions that
agitated the public and in none has this
paper done nobler work than in civil
service reform. There has never been
any question as to its position, which
has been exprest with plainness, with
avowed moral purpose and not a little

acerbity. Later *The Nation* was attached to the *Evening Post* and if its influence has been less of late years it is because its idealism has permeated journalism and civil service reform has been so far achieved.

In this respect its influence may be compared with that of Johns Hopkins University, which was unique in its day, but is so no longer. As Tennyson said,

"Most can raise the flowers now
For all have got the seed."

Fifty Years of American Idealism, by Gustav Pollak. Houghton, Mifflin. $2.50.

THREE SORTS OF WAR BOOKS

As war books flow from the presses, they may be thus classified: military, war correspondent, civilian. Sometimes one overlaps the other, as is the case in *War Pictures*, by Ian Malcolm, whose Red Cross work occasionally induces the military view, but what he writes of chief note is from the civilian outlook. Some personal intimacy with the German Imperial Family while an attaché at Berlin enables him to recount an informal interview with the Crown Prince; lay the blame for the war on that headstrong young man, together with the military party; absolve the Emperor from a wilful design to bring it about. He relates much about Thomas Atkins in France, and condemns those English "groups" without "spirituality or imagination" who seem utterly incapable of rising to the courageous optimism of the front.

With Our Army in Flanders, by G. Valentine Williams, "war correspondent," but not of the best. The newsgatherer tells too much of what he thinks, instead of what he sees. Cut to half the length the pith of the book might be apparent.

For those whom the doctor has positively forbidden the reading of war books, we can heartily recommend the Rev. E. J. Hardy's *The British Soldier*. With entire truth Mr. Hardy reveals the British soldier, from the view of a chaplain of the forces. His sub-title is Courage and Humour. He refrains from German abuse, and, in place of it, notes instances of chivalrous conduct on the part of his country's enemy.

For a description of what apparently the author did not witness, *The Undying Story*, by W. Douglas Newton, is well done. But his effort lacks the supreme quality of human feeling. He does not grasp the comradeship of arms; he has not heard with ears tuned rightly the singing of French and German national anthems as men go to their death; he seems not to know that deeds of chivalry and courage lie on both sides of the fighting line. Of such matters are composed the truly great war story. A brave soldier once wrote an undying work. It contains a panegyric on arms, worth re-reading as singularly modern in soldierly spirit. His name was Cervantes.

It is not until page 125 of *A Surgeon in Khaki* that the author, Arthur Anderson Martin, M.D., seems to realize what the reader expects from him. Marching, camping and fighting he

might have left to others, since when he does settle down to the surgeon's work in warfare his book becomes conspicuously informing. He describes the lack of organization in the British Medical Service, and difficulties of relieving the wounded without proper appliances. From personal observation he concludes that men over forty, with little previous physical training, can endure hardships at least as well as men much younger.

Stanley Washburn's second volume *In the Russian Campaign* begins with the Russian capture of Przemysl. At the outset, while mindful of subsequent events, he affirms his conviction of the final victory of Russian arms. This he believes because of the long enduring qualities of the Russian soldier, and the newly united pride of race felt by the Russian people. He notes a great national awakening to the consciousness that Russia at last marches forward to a worthy destiny. He emphasizes the fraternal relations between Russian officers and men, and quotes an American doctor in high praise of their stoical resistance when wounded.

Part ownership of the New York *World* has deprived that paper of Ralph Pulitzer's services as a first rate war correspondent. His little volume *Over the Front in an Aeroplane* gathers much interesting material, without even suggesting the manner of a text book. A graphic description of a flight to the firing line is followed by numerous scenes at the front, incidents of moment, and a curious explanation of how Von Kluck missed his chance of Paris. This is a book worth while slipping in your grip for a railway journey.

War Pictures, by Ian Malcolm. Dutton. $2. *With Our Army in Flanders,* by G. Valentine Williams. Longmans, Green. $3.50. *The British Soldier,* by E. J. Hardy. London: Fisher Unwin. *The Undying Story,* by W. Douglas Newton. Dutton. $1.55. *A Surgeon in Khaki,* by A. A. Martin, M.D. Longmans, Green. $3. *In the Russian Campaign,* by Stanley Washburn. Scribner. $2. *Over the Front in an Aeroplane,* by Ralph Pulitzer. Harper. $1.

THE PITTSBURGH SURVEY

Of the final two volumes of the report on the Pittsburgh Survey, *The Pittsburgh District* should properly precede the others. It contains three main parts: the Community, dealing with descriptive and historical matter; Civic Conditions, relating to housing, health, taxation and administration from the civic side; and Children and the City, with special chapters on the different child-welfare agencies.

The chief divisions of *Wage-earning Pittsburgh* deal with the Community and Workshop, Race Studies, Industry (kinds of occupations, wages, hours, conditions, factory inspection, industrial hygiene, child labor), and "The Reverse Side"—that is, the under side, beggars, prostitutes, yeggs, police problems and police opportunities.

Much of the material in these volumes has already appeared in magazines, special reports, and in papers before various gatherings. The tables, charts, maps and pictures, and the distinctively human and social tone set a standard for work of this kind. The mechanical side is of the same high quality that characterizes the other publications of the Russell Sage Foundation.

The Pittsburgh District; Wage Earning Pittsburgh. Survey Associates. $2.50 each.

OUR ISLAND PROTÉGÉE

Cuba Old and New is a somewhat discursive description and history of the island by A. G. Robinson, who has been familiar with it for nearly twenty years. The photographs by the same are rather better than the text.
Longmans, Green. $1.75.

LINCOLN

A very interesting collection of poems on the great President has been made by Osborn H. Oldroyd in *The Poet's Lincoln.* The illustrations are many and for the most part Lincoln portaits, which will give the book an especial value to those who cannot readily come at these pictures.
Washington, D. C.: O. H. Oldroyd. $1.

PEACE LITERATURE

All readers and debaters interested in the problems of the war and their possible solution should procure the bulletin on *Peace Literature of the War* sent free by the American Association for International Conciliation, New York. It contains a list of references to the best books and periodicals on the subject.

DITCHES, DERRICKS AND DREAMS

Sketches of the romance of industry and the human interest of manufacture give us, in impressionistic pictures, a new viewpoint of *America at Work,* a vision of the world significance of her labor and the glory of its achievement. Joseph Husband writes of industry as many men have written of war—as a spur to the imagination and a stirring call to an ideal.
Houghton, Mifflin. $1.

AMATEUR THEATRICALS

Constance d'Arcey Mackay has prepared a much needed practical handbook in stage craft. Simplicity and economy are kept in view thruout *Costume and Scenery for Amateurs.* There are descriptions of typical costumes, for different nationalities, epochs and callings, designs for simple scenery and furnishings and directions for an outdoor Greek stage.
Holt. $1.75.

MINE AND THINE

Dr. Healy, of the Psychopathic Institute, Juvenile Court, Chicago, in *Honesty,* records skillful analyses of instances of dishonesty in children showing the substitutions and sublimations involved. He is more effective in case records than in general exposition, but makes clear the complexity of apparently simple problems, the personal habit and social responsibility factors in acquiring this trait.
Indianapolis: Bobbs-Merrill. $1.

COLLEGIATE BOOK PLATES

The subject of institutional bookplates has been happily considered by Harry Parker Ward, in *Some American College Bookplates.* The strength of the volume lies, however, in its illustrative reproduction of many bookplates of the various colleges, some of which are in color. The admirable list of bookplate literature, and of the names and addresses of the leading bookplate designers, will be useful to amateurs and collectors.
Columbus, Ohio: Champlin Printing Co. $4.

THE STOICS

Prof. Gilbert Murray demonstrates his personal appeal by draping it about the great names of *The Stoic Philosophy,* and further negotiates successfully a precarious correlation of a system of thought with social conditions and human nature. But he cannot resist the temptation to drag in at the end his psychological anthropology, which even the fine poetry on a "Friend behind phenomena" who dwells "in the great spaces between the stars" will not excuse.
Putnam. 75 cents.

INDEPENDENT CORPORATION

The annual meeting of the stockholders of Independent Corporation, will be held at the office of the corporation, 119 West Fortieth street, Borough of Manhattan, City of New York, on Wednesday, February 23, 1916, at eleven o'clock in the forenoon for the election of directors and for the transaction of such further business as may properly come before the meeting.
By order of the Board of Directors.
FREDERIC D. DICKINSON, Secretary
Dated, New York, January 24, 1916.

DIVIDENDS

LIGGETT & MYERS TOBACCO CO.
St. Louis, Mo., February 2, 1916.
A quarterly dividend of three per cent. (3%) was this day declared upon the Common Stock of Liggett & Myers Tobacco Company, payable on March 1, 1916, to Common stockholders of record at the close of business on February 18, 1916. Checks will be mailed.
T. T. ANDERSON, Treasurer

LIGGETT & MYERS TOBACCO CO.
St. Louis, Mo., February 2, 1916.
The Transfer Books of the Preferred and Common stock of Liggett & Myers Tobacco Company will be closed at 3 o'clock P. M., on the 18th day of February, 1916, for the purposes of Common dividend this day declared and the Annual Meeting of the stockholders of the Company, to be held on the 13th day of March, 1916, and be reopened at 10 o'clock A. M., on the 14th day of March, 1916.
E. H. THURSTON, Secretary

NILES-BEMENT-POND COMPANY
New York, February 9, 1916.
The Board of Directors of NILES-BEMENT-POND COMPANY has this day declared the regular quarterly dividend of ONE AND ONE-HALF PER CENT. upon the PREFERRED STOCK of the Company, payable February 15, 1916.
The transfer books will close at 3 o'clock in the afternoon of February 9, 1916, and will reopen at 10 o'clock in the forenoon of February 16, 1916.
JOHN B. CORNELL, Treasurer

NILES-BEMENT-POND COMPANY
New York, February 9, 1916.
The Board of Directors of NILES-BEMENT-POND COMPANY has this day declared the regular quarterly dividend of ONE AND ONE-HALF PER CENT. upon the COMMON STOCK of the Company, payable March 21, 1916.
The transfer books will close at 3 o'clock in the afternoon of March 7, 1916, and will reopen at 10 o'clock in the forenoon of March 21, 1916.
JOHN B. CORNELL, Treasurer

The Market Place

THE NEW STEEL MERGER

When the Midvale Steel Company was bought last summer by William Ellis Corey, former president of the United States Steel Corporation, and a group of bankers and capitalists, it was understood that a new association of steel and munition companies was to be made. The new president of the company, Alvah C. Dinkey, had been president of the Carnegie Steel Company for several years. He resigned to become the head of the Midvale. In October the Midvale Steel and Ordnance Company, with an authorized capital of $100,000,000, was incorporated in Delaware. It took over the original Midvale company and acquired several smaller companies, the Coatesville Rolling Mill Company included. The Remington Arms Company, which has orders for 2,000,000 rifles, is a part of the new holding corporation, whose president is Mr. Corey, while Mr. Dinkey is vice-president. There is a very strong board, including Frank A. Vanderlip, president of the National City Bank; President Sabin, of the Guaranty Trust Company; President Wiggin, of the Chase National Bank; Percy A. Rockefeller, largely interested in the Union Metallic Cartridge Company and the Remington Company.

It became known last week that the new Midvale had bought control of the Cambria Steel Company, agreeing to pay $81 a share for its 900,000 shares of stock. This purchase followed the failure of negotiations for acquisition of the Lackawanna Steel Company and the Youngstown Sheet and Tube Company. Not long ago Dr. J. L. Replogle, for himself and others, bought from the Pennsylvania Railroad Company 240,000 Cambria shares at $60, and in the open market 110,000 more shares at about $70. It is understood that W. H. Donner, Cambria's president, had paid $50 a share to the railroad company for 112,000 shares. The profits of these buyers now exceed $9,000,000. To obtain the money which is to be paid for the Cambria stock the Midvale will issue $50,000,000 of twenty-year five per cent bonds and offer to stockholders at $60 a share $25,000,000 of its capital stock which is now in the treasury. The price in the curb market is about $69.

Some expect that the Lackawanna and Pennsylvania Steel companies will be brought into the association. Be-

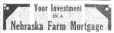

cause Mr. Rockefeller is on the board, there are predictions that the Colorado Fuel and Iron Company may come in. It is said that the Midvale, which has been making shells for the French Government, has orders enough to keep its works going at full capacity for the remainder of this year. The Remington Company has begun to make deliveries on its rifle contract. A few shares of the original Midvale Company were not bought by Mr. Corey and his associates, and 100 of them were sold at auction last week for $350 a share. The price paid by Mr. Corey is said to have been about $225. Acquisition of the Cambria gives to the Midvale control of valuable iron ore properties in the Lake Superior district. It is reported that thus far the Government has found no warrant for proceeding against the new association under the Anti-Trust law.

NATIONAL REVENUE

While the reduction of the value of our imports last year was not large, the customs revenue derived from those that were dutiable declined, on account of the war, from $283,700,000 to $205,800,000, according to a report issued recently by the Government. This loss of about $78,000,000, or 27½ per cent, must be taken into account in all plans for raising sufficient revenue for the Government's ordinary expenses, as well as for the proposed enlargement of the army and the navy. The average customs revenue for the last twenty years has been a little more than $257,000,000, and the highest point was reached in 1907, when the sum collected was $329,500,000.

This reduction, as well as the increase of expenses involved in the new defense projects, has had weight in leading the Administration to oppose removal of the present duty on sugar, which yielded $49,000,000 last year. The new special taxes on gasoline, automobiles, iron, steel and bank checks, proposed by President Wilson and Secretary McAdoo, have encountered formidable opposition on the Democratic side in Congress, where the party leaders now intend to obtain the needed additional revenue by increasing the income tax rate, without lowering the exemption limit, and by a tax on munitions.

Kansas spent $37,000,000 for motor cars last year.

The average price of finished steel products is now the highest in fifteen years, and forty per cent above the average for the year 1914.

Sales of copper at 27 cents were made last week, and an advance to 28 was expected. At 27 cents the price exceeds the previous high record, which was 26¼.

Annual reports of munition companies show how large last year's profits were. The Winchester Arms Company had net profits of $4,652,000 on a gross business of about $20,000,000. The Hercules Powder Company had net earnings of $4,992,000, against $1,434,000 in 1914, and the net of the Atlas Powder Company rose from $294,000 to $1,705,000.

The following dividends are announced: Liggett & Myers Tobacco Company, common, quarterly, 3 per cent, payable March 1. Niles-Bement-Pond Company, preferred, quarterly, 1¾ per cent, payable February 15; common, quarterly, 1½ per cent, payable March 21.

Insurance

Conducted by

W. E. UNDERWOOD

LOW-PRICED ACCIDENT POLICIES

This department is constantly in receipt of inquiries from readers respecting the value of certain low-priced accident policies offered by some companies. Sometimes I get the impression that my correspondents regard these contracts as equal in coverage to the policies for which $25 and $30 a year are charged, but are prompted to make inquiries because of the seeming great difference in prices, perhaps suspecting that the companies offering the cheaper forms are financially unreliable. This is an error. Different combinations of benefits are made and the premium charges conform—the smaller the charge, the less one gets. The lower priced policies have many exceptions, limitations and restrictions. There are many accident associations furnishing insurance at a comparatively low rate; sometimes their policies contain all the contract, but more often the latter is governed by the association's by-laws, copies of which insured members seldom possess, which can be, and not infrequently are, altered and amended without their knowledge. These associations render good service at the price paid—and that is the point—one gets what one pays for, not more nor less. The man who has some special policy at $5 or $6 a year is not warranted in assuming that he has the same quantity of protection as is furnished under a contract costing $25 a year. So with the coöperative association policies at from $9 to $12 a year. As I have frequently observed, there are no bargains in insurance.

J. H. K., Seattle, Wash.—Unless a parent is wholly or partially dependent on a child, he has no insurable interest in its life. Ordinarily the death of a child works no financial loss—aside from the expenses of burial—on a parent. Industrial insurance is designed to cover that expense, and that is its principal merit. While I cannot make a positive statement, there being so many companies now, I do not believe any company would issue a policy on the life of a dependent child for the amounts you name. Some companies issue endowments on young children, payable as such only if they survive the endowment period. These policies may be had without premium return or with premium return in case the child does not survive the period. As to paying industrial premiums annually or semi-annually instead of weekly, consult an agent of any of the companies you mention.

H. N. C., Pittsburgh, Pa.—Am indebted to you for information that the Standard Life Insurance Company of Pittsburgh writes a special policy for total abstainers. The Security Mutual of Binghamton, N. Y., and the Peoria Life of Peoria issue similar policies.

FACTS arguments, briefs for debates. Outlines, literary, historical, scientific and other material for club papers, orations, speeches and lectures. BUREAU OF RESEARCH, 318 E. 5th St., New Albany, Ind.

Journalism As An Aid To History Teaching

By Edwin E. Slosson, Ph. D.

Literary Editor of The Independent

Associate in the School of Journalism. Columbia University

This address, which was given before the History Section of the New York State Teachers' Association at Rochester, November 23, 1915, has been published in pamphlet form and will be furnished free to teachers—Write to W. W. Ferrin, 119 West 40th Street, New York.

HISTORY AND ENGLISH

WEEKLY LESSON PLAN FOR HISTORY, CIVICS AND ECONOMICS, BASED ON THE INDEPENDENT, FEBRUARY 14, 1916. PREPARED BY ARTHUR M. WOLFSON, PRINCIPAL OF THE JULIA RICHMAN HIGH SCHOOL, NEW YORK CITY.

AMERICAN HISTORY AND CIVICS

I. The Territorial Expansion of the United States.

A. Read (1) "Lower California," page 227.
B. Look up the acquisition of territory by the United States from 1783 to 1848.
C. Study the history of the negotiations which led to the treaty of Guadalupe Hidalgo (1848) and those which led to the Gadsden Purchase (1853).
D. Why was the "slave power" in favor of the acquisition of territory from Mexico? the New Englanders opposed to it?
E. Investigate the facts concerning the "Magdalena Bay Incident" and discuss the present movement toward the "rectification of our Mexican frontier" in the light of this incident.
F. Do you agree with the author of this article in his conclusions?

II. The Issue of Preparedness.

A. Look over your notes on "The Army and Navy of the United States," based on the issue of The Independent of Feb. 7th.
B. Read (1) "The President's Tour," pages 216-217.
(2) "The President's Speeches," "In Iowa, Kansas and Missouri," page 221.
C. What is the present size and equipment of the United States army and navy?
D. What are the various proposals offered for increasing the army and navy?
E. What are the reasons given by the president in his speeches for favoring a larger army and a larger navy? Are his reasons good?

III. The Philippine Government Bill.

A. Look over your notes on "The Philippine Islands and their Relation to the United States," based on the issue of The Independent of Feb. 7th.
B. Read (1) "Independence or Self Government," pages 217-218.
(2) "Philippine Independence," page 222.
C. What does the writer mean by the paragraph on page 218 beginning, "The peoples of Canada and Australia have self government without independence"?
D. Upon what facts does he base the statement: "The American Revolution had its origin in the intense conviction," etc.?
E. What are the provisions of the present "Philippine Bill"? What further steps are necessary if it is to become a law?

IV. The proposed Treaties with Colombia, Nicaragua, and Hayti.

A. Read (1) "Treaties Favorably Reported," page 222.
B. Read Article II., section 2, clause 2, of the Constitution.
C. Look up the history of the negotiations with Colombia in 1901-1903 and the Panama Revolution of 1903.
D. Look up the history of the proposed Isthmian canal by way of the Nicaraguan route.
E. In view of the fact that the United States already owns the Panama Canal, why do we propose to pay $3,000,000 for the exclusive right to construct a canal over the Nicaraguan route?
F. When and under what circumstances did "the powers of a financial protectorate" in Hayti begin?

V. Municipal Improvements in the United States.

A. Read (1) "The City of the Future," page 231.
B. How far has your city progressed toward the ideal described?
C. Give in detail the provisions which are made in your city for some three or four of the things indicated in the article.

EUROPEAN HISTORY

I. The Destruction of Commerce During a War.

A. Read (1) "The Arrival of the 'Appam'."
(2) "The Mysterious Raider,"
(3) "The 'Appam' Case," page 210.
B. What methods are legitimate under international law for destroying an enemy's commerce?
C. What method was legitimate during the Napoleonic Wars which is forbidden to civilized nations at the present time?
D. What rights has the vessel of a belligerent in a neutral port? Does the "Appam" come under this right?

II. European War in Asia.

A. Look up your notes on "The Interest of England and Russia in the Tigris Valley," based on the issue of The Independent of Feb. 7th.
B. Read (1) "The War in Asia," page 220.
C. Locate the places mentioned in the article on a map. Are the Russians and English advancing in their campaign?

ECONOMICS

I. Foreign Trade.

A. Read (1) "Our Great Foreign Trade," page 244.
B. What has caused the rapid change in the "balance of trade"?
C. What were the chief articles of export and import before the beginning of the war? What are they now?
D. What is the relation between the "gold movement" and foreign trade?
E. Study the figures given concerning the present trade with South America. Upon what does the future of this trade depend?

Teachers realize that they have not done their full duty when they have personally conducted their students down the well-beaten paths of History and Literature unless they have also shown them how to use the History and Literature of the future, which the newspapers and magazines will provide. The day when it was necessary to present extended arguments in favor of the use of a weekly magazine like The Independent in the teaching of Civics, Economics, History, and English has already passed. It is also decided in the minds of the majority that a weekly journal is far superior to the newspapers or monthly magazines for class room use. Several thousand teachers are agreed that there is no better medium for arousing interest in the social sciences, and no better laboratory material than The Independent presents. The human mind is stimulated by things which are immediate and familiar. Present day interest in the affairs of Europe, for example, is enormous. Thousands of copies of books, maps, and pictures are purchased each week. The reason for this interest is obvious. The task of the teacher is easy; all that he needs is a proper method of presenting the facts.

The Independent is already being used as laboratory material, but the laboratory manual has thus far been lacking and we propose in future to furnish such a manual each week. By means of the outlines, topics and references furnished, the teacher can easily make his assignments definite and exact.

We advise the teacher to allow two or three days to elapse between the assignment of topics and the class recitation in order that students may have adequate opportunity for study and thought. We advise him to check up results quite as carefully as though he were a teacher of Biology, Physics or Chemistry. Note book work in connection with laboratory exercises in Current Topics and English is quite as essential as it is in science. Haphazard, unprepared, discussions and unverified assertions about History, Economics, Civics or English are quite as vicious as guesses in physical sciences, and should not be allowed.

Hundreds of instructors have told us that The Independent has made their work more interesting and more fruitful. This new arrangement of mailing a lesson plan giving outlines, topics and references should make the work easier and still more interesting. We have printed on this page a sample set of these "lesson plans" based on the February 14th issue. These lesson plans are equally well adapted for the use of clubs and private classes for they make the study of current events more interesting and profitable, and greatly relieve the labor of the leader.

To secure a copy of either or both of these weekly lesson plans it is only necessary for you to use the coupon below and we shall gladly mail a copy each week without expense to you.

W. W. Ferrin, The Independent,
119 West 40th Street, New York:
Without cost to me, please mail each week your Lesson Plans for {English / History} as outlined above.
Name ....
School ....
City ....State ....

WEEKLY LESSON PLAN FOR ENGLISH, BASED ON THE INDEPENDENT, FEBRUARY 14, 1916, PREPARED BY FREDERICK HOUK LAW, HEAD OF THE ENGLISH DEPARTMENT, STUYVESANT HIGH SCHOOL, NEW YORK CITY.

Section I. The Story of the Week.

1. Write a story of imaginary adventures in connection with the capture of the "Appam" in the style of Jim Hawkins in *TREASURE ISLAND.*
2. Prepare an argument for or against the use of Zeppelins in war.
3. What is the plan of the article on The War in Asia?
4. What method has The Independent followed in reporting the series of speeches delivered by President Wilson?
5. Which article in The Story of the Week is the best written? Write a similar article concerning some school event.
6. Study the methods of condensation evident in the articles on page 224. Write a condensed article concerning an important school event.

Section II. Editorial Articles.

1. How does the article on The President's Tour, Page 216, differ from the article on The President's Speeches, Page 221? Write a brief of The President's Tour.
2. Study the article on Independence or self Government. Prepare a debate on the subject of Philippine Independence. See Page 234.
3. Point out the topic sentences in the article on The Non-Jewish Sabbath.

Section III. Shakespeare.

1. What reasons does the article, Three Hundred Years After, (Page 224) assign for Shakespeare's abiding popularity? What is the purpose of the article?
2. Write an outline of the article on Shakespeare the Man.
3. Give the principal facts in Shakespeare's life.
4. What does the article tell us concerning the personality of Shakespeare?
5. How did Shakespeare gain his education?
6. What was Shakespeare's attitude toward formal education?
7. What shows us that Shakespeare was a lover of music?
8. Explain the allusions to Romeo and Juliet, Macbeth, Othello, King Lear, Richard III, King John.
9. Since the quotations give the thoughts of characters in Shakespeare's plays, how can they be said to give Shakespeare's own thoughts?
10. In what sort of place was Shakespeare born?
11. What was the effect of his early surroundings?
12. Make a list of the plays referred to in this article. How many have you read? How many are now played on the stage?
13. What is Shakespeare's attitude toward nature?
14. Comment on Shakespeare's patriotism.
15. What types of humor are employed by him?
16. What is said of Shakespeare's sympathy?
17. Who was Ben Jonson? Why is his opinion valuable?
18. What is the moral effect of Shakespeare's plays?
19. In what ways is Shakespeare a philosopher?
20. Explain the various quotations in the article.
21. How does the article make you feel toward Shakespeare?
22. Ask your librarian for some of the books recommended for further reading.
23. Read some of the plays mentioned in this article.

Section IV. Leading Articles.

1. Point out unusually effective words in the article on Confessions of a Peace Pilgrim. Point out unusually effective sentences. Do you approve or disapprove of the paragraph structure? Why? How does the style differ from that of Old Winter in His Home? Which style do you prefer? Give reasons.
2. Point out various methods of exposition in the article on Lower California. How does the author prove that the acquisition of Lower California is necessary? Point out the course of thought-development in the article. Give an account of the life and work of Daniel Webster.
3. Comment on the introductory paragraph of the article on What Young Ireland Needs. What means does the author take to present his thought? What gives the article its peculiarly forceful effect?
4. Old Winter in His Home is an excellent example of essay writing. How does it differ from the article on Lower California? What is the spirit of the article? How does the author make his spirit appeal to us? Give the meanings of the following words: beaker, vagaries, shrewish, chic, puttees, looming, quondam, ignominy, mettle, Druid, fostering. Who is "Van Dyke" and what is the story of "The First Christmas Tree?" Tell the story of Loki and Baldur the Beautiful. Which is the best paragraph of the essay? Point out unusually effective adjectives. What words are used colloquially? What is their effect?

Section V. Poetry.

1. What is the thought of the poem called The Charge? What war does the poem concern? Why does the author use figurative language? What is meant by the words: "Truth again flung out her ensign before men?" Define the following words: grim, frenzied, cults, gore, ruthless, pinnacle, carnage, ensign.

Section VI. Miscellaneous Articles.

1. Make a careful study of the debate plans on Page 234. How many principal divisions are suggested? Point out methods of proof.
2. Which is the best written book-review? Write a review of a book you have read.
3. Write a description based on any picture in this number of The Independent.

The Independent

FOR SIXTY-SEVEN YEARS THE
FORWARD-LOOKING WEEKLY OF AMERICA

THE . CHAUTAUQUAN
Merged with The Independent June 1, 1914

FEBRUARY 28, 1916

OWNED AND PUBLISHED BY
THE INDEPENDENT CORPORATION, AT
119 WEST FORTIETH STREET, NEW YORK
WILLIAM B. HOWLAND, PRESIDENT
FREDERIC E. DICKINSON, TREASURER

WILLIAM HAYES WARD
HONORARY EDITOR

EDITOR: HAMILTON HOLT
ASSOCIATE EDITOR: HAROLD J. HOWLAND
LITERARY EDITOR: EDWIN E. SLOSSON

PUBLISHER: KARL V. S. HOWLAND

ONE YEAR, THREE DOLLARS

SINGLE COPIES, TEN CENTS

Postage to foreign countries in Universal Postal
Union, $1.75 a year extra; to Canada, $1 extra.
Instructions for renewal, discontinuance or
change of address should be sent two weeks
before the date they are to go into effect. Both
the old and the new address must be given.

We welcome contributions, but writers who
wish their articles returned, if not accepted,
should send a stamped and addrest envelope. No responsibility is assumed by The
Independent for the loss or non-return of
manuscripts, tho all due care will be exercised.

Entered at New York Post Office as Second
Class Matter

Copyright, 1916, by The Independent

Address all Communications to
THE INDEPENDENT
119 West Fortieth Street, New York

CONTENTS

JUST A WORD

The next issue of The Independent
—March 6—will be the Little Gardens
Number, with a colorful cover, suggestive of springtime. Experts on gardening will give practical advice to the
amateur on Planting Flowers and
Shrubs—What, Where and When, How
to Grow Vegetables in the Backyard,
and What Tools are the Most
Useful?

Readers of The Independent have enjoyed for some time the whimsical
humor of Edwin E. Slosson, which has
appeared at frequent intervals under
the title of "A Number of Things." Now
we plan to publish regularly the contributions of two other genial commentators on American life, one representative of New York City and the
other of the Western small town point
of view.

John Kendrick Bangs, the author of
A Houseboat on the Styx and fifty-five
other varieties of popular books, will
introduce the Genial Philosopher to our
readers in a delightful essay on his
novel theories for the utilization of one
of our greatest natural resources—
Noise.

Ed Howe (the Ed stands for both
Edgar and Editor) has spent fifty
years of his life in a printing office,
writing and publishing the gossipy
"human interest" news that people the
world over love to read. He has found
time, however, to write several books on
the side. His best known piece of
fiction, The Story of a Country Town,
was said by Mark Twain to be the best
American novel since The Scarlet Letter. His contribution to The Independent will appear in an early issue.

Each of these three page features
will be published once a month.

SCENERY OR SPEED?

The five-mile Canadian Pacific tunnel whose western portal, three miles
west of Glacier, is pictured on another
page, will cut four and a half miles out
of the main line and reduce the stretch
of maximum-grade track (2.2 feet in
the hundred) from 22.15 miles to 6.61.
But in so doing it eliminates two picturesque loops which have delighted
tourists, including the famous horse-
shoe from which the Great Illecillewaet
Glacier is visible.

A new method of construction has
made this a speedy piece of building.
A "pioneer bore," seven feet by nine,
was first put thru, paralleling the main
tunnel route. This carried pipes and
wires, and from side shafts run out of
this work was done on the large
bore at many points simultaneously.
The advance headings of the main
tunnel met in December. The tunnel
will be completed at the beginning of
1917, or possibly earlier. In the pioneer tunnel a world's record for hard-
rock boring, 932 feet in one month,
was made in January, 1915.

REMARKABLE REMARKS

W. H. TAFT—I shrink from seeing my
views in print.

KING CONSTANTINE—I have always
played safe.

COLONEL HOUSE—President Wilson is a
great man.

CLARK HOWELL—Bryan will not work
in double harness.

LINDLEY M. GARRISON—I shall not
make myself vocal.

LILLIAN RUSSELL—Life is one long
round of masquerading.

HENRY HOLT—It takes at least a year
to write a good novel.

EDWARD P. MITCHELL—The dodunk is
not extinct like the dodo.

CONGRESSMAN CARY—A "dry" national
capital would be a menace to society.

GEORGE ADE—You can lead a boy to
college, but you can't make him think.

DR. DAVID STARR JORDAN—A low-brow
is only one degree removed from a roughneck.

WOODROW WILSON—I hope every man
in public life will get what is coming to
him.

SENATOR JOHN SHARP WILLIAMS—The
British Empire will probably be wrecked
some day.

COMMISSIONER OF HEALTH EMERSON—
There were 3000 dog fights in New York
last year.

GENERAL LEONARD WOOD—This much I
know—our war will be with a power
of the first class.

ED. HOWE—We had eight guests for dinner Christmas day; not one of them got a
spot on the table cloth.

CONGRESSMAN MOORE—The panic of
1907 is the only thread that the Democrats
have to hang their hats on.

CONGRESSMAN "CYCLONE" DAVIS—Democrats rarely put up at anything higher
than two-dollar-a-day hotels.

ELIHU ROOT—The government which
shakes its fist first and its finger afterward,
falls into contempt.

REV. G. H. TOOP—The Protestant Episcopal Church is probably nearer to a deep
sundering split than ever before.

LAURA JEAN LIBBY—When the man
pops the question, be it in ever so slipshod
a manner, the girl is ready to give her
consent.

VOLUME 85   FEBRUARY 28, 1916   NUMBER 3508

THE KEYNOTE OF THE OPPOSITION

THE speech of Elihu Root as temporary chairman of the unofficial Republican Convention in New York State has every appearance of sounding the keynote for the approaching presidential campaign. It is a speech remarkable for its lucidity, its forcefulness and the restrained passion with which it arraigns the course of action of President Wilson and the Democratic party. The gravamen of the charge which Mr. Root brings to the President's door is the failure of the Administration's foreign policy. It concerns itself with two subjects—our course toward Mexico and our course toward the Great War

In both of these directions Mr. Root finds the President's policy to have been weak, vacillating and stultifying.

In the disturbed condition in Mexico when Mr. Wilson took office the duty of the President of the United States, says the former senior Senator from New York, was a double one. First, to use his powers as President to secure protection for the lives and property of Americans in Mexico; and, second, to respect the independence of Mexico and to refrain from all interference with its internal affairs.

President Wilson, in the belief of Mr. Root, failed to observe either of these duties. He interfered to aid one faction in civil strife against another; and he ignored and condoned the murder of American men and women, the rape of American women, and the destruction of American property. More than fifty American soldiers, in uniform, on duty, have been shot and killed and wounded across the border by soldiers belonging to one or another faction in the Mexican civil strife, and no attention has been paid to it by the American Government. While ignoring these assaults upon the rights to life and property of American citizens, the President has, in Mr. Root's view, made war upon Mexico, ostensibly to secure reparation for an insult to the American flag, but actually in order to support the faction in which Mr. Wilson believed against the man in power, whom Mr. Wilson adjudged to be a usurper. The results of this course of action, says Mr. Root, were most unfortunate. He adds in explanation:

If our Government had sent an armed force into Mexico to protect American life and honor we might have been opposed, but we should have been understood and respected by the people of Mexico, because they would have realized that we were acting within our international rights and performing a nation's duty for the protection of its own people; but when the President sent an armed force into Mexico to determine the Mexican presidential succession he created resentment and distrust of motives among all classes and sections of the American people.

. . . . .

Who can interfere in a quarrel and help some contestants and destroy others and then absolve himself from responsibility for the results? It is not by force of circumstances

over which we had no control, but largely because the American administration intervened by force to control the internal affairs of that country instead of asserting and maintaining American rights that we have been brought to our present pass of confusion and humiliation over Mexico.

This is the one great failure in foreign policy that Mr. Root charges against President Wilson. The other relates to our relations with the warring nations of Europe. In the President's conduct of these relations Mr. Root finds three fundamental errors:

First, the lack of foresight to make timely provision for backing up American diplomacy by actual or assured military or naval force;

Second, the forfeiture of the world's respect for our assertion of rights by pursuing the policy of making threats and failing to make them good;

Third, a loss of the moral forces of the civilized world thru failure to truly interpret to the world the spirit of the American democracy in its attitude toward the terrible events which accompanied the early stages of the war.

To put the matter concretely, Mr. Root believes, in the first place, that the President should have taken the lead in a movement for military and naval preparedness immediately upon the outbreak of the war, instead of waiting until an aroused public opinion had forced him to acquiesce in such a movement then already under way. He believes, in the second place, that the President should have acted more promptly, more forcefully, and more decisively in following up his original declaration to Germany that she would be held to a strict accountability for the destruction of American ships and lives by German submarines. In criticizing the course of Mr. Wilson in this regard, Mr. Root uses the picturesque language: "No man should draw a pistol who dares not shoot. The government that shakes its fist first and its finger afterward falls into contempt." In the third place he believes that the President should have protested solemnly and vigorously against the violation by the German arms of the neutrality of Belgium. His conception of the effect of such an action is set forth thus:

It was not necessary that the United States should go to war in defense of the violated law. A single official expression by the Government of the United States, a single sentence denying assent and recording disapproval of what Germany did in Belgium would have given to the people of America that leadership to which they were entitled in their earnest groping for the light.

It would have ranged behind American leadership the conscience and morality of the neutral world. It would have brought to American diplomacy the respect and strength of loyalty to a great cause.

This constitutes a strong indictment of the Wilson administration. Its utterance by Elihu Root in this impressive fashion is a significant sign of the direction in which the currents of thought in the national opposition are running. For it is precisely what Theodore Roosevelt has been saying with vigor for some time. Allowing for differences of temperament and of mental make-up the statements of their respective beliefs by the two arch antagonists of the Republican National Convention of 1912 are identical.

The two streams of Republican thought and membership which then and there violently diverged are running together again. There is every reason in the coming campaign to expect a unified opposition to the aspiration of the Democratic party for a continuance in power.

As The Independent has said before, such a united opposition will be a benefit to the nation. It is not good for the party in power, no matter which party it is, to be weakly and ineffectively opposed. It weakens its sense of responsibility, and tends to make it forgetful of its duty to the people. A fortiori, a flabby or divided opposition is a detriment to the interests of the country.

On the merits of Mr. Root's indictment, the case is not so clear. The Independent agrees with Mr. Root in his belief that the American people missed a great opportunity when their Government did not enter a solemn protest against the German violation of the neutrality of Belgium. As early as August, 1914, our special representative in Belgium, Major Seaman, in a cable article from Antwerp, urged the President to take the same action which Mr. Root now says he should have taken. It agrees with him that the controversy with Germany over the killing of Americans by submarine attacks—especially in the "Lusitania" case—could and should have been prest with more firmness and with greater insistence on a prompt and full compliance with American demands. It believes that the capture and evacuation of Vera Cruz was a series of mistakes, that Americans in Mexico have not been afforded the adequate protection to which they are entitled, and that the killing of fifty American soldiers on duty on American soil called for more drastic action than watchful waiting.

But we believe that the President, in bending every effort to keep the United States out of war, whether in this hemisphere or the other, was following the dominant desire of the American people. In trying faithfully to carry out that desire, Mr. Wilson has had a terribly difficult task to perform. He has kept us out of war thus far—except to the degree that the capture of Vera Cruz constituted an act of war. In so doing he has been compelled to make some sacrifices of American interests. Whether another man of different temperament and different mental equipment could have accomplished the same result with fewer sacrifices is an open question.

In the early months of the war the public opinion of the United States was emphatic in approval of the President's determination to keep this country out of war even at some sacrifice. Has this sentiment persisted? There are indications that it has changed and is changing. Mr. Root believes that it ought to make a complete about face. Only the result of the campaign will show how complete the change is to be.

THE NICARAGUA TREATY

THE Senate is to be congratulated upon its ratification of the treaty with Nicaragua by the handsome majority of 55 to 18. The House of Representatives, when called upon to do so, should pass without undue delay or debate the three million dollar appropriation which, according to the treaty, is to be expended "for the advancement of the welfare of Nicaragua" in such ways as our Government may approve. It is questionable if the House has a constitutional right to refuse to make any appropriation necessary for carrying out a treaty, and certainly it would be unwise to impede the passage of such a bill in these critical times.

The Nicaragua treaty is merely one more of the many efforts we have made in the last sixty-five years to rectify that most unfortunate blunder of American diplomacy, the Clayton-Bulwer treaty. If the new treaty is ratified we will be nearly, tho not quite, as well off as we were in 1849, when both Nicaragua and Honduras consented to cede to us the canal route and its terminal, Fonseca Bay. But before these treaties were ratified a British fleet sailed into Fonseca Bay and took possession of what we claimed as our property.

Since the British then held both sides of the isthmus of Nicaragua we were powerless to do anything without their consent, so we promised, by the Clayton-Bulwer treaty, to give them equal rights over any canal or railroad that we should construct at any time in the future across Nicaragua, Panama, Tehauntepec or anywhere else. It is this promise, carried over in an attenuated form into the Hay-Pauncefote treaty, that is bothering us yet whenever we want to settle canal tolls or arrange our difficulty with Colombia.

Another and even more serious embarrassment has resulted from the Clayton-Bulwer treaty. According to its provisions the United States was never to occupy, fortify, colonize or assume any dominion over any part of Central America, and at the same time the United States was required to acquiesce in all the British holdings and claims in Central America. Now, Great Britain had, by the treaty of Versailles in 1786, renounced all claims to sovereignty in Central America, and, as our Government repeatedly pointed out, her continued occupation of the Caribbean coast was in direct violation of this treaty. Nevertheless, Great Britain ignored our protests and holds Honduras to this day.

Personally, we Americans have no objection to the British holding Honduras. To be sure, she has no title to it, but then most land tenures are equally illegal when you go back far enough. The original title deeds to Manhattan Island are, we fear, not on file at the City Hall. The natives of Honduras are doubtless better off under British administration than if they were nominally free and independent. Our last attempt to dispossess the British was when we bombarded Greytown at the eastern end of the proposed Nicaragua canal. Our feeling toward Great Britain has become, on account of our sympathy with her side in the war, more friendly than it has ever been since the Revolution, and it would be absurd to suppose that we should now or in the future revive our old contention against the British occupation of Honduras. We are never likely to submit to The Hague Court or to "the dread arbitrament of war" the unsolved question on which the British claim in its origin depended: whether it was a crown or a cocked hat which Charles II gave to Oldman, chief of the Mosquito Indians.

But the question of the British claim to Honduras and our acquiescence in it has a present interest in that it is claimed by some to invalidate the Monroe Doctrine. When we talk of the Monroe Doctrine to our Latin-American friends they are apt to reply: "The Monroe Doctrine no longer exists. It was abrogated in 1850 by the Clayton-Bulwer treaty, when Great Britain was permitted to extend her colonial possessions in Central America."

It is not easy to meet this Latin-American argument,

especially since the British Government seemed to take the same view of it, for four years after the conclusion of that treaty Lord Clarendon, the British Foreign Minister, declared that Great Britain did not recognize the Monroe Doctrine as international law. Doubtless it is just as well to let it go at that and regard the Monroe Doctrine as merely our own national policy, which we have pursued with tolerable persistency for many years and seem likely to continue indefinitely.

If we so regard it we need not care whether the Clayton-Bulwer treaty was a violation of it or not. But at any rate the Clayton-Bulwer treaty got us into a terrible tangle from which the new Nicaragua treaty will help to extricate us.

THE NOMINATION OF MR. BRANDEIS

THE subcommittee of the Senate has been hearing testimony all the week for and against the confirmation of Mr. Brandeis to the Supreme Court. This is as it should be. If Mr. Brandeis, for any reason, is unfitted to occupy the exalted office to which the President has nominated him, now is the time to know it. If, on the other hand, the charges against him are without real foundation, as we firmly believe, then his name will be cleared once and for all. Reports from Washington now indicate that the opposition in the Senate is crumbling. This gives us no surprize, for the adverse testimony so far given is based more on hearsay than on direct evidence. On the other hand, there is abundant personal testimony to his integrity as well as to his judicial temperament. We trust that the Senate will confirm the nomination without delay.

A MISTAKE IN CHEMISTRY

IT was such a little mistake. A critical teacher might mark it "five off" on a chemistry quiz. But a little mistake made by big people may be a big blunder. It all happened because the British Government is composed of able lawyers, metaphysicians, authors, military men and gentlemen of leisure, but not a scientist among them. Oxford seven, Cambridge six, scattering seven, so the cabinet stands—quite the usual and proper thing, according to British traditions, except that the unsettled state of politics necessitated the admission to this inner circle of an unusual number of men from scrub colleges or from no college at all, like Kitchener and Lloyd-George.

Upon these distinguished gentlemen, none of whose hands had ever been soiled with soot or stained with nitric acid, was unexpectedly thrust the unpleasant duty of making war upon a people quite exceptionally proficient in chemistry. They undertook to cut off from the enemy all materials necessary for munition and nutrition.

Now, the smokeless powder and high explosives which have revolutionized warfare are mostly made from cotton and glycerine by the action of nitric acid. On account of the demand for munitions the price of glycerine jumped from fifteen to fifty-five cents a pound. Since cotton was chiefly used in England for the manufacture of cloth it does not seem to have occurred to the British Ministers that the wicked Germans were using it extensively for nefarious purposes. The chemists of England, not being represented in the Government, had to organize mass meetings and write letters to the papers to persuade the Government to put an embargo on the importation of cotton into Germany.

Glycerine was, of course, put on the contraband list. So were all fats and oils used for food. But what reason could there be for shutting out soap fats? If "the Huns" wanted to adopt the Englishman's "bawth" would it not be wrong to hinder them? But when the trade reports of the first year of war came in it appeared that the Germans had taken to the use of soap to an astonishing extent. Fish oils, copra, rancid fats, all sorts of stuff good for nothing but soap and axle grease were being imported in large quantities from Holland and Scandinavia. The Cabinet then looked into the matter and discovered to their surprize that glycerine is a by-product of soap making.

So finally His Majesty's Ministers perceived that the Germans had been taking an unfair advantage of their ignorance of chemistry and the Attorney General, Sir John Simon, gravely stated to the Commons that, since it had "recently been discovered" that glycerine could be obtained from fat, the importation by Germany even of inedible fats would be henceforth prevented. If a speaker in Parliament uses a false quantity in a Latin quotation he gets a general ha-ha, but nobody cracked a smile when the Attorney General announced as "a recent discovery" an experiment which was first performed by Scheele in 1779 and included in the list of exercizes for pupils in elementary science. Of course, cabinet ministers cannot be expected to know everything, but the lack of somebody about the shop who knew that handy bit of information must have cost the Allies many thousand lives.

In consequence of this and similar humiliating blunders during the war the leading scientific men of England have organized a committee to effect a revolution of the educational system of the country by overthrowing the monopoly of the classics and admitting science to an equal footing. They point out that Sandhurst, the British West Point, "is probably the only military institution in Europe where science is not included in the curriculum." In the navy some knowledge of science is expected, but not in the army. Now, the British navy has driven its foes from the sea, but the British army has nowhere achieved a signal success in eighteen months of war.

But even with these terrible lessons in view the reformers do not seem likely to succeed. To overthrow the classics is as difficult as to overthrow the monarchy. In fact, they are regarded as much the same thing. The leading speaker before a session of the British classical association held since the war began brought forward as one of the chief arguments for the present system that the study of the classics proves the impracticability of republics, and so strengthens the monarchy. The same view is held in Russia, where science is excluded or minimized in the schools because of its supposed democratic tendencies.

But the classicists have another argument; namely, that science is a dangerous thing, for see what it has made of the Germans! As one of them puts it in the London Times: "A lover of 'the humanities' might, perhaps, urge that 'science' when put to service of the devil —Milton's Satan has a Teutonic delight in explosives— is today working more human misery than was ever wrought by pedants and the Latin grammar." Evidently the British scientists made a mistake in tact when they held up Germany as a model for their educational reform. In the sixteenth century, when England refused to adopt the reformed calendar of Gregory XIII, it was wittily said that the English would rather disagree with the solar system than agree with the Pope. So now it appears that they are inclined to take pride in their neglect of what has been called "a German science." But somebody should remind the classicists of *Fas est et ab hoste doceri.*

MAKING ALIENS INTO CITIZENS

WE have a way of doing things in America "when we think of them," and our thinking is spasmodic. The method leaves much to be desired. It cannot be described as businesslike. It offers a sharp contrast, for example, to those well-considered, planned-ahead programs and day-by-day ploddings according to schedule, which we are beginning to associate with the word "efficiency."

Naturally enough, our habit of thinking about things when something excites us, and then working at them furiously until we get interested in something else, has been made worse and more absurd by the onset of new dangers, interests and responsibilities let loose by the upheaval in Europe. We ought to have been busy with a rational scheme of preparedness twenty years ago. It ought to have been firmly advanced toward realization ten years ago. It should have included educational, commercial and industrial preparedness, and a vast amount of preparedness in social efficiency, as well as preparedness of the military and naval sort. Now, we are jumping into the business much as a lot of respectable villagers in pajamas jump into amateur fire-fighting when a midnight conflagration breaks out. That we shall do the thing in the wrong way, in the most wasteful way, and get a minimum result, is a safe bet, with odds 90 to 10. In like manner, there is every indication that we shall deal emotionally, thoughtlessly and more or less ridiculously with the practical problem of converting our millions of unnaturalized aliens into Americanized American citizens.

aliens in America wo ld not take the trouble to learn our language must inevitably suffer in mind and estate. He should be told that his chances of economic betterment will greatly improve if in good faith he takes steps to become a citizen. Lawyers may properly give preference and precedence to citizens: it is sound policy from every point of view—political and economic.

All this, however, a different thing from "drawing the line" at the alien. Drawing the line and bringing pressure to bear are confounded only by men who do not make a practice of thinking their problems thru. Drawing the line is hasty action, it is ill considered. it cannot be lived up to, and when its impossibility becomes manifest it is abandoned and everything goes back to the old *laisse-faire* indifference. Bringing pressure to bear is a businesslike, day-by-day proceeding. It demands knowledge, science, adjustment, adaptation of means to ends. Not until short of persistent, patiently applied pressure will convert our alien population into American citizens that are Americanized in heart and mind, and not in name only.

We are thoroly in sympathy with the demand for Americanization. As a people we are a mechanical mixture of incongruous elements, and it will be generations before we shall become a consistent blend of the good qualities that exist potentially in our alien nationalities. We firmly believe that a well-considered, broadly planned, persistent effort should be made by patriotic Americans in every part of the country to further the work of assimilation and blending. We cannot expect to be an efficient nation, a nation with a mind of its own, formulating and maintaining great policies and respected by the world, unless we become more homogeneous and united than we now are. But let us have done with spasms and fads. Let us look at our task like grown up, reasoning men, and tackle it in a businesslike way.

MUSIC OR MOVIES?

IT was bound to happen. You cannot mix movies and opera with impunity. It's like expecting Bryan and Boadicea to live happily together. In the movies you act as much as possible, to the accompaniment of music. In the opera you act as little as possible, also to the accompaniment of music.

Mrs. Lou-Tellegen otherwise Geraldine Farrar, has been doing Carmen for the movies. Last week she did Carmen at the Metropolitan for the first time after her sojourn with strange gods, and her performance set the critics' tongues to wagging furiously. She not only introduced "a lively wrestling bout in which she threw her opponent easily and had all but succeeded in plucking out handfuls of her air when the rude soldiers intervened," but, according to gossip, slapped Caruso's face and clung to him so violently that he was obliged to pinion her in order to be able to sing, and half threw her to the floor when he had finished. Then, in the wings, he inquired, with all the hauteur of which a million-dollar throat (or is it a billon?) is capable: "Do you think this is an opera house, or a cinema?"

There is the question flung in the face of operatic art. Shall opera be cinemized? For ourselves, we say Amen. If every impresario sent his singers to school to the movies there might be a spice of ginger in the wooden lovers and mollycodie fighting men that cumber the boards today.

THE STORY OF THE WEEK

The Caucasian Campaign — The most signal victory of the Russians in Asia since the war began is the capture of the Turkish stronghold of Erzerum. There are two remarkable things about it; first, that Erzerum was not taken a year ago, and, second, that it should have been taken now. When the war between Russia and Turkey began in November, 1914, it was generally expected that Erzerum would soon fall into the hands of the invaders; in fact there were rumors that they had captured it. It lies only fifty miles from the frontier of the Russian Transcaucasian province and the Russians had years before prepared for an advance in this direction by running a military railroad from the fortress of Kars to Sarikamish, on the frontier directly opposite Erzerum.

The Turks tried to forestall the Russian invasion by taking the initiative and seizing the railroad. But they were severely defeated at Sarikamish and thrown back into their own country. The Russians pursued the fleeing troops to the chain of forts in front of Erzerum, but there they stopped and made no serious effort to break the barrier, altho it was then feebly fortified and ill-prepared for defense. A vigorous attack would probably have carried it, but at that time the Russians needed all their men and more munitions to check the German invasion of Poland. It was supposed in 1914 that the war would be decided in Europe and neither side took much interest in Asia.

Now it is felt to be different. On all the European fronts, Belgium, France, Italy, Galicia, Greece and Russia, the armies of both sides occupy entrenched positions which it seems impossible to break thru. Albania is the only European field where the war has not settled down into a state of siege. So attention is being directed toward Asia and Africa, where large territorial gains are still attainable. In Africa the French and British have completed the occupation of German Kamerun, and the British have undertaken the conquest of German East Africa. In Asia joint operations against the Turks are being conducted from three points; the British northward from the Persian Gulf, the Russians southward from the Caspian and the Caucasus.

Last fall, when the Grand Duke Nicholas was removed from the supreme command of the Russian armies and sent to the Caucasus, it was commonly supposed that this meant banishment in disgrace for his failure to save Poland. But now it seems rather as he was being given an opportunity to retrieve his reputation by conducting the most important campaign of the winter. At any rate that is what he has done, for his swift advance and speedy capture of Erzerum is a brilliant feat of arms, comparable to his Galician campaign of a year ago when he captured Przemysl and stormed the crest of the Carpathians. In fact the Russians seem to fight best in cold weather. Erzerum was captured when the mercury was thirty degrees below zero and the mountain passes filled with snow.

To Capture Erzerum — The news of the fall of Erzerum was as much of a surprise to the outside world as the fall of Namur and Antwerp at the beginning of the war. It, of course, anticipated that the place would eventually succumb to the Russian attack. The old adage, "a city beged is a city taken," was never so true as today. These antiquated forts could not be expected to withstand the heavy artillery which the Russians succeeded in bringing thru the mountains. But on the other hand the Turks had had a year in which to prepare for the Russian attack with the assistance of German engineers and under the direction of one of the most renowned of contemporary strategists, Field Marshal von der Goltz. The chain of forts which had been erected before the war for the protection of Erzerum against the Russians extended from fifteen miles north to five miles south of the city. They were garrisoned, it is said, by four army corps of Turkish troops, amounting to more than 100,000 men. Provisions and munitions for a long siege had been laid in. According to the Petrograd report, which is the sole source of information, there were 467 guns in the outer forts, 374 in the central forts and 200 field guns. Most of these arms and supplies were taken intact by the Russians, for the Turks appear to have given up all hope of holding Erzerum as soon as the outer forts fell, and to have confined their efforts to getting the troops safely away. This they seem to have accomplished, for the early report that the Russians captured 100,000 or 40,000 Turks in Erzerum was later discredited. Such prisoners as the Russians took were either the small garrison left in the inner forts as a rearguard or the regiments they overtook in following up the retreat.

The Russian attack was carried out by three columns directed at the northern, central and southern forts of the chain. On January 29, after a brief bombardment, the most distant of the Erzerum forts, Kara Gobek, eighteen miles northeast of the city, was carried by assault. On the following night Fort Tafta, twelve miles out in this direction, was stormed. The forts on the Palandoken mountains, southeast of

THE CAPTURE OF ERZERUM

The Russian Army of the Caucasus has taken Erzerum, the chief Turkish stronghold on the eastern front. Being relieved from danger in this quarter the Russians may move on southward from Lake Van and rescue the British, who are besieged at Kut-el-Amara

held up Germany as a model for their educational reform. In the sixteenth century, when England refused to adopt the reformed calendar of Gregory XIII, it was wittily said that the English would rather disagree with the solar system than agree with the Pope. So now it appears that they are inclined to take pride in their neglect of what has been called "a German science." But somebody should remind the classicists of *Fas est et ab hoste doceri.*

MAKING ALIENS INTO CITIZENS

WE have a way of doing things in America "when we think of them," and our thinking is spasmodic. The method leaves much to be desired. It cannot be described as businesslike. It offers a sharp contrast, for example, to those well-considered, planned-ahead programs and day-by-day ploddings according to schedule, which we are beginning to associate with the word "efficiency."

Naturally enough, our habit of thinking about things when something excites us, and then working at them furiously until we get interested in something else, has been made worse and more absurd by the onset of new dangers, interests and responsibilities let loose by the upheaval in Europe. We ought to have been busy with a rational scheme of preparedness twenty years ago. It ought to have been well advanced toward realization ten years ago. It should have included educational, commercial and industrial preparedness, and a vast amount of preparedness in social efficiency, as well as preparedness of the military and naval sort. Now, we are jumping into the business much as a lot of respectable villagers in pajamas jump into amateur fire-fighting when a midnight conflagration breaks out. That we shall do the thing in the wrong way, in the most wasteful way, and get a minimum result, is a safe bet, with odds 90 to 10. In like manner, there is every indication that we shall deal emotionally, thoughtlessly and more or less ridiculously with the practical problem of converting our millions of unnaturalized aliens into Americanized American citizens.

A generation has gone by since our attention was called to the importance of assimilation in its relation to naturalization, and of naturalization in its relation to political solidarity, by such events as the Sand Lots disturbances in San Francisco, the ill feeling over the attempted substitution of German for English in Wisconsin public schools, and the killing of unnaturalized Italians in New Orleans, which made us beholden to Italy. But nothing deserving to be called thought-out and systematic effort has been attempted. We have drifted along in our happy-go-lucky fashion, until now, with the zeal of camp-meeting converts, we throw ourselves into a feverish campaign of Americanization.

Of course we shall commit all the excesses of virtue unrestrained by common sense. We shall forget that assimilation is not a machine-made product. Assimilation takes time, and it cannot be hurried. And we shall not only be foolish, we shall be unjust.

Pressure of various kinds should be applied in a great variety of ways to the alien. He should be compelled to choose between American citizenship and certain real disabilities and hardships. He should be made to understand that our hospitality is hospitality, and not largesse. He should be assisted to discover quickly that

aliens in America who do not take the trouble to learn our language must inevitably suffer in mind and estate. He should be told that his chances of economic betterment will greatly improve if in good faith he takes steps to become a citizen. Employers may properly give preference and precedence to citizens; it is sound policy from every point of view—political and economic.

All this, however, is a different thing from "drawing the line" at the alien. Drawing the line and bringing pressure to bear are confounded only by men who do not make a practice of thinking their problems thru. Drawing the line is a hasty action, it is ill considered, it cannot be lived up to, and when its impossibility becomes manifest it is abandoned and everything goes back to the old *laissez-faire* indifference. Bringing pressure to bear is a businesslike, day-by-day proceeding. It demands knowledge, patience, adjustment, adaptation of means to ends. Nothing short of persistent, patiently applied pressure will convert our alien population into American citizens that are Americanized in heart and mind, and not in name only.

We are thoroly in sympathy with the demand for Americanization. As a people we are a mechanical mixture of incongruous elements, and it will be generations before we shall become a consistent blend of the good qualities that exist potentially in our alien nationalities. We firmly believe that well-considered, broadly planned, persistent effort should be made by patriotic Americans in every part of the country to further the work of assimilation and blending. We cannot expect to be an efficient nation, a nation with a mind of its own, formulating and maintaining great policies and respected by the world, unless we become more homogeneous and united than we now are. But let us have done with spasms and fads. Let us look at our task like grown up, reasoning men, and handle it in a businesslike way.

MUSIC OR MOVIES?

IT was bound to happen. You cannot mix movies and opera with impunity. It's like expecting Bryan and Boadicea to live happily together. In the movies you act as much as possible, to the accompaniment of music. In the opera you act as little as possible, also to the accompaniment of music.

Mrs. Lou-Tellegen, otherwise Geraldine Farrar, has been doing Carmen for the movies. Last week she did Carmen at the Metropolitan for the first time after her sojourn with strange gods, and her performance set the critics' tongues to wagging furiously. She not only introduced "a lively wrestling bout in which she threw her opponent easily and had all but succeeded in plucking out handfuls of her hair when the rude soldiers intervened," but, according to gossip, slapped Caruso's face and clung to him so violently that he was obliged to pinion her in order to be able to sing, and half threw her to the floor when he had finished. Then, in the wings, he inquired, with all the hauteur of which a million-dollar throat (or is it a billion?) is capable: "Do you think this is an opera house, or a cinema?"

There is the question flung in the face of operatic art. Shall opera be cinematized? For ourselves, we say Amen. If every impresario sent his singers to school to the movies there might be a spice of ginger in the wooden lovers and mollycoddle fighting men that cumber the boards today.

THE STORY OF THE WEEK

The Caucasian Campaign The most signal victory of the Russians in Asia since the war began is the capture of the Turkish stronghold of Erzerum. There are two remarkable things about it; first, that Erzerum was not taken a year ago, and, second, that it should have been taken now. When the war between Russia and Turkey began in November, 1914, it was generally expected that Erzerum would soon fall into the hands of the invaders; in fact there were rumors that they had captured it. It lies only fifty miles from the frontier of the Russian Transcaucasian province and the Russians had years before prepared for an advance in this direction by running a military railroad from the fortress of Kars to Sarikamish, on the frontier directly opposite Erzerum.

The Turks tried to forestall the Russian invasion by taking the initiative and seizing the railroad. But they were severely defeated at Sarikamish, and thrown back into their own country. The Russians pursued the fleeing troops to the chain of forts in front of Erzerum, but there they stopped and made no serious effort to break the barrier, altho it was then feebly fortified and ill-prepared for defense. A vigorous attack would probably have carried it, but at that time the Russians needed all their men and more munitions to check the German invasion of Poland. It was supposed in 1914 that the war would be decided in Europe and neither side took much interest in Asia.

Now it is felt to be different. On all the European fronts, Belgium, France, Italy, Galicia, Greece and Russia, the armies of both sides occupy entrenched positions which it seems impossible to break thru. Albania is the only European field where the war has not settled down into a state of siege. So attention is being directed toward Asia and Africa, where large territorial gains are still attainable. In Africa the French and British have completed the occupation of German Kamerun, and the British have undertaken the conquest of German East Africa. In Asia joint operations against the Turks are being conducted from three points; the British northward from the Persian Gulf, the Russians southward from the Caspian and the Caucasus.

Last fall, when the Grand Duke Nicholas was removed from the supreme command of the Russian armies and sent to the Caucasus, it was commonly supposed that this meant banishment in disgrace because of his failure to save Poland. But now it seems rather that he was being given an opportunity to retrieve his reputation by conducting the most important campaign of the winter. At any rate that is what he has done, for his swift advance and speedy capture of Erzerum is a brilliant feat of arms, comparable to his Galician campaign of a year ago when he captured Przemysl and stormed the crest of the Carpathians. In fact this, like the Galician campaign, was fought best in cold weather. Erzerum was captured when the mercury was thirty degrees below zero and the mountain passes filled with snow.

The Capture of Erzerum The news of the fall of Erzerum was as much of a surprize to the outside world as the fall of Namur and Antwerp at the beginning of the war. It was, of course, anticipated that the place would eventually succumb to the Russian attack. The old adage, "a city besieged is a city taken," was never so true as today. These antiquated forts could not be expected to withstand the heavy artillery which the Russians succeeded in bringing thru the mountains. But on the other hand the Turks had had a year in which to prepare for the Russian attack with the assistance of German engineers and under the direction of one of the most renowned of contemporary strategists, Field Marshal von der Goltz. The chain of forts which had been erected before the war for the protection of Erzerum against the Russians extended from fifteen miles north to five miles south of the city. They were garrisoned, it is said, by four army corps of Turkish troops, amounting to more than 100,000 men. Provisions and munitions for a long siege had been laid in. According to the Petrograd report, which is the sole source of information, there were 467 guns in the outer forts, 374 in the central forts and 200 field guns. Most of these arms and supplies were taken intact by the Russians, for the Turks appear to have given up all hope of holding Erzerum as soon as the outer forts fell, and to have confined their efforts to getting the troops safely away. This they seem to have accomplished, for the early report that the Russians captured 100,000 or 40,000 Turks in Erzerum was later discredited. Such prisoners as the Russians took were either the small garrison left in the inner forts as a rearguard or the regiments they overtook in following up the retreat.

The Russian attack was carried out by three columns directed at the northern, central and southern forts of the chain. On January 29, after a brief bombardment, the most distant of the Erzerum forts, Kara Gobek, eighteen miles northeast of the city, was carried by assault. On the following night Fort Tafta, twelve miles out in this direction, was stormed. The forts on the Palandoken mountains, southeast of

THE CAPTURE OF ERZERUM

The Russian Army of the Caucasus has taken Erzerum, the chief Turkish stronghold on the eastern front. Being relieved from danger in this quarter the Russians may move on southward from Lake Van and rescue the British, who are besieged at Kut-el-Amara.

the city, were enveloped and taken in the same way, and the frontal attacks were equally successful. The Turkish commandant, Ekved Pevzi Pasha, then began the evacuation of the city, which was accomplished before the inner chain of forts were taken.

The Effect of the Russian Victory The situation has been decidedly altered by the capture of Erzerum, because this was the only stronghold in eastern Turkey. Doubtless the retreating Turks can make a stand in the mountains to the west, but there is no reason why the Russians should attempt to pursue them further in this direction when there are more promising fields to the north and south. Only a hundred miles northwest of Erzerum is the ancient city of Trebizond, where Xenophon's Greeks first saw the sea. This has several times been bombarded by the Russian warships and now a landing has been made about fifteen miles to the east. With this port once in their possession the Russians will have as secure a hold on the southern littoral of the Black Sea as they have on the northern and eastern. There seems little chance of the Turks retaking Erzerum, for it is over six hundred miles from Constantinople and there are no railroads leading toward it, while the Russians have the railroad from Kars coming within eighty miles on the northeast and are likely soon to have the port of Trebizond on the northwest.

Twice before, in 1828 and 1878, the Russians took Erzerum from the Turks and both times they were forced by Great Britain to restore it. This time, being allied with Great Britain, Russia will doubtless hold it unless the Allies are defeated. The extension of Russian sovereignty over this territory would mean the suppression of the American schools, hospitals and churches unless Russia could be compelled to change her historic policy for one of toleration. All thru this part of Armenia American missionaries, doctors and teachers have been active for many years. In Erzerum there is a school for boys and another for girls. The American Board

had five stationed there, the Reverend Robert E. Stapleton and his wife, Dr. E. P. Case, Miss Atkins and Miss Sherman.

The Turks have been engaged in clearing the Armenians out of the region into which the Russians are now advancing because the Armenians favored the Russians. In the course of these repulsions and deportations hundreds of thousands of Armenian Christians have been murdered or perished by the way. Our Government has addrest a note of protest to the Ottoman Government, said to be in substance as follows:

The American people have been deeply stirred by the fate of the Christians ruthlessly slaughtered in Armenia. The Government of the United States, having received precise official information of the occurrences, no longer can doubt that authorities of the Turkish Government are responsible for hitherto unparalleled atrocities, which have shocked the civilized world.

The United States is prompted to express to the Turkish Government the confidence that the authors of the atrocities will be punished.

Furthermore, the United States, actuated by a wholly disinterested desire to uphold the principles of justice and humanity, protests against the toleration of such occurrences and gives warning that in the event of a repetition thereof the American Government will be compelled to take action of a more drastic character.

The Russian Movement Southward The Russian army which passed south of Erzerum is reported to have reached the city of Mush, fifty miles west of Lake Van. This would indicate that the Russians intended to push on in this direction until they cut the line of Turkish communications with Bagdad and Persia. The German Bagdad railroad has probably been completed to a point about half way between Aleppo and Mosul. At Mosul troops and supplies are presumably transhipped to river steamers to be sent down the Tigris to Bagdad or to Samara, which is connected with Bagdad by rail.

But the Russians south of Lake Van are within a hundred miles of Mosul and may be able soon to reach the Tigris and perhaps to attack Bagdad from the north while the British at-

tack from the south. At present the British expedition under General Townshend which attempted to reach Bagdad is invested by a Turkish force at Kut-el-Amara, a hundred miles down the river, while the relief expedition under General Aylmer is held up at Sheikh Said, about thirty-five miles below.

More alarming still is the report that the third British expedition under General Brooking, which had gone up the Euphrates River as far as Nasirjeh, is also in trouble. It appears that by moving north from this point was frustrated by the Turks and that they have recaptured Nasirjeh. If the Turks should be strong enough to follow up their success and attack the British base at Kurna, where the two rivers join, it might involve the loss of all the British expeditions.

It seems, then, that if the British are to be rescued from their dangerous predicament on the Tigris, the Russians must come to their rescue. This they are evidently doing with astonishing celerity considering the character of the country and the state of the weather. The remnants of the Turkish army are retreating rapidly toward the Tigris, but several detachments have been overtaken and captured by the Cossacks. From Lake Van and Lake Urmia they are covering the territory to the south and west.

The Swedish Protest The Swedish Government has been urging our Government to unite with it and other neutral nations in opposing British interference with neutral mails and commerce. The latest Swedish note calls our attention to increasing violation by Great Britain of the rules of international law which concern the protection of neutral commerce and navigation and says:

Of late the British authorities have violated the mail traffic. Parcel post from one neutral country to another is being unloaded in British ports and the contents are being seized. While parcel post is not protected thru The Hague Postal Convention, it nevertheless seems to his Majesty's Government that the British procedure, in the form and extensiveness practised, would

© Underwood & Underwood

CAMEL CAVALRY
A British mounted regiment leaving Cairo for desert service in defense of the Suez Canal, where the Germans are still awaited

Underwood & Underwood

GERMAN AND RUSSIAN

be invalid even with regard to ordinary express goods, and that this seems particularly evident when the seizure of parcel post is directed against a means of conveyance under guarantee of sovereign powers. Besides, great personal inconvenience is connected with seizure of this kind.

However, England's present practise of censoring also first-class mail, sent by neutral vessels from one neutral country to another, is an even greater violation of the rights accorded neutral powers by the rules of international law. It is not necessary to particularly point out how contrary this practise is to the stipulations in the above-mentioned Hague Convention, which stipulations or rules must be considered to have been in existence even before the promulgation of this convention.

As a measure of reprisal for interference with the Swedish mails the Swedish Government is holding up the British mail passing thru Sweden. It is said that there are in Gothenburg 58,000 parcels bound for England which have been detained on this account. Since Sweden is the chief channel of communication between England and Russia, she is in a position to cause the Allies serious inconvenience if driven to take a hostile attitude.

The Swedish Government seems disposed to acquiesce in the distinction which Germany is seeking to establish between armed and unarmed merchantmen, for it has formally warned all Swedish subjects against traveling on armed merchant vessels after February 29. The German Government announced that after this date armed merchant vessels would be torpedoed without warning.

Secretary Lansing has declined to join with Sweden or other neutral powers in any joint action such as has been proposed. He has stated it as the opinion of the American Government that merchant vessels should not be armed, but this does not imply assent to the German proposal to sink armed merchantmen at sight. Where Italian and British merchantmen have been permitted to leave our ports armed it has been on the assurance that their guns would be used solely for defensive purposes.

German Attack at Ypres The old Flemish town of Ypres, about which some of the fiercest fighting of last year occurred, is again the chief theater of action. The Germans attacked the British lines southeast of Ypres along a front of nearly two miles and succeeded in gaining possession of some six or eight hundred yards of first line trenches. This gain was made by a heavy bombardment and the explosion of five mines from tunnels which had been run beneath the British trenches. The efforts of the British to regain the position have been so far unavailing. This ground has changed so many times that it has become known as "the international trench." The Canadian troops are standing the brunt of the German attack on the Ypres front. It is rumored that the Germans are running many troop trains thru Belgium to this sector in preparation of a heavy drive against the British lines. North of Ypres on the Yser Canal the Germans have also carried a few hundred yards of British trenches.

The Entente Powers have informed Belgium that they will not cease hostilities until Belgium's political and economic independence is reëstablished and that Belgium will be called upon to take part in the peace negotiations.

For a Canal Monopoly A long step toward giving the United States control of all interoceanic canal routes thru Central America was taken on February 18, when the Senate, by a vote of 55 to 18, ratified the Bryan treaty with Nicaragua. The treaty gives this country in perpetuity

The unencumbered exclusive rights necessary and convenient to the construction, operation and maintenance of an interoceanic canal by way of the San Juan River and the Great Lake of Nicaragua or by way of any other route over Nicaraguan territory,

together with a ninety-nine year leasehold, which may be renewed, of Great Corn Island and Little Corn Island, in the Caribbean Sea east of the Nicaraguan coast, and a naval base on the Gulf of Fonseca to be selected by the United States.

The compensation to Nicaragua is $3,000,000, to be spent under the supervision of the United States for Nicaragua's debt or other public uses. This Government will choose the banks where the money is to be deposited and disbursements are to be made only with the approval of the Secretary of State or his appointee. In order to meet the objections of Costa Rica, Salvador and Honduras to various provisions, the ratification resolution contained a proviso expressly declaring that nothing in the treaty was "intended to affect any existing right" of the three states.

The statement that Germany had outbid the United States in its efforts to get control of this route was used in the Senate as an argument for ratification. Forty Democrats and fifteen Republicans were counted in favor of the treaty. Opposed were five Democrats and thirteen Republicans. General Chamorro, Nicaraguan Minister, expects his government to ratify the treaty promptly.

The Nicaragua Project When this is done the negotiations of half a century will be completed. In 1849 Nicaragua gave us the exclusive right to construct a canal thru her territory and ceded us Tiger Island in the Gulf of Fonseca, but Great Britain objected, seized the island, and forced us to negotiate the Clayton-Bulwer Treaty which provided that neither nation should control the isthmian canal. The Hay-Pauncefote Treaty in 1901 modified this restriction and left the United States free to build a canal by either the Nicaragua or Panama route. A private American company was already at work at Nicaragua, but the panic of 1893 put it out of business. In 1900 the Isthmian Canal Commission reported in favor of this route, and the House of Representatives had actually passed a bill author-

Underwood & Underwood

HAVING THE TIME OF THEIR LIVES

Tho war has dealt cruelly with Serbia, it does bring the most exciting sights and sounds for the edification of the primitive folk to whom this expressive row of heads belongs

ONE ASPECT OF PREPAREDNESS THAT FINDS WIDE APPROVAL

izing the construction of the Nicaragua canal by the Government when the Panama Company reduced its price, which led the commission and Congress to decide on the present route.

Late in President Taft's administration a treaty substantially the same as the one just ratified was negotiated. It failed of ratification, and after Secretary Bryan had added provisions for a protectorate it was still less liked by the Senate. In the summer of 1914 the present treaty, without the protectorate clause, was submitted, but the Senate, after an investigation, adjourned without ratifying it.

The Isthmian Canal Commission estimated the cost of the Nicaraguan canal at $180,000,000, less than half what the Panama Canal has cost, and it was therefore within the bounds of possibility that some other nation would build a competing canal if we did not secure a permanent option. The Atrato River route, thru Colombia, is still not under our control. The Gulf of Fonseca offers one of the very few good harbors on the Pacific coast. Nicaragua has been financially embarrassed for a long time, and the $3,000,000 will materially aid her.

Other Treaties The Haytian treaty providing for a virtual protectorate, the terms of which were reported in detail in these pages last week, was to be considered next. Some

of its provisions are already in force, by agreement with Hayti, and the Senate was expected to ratify it.

The Colombian question, however, which has stood in the way of Pan-American concord for twelve years, seems as far from adjustment as ever. The action of the Senate Committee on Foreign Relations in reducing the indemnity to Colombia from $25,000,000 to $15,000,000 and practically nullifying the American apology by softening it into an expression of mutual regret, is bitterly resented in Colombia. The Colombian minister at Washington, Julio Betancourt, has asked for leave of absence, which may be made a permanent withdrawal if the original treaty fails of ratification, and Colombia has notified this Government that she will not accept the revised convention. It is said that Colombia may withdraw from the Pan-American Union and that other Latin-American countries are likely to support her protest.

It is not thought that the treaty even in its present form can secure the necessary two-thirds vote in the Senate.

The Work of Congress Altho the House Committee on Rivers and Harbors was committed to a program of merely continuing work on existing projects, a new undertaking—an appropriation for the improvement of New York Harbor—was included in the Rivers and Harbors

bill, after a hot fight, before it was reported on February 16. The $200,000 now voted, with $500,000 to come, is to be used to clear a 35-foot channel in the East River from the Hudson River to the Navy Yard. It is endorsed by Secretary Daniels as a defense measure, and President Wilson's approval carried it thru, altho the Republican minority opposed what they called the President's interference, for political reasons, in the committee's work. The bill carries a total appropriation of $39,608,410, of which $6,000,000 is for the Mississippi River.

The Democratic House caucus, by a vote of 84 to 20, ten members refusing to be bound, has committed the party to a repeal of the free sugar provision of the Underwood tariff law. This will continue in force the present tax of about one cent a pound, which would have ceased automatically on May 1. The Democratic explanation of this reversal of a party policy is that the unforeseen emergency of the war makes it necessary to retain the $40,000,000 of revenue from this source. The Ways and Means Committee is therefore including this provision in the Omnibus Revenue Bill which was nearly completed last week. The bill will probably provide for a lowering of the exemption and raising of the surtax in the income tax law, and the establishment of a tariff commission.

Action on the Susan B. Anthony

amendment to the Constitution, granting nation-wide woman suffrage, has been postponed nearly a year. The House Judiciary Committee voted on February 15 to defer consideration of the measure till December 14, 1916. By a tie vote the prohibition amendment was still left before the committee.

Before the House Committee on Naval Affairs, which is framing the naval part of the defense program, Rear Admiral Grant, Chief of Submarines, U. S. N., urged the need of a fleet of 183 submersibles, three divisions of six each to cruise with the Atlantic fleet, two with the Pacific, and the remainder to work from numerous shore bases. At present twenty-seven submarines are ready for war service, ten more are laid up, and thirty-five are building or authorized. The House Committee on Military Affairs was told last week that the coast fortifications of the country lack 52 per cent of the men necessary to man them according to the plans of the War Department.

An investigation into the possibility of government ownership and operation of all public utilities engaged in interstate commerce is sought in a bill introduced by Senator Newlands, of Nevada, chairman of the Committee on Interstate Commerce. In the form of an amendment to a bill providing a joint committee to study traffic conditions, the proposal was approved by the Senate by a vote of 39 to 22.

Killed in Mexico Secretary Lansing has replied to the Senate's sweeping request for information on the history and present status of our relations with Mexico. In January, on the motion of Mr. Fall, Republican, of New Mexico, who has been the Administration's bitterest critic on the subject of Mexico, ten questions were asked, and the Administration now replies to all but one. The request for all reports from the Brazilian Minister who has cared for American interests at

© *Underwood & Underwood*
WHERE TWO WAR CARGOES BURNED
The "Bolton Castle" and "Pacific," loading with supplies for the Russian government, were burned at dock on February 16, together with the pier in Brooklyn, where they lay. There was suspicion of a bomb plot, but it was found that crost wires started the fire

Mexico City while we were without diplomatic representative there, and from our consular representatives and other informants, was refused. Secretary Lansing explained that the information in these thousands of documents was highly confidential and could not·be made public without destroying the usefulness of the Government's correspondents.

There have been 76 Americans killed in Mexico in the last three years, 24 from causes attributed directly to the revolution, to which may be added eight deaths in the Cumbre tunnel disaster, and 44 by bandits, Indians and civilians. In the years 1910, 1911 and 1912, with less widespread disorder, the total had been 47. Twenty civilian Americans, 16 American soldiers and 92 Mexicans were killed on the American side of the border in 1913-15.

Secretary Lansing defined the present authority in Mexico as a *de facto*, not a constitutional, government, "established by a military power, which has definitely committed itself to the holding of popular elections upon the restoration of peace." In answering the inquiry as to the circumstances surrounding the recognition of Carranza, he emphasized the fact that when the Seven Diplomats invited the Mexican chiefs to confer, all the Villistas replied separately, while all the Carranzista leaders referred the question to the First Chief, and continues:

The inference to be drawn was plain. On the one hand there seemed to be no central organization among the Villista forces, while, on the other hand, submission to a central authority was evidenced in the replies of the Carranzistas. The unity and loyalty of the Carranzistas appeared to indicate the ultimate triumph of that faction, especially as the Carranzista forces were then in control of approximately seventy-five per cent of the territory of Mexico.

On these grounds the decision to recognize Carranza was reached. As to the power and determination of Carranza's government to maintain order, he declares that

The *de facto* Government is now in control of all but a few sections of Mexico and that, bearing in mind that the nation is just emerging from years of domestic strife, it may be said that within the territory which it controls it is affording in all the circumstances reasonably adequate protection to the lives and property of American citizens, and it is taking steps to extend its authority over and to restore order in sections now in the hands of the hostile factions.

Papers relating to Carranza's guarantee of the payment of claims, religious freedom and personal liberty and to the seizure and evacuation of Vera Cruz accompanied the note. It is thought that the principal object of Senator Fall's resolution was to get the correspondence which the Administration declines to release. Now that the formal reply has been received, the Senate is expected to proceed to consider the nomination of Henry P. Fletcher as Ambassador to Mexico.

© *Medem Photo Service*
SEEKING COMFORT IN SERVING THE STATE
War widows in Paris on their way to the War College to train as auxiliary troops

THE BEST THING IN YOUR TOWN—FIRST PRIZE ARTICLE

LA GRANGE INDICATOR

LA GRANGE: THE CITY OF MINERAL SPRINGS

Vol. XXIII.   LA GRANGE, MISSOURI, THURSDAY, FEBRUARY 3, 1916   No 48

CONSOLIDATION IDEA SWEEPS COUNTY	STUDENTS' PROGRAM WAS ENJOYED	BOLD NELS DARLING WAKED 'EM UP	MEMBER OF PIONEER FAMILY GONE	FEAR RESULT OF "PREPAREDNESS"
Maywood District election Called—Durham Votes Saturday—Taylor's Plans Maturing—Monticello Investigating. Notices will be posted Friday in the districts interested, calling for a special to vote the question of a	Joint Session of Literary Societies—Domestic Science Pupils' Sandwiches Sampled—College Notes On Friday evening, January 28, the Aurora, Philomathean and Shakespearean societies assembled in joint	Noted Lecturer Startled Audience With Unvarnished Truth in Address on "Community Interests" The greatest shaking up this town has had in many	Death Calls Joseph Cottrell in his Seventy-ninth Year. Un	Farmers Petition Representatives at Washington to Oppose Increased Armament—West Hamilton Sales Stopped One hundred and fifty men of Van Mile and surrounding neighborhoods, who fear the future effect upon in-

T HE most wholesome single influence in our town is what George Fitch calls The Homeburg Democrat, which in this instance is the LaGrange Indicator. It is published by a pair of brothers commonly known hereabouts as the Painter boys, and we are proud to call it the best newspaper in the county. In fact, LaGrange has tried to become famous as a place of mineral water and summer resorts, and as the boyhood home of Vice-President Marshall, and has failed at all three. But it is known all over the state among the newspaper fraternity for the character of the paper it supports. Our twenty-two year old editor has already had his name coupled with the Frankensteins of Missouri. And there are reasons.

Not the least of these is the frank and straightforward way in which the Indicator acts as the guardian of the common weal. It defends everyone and everything that is being abused. And yet it keeps above the muckraking spirit of so many small weeklies which attempt reform. This town of ours has a typical set of genuine Missouri petty politicians who do nothing of their own initiative, partly because they do not know how, and partly because they are afraid they will make enemies. When our editor finds that a city ordinance is not being enforced, the text of the ordinance is printed in big type across three columns of the "personals" page like this:

Is Your Son A Lawbreaker?

> CITY ORDINANCES, Section 428
> —Any person who shall kill, wound or attempt to kill or wound by the use of firearms, bow and arrow, pelting with stones or other missiles, OR OTHERWISE, any bird within the city limits, or throw stones, clubs or other missiles at any bird within any private grounds or public park, squares or grounds, or enter upon any private enclosure or public grounds belonging to the city, for the purpose of doing any act prohibited in this section, shall forfeit and pay a fine of not less than two, nor more than ten dollars for each offense.

Do you know what your boy is doing with that air rifle?

300

BY REV. DAVID R. PIPER

And on the first page of the same issue a paragraph on the enforcement of the law appears, in which the name of the responsible official is unobtrusively but suggestively inserted. The good people of the town awake, and the marshal, who, like all other marshals, wants to be sheriff, swallows his grouch at the editor, and begins to show signs of life. The thing is done and everybody is happy; there are no petty quarrels and no political fights are precipitated.

Advertising is what makes a country newspaper pay—if it does happen to pay! And yet these Painter boys have a way of donating whole yards of perfectly good white space to causes of social and religious betterment. Last April they began to give the best space in their paper to a series of Go-to-Church appeals, a three-column ten-inch space each week. At the lower right hand corner of each insertion appeared this caption: "The above advertisement has been arranged for by men interested in all La Grange churches." The truth was that the only men "interested" were the two Painter boys. They decided that the half a dozen dead or dying churches needed to be resurrected into life. They composed the copy and donated the space, and so got back of religion in "Homeburg." This agitation was kept up during the hottest of the summer months, and the resulting total Sunday School attendance was probably never so great in any two months in the history of the town as during this period. Church advertising is no longer unique, but editorial initiative in these matters is. That makes another reason why the Indicator is the best thing in our town.

But the biggest reason is to be found in its editorials. They are not mere political harangues. They do not simply echo the opinions of other journals. They reflect the life of the community. They are written under the inspiration of local scenes and events. They bear a message of cheer

and moral stimulus. They make one see the beauty and the possibilities of good in the life of this sleepy old river town. In the days of disappointment and calamity they give one courage to hold on.

This season the old Father of Waters asserted his might. He came out over the rich wheat-fields and corn-lands of the bottoms, which promised to yield the most miraculous crop in a lifetime, and carried away or destroyed thousands of acres of harvests. Then, if ever, was the propitious time to write a calamity editorial. But no, it is courage men need. Out comes the Indicator after the flood, and here on page 3 is one of the greatest editorials ever written by a country scribe:

For years men have gambled against the rise and fall of the Mississippi River. Time after time they have gone back with new hopes to rebuild their possessions and gamble against other floods. We in LaGrange have seen men leave their upland refuges as soon as the waters recede and go back with their families to the house of the bottom land. Call it the "fever"—say if you will that it is the same instinct that impels a man to put his last dollar on a good "hand"; in any event it is the hope that springs eternal—sometimes infernal—of making those rich acres yield their most bountiful some day. An uplander might farm several years in the bottom and come out. But let him pass thru the baptism of one flood and he is lost to the hills forever. He begins to think what he might have done with a normal stage of the river. The richness of the black soil and its future fabulous yields lure him to day dreams. Nothing but death can remove him. Courageous, contented, happy-go-lucky men these bottom farmers have been. Always they have lost with a smile and have gone back with no tears for the past.

Could any bottom farmer, his year's work gone for nothing, his life till another harvest dependent upon his credit at the bank, keep his case of blues after reading that?

Is it any wonder that such editorials as these in our Homeburg Democrat are copied in the St. Louis papers, and recopied in the East? This is why we love it. It stands by us thru thick and thin. It is the best thing in our town.

La Grange, Missouri

WHY NOT SWAP THE PHILIPPINES FOR SOMETHING NEARER HOME?

BY EDWIN E. SLOSSON

AS the holder of a 101,000,000th undivided interest in the Philippines I have been puzzled like the other stockholders in the question of their disposition. To make them "free and independent" is something that Congress could not do if it wanted to. There are, I presume, a hundred thousand tropical islands in the world and not one of them is "free and independent" unless you consider Santo Domingo and Cuba so. All we could do would be to transfer them directly or indirectly to another power, say, England, Germany or Japan. Of the three we should, most of us, prefer to entrust the Filipinos to the first.

But if we relinquish the Philippines we must get an equivalent somewhere, for the development of transportation and tropical agriculture in recent years has shown that the prosperity of a commercial country is dependent upon the possession of extensive territory in the tropics. My Yankee blood suggested a swap. Has Great Britain any tropical possession near to us which would be a fair trade for the distant Philippines? I twirled the globe on my desk. Yes, there was British Guiana or Demerara lying in about the same latitude and as near as I could see about the same size. I had never been to Demerara. None of my kinfolk ever had. None of my friends. Nobody I ever knew of. That was a sufficient reason for wanting to go there. The unknown is always attractive. The sight of an unknown name on the map excites the appetite as does an à-la-something-new on the menu. Now I might have twirled the globe a dozen times and stopped it with a finger touch without hitting

upon a spot which I knew less about than Demerara. The polar regions north and south are familiar to us from the movies. The Forbidden City

EL DORADO
The Golden Land of British Guiana needs American capital to develop its vast resources. Col. Roosevelt is now journeying over the same route that Dr. Slosson took

of Lhasa has been entered by Colonel Younghusband and his attendant photographers. Roosevelt has removed the doubt that hung about the tributaries of the Amazon. But I beat him to Demerara by eight months.

It was with all the rare delight of the discoverer of an unknown land that I approached the shores of Demerara. To be sure there were people already living there when I came. But then so there were when Sir Walter Ralegh discovered it in 1595. In fact, the city of Georgetown, spacious and imposing as it is, cannot compare with the magnificence of the city of Manoa as Ralegh imagined it. Here dwelt El Dorado, the Golden King, in a paradise for which lapidary work rivaled the New Jerusalem and for conviviality surpassed Valhalla.

Ralegh outrivaled Othello in his tales

Of the Cannibals that each other eat,
The Anthropophagi and men whose heads
Do grow beneath their shoulders.

"They are reported," says Sir Walter, "to have eyes in their shoulders and mouthes in the middle of their breasts and that a long traine of haire groweth backward betweene their shoulders."

But, as it happened, Sir Walter Ralegh, instead of discovering the headless men became one himself. He was in advance of his age. He would have made a fine yellow journalist. And I may say at once that any one taking Hakluyt as a Baedeker will be disappointed, tho, on the whole, agreeably disappointed.

When on the sixteenth day from New York the "Guiana" steamed up the Demerara River to Georgetown the first thing I saw, down by the sea wall, was a cricket ground, that world-wide British cricket ground on which the sun never sets. Towering in the distance was an Episcopalian cathedral, and when I went to the hotel I found my window looked out upon the Carnegie Library. In the shop windows were the signs of American cereals and cameras mingled in Anglo-Saxon amity with those of British beef tea and marmalade. Along the street in front there marched a train of turbaned Hindus as sandwich men, bearing billboards that announced that a most sensational and scandalous film portraying "The Lure of New York" was to be seen that night at the Electric Theater and what films at the Empire on payment of twelve cents. Prices are quoted in dollars and

WHAT RALEGH SAID I SHOULD SEE
According to Sir Walter Ralegh, headless men and amazons inhabited Demerara

BUT WHAT I REALLY SAW
Was a file of Hindu sandwiches marching down a city street advertising the movies

cents; payment is made in pounds, shillings and pence. The process of conversion requires more arithmetical agility than I, possess, so I always pocketed without question the change that was handed me, generally more than I expected and often less than I deserved.

I did not see any of the headless Ewiapanos, but all the other races of mankind are, I feel sure, represented in Demerara. The Stabroek Market is a museum of living ethnography. East and West have met here. Asia and Africa have combined to people Guiana, and to crowd out America and Europe. The aborigines form about 2⅓ per cent of the population and are decreasing. The Europeans form about 5 per cent and are decreasing. The rest of the population is almost equally divided between negroes and East Indians, and they are increasing. The irony of it is that both these races which are crowding out the whites have been brought here by the whites for their own selfish purposes.

When the negroes were emancipated in 1838 they refused to work on the sugar estates, at least for such wages as the planters could pay them. So India was drawn upon and ever since has been the chief supply of cheap labor. At first the Indian coolies were brought under an indenture system which the Anti-Slavery Society of England regarded not without reason as being little better than the old slave trade, but these conditions have been in the course of time reformed until now the interests of the immigrants are very carefully watched over by a paternal government. The Indians are imported by the planters under indentures which bind them to remain on the estate for five years and in the colony for five more. At the end of that time they may return to India by paying half fare. To get an able-bodied laborer under this system costs the planter about a hundred dollars. The employer is obliged to provide free lodgings of a prescribed type and free medical attendance and to pay a minimum wage of a shilling a day.

But no matter how little an East Indian earns he lives on a little less, so that by the time his five years are up he may be able to embark in busi-

THE RESIDENCES IN GEORGETOWN ARE PLEASANTLY ADAPTED TO THE TROPICAL CLIMATE

A VILLAGE OF NEGRO LABORERS ON A SUGAR PLANTATION IN DEMERARA

ness or till a rice field of his own. In slavery days the planters used to destroy the rice plantations started by runaway negroes in the bush. Now they encourage the industry and more rice is grown than is needed to supply the colony. It is being exported at the rate of sixteen million pounds a year, most of it grown by hand labor on the little patches owned by the East Indians, altho recently an American company has put in five thousand acres of rice to be cultivated by machinery.

The windows of the Chinese shops on Water street are filled with the brass idols of the Hindu pantheon, made doubtless in Birmingham. In the coolie quarters these Hindu temples and Mohammedan mosques are provided just as there are hospitals and schools. I visited a mosque on the road to the sugar factory, a plain board building with crescents painted on the front and nothing inside but matting, rugs and a copy of the Koran, not half so real-like and impressive as the mosque of any "Street of Cairo" in America. The sacristan, muezzin or whatever the name of a mosque-manager is, instructed me on entering to leave on my hat and take off my shoes. He took occasion to explain that this was a much more sensible custom than the Christian because leaving on a

hat does no harm to anybody, while leaving on the shoes carries into the sacred place the filth of the street.

Shoes seem to be the last article of civilized apparel to be adopted, tho one would think they would be the first in this land of centipedes, tarantulas and chiggers. The two races can usually be distinguished by their dress. If you see a man with trousers but no shirt he is a negro. If he wears a shirt but no trousers he is an East Indian. Those who are white or aspire to be considered so wear both. A costume much in vogue is that of Kipling's "Gunga Din":

The uniform 'e wore
Was nothin' much before,
An' rather less than 'arf
     o' that be'ind.

The negroes saunter down the middle of the street in chattering, laughing groups. The Indian slips by singly and swiftly, slim and silent, like an afternoon shadow in a shroud. The negro walks flatfooted. The Indian steps on the ball of his foot, delicately, mincingly, like a cat on a cook-stove.

Two paces behind him walks his wife, small and graceful, wearing a gaily embroidered jacket with a green or pink scarf draped about her head and body. There is a nose-ring hanging down over her upper lip or a gold rosette in the side of the left nostril, a style no more disfiguring and grotesque than the earring, which I see still worn in New York. Her forearm is loaded with silver bracelets or soldered into a silver tube reaching from the wrist almost to the elbow. This is the East Indian substitute for a savings bank. You can estimate the wealth of the man by the number of rings on his wife's arms, just as in New York you estimate it by the size of the wife's diamonds. In case of a financial crisis the silver like the diamonds may be cashed for current expenses. But what seemed most strange to me was that the Demerara woman has a baby in her arms instead of the dog that the New York woman carries.

I was forced to make constant comparisons between New York and Demerara not merely because they were the terminals of my vacation voyage, but because they were once considered of about equal value. Two hundred and fifty years ago the Dutch traded off New Netherland, which we call New York, for Guiana and chuckled at their shrewdness in beating the British at the bargain, for they could not imagine that the northern trading post could ever equal in value this spacious and fertile paradise. After the British lost the North American colony, in the course of a misunderstanding between King George and George Washington, they went and took Demerara from the Dutch. In 1796 the three colonies of Berbice on the east, Essequibo on the west and Demerara in the middle were united to form British Guiana.

Of course it seems absurd now to compare New York and British Guiana as territorial equivalents, but Gabriel's trump has not yet sounded and real estate values have a way of going up and down in the queerest way. New Netherland, that is to say, Manhattan Island and the Hudson valley, has about all the population it can comfortably hold and much more than it can support, while British Guiana is still practically empty. It is nearly the size of Oregon, but Oregon has already more than twice its population and is clamoring for more. Besides, the tropics can maintain a much denser population than northern lands. If British Guiana were as thickly settled as the neighboring island of Barbados, that is, 1034 to the square mile, it would have a population of 93,-000,000, which is more than the United States had at the last census. It is not at all impossible, tho it may be undesirable, that British Guiana should have as dense a population, for the climate is much the same and the soil is in most parts as productive.

But Guiana has been a sink for population. Up to a hundred years ago the forcible importation of negroes was necessary to keep up the supply of labor, and later the influx from India took its place. Now, however, the advance of sanitary science has abolished the endemic yellow fever and pointed the way to the possible abolition of typhoid and malarial fevers. In 1912, for the first time in the history of the colony, the birth rate surpassed the death rate. The improve-

ment here, as elsewhere, has chiefly been due to the reduction of infant mortality.

"The conquest of the tropics," of which we hear so much, is not yet an accomplished fact, but enough has been done, in Panama and India, for example, to show that most if not all the disabilities of the climate can be overcome. The white can, it appears, live in the tropics, but it requires more intelligence to live there, a condition of excellent promise for the future. But for the present—well, it was put best by a hale and active septuagenarian of Demerara, who said to me: "Englishmen come out here and drink and drink and drink and die, and then write home to their folks that the climate killed them."

The climate is officially stated in the *Handbook of British Guiana* to be "a delightful one even for the tropics," whatever that may mean. Then it goes on to prove it by statistics, from which it appears that the mercury sticks as close to 80° F. as a timid child to its mother. A variation of five degrees either way is uncommon, night or day, summer or winter. A Demeraran never has to wonder what the weather is going to be. He knows. The sun gets in six to ten hours of shining almost every day in the year and the rainfall measures up to one hundred inches.

ANOTHER NIAGARA
The Kaieteur Falls on the Potaro River, a tributary of the Essequibo River, are nearly five times as high as Niagara and about four hundred feet wide, but they are rarely visited by tourists because there is no railroad leading into the interior

The Demerara River is as muddy as the Mississippi and yellows the ocean for miles about its mouth. We are officially informed by the *Handbook* that "the depth of water on the bar is sufficient to allow of large vessels crossing with ease and security." This is doubtless true if the "large vessel" is spread out on top of the water. If it draws more than nine feet of water and tries to get into the harbor at low tide it has to plow thru the mud on the bottom.

The country is flat so far as the eye can see from the ocean, but in the interior there are first wooded hills, then plateaus and finally mountains. The upland savannas are said to offer as good pasturage as the plains of Argentina and it is expected that as soon as the hinterland is opened up by rail it will provide the beef for the markets of England and the United States. Here, too, cotton can be grown and coffee, tobacco, rubber, and all sorts of fruits. Then there are great attractions to the tourist in these inaccessible regions. Sir Walter Egerton, Governor of British Guiana, who has been over the route, estimates the cost of a railroad from the coast to the southern boundary would be a million and a quarter pounds. The distance is about 380 miles, and then if the Brazilian Government would build a railroad from Manaos to meet it, a distance of 300 miles, there would be a thru route from the Caribbean Sea to the Amazon and ultimately to Rio Janeiro and Buenos Aires. This is a project to rival Cecil Rhodes's scheme of a Cape-to-Cairo railroad and perhaps more remote from realization. For Brazil has no money and if she had would not be inclined to spend it in draining the hidden wealth of the hinterland to a British port. The British part of the project, which would be practical and profitable, has been postponed indefinitely by the war. American capitalists have, it is said, offered to construct a railroad into the interior, but they want more land as a bonus than the Government is willing to give them.

A country of such extent and resources as British Guiana cannot remain undeveloped much longer. I'm as confident as

Ralegh and there's bound to be a boom, but I'm as uncertain as was he when it will come. The colony is doing well as it is, now that its sugar is in demand owing to the shutting off of German beet sugar and the lowering of the American tariff bars. Anthony Trollope says of Demerara that "the Government is a mild despotism tempered by sugar." Some of the people would put it "an absolute despotism of sugar," for they gave me to infer that the factory had more power than the Government House. But whoever runs the country seems to do it well enough.

According to Trollope, "The men in Demerara are never angry and the women are never cross. The only people who do not thrive are the doctors." On the authority of personal observation and experience—for I lived in Demerara from Saturday to Monday—I can contradict all three of these statements. He goes on to say: "When I settle out of England . . . British Guiana shall be the land of my adoption." With this I have no quarrel. For he might easily have made a worse choice of residence. When I returned to New York I

> ## A BARGAIN FOR BOTH
>
> *Why not exchange the American Philippines for British Guiana, West Indies and Honduras?*
> *Their area is nearly the same.*
> *They lie in much the same latitudes.*
> *Both contain immense undeveloped resources.*
> *The Philippines are far away from us, and the British Caribbean possessions are far away from England. But the Philippines come within thirty miles of British territory and the British West Indies come within forty miles of American territory.*
> *Under either flag the people would be protected, their welfare provided for, their prosperity promoted, and their present self-government maintained and extended.*
> *More Americans and Englishmen voluntarily exchange citizenship in a few years than would be involved in this transfer of territory.*
> *The danger of war would be lessened.*
> *The cost of the navy would be reduced.*
> *The commercial advantages to all the countries concerned would be incalculable.*

found the thermometer ten degrees above what I had seen it in South America. I got one mosquito bite in Demerara. I got five coming up New York Bay.

My week-end in Demerara was a success. I wondered why I had not gone there before since it is so interesting and so near. The Philippines are still closer to Australia and would form a natural extension of the territory in New Guinea which the Australians have recently taken from the Germans. Under the humane and efficient rule of the Aus-

tralians the Philippines would prosper and the interests of the natives would be safeguarded. On the other hand, our experience in the Philippines, Porto Rico and the Canal Zone has shown that we can be trusted with colonies, for we better the British in some respects, such as education and sanitation. The acquisition of British Guiana by the United States would bring about an influx of capital and a development of the resources of the country which otherwise will be indefinitely delayed.

Intrinsically the Philippines are vastly more valuable. But on account of their situation they are less valuable to us than Demerara would be. To make the bargain more nearly equal and to complete the territorial readjustment the British West Indies and Honduras should be included. That would still leave the advantage on the British side, for the area of the Philippines is 120,000 square miles and their population 9,000,000, while the area of British Guiana, Honduras and West Indies is 111,000 and their population 2,100,000.

Why not swap?

RECOMPENSE
BY EDWARD BLISS REED

Where the green fir-tips meet the sapphire sky,
　A gull, cloud-white,
Careless of earth, floats insolently by.
　In the warm light.

Still, imperturbable, it holds a course
　To lands unknown,
And scornful of the south-wind's gathering force
　It sails alone,

Seeing unmoved the noon's exultant glow,
　The evening's grief,
The wind-swept waves that crumble into snow
　Upon the reef.

The ships becalmed or scudding for the shore
　In wind and rain,
Alluring isles—all these it passes o'er
　In calm disdain.

Deep in the woods, the sea left far behind,
　I listen long,
Searching in ambush, yet in vain, to find
　Who sings that song.

I know those notes pure as the brooks that gush
　Down Alpine vale;
Enchantress of the woods, the hermit-thrush,
　Our nightingale.

Its world a forest bough; here in the shade
　It sings unseen
The magic songs a yearning lover made
　To charm a queen.

The ocean-wandering gull from all his quest
　Can nothing bring.
You have the world within your throbbing breast,
　For you can sing.

THE LONGEST RAILROAD TUNNEL IN AMERICA

ROGER'S PASS TUNNEL, FIVE MILES LONG, WILL CARRY THE CANADIAN
PACIFIC RAILROAD UNDER MT. MACDONALD IN THE SELKIRKS
OF BRITISH COLUMBIA. SEE PAGE 289

k Your Doctor

ealthfulness, nutritive value and digest-
d made with Royal Baking Powder as
food made with baking powders con-
dients of mineral origin, such as alum
. Royal Baking Powder is made from
artar, which is derived from grapes.

a healthful fruit origin,
od element, as distin-
n mineral substitutes
per baking powders.
y eminent scientists,
n record to the effect
ctory baking powder
ration of food it never
r quality for low price.

ING POWDER

no alum—no phosphate

M. William Shak-ſpeare:

EIGHT PAPERS BY FREDERICK HOUK LAW
IN OBSERVANCE OF THE THREE HUNDREDTH
ANNIVERSARY OF SHAKESPEARE'S DEATH

The Comedies: Plays of Fun and Fancy

SHAKESPEARE'S plays are full of fun and laughter, sometimes having the spirit of schoolboys playing jokes and hurrahing at nonsense; sometimes the happy spirit that characterizes people set free for a time from the cares of life, and sometimes a kind of sober fun that recognizes sadness, but smiles in spite of everything.

In certain comedies, like "The Comedy of Errors" and "The Taming of the Shrew," Shakespeare's humor is more boisterous than elsewhere, as tho he had resolved to write "Even to the world's pleasure, and the increase of laughter." Such plays are written without deep searching into character. They turn on unusual and surprizing events, and ring with the laughter of a hearty young man, not wholly thoughtless, but more ready to laugh than to moralize. They have the spirit of the rogue Autolycus in his song:

Jog on, jog on, the foot-path way,
   And merrily hent the stile-a;
A merry heart goes all the day,
   Your sad tires in a mile-a.

The spirit of joyous comedy makes the plays so delightful that we do not expect them to give us much of poetry or lofty thought. We read them for their buoyant fun.

In some comedies, like "Love's Labour's Lost" and "A Midsummer Night's Dream," Shakespeare gave his happy imagination full scope. In such plays he looked upon the world, not so much as a reality, as something interesting, whimsical, a subject for humor; and upon the serious side of life as something far-off and strange—a subject for poetry, perhaps, but not a stern fact. In such a comedy as "A Midsummer Night's Dream" he plays with life, while his

Imagination bodies forth
The forms of things unknown.

A small group of plays echoing with loud laughter, and rough and boy-like in humor, with some others that are redolent with idle imagination, fancy and dreams, is the product of Shakespeare's young manhood before he had felt the gripping hand of reality. In the period in which he produced these merry plays he wrote some other and darker plays as well, but in them, too, he looked upon life as a pageant rather than a mystery, writing, it is true, some cruel and gruesome plays, but regarding event rather than soul, and looking upon history as

The tide of pomp
That beats upon the high shore of this world.

It is only natural that Shakespeare, as a young man, should be far more interested in plot than in character, far more interested in what his characters do than in what they really are, far more ready to play upon words, and to revel in puns, conceits and tricks of style.

"In the very May-morn of his youth" when Shakespeare was between twenty-six and thirty-three years old, he wrote the hilarious "Comedy of Errors," the boisterous "Taming of the Shrew," the happy-go-lucky "Henry IV," Part I and Part II, and its sequel, "The Merry Wives of Windsor," the lively "Love's Labour's Lost," the romantic "Two Gentlemen of Verona" and the fanciful "Midsummer Night's Dream."

Anyone who would look into Shakespeare's plays for mere amusement, and the delight of escaping from the too-stern world around him, should read any of the eight comedies written in Shakespeare's early manhood. It is altogether probable that they have created more laughter than any other plays ever written. They rest most largely upon the surprize of events, and deal very little with character analysis.

The "Comedy of Errors" is little more than a hit-or-miss, slap-stick farce from beginning to end, with just a relieving touch of the romantic and the serious. The more tragic element is introduced in the story of unfortunate, old Aegeon who, after years of fruitless search, at last finds his wife and two sons at a moment when he thinks he has been sentenced to death. In his story there is a hint of the greater power, rising from a rare combination of inner nature and action, that characterizes Shakespeare's more distinguished plays. The "Comedy of Errors" is practically all action. Twin brothers and their twin servants are so taken for one another that they hardly recognize themselves. The wives of the married claim the unmarried as their husbands; one twin receives money due the other, and the servants are beaten for each other's faults. Such material is not the material for character drawing. It is the subject of farce, but Shakespeare has touched even this broad canvas of laughter with a refining hand.

"The Taming of the Shrew" is somewhat the same sort of play, but it has a greater element of character and a finer spirit of romance. Like many of Shakespeare's plays, it is complex in structure, having three distinct stories. One is that of the drunken tinker, Christopher Sly, who, picked up by a rich lord and his

SHAKESPEARE!

The Zoust or Soest portrait, painted by Gerard Soest, born twenty-one years after Shakespeare's death, is identified with the poet "only on fanciful grounds"

servants, is put into an elegant bed in a near-by castle and told that he is not himself but someone else! Another is the story of Baptista's daughter Bianca, who outwits her father and two unwelcome suitors by receiving her lover disguised as a teacher of languages. The third story is that of Baptista's other daughter, Katharina the Shrew, whose seemingly irrepressible temper had terrified everyone around her till Petruchio, a gay-hearted young man from Verona, marries her against her will. Such a play is of course an action-play, but it turns very pleasantly in the direction of character. It has many of the farcical elements of the "Comedy of Errors," but it also has a delightful whimsicality and many touches of gentle romance.

The two parts of "Henry IV" and "The Merry Wives of Windsor" likewise contain the element of rough, farcical humor, but they also give still stronger character portrayal. Henry IV is a combination of history-play and farce-comedy, presenting on the one side the tragic story of Henry IV struggling against rebellious subjects, and on the other the low-comedy story of Falstaff, an irresponsible tavern roisterer. The young Prince Hal appears in both stories and brings them into harmony, at first being little more than a careless, jesting, prank-playing companion of the too-good-hearted and over-bibulous Falstaff, but rising, when real responsibility comes, into a serious-minded king. In "Henry V" the story of Falstaff is brought to a close when we learn that he died "Like any christom child" and "babbled of green fields." The story of Prince Hal develops into heroic proportions in the epic-like account of Henry the Fifth's victories over the French. The entire story of Prince Hal, given in three plays, is not unlike Shakespeare's own life-story, a development from somewhat wild, mischief-making days into genuine greatness. Some have chosen to consider the story of Prince Hal as partly autobiographical.

In "Henry IV" the character interest is important. There is the pathetic Henry IV mourning his failure to attain happiness, and finding how "uneasy lies the head that wears a crown." There is the quick-tempered, over-zealous Hotspur, whose boy-like passion sweeps us with him, but who, in spite of his seeming greatness, lacks the broad manhood of Prince Hal, whom he despises. Most notable of all, there is Falstaff, the most laughable character Shakespeare ever conceived—a fat, jolly knight, too fond of drink, too fond of idle sport, but always the soul of good humor

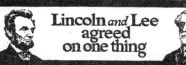

"BUT FOR MY BONNY KATE, SHE MUST WITH ME"

Act iii, Sc. 2, of "The Taming of the Shrew." Petruchio, Katharina and Bianca just after Petruchio has married Kate. One of the plates from Boydell's "Shakespeare Prints" published in 1805 in two huge volumes after Alderman Boydell had commissioned many painters, including several academicians like Wheatley, who painted this, to illustrate Shakespeare and had established a Shakespeare gallery in London

and friendliness. Falstaff is the most audacious, the most laughable, and the most lovable of all Shakespeare's comic characters.

"Love's Labour's Lost" and "The Two Gentlemen of Verona" have less of the boisterous and more of unreality. In the first a king and three lords withdraw from the busy world, but when a French princess and her three ladies intrude, study gives way to love! In the same play is the story of the fantastic Don Armado and some ignorant country people who make ridiculous attempts to present a play. Just then the Princess' father dies, the happy company must separate, and all love's labor is lost. In the second, a loyal girl named Julia, disguised as a boy, follows her faithless lover to Milan and regains his love. Her lover's friend, treacherously thwarted from a romantic elopement, becomes leader of a band of outlaws—and there with him, in the good, free wood, all the characters are at last happily united. Such stories are the light romances of youth, the play of events under the light of love, with little of seriousness, and much of sparkling wit.

"Love's Labour's Lost," like "Henry IV," has interesting passages that

310

may refer to Shakespeare's personality. The dramatist had come down to London from a country village, and he had gained education by experience rather than by study. In this play he ridicules continuous study as something that blinds one to the world, and extols experience.

BOOKS FOR FURTHER READING

Edward Dowden: *Shakespeare as a Comic Dramatist*; J. Weiss, *Wit, Humour and Shakespeare*; O. F. Adams, *Motley Jest*; *Shakespeare Diversions*; J. Bennett, *Master Skylark*; H. A. Gerber, *Stories of Shakespeare's Comedies*; F. A. Britton, *Shakespearean Fairy Tales*; W. H. Fleming, *Shakespeare's Plots*; C. Ransome, *Short Sketches of Shakespeare's Plots*; M. McLeod, *Shakespeare Story Book*; L. G. Hufford, *Shakespeare in Tale and Verse.*

Small have continual plodders ever won,
Save base authority from others' books.

In such a song as that which closes the play we find the heart of the country boy:

When icicles hang by the wall,
  And Dick the shepherd blows his nail,
And Tom bears logs into the hall,
When blood is nipp'd and ways be foul,
Then nightly sings the staring owl,
Tu-whit; tu-who, a merry note.

"A Midsummer Night's Dream" combines the buffoonery, story-telling, and romance of the other plays with a poetic beauty of its own. The whole play is fantastic, dreamlike, "Like far-off mountains turned into clouds." It is a play of love and laughter and fairyland and is fitly named.

At about the time when Shakespeare wrote these plays he also wrote other and sadder plays, but in them, as in these, he showed love for story, and delight in playing upon words. He had not yet risen to the greater hights of character, of poetry, and of philosophy. The early comedies, showing the quick, interested and care-free heart of the young Shakespeare, make a delightful introduction to the greater plays.

MOVIES INSTEAD OF SALOONS

BY CHARLES STELZLE

WHEN saloon-keepers organize to fight motion picture houses it is a sign that the picture shows are either very, very bad, or very, very good—that they are so much *worse* than the saloon that even a saloon-keeper cannot stand for them, or else that they are so much better than the saloon that they threaten to injure the saloon-keeper's business.

There is no doubt that the latter is the actual situation. Nothing in social and recreational life is doing more to furnish a saloon substitute than the motion picture house. And furnishing a saloon substitute isn't the comparatively easy task that most people think it to be.

There can be no real substitute for the saloon for those who now find their chief pleasure there. An institution which has in it so many serious objections, many of which constitute its main charm and attractiveness for those who patronize it, cannot very well be duplicated—*minus* all these features, and still be a success. The best that can be done is to try to discover what are the really good features of the saloon, and then to incorporate them in existing agencies or organize new ones.

Several outstanding peculiarities immediately strike one as the saloon is studied. In the first place, there is the perfectly natural way in which the saloon is conducted. There's nothing strained about it. Men aren't made *too* welcome. Few restrictions are imposed. Those who conduct the place make themselves as inconspicuous and as unobtrusive as they can. Those who patronize the saloon usually have nothing special *done* for them. They pay for what they get, and they do it cheerfully—often hilariously. There's a spirit of democracy about the saloon which is tremendously appealing. A five cent piece places the average man upon an equality with everybody else in the place; the music helps to produce a cheerful atmosphere.

The motion picture house possesses all of these virtues and many others besides. Here is

The motion picture show, once suspected of being the enemy of morality and as such subjected to unprecedented restrictions and censorship, is now generally recognized as a valuable educational agency and as a dreaded competitor of the saloon. Mr. Stelzle, machinist, sociologist and Presbyterian preacher, here explains the reason for its popularity among the working classes.—THE EDITOR.

found the free normal atmosphere to which the average man is accustomed. Attentions are not forced upon him. There's no one at the door to bid him an embarrassing welcome or speed him a confusing farewell. He doesn't have to talk about himself and his affairs, or about his family. The average workingman is about as shy a creature out of his natural element as one can find anywhere. In the motion picture house he may come and go in the dark. He isn't compelled to wear good clothes—he doesn't even have to change his shirt or put on a stiff linen collar. He can come just as he is. To the average workingman "dressing up" is an intolerable burden. When a man hugs the little red ticket that is flipped at him thru that cleverly contrived machine in the selling booth in front of the picture house he takes it with a feeling of independence, and passes into the show with his head up.

Furthermore, he can take his wife and children. He cannot take them to the saloon. The workingman can afford to take his family to the picture show, because it usually costs him no more than if he spent the evening in a saloon. And he feels a lot better for it the morning after. This often induces him to try it again. A few such experiences and the entire family are regular customers at the motion picture house.

Whereas in the saloon the evening is usually spent in an inane or worse manner, the modern motion picture show has in it a distinct educational advantage, and the education comes in a form which is palatable and easily digested. The mind isn't taxed unduly. The workingman really hasn't much mind left at the end of an average day's work. Also even the comparatively popular educational films are interspersed with others of a dramatic or humorous character. Sometimes the dramatic picture has an element of moral or ethical teaching which is decidedly wholesome. The cheap, harmful film is rapidly disappearing even from the cheaper houses. The entire film business is on the up grade.

To what extent the church or the school may engage in the motion picture business depends upon the character of the neighborhood, the ability to finance properly such an enterprise, the opportunity for making a selection of the right kind of films, and some other questions which may be peculiar to the locality or the organization attempting it. But principally, it is a matter of conducting the enterprise in a business-like manner, for running a motion picture show is no job for amateurs —it requires specialization and experience, which, however, may be acquired by educational and religious institutions if brains and energy are put into the task. Chiefly, one must have studied the element of human nature.

New York City

LO AND BEHOLD

BY ELLIS O. JONES

See the War Expert!

Yes, what a solemn-looking, wrinkle-browed, Atlas-like individual he is. What is the War Expert doing?

The War Expert is making sapient and pregnant observations about the war.

Does the War Expert take himself seriously?

Oh, yes, very seriously indeed. He finds it absolutely impossible to admit of the slightest chance of his being wrong in any particular.

How did the War Expert become a War Expert?

By being willing to draw the most infinitely far-reaching conclusions from the most scant and unreliable data and to assert these conclusions in a positive and scholarly manner.

Is this the only War Expert there is?

Oh, no. The woods are full of them and the newspapers are full of them and the highways and byways are full of them.

How interesting. Do the War Experts agree with each other?

Oh, no. One of the essentials of a true and trustworthy War Expert is that he shall agree with no other War Expert as to the least detail whatsoever.

New York City

Bird Spies

The pigeon of war, first cousin once removed of the dove of peace, has become an important factor in modern warfare.

His special value is as a photographer, a messenger and a spy. Equipped with a camera peculiarly designed for his purpose, he can dodge shells and aeroplanes' and penetrate the enemy's lines until their innermost secrets are recorded by his lens.

The tiny camera is fastened under the bird's body, where it will not impede flying. Its shutter works automatically.

The birds are trained as ordinary carrier pigeons—in fact they are still used to some extent to carry messages—but it is as scouts that they have become indispensable to practically every army in Europe. The French have made the most thoro tests of the war pigeons' efficiency and their conclusions have resulted in the addition of many automobile pigeon houses to the general army equipment.

Whether or not the birds accustomed to carrying cameras and dispatches can be induced to substitute the olive branch is an interesting subject for speculation.

Medem Photo Service   FRENCH ARMY PIGEONS
They travel by automobile and have a commissariat all their own

Record Speed and Endurance

The repeating "Autophone" is the latest thing in talking machines. It is just what its name suggests, a talking machine equipped with a device upon which twelve cylindrical records may be placed at one time. After these records have been placed in position the patent reproducer is placed at the starting point; the case is closed and the powerful spring, which will run for a half hour with one winding, is tightened. Simply pulling out a pin starts the mechanism to working and it requires no further attention for half an hour or more. The machinery has been so arranged that just as soon as one record has been finished the arm holding the diamond point reproducer is automatically carried back to the starting point, and the wheel holding the records turned around one notch, whereupon everything is in readiness for the playing of another selection. At the given instant the point of the reproducer is dropt upon the record and selection No. 2 begins.

A sufficient number of records may be placed in this machine to provide a program sixty-five minutes long. After one record ends it takes the machine

just a minute and a half to get in position to begin the next. When one set of records has been played it takes but five minutes to change the entire set and to have the machine again in motion.

The Census Bureau

Probably few people visit Washington and look over the different departments of Government activity without a sense of wonder and a query as to

Albert Marple
AN HOUR'S CONTINUOUS CONCERT

whether after all it is worth while. Especially is this true in regard to some of the bureaus, such as the Census Bureau, which do not bulk as large in the public eye as do the departments of War, Navy, State, Agriculture, etc.

Yet when one looks into the detail more closely it becomes evident that there is no other bureau which touches the national life at so many and such vital points. Its reports decide the apportionment of members of Congress among the states, and without its testimony ho new state can be admitted to the Union. Upon its figures are based our immigration laws.

Business men look to its reports on manufactures, agriculture, transportation, electrical industries for suggestions as to investment. The Cotton Exchange watches with feverish anxiety for its monthly reports and municipalities use its financial statistics of cities for testimony as to the best methods of accounting.

It registers the number of the insane, of criminals in prison, of paupers in almshouses, of inmates of benevolent institutions, of members of the different denominational bodies. It tells the number of persons in different occupations, business, agriculture, manufactures, mining, the professions; records the births and deaths wherever there are registration areas and reports on the prevalence of divorce.

Its volumes pour in an almost unending stream from the Government Printing Office and can be had, except in a few cases, by any American citizen for the asking.

The Shark in Commerce

Products obtained from the shark are both numerous and valuable. Shark fins furnish a jelly that makes a delicious soup, for which there is an excellent market wherever Chinese are to be found.

The shark's liver gives a clear oil excellently adapted for the lubrication of the parts of watches, clocks and fine guns. This oil is held in some quarters in as high esteem as is the oil obtained from porpoise and dogfish liver, long claimed to be the finest of animal oils.

Shark skin is of great value. It is of a beautiful burnished gray or bluish color, and at first glance looks like finely grained leather because of the tiny prickles plentifully set one way. There are so many of these prickles, quite invisible to the naked eye, that the effect afforded the dried skin is one of rich beauty, a quality that renders it particularly valuable.

Even the bones of sharks are useful. The spine is in demand by the manufacturers of curious walking-sticks. They pass a thin malacca or steel rod thru the round, polished vertebrae, and the result is a cane that sells for a high price. The shark-spine stick is a great favorite in Germany.

How They Have Grown

The Woman's Club, it seems, is one of those institutions which we have always had. To be sure, the number of them has grown exceedingly since the early days. There are at present over 2000 women's clubs in America alone.

But in 600 B. C. there was only one in the world and that was in Greece, founded by a lady named Sappho, who instructed the club in versification and the appreciation of literature.

In the fifth century B. C., Aspasia, unofficial political adviser to Pericles, started another club for the intellectual improvement of Greek women.

There are records, too, of women's clubs in early Greece, which met to discuss municipal questions and which voted funds for the erection of statues and monuments in honor of distinguished men—in those unenlightened days the monuments were all to men.

Africa came next in the development of women's clubs—its most notable the one at Alexandria, where Hypatia, one of the foremost mathematicians and philosophers of her time, taught the studious women of Egypt. Contrary to modern custom, the men begged permission to join, and astronomers, philosophers, statesmen and scholars were admitted regardless of sex.

The first club organizer in America was Anne Hutchinson, who came to New England in 1634 and formed circles of women to discuss the sermons of the day and other matters of religion. The interest in these discussions brought the men of that colony to their sessions, too, and finally caused the banishment of Anne Hutchinson.

That put a stop to women's clubs for nearly a century. The next attempt was made in 1818, again in Boston, when an organization called The Gleaners came into existence. This was composed of unmarried women, who met to discuss questions of the proper attitude to be maintained toward gentlemen. With the marriage of all the members the club ceased to exist.

Women's clubs spread thruout the country after that. Illinois, Ohio, Indiana, and Michigan followed the lead of Massachusetts—one of the most flourishing of their ventures was the Minerva Club of New Harmony, started by Mrs. Constance Fauntleroy Runice.

But all of these were more or less "feelers," preliminary to the actual beginning of the woman's club movement in the United States. The New England Women's Club in Boston and the Sorosis Club in New York, both founded in 1868, laid the foundation for the organization of women's clubs today, in which they are still active leaders.

"THE SHEPHERD IN THE DISTANCE." A PANTOMIME WRITTEN, DESIGNED, ACTED, PRODUCED BY WASHINGTON SQUARE PLAYERS

TWO LITTLE THEATERS GROW UP

BY HANNAH WHITE

PRACTICALLY everyone, with the possible exception of theatrical managers, has a theory for the ideal theater—a place for something more than dramatized best sellers and vehicles drawn exclusively by stars. And in consequence amateur companies and "little theaters" have sprung up all over the country, most of them leaping into the experiment with complete abandonment of tradition and frequently finding, when they stop to look, that the sum total of their achievement is a difference without a distinction.

Two exceptions, both in New York City, have succeeded during the present theatrical season in establishing themselves as forces to be reckoned with in the future of the American stage. Both are democratic ventures, both are presenting plays that have no appeal to the commercial manager, both are giving their attention exclusively to the stage and forgetting the box office, both are interested in stimulating and developing new and artistic methods of acting and producing—and both are winning out

It was just a year ago that the Washington Square Players, "that valorous band that came out of nowhere late last winter and settled down quietly to the business of taking the curse off the word amateur," presented their first program of four one-act plays to an audience of 299 people at the Bandbox Theater.

Their capital was exactly nothing, their stock in trade boundless enthusiasm, in-

314

defatigable energy and a wide variety of talents. And next morning the newspapers heralded their production as "the most novel theatrical opening ever seen in this city," "a stimulus and suggestion for all who are concerned with the drama."

Thruout the rest of the season they played three or four times a week to a house sold out in advance for every performance, giving in all fourteen new plays by American writers and

THE NEIGHBORHOOD PLAYHOUSE
Where the heritage of the immigrant is furthering our artistic ideals

three by foreign authors. The entire staff, the press representative and all the actors contributed their services. All seats were sold at fifty cents.

Now the theater is leased for eight performances a week, a part of the seats are sold at $1, and a living wage is paid to each of the actors and producers who form the nucleus of the company. Second only to their achievement of artistically worthwhile productions is the Washington Square Players' record of paying as they go and even putting aside a surplus for further experiments. The company even hopes this spring to be able to make a tour of New England and of the Middle West.

The secret of their success is in the personnel of the Washington Square Players —so-called because they live in Greenwich Village, "the Quartier Latin—minus the Latin—of New York." They are all young and they are all idealists. They have convictions and they have the courage to carry them out. Their convention is unconventionality and their motto Dare!

Moreover, they are willing to work hard—as actors, playwrights, producers, designers and, in a pinch, ticket-sellers or scene-shifters, all at once. For one person to write, for instance, the first play of a bill, to take the leading part in the next, and to design the costumes or direct the production of the third seems quite possible to them. Even the publicity manager may rush from lobby to stage to "supe" when the business calls for "a throng of passersby."

The selection of plays has been particularly happy. Aside from their individual merits they have been chosen to present interesting contrasts and to include a wide range of modern dramatists.

But it is in the creation of artistic stage settings, daringly impressionistic, that the Washington Square Players have made their most important contribution to dramatic progress. Colors have been used as never before to register ideas. The audience gasps when the curtain goes up, but it applauds, too; and before a word is spoken the atmosphere of the play is established and the imagination of each spectator is in good working order.

"Art for art's sake" has been quoted as the slogan of the Washington Square Players. Art for the people's sake sums up fairly well the purpose of the second successful dramatic experiment in New York, the Neighborhood Playhouse. It too was opened in February, 1915—the outcome of the work of the festival and dramatic groups of the famous Henry Street Settlement.

For nine years these groups have presented festivals and pantomimes in the gymnasium of the settlement, developing their possibilities until they were able to form a dramatic club—The Neighborhood Players—which did so well that they were given a little theater, offering every facility for artistic productions.

"Jephthah's Daughter," a Biblical festival, opened the playhouse with a performance beautiful in itself and significant both as a reminder of our indebtedness to Jewish literature and art and as a demonstration of the potential talent of the East Side. Seventy-eight young people were in the cast, and many more, as craftsmen, composers, painters, and musicians, seamstresses, and producers, had a share in the production.

During the year a half dozen plays, chosen for their educational value as well as for their dramatic possibilities, have been produced. The Thanksgiving Festival, an elaborate pageant, which brought out the musical as well as the dramatic ability of the company, was the most successful production of the year. To the East Side it was an interpretative festival, which they appreciated as participators. But the rest of New York found it a delightful entertainment.

The Thanksgiving Festival typifies the aim of the Neighborhood Playhouse, "to recapture and hold something of the poetry and idealism that belong to its people and open the door of opportunity for messages in drama, picture, story and song."

THE NEW BOOKS

RUPERT BROOKE IN AMERICA

There are two main streams in Rupert Brooke's poems: a keen and frequently ironical analysis of some phases of emotion, and a tingling freshness of sense-experience, exprest alike with the greatest pungency and beauty of phrase. In the *Letters from America*, which adds one to the small group of books by and about the vivid young Englishman, there is little of the searching analysis of men's hearts, but a great wealth of things and the appearances of things, pictured and discussed with that same piercingly suggestive diction.

Brooke left England in May, 1913, to visit the United States, Canada, and the South Seas, and was away until the beginning of June, 1914. Thirteen travel letters were written to the *Westminster Gazette*, and one other paper appeared in the *New Statesman;* and these have been collected, together with an additional essay, of which more later, by Brooke's close friend, Edward Marsh, who is also preparing a memoir and such posthumous matter as still awaits publication. Henry James supplies a preface.

It is fortunate that the poet's chief concern is not with the United States, but with Canada. He was so finely linked up with the English heritage, as Mr. James points out, that his reactions to the half-English Dominion would naturally be more interesting than his impressions of our own country, and his curiosity as to the surfaces of things quite dominates the brief attention he gives to New York and Boston, which alone are treated in these rapid and frankly casual sketches. Mr. James remarks:

We feel him not a little lost and lonely and stranded in the New York pandemonium—obliged to throw himself upon skyscrapers and the overspread blackness pricked out in a flickering fury of imaged advertisement for want of some more interesting view of character and manners. We long to take him by the hand and show him finer lights—eyes of but meaner range, after all, being adequate to the gape at the vertical business blocks and the lurid skyclamour for more dollars. We feel in a manner his sensibility wasted and would fain turn it on to the capture of deeper meanings.

Most interesting among the American observations is Brooke's impression of a Harvard commencement. Here there is some balm—but not much—for the friendly contempt which he pours upon New York and the typical American.

Brooke saw Canada when the flush of the Great Speculation which made the Dominion a nation of real estate dealers had not yet died away, killed by the collapse of land values. So he speaks with amusement and some scorn of the booster and the land trader. "To boost," he says, "is to commend outrageously." And there is a delicious account of an encounter with two boosters.

I traveled from Edmonton to Calgary in the company of a citizen of Edmonton and a citizen of Calgary. Hour after hour they disputed. Land in Calgary had risen from five dollars to three hundred; but in Edmonton from three to five thousand. Edmonton had grown from thirty persons to forty thousand in twenty years; but Calgary from twenty to thirty thousand in twelve. . . . "Where"—as a respite—"did I come from?" I had to tell them, not without shame, that my own town of Grantchester, having numbered three hundred at the time of Julius Caesar's landing, had risen rapidly to nearly four by Doomsday Book, but was now declined to three-fifty. They seemed perplexed and angry.

The dry humor which flavors this is much in evidence thruout the book. The often repellant irony which one finds in the poems is softened, and, oddly enough, Brooke finds in all his travels here no such distressing grotesqueries as some of the poems exhibit. One piece of quaintly phrased characterization must be quoted:

His mind was even more childlike and transparent than is usual with business men. The observer could see thoughts slowly floating into it, like carp in a pond. When they got near the surface, by a purely automatic process they found utterance.

To suggest that humor is the predominant strain in the book would be an in-

justice to the poet in the man. There are places where the sheer beauty of the description and the delicacy of the comment would be hard to surpass in the whole range of English writing. Particularly in telling of the Northwest, where Brooke got to the frontier and the mountains, and of Samoa, does the poet break away from the journalist—tho either rôle sits well on him. A few papers come to their conclusion with a lovely falling cadence that recalls Ruskin.

The last chapter, somewhat unhappily called "An Unusual Young Man," ties the book to the war by presenting what purports to be a straightforward record of a young man's mental processes when he came home from at Great War. It is, of course, autobiographical, and it adds interestingly to the distinctive literature of this war—the literature that attempts to study the impact of war upon the individual.

Of the preface by Mr. James one is inclined to say little, remembering the blow that has fallen upon him. There is a subtle study of the relation between Brooke and his heritage and environment, but that curious style which was once a matter of admirable, tho often tedious precision, has here lost itself in a sad welter of words.

Letters from America, by Rupert Brooke. New York: Scribner. $1.25.

A DAUNTLESS LADY

In *Life and Gabriella*, by Ellen Glasgow, there is a duel between the two, and, at first, Life appears to have conquered the bright, spirited girl. But Gabriella has courage as well as spirit and the gift of doing one thing well, which is the best gift the fairies can bring to the cradle of any child. Miss Glasgow contrasts Richmond in the middle nineties and its spare and Spartan living, with New York in its growing extravagance. The effort of the less opulent people in both cities to keep up appearances is a sordid struggle to which she does full justice. Gabriella's escape into the business world, and her career as a successful woman of affairs, add the romance of trade to the story of social and domestic complications. The heroine who can throw aside her home worries by a plunge into practical finance, is happier than the lady of older fiction who could only sit by the fire and weep—and she is more interesting.

Doubleday, Page. $1.35.

AMERICA EXPLAINED

The lectures delivered in 1914 by President Arthur Twining Hadley of Yale University at Oxford and the University of Virginia have now been published in *Undercurrents in American Politics*. The analysis of the realities of American political life is more searching and complete than would be expected from the brief compass of the

· 316

book. President Hadley says little of the formal changes of law and constitution and much of the purely extra-legal features of our political machinery; the party organization, the power of the boss, the spoils system and the reform movements. The influence of economic factors upon legislation and administration is stressed; the author even venturing the statement that "the whole American political and social system is based on industrial property right, far more completely than has ever been the case in any European country."

Undercurrents in American Politics, by Arthur Twining Hadley. Yale University Press. $1.35.

SONGS OF WAR AND PEACE

Glorious indeed is the *Vision of War,* as Lincoln Colcord sees it. Here is an idealization, not so much of war, as the martial spirit. "The actual fighting is not of the least importance. . . . The willingness to be killed is the only vital issue." Which is greater, Mr. Colcord asks, the Belgium of peace and plenty and the Congo atrocities, or the devastated Belgium of today? Mr. Colcord's use of free verse is as forceful as Whitman's, and his vision is as wide.

Songs of Brittany by Theodore Botrel has been a favorite of the soldiers in the trenches. Elizabeth S. Dickerman has translated for us his first volume, published in 1897. His songs are the stuff of which folk-lore is made. They are simple; they are patriotic; they are religious; and, occasionally, as in The Prude, who boasts that she does not go walking with the village lads—because "I am not asked, you know"—whimsical.

A volume of unusual merit is *Prayer for Peace and Other Poems,* by William Samuel Johnson. The opening poem, Prayer for Peace, strikes a high note that is sustained thruout. The Poor Little Guy is a fine plea for those who suffer most from war. A La Soiree Musicale is a triolet of rare grace.

Songs to Save a Soul, by a new English poet, Irene Rutherford McLeod, went into its fourth edition in England in a few months. There is a freshness and charm about the volume that is the result not only of its splendid lines but of its varied themes. The opening poem, Soft Places, is typical of the mystical strain that runs thruout. Lone Dog is the cry of a rebel; the note struck is akin to that of Masefield, who, by the way, has helped greatly to render the author her due.

The *Collected Poems* of Condé Benoist Pallen is a volume of distinctive verse by a Catholic poet. The book has none of the harshness of our modern verse; it is the work of a scholar and a classicist. There is the flavor of Fitzgerald in The New Rubaiyat; something of Milton in Maria Immaculata; and The Death of Sir Launcelot shows Tennyson's Influence.

Charles Erskine Scott Wood's chief claim to fame heretofore has been as a writer of the famous (or infamous, if you will) "Heavenly Dialogs" for *Masses.* In *The Poet in the Desert,* however, he has produced literature.

CONSTIPATION IN CHILDREN

D O you realize how often the foundations of ill health are laid in early childhood—by the neglect of parents who fail to guard their children from the dangers of the constipation habit?

Children should not be given cathartics and strong purges. They weaken the *natural* processes of evacuation and are dangerously habit-forming.

A far safer and saner means of securing normal bowel movements is the use of **Nujol**, which eminent physicians both in this country and abroad are now prescribing.

Nujol is not a laxative, but acts in effect as a mechanical lubricant, preventing the contents of the intestines from becoming hard, and so promoting healthy and regular bowel activity.

Most druggists carry **Nujol**, which is sold only in pint bottles packed in cartons bearing the **Nujol** trademark. If your druggist does not carry **Nujol**, accept no substitute. We will send a pint bottle prepaid to any point in the United States on receipt of 75c—money order or stamps.

Write for booklet, "The Rational Treatment of Constipation."

Address Department 19.

STANDARD OIL COMPANY
(New Jersey)

Bayonne　　　　New Jersey

Nujol

REG. U.S. PAT. OFF.

Approved by
Harvey W. Wiley, Director of
Good Housekeeping, Bureau of
Foods, Sanitation and Health.

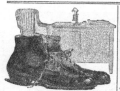
The most violent opponent of free verse will hesitate to say that this is not poetry. In a splendid tribute to the Desert, wherein the Poet talks with Truth, Mr. Wood makes a notable addition to our American verse.

Vision of War, by Lincoln Colcord. Macmillan. $1.25. *Songs of Brittany,* by Theodore Botrel. Boston: Badger. $1. *Prayer for Peace and Other Poems,* by William Samuel Johnson. Kennerley, $1.25. *Songs to Save a Soul,* by Irene Rutherford McLeod. Huebsch, $1. *Collected Poems,* by Condé Benoist Pallen. Kennedy, $1.25. *The Poet in the Desert,* by Charles Erskine Scott Wood. Oregon: F. W. Baltes. $1.

GIVING THE BABY A GOOD START

Sensible suggestions on the care of young children never come amiss to the inexperienced but loving, conscientious mother. *The Baby's First Two Years,* by Richard M. Smith, M.D., may be recommended as certain to be helpful.

Houghton, Mifflin, 75 cents.

NATIONAL QUESTIONS

The current issue of the *University Debate Annual* contains debates on the Income of the Army and Navy, the Monroe Doctrine, the Minimum Wage, Government Ownership of Telephone and Telegraph, Socialistic Control of the Means of Production and Exchange, and Single Tax.

White Plains, N. Y.: Wilson. $1.50.

POPULAR SCIENCE

An uncommonly attractive collection of miscellaneous information is that of the *Book of Progress,* which all boys and girls and many grown folk would enjoy and profit by. Compiled by A. A. Hopkins from the last five years of the Scientific American, the papers are trustworthy as well as interesting.

N. Y.: Cricks Publishing Corporation. 3 v. $9.

ST. PAUL

The new volume on *Paul and His Epistles,* by Professor D. A. Hayes, is full of learning vigorously exprest, but lacks freshness of view and historical insight. The author stands in fear of the older commentators and has given us a strange mixture of scholasticism, traditionalism and modern learning.

Methodist Book Concern. $2.

THE GANG AT SUNDAY SCHOOL

In *Fishers of Boys* William McCormick gives sound advice to religious workers and parents. He has found that boys can be reached best through the gang, and he presents his case in a breezy readable manner. Boys are influenced more by a great baseball player's opinion of religion than by the Old Testament Prophets and a Golden Text.

Doran. $1.

OUR NEW HIGHWAY

Thirty-one beautiful plates, by a new process of color photography, make C. Lancaster's pamphlet on *The Columbia, America's Greatest Highway,* a notable little publication. Mr. Lancaster was chief engineer in laying out the road that runs thru the Cascade Mountains to the sea, and he knows well the wonderful region, its geology, its Indian legends, its tales of settlement days.

Portland, Ore.: S. C. Lancaster. $2.50.

THE BEST OF THE MODERNS

The *Trail of the Torch,* by Paul Hervieu, perhaps today the greatest of French dramatists, has now been included in the Drama League Series. The capable translation is by John Alan Haughton. Hervieu's art is here at its best, and the austerity and intensity of the emotional appeal is brought home, whether or not we sympathize with the problem the author has presented after the French fashion.

Doubleday, Page. 75 cents.

HOPE

Professor George Trumbull Ladd has followed his inquiries into the possibilities of knowledge, moral values, and faith by a new volume, the last of the series, entitled *What May I Hope?* With delibera-

tion and sound reasoning he outlines the essence and ground of hope, its practical use and value, and its objects in the moral and social realms, and points out the basis upon which humanity rises to the assurance of immortal life

Longmans, Green. $1.50.

THE DIFFICULT ART OF GROWING UP

Exercise, air, rest, food and "the control of inner force" are Mr. Moore's essentials in *Keeping in Condition, a Handbook on Training for Older Boys.* Worry, colds, constipation, are among the dangers that check full growth and participation in race and national progress. The sex life is placed normally among other functions and conservatively treated.

Macmillan. 75 cents.

THE PURITAN LEGACY

In a series of readable historical sketches James Phinney Munroe shows the strength and possibilities of that often maligned quality, *The New England Conscience.* He also discusses democracy and woman suffrage; gives a most interesting description of the Middle West, the Heart of the United States from a New England standpoint; and endeavors, not very convincingly, to show the basic relation between the New England Conscience and the Eternal Feminine.

Boston: Badger. $1.25.

SUGAR-COATED HISTORY

The twenty-third edition of Gertrude Atherton's biographical story of Alexander Hamilton, *The Conqueror,* proves the popularity of a book which combines authentic history with an intensely interesting novel. The personality of "the greatest of constructive American statesmen, on the wheels of whose work this country still travels" is portrayed with enthusiastic appreciation of the power of his intellect and the scope of his career.

Stokes. $1.50.

FOR WOMEN AND BY WOMEN

The middle of the nineteenth century saw the beginning of many movements, few of them more important than the founding of the Young Women's Christian Association. In 1866, *Fifty Years of Association Work Among Young Women,* by Elizabeth Wilson, tells the story of its phenomenal growth and gives an adequate and accurate survey of its varied activities.

New York: National Board Y. W. C. A. $1.35.

EDUCATIONAL PHILOSOPHY

The essays in *The Meaning of Education,* by Nicholas Murray Butler, an enlargement of the book of the same title published in 1898, illustrate happily the saying that everyone is a radical in his own specialty. A typically incisive remark, to be taken to heart in all normal schools, is as follows: "Some of the books and periodicals that purport to deal with education make me regret the invention of printing; . . . they cannot be read without subtracting from the sum of human knowledge."

Scribner. $1.50.

WHAT IS THE MATTER WITH AMERICA!

When you have finished Van Wyck Brooks's *America's Coming of Age* you know that our country badly needs "something" in her life and literature. You have a general conception of that "something," but not the remotest idea how it is to be obtained. But you have come in contact with many ideas worth meeting. Some you receive with joy, others you repudiate, nearly all arrest your attention because of their felicitous phrasing.

Huebsch. $1.

MOUNTAIN BLOSSOMS

This untechnical, yet carefully made, handbook, *Wild Flowers of the North American Mountains,* by Julia W. Henshaw, will be extremely useful to every tourist to the national parks among the Rockies and the coast ranges, as well as to residents of those regions. The flowers are arranged in groups according to their most conspicuous color; and there are scores of the most helpful as well as pleasing illustrations from photographs, including twenty in colors.

McBride. $2.50.

EFFICIENCY QUESTION BOX

CONDUCTED BY

EDWARD EARLE PURINTON

DIRECTOR OF THE

INDEPENDENT EFFICIENCY SERVICE

210. Mr. R. W. D., Oregon. "I am a stenographer and executive in the Government service. I don't feel energetic and enthusiastically interested as I should be. When I do occasionally get enthusiastic and begin to hurry I make mistakes and lose my bearings. I want to learn to think and do things quickly, but accurately and thoroly. Health good, no bad habits. Kindly make suggestions."

You should learn scientific management. Ask Efficiency Press Syndicate, Woolworth Building, New York, for list of books on the subject. The key to your problem lies in planning your day ahead, thinking out each move on a standardized time schedule, in advance of making it. To increase energy, take a good course in physical exercise—answer all such advertisements in a copy of *Physical Culture* magazine, Flatiron Building, New York; and of *Health Culture*, Passaic, New Jersey. A Government job tends to stagnation. Get a future where you are, and get it in mind—or get out.

211. Mrs. H. B. C., California. "(a) Does an active child of twelve need as much food as an adult doing sedentary work? (b) Have the Fletcher or Chittenden standards been tried out on children? (c) Is not the danger of underfeeding as great as that of overfeeding, with the growing organism? (d) Is it advisable to measure and limit a growing child who is healthy and on plain rations? (e) Can you refer me to authorities on the scientific feeding of children? The new standards and ideals seem to apply mostly to adults."

(a) Probably yes. (b) Not so far as we know—and we devoutly hope they never will be. Fletcher and Chittenden were meant to guide grown-ups, not children. (c) Yes. Read Crighton-Browne's "Parsimony in Nutrition." (d) Hardly ever. Teach the children to eat slowly, regularly, and only at meal time, then allow natural hunger to operate unmolested. (e) We do not consider anybody a final authority. But we suggest gladly a few names of leading investigators: Dr. J. H. Kellogg, Battle Creek, Mich.; Prof. L. B. Allyn, Westfield, Mass.; Dr. J. H. Tilden, Denver, Colorado; Dr. H. Lindlahr, Ashland Boulevard, Chicago; Eugene Christian, 213 West Seventy-ninth Street, New York; Editor of *National Food Magazine*, 45 West Thirty-fourth Street, New York; Bernarr Macfadden, Flatiron Building, New York; School Lunch Committee of Child Hygiene Bureau, New York City Board of Health.

212. Mr. J. S. F., Brooklyn. "I am ambitious to become a lecturer. I have given successfully a few informal talks on travel subjects. How would you advise me to perfect myself, and to secure a position as a lecturer on serious subjects?"

Without knowing you we cannot advise you how to perfect yourself in anything. But your first step, doubtless, will be to find what successful speakers are doing. Learn of their topics, methods, itineraries, and apply the lessons to yourself. Obtain descriptive literature of the lectures of Chautauqua Institution, Chautauqua, New York; Burton Holmes Travelogues, 156 Fifth Avenue, New York City; J. B. Pond Lyceum Bureau, 1 Madison Avenue, New York City; League for Political Education, 147 West Forty-eighth Street, New York City; West Side Y. M. C. A., 318 West Fifty-seventh Street; Bureau of Lectures, New York City Board of Education, 157 East Sixty-seventh Street.

Have you a real message to give? Don't try to be a lecturer without it. Become a recognized authority in some special field—and you will be asked to tell about your work. Investigate the Kaiser Course in Public Speaking, managed by Funk and Wagnalls, 390 Fourth Avenue, New York —and improve your delivery.

213. Mr. G. S. H., Michigan. "We were very much interested in your Independent article for October 25, on 'Efficiency in the Factory.' One of the bits of advice given in this article was to consult an expert. You mention organizations such as The American Institute of Consulting Engineers and The American Society of Mechanical Engineers. The writer would appreciate it highly if you would mention the location of these societies, so that we might write to them for information."

Address the American Institute of Consulting Engineers at 35 Nassau Street, New York; The American Society of Mechanical Engineers at 29 West Thirty-ninth Street, New York.

214. Mr. H. W. H., New York City. "Does not efficiency minimize physical effort? Do not people doing least physical work have smallest families? Therefore would not efficiency on a large scale tend toward race-suicide?"

Your logic is faulty. The really efficient person thinks—first, last and all the time. The parents who think save their children from the terrible infant mortality, vice and crime that destroy hundreds of thousands of children every year. This saving should more than offset the lower rate of birth resulting from the hypothetical physical apathy of a race of efficient people. It may be that one man in 10,000 is truly efficient, and one woman in 50,000. The condition is not yet epidemic, and should cause no alarm.

215. Prof. M. A. Alabama. "I am twenty-six years old, a supervisor in the city schools; seem to be highly respected, and to discharge my duties satisfactorily. But I feel that I do not know anything, and have never learned how to think, to study, to concentrate, to analyze or compare. I cannot make a systematic study of myself, my talents or opportunities. Where can I obtain knowledge of experimental psychology, character analysis, vocational guidance, human nature, self-discovery and self-improvement? How can I secure a copy of your article 'What Is Efficiency,' and what will be the cost?"

If you have been reading the Question Box regularly, and continue to do so, you will find many of your queries answered in replies to others. What you want is a new educational system applied to yourself —twenty years after it should have been started. The new system is woefully needed, but we cannot produce it in a few lines of a magazine column. The article "What Is Efficiency," price 10 cents, may be had from The Independent.

216. A Reader in the West. "I am forty years old, married, no children. Was in office and banking; but thru failure of an irrigation project I lost everything, and am $4400 in debt. A year ago I went into life insurance, am now state manager, making a living, and reducing my indebtedness about $500 a year. I don't want to go into bankruptcy, but cannot pay off my debts in many years at this rate, with no prospect of saving money at all. My wife and I are both studying Spanish. We would go anywhere, to rebuild our fortunes. Are there opportunities in the new companies now being formed for the development of South American trade? If so, where can I learn of them?"

Write the Secretary of the American International Corporation, 120 Broadway, New York; The Exporter's Review, 80 Broad street; Exporters' and Importers' Journal, 17 State street; South American Export and Import Company, 24 Stone street; South American Publishing Company, 1 Broadway; South American Trade and Finance Company, 149 Broadway. Then apply to officials of the firms doing business in South America, whose names you will have secured. Tell those men what you have done—a man who can rise to be state manager of a business in a year or service has a right to be heard!

Why wouldn't your own life insurance company send you to South America, and put you in charge of a good territory when you had mastered local details? Ask your company about this.

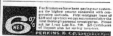

217. A Reader in Connecticut. "Can you advise me in regard to obtaining a position in the office of an architect or building superintendent? I have been a teacher and social worker, but my natural bent is toward architecture and building. Am a college graduate, and a hard worker; have been told that in regard to building problems I have an unusually practical mind. Am now taking a correspondence course, with the I. C. S. of Scranton, and would appreciate and give loyal service to an employer who would grant me the opportunity of working for him while finishing the course."

You are on the right track, with the right idea. Congratulations. We offer several suggestions. Ask the I. C. S. for a list of their old architectural graduates in your vicinity, who might have an opening in their office. Put an advertisement in a trade journal—send for copies of these, and look them over: *Architecture*, 527 Fifth avenue; *Architectural Record*, 119 West Fortieth street; *Architecture and Building*, 23 Warren street; *Building Age*, 239 West Thirty-ninth street; all of New York. Obtain particulars of their work—then use to advantage—from Architects' Bureau Technical Service, 105 West Fortieth street; Architects and Builders' Index, 340 Madison avenue; Architectural League of New York, 215 West Fifty-seventh street; Building Trades Employers' Association, 30 West Thirty-third street; all of New York. From this data compile list of possible employers; send to each a brief, strong letter, typewritten, presenting your ambitions and qualifications.

218. Mrs. L. C., District of Columbia. "(a) How would you plan a home so that all five bedrooms may have the morning sun? (b) Should a wife and mother leave her home for half the day, in order to do outside work, even if she has a good maid, when the result is a scattering of the family and few home evenings? I have been watching several cases where outside interests of women cause home inefficiency, and should like your opinion. Other women readers of The Independent join me in this request."

(a) Put the very young, old or weakly members of the family in rooms exposed to the morning sun, and the rest in sleeping chambers with a clear Western exposure. For an average healthy person the rays of the afternoon sun, if direct from noon to night, should be sufficient for home hygiene.

(b) Some modern club women err on the side of preferring the limelight to the heart-glow. When the price of publicity is domesticity, a woman will find it a bad bargain. What is the objection, however, to a useful public service or business for a woman if she is absent from home during office hours only, when husband and children are at work and at school? The typical woman publicist needs heading off, but every woman should have something of a career. See page 343 of my book "Efficient Living," for an extended answer.

219. Miss O. D. R., Ohio. "(a) Can you give me the address of a news clipping agency? I wish to have clippings from magazines on specified subjects, but am unable to find the address of any agency. (b) Will you kindly suggest a subject for a high school senior girl's oration to be given in a literary contest? My opponents will write upon the subjects, 'Pan-American Union' and 'The Value of the Chautauqua.' I shall greatly appreciate your favor."

(a) Among the leading press clipping bureaus are the following: The *Atlas*, 218 East Forty-second Street; Burrette's, 60 Warren Street; Luce's, 88 Park Place; Romeike's, 106 Seventh Avenue; National Press Intelligence Company, 119 West Fortieth; all of New York City.

(b) Do you want merely to win the contest—or to give an oration that shall be of most benefit to your hearers and yourself? Analyze your motive and aim. One of these topics would be good: "Finding Your Vocation"; "Woman's Work"; "National Preparedness and Individual Responsibility"; "Should a High School Graduate Go Thru College?" "Social Service and the New Age"; "The Science of Home Building"; "Great Lessons from the Great War." Take a subject that *appeals to your heart*—then fill your brain with facts—then write yourself into your production.

The Joy of Owning a Boat

MOTOR BOATING is the greatest sport in the world—it's healthful, it's enjoyable—it's invigorating. Again, for 1916, over 100 leading Boat Builders in various parts of the United States and Canada have joined with the Gray Motor Company in issuing a catalog of *specialized boats*, telling where you can buy the kind of boat you want at the price you want to pay—also giving you the name and address of the leading boat builder nearest your locality.

Boats a Girl Can Operate

The boats shown in this catalog are powered with Guaranteed Gray Motors, self-starting, clean and reliable—making motor boating a real pleasure for "Milady."

GRAY MOTOR COMPANY
356 Gray Motor Bldg.   Detroit, Mich.

DEBATING SOCIETIES

The Single Six-Year Term for President.
The Death Penalty.
Price Maintenance.
Minimum Wage Legislation.
Mothers' Pensions.
Who is Responsible for the War?
Government Owned Merchant Marine.
Shall We Enlarge the Army?
Convict Labor In the United States.
The Problem of The Trusts.
The Monroe Doctrine.
Military Training For College Students.
An Embargo On Arms.
Mexico and The United States.

Both sides of all these fourteen debates will be furnished for only 25 cents.

THE INDEPENDENT
119 West 40th St.   New York

---

recognized authority in some special field—and you will be asked to tell about your work. Investigate the Kleiser Course in Public Speaking, managed by Funk and Wagnalls, 360 Fourth Avenue, New York—and improve your delivery.

213. Mr. G. S. H., Michigan. "We were very much interested in your Independent article for October 25, on 'Efficiency in the Factory.' One of the bits of advice given in the article was to consult an expert. You mention organizations such as the American Institute of Consulting Engineers and The American Society of Mechanical Engineers. The writer would appreciate it highly if you would mention the location of those societies, so that we might write to them for information."

Address the American Institute of Consulting Engineers at 35 Nassau Street, New York; The American Society of Mechanical Engineers at 25 West Thirty-ninth Street, New York.

214. Mr. H. W. R., New York City. "Does not efficiency minimize physical effort? Do not people doing least physical work have smallest families? Therefore would not efficiency, on a large scale tend toward race suicide?"

Your logic is faulty. The really efficient person thinks—first and last and all the time. The parents who think save their children from the terrible infant mortality, vice and crime that destroy hundreds of thousands of children every year. This saving should more than offset the lower rate of birth resulting from the hypothetical physical apathy of a race of efficient people. If may be that one man in 10,000 is truly efficient, and one woman in 30,000. The condition is not yet epidemic, and should cause no alarm.

215. Prof. M. A., Alabama. "I am twenty-six years old, a supervisor in the city schools; seem to be highly respected, and to discharge my duties satisfactorily. But I feel that I do not know anything, and have never learned how to think, to study, to concentrate, to analyze or compare. I cannot make a systematic study of myself; my talents or opportunities. Where can I obtain knowledge of experimental psychology, character analysis, vocational guidance, human nature, self-discovery and self-improvement? How can I secure a copy of your article 'What Is Efficiency,' and what will be the cost?"

If you have been reading the Question Box regularly, and continue to do so, you will find many of your queries answered in replies to others. What you want is a true educational system applied to yourself—twenty years after it should have been started. The new system is woefully needed, but we cannot produce it in a few lines of a magazine column. The article "What Is Efficiency," price 10 cents, may be had from The Independent.

216. A Reader in the West. "I am forty years old, married, no children. Was in office and banking; but thru failure of an irrigation project I lost everything, and am $5000 in debt. A year ago I went into life insurance, am now state manager, making a living, and reducing my indebtedness about $500 a year. I don't want to go into bankruptcy, but cannot pay off my debts in many years at this rate, with no prospect of saving money at all. My wife and I are both studying Spanish. We would go anywhere, to rebuild our fortunes. Are there opportunities in the new companies now being formed for the development of South American trade? If so, where can I learn of them?"

Write the Secretary of the American International Corporation, 120 Broadway, New York; The Exporter's Review, 80 Broad street; Exporters' and Importers' Journal, 17 State street; South American Export and Import Company, 24 Stone street; South American Publishing Company, 1 Broadway; South American Trade and Finance Company, 149 Broadway. Then apply to officials of the firms doing business in South America, whose names you will have secured. Tell these men what you have done—a man who can rise to be state manager of his business in a year of service has a right to be heard!

Why wouldn't your own life insurance company send you to South America, and put you in charge of a good territory when you had mastered local details? Ask your company about this.

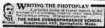

217. A Reader in Connecticut. "Can you advise me in regard to obtaining a position in the office of an architect or building superintendent? I have been a teacher and social worker, but my natural bent is toward architecture and building. Am a college graduate, and a hard worker; have been told that in regard to building problems I have an unusually practical mind. Am now taking a correspondence course, with the I. C. S. of Scranton, and would appreciate and give loyal service to an emp'oyer who would grant me the opportunity of working for him while finishing the course."

You are on the right track, with the right idea. Congratulations. We offer several suggestions. Ask the I. C. S. for a list of their old architectural graduates in your vicinity, who might have an opening in their office. Put an advertisement in a trade journal—send for copies of these, and look them over: Architecture, 527 Fifth avenue; Architectural Record, 119 West Fortieth street; Architecture and Building, 23 Warren street; Building Age, 239 West Thirtyninth street; all of New York. Obtain particulars of their work—then use to advantage—from Architects' Bureau Technical Service. 105 West Fortieth street; Architects and Builders' Index, 340 Madison avenue; Architectural League of New York, 215 West Fifty-seventh street; Building Trades Employers' Association, 30 West Thirty-third street; all of New York. From this data compile list of possible employers; send to each a brief, strong letter, typewritten, presenting your ambitions and qualifications.

218. Mrs. L. C., District of Columbia. "(a) How would you plan a home so that all five bedrooms may have the morning sun? (b) Should a wife and mother leave her home for half the day, in order to do outside work, even if she has a good maid, when the result is a scattering of the family and few home evenings? I have been watching several cases where outside interests of women cause home inefficiency, and should like your opinion. Other women readers of The Independent join me in this request."

(a) Put the very young, old or weakly members of the family in rooms exposed to the morning sun, and the rest in sleeping chambers with a clear Western exposure. For an average healthy person the rays of the afternoon sun, if direct from noon to night, should be sufficient for home hygiene.

(b) Some modern club women err on the side of preferring the limelight to the heart-glow. When the price of publicity is domesticity, a woman will find it a bad bargain. What is the objection, however, to a useful public service or business for a woman if she is absent from home during office hours only, when husband and children are at work and at school? The typical woman publicist needs heading off, but every woman should have something of a career. See page 343 of my book "Efficient Living," for an extended answer.

219. Miss O. D. R., Ohio. "(a) Can you give me the address of a news clipping agency? I wish to have clippings from magazines on specified subjects, but am unable to find the address of any agency. (b) Will you kindly suggest a subject for a high school senior girl's oration to be given in a literary contest? My opponents will write upon the subjects, 'Pan-American Union' and 'The Value of the Chautauqua.' I shall greatly appreciate your favor."

(a) Among the leading press clipping bureaus are the following: The Atlas, 218 East Forty-second Street; Burrette's, 60 Warren Street; Luce's, 88 Park Place; Romeike's, 106 Seventh Avenue; National Press Intelligence Company, 119 West Fortieth; all of New York City.

(b) Do you want merely to win the contest—or to give an oration that shall be of most benefit to your hearers and yourself? Analyze your motive and aim. One of these topics should be good: "Finding Your Vocation"; "Woman's Work"; "National Preparedness and Individual Responsibility"; "Should a High School Graduate Go Thru College?"; "Social Service and the New Age"; "The Science of Home Building"; "Great Lessons from the Great War." Take a subject that appeals to your heart—then fill your brain with facts—then write yourself into your production.

The Joy of Owning a Boat

MOTOR BOATING is the greatest sport in the world—it's healthful, it's enjoyable—it's invigorating. Again, for 1916, over 100 leading Boat Builders in various parts of the United States and Canada have joined with the Gray Motor Company in issuing a catalog of specialized boats, telling where you can buy the kind of boat you want at the price you want to pay—also giving you the name and address of the leading boat builder nearest your locality.

Boats a Girl Can Operate

The boats shown in this catalog are powered with Guaranteed Gray Motors, self-starting, clean and reliable—making motor boating a real pleasure for "Milady."

GRAY MOTOR COMPANY
356 Gray Motor Bldg.   Detroit, Mich.

BOTH SIDES

We have prepared fourteen briefs for debate on important questions of the day for the use of Schools, Debating Societies and Lyceums. Price 25 cents.

THE INDEPENDENT   119 West 40th St., New York

PEBBLES

Wait for the big show! At Chicago, June 7! Two rings!—*Indianapolis News.*

President Wilson is sure to go down in history as a man of international note.—*Christian Home and School.*

If the optimistic expectations of all of Europe are realized, there won't be any Europe left.—*Washington Post.*

A London editor lets us know that England will never permit Germany to capture America. Thanks, awfully.—*Galveston News.*

"Brevity is the soul of wit," observed the sage.
"Maybe," replied the fool, "but I never feel very witty when I am short."—*Milwaukee Sentinel.*

Summing things up in general, one may say that the two heroes of the year who have kept their following are Field Marshal von Hindenburg and Charlie Chaplin.—*Chicago Daily News.*

In his recent talk about satirists, Mr. Bliss Perry omitted mention of Robert Browning, author of the greatest satirical line ever written—"All's right with the world."—*New York Tribune.*

Germans complain that American ammunition is more deadly than that of French and English make, which after all may not be an unfortunate discovery for foreigners to make.—*Boston Transcript.*

No longer can there be any doubt about the horrors of war. Garet Garrett, correspondent of the *Times*, writes that the cost of living in Berlin is as high as it is in New York.—*New York Morning Telegraph.*

Germany, however, may be able to extract some consolation from the exchange situation. If a mark isn't worth as much as it used to be, then she doesn't owe as much to herself as she thought she did.—*Indianapolis News.*

These are days of efficiency and efficiency talk, and it is said that at the next meeting of the Poetry Society—which has some motorist members—the question for discussion will be, "How Many Lines Do You Get Out of a Gallon of Ink?"—*New York Tribune.*

A scene in Stockport.
Recruiting Officer to Passing Workman: "Now, sir, what do you say to fighting for your country?"
P. W.: "Nay, lad. I don't want to fight."
R. O.: "Don't want to fight. Where would the war be if every one spoke like you?"
P. W.: "I suppose ther'd be no war."—*Labour Leader.*

PROM-TUNE PANTOUM

Prom. talk is certainly Art!
"*My*, what a wonderful floor!"
"*Of course* Mr. Jones may have part."
"I've never been up here before."

"Mr. what a *wonderful* floor!"
"The orchestra's perfectly fine."
"I've never been up here before."
"Another? How *nice!* Number nine?"

"The orchestra's perfectly *fine.*"
"You say those are Freshmen up there?"
"Another? How nice! Number *nine?*"
"My goodness, just *look* at my hair!"

"You say those are *Freshmen* up there?"
"*That* thing? Is *that* the Yale shell?"
"My goodness just look at my *hair!*"
"I'm having the 't of my l."

"That thing? Is that the *Yale* shell?"
"You *college* boys must have such larks!"
"I'm having the 't of my l."
"I hear you get wonderful marks."

"You college boys must have *such* larks!"
"*Of course* Mr. Jones may have *part.*"
"I hear you get *wonderful* marks."

Prom. talk is certainly Art.
—*Yale Record.*

SANATORIUMS

Insurance

Conducted by

W. E. UNDERWOOD

HELPLESS OLD AGE

One of my correspondents, agreeing with a recent statement of mine to the effect that helpless old age is worse than death, wants to know what material benefit a small annuity resulting from a very limited amount of life insurance would be, adding that most men are poor and therefore financially unable to maintain any considerable sum of insurance during a period of thirty or forty years.

I will have to admit that something cannot be made from nothing. The fundamental defect lies in the fact that most men do not commence building a life insurance reserve for themselves early enough. Young people should be trained to regard that form of thrift as a necessity. Comparatively few young unmarried men carry life insurance. They squander in social pleasures enough money every year to carry from $1000 to $5000 insurance. Then they marry and, if conscientious, commence being drudges with, in most cases, just enough insurance protection to pay doctors' bills, funeral expenses and a few hundred dollars for their widows.

They should commence at the age of eighteen or twenty to accumulate life insurance equities, adding new policies as circumstances and means permit. I will not stickle at the kind of policies taken, altho I believe in endowments for the young. All old line legal reserve insurance is endowment insurance. The ordinary life policy is an endowment at age ninety-six; all the others, except term and special contracts, are endowments at earlier ages. Let them take any plan they prefer; but take it and keep it. Keep it even tho their families outlive the need for it. Keep it as a part of their own support in old age.

J. R. P., Princeton, Fla.—If you can get it, take your cash value; if not accept the paid-up insurance. Don't pay any more money into the concern.

C. O. H., Marengo, Ill.—The Ancient Order of Gleaners of Detroit is not a life insurance company; it is a fraternal assessment concern charging inadequate rates. The Union Central is a strong old line company paying good dividends to policyholders, the only criticism adverse to it being the capitalization of $100,000 of its surplus in 1908. The Equitable of Iowa is a good average company with many superiors.

H. H. M., Columbia, Mo.—The latest figures available for both companies are those of December 31, 1914. Postal: Assets, $9,613,849; surplus to policyholders consists of $100,000 capital and $129,882 net surplus; total, $229,882. Kansas City Life: Assets, $4,053,950; policyholders surplus, $346,597, including $100,000 capital. Measured by service to policyholders neither of them compare favorably with the leading well established mutual companies.

A Number of Things

by

Edwin E. Slosson

DEFEAT OF THE TEN COMMANDMENTS!

Mosaic Laws Voted Down on Referendum by Decisive Majorities.

SINAI, 2000 B. C.—Some surprise has been exprest in political circles that every article of the Decalog recently submitted to popular referendum was defeated, altho each was voted upon independently and several had a considerable measure of influential support during the recent campaign. The first two commandments had against them a strong body of opinion among persons who feared that they might lead to an alliance between church and state. The first, however, ran far ahead of the second, which had against it the Sculptors' Union and all the artists, with the single exception of the Futurists, who supported the commandment on the ground that they were guiltless of making anything in the likeness of anything that is in Heaven above, or that is in the earth beneath, or that is in the waters under the earth. The third commandment was doomed from the start by the cry that it was an interference with freedom of speech. In the precinct of Billingsgate it did not receive a single vote. The fourth commandment was downed by the untiring efforts of the Anti-Blue Law League. Like the fifth, it received a certain amount of support in the rural districts, but not enough to overcome the negative majority returned by the great centers of population.

The defeat of the sixth amendment had not been anticipated. Of course, much of the majority against it is to be ascribed to fraud and intimidation in the so-called "gunmen". districts, but there seems to have been a feeling also even in the most conservative circles, that a commandment which was all very well, in time of peace might weaken the nation in case of war. The seventh commandment, loudly denounced as "Comstockery" and "Puritanism," lost out by a three to one vote. Sodom and Gomorrah reported less than ten votes in its favor, altho a prominent man had exprest the hope that peradventure fifty might be found in the Twin Cities. The eighth commandment had been expected to carry in spite of the powerful opposition of the Burglar Amalgamation. What seems to have killed it was the fear lest the Supreme Court might construe the law in a sense broad enough to include the operations of high finance.

The defeat of the eighth commandment involved the defeat of the tenth, which also had against it the organized opposition of the Socialist party. The ninth commandment seems to have been beaten on the face of the returns, probably owing to the campaign conducted against it by a large section of the press. The professional politicians gave it no support and are said to have secretly instructed their henchmen to vote it down on the ground that it would take the life out of politics.

It is not thought that the precincts still to hear from will make a great change in the result. The electorate is in a very conservative mood and is not disposed to welcome changes. As Rameses, boss of Upper and Lower Egypt, told our reporter last evening: "The present is not the time for tinkering with the constitution."

"Kubla Khan" is no dream. I mean to say, the incident was not fictitious, or at least not impossible. I once dreamed of reading a new play in a volume of Shakespeare, "The Man from Araucania"; not equal, I confess, to the best in the book, but ranking somewhere between "Titus Andronicus" and "Hamlet."

And the other day I took home Master's "Spoon River Anthology" for my wife to read. She read it—all the evening, and dreamed about it all night, her thoughts naturally falling into that infectious rhythm—if rhythm it may be called. In the morning she wrote down what she could remember of her dream critique and here it is:

ANTHOLOGY IN A COUNTRY CHURCHYARD

No, I don't like your Spoon River Anthology,
Lee Master's long line of too loquacious corpses
Lying at length in a quiet country churchyard
Who lift their hideous heads from their decaying pillows
And address a few remarks to the world in general.
I tell you those people aren't dead, to begin with!
They haven't the pulseless calm of immortality.
Then, I don't like the way they talk to each other;
When they talk to *me* I bitterly resent it.
To be frank, I don't like their society;
Dead or alive they are equally detestable.
Where are the good people buried in that graveyard?
There must a lot of them live in Spoon River—
Grey warriors of the Lord—
Children like flowers—
Boys and girls with their eyes full of visions—
Mothers who were sweet and calm and sensible.
Perhaps they are in heaven, and these earth-bound spirits,
Lingering around and watching their own corruption.
Coiling like rattlesnakes around their own headstones,
Are all that are left in Spoon River graveyard.
Then I don't like it because it isn't poetry
Nor metrical prose nor anything musical,
All of its cadences are humpy—like the graveyard!
He tried to be a Whitman with a touch of Rabelais;
But Whitman sometimes has a mighty music
Like the roar of the sea
(Or the thunder of the elevated),

Reminding us at times of his own Wild Trumpeter.
Oh, how I dread a set of Spoon Rivers,
A lot of little Whitmans without any music,
A herd of Rabelaises without any genius,
Spoiling white paper and mussing up the universe . . .
It gives one a taste for annihilation!

Our prayers and pious injunctions will need some verbal modifications to fit the conditions of modern warfare. The Gallipoli correspondent of the London *Times*, Ashmead Bartlett, quotes what the censor found in the letter of a young bluejacket:

Mother, it is sometimes very hot out here when the shells are dropping all about you and the submarines are hovering round, and you may strike a mine at any minute. At first I was a bit scared, but I remembered the words of the *padre* last Sunday, when he said:—"Men, men, in times of trial and danger look upwards." I did look upwards, mother, and if there wasn't a blooming aeroplane dropping bombs on us!

Now that the season of the Tercentenary approaches we set ourselves sternly to the duty of remembering Shakespeare or recollecting him as the case may be. We write about him or read about him; in his honor we recite, we sing, we dance, we act, we paint, we pageant, each according to his own talents or ambition. The whole country has become one great Shakespeare Memorial Society such as Chesterton wrote about:

While the vain world careless sped
Unheeding the heroic name—
The souls most fed with Shakespeare's flame
Remembering him like anything . . .
They stuck like limpets to the spot,
Lest they forgot, lest they forgot.

I don't want to be unjust to the Germans, but I must say that it sometimes seems to me, tho I may be mistaken, that they—of course I don't mean all of them—are a trifle wanting in tact, or perhaps I should put it, somewhat deficient in the comprehension of the psychology of foreigners. One of the things which leads me to this conclusion is that *The Continental Times*, which is published in Berlin for the purpose of enlisting American sympathy for the German cause, brings forward as one of the evidences of Germany's unerring uprightness the fact that she took the side of Spain in the Spanish-American war.

In Gladstone's time the English used to talk about the "Bulgarian atrocities." In Asquith's time they talk about the "atrocious Bulgarians." .

More and more the members of the British cabinet are coming to say: "Let George do it," referring, of course, not to George V of England, but to George I of Wales.

With most audiences a thing needs to be said twice; once to open their heads and once to fill them.

All debts are divided into two classes; "honest debts" and "debts of honor."

The Independent

FOR SIXTY-SEVEN YEARS THE
FORWARD-LOOKING WEEKLY OF AMERICA

THE CHAUTAUQUAN
Merged with The Independent June 1, 1914

MARCH 6, 1916

OWNED AND PUBLISHED BY
THE INDEPENDENT CORPORATION, AT
119 WEST FORTIETH STREET, NEW YORK
WILLIAM B. HOWLAND, PRESIDENT
FREDERIC E. DICKINSON, TREASURER

WILLIAM HAYES WARD
HONORARY EDITOR

EDITOR: HAMILTON HOLT
ASSOCIATE EDITOR: HAROLD J. HOWLAND
LITERARY EDITOR: EDWIN E. SLOSSON

PUBLISHER: KARL V. S. HOWLAND

ONE YEAR, THREE DOLLARS

SINGLE COPIES, TEN CENTS

Postage to foreign countries in Universal Postal
Union, $1.75 a year extra; to Canada, $1 extra
Instructions for renewal, discontinuance or
change of address should be sent two weeks
before the date they are to go into effect. Both
the old and the new address must be given.

We welcome contributions, but writers who
wish their articles returned, if not accepted,
should send a stamped and addrest envelope. No responsibility is assumed by The
Independent for the loss or non-return of
manuscripts, tho all due care will be exercised.

Entered at New York Post Office as Second
Class Matter

Copyright, 1916, by The Independent

Address all Communications to
THE INDEPENDENT
119 West Fortieth Street, New York

CONTENTS

ASSISTED PLAGIARISM

In The Independent for February 21 was published a splendid poem entitled "My Battle Prayer." It was credited to F. F. V. We have since discovered that the poem was actually written by Theodosia Garrison and published in a volume of verse from her pen entitled "The Earth Cry and Other Poems."

This all looks like a flagrant piece of plagiarism.

But we are glad to record that it was unconscious plagiarism—perhaps assisted plagiarism would be the better phrase. The poem was sent to The Independent by an old and valued contributor, with the statement that it was the work of a protegé of hers, and was sent without his knowledge. It now appears that this fairy godmother found the verses among the papers of her protegé and in his handwriting, liked it, and sent it off to the editor forthwith in the hope of springing a pleasant surprise upon the young and bashful poet. It is probable that he will be surprized when he sees the poem in print, with his initials attached, tho perhaps not quite pleasantly.

The Independent and the fairy godmother deeply regret the injustice that has been done to Mrs. Garrison by this absurd bit of plagiarism. The moral seems to be that poets ought not to copy other poets' work and leave it around unsigned; that fairy godmothers can be too cleverly benevolent; and that editors ought to be omniscient.—*The Editor.*

REMARKABLE REMARKS

WOODROW WILSON—I love peace.

ED. HOWE—Millions of women are too "churchy."

HON. WILLIAM BARNES—Never give a bully a stick.

LORD BERESFORD—Brilliant retreats will not win the war.

LILLIAN RUSSELL—More women than men suffer from cold feet.

VERNON CASTLE—It was Broadway that made an American out of me.

WILLIAM ALLEN WHITE—The reformer with a past never gets beyond second base.

CONGRESSMAN FREAR—Congress is constantly straining at gnats and swallowing camels.

JUSTICE HUGHES—I do not feel that I have any right to take part in political discussion.

GRAND DUKE NICHOLAS—God has granted to the brave troops such great help that Erzerum has fallen.

VICTOR MURDOCK—Before July, maybe by April, half of London will be destroyed by a great Zeppelin attack.

YUAN SHI-KAI—To perform the ceremony of enthronement at this juncture would set our heart on thorns.

TUDOR JENKS—What is the use in filling a boy's head with geographical knowledge when he can buy an atlas for a quarter?

ADELINE E. BROWNING—The day when women looked up to men and thought them infallible has passed away never to return.

SENATOR CHAMBERLAIN—There is not in the diplomatic history of the United States a single instance in which we did not get the worst of it.

HELEN KELLER—A dollar that is not being used to exploit some human being is not fulfilling its purpose in the capitalist's scheme of things.

W. J. BRYAN—If we had been as well prepared as some now ask us to be we would be in the war today shouting for blood as lustily as any of them.

BILLY SUNDAY—We want to fight like old Michiah, not like hog-joweled, weasel-eyed, sponge-columned, mushy-fisted, jelly-spined, pussy-footed, charlotte-russed Christians.

GENERAL NELSON A. MILES—If 500,000 men were landed on either of our coasts and we were not able to raise enough men to drive them out, I would want to move to another country.

CHARLES RANN KENNEDY—We don't want literature used as a sugar coating around the illuminating lesson that God loves little Willie becuase he fed the dickie birds and didn't say "damn."

H. G. WELLS—All the belligerent countries of the world are at the present moment quietly, steadily and progressively going bankrupt and the mass of people are not even aware of this process of insolvency.

THE NEW PLAYS

Erstwhile Susan. Mrs. Fiske, with a background of Dutch Pennsylvania and the rest of the cast. An odd little comedy, very well played. (Gaiety.)

Maude Adams is at her best in *The Little Minister*—an excellent revival of a popular play. Probably the most enjoyable production in New York. (Empire.)

The Cinderella Man. Fairy-story love-comedy in situations of one syllable. Some amusing lines and, in the minor rôle of a decayed gentleman's gentleman, a capital bit of acting. (Hudson.)

Margaret Schiller. A war tragedy in which Elsie Ferguson, in the title rôle, plays the part of a German spy in the English Prime Minister's home. Morbid, lugubrious, but excellent cast. (New Amsterdam.)

The Melody of Youth. A delightful comedy of Irish romance—with harp accompaniment. The usual love story is enlivened by really funny character parts. Brandon Tynan is both author and hero. (Fulton.)

Yellow journalism is rampant in *The Earth,* a play of interesting character development, tho somewhat hackneyed plot. Ably acted by Grace George and her company. Thoroly entertaining. (The Playhouse.)

Just a Woman, by Eugene Walter, proves it still possible to construct a trial scene that will suprize even the blasé New York audience. Drama of Pittsburgh mines and millionaires with anti-divorce moral. (Forty-eighth Street.)

The Fear Market. Dramatization of a celebrated case of society blackmail by Amélie Rives. Princess Troubetzkoy—and obviously others. A queer mixture. Conventional plot and unconventional people. Good acting and poor. (Booth.)

The Gorham Trade-Mark
is the Author's Name

A name may be one of two kinds — it may be the name of the maker, or it may be the name of a sponsor for the maker.

The Gorham Company always uses its own trade-mark on its own productions and that trade-mark is no more in need of a sponsor than Shakespeare is.

The famous Gorham Trade-mark on Sterling Silverware

STERLING

is the name of the author, and is an inviolable guarantee that it is a Gorham production. To this rule there are no exceptions, for we affix our trade-mark to nothing which is not the work of our hands nor produce anything whose authorship we are not proud to acknowledge.

In silverware for service, for sentiment, and for ornament, there is both added lustre and added value in the classic indentation of the Gorham insignia.

GORHAM STERLING SILVERWARE is for sale by leading jewelers everywhere.

THE GORHAM COMPANY
Silversmiths and Goldsmiths
NEW YORK
Works: Providence ~ New York

COPYRIGHT 1916

The Independent

VOLUME 85   MARCH 6, 1916   NUMBER 3509

OUR DUTY IS CLEAR

THE letter of President Wilson to Senator Stone should be read by the German Government with grave attention. It will do much to remove any doubt—or hope—that may have been cherished in Berlin as to the purpose of the United States to uphold in full measure American rights upon the sea.

The letter should be read with approval and gratification by the American people. It will assure them again that their President is stedfast in seeking the difficult middle course between war on the one hand and national dishonor on the other.

The President does not use the word "honor" in any careless or distorted sense. It has been well said that "all honor's wounds are self-inflicted." A man's enemy cannot dishonor him, nor can anything outside himself. But often the act of his neighbor confronts him with a situation in which he must choose between the honorable course and the dishonorable. It is his choice that protects his honor or tarnishes it. But it is the act of his neighbor that has forced him to the choice.

For Germany to kill American citizens wantonly is in itself no stain upon our honor. But for the United States to acquiesce in the continuance of such wanton killing would smirch our honor beyond cleansing.

This fact the President recognizes to the full. He has no intention of permitting such dishonor to come to the American people thru any act or omission of his.

Mr. Wilson in his letter reiterates with emphasis two fundamentals upon which he is determined. On the one hand he says: "I shall do everything in my power to keep the United States out of war." In so saying he is correctly interpreting the earnest desire of the American people.

On the other hand he says: "I cannot consent to any abridgment of the rights of American citizens in any respect." The American people will uphold him no less definitely in this position.

The latest cloud upon our international horizon comes from the announced intention of Germany and Austria to treat armed merchantmen as vessels of war, subject to destruction on sight. We comment on this subject on another page. The President's statement of the underlying principle is unescapable. He says: "No nation, no group of nations, has the right while war is in progress to alter or disregard the principles which all nations have agreed upon in mitigation of the horrors and sufferings of war; and if the clear rights of American citizens should ever unhappily be abridged or denied by any such action, we should, it seems to me, have in honor no choice as to what our own course should be."

President Wilson has rightly adjudged the two great responsibilities that are his so long as the Great War continues to rage. He must keep the United States out of the war just as long as it is possible to do so without dishonor. He must maintain the rights of American citizens against every assault from without. In so doing he will be serving not only the American people but the cause of humanity and the world.

THE GERMAN WAY

THE chief thing that has been disclosed about German strategy is that it is *German* strategy, not anybody else's. Altho the military experts of their adversaries have repeatedly pointed out that their methods are unsound, the Germans continue to use them, and, on the whole, continue to win. We learn from British studies of the campaign of 1914 that if General von Kluck had not got cold feet he might have taken Calais or even Paris, that the French army in Alsace and the British army at Mons might have been annihilated if the Germans had only followed up their advantage. Our own Richard Harding Davis tells us that they missed the chance of their lives in stopping at the Serbo-Greek frontier when by pushing on they might have captured Salonica before the Allies could fortify and be reinforced.

All this may be quite true, but anyhow it is not the German way. They lay their plans, arrange their train dispatcher's chart, mass their men and munitions, then they strike where and when they choose without much regard to what the enemy is doing. If they fail they try again, at the same point or some other, whenever they get good and ready, not before. They stick to their maxim, "the best defensive is an offensive," and so far have usually succeeded in keeping the initiative in their own hands on all fronts, and forcing their adversaries to meet their moves.

Also to meet their feints. Somehow, in spite of the censorship, the German papers a few months ago were saying a lot about the preparations which were being made for an attack on Salonica. Accordingly, some 350,000 French and British troops were sent to Salonica, where the Bulgars are keeping watch over them. Next we heard much of a combined Turkish and German army which was being assembled in Palestine for a drive at Suez. Consequently the British have sent, say, 500,000 troops to Egypt. Then the British armies on the Tigris were attacked and reinforcements had to be sent to the Persian Gulf.

Having then got the French and British troops scattered as widely as possible over Europe, Asia and Africa, the Germans began their offensive in France and

Belgium by attacks near Lens, next south of the Somme, later at Ypres, then in the Champagne, and finally what seems to be their most serious and certainly is their most successful effort, the attack on Verdun.

We do not mean to imply that the Allied generals are stupid and have been outwitted by a common trick. They could hardly have done otherwise than scatter their forces, for they had to meet each threatened attack, or it might have become more than a threat. This is simply the advantage which the attacking party always has in forcing the game, and that is why the Germans prefer to attack, notwithstanding the fact that the newspaper strategists of England and America demonstrated—to their own satisfaction—that the Germans were getting so short of men that their best plan was to keep to the shelter of their trenches and prepare, as best they might, to meet the spring drive of the French and British armies. The argument certainly sounded reasonable, but the Germans evidently reasoned otherwise. Instead of saving their men they have thrown them in the old mass formation against one of the strongest of the barrier fortresses on the French frontier, Verdun. We are told from the French reports that the Germans are losing frightfully, and we may well believe it. But when they attempt to estimate the German losses—175,000 is the latest figure—we should be skeptical. We have not forgotten that in August, 1914, the Allies were similarly shocked at German callousness in sacrificing 25,000, even 40,000, men in the attack on Liège. Their sympathetic feelings must have been relieved later when they learned that the German forces actually engaged in that forty-hour fight were not so great as the number supposed to be killed, and that enough of them were left alive to go on to the next town.

It seems indeed a desperate venture at this late day to assault Verdun, a fortress of the first class, on which the French military engineers had labored for forty years, and which they have had a year and a half to strengthen in accordance with the lessons of the Great War. It stands in the midst of a tangle of hills and woods astride the River Meuse, a river that has often run with blood from Cæsar's to the Kaiser's time. The names of the towns along its banks in its course from the hills of France thru the valleys of Belgium to the sea of Holland read like a battle roll: St. Mihiel, Verdun, Sedan, Mezières, Dinant, Namur, Liège. The Meuse is the moat of France. If the Germans should cross it—well, there are still the Aisne and the Marne between them and Paris.

A LESSON FROM CANADA

CANADA, being the nearest country to ours both geographically and psychologically, is the one from which we can derive most instruction on such questions as preparedness. In 1911 England found it necessary for the first time in her history to call upon her overseas dominions to aid her in preparing for an anticipated war. The British navy during the ten years preceding had been gradually withdrawn from all parts of the world, even from the Mediterranean, and concentrated in the North Sea to meet the German menace. This left the dominions unprotected, and besides it was questionable whether the British Navy would be adequate to fulfill the task assigned to it in the Entente plan of campaign. According to the understanding with France,

Great Britain was not expected to do more on land at the outset than to send an expeditionary force of 160,000 men to the continent. This was to be under the command of Sir John French, who had for several years been making a thoro study of his future battlefields in France and Belgium. Aside from this moderate participation in the military operations, England's part was to defend herself and the north coast of France and to police all the seas outside the Mediterranean, which was entrusted to the French Navy, and the North Pacific, which was entrusted to the Japanese. For this stupendous task England increased her naval expenditure by fifty per cent, but still found herself unable to keep up her rate of naval increase to what she had determined was the essential margin of safety, that is, twice the strength of the German. Accordingly a strong hint was given to the dominions that their aid was needed.

But the dominions were far from Europe and did not realize the international complications and obligations in which the mother country had become involved. So the British Government took the unprecedented step of inviting the colonial premiers and defense ministers to London in order that Mr. Asquith and Sir Edward Grey might explain to them personally and privately the foreign policy of England and her treaties and international understandings. What was revealed to the colonial representatives at the Imperial conference of 1911 will not be known to the world until the passage of years removes the ban of secrecy. But whatever it was we know that the premiers, one and all, without regard to party or previous opinion, went back home convinced that the Empire was threatened with imminent danger of war with Germany, and, one and all, they used their best efforts to induce their people to prepare for it.

The Premier of Canada was perhaps most outspoken. In his historic speech of December 5, 1912, asking Parliament for an "emergency contribution" of $35,000,000 for the construction of three dreadnoughts, he said:

These ships are urgently required *within two or three years at the outside* for rendering aid upon which may depend the Empire's future existence. . . . If we should neglect the duty which I conceive we owe to ourselves and if irreparable disaster should ensue, what will be our future destiny? Obviously as an independent nation or as an important part of the great neighboring republic.

And he went on to explain that as a part of the United States the Canadians would have to pay three times as much per capita for a navy that afforded vastly inferior protection.

But the Canadian people refused to accept Mr. Borden's word that the danger was imminent and he could not convince them without betraying the confidence of the British Government and revealing to the enemy the secret policy not only of Great Britain, but of her Allies. So the Canadian parliament refused the appropriation for the dreadnoughts.

How their refusal disappointed the mother country may be seen from what that most witty of Canadians, Stephen Leacock, wrote in the *National Review* in 1913:

The patriotic Canadian hangs his head to blush. He recalls with shame the plaudits of the British press six months ago. He remembers Canada enthusiastically depicted as a Viking's daughter, a sea-lion, as a sea-horse, as a sea-anything. Now it turns out that the Dominion is not a sea-lion, but a mud turtle and has crawled back on its back. The sea-lion has a cub that can't swim. The Viking's daughter is sea-sick. It appears that she came from Alberta and had never been off the ranch in her life. The trident of Britannia is exchanged for the pitchfork of the Albertan agriculturist.

Now a number of lessons may be drawn from this. The preparedness people may point out that because the Canadians declined to contribute $35,000,000 for defense in 1913, they had to pay $150,000,000 for war in 1915 and more to follow. The anti-preparedness people may argue that you never can tell what sort of preparation is going to be needed; that the British navy, which the Canadians were asked to aid, has proved more than adequate while they have had to raise an army which England did not expect to want.

But the lesson which seems to us most clear and significant is that in a democracy you have to explain what you want a thing for before you can get it. Now that the Canadians know why their help is needed no part of the empire is more generous with money and men. Professor Leacock no longer has to blush for his countrymen. The man from Alberta is like the man from Missouri; he has to be shown. Every cross-roads politician will admit that the President has access to information which he knows not of, but yet he will not vote money on such unrevealed evidence. Because the American people have not responded enthusiastically to Mr. Wilson's appeal for the biggest navy in the world and an army to match, there are some Americans who, like Leacock, blush with shame. Now we believe that the people of these states are no more cowardly than the Canadians, but, like the Canadians, it will never be possible for the President to get them to respond to his appeals for any very great increase in military power unless he is at liberty to make public the reasons for his opinion.

DRAMATIC COMMENDATION

THE theatrical managers of New York, by excluding the critics who found fault with their plays, have destroyed the last vestige of faith which the public has placed in dramatic criticism. It has long been known that the managers held a whip over the newspapers thru their advertising and they are suspected of having caused the dismissal of more than one New York critic because of adverse opinions. But still some newspaper publishers had the nerve to stand by their critics, so the managers went further and refused to allow the men who had attacked their productions from entering their theaters even when presenting purchased tickets at the door. Their right to exclude persons on this ground was contested in the courts, but has just been confirmed by the New York Court of Appeals, which holds that so long as it was not discrimination because of race, creed or color, the theater owner could shut out whomsoever he pleased.

To the non-legal mind it would seem that excluding a man from a theater because it was feared that he would not like the play was as much an infringement on personal rights as excluding him because he was a Baptist or a negro. And if it is illegal to discriminate on racial grounds, why is it that the orchestra seats are all sold out when a gentleman of color wants to buy one?

The decision that a theater may exclude an unappreciative critic may be good law, but it is not so surely good policy. Theatrical managers have been complaining that many of their best plays failed because people would not turn out during the first week or two. Now it will be worse than ever because nobody will want to risk his money on a new play from what the news-paper says of it. If the reviewer calls it a good play, that may indeed be his opinion, but we shall doubt it because we know that if he called it a bad play he might never get a chance to see another. Henceforth we shall have not independent criticism but compulsory commendation.

THE FAT IN THE FIRE

AN interesting story comes to us thru private channels from Holland. There have been destructive floods in that submarine country. Great numbers of fine cattle have been drowned.

Forthwith government agents swarmed over the border from Germany, bought up the carcasses by wholesale and lugged them off home.

Now this may show that the German people were starving. Or it may merely show that the German army was getting ready for the drive on Verdun. For cattle yield fats, and fats give up glycerine, and out of glycerine come modern explosives.

In any case, it shows that the German Government is still wide awake.

GERMANY COUNTERS

THE United States insists that if Germany attacks an enemy's merchant or passenger vessel on which there is any American citizen, she must allow time for those on board to escape with their lives. Germany replies that she will yield and then announces that if any such vessel has guns mounted for defense it will be held to be a ship of war, to be attacked and destroyed without notice.

Of course the United States can never assent to this doctrine. A ship of war is made for offense; its purpose is to destroy. A merchant vessel has no purpose of offense. Its aim is to get away, to keep out of danger; if it has a gun on deck it can use it only for its own protection, and when it cannot escape. The submarine is the hunter, nothing else, while the merchant vessel is the prey, and to deny it the right of self-defense in extremity contradicts all honorable warfare.

Let us suppose that a submarine steals up to a merchant vessel unseen in the open ocean and sinks it in ten minutes with all on board. That is what it was built for and under orders has done. When called to account its officer and the government behind him say the vessel was armed. Who knows whether it was true? It may have been unarmed. There is every opportunity for error, intentional or unintentional. It is the easiest thing in the world to say that it was armed and thus evade all responsibility for its destruction.

Of course, under the accepted rules of international law, if a merchantman, when hailed by a belligerent warship and ordered to stop, either flees or resists, it may be sunk without further ado. But the mere presence on board the merchantman of a gun or guns suitable for defense does not subject it to this peril provided it does not actually resist resistance.

This announcement on the part of Germany of an intention to sink armed merchantmen without warning is only the old contention in a new guise. In the correspondence over the "Lusitania" case, Germany originally maintained that the submarine, because it is vulnerable and small in capacity, was not to be bound by the ordi-

narily accepted rules of international law. From this contention Germany has been obliged to recede. She will be equally obliged to recede from the present contention. A merchant vessel with a small gun mounted on her stern for defense is only dangerous to the submarine because the submarine is an especially vulnerable type of ship. This limitation on the part of the submarine cannot be advanced with success by Germany as a reason why this particular boat should be granted especial license of action.

THE COLLEGE GIRL'S BUDGET

FROM the statistics of student expenditures, recently collected by the dean of Smith College, come two somewhat unexpected and thoroly praiseworthy conclusions: the average student spends in all $765.55 during the college year; fifty-six per cent of the students spend less than that.

Such an allowance would hardly buy hats for the debutante, even the wage-earner would find that it necessitated strict economy, and at many a boarding school it might just about cover the cost of board and tuition. College—the girl's college, that is—seems to have monopolized the low cost of living happily; and never to have had due credit for its achievement.

Moreover, 87.6 per cent of the average Smith girl's money is spent for necessities, while 8.2 per cent goes for pleasure (in which category the dean, not the student, puts dues for clubs and societies and contributions to church and charity), and 4.2 per cent for books and stationery.

The popular theory that college girls spend most of their time and money on pleasure is put out of commission by the announcement that "recreation, hospitality and extra food" cost the average girl $35.09 a year—no one can ever again accuse her of undue emphasis on frivolity and fudge.

In the face of ever-increasing alarms at the extravagance of American women it is reassuring to find the students of our largest woman's college spending so sanely.

NOAH DID NOT EAT THE APPLE

A TABLET in the Museum of the University of Pennsylvania, lately published by Professor Langdon of Oxford University, is creating a lively discussion among oriental scholars. It is written in the older of the two languages found on the inscriptions, the Sumerian, and is not easy to translate. Professor Langdon announced it as containing a story of the Babylonian Paradise, Noah and the Flood—Noah, according to him, being also the first man who disobeyed the command of the god in eating of the forbidden plant, which he identified as cassia. In England, Professor Sayce and Dr. T. G. Pincher, both competent scholars, have published comments and criticisms of Professor Langdon's work, recognizing the bearing of this very ancient inscription upon the account of the Creation and Flood as given in Genesis. When Professor Langdon's translation and commentary were published, the newspapers made much of it, and told their readers how Moses was mistaken in supposing Adam to have eaten the forbidden fruit, for this record, much older than Moses, made it out to be Noah.

Now Professor Morris Jastrow, Jr., of the University

of Pennsylvania, a most competent scholar, having the tablet in his own hands, publishes a preliminary paper on the subject in which he seems to prove that Professor Langdon was very hasty in drawing his conclusions. He does not find any flood on the tablet, nor any forbidden fruit, altho the cassia plant is there mentioned with other plants allowed for man's use. Really the tablet is of more importance in the history of early religion than Professor Langdon had supposed. Two years ago Dr. Poebel found in the same museum collection another tablet which gave a definite account of the Flood, and it now appears that that was number two in a series of which Professor Langdon's tablet is number one.

According to Professor Jastrow the new tablet begins with the organization of Nature to fit it for the habitation of man by the provision of rivers and canals and even cities created by Anu-Enlil, who represents the combined god of Heaven and god of Earth. Very much as in the second account of the Creation as given in Genesis beginning Chap. 2:5, Yahveh Elohim, the Lord God, is said to have prepared the earth for vegetation by causing a mist to water the earth, so in the new tablet Ea, the god of waters, irrigates the land copiously and abundant vegetation results. Then follows the appearance of man and the god presents him with all useful plants and fruits and gives them names, among them the cassia. What Professor Langdon took to be a peaceful condition in Eden before the Flood, Professor Jastrow finds to be a description of the state of absolute quietude before birds and beasts of prey had been created; and what Professor Langdon took to be the account of the Flood, he interprets as the beginning of irrigation with the resulting fertility.

As there is on this tablet no account of the Flood, there is equally no Babylonian Noah; for the second tablet, previously published by Dr. Poebel, continues the story with the subsequent flood, and the escape in a boat and the sacrifice of offerings to the gods exactly as in the Biblical order. It is hoped that other fragments of the same series will add further details of this very interesting myth which represents one, called the Sumerian, of the two versions current in ancient Babylonia, while the other, the Semitic or Accadian version, represented nature beginning with a chaos of water and watery monsters reduced to order by the god, as in the first chapter in Genesis. The two tablets here described were written about 2000 B. C., but the myth must have been much older.

The interpretation which made cassia the forbidden plant was seductive, but must be given up. Under the modern name of senna, it is the oldest of all known medicines, and its leaves are kept in every drug store, being administered as a cathartic. It is prescribed in Babylonian medical documents, among other things, for intoxication; indeed, the name cassia has come down to us thru the Greek from the Babylonian *kasu*.

It is forty years since the lamented George Smith startled the religious world with the discovery on Assyrian tablets of a detailed poetical story of the Flood wonderfully like that in Genesis, but those tablets were comparatively late, not much more than 600 B. C. We are now able to trace back the legends of the Creation and the Flood to a period long before the composition of the book of Genesis. It is a matter for congratulation that American research is filling out the ancient story, but there is much more yet to be discovered.

THE STORY OF THE WEEK

The Gateway to Paris

The significance of the German attack upon Verdun may be seen from any map or history of France. A straight line is the shortest distance between two points. On the line between Metz and Paris stands the fortress of Verdun. The reason why the Germans did not go straight from Metz to Paris is because Verdun was in the way. They went to the north of it instead, thru Belgium, tho that act made it certain that England would be counted among their enemies and that neutral nations would be alienated.

This was bad policy from a political point of view and it may now be questioned whether it was good policy from a military point of view. To be sure the Germans cut thru the defenses of Belgium and the northern French frontier with surprising ease, but they failed to reach their goal; and one must wonder whether they would not have broken thru the Verdun gateway in August, 1914, if they had expended on the Meuse the million lives they have sacrificed since on the Marne, the Aisne, the Somme and the Yser. If they can come anywhere near taking Verdun now they could certainly have taken it then, for its defenses have been enormously strengthened and the French artillery become more efficient in the eighteen months since.

But the Germans took what they regarded as the easiest way, and they forced the Belgian Meuse at Liège and Namur instead of the French Meuse at Verdun. While General von Kluck was making his grand sweep with the German right the Crown Prince with the central army was expected to come down between Verdun and Rheims and enter Paris by a triumphal march along the Champs Elysées. But the Crown Prince failed to arrive in time to fit his army as the keystone into the German

---

THE GREAT WAR

February 21—Germans advance upon Verdun. Turks evacuate Bitlis, Armenia.

February 22—Czar opens Duma in person for the first time. British steamer "Westburn" brought to Teneriffe as German prize.

February 23—Germans take Brabant and Ornes. Portugal seizes German ships.

February 24—Germans take Fort de Douaumont, five miles north of Verdun. Russians bombard Black Sea coast near Sinope.

February 25—Russians take Kermanshah, Persia. Kuropatkin made commander-in-chief of Russian armies in the north.

February 26—Italians evacuate Durazzo, Albania. Germans take Champneuville.

February 27—P. & O. liner "Maloja" sunk by mine near Dover. Germany again warns public that armed vessels will be attacked by submarines after March 1.

---

arch. General de Castelnau met him on September 6 with a curtain of fire from the French 75's, and the German troops instead of advancing, fell back twenty-five miles over night. This threw out the German plan of campaign and von Kluck had to let Paris go and swing around to the left to close up the gap in the line caused by the retreat of the Crown Prince.

There were rumors at the time that the Crown Prince had been scolded by the Kaiser for incapacity, that he had been dismissed in disgrace, that he had been shot, that he had committed suicide, but whatever the trouble, whether he was blamed or was not to blame, he has now a chance to retrieve his reputation, for he is nominally leader of the army again attacking Verdun.

The Verdun Fortress

The Franco - German war of 1870 revolved about Verdun. At Sedan, a little further down the Meuse River, Napoleon III and his army were captured. At Metz, to east, Marshal Bazaine and his army were captured. And Verdun itself succumbed to a three weeks' siege and a bombardment from the nearby hills which the French are now defending against the Germans.

Five years after the war the French set about the task of fortifying their eastern frontier to prevent a recurrence of the debacle. A chain of fortresses was constructed along the ridge of the Meuse and Moselle from Verdun to Toul and from Epinal to Belfort. This fortified wall was supposed to be impregnable and so far has proved to be. At St. Mihiel, twenty miles south of Verdun, the Germans have succeeded in taking one of the minor forts of the barrier chain, Fort du Camp des Romains, but even here they have not been able to maintain a hold on the western bank of the Meuse.

Verdun is protected on the western side by the forest of Argonne, which the French have held against furious and oft-repeated attacks from the first of September, 1914, to the present. Between these two points, St. Mihiel on the south and Varennes on the west, there is a gap of some twenty-five miles which the Germans have not been able to close. Verdun has, therefore, never been completely invested, but has remained in easy reach by rail from Paris, 150 miles west. It has always been possible to supply the garrison with everything needed in the way of provisions, ammunition and reinforcements and the fortifications have been thoroly reconstructed during the past year and a half.

Verdun was before the war ranked

Underwood & Underwood

SHAM FIGHTING IN REAL WAR

A dummy battery arranged by the Russians on a snow-covered raft to draw the German fire and thus waste German ammunition. Such a ruse is often used, also, to get the range of enemy batteries

331

as a "fortress of the first class," that is to say, it constituted an "entrenched camp" within which a large army could find protection. The town itself is of no great importance. Its population in peace time is only 20,000 and these mostly military. But within a radius of five miles there are some forty distinct forts so placed as to protect one another and connected by sunken railways. Of course the exact number, strength and location of these fortifications are known only to the French military authorities.

The Verdun forts before the war were constructed on the same general plans as those of Liège and Namur. The guns were placed in movable steel cupolas, shaped like an inverted saucer, and protected by a ring of concrete so heavy as to be invulnerable to the artillery of the time. But a shell filled with a modern high explosive dropt on one of these cupolas does not glance off, but explodes. The concrete and steel structure is blasted to pieces and the gunners crushed or suffocated by the gas evolved. This is why Liège and Namur were taken within two days after the twenty-eight-centimeter guns had been brought to bear upon them. The cupola is so low and so tinted as to be invisible at a distance, but the aeroplane can locate it by photographing it from above and once its range is found it is sure in time to be shattered by a shell. A gun on caterpillar wheels behind a simple sand pile is safer than in the best fortress Vauban designed.

It is understood that General Sarrail, when he was in command at Verdun, took many of the big guns from the cupolas and hid them in the ravines and among the trees and behind the rocks of the hills round about. The artillery mounted on trucks can be moved back and forth along a track whenever the enemy gets their range and, on the other hand, they can drop their shells on any point of the accurately mapped area thru which the enemy must advance.

The Battle of Verdun It seems that the recent attacks upon the French and British positions in the west were intended to divert attention from the eastern end of the line toward which the German drive was to be directed. The bombardment of the French lines north of Verdun began on Monday, February 21, but the work of preparation had been actively going on ever since December. Railroad lines had been run to the front, munition factories established close by and artillery brought from Serbia and Russia. Seven army corps were assembled which, together with the army already there, probably brought up the number to four or five hundred thousand.

The Kaiser came to inspire his troops with his presence and superintended a dress rehearsal of the attack in which each division took the position assigned to it and was lectured on the part it was to play. A map of the Verdun fortifications, on a scale of 1 to 2000, pre-

pared from photographs taken by aeroplanes, was distributed to every soldier. Field Marshal Count von Häseler, former commandant at Metz, is now acting as adviser to the Crown Prince.

The Germans' line of attack extended from west of the Meuse to the Orne on the east, a distance of twenty-five miles, but as the French drew in their wings the front narrowed to seven miles. The Germans adhered to their old tactics of mass formation and assigned ten men to every yard of front. The machine guns mowed them down like grass but could not fire fast enough to stop the charge. According to the French report the Germans have lost 175,000 men, but such estimates are notoriously unreliable. The German reports state that their losses were "normal" and the French losses much greater. The French claim the capture of 10,000 prisoners and many guns.

The main drive came straight south toward Verdun and was successful all along the front. By the end of the week the Germans had gained about four miles, a greater shift in the line than has been made by either side for a year. The German right first advanced up the eastern bank of the Meuse from Consenvoye to Brabant and later on to Champneuville. The center carried the Forest of Caures and advanced beyond Beaumont; the left advanced from Gremilly to Ornes and attacked the fortifications on the Côte de Poivre (Pepper Ridge).

After fighting their way thru the

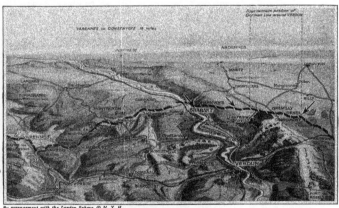

By arrangement with the London Sphere, ⓒ N. Y. H.   THE NEW GERMAN DRIVE

The spring campaign has opened with a furious attack on Verdun, the corner fortress of the French defenses on the German frontier. During the past year and a half the Germans have made many efforts to surround Verdun by advances from the west and south. Now they have struck a blow directly at the fortress from the north and have penetrated several miles inside the French lines. Verdun is protected by a dozen strong forts and innumerable batteries entrenched among the woods and hills. The Germans have taken Brabant and Champneuville on the Meuse, Caures Forest in the center and the Fort of Douaumont on the high ridge to the east

outer zone the Germans encountered the most northerly of the permanent forts, Donaumont. This was of the concrete and cupola type and stands upon a hight overlooking the eastern frontier for a distance of twenty miles. In front of it the land had been graded to a slope of five degrees and smoothed and sodded like a putting green for 3000 yards so that an advancing foe would not find the least shelter. The Germans smashed the fort with four shells from their long range howitzers and then took it by storm. The French are striving to regain this dominating point by furious counter-attacks.

Since the Germans are now within four or five miles of Verdun they could bombard the town at any time. But that alone would be of little use, for their object is not to take Verdun but to dislodge the French army from this region. A heavy fall of snow has added to the difficulty and discomfort of the campaign.

The Mysterious "Möwe"

On the Sea which sent the "Appam" to Norfolk has sent another prize to the Canaries. The British steamer "Westburn" appeared at the port of Santa Cruz de Teneriffe flying a German naval ensign and in charge of a German prize crew of eight. The "Westburn" had left Liverpool on January 21 for Buenos Aires. On the vessel were 206 prisoners taken from seven vessels, six of them British and one Belgian, all of which had presumably been captured by the German raider "Möwe." The crew of the "Clan MacTavish," part of whom were on the "Appam," was also represented on the "Westburn." The other vessels were the "Flamenco," "Horace," "Cambridge" ("Corbridge?"), "Edinburgh," "Belgian" and "Luxemburg." These are mostly freight steamers of two to three thousand tons. After landing his prisoners the German captain took the vessel out to the three mile limit and there sunk her to prevent her from falling into the hands of the British cruiser waiting there for that purpose. Then he returned with his crew in a boat to Santa Cruz where they will be interned by the Spanish authorities.

The Portuguese Government has seized all of the German and Austrian ships which have been lying in the Tagus River at Lisbon since the war began. There were thirty-six of these vessels, some of them of over 8000 tons. The Portuguese warships trained their guns upon the ships and the crews were ordered to leave the vessel within three hours, when the Portuguese flag was raised and saluted with twenty-one guns. The Portuguese Government explains that this seizure is not to be regarded as an aĉt of war and that the owners' rights will be respected. It remains to be seen how Germany will regard it. The position of Portugal is peculiar. She is allied to England and under obligation to send her 10,000 troops on demand. The Portuguese Congress has voted to coöperate with the Allies and in the Portuguese African colony of Angola the Germans have

© *International Film Service*

AN OBJECT LESSON IN CITY DEFACEMENT

The balloon shows the location and hight of the smokestacks of the proposed power plant, which will permanently disfigure Washington if it is built. It would block the parkway along Washington Channel, which is an integral part of the Washington city plan. The Senate has adopted the conference report authorizing its construction, but a stiff fight is being waged by the American Civic Association and national bodies of architects and artists against this stupid attack on the beauty of the Capital City

come into conflict with the Portuguese yet war has never been declared.

The British steamship "Maloja" of the Peninsular and Oriental Line struck a mine two miles from Dover and sank in half an hour. The loss of life is said to be 150. It is not known whether the mines were British or German.

War Crisis in Congress

There was evidence, on the 23d, of a serious and menacing revolt in Congress, especially in the House, against the President with respect to his policy concerning the proclaimed determination to sink armed merchantmen without warning, even if the armament were only for defense. Germany was to take this course on and after March 1. Secretary Lansing had suggested to the Allies an agreement which might cause a modification of the German purpose, but they had not replied. There was danger, at the beginning of the week, that the subject would be discussed in Congress. At that time, however, the danger seemed imminent in the Senate, rather than in the House, because a group of Senators, including Mr. Gore and Mr. Hoke Smith, were inclined to support resolutions designed to prevent Americans from taking passage on steamships owned by the belligerent nations. On the 21st Mr. Wilson had a conference with Senator Stone, chairman of the Senate committee; Senator Kern, Democratic leader, and Representative Flood, chairman of the House committee. The situation in the Senate was considered. Mr. Wilson was firm in opposition to resolutions of warning or exclusion, and rejected any proposition to relieve him of responsibility.

Two days later there was a panicky revolt in the House, where many feared that the President's attitude and policy would compel a severance of diplomatic relations with Germany and draw us into the war. Democratic leaders told Mr. Wilson that if he did not agree to warn Americans to avoid belligerents' ships the House would pass a resolu-

tion of warning by a great majority. Mr. McLemore, of Texas, had introduced a resolution directing that such warning be issued by the Government, and all the members of the House Committee on Foreign Affairs were said to be in favor of it. The President was to have forty-eight hours to consider the crisis, but it was thought that action could not be deferred after that allowance of time. While it was asserted that a resolution like Mr. McLemore's would be passed by a vote of four to one in the House, there were indications that it would not have a majority in the Senate, where Mr. Stone and others, altho in favor of excluding Americans from the ships, were unwilling to interfere with the President and were seeking to restrain others who objected to his policy. It was decided by the Democrats in the House that Speaker Clark, Floor Leader Kitchin and Chairman Flood should go to the President on the 25th, and give him information as to the attitude of the House.

The President's Letter

Mr. Wilson did not wait for them, but on the night of the 24th gave to the press a letter sent to him that day by Senator Stone, with his reply. The Senator had undertaken in his letter to set forth the President's position. In brief it was that the Allies would be within their rights under international law if they should insist upon arming their merchant ships for defense; that he would allow such ships to be cleared from our ports; that he opposed the taking by our Government of definite steps to prevent American citizens from going on armed merchant vessels; and that he would hold Germany to strict account if a German warship should fire upon an armed merchant ship bearing American passengers. Members of both Houses, he said, He had urged them to keep cool and not to affect the diplomatic situation by hasty action. He intended to stand by

No Abridgment of American Rights
President Wilson's Letter to Senator Stone

THE WHITE HOUSE,
Washington, February 24, 1916.

My Dear Senator—I very warmly appreciate your kind and frank letter of today and feel that it calls for an equally frank reply.

You are right in assuming that I shall do everything in my power to keep the United States out of war. I think the country will feel no uneasiness about my course in that respect. Thru many anxious months I have striven for that object, amidst difficulties more manifold than can have been apparent upon the surface, and so far I have succeeded. I do not doubt that I shall continue to succeed. The course which the Central European Powers have announced their intention of following in the future with regard to undersea warfare seems for the moment to threaten insuperable obstacles, but its apparent meaning is so manifestly inconsistent with explicit assurances recently given us by those powers with regard to their treatment of merchant vessels on the high seas that I must believe that explanations will presently ensue which will put a different aspect upon it. We have had no reason to question their good faith or their fidelity to their promises in the past, and I for one feel confident that we shall have none in the future.

But in any event our duty is clear. No nation, no group of nations, has the right while war is in progress to alter or disregard the principles which all nations have agreed upon in mitigation of the horrors and sufferings of war; and if the clear rights of American citizens should ever unhappily be abridged or denied by any such action we should, it seems to me, have in honor no choice as to what our own course should be.

For my own part, I cannot consent to any abridgment of the rights of American citizens in any respect. The honor and self-respect of the nation are involved. We covet peace, and shall preserve it at any cost but the loss of honor. To forbid our people to exercise their rights for fear we might be called upon to vindicate them would be a deep humiliation indeed. It would be an implicit, all but an explicit, acquiescence in the violation of the rights of mankind everywhere, and of whatever nation or allegiance. It would be a deliberate abdication of our hitherto proud position as spokesmen, even amidst the turmoil of war, for the law and the right. It would make everything this Government has attempted, and everything that it has achieved during this terrible struggle of nations, meaningless and futile.

It is important to reflect that if in this instance we allowed expediency to take the place of principle the door would inevitably be opened to still further concessions. Once accept a single abatement of right, and many other humiliations would certainly follow, and the whole fine fabric of international law might crumble under our hands piece by piece. What we are contending for in this matter is of the very essence of the things that have made America a sovereign nation. She cannot yield them without conceding her own impotency as a nation, and making virtual surrender of her independent position among the nations of the world.

I am speaking, my dear Senator, in deep solemnity, without heat, with a clear consciousness of the high responsibilities of my office, and as your sincere and devoted friend. If we should unhappily differ, we shall differ as friends; but where issues so momentous as these are involved we must, just because we are friends, speak our minds without reservation. Faithfully yours,

WOODROW WILSON.

To Hon. William J. Stone,
United States Senate.

the President, and was unwilling to disagree with him, but he found it difficult to consent to plunge the nation into war because of the unreasonable obstinacy of any of the Powers, or the foolhardiness and moral treason of Americans who risked their lives on armed belligerent ships.

The President replying, defined his position emphatically and clearly, pointing out his reasons for refusing to warn American citizens against a course that was manifestly within their rights, or to countenance such a warning. The letter is printed above.

The Effect of It

Speaker Clark, Mr. Kitchin and Mr. Flood talked with the President on the 25th, but there had been a change in the temper of the House, owing to his letter. Mr. McLemore said that, on the advice of friends, he had decided not to ask the committee for action on his resolution. The President should have ample time, he thought, to complete his negotiations. Mr. Foster, who had intended to introduce a similar resolution, withheld it, for reasons like those given by Mr. McLemore. The revolt was under control, but the Speaker assured Mr. Wilson that a resolution of warning or exclusion would be passed by a

vote of two to one if a change for the worse in the attitude of Germany should bring it before the House. At present, however, no such resolution will be reported from the House committee. Nor is the Senate committee disposed to vote for any warning. Mr. Gore has introduced two resolutions with long preambles, and has published statements about them, but the resolutions will not receive committee approval.

Mr. Bryan exerted his influence in support of the proposed legislative action which the President opposed. In a telegram to Representative Bailey, of Pennsylvania, on the 24th, he exprest an earnest hope that Congress would forbid the granting of passports "to Americans traveling on belligerent ships," and withhold "clearance from belligerent ships carrying American passengers." No citizen, he added, should be permitted to endanger the peace of our nation, which would probably be the mediator "when the time for mediation comes." It would be a crime against civilization to become involved in this war and "thus to loan our army and navy to a European monarch to use in settling his quarrels." At the end of the week there was no indication of a renewal of excitement in Congress.

The Treaties

Action upon the pending treaty with Colombia has been delayed not only by the exprest objection of Colombia to the changes made by the Senate committee, but also by consideration in the House of the constitutional power of that branch of Congress to participate in the action. This question has been raised by Representative Moore, of Pennsylvania, and a resolution introduced by him, providing for an inquiry as to this power, has been sent to the Ways and Means Committee. As the Constitution says that revenue legislation shall originate in the House, Mr. Moore points out that the treaty remits import duties on Colombian products brought into the Panama Canal Zone, and also the canal tolls on Colombian ships. James T. Du Bois, formerly Minister to Colombia, has published an attack upon the treaty in its present form. The greater part of his statement relates to the connection of our Government with the secession of Panama. He urges that the treaty as originally negotiated should be ratified. "To amend it as now proposed," he says, "will be disastrous to the cause of justice and the hope of an enduring and uplifting Pan-Americanism, leaving the only real injustice we have ever perpetrated against the Latin-American race as a festering wound." Ratification of the treaty as it stands is not expected.

A public meeting, to express a protest against the treaty of Nicaragua, recently ratified by a vote of 55 to 18, was held last week in the capital of Salvador. Dr. Castrillo, who, as Minister to the United States, participated in the treaty negotiations, was present, and there were such manifestations of hostility toward him that it was necessary to give him police protection. Salvador Diaz, formerly judge of Nicaragua's Supreme Court and Minister of the Interior, has published an attack upon the treaty. He calls it "a disreputable and dishonorable transaction" and "a blow against the rights of Costa Rica, Salvador and Honduras." "Our people," he says, "are deceiving themselves. You have only two courses to follow—to conquer us frankly, ruthlessly, Germany-like, crushing the national spirit and natural pride of our race—or you must treat us squarely on an equal footing, without hurting our patriotic feelings, as good and honest friends ought to do. But this cowardly and treacherous conquest, by buying with your dollars miserable politicians accidentally in power, will give you only a temporary success."

Labor Questions

Negotiations for a settlement of the wage controversies in the coal mining industry were continued last week. The bituminous miners ask for an eight-hour day and an increase averaging about 10 per cent. Their agreement with the operators, or mine-owners, will expire on March 31. The anthracite miners also seek a new agreement, beginning on that date. They ask for an eight-hour day, an increase of 20 per cent, and recognition of their union. Such changes, the operators say, would largely increase the selling price of coal. After a conference, in which about twenty-five representatives of each side took part, committees were appointed. Four operators and four union men undertook to consider the question, and to report at another conference. The meeting was a quiet and peaceful one, and the president of the union exprest his appreciation of the manner in which the demands were received.

About 50,000 ballots have been sent to headquarters by the 400,000 members of the four great railroad unions. They indicate practically unanimous approval of the demands which are to be made. These include an eight-hour day, with time and a half for overtime.

A menacing strike of the employees of the American Brass Company, in Ansonia, Connecticut, and of the employees of other manufacturers there and in neighboring towns, was settled at the end of last week. There was danger that all the factories in that part of the state would be closed. The strikers demanded a reduction of hours, an increase of 5 cents an hour, and time and a half for overtime. Eight nationalities were represented in the strikers' ranks, and their leader was a youth named Grotol, a pupil in the high school, who, it is said, can speak seven languages. The factories have been at work on war orders. An offer of 10 per cent, with full pay for a half holiday on Saturday, was rejected. A settlement was reached by giving an increase of 15 per cent, with time and a half for all overtime and full pay for the half holiday. Thousands of rejoicing workmen took part in a parade.

The Danish Islands Owing to a strike of the native agricultural laborers on the island of St. Croix, Danish West Indies, the question of the sale of the Danish islands has been raised again in Copenhagen. By this strike, in which about 10,000 men demand an increase of wages, the sugar industry has been paralyzed. Owners of plantations have taken their families to the towns for safety. Martial law has been declared in the cities. M. Hageman, the wealthiest of the planters, has published in Denmark a pamphlet in which he favors a sale of the islands, taking a pessimistic view of their future under Danish rule. The population is decreasing, he says, and the infant mortality, due to bad sanitary conditions, has risen to 63½ per cent.

The prevailing belief in Copenhagen, it is said, is that the Danish Parliament will vote for a sale of the islands if the question comes before it, but will ask more than the sum named, about $4,300,000, in the agreement of 1902, ratified here but rejected by the upper House in Copenhagen.

Mexico The nomination of Henry Prather Fletcher to be Ambassador to Mexico was reported from the Senate Committee last week, two of the fourteen members opposing it, and was confirmed by a vote

of 49 to 16. Mr. Fletcher is now Minister to Chile. Carranza's army has not yet captured Villa, whose forces are said to be increasing. Owing to the record of failures, Carranza has sent new leaders to the north and ordered a new campaign under their direction. In the south, General Gonzales is at the head of a new movement against Zapata in the state of Morelos, and it is reported that one of Zapata's officers, General Pacheco, with 10,000 men, has offered to surrender. Carranza proposes to reduce his army, saying that he now has 100,000 men, and to increase the salaries of all employees in the civil service. He is planning a new currency system and proposes to establish a national bank in which the Government shall have an interest of one-third, while existing banks shall have the remainder.

On the anniversary of the arrest of President Madero, Carranza opened a public library and night school in Colima, for the working men. The library and school are in the Church of Santa Maria. In the course of the exercises,

Luis Cabrera, Minister of the Interior, defined the Government's attitude toward the Catholic Church. There were in Colima, he said, many more churches than were needed, and to use one of them in this way was only an act of justice. There were not enough schools, and to avoid loss of time in erecting a building the Government took this church structure and turned it into a school. The Catholics had been so busy building churches that they had found no time to build school houses. There was to be religious liber-ty, and the Protestant religion would be encouraged. The Government was against the abuses committed by churches and priests, and the priests must not interfere with politics. The Spanish Consul at Monterey protested against the deportation of a priest, and was ordered to leave the country within twenty-four hours. He is now in Texas. Senator Fall asserts that he has the names of sixty-seven Americans killed in Mexico who were not included in the list sent to the Senate by Secretary Lansing.

© *International Film*   RESULTING IN —— MORE INVESTIGATIONS

Ten persons were killed when a local train crashed into a stalled express on the New York, New Haven and Hartford Railroad near Milford, Connecticut, on February 22. It is thought that the engineer of the local, who passed a precautionary and a danger signal at high speed, may have been talking with a companion, who was riding in the cab contrary to railroad regulations

COUNTRY LIVING IN THE NEXT GENERATION

BY LIBERTY HYDE BAILEY

E have had much prophecy of the new country life, perhaps most of it of things hoped for rather than of things foreseen. We are not dealing with a trade or an occupation, but with a human situation under thousands of conditions and over thousands of miles of differently developed regions. It is not a simple matter, therefore, to meet the editor's demand for a forecast of country life in the coming generation. One cannot be too confident; and yet there are certain. considerations that lead one to rather definite conclusions, for the fundamental principles in the reshaping of country life have now been formulated.

We are confronted by any number of movements and new developments, varied, apparently disconnected, sometimes disconcerting; we are not able to judge them unless we are aware that all of them (at least all that promise very much) are applications and outcomes of the principles of action that the prophets have stated with clearness; and out of these underlying formulations other applications will come.

The teaching in the colleges of agriculture has taken hold and has found a hearing. The students have become numerous enough to have a voice among the people, and to influence public opinion. The constant precept upon precept, with many thousands of examples, have had their cumulative effect. More knowledge was demanded and the experiment stations were established. The press has disseminated the new teaching. Political ideas have turned countryward after long concentration on urban and consolidated affairs. The economic world has recognized its dependence on its agricultural basis. Lately the demand for dissemination of knowledge has taken shape in the national and state coöperative extension system, which is a new application in politics as well as in agriculture and its kindred subjects.

In this span of fifty years, there have been a good number of prophets. For the moment, all we can do is to mention a half dozen and more lines of development that one may

Whenever one thinks of country life betterment he thinks of Liberty H. Bailey. Brought up on a farm, a graduate of the Michigan Agricultural College, an apprentice to the botanist Asa Gray, a teacher in the Michigan and Cornell Agricultural Colleges, for ten years director of the New York State College of Agriculture (Cornell), head of the Roosevelt Commission on Country Life, and author of so many books and other writings on agriculture and country life that if we should list them all here there would be little room left for the article—Liberty H. Bailey was the logical man to write about the farmers of the next generation, and here he has done it.—THE EDITOR.

project with little hazard. Even when these lines deal with rather special problems of agriculture, they are nevertheless all movements in the large, because they affect profoundly the welfare of the vast range of people producing the initial supplies and touch so quickly our occupancy of the planet; they all have their direct bearing on our political system, for there can be no real democracy without free and useful access to the earth.

Let us hope that the next generation will have passed the epoch of land exploitation, of fantastic back-to-the-farm movements, of the reporter's write-up, of the exaggeration of the results of science-work, and of the general foolishness that follows a new kind of development.

THE FARMER HAS BEGUN TO MOVE FORWARD

WITH the ground thus cleared, we may proceed with our forecast. It will not be necessary to speak specially of many agitations now before the country, not even of rural credits or of schemes of distribution; these are but processes. Nor will it profit us here to discuss the necessary increase in production, as the country grows, for this will be met by the working out of plain economic laws if their operation is not retarded by extraneous factors beyond the control of the farmer.

It requires no foresight to note the inevitable tendency, in the business of farming, to incorporate the findings of patient enquiry into it and to make it meet the commercial and ed-

ucational conditions of its time. It is no longer stationary: this itself is a great gain and makes other developments possible. This development is not the direct application of discoveries of science to existing methods, as the outsider thinks, but a making over of the business, in the way of a new organization of it, a rational approach to the subject, a more effective way of attacking the problem, a better relationship of the farm to the community. The farmer rapidly becomes a more resourceful man. This gives him a better place in society, increases his responsibility and his influence. The next generation will find the farmer occupying a still more important position in reference to other pursuits and affairs, as a necessary result of his increasing mastery of his occupation. On this possibility all other developments rest.

THE CONSERVATION OF TIME

EVERY part of the occupation of farming will be better performed. This will mean better care of the land, better cropping schemes, better crops and animals, more improved methods in every direction, more careful attention to upkeep, a bigger grasp of the business.

It has been necessary to eliminate much of the old farm method in order to clear the way for the new. We have also been undergoing a process of assorting the people, to determine who will make the farmers that we need; this process is not yet completed. Some of the redirections will be striking. I look for a very marked change of attitude in the man toward the use of his own time. To save time is more important than to save coal or to conserve water-power. It releases energy for much good work. The farmer has not thought of his time as valuable, in the sense in which the investigator or the business man or the professional man conceives it. Bear in mind that I am not thinking of an eight-hour day or any formal time-serving. The sun does not work on an eight-hour basis. The farmer will save his minutes, that he may use them intellectually. He must do this if he is to make use of the new literature that is made for him and of which much more is yet to come. He will find increasing satisfactions in the intellectual concept of his business. The number of well-trained young folk now establishing themselves on farms insures this result. This mastery will make him a more efficient man in all public and community work, and it will give him more time for service. This will be an outstanding mark of the time just ahead of us.

Much of this energy will be expended in local betterment as well as in better practise on the farm itself. Another generation should find us with few highways of the old kind; the highway advertising has already mostly gone and the remainder will go; a new building construction will develop, and it is to be hoped that house architecture will improve and that the present hideous milk-station and creamery and similar construction will perish; scenic and landscape effects will receive new attention; mechanical and physical aids to the business will be extended. Inside the home, the development of labor-saving devices and machines will necessarily be marked, and we are to expect as radical a redirection of activities therein as has taken place in the past generation in the fields and barns. The woman of the farm, as well as the man, is to organize and economize her time; this is her most essential emancipation.

The physical and outward improvement of the farming regions will necessarily come slowly, so slowly and gradually that some of us may not recognize it, but it is already well under way. The first necessity is to stimulate a new ambition for excellence in agricultural operations, to arouse a new purpose on the part of the countryman as affecting his own life, to discover local potential leadership. All permanent movements begin with folks; the change in attitude in most country districts is even now very marked and significant. The human reactions are to be more important than the physical improvements.

Many marked discoveries will be made and many new inventions; but the great problem before the farmer of the next generation is to incorporate the accumulating knowledge into a scheme of life.

THE BASIS OF OCCUPANCY—NO PEASANTRY HERE

FOR all that we can see, and certainly in the immediate future, the farmer will live separately on his land as an individual owner. The tendency of affairs and of events is against the socialization of agriculture, if by that we mean the common ownership of land and of tools of production. Of coöperation we are to see a great extension, and the social

instinct is growing in rural districts; but I see no sign of any fundamental change in the basis of land occupancy. The dispersive and separatist movements are, in fact, the significant marks of our day so far as agriculture is concerned, and I think that in the nature of the case these movements must continue. The farm is too directly controlled by the processes of nature to make a theoretic socialistic scheme applicable. The attempts at partitioned social rural life have been failures either socially or agriculturally. The dispersive movements to which I refer are the extension of improved highways, of delivery of mails, of telephones and telegraphs, of farm bureau enterprises, of demonstration tests, of rural societies, of the general application of intelligence to localities and to the separate farmer. These all make for the establishing of a man independently on his land, keeping him there, making him master of his individual problem for which he himself must be responsible. This is essential to good farming, to the economy of time and energy, to the meeting of the problems set by nature.

It is here that those persons who fear the coming of a peasantry in American agriculture are in error. That a man is poor and a hard hand-worker on a small area does not indicate that he is a peasant or in danger of becoming a peasant. The notion that every farmer shall live by his own labor on a little piece of land highly tilled, has produced much harm and ought to be combatted; but peasantry is of a very different order. The tenancy problem is indeed a difficult one for the moment, but in the United States it is not a peasantry problem.

Peasantry is historically a question of social rank and of civil subjugation. It is founded on the assumption that there are necessary class strata. Peasants have been much restricted in their privileges and even in their political and civic rights. These rights they have been acquiring, laboriously; and even when they acquire them they may not be able to turn them to much account because of the social sentiment against them. Now, in a democracy like the United States, the people are guaranteed all their civil, judicial and political rights by the law of the land and by the very constitution of the state. The wide extension of education preserves these rights, which are in themselves inalienable, against encroachment and always stimulates the people to self-assertion.

The American political movement is naturally away from peasantry. It has been so from the first, except as

regards slavery. The question of the small farm, worked by the family, is quite another problem. We are not to look, in the next generation, for a community of small land-owners. The present general basis of occupancy is likely to stand, with necessary adaptation, for a long time to come; and, in fact, I can not clearly foresee a different or a better basis than will develop naturally from the present situation.

The position of the American working farmer is unusually good, in these regards. I find it difficult to make my friends and correspondents in other countries understand what I mean when I speak of the place that he may occupy. The restricted lot of the peasant, grounded in centuries of repression, is foreign to our whole philosophy. Therefore do we bear extra and special responsibility to develop our entire self-governing system, extending even to the range that rests on the earth. One is liable to over-stress the promise of one's own situation; but I think it not too much to say that here in North America do we have the opportunity to develop the best land occupancy yet known: this, at all events, is essential if we are to have a real democracy.

THE BUSINESS AND COMMERCIAL SITUATION

THE separate man is always at a disadvantage in dealing with organized men. This has been specially marked in the case of the farmer. His investment is tied up in land and its improvements, and in a kind of personal property that cannot be easily transferred to other business. He has been obliged to stand while others have moved. He has suffered from the vampirism of intrenched and interlocked interests. His traditions are also conservative. His terms of buying and of selling are not comparable. He takes not only the risk of production, but also to a large extent the risk in the selling even when the selling is the business and ought to be the risk of others.

It is desirable for many reasons that the farmer remain separate. Government ought so to protect him as to allow him to maintain his detachment. The general regulation of markets and distribution, of facilities for credit, and of commercial situations, should safeguard him and obviate the necessity of organizing producers as against distributors and consumers. The marketing problem must be solved on the basis of a public utility and in the interest of all men. Class organization for protection is a very dangerous thing in a democracy.

Nevertheless, the coming generation will undoubtedly see a very marked defensive movement on the part of farmers. This will have the immediate effect of bringing the farmer directly into the general business or commercial sphere, making him a personal factor to be reckoned with. Even if for protection, this organization will have great effect in broadening his interests and also in introducing public policies that are founded on the underlying moralities of nature.

The commercial or trading enterprises will extend far and wide into the open country. There is indication that small manufacturing units will again prosper for certain products. Certainly many of the industrial pursuits will continue to seek small and open settlements and we shall see an increasing industrializing of the open country. With the extension of invention and the installation of power, the farmer will himself introduce more mechanical processes and probably he will even manufacture some of his supplies again. The latter field is now essentially untouched.

These industrial and other movements will increase the importance of the country village and will also make considerable shift in villages. We are coming to the day of the country town—not to the European peasant hamlet,—but that is quite another matter.

NEW INFORMATION—THE RURAL PERIODICAL

FOR ages the basis of information in the farming occupations has been almost invariable: the slowly accumulating results of hard experience, the sense of the barriers imposed by society, the climate and the weather, the neighborhood gossip, the recurring work, the state of the crops told as a matter of news.

Suddenly a new range of fact and outlook is presented, as if the curtains were rolled back before a strange world. To absorb any part of this information means a new way of thinking. The old ways begin to break down, and another generation, with a folk in large part differently trained, will find new intellectual interests well established in every countryside.

The crops and animals take on a novel and large significance. Witness the wholesome competition in corn-growing, potato-growing, in boys' and girls' clubs for the growing of crops, in the rising standards of excellence in agricultural products, in the organizing of societies of growers of the different crops and animals.

These intellectual interests extend

THIS series was begun with William Allen White's article, "Government of the People, by the People, for the People," in our issue of February 7. The next article, THE NEXT GENERATION IN AMERICAN BUSINESS, by Elbert H. Gary, president of the United States Steel Corporation, is to be published on March 27.

---

to the situations and also to the human materials. Witness the revival of interest in the rural school, in church extension, in farm bureau movements, in demonstrations and tests, fairs, recreation, lectures, community service. The rural community begins not only to see itself but to evaluate its enterprises in relation to society as a whole.

The accumulating information on every kind of rural subject will, of course, make the new farmer. He will want new intellectual aids. The technical bulletins have come, for such as want them. The books are coming, altho we still lack a truthful artistic literature of the farm situation.

Immediately before us is the need of a new or an improved periodical agency for the dissemination of information. The prevailing type of local country newspaper will not do. Its content is largely imported or inapplicable. It lacks inspiration. It lives too much on outside advertisement—sometimes of very doubtful character—and on political and exotic means of support. It may not really represent its region, or live on it. In a region in which there is apparently no advertising support, a local breeder's society will organize, for example, and establish a journal; and it will find advertising patronage from those who have animals to sell or to exchange. A grange periodical may develop a good support, for every progressive farmer has something to sell. We already begin to see a new periodical literature in the journals published regularly by farm bureaus, clubs, and also in the monthly periodicals issued by students in the colleges of agriculture and which have now become a class by themselves. The "news" is to be less a printing of personal gossip than a record of the real progress of the region: who has built a new barn, and the plans that went into it; who has purchased a pure-bred animal, and why; who has tried a new method, and the results; who has given a lecture or demonstration, and what was said; who has installed a system of drainage, and how; the year's crop movements, and the reasons.

Whether this type of information is to be combined in fair proportion and with understanding in the usual local country newspaper or whether a different kind of publication is to arise, we cannot foresee; but a new periodical local literature is coming.

LEADERSHIP—THE COUNTRY CAREER

WE begin to rejoice that such of the old political leadership as is founded on favoritism, self-interest, agreements and deals, is doomed. We know that the handwriting is on the wall. Never do I see a farm bureau agent going directly about his work and founding it on merit and fact, but I am conscious of the shift of the old initiative to new shoulders. The new district or county superintendent of schools is a vitalizing force, and his freedom from political control constantly becomes more secure. Many other agents, so far as they are based on the needs of the community and are not serving for personal ends, represent leadership forces now working in town and country alike. The new information cannot be applied to rural conditions without this kind of guidance. Undoubtedly we shall find the political leadership taking on new intentions and using the essential facts of the region for its basis.

The problem of the centuries has been to cause the people on the land to act and to express themselves. Under the stimulus of new knowledge and of many changed conditions this free action will come about, and it will make itself felt in the nation in the coming half century. This will not only bring a reaction directly on public policies, but will develop policies and institutions of its own. The farmers will take their particular problems in their own hands and will organize their own forces. There is every indication that the partizan politician cannot long hold the rural people for his ends: these people now have too many examples of other kinds of leadership.

Careers are now possible and even inviting for young men and women in the open country. These are not so much commercial careers, in the big sense in which we now measure them, as opportunities to establish a well-rounded occupation and business, to develop a high type of home life, and to render a useful service. The open country is to have more affairs and more interests. There will be greater diversity in its life. There will also be better rewards for the labor expended. The intellectual standards of excellence will very definitely include rural attainments as well as urban attainments.

Ithaca, New York

WHERE THEY ACTUALLY HAVE PREPAREDNESS—THE REMINGTON ARMS PLANT AT BRIDGEPORT, CONNECTICUT

AMERICA ARMING THE ALLIES

BY SYDNEY BROOKS

HARNESS Aladdin in the service of Mars and you get Remington's. By Remington's I mean the Remington Arms and Ammunition Company and the Union Metallic Cartridge Company. They are both under a single proprietorship; they are both situated at Bridgeport, Connecticut, and both within the last year have enormously expanded to meet the demands of the struggle in Europe. Who could have foreseen that a policy initiated in Potsdam would dislocate the life and industries of a New England townlet three thousand miles and more away, perhaps treble its population, and convert one of its factories into the largest small arms and ammunition plant in the world? That is what has actually happened; and if it isn't romance, then I for one don't know what romance is.

But such things do not happen by themselves. This is no affair of impersonal causes at one end of the scale and automatic consequences at the other. Somewhere in between you may be sure there is a man. Even in tales of magic you cannot dispense with the human agency. There must always be someone to wave the wand and rub the lamp. Remington's, I dare say, might even now be turning out nothing but its famous sporting weapons, might have no industrial interest whatever in the European war, were it not for one man. That man, of course, is Mr. Marcellus Hartley Dodge, the owner of the concern. Mr. Dodge was in Germany when the war broke out. He made his way to Paris and thence to London. He talked with his agents; he learned from them, probably long before we in England realized it ourselves, the deficiencies of the Allies in small

Independent readers have long been familiar with the illuminating articles on English and Continental affairs which Mr. Brooks has sent us from London. He has been a frequent visitor to America and is now again in this country for a few weeks renewing acquaintances and observing the reactions of the United States to the Great War.—THE EDITOR.

arms and ammunition; he saw his prodigious, his positively staggering, chance, and he seized it with both hands.

On the spot and with no specific contract that would justify any such enterprise, he made up his mind to build as an adjunct to the old Remington foundation an entirely new plant for supplying rifles, bayonets, shell cases and cartridges, to make it the largest and best of its kind and to have it working in record time. Nothing less than that would content him or meet the emergency which he was one of the first to foresee. In little more than a month after his return to America the contracts were all signed; the first sod was turned in December, 1914; in the following March work began on the main buildings, and in less than eight months, that is to say by the middle of last November, they were all completed and seventy-five per cent of the machinery was installed and in operation. But Mr. Dodge had not spent some $12,000,000 in less than a year to receive in return makeshift, jerry-built works. This new plant of his is meant to last. It is the product of the war only in the sense that the war furnished the occasion for its construction and the means where-

with to run it. But it will long outlive the immediate chance and need that brought it into being, and when the war orders cease, and if nothing from the United States Government is forthcoming to take their place, only a very slight adaptation will be necessary to convert its machinery to ordinary commercial uses.

To put up a plant with a floor area of about 1,500,000 square feet is one thing, tho I think a very big thing. To get the men to manage, superintend and work is another and a much more difficult thing. And in this case it was peculiarly difficult because the industry was a strange one. Until Mr. Dodge launched out, there was practically no private firm in the country that manufactured military arms and ammunition; most of the men who understood the business were in the Government arsenals; there was only a limited amount of the right sort of machinery; and side by side with the erection of the plant had to go the collection and training of a small army of skilled mechanics. Mr. Dodge has done more than set up a new factory; he has enriched the United States with a new industry; and he has furnished in addition a model example of how it should be carried on.

I will not attempt anything more than the purest description of the plant. It consists of thirteen main buildings, each five stories high, over sixty feet wide and over 270 in length, connected thru their centers —much as a skewer impales a row of kidneys—by a dozen service buildings of equal hight, but some eighty feet long by fifty in breadth. Standing on any floor in any of the service buildings one can thus look backwards or forwards from one end of

Nevertheless, the coming generation will undoubtedly see a very marked defensive movement on the part of farmers. This will have the immediate effect of bringing the farmer directly into the general business or commercial sphere, making him a personal factor to be reckoned with. Even if for protection, this organization will have great effect in broadening his interests and also in introducing public policies that are founded on the underlying moralities of nature.

The commercial or trading enterprises will extend far and wide into the open country. There is indication that small manufacturing units will again prosper for certain products. Certainly many of the industrial pursuits will continue to seek small and open settlements and we shall see an increasing industrializing of the open country. With the extension of invention and the installation of power, the farmer will himself introduce more mechanical processes and probably he will even manufacture some of his supplies again. The latter field is now essentially untouched.

These industrial and other movements will increase the importance of the country village and will also make considerable shift in villages. We are coming to the day of the country town—not to the European peasant hamlet,—but that is quite another matter.

NEW INFORMATION—THE RURAL PERIODICAL

FOR ages the basis of information in the farming occupations has been almost invariable: the slowly accumulating results of hard experience, the sense of the barriers imposed by society, the climate and the weather, the neighborhood gossip, the recurring work, the state of the crops told as a matter of news.

Suddenly a new range of fact and outlook is presented, as if the curtains were rolled back before a strange world. To absorb any part of this information means a new way of thinking. The old ways begin to break down, and another generation, with a folk in large part differently trained, will find new intellectual interests well established in every countryside.

The crops and animals take on a novel and large significance. Witness the wholesome competition in corn-growing, potato-growing, in boys' and girls' clubs for the growing of crops, in the rising standards of excellence in agricultural products, in the organizing of societies of growers of the different crops and animals.

These intellectual interests extend

THIS series was begun with William Allen White's article, "Government of the People, by the People, for the People," in our issue of February 7. The next article, THE NEXT GENERATION IN AMERICAN BUSINESS, by Elbert H. Gary, president of the United States Steel Corporation, is to be published on March 27.

---

to the situations and also to the human materials. Witness the revival of interest in the rural school, in church extension, in farm bureau movements, in demonstrations and tests, fairs, recreation, lectures, community service. The rural community begins not only to see itself but to evaluate its enterprises in relation to society as a whole.

The accumulating information on every kind of rural subject will, of course, make the new farmer. He will want new intellectual aids. The technical bulletins have come, for such as want them. The books are coming, altho we still lack a truthful artistic literature of the farm situation.

Immediately before us is the need of a new or an improved periodical agency for the dissemination of information. The prevailing type of local country newspaper will not do. Its content is largely imported or inapplicable. It lacks inspiration. It lives too much on outside advertisement—sometimes of very doubtful character — and on political and exotic means of support. It may not really represent its region, or live on it. In a region in which there is apparently no advertising support, a local breeder's society will organize, for example, and establish a journal; and it will find advertising patronage from those who have animals to sell or to exchange. A grange periodical may develop a good support, for every progressive farmer has something to sell. We already begin to see a new periodical literature in the journals published regularly by farm bureaus, clubs, and also in the monthly periodicals issued by students in the colleges of agriculture and which have now become a class by themselves. The "news" is to be less a printing of personal gossip than a record of the real progress of the region: who has built a new barn, and the plans that went into it; who has purchased a pure-bred animal, and why; who has tried a new method, and the results; who has given a lecture or demonstration, and what was said; who has installed a system of drainage, and how; the year's crop movements, and the reasons.

Whether this type of information is to be combined in fair proportion and with understanding in the usual local country newspaper or whether a different kind of publication is to arise, we cannot foresee; but a new periodical local literature is coming.

LEADERSHIP—THE COUNTRY CAREER

WE begin to rejoice that such of the old political leadership as is founded on favoritism, self-interest, agreements and deals, is doomed. We know that the handwriting is on the wall. Never do I see a farm bureau agent going directly about his work and founding it on merit and fact, but I am conscious of the shift of the old initiative to new shoulders. The new district or county superintendent of schools is a vitalizing force, and his freedom from political control constantly becomes more secure. Many other agents, so far as they are based on the needs of the community and are not serving for personal ends, represent leadership-forces now working in town and country alike. The new information cannot be applied to rural conditions without this kind of guidance. Undoubtedly we shall find the political leadership taking on new intentions and using the essential facts of the region for its basis.

The problem of the centuries has been to cause the people on the land to act and to express themselves. Under the stimulus of new knowledge and of many changed conditions this free action will come about, and it will make itself felt in the nation in the coming half century. This will not only bring a reaction directly on public policies, but will develop policies and institutions of its own. The farmers will take their particular problems in their own hands and will organize their own forces. There is every indication that the partisan politician cannot long hold the rural people for his ends: these people now have too many examples of other kinds of leadership.

Careers are now possible and even inviting for young men and women in the open country. These are not so much commercial careers, in the big sense in which we now measure them, as opportunities to establish a well-rounded occupation and business, to develop a high type of home life, and to render a useful service. The open country is to have more affairs and more interests. There will be greater diversity in its life. There will also be better rewards for the labor expended. The intellectual standards of excellence will very definitely include rural attainments as well as urban attainments.

Ithaca, New York

WHERE THEY ACTUALLY HAVE PREPAREDNESS—THE REMINGTON ARMS PLANT AT BRIDGEPORT, CONNECTICUT

AMERICA ARMING THE ALLIES

BY SYDNEY BROOKS

HARNESS Aladdin in the service of Mars and you get Remington's. By Remington's I mean the Remington Arms and Ammunition Company and the Union Metallic Cartridge Company. They are both under a single proprietorship; they are both situated at Bridgeport, Connecticut, and both within the last year have enormously expanded to meet the demands of the struggle in Europe. Who could have foreseen that a policy initiated in Potsdam would dislocate the life and industries of a New England town—let three thousand miles and more away, perhaps treble its population, and convert one of its factories into the largest small arms and ammunition plant in the world? That is what has actually happened; and if it isn't romance, then I for one don't know what romance is.

But such things do not happen by themselves. This is no affair of impersonal causes at one end of the scale and automatic consequences at the other. Somewhere in between you may be sure there is a man. Even in tales of magic you cannot dispense with the human agency. There must always be someone to wave the wand and rub the lamp. Remington's, I dare say, might even now be turning out nothing but its famous sporting weapons, might have no industrial interest whatever in the European war, were it not for one man. That man, of course, is Mr. Marcellus Hartley Dodge, the owner of the concern. Mr. Dodge was in Germany when the war broke out. He made his way to Paris and thence to London. He talked with his agents; he learned from them, probably long before we in England realized it ourselves, the deficiencies of the Allies in small

Independent readers have long been familiar with the illuminating articles on English and Continental affairs which Mr. Brooks has sent us from London. He has been a frequent visitor to America and is now again in this country for a few weeks renewing acquaintances and observing the reactions of the United States to the Great War.—THE EDITOR.

arms and ammunition; he saw his prodigious, his positively staggering, chance, and he seized it with both hands.

On the spot and with no specific contract that would justify any such enterprise, he made up his mind to build as an adjunct to the old Remington foundation an entirely new plant for supplying rifles, bayonets, shell cases and cartridges, to make it the largest and best of its kind and to have it working in record time. Nothing less than that would content him or meet the emergency which he was one of the first to foresee. In little more than a month after his return to America the contracts were all signed; the first sod was turned in December, 1914; in the following March work began on the main buildings, and in less than eight months, that is to say by the middle of last November, they were all completed and seventy-five per cent of the machinery was installed and in operation. But Mr. Dodge had not spent some $12,000,000 in less than a year to receive in return makeshift, jerry-built works. This new plant of his is meant to last. It is the product of the war only in the sense that the war furnished the occasion for its construction and the means where-

with to run it. But it will long outlive the immediate chance and need that brought it into being, and when the war orders cease, and if nothing from the United States Government is forthcoming to take their place, only a very slight adaptation will be necessary to convert its machinery to ordinary commercial uses.

To put up a plant with a floor area of about 1,500,000 square feet is one thing, tho I think a very big thing. To get the men to manage, superintend and work is another and a much more difficult thing. And in this case it was peculiarly difficult because the industry was a strange one. Until Mr. Dodge launched out, there was practically no private firm in the country that manufactured military arms and ammunition; most of the men who understood the business were in the Government arsenals; there was only a limited amount of the right sort of machinery; and side by side with the erection of the plant had to go the collection and training of a small army of skilled mechanics. Mr. Dodge has done more than set up a new factory; he has enriched the United States with a new industry; and he has furnished in addition a model example of how it should be carried on.

I will not attempt anything more than the purest description of the plant. It consists of thirteen main buildings, each five stories high, over sixty feet wide and over 270 in length, connected thru their centers —much as a skewer impales a row of kidneys—by a dozen service buildings of equal hight, but some eighty feet long by fifty in breadth. Standing on any floor in any of the service buildings one can thus look backwards or forwards, from one end of

Nevertheless, the coming generation will undoubtedly see a very marked defensive movement on the part of farmers. This will have the immediate effect of bringing the farmer directly into the general business or commercial sphere, making him a personal factor to be reckoned with. Even if for protection, this organization will have great effect in broadening his interests and also in introducing public policies that are founded on the underlying moralities of nature.

The commercial or trading enterprises will extend far and wide into the open country. There is indication that small manufacturing units will again prosper for certain products. Certainly many of the industrial pursuits will continue to seek small and open settlements and we shall see an increasing industrializing of the open country. With the extension of invention and the installation of power, the farmer will himself introduce more mechanical processes and probably he will even manufacture some of his supplies again. The latter field is now essentially untouched.

These industrial and other movements will increase the importance of the country village and will also make considerable shift in villages. We are coming to the day of the country town—not to the European peasant hamlet,—but that is quite another matter.

NEW INFORMATION—THE RURAL PERIODICAL

FOR ages the basis of information in the farming occupations has been almost invariable: the slowly accumulating results of hard experience, the sense of the barriers imposed by society, the climate and the weather, the neighborhood gossip, the recurring work, the state of the crops told as a matter of news.

Suddenly a new range of fact and outlook is presented, as if the curtains were rolled back before a strange world. To absorb any part of this information means a new way of thinking. The old ways begin to break down, and another generation, with a folk in large part differently trained, will find new intellectual interests well established in every countryside.

The crops and animals take on a novel and large significance. Witness the wholesome competition in corn-growing, potato-growing, in boys' and girls' clubs for the growing of crops, in the rising standards of excellence in agricultural products, in the organizing of societies of growers of the different crops and animals.

These intellectual interests extend

THIS series was begun with William Allen White's article, "Government of the People, by the People, for the People," in our issue of February 7. The next article, THE NEXT GENERATION IN AMERICAN BUSINESS, by Elbert H. Gary, president of the United States Steel Corporation, is to be published on March 27.

to the situations and also to the human materials. Witness the revival of interest in the rural school, in church extension, in farm bureau movements, in demonstrations and tests, fairs, recreation, lectures, community service. The rural community begins not only to see itself but to evaluate its enterprises in relation to society as a whole.

The accumulating information on every kind of rural subject will, of course, make the new farmer. He will want new intellectual aids. The technical bulletins have come, for such as want them. The books are coming, altho we still lack a truthful artistic literature of the farm situation.

Immediately before us is the need of a new or an improved periodical agency for the dissemination of information. The prevailing type of local country newspaper will not do. Its content is largely imported or inapplicable. It lacks inspiration. It lives too much on outside advertisement—sometimes of very doubtful character—and on political and exotic means of support. It may not really represent its region, or live on it. In a region in which there is apparently no advertising support, a local breeder's society will organize, for example, and establish a journal; and it will find advertising patronage from those who have animals to sell or to exchange. A grange periodical may develop a good support, for every progressive farmer has something to sell. We already begin to see a new periodical literature in the journals published regularly by farm bureaus, clubs, and also in the monthly periodicals issued by students in the colleges of agriculture and which have now become a class by themselves. The "news" is to be less a printing of personal gossip than a record of the real progress of the region: who has built a new barn, and the plans that went into it; who has purchased a pure-bred animal, and why; who has tried a new method, and the results; who has given a lecture or demonstration, and what was said; who has installed a system of drainage, and how; the year's crop movements, and the reasons.

Whether this type of information is to be combined in fair proportion and with understanding in the usual local country newspaper or whether a different kind of publication is to arise, we cannot foresee; but a new periodical local literature is coming.

LEADERSHIP—THE COUNTRY CAREER

WE begin to rejoice that such of the old political leadership as is founded on favoritism, self-interest, agreements and deals, is doomed. We know that the handwriting is on the wall. Never do I see a farm bureau agent going directly about his work and founding it on merit and fact, but I am conscious of the shift of the old initiative to new shoulders. The new district or county superintendent of schools is a vitalizing force, and his freedom from political control constantly becomes more secure. Many other agents, so far as they are based on the needs of the community and are not serving for personal ends, represent leadership forces now working in town and country alike. The new information cannot be applied to rural conditions without this kind of guidance. Undoubtedly we shall find the political leadership taking on new intentions and using the essential facts of the region for its basis.

The problem of the centuries has been to cause the people on the land to act and to express themselves. Under the stimulus of new knowledge and of many changed conditions this free action will come about, and it will make itself felt in the nation in the coming half century. This will not only bring a reaction directly on public policies, but will develop policies and institutions of its own. The farmers will take their particular problems in their own hands and will organize their own forces. There is every indication that the partizan politician cannot long hold the rural people for his ends: these people now have too many examples of other kinds of leadership.

Careers are now possible and even inviting for young men and women in the open country. These are not so much commercial careers, in the big sense in which we now measure them, as opportunities to establish a well-rounded occupation and business, to develop a high type of home life, and to render a useful service. The open country is to have more affairs and more interests. There will be greater diversity in its life. There will also be better rewards for the labor expended. The intellectual standards of excellence will very definitely include rural attainments as well as urban attainments.

Ithaca, New York

WHERE THEY ACTUALLY HAVE PREPAREDNESS—THE REMINGTON ARMS PLANT AT BRIDGEPORT, CONNECTICUT

AMERICA ARMING THE ALLIES

BY SYDNEY BROOKS

HARNESS Aladdin in the service of Mars and you get Remington's. By Remington's I mean the Remington Arms and Ammunition Company and the Union Metallic Cartridge Company. They are both under a single proprietorship; they are both situated at Bridgeport, Connecticut, and both within the last year have enormously expanded to meet the demands of the struggle in Europe. Who could have foreseen that a policy initiated in Potsdam would dislocate the life and industries of a New England townlet three thousand miles and more away, perhaps treble its population, and convert one of its factories into the largest small arms and ammunition plant in the world? That is what has actually happened; and if it isn't romance, then I for one don't know what romance is.

But such things do not happen by themselves. This is no affair of impersonal causes at one end of the scale and automatic consequences at the other. Somewhere in between you may be sure there is a man. Even in tales of magic you cannot dispense with the human agency. There must always be someone to wave the wand and rub the lamp. Remington's, I dare say, might even now be turning out nothing but its famous sporting weapons, might have no industrial interest whatever in the European war, were it not for one man. That man, of course, is Mr. Marcellus Hartley Dodge, the owner of the concern. Mr. Dodge was in Germany when the war broke out. He made his way to Paris and thence to London. He talked with his agents; he learned from them, probably long before we in England realized it ourselves, the deficiencies of the Allies in small

Independent readers have long been familiar with the illuminating articles on English and Continental affairs which Mr. Brooks has sent us from London. He has been a frequent visitor to America and is now again in this country for a few weeks renewing acquaintances and observing the reactions of the United States to the Great War.—THE EDITOR.

arms and ammunition; he saw his prodigious, his positively staggering, chance, and he seized it with both hands.

On the spot and with no specific contract that would justify any such enterprise, he made up his mind to build as an adjunct to the old Remington foundation an entirely new plant for supplying rifles, bayonets, shell cases and cartridges, to make it the largest and best of its kind and to have it working in record time. Nothing less than that would content him or meet the emergency which he was one of the first to foresee. In little more than a month after his return to America the contracts were all signed; the first sod was turned in December, 1914; in the following March work began on the main buildings, and in less than eight months, that is to say by the middle of last November, they were all completed and seventy-five per cent of the machinery was installed and in operation. But Mr. Dodge had not spent some $12,000,000 in less than a year to receive in return makeshift, jerry-built works. This new plant of his is meant to last. It is the product of the war only in the sense that the war furnished the occasion for its construction and the means where-

with to run it. But it will long outlive the immediate chance and need that brought it into being, and when the war orders cease, and if nothing from the United States Government is forthcoming to take their place, only a very slight adaptation will be necessary to convert its machinery to ordinary commercial uses.

To put up a plant with a floor area of about 1,500,000 square feet is one thing, tho I think a very big thing. To get the men to manage, superintend and work is another and a much more difficult thing. And in this case it was peculiarly difficult because the industry was a strange one. Until Mr. Dodge launched out, there was practically no private firm in the country that manufactured military arms and ammunition; most of the men who understood the business were in the Government arsenals; there was only a limited amount of the right sort of machinery; and side by side with the erection of the plant had to go the collection and training of a small army of skilled mechanics. Mr. Dodge has done more than set up a new factory; he has enriched the United States with a new industry; and he has furnished in addition a model example of how it should be carried on.

I will not attempt anything more than the purest description of the plant. It consists of thirteen main buildings, each five stories high, over sixty feet wide and over 270 in length, connected thru their centers —much as a skewer impales a row of kidneys—by a dozen service buildings of equal hight, but some eighty feet long by fifty in breadth. Standing on any floor in any of the service buildings one can thus look backwards or forwards from one end of the plant to the other, down a vista of a third of a mile. It seemed to me a scheme of construction admirable alike for its efficiency and its healthfulness. The service buildings are real service buildings, consisting as they do, on each floor and immediately adjacent to the workshops, of locker rooms, toilets, hot and cold lavatories and notice-boards whose contents are a standing testimony to the thought and care the management has taken for the health and comfort and amusements of the employees. The hospital with its scientific equipment, the elaborate machinery for gathering up dust, the restaurant where over 800 employees can be seated at once, the portable kitchens, the power house that at a pinch could supply a city of over 150,000 people with light and heat, the employment office where some 500 applicants are examined and sifted every day, the force of 300 guards keeping watch over every entrance, the welfare work which is under the direction of a man who for four years had charge of similar duties at Panama, the building and housing schemes which the company has undertaken to provide homes for the 18,000 employees that are already on the Bridgeport payrolls and for the other 16,000 or 18,000 that it expects to take on, the whole clean and spacious atmosphere of the works and the skill and contented busyness of the workers—all this made a deep and something more than a favorable impression upon me. I am not thinking so much of prodigious and unprecedented output, of the speed with which it is working up to a production of 5000 rifles, over 10,000 shell cases and nearly 4,000,000 cartridges a day, but of the liberal and enlightened spirit which informs the efficiency of the entire enterprise.

There are some reflections that an Englishman who is more than merely interested in America cannot banish from his mind as he goes the rounds of such an establishment. One of them is the fact that while Congress debates preparedness and the press argues it to and fro there in Bridgeport they actually have it. And it is the sort of preparedness of which, if British experience in this war goes for anything, neither you in America nor any other country can have too much. The plant that Mr. Dodge has erected is a national asset and a national safeguard. What do you imagine we in England would not have given when the war burst upon us to have possest a factory on such a scale and with such an equipment? What would not Russia give even today to possess anything like it? One of the most obvious lessons of the war is that while men will always be forthcoming in abundance it takes an immense effort and wastes many crucial months to arm them.

You cannot turn out arms and ammunition in a day. It is a highly skilled and extremely delicate form of manufacture. There are anywhere from eighty to a hundred and thirty separate parts in a modern rifle; it takes over sixty different operations to make even a gunstock; you have to work down to a thousandth of an inch; and I do not suppose that any plant could be erected and could produce 5000 rifles a day, in less than eighteen months. I do not know how it may be with you in America, but certainly any other country in which such a factory as Remington's existed would make it a point of public policy to conserve it, to feed it, to keep it instantly ready against the hour of need. When your time comes, and one must be blind indeed not to see that it is fast approaching, you will be grateful for what is now being done at Bridgeport.

Yet so far from being appreciative the general attitude of the American people toward this new munitions industry seems to be suspicious, reserved, and even hostile. I hear talk of an embargo and talk of a special tax on the manufacture of arms. There seems positively to be an idea that a plant such as Remington's draws its strength from within and is independent of other industries and other sections of the country. The truth is, of course, that pretty nearly all parts of the Union have contributed to its upbuilding and share in and profit by its success. At Remington's they draw their steel from Pennsylvania, New York and New England; their walnut for the gunstocks from the Middle West and South; their ordinary lumber from the North; their copper from Montana, Utah and Arizona; their spelter from Pennsylvania, Illinois and Missouri; their machinery from New England, the south as far as Delaware, the northern states and the Middle West; their lead from Missouri and Illinois; their oils and greases from Oklahoma and Texas; their coal from Pennsylvania; their paper from the states between New England and Wisconsin; their chemicals from all over the Union wherever they are to be bought; their cement and bricks from Pennsylvania and New York; their hardware and leather from the regions lying between New England on the one hand and Chicago on the other. All these states and all these industries would be directly and immediately affected were any policy to be aimed at Bridgeport on the supposition that its consequences could be confined to Bridgeport. It is, I admit, no concern of mine, but I could not help wishing that all Americans might have enjoyed my privilege of going thru the Remington plant, observing with their own eyes its extraordinary efficiency, and realizing by visible demonstration the breadth and closeness of its connections with other industries and other states. Such an experience, I conceive, would make them proud. And it would also make them hesitate.

New York City

THE SEEING EYE

BY MARGARET L. FARRAND

A curve in the road and a hillside
Clear cut against the sky;
A tall tree tossed by the autumn wind,
And a white cloud riding high;
Ten men went along that road;
And all but one passed by.

He saw the hill and the tree and the cloud
With an artist's mind and eye;
And he put them down on canvas—
For the other nine men to buy.

M. William Shak-ſpeare:

EIGHT PAPERS BY FREDERICK HOUK LAW
IN OBSERVANCE OF THE THREE HUNDREDTH
ANNIVERSARY OF SHAKESPEARE'S DEATH

The Comedies: Plays of Joy and Contemplation

TWELVE of Shakespeare's plays, delighting in life's humors, and dealing meditatively with life's problems, are at once joyous and inspiring. Boisterous action and brilliant wit yield place to more thoughtful characteristics. There is a greater mastery over word and phrase, a finer poetry, and a richer content. In these plays the characters are so lovingly drawn that they appeal to us as intrinsically human. What they do is of small importance compared with what they are. Portia, Rosalind, Viola, Imogen—these are so real that in thinking of their charm we forget the events thru which they move. Nor is it reality alone that marks the characters of these great comedies. Spirit, atmosphere, attitude toward life—call it what we will—something intangible draws us toward these plays as toward a revelation of life. Shakespeare was between thirty-two and forty when he wrote "The Merchant of Venice," "Much Ado About Nothing," "As You Like It," "Twelfth Night," "Henry V," "All's Well That Ends Well," "Measure for Measure" and "Troilus and Cressida." He was within a few years of his death when he wrote "Pericles," "Cymbeline," "The Tempest" and "The Winter's Tale." In this group of twelve plays we feel sure we have the great writer's happiest thoughts concerning life.

"The web of our life is of a mingled yarn, good and ill together," says the First Lord in "All's Well That Ends Well," and such, in fact, is the message of Shakespeare's comedies, for all touch upon serious events, and some closely approach tragedy. But this message is less important than that conveyed by the Duke in "Measure for Measure," when he says:

Spirits are not finely touch'd,
But to fine issues.

Shakespeare's view of life, when considered as a whole, is altogether noble. His interest lay in man's mastery of event, that is, in the development of lofty manhood. In his comedies, therefore, we find spirits rising "to fine issues"—and this it is, combined with convincing reality and beauty of expression, that makes Shakespeare's comedies great.

"The Merchant of Venice" is admirable as an introduction to the greater comedies. The reader delights in the romantic story of Portia, the rich heiress, who must marry the man who chooses a certain casket. He finds interest in the story of wayward Jessica, who, putting on boy's apparel, elopes with her favored lover. He laughs at the story of how disguised wives obtain rings from their husbands, whom they afterward taunt for weakness. But these interests are slight compared with the surpassing interest in the story of the money-lender who made a hard bond in order to gain revenge, and found himself caught in his own wickedness.

"Much Ado About Nothing" likewise approaches tragedy. On the one side is the story of how Benedick, having sworn never to marry, is tricked into love. On the other is the story of how the villainous Don John so inspires Claudio with jealousy that he rejects the gentle Hero and apparently drives her to death. The absurd constable Dogberry, who is almost as laughable as Falstaff, finds out the rascality of Don John, and all ends happily, "much ado" having been made "about nothing." The irrepressible liveliness, mischief, wit, sauciness and good heart of Beatrice, whom Benedick is led to love, make her the most delightful person in the play. In her charming pertness we forget wickedness, jealousy and rage, and gain something of her gladness in being alive.

"As You Like It" is another play sparkling with joy in life, but with serious thought underlying its good spirit. A banished duke and his followers, two court ladies and a jester, and a young man with a faithful old servant, all fleeing from ill-treatment in the great world, come together in the Forest of Arden. There, with rustics whom they meet, they live a care-free life, hunting, jesting, playing at love, philosophizing, and learning that life, whether in court or forest, is "as you like it." A flood of sunshine comes to us with the utterly charming personality of Rosalind.

"Twelfth Night," taking its name from the joyful twelfth night after Christmas, is another play of mingled poetry and laughter, and is set in the no-man's land of Illyria. The quick-minded Viola is one of Shakespeare's most charming women. The play is charmingly romantic, sparkling with humor, filled with a kindly satire, full of delightful characterization, and touched with beautiful poetry, as is shown by the Duke's speech in the first scene:

If music be the food of love, play on:
Give me excess of it, that, surfeiting,
The appetite may sicken and so die.
That strain again! it had a dying fall:
O, it came o'er my ear like the sweet sound,
That breathes upon a bank of violets,
Stealing and giving odor!

"Henry V," like "Henry IV," is a combination of heroic chronicle and ludicrous comedy. At one time we follow the fortunes of the heroic, patriotic English king, who leads a weakened army against tremendous odds to a noble victory. The play shows us the king's agony of soul, when, moved by the great responsibility of his position, he prays for his men just before the battle. He is an ideal of strength and manly leadership, saying in the face of what might have been fear:

We are in great danger;
The greater therefore should our courage be.

The play has two divisions of comedy, one centering around a group of low-comedy characters, some of whom speak in dialect; and the other centering around the king. The scene in which he courts the Princess Katharine of France is as humorous and as charming a scene as Shakespeare ever wrote.

Take me by the hand, and say, "Harry of England, I am thine;" which

Sarony

PORTIA

HELENA MODJESKA, THE POLISH ACTRESS, WHO CAME TO AMERICA AFTER WINNING HIGH DISTINCTION IN WARSAW, AND ACTED SHAKESPEARE HERE IN THE LATE SEVENTIES, EIGHTIES AND NINETIES. WILLIAM WINTER SAYS THAT SHE "GAVE A DELICIOUS IMPERSONATION OF PORTIA, . . . SHE SPECIALLY REVEALED, AND EXULTED IN, THE TENDER, ARDENT, INTRINSIC WOMANHOOD OF THAT GOLDEN GIRL OF ITALY"

word thou shalt no sooner bless mine ear withal, but I will tell thee aloud, "England is thine, Ireland is thine, France is thine, and Henry Plantagenet is thine." . . . Come, your answer in broken music; for thy voice is music and thy English broken.

"All's Well That Ends Well" creates strong character interest in its resolute young heroine, Helena, a woman who is not only mistress of herself, but also of all events and conditions that confront her. By her cleverness she wins the husband she desires; when he flouts her and leaves for a distant land she follows, and, in a series of events, masters circumstance and gains his regard. The personality of this charmingly strong woman is so well presented that Coleridge has called her "Shakespeare's loveliest character." The play "ends well" because Helena had force to master events. As she says:

Our remedies oft in ourselves do lie,
Which we ascribe to heaven: the fated sky
Gives us free scope, only doth backward pull
Our slow designs when we ourselves are dull.

"Measure for Measure," like "The Merchant of Venice," concerns the thought of mercy, the events of the play leading one to see that "measure" should not be given for "measure," but that mercy should temper justice. With such a theme it is natural that the play should approach the tragic, and should have much depth of thought. Dealing as it does with man's wrong doing and lack of mercy it is sometimes satirical:

Man, proud man,
Drest in a little brief authority,
Most ignorant of what he's most assured,
His glassy essence, like an angry ape,
Plays such fantastic tricks before high heaven
As make the angels weep.

In the pure-minded Isabella, who, rather than sacrifice honor, would let her brother die, we have another of Shakespeare's noblest women.

"Troilus and Cressida," telling the story of how the Trojan warrior, Troilus, gave his love to the unworthy Cressida, is even more satirical. Its interest is so little in story and so much in thought that some have called it "Shakespeare's wisest play." The thought that life fails to fulfil all its promises is not pleasant, but the play has other themes as well.

The remaining plays, "Pericles," "Cymbeline," "The Tempest," and "The Winter's Tale," are as bright and kindly as "All's Well That Ends Well," "Measure for Measure" and "Troilus and Cressida" are dark and satirical. Before he wrote these last comedies Shakespeare had lived himself into the souls of the powerfully drawn characters of the great tragedies—Hamlet, Othello, Lear, and Macbeth. Now, as tho the time of satire, bitterness and tragic struggle had passed, he turned to joyful romance made wise by experience.

In "Pericles, Prince of Tyre," he tells the imaginative story of how Pericles surprizingly found his long-lost wife and daughter. Interest in event once more comes to the front, tempered by beautifully poetic meditations. It is supposed that Shakespeare wrote only a part of the play, his work beginning in the opening scene of the third act with the powerful description of a storm at sea:

Thou god of this great vast, rebuke these surges,
Which wash both heaven and hell . . .
O, still
Thy deafening, dreadful thunders . . .
The seaman's whistle
Is as a whisper in the ears of death,
Unheard.

There is an especial charm in that part of the play ascribed to Shakespeare, for it deals almost entirely with the tender story of the sea-born Marina and her meeting with the father from whom she had been separated.

"Cymbeline" is another romance that tells of restoration from seeming death. Imogen's pitiable adventures, her meeting with her lost brothers, and her recovery of her husband's love, make excellent story material. A charming, beautiful and noble woman, she is a high example of faithfulness and purity. It is this play that contains the famous song:

Fear no more the heat o' the sun,
Nor the furious winter's rages;
Thou thy worldly task hast done,
Home art gone and ta'en thy wages:
Golden lads and girls all must,
As chimney-sweepers, come to dust.

"The Tempest," a play combining dramatic power, poetry and wisdom, is like "A Midsummer Night's Dream" in dealing with magic, but it has a deeper purpose. In its story of Prospero, the magician, living on a mysterious island where he has at his command a bright spirit named Ariel, and a lumpish being called Caliban, some have seen Shakespeare, the magician of the drama, whose intention to abandon play writing may be set forth in the lines:

I'll break my staff,
Bury it certain fathoms in the earth,
And deeper than did ever plummet sound
I'll drown my book.

Full of wisely beautiful poetry and fascinating in its imaginative story, "The Tempest" is thoroly delightful. Its thought centers around the conception that true freedom is neither license nor stern restraint, but sympathetic adaptation. Prospero, free to torment those who had kept him from his dukedom, finds a higher freedom in mercy, saying to Ariel:

Hast thou, which art but air, a touch, a feeling,
Of their afflictions, and shall not myself,
One of their kind, that relish all as sharply,
Passion as they, be kindlier moved than thou art?
Though with their high wrongs I am struck to the quick,
Yet with my nobler reason 'gainst my fury
Do I take part: the rarer action is
In virtue than in vengeance.

His best self demands a noble life in the world rather than supremacy on a lonely island.

In "The Winter's Tale," Shakespeare's last play, there is also a wealth of wisdom, poetry and characterization. Its story of how Leontes' wife and daughter are restored to his love is interestingly romantic. Best of all is its delightful spirit of outdoor life—strong-limbed youth, charming girlhood, shepherds shearing their sheep, and country festivities, all entering into the play. No one who reads it will forget the surprize that ends the play, nor will he forget Perdita's charm, nor Autolycus' lovable rascality. The play has the happy spirit of the jolly rogue in his song:

When daffodils begin to peer,
With heigh! the doxy over the dale,
Why, then comes in the sweet o' the year;
For the red blood reigns in the winter's pale.

Shakespeare's comedies, taken as a whole, form a complete round of humor, beginning with boisterous plays of event and ready dialogue; proceeding thru plays in which rich imagination finds expression in suggestive verse; dropping for a time into satire that takes full cognizance of the ills of life; and ending at last in mellow romance, as tho the good, sweet breath of the Stratford fields had driven away all the somber thoughts that London life may have created.

BOOKS FOR FURTHER READING

E. Bland, edited by E. T. Roe: Twenty Beautiful Stories from Shakespeare; H. S. Morris: Tales from Shakespeare; W. C. Jerrold: Descriptive Index to Shakespeare's Characters in Shakespeare's Words; A. B. Jameson: Shakespeare's Heroines; M. C. Clarke: Girlhood of Shakespeare's Heroines; M. M. McKenney: Studies of Shakespeare's Women; H. F. Martin: Some of Shakespeare's Female Characters; F. Harris: Women of Shakespeare; A. P. Wright: Children of Shakespeare; Alice S. Hoffman: The Children's Shakespeare.

BOTH SIDES A DEBATE

INDEPENDENCE OF THE PHILIPPINES

RESOLVED, That the United States should within the next four years grant the Philippines their independence.

SINCE the United States gained possession of the Philippines in 1898 four ways of treating them have been suggested: to sell the Islands, to establish a protectorate, to retain them permanently, and to grant them independence. The Clark amendment directing the President to withdraw American sovereignty within four years was approved by the Senate, February 2, 1916. This brief was prepared by R. S. Fulton.

BRIEF FOR THE AFFIRMATIVE

I. The Philippines should be granted independence in four years for moral reasons.
  A. The United States had no right to establish sovereignty.
    1. A mandate of international law declares that "No nation has a right to obtain by purchase or acquisition sovereignty over a people which is not actually exercised by the country which undertakes to convey or yield it."
    2. Spain had no right to give us a title to the Philippines. (a) She was not exercising sovereignty over them. (1) The natives, except in Manila, had overthrown the power of Spain.
  B. Our indefinite policy is destroying the confidence of the Filipinos.
    1. Our Government is expected to give them independence. (a) Preparation of the Filipinos for self-government was the policy of President McKinley, President Roosevelt, Governor Taft, Governor General Wright, Governor General Ide, and all their successors. (b) Democrats have advocated independence for the Filipinos.
  C. They desire independence.
    1. Petitions for independence repeatedly presented to Congress by them.
    2. In 1907, the National Party, standing for immediate independence, at the first election for assemblymen elected sixty-six out of eighty-one members.
  D. Possession unjust to Filipinos.
    1. Deprives them of self-government.
    2. Keeps them in servitude. (a) Destroys incentive to self-government.
    B. We cannot govern them well.
    1. The natives distrust us.
II. They will be competent to maintain a stable government in four years.
  A. They are now homogeneous.
    1. A unit in temperament. (a) Report of fourteen governors in 1903. (b) They are peaceable, law-abiding people.
    2. A unit ethnographically. (a) The same characteristics and customs due to same civilization for three centuries.
    3. They have made a united effort for freedom. (a) In the wars against Spain and the United States.
    4. A unit politically. (a) They vote for party rather than tribe.
    5. More homogeneous in race and religion than Americans. (a) All Malay stock. (b) Ninety-four per cent Catholics.
    6. A unit geographically. (a) Drawn together by communication and transportation. (1) Under American control wagon roads extended from 300 to 500 miles by Philippine capital and labor. (2) Railroads extended from 128 to 611 miles. (3) Seven thousand five hundred miles of telegraph and cable lines with a forty per cent annual increase.
    B. English is becoming the language.
    C. They have few criminals.
    D. Their material progress is satisfactory. (a) They now produce $23,000,000 worth of exports. (b) They use modern

methods of production. (c) Their municipalities provide improvements.
    E. Social progress.
    1. Sanitation.
    F. Education.
    1. The Filipinos intensely desire education. (a) Without legal compulsion 500,000 children attend public schools. (b) Cost of education paid by taxes.
    2. 4404 schools in the Islands.
    G. They can establish law and order.
    1. Natives have shown ability in government. (a) Seven thousand three hundred and ninety-four Filipino officers in government service. (b) Three justices of Supreme Court are natives. (c) For many years people have elected good governors. (d) Out of 12,340 officials in the Islands 12,190 are natives.
III. Independence should be granted for military reasons.
  A. Islands a burden in time of peace.
    1. A large army necessary.
    2. A strong Pacific fleet.
    3. Expensive military stations.
    B. Retention dangerous in war.
    1. Opinion of military authorities.
    2. Not easily defended. (a) An extensive seacoast. (b) Seven thousand miles from our base of supplies.
IV. Economic reasons.
  A. They can bear economic burden of independence
    1. Now maintaining their government.
    2. Financial condition easily strengthened. (a) Lowest tax rate in the world. (b) Indebtedness per capita is low.
    B. Retention an economic burden to U. S.
    1. U. S. military and naval expenditures there $26,000,000.

BRIEF FOR THE NEGATIVE

I. Philippines should not be granted independence in four years for moral reasons.
  A. We have not deprived Filipinos of their rights.
    1. Our Government better than they would have otherwise had.
    B. Majority of Filipinos do not desire immediate independence.
    1. They realize progress is faster under American rule.
    C. Our promise not binding. Freeing of Philippines a matter for Congress.
    D. Independence in four years unjust.
    1. We owe them a stable government.
    2. To retain the Islands the only way.
    E. They cannot be given to foreign power. (b) Protectorate not advisable.
II. Filipinos cannot within four years maintain stable government.
  A. They lack power of initiative.
    1. No great leaders.
    (a) Rizal, their writer, and Aguinaldo, their warrior, not pure Filipinos. (b) Ninety-eight per cent of pure Filipinos have accomplished little.
    B. They cannot be unified so soon.
    1. Many different tribes.
    2. Tribes living together for centuries never intermixed.
    3. No common language.
    4. Cannot be assimilated. (a) Limited transportation. (b) Press reaches few.
    C. Too illiterate.
    1. A half million wild savages.
    2. Only twenty per cent literate.
    3. Only three per cent read English.
    4. Not enough competent voters can be produced. (a) One child in four attends school. (b) Ninety-five per cent in primary grades. (c) One out of two hundred enters high school.
    D. Natives have shown incapacity in government.

    1. Municipal and national politics. (a) Candidates make appeals for votes which would insult American voter. (b) Radical parties defeated conservative. (c) Ignorant or corrupt officials elected.
    2. Masses may be exploited by rich.
    3. Natives untrustworthy. (a) Think public office private property of holder.
    4. Good government in Philippines result of American control. (a) Protected the ignorant. (b) Prevented revolution. (c) Furnished the initiative.
III. Independence should not be granted for military and naval reasons.
  A. Islands beneficial to us in peace. Permanent Eastern base for our fleet.
    B. Islands advantageous in war.
    1. Coaling and supply station.
    2. Place to mobilize an army. (a) The natives a strong fighting force. (b) Rich natural resources.
    C. Permanent possession advantageous to Islands.
    1. Domestic tranquillity.
    2. Protection from foreign foes.
V. Economic reasons.
  A. Economic burden too great.
    1. Insular government lately has not met expenses. (a) In 1915 many schools closed for lack of funds.
    2. Present financial stringency.
    3. Additional expenditures necessary for internal improvements. (a) School system should be extended. (b) More roads and railroads needed.
    4. Expenditures necessary for army and navy.
    B. Retention of the Islands will not be great expense to us.
    1. Only expense is for soldiers.
    2. Military expense can be reduced by substituting more native soldiers.

REFERENCES

General

Atlantic Monthly, 103:299-309, February, 1909. Barrows, David Prescott: *A Decade of American Government in the Philippines, 1903-1913*, Yonkers-on-Hudson, N. J. World Book Company, 1914. *Congressional Record*, 64th Congress, 1st Session, 53:1728-1744, January 26; 1865-1870, January 28, 1916. *Everybody's Magazine*, 19:640a-640b, November, 1908. *Independent*, 74:1070-1071, May 15, 1913; 1377-1383, June 19, 1913, 79:89-90, July 20; 80:50-51, October 12; 237-239, November 16, 1914. Jernegan, Prescott F.: *The Philippine Citizen* (fourth edition), Manila, Philippine Education Company, 1914. *Literary Digest*, 45:1045-1047, December 7, 1912. *North American Review*, 179:289-300, August, 1914 199:165-73, January, 1914. *Outlook*, 101:142-145, May 25, 1912; 106:664-666, March 28, 1914. Teich, Emma Louise, comp. *Selected Articles on Independence for the Philippines*, Minneapolis, The H. W. Wilson Company, 1913.

Affirmative

Atlantic Monthly, 110:649-662, November, 1912. *Century Magazine*, 87:422-438, January, 1914. *Congressional Record*, 64th Congress, 1st Session, 53:834-846, January 7; 861-880, January 10; 932-936, January 11, 1916. *Independent*, 72:96-96, January 11, 1912. *North American Review*, 194:135-149, January, 1911; 195:965-977, June 21, 1907; 199:708-718, May, 1909. *Nation*, 70:50, January 18, 1900; 82:47-48, January 18, 1906; 95:474-5, November 21, 1912. *Outlook*, 91:75-83, January 9, 1909; 105:132-136, September 20, 1913.

Negative

Congressional Record, 63d Congress, 2d Session, 51: 13148-13146 (No. 180 current file), June 14, 1914; 17841-17842, October 6; 18531-18532, October 19; 18787-18789, October 21, 1914. *Congressional Record*, 64th Congress, 1st Session, 53:725-727, January 7; 1318-1324, January 17; 1908-1912, January 28; 1866-1868, January 28; 1985-1986, January 29, 1916. *Forum*, 51:187-192, February, 1914. *Literary Digest*, 45:1163-1164, December 21, 1912. *Living Age*, 251:516-525, December 1, 1906. *Munsey's Magazine*, 33:139-143, May, 1905. *National Monthly*, 38:755-759, August, 1913. *Overland Monthly*, n. s. v. 59:62-69, January, 1912. *Outlook*, 102:602-604, November 23, 1912; 108:357-369, October 14, 1914. *World's Work*, 27:256, January, 1914.

LITTLE GARDENS

THREE BRIEF PRACTICAL TALKS TO PEOPLE WHO HAVE BACKYARDS AND WANT TO USE THEM

A SIMPLE HARDY BORDER   A GARDEN OF ANNUALS
THE BACKYARD VEGETABLE GARDEN

Flowers are not luxuries—they are as essential to a house as dress is to a woman. They belong to the category of necessities such as bath and breakfast, rather than to that of superfluities like clubs and candy—and they cost less. To live up in the country, or even the half-country, and not be surrounded with flowers is an anomaly. Every suburban house should have, if not a garden, then blooms and greenery, color and background.

There is a great deal of flat green in our suburbs and of uniformity in the neat, cold grass plots, but not enough warmth, lights and shadows, and variety.

The size of our place and of our pocketbook are the first points to consider in laying out our lot or back yard. But even if the start must be small we know that year by year we can add a few plants or a new shrub, and have the delight of watching the growth of our garden.

A SIMPLE HARDY BORDER

Cost of Plants, Ten to Fifteen Dollars

A BORDER of hardy perennials is the most satisfactory start to make in laying out a small lot, for, while we need never add to it, we can at any time build a garden around it. First look for a background. Flowers need to be thrown into relief. The house makes a good one, or a fence or wall; a green hedge or row of shrubs is even better. Do not make beds of flowers in the middle of the lawn, or stiffly bordering the sides of the entrance road. Choose, rather, the south or east side of the house, or one side of the boundary line, especially if there is a hedge or fence.

We will make a border of ninety square feet, arranging it according to our taste and needs. It may be four feet wide and twenty-two feet long, or if we want more length we can make it three feet wide and thirty feet long. The last would make the best looking border. Place stakes at the corners, and draw a line of twine taut from stake to stake. Cut the sod close to the twine with a square spade, lift the sod in sections and lay to one side, then dig down eighteen inches or two feet. As some plants need a deep bed it is as well to make it two feet. Put a layer of pebbles or broken stone at the bottom for drainage, and the sods next. If the soil is clayey mix it with one-fourth sand. About one-fourth of well-rotted manure ($2.00 a ton) should be mixt with the earth and thoroly pulverized so that there will be no lumps. Fill in the ditch and pile the earth several inches higher than the surrounding ground, to allow for

shrinkage. The top layer should be a rich garden soil or top soil. This border should be made as early in the spring as it is possible to work the soil, and allowed to stand and settle before planting. All the plants will not be put in at the same time, as some should be set out in the spring and others in the fall. It would be an advantage to prepare the bed six months before the planting is to be done.

By using entirely small plants one can get the quickest results with a minimum of work.

The accompanying diagram shows a border thirty feet long and three feet wide. At the back of the border, plant at each end three Oriental poppies of the Mammoth or Goliath variety, a gorgeous splash of scarlet with black center. Start six inches from the outer edge of the bed and set the plants one foot apart. These perennial poppies will self-sow and increase in numbers until in a few years it will be necessary to transplant them. In three years they may also be taken up and divided, so that the original six will soon grow to a hundred.

Next to the poppies plant a group of three phloxes at each end of the border and on the back line. Select the clear and pure colored varieties of phloxes, the white and salmon pink, and have each group of one variety. The Frau Anton Buchner, Amazone and Anna Crozy are large pure white varieties, the Pantheon is carmine rose, and the Molière a clear salmon pink.

Having planted the poppies and phloxes at the two ends, this will leave

about seventeen feet in the center of the back line for a dozen hardy Pompon chrysanthemums, set about a foot and a half apart or a little less. The "aster" flowered type is more picturesque than the button varieties. The Fairy Queen, pink, and the Julia Lagravere, garnet, make good fall colorings, and the Sunshine is good for a yellow.

In front of the back row, with a foot between, plant at each end a group of six Anemone Japonica, the loveliest of the fall perennials. Select the Whirlwind, which is a charming white variety, and either the Queen Charlotte or Rosea Superba for a pink, and set them about fifteen inches apart. In the center of this line plant one dozen delphiniums, one foot apart—six of the light blue Belladonna, and six of the dark blue Formosum varieties. They will grow three or four feet high, and if the first stalks are cut off while still in bloom, they will make a second blooming, and stretch the flowering season from June to September. When the flower stalks are cut down, stir in a handful of bone meal at the roots.

The front line will be divided into three sections. At each end have a group of six Aquilegia (columbines), planted one foot apart. This graceful and spirited flower grows freely to a hight of about two and a half feet, and its delicate colorings blend with almost any flower. The Canadensis is an early blooming variety and the Californica a later flowering kind.

The center of the front line may be filled with spring flowering bulbs, and

PERENNIAL BORDER, 30 FEET LONG, 3 FEET WIDE

3 Oriental Poppies	3 Phloxes	Plant 25 Gesneriana Tulips on back line		5 Phloxes	3 Oriental Poppies
		12 Hardy Pompon Chrysanthemums			
6 Anemone Japonica		12 Delphinium Formosum and Belladonna		6 Anemone Japonica	
6 Aquilegia		25 Tulips 50 Narcisus		6 Aquilegia	

as these may be planted five or six inches apart, the space will allow of a double row in front of the delphiniums. Fifty of the late-blooming cottage tulips, the gorgeous Gesneriana spathulata, and the white Innocence or La Candeur, will make an effective line of bloom. Along the entire front line plant fifty narcissus of the trumpet varieties, the Golden Spur, Emperor and Empress.

Bulbs should be planted about five or six inches deep, and each one set in a handful of sand, to avoid any danger of contact with the manure.

The narcissus should be planted in September, as they make an early growth in the spring; tulips may be planted in October or as late as November. When all the bulbs are planted, rake the surface carefully and evenly. As the perennial plants may all be set out in the spring, the space for the bulbs would be vacant the first summer, and seeds of annuals could be sown for temporary bloom.

Anemones may be planted the middle of April, chrysanthemums the last of April, and the other perennials by the middle of May. The best time for planting delphinium is the spring, but columbines, Oriental poppies and phloxes may be planted in September. Every two or three years these perennial plants should be lifted and divided, and a new border started.

In winter the border should be covered with a light mulch of leaves or garden muck, but the phloxes will need a mulch of manure. And when the plants are first set out they must be watered in the late afternoon.

An outlay of $15.00 would make a border four feet wide or 120 square feet, and one could add to the other plants a half dozen herbaceous peonies

LIST OF PERENNIAL PLANTS FOR BORDER

Quantity	Name	Variety	Description	Time of Bloom	Price	Total Cost
½ doz.	Oriental Poppies	Mammoth	Scarlet with black blotch at base of petals	June	$1.25	
½ doz.	Hardy Phloxes	Amazone, Moliere, Pantheon	Pure white and pure salmon crimson	July and August	.75	
1 doz.	Chrysanthemums	Fairy Queen, Julia Lagravere, Sunshine	Pink, Garnet, Yellow	October	1.00	
1 doz.	Anemone Japonica	Whirlwind, Queen Charlotte	White, Pink	Sept. and Oct	1.50	
½ doz.	Delphinium Delphinium	Formosum, Belladonna	Dark blue, Light blue	June to Sept.	.75 1.25	
1 doz.	Aquilegia (Columbine)	Canadensis, Californica, Coerulea	Early blooming, Later blooming, Blue and white	May, June, June	1.50	
50	Tulips	Gesneriana Spathulata, Innocence	Crimson, White	May	1.00	
50	Narcissus	Golden Spur, Emperor, Empress	Yellow	April	1.00	—$10.00
½ doz.	Herbaceous Peonies	Festiva Maxima, Delicatissima, Felix Crousse, Md. Chéreau	White, Pink, Brilliant red, White edged blue	June, May	2.50 2.50	5.00
50	German Iris	Orientalis, Queen of May, etc.	Blue, Rose			$15.00

LIST OF ANNUAL FLOWER SEEDS FOR SUMMER AND AUTUMN GARDEN

Quantity	Name	Variety	Color	Time of Bloom	Price
1 Pkt.	Alyssum (edging)	Little gem	White		.10
1 Pkt.	Alyssum (edging)	White Fleece	White		.10
1 Pkt.	Anchusa	Capensis	Azure blue	July and August	.10
1 Pkt.	Anchusa	Farquahar's annual blue	Dark blue		.10
1 Pkt.	Arkemisia	Saccorum viridis	Foliage plant		.15
4 Pkt.	Antirrhinum	4 varieties	Rose, white, yellow	August	.40
2 Pkt.	Asters	Late-branching	Two colors	September	.20
2 Pkt.	Asters	Asterum	Two colors	August	.30
1 Pkt.	Calendula	Meteor	Yellow and orange	June to November	.05
1 Pkt.	Calendula	Orange King	Dark orange	June to November	.05
2 Pkt.	Coreopsis	Golden, Wave, etc.	Yellow and red		.10
2 Pkt.	Campanula	Attica and Macrostyla	Violet and white		.30
2 Pkt.	Candytuft (edging)	2 varieties	White, pink or rose	July or August	.20
3 Pkt.	Carnation Marguerite	3 varieties	White, yellow and pink or red	July to frost	.30
2 Pkt.	Chrysanthemum, annual	2 double varieties	White and red	September	.20
2 Pkt.	Cosmos	Lady Lenox	Pink and white	June to frost	.40
4 Pkt.	Dianthus	4 varieties	Many colors	June to frost	.40
1 Pkt.	Eschscholtzia	California	Yellow	June to frost	.05
1 Pkt.	Eschscholtzia	Rose Cardinal	Rose colored	June to frost	.05
1 Pkt.	Ornamental grass	Bromus brizae formis	White and pink		.15
2 Pkt.	Gypsophila	Grandiflora and rosea	Purple, pink, lilac, blue, white		.15
	Larkspur	Invincible	Scarlet		.15
¼ Oz.	Lavatera (Mallow)	Rosea Splendens	Rosy pink	All summer	.40
¼ Oz.	Lavatera	Alba Splendens	Pearly white	All summer	.40
¼ Oz.	Mignonette	Farquahar's Giant	Reddish green		.50
1 Pkt.	Marigold	Double French	Yellow and brown		.10
1 Pkt.	Marigold	Double African	Yellow		.10
1 Oz.	Nasturtium	Tall or Running	Rainbow Mixture	All summer	.30
1 Pkt.	Nasturtium	Dwarf, Mixed	Crimson	All summer	.20
1 Pkt.	Nicotiana	Affinis Hybrids	Rose, violet, white	August	.10
1 Pkt.	Pansies	Giant, Mixed		All summer	.25
1 Pkt.	Pansies	Cassier's Mixture		All summer	.25
1 Pkt.	Violas	Mixed	All colors	All summer	.10
2 Pkt.	Phlox Drummondi		Salmon, white	July to Fall	.20
1 Pkt.	Phlox Drummondi	Isabelliana	Yellow	July to Fall	.15
1 Pkt.	Phlox Drummondi	Chamois-rose	Shell pink	July to Fall	.10
1 Pkt.	Poppies	Shirley	Salmon and pink	August	.20
3 Pkt.	Poppies	Carnation-flowered	Gray, lilac, scarlet		.15
1 Pkt.	Racinus	Borboniensis Arboreus	Purple foliage		.05
1 Pkt.	Racinus	Sanguineus	Reddish purple		.05
1 Pkt.	Salvia	Patens	Bright blue		.25
4 Pkt.	Stocks	Giant Ten Week	Different colors		.60
4 Pkt.	Stocks	Cut-and-Come-Again	Different colors		.60
¼ Oz.	Sunflowers	Primrose Queen	Yellow		.20
¼ Oz.	Sunflowers	Cucumeri Foliers	Golden yellow		.40
1 Pkt.	Zinnias	Colossal and Dwarf	Different shades		.05
					$10.00

To equal the Cadillac
is the universal ambition

THERE is great gratification for the Cadillac owner in this fact:
That the highest aim of the serious minded manufacturer is to approximate
Cadillac performance.

Consciously or unconsciously, engineers are constantly inspired by the characteristics which distinguish the Cadillac Eight-Cylinder engine.

Consciously or unconsciously, automobile salesmanship—both oral and printed
—endeavors to emphasize the claim that other cars possess these Cadillac
qualities.

Consciously or unconsciously, that salesmanship continually endeavors to
emphasize the very things for which the Cadillac engine is famous.

Other types sometimes claim equality and sometimes superiority, but consciously or unconsciously, it is always the Cadillac standard which they claim
to equal or to surpass.

Fewer cylinders or more cylinders, they apparently have but one criterion, and
that is the Cadillac V-type Eight-Cylinder criterion—forgetful of the fact
that the high development of the Cadillac engine is only one fine phase of
Cadillac performance.

It is well to remember that this has always been true—since the infant days of
the industry.

Cadillac quality and Cadillac performance have frequently been on the very
verge of being surpassed—according to the enthusiastic advertising and sales.
manship of other cars.

The Cadillac market has always been *about* to be taken by storm.

But somehow, the Cadillac market continues to increase in volume and in
enthusiasm, year after year.

Meanwhile, ambitious aspirants for comparison with the Cadillac have fallen
away—one by one—and taken their places in a lower price class.

The simple truth is, that the beautiful riding qualities which make the Cadillac
owner almost forget that he is in a motor car, represent the very uttermost
that has yet been accomplished.

Styles and Prices

Standard Seven passenger car. Five passenger Salon and Roadster. $2080. Three passenger Victoria. $2400. Four passenger
Coupe, $2800. Five passenger Brougham, $2950. Seven passenger Limousine. $3450. Berlin. $3600
Prices include standard equipment. F. O. B. Detroit.

Cadillac Motor Car Co. Detroit. Mich.

Try this easy way to clear your skin

Bathe your face for several minutes with Resinol Soap and warm water, working the creamy lather into the skin gently with the finger tips. Then wash off with more Resinol Soap and warm water, finishing with a dash of cold water to close the pores.

Do this once or twice a day, and you will be astonished how quickly the healing, antiseptic Resinol medication soothes and cleanses the pores, lessens the tendency to pimples, and leaves the complexion clear fresh and velvety.

If the skin is in bad condition through neglect or an unwise use of cosmetics, apply a little Resinol Ointment* and let it remain on ten minutes before the final washing with Resinol Soap.

Resinol Soap contains no harsh, drying alkali, and is not artificially colored; its rich brown being entirely due to the Resinol balsams in it. Sold by all druggists and dealers in toilet goods. For trial free, write to Dept. 7-C, Resinol, Baltimore, Md.

*Physicians have prescribed Resinol Ointment for over twenty years in the treatment of skin and scalp affections.

Men with tender faces find the rich lather of Resinol Shaving Stick delightfully soothing.

of the Festina Maxima, white, and Delicatissima, pink, or Felix Crousse, brilliant red, varieties. Get freshly dug and strong two-year-old roots; plant them in early September, and set so that the tip of the crown will be covered with two inches of soil. Mulch them lightly when newly planted. Then too, one could have fifty of the beautiful German and other Rhizomatous irises, which, unlike the tulips and narcissus, may be planted early in May. Iris bulbs should be set a foot apart, putting a handful of sand in the hole, and covering the bulb with sand. As for varieties, it is difficult to make a limited selection among the many good ones. Md. Chéreau, Florentina alba, Orientalis, Innocenza, Palida, Queen of May for the light blues, whites and rose; Purple King, a dark purple; Aurea and Darius for the yellow.

Never buy "mixtures" or "varieties" of bulbs or seeds; order a few named varieties, and plan to have masses of one or two colors instead of mixtures of many.

If time and labor are of no account one may have two borders instead of one at the same cost by raising perennials from seeds. The seeds should be sown in rows in a prepared nursery bed, in June or July, transplanted to the border in September, and the following spring they will bloom.

A GARDEN OF ANNUALS

To Cost Ten Dollars

For a summer and early fall garden, annuals give a larger return on the investment than any other form of planting. They also require more care and judgment in arrangement. We must give them light and shade, perspective, and some green for a backing.

A large number of annuals may be grown from seed in the border where they are to bloom, but for those who have cold frames it will be better to start them early and transplant them to the border in June. For sowing seeds out of doors in the vicinity of New York, the first of May is a safe date; if sown as early as April there might be danger that they would rot in the ground, and fewer would germinate. In the north and in higher altitudes seeds should not be sown until June. The majority of the annuals have a long period of bloom, but a few flower only for a few weeks, and of these it is well to make two periods of sowing to give successive bloom. Sow Candytuft, Mignonette, Poppies in May and again in July.

The borders should be prepared as soon as frost is out of the ground. They need not be spaded deeper than a foot, but the surface of the bed should be raised several inches above the ground level, the earth broken up and pulverized, and raked very fine on top. The soil should be loose, friable, and mellow. If the earth is clayey, mix it with one-fourth sand; if it is soggy, mix in some lime. A moderate amount of cow manure should be used as fertilizer. If the borders are prepared the previous season the manure may be mixt thruout the earth, but if the planting is done the same season the manure must not come in contact with the seeds.

The most expeditious way is to draw furrows six inches deep in the borders where the flowers are to grow. Fill the bottom of the furrow with cow manure; cover this with five inches of earth, prest smooth, then sow the seeds evenly and thinly, and sprinkle over them a little fine soil. Press the surface gently with a board, and water. When the small plants come up, they should be thinned out to strengthen those that are left.

The majority of garden borders should be curving and irregular. Arrange for the higher growing annuals to be at the back, such as Nicotiana, Larkspur, the branching Asters, Cosmos, the tall Snapdragons, Lavatera, Salvia, Sunflowers, and edge the front line with Pansies, Violas, the dwarf Alyssum, or Candytuft. The intermediate space between the high flowers at the back and the front edging may be filled in with medium growing plants: Calendulas and Coreopsis, the lovely Bell-Flower and the double blue Bachelor's Button, Pinks, California Poppies and Shirley Poppies, Baby's Breath and Butterfly Flower, Marigolds, Nasturtiums, possibly the annual Phlox, and surely the beautiful Stocks, the Zinnias which last late in the autumn, and Mignonette.

Another caution is in the matter of color arrangement. For planting in the borders near the house, try to select the flowers of delicate and cool colorings in lavenders, blues, whites, and pinks. The vivid yellows, the strong reds, and the coarser flowers are effective in the distance, especially with the contrast of green.

A word about some of the annuals. The California Poppies and Cornflowers re-seed themselves year after year; but do not allow all the blooms to go to seed as that shortens the flowering season. Nasturtiums serve as low climbers, have a dense foliage, and fill in ugly places Both the annual Poppies and Nasturtiums do not bear transplanting and should be sown in the border. Cosmos is a rampant grower and suits the shrubbery. Salvia in its scarlet dress awears at everything and should be given a sabbatical year; choose, rather, the blue Salvia, Harminum Violacea, and combine it with white or yellow. Carnation Marguerite with a slight protection of leaves thru the winter will bloom the following spring. Almost all annuals like the sun, but Violas prefer a partly shaded situation.

Two foliage plants, Artemisia and Racinus, grow rapidly and will serve for backgrounds. The list of good annuals is almost discouraging in its length. It is preferable to have fewer varieties and a good mass of bloom of one kind. I have made a list of about twenty-eight satisfactory annuals, and from these one could easily select fifteen or twenty varieties for a small

garden. The main point to keep in mind is to separate colors that clash.

Have a few beds or borders planted with two colors, such as blue and white, blue and yellow, or several shades of the rich oranges, maroons, and yellows. But one may have masses of many colored flowers in a long border by combining the purples, whites, violets and pale yellows, then the blues and deeper yellows; the pinks and lavenders may be in the same bed, but not near deeper yellows; the pinks and lavenders really difficult to manage is red in all its shades, and these may be helped by the mixture of white and of green. It is a safe rule never to have magenta.

I have not listed the Sweet Pea, as that is essentially a cutting flower and not a garden plant. Select only a few shades of Sweet Peas. A mellow soil and mulching are requisites. Sow the seeds as early as possible in drills about five inches deep. At first cover the seeds with a couple of inches of soil, but when the plants have shown a few inches of growth cover again with earth almost to the top of the drill. A thoro watering, and then a good mulch will keep the plants moist. Thin out so that the plants are about eight inches apart.

THE BACK YARD VEGETABLE GARDEN

The backyard garden need not be large. Suppose it be only 25 feet square. Such a garden well tilled should produce a bushel of string beans (Stringless Green pod), a dozen Savoy cabbages, a bushel of ripe tomatoes, a dozen stalks of celery (Golden Self-Blanching), half a dozen plants of Lucullus Swiss chard, two full meals of peas (American Wonder), two dozen beets (Detroit), ten dozen turnips and a constant succession of lettuce and radishes all summer, growing May King lettuce first and then Big Boston.

Double the size of the garden and more of the above vegetables may be grown, along with ten dozen ears of Golden Bantam corn, two dozen green onions, a bushel of Kidney wax beans, a dozen English vegetable marrows (bush variety), 25-foot row each of parsnips and salsify to dig in the Spring. Double the size of the garden once more and there will be room enough for an asparagus bed, four or five rhubarb plants, a few plants of Witloof chicory for winter forcing, and two dozen everbearing strawberry plants, as well as six poles of Kentucky Wonder or Old Homestead pole beans, a dozen heads of Chinese cabbage (Pe Tsai), a dozen plants of Brussels sprouts, five hills of Davis Perfect cucumber, half a dozen plants of green curled kale for late Fall greens and possibly half a dozen hills of muskmelons trained out on the grass or along the fence.

If amateurs would plan out their gardens before they started to sow the seeds, they would reap bigger crops and fewer disappointments. Also, if they would buy their seeds of reliable seedsmen, they would grow better vegetables. This latter warning is unusually important this season, for many seeds are scarce.

It pays to get down on the floor with a big sheet of wrapping paper and make a regulation plan of the backyard garden. If corn nad pole beans are to be grown, they should have a place at the rear. Permanent crops like asparagus and rhubarb will need a little space at one side, where they will be out of the way when the garden is plowed. Forty asparagus plants and four of rhubarb will supply the average family.

Rotation of crops is needed to economize plant food and help avoid plant diseases. Tomatoes, lettuce and cabbages, for example, may be planted this season where peas and beans grew last. Double cropping will double the total yield. That means that beets, cabbage or celery will go in as soon as early peas are off, that turnips will follow early beets and that lettuce will be sown wherever a vacant space appears. Of course these are only illustrations; many garden-makers get their crops from a few square feet of backyard soil.

It is a wise plan to start peas, beans, corn, radishes, beets and lettuce at intervals of a week or ten days all thru the Spring. Then there will be a long season of each kind. Parsnips and salsify require the whole season for their growth and are best placed at the further end of the garden. These two vegetables should be left all winter, and dug in Spring as soon as frost is out. The seeds of parsnips, salsify and carrots are slow to germinate. To prevent weeds getting a long start before the first shoots appear, sow a few radish seeds at the same time. They will mark the rows for the wheel hoe. If the soil in the furrows is soaked with water before the seeds are sown, germination will be hastened by several days.

The earliest seeds to go in are peas, radishes, lettuce and spinach, which may be planted as soon as the soil is fit to work. Gradus, one of the best sorts of wrinkled pea, may be planted first and then American Wonder put in at ten-day intervals. Most of the common radish varieties are good, but there is a great difference in lettuce, with May King among the best for early use. The very best way to grow lettuce all summer is to make a cold frame, even tho there be no glass for it. Big Boston planted and grown to maturity in a cold frame will head beautifully in the hottest weather, while it will go to seed in the open ground or refuse to grow at all. And if a glass sash be used on the frame, both lettuce and radishes may be eaten by the time seed sown outside has broken the ground.

PLANTING TABLE FOR VEGETABLES

Name	When to Plant	Distance Apart in Rows	Amount	When Ready (Days)
Beans, dwarf	May-August	3 in.	1 qt. 100 ft.	45-75
Beans, pole	May-June	3 ft.	1 qt. 100 hills.	65-100
Beets	April-July	4 in.	oz. 50 ft.	60-75
Cabbage	April-June	2 ft.	oz. 100 ft.	100
Carrots	April-June	4 in.	oz. 100 ft.	75-100
Celery	April	6 in.	oz. 100 ft.	125
Corn	May-June	1 ft.	1 pt. 100 ft.	60-100
Cucumbers	May-July	4 ft.	oz. 15 hills.	60-85
Lettuce	April-August	1 ft.	oz. 100 ft.	30-60
Melon, musk	May-June	4 ft.	oz. 15 hills.	120
Melon, water	May-June	8 ft.	oz. 15 hills.	110
Parsley	April-May	4 in.	oz. 75 ft.	45
Parsnip	April	6 in.	oz. 100 ft.	140
Peas	April-May	2 in.	pt. 50 ft.	40-80
Pumpkins	May-June	5 ft.	oz. 50 hills.	115
Radish	April-September	3 in.	oz. 50 ft.	25-40
Salsify	April	6 in.	oz. 50 ft.	130
Spinach	April-September	4 in.	oz. 50 ft.	60
Squash, summer	May-July	4 ft.	oz. 25 hills.	60-75
Squash, winter	May-June	8 ft.	oz. 25 hills.	100
Tomato	June	3 ft.	oz. 100 hills.	125
Turnip	April-August	6 in.	oz. 100 ft.	60

Golden Bantam is unsurpassed among the varieties of corn. It is very early and may be planted in furrows rather than hills. Cultivation should be shallow to avoid disturbing the roots, which grow very near the surface of the ground.

Tomatoes in the backyard garden are best trained to stakes or supported on frames to economize space and keep the fruit clean. When you set out tomato plants which have long, spindling stalks, if a shallow trench be scooped out and a large part of the stalk bent lengthwise and buried along with the roots, scores of new rootlets will be formed and the strength of the plant greatly increased. Tomatoes may be stimulated by sinking a tin can in the ground at the base of each plant and partly filling it with manure, holes having first been made in the sides of the can. When water is poured into the cans, the roots will get a fertilizer that they can use immediately.

Several vegetables not often seen in American gardens deserve mention. One is the Chinese cabbage catalogued as Pe Tsai, which looks more like a head of cos lettuce than it does like a cabbage. It makes a delicious salad when served raw with French dressing or even with sugar and is very easy to grow, altho it likes cool weather. People who are fond of summer squashes will have a treat when they indulge in the new English vegetable marrows, which are splendid in every way and even make good midsummer substitutes for pumpkin pie. The bush varieties are best for the backyard garden. Then there is martynia, which makes the best of pickles and grows in sections where cucumbers usually succumb to the blight. Finally there is Scotch kale, a Fall green of wonderful hardiness which will last in the garden till Christmas.

In addition to steady cultivation, the backyard garden will need fertilizers and water. Without doubt the best fertilizer is stable manure broadcasted and plowed under. Five dollars' worth will go a long ways. Two dollars may possibly be spent for a ready-mixed garden fertilizer to use in the rows and a little nitrate of soda to dig into the ground around backyard seedlings and to force tomatoes just as the fruit begins to turn. A water system will greatly increase the yield of any garden and likewise reduce the labor. A very satisfactory equipment can be obtained for from five to ten dollars.

PEBBLES

The first duty of a Mexican executive is to execute.—*Brooklyn Eagle.*

"Jinks is a born poet."
"That's no reason why he shouldn't try to make something of himself."—*Boston Transcript.*

"Mummy, God doesn't love me!"
"What nonsense, Harry boy; how can you say such things?"
"It's true, Mummy. I tried Him with a daisy."—*Sydney Bulletin.*

Dad—No. I won't have my daughter tied to a stupid fool for life!
He—Then don't you think you'd better let me take her off your hands?—*Penn. State Froth.*

"What on earth are two Zepps on a cloud?" she asked. "That's the order I've just taken from the last soldier to come in, and I won't tell him to translate." Whereupon she proudly served him with two sausages and a poached egg."—*Weekly Dispatch.*

First Bridge Fiend—I once knew a man who had thirteen trumps and never took a trick.
Second Bridge Fiend—How so?
First Bridge Fiend—His partner led an ace, he trumped; and then his partner threw him out of the window.—*Brunonian.*

Sardines preserved in oil and rubber cement have been added to products, the exportation of which from Norway is prohibited.—*From the Daily Consular and Trade Reports.*
If the lack of sardines preserved in rubber cement is going to inconvenience you, there is always the English muffin.—*New York Tribune.*

A certain college president wore sidewhiskers. Whenever he suggested removing them, there was a division of opinion in the family. One morning he entered his wife's dressing-room razor in hand, with his right cheek shaved smooth.
"How do you like it, my dear?" he asked.
"If you think it looks well, I will shave the other side, too."—*Facts and Fancies.*

The New Books

SECRET DIPLOMACY

In the *Revelations of an International Spy*, Mr. "I. T. T. Lincoln" gives a lively account of the espionage and counter-espionage preceding the war and especially the efforts of the certain Liberal leaders in England to uncover and thwart the anti-German policy of Sir Edward Grey which they feared would lead to war. The "revelations" are, on the whole, rather of the author's own psychology, albeit unconscious, than of the entanglements of European diplomacy. Big portions of the book are bland self-description, and give an occasional glimpse of I. T. T. Lincoln that is more vivid than he appears himself to know. The egotism is intentional enough when he says that, of the two strains in his nature, one is a "craving for excitement, a passion for deduction and analysis, and a love of applause that overshadows all other leadings." We cannot find much to support the supplementary claim to have "the quiet fervor of the mystic and the imaginative sensitiveness of the artist"! A man who can let go in this wise over his own qualities, and who can pride himself on the showing of this book as having been employed "in some of the most momentous diplomatic moves between 1906 and 1911, with entire and unqualified success," is not unlikely, of course, to think Sir Edward Grey "very clever, reticent, but shallow" by comparison. One is more and more curious to know what manner of man it is that can, on the strength of this outstanding quality of self-confidence and esteem, bluff his way into the House of Commons and the pages of *Punch*, secure the assistance of philanthropists, statesmen and diplomatists sufficient to further a generous scheme of personal exaltation, not omitting the fun of taking part in the melodrama of Continental high life, and finally come to attempt, with the same delicious complacency, the undoing of the country whose guest he had been for years.

Apart from their autobiographical interest, the "revelations" have, as it appears to us, little importance. There is far more of diplomatic generalities than of fresh, corroborated testimony. Aside from the documents he alleges he obtained from the French permanent official, "M. Legrange," regarding Anglo-French-Belgian military and naval consultations prior to the war (and which, incidentally, have since the war began been admitted by Sir Edward Grey in Parliament) there is not a single instance in which Lincoln gives anything beyond his own word and an appeal to the "secret and unofficial" archives of the Foreign Office to back

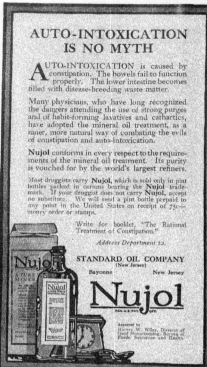
his assertions. The bulk of the book might have been written by anyone familiar with what he would probably call "the gossip of the European Embassies." There are many such people, and a large part of the secrets he reveals have been known or guessed by the outside world. A delightful naïveté is in the solemn reproductions of the formal letters of introduction which prove him—he would have us believe—to have been "in close personal touch" with the highest British diplomats and statesmen. Any British M. P. could have obtained such letters under similar circumstances, and that Lincoln should regard them as so convincing is not less amusing or amazing than his account of the anti-Government progressive whose offer formed the basis, if we accept his word, of Lincoln's curiously-motived espionage campaign. It is quite clear that he hints at Dalziel as his employer "D," but (aside from the manifest improbability of Sir Henry choosing an Hungarian Jew as a pro-British agent in such an undertaking), the bottom is knocked out of the innuendo by the simple fact of there having been no tangible result, in England, from Lincoln's "discoveries." If Sir Henry Dalziel had actually learned of the Anglo-French military understanding prior to the war there cannot be the least doubt that a corresponding movement, altho perhaps discreet, would have occurred in the British press, and *Reynold's* would probably not have been even discreet!

Revelations of an International Spy, by I. T. T. Lincoln. McBride. $1.50.

A HERO OF PEACE

Stephen Chalmers' appreciation of Dr. Trudeau, published in the *Atlantic* directly after the death of the great leader in the war on tuberculosis, is the nucleus of *The Beloved Physician*, which describes the doctor as he was known to his patients and seen by his friends and townsfolk. The introduction is taken from his last address to his fellow physicians, made when he was hardly able to stand, and, characteristically, on optimism. No better word could be found for the keynote of the *Autobiography*, which he was with difficulty persuaded to write during this last year. It is of course a book of prime importance to the medical profession in this land and abroad, and of especial interest to the thousands who have been brought in contact with the wonderful work at Saranac Lake. But aside from medical and personal interest, it is a singularly delightful and, despite its tragedies, singularly happy biography. Written with the utmost simplicity and directness, it recounts a life, after its somewhat romantic youth, of no dramatic events. But it draws a picture of a man whose strength lay in never knowing when he was beaten, of a man so absorbed in his vision that he was unconscious of the magnitude of his task, and moreover equally unconscious of his own power. The wisdom, the generosity, the devotion of his friends is the theme of every page, and he appeared to himself as simply "doing the next thing." It is only by reading between the lines that one finds the self-sacrificing scientist, the dauntless leader of the forlorn hope, to whom the world owes so mighty a debt.

The Beloved Physician, by Stephen Chalmers. Houghton, Mifflin. $1. *An Autobiography*, by Edward Livingston Trudeau. Doubleday, Page. $2.

IRISH VERSE

With his whimsical prose fantasies, "The Crock of Gold" and "Demi-gods," James Stephens pleased his readers, and charmed or disarmed his critics. There was a racy Irish flavor to his wit, an unction in his drollery, and a spell in his mystifications that tickled the literary palate. None knew, to be sure, what he meant or where he was "at." But what then? He was amusing; that sufficed. His Irish fancy in full career was an arresting spectacle, and so engaging were his performances in general that grave reviewers encouraged him to cut what imaginative capers he chose, and assured him of an audience, however queer the themes on which he might choose to fiddle his eccentric harmonics. When, in the essays and stories of "Here Are Ladies," he spoke directly and lucidly, he still kept in the good graces of his hearers. But a liking for this author drawn from the books mentioned can hardly fail to moult a feather after a perusal of his latest collection of verse, *The Rocky Road to Dublin*. In that slender volume of lean lyrics, Mr. Stephens, remembering both Blake and Stevenson, and aiming at a childlike simplicity and naïveté, achieves chiefly childishness and fatuity. The diction of these facile rimes sinks continually to the dead levels of prosaic commonplace; there is little music in them; and there is no evidence of the sensitive or exacting literary conscience.

The Rocky Road to Dublin, by James Stephens. Macmillan. $1.

A GENTLER WEST

A delightful, delicate, life-like story of three dogs, three children, three men, some of them from Ireland, is *The Glory and the Dream*, by Anna Preston. Whether or not children will appreciate the charm and the humor and the pathos of Michael, aged six, grown folk will.

Heubsch. $1.25.

WHICH SCHOOL?

A most useful annual is the *Handbook of the Best Private Schools*, prepared by Porter E. Sargent. Boarding, day, and special schools and camps in the United States and Canada are listed, and careful investigation has gone to the preparation of this list and the discriminating descriptions.

Porter E. Sargent, 50 Congress street, Boston. $2.

DOGS

Of course Scott figures in *Your Dog and My Dog*, the anthology compiled by Lincoln Newton Kinnicutt. Gilder's sounding hexameters to Leo, too, are here, and others well known. One is particularly pleased to be introduced to Celia Duffin's sympathetic verse An Old Dog, and Sir Bat Pars, Mrs. Eden's delightful description of an ancient English almshouse and its dog.

Houghton, Mifflin. $1.

AS PARIS WAS

Among the many books from the other side that bear a year-old date and so miss notice in the year's art books, is a cheaper edition of *The Color of Paris*, with its essays by gentlemen of the Académe Gon-

Independent Opinions

Many of our readers apparently regard this periodical as a sort of "Independent Primary," for we keep getting presidential nominations:

An allusion to presidential possibilities in the last paragraph of your amusing editorial "A la carte," in the issue for January 31, impels me to add a further word. And that is concerning my astonishment that no one has yet mentioned the name of ex-Governor and ex-Ambassador Myron T. Herrick of Ohio as a strong candidate for presidential nomination by the Republican party this year. Let any one read Eric Fisher Wood's "Note-book of an Attaché" with its vivid presentation of Mr. Herrick's ability and wisdom in handling that unforeseen work in Paris, early in the war, then see if any doubt can remain that he is better fitted than any man in America to deal with the most important questions soon to press for solution. Why not replace your jesting reference to another university president with a genuine "boom" for ex-Governor Herrick?

A. B. JACKSON

North Adams, Massachusetts

I am writing you to express my high estimate of the article by Mr. Darwin P. Kingsley in your issue of January 31, 1916, on "The World's Fundamental Error."

That it may have the wider reading it deserves, I beg leave to suggest its publication in pamphlet form.

L. W. KEISTER

Los Angeles, California

The address of Mr. Darwin P. Kingsley is remarkably able and shows him to be a man with the proper American world vision. Our country sorely needs such a man in her political affairs. It would be interesting to have him give his views as to the internal needs of the United States with the same fearlessness and lucidity. I am persuaded they would prove true to the crying need for a strong but just man at the head of our national Government. Why can't The Independent suggest that the Republican party nominate him for President?

ASHLEY J. THOMPSON

Alameda, California

Mr. Kingsley's address in pamphlet form may be obtained free by writing to Mr. Darwin P. Kingsley's secretary, New York Life Insurance Company, 346 Broadway, New York City. We respectfully refer the proposed nomination to the Republican primaries.

On the puzzling question of our naval strength we have received the following interesting information from Mr. Green, of Iowa, a member of the Committee on Ways and Means:

I observe in the February 14 issue of your magazine, an inquiry from a reader as to whether the United States is building battleships of the twenty-five knot class similar to the "Queen Elizabeth" of the British navy. In your reply you seem to assume that our ships built about the same time are defective by reason of not having equal speed, and that a change will be made in our new dreadnaughts in this respect.

If such an impression was intended to be conveyed it is erroneous as to our ships now building. There is much difference in expert opinion as to what speed battleships ought to have, and after having tried out the "Queen Elizabeth" class the British Government has gone back in its later vessels to a type corresponding to that of our

Don't Go Through Life
Loaded Down With a Millstone!

How can you expect to be happy, healthy or successful when you are continually handicapped by mild forms of disease? Why don't you double your margin of safety against this over-powering handicap? The life work of a Man-Builder tells how. 5 volumes, 3000 pages, sent free on approval, not a penny in advance—just mail the coupon.

THINK of the first ten men that come to mind and you will find that nine of them at some time or other were "down in the dumps." Think back to your own case and you will find that time and again you have felt that there was "something wrong" with you—yet you didn't know what it was. The reason most people feel that way is simply because we haven't enough *Reserve* health. We have barely enough energy and stamina to carry us through the ordinary day's work. Just the minute there is any *extra* strain, mental or physical, we topple over the brink and find ourselves handicapped by *partial* sickness. Isn't that true?

Everybody knows that physical well being is the mother of mental well being. If your body is full of *super-health*—if you have great reserve energy—you are irresistible! Nothing daunts you!

The biggest tasks melt under your Power. You solve problems with amazing speed, with uncanny judgment. You simply sweep everything from your path to success and victory. And still, knowing this, most men pay more attention to machines *made of iron and steel* than they do to their own throbbing *h u m a n* machine. They work and *work* and WORK—yet they have nothing to show for their labors except a weakened, run-down body almost ready for the scrap pile. You haven't the smashing, driving *power* now so necessary to win life's battles. You are only of *average* health and vitality so you achieve only average success—or less.

The problem of getting and keeping the human organism "fit as a fiddle" has been the life-study of Bernarr Macfadden. His mother was a consumptive. Both mother and father died before he was eight years old. Himself weak, frail, cringing, he was marked as a victim of heredity—a certain consumptive—a sure failure at living. Yet today Bernarr Macfadden's name is a synonym for health and all that health means. He is the most vitally healthy and energetic man you could see in a year's travel. He has lectured and written to millions during the past 20 years and so wonderful have been the results of his work that by some they are considered almost miraculous. Time after time he has pointed out the Right Road to men and women who had given up all hope after disheartening, discouraging experiences with drugs and medicines.

And now Mr. Macfadden has written down the results of his life's experience. Macfadden's Encyclopedia of Physical Culture is beyond question the greatest work ever attempted on this intensely and vitally interesting subject. It contains what you *want to know* about every phase of your constantly working engine. Its information will make a new man of you—a new kind of being, divorced from your present half-alive, half-efficient self!

Read, above, a partial list of what these marvelous books contain. There are nearly 3000 pages in the five volumes—and over 1300 illustrations. Hundreds of illustrations are from photographs, many are printed in colors and the truly wonderful dissectible manikins will fascinate you. Everything about every possible ailment, about diet, about sleep, work, play, sex, fasting, development of every organ of the body—these and a thousand and one other subjects are treated in the most intimate personal way. Everything is written in the author's simple style—amazingly easy for anyone to understand.

THE five massive volumes comprising this Great Encyclopedia of Physical Culture contains in complete form for ready reference: (1) A Complete work on Anatomy. (2) A Physiology in plain language. (3) A comprehensive handbook on Diet. (4) A complete Cook Book. (5) A Book on Exercise in Relation to Health. (6) A hand-book on Gymnastics. (7) A book of Indoor and Outdoor Exercises—complete course in Boxing, Wrestling, etc. (8) Handsome colored charts and instructions for Developing a Powerful Physique. (9) The most complete work on Fasting ever published. (10) A comprehensive work on Hydrotherapy. (11) A book on Mechanical Therapeutics. (12) A thorough work on First Aid. (13) A lavishly illustrated work on Diagnosis. (14) A book on Home Treatment for all Diseases. (15) An Anatomy of the Sexual Organs. (16) Their Cause and Cure. (17) Rules for Happy Marriage and Parenthood. (18) A complete work on the Training of Children. (20) A complete hand-book on Beauty-Culture.

These five massive books—volumes that will be consulted more frequently than any other books you have or can get—these masterpieces that bring you so much in health, in personal power, in energy—will be sent to you for examination without a penny deposit. We know what you will say when you open these volumes—we know you will never let these books get out of your home. Others in every walk of life who now have them would not take five times their cost if unable to obtain another set.

We want you to see and read these books for five days—then send the entire set back. But if you want to keep the books—if you feel that the life-lengthening, health-and-energy-giving secrets it contains are *invaluable* to you, send us $1.00 in 10 days and the balance in small monthly payments that you will hardly notice. This offer is *special*, and for a limited time. Miss this opportunity and it is gone forever. Never again will you have so much information offered you—information that concerns your most precious possession—at these prices or on these easy terms. The cost of paper, printing and binding has gone up 20 per cent. since these books were printed and as soon as the present edition is exhausted new prices must come into effect. At this price, now, we will also include a year's subscription to Physical Culture Magazine, which contains every month over a hundred pages of matter akin to health and self-betterment.

In the 3,000 pages—in the thousands upon thousands of articles—if you get only fifty life-juvenating, health-mastering ideas you will have gained a hundred times their cost in personal benefit and profit—yet there is no reason why you should not find some valuable fact that you can *apply to yourself* EVERY DAY.

Send no money. Just mail the coupon and the *entire set*, together with the latest copy of Physical Culture Magazine, will be sent postage prepaid. There is no obligation on your part to keep the books or make any payments—we merely want you to EXAMINE them at our risk. Address Physical Culture Publishing Co., 1123 Flatiron Building, New York.

own navy, having a speed of about twenty-two knots.

An increase in speed is always obtained at a sacrifice either in armor or armament—usually of the latter. The much vaunted battle cruisers with their great speed are so lightly armored that they would be no match in battle for some of our later battleships, to say nothing of our dreadnaughts. Of course, they can run away or rush out for scouting expeditions; destroy or drive the enemies, scouts and armored cruisers off the sea, and serve many other purposes; but so far their value in fleet contests where battleships are engaged has not been shown. In the North Sea battle they overtook and with the aid of torpedo craft sunk the "Bluecher." The German battle cruisers were not strong enough to fight, but were fast enough to get away. Much has been made of speed in connection with this exploit, but had the "Bluecher" been supported by the slower but more powerful dreadnaughts a different story would have been told. The "Bluecher" was said to be faster than any of our battleships or dreadnaughts. So it was, being merely an armored cruiser—an altogether different type of vessel. While the "Bluecher" was the largest and most powerful armored cruiser that Germany possessed, we have four of equal speed, which are more powerful in both armor and armament, any one of which would have overmatched the "Bluecher."

Our new dreadnaughts, now building, or to be built, are of only twenty and one-half knots speed, but it is understood, altho no final details are given out, that they are to carry heavier armor than any vessel afloat, and it is well known they will deliver a heavier broadside. Experts are practically agreed that power in these two respects will constitute the most important factor in future naval actions.

         WILLIAM R. GREEN
House of Representatives, Washington

The apostles of preparedness are making extensive use of the most powerful organ of propaganda, the movies. How the pacifists feel about it may be seen from the following:

The "Battle Cry of Peace" is particularly well adapted to deceiving the unreflecting; arousing a false and cheap patriotism, and bringing into disrepute the courageous souls, who in the face of ridicule and contumely, are laboring for the sanity of our beloved country. To a city composed largely of factory operatives who by virtue of necessity cannot stop long enough to think "The Battle Cry of Peace" with its lurid ghastliness is a veritable menace, and the victims thereof do not follow to the only logical conclusion that after being shown (by the picture) the unspeakable havoc wrought by the big guns and air fiends Americans are actually being urged to support the hellish work of creating more devils to demolish and maim and corrode and this under the guise of "preparedness." Even were this so-called "preparedness" genuine, the crime would not be so great, but to insult the already exploited "laboring man and woman" with the thinly veiled commercial scheme which underlies this pseudo "preparedness," to cheat with screen statements concerning "enemies" which have never materialized, to lure them into the meshes of "big business" under the guise of "danger to hearth and home," seems the acme of cowardly enterprise.

The little tow-headed baby, warrior in embryo, who during a lull in the battle (?), turned to me with "I like the war pictures best," spoke more eloquently and alas! more sadly than he knew.

         S. G. HARRINGTON
Jamestown, N. Y.

It is a pleasant surprize—for it is not too common—to find that the "new woman" in her most provocative mood meets with approval from one who signs herself as of a former genera-

tion. She is not shocked, it seems, by anything in the article except its English. Being an author herself, she cannot condone inaccuracy in the use of words:

I have read with interest the article by Elinor Byrns in your January 10th number, entitled "I Resolve To Be Restless"; but protest that she has made use of the wrong word. Instead of restless she should have said: "I am an active woman. Almost all of my chosen companions are active women . . . activity keeps us well. We have no time to imagine ourselves ill . . . activity makes us happy."

I know this young woman and know of her chosen associates. They are doing good work in the world. They are not restless, they have poise, continuity of purpose, close application to business and persistence in working for the right. They are of the new period. Women have scarcely a generation of emancipation, but these women see things to be done and valiantly take up the work for humanity. They purpose to have a university education, and make the sacrifice necessary to secure it. They love a home of their own, whether married or single, and are willing to work to maintain it. They recognize that wrongs exist and forego leisure to right them. They read more, think more, touch life at more points than women of idleness. They are more virile, more vivacious, more interesting than men and women who say "I will take mine ease in mine inn." There are too many vital movements awaiting assistance for them to grow fidgety and restless or succumb to ennui. Besides individual development and cultural studies there is settlement work, and suffrage agitation, picketing, and housekeeping to be done.

No, these young women are not restless or they would not have the concentration to accomplish so much. It is industry, activity. It is the result of vigor of mind and body. Our great-grandmothers displayed the same traits when they capably carried on the multitudinous duties of home manufacturing, nursing, gardening, bearing and rearing families, giving lady bountiful ministrations, and dispensing hospitality.

New York   A GRANDMOTHER

The article of January 10 by Professor Giddings, entitled "Which Do You Prefer?" brought out many letters of criticism. Here is one from the associate editor of *The Minneapolis Journal:*

My first whipping at school was at age six. Three of us children had gone for wild plums during the intermission and were tardy in returning. Before the whip descended the school ma'am asked the question: "Which would you rather have, plums or a whipping?"

Never since then have I heard a school teacher ask so foolish a question till Professor Giddings spoke. Where would Professor Giddings rather be today, trampling Belgium under orders of Prussian professional killers, or in America, where, if a President is a little too feeble, one has full liberty to help get a stronger one?

I do not fully agree with Professor Giddings in his indictment of President Wilson. Wilson's head and heart plus Teddy's teeth would just about suit me.

MILTON O. NELSON

Minneapolis, Minnesota

As to Professor Giddings' summary of the characteristics of Emperor William and President Wilson, I'd rather be a kitten and cry 'mew' than subscribe to either, representing as they do, respectively, the two far extremes—the one the very limits of savagery and perfidy; the other the milk-and-water, word-building bluffer and mollycoddle.

I look forward with a peculiar anxiety to the November election wondering what we—the great American people as we are pleased to style ourselves—will do. I shall certainly hang my head with shame if the policy of the present administration is sustained.

New York   B. B. DAVIDSON

THE MARKET PLACE

A REVIEW OF FINANCE AND TRADE

THE INVESTOR'S SERVICE

The Independent is now offering a Service for Investors in which personal attention will be given to the desires of its subscribers for information in regard to investments of all kinds. We cannot of course decide for our readers where they should put their savings and will not undertake the responsibility of recommending specific securities to any individual. But we ask our readers to write to us frankly and this Department will give them by letter or thru the columns of The Independent such impartial information as may assist them in making a wise decision for themselves.

BUYING BONDS AS BUSINESS INSURANCE

BUSINESS men carry fire insurance, casualty insurance, health insurance, life insurance, burglary insurance and insurance of other sorts, but how many insure themselves against embarrassment during a period of money stringency? Right now we are in the midst of great business activity with large profits pouring into the coffers of great and small business men of certain classes. Will it continue?

For every period like 1906 or 1915 we have a year like 1893 or 1907, when the best of firms found that banks were unwilling to lend funds excepting upon deposit of good collateral; prime bonds like underlying railroad issues, the best municipals and in some cases those of industrial and public utility corporations. Commercial or manufacturing concerns carry large stocks of merchandise, raw material and supplies and own real estate, plants and machinery worth thousands; all have ordinarily sufficient cash to meet current requirements or can borrow it, but how many firms have a strong, live reserve fund against a possible money stringency at a time when cold cash is a matter of life and death to the organization? How many concerns have a reserve that would enable the president to go to a bank during a period of depression and borrow a substantial sum when his competitors were being refused?

In other words, how many firms invest a part of their surplus, a percentage of their weekly or monthly pay-roll in prime, marketable securities? The suggestion is not, of course, advanced here as a new one. But it is one that is very easily "pigeon-holed" by busy executives in favor of other matters of immediate interest, such as additions to plant. Nevertheless, in these prosperous times the matter of a reserve fund should receive more than passing notice even at the expense of increased dividend declarations. A concern can, of course, deposit its reserve fund in a bank at 2 per cent or 3 per cent interest, but with a large amount of cash available by the mere signing of a check, there is always the temptation to make expenditures for one thing or another that might not arise were the funds invested in prime securities.

Of course, ready marketability is an expensive feature in an investment inasmuch as it is not possible to find bonds that combine safety and ready marketability with high yield. Therefore, bonds that possess the degree of safety and marketability that makes them eligible for a business reserve fund rarely yield over 4.75 per cent. The best grades of investment bonds have not only a market on the New York Stock Exchange, but on many of the European exchanges; they also have a market in the other American exchanges and are dealt in "over the counter" in the large financial centers.

Bonds of this class include those of railroads, municipalities, industrial and public utility corporations. When it is stated that such bonds should yield not over 4.75 per cent in order to be eligible, even the reader who is not at all initiated will realize that only the securities of the highest grade are included. There are many railroad, municipal, industrial and public utility bonds that are reasonably safe that yield as high as 5½ per cent, but, obviously, they are not so desirable as securities yielding 4.75 per cent or less and would not have the same degree of marketability during a depression as higher grade bonds.

Short term notes of strong corporations or municipalities are in demand for this purpose. Obligations of corporations known to be in a flourishing condition usually sell at very near par value, and it is assumed that they will be paid off at par upon maturity; the yield is in most cases greater than that paid by banks upon deposits. These notes are secured by collateral such as stocks or first mortgage bonds or are absolutely unsecured credit obligations; they are often in the form of receivers' certificates taking precedence over first mortgage bonds. When bought with

BONDS SUITABLE FOR THE RESERVE FUND OF A BUSINESS HOUSE

			Approximate Yield, Per cent
Railroads			
Atchison, Topeka & Santa Fe Ry., General Mtge.	4s	1995	4.23
Atlantic Coast Line Ry., Consol	4s	1952	4.42
Baltimore & Ohio R. R., First	4s	1948	4.49
Chicago, Burlington & Quincy R. R., General	4s	1958	4.31
Chicago, Milwaukee & St. Paul Ry., General	4½s	1989	4.35
Chicago & North Western Ry., General	4s	1987	4.24
Delaware & Hudson Co., First Ref	4s	1943	4.19
Great Northern Ry., First Ref	4¼s	1961	4.26
Louisville & Nashville R. R., General	6s	1930	4.81
Minn., St. Paul & S. Ste. Marie Ry., Consol	5s	1938	4.46
New York Central R. R., First	3½s	1997	4.25
New York Central, Lake Shore, First	3½s	1997	4.14
Norfolk & Western Ry., Consol	4s	1996	4.28
Northern Pacific Ry., Prior Lien	4s	1997	4.27
Pennsylvania R. R., Consol	4s	1948	4.03
Southern Pacific Co., First Ref	4s	1955	4.51
Union Pacific R. R., First	4s	1947	4.13
Municipals			
City of Baltimore, Md	3¼s	1927	4.00
City of Buffalo, N. Y	4½s	1926-65	3.85
State of California	4s	1926-65	3.90
City of Chicago, Ill	4s	1924-30	3.90
City of Hoboken, N. J	4½s	1946	4.00
City of Los Angeles, Calif	4½s	1924-27	4.15
City of Memphis, Tenn	4½s	1942-49	4.25
City of Newark, N. J	4½s	1944	4.00
State of New York	4½s	1964	3.80
Township of Raleigh, N. C	5s	1946	4.37
City of St. Paul, Minn	4½s	1918	3.25
Sioux City, Iowa	4½s	1932-34	4.00
State of Tennessee	4½s	1927	3.95
City of Trenton, N. J	4½s	1946	4.00
Industrials and Public Utilities			
American Telephone & Telegraph, Coll. Tr	4s	1929	4.75
Brooklyn Rapid Transit, First	5s	1945	4.79
Brooklyn Union Gas Co., First	5s	1945	4.67
General Electric, Debenture	5s	1952	4.72
Laclede Gas Light, First	5s	1919	4.41
Manhattan Railway (N. Y.), Consol	4s	1990	4.37
Milwaukee Gas Light, First	4s	1927	4.75
New York Telephone, First	4½s	1939	4.57
Pacific Telephone & Telegraph, First	5s	1937	4.93
U. S. Steel Corporation, S. F	5s	1963	4.73
Western Union Telegraph, Funding	4½s	1950	4.77

discrimination, short term notes form a desirable holding for a reserve fund.

A firm having a larger cash surplus than it could keep actively engaged in its own business could invest profitably a part of it in sound securities. A concern not having a large cash surplus might at some time, even when no depression existed, be pressed for funds and be unable to secure them thru lack of collateral. Any firm that has experienced the lack of funds when thousands of dollars in obligations were coming due in a few days, when the pay roll was also to be made, should prepare *now* for hard times by setting aside 2 per cent or 5 per cent or 10 per cent of its pay roll each week in order to provide an insurance fund against lack of ready money during a depression.

A manufacturing concern with a pay roll of $2500 weekly might find it possible to invest $250 weekly in prime securities, so that at the end of the year it would have $13,000 invested. It might be able to invest a much larger sum, all depending upon how great were its profits and how much in dividends its stockholders expected. Inasmuch as a depression occurs about every seven years, if such a fund were started now, by 1923 a corporation should find itself the proud possessor of $91,000 invested in prime securities and no great effort expended. If the securities were purchased under par, the sum would be much larger, and still larger if interest on the securities owned were added to the cash to be invested. The fund may be $10 per week for a small firm or $1000 a week for a large one, the principle being identical. Any concern that can count among its quick assets a few thousand dollars or a hundred thousand dollars in the *best* securities can command respect at a bank president's office at any time.

When such a proposition has been advanced to the head of a large business, the retort has often been that the firm's money was "all tied up in the business," or "why should we invest at 4½ per cent when we can earn 15 per cent in our own business?" or, "we need improvements to our plant," etc. Nevertheless, skeptics who failed at first to see the light are now forbearing to place funds in their business at 15 per cent and buying bonds which yield but 4½ per cent because 15 per cent today may not be an asset ten years hence when the bank president turns a deaf ear to pleas for money on unsecured paper.

Look over the holdings of savings banks, insurance companies, institutions and successfully managed corporations; what sort of investments do you find? There are mortgages yielding from 4½ to 6 per cent, not readily marketable; various corporation bonds yielding 5 to 6 per cent, not readily marketable during a depression excepting at a sacrifice; prime railroad, municipal, industrial and public utility bonds yielding from 4 to 4.75 per cent, easily marketable at all times with little sacrifice, or always available as collateral. Why do concerns like these invest in bonds yielding but 4 per cent when they could place all of their funds in securities yielding 6 per cent? The reply is obvious.

DIVIDENDS

THE MARKET PLACE
A REVIEW OF FINANCE AND TRADE

BUYING BONDS AS BUSINESS INSURANCE

BUSINESS men carry fire insurance, casualty insurance, health insurance, life insurance, burglary insurance and insurance of other sorts, but how many insure themselves against embarrassment during a period of money stringency? Right now we are in the midst of great business activity with large profits pouring into the coffers of great and small business men of certain classes. Will it continue?

For every period like 1906 or 1915 we have a year like 1893 or 1907, when the best of firms found that banks were unwilling to lend funds excepting upon deposit of good collateral; prime bonds like underlying railroad issues, the best municipal and in some cases those of industrial and public utility corporations. Commercial or manufacturing concerns carry large stocks of merchandise, raw material and supplies and own real estate, plants and machinery worth thousands; all have ordinarily sufficient cash to meet current requirements or can borrow it, but how many firms have a strong, live reserve fund against a possible money stringency at a time when cold cash is a matter of life and death to the organization? How many concerns have a reserve that would enable the president to go to a bank during a period of depression and borrow a substantial sum when his competitors were being refused?

In other words, how many firms invest a part of their surplus, a percentage of their weekly or monthly pay-roll in prime, marketable securities? The suggestion is not, of course, advanced here as a new one. But it is one that is very easily "pigeon-holed" by busy executives in favor of other matters of immediate interest, such as additions to plant. Nevertheless, in these prosperous times the matter of a reserve fund should receive more than passing notice even at the expense of increased dividend declarations. A concern can, of course, deposit its reserve fund in a bank at 2 per cent or 3 per cent interest, but with a large amount of cash available by the mere signing of a check, there is always the temptation to make expenditures for one thing or another that might not arise were the funds invested in prime securities.

Of course, ready marketability is an expensive feature in an investment inasmuch as it is not possible to find bonds that combine safety and ready marketability with high yield. Therefore, bonds that possess the degree of safety and marketability that makes them eligible for a business reserve fund rarely yield over 4.75 per cent. The best grades of investment bonds have not only a market on the New York Stock Exchange, but on many of the European exchanges; they also have a market in the other American exchanges and are dealt in "over the counter" in the large financial centers. Bonds of this class include those of railroads, municipalities, industrial and public utility corporations. When it is stated that such bonds should yield not over 4.75 per cent in order to be eligible, even the reader who is not at all initiated will realize that only the securities of the highest grade are included. There are many railroad, municipal, industrial and public utility bonds that are reasonably safe that yield as high as 5½ per cent, but, obviously, they are not so desirable as securities yielding 4.75 per cent or less and would not have the same degree of marketability during a depression as higher grade bonds.

Short term notes of strong corporations or municipalities are in demand for this purpose. Obligations of corporations known to be in a flourishing condition usually sell at very near par value, and it is assumed that they will be paid off at par upon maturity; the yield is in most cases greater than that paid by banks upon deposits. These notes are secured by collateral such as stocks or first mortgage bonds or are absolutely unsecured credit obligations; they are often in the form of receivers' certificates taking precedence over first mortgage bonds. When bought with

BONDS SUITABLE FOR THE RESERVE FUND OF A BUSINESS HOUSE

		Approximate Yield, Per cent
Railroads		
Atchison, Topeka & Santa Fe Ry., General Mtge..4s	1995	4.23
Atlantic Coast Line Ry., Consol................4s	1952	4.42
Baltimore & Ohio R. R., First.................4s	1948	4.49
Chicago, Burlington & Quincy R. R., General...4s	1958	4.31
Chicago, Milwaukee & St. Paul Ry., General....4½s	1989	4.35
Chicago & North Western Ry., General..........4s	1987	4.24
Delaware & Hudson Co., First Ref.............4s	1943	4.19
Great Northern Ry., First Ref................4½s	1961	4.26
Louisville & Nashville R. R., General.........6s	1930	4.31
Minn., St. Paul & S. Ste. Marie Ry., Consol...5s	1938	4.46
New York Central R. R., First................3½s	1997	4.25
New York Central, Lake Shore, First...........3½s	1997	4.14
Norfolk & Western Ry., Consol................4s	1996	4.28
Northern Pacific Ry., Prior Lien.............4s	1997	4.27
Pennsylvania R. R., Consol...................4s	1948	4.03
Southern Pacific Co., First Ref..............4s	1955	4.51
Union Pacific R. R., First...................4s	1947	4.13
Municipals		
City of Baltimore, Md.......................3½s	1927	4.00
City of Buffalo, N. Y.......................4½s	1926-65	3.85
State of California.........................4s	1926-65	3.90
City of Chicago, Ill........................4s	1924-30	3.50
City of Hoboken, N. J.......................4½s	1946	4.00
City of Los Angeles, Calif..................4½s	1924-27	4.15
City of Memphis, Tenn.......................4½s	1942-49	4.25
City of Newark, N. J........................4½s	1944	4.00
State of New York...........................4½s	1964	3.80
Township of Raleigh, N. C...................4½s	1946	4.37
City of St. Paul, Minn......................4½s	1918	3.25
Sioux City, Iowa............................4½s	1932-34	4.00
State of Tennessee..........................4½s	1927	3.95
City of Trenton, N. J.......................4½s	1946	4.00
Industrials and Public Utilities		
American Telephone & Telegraph, Coll. Tr.....4s	1929	4.75
Brooklyn Rapid Transit, First...............5s	1945	4.79
Brooklyn Union Gas Co., First...............5s	1945	4.67
General Electric, Debenture.................5s	1952	4.72
Laclede Gas Light, First....................5s	1919	4.41
Manhattan Railway (N. Y.), Consol...........4s	1990	4.37
Milwaukee Gas Light, First..................4s	1927	4.75
New York Telephone, First...................4½s	1939	4.57
Pacific Telephone & Telegraph, First.........5s	1937	4.93
U. S. Steel Corporation, S. F...............5s	1963	4.73
Western Union Telegraph, Funding............4½s	1950	4.77

discrimination, short term notes form a desirable holding for a reserve fund.

A firm having a larger cash surplus than it could keep actively engaged in its own business could invest profitably a part of it in sound securities. A concern not having a large cash surplus might at some time, even, when no depression existed, be pressed for funds and be unable to secure them thru lack of collateral. Any firm that has experienced the lack of funds when thousands of dollars in obligations were coming due in a few days, when the pay roll was also to be made, should prepare *now* for hard times by setting aside 2 per cent or 5 per cent or 10 per cent of its pay roll each week in order to provide an insurance fund against lack of ready money during a depression.

A manufacturing concern with a pay roll of $2500 weekly might find it possible to invest $250 weekly in prime securities, so that at the end of the year it would have $13,000 invested. It might be able to invest a much larger sum, all depending upon how great were its profits and how much in dividends its stockholders expected. Inasmuch as a depression occurs about every seven years, if such a fund were started now, by 1923 a corporation should find itself the proud possessor of $91,000 invested in prime securities and no great effort expended. If the securities were purchased under par, the sum would be much larger, and still larger if interest on the securities owned were added to the cash to be invested. The fund may be $10 per week for a small firm or $1000 a week for a large one, the principle being identical. Any concern that can count among its quick assets a few thousand dollars or a hundred thousand dollars in the *best* securities can command respect at a bank president's office at any time.

When such a proposition has been advanced to the head of a large business, the retort has often been that the firm's money was "all tied up in the business," or "why should we invest at 4½ per cent when we can earn 15 per cent in our own business?" or, "we need improvements to our plant," etc. Nevertheless, skeptics who failed at first to see the light are now forbearing to place funds in their business at 15 per cent and buying bonds which yield but 4½ per cent because 15 per cent today may not be an asset ten years hence when the bank president turns a deaf ear to pleas for money on unsecured paper.

Look over the holdings of savings banks, insurance companies, institutions and successfully managed corporations; what sort of investments do you find? There are mortgages yielding from 4½ to 6 per cent, not readily marketable; various corporation bonds yielding 5 to 6 per cent, not readily marketable during a depression excepting at a sacrifice; prime railroad, municipal, industrial and public utility bonds yielding from 4 to 4.75 per cent, easily marketable at all times with little sacrifice, or always available as collateral. Why do concerns like these invest in bonds yielding but 4 per cent when they could place all of their funds in securities yielding 6 per cent? The reply is obvious.

Insurance
Conducted by
W. E. UNDERWOOD

MUTUAL BENEFIT'S EXTRA DIVIDEND

In their report to members of the company made in January the management of the Mutual Benefit Life Insurance Company of Newark, N. J., announce that in addition to the regular dividend of $5,784,890 apportioned for distribution among policyholders in 1916 a further sum, equalling $1,156,978, will be paid. Every policy entitled to a regular dividend will be credited with a bonus amounting to 20 per cent thereof, both of which will be payable at the same time. This company paid supplementary dividends in 1910, 1913 and 1914, and raised the percentage rate of its dividends in 1909, 1911 and 1914. All new benefits, privileges and profits adopted from time to time by the Mutual Benefit are made retroactive, thus including the oldest policies with the latest issued.

CRITICISM OF A SORT

Sometimes, not very often, I am happy to report, I receive from readers of The Independent letters of a studied controversial character, taking issue with some fact or opinion previously stated by me. As my readers certainly realize, a satisfactory discussion of any disputed question would be utterly impracticable in the limited space devoted to this department. There are occasions when I hungrily yearn for the room and time to answer, if not refute, some of the few criticisms fired at me.

There lies before me an unpleasing letter from a member of the clergy at Morris, Ill., who tells me he is a policyholder in the Metropolitan Life; that succeeding the mutualization of that company he was told by one of its agents that his premium would be lower thru dividend earnings; and that altho more than a year has elapsed his premium remains at the old rate. He asks me if I do not think the company is overlong in getting to its premium abatements; and then adds that he thinks he notices a tendency on my part to defend the big companies. In presenting his position I have softened his attitude by abandoning the unlovely terminology he employs.

The transformation of the Metropolitan from a stock to a mutual company was only completed in January, 1915; therefore, I do not think it as yet censurable for its refusal to declare dividends on any particular policy or class of policies. Knowing, as I do, that for many years prior to its mutualization this company voluntarily distributed dividends to its industrial policyholders under policies which by their terms

specifically excluded them from sharing in dividends, I am prepared to believe that it is now acting justly and honestly with this clergyman. He holds a non-participating policy; that is to say, he is paying a premium which is substantially lower than that charged by a mutual company for the same amount and plan. I believe his policy will earn dividends; necessarily, they must be small, because stock premiums are close to net cost; and I am confident that he will receive them in conformity with such plans as the company uses in calculating and distributing dividends.

There is no disposition in this department to defend anything but the interests of the insuring public. Careful effort is made to procure and present reliable information. Such advice as is tendered by request is founded on the knowledge and experience of the conductor of the department.

J. H. A., Punta Gorda, Fla.—The Presbyterian Ministers' Fund of Philadelphia is a sound, well managed old line life insurance company, ranking with the best in its service to policyholders.

F. J. D., Baraga, Mich.—The Great Northern Life Insurance Company of Wausau, Wis., is a stock company writing non-participating policies exclusively. It is financially sound and well managed.

J. L. H., McCutchenville, O.—Presbyterian Ministers' Fund is first class. You will be justified under the circumstances in using annual dividends in reduction of premiums. Your Columbus Mutual accident contract is limited in benefits at the price, but all right.

G. C. A., Modesto, Calif.—I regard a stock investment in a comparatively new life insurance company as a venture, one that is more often unprofitable than profitable. The financial condition of the Western States Life is satisfactory, its net surplus being about $117,000 a year ago. Later figures as yet unavailable.

E. A. H., Richmond Hill, N. Y.—There is an Commercial Casualty Company domiciled at Philadelphia; the circular you send was issued by the Commercial of Newark, N. J., which is a sound and reliable company. The policy offered at $6 a year is of the restricted kind. See article on that subject in The Independent of February 21.

S. A., Salisbury, Md.—As yet I have not seen the balance sheet of the Columbian National Life for the year ending December 31, 1915, but it will doubtless show that satisfactory progress was made. The company is financially sound and its management is capable. You may unhesitatingly accept its representations respecting any policy contract it offers.

F. M. McC., Bayard, Iowa.—The Standard Life of Des Moines, tho young and small financially, is organized and doing business on sound lines and has a good reputation. Its sixty-days clause respecting claim settlements should be eliminated, and its application blank should be so revised as that the statements made by applicants would appear as representations and not as warranties.

J. D. P., Tulsa, Okla.—As I have stated in this department on a number of occasions, a life insurance policy reserve calculated on any basis that does not conform with the standard set by the laws for old line legal reserve companies, will finally prove to be inadequate. Consequently, I do not believe that the mathematical system employed by the Guarantee Fund Life is correct. All of the regular life companies write term policies. I don't know that policies are issued exclusively on hands and eyes, but indemnity of that kind is included in nearly all accident policies.

The Independent

FOR SIXTY-SEVEN YEARS THE FORWARD-LOOKING WEEKLY OF AMERICA

THE CHAUTAUQUAN

Merged with The Independent June 1, 1914

MARCH 13, 1916

OWNED AND PUBLISHED· BY THE INDEPENDENT CORPORATION, AT 119 WEST FORTIETH STREET, NEW YORK
WILLIAM B. HOWLAND, PRESIDENT
FREDERIC E. DICKINSON, TREASURER

WILLIAM HAYES WARD
HONORARY EDITOR

EDITOR: HAMILTON HOLT
ASSOCIATE EDITOR: HAROLD J. HOWLAND
LITERARY EDITOR: EDWIN E. SLOSSON

PUBLISHER: KARL V. S. HOWLAND

ONE YEAR, THREE DOLLARS

SINGLE COPIES, TEN CENTS

Postage to foreign countries in Universal Postal Union, $1.75 a year extra; to Canada, $1 extra. Instructions for renewal, discontinuance or change of address should be sent two weeks before the date they are to go into effect. Both the old and the new address must be given.

We welcome contributions, but writers who wish their articles returned, if not accepted, should send a stamped and addrest envelope. No responsibility is assumed by The Independent for the loss or non-return of manuscripts, tho all due care will be exercised.

Entered at New York Post Office as Second Class Matter

Copyright, 1916, by The Independent

Address all Communications to
THE INDEPENDENT
119 West Fortieth Street, New York

CONTENTS

IN THE YELLOWSTONE

The exceptionally heavy snowfall this winter has deprived the wild animals in the Yellowstone region of the Rockies of their usual feeding grounds and has driven them down by thousands to take refuge in the Park.

At Gardiner, Montana, immense herds of antelope, elk, mountain sheep and deer have been· saved from starvation by the Government supplies of alfalfa hay; and have made themselves thoroly at home in the hills near the entrance to the Park. The scene is one of unusual interest, remarkable enough to attract tourists and photographers from all over the country. One of the finest photographs—a big elk challenging the crmera—appears on the cover of The Independent for this issue.

A SAPPER'S STORY

From the German side we get little news of the Verdun battle except announcements of the kilometers gained, guns captured and strategic points obtained. But the French papers publish many personal narratives which give one a better idea of what is happening at Verdun than any figures can give. Here, for instance, is the story of a man who exploded one of the mines which caused havoc to the Germans.

We were in a front line trench on the slope of Côte du Poivre. The captain sent me forward to a small shelter in the open, where the electric contact which led to a mine field had been placed. I crawled thru it along a narrow tunnel without mishap. Thru a slit I looked out on the battlefield as thru the opening in a theater curtain. I saw the Germans, after long wait-

ing, march forward in good order. They thought from their observation that the bombardment had sufficiently devastated our trenches, but they were unable to see that our men had held firm and were making fresh trenches and using shell craters. The Germans were 290 yards from my post when our rifles and machine guns opened fire. They were taken by surprize and crouched down. When the order was passed along their line to advance they began to sing "The Watch on the Rhine" and dashed forward.

My heart beat madly. They were over the mine at last. I touched the button. An infernal fountain seemed to shoot up in the midst of the mass of men in gray with a great whirl of smoke. I saw men go up bodily, as if from the crater of a volcano. The attack was stopped.

CARMEN SYLVA

The death of Carmen Sylva, Queen Elizabeth of Rumania, not only removes from the royal family of Europe one of its kindliest members, but takes from the roll of Independent contributors one of its oldest names. We reprint a "folk song," from her pen, translated from the Rumanian, which appeared in our columns on May 30, 1889, but which has once more become especially significant.

I AM CONTENTED

I had a spindle of hazelwood;
The spindle fell into the water by the mill.
And never hath the water brought it back again.

The soldier said, as he was called to die:
"I am contented;
But tell my mother in the village,
My sweetheart in the cottage,
To pray for me with folded hands."

The soldier's dead; his mother and his sweetheart—
They pray for him with folded hands.
They dug his grave upon the battle-field,
And all the earth was red
Wherein they laid him.
The sun beheld him thus, and said:
"I am contented."

And flowers clustered on his grave
And were contented here to bloom.
And when the wind would roar
Among the trees,
Then asked the soldier from his deep, dark grave:
"Was it the flag that fluttered?"
"Nay!" said the wind; "my gallant hero.
Nay; thou hast died in battle, but the flag
Hath won the day. Thy comrades
Have carried it away full happily."
Then said the soldier from his deep, dark grave:
"I am contented."

And then he hearkened to the wandering
Of herds and shepherds, and he asked:
"Is that the din of battle?"
"Nay!" said they; "nay, my gallant hero;
For thou art dead; the war is over;
Thy fatherland is free and happy."
Then said the soldier from his deep, dark grave:
"I am contented."

And then he hearkened to the lovers' laughter:
And thus the soldier asked:
"Are these the people's voices, who remember me?"
"Nay!" spake the lovers; "nay, my gallant hero.
For we are they who never do remember:
For spring hath come, and all the earth is smiling.
We must part first."
Then said the soldier from his deep, dark grave:
"I am contented."

I had a spindle of hazelwood;
It fell into the water by the mill.
And never did the water bring it back again.

The Independent

In announcing a series of Shakespeare contests, not only becomes a prominent factor in the nation-wide SHAKESPEARE TERCENTENARY CELEBRATIONS—but also serves to bring sharply to public notice the pronounced merits both textual and mechanical of the famous

BOOKLOVERS SHAKESPEARE

This year, the three hundredth anniversary of the death of the World's Master Writer is being commemorated everywhere—by masques, pageants, plays, monuments—but the most fitting way to pay tribute to his matchless genius is to possess oneself of the literary treasures he has left to the world for all time. Nowhere else will one find such bubbling humor, sincere pathos, stern tragedy—every height and depth of emotion—as in these wonderful plays.

Every home needs a good Shakespeare, and the BOOKLOVERS qualifies in many important features as the best. That is why nearly two million copies have been sold in the last ten years—far outranking any other edition ever published.

The BOOKLOVERS is widely commended as the best equipped edition ever offered the general public. It contains 7,000 pages, including every word that Shakespeare wrote—also every possible aid to the reader for his fuller understanding and enjoyment. Here are two sets of notes, one for general use, the other at the back for the most exhaustive study. Here are glossaries, comments, arguments, indices and full biography. The reading page is large and clear, and every manufacturing detail of the highest grade. There are 90 full-page plates in color, and over 400 other illustrations. The bindings are charming, the volumes of convenient size. Every new reader is delighted with this attractive edition.

A New Edition at Practically Half Price

No Other Edition Has These Special Features

Topical Index
in which you can find instantly any desired passage in the plays and poems.

Critical Comments
on the plays and characters. They are selected from the writings of world-famed Shakespearean scholars.

Glossaries
A complete one in each volume explaining every difficult, doubtful or obsolete word.

Two Sets of Notes
One for the general reader and a supplementary set for students.

Arguments
These give a condensed story of each play.

Study Methods
which furnish the equivalent of a college course of Shakespearean study.

Life of Shakespeare
by Dr. Israel Gollancz, with critical essays by Walter Bagehot, Leslie Stephen, Thomas Spencer Baynes and Richard Grant White.

Until this year the BOOKLOVERS SHAKESPEARE was in 40 thick-paper volumes. Now as a crowning achievement we have compressed this into 20 beautiful thin-paper books—retaining every single feature of the old edition and adding others. But the great saving in binding (20 volumes instead of 40) has enabled us to cut the price nearly in two. Instead of $35 and $50, the old prices—see the low prices in the coupon. Subject to advance when this edition is exhausted.

We cannot describe the beauty and the utility of this wonderful Shakespeare—or its wonderful notes and special aids to the reader—in an advertisement. WE WANT YOU TO SEE THESE BOOKS FOR YOURSELF AT OUR EXPENSE. You take no risk as you do not order until you do see them. No agent will be sent. The books are their own best witnesses. If you don't like them—send them back, also at our expense. That's the way we have dealt with thousands of pleased customers.

Readers For Pleasure—And Contestants For *The Independent* Prizes Will Alike Want The BOOKLOVERS

One could scarcely imagine a more perfectly equipped edition for home use—for the pleasure of the evening by the fireside, revelling in these great plots for the sheer joy of them —or for the more ambitious student of the text who will find in this one set of books every possible incentive and aid. The present special offer saves you nearly one-half on the former price of these great books—brings the full set for your personal examination—and allows you to pay for them at the rate of only a few cents a day. So why hesitate?

This entire, beautiful set will be sent you on approval prepaid—If you send Coupon at once

I. 8-13-16

APPROVAL COUPON

THE UNIVERSITY SOCIETY, Inc.
44 East 23d Street, New York

Send me on approval, charges prepaid, a complete set of your new Booklovers Shakespeare, 20 volumes, art cloth. If the books are satisfactory, I agree to pay you $1 within five days and $2 a month till the special price of $19.80 is paid.* If I do not like the books, I shall notify you and hold subject to order.

.... NAME

.... ADDRESS

.... OCCUPATION

*Most readers prefer the luxurious full limp leather binding. We recommend it. To obtain it, change $19.80 to $29.80.

20 Handy Size volumes—5x7¼ in.—7,000 pages—400 pictures—90 full-page illustrations in 6 to 12 colors—clear type —bible paper—flexible books stamped in gold.

The Independent

| VOLUME 85 | MARCH 13, 1916 | NUMBER 3510 |

K I N G S

By G. Bernard Shaw

We sent G. B. S. a copy of the editorial entitled, "And There Shall Be No More Kings," in The Independent of March 22, 1915, and the following, penned on the margin of the clipping, in his careful handwriting, is his comment on what he calls "a wise and timely article."

THIS war raises in an acute form the whole question of Republicanism versus German dynasticism. After the mischief done by Franz Josef's second childhood as displayed in his launching the forty-eight-hour ultimatum to Serbia before the Kaiser could return from Stockholm, the world has the right—indeed the duty—to demand that monarchies shall at least be subject to superannuation as well as to constitutional limitation.

All recent historical research has shown that the position of a King, even in a jealously limited monarchy like the British, makes him so strong that George III, who was childish when he was not under restraint as an admitted lunatic, was uncontrollable by the strongest body of statesmen the eighteenth century produced. It is undoubtedly inconvenient that the head of the State should be selected at short intervals; but it does not follow that he (or she) should be an unqualified person or hold office for life or be a member of a dynasty.

I may add that if the policy of dismembering the Central Empires by making separate national States of Bohemia, Poland and Hungary, and making Serbia include Bosnia and Herzegovina, is seriously put forward, it would involve making them Republics; for if they were Kingdoms their thrones would be occupied by cousins of the Hohenzollerns, Hapsburgs and Romanoffs, strengthening the German hegemony instead of restraining it.

London

THE PRESIDENT AND THE RECALCITRANT DEMOCRATS

IN a time of great national stress the President can hardly have a more serious obstacle to contend with than a division in his own party. A spirited and effective opposition is not such a bad thing; it keeps the issue clear and sharpens responsibility. But disunity in the leader's own following threatens to cut the very ground from under his feet.

With such a situation President Wilson has had to contend for nearly a year. During all that time conditions in the field of foreign relations have been continuously acute. There has been imminent every day the possibility that the United States might become involved in the Great War.

In the early months of that year the President was embarrassed by the presence in the chief place in his Cabinet of a man who did not see eye to eye with him on fundamental questions of foreign policy. The story persists, without denial, that when the first "Lusitania" note went to Germany, signed with the name of Mr. Bryan, then Secretary of State, Mr. Bryan himself told the Austrian Ambassador in private conversation that the stern tone of the note was intended for effect at home and not abroad. A condition of affairs which made possible such an act was obviously intolerable. But it persisted until it was resolved a month after the sinking of the "Lusitania" by Mr. Bryan's resignation.

Now an equally serious situation confronts Mr. Wilson. Some of his party associates in Congress have proposed to have Congress lay down a different principle in relation to the protection of American citizens upon the high seas from that which the President has consistently asserted in his dealings with the nations at war. Not only was this proposal of certain leading Democrats in Congress a direct assault upon the President's foreign policy; it was an attempt to weaken international law. The immediate effect of it was to give aid and comfort to those European governments which have also been attempting to reconstruct the recognized rules of international law to fit the exigencies of their peculiar position upon the sea. The President straightway found himself hampered in his dealings with Germany and felt a new confidence in the attitude of his diplomatic antagonists born of a not unnatural belief that the President was not supported by a united party, to say nothing of a united nation.

Mr. Wilson did not waver. He took a straightforward course in dealing with this attempt to scuttle his foreign policy. He called upon his associates in Congress to bring the matter to a direct vote, and thus to put the Congress on record in support of the course which he was pursuing.

There are two good reasons why the Congress should have met the President's request frankly and given him the vote of confidence which he asked. In the first place, Congress—and the nation—ought to support the President at every crisis in our foreign relations, unless and until he goes so flagrantly wrong that the national honor or the national safety is clearly imperiled.

In the second place, the President is right. The advocates in Congress of the proposal to warn American citizens not to travel upon armed merchant ships belonging to belligerent powers would have the United States Government attempt to evade its primary duty of protecting its citizens upon the seas in the hope that by so doing the possible danger of war would be minimized. The motive is commendable. No American wants the United States to enter the war. But the act itself would be indefensible. To have the American Government deliberately abjure what is a cardinal duty of every sovereign nation would be a national disgrace.

President Wilson has consistently sought two ends. He has striven to keep the United States out of the Great War. He has labored to uphold the recognized and incontrovertible rights of American citizens against every assault. In so doing he has had to pursue that perilous middle path which subjects him who travels it to attack from both sides. There are those who assail him because he has been too anxious to keep the nation out of war. They are to be found chiefly in the opposition. There are those who accuse him of not trying hard enough to keep the nation out of war. They are largely those of his own party. In this difficult situation Mr. Wilson has steered a straight course. He deserves the support of Congress and of the nation. If he loses either, his dual task will become insurmountably hard. Neither the safety of the United States nor its honor will be secure.

OUR LATEST PROTÉGÉE

THE Senate has ratified the Haytian treaty with commendable promptness and unanimity. By this act the United States formally assumes responsibility for the maintenance of the financial integrity and civil order of the Republic of Hayti and so will exercize over the western third of the island somewhat the same oversight as she has exercized for the past eight years over the Dominican two-thirds.

The treaty has been so modified as to be inoffensive to Haytian pride. It calls for coöperation rather than dictation on our part and we have voluntarily withdrawn our demand for Mole St. Nicholas as a naval station. The republic is to be policed by a native constabulary; under American officers at first, but these are to be replaced by native officers as they are found qualified. An American financial adviser will control the collection of the revenue and its expenditures and keep the republic from sinking deeper into debt. In Santo Domingo our administrators found it possible to scale down the extravagant obligations which that Government had incurred and doubtless it will be found in Hayti that a part of its $40,000,000 debt is invalid.

The intervention of the United States came just in the nick of time to save Hayti from bankruptcy, anarchy and conquest. France and Germany before the war were both eager to foreclose and take possession of the island and even since the war began their representatives in Hayti have worked together to thwart the plans of the United States. Revolution had followed revolution. There have been six presidents in the last two or three years, Oreste, Zamor, Théodore, Sam, Bobo, and Dartiguenave. When Sam usurped the presidential power a year ago our Government refused to recognize him as it refused to recognize Huerta and with still better reason. We refused to allow him to get hold of the half million dollars in gold which the Bank of Hayti had sent to New York for safe keeping. But France and Germany promptly recognized him and France offered him a loan of a million or more, altho France needs all her money for the war.

But when Sam arrested 160 of the prominent citizens of Hayti, put them in prison and there murdered them, the storm broke. Sam took refuge in the French Legation, but the mob invaded the Legation, dragged out Sam, killed and dismembered him and carried parts of his body on pikes thru the street, a French revolution in black. Then Admiral Caperton stepped in and the American marines landed at Cap-Haitien August 1, 1915, soon restored order with very little bloodshed.

In spite of the turbulent spirit of the people it is not probable that there will be any great difficulty in preventing future outbreaks of disorder. But that is the least of our obligations. Our most difficult duty will be to assist in the administration of affairs so that the people may be trained in paths of peaceful industry. Here we should heed the wise counsels of Booker T. Washington, who, tho dead, may yet speak to us. In an article published shortly before he left us he said:

I hope the United States will not pursue a mere negative policy in Hayti, that is, a policy of controlling the customs and what not, without going further in progressive, constructive directions. In a word, the United States now has an opportunity to do a big piece of fine work for Hayti in the way of education, something the island has never had. I hope some way will be provided by which a portion of the revenues will be used in giving the people a thoro up-to-date system of common school, agricultural and industrial education. Here is an excellent opportunity for some of the young colored men and women of the United States who have been educated in the best methods of education in this country to go to Hayti and help their fellows. Here is an opportunity for some of the most promising Haytian boys and girls to be sent to schools in the United States. Here is an opportunity for us to use our influence and power in giving the Haytians something they have never had, and that is education, real education. At least ninety-five per cent of the people, as I have said, are unlettered and ignorant so far as books are concerned.

In carrying all these suggestions into practise, let me repeat again and again that we will have to be patient with Hayti. We ought to be patient. We are big enough and strong enough to be patient, not arbitrary and force-compelling in our relations with her.

Also, we ought to be careful in the class of white men sent to Hayti as officials. Here is the first experience American white people have had to live and work in a black man's country, with black men and women. This is quite a different thing from living in what is called a "white man's country." Every Haytian would rather be swept from the face of the earth than give up his independence or his country. He does not wish the dominance of the white man. They are a proud people, albeit an ignorant people, often mistaken in their ideals and methods, but nevertheless a proud people determined to preserve the independence won by their ancestors in the face of great odds. The average American white man is not fitted to work with these Haytians. The average army officer, or naval officer, the average white soldier or white marine, is not fitted to live and work among these Haytians. The racial lines which are drawn in this and other countries will not be tolerated in Hayti, and American white men who go there should understand this. They must fit themselves to live with men in a black man's country if they want to live there and work there and have any influence there.

This means that we should have no more letters from Washington such as Secretary Bryan wrote to Mr. Vick, American Receiver of Customs in Santo Domingo: "Can you let me know what positions you have at your disposal with which to reward deserving Democrats?"

The suggestion of Booker Washington that we send to Hayti some of our educated negroes is a good one. When the first contingent of colored troops landed at Manila, one of the American soldiers on the dock called out:

"Why, hello, Sambo, what are you doing here?"

And the negro soldier aptly replied:

"I'se helping bear the white man's burden, sah."

Now in our new undertaking the new generation of colored people trained in practical lines and habits of industry can do better service for us than fighting. A social settlement of Tuskegee alumni would accomplish more for the regeneration of the island than a regiment of soldiers or a hundred officeholders chosen from "deserving Democrats."

THE ARRIVAL OF THE CHAUFFEUSE

THE departure of a large proportion of the able-bodied men to the front has opened many avenues to women in England and France. One of these is the demand for feminine motorists. In the Wanted columns of the London *Times* one often sees an advertisement for a "chauffeuse-companion" from some lady who, in the absence of men folk and mechanician, desires a young woman to go about with her and drive the car. To meet this new demand schools of motoring have been opened on Piccadilly in which women are taught not only to run an automobile but to take the engine apart, replace tires and make minor repairs. It probably will be found that women are not so devoid of mechanical ability as has been supposed, and the duties of a chauffeuse are not likely to be any more arduous or unwholesome than the confinement at hard labor in kitchen or factory, to which many women are now condemned for life.

THE CULTIVATION OF OBLIVIOUSNESS

THE art of seeing things is one which educators have always commended and tried to train, but the city man needs nowadays to learn how not to see things. Our streets are turned at night into continuous Fourth of July celebrations wherein electric fireworks flare and flash and flame. Glowworms crawl up and down the front of the buildings. Zigzag lightning strikes a signboard. Words are spelled out letter by letter or written with an invisible pen or race across the skyline of a block. Fiery highballs are continually compounded. Bottles pour out a ceaseless flood of sparkling beverage. A mammoth squirrel runs unweariedly in his whirling cage. A four-story Highlander dances flings eternally. A gigantic kitten plays with a Ferris-wheel spool and then leaps with one bound to the top of a skyscraper. An eagle, the size of Sinbad's roc, flaps its wings and soars aloft and then returns to roost.

Amid all this glare and flare and flicker the weary workman plods his homeward way, thinking of nought but supper. The pleasure seekers thread their way thru the maze in complete unconsciousness of the rainbow lights on every side. They might not be able to tell you the name of a single one of the signs which have been flashed upon them. They have looked at them but not perceived them. They have seen them only to shut them out of their inner sight. They have found it necessary thus to blind their conscious vision in order to attend to their own affairs. The failure to cultivate obliviousness may involve the penalty of death. The automobiles show no mercy to the startled stranger who stops an instant in the midst of the street to look at a Ben Hur chariot race.

The mental mechanism by which these sights are shunted off must be a curious thing. It is perhaps the same as the Freudian censor who shields the self from unpleasant thoughts, a sort of office boy who keeps unwelcome visitors from bothering the boss. And so the struggle goes on incessantly between the advertiser who is trying to attract our attention and the guardian of the gate whose business it is to keep our attention from being distracted. In this contest the ultimate victory lies with the defense. To dazzle our eyes is to blind them, and the signboard that we are at first forced to see becomes the easiest to avoid in the future. The consciousness becomes callous and we are protected from further disturbance by a sort of induration of the intellect. So it comes that the city man pays no more attention to a tungsten film in nitrogen or a cascade of colored lights than the countryman pays to Venus in the heavens or the fireflies in the grass.

AN AMERICAN SCRAP OF PAPER?

MR. MOORFIELD STOREY is a lawyer of Boston distinction and known outside of the shadow of the gilded dome as president of the Anti-Imperialist League; his speeches at the annual meetings of the League, for which meetings ample space is found in a club room on Jay street, are duly reported in the press. His annual address last week is distinguished by the charge that in its treatment of the Philippine people the United States is "getting dangerously near the 'scrap of paper doctrine,'" and that "surely no American with a conscience should be willing to adopt this or sell his country's honor for money."

Surely no conscientious American would adopt the "scrap of paper" policy or sell his country's honor for money. But how is it that we have come into such dangerous proximity to this hateful doctrine? What treaty have we threatened to break? Surely no treaty that concerns the Philippines. Under the treaty with Spain the Philippine Islands came into our possession and we have never promised to give them up. To be sure, a Democratic convention did make the pledge, but that is not the United States. It is true also that the United States Senate has approved a bill proposing on a given date to give the Islands their independence, but the Senate is not the United States. To pledge the United States requires the action of the popular House of Representatives as well, and the assent of the President, and that the bill will pass the House there is little reason to fear despite the Democratic platform. Either House of Congress is liable to do a foolish and hasty thing, but the other House can generally be trusted to correct the blunder. So near a new Presidential election, the House of Representatives will find a way to bury the Senate Bill.

So far from approaching a dishonorable "scrap of paper" policy, should we hold the Philippines, it would be most disgraceful and cowardly to absolve ourselves from responsibility for them. It is not true that we hold the Philippines by selling our honor for money; we hold them for the good of their people, for their advantage and at our expense. We are doing it to give the Philippines both peace and liberty, but not yet to promise them independence. Liberty and independence are dif-

ferent things. The people of New York state have freedom and liberty, but not independence. They are under the government of the nation. The Philippine Islands are now very much in the same condition that the people of Oklahoma were before Oklahoma became a state. Their people govern themselves. They choose their own mayors. They enact their own laws. They are represented in their highest courts and in the highest commission that governs them. The United States government can veto any unwise law they enact, just as any bill passed by the Oklahoma territorial legislature could have been vetoed. In the government of the Philippines there is no imperialism, no tyranny, but a good and sufficient measure of liberty, and we do not believe that the Philippine people wish to lose the protection of the United States, to lose their liberty, with the serious danger of becoming, like Formosa, subject to a neighboring island power. For the peace, the liberty, the self-government, and the happy civilization of the Philippine Islands, the United States has made itself responsible. To this it has in every way pledged itself. For this it has assumed a task of grand altruism, as real and generous altruism as that for which the Church sends missionaries to lands of dark ignorance and superstition; and now

> To doubt would be disloyalty,
> To falter would be sin.

WHERE PUBLIC BUILDINGS ARE NEEDED

TO the casual visitor Washington seems full of Government buildings. There are first the Capitol, with its Senate and House Office buildings; the Congressional Library, and the White House. Then come the Department buildings, the Treasury; the State, War, and Navy; the Interior; the Pension, and Patent buildings; the Printery; the Bureau of Engraving and Printing. These, however, are so inadequate that almost all overflow into rented offices, while three Departments—Justice, Commerce, and Labor—and a large number of Bureaus and Commissions are obliged to rent buildings, floors, or suites in office buildings, wherever they can. Among these are the Geological Survey, the Reclamation and Forestry Services, the Bureaus of Plant and Animal Industry, the Civil Service and Interstate Commerce Commissions, the Bureau of Mines, and a number of subordinate sections.

The result is inefficiency in administration, great danger of loss from fire or poor storage, and unnecessary expense. Many of these offices are so far from the headquarters of the Department to which they belong that adequate supervision is impossible. Not one of these rented buildings or offices, either in its construction or location can, even by courtesy, be regarded as fire proof. The invaluable records of the Geological Survey, the Reclamation and Forestry Services, the Bureau of the Census, the Passport Office, the Court of Claims, may go up in smoke almost any day, while the Patent and Land offices, and the Treasury Department are so crowded that it is impossible to keep their files in anything like decent condition.

The total rental for this next year is estimated at over $600,000. For $12,000,000 at the most, in bonds bearing not over $400,000 in interest, it is estimated that the whole work could be amply provided for. Even if more were needed, or the repairs and upkeep brought the annual sum up to the present figure, the gain in safety and efficiency would be enormous.

Why is it not done? These facts are perfectly well known to Government officials and to Congress. They have been stated repeatedly in the House and Senate. Meetings of scientific associations have many times emphasized the need. A few years ago, under their pressure, land was bought for three Department buildings. Not a step has been taken for their erection. Why? Popular judgment says that certain real estate interests would suffer from the lapse of rentals. There are no votes to be affected by the necessary appropriations. No Congressman will incur danger of not being re-elected because he does not vote for the appropriations. There is no "pork" in it, as there is in a Public Buildings bill for erecting massive court houses and florid postoffices in frontier towns. For the District of Columbia has no representative in Congress. That Government property is endangered, that Government work is hampered, that Government clerks suffer,. means nothing to any but a very few. Not until the people of the country demand adequate provision will it be provided. What will wake them up?

FROM A PIRATE'S WINDOW

PUBLIC attention is once more directed toward the Danish West Indies by the visit of ex-President Roosevelt and the rumor that Denmark might in these troublous times be more willing to sell us the islands than she was when last we tried to buy them. In our issue of December 27,·1915, we told how nearly the United States came to getting them in 1868 and in 1902. In discussing the question of annexation much stress has always been laid upon the commercial and naval advantages of the acquisitions. But to us, looking at the matter from the point of view of a penman instead of a seaman, it seems that the romantic history which would be thrown in with the islands would be worth a lot.

The harbor of St. Thomas, big tho it be, is chockful of good stories of the pirates and blockade runners who made it their headquarters from the time of Columbus to that of Jefferson Davis. The beautiful view of "the Gibraltar of America," which we publish on another page, is appropriately taken from the tower which tradition assigns to Black Beard, as ferocious a pirate as ever delighted the innocent mind of childhood.

The feature that gave to Edward Leach his *nom de guerre* was the jet black beard which began close under his eyes and extended down so far that he braided it and hung it over his ears when actively engaged in his profession. Two lighted fuses ready for the matchlocks were stuck in his shaggy hair and glowed like fiery eyes in the dark. With a cutlass in his right hand, a pistol in his left, and five other pistols stuck in his belt he was the picture of preparedness.

Not content with preparing for this life he devised an ingenious method of inuring his crew to their life to come by what he called "making a hell of our own." In this game all parties went down into the hold and closed the hatches. Then they lit pots of brimstone precisely as the quarantine doctor does nowadays when he fumigates a ship. The man who could stand it longest without suffocating was the winner, and it was Black Beard who came up last to breathe.

Another of his diversions when in a merry mood after dinner was to blow out the candles and shoot right and left under the table to see how many legs he could hit.

Naturally such a fascinating man would be a great favorite with the ladies, as we may judge by the fact that he had married his fourteenth wife when his career came to an untimely end thru the influence of the Governor of Virginia, who in 1718 offered a prize of 140 pounds for him dead or alive. The details of his last fight we forbear to transcribe lest librarians who seem to have acquired the notion that pirate stories are not suited to the young should ·exclude The Independent from their reading rooms. Suffice it to say that he was not taken alive, and that when the "Pearl" returned to the port of Bath Town, North Carolina, a ·black beard was dangling from her bowsprit. Owing to the unavoidable absence of the leading actor the pirates taking part in that Friday's hanging numbered unluckily thirteen.

Of course we agree with the watchful librarians that such stories are unwholesome for the adolescent mind. Therefore we warn our youthful readers that if they should ever happen upon such books as Johnson's "History of the Pyrates" or Esquemeling's "Buccaneers of America," they should return them to the shelves unopened.

But when the United States acquires St. Thomas and the tide of tourists turns that way, we should like to have the postcard rights for Black Beard's Tower.

THE HERITAGE OF HATE

IT is greatly to the credit of the generous and placable Irish people that they have so readily forgiven England for its centuries of injustice and oppression. They promised loyalty and goodwill if they were allowed their own Parliament and self-government. This was granted, and they have kept their word. They have sent 142,000 of their sons to the war front to stand beside their Welsh, Scotch and English brothers, all offered voluntarily without compulsion or draft, and they are adding to the number a thousand a week; and the Irish members of Parliament are as loyal as any others.

The same generous and forgiving spirit characterizes the great majority of those in this country of Irish birth or descent. There is a multitude of branches in this country of the United Irish League and of the Ancient Order of Hibernians, with many other Irish benevolent societies. These are federated under an executive committee, which has just issued an admirable series of resolutions declaring their sympathy with the people of Ireland and their condemnation of a certain number of Irishmen in this country of the Clan-Na-Gael type, and their sons born here, who are cultivating an inheritance of hate against England. The resolutions declare that Irish-Americans are Americans first and last and all the time, and that it is not their will to make trouble for the President in his present contention.

We have observed that there are a few Irish papers, even religious papers, of which the *Sacred Heart Review*, of Boston, is an example, which cannot forgive or forget. We cannot believe that it is because they love Germany more, but because they hate England implacably, that they disparage the cause for which Ireland is engaged with the whole British people. It is a mean spirit and far from the Irish nature to hug the heritage of hate.

THE STORY OF THE WEEK

THE GREAT WAR

The Second Week at Verdun In their attack upon the entrenched camp of Verdun the Germans have continued to gain, tho not so rapidly as during the first week. The operations have developed sufficiently for the plan of campaign to be seen. The battle opened at half past eight in the morning of February 21 by the bombardment of the northernmost line of the French trenches. The amount of ammunition expended was probably greater than in any former engagement of the Great War, and of course there is nothing in the previous history of the world to compare with it. Under this furious fire the trees were mowed down as with a scythe, the barbed wire entanglements swept away, the parapets leveled and the trenches filled.

Then followed a series of infantry attacks which in a few days brought the German lines southward three or four miles along a ten mile front. The French retired from these outlying positions as soon as they became obviously untenable; so the number of prisoners taken was comparatively small, 17,000 being all the Germans claim. But the retiring forces took a terrible revenge, for whenever a position was evacuated the adjoining batteries concentrated their fire upon it and the explosion of mines underneath ground occupied by the advancing Germans wiped out a regiment at a time.

During the first ten days the Germans launched twenty-six infantry assaults, each composed of several lines. Their gains about Verdun amount to over a hundred square miles, which is five times as much as the French won in their Champagne drive of last fall. Among the booty taken in the French entrenchments are specified 115 cannon and 161 machine guns.

The German attack from the north culminated in the capture of the Fort de Douaumont last week. Since then their attention has been directed to the west and east of this point. To the west they took Champneuville and cleared the French from the bend of the Meuse. The French lines on the western side of the Meuse have also been bombarded between the river and the town of Malancourt. The hills on this side of the river are lower than those on the right side, but their batteries flank the line along which the Germans must advance toward Verdun.

The attack upon Verdun from the east this week resulted in greater territorial gains to the Germans than that from the north last week, but is not so striking an achievement, for it has only carried them over the Woevre plain to the edge of the plateau on which the permanent fortifications of Verdun are constructed. Their gains on this side, however, put them in possession of most of the railroad which runs below the range of hills from Vaux to Fresnes. The mud has prevented them from bringing up their big guns on this side.

Most of the French despatches describe the German losses as appalling.

Their estimates range from 100,000 to 300,000. On the other hand, the Germans deny any excessive losses and the Paris correspondent of the London *Times* says that the slaughter on neither side has been so great as when the Germans attacked the British lines in Flanders or the French lines in Artois. All the civilians have been sent out of Verdun.

The defense of Verdun has been entrusted to General Petain, who was suddenly called from the Champagne to take charge. He is one of the new commanders whom the war has made. In June, 1914, he was only a colonel and about to retire since he was sixty. But at Charleroi he showed his ability and is now recognized as one of the most energetic and skillful of the French generals.

The Struggle for Douaumont The focus of the battle of Verdun has been for the past fortnight the Fort de Douaumont and the story of its attack and defense will doubtless be the theme of strategic study and pictorial art for more than one generation to come. The wedge

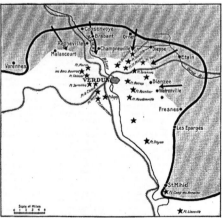

THE FIERCEST FIGHT IN HISTORY

It appears from present reports that the attack upon Verdun is unprecedented for strength of defense and violence of assault and it may prove to be the decisive battle of the war. The Germans advanced nearly four miles in the first four days and captured Fort Douaumont, which stands on a hill overlooking the surrounding country and is only five miles from Verdun. The next German attack came from the eastern side between Etain and Fresnes and was carried as far as the ridge on which stands Fort Vaux. A third attack from the western side near Malancourt is reported. The heavy line shows the German position before the present attack; the shaded portion shows the territory they now hold

which the Germans have driven into the heart of the Verdun defenses from the north had a base of ten miles, but narrowed down to a point at Douaumont. The importance of this position lies in the fact that it stands upon the ridge leading toward Verdun. The ground in front of it had been cleared of trees, but covered with traps and tangles. The ravines which approached Douaumont on either side were of course raked by the guns of the fort. Its altitude is about 1200 feet, and it commands a view of the city of Verdun only five miles south.

The Kaiser entrusted the post of honor and danger at the apex of the German wedge to his "brave Brandenburgers," men from the heart of Prussia, who from the time of Frederick the Great have formed the nucleus of the German army. It was the Brandenburgers who captured Verdun in 1792 and led the attack on Liège in 1914.

After the steel and concrete cupolas of the Douaumont fort had been smashed by four well-placed shells the Brandenburgers charged and in spite of heavy losses from the fire of neighboring batteries they captured the fort. A French soldier thus describes the assault:

Some Boche infantry were creeping up a narrow ravine on the right front, others were crawling thru the wood directly before the position. Suddenly they surged forward in a gray mass from both quarters at once. There must have been 5000 in the ravine and perhaps 20,000 from the wood. As the former reached the plateau a single shell burst right among them, flinging pieces in all directions. The front was enveloped in a storm of shells, fragments of men, and lumps of earth.

Thru the smoke one could see them advancing, heads down, as if sheltering themselves from rain. Soon the ravine head was choked with bodies. Others tried to clamber over and kept rolling down the hillside. The heaps of dead gave us a more effective barricade than our own intrenchments. They simply could not pass. But in front, where the slaughter was even greater, they came on incessantly.

Truly, they are brave, those Boches. I would never have believed that human beings could face such a terrific fire. Yet they knew it was certain death, for the wounded were stifled under corpses or torn in pieces by fresh shells.

Wave after wave advanced. At last they reached the spot where our fortifications had been on the spur of the hill, and began piling up bodies to protect them from our fire. Douaumont was theirs, but at ghastly cost.

But the real struggle took place not over the fort, but over the village of Douaumont. This is a group of some fifty houses a little in front of the fort and a hundred feet lower. The French also brought here their crack troops, those who had been foremost in the Champagne drive. They ran around the fort from both sides and took possession of the village. The Brandenburg regiment was then virtually besieged and for the next ten days had little or no relief from the outside. The Germans made desperate efforts to come to their rescue, but the village had been previously prepared for defense by tunnels and mines and was protected by concealed batteries on each side. The Germans tried assaults by day and assaults by night. suffocating gases and

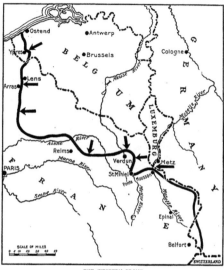

THE WESTERN FRONT

The strategic importance of Verdun is shown by this map. It is the cornerstone of the French defenses. But while the Germans seem to be concentrating their main efforts on this fortress, they have also taken the offensive at various other points as indicated by the arrows, especially in the Champagne region near Reims, in the Artois region near Lens and Arras. At Ypres the British have not only recovered the "international trench" recently taken by the Germans, but have penetrated their first line of fortifications

streams of fire, long-range bombardment and hand grenades, and have finally, it seems, succeeded in occupying the village of Douaumont or rather the ruins of it.

The Russians in Asia　By the capture of Erzerum the Russians did not, as was at first reported, take the entire Turkish army prisoner, but they got enough of it to seriously weaken the opposition. According to the official Russian report they captured 235 officers and 12,753 men, besides 325 guns and large stores of arms and supplies. The town was practically uninjured, altho the Turks before evacuating blew up a few of the government buildings and some of the military depots.

The retreating Turks are being pursued in all directions. To the south the Russians have reached Mush and captured Bitlis, a hundred miles from Erzerum and only fifty miles from the Tigris. To the west they have reached Ashkale, forty miles away. To the north they have advanced about the same dis-

tance, which brings them half way to the Black Sea. Another column moving westward along the coast is near Rize, thirty-five miles from Trebizond. In Byzantine times the Greek city of Trebizond was the first important stronghold on the coast, but now it could not be expected to hold out against a Russian attack from both land and sea. Another ancient Greek colony of the Black Sea coast, Sinope, was shelled last week by the Russian fleet.

In Persia also the Russians are meeting with success. They defeated the Turks, Kurds and Persians in the passes between Hamadan and Kermanshah and have taken that town. Kermanshah is the most important trading center on the caravan route between Bagdad and Teheran. This brings the Russians within about 150 miles from Kut-el-Amara, on the Tigris, where the British under General Townshend is besieged.

This expedition is so closely invested by the Turks that it has not been able to get any supplies for two months except such as could be brought by aeroplane. Communication is kept up by

THE GUNS THAT CAUSE THE TROUBLE

This photograph of the Italian S.S. "Verona" shows how and where the defensive armament of a merchantman is likely to be placed. Germany's announced intention to regard vessels so equipped as subject to attack without warning has reopened the submarine controversy and threatened to rupture the Democratic party

wireless with General Aylmer's expedition some twenty miles down the river. Altho to a civilian General Townshend would seem to be in a distressing plight, he seems to be in good spirits. When asked by wireless what he was doing and what he wanted he replied that he was planting vegetable seeds and wanted some new needles for his phonograph. The needles will be dispatched by aerial post.

The New Russian Premier

Boris Vladimirovitch Sturmer, the new Russian Premier, first became identified with the Russian Court in 1878, and since then has remained one of the "inner circle" of that court, participating in all secret councils, and never losing favor with the three emperors he served.

In 1902, as General Director of the Ministry of Interior, M. Sturmer became closely associated with Sypiagyn, Minister of Interior, who has written some of the bloodiest pages in the history of Russia. In 1903, the famous Von Plehve dispatched him to wreck the liberal Tver Zemstvo, which he faithfully accomplished. Von Plehve made no step of importance without having first consulted the present Premier, and the latter quite often served him as a tool in the fight with the rising tide of liberalism in Russia. As a reward, M. Sturmer, from Directorship of the Ministry of the Interior, was elevated in 1904 to the position of member of the Council of the Empire, a procedure unusual in the annals of the Russian Government.

As a member of the Council (Russia's House of Lords), M. Sturmer has not distinguished himself in any capacity. He occupies a seat at the extreme right of the house. Thruout the last twelve years, perhaps the most tempestuous period in Russian history, he kept aloof from the raging currents of the social and political life of the country. In the last five years he had not spoken even a word from the floor of the Council of the Empire. He has, however, remained closely affiliated with the reactionary forces in the background of the court, and was regarded in Russia as the truest and most typical representative of the Petrograd bureaucracy.

His appointment to the Premiership came as a complete surprize to the Russian public, which saw in it a victory of the reactionary forces in the court which advocate a peace with Germany. The leaders of the Duma are said to have refused to accept the invitation of the new Premier to confer with him. This was an unprecedented act in Russian parliamentary life. The *Novoye Vremya*, the well informed conservative paper of Petrograd, was also taken by surprize, as it acknowledges in its editorial columns its ignorance of the new Premier's present political views. The muzzled liberal press saw but an ominous warning in his appointment.

Since the beginning of the war public opinion in Russia has not been stirred as deeply as by the appointment of M. Sturmer. To appease it, he hastened to call together representatives of the press and make some promises as to "internal reorganization" and reforms. This and his subsequent address at the opening of the Duma, in which he assured the country that Russia was resolved to fight the war till a decisive

victory over the enemy is won, has to a great extent calmed the masses, tho it has not entirely erased the distrust from their minds.

Maritime Warfare

After March 1, according to the announcement of the German Government, the German submarines would begin to attack armed merchant ships without warning. The German contention is that its previous promise not to sink liners without warning and providing for the safety of passengers does not apply to armed vessels. It is held that it is absurd to require that a submarine approach, hail and search a vessel which is known to carry a gun big enough to disable the submarine with a single shot at a distance of a mile or more, especially if the merchant vessel is under instructions to open fire. This, according to the German Government, is the case with British merchantmen and they quote in evidence from the instructions found on the British steamer "Woodfield":

> If a submarine is obviously pursuing a ship by day, and it is evident to the master that she has hostile intentions, the ship pursued should open fire in self-defense, notwithstanding the submarine may not have committed a definite hostile act, such as firing a gun or torpedo.

On the other hand the British Government claims that its merchantmen are armed solely for defense and makes public the instructions from which we quote in another column. The British note, however, explains that these instructions have been repeatedly modified so it is possible that the copy captured by the Germans may be one of the earlier set of regulations.

The British explain that they can put no confidence in the German promise not to attack unarmed vessels because that has been done right along. In proof of this the Admiralty publishes a list

BORIS STURMER

The new Russian premier is a reactionary whose war policy is a matter of doubt

of fifty-four unarmed vessels which have been sunk by German submarines without warning. Fourteen of these are neutrals; two American (the "Gulflight" and "Nebraskan"), four Norwegian, four Swedish, and one each Dutch, Danish, Greek and Portuguese. Of the nine vessels sunk by the German submarines on March 1 and 2, when the new German submarine policy came into effect, none is known to be armed.

The French auxiliary cruiser "Provence," which was sunk in the Mediterranean on February 26, had on board nearly four thousand men, and of these, according to the French Ministry of Marine, 3130 were drowned. This is more than ever were lost before in the sinking of any ship. In the "Lusitania," 1198 lives were lost, and in the "Titanic," 1595. The "Provence" was a converted liner used as a transport and carried eleven cannon. No submarine was seen.

The Peninsular and Oriental liner "Maloja," sunk within sight of Dover on February 27, was found by the coroner's jury to have struck a mine, altho the chief officer testified that he believed she was torpedoed by a submarine. There were 169 lives lost.

Following the example of Portugal which last week seized all the German ships in her harbors, Italy has taken over thirty-four of the thirty-seven German ships in Italian ports. Germany has protested against the seizures and may declare war against Portugal and Italy, neither of which is yet nominally included among her enemies altho Portugal is allied with England and Italy is at war with Austria.

The German sea raider "Möwe" is reported safely back "in a home port," presumably Wilhelmshafen. She brought in $250,000 in gold bars taken from the "Appam," which she sent to Newport News. She had on board 402 prisoners, from the officers, soldiers and crews of the fifteen vessels she cap-

© *Harris & Ewing*

HOUSE LEADERS WHO WARNED THE PRESIDENT

From left to right, Chairman Flood of the House Committee on Foreign Affairs, Speaker Clark and Majority Leader Kitchin. They told President Wilson that a large majority of the Representatives favored a resolution warning Americans not to travel on armed belligerent merchant men. Before the matter came to a vote the temper of the House had changed

tured. Besides those previously reported she had taken the British steamers "Saxon Prince" and "Maroni," and had sunk by her mines the British battleship "King Edward VII." The commander of the "Möwe," Burgrave Count Dohna-Schlodien, has been awarded the Iron Cross by the Kaiser.

War Problems in Congress — At the beginning of last week, the tension at Washington was slightly relieved by assurances that Germany would not sink merchantmen without warning unless there was proof that they were armed. But, on the 29th, Mr. Wilson caused surprize in Congress by what was virtually a challenge. In a letter to Mr. Pou, the acting chairman of the House's powerful Committee on Rules, he practically demanded a vote at once on the pending McLemore resolution, which warns Americans not to go on the ships of belligerents. He called the attention of the committee, he said, to a matter of grave consequence to the country. Industrious use was being made in foreign capitals of the report that there were divided counsels in Congress in regard to the Government's foreign policy. He believed that the report was false, but so long as it was credited anywhere it could not fail to do the greatest harm and expose the country to the most serious risks. And so he felt justified in urging an early vote on the resolutions concerning travel on armed merchantmen, in order that there might be full discussion at once, and that all doubts might be swept away.

The House leaders pleaded for delay, and it was suggested as a compromise that a resolution of confidence in the President be adopted. But Mr. Wilson made it very plain that he would be satisfied with no compromise. In the House there was confusion. Many wanted a resolution of confidence accompanied by a warning to travelers. Some feared that a vote on the McLemore resolution would show a very large minority in favor of it. In the Senate, where Mr. Gore's similar resolution was pending, there was a disposition to wait for the House.

British Orders to Armed Merchantmen

The German Government claims the right to sink armed merchantmen without warning on the ground that vessels had been instructed by the British Admiralty to open fire upon submarines approaching for the purpose of exercising the right of search. The British Admiralty made public on March 2, 1916, the instructions issued on October 20, 1915, and now prevailing. The rules covering the points in dispute are as follows:

The right of the crew of a merchant vessel to forcibly resist visit and search and fight in self-defense is well recognized in international law and expressly admitted by the German prize regulations in an addendum issued June, 1914, at a time when it was known that numerous merchant vessels were being armed for self-defense.

Armament is supplied solely for the purpose of resisting attack by an armed enemy vessel and must not be used for any other purpose whatsoever.

The status of a British armed merchant vessel cannot be changed upon the high seas.

The armament is supplied for the purpose of defense only. The object of the master should be to avoid action whenever possible.

Experience has shown that hostile submarines and aircraft have frequently attacked merchant vessels without warning. It is important, therefore, that craft of this description should not be allowed to approach to short range, at which a torpedo or bomb launched without notice would almost certainly be effective. British and allied submarines and aircraft have orders not to approach merchant vessels. Consequently it may be presumed that any submarine or aircraft which deliberately approaches or pursues a merchant vessel does so with hostile intention. In such cases fire may be opened in self-defense in order to prevent the hostile craft from closing to a range at which resistance to a sudden attack with bomb or torpedo would be impossible.

Defensively armed merchant ships are forbidden to adopt any form of disguise which might cause them to be mistaken for neutral ships.

A contest in the Senate was precipitated, however, on the 2d, by a statement from Mr. Stone as to his own position, and by a speech from Mr. Gore. Mr. Stone, who, as chairman of the Foreign Relations Committee, has sought to prevent action upon resolutions of warning, said it was distressing to disagree with the President, but he desired to save the country from the consequences of the recklessness of foolhardy Americans. Mr. Lodge supported the President, who, he said, ought to have a vote on the question. Mr. Williams opposed any evasion. The only danger of war, he said, was in the hampering and embarrassment of the President. Mr. Gore exprest his disapproval of the madcaps who travel on armed merchantmen. He had heard, he added, that the President had recently said to Senators or Representatives that the loss of American lives on a merchantmen sunk by a German submarine would probably cause severance of diplomatic relations with Germany; that this would probably be followed by war; and that participation in the war by the United States might not be wholly an evil, because it would end the great conflict by midsummer and thus be of great service to civilization.

Mr. Stone at once denied that he had heard the President say anything of this kind. Other Senators made similar disclaimers, and an unqualified denial from the Wh'te House was published a few hours later. No action upon the resolutions was taken that day in the Senate.

The Gore Resolution Tabled   Mr. Gore's resolution was taken up in the Senate on the following day, a motion to lay it on the table having been made. Before the votes were cast he modified the resolution by an amendment or substitution, at variance with the long preamble and the original proposition. This substituted clause asserted that the sinking of a merchantman by a submarine without warning, with an accompanying loss of American lives, would be just and sufficient cause for war with Germany. The motion called for the tabling of the Gore resolution and all substitutes, and there was no debate before the votes were counted. By a vote of 68 to 14 the resolution was laid on the table. Mr. Jones, Republican, had withdrawn his similar resolution. In the affirmative were 49 Democrats and 19 Republicans. Those voting on the other side were Democrats (Mr. O'Gorman and Mr. Chamberlain), and 12 Republicans. Mr. Gore's vote for tabling his own resolution showed his attitude toward the substitute clause which he had inserted. Several who voted against tabling were not in favor of either the original or the modified resolution. They were displeased because there had been no opportunity for debate. And the modification had obscured the issue.

In the House the Committee on Foreign Affairs decided to report a recommendation that the McLemore resolution be laid on the table, with the adoption of a statement that the conduct of diplomatic negotiations should be left with the President, who would report to Congress if his power should be exhausted. It is understood that a majority of the committee are in favor of a warning to American travelers, but are unwilling to embarrass the President. There was expectation that action would be taken on the 4th, but a vote was postponed. This delay was disappointing to Mr. Wilson, for the Senate's action was regarded as indecisive, and there will be further debate in that branch on resolutions like Mr. Gore's, which have been introduced since his was tabled.

Protectorate for Hayti   The treaty or agreement which gives to the United States for at least ten years wide powers of supervision over the internal affairs and foreign relations of Hayti was ratified in our Senate last week without a dissenting vote. Certain provisions of it were already in effect, with Hayti's consent. The treaty is a long one. At the beginning it says that the United States is in sympathy with Hayti's desire to improve the condition of its finances, preserve peace, and develop the country's resources; and will assist the Haytian Government in developing agriculture, mining and commerce, and also in placing the republic's finances on a firm basis.

All customs duties on imports and exports are to be collected by a General Receiver nominated by our President and appointed by the President of Hayti, and in the same way there is to be appointed a Financial Adviser, who shall devise an adequate system of public accounting, aid in increasing the revenues, inquire into the validity of Hayti's debts, and take other action, in association with the Minister of Finance, for the republic's welfare and prosperity. These two officers (who will be Americans) are to have full protection ·in the use of the power thus conferred. The republic's debts are to be classified in a comprehensive statement, showing the sinking fund required for the final discharge of them. The sums collected are to be used, first, for the payment of the salaries and expenses of the General Receiver and the Financial Adviser and their assistants; second, for the interest and sinking fund of the public debt; third, for maintenance of the new constabulary; and, fourth, for the Government's current expenses.

This constabulary is to be both urban and rural. Composed of natives, its officers will be Americans nominated by our President. But these are to be replaced ultimately by Haytians found, upon examination by an American board, to be properly qualified. The constabulary is to have supervision and control of arms and ammunition, military supplies, and the traffic therein. Hayti agrees not to increase its public debt without the consent of our President, or to contract any debt unless the surplus revenue is sufficient to pay interest and provide a sinking fund. It is also agreed that Hayti will not, without our President's consent, so modify her customs duties that the revenue will be reduced. Hayti is bound not to surrender any part of her territory by sale or lease to any foreign Power, and will not make with any foreign Power a treaty that can impair her independence. All foreign claims against Hayti are to be settled by arbitration, under an agreement with the United States. Sanitary improvements are to be made under the direction of an engineer nominated by our President.

There may be intervention. "Should the necessity occur," says the treaty, "the United States will lend efficient aid for the preservation of Haytian independence, and the maintenance of a Government adequate for the protection of life, property, and individual liberty." The term of the agreement is ten years, but ten years more are to be added "if, for specific reasons presented by either high contracting party, the purpose of this treaty has not been fully accomplished."

AT THE STORM CENTER

Senator Stone, of Missouri, chairman of the Committee on Foreign Relations, disagrees with the President as to the status of armed merchantmen, but has labored to prevent any action by the Senate which would embarrass the Executive. It was his letter to which President Wilson replied with so emphatic a statement of his policy

FROM STATE TO STATE

ALABAMA: As a means of attracting immigration to this state, Emmet A. Jones, chief of the Immigration and Markets Bureau, has compiled what he calls "The Alabama Land Book." It is said to answer every question that any prospective settler can reasonably ask concerning not only the lands of different sections, but the roads, schools, churches, public improvements, taxes, towns and general character of each region. For the publication and nation-wide distribution of this book Governor Henderson, State Treasurer Lancaster and Commissioner of Agriculture and Industries Wade have consented to act as trustees, without compensation, of a fund to be raised by private subscription, and Mr. Jones has agreed to serve, also without compensation, as secretary and treasurer.

ARKANSAS: A movement is on foot in Sebastian, Crawford, Washington and Benton counties for a first-class modern highway from Ft. Smith thru Winslow, Fayetteville and Rogers to the Missouri border, where it is to connect with the great system of roads in that state and, by the Santa Fé trail, with points east and west. The section of the road in Arkansas is to be known as "The Ozark Trail."

IOWA: This state is making systematic and determined war upon rats. Dairy and food inspectors are calling upon all dealers in edibles to compare their cellars and other storing places. They say they find that merchants generally willing to comply with this requirement. In some cases it has been necessary for the courts to compel them to. It is the declared purpose of the state authorities to persist in this work until every citizen may feel assured that all food offered for sale is not only unadulterated, but is secure against vermin.

KANSAS: The recently increased demand for potash and the high prices it commands have induced many Kansans to set up a search for it in their state. It has been demonstrated that potash deposits are likely to be found where salt and gypsum abound, and since Kansas has a profusion of both these substances, United States Senator Curtis is hopeful that the Federal authorities will include his state in the investigations for potash now being made in Utah, Texas and other promising states.

LOUISIANA: The recent investigations of the Bureau of Plant Industry of the United States Department of Commerce into possible uses of the water hyacinth have been interesting to the people of this state. This troublesome plant propagates very rapidly, chiefly by off-shoots, and soon chokes up any stream in which it gains a roothold. The length of its stem and its fibrous nature suggested that it might be used as a substitute for jute, but investigation has shown that the fiber

is too short and too irregular for spinning. It has been learned, however, that the plant makes fairly good forage for cattle.

MAINE: The State Highway Commission is working out a plan to have the principal trunk highway of every town in the state patrolled by men who will devote their entire time from early spring to late fall to keeping the roads in the best possible condition. It is estimated that this will require about 500 patrolmen, but it is pointed out that it will mean the rehabilitation of hundreds of miles of highway now rapidly going to ruin for lack of maintenance.

MASSACHUSETTS: Altho this is one of the most thickly populated states in the Union, it contains tens of thousands of acres of barren lands which have lain idle since they were long ago denuded of their forests. Now the state purposes to renew these forests. The State Forester reports 7,000,000 young trees in the state nurseries, 1,000,000 of which are to be planted this spring. Next year the number will be increased to 3,000,000, and it is expected that eventually a total of 15,000,000 trees will be planted every year. While the preliminary work is expensive, the state authorities believe that the investment will ultimately prove very profitable.

MINNESOTA: The Minnesota Art Commission recently began a movement for the bettering of farmers and villagers in this state. Several plans for model farm houses of varying cost were sent to about 1,000,000 farmers thruout the state. As a result the commission has been deluged with requests for information, which are being answered by the Minnesota Chapter of the American Institute of Architects, giving its services freely thru the art commission. Fifty plans for model village houses to cost $3000 each have been prepared and are being sent out for the bare cost of making the blue prints. The responses indicate that rural Minnesota is soon to have hundreds, if not thousands, of new, artistic homes.

MISSOURI: The walnut timber trade, which is of great importance to many Missouri land owners, has had its full share of ups and downs. A generation ago most of the furniture in this country was made of walnut. Then, as our population grew and the demands increased, the big manufacturers, fearing that walnut would soon be exhausted, created a fashion for other woods. That made it necessary for walnut growers to seek another market, so they laboriously built up a trade with Europe, especially with Germany and Austria. Then the war put a stop to those exports, and for more than a year there was practically no market anywhere for walnut. Now every owner of a walnut grove is busy trying to supply the demand for gun stocks. Two Kansas City concerns are sawing

up more than 300 carloads of walnut logs a month, turning out 5000 gun stocks a day.

MONTANA: According to preliminary estimates made by the United States Geological Survey the value of the output of gold, silver, copper, lead and zinc from Montana mines in 1915 was nearly $87,000,000, an increase of more than 81 per cent over the total value of output of the same metals in 1914, which was $47,849,747. The greater quantities of all these metals, especially lead and zinc, were produced, the increase in value was due principally to higher prices. The mine output of lead increased from 9,656,608 pounds in 1914 to more than 14,000,000 pounds in 1915, and that of zinc from 111,580,544 pounds (figured as spelter) in 1914 to 184,086,000 pounds in 1915.

NEVADA: An epidemic of rabies, said to have been caused by mad coyotes, has been spreading so rapidly in Nevada that the state and local authorities and almost the entire citizenry of some counties have been unable to cope with it. Large numbers of wild animals and dogs, and not less than 500,000 head of sheep, cattle and horses have been destroyed by this scourge. So serious has the epidemic become that neighboring states are fortifying against it and the Federal Government has sent aid. The intention is to exterminate the coyote family.

NEW YORK: At a recent largely attended meeting of the Penn Yan Grange the question of incorporating farms was seriously discussed, many members favoring the plan and expressing the opinion that it would soon be adopted. Mr. Francis E. Hoyt strongly advocated it, pointing out many advantages to be gained if, say, fifty farmers, each with 100 acres worth $200 an acre, should combine and operate a farm of 5000 acres with a capital of $1,000,000 on a wholesale scale, breeding horses or specializing in fine cattle, grains, etc. Theo, said he, modern farm implements and tractors, now beyond the purchase of the average farmer, could be used, the help problem would be solved and conditions which make for the instability of prices be eliminated.

NORTH CAROLINA: The immense power plant at Badeu in this state, after many vicissitudes, is at last to become one of the most important industrial centers in the South. It was originally promoted as a commercial hydro-electric proposition by a Pittsburgh company which went into the hands of a receiver. About three years ago the plant was taken over by the Southern Aluminum Company, organized by French bankers. Considerable development work had been done on the plant, which was planned to cost over $10,000,000, when the European war put a stop to it. Now peace war put a stop to it. The Aluminum Company of America has secured control and begun carrying out an even

larger plan of development. The partially constructed hydro-electric and aluminum reduction plants will be completed at once. It is said they will give employment to several thousand.

TENNESSEE: Within a short time Tennessee has raised herself from the third to the seventh state in percentage of illiterate population. A considerable measure of this improvement has been due to the intelligent and energetic efforts of Prof. John R. Brown, the state rural school agent. Yet he is far from satisfied with the situation, and is pressing for longer terms, better equipment and more efficient teachers. He is convinced that fewer instead of more rural schools are needed. Consolidation of these schools, he says, means better buildings, better equipment and more money with which to keep the schools open for nine months. In twenty-one counties he has succeeded in effecting such consolidations, and the results, he asserts, have been good.

UTAH: The Utah Chamber of Commerce has been organized to advertise every resource and industry of every section of the state. It will have four general departments: County exhibits, publicity, general exhibits and public intercourse. Under the first head each county will maintain a display of its representative products, mineral, manufactured, agricultural, etc., together with maps, pictures, literature and data needful for the information of persons seeking homes or investments. The publicity department will conduct a systematic national advertising campaign, while the department of public intercourse will seek to bring the county and general exhibits to the attention of all tourists, school children and the public.

WEST VIRGINIA: The perennial if not everlasting controversy over West Virginia's share in Virginia's ante bellum debt has perhaps engaged more legal talent for less pay than any other pecuniary case ever tried in America. The latest citation of authorities by a leading member of the West Virginia Bar Association seems to leave no room for doubt that, altho the Supreme Court of the United States has decreed that West Virginia must pay some $12,000,000, there is no lawful way in which that decree can be enforced.

WYOMING: Definite steps are being taken for the establishment in this state of what is expected to be the greatest game preserve in the United States. Wyoming, with its wide plains, long ranges of foothills, lofty mountains, immense forests and numerous lakes and streams, is an ideal habitat of wild creatures, especially large game animals. The plan as proposed is to set apart a vast area as a preserve, with a considerable portion of it reserved as a perpetual refuge in which it shall be unlawful to kill any creature not of a predatory nature.

377

WHAT WOMEN KNOW ABOUT MEN

BY IRVING BACHELLER

AUTHOR OF "EBEN HOLDEN," "DRI AND I," "KEEPING UP WITH LIZZIE"

THE old rib theory glorifies man in reducing woman to a kind of paring off his finger nail. In those days nobody tried to understand women. Why should they? It was only necessary that women should understand men and so keep their heads from being broken.

Here is a fundamental point in the proper understanding of woman: she has always understood man because it was unsafe to misunderstand him.

The rib theory is too forced either for credible history or good fiction or reconcilement with the processes of nature, which it completely reverses. If we were permitted to believe that woman was fashioned first we spare Adam that needless and incredible bit of violence and found the Old and New Testaments on two sublime and harmonious miracles of birth.

The story of the fall has never satisfied my sense of fairness. Any good judge of human nature would lean to the theory that Eve became weary of seeing Adam lying idly about and probably littering up the place. So she cunningly devised a way of getting him a permanent job. The secret was committed to her daughters and went on down the line, and so the sons of Adam have been busy ever since.

From the beginning men have invented many fictions about women. They enslaved and married them *en masse*. They held the club. They commanded the legions jointly with the Lord. The Lord had tacitly accepted the honor. Therefore it was so. No man dared deny it. Their treasuries were filled with fiat money, their souls with fiat virtue. Thus equipped they began to practise generosity. Woman was its first victim. She became a confirmed receiver. Men like to be generous. It makes them feel good and great. It is a common form of masculine dissipation. Many wars have been caused by the feeling on the part of some king that he needed larger accommodation for his generosity. He wanted more people to be indebted to him for the privilege of living.

For ages men have used women for receivers of generosity and sayers of gratitude. In Europe even now a woman is largely dependent on the generosity of her husband. Man has always misunderstood both the needs and desires of woman. With his well-known generosity he has at sundry times conferred upon her many kinds of distinction, including that of be-

378

ing an incipient angel. What she needed and desired and dared not demand was the chance to be a human being. Man conferred upon her silks and jewels and laces and slaves and flattery and inferiority. At best she was an ignorant and beautiful plaything, who achieved her ends by subtlety and cunning.

If there were any trouble you had to *chercher la femme*. It was never necessary to *chercher l'homme*. The man was always in evidence. The woman had some sense of shame. She had to have it, being aware that if the facts were known it would be all up with her, while he could wipe it off the slate with some magnificent stroke of generosity. He thought that her lack of courage and frankness signalized a nature essentially base. Here was the first great misunderstanding.

There was only one part of life where a woman had any chance of respect. It was down among the toilers, where heavy tasks gave her strength and destroyed her beauty; where men had no leisure—for leisure among men generally brought trouble to women. There she was a human being and not a bedizened plaything. There appeared the first really great mother of whom we have any record.

Whatever else we may say of her she was blessed above all women in her understanding of the terrified children of the empire—in her sympathy, in her passion, in her vision. She gave to her son, returning day by day to that humble home weary from his tasks—her soul. It was a full and beautiful soul. When the qualities of a strong woman join those of a rugged man in the same body and spirit—when the tenderness of the one softens and directs the strength of the other—then have we the foundation of miracles. Only that type of man understands woman and gives her the sympathy and honor she deserves. Whatever else we may say of Him, that son of the great mother in Galilee was the first man who understood women.

He put them on a new footing, and not yet have women learned how immeasurably sacred he made the office of motherhood.

So, then, let us be sure that we understand this much about woman —no man was ever really great who had not in some measure within him the qualities of womanhood. Alexander and Cæsar and Napoleon were monsters—nothing more. The man

who shows only strength and a talent for spreading terror and destruction is on a plane with the submarine and the howitzer.

Now we are in the immediate neighborhood of one big fact about men and women. The spirit of either sex can never be fully great until the other has contributed to its content.

Some women have achieved greatness, and how? Was it not by filling mind and body with the strength and firmness and courage of manhood? The greatest human being I ever saw was a mountain woman with the strength of a man in heart and sinews. Strong to endure great tasks in the midst of poverty, she was the tenderest and most unselfish creature I have known. The greatest women the world has seen, probably, were the wives of the pioneers who made America. They were mostly strong-armed, broad-backed, big-shouldered women who could do and dare, and yet they were the tenderest of mothers. Many of them had a certain beauty of countenance hard to define, for it was not a thing of form or color. Out of their bodies came the new children of light and went to their tasks—Washington, Webster, Whittier, Lincoln, Grant, Greeley, Beecher and their like. Here in America our eyes have seen true womanhood. New ideals set in immortal phrases, the silent drum, the stilled cannon, the forgiven foe, the freed slave, the onmoving hosts of democracy celebrate her greatness.

Men are largely what their mothers make them, working on the tender soul of childhood; women are largely what men make them in the season of youth and beauty. It all goes back to the mother. She is the barometer of morality. Paint, idleness and peroxidity are storm signs on the dial.

Therefore I think that I understand this much about woman: she carries the flag in the front rank. She is the chief servant making the hand and spirit which are strong in peace and irresistible in war. All that is she, or a shirk, a gadder, a whister, a peacock, a leader in great debacles.

To condemn the beauty and pride of woman is treason to the human race. They are as natural as the summer shine of a bird, but they have led to the worst of all misunderstandings. It is that of women regarding themselves.

Riverside, Connecticut

WHAT MEN KNOW ABOUT WOMEN

BY CORRA HARRIS

AUTHOR OF "THE CIRCUIT RIDER'S WIFE," "THE RECORDING ANGEL," "THE CO-CITIZENS"

DO men understand women? They do. This is the reason why they say they do not. Thus are they absolved from so many responsibilities toward women. They evade them.

The unjust judge said, "Because this woman troubleth me, I will avenge her"—not because he considered the righteousness of her cause, but to be rid of her. To this day the same man in every man often does what a woman wants him to do, not because he ought to do it, but because he understands her and knows this is the only way to be rid of her, "lest by her continual coming she weary me." A woman can weary a man sooner by demanding justice of him than if she asked anything else, because he knows exactly how importunate she is.

If men admitted the truth once and for all, that they do understand women, they would be forced by their own confession to act up to their enlightenment, or be stultified before the bar of their own conscience. This would precipitate the greatest revolution in the history of man (there is no history of woman!). He would be compelled to provide a place for her commensurate with his by changing all the laws he has made, forms of government, social and economic conditions, and his own standards of morals. It is easier to keep on pretending that he does not understand her.

He hails her as the sweet goddess of charming mysteries by way of throwing dust in the eyes of the goddess, not because he really regards her as mysterious. And he has practised this method so long, for so many, many centuries, that he has finally convinced woman herself that she is a vague, amorphous creature not yet sufficiently evolved from the unknown for it to be possible to understand her. So she takes it out on him by being "importunate." She wants this or that. She is always wanting something. And she has learned that she can get it, not by demanding intelligent justice, but by "troubling" him.

Still, she has her moments of suspicion, when weeping or some lightning flash of anger clears the dust from her eyes. She knows then that she is not the cryptic, smiling sphinx of his romantic protestations, but that generous fool who shared too graciously the first fruit of knowledge with him in the Garden. She took one bite and gave him the rest

because it was "good." She should have eaten it all. The uneven division has been bad for her ever since, gave him the advantage in wisdom and this matter of understanding.

"Why, oh! why, then, doesn't he understand *me?*" she is forever complaining.

He does, my dear. He only pretends ignorance. He knows your frantic uprisings and despairing down sittings, your little east from your farther west. He knows early in the morning whether your weather will be fair or cloudy that day. He knows by that pale mewing face of yours before you suspect your own intentions that you will make him and yourself and the cat unhappy that day, because you are feeling for some reason so keenly the sorrow of being misunderstood. But not for worlds would he relieve the tension by saying:

"I understand, my dear, exactly how it feels to be a woman with the zodiac of your emotions scattered to the four winds."

He knows when you are getting ready to raise your banner and lead a world movement, knew it long before you did.

First, you study Browning because you are not understood. This pulls the neck of your soul, by the pain of which you discover that something is wrong. And when something is wrong it is bound to be man, and, if it is man, Browning is not equal to your emergency. Forthwith you discard him, all poets, and study "social unrest," economics, parliamentary law, until you find that you are the victim of it all. Then comes your World Movement, tramping up Fifth Avenue or some other avenue—and that is as far as it gets. You can move the world three times over without moving man once. You must get back home in time for dinner, to make sure that everything is in order, comfortable for *him.* He knows that, understands you perfectly, and your little rubber string excursion. And he is not troubled, because, bless you, you've got to come back home to him. And he is so stupid. You are obliged to forgive him for not understanding how it is with you.

This is the strength of his position; woman absolves him from his responsibility by accepting his solemnly reiterated excuse of his inability to comprehend her. You cannot hold an idiot responsible. He understands that. Besides, to feel that, as

a woman, one is incomprehensible, appeals to the vanity. He understands that point, too. It is shrewdly taken.

The rub comes here: women really do *not* understand men. Not only that, but they literally crave to be deceived by men. The one perfectly happy woman, if such a being exists, is the one who is in complete ignorance of man. This is, from his point of view, an exceedingly satisfactory state for her.

No one ever heard of a man who has past the sophomoric stage of personal revelations, when he has nothing to reveal but his adolescence, who ever complained because women do not understand him. On the contrary, if they did, he would feel that some violence had been done him, and he would immediately change his disguise.

If women gave more attention to the study of man, less to his representations of himself, of his laws and standards and all the other dust he stirs up to conceal himself, his motives and purposes, from her—there would be something doing in the world. He is not a rogue, nor a criminal, nor selfish, nor mean, he is simply the one sex there is in the human or any other specie. And you cannot get around that with all the thinking and doing that can be thought or done. This is the secret which explains the whole phenomenon of man, including woman. So far it has never been acknowledged nor recognized.

Women know much about him. They know what he likes and does not like, how far they can "trouble" him, and when to stop. But at last this outside, incidental knowledge amounts to nothing, no more than knowing his food, habits, and the measure of his clothes. For they do not know *him,* nor recognize him as the other part of themselves. This is a mistake which he never makes. Whenever he considers woman, he is himself the standard, and he considers her only in relation to himself, what he needs, what he will have of her, more particularly what she cannot give and what he does not want of her, and nothing else.

This is why things are as they are. Men do understand women, and women do not understand men. If the order is ever changed, then men will do it, and the women will not do it, because they do not grasp and will not admit that mastering phenomenon of the one sex.

The Valley, Georgia

SHALL THE UNITED STATES OWN THIS HARBOR?

THE HARBOR OF CHARLOTTE AMALIE IN THE ISLAND OF ST. THOMAS IS ONE OF THE MOST BEAUTIFUL AND CONVENIENT IN THE WEST INDIES. THIS VIEW IS TAKEN FROM BLACKBEARD'S CASTLE, A PIRATE STRONGHOLD. IN THE HARBOR MAY BE SEEN A HAMBURG-AMERICAN LINER, CAUGHT HERE BY THE OUTBREAK OF THE WAR. RECENT LABOR TROUBLES IN THESE DANISH ISLANDS HAVE CAUSED RENEWED TALK OF A SALE TO THIS COUNTRY. SEE EDITORIAL COMMENT

COURAGE, MON VIEUX!

HOW ADRIENNE, OF PROVENCE, REVEALED THE SPIRIT OF FRANCE

BY HENRY G. DODGE

IT was there at the station in Marseilles that we saw the thing which shall surely live longest in our memories, which—more than all the battlefields and hospitals in France—brought us face to face with the realization of what war really costs.

As we drove up we found the square packed with waiting ambulances and automobiles driven by soldier chauffeurs. A number of the *grands blessés*, or the badly wounded, had just arrived from Geneva by way of Lyons, and were being unloaded here for distribution thruout Provence. They were a part of the great exchange of crippled prisoners that is continually going on between France and Germany, thru the intermediary of neutral Switzerland. Tho entirely recovered, no one of them will ever fight again, for it is only the hopelessly crippled who are exchanged.

We stood by the station entrance and watched them cross the narrow platform to the line of ambulances backed up to the curb. They came out of the door, a pitiful company, a hundred strong, and each man had lost a leg or an arm. Behind those who were walking or hobbling on crutches or canes came a line of wheel chairs with those who had lost both legs; and behind them—the blind.

I DO not know if other wars have left in their wake so much of that most hopeless of afflictions—blindness, but it is the most terrible and impressive result of this war. A dozen of these poor sightless heroes, each supported by two orderlies, came thru the door of the station, out into the sunlit square. They felt the warm glow of the Provencal autumn, but they would never see its brilliance again. Their Provence, the "Empire of the Sun" as its children love to call it, could now only give to them its soft airs, its familiar sounds, and the warmth of its summer days. The brilliance of its mornings and the beauties of its nights, its rugged Alps and its lordly Rhône, and the sparkling blue of its Mediterranean, are to be no more for them.

The waiting crowd, silent and with uncovered heads, as if at mass, made a lane thru which the blind soldiers came. They stumbled over the flagging and down the steps with groping feet, and always, tho the order-lies guided them by the arms, their hands were stretched before them, open wide; hopeless, hesitating hands, distrustful of the dark.

The last in line was a handsome boy not over twenty-one, a sub-lieutenant of the Chasseurs d'Afrique. His fair hair was pushed back from his forehead by the black bandage over his eyes, his red fez was tipped to one side by another dressing on his head—and his right sleeve was empty. And tho there glittered on his breast the Military Medal and the Cross of the Legion of Honor, pinned there when he had crost the Swiss border into France, he was trembling over and over and over, "J'ai peur, j'ai peur, j'ai peur"—"I'm afraid, I'm afraid, I'm afraid." France had given him all she could—but he was afraid of the dark.

AND then that happened which changed the whole gruesome picture of horror and misery into something sublime.

A girl stepped out of the crowd to the boy's side, put her arm about his waist, and took his groping hand in hers. She was no more than sixteen, beautiful with the dark, splendid, Greek beauty of the women of Provence—a girl of the people, who looked as tho she might have come into Marseilles that day from the country with her cartload of garden truck.

"Courage, mon vieux," we heard her say, and the boy could feel, I am sure, the smile in her voice; even tho he could not see, as we could, her smiling and compassionate eyes. "Do not have fear. Let me walk with you."

The orderly saluted and unhesitatingly stepped aside. The boy turned his bandaged eyes toward the girl and, as he felt the protecting arm about his waist and the strong hand closing over his, his trembling ceased, his shoulders went back, and what had been a terrified child became a soldier again. It was the woman's touch that he had been needing—the hand and the word of encouragement of a woman of his own France—during the agonizing days in the hospital, and the long terrifying train journey in the darkness.

"Courage, mon vieux!" It was the spur to make him a soldier again. One does not show fear before a woman. He took the few steps across the pavement to the waiting ambulance with steady and confident feet, his head turned always toward the sound of the voice at his side, and as he walked he smiled into the girl's face. How long it had been since he had smiled!

They came to the curb; and as she released his arm and an orderly stood ready to guide his foot to the step of the ambulance, he turned to the girl and paused a moment, with trembling lips. He raised his hand half way to the salute, and stopped.

"What do you call yourself, my friend?" he said.

"Adrienne, my lieutenant," she replied softly, still smiling. There was no trace of coquetry in her voice or in her bearing. She stood, slim and straight, before him, like a soldier before his superior officer.

The boy whipped off the red fez from his blond head and tucked it under the empty sleeve pinned to his breast. His hand went out and found her shoulder, as she instinctively stepped nearer to him, a look of incredulous wonder upon her uplifted face.

"Merci, Adrienne," he said huskily, and bent and kissed her upon both cheeks.

THE little peasant drew herself up like a queen, but her eyes were full of tears and for a moment she could not speak. Then, tremblingly but proudly:

"Merci, mon lieutenant."

Her hands were clasped together upon her breast and on her face was the look of Jeanne d'Arc standing before the Vision. The boy took his seat in the ambulance and as it swung away from the curb his hand went to the salute, and his bandaged eyes turned toward the spot where she was standing. And until the car disappeared into the traffic beyond the station gates we could still see his erect figure and his hand raised to his forehead.

The girl stood motionless, looking after him, until he was out of sight, her face transfigured and her dark eyes still brilliant with tears. She had not been kissed; she had been decorated, and she wore the red badge of her glory in her flaming cheeks as proudly as the blind boy soldier wore the red ribbon of the Legion of Honor upon his breast.

M. William Shak-Ipeare:

EIGHT PAPERS BY FREDERICK HOUK LAW
IN OBSERVANCE OF THE THREE HUNDREDTH
ANNIVERSARY OF SHAKESPEARE'S DEATH

The Tragedies: Plays of Romance and War

HAKESPEARE was no exception to the truth pronounced in "The Two Gentlemen of Verona," that "Experience is by industry achieved and perfected by the swift course of time." He gained his success not by genius alone, but also by work—hard and patient work that, by repeated trials, made way for him to the hights of tragic power. If some one had asked him how he had gained the ability to write "Hamlet," "Othello," "King Lear" and "Macbeth," he might have answered in the words of one of his characters: "I have labored with all my wits, my pains and strong endeavors." Shakespeare's great tragedies, masterpieces in the world's literature, were not produced without preliminary attempts at tragic writing. The surprizing excellence of his first efforts is strong evidence of his natural genius.

Between the ages of twenty-four and thirty-one Shakespeare wrote in "Romeo and Juliet" a passionate tragedy of youth; in "Titus Andronicus" a terrible tragedy of blood; and in "Henry VI," Part I, Part II, and Part III, "Richard II," "Richard III," and "King John," a series of chronicle plays that concern the romantic tragedies of great English rulers. All these plays, in spite of great story interest, put the emphasis on character, pointing the way toward the searching character analysis of the great tragedies. To Shakespeare, even in the beginning of his dramatic work, men appeared as more than puppets tossed about by fate; in part, at least, they were makers of their own destinies.

There is a kind of character in thy life,
That to the observer doth thy history
Fully unfold.

In some respects "Romeo and Juliet" is the most pleasing of all of Shakespeare's tragedies. It is a play of summer, and youth, and love, a play of misty moonlit nights in medieval Verona, with the breath of roses blowing over old gardens, telling:

How silver-sweet sound lovers' tongues
    by night,
Like softest music to attending ears.

and at another time saying

Violent delights have violents ends
And in their triumph die.

Romeo, a Montague, falls in love with Juliet, a Capulet, between whose family and his own there is deadly enmity. On the heads of this "pair of star-cross'd lovers" fall the baneful results of their parents' discords. Shakespeare wrote this play of love and rapid action with all the poetry of youth, for he himself was then less than twenty-seven. Interested as he was in unfolding a romantic story, he did not fail to make his characters real. In Juliet particularly he presented an altogether charming example of womanly love, forethought, faithfulness and daring.

"Titus Andronicus" is so different from "Romeo and Juliet" that we are glad to believe that Shakespeare had hardly any part in writing it. In place of romantic imagination and rich poetry there is a series of shocking events, with little attempt to fasten attention on anything but gruesome detail. Nowhere else in Shakespeare can we read of such deeds of horror as those enacted by the Roman general, Titus Andronicus, in revenge for wrongs done to his daughter Lavinia. Undoubtedly Shakespeare, when about twenty-five years old, felt the attraction of an old tragedy of vivid action, and recast it for his company. The play as a whole is strikingly different from the rest of Shakespeare's tragedies, but here and there, like glittering jewels on black velvet, there stand out against the dark background of crime some passages that are wholly typical of Shakespeare:

The hunt is up, the morn is bright and
    grey,
The fields are fragrant, and the woods
    are green.
The birds chant melody on every bush;
The snake lies rolled in the cheerful
    sun;

The green leaves quiver with the cooling wind,
And make a chequer'd shadow on the ground.

It is far easier to think that the young man who had just come down into London from the country peace of Stratford wrote such lines as these than it is to think that he wrote of the heartlessness of cruel Tamora, or of the fiendish revenge of Titus Andronicus.

"Romeo and Juliet" is a tragedy of love; "Titus Andronicus" is a tragedy of blood; and "Henry VI," Part I, Part II, and Part III, "Richard II," "Richard III," and "King John," are tragedies of history. In Shakespeare's time, because England was thrilling with sense of national greatness, the history play was widely popular. Men had strong interest in hearing of the great deeds of their fellow-countrymen, and, in particular, of the lives of noblemen and kings, the nation's leaders in times of crisis. They knew that in such men the common ideals of their people were crystallized. They felt that the lives of the great represented humanity in magnified form. In the triumph or the tragedy of the nobility the common people found their own best souls. Royalty might represent all that is ideal, and right to kingship might rest upon the possession of

The king-becoming graces,
As justice, verity, temperance, stableness,
Bounty, perseverance, mercy, loveliness,
Devotion, patience, courage, fortitude.

In stories of the rise or the fall of kings the people of Shakespeare's time were, in reality, considering the rise or the fall of humanity, as it keeps true to ideals or swerves from them.

They found an especial pathos in the fact that kings, great as they were, had no escape from common ills.

Within the hollow crown
That rounds the mortal temples of a
    king,
Keeps Death his court, and there the
    antic sits,
Scoffing his state and grinning at his
    pomp.

382

EDMUND KEAN AS RICHARD III

THE ELDER KEAN (1787-1833) WAS THE OUTSTANDING SHAKESPEAREAN ACTOR OF THE FIRST HALF OF THE NINETEENTH CENTURY. HIS FIRST
APPEARANCE AT DRURY LANE WAS IN 1814, AND BYRON, WHO SAW HIM IN THIS ROLE THAT YEAR, WROTE A FERVID
APPRECIATION OF HIS ACTING. COLERIDGE SAID THAT TO SEE HIM ACT WAS LIKE "READING SHAKESPEARE
BY FLASHES OF LIGHTNING." HIS SON, CHARLES KEAN, PLAYED SHAKESPEARE AFTER 1850

Allowing him a breath, a little scene,
To monarchize, be fear'd and kill with
   looks,
Infusing him with self and vain conceit,
As if this flesh which walls about our
   life
Were brass impregnable.

They found consolation for their own humbler lives by considering the responsibilities and misfortunes of kingship, that led Henry IV to say, "Uneasy lies the head that wears a crown." They would hear to the full the story of royalty so that their own lives might catch something of the national greatness, and gain satisfaction in lowliness.

Let us sit upon the ground,
And tell sad stories of the death of
   kings:—
How some have been depos'd, some
   slain in war,
Some haunted by the ghosts they have
   depos'd,
Some poison'd by their wives, some
   sleeping kill'd,
All murder'd.

They would know the irony of greatness, the king living in seeming happiness,

His viands sparkling in a golden cup,
His body couched in a curious bed,
When care, mistrust, and treason waits
   on him.

Beside this they would place the happiness of some care-free humble life, such as that of the shepherd who has

His cold, thin drink out of his leathern
   bottle,
His wonted sleep under a fresh tree's
   shade,
All which secure and sweetly he enjoys.

It was a great day for London, and for English literature, when Shakespeare, at about the age of twenty-seven, united with some other dramatists in writing three plays on the life and times of Henry VI. The writers had the practical aim of giving dramatic life to old material. Taking some earlier plays on the same subject they made them over, adding reality, power and beauty. The first play tells of the brave deeds of Talbot and the English lords fighting in that French war in which Joan of Arc played so great a part. The play is highly patriotic and full of the strong spirit shown in old Talbot's account of the death of his son:

When he perceived me shrink and on
   my knee,
His bloody sword he brandish'd o'er
   me,
And, like a hungry lion, did commence
Rough deeds of rage and stern impa-
   tience;
But when my angry guardant stood
   alone,
Tendering my ruin and assail'd of none,
Dizzy-eyed fury and great rage of
   heart
Suddenly made him from my side to
   start
Into the clustering battle of the
   French;

And in that sea of blood my boy did
   drench
His over-mounting spirit, and there
   died!

The second play tells of the overthrow of the powerful Duke of Gloucester; of the tragic love story of Queen Margaret and the Duke of Suffolk; and of Jack Cade's rebellion. It is far more spirited than the first, and far more interesting in its characterization. Eleanor, Duchess of Gloucester, is not unlike Lady Macbeth in unscrupulous ambition; and Queen Margaret, with her jealousy and passion, is a memorable character.

The third play concerns the wicked deeds of Richard, Duke of Gloucester, afterward Richard III, and more particularly his murder of King Henry. The fiendish and courageous Queen Margaret is in strong contrast with the weak king, who creeps from the battle and moans, "Would I were dead! if God's good will were so!" Such plays as these, with vivid stories of heroic action, must have taken London by storm. They were a triumph for the young Shakespeare just entering upon his dramatic career.

"Richard II" tells another tragedy of history. The strong, self-willed, ambitious Bolingbroke—a man of action and genuine power—takes the throne from the unscrupulous dreamer, Richard II. The play has much manly spirit and an ardent patriotism, as well as far more poetry than appears in most of the historical plays.

"Richard III" and "King John" have great dramatic interest because of strong characterization. In somewhat leaving the method of the chronicle and centering all attention on some one powerful character each play approaches the method of the great tragedies. Richard III, putting himself against society, wages a titanic battle against the forces of right. Hated and deformed, he outwits his enemies and send them, one by one, to bloody deaths until, at last, he rises to royalty. Giant as he is in intellect, he is no match for the

BOOKS FOR FURTHER READING

W. H. Fleming: How to Study Shakespeare; A. H. Tolman: Questions on Shakespeare; A. T. Quiller-Couch: Historical Tales from Shakespeare; C. S. Terry: Shakespeare the Historian; B. E. Warner: English History in Shakespeare's Plays; A. S. G. Canning: Thoughts on Shakespeare's Historical Plays; W. D. Briggs: The Chronicle History, a Study in Dramatic Development; S. Davey: The Relation of Poetry to History, with Special Reference to Shakespeare's Historical Plays; J. C. Collins: Studies in Shakespeare; W. G. Boswell-Stone: Shakespeare's Holinshed.

stern forces of retribution, chief of which is that inner force so strongly shown in Macbeth. In the midst of battle it is not man he fears, but himself:

My conscience hath a thousand several
   tongues,
And every tongue brings in a several
   tale,
And every tale condemns me for a
   villain.

"King John" is another history play of direct purpose and strong characterization. John, having stolen his throne, makes a hopeless effort to keep it against his enemies. Once again Shakespeare shows that evil can never gain lasting power, and that conscience, if nought else, brings sure punishment. King John, in mental agony, says:

My nobles leave me; and my state is
   braved,
Even at my gates, with ranks of foreign
   powers:
Nay, in the body of this fleshly land,
This kingdom, this confine of blood and
   breath,
Hostility and civic tumult reigns
Between my conscience and my cousin's
   death.

In this play are three of Shakespeare's most notable characters: John, with contemptible meanness of spirit; Constance, with beautiful mother-love; and Faulconbridge, scorning baseness, and showing English dash and patriotic ardor that undoubtedly represents Shakespeare's ideal of a noble man of action. Powerful in conception, dramatic in arrangement, realistic in its characters, and touching in its pathos, "King John" is without doubt one of the greatest of Shakespeare's plays.

Shakespeare had probably sketched "Henry VIII" before his retirement to Stratford, but he left its completion to John Fletcher. The play that we have is a series of spectacular incidents showing pompous court life. Its theme is highly appealing, for it shows the pathos of earthly greatness. The dignified and noble Queen Katharine is driven from the King's side, and the rich, cunning and ambitious Cardinal Wolsey falls from power, saying nobly:

Had I but served my God with half the
   zeal
I served my king, he would not in mine
   age
Have left me naked to mine enemies.

"Romeo and Juliet," "Titus Andronicus," and the history plays—so many "Mirrors for Kings"—show Shakespeare's interest in tragic story largely for the story's sake. They show, most of all, his certain development toward searching analysis of the inner nature. They are the stepping stones by which he advanced toward ability to produce the great tragedies.

Our Increasing Population

Census Bureau experts estimate that the population of the United States on January 1 was 101,208,315, and that by July 1 next will be 102,017,302. On July 1 last year they figured the population at 100,399,318.

On the basis of the rate of increase between the 1900 and the 1910 censuses the bureau estimates that there is an increase of 808,997 in the population of the United States every six months, or an annual increase of 1,617,994. The census estimate is that the population of the country is increasing at the rate of 4433 a day—184 every hour and 3 1-15 persons every minute.

Western states have led in growth, Washington heading the list, with Oklahoma, Nevada, North Dakota, and New Mexico following in the order named.

Forward to the Land

An organization to get people out of the cities by teaching them how to make farming both profitable and pleasant, and by establishing them in coöperative agricultural colonies thruout the country, is the Forward-to-the-Land League, which has its headquarters in New York City.

It has opened evening classes in gardening, poultry-raising, dairying, etc., in many of the large cities, where experts are prepared to give unbiased advice regarding location and the purchase or rental of land to any who are genuinely interested. At present a large tract of land in Florida is open for inspection and land-owners in many other states have declared their willingness to equip for colonization according to the high standards recommended by the League.

Emphasis is continually put on the necessity of colonization. The small individual farm has proved over and over again that it does not pay, since it cannot command adequate marketing facilities. Co-operative management of fifty farms as a business unit, with an agricultural instructor and a market expert, is the League's advice.

The new type of rural school, with ten-acre garden and auditorium for social activities of the "grown-ups" is stipulated; and a rural Y. M. C. A. secretary and an engineer

Underwood & Underwood

A MOTOR BOAT FOR ICE

This ice-boat, equipped with an aeroplane drive motor, was shown at the St. Paul Outdoor Sports Carnival. It is capable of much higher speed than the usual type of sloop-rigged ice-boat, which is dependent on the wind for its power

from the department of sanitary survey are sent with each colony.

Dr. Thomas Nixon Carver, professor of Rural Economics at Harvard University, has just accepted the directorship of rural organization in the League. He plans to visit each colony long

A FIRE-ESCAPE FOR HORSES

© *International Film Service*

WHEN A FIRE BURNS THE CORD WHICH RUNS UNDER THE WINDOWS, THE LEVERS DROP, THE FIRE ALARM SOUNDS, AND——

© *International Film Service*

THE DOORS OPEN AND THE HORSES RUN OUT

enough to get it in good working order. The plan sounds Utopian, but it has already shown its practicability to some extent.

A Fire Drill for Horses

By means of an arrangement of levers, invented by John Batty, of Los Angeles, horses are not only given a chance to escape when their stable catches fire, but they are actually taught how to do it.

The stables are built so that the horses are all headed toward the doors, which, of course, swing outward.

The invention works on the theory that any dangerous fire would burn the fusible cord stretched along the top of the doors and thereby release the levers which it holds in place. When these levers drop they throw open the doors of the stalls.

In order to make the horses take advantage of their automatic release a terrific clanging of gongs sounds an alarm as soon as the doors open. The noise is supposed to frighten the horses into running away from it, and consequently from the fire.

As yet no real fire has tested the invention. But at the Cudahy estate in Los Angeles, where the apparatus has been installed, there have been several fire drills in which both machinery and horses have done their part to perfection.

An Egyptian Tomb in New York

Perneb, a high dignitary of the Egyptian court, lived some 4000 years too early to spend his money in New York. So he built a costly tomb, near the royal pyramid in the cemetery of Memphis, stocked it with provisions and decorated it as a worthy dwelling place for his body and a memorial to his name.

Thru the centuries it has been successively a monument, a storehouse, a robbers' cave, a quarry, and now a Fifth avenue residence—erected in the north end of the entrance hall of the Metropolitan Museum.

It is the first Egyptian tomb to be so perfectly transplanted and reconstructed. The colors of the decorations are still bright and most of the stones are whole. On the outer walls, on either side of the entrance, are colored portraits of Perneb, and inside, his statue, carved

385

Feature Photo Service
AN ELEVATOR IN THE ALPS

from cedar. It was the belief of those days that if the body were removed from the tomb the soul would be lost, but a chance of rehabilitation was given it if it chose to enter the statue.

Outside the real tomb, as it stands in the Museum, is a miniature reproduction which shows the complete structure in detail. The tomb proper, containing the sarcophagus, was sunk in the rock over fifty feet below the building. Originally it was covered with circular blocks of stone and tightly sealed.

In the superstructure is the chapel, or offering chamber, covered with elaborate pictures of the offerings and representing the earthly pleasures and activities of the owner. This chamber opens on the main entrance, but at right angles to it, so as to elude the evil spirits.

Near it, and entirely inaccessible, is the secret statue chamber or "serdab," into which only the spirit of the deceased was supposed to enter.

As it stands in the Metropolitan Museum the inner walls of Perneb's tomb are all protected by glass and lighted from above. It is the gift of Edward S. Harkness, one of the trustees of the Museum.

For Smaller Electrical Machines

By the use of a new material, discovered at the Engineering Experiment Station of the University of Illinois, many electrical machines in common use may be made smaller and more compact without sacrificing strength or power capacity. The material is a compound of silicon and iron produced by fusing in a vacuum, a process which effectually eliminates all impurities in the iron and makes it possible to procure an alloy of exact porportions.

The magnetic permeability of the new material, or the ease with which it may be magnetized electrically, is

ten to fifteen times greater than that of commercial iron or steel now employed, while its hysteresis loss, or the electric energy which must be supplied in order to reverse its magnetism, is only one-eighth as great. In dynamos, transformers, loading coils in telephone circuits, electrical testing machinery and ,numerous other electrical machines, the new vacuum alloy will make possible economies in cost and size, and will increase the range of usefulness of such machinery.

T. D. Yensen, the discoverer of the new material, is a Norwegian by birth. He is a Research Assistant Professor at the University of Illinois. The experiments leading to the discovery have occupied a period of nearly three years.

Going Up!

The Bürgenstock Hotel, overlooking Lake Lucerne, is perched on the top of a cliff, 2880 feet above sea level. And the nearest railroad station is on the shore of the lake—nearly 1500 feet below.

Making connections is obviously difficult. A road is impossible and airships rather expensive. But the missing link has finally been forged in the shape of an enormous lift, standing straight out from the edge of the cliff and fastened to it at intervals by framework and bridges. It is run by electricity and the cage is suspended by cables which run over a pulley at the top.

The schedule of trips is adapted to the railroad time-table. The elevator leaves "on arrival of connections" or whenever there is a special demand for its service. It is run primarily for the convenience of the Hotel Bürgenstock.

Probably it is the only elevator in the world which combines esthetic pleasure with utility. As an observation tower it offers a panoramic view of the Swiss lakes and surrounding country that is almost as perfect as that from an aeroplane.

Information by Machinery

A mechanical directory, the object of which is to convey information concerning leading business and professional men and companies in one city to persons who happen to be situated in another, has been invented by William C. Cutler, of Los Angeles, California. Its

operation and the results to be obtained from this device are unique.

For instance, should a person be located in the northern part of California and desire the address of and information concerning a business and professional man in Los Angeles, all that person would need do would be to step on the platform, turn the pointer to the word "Los Angeles," and push the dial button. Instantly the large directory card representing Los Angeles would appear under the glass front of the card space. By simply remaining on the platform the operator retains the directory card before him, but the moment he takes his weight from the platform the card is automatically returned to its original position within the lower part of the case.

This case is about six feet high, two feet wide and a foot thick. Its display space is 18x22 inches, which permits the insertion of names, addresses and information concerning several hundred business men in each city.

Not only can this device be used in the manner herewith described, but it may profitably be used in connection with banks, newspaper offices, business establishments, etc. It takes a weight of but thirty pounds upon the platform to operate the machine, and its operation, after the button is prest, is practically instantaneous. Any number of cards from one to a hundred may be placed in the machine at one time.

Albert Marple
INFORMATION WHILE YOU WEIGHT

HOW TREE PLAYS SHAKESPEARE

BY MONTROSE J. MOSES

AUTHOR OF "FAMOUS ACTOR-FAMILIES OF AMERICA," "THE AMERICAN DRAMATIST"

SINCE 1887, Sir Herbert Tree has been one of the leading actor-managers of London. He has produced various plays of a melo-dramatic and romantic character, varying all the way from "Jim, the Penman," "Partners" and "Captain Swift" to "Fedora," "Trilby," "The Musketeers and "The Darling of the Gods." When he leased the Hay-market Theater, he produced Maeter-linck's "The·Intruder," won success in Ibsen's "The Enemy of the Peo-ple," and gave a spirited revival of Wilde's "A Woman of No Impor-tance." But his greatest claim to recognition was the standard of his Shakespearean productions.

When he visited America some twenty years ago, he was known to the play-going world as Mr. H. Beerbohm Tree. Since that time, the London public has come to regard him almost as a national institution, and for his great services to the art of the theater he has been knighted, adding another name to the list of titled actors, including Forbes-Rob-ertson, John Hare, and George Alex-ander.

Sir Herbert comes to New York now, for a season beginning March 14, as an exponent of no "new" art, but as the upholder of a generous policy started in years gone by by Charles Kean, and brought to such extravagant perfection by the late Sir Henry Irving. Instead of offer-ing, during his Tercentenary season of Shakespeare here in America startling examples of "new" scenery, where decoration and symbolism play a large part; instead of show-ing himself to be under the same spell as that which prompted Mr. Granville Barker last season to give his fantastic setting of "Midsummer Night's Dream"; he brings with him a solidly, splendidly pictured pageant of "Henry VIII," and equally color-ful productions of "Richard II," "The Merchant of Venice," and "The Merry Wives of Windsor."

If Sir Herbert had done nothing more than present Shakespeare fair-ly well, he would have gained some reputation for the mere fact that he had had sufficient courage and con-viction to appear in seventeen of the plays. But in all of these productions he scored because of the beauty of the scene and the excellence of the acting. Supporters of the Eliza-bethan Stage Society registered com-plaint that Mr. Tree was smothering Shakespeare in unnecessary para-phernalia. They urged that one should present Shakespeare simply and crudely as he was given in Eliza-bethan days.

Such a claim was a challenge to Sir Herbert, and then and there be-gan a battle of words which has been carried on ever since. If we consult Miss Ellen Terry's charming "Mem-oirs," we will find mention of Tree's production of "The Merry Wives of Windsor," where she asserts that the actor-manager spent most of his time inventing "new" business of a humorous character for herself and for Mrs. Kendal. This is one of the ways in which Mr. Tree revivifies Shakespeare for modern audiences. He does not believe in becoming a slave to convention; he scouts any idea of becoming either archeological or academic. What he strives for is illusion, and he has declared more than once that he has taken his cue from Shakespeare's own stage direc-tions. He spares no expense in order to gain truth in atmosphere and gorgeousness in spectacle.

Most of his productions, since he built for himself a theater which he calls "His Majesty's," have been on a stupendous scale. He likes to strive for pictorial effect. That, in all prob-ability, attracted him to the late

SIR HERBERT AS CARDINAL WOLSEY

Stephen Phillips, whose "Nero" and "Ulysses" he gave in magnificent fashion. London theatergoers have become so used to his extravagance that when he appears in anything slight, they regard it as unworthy of him.

Like his brother, Max Beerbohm, who succeeded Bernard Shaw as dra-matic critic on *The Saturday Review,* Sir Herbert Tree possesses a facile pen, and in his book, "Thoughts and Afterthoughts," he is not only epigrammatic regarding life in gen-eral, but he is very pronounced in his declarations regarding the way in which Shakespeare should be pro-duced. He says:

The public of today demands that, if acted at all, Shakespeare shall be pre-sented with all the resources of the theater of our time—that he shall be treated, not as a dead author, speaking a dead language, but as a living force speaking with the voice of a living humanity.

He is frank in his confession that tho he has been extravagant in his preparations, every production of his has been profitable. After he had been attacked for his realism in "The Tempest," he came forth with a dec-laration that of all Shakespeare's plays demanding the resources of the modern stage, this was the most ex-acting. He showed in an analytical paper how the stage directions in the play called for even more detail than he was capable of supplying. But, as an "Afterthought," he added that the tendency toward simplicity is the modern demand, and he has found that in his performance of "Hamlet," for example, he can get more sugges-tive effects by the use of simple cur-tains than by cluttering the stage with unnecessary trappings for pic-torial interest. In other words, the stage is now groping toward spirit-ual effects, or moods.

"Henry VIII," which has not been seen in America for many a year, will be done by Sir Herbert, who plays Wolsey in the Irving style; there will be no Urban, Reinhardt or Gordon Craig concessions. Mr. Tree embroiders his pictures; his is a taste that tries to suggest what oth-ers would leave to the imagination. Without discounting the modern au-dience, he has always held that the present age is not as fresh as the Elizabethan in its power to conjure up a scene mentally and requires a setting as rich as the lines suggest. Of course to this he adds his per-sonality as an actor. Even as Irving used to cast his plays to the highest

387

point of excellence, so does Sir Herbert. As an actor-manager, he tries to overcome the prejudice against his "species," where everyone believes that a play is pared and shifted about until the whole substance of it falls upon the shoulders of the "star." But the very fact that as his opening bill he has selected "Henry VIII," with all its pageantry, is measure of his taste; undoubtedly he will go down in English dramatic history as the successor of Irving. It is his love for spectacle, no doubt, among other things, that induced him to come to America, and to appear in a gigantic moving-picture production of "Macbeth"—a production which in scope and pictorial splendor will vie with "The Birth of a Nation."

Put his portrait gallery in a row —the lean, tall figure of Svengali (for Sir Herbert is over six feet in hight), the crouching devilish person of Fagin, the majestic austerity of Wolsey, the sensuous insolence of Nero, the coxcombery of Malvolio, the military bearing of Colonel Newcome—were it not for the fact that in whatever he undertakes, Sir Herbert has a mannerism of voice which betrays him as one and the same person, he would be the foremost character actor of his time. As it is, not only do his productions vie with Royal Academy canvases, but he himself, in bearing and in gesture, shows how uppermost in his mind is the pictorial effect. And he claims that his palette is the identical one Shakespeare would have used had he been alive today. Thus does he brave the Elizabethan Stage Society, and the modern movement of which Gordon Craig was virtually the founder.

New York City

"Mexico for the Mexicans." Serves them right.—*Chattanooga News.*

It's to be "America first" if we are to make America last.—*Philadelphia North American.*

A politician's idea of a demagog is a man who is making a bigger hit with the public than he is.—*Boston Transcript.*

"How much are your four-dollar shoes?" asked the smart one.
"Two dollars a foot," replied the salesman, wearily.—*Judge.*

He—"I heard that Griggs wrote that wonderful poem while two cats were fighting outside of his window."
She—"I wonder how he did it."
He—"Probably the mews inspired him."
—*Lampoon.*

Our notion of a careful sweeper is the one employed by the Washington Terminal, Washington, D. C. Among the articles found, a list of which appears in the *Washington Post*, is "1 needle."—*New York Tribune.*

Cheerful One (to newcomer, on being asked what the trenches are like)—If yer stands up yer get sniped; if yer keeps down yer gets drowned; if yer moves about yer gets shelled, and if yer stands still yer gets court-martialled for frost-bite.—*Punch.*

EVERY MOMENT
A PLEASANTER
MOMENT ⸗ EVERY
MILE A SMOOTHER
STEADIER MILE ⸗
EVERY HOUR AN HOUR
OF GREATER EASE

THE NEW BOOKS

THE PEACE PROTOCOL

Seventy per cent of the clothing worn by American women is manufactured in New York City. This metropolitan part of the trade is capitalized at $100,000,000 and employs over 100,000 workers. It is largely a Hebrew industry both on the side of employer and employed. It is divided into half a dozen branches. The cloak, suit and skirt branch is the most powerful. In 1910 a great strike took place in this branch. Owing largely to the conciliatory efforts of the great-hearted Boston lawyer, Louis D. Brandeis, the strike was settled. But the chief difficulty arose over the question of the open versus the closed shop. A deadlock ensued. Mr. Brandeis suggested his famous compromise of the preferential union shop. This was finally accepted and in order that the industry might be protected from the recurrence of strikes and lockouts, a trade agreement was entered into, known as the Peace Protocol, which, in our judgment, is the longest step yet taken in the United States toward the goal of industrial peace, and which can be compared in industrial significance only with the Compulsory Arbitration Law of New Zealand and the Compulsory Investigation Act of Canada.

The Protocol was intended to perform four main purposes: First, to raise the general standards of the industry and to make them uniform; second, to strengthen both the Employers' Association and the Union; third, to insure the worker just, reasonable and fair treatment on the part of the employer; and fourth, to inaugurate in the industry the principle of industrial democracy, i. e., to make a beginning of joint control and joint responsibility on the part of both employers and employees in their common enterprise.

The Protocol has been successful beyond expectation. It has had its setbacks and vicissitudes, of course, but it is steadily going ahead. It has now been copied in the dress and waist industry of New York, the clothing and cloak making industries in Chicago, the cloak and dress and waist industries in Boston and in Philadelphia. In New York it was also followed in three other branches of the needle-working industry—the misses and children's wear, wrappers and kimonos, and muslin underwear.

To Mr. Brandeis more than any one else real credit must ever be due for initiating the Protocol. But the men upon whom have devolved the chief burden of working out its provisions are the attorneys for the Manufacturers Association and for the Union. Of these Mr. Julius Henry Cohen, the attorney for the manufacturers, has been the most active and thorogoing. He knows probably better than any one else the history and philosophy of the Protocol, and it is fair to say that his mind has been the constructive force in upholding its manifold provisions.

Accordingly when his volume, *Law and Order in Industry*, came to our desk we were prepared for something unusually good. We were not disappointed. Mr. Cohen has not only given us a history and philosophy of the Protocol, but he offers a constructive plan for the enlargement of its scope that is worth the serious attention of economists and statesmen. And not the least worthy of mention is the fact that Mr. Cohen is the possessor of a literary style that we commend with earnest solicitude to the average brief writer. Consequently we have here an intensely interesting pioneer treatise on a novel and highly significant forward movement in American life that is a credit to American scholarship and industrial statesmanship.

We have not the space to recapitulate Mr. Cohen's thesis, argument or conclusions; suffice it to say his facts are trustworthy, his statements of controversial questions impartial and his inferences in the main sound. The book is a distinct contribution to the science of social relations and as such should have a wide reading both here and abroad.

Law and Order in Industry, by Julius Henry Cohen. Macmillan. $1.60.

CHESTERTONIAN HISTORY

Everybody who likes G. K. Chesterton has wished that he might be induced to follow the example of Charles Dickens and write a Child's History of England. When a literary man of wayward genius undertakes to interpret and record the story of his country the result is almost always worth while. We do not get the white sunlight of impartiality, but we get a beautiful rainbow of prejudices, personal opinions and mystical insight. Chesterton has still to write us a complete English history, but he has dealt faithfully with about a century and a half of it in his latest book, *The Crimes of England*. It is due to him to say that the unhistorical character of the work is caused rather by partizan emphasis than by any inaccuracy of detail. Rarely if ever has Chesterton written with such care for his facts, and, as for his transcendental interpretation of them, he has as much warrant to philosophize as Carlyle or Taine or any other literary historian. But one does tend to get the impression from the book that only Prussians had ever incurred the scriptural curse on him who removes his neighbor's landmark.

For the "crimes of England" are really the crimes of Prussia, and England's guilt is summed up in the phrase that English politics has been devoted ever since the time of Frederick the Great to "the belittlement of France and the gross exaggeration of Germany." Chesterton denounces the part played by his country in the wars of Frederick the Great, in the Napoleonic struggles, in the repression of Ireland, in tolerating Bismarck's schemes of aggrandizement, only to bring into darker relief the wickedness of the state which used England thruout all these years as a catspaw. Yet the indictment of England as Prussia's accomplice is delivered in very sharp terms; so far as Chesterton shows bias it is pro-French or pro-Irish rather than pro-British. He really believes that the war is an epic struggle between the old soul of Christendom, most clearly incarnated in the Roman Catholic nations, and a blast of sinister materialism from the wastes and forests of Brandenburg. In this belief he writes not only seriously, but soberly, as befits the great hour, and concludes his book with a vivid and moving description of the Battle of the Marne which has in it a world of eloquence and no "cleverness" at all.

The Crimes of England, by Gilbert K. Chesterton. Lane. $1.

MODERN FRENCH POETRY

Six French Poets of the great epoch in French literature, which the war brought to its untimely end, are studied, translated, and explained by Amy Lowell in a series of brilliant essays, each prefaced by a portrait of the poet and generously interspersed with quotations of his best work. Miss Lowell's own delightful style and her keenly appreciative comments add much to the pleasure of reading the poems, and her particularly happy translations accomplish the difficult art of keeping the spirit of a French poem in an English dress.

Six French Poets, by Amy Lowell. Macmillan. $2.50.

RELIGION IN INDIA

Professor Pratt of Williams College, author of "The Psychology of Religious Belief," visited India in order to learn at first hand not merely what are the documents on which the religions of India are based but what in actual life is their influence upon their adherents and what is the nature of their religious experience. The fruit of this study is *India and Its Faiths*. He did not avoid the missionaries and foreign teachers, but he sought especially to meet the native representatives of Hinduism, and Buddhism, as well as Mohammedans, Parsees, Jainas and Sikhs. As he studied these religions as one not interested in proselyting, but in their philosophical aspect, he was quick to see their spiritual content and to recognize what is good in them. We have a fair statement here of their doctrinal beliefs but particularly of their influence on life and character. He dwells on the passive side of religious experience, the value of meditation which so far takes the place of that active service which is the

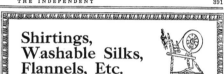

mark of Christianity. He does not dwell on the grosser side of Indian religions, so that one is startled when he comes across a scathing description of the morals of the Brahmin priests. The author discovers the immense influence which Christianity has already had in creating reformed sects, such as the Brahm Somaj and the Adya Somaj. These reformed sects abjure caste and deny the subjection of women. Professor Pratt finds that among the great obstacles to the spread of Christianity are the bad morals of Europeans, and the hateful war which, devastating the world, makes it appear that Christianity is inferior to Buddhism and Hinduism, and the ultra-conservative teachings of many missionaries. The book is well worth careful reading.

India and Its Faiths, a Traveler's Record, by James Bissett Pratt. Houghton, Mifflin. $4.

AUX ARMES

Eric Fisher Wood's book with the somber prophetic title *The Writing on the Wall* is the most important of the later contributions to the momentous question of Preparedness. It is important because its author, tho a layman writing for laymen, has had singular opportunity to know what war is today, for he has traveled freely with the best credentials, a messenger among the warring nations. In America he has conferred with our military and naval authorities and been accepted by them as an expert. In short he is in an unofficial way a spokesman of their views. He appeals for better discipline in army and navy, for immediate supplies of mines, ammunition, armored motors and the like that would be needed to repel an attempted invasion should the kaleidoscope of fate in some quick turn produce one, and he advocates, as do others, the introduction of the Swiss and Australian systems of national defense. In an appendix, Mr. Wood quotes concretely the opinions of many prominent citizens.

If we are unprepared and should be prepared, no doubt we should be thoroly prepared. This is the starting point of General Woodhull; a veteran volunteer of the Civil War. He considers that modern conditions, efficiency and suddenness of attack prohibit reliance on volunteers. Nor does he have confidence in a citizen soldiery as he reads Secretary Garrison's plan. He would increase West Point's capacity from seven hundred men to thirty-six hundred, thereby having officers enough, some in reserve, some in the standing army, whom he would place at 200,000 men, raised and maintained under a conscription system, which he regards as not only necessary and just, but the only possible efficient method. A reserve army of 800,000 would be the natural result. He regards the Panama Canal and the Philippines as danger spots—and it is true that in the splendid isolation of earlier days we had to consider neither.

But while we are thinking of an enlargement of the army, a view of the *U. S. Army from the Inside* comes to us from Van C. Kirkpatrick. It is brief and direct and it scores the army severely for gambling, drunkenness, the Scarlet Woman and laziness. This little pamphlet advocates an army half as large as that we have now, double pay, equality between men and officers and an aroused public conscience. It approves an increase of the National Guard and citizens' training camps. University military training is also suggested to take the place of fees for other tuition. The author was for five years in the army.

The Writing on the Wall; The Nation on Trial, by Eric Fisher Wood. Century. $1. *West Point in Our Next War; The Only Way to Create and to Maintain an Army*, by Maxwell Van Zandt Woodhull. Putnam. $1.25. *The U. S. Army from the Inside*, by Van C. Kirkpatrick, Caldwell, Idaho. 10 cents.

A COWARD WHO DARED

Out of the Great War will come many studies in the psychology of the man under fire. *The Belfry*, by May Sinclair, is a notable one, and it is more than a study of the war in Belgium of which the author writes with sure knowledge, it is also a great novel. Two-thirds of the book is given to making us acquainted with a group of characters, so unusual, so individualized, and so interesting, that we follow them into the war zone with the breathless anxiety of relatives or, at least, of lifelong friends. The central figure, the novelist, Tasker Jevons, who moves heaven and earth to reach the front—just *because* he is afraid to go there—is one of Miss Sinclair's subtlest studies of character. He is by turns, exasperating and lovable; a snob and a genius; a coward and a hero. His incredible courage in Belgium is not more magnificent than his fight against his horror of going there. The man of superior intellect and imagination, who can visualize danger with exceptional vividness, always is at the disadvantage of his qualities, and might well pray to be made stupid when he goes to war. And thru those hurried, incredible war scenes in Belgium, The Belfry of Bruges stands as a symbol of a love that greatly dared, of aspiration, and of ultimate peace between warring nations and riven classes of men.

The Belfry, by May Sinclair. Macmillan. $1.35.

ADVENTURES

White Tiger, by H. M. Rideout, is a tale of the experiences of a lad just out of college, sent by his uncle to the family tin mines of the Dutch East Indies, where follow mysterious adventures in a new setting.

Duffield. $1.

WINTER PLAYGROUNDS

The Lesser Antilles form a pleasure ground within reach but little visited. *The Isles of Spice and Palm*, A. Hyatt Verrill calls them, and describes with enthusiasm the scenery, the quaint customs and the foreign ways of the Barbadoes, of St. Thomas, of Saba, "strangest of all islands," of Trinidad and Surinam, "quaintest spot in America."

Appleton. $1.25.

ANOTHER MESALLIANCE

In *The Strangers' Wedding*, W. L. George forgets that most marriages are just that—the union of two strangers; and with a little more patience and a little more love, his ill-assorted couple might have won happiness, as the majority of married folk do. However the distance between an Oxford man and a London laun-

dress is difficult to bridge, and the readjustments are painful processes of growth and disillusionment. The story is cleverly told and is a subtle satire on the English *mores* it depicts.

Boston: Little, Brown. $1.25.

CAUSES OF PROGRESS

Dr. Lucius M. Bristol's *Social Adaptation* is a very comprehensive survey of the views of modern sociologists in America and Europe who have considered the question of adaptation to the environment as a means to social progress.

Harvard University Press. $2.

FROM POLAND

Tales by Polish Authors, translated by Else Benecke. Sienkiewics is the only one of the four authors represented in this group of powerful, touching stories known to English readers. Two have been Siberian exiles and write of the Siberian life and of the Yakut Indians.

Longmans, Green. $1.25.

THE MOST INTERESTING AMERICAN

For a thoroly attractive description of Theodore Roosevelt, one that will show those who do not admire him the undoubted and powerful charm he has for his friends and followers, read Julian Street's little book, *The Most Interesting American*.

Century. 50 cents.

FAMOUS ACTRESSES

Forest Izard is the author of two books that will attract lovers of the stage, *Sarah Bernhardt, an Appreciation*, is a critical study of her personality and art. *Heroines of the Stage* contains biographical accounts of Rehan, Terry, Marlowe, Adams, Duse and other favorites of this and the last generation.

Sturgis & Walton. 50 cents and $1.50.

POETRY WELL CHOSEN

The Leading English Poets from Chaucer to Browning, edited with introduction, biographies and glossary, by Lucius Hudson Holt, is a rather comprehensive order for one book to fill. By a wise recognition of its own limitations, however, this anthology does succeed in living up to its title. Only the best-known poets of the period are included and an unusually liberal amount of each author's work is given.

Houghton, Mifflin. $2.25.

EVERYMAN'S

The editors of Everyman's Library are amazingly clever in the choice of books that one has wished in vain to find in cheap edition. Among the recent issues in Green's *Short History of the English People*; Margaret, Duchess of Newcastle's *Life of the First Duke of Newcastle*, a quaint and charming classic; and Penn's *Peace of Europe*, which fits the times. Volumes of Gogol, Balzac and Ibsen are added to the fiction and drama series.

Dutton. Cloth 35 cents, leather 75 cents.

HOLLYHOCKS ALL IN A ROW

Here is a wonderful picture book, with superb colored plates interspersed among near two hundred half-tones. *The Beautiful Gardens of America*, by Louise Shelton, is calculated to turn the head of any townswoman. Gardens of the North—as far North as Alaska—South, East and West are framed in evergreens, set by ponds, punctuated by cactus. It is good to see there is such elaborately ordered beauty here and there in this still rough land.

Scribner. $5.

THE DIGESTION OF PROTEIN

Not many years ago food chemists and physiologists were content to lump everything containing nitrogen into one bundle labeled "proteids" and assumed to be of equal value. How much fine research work has been done recently in this field may be seen from Prof. Frank P. Underhill's summary of the results in *The Physiology of the Amino Acids*. It is now probably possible to support life entirely on artificial fats, carbohydrates and amino acids made out of the elements in the laboratory.

Yale University Press. $1.85.

MR. PURINTON'S EFFICIENCY QUESTION BOX

220. Mr. L. S., Michigan. "In your efficiency article for November 22, you tell how to become an efficient optimist. Can you suggest books which would be helpful in cultivating hope, faith, perseverance, independence, courage, and other necessary faculties and qualities of the mind? Also kindly name books for the attainment of health and the banishment of poverty."

There are so many good books for your purpose that we hardly know which to suggest. However, you might start with these: "Health and Happiness," by Bishop Samuel Fallows; "Story of My Life," by Helen Keller; "Pollyanna," by Eleanor H. Porter; "As a Man Thinketh," by James Allen; "Thought Force," by William Walker Atkinson; "Power, Peace and Plenty," by Orison Swett Marden.

Books on health have been cited frequently in these columns. Books for improvement of your finances: "Why I Believe in Poverty," by Edward Bok; "The Book of Thrift," by T. D. MacGregor; "Overcoming Poverty," by Bruce Maclelland. These volumes may all be obtained thru Efficiency Press Syndicate, Woolworth Building, New York.

221. Mr. B. B. T., Maine. "Kindly advise me as to the best course to pursue in my profession. Am graduate in Electrical Engineering; for past three years have been in a machine shop, getting the practical side. But the army is my ambition; have been lieutenant in militia; wonder if I could use my education to better advantage where I am, or should I prepare to qualify for a commission?"

The United States Army has employment for engineers, therefore you should find entrance easier because of your experience. Write the United States Military Academy, West Point, New York, for details of the preparation required of candidates for the army.

But there is not much future—educational, industrial, financial or moral, in the average life of an army officer. The training is fine—but the goal futile. You may be a born soldier; if you are, you belong in the army; otherwise, better stick to your job.

222. Miss H. M. B., Minnesota. "Your articles have interested me very much, and you may be able to help me. I am a college graduate, twenty-five years of age; prepared myself for teaching, but feel that I am not suited for that work. I should like to become a private secretary, but am a poor speller, do not express myself clearly, and do not know how to secure a position as secretary. Please advise me regarding secretarial work."

Addresses of secretarial schools were given October 4, 1915, in reply to Question Box query 160. Why not plan to enter the field of social service? The possibilities for usefulness are very great, and the work would combine tutorial and secretarial activities. Write for details, to the School of Civics and Philanthropy, Michigan avenue, Chicago; the Associated Charities Training School for Social Service, Cleveland, Ohio; the School of Philanthropy, 105 East Twenty-second street, New York.

223. Mrs. A. B. C., Missouri. "I am a woman of forty, have taught, most of my life, am now at the head of the Household Arts Department in a college for young women. There seems to be a demand for this line of work, yet so few heads of schools see the value of good experienced teachers. How can I reach a broader field, and grow to be more useful? I have not been successful in applying thru agencies."

You have a great opportunity right where you are. Find it, and use it. Mrs. Rohrer, Miss Farmer, Mrs. Pattison, Mrs. Frederick, and other women have made themselves national authorities in domestic science—and with poorer chances than you enjoy. Prof. L. B. Allyn of Westfield,

1775   *1916*

We Are Prepared

Within the wide boundaries of our country, embracing more than three million square miles, dwell a hundred million people.

They live in cities, towns, villages, hamlets and remote farms. They are separated by broad rivers, rugged mountains and arid deserts.

The concerted action of this far-flung population is dependent upon a common understanding.

Only by a quick, simple and unfailing means of intercommunication could our people be instantly united in any cause.

In its wonderful preparedness to inform its citizens of a national need, the United States stands alone and unequaled. It can command the entire Bell Telephone System, which

completely covers our country with its network of wires.

This marvelous system is the result of keen foresight and persistent effort on the part of telephone specialists, who have endeavored from the first to provide a means of communication embracing our whole country, connecting every state and every community, to its last individual unit.

The Bell System is a distinctly American achievement, made by Americans for Americans, and its like is not to be found in all the world.

Through it, our entire population may be promptly organized for united action in any national movement, whether it be for peace, prosperity, philanthropy or armed protection.

AMERICAN TELEPHONE AND TELEGRAPH COMPANY
AND ASSOCIATED COMPANIES

One Policy   *One System*   *Universal Service*

Journalism As An Aid To History Teaching

By EDWIN E. SLOSSON, Ph.D., Literary Editor of The Independent
Associate in the School of Journalism, Columbia University

This address, which was given before the History Section of the New York State Teachers' Association at Rochester, November 23, 1915, has been published in pamphlet form and will be furnished free to teachers—Write to W. W. Ferrin, 119 West 40th Street, New York.

Mass., founded a national pure food movement by the original work he did among his classes in food chemistry. Wake up, and build up, your own classes, neighbors and friends on domestic science lines—then your field will broaden of itself. Write for literature of American School of Home Economics, Chicago; of Domestic Engineering Company, 200 Fifth Avenue, New York; of Mrs. Mary Pattison's Household Experiment Station, Colonia, New Jersey; of Associated Clubs of Domestic Science, 45 West Thirty-fourth Street, New York; of West Virginia University Agricultural Extension Department, Morgantown, West Va.; of United States Department of Agriculture, Washington, D. C.

224. Miss A. S., Pennsylvania. "Are there institutions for persons mentally deficient from childhood? A woman of thirty-five has been neglected all her life, she cannot do much more than knit and perform simple household duties when properly directed. She has gotten certain fixed ideas and notions which are undermining her health. If you can suggest an institution to aid her, your advice will be gratefully received by an appreciative reader of The Independent Efficiency articles."

There are various institutions and methods for cases of this kind; with hundreds of records of cure or partial relief, to encourage the friends of those who are mentally deficient. The choice of an institution depends on local and personal conditions. Hence we would refer you to a number of places where you may find the knowledge you seek: Neurological Institute, 149 East Sixty-seventh street; Department of Psychiatric Institute, Ward's Island; *Journal of Nervous and Mental Diseases*, 64 West Fifty-sixth street; all of New York City.

225. Prof. H. J. F., Tennessee. "I am a school teacher, and am making good in this work; finished college at the head of my class, I desire to become a lawyer. Should I try to be one; if so, in what class? Will you give practical advice concerning the cultivation of alertness and quickness in thinking? It seems hard and awkward for me to change rapidly from one line of thought to another. Would this handicap me as a lawyer?"

It would handicap you greatly as a pleader in court, but not necessarily as a counsellor. We would urge you not to resign your position, if you depend on it for support; but to study law by correspondence—a number of mail courses have been advertised in The Independent; and to find an opening in a law office while teaching. First consult one of the character analysts, mentioned frequently in the Question Box. A man successful in any field of work should wait long and think hard before changing to another field.

The time-study and motion-study phases of scientific management should quicken your thought in action; a good course in public speaking should serve perhaps better.

226. Mr. N. T., Delaware. "In your estimation what field opens up the best inducements for a young man? Does mechanical engineering offer good returns from both a financial and physical standpoint? Would you advise one to study for such, if interested?"

I don't like your emphasis on "inducements"—apparently you consider the selfish returns the most important. Of course you should want to make money; but in all good work the aim and ideal of service comes ahead of the salary. A man receives most where he serves best.

You are likely to succeed in any work that greatly interests you. Consult an experienced character analyst—names were given, Question Box for January 31; also familiarize yourself with magazines and books in Mechanical Engineering, before deciding on this vocation. Secure copies of *Engineering Magazine*, 140 Nassau street; *Engineering News*, Tenth avenue and Thirty-sixth street; *Engineering Record*, 239 West Thirty-ninth street; *Engineering Graphic*, 20 Broad street; all of New York. Write also the Librarian, Engineering Societies, 29 West Thirty-ninth street, for names of books, and the Secretary, Engineers' Club, 32 West Fortieth street, for data that might be helpful.

The Market Place

THE RAILROADS

Great congestion of freight in the vicinity of northeastern ports continues to present a problem which the railroads have been unable to solve. The American Railway Association, at a recent meeting of its leading officers, took action which may have some effect, and the Interstate Commerce Commission has given notice that it desires to hear the opinions of railroad men and shippers at a conference in Washington on the 6th and 7th. While the Commission has no direct authority to apply remedies, it hopes that relief will be obtained by an agreement of the interests involved. At the meeting of the Railway Association it was decided that roads east of Chicago should deliver to Western lines twenty per cent more box freight cars than they receive from them. There is a marked shortage of cars in the West. The roads in that part of the country hold only ninety per cent of the cars which they own, while the Eastern roads have thirteen per cent more than they are entitled to by ownership. In New England the excess is forty-three per cent.

It is well known that the congestion is due almost wholly to the export trade in war supplies, altho it appears that nearly three-quarters of the Pennsylvania Company's 11,896 loaded cars held in the vicinity of Philadelphia carry goods for local delivery and not for other ports. Delay in unloading at New York and other ports is due to several causes. Many of the ships are not so well fitted to receive the freight as a majority of ocean freight carriers are in normal times. Therefore the work of transferring the freight takes much time. And ships which were to take certain kinds of freight have unexpectedly been commandeered by Governments. At the munition factories, especially those in New England, the railroad men say, there is great delay in unloading raw material from cars, and in many places manufacturers who fear a strike at the mines have been ordering unusually large supplies of coal. This has reduced the number of cars available for other freight. While certain manufacturers in New England unload their raw material slowly, others, unable to get cars, are bringing raw material from New York and other points to their factories on automobile trucks.

The great volume of freight which has caused this congestion has largely increased the gross revenue and net

earnings of the roads. This is proved by their reports. The returns from 476 roads (248,437 miles) for the month of December last shows an increase of $62,438,000, or twenty-seven per cent, in gross revenue, and of $44,692,000, or seventy-three per cent, in net profits, when comparison is made with December, 1914. The Pennsylvania's report shows, for the calendar year, a gain of nearly $15,000,000 in gross, and one of $8,334,000, or more than twenty per cent. in net, the net being equal to 8¾ per cent on the capital stock, against 6¾ in the preceding year. But railroad gains, as a rule, did not begin to appear until last September. Reports issued last week show what several roads were doing in January. The Pennsylvania's increases were nearly $8,000,000, or thirty-one per cent, in gross, and an advance for the net from less than $2,000,000 to $7,048,000. Gross revenue on the New York Central in the same month showed a gain of $6,000,000, or thirty-one per cent, the net rose from $3,085,000 to $7,720,000, or 150 per cent.

While the railroads are doing a large and profitable business, it must be borne in mind that the demand for the war supplies which they are carrying has very considerably increased the prices which they must pay for new equipment and maintenance. In his recent address to the stockholders of the Lackawanna, President Truesdale remarked that if the war should suddenly end, the business of the railways would drop off quickly. "It is difficult, therefore," said he, "to plan for the future with any degree of certainty, and in view of the high prices of labor and all commodities a conservative course would seem the wisest for railway companies to pursue."

Prices of railroad shares in the stock market have not moved in accordance with the evidence of increased profits. The causes of restraint have been the uncertainty to which Mr. Truesdale referred, the effect of our international complications upon the entire market, continued sale of English and other foreign holdings of our railroad securities on the New York Stock Exchange, and the menace of a possible general strike in May. A peaceful settlement of the coming wage controversy would considerably increase the companies' expenses for labor.

===

Three copper mining companies and a company that produces zinc increased, last week, their regular quarterly or extra dividends. The price of copper, from 27 to 28 cents a pound, depending partly upon the time of delivery, is now higher than it has been at any other time in the last forty-three years.

===

The following dividends are announced:
Liggett & Myers Tobacco Company, 1¾ per cent, payable April 1.
Electric Storage Battery Company, 1 per cent on both common and preferred, payable April 1.
Ray Consolidated Copper Company, quarterly, 60 cents per share, payable March 31.
American Can Company, preferred, quarterly, 1¾ per cent, payable April 1.
Federal Mining and Smelting Company, preferred, 1 per cent, payable March 15.
Mergenthaler Linotype Company, quarterly, 2¾ per cent, payable March 31.

Insurance
Conducted by
W. E. UNDERWOOD

CONTINENTAL LIFE OF UTAH

Recent inquiries touching the financial condition and management of the Continental Life Insurance Company of Salt Lake City make timely the information just promulgated by the Insurance Departments of Colorado, Wyoming and Utah, the examiners of which recently completed an investigation into its affairs. Two changes have occurred in the management of this company within the past three years. The parties preceding the present management, which assumed control in 1914, evidently conducted the business in an extravagant, probably in a reckless, manner. Since that time, while expenses have been above normal, there has been much improvement. The examiners state that the men now in charge of the company are of good repute and possess ability, and that they realize the seriousness of the task they have undertaken in endeavoring to remedy the defects resulting from the mistakes of their predecessors.

This company writes both participating and non-participating insurance. Its participating business is on the annual dividend and deferred dividend plans. Its existing deferred dividend policies have little or no dividend reserves behind them. My advice to those taking insurance in the company is to confine themselves to the acceptance of non-participating policies.

The financial condition of the company on October 31, 1915, as found by the examiners, was as follows: Assets, $1,477,846; total liabilities, except capital stock, $1,223,979; capital stock, $208,875; net surplus, $44,992.

M. T. H., Warren, O.—In the long run you will find the Connecticut Mutual much the cheaper. It is incomparably a better company than the other.

H. C. L., New York City—You have a line of life insurance considerably above the average in amount and excellent as to character of companies. Advise against replacing any of the policies now.

N. H. E., Alliance, O.—Some of the casualty companies may issue health policies on women beyond the age of forty-five, but I do not know of any. Perhaps some of our readers among agents or company officials could help us. Names of companies issuing such policies, if any, will be printed in this department on receipt.

C. L. R., Union Mills, Ind.—The fact that the agent of the Association is urging the holders of old line companies to lapse their policies and sacrifice valuable equities, for the purpose of enabling him to gather in commissions by rewriting them in his institution, is enough to discredit him and it. His association does not maintain an adequate legal reserve, and its policyholders who live long enough will have to pay for the mistake.

SCHOOLS

JOHN KENDRICK BANGS
Presents THE GENIAL PHILOSOPHER

"I OBSERVE with interest," began the genial Philosopher.

"Never mind about the interest," interrupted the Cynical Sciolist. "Give us the principle."

"I observe with very great interest," repeated the Genial Philosopher, "that my friend, the Secretary of the Treasury, in order to make up for the general bustification of this nation in respect to spare change, which Uncle Sam seems to need to the tune of $112,-000,000, proposes an increase of the income tax, and a tax upon gasoline, and one upon crude and refined oils. He has also got his eye upon sugar to sweeten the treasury."

"O well, what of it?" said the Cynical Sciolist wearily. "Let others worry—I shan't. I can't qualify for the privileges of the income tax under the most favorable exemptions. Having no motor car I don't use gasoline. I neither burn nor drink oil, crude or refined, confining my attention solely to cod-liver; and since I took to drinking hot water instead of tea and coffee I don't use sugar. Wherefore, pile the taxes on. Let 'em rise, mount, climb, and soar, until they look like Barbarossa piled on Perihelion—it's all the same to me."

"That is the comfortable view of taxation that most people take who pay taxes without knowing it," said the Genial Philosopher, "but it was not of them that I intended to speak, tho I must confess they are a class deserving of considerable attention—the man who rejoices that he derives all the benefits of modern civilization without paying for them; the Something For Nothing man. We all know him—the Hitch-Behind Citizen, beating his way on the Public Ice-Wagon, as it were, just as we old New Yorkers used to sneak rides on the real ice-wagons in our boyhood days when New York was a pleasant little Village, filled with human beings. No—this is too pleasant a morning to discuss the Tax-Dodger, high or low. What interested me when I read the Secretary's program was the possibility that flashed across my mind of a Double Function of Taxation. Primarily, of course, taxation was invented to increase the public revenue, and short of a scheme of general confiscation of the gross earnings of humanity, it is the best method yet devised for the purpose. But why should it not also exercise the function of suppressing Nuisances, and Viciousness, and the crudeness and vulgarities of life?

"For instance, one of the curses of modern civilization is NOISE. We have made great progress in this country along many lines of industry, but I do not think I exaggerate when I say that in general Sonority we are the Grand High Stentors of All the Ages. In things obstreperantly fulminate it requires undiscovered superlatives in clangor fitly to describe the quality of our hullaballoonacy. The man who invented the phrase that this or that was noised abroad must have had a prevision of conditions in these United States of America in this year of grace 1916. The gum-shoe, the pussy-foot, the muffled thing, the subtleties of the inaudible, are coming to be strangers in our midst. Our Detectives go about their work with megaphones, and the brass-band is ever with us. Conversation even in exclusive circles is conducted on lines of a shrill fortissimo series of rising crescendos in order that it may surmount the alpine heights of the general vocal bombilation."

"Can't you as a special favor to me commute some of your sentences?" pleaded the Cynical Sciolist, clutching his forehead in his hands.

"Certainly—we live in an Age of Holler," said the Genial Philosopher. "Wherever we go it is noise, NOISE, NOISE. A poet friend of mine has recently taken desk-room in a boiler-riveting establishment so that he may have at least one spot in which to write his Odes, Sonnets, Triolets, and Limericks, in comparative quiet; and my cousin, Billie Binks, has actually reached a point in his life where he has got so used to noise that he can't sleep when it stops; and consequently he has a frieze of a hundred and twenty alarm clocks on a shelf running around his bedroom to bang away every two minutes during the night in order that no untoward silences may break in to destroy his slumbers. In short, my friend, life has become just one alarm thing after another."

"So I have heard," said the Cynical Sciolist, "but what of it?"

"Why not make of Taxation a sort of Soft-Pedal on the general Jangle?"

"You mean to tax unnecessary noises?"

"I mean to tax all noises," said the Genial Philosopher. "Who shall say what noises are necessary, and what noises are unnecessary? What is one man's noise may turn out to be another man's necessity, and it would never do under our present political system to make differentiations in noises which politicians seeking the emoluments of public office could use as the basis of further demagogic appeals. No, tax 'em all. Why think about it just a moment. If Congress were to pass an act requiring that on and after April the first every maker of noises in this land shall pay a tax of one cent per noise on each and every noise projected by himself on the public ear, either necessary or unnecessary, during the day, the revenue would be enormous, and the word Deficit would become obsolete. We have in round figures a hundred million people in this country who average I should say not less than one hundred noises per capita per diem, or 36,500,000,000,000 noises a year. Fig-

ure that out on a basis of one cent apiece, and you have a revenue of $36,-500,000,000. Figure also the value of such a tax in the suppression of the tendency. If every noisy person in the land realized that he was compelled by law to put a one cent stamp, figuratively speaking, on every noise he made, I fancy he'd calm down a bit, and reduce his output materially; say possibly fifty per cent, which even then would give the Government a revenue of $18,250,000,000, to say nothing of the blest relief to the public eardrum. There might also be certain exemptions for five or six years until the people had learned how to be quiet. This of course would result in a further reduction of the gross revenue, another fifty per cent perhaps, leaving the total at $9,125,000,000, but that would be an income which even a modern Congress would find difficulty in appropriating."

"I don't see exactly how you would be able to establish the accuracy of the returns," said the Cynical Sciolist, shaking his head doubtfully. "Who's going to keep track of these Noises? Do you propose that every citizen shall carry a sort of Noise Register on his chest?"

"That is a point that will have to be worked out by an Auxiliary Board of Inventors," said the Genial Philosopher. "If the Navy Department is permitted to mobilize the Inventors I don't see why the Treasury Department can't do the same thing. Anyhow if our Government would go in for the Double Function System of Taxation, and use taxes not only for the purpose of raising revenue, but for the suppression of Nuisances as well, taxing over-crowded trolley and subway cars; taxing the Gum-Chewing hordes according to the density of the obnoxious perfumes they breathe into the air; taxing persons who carry lighted imperfectos into vehicles, so much per pipe, cigar, or cigaret; taxing burglars ninety per cent on the swag they accumulate; taxing people who come late to the theater fifteen cents per minute; taxing every fake item of war news that appears in the newspapers thirty cents a line; and confiscating all tips paid to persons who earn them only by a supercilious inattention to the payor—well, my friend, Uncle Sam would be able to drop all other kinds of taxes altogether; build three more Panama Canals, one for traffic, one for slides, and one to hold in reserve for emergencies; maintain an Army and Navy big enough to defend our Planet against invasion by the unscrupulous hordes of the Milky Way; meet the highest expectations of the Pork Seekers the country over, and still have enough left to look his Creditors in the face on pay day. Eh? What?"

"It sounds good," said the Cynical Sciolist, "but I am not ready yet offhand to classify it. It may come under the head of mere NOISE after all."

400

The Independent

FOR SIXTY-SEVEN YEARS THE
FORWARD-LOOKING WEEKLY OF AMERICA

THE   CHAUTAUQUAN
Merged with The Independent June 1, 1914

MARCH   20,   1916

OWNED   AND   PUBLISHED   BY
THE INDEPENDENT CORPORATION, AT
119 WEST FORTIETH STREET, NEW YORK
WILLIAM   B.   HOWLAND,   PRESIDENT
FREDERIC E. DICKINSON, TREASURER

WILLIAM   HAYES   WARD
HONORARY EDITOR

EDITOR: HAMILTON HOLT
ASSOCIATE EDITOR: HAROLD J. HOWLAND
LITERARY EDITOR: EDWIN E. SLOSSON

PUBLISHER: KARL V. S. HOWLAND

ONE   YEAR,   THREE   DOLLARS

SINGLE   COPIES,   TEN   CENTS

Postage to foreign countries in Universal Postal
Union, $1.75 a year extra; to Canada, $1 extra.
Instructions for renewal, discontinuance or
change of address should be sent two weeks
before the date they are to go into effect. Both
the old and the new address must be given.

We welcome contributions, but writers who
wish their articles returned, if not accepted,
should send a stamped and addrest envelope. No responsibility is assumed by The
Independent for the loss or non-return of
manuscripts, tho all due care will be exercised.

Entered at New York Post Office as Second
Class Matter

Copyright, 1916, by The Independent

Address all Communications to
THE   INDEPENDENT
119   West   Fortieth   Street,   New   York

CONTENTS

THE GREAT GRAY CARPET

A young French soldier of the class of 1914, who was wounded in the battle of Verdun, gives this vivid account of the German attack on the fortress:

"As for the cannonade, it was a regular deluge. Our trenches were demolished as if they had been deliberately turned upside down by a giant hand. After six hours of that there was nothing left to defend, so we retired to the support trenches near Anglomont. We had to crawl, and, what with shell holes, corpses, and barbed wire, it was no trip in a sleeping car.

"Then the enemy began to advance. They looked like a big gray carpet being unrolled over the country. Our guns had the range exactly, but the gaps filled up as by magic.

"We opened fire at 200 yards. I guess there were few misses at that close, but we might as well have been firing peas. They never even hesitated.

"Then our mitrailleuses got going. That was different. Whole rows of the enemy toppled over like corn under the scythe. They stopped; then we charged with the bayonet. They died just like sheep, almost without resistance."—*New York Times.*

"GASSED"—PIERRE LOTI

A place of horror which one would think Dante had imagined. The air is heavy—stifling; two or three little night lamps, which look as if they were afraid of giving too much light, hardly pierce the hot, smoky darkness which smells of fever and sweat. Busy people are whispering anxiously. But you hear, more than all, agonized gaspings. These gaspings escape from a number of little beds drawn up close together on which are distinguished human forms, above all, chests, chests that are heaving too strongly, too rapidly, and that raise the sheets as if the hour of the death rattle had already come.

It is one of our hospitals on the battle line, improvised as well as was possible on the morrow of one of the most infernal of German abominations; all these children of France, who look as if they are at the last gasp, were so terribly injured that it was impossible to carry them further away.

But, why this heat, which the stoves send forth and which makes breathing almost impossible? The reason is that it cannot be too hot fer asphyxiated lungs. And this darkness, why this darkness? It is because the barbarians are there in their burrows, quite close

to this village, whose houses and church tower they have more than once amused themselves by pounding with their shells. Every moment nurses bring huge, black, air balloons, and those who are struggling in agony stretch out their poor hands to beg for them; it is oxygen, which makes them breathe better and suffer less. Many of them have these black air balloons resting on their panting chests, and in their mouths they greedily hold the tubes thru which the saving gas escapes; you would say that they were great children with milk bottles; this throws a sort of grotesque buffoonery over these scenes of horror.

Thank God, they will save almost all of them! As soon as they can be moved they will be taken away from this hell of the battle front, where the Kaiser's shrapnels fall so willingly, even on the dying; they will be laid more comfortably in quiet hospitals, where they will still suffer much, indeed, for a week, a fortnight, a month, but which they will presently leave, more cautious, more prudent, and eager to return to the fight.

But the next time they will not be caught, neither these men, nor any of our soldiers; with masks hermetically sealed they will stand immovable around heaps of fagots prepared beforehand, the sudden flames of which neutralize the poisons in the air, and there will be no result beyond an hour of discomfort, painful to pass thru, but almost always without fatal consequences.—*New York Times.*

P E B B L E S

Next to the new minister's wife the silk hat is the object of the most suspicion in the small town.—*Kansas City Star.*

Well, the President seems to have stated, in no u. t., his attitude on preparedness. And what will Mr. Hearst's cartoonists do now, poor things?—*New York Tribune.*

If you think you are pretty well read in world-literature, how does it strike your complacency to learn that the Nobel prizes for literature have been awarded to Romain Rolland, Henrik Pontoppidan, Troefs Lundasve, and Verner von Heidenstam?—*Kansas City Star.*

He was enormous, with offensively prominent, milk-blue eyes, and a disorderly beard, garishly red but trimmed at the temples with white.—*The New Republic.*

You might say that that was a high-brow beard, such as you might expect to find growing in the New Republic.—*New York Tribune.*

Two little fleas sat on a rock
  And one to the other said :
"I have no place to hang my hat
  Since my old dog is dead.
I've traveled the wide world over,
  And farther will I roam.
But the first darn dog that shows his face
  Will be my Home Sweet Home !"
        —*Awgwan.*

, The grouch was dissatisfied with the letter which his stenographer presented for his signature. He signed, but made her put it back into the machine and add: P. S.—Dictated to a poor stenographer.

She folded the letter and put it in the envelope, but no sooner was her employer's back turned than she took it out and added : P. S.—No. 2. The reason I am so poor is because he pays me only $6 per week.—*Collier's.*

The Independent

VOLUME 85   MARCH 20, 1916   NUMBER 3511

© Harris & Ewing

THE DEFENDER OF THE FRONTIER

GENERAL FREDERICK FUNSTON, WHO HAS CHARGE OF THE PUNITIVE EXPEDITION INTO MEXICO, HAS HAD A LONG EXPERIENCE IN THIS SORT OF FIGHTING. HE GOT HIS MILITARY TRAINING, NOT AT WEST POINT, BUT IN THE CUBAN ARMY, FIGHTING THE SPANIARDS IN 1896. WHEN OUR WAR WITH SPAIN BROKE OUT HE WENT TO THE PHILIPPINES, WHERE HIS DARING CAPTURE OF AGUINALDO PUT AN END TO THE FILIPINO REBELLION

WE CAN WAIT NO LONGER

THE murderous raid upon the town of Columbus in New Mexico by the organized and lawless crew of Francisco Villa, the Mexican desperado, was the last straw. We could wait no longer. We might watch no more.

Year after year we have suffered in unbelievable forbearance the wanton destruction of American property in Mexico, the slaying by predatory bands of law-abiding American citizens there, and even the killing, by shots fired across the border, of American soldiers upon American soil performing their allotted duty of patient vigilance. Under intolerable provocation we have held our hand.

But the hour struck. American soil was invaded. American sovereignty was flouted. The American nation was defied. We could not in honor submit longer to insult and wanton injury.

The murderer Villa and his fellow bandits must be punished. Carranza, the recognized ruler of Mexico, cannot do it. His impotence in Northern Mexico is beyond dispute. The United States Government must perform the task itself. Its armed forces must seek out the murderers of Columbus and put them to death. They must follow the trail wherever it leads; they must use whatever means are necessary to bring the guilty to book.

We are not waging war; we are administering justice. We shall not assail the rights of any other people; we shall merely defend our own. To do less would be national dishonor.

This is the second time during the present administration that the policy of watchful waiting has been laid aside. Two years ago the armed forces of the United States attacked and captured the city of Vera Cruz. But the purpose for which it was captured was never accomplished. After seven months of occupation our forces withdrew with no better reason than existed for the original capture of the city. The first act in the drama of Vera Cruz was a mistake; the second was a more serious one.

We must not make the same mistake again. The punishment of Villa and his band is our present duty; but a greater lies behind. Peace and good order must be established in Northern Mexico. Our southern border must be made inviolable. We must do for that anarchic region across the Rio Grande what the helpless Carranza cannot—and apparently will not try to—do. Our troops must not come home until the lives and property of American citizens are safe not only along the border but in those parts of Mexico where the *de facto* Mexican Government is powerless.

THE MEANING OF VERDUN

WHATEVER may be the outcome of the battle which has been raging for three weeks at Verdun, this furious onslaught by the Germans upon the foremost fortress of France is obviously one of the most important operations of the war. If the Germans succeed they will have broken thru the strongest barrier between them and Paris. If they fail they will have sacrificed their precious men and munitions in vain and will suffer a loss of prestige that will seriously impair their chances of winning the war. Such a bold enterprise of what seemed a hopeless undertaking can be justified only by success. What they have so far accomplished, the gain of a hundred square miles of strongly fortified ground, is indeed a striking triumph of courage and preparedness, but in itself avails them nothing, for it merely reinforces the lesson already learned from the attacks of the Germans at Ypres, of the British and French at Lens and of the French in Champagne; that is, that it is possible to smash in the front of any line, but not to break thru it so long as it is ably defended. According to the British press correspondent the French and British have more than twenty miles of trenches to every mile of front or 10,000 miles altogether.

Even the capture of Verdun would, therefore, not mean that the Germans could repeat the advance toward Paris which they undertook in August, 1914. Paris is 150 miles from Verdun and the invaders might be stopped or held at any point as well as they have been in the mud-flats of Flanders or the valley of the Suippe. It all depends upon what power of resistance the French still possess and what support the British can give them.

The dispatches from France claim that the French were well aware of the plan of the Germans to attack Verdun. But if the French were not surprized they certainly were not fully prepared. General Sarrail, who

defended Verdun previously and who had reconstructed its fortifications in accordance with the lesson of Liège and Namur, was in Salonica, and General Petain, who was holding the Champagne line, was called from his bed in the night and had to take command of Verdun at two hours' notice. We hear of Australians and Canadians assisting in the defense of the fortress; also that the British have extended their line in Artois to replace the French troops who have been sent to Verdun. This indicates that the French have not been able to defend Verdun with the troops already there or by their reserves behind the line, but have been obliged to make some radical and sudden rearrangements at the front.

If the German objective is Paris one would suppose that they would have attempted to break thru on the Aisne, where they are only fifty miles away and there are no permanent fortifications to prevent, rather than on the Meuse, a hundred and fifty miles away, which the French have been for thirty years engaged in fortifying. Perhaps that is the very reason why they struck at the Meuse instead of the Aisne. The strength of Verdun lies in its location among the river bluffs and in the recently constructed entrenchments and concealed batteries. The millions which were expended in the impregnable steel and concrete cupolas were worse than wasted. The fort of Douaumont was smashed by three shells; the village of Douaumont held out for a week. How little such rapid reduction of permanent fortifications was anticipated, at least by the Allies, may be seen from the very thoro article on "Fortification and Siegecraft" in the *Encyclopedia Britannica*, published in 1911. We quote a few sentences:

At the present day little military importance is attached to bombardment, since under modern conditions it cannot do much real harm.

To stop a single shell of any siege caliber in use at present five feet of good concrete would be enough.

The cupolas can hardly be considered ideal targets and the probability is that they would hold their own against both direct and indirect fire for a long time.

Since this article was written by Colonel Jackson, Instructor in Fortification at Woolwich and Assistant Director of Fortifications in the War Office, it may be taken as representing the opinion of the British military experts at the opening of the war and so may account for the failure of the Allies to reach Belgium until after Liège and Namur had fallen.

The German authorities on the contrary held that it was better to put money into men and guns than into armored turrets, so they constructed few fortresses. Maybe these can be taken as easily as the French, Belgian and Russian, but so far the Allies have not had a chance to try because the German army has stood in the way.

It would be a strange historical coincidence if Verdun should prove the turning point of the war, for it was at Verdun that France and Germany first were parted. By the Treaty of Verdun in the year 843 the kingdom of Louis the Pious was divided among his three sons; Louis the German taking the right bank of the Rhine; Charles the Bold taking the Seine valley, and Lothair taking the valley of the Meuse. The kingdom of Louis became Germany; the kingdom of Charles became France and these two have been quarreling for a thousand years over the kingdom of Lothair, which lay between.

In all these wars Verdun has figured prominently. The Germans held it in the tenth century. The French regained it in the sixteenth. In 1792 Verdun was besieged by the Duke of Brunswick with a coalition force of Prussians, Austrians, Italians and French *emigrés*. The fortress succumbed after so feeble a resistance that the commandant, Colonel Beaurepaire, shot himself from chagrin. The inhabitants greeted the conquerors with joy and young girls strewed flowers in the path of the Prussians as they marched thru the streets. When the revolutionary forces regained the city these girls were put to death for treason.

Next time the Germans came, in 1870, Verdun was commanded by a man with a Franco-German name, Guérin de Waldersbach, and he held out till after the fall of Metz, altho Verdun was three times invested and bombarded. On the hills where the Germans then placed their guns the French after the war built the inner ring of forts about Verdun. Later as the range of guns increased they put fortifications on the outer hills, such as Douaumont and Vaux, which the Germans have now destroyed.

The attack upon Verdun was probably instigated as much by political as by military strategy. The Germans may be thinking not so much of capturing Paris as of holding Constantinople and of winning Bucharest. Whether or not they succeed at Verdun they have, by taking the offensive in the early spring at a distant part of the line, disarranged the plans of the Allies for a spring drive at the Belgian end. This may give the Germans time enough to carry out their own plans, whether these be another drive at Calais, a further invasion of Russia, an attack upon the Suez Canal, a raid by the fleet or something less obvious. At any rate the Germans have "got the move" in this game of war by their assault at Verdun.

THE UNPREPAREDNESS OF THE BRITISH PEOPLE

EVER since the war began various members of the British Government have come out with statements that they had long believed that war with Germany was imminent, if not inevitable, and that England was in duty bound to intervene in case Belgium was invaded. Sir Edward Grey in his speech of August 6, 1914, convinced the House of Commons, even those members most reluctant to accept it, that England had been ever since 1906 and more definitely since 1911 under the strongest moral obligations to join with France in the war.

But the more clear it is made that the Government anticipated the war and regarded British participation as unavoidable, the more clear it appears that there was a wide difference between the British Government and the British people, even the well informed, as to England's obligations toward Belgium and the advisability of her entering upon a continental war. For instance, the University Extension Manual on *English Colonization and Empire*, prepared in 1890 to instruct the people on Britain's history and foreign policy, states:

As it stands now, it is difficult to imagine any purely European difficulty arising that would call us to arm. An attack upon Belgium hardly would do so, nor upon Denmark, nor even Holland; if they cannot stand alone it is difficult to persuade us now that Britain ought to prop them up, even if it were possible.

In a speech of May 7, 1913, the Right Honorable L. V. Harcourt said:

I can conceive of no circumstances in which continental operations by our troops would not be a crime against the people of this country.

That same year an ex-Lord Chancellor, the Earl of Loreburn, declared:

That any British Government would be so guilty toward our own country as to take up arms in a foreign quarrel is more than I can believe. To say so appears to me a duty not less to ourselves than to Continental Powers.

And on the morning of the day when England declared war with Germany the *Manchester Guardian* exprest for the last time this view:

If and when England joins in the war it will be too late to discuss its policy. Meanwhile we hold it to be a patriotic duty for all good citizens to oppose to the utmost the participation of this country in the greatest crime of our time.

Such opinions could be multiplied indefinitely. These are merely a few that we have happened upon. We quote them, not to prove that the British Government entrapped the people into war, but to show how great a misunderstanding may exist for years between Government and people as to the policy and obligations of a country. And if such a condition prevails in a nation where the people take an active interest in foreign politics and where the administration is under direct parliamentary control, a similar misunderstanding could exist in a country where the people are little concerned with foreign affairs and where the administration is independent and irremovable.

We do not go so far as to say with some that all secret negotiations must be abolished and the people be allowed to vote on a declaration of war. Secret diplomacy is a decided advantage in international bargaining and a nation which had to hold a referendum before it began to fight would most likely be beaten before the returns were in.

But it seems to us that the war clearly teaches the desirability of a greater frankness and a better understanding between a government and its people if, when the crisis comes, they are to act together. We believe also that more publicity in the discussion of foreign policies would tend to prevent wars. It is, for instance, a disputed point whether Germany would have abstained from war if she had known that the British Government was determined to come to the aid of Belgium. But we may be sure that if she had known that the British people were either in accord with their Government on this point or were prepared to give it their loyal support without regard to their previous opinions, as they have, Germany would have shown greater hesitation about engaging Great Britain in war. Such considerations go a good way toward counterbalancing the advantages of a secret diplomacy and an instantaneous initiative.

THE BIBLE SOCIETY CENTENNIAL

THE oldest Bible Society in the world apart from the Christian Church is the British and Foreign Bible Society organized in 1804. Among the incidents which seem to show the need for such a society was one, much repeated at the time, of a Welsh woman who walked twenty-five miles barefoot to buy a Bible for which she had been saving up money for eight years. The American Bible Society followed in 1816, and these two societies have covered the world with their agencies. In a single year the American Bible Society issued six and one-half millions of Bibles and the British society over ten millions. There are twenty-five Bible societies, American and European, and about nine-tenths of the issues of the Bible printed the world over are produced by five societies in Great Britain and the United States. Their purpose is by their agencies to supply Bibles by sale or gift to every Christian family in the world.

For several years before 1816 there had been organized local societies for the distribution of the Bible, and in that year their representatives from ten states met in New York to organize a National Society. They made Elias Boudinot its first president. In 1783 as President of Congress he had signed the Treaty of Peace with Great Britain after the Revolutionary War. John Jay was the second president, and John Quincy Adams one of the first vice-presidents. A provision in its constitution rendered it possible for all Protestant denominations to unite in its support; namely, that the Bible should be printed without note or comment. To be sure this was not literally observed, for the familiar headings to the chapters were retained, and these in the Song of Solomon interpreted the "Beloved" and his "Love" as Christ and the Church, and we recall the difficulty which Dr. R. S. Storrs and his committee had in securing the issue of an edition in which these comments were omitted. There was a similar long hesitation before the society ventured to issue the Revised Version in its American Revision.

It is not our purpose here to go deeply into the statistics of the work of the American Bible Society. Its receipts in its first year were less than one thousand dollars, while its appropriations for the last year were $652,300, and its endowment is nearly two and a half millions. During the last twelve months Bibles were issued in ninety-two languages and dialects other than English, among which we note 214,189 copies in Spanish, 97,138 in Italian, 32,971 in German, 31,610 in

Polish. There is not a language of any part of the world where American missionaries are working for which the American Society does not supply Bibles.

The Bible is not a fetish. The possession of a Bible does not make a family Christian. There were large bodies of Christians before one book in our New Testament was written. But the Bible is the symbol of the Christian faith, the source of history and teaching and without the written word as its foundation the structure would have fallen. We need not worship the Bible in the way that our fathers did, as if like the image of Diana it had fallen down from Heaven, infallible in its history and its teaching, and as if God had since given us no instructor in religion. But any imperfections or errors which scholars may find cannot affect the fact that it is from the teachings of Jesus and His Apostles as recorded in the Bible that the mightiest influence has come for the regeneration of the world. We have good reason to believe that far from being supplanted, the Christian faith, resting upon the Bible, is sure to cover the world. Those who carry that Christian faith to the nations will first hold out in their hand the book which for a hundred years our American Bible Society has been putting within the easy reach of all people of every civilized and savage tongue.

AN AMERICAN DIPLOMAT

THE United States has not always had the reputation of providing trained and cultured representatives in its diplomatic posts. Indeed we have heard much of our "shirtsleeve diplomacy," but certainly in the fearful strain which has come upon our ambassadors and ministers abroad during the present war we have good reason to feel satisfaction. Every report that comes back from the field of war tells us that they have been equal to the strain of an unusual responsibility. Two of them especially who are now taking a vacation at home, Mr. Gerard and Mr. Morgenthau, are receiving unusual and well deserved honor, in acknowledgment of their distinguished success in very difficult fields.

It has lately come to be known that Mr. Morgenthau shortly before the opening of the European war was the recipient of an unusual and quite unconventional invitation from the Turkish Goverment to which he was accredited. He is an experienced and accomplished business man from New York, a member of many directorates, and on reaching Constantinople he soon showed himself interested in the business affairs of the country, and members of the Turkish Cabinet sought his advice. When he replied that he had been so short a time in the country that he was not yet acquainted with its conditions they made it convenient for him under the most favorable auspices to visit Palestine and Syria and portions of Asia Minor. To his surprize on his return they asked him to join the Cabinet as Minister of Commerce and Agriculture. He told them that he regarded his present position as Ambassador as more important. Whereupon he was told with all seriousness that he might yet hold the double position of Turkish Cabinet Minister and American Ambassador. It will be remembered that Mr. Morgenthau is a Jew, and he has a German name; but he is first and last an American. We get the spirit of an American diplomat from his reply when welcomed on his return by a thousand members of the Merchants' Association:

My task was a comparatively easy one, because I went out there every inch an American and every bit possest of American ideas and brought up in this school where we all sit down together, whether we be Protestants or Catholics or Jews, and are devoid of prejudice. I did not devote my time in a snobbish way and associate with Marquises and Dukes and the Barons and the ladies of the Diplomatic Corps, for I felt that I had gone there as an American representative, as an American merchant to help the country, and I tried to do it.

When the various representatives of countries came together, whether representatives of the Zionist movement or from the Jewish community or Armenians or the Grand Rabbi or the Bishop of the Greek Church, I made known to them that I was ready to receive them as a brother, not as a high-class diplomat who had to look up precedents on how to receive them or how he should talk or who should talk first. I met them on an equal basis.

The great American influence in Turkey is educational and missionary, and the three great American colleges in Turkey are enthusiastic in their admiration for him, and declare that no one could have better served their interests, or the interests as well of all the suffering races of Turkey. He returns to get a fresh dose of Americanism, and he tells us that every diplomat ought to return home once every year or two to freshen his patriotism.

VOLUNTEER AND REGULAR

IN these stirring days, when the voice of the militarist is heard in the land, and we are solemnly warned that only a great standing army can save us from invasion, it is refreshing to turn back to the "Reminiscences of Carl Schurz" and read that great hyphenated citizen's opinion of the American volunteer soldier.

Says Mr. Schurz in volume III, page 121:

Some years later, when I visited Germany again and met the Chancellor, Prince Bismarck, as well as several generals of the Prussian army who had studied the history of our Civil War, they plied me with questions about the organization, the spirit, and the efficiency of our volunteer army. What I told them was substantially what I have put into these pages. It amused them immensely, but, accustomed as they were to judge everything by the high standard of professional instruction and discipline of the Prussian army, they seemed unable to understand how an army like ours could fight. How would it cope with any of the regular armies of European powers arrayed against it on anything like equal terms in point of numbers?

They listened to me with a polite smile when I exprest the opinion that no country had human material superior to ours as regards physical development, intelligence, and martial spirit; that in the long run our volunteers could outmarch any European troops, and surpass them in the endurance of any sort of fatigue; that our volunteers, with incredible skill and rapidity, would build roads, and extemporize serviceable railway bridges and viaducts, with nothing but nails and tools, such as axes and saws and hammers and picks and shovels, and pine trees near at hand, and a clever engineer to guide them—I had seen them do it—and that they would construct temporary entrenchments and defenses almost without tools—I had seen them do that, too, many times—and that, in my opinion, they would, in a conflict with a European army, perhaps at the beginning of a campaign suffer some reverses by the superiority of European drill and discipline, but soon become acquainted with the tactics of their adversaries, and prove decidedly superior in the long run, especially if the contest were to be fought out on American soil.

Here is the secret of it, which the European mind, unacquainted with the genius of this country, finds it difficult to understand: Owing to the educational power of free institutions, many things are accomplished in America without much drill and discipline, for which in Europe very much drill and discipline is required.

As to the bravery of the American soldier, Northern as well as Southern, volunteer as well as regular, there can hardly be two opinions. He will not suffer, but rather profit, by any comparison with any other. In his courage

there is a peculiar element of national pride. But I must confess that my war experience has destroyed some youthful illusions as to the romantic aspect of bravery or heroism in battle. . . .

Mr. Schurz knew what he was talking about. He received his military training in the German army and then, after he emigrated to the United States, enlisted as a volunteer in our Northern army. We need only add that the American volunteer is generally supposed to have given a pretty good account of himself in every war in which the United States has been engaged. At least such is the popular impression.

But lest it be claimed that modern warfare has now so changed conditions that no volunteer army can hope to cope with the technically trained, highly seasoned regulars of a modern militaristic state, we venture to point to the Canadians, whose volunteer army has stood steadfast without fear or faltering against the most excellently trained army the world has ever seen. The Canadian volunteer today fears no man on earth. Would his American cousin prove a whit less valiant fighter in the trenches?

THE GOAL OF HOUSEHOLD EFFICIENCY

WHAT is the ultimate end and aim of the movement for household efficiency? Is it to make the home a better place to live in or an easier place to get away from?

On another page we print the first of a series of four articles by Martha Bensley Bruère on different phases of this interesting question. Mrs. Bruère sums up her subject in the phrase, "The Habits of Women Under Domestication," and presents her thesis something in this form:

Most teachers in domestic science and most people who speak and write on the subject of household efficiency take the attitude that the result of increased efficiency in housekeeping will be to reduce the cost of living, to make domesticity more satisfying to women, and to keep the home the center of community life. None of these things will inevitably follow. The real object of increasing home efficiency is to get rid of housework—to transform as much as possible of it into community work, and to boil down the rest to an irreducible minimum, so that women may have a chance to do some of the other things, from regulating the gas supply to supervising the schools, that need to be done in a country that is trying to become a democracy. For no interest in clubs, sports or society, no suffrage agitation or feminist propaganda will so effectually undomesticate and socialize women as the simple expedient of cutting the cable of household drudgery that has hitherto tied them to the house. Every new apparatus for house cleaning, every satisfactory prepared food, every laundry which washes the clothes as well as "Maggie" at the wash tub, every invention from the electric egg-beater to the machine to darn stockings is a direct step toward women's political, social and industrial enfranchisement for a larger usefulness.

This point of view has something a little startling about it. But that should be no reason for assuming it to be unsound—nor, for that matter, for assuming it to be sound. Many of the readers of The Independent will doubtless have ideas of their own on this point. We shall be glad to welcome expressions of any opinions that they may have on the subject as the series progresses.

Villa's Attack Upon
Columbus

... soldiers of the regular army. The force is ordered to capture General Francisco Villa, dead or alive and to punish or capture the bandits whom he has been seeking. Relief has been ordered ... the war because of Villa's massacre of the United States and his attack upon the people of the town of Columbus in New Mexico. In the dark, at half past four in the morning of the 9th, Villa at the head of 1500 of his men, suddenly attacked Columbus and the army post of three troops of cavalry. Their version was that of assassins who arrived to merely Residents were murdered at the town of their homes. The soldiers of a town was dragged from a sick bed and put to death. The mob had been applied to his body, and his body was thrown onto the flames to be consumed. A druggist was killed in his store. The husband of a guest in the town was torn from the arms of his wife, who was striving to save him, and murdered five minutes later. He was a delegate to the State building school Convention. One of the victims was Dr. Hart, an inspector of the Bureau of Animal Industry in the Department of Agriculture.

Eight civilians were killed, and nine soldiers of our army. Many buildings were burned. But when the Mexicans withdrew, after a stay of two hours, they left the bodies of twenty-seven of their men in the streets. One of these was the body of Pablo Lopez, second in command to Villa, and the leader of the bandits who murdered sixteen Americans at Santa Ysabel.

Simon, commander of the American cavalry post, had his revolver shot from his hand.

When the bandits withdrew from Columbus they were pursued by 194 cavalrymen, who followed them for five miles on Mexican soil. There was more fighting, and it is reported that not less than forty of the Villistas were killed, while the cavalry lost only one man. The bodies of forty-seven Mexicans have been buried or burned, this number including the twenty-seven found in Columbus. At 11 o'clock in the morning the pursuing cavalry returned.

It is now known that Villa had spied on Columbus on the 9th. They scanned the cavalry camp and reported the number of soldiers in it. When the attack was made, Villa cut the telegraph and telephone wires, and no warning could be given to other American soldiers along the border. He had missed the American authorities by a telegram, on the 9th, saying that he was at Nogales ranch, forty-four miles south of Columbus, and by causing the publication of reports that he was seeking a conference with officers of our army. Just before the attack, however, he had looted the ranch of an American land company at Palomas, killed four Americans there and burned their bodies. And he brought with him to Columbus, where she was set free, the widow of a murdered American. She had been a prisoner for nine days. Villa asserted, she says, that if possible he would kill all the Americans, men, women and children, and that he would have the aid of Japan and Germany. In addition to the 1500 men whom he led to Columbus he had about 1600 whom he had left a few miles south of the boundary.

Our Punitive Expedition

The news carried much indignation in Washington, where the President and his Cabinet at once began to plan the course our Government would take. It was the first day of Mr. Baker's service as Secretary of War. It is understood that Mr. Wilson promptly informed Señor Arredondo, Carranza's Ambassador, that our army would be used in Mexico for the capture of Villa, with or without Carranza's consent. Arredondo replied it is said, that he would advise Carranza not to object or interfere. It was thought that at least 5000 men would be required. At Columbus there were only 354. Scattered along the border were 19,966. On the 11th it was decided that a punitive expedition should go into Mexico at once. General Funston, who captured Aguinaldo in the Philippines, was to be in command, with full responsibility and a free hand, but the leader in the field was to be General John J. Pershing, another officer who has served in the Philippines. The sole object of the measure was, of course, to be the capture of Villa and his forces. As General Funston has asked that publicity be avoided, the official statements have been brief. The first official announcement, on the 10th, was as follows:

An adequate force will be sent at once in pursuit of Villa, with the single object of capturing him and putting a stop to his forays. This can and will be done in entirely friendly aid of the constituted authorities in Mexico, and with scrupulous respect for the sovereignty of that republic.

General Funston said that day in a message that unless Villa should be relentlessly pursued and his forces scattered he would continue his raids. As Carranza's troops were accomplishing nothing, but were guilty of apathy and gross inefficiency, it would be unwise to fritter away the whole available American force by guarding towns, ranches and railroads, because Villa could strike with 2500 men at any point on the border. On the 11th, Secretary Baker said that General Funston was free to move his expeditionary force across the border at any time, and to use it at his own discretion. As soon as the crossing had been made, this fact would be given to the public. In the absence of official information it was understood that there would be three columns, one starting from El Paso, one from Agua Prieta, and one from some western point, and that the three were to converge. Carranza has sent 1200 men to Palomas, and Calles, his Governor of Sonora, has promised to guard passes westward which Villa might desire to use. The 400 Mormon colonists at Casas Grandes have been in danger. Villa intended to attack them, and a part of his force was recently only 30 miles from the place.

Carranza sent to Secretary Lansing,

THE WAR AREA IN MEXICO

Villa raided Columbus, New Mexico, from Boca Grande. The border patrol of the United States Army stretches along the entire frontier from the Gulf of Mexico to the Colorado River. The country south of the Mexican border here is almost entirely mountainous and arid

GET VILLA—DEAD OR ALIVE

on the 10th, a long message in which he expresses regret for the "lamentable incident" at Columbus, and says it was similar to the attacks made by one Indians about the year 1836, and at later dates, upon the Mexican people in Sonora and Chihuahua, when many murders were committed. As there were agreements then permitting the armed forces of either country to cross into the territory of the other, he asks that his forces be allowed to cross in pursuit of Villa, "acknowledging this reciprocity in regard to American forces crossing into Mexican territory."

Our Congress supports the President in his course. At meetings of the House Committee approval had been express. Mr. Mann, Republican, introduced a resolution declaring that the President was justified in the proposed use of armed forces. In the Senate Committee there was informal approval. It was held that the consent of Congress was not needed, as war was not involved. Senator Fall introduced a resolution authorizing the use of our armed forces in Mexico and calling for 500,000 volunteers. One from Senator McCumber says that Mexico has no Government capable of punishing Villa, and that the force sent after Villa by us should be large enough to overcome opposition "from any source."

Wages and Strikes — As a result of the conferences in New York between the miners and their employers, the bituminous miners, nearly 300,000 in number, have obtained nearly all they demanded. An agreement had been signed which goes into effect on April 1 and will be in force for two years. It gives a wage increase of from 5 to 13½ per cent, and this will add $4,000,000 to the annual cost of production. A price increase of 12 cents a ton will be required, it is said. The wage increase for miners ranges from 18 to 26 cents a day, and the addition for day laborers is from 10 to 16 cents. A settlement for the anthracite miners has not been reached. They ask for an increase of twenty per cent, an eight-hour day, and recognition of the union. Their employers say that compliance with the demands would increase the annual cost of production by $23,000,000. More than eighty per cent of the 100,000 members of the four railroad unions have voted for the demands which are soon to be laid before all the companies, and which, the companies say, call for an addition of $100,000,000 to the annual expenditures. Already the telegraphers and trackmen of two roads are on strike.

There was news, last week, of many strikes. In Buffalo more than twenty factories are affected by a strike of 7500 machinists, who ask for an eight hour day, with time and a half for overtime and a minimum of 40 cents an hour. Higher wages are demanded by 5000 strikers at the Massachusetts and New Hampshire quarries. In Baltimore, 7000 strikers from the garment makers' factories took part in a riot, and 118, several women among them, were arrested. There were arrests also in Shelton, Connecticut, where girl strikers from a corset factory attacked with eggs and pepper the girls who remained at work. About 2000 men employed in three or four factories at Passaic, N.

J., are out for an increase of 20 or 25 per cent. At the fertilizer works in Roosevelt, N. J., where two men were killed in a strike last year, 300 are out, demanding an increase of 18 cents a day. At Washington the street cars were tied up for two days by a strike of 1200 of the 1500 employees. Service was resumed after an agreement to submit the dispute to arbitrators had been reached. The men demand an increase from 22½ to 30 cents an hour and other changes.

Fresh gunmen have been used in the garment workers' strike at New York. Three men arrested for attacking guards stationed in front of one factory to protect girls remaining at work confess that they had been employed by a representative of the union to shoot the guards. The price was to be $100 for each guard shot. They had wounded one, named Benjamin Weinstein. These strikers ask for a week of fifty hours, with a wage increase ranging from 15 to 25 per cent.

All the employees of the hand window glass factories (six states are affected) are to have a wage increase of 7½ per cent. In East St. Louis, 6000 men employed by the Armour and other packing companies get an increase of $3,000 a week. The pay of 5000 men at the Cramp shipyards, where there is work for two years on hand, has been increased by 10 per cent. Representatives of the canning factories in the State of New York ask the officials in industrial Commission to exempt them during the canning season from the requirements of the laws regulating hours of work for women and children. They call for a limit of twelve hours

THE STORY OF THE WEEK

Villa's Attack Upon Columbus

Our Government has sent into Mexico about 5000 soldiers of the regular army. This force is ordered to capture General Francisco Villa, dead or alive, and to punish or disperse the bandits whom he has been leading. Mexico has been invaded in this way because of Villa's invasion of the United States and his attack upon the people of the town of Columbus in New Mexico. In the dark, at half past four in the morning, on the 9th, Villa, at the head of 1500 of his men, suddenly attacked Columbus and the camp there of three troops of cavalry. Their conduct was that of assassins who showed no mercy. Residents were murdered at the doors of their houses. The landlord of a hotel was dragged from a sick bed and put to death. The torch had been applied to his hotel, and his body was thrown into the flames, to be consumed. A druggist was killed in his store. The husband of a guest in the hotel was torn from the arms of his wife, who was striving to save him, and murdered five minutes later. He was a delegate to the State Sunday School Convention. One of the victims was Dr. Hart, an Inspector of the Bureau of Animal Industry in the Department of Agriculture.

Eight civilians were killed, and nine soldiers of our army. Many buildings were burned. But when the Mexicans withdrew, after a stay of two hours, they left the bodies of twenty-seven of their men in the streets. One of these was the body of Pablo Lopez, second in command to Villa, and the leader of the bandits who murdered nineteen Americans at Santa Ysobel. Colonel Slocum, commander of the American cavalrymen, had his revolver shot from his hand.

When the bandits withdrew from Columbus they were pursued by 250 cavalrymen, who followed them for five miles on Mexican soil. There was more fighting, and it is reported that not less than forty of the Villistas were killed, altho the cavalry lost only one man. The bodies of fifty-seven Mexicans have been buried or burned, this number including the twenty-seven found in Columbus. At 10 o'clock in the morning the pursuing cavalry returned.

It is now known that Villa had spies in Columbus on the 7th. They located the cavalry camp and reported the number of soldiers in it. When the attack was made, Villa cut the telegraph and telephone wires, and no warning could be given to other American soldiers along the border. He had misled the American authorities by a telegram, on the 8th, saying that he was at Nogales ranch, forty-four miles south of Columbus, and by causing the publication of reports that he was seeking a conference with officers of our army. Just before the attack, however, he had looted the ranch of an American land company at Palomas, killed four Americans there and burned their bodies. And he brought with him to Columbus, where she was set free, the widow of a murdered American. She had been a prisoner for nine days. Villa asserted, she says, that if possible he would kill all the Americans, men, women and children, and that he would have the aid of Japan and Germany. In addition to the 1500 men whom he led to Columbus he had about 1000 whom he had left a few miles south of the boundary.

Our Punitive Expedition

The news excited much indignation in Washington, where the President and his Cabinet at once began to plan the course our Government would take. It was the first day of Mr. Baker's service as Secretary of War. It is understood that Mr. Wilson promptly informed Señor Arredondo, Carranza's Ambassador, that our army would be used in Mexico for the capture of Villa, with or without Carranza's consent. Arredondo replied, it is said, that he would advise Carranza not to object or interfere. It was thought that at least 5000 men would be required. At Columbus there were only 350. Scattered along the border were 19,000. On the 10th it was decided that a punitive expedition should go into Mexico at once. General Funston, who captured Aguinaldo in the Philippines, was to be in command, with full responsibility and a free hand, but the leader in the field was to be General John J. Pershing, another officer who has served in the Philippines. The sole object of the movement was, of course, to be the capture of Villa and his forces. As General Funston has asked that publicity be avoided, the official statements have been brief. The first official announcement, on the 10th, was as follows:

An adequate force will be sent at once in pursuit of Villa, with the single object of capturing him and putting a stop to his forays. This can and will be done in entirely friendly aid of the constituted authorities in Mexico, and with scrupulous respect for the sovereignty of that republic.

General Funston said that day in a message that unless Villa should be relentlessly pursued and his forces scattered he would continue his raids. As Carranza's troops were accomplishing nothing, but were guilty of apathy and gross inefficiency, it would be unwise to fritter away the whole available American force by guarding towns, ranches and railroads, because Villa could strike with 3000 men at any point on the border. On the 11th, Secretary Baker said that General Funston was free to move his expeditionary force across the border at any time, and to use it at his own discretion. As soon as the crossing had been made, this fact would be given to the public. In the absence of official information it was understood that there would be three columns, one starting from El Paso, one from Agua Prieta, and one from some western point, and that the three were to converge. Carranza has sent 1200 men to Palomas, and Calles, his Governor of Sonora, has promised to guard passes westward which Villa might desire to use. The 400 Mormon colonists at Casas Grandes have been in danger. Villa intended to attack them, and a part of his force was recently only 30 miles from the place.

Carranza sent to Secretary Lansing,

THE WAR AREA IN MEXICO

Villa raided Columbus, New Mexico, from Boca Grande. The border patrol of the United States Army stretches along the entire frontier from the Gulf of Mexico to the Colorado River. The country south of the Mexican border here is almost entirely mountainous and arid

Kirby in New York World

THE RATTLESNAKE

Peass in Newark (N. J.) Evening News

GO GET 'EM

GET VILLA—DEAD OR ALIVE

on the 10th, a long message in which he expresses regret for the "lamentable incident" at Columbus, and says it was similar to the attacks made by our Indians about the year 1880, and at later dates, upon the Mexican people in Sonora and Chihuahua, when many murders were committed. As there were agreements then permitting the armed forces of either country to cross into the territory of the other, he asks that his forces be allowed to cross in pursuit of Villa, "acknowledging due reciprocity in regard to American forces crossing into Mexican territory."

Our Congress supports the President in his course. At meetings of the House Committee approval has been exprest. Mr. Mott, Republican, introduced a resolution declaring that the President was justified in the proposed use of armed forces. In the Senate Committee there was informal approval. It was held that the consent of Congress was not needed, as war was not involved. Senator Fall introduced a resolution authorizing the use of our armed forces in Mexico and calling for 500,000 volunteers. One from Senator McCumber says that Mexico has no Government capable of punishing Villa, and that the force sent after Villa by us should be large enough to overcome opposition "from any source."

Wages and Strikes As a result of the conferences in New York between the miners and their employees, the bituminous miners, nearly 300,000 in number, have obtained nearly all they demanded. An agreement has been signed which goes into effect on April 1 and will be in

force for two years. It gives a wage increase of from 5 to 13½ per cent, and this will add $8,000,000 to the annual cost of production. A price increase of 12 cents a ton will be required, it is said. The wage increase for miners ranges from 18 to 28 cents a day, and the addition for day laborers is from 10 to 16 cents. A settlement for the anthracite miners has not been reached. They ask for an increase of twenty per cent, an eight-hour day, and recognition of the union. Their employers say that compliance with the demands would increase the annual cost of production by $23,000,000. More than eighty per cent of the 400,000 members of the four railroad unions have voted for the demands which are soon to be laid before all the companies, and which, the companies say, call for an addition of $100,000,000 to the annual expenditures. Already the telegraphers and trackmen of two roads are on strike.

There was news, last week, of many strikes. In Buffalo more than twenty factories are affected by a strike of 7500 machinists, who ask for an eight-hour day, with time and a half for overtime and a minimum of 40 cents an hour. Higher wages are demanded by 5000 strikers at the Massachusetts and New Hampshire quarries. In Baltimore, 7000 strikers from the garment makers' factories took part in a riot, and 116, several women among them, were arrested. There were arrests also in Shelton, Connecticut, where girl strikers from a corset factory attacked with eggs and pepper the girls who remained at work. About 2000 men employed in three or four factories at Passaic, N.

J., are out for an increase of 20 or 25 per cent. At the fertilizer works in Roosevelt, N. J., where two men were killed in a strike last year, 900 are out, demanding an increase of 18 cents a day. At Washington the street cars were tied up for two days by a strike of 1200 of the 1500 employees. Service was resumed after an agreement to submit the dispute to arbitrators had been reached. The men demand an increase from 22½ to 30 cents an hour and other changes.

Hired gunmen have been used in the garment workers' strike at New York. Three men arrested for attacking guards stationed in front of one factory to protect girls remaining at work confest that they had been employed by a representative of the union to shoot the guards. The price was to be $100 for each guard shot. They had wounded one, named Benjamin Weinstein. These strikers ask for a week of fifty hours, with a wage increase ranging from 15 to 25 per cent.

All the employees of the hand window glass factories (six states are affected) are to have a wage increase of 7½ per cent. In East St. Louis, 5000 men employed by the Armour and other packing companies get an increase of $3000 a week. The pay of 5000 men at the Cramp shipyards, where there is work for two years on hand, has been increased by 10 per cent. Representatives of the canning factories in the State of New York ask the State's Industrial Commission to exempt them during the canning season from the requirements of the laws regulating hours of work for women and children. They call for a limit of twelve hours.

President Gompers, of the Federation of Labor, has been urging the public school teachers in New York City to form a union and affiliate with the national organization.

The Warning Resolutions After the tabling of the Gore resolution in the Senate, action in the House upon the McLemore resolution, warning Americans not to take passage on the ships of the belligerent nations, was delayed until the 7th. The Rules Committee proposed that there should be debate for an hour and a half on its reported plan, and for four hours on the motion to table. There had been some misgivings as to the result, but the first test, a vote of 256 to 160 in favor of ordering the previous question, reassured the supporters of the President. On the adoption of the rule or plan the vote was 271 to 138, and after a debate in which the speeches were short the McLemore warning resolution was tabled by a vote of 276 to 142. In the affirmative were 182 Democrats and 93 Republicans, and on the other side 33 Democrats and 102 Republicans were counted. The record was quite emphatic against any interference with the President's treatment of the issue involved, and it is not expected that the question will be raised again.

A day or two earlier a collection of letters and reports had been published which tended to show that the German-American Alliance had been interested in a lobby at Washington, engaged in suggesting the introduction of such resolutions and in promoting the adoption of them.

Representative Page, of North Carolina, a brother of the Ambassador to Great Britain, has given notice that he will retire at the end of his present term because he cannot support the President's foreign policy. His conscience would not permit him to vote against a resolution of warning, and he thinks all semblance of neutrality here was destroyed when our Government failed to express disapproval of the $500,000,000 Anglo-French loan. For similar reasons, and because he opposes the defense or preparedness program, Representative Kitchin, Democratic floor leader, it is said, will retire. Another Democrat, Representative Sherwood, of Ohio, will go because he is at variance with the President as to a warning and also concerning the defense bills.

In the Senate, Mr. McCumber, Republican, withdrew his resolution of warning, which resembled Mr. Gore's, saying he thought Americans had been warned effectively and that it might embarrass the President in his negotiations. Senator Vardaman, in a speech, defended the Gore resolution, attacked the manufacturers of munitions and said the press advocates of preparedness were patriots for pelf. Senator Stone said he had had a frank talk with the President, whose supreme wish was to avoid the calamity of war.

The nominations of Newton D. Baker, to be Secretary of War; David R. Francis, to be Ambassador to Russia, and Joseph H. Shea, of Indiana, to be Ambassador to Chile, have been confirmed. Mr. Baker, a lawyer, formerly Mayor of Cleveland, was a supporter and assistant of the late Mayor Tom L. Johnson, and has not been regarded as an advocate of the defense program. Mr. Francis was a member of President Cleveland's Cabinet.

Trust Cases In Youngstown, Ohio, a grand jury has indicted the United Steel Corporation, the Republican Iron and Steel Company, the Carnegie Steel Company, the Youngstown Sheet and Tube Company, two other steel companies, and Judge E. H. Gary, chairman of the Steel Corporation's board, for conspiracy, in violation of Ohio's Anti-Trust law, to fix the rate of wages in the steel industry. The indictment follows an investigation concerning the strike riots at East Youngstown in January, when several persons were killed and $1,000,000 worth of property was destroyed. It appears that the conspiracy, if there was one, was for the purpose of increasing wages, for the complaint is based upon the fact that an announced increase of 10 per cent by the Corporation was followed within two days by a similar increase at the works of the other five accused companies. The county prosecutor says Judge Gary was indicted because he is the dictator of the steel industry. Judge Gary says the indictment is an outrage, and that there are no facts to justify it.

The Eastman Kodak Company has appealed from the decision of the Federal District Court, which held that the company is an illegal monopoly and ordered the dissolution of it. The company is willing to discontinue certain trade practises as to which complaint was made, but will oppose dissolution. Probably a year will elapse before the appeal can be taken up at Washington.

In an interesting decision announced at Baltimore by Judge Rose, of the United States District Court, in the suit of the Government, under the Anti-Trust law, for dissolution of the American Can Company, it

Kirby in New York World
A STRATEGIC RETIREMENT

Carter in New York Evening Sun
IT CAN'T BE DONE

CONGRESS REFUSES TO SCUTTLE AMERICAN RIGHTS

© International News

IN COMMAND AT COLUMBUS

Colonel Herbert J. Slocum was commanding the Thirteenth United States Cavalry at Columbus, New Mexico, when Villa took that town by surprise on the morning of March 9. As he ran out of his house at the first alarm the Mexicans were already so close that his revolver was shot from his hand. Colonel Slocum is a nephew of Mrs. Russell Sage. Up to 1914 he had been in Cuba, where he organized the Rurales for the Cuban Government

is held that, altho the company had its origin in unlawful acts and thereby acquired power which may be harmful, it has for some time past "used that power on the whole rather for weal than for wo." It is impossible, Judge Rose says, to put things back, in this industry, where they were in 1901, and probably highly undesirable if it were possible. The company's power is great, but it is limited by a large volume of actual competition. Those in the trade do not complain and do not want a dissolution. It is "doubtful whether dissolution would profit any one."

Judge Rose is "frankly reluctant to destroy so finely adjusted an industrial machine." The situation which existed before the company or combination was formed cannot be restored. The Government, he continues, fears that the company "will hereafter, to the public prejudice, dangerously use the strength which it gained by its original law-breaking." Therefore he decided to retain the bill of complaint, without ordering a dissolution, but reserving the right to do this if hereafter it shall appear that the company's power is being used to the injury of the public, or has given the company so great control over the industry as to make dissolution expedient. This is the first decision of its kind in the record of cases under the Anti-Trust law.

The Thirteenth Belligerent

At half past three on the afternoon of March 9, Germany declared war upon Portugal. Virtually, however, the two countries have been in a state of war since February 23,

when the Portuguese Government, at the request of England, seized all of the German ships in Portuguese waters. There were thirty-six German steamers at Lisbon and eight at St. Vincent, Cape Verde Islands, thus appropriated. The German Government protested against this as an illegal and unfriendly act and called attention to other violations of neutrality such as the use of Portuguese ports by British warships, the permission granted to British troops to cross the colony of Mozambique in order to attack German East Africa, the fighting on the frontier of Angola and German Southwest Africa, and the employment of Madeira as a naval base by the British.

The position of Portugal has indeed been anomalous, for she was virtually allied with Great Britain when the war broke out and under treaty obligations to supply 10,000 troops at any time they were requested. This alliance and obligation were confirmed by the Portuguese Parliament in August, 1914, but no hostilities have taken place except in the African colonies and that soon ceased.

By the seizure of the German shipping Portugal multiplies her merchant marine by three and will be able to relieve the embarrassment which the interruption of Portuguese commerce has caused the country. The German ships may also be used for the transportation of British troops, and in many other ways the participation of Portugal in the war will be of great advantage to Great Britain apart from the army, which on a peace footing numbers 32,-000; on a war footing 183,000. The value of these troops is questionable, but they could, no doubt, be made useful either in France or in the conquest

© 1900 J. C. Strauss

AMBASSADOR TO RUSSIA

David R. Francis, who has been Mayor of St. Louis, Governor of Missouri, and Secretary of the Interior under President Cleveland. He is a grain merchant of St. Louis

THE DEAN OF DRAMATIC CRITICS

In honor of William Winter, who is eighty this year, a great number of distinguished men and women—the President and ex-Presidents of the nation, publicists and artists in all fields—asked his permission to give a testimonial performance at the Century Theater in New York on March 14. Mr. Winter is a poet, author, dramatic critic and editor, and has been a regular contributor to magazines and newspapers since 1852. From 1865 to 1909 he was dramatic critic for the New York Tribune, and it is as a loving exponent of the finest standards of dramatic art, and a strong force for the maintenance of the dignity and purity of the stage, that he commands such widespread loyalty and affection

of German East Africa, which General Smuts is now undertaking.

This brings the number of nations formally taking part in the war up to thirteen, Great Britain, France, Russia, Belgium, Italy, Serbia, Montenegro, Japan and Portugal on one side and Germany, Austria-Hungary, Turkey and Bulgaria on the other. Besides these the war has extended into the territories of five other countries, Luxemburg, Albania, Greece, Persia and China.

Russian Conquest of Armenia

The most spectacular and quite possibly the most important campaign at present is the Russian invasion of Turkey from the Caucasus. Since the loss of Erzerum the Turks have offered no resistance to the Russian troops who are moving north, west and south from that city. On the Black Sea coast, north of Erzerum, the Russians have landed forces which are marching westward to take the city of Trebizond, the principal city on the south coast of the Black Sea. They have already reached Rize, the nearest town to Trebizond and only forty miles away.

South of Erzerum the Russians have possession of all shores of Lake Van and by the capture of Bitlis, a fortified town twenty miles west of the lake, they have come within less than fifty miles from the Tigris. Whether from this point they will go down the river to Mosul or up the river to Diarbekr remains to be seen. If they go downstream they may be able to reach Bagdad and make connections with the British, who for more than a year have been trying to force their way up the Tigris to Bagdad. The advance detachment of the British army under General Townshend has been since last November besieged at Kut-el-Amara, over a hundred miles below, but now it is announced that the relief expedition under General Aylmer, which started the first of the year, has got within seven miles of Kut. Between the two British forces the Turks are occupying a fortified position, but this barrier may soon be broken down and then the combined forces may resume their advance on Bagdad. This time the Ottoman opposition will probably not be so strong as it was last fall because the Russians from Erzerum are threatening and may even have interrupted the line of communication with Constantinople.

The Russian advance has also checked any plans which may have been made at Constantinople for an attack upon Suez. If the Russians can go on twice as far as they have already gone they will reach Aleppo, which is the railroad junction for the line that runs east toward Bagdad and the one that runs south toward Jerusalem and Egypt. From Aleppo to the Gulf of Alexandretta is only about fifty miles farther and the French and British warships in the Mediterranean could land troops in Alexandretta at any time, to make connection with the Russian forces coming overland from the Caucasus.

This would cut the Ottoman empire in two and leave the three powers free to divide up Turkey and Persia to suit themselves. It has long been surmized that whenever the time came for a partition of these regions that Great Britain was to get Egypt, Arabia, Mesopotamia and southern Persia, Russia was to get northern Persia and Armenia with a southern port at Alexandretta, if not Constantinople, and France was to get Syria. These territories are now rapidly passing into the possession of the Powers to which they are supposed to have been allotted.

The Assault on Fort Vaux
The attack on Verdun began with an advance of the German center directly north of the town. That was carried as far as Fort Douaumont, five miles from Verdun. This was followed by a swing of the left which brought the German line up Fort Vaux, five miles to the east. The third movement is the advance of the right wing on the west bank of the Meuse River. If this meets with equal success the Germans will have Verdun closely encircled on three sides and every part of it will be under fire as soon as they get their big

THE GREAT WAR

March 6—Germans take Forges, west of Meuse. Russians advance twenty-seven miles beyond Kermanshah, Persia.

March 7—Germans attack Vaux and takes Fresnes and Regnéville, near Verdun. Admiralty announces that British navy is stronger by 1,000,-000 tons than before the war.

March 8—French regain Bois des Corbeaux. Austrians closing in on Avlona, Albania.

March 9—War declared between Portugal and Germany. Norwegian bark "Silicea" with seven Americans on board torpedoed without warning.

March 10—Russians land at Rize, forty miles east of Trebizond. Germans take French lines near Rheims.

March 11—Germans gain trenches on Dead Man's Hill. Portuguese cabinet resigns.

March 12—Russians reach Karind, Persia, 110 miles from Bagdad. Italians resume bombardment of Görz.

guns established on these new positions. When this is done the eventual reduction of the fortress would be inevitable, provided, of course, that the French do not launch a serious counter-offensive and that the Germans do not run short of men and ammunition before accomplishing their purpose.

As to this question of how long the Germans can afford to keep up an offensive on such a gigantic scale there is room for wide difference of opinion. From the Allies side we hear that the Germans are every day suffering enormous losses, that they have already used up two-thirds of the 300,000 men engaged, and that their assaults are growing constantly weaker. For instance this is the way the correspondent of the London *Daily Mail* reports his observations of the new battle at Vaux:

Not since the battle of Verdun began have the German losses been so terrible as in yesterday's fighting. Whole brigades which went into action against Douaumont, Vaux village and Vaux fort were practically wiped out of existence and most of the German units engaged lost two-thirds of their strength.

They suffered heavily, as always, in fighting the French infantryman, marvelous with the bayonet, and the Zouaves, Turcos and Senegalese, who figured prominently in yesterday's engagement, like demons let loose, as they drove their bayonets home with an overarm plunging stroke. Unlike British and French infantrymen, who usually thrust upwards, the French African troops raise their rifles above their heads, and with the whole weight of the body bring it down with a thrust which sends the bayonet thru the opponent. The Germans suffered even more cruelly from the French artillery and machine guns.

On Wednesday the Germans gained a footing for less than an hour in the streets of Vaux, but they could not withstand the cyclonic rush with which the French counter attacked, and when the latter paused for breath the German dead and dying lay in heaps where they had fallen. Another fruitless German attack was led against the trenches lining Hill 600, on which Vaux fort stands. Here the Germans met with even less success, for they never reached the trenches, but were mown down almost to a man.

THE LOOKOUT—WATCHING THE ITALIANS IN THE VALLEY FROM AN AUSTRIAN OUTPOST

It was categorically denied by the French Foreign Office that the Germans had captured the village or had even attacked the fort at that time. But it is now acknowledged by the French that the Germans have possession of the village and also the slope of the fort.

Other forts on the same ridge as Vaux, such as Moulainville, Tavannes, and Eix, have been bombarded, and further south the village of Fresnes has been taken by the Germans.

The Battle of Crows' Wood The fighting on the western side of the Meuse is very different and perhaps even more important than that on the eastern, for a sufficient advance here would cut off Verdun, which so far is kept in communication with Paris by railroad trains and a double stream of automobiles. As will be seen from the map the river pursues a very winding course below Verdun. In one of its westward loops is the village of Champneuville, which the Germans took last week. Just below this the Meuse makes a curve to the east around the villages of Forges and Regnéville, which the Germans have taken this week.

But to go farther was no easy matter for the way was barred by two strongly fortified hights, Côte de l'Oie and Le Mort Homme, or, to put them into English, Goose Ridge and Dead Man's Hill. Both are over eight hundred feet high and dominate the plain and ravines across which the Germans had to advance. They stand about two miles apart and the lower hills between are covered with timber known as the Bois des Corbeaux or Crows' Wood. Barbed wire stretched from tree to tree had made of it a veritable crow's-nest entanglement and concealed batteries covered all approaches.

In spite of these obstacles, however, the Germans succeeded in penetrating Crows' Wood and by Tuesday night held virtually the whole of it and were beginning to ascend the slop of Goose Ridge. But the French drove them out by raking the woods with their 75's and then charging with infantry. Later the Germans again gained the wood and now threaten the French line south of Bethincourt.

Berlin claims the capture in the fighting about Verdun of 26,472 unwounded prisoners, 41 heavy guns, 148 field pieces and 232 machine guns. The French deny that the German gains are so great as this.

The German activity is not confined to Verdun but extends east. Along the Aisne River they took three-quarters of a mile of French trenches, part of which the French regained.

THE DEFENDER OF VERDUN
General Petain, called on two hours' notice to take command at the threatened fortress. He was an obscure officer before the war, but proved his fitness in the fighting at Charleroi and has won rapid promotion

On the other hand unofficial reports from Berlin claim that the German losses at Verdun amount to "only a few thousand." According to the British version, the Brandenburgers, who stormed Fort Douaumont, lost 40,000 of their number, but the official casualty list gives the loss as only 202 of whom fifty were killed.

There is also a great discrepancy between the accounts of the early operations at Vaux. The German headquarters reported with unusual definiteness that

in the Woevre district the village and armored fort of Vaux, with numerous adjoining fortified positions, were captured in a glorious night attack, after thoro artillery preparation, by the Posen reserve regiments Nos. 6 and 19, under the leadership of the commander of the Ninth Reserve Division of infantry, General von Guretsky Cornitz.

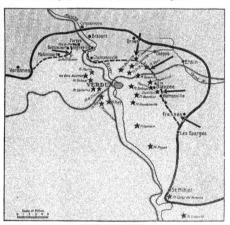

CLOSING IN ON VERDUN

The Germans have gained ground successively on the north, the east and the west of the fortress and now are within five miles of the town at several points. During the past week they have taken Fresnes and demolished the fort of Vaux on the east, while on the western side they have penetrated the wood that lies between the two hills of Côte de l'Oie and Le Mort Homme. This attack from the west was the last to develop and shows the Germans attempting to complete their semi-circle of siege guns. The shaded area shows the ground now held by the Germans. The solid line is their position before the recent attack; the dotted line is their present front

Heise © Lawrence-Ripley

I have always been a peace advocate. I believe in peace and in the proper enforcement of the laws of peace—by force, if necessary

NEWTON D. BAKER
SECRETARY OF WAR

BAKER: TRAINED ADMINISTRATOR

BY FREDERIC C. HOWE

COMMISSIONER OF IMMIGRATION AT THE PORT OF NEW YORK

FEW men in public life more completely refute the opinion commonly held that democracy involves the commonplace and will not tolerate the expert trained official than Newton D. Baker, the new appointee to the portfolio of war. For few men in America are more thoroly prepared for public life, and few men have had a longer, more progressive and more fruitful career, measured by achievement, than the most recently appointed member of President Wilson's Cabinet. Probably the increasing number of trained men who are finding their way into municipal, state and Federal service is the best evidence of the changing character of our politics.

Mr. Baker has been in the public service almost continuously since his graduation from Johns Hopkins University in 1892, where he took his Bachelor degree, and Washington and Lee, where he completed his law studies. Trained for the law and really interested in the profession, he has been called from it repeatedly from the moment he returned to his native town of Martinsburg, West Virginia, down to the present. He was first appointed private secretary for Postmaster-General Wilson, the author of the Wilson Tariff Bill. Leaving that position, he was induced to go to Cleveland, Ohio, as a larger field for professional work. Almost immediately after arriving there he was appointed assistant solicitor in the City Law Department, and upon the election of Tom L. Johnson as Mayor in 1901 he was appointed city solicitor. This position he filled for eight years. It was an experience that would train any man in the most difficult legal problems, in the most complex administrative difficulties, for these were years of strenuous city building in Cleveland, in which the old traditions of spoils politics and corrupt control by public service corporations were being shattered, and the foundations of a new type of city government were being laid.

Mr. Baker was not only the city solicitor, he was the close confidential adviser of Mayor Johnson in his struggle to free the city from the public utility interests controlled by Hanna and other politicians. The street railway franchises were expiring. The companies desired their renewal. They refused to grant satisfactory terms. Mayor Johnson insisted that his experience had demonstrated that three cents was a reasonable charge for carrying passengers. And this was his rallying political cry. The issue was as to whether Cleveland really owned its streets. It seems a simple one, yet all the intrenched privileges of the state were bent on denial of this right. Year after year the struggle waged. Probably twenty elections turned around that issue.

At the end of eight years of struggle the street railways finally capitulated. They were driven to accept a three-cent fare. This fare has continued, with only occasional interruptions when it has been necessary to add one cent for a transfer to tide over periods of hard times which were reflected in the companies' earnings. Thru this reduction in fares the car riders of Cleveland have been saved from $2,500,000 to $3,000,000 every year.

On the death of Mayor Johnson, Mr. Baker was recognized as his logical successor. He was elected mayor by a majority of 15,000, a large part of his support coming from districts which had been most antagonistic to Mayor Johnson and his program. The program of municipal ownership had been freed from many obstacles, and Mayor Baker was first elected on an issue of municipal ownership of the electric lighting plant. A $2,000,000 plant was approved by the voters. It was subsequently erected. Electric lighting rates were immediately reduced to a maximum of three cents and a minimum of one-half cent per kilowatt hour. Even on these charges the municipal plant has proven a great success; it has not only earned all operating and fixed charges, but a substantial surplus as well.

These dominating issues being out of the way, Mayor Baker turned to other lines of municipal activity. Under the provisions of the Constitution the cities of Ohio were authorized to draft their own charters. A charter commission was appointed of fifteen men. It was a really representative and distinguished commission. It sat for several months, and finally reported back a model democratic charter, which was subsequently approved by the people. Under this charter Mr. Baker was elected mayor for a second term, which expired January 1, 1916.

During the years of his administration Cleveland took rank as probably the best governed city in America. A splendid project of grouping all the public buildings was adopted. Similar plans were carried thru in the surrounding territory, so that Cleveland has now provided wonderful suburban developments capable of accommodating probably half a million people. Other great projects were the completion of the water works system, the building of splendid bridges over the Cuyahoga River, the completion of the park system, and negotiations for the acquisition of a large part of its lake front to be used for municipal docks and terminals.

This is but indicative of the big visioned development which it has fallen to Mr. Baker's lot to carry thru. It has trained him in the handling of big projects; it has familiarized him with men and methods, and the interests which menace the nation no less than the city and the state. It has been a training involving just such large administrative and legislative measures as the administration of the portfolio of war presents.

At the expiration of his second term as mayor, Mr. Baker declined to be a candidate for reëlection. He desired to return to the law. He is recognized as a great orator and he is an orator of the scholarly type. At the Baltimore convention which placed Mr. Wilson in nomination he delivered an address recognized as one of the most brilliant of the convention, and his activities on behalf of Mr. Wilson contributed greatly to his nomination.

Mr. Baker is one of the few men in politics who keeps all of his academic enthusiasms alive. He is a constant reader and has a remarkable memory. He is interested in many social activities. For several years he was president of the Phi Gamma Delta Fraternity, which he joined at Johns Hopkins when he was a student under Woodrow Wilson. He has recently been elected national president of the National Consumers' League. While mayor he gave a great deal of attention to many social activities for the amelioration of housing, living and recreational conditions in the city.

According to the press Mr. Baker, who at forty-four is the youngest member of the Cabinet, is said to be profoundly interested in peace. He has, however, exprest approval of the President's preparedness program, and if the news accounts may be accepted as correct, we may assume that he is for preparedness for defense and the conduct of the War Department as an aid to the preservation of peace, rather than as an instrumentality for easy war.

Ellis Island, New York

415

WHY GIRLS SHOULD NOT BE TAUGHT TO DO HOUSEWORK

BY MARTHA BENSLEY BRUÈRE

OF all the inconsequent recommendations for the general instruction of girls, none is so recklessly handed about as the advice to teach them domestic science. It is the impressive Podsnappean wave of the educational arm intended to solve the girl as an economic problem. When housework required practically all the time of every woman it might have been an adequate solution. Then female seminaries and even colleges taught it as a matter of course, but as woman's opportunities broadened it was dropt. Now enlarged, elaborated and insistent, it is being brought back into education from the grade into education under the guise of vocational training.

Why?

Thru the mistaken idea that we need more and better housekeepers! We do not. The more women who must make housework their profession, the more backward we are in industrial organization and the less able to protect the family. What we do need is more and better community servants. So far as under the guise of domestic science women are trained for restaurant keepers, laundry supervisors, pure food experts and the hundred other forms of community service, that study justifies itself. But then it has become *community*, not *domestic* science. So far as it trains them to be their own or some one else's domestic servant it is not valuable, for housework is obsolescent. In a perfect progression from the mountain cabin, where the woman has no time for anything but housework, to the city apartment hotel, where her duties consist of checking the monthly bill, the need for training in domestic science proper is vanishing away. And even when a city woman chooses to "keep house," her housework has reached a minimum which no one has yet presumed to call irreducible.

It seems necessary to remind ourselves that we are living under a form of government that is trying to become a democracy, and that democracy implies that every adult human being shall put in a full time job for life of real work—not merely keep busy; and that real work is doing something that needs to be done. If a girl expects to do housework in her own home, under modern conditions that should not take more than one-fifth of her time. If she plans to make housework a paid profession,

416

This article is the first of a series on "The Habits of Women under Domestication," written for The Independent by Mrs. Martha Bensley Bruère, a graduate of Vassar College, and the author of numerous books and articles on efficiency for women. Among them are "Experiences of a Nursery Governess," the record of Mrs. Bruère's own experiments in that profession, and "Increasing Home Efficiency," written with her husband, Robert W. Bruère. Mrs. Bruère is an active worker for woman suffrage and for socialism.—THE EDITOR.

then she is going into domestic service. It would be a great gain if the vociferous advocates of universal conscription into the ranks of houseworkers would open their dictionaries, and, while holding the left forefinger on the definition of "education" as "to train for the duties of life," would turn to the last census, which shows that nearly one-fifth of those who find their life duty in manufactures are women; that in places eighty per cent of the teaching force are women, and that vast numbers of women are engaged in business, commerce, the professions and agriculture. They should also look up the table which shows that in the larger cities nearly one-fifth of the women who work are married. Obviously housework is no longer inevitable even if one is a female and married and a housekeeper. It is in fact increasingly improbable.

And there are other adverse reasons. When practised as a profession housework is the most dangerous trade for a woman. The Government investigations made by Miss Conyngton of industrial centers, the reports of correctional institutions, and the recent Chicago investigation all show that a larger percentage of criminal women come from domestic service than from any other occupation, in some places a higher percentage than from all other occupations combined. And in spite of seemingly high wages it is not profitable. I examined the records for two months of a great institution for the care of paupers—ninety-four per cent of the women admitted had been domestic servants. Why train girls for a dangerous trade where they may confidently contemplate a dependent old age?

Some urge domestic science as a cultural study—discipline for the mind like higher mathematics. This

is true of the scientific basis on which domestic as well as other science rests. But the knowledge of housework as commonly imparted to the young has about as much cultural value as speech imparted to a parrot. I found in a city public school rows of little girls putting squares of calico together with a fine "over and over" stitch to make a patchwork quilt. They raised the picture of myself as a little girl being taught that same work by a mother who never made a patchwork quilt in her life, but who had been taught the method by my grandmother who did in her day produce masterpieces. There have been some four generations of girls taught to make patchwork quilts since the world took to sleeping under blankets, and in the name of domestic science it is still going on. They say that patchwork is "good to learn on." Learn what? If those rows of industrious little girls earn a living by sewing they will not use the "over and over" seam stitch nor anything more closely resembling it than can be produced by a power machine. Learning to make patchwork has ceased to be a training for life and become an experiment in archeology.

And yet how easily the houseworking child makes the glad parent."

"Annie can make a two egg cake and—why I couldn't buy better anywhere!"

"Hazel's been taught to make biscuits and her father's *so* pleased!"

But under questioning neither Annie nor Hazel showed any knowledge of how to make a cake when only one egg was present, or knew what happened when a biscuit rose. I asked the same questions of a girl who was deep in chemistry, but quite innocent of its domestic application.

"Let me see what's inside a biscuit," she said, and got the family cook book. Then she looked up the chemical composition of baking powder, and told me. She proved also quite as able to make biscuits as to perform any other chemical experiment. Her scientific training made her able to cook quite incidentally. She was beginning on the sort of education which is the basis for housework as well as for most other occupations and was also getting a physical training for any work—an education which would poise her as lightly as a boxer on her industrial toes, ready to jump either way. For every woman who knows chemistry and physics, who owns a good cook book, who can measure by weight and quantity and can watch the clock, can cook. She may be awkward about it at first, but so is the best trained cook if she is out of practise or in a strange kitchen where the pots and pans are in unaccustomed places, the egg beater hanging beside the stove instead of reposing in the table drawer, the drip board on the left instead of the right side of the sink.

It is fortunate that here and there this scientific training is taking hold of the schools and colleges in spite of the emphasis placed on the narrow form of domestic science. For those who are distractedly advocating housework as a safe and sound study for girls who must—such is the insistent nature of the female—be taught something, but who should be tenderly blocked in their inherent tendency to abandon domesticity, are not furthering the interests of the family by any means

And in the face of the fact that housework is dangerous, leads to dependency and is decreasingly needed, is it not possible that those who want girls trained for safe and lucrative occupations are not enemies of society? That those who feel that a girl may be educated to some career in addition to matrimony are not traitors to the child? That those who believe in undomesticating woman in order that she may be socialized are not attacking the state?

New York City

THE THAW

BY O. WARREN SMITH

SPRING is imminent. Somewhere the robins, blue birds, meadowlarks and song sparrows—spring makers—are advancing northward. What's that? How do I know? Have patience and I will explain.

Recently, while the snow lay almost four feet deep in the swamp, I received a "wireless" which set my heart a-bounding. Nothing more or less than a common sapsucker beating the long-roll to the South-Wind upon a resounding dead branch. How the hollow sound awakened the long silent echoes of the swamp, until the very air seemed to pulsate with the gladsome music. Yes, I call it just that—"music."

For two days of zero weather that bird drummed away with all the faith of your true optimist, until I felt like shouting encouragingly, "Keep it up and you will win out."

The swamp was calling me, but I waited. Upon the fourth day after I noticed the drumming, a slight change was discoverable, a certain indefinable, intangible something had crept into the atmosphere. The sapsucker, half crazed with delight, beat the long-roll in double time until all the woodpeckers took up the refrain and my swamp fairly pulsated with the rolling, throbbing sound.

I am never tired of watching the transforming miracles of falling snow, over night accomplishing wonders beyond the power of pen to describe; but a warm south wind will change the face of nature in a few short hours, destroying fantastic snow-drifts and liberating ice-bound creeks. A few warm days and the snow settles rapidly. Listening, you can hear a low "seep, seep," the swan song of the snow. When the water begins to run in the sleigh tracks we know that winter is all but defeated.

Did you ever notice how restless the farmer's cattle become as soon as the spring thaw sets in in earnest? They are no longer satisfied to feed in the comfortable barn-yards, but must go out into the fields, where they stand, knee-deep in the heavy snow, and gaze out upon their buried feeding grounds. Why is it? What memories of bygone days haunt them? I, too, am conscious of a desire to explore the woods and fields. I needs must up and away. I, too, must respond to the insistent invitation of the sapsucker's long-roll. Is it just an animal joy in the return of warm days, or is it a sub-conscious memory of hairy ancestors, illy protected against the cold, rejoicing once more in life? I leave that for the reader's speculation.

There are two birds I look for these warming March days, precursors of the real spring birds. The first is a constant dweller in the north; no winter is too cold for him; and yet the first hint of thaw sets his blood a-bounding, and puts a new note in his throat. Down in the thick swamps, where the sapsucker and his relatives spend the winter, a little black and white bird feels the urge of spring time and changes his note from "chick-a-dee-dee" to "phoebe-e-e." Not uncommonly people will inform me that they have heard a phoebe long before that bird has even thought of journeying northward; knowing what they have heard, I only smile and look interested. If you have not heard the March phoebe note of the chickadee you have missed something well worth while.

The other bird that helps to bring the spring, blazes a trail as it were for the bluebirds and robins, is that bird of mystery, the prairie horned lark, which appears in Wisconsin in mid-February or March. Its whistle —one cannot call it a song—while not very musical is decidedly cheery. Usually these birds are found in pairs, tho once in a while I find them in flocks of half a dozen. There is no mistaking the bird; the two little tufts of feathers, or horns, upon either side of the head are sufficient to identify it. To a great many people they are just "sparrows," as every brown or indeterminate bird is. Nevertheless our inconspicuous early visitor and summer resident is a true lark, something which can not be said of our well-beloved "spring of the year" bird, for the meadowlark belongs to the blackbird family and is not a lark at all.

Those are the two birds I think of in connection with the first thaw, perhaps there is some connection between them and the long-roll of the sapsucker. Honestly, I believe that I owe the thaw itself to the drumming of that "wicked woodpecker," my "bird of faith."

As I sit here in my pleasant study I can hear the puffing of busy switch-engines down in the yards, the throb of the machinery on the coal-docks, the rat-a-tat-tat" of many busy hammers; yet over all, under all and thru all, I can hear the sound of the woodpecker's long-roll, beating a knell to dying winter. Now I would hear the gladsome sound if I were incarcerated in a cell of solid masonry. What I hear depends largely upon what I am prepared to hear. If I let the sounds of the busy world shut out the higher music, whose fault is it?

Come, are you not conscious of a desire to wander, to get away from the noise and hurly-burly of the town? Have you not heard the long-roll of the sapsucker? Do not wait for spring or summer to journey a-field. Now, while the creeks are beginning to rejoice in regained freedom, and the chickadee to call "phoebe-e-e," take a day off. You need it.

And it was only the long-roll of a sapsucker.

Washburn, Wisconsin

M. William Shak-fpeare:

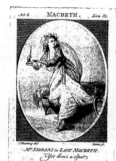

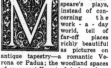

M. William Shak-ſpeare:

EIGHT PAPERS BY FREDERICK HOUK LAW
IN OBSERVANCE OF THE THREE HUNDREDTH
ANNIVERSARY OF SHAKESPEARE'S DEATH

The Tragedies: Plays of Character and Pathos

Act 2.   MACBETH.   Line 33.

Mᵣˢ. SIDDONS in LADY MACBETH.

Mrs. Sarah Siddons (1755-1831), sister of John Philip Kemple, first played Lady Macbeth in London in 1785. No other English actress has so completely dominated the stage of her own day. From an old print

MANY of Shakespeare's plays, instead of concerning the work - a - day world, tell of far-off places richly beautiful as pictures on antique tapestry—a romantic Verona or Padua; the woodland spaces of an unreal Forest of Arden, where life is jest and song; or a forest-bounded Athens, where a medieval court, English fairies, clownish workmen, and wandering lovers move in the shades of dream. The scenes of many comedies, Ephesus, Messina, Rousillon, Navarre, Illyria, are little more than suggestive names in the land of romance, "Too flattering sweet to be substantial."

Altho the English scenes in the histories, London, Gloucestershire, Pomfret, Shrewsbury, Westminster, show something more of the stern realities of life, they are principally

418

a setting for one mighty pageant of kings and queens, and for a series of events that unroll in vividly dramatic form, wakening once more the memory of desperate battles and the deeds of forgotten years.

As a young man, Shakespeare was most interested in event, delighting in the hearty laughter of "The Comedy of Errors," the practical jokes of "Henry IV," the idyllic story-life of "Love's Labour's Lost," and the romantic tragedy of "Romeo and Juliet." And yet, even in his earliest plays, reality treads upon the heels of romance, and the deeper, inner life begins to take the place of outward event. Juliet warns Romeo that their love is

Too rash, too unadvised, too sudden,
Too like the lightning, which does cease
    to be
Ere one can say "It lightens."

Henry VI, in the bedchamber of a dying man, says:

Ah, what a sign it is of evil life,
Where death's approach is seen so
    terrible . . .
Forbear to judge, for we are sinners
    all.
Close up his eyes and draw the curtain
    close;
And let us all to meditation.

Jacques, in "As You Like It," looks upon life thru the eyes of satire and says:

All the world's a stage,
And all the men and women merely
    players.

He suggests that life, even if lived thru honorable days, ends at last in "second childishness and mere oblivion."

In spite of Shakespeare's interest in the far-off days of romance and war, people of the everyday Elizabethan world come into his plays: ignorant members of the watch; servants busy with the preparation of a feast; a gross-minded talkative nurse; hired murderers not wholly dead to sympathy; Scotchmen and Welshmen speaking dialect; carriers busy in an inn-yard; parsons; physicians; justices—in fact, the world of reality as opposed to the world of romance.

Into the midst of comedy scenes breaks noble poetry. A boisterous passage in "The Taming of the Shrew" suddenly gives place to this:

'Tis the mind that makes the body rich;
And as the sun breaks thru the darkest
    clouds,
So honour peereth in the meanest habit.

At about thirty-seven years old, as tho he had not found the world of romance wholly satisfactory, and as tho the reality of life had prest in upon his dreams and made him almost bitter against the false existence of outward action in the story-world, Shakespeare wrote comedies far more thoughtful than those that had preceded, touched with satire, and darker in meaning. No one knows exactly what it was that changed the current of Shakespeare's thought. Perhaps it was years of experience in an active city; perhaps it was the death of his little son Hamnet, and the succeeding death of his own father; perhaps it was some experience of which we have no knowledge—at any rate, Shakespeare turned from light-hearted imagination to a consideration of that greatest of all realities—the human soul, saying, as it were:

I will find
Where truth is hid, tho it were hid
    indeed
Within the center.

Some of Shakespeare's comedies find solution in fortuitous event; the great tragedies are immutably final. Two comedies, for example, "Much Ado About Nothing" and "Measure for Measure," end happily in surprizing event. In the first, Claudio, thinking that his injustice has killed Hero, agrees to marry her cousin—and finds the "cousin" no other than Hero herself! In the second, Angelo and Isabella think that one whom they love has been executed—but, when they no longer hope, they see a form unveiled, and behold their friend alive! The results of the great tragedies are decisive and beyond recall. Lear moans for Cordelia, whom he has lost, and says in vain: "I might have saved her; now she's gone forever!"

Othello, learning of the innocence of Desdemona, whom he has murdered, has no relief except in his bitter cry: "O fool! fool! fool!"

Lady Macbeth, and Macbeth, having killed Duncan, could never recall him to life. The one mourns hopelessly in her sleep:

Here's the smell of blood still: All the perfumes of Arabia will not sweeten this little hand.

The other goes from crime to crime, knowing that no unmuffling would ever reveal a living Duncan or a restored Banquo, and realizing that his old heroic high-mindedness had gone forever. Thus, faced by reality, he says:

I 'gin to be a-weary of the sun,
And wish the estate o' the world were now undone!

The great tragedies are tragedies of actuality, whose irresistible force makes them great. In such plays the characters, face to face with choice, solve their own fates. They move, thru wavering resolutions, to an apparent brute mastery over the deep, unmoved machinery of existence. Finally, they confront the eternal verities, and find no relief except in madness or death.

"Julius Caesar" shows us, in Brutus, a man whose failure to understand the actual world brings him to destruction. Brutus is a man above reproach, a kindly master, a devoted friend, a faithful husband, and a high-minded patriot; but he is also an idealist living outside the world of fact. His ignorance of life makes him a ready instrument for the unscrupulous villain, Cassius, who confronts him with the apparent necessity of killing Caesar or being false to Rome. Thus led to kill his best friend, he fails again and does not recognize the worldly wisdom of shrewd Marc Antony, who stirs against him the retribution of Rome. Brutus' virtues are so many, his character so noble, that he awakens our deepest sympathy.

"Hamlet" also is the tragedy of a man incapable of practical action. Hamlet, a Danish Prince, called upon to revenge his father's murder, so wavers between thought and deed that he brings others, as well as himself, into a circle of death. Polonius, killed behind the arras; Ophelia, driven to madness and death; Rosenkrantz and Guildenstern sent to execution; and Laertes, dying with Hamlet when revenge has been achieved, make Hamlet's own tragedy of irresolution all the greater. Hamlet is as much a man of introspection as Brutus is a man of ideals. His wonderful meditations reveal a depth of philosophic nature that lifts us into sympathy with this man of thought, called upon by fate to carry out action for which his nature is not fitted. He judges himself, and emphasizes the need of strong, decisive action, when he says:

The native hue of resolution
Is sicklied o'er with the pale cast of thought.

The remaining tragedies, "Othello," "Macbeth," "King Lear," "Antony and Cleopatra," "Coriolanus," and "Timon of Athens," instead of showing men unfit for the world of practical reality, tell of those who yield to overmastering passions, and thus, by action, make themselves unfit for a moral world. Othello yields to jealousy; Macbeth to unrighteous ambition; King Lear to self-will; Antony to pleasure-seeking love; Coriolanus to self-centered pride, and Timon to anger and disgust. All are strong characters, their tragedies being great in proportion to their greatness of nature.

"Othello" is a tragedy of jealous love. The Moor, Othello, telling of

Battles, sieges, fortunes. . . .
Of moving accidents by flood and field,
Of hair-breadth 'scapes i' the imminent deadly breach,

unconsciously wins the love of Desdemona, daughter of Brabantio, a Senator of Venice. Then Iago, one of his officers, in a spirit of revenge, spurs him to an unfounded jealousy. He yields, and strangles Desdemona, allowing passion to overcome his noble nature. The deed has no sooner been accomplished than the truth of Desdemona's innocence is flashed upon him. He realizes the wrong he

Mr GARRICK in Four of his Principal Tragic Characters.

David Garrick (1717-1779) made his first prominent London appearance in 1741, as Richard III, and from then to 1776, as actor, playwright and manager (he controlled Drury Lane), he was the most important dramatic personage in England. His roles included seventeen Shakespearean parts, and he produced—with more or less fidelity to the original text—twenty-four of the plays at Drury Lane

has done to her and to himself, and cries in agony:

O cursed slave!
Whip me, ye devils . . .
Blow me about in winds . . .
O Desdemona! Desdemona! dead!
Oh! Oh! Oh!

A single flaw could destroy a noble soul, whose appealing greatness makes the tragedy convincingly powerful.

"Macbeth" is another tragedy of true greatness ruined by a line of weakness. Macbeth, one of the boldest and most ardent of King Duncan's generals, is led by his success to desire Duncan's throne. Goaded on by his secret ambitions, and the help of an understanding wife, he kills his king. Then, to cover his sin, he kills Banquo, his fellow-general, and moves from crime to crime until he meets death gladly, realizing that he has made of life

A tale
Told by an idiot, full of sound and fury,
Signifying nothing.

If Macbeth had been an ordinary murderer we should have slight interest in the tragedy. His overmastering power, introspective nature, and ever-punishing conscience stirs us to the keenest sympathy. In the wreck of his life, caused by his own evil-doing, he says:

I have liv'd long enough: my way of life
Is fall'n into the sear, the yellow leaf;
And that which should accompany old age,
As honor, love, obedience, troops of friends,
I must not look to have; but, in their stead,
Curses, not loud but deep, mouth-honor, breath,
Which the poor heart would fain deny, and dare not.

In the fall of such a man there is all the awe-inspiring power, and something of the glory, of a burning city.

"King Lear" is a terrible story of self-will, narrowed affections, and misdirected love. King Lear, a doting old man on whom madness is slowly closing in, gives his love to his flattering daughters, Goneril and Regan, and curses Cordelia, the one daughter who loves him too much to flatter. In the same play, parallel with the story of Lear and lighting it by contrast, is the story of the Earl of Gloucester, who trusts a deceitful son and drives away one who is virtuous. In both cases the favored children turn against their parents and bring them into wretched agony. Lear, driven from home, old, white-haired, bereft of reason, rages in a midnight storm; Gloucester, cruelly blinded, is turned upon the world. In the all-enshrouding gloom is the bright gleam of faithfulness in Lear's court fool, who follows his old master; and the beauty of Cordelia's love for her unfortunate father. In the words of the King of France, her lover, one thinks of Cordelia as

Most rich, being poor;
Most choice, forsaken; and most loved, despised!

"Antony and Cleopatra," "Coriolanus," and "Timon of Athens," are less gripping in power. The first, richly powerful in language, and superbly strong in characterization, is a romantic story of glowing color and passion, telling of the ruin of a great man who devoted himself to

BOOKS FOR FURTHER READING

H. A. Guerber: *Stories of Shakespeare's Tragedies;* A. C. Bradley: *Shakespearean Tragedy;* G. Fletcher: *Character Studies in Macbeth;* A. H. Tolman: *Views About Hamlet, and Other Essays;* C. E. L. Wingate: *Shakespeare's Heroes on the Stage;* S. A. Brooke: *On Ten Plays of Shakespeare;* G. N. Boardman: *Shakespeare: Five Lectures;* A. C. Swinburne: *Three Plays of Shakespeare;* R. G. White: *Studies in Shakespeare;* G. E. Woodberry: *Great Writers;* J. Stalker: *How to Read Shakespeare.*

pleasure rather than to moral duty. As in the other tragedies the pathos is not in mere event, but in the downfall of noble manhood. When both Antony and Cleopatra are dead Caesar says:

High events as these
Strike those that make them; and their story is
No less in pity than his glory which
Brought them to be lamented.

The second play, "Coriolanus," tells of a proud, quick-tempered Roman noble whose contempt of the people's rights led him to unite with the enemies of Rome. Even among them he did not subdue his pride and temper, and so he met death at their hands at a moment when his wife and his mother had somewhat softened his haughty spirit. His character is well given by the Volscian general, who says:

He could not
Carry his honors even: whether 'twas pride,
Which out of daily fortune ever taints
The happy man; whether defect of judgment . . .
. . . Or whether nature . . .
As he hath spices of them all, not all,—
For I dare so far free him—made him fear'd,
So hated, and so banish'd.

"Timon of Athens," written only in part by Shakespeare, tells of a man of extraordinary generosity and friendliness, who found that wealth brings flattery and that friends are sometimes false. Angered so that he was willing to die rather than live among liars, he forsook the world.

The greatest of Shakespeare's tragedies have such dramatic intensity and moral grandeur that they "purge the soul thru pity and fear." They are human studies, vivid, soul-deep, appealing directly to the heart of every reader because every reader feels within his own breast passions that ally him with Shakespeare's great protagonists.

MY GRAND AUNT'S PATCHWORK QUILT

BY FLORENCE RIPLEY MASTIN

Sedate and silent little quilt of mine,
    What wonder that I dream 'neath thy caress?
Soft forms sway phantom-like in curve and line,—
    Thy flower bright patches shimmer into dress!

Within this bit of silk as blue as May,
    A little girl in hoops is curtsying low.
Her lover dons that velvet on the day
    When all the blossoms of the Springtide blow.

Such snowy satin sheathes a lily maid
    As fair as one in Astolat who died;
And, mischief in jade green, some lad is paid
    Who steals a kiss while sitting by thy side!

O stern old maid, in sober, Sabbath brown
    Of silk magnificent that stands alone,—

I see thee look askance upon the gown,
    Peach colored, in the pew beside thine own!

And now, behold, within that sapphire square,
    As dusky as the blue of summer night,
Beribboned masters pledging to their fair
    In foaming tankards till the dawn is white!

Hark how the music of the minuet
    Calls from the dim brocade each shadowy face.
It seems as tho they all were living yet,
    Pale lovers swaying slow with stately grace.

Dear little grand aunt in the silver grey,
    Unconscious of thy patchwork wizardry,
Thy placid hands have summoned yesterday
    Down pansy 'broidered paths of dreams to me.

THE EFFICIENT HOUSEWIFE

BY EDWARD EARLE PURINTON

DIRECTOR OF THE INDEPENDENT EFFICIENCY SERVICE

THE leading citizen of the world is the housewife. A bold, new appraisal of the values of the world is to be made by the women of the twentieth century. The guide for the race to come is the scientific housewife. In the shaping of her hands lie the gifts of heart, brain and body that shall belong to the children of tomorrow.

The housewife is the first keeper of a man's morals. Fat body, lean soul. Sick body, frail soul. Weak body, numb soul. Coarse body, hurt soul. The care of the body, for her husband, her children and herself, is a moral responsibility second to none, which every housewife must meet fairly and discharge fully, or be derelict.

Further, a man's capacity for work and a child's for study, analyzed and traced to their source, depend largely on the home regimen directed by the wife and mother. Given the right home care, a man may work two hours longer a day, with less fatigue and more enjoyment. His alertness, decisiveness, energy, accuracy and endurance will be increased from ten to forty per cent by science in the home. I have seen a man's output of work doubled by the reorganization of his household.

Experts declare that seventy per cent of the school children of the United States are physically defective; that a large proportion of backwardness and dulness may be ascribed to this oft-unsuspected state of chronic ill health; and that the causes reside principally in the home factors of food and drink, sanitation, ventilation, clothing, baths, exercize, and other daily features of home life. The housewives of America, if they would learn their profession, could save to their families at least $500,-000,000 a year—now being wasted in hospitals, asylums, sanitariums and drug-stores.

To the average woman, the bed-rock reason for mastering the new art of household engineering lies in the reduction of her home cares, periods of hurry and worry, exactions of the daily budget, hours of toil and fatigue. And a neat and clever, prompt and cheerful, wholesome and economical housewife is much more attractive to her husband! (That is, if she does not forget to be his sweetheart first.)

There are more people engaged in some branch of household work than in any other trade or profession. The number in the United States has been conservatively reckoned at 20,-000,000. Among this great body of workers the dearth of scientific knowledge is appalling. My work has brought me in touch with many thou-

---

The $100,000 Man Who Went to School Again

This is an inspiring story of a big-minded business man. Despite his wide experience, despite his huge income, he left his business for a year while he *learned the fundamental principles* b e h i n d the problems of his complicated business.

Many Big Men Doing the Same

The brainiest men in America today are doing what he did, for exactly the same reason he did it. The only difference is that they do not now have to leave their business as this man did. Instead, the Alexander Hamilton Institute now brings this business training right to their desks or to their home reading tables.

The Advisory Council

Judge E. H. Gary, Chairman of the U. S. Steel Corporation; Frank A. Vanderlip, President of the National City Bank; John Hays Hammond, the great engineer; Joseph French Johnson, Dean of the New York University School of Commerce; and Jeremiah W. Jenks, the statistician and economist, compose the Advisory Council.

How Men Make Good

What our Modern Business Course and Service has done for its 35,000 subscribers will probably never be known in its entirety. But daily there filter into the headquarters in New York many intensely human stories, showing how men are helped. One day you hear of a brilliant lad of twenty-two, in a big New York Bank, rising to a $9,500 job and giving credit to the Institute for his success. The next day a factory manager writes that the Course has just helped him save his firm $7,000 a year, and that a "fair slice" of this went to increase his salary. Or a man in a western concern tells how he saved the firm $37,000 a year *by one suggestion*, and what happened then to *his salary*.

These are only typical cases. There are literally hundreds of them described in the 128 page book, "Forging Ahead in Business," a copy of which will be sent you, *free*.

ALEXANDER HAMILTON INSTITUTE
294 Astor Place   New York City

Send me "Forging Ahead in Business"—FREE

Name.................................

Business
Address..............................

Business
Position.............................

---

sands of women whose labor and love is for the home;—but I have not met a dozen housewives who really knew their business.

There are in this country approximately 150,000 doctors; and at least 150 schools where the doctor's profession may be studied. Equal provision for training those occupied in the household would require 20,000 schools of domestic science in America! We have perhaps *twenty* good institutions of household engineering—for *twenty million* people in urgent need of schooling. Was there ever a greater field for applied efficiency?

I would here interject a word of preface. No mere man, tho he be a Solomon of domestic lore, could ever persuade , an orthodox housekeeper that he knew her business better than she did. Therefore, modestly and becomingly, I would state that, in preparing this paper, I have consulted various women authorities considered among the best in the world. Housekeeping is a hard job—a much harder job than the ordinary *man* ever tackled. But the way to make a hard job an easy one is to put some education into it. Therefore, while agreeing with the housekeeper as to the difficulty of her problems, I hold the average man's view that they *need not* be difficult.

To introduce our theme, let us borrow a printer's term and produce a "lay-out" of the matter before us. In approaching any kind of work, the initial move is to build an outline of the duties and functions of the worker, and their relations to each other, to the worker, and to those affected by the work.

WIFE, MOTHER, HOUSEKEEPER

AN efficient housewife is three women—a wife, a mother, and a housekeeper. Now being a wife is an art, being a mother is a profession, and being a housekeeper is a business. The art, the profession and the business must be learned separately and completely, then so united as to create a perfect mosaic of labor, life and character. Most of a woman's troubles and perplexities at home are but the failure to realize and observe this classification of her duties and opportunities. We must here limit ourselves to the discussion of the factors in efficient housekeeping only, but we wish it thoroly understood that when a wife has become an efficient housekeeper, she is still but a third of an efficient woman.

The *complexity* of household management is the real problem to be solved. How can any mortal be a sanitary expert, a hygienist, a psychologist, a purchasing agent, a sartorial counsel, a seamstress, a dietetic physician, a director of employees, a kindergarten supervisor, a household financier, a nerveless mechanism, a hostess, a helpmeet 'and a beautiful lady of leisure—all at the same time? Yet these are only a few of the multiple individuals the average man expects his wife to be—and her salary nothing but the supernal joy of waiting on him. Is a housewife more foolish for not learning her business, or a husband more foolish for not being willing to pay her a salary when she does learn her business?

SAVE

MANY a housekeeper could learn to save $100 to $300 a year by adopting scientific methods of marketing. The Commissioner of Weights and Measures of New York City declares the people of New York are cheated out of $50,000,000 a year, by means of the false weights and measures, imitations and substitutions, and other swindling devices in daily use by New York butchers, grocers, bakers, delicatesseners, and other shopmen who ought to be in jail. More money is wasted thru negligence and ignorance on the part of the housewife. Let us give one example—out of scores of similar cases.

Lamb chops and leg of lamb cost about the same. The chops are nearly half bone—why pay for the bone? Also the leg of lamb remaining from the first meal can be served again, revamped or disguised; but the chops left over cannot be safely put in hash and called by a French name used for an alias. Why waste perfectly good money on porterhouse steak because it sounds elite, when it costs fifty per cent more than other good cuts whose protein equivalent is almost the same? Why imagine that you need expensive meats at all? An order of steak for a small family costs, we will say, fifty cents. This makes one meal. For fifty cents you can buy two or three meals of fish; and four or five meals of nuts, legumes, cheese or grains. If you are feeding your imagination, you will go on buying steak; if you are feeding your stomach, you will buy mostly something else.

Other examples of economy: A ten-cent box of whole wheat crackers will yield more nourishment than two ten-cent loaves of ordinary white bread. For most sweetening purposes, "brown" sugar is better than granulated, and costs less. Home-made grape juice can be put up for about eight cents per pint—the store price is twenty-five cents. A barrel of apples in season from Oregon, a crate of oranges and grape-fruit from Florida, may be purchased at a saving of twenty to forty per cent on each piece—and a large supply of fruit the whole year round is a mighty good investment for any family. The cost of nearly all the articles of home consumption may be reduced, yet the quality improved, if you know when, where and how to buy.

PLAN THE MENU

A COMPLETE scientific table of food values, covering all the articles of home use, and specifying both hygienic and economic percentage, should be the constant guide of the housekeeper. A balanced menu is fundamental to health. And no one ever happened on a balanced menu system —it has to be studied out. I know people who have cut down their druggist and doctor bills by two-thirds, merely thru applying some dietetic wisdom. There is a fascination, moreover, in learning how far you can make a dollar go in the kitchen. Five ounces of cornmeal, costing about one cent, offer as much nutrition as ten eggs, costing twenty to thirty cents. When you learn a few hundred facts like this, and base your marketing on these principles, you will come to enjoy your work as everybody does who is expert and masterful. How to like your work better: *Do* it better.

This means also, do it more easily. I judge that the typical American housewife wastes nervous energy to a wholly unnecessary degree every day. This explains why she frets and scolds, and why she is too tired to greet her husband with a smile when he comes home from work. She must learn to adopt the general truths of scientific management, and to save her time and strength as well as her husband's money. Theoretically, the operations of the household should all be standardized, in respect to motion, time and sequence. But as the homes of today were constructed by men architects and builders, who had no scientific knowledge of household engineering, the usual arrangement of the kitchen, pantry, dining-room and cupboards makes a perfect "routing" system next to impossible. A man can no more be the sole architect of a home than a woman could be of a factory. A woman specialist—a domestic science engineer, should be consulted before any home has the foundation laid. Such mechanical devices as the speaking tube and dumbwaiter connecting different floors and saving many trips a day up and down stairs, or the belt line tray carrier from kitchen to dining-table which brings all dishes to and from the meal in one operation, cost little when embodied in the first plans of a house; their upkeep is almost nil.

The Fascination of the New Housekeeping

THAT is how members speak of the everyday humdrum tasks of the home when they get into the new correspondence course, HOUSEHOLD ENGINEERING, SCIENTIFIC MANAGEMENT IN THE HOME.

The new "scientific management" is really nothing very perplexing or difficult, but the results of its application in all industries have been *truly marvelous*.

This course applied to housekeeping will actually produce results *just as unbelievable*. It will save up to a third or more of the time spent in housekeeping. The housework will go more smoothly with less effort. It will be done better with a considerable saving of expense.

Even more important, the course gives to housekeeping fresh, live interest—changes indifference to enthusiasm—brings about the splendid efficiency attitude of mind that masters all difficulties. It is an inspiration to beginners, the way out for the discouraged and the next step forward for experienced housekeepers.

The author Mrs. Christine Frederick is a pioneer worker in this field. The twelve years' experience in correspondence instruction and the reputation of the American School of Home Economics is back of this course.

"Household Engineering" is divided into twelve (12) Parts or lessons as follows:

1. THE LABOR-SAVING KITCHEN.
2. PLANS AND METHODS IN HOUSEWORK.
3. HELPFUL HOUSEHOLD TOOLS.
4. METHODS OF CLEANING.
5. FOOD PLANNING FOR THE FAMILY.
6. THE PRACTICAL LAUNDRY.
7. FAMILY FINANCING AND RECORDS.
8. ECONOMICAL HOUSEHOLD PURCHASING.
9. HOUSE PLANNING AND SANITATION.
10. THE SERVANTLESS HOUSEHOLD.
11. MANAGEMENT OF HOUSEHOLD SERVANTS.
12. THE HOMEMAKER'S PERSONAL EFFICIENCY.

These lesson books contain 40 to 60 pages, very liberally illustrated and attractively bound. The Reports sent in are read by Mrs. Frederick or her assistants, graded, all questions answered and returned. The lessons are sent one a month for a year—wonderfully interesting continued story on the NEW ART OF SCIENTIFIC HOUSEKEEPING.

All who are interested in housekeeping, or who would like help in their problems, or who wish to make progress in their life work are invited to enroll (for a month only) *free of charge*. Send a post card or note as follows or clip:

But in all efficiency work, our aim is to turn limitations into opportunities; and the faulty arrangement of a house merely gives the housewife a better chance to use her wits in her own behalf.

PLAN THE DAY

Planning the day ahead is a fundamental factor in good housekeeping. A schedule of the duties and responsibilities for each member of the family, and each day in the week, should be lettered attractively, posted conspicuously, and observed minutely. A good business man has the entire business day mapped out in advance. A good housekeeper does likewise, finishing each bit of work in its allotted time, and proceeding calmly and quietly from one memorandum to another, without the nerve strain and emotional panic that result from hodge-podge habits of work. A housewife's first need is to get over being a hodge-podger.

Meals can be scheduled and ordered a week in advance, and the whole job done at one time. This method not only helps the maid, the grocer and the butcher to avoid haste and errors, but provides for the complete utilization of "leftovers," and relieves the mind of the housekeeper from the everlasting bother of having to think always what the family can eat next. The bargain-day shopping, the sessions with milliner and dressmaker, the attendance at social functions, the care of the children, the philanthropic work, everything that a modern woman does and wants to do, may be so effectively reduced to a system that worry and fatigue are banished, and duties become delights. I am theorizing or sentimentalizing? I am not—I have seen it done.

Many a housewife walks ten miles a day, in pursuing her vocation. Has she fitted all her house shoes with rubber heels? Has she tried openwork sandals for home wear, in place of shoes? Does she know that cushion felt slippers are made so easy that you hardly think you have anything on your feet, but so durable that they wear as long as leather shoes? Further; does the housewife suspend all her clothing from the shoulders, none from the waist? Can she forego the corset, and every other tight garment, while at work? Has she learned how to look attractive, and feel comfortable, both at the same time? Is it her daily custom to go to her rooms, give orders not to be disturbed, and relax entirely for a half hour each afternoon? A few dozen questions like these will show the housewife whether she is, or is not, fully conserving her energies.

USE HELPFUL MACHINERY

The best hardware, housefurnishing, and department stores now handle an assortment of devices, tools, and implements for saving labor, time, health and money in the home. To women folk living in the country, many of these utensils are offered by mail-order houses. We can mention here but a small number of these aids to easy and effective housekeeping: Fireless cook-

er, with recipe book and instructions for saving time, care and fuel; kitchen cabinet, for eliminating much of the standing and walking work, and enabling you to sit comfortably with most of your dishes and supplies in reach; sanitary window-ventilator that keeps out dust and germs, rain, snow and drafts; oiled mop and duster, for settling the dirt instead of scattering it; safety clothes-line, non-stretching, nonstaining, non-raveling, warranted to keep clothes from blowing away; dishpan that fits into the sink and protects it while accommodating all the dishes at once; tea wagon to save steps; paper towels for bathroom and kitchen; sanitary cleaning brushes for specific uses, to fit cracks, corners and curved surfaces; meat perforator to make "round steak as tender as porterhouse"; nutcrackers that deliver kernels whole; glass dishes for baking, that let you watch the process going on inside, then serve food in same dish, and wash easily; duplex bulb for electric light, that regulates amount of current used, with light bills and eye strain reduced fifty per cent; guaranteed aluminum cooking utensils, to prevent scorching and retain full flavor of food; family clothes washing machine, electric or water power, that does not break buttons, tear clothing or fray edges of garments.

Among the new manufactures and inventions for making housework a joy instead of a nuisance are the varied and appealing forms of electrical contrivance now available, and growing more and more economical. A few examples: The electric ironing machine and washing machine which make washing day and ironing day one and the same by saving hours of time and pounds of former drudgery. The electric vacuum cleaner; the dish-washer that cleanses, rinses and dries the table dishes for an average family in less than five minutes; the sewing machine motor, that enables you to complete a day's sewing in a few hours with scarcely any fatigue; the portable desk lamp and floor lamp, for directing the most concentrated light wherever needed, while protecting the eyes from the glare; the water heater; the "sad" iron—not sad in this case; the toaster stove; the warming pad; the rotary fan; the pocket searchlight; the household interphone.

EMPLOYEE—NOT SERVANT

But the human element, in domestic science as in all applied science, takes precedence over the material adjuncts. I refer now to the housemaid, and to the storekeeper, on whose coöperation the mistress of the home has to depend for a large degree of her success. The loyal, energetic, enthusiastic team work that makes a business project forge ahead is conspicuously absent in the home régime. Did you ever see a housemaid illumined with ardor and joy in her work, and so faithful and devoted that she clung to her mistress ten or twenty years without a murmur? If not, why not? Did you ever see a grocer who respected the business acumen of

Are You a Vegetarian?

Do you know what "Vegetarianism" is?

"No."

Then you should find out.

Because—

It is far more—means far more—than you can think, until you actually know just what, and all, it is and means.

How can you find out about "vegetarianism"?

Easily enough.

Write your name and address in the coupon margin, cut or tear it out and mail it at once.

And you will receive, by return post, without obligation, fully postpaid, a copy of the vegetarian magazine—GOOD HEALTH—and much other interesting information—information you will be glad to have, because it will help you to get more out of life.

In the vegetarian diet there are *over seven hundred* recipes. Think of it!

Wouldn't you like to know about them?

Then send the coupon.

No Money—Just This Coupon

GOOD HEALTH PUBLISHING CO., 303 Main St., Battle Creek, Mich.

Send me without obligation, the current number of GOOD HEALTH, fully postpaid.

Name_____

Address_____

the housewife as much as that of her
husband? If not, why not?

The cure for the "servant" problem
is to realize that there *is* no servant.
There is an employee—but no servant.
What the housemaid objects to is being
called, classed and treated as a servant.
When she does her work right, she is
an artist. But, ordinarily, she is an out-
cast in the family. She is promptly
banished to a cold, ugly, dreary attic
room; she is robbed of the home ties
and sense of personal ownership that
every woman craves; she is run thru
a mill of monotony, slavery and
drudgery, with no chance of promotion
or advancement; she is forced to work
at any or all hours of the day or
night; she has for an employer a mistress who knows neither her own business nor that of the maid, but who
gives orders with the air of omnis-
cience and the finality of fate; she cannot have Sundays or legal holidays to
herself, as other employees rightfully
demand; she loses caste everywhere because of being a "domestic"; she receives in cash only a half to a third of
what she might expect, sooner or later,
in other lines of work; and she has no
compensations for all these drawbacks
and discouragements.

Do you have trouble in getting, keeping or managing a maid? Then it might
be well to ask yourself how many of
the usual defects in the household employment relation you have discerned,
acknowledged and corrected. Also, if
your butcher, grocer, ice-man or plumber treats you badly, you have yourself
to blame. A shopkeeper would not dare
to cheat or maltreat a first-class business man; why should he dare to cheat
or maltreat you? We are always discounted in being disrespected—no matter who does the disrespecting.

I can only suggest briefly and roughly in this article a few of the most
important branches and phases of domestic engineering.

HOW TO LEARN

To the progressive housewife determined to know her business, I would
recommend one or more of these five
channels of knowledge now open to her.
(1) Books and magazines for the home
and the home-maker; (2) Bulletins and
reports from leading experts and national organizations; (3) Personal
courses in all branches of household
management and maids; (4) The direct
management for mothers, daughters
and maids; (4) The direct service and
counsel of a qualified domestic engineer; (5) The aid of agricultural colleges and extension departments of
state universities in many localities of
the United States.

I have before me a recent announcement from the household science department of the University of Illinois,
stating that a demonstration car will
be sent to clubs and organizations of
women thruout Illinois, for the purpose
of showing the newer methods of housekeeping in actual operation. No matter where you live, nor how little you
have to live on, you can learn how to
live better, and make life easier and
happier.

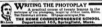

The New Books

BRITISH HUMOR

Some Americans think that they do not like British humor. That is because they expect it to be like American humor. They might as well dislike the charming Surrey hills because they are not the Rocky Mountains. American humor is original, quick and striking; it insists on your attention like a lively terrier. British humor is quiet and confident; it sits and purrs by the fire until you come and stroke it. It is an acquired taste, but it is worth acquiring. A good way to begin is with *Happy Days*, a collection of A. A. Milne's contributions to *Punch*. Do not begin at the beginning. Margery is the most English part of the book, and should be worked up to gradually. Begin with the Little Plays for Amateurs. No one who has ever trod the boards can fail to appreciate such a bit as this:

"Henry—Who is the lucky little lady?

"George (taking out a picture postcard of the British Museum and kissing it passionately)—Isobel Barclay!"

Then read The Making of a Christmas Story, and then the charming little sketches about the spaniel, Chum, and then—well, then you may read the rest in any order you please; you are probably well advanced toward a proper appreciation of British humor.

Happy Days, by A. A. Milne. Doran. $1.25.

THE SACRIFICE OF BELGIUM

Belgium has a double claim upon the sympathy of the world in that she has suffered both a legal wrong and an undeserved injury. The former aspect of the case of Belgium, the violation of territorial neutrality, has occupied more public attention than, relatively to other features of the war, it deserved, considering first that the German Chancellor admitted at the start that it was wrong and, second, that Great Britain would have gone into the war anyway, even if Germany had kept out of Belgium.

But those who wish to acquaint themselves with both sides of the question will find it ably argued by the two books before us. In *The Neutrality of Belgium*, Alexander Fuehr, LL.D., presents the German side of it. He shows that the binding force of the treaty of 1838 guaranteeing the perpetual neutrality of Belgium has been questioned at various times by British, French and Belgian writers; that Palmerston, Gladstone, Derby and Stanley did not regard England as obligated to intervene to defend it and that in 1887 both Liberal and Tory papers took this view. He reproduces in facsimile the secret papers discovered in Brussels by the Germans, showing that plans had been

If your floors could show the steps you waste

If a tally could be kept of all your trips up and down stairs; if all the footsteps you take to find the maid and all her steps in coming to you could be counted, what a waste of time and energy would be revealed! The more convenient way—the approved method—of home management is to connect rooms or floors by means of

Western Electric Inter-phones

These inexpensive little time savers are adaptable to any home, old or new. They are easily installed. They can be placed anywhere. A set, as illustrated, connecting any two points, costs only $15, and can be put in by any competent electrician without disfiguring the walls.

You surely need this great convenience. If your local electrical store cannot supply you, we will ship the outfit by parcel post, with full directions for installing.

Write for our illustrated booklet, "The Way of Convenience." Ask for Booklet No. 33-BJ.

WESTERN ELECTRIC COMPANY, Inc.

463 West Street, New York
500 S. Clinton Street, Chicago

Houses in all Principal Cities

"Wire Your Home" Month, Mar. 15—Apr 15

made by Belgium for British military coöperation in case of an invasion by Germany. The British Military Attaché told the Belgian Chief of Staff in 1912 that British troops would be landed in Belgium in such a case immediately even if Belgium did not ask for them or consent to their coming. In August, 1911, according to Lord Roberts the British fleet had its torpedo nets down and "our expeditionary force was held in equal readiness instantly to embark for Flanders." From this Dr. Fuehr argues that Belgium had forfeited her guarantee of neutrality by 1905, and that in any case Germany was justified according to international law in crossing Belgium by right of military necessity.

In opposition to this is *Belgium Neutral and Loyal*, by Emile Waxweiler, Director of the Solway Institute of Sociology at Brussels. He, tho a Belgian, is much more moderate in his language and fair-minded in his argument than most English and American advocates of the cause of Belgium. He points out that neutrality was imposed upon Belgium by the Powers for their own interests, and that it was their duty to defend it. He frankly admits that the German troops were in some cases fired upon by civilians, but he denies that there was any such opposition as would justify the German reprisals, and he disproves the rumors of Belgian cruelty to German wounded.

Emile Verhaeren is one of the few Belgian authors, except Maeterlinck, known to the outside world and none is better qualified to voice *Belgium's Agony*. Three new poems are given in the original, *La Belgique sanglante*, *Ceux de Liège* and *Guillaume II*. The prose portions of the book are translated with sufficient skill to convey the fire and force of the original French in which he laments his country's wrongs and denounces her enemy. Here is a passage from the chapter on Germany Uncivilizable:

With what clumsy violence does the German conqueror impose himself on the lands he wins. France, in fifty years, has made herself beloved in Savoy; in two centuries she assimilated Lille, Dunkirk, Strasburg and Alsace. England in a few decades has attached to herself Egypt and South Africa. But Germany is still a hated name alike in Poland, Schleswig and Alsace-Lorraine. Wherever she goes, she is unwanted. She knows only the way to tear apart; not the way to unite and heal. Her proclamations shrivel the human mind as frost shrivels plants. She can neither attract, nor tempt, nor civilize, because she has herself no deep spiritual force. Europe, under the successive hegemony of Athens, Rome, and Paris, has been the noblest home of human progress and development. Under German domination she will drift dismally into a gloomy officialdom, organized and drilled by a tyrannous ruling caste.

If there is any one yet unconvinced that the German advance thru Belgium was marked by official tyranny, violations of rules of war and unwarranted cruelty the collection of texts and documents entitled, *Belgium and Germany*, should be brought to his attention. Here are facsimiles from the diaries of German soldiers telling of their atrocities, photographs of buildings destroyed and

of civilians shot, lists of the victims and reproductions of the German proclamations threatening and announcing the burning of towns and the shooting of hostages but, on the other hand, if we accept these documents as evidence of German misdeeds we cannot altogether disregard them when they accuse the Belgians of sniping, using dumdum bullets, etc.

Two little volumes of eye-witness testimony are at hand, one, *The Truth About Louvain*, by a Belgian, René Chambry, the other, *The Germans in Belgium*, by a neutral, Professor Grondys, of Dordrecht, Holland. The latter is especially interesting since it is the narrative of his personal observations in Louvain, Ghent and Brussels. He tells of German kindness and courtesy as well as of German cruelty and unmannerliness.

The peaceful community of Irish nuns which had for two hundred and fifty years been established at Ypres found itself suddenly the center of the fiercest war of history. Their experiences under bombardment from Krupp guns and aeroplanes are well narrated in *The Irish Nuns at Ypres*.

Most of us have felt the need of a better comprehension of the background of Belgium since that country has been thrust into this unhappy prominence. The *Short History of Belgium*, by Professor Van der Essen, of the University of Louvain, admirably fits this need, for in brief and readable form it tells the story of the country from the time of Caesar to recent times. It does not touch upon the present war and seems unmoved by its animosities.

The Neutrality of Belgium, by Alexander Fuehr. Funk & Wagnalls. $1.50. *Belgium Neutral and Loyal*, by Emile Waxweiler. Putnam. $1.25. *Belgium's Agony*, by Emile Verhaeren. Houghton, Mifflin. $1.25. *Belgium and Germany*, by Henri Davignon. Thomas Nelson. 25 cents. *The Truth About Louvain*, by René Chambry. Doran. 25 cents. *The Germans in Belgium*, by L. H. Grondys. Appleton. 50 cents. *The Irish Nuns at Ypres*, by D. M. C. Dutton. $1.25. *A Short History of Belgium*, by Léon Van der Essen. Univ. of Chicago Press. $1.

TROUT SEASON

Let no one be kept by the color of the cover from sending to his fisherman friend, with the first hint of spring, Bliss Perry's delightful little essay, *Fishing with a Worm*.

Houghton, Mifflin. 50 cents.

LESSONS IN LEADERSHIP

A suggestive little book for the use of all people who have the care and training of groups of young girls, is *Leaders of Girls*, by Clara Ewing Espey, and any troubled teacher or welfare worker should find it helpful.

Abingdon Press. 75 cents.

THE TRAIL OF THE TICKER

To those who love to read of the romance of 'the street'" Edwin Lefevre's *Wall Street Stories* will furnish many pleasurable thrills. These character studies, anecdotes and descriptions are a graphic presentation of the human side of the noisy, tragic, busy world of speculation.

Harper. $1.

PULPIT AND PEN

Albert Currier's *Biographical and Literary Studies* contain a simple, comprehensive presentation of four great preachers, Augustine, Fuller, Herbert and Knox, and suggestive essays on *Imagination in Preaching* and the *Psychological Value of Self-Forgetfulness*. The questionable taste of the title: Where is Charlie? prejudices

DIVIDENDS

the reader in advance against the discussion of immortality. Thruout the book a heaven and hell theology and a painful fondness for quotation are redeemed by sincerity and earnestness of purpose.

Boston: The Pilgrim Press. $1.50.

MEMORIES OF THE STAGE

Kate Ryan's recollections of *Old Boston Museum Days* date from 1832 when a young girl, entirely untrained, she walked into the Boston playhouse and demanded a position. A position she won and held to the close of the house in 1893. The book has not only anecdotes of famous actors, but is of especial interest as the story of a successful stock company.

Boston: Little, Brown. $1.50.

ALASKA IN VERSE

The Independent first published some of the thoughtful poems now gathered in R. G. Taber's *Stray Gold*. Much of the book, however, is later work, the fruit of years in the north; dramatic incidents in the miner's life and a group of Esquimaux legends. The Song of Azrael is an excellent example of Mr. Taber's forceful irregular verse and To Fit a Clown a delightful satire.

St. Paul, Minn.: Stationery and Book Co.

THE CHANT OF LOVE FOR ENGLAND

Most of Helen Grey Cone's new volume, *The Chant of Love for England*, has been published before in book form, but among the new poems are three born of the war: the title poem; the noble lines in memory of the sons of Mr Dent, the publisher; and a splendid lyric, Soldiers of the Light. The collection closes with the ode to Lincoln, which is worthy to stand with that small group of real poems to his memory.

Dutton. $1.

EVOLUTION OF THE VARIETY

How far the vaudeville stage has evolved from the days of blackface comedians and low-brow comedy may be glimpsed from *Writing for the Vaudeville Stage*, by Brett Page. Here in more than 600 pages is well reasoned instruction how to write and sell playlets, monologs, two act burlesques, musical comedies, and songs, together with working models from some of the more successful vaudeville authors.

Home Correspondence School. $2.

ART AND PHILOSOPHY

Professor L. W. Flaccus has a refreshing gift of saying what he means and leaving one with a definite impression. In *Artists and Thinkers* he proposes a question, a question impossible to answer, he assures his readers, but well worth considering: Is the Artist a Thinker and the Thinker an Artist? On this as a framework he builds excellent studies of three artists: Rodin, Maeterlink, Wagner; and three thinkers: Hegel, Tolstoy, Nietzsche.

Longmans, Green. $1.25.

AMATEUR DRAMATICS

Written for a congenial group of amateur actors, Mary Aldis's *Plays for Small Stages* should be of value to similar organizations, not for their intrinsic worth, but as suggesting lines along which to work. The plays are simple in setting, relying for their effects on dialogue and the interplay of character. They make the average amateur feel: "I could write a better play on those same lines myself"; and that is a feeling worth cultivating.

Duffield. $1.25.

A HARRIMAN VINDICATION

In the *Chicago and Alton Case* George Kennan has reviewed the Interstate Commerce Commission's investigation of Mr. Harriman's reorganization of the Chicago and Alton Railroad and the criticism that ran with and followed the investigation. It is a good comment on investigations and on critical methods, a good defense of Mr. Harriman and his hundred financial associates who, with a widely approved scheme, improved the road greatly both physically and as an investment—tho it met misfortune later.

Garden City, N. Y. The Country Life Press.

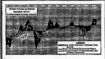

Insurance

Conducted by—

W. E. UNDERWOOD

TWO LARGEST IN THEIR LINE

Included among the very few insurance companies which have published their balance sheets as of date December 31, 1915, are the two largest of their class in the world: the New York Life and the Home Insurance Company. The New York Life begins the year with total resources aggregating $822,917,850 and surplus of $123,564,466. While the Home is not the largest insurance company writing fire insurance, there being a number of British companies with greater resources transacting all the various lines, it is undoubtedly the largest in point of assets confining its activities to fire insurance alone. The Home ended the year 1915 with total assets of $37,982,744 and a policyholders' surplus of $19,536,177.

E. F. B., Grove City—See answer to E. A. H. in The Independent for March 6, 1916.

C. H. F., Lafayette, N. Y.—It is my opinion that a twenty-year endowment is one of the best forms of life insurance a young man of twenty-one can carry. The company is reliable.

M. B. B., Palestine, Tex.—As between the Illinois Bankers' Life Association and the Postal Life, take the latter. There is reserve security behind the Postal. The mathematics of the other are faulty.

J. F. J., Waukesha, Wis.—You are probably referring to group insurance. Your data are insufficient to enable me to aid you in finding the article you are hunting. For information respecting group insurance, write Equitable Life Assurance Society, 120 Broadway, New York, N. Y.

E. E. H., Oxford, O.—For its age, the company is of good average quality. Considering all your circumstances, would advise you to take ordinary life (instead of endowment) insurance. You have a dependent who needs protection. You can get twice as much in the way of a policy for the same premium. Put it in one of the old, well established companies with a good annual dividend record.

D. D. J., St. Louis, Mo.—As investments for profit, stock in new insurance companies may be classed as pure speculations. They may turn out well; a few do; most of them are failures. I should say that the necessity to increase the premium rates on life insurance policies is an indication that the persons calculating the inadequate rates are incompetent. A properly managed new life company would not earn a dividend for its stockholders under five years.

J. G. C., Clifton, Ariz.—The Western Mutual Life Association of Los Angeles, California, is an assessment organization, collecting from its members only an amount sufficient to pay current death losses and expenses. Funds requisite to offset the increasing age of the membership are not accumulated and the total net assets of about $600,000 are obviously inadequate if used as a reserve to protect the $15,000,000 of outstanding insurance. The cost to members must inevitably increase. The New York Life policy will be the more economical in the long run.

"Standard" Built-in Baths

insure pride of ownership, satisfaction in service and an every-day appreciation of the bathroom because it is modern and right.

The up-to-date home deserves a Built-in Bath, together with other "Standard" Plumbing Fixtures for bathroom, kitchen and laundry.

The use of a "Standard" Built-in Bath is like bathing in a china dish. The beauty of "Standard" equipment, together with its sterling worth, mean the <u>correct</u> solution of your plumbing problem.

Ask your architect or plumber about it, or see these fixtures at any "Standard" showroom. The green and gold guarantee label identifies the genuine. Write for a copy of "Modern Bathrooms."

Standard Sanitary Mfg. Co.

DEPT. M, PITTSBURGH

Visit any of these "Standard" Showrooms

NEW YORK	35 W. 31ST	YOUNGSTOWN	N. CHAMPION
BOSTON	186 DEVONSHIRE	ERIE	128 W. TWELFTH
PHILADELPHIA	1215 WALNUT	LOS ANGELES	MESQUIT AT SEVENTH
WASHINGTON	SOUTHERN BLDG.	LOUISVILLE	319 W. MAIN
PITTSBURGH	106 SIXTH	NASHVILLE	315 S. TENTH
CHICAGO	900 S. MICHIGAN	NEW ORLEANS	846 BARONNE
ST. LOUIS	100 N. FOURTH	HOUSTON	PRESTON & SMITH
CLEVELAND	4409 EUCLID	DALLAS	1200 JACKSON
CINCINNATI	633 WALNUT	SAN ANTONIO	312 LOSOYA
TOLEDO	311-321 ERIE	FORT WORTH	FRONT & JONES
COLUMBUS	248-255 S. THIRD	TORONTO, CAN.	59 E. RICHMOND
		HAMILTON, CAN.	20 W. JACKSON

THE MARKET PLACE
A REVIEW OF FINANCE AND TRADE

WAR SUPPLIES

There were rumors last week that several new orders for munitions had been placed in this country by the Allies, but evidence was produced concerning only one, an order for $5,775,000 worth of eight-inch shells, given to four Western manufacturing companies that are not widely known. Many of the Eastern companies are busily engaged on orders placed several months ago. For example, work on the Westinghouse Air Brake Company's orders will not be complete until the beginning of August. New orders for shells are expected in Canada, where the British Government's expenditures for such ammunition this month will be $25,000,000, a sum which is advanced by the Government of the Dominion. Large quantities of shells are needed. This is shown by the estimate that more than $50,000,000 worth have been used in the Verdun battles.

Large shipments of munitions and other supplies have recently been made from New York. In thirty-six hours, beginning on March 3, nine ships sailed with cargoes of this kind, the total being 55,000 tons. In the list were several liners withdrawn from the British naval service for this work. Only one of the nine was armed, and only three carried passengers. The shipments included shells, cartridge cases, bayonets, rifles, revolvers, fuses, toluol, copper, brass, steel, aeroplanes, automobiles, alcohol, powder, dynamite, wire, spelter, and 1257 horses.

The British Government bought $6,000,000 worth of sugar here last week. In association with the French Government it has recently purchased great quantities of wheat elsewhere, paying $16,000,000 in Australia, $20,000,000 in Argentina, and $50,000,000 in Rumania. It is estimated that the Allies now own or control 323,000,000 quarters, while the neutrals have 189,000,000, and 56,000,000 are assigned to Germany, Austria and the minor nations associated with them. These large British and French purchases abroad have in some measure affected our wheat market.

OUR FOREIGN TRADE

Our exports in January, $335,535,000, were less by $17,000,000 than those of December (which had never been equaled), but there was an increase of $12,000,000 in the value of imports. Those who watch the course of our foreign trade are accustomed to look for the excess of exports over imports. In January it was $151,343,000. December, with an excess of $187,459,000, still holds the record. The extraordinary growth and amount of this balance in favor of the United States are shown when the figures for the seven months ending with January are considered, and when comparisons with the trade reports of past years are made. For

432

those seven months the excess was $1,084,333,000, a sum nearly equal to half of the exports. In the corresponding months of 1915 the excess was only $403,000,000, and $454,000,000 was the amount for 1913. Official figures for the entire calendar year of 1915 were published last week by the Government. The exports were $3,486,015,000—an increase of nearly $1,500,000,000, or about seventy per cent—over those of 1914, and the imports were $1,779,794,000. Little change in the value of imports was shown, the reduction having been less than $10,000,000.

The great increase of our exports has been due mainly, of course, to the shipment of war supplies to the Allies in Europe, but there has also been a large increase of our sales to South America, China, the British East Indies, Australia and New Zealand. Our imports from those countries, also, have grown. Comparisons between the transactions of last December and those of December, 1914, show how great has been the advance in the values of exported war supplies. Explosives rose from $2,200,000 to $46,000,000; manufactures of iron and steel, partly for use in making ammunition, from $15,000,000 to $45,000,000, and copper from $7,000,000 to $16,000,000, while the shipments of brass were multiplied by ten, growing from $900,000 to $9,000,000. It is estimated that the value of ammunition, other explosives and firearms sent to Europe from this country since the beginning of the war has been $201,679,000.

COPPER AND STEEL

It is estimated that if the present prices of copper, from 27 to 28 cents a pound, are maintained thruout the year, our producers will receive in 1916 about $200,000,000 more than was paid to them in 1915.

On the 2d, the members of the London Metal Exchange decided to suspend trading in all metals except tin. This action was taken in obedience to the following order issued by the British Government:

It shall be unlawful for any person to sell or buy, or to offer to sell or buy, iron, steel, copper, zinc, brass, antimony, nickel, tungsten, molybdenum, ferro-alloys, or any other metal specified by the Ministry of Munitions as necessary for the production of any war material, unless the metal is in the possession of the seller or in course of production for him: and, in the case of the buyer, unless the purchase is made for the actual consumers.

This suspension in London will not appreciably affect our market. The price of copper is determined in this country. For this metal, and also for lead and spelter, England must depend mainly upon the United States. There has been a partial resumption of business on the Exchange, under an agreement with the Minister of Munitions concerning prices.

Since the beginning of the year, the prices of steel products have been rising steadily. Additions were made last week. The average for all is now about $49 a ton, against $30 one year ago. But the increase in twelve months for several prominent products has been almost 100 per cent. This is true of steel billets and sheet bars. Never before has the output of the mills been so large or sold so far ahead. While the largest tonnage demands at the present time are for shrapnel steel—and there are inquiries for several million shells from Russia and Great Britain—the shipyards are calling for large quantities of the metal. In this country there are now 334 ships under contract, 275 of them for the merchant service, and 59 for our Government. There is much ship-building for foreign owners. Since January 1 orders for 43 ships have been given.

All the orders placed at the steel mills since that date amount to 4,000,000 tons, and have a value of $240,000,000. They include about $30,000,000 worth of locomotives and cars. Much of the steel is to go abroad in one form or another. It is estimated that about 15 per cent of our steel output is now exported.

An addition of about 600,000 tons to the Steel Corporation's total of unfilled orders was expected at the end of last week, but the official statement showed an increase of 648,199 tons, and a new high record was made. February's output of pig iron, 3,087,212 tons, was a little less than the product in December and in January, but February is a short month, and the daily average at the furnaces was the largest ever known. We are now making pig iron at the unprecedented rate of 39,500,000 tons a year.

Several new plants are to be built, or existing plants are to be enlarged, with a part of the steel industry's surplus earnings. The Corporation has decided to use $25,000,000 in making a new mill at Gary, Ind., where it has already invested $65,000,000. And during the last six months $28,000,000 has been set aside for development work. A large mill may be erected in Canada. The Bethlehem Steel Company will spend $25,000,000 for additions and improvements at the Sparrows Point plant of the recently acquired Maryland Steel Company.

The following dividends are announced:
Manila Electric and Lighting Corporation, quarterly, 1½ per cent, payable April 1.
American Car and Foundry Company, preferred, 1¾ per cent; common, ½ per cent; both payable April 1.
Utah Copper Company, quarterly, $1.50 per share; extra dividend, $1 per share; both payable March 31.
United Shoe Machinery Corporation, preferred, quarterly, 1½ per cent per share; common, quarterly, 2 per cent per share; both payable April 5.
American Agricultural Chemical Company, preferred, quarterly, 1½ per cent; common, quarterly, 1 per cent; both payable April 15.

The Independent

FOR SIXTY-SEVEN YEARS THE
FORWARD-LOOKING WEEKLY OF AMERICA

THE CHAUTAUQUAN
Merged with The Independent June 1, 1914

MARCH 27, 1916

OWNED AND PUBLISHED BY
THE INDEPENDENT CORPORATION, AT
119 WEST FORTIETH STREET, NEW YORK
WILLIAM B. HOWLAND, PRESIDENT
FREDERIC E. DICKINSON, TREASURER

WILLIAM HAYES WARD
HONORARY EDITOR

EDITOR: HAMILTON HOLT
ASSOCIATE EDITOR: HAROLD J. HOWLAND
LITERARY EDITOR: EDWIN E. SLOSSON
PUBLISHER: KARL V. S. HOWLAND

ONE YEAR, THREE DOLLARS

SINGLE COPIES, TEN CENTS

Postage to foreign countries in Universal Postal
Union, $1.75 a year extra; to Canada, $1 extra.
Instructions for renewal, discontinuance or
change of address should be sent two weeks
before the date they are to go into effect. Both
the old and the new address must be given.

We welcome contributions, but writers who
wish their articles returned, if not accepted,
should send a stamped and addrest envelope. No responsibility is assumed by The
Independent for the loss or non-return of
manuscripts, tho all due care will be exercised.

Entered at New York Post Office as Second
Class Matter

Copyright, 1916, by The Independent

Address all Communications to
THE INDEPENDENT
119 West Fortieth Street, New York

CONTENTS

JUST A WORD

The striking photograph of a bronze
statue, "The Pour," which appears on
the cover of The Independent for this
issue, is reproduced thru the courtesy of
the Damascus Bronze Company, in
whose offices at Pittsburgh the statue
is exhibited, and which holds the copyright.

A MENTAL INVENTORY

Some of our readers are writing in
to know when the next information test
will appear. Owing to the press of other
matters, etc., etc.—but here it is. As
usual we borrow it from our Friends.
It is the custom of the Quaker schools
to put to their pupils once a year a set
of questions designed to show the range
of their reading and their familiarity
with terms occurring commonly in
books and newspapers. They prospect,
so to speak, the minds of the boys and
girls by running down the diamond drill
into their apperceptive basis. The following list of 100 questions has been
prepared from the General Information
Tests used recently in the Germantown
Friends' School and the Friends' School
of Baltimore, by eliminating those questions depending upon local events and
observation. It is a useful sort of examination, for there is no possibility of
cramming for it. Try it out on your students, club members, friends and other
willing or defenseless individuals. Next
month we will publish the answers, but
do not send us the papers. Grading examination papers is not the sort of
thing one does for fun, and we are not
paid for it.

GENERAL INFORMATION TEST
GERMANTOWN FRIENDS' SCHOOL
Second Month 11, 1916

Name: 1. The President of the United
States. 2. The Secretary of State. 3. The
Speaker of the House of Representatives.
4. The Secretary of the Navy. 5. The mayor
of your town. 6. The Governor of your
state. 7. The President of Mexico. 8. The
president of Mount Holyoke. 9. The president of Columbia University. 10. The Great
Commoner. 11. The Iron Duke. 12. Old
Scratch. 13. The Wizard of Menlo Park.
14. The European countries not engaged in
the present war. 15. The countries between
which the "Alabama" case was arbitrat-
ed. 16. The Hoosier Poet. 17. The Harvard
professor who won the latest Nobel prize
for chemistry. 18. The world's most famous
tenor. 19. A European possession on the
mainland of South America. 20. The Senators from your state. 21. The book in the
Bible in which the Ten Commandments
are found. 22. The two great powers whose
boundary has remained unfortified for over
100 years. 23. The city in which the Democratic convention of 1916 is to be held.
24. The city in which the Republican convention of 1916 is to be held. 25. The Lone
Star State.
Locate when possible; otherwise explain:
26. The Black Forest. 27. The Green
Mountains. 28. The Golden Rule. 29. The
Black Hand. 30. The Scarlet Letter. 31.
Yellow journalism. 32. The White Ribbon
33. A blue stocking.
What do the following mean: 34. S. O. S.
35. S. P. C. A. 36. B. & O. 37. cf. 38.
A.D. 39. B.B.
What part of the following plants do we
use: 40. Almonds. 41. Sweet potatoes. 42.
Irish potatoes. 43. Cinnamon. 44. Cloves.
Give the author of the following book or
quotation: 45. "Judge not that ye be not
judged." 46. "A Man without a Country."
47. "A Comedy of Errors." 48. "A Christmas Carol." 49. The Koran. 50. "Captains
Courageous." 51. "The Little Minister."
52. "Bless the Lord, O my soul; and all
that is within me, bless his holy name." 53.
"Don't give too much for the whistle." 54.
"The Rubaiyat of Omar Khayyam." 55.
Out of the trenches by Christmas.
To what country is each of the following ambassador: 56. Graf von Bernstorff.
57. Brand Whitlock. 58. Henry van Dyke.
59. Walter H. Page.
Show the difference in meaning between
the following: 60. Feminist and effeminate.
61. Direct taxation and indirect taxation.
62. Custom-house and clearing-house. 63.
Indulging in personalities and having personality. 64. Diadem and diaphragm.
Explain: 65. Mardi Gras. 66. Sublime
Porte. 67. White Wings. 68. Old Faithful.
69. Adam's ale. 70. Hyphenated American.
State some interesting fact about each
of the following: 71. Booker T. Washington. 72. Anna Howard Shaw. 73. George
Fox. 74. Lewis Carroll. 75. Fritz Kreisler.
76. Sir Edward Grey. 77. Joseph Pennell.
78. Sarah Bernhardt. 79. Venizelos. 80.
Thomas Mott Osborne. 81. John R. Mott.
82. William Dean Howells. 83. Charles E.
Hughes. 84. Sir Douglas Haig.
Miscellaneous: 85. What two bodies of
water are connected by the Dardanelles?
86. Why is a German submarine called a
U-boat? 87. What is "the Christ of the
Andes"? 88. What is the aim of workmen's
compensation laws? 89. To what city was
Paul of Tarsus going when he saw the
vision? 90. What story by Robert Louis
Stevenson is a study in dual personality?
91. What city was the seat of our Government in 1783? 92. What is the motto of the
Boy Scouts? 93. What league was formally organized on June 17, 1915, in Independence Hall, Philadelphia? 94. Who discovered radium? 95. Which foreign nation exerts the greatest influence upon China? 96.
On what island were United States marines
recently landed to restore order? 97. What
Welshman is Minister of Munitions in
Great Britain? 98. What is meant by conscription? 99. Which of the four seasons
is now being experienced in Australia? 100.
In what direction from the North Pole is
Alaska?

The Independent

VOLUME 85   MARCH 27, 1916   NUMBER 3512

THE COLONEL
COMES BACK

See HOW I SWUNG BACK
TO TEDDY. *Page 440*

WHAT WE MUST DO IN MEXICO

AFTER a week of preparation, the punitive expedition against Villa and the sackers of Columbus is well under way. It sets out upon its mission with the express acquiescence of the *de facto* government of Mexico. Before acquiescing in the action of the United States army, Señor Carranza stipulated that reciprocal permission should be given to Mexican forces to pursue raiders across the American border if occasion should ever arise. President Wilson promptly agreed to the Mexican suggestion. In so doing he made it perfectly clear that the conditions must be precisely parallel. He declared that permission was readily granted for military forces of the *de facto* government of Mexico "to cross the international boundary in pursuit of lawless bands of armed men who have entered Mexico from the United States, committed outrages on Mexican soil, and fled into the United States."

So the pursuit of Villa goes vigorously on. It is not yet clear to what extent there will be active and efficient coöperation by the Carranza forces. Such coöperation would doubtless be of value; but whether it is forthcoming or not, the task of punishing Villa and suppressing the activities of similar lawless bands must be carried thru to the end. "Thoro" must be the slogan.

Meanwhile it must not be forgotten that our purpose is not to be confined within the four corners of the idea of vengeance or even of retribution. Villa must be punished. But we are not to stop there. In his reply to Carranza the President gives admirable expression to this larger duty. The privilege of sending our armies into Mexico, he says, will be exercized "in the hope and confident expectation that . . . lawlessness will be eradicated and peace and order maintained in the territories of the United States and Mexico contiguous to the international boundary." To this important purpose the energies of the United States must be bent. We must not recall our forces until this end is accomplished.

The Senate has unanimously adopted a concurrent resolution—which must be also passed by the House to become effective—approving the action of the President in sending the expedition against Villa. In the resolution the Senate "joins with the President in declaring that such military expedition shall not be permitted to encroach in any degree upon the sovereignty of Mexico or to interfere in any manner with the domestic affairs of the Mexican people." This is a good declaration, provided it is interpreted broadly and sanely. We have no purpose of aggression against the people of Mexico. We intend no assault upon their sovereignty. But the duty of making American life and property safe which has been thrust upon us by the impotence of the Mexican people themselves is one which we must perform with all thoroness. We must not tie our hands by any declaration which means that we may be expected to relax our efforts before this end is accomplished.

THE MYSTERY OF THE ALTRURIAN BATTLESHIP

THE other day a curious craft bobbed up at Washington, a semi-submersible torpedo-battleship of unprecedented speed and power, capable, it seems, of putting out of action a fleet of the old-fashioned dreadnoughts. This vessel was introduced by Captain Sims, of the new battleship "Nevada," in his testimony before the House Naval Committee, and he credits its invention to Commander Schofield.

Now we are particularly glad to see the torpedo-battleship come to the surface again, because we have been wondering what had become of it. It appeared out of nowhere in The Independent of September 30, 1909, and, after making some commotion in naval circles, vanished into the limbo of forgotten things. All we know about it was what was told by Park Benjamin in the article of that date on "The New Altrurian Battleship." From this it appears that the Republic of Altruria, tired of having to compete with "the Bullonians and the Crapaudians and the Dagoes and the savage tribes which once annihilated the legions of Varus" in the construction of bigger and more expensive battleships, set its wits to work to invent a new kind of craft that could knock them all out —and did it. This is the description of it:

Now the Altrurian vessel looked a good deal like a "whale back," such as one sees on the Great Lakes, only she was longer and narrower, say 500 feet in length and perhaps not over 30 or 40 feet in beam. Her deck, which curved over on each side, rose at the highest barely 3 feet above the water and was armored. Nothing showed on it except a low conning tower and a periscope tube, which, as is now common in torpedo boats and submarines, projected the picture of her surroundings upon the whitened table in front of the helmsman far below the water line. Her frames were of light but excessively strong steel, some one of the odd alloys which have lately been invented, and they were filled in with immensely strong but again light compressed paper pulp. Oil carried in her double bottom supplied the fuel for her tremendously powerful internal combustion engines, which drove a multiplicity of propellers, and gave her a speed of at least 35 knots per hour. Her sole armament was ten fish torpedoes on each side, each delivered from a separate water-tight compartment, each capable of going straight for 4000 yards under water, and at a speed of perhaps 37 knots, and in the racks adjacent to each torpedo tube were six spare torpedoes. The absence of guns and of all armor except the protective deck, together with the light construction of the hull, rendered it possible to give to the gas engines the high power noted, not only for a sudden dash, but for comparatively long periods of time, and while the vessel was driving ahead, a peculiar formation of her bow sent the sea over her for a depth probably sufficient to cause any projectile striking her at the necessarily low angle to glance and ricochet from her deck without penetration. The Altrurians found that they could build six vessels like that for the cost of one dreadnought, and that she needed for her management less than one-fifth of a dreadnought crew. And because of her speed she could lie far off from the fleet and arrive close at hand at any desired moment, say in thick or foggy weather, or when the fleet was threading narrow straits, or otherwise navigating troublesome waters.

This corresponds closely to Captain Sims' subsea battleship, even in details, so it seems that there must be open sea between Altruria and the United States, altho the two countries are evidently far apart, since it takes seven years to make the passage. This may give a clue to the location of that unknown land which Howells describes so attractively in his "Traveler from Altruria."

But a more important possibility is that the "Altrurian" or her sister ships may have got to Kiel as well as Washington. If von Tirpitz or rather von Capelle has some of these up his sleeve it may go far toward neutralizing the advantage of two to one in dreadnoughts which the British now have over the Germans.

DO IT WELL

BACK of all achievement, personal and national, is Will; but the determination to achieve needs skilful directing. "Efficiency" is the science of guiding human endeavor, with the minimum of waste, to the best possible results. Everywhere is the desire to achieve, and every day the thought is growing that half life's problem is to know the simplest, quickest and most satisfactory way of doing things.

No doubt can exist as to America's constructive vitality: there is already proof of it in a coast-to-coast chain of accomplishment, in which the Woolworth Building and the Panama Canal are but two of the "outward and visible" links. And only the threshold has been crost. None can forecast the future, but it is clear that enormous possibilities wait upon the ability of Americans to develop further, in a hundred different directions, the science of achievement as well as its spirit. In every sphere "the better method" is being sought, and the urge toward improvement affects the intimate home life of America's myriad units no less than their composite life as a community and nation.

The National Institute of Efficiency, the organization of which is reported in this issue, has come into being, as the name implies, as a part of the rapidly growing movement toward the increased effectiveness which, beginning with the individual, can become nation-wide in extent. Its endeavor will be to focus some of the attempts that are already being made to develop personal efficiency in its many aspects, as well as to encourage, by every fitting means, the acquirement of fresh knowledge leading in the same direction.

"The man is the nation," and the National Institute of Efficiency is organized in the belief that the future lies with the nation, no less than the individual, that has learned to Do It Well.

THE COLLAPSE OF A PERSECUTION

THOMAS MOTT OSBORNE, humanitarian warden of Sing Sing prison, has been acquitted of one of the charges against him in quick time. Before the defense had presented any evidence whatever, the judge directed a verdict of acquittal. The charge was perjury. The specifications were that in an investigation of conditions in the prison made by a member of the State Prison Commission the warden evaded questions as to the existence of cases of immorality among the convicts.

The judge summarily disposed of the charge by declaring that the investigation by a single member of the commission acting on his own initiative was not authorized by the law. The investigator, therefore, could not administer a valid oath, and a witness could not commit perjury in testifying before him.

The judge further declared that Mr. Osborne did not wilfully deceive the investigator, because the latter already knew from other witnesses, and the warden knew that he knew, that there had been cases of immorality among the prisoners. The judge further explained, with implied approval, why Mr. Osborne evaded the questions about immorality. He said:

The defendant's refusal to answer and his evasive replies were to keep good the promises he made to the men when they confest to him their offenses and received their punishment under the prison management; namely, that they would not be subject to further punishment therefor,

and that he would go to jail rather than betray their confidence.

The summary termination of the case by judicial decree is all the more gratifying, in that it is not the result of a technicality. "The question," said the judge, "goes to the very heart of the case."

Another indictment hangs over Mr. Osborne. In that one appears the charge of personal immorality. The warden and his attorneys press for an immediate trial, but the district attorney shuffles and delays as he has done thruout the case. As the matter proceeds, the indications become stronger and stronger that there is malevolent animus back of the prosecution. Mr. Osborne should have his second day in court without delay. There is no reason to fear that he will emerge from it less triumphantly than from the first.

Meanwhile, the inmates of Sing Sing greet the news of the warden's acquittal with boisterous applause. Their rejoicing at his exoneration is not the least evidence of his success in his whole-hearted attempt to treat criminals like men—and so help them to become men again.

THE BETTER HALF OF MEXICO

NOT all the news from Mexico is bad. For while the men are raiding and fighting, the women of Mexico have held a congress to advocate "a new system of moral and religious education." Over a thousand delegates, representing all sections of the republic, met recently in Mérida, in the province of Yucatan. They suggested measures for the enfranchisement of women and the betterment of her condition socially; they discussed progress and culture for women and for the state; and they made practical plans for acting upon the inspiration which the convention gave.

It is a striking illustration of the possible value of women in government. Mexican leaders have been for years floundering in the midst of petty revolutions and personal recriminations. They have seen no wise way out. But Mexico's women have taken a real step toward democracy and an orderly government for their country.

Naturally they urge the necessity of woman suffrage as a basis for their work. When popular suffrage is established in Mexico—as it must be if the republic is to prove worthy of the name—it will be the women who have earned the right to vote rather than the men. But perhaps they will succeed in getting it for both sexes.

WELL DONE, ST. LOUIS!

THE great city of St. Louis has voted three to one that hereafter negroes shall not move into blocks in which seventy-five per cent or more of the houses are occupied by whites, and that whites shall not move into blocks in which seventy-five per cent or more of the houses are occupied by negroes.

This is excellent as far as it goes, but why stop there? Would it not be a good plan to reserve the streets in which over seventy-five per cent of the traffic is white entirely to whites, and the streets—if there be any—in which over seventy-five per cent of the traffic is colored to the colored. If this works without injustice or friction, then St. Louis might pass an ordinance requiring the two races to eat different food, to wear different styles of clothes, and to think different thoughts.

We respectfully suggest that the fair city of St. Louis

send a commission to India to investigate and report on the admirable caste system prevailing there. It will evidently need all the light it can get in working out the broad and humane policy it has now begun.

COME BACK

COLONEL ROOSEVELT is back. He is back from his trip to the Spanish Main; and he is back on the front page of the newspapers.

There is only one man who shares with him the popular interest as possible opposition candidate for President—Mr. Justice Hughes. Local politicians are vociferating the names of favorite sons like Root, McCall, Estabrook, Sherman, Burton, Hadley, Brumbaugh, Borah, Fairbanks.

But the public will not listen. They talk only of Hughes and Roosevelt—with varying emphasis. Some like one, some the other. Some like neither, but make a wry face and admit that the one (or the other, as the case may be) must be nominated in order "to beat Wilson."

The recrudescence of Mr. Roosevelt as a figure of political prominence is an interesting phenomenon. One phase of it is set forth on another page, where a young business man explains how he "swung back to Teddy."

The Colonel cannot be kept for long at a time off the front page because he persists in doing and saying things that challenge attention. You may admire him or you may disapprove of him; you may hate him or you may love him. But you cannot ignore him.

He has an uncanny faculty for knowing what the people are going to be interested in, and talking about it first. When he begins to talk about it, they listen. Then they begin to talk about it, too, according to their several kinds—with acclamation or vituperation. Never with indifference.

The Colonel is bound to be an increasingly interesting figure until the seventh of June. And after? That depends.

Anyhow, he has come back.

SHAKESPEARE IN MAGNIFICENCE

SHAKESPEARE'S "Henry the Eighth" is not a closely knit, logical drama. It might appropriately be called "Scenes from the Life of a King, and His Court." But the scenes are splendidly pictorial, and one or two of them somberly dramatic. It is not a great play, but it can be made a great spectacle.

This feat has been accomplished in rich measure by Sir Herbert Beerbohm Tree in his production at the New Amsterdam Theater in New York. It is a series of superbly decorative pictures, splashed upon the canvas of a huge stage with a lavish hand and colorful brush.

As a pageant it is even better than the best of the "movies." One can hardly say more than that in these latter days.

But it is something more. There are two pieces of characterization in the present production that rank high as examples of the actors' art.

American audiences have learned to expect great things from Edith Wynne Matthison. Once more they are not disappointed. As Henry's queen, Katherine, she is a lovely, tragic, heart-breaking figure. Not less effective is the Henry of Lyn Harding. The sensual, heartless buffoon of a king straddles before us "in his habit as he lived."

One would like to add a third great characterization to the list. But candor forbids. Sir Herbert's Wolsey misses greatness by the breadth of a voice. Tree is a master producer and a sound actor, but his own medium is not equal to his conception of the part he plays.

But this is ungenerous criticism. We owe him great thanks for so magnificent and artistic a production.

A NEGRO NONCONFORMIST

AN eleven-year-old colored boy in Des Moines has been brought before the Juvenile Court because he refused to salute the American flag. He declares that he will salute "nobody or nothing" but his God. His parents approve his stand.

Several such cases of refusal to conform to this new patriotic ceremony have occurred in various parts of the country, so it is well to consider the principle involved in the question. Assuming that this is a case of real conscientious scruple and not wilful disobedience or caprice, it seems to us clear that the boy is wrong in his opinion and right in his action. To most of us the salute to the flag seems a beautiful and appropriate way of expressing our loyalty to our country and our allegiance to our government. But we can easily understand that to some it might seem a bit of patriotic superstition and therefore wrong. To compel outward conformity in such a case would be to inculcate hypocrisy, and any teacher or magistrate who should use his power to such an evil purpose should himself be brought before the court. The more anxious we are to inculcate a real spirit of reverence to the flag as a symbol of our nation the more careful we should be to prevent its becoming an empty form or false pretense, and to avoid making unnecessary martyrs of conscientious dissenters.

In New Jersey not long ago a boy got into trouble with the authorities for refusal to take part in the flag ceremony, and it turned out that he was a Canadian. Of course, a foreigner who has no intention of becoming a citizen could not be expected to say: "I pledge allegiance to this flag and to the republic for which it stands," or anything of the kind. Instead of being compelled to take such a pledge he should never have been allowed to do so. But the true born Britisher may without disloyalty raise his hat to the American flag or even join in the singing of the "Star Spangled Banner." We will not in that case regard it as discourteous in him if he omits to vote the lines so uncomplimentary to him and the Hessians:

Their blood has washed out their foul footsteps' pollution.
No refuge could save the hireling and slave
From the terror of flight or the gloom of the grave.

On the other hand, the American does not renounce his republicanism when he joins his British cousins in singing "God Save the King." There are some, we know, who on such occasions surreptitiously substitute the words of "America" or who modify them to "God Save Their King," but such we regard as overscrupulous.

The modern trend is toward conformity to the customs of the community in which one happens to be as a matter of propriety and without sacrifice of principle. To be continually objecting to forms one does not like or believe in makes one obnoxious, and, besides, a conspicuous act of disapproval often gives to the ceremony an importance and significance which it does not actually possess in the minds of its adherents. The Quakers of our acquaintance are as quick to raise the hat as any worldling, yet their forefathers would have gone to the stake rather than do such reverence to a human being.

But we must deal gently with those who decline to adopt this modern attitude and who cannot look at the question in this light. The willingness to make personal sacrifices for private convictions is all too rare nowadays to be crushed out when it appears. The question is often a vital one. Many a Chinese Christian has gone to his death rather than kowtow to the tablet of Confucius, and we honor them for it. Yet we do not believe that they were necessarily more conscientious than those who choose to interpret the ceremony not as an act of worship but as the homage due to the memory of a great and good man. Since the war began the oath required of British recruits has been changed to read: "I swear by Almighty God." This is keeping out of the army both conscientious infidels and conscientious Quakers, who are willing to give their lives for their country but refuse to say what they do not believe. Such men are needed in the British army—and elsewhere.

So let us not be hard upon little Hubert Eaves, of Des Moines, wrong-headed and pig-headed tho he may be. If he is as scrupulous in big things as he is in this comparatively little thing he will make a good citizen, even tho he may never doff his hat to the flag or stand when the national anthem is played. Such acts are valueless unless voluntary.

Very likely, if we got at the bottom of it, we should find that Hubert had been led astray by the reading of pernicious literature such as the story of William Tell. If that is the case, we are glad he refrained from using the teacher as a target for his bow and arrow. When he grows older he will learn that Third Reader heroes are to be admired, not imitated, and that there is a difference between an Austrian duke's hat and our own flag.

PREPAREDNESS IN THE SCHOOLS

WE have pointed out the objections to military training in the public schools. It should not be necessary to explain that our objections apply only to military training in a technical sense of the term, and not to those exercises and disciplines that are proper elements of any sound education, preparatory to a responsible citizenship. As we do not propose to have our actual contention in this matter distorted or perverted by parties who will not or who cannot make valid discriminations we shall take the trouble to present certain distinctinctions explicitly enough to remove all excuse for misunderstanding.

The essentials of technical military training are drill in the manual of arms, organization by military units, and specific instruction and practice in military operations. The public schools, we contend, are not the place for these exercizes and schemes of organization.

On the other hand, there are disciplines that are essential to the making of good soldiers which also are essential to the making of self-reliant men and women, good members of society and good citizens. These exercizes the schools should give with firmness of discipline and under intelligent direction.

First among these measures of preparedness for sound and dutiful living is physical training, as rigorous, as scientific, as the most urgent military necessity could call for. Not only should all school pupils be taught habits of proper care of their bodily health and made to perform the ordinary gymnastic work, they also should be held strictly to the achievement of specific accomplishment, namely, to carry themselves properly, to endure marching, to swim, to handle the tools that pertain to emergency situations, as ax, pick and spade. The spirit and the method of such instruction is totally different, as every well-informed person knows, from the spirit and the method that go into a feverish training for doing athletic "stunts." The public school athletic activities that have been developed in New York City under the enthusiastic supervision of General Wingate and of Dr. Crampton afford suggestions that are well worth the serious study by other communities.

In the second place, public school pupils should be taught respect for authority, decorum, and obedience. The extent to which rowdyism and hoodlumism prevail in America is not only a national disgrace, it is an incontrovertible evidence of indifference to a serious situation which includes wastage of energy and a general state of inefficiency. We let children grow up without respect for their elders and without courtesy toward one another. Those educators who see in an insistence upon deference and obedience a survival of the obsequiousness of subject classes to the socially powerful are blind to some of the most essential facts of life. Obedience of the weak to the powerful is not the only or the most important obedience in human society. If we are to have collective effort, organized activity and the achievements which are possible only thru a proper functioning of society, respect for experience, obedience to accredited leaders and to group law are far more essential than is any obsequiousness of the subordinated to the dominating element in the despotic state. They are facts of sound economy, of efficiency, of moral steadiness, and of self-command.

Finally, there should be stimulation of initiative and training in self-reliance. We believe that one of the most costly and lamentable fallacies in prevalent educational philosophy is the assumption that there is a necessary conflict between an old-fashioned discipline which included an insistence upon acquisition, obedience and facility, on the one hand, and, on the other hand, the encouragement of curiosity, the strengthening of powers of observation and invention, and the development of self-reliance. There is no such conflict except in the imagination of pedagogic partizans. There is no good reason why all that has been best in the older schemes of education should not be conserved and combined with all that is good in the so-called Gary plan. Also our educational scheme should include practically all of the activities that have been developed in the Boy Scout movement.

When pupils leave the public schools they should be ready for the further disciplines of peace or the further disciplines of war as fate shall require of them. They should be physically sound and be masters of the important physical activities. They should be obedient, respectful and law-abiding. They should have acquired sound knowledge and facility in applying it. They should also be independent, inventive and resourceful. To think of this ideal as beyond attainment or even as of prohibitive difficulty or costliness, is absurd and inexcusable. If we do not demand its realization it is because we are unawake, indifferent and ineffective.

THE STORY OF THE WEEK

Our Soldiers in Mexico The troops of our punitive expedition crost the boundary and entered Mexico on the 15th, General Pershing commanding one column that started from Columbus, New Mexico, while another, entering at a point further west, was led by Colonel Dodd. The entire number was a little more than 4000, but it is said that between 7000 and 8000 American soldiers are in Mexico now. General Pershing's force was joined by a party of Carranza's soldiers, several of whom were used as scouts, altho this is denied by General Gavira, the Carranza commander at Juarez. Villa had gone southward. On the 18th he was about 110 miles southeast of Casas Grandes, and 100 miles in advance of the American troops. Carranza, who had about 5000 men in Chihuahua, ordered reinforcements, and 20,000 men were said to be on their way north.

When it was reported that our troops were about to enter Casas Grandes, General Gavira telegraphed an order that they should not be permitted to do so. For a time there was danger of a collision, but our Government gave notice that its forces would not occupy any towns, whereupon Gavira said the crisis had passed. He had exprest disapproval of the admission of American troops, and had feared that our soldiers would be attacked by "snipers" if they should enter Casas Grandes, or even pass thru the place. The fact that they had entered Mexico without being molested he regarded as a supreme tribute to the Mexican people's confidence in Carranza. Colonel Slocum, who was in command at Columbus when Villa attacked the town, has offered a reward of $50,000 for the capture of Villa, and about $50,000 more has been offered by American ranchmen in Northern Mexico.

Our Government, on the 13th, accepted Carranza's proposal that there should be reciprocity in crossing the boundary. It "readily granted permission for military forces of the de facto Government of Mexico" to cross in pursuit of "lawless bands of armed men who have entered Mexico from the United States, committed outrages on Mexican soil, and fled into the United States," on the understanding that a reciprocal privilege should be given to our forces. Gratification was exprest because Carranza had shown "so cordial and friendly a spirit of coöperation." At the same time Secretary Lansing issued a statement in which he said that, to remove any misapprehension that might exist here or in Mexico, the President had authorized him to give the public assurance that the military operations would be scrupulously confined" to the pursuit of Villa, and "in no circumstances would be suffered to infringe in any degree upon the sovereignty of Mexico or develop into intervention of any kind in the internal affairs of our sister republic." On the contrary, what we were doing was "deliberately intended to preclude the possibility of intervention."

Carranza at once ordered his forces to coöperate with our soldiers, and a similar order was sent to the border garrisons by General Obregon, his new Minister of War. Carranza also published a statement in which he said that there was no longer any danger of international complications. At the Mexican capital and in Queretaro there were parades, with cannon salutes and the ringing of church bells. Placards asserted that Carranza was the savior of Mexico's honor. From a large meeting in Vera Cruz a message of congratulation was sent to President Wilson. But there were disquieting reports from many places in Mexico. Carranza's troops in Juarez were angry, and Americans were insulted there. Our consul at Torreon, Mr. Williams, with eighty-six American residents, came to Texas because Torreon was no longer safe. There was trouble in Tampico.

To many Mexicans, Villa was a hero, and they had no confidence in the assurances given by our Government.

Action Taken in Congress On the day when Carranza's request for reciprocity in crossing was granted, Mr. Wilson urged the leaders in Congress to prevent delay in the consideration and enactment of the pending defense bills. During a debate in the Senate, Mr. Borah and Mr. Warren, Republicans, heartily supported him and argued against delay. Mr. Borah remarked that the result of the movement against Villa could not be foreseen. On the Democratic side, Mr. Myers said the present army was large enough, but he was met by a chorus of protests. He assumed that we had 100,000 men. Mr. Chamberlain said that in the continental United States there were only 35,000, and that only half of these were available for service in Mexico. Mr. Borah exprest the opinion that we might need 50,000 or 100,000.

At the urgent request of the President, on the following day, the House passed a resolution authorizing him to increase the army to the maximum permitted by existing law. The vote was 236 to 1, Meyer London, Socialist, being the only member in the negative. It was shown that our mobile army was composed of 36,433 men, not including the coast artillery, and that only 34,510 were available for service in Mexico. There have been 19,000 on the border. Mr. Hay said that many in the militia had volunteered, but he thought it would be better to enlarge the regular army. The same resolution was adopted in the Senate by unanimous vote.

Two days later, Senator La Follette, with the knowledge and approval of President Wilson, introduced a concurrent resolution, in which, after preambles referring to the assurances already given by the President and Secretary Lansing to Carranza, the use of the

ACTIVITY ON THE BORDER
Two columns of American troops, cavalry with some artillery, have already crost over into Mexico hunting Villa

THE AMERICAN PURSUIT OF VILLA

As The Independent goes to press the cavalry column commanded by General Pershing, which started from Columbus, is reported to be beyond Casas Grandes, and moving southwest, 133+ miles from the border. Villa is said to be near Hablcora—about where a line drawn thru Palomas and Casas Grandes would intersect the Sierra Madre. Carranza forces are said to hold all the passes thru these mountains

armed forces for the sole purpose of apprehending and punishing Villa and his lawless band was approved by Congress, which extended to the de facto Government of Mexico and to the Mexican people assurances that this was the only object of the punitive expedition, and that "Congress, in approving this use of the armed forces of the United States, joins the President in declaring that this military expedition shall not be permitted to encroach in any degree upon the sovereignty of Mexico or to interfere in any manner with the domestic affairs of the Mexican people." Without debate the resolution was adopted by a unanimous vote. Mr. Fall, of New Mexico, was absent. After his return he said that if he had been present he would have registered his complete disapproval of the resolution, and would have opposed the adoption of it. Similar action upon the resolution in the House within a few days was expected. It is understood that our Government has given large orders for munitions to several companies that have been at work on foreign contracts.

The Army Bills   There has been debate in the House on the bill reported by Mr. Hay for enlarging the army, and in the Senate a bill of the same general character has been reported from committee. The House bill provides for a regular army of 140,000 men, and empowers the President to make the total 170,000 in an emergency. In the Senate bill provision is made for an army of 194,000 in time of peace, with a war increase to 236,000. Both bills call for a federalization of the militia, but the plan in the House bill is held by some to be at variance with the Constitution. In addition, the Senate bill proposes something resembling the Continental Army which was a feature of the plan supported by Secretary Garrison. Both bills largely increase the number of West Point cadets.

Representative Gardner read a letter, signed by Mr. Baker, the new Secretary of War, severely criticizing the Hay bill and the committee's statements in support of it. This letter, it has been shown, was prepared in the War College, and signed by Mr. Baker as a matter of routine. Mr. Hay declared that his bill was satisfactory to the President. The Senate has passed a bill appropriating $2,065,000 to be used in equipping the Puget Sound Navy Yard for the construction of battleships.

The Sugar Duty Retained   It was provided in the Underwood tariff law that the duty on sugar should be removed in May of this year. Because more revenue is needed, on account of the great war, it was decided some time ago at Washington that this part of the tariff law should be repealed. On the 16th a resolution repealing it was adopted in the House by a vote of 346 to 14. Those in the negative were thirteen Democrats and the only Socialist member, Mr. Meyer London. There will be concurrence in the Senate, and by this action of Congress there will be retained $44,000,-000 of annual revenue. Preceding the vote in the House there were seven hours of tariff debate.

The respective merits or demerits of the Payne-Aldrich and Underwood tariff laws were the subject of much talk. Democrats were accused by Republicans of reversing their policy as to "free sugar." Among the Democrats who voted against repeal were Mr. Tavenner and Mr. Buchanan, of Illinois, and Mr. Bailey, of Pennsylvania, an intimate friend of Mr. Bryan. Several of the opponents said that they could not vote against removal of the duty after telling the voters in their districts that removal was one of the Democratic party's most notable achievements. The duty is a little more than one cent a pound. Mr. Bailey has introduced a bill providing for complete free trade with any country in South America or Central America that will adopt the same policy with respect to imports from the United States.

Democratic leaders in the House intend to present for action a bill creat-

American Press

WHERE VILLA SEALED HIS DOOM

Ruins of the Commercial Hotel at Columbus, New Mexico, raided by Villa. Six Americans were killed in this building and it was fired by the bandits

© Paul Thompson   IN SERRIED RANKS THE POETS STOOD

At the Civic Forum dinner in New York last week most of the better known poets of this country and some of England were guests. A few of them are here, gathered around Masefield, in whose honor the literary dress parade was held. Standing, from the left, Lawrence Housman, Witter Bynner, Percy Mackaye, Edwin Markham, Cale Young Rice, Louis Untermeyer, Vachel Lindsay. Seated, Amy Lowell, Josephine Daskam Bacon, John Masefield, Alfred Noyes

ing a tariff commission of the kind suggested by President Wilson, certain changes in duties relating to dyestuffs, and the provisions proposed by Secretary Redfield for protection against the "dumping" of European products on our market at very low prices after the war. Some increase of the present duties on dyestuffs will be proposed, but the additions will not be so great as those recommended in the schedule submitted by the American Chemical Society. The taxes of the war revenue law will be continued, the stamp taxes excepted, and the bill will include the projected increase of the income tax.

Trust and Rebate Cases Three and one-half years ago the Government brought suit against the Association of Billposters of the United States and Canada, under the Sherman Anti-Trust law, asking for a dissolution. In Chicago, last week, Judge Landis, of the Federal court, decided that the association was an illegal combination in restraint of trade. Execution of an order for dissolution was deferred for sixty days, to give time for an appeal to the Supreme Court. The Government charged that the association, since it was formed in 1891, had sought in many ways to crush competition. It had admitted to membership, the Government asserted, only one person or firm in each town; had declined to serve advertisers who gave work to those who were not members; had established uniform prices; had driven out of business lithographers who worked for those outside, and had formed an alliance with a dozen prominent advertising agencies, by means of which its ability to injure competitors was increased.

Judge Gary, of the Steel Corporation, and the steel companies indicted at Youngstown, Ohio, for violating Ohio's Anti-Trust law by conspiring or agreeing to increase wages, have moved that the indictment be quashed, saying that it does not show how the alleged agreement was carried out. The charge was based upon the fact that within two days all the accused

companies increased the wages of their workmen by 10 per cent. The business men of Youngstown regret that the companies (one of them being the Steel Corporation) were indicted, fearing that Youngstown will not be in the list of places where the companies are to spend large sums for those extensions and improvements which the great prosperity of the steel industry demands. The Government, which was to submit at Washington, on March 15, its appeal from the decision in favor of the Steel Corporation (in the suit for dissolution) has asked that the time limit be extended until July 15.

Following the decision which required the New Jersey Central Railroad Company to pay a fine of $200,-000 for giving rebates to the Lehigh Coal and Navigation Company, a Federal court has now found the latter company guilty of soliciting and receiving the rebates. As the company was convicted on twenty-seven counts, the maximum fine permitted by the law is $540,000, but the jury recommended clemency. It has been pointed out that the Government is authorized to sue for three times the sum involved in the rebates, or for several millions of dollars. There are no indications, however, that it will take such action.

Wages and Strikes Altho the bituminous coal miners have been successful in conferences with their employers, and have gained a wage increase that will add $8,000,-000 to the annual cost of production, a settlement with the anthracite miners has not been reached. They ask for a wage increase of twenty per cent, an eight-hour day, and recognition of the union. Their employers, who assert that the proposed wage increase would add $23,000,000 to the annual cost of their labor, say that the cost of production has already been considerably increased by the high prices of explosives used in mining, this advance having been due to the war. It is said that they will not recognize the union. Many real estate, civic and commercial organizations, led by the New York Real Estate Board, have sent letters to Presi-

dent Wilson and members of the Senate and the House, asking that an investigation concerning the coal industry, with especial reference to distribution and prices, be made by a Federal commission. Such an inquiry, they say, might prevent a strike.

In New York City, 1000 public school teachers have formed a union, to be affiliated with the American Federation of Labor. Among the speakers at their meeting were Miss Haley, who organized the teachers' union in Chicago, and a representative of the Federation. At a meeting of 800 actors in New York there was a unanimous vote in favor of organizing a union, to be associated with the Federation. Meetings at which similar action was taken were held on the same day in Boston, Chicago and Philadelphia.

Twenty thousand painters, paperhangers and decorators in New York have voted to strike for a daily wage of $5. Those in Brooklyn are to go out on April 1, and those in other parts of the city one month earlier. It is said that about 20,000 in other Eastern cities will begin a strike on April 1, and it is expected that 6000 tailors in New York will decide to take the same course in the early weeks of April. Twenty-seven shops in New York are still closed, on account of the strike of cloak and suit makers, but the 8000 workers in the embroidery trade, after being on strike for nearly six weeks, have returned to work, having gained a wage increase of about ten per cent, a week of fifty-two hours, and a plan for the settlement of grievances, with final appeal to an arbitration board. Additional strikes have closed several factories in Passaic, N. J., where about 4000 employees are out. The demand is for a wage increase of 15 or 25 per cent. A few have accepted ten per cent and returned to work.

The Progress of Woman Suffrage The New York State Assembly has passed by a vote of more than three to one the woman suffrage bill providing for a referendum on the Constitutional amendment. The majority in favor of the measure was larger than even the most optimistic suffrage predictions—109 for the referendum and only thirty-one against it.

In the New York Senate, however, an entirely different attitude toward woman suffrage is being shown. By a program of procrastination and obstructionist tactics the Judiciary Committee is putting off its report on the Whitney-Brereton bill, in spite of the fact that eight of the thirteen members of the committee have declared themselves in favor of it. Senator Elon Brown, chairman of the Judiciary Committee, is held responsible for the successive delays, tho he has tacitly promised a report of the bill by announcing that he will vote against it when it comes before the Senate.

At an indignation mass-meeting in Cooper Union both men and women suffragists of New York City voiced their protest against this inaction.

In Congress the question of nation-wide woman suffrage has been promised a hearing as the special order of business on March 28. Lobbyists from all over the country, armed with petitions, letters, and telegrams from constituents "back home," are urging a favorable consideration of the Federal Suffrage amendment. The women voters of Illinois have sent to Congressman Kitchin a petition bearing twenty-one feet of signatures in its favor. Most of the members of the Judiciary Committee have promised to support the amendment.

The Fourth Week of Verdun During each of the first three weeks of the attack on Verdun the Germans made definite advances, first on the north, then on the east and lastly on the west. During the past week on the contrary they have made no perceptible progress altho they have attacked on both the eastern and western sides.

On the western side of the Meuse the Germans last week obtained a lodgement in Crows' Wood (Bois des Corbeaux) which lies between the hights of Le Mort Homme (Dead Man's Hill) and Côte de l'Oie (Goose Ridge). These are isolated elevations commanding the railroad, which runs along the left bank of the river, and the route along which the Germans must advance if they are to encircle Verdun on the western side. The French, fully realizing the importance of holding these positions, had banked here their famous 75 millimeter field guns. Met by this withering fire the German troops were mowed down before they got half way up the slope of Goose Ridge.

Their assault on Dead Man's Hill promised to be more successful. After a terrific bombardment of ten French trenches, lasting more than twenty-four hours, the Silesians charged the hill from Crows' Wood in three separate columns. Line after line swept up the slope, a hundred yards apart, the men standing so close in the line that they could have clasped hands. In crossing the open they were exposed not only to the fire of the batteries they were assaulting, but to an enfilading fire from the neighboring hights. Nevertheless they succeeded in gaining some two hundred yards of the outermost French trenches and captured a thousand prisoners. Apparently they were not able to hold these gains for at the end of the week the French official report claimed complete possession of Dead Man's Hill.

On the eastern side of the Verdun complex the German bombardment and assaults were directed at the fort and village of Vaux. But the attacking troops were driven back by the French curtain of fire, leaving, it is said, thousands of their dead on the field.

Airy Navies The battle of Verdun, unprecedented in the amount of ammunition expended and probably also in the numbers slain, is unique in another respect as the first time in history that aeroplanes have taken an active part in the fighting. They are employed not only against

other planes, but against troops. When the Germans were bringing up a battery to shell Pepper Ridge (Côte du Poivre) an air squadron swooped down upon them and dropt bombs from an altitude of less than a thousand feet. The first series of bombs killed nine horses and thirty men. With other horses wounded and frightened the guns could not be moved and the soldiers abandoned them and ran to cover.

In one day the French reported twenty aerial engagements in the area northeast of Verdun. Sometimes these are duels, sometimes a score of avions participate. The new German "dreadnought of the air," the Fokker biplane, turns out to be not so invincible as was feared at first.

The most famous of French airmen is Sub-Lieutenant George Guynemer. He is barely twenty-one and at the outbreak of the war was a high school student. He offered himself for the army, but was rejected by the examining board. Then he set himself to learn flying and last August obtained his pilot's license. In December he brought down his first German Fokker, and since then he has devoted himself to single combats with the German aeroplanes. He flies alone and acts both as pilot and gunner. In one of these duels he chased the German to a hight of two miles, where the air was so cold that his machine gun would not work because of the freezing of the oil. But Guynemer dashed against the German machine and both fell. The German aeroplane was crushed on the ground, but Guynemer recovered control at a hight of 1500 feet and alighted

safely. For his exploits he has been awarded the Legion of Honor, the Military Medal and the War Cross. On the ribbon of the cross are embroidered eight palms, one for each German aeroplane that he has brought down. According to a Swiss report he has been shot by a German aviator and wounded in the face and left arm.

Doubtless one reason why the German onslaught on Verdun has slackened is because the French air raids have interfered with the lines of communications to the supply depots in the rear. The army which is attacking Fort de Vaux receives its ammunition and reinforcements by means of the railroad that runs via Conflans to Metz. But one night last week a squadron of seventeen French aeroplanes from Verdun flew over this line, dropping forty large caliber shells on the station at Conflans and fourteen on the station at Metz. All the aviators returned to base unharmed. On another night forty-two shells were dropt on the station at Brieulles which feeds the northern sector of the investing force.

Mülhausen was raided by a French air squadron of twenty-three machines bent on destroying the railroad station and aviation camp. According to the German report four of the French aeroplanes were brought down. Seven of the inhabitants of Mülhausen were killed and thirteen injured. One soldier is reported killed.

Four German seaplanes flew over Kent at a hight of over a mile. A British monoplane pursued them out to sea and brought down one of them, the first

Mishkin

SHAKESPEARE SUPERBLY PLAYED
In the production of "Henry the Eighth," made by Sir Herbert Beerbohm Tree, a high level of dramatic characterization is reached by Edith Wynne Matthison as Katharine and Lyn Harding as Henry. We comment editorially on the production elsewhere in this issue

THE GREAT WAR

March 13—Germans and British fight over Hohenzollern Redoubt near La Bassee. Turks report British loss of 5000 in Tigris.

March 14—Germans attack Dead Man's Hill, west of Verdun. Senussi defeated on Egyptian frontier.

March 15—Austrians attack Italian attacks on San Marino, near Görz with heavy loss. Dutch liner "Tubantia" sunk.

March 16—Admiral von Tirpitz retires from Ministry of Marine. General Roques succeeds General Gallieni as French Minister of War.

March 17—Germans repulsed at Vaux, east of Verdun. Antonio Almeida becomes Premier of Portuguese war ministry.

March 18—Dutch liner "Palembung" sunk. Seventeen French aeroplanes bombard Conflans and Metz.

March 19—Forty French aeroplanes raid Alsace-Lorraine, killing seven civilians. Four German aeroplanes raid England, killing nine civilians.

time the British aviators have succeeded in inflicting any damage on the air raiders. One bomb dropt on an orphan asylum. The total losses were three men, one woman and five children killed; seventeen men, five women and nine children injured.

Retirement of Gallieni

General Joseph Gallieni, who last-fall succeeded M. Millerand as Minister of War, has now resigned that post by advice of his physicians. There have been rumors of his disagreement with Generalissimo Joffre, but we need not question that the strain of his tremendous exertions have been too much for his sixty-six years. It was he who organized the defenses of Paris in August, 1914, and gave the first check to General von Kluck's advancing army.

His successor in charge of the war department is General Pierre Augustus Roques, who is, like Joffre, an engineer and a southerner, and served with Joffre in Tangking and Madagascar. The splendid record which the French have made in the air is largely due to General Roques, for as Inspector General of Aeronautics, 1910-1912, he devoted himself to the development of the aerial arm. For his distinguished services in the fall of 1914 he was placed at the head of the First Army. He has six years the advantage of General Gallieni in the matter of age.

The repulse of the Germans at Verdun has greatly encouraged the French and they speak now with more confidence not merely of their ultimate victory, but of its speedy coming. The Minister of Finance, Alexandre Ribot, in presenting the budget to the French Chamber of Deputies, said:

We can say without exaggeration, without illusion and without vain optimism that we now see the end of this horrible war.

The new budget calls for an appropriation of $1,560,000,000 for the second quarter of 1916. This will bring the total French expenditure on the war to $7,400,000,000 by the end of June. The daily expenditure has risen to $17,400,000.

M. Ribot recommended the curtailment of all luxuries and the sale of American securities:

We must look thru our portfolios of foreign securities and send to the United States all we are able to pick up in the French market of securities negotiable there. The total amount of American securities is not as large as we could wish.

The Teutonic Neptune

The resignation of Admiral von Tirpitz as Imperial M i n i s t e r of Marine is doubtless one of the crucial events of the war tho what are its reasons and what will be its effect upon the German naval policy must remain for the present a matter of speculation. It was he who developed the giant submarines which were to shut off England's commerce and he has bitterly opposed all restrictions of their power of attack upon merchant shipping. It is also rumored that the Kaiser has been dissatisfied with him because of the inactivity of the German fleet.

Whatever may be the judgment of the future upon the effect of his activities it cannot be denied that few men have had a greater influence upon the course of history than Admiral von Tirpitz. The present war is essentially a struggle between Germany and Great Britain for the mastery of the sea and it is thru the efforts of Tirpitz that the German navy was created. While still a boy he acquired a great admiration for England and was seized with the desire to have Germany emulate her naval prowess. In 1898, when the Kaiser, largely under the influence of Admiral Mahan's "Influence of the Sea Power on History," came to the conclusion that "the future of Germany lay on the sea," he called upon Tirpitz to put this policy into effect.

From 1898 to the present Admiral von Tirpitz has remained in power and by his indomitable will has overcome all opposition. His first naval bill in 1900 called for a program almost as ambitious as that announced by President Wilson in his western speeches:

Germany must have a fleet of such strength that a war even against the mightiest naval Power would involve such risks as to threaten the supremacy of that Power.

The year before the naval appropriation has been thirty millions a year, but by the time the war broke out he had forced the Reichstag to provide $115,-000,000 a year, and the German navy had been raised to the rank of the second in the world.

"Silius" and "Tubantia"

The sinking of two unarmed neutral vessels within a week has revived the discussion of the question of Germany's submarines. There is, however, no clear evidence as to the cause of the disaster in either case. The "Silius" was a Norwegian bark carrying grain from New York to France. She had arrived at her destination and was anchored in Havre Roads when in the middle of the night she was blown up by an explosion. The French steamship "Louisiane," close by, had been sunk a half hour earlier. The "Silius" carried a crew of seventeen of whom seven were Americans. All of the Americans were saved, tho one was wounded. The German Government has denied that any of its submarines were concerned in the sinking of the "Silius." The channel where she lay was only thirty feet deep and no submarine has ever been known to attack in such shallow water, so it seems more likely to have been a floating mine. Since the American sailors being members of a Norwegian crew were under the authority and protection of Norway, and since the disaster occurred in French waters over which the United States has no jurisdiction, it is not probable that our Government will take any action in the case, tho if the "Silius" should prove to have been sunk by a German submarine it would increase the distrust of Germany's pledges not to attack unarmed merchantmen.

The other case is somewhat similar. The Holland-Lloyd liner "Tubantia" was struck amidships nine feet below the water line early in the morning off Noordhinder Lightship. She had left Amsterdam for Buenos Aires with 80 passengers and a crew of 300. All on board except four were rescued by Dutch torpedo boats.

The anti-German feeling in Holland was intensified by the sinking of a second Dutch liner three days later. The "Palembang," bound for Java, was struck by a torpedo off the Essex coast and sank in nine minutes. All of the crew were saved, altho nine were injured by the explosion.

THIS CHECK WAS PASSED IN NEW YORK LAST WEEK

It was part of the payment of $50,000,000 for the issue of Midvale Steel convertible five per cent bonds recently sold to a New York banking syndicate. Only two larger checks are on record, the largest being for $62,075,000.

NATIONAL INSTITUTE OF EFFICIENCY

YESTERDAY "Efficiency" was a suspected term. Today it stands as a beacon light to which thousands, in every walk of life, are looking hopefully. Tomorrow it is destined to be the very key-note of personal and national activity. Efficiency is no longer a vogue, but a principle. Its claim on the future is inevitable, and no less certain are the enormous results that must spring from its application. Even from day to day there is better understanding of what Efficiency means in its widest aspect, and how vastly greater is its field than any successful experiment in motion-economy or a newly found instrument for labor-saving—however valuable these may be within their limited sphere. Rather than representing the source of technical devices and "smart" business methods, Efficiency is seen to be the path down which every ambition, however lofty, must work to its goal. The word is coming to embody the very spirit of attainment.

Five factors are involved in all great work: material, machines or tools, methods, money, and man, and the greatest by far is the man. Minute study has already been devoted to the first four, and specially to machines and methods. But the experts have given less attention to the most important factor. Scores of organizations, local and national, are doing valuable service for Efficiency, but hitherto none has emphasized fully the intimately personal application of the Efficiency Idea. The domain of Efficiency stretches, potentially, far beyond the routine side of the workaday world. Centering first in the individual, it may and should permeate every science and art contributing to the advance of American civilization. It is in the spirit of this belief that a new organization—destined, its originators hope, to materially serve the movement toward Efficiency—has been brought into being.

On Lincoln's birthday, the 12th of February, there was incorporated, under the educational laws of the District of Columbia, the National Institute of Efficiency, and on Saturday, March 11th, the organizing meeting of the Board of Governors was held at the Aero Club of America, New York. Those who were present, representing widely varied fields of activity, were at one in their conviction that Efficiency is the commanding need of the nation, and the Institute is dedicated to the proposition that human Efficiency—the Efficiency of the individual—lies at the foundation of all great work, in government, in business, in the home. Its purpose is therefore to promote Efficiency in the individual, to popularize its practise, and to develop personal Efficiency as applied to every problem of life. Accordingly its aim will be to make available and of practical value to the average man the best results attending the work of experts in the universities, laboratories, factories, studios, and even the playing-fields of the country.

From the list of Governors of the new Institute, given below, can be gauged the breadth of the movement of which the organization should become the instrument:

Mr. Gutzon Borglum, Sculptor and Publicist.
Hon. Melvil Dewey, President of the Efficiency Society.
Mr. William F. Dix, Secretary of the Mutual Life Insurance Company.
Dr. Henry Sturgis Drinker, President of Lehigh University.
Hon. John H. Finley, Commissioner of Education of the State of New York.
Hon. Philip H. Gadsden, President of the Charleston Consolidated Railway and Lighting Company.
Hon. John Hays Hammond, Mining Engineer and Diplomat.
Hon. Job E. Hedges, Lawyer and Statesman.

Mr. Henry B. Joy, President of the Lincoln Highway Association and of the Packard Motor Car Company.
Mr. Curtis J. Mar, President of the Efficiency Publishing Company.
Mr. J. Horace McFarland, President of the American Civic Association.
Hon. Truman H. Newberry, ex-Secretary U. S. Navy.
Hon. Alton B. Parker, former Chief Justice of the Court of Appeals of New York.
Admiral Robert E. Peary, Explorer, and discoverer of the North Pole.
Hon. Herbert W. Rice, President of the U. S. Gutta Percha Paint Company.
Hon. John A. Stewart, Chairman of the Executive Committee of the American Peace Centenary Association.
Hon. Conrad H. Syme, Corporation Counsel of the City of Washington.
Mr. Richard B. Watrous, Secretary of the American Civic Association.
Hon. William R. Willcox, former Chairman of the Public Service Commission of New York.
Mr. Henry A. Wise Wood, President of the American Society of Aeronautic Engineers.
Major General Leonard Wood, United States Army.

The by-laws of the Institute were adopted and the following officers elected for the coming year: William B. Howland, president; Alton B. Parker, vice-president; Richard B. Watrous, secretary; Herbert W. Rice, treasurer.

With the work for which the National Institute of Efficiency has been established The Independent has been conspicuously identified, especially during the past year, and it has now been chosen by the Board of Governors as the official organ of the Institute.

The Independent entered actively upon its Efficiency crusade a year ago last November, with an article on "Efficiency and Life," by Edward Earle Purinton. This was followed by the discussion of various phases of Efficiency by men of power and achievement, such as Elbert H. Gary, William R. Willcox, John Purroy Mitchel, Harrington Emerson, John Wanamaker, Frank A. Vanderlip, Louis D. Brandeis, F. C. Henderschott, Luther Halsey Gulick and Charles W. Eliot. Mr. Purinton's article was accompanied by a "Personal Efficiency Test," affording opportunity for showing in terms of percentage the effectiveness of the individual. Mr. Purinton's articles, and especially the Efficiency Test, attracted very wide attention. With these articles and tests originated The Independent's Efficiency Service, under Mr. Purinton's charge, which has been of practical use to a great number of people in all walks of life.

Mr. Purinton has been selected by the Board of Governors of the Institute as the Chairman of its Editorial Board, which, in coöperation with the Institute Committees, has before it the task of presenting the most recent findings of a science that is daily extending its boundaries. There is no last word in Efficiency. Able minds are constantly coming upon improved means of meeting specific needs in their individual life work. Data accumulates faster than it can be used, and needs only careful correlation to transmute it into the concrete stuff of self-improvement. In this fact is to be found the goal, no less than the origin, of the Institute. Such a goal, in face of the complexity of modern life, is beyond any single individual, but to a body of the scope of the National Institute of Efficiency it would appear as possible of attainment as it is desirable. And the names of those identified with the Institute's future stand, meanwhile, as assurance that great and varied ability will be brought to the matter in hand.

445

ELBERT H. GARY
CHAIRMAN OF THE BOARD OF DIRECTORS
OF THE UNITED STATES STEEL
CORPORATION

BUSINESS TO-MORROW

BY ELBERT H. GARY

CHAIRMAN OF THE UNITED STATES STEEL CORPORATION

HAT changes the next generation will see in American business and industry no one can tell. There has probably never been a time when the forecasting of the future was more difficult and hazardous. As a result of the great war the entire civilized world is confronted with economic and political conditions that have no parallel in history.

It is true that we in America have been less directly affected than the peoples of the belligerent nations. But the whole fabric of modern industrial civilization has become too closely woven to permit of any civilized nation escaping some share in the consequences of this epochal world war.

Not even of the immediate future can we speak with any feeling of certainty. This war will end some time, of course, and it is my personal opinion that it will be ended sooner than most people think—by the economic exhaustion of the belligerents, if in no other way. One thing seems fairly sure. Whenever peace comes American business men must be prepared to face, temporarily at least, a falling off in our present enormous export trade. Moreover, the purchasing power of the whole world will have been greatly reduced, and in all the markets of the world there will be the keenest kind of competition based on cheap labor and low costs. Most of the foreign manufacturing countries, if not all of them, will protect themselves from destructive competition by tariff provisions, and we should even now be giving careful thought to this subject. So far as possible the entire question should be removed from politics. A scientific study of the facts should be made, and based on that study there should be evolved a tariff system that will be adequate—no more and no less—for the protection of our manufacturers and wage earners.

The plain dictates of common sense bid us to make these preparations. The transition from war to peace must necessarily entail a period of economic readjustment that will bring radical changes in volume and prices to most lines of business. There is some danger at present of overproduction, overextension of credit and liabilities and over confidence. We should proceed

Judge Gary—he sat on the bench for two terms in Du Page and Cook counties, Illinois—had practised law for twenty-five years and had been president of the Federal Steel Company for several years when the United States Steel Corporation was formed in 1901. He was an active participant in its organization and became chairman of the Board of Directors and of the Finance Committee. In this position—which is one of the half dozen most responsible in the financial and industrial world—Judge Gary has stood for many years as a leading spokesman of progressive business.—THE EDITOR.

with caution, but with faith in the great future of our country.

HOW SHOULD YOUNG MEN TRAIN FOR THE FUTURE?

IT is, in truth, with the next generation of American business men that some of the greatest problems and opportunities of American history lie, and it would serve a more useful purpose here to point out what, in my opinion, these problems and opportunities are, and how the young men of today may best prepare to meet them, than to attempt to forecast the future. I address myself, therefore, primarily to the ambitious young men who are shortly to enter business and are now seeking to obtain the training that will best fit them for successful careers.

Before there can be any intelligent discussion of what nowadays constitutes the right sort of educational training for a successful business career we must have an accurate conception of the service requirements of modern commerce and industry. They are very different from what they were when I was a young man. The past thirty or forty years have seen amazing changes in practically every line of industry. This is an age of vast coöperative organization, of large scale production going hand in hand with minute scientific economies in every process of manufacture. It is an age of great machinery and enormous mills and factories where armies of men labor under the efficient direction of technical experts. Above all it is an age of specialization. No man can expect to go very far in modern commerce or industry unless he is a specialist in some line or other.

Now what training does the young

man of today get to prepare him for these bewilderingly complicated activities of modern business? The average American has always very properly looked for the foundation of his educational training in the public schools. How, then, do our public schools, in the education they give, measure up to the service requirements of modern commerce and industry?

Not, I fear, to the extent which might reasonably be expected. There may have been a time when the preparation given by the public schools of the country was really adequate for business life. But of the average public school that cannot be truly said today. It is because this question seems vitally important to me that I have been so deeply interested in the splendid work done by Mr. William Wirt in the public schools of Gary, Indiana.

The Gary plan has been too thoroly discussed in newspapers and magazines to need any description here. But I want to say that in my opinion Mr. Wirt's work is the first successful attempt to bring the teaching in public schools into any real adjustment with the conditions of life in modern industrial communities. The children get everything of any practical value that is taught in the ordinary public school, and in addition acquire most of the advantages of a thoro vocational training. The boys in the cabinet and furniture shops, in the printing establishments, foundries, and so on, are obtaining practical experience that will be invaluable to them in later life, and, what is even more important, they have an opportunity to learn along what lines their real talents lie.

The young men who enter the business life of the next generation with such a training as this will be fortunate, indeed, and it has been a great pleasure to me to learn how extensively Mr. Wirt's work is being imitated in many other cities of the country.

COLLEGIATE, TECHNICAL, AND MILITARY EDUCATION

FREQUENTLY I have been asked whether I think a college education is worth the time and money necessary to obtain it. This depends on what is meant by a college education, and also on the standard of value by which it is to be judged. It is a pleasant thing to have, and if one is young enough and has time

447

and money enough, a very desirable thing. But considered solely as a money investment with a view to adding to the earning power, I rather doubt if the average college course in the liberal arts is entitled to all the credit it sometimes receives, tho it is important and should have consideration.

The case is different with the technical education obtained in the scientific departments of many of our larger universities and in such institutions as Lafayette, Pittsburgh University, Stevens, Lehigh and the Massachusetts Institute of Technology. Their graduates have a highly specialized knowledge that is immediately saleable, and if a young man can by any means obtain such a technical education I should say that he would be well-advised to do so. In fact I believe that this kind of specialized training will in increasing measure become the quickest road to success in practical business of the future.

It seems clear that the future safety of our country will require that a far greater number of our young men should have some degree of military training. In this connection I may say that from the standpoint of an employer I am a thoro believer in the value of such training. It teaches discipline, resourcefulness, order, and system, and one learns to be a gentleman. It tends to make one an honorable citizen. I would, therefore, add to the ideal education for the young business man of the next generation some degree of military training.

Let us now sum up the qualifications with which our young man will enter upon his business career. He will, or should, have had the ground work of a good up-to-date public school education. The elements which are practical to everyday business life, including spelling, writing, grammar and arithmetic, should be emphasized. He will have had enough vocational training to enable him to decide upon the line of business that will give the best scope to his natural talents. He will have had the specialized technical education that will best fit him to succeed in that particular line. He will have the soldierly virtues of order and system, and a habit of prompt obedience to discipline.

Is there any prominent employer who would not be glad to have such a young man enter his service?

This, of course, represents my conception of the ideal educational

---

THIS is the third in The Independent's series of articles by men and women of large achievement on "The Next Generation in American Life." The next to come will be published in the Easter Number, April 10, when Shailer Matthews, D.D., dean of the Divinity School of the University of Chicago and president of the Federal Council of Churches, will write on RELIGION, THE CHURCH AND THE PEOPLE.

---

training for business which, unfortunately, comparatively few young men of today have an opportunity even to approximate. But it marks the educational goal of what we of the older generation should strive to give and they of the coming generation to obtain.

BIG BUSINESS IS HERE TO STAY

FOR, be it remembered, that for good or ill, we have become a great industrial nation, and among the most important problems which the next generation will have to solve are economic and industrial problems. Upon the common sense and breadth of vision of the business men of the next generation much will depend. We cannot turn the hands of the clock backward. Coöperative organization and large scale production are here to stay because they mean greater economy of production and greater and more successful business. Yet the great opportunities given to large aggregations of wealth to succeed, to prosper, to construct and to benefit entail equally great opportunities to do harm, and this necessarily means that there should be in this country such governmental regulation as will protect business men in anything they do that is good and prevent them from doing anything that is harmful. It is easy to state such a theory of governmental regulation in broad and general terms, but much more difficult to work out the specific and practical applications of that theory. However, the subject should have the best thought of all thinking men.

It is because the future offers such great opportunities for work of national importance in solving these and other similar problems that I believe the service of the great corporations will become increasingly attractive to young men of the coming generation. Even in the past few years it seems to me that we have seen the leaven working. People are not so eager as they once were to make the standards of modern industry the rule-of-thumb of a past generation. Of recent years there has been a very much better feeling between capital and labor. More and more the corporations are disposed to deal fairly and generously with their employees, and perhaps conditions in this respect may still further improve.

The alert and enterprising young man of today is coming more and more to realize that the service of the large corporation offers the greatest facilities and opportunities for a man's progress and advancement, that his association with other keen and ambitious men makes for his own development—in a word, that competition in this respect is desirable. And I can truly say from my own experience that I believe the men connected with the United States Steel Corporation have done better for themselves on an average than they could possibly have done by going into business for themselves.

One of the most satisfactory developments of recent years in the business of our own corporation has been the success that has attended our profit sharing plan and stock ownership by employees. I look to see a great development of this idea in American industry of the future, and I believe it will bring with it a continuous improvement in the relations between capital and labor.

This, then, is a brief outline of what seem to me to be the problems and opportunities that lie before the business men of the next generation. I think there has never been a time when the young man entering business has had greater opportunities for his own development and for service to his fellow men. We have here the greatest country in the world with the greatest natural resources and the greatest possibilities of development. The young men of the next generation in American business have every right to be both hopeful and confident. Success or failure depends upon themselves.

New York City

A BIT OF SPRING
BY MARGARET L. FARRAND

A river flowing swift and blue and still;
   Brown fields just touched by finger tips of spring;
Soft, drifting clouds above a little hill;
   Then hark! I hear the first song-sparrow sing.

HOW I SWUNG BACK TO TEDDY

BY A YOUNG BUSINESS MAN

I HAVE swung back to Teddy. I have completed the circle, or nearly completed it, and am back again almost where I started. I have passed thru every stage of feeling toward him — hero worship, admiration mingled with mild criticism, severer criticism, impatience, distrust, bitter criticism—almost hatred—then indifference, a slowly growing confidence, finally new admiration and respect. I can never worship him again as I did in college: but I am ready to give him the White House for four years more.

The only excuse for writing this is that thousands of other young fellows like me must have gone—are now or going—thru the same process. I have an idea that by June there may be enough of us to put him at the top of the ticket again.

I REMEMBER the first time I ever saw him. I was a Sophomore. Our little New England college was stampeded by a scarlet fever scare and the authorities decided to close up for two weeks until everything could be thoroly fumigated. I went to Boston; and that evening the papers announced that Teddy would arrive at the Back Bay Station next morning. He was coming to visit Theodore, Jr., at Harvard and his train was scheduled to arrive at 5:45.

At 5 o'clock I got out of bed and started for the station. It was bitter cold, eight below zero; yet the station was already full of people when I arrived, and I was prest out into the street. There I stood for forty minutes—and finally Teddy arrived.

He stepped out of the station and into a waiting carriage, waved his hat to us, and vanished—all in a minute. I was left with nothing to show for my forty minutes' wait but an incipient case of chilblains; yet I felt repaid. "Lord, what a man!" I kept saying to myself, "What a ruler! Line up the kings and emperors of the world beside him and he would stand out among them like a giant among pygmies. He's the best we've got, and we don't need to be ashamed of him anywhere. He typifies us: he represents us to the world the way we like to think of ourselves — big, and strong, and square, a little loud maybe, but absolutely self-confident and able to stand up with the best of them." I threw back my chest, and all that day I had a curious warm glow around my heart at the thought that I was an American.

I have seen Mr. Taft and Mr. Wilson several times, and neither of them ever left any such feeling with me. Perhaps it is because I am older; perhaps I can never feel the same about any President as I did about my first; perhaps I know too much now about the way Presidents are made, and the influences that act on them. And yet I don't know—I passed Teddy again on Madison avenue, New York, last week, and—but that comes later.

BUT during Teddy's last year in the White House my enthusiasm began to wane. He was terribly loud and overbearing, it seemed to me, forever running out onto the front porch and denouncing some one as a "liar" at the top of his voice. I began to be a bit glad that his time was almost thru. "He's done a big work," I said to myself, "but he's getting tired; it's time for him to step down and discover that the country can, somehow, get along without him."

And then he did the one thing for which I can never forgive him. He had fought our battles, he had spent his life in telling us how highly he regarded us as common people, but when it came to a showdown he failed us. He was willing to fight our battles, but he didn't trust us to select a President for ourselves. If there was any other man in the United States who had thought of Taft for President—except Brother Charlie—I never heard of it. Most of the folks out in my section were getting ready to cheer their heads off for Hughes. Then Teddy stepped in to tell us that we couldn't have Hughes or anybody except Taft. I went out to Chicago to the convention and got appointed an Assistant Sergeant-at-Arms along with a thousand others. And the cheers of those delegates for Taft reminded me of a crowd of medical students at an inquest. There was just about the same unbridled enthusiasm.

Teddy's stock was pretty low with me when he sailed for Africa. But when he came back across Europe, the old feeling of pride surged thru me all over again. I just chuckled when he told the French that they ought to raise larger families; when he lectured the English on their bullheaded muddling in Egypt, and I could picture to myself those polished gentlemen leaving the hall and saying, "Extraordinary, y'know. A quite impossible person—quite." But none of them ever said it to his face. They may have grumbled about him after he left, but while he was there he was the whole show. He was Us

typified—all our brashness and rudeness, and bluster, but all our straightforward hard-hitting sincerity, too. I never liked him more in my life.

Then came the 1912 campaign, and his stock sunk out of sight with me. I was at that Chicago convention, too. I didn't like the stuff the Old Guard pulled, but I didn't think his managers covered themselves with glory either. They brought in a couple of hundred contesting delegations and admitted afterward that only a score or so of the contests had any merit whatever. They were fighting the devil with fire, and both sides disgusted me.

Then when Taft and Teddy started beating each other around the country, dragging the presidency thru the mud, I cried, "A curse on both your houses," and voted for Wilson. It wasn't that I loved Woodrow more, but that I felt that the whole Republican outfit was spoiling for a good sound beating—and I did all that the Constitution allows any one citizen to do.

SINCE the day the warships sailed for Vera Cruz, my respect for Teddy has been coming back. Apparently no one in Washington knows just why the warships did sail; nor why, being down there, they turned around and came back. But the Mexicans know. They say that the reason we never ventured beyond Vera Cruz was because we were afraid. And all South America thinks the same. We may have gained "friendship" by our "What do you think we ought to do about this?" policy, but we have certainly sacrificed respect. And in dealing with the Latin races I would feel safer with a little less protestation and a little more of the fear of a righteous wrath.

Teddy knew how to deal with them. I have been reading the diplomatic history of his presidency during the past year; and I've just finished it off by reading the "Life of John Hay." The most heeded voice in the world in 1904-8 was the voice that spoke for America from Washington, D. C.

John Hay's life tells of the time when Germany was ready to seize the ports of Venezuela and hold them until certain claims were satisfied. Teddy called the German ambassador in and said to him:

"I should like the Kaiser to invite me to arbitrate between Germany and Venezuela."

"Oh, impossible," said the ambas-

449

THE COLONEL ON THE CAMPAIGN

From a Statement Issued at Trinidad on March 9

I WILL not enter into any fight for the nomination and I will not permit any factional fight to be made in my behalf. Indeed, I will go further and say that it would be a mistake to nominate me unless the country has in its mood something of the heroic; unless it feels not only like devoting itself to ideals, but to the purpose measurably to realize those ideals in action.

This is one of those rare times which come only at long intervals in a nation's history, when the action taken determines the life of the generations that follow. Such times were those from 1776 to 1789, in the days of Washington, and from 1858 to 1865, in the days of Lincoln.

It is for us of today to grapple with the tremendous national and international problems of our own hour in the spirit and with the ability shown by those who upheld the hands of Washington and Lincoln.

Whether we do or do not accomplish this feat will largely depend on the action taken at the Republican and Progressive National Conventions next June. Nothing is to be hoped from the present Administration, and the struggles between the President and his party leaders in Congress are today merely struggles as to whether the nation shall see its Governmental representatives adopt an attitude of a little more or a little less hypocrisy, and follow a policy of slightly greater or slightly lesser baseness. . . .

We must clarify and define our policies. We must show that our belief in our governmental ideas is so real that we wish to make them count in the world at large and to make the necessary sacrifice in order that they shall count surely.

sador. "The Kaiser has made up his mind, and cannot change."

"All right," said Teddy, "you might tell him in that case that if he does not invite me to arbitrate within ten days, I shall have Admiral Dewey sail for Venezuela ten days from tomorrow."

The ambassador blustered, but Teddy was firm.

"I am not arguing the matter," he said, "for we have had arguments and they got us nowhere. I am simply giving you some information that you may want to pass on to Berlin."

A day or two later the ambassador called again; he talked of various things, but said nothing about Venezuela. As he rose to leave Teddy said, "What about Venezuela?"

"I have had no instructions," the ambassador replied.

"In that case," said Teddy, "you might inform the Kaiser that if within thirty-six hours I receive a request from him to act as arbitrator, I will the following day publicly praise him to the world as the friend of peace. If I do not receive such a request I shall have Dewey sail three days earlier than I told you last. Good day."

The next afternoon the ambassador called with a formal request from the Kaiser that Mr. Roosevelt consent to arbitrate the difference between Germany and Venezuela, and the morning papers of the following day contained Teddy's wholehearted praise of His Majesty, the friend of peace.

Some newspapers have said that if Teddy had been President he would have settled the "Lusitania" matter within forty-eight hours. It may be a foolish idea, but I believe that if Teddy had been there the "Lusitania" would never have been sunk. I have an idea that when that German warning appeared in the newspapers, Teddy would have had Bernstorff in and said, "If any passenger ship is torpedoed, without warning, and Americans are killed, you may call here at once for your passports. They will be ready."

Maybe not; but I think so.

I MISS the *esprit de corps* that used to be in Washington when Teddy was there. The fellows he appointed would have died for him. The Congressmen hated him in secret, and denounced him in the cloak-rooms, but they redeemed the party's pledges and got thru with the public business just the same. There was an atmosphere of efficiency and achievement; you felt it as soon as you got off the train. Now—perhaps I imagine it—but Washington seems to me a dreary sort of place. Nobody sees the President; he has no friends. He draws himself off into a closet and there decides the country's fate alone. And Congress meanwhile muddles about, introducing pension bills—without plan, without leadership, without vision.

I may be wrong. I am not "on the inside." I merely give the impression of a business man whose business takes him frequently to the national capital.

I am for Wilson in all his effort to stir up a national defense sentiment; but I think he is nine months late. When we took Mason and Slidell off that English ship in the Civil War, England demanded that we release them at once; and in the same breath gave orders to her army and navy to strip for action. We gave them back, too.

When the "Lusitania" sank, it would have been easy to put us in shape to guard our own rights and the rights of the neutrals of the world. And we would not have been compelled to fight either. But now—the President's speeches seem to me somehow pathetic. "I'm at the end of my rope," he says in effect, "I don't know what to do. I can't make Congress act, and you must help me." I'm for him in his effort: I certainly will do my little share to boost along his preparedness efforts. But he talks and acts to me like a man who was in about as deep as he could go. I'd like to see some one in Washington who never discovered that he had any limitations; who knows how to handle men as well as a pen.

I passed Teddy on Madison avenue the other day. He has grown fat; he dresses a little better than he used to—but he looked wonderfully fit. If there were a younger man in the Republican party I would prefer him. But—and this seems to me the disheartening, almost disgraceful thing —I don't see a single other man of presidential size in the whole party, barring Hughes, who has barred himself. Perhaps that's the price we pay for democracy, for the direct primary, and all the rest. I do not know. But this I do know, that if ever we needed a super-man in Washington we shall need him during the next four years. I get the feeling in Washington now of a lot of mediocre men running about in circles because they do not hear their master's voice.

And I've swung back to Teddy again. It makes me blush with shame to think that there is not another masterful American to whom we can turn. But who is there?

THE DELEGATES AT THE CANAL

PAN-AMERICAN CHRISTIANITY

BY CHARLES CLAYTON MORRISON

EDITOR OF "THE CHRISTIAN CENTURY"

A GATHERING that now promises to take its place in the history of Christian progress as the most significant and far-reaching ever held by the religious forces of the Western Hemisphere came to its close in the city of Panama on February 20. It was called a Congress on Christian Work in Latin-America. Representatives of the religious life of every republic of the hemisphere were present, as well as of Great Britain, Spain and Italy—304 all told. There were 145 Latin-Americans, and 159 from the United States, Canada, England, Spain and Italy. Twenty-one nations were represented. The Congress was tri-lingual, delegates speaking in Spanish, Portuguese or English as they preferred. These men and women were the most prominent leaders of the Christian denominations of the United States and the Latin-American Republics. Their purpose was to consider the moral and religious conditions of Latin-America, with a view to bringing into coöperation the religious forces of the whole hemisphere.

No such undertaking was ever projected before. It rose above denominational and merely national lines. It took into account the fact—a new fact since the opening of the Panama Canal and the demoralization of overseas commerce by the European war—that the Americas of both Latin and Anglo-Saxon culture are to be drawn, in the near future, into most intimate commercial, economic and political relationships. This fact brings to religion both an opportunity and a duty. Tho the idea of this gathering originated with the leaders of the missionary work of

Protestantism, the invitation calling the Congress together was not limited to Protestant churches, but was formulated so as to include Roman Catholicism as well, should representatives of that communion choose to attend. "All communions or organizations which accept Jesus Christ as Divine Saviour and Lord and the Holy Scriptures of the Old and New Testaments as the revealed Word of God, and whose purpose is to make the will of Christ prevail in Latin-America, are cordially invited to participate in the Panama Congress and will be heartily welcomed"—thus ran the invitation. It was stated yet more definitely that, "In the matter of Christian service we will welcome the coöperation of any who are willing to coöperate in any part of the Christian program. We should not demand union with us in all our work as the condition of accepting allies for any part of it."

THE time and place of the Congress were psychologically strategic. Panama with its marvelous canal is in the eye of the world. One was struck at every turn with obvious analogies between the thing that man's genius has wrought on this Isthmus and the thing that the Church of Christ now undertakes to accomplish in Latin-America.

It was the idea of the spiritual coöperation of all the Americas that lay at the basis of the deliberations of the Panama Congress. The assumption of racial superiority that is implicit in much of our Anglo-Saxon missionary work was consciously and expressly disavowed. Indeed the word "missionary" was used

very infrequently. The republics of Latin-America are, of course, nominally, at least, Christian lands, tho the word Christian has not quite the same significance that it has in Protestant countries. In Latin-America the word is almost synonymous with human being. The antithesis of Christian is "dog." It was felt that the conventional nomenclature of the missionary enterprize would both affront and needlessly wound the sensibilities of Latin-Americans, and make them yet more inaccessible to the truth of the Christian Gospel. Upon the minds of the delegates themselves the reflex action of their effort to state their purpose in terms that would do full justice to the people whose coöperation they desired cannot but result in an increase of tolerance and interracial sympathy—two qualities which Anglo-Saxon Christians seem able to attain only with a great deal of difficulty.

For ten days the Congress held three sessions daily, discussing eight elaborate reports submitted by as many commissions, and covering the many problems related to the moral and religious progress of the lands of Latin-America. These commissions were composed of leading scholars of Latin-America and of North America—men like President Henry Churchill King, of Oberlin College; Professor William Adams Brown, of Union Theological Seminary; Professor Ernest DeWitt Burton, of the University of Chicago; President Charles T. Paul, of the College of Missions, Indianapolis; President William Douglas Mac-Kenzie, of Hartford Theological Seminary; Professor Erasmo Braga, of the Presbyterian Theological

451

Seminary and the State Gymnasium of Brazil; Professor Eduardo Monteverde, of the University of Montevideo; Professor Eduardo Pereira, of the Independent Presbyterian Theological Seminary of Brazil; Principal Webster E. Browning, of the Instituto Ingles of Santiago, Chile—to mention only a few names. The field was divided into eight sections—General Survey, the Message and Method of Evangelical Christianity, Literature, Education, Women's Work for Women, the Coöperation and Unity of the Christian Forces, the Evangelical Church in the Latin-American Field, and the Church at the Home Base. The reports of these eight commissions represent a year and a half of the most thoro study of social and religious conditions in the Latin countries of this hemisphere that has ever been undertaken.

THERE are four features of first-rank significance which, in my opinion, give historic distinction to the Panama Congress. First, this gathering has, for the first time since the Reformation, brought into the consciousness of the Protestant churches the need of defining a constructive attitude in relation to Roman Catholicism. Protestantism has always been more or less belligerent in its attitude, continuing the heritage received from the days of the great Protest. This has been partly responsible for a certain narrowing of the spirit of the evangelical churches, as any negative temper is bound to do. But now, facing a continent of entrenched Catholicism, the Protestant forces have been thrown back upon their basic principles and compelled to construct a positive method of procedure by means of which their missionaries might enter this already preëmpted field, and carry to a progressive consummation the ends and aims of New Testament religion.

A beginning at such a constructive program was made at this Congress, but not without difficulty. A few delegates came breathing out the usual threatenings and slaughter against the Catholic institution. Other representatives of the evangelical churches, mainly missionaries from the field, declined to attend the Congress because they conceived the constructive path chosen by the preparation committees as a path of compromise with Rome. The whole spirit of the ten days' sessions apparently satisfied all who came with this conception in their minds that it was groundless. Few left Panama who had not been convinced of the more excellent way.

The Congress gave evidence of the beginning and growth of a science of missions. The need of such a science is being constantly felt by all Christian leaders who have been trained in the use of scientific methods in other departments of research and practical life. In the past the work of missions has been conceived as a very simple task, calling mainly for consecrated preachers to go forth among the non-Christian peoples, telling the story of the Gospel as it was revealed in the Scriptures, and offering salvation to those who believed it. This, of course, is mission work in its essence. But with the doing of this essential and simple thing there have grown up a complex body of problems and tasks which have not until now begun to be grouped together in any systematic fashion. The World Missionary Conference at Edinburgh in 1910 was the first conscious attempt made to systematize in any scientific way the work of missions. Basing its study upon the results attained at Edinburgh, the Panama Congress has carried the process several very positive steps further. The method of the Panama gathering was that of a comprehensive induction of the facts and a fair facing of them. It analyzed and tried to understand the Latin-American mind that it might find the natural and most direct way of approach for the utterance of the evangelical message. And it brought to the point of clear definition the end and aim of all Christian mission work—the development of a free, indigenous Church of Christ in the countries where mission work was done. The implications of this conception of missionary purpose are many and very significant.

A THIRD feature of the Congress was its marked sympathy with modern scholarship. This was a characteristic which no observer could fail to see. The most influential speakers in the Congress were men of the modern spirit. Probably President Henry Churchill King's frank criticism of those missionaries who declared that no one who has anything to do with evolution or historical criticism can be a Christian brought as pronounced a response from the delegates as any utterance from the platform. And when Dr. King went on to say that he knew of nothing in modern science that need stand in the way of the heartiest acceptance of Christ, his words were greeted with the kind of applause that many of his hearers had deep convictions on the subject.

This feature of the Congress con-

trasted sharply with the still too-popular notion that mission work can find its motives only in the dogmatic theology of the older orthodoxy. It is becoming clear that there are rich missionary motives of ample power implicit in the view of the world and of life which modern scholarship is inculcating.

FINALLY, the Panama Congress, like the conference at Edinburgh, brought into bold relief the weakness and shame of the Protestant sectarian divisions and the need of Christian unity. Most of the problems discussed came back to this. The presence of overlapping and competing denominational activities in parts of the mission field, while great sections were entirely neglected, was again and again characterized as a scandal and a sin. More than one speaker pleaded for the right of the young Church in the Latin-American nations to divide—if it must divide—on issues of its own choosing rather than to have our Anglo-Saxon divisions thrust upon it. Efforts will be made as a result of the Congress to unify the various evangelical forces in the various countries, by merging those now divided, by partitioning the territory among the various denominations, and by other means. Already a partitioning of the territory of the whole of Mexico has been agreed upon, and it is expected that future work in that country will follow the lines of the new arrangement.

The perception of this obvious weakness of denominationalism on the field of missions is bringing to the mind of churchmen an answering awareness of the weakness of denominationalism in the Church at home. One speaker, in discussing the question of Church unity, turned to the chairman, Dr. Speer, reminding him of a statement he had heard him make some two years ago to the effect that by the end of the century there would be no Presbyterian Church at all. He asked the chairman whether he was still of the same mind. "I am," promptly replied Dr. Speer, "except that I would now shorten the time."

This feeling that our present denominational order of the Church must give place to another order wherein the prayer of Christ for the unity of His followers may be answered, was one of the most pervasive sentiments of the Panama Congress, as it is of any meeting of present-day missionary leaders. For the conviction is steadily deepening that only a united Church can evangelize the world.

On board S. S. Huallaga

OUR BIGGEST NEED IN MEXICO

BY HENRY WOODHOUSE

EDITOR OF "FLYING," GOVERNOR OF THE AERO CLUB OF AMERICA

THAT the American Eagle needs wings—a substantial aeronautical service—is a matter in which both preparationists and pacifists agree. It is about the only thing on which the different factions of the present Congress do not disagree, and the only reason why the military programs proposed for this year do not include an appropriation of $25,000,000 for aeronautics is undoubtedly that the shortage of officers in the Army would make it impossible to get the necessary officers.

Coming down from what ought to be to what is, we find with a shock that there are only eight aeroplanes available for service at the Mexican border, at a time when 100 aeroplanes could quickly do the work which it may take 25,000 soldiers to do. It is evident from the statement of General Funston that a large number of aviators are needed as soon as operations begin. Only aviators can scout over Mexican territory with little danger. Others, General Funston states, will face death.

The Secretary of War has ordered General Scott to instruct General Funston to use as far as possible the squadron of aeroplanes of the Army. This consists of eight biplanes, equipped with ninety horsepower motors, which, on account of their low power, could not climb fast enough in case of emergency, the Mexican atmosphere being so rare as to require high-powered aeroplanes.

Mr. Alan R. Hawley, president of the Aero Club of America, at 297 Madison avenue, New York City, very aptly summarizes the need thus:

An immediate appropriation of $1,000,000 to at once properly equip four aeroplane squadrons with the necessary high-powered aeroplanes may save the lives of 10,000 American soldiers on the Mexican border. There should be three aeroplanes available for every aviator now at the Mexican border, which is the number of aeroplanes allowed to each aviator in Europe, and three more squadrons should also immediately be put in readiness. A hundred high-powered aeroplanes would make it possible to round up Villa and his band in a very short time, where it might take thousands of men a long time with considerable losses to attain the same end.

Every aeroplane being worth a thousand soldiers in the Mexican campaign, the Aero Club of America is mobilizing the licensed aviators available, equipping them with high-powered aeroplanes, and keeping them in readiness to answer the call of the War Department, which will gladly avail itself of this reserve in case of need. It will cost between $400 and $750 to train each aviator, and $8000 or $10,000 each for the high-powered military aeroplanes.

Eight trained aviators have already been mobilized, and are being trained on high-powered aeroplanes. One hundred thousand dollars is now being raised by public subscription to buy suitable military aeroplanes which will be turned over with the aviators to the War Department, to be given to the militia of different states after the Mexican campaign.

The officials of the club are quite frank in stating that Congress should be the agency to do this. But they realize that if they wait for Congress to do its duty, they may find that

thousands of American lives will be lost first for lack of adequate protection. There are no funds available at present for this purpose for the Army, and the next appropriation, not yet sanctioned by Congress, will not become available until June 30!

The most unfortunate situation is also that the Army is so extremely short of officers for all branches of the service that it cannot increase the air service without hampering other arms. Last year Congress allowed sixty officers for aviation, but it was impossible to obtain them. Until Congress authorizes a substantial increase of the Army, the only relief can be had by equipping the militia with aeroplanes, and that is what the National Aeroplane Fund was instituted to do.

Unfortunately, the Navy is no better off. It has only about a dozen aeroplanes available, and twenty or so ordered, many of which will be needed to replace the machines which are now in commission.

In the short period of eight months, the Aero Club of America has succeeded in supplying funds for twenty-four states to begin to organize aviation detachments in the militia. In some states, as in the case of New York, the National Guard and the First and Second Battalions of the Naval Militia have already been presented with aeroplanes and means for training aviators. The American Eagle is growing wings—but money raised thru public subscriptions, not appropriated by the nation, is paying for their growth.

New York City

C. O. Lee, San Antonio

THE FIRST U. S. AEROPLANE SQUADRON—NOW IN ACTIVE SERVICE SOMEWHERE IN MEXICO

M. William Shak-fpeare:

EIGHT PAPERS BY FREDERICK HOUK LAW
IN OBSERVANCE OF THE THREE HUNDREDTH
ANNIVERSARY OF SHAKESPEARE'S DEATH

Shakespeare Today

 NEARLY a hundred years ago John Wilson, a celebrated professor of Moral Philosophy in the University of Edinburgh, spoke of England's great poet in words which we can echo today:

Shakespeare is of no age. He speaks a language which thrills in our blood in spite of the separation of two hundred years. His thoughts, passions, feelings, strains of fancy, all are of this day as they were of his own; and his genius may be contemporary with the mind of every generation for a thousand years to come.

Thomas Carlyle, in *Heroes and Hero Worship*, says much the same thing in even more forceful language:

This king, Shakespeare, does not he shine in crowned sovereignty over us all, as the noblest, gentlest, yet strongest of rallying signs; indestructible; really more valuable in that point of view than any other means or appliance whatsoever? We can fancy him as radiant aloft over all the nations of Englishmen a thousand years hence.

Our own great American essayist, Ralph Waldo Emerson, likewise bears witness to the importance of Shakespeare's contribution to life

Far from Shakespeare's being the least known, he is the one person, in all modern history, known to us. What point of morals, of manners, of economy, of philosophy, of religion, of taste of the conduct of life, has he not settled? What mystery has he not signified his knowledge of? What office, or function, or district of man's work, has he not remembered? What king has he not taught state, as Talma taught Napoleon? What maiden has not found him finer than her delicacy? What lover has he not outloved? What sage has he not outseen? What gentleman has he not instructed in the rudeness of his behavior?

The words of such great men are impressive evidence of the value of Shakespeare's gift to the world. To their testimony might be added that of thousands upon thousands of others who have felt Shakespeare's power. In fact, the opinions of three

hundred years unite in extolling the work of the great English dramatist.

For many years thoughtful people have called Shakespeare and the Bible the two greatest literary influences that have entered into the lives of the race. While the influence of Shakespeare, like that of the Bible, is to be felt rather than measured, there are many tangible proofs of his vitality as a present-day force.

In the drama Shakespeare has surpassed all other influences. Out of 1500 new plays produced in the Elizabethan period, his plays are practically the only ones that are produced today. In view of all the changes that have taken place in the last 300 years it is astonishing that any play written so long ago should still have stage-life. How much more astonishing is it that at least twenty-six of the thirty-seven plays commonly attributed to Shakespeare have been acted within the last quarter of a century! Some of these plays have been presented repeatedly, "The Merchant of Venice," for example, appearing on the stage over 100,000 times and producing receipts of over $35,000,000!

The drawing power of Shakespeare's plays is remarkable. In one year Sir Henry Irving played Hamlet 200 successive times, and in another year, 108 times. The same actor gave 250 consecutive performances of "The Merchant of Venice"; 212 of "Much Ado About Nothing"; and 130 of "Romeo and Juliet." Since no year passes in which it is not possible to see elaborate productions of Shakespearean plays, as well as a great number of amateur presentations, it must be true that actors and managers alike recognize public interest in the plays of Shakespeare.

In spite of the frequency with which the plays are presented the rewards are great. Edwin Booth, with a repertory of eleven Shakespearean plays and five others, made great expenditures and endured various losses, but left a fortune of $605,000!

Between 1887 and 1899 Daly's Theater produced nine Shakespearean plays, from which there was a gross income of $2,000,000! Between 1878 and 1905 the Lyceum Theater, one-third of whose plays were Shakespearean, had a gross income of $10,500,000! In 1910 the Shakespearean productions in which Julia Marlowe and E. H. Sothern took parts had average gross receipts of $16,000 per week! In four weeks at the Academy of Music the Shakespearean plays in which Robert Mantell took the leading part brought in an average gross income of $10,000 per week!

If Shakespeare has been a maker of money for actors and managers he has been an even greater maker of reputations, for the greatest fame in the world of acting has gone to those who have made successes in Shakespearean parts. The list of names that might be mentioned is astonishingly long. In the past are the great names of Robert Burbage, Colley Cibber, Mrs. Siddons, David Garrick, John Philip Kemble, Edmund Kean, Junius Booth, William C. Macready, Edwin Forest, and Edwin Booth. In our time Henry Irving and Johnston Forbes-Robertson were knighted for excellence in Shakespearean parts. Among other recent actors to gain fame in Shakespearean parts are Herbert Beerbohm-Tree, John Drew, Richard Mansfield, Robert Mantell, E. H. Sothern, Tyrone Powers, William Faversham, and Ben Greet. The number of Shakespearean actresses is even greater, among them being Charlotte Cushman, Mary Anderson, Mme. Modjeska, Sara Bernhardt, Mrs. Patrick Campbell, Ada Rehan, Ellen Terry, Julia Marlowe, Viola Allen, Henrietta Crossman, and Margaret Anglin. It is a notable fact that so many actors and actresses should wish to present Shakespeare's characters.

In the world of books Shakespeare has gained an equally important place. The last edition of the *Encyclopedia Britannica* gives fifty col-

454

Sarony

EDWIN BOOTH AS HAMLET

THE GREATEST OF AMERICAN ACTORS (1833-1893) FIRST PLAYED HAMLET IN SAN FRANCISCO IN 1853. HE WAS BY PHYSIQUE AND TEMPERAMENT PARTICU-

umns of fine print to matter concerning Shakespeare. *The United States Catalogue,* in its list of Shakespearean books now on sale in the United States, prints thirty-five columns of fine print with an average of fifty books to a column! Magazines and newspapers print hundreds of Shakespeare articles. All this shows an immense public interest in Shakespeare. In fact, the demand for Shakespeare's works is so great that there are now on sale in the United States alone no less than 130 editions of his complete plays and poems, besides a great number of editions of separate plays, abridged plays, adaptations of plays and special versions.

The interest, instead of being confined to English-speaking people, is world-wide. Shakespeare's plays have been translated into the languages of the civilized world, and exert a powerful influence in disseminating the ideals of the English race. They are read with the greatest interest in Germany, France, Italy, Spain, Greece, Holland, Russia, Poland, Finland, Denmark, Norway, Sweden —in fact, in every land where there is literature at all. The plays have been acted in China and in Japan, and they have been translated into such strange languages as Marathi, Urdu, and Canarese.

In Germany especially the influence of Shakespeare is very great. Goethe, the foremost German writer, once wrote:

I do not remember that any book or person or event in my life ever made so great an impression upon me as the plays of Shakespeare.

Some of the most painstaking studies of Shakespearean subjects have been made by German scholars, and the number of books written in German concerning Shakespeare is remarkably great. The plays are acted very frequently in Germany, twenty-six of them being put on the stage in 1911, and "Othello" being presented 158 times!

One of the powerful influences that makes Shakespeare a leader in present-day thought is the attention given to his works in educational institutions. Practically every school and college in the United States includes Shakespeare in its course of study. Every year this immense army of young students gains mental and spiritual strength from Shakespeare's plays, a strength that is carried out into the thought and action of national life.

Books of quotations, such as Bartlett's, Bennett's, or Hoyt and Ward's, and such special books as Routledge's *Quotations from Shakespeare,* Morgan's *The Mind of Shakespeare,* and Stearns's *The Shakespeare Treasury* show how thoroly Shakespearean phrases have permeated our common speech.

In the world of music Shakespeare has given inspiration to some of the world's greatest composers, Rossini writing "Otello," Schubert giving music for such songs as "Hark, Hark, the Lark!" Mendelssohn composing his beautiful "Midsummer Night's Dream," Schumann planning a "Hamlet," Verdi producing "Macbeth," "Otello," and "Falstaff," and Saint-Saëns his "Henry VIII."

Many great painters have devoted time to Shakespearean subjects, among them being Sir Joshua Reynolds, Hogarth, Romney, Sir John Gilbert, George Cruikshank, Sir John Millais, Holman Hunt, Sir Frederick Leighton, Washington Allston, Eduard Grutzner, Frederick Barth, Walter Crane, and Edward A. Abbey. Thousands upon thousands of pictures and engravings of all kinds have been made by artists more or less distinguished. John Boydell spent $1,750,000 in preparing a collection of Shakespearean engravings!

Great sculptors likewise have turned their attention to Shakespeare as a theme for art, among them being Roubillac, John Bacon, Lord Ronald Gower, William R. O'Donnovan, J. E. Carew, P. J. Chardigny, of Paris; M. Paul Fournier, of Paris; Augusto Possaglio, of Florence; R. S. Greenough, Frederick MacMonnies, J. Q. A. Ward, and William Ordway Partridge.

Important statues of Shakespeare stand in various cities of the world. They are to be found in Stratford-on-Avon, in London, in Birmingham, in Central Park, New York; in Lincoln Park, Chicago; in the Library of Congress in Washington; in Paris, France; in Weimar, Germany, and in the Castle of Kronborg in Denmark.

It is by no means necessary that a person shall have read Shakespeare

BOOKS FOR FURTHER READING

H. Copley Greene: *The Wisdom of Shakespeare*; C. S. Ward: *Wit, Wisdom and Beauties of Shakespeare*; A. Davenport: *Leadership of Shakespeare*; F. C. Sharp: *Shakespeare's Portrayal of the Moral Life*; H. S. Bowden: *The Religion of Shakespeare*; G. Arbuthnot: *Shakespeare Sermons*; J. D. E. Spaeth: *Living Problems in Shakespeare*; S. L. Lee: *Shakespeare and the Modern Stage*; William Winter: *Shakespeare on the Stage*; R. G. Moulton: *Shakespeare as a Dramatic Thinker*; W. J. Rolfe: *Golden Texts from the Works of Shakespeare*; N. C. Clarke, edited by W. J. Rolfe: *Shakespeare Proverbs*; Ben Greet: *Shakespeare a Child Can Read and Act.*

to feel his influence. The frequency of quotation from the plays has made many of the longer passages familiar to people who know nothing more of his works. Whether people know it or not, Shakespeare has entered profoundly into daily thought. Some of his lines are on every one's lips. Think only of: "All that glitters is not gold"; "Tell truth and shame the devil"; "Uneasy lies the head that wears a crown"; "A man can die but once"; "He jests at scars that never felt a wound"; "The wish was father to the thought"; "Brevity is the soul of wit"; "I am a man more sinned against than sinning"; "There's a divinity that shapes our ends"; "All's well that ends well"; "The weakest goes to the wall." Shakespeare's use of certain terse expressions has aided in fixing them as permanent possessions of the language, some of them being: "I dote on his very absence"; "In the twinkling of an eye"; "My cake is dough"; "A poor, lone woman"; "A dish fit for the gods."

It is evident that Shakespeare's influence upon the modern world can be demonstrated in very tangible fashion. Because of that influence millions of dollars are exchanged yearly, and countless numbers of people devote themselves in one way or another to work in connection with Shakespeare.

From the point of view of the intangible, Shakespeare, outside of the Bible, is the greatest spiritual force in literature. His plays uphold the ideals of right living and high thinking, the unchanging, eternal laws of life. They show that lack of moral restraint brings the certain punishment of conscience, and very frequently the punishment inflicted by human society. They show that true nobility lies neither in rank nor in wealth, but in noble character. They broaden the mind by a sane and liberal view of life, creating sympathy for all types of people, opening the eyes to the charms of nature, and inducing meditation on all that exists. They strengthen the love of liberty, justice, mercy, fair-play, kindness, peace, modesty, temperance, courage, and manliness—in fact, of all that is noble and good. Shakespeare's plays hold their high position because they come so close in spirit to the highest ideals of the race. Their influence on present-day thought and action is strong beyond estimation.

THE FURROWS

Last year we ploughed the furrows straight,
 together, Jean and I,
When down the Flanders Road a lark was
 singing sweet and high,
With Paris white and beautiful, a mirage
 in the sky.

This year in kepis smart and red and jacket
 short and blue
My Jean toward the trenches went to help
 his country thro';
Alone I drive the sleek white ox along the
 fields he knew.

Soft o'er a stretch of fallow ground the
 tender spring grass waves,
I toil with anxious care today (for care a
 sick heart saves),
Yet cannot keep the furrows straight.
 There are too many graves.
   —M. Forrest in the Toronto Globe.

The New Books

IN JAPAN

From Japanese presses have recently come to this country two interesting specimens of book making. One, *Suiko-iko*, is the memorial volume of the writings and speeches of Mr. Midzumo, for seven years consul general at New York, whose American friends will be interested in the photographs that illustrate the pages, even tho all they can read will be the few addresses delivered in America and printed in English at the close of the volume. The other, an attractive little book illustrated by a few colored prints, is the *Imperial Japanese Poems of the Meiji Era*. These Royal poems are for the most part single stanzas, each gracefully expressing a sound moral. The English translation is printed opposite the decorative Japanese characters. Less charming than these books in silk and crêpe is Ernest Wilson Clement's *Short History of Japan*, but it gives swiftly and clearly an account of what is known of the centuries before the Meiji Era and of the changes that have taken place under the late Emperor. *The Mikado, Institution and Person* is at once a more detailed and less complete study. William Elliot Griffis considers the legendary period, but leaving out the Samurai, who were for centuries the actual rulers, he treats of the active life of the kingdom only after the middle of the nineteenth century and the fall of the Samurai. The accounts of the internal affairs from that time on and of the personality of the late Mikado are full and enthusiastic. *The Working Women of Japan* is a sad enough description of piteous and shocking conditions by Sidney L. Gulick, of Doshisha University, who is in a position to know whereof he writes. The little leaven that begins to lighten this heavy mass of human misery comes from the efforts of one poor workman, Shinjoro Omoto. There is a chapter on the Geisha girls, on the rural workers and on recent legislation. Worlds away from these somber pages is the *Flower Art of Japan*, by Mary Averill, a delightful book on a fascinating subject. Its explanations of combinations and symbolism are clear and simple. Its hundred illustrations, mostly in line, show the methods of preparation and arrangement. For a beginning in the study of line and composition one could hardly find a better introduction than this Japanese flower art.

In *The Students of Asia*, G. Sherwood Eddy gives accounts of the educational movements in India, China, and Japan started by the work of Christian missionaries and fostered by contact with western civilization. The

extent of the western spirit in Oriental education will astonish those who have not kept track of the swiftly changing East. Mr. Eddy was Mr. John R. Mott's companion in the recent journey for the Y. M. C. A. to the student bodies all over the world and his analyses of conditions and tendencies are made upon broad and thoro knowledge of conditions in Eastern lands.

The Japan Society of America has published a symposium of addresses by various eminent Japanese setting forth the ideals and the policies of Japan and entitled *Japan to America*. The topics cover a wide range from commercial methods and international ambitions to translations from Eastern literature and Christianity in Japan. An especially interesting paper is that on the moral code of the great Japanese educator, Fukuzawa.

Tho thete has been a guide for travelers in Japan, there has been none for China, Korea and Manchuria till the publication of the four volumes of the Official Guide to Eastern Asia, *China, Manchuria and Chôsen, and Northeastern and Southwestern Japan*. Tho stout and handy like our Baedekers, even a guide book made in Japan has charm. The smallest illustrations are clear, the colored frontispieces delightful, and the maps are beautiful instead of garish.

A Short History of Japan, by Ernest Wilson Clement. Univ. of Chicago Press. $1. *The Mikado, Institution and Person*, by William Elliot Griffis. Princeton Univ. Press. $1.50. *Working Women of Japan*, by Sidney L. Gulick. Missionary Education Movement. 50 cents. *The Flower Art of Japan*, by Mary Averill. Lane. $1.30. *The Students of Asia*, by G. Sherwood Eddy. Student Volunteer Movement. 50 cents. *Japan to America*. Putnam. $1.25. *The Official Guide to Eastern Asia*, 4 vols. Tokyo: Imperial Japanese Government Railways.

A LEAGUE OF PEACE

Mr. Hobson is one of that masterful little band of English federationists who, with Lord Bryce, A. Lowes Dickinson, Aneurin Williams and others, is now devoting his time to working out the basis for a durable peace when the Great War ends. *Towards International Government* is a plea for a League of Peace, with legislative, judicial and executive branches all backed up by force. Altho the idea has already been treated in several striking magazine articles both here and abroad, this is the first book to be published on the subject.

The author presents a well thought out and detailed plan. He sees the coming of the new order and urges it with all the charm and erudition that a cultivated Englishman can bring to such a task. He has the enthusiasm of the devotee and yet is not blinded to the tremendous difficulties to be overcome before the goal is reached.

Mr. Hobson's League is strikingly like the proposals of the American branch of the League to Enforce Peace, promulgated a Declaration of Interdependence at Independence Hall, Philadelphia, last June. All of which goes to show that when the time is ripe for an idea to be born whether in the realm of science or government, the light is vouchsafed almost simultaneously to

different men working independently in different places.

Nobody who is seriously interested in seeing that this war ends all war can afford to ignore this scholarly and statesmanlike volume. Altho it is the pioneer work in the field, it is pretty nearly the last word on the subject, at least as far as the theory of the League of Peace is concerned.

Towards International Government, by J. A. Hobson. Macmillan. $1.

THEORIES AND THRILLS

Marriage, thinks Henry Kitchell Webster, is *The Real Adventure* of life, "the essential adventureness of which no amount of cautious thought taken in advance could modify." And he proceeds to prove the theory in an entertaining story of how one woman tried it, forced by the circumstances of the adventure to win her way successively as the perfect hostess in high society; as a chorus girl; after the show left her stranded "on the road," as a small town milliner; and at length as a successful costume designer in New York.

All of which is due to her insistence on economic independence, theoretically accepted and practically denied by her husband. Only after she has "made good" as an individual does she come to the realization that "there's a real job just in being successfully the wife of a successful man." It is a tale full of real people who are trying life from nearly every angle and whose comments on their experiences offer keen suggestions for a fairly workable philosophy. The conclusions it reaches ring true, and the intrinsic interest of the plot holds the reader's close attention in spite of the rather excessive length of the story, somewhat overgarnished with adjectives and author's digressions.

The Real Adventure, by Henry Kitchell Webster. Indianapolis. Bobbs-Merrill. $1.50.

THE CRITICAL YEARS

The years during which a human animal becomes civilized—or not, as the case may be—are coming to receive an increasing share of attention from all who have to do with human beings in the process of development. The reprinting of Dr. Slaughter's *The Adolescent* from the English edition of five years ago should be of great benefit to those who have to do with young men and women in the *becoming.* Dr. Slaughter has succeeded in doing two unusual things: he has condensed the significant facts about the mental and moral characteristics of the adolescent into a small book of a hundred pages; and he has presented his concentrated extract in a most readable, and sometimes even entertaining way. There are shreds and remnants of a lingering Darwinism thruout the text, but the essentials are up to the best thought and scholarship on the main subject.

The same period of life is discussed from the physician's point of view in Dr. Louis Starr's *The Adolescent Period.* The emphasis is here naturally on the physical side—growth, the development of the muscular system,

Joy just hangs on every puff

How a pipe of "Tux" does bubble over with good cheer and sunny comfort! There's something about the mellow taste of "Tux" that stirs a smoker's soul. It gets into his inside works, sweetens his disposition, and gives him that perky, chesty feeling, like a high-stepper trotting down the avenue.

Tuxedo
The Perfect Tobacco for Pipe and Cigarette

Men who never smoked a pipe before are now smoking Tuxedo, because they have found that Tuxedo is the mildest tobacco made, and that it is the one tobacco that never irritates mouth, throat or nerves.

You simply *cannot* get another tobacco made by the "Tuxedo Process"—and that's the original of all processes for removing every trace of harshness and bite from the tobacco. It has been widely imitated, but never duplicated.

Try Tuxedo for a week, and you'll get acquainted with the sweetest, mildest, mellowest smoke in the world.

YOU CAN BUY TUXEDO EVERYWHERE

Convenient, glassine wrapped, moisture-proof pouch . . **5c**

Famous green tin with gold lettering, curved to fit pocket **10c**

In Tin Humidors, 40c and 80c
In Glass Humidors, 50c and 90c

THE AMERICAN TOBACCO COMPANY

Shakespeare's Portrait

While our limited supply lasts we
will mail in a tube suitable for framing an excellent reproduction on
heavy cameo paper of Leopold Flameng's etching of the famous Chandos
portrait of Shakespeare. Send six
two-cent stamps to cover cost of
wrapping and mailing.

THE INDEPENDENT
Shakespeare Dept., 119 W. 40th St., N. Y.

---

physical education, the diseases of
adolescence, etc. There is a brief discussion of the "faults" of adolescence,
in which some of the normal symptoms
of youth are treated from the point of
view of the offensive and criminal and
otherwise undesirable forms that they
may take. These two books supplement
each other in a practical way.

The Adolescent, by J. W. Slaughter. Macmillan. 60 cents. *The Adolescent Period*, by Louis
Starr. Philadelphia: Blakiston. $1.

TOMMY ATKINS

Ian Hay has written a delightfully
witty account of the life in a training
camp of Kitchener's first army, *The
First Hundred Thousand*. The writer,
who before he became an officer in a
Scotch regiment was a novelist describes his own experiences, and there
is a smile in almost every paragraph
and a laugh on every page, so keen is
his eye for the amusing side of their
troubles and privations. One gains a
vivid idea of exactly what happens to
the recruit thru the long months of
training before he is sent to the front.
The reader lives with Tommy Atkins
in camp, on parade, on the march and
in sham battles, and then he goes to the
front, where the fun suddenly ceases
and he is face to face with real war.
It is a most illuminating and interesting book, with true literary value—a
book to read and to keep.

The First Hundred Thousand, by Ian Hay.
Houghton, Mifflin. $1.50.

SOCIALISM AND THE CHURCH

John Spargo, one of the most persuasive and tolerant of all the expound-
ers of Socialist thought, extends the
olive branch to the Christian churches
in his recent study of *Marxian Socialism and Religion*. He does not attempt
to minimize the magnitude of the historic quarrel between the party and the
church. "In the average religious paper," he admits, "the most bitter,
brutal, stupid and false charges against
Socialism and its advocates are to be
found with a frequency which precludes
the suggestion of accident as an explanation. In the Socialist papers, with
equal frequency, charges just as brutal,
stupid and false are hurled against religion and all its associations." But this
unfortunate state of affairs is due, Mr.
Spargo thinks, not to anything inherent in Socialist doctrine, but to the unwise political attitude of some established churches, notably the Roman
Catholic, and the coincidence of the rise
of Socialism with the materialist trend
of thought among the educated classes
in the middle of the last century. With
great ingenuity he shows that even the
materialistic conception of history, the
only Marxian dogma which seems on
the face of it irreconcilable with Christian teaching, may be made to bear a
religious interpretation. Why should not
the progress of industry and the shifting phases of the class struggle be
God's way of working out the evolution
of humanity? The query"thus put Mr.
Spargo regards as unanswerable. It is
certainly most strange that every right
or wrong attempt to explain how things
come about should be regarded, equally

by those who champion the new theory and by those who attack it, as a denial that the newly explained law of nature may be also a manifestation of the will of God.

Marxian Socialism and Religion, by John Spargo. Huebsch. $1.

EFFICIENCY INVESTMENT

Eight minutes a day to keep in condition! Dr. W. J. Cromie in *Keeping Physically Fit* gives single stick, towel and no apparatus exercises for busy men, nervous women, and growing children.

Macmillan. $1.

NEW ENGLAND STORIES

Annie Trumbull Slosson's work is sure to be delicate, full of mystical meaning, of pathos and yet of hopefulness. In *Puzzled Souls* the opening dog story is too pathetic, but Old Home Day is a fine, weird fancy, and the tale of the boy who became an infidel is an interesting study in child psychology.

Philadelphia: S. S. Times. 75 cents.

THE SPIRIT OF ENGLAND

The Spirit of England, by George W. E. Russell, would seem to be mainly a political apology for his passing from a convinced pacificist to a volunteer militarist. To satisfy this end he wanders into every land, and calls to witness a host of authorities. Directness is hardly one of his gifts, and clarity shines none too brilliantly thru the bewildering maze of his pages.

Dutton. $1.25.

AN ANTHOLOGY

In striking contrast to the war poems of the day is *The Quiet Hour*, a collection that has been selected and arranged by FitzRoy Carrington under the seven headings, Cradle Songs, Infancy, Childhood, Night, Sleep, Charms, and Dirges. Mr. Carrington gleans not from the great poets alone, but gives us much worth while from minor singers.

Houghton, Mifflin. 75 cents.

THE BEAUTY OF WONDER

Superficially reminiscent of Kenneth Grahame, but with more of philosophy and of mystical fancy, Algernon Blackwood's story of children, *An Extra Day*, is full of beauty and originality. It should be loved of all child lovers and indeed of all, for whom the poetry of life is as real as its tasks and its pleasures.

Macmillan. $1.35.

ETHICS IN SERVICE

The Page Lectures at Yale, delivered last year by Mr. Taft, are now published under the title, *Ethics in Service*. Two of these explain his convictions as to various political and social reforms, one is a genial discussion of the Presidential office. Those most valuable are on the bar, its history and its standards, giving the ideals of the profession as they appear to this highminded and able member of the profession.

Yale Univ. Press. $1.

EUROPA'S FAIRY BOOK

Joseph Jacobs, whose untimely death took place in January, had collected and retold certain selected European Folk-Tales that he had found practically identical in all continental countries, under the title of *Europa's Fairy Tales*. In them he followed in general the admirable plan used in his "English Fairy Tales." The Master Thief, Beauty and the Beast, Androcles and the Lion, and others, less familiar, appear in the present collection. The illustrations are by John D. Batten.

Putnam. $1.25.

A ROMAN SKEPTIC

The second of the seven volumes of the works of *Lucian* in the Loeb Classical Library is now out. This contains the dialogs which gave Lucian the reputation of a skeptic and in which he ridicules the gods. In one of them a philosopher cross-questions Jupiter and shows that he is a helpless pretender. His arguments on fate and destiny and the prevalence of evil and

The Value of Sanatogen to The Man who Works His Brain

"Without albumen, no life; without phosphorus, no thought"—so runs a famous saying.

True, the healthy body gets enough albumen and phosphorus from the daily food, but an overtaxed brain and nervous system will run short of these vital substances because the demand outruns the normal supply. Then we have fatigue, depression—and worse, if nothing be done.

It is *then* that Sanatogen is of splendid aid. Combining purest albumen and organic phosphorus in chemical union, Sanatogen takes to the fundamental sources of nervous and mental efficiency just the elements needed. It supplies these elements quickly and without strain upon digestion, giving the depleted cells real nutriment, real sustenance and no false stimulation.

The result of this is well epitomized by Sir Gilbert Parker when he writes, "Sanatogen to my mind is a true food-tonic, giving fresh vigor to the overworked body and mind." And by Arnold Bennett, who tersely reports, "The effect of Sanatogen upon the nervous system is simply wonderful."

It is good to remember that the medical profession has set the seal of approval upon the value of Sanatogen—no less than 21,000 doctors have written letters endorsing its value.

Should not the knowledge of these facts create the conviction that *Sanatogen will also help you?*

Grand Prize, International Congress of Medicine, London, 1913.

Sanatogen is sold by good druggists everywhere, in sizes from $1.00 up

THE FOOD-TONIC APPROVED BY SCIENCE

Sanatogen

ENDORSED BY OVER 21,000 PHYSICIANS

Send for *"The Art of Living"*—a charming little book by Richard Le Gallienne, the popular poet-author, touching on Sanatogen's kindly help and giving other interesting aids in the quest for contentment and better health. This book is free. Tear this off—as a reminder to write

THE BAUER CHEMICAL CO.,   26R Irving Place, New York.

wrong in the world under the permission of Heaven have a very modern sound. The visits to Hades and jollying of Charon and Hermes are quite a contrast to the interviews of Ulysses and Æneas in the lower world.
Macmillan. $1.50.

BONAPARTE

Most vividly written is James Morgan's *In the Footsteps of Napoleon*. It enters little into the discussion of details of campaigns, or the causes and results of that marvelous career. It is rather the story, dramatically, but not sensationally told, of the man Napoleon, with special regard to the setting of the critical events, for which setting the author has journeyed to all the scenes of the Napoleonic drama.
Macmillan. $2.50.

AN IRISH JAUNTING-CAR

"'Tis a quare world, an' judgin' from the preparations they're making for it, the next wan will be quarer," says Jerry of Alexis Roche's *Journeys with Jerry the Jarvey*. His stories of the "quare" people he has known in this "quare world" are Irish thru and thru, and hence delightful. Filled with excellent material, the book is marred by unskilful handling. A judicious omission of the broader bits of humor would also be an improvement.
Dutton. $1.35.

BELGIAN LEGEND AND BUILDING

The most attractive book on Belgium out lately seems to us Mrs. Champney's *Romance of Old Belgium*. The first stories purport to be from a hidden manuscript of Froissart, discovered on the destruction of a monastery by German shells. Later tales are historical. There is a chapter by Frère Champney on the characteristic architecture of this land. The illustrations are peculiarly apt to the text, varied and delightful.
Putnam. $2.50.

THREE PLAYS

In the three plays included in the sixth volume of Hauptmann's works is shown again the dramatist's tremendous grasp of human nature. In "The Maidens of the Mountains he shows a group of people who live and love and dream, and being modern, know that they dream. Griselda is the medieval legend retold with the keenest psychological insight, yet subtly touched with poetry. Gabriel Schilling's Flight is a brilliant analysis of the relations of the sexes.
Huebsch. $1.50.

NOT FOR LAYMEN

Consumption and Its Cure by Physical Exercises propounds a theory directly at variance with the methods that in the past twenty-five years have made such progress in combating this frightful disease. The author, Filip Sylvan, M.D., is an English doctor, and his record of cases extends over five years, so that the book will be of interest to physicians, but patients cannot be too strongly warned against trying without medical advice to treat themselves by its suggestions.
Dutton. $1.25.

A ROMANCE OF LABOR

In the third part of *Pelle the Conqueror, The Great Struggle*, Martin Nexö depicts the development of the social conscience in Pelle and his work in Copenhagen as a labor leader convinced that the salvation of the poor lies in their consolidation. Despite a somewhat unnecessary coarseness, despite the exceeding badness of the translation, the book is worth reading for its exposition, from the workingman's point of view, of the methods and purposes of organized labor.
Holt. $1.40.

MEXICO

Adventures in Mexico is an Englishman's account of his journey, thru that country in 1846, George Ruxton gives lively and picturesque descriptions of the country and people, descriptions which might have been written today so little have conditions changed. He admires the women and the natural scenery, but cannot say enough in

disparagement of the men and the towns. The book abounds in hairbreadth escapes and doughty deeds on the part of the hero-author.

Outing Publishing Co. $1.

AROUND THE MEDITERRANEAN

The new edition of E. Reynolds-Ball's *Mediterranean Winter Resorts* is revised and in part rewritten. This is an excellent practical guide book for Egypt and north-ern Africa as well as the Riviera and Italy.

Dutton. $1.75.

TURKISH WOMEN

Much romance regarding the Oriental harems is exploded in Elizabeth Cooper's present book. *The Harem and the Purdah.* Into its pages she has crowded much of first hand information. The manners and social ideas that have led to the harem as an institution are considered and much new light is incidentally but entertainingly shed upon the social East.

Century. $3.

COMPETENT OFFICE WORK

Business psychology, in so far as it con-cerns the employer, and the running of the well-ordered and systematic office, is ad-mirably presented in *The Efficient Secre-tary*, by Ellen Lane Spencer. Its terse and lucid manner, its special reference to the so-called unessential details, and its direct appeal, make it of value to those who as-pire to "success and financial reward."

Stokes. $1.

A LAPSE INTO THE VICTORIAN

It is hard to associate the Compton Mac-kenzie of "Youth's Encounter" and "Car-nival" with the anemic *Plashers Mead.* Abandoning the gay adventuring into life which made the earlier novels fascinating, he has here lapsed into the silly, idyllic love story, a story, says the publisher's notice, "enhanced by the perfect setting of an in-comparable English landscape"—and about as lifelike.

Harper. $1.35.

HOKUSAI IN NEW YORK

A noteworthy exhibition of old Jap-anese color prints, of the so-called Ukiyo-e School, as executed by the great and incomparable Hokusai, and which took five years to assemble, has just been held at the Yamanaka Gal-lery in New York City. The work of some of the master's pupils was also included.

There is a growing appreciation of Oriental art in this country, and par-ticularly that produced by the Japanese artist. It makes a strong appeal to con-noisseurs and fine impressions of chromoxylographic work, the cost of which, when issued, was but trifling, now often fetch hundreds, and some-times thousands of dollars at the great sales.

The Japanese myth and legend, the folk tales, with which Hokusai and his brother artists love to deal, are so vio-lently unlike the Occidental myths that the color prints of Japan take on a charm that is all their own. This ap-plies with special force to the pictures by Hokusai, whose sense of humor was very strong.

The wide range of subjects that oc-cupied this Japanese master during his long and busy life (1760-1849) was highly interesting. His famous "Wave" print was represented by a magnificent example, in fine color and in clear im-pression. His various prints of Fuji (sacred mountain), his waterfalls, his bridges, his fishes and birds, his genres, and his flower pieces were all selected gems.

THE MARKET PLACE
A REVIEW OF FINANCE AND TRADE

THE NEW YEAR IN FINANCE AND TRADE

BY FRANK D. ROOT

INDUSTRIAL conditions in the United States at the beginning of the present year were highly favorable. In 1915 there had been a notable revival of activity and a great increase of trade profits. The output of pig iron had been doubled. Steel mills, only sixty per cent of whose capacity was in use during the year's first month, were overwhelmed with orders in December, and their output was sold far ahead. Net earnings of the great Steel Corporation had risen from less than $11,000,000 in the last quarter of 1914, and only $12,500,000 in the first quarter of 1915, to $51,000,000 in the fourth quarter, and the suspended dividend on the common stock was about to be restored. The price of copper had advanced from 13 to 20 cents a pound, and that of cotton from 7¾ to 12½ cents. For about four months the railroads had been carrying so much freight that a remarkable congestion of loaded cars was to be seen at our north Atlantic ports. Unprecedented exports were making a great trade balance in our favor. Crops had been very large. Our gold imports had exceeded exports by $420,000,000, and we had loaned more than $1,000,000,000 to foreign nations.

In the first two and one-half months of the new year this prosperity has continued. There has been no change to our disadvantage in the conditions prevailing at the end of 1915. The earnings of our railroads have been growing. New high records have been made in the iron and steel industry, where there have been additions to prices every week. The net earnings of the Steel Corporation are at the rate of about $240,000,000 a year. The daily average of output at the iron furnaces in February had never been equaled. Exports are still making a great excess in our favor. Many companies that are at work on war orders have declared large extra dividends. Fifty industrial corporations have reported, for the year 1915, earnings of 31.4 per cent, against ten per cent in the preceding twelve months, and this list does not include several whose gains have been extraordinary, because their reports have not yet been given to the public. Our shipyards have orders that will keep them busy for two years. Under contract there are 334 ships—275 for the merchant service and fifty-nine for the Government—and orders for forty-three have been given since January 1. Many are for foreign owners. The price of copper, 27½ cents a pound, is the highest in forty-three years, and if it is maintained our producers of this metal will receive this year $200,000,000 more than was paid to them in 1915.

But the gains have not, as a rule, been accompanied by higher prices in the market for securities. At the close of last year, large additions had been made (as our tables show) to the market values of railroad stocks, and there had been extraordinary advances for the shares of war order companies, with Bethlehem Steel and General Motors at the top of the list. In the first two and one-half months of 1916 the leading railway stocks have shown net losses ranging from 3½ to 5⅝ points, and in the field of war order shares there has been no uniformity of movement. Losses are seen there as well as gains. A revival of speculative activity on the Stock Exchange during the last two or three weeks tends to make higher prices.

IRON AND STEEL

The output of pig iron, which in 1915 had grown from an average of about 1,500,000 tons a month in the first two months to 3,203,000 in December, was 3,188,000 in January and 3,087,000 in the short month of February, when, as has been said, the daily average at the furnaces was the largest ever known. The United States is now making iron at the rate of nearly 40,000,000 tons a year. The average price of steel prod-

COURSE OF RAILROAD STOCKS

	Net Change in 1914	Net Change in 1915	Opening, 1916	Net Change in 1916 to March 15
Atchison	— ½	+15½	108	— 4½
B. & Ohio	—24⅝	+17⅞	95	— 5¾
Can. Pac.	—53	+29	182	—14⅞
St. Paul	—13	+14⅛	101	— 5¼
Northwestern	— 5½	+13	134½	— 7½
Del. & Hud	— 9¾	+12½	153½	— 1
Gt. Northern	—13¼	+14⅜	126¼	— 3⅜
Lehigh	—19¾	+17⅜	81¼	— 2¼
M., K. & Tex.	—10½	— 1⅝	6⅛	— 2¼
Mo. Pac.	—17	— 3¼	4⅛	+ ¾
N. Y. Central	— 8⅛	+26	109½	— 3¾
North. Pac.	— 9⅛	+18⅜	118	— 3⅝
Pennsylvania	— 5	+ 6⅞	59	— 1⅛
Reading	—24⅞	+12½	83	+ 5
So. Pac.	— 6¾	+21⅞	102½	— 2⅞
Un. Pac.	—39⅛	+23⅝	138	— 3⅝

STEEL CORPORATION'S NET EARNINGS, BY QUARTERS

	1915	1914	1913
First	$12,458,159	$17,994,351	$34,426,801
Second	27,950,055	20,457,596	41,219,813
Third	38,718,644	22,276,002	38,450,400
Fourth	51,232,788	10,933,170	23,084,331
	$130,359,646	$71,661,149	$137,181,345

FOREIGN TRADE

The excess of our exports over imports continues to be very large. A high record was made in December. The official figures for February are not yet available. The excess since the beginning of the war and up to the end of January was $2,184,185,941.

1915—	Exports	Imports	Excess of Exports
January	$267,879,313	$122,148,317	$145,730,996
February	299,805,869	125,123,391	174,682,478
March	296,611,852	157,982,016	138,629,836
April	294,745,913	160,576,106	134,169,807
May	274,218,142	142,284,851	132,033,291
June	268,547,416	157,695,140	110,852,276
July	268,974,610	143,244,737	125,729,873
August	261,025,230	141,804,202	119,221,028
September	300,676,822	151,236,026	149,440,796
October	328,018,300	149,172,729	178,845,671
November	327,670,413	155,496,675	172,173,738
December	359,306,492	171,832,505	187,473,987
Tot., 12 mos.	3,547,480,372	1,778,596,695	1,768,883,677
1916—			
January	335,535,303	184,192,299	151,343,004

WAR ORDER STOCKS

	1914 Low	1914 High	1915 High	1915 Net Change	Opening, 1916	Net Change in 1916 to March 15
Am. Can.	19¼	35⅛	49⅜	+ 36½	60½	+ 2
Allis-Chalmers	6	14¼	68½	+ 23⅜	31	+ 1⅜
Am. Car. & Foundry	42½	53½	98	+ 33¾	77	— 4½
Am. Locomotive	20½	37½	74⅜	+ 46⅜	68⅛	+12⅜
Am. Smelting	50¼	71⅛	101⅞	+ 51⅞	106⅝	— 4½
Anaconda	24¼	38¼	91⅝	+ 40⅜	90	— 2¾
Baldwin Locomotive	38½	52⅜	154½	+ 77⅞	115½	— 4⅛
Beth. Steel	29½	46½	600	+425¾	450	+67½
Gen. Electric	137½	150⅝	185½	+ 34¾	174½	— 4
Gen. Motors	37⅞	99	535	+443	495	—20
Maxwell	14½	15¼	92	+ 58⅝	75	—12⅞
Nat. Lead	40	52	70¾	+ 18¾	66	+ 1½
N. Y. Air Brake	58	69	164¼	+ 75	139½	+ 9¾
Pressed Steel Car	26¾	46	78¼	+ 29⅞	64	— 6½
Studebaker	20	36¼	195	+128⅞	163½	—17
Indus. Alcohol	15	20	129¾	+101	127	+28½
U. S. Steel	48	67¼	88⅜	+ 37⅛	87⅞	— 1⅝

COURSE OF THE BOND MARKET

	Net change in 1915	Net change in 1916 to March 15
Government 4s	+ 5/8	+1 3/8
Panama Canal 3s	+2 1/4	+ 1/2
Atchison gen. 4s	+2 1/2	+ 3/8
B. & O. gold 4s	+2 1/4	+ 3/8
Burlington 4s	+3 3/8	+ 1/4
St. Paul gen. 4s	+2 1/4	+ 1/4
Northwestern gen. 4s	+5 1/4	—1 1/4
D. & R. G. 4s	+4	—2
N. Y. Cent. deb. 4s	+6 7/8	— 3/8
Northern Pacific 4s	+4	+ 5/8
Reading gen. 4s	+1 1/2	— 1/4
So. Pacific conv. 4s	+9 1/2	—1
Union Pacific 4s	+2 3/4	+ 1/4
Interboro 5s	+2 3/8	— 3/8
Am. Tel. & Tel. 4s	+4 1/2	+1
N. Y. Telephone 4 1/2s	+3 1/4	+ 1/4
U. S. Steel 5s	+3 1/2	+ 1/4

ucts is $49 a ton, against $30 one year ago. For some of them the advance has been more than 100 per cent. Bessemer billets at Pittsburgh are now $45, and last week's addition was $5. One year ago the price was $19.50. Sheet bars have risen from $20.50 to $45. Many enlargements of plant have been ordered, and there are to be 91 new open-hearth furnaces, with an annual capacity of 4,250,000 tons of ingots.

After an official report had shown that the Steel Corporation's net earnings for the December quarter were $51,232,000, the 5 per cent dividend on the company's common shares was restored. It was decided in that quarter that $70,000,000 out of the earnings should be expended for new construction, including $25,000,000 for a mill at Gary, Indiana. The number of the Corporation's employees increased from 141,000 in January of last year to 227,000 in December. A wage increase of 10 per cent, ordered for February, adds $14,000,000 to the annual cost of labor. Net earnings at the rate of $240,000,000 a year will leave $130,000,000 free to be used for improvements or in other ways. It is expected that the Bethlehem Steel Company will expend $25,000,000 upon the Sparrow's Point plant of the Maryland Steel Company, which it recently acquired, and that the new Midvale Company will devote $10,000,000 to improvements and extensions.

RAILROAD GAINS

Notable gains for the railroads began to appear in the first weeks of last September. Up to that time the roads had not been doing well. New construction for the year was only 933 miles, the smallest addition made since 1864, and in October 41,988 miles of road, or about one-sixth of the whole number, were in the hands of receivers. But there was a reduction to 36,661 miles before the year closed. In the last four months of 1915 the roads handled more freight than ever before. Their earnings, of course, have shown large increases. No complete report for recent months can be obtained, but such official statements as have been published are in agreement as to the growth of business and profits.

In November, about one-third of the mileage, according to the Interstate Commerce Commission's returns, showed an increase of 31 per cent in gross revenue and of 84 per cent in net earnings. In the East the net advanced from $351 to $713 per mile. The New York Central's net rose from $5,067,000 to $11,461,000. In December returns from a large part of the mileage pointed to a gain of 27 per cent in gross and $44,000,000, or 73 per cent, in net. January gave the Pennsylvania road a gross increase of nearly $8,000,000, or 31 per cent, with a remarkable gain in net, which rose from $1,931,000 to $7,048,000. In the same month the New York Central's net earnings advanced from $4,274,000 to $8,903,000. For those roads whose reports for February have been made known, the increase of gross receipts has been about 21 per cent.

Prices of shares in the stock market have not been in accord with such an exhibition of profits, for, as has been said, these prices have been reduced by several causes. As the great growth of freight traffic is due mainly to the transportation of war supplies, it would be checked sharply if the war should suddenly and unexpectedly end. This is not overlooked in the stock market. And there is the menace of a great strike if the demands of the 400,000 members of the four unions are rejected. The companies say that compliance with these demands would cost the roads $100,000,000 a year. As at least a part of the desired wage increase will be granted, by arbitration or otherwise, a considerable addition to the roads' expenses cannot be avoided.

Congestion of unloaded cars is most noticeable at New York. For several reasons that port is attractive to those engaged in the foreign trade. It offers a comparatively short route, its banking facilities and provisions for foreign credits are unequaled in this country, and it has been the foremost port for the reception of imports, which are nearly six times the quantity taken in at any other place. Its exports have risen from $864,000,000 in 1914 to $1,785,000,000 in 1915, which is more than one-half of the entire shipments from the United States. But many of

OUTPUT OF PIG IRON, TONS

1908	15,936,018
1909	25,795,471
1910	27,298,545
1911	23,649,547
1912	29,727,137
1913	30,724,581
1914	23,049,792

1915

January	1,601,421
February	1,674,771
March	2,063,834
April	2,116,494
May	2,261,470
June	2,380,827
July	2,563,420
August	2,770,647
September	2,852,561
October	3,125,491
November	3,037,308
December	3,203,322
	29,682,566

1916

January	3,185,121
February	3,087,212

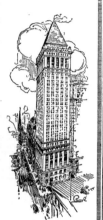

---

the ships now taking cargoes there are not well fitted for the trade, and the work of loading them from cars is done slowly. Ships ordered to take cargoes have been suddenly withdrawn by foreign governments for other service in the war. Our own munition companies, not fully equipped for the increase of their production, have been very slow in unloading the cars carrying their raw material, and some of them, fearing a strike of coal miners, have used many cars by their large orders for coal. Western railroads have only 90 per cent of the cars they own. In the East there is an excess of 13 per cent, which is increased to 44 per cent in New England. And so the American Railway Association has ordered that Eastern roads deliver to roads in the West 20 per cent more freight cars than they receive from them. But this has not solved the congestion problem, as to which the Interstate Commerce Commission is now taking testimony.

FOREIGN TRADE

Our exports in the calendar year 1915 exceeded our imports by $1,768,000,000, which was not far below the entire exports, $2,113,624,000, of 1914, and may be compared with an export excess of only $325,000,000 in that year. December's exports and excess made new high records. Our imports have been only slightly affected by the war. Last year they were only a few millions below those of 1914 or 1913. The reduction was less than 1 per cent. The excess of exports over imports for the seven months that ended with January was $1,084,333,000, or two and one-half times the excess in the corresponding period one year earlier. Our net gain in gold imported was $420,000,000 in 1915, against a net loss of $165,000,000 in 1914. Shipments of war supplies have recently been very large, despite the delays for which the railroads are criticised. And on several of the largest orders there have been no shipments. Exports of food have been nearly equal to those of war material. Our sales of breadstuffs and dairy products to foreign countries rose from $330,000,000 in 1913, which was a normal year, to $760,000,000 in 1915. Our trade with South America, China, the British East Indies, Australia and New Zealand has been growing. Both exports to and imports from South America show an increase of about 40 per cent. Probably this gain can be retained after the war only by satisfying local preferences concerning goods, accepting South American credit customs, and investing United States capital in South American undertakings.

THE STOCK MARKET

Prices of securities on the Stock Exchange have not moved in accord with the prevailing favorable financial and industrial conditions. In January the market was not a broad one. There were signs that the outside public's speculation in war order shares had been checked. The market was not stimulated by the resumption of the dividends on United States Steel common, the declaration of a dividend of 30 per cent on Bethlehem Steel common (with a wage increase of 10 per cent), the increase of the St. Paul dividend from 4 to 5 per cent, or the good reports of railroad earnings. Bethlehem common sold at 46 in January a year ago, and at 600 in October last. The price is now in the neighborhood of 530. Some traders were nervous and apprehensive on account of President Wilson's utterances during his tour in the West. Restraint was caused by the railway employees' demand for higher wages, and the sale of American securities day after day by English owners. Since the beginning of the war the number of Steel common shares held abroad has been reduced from 1,285,626 to 696,631, the sales amounting to about $51,000,-000. American securities were coming across the Atlantic every week, and sales were made by the British Government of those taken from owners under the provisions of the mobilization plan.

In February the market was even more narrow. The course of prices was affected by the submarine controversy with Germany and by indications that President Wilson might not be supported by his party in Congress. The downward tendency was not checked by many extra dividends which munition and copper companies announced. But in March, after the warning resolutions had been tabled in Congress, the market broadened, and the 14th was a million-share day. There were some signs that the public was again buying war order shares. Villa's raid in Columbus, and the sending of a punitive expedition into Mexico by our government, exerted no depressing influence, and, as a rule, no one ventured to predict the effect of the Verdun battles or any international complications that might appear.

The price of wheat has declined at Chicago since January 1 from $1.25 to $1.08. Exports for the seven months ending with January were much less than those of the corresponding months a year earlier. Farm reserves are unexpectedly large, 241,000,000 bushels, against 153,000,000 one year ago.

Our new loans are $5,000,000 to Norway and $15,000,000 to Argentina, making a total of $79,500,000 to the latter country. The supplementary Anglo-French credit of $50,000,000, arranged by groups of banks and based upon collateral deposited in the Bank of England, is now effective. A syndicate of bankers in New York will loan $75,-000,000 to Canada. There may be a French loan, but the proposed loan of $60,000,000 to Russia appears to have been laid aside.

Reports concerning general trade are favorable, the iron and steel industry is breaking all previous records, metal prices are high, railroad traffic is large and profitable, the woolen and cotton mills are busily employed, and the encouraging conditions seen at the end of last year have not been impaired. The approaching wage controversy on the railroads may cause disturbance, and the situation may be unfortunately affected by international disagreements.

Independent Opinions

A part of the British press is urging that German ships and German goods be permanently debarred from the entire British empire. A pledge of perpetual boycott against Germany is reported to have received millions of signatures. The business manager of the Pasadena Water Department sees danger in this policy:

The talk by the Allies of demolishing German militarism is entirely reasonable, but they go further and propose a system of tariffs that would shut out Germany from the fields of commerce to a very large extent. The peace-loving industrial element in Germany has been made to believe that they are fighting not an offensive war, but a war in defense of the national existence, and it has been concealed from them that the present great war was brought about by the Kaiser and other militarists thinking conditions were ripe to conquer Europe and later the world. This talk of barring out Germany from commercial business after the war will only confirm industrial Germany in their present belief as stated above, and will weld the nation into a more solid mass, if possible, than now.

On the other hand, if it was published abroad that only German militarism was to be blotted out and that German commerce was to have a fair field with no handicap, I do not doubt that very many Germans who are already quite tired of the war would heartily endorse the program. Threats against the commercial life of the nation can only prolong the war.

WILLIAM SELBIE

Pasadena, California

That article in The Independent of January 24, on "Shall the United States Protect Its Citizens?" is certainly "the limit." Send an army into poor, bleeding Mexico because a few adventurers have been killed—or *because Mexico is a weak nation?* but let Germany kill American citizens by the score and keep on sending another friendly remonstrance! And in The Independent!   R. S. LINDSAY

Congregational Manse, York, Nebraska

Nevertheless we still believe that it is the business of Uncle Sam to police Mexico rather than to police Europe.

In regard to the question of immigration and assimilation discussed in our editorial of January 17 on "No Disunited States," we have an interesting communication from the editor of *Il Carroccio*, the only Italian monthly magazine published in the United States:

Don't you think that the political and educational problems of the United States which embrace the naturalization question would be better resolved than the artificial change of nationality, by means of a more just treatment of the foreigners in whom the Americans see nothing else but an inferior element to be educated, to be protected, to serve afterward, with their number and labor, in constituting a large American body without soul? If the Americans would treat the foreigners as their equals—if they would respect their nationality—if their high principles of democracy, of humanity and of education, added to the economic fortunes by them possessed, would aid and elevate the less fortunate foreigners—if they would see in them instead of *American Citizens* prey of political parties—foreign citizens respectful of the laws and of the customs of their adopted country (because a citizen is a *good citizen* either in New York, London, Paris or Rome)—then, among *true Americans* and foreigners, political and social ties would be more sincere and stronger than the present, founded on friendly relations, on the coöperation of labor and on the reciprocal help for their own common welfare and that of humanity.

The American institutions would not walk on the mined territory of the *hyphen* and the foreign collectivity would be spared the suffering, the tragedy which now troubles the soul of the German-Americans.

I think that among the immense horrors, the European war has been a great lesson to the United States. It has placed them before the abyss in which they were precipitating and which has been excavated by their own hands: that of proceeding to denationalize the people who can never abandon their *most obscure impulses, the original qualities of their mind* and in which the spirit of superiority shown by the Americans and the differences of treatment at disadvantage to· the foreigners, exasperate their nationalism to a fanatic pitch. Better few good Americans of certain, immovable faith, than many *naturalized* on which you cannot depend in the hour of defense.

New York City　　AGOSTINA DE BIASI

We never expected to hear Oklahoma disclaim credit for any legislative innovation, as in this letter:

In your able and interesting "Both Sides of a Debate," in The Independent for January 24, occurs this statement: "The first state to establish the office (of Public Defender) was Oklahoma, in 1911."

This is "news" to your Oklahoma readers. It is true that Dr. J. H. Stolper, in 1911-12, attorney for Kate Barnard, Commissioner of Charities, assumed this title, but it was mere assumption. The office of Public Defender has never, nor does it now exist, in the state of Oklahoma.

Okmulgee, Oklahoma　　E. RISOR

Our correspondent seems to have overlooked the fact, however, that in March, 1911, the Legislature of Oklahoma did pass an act creating the office of Public Defender of the State of Oklahoma to be appointed by the Commissioner of Charities and Correction (Section 8101 of the Revised Laws of Oklahoma as amended by chapter 25 of the Laws of 1911). The bill was vetoed by the Governor, but it was claimed that the veto was too late, and that the bill became a law without the Governor's approval. The existence of the office has, in fact, been recognized by the County Court of Okmulgee County, by the Criminal Court of Appeals, and by the Supreme Court of the State (33 Okla., 526).

It is true that the office as constituted in Oklahoma differs widely from the familiar type seen in Los Angeles, for it deals only with suits involving "minor orphans, defectives, dependents and delinquents" and with "such other duties as the Commissioner of Charities and Corrections may authorize."

A letter which we quoted in this department on January 17 included the sentence: "If he is sincere we can respect the antagonist quite as much as the contagonist." But the rector of Saint Mary's School objects to the way our correspondent coins the word.

If you must do it, please do not bridize. Try *synagonist.* GEORGE W. LAY
Raleigh, North Carolina

INSURANCE

CONDUCTED BY W. E. UNDERWOOD

BRIEF REVIEW OF FIRE INSURANCE

One hundred and thirty-five American and sixty foreign fire insurance companies reporting to the New York Insurance Department, representing a combined capital of $106,500,000, closed the year 1915 with combined total assets of $701,515,432, a gain in that item of $36,654,826; and a combined total net surplus of $281,329,493, representing a gain of $30,891,575.

During the year 1915 these 195 companies received total premiums of $353,919,023, a sum larger than the year before by $17,260,484; a total income of $382,860,875, a gain of $14,667,882—indicating, however, a decrease in income from sources other than premiums of $2,592,602. The total losses paid were $193,515,307, an increase over 1914 of $2,173,970. The total disbursements were $333,987,732, less than the previous year by $5,221,615.

There are perhaps 250 stock companies in the United States. That the average experience of those, the figures of which are quoted, is applicable to all it is impossible to assert, but the chances are rather in favor of than against that assumption. It is a vast improvement on the record of 1914, when the net surplus fell off nearly $6,000,000, and the ratio of losses paid to premiums received was between five and six per cent greater.

After paying $14,440,153 in dividends to stockholders, the total disbursements, including the losses as noted, were $333,987,732, as against a total income of $382,860,875, showing an excess of income of $48,873,143. Losses and dividends absorbed a total of $207,955,460, indicating that the total general expenses were $126,032,272, or about thirty-five per cent of the premium income. While this ratio of management expense will probably be found on more detailed calculation to show a decrease as compared to previous years, it is yet too high, due mainly perhaps to the inherent defects of the agency system as now organized and operated.

Thus far, 1916 has not opened auspiciously for the companies, if we are to judge their experience by such records as are kept of the general fire waste. According to the figures compiled daily by the *Journal of Commerce and Commercial Bulletin*, the fire loss in January this year exceeded that of the same month last year by $1,362,750, while the excess of February, 1916, over February, 1915, aggregated $11,670,000, the total of the two months, each year, being: 1916, $46,203,220; 1915, $33,161,370. This unevenness of experience, one year with another, is seemingly an ineradicable difficulty in the business of fire insurance, one which renders it more completely dependent on the laws of average than perhaps any other branch of insurance.

474

Out of these erratic fluctuations, in part, arise many of the insoluble problems of rate-making. There is no sort of dependable constancy in the loss factor. As may readily be concluded the only safety in computing premium income lies in using an experience covering the longest practicable period; the greater the number of years contributing it the better. The older and larger companies are better equipped to withstand these sudden and sometimes disastrous rises in the loss ratio. The income from their great invested assets is a second line of defense against violent assaults by fire, and enables them at the same time to pay good dividends to their stockholders and pile up heavy reserve and surplus funds. It is the lack of this resource which renders the success of new companies so precarious and places almost within the realm of speculation investments in their stocks.

A GLANCE AT THE LIFE INSURANCE FIELD

It is quite probable that the volume of new life insurance written this year in the United States will not only exceed the figures of 1915, but will greatly surpass all previous records, even those of the years immediately preceding 1905, when the Armstrong Committee investigation brought it close to a dead stop. Prior to that event, under the stimulus of extravagant commissions to agents, rebating and fascinating estimates of ten, fifteen and twenty-year deferred dividend bait, the year-end totals soared, the biggest companies leading the way with between $300,000,000 and $400,000,000 each. There were not so many companies then, but all save a few were operating under tremendous pressure and rolling up big totals.

Present conditions are immeasurably better. Business is more carefully written and will remain in force longer. Net gains in insurance in force now, regarded from a commercial viewpoint, should be worth two or three times their former value.

Before me lies a compilation of the principal items of 188 life companies

for the year ending December 31, 1915. Of these only six issued and were paid for more than $100,000,000 each. The companies and round amounts follow: Metropolitan, $256,000,000; New York Life, $228,000,000; Prudential, $195,000,000; Equitable, $164,000,000; Mutual Life, $160,000,000; Northwestern Mutual, $132,000,000. In addition, it must be noted that the Metropolitan and Prudential figures represent Ordinary business only, and that their Industrial totalled, respectively, $327,000,000 and $385,000,000.

Lacking sufficient time on this occasion to make a detailed computation of the figures of all the companies, I have been able to approximate the total and find that the 188 companies wrote new business in 1915 aggregating about $2,623,000,000. Large as this seems, it is equal to but $26.23 per capita of the population. If we estimate the insurable adult population at one-fifth the whole, it represents an average of but $131.15 apiece. From these facts one may easily imagine the acreage, as a farmer would say, yet open to intensive cultivation by our enterprising and ubiquitous friends, the insurance agents.

Many of the companies included in this résumé are superfluous. Perhaps three-fourths of them are under ten years of age. The greater number of them wrote between $1,000,000 and $2,000,000 new business, which means new premiums of from $30,000 to $60,000 a year. They are generally of the class using what are known as "first-year preliminary term" or "modified preliminary term" reserves, which, tho entirely safe, are below standard and only resorted to as a means of increasing the amount available for first-year expenses. It is difficult to believe that a large number of them will not be eliminated during the next ten years by competition, plus their own mediocre managements. It is my observation that there are many men connected with the lesser and newer life companies who have much to learn about life insurance management, men who will eventually land in occupations better suited to their abilities.

The promotion of new companies was a dull trade in 1915, confirming the impression prevalent for several years past that the investing public was growing cold to that line of speculation. A sum estimated at from $50,000,000 to $60,000,000 is alleged to have been lost by the stockholders in companies organized and retired within the past ten years. To this must be added other millions locked up in companies of the same period and class which are destined to failure of one sort or another—by which is meant flat insolvency or retirement by reinsurance.

Business and trade reports made at different times since this year commenced indicate increased activity for at least another twelvemonth, whether the European war does or does not cease within that period. The life companies and their agents are redoubling their efforts to improve the opportunities which are afforded by the prevailing trade expansion. They are estimating a volume of new business considerably in excess of that of 1915 and they realized the expectation in January and February.

EVOLUTION OF THE ACCIDENT BUSINESS

The outstanding feature at present in the evolutionary processes of the casualty business involves the changes which are taking place in the accident policy. Readers will understand that the use of the term casualty business is descriptive of that branch of insurance, multiple in its purposes, which provides indemnities by the same company against loss or damage thru accidental causes to the person (accident insurance), all forms of liability, breakage of plate glass, burglary and theft, etc. The personal accident policy has always provided a principal sum against accidental death in addition to weekly indemnities for accidental injuries.

For a number of reasons, the provision of the principal sum against death is losing its popularity with some companies. In some sections of the country losses due to this benefit are and have been inordinate. Much trouble under it is due to deaths by suicide. Compared with the cost of life insurance, $1000 of accident insurance is extremely small, not more than one-tenth on the average, and it has been satisfactorily settled in many cases that persons have deliberately loaded up with accident insurance preparatory to killing themselves. Generally, the matter has been so managed that the companies could not successfully defeat the claim.

Another impelling motive for the exclusion of the death indemnity from the accident contract results from the inclusion of that benefit of late in the policies of a number of life companies. Some of the latter are now doubling the amount of the life policy if death occurs as the result of violent and accidental means, the simple face being payable for natural death. In short, there are numerous evidences leading to the conclusion that the life companies will eventually cover everything now included in the accident policies.

W. A. D., Deer Creek, Ill.—Without prejudice to the other company you name, which in every respect is a most excellent one, after considering all the circumstances, I am of the opinion the Presbyterian Ministers' Fund would be the better choice. Assuming that you have dependents, I would not advise one in your profession on your salary to take a twenty-year endowment. If you are without dependents who need protection in the event of your death, the endowment is preferable. But if protection now is a consideration take two or two and a half times the amount of the proposed endowment in ordinary life. An endowment in the Fund for $1000 would cost you about $46 a year and have a final cash value of $1000. For about $44 a year you can get $2000 ordinary life which in twenty years will have a cash value of about $560. But you will have had double the amount of protection.

A Number of Things

by Edwin E. Slosson

One of the best source books in psychology is the personal column of the London *Times*. Here is a sample lesson:

WILL ANY DOG LOVER give TOWN HOME to fascinating mongrel-like, small, unshaved POODLE, 12 months? Unusually affectionate, intelligent. Follows to heel; sleeps out.—Circumstances only compel mistress to part.—Box R. 903, The Times.

One would think that under the circumstances the love and care here lavished upon a mongrel-like poodle had better be bestowed upon a small unshaved Belgian baby who might prove equally affectionate, intelligent and fascinating. But there's no accounting for tastes as the old lady said when she kissed the cow.

The "lost art of letter-writing" seems to be reviving under the influence of the war.

YOUNG ENGLISH WOMAN would be glad to CORRESPOND with lonely or wounded officers.—Box D.562, The Times.

FIELD OFFICER (in England) lonely, would greatly appreciate CORRESPONDENCE.—Box B.926, The Times.

A GIRL will Gladly WRITE cheerful LETTERS to a LONELY or WOUNDED OFFICER.—Box D.87, The Times.

LADY will WRITE CHEERFUL LETTERS to LONELY or WOUNDED OFFICER.—Reply L. Y. D., 48, Haymarket, W.

Now which do you suppose the lonely field officer wrote to, the lady, the woman or the girl?

GOLF.—Young wounded Officer desires to stay in country house (PAYING GUEST?) and have companion for golf.—Box S.940, The Times.

I'm glad that the young officer's wounds do not put him off his game, but what does this questionable paying guest mean by his intrusion?

WOULD any REGIMENT like as GIFT from a lady a little TAME WHITE PIG for a mascot? Two months old; hand fed; very affectionate.—Box D.565, The Times.

It's a long way to Tipperary.

Some said I was sacrilegious when in the issue of January 31 I ventured to suggest that Ezekiel might serve as a political platform. This surprised me because I had supposed that the prophets intended their sermons to have a political bearing and that they were not altogether out of date yet. But I am comforted to find that the editor of *Bible Study*, the monthly of the Bible Teachers' Training School, is not shocked by my remarks:

The Bible is a book of affairs. It is able to take care of itself. I like to see evidences that it is being used. I even think that the versatile writer of A Number of Things, in The Independent, will stimulate many to read Ezekiel for profit, and that perhaps his "take off" of the recent illustrious interpreters of the passage about Ezekiel's watchman may lead these gentlemen to study the context and discover how wide of the mark they came in their use of the same. Ezekiel does stand for preparedness there. But it is of a kind different from that advocated by the current interpretation. Read for yourself and see.

At a meeting of the authors and artists of France held in the Sorbonne to express their gratitude for the many forms of hospital and relief work supported by Americans, a poem written for the occasion by Mme. Daniel-Lesueur was recited by M. Mounet-Sully, the dean of the Comédie Française. I quote the first half of it, together with a translation which my son, Preston W. Slosson, has made for me.

AUX ÉTATS-UNIS D'AMÉRIQUE

Etats-Unis, creuset formidable des races!
Jeune univers, qui fleurit en tes espaces
Une nouvelle humanité,
Le monde en tes sillons lança tant d'énergie
Que ton Peuple naissant, moisson bientôt surgie,
Eut pour premier cri: "Liberté!"

Quel écho! quel frisson sur l'Océan sonore!
Notre France éblouie acclama ton aurore,
Ton drapeau fut notre drapeau.
Avant nos trois couleurs, voici tes treize étoiles!
Et voici, sur la nef où palpitent les voiles,
La Fayette avec Rochambeau.

Tu n'as pas oublié ton acte de naissance
Signé de ces deux noms. Car la reconnaissance,
Pesante au faible, est douce au fort.
Près du grand Washington, notre beau La Fayette
Avec sa martiale et fine silhouette,
Est sur ton cœur, comme un trésor.

Et tu t'es souvenue hier, quand sa Patrie
La France, menacée, indomptable, meurtrie,
Luttant pour vivre encor demain.
Reprenait pied à pied sa terre, ses collines,
Ses bois, ses prés sanglants, ses villes en ruines—
Vers elle, tu tendis la main.

Une main désarmée, une main pacifique.
Car l'équité du Neutre, ô loyale Amérique!
Est intacte en ta bonne foi.
Mais la pitié n'est pas contrebande de guerre.
Quand nos petits enfants souffrent, ils ont deux mères:
Une en France, l'autre—chez Toi.

TO THE UNITED STATES OF AMERICA

United States, world's melting pot thou art!
Young universe, that flowerest in each part
With fresh humanity;
The nations poured into thy furrows all their strength
That thy people, grown to harvest, might at length
Choose the watchword "Liberty"!

That cry resounded till the ocean shook,
France cheered thy dawn, and thine own colors took
In her bright flag to glow.
Lending the tricolor behold the thirteen stars,
And on swift ships beneath the groaning spars,
La Fayette and Rochambeau!

Remembrance of these friends cannot but last;
Only the weak lose memory of the past,
The strong do not forget.
Next to thy Washington, who may hold favored place
Within thy heart but he, with his fine martial face—
Our own good La Fayette?

Thou didst recall their homeland yesterday,
When fair France, menaced, stricken sore, at bay,
Struggled to breathe and stand;
Reconquering foot by foot her land, her hills, her wealds,
Her ruined towns, her desolated blood-drenched fields—
To her didst thou reach out thy hand.

An unarmed hand in peaceful friendship proffered;
No insult to neutrality is offered,
By that gesture proud and free.
But pity is not contraband of war. And thus
Our suffering children find two mothers; one with us;
The other is with thee.

The Mesopotamian Valley, up which the British expedition from the Persian Gulf has made its way, is, according to tradition, man's first—and last —paradise. But Tommy Atkins, toiling thru the sand under a blazing sun, fighting fleas and flies as well as Turks and Arabs, did not find the country Edenic. One night when the troops were trying to sleep one soldier was heard to say to another: "'Ere, Bill, if this is the Garden of Eden, I wonder what Adam and Eve did with these 'ere mosquitos a-buzzin' around 'em."

Ravenna. O. Feb 29th 1916
Editor of Independent. New York.
Dear Ed. You should have a heart to heart, fatherly talk with that man.Slosson.
He certainly was "spoiling white paper and mussing up the universe" when he wrote. "Anthology in a country church yard" as a rediculous criticism of Masters great work "Spoon River Anthology." He is ashamed of it himself, for he laid it to his defenseless wife, poor thing.
And, Dear Ed. You had better watch out, or he will be trying to break into print with that play he has written, which he is so modest (?) as to confess is not equal to the *best* of Shakespears work.
Do! do! hand him off Mr Editor if you can, or he will give us "a taste for annihilation."
Hopefully Yours
E. C. CARIS

There! I always get into trouble whenever I tell the truth. Nevertheless I stick to both points. My dream play was *not* equal to Shakespeare's best and my wife *did* dream the Spoon River poem. But I would remind the indignant correspondent that it was published, not as a literary criticism, but as a psychological curiosity. If "dreams go by contraries" we should infer that Mrs. Slosson's real opinion of Masters' masterpiece was quite the opposite. But what man can fathom a woman's mind, let alone his subliminal? .

The Germans claim to be the true disciples of Shakespeare. I wonder if they have read "Henry V:"

When lenity and cruelty play for a kingdom, the gentler gamester is the soonest winner.

I notice that the chauffeurs are more careful to blanket their engines in cold weather than the drivers are their horses. The machine does not arouse compassion like the animal, but somehow it gets more care.

The Independent

VOLUME LXXXVI

APRIL—JUNE
1916

INDEPENDENT CORPORATION
NEW YORK

THE INDEPENDENT

Index for Volume LXXXVI (April to June, 1916)

(Ed., Editorial; Week, The Story of the Week; Rev., Book Review; M. P., The Market Place; Pic., Picture)

The Independent

FOR SIXTY-SEVEN YEARS THE
FORWARD-LOOKING WEEKLY OF AMERICA

THE　　CHAUTAUQUAN
Merged with The Independent June 1, 1914

APRIL　　3,　　1916

OWNED AND PUBLISHED BY
THE INDEPENDENT CORPORATION, AT
119 WEST FORTIETH STREET, NEW YORK
WILLIAM B. HOWLAND, PRESIDENT
FREDERIC E. DICKINSON, TREASURER

WILLIAM HAYES WARD
HONORARY EDITOR

EDITOR: HAMILTON HOLT
ASSOCIATE EDITOR: HAROLD J. HOWLAND
LITERARY EDITOR: EDWIN E. SLOSSON

PUBLISHER: KARL V. S. HOWLAND

ONE YEAR, THREE DOLLARS

SINGLE COPIES, TEN CENTS

Postage to foreign countries in Universal Postal
Union, $1.75 a year extra; to Canada, $1 extra.
Instructions for renewal, discontinuance or
change of address should be sent two weeks
before the date they are to go into effect. Both
the old and the new address must be given.

We welcome contributions, but writers who
wish their articles returned, if not accepted,
should send a stamped and address envelope. No responsibility is assumed by The
Independent for the loss or non-return of
manuscripts, tho all due care will be exercised.

Entered at New York Post Office as Second
Class Matter

Copyright, 1916, by The Independent

Address all communications to
THE INDEPENDENT
119 West Fortieth Street, New York

CONTENTS

REMARKABLE REMARKS

SENATOR NEWLANDS—"Uncle Sam" is
a myth.

GEN. FUNSTON—I don't believe in swivel
chair campaigning.

BILLY SUNDAY—The world needs a
panic in religion.

SIR EDWARD CARSON—The real Irishman loves peace.

SENATOR THOMPSON—There are no idle
men in Kansas.

HERBERT KAUFMAN—Quit thinking with
dead men's minds.

JESS WILLARD—I am pretty well fixed
in this world's goods.

DAVID LLOYD-GEORGE—What you spare
in money you spill in blood.

THEODORE ROOSEVELT—Nothing is to be
hoped from the present Administration.

WOODROW WILSON—It is very difficult
to think when so many people are talking.

SENATOR CHAMBERLAIN—After this war
is over we shall not have a friend in the
world.

MAYOR MITCHEL—New York has been
too self-centered to have a real community spirit.

BONAR LAW—The Mother Country is
old, but the spirit of the British Empire
is young.

RUTH ST. DENIS—To be a good dancer
a man must have a certain amount of the
feminine in him.

PROF. BRANDER MATTHEWS—A high-
brow is a person who is educated beyond
his intelligence.

PROF. J. MCKEEN CATTELL—When we
embroider with gold braid we are likely to
bind with red tape.

ED. HOWE—The King of Belgium
amounts to about as little now as the king
in a pack of cards.

JUDGE JOHN S. SNOOK—My experience
in hearing divorce cases is that half the
trouble comes from money.

MARTIN W. BARR. M. D.—There are in
our country at least 328,000 mental and
moral defectives at large.

LORD NORTHCLIFFE—I never have hesitated to state my profound admiration for
the Germans as domestic servants.

VICE-PRESIDENT MARSHALL—As the
present writes of Abraham Lincoln, the
future will write of Woodrow Wilson.

MR. PURINTON'S
EFFICIENCY
QUESTION BOX

227. Mr. R. B. S., Washington. "Can you tell
me where I can get the necessary training to
become an efficiency engineer, so as to be the
best in my profession? This is what I most want
to become. I am a high school senior, nineteen
years of age."

The profession of efficiency engineer
is so new that methods for learning
it have not been standardized. Most of
the experts are men past thirty-five, who
have gradually evolved thru experience in
advertising, salesmanship, accountancy, or
other branches of business. You might follow this course; or else connect with a
firm of *good* experts in New York, Chicago,
or some other large city—see classified
business telephone directory for names, under title "Engineers" and sub-title "Efficiency."

Other suggestions. Write Efficiency Press
Syndicate, Woolworth Building, New York,
for a list of a dozen modern books on
Efficiency. Look over *The Efficiency Magazine*, 260 Broadway, New York. Investigate the Efficiency Society, 41 Park Row,
New York. Read my book, *Efficient Living*, obtainable from the Independent.
Watch these columns for future announcements.

228. Mr. R. E. O., New Jersey. "Is it possible
to develop leadership? I find that I am a very
good follower, but am never able to get my
views adopted. When I am with other men, I
follow their suggestions. Why can't I be a
leader?"

Perhaps you were not meant to be a
leader. Think what a bedlam this world
would be, if every man were a leader.
Never mind about getting your "views
adopted." Think rather, how to *act* on your
own *convictions*. Get a copy of my "Triumph of the Man Who Acts," carry it with
you, read and re-read it till you make it a
part of you. Study also Dr. Katherine
Blackford's book, *Analyzing Character*,
and find where your weakness lies. The
books can be had from the Efficiency Press
Syndicate, 233 Broadway, New York City.

229. Miss A. H., New York City. "Your article of some months ago on 'The Efficient Man's
Money' so interested me that I should like to
get on an efficient financial basis myself. Will
you kindly suggest a proper division for a $1400
income? I am a college graduate, have few social duties, no one dependent on me; am obliged
to dress well during business hours."

Local and personal conditions always
preclude an exact standardizing of a yearly
budget. We should say, however, that yours
might be, roughly, as follows:

Clothing, $300; board, $260; lodging,
$180; church and philanthropy, $140; savings and insurance, $350; books and mag-
azines, pleasure and recreation, $70; car-
fare, laundry, upkeep and incidentals, $100.
Total, $1400.

230. Mr. O. A. S., Texas. "(a) Should a boy
decide what he wants to be and do in life before
he leaves high school? (b) If so, how shall he
come to a decision?"

(a) Vocational experts differ on this
point. Some boys know intuitively their
life work, at ten years of age; and certain
great men did not find their life work till
they were past thirty. The best course seems
to be for a boy to learn all there is to learn
about vocational guidance, and make such
tests for himself as are practicable, while
still in the high school; then to have some
trial experiences in real life before determining finally what his career shall be. Get
three or four good books on vocational guidance, study them carefully—then ask us
more questions if you like.

(b) See answer to query No. 197 in Efficiency Question Box for January 31, 1916.
Write these experts, and consult with any
that appeal to you.

The Independent

VOLUME 86   APRIL 3, 1916   NUMBER 3513

© International Film Service

TO SWEEP OUT THE MEXICAN CANYONS

A PORTABLE MACHINE GUN OF THE SORT THAT THE PUNITIVE FORCES IN MEXICO WILL USE AGAINST VILLA AND HIS BANDIT TROOPS. THE BENET-
MERCIER GUNS NOW IN USE, ONE OF WHICH "JAMMED" AT COLUMBUS, ARE TO BE REPLACED BY A MECHANICAL-RECOIL
TYPE, THE VICKERS GUN, BUT THE WAR DELAYED DELIVERY TO THE UNITED STATES ARMY

NO INTERCOURSE WITH PLEDGE-BREAKERS

IF the Channel steamer "Sussex" was struck by a German torpedo, how can we trust Germany longer?

The "Sussex" is purely a passenger vessel. She mounts no guns, carries no munitions. Her 436 passengers were largely women and children.

The "Sussex" was not warned. She was not ordered to stop. The noncombatants on board were given no opportunity to seek safety.

If she was struck by a torpedo—and the evidence all points in that direction, tho the German evidence should be heard before the question is finally adjudged—there are no extenuating circumstances. None of the excuses that the German Government has concocted from time to time in defense of its submarine warfare is here present. The attack upon the "Sussex" is a plain violation of the principles of international law and the rules of war as interpreted by the rest of the world. But it is more than that. It is a clear infraction of the rules which Germany has agreed to in the course of the submarine controversy with this country.

If it was a torpedo, Germany has broken her pledged word to the United States. It makes no difference whether any American life was lost or not. There were Americans on board. As President Wilson has repeatedly pointed out to the German Government, putting American lives in jeopardy is a violation of American rights just as much as the taking of American lives. It is only a matter of degree. Murder is one crime; but attempted murder is another.

When one nation does not keep its word solemnly given to another nation, by that act the fabric of friendly intercourse is torn asunder.

We can have no intercourse with those who pledge us their word and falsely break it.

PEACE—ON WHAT TERMS?

THERE are rumors of coming peace in the air. Where their source and what their authority nobody knows. But we know that they spring from the secret wish of all the peoples that this awful era be brought to an end. The war is so disastrous to all concerned that there will be but comparatively little difference in the long run between the victor and the vanquished. Neither side can possibly gain enough to pay for another year of war. Any reasonable peace terms accepted now would be better than any future triumph.

In every belligerent country the people are beginning to ask the question, which should have been answered at the beginning, "What are we fighting for?" No definite answer has been vouchsafed by any government, so the people are beginning to answer it for themselves, and they answer it so variously that their peace terms sometimes overlap their enemy's. That is to say the most moderate factions of both sides have not merely met, but passed each other. For instance, some Germans are willing to concede more favorable terms than some Englishmen are determined to demand and *vice versa*. On the other hand, the extremists on both sides are getting more extravagant in their demands and so further apart every day.

Let us consider some of the peace terms which have been voiced in England and Germany. Disregarding extravagant and irresponsible utterances, let us take as a specimen of the extreme British terms the demands formulated by the *National Review* as the minimum to be imposed on Germany in case she is defeated. These are in brief that Belgium be fully compensated for all losses direct or indirect, and granted $2,500,000,000 besides; that Russia, France and Serbia be fully compensated on the same scale; that all territories acquired by Germany anywhere in the world be confiscated; that Prussia be permanently crushed and crippled; that German trade be rigidly restricted, and that those responsible for the war be publicly executed.

Now whether these demands are just or unjust need not concern us because they are obviously incompatible and impossible. No one nation even in the light of its prosperity could pay for all the losses, direct and indirect, of all the belligerent countries, and certainly not Germany if deprived of both her colonies and commercial privileges. It will be impossible to get any money out of Germany unless she is allowed to make money either thru foreign commerce or by the development of her African possessions. There is not enough gold in Germany or the world to pay such an indemnity. It could only be paid in goods, that is, thru foreign commerce.

The permanent restriction of German trade is the question that receives most attention in the British press. It is proposed, for instance, to shut out German shipping from any ports of the British empire, to prohibit the importation of any German-made goods even thru neutral countries, to require passports of all travelers so that Germans may be "treated like lepers" wherever they go, to confiscate German patents and the funds left by Cecil Rhodes to educate German boys at Oxford, etc. The movement has received official recognition and delegates of the British Government are now conferring with the representatives of France to devise some form of commercial alliance to follow the present military alliance. This action has alarmed the free-traders, but Premier Asquith has endeavored to allay their anxiety by stating that no measures involving a break with England's traditional policy will be taken without parliamentary approval. It will be interesting to see what measures can be devised that will not violate the principle of free-trade.

It will in any case be difficult for the Allies to cripple German trade without crippling their own. To take only one instance, Antwerp has been brought to rank as one of the world's greatest seaports largely thru German money and German trade. If these were shut out from Antwerp it would be a greater financial blow to Belgium than the German invasion.

When Premier Asquith was recently questioned in

Parliament by Mr. Snowdon and Mr. Trevelyan as to the British terms of peace he replied by repeating what he had said at the beginning of the war:

We shall never sheath the sword, which we have not lightly drawn, until Belgium recovers in full measure all, and more than all, that she sacrificed; until France is adequately secured against menace of aggression; until the rights of the smaller nationalities of Europe are placed upon an unassailable foundation, and until the military domination of Prussia is wholly and finally destroyed.

This naturally was too indefinite to satisfy his interlocutors, who wanted these aims translated into concrete terms. In default, then, of any official interpretation of the Premier's statement we may consider that given by the Right Honorable C. F. G. Masterman, who is believed to express the government's views. According to Mr. Masterman the British minimum must include the following: Germany to pay an indemnity to Belgium sufficient to rebuild her cities, restore her industries and compensate for her disabled and dead; France to receive Alsace-Lorraine, and all territory up to the Rhine as well as an indemnity; Denmark to get back Schleswig; German, Austrian and Russian Poland to be reunited under the Czar; Italy to get the whole of Italia Irredenta; the Turkish empire to be partitioned; Bosnia and Herzegovina given to Serbia; the German fleet sunk or divided up among the Allies; all the Zeppelins to be burned; and the German colonies to be given to those who have conquered them, Australia, New Zealand and South Africa.

These demands are certainly moderate compared with some we have mentioned, but there are Englishmen who would offer their beaten foe more generous terms still. They talk of the necessity of England's coming out "with clean hands" without acquiring any territorial or trade advantages, and they would have Germany given back her colonies and her shipping admitted on equal terms to British ports.

This group of British conciliationists may be matched on the other side of the fence by the *Bund Neues Vaterland*, which is opposed to the annexation of any conquered territory by Germany and ridicules the idea that any permanent weakening of England and Russia would be an advantage to Germany. The New Fatherland Union petitioned for the suppression of the annexationist movement that is championed by a combination of six agricultural and industrial associations. These associations protest against a premature peace and assert that, since the enemies of Germany declare that she must be wiped out from the list of great powers, the safety of the empire can only be assured by the extension of its bounds to include territory of strategic and economic importance on each side. In order to secure an outlet to the Atlantic they desire the acquisition of the French coast as far as the Somme, also the fortresses of Verdun and Belfort, the chief coal and iron districts of France would thus pass into the hands of Germans and France would be left to indemnify the proprietors. Belgium is to form part of the same economic, postal and financial system as the rest of the empire. This would ensure the prosperity of German industries. To satisfy her agricultural needs Germany must annex the Russian border provinces on the Baltic and to the south.

Some of the German papers go beyond this and demand the annexation of Belgium; the surrender by England of Egypt, Uganda and Nigeria; India to become a German protectorate; Russia to lose Finland, Poland, Bessarabia and Crimea.

Such extreme demands as these are, like those of the *National Review* on the British side, not to be taken seriously. The real German minimum is undoubtedly much more moderate. What it is cannot of course be told exactly, but it has been pretty clearly intimated more than once that the German Government is willing to make peace on some such terms as these: the evacuation of Belgium and France; the cession or purchase of Belgian and French Congo; the restoration of the Kingdom of Poland under a German prince; the transfer to Germany of the Russian debt to France; the establishment of the freedom of the seas for commerce, travel, mails and cable communication in time of peace and war under international guarantee; and equality of trading rights in all ports and colonies. It has been recently rumored that Germany is willing to cede part of Lorraine to France, to grant autonomy to Alsace and to pay an indemnity to Belgium.

Such, then, are opposing demands in both their extreme and more moderate forms. On their face value of course they seem irreconcilable, but we must remember that "nothing is ever served as hot as it is cooked." Besides it is apparent that the objects which the opposing parties most earnestly desire are not the same. The Allies are most intent upon getting the Germans out of France and Belgium. Germany is most concerned over her future opportunities for commercial and colonial expansion.

But so long as neither party is clearly victorious and both parties fear that it will be taken as a sign of weakening to mention the conditions of peace, there seems to be no hope of getting them even to consider the possibility of coming to an agreement.

NO TASK FOR CONGRESS

THE United States Government is a big shipper on American railroads. What it ships is not freight, but mail matter. This is a distinction, but hardly an essential difference. Why should there be any difference in the manner of fixing the rates to be paid for the transportation of the two kinds of matter?

In the old days, the railroads themselves determined how much the shippers of freight should pay for the carriage of their freight. This came in time to be recognized as manifestly unfair to the shippers. For there was a perfectly natural tendency on the part of the railroads to charge "all the traffic would bear." The Interstate Commerce Commission was accordingly entrusted with the final determination of freight rates.

But in the case of mail matter the old condition remains, tho in even more unfair form. For the rates are determined by the shipper. The railroads have nothing whatever to say about it. The rates of railway mail pay are decreed by Congress.

This is flagrantly unjust. The party that pays the bills should not in fairness and good conscience be the one also to make the prices; any more than the public servant should be the one to set the price upon the service it renders to the public.

The matter is brought concretely before the country by a rider upon the Post Office Appropriation bill now before Congress changing the basis of fixing the compensation of the railroads for carrying the mails from one of weight to one of space. The purpose of it is to cut down the amount paid to the railroads. That the change would be an unfair one is one good argument against the rider. But a more fundamental argument against it is that Congress ought not to fix the rates at all.

The case was set forth convincingly before the Senate Committee on Post Offices and Post Roads by President Rea of the Pennsylvania Railroad:

Turn the whole matter over to the Interstate Commerce Commission. Let the commission study it carefully and then advise Congress as to what changes are required in the method of pay or the rates in order to do justice to both the railroads and the Post Office Department. The question of pay for carrying the mails and parcel post has become a most intricate study in rates. The Interstate Commerce Commission is the nation's expert body on rates, and was created by Congress to serve that purpose. It is better fitted than any other branch of the Government to reach a fair conclusion. Both the railroads and the Government, I am sure, would be willing to abide by its judgment.

Another aspect of the case was presented by President Smith of the New York Central Lines:

The Government is all powerful. It can inflict upon the railroads rates that will be unprofitable to them. It can compel the roads to carry business at a loss. Whatever losses are forced upon the roads, however, will be felt by the travelling public, the shippers and the stockholders. The railroad managers are merely trustees. We are here to protect thousands of owners of these properties. If the Government insists upon getting service below cost to the railroads, this money, taken out of the funds of the roads, must be met somewhere and somehow. Either the freight or passenger service must bear the burden, or else the stockholders. All that we ask is fair play. The Government has intrusted other problems of railroad management to the Interstate Commerce Commission and it should, we think, entrust this one to that body for fair consideration.

The request of the railroads is reasonable, logical and fair. Congress ought not to fix railroad rates—even for the carriage of the mails.

CALIFORNIA REPEATS

CALIFORNIA refuses to be silent about one absorbing topic—California.

The Great Northwest, the Prairies, the Electric City, the Historic South, gather themselves together, burst forth in a gigantic fair, dominate for a few months the papers and magazines and travel bureaus, flood the land with pictures and real estate pabulum, and then, lingering for a little time in the movies and Chautauquas, sink back into that comparative obscurity which, in this land of universal self-exploitation, overtakes everything which does not advertise extravagantly.

Not so California.

Not only did she insist on the double-barreled publicity of two expositions in 1915, but she has now begun all over again. The Panama-California Exposition at San Diego, adding "International" to its name and inheriting some of the finest exhibits from the defunct Panama-Pacific Exposition, has been reopened, with more of the gala excitement which seems to be a habit on the coast, to run thruout 1916.

Perhaps the city by the Harbor of the Sun hopes thus to come fully into its heritage, now that the competition of its big neighbor to the north is ended. But will Los Angeles sit supinely by and let its little rival take the lion's share of the nation's attention for another year? We begin to suspect that 1915 saw the beginning of an endless series of expositions, and that California will never break her habit of inviting the world to peek into her mirror.

ON THE CONTRARY, GENTLEMEN

WILLIAM H. TAFT, Elihu Root, Joseph H. Choate, and Simeon E. Baldwin do not approve of the appointment of Louis Brandeis to the United States Supreme Court. They feel it their painful duty to declare that in view of his "reputation, character and professional career" he is not a "fit person" to sit on that exalted bench.

We respectfully dissent—and vigorously. Louis Brandeis is an eminently fit person to be a member of the highest court in the land. And for three reasons:

Because of his reputation for fearlessness, sanity and clear-headedness.

Because of his character, notable for integrity, unselfishness and human sympathy.

Because of his professional career, marked by antagonism to predatory special interests, devotion to the public welfare, loyalty to the interests of the weak and the opprest.

It is true Mr. Brandeis is not a conservative (which is probably what his distinguished critics really meant). But just for that reason he will find himself thoroly at home side by side with such men as Mr. Justice Holmes and Mr. Justice Hughes. The Supreme Court needs just such a man.

A REPUBLIC AGAIN

IN our editorial of December 20 last on "The Betrayal of the Republic" we express the opinion and the hope that the Chinese republicans would not tamely submit to Yuan's usurpation of the throne. We are glad to see that they did act quickly and effectively. With six provinces in open revolt and a republican army marching toward Peking, Yuan Shih-kai has discovered that he had misinterpreted the will of the people—as exprest by his sycophants—so he cancels his former decree restoring the monarchy and signs himself president instead of emperor.

As a matter of fact he is neither president or emperor. He is plain dictator, or, in the primary sense of the word, a tyrant, that is, an illegal autocrat. This would not necessarily imply that he is a bad man or the wrong man for the place. The Greek tyrants were often true patriots. "The tyrant of the Chersonese was Freedom's best and bravest friend," says Byron. But for most of them the possession of unlimited power proved too much of a temptation, so they exercised it "tyrannically" and tried to pass it down to their descendants. This, we fear, is the case with Yuan Shih-kai. To oppose him is to risk one's head if within his reach, and his assumption of imperial state is meaningless unless he designed to fasten upon China a new dynasty.

If Yuan were only trustworthy he would be just the man to guide China in her transition stage from despotism to republicanism, for he is possest of remarkable administrative ability and political skill. But his shifty past will prevent any one from putting confidence in the sincerity of his new turnabout.

The one encouraging feature about it all is that Yuan both in assuming and in relinquishing the crown takes pains to explain that he is acting in accordance with the will of the people as he understands it. He does not claim, like the Kaiser, to rule by divine right, nor does he question the right of the people to depose him for unfaithfulness to duty.

The Chinese revolutionists have the best of authority for their revolt. The ideal of government, according to Confucius, is

The display of justice, the realization of sincerity, the exposition of errors, the exemplification of benevolence and the discussion of courtesy and the manifestation of all the fundamental virtues. If any ruler, having position and power, will not follow this course he should be driven out by the people as a public enemy.

A people in whom such principles are thoroly engrained ought to make good material for a republic. We hope that they will continue without faltering along the road they have entered upon until finally they realize the Golden Age prophesied by Confucius, when the people shall rule, police be unnecessary, and peace reign thruout the world.

THE RUSSIAN DRIVE

ON the western front the spring campaign began with a German offensive. On the eastern front the Russians have taken the offensive. In France the Germans are confining their attack to the fortress of Verdun, but on the other side the Russians have assaulted the German entrenchments at no less than four points of the 700-mile line between Riga and Rumania. This line represents the high-water mark of the German invasion of Russia last fall. It was evidently chosen in advance as the most defensible position attainable, and each army halted as it drew up on the line like a company of soldiers forming for inspection. At points where some German troops had got ahead of the others they were drawn back to the lines. This line, except for local irregularities, runs almost straight north and south from the Dvina to the Pruth. It is therefore very nearly the shortest distance between these two points, and is shorter by a third than the line which the Germans and Austrians would have had to defend if they had stayed within their own national boundaries. That is to say, they have shortened their front instead of lengthening it by their invasion of Russia, notwithstanding the fact that the upper end has been extended 200 miles northward. The German line was so drawn as to include most of the railroad running north to Petrograd, so they have a railroad not far behind their front, while on the Russian side the only north and south railroad is 150 miles east of their front.

But while the line along which the Germans established their winter quarters was, on the whole, excellently adapted for defensive purposes, they failed at two points to secure strategic positions, as may be seen from the map upon another page. These weak places are near the ends of the line. At the southern end the Austrians were not able to free their country altogether from the invaders. The Russians held on stoutly to the corner of Galicia north of Dniester and to the fortress of Rovno, just inside the Russian frontier. On the northern end of the line the Germans were not able to capture the important cities of Riga and Dvinsk. The German front makes a curve around these cities, tho between them the line reaches up to the Dvina River at Jacobstadt and Friedrichstadt.

Now, what the Russians have done is simply to strike at these two defective sectors in the German line of defense. They have attacked on the southern end in Galicia

and on the northern end at Jacobstadt as well as south of Dvinsk. If the Russians succeed in the South they may be able to reinvade Bukovina and Galicia, in which case Rumania might join with them in an attack upon Hungary. If the Russians succeed in the north the Germans may be compelled to evacuate the Baltic provinces.

It is, of course, too early to determine the strength of the Russian offensive. They have gained at all points, but that simply demonstrates that the German front trenches, like any other, can be taken if enough men and ammunition can be brought against them. Of men Russia has no lack, and her supply of ammunition has been replenished during the winter from Japan and the United States.

On the other hand, the Germans have presumably withdrawn from the Russian front for use in France all the men they think can be spared without letting the Russians thru. But unless the Germans have changed their tactics they will not remain behind their entrenchments until they are routed out by the Russians, but will prefer to take the offensive even against heavy odds, because this enables them to choose their own time and battlefield. If their attack on Verdun, whether successful or not, has sufficiently disarranged the plans of the Allies, so that their spring drive has to be postponed, the Germans will have a chance to make an attack on the Russian side or at some other point in the French line. According to the military correspondent of the London *Times*, the Germans have 118 divisions on the western front. Now there have been reported as engaged at Verdun only eighteen or twenty divisions. Where the rest are or what they are held in reserve for, is a matter of surmise.

So far the campaign of 1916 opens in the same way as the campaigns of 1914 and 1915, that is, with the Germans on the offensive in the west and on the defensive in the east. If the present campaign follows the same course as the others, we may expect to see the Germans shortly becoming less active in France and more active in Russia. Formerly they were able to shuttle their troops back and forth from one front to the other as needed, because there was no coordination between the Allies. Now, however, the operations of the Allied armies are conducted in accordance with the plans of a joint staff at Paris, so they should be able to combine their efforts and exert a crushing pressure upon the Central Powers.

NEXT YEAR!

THE half million men of New York state who voted for woman suffrage last fall are likely to have another chance next year. The bill providing for another referendum on the constitutional amendment has already passed the Assembly by a vote of more than three to one. It has been withheld from vote in the Senate by a recalcitrant party leader. But this Mrs. Partington can hardly sweep back the sea. Suffrage is becoming too popular a cause to make it healthy for politicians to oppose it.

The bill must pass one more legislature, after this one. Then the people—no, the men—will have a chance at the question.

There is no doubt of the outcome. The tide is making fast.

THE STORY OF THE WEEK

The Pursuit of Villa
It was asserted at the beginning of last week that Villa and his band were surrounded and would be captured within a few days. They were in the vicinity of Namiquipa, with Carranza forces on the east and on the south, while our troops were advancing from the north. The bandit leader could escape only by way of passes thru the mountains westward. General Calles had promised to guard these. On his way southward Villa had left thirty of his wounded men, who were found by our troops. His forces were in several bands. One of them held up and robbed a train at Moctezuma, eighty-five miles northeast of Namiquipa. Another was attacked and defeated by General Cano, of the Carranza army. At the end of the week it was expected at Washington and by Carranza's War Minister that Villa would soon be forced to surrender. He had withdrawn westward into a canyon. But it was admitted that the country was one with which he had been familiar for many years, and that it presented many difficulties to a pursuing force. Two of the eight aeroplanes that started from Columbus with our troops went astray, but both aviators were rescued. One of them had been alone in the desert for eighty-four hours.

For a time there was much anxiety because of reports and apparently authoritative assertions that parts of Carranza's army had revolted and gone over to Villa. It was known also that many of the Carranza soldiers in the north were recently under Villa's command, and had come to Carranza in response to his offer of amnesty, a small sum of money for each man, and free transportation to his home if he should choose to go there. Some were deserting because they were paid in Mexican money which is now worth, in gold, only 6 per cent of its face value. On the 22d it was declared in reports from Columbus and elsewhere that General Luis Herrera, with 2000 men, had turned from Carranza and joined Villa. Herrera was recently military governor of Chihuahua, but had been removed from this office for misbehavior. He is well known in the north, where he and his brother, Maclovio, served under Madero and for a time were with Villa. When our forces took possession of Vera Cruz, he issued a bitter anti-American proclamation, urging all Mexicans to drive out the invaders. The story about his alleged revolt said that it followed a banquet in Chihuahua City, at which he read the old proclamation and remarked that he had not changed his mind.

But other Carranza officers promptly declared that Herrera was still loyal to the First Chief. Such testimony was given by Enriquez, the civil governor of Chihuahua, and on the 23d Herrera, in a telegram to General Gavira, at Juarez, asked that officer to deny emphatically in his name the "rumor circulated by reactionaries" that he had gone over to Villa. There were reports, however, that he opposed the admission of American troops, and it was thought at Washington that his attitude was not wholly satisfactory.

Along the border there was some uneasiness. The people of Presidio, Texas, across the line from Ojinaga, appealed to our forces for protection. And telegrams were sent to members of Congress from Douglas, on the border in Arizona. Disquieting reports from Tampico led our government to send the battleship "Kentucky" to that port.

The Question at Washington
On the day when the report about Herrera was denied, Mr. Johnson, of South Dakota, read in the Senate a telegram from a constituent who offered 100 volunteers for service in Mexico. Senator Stone said that this action was ill-advised, as the situation in Mexico was somewhat critical. Men who sent such telegrams ought to know that the enlistment of 20,000 men, for the regular army, had recently been authorized. The telegram should, in his opinion, have been turned over to the War Department. Senator Smoot said he had sent to the department several of the same kind which he had received from Utah. Senator Sherman, of Illinois, who had introduced a resolution authorizing the President to call for 50,000 volunteers, complained when objection to consideration of it was made, saying that if the blood of our soldiers should hereafter cry to us from the sands of Mexico we should remember this delaying action in the Senate. On the same day Mr. Scott, of Pennsylvania, introduced in the House a resolution calling for an appropriation of $50,000 to be used in offering a reward for Villa's body.

Mr. Wilson and the Cabinet decided that it was not necessary to seek the aid of the militia. Secretary Lansing said to the press that alarming stories had been circulated by persons who desired intervention. They could have no other purpose than to inflame the minds of the Mexican people. It was known in Washington that our government believed that these tales were spread abroad by persons having property interests in Mexico. Secretary Baker said that no hostile shot had been fired at our troops. Some said that the story about Herrera had been started by George C. Carothers, who for two years was with Villa as a representative of the State Department, but Mr. Carothers, now in El Paso, published a denial.

In the Senate on the 24th there was a bitter debate. Mr. Borah read a telegram from an attorney in Douglas, Arizona, named Richardson, saying that Carranza had 3000 cavalry and forty cannon very near that town, with 7000 more not far away. The place was not defended, and he called for help. Mr. Stone denounced the Sherman resolution for 50,000 volunteers, and criticized the reading of such telegrams, remarking that if a man were obsessed with the idea that he was running for the Presidency he was apt to indulge in vain delusions. Many persons in and out of Mexico were trying to excite and mislead the Mexican people by inducing them to believe that

STILL FARTHER INTO MEXICO

Using Casas Grandes as an advanced base, the American troops in pursuit of Villa have been thrown out in fan-shape to the south in the attempt to catch the outlaw before he can reach the mountains. He was thought to be trapped near Namiquipa, but seems to have defeated the Carranzistas there and to have broken thru the ring of pursuers. Col. Dodd is keeping his cavalry hot on Villa's trail

the United States would attack the sovereignty of Mexico and take its territory. But the President by proclamation, and Congress by resolution, had disavowed such a purpose. Mr. Sherman, in his opinion, ought not to have introduced a resolution which was virtually a threat. He believed, as the President and Secretary Baker did, that our troops were not in danger.

That night, the President, over his signature, issued a statement. He had asked the news agencies, he said, to assist the Administration in keeping before the people of this country and the distrest and sensitive people of Mexico our agreement with Carranza and the sole purpose of the expedition. He desired to impress upon both peoples the fact that the expedition was simply a punitive measure, aimed solely at the elimination of the marauders who raided Columbus. He warned our people that there were persons all along the border actively engaged in originating and circulating rumors of the most sensational and disturbing character, wholly unjustifiable by the facts. The object of this traffic in falsehood was to create intolerable friction between the two governments, and to bring about intervention in the interest of certain American owners of Mexican properties. They could not be successful so long as sane and honorable men were in control of our government, but unnecessary bloodshed might result and the relation between the two governments might be embarrassed. Our people should know the sinister and unscrupulous influences that were afoot, and be on their guard against crediting any story coming from the border. Those disseminating the news should test the source and authenticity of every such report.

The Republican senators in conference considered a resolution declaring that no effort to protect Americans on the border should be spared, but took no definite action. Mr. Richardson's telegram from Douglas has been denounced by the Mayor of Douglas and the local Chamber of Commerce as a falsehood.

Passage of the Army Bill

The House bill for reorganizing and enlarging the army, known as the Hay bill, was passed last week by a vote of 402 to 2, the two members in the negative being Meyer London, of New York, Socialist, and Frederick A. Britten, Republican, of Illinois, who explained that, in his opinion, the bill did not go far enough. Mr. Kahn's amendment, making the enlarged army 220,000 men instead of 140,000, which had been lost in committee of the whole by a vote of 103 to 183, was rejected again, but the final and decisive vote of 191 to 213 showed so small a majority against it that the coming compromise in conference (after the passage of the Senate bill) will probably provide for more than 140,000 men. The number in the Senate bill is 178,000. Party lines were not observed, for on this amendment 34 Republicans voted against an army of 220,000, and 33 Democrats for it.

By an amendment the Hay bill's term of enlistment was shortened. It provides that after one year of honorable and efficient service an enlisted man may be furloughed to the regular army reserve for six years. In the Hay bill the term was three years, with four in the reserve. There is also a new provision authorizing the President to call out this reserve (which in four years will amount to 60,000 men) without first getting the consent of Congress. By another amendment authority is given for detailing officers of the regular army as instructors at any school or college where a cadet corps of more than 100 students is maintained. The conditions are that the student shall have three hours a week of training for two years, and five hours a week for the succeeding two years. After graduation he serves for six months with the regular army and then is placed in the officers' reserve, bound to respond to a call at any time within ten years. It is estimated that in this way an officers' reserve of 50,000 will be created. Our government is authorized, by another amendment, to procure a supply of tools and drawings that would be required for the immediate manufacture of arms and ammunition sufficient for the army, and to keep a list of manufacturing plants available for the production of such supplies. All provision for appropriations or inquiry relating to a nitrate plant were stricken out, and the Senate's plan for a volunteer army, resembling ex-Secretary Garrison's Continental Army of 400,000, was rejected.

The Senate, with only two dissenting votes, has passed a bill which doubles the number of West Point cadets. Senator Works, in a speech last week, opposed any increase of the army or the navy, saying that the plea for increased defenses came from capitalists and the newspapers they had subsidized. By a vote of 58 to 23 the Senate has passed a bill authorizing the expenditure of $11,000,000 for the purchase or construction of a government armor plate factory.

© *Underwood & Underwood*

THEY'RE FOOT-SLOG-SLOGGING IT THRU MEXICO

The first part of the march thru Chihuahua was over country like this, hard going for both men and horses. Rutted rails thru the sand are the only roads for the motor trucks which bring up supplies from the base at Columbus

Fires and Storms

Fires in southern cities last week caused a loss of not less than $11,500,000 and deprived 14,000 persons of their homes. On the 21st, at Paris, Texas, a fire that started in a cotton compress quickly made a path three or four blocks wide to the residential district. Thirty blocks of buildings were burned, and of 140 business structures only fifteen were left standing. Virtually the entire business section was destroyed, and with it the main part of the residential section. Only one life was lost, but the property loss was $5,000,000. Their homes were taken from 8000 persons. The care of these presented a difficult problem, because all the hotels, restaurants and grocery stores had been burned. Paris takes its water from a storage lake, six miles away. It is brought to the city by electrical force. But the electric power plant was burned, and with it the central fire station.

On the following day, a fire in Augusta, Georgia, starting in the elevator shaft of a drygoods store, swept over an area of one and one-quarter square miles, destroying ten business blocks and twenty blocks of residences. Among the buildings burned was St. Paul's Episcopal Church, 135 years old, and the homes of the two local newspapers. One life was lost, and the property loss was $5,000,000, including $2,000,000 worth of cotton. There are 3000 homeless residents.

In Nashville, Tennessee, on the 22d, a burning ball of yarn thrown by a boy into dry grass on a vacant lot started a fire that swept over thirty-five residence blocks, destroyed 600 buildings, and caused a loss of $1,500,000. Here 3000 persons lost their homes. The 1400 pupils in a school were saved by the fire drill only a short time before the destruction of their school house. Four churches were burned.

It was also on the 22d that a hurricane swept across four states in the Middle West. At first there was an electric storm. This was followed by sleet and snow. Ten persons were

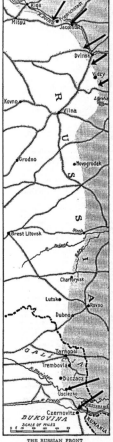

THE RUSSIAN FRONT

All winter the Russian battle line has stood as here drawn on the edge of the shaded area. Now the Russians are attacking the German entrenchments at the points indicated by arrows

killed, five of them in Northern Indiana, where a railway train was blown from the track. Churches and houses were destroyed, and the losses were about $3,000,000.

Orders for War Supplies The largest war order recently placed on this side of the Atlantic is one for $91,000,000 worth of beef stew, in 600,000,000 one pound cans. It was given by the British Government to The Imperial Canneries, Limited, of Montreal, a new company, but the greater part of the material must be supplied in the United States. Contracts for 490,000,000 pounds have already been made, and only 60,000,000 are held by Canadian companies. In this country there is a wide distribution, the largest assignment being to a Philadelphia company, which undertakes to deliver 125,000,000 pounds within twelve months. The price paid is about $1.75 per dozen cans, and the profit is said to be 60 cents. The 300,000,000 pounds of beef required will be supplied by three Chicago companies, the Armours and Swifts included, and nearly all the cans will be procured from the American Can Company. About 10,000,000 cans will be delivered every week for the use of the British army.

It is estimated by the Canadian Bank of Commerce that the war orders given to Canada this year will amount to about $600,000,000. But much of the material will be supplied in this country. Canada's Munitions Board placed orders for $200,000,000 last week. In a circular letter the bank says:

War has made many homes desolate, but it has filled the bread baskets of our workers. It is extremely difficult to estimate the economic results of the long struggle in Canada. Had it not been for the war many of our plants would be idle, as the result of the world-wide depression, which included Canada in its sweep. Those plants which were able to make war supplies not only weathered the storm, but made enormous profits and have made themselves secure for the future by building up large cash reserves.

At the Pittsburgh steel mills there is a continuous demand for the forms of steel that are used in making shells. This demand comes from neutrals as well as belligerents. Large quantities are sought by Spain and Rumania. The orders in sight call for more than 400,-000 tons of steel. There is great congestion at the northern Russian ports of Archangel and Kola, with no prospect of relief in the immediate future. At or near Archangel about 100 ships carrying war supplies are frozen in, waiting for spring to permit unloading. At Vladivostok, on the Pacific coast, there is also great congestion, but a part of the war supplies will hereafter be diverted to the port of Nikolayevsk, at the mouth of the Amur River.

The Sinking of the "Sussex" Before the war it was anticipated by both the British and German experts that the German torpedo boats would make the Channel crossing perilous if not impossible. But the British Admiralty have succeeded in preventing this some-

how, whether by steel nets, patrol boats or mines is not known to the public, so that millions of troops and passengers have been carried back and forth for the past twenty months with almost no losses.

But in their new submarine campaign the Germans are more successful in interfering with cross-Channel traffic. Their latest victim is the British steamer "Sussex," which was torpedoed in mid-Channel on the afternoon of the 24th on her way from Folkestone to Dieppe. She had on board about 380 passengers, mostly French, but with many British and some thirty Americans. The explosion shattered the fore part of the vessel and brought down the mast, thus putting the wireless out of commission. Some fifty persons lost their lives, among them probably one or more Americans. Several of the passengers were killed or wounded by the explosions. Others were drowned. Five boats were launched, but after an hour, as the ship did not seem to be sinking, these people were taken on board again. About midnight a French trawler happened to sight the "Sussex" and took off most of the surviving women and children, and a British destroyer took the other passengers back to Dover. Among the prominent Americans on board were Prof. J. Mark Baldwin, the psychologist, with his wife and daughter; Edward Marshall, journalist; J. D. Armitage, treasurer of a cotton goods manufacturing company; E. H. Huxley, president of a rubber company, and Wilder G. Penfield, Rhodes scholar from Wisconsin.

The British Admiralty announces the loss of the Dominion liner "Englishman" by a torpedo, but does not state where or when the disaster occurred. She was carrying horses for the Northwestern Trading Company of New York. There were 111 persons on board, among them four Americans in care of the horses. Eighteen persons are still unaccounted for.

The Russian Campaign The Russians opened the spring campaign by attacks upon the northern and southern sections of the German line and appear to have made gains at several points tho so far there is nothing to indicate that the German position is seriously endangered. In the south their object is to take Czernovitz, the capital of the Austrian duchy of Bukovina. Twice already in the present war the Russians have captured Czernovitz but have later been driven out. It is not a fortified city and both parties have promptly evacuated it whenever the surrounding defenses have been taken. Czernovitz lies just south of the Pruth River, eleven miles from the Russian border and only eight miles from the Rumanian.

On the northern side Czernovitz is protected by the Dniester River, which the Russians are now trying to cross. The first step in this direction has been taken in the capture of the bridgehead at Usciezko by a vigorous Russian attack. This position on the northern bank of the river was strongly fortified and had resisted the Russians for the last six months. But on Sunday morning a breach 400 yards wide was made in the Austrian trenches by mine explosions. The garrison, tho said to have been outnumbered eight to one, held out all day and then began to withdraw to the southern bank in boats. But the Russian artillery was brought to bear upon the transports and cut off the garrison from retreat in this direction. So the commander, Colonel Pflanch, took the daring alternative of cutting his way thru the investing troops. In this he was successful and with the remnants of the garrison he joined the Russian forces on the hills to the northwest.

In the Riga region the German advance in the direction of Petrograd was halted on the Dvina River. Here they hold the southern bank for about twenty-five miles between the old German cities of Jacobstadt and Friedrichstadt. The strategical importance of this position may be seen from the map and from the editorial on "The Russian Drive." To push back the German salient on the Dvina is manifestly the first step toward the relief of the two cities on each side, Riga on the west and Dvinsk on the east. The Russians attacked here with fresh Siberian troops and an abundance of artillery as well as projectiles containing asphyxiating and poisonous gases. At first it seems the Russians made some inroads upon the German entrenchments, but their later efforts, according to the Berlin account, were unsuccessful and they suffered heavy losses.

South of Dvinsk, in the neighborhood of Vidzy and Lake Narotch, the Russians began attack on March 19. The Germans say that more than 50,-000 shells, mostly of large caliber, were showered on a short front and that the Russians captured a hundred yards of trenches which were regained by the Germans.

On the Meuse   The Germans continue to make gains in the vicinity of Verdun. Their latest attack is directed still further to the west than their last week's operations. Their first efforts were directed against the northern and eastern fortifications of Verdun. Then they turned their attention toward the defenses on the western side of the Meuse River. Here they penetrated Crows' Wood and then, according to their reports, captured the hills that stand on either side of the forest, Goose Ridge and Dead Man's Hill. The French, however, deny that the Germans hold or ever did have possession of Dead Man's Hill. The dispute seems to turn upon which particular crest is entitled to that ill-omened designation.

The point now attacked by the Germans is about three miles to the west of Dead Man's Hill. Here they have taken the wooded hills which lie between Malancourt and Avocourt. This advances their line about two miles and brings them within five miles of the railroad which feeds Verdun. Obviously further gains in this direction might bring about the isolation of the fortress.

By this advance the French forces between Bethincourt and Malancourt are hemmed in on three sides and presumably rendered untenable. The Germans claim that their gains in the Avocourt region brought them in unwounded prisoners to the number of 2914 men and fifty officers. The French claim that the German casualty lists are utterly unreliable and to prove it they allege that the total losses in killed, wounded and missing reported by the Germans from certain corps do not equal the number of German prisoners taken by the French at the time. If this charge is true it would invalidate the estimates of German losses given in the table below.

In their recent attacks the Germans have made extensive use of their *Flammenwerfer*, which throw streams of blazing oil on the opposing trenches. These are operated like a portable fire extinguisher and carried by men who move forward with the charging line. But a shell from a French 75 striking one of the reservoirs scatters the flaming fluid over the German soldiers and burns them alive. For protection against the fire-throwers the French wear masks and shelter themselves behind big oblong shields of wickerwork coated with clay.

Chinese Republic Restored   On December 11, President Yuan Shih-kai announced that in obedience to the will of the people, as exprest by the provincial dignitaries whom he consulted, he would assume the throne as Emperor of China. But this announcement was the signal for a revolt which originated, like the revolution which overthrew the Manchu dynasty, in the southern provinces. The official reports have announced successive victories of the government troops over the rebels, but nevertheless the insurrection spread until, according to the statements of the Chinese republicans in the United States, six provinces had been involved. At the head of the republican army is General Tang Chi-yao, Governor of Yunnan province.

The real forces and motives concerned in these sudden reversals of Yuan's attitude are impossible to determine from what has been made public. It is known that Japan has strongly opposed the restoration of the empire. It is surmised that Germany has secretly favored it. Yuan, in his edict of March 23, reëstablishing the republic, explains that he consented to become Emperor with great reluctance and misgivings at the urgent solicitation of the Council of State. We quote from his explanation:

The representatives of the convention unanimously decided on a monarchical gov-

© *Underwood & Underwood*

EVEN THE MULES GO WRONG IN MEXICO

The driver of this field piece is having trouble with his team, but Battery B of the Sixth Field Artillery, forming part of Pershing's flying column, covered the first 110 miles of the march thru Chihuahua brilliantly, reaching camp only an hour and a half after the cavalry, which made the distance in twenty-two hours' marching time

ernment and elected me Emperor. Since the sovereignty of the country was vested in citizens and the decision made by the entire body of representatives, there was no room left to me for further discussion.

Nevertheless, I was convinced that my sudden elevation to the throne would constitute a violation of my oath, leaving me unable to explain myself. The Council of State, however, was firm and stated that the oath of the chief executive was based on his position and should be observed or discarded according to the will of the people. Their arguments were so irresistible that there was no excuse for me to decline their offer. Using preparations as a pretext, I took no steps to carry out their program actually.

When the trouble in Yunnan and Kweichow arose, I issued a mandate postponing the measure and forbidding the presentation of petitions praying for my enthronement. Then I hastened the convocation of the Council in order to secure various views, hoping to revert to the original state of affairs. Being a man of bitter experiences, I cared for nothing but the salvation of my country. A section of the people, however, suspected me of harboring a desire for great power and privileges. Thus difference in thought has created an exceedingly dangerous situation.

I have myself to blame for my lack of virtue. Why should I blame others? The people have been thrown into misery. The soldiers have been made to bear hardships. Commerce has declined. Taking this condition into consideration, I feel exceedingly sorry.

Thus I hope to imitate the example of the sincerity of the ancients by shouldering myself all the blame, so that my action will fall in line with the spirit of humanity, which is the expression of the will of Heaven.

In this self-deprecatory phraseology Yuan is merely following the traditional custom of China according to which the Emperor always assumes the blame for anything that goes wrong in the country, even earthquakes and floods.

An Estimate of the Armies For the benefit of the many readers who write to us asking about the losses of the war and the number of men now available we publish the accompanying table. It appeared in the February number of the journal of the Union of Democratic Control, London, and seems to have been calculated with care. It must be remembered, however, that no government

gives out the number of its troops or of its net losses. The British and German governments alone publish casualty lists, but it is not known how many of the wounded and missing return to the ranks. The compiler of this table assumes that twenty per cent of the wounded die or are permanently disabled. It is also assumed that five per cent of the army are sick or temporarily incapacitated. These estimates added to the killed and missing give the figures in the column headed "Wastage." According to this the percentage of wastage to the original number of troops is for the various nations: Russia, 47; Austria, 42; Germany, 36.2; France, 33; Turkey, 26; Britain, 23; Italy, 16; and Bulgaria, 10.

Comparing these with the estimates from various sources published in The Independent of February 21, we see that the compiler of the U. D. C. table has added 275,000 to the German losses as estimated by the British War Office from the German casualty lists. The reason given for this increase of the estimate of the German losses is that the lists issued by the other German states outside Prussia are belated. If, however, we take the British War Office summation of the German casualty lists without making this correction, the German wastage up to the first of January would be 1,423,000 instead of 1,659,000 and the percentage of wastage would be 29.3 instead of 34.2. These figures seem more probable than those given in the table, for the March statement of the British War Office gives the total German losses during January and February, according to the German casualty lists, as 131,430. If this is correct the addition of 275,000 to German losses on the ground of belated lists is far too great.

On the other hand, the compiler of the table has not used the statement of French losses made by M. Longuet, member of the Chamber of Deputies for Paris, at the Bristol Labor Conference. According to this, which is the nearest to an official estimate that we have, the French losses have been 800,000 dead,

© International Film Service

THE SUCCESSOR OF VON TIRPITZ
Admiral Edward K. von Capelle, now in charge of the German fleet and directly responsible for the action of German submarines

1,400,000 wounded and 300,000 prisoners. If these figures are adopted the French wastage would be 1,560,000 instead of 1,188,000 and the percentage of wastage would be 43.3 instead of 33.

In the absence of more authentic data we should mention a report which comes by way of Amsterdam and Berlin purporting to give the figures that General Gallieni presented in confidence at a recent military conference. According to this the Minister of War estimated the total French losses at 2,500,000 up to March 11. Of these 600,000 are dead, 400,000 severely wounded and 300,000 missing. If this is anywhere near correct the French and British have lost more in France than the Germans on all fronts.

It is rumored that a Petrograd compilation of the Russian losses for 1915 made them out as: Killed in battle, 387,918; dead from wounds, 192,300; dead in hospitals, 274,175; wounded, 783,438; missing, including captured, 954,813. This if augmented by the losses in 1914 would not be far from the figure in the table. But it is obviously impossible to make any reliable estimates even in the case of Germany and France, while, of course, for such countries as Russia and Turkey the data is still more indefinite.

According to the table the permanent loss to the belligerent countries is about 8,000,000 men. At the beginning of the war the armies of the Entente Allies stood toward those of the Central Powers as 167 is to 100; at the beginning of 1916 they stood as 142 is to 100, a loss of strength of the Allies relative to the Central Powers of 25 per cent.

ESTIMATE OF BELLIGERENT ARMIES IN JANUARY 1916
(Thousands omitted; e.g. 6,800 stands for 6,800,000)

Nations	Population in Millions	Armed Full Strength	Line Troops Outside War Area	Available Armies June, 1915	Wastage % Out of Table	Permanent	Additions to Cover Wastage and to Strengthen	Armies Jan 1916	Original Armies and Losses Based Since
Russia	170	6,800	600	6,200	2,940	3,260	3,200	6,460	10,000
France	45	3,750	150	3,600	1,188	2,412	750	3,162	4,500
Britain	55	1,900	400	1,500	347	1,153	1,400	2,553	3,300
Italy	34	1,500	100	1,400	221	1,180	500	1,680	2,000
Belgium	7½	280	...	280	200	80	...	80	280
Serbia.Mont.	5	450	20	430	360	70	...	70	450
	316½	14,680	1,270	13,410	5,255	8,155	5,850	14,005	20,530
Germany	68	5,000	150	4,850	1,659	3,191	1,800	4,991	6,800
Austria	52	2,750	100	2,650	1,128	1,522	1,800	3,322	4,550
Turkey	20	550	50	500	130	370	700	1,070	1,250
Bulgaria	5½	500	50	450	46	404	50	454	550
	145½	8,800	300	8,000	2,917	5,083	4,300	9,837	13,150

THE DEMOCRATS SHOULD WIN

A FORECAST OF THE 1916 ELECTION

BY WILLIAM JENNINGS BRYAN

NO one who has had any considerable experience in politics will risk an opinion on platforms very far in advance of the conventions, especially at a time like this when the situation is undergoing constant change. Who could have foreseen in 1912 the problems with which the Administration has had to deal? And who could have predicted a year ago the changes which have taken place in the opinions of men within the last twelve months? The qualifying phrase, "other things being equal," affords some protection, but, as other things are never equal, forecasts are always subject to discount. If the campaign of 1916 could be fought upon the party's remarkable record of achievement, a Democratic victory ought to be reasonably sure; but even then, it would be necessary to remember that we won in 1912 not because our party secured a majority of the votes cast, but because the opposition was divided into two almost equal factions.

There are three factors which must be taken into consideration in our calculations respecting the outcome of the Presidential election of 1916; first, the impression made by the domestic policies of the Administration; second, the impression made by the foreign policies of the Administration, and third, the unity or lack of unity in the Republican party.

The Democratic party can with confidence submit its claims upon a number of important reforms.

First: The popular election of Senators. This is a reform of the first magnitude; a reform in the methods of government which could n o t have been achieved a g o without vast bloodshed. The Democratic party began the fight for this reform in Congress in 1892; it embodied a demand for it in its platform in 1900, 1904, and in 1908, and in 1912 endorsed the amendment which was then before the states f o r ratification. T h e Republican party never endorsed this reform in a n y platform

prior to its submission, and as late as 1908 overwhelmingly defeated a resolution approving it. The people ought to give the Democratic party credit for thus opening the way to other reforms.

Second: The Democratic party reformed the rules of Congress and gave to the House of Representatives real representative government. The people ought to give the party credit for this reform also.

Third: The Democratic party reduced the tariff and put upon the statute books the best revenue law which the country has had in fifty years. The tariff law included an income tax and the Democratic party can claim credit not only for the income tax law, but also for the fact that the Constitution has been so amended as to authorize an income tax. In 1894 a Democratic Congress enacted an income tax law, but the law was declared unconstitutional by a divided court, one judge changing his mind between two hearings of the case. The Democratic party then proceeded to agitate for an amendment

to the Constitution, specifically authorizing an income tax, and, while the necessary amendment was submitted under a Republican administration, it came as a result of Democratic labors and was really submitted for the purpose of preventing an income tax. The Republican leaders who assisted in securing the submission of the amendment did it to defeat a bill providing for an income tax and did not expect the amendment to be ratified; they were caught in their own trap.

Fourth: The Democratic party is entitled to credit for the new currency law. The Republicans had talked currency reforms for twenty years, but did nothing; the Democrats went to work and brought about a change which gives us the best currency law we have ever had. It vindicates the right of the government to issue paper money; it destroys the monopoly which the national banks have held of favor from the Federal Government; it takes from Wall Street its controlling influence as a money center and establishes twelve financial centers in different parts of the country, all linked together at Washington and controlled by responsible government officials. The Democratic party has a right to expect gratitude from the business world, which has been released from the grip of the money trust, and from the political world, which has been set free from the tyranny of a few money magnates.

Fifth: The Democratic party deserves credit for having entered upon a program which contemplates the complete overthrow of the principle of private monopoly; it has already made a start and is building upon the only sure foundation, namely, that a private monopoly is indefensible and intolerable. Its services ought to be appreciated by the s m a l l e r corporations which find an added sense of security in the anti-trust laws already passed.

Sixth: The Democratic party deserves credit for the enactment of the

© International Film Service

TWO DEMOCRATS

13

long promised measure giving to the Filipinos the promise of independence, thus answering the charges that have been made against our national purpose and restoring to us freedom to proclaim to the world the doctrine that governments derive their just powers from the consent of the governed and not from superior force.

Seventh: These are some of the substantial results of harmonious coöperation between a Democratic President, a Democratic Senate and a Democratic House. During the accomplishment of these domestic reforms the Administration has been dealing with diplomatic problems of great delicacy. It deserves credit for having resisted the demands of those who tried to force the Government into intervention in Mexico. The policy of "watchful waiting" has saved us untold loss in life and money, and it is not improbable that by refusing to intervene this nation escaped the awful responsibility of starting the European war.

Eighth: The Democratic party deserves credit also for the fact that it has not allowed the country to be drawn into the European war, altho the course of neutrality has been beset by many difficulties. Our nation has suffered at the hands of both sides, but the injuries were not intended against us, they were incidental to the war.

Ninth: This Administration has very much improved our relations with Latin America. A policy of friendly coöperation has been substituted for dollar diplomacy, the legations in Argentina and Chile have been raised to embassies, the offer of mediation tendered by Brazil, Argentina and Chile was accepted in the dispute with Mexico, important treaties have been negotiated with Nicaragua, Colombia and Hayti, and all South and Central America has been brought to the cordial support of the Monroe Doctrine.

> CREDIT THESE ACHIEVEMENTS TO THE DEMOCRATS, SAYS MR. BRYAN
>
> 1. Popular election of Senators.
> 2. Reform of Congressional procedure.
> 3. Reform of tariff.
> 4. Currency reform.
> 5. Anti-monopoly laws.
> 6. Promise of independence to Filipinos.
> 7. Avoidance of war in Mexico.
> 8. Neutrality in the Great War.
> 9. Improved Pan-American relations.
> 10. Arbitration treaties.

Tenth: The Democratic party deserves credit for the negotiation, by this Administration, of thirty treaties, on a new plan, providing for investigation by an international tribunal of all disputes of every kind before any declaration of war or commencement of hostilities. These treaties are with nations exercising authority over one billion, three hundred million people, or three-fourths of the inhabitants of the world, and make war between the contracting parties a remote possibility.

On the subject of preparedness the record of the party has not yet been made up. The President has announced a program and made a nonpartizan appeal in its behalf. According to present prospects it cannot succeed as a party measure in the form in which he asks it. If he succeeds in securing the appropriations which he asks, it will in all probability be by the aid of the Republicans. The Democratic party cannot, therefore, expect gratitude from those who look upon the policy with favor, or be held responsible for it by those who oppose it.

It is too early to measure the advantage or disadvantage of the program to the party, if the Democrats in Congress secure the President's consent to a modification of his program.

The third element of uncertainty cannot be weighed until the Republican convention or conventions have met. If the two wings of the Republican party unite upon a candidate acceptable to both, the Republican chances will be greatly improved, and it follows that the Democratic prospects will brighten in proportion as there is discord in the Republican ranks. It now looks as if the Progressives were determined to return to the Republican party almost without condition, altho they will, of course, secure as favorable terms as possible. The Democratic party has been so progressive that it ought to appeal strongly to that portion of the Progressive party which acted upon conviction rather than upon personal affection for the Progressive candidate, but the number of recruits thus far won from the progressive Republicans is not encouraging—in fact it is disappointing. The reunion of these elements so bitterly hostile to each other four years ago illustrates anew the strength of party ties and the difficulty of drawing permanently from one of the leading parties any considerable element of its membership.

Man's opinion of what is to be is part wish and part environment, and I cannot claim freedom from the influence of either wish or environment when I construe the prospects to favor Democratic success. Believing that the party has earned the confidence of the public, and should therefore receive it, I believe Democratic success probable. The party has done good where the Republicans would have done harm, and wherever it has failed at all, the Republicans have failed more signally.

Lincoln, Nebraska

EARTH-BORN
BY LOUISE MOREY BOWMAN

Do you think God will make us forget—
    When we wake up in Heaven—
All the queer, little, earth-fashioned things
That are sacred as archangels' wings
    Or the stars that are seven?
Our books, our green china with posies,
My white wedding-gown with its roses,
    The candles we light
    In our wee house at night,
Your father's old clock with its wise, friendly face,
And my mother's old lace—
Do you think Love can ever forget?

Yes, count me a lover of Earth
With its tears or its mirth;
Its wine that is bitter or bread that is sweet—
With the pink apple trees and the brown honey bees,
    With the far purple lands,
    And the warm, golden sands—
And its queer, little, love-hallowed things
That are sacred as archangels' wings
    Or the stars that are seven!

Do you think God will make us forget
    When we wake up in Heaven?

HOME VS. FAMILY

BY MARTHA BENSLEY BRUÈRE

"MY wife," said a harassed commuter, "wants to live on a street with trees and not too far from the next house. She loves to sit on her veranda and see her friends sitting on their verandas with their embroidery. She is all wrapt up in her home."

And she was! A perfectly domesticated woman!

A slow brook spread out under the arching trees at the edge of their suburb into a vivid green marsh with still pools and cat-tail thickets—an open-armed refuge for rubbish, tin cans, mosquitoes and the village gang. A number of families had recovered their ancestral silver and parts of the plumbing from its depths, and several village boys had been sent up to the state reformatory in consequence. A group of women, imprest by the idea that the village spirit rather than the boys needed reforming, called on the commuter's wife to help convert the marsh into a playground.

Impossible! What time had an "old-fashioned mother" for things outside her home? She was doing her whole duty even as it had come down to her, for on her center table was her treasured *mark of place*—a record of the State Historial Society containing her family tree—showing how her pioneer ancestress made the little white homstead on the road-edge of the farm her husband got from the government, a defense against all the frontier enemies from wolves to wickedness. She had made the family clothes—at home. Prepared their food—at home. Stored supplies for the winter, books for school, seed for the spring planting, entertained her friends, expended her esthetic impulses, developed her powers of invention and energy of accumulation —all at home.

Quite justly the *Ladies' Friend* declared of the women of that day: "If a woman does not know the various work of a house she may as well know nothing, for that is her express vocation."

But that was in 1838. Today it should be rewritten: "If a woman does not know the various work of the community thru which the modern family must be conserved, she may as well know nothing, for that is her express vocation."

But that commuter's wife could not have rewritten it! She had only read the surface fact that her revered ancestress stayed in her home. She had quite missed her democratic gospel of work for everybody thru which the family had been made

In The Independent of March 20, Mrs. Bruère began a series of articles on "The Habits of Women Under Domestication." This is the second paper, to be followed by "The Waste of Saving" and "Pernicious Heirlooms."—THE EDITOR.

into a unit worthy to build into the nation. Most of the work for her family was done thru the community. She earned about a quarter of a meager living by the two hours a day which was the maximum she needed to spend on indispensable housework. The rest of her time she devoted to remaining in a state of domestication, a decoration in her husband's button-hole, a symbol of his prosperity, of his ability to indulge in conspicuous waste.

And if a man cannot afford such a luxury?

Two men were walking behind me.

"Frankly I like it," said one. "She makes a comfortable home for me and I haven't any bother or responsibility about it. If we were married you couldn't tell what I'd let myself in for—there'd be no end to my responsibility."

They passed me at the corner— well washed business men of the class who make three or four thousand a year—were they not the perfect parallel, possibly the resultant, of such as the lady who embroidered? These men knew that marriage to a domesticated woman of their own class meant the permanent support of a home, and of a woman who earned no money "so long as you both shall live" and that all the force of the law and of public opinion would hold them to their contract.

The other day a happy married woman busy serving the family thru the community said to me:

"Do you realize how difficult it is for a really domestic woman to either acquire or retain a husband? Who are the old maids we know? Chiefly the thoroly domesticated women. Who are the unhappy wives and those who sue their husbands for alimony? Women devoted to the home and to nothing else. Any woman devoting herself to Causes or Propaganda, or holding down a steady job, can choose among a dozen men."

And it's true! The woman who expects to make her living in domestication is in a precarious position now that society is offering the material comforts of which she was once the sole dispenser for far less than she can produce them. Not that marriage is to be regarded as an end in itself,

exactly, but it does seem to be a means to the permanence of the community. Certainly a democracy is a most unfavorable habitat for the sort of personal dependent which the domesticated woman has become, for a democracy implies that the consideration in which every one is held— yes, her very life itself—depends on her ability to perform some useful service, not on her willingness to seem busy. And the home-bound woman has forgotten the democratic gospel of work for everyone, and abandoned the Woman's Sphere— which is always in the place where the interests of the family must be served. It is in vain that she thinks to retain her usefulness by any devotion to the new science of household efficiency. Every magazine that tells of easier ways to do housework, every home economics course and domestic science school that teaches not how much work can be corralled on the fireside, but how much can be banished from it, helps to make the home duties behind which the domesticated woman is hiding, so trifling that they wouldn't conceal a cat. Every labor-saving device or increase in public service helps to shift the center of interest from the home to the community, so that democracy may replace domestication.

Not that to discontinue the home is in any sense the work of the un-domesticated woman, but to stop canonizing it and to put it in its place as one of many family servants, and to force the woman to become the helpmeet of her husband in making the community, which has become the home of their children, a proper place for them to live in.

In spite of the incredible numbers of such shirkers as the commuter's wife, especially among the middle class, there are signs everywhere that the domesticated woman is laying down her embroidery and taking up her job of family conservation in the only way it can now be done—thru the community. She is making investigations and fighting for laws which will give to all families together what she could never assure her own household by working at home.

All sorts of forward cries are coming from these women in the course of their undomestication—"Rights of Children," "More and Better Babies," "The Solidarity of the Family" and "On to Democracy." But among them all not the most apprehensive ear can detect the faintest whisper of "Back to the Home!"

New York City

HOPEDALE'S GLORIFIED MILL-POND

ANOTHER PRIZE ARTICLE IN THE BEST THING IN YOUR TOWN CONTEST

BY JAMES CHURCH ALVORD

HOPEDALE, Massachusetts, has been "done to death," in the stock phrase of those who write and those who publish. After living in the village for four years I found that it was known by Germans, Italians, Englishmen and Frenchmen for its model homes, its paternal government, its famous strike against some of the conditions appertaining to paternalism. But there is one thing which, strangely, has never been cataloged abroad—this is its glorified mill-pond.

A mill-pond is an ugly spot, God wot. Never was an uglier pond than the bare, bulrush-shored, mucky stretch of bog and water which nestled, up to 1898, right in the heart of this community. From this dingy morass clouds of mosquitos arose each night to swoop down upon the unhappy inhabitants.

But in one famous day and year at the annual town meeting a few progressive souls advocated, as they had for a decade, "the purchase of about five acres for a town park" and succeeded. The town annually appropriates $2500 for the care of the park, and the sale of trees brings in five hundred or so more. There has always been at the head of the work a scientifically-trained forester. The present man has held his place for thirteen years and is an artist in his line. His one ambition has been to keep the park with so carefully careless a grace that the casual visitor shall declare "nature did it all." Nature did—mighty little.

The first care of the committee was to attend to the immediate needs of the community; so an extra appropriation of twenty-five hundred was voted. The worst part of the swamp-land, immediately under the noses of the villagers, was drained with catch-basins, a hedge of shrubbery was set about, and a field for football and baseball, as well as a bandstand, was built. An annual field day for athletic and aquatic sports has increased the interest of all in this portion of the park. Gradually too this end, into which a bit of orderly, artificial, decoration was allowed to creep, was fitted up for the recreation of the toilers. There is a bath-house, a shore of imported seasand, and wharfs for boats and canoes. Unfortunately a group of small boathouses have grown up, sheds of the shed-iest type; but their days are numbered.

Then slowly with the years began the work of transforming a hideous muck-hole to a lovely plaisance. The lakelet was drained, dead trees removed, boulders blasted; but the artistic sense sufficed and an ancient stone-fence, cutting under the waters, has been left. In a drought it makes an exciting bit to negotiate in a boat, yet is so lovely, so odd, that nobody complains. Huge lilies, a pink-stained variety and native to the pond, were encouraged; the lotus has begun to bloom in sheltered nooks. The townsfolk gather these blossoms by huge armfuls every morning, every social occasion overflows with them, and the two pulpits droop under their burden every Sabbath; but the supply never fails.

The appreciation of the people for their own work is immense. They own boats and canoes almost to a man—and a woman, and vote enthusiastically for the efforts at mosquito-extermination, while the attempt to induce the wild natives of the woods to seek refuge here is encouraged by everybody. The result is that squirrel, peasants, quail, rabbits, as well as all the common, and uncommon, birds have learned that in this park is safety from the volley of the gun.

From the nearer end of the water pleasant glimpses show the huge factory looming up like some medieval factory and houses "beside the pond" are in wide demand. Only the very fortunate obtain one right on the shore and, having obtained one, never let it go.

The whole morale of the village is raised and transfigured by Hopedale's glorified mill-pond.

Littleton, Massachusetts

M. William Shak-ſpeare:

EIGHT PAPERS BY FREDERICK HOUK LAW
IN OBSERVANCE OF THE THREE HUNDREDTH
ANNIVERSARY OF SHAKESPEARE'S DEATH

Why Everybody Should Read Shakespeare

IT is not necessary to travel, nor is it necessary to read Shakespeare, but who would not come into touch with what, for centuries, has uplifted and inspired the thoughts of men! Who wishes to lead a narrow existence when the door of opportunity is open! A man may stay all his life in some flat region remote from the sea—never once reading the works of the great dramatist—and still be noble at heart. But he will be a wiser and better man if he looks upon the sea and the mountains, and better still if he reads the plays of Shakespeare, for Shakespeare is as great a fact as the Alps or the Atlantic.

Many thoughtful men have said that if a person were to read no other books than the Bible and Shakespeare he would read enough to uplift his mind, and to raise his soul into communion with the heart of life. To neglect either is to shut out two of the world's finest sources of inspiration.

The best reason for reading Shakespeare is his universality, that is, the fact that he is interesting in different ages and to all classes of people. The interest that attracts one may not be the interest that attracts another. To one he may appeal as a story-teller; to another as a writer who pictured all kinds of human character in every imaginable situation; to another as a philosopher who fully understood and exprest the depths of the human heart; and to another as a poet who had wonderful command of suggestive word and phrase, and whose high and beautiful thought declares our own best emotions and aspirations. Shakespeare's many-sided interest, his expression of the common life-thoughts of the world, and the uplift that comes with his work make him a writer whom all kinds of readers instinctively like.

No one has told more interesting stories than Shakespeare. Every plot tells of something unusual, or surprizing, that immediately awakens interest; as is indicated if we make use of subordinate titles such as "The Comedy of Errors," or the story of the two pairs of twins who got mixt up; "Henry IV," or the story of the happy-go-lucky prince and the fat rascal; "As You Like It," or the story of two girls and a fool who ran away to the woods; "Much Ado About Nothing," or what happened to the man who said he would never marry; "Macbeth," or the story of the man who wished to be great even if he broke all the ten commandments; "The Merchant of Venice," or the money-lender caught in the terms of his own bond; "Cym-

THE WARD STATUE
The work of J. Q. A. Ward, made in 1892. It stands in Central Park, New York

beline," or how the supposedly dead princess came to life and found her long-lost brothers.

Shakespeare's plays are peculiarly fitted to stimulate the imagination, for they tell us just enough to make our minds creative. As we read, there come before our eyes wonderful scenes such as that of the view from the cliff in King Lear:

Come on, sir; here's the place; stand
    still. How fearful
And dizzy 'tis to cast one's eyes so low!
The crows and choughs that wing the
    midway air
Show scarce so gross as beetles: half
    way down
Hangs one that gathers sampire, dread-
    ful trade!
Methinks he seems no bigger than his
    head.
The fishermen, that walk upon the
    beach,
Appear like mice; and yond tall anchor-
    ing bark,
Diminish'd to her cock; her cock, a
    buoy
Almost too small for sight. The mur-
    muring surge,
That on the unnumber'd idle pebbles
    chafes,
Cannot be heard so high. I'll look no
    more;
Lest my brain turn, and the deficient
    sight
Topple down headlong.

How vividly, and in a few lines, Shakespeare brings before us a great scene of battle, with the young Black Prince fighting his ever-remembered battle while his father, the king, looks on in pride:

Edward the Black Prince,
. . . On the French ground play'd
    a tragedy,
Making defeat on the full power of
    France,
Whiles his most mighty father on a hill
Stood smiling to behold his lion's whelp
Forage in blood of French nobility.
O noble English, that could entertain
With half their forces the full pride
    of France,
And let another half stand laughing
    by,
All out of work and cold for action!

In play after play his magic brings before us the rich interiors of palaces, the depths of castle dungeons, inns and streets and woodland scenes, making our imaginations, as we read, ever more and more creative and able to give

To airy nothing
A local habitation and a name.

Most of all, Shakespeare makes us intimately acquainted with characters who are so real, so human, that they cease to be "book-people" and become living realities. Some, like Bolingbroke or Macbeth, are men ambitious for power, whose hearts we read

As a book where men
May read strange matters.

Some are great leaders, like Henry V, who, in stress and danger, bound his men to himself like brothers and found victory by spirit rather than by strength:

We few, we happy few, we band of
    brothers;
For he today that sheds his blood with
    me
Shall be my brother: be he ne'er so
    vile,
This day shall gentle his condition;
And gentlemen in England now abed
Shall think themselves accurs'd they
    were not here,
And hold their manhoods cheap whiles
    any speaks
That fought with us upon Saint Cris-
    pin's day.

Some, like Richard III, or King John, are men of evil lives, but gifted with mental power and strength; while others are base villains despised by the very men who make them their tools. Thus Macbeth says contemptuously to the murderers he has hired:

Ay, in the catalogue ye go for men;
As hounds and greyhounds, mongrels,
    spaniels, curs,

Shoughs, water-rugs, and demi-wolves,
    are clept
All by the name of dogs!

Some, like Faulconbridge in "King John," are heroes of admirable dash and ardor; others, like Hotspur, are men of fire. Some, like Richard II or King Lear, are great sufferers, rousing our hearts to pity. Some, like Rosalind or Viola, are beautiful, laughing, clever young women, fascinating us with an eternal youth. Some, like Cordelia or Imogen, are high-hearted women whose nobility lives forever. There are prattling children like Arthur in "King John"; common people in inns and country towns—like Justice Shallow in "Henry IV"—and all these characters grip us with interest. In their living reality is one of the main reasons for reading Shakespeare.

Shakespeare's humor, more than the humor of any other English author, has awakened laughter. Some plays, like "The Comedy of Errors" and "The Merry Wives of Windsor," are largely farcical. Who would not laugh at "The Taming of the Shrew," or at the comic parts of "Henry IV," of which Johnson said: "Perhaps no author has ever, in two plays, afforded so much delight"? In most of Shakespeare's work humor plays a large part.

There is no author who appeals more deeply to our sympathies. Shakespeare leads us to feel the pathos of broken lives and to realize that tragedy is not in empty event, but in the fall of a soul. There is a note of kindly sympathy thruout the plays, as when Brutus, in "Julius Caesar," says to his boy Lucius:

Poor knave, I blame thee not; thou
    art o'er-watched.

Even in the stern tragedy of "Macbeth" a Messenger, probably no other than one of Macbeth's hired villains, says in warning to Lady Macduff:

Be not found here: hence, with your
    little ones!
To fright you thus, methinks, I am too
    savage;
To do worse to you were fell cruelty!

The underlying humanity of Shakespeare inevitably softens the hearts of those who read.

There is a world of moral uplift to be gained from reading the great plays. They lead one to a love of the good outdoor world where one may find:

Tongues in trees, books in the run-
    ning brooks,
Sermons in stones and good in every-
    thing.

Most of all, the plays lead to self-mastery, for they are crowded with precepts based upon the wisdom of the ages.

Love all, trust a few,
Do wrong to none.

Was there ever a better maxim? But Polonius in "Hamlet" has more to say:

Be thou familiar, but by no means
    vulgar.
Those friends thou hast, and their
    adoption tried,
Grapple them to thy soul with hoops
    of steel. . . .
Give every man thine ear, but few thy
    voice;
Take each man's censure, but reserve
    thy judgment.
Costly thy habit as thy purse can buy,
But not expressed in fancy; rich, not
    gaudy;
For the apparel oft proclaims the
    man. . . .
Neither a borrower nor a lender be;
For loan oft loses both itself and
    friend. . . .
This above all: to thine own self be
    true,
And it must follow, as the night the
    day,
Thou canst not then be false to any
    man.

With over-love of gold, and of drink, two of the world's besetting sins, Shakespeare had little patience. Romeo, giving gold in payment for poison, says to the apothecary:

There is thy gold, worse poison to
    men's souls,
Doing more murders in this loathsome
    world
Than these poor compounds.

And Cassio in "Othello" exclaims:

O, that men should put an enemy in their mouths, to steal away their brains! that we should with joy, revel, pleasure, and applause, transform ourselves into beasts!

SHAKESPEARE'S BIRTHPLACE AT STRATFORD

It is not known in which half of the double house Shakespeare was born. This old print shows the buildings as they were before they were bought by subscribers and restored to something like their original aspect, in 1847. The two buildings, which Shakespeare's father had thrown together, were separated before Shakespeare's death, one-half becoming an inn, while the other, early in the last century, served for a time as a butcher's shop. Since 1891 the property has been held by trustees on behalf of the nation

Of temperance, Shakespeare has old Adam, in "As You Like It," say:

Though I look old, yet I am strong and
     lusty:
For in my youth I never did apply
Hot and rebellious liquors in my blood;
Nor did not with unbashful forehead
     woo
The means of weakness and debility;
Therefore my age is as a lusty winter,
Frosty, but kindly.

The plays teach one not to regard misfortune as wholly evil but rather as a means to something better. Cordelia, in "King Lear," dies miserably, but she has proved a noble womanhood.

Sweet are the uses of adversity;
Which, like the toad, ugly and ven-
     omous,
Wears yet a precious jewel in his
     head.

No one can read Shakespeare without being more staunchly a patriot. Old Siward, in "Macbeth," on being told that his dearly loved son had died nobly in battle, said:

     Why then God's soldier be he!
Had I as many sons as I have hairs,
I would not wish them to a fairer
     death!

Shakespeare's ardent love of country, displayed in so many of his plays, made him awake to the necessity of national defense,

For peace itself should not so dull a
     kingdom,
Though war nor known quarrel were
     in question,
But that defenses, musters, prepara-
     tions,
Should be maintain'd.

To read Shakespeare is to learn reverence for self, and reverence for God. The moral teaching of Shakespeare is summed up in Hotspur's words in "Henry IV":

O gentlemen, the time of life is short;
To spend that shortness basely were too
     long.

The deeply-religious note in Shakespeare is evident to all who read his plays. An overhanging presence of something beyond the world of men is felt in all of Shakespeare's serious work. There is even, at times, a childlike expression of religious faith, as in Richmond's prayer in "Richard III":

O Thou, whose captain I account my-
     self . . .
To thee I do commend my watchful
     soul,
Ere I let fall the windows of mine eyes;
Sleeping and waking, O, defend me
     still!

From a mere worldly point of view everyone wishes to read the plays of Shakespeare. There is a volume of information in the historical plays, and of material for thought in all. Knowledge of the plays explains a host of allusions met in daily reading, and in the worlds of music and of art. Shakespeare's marvelous vocabulary of fifteen thousand different words opens up the mines of English. His suggestive phrases, sweeping sentences, glowing rhetoric and lofty poetry reveal the power of language.

Everyone wishes to know an author who is so much a topic of conversation, so great an influence in literature, so supremely the poet of all who speak English, and so loved by the people of all nations into whose languages his works have been translated.

Everyone wishes to know that author, who, by giving to all men—however limited and confined their lives may be—a kind of vicarious experience, has done so much to broaden sympathy and to increase the conception and understanding of life.

THE KESSELSTADT "DEATH MASK"
This cast appeared in 1849 in a rag-shop in Mainz, Germany, where it was bought by Dr. Ludwig Becker. It bears the inscription + A° Dm 1616, and Becker thought it a death mask of Shakespeare. It was supposed to have been the possession of Count Kesselstadt, and is now exhibited at Darmstadt. Its authenticity has never been proved

BOOKS FOR FURTHER READING

The Shakespeare Treasury, by Charles W. Stearns; William Shakespeare, Poet, Dramatist and Man, by H. W. Mabie; What is Shakespeare? by L. A. Sherman; Shakespeare as a Playwright, by Brander Matthews; Shakespeare as a Dramatic Artist, by R. G. Moulton; Introduction to Shakespeare, by Edward Dowden; Shakespeare's Heroines, by Mrs. Anna Jameson; Tales from Shakespeare, by Charles and Mary Lamb; The Moral System of Shakespeare, by R. G. Moulton; The Religious Belief of Shakespeare, by J. Countermine.

LEAD, KINDLY LIGHT

BY LOUISE DUNHAM GOLDSBERRY

Lead, Kindly Light, the bells are softly telling,
     Till night be gone;
In many a heart the silent song is welling—
     Lead Thou me on;
Oh bells! That sing the hymns my mother sung—
Oh bells! That sing the hymns my mother sung—
     Lead Thou me on!

Life's cup I lift, with braver lips to drain it,
     For that ye sing;
My cross I kiss nor may I dare disdain it,
     Whate'er it bring;
Oh bells! Ye voice the voice of one passed on!
Oh bells! Till night be gone—Till night be gone!

I hear the grasses o'er a dead face growing
     Beyond your song;
From out the years, my mother's sweet eyes
     showing—
     And night is gone;
Oh bells! That sing above the rain and cold!
Oh bells! That sing ajar the gates of gold!

Lead, Kindly Light, the bells are softly pealing—
     Lead Thou me on;
A child again against her heart-beats kneeling—
     Till night be gone;
Oh bells; That sing the gracious story on—
Oh bells! Till night be gone—Till night be gone!

THE CAVALRY ARE HOT ON VILLA'S TRAIL. PE

A SKIRMISH LINE IN THE MOUNTAINS. OVER ROUGH C(

Making Parents Efficient

The recent nation-wide celebration of "Better Babies Week"—advertised from the pulpit and at the movies, explained in schools and woman's clubs and newspapers—is due to the efforts of one woman, Miss Julia C. Lathrop, Chief of the Children's Bureau, under the United States Department of Labor.

For over three years Miss Lathrop has directed the Government's campaign against infant mortality, gathering statistics and directing popular education.

"The vast resources of unused information which the Government already possesses," she says, "indicate clearly our national neglect—in a field where it is complacently taken for granted that our emotions and personal interest guarantee our efficient attention."

Miss Lathrop believes in publicity as a sort of general alarm clock. She publishes the facts: that one in eight of all the babies born in the United States dies before it is a year old; that in some parts of the country this proportion reaches one in three. Then she puts it up to the people to carry thru the necessary reforms.

"No city or town should fail to provide instructive nursing service, and to pay constant heed to the problems of hygiene and sanitation, of proper housing and of recreation spaces, since all these immediately affect the welfare of infants.

"In every county there should be a health-teaching center.

"Give the work of the woman head of the household the status of a profession."

These are some of the salient points in the publicity campaign of the Chief of the Children's Bureau; and they make up a platform of revolutionary reforms well worth considering. For Miss Lathrop is not talking at random. Her theories have the weight of thirty-five years of practical experience in social work behind them.

After her graduation from Vassar College in 1880, she returned to her native state and became a resident worker at Hull House, Chicago. For twelve years she was a member of the Illinois State Board of Charities. Her constant emphasis on construction rather than on patchwork made Miss Lathrop's appointment as chief of the newly organized Children's Bureau a particularly fortunate one.

When the Press Helped the Plow

From a small daily paper in Ohio, W. C. Deming came to Cheyenne, Wyoming, to become editor of the *Wyoming Daily Tribune*—and incidentally to revolutionize the ideas of an entire state.

Very early he became interested in Wyoming's agricultural possibilities.

© *G. V. Buck, Washington*

SHE CARES FOR U. S. CHILDREN

Few, if any, of the town people had given the subject any thought. Occasionally a ranchman would plant a patch of potatoes or a dab of oats; but they received practically no attention. Whenever the editor of the *Wyoming Tribune* observed the slightest evidence of farming he "wrote it up," even to flower gardens, irrigated with a hose.

In 1904, as chairman of the program committee of a young men's club, he asked Hon. C. T. Johnston, the state engineer, now professor of irrigation at Ann Arbor, to prepare a paper on the

WYOMING FARMERS THANK THIS MAN

subject "Is Farming Around Cheyenne Practicable?" Mr. Johnston, after an exhaustive study of the Campbell System of Dry Farming, rendered a favorable verdict. The club at once engaged Dr. V. T. Cooke, a practical dry farmer, purchased a four hundred acre tract of land near Cheyenne, and started to work. That was in 1905, when dry farming was a joke and a by-word. But Dr. Cooke never had a crop failure.

Homesteaders began to flock into Wyoming by the hundreds. The result is that within a radius of eighty miles of Cheyenne today there are three thousand small farms. The mean rainfall is 14 inches, but wheat and oats frequently yield thirty bushels per acre. There are ten grain elevators in southeastern Wyoming; a big flour mill in Cheyenne, a large farming community, and the people say it was Deming's faith and vision that did it.

Astronomer of Two Hemispheres

The oldest of our state universities and the youngest of the universities of Argentina have formed a unique sort of partnership to increase their efficiency in astronomical research. The observatories of Michigan and La Plata have been for the last few years under the management of a single astronomer and their telescopes working in harmony command both hemispheres of the heavens.

Professor W. J. Hussey is doubtless the first man to attempt to occupy chairs in two universities nine thousand miles apart. But Professor Hussey is not unused to attempting the unusual. He has been at it all his life. A farmer boy does not work his own way to the front rank of stellar discoveries at the age of forty-nine without exceptional initiative and ability. He started in life with no apparent advantages toward such a career, except perhaps Quaker ancestry and a book-loving father; two factors which appear with significant frequency in the biographies of famous Americans.

He took the engineering course at Ann Arbor, working summers on railroad construction in Wyoming and Kansas to get money to carry him thru the winter. One summer he was ordered to report to the superintendent at Mankato, Kansas, to be sent into the field. Entering the office he found the superintendent out and while waiting his orderly mind was so much distressed by the confusion in the office that he busied himself cleaning up and setting things to rights. When the superintendent came back and saw the transformation he gave the young man a position in the office instead of sending him out on the road. This incident sounds like a story from the Rollo books, but it's true, nevertheless.

At the Lick Observatory on Mount Hamilton he began the discoveries which brought him an international

22

THE DISCOVERER OF TWIN STARS

reputation. Upon the publication of his work on the double stars observed at Pultowa, Russia, and of his systematic observations of the satellites of Saturn for many years, he was elected to membership in the Royal Astronomical Society of London and awarded the Lalande gold medal by the Paris Academy of Science. He has devoted himself especially to double stars and has discovered 1400 such systems previously unknown. He has found that about one star out of every eighteen is really double. To distinguish between two such stars, which are less than two seconds of arc apart, is as difficult as it would be to distinguish two pinheads placed side by side at a distance of two miles.

From Blackstone to Botany

Frank Pellett was sick of the dull grind of the legal mill, the eternal wrangling over admissible evidence, precedent, and the mass of technicalities that too often obscure justice. Altho he was a successful attorney, his interest was in outdoor things, and whenever he could steal away from his office, he wandered along the shady roads, studying the native wild flowers.

Finally the impulse grew too strong to be resisted. Law seemed like an unendurable bondage, and so he simply "chucked" it, leaving a secure profession for the precarious career of a nature student.

His first active work was an effort to conserve the wild flowers of his own

state, Iowa, and he set the example by allowing eleven of the twelve acres that constitute his farm to run wild. It is a veritable flower farm, and is replenished until it includes specimens of nearly all the lovely things that grew there before the pioneers first broke the soil. In this living botanical collection are golden rod, trillium, Virginia water-leaf, Solomon seal, starry campion, and scores of blossoming plants with names that read like a spring lyric.

Fortunately, when a man loves to do a certain kind of work, he can as a rule find a way to make it so useful that the world will pay him for doing it. The ex-attorney discovered so many valuable things in connection with his studies of birds, flowers and insects that he was appointed State Apiarist, and bee culture and the checking of diseases that menace the hives became a prominent feature of his duties.

Valuable results of Mr. Pellett's observation of wild life are the facts he discovered concerning birds and insects that are beneficial to the farmer. His is research work, with all outdoors as a laboratory.

Pit Boy and Prime Minister

Thirty years ago a young coal miner left his home in Kilmarnock, Scotland, for the antipodes, because he had been blacklisted by the mine owners on account of his activity in a strike. Today he has gone back to the Mother Country as the official representative of the Commonwealth of Australia. In the period between he has taken a leading part in shaping the industrial and political system of a country as large as the United Kingdom. Three times since the formation of the Australian federation at the beginning of the century he has been called to preside over its destinies as prime minister, for he is recognized as the ablest statesman in the Labor party.

It was his preparedness policy that carried him into power at the last election, in September, 1914. The campaign was at its hight and the Liberal party, then in power, seemed likely to win when the war broke out. This new issue turned the tide, and the Laborites secured such a heavy vote as to give them

THE INSPECTOR OF IOWA'S BEES

THE HIGH COMMISSIONER FOR AUSTRALIA

a big majority in the House and almost a monopoly of the Senate. The reason for this Labor landslide was largely that Fisher and his party had established in 1910 the system of compulsory military training in Australia, and it was felt that the men who had prepared the country for the war should have charge of it during the war.

Those who have feared that the accession of the Labor party to power would bring into office a lot of rowdy and fanatical and impractical agitators would be surprized to find Australia's Labor premier a quiet, self-possest and efficient administrator, who wins the respect of his bitterest opponents. He began work as a pit boy at the age of eleven and was only twenty-three when he was forced to leave Britain.

He had been for twenty years a miner in Queensland when he first entered Parliament. Since then he has carried out an extensive program of social reform and national development, establishing a national bank, extending the state railroads, providing pensions for invalids and bounties for babies, and founding a federal capital at Canberra. One of his hardest fights has been to check the Australian propensity to borrow money from England even for such purposes as paying the interest on previous loans. He has always insisted that not only current expenses, but also the cost of armament and of public works, should be paid for at the time by taxation.

The New Books

REMEMBERING THE JEWEL CITY

"That was a dream worth building," says San Francisco of her Exposition, in the words of one of the many memorialists, commentators and rhapsodists who are still keeping western —and some eastern—presses hot with exposition literature. It may have vanished like a dream, but there was never a dream more luxuriously perpetuated, and with nearly a hundred and fifty titles already accumulated in a bibliography of the art and architecture of the two California fairs no one who wants a guide for his memories of those sunny courts need go without. The picture, of course, is what one wants to keep, and whatever the text may be these books are sure to have photographs beautifully reproduced.

We have already noticed Mr. Neuhaus' "The Art of the Exposition" and "The Galleries of the Exposition." Paul Elder publishes in similar dress *The Architecture and Landscape Gardening of the Exposition*. Once past the introduction, with its alarming remark that at San Francisco one could see "architecture nestling like flamingoes with fine feathers unfurled within a green setting," there is a wealth of photographs with appreciative and informing captions. A detail of the subject is expanded in a luxurious booklet on the *Palace of Fine Arts and Lagoon*, in which Bernard P. Maybeck, the architect, tells his purpose and method in planning this most beautiful of all exposition buildings. As a thumbnail commentary on architecture this has a more general significance than most of the exposition books.

The passing of *The Evanescent City*, "fleeting as all fair things and, fleeting, dear," is George Sterling's inspiration for a delicate piece of verse under that title; while the beauty of the communal enterprise, rather than its product, interests Louis J. Stellmann, who gives the name *That Was a Dream Worth Building* to his pleasant specimen of that ecstatic English that is California's native tongue.

Christian Brinton's *Impressions of the Art at the Panama-Pacific Exposition* adds to a remarkably good set of reproductions from paintings exhibited in San Francisco critical comment on them and on the two expositions as artistic units, and an interesting essay on "The Modern Spirit in Contemporary Painting." Mr. Brinton confesses that the "congenital penchant for hyperbole which obtains west of the Mississippi" led him to be cautious. The bibliography already referred to is found here.

When you find the house sold out, you want to see the play twice as much.

When they promptly hand you two front seats, you wonder if you want to see it at all. That's human nature. The crowd confirms your judgment.

So with Kelly-Springfield Tires. The demand is so great that loyal users often have to wait. We are sorry to disappoint, but glad that the tires have made so good. Now we're very busy trying to avoid further disappointments.

Kelly–Springfield
Automobile Tires–Hand Made

CATCHING up with such a demand as we have had for Kelly-Springfield Tires is not easy.

In 1915 we doubled our output. Still we could have sold twice as many tires as we made. The demand is increasing steadily.

Were we making machine-made tires it would be an easy matter to go out and buy a factory. In a few months' time we could be turning out a multiple product.

But we are not making machine-made tires. If we were we could not give the mileage which is responsible for your extraordinary demands on us. You want the tires only because they have made so good.

It is the hand-made process which is responsible for the service which the tire yields—the care exercised in making them.

We have bought a new factory. We are about to build another. But it takes time to train hands to make our tires. Ordinary workmen cannot do it.

So time is necessary to effect an increase without lowering the standard of our product.

We are sorry that temporarily you must be disappointed if you wait to buy Kelly-Springfield Tires until you need them.

You can avoid this difficulty if you will anticipate your wants. Order your tires from your supply man a week before you need them and he can have them for you by the time you want them.

You have proved that they are worth waiting for. A little foresight will pay you well.

Kelly-Springfield Tire Co.
Factories in Akron and Wooster, Ohio
Executive Offices: B'way and 57th St., New York
Send 10 cents for the new game, "Going to Market"

The Palace of Fine Arts has been kept open for a four months' post-Exposition season, and a *Brief Guide* to the new collection has been issued by the San Francisco Art Association, which will also publish an illustrated catalog.

The Architecture and Landscape Gardening of the Exposition, Introduction by Louis C. Mullgardt. San Francisco: Paul Elder & Co. $2. *Palace of Fine Arts and Lagoon*, by Bernard R. Maybeck. Paul Elder & Co. 50 cents. *The Exantecent City*, by George Sterling. San Francisco: A. M. Robertson. 75 cents. *That Was a Dream Worth Building*, by Louis J. Stellmann. San Francisco: H. S. Crocker Co. $1. *Impressions of the Art of the Panama-Pacific Exposition*, by Christian Brinton. New York: John Lane Company. $3. *Brief Guide to the Palace of Fine Arts*, by Michael Williams. San Francisco Art Association. 25 cents.

THE EAST AND THE WEST

What the reviewer would say of *A City of the Dawn* has already been said by Mr. Arthur C. Benson in his introduction to this most uncommon book by his pupil and friend, Robert Keable, an Anglican priest, for some while missionary in Mombasa. It is a study of that region, of its people, its life, its thought, and the reaction of all these upon the western and the Christian mind. As a book of travel, merely, it has a charm in which most descriptions of foreign lands are oddly lacking. The people are not queer figures hurrying across a movie screen. The barber, the coffee seller, the Vessel Unto Dishonour, Old Sylvester, these are human beings like ourselves, neither curiosities nor souls to be saved. Yet we feel the appalling sense of hopelessness and helplessness that any thoughtful man must feel before the immeasurable mass of brutality and wretchedness; and also sympathy, affection even, for the childlike and fine qualities that show thru sordidness and ignorance. A bit of real literature has been produced out of what we have learned to count, for that purpose, the unpromising material of the missionary experience. Mr. Keable has the eye that sees, the mind that takes nothing for granted, and he has as well the English of the scholar and the poet. But the force and the appeal of his pages lie first in his absolute sincerity and frankness. In the priest is never lost the entirely human English gentleman, with all his fastidiousness, his sense of fitness—and his sense of humor.

A City of the Dawn, by Robert Keable. Dutton. $1.50.

OUR PERILOUS ISOLATION

Professor Roland G. Usher, author of "Pan-Germanism" and "Pan-Americanism," undertakes to show in *The Challenge of the Future* that the nation has come to the parting of the ways and must either maintain its diplomatic isolation with an armament as formidable as Germany's or seek a friend abroad. "A policy of isolation, based upon anachronism and an anomaly, is a living international falsehood, a denial of the plain facts of international relationship, a policy based upon an obvious blindness to realities. The United States is a part of the world. The fact may be ignored, but not changed; we have merely the right to decide the form which our recognition of this relationship shall take." But, not being much of an idealist, Professor Usher does not suggest a general league of peace as the alternative to the continuance of our separate sovereignty; such is for the distant future. He desires an open alliance with Great Britain, not on grounds of sentiment or sympathy, but because that power thru its command of the seas would strengthen our international position and because the diplomatic interests of the two powers happen to harmonize sufficiently to make such an alliance feasible.

Many other suggestions of policy are made in this book, for in no previous work has the author given so much of his own reaction to the facts of the world situation. He would have us abandon the Monroe Doctrine for South America, but establish a very strict control over the international affairs of the backward Central American and insular republics. Japan should be given a free hand to develop the resources of China. The American army and navy should be increased to the point which will rank America as a powerful member of the "concert." Above all, we must prepare economically to meet the fierce commercial competition awaiting us after the war.

The Challenge of the Future, by Roland G. Usher. Houghton, Mifflin. $1.75.

INTERNATIONAL AGREEMENT

Mr. Lippmann in his *Stakes of Diplomacy* makes some interesting proposals for the avoidance of war. His main thesis is that European questions, even issues like Alsace-Lorraine and Italia Irridenta, are no longer causes of war. Of course there is still the friction of inflated nationalisms, but the conflict comes rather as a result of the commercial struggle to organize the backward places of the earth. The present war, and its immediate predecessors, grew out of the "Balkan question," with their primary cause in the disintegration of the Turkish Empire. Morocco, Tunis, Egypt, the Sudan, China, Persia, all are synonymous with Europe's narrow escapes.

The greatest indictment of the pacifists is their failure to grasp this essential point, and to safeguard these danger zones, just as the failure of the panaceas for war result from dealing with the issues that lead to war only after they have reached an inflamed stage. To avoid war it is proposed to organize the world's danger zones under international commissions on the model of the Algeciras Conference, which, had it been successful, "would have been more important than all The Hague rules about how to fight in 'civilized fashion,' all the arbitration treaties, all the reduction of armament proposals with which the earth is deluged."

In case of Entente victory, organize a "series of local world governments," each charged with some one of the world problems" for Morocco, for the Congo, for the Balkan Peninsula, for China, perhaps for Constantinople, and for certain of the countries on the Caribbean Sea; bind the local governments

to this "internation" by the withdrawal of the protection of the national flag of each and by the self-interests of powerful groups, as Professor Beard shows Hamilton rallied the interests of the American colonists 'round the Constitution. Allow the interference of no outside nation in the affairs of the administered territory, such as ruined the Morocco experiment, and Mr. Lippmann believes that most international friction will disappear.

The book is packed full of ideas, handled in an incisive and confident style; unfortunately the author has a habit of laying down as a fact what often needs more than a fiat to make it so. A further criticism might be the lack of historical evidence or parallel. But as a measure of the man, *The Stakes of Diplomacy* casts a much longer shadow than either his "Drift and Mastery" or "A Preface to Politics."

The Stakes of Diplomacy, by Walter Lippmann. Holt. $1.25.

SCHOOLS AND FAMILIES

A practical school man with a philosophy of education "learned chiefly from Socrates and Plato," yet able to see the defects of the doctrine of general discipline and to find a place for the Courtis tests and Ayres scale, Professor Moore, author of *What Is Education,* shows best his thinking in chapters on "Learning by and for doing," "Learning by problem getting," and "Organization by selection." *Financing the Public Schools,* by Earle Clark, shows that Cleveland in a group of eighteen large cities spends more than the average city for important business purposes and less for important educational purposes. The interpretation of revenue, expenditure, administration and control problems is well made. Mr. Perry's report on *Educational Extension* is more popularly written and its facts and plans serve equally well Cleveland's new Division of School Extension and the citizen anywhere who seeks the meaning and justification of community education responsibilities. Dr. Johnson shows the *Education Through Recreation* of 14,000 Cleveland children on one June day and in habitual play interests from wrestling and fishing to the movies, and makes suggestions for a more satisfactory recreation program.

Elizabeth Harrison's earlier book, "A Study in Child Nature," included a chapter on punishment, which has developed into her new volume, *When Children Err.* This is a helpful interpretation of concrete ethical situations from the author's broad experience back to Plato. Dr. Forbush provides a course of study for classes in *Child Study and Training,* but individual parents, day and Sunday school teachers will find it useful. The periods of childhood, types of children, psychological and social problems are followed in statement by laboratory experiments ranging from hidden longings, play and prayer to the movies and the gang.

A view of *The American School,* public and private, by a master at Groton, presents a reflection on past development and present tendencies leading to "the school of tomorrow." Mr. Hinchman's central idea is "growth by production." His proposal to reduce beginning salaries in order to increase those farther on is likely to lead to misunderstanding. Allegheny College celebrated its centenary by a program of addresses on the status and future of *The American College*. Five speakers dealt with the curriculum—the old and the new humanities, science, professions, practical affairs. *The Child in Human Progress* is a record of the tragedy of childhood, tracing the line from animal relationships, human marriage and sacrifice, legal protection in Rome, the Napoleonic recognition of state responsibility, the horrors of factory exploitation, to the work of present day child protection. The book's culmination in the honoring of a single society narrows the interpretation of the present period, without, however, limiting the significance of Mr. George H. Payne's historical study.

Dr. Goodsell contributes a much needed background for the discussion of such urgent problems as birth control, divorce, woman's economic status, seasonal occupation, widows' pensions, in *The Family as a Social and Educational Institution*. Even better than the historical treatment of the family is the frank yet fairly conservative comparison of current theories of adjustment and reconstruction of family relationships.

What Is Education, by Ernest Carroll Moore. Ginn. $1.25. *Financing the Public Schools*, by Earle Clark. *Educational Extension*, by Clarence Arthur Perry. *Education Through Recreation*, by George E. Johnson. Cleveland Foundation. 25 cents each. *When Children Err*, by Elizabeth Harrison. Chicago: National Kindergarten College. $1. *Child Study and Child Training*, ed. by Wm. Byron Forbush, Scribner's. $1. *The American School*, by Walter S. Hinchman. Doubleday, Page. $1. *The American College*, by William H. Crawford, Holt. $1.25. *The Child in Human Progress*, by George H. Payne. Putnam. $2.50. *The Family as a Social and Educational Institution*, by Willystine Goodsell. Macmillan. $2.

SUCCESS

Optimism is, of course, the note of all Orison Swett Marden's Efficiency Books. *The Victorious Attitude* explains the effect produced on one's self and on others by the successful, fearless manner and the hopeful outlook.

Crowell. $1.

WAR RELIEF

The most beautiful of all the war relief publications is *The Book of the Homeless*, edited by Edith Wharton. It is a brilliant mosaic of story, verse, pictures and music, contributed by Jofre, Maeterlinck, Galsworthy, Bakst, Benoit, Henry James, Rupert Brooke, Rodin and other famous representatives of the arts of peace and of war in America and the Allied Nations.

Scribner. $5.

FIFTEEN RULES OF HYGIENE

The service of the Life Extension Institute in emphasizing sane living and especially periodical physical examinations is furthered in *How to Live*, by Irving Fisher and Director Fisk. Fifteen brief formulas under Air, Food, Poisons and Activity summarize the chapters. The appended notes direct to material on Food, Underand Over-weight, Alcohol, Degenerative Diseases, etc.

Funk & Wagnalls. $1.

A NOVEL NOVEL

To "Allah, Source of All Glad Surprizes" Bildad, the *Quill-Driver* sings praise for the many adventures that enlivened his path and from which he is miraculously rescued with unfailing regu-

---

FOUR OUTSTANDING SPRING NOVELS

Unusual Stories by Leading Authors

JACK LONDON'S

New Novel

"*A novel of large significance and unquestionable interest.*"

The Little Lady of the Big House

"Executed with the fine finish of an indisputable master . . . He has written as only a real man can write of real men. . . . Almost one is tempted to declare that now at last the great American novel has been written. One of them at least, one may safely venture to say, has been brought into being."—*Book News Monthly*.

Ready April 5. $1.50

MAY SINCLAIR'S

New Novel

"*A really successful novel.*"

The Belfry

"A perfect, composite picture of real human beings amid the stress of present-day events and emotions. . . . A fascinatingly interesting story. Better in scheme and motive and characterization even than 'The Combined Maze.'"—*Boston Transcript*.

Already Fourth Edition. $1.35

NATHAN KUSSY'S

New Novel

"*A masterful piece of writing.*"

The Abyss

"Remarkable for its material, manner and absolute harmony of substance and style. Strange and convincing. Contains not one dull or unnecessary word."—*Chicago Herald*.

$1.50

MARY S. WATTS'

New Novel

"*Mrs. Watts is in the front rank of American novelists.*"

The Rudder

A story of convincing reality, vivid and of unfailing interest, told with that charm of manner, humor and insight that have always been found in Mrs. Watts' novels.

Now ready. $1.50

THE MACMILLAN COMPANY, *Publishers*, NEW YORK

The Story of an Old Man Who Recovered His Youth

At Fifty, Sanford Bennett Was an Old Man. Today, at Seventy-five, He Is Younger Than Most Men at Thirty. How He Did It.

By PAUL MILLER

MOST of us number among our acquaintances men of advanced age who seem to have maintained their youth to a remarkable degree, but the case of Sanford Bennett is perhaps the most interesting and remarkable on record.

When he was fifty years old, Sanford Bennett was a mere shell of a man. His face was lined with suffering and his body well nigh useless. As he says himself, he was a worn out, decrepit old man. He had even lost most of his hair and his eyes were so weak that he read with difficulty.

Could you see Sanford Bennett today at the age of seventy-five you would believe that a miracle had come to pass.

Big chested, erect, with the step and enthusiasm of a youngster, a face which looks as though it had never known a worry, eyes clear and strong—a full crop of hair, although it is white—Sanford Bennett today is the picture of health. He has forgotten that he ever had an ache or a pain.

Unlike other men who manage to keep young after the fiftieth milestone of life, Sanford Bennett had a doubly hard task on his hands. It wasn't merely a case of maintaining youth—he had to reconstruct a body that had already become old and feeble.

So much attention was attracted by Sanford Bennett's transformation from an old man to a young one, which was accomplished without drugs or medicines of any kind, that

Sanford Bennett at 50

Sanford Bennett at 75

he was induced by his friends to write a book and pass on to others the methods he used.

This he has done under the title of "Old Age, Its Cause and Prevention," in which he outlines exactly how he achieved his return to youth, so that any one can follow his methods, which, like most everything else really effective, are in reality very simple and easy.

I cannot go into Sanford Bennett's system at any length here, but there is a brochure that the publishers will be glad to send free to any reader of this magazine, which describes the book and cites some of the astonishing results others have secured by following Bennett's ideas.

Merely write a letter or postal saying, "Please send me your Free Booklet describing Sanford Bennett's book," and address it to Physical Culture Publishing Company, 3424 Flatiron Building, New York, and I am authorized to say they will honor your request at once.

Sanford Bennett has done so much not only for himself but for thousands of others who are following his suggestions that I believe you will find it well worth while to investigate further and at least acquire a knowledge of his remarkable methods for prolonging the health and energy of youth, particularly when sending for the free brochure puts you under no obligation whatever.

larity. However the rescues are the only foreseen occurrences in the highly diverting autobiography of this Child of Enterprise —a tale of fantastic humor and Arabian Nights surprises, told with delightful originality by William Caine.
                                    Lane. $1.25.

BANTU AND SUDANIAN

A book of curious interest to philologists and of practical use to missionaries and those whom business or adventure lead to the dark continent, is *The Language Families of Africa*, by Alice Werner.
London: Society for Promoting Christian Knowledge. 75 cents.

THE ROMAN CHURCH

In the *Dogmatic Series* of five small books, Roderick MacEachen explains simply and clearly for laymen the Roman Catholic tenets. The work is introduced by Cardinal Gibbons, and, the written for Catholics, will fit the need of Protestants who want to know precisely what their Romanist brethren believe.
Wheeling, W. Va. Cath. Book. Co. 5 vol. $2.

HOW WE KNOW

Professor Douglas Clyde Macintosh in *The Problem of Knowledge* gives an exhaustive and systematized classification of modern theories in epistemology, together with a brief criticism and the historical setting of each. The range of subject matter, however, which is covered in detail in 496 pages would be better adapted to as many volumes.
                                Macmillan. $2.50.

A SOUTHERN BAPTIST

Dr. William E. Hatcher, for fifty years, a leader of the Baptist Church in the South, is one of those fellow-citizens of whom we have reason to be proud, for he made his own way from deep poverty and discouragement to usefulness and eminence. His life, by E. B. Hatcher, shows a lovable man, of strong will, immense energy, humor and sympathy.
                        W. C. Hall. Richmond, Va. $2.50.

THE SUPERNATURAL IN THE DRAMA

This unique study of *The Supernatural in Tragedy*, by Charles E. Whitmore, treats the subject from the historical and the critical viewpoints. It tells of the use of the supernatural by tragic writers of all ages, from Æschylus and Seneca thru the medieval period and the Renaissance to Maeterlinck, Ibsen and d'Annunzio, and discusses its general place and value in the drama.
                    Harvard University Press. $1.75.

1870—1914

There is a startling similarity between the destruction of Louvain and the bombardment of the Alsatian capitol during the Franco-Prussian War as it is described by Paul and Victor Marguerite in *Strasbourg*. Written many years before the outbreak of the present war, the book has just been translated into English by S. G. Tallentyre. The tale is terrible yet beautiful in its portrayal of courage and hopeless patriotism.
                                    Dutton. $1.35.

VOTING TRUSTS

It is an astute business man who understands corporations and their possibilities. Among these is the *Voting Trust*, whereby a number of stockholders pool their voting power. This is useful, at times necessary, but like all powers, possible of abuse. Harry A. Cushing has written a clear statement of its history, purpose and development, basing his account on leading cases and on many examples of the documents used in this method of corporate management.
                                Macmillan. $1.50.

BABYLONIA AND JUDAISM

Babylonian Texts in the Yale Oriental Series contains a selection of fifty-three out of some eight thousand tablets and other Babylonian inscriptions in the Yale collection, translated and edited by Professor A. T. Clay. These inscriptions go back to the most archaic period, and offer new evidence to support the contention of late gaining adherents that the religion and culture of the Hebrews had their origin not in Babylonia, but in the Amorite region of Palestine and Syria and were imported thence to Babylonia.

Yale University Press. $6.

HOW TO BUY

Purchasing is a study of the methods of buying intelligently, efficiently and economically, and of keeping track of purchases. The ideas are applicable to a small business, tho written by one who deals with large orders, H. B. Twyfford, of the Otis Elevator Company.

Van Nostrand. $3.

19TH CENTURY LITERATURE

The latest volume of the Cambridge history of English literature, *The Romantic Revival*, is the work of a large group of scholars, each an authority on the subject with which he deals. This composite authorship makes it possible for each phase of the literary history of the period to be treated with a depth of insight and catholicity rarely attainable in the work of an individual. Much valuable new material is presented on heretofore neglected topics.

Putnam. $2.50.

VERSE TO ORDER

Pretty good are the jingles from all sorts of folk whose notability is their only common characteristic, and the reason for their being asked to contribute to this amusing volume of *Little Verses with Big Names*. Not all the rimes are for children, but so many, and the best, are that the fat book will be no misfit in a youngster's library, while the price will go to help some sick baby.

Doran. $2.

OVER CROWDS

Of practical application in the matter of understanding and influencing public opinion are the theories set forth in *The Crowd in Peace and War*, Sir Martin Conway's at once popular and thoughtful discussion of the difference between the group and the individual character. If the first chapters leave one feeling the helplessness of the individual before the crowd, one lays down the book with a clearer understanding of the causes of group feeling and action, and of the direction in which one must move to produce effect on mass opinion.

Longmans, Green. $1.75.

THE MAKING OF CRIMINALS

Seventeen Years in the Underworld is a straightforward narrative of the opportunities society provided for making a criminal out of a promising boy of fifteen. Pool rooms, jail, reformatory, penitentiary, the lonesome lad and the lure of the underworld are presented without prejudice or bitterness. Wellington Scott, the name assumed for this writing, is at his best recounting the coming into his life of two real men and the place made for himself since that time.

Abingdon Press. 50 cents.

HIGH PRICE OF LIVING

Dr. Fabian Franklin in the *Cost of Living* gives an unusually lucid explanation of the economic factors involved in the fluctuation of prices, and of the effects of such fluctuation upon various classes of people. The quantity theory of money, and that of a multiple standard and compensated money units are set forth with concrete examples that will help many people to a better understanding of these perplexing problems.

Doubleday, Page. $1.

VIRGIL'S PASTORAL POETRY

Virgil's pastoral poetry represents, in some respects more vividly than the "Æneid," the poet's profound preoccupation with the duties and possibilities of Roman life. Its sublimated and purposeful picture of rural labor receives at the hands of the late Theodore Chickering Williams at once a scholarly and musical translation. The sensitive blank verse of the rendering of the *Georgics* and *Eclogues* retains to an extraordinary degree the majesty and serenity of the original.

Harvard University Press. $1.

PEBBLES

One hopeful sign is that there are fewer new books dealing with the causes of the war and more discussing what is to happen afterward.—*San Francisco Chronicle.*

Little Holland finds compensation for its troubles as a neutral. The Holland-American Steamship Company's dividend for 1915 was fifty per cent. In 1914 it was seventeen.—*Boston Herald.*

Dentist—Open wider, please—wider.
Patient—A—A—A—Ah.
Dentist (inserting rubber gag, towel and sponge)—How's your family?—*Harvard Lampoon.*

"One of the mysteries of journalism." remarks a newspaper, "is why they persist in printing the chess news on the sporting page." Still another mystery of journalism is why they persist in printing the chess news.—*Puck.*

Captain—"What's he charged with, Casey?"
Officer—"I don't know the regular name fer it, captain; but I caught him a-flirtin' in the park."
Captain—"Ah, that's impersonatin' an officer."—*Judge.*

The British debt, March 1, will be close to $11,000,000,000. Terrible! Almost $240 per capita! At this rate it will soon reach the gross debt of New York City, which was nearly $300 per capita, June 30, if reckoned from the last general census in the same manner.—*New York World.*

A lawyer who was sometimes forgetful, having been engaged to plead the cause of an offender, began by saying: "I know the prisoner at the bar, and he bears the character of being a most consummate and impudent scoundrel." Here somebody whispered to him that the prisoner was his client, when he immediately continued: "But what great and good man ever lived who was not calumniated by many of his contemporaries?"—*Case and Comment.*

A professor in an educational institution of the city was examining some students in hygienic science.
"The great city agglomerations vitiate the atmosphere," he said. "Morbiferous germs, escaping from inhabited interiors, contaminate the air round about. In the country, however, the atmosphere remains pure. Why is that, Jones?"
"Because," said Jones, "the people in the country never open their windows."—*Tit-Bits.*

"Children," said the Sunday school superintendent, "this picture illustrates to-day's lesson! Lot was warned to take his wife and daughters and flee out of Sodom. Here is Lot and his daughters, with his wife just behind them; and there is Sodom in the background. Now has any girl or boy a question before we take up the study of the lesson? Well, Susie?"
"Pleathe, thir," lisped the latest graduate from the infant class, "where ith the flea?"—*Harper's Magazine.*

GUIDE TO LEADING STATES

Connecticut: The home of the original Yankee, now peopled by insurance agents and New Haven officials who are trying to live down the past. Also where pure Havanas come from.

Illinois: A piece of land held in reserve by the city of Chicago for future golf links.

Massachusetts: The alleged home of the highbrow. In reality, a voting booth for newly landed immigrants.

New York: A small body of fans, entirely surrounded by debt.

New Jersey: A place that once had a reputation for good roads, bad corporations and Woodrow Wilson; now living on its past.

California: A part of Japan, temporarily held by the United States.

Ohio: A place where the presidential candidates don't come from.—*Life.*

Independent Opinions

So long as we talk about the inhabitants of Mars and the intentions of the Kaiser, we are safe, because nobody knows anything more about such questions than we do. But whenever we get down to solid earth and talk about topics of the common or garden variety we are likely to hear from our readers, some of whom know more than our authors—or think they do, which amounts to the same thing.

May I be tolerated with a couple of heretical statements on the "Vegetable Garden," of March 6?

1. There is a still better sweet corn than Golden Bantam, of the same season. It is the Early Catawba. Planted the same day with Bantam, it is ready for use three or four days ahead. In color when ripe it is exactly like Catawba grapes. When just ready for cooking it is milk white.

2. The best time for using parsnips is not in the spring (I defy the old notion), but in September, October and November. Take them when the size of a fountain pen, even in August, and they are unsurpassed by any other vegetable.

           JOHN G. ROBERTS
Syracuse, New York

Here follows a letter which we dare not provide with an "introduction":

Secretary Garrison writes a clear, concise, carefully considered letter of about 1000 words to President Wilson. The President answers with a clear, concise, carefully considered letter of about 600 words. The busy Washington correspondent of a great New York newspaper rips off 3000 words of ill-considered and confusing "introduction," telling us what the letters contain. Then follow the letters themselves. After which the editors, if you ask them, will mournfully tell you that they haven't room for half the interesting news of the day.

Brooklyn   WILLIS BROOKS

An item in our issue of December 20 on what a cent's worth of electricity would do in the way of cooking or work was intended to give the unscientific reader a tangible idea of that indefinite entity, the kilowatt-hour, which he has to pay for, but can never quite grasp. The customary price of ten to twelve cents was assumed, tho not specified. A Kansas City engineer points out, however, that our contributor was neither accurate nor definite enough in his calculations:

In the first place, nothing is stated as to the price or rate at which the current is supposed to be sold, and this may vary for domestic use from 1½ to 2 cents to as high as 15 or even 20 cents per kilowatt-hour, depending on many conditions. Therefore to say a cent's worth will accomplish all these results is like saying that a cent's worth of candy will fill up a white child three years old and a black one five years old, and will just fill a wooden box two by three by six inches, or tin box four by two inches.

Notice, please, that raising 250 gallons of water 100 feet means mechanical *work*, a definite number of "foot-pounds," approximately 208,333. And a unit of work is the

The Highest Choice

D^O not let it be merely a question of initial cost when you make your choice of pianos. The matchless music of the Steinway has lifted it above the "price" atmosphere for all time.

It is true, the Steinway does cost a little more. But no one who owns a Steinway has ever a shadow of regret for the price paid. It is but little higher than the cost of other pianos, and the Steinway carries within its perfect mechanism the guarantee of a satisfaction beyond all price.

For more than three-score years it has been the ideal of the greatest music masters of their day. So the Steinway must command your respectful attention before your choice is made.

Write for illustrated literature about the

STEINWAY

STEINWAY & SONS, STEINWAY HALL
107-109 EAST FOURTEENTH STREET, NEW YORK
Subway Express Station at the Door

"Pretty soft for him"

The price of electricity to raise the ten tons twelve feet with one cent's worth would have to be 11 cents per kilowatt-hour. At 10 cents per kilowatt-hour a common domestic rate the ten tons could be raised 13.2 feet, resistance neglected. The rate at which one cent would raise the 250 gallons 100 feet would be closely 12.07 cents per kilowatt-hour.

W. K. PALMER.

Kansas City, Missouri

A useful purpose might be served by opening a discussion on the question, "On what terms ought peace to be made?" We all know that peace must be made, and the only question is when and on what terms. Yet on both sides there is a disposition to close the ears to the discussion of terms. "We will not make terms" is a common expression. It can be easily understood that each group of combatants is unwilling to make a proposal lest it should be taken for a sign of weakness. Naturally, also, the Government of the United States is unwilling to make a proposal which might be met with a snub.

But this objection would not apply to an open discussion in The Independent. We have heard enough discussion as to who is to blame; we have also heard many proposals as to what ought to be done after the war. But there has been practically no discussion as to how to end the war. If a score of proposals were made as to terms and compared and discussed, substantial progress might be made. DIPLOMACY

New York City

We started such a discussion on November 29, in the article, "What Are You Fighting For?" where we brought together what has been put forward, officially and unofficial, as the terms of the several belligerents. When the more extravagant of these have been eliminated and the rest reduced to concrete terms, they are seen to be not so far apart, after all. Certainly they are not more difficult to reconcile than many an international disagreement that has been settled by amicable negotiation or arbitration. But when both parties are fighting mad, what are you going to do about it? At present the sole aim of each belligerent is simply to lick the other.

The efforts to bring the churches together on a common creed have had little success. Perhaps better results may be obtained if the attempt is made to bring them together on a financial basis. The "federated fair" seems to be a step in that direction.

Most churches have to resort to moneymaking schemes. In small towns where there are several churches of as many denominations, it is always a difficult matter to present their financial projects from conflicting in the matter of convenient dates and places. Sharp competition and even bitter hostilities are aroused and the saying that most American villages have several churches only a stone's throw apart becomes more than a simile.

Middlebury churches are doing away with that sort of thing. Three years ago, as an experiment, the Protestant churches of this town held a federated fair in the town hall. It was such a success financially and socially that the plan has been continued and the churches have established a permanent Fair Association. The

---

division of profits is on terms of equal shares after expenses are paid.

It may be a far cry from federated church fairs to church federation, but it certainly is a step in that direction. There is nothing more unifying than a common financial interest. We find that we can work together harmoniously and we have become better acquainted socially than we could have, in any other way. The effect has been most wholesome in our community life as an example of federated effort in church life. Years of occasional union religious services have not succeeded in bringing the churches into such intimate friendliness as has the federated fair.

HARRIET G. COCKRAN

Middlebury, Vermont

Your assumption in "The Heritage of Hate" editorial of March 13, that the Catholic Irish—who form 95 per cent of the Nationalist or Home Rule party—are enlisting in great numbers for the defense of the Empire is quite erroneous.

The census of 1911 shows that Ireland contained nine and seven tenths of the population of the British Isles. Since the outbreak of the war 4,000,000 men in the United Kingdom have volunteered for service and of these less than 100,000 enrolled in Ireland. Of these 40 per cent (Protestant Irish) are anti-Home Rule. So that less than 60,000 Home Rulers have joined the colors. Based on 74 per cent (Catholic Irish) of its population. Ireland should have sent 287,000 men to the front, as representative of the Nationalist sentiment.

The population of England proper is 75 per cent of the total population of the British Isles, yet 90 per cent of the new army was born there. Of the first Canadian contingent 70 per cent were born in England.

The man today who is doing the fighting in the British Army is the Englishman born. He has been so modest about it that it is assumed by most Americans that Irishmen, Scotchmen, Canadians, etc., are doing all the dying. Since the beginning of the war I have read in the London *Times* the daily record of killed and wounded and the vast preponderance of English names clearly shows that the Englishman is in the forefront of battle.

With regard to the navy, the Irish make a still poorer showing—less than 5 per cent being born in Ireland. I do not wish thus to disparage the Irish people, for their valor is well established, but to do justice to those men of the English race who today as never before are freely offering their lives to the service of their country.

JOHN RHODES

New York City

We did not say or assume that the Irish Catholics were enlisting in as great a proportion as the Irish Protestants or the English. The recent meeting at the Hotel Astor showed that there was, as we said, an irreconcilable faction who maintained "The Heritage of Hate." An Irishman recently in London speaks of "the absolute conviction of the Scotch, Irish and Welsh troops, as well as of all the colonial troops, that they are deliberately sacrificed in battle, in order to spare the English regiments." As our correspondent points out, an examination of the casualty lists does not confirm this charge.

Such jealousies and mutual mistrust are unwarranted and unfortunate. After living together for two thousand years, the people of the United Kingdom should be united. However much Ireland has been wronged in the past, she has recently been treated with wisdom and generosity. Her grievances in regard to land and local government are being removed and she should not allow her ancient resentment to interfere with future prosperity.

THE MARKET PLACE
A REVIEW OF FINANCE AND TRADE

RAILROAD EQUIPMENT OBLIGATIONS

PRIVATE investors of small means are not so well acquainted with railroad equipment bonds as they are with first mortgage railroad and public utility bonds or with stocks. Bonds secured by equipment have often been regarded in the same light as chattel mortgages on movable property, altho the analogy is not fair, as equipment is highly productive while ordinary chattels are usually not.

Incidentally there is overlooked the fact that cars and locomotives form a *most vital part* of a railroad's property without which it could not operate. It is absolutely essential that a railroad acquire new equipment from time to time as old cars are scrapped or new cars are needed. The most approved method of financing such purchases is by the issuance of bonds maturing in series during the life of the property covered.

The original equipment bond as now known was really the product of the weak financial condition of a few railroads during the early seventies and the absence of proper provisions in railroad mortgages of that time for the issuance of bonds for equipment. Bonds could have been issued under the mortgages, but there were no provisions for depreciation of the equipment and replacement when it had no value for operating purposes. Some prudent railroad men of the period cited saw the advantages of a "pay-as-you-go" policy rather than the issuance of long term bonds for short-lived property, and the equipment bond maturing serially was the result.

The life of a wooden car is estimated at about seventeen years, while a steel car lasts twenty or more. Most cars are now made of steel, or wood with steel under-frame. Having in mind the extinction of the equipment debt prior to the time when the property begins to depreciate, a railroad company wishing to purchase equipment will pay from 10 to 25 per cent of the cost price in cash and issue bonds for the remainder. The bonds usually mature in semi-annual series amounting to 5 per cent of the total authorized issue. In this manner, by the time the property has depreciated 50 per cent the entire issue of bonds will have been re-

tired and the railroad will still have five or ten additional years' use out of its equipment.

There are several plans for the issuance of railroad equipment obligations. One provides for the direct purchase of equipment by a railroad and the issuance of bonds to the extent of 75 to 90 per cent of the purchase price. The bonds are secured by a first lien on the equipment in favor of a trustee. They are a direct obligation of the railroad and mature in series of 5 per cent of the total amount at each semi-annual interest period; title to the equipment remains absolutely with the trustee until the last series of bonds has matured and been retired. At this juncture, absolute title reverts to the railroad company. As the amount of equipment bonds decreases, the equity for the outstanding bonds increases correspondingly. At the time the final payment is made the equipment is worth a much greater sum than that represented by the last series of bonds. These are straight equipment bonds.

Car trust bonds or car trust certificates differ somewhat, the former secured by an agreement of conditional sale and the latter representing a beneficial interest in a lease. Under the conditional sale a manufacturing company will transfer the title to equipment to a trust company, allowing the purchasing railroad use of the cars or locomotives upon payment of interest on the amount of bonds outstanding plus an instalment of 5 per cent of the principal at each semi-annual period. When the amount of instalments paid totals that of the original issue of bonds, the title is transferred to the railroad company by the trustee. Car trust bonds are se-

cured by the contract of conditional sale and are the direct obligation of the railroad issuing them.

Car trust certificates issued under the "Philadelphia Plan" are very generally used for financing a railroad's equipment requirements. Under this plan an agreement is made for the purchase of equipment between a railroad company, a trust company and certain third parties. A lease of the equipment is made by the trustee with the railroad, title remaining with the trustee, and certificates of beneficial interest in the lease are issued to investors. The railroad agrees under the lease to pay semi-annual interest on the certificates outstanding and serial instalments of principal as they mature, usually semi-annually. When the entire issue of certificates has been retired, title is vested in the railroad company. The principal and interest on the certificates are guaranteed by the railroad company by endorsement.

Conditional sales are not recognized in Pennsylvania as a proper means of issuing equipment bonds, so the lease method is used. Car trust certificates issued by a Pennsylvania corporation, trustee or equipment association are free of state taxes in Pennsylvania to resident owners when the railroad issuing the certificates agrees to refund the tax.

As equipment deteriorates and is liable to be destroyed by fire, flood or wreck, holders of equipment obligations must be safeguarded. Provisions are included in the trust agreement to the effect that during the life of the bonds the equipment is to be kept insured against loss and that the railroad company must replace any part or all of such equipment as may be damaged or destroyed. Many indentures provide that the railroad company must furnish a statement to the trustee each year, or oftener if required, setting forth the true physical condition of the

| | | | Approximate Yields | |
| | | Rate of | At the | At the |
	Maturity	Interest	Bid Price	Asked Price
Atlantic Coast Line	1916-23	4-4½	4.30	4.10
Baltimore & Ohio	1916-23	4½	4.30	4.10
Buff., Roch. & Pittsb.	1916-30	4½-5	4.50	4.15
Canadian Pacific	1916-28	4½	4.50	4.20
Car., Clinch. & Ohio	1916-24	5	4.60	4.35
Chesapeake & Ohio	1916-24	4½	4.40	4.20
Chicago & Alton	1916-20	4½	5.25	4.75
Chicago & Northwest.	1916-23	4½	4.20	4.00
Chi., St. L. & New Or.	1916-24	5	4.35	4.12
Cleve., C., C. & St. L.	1916-29	5	4.55	4.20
Delaware & Hudson	1922	4½	4.20	4.10
Erie	1916-23	4½-5	4.55	4.25
Hocking Valley	1916-23	4-5	4.40	4.20
Illinois Central	1916-24	4½	4.25	4.12
Louisville & Nashville	1916-23	5	4.20	4.00
N. Y. Central Lines	1916-28	4½-5	4.40	4.20
Norfolk & Western	1916-24	4½	4.20	4.00
N. Y., N. H. & H.	1916-26	6	4.40	4.20
Penna. Gen. Freight.	1916-23	4-4½	4.20	4.00
St. L. Iron M'n & Sou.	1916-24	5	5.38	4.88
Seaboard Air Line	1916-23	5	4.60	4.25
Southern Pacific	1916-23	4½	4.30	4.10
Southern Railway	1916-24	4½-5	4.55	4.25

equipment secured by the bonds or certificates. For identification each car or locomotive is distinguished by a plate attached to its side stating that it is the property of so and so as trustee.

While rolling stock usually represents about one-fifth of a railroad's total investment, it is the most important revenue-producing part of the property owned. Equipment includes locomotives, passenger and freight cars, mail cars, baggage cars, crane cars, snow plows, refrigerator cars, tank cars, car ferries, etc. The courts have recognized that a railroad in receivership must not default on the principal or interest on equipment obligations inasmuch as the loss of its equipment would seriously cripple its earning capacity. In most cases on record the interest on such bonds has been paid even when interest on first mortgage bonds was in default. During the crisis of 1893-1896 over 100,000 miles of railroad was in the hands of receivers, yet it is stated that not a dollar was lost by holders of equipment securities.

The mortgage bondholders of a company in receivership recognize, of course, that as the equipment bonds are retired the less interest there is to pay, and their equity in the property increases proportionately. In current reorganizations many mortgage bonds are either being scaled down or else compelled to accept junior bonds, or even stocks, while equipment obligations are nearly always provided for by a cash payment.

On account of their short maturity, rarely over fifteen years, equipment bonds have a very good market and do not fluctuate greatly in price. A favorable factor is that the value of the equipment is known at the outset and the investor can easily figure what equity he has above the total issue of bonds. If, for instance, he purchases a bond of an issue of $800,000 against equipment costing $1,000,000, he knows that there is 20 per cent in value over his bonds. Also, that in five years, if his bonds are for a longer term, he will have an equity of 50 per cent and can feel assured that his principal is safe aside from the guarantee or direct obligation on the part of the railroad company.

The most discriminating investors are attracted by the soundness of equipment obligations and large amounts are purchased by banks, institutions and insurance companies. The Equitable Life, New York Life, Mutual Life and Prudential Life are among the prominent insurance companies that report very large holdings of these bonds. The amount held by investors today is placed at about $550,000,000, while in 1890 there were less than $50,000,000 outstanding. For the convenience of the investor some of the best issues are listed on the preceding page, together with maturity dates and approximate yields.

The following dividends are announced:
Liggett & Myers Tobacco Company, common, extra, 4 per cent, payable April 1.
D. C. Heath & Co. preferred, quarterly, 1¾ per cent, payable April 1.

Insurance
Conducted by
W. E. UNDERWOOD

PARTICIPATING AND NON-PARTICIPATING LIFE INSURANCE

A request comes from a reader in Indianapolis for my "opinion as to the relative value of participating and non-participating life insurance." In complying, I wish it understood that in expressing a choice of one, I do not in the slightest degree abridge the value or the merits of the other. As between the two, I am a mutualist.

Insurance is a loss-distributing system. That is a fundamental fact. In life insurance we know that the loss will certainly occur, for men always die. In addition to the loss claims, money is required to run the system. The persons insured furnish all these funds. To those interested, then, life insurance is an expense. That being true, it is desirable it should be reduced to a safe minimum.

A capably managed mutual company can achieve that end; a non-participating company cannot. Its expense will be greater than the irreducible minimum to the extent of the sum paid stockholders on their investments in the company's capital.

It does not follow from this that any mutual company has as yet reduced the net cost of the service to the lowest point consistent with safety; nor does it mean that no stock company is furnishing it at a cost below that paid by the policyholders in some mutual companies. The best managed mutuals improve in this respect every year; the best managed stock companies do better than a number of mutuals. But, given managements of equal skill, experience and business ability, one operating a mutual and the other a stock company, the lower net cost rate to policyholders will be attained by the mutual, because the dividends to stockholders will be an expense factor in the latter which is absent in the former.

In considering this question it is essential that the human element involved be kept in mind. In the last analysis, we will find that the interests of policyholders in every insurance company are largely dependent on the personal character of the few men running them. Splendid ability is not enough. They must inherently possess a fine quality of morality and a sense of duty to accepted trusts that is beyond the reach of temptation. As a matter of fact, that is one of the principal differences between companies. The directors, officers and representatives who are concerned too often about their individual promotion or financial gain lack that sturdiness of character necessary to the faithful steward. It is enough for such

---

DIVIDENDS

AMERICAN TELEPHONE AND TELEGRAPH COMPANY

A dividend of Two Dollars per share will be paid on Saturday, April 15, 1916, to stockholders of record at the close of business on Friday, March 31, 1916.
    G. D. MILNE, Treasurer.

UNITED FRUIT COMPANY
DIVIDEND NO. 67

A quarterly dividend of two per cent. (two dollars per share) on the capital stock of this Company has been declared, payable on April 15, 1916, at the office of the Company, 131 State street, Boston, Mass., to stockholders of record at the close of business on March 24, 1916.

The said dividend is not payable on shares subscribed for under the terms of the Company's circular letter to stockholders dated January 21, 1916.   JOHN W. DAMON, Assistant Treasurer

---

WESTINGHOUSE ELECTRIC
& MANUFACTURING COMPANY

A quarterly dividend of 1¾% (87½ cents per share), on the PREFERRED stock of this Company will be paid April 15, 1916.

A dividend of 1½% (75 cents per share) on the COMMON stock of this Company for the quarter ending March 31, 1916, will be paid April 29, 1916.

Both dividends are payable to stockholders of record as of March 31, 1916.
    H. D. SHUTE, Treasurer
New York, March 22, 1916.

D. C. HEATH & COMPANY
BOSTON
Preferred Stock

The regular quarterly dividend of one and three-quarters per cent. has been declared by the Directors of this Corporation, payable April 1, 1916, to preferred stockholders of record March 25, 1916. Checks will be mailed.
    WINFIELD S. SMYTH, Treasurer

STANDARD MILLING COMPANY
40 Wall Street
PREFERRED STOCK DIVIDEND NO. 28

New York City, March 22, 1916.
The Directors of this Company have today declared a dividend of TWO AND ONE-HALF (2½%) PER CENT. from the earnings of the Company upon the Preferred Stock, payable April 15, 1916, at the office of the Company, to the Preferred Stockholders of record on April 5, 1916. The transfer books of the Preferred Stock will be closed on April 5, 1916, at three o'clock p. m., and opened on April 17, 1916, at ten o'clock a. m.
    JOS. A. KNOX, Treasurer

a one that he performs his duty with rigid fidelity, without regard to the reward he is to receive. In most cases he will come into all that is justly his. This is not always true, for I have evidence of several exceptions, due to the fact, however, that the faithful man was overruled by associates more powerful and less just than he. In such cases, the latter is feared, distrusted and, as far as may be, forced out of the councils of his fellow-managers, while his participation in affairs is reduced to a minimum.

Personally I prefer, when asked to indicate a choice, participating to non-participating life insurance; but I have no strong objections to urge to the latter when furnished by a company of proper financial condition conducted by men of proved good moral and business character. The policyholder who takes a non-participating policy should understand that the premium he is paying is ten, twelve, sometimes fifteen per cent lower than he would pay for a participating policy; and for that reason he will get no dividends. In other words, that there will never be any reduction in the amount of his annual premium. Beyond that, and the additional fact that the company is controlled by stockholders who have the power, rarely exercised, of inflicting injury on the interests of policyholders, there is no difference requiring consideration.

Mutual companies can be mismanaged and the interests of their members, as we saw by the New York legislative investigation of 1905, can be hurt; but if the state insurance departments, with their unlimited power of visitation and examination, do their duty properly, the irregularities of managements can be quickly detected and promptly suppresst.

Stock companies should be restricted to the transaction of non-participating life insurance, and all mutual companies should be prohibited from issuing non-participating policies. The two classes should never be mixed in the same company. Mutual policyholders are members and owners of the company; policyholders in a stock company are buyers from the owners, the stockholders.

It is not a question of security in either case. Most companies now are good for their death losses at any time. The laws governing reserves and the supervision exercised by the states put that point almost beyond the shadow of a doubt. It is a question of net cost during a term of years; a question of skilful and honest management; a question of permanent immunity against dereliction of duty, incapacity and personal cupidity.

N. C. H. Rolfs, Mo.—The market value of stock in a life insurance company is impossible of ascertainment. It is generally held by a comparatively small number of persons and is never listed on any of the exchanges. I judge from such indications as are available in its reports that the Missouri State Life is in a prosperous condition, but am in no position to prophesy the value or future income of its stock to investors.

THE CITY
MANAGER PLAN

*Resolved, That all American cities
should adopt the Dayton, Ohio, City
Manager Plan of municipal government.*

The City Manager Plan of municipal government has been developing rapidly for the past few years. Sumter, South Carolina, put it into effect in January, 1913. Since this date twenty-five cities and towns, of which Dayton, Ohio, is the largest, have adopted city manager government. This brief was prepared by R. S. Fulton.

AFFIRMATIVE

I. Dayton Plan offers safest means for municipal government.
  A. It approaches nearest to successful German system.
    B. Preferable to Mayor and council.
    1. Ex-President Eliot and James Bryce call ward system "dead failure."
    2. Dayton Plan fixes responsibility.
    3. Brings expert men to its service.
    4. Establishes continuity in office.
      (a) Two members, then three members, of board of commissioners, are elected every alternate two years.
      (b) City manager is appointed for indefinite time.
    5. Destroys ward lines and patronage.
  C. Superior to commission system.
    1. Retains and adds to merits of commission system.
      (a) Retains idea of responsible elected legislative body.
      (b) Attains unification of powers.
      (c) Adds expert men and permanent force of trained executives.
    2. Concentrates responsibility for administrative work in city manager.
    3. In commission system responsibility for administrative work is divided.
    4. Unlike commission system it separates legislative and executive functions.
II. Proposed plan sound in theory.
  A. Basic principles of Dayton Charter are sound.
    1. Five commissioners elected on nonpartisan ballot from city as whole constitute legislative body.
    2. These commissioners can be recalled by voters thru initiative, referendum.
    3. Administrative functions delegated to city manager.
    4. Manager holds universal appointive power over administrative department.
    5. Charter provides for scientific methods of business:
      (a) Detailed budget.
      (b) Accounting system.
      (c) Time reports.
      (d) Uniform departmental reports.
      (e) Service records.
      (f) Centralized purchasing.
      (g) Modern appliances for street cleaning.
      (h) Public welfare department.
    B. Makes municipal government like business organization.
      1. Citizen represents shareholder.
      2. Commissioners represent directors.
      3. City manager represents manager.
      4. Departmental heads are aids to manager.
    C. Eliminates politics.
      1. Manager need not be city resident.
      2. He is appointed for his merits.
      3. Departmental heads are appointed for ability.
      4. Commissioners are elected on nonpartisan ticket.
    D. Manager cannot become autocratic.
      1. He is subject to public control thru initiative, referendum, recall.
      2. Holds office at will of commissioners.
      3. Power of manager to dismiss and

appoint employees is guided by merit system of civil service.
  E. May be applied to cities of any size.
    1. Functions of municipal corporation, as in Dayton, can be performed by departments in which heads are in direct touch with manager.
    2. Council can be large in large cities and small in small cities.
    3. Council may be elected at large, or by districts, or by proportional representation by means of short ballot.
    4. Corporations regardless of size are built upon principles like in Dayton Charter.
III. Proposed plan has been a success.
  A. Successful in Dayton.
    1. Given new and efficient service.
      (a) In 1914 gave $140,000 worth of new service.
      (b) Regenerated city socially and morally.
      (c) New improvements made.
      (d) Better city administration.
      (e) Reorganized the departments.
      (f) Has kept expenditures to income.
      (g) Collected taxes more efficiently.
      (h) Put municipal credit above par.
      (i) Saved money for taxpayer.
    B. A success in other cities.
      1. Floating debts wiped out.
        (a) In Springfield, Ohio, $100,000.
        (b) In La Grande, Oregon, $35,000.
      2. Kept disbursements within appropriations.
      3. Lowered tax rates.
      4. Increased service.
      5. Resulted in savings.
        (a) In first year under new plan Springfield saved $50,000.
        (b) Cadillac, Mich., saved thirteen per cent of its annual running expenses.

NEGATIVE

I. Proposed plan not most feasible method.
  A. Inferior to commission system.
    1. None of commission governed cities, except Amarillo, Texas, have changed over to Dayton Plan.
    2. Gives too much power to one man.
    3. Commission system divides administrative work among commissioners.
    4. Greater opportunity for shifting responsibility than commission system.
      (a) Commission system places responsibility directly upon commissioners.
      (b) Manager plan enables commissioners to shift responsibility.
        (1) People hold commissioners responsible for administrative work of city.
        (2) Commissioners in turn held manager responsible.
        (3) Recall of manager by people diverts responsibility from commissioners.
    5. Its commissioners will give less efficient service.
      (a) Commission system gives its commissioners adequate compensation.
      (b) Manager plan gives its commissioners little or no compensation.
      (c) Commission system requires its commissioners to devote all their time to municipal work.
      (d) Manager plan requires only part of commissioners' time.
    B. Many American cities have rejected manager plan.
II. Proposed plan not sound in theory.
  A. Dayton Charter contains radical provisions.
    1. Compels manager to serve two masters.
      (a) He is subjected to popular recall.
      (b) Holds office at will of commissioners.
    2. Gives too much work to manager.

B. Initiative, referendum, recall—integral parts of system are radical.
    1. Average citizen has neither time nor training for wise law making.
    C. Not democratic.
      1. Most important officer is appointed.
      D. Faction may elect most incapable member of commission mayor.
      1. Charter provides that commissioner who receives highest vote at election when three commissioners are chosen shall be mayor.
      E. Contention that manager will remain permanently in office is false.
      1. To dismiss a manager, commissioners are not required to prefer formal charges or give him public hearing.
      F. Relation between manager and commission will result in friction.
      1. Commissioners will interfere unduly.
      2. Expert manager may become impatient with amateur commissioners.
      G. Argument that proposed plan will eliminate politics is absurd.
      1. If commissioners happen to be members of same party, they are apt to appoint partisan managers.
      2. Manager in turn apt to appoint men from his party.
III. Proposed plan not a success.
      A. Has not been in operation long enough to demonstrate its merits.
      B. Saving money no proof of success.
      C. In Dayton many reforms secured under new plan are results of additional expenditures.
      1. Operating expenditures for first year of new plan were $77,709 more than for previous year.
      D. In many cities there has been friction between managers and commission.
      1. In Sumter, S. C., commissioners made first city manager helpless.
        (a) In place of coöperating with manager they dealt with subordinates.
      2. In Phœnix, Arizona, friction between commissioners and manager threw city government into state of disorder.

REFERENCES

General

American City, 8:373-380, April, 1913. *American Municipalities*, 27:51, May, 1914. *American Political Science Review*, 7:653-655, November, 1913; 9:504-506, 561-563, August, 1915. *American Review of Reviews*, 47:599-602, May, 1913; 49:144-145, February, 1914. *Collier's Weekly*, 52:5-6, January 3, 1914; 56:9-10, October 16, 1915. *California Outlook*, 13:10-11, October 25, 1913. *Engineering and Contracting*, 39:565-566, May 21, 1913. *Engineering Record*, 70:222, August 22, 1914. *Literary Digest*, 47:303, August 30, 1913; 51:199-200, July 31, 483, September 25, 1915. *National Municipal Review*, 2:76-81, January, 693-644, October, 1913; 3:113-116, January, 1914. *The Short Ballot Bulletin*, monthly (383 Fourth Ave., New York), contains frequent lists of commission-managed cities.

Affirmative

American City, 9:25-27, July; 523-525, December, 1913; 11:11-13, July, 1914. *American Municipalities*, 26:113-114, January; 27:55-60, May; 13, June, 1914. *American Political Science Review*, 9:495-504, August, 1915. *American Review of Reviews*, 49:714-717, June, 1914. *Engineering News*, 71:831-832, April 16, 1914. *Equity*, 16:207-208, October, 1914. *Literary Digest*, 48:147-148, January 24; 51:199-200, July 31, 1915. *Municipal Journal*, 36:622-625, June 4; 37:11, July 2, 1914. *Municipal World*, 24:84, April, 1914. *National Municipal Review*, 4:371-382, July, 1915. *Outlook*, 104:887-889, August 23, 1913. *Pacific Municipalities*, 28:356-362, July; 578-584, November, 1914. *Independent*, 80:433, December 21, 1914.

Negative

American City, 10:27-38, January, 1914. *American Political Science Review*, 8:602-13, November, 1914. *National Municipal Review*, 3:148, January; 3:95-97, January, 1914. Toulmin, H. A. Jr., *The City Manager—a New Profession*. New York: D. Appleton & Co., 1915, pp. 162-166, 222-237, 250-253, 262-264.

The Independent

FOR SIXTY-SEVEN YEARS THE
FORWARD-LOOKING WEEKLY OF AMERICA

THE　CHAUTAUQUAN
Merged with The Independent June 1, 1914

APRIL,　10,　1916

OWNED AND PUBLISHED BY
THE INDEPENDENT CORPORATION, AT
119 WEST FORTIETH STREET, NEW YORK
WILLIAM B. HOWLAND, PRESIDENT
FREDERIC E. DICKINSON, TREASURER

WILLIAM HAYES WARD
HONORARY EDITOR

EDITOR: HAMILTON HOLT
ASSOCIATE EDITOR: HAROLD J. HOWLAND
LITERARY EDITOR: EDWIN E. SLOSSON

PUBLISHER: KARL V. S. HOWLAND

ONE YEAR, THREE DOLLARS

SINGLE COPIES, TEN CENTS

Postage to foreign countries in Universal Postal
Union, $1.75 a year extra; to Canada, $1 extra.
Instructions for renewal, discontinuance or
change of address should be sent two weeks
before the date they are to go into effect. Both
the old and the new address must be given.

We welcome contributions, but writers who
wish their articles returned, if not accepted,
should send a stamped and addressed envelope. No responsibility is assumed by The
Independent for the loss or non-return of
manuscripts, tho all due care will be exercised.

Entered at New York Post Office as Second
Class Matter

Copyright, 1916, by The Independent

Address all Communications to
THE INDEPENDENT
119 West Fortieth Street, New York

CONTENTS

TURNING THE TABLES

Teachers are much given to lecturing
their students on intellectual honesty.
But there is, apparently, something to
be said on the other side, and it is said
by *Challenge*, the new intercollegiate
periodical of radical thought and
criticism, published by students of Columbia and elsewhere. A reformed
form of university catalog is proposed
by one of the editors of *Challenge*, Preston W. Slosson.:

CANDOR UNIVERSITY

The president reports to the trustees
another successful year. Owing to the
munitions boom and the death of several
wealthy men during the influenza epidemic
our receipts have been larger than usual
and we have been able to erect two fine
new buildings and even (what is most remarkable) to spend a little on instruction.
There have been no scandals, and the only
ebullitions of free speech in the faculty
have been such as rather to advertise than
to discredit the university. In the field of
scholarship we have produced many works
of research and instruction. Nine-tenths of
them will serve no useful purpose here or
hereafter, but they look well in the report.
In the more important field of athletics
our unfortunate reverses in baseball have
been more than compensated by a successful season in crew, track and football. In
view of all these facts I feel emboldened to
ask for a lot more money, and if you can't
get it anywhere else, to pay up yourselves.
　　　　　—*President's Report, 1916.*

The student must obey the requirements
of the catalog with implicit obedience if
he hopes to get a degree. He must also keep
in mind, however, that the interpretation
of these rules is very elastic, for it is a
poor rule that won't stretch both ways.
　　　　　—*Catalog, 1916.*

COURSES ANNOUNCED

Professor Osmosis Foliage offers Botany
99-100 to graduate students. At least eight
students must elect this course, and since
no more than six have elected it any previous year, he feels safe.

History F3-F4—Professor Joffre Mackensen. This course is supposed to deal with
the Evolution of Law in Modern History.
By April it will have reached only the
tenth century A. D. because the professor's
hobby is Hittite Jurisprudence.

Sociology X8-Y9—This course is to enable Professor Malthus Marx (M.A.) to
get material for his thesis in which he
develops a completely new terminology for
quite old concepts. If you like that sort of
thing that's the sort of thing you like.

Greek 1-2—Offered by Professor Jones
and Mr. Smith (Jones's text book used).
It is worth noting that Mr. Smith never
gives anybody marks as high as Professor
Jones gives to half his class.—*Verb. sap.
sat.*

Philosophy 4-11-44—Comes at 5 o'clock.
Placed at this awkward hour because it
is a snap course and the authorities don't
want everybody to be taking it. For the
same reason it is held on the top floor of
College Hall and nobody is allowed to use
the elevator.

REMARKABLE REMARKS

JESS WILLARD—I draw the color line.

MRS. HENRY SYMES—Never refuse soup.

W. H. TAFT—The general primary is a
fraud.

THEODORE ROOSEVELT—June is a long
way off.

AMY LOWELL—No city is greater than
its poets.

YUAN SHIH-KAI—China is racing to perdition.

THOMAS A. EDISON—The instincts of
women are good.

JOHN MASEFIELD—The American is the
Englishman set free.

"BUGS" BAER—Every man has a lot of
influence with himself.

KING PETER—This war is the supreme
last effort of feudalism.

GEORGE W. PERKINS—We as a nation
are unprepared for peace.

THE DUKE OF MANCHESTER—There are
good and bad noblemen.

ED. HOWE—I never knew a retail gro-
ceryman who became rich.

NICHOLAS MURRAY BUTLER — Europe
has been at war for years.

POPE BENEDICT—This appears to us as
the suicide of civilized Europe.

SECRETARY OF WAR BAKER—The Democratic party is a dismal failure.

ADMIRAL KNIGHT—I am not so sure we
will never have a war with England.

RABINDRANATH TAGORE—Because I love
this life I know I shall love death as well.

LONGWORTH GREEN—I would follow
Theodore Roosevelt into the depths of hell.

G. K. CHESTERTON—The battle of Waterloo was not won on Eton's playing fields.

EMPEROR WILLIAM—Only one is master
within the empire, and I will tolerate no
other.

J. PIERPONT MORGAN—They don't seem
to be suffering from any lack of money over
there.

BILLY SUNDAY—If Martin Luther were
here, he would say: Go to it, Bill, I'm
with you.

GOVERNOR WHITMAN—To say that I
have no thought of the presidency would
be an untruth.

FELIX TUMULTY—It is the expedient
thing for the politicians to get on the suffrage band wagon.

PROF. WILLIAM LYON PHELPS—The
greatest compliment an author can receive
is to have his words repeated without quotation marks.

FRANCISCO VILLA—Uncle Sam's beard
and Carranza's whiskers have been plaited
together to make a rope with which to hang
the hopes of Mexico.

PASTOR FRITZ PHILIPPI OF BERLIN—
On Germany is laid the Divine command
to bring about the destruction of those who
are the personification of evil.

Her Second Childhood

Eating the simple, nutritious foods that keep the mind buoyant and the arteries soft and pliable is the surest road to the bounding, exuberant health of children. You can postpone Old Age through the constant companionship of children and through eating the simple, natural and well-cooked foods.

Shredded Wheat

supplies in well balanced proportion the greatest amount of nutriment with the least tax upon the digestive organs. It contains all the material for replenishing the daily waste of tissue and at the same time supplies a laxative element that keeps the colon clean. A food for all ages—for babies, mothers and grandmothers—for invalids and athletes —for outdoor men and indoor men.

Being ready-cooked and ready-to-serve, it is easy to prepare with Shredded Wheat a delicious, nourishing meal in a few moments. Always heat the Biscuit in the oven to restore its crispness. Serve with hot or cold milk, adding a little cream and salt. Delicious for any meal with sliced bananas, baked apples or other fruits.

Made only by
The Shredded Wheat Company, Niagara Falls, N. Y.

The Independent

VOLUME 86   APRIL 10, 1916   NUMBER 3514

EARTH'S EASTER FAITH

IT is a holy legend that when Jesus was born in Bethlehem of Judea all the demons of war fled in affright to their nether caves. The gates of Janus were shut, for no squadrons passed thru to fight the world over. The angels flocked down and filled the plain with songs of glad peace among goodwilling men, while the very crystalline spheres that bear the stars of heaven rang like cymbals in silver chime, for heaven had come down to dwell forever on earth with men. But Jesus and the virgin mother fled to Egypt and then to Nazareth and thence to Calvary's cross; and cruel Moloch with all his sullen crew recovered courage and remounted their old thrones in their old temples.

Jesus rose from the grave, but earth was slow to know her Easter morn. One said, "The Lord is risen" and another replied, "He is risen indeed and has appeared unto Simon," but Rome knew it not, and Janus opened wider his gates. So the centuries have moved on and the sanctities of heaven still stand thick as stars in their station about the throne of God, for the Easter hope still lingers while the weary earth waits for the time when heaven shall come down again to take its promised rest with men.

Sight is blind, but faith's celestial hope shines inward and sees things invisible to mortal sight; she sees beyond and thru the cannon smoke the gleam of the New Jerusalem, and above the roar of battle she hears the Easter joy.

Never till now out of the gates of war have such thickset legions hasted before. It must be that two thousand years of wrong are close to their end and the bottomless pit of war will be closed and locked fast, while out of heaven Truth and Justice shall descend to dwell with men, and a scrap of paper with the nations' promises engrossed upon it shall be strong enough to bind the world in one, while bayonets and mortars and sea-planes and Zeppelins and super-dreadnoughts are flung into the scrap-heap of ancient history or fly with monarchies and despotisms and other follies into the limbo at the back side of the world.

WATER POWER, ELECTRICITY AND THE PUBLIC INTEREST

AFTER steam, electricity. After coal, water power. So runs the course of industrial progress.

We are well embarked upon the electrical age. We have only taken the first step into the age of water powers.

Four years ago (unfortunately, no later figures are available), thirty million horse power of electrical power were in use in the United States. Of this less than one-sixth was created by the use of the energy of falling waters.

Nearly five million horse power of electricity were being generated by water power for industrial uses. But the estimated potential water power resources of the whole country were somewhere between a minimum of twenty-eight million horse power and a maximum of fifty-four million horse power. There is available for development from six to eleven times as much water power as was then being used for industrial and commercial purposes.

How shall we go about to avail ourselves of this vast natural resource? No more important problem of national development on the material side lies before us as a people. Power is the prime requisite of modern industry; and as a source of power falling water is unique. It is perennial. You burn coal to make steam to generate electricity to turn the wheels of a mill, and the coal is gone. You must dig other coal out of the earth and begin over again. Some day your coal will be all gone. You harness your electric generator to a wheel turned by a waterfall and generate your electricity;

and tomorrow other water has taken its place, and the day after and next week and next year, and so on forever. The water will work for you and never tire, never give out.

On another page we print an article which describes in graphic style the industrial possibilities of electrical power. They run from the electric range in the kitchen and the electrically driven sewing machine to the extraction of nitrogen from the air for the making of fertilizers for the farm and high explosives for national defense. With such great resources awaiting utilization and such manifold uses to which the power can be profitably applied, the way should be opened as rapidly as possible for their development. To this end new legislation is necessary.

Two bills are now before Congress—the Shields bill and the Ferris bill—looking toward such development. The Ferris bill deals with water powers in national forests; the Shields bill with water powers on navigable streams.

The purpose of both bills is in essence good. But each bill contains provisions which would give away too much that belongs to the public and that ought to be retained in public ownership and control.

The case against these bills as they now stand has been set forth by Gifford Pinchot, the father of the conservation movement:

The Shields bill, now before the Senate, gives to the power interests without compensation the use of water power on navigable streams. The amount of water power these streams will supply is larger by far than all the power of every kind now in use in the United States. It pretends to, but does not, enable the people to take back their own property at the end of fifty years, for in order to do so, under the bill, the government would have to pay the unearned increment, and to take over whole lighting systems of cities and whole manufacturing plants. Private corporations are authorized to seize upon any land, private or public, they choose to condemn.

Bills which gave away public water powers without due compensation were vetoed by President Roosevelt and President Taft. The Shields bill would do precisely the same thing today.

Another water power bill, the Ferris bill, relating to the public lands and national forests, was in the main a good bill as it passed the House. As reported to the Senate, it encourages monopoly by permitting a corporation to take as many public water power sites as it may please. Under it the corporations could not even be kept from fastening upon the Grand Canyon, the greatest natural wonder on this continent. This bill takes the care of water powers on national forests from the experienced and competent Forest Service, and gives it to the Interior Department, thus entailing duplication and needless expense.

We are not so much concerned as is Mr. Pinchot over the prospect of a monopoly in water powers and electrical generation. As Mr. Easton points out on 'another page, the electrical power business is a natural monopoly; and the way to deal with a natural monopoly is not to try to prohibit it, but to control it. Aside from this criticism of the bills, however, Mr. Pinchot's points seem well taken. It is a great pity that the praiseworthy attempt to open up this great natural resource to general usefulness should be thus accompanied by an attempt to loosen the public control and to grant undue privileges to private interests. Private capital which is prepared to undertake the pioneer work of developing a new industrial field ought in fairness and in the general interest to be treated with generosity. But such generosity need not be so lavish as to be shortsighted. If we give away in haste now too much in order to encourage the bringing into use of the water powers of the country, we shall repent at leisure when the pioneer period is over.

Legislation embodying the basic principles of the Ferris and the Shields bills ought to be passed by Congress without delay. But the unsound details of both these bills should be ruthlessly cut out. If Congress passes the bills in their present form, much of the splendid work that was involved in the conservation movement will have been in vain.

AN OBSTACLE TO PEACE

LAST week we discussed the terms of peace which had been suggested by various responsible and irresponsible parties in the belligerent countries. Some of them are not irreconcilable, but there is one serious difficulty in the way of coming to terms, and that is the agreement among the Allies that none of them shall negotiate terms of peace without the approval of all of the others. This pact has been signed by Great Britain, France, Italy, Belgium, Japan and Russia. Besides these the Allies must consider the claims of Serbia, Montenegro and Portugal, which have taken part in the conflict, and of Greece, Persia and Albania, which have without resistance permitted the Allies to use their territory for purposes of warfare. Now the interests and ambitions of these twelve nations are quite as much at variance with each other as they are with those of the Teutonic Powers. It is literally impossible to devise a form of settlement which would be satisfactory to all of them even if the Allies should win so complete a victory as to be able to dictate any terms they liked.

Yet, according to the agreement, no peace can be concluded except by the consent of each and every one of the Allied Powers. It would seem, then, that this pact, while it has united and strengthened the Allies, will inevitably tend to prolong the war.

Suppose, for instance, that the French and British succeed in driving the Germans out of France and Belgium. Will they go on fighting for another year or so in order that Russia may gain Constantinople, Serbia may gain Croatia, and Italy may gain the Tyrol? These territories have never belonged to Russia, Serbia and Italy, but they are now fighting for them and would certainly not be content with any peace which did not secure them.

Or, to take another hypothetical case, suppose Germany should declare her willingness without more ado to relinquish and indemnify Belgium, France and Russia, but insisted upon getting back German Southwest Africa. These three Powers would undoubtedly be disposed to accept the offer. England also might think that this arid land was not worth much longer fighting at a cost of $20,000,000 a day. But how could the London Government induce the Boers to surrender to Germany the country which they have conquered at their own expense in men and money? And if General Smuts succeeds in conquering German East Africa this also will be removed from the available trading stock in case peace has to be made by any kind of bargaining process.

It is easy enough to start a war. A Serbian youth with a revolver in his hand could do it. But to stop a war such as this will puzzle the wisest brains of the world.

PRIVATE ENTERPRISE NOT DOWNED YET

AT a political club luncheon a Wall Street business man, discussing effects of the European war upon the financial future of America, characterized the industrial and economic organization of Germany as the most efficient ever devised by a nation, and a United States Senator, continuing the discussion, suggested that "a most ominous result of this war" may be the nationalization of industry in the German Empire.

These opinions were not pro-German utterances. They were the judgments of men whose sympathies are with the enemies of the nation whose efficiency was recognized. They sound strange in a land where, hitherto, business men and politicians have tirelessly "exposed" the unfitness of government to carry on business, and the mischievousness of governmental "meddling" in industry.

To offset the heresy of Mr. Kies and Senator Burton, Mr. Sydney Brooks has been pointing out the danger of giving over to a government the manufacture of munitions of war, an industry which not a few individualists would surrender to the state, along with the coinage of money and the handling of the mails. Mr. Brooks reviews England's experience since the summer of 1914, and shows that the situation would have been desperate but for the resources of private enterprise, which Mr. Lloyd-George had the wisdom to foster and to commandeer.

There has been a great deal of premature assumption that the war has demonstrated the truth of the socialist contention, or of the Bismarckian state-socialist assumption, that a comprehensive public organization and control of industry and commerce are more economical and immensely more efficient than an individualistic system.

The war is not over yet, and, above all, the economic recuperation from its devastations has not yet begun. The reliance of France and England is chiefly on the wealth, the initiative, and adaptability of a social order in which private enterprise is largely left free. There is every indication now that this social order as developed in Western Europe and the United States is proving more adequate to the demands made upon it than the paternalism of Germany is.

It will be well to suspend judgment until, as we say at election time, the returns are all in. Perhaps it will appear that in this matter, as in so many other practical affairs, the extremists are unsafe guides. Perhaps the nation which is careful not to destroy the splendid energy, the inventiveness and the fine flexibility of individual enterprise, but which, thru governmental action, coördinates it, regulates it with reference to the conservation of resources, to the needs of different regions and to the just claims of all citizens, and, in time of danger, commandeers its products, may in the long run give the best account of itself.

======

CONGRESSIONAL AND COLLEGIATE ETHICS

CONGRESS has again voted that we the people pay them the substantial and agreeable sum of 20 cents a mile whenever they travel to and from the capital on our business.

And we once heard of a board of trustees of a certain college (name deleted by the censor) who voted themselves honorary degrees.

SANCTA SIMPLICITAS

FOR religious simpleness, not to say silliness, commend us to a law recently enacted by the New Jersey Legislature and signed by the Governor. It is so grotesque that it might seem that it was a joke perpetrated on the people of the state. A bill was introduced requiring that in the public schools of the state three verses from the Bible should be read every day. Of course that raised a religious row. It was to be presumed that the reading would be from the Protestant version of the Bible and the Catholics objected. It was also thought likely that the verses might be taken from the New Testament and to that the Jews objected. Whereupon the bill was amended so as to take the verses from the Old Testament, and in that form it was passed, so the veracious papers tell us. It would seem then that in politics the Catholics do not count as much as the Jews.

This story illustrates the absurdity of trying to make the state teach religion. The only reason for requiring passages from the Bible to be read in public schools is to teach reverence for the Bible as a book of religion. The public schools are for the children, for all the children, Jew or Gentile, Protestant or Catholic, Christian or Pagan. To impose the religion of one section of the people upon all children would be an interference with parental authority and right worth fighting against. Religion is a matter between man and God, not between man and the state. We would not trust the state to teach religion, not even our own religion. In the very interest of religion we would resent the impertinence of

the state in meddling with religion in the schools as much as in our factories.

What a farce such a law could be made by an irreverent teacher!

======

THOSE MUZZLED SEA DOGS

SOME good people are greatly excited because Secretary Daniels will not permit the naval officers to go on the Chautauqua platforms and write magazine articles to accelerate public opinion for preparedness. The country, they say, is entitled to the best expert opinion available on the subject.

So it is. But they seem to forget that Congress every year is accustomed to call the chief officers of the army and navy before it for advice when the military bills come up for discussion. The people and the press have free access to the hearings at the time and to the printed testimony afterwards. They can always learn exactly what the army and navy want.

But it is no more proper, say, for Admiral Fiske to go about the country telling the people how many battleships they should require Congress to authorize, than it would be for Ambassador Gerard to go on the stump to force Congress to appropriate money to erect a new embassy for the American Ambassador in Berlin.

WHAT ARE LUXURIES?

THE British Government, besides its other embarrassments, has now to decide one of the most puzzling questions of economics, namely, where is the dividing line between necessities and luxuries to be drawn? Because the ships are all needed to supply the army and because of the desire to keep money in the country, the British Board of Trade is rapidly extending its list of prohibited imports. Among the commodities which may not be imported even from the British colonies without special license are practically all kinds of china ware, hardware, wooden ware, basket ware, yarns, soaps, playing cards, toys, musical instruments, cutlery and automobiles for private use. War devours theories as it does everything else, so it is not surprising to find free-trade England in this emergency going far beyond the wildest dreams of protectionism.

Besides putting an embargo on imported superfluities the editors and the ministers (both political and ecclesiastical) are preaching the duty of economy and holding up for emulation the almost forgotten virtue of thrift. They even in some cases go so far as to set an example to the commonalty. For instance, Reginald McKenna, who as Chancellor of the Exchequer doubtless realizes better than his colleagues the necessity of cutting down expenses, has given up his motor car and may daily be seen and admired walking to Parliament and council meetings—and in so doing, it would seem, wasting many of the hours for which his country pays him handsomely. But is the reason why he does not take a train or the tuppenny tube that he wants to save yet more money, or to set a still better example?

But in the articles specified as dispensable luxuries in the embargo lists and in most of the exhortations to economy, there is one curious omission, that is, alcoholic liquors. The possible savings and benefits to be derived by a temporary abstinence from these enticing beverages are not talked about much except by certain unfashionable and fanatical sects known as nonconformists and certain disagreeable people like Lloyd George. But Lloyd George, when last year he said that drink was as great a danger to the country as the Germans, got speedily squelched. He was hit from both sides—from the laboring classes, who considered themselves insulted, and from the peerage—commonly called the beerage—who thought their craft was in danger. Since then he has kept his mouth shut, no easy thing for him, so evidently he was hard hit.

It did occur to some British statesmen that the country might without serious injury get along for a while on beer and whisky without importing champagne and other expensive wines. But as soon as it was mentioned a great howl came from across the Channel. France gave unmistakable evidence that she would regard it as an unfriendly act if an embargo were put on her most profitable export. So that project was dropt.

One bishop ventured to suggest to his clergy that they might well leave off liquor during the war, but straightway the church papers were filled with letters from indignant vicars and dons, who protested against such an interference with their dietary. The King, who took the pledge for the war and banished all intoxicants from the palace, has relapsed, on the advice of physicians, since his accident, tho why they should think wine would make him stick on his horse better is not clear.

But it does not matter, because his loyal subjects declined to follow his example of abstinence. On the contrary, they spent $87,480,000 more on alcoholic beverages in 1915 than they did in 1914. Their drink bill for last year was $909,790,000, and probably they are now spending a billion dollars a year on something which many people in the United States and England manage to get along without. The war has cost Great Britain about $7,500,000,000. If we subtract from this the loans to other countries, which will presumably be repaid, and the money spent on feeding the soldiers, who would have had to be fed and clothed anyhow, tho not so well in time of peace, we should have left, using the estimate of Sir George Paish, a net loss to the country of about $2,500,000,000. If, then, Great Britain should go dry, as Russia has, its total war losses could be paid up within the next three years, not allowing anything for the gain in industrial efficiency and the saving from the crime and impaired health which incidentally results from the consumption of a billion dollars' worth of liquor a year.

THE SHIP OF THE DESERT

IT is now in order for one of our modern manufacturers of folklore to write the story of "How the Camel's Nose Was Put Out of Joint." The war has proved that the true "ship of the desert" is the automobile. The arid plateaus of German Southwest Africa were overrun by General Botha with an army on wheels propelled by gasoline. The rapid advance of the Russians from the Caspian to Kermanshah was accomplished by means of the motor car. On the other hand, the British who were to come up from the Persian Gulf to meet them depended on the old-fashioned camel trains. But the camels were stampeded and captured or killed by the Arabs so the British expedition was left stranded while the Russians still sweep on thru the Persian desert. The French have found the Sahara no barrier to their advance toward Timbuktu and the tourist may

now traverse the dead heart of Australia where many a pioneer has laid him down to die.

Poor old camel! He thought he held the record for speed and endurance when he could carry his rider at the rate of fifty miles a day for five days without drinking. But the automobile can go as far in an hour as the camel in a day. Possibly in thick sand a padded foot may have an advantage over a pneumatic tire, but it is evident that the day of the camel has gone. Some three thousand years he has been in the service of man, but nobody loves him and all will be glad to get rid of the ugly, stupid, awkward, vicious and ill-smelling brute. Henceforth his place is in the zoölogical garden, where he may survive to convince future generations that there really was such an animal. The gasoline motor sometimes acts badly and smells likewise, but it is more dependable and lovable than the camel.

IN JUSTICE TO MR. BRYAN

IN a recent editorial in these pages the statement was made that "the story persists, without denial, that when the first 'Lusitania' note went to Germany, signed with the name of Mr. Bryan, then Secretary of State, Mr. Bryan himself told the Austrian Ambassador in private conversation that the stern tone of the note was intended for effect at home and not abroad."

We are in receipt of a letter from Mrs. Bryan, in which she assures us that the statement is not true, and that it has been officially denied not only by Mr. Bryan but by the Austrian Ambassador.

We deeply regret that these denials had escaped our attention, and that in reporting the widely accepted allegation without being more certain of its accuracy we have done Mr. Bryan a deep injustice.

PROFITEERING

CANADA, that "young" country where one can still pioneer, and where there is a nice blend of imperial loyalty and hearty democracy, is having her troubles with a political disease from which we in this country are, we hope, slowly recovering. Graft and rumors of graft fill the newspapers—not in one province alone, nor in small matters. There seems to have been railway graft in Alberta, public building graft in Manitoba, and munitions graft in the Dominion Government.

The Toronto *Globe*, reporting the charges brought against the shell committee which contracted for munitions, calls attention to "damning evidence of *profiteering*." That is a bad business, but a good word. It means, we take it, something which bears the same relation to legitimate industry that privateering bears to legitimate commerce. To privateer is to make exorbitant profits by capturing loaded ships; to profiteer is to get the same results by capturing loaded contracts.

Perhaps the word has a wider application. There is profiteering whenever by force—economic as well as political—extravagant profits are being made at the expense of legitimate traders, whether the victims be taxpayers, or employees, or consumers. The average man of today will not accept the theory that private profits are wrong; but he does sympathize with those who attack the unreasonable wealth of men who are notoriously getting more than their share. He objects to profiteering, and sooner or later he will stop it.

Villa's Band Routed

Villa, on March 27, attacked the town of Guerrero, overcame the Carranza garrison, put to death 172 of his prisoners and held others under guard, intending to kill them. Two days later, at an early hour in the morning, his soldiers were surprized and routed by a flying detachment of American troops, the Seventh and Tenth Cavalry, commanded by Colonel George A. Dodd. There were about 400 of these troopers, and, led by an officer nearly sixty-four years old, who is to go on the retired list in July next, they had ridden fifty-five miles in seventeen hours, over a rough country. Altho they were weary they at once charged upon Villa's force, which exceeded 500, fought a running fight for five hours, and then pursued the bandits for ten miles. Probably they were glad to take a little rest when they knew that the Villa men had been scattered and were seeking refuge in the mountains. Colonel Dodd's cavalrymen killed sixty of the Villa band. The bodies of thirty were left at Guerrero, and the bodies of as many more were found at various places in the ten-mile chase. And not one American lost his life. Only four of our troopers were wounded, and their injuries are not of a dangerous character. Among the Mexicans killed was General Eliseo Hernandez, commanding in Villa's place because the bandit chief was disabled.

During the attack upon Guerrero, two days earlier, one of Villa's legs was broken, and one of his hips was shattered by a bullet. When his men were surprized by Colonel Dodd, he was in a tent. At once his guards placed him in a carriage, and he was taken away. On the following day the tracks made by this carriage were found by the pursuing Americans, and it was expected that he would soon be captured. Colonel Dodd liberated the Carranza soldiers who had been held for execution. The scene of this affair, so creditable to our troops, is a broad valley at the head of the Santa Maria River. On the west are the foothills of the Continental Divide, and on the east a trail leads to Santa Ysobel, where, some weeks ago, a party of Villa soldiers murdered eighteen Americans. "With Villa permanently disabled," said General Pershing in his brief report, "Lopez wounded and Hernandez dead, the blow to Villa's band is a serious one." When Colonel Dodd attacked Villa's forces, our troops had been in Mexico just two weeks.

It is now known that Villa had tortured and then put to death at Minaca, ten miles southeast of Guerrero, five Americans, one German and one Englishman. Among the American victims was Dr. A. T. Stell, a practicing physician who had gone to Mexico from New Orleans. Another was the owner of a ranch. Villa had also tortured and killed a family of five Mexicans because they had been on friendly terms with American ranchmen, to whom they sold supplies.

Other News About Mexico

After long delay, Carranza permitted the use of the Mexican railroads for the transportation of supplies, but under restrictions which forbid the presence of guards on the trains and provide that the supplies must be shipped from one American to another, neither of whom is directly connected with the army. Supplies have been forwarded on auto trucks, of which there are 108 in service, and the government has ordered fifty-four more. Felix Diaz has landed on the Gulf coast of Mexico with a small force. It is said that he has strong financial support and will be assisted by troops from Oaxaca. Large purchases of arms and ammunition for his use have been made in this country, and it is understood that these supplies are to be shipped by way of some port in the West Indies. A considerable number of men in his service have crossed the boundary from Guatemala.

Carranza and his Cabinet are seriously considering a movement for the confiscation of all the property of Catholic priests in Mexico, and the sale of this property to obtain a reserve for the forthcoming new issue of currency. The value of the present currency has fallen to about three cents on the dollar. A decree recently issued says that the goods of merchants who refuse to take it will be seized and sold at auction for the benefit of the government. Merchants who go out of business on account of the condition of the currency will be treated in the same way. A strike of street railway employees in the Mexican capital, for a sixty per cent increase of pay, we suppress last week by Carranza's troops. The men were forced to resume work, and it is said that fourteen promoters of the strike, now under arrest, will be shot.

The adjourned meeting of the Republican senators at Washington followed the publication of President Wilson's statement about the circulation of false reports along the border designed to bring about intervention in the interest of certain American owners of Mexican properties. At this deferred conference no action was taken, the senators deciding that they would await

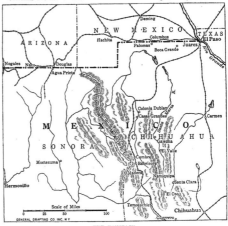

THE HAYSTACK

After Villa's forces were fought and beaten by Colonel Dodd's cavalry at Guerrero last Wednesday the American troopers pushed on in a northwesterly direction to find the bandit himself. Abundant rumors of his whereabouts had not led to any definite discovery at the time when The Independent went to press, and nothing was known except that Villa was somewhere in the mountainous country around Guerrero—the proverbial needle in the haystack. The Mexican Northwestern Railroad, passing thru Madera and Temosachic, is carrying American supplies

Harding in Brooklyn Eagle
THE "NET"
Carranza's troops seem to be able to "encircle" Villa, but not to keep him encircled

Westerman in Columbus (Ohio) Dispatch
"WITH UNITED STATES AID"
Our troops have been "helping Mexico" by beating Villa after he had beaten Carranzistas

Harding in Brooklyn Eagle
FORBIDDEN?
Have we obtained Carranza's permission for our soldiers to smoke while in Mexico?

Carter in New York Evening Sun
SHIFTING SANDS

developments. In a report or statement published by Senator Gallinger it was said that the senators did not intend to interfere with the President, but were anxious that the punitive expedition should be protected and the border guarded, even if it should be necessary to use the militia for that purpose. Our government, Mr. Gallinger added, had not protected American citizens on one side of the line or the other. Mr. Roosevelt published a statement in criticism of the one issued by the President, saying that the charges about American owners of Mexican properties were utterly baseless. Senator Fall, at El Paso, insisted that the President should make known the names of the men he had in mind, as he was misrepresenting the people of the border.

Wages and Strikes The demands of the four great railroad unions, which have about 400,000 members, were formally presented to all the railroad companies of the United States on March 30, and the companies are required to reply before April 29. They have suggested a conference. The demands are for an eight-

hour day and time and a half for all overtime. It is asserted by the companies that the present rates of pay, fixed by mediation and arbitration, are adequate. They present certain counter-claims which were brought up at a wage controversy in 1914 and then withdrawn by them at the request of President Wilson. These relate to conditions which, it is said, cause double payment for some kinds of work. The companies declare that if the demands should be granted their annual expenses would be increased by $100,000,000. Prominent representatives of the unions say that there will be "a fight to a finish." Last week the Switchmen's Union joined the other four unions in making the demands.

In the anthracite coal case no settlement has been reached, but the term of the existing agreement has been prolonged until the end of the negotiations. It is understood that the companies will decline to recognize the union or to grant the demanded wage increase of 20 per cent, with an eight-hour day. They may consent to give an increase of 5 per cent, with an eight-hour day, and some say the men would accept 10 per cent. There may be a strike of 50,000 bituminous coal miners in the central Pennsylvania district, as the agreement recently signed for Illinois, Indiana, West Virginia, Ohio and the Pittsburgh district does not include them, and their demand for a wage increase has been rejected.

A strike of 25,000 silk mill workers in Paterson, New Jersey, has been averted by the action of the mill owners. The demand of the employees was for a nine-hour day. At first the owners offered nine and one half hours from May 1, and a reduction to nine hours on November 1. This was rejected. As a strike one week later was promised, the owners yielded. The controversy recalled the memorable strike of three years ago when several persons were killed and the losses of the manufacturers amounted to $10,000,000. One

of the owners, who has a large and fine mill, offered last week to turn the entire property over to his employees on condition that they would guarantee to him 8 per cent on his investment.

Several strikes of street railway employees are in progress. In Toledo the cars were tied up because the company would not permit its men to wear the badges of their new union. A strike in Newark, New Jersey, has not prevented use of the cars. In Wilkesbarre, Pennsylvania, where there has been a strike for a long time, twelve cars were destroyed and seven wrecked last week by mobs of strikers. For two days there was great disorder, but no one was arrested. A bill pending at Albany for the creation of a state constabulary has been opposed by labor leaders, who denounced the constabulary of Pennsylvania, saying that New York ought not to have a similar force of "Cossacks." The bill is supported by the Chambers of Commerce in the state, and by mayors of leading cities.

There may soon be a strike of 200,000 men in the building trades at New York, where 8000 painters are out, demanding an increase from $4 to $5 a day. Employers point to the high cost of building materials. A thousand hardware workmen in Torrington, Connecticut, who went on strike for an addition of 10 per cent, were successful at the end of two days. In or near Philadelphia wage advances for about 8000 employees in half a dozen manufacturing plants have recently been granted. The General Electric Company has decided to give bonuses amounting to more than $3,000,000 in the form of 5 per cent of the annual pay of all employees who have been in its service five years, about 50,000 persons.

Trust Cases The indictments found at Youngstown, Ohio, against the United States Steel Corporation, the Carnegie Steel Company, four other steel companies, and Judge E. H. Gary, chairman of the Steel Corporation, have been quashed, upon the defendant's motion. The companies were accused of violating Ohio's Anti-Trust law because they increased the wages of their employees by 10 per cent. This advance having been granted by the Steel Corporation, the other companies took similar action within two days. Here, the grand jury and local prosecutor said, was evidence of a combination to fix wages. Judge Anderson said that labor could no longer be regarded as a commodity, and that the indictments were defective because they were not confined to alleged offenses committed in the state, and conflicted with Federal statutes and authority.

Arguments have recently been made, at New York, in the suit for the dissolution of the Corn Products Refining Company, which makes glucose and starch. The company in its defense asserted that it was not an unlawful combination, and pointed to the fact that while its annual output of glucose had fallen from 414,000,000 pounds in 1907 to 219,000,000 in 1914, that of its competitors had risen in the same time from 34,000,000 to 292,000,000 pounds. The presiding judge said that while the company appeared to have been formed, for purposes at variance with the Sherman act, and altho its methods at times in the past had been illegal, he thought these methods had been laid aside. It had failed, he added, to monopolize the production of glucose and starch, and it was impossible to make such a monopoly. His remarks indicated that the judgment of the court would not be a severe one.

In the similar case against the American Can Company, the presiding judge recently withheld a decree of dissolution and permitted the company to carry on its business, future action being conditioned upon its good behavior. But the government now asks for a definite decision, in order that an appeal may be taken if the decision is finally against dissolution.

Immigration Bill Passed The Burnett Immigration bill, with its literacy test, was passed in the House last week by a vote of 308 to 87. This bill, on account of the test included, was vetoed by President Taft, and again by President Wilson. In the Senate the second veto was overridden, but the majority in the House was less than the required two-thirds by about a dozen votes. The majority on passage last week was so large, however, that a veto this year promises to be ineffective. The literacy test excludes "all aliens over sixteen years of age, physically capable of reading, who cannot read the English language, or some other language or dialect, including Hebrew or Yiddish; provided, that any admissible alien or any alien heretofore or hereafter legally admitted, or any citizen of the United States, may bring in or send for his father or grandfather, over fifty-five years of age, his wife, his mother, his grandmother, or his unmarried or widowed daughter, if otherwise admissible, whether such relative can read or not, and such relative shall be permitted to enter."

To the classes now excluded the bill adds stowaways, vagrants, sufferers from tuberculosis, those who advocate the unlawful destruction of property, Hindoos, and "persons of constitutional psychopathic inferiority." The head tax is increased from $4 to $8, and the penalties imposed on steamship companies for bringing defectives are made heavier than they are now.

Other Questions in Congress In the House Judiciary Committee, by a vote of 10 to 9, consideration of the proposed constitutional amendments for woman suffrage and prohibition has been postponed indefinitely. The advocates of woman suffrage will now strive to gain support for their amendment in the new national party platforms. The Senate Finance Committee has reported a substitute for the House resolution repealing the provision of existing law which puts sugar on the free list. This substitute provides that the duty be retained until 1920. Mr. Rainey, Democrat, has introduced a bill supported by a majority of the Ways and Means Committee, and approved by the President, for the creation of a permanent and non-partisan Tariff Commission of six members, empowered to make thoro investigations.

By a vote of 3 to 2, the subcommittee which has been considering the nomination of Louis D. Brandeis for the Supreme Court has reported in favor of confirmation.

Russians Repulsed at Riga The Russian attack on Hindenburg's lines east of Riga, which we mentioned last week, appears to have come to an end after ten days of hard fighting without any material gains. While the eyes of the world have been fixed on France the Russian front has been rather ignored, yet, according to the German account, the operations here have been far more bloody than at Verdun. The German War Office estimates that more than half a million men were engaged in the offensive and that the Russian losses amount to 140,000. Of course, esti-

© International Film Service

ON THRU THE MEXICAN CACTUS COUNTRY
The Sixteenth Infantry in the longest march of the campaign, traveling twenty-six miles on March 21 to a camp at Corralitos ranch

mates of enemy losses in a case like this where the ground has not been gained are very uncertain, and this seems almost incredible, but since the German official reports have on the whole been quite free from sensational exaggeration the figures may be taken at least to indicate the severity of the conflict in the opinion of one of the combatants.

A copy of the general order issued to the Russian army on the eve of the offensive calls upon the troops in the name of the Czar to advance and drive the enemy beyond the frontier. It is surmised that the reason why the Russians took the initiative at such an unfavorable season was to draw off the Germans from the western front and thus relieve the pressure on Verdun. If so the effort does not seem to have accomplished its object.

But, on the other hand, we might say that the season forced the fighting when the spring thaw flooded the trenches along the Dvina River and in the swamps about Dvinsk both parties struggled to hold or gain the higher ground because of the advantage it would give when the floods retired.

Mining on the British Front The British lines have been extended some twenty-five miles to the south to replace the French who have been sent to Verdun. The British signalized their arrival in the new field by exploding a mine under the German trenches near La Boiselle. Further north near Hulluch the Germans undermined and blew up the British trenches but they did not gain much for the British took possession of the crater.

Still further north in the old battlefield of Ypres, where German and British troops have been fighting for a year and a half, the British mining operations were more successful. At St. Eloi, two miles south of Ypres, the British blew up more than a hundred yards of trenches, then the Northumberland and Royal Fusiliers charged and carried front and second trenches for a distance of 600 yards. As soon as they had broken into the German trenches the British soldiers scurried thru them to pick up stray prisoners and succeeded in taking 170 of them. At one point an officer found two fusiliers who had laid their rifles on the ground and were fighting with their fists for the possession of a German prisoner whom both claimed.

Malancourt and Vaux During the past week the Germans have taken a village on each side of Verdun, five miles east, and Malancourt, ten miles west. Fort de Vaux was smashed to pieces by the German shells two weeks ago, but, as in the case of Douaumont, the village, sheltered in the ravine, held out longer than the fort on the hilltop. On the last night in March the Germans in large mass charged the French salient at Vaux from north and south simultaneously but were checked before they reached the French lines. But a second charge followed immediately and after a hot fight among the houses the Germans obtained possession of the place. They followed this up on the following day by penetrating the woods lying between Vaux and Douaumont.

The advance upon Verdun from the north has hitherto been prevented because the French guns on the hights to the west of the Meuse River enfiladed the plateau along which the Germans must pass to reach the city. They have accordingly been resting in this sector for the last fortnight while they gained these dominant positions. Côte de l'Oie, or Goose Ridge, the nearest of these to the river, is now in German hands, and they also hold part if not all of the next hight, Le Mort Homme or Dead Man's Hill, as well as the forest between Bois des Corbeaux or Crows' Wood.

Two miles further west is the village of Malancourt, which the Germans took by storm on Thursday night. Since this village, like Vaux, forms a French salient the Germans were able to assault it from west, north and east. A single battalion of infantry held the place in the first attack against assailants twenty times their number. But a second assault was made two hours later and forced an entrance thru the French defenses on the left. The house-to-house fighting continued till dawn. The Germans took here 328 unwounded prisoners.

British Strikes The big guns urgently needed by the army in France for the summer campaign are being held up by a strike in munition factories on the Clyde. This is not a mere case of local dissatisfaction with wages but an organized effort to force the government to give up conscription and repeal the act placing the munition works under government control. The union authorities and the parliamentary representatives of the Labor party are opposed to the strike, but the movement is instigated by a union inside the union under the management of the Clyde Workers' Committee. About 1700 men went out. The government for the first time used the powers conferred upon it by the munitions act, fining twenty-two of the strikers $25 apiece and banishing nine of the leaders from the district. This, however, only increased the resentment of the men and most of them are still out.

Another strike of more extensive character has broken out on the Mersey River where 10,000 dock workers have gone out. This threatens to tie up the shipping of Liverpool, which is now the most important as it is the most secluded port in the British Isles. The decision of the arbitrators was rejected by the men as not sufficiently meeting their demands. Later, however, part of the men returned to work.

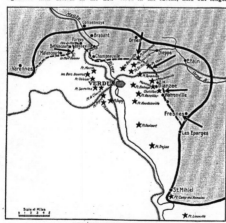

THE INVESTMENT OF VERDUN

Slowly but so far without any serious setback the German forces are closing in upon the chief fortress of the French frontier. On the north and east their lines have been brought within easy gunshot of the city and now on the west side of the Meuse they are steadily advancing. Last week they captured Malancourt and they have gained a lodgment on the hill of Le Mort Homme. It seems impossible for the French to hold on much longer to the salient which projects between Dead Man's Hill and the Meuse. The shaded area is that now held by the Germans. The solid black line is their former position

Air Raids on England

On the night of March 31 five Zeppelins crossed the sea and sailed over the eastern counties by different routes. Ninety bombs were dropt, causing the death of twenty-eight persons and the wounding of forty-four. One of the Zeppelins was brought down by the land guns and fell into the mouth of the Thames. The crew, seventeen uninjured and four badly wounded, were taken from the wreckage by the trawler "Olivine."

This makes thirty-one air raids on England which have been reported, and probably there are others of which the censor has supprest mention. That there was at least one such came to light in the course of the parliamentary debate of March 28 when Mr. Tennant, Under Secretary for War, virtually admitted that Zeppelins had approached the coast on the night of March 19. It had been supposed that the German air squadron that night consisted of four seaplanes only.

According to a statement of Premier Asquith on March 10 the air raids made up to that time had caused the death of 127 men, ninety-two women and fifty-seven children. The bombardment of the coast by the German fleet killed forty-nine men, thirty-nine women and thirty-nine children. Besides these some 2750 other noncombatants had lost their lives on British merchantmen and fishing vessels, making altogether about 3153 civilians killed since the war began. The military casualties and damage are not reported. In the House of Lords recently it was stated in one case a great munitions works was missed by a few yards, and that one of the most important machine shops had an equally narrow escape. The German reports claim that in the raid of March 5 on Hull a magazine was blown up, a provision depot destroyed, the docks damaged and the warships hit.

The Zeppelins fly at a height of 7000 to 15,000 feet and at a speed of thirty-five to seventy miles an hour. The most recent type of Zeppelin is nearly 600 feet long and can travel about 2000 miles from its base. The German aeronautic bases in Belgium are only 160 miles from London. The British aircraft guns have a range of only 5000 feet upward, so the Zeppelins are mostly out of their reach and have hitherto escaped.

The growing dissatisfaction of the people with the government for its failure to protect the country against the German air raids found expression in the election to Parliament of Noel Pemberton-Billing, a former Flight Lieutenant. He ran independently on this issue and beat the Coalition candidate, who had the support of both party machines. He declares that there are aeroplanes and pilots enough in the country to exterminate the Zeppelins if the government would only set them at it. Now that a Zeppelin has been actually captured the criticism of the government will doubtless be less acrid.

The British have begun to retaliate by raiding the German hangars in Schleswig-Holstein, east of the island of Sylt. Five seaplanes were escorted by cruisers to a convenient point off the German coast and there launched. Whether they did any damage or not is not known, but three of the machines were brought down on the island.

Salonica Attacked by Air

When the French and British evacuated Serbia and retired behind the Greek boundary the pursuit stopped because the Germans and Bulgars were reluctant to trespass upon Greek soil. But the Allied barracks, ships and fortifications at Salonica are reachable by air, so it is not surprising that with the advent of spring the Zeppelins and Fokkers have been paying frequent visits to the enemy's camp. It is only forty miles from the Serbian frontier to Salonica, so the German aircraft can make the round trip in an hour and a half. The French avions are not backward about returning the flying visits of the Germans. On March 24 a squadron of twenty-three French aeroplanes shelled the Bulgar positions west of Lake Doiran, losing two machines. One of them fell into the lake and the other was brought down on land, so close to the Greek border that the pilot could escape into the Allied lines after burning his machine.

On the 27th a squadron of German aeroplanes flew over Salonica and dropped bombs upon the barracks, magazines and railroad yards. According to the German report twenty tons of explosives were detonated and twenty-seven cars loaded with war material were destroyed. The same report states that 200 French and British soldiers were killed. In the French report no mention is made of any soldiers killed, but it is said instead that the bombs killed twenty Greek civilians and wounded thirty or forty more. It is also claimed that four out of the seven German aeroplanes were brought down.

The Greek Government has protested to the Central Powers against the aerial bombardment of Salonica and also presented a bill to General Sarrail, commander of the Anglo-British troops, for the damages, amounting to over a million dollars, due to the air raids which the presence of the Allied troops has caused. Payment was refused by General Sarrail, who said he was responsible only for damages caused by the Allies and advised Greece to send the bill to Germany.

Avlona, which is the only port on the Albanian coast now held by the Italians since their evacuation of Durazzo, has also suffered from aeroplane bombs.

Kirby in New York World

THE SAME OLD CROOK

Kirby in New York World

STILL OUT OF REACH

Wood in Philadelphia Public Ledger

BETWEEN THE DEVIL AND THE DEEP SEA

FROM STATE TO STATE

ARIZONA: When Judge Baxter, of the Superior Court, recently held that under the Webb-Kenyon act liquor could not be lawfully brought into this state even for personal use, it was declared that Arizona had the most drastic prohibition law in the Union. Now the Supreme Court of the state holds that Judge Baxter erred, and that "it is not unlawful in Arizona to have or to personally use intoxicating liquors." It is said that this decision, by relieving sheriffs of the task of watching all the shipments of liquor to the state, will give them more time for preventing illicit sales.

CALIFORNIA: The Pacific Traffic League has been organized in San Francisco. Its membership includes officials in charge of the regularly organized traffic bureaus, associations and chambers of commerce throout practically all the territory west of the Sierra Nevada and Cascade Mountains. Some of its purposes are: to increase the Interstate Commerce Commission to nine members and provide that three of those members shall hold regular hearings on the Pacific Coast instead of, as now, sending a mere "examiner" there; to secure notification of proposed changes in rates and the publication of the transcontinental docket in advance, and generally "to advance fair dealings and promote, conserve and protect the commercial and transportation interests of the Pacific Coast."

COLORADO: It is said that, thru the efforts of Prof. B. C. Buffum, of Wyoming, emmer is likely to become one of the most important crops of Colorado, especially of the non-irrigated districts in the eastern part of the state. Emmer is an original type of wheat which grows wild in Palestine. There it has a sharp spinelike beard which clogs threshing machines and causes sore mouths among cattle, but Professor Buffum has succeeded in producing a beardless emmer, and Colorado farmers who have grown it without irrigation are delighted with the results. On about 2000 acres the average yield has been from forty to fifty bushels an acre, and it has run as high as seventy-five bushels. As stock feed they say it is superior to oats and produces much more heavily. It is also useful for making a very nutritious black bread.

CONNECTICUT: Brief interviews were recently held with a large number of parents of Hartford school children on the subject of introducing military training into the public schools. The purpose was to get the opinions of representative parents not only of different nationalities, but also of various occupational walks and social grades. The poll covered eight nationalities and most vocational fields, from the professional man to the day laborer. The result showed that about seventy-two per cent of the interviewed parents favored the military training for school children.

IDAHO: The Bannock County Republican Voters' Information League is something new under the sun, at least in Idaho. This organization, formed by a large number of non-office-seeking Republicans who desire good candidates for their party, purposes, it is said, to supply positively truthful information concerning all candidates, county, state or national, who may seek the suffrage of Republican voters under the direct primary laws. It is predicted that the league will soon be extended throuot the state, and that so long as it remains in the hands of its present class of members it will be of real service to the people and therefore to its party.

INDIANA: The second annual "Safety First" week, under the auspices of the Indianapolis Chamber of Commerce, has been celebrated with widespread enthusiasm. In Indianapolis the first three days were devoted to public meetings which were addrest by experts in reducing the number of accidents in streets, shops, on railroads and elsewhere. Clergymen took "safety" for their texts, schools made a specialty of teaching it, the city was placarded until the city was placarded with red glow window, vehicle and even from the sky, since Boy Scouts flew kites from which great streamers of caution waved. Practically every civic, social and industrial organization in the city gave the greater part of the week to aiding the propaganda.

MISSISSIPPI: In the hope of inducing the Jackson Memorial Highway Association to lay its route thru Mississippi, the people of this state are stirring themselves as never before in the matter of making good roads. Nearly every county is working to make a good showing before the pathfinding committee comes to make its decision.

NEW JERSEY: A bill to regulate flying machines and undersea craft has been introduced in the New Jersey Senate. This is the first measure of the kind ever proposed in any of the states. Recent reports that planes have been seen hovering above munition plants and that submarines have been plying in waters near such plants have made it seem advisable to place these craft under restrictions which would make their owners responsible for their presence in forbidden localities. It is believed the bill will be put thru speedily.

NEW MEXICO: Few if any states in the Union can show as great increase in wealth production in the past fifteen years as New Mexico. In 1900 the taxable assessment of the state was $42,000,000; now it is $305,-000,000. Then its population was 195,000; now it is 425,000. In the meantime the number of farms has increased from 12,-311, valued at $53,767,824, to 45,000, valued at more than $250,000,000. The production of

eggs has increased in value from $157,000 in 1900 to $750,000 in 1915; of manufactured articles, from $2,161,000 to more than $10,000,000. The production of its mines in 1915 exceeded $20,-000,000 in value, surpassing that of any other year in the state's history. The total value of the products of its mines, farms, ranches, factories, home industries and its ten million acres of forest area is said to have exceeded $100,000,000 in the past year.

OKLAHOMA: With a view not only to beautifying the city, but also to encouraging young boys and girls to learn gardening, Mayor Overholser, of Oklahoma City, has instituted a contest for a five-passenger automobile which he is to give and several cash prizes to be offered by other citizens. An exchange has been established where property owners may list vacant lots and where boys and girls may apply for the privilege of cultivating them. Within the city limits there are hundreds of vacant lots. It is Mayor Overholser's hope that practically all the owners will grant to the children the privilege of turning these worse than waste places into beauty spots, productive, in the aggregate, of considerable wealth.

OREGON: This state, thru Attorney General Brown, is to take a hand in the Utah case now pending in the United States Supreme Court in which the issue of state or Federal control of water power on public lands is at stake. It is estimated that more than 20,000,-000 horsepower is running to waste in the Pacific Northwest, while only 700,000 horsepower has been developed. Nearly all this undeveloped water power is under the control of the Federal Government which, is permitting it to go to waste, while fuel supplies, used in its stead, are being exhausted. Those who favor state control say that under it not only a large part of this power would be developed by private capital, but the flood waters of the Columbia River alone would be used for reclaiming 2,000,000 acres of arid and semi-arid land.

RHODE ISLAND: A large number of farmers in this state are taking steps toward coöperation as a means of following out the suggestions made by the Commission of Agricultural Inquiry in its first report to the General Assembly. The commission' urged the need not so much of increased production as of better methods of marketing and distributing. Last year the value of Rhode Island's agricultural products was about $9,000,000, yet, the commission says, the farmers as a class are not making money, altho knowledge of how to increase production has been spread among them. The remedy, it is believed, lies in eliminating much duplication of effort and in reaching the consumer by a more direct and economical route; and this, they think, can best be accomplished by unit-

ing and employing their own marketing and distributing machinery.

SOUTH DAKOTA: The decision of Congress to continue indefinitely the duty on sugar has caused a revival of effort on the part of South Dakota men to establish at least one beet sugar factory in this state. Information gathered from neighboring states where such factories have been established shows that all are making money and that farmers in the vicinity of them are finding sugar beets one of the most remunerative crops they can raise. It is likely that South Dakota will soon have such a factory. A preliminary canvass of farmers has convinced the projectors that a sufficient quantity of beets would be produced to insure its success.

TEXAS: Governor Ferguson and a large number of prominent citizens of all parts of this state journeyed to old Washington on the Brazos, March 2, to celebrate the eightieth anniversary of the signing of the Texas declaration of independence. Washington, which is now almost deserted, was twice the capital of the Republic of Texas—the first and the last capital. Fifty acres of land there have been purchased for a state park. Near the center of this tract stands a simple granite shaft commemorating the signing of the declaration and the establishment of the Lone Star republic.

VERMONT: By the purchase of an additional tract of 2000 acres on the east side of Mt. Mansfield the Mansfield state forest has been increased to a total area of 5000 acres. It thus becomes not only the largest state forest in Vermont, but, excepting the Crawford Notch forest in New Hampshire, the largest in New England. A considerable portion of the summit of the mountain is owned by the University of Vermont, which insures the preservation of one of New England's greatest scenic attractions and makes possible a demonstration of practical forestry under the direction of the State Forester. A movement is already on foot for opening fine automobile roads thru Smugglers' Notch and Nebraska Notch.

VIRGINIA: The House of Delegates has defeated the bill, recently passed by the Senate, providing for the establishment of a coördinate college for women at the University of Virginia. The House vote was forty-six to forty-eight, the same majority against the measure that the Senate gave in its favor. The chief argument against the bill was that the state should discharge its obligations to the children by giving needed assistance to the graded schools of the rural districts before spending money "to keep up a college for a few well-to-do young women who are abundantly able to procure whatever extra educational advantages they may desire in addition to those now furnished by the state in its high schools and normals."

A RELIGION FOR DEMOCRACY

BY SHAILER MATHEWS

PRESIDENT OF THE FEDERAL COUNCIL OF THE CHURCHES OF CHRIST OF AMERICA

THE rôle of a prophet is always risky. The currents of history on which we move are so confused that it is difficult to pick out infallibly the main stream. In religion this is particularly the case, for there never was a time when the world was more busily engaged in recasting its religious thoughts and operations. Yet certain tendencies are undeniable, and may serve as a nucleus for a reasonable forecast of the next generation.

Christianity is both an asset and a problem. It is an asset to the degree in which men put it into actual operation, be the temporary cost never so great. It is a problem when one balks at the sacrifice it involves or questions its ideals. It is from each of these two points of view that our present religious situation must be approached if we are to forecast the future.

When the People repudiate a religion, that religion dies. If a religion is repudiated, it is because its institutions and teachings have been outgrown. Greek mythology was not disproved; it died of being ignored. Greek men became better than their gods and preferred to worship Jesus than to undertake to convert Zeus. There are those who say that the same future awaits Christianity. I cannot so believe. Christian ideals are immeasurably superior to social practices and unless we frankly reject these ideals and turn to the worship of some Baal of economic efficiency, we shall still look forward, rather than back, to Jesus.

THE CHURCH MUST BECOME DEMOCRATIC

YET so far as Christianity during the next third of a century is concerned, all prophecy must be discriminating. The past of Christianity would argue that the immediate future will see a larger assimilation of the ideals of Jesus, and that Christianity as a socialized religion will increasingly stand for the gospel *of* Jesus as the ethical heart of the gospel *about* Jesus. But new conditions which the present war will produce will demand a more precise and direct application of the teaching of Jesus to the People. Whether the immediate effect of the war will be to hinder or aid democracy, democracy holds the ultimate future. This tremendous fact sets new problems for the Christianity of this generation. Those which concern the church as a social institution are evident. However much we may differ with those radicals who hold that Christianity was originally a proletarian movement in the Roman Empire which found itself at last checkmated by the rise of an ecclesiastical aristocracy, the history of the last nineteen centuries shows plainly that great groups of Christians have not been democratic. Wherever there have emerged priests or officials claiming superior privilege in the presence of God, the People have been subordinated. The Reformation was a movement toward ecclesiastical democracy in that it denied special priestly privileges to the clergy, but distinctions none the less have been drawn in Protestantism between priest and laymen.

Furthermore the organization of state churches served to perpetuate the clergy as a special class with an official status not enjoyed by the rank and file of church members. The appearance of independents like the Anabaptists on the continent of Europe and various groups of nonconformist Christians in England and America marked the spread of democratic tendencies, but even in these churches the position of women has been one of ecclesiastical inferiority.

That some men should have special duties within the church is, it is true, imperative for institutional efficiency; and such a grouping is by no means inconsistent with truly democratic ideals. But this conception is even yet only partially held, and the democratic movement looks with ill-concealed suspicion upon an institution in which ancient inequalities of society persist, and in which there is also an alignment with the capitalistic group. This alignment is by no means to be pressed so far as the literature of radical democracy affirms, but socialist propagandists are not altogether without justification in their identification of Protestantism with capitalistic sympathies. If the churches are increasingly to reach the people, they must grow democratic.

The second difficulty which democracy must face in the Christianity of the next few years is less obvious. It has to do with the terms and concepts of Christian theology. The social mind of each of the great creative epochs of western history has exprest itself in all aspects of human affairs, but especially in religious thinking. Speaking in general terms our theological systems have been transcendentalized politics. God has been conceived of as a sovereign, who gives laws to his subjects; and they are punished or rewarded in proportion to their obedience. Reconciliation between God and man has always been set forth in terms of forensic justification, and doctrines of atonement since that of Anselm have conformed to political experience.

This conception of religion under the forms of monarchy is sure to furnish difficulty for the religion of a growing democracy. Our inherited orthodoxy, shaped up as it was under the influence of the political practices and theories of empire and monarchy, is already with difficulty appreciated and understood by men under the domination of democratic ideals in both state and industry. How can a social order accustomed to elect its government grasp the full meaning of terms which exprest the religious beliefs of men accustomed to government as something superimposed upon the people? How can a democrat in politics and society be a monarchist in religion?

WHAT CAN CHRISTIANITY GIVE LABOR?

THIS difficulty which a rising democracy finds when it faces religion is by no means insuperable, but is more than mere speculation. The general disinclination of socialists and representatives of the People to find satisfaction in the church is due not so much to a turning against God and fundamental religious concepts as against our inherited ecclesiasticism. That may be one reason why working people are more ready to honor Jesus than the church. Much as church members may shrink from admitting the statement, the people at large, particularly in so far as they are wage earners, are growing indifferent, if not unfriendly, toward organized Christianity, both Protestant and Catholic.

I am by no means saying that this indifference cannot be dispelled by wise planning and action. But the modern church, whether it be Protestant, Roman Catholic or Greek Catholic, cannot afford to overlook the deep-seated cause of the present situation.

Christianity is endeavoring to satisfy the religious needs of a developing industrial democracy with the forms and teachings begotten of that monarchial system against which democrats of all shades and countries are in revolt. In the new era already opening, the consequent tension is likely to become more acute.

Many attacks made upon organized Christianity by the representatives of popular movements seem to me to be thoroly unjustifiable, the result of misunderstanding often as wilful as it is inexplicable. But after one has thus made all necessary allowances, the fact remains that organized Christianity in all its branches faces the distinct and vital problem of adjusting itself to the religious needs of a world that is reorganizing itself in the interest of the people rather than in that of the classes. Thirty—yes even five years hence we shall see this more clearly than today.

CHRISTIANITY MUST NOT BE A CLASS MOVEMENT

I CAN conceive of no greater misfortune to both Christianity and the social order than to have organized Christianity become a class movement. Such a misfortune would carry with it a train of other misfortunes, not the least of which would be the identification of the church with the capitalistic classes. Such an identification would mean that our social morality would develop apart from our religion, and democracy itself would be deprived of forces both conservative and inspirational which it already greatly needs.

It is sometimes said that the people as a whole are possessed of a religion superior to that of the church. The laborer's loyalty to his union, his hatred of scabs and his determination to better his conditions thru his union are often contrasted with the moral force of the churches to the discredit of the latter. Much as we who are devoted to the church dislike admitting the force of the argument, it is undoubtedly true that the labor movement has a much stronger hold upon the masses of wage-earners than have the Protestant churches. The explanation of this is not difficult in view of all the facts, but it becomes clearer when one recalls that the ideals of the labor union are essentially those of *gaining* and enforcing

rights, while the ideals of Christianity are professedly those of *giving* justice to those who have not shared equitably in social privileges. Christianity as it originated and was embodied in Jesus was essentially more concerned to give justice than to demand rights. The Christian movement ought to be loyal to this sacrificial fraternalism.

Democracy must be leavened by the social spirit exprest in the teaching of Jesus if it is not to develop a new form of aristocracy or a new bourgeois emphasis upon rights as over against duties. The church can and must leaven the changing order with the ideals of Jesus. But it must itself first be so leavened.

With these ideals the recognition of a superiority of one social class to another is impossible. A consistent follower of Jesus does not judge others by their occupations, their relative wealth, their birth, or their nationality. In Christ they are all one. From this unity should spring the sense of mutual respect for each other that the search for rights tends to deaden. Unless signs fail, democracy itself, at least in certain of its industrial expressions, is seriously in danger of developing the same relentless pursuit of rights as characterizes the capitalism it attacks. Whether or not the ideals of Jesus are consistent with economic inequalities, whether or not the compulsion to labor that now lies in these inequalities would be any less dangerous if exprest in an absolute democracy, may well be open questions, but the obligation of the Christian Church to propagate the spirit of sacrificial fraternity is undeniable. That must be the first step in the evangelizing of our future democracy.

HOW WILL THE CHURCH EXERT ITS INFLUENCE?

THESE considerations, however, may seem to leave the matter in the region of general theory. To a certain extent this is true. Yet general theories are by no means to be despised. It may be that the largest service that any institution can render its day is to develop general sympathies and attitudes of mind in advance of actual activities. If the present generation can be trained to a moral sensitiveness to the ideals for which the church professedly stands, it can be trusted to use expert advice in industrial organisation and political legislation of the future. It certainly is not and will not be the business of the church to enter politics. In the same proportion as religious institutions become identified with governmental processes

are they apt to lose the sense of the primacy of the spiritual and become engrossed in political maneuvers. It would be lamentable if the effort to evangelize our modern social order had any such outcome.

But Christians will do that which a church must avoid. By the readjusting both of their formulas and of their activities, churches should make their members sensitive to the immediacy of religious needs and also to the bearing of Christian ideals upon our industrial and political future. Organized Christianity has the agencies for such moral education. Sunday Schools might become, and I believe are becoming, agencies for teaching a religion which is something more than a knowledge of a list of the names of the books of the Bible and of denominational theologies. In so far as a Sunday School is now really fulfilling its function, it is teaching the young to see that the ideal life must express itself in social activity, and that love is vicarious social-mindedness. In this way as well as in others the churches are increasingly serving the cause of our future democracy.

This type of religious teaching is not as sensitive to doctrinal precision as was the older non-social instruction. It is, however, more than an appeal for "social service" and is no less true to the fundamental principles which constitute real Christianity. But just as we are coming to see that the teachings of Christ are quite as important as the teachings of the church about Christ, are we also coming to see that a generation which regards religion only as a means of gaining salvation in a future life is not as thoroly democratic as one trained to see that the supreme accomplishment of life is the individual who by God's grace has grown sacrificially fraternal and Christlike. When once society is convinced that a Christlike individuality is an ultimate good, it will more easily realize that economic efficiency is a secondary good. Wealth will become a servant rather than the master of human welfare. It is not reckless prophesying to say that already the great currents of church life are setting in this direction.

THE SOCIAL GOSPEL

BUT the course of events during the next generation will demand that the church become something more than an inculcator of ideals among the people. It must be also a servant of the people's welfare. It must practise what it preaches. It must see in society opportunities not only for heralding the wealth of human life, but it must also undertake

SHAILER MATHEWS

DEAN OF THE DIVINITY SCHOOL OF THE UNIVERSITY OF CHICAGO, PRESIDENT OF THE FEDERAL COUNCIL
OF CHURCHES OF CHRIST IN AMERICA, AUTHOR OF "THE SOCIAL TEACHING OF
JESUS," "THE CHURCH AND THE CHANGING ORDER"

to benefit human life by its own operations. It is easy for radicals who are impatient of social transformation and want social revolutions to say that the church is so hopelessly degenerate as to be on the point of being replaced by some other as yet unknown movement. From my knowledge of the churches of the United States I am convinced that the next few decades will show that such an opinion is born of ignorance and hypercriticism. The problems which rise from democracy are felt by the leaders of organized Christians quite as truly as by those not within the church.

A lady whose work has been of large significance in the field of industrial reform once said to me, "Tell me about the church. Is it really dying?" I asked her how long since she had attended church. She finally was able to recall one or two occasions during the past ten years. I had the satisfaction of telling her of the Commission in Social Service of the Federal Council of the Churches of Christ in America, of the other commissions of the various denominations, of how local federations of churches have engaged in reform, of efforts being made by Christian people backed by the denominations to bring about legislation in behalf of child workers. The list might be even more extended. Organized Christianity of all sorts is deliberately shaping itself to meet the conditions of our new sense of the People's rights. It has not gone as far as it will go, but it has made a definite beginning. At least it is seeing that spiritual life is and must be social; giving justice as truly as caring for the victims of injustice.

There is apprehension on the part of some church leaders that this attempt to socialize the purpose of the Gospel will transform a church from a religious institution to an agency of charity or of recreation. That there may be such a danger need not be denied, but here again, within the most recent past, there has been a stabilizing of ecclesiastical purpose and a clearer perception that all agencies with which the church seeks to minister to the social needs of its community are secondary to its primary task of stimulating the spiritual ambitions and sympathies of the community. The Social Gospel, about which we hear sometimes such bitter words from those who believe that Christianity needs only to rescue rather than to save, is not another gospel. It is simply the application of Christianity to social forces as intelligently as it has been and is being applied to individuals. Thirty years hence the results of such an

THIS is the fourth article in The Independent's series on "The Next Generation in American Life." In a May number will appear the fifth: THE EXPANSION OF POPULAR EDUCATION, by George E. Vincent, who as Chancellor of Chautauqua Institution and President of the University of Minnesota, has worked largely to bring about the changes which he discusses.

extension of the Gospel will be reckoned as supreme social assets.

THE CHURCH MOVES FORWARD

MUCH of the tension between the People and the churches is born of mutual criticism. Rhetorical exaggerations were never less needed than at the present time. The church from the point of view of democracy is no more subject to criticism than is democracy from the point of view of genuine Christianity. If the church can be charged with emphasizing mere other-worldliness, democracy can be charged with a leaning towards mere economic interests. But both criticisms I believe to be unbalanced.

The day is past when the church is becoming more aristocratic. There is within its organization a distinct movement toward equality. Women and laymen are gaining influence even in those churches which most sharply distinguish between the clergy and the laity. Everywhere there is emerging a feeling as to the true obligations of the church. Within a few days I have heard of four towns in such widely separated regions as Texas, Kansas, Illinois and New York in which small churches in the country are ministering to the community actively and wisely. The coöperation between state universities and churches is growing closer. Feelings of mutual suspicion, if they ever existed, are rapidly disappearing, and thruout the country districts as well as in the great cities, there is coming to be a more distinct perception on the part of the church that if it is to be spiritually efficient it must minister to all those real needs of its community to which the community itself does not attend.

As I look back over the last twenty years I am imprest with the change which has come over the spirit of organized Christianity in these respects. I do not find that Christianity has grown less interested in spiritual truths. On the contrary the men I know who are most devoted to the social gospel are those who are

emphasizing the need of spirituality. It would not be difficult to mention scores of clergymen who not only lead the wider ministry of their churches to the needs of the people, but who are endeavoring to make the people themselves feel that man shall not live by bread alone but by the word of God.

WHEN DEMOCRACY AND RELIGION JOIN HANDS

ALTOGETHER, therefore, looking forward from a wide survey of the actual life of the American churches, I feel there is abundant ground for hope. True, there are reactionary groups with apparently unlimited funds at their disposal who are endeavoring to combat this effort to make Christianity recognize today's social needs. But such groups themselves cannot escape the general tendency and are enforcing their message of a living and forgiving God by social service to the people of great cities. In the future I believe the two wings of Christian evangelism will come to understand each other better. And thus understanding each other they will unite to bring Jesus Christ and His Gospel not only to individuals as they stand related directly to God, but also as they stand related to His immanent will in society. A real reliance upon God for help and a life in accordance with His purposes will find expression in forms and agencies thru which regenerate lives shall function socially. The People in their search for larger corporate self-expression will thereby be enabled to move more readily and surely toward not only a larger economic freedom, but also that freedom of the spirit which is born of a trust in the Heavenly Father.

Those of us who may not live to see this better day when religion and democracy shall come to a mutual understanding, can yet rejoice to have a share in preparing for its coming. Our religious life is certainly moving forward and we are organizing ideals and teachings and institutions which will make the religion of the future less a system of dogmatics and more a form of rational living. God and Christ will mean even more to the democrat of thirty years hence than they mean to us today. And altho my convictions may be too highly colored by my hopes, I dare predict that the men and women who shall be shaping public opinion and public policies in the next generation will admit more readily the practicability of Jesus' teaching as to the good sense of love and the foolishness of appeals to force.

Chicago

WHEN THE WATER WORKS FOR US

BY WILLIAM H. EASTON

EVER since George Westinghouse proved that electricity could be transmitted commercially a thousand miles as easily as a thousand feet men have been dreaming of the day when this mysterious force would become the Universal Servant of mankind—when it would be available everywhere and would be cheap enough to be used for every possible purpose. These dreams, tho inspired by true scientific insight, have so far remained mere castles in the air, for in spite of the great development of electricity it is not cheap, except in a few favored places, and it is available only in restricted areas.

But today these dreams bid fair to become true. For years conditions have been quietly shaping themselves—so quietly as to be marked by but a few—and now suddenly we have awakened to the fact that the day of universal electricity is about to dawn. All the means are now at hand. We are able to generate electricity in any quantity, transmit it any distance, and utilize it in innumerable ways. And most important of all, we have the power wherewith to generate it; for more than thirty million horsepower of inexhaustible water power is available in the United States. Today this great supply of energy wastes itself in idleness; tomorrow it will be working for you and me, making our lives safer and happier, reducing the cost of our living, and increasing our resources by an incalculable amount. But it will occur to you that this power has existed here for centuries. Why has it not been developed on a large scale before now? There have been two main obstacles to this development, one legal and the other commercial, and it is because these obstacles have been, or promise to be, successfully removed that we can now look forward to universal electricity.

THE legal obstacle is an inheritance from days gone by. Quite properly at the time, Congress passed various laws that put a stop to the erection of power plants on navigable streams and in government reservations. Now it so happens that practically all the available water power is situated in these restricted locations, and as a result its use has been prevented. For example, a large electro-chemical plant, after having obtained all the power from Niagara it could get, desired to expand. Nowhere in the United States could it obtain a sufficient amount of power because of our adverse laws. Finally it actually decided to build its new plant in Norway, so that America is deprived of the benefits of a huge investment. Conditions have, however, changed radically since these laws were passed. Our government clearly recognizes this fact and Congress is now considering legislation that will permit the use of water power, and at the same time safeguard the interests of the people, prevent monopolization, and insure unobstructed navigation.

The solution of the commercial problems that clears the way for universal electrification is best shown by the following illustration: Suppose there are five water powers well distributed thruout a state the size of Pennsylvania, and each is near a city of some size. The older practise would have been to develop each of these powers separately and transmit the electricity to the nearest city. Owing to conditions too technical to discuss in this article, it is possible that none of these developments would have been very successful commercially. Many experiences of this sort turned engineers to the steam engine for generating electricity in large amounts—and the steam engine can never produce universal electricity. But now our engineers know that if all five water powers are joined together into a single system, which supplies all five communities, power of great reliability and low cost can be produced. And note this point especially: By the older method no one could obtain power unless he was located in or near the city or on the line between the city and the plant; but by the new method, all five plants would be inter-connected with a complex network of power lines which would be so arranged that nearly every one in the state would be reached.

Such networks will make our

AT THE ALABAMA POWER COMPANY'S DAM. THIS IS THE FORCE THAT WILL ELECTRIFY CIVILIZATION

dream of universal electricity come true. Their main source of power will be water, but every other supply of cheap power will contribute its share—the waste gases of blast furnaces, the culm piles of the anthracite regions, soft coal at the pit's mouth—and the result will be electricity at a fraction of the present cost. No demand for power will be too great for the capacity of these systems, no need too small to be supplied. The great railroad and the lamp in a miner's hat will each draw freely from the immense supply.

BUT after all, what will universal electricity do for us? What shall we personally gain from it? Let us answer this question without calling upon our imagination. Let us not consider what wonderful things may be brought into existence twenty years from now, but simply review a few of the more interesting applications of electricity that are in actual practical use today.

First, in our homes. In the day of universal electricity every one will have electric light—the clean, safe, cool, convenient light, that is always ready without the slightest thought or effort on the part of the housekeeper. But electric light is a small part of the service electricity will offer us. Electric cooking and heating are as superior to our present methods as the electric light is to the kerosene oil lamp. Imagine cooking without flame or smoke, on a range that will automatically start at any desired time, heat up to any desired temperature, and then hold that temperature until the food is cooked. No need for the housewife to live in the kitchen; no early rising for breakfast; no interference with afternoon pleasures to prepare dinner. And no servants needed, either. And as for heating, if you have shoveled coal and ashes; if you have fought a stubborn fire with the thermometer at zero; if you have feared for the safety of your house because something has gone wrong; would you not welcome a heating system that requires only the turn of a switch and keeps the temperature of each room at an exact point all winter long regardless of the weather? You can have all these things now if you will pay the price for the current, and every one will have them in the days of universal electricity.

But electricity will do more than light, cook and heat. It will wash your clothes, wring and iron them; sweep your floors; do your sewing; wash your dishes and dry them; grind your tools; polish your knives; curl your hair. And it will banish ice as well as fire from our homes. In place of the damp, germ-infested ice box will be a clean, dry, sanitary refrigerator, operated by a little motor. And remember, these things will be enjoyed not only in the luxurious city apartment, but also on the remotest farm.

THE benefits of universal electricity will not stop in the farmer's home. His most troublesome problems at present are the difficulty of obtaining sufficient help, his dependence on nature for rain at the proper times, and the high cost of keeping his soil fertile. Let us see how electricity can solve these problems.

Electricity is not only the Universal Servant, it is also the great Hired Man. The electric motor is the ideal source of farm power. It is small and light so that it is easily portable; it requires practically no attention; and it is absolutely safe even around hay and other inflammable substances. Electric motors will do all the work around the farm, even to milking the cows and cleaning the horses, so that the need for human help will be cut down to a minimum.

Irrigation becomes a simple matter with cheap electric power. The electric pumps can be placed anywhere, started and stopped from the house or barn, and need be visited but once a week for inspection. Even in the moist climate of the East a prolonged dry spell at the wrong season will spell ruin at present—but never with universal electricity.

As for fertilizer, nitrogenous matter is one of the vital elements that must be returned to the soil. Today the farmer is dependent for nitrogen on animal refuse or the nitrate beds of South America. But electricity has the power of forcing the nitrogen of the air into combinations suitable for use as fertilizer. The raw materials for this process are universal and cost nothing, and if sufficient amounts of cheap electric power are available, the fertilizer problem is solved.

As an inevitable result of these various improvements, more land will bear crops, larger crops will be produced per acre, and the cost of production will be greatly reduced. Millions of acres of desert, where now no man can live, will blossom with harvests, support millions in comfort, and supply food for millions more. Will this not reduce the cost of our living?

In the field of transportation electricity is proving itself the ideal motive power. Today many railroads are using electricity at a compara-

tively high cost to operate their most difficult divisions—mountain passes, tunnels, suburban lines, and main lines with heavy traffic—because it reduces expenses, increases speed and safety, and eliminates many causes of delay. How they will benefit from cheap and universal electric power! At the same time, trolley systems will naturally multiply, and electric automobiles will laugh at forty-cent gasoline.

FROM another standpoint failure to make full use of our water power is foolhardy, not to say criminal. Our water power is inexhaustible; our coal, gas, and oil are not. Why should we let the water go to waste and continue to consume our precious and never-to-be replaced fuel? The substitution of twenty million horsepower of water for steam would mean the conservation of $225,000,000 worth of coal *a year*.

It is not necessary to point out the value of cheap electricity as power for manufacturing and mining; the fact is obvious. In addition, great electro-chemical industries will arise, employing large numbers of workmen and producing certain substances that can be obtained in no other way or only at a high cost. Mention has already been made of fertilizer; there are also aluminum, caustic soda, chlorin and carborundum, among many others. The electric refining of iron and steel will probably revolutionize our most important industry, to the benefit of every person in existence.

Nor must we overlook the question of national defense. Today we are absolutely dependent on Chile for our supplies of the nitrates from which to manufacture gunpowder and every other explosive. What would be our position if we lost command of the sea and our reserve supply of nitrates gave out? No amount of preparedness in men, ships, or weapons could save us if we could not manufacture ammunition. And yet, as we have seen, electricity can make the essential ingredient, the nitrogen compounds, from the air. But nitrate plants cannot be built overnight, so they must be built for commercial purposes during times of peace to be ready for war; and for this, cheap electricity is essential.

It would seem, therefore, that we are about to enter upon a new era. The change will of course come gradually, but you and I will probably see the first steps, and if we live until 1950 we will undoubtedly look upon the year 1916 much as we now do upon the year 1840. The Age of Electricity is dawning.

New York City

THE HOURGLASS ON THE YELLOW SANDS

Joseph Urban, the scenic producer of the Shakespeare Masque, has designed this great hourglass to stand on the circular stage thruout the performance, to symbolize the passage of time in the art of the theater. The Spirit of Time rises on this altar to present the epilogue

THE SHAKESPEARE MASQUE

BY PERCY MACKAYE

THE tercentenary of Shakespeare's death—an occasion of international significance—can have no international celebration in Europe. It is, then, fitting that here in America, New York, the most cosmopolitan city of the world, should do honor to the supreme master of the art of the theater. Representatives of at least ten of the nationalities of this country, nationalities with which Shakespeare peopled his plays, will, it is hoped, be represented in the memorial masque in which New York's celebration will center.

By drawing in this manner from isolated groups of this great city—groups which ordinarily hardly know of each other's existence—the Tercentenary Committee hopes to effect the beginnings of that rare phenomenon known as "civic consciousness." But the community festival consists also of hundreds of local celebrations held in the schools, settlements, dramatic clubs, literary societies and the like, all of which contribute their part to the great whole.

In all, there will be the greater part of a million people thus actively engaged in the celebration. From among the many participants in the smaller celebrations, and from many widely divergent groups, will be selected the community actors for the Masque, which, with its interludes will be enacted for five performances on the evenings of May 23 to 27, in the New York City College Stadium, reconstructed temporarily to seat 20,000 spectators.

"Caliban, by the Yellow Sands,"

the Shakespeare Memorial Masque, seeks to honor Shakespeare by honoring the art of which he was master. It takes as its principal characters certain personages out of Shakespeare's play, "The Tempest." In the text these characters are developed for the purposes of the Masque so as to enact their own symbolic drama of the regeneration of brute man under the ennobling influences of the art of the theater.

In the first scene (the prologue) Caliban, a deformed creature, half man, half brute, is worshiping his father, the god-idol Setebos (half tiger, half toad), divinity of the Magic Isle of the "Yellow Sands." Miranda enters. Caliban, enchanted by the sight of this strange loveliness, approaches her, sniffing and staring in wonder:

Caliban
Hath feet
And hair; hath bright hair shineth like a fish's tail;
Hath mouth, and maketh small, sweet noises.
(He sniffs nearer; then howls strangely)
Spring in the air: Oho!

Miranda
Alas, poor creature! Who hath hurt thee?

Caliban
Hurt?
Who hurteth God? Am seed of Setebos;
Am Caliban: the world is all mine isle:
Kill what I please, and play with what I please:
So, yonder, play with him: pull out his wings
And put 'em back to grow. . . .
Where be *thy* wings,
Spring—i'—the—air? . . . .
. . . The moon hath a face

And smileth on the lily pools, but hath No lily body withal; thy body is All lilies and the smell of lily buds, And thy round face a pool of moonbeams.

As Caliban's wooing becomes more insistent, Prospero, her father, appears and by his magic power quells the man-brute, and dethrones Setebos. He appoints the good Ariel to train Caliban's spirit to nobler uses. With this purpose he conjures the historic pageant of the art of the theater. Thus begins the first interlude—the dramatic art of antiquity.

The three interludes and the epilogue, in which the trained amateurs participate, present thru rituals of pageantry and music varied forms of the dramatic art of past ages, culminating in the Elizabethan. The action is centered about the character of Caliban, which develops toward human self-consciousness under the influence of the "mirror held to nature." Bound in Prospero's power, he hears the call of the Priest, Lust, but Prospero tells him that Ariel will tutor him in the arts of civilization:

Come, Caliban: behold thy tutor.
Behind these curtains he will show thee now
More than thy nature dreams on. If thou obey him
And learn mine art, thou shalt go free like him.
If not, thou shalt be spitted on a tooth
More sharp than Setebos. What sayest?
Caliban (cringing)
Lord,
Art Cock o' the world, and Caliban thy worm;
Yea, only beggeth thee crow no more, nor set
They dancing dogs to bark at him.

MR. MACKAYE IN CHARGE
The author of the masque is directing a rehearsal in the snow-covered stadium. He has already made notable contributions to American pageantry and poetic drama—such as "Jeanne d'Arc," "Sanctuary," and the Masque of St. Louis.

Prospero

Tush, fool:
Wilt thou obey?

Caliban

Obeyeth both of you.

Then appears, on the inner stage, the scene in Shakespeare's "Antony and Cleopatra," in which the lovers meet after the battle of Actium. It disappears, and Caliban exclaims:

Ho, light! All's smother; 'tis gone!
   Yo—yo, all gone—
Cloud-swallowed, all! Ah, woman,
   snake-bright queen,
Thou wonder-thing, come back! Ah,
   where—where—where?

Caliban, after beholding scenes from "Troilus and Cressida" and "Julius Cæsar," becomes overweening, and conspires with Lust to snatch Prospero's magic staff. Grasping it, he staggers and sways wildly, as tho being shocked by an invisible force, crying:

Now am *I* lord of lightenings: Lo,
   mine art
Shaketh the throne of Prospero. Awake,
Imperial Rome! Return, ye snake-
   bright women
Of Troy and Egypt! Stain these yellow
   sands
Wine-red with spillings of your
   wreathed bowls,
And let the orgied priests of revel
   reign. . . .

The mob which he gathers about him, a Roman rabble, clambers over the stage, but a great cross, appearing high above, stops them. The rab-

ble is revealed as the powers of Setebos. Thus the Christian Church arrests the degeneration of the civilized world, and Caliban is once more overpowered, and exclaims:

      Yea, methought to be
His artist, and make dream-things of
   mine own
Like Ariel his spirits, yet now—am
   mud.

      Then, in the second interlude, the art of the theater in medieval Germany, France, Spain and Italy appears in symbolic ritual. The pageant, summoned by Prospero, continues with scenes from "Hamlet," "Romeo and Juliet," "The Merchant of Venice" and "A Winter's Tale." Once more carried away by the enchantment, Caliban, in conspiracy with the second priest, Death, seeks the scroll of Prospero. His gray hordes, hatted and garbed like Puritans, wrest the prize from its proper hands, but withdraw in the face of the merrymakers of Elizabethan England, who now appear and dance the May-pole dances of the third interlude.

Caliban has thus twice betrayed his trust, but he is granted yet another chance. He witnesses scenes from "As You Like It," "The Merry Wives of Windsor" and "Henry V." Still again, under the influence of the third priest, War, he leads his mob to capture Miranda and the spirits of Ariel. Then Prospero, who, unhooded, is revealed in the form of the spirit of Shakespeare himself,

summons a final pageant of the creative forces of the theater in all ages—the great actors from Roscius to Irving, the great dramatists from Æschylus to Ibsen, and symbolic groups representing the great theaters, from that of Dionysus to the Comédie Française. And Caliban, groping and dazed, comes forth and in a voice hoarse with feeling says:

Thy tempest blindeth me: Thy beauty
   baffles. . . .
A little have I crawled, a little only
Out of mine ancient cave. All that I
   build
I botch: all that I do destroyeth my
   dream.
Yet—yet I yearn to build, to be thine
   Artist
And stablish this thine Earth among
   the Stars.

DESIGNING A COSTUME FOR THE MASQUE
Mrs. John W. Alexander, whose husband left so deep an impress on American art, is designing the two thousand costumes which will help to make the Shakespeare Masque beautiful. The picture suggests how splendid these will be

SAVING—A VICE OR A VIRTUE?

THE CONTRADICTORY OPINIONS OF TWO HOUSEKEEPERS

Pearl Grace Loehr

MRS. BRUERE

Harris & Ewing

MRS. THOMPSON

THE WASTE OF SAVING

BY

MARTHA BENSLEY BRUÈRE

cestress laid by a cave full of summer food to steal her family thru the winter? And from then till now, thru all the intervening ages when there wasn't enough of anything to go round, and when women not being earners could only add to the family security by saving, unremitting individual thrift was an important feminine virtue.

But those thrifty ancestresses of ours are dead, and we have come on a time when the work of saving, like the work of making cloth or books or flour, can be more effectively done by the community than by the individual. It is time for that habit of individual petty saving to be transplanted to the community garden.

For consider its workings when unhampered by the reasoning powers! "Mother" carries what the carver has left of a roast shoulder of lamb into a bright light, puts on her glasses and with a small sharp knife extracts from the interstices of the bones from one-half to two-thirds of a pound of edible fragments. She adds a green pepper, an onion, four cold potatoes, some dry bread and any appropriate trifles she finds in the refrigerator, puts the whole thru the meat chopper, breaks in two eggs and molds it into a loaf. If she is practised and quick she can perform the feat with the necessary preparation and cleaning up afterward in forty-five minutes, tho she must be on hand to baste the roast at appropriate intervals. Today the butcher quoted 26 cents as the price of lamb, so "mother" probably saves 15 cents by her endeavor—and a well-trained family will often accept the result as nourishment. But if "mother" had dropt the lamb bones with their ad-

This is the third article in Mrs. Bruère's series on what she calls "The Habits of Women Under Domestication." In an early number "Pernicious Heirlooms" will conclude the series.—THE EDITOR.

"BUT have you considered," a life insurance agent urged a friend of ours, "that some time you may not be earning as much as you are now? That when you are old——"

"My dear sir, what are the almshouses for?"

It is reported that the agent went away.

"And you know Wellford really meant it!" is every one's comment, which is praise or blame, according to the understanding of the speaker. Some feel that he is showing a wise altruistic courage, others that he is a prey to selfish folly. Few realize that Mr. Wellford knows he cannot afford to hamper his present usefulness by attempting personally to save money. Can the rest of us?

The answer to this question depends on the stage of civilization in which we are living. I say "we," meaning particularly women whose business is the vanishing one of housekeeping. Strict economy of money and things is expected of us as a class virtue, and usually we practise it. During the long ages when the business of housekeeping developed, its side partner, the Habit of Saving, was grained deep into womankind, and became perhaps the highest of the virtues. Was it not a great day for the race, still a bit uncertain on its hind legs and reminiscent of the tree tops, when some provident an-

hering meat first into the soup kettle, and later into the garbage can, she would have spent two minutes of time and thrown away some seven cents' worth of nourishment. Would that seven cents have been wasted?

The Commissioner of Street Cleaning for New York City has just told me that the refuse from the city has a gross value of about $4 a ton and that, altho the cost of saving it is from $2 to $3, there is still so large a profit that the latest contract for garbage disposal nets the city $180,-000 a year.

I can already hear some New York housewife crying wrathfully:

"What good does that $180,000 do me? I don't get any of it back!"

Madam, if you don't it is your own fault. That saving is for the benefit of us all. Come out of domestication and take your seven cents' worth of the advantages which $180,000 will give the community!

It is the tragedy of domestic saving that it is most prevalent in the middle class, which ought to know better. According to the best statistics which I have been able to put together people who have a little leeway above the requirements of decent living save about $300 per year per family. And at what a community cost is it done!

A lady, blooming like a scentless plant in a window box, has just confided to me that she has saved enough

· 61

out of her housekeeping to provide for her old age. For more than thirty years she has run her ménage on the principle the Japanese use to grow their miniature gardens—each plant and tree is given, not all that it can advantageously assimilate, but the least that can be made to do. One would rise from her table with the taste of saved pennies in the mouth. And it wasn't only food—clothes, furniture, education, even the family doctor—all were the least expensive that could be made to do. If she had not looked upon matrimony as an opportunity to retire from industry, might she not have earned as much as she had saved? Might she not have expanded under a series of fresh impressions instead of shriveling mentally like a starved apple on a sapless tree? For not a thing has she done for the community but refrain from becoming a public charge—in money. In mental and physical inertia she has become a drag on the wheels of progress.

Then is our housekeeping to be deliberately wasteful?

Indeed no! Let us get what we need at the least price we can pay for it, but remembering that there are more coinages than money to buy with. We must determine whether money is more precious than muscle, legal tender more to be saved than brains, mere dollars and cents than time, material things than the effort it takes to conserve them. The crux of the matter is to determine the cost of the individual saving of money in terms of the other measures of value, and to balance money saving against money earning both in its financial outcome and in its effect on ourselves—and this is a very difficult thing for women trained to think economy a virtue in itself to do.

Under domestication woman is blind to the fact that if she becomes part of a great community movement to control the meat packing industry, she will not have to stay at home and try out beef fat; if she puts her mending and sewing—yes, even the darning of the family socks, which can now be done by machinery—into the hands of industry she need not lie awake nights planning to cut a middy blouse for Ellen out of her aunt's old dolman in order to save a yard and a half of cotton duck, but can take up some form of earning to which she is suited. For now that material things are plenty and cheap, and labor and thought are dear, it is up to her to save the most valuable—and not to forget in the process that her own development is a commercial asset, to be fed and increased, not perpetually denied. We must indeed continue to save, but collectively thru organized society rather than individually in the home, for in a modern state the aggregate of our common savings, not our individual hoards, is the measure of our civilization.

Besides we already have a minimum provision of the things we're saving for. We are secure against actual hunger and cold, against utter neglect in sickness, against complete illiteracy, against starvation in our old age. We have not provided ourselves with these things adequately nor with honor, but the combined effort it would take to make this provision adequate for all the families in the land, is out of all proportion small compared with the individual effort that goes into the attempt to make uncertain provision for the families of a few. Shaw says that we all need pensions for life—and then to be forced to earn them. Wouldn't it be a strong drive toward democracy! The pension for life earned under compulsion would give ease of mind to generations, for insurance companies may be mismanaged, and stock companies may fail, but the government, which is ourselves, goes on forever. And for those "solitaries" whom age finds ungathered into families there may come, instead of the almshouse, the Community Club, where such public servants as Mr. Wellford can live, not in dependence, but on the deferred payments for services they have stored to their credit during a long life.

Is it not high time that we women allowed our old virtue of domestic saving to be socialized along with our other individualistic virtues of industry and mercy and love? Time we tried to make ourselves contemporary?

New York City

THE SAVING OF WASTE

BY FLORA McDONALD THOMPSON

THE prevention of waste, the promotion of household economy, is the "better half" of preparedness.

Competent authorities proclaim that there is need of mobilizing the industrial forces of the United States. This means mobilizing the housewives of the country, too, and I propose that we get ready. I propose that we practise and perfect domestic economy as a patriotic duty—because we are good citizens.

This sort of efficiency has served the Germans admirably in the present war. Great Britain is just waking up to its importance and has begun an Anti-Waste Campaign, concerning which the Princess Louise said, "Under pressure of this terrible war the importance of domestic economy to the people and its value to the country is now very widely recognized, but there is still much waste in our kitchens, and it is by education and training that we have to

As president of the Housekeepers' Alliance in Washington, D. C., Mrs. Flora McDonald Thompson leads a nation-wide campaign for household economy.—THE EDITOR.

correct these national faults." The London *Illustrated News* calls attention to the "mischievous amateur spirit" in which women undertake housework, and remarks on the misfortune it is that women carry this same spirit into other work.

In France, on the other hand, the women, being perfectly trained in housework, have replaced their men in industry, in business, in the railroads, in the government, with no appreciable disturbance of the economic or public order. In short, the war in Europe, with terrible precision, defines housewifely ability as the necessary base of the good citizenship of women; it shows how inseparably domestic economy is allied with the maintenance of industry and of the defense of the nation.

The Housekeepers' Alliance now proposes to make war on waste. We are not going to talk; we mean to do things. We confidently expect a great many men and women, who have never before considered housekeeping their business, to join with us in this campaign of household economy and to make our efforts real and practical.

Here is an all-inclusive woman's movement—making the most of our homes. What we save in the kitchen comes back to us in the form of increased resources for the happiness and productivity of all.

The American woman who makes up her mind can do anything she pleases. Let us make up our minds to do our part in the preparedness of the nation. Let us prevent waste. Let us promote efficiency in the household.

Washington, D. C.

ONLY THE CADILLAC RIDES LIKE THE CADILLAC

IT is still unique in the large number of parts and operations ground to the accuracy of a thousandth and the fraction of a thousandth part of an inch.

It is still unique in that standardization which insists that every essential part be exactly like every other part of its kind.

It is still unique in the extent to which friction is eliminated from its working parts.

It is still unique in that alignment which makes for the harmonious action of its units.

It is still unique in its balance and in the scientific allotment of its weight.

It is still unique in those qualities which make for year after year of dependable service.

It is still unique in the characteristics which makes a fact of the phrase:———————

ONLY THE CADILLAC RIDES LIKE THE CADILLAC

PURE CREAM OF TARTAR

NO LIME PHOSPHATE

NO ALUM

P CREA TA

NO ALUM

NO LIME PHOSPHATE

Pure Food

on the home table is a matter of intelligent study and careful buying on the part of the housewife. The healthful quality of biscuits, cake and other flour foods is largely determined by the ingredients of the baking powder with which they are made.

This is the important reason why the pure food laws of most states demand that the ingredients of baking powders shall be clearly stated on the label of the package.

ROYAL Baking Powder

NO ALUM

PURE CREAM OF TARTAR

NO LIME PHOSPHATE

PURE CREAM OF TARTAR

Good Health

is the natural result of the proper selection of food ingredients.

Mothers and housekeepers who are well informed do not accept inferior baking powders, made from alum or phosphate.

They insist on Royal Baking Powder, which is free from these mineral substitutes because it is made from Cream of Tartar, a pure, healthful fruit product, which is derived from ripe grapes.

Absolutely PURE

THE STORY OF GOOD FRIDAY

THE retelling of the story of Good Friday is no task for small men. John Masefield brings to the undertaking a vigor of expression, a fidelity to humanity, and a homely, flexible versification which make the dramatic poem which gives the name to his new volume, *Good Friday, and Other Poems*, a notable addition to a body of verse already more distinctive and important, perhaps, than that of any other living English poet.

It is rightly called a dramatic poem. It is not, properly speaking, poetic drama. In structure it is narrative rather than dramatic; the limits and incidents are determined rather by the original story, with which the poet has taken few liberties, than by considerations of dramatic unity.

But Masefield has woven on the threads of the Bible record a vivid tapestry of the forces and counter-forces, the political rivalries, the personal interactions, the ironies and the passions of that day. His Pilate is beautifully characterized, his Herod and Pilate's wife very real, his Voices grimly true to the mob everywhere.

He has chosen to subordinate the scene which has figured so largely in Christian art, the "Ecce Homo," but in the story of Golgotha, put in the mouth of the centurion, he has written a picture which it would be hard to surpass.

> We nailed him there
> Aloft, between the thieves, in the broad air.
> The rabble and the readers mocked with oaths;
> The hangman's squad were dicing for his clothes.
> The two thieves jeered at him. Then it grew dark,
> Till the noon sun was dwindled to a spark.
> And one by one the mocking mouths fell still.
> We were alone on the accursed hill
> And we went still, not even the dice clicked,
> Only the heavy blood-gouts dropped and ticked
> On to the stone: the hill is all bald stone.
> And now and then the hangers gave a groan.
> Up in the dark, three shapes with arms outspread.
> The blood-drops spat to show how slow they bled.
> They rose up black against the ghastly sky,
> God, Lord, it is a slow way to make die
> A man, a strong man, who can beget men.
> Then there would come another groan, and then
> One of those thieves (tough camelers those two)
> Would curse the teacher from lips bitten through
> And the other bid him let the teacher be.
> I have stood much, but this thing daunted me.
> The dark, the livid light, and long loud groans
> One on another, coming from their bones.
> And it got darker and a glare began
> Like the sky burning up above the man.
> The hangman's squad stood easy on their spears
> And the air moaned, and women were in tears.
> While still between his groans the robber cursed . . .

While the prevailing impression of the poem is its keen homeliness and reality, and the accuracy with which Masefield has suggested the human background of the tragedy, the closing note—as has sometimes happened before in his work—is vague and over-lyrical. The "Madman" is not a part of the picture; nor is he satisfying as a mouthpiece for the spiritual message. The poem is so intensely human that the highly poetized distillation of the sacrifice-theme into a sort of beauty-worship is quite inadequate.

One thinks of "The Terrible Meek" in reading this. In every respect save dramatic force and coherence Mr. Masefield's treatment of the Crucifixion is the finer. He gets naturalness without the exaggerated crudity which Mr. Kennedy uses; his canvas is, by choice, broader; his figures more lifelike. But where Mr. Kennedy errs in one direction Mr. Masefield goes to the other extreme. If "The Terrible Meek" is too argumentative, *Good Friday* disappoints because it is too vague. But it is an impressive achievement.

The rest of the book is given to a loosely-joined sonnet sequence and a short poem of similar tenor. These philosophial musings on beauty, mortality and wisdom, elaborately metaphorical, sometimes turgid, often ragged in form, are a far cry from the "Salt Water Ballads," the long narratives and the dramas to which Masefield has recently been devoting himself.

As a whole they are hardly successful. Metrically they are just what one would expect from a Masefield turned sonneteer—sonnets reduced to the lowest terms. Elizabethan in form, of course, for he would not be likely to choose the Italian intricacies, they lack in most cases even the epigrammatic thrust which men of Shakespeare's age gave to the final couplet. In thought they are of unequal interest; the most appealing, as well as the most beautiful in form, are two or three superb sonnets dealing with the thought that

> Wherever beauty has been quick in clay
> Some effluence of it lives, a spirit dwells,
> Beauty that death can never take away.

Taken together they reveal a new Masefield, but a Masefield not entirely articulate.

Good Friday, and Other Poems, by John Masefield. Macmillan. $1.25.

MIDSUMMER FICTION IN APRIL

THE fiction of the last few weeks is a little in advance of the season. It is the sort of material which publishers are accustomed to offer to the public for "vacation reading," meaning thereby a book which will while away a sunny hour with the least possible exertion on the part of the reader.

Belle K. Maniates' *Mildew Manse* is admirably adapted for this purpose. There is a likeable, happy-go-lucky family with rich friends who provide work for the eldest son, tents for the boys, a husband for the daughter and a phonograph for the mother. There is the eternal mortgage on the old home. There is the young heroine who boards with the Haphazard family, who tells the story in quite impossible letters to her father and who embarks upon a ridiculous but entertaining business enterprise. Also there is a love affair on every page.

Likewise afflicted with a mortgage is a new book by the author of "Pollyanna." Eleanor H. Porter has taken a trumped-up situation, a threadbare plot, some commonplace characters, and by virtue of David, *Just David*, has made a charming story. David is endowed with goodness which should make him a prig, but renders him delightful; with a simplicity which should render him an idiot, but makes him fascinatingly naïve; with a musical ability which should be incredible, but is not. In short, he is a perfectly real impossible character. Quite the contrary is

Sylvia Chatfield Bates's *Geranium Lady*, who accomplishes the feat of being attractive with a red geranium in her hair. She has moreover a disinclination to explain herself to her naval lieutenant lover which serves to produce a fairly good plot.

If one likes skilful character drawing, pleasant comedy, clever, almost too clever, talk, and truthfully amusingly depicted contrasts of two generations, read *Some Elderly People and Their Young Friends*, by S. Macnaughtan, which takes one into the pleasant, easy, English social life, beloved of the novelist of manners.

The publishers present Carolyn Wells's *The Curved Blades* as "an old-fashioned detective story." It is. Fleming Stone is the orthodox sleuth. The plot is elaborate and fantastic enough to "hold the reader breathless to the last chapter." There are plenty of possible murderers. The heroine is beautiful, if not agreeable. But Miss Wells's knowledge of coroners' inquests and legal proceedings is limited.

It is surprising that any novelist can be as devoted to common sense as is Mrs. Watts and still be so interesting. Here at least is no midsummer fantasy. *The Rudder* is full of the same shrewd delineation of ordinary people, the same good-natured irony, the same frank use of homely detail, and above all the same persistent Ben Franklinism that one found in "Van Cleve" and "Jennie Cushing." Again there is a

selfish and inept woman (a little too black for belief, this time), and again the good old-fashioned contrast between shiftlessness and self-reliance. But the center of the stage is held by newer figures. The flashing heroine is a fine and convincing piece of portraiture, and except for a superfluous and obvious love-story, which provides a smooth ending for the book, the whole novel—broader and better balanced than the others—is a well-constructed picture of thoroly interesting people. Only once does Mrs. Watts become noticeably talky, and if her contribution to the labor question is neither original nor conclusive—neither is Ben Franklinism.

It is refreshing to leave well trodden ways for a new field of fiction. In *Cam Clarke*, John H. Walsh describes two things well: a frontier town and the boyhood of a railroad magnate. Washtucna, Washington, is not altogether prepossessing, but its worship of Mrs. Sarah Clarke, its kindliness, hospitality and fair play go far to offset its chronic state of drunkenness and its somewhat free use of revolvers. The town and Cam are described with directness, insight, a nice sense of proportion and an agreeable cynicism. It is an unusual story, unusually written, and well worth reading.

Mildew Manse, by Belle K. Maniates. Boston: Little, Brown. $1. *Just David*, by Eleanor H. Porter. Houghton, Mifflin. $1.25. *The Geranium Lady*, by Sylvia Chatfield Bates. Duffield. $1.25. *Some Elderly People and Their Young Friends*, by S. Macnaughtan. Dutton. $1.35. *The Curved Blades*, by Carolyn Wells. Philadelphia: Lippincott. $1.35. *The Rudder*, by Mary S. Watts. Macmillan. $1.50. *Cam Clarke*, by John H. Walsh. Macmillan. $1.35.

FROM WAR CORRESPONDENTS

When a complete history of the European war comes to be written a complimentary chapter will be due justly to the American correspondent. His narratives of this greatest human cataclysm come one after the other intense with vitality, keenness of vision, and alertness to grasp an essential fact enveloped in the onsweep of mighty events. This we write after reading every line of Arthur Sweetser's *Roadside Glimpses of the Great War*. This war correspondent is already well known to readers of The Independent.

To begin with he was not a member of the now familiar personally conducted party to the front. He simply had to be where "world history" was being made, and thither he went on a bicycle in spite of rules, rebuffs and the assurance he would be made prisoner and probably shot. It is his clear, independent view of the reality of war, obtained in a series of extraordinary adventures while chasing elusive French and German fronts, which makes his book illuminating for those occupied with the prevailing topic of American preparedness. Thus, after the German blow fell, Mr. Sweetser found in the French provincial cities of the north and among the peasants as complete a lack of the spirit of preparedness, as great a panic, as if France had failed to add a regiment or gun to her military organization since 1870. Here one may speculate

BEHOLD THE WOMAN!

By T. EVERETT HARRÉ

$1.35 net. Postage extra

"May justly be said to surpass in vividness, reality and human appeal any novel of recent years. Its true predecessors are 'Quo Vadis,' 'Ben Hur,' 'Salammbo,' 'Hypatia.' It is a novel of powerful religious significance, and bears a message for every man and woman."

In the character of Mary, the powerful Alexandrian courtesan whose beauty was "the glory of Egypt," the author presents the struggle of womanhood in its integrity and nobility with man's age-long exploitation, and interprets that eternal struggle which is today finding one of its expressions in the feminist movement.

It is the absorbing story of a woman's quest of love amid the vices and excesses of an age when wantonness was an art and a woman became eminent only through her shame, and of this woman's finding redemption in the divine love that in all ages knows not utter condemnation, but is all forgiving because all knowing.

A novel teeming with the turbulent excitement, intrigue and romance of the most splendid and licentious age of the world. The Time is the final conflict between Paganism and Christianity.

THE CURVED BLADES

By CAROLYN WELLS

Frontispiece by Gayle Hoskins. $1.35 net. Postage extra.

FLEMING STONE in a murder mystery as calculating and cruel as it was hidden, which he unravels through a maze of misleading evidence. Those who have followed the career of Stone will enjoy heartily the falling in love of the great sleuth. It is his first affair and is as appealing as the mystery of the murder of Miss Lucy Carrington is baffling.

THE FINDING OF JASPER HOLT

By GRACE L. H. LUTZ

Author of "Miranda," "Lo, Michael!" "Marcia Schuyler," etc., etc.

Three illustrations in color by E. F. Bayha. $1.25 net. Postage extra.

A love story of a Western man and an Eastern woman. To rise to the occasion he needs the agencies of an exciting railroad accident, a horse race and loads of beautiful roses from his own garden; but he succeeds and the reader rejoices. Mrs. Lutz's heart and humor are on every page.

A MAN'S REACH

By SALLY NELSON ROBINS

Three illustrations in color by Edmund Frederick. $1.25 net. Postage extra.

Governor Stuart, of Virginia:
"I have much pleasure in commending it to the thousands who must be interested in the vital thought suggested by the title."

THE CONQUEST

By SIDNEY L. NYBURG

Author of "The Final Verdict."

$1.25 net. Postage extra.

Boston Transcript:
"Originality and dramatic strength are marked in many pages of this novel."

ADAM'S GARDEN

By NINA WILCOX PUTNAM

Frontispiece in color by H. Weston Taylor. $1.25 net. Postage extra.

Adam's fate was to work out his salvation and win his girl by raising flowers upon a vacant city lot, surrounded by cats and dogs, dwelling with crusty, humorous curmudgeons who drift in from everywhere, having a feud with a thug, and being desperately loved by an unfortunate girl. A big story with humanity its theme.

A PENNELL VOLUME
NIGHTS

Rome, Venice—in the Aesthetic Eighties. Paris, London—in the Fighting Nineties. By ELIZABETH ROBINS PENNELL. *Sixteen to Eighteen Illustrations from Photographs and Etchings. $3.00 net. Postage extra.*

The pleasure of association with equally famous literary and artistic friends has been the good fortune of the Pennells. In this absorbing book there is the inside history of an enthralling period; and an acquaintanceship with those who made it what it was: Beardsley, Henley, Harland, Editor of "The Yellow Book," Whistler, etc. The illustrations, photographs and some of the etchings by Joseph Pennell are unusual.

FUNDAMENTALS OF MILITARY SERVICE

Prepared under the supervision of MAJOR-GENERAL LEONARD WOOD. By CAPTAIN LINCOLN, C. ANDREWS, U. S. CAVALRY. *Limp Leather. $1.50 net. Postage extra.*

This will be the text-book in the summer training camps of the Eastern Army Division. It should be read by all classes, not only those who wish to equip themselves for military courses, but also those who will wish to be ready for any eventuality. It describes in detail the military service in all branches of the army.

whether the same effect in similar circumstances would be produced upon a whole nation, such as the Germans, governed and imbued with military principles in all branches of effort.

A follower in the wake of Von Kluck's army, he grants, from observation, that its all forceful advance was conducted, for the most part, according to the rules of war, which of unhappy necessity cover devastation, ruin and bloodshed. Otherwise he does not hold the Germans were outrageously severe with the French civil population. What happened to him when he did pedal down into German headquarters at Valenciennes with a dubious pretext for being there—and thereafter—will hold the reader's tense interest until the end of the last chapter. The inevitable bagging of the American newspaper man and the resulting puzzle as to what is to be done with such an extraordinary individual are the sole gleams of comedy in unending tales of horror. As Baron von Mumm Schwartzenstein is quoted as saying in Horace Green's *The Log of a Noncombatant*, "You see, we were prepared for everysing—except ze invasion of ze American newspaperman. When he iss out of sight, zen we do not feel secure." Precisely! How is the military mind to deal with men, apparently crazy, who arrive at battle fronts in taxis, on bicycles, on foot, in straw hats, without proper credentials, and with sublime innocence demanding passes to impossible places because they prefer not being shot on their unwelcome travels. That the Germans were able to appreciate the jest of it is evident from roars of Teutonic laughter, but the French were in no humor to recall touches of Molière.

Mr. Green is, however, serious enough in his wanderings thru Belgium previous to the siege of Antwerp, and on a side trip to Germany, and back to the last Belgian fortress for its investment and capture. He throws an impartial light on the subject of German atrocities. When in Belgium he exerted effort to reach the sources of such stories, and states that, excepting a few detached cases which are likely to occur in any war, and should not be charged to wilful brutality on the part of the German military authorities, the reports were widely exaggerated. He reaffirms this in an appendix after reading the Bryce report, tho previously he intimates there may have been truth in sinister remarks let drop by Germans of British military prisoners ill treated by their captors and summarily executed. If these are ever proved, then indeed would lie a charge without defense or palliation.

In journalistic contrast we come to Arnold Bennett's *Over There*. It is evident that Mr. Bennett's intimacy with soldiers and knowledge of military affairs has been extremely limited. Moreover, he seems unable to draw near to or more than half comprehend either with the requisite sympathetic feeling —the broad vision—needful in a satisfactory witness of the greatest human drama. While he discusses interestingly the British military organization

J. B. LIPPINCOTT COMPANY PUBLISHERS PHILADELPHIA

A NEW LIFE

FOR YOU

In Six Short Months I Can Remake You. Men and Women, Your Destiny Is in Your Own Hands

WHAT IS YOUR EARNING POWER?

Your Position in the World
Your Facial Appearance and Ex-pression
Your Health, Strength and Vim
Your Power to Control and Lead Others

Your Physique and Symmetry
Your Power to Control Your Thoughts
Your Control of Your Body and Habits
Your Faculties of Reasoning

**THESE ARE ALL WITHIN YOUR POWER TO RULE.
AND SO FRAME YOUR FUTURE**

The Start

The Start

Have you considered why it is some men and women succeed while others fail? Have you considered why some businesses go up by leaps and bounds while others come down by leaps and bounds? Have you considered why some people are content with a menial position and poverty as a reward in old age? Have you considered why some people enjoy good health while others are never ill but never well? Have you considered why some people are handsome and full of expression while others are faded and expressionless? Now, there MUST be a cause for all this. THERE IS: The law of cause and effect teaches us this. **But what is this cause?** I will tell you. Success and Failure depend upon—(1) Your Mental Condition. (2) Your Physical Condition. (3) Your Facial and Outward Expression. (4) Your Knowledge as to how to apply what you know. The vividness, ingenuity and inventiveness of your thoughts depend upon the quickness of your brain to generate nerve power, while these in turn are dependent upon the richness of your blood, the sureness of your disposition, the sureness of your concentration, the strength of your will, and the reliability of your memory. It is the harmonious development of **all these that ensures Success.** The Nicholson-Wase Mail Course of Mental and Physical Efficiency trains the entire person. IT FITS YOU FOR A BETTER BUSINESS AND SOCIAL POSITION IN LIFE. —IN FACT, IT MAKES YOU LORD OF YOURSELF.

This Course Gives You { Virility of Speech — Power to Combat Difficulties as they arise — Shrewdness in Business — Strength of Purpose — Power of Observation — Retentive Memory — Power of Facial Expression — Graceful Carriage — Strong Nerves and a Balanced System.

**IT TRAINS YOU
FOR SELF-POSSESSION**

**IT MAKES YOU
STRONG AND INTELLIGENT**

Third Month

Third Month

You are not a Creature of Circumstances, you are just what you make yourself. Have you ever thought of what Mental Force really is? Have you estimated the amount of force that you can generate and keep going for twenty-four hours? Do you know this force is responsible for your health? Seeing this is so, do you suppose your EARNING POWER IS AT ITS BEST WHEN YOUR CREATIVE POWER IS AT ITS WORST? Of course you don't. To develop your Earning Power you must know how to generate Mental Force. Now I wish to make a proposal to you. Suppose you had you have little time on your hands, suppose you feel equally certain you ought to be earning more money; and suppose it were possible for someone to take you in hand and teach you how to succeed. And then, on top of this, suppose it were only going to take a few minutes daily out of your time, would you accept this offer? I am sure you would. Now, this is exactly what I am offering you today. I will send you free my explanatory Booklet, which will tell you all about it; also full detailed Folder Synopsis, giving you the outlines of each of the 52 lessons. Write to me at once. Write today. Fill in the Coupon. Get a pencil and DO IT NOW! Your dividend is waiting!

THE NICHOLSON-WASE MENTAL AND PHYSICAL EFFICIENCY TRAINING COURSE

Longacre Building, 1476 Broadway, New York

Sixth Month

Sixth Month

PERFECT WOMANHOOD

How about the women who succeed? What are the qualities that make success for them? Why, it is just that indefinable "something" that we call Personality, or Magnetism. That's it! Appearance and Character, a developed mind in an attractive-looking body. Perhaps the most important class to which we have to appeal is the housewife—she who rocks the cradle truly rules the world. Do you wish to develop that tact and sweetness of character that makes you firm but kind,

loved and loving, with the foresight to control the home and hearth, making it your little world of happiness? A healthy and genial appearance, intelligence, quickness of thought and an understanding, capable, and sympathetic intuition—all these go further than merely educational Training.

You may **appear** outwardly to be all right, and yet you know you are not at your best. I will show you the reason, and how to overcome it.

Cave Life or Civilization

Civilized man is distinguished from the cave man by his habit of co-operation.

The cave man lived for and by himself; independent of others, but always in danger from natural laws.

To the extent that we assist one another, dividing up the tasks, we increase our capacity for production, and attain the advantages of civilization.

We may sometimes disregard our dependence on others. But suppose the farmer, for example, undertook to live strictly by his own efforts. He might eke out an existence, but it would not be a civilized existence nor would it satisfy him.

He needs better food and clothes and shelter and implements than he could provide unassisted. He requires a market for his surplus products, and the means of transportation and exchange.

He should not forget who makes his clothes, his shoes, his tools, his vehicles and his tableware, or who mines his metals, or who provides his pepper and salt, his books and papers, or who furnishes the ready means of transportation and exchange whereby his myriad wants are supplied.

Neither should he forget that the more he assists others the more they can assist him.

Take the telephone specialists of the Bell System: the more efficient they are, the more effectively the farmer and every other human factor of civilization can provide for their own needs and comforts.

Or take our government, entrusted with the task of regulating, controlling and protecting a hundred million people. It is to the advantage of everyone that the government shall be so efficient in its special task that all of us may perform our duties under the most favorable conditions. Interdependence means civilized existence.

**AMERICAN TELEPHONE AND TELEGRAPH COMPANY
AND ASSOCIATED COMPANIES**

One Policy   One System   Universal Service

—particularly its transport service—it is unfortunate that his personal attitude toward soldiers suggests remoteness if not superiority. It is toward the end of Mr. Bennett's book that an incident occurs which reveals the author as not quite the type of man to mingle with and report upon the soldiers of his country. Mr. Bennett found himself alone temporarily in the ruined square of Ypres. Two Tommies strolled upon the scene. "I had a wish to accost them, but Englishmen do not do these things, even in Ypres. They glanced casually at me, I glanced casually at them, carefully pretending that the circumstances of my situation were entirely ordinary." Mr. Bennett is mistaken. All Englishmen are not of that narrow social creed. In another book, "A Surgeon in Khaki," is told the story of the old English clergyman —a dignitary of his church—drawn to the same scenes, and straight to the hearts of British and Belgian soldiers by simple democratic acts of kindness. He, too, of his own volition was "under fire," but it was to rescue, help and comfort the stricken soldiers thruout a long night in a place of unthinkable horror.

As the official British observer it is presumably Bernard Parés' part in *Day by Day With the Russian Army* to show what a wonderful uplift has taken place in Russia during the last ten years. Consequently everybody and everything in Russia are admirable. The book is a kind of grand full-dress parade, into which even the American correspondent steps as an "eminent" personage. It is such a novel role for him in the war that this time he surely must have been a bit rattled. But after discounting Mr. Parés' position one gathers that unquestionably a new era of freedom and fraternity has opened in Russian political and social life. Much of the ground traversed by Mr. Parés—Galicia and Poland—is now familiar, and he adds little new in this respect. But numerous opportunities to discuss the origin of the war with Austrian and German prisoners yield an interesting conflict of popular opinion in those countries, and as a companion to similar works the book is valuable for the political and military student.

Roadside Glimpses of the Great War, by Arthur Sweetser. Macmillan. $1.25. *Log of a Noncombatant,* by Horace Green. Houghton, Mifflin. $1.25. *Over There,* by Arnold Bennett. Doran. $1.25. *Day by Day with the Russian Army,* by Bernard Parés. Houghton, Mifflin. $2.50.

NINETY YEARS

Certainly one of the most interesting records of a literary life ever published is that of *Julia Ward Howe* written by her daughters. That life ran from 1819 to 1910. Its youth was spent in the dignified society formed by the families of New York's great merchants of the thirties and forties. Its later years belonged to the literary circle of Boston. But quite aside from her surroundings Mrs. Howe was a commanding figure—a woman of uncommon ability and power and of great charm. She sprang into fame with the writing of the "Battle Hymn of the Republic." That remarkable poem, born in a dream, seems the sudden fruition of tremendous conviction and enthusiasm, for, with this exception, delightful as is some of Mrs. Howe's verse, she is greater in personality than as a poet.

A student always, one finds her seizing time during a visit to Rome to study Hebrew with some learned Jew whom she had the fortune to meet. With six children to care for, and to care for with untiring devotion and sympathy, as the pictures of that busy, happy household show, she determined to master philosophy and took up Kant, Hegel, Fichte in turn. It was no small matter, in the sixties, for a woman reared in her conservative circle, the head of a complicated household, to start out in the public work to which she felt herself called. It was not long, however, before her philosophical and ethical lectures, brought her into the field of practical organization and for thirty years she was in the forefront of the movements for the widening of opportunities for women and the aid of the oppressed. One incident shows her characteristic spirit. Starting in a heavy storm for a lecture in Salem, she and the hackman rolled together down the steps. "Oh, Mrs. Howe," cried the terrified man finding her already on her feet when he picked himself up, "let me help you into the house." "Nonsense," was the reply, "I have just time to catch my train." She was then seventy-six.

Over these pages plays a never failing humor, while the always entertaining reminiscences include literally almost every one of note in the literary world of England, Italy and this country for three-quarters of a century.

Julia Ward Howe, 1819-1910, by Laura E. Richards and Maud Howe Elliott. Houghton, Mifflin. $4.

STORIES OF MEN AND THE SEA

There are many reasons for reading Joseph Conrad's latest book, a collection of four short stories. But aside from their beauty of style, their interest of plot, their skill in character portrayal and their keen psychological insight, most people will read *Within the Tides* just because they are good stories—stories of the sort that compel attention from start to finish.

All four are stories of adventure. If the author did not emphasize so clearly the mental, instead of the physical conflicts, they would be blood and thunder tales of mystery and murder. But their interest centers in personality more than in plot, and in each case the character of one man is formed by the incidents of the story.

Because of the Dollars is perhaps the most forceful—in plot it somewhat resembles Mr. Conrad's recent novel "Victory." The Partner is a tale of deep-dyed conspiracy on the high seas; villain is matched against villain and both meet inevitable defeat. In the Inn of the Two Witches is a remarkable description of a man's terror, "a deadly, chilly languor spreading over his limbs—as if his flesh had been wet plaster stiffening slowly about his ribs."

The longest of these stories, The Planter of Malata, has the least action.

SPEED UP!

Whether you are big or little, old or young, president or apprentice, you must SPEED up or GIVE up.

Competition is *desperate*, progress swift beyond precedent, the *best* opportunities *home-made*. SPEED UP!

HOW?

The prime essential of speed is KNOWLEDGE. Energy, initiative, loyalty *alone* are of little avail—you must KNOW. And when emergencies arise you must know INSTANTLY *how* to handle them.

But it takes *time* to acquire knowledge and time is *precious*. Libraries are not always available, college or technical courses often beyond reach. What is to be done?

You must have a good *encyclopædia* at hand. It contains the knowledge of the whole world condensed in tangible form for instant use. It is the *quickest* question-answerer known. It will help you to "speed up" better than any other one medium. It has been the *chief educator* of many a successful man and woman. It is *necessary* to *all* and *always* necessary.

But THE DAY is today—yesterday is *dead*, tomorrow will *never* come. You must have at hand the *knowledge of today*. Your encyclopædia must be *up-to-date*. It's as foolish for you to depend for success on a *short-range* encyclopædia as for a warship commander to expect to win with *short-range* guns. Stop and *think!* When, in the world's history, has such wonderful progress been made, when have such sweeping changes taken place, as in the *last few years?* Can you *afford* to have an encyclopædia that is *silent* on these vital facts? NO! The *latest* authoritative ency. clopædia is the *only* one that is *safe* for you to buy. Which *is* this one invaluable and indispensable reference work? The

New International Encyclopædia
SECOND EDITION

It is being published NOW. Therefore, it is *up-to-date.*

It is years later than any other reference work. Hence it is the *only* up-to-date encyclopedia.

Its preparation is in charge of two of the most brilliant and experienced cyclopedians of the day.

Its long list of contributors includes the foremost authorities on every subject of human interest.

Its publication is in the hands of Dodd, Mead & Co., Inc., publishers for over 75 years.

It is *complete*. It contains the world's knowledge from the dawn of history.

It contains 80,000 articles—*33 per cent.* more than any other encyclopedia.

Its articles are arranged *alphabetically*—a wonderful saving of time—you can thus turn *instantly* to the desired information.

It is an *American* production throughout—editorially and mechanically.

It has been pronounced the *"best and fullest"* for American readers and American interests.

Yet it gives intelligent, impartial, comprehensive consideration to all *foreign* topics.

It is the best and most *profusely illustrated* reference work in existence.

It contains *more* and *better* maps than any other encyclopedia.

The print is from special, new type and is a pleasure to read.

The work is written in clear, interesting language that you can *understand*.

It is never *prosy* nor *verbose*, its articles containing not a word too little nor too much.

Its 24 volumes are as *convenient* in size as a standard magazine and almost as *light* in weight.

The paper was made *especially* for this Second Edition and is *thin* but *opaque*, *light* but *tough* and *durable*.

This encyclopedia is *easy to buy*—a small first payment places the work in your *immediate possession*; small monthly remittances complete the transaction.

And *after* you buy this encyclopædia, USE It. Don't forget that an encyclopædia *in hand* is worthy twenty on the *shelf*.

But you can best judge all these points for yourself—we'll send you a volume of the New International Encyclopedia for examination absolutely without obligation.

Write your name and address on the information blank and mail it to

Dodd, Mead & Co., Inc., Publishers, 449 Fourth Avenue, New York

Send me full information regarding your SECOND EDITION OF THE NEW INTERNATIONAL ENCYCLOPÆDIA, with details of Special Price, etc.

Name .... Occupation ....

Business Address .... Residence ....

Town .... State .... Ind. 4-10-16

INDOORS AND OUT

Raffia Basketry as a Fine Art, by Gertrude and Mildred Ashley. A text book on basketmaking that carries the learner from the beginnings to the most beautiful and complicated weavings.

Deerfield, Mass.: Ashley. $2.

Spring herself is in the pictures and the names looking out from the pages of Harriet L. Keeler's fourth nature book, *Our Early Wild Flowers* is an uncommonly attractive as well as dependable pocket guide.

Scribner. $1.

Unless one must have specific directions for the care of plants, no more suggestive book on gardening can be found than *Some Old Time Gardens* by Alice Morse Earle, of which a new printing is just issued.

Macmillan. $2.

Indoor Merry-Making and Table Decoration, by Adler Mendel, contains suggestions for home entertainment on various festivals, including St. Valentine's Day, Hallowe'en, a Mother Goose Party, a Suffrage Party, and added chapters of riddles and games.

Boston: Wilde. $1.

The *A B C of Vegetable Growing*, by E. E. Rexford, is a handy little guide to the culture of most of our vegetables and small fruits, the making of the hotbed and storage for winter, with an introduction that invites the attention of women and children to garden work.

Harper. 50 cents.

The Belgian Cook-Book, by Mrs. Brian Luck, contains, besides some receipts like sausage and fried apples, so familiar that they must have been brought from the Continent to the New World by the settlers, many quite new and tempting, as Hoche Pot, which is "delicious and makes a dinner."

Dutton. $1.

It tells the love story of a man of extraordinary leadership, purposeful, imaginative, reticent, who refused to be satisfied with less than his ideal and so "set out calmly to swim beyond the confines of life, with a steady stroke, his eyes fixed on a star!"

Some of us have always appreciated Mr. Conrad's books; more of us perhaps have bowed to the dictum of authoritative opinion and read them because we have been told to like them; a few may even have refused to agree with the critics. But here are stories that must claim the approval of the "average reader" as well as of the literary connoisseur.

Within the Tides, by Joseph Conrad. Doubleday, Page. $1.35.

A SONG OF THE PIONEERS.

Of American poets of the younger generation several are more widely known and find their way more often into print than John G. Neihardt, but those who have been fortunate enough to make the acquaintance of his first two volumes of verse, "A Bundle of Myrrh" and "Man-Song," will probably agree that at his best Mr. Neihardt is exceedingly good. To our thinking his lyric work excels his narrative poetry, to which latter kind the present volume, *The Song of Hugh Glass*, belongs. Hugh Glass sings of the daring of those pioneers of the American fur trade whom Mr. Neihardt declares every way fit for the heroic roles of poetry of an epic cast. One of them he has made the hero of his own poem. In choosing to tell his story in heroic couplets, he has once more demonstrated that the "rocking-horse metre" has by no means outlived its usefulness, but, that, in the hands of one with a gift for musical and varied cadence—and Mr. Neihardt has this gift conspicuously—it serves as an admirable vehicle for narrative poetry. *The Song of Hugh Glass* carries the reader into the world of the pioneer and the Indian fighter; it records typical incidents and adventures of that world; it paints with a sure hand the wild beauty of the setting of the story; and it does all this in a truly poetic narrative.

The Song of Hugh Glass, by John G. Neihardt. Macmillan. $1.

PLAYS TO READ AND ACT

In a four volume memorial edition of *Plays*, by Clyde Fitch, have been collected his most popular works, such as Beau Brummel, The Girl with the Green Eyes, Barbara Frietchie and Captain Jinks. They were written for the stage, but many of them adjust themselves very easily to the library.

Boston: Little, Brown. $1.50 each.

The Unchastened Woman, still playing in New York, is counted as one of the most successful plays of the season. But it needs the skill of Emily Stevens' acting as well as that of Louis Kaufman Anspacher's writing to present its full interest. Much of its clever characterization and dramatic force are lost in print.

Stokes. $1.25.

St. John G. Ervine has won fame as the author of novels, short stories and essays. In his latest book, a play, *John Ferguson*, the literary quality is emphasized at the expense of the dramatic. There is plenty of action and the situations are well planned, but the author cannot resist long explanations, extremely interesting to the reader, which have no place on the stage.

Macmillan. $1.

The Arrow-Maker, by Mary Austin, is an elaborate drama of Indian customs and psychology, carefully authentic in its presentation of the aboriginal community and yet modern in its discussion of "the struggle of Femininity to recapture its right to serve and still to serve with whatever powers and possessions it finds itself endowed." The play is particularly readable.

Houghton, Mifflin. 75 cents.

A group of one-act plays—obviously intended to be acted, and yet well worth reading—is *Confessional and Other American Plays*, by Percival Wilde. The subjects are those of most interest today, the treatment is fresh and sincere, and the author shows a keen sense of dramatic values. One of these plays, According to Darwin, is announced for performance in New York shortly.

Holt. $1.20.

The saving grace of humor kept Anton Tchekoff from the depths of morbid psychology that characterizes so many of the foremost Russian writers, and enabled him to write plays which, in spite of their emphasis on ideas rather than actions, have found favor on both the English and the American stage. The *Second Series of Plays*, just translated by Julius West, includes The Bear, which was produced this season by the Washington Square Players in New York.

Scribner. $1.50.

Independent Opinions

The "Young Business Man" who confest a change of heart in regard to T. R. evidently voiced the feelings of more than himself.

I have read with much interest and sympathy the article in your March 27 issue, entitled "How I Swung Back to Teddy." The author of this article has spoken for a multitude of voters. I would like to communicate with the author directly. I believe the delegates to the Republican National Convention which were elected in Minnesota this month will ultimately support Mr. Roosevelt.   CHAS. S. MARDEN

Moorhead, Minnesota

Your young business man of this week's issue in the language of the street, has nothing on me. I was among those who howled with delight when Wilson won in 1912. Oh, for the "two-fisted strong man" who acts first and lets the other fellow compose the unanswerable argument. I have always been a Democrat, but I am willing and anxious to take off my coat and spend the hot weather campaigning for "Teddy."

DEMOCRATICUS

University Alabama

Being attracted by the article from a "Young Business Man," I submit a few condensed thoughts, from one who has not yet "Swung back to Teddy." I feel safe in saying that my admiration for Teddy was no less than that of this Prodigal Son, and while his argument is of a convincing tenor, I must still remain hostile. Differing from Young Business Man, I can forgive Teddy for giving us Taft, even as a failure, but cannot forgive him for his treatment of Taft—tho not because he was Taft. Finding little in the present administration to commend, I should not point to the return of our warships from Vera Cruz for especial demerit, even tho the expedition, fraught with fatalities, was suggestive of the traditional elements of the "False Alarm." Huerta was forced to flee, and be being the only "Government" at that particular time, we could find no one to grapple with, unless it be the Hot man on the street—so we came home. The ironic reference to Taft's availability rather disappoints the reader, on recalling the series of speeches which Teddy acknowledged greatly helped him in 1904, to say nothing of Mr. Taft's work in the Philippines and secretaryship of war, that made him a national, popular figure. Young Business Man's pessimistic view about the office of chief executive is exaggerated, but why not make a heroic effort now with Colonel Roosevelt in the ranks and not in the race, and land Hughes, or, perhaps a less known man. This country has elected so small man President and will not.

ISAAC BOWER

Atlantic City, New Jersey

I have lived in this city for over thirty-five years. I saw the C. & N. W. depot built, also the water tower, and if the picture on page 222 of the issue of February 14, 1916, showing the crowd who turned out to see President Wilson, is not Racine rather than Waukegan, I am very much mistaken.

WILLIAM A. LUNN

Racine, Wisconsin

You are not very much mistaken. We are. The photograph came to us labeled wrong, and not being as familiar with the Racine depot as our correspondent we published it as marked.

Here is a letter which we must admit is rather belated. And it is our fault, too. When received, last December, it was timely. But we could not publish it then because we got so many similar remonstrances against our criticism of Yuan Shih-kai for making himself emperor. Chinese students and American professors rushed to the defense of Yuan against our aspersions and argued that an emperor was just what was needed to make China tranquil and strong.

Barely three months have passed and China is not more tranquil and strong, but more turbulent and weak. So Yuan has, quite wisely, changed his mind again. It must be a great grief to President Goodnow to find his advice disregarded as soon as he left Peking for Johns Hopkins. We are assuming, of course, the truth of the official announcement of the Peking Government last year, that it was upon the recommendation of Dr. Goodnow in his capacity of constitutional councillor to the Chinese Republic that President Yuan became emperor.

But this letter from which we now propose to quote is belated, the restoration of the republic has, as our readers will agree, made views exprest in the following letter even more interesting and significant than if they had been published last December. We hope that President ex-Emperor Yuan will pardon the expression of the views which were so recently his own and will not treat Mr. Wang, whoever he may be, as rudely as he has some of his other political opponents.

I disagree, with you that by accepting the crown President Yuan Shih-kai has betrayed all parties which have trusted him. The Republic is given up out of sheer necessity and on account of the peculiar situation in which China finds herself today, for which Mr. Yuan is not responsible.

The restoration of peace and stable government in China have been largely due to the strong personality of the man now at the head of the state. Good citizens feared that the passing away of Mr. Yuan might also mean disappearance of the settled government and the return of chaos and disturbance and then foreign intervention. Recognizing the limitation of the present regime and the peculiar situation in our country, a large majority of the intelligent Chinese who wanted to strengthen their national administration started the monarchical movement. They well knew the reestablishment of monarchy was more an alteration in the name of things than in realities, and if Mr. Yuan, who is master of the situation, could permanently assert his power the better would be the chances of definite improvement in the prospects of China in future. When all these facts are taken into consideration, they are wise in making President Yuan emperor.

WANG SHIH-YOUNG

Washington, D. C.

Will you kindly call and get my Independent of February 21? It contains no "Pebbles!" Oh, yes, I saw an article about Will Shakespeare, and Armor Plate, and The Nose of the Camel; and something relative to S. Bernhardt, and ditto Mr. "A. Columbus," and ditto Arnold Bennett's something; and two or three pages about War in Africa; and a touch on Office Efficiency, by Ed. Earle Purinton; and lots of things about books and Insurance and dividends; and on advertisement intimating that men do not know how to shave; and bushels and bushels and bushels of other stuff, but nary a Pebble! I must have pebbles. They are first aid to digestion.   O. L. DOTY

Cleveland, Ohio

If You Would Be Successful Look to Your Food

By Arthur True Buswell, M.D.

AT first glance it seems a far cry from the eating question to business success, yet successful executives all over the country are proving that the foods we eat have a distinct relation to our mental efficiency and consequent material prosperity.

When simmered down, personal efficiency—the "power to do"—is intimately connected with our physical state. If we are full of vitality, abounding in surplus, energy, bubbling with the enthusiasm of perfect health, our minds are keener, more alert and we are able to accomplish things that would be impossible without the smashing mental power with which great physical vitality endows us.

That the foods we eat have the power to make or mar us physically and mentally seems to have been conclusively proven by Eugene Christian, the noted food specialist.

Twenty years ago Eugene Christian was at death's door. Suffering from acute stomach disorders, he consulted leading specialists without relief. Educated as a doctor, his brother physicians could offer him no hope. He finally went out on a farm supposedly to die, but in reality to try to save himself.

Here he commenced studying the chemistry of foods and their relation to the human organism and as a result of what he learned, without drugs or medicines, he literally *ate his way back to perfect health* in a remarkably short space of time.

Today, Eugene Christian is in his fifty-fifth year, yet he has more physical and mental energy—more enthusiasm than the average boy in his 'teens. He fairly radiates health and vitality.

According to Christian, the secret of eating for health and efficiency lies in knowing how to select and combine or balance our foods more than to any other thing. This does not mean that we have to eat foods we don't enjoy, or to which we are not accustomed—it merely means that at each meal we should eat the things that go to make up a constructive whole. Christian regards the human stomach as a furnace and food as the fuel, and he says that some of the combinations of food we eat every day are as dangerous as wet leaves, sawdust, mud and a little dynamite would be for a furnace. No wonder 90% of all sickness originates in the digestive tract!

On the other hand, other combinations of equally delicious foods furnish maximum physical and mental power with a minimum of waste.

In order that business men and women or, in fact, anyone interested in increasing their health and personal efficiency, may follow Christian's methods, the Corrective Eating Society has published a little course of lessons written by Eugene Christian out of his 20 years' experience in personally treating about 23,000 people.

Technical terms have been avoided and every point is explained so that there can be no possible misunderstanding. Reasons are given for every recommendation, based upon actual results secured in the author's many years of practice. The course also includes actual menus for breakfast, luncheon and dinner, curative as well as corrective, covering every condition of health and sickness for all ages from infancy to old age and for all occupations, climates and seasons.

If you would like to see the 24 Little Lessons in Corrective Eating written by Eugene Christian, simply write The Corrective Eating Society, 44 Hunter Ave., Maywood, N. J. It is not necessary to enclose any money with your request. Merely ask them to send the lessons for five days' free examination with the understanding that you will either return the lessons within that time or remit $3, the small fee asked.

There are, of course, some who will doubt the efficacy of Corrective Eating and its direct bearing on personal efficiency, but I am certain their objections will be quickly removed once they examine Christian's Course. Anyway, you are obligating yourself in no way by accepting the society's generous offer which enables you to investigate its wonderful work before you pay for the lessons. If the more than 300 pages contained in the course yield but one single suggestion that will bring greater physical and mental energy, or make you more clear headed at the office—you will get many times the cost of the course back in personal benefit—yet hundreds write the Society that they find vital helpfulness on every page.

I suggest that you clip out and mail the following form instead of writing a letter, as this is a copy of the official blank adopted by the Society and will be honored at once.

CORRECTIVE EATING SOCIETY, INC.,
44 Hunter Ave., Maywood, N. J.

You may send me prepaid a copy of Corrective Eating in 24 Lessons. I will either remail these to you in five days or send you $3.

NAME ....

ADDRESS ....

That is what happens to us whenever we leave out any one of our many departments. Somebody is sure to write in and say that the magazine isn't worth shucks without it. That is the reason we have so many departments. Some readers like one and some another, and none probably finds them all equally interesting. But we suspect that more of our readers than would be willing to confess it, have an avian appetite for pebbles. Youth is more frank in expressing its likes. In visiting a school where The Independent is used as a text-book the teacher told us how interested the pupils were in the periodical. Unable to conceal our pleasure at this and hoping to get more specific praise, we turned to the school and asked: "What part of The Independent interests you most? What page do you turn to first?" And the answer came in chorus from all over the room, "Pebbles!" This being the only part of the periodical that is not original, we should naturally have preferred some other selection, but nobody ought to ask a question of a school-room unless he is prepared to listen to the truth.

If we needed further proof that "Pebbles" are read—and carefully at that—we should find it in the following:

In regard to your article printed in the "Pebbles" column, I will say that you are entirely wrong as to the location and nickname of the L. K. & W., as it runs thru Clay Center, Kansas, and is owned by the Union Pacific Railway, and it is called the Little Kansas Wiggler.
DONALD P. BARNES
Clay Center, Kansas
P. S.—I am a twelve year old reader of your paper and sincerely hope you will take no offense.
P. P. S.—Let no man rob Kansas of her treasures.

No, we do not take offense and we do not intend to rob Kansas of her treasures, and we hope that Donald will continue to aid the advancement of editorial accuracy by viewing his periodicals "with a cricket's eye."

One of the little nations overrun by the war has been almost ignored by the outside world. Albania, which the European powers less than three years ago pledged themselves to protect, has been invaded by the troops of all the neighboring countries, Greece, Italy, Germany, Austria, Serbia, Montenegro and Bulgaria. The people had been previously reduced to destitution by the two Balkan wars and now that the invading soldiers have seized their provisions they are in danger of general starvation. The relief ship which was sent to their relief was shut out by the Italian Government, which is maintaining an illegal blockade of Albanian ports. To get these facts before the American public an association, The Friends of Albanian Independence, has been formed. From its publicity manager we receive the following:

If the territory of Albania is given to any other race than its legitimate owners, from their almost impregnable mountains, the warlike Albanians will maintain such a desperate resistance that it could only be ended by their extermination. The civilized world ought not to allow these descendants of the ancient Ilyrians and Pelasgians to perish, for in the days when they had a fair chance, they made contributions to the world's welfare which show that their natural abilities are high. Under the banner of Scanderbeg—a black double-headed eagle on a red background, they beat back the Turk in the fifteenth century, and their race has produced Pyrrhus, Alexander the Great, Saint Jerome, Constantine, five other Roman emperors, Pope Clement XI, Crispi, Marco Bozzaris and other heroes of the Greek war for independence.

Albania occupies such a strategic position that it is coveted by all of the neighboring races, but none of them would be willing to see it possest by any rival. Hence the surrender of Albania to any one race, or any possible division of it among several races, would cause such national and racial jealousies to arise in the Balkans, that another Balkan war would be inevitable which might again embroil all Europe.

Among those who have enrolled themselves as The Friends of Albanian Independence are Miss Jane Addams, of Hull House, Chicago; Prof. Emily G. Balch, of Wellesley; Mr. George W. Coleman, of the Ford Hall Foundation, Boston, Massachusetts; Prof. Samuel T. Dutton, of the World Peace Foundation, New York City; Doctor Charles Eastman (Ohioyesa), of Amherst, Massachusetts; Mr. Charles Wellington Furlong, the explorer, of Boston, Massachusetts; Mrs. Mary Antin Graham, of Scarsdale, New York; Mr. Hamilton Holt, of The Independent; Mrs. Haviland H. Lund, of the National Forward to the Land League, New York City; Dean Kelly Miller, of Howard University; Miss Mary White Ovington, of Brooklyn, New York; Prof. Herschel Parker, of New York City; Prof. Edward A. Steiner, of Grinnell, Iowa; Prof. Radoslay A. Tsanoff of Rice Institute, Houston, Texas; Mr Oswald Garrison Villard, of the New York Evening Post; Mr. George Fred Williams, Ambassador to Greece; and Doctor Evangeline Young of the Boston School of Eugenics.

Information may be obtained from Mr. John Adams, editor of the Albanian Era, of 1412 South Halstead street, Chicago, or from Kol Tronnara, secretary of the Pan-Albanian Federation "Vatra," at 67 Compton street, Boston, or from the undersigned.
JOSEPH F. GOULD
Elbowoods, North Dakota

Whenever we let slip in the word "first" or "new" in reference to municipal institutions we are sure to get letters claiming prior credit for some other locality, which is, of course, gratifying because it shows how close is the race between our progressive towns. When we referred to the circulation of player rolls by the St. Louis Public Library as "a new experiment" we learned that several libraries had the department in operation:

The Evanston Public Library has circulated pianola rolls since April 3, 1908. The Sadie Knowland Coe music room, which was opened April 2, 1908, now contains almost 2000 books, opera scores and sheet music; and about 575 pianola rolls. The room has contained since its opening a Weber pianola-piano, the pianola being open for use at certain periods of every day, the piano available at any time during library hours.

The collection is available for reference use at all times during library hours, and books, printed music and music rolls may be drawn upon borrower's cards. Only works of permanent musical value are included in this collection, which has proved of inestimable value in bringing a knowledge and love of the works of the masters of music to scores of people whose opportunities for musical culture have been very limited.
MARY B. LINDSAY.
Evanston, Illinois

MR. PURINTON'S EFFICIENCY QUESTION BOX

231. Mr. S. C., Missouri. "(a) On pages 343-347 of your book *Efficient Living* are answers to a question on woman's economic independence. Please advise me in what number of The Independent these pages were originally published, as I wish a copy for a friend who needs the broad view they contain. (b) My grade is only 60 per cent on your Personal Efficiency Test. Can you outline a course of reading and self-discipline to put me in the nineties' grade?"

(a) This material never appeared in The Independent like much of the contents of the book; it was taken from my personal answers to personal questions.

(b) I will note a few of your weak points on the chart. For knowledge of scientific management, of your own greatest power (character analysis), and of habitual optimism, see references in back files of the Question Box. For inventory of your mental and moral traits see "Efficiency Mind Builder," on page 257 of the book "Efficient Living." For suggestions on slow eating, see Horace Fletcher's various books. For health information, get sample copies of health magazines mentioned previously in Question Box, and answer the best advertisements.

232. Mr. C. E. F., Arizona. "Please tell me where I can obtain information as follows: (a) Regarding methods of industrial work in schools having the so-called 'self-help' departments; (b) regarding the shop-school plan to which you recently referred as being tried out in New York; (c) regarding the proposed Rural Credits legislation."

(a) Self-help features in college and universities are generally conducted by the Y. M. C. A. or Y. W. C. A. of each institution, not connected organically with the school. For general information apply to Intercollegiate Branch, Y. M. C. A., 554 West 114th street, or to National Board, Y. W. C. A., 600 Lexington avenue; both New York City.

(b) Write to the United States Commissioner of Education, Washington, D. C.; also the New York City Board of Education, Park avenue and Fifty-ninth street, New York; also Superintendent Wirt, of the City Schools of Gary, Indiana, the latter for details of the "Gary Plan."

(c) Your local bank officials probably could inform you. If not, write American Bankers' Association, 5 Nassau street, New York City. Experts consider Dr. John Lee Coulter, of the West Virginia University, an authority on rural credits; address Morgantown, West Virginia.

233. Rev. F. E. D., Vermont. "Will you put me in the way of finding literature on the subject of the improvements that have been made, especially in *morals*, in this country, since the days of the fathers? I want to show the advance on all lines, in a lecture on the subject."

Apply to Church Literature Press, No. 2 Bible House; American Social Hygiene Association, 105 West Fortieth street; Society for Ethical Culture, 2 West Sixty-fourth street; American Institute of Social Service. Bible House; G. P. Putnam's Sons. 2 West Forty-fifth street; Fleming H. Revell Company, 158 Fifth avenue; all of New York City.

234. Miss B. W., Georgia. "I look after out-of-town collections for a manufacturer, and would like to find some new ways to say *Please remit*. We want short, courteous letters. Can you suggest any books to help along this line?"

We don't believe much in stereotyped business letters. They are usually about as effective as marriage proposals made out of a book. You can, however, learn the correct *principles* from an authority, and then put your own personality into your business forms. A few possible aids: "How to

Write a Business Letter," "Golden Rule Collection Letters," "How to Collect Accounts," "Pointers on the Collection Business," "Debt Reminders," "Business Correspondence." These books can be secured from the Efficiency Press Syndicate, 233 Broadway, New York City.

---

235. Mr. E. S. C., Vermont. "Where can I obtain literature or any information on The Fourth Dimension?"

Ask the Professor of Mathematics of your State University; also the Searchlight Information Library Company, 450 Fourth avenue, New York City. Manning's *Fourth Dimension Simply Explained*, published by Munn & Co., 233 Broadway, New York, is helpful.

---

236. Mr. G. L. W., Pennsylvania. "As a constant brain-worker, I am often troubled with brain fag, headaches, etc. I have an idea that the brain is undernourished, but don't know what to eat for the condition of anemia. Is fish a good brain food? I have heard it contains phosphorus."

It is by no means certain that your brain is undernourished. Your head troubles may come from any one of a number of other causes. Are you sure that your eyes are all right? Is your digestion in good order? Do you take enough exercise? Are your habits of living, to say nothing of your habits of work, rational and sensible? Do you drink plenty of water? There is no such thing as a brain food any more than there is an ear food or a hand food. The phosphorescent glow on a fish pertains to the scales. Must we then eat the fish scales, in order to become brainy? If you lead as sensible and well-regulated a life as you know how, not burning the candle at both ends, or indulging yourself in any direction, and the brain fag and headaches continue, you probably ought to consult a doctor. Are you sure that it is the work that you do which tires your brain, and not the fact that you come to your work with your brain already handicapped by some of the things you have done outside of your work?

---

237. Miss E. C. W., New York City. "Please advise me as to the best way to sell some oil paintings done by a Belgian prisoner of war. The paintings bear the name of the camp and the date."

Apply to Fifth Avenue Auction Rooms, 341 Fourth avenue; also to Merwin Sales Company, 16 East Fortieth street; also to Charles J. Darling and Company, 623 Sixth avenue; also to John J. Morris, 623 Sixth avenue; all of New York. If none of these firms can sell your paintings to your satisfaction, look up "Art Goods" dealers and "Picture Importers" in the business directory called the *Red Book* of New York, on view at almost any large hotel or drug store—publisher, Reuben H. Donnelly, 227 Fulton street.

---

238. Mr. J. C. C., New York. "After reading your articles on efficiency, I am very much interested in the subject. I am taking a special course in the arts department of a leading university, but feel that I am not working as effectively as I should. My schedule includes English History, Nineteenth Century Poetry, Astronomy, Debating, Shakespeare, and International Law. Could this be improved? Have you written any books that would help me secure efficient training for life?"

Your study curriculum is open for improvement. Why take Shakespeare and Nineteenth Century Poetry simultaneously? Does your life work prove the need for Debating and International Law? It may —but ask yourself how and why. A modicum of English History may be desirable. Astronomy is of doubtful value.

Like most "classical" students, you are neglecting the practical side of education. We would suggest that you quietly fade away from the Arts department a few hours each week, and learn how to handle your bodily machine.

Yes, you would probably find some help in my books; particularly *Efficient Living*, and Five Efficiency Booklets, obtainable from Efficiency Press Syndicate, Woolworth Building, New York.

PEBBLES

The most important spring opening thus far announced is the Panama Canal.—*New York Tribune.*

This is also the season when a town man would like to be a farmer if he didn't have to farm a great deal.—*Atchison (Kansas) Globe.*

Free soup kitchens would unite all Mexican factions. This is philosophy, not a superficial suggestion.—*Brooklyn Daily Eagle.*

Colonel Roosevelt insists that we "must make disorderly nations behave." The dickens of it is, Colonel, that there's such an infernal lot of 'em just at present.—*New York Sun.*

Australian Preacher: "Brethren and sistern, these is stirring times we do be livin' in. But we should remember the words of the Good Old Book, where it do say 'England expects that every man this day will do es duty.'"—*Sydney Bulletin.*

RIMES OF THE TIMES
He thinks he sees upon a hill a
Disheveled guy that looks like Villa,
But even as the guy he scans, a
Sharpshooter cries,　　　"Why, that's Carranza!"
　　　　　　　　　Cleveland Leader.

"Say, Alabama is a dry state, isn't it?".
"Sure."
"But when I was there I saw several negroes who were intoxicated."
"Well, of course, they can't stop the sale of that awful onion gin entirely."—*Cornell Widow.*

Officer to Tommy, who has been using the whip freely:—
"Don't beat him; talk to him, man—talk to him."
Tommy to horse, by way of opening the conversation:—
"I coom from Manchester."—*Punch.*

"How quickly some of those immigrants assimilate our ideas and methods!"
"As for instance?"
"Well, I asked my Italian barber if he was going home to fight and he said he wasn't; that he had paired with an Austrian in the next block."—*Boston Transcript.*

I remember, I remember
　When Funston wasn't It.
When he among the Generals
　Was not allowed to sit.
He was a most ambitious chap—
　At nothing would he balk,
But then, as now, I well recall,
　He was too prone to talk.
　　　　　—*Cleveland Leader.*

In thinking of neutrals, I can't help thinking of two boys who stood the other day and watched an enormous safe being raised up to the twenty-sixth story of a skyscraper.
The boys watched the safe rise slowly, dangling at the end of its wire rope, and when it reached the twentieth story the older lad turned away in disgust.
"Come on, Joe," he said. "We might as well move on. They ain't a-goin' to let her drop."—*Indianapolis News.*

Mr. Binks had invested $500 in Colossal Steel stock. The War-Bride fever was upon him. One hour after making his investment he dropped into an office to see how many points his stock had gained. He grabbed the tape that flowed from the ticker and hunted for Colossal Steel. This is what he found:

"OWSMULXZ. SWWW. MY.54‡‡‡‡‡‡
LMWNYCCK. -11S4‡‡‡‡‡‡ .....UKWNA-
AEVYYYYNAAEWN'NNNCMY 1‡‡‡ CC
WHULEDLOWWWWWPUUU—‡ P 4‡‡
‡‡ Y 604‡‡—CJY.—WJYNAAUVYYY-
YIIULZZHUUUU 76 ‡‡‡‡—54‡‡‡"

One hour later strong men led Mr. Binks away and locked him up in a padded cell.—*Cincinnati Enquirer.*

The Market Place

THE RAILROADS

Recent reports show no reaction in the favorable movement of railroad gross revenue and net earnings. Owing to the improved conditions and increase of profits, large orders for equipment have been given to the steel mills. Since March 1, orders for 900,000 tons of rails have been placed, but these, as a rule, are for delivery next year. The companies have also ordered, since the first day of the year, 1200 locomotives, and this number, in three months, may be compared with 2000 in the entire year 1915.

One result of the hearings before the Interstate Commerce Commission concerning the continuing severe congestion of freight at and near Eastern ports has been the forming of an association by fifteen prominent companies whose roads lead to New York, Boston, Philadelphia and Baltimore, with an embargo committee whose power is represented by an executive committee composed of six presidents and Commissioner Clark, of the Interstate Commerce Commission. With the coöperation of shippers and the support of Federal authority, these officers hope to make plans for relief. But the problems presented by freight congestion are regarded as of much less importance than the one which more than 400,000 employees ask the companies to consider. Their demands, which, the companies say, could be granted only at a cost of $100,000,000 a year, have been formally submitted, and before April 28 the roads must reply.

FOREIGN LOANS

Subscriptions for the new loan of $75,000,000 to the Canadian Government, offered to the public here by J. P. Morgan & Co., the National City Bank, the Guaranty Trust Company, Brown Brothers & Co., Harris, Forbes & Co., and the Bank of Montreal, were four or five times the amount named, and the bonds have been selling at a premium in the New York market. They are in three classes—five years, ten years, and fifteen years, the interest rate being five per cent. Those having a term of fifteen years were the most attractive to investors. They were offered at 94.94, and have been sold, since the original offering, at 97%. Sales of the ten-year bonds, originally offered at 97.13 by the banking syndicate, have been made at 97%. The bonds are free from all present or future taxes imposed by the Canadian Government, in-

REPORT OF THE CONDITION OF THE

New York Life Insurance & Trust Company

at the close of business on the 17th day of March, 1916:

RESOURCES

Stock and bond investments, viz.:	
Public securities (book value, $3,506,638), market value..	$3,416,981.02
Private securities (book value, $14,051,389.97), market value	14,282,585.56
Real estate owned........	1,954,695.94
Mortgages owned	4,742,410.55
Loans and discounts secured by other collateral	2,625,618.05
Loans, discounts, and bills purchased not secured by collateral	12,685,645.97
Overdrafts, secured	63,893.53
Due from approved remote depositaries, less amount of offsets	1,097,723.79
Specie	3,036,590.00
United States legal tender notes and notes of national banks..	100,410.00
Other assets, viz.:	
Accrued interest entered on books at close of business on above date	504,929.43
Accrued interest not entered on books at close of business on above date	
Suspense account	74,538.68
	186,610.88
Total	$45,690,634.40

LIABILITIES

Capital stock	$1,000,000.00
Surplus on market values:	
Surplus fund	3,075,882.07
Undivided profits	181,964.79
Surplus on book values	3,834,343.40
Deposits:	
Preferred, as follows:	
Due New York State savings banks	438,923.29
Other deposits due as executor, administrator, guardian, receiver, trustee, committee, or depositary..	2,506,653.22
Not preferred, as follows:	
Deposits subject to check (on 10 days' notice)	26,668,780.98
Demand certificates of deposit	1,682,000.00
Other certificates of deposit (on 10 days' notice)	4,324,109.33
Due trust companies, banks, and bankers	1,363,857.86
Other liabilities, viz.:	
General account interest....	332,455.11
Annuities	2,392,768.67
Life insurance	360,822.44
Reserves for taxes, expenses, etc.	41,100.00
Accrued interest entered on books at close of business on above date	339,468.19
Accrued interest not entered on books at close of business on above date....	58,035.13
Contingent account	2,374.71
Estimated unearned discounts	81,438.69
Total	$45,690,634.40

AN INCOME FOR LIFE

---

come tax included. It is understood that at least a part of the money will be used in advances to the British Government for the payment of obligations for munitions and other war supplies. As a considerable portion of the supplies for which orders are placed in Canada is obtained on this side of the boundary, by means of subcontracts, part of the proceeds of the loan will be expended in the United States.

Carlos Castro, a member of the City Council of San José, the capital of Costa Rica, has come to New York to negotiate a loan of $2,000,000 for that city. The money is needed for street paving, enlargement of the water supply plant, garbage disposal and other municipal improvements. In the past Costa Rica has borrowed in London or Paris. Now she turns to New York. If the money is procured here, the materials required for the projected improvements will be bought in the United States.

The new loan to Argentina is $15,-000,000, and the money was provided by the Guaranty Trust Company, which made a public offering of the securities. Since the beginning of the war, Argentina has borrowed $79,500,-000 here, including $25,000,000 last May, represented by five-year notes. Her loans were formerly obtained in London. It is reported that there have been preliminary negotiations for a new loan of $200,000,000 to France, the term to be three years, and the rate five per cent. Funds have been deposited here for the redemption of the $30,000,000 of French bonds which fall due on April 1. Nothing is heard about the proposed loan of $75,000,000 or $100,-000,000 to Russia. Our loans to foreign borrowers since the beginning of the war amount to about $1,100,000,000. This total includes $240,000,000 to the Canadian Government and to provinces and municipalities in Canada.

WAR SUPPLY ORDERS

The largest of the war orders recently reported is one for $70,000,000 worth of submarines, which the Submarine Boat Corporation has undertaken to build for the Russian Government. But the work is to be done in Russian shipyards, under the supervision of officers of the company. There are to be 200 submarines forty-five feet long which can be carried on the decks of battleships. The cost of each will be about $200,000. In addition the contract calls for fifty larger boats at $600,000. The company will receive 7½ per cent of the entire cost, or $5,-250,000. It has recently taken an order for eight boats, at $650,000 each, from another foreign government, and is said to have on its books contracts amounting to $150,000,000.

Large sales of sugar have been made to the belligerents at rising prices. Italy has bought 20,000 tons. Exports of refined sugar to Great Britain in January and February were 52,000 tons, altho not a pound was shipped to that country in the corresponding months of 1915. Purchases of $15,000,000 worth of leather have been made by the British

---

DIVIDENDS

AMERICAN TELEPHONE AND TELEGRAPH COMPANY

A dividend of Two Dollars per share will be paid on Saturday, April 15, 1916, to stockholders of record at the close of business on Friday, March 31, 1916.

G. D. MILNE, Treasurer.

BOTH SIDES

Send 25 cents for pamphlet containing fourteen briefs for debate on important questions.

THE INDEPENDENT, 119 W. 40th St., N.Y.

Moving This Spring?

Do not change your place of residence without telling us your new
address, so that you will continue to
enjoy The Independent without interruption. Be sure to give us your
old address too, and let us know if
possible about three weeks ahead.

THE INDEPENDENT

and French governments, as material
for 10,000,000 pairs of shoes. Companies in Portland, Oregon, have been
asked to submit bids for 8,000,000 feet
of lumber, in forms suitable for trench
posts and pickets. The French Government has bought 25,000,000 pounds of
copper at a price between 27 and 27½
cents a pound. This is the largest order
of the kind since the notable one of the
British Government, a few months ago,
for 135,000,000 pounds. Orders for steel
to be used in making shells are frequently reported, and one from the
British Government for 200,000 high
explosive shells was made known last
week.

INTERNATIONAL TRADE

Since the beginning of the year there
has been a noticeable increase of our
imports, while, as is well known, our
exports have continued to be very
large. Imports in January were $184,-
000,000, against $122,000,000 in Jan-
uary, one year earlier. But the gain
for the seven months that ended with
January was only $16,000,000. Official
figures as to the exports in February
are not yet available, but from the port
of New York alone they were $216,-
500,000, against $182,500,000 in Jan-
uary. The value of shipments of firearms and explosives rose from $31,-
451,000 in the year's first month to
nearly $48,000,000 in the second. Ex-
ports of war supplies have been growing. In the last week of March eighteen
ships loaded with them sailed from
New York. There has been a great increase of the exports of gunpowder. In
the year 1914 the value of the shipments was only $289,000, but in 1915
it was $66,346,000, the average price
per pound advancing from 33 cents in
the first of these years to 79 cents in
the second. At the present time the
quantities going out are very large. Deliveries on a great scale began in November, and 44,000,000 pounds were exported in that month and December,
the price rising to 87 cents. Powder companies have declared great dividends.

In the harbor of Kola, on the north
coast of Russia, there are about 100
loaded ships, waiting, with ships at several Norwegian ports, for the opening
of the port of Archangel, which may be
icebound until June. The new railroad
from Kola to Petrograd will not be completed this year, it is said. Munitions
recently received in Russia have
crossed the Pacific and been carried on
the Siberian railroad. More than forty
ships from New York are now on their
way to Vladivostok. There are said
to be about 300 ships, in all, now bound
for Russia and loaded with munitions,
their cargoes amounting to nearly
1,000,000 tons. As the freight charges
are high, the cost of transportation to
the war front is estimated at more than
$75,000,000.

The following dividends are announced:
United Fruit Company, quarterly, 2 per cent,
payable April 15.
Otis Elevator Company, preferred, quarterly,
$1.50 per share; common, quarterly, $1.25; payable April 15.
American Telephone and Telegraph Company,
$2 per share, payable April 15.
Standard Milling Company, preferred, 2½ per
cent, payable April 15.

"Pretty soft for him"

OF course, it's pretty soft for the man who has made good. But, if you look behind for the real cause of his success, you'll find that luck played *no* part whatever—TRAINING did it. Yes, TRAINING secured through spare-time study. TRAINING is the *big* difference between you and the man who holds down the sort of job you'd like to have. Don't worry because others get ahead. Train yourself with the help of the International Correspondence Schools for the job you have in mind and you can do as well or even better.

Tens of thousands of men, at one time no better off than you, *now* hold good jobs as the direct result of I. C. S. training. These men simply wouldn't stay down. You're a man capable of doing bigger things. Make up your mind to do them. But get started. Every minute gained brings your success so much nearer. Mark and mail this coupon now.

I. C. S., Box 4504, Scranton, Pa.

--- TEAR OUT HERE ---

Insurance

Conducted by

W. E. UNDERWOOD

SOUTH CAROLINA LAW

For some years past the attitude of the Insurance Commissioner of South Carolina toward associated effort by fire insurance companies has been unfriendly. He doubtless regards the use of uniform rates and one code of practise by a number of companies as the exercise of monopolistic powers. Nearly all the fire insurance companies operating in South Carolina are members of the Southeastern Underwriters' Association, an organization which employs an efficient staff of expert inspectors to make periodical examinations of all the physical hazards in several of the Southern states on the Atlantic seaboard. From their reports, under properly formulated schedules, based on the combined experience of the companies in that territory, rates are made.

After years of agitation in political circles there the South Carolina Legislature has enacted a law proscribing the activities of the Southeastern Underwriters' Association and prohibiting the companies from making any agreement as to rates and practises. One clause of the law requires that some office or agent of each company who resides in the state, shall file an affidavit with the Insurance Department once a year stating that his company has not transgressed the law during the preceding twelve months. Every violation of the law is doubly penalized with a fine of from $100 to $1000 and imprisonment in the state prison for one year, but the imprisonment may be, in the direction of the court, reduced to from one month to one year in a jail.

Another provision of the law empowers the Insurance Commissioner to review any rate fixed by a company and to determine whether it is unjust or discriminatory. If he finds against the rate fixed he may order it changed. The relations of agents to each other are in the same manner rigorously regulated.

This policy of repression and proscription, new in South Carolina, has been tried out and been proven a failure in a few other states. Fire insurance companies, for the sake of the agency organizations built up at great expense thru years of effort, have submitted to injurious legislation in various Western and Southern states, clinging to the hope that time would remedy the conditions. But there is a point beyond which they dare not go in that direction. This was shown in their withdrawal from Missouri about two years ago.

As one who has worked in and believes he understands the fundamental principles under which the business of fire insurance operates, I say to the readers of The Independent that not only is it essential to the security of policyholders that rates be adequate, including not only ability to yield a profit as well as to pay losses, but that it is impossible properly to calculate those rates except upon the extensive data alone possest by the companies. It is idle to talk about discriminatory rates; there are not two physical hazards precisely alike. A thousand factors are involved, and the same number and kind will not be present in any two risks.

Insurance is a service, not a product. Its cost to the user is mainly determined by the losses incurred. In fact, insurance is nothing more than the medium thru which losses are distributed among the persons insured. With these truths in mind, does it not seem rather absurd to endow a state official who possesses no practical knowledge, no experience, no data, with the power to change rates calculated by insurance experts from records accumulated during many years?

Unless I am very much mistaken, the fire insurance companies cannot safely transact business in South Carolina under its new law and will probably withdraw from that state. That is one step toward self-preservation still remaining to them.

F. J. S., Ithaca, N. Y.—Under the circumstances, I am of the opinion that $4000 or $5000 of life insurance is too much for a young man who is several hundred dollars in debt and just starting in life. Take $2000 ordinary life in some good dividend-paying old line company.

J. H. T., La Grande, Ore.—Without the aid of a constantly accumulating reserve no life insurance plan is practicable. It must be a full reserve, mathematically ascertained, based on a standard mortality table and a minimum rate of interest. Otherwise the rate must gradually rise to a prohibitive point.

J. E. W., Laramie, Wyo.—By applying to the Insurance Department of any state you can procure a list of all the insurance companies doing business in that state. If you wish a list of all the companies in the United States you will either have to write to the insurance departments of all the states or subscribe for a volume of reports furnished by one of the publishing houses engaged in that work. The latter, however, are expensive, for they contain a vast quantity of other information.

J. G. H., Lakeport, Calif.—A report before me touching on the so-called reserve fund of the Woodmen of the World, Pacific Jurisdiction, states that "the surplus . . . is shown only because the order does not charge among the liabilities a reserve to provide for the increasing cost of insurance due to the increasing age of the member and the corresponding increase in the mortality rate. The reserve (such as used by life companies), if charged, would much more than offset this 'surplus' and would leave a large deficiency." That means that rates must necessarily go up. The Penn Mutual is an excellent company. Your age, circumstances and income considered, I would advise you to choose from among the policies you name the twenty-year endowment. As a policyholders' company the Penn Mutual ranks higher than the Missouri State Life.

A Number of Things
by
Edwin E. Slosson

THERE'S nothing I admire more than courage and nothing I lament more than my lack of it in the great emergencies of life. Not long ago I attended—in honor of somebody who needed honoring or in furtherance of some cause which needed furthering—one of those feasts of Tantalus to which New Yorkers are addicted. The guests are seated at tables by tens and have placed before them at intervals dishes of the choicest food, which they are permitted to look at and taste, but before they can satisfy the appetite the plates are snatched away by a swarm of harpies in swallowtails. Now a good dinner demands and deserves both time and attention, but it can get neither at these big banquets because there is always some one at the speakers' table or by your side who wants to talk.

On this occasion I saw before me a salad of a sort in which I most delight, one of those wonderful confections to which all nature contributes; fruit, fish, flesh and fowl; nuts plucked from the tallest trees, crustacean drawn from the ocean bed; all flavors and savors combined and commingled in artistic confusion; harmonies and dissonances, strong chords and subtle overtones, a veritable Strauss symphony of the palate, something that would be treasured in the memory long after the last lingering taste had left the mouth. Over this mountain of pleasure there flowed a creamy lava, the making of which had required joint genius of the whole coalition cabinet of the kitchen, "the spendthrift for oil, the miser for vinegar, the councillor for salt and the madman to stir it up."

It seemed a shame to spoil such a masterpiece of culinary art, but my appetite overcame my awe and I timidly touched the edge of it with my fork, even as the bather steps first into the ripples on the beach in order to anticipate and postpone the pleasure of the plunge. The taste confirmed all of the expectations which the sight had aroused. But just at this critical moment the man on the right asked me a question on a subject that I knew about or thought I did, which amounts to the same thing. I replied with eagerness and eloquence, my eyes enlivened and my voice made musical by the thought of the plateful of bliss before me. This is, of course, a hypothetic objectivization of a subjective impression. Not having a mirror and a phonograph

at hand I was unable to prove that my manner corresponded with my idea of it. But it does not matter about that now.

I answered my right hand neighbor as briefly as the importance of the subject and the extent of my own knowledge of it would permit, then turned to the Salad of the Four Seasons, but to my dismay it was being withdrawn by a stealthy hand reached over my shoulder. I made no outcry. I stifled my emotion and submitted meekly to the wrong. I knew no other way. Lost property may sometimes be recovered, even lost health or a lost wife. But for a missed meal there is no possible recompense in this world and I fear not in the next, for even omnipotence seems to be subject to the limitations of chronology.

I turned to my neighbor on the left. He had eaten half his salad, but I saw the hand of destiny had already seized the edge of the plate. But while I watched with unsympathetic eyes, for misery loves company, I saw the hand of destiny slip. The plate stuck fast to the table as the fastened with the glue which the man on the street corner uses when he hangs cannon balls to his broken crockery. My friend held the inner edge of the plate firmly gripped between the thumb and the knuckle of the forefinger of his left hand and he looked up with a malicious grin at the Great Stone Face as he chuckled:

"You didn't get it that time, did you?"

As the waiter stalked off with other plates echeloned on his arm, I could have hung my hat on his nose if it had not been taken from me by the hallway robber.

I knew then that I had the honor of sitting beside the bravest man in the world. I looked upon him with admiration and envy as he finished the salad to the last delectable drop. He did not offer to share it with me, altho he must have seen the hunger in my eyes. But I did not complain. I knew I did not deserve it. None but the brave deserve the fare.

———

Humor, say the Freudians, is the disguised expression of a supprest wish. Perhaps there's something in this theory. At any rate, humor often serves as a safety-valve for emotions which otherwise might make trouble. Whenever two nations or two persons stop making fun of each other look out for blows.

Our little tiff with Germany over the partition of the Pacific some twenty years ago worked itself off in comic verse, which is much better than slinging shrapnel. Admiral Coghlan started it going on this side-track by his:

HOCH DER KAISER!

Der Kaiser of die Fatherland
And God on high all dings command.
Ve two—ach, don't you understand,
Myself—und Gott.

Vile some men sing der power divine,
Mein soldiers sing: "Der Wacht am Rhein."
Und drink der health in Rhenisch wine
Of me—und Gott.

The Germans replied with a volley of verses quite as bad:

HOCH DER PRASIDENT!

Der Teddy 'Roosevelt bin ich ja,
Rauhreiter-Präsident,
In Deutschland und Amerika
Ein jedes Kind mich kennt.

Verletzet nie Monroes Doktrin
Sonst mach' ich gleich mobil,
Ich selbst ich stürme nach Berlin,
Held Dewey dampft nach Kiel.

And that was all there was to it; no high explosives, no torpedoes, no poison gases, merely hot air.

———

Time was when it was considered as disreputable to employ a tutor as to use a pony. Coaching was carried on in the woods or behind blanketed windows at dead of night. Later when it was realized that professors could not be expected to waste their time in teaching or students in studying, tutoring became recognized as an honorable and indispensable occupation, but those who practised it were slow to adopt up-to-date methods of pushing their business. They confined their efforts to the private circulation of neat copperplate visiting cards in the lower left corner of which one could discern with aid of a monocle the word MATHEMATICS or GREEK in the same small caps as are used by a fashionable hostess for MUSIC or DANCING or SKATING on her invitations.

But now the tutor has come to realize his own importance and learned how to impress it upon the public. In the Columbia daily I find an ad striking enough to stop an automobile, and from a Harvard man, too:

STOP! LOOK! LISTEN!
Stop flunking Mathematics. Look me up. Listen to my advice. I have taught Differential and Integral Calculus, Analytic Geometry, College Algebra and Trigonometry for several years, and have also wide experience as a tutor. Who am I? Ask your professor of Mathematics. F. S. Nowlan, A. M. (Harvard). Telephone Morn. 8920.

The distrest student has also adopted modern publicity methods for sending out his S. O. S. calls:

LOGIC TUTOR WANTED—A PATIENT, slow-speaking, flegmatic philosopher, who knows Jevons backwards, and who can sympathetically inject his definite practical knowledge into an eager mind, too busy to puzzle out the subject alone. Professors not satisfactory. Student will meet Tutor at University Tuesdays and Fridays between 5:30-7 p. m. State in own handwriting, age, sex, weight and terms. D., Spectator Office.

———

Some people have not taken as active a part in the discussion of the Balkan situation as they would like because they were uncertain as to the proper pronunciation of that city which in Bible times used to be called Thessalonica. But they should not worry. They can hardly miss it. The "Salonika correspondent" of The Near East gives the local usage:

If you are a Greek you will call it "Thessaloni'ki," if a Turk "Sela'nik," if a Frenchman "Saloni'que," if an American "Saloni'ki," but if you are an Englishman —or a Scotchman or Irishman, for the matter of that—you will call it "Salon'ika," or, as some people write it, "Salon'ica."

The Independent

FOR SIXTY-SEVEN YEARS THE
FORWARD-LOOKING WEEKLY OF AMERICA

THE   CHAUTAUQUAN
Merged with The Independent June 1, 1914

APRIL   17,   1916

OWNED   AND   PUBLISHED   BY
THE INDEPENDENT CORPORATION, AT
119 WEST FORTIETH STREET, NEW YORK
WILLIAM B. HOWLAND, PRESIDENT
FREDERIC E. DICKINSON, TREASURER

WILLIAM   HAYES   WARD
HONORARY EDITOR

EDITOR: HAMILTON HOLT
ASSOCIATE EDITOR: HAROLD J. HOWLAND
LITERARY EDITOR: EDWIN E. SLOSSON

PUBLISHER: KARL V. S. HOWLAND

ONE YEAR, THREE DOLLARS

SINGLE COPIES, TEN CENTS

Postage to foreign countries in Universal Postal
Union, $1.75 a year extra; to Canada, $1 extra.
Instructions for renewal, discontinuance or
change of address should be sent two weeks
before the date they are to go into effect. Both
the old and the new address must be given.

We welcome contributions, but writers who
wish their articles returned, if not accepted,
should send a stamped and address envelope. No responsibility is assumed by The
Independent for the loss or non-return of
manuscripts, tho all due care will be exercised.

Entered at New York Post Office as Second
Class Matter

Copyright, 1916, by The Independent

Address all Communications to
T H E   I N D E P E N D E N T
119   West   Fortieth   Street,   New   York

CONTENTS

JUST A WORD

Auguste Rodin, whose best-known statue "Le Penseur" is reproduced on the cover of The Independent, has recently given to the French Government his entire collection of art works, and his mansion in Paris, which is to be made into a public museum for their exhibition. All his own sculpture and sketches, accumulated thru forty years of work, are represented in this collection. It also includes some notable examples of antique statuary.

We publish the photograph of a bronze cast of "Le Penseur" thru the courtesy of the Metropolitan Museum in New York City, which devotes one of its galleries to Rodin's work.

REMARKABLE REMARKS

E. H. SOTHERN—I prefer to snuff out.

THEDA BARA—I vampire to save souls.

DR. D. A. SARGENT—Fat is uninvested capital.

COL. HOUSE—Europe is always interesting.

LEW FIELDS—The Bowery is a fine old street.

ELSIE JANIS—I am still in the old maids' row.

BENNIE KAUFF—Say, who is this guy Ty Cobb, any how?

M. CLEMENCEAU—Wilson and his correspondent Wilhelm.

FRANCISCO VILLA—Americans will be shown no quarter.

DR. M. S. GREGORY—Every where I look I see signs of insanity.

AMBASSADOR MORGENTHAU—The missionaries have the right idea.

W. H. TAFT—I am afraid that some time this country will get a jolt.

KING GEORGE—The spirit of My allies and My people remains stedfast.

MRS. JOHN ASTOR—The English I think feel closer to us than we to them.

MRS. J. TERWILLIGER TARPON—I did not raise my husband to be a highbrow.

SENATOR JOHN SHARP WILLIAMS—We are the most egotistical people in the world.

MRS. O. H. P. BELMONT—It is time for us women to have a civilization of our own.

EVANGELIST MUNHALL—The curse of the Methodist Episcopal Church is her politics.

REV. S. PARKS CADMAN—Duty is the most fascinating pursuit for a healthy spirit.

PROF. R. L. GARNER—Once a gorilla takes a wife he cuts out the clubs and everything.

W. J. BRYAN—I will not allow anybody to drag me into a discussion of the presidential situation.

E. PHILIP PRINGLE—Pajamas cut you in two with the waist string, but the night shirt works up and leaves you cold.

G. K. CHESTERTON—The Prussian professors would defend cannibalism if they were allowed to call it Anthropophagy.

MARY PICKFORD—Some day I am going to study the history of art, as I feel it should be the part of every woman's education.

VICE-PRESIDENT MARSHALL—A member of the Supreme Court is a vestal virgin trimming the lamps at the altar of equal and exact justice.

GEORGE HAVEN PUTNAM—It is true I was born in England. But I am no more an Englishman than kittens born in an oven are biscuits.

WOODROW WILSON—I have sometimes been very much chagrined in seeing myself in the motion pictures. I have often wondered if I really was that kind of a "guy."

JAMES J. HILL—When the war is over the question confronting American wage-earners will be that of finding a market for their labor instead of fixing a price for it.

PROF. ERNST HAECKEL—The average course which the history of humanity follows is like the famous Eeblernach dancing processions, three steps forward, two steps backward.

BILLY SUNDAY—I have been in some churches where I could see the icicles hanging from the chandeliers, the frost on the walls, and where I felt like skating down the aisles.

GEORGE ADE—In the good old days, if most of the principals curled up and Died in the last act, the play was a Tragedy. If they stood in a line and Bowed, the play was a Comedy.

THE NEW PLAYS

The Great Pursuit is an ill constructed play, undecided whether to be tragedy or farce, but redeemed by most admirable acting, especially in the lighter parts. (Shubert.)

Captain Brassbound's Conversion. Grace George and her repertory company in one of Bernard Shaw's near masterpieces. Well-staged, well-played and entertaining. (Playhouse.)

The Blue Envelope. One of those old-fashioned farces where there are six doors opening into the scene and somebody behind each who does not want the others to see him or her; so they keep dodging in and out. (Cort.)

Lou-Tellegen does some excellent acting as *A King of Nowhere*—Celtic cousin of Henry VIII. The play has more histrionic than historic value. An expert fencing match adds to its entertainment. (Thirty-ninth Street.)

Merry Wives of Windsor. Mr. Hackett's production catches very happily the elate, sparkling atmosphere of the best in Shakespearean comedy. Scrupulous but thoroly vivacious acting, with a highly convincing Falstaff. (Criterion.)

The Washington Square Players give a varied bill—posteresque French farce, negro psychology, "The Age of Reason," in which children satirize parental platitudes, and "The Magical City," an emotional play, well acted. (Bandbox.)

The Heart of Wetona. An Oklahoma Comanche Belasco play. The villain is a white cur whom everybody on the stage and off wants to shoot. The heroine is an Indian ingenue who draws handkerchiefs from everybody's pocket. (Lyceum.)

Pay-Day is a novel sort of parody on a supposedly typical moving picture thriller. Part of it is presented on the screen and then the curtain rises and the act continues behind the footlights. Satirical, sardonic and slushful extravaganza. (Booth.)

A Number of Things
by
Edwin E. Slosson

THERE'S nothing I admire more than courage and nothing I lament more than my lack of it in the great emergencies of life. Not long ago I attended—in honor of somebody who needed honoring or in furtherance of some cause which needed furthering—one of those feasts of Tantalus to which New Yorkers are addicted. The guests are seated at tables by tens and have placed before them at intervals dishes of the choicest food, which they are permitted to look at and taste, but before they can satisfy the appetite the plates are snatched away by a swarm of harpies in swallowtails. Now a good dinner demands and deserves both time and attention, but it can get neither at these big banquets because there is always some one at the speakers' table or by your side who wants to talk.

On this occasion I saw before me a salad of a sort in which I most delight, one of those wonderful confections to which all nature contributes; fruit, fish, flesh and fowl; nuts plucked from the tallest trees, crustacean drawn from the ocean bed; all flavors and savors combined and commingled in artistic confusion; harmonies and dissonances, strong chords and subtle overtones, a veritable Strauss symphony of the palate, something that would be treasured in the memory long after the last lingering taste had left the mouth. Over this mountain of pleasure there flowed a creamy lava, the making of which had required joint genius of the whole coalition cabinet of the kitchen, "the spendthrift for oil, the miser for vinegar, the councillor for salt and the madman to stir it up."

It seemed a shame to spoil such a masterpiece of culinary art, but my appetite overcame my awe and I timidly touched the edge of it with my fork, even as the bather steps first into the ripples on the beach in order to anticipate and postpone the pleasure of the plunge. The taste confirmed all of the expectations which the sight had aroused. But just at this critical moment the man on the right asked me a question on a subject that I knew about or thought I did, which amounts to the same thing. I replied with eagerness and eloquence, my eyes enlivened and my voice made musical by the thought of the plateful of bliss before me. This is, of course, a hypothetic objectivization of a subjective impression. Not having a mirror and a phonograph

at hand I was unable to prove that my manner corresponded with my idea of it. But it does not matter about that now.

I answered my right hand neighbor as briefly as the importance of the subject and the extent of my own knowledge of it would permit, then turned to the Salad of the Four Seasons, but to my dismay it was being withdrawn by a stealthy hand reached over my shoulder. I made no outcry. I stifled my emotion and submitted meekly to the wrong. I knew no other way. Lost property may sometimes be recovered, even lost health or a lost wife. But for a missed meal there is no possible recompense in this world and I fear not in the next, for even omnipotence seems to be subject to the limitations of chronology.

I turned to my neighbor on the left. He had eaten half his salad, but I saw the hand of destiny had already seized the edge of the plate. But while I watched with unsympathetic eyes, for misery loves company, I saw the hand of destiny slip. The plate stuck fast to the table as tho fastened with the glue which the man on the street corner uses when he hangs cannon balls to his broken crockery. My friend held the inner edge of the plate firmly gripped between the thumb and the knuckle of the forefinger of his left hand and he looked up with a malicious grin at the Great Stone Face as he chuckled:

"You didn't get it that time, did you?"

As the waiter stalked off with other plates echeloned on his arm, I could have hung my hat on his nose if it had not been taken from me by the hallway robber.

I knew then that I had the honor of sitting beside the bravest man in the world. I looked upon him with admiration and envy as he finished the salad to the last delectable drop. He did not offer to share it with me, altho he must have seen the hunger in my eyes. But I did not complain. I knew I did not deserve it. None but the brave deserve the fare.

Humor, say the Freudians, is the disguised expression of a supprest wish. Perhaps there's something in this theory. At any rate, humor often serves as a safety-valve for emotions which otherwise might make trouble. Whenever two nations or two persons stop making fun of each other look out for blows.

Our little tiff with Germany over the partition of the Pacific some twenty years ago worked itself off in comic verse, which is much better than slinging shrapnel. Admiral Coghlan started it going on this side-track by his:

HOCH DER KAISER!

Der Kaiser of das Fatherland
And God on high all dings command.
Ve two—ach, don't you understand,
Myself—und Gott.
. . . .
Vile some men sing der power divine,
Mein soldiers sing: "Der Wacht am Rhein,"
Und drink der health in Rhenisch wine
Of me—und Gott.

The Germans replied with a volley of verses quite as bad:

HOCH DER PRASIDENT!

Der Teddy Roosevelt bin ich ja,
Raubreiter-Präsident.
In Deutschland und Amerika
Ein jedes Kind mich kennt.

Verletzet nie Monroes Doktrin
Sonst mach' ich gleich mobil,
Ich selbst ich stürme nach Berlin,
Held Dewey dampft nach Kiel.

And that was all there was to it; no high explosives, no torpedoes, no poison gases, merely hot air.

Time was when it was considered as disreputable to employ a tutor as to use a pony. Coaching was carried on in the woods or behind blanketed windows at dead of night. Later when it was realized that professors could not be expected to waste their time in teaching or students in studying, tutoring became recognized as an honorable and indispensable occupation, but those who practised it were slow to adopt up-to-date methods of pushing their business. They confined their efforts to the private circulation of neat copperplate visiting cards in the lower left corner of which one could discern with aid of a monocle the word MATHEMATICS or GREEK in the same small caps as are used by a fashionable hostess for MUSIC or DANCING or SKATING on her invitations.

But now the tutor has come to realize his own importance and learned how to impress it upon the public. In the Columbia daily I find an ad striking enough to stop an automobile, and from a Harvard man, too:

STOP! LOOK! LISTEN!
Stop flunking Mathematics. Look me up. Listen to my advice. I have taught Differential and Integral Calculus, Analytic Geometry, College Algebra and Trigonometry for several years, and have also wide experience as a tutor. Who am I? Ask your professor of Mathematics. F. S. Nowlan, A. M. (Harvard). Telephone Morn. 8920.

The distrest student has also adopted modern publicity methods for sending out his S. O. S. calls:

LOGIC TUTOR WANTED—A PATIENT, slow-speaking, flegmatic philosopher, who knows Jevons backwards, and who can sympathetically inject his definite practical knowledge into an eager mind, too busy to puzzle out the subject alone. Professors not satisfactory. Student will meet Tutor at University Tuesdays and Fridays between 5:30-7 p. m. State in own handwriting, age, sex, weight and terms. D., Spectator Office.

Some people have not taken as active a part in the discussion of the Balkan situation as they would like because they are uncertain as to the proper pronunciation of that city which in Bible times used to be called Thessalonica. But they should not worry. They can hardly miss it. The "Salonika correspondent" of The Near East gives the local usage:

"If you are a Greek you will call it 'Thessaloniki,' if a Turk 'Sela'nik,' if a Frenchman 'Saloníque,' if an American 'Saloni'ki,' but if you are an Englishman —or a Scotchman or Irishman, for the matter of that—you will call it 'Salon'ika,' or, as some people write it, 'Salon'ica.'"

The Independent

FOR SIXTY-SEVEN YEARS THE
FORWARD-LOOKING WEEKLY OF AMERICA

THE   CHAUTAUQUAN
Merged with The Independent June 1, 1914

A P R I L   1 7,   1 9 1 6

OWNED AND PUBLISHED BY
THE INDEPENDENT CORPORATION, AT
119 WEST FORTIETH STREET, NEW YORK
WILLIAM   B.   HOWLAND,   PRESIDENT
FREDERIC E. DICKINSON, TREASURER

W I L L I A M   H A Y E S   W A R D
HONORARY EDITOR

EDITOR: HAMILTON HOLT
ASSOCIATE EDITOR: HAROLD J. HOWLAND
LITERARY EDITOR: EDWIN E. SLOSSON

PUBLISHER: KARL V. S. HOWLAND

ONE   YEAR,   THREE   DOLLARS

SINGLE   COPIES,   TEN   CENTS

Postage to foreign countries in Universal Postal
Union, $1.75 a year extra; to Canada, $1 extra.
Instructions for renewal, discontinuance or
change of address should be sent two weeks
before the date they are to go into effect. Both
the old and the new address must be given.

We welcome contributions, but writers who
wish their articles returned, if not accepted,
should send a stamped and addrest envelope. No responsibility is assumed by The
Independent for the loss or non-return of
manuscripts, tho all due care will be exercised.

Entered at New York Post Office as Second
Class Matter

Copyright,   1916,   by   The   Independent

Address all Communications to
THE   INDEPENDENT
119 West Fortieth Street, New York

C O N T E N T S

J U S T   A   W O R D

Auguste Rodin, whose best-known
statue "Le Penseur" is reproduced on
the cover of The Independent, has recently given to the French Government
his entire collection of art works, and
his mansion in Paris, which is to be
made into a public museum for their
exhibition. All his own sculpture and
sketches, accumulated thru forty years
of work, are represented in this collection. It also includes some notable examples of antique statuary.

We publish the photograph of a
bronze cast of "Le Penseur" thru the
courtesy of the Metropolitan Museum
in New York City, which devotes one
of its galleries to Rodin's work.

REMARKABLE REMARKS

E. H. SOTHERN—I prefer to snuff out.

THEDA BARA—I vampire to save souls.

DR. D. A. SARGENT—Fat is uninvested
capital.

COL. HOUSE—Europe is always interesting.

LEW FIELDS—The Bowery is a fine old
street.

ELSIE JANIS—I am still in the old
maids' row.

BENNIE KAUFF—Say, who is this guy
Ty Cobb, any how?

M. CLEMENCEAU—Wilson and his co-
respondent Wilhelm.

FRANCISCO VILLA—Americans will be
shown no quarter.

DR. M. S. GREGORY—Every where I look
I see signs of insanity.

AMBASSADOR MORGENTHAU—The missionaries have the right idea.

W. H. TAFT—I am afraid that some
time this country will get a jolt.

KING GEORGE—The spirit of My allies
and My people remains stedfast.

MRS. JOHN ASTOR—The English I think
feel closer to us than we to them.

MRS. J. TERWILLIGER TARPON—I did
not raise my husband to be a highbrow.

SENATOR JOHN SHARP WILLIAMS—We
are the most egotistical people in the world.

MRS. O. H. P. BELMONT—It is time for
us women to have a civilization of our
own.

EVANGELIST MUNHALL—The curse of
the Methodist Episcopal Church is her politics.

REV. S. PARKES CADMAN—Duty is the
most fascinating pursuit for a healthy
spirit.

PROF. R. L. GARNER—Once a gorilla
takes a wife he cuts out the clubs and
everything.

W. J. BRYAN—I will not allow anybody
to drag me into a discussion of the presidential situation.

E. PHILIP PRINGLE—Pajamas cut you in
two with the waist strong, but the night
shirt works up and leaves you cold.

G. K. CHESTERTON—The Prussian professors would defend cannibalism if they
were allowed to call it Anthropophagy.

MARY PICKFORD—Some day I am going
to study the history of art, as I feel it
should be the part of every woman's education.

VICE-PRESIDENT MARSHALL—A member
of the Supreme Court is a vestal virgin
trimming the lamps at the altar of equal
and exact justice.

GEORGE HAVEN PUTNAM—It is true I
was born in England. But I am no more
an Englishman than kittens born in an
oven are biscuits.

WOODROW WILSON—I have sometimes
been very much chagrined in seeing myself
in the motion pictures. I have often wondered if I really was that kind of a "guy."

JAMES J. HILL—When the war is over
the question confronting American wage-
earners will be that of finding a market
for their labor instead of fixing a price
for it.

PROF. ERNST HAECKEL—The average
course which the history of humanity follows is like the famous Eckhernach dancing
processions, three steps forward, two steps
backward.

BILLY SUNDAY—I have been in some
churches where I could see the icicles
hanging from the chandeliers, the frost on
the walls, and where I felt like skating
down the aisles.

GEORGE ADE—In the good old days, if
most of the principals curled up and Died
in the last act, the play was a Tragedy.
If they stood in a line and Bowed, the play
was a Comedy.

THE NEW PLAYS

The Great Pursuit is an ill constructed
play, undecided whether to be tragedy or
farce, but redeemed by most admirable acting, especially in the lighter parts. (Shubert.)

Captain Brassbound's Conversion. Grace
George and her repertory company in one
of Bernard Shaw's near masterpieces. Well-
staged, well-played and entertaining. (Playhouse.)

The Blue Envelope. One of those old-
fashioned farces where there are six doors
opening into the scene and somebody behind each who does not want the others to
see him or her; so they keep dodging in and
out. (Cort.)

Lou-Tellegen does some excellent acting
as *A King of Nowhere*—Celtic cousin of
Henry VIII. The play has more histrionic
than historic value. An expert fencing
match adds to its entertainment. (Thirty-
ninth Street.)

Merry Wives of Windsor. Mr. Hackett's
production enriches very happily the elate,
sparkling atmosphere of the best in Shakespearean comedy. Scrupulous but thoroly
vivacious acting, with a highly convincing
Falstaff. (Criterion.)

The *Washington Square Players* give a
varied bill—postоresque French farce,
negro psychology, "The Age of Reason," in
which children satirize parental platitudes,
and "The Magical City," an emotional
play, well acted. (Bandbox.)

The Heart of Wetona. An Oklahoma
Comanche Belasco play. The villain is a
white curr whom everybody on the stage
and off wants to shoot. The heroine is an
Indian ingenue who draws handkerchiefs
from everybody's pocket. (Lyceum.)

Pay-Day is a novel sort of parody on
a supposedly typical moving picture thriller. Part of it is presented on the screen
and then the curtain rises and the act
continues behind the footlights. Satirical,
sardonic and slushful extravaganza.
(Booth.)

The Independent

| VOLUME 86 | APRIL 17, 1916 | NUMBER 3515 |

Paul Thompson

DODD OF "DODD'S RIDE"

A SEVENTEEN-HOUR RIDE WITH A FIGHT AT THE END OF IT ADDS ANOTHER CHAPTER TO THE RECORD OF OUR FAMOUS CAVALRY REGIMENTS. WHITE AND BLACK, THE SEVENTH AND THE TENTH CAVALRY, THEY RODE NECK AND NECK IN PURSUIT OF THE BANDIT, VILLA, AND THEIR LEADER WAS COLONEL GEORGE A. DODD, WHO IS BILLED FOR RETIREMENT NEXT JULY BECAUSE HE WILL BE SIXTY-FOUR AND THEREFORE PRESUMABLY DECREPIT

WILL HOLLAND HAVE TO FIGHT GERMANY?

THERE is great and manifest uneasiness in Holland, the uneasiness of a small, weak Power wedged in between two powerful belligerents. For many days past the papers have been full of rumors of Dutch mobilization, of the closing of the frontier, of dangers threatening the people of the Netherlands both from the Allies and the Germans. On the one hand it is reported that Great Britain and France are determined to put an end to a situation which has made Holland the chief clearing-house for German imports, and that they would really prefer the Dutch to be openly ranged on the side of their enemies. On the other hand, it is said that Germany believes that the British meditate a landing in Holland in order to strike at the Teutonic flank and that in this belief she is demanding permission to send German troops to reinforce the Dutch army. A further report makes nonsense of both these suppositions by suggesting that the recent sinking of the "Tubantia" and other Dutch vessels is a part of a deliberate German plan to drive Holland into the war. Finally, the real root of Dutch perturbation is declared to be a fear that a successful Allied offensive may lead to a violation of Dutch neutrality.

Which of these delightfully contradictory rumors is the most credible? From which side have the Dutch most to fear? The answer is clear to any one who looks at the broad, determining facts. It is from the Germans and from them alone that the Dutch have anything to fear. That the British or the French would dream of duplicating the infamy of Germany's occupation of Belgium by an invasion of Holland is unthinkable. That the Allies who already have their hands sufficiently full are thinking of adding Holland to the list of their opponents that they might thereby be legally empowered to blockade the Dutch coast, seems on the face of it not less fantastic. The conclusion, therefore, is irresistible that it is on Germany's policy today and on her possible action in the future that Dutch apprehensions turn. And this conclusion is buttressed by official German utterances in the past and by the pressure which Germany will increasingly feel to invoke once again the "necessity" which "knows no law."

WHEN the German Chancellor at the beginning of the war declared in effect that Belgium would be of little value to Germany unless a considerable slice of Holland were thrown in, he said a very significant thing. Its significance so far has been obscured by the German successes on land. The Kaiser up to now has had no occasion to treat Holland as he treated Belgium. But as soon as the tide begins to turn and the hopelessness of a final victory is driven into the mind of the ruling caste, the position of Holland, instead of being more secure, will be less so. It will be less so because in proportion as the possibility of defeat becomes a probability, and the probability a certainty, the Germans, or the governing clique in Germany, will be tempted, if not compelled, to gather in all the counters they can lay hands on to bargain with in the day of settlement. The harder Germany is prest along her present fronts the more will she be driven to recoup herself elsewhere. That is why the sinking of these Dutch steamers has a

sinister air. That is why the talk of a deliberate attempt on Germany's part to goad Holland into the war cannot be dismissed as meaningless. That also is why among the conceivable developments of this conflict a German invasion of Holland has to be taken into account.

If a handful of soldiers, Junkers and blood-and-iron statesmen decide that German interests require the occupation of Holland, Holland will be occupied. The considerations that will guide them will be of the simplest character. That Antwerp is useless without the full control of the Scheldt; that now or never is the time to settle the question of the Rhine; that 400,000 Dutchmen present an easier military problem than 1,000,000 Englishmen with vast reserves in the background; that the seizure of Holland, besides facilitating the prosecution of the naval war against England, would immensely strengthen the hands of German diplomacy when the terms of peace come to be discussed—such are the sort of arguments that will count in deciding this issue. And behind them and perhaps governing them all will be the desperation of the official hierarchy, fighting to the last for its powers and privileges, and acutely conscious that its knell has sounded unless it can show that the sacrifices it has exacted from the German people have resulted in some solid, tangible gains.

ONE must remember, too, that the incorporation of Holland in the German Empire has long been an object of Pan-German policy; that all Germans are Pan-Germans at heart; and that the Pan-German program, officially repudiated at the outset, is very apt to be officially adopted in the sequel. The German Jingoes have never acquiesced in Dutch control of the Lower Rhine. That the mouth of the German Tiber should be in the hands of strangers, that a small and weak people should sit astride of Germany's busiest river, is as vexatious an anomaly as tho the mouth of the Mississippi were still in Spanish hands. It bars Germany out from the full freedom of the North Sea. It places her in the intolerable position of a man denied a key to his own front door. It makes of the short and difficult coast line between Holland and Denmark virtually the sole effective channel for the commerce of that great empire.

The Dutch have been warned time and again that this cannot endure, that Germany sooner or later must advance to her "natural" confines, and that an end would eventually have to be made of a situation which allowed Holland to share in the advantages of German progress without sharing in its burdens.

It has been of little avail. The Dutch are not willing to give up Free Trade; they foresee that an economic union with Germany foreshadows a complete political subserviency to Berlin; they intensely dislike the German militarist and bureaucratic spirit; they are far more conscious of the points of character, speech and manners that differentiate than of those that tend to unite the two peoples; and they cling with a hardy pride to the memories of the greatness of their past.

But the idea that Holland cramps Germany's development and shuts her off from much that she vitally needs for the protection of her security and the full utilization of her strength is one that has taken deep root in the German mind. The necessity which knows no law may again be invoked to use that idea as the justification for further aggression. The Dutch at any rate do well to stand by their dykes and their guns in a state of instant preparedness. For them, more than for almost any other neutral, the war has been an incessant and imminent anxiety. Their difficulties and their dangers both increase as it nears its climax and the prospect of Germany striking out blindly in defeat to save whatever she can from the wreckage of her original hopes draws nearer and nearer.

THE GERMAN OPPOSITION

WHEN the Reichstag first assembled after the war broke out, one solitary Socialist voted against the war budget. Later on in the year 14 Socialists opposed war credits. In December, 1915, the number had risen to 20. Now 33 Socialists have voted against disciplining a member who declared "We cannot bring our enemies to their knees any more than they can Germany."

These 33 Socialists represent a million and a quarter of the Socialist votes. Can it be presumed that such a large proportion of the most intelligent people in Germany are beginning to get tired of the war? We shall see.

WHO WANTS WAR?

WE suppose there is not a responsible person in the whole United States who believes that our preparedness movement is designed for the purpose of waging an aggressive war upon Japan. We suppose likewise there is not a responsible person in all Japan who believes that the Japanese preparedness movement is for the purpose of waging an aggressive war upon the United States.

Yet there are sane people in America who believe Japan is preparing to attack us, and there are likewise sane people in Japan who believe the United States is going to attack them.

For instance, *The Chicago Tribune* not many days ago gave some of its valuable space to the report of a speech made by one John Maynard Harlan—"a candidate-at-large to the Republican National Convention"—who told a Champaign, Illinois, audience that

Japan could within a comparatively short time place 100,000 troops in Chicago. They could easily bring over small river boats "in the knock-down," put them together at New Orleans, after capturing that port, and steam up the Mississippi River at their leisure, taking cities and towns en route.

We presume the Japanese would come to New Orleans via the Panama Canal, altho so far we have found it rather difficult to traverse it ourselves.

Such a news item must seem about as absurd to the Japanese as the following editorial in the March issue of the *Japan Magazine* seems to us. Remember that the *Japan Magazine* is a reputable and responsible journal:

The Tokyo *Nichinichi* is quite alarmed at America's program of army and navy expansion, which, it says, attracts the attention of the world. Why does the United States require such enormous defenses? Some may say that America is preparing against Germany after the war; but so long as she maintains amicable relations with England she can have nothing to fear in that direction. No; America's objective is in another direction. She wants to command a big navy on the Pacific and play a striking rôle in the Orient. Japan, which holds the key to the peace of the Far East should not neglect to keep a sharp eye on American

policy. No amount of peace talk can alleviate Japan's anxiety over America's determination for a big navy. President Wilson seems to support the Monroe Doctrine, but if America has an ambition to play a leading part in Oriental affairs it is inconsistent with the Monroe Doctrine. There is no doubt that the aim of the American Government is to secure a foremost position in the Far East and the American people are determined to extend their concessions in this direction. In carrying out such a program how can America avoid conflict with Japan? This is what we fear. Japan has brought herself to the present position at enormous expense; and the position must be maintained at all costs; but how is she to do so in the face of American ambition?

If each nation now would only give the other the credit of being as unwilling to take offensive measures as it knows itself to be, all this disheartening war talk would cease. Or are there sinister influences working underground to bring about unfriendly relations between Japan and America? It would almost seem so.

A FILM OF WAGNER

THE Germans, under the maternal care of necessity, are developing their own resources. They are making nitrates from the air, cotton from wood and rubber from potatoes. Thru the assiduous watchfulness of their dearest foes they are protected from the temptation of wasting their money on foreign luxuries such as the American movies. Our Wild West films have always been highly appreciated in Europe for their educational value in giving a true picture of American life. There are, of course, brands of cowboy films made-in-Germany, but somehow the sight of an actor in chaps climbing to the top of his mount by the aid of a horse-block, and afterwards holding on by the aid of a saddle horn, does not convey the thrill of the genuine even to the unsophisticated European.

But now, deprived as they are of broncho-busters and suffering for lack of Charlie Chaplin and Mary Pickford, the Germans have been obliged to fall back upon such native talent as they do possess; so they have put Wagner on the screen. "Lohengrin" is the first to be filmed, and it is said to be a great success. The orchestra leader watches the screen and keeps the music in time to the action. It is also produced without an orchestra by the use of a synchronized phonograph.

This is a development of the music drama that would have delighted Wagner. His ambitions transcended the limitations of the stage of his day, and attempting the impossible in scenic effects he sometimes achieves the absurd. Even the devout Wagnerite can scarcely suppress a snicker at the sight of the gods crowded together on the gang plank running into the back screen which is supposed to represent the rainbow bridge leading to Valhalla. The Rhine maidens have always protested that they could not sing while hanging head down from the flies. The dragon has never been able to frighten a school girl. The castle of Klingsor does not vanish, but folds up and moves off with many a creak and rumble.

Now the magic of the movies can make visible the wildest of these dreams of Wagner. He did the best he could with such machinery as he had to get cinema effects. In the ride of the valkyries he used the stereopticon. In "Parsifal" he employed the panorama to produce moving scenery. But real giants and dwarfs were not to be obtained at any price, and it too often happened that the best singers did not look the part and could not act.

But now the Elsa need not appear as a too robust and

over-mature prima donna and Lohengrin can really look the swan knight. Beside this the film-opera has another advantage at the present time; it does not take men from the front. The actors may be filmed on a furlough and then continue to play their rôles in all parts of the empire while they are fighting or have fallen at Riga or Verdun.

ILLITERATE HUMBUGGERY

THE United States Congress will again pass a bill forbidding the admission of illiterates into this country, and again the President will veto it, altho there is some fear that it will be passed over his veto. The bill is a pretense and a humbug. It deceives nobody. No one is afraid of any danger from the admission of immigrants who cannot read and write. The object of the bill is to shut out immigrants, as many as possible, whether they can read or not. What is feared is that they will work and earn money and divide jobs with those already here. It is a very shortsighted policy. Every able-bodied immigrant, willing to work, adds so much to the wealth of the country, benefiting others as well as himself. Opposition to immigrant labor is as unreasonable as opposition to the introduction of machinery.

It is a part of the argument in favor of exclusion that the end of the war will bring to us an avalanche of ignorant immigration. That is far from likely. Workmen will be in demand abroad and money will be scarce to pay the passage. Passenger agents expect much more that the drift will be in the opposite direction. Tens of thousands will be taking steerage passage to visit their old homes and help their relatives. This talk about a flood of invasion is but a part of the pretense to help an unworthy cause.

AN ARMY STRIKE

AUSTRALIA used to be held up to us for our shame and emulation as "a country without strikes." But later, like all model children, it fell from grace, for in spite of its admirable machinery for the settlement of industrial disputes, the men would strike even on trivial occasions and against the decisions of their own tribunals. Now, it appears, "the right to strike" has been extended to a form of service which has, in theory at least, hitherto been exempt, that is the army. The recruits in the training camp near Sydney, who were being prepared to go to the front, decided that forty hours of drill per week was an intolerable imposition, tho it seems to be well within the limits of the eight hour law. So they went on strike and, seizing the railway trains, went to Sydney by the thousands. After looting the saloons they proceeded to paint the town red, and the 2000 men on police and picket duty were powerless to control them. Finally the labor government did what every other government, be it autocratic, aristocratic or bourgeois, has been obliged to do under similar circumstances, it put down the rioters by force. A regiment of loyal troops was sent to the scene of disturbance, cleared the streets by bayonet and cavalry charges and finally used ball cartridges on the mob at the Grand Central Station, killing one and wounding eight.

We used to be told that when the people owned the industries and determined for themselves the wages and conditions of labor, that work would be done with

good will and efficiency. But in Australia, where the state owns and manages the railroads, and where the state is merely the political branch of the labor unions, the old ca' canny policy still prevails. In the workshops of the state railroads of New South Wales the following placards were printed and posted:

> Don't scab upon the unemployed by working hard. Slow work means more jobs—more jobs mean less unemployed—less competition means higher wages, less work, more pay. Slow down! Slow down! Don't be slaves!

With such admonitions reinforcing the natural disposition of all human beings to work as little as possible, it is no wonder that the efficiency of the service fails to meet the demands of the times.

Obviously the labor union rules and the labor union spirit are serious handicaps when it comes to war. It would be decidedly inconvenient if the first line troops should stop work and throw down their tools when their eight hours were up, or if they should adopt sabotage methods and jam their machine guns. Strikes among soldiers, formerly called "mutinies," have been known in all ages; the Pretorian Guards in the later days of the Roman Empire were much given to them, and the "slow down!" tactics of the Australian workshops are what has long been known as "soldiering." Such spirit and methods are really just as much of a detriment to a nation in time of peace as in time of war, tho the injury is not so conspicuous. The labor movement has done much in Australia and elsewhere for the advancement of wages and improvement of conditions, but it has failed to secure efficiency except by the adoption of the measures it condemns.

A HUNDRED YEARS AFTER

MASSACHUSETTS is not what it was early in the last century. It seems more than a hundred years ago that a mob of Protestants angrily demolished a Catholic convent in Charlestown, Massachusetts. Catholics were few then in the state and they did not try to rebuild it, but left the ruins as a monument of the malignity of Protestantism toward Catholic Christianity. We think we are living in a better world now when religious bigotry is vanishing away; and yet last week in Haverhill, Massachusetts, on two successive nights an angry mob of many thousands attacked the City Hall, smashed windows and doors, overpowered the police, injured and attempted to kill citizens and officers of the law, and so terrorized the city that the Governor had to call on the militia for protection. And it was a religious riot, only the conditions were reversed. It was the Catholics that composed the mob. Massachusetts cities are ruled by Catholics now; they have the population.

A foolish, reckless man who called himself an ex-priest had announced that he would make an address against giving public funds for parochial schools. We presume it was viciously intended to excite religious hatred. The proper way to treat it would have been with contempt. Those who did not like it should have stayed away and allowed him to speak to empty benches. Instead of that they advertised the lecturer and disgraced themselves, their city and their church. Here and now, in the early twentieth century, they rivaled the Charlestown mob of the early nineteenth century. There is nothing to choose.

We have no word to say against parochial schools. If parents wish to send their children to a religious school they have a perfect right to do so. If parochial schools are better than public schools it will appear in the product. If the public schools are the better that will come in evidence. *Probat ambulando.* The teachers in our public schools are a noble body of men and women, and the same can be said of the Sisters and Brothers who teach in the religious schools. They can live side by side in peace and if they are well taught their graduate pupils will be all fellow-citizens together, and love law and detest riot.

TOMMY ATKINS' REPUTATION

THE British army is not only bigger than ever before, but it is better behaved. At least it is supposed to be and anybody who insinuates to the contrary goes to jail. A London periodical, the *Bystander*, has been prosecuted for publishing a cartoon in which a British soldier is represented lying drunk on the ground "somewhere in France." The mere suggestion that any one of Kitchener's four million could so demean himself was held to be an actionable libel upon the army.

We congratulate Great Britain upon the high character of its soldiery, assuming, of course, that it was a case of false libel and that the cartoon could not have been drawn from life. Such a great improvement in so short a time is as remarkable as it is commendable. It was, if we remember aright, not many years ago when Kipling was amusing the British public with plain tales and barrack-room ballads to which this cartoon might have served as illustration. This most patriotic of poets also wrote verses in praise of loot and told how the sentry shut his eye when the officer rode past upon his sword. Now all that is over and forgotten, and Kipling, if he dare to write such nonsense nowadays, would be apt to find himself in prison instead of in the hall of fame.

But there is still another vice than drinking which Shakespeare and others have intimated was characteristic of the soldier. We mean profanity. It was at one time whispered about in England that "our army swore terribly in Flanders." The army is in Flanders again. The provocation is quite as great. Does Tommy Atkins resist the temptation nowadays? That is what we want to know, but we cannot think of any way of finding out except by publishing a cartoon of a British soldier with an oath coming out of his mouth. Then if we were sued for libel we should have to assume that Kitchener had indeed a model army.

IMPARTIALITY AND NEUTRALITY

THE two words *impartiality* and *neutrality* do not mean the same thing. In fact they are very different. One is positive and the other negative. One a word of strength, the other a word of weakness.

It is the business of a judge to be impartial, but not to be neutral. His business is to decide, to pronounce acquittal or guilt and punishment. He has to take sides. He must impartially acquit or convict. The position of a neutral is very different; he is an onlooker, nothing else. He has no passion, no sentiment, no judgment, or if he has he keeps it to himself and "roots" for neither side. Impartiality is the attitude of an intelli-

gent, self-respecting man, while neutrality is the attitude of the brutes about the ring of a dog-fight.

Unfortunately action and feeling cannot always go together. In the present terrible war it is the business of every intelligent citizen to be impartial, to commend or to condemn; he must do it if he has a conscience; he cannot be neutral; but it is different with what are called neutral states. The neutral nations must stand about the dog-pit and restrain their individual feeling and give equal show to the combatants. That is what we are trying to do.

Yet not wholly neutral. Neutrality has its limit. The game of war must be played by its rules, and even President Wilson has found it necessary at times to rise above the level of dead neutrality into the hight of impartiality. If our Government did not protest impartially when Germany broke its pledged faith and invaded Belgium, it has at least strongly condemned the murder of innocent passengers of the "Lusitania" and a succession of other similar crimes. Our Government is finding it very hard to maintain the attitude of neutrality.

The most unhappy position is that of the Pope of Rome. Benedict XV is head of the Catholic Church the world over, and nearly all his spiritual subjects are fighting on one side or the other. Shall he be impartial or shall he be neutral? That depends upon whether he considers himself a temporal and political or a religious and spiritual potentate. If he is the teacher of the world's religion and morals it is his business to speak strongly and impartially in favor of what he sees to be justice, as does Cardinal Mercier. If, on the other hand, he considers first his political interest to maintain his position between the warring camps and offend neither, he will prudently declaim on the evils of war, the duty of seeking peace and the maintenance of a Christian spirit on the part of those who are killing each other.

A SECOND CANAL

THE United States Government has constructed a great Panama Canal. It now has the right, by treaty with Nicaragua, to dig the second great canal which one day must connect the Atlantic and the Pacific Oceans. Our Government ought forthwith to begin planning for its construction.

The United States built the canal at Panama, after great question between the route and that by Lake Nicaragua. We have finished the Canal, opened it to the trade of the world, and have had to close and reopen it more than once on account of persistent slides.

We need just now and may sorely need at any time in the future a second Canal. Of course we hope to control the slides, and we probably shall. Then there is the certainty of congestion some day from enormous and growing traffic that will eventually require two channels. The Nicaragua Canal will save about a thousand miles of travel to vessels from New York to San Francisco or Portland. We have the engineers, we have the machinery, and it would be the part of wisdom immediately to confirm our option, undertaking the preliminary work. It will relieve us from possible political complications later and will permanently and completely ensure American influence thruout Central America.

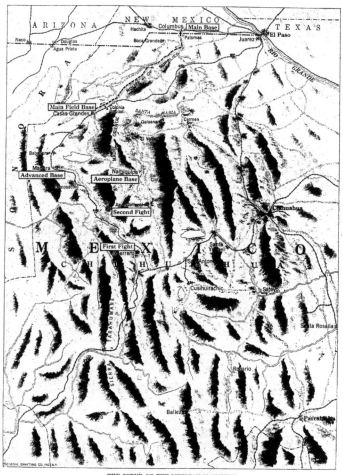

THE SCENE OF THE MEXICAN MAN-HUNT

VILLA, AS THE INDEPENDENT GOES TO PRESS, IS BELIEVED TO BE
ON HIS WAY TO PARRAL, AND DODD'S CAVALRY
HAS GONE BEYOND SATEVO

THE STORY OF THE WEEK

On Villa's Trail

The pursuit of Villa and his band has gone on during the past week persistently but uneventfully. It seems certain that the bandit is really wounded so seriously that he is being carried in a litter by his men. After the rout by Colonel Dodd's cavalry of Villa's force which had attacked Guerrero, the bandits continued to flee south toward Parral. Two or three small encounters with American and Carranzista troops somewhat depleted their numbers; but it was soon reported that the bandit's force was being swelled again, tho whether voluntarily or by conscription is not known. American cavalry is hot on Villa's trail south of Satevo, and General Pershing has left his headquarters at the San Geronimo ranch and gone south to Satevo.

The American line into Mexico has been extended over 400 miles, and the problem of transportation of food, forage, ammunition and other supplies grows steadily more difficult. The State Department has tried to negotiate an agreement with General Carranza for the use of the Mexican railways for sending these necessary stores nearer to the forces in the field. But the *de facto* President has shown his usual spirit of obstinate arrogance, and declined to accede to this eminently proper request. The expedient has been tried of having shipments of army supplies made to private traders in Chihuahua for transfer by them to the quartermasters in the field. The question is also under consideration of establishing a new line of transportation direct from Presidio and Ojinaga on the border to Chihuahua. This line would be only about half the length of the present one from El Paso and Juarez.

Excitement was caused last week by rumors than there was an intention of withdrawing the forces in Mexico before Villa was captured. It was promptly allayed, however, by the declaration of the Secretary of War that the rumors were quite without foundation. Mr. Baker said, "The object of the expedition . . . has never been changed. No other orders have been given and the expedition is busily pursuing that object now with what, I hope, is a fair chance of early success." The original object of the expedition has been twice explicitly stated by President Wilson. On March 10 he said, "An adequate force will be at once in pursuit of Villa with the single object of capturing him and putting an end to his forays." On March 25 he reiterated this in these words, "The expedition into Mexico was ordered under an agreement with the *de facto* Government of Mexico, for the single purpose of taking the bandit, Villa, whose forces have actually invaded the territory of the United States." There is no reason to suppose that the Administration has any thought whatever of deviating from this purpose until it is accomplished.

The Reorganization of the Army

The Senate has agreed to vote on the Army Reorganization bill on Tuesday, April 18. The Legislative, Executive and Judicial Appropriation bills were passed last week to make way for the Army bill. Next came the bill continuing the sugar duties. Then from Tuesday of this week, the Army bill has the right of way.

There are two hotly contested points in this bill—the provision for increasing the pay of the National Guard, and the national volunteer reserve provision. The latter escaped elimination from the bill in Committee of the Whole by the narrowest of margins. Thirty-four votes were cast in favor of throwing it out, and only thirty-six in favor of retaining it. The motion to discard it will almost certainly be renewed and the margin of safety is so slight as to afford the supporters of the provision scant sense of security. The votes for retaining the section were quite evenly divided between the two parties — seventeen Republican and nineteen Democratic—while on the negative side the preponderance of Democratic votes was decidedly greater —thirty-four Democratic to ten Republican. Obviously the question of army reorganization is cutting squarely across party lines.

The conflict between these two provisions of the Army bill is a straight out disagreement as to fundamental principles. Under the section in question the reserve force behind the regular army would be a national organization at the command of national authority at all times, made up of national volunteers, trained and prepared under exclusive Federal authority. Its members would be drawn from their usual employments for only a small part of the year, unless needed for actual service.

In this respect the national volunteer reserve plan is like that for additional support for the National Guard; but in the other respects it is entirely different. The National Guard comprises forty-eight separate forces, each primarily under the control of a single state, and available for Federal service only in certain limited contingencies. The militia may be used by the Federal Government only to enforce Federal law within the states, to suppress insurrection or to repel invasion in time of war.

The movement to substitute additional financial support for the state militia for the plan to create a national volunteer reserve has been strongly assailed as tainted with a "pork-barrel" quality. It is asserted that a strong lobby is maintained by the National Guard organizations of the country for the purpose of influencing the army legislation in the direction of increased financial profit for state militiamen. Senator Chamberlain, of Oregon, chairman of the Senate Committee on Military Affairs, declared in the Senate that the lobbying which militiamen were doing almost inclined him to "put the Guard out of business."

The Army bill, as it passed the House, contained the additional pay for the National Guard feature, without the National volunteer reserve plan. The conflict between the two proposals will doubtless be threshed out in conference, as will the difference between the House and the Senate as to the size of the enlarged regular army. The House bill provides for 140,000 men; the Senate bill for 178,000.

© *Underwood & Underwood*

THE CENSOR

N. O. C. Brunnell, who censors despatches at Columbus. This is an interesting experiment in our own army with military methods which the Great War has made commonplace

© *International Film Service*

THE WIRELESS STATION THAT FOLDS UP
These fish-pole sections are fitted together to make the 103-foot rod shown in the illustration below

Mr. Roosevelt's Platform

There is one outstanding fact about Theodore Roosevelt. No one has to take him on faith. He is wont to let it be known in no uncertain terms just where he stands—and where he thinks the rest of us ought to stand—on the important questions that confront the nation. To a group of political visitors at Oyster Bay the other day he made it emphatically clear just what any political party that contemplated nominating him for the Presidency would have to expect. The subject was broached by a prospective delegate to the Republican National Convention, who said: "You know, Colonel, I may make up my mind that we will have to nominate you."

The response was characteristically instantaneous: "Let me give you a piece of advice. If you have any doubt on the subject do not nominate me. Get it perfectly clear in your head that if you nominate me it mustn't be because you think it is in my interest, but because you think it is in your interest and the interest of the Republican party, and because you think it to the interest of the United States to do so."

This is good doctrine. It is the only possible basis on which a candidate for the Presidency—or, indeed, for any office—should be selected.

Mr. Roosevelt thereupon proceeded to outline his beliefs as to the paramount issues before the people of the United States at the present time. He prefaced this statement of his creed with the almost superfluous warning, "Don't you do it if you expect me to pussy-foot on any single issue I have raised." The Colonel, whatever else he may be, is no pussy-foot. The first item in the Rooseveltian creed is Americanism and no hyphenism.

Don't be for me unless you are prepared to say that every citizen of this country has got to be pro-United States, first, last and all the time, and no pro-anything else at all, and that we stand for every good American everywhere, whatever his birth-place or creed, and wherever he now lives, and that in return we demand that he be an American and nothing else, with no hyphen about him.

Every American citizen must be for America first and for no other country even second, and he hasn't any right to be in the United States at all if he has any divided loyalty between this country and any other.

I don't care a rap for the man's creed or birthplace or national origin, so long as he is straight United States. I am for him if he is straight United States, and if he isn't I am against him.

The second item sets forth his views on war:

I am not for war; on the contrary, I abhor an unjust or a wanton war, and I would use every honorable expedient to avoid even a just war. But I feel with all my heart that you don't, in the long run, avoid war by making other people believe that you are afraid to fight for your own rights.

Uncle Sam must never wrong the weak: he must never insult any one or wantonly give cause of offense to either the weak or the strong.

The last item deals, of course, with preparedness:

And don't you nominate me unless you are prepared to take the position that Uncle Sam is to be strong enough to defend his rights and to defend every one of his people wherever those people are, and he can't be strong enough unless he prepares in advance. . . . The squarest possible way to enable him to keep the peace and to keep it on terms that will enable Americans to hold their heads high and not hang them in shame is to be prepared in advance—and I mean prepared in his own soul as well as with his army and navy—that when he says anything the rest of the world will known that he means it, and that he can make it good.

Don't you try to nominate me unless you think that is the policy that ought to be followed out, and followed out for your sake as much as for mine, and for the sake of the rest of us here in the United States, and don't forget that isn't a course that provokes war; it is the only course that, in the long run, prevents war, and secures national self-respect and guarantees the honor of this country, and the rights of its citizens wherever they may be.

So there we have the Theodore Roosevelt of the present day. If the Republican party wants a man for President who holds such views, and holds them, as he would say, not "tepidly," it knows where to find him.

Elihu Root for President

Seventy-five prominent Republicans of New York State, including a score of delegates to the National Convention, have issued a public indorsement of Elihu Root for the Republican nomination for President. In their pronouncement they set him forth as "the ablest living American." The platform upon which they propose him to their fellow Republicans is, like the Roosevelt platform, one of Americanism and preparedness. The seventy-five include among their number Nicholas Murray Butler, Cornelius N. Bliss, Otto Bannard, Joseph H. Choate, Chauncey M. Depew, Job E. Hedges, John G. Milburn, William A. Prendergast, James R. Sheffield, Henry L. Stimson and Senator James W. Wadsworth, Jr. They include, as is perfectly natural, many well-known lawyers, and on the whole the membership is distinctly conservative. Their statement is as follows:

Elihu Root is the ablest living American.

The next four years will be critical in the life and influence of the people of the United States. New and vitally important problems confront the American people. Not only the domestic questions of national prosperity, of economic and industrial readjustment of the social welfare and of the

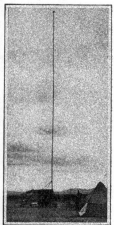

© *International Film Service*

A FIELD WIRELESS STATION
The army in Mexico keeps in touch with the base at Columbus by a combination of aeroplane courier service, wireless, and field telegraph

IT'S A LONG DRIVE AND A DANGEROUS ONE

The refusal of the Mexican Government to allow any but the most indirect and inadequate use of the Mexican Northwestern Railway for the transport of supplies to the punitive force has forced the army to rely on motor trucks. From Columbus to Guerrero is 300 miles

best use of our natural resources are pressing for solution, but the international policy of the nation is now to be defined in terms of present-day needs and relations.

At this time the nation requires its best trained, most experienced and most thoroly tested leader in the highest executive office. After sixteen years of devoted public service as Secretary of War, Secretary of State and Senator of the United States, Elihu Root stands preëminent among contemporary Americans as a constructive, farsighted and forward-facing statesman. While he has declined to become a candidate for even the highest political office, yet if nominated for the Presidency by the coming national convention at Chicago his sense of public duty must compel his acceptance.

As Americans, believing in an American policy at home and abroad and in proper preparation to express and to defend such a policy, we favor the nomination of Elihu Root for the Presidency of the United States.

The main plank in the Root platform, as here suggested, and as more fully set forth by Mr. Root himself in his speech at the Republican State Convention recently, is little different from that of Mr. Roosevelt. In choosing between the two men, the Republican party will have to be guided by other considerations—such as age, type of mind, temperament, fundamental convictions on domestic problems, associations, availability, popularity.

Meanwhile, Mr. Justice Hughes, the third in the trio of Republican possibilities, goes on administering justice on the Supreme Court bench—and says nothing, in both of which activities he is an adept. The Republican State Committee at a recent meeting adopted a resolution calling for the nomination of "a tried Republican, on whose record and character the nation can rely as a guarantee of wise statesmanship in the management of foreign and domestic affairs." State Senator Ogden Mills, who offered the resolution, declared, after the meeting, that this was a Hughes resolution—he himself being for Justice Hughes "first, last and all the time." Senator Wadsworth, however, who also voted for the resolution, declared, "We are our first, second and third choice for President."

Canadian War Graft

Canada's united support of the Great War, which has made possible a remarkable response to the Empire's need, is rudely threatened by

charges of huge war graft in the making of munitions, which may involve Major General Sir Sam Hughes, Minister of Militia.

Six weeks after the war began a Dominion Shell Committee was formed to take charge of the manufacture of munitions for the Canadian and British governments. It was later superseded by an Imperial Munitions Board, but its contracts, totaling more than $300,000,000, are now under fire from the Liberal Opposition in the Dominion Parliament.

On March 28 documentary evidence of graft was offered in a Parliamentary debate at Ottawa by George W. Kyte, a Liberal member from Nova Scotia. He declared that thru the influence of Honorary Colonel J. Wesley Allison, a friend of General Hughes and publicly praised by him, four contracts for fuses, cartridge cases and picric acid had been so manipulated as to return a profit of over a million and a half dollars to Allison, his associates and the manufacturer. It is said that two orders for fuses, worth $23,000,000, were placed with mushroom companies in the United States, companies which had neither adequate capital nor facilities for manufacture. Deliveries were therefore much delayed, and there is widespread indignation at the injury which may thus have been done to Canadian soldiers overseas.

Colonel Allison could not be reached when the charges were made, but it developed that he had been to Florida and was slowly traveling home. Sir Sam is in England, where he reviewed the Canadian troops on April 3, and tho he has cabled a flat denial of improper conduct, his return is anxiously awaited by his associates in the government.

Sir Wilfrid Laurier, Opposition leader at Ottawa, demanded an unlimited investigation of the Shell Committee contracts by Parliamentary commission. This the Government declined to grant, but by an Order in Council a Royal Commission has been appointed to sift the charges relating to the four contracts mentioned and make such other investigations as further orders in council may require. Sir Wilfrid's motion was defeated by party vote. Sir William Meredith, Chief Justice of On-

tario, and Justice L. P. Duff, of the Supreme Court of Canada, are the commissioners.

The "Sussex" Question

The sinking of the "Sussex" seemed at first likely to bring to a head the dispute between Germany and the United States over the use of submarines, and it has been rumored from Washington that our government was about to break off diplomatic relations on the ground that Germany had violated her pledge not to attack liners without warning. But the evidence of German responsibility is not so complete as one would like if the case is to be made the ground for action leading to a severance of relations and possibly to war. In the first place nobody on board the "Sussex" saw a submarine or a periscope, altho it was in the afternoon of a clear day. The captain and several others, however, report having seen the wake of a torpedo a few seconds before the explosion. The captain when he saw this gave orders to swing the ship, but this was done too late to dodge it.

The "Sussex" was a regular packet steamer plying between Folkestone and Dieppe. She was unarmed and carried no munitions. There were aboard on the day of the disaster, March 24, about 350 passengers and a crew of fifty-three. Of these there were about fifty who lost their lives, among them many women and children. None of the Americans on board was killed, but two were badly wounded, George Crocker and Miss Elizabeth Baldwin, daughter of Professor Mark Baldwin, the psychologist.

Fragments of metal found on board the "Sussex" and supposed to come from the torpedo have been sent to Washington for examination. These are said to be of phosphor-bronze not used in any torpedoes than the German.

Against this evidence there is the positive denial of the German Government that the "Sussex" was sunk by a German torpedo. It is stated by Berlin that all the craft which might possibly have been involved in an attack on the "Sussex" have now reported, and that the reports of their commanders make it certain that no German submarine or warship is responsible.

The German Government denies that it has relaxed its rules to submarine commanders, and it reaffirms its responsibility in case its instructions are violated. Dr. Alfred Zimmermann, Under Secretary for Foreign Affairs, gave out on April 6 this statement as to Germany's policy:

If German submarines have made, or should make, an attack on unarmed and unresisting passenger steamers without warning their action would constitute an error in violation of the German Admiralty's explicit orders made in pursuance of her promise to the United States. In all cases of such errors Germany would not hesitate to accept the consequences and make all suitable amends.

The Chancellor's Speech   The address of Chancellor von Bethmann - Hollweg to the Reichstag is one of the most important official utterances of the war, since it bore upon such important questions as Germany's policy in regard to submarine warfare, the Monroe Doctrine and the future of Belgium and Poland. He began by a review of the military situation and showed what great gains had been made in Galicia, Russia, Serbia, Montenegro, Albania, Gallipoli and Asia since his Reichstag address of a year ago. He claimed that the food supply in most cases was sufficient and even tho the shortage of meat should lower its consumption to the level of the seventies, yet the Germans were strong in those days as their adversaries will remember.

He declared that neither Germany nor Austria-Hungary had intended to touch the Polish question, but since they had been forced into it they would see that neither the Poles, the Lithuanians nor the Livonians of the Baltic should ever be delivered into the hands of reactionary Russia. He denounced as "the silliest of imputations" the report that at the end of the war Germany intended to rush to America and conquer Canada, or had any intention of acquiring any territory in Brazil or any other part of America whatsoever.

On the submarine question he said:

No fair-minded neutral, no matter whether he favors us or not, can doubt our right to defend ourselves against this war of starvation, which is contrary to international law. No one can ask us to permit our arms of defense to be wrested from our hands. We use them, and must use them. We respect legitimate rights of neutral trade and commerce, but we have a right to expect that this will be appreciated, and that our right and our duty be recognized—to use all means against this policy of starvation, which is a jeering insult not only to all laws of nations, but also to the plainest duties of humanity.

An insurmountable obstacle to peace was the declaration by Premier Asquith that the Allies "shall never sheathe the sword . . . until the military domination of Prussia is wholly and finally destroyed." On this point the Chancellor said:

Let us suppose I suggest to Mr. Asquith to sit down with me at a table and examine the possibilities of peace, and Mr. Asquith begins with a claim of definitive and complete destruction of Prussia's military power. The conversation would be ended before it began. To these peace conditions only one answer would be left, and this answer our sword must give.

THE GREAT WAR

April 3—Parliament called upon to meet war expenses of $25,000,000 a day. General Smuts captures stronghold in German East Africa.

April 4—Germans take offensive on northern part of Russian front. British relief force within twenty-three miles of Kut-el-Amara.

April 5—German Chancellor discusses peace terms before Reichstag. Germans take village of Haucourt.

April 6—Zeppelin raid on England kills one child. Canadians repulse German attacks at St. Eloi.

April 7—Turks holding Russians northwest of Erzerum. British steamer "Kent" torpedoed, fifty drowned.

April 8—Austrian attack on Monte Nero repulsed by Italians. Holland strengthens army and defenses.

April 9—Germany denies sinking the "Sussex." French evacuate Bethincourt.

If our adversaries want to continue the slaughter of human beings and the devastation of Europe theirs will be the guilt, and we shall have to stand it as men.

German Peace Terms   The passages in the German Chancellor's speech which have attracted most attention are those in which he discusses the future of Belgium and the possibilities of peace. Since this is the first time the aims of Germany have been so definitely and officially formulated we quote his words:

We fight for our existence and for our future. For Germany and not for space in a foreign country are Germany's sons bleeding and dying on the battlefield. Every one among us knows this, and it makes our hearts and nerves so strong. This moral force strengthens our will in order not only to weather the storm, but also to achieve final victory.

Harding in Brooklyn Eagle

USED UP!

We have so often turned the other cheek to Germany that we may not have the face to do it again

Our enemies wish to destroy united, free Germany. They desire that Germany shall be again as weak as during past centuries, a prey of all lusts of domination of her neighbors and the scapegoat of Europe, beaten back forever in the dominion of economic evolution, even after the war. That is what our enemies mean when they speak of definite destruction of Prussia's military power.

And what is our intention? The sense and aim of this war is for us the creation of a Germany so firmly united, so strongly protected, that no one ever will feel the temptation to annihilate us, that every one in the world will concede to us the right of free exercise of our peaceful endeavors. This Germany, and not the destruction of other races, is what we wish. Our aim is the lasting rescue of the European continent, which is now shaken to its very foundations.

After the war there must be another Belgium. We must create real guarantees that Belgium shall never be a Franco-British vassal; never again shall be used as a military or economic fortification against Germany. Also in this respect things cannot be as they were before. Also here Germany cannot sacrifice the supprest Flemish race, but must assure for them sound evolution which corresponds to their rich natural gifts, which is based on their mother tongue and follows their Netherlandish character.

We want neighbors that do not form coalitions against us, but with whom we collaborate and who collaborate with us to our mutual advantage. Remembrance of this war will still echo in the sadly tried Belgian country, but we shall never allow that this will be a new source of wars—shall not allow it in our mutual interest.

Financing the War   The fourth popular loan for the support of the war in Germany brought in subscriptions amounting to over $2,500,000,000. The German Secretary of the Treasury, Dr. Karl Helfferich, announces with pride that:

Germany is the only belligerent power which has covered her total war expenditures by long term loans. That a nation of 70,000,000, cut off from the outer world by arbitrary acts in conflict with international law, should have borne for twenty months the heavy burden of the war, and should now again be offering to the Fatherland more than 10,000,000,000 marks, is proof of greatness beyond praise of words.

The ordinary expenses of the German Government exclusive of the military operations have risen from $875,-000,000 for the year 1913-1914 to $1,375,000,000 for the current year. Since the closing of the custom houses and the curtailment of industry have cut off a large part of the national revenue it has become necessary to resort to new taxation. This takes the form of an impost on profits ranging in the case of an individual from 5 to 25 per cent and in the case of a corporation from 10 to 30 per cent.

In France the total appropriations made from August 1, 1914, to July 1, 1916, will amount to $9,410,000,000, of which $7,400,000,000 is for military purposes. France has shared with England the burden of financing the lesser Allies. The Budget for the second quarter of 1916 includes $120,000,000 to Belgium, $33,000,000 to Serbia, $1,000,000 to Greece and $80,000 to Montenegro.

In Russia the cost of the war is reported as $4,000,000,000 in 1915 and $5,500,000,000 in 1916. The prohibition of vodka, formerly a government

Weed in Philadelphia Public Ledger
THE GRIST

Starrett in New York Tribune
THE HOLLAND BORDER
HOLLAND IS READY

Harding in Brooklyn Eagle
"I'M NO UNCLE SAM!"

monopoly, meant a loss in revenue of $345,000,000 a year, but according to the Minister of Finance this is more than compensated by the gains to the people from this compulsory temperance.

The expenditures of Great Britain for the army alone now amount to $15,000,000 a day. The number of articles of apparel such as tunics, boots, etc., provided for the army since the war began amounts to 117,000,000, and the military stores consumed would have sufficed the British army at its former strength for 140 years.

The Meaning of Verdun The German attack upon the entrenched camp of Verdun, the strongest of the French frontier fortresses, began on February 21 and has been actively pushed ever since. This, however, does not mean that the fighting has been incessant all along the line or at any one point. On the contrary, the point of attack has shifted from one sector of the great circle to another, while the rest of the line is quiescent except for occasional skirmishes and the almost constant artillery duels. The fact the Germans have not stuck to one point and followed up their advantage where they have gained one does not, as it is sometimes interpreted, indicate that their assault has failed and that they have given up hope of success at that point and so turned in despair to another. The conditions of modern warfare make it impossible to break thru a fortified line at a single point and then continue the advance indefinitely as might have been done formerly. On the contrary it is essential that the line of attack be kept as nearly straight or as smoothly curved as the nature of the ground will permit and both sides are constantly engaged in smoothing out—in their own interest—the line that separates them. Such instruments of reconnaissance as the aeroplane and the captive balloon and such instruments of communication as the telephone, the helio-

graph and the wireless have made a "surprize attack" on a large scale almost impossible, and with modern organization and railroad and motor transportation there need be no "weak point" of a fatal character. If, for instance a German column should by some chance have hit upon a poorly defended point and been able to advance a mile or so inside the French line, the troops would doubtless be recalled unless they happened to have secured some dominant position or there seemed some prospect of bringing up to them the attacking line on both sides. For a body of troops occupying such a salient is subjected to fire on right and left and front from artillery miles away over an accurately measured range and the troops would be in danger of being killed or cut off.

Besides this a modern battle must be intermittent because of the necessity of reinforcing and replacing the men at the front and bringing up a new supply of ammunition to replenish the enormous waste. Even with the best of transportation facilities it is impossible to accumulate enough shells in advance at a given point and move them forward rapidly enough to allow of a continuous advance even against ineffectual opposition.

Now in the battle of Verdun the element of surprize has not entered except possibly in the first onslaught when the Germans within a few days advanced nearly four miles and took the fort of Douaumont. The French, at any rate, have made no mistakes but have stoutly contested every foot of ground, for they are supplied with plenty of ammunition and with artillery which is the admiration of their enemies. But this very fact makes the German attack seem all the more alarming. If the French, for all their skill and courage, are constantly being driven out of their entrenched positions, what assurance have they that the Germans will not eventually reach Verdun?

This assurance they find in the Ger-

man losses, and they believe that it will be impossible for the Germans to keep up the attack much longer. A semi-official estimate emanating from Paris gives the number of German troops which have been brought against Verdun as 450,000 and their casualties up to April 1 as more than 200,000. Such losses are indeed unprecedented in the history of warfare and certainly Germany could not afford to pay such a rate for the five miles which they have yet to make before they get to Verdun.

The Germans on the other hand claim that their losses are not excessive. Certainly they manifest no external evidences of discouragement and they still continue to gain, tho slowly. Last week they took the village of Haucourt, which lies just south of Malancourt. They also stormed the ridge beyond, capturing over a mile of French trenches and 714 unwounded prisoners. Their next objective in this quarter is probably Hill 304, which stands next to Le Mort Homme, still claimed by both sides. The French have been obliged to evacuate their salient at Bethincourt to avoid being cut off and to straighten their line.

The Battle of St. Eloi It is believed that the Germans have more troops massed in front of the British lines in Flanders than they have at Verdun and it is surmised that they may intend to make their main offensive in the west instead of on the Meuse. So far the chief center of activity on the west has been at the village of St. Eloi near the famous Belgian city of Ypres. Here the Canadians are posted and have made themselves conspicuous by their skill in tunneling and their daring in following up the vantage gained by their mine explosions. On March 27 they blew up the front trenches of the German line and establisht themselves in the craters. Ever since then the Germans have been trying to dislodge the Canadians from their crater forts but they have only succeeded in regaining one of them.

THE UNITED STATES MUST FIGHT

BY SYDNEY BROOKS

THERE are, roughly, four ways in which the present war can be brought to an end. First, peace would come speedily if the United States entered the conflict. Secondly, it would come more speedily still if a British defeat at sea destroyed the pivot of the whole Alliance. Thirdly, in the judgment of some good observers, the military force is to be so quickened, and we are destined during the spring and summer to see such terrific slaughter on all the fronts, that hostilities will be over by the winter thru the sheer exhaustion of the combatants. Fourthly—and this perhaps is the general British view—there is nothing for it but to go on killing German soldiers and applying the maximum of economic pressure to the German people until the military authorities are convinced by their losses in men and the civilians by their privations that the strain can no longer be maintained. When that point will be reached is, of course, a matter rather of guesswork than of mathematical calculation. Personally I do not see how the process of attrition can by itself end the war before the autumn of 1917.

Of these four alternatives the intervention of the United States is the only one I am at present concerned with. For myself I have not the slightest doubt that you are coming into the war. That is not the view that is most widely held in England. The vast majority of my countrymen neither expect American intervention nor desire it, except on one condition, that it proceed from America's own conception of her highest and final interests in this matter. There has never that I know of been any disposition in England to quarrel with or to criticize the official policy of neutrality adopted at Washington. At the beginning of the war neutrality was the obviously proper and sensible line for the United States to follow. Every one in Great Britain admitted as much; no one contemplated anything else. There was, it is true, some good-humored surprise when the President attempted to expand the program of official neutrality into a rule of private thought and conduct; but to neutrality itself, as the policy of the United States Government, nobody took or could take the slightest objection. The war was not an American war; the issues at stake were not specifically American issues; there seemed every reason to hope that the United States could hold honorably aloof.

102

There is no need to introduce Mr. Brooks to Independent readers. But this article—with its sharp and disquieting forecast of America's entry into the Great War—is more than the mere expression of an observant journalist's opinion, colored by the natural hope of an Englishman that the United States will aid the Allies. In the last few weeks Mr. Brooks has had exceptional opportunities to learn from American officials and public men just what trend affairs are taking, and what he has to say on the subject merits serious and thoughtful consideration.—THE EDITOR.

Nor even now would any Englishman desire to see America drawn into it, except, as I have said, under the constraint of purely American interests and in order to fulfil her own idea of what her honor, her dignity and her duty as one of the great pillars of democracy demand. Were the United States on her own initiative to throw in her lot with the Allies, then, indeed, every Englishman would hail her advent into the arena with a great shout of joy, would feel that the dearest wish of his heart had been realized in the mere fact of a working coöperation between all the English-speaking peoples, would say—and would be right in saying—that now at last the only possible foundations of a lasting peace had been well and truly laid. But that, as every one in Britain recognizes, is a matter for Americans to decide in their own way and at their own time. From first to last in this war I do not think you will be able to point to a single line in the British press or a single utterance of any British statesman that savored of the impertinence of urging the United States to abandon her neutrality or that tendered any advice whatever on the subject.

IF America is satisfied to remain outside, we in England are content to have her do so. We do not need the naval or military assistance of the United States to win this war. We can and we shall save civilization, if we have to, without her. For themselves the Allies want nothing from America beyond what their command of the seas enables them at this moment to receive—arms, food, raw material, equipment of all kinds; and in regard to many of these necessaries they will very soon be independent of any sources of supply but their own. We do not seek American intervention for our

own sakes; we are confident we can dispense with it; at the same time if it came we should passionately welcome it—not for its effect on the present war alone, but because we should see in America's emergence into the world as an Ally among Allies the one sure and certain guarantee of future peace.

BUT there are different kinds of neutrality and it would be absurd to pretend that the kind adopted by the United States Government has met with universal acceptance in England. There is a large and sober body of British opinion, friendly to the United States by instinct and conviction, that has found American diplomacy during the past year and a half a difficult pill to swallow.

If I were asked for a summary of what in British eyes have appeared to be its deficiencies I should point to the speech delivered by Mr. Root on February 15. Englishmen have rightly refrained from saying the things that Mr. Root as an American was free to say. Indeed one of the pleasantest surprises that awaits an English visitor to the United States these days is to discover how mild is British dissatisfaction with the foreign policy of the Administration, and in what scrupulously temperate language it finds utterance, as compared with the full-blooded ferocity of American comment. But it seems clear to me that Mr. Root and the general run of Englishmen approach this question from approximately the same angle. Both feel that in what has been done and left undone at Washington there has been a failure to embody and interpret the best American sentiment. Both feel that it is the American people themselves and not the Allies who have the most cause to complain of and to be chagrined by the Administration's acts of commission and omission.

But it would be very easy to exaggerate the extent to which British opinion has thereby been adversely affected. Toward the American people there is thruout the British Isles, and there will continue to be, nothing but the utmost friendliness and sympathy. We know how many thousands of Americans have enlisted in the Allied armies. We know of their work in succoring the wounded. We know of that increasing stream of gifts in money and kindly service that flows eastward from the United States. And above all we know that the heart of America is with us. Knowing all this we do not allow trivial clashes of opinion between our respective governments to disturb us unduly. Rightly or wrongly we distinguish between popular sentiment in the United States and official neutrality. We are not blind to President Wilson's difficulties. Some of us, I imagine, make even greater allowance for them than do his own countrymen. If at times the actions and attitude of the American Government have disconcerted us it has not been solely, or even mainly, on our own account. It has been because those actions and that attitude have struck us as falling below our ideal of what the United States is and stands for. We have no specific grievances against Washington. We retain to the full that goodwill toward America and Americans that is now an inseparable element not merely of British policy, but of the British consciousness. The only thing that infuriates us is to hear Americans say, as I have often heard them say, that the events of the past eighteen months have left the United States without a single friend in Europe. The United States will always have a close friend and a faithful friend in England. And at a crisis, if America ever finds herself in a tight corner, that friendship will not be found wanting. Even in the convulsive fluidity of world-politics as they are today and as they are likely to continue for some time to come, that at least is a fixed and stable point.

ON what then do I base my conviction that you must shortly enter the war? I base it on the inherent conditions of the case. The last hope of reaching any satisfactory agreement with Germany on the issues of submarine warfare has by now, I should imagine, been pretty well exploded. No one can any longer cling to it. No one in Washington does cling to it. It has gone down in a welter of broken pledges and repudiated assurances. Germany, it is perfectly obvious, intends to go on torpedoing all the merchant vessels that her submarines can get at, armed or unarmed, and wholly irrespective of the nationality of the passengers on board. Any day an incident may happen comparable to Villa's raid on Columbus. Any day you may be forced into the European war as you have been forced into Mexico, reluctantly, in spite of yourselves, as the result of some intolerable outrage. You have suffered in the last eighteen months at Germany's hands a series of unexampled affronts and you have suffered them with unexampled patience. But there are limits to American patience. Villa overstepped them. Germany

likewise will overstep them. It may be tomorrow, it may be next week or the week after, but that eventually, and before very long, Mr. Wilson will have no option but to hand Count Bernstorff his passports and recall Mr. Gerard from Berlin is, in my judgment, beyond question. And that sooner or later means war.

AMERICANS have frequently said to me, "Are we not doing a greater service to the Allies by staying out of the war than we should be doing by coming in?" They are thinking chiefly of the supply of munitions and of the inevitable demands upon the domestic output if the United States were to raise an army on the European scale. Well, I have seen more than a little of what America is doing in the way of munitions, and it commands my immense gratitude, my unbounded admiration. The way in which, under the direction of Messrs. Morgan & Co., American manufacturers have been organized for the production of war material, and the zeal and efficiency with which they have thrown themselves into the industry, are a record of which every American might well be proud. At the same time only the fringe of the country's industrial resources has been brought into play and under government encouragement and control the output could be increased well-nigh indefinitely. That is one consideration. Another is that the British Government, British manufacturers and the British workingmen by magnificent efforts have by now all but made good our original deficiencies and that the Allies before long will be comparatively independent of American shells, guns, rifles and cartridges. I always therefore beg my American friends who are apprehensive on the score of munitions not to be deterred from entering the war on that account; and I always add that the participation of the United States, by its effect on such neutrals as are still hesitating, by its shattering demonstration of the final impossibility of a Teutonic triumph, and by its immediate easing of the Allied financial situation, would be a commanding asset, and more than any other single factor, always excepting the almost unthinkable contingency of the destruction of the British seapower, would shorten the war. Work out the effects of a proclamation by President Wilson calling for the enlistment of 1,000,000 men and of another proclamation placing the entire engineering trade of the country under government direction and dedicating it to the production of munitions, and the enormous importance

to all the belligerents of American intervention will be very soon apparent.

But if I were an American I should like to see my country enter the war not to avenge the loss of American lives, not to reinforce the Allies, not to ward off the menace to American political and strategical interests that is implicit on a German victory, but on other and wider and nobler grounds. I should like to see it enter the war, first of all, on the score of humanity and in the sure knowledge that American intervention would lessen, and possibly avert, the most appalling slaughter, the most hideous mass of waste and misery, that ever threatened to devastate the world. I should like to see it enter the war, secondly, because democracy is at death-grips with militarism and absolutism and because every principle of right-dealing between nations, and, indeed, the whole form and temper of civilization, are at stake in the struggle. I should like it, finally, to enter the war because only by so doing can the United States help to start the world on a new and saner path and to erect and support an enduring fabric of peace.

PEACE, democracy, humanity— no nation every had a nobler call to arms than these causes. As an Englishman, who has loved and studied and done what he could to interpret America for the past twenty years, I refuse to share the misgivings and lamentations of many of my American friends. I believe that the great issues I have named are powerful to touch the conscience and idealism of the American people. I believe that in no land is a leader who appeals to what is best and least material and most self-sacrificing in human nature more certain of a national response. I believe that the fundamental passion of America is to serve the world at whatever cost to herself. But there never has been in all history such an opportunity for service as now, or so clear and insistent a summons to the faith and vision of American statesmanship—the aspiring spirit of the American people. You will come into the war in any event. What I hope and pray is that you may not drift into it on some minor and merely national pretext and with incoherent aims, but will take your stand deliberately as befits the splendor of the American nation proclaiming its resolve to rescue humanity, to safeguard democracy, and to lay broad and deep the foundations of future peace.

New York City

THE WESTERN GATEWAY TO
FROM SOSA HILL ONE GETS A VIEW OF THE PACIFIC ENTRANCE TO THE PANAMA CANAL FROM BALBO
IS THE PRADO, AN ASPHALTIC CONCRETE DRIVE BETWEEN A DOUBLE ROW OF NEW
LIKELY TO BECOME ONE OF THE WORLD'S GREAT SHIPPING PORTS.

LANTIC OCEAN IS REOPENED

FIRST LOCKS AT MIRAFLORES, THE ADMINISTRATION BUILDING IS IN THE CENTER AND TO THE LEFT
WHICH WILL FORM THE NUCLEUS OF THE FUTURE CITY OF BALBOA, WHICH SEEMS
WAS REOPENED ON APRIL 15 AND IS AGAIN READY FOR BUSINESS

PERNICIOUS HEIRLOOMS

BY MARTHA BENSLEY BRUÈRE

With this article Mrs. Bruère ends the series of studies of "The Habits of Women Under Domestication," which was begun in The Independent on March 20.—THE EDITOR.

DOES a frog serenely sunning himself, drawing dry air into a newly acquired pair of lungs, choosing luxuriously which one of four available legs he shall scratch himself with, have any of the habits of his recent gray-green world where a cold fluid surged thru his gill slits and he was all bulbous head and vibrant tail? Sometimes he does bring a bit of his tadpole appendage to land, but that is a purely material hang-over and soon discarded. If he brings tadpole habits will they not make him a less efficient frog? Will not a tadpole mind hamper him more than a tadpole tail?

Almost as suddenly as a frog passes from water to land, we have passed from the old civilization, where for the race as a whole there was not enough of anything, to the new time where, thanks to machine production, scientific agriculture, quick transportation, and especially to the rise of the democratic ideal, there can be enough for every one. And we—the women especially, who thru domestication were very perfectly adapted to the earlier stage of privation—have brought over into the age of prosperity a vast number of possessions. The actual material heirlooms are not a serious menace. Great-grandfather's clock does not greatly hamper us unless it prevents our buying a new and more accurate timepiece. But under the slow civilization that was controlled by a perpetual community deficit, women acquired the appropriate habits of toil, economy, self-sacrifice, an incredible patience, and a fixity of mind which mitigated the pressure; and they are still trailing these hampering tadpole habits and ideals. Most terrible of all, they still have minds set in the mold of another civilization, to which our modern working hypothesis, that all change is probably good, is quite incomprehensible.

It would seem that only thru youth are women able to free themselves from this backward drag. Then, while they can feel the pull of the future, things are not good or desirable to them because they have always been, but because they are about to be. Instead of memories, they are governed by hopes. They are plastic things, and for this reason they are able to do the work of a fast changing civilization—able to learn the governing conditions of the new age of plenty and act on them—able, so long as they are young, to beat back their inheritances.

Shall not a frog remain a frog? If women are to give their full value to this modern world, they must learn to keep at least so much of youth as its plasticity, in order that they may adapt themselves to the continual change which is the governing factor of the civilization of prosperity. But to remain plastic requires the most unceasing vigilance, the firm refusal to take any tradition for granted, even that of our own personal experience, and most particularly to avoid accepting heirlooms of thought and practise in what is still woman's most common occupation—housekeeping. For there is no more insistent beckoning to a fixed mind than domestication. It was under the controlling power of a perpetual social deficit that our whole theory and practise of housekeeping was developed, and it is in that field that pernicious inheritances have us most closely entangled. To realize that the past is dead—all of it—is practically impossible till we have learned to think in terms of change rather than permanence. And even while we are acting on this knowledge, the dead world mysteriously rises ready to "set" our minds again like jelly in a mold!

Quite recently I fought with this ghost as raised by an antiquated household equipment — treasured heirlooms lovingly preserved. Without the possibility of rescue I was dropt into a white cottage on a hillside, and housework, which had been under my feet, rose up and attacked me. From the time when I started the wood stove in the morning, thru all the sweeping and cleaning, cooking and sewing of the day, my mind had to adjust itself to machinery developed on the basic concept of saving everything but human work. The heirlooms from the civilization of poverty and self-sacrifice produced the inoperative mind which was content to endure them. The potatoes for Monday, for Tuesday, for Wednesday, all equally bulbous, equally brown and susceptible of the same number of ways of cooking, were kept in an ancestral bin where it was best for them, but not most convenient for me. The lingering routine of bringing water from the well offered after the first time no mental stimulus whatever; neither did

sweeping out the corners of the same rooms with the same broom, or scrubbing the dirt from the same shirtwaists on the same washboard in the same tub. The combination of all these monotonies made up a stifling routine that filled the day; and which, with that equipment, there was no avoiding.

It was not that the work was hard —to run a typewriter all day is more fatiguing; it was not the isolation; it was the fact that there was no new use for my brain in these changeless surroundings; nothing for it to do but become fixed. By just so much as I grew to do these things without change, did change become more difficult for me. If I had stayed there long enough I would have reverted to the past and become unable to fit into modern civilization.

I knew once a little Swedish woman, who, having been taught housekeeping by her mother, who was very poor, could never be brought to beat eggs with anything more efficient than a fork. Her mind had "set" so that she could not think in terms of even a hand driven egg-beater, much less of an electric one. And because her inherited ideas, formed under the stress of poverty, would not let her do housework in the most efficient way—would not in fact, permit her to let go of most of the details of it —she was less valuable as a housekeeper and a human being than she might have been. Her inherited training had fossilized her mind.

If we could only act on the theory that anything left to us from the past, whether an idea or a thing, has got to prove its present value before we accept it, and that anything new has got to prove itself worthless before we pass it by, we might stay these ossifying mental processes.

For it is obvious that our work of family conservation cannot be performed by antiquarians. We can do nothing for the families of the past; our work is in the present, for the future, and it cannot be performed by inherited mental processes or by machinery designed for dead occupations. We are working our civilization out in a new set of interchangeable parts, and the attempt to use old ones makes the whole run wobbly. It is important to realize that if an idea or a habit was inevitable in great-grandmother, it is better dispensed with by her descendants, and to act on the conviction that if a habit was perfectly adapted to the needs of a tadpole it is by that very fact unadapted to the needs of a frog.

New York City

CLIMBING THE ROCKIES BY ELECTRICITY

A LONG STEP TOWARD A NEW ERA OF RAILROADING

OVER the Rockies by electricity! That is possible, now that the biggest piece of railroad electrification on the continent has been completed by the Chicago, Milwaukee and St. Paul Railway.

Four hundred and forty miles of track, from Harlowton, Montana, to Avery, Idaho, clean thru the three ridges that make up the Rockies, over the back of the continent at a hight of 6300 feet, have been prepared for the heavy electric tractors that will displace the steam locomotives. Already 115 miles are in operation, between Three Forks and Dear Lodge—the section which includes the Continental Divide.

The electric locomotives draw heavier trains, at higher speed, than the old ones, over grades where the line climbs as much as 115½ feet in a mile. They are leviathans; each weighing 284 tons, with a length of 112 feet 8 inches. Each is more than 10 per cent more powerful than the modern Mallet steam locomotive. Mountain streams, with their tremendous head of water, are tapped at various points in Montana to create the current. The railroad buys its power from the Montana Power Company, which has its main plant at Great Falls. Fourteen sub-stations along the railroad receive the electricity in 100,000-volt alternating current, reduce it from 100,000 to 2300 volts, still alternating current, and then by the use of motor-generator sets at each sub-station, consisting of one alternating current motor driving two direct current generators, change it to a direct current of 3000 volts. This is nearly six times the voltage used in ordinary street railway work.

So much for the way the trains climb the mountains. But they behave surprisingly as they slip down the other side. The motion of the train as it slides down hill is used to make the reversed motors generate more electricity. This serves as a braking system, so that the air-brake is not needed except for emergency or to stop the train, and new current is actually turned back into the trolley wires to be used as needed by other trains. From a quarter to a half of the current used up on one side of the mountains is thus restored on the other side by "regenerative braking."

Why should steam give way to the new power?

For many reasons — all lumped under the familiar term "efficiency." It is cheaper—you get more power for your money. When a steam locomotive stops at a station or at a division point where locomotives are changed, it goes right on burning coal; it uses indeed 80 per cent of the fuel that it requires when it is at work drawing the train. The electric locomotive uses power only when it moves. The steam locomotive loses heat—and hence power—in cold weather. The electric works better then than at any other time and has power enough to buck the heaviest snowdrifts. The old engine had to be inspected and groomed at the end of each division—every hundred miles or so. The new one runs a thousand miles without needing inspection. Coal has to be hauled; electricity requires no fuel trains. The electric train is clean, noiseless, "jerkless." Electrifying one track, the railroad officials believe, will increase the efficiency of the mountain division as much as tho the line had been double-tracked.

THE GIANT OIL SWITCHES
The current under the enormous pressure of 100,000 volts is controlled by oil insulation

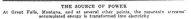

THE SOURCE OF POWER
At Great Falls, Montana, and at several other points, the mountain streams' accumulated energy is transformed into electricity

CONCENTRATE!

BY EDWARD EARLE PURINTON

DIRECTOR OF THE INDEPENDENT EFFICIENCY SERVICE

TO every one of the boons of life, the short cut is concentration. No matter what the goal ahead of us may be, the first step is to find and follow the path of concentration. Out of the blind thicket of human destiny, that surrounds, tangles and impedes the great majority of us, the one clear, open, swift way to freedom is the path of concentration. What do you need most? Health—money—power—leisure—friends—counsellors—advantages—opportunities? Learn to concentrate, and whatever you need most will come to you. The law never fails.

I am not talking metaphysics. Indeed my first duty is to rescue the word *concentration* from the mouths of metaphysicians. Nowadays nearly every city in America has a fluttering bevy of self-styled metaphysical teachers who would, for a suitable honorarium, induce you to "practise concentration" by sitting vague and vapid in a "concentration class," or fixing a rapt gaze on a crystal ball, or doing some other fancy exhibition stunt. This brand of concentration is not the one I am writing about.

Suppose you are riding east, on a New Jersey road, fifty miles out of New York. You meet a man walking west. He is gaunt, begrimed, unshaven, unwashed. He hobbles on a twisted cane. His clothes are torn. He looks the picture of hunger, friendlessness and woe.

You are moved with pity. You stop and ask him, "Why so forlorn?" He answers, "I have no friends, no money and no food." You ask him, "Where are you going?" He answers, "I don't know." You ask h'm, "Why did you leave the city?" He answers, "I forget the reason just now." You ask him, "How long are you going on like this?" He answers, "Till I drop from weariness or fall ill—then some one may give me a lift." What do you do? You buy the man a meal, ring up the police station, have him taken to the psychopathic ward of the nearest hospital, and try to locate his relatives or friends.

On the road of destiny the average man is walking west. In the mental geography on the map of his mind, he is aimless and powerless as a ragged, starving tramp. He hobbles on a twisted cane of tradition, habit or misinformation. He hasn't enough mental food to keep him nourished—and most of what he has wouldn't pass a pure food inspector. He follows a rut of routine, looking neither ahead nor above. His psychic raiment

is mud and tatters. His moral expression is meaningless, like that of a man with a wandering mind. He does not know where he is going, or why he is going anywhere. He is waiting for some one to give him a lift—or send him to a hospital. Why all this vacuity, poverty, tragedy, in the life journey of the average man? *Loss of the power, loss of the path, of concentration.*

Is the picture overdrawn? From reading thousands of letters, by men like this, I say it is not. Four persons out of five that you meet are mentally and spiritually lost. They have never found themselves, nor their place and work in life. Lacking a goal, they lack the grit and gumption that a man with a goal has to get. Their actions, thoughts and emotions are at loose ends—kite tails flying in the breeze. A man's career is but the measure of his concentration.

WHAT DOES IT MEAN?

LET us define our word. Concentration is the science of knowing what we want most to do, have and be; the art of achieving it; and the habit of forgetting it.

The prime essential is a fixed goal. A good example here is the racing crew of a big eastern university. Every member of the crew knows just where he must end the race and land the boat; he has learned to time his stroke to the fraction of a second; he has stripped away every ounce of superfluous clothing—he has for weeks lived on simple fare selected by science; he has fully mastered the principles and methods of team work.

Just where am I going to be at the end of the race of life—or five, or ten, or twenty years from now? Have I a definite picture of the goal in my mind? Have I chosen, and proved, the shortest, easiest and best way to that goal? Am I working every day, every hour, with this in view? Are all the useless things left behind? Is every act in working hours properly, regularly timed, so that my daily output is sure to equal my maximum? Do all my habits of life speed me on to my goal—or do some of them handicap me? Is every one of my working associates eager to help me win? If not, why not—and where am I now? Have I advanced all that was possible? Have others advanced more? Do I know the causes of my slowness in progressing? How shall I remove the obstacles, in my surroundings and myself? These are a few of the questions for every alert

man or woman to face bravely and settle fairly, as initial steps on the road of concentration.

Before one attempts to concentrate, he should have his greatest, finest, strongest desire shape and designate the exact goal that he would reach thru concentration. Then he should line up his present system of work, thought, and home life with his ultimate goal, to such an extent that he can see how every move he takes puts him forward. Then he should make his will a power so firm, prompt, resistless, that he does precisely and fully whatever he sets out to do. Then, he is prepared to learn to concentrate. A difficult program? Surely, and gladly. What are we here for if not to face hard jobs with a smile? What keeps a man small is the habit of looking for easy things.

There is, however, a shorter, easier way. Few people have learned how to plan, foresee, and lay out their lives, from here and now to the larger place ahead. It will suffice, temporarily, to learn to concentrate by doing our daily work—whatever it is, more thoroly, quickly, easily, and thoughtfully. Suppose, for example, you are a stenographer. Your first concentration exercize will be to make every letter, manuscript and memorandum *perfect*—so as not to waste a moment of your chief's time in the location and correction of your mistakes. When you have made every piece of work faultless during a whole day, try it for two days—three days—a week. Having attained a perfect record for a week, you can then focus on speed. Without losing in accuracy, you should be able to gain perhaps thirty per cent in rapidity, merely by ceaseless practise in mental and manual concentration. There are new books and systems to aid you here. Find them, and study them. Your next object will naturally be an easier way of doing the work you have made better and faster. Modifications of scientific management, and service departments of the large typewriter companies, should save you needless motions and responsibilities. Then you may begin to *think for your company*, especially in relation to your desk and departments, for increasing the sales and decreasing the costs. Now if you are an ordinary stenographer, you have never practised *any* of these four kinds of concentration exercize—that is why you remain an ordinary stenographer. Promotion follows concentration.

EFFICIENCY CONCENTRATION TEST

FOR ANY MAN OR WOMAN BETWEEN
15 AND 55 YEARS OF AGE

DIRECTIONS. Read first this article. If any point is not clear, talk it over with some friend who is a logical, deep thinker. On the basis of the article, interpret and answer the following questions. Where the answer is Yes, write numeral 10 in blank space on dotted line. Where the answer is No, leave space between 1 and 10 expressing degree of assurance. Don't favor yourself—make each numeral too low rather than too high. Add column of numerals for your percentage in concentration, so far as the test goes. This test shows the general aim of Mr. Purinton's efficiency work—to apply to every one, starting with himself, the rules and principles followed by the world's leaders in attaining their goal. On this test, the grade of a really big man or woman would be perhaps eighty per cent, while that of the average person might be not more than twenty-five per cent. If your grade, honestly reckoned, is 40 or 50 per cent, you are probably ahead of the majority, but still far behind the leaders.

1. Have you a great ultimate achievement, based on your talents, clearly pictured in mind for ten or twenty years hence? ....

2. Do you know how to work toward your goal, and is every day's work put minutely in line with your advancement? ....

3. Have you a surplus of energy, so that you are never tired, vexed or despondent?................. ......

4. Can you think or work so hard, five hours at a stretch, that you forget to eat or sleep or answer the door-bell? ....

5. Do you spend at least a half hour every day in planning your future, studying your work, and improving yourself? ....

6. Is your earning capacity regularly increasing at a substantial rate? ....

7. Have you read at least two modern books on the principles and methods of concentration?............ ......

8. Have you learned how to make use of all the functions of your mind?............................ ......

9. Do you always tackle the hardest job first, and choose hard jobs in preference to easy ones?.......... ......

10. Are you so sure of final success that nothing and nobody can discourage you; and when everything seems to go wrong, you calmly forge ahead with even greater strength and determination?...... ......

Copyright, 1916, by
Edward Earle Purinton

Total equals your approximate grade in
the knowledge and use of concentration.

Lloyd-George has become the first man of England. Apparently the war crisis made him such; but really his own concentration habits made him. He was a poor, alien boy, without friends, influence or opportunity. Worse—he was violently opposed by the political, financial and ecclesiastical authorities who froze careers with a frown. But only fluid minds can be frozen, and Lloyd-George had his mind set. He resolved to know what were the great problems of the nation, and how they could be solved. Nothing else mattered. Anything materializes when nothing else matters. And the first place in the realm was given the man who had given the realm first place in his thought.

All great men are masters of concentration. And any man will be great when he has learned to be master of concentration. The texture of the brain counts for little. The size of the brain counts for less; the *use* of the brain counts for the measure of human power. Concentration is merely intensive farming of the mind; and what the scientific farmer can do for and with his crops, the scientific thinker can do for and with his thoughts. We have today the new agriculture, we shall have tomorrow the new menticulture. The barren mind, as the barren field, is merely one that has not been cultivated. And the output of any mind, as of any field, can be doubled by the right methods of cultivation.

A number of books now available discuss the metaphysical side of concentration more or less truthfully and impressively. But the majority of these neglect the practical side. Out of perhaps fifty fundamental factors in the science and art of concentration, I would here dwell briefly on ten of the most important. If you incorporate only these ten in your daily habit of thought, work and life, you should eventually double your power of mind—and your productivity, happiness and usefulness.

WHAT YOU NEED

FIRST. *A focus of taste and talent.* Always concentrate on something you want to do, and may reasonably hope to do well in course of time. There is a group of things, different but related, which every man or woman could perform with unusual skill when trained and experienced. Learn your vocational group of inherent possibilities, and confine to this group your exercizes in concentration. The prime focus of our will should be our work; and our work, to succeed, must literally be ourselves. It is not true, as we are told by certain peddlers of metaphysics, that we can always be what we mean to be. It is true that we can be what we were meant to be! The first move in concentration is to find what we were meant to be.

2. *A clear, firm and useful ambition, both ultimate and immediate.*

Have you learned how to use mental photography? The world's most powerful camera is the human mind; a picture of our desired achievement there scientifically produced will outlive and outreach a hundred photographs of our face by a mechanical instrument. The purpose of concentration is creation; therefore we must know exactly what we want to create, what motive is back of it, what use ahead of it. To concentrate without a present object is to cheat your client or employer; to concentrate without a future object is to cheat yourself. Haphazard work is the universal bane, whether in commerce, education or religion.

3. *A surplus of energy, and control of the sources of vitality.* The mind that creates must be a self-renewing dynamo of impelling, animating, electrifying thought. Physical health is the basis. Whether you put your whole self into your brain and evolve a masterpiece of music or invention, or whether you put your whole self into your fingers and weave a rare fabric or weld a steel frame of a thirty-story building, your power of concentration depends on how healthy you are. Get a physique, or your mind will crack under the strain of prolonged, intense concentration, which to a master worker ends in exhaustion. You must eat and bathe and exercize and sleep with vitality in view. You can't live an ordinary life and do extraordi-

109

nary work. Have you developed a satisfactory system of creating and conserving your maximum of energy?

4. *A regular concentration habit, both mental and manual.* When you lie in bed a few weeks, you can hardly walk. To walk right, you must walk every day. So, to think right, you must think every day; and toward a given point, as you walk. If a man started for the postoffice, then decided to go to church, then got a notion to visit the blacksmith shop, and finally went home without reaching anywhere, you would call him feeble-minded. Yet the whole thought-world is a realm of wandering minds—we merely do not see them wander. Can you think so hard on a plan or purpose or piece of work that you forget to eat and sleep, don't know whether it is today, yesterday or tomorrow, and feel concern about nothing in the universe but the all-absorbing thing you are doing? If you can, you are on the road to somewhere; if you can't, you are a mental and moral idler, with an empty future like your empty past.

Learn to spend at least a half-hour each day fostering and strengthening your life purpose, by a period of intense, original, constructive thought on the best and quickest ways of reaching your goal. And form the habit of doing *everything* promptly, thoroly, scientifically. When I throw a fistful of discarded papers at the waste-basket, and the wad fails to hit, I get up and walk over and place the consignment where it belongs. Not to be neat, bless your heart—a man too neat is an unmanly mixture of ladylikeness and nothingness; but rather to keep in trim the wholesome habit of hitting what I aim for.

5. *A proper observance of time and place.* For concentration of mind the best time seems the early morning, when brain is clearest, body strongest. And the best place is wherever you can be in silence and solitude. Great thoughts are crushed by the crowd. But for concentration of *body*, the turmoil of business competition seems required—in their manual skill men are naturally gregarious.

6. *A punctilious regard to the physiology of thought.* The brain is mostly blood. Hence a copious and ready supply of rich, pure blood is the first essential to powerful thought. Do not try to concentrate when physically tired, or less than two hours after a full meal. Give brain and nerve foods a large place in your diet. Learn to think at home in a bathrobe and sandals—every bit of tight clothing serves to congest the blood and retard its passage to the brain. Consider also the matter of posture; lie flat if that helps you to think hard.

7. *A systematic study of practical psychology.* A thinker must know the mind as an electrical engineer knows the dynamo, not for the sake of the theoretical knowledge, but so as to get the greatest service out of the mechanism.

8. *A balanced life.* The strain of holding the mind on a tension must be offset by frequent periods of absolute relaxation; with such aids to carefreeness as music, a romp with the children, a bit of gardening, or a long tramp. The ordinary man must learn to be a firebrand—the extraordinary man must learn to be a vegetable. Kindly, however, do not try to be a vegetable until you know you are a firebrand, as the supply of human vegetables now gluts the market.

9. *A dauntless perseverance.* You may need forty years to work out your life purpose. What of it? The holding of the purpose makes you strong, and that is really the mission of the purpose. Ten thousand obstacles may hinder you. No matter—the fiends plague and fates besiege only the man of power. You are stronger than they, as soon as you know you are. Even your old friends may turn from you, misunderstand you, join against you, as you fare on and up. Keep smiling—new and better friends are waiting. Everything you try to do may seem to go wrong, and whelm you in failure—only that you may learn to survive success thru learning to survive failure.

10. *A never-failing fund of optimism.* The road of concentration, as you may have surmized, is not necessarily a boulevard of roses. But the real people travel here, and the real rewards lie ahead on this road. Besides, this road gets easier and easier, while the road of inertia gets harder and harder. A man doesn't know what life is for till he tries to do something his neighbors say can't be done. Concentration is the science of removing the word "can't" from the mind. When this has been performed—this necessary operation on the intellect—such a new array of opportunities will be manifest that no pessimist can live in their presence. Accordingly we say: Become an optimist now, that you may feel at home with the triumphant workers when they gather at the goal of their ambitions. Only the optimist *sees* opportunities. And the road of concentration is the world's highway of opportunities.

SEE THE ROYAL FAMILY!

BY ELLIS O. JONES

SEE and behold the Royal Family! Yes. What a scrumptious, effulgent and withal perfectly useless Royal Family it is. What is the Royal Family doing?

The Royal Family is regaling itself with a certain form of mortal combat called war. That is to say, the Royal Family is fighting.

Ah, but is it not unseemly and altogether *infra dig* for the Royal Family to fight?

Oh, but you must remember that the Royal Family does not engage in the fight *in propria persona.*

No? How can that be?

The Royal Family would no more think of doing its own fighting than of shining its own shoes or currying its own horses or running its own automobile or buttoning itself up the back.

How then does the Royal Family get its fighting done?

By the use of a carefully selected body of men called soldiers and sailors.

Whenever a Royal Family picks a quarrel with some other Royal Family, it is only necessary to order out these carefully drilled soldiers and sailors and have them shoot each other with great zeal, vigor and diligence.

But isn't it rather difficult to get men to engage in such a dangerous occupation?

Not at all. It is very easy. Of all the occupations under the sun, that of soldiers and sailors is the poorest paid and they are usually ill treated into the bargain.

It is incredible. How long has it been that way?

It has been that way for a very long time.

How long will it be that way?

As long as hard-working citizens cherish the notion that idle Royal Families are worth fighting for.

New York City

Take a
KODAK
with you.

EASTMAN KODAK COMPANY,

Catalog free at your dealer's, or by mail.   ROCHESTER, N. Y., *The Kodak City.*

SHALL WE SWAP?

SOME COMMENTS ON THE PROPOSAL TO EXCHANGE THE PHILIPPINES FOR THE BRITISH TROPICAL POSSESSIONS

IN describing his visit to British Guiana in our issue of February 28, Edwin E. Slosson suggested that if the Administration and Congress were determined to relinquish the Philippines it would be better to trade them off for British Guiana, Honduras and West Indies rather than turn them adrift in an unfriendly world. As might be expected such a radical proposal aroused considerable criticism and we print below some of the letters we have received on the subject.

We quote first from Professor Elwood Mead, who was for many years in charge of the irrigation service of Victoria, Australia:

The more one considers the novel suggestion of Dr. Slosson the more advantageous it appears. This country could develop and protect British Guinea with few of the hazards and expenses that must always go with the control of the Philippines.

It would seem that the exchange would benefit Great Britain in equal measure. There is a profitable and rapidly growing trade between Australia and the Philippines. The relations of both parties would be more satisfactory if both countries were under the same government, with tariff restrictions and trade jealousies wholly eliminated. Australia is the nearest supply point for the Philippines for agricultural products not now produced there and which can be grown more cheaply in temperate climates. It would only add one more to the immense island possessions of Great Britain and lessen rather than increase the difficulties of administration.

So far as the Philippine people are concerned, this transfer would be to their advantage. While we have done much for the country, we cannot yet claim to have reached there the certainty and efficiency in the administration of outside countries that Great Britain has shown in the control of adjacent island areas. In both political and economic equality the countries under British rule are better off than under any other government, and the sentimental political freedom which turning these islands adrift to their own inexperienced management is supposed to make possible would never be realized. To do this is simply to connive at their spoliation, either from lawless elements at home or by the greedy countries that surround them.

I hope therefore that this proposal will become more than a matter of speculative discussion.

ELWOOD MEAD
University of California

There are, as stated in Dr. Slosson's article, some advantages which might be derived from such a trade, but there are also some very pertinent arguments against the plan as well as some practical difficulties in its realization.

1. It takes two to make a bargain, and it is hardly conceivable that England would be willing to relinquish her foothold in Latin-America.

2. We now have possessions in and

about the Caribbean sea sufficient for our strategic purposes and I fear that the South American Republics, with whom we are trying to form a closer union, but to whom our motives have heretofore been an object of suspicion, will look with great disfavor upon any further attempt by us to acquire territory in those sections.

3. The Philippines are very desirable as a base for operations in the event of war with one of the Pacific nations. It has been argued by many that the islands are particularly susceptible to attack, but Corrigedor, at the opening of Manila bay, is now one of the world's great fortifications and were a nation to direct toward that port an army and a fleet large enough to even hope to take it, the force remaining for invasion of our home shores would be materially weakened.

4. England, together with the other European nations, has scoffed at our attempt to educate and give self-government to the Filipinos, and has laughed at our "Little Brown Brother Policy." Shall we leave, half-finished, our experiment in altruism, admitting our defeat, giving over the benefits of education, sanitation, public works to a nation whose policy has too frequently been exploitation, and go to another part of the world and start over again?

5. Since 1899, our motto has been "The Philippines for the Filipinos," and we have promised them self-government as fast as they could fit themselves for it and, ultimately, independence. Such a trade as suggested by Dr. Slosson would be a direct violation of that promise, for we could certainly not dictate to England her policy of administration of the islands nor could we bind her to ever give them up. It will, in my opinion, be a long time before the hope of independence can be fulfilled, and I am not at all sure but that such a government as would be given them by England would be better than any they would ever give themselves. Nevertheless, we have given our word to the Filipinos and we are in honor bound to, if possible, see that this pledge is redeemed.

Bearing in mind that we have promised independence to the Filipino *people* and not merely to a little group of politicians, I greatly deplore the recent action of the United States Senate to whom these arguments seem to have no weight.

DEAN A. WORCESTER
University of New Mexico

Mr. Bowen, former American Minister to Persia and to Venezuela, comments as follows:

Dr. Slosson's plan, if it could be carried out, would relieve us of a great burden in the Pacific and would add very much to our power and prestige in the Atlantic; but we cannot consider it seriously, for we have made many promises, express and implied, to the Filipinos to the effect that in due course of time we would give to them their independence. That they would ever consent to be bargained away to another Power, or that an enlightened people such as the British are, would, in view of all the circumstances, attempt to incorporate them into the British Empire without their consent is hardly sup-

posable. Furthermore the great war now raging in Europe has so intensified the patriotism and loyalty of all British subjects, and our weak and wavering course toward Germany has derogated so much from our dignity as a nation, that she inhabitants of the British possessions Dr. Slosson proposes should be exchanged for the Philippines would undoubtedly elect to retain their present allegiance, and Great Britain could not do otherwise than respect their wishes even if she wished to make the exchange. In short, Dr. Slosson's plan would be favorable only to our own interests. The Filipinos would lose by it, as they would lose the hope of receiving what is dearest to their hearts—their independence. Great Britain would lose by it, for she would have to shoulder our burden in the East, and lose possessions of little account that are of very great value to her, and the inhabitants of those possessions would lose by it, as they would be transferred to a Power that has not adequate forces to protect them, and that had not even spirit enough to break off friendly relations with Germany when she horrified the whole civilized world with her malignant atrocities on land and her murderous outrages on the sea.

HERBERT W. BOWEN
Woodstock, Connecticut

A much more ambitious proposal than that suggested by Dr. Slosson was brought forward by Charles W. Sherrill, of New York, former Minister to Argentina, in an address before the University of Buffalo, October 20, 1915, and at a banquet given in Washington, December 30, 1915, by the Carnegie Endowment for International Peace to the American Society of International Law, the American Political Science Association, the American Society for the Judicial Settlement of International Disputes and Section VI of the Pan-American Scientific Congress. We quote from the latter speech:

Our possession of the Philippines does not true up to the underlying ideas of the Monroe Doctrine. But neither does the possession by Denmark, Holland, France and England of colonies in this hemisphere? Why not set one of these discordant facts off against the other, and trade the Philippine Islands for all European possessions to the south of us, and then turn the Guianas and British Honduras into free republics, return the Falkland Islands to Argentina, and take under our flag the West Indian Islands, so important to the defense of the Panama Canal. Thus at one step would we eliminate Japanese distrust caused by our holding the Philippines, honorably release us from the responsibility for those distant islands, complete the protection from European entanglements initiated by Monroe's protest against additional European colonization, and, finally, free us from European military bases near the Panama Canal.

In his book "Modernizing the Monroe Doctrine" just published by Houghton, Mifflin, Mr. Sherrill de-

112

velops his idea that the United States should coöperate with other American republics to free all American territory south of us from the cloud of European sovereignty.

The official spokesman for the Filipinos is the Resident Commissioner, Mr. Quezon. He desires independence, pure and simple, but that, in our opinion, is an impossibility under present circumstances, whether it is a desirability or not.

I hardly need to tell you that I am against this proposition. I deny the moral right of the United States to dispose in this way of the Philippine Islands, I contend that the only thing that the American Government can do in regard to the Philippines consistently both with the ideals of the American people and the principles of justice and morality is to grant the Philippines independence.   MANUEL L. QUEZON
House of Representatives

Dean Kinley of the University of Illinois has several times represented the United States at South American conferences:

On the whole, I think the balance of argument is against his proposal. The exchange would be an advantage to us because it would somewhat consolidate our possessions and would take us out of a position in the Pacific which in some degree arouses the resentment of other countries. But I cannot see that the inclusion into our citizenship of the population of these British possessions would be a greater advantage to us than the inclusion of the Filipinos. To my mind, the positive disadvantages of the exchange would be two. The most important would be the effect on public opinion in South and Central America. The step would undoubtedly be regarded by some as another advance towards domination of the political destiny of the southern continent. Moreover, it seems to me that it would be as a shirking of a duty to the Philippines which, fortunately or unfortunately, has become ours; and it would be a shirking of international responsibilities which, as the possessor of the Philippine Islands, and as a member of the family of nations, we are morally bound to carry.   DAVID KINLEY
University of Illinois

We would remind our readers that the author of the article under discussion made the proposal of a trade with Great Britain merely as a preferential alternative to the measure which the President and Senate approves, for abandoning the Philippines altogether. This would mean their speedy acquisition by some one of the world Powers. The question of our right to transfer the islands to another sovereignty is relevant. A quit-claim deed from the United States is all that any Power would ask, and this the Administration is proposing to pass.

I have been an active Anti-Imperialist since our taking of the Philippines and only stronger in my convictions as the years go by, that people should decide for themselves upon their government, and neither Great Britain nor this country have any right to transfer

ORIGINALLY   NOW, AS TREATED WITH RICES GLOSS MILL WHITE

The most remarkable factory in the United States

THE old Lippitt Mill, at Lippitt Village, R. I., is the oldest cotton mill in continuous operation in this country. Though built in an era when factories were dark as dungeons, today this plant is fairly flooded with daylight. Visitors to this old mill are first struck by the unusual brightness and cheerfulness of the interior. In this respect it compares favorably with any modern plant although the windows are small and the only other lighting is by kerosene lamps.

The secret of this bright interior is that *the ceilings and walls have been treated with Rice's Gloss Mill White.*

INCREASES DAYLIGHT 19% TO 36%

In this plant as in 3,000 others, Rice's has increased the amount of daylight from 19% to 36%. It helps the workmen see better—do more and better work. It also saves big money in painting bills, and vastly improves sanitary conditions, in a way that the Lippitt Mill well illustrates.

(Reg. U. S. Pat. Off.)

MANY OLD LAYERS OF WHITEWASH

In this old mill, during the past century, literally scores of layers of whitewash had been applied. This was continually flaking off, and necessitated continual and costly repainting. *By the Rice Method, Rice's Gloss Mill White was used.* Flaking and scaling is now a thing of the past. Repainting will not be necessary *for years.* The original. There is no substitute.

TRY IT UNDER OUR GUARANTEE

Rice's is an oil paint, but it does not yellow like ordinary oil paints. It gives a glossy, tilelike white finish, at no more expense than lead and oil paint. Every user is protected by the Rice guarantee.

Write for our book "More Light"

RICE'S GLOSS MILL WHITE

U. S. Gutta Percha Paint Co.
30 Dudley St.,   Providence, R. I.

Barreled Sunlight

sovereignty over either Guiana or the Philippines.

GEORGE FOSTER PEABODY
Saratoga Springs, New York

Dr. Slosson's article, as a journal of travel, is very entertaining. His pictures of scenes and conditions in British Guiana are drawn with a skilful pen, at once interesting and instructive. But his proposition to swap the Philippines for the British West Indies and British Guiana cannot seriously be entertained. Immediately is raised the question of the moral status of our title to the islands and consequently of our right to enter into any such negotiation. If we hold to the declaration that governments derive their just powers from the consent of the governed, then we have no title, and we cannot in conscience swap something the ownership of which is not clearly and morally vested in us.   JOHN F. SHAFROTH

Chairman of the Committee on Pacific Islands and Porto Rico, United States Senate

Professor Usher's "Pan-Germanism," appearing just before the war, gave him an international reputation which he has confirmed by his "Pan-Americanism," dealing with the larger aspects of the Monroe Doctrine:

I am of the opinion that the Philippines are not a very desirable commercial possession of the United States, and are likely, rather sooner than later, to involve us in regrettable trouble with Japan. I am therefore in favor of ridding ourselves of this possession if we can do it honorably both to ourselves and to the Filipinos. Whether the exchange proposed by Dr. Slosson with Great Britain is practical, I am inclined to doubt, and should myself feel that Jamaica is the British territory we wish to acquire rather than Guiana and the smaller islands. It is not, however, Great Britain which covets the Philippines, but Japan, and I should feel that the sale of the Philippines to Japan for even a nominal sum would be better statecraft than the more cavalier treatment which the pending legislation would sanction.

ROLAND G. USHER
Washington University, St. Louis

Professor Shepherd of Columbia is known widely thru his handy little volume on "Latin America":

Tho I doubt the historicity of Dr. Slosson's version of the swap of 1667, I am much inclined to favor the arrangement he proposes for 1916, or as soon thereafter as practicable. But in order to lessen still further the disparity between our end and the British end of the compact, I would suggest the inclusion of the Bermudas also. Turning over the Philippines to a party not so disinterested, perhaps, as ourselves, and receiving in exchange what we can use to better advantage and situated near our own shores, would be a bargain altogether desirable. Strategy, economies and common sense approve it. Here in the Americas the United States has two continents and numerous islands in which to apply its future energies to the mutual welfare of all concerned. The Monroe Doctrine is not elastic, and the Federal Constitution not amphibious enough to make them properly applicable to adventures in Australasia.   WILLIAM R. SHEPHERD
Columbia University

What Is Auto-Intoxication—and How to Prevent It

By C. G. PERCIVAL, M.D.

PERHAPS the best definition I have ever noted of Auto-Intoxication is "Self-intoxication, or poisoning by compounds produced internally by one's self." This definition is clearly intelligible because it puts Auto-Intoxication exactly where it belongs; takes it away from the obscure and easily misunderstood, and brings it into the light as an enervating, virulent, poisonous ailment.

It is probably the most insidious of all complaints, because its first indications are that we feel a little below par, sluggish, dispirited, etc., and we are apt to delude ourselves that it may be the weather, a little overwork or the need for a rest—

But once let it get a good hold through nonattention to the real cause, and a nervous condition is apt to develop which it will take months to correct. Not alone that, but Auto-Intoxication so weakens the foundation of the entire system to resist disease, that if any is prevalent at the time or if any organ of the body is below par, a more or less serious derangement is sure to follow—

The ailments which have been commonly, almost habitually traced to Auto-Intoxication, are—Languor, Headache, Insomnia, Biliousness, Melancholia, Nervous Prostration, Digestive troubles, Eruptions of the skin, Rheumatism, Neuralgia, Kidney Disturbance, Liver Troubles.

There are several conditions which may produce Auto-Intoxication, but by far the most common and prevalent one is the accumulation of waste in the colon, caused by insufficient exercise, improper food, or more food than Nature can take care of under our present mode of living.

I wonder if you realize how prevalent this most common cause of Auto-Intoxication really is—the clearest proof of it is that one would be entirely safe in stating that there are more drugs consumed in an effort to correct this complaint than for all other human ills combined—it is indeed universal and if it were once conquered, in the words of the famous Medical Scientist, Professor Eli Metchnikoff, "The length of our lives would be nearly doubled."

He has specifically stated that if our colons were removed in early infancy we would in all probability live to the age of 150 years.

That is because the waste which accumulates in the colon is extremely poisonous, and the blood, as it flows through the walls of the colon, absorbs these poisons until it is permeated with them—Have you ever, when bilious, experienced a tingling sensation apparent even above the dormant sensation which biliousness creates? I have, and that is Auto-Intoxication way above the danger point.

Now, if laxative drugs were thorough in removing this waste, there could be no arraignment against them—

But they are at best, only partially effective and temporary in their results, and if persisted in soon cease to be effective at all. Their effect is, at best, the forcing of the system to throw off a noxious element and they therefore "jolt" Nature instead of assisting her.

There is, however, a method of eliminating this waste which has been perfected recently after many years of practice and study which might be aptly termed a Nature Remedy. This is the cleansing of the Colon its entire length at reasonable periods by means of an internal bath in which simple warm water and a harmless antiseptic are used.

This system already has over half a million enthusiastic users and advocates, who have found it the one effective and harmless preventive of Auto-Intoxication, and a resulting means of consistently keeping them clear in brain, bright in spirits, enthusiastic in their work, and most capable in its performance.

The one great merit about this method, aside from the fact that it is so effectual, is that no one can quarrel with it, because it is so simple and natural. It is, as it is called, nothing but a bath scientifically applied. All physicians have for years commonly recommended old-fashioned Internal Baths and the only distinction between them is that the newer method is infinitely more thorough, wherefore it would seem that one could hardly fail to recommend it without stultifying himself, could he?

As a matter of fact, I know that many of the most enlightened and successful specialists are constantly prescribing it to their patients.

The physician who has been responsible for this perfected method of Internal Bathing was himself an invalid twenty-five years ago. Medicine had failed and he tried the old-fashioned Internal Bath. It benefited him, but was only partially effective. Encouraged by this progress, however, he improved the manner of administering it, and as this improved so did his health.

Hence, for twenty-five years, he has made this his life's study and practice until to-day this long experience is represented in the "J. B. L. Cascade." During all these years of specializing as may be readily appreciated, most interesting and valuable knowledge was gleaned, and this practical knowledge is all summed up in a most interesting way and will be sent to you on request without cost or other obligations, if you will simply address Chas. A. Tyrrell, M.D., 134 West 65th Street, New York, and mention having read this article in The Independent.

The inclination of this age is to keep as far away from Medicine as possible and still keep healthy and capable. Physicians agree that ninety-five per cent of human ailments is caused by Auto-Intoxication.

These two facts should be sufficient to incline every one to at least write for this little book and read what it has to say on the subject.—*Advertisement.*

The New Books

ARMS AND THE SOCIALIST

The Future of Democracy, by H. M. Hyndman, the leader of British Marxism, represents the views of those English Socialists who support the war without supporting the government. Mr. Hyndman regards a German victory as the greatest possible menace to democracy and social reform; desires the British to adopt universal military service on the Swiss model; and, like his fellow Socialist, Bernard Shaw, thinks that the United States also should follow the path of preparedness. "If the Great Republic," he says "were in possession of a sufficient army and an adequate navy, the attitude of the American President, alike toward our enemy, Germany, and our ally, Japan, would be very different from what it now is." On the other hand, he views the coalition government with the deepest suspicion, as at once cringing to the capitalists and oppressive to the working men; "we are at the mercy, not of one powerful and capable, if obnoxious dictator, but of a series of petty despots and jacks-in-office, who take advantage of the truce in party politics and the general desire not to embarrass the Government, to imperil and attack our ancestral liberties in every direction."

The Future of Democracy, by H. M. Hyndman. Scribner. $1.

MADE IN AMERICA

If you would be Colonial, first know *The Colonial House* as she is built, lest you fall into error and encourage large meshed trellises to clamber over a doorway of 1800 simplicity or permit an Italian pergola to coquette with a gambrel roof. Joseph Everett Chandler in his readable volume will educate you in the periods of Colonial development in a most pleasing fashion and pilot you safely past the architectural pitfalls of your own ambition.

McBride. $2.50.

RUSSIAN MELODIES FOR AMERICAN PIANOS

At first reading *Modern Russian Piano Music* is discouraging. The elusive themes leap nonchalantly from bass to treble, and it takes not only nimble fingers, but nimble musical wit to follow them. But they respond to a little study, and minor melodies of unique tone-color emerge from the disconcerting accidentals. As Constantin von Sternberg says in the preface to these two volumes of the Musicians' Library: "Russian music furnishes a strong illustration of the great difference between natural dignified modernity and its frenzied caricature, called modernism."

Ditson. $1.50 each.

THE BENEFITS OF MONOPOLY

In *Anthracite*, Scott Nearing describes the system of monopoly ownership in natural resources, drawing his illustrations from the coal business, and shows how the consumer, the worker and the owner fare under the system. There is a study of the strike of 1912, with the analysis of the net results to the three parties at interest. In short, his argument is that monopoly al-

ways leads to ends that are in conflict with the best interests of society. The benefits accrue to the owners only, and the rest of us pay the bills.

Philadelphia: John C. Winston. $1.

TRICKS FOR TRAMPERS

Every experienced campaigner in the woods feels an impulse to save others work and worry by giving them the benefit of what he has learned. In Emerson Hough's *Out of Doors* a most complete book of this sort is presented, and every one who thinks of a walking-tour, or a camping-trip, or a shooting-excursion in either lowlands or highlands, will do well to read it.

Appleton. $1.25.

THEORIES OF ART

Raley Husted Bell pretentiously calls his book on *The Philosophy of Painting* a study of the development of the art from prehistoric, to modern times. Yet he altogether misses the opportunity offered him to discuss futuristic art, and ends his survey with the Impressionists. The book, while readable enough, and containing much information, falls far short of any realization of its lofty promise.

Putnam. $1.25.

SPANISH COLONIAL ADMINISTRATION

The splendid research work being done in western history by the University of California is evidenced by the handsome volume on *Texas in the Middle Eighteenth Century* by Prof. H. E. Bolton. This is based not only upon the study of manuscripts in the archives of Mexico City, Sevilla and Austin, but upon twenty-five thousand miles of travel by train, horse and foot in search of material and verification of sites.

University of California. $3.25.

A MUSICAL POT-POURRI

A collection of "favorites" is usually disappointing, but Julia Culp's two volumes of *My Favorite Songs,* the second of which now appears, are representative enough to be well worth possessing. They have an unusually wide range, with emphasis on the German group, comprizing many well-known songs common to concert singers in general, and others that seem especially part of the musical personality of the Dutch Lieder singer.

Ditson. $1 each.

"LES MISERABLES" IN LITTLE

Les Miserables in a small pocket volume seems a miracle, but the editor responsible for the abridgement has done his work so judiciously that we venture to say one unsequainted with the original might never discover that he was not here perusing a work complete in itself. The edition includes a helpful introduction and notes that elucidate obscure matters, and also explains many things that insufficiently explain themselves.

Macmillan. 25 cents.

PENNSYLVANIA'S DEPENDENT CHILDREN

A Study of Child Welfare Work in Pennsylvania, by a committee of the State Conference of Charities, under the direction of Dr. William H. Slingerland, condenses a great deal of important information about the opportunities for dependent children. The constructive suggestions will be helpful to all engaged in social work with children, wherever situated. Comparisons with methods and accomplishment in other states give balance and practical outlook to the study.

Russell Sage Foundation. $2.

REALISM VS. ROMANCE

The Miseralea One is a romantic drama of the sixteenth century set in admirable blank verse. The realist would think to dismiss it by the epithet, "sentimental." But then the chief failure of the realist is his blind spot on the side of the heart. Sentiment is just as solid a reality in this human world as viciousness. Too much of either is quite as bad as too much of the other. In Ann Cleveland Cheney's play there is no realism, and not too much romance.

Stokes. $1.

Insurance
Conducted by
W. E. UNDERWOOD

A GREAT ACHIEVEMENT

Considered merely from the viewpoint of a commercial achievement, the business-getting record of the Metropolitan Life Insurance Company in 1915 may be described as something more than notable. The new insurance written aggregated $592,800,860. Even those who know nothing of a working life insurance organization must have a measurable idea of the energy, skill and acumen that produces a result so prodigious. Seasoned veterans, who know and understand every cog in the agency machine, are struck with admiration for the system which in a single year can produce without strain at any point six-tenths of a billion of new insurance of which three-fifths consists of industrial policies averaging less than $150 each. On January 1, the Metropolitan had in force 15,-832,885 policies for $3,196,491,344.

J. L. Harvey, N. D.—The financial condition of the Postal Life warrants the statement that its policies are fully secured. I presume the policies of the Brotherhood of All Railway Employees cover for sickness and accidental injuries only. I have no data respecting the organization, but you can get its figures by writing to the Insurance Department, Springfield, Ill. I presume a citizen who desires a policy in a company not operating in his state could procure it by applying directly (without the intervention of an agent) to the home office of the company. No first-class company would issue a policy that did not cover from date.

F. R. M., Cimarron, Kans.—It is difficult to express an opinion of the Pioneer Life of Kansas City, Missouri, that would be mutually satisfactory. The company seems to have changed managements five times since organization in 1907; its capital was once officially declared impaired; its capital has been increased and decreased several times and, taking altogether, it seems to have experienced many difficulties. On January 1, its assets were $403,472; its surplus, $160,181. Its insurance in force, $2,338,980, is $217,243 less than the year before. I think it is in better shape now than ever it has been previously, but what its future will be is difficult of determination at this time.

L. L. H., Hanover, Ind.—The Illinois Bankers' Life Association of Monmouth, Illinois, does business on the assessment plan. It maintains a graduate fund composed of contributions from applicants, based on age, with the object of providing for claims in excess of the amount realized on a call of 30 per cent for mortuary purposes. But to life insurance mathematicians this fund is inadequate for the purposes of a reserve to meet increasing cost due to the increasing age of the membership, with the result that ultimately the members will have to submit to heavier assessments. No scheme of life insurance which ignores the accumulation of a reserve scientifically calculated on a standard mortality table can result in a level premium and guaranteed security to policyholders.

THE MARKET PLACE

THE FLOOD TIDE OF FOREIGN TRADE

The foreign trade figures for February, in spite of the shortness of the month, show continued increase. Imports amounted to $193,935,117, nine and a half million dollars more than in January, and sixty-eight million dollars more than in February of last year. Exports were more than twice as great, $409,836,525. This was an increase over the highest preceding month, December last, of more than fifty million dollars; and over the corresponding month of last year of one hundred and ten millions, or more than one-third. The favorable trade balance was a record figure, $215,-901,408.

For the eight months of the fiscal year the increase in imports over the preceding year was $235,452,481; but the increase in exports was $951,835,-553—a gain of thirty-seven per cent. The excess of exports over imports was $1,295,217,462, considerably more than double the excess for the corresponding months a year ago.

These are the most astounding figures in our trade history. While no definite information is yet forthcoming it is clear that the great excess of exports is due to munitions and other supplies for the warring nations. This excess of exports is paid for by loans to foreign governments and by securities returned here for sale. It is a curious fact that during February there was no balance of gold coming here in adjustment of the foreign exchange situation; in fact, we exported more than twice as much as came in.

Only one thing can happen when the close of the war brings this abnormally favorable condition to a sudden end—a reaction which will require all our wisdom and ingenuity to meet.

THE WINTER WHEAT CROP

It is a dozen years since the Department of Agriculture's first report of the season on the winter wheat crop has been as pessimistic as it is this year. The estimate, which has just been made public, gives a "condition percentage" of 78.3 per cent. In 1904 the estimate was 76.5, but every year since it has been so much higher that the ten-year average is 87.3. A year ago the percentage was 88.8, and in April, 1914, it had reached the remarkable level of 95.6.

The Department gives the "harvest indication," based upon this "condition percentage," as 495,000,000 bushels. This April indication is, of course, not a thoroly safe guide to the actual harvest; for in 1915 there was harvested 36,000,000 bushels more than was estimated in April, and in 1914 65,000,000 bushels more than the early estimate.

But even making all allowances for the increases over the present estimate that are probable, it is clear that the winter wheat crop this year is to be much below any crop since the war began.

The government estimate on this important crop, however far it may prove to be from the final outcome, is of great interest in view of the tremendous influence of the two great wheat crops of last year and the year before upon the balance of trade and our national prosperity.

AN ASSAULT UPON DECENT BUSINESS

A thoroly vicious law dealing with the affairs of corporations has been enacted by the Legislature of New York state and signed by the Governor. It provides that the list of stockholders of any corporation is to be open for inspection only to a stockholder holding more than five per cent of the stock of the corporation and to such a stockholder only after six months of stock ownership. For such an assault upon the rights of the small stockholder there can be no justification. The law will deprive many of the owners of a business of the right to important knowledge as to the affairs of the business. It will keep many of the partners in a business from knowing who the other partners are. It puts a premium upon underhandedness and secret manipulation.

The *Wall Street Journal* has picturesquely described the measure as "conceived in iniquity, born in secrecy, passed in ignorance and signed by the Governor in callous indifference to anything but his own political fortunes."

No legitimate and honest corporation needs or desires to carry on its business under such baleful obscurity. The facts as to the actual ownership of any corporation are the legitimate property not only of every stockholder, but of the public as well. The business whose owners fear the light is a legitimate object of suspicion. For the state to aid and abet such men in their desire for secrecy is a betrayal of the public welfare. It is an affront to every decent business interest.

The following dividends are announced:
The New York Central Railroad, $1.25 per share, payable May 1.
American Brake Shoe and Foundry Company, preferred, quarterly, 2 per cent; common, quarterly, 1¾ per cent; both payable March 31.
Westinghouse Electric and Manufacturing Company, preferred, quarterly, 1¾ per cent, payable April 15; common, quarterly, 1½ per cent, payable April 29.
American Light and Traction Company, preferred, 1¾ per cent; common, 2½ per cent, and 2½ shares common stock on every 100 shares
Pacific Gas and Electric Company, common, $1.25 per share, payable April 15.
The Niagara Falls Power Company, $2 per share, payable on and after April 15.

Department Store Training

"I sold three times the amount of the girl next to me," Mrs. Lucinda W. Price says in *The Bookman*, in telling how a self-imposed turn at the counter of a big department store led to her founding the School of Salesmanship in connection with the Women's Educational and Industrial Union, of Boston. "It was partly because I was interested in serving the public; she was interested in getting her salary." As the result of finding, first-hand, the needs of department store employees and the vast possibilities of more efficient service, Mrs. Price was able to organize lessons in selling methods, arithmetic, applied physical education, textiles, design, hygiene and the elements of economics, with an advisory committee composed of the heads of Boston stores, who have taken up the movement vigorously. Girls actually working in the Boston stores are taking the lessons mentioned; another branch of the school's activity is to equip college graduates for training department store employees. Applied psychology, economics, textiles, and the principles of education form part of the curriculum of this class of students, who, on the practical side, learn their business by going as saleghirls into the large stores. Fully trained graduates are working, as a result, in New York, Cleveland, Atlanta, Newark, San Francisco, Milwaukee, Denver and Toledo. "For the college girl who has the vision of service," says Mrs. Price, "no greater field than this can be found." In New York the Board of Education and the University have agreed to develop, as part of the regular work, the plan of the Department Store Educational Association, under which 336 saleswomen from one store alone have already taken courses.

An Inventory of Industry

Prominent among the many steps that are being taken toward Preparedness—the topical name for national efficiency—is likely to be the preparation of a thoro inventory of American industry, for the first time in the country's history. Three hundred thousand qualified engineers, according to the plan, will combine in the undertaking, which is part of the scheme for stimulating the Preparedness Idea planned by the Associated Advertising Clubs of the World. With the sanction of President Wilson, the organization, representing American business at every point, placed its services at the disposal of the Committee on Industrial Preparedness, that will assist thru a committee of leading publishers and advertising experts and a big campaign in the press. "It is vitally necessary," says Mr. Howard E. Coffin, "that American industry be made aware of the part it must play in our national defense.

120

Our whole conception of warfare has changed almost overnight. We are confronted with the need for interlocking the military and industrial elements in one great working organization, and that is the work before us."

Art and the Poster

The efficient poster is not a thing of screaming colors and harsh lines—this is the proposition which the Pennsylvania School of Industrial Art is seeking to prove by an exhibition at which will be shown some of the latest and most successful attempts to combine artistic and publicity values. The exhibition reflects a growing body of opinion among advertisers in favor of billboards, posters and other illustrative advertising that shall strike the imagination as well as the retina, and one of the principal exhibits is to be the $1000 prize poster designed by Adolph Treidler for the Newark, New Jersey, anniversary celebration.

The New Way in Railroad Telegraphy

Mr. Andrew Carnegie, at the age of fifteen years, was working as a telegraph operator on the Pennsylvania Railroad, a fact which gives point to the effort which the company is making to popularize this branch of its operative work. The railroad is up against the pulling power of big wages offered by the flourishing munitions works of the state, but results are looked for from an offer to teach telegraphy free at the company's school at Bedford, where, in addition to every facility on the theoretical side of the work, there has been erected a miniature railroad, with tiny trains operated by electricity. In cabins arranged round the track pupils learn how to do their share in the work of traffic regulation, seeing meanwhile the actual effect of their duties. With proficient scholars the miniature trains run to schedule time, and literally as smoothly as clockwork, but an error may produce a bloodless disaster that effectively warns the would-be telegrapher of his responsibility.

A Better St. Paul

The Association of Commerce of St. Paul is considering a plan of reorganizing with a view to greater efficiency and making St. Paul "a better city in which to live, and a more productive community in which to transact business." The scheme, which is exhaustive in its consideration of the life of the city, aims to enroll all classes who may conceivably help toward the general improvement. Three divisions of the association's work are contemplated: one for dealing with public affairs, embracing every economic problem of the city, from housing conditions and street planning to recreation facilities and the administration of charities; another for the advancement of business and for such matters as labor welfare, trade expansion and transportation difficulties; and a third for the administration of the association itself. The movement aims: ". . . to inculcate among our citizens a higher appreciation of the value to the individual of disinterested community service and a keener understanding of community problems; . . . to perfect a central clearing-house of information having to do with civic, commercial and industrial St. Paul."

A Columbus of the Air

What is the goal of efficiency in the matter of aerial science? Mr. Rodman Wanamaker gives the answer in a letter to Mr. Alan R. Hawley, president of the Aero Club of America, printed in full in the *Aerial Age*. He believes that not until one of our great oceans is crossed in a single flight will aviation have met the supreme test, and he is having built another aircraft specially designed for alighting on and rising from rough seas, and fitted for a transatlantic flight. It is now under construction and when complete will be thoroly tested at the Atlantic Coast Aeronautical Station at Newport News. "The crossing of the Atlantic Ocean in one flight," Mr. Wanamaker writes, "is, to my mind, as important to aerial navigation as was the voyage of Columbus to transportation by water. What man can do once, he can do any number of times. Once the Atlantic is crossed in a single flight of an airship, there will soon follow regular transatlantic trips and a fixed, safe transatlantic passenger air line. The crossing of the Atlantic by air is not a matter merely of initiative, nor of daring, nor even of skill; it is a problem of science." It is understood that the design of the new craft is absolutely different from anything else constructed so far, is an entirely new departure in design and construction, and will be the largest aircraft every built, and also that this craft will be equipped with six twelve-cylinder motors of 300 horsepower each, or 1800 horsepower, and will be capable of making a speed of about 100 miles an hour, with a crew of six people, the fuel, instruments, provisions and equipment necessary for the transatlantic flight, which it is expected will be made by this craft in about thirty hours.

Following Mr. Wanamaker's announcement, the Aero Club of America has sent a cable to the Royal Aero Club of Great Britain and to Lord Northcliffe advising of Mr. Wanamaker's project, and inquiring whether the $50,-000 prize for a cross-Atlantic flight offered by Lord Northcliffe is still open. His reply was, "Yes, after the war."

The Independent

FOR SIXTY-SEVEN YEARS THE
FORWARD-LOOKING WEEKLY OF AMERICA

THE CHAUTAUQUAN
Merged with The Independent June 1, 1914

APRIL 24, 1916

OWNED AND PUBLISHED BY
THE INDEPENDENT CORPORATION, AT
119 WEST FORTIETH STREET, NEW YORK
WILLIAM B. HOWLAND, PRESIDENT
FREDERIC E. DICKINSON, TREASURER

WILLIAM HAYES WARD
HONORARY EDITOR

EDITOR: HAMILTON HOLT
ASSOCIATE EDITOR: HAROLD J. HOWLAND
LITERARY EDITOR: EDWIN E. SLOSSON

PUBLISHER: KARL V. S. HOWLAND

ONE YEAR, THREE DOLLARS

SINGLE COPIES, TEN CENTS

Postage to foreign countries in Universal Postal
Union, $1.75 a year extra; to Canada, $1 extra.
Instructions for renewal, discontinuance or
change of address should be sent two weeks
before the date they are to go into effect. Both
the old and the new address must be given.

We welcome contributions, but writers who
wish their articles returned, if not accepted,
should send a stamped and addrest envelope. No responsibility is assumed by The
Independent for the loss or non-return of
manuscripts, tho all due care will be exercised.

Entered at New York Post Office as Second
Class Matter

Copyright, 1916, by The Independent

Address all Communications to
THE INDEPENDENT
119 West Fortieth Street, New York

CONTENTS

VOX CLAMANTIS

*"Rattle and clatter and clank and whirr,"
And it's long and long the day is.*
From earliest morn to late at night,
And all night long, the self-same song—
"Rattle and clank and whirr,"
Day in, day out, all day, all night—
"Rattle and clank and whirr";
With faces tight, with all our might—
"Rattle and clank and whirr";
We may not stop and we dare not err;
Our men are risking their lives out there,
And we at home must do our share;—
But it's long and long the day is.
We'll break if we must, but we cannot spare
A thought for ourselves, or the kids, or
  care;
For it's *"Rattle and clatter and clank and
  whirr."*
Our men are giving their lives out there.
And we'll give ours, we will do our share—
"Rattle and clank and whirr."

Are our faces grave, and our eyes intent?
Is every ounce that is in us bent
On the uttermost pitch of accomplishment?
Tho it's long and long the day is!
Ah—we know what it means if we fool or
  slack;
—A rifle jammed—and one comes not back,
And we never forget—it's for us they gave.
And so we will slave, and slave, and slave,
Lest the men at the front should rue it.
Their all they gave, and their lives we'll
  save,
If the hardest of work can do it;—
But it's long and long the day is.

Eight hours, ten hours, twelve hours'
  shift—
Oh, it's long and long the day is!
Up before light, and home in the night.
That is our share in the desperate fight,
And it's long and long the day is!
Backs and arms and heads that ache;
Eyes over-tired and legs that shake;
And hearts full nigh to burst and break:—
Oh, it's long and long the day is!
Week in, week out, not a second to spare,
But tho it should kill us we'll do our share,

For the sake of the lads who have gone out
  there
For the sake of us others to do and dare;—
"Rattle and clatter and clank and whirr,"
And thousands of wheels a-spinning—
Spinning Death for the men of wrath.
Spinning Death for the broken troth,
—And Life, and a New Beginning.
Was there ever, since ever the world was
  made,
Such a horrible trade for a peace-loving
  maid,
And such wonderful, terrible spinning?

Oh, it's dreary work and it's weary work,
But none of us all will fail or shirk;—
Not women's work—that should make, not
  mar,
But the Devil drives when the world's at
  war;—
And it's long and long the day is.
And YOU can help us in many a way,
You others, who have not to be in the fray;
For it's your men, too, we are working to
  save,
Your bravest and best, just as we did, you
  gave;
But it's all giving now, if we'd safeguard
  the rest,
And make a sure end of this horrible waste.
We ask you to help us to lessen the stress
Of these days of unnatural weariness,
There are plenty of ways for you to express
The warmth of your hearts and your
  thoughtfulness—
*For it's weary and weary our way is,
And it's long, long, long, the day is.*

We're not slacking,
Tho we lack,
You're not lacking—
Will you slack?

—By John Oxenham, in the *London Times*
  (Copyright)

REMARKABLE REMARKS

"BUGS" BAER—The only cure for golf is
golf.

SENATOR VARDAMAN—The President
has written some good books.

SENATOR SHERMAN—The country is sur-
feited with phrase-makers.

AMY LOWELL—I wish that newspapers
did not try to review books.

SENATOR SMOOT—The American garbage
can is the fattest in the world.

PUGILIST MORAN—There's a lot of
money in that Billy Sunday game.

MARION HARLAND—Few of us escape
the well meant gifts we do not wish.

COMMISSIONER OF HEALTH EMERSON—
Dogs are not necessary to a cultivated existence.

YUAN SHIH-KAI—Owing to our lack of
virtue we are unable to win the will of
heaven.

WOODROW WILSON—Have you the courage to go in? Have you the courage to
come out?

S. STANWOOD MENKEN—Internationalism as a practical possibility is dead for
our generation.

ARTHUR CHAPMAN—Impressive office
furniture can often carry an unimpressive
man to success.

ANNE RITTENHOUSE—It looks as tho the
majority of bathing suits will be parade
uniforms this summer.

SENATOR BURTON—It is impossible to
contemplate the future of America without
a feeling of enthusiasm.

W. H. TAFT—Railroads have themselves to blame for the condition in which
they now find themselves.

GEN. NELSON A. MILES—I would match
a volunteer American defending his liberties and his government against any German soldier.

WILLIAM RANDOLPH HEARST—The press
of New York City and New York State
should unite in an effort to maintain the
moral standards.

THE PRESTIGE OF A MOTOR CAR no longer depends upon mere name, surrounded by a fictitious atmosphere of aristocracy.

The only aristocracy in motor cars, now, is an aristocracy of merit.

It is true that the ownership of a Cadillac carries a distinct social value in every community.

But it is the *character of the car* which sheds lustre on the Cadillac name—not the name which confers lustre on the car.

Intent upon the more serious purpose of making the Cadillac as good a motor car can be made, this Company has paid scant attention to any other part of the case.

Social distinction came to Cadillac as an afterresult. It was earned by the owners themselves—an appreciation of its sterling quality.

Each added new number to the number to pay, but who became to what the became rapid ased.

Each lure grew

It is the proof

Neither nor on a r

The w and p

In the world distir

The Independent

| VOLUME 86 | APRIL 24, 1916 | NUMBER 3516 |

WHAT SANK THE "SUSSEX"?

THE German note on the attack pon the British Channel steamer "Sussex" psents what is either an astounding coincidenc or a disgraceful attempt at evasion.

The German Government admits tha on the day the "Sussex" was damaged a German subrrine torpedoed in the English Channel a vessel whict the submarine commander assumed from outward apparances to be a British mine layer; but it asserts tha this could not have been the "Sussex." In support of t s contention it offers in evidence a sketch of the torpeded vessel made by the captain of the submarine, and, fc comparison, a newspaper picture of the "Sussex."

Observe, now, the remarkable coincidnce. The "Sussex" was damaged in the Channel beteen Folkestone and Dieppe; so was the vessel admitte to have been torpedoed. The disaster to the "Sussex' happened at a few minutes before four on the afternoo of March 24; so did the torpedoing confest to by Genany. The forward part of the "Sussex" was wrecke by the explosion; the same part of the strange vessl was wrecked by the German torpedo.

Was the vesel that the German commader torpedoed on sight, without warning, with no defiite knowledge of its identity or character, the "Sussex' If it was not, the coincidence verges upon the miraculos?

If it was the "Sussex," our course is ear. The incident proves once for all that Germany is ot keeping her word to us. It shows that the "scrap of per" habit is too deeply ingrained to be eradicated. We an trust Germany no longer. Our friendly relations mt have an end.

The German Government calmly suggescs a reference of the disputed facts in the case to an intnational commission of inquiry in accordance with th Hague Convention for the Pacific Settlement of Int national Disputes. This is a plausible proposal. The Sussex" case, considered alone by itself, is exactly thecind that the Commission of Inquiry was intended totake care of.

It involves primarily a disagreement as to facts. Was the "Sussex" sunk by a German torpedo, or was it not? That is the question.

But it is not necessarily the whole question. If the "Sussex" struck a mine, of course the determination of that fact would automatically close the case, so far as the United States is concerned. But if the boat was torpedoed, it is not merely a question of apology and disavowal and reparation. There is involved a broken pledge on the part of the German Government, a violation of plighted faith. Such a breach between two nations cannot be healed by mere expressions of regret or cold payments of money.

Nevertheless, if the evidence at the   he United States Government is not suffi us beyond a reasonable doubt that the ". pedoed, it would be well to accept the Ge. on one condition. Germany must give the i. guarantees that, pending the report of the she will give up her submarine warfare aga. chant ships in its entirety. For in that warfare, . admittedly caried on by the German navy, there ai. many chances for mistakes and unfortunate accidents.

If Germany is to go on torpedoing merchantmen will, we must come to our own conclusion as to th facts in such a case as that of the "Sussex." Under such conditions Germany could not come into court with clean hands.

But the belief is irresistible that the German proposal is not made in good faith. It comes too late in the day. It bears too much the look of one more move to gain time and to postpone the day of reckoning.

If our government becomes convinced that the "Sussex" was in fact sunk by a German torpedo, that day of reckoning should come swiftly. Diplomatic relations should be severed without parley. We cannot live on terms of friendly harmony with a people who make it impossible for us to trust their word.

LABOR, LAW AND LIFE

ONE of the most vitally important questions of our present day world is that of th relation of industry to the common ife and the general welfare. This question, with evr increasing insistence, is urging itself upon the hought and enlisting the activity of students everyhere of the social problem. With greater and greater lequency it is engaging the attention of our legislatures d our courts. Step by step the domain of the old argant theory that industry is a private matter between he employer and the laborer has been invaded. The victious invader has been the dawning realization that industry is a matter of public concern and that the condition of the great mass of mankind that works with the hands is of vital interest to the community and to all mankind.

The trunk line of this invasion has been the public control of the hours of labor. The forces of progress in this country have now reached a crucial point in the ad. vance. If this point can be successfully assaulted, the way will be opened for a complete conquest, by the powers of enlightenment, of the benighted kingdom of industrial exploitation of the workers.

THE PRESTIGE OF A MOTOR CAR no longer depends upon a mere name, surrounded by a fictitious atmosphere of aristocracy.

The only aristocracy in motor cars, now, is an aristocracy of merit.

It is true that the ownership of a Cadillac carries a distinct social value in every community.

But it is the *character of the car* which sheds lustre on the Cadillac name—not the name which confers lustre on the car.

Intent upon the more serious purpose of making the Cadillac as good as a motor car can be made, this Company has paid scant attention to any other aspect of the case.

Social distinction came to the Cadillac as an after-result. It was conferred by the owners themselves—as an appreciation of its more sterling qualities.

Each year the number of those amply able to pay more, but who prefer the Cadillac because of what the Cadillac is, has rapidly increased.

Each year the lure of a mere name has grown less.

It is the age-old process at work.

Neither a man, nor a motor car. can live on a name alone.

The world demands deeds from the one, and performance from the other.

In the working-out of that process, the world has bestowed greater and greater distinction upon the Cadillac.

The Independent

| VOLUME 86 | APRIL 24, 1916 | NUMBER 3516 |

WHAT SANK THE "SUSSEX"?

THE German note on the attack upon the British Channel steamer "Sussex" presents what is either an astounding coincidence or a disgraceful attempt at evasion.

The German Government admits that on the day the "Sussex" was damaged a German submarine torpedoed in the English Channel a vessel which the submarine commander assumed from outward appearances to be a British mine layer; but it asserts that this could not have been the "Sussex." In support of this contention it offers in evidence a sketch of the torpedoed vessel made by the captain of the submarine, and, for comparison, a newspaper picture of the "Sussex."

Observe, now, the remarkable coincidence. The "Sussex" was damaged in the Channel between Folkestone and Dieppe; so was the vessel admitted to have been torpedoed. The disaster to the "Sussex" happened at a few minutes before four on the afternoon of March 24; so did the torpedoing confest to by Germany. The forward part of the "Sussex" was wrecked by the explosion; the same part of the strange vessel was wrecked by the German torpedo.

Was the vessel that the German commander torpedoed on sight, without warning, with no definite knowledge of its identity or character, the "Sussex"? If it was not, the coincidence verges upon the miraculous?

If it was the "Sussex," our course is clear. The incident proves once for all that Germany is not keeping her word to us. It shows that the "scrap of paper" habit is too deeply ingrained to be eradicated. We can trust Germany no longer. Our friendly relations must have an end.

The German Government calmly suggests a reference of the disputed facts in the case to an international commission of inquiry in accordance with the Hague Convention for the Pacific Settlement of International Disputes. This is a plausible proposal. The "Sussex" case, considered alone by itself, is exactly the kind that the Commission of Inquiry was intended to take care of.

It involves primarily a disagreement as to facts. Was the "Sussex" sunk by a German torpedo, or was it not? That is the question.

But it is not necessarily the whole question. If the "Sussex" struck a mine, of course the determination of that fact would automatically close the case, so far as the United States is concerned. But if the boat was torpedoed, it is not merely a question of apology and disavowal and reparation. There is involved a broken pledge on the part of the German Government, a violation of plighted faith. Such a breach between two nations cannot be healed by mere expressions of regret or cold payments of money.

Nevertheless, if the evidence at the command of the United States Government is not sufficient to convince us beyond a reasonable doubt that the "Sussex" was torpedoed, it would be well to accept the German proposal, on one condition. Germany must give the most complete guarantees that, pending the report of the commission, she will give up her submarine warfare against merchant ships in its entirety. For in that warfare, as now admittedly caried on by the German navy, there are too many chances for mistakes and unfortunate accidents.

If Germany is to go on torpedoing merchantmen at will, we must come to our own conclusion as to the facts in such a case as that of the "Sussex." Under such conditions Germany could not come into court with clean hands.

But the belief is irresistible that the German proposal is not made in good faith. It comes too late in the day. It bears too much the look of one more move to gain time and to postpone the day of reckoning.

If our government becomes convinced that the "Sussex" was in fact sunk by a German torpedo, that day of reckoning should come swiftly. Diplomatic relations should be severed without parley. We cannot live on terms of friendly harmony with a people who make it impossible for us to trust their word.

LABOR, LAW AND LIFE

ONE of the most vitally important questions of our present day world is that of the relation of conditions of industry to the common life and the general welfare. This question, with ever increasing insistence, is urging itself upon the thought and enlisting the activity of students everywhere of the social problem. With greater and greater frequency it is engaging the attention of our legislatures and our courts. Step by step the domain of the old arrogant theory that industry is a private matter between the employer and the laborer has been invaded. The victorious invader

has been the dawning realization that industry is a matter of public concern and that the condition of the great mass of mankind that works with the hands is of vital interest to the community and to all mankind.

The trunk line of this invasion has been the public control of the hours of labor. The forces of progress in this country have now reached a crucial point in the advance. If this point can be successfully assaulted, the way will be opened for a complete conquest, by the powers of enlightenment, of the benighted kingdom of industrial exploitation of the workers.

A case is now being argued before the Supreme Court of the United States, the decision of which will determine whether the next step is to be forward or back. It is to test the constitutionality of the Oregon Ten Hour Law. The phraseology of the law is so unusual and so significant that we quote its principal provisions:

Section 1.—It is the public policy of the state of Oregon that no person shall be hired, nor permitted to work for wages, under any conditions or terms, for longer hours or days of service than is consistent with his health and physical well-being and ability to promote the general welfare by his increasing usefulness as a healthy and intelligent citizen. It is hereby declared that the working of any person more than ten hours in one day, in any mill, factory, or manufacturing establishment is injurious to the physical health and well-being of such person, and tends to prevent him from acquiring that degree of intelligence that is necessary to make him a useful and desirable citizen of the state.
Section 2.—No person shall be employed in any mill, factory, or manufacturing establishment in this state more than ten hours in any one day. . . .

The constitutionality of the law is assailed under the Fourteenth Amendment to the Federal Constitution, which provides that no state shall "deprive any person of life, liberty or property, without due process of law." Its constitutionality is defended under the police power of the state. The liberty of contract guaranteed by the Constitution is subject to modification by reasonable regulations imposed by the Legislature on behalf of the general welfare. The only limit to such modification is that it shall be actually reasonable and not arbitrary.

It is an interesting development in the judicial attitude that cases like the present, concerned with industrial conditions, have come more and more to be considered as questions not of law but of fact. Is the legislation in question as a matter of fact a reasonable exercize of the police power as applied to the conditions which actually exist in the industries involved? This is the question which the Court has to decide in any case like the one now before it.

This has led to a new method of arguing such cases, invented by Mr. Louis D. Brandeis, whose appointment to the Supreme Court still awaits confirmation. It consists in presenting a mass of evidence and authoritative opinion in support of the thesis that the conditions legislated against are actually detrimental and a danger to the public welfare.

The law in the case needs no arguing: it is too well established by decisions of courts thruout the country and of the Supreme Court itself. It is only the facts that need to be determined. In a previous case—that of the California law establishing an eight hour day for women in certain industries, which the Supreme Court sustained just a year ago—the Court reasserted the principle that it is the function and the duty of the Legislature to determine the need, the expediency and the wisdom of the law as a protection of the public welfare, and that the function of the court is limited to the determination whether in view of the actual facts in each case the Legislature acted arbitrarily.

In the present case the Attorney General of Oregon had retained the services of Mr. Brandeis for the preparation of the case on appeal. When Mr. Brandeis was appointed to the Supreme bench, he of course retired from the case, and Professor Felix Frankfurter, of the Harvard Law School, one of the most brilliant of the younger generation of American lawyers, was retained in his place. In the preparation of their brief these gentlemen have had the able and expert assistance of Miss Josephine Goldmark, publication secretary of the National Consumers' League.

It has long been accepted, not only by the courts but generally, that it is a legitimate function of government to protect by legislation the health of workers in dangerous trades. The contention of the brief is that all occupations are dangerous where the hours of work are too long. In all industries a permanent predisposition to disease and premature death exists in the common phenomena of fatigue and exhaustion. This is a danger common to all workers, even under good working conditions, and all manufacturing industries. Excessive hours of work produce over-fatigue and the results of over-fatigue are lessened efficiency, increased susceptibility to disease, particularly the so-called degenerative diseases of the heart, blood vessels and kidneys, weakening of the moral fiber, and general deterioration.

Beside these general factors of danger to the workers, other dangers of environment are found to be common to many trades. It was formerly supposed that injurious substances, such as mineral and vegetable dusts, fluff, gases, fumes and industrial poisons, were menaces to the health of the workers in only a few dangerous occupations. It is now known that one or another of these deleterious substances is to be found present in most of the important branches of manufacture. They constitute hazards not only in a few special trades, but almost universally. In addition to these specific dangers there are numerous general industrial hazards common to practically all manufacturing industries. They include bad air, humidity, extremes of heat and cold, noise, bad lighting, vibration, and other similar conditions. Not all these injurious factors are ordinarily found in conjunction in every industry; but one or more of them is operative in nearly every manufacturing industry. Investigation has proved that these general incidents of factory life predispose to the more rapid onset of disease. They thus undermine the workers' powers of resistance and constitute causes of premature deterioration.

The brief in the present case presents an impressive array of evidence, drawn from the experience of countries all over the world, in support of the thesis which we have all too inadequately stated here. It marshals an array of facts that is overwhelming.

The decision in this case will be awaited with the greatest eagerness by all those who realize the importance to the welfare of the whole community of legislative protection of the workers against unhealthful and oppressive conditions of labor.

RECONSTITUTING THE BRITISH EMPIRE

THE unwritten constitution of Great Britain has received a severe jolt. The Little Englanders were content, as they always have been, with an automatic and imperceptible evolution of political institutions "broadening slowly down from precedent to precedent." But the people who live in the "British Isles" lying on the southern side of the world care nothing for precedents, and they share the American aversion to "taxation without representation." Three years before the war Sir Joseph Ward, then Prime Minister of New Zealand, shocked London by suggesting that the foreign policy of the empire ought no longer to be managed exclusively by a small group of Englishmen, but that the self-governing dominions ought to have something to say about it. This unconventional proposal naturally excited considerable amusement, but, out of regard for the feelings of the New Zealander, the English quietly ignored it.

But such polite obliviousness will no longer suffice. Australia has sent two men to England who are accustomed to speaking their mind and who are doing it, ex-Premier Fisher and present Premier Hughes, both leaders of the Labor party.

In 1911 Premier Fisher and his Minister of Defense, Senator Pearce, were called to London with the representatives from the other dominions in order that Premier Asquith and Sir Edward Grey might explain to them the foreign policy of Great Britain and urge them to more active measures in preparation for the coming conflict. Mr. Fisher was deeply imprest, and when he went back used all his influence with the party and the people to put thru measures for a greater army and navy. As soon as he came into power again, in September, 1914, he declared in favor of "standing with the empire to the last man and the last penny," and he has kept his word.

But while he has thus pledged the support of Australia to the Mother Country, he has at the same time insisted that the dominions ought to have something to say about the foreign policy which they are asked to support, and about the terms of peace at the end of the war. But his request early in 1915 that an Imperial Conference be called to consider such questions was curtly declined by the British Government, which still adhered to its old policy of refusing the colonies any share in governing the empire of which they are members.

Now Mr. Fisher has come back to England as High Commissioner of the Australian Commonwealth. Almost as soon as he landed he called attention to the curious circumstance that, if he had remained a poor miner in Scotland, where he was born, he would have had some influence over questions of imperial policy, because he could have heckled his representative in Parliament and voted for or against him on that ground. But, he says:

I went to Australia. I have been Prime Minister. But all the time I have had no say whatever about Imperial policy —no say whatever.

Now, that can't go on. There must be some change.

So, too, Sir Robert Borden, Prime Minister of Canada, has declared that "never again" will Canada take part in a British war unless she has something to say about its causes and results.

But Premier Hughes has gone further. Hearing that a conference of the Allies was to be held in Paris the last of April to consider the advisability of a customs union and other measures by which German trade could be kept down after the war, the Australian Premier coolly asked to be admitted to the conference. This suggestion was, as we might suppose, received with pained surprise. It was politely pointed out to him that Australia was not one of the Allied Powers and that it would be manifestly improper to admit the Premier of Australia and not the Premier of Canada, who, it appears, did not want to be included. But Mr. Hughes persisted and he carried his point. He will attend the conference on commercial strategy, and it would be interesting to know—tho we are not likely to—what he will say. At any rate, we know that he will not be likely to say the same things about tariffs, labor, defense and the

like as would be said for him by Mr. Asquith and Sir Edward Grey.

It seems quite possible that when President Lowell gets out a new edition of his great work on "The Government of England" he will begin a new chapter with Mr. Hughes's arrival at Paris.

THE DIABOLICAL JAPANESE

OF course, you have heard of the 100,000 trained Japanese soldiers now in the United States disguised as farmers, artizans, students and domestic servants, going about seeking whom they may devour and prepared at a given signal to unite and seize the United States. Well, the statistics of the Japanese in the country for 1914 are now available, and the most alarming prophecies are confirmed. It seems that there were 99,321 Japanese scattered thruout the country in 1914, of whom 70,303 were men, 14,876 women, and 14,142 children. Of these 70,303 mature men about fourteen per cent were born in the United States and therefore have not served in the Japanese army. Moreover, the men are decreasing in numbers steadily, to say nothing of getting older and past military age all the time. In 1906 eighty-eight per cent of the Japanese in California were men; in 1914 only sixty-six per cent. Since 1908, when the Japanese population was at its maximum, over 10,000 more Japanese have left our shores than have come here. Thus the Japanese menace proves more horrendous as each new fact is unfolded. We can well applaud the brave Chamber of Commerce of Los Angeles which has just memorialized Congress for a "national rural reserve" of 5,000,000, and a permanent force stationed on the Pacific slope of 500,000 troops "fully equipped and officered" and "ready for instant military service."

COLLECTIVE VS. COMPETITIVE ARMAMENTS

NATIONAL preparedness is a necessary evil. It is necessary because the world is politically unorganized and each nation is the sole custodian of its own security. It is an evil, because it is costly, wasteful, subversive of the golden rule, and is apt to result in the very resort to force it is intended to prevent.

As long as each nation lives under the delusion that it can protect itself against all, as long as it believes in the mathematically impossible policy of having a greater force than any other nation, the United States has got to "play the game" with the rest.

The system is analogous to cut-throat competition in railroads. If one road selfishly lowers rates, thinking thereby to get the other's business, the competitor must follow suit whether he wants to or not. As a result, both roads are worse off than before. So if one nation thinks to gain advantage over a neighbor by greater preparedness, the other must prepare likewise or risk being conquered.

This is why The Independent is for preparedness, and yet deplores preparedness. If we stand for preparedness —moderate and unhysterical tho it be—we do so only as a stop-gap until the whole competitive system of armaments is abolished. This, we admit, is no small task. But there can be no doubt but that once the world has sense enough to substitute the collective system of armaments under a League to Enforce Peace for the competitive system of armaments, under which the world now so grievously suffers, we shall have devised a scientific formula for changing the colossal rival armaments of the world into a true international police, and that will mean their inevitable reduction. For if a recalcitrant nation cannot hope to create a large enough force "to lick all creation," and if a law-abiding nation can be certain to be backed up in its just actions by an overwhelming world force, there will be no incentive to increase armaments and every incentive to decrease them.

Let the United States, then, proclaim to the world that it is ready to join with other nations in a League to Enforce Peace. In the meantime, let us heed the lessons taught by the present war and put our military house in order.

National preparedness is a necessary evil. International preparedness is a necessary good.

UNIVERSITY MANAGEMENT

IF there be a Professors' Almanac like to the old Farmers' Almanac, it would have strung down the April page: "About—this—time—look—out—for—squalls." For every spring we hear complaints about the tyranny of university authorities and attempted interference with free speech. Last year the chief storm centers were Pennsylvania, Utah, Dartmouth, Colorado, Lafayette and Minnesota. This year trouble is reported from about as many more places, and the season is young. For instance, the German-American Alliance of Cincinnati demands the suppression of President Dabney because he "attempts to foist his dangerous notions, personal fallacies and national antipathies upon the community and to turn the tide of opinion to his own liking." The chief ground of complaint seems to be the publication of a private letter which the president of Cincinnati University wrote to a kinsman of his wife's, Congressman Cantrill, urging him to support President Wilson on the question of warning passengers against armed liners. Evidently if a public man in Cincinnati has any private opinions that are not pro-German he had better beware how he puts them on paper.

We may match the sample of German intolerance by a piece of British intolerance from the other side of the ocean. The Rev. Dr. Edward Lyttelton, the honored headmaster of Eton College, has been compelled to resign because, as the dispatch naively states, he exprest the opinion "that it was the duty of Great Britain to extend the principles of Christian charity to Germany."

From Oregon we hear that J. Willis Jefferies has been dismissed from the Franklin High School of Portland because he preferred The Independent and other periodicals to the grammar and rhetoric books in the teaching of English. There are, we have good reason to believe, several thousand teachers in the United States who are guilty of the same crime, but we will never tell on them.

The most serious affair, however, is an insurrection in Bryn Mawr against the rule of President M. Carey Thomas, who is accused of autocratic and dictatorial methods by many of the faculty, alumnæ and students. This outbreak is no surprize, for the trouble has been brewing for many years, and now that it has become public it will probably result in a reorganization of the institution on a more satisfactory basis.

That has been the result in the neighboring University of Pennsylvania. The dismissal of Professor Scott Nearing, which we discussed on July 5 of last year in the editorial on "The Rights of Professors and Students," aroused such indignation among the alumni and public that the university trustees amended the statutes so as to provide for consultation with representatives of the faculty before a professor is removed. This is a great step in advance and will do much to unify the university and to restore confidence in its management.

It is not safe to assume, as the public is apt to do whenever a professor is removed, that the administration is altogether to blame. Such cases are never so simple as they seem to outsiders, but are always complicated by personal factors and conflicting educational ideals. The university authorities should scrupulously avoid all forms of interference with freedom of speech, but, on the other hand, the teacher should remember that he also is under obligation to the institution as to the way in which he exercises that freedom. The best statement we have seen of this reciprocal obligation is contained in the report of the Committee on Academic Freedom and Academic Tenure of the American Association of University Professors, vulgarly known as the "Professors' Trade Union" :

The claim to freedom of teaching is made in the interest of the integrity and of the progress of scientific inquiry; it is, therefore, only those who carry on their work in the temper of the scientific inquirer who may justly assert this claim. The liberty of the scholar within the university to set forth his conclusions, be they what they may, is conditioned by their being conclusions gained by a scholar's method and held in a scholar's spirit; that is to say, they must be the fruits of competent and patient and sincere inquiry, and they should be set forth with dignity, courtesy, and temperateness of language. The university teacher, in giving instruction upon controversial matters, while he is under no obligation to hide his own opinion under a mountain of equivocal verbiage, should, if he is fit for his position, be a person of a fair and judicial mind; he should, in dealing with such subjects, set forth justly, without suppression or innuendo, the divergent opinions of other investigators; he should cause his students to become familiar with the best published expressions of the great historic types of doctrine upon the questions at issue; and he should, above all, remember that his business is not to provide his students with ready-made conclusions, but to train them to think for themselves, and to provide them access to those materials which they need if they are to think intelligently.

If all professors would live up to the ideal thus formulated by their representatives there would be fewer cases of tyrannical action on the part of university authorities, and when such a case did occur public opinion would be unanimous in condemning it.

SHAKESPEARE HARD AT IT

THE other day Ellen Terry helped the Lord Mayor of London to pack—with due pomp and ceremony—a consignment of Shakespeare tercentenary badges to be sent to Canada.

These 750,000 buttons for Canadian buttonholes would seem to indicate an admirable loyalty on the part of this active youngster of a nation to the memory of an old-country poet. It is not literature, however, but philanthropy that is at the bottom of the nation-wide decoration. The Shakespeare buttons are to be sold for the benefit of the British Red Cross, Belgian Relief, and the League of Mercy.

So for a small investment one can honor Shakespeare, comfort a wounded Tommy Atkins, and feed a Belgian baby, all at one stroke. It is a bargain tag-day.

The quality of mercy is not strained. But can one say as much for the memory of Shakespeare?

THE STORY OF THE WEEK

Carranza Wants Us to Withdraw

General Carranza has address a note to the American Government formally protesting against the continuance of American troops in Mexico in pursuit of Villa. The de facto President of Mexico declares that the expedition into Mexico was undertaken under a misapprehension by the American Government of the position of the Mexican Government as set forth in General Carranza's note of March 10. He admits that the action in dispatching the troops in pursuit of Villa was taken in good faith; but asserts that he had no intention of agreeing to such an act in the present case.

The purpose of the original Mexican note was, Carranza now says, to submit a proposal for an agreement under which American or Mexican troops, as the case might be, could cross the boundary line in pursuit of bandits if "unfortunately, there should be repeated along the border acts like those committed in Columbus." The note of last week further declared that the Mexican Government had judged from the first that the Columbus incident, because some time had passed since it had occurred, could not be considered an occasion for the sending of troops into Mexico. Since the subsequent attempts to frame a formal agreement or protocol regulating the reciprocal passage of troops across the border had proved unsuccessful, the Mexican Government now asserts that it "judges it convenient to suspend for the present all discussion or negotiations in this particular or founded on the circumstance that the expedition sent by the United States Government to pursue Villa is without foundation in virtue of the non-existence of a previous agreement, formal and definite." The delivery of the note to Secretary Lansing was regarded by General Carranza as "ending negotiations for a reciprocal passing of troops and asking for disoccupation of the territory occupied by American troops in view of Villa's party having been destroyed."

The Protocol Negotiations

Subsequent to the receipt of the Carranza note, the State Department made public all the previous correspondence between the two governments looking toward the making of a formal agreement. The Mexican Government, in its proposals, suggested severe limitations in several particulars to the sending of any punitive expedition. The expedition must not exceed 1000 men; it must be composed only of cavalry, with no infantry or artillery. The cavalry, however, might be accompanied by machine guns. The pursuit must not be carried further than forty miles across the boundary line, and must be discontinued and the troops withdrawn within five days, "except in unusual cases."

The pursuing forces are not to cross the line within six miles of any town on the border, or to occupy any city or town in the country they have entered. It was further proposed that clashes between troops of the two governments "thru errors or indiscretions of commanders" should not be considered sufficient to hold the government of the offenders responsible; nor could attacks upon the pursuing forces by the inhabitants operate to impose responsibility upon their government.

To these proposals the American

Starrett in New York Tribune
"I GOT IT!"

Harding in Brooklyn Eagle
STRICT NEUTRALITY
Never mind, Carranza has not given the Villistas permission to use the railways, either

State Department returned counter proposals, disposing of most of the limitations suggested with the exception of those relating to the point on the border where the line should be crost, the occupation of towns, and the length of time these forces should remain within the entered country. The length of time under this last provision was proposed to be lengthened to fifteen days, subject to a special agreement for its extension. A request was added to the American reply for the consideration of the Columbus case as falling outside the limits of the protocol and therefore not subject to the limitations contained in the proposed agreement.

To these counter proposals General Carranza declined to agree and the negotiations therefore came to an end.

The Needle and Haystack Hunt

Meanwhile the troops of General Pershing were pushing on along the supposed trail of Villa. More than 400 miles over the boundary line they were well beyond easy communication with their base at the border, and their movements were taking place behind a dense haze of remoteness, accentuated doubtless by the rigorous censorship. Thus this mist came last week the story that Villa had died and been buried in a lonely grave in the mountains. According to the tale, the body was exhumed and started on its way to Chihuahua for definite identification.

A report by Robert Dunn, special correspondent of the New York *Tribune*, gives an interesting picture of the chase as it has now developed:

With the prospects for the capture of Villa apparently no better than they have been since the battle at Guerrero, the campaign has entered into still another new phase—a process of minute search and elimination. Every adobe, every clump of tangled undergrowth that may afford a refuge, is examined in quest of Villa and his generals.

Dramatic night sleuthing and dangerous day combing of arroyos, mesas and canyons have marked the work of our column. Much of the night the men are in the saddle, tumbling into well-earned slumber with the advent of broad day, and buckling again to their work before the afternoon sun has permitted the first faint touches of the evening chill to steal upon them.

Recently three villages were surrounded and searched in the dead of the night, for here we are hot on the trail of Pablo Lopez, and perhaps of Villa himself. In one of these villages our native scout, formerly a Diaz colonel, reported Lopez in hiding. He had been to visit his parents there the night before, our scout had learned, and it was expected he would return again from his hiding place in the hills—a cave, located the villagers knew not where.

At dusk the village in which Lopez's parents live (I am not permitted to write names of places or positions) was surrounded. When the place had grown silent, cavalrymen clattered from door to door, arousing the sleepily protesting inhabitants, searching every hovel, pokin, even into ovens and straw piles. Lopez, warned, doubtless slept on in his cave bed, and

127.

Cesare in New York Sun
GERMAN SUBMARINE COMMANDER'S ACCURATE CONCEPTION OF BOAT HE BLEW UP

Kirby in New York World
FROM ALL SIDES

Starrett in New York Tribune
JOB: "THERE, YOU WEAR IT!"

morning again found our men, irritable and tired, ready for camp and rest.

. . . We were again in the saddle at dusk, halting a brief spell beyond the ranch and dismounting. . . . In the light of the half moon the whole world seemed immersed in a single coloring of silver gray. For a silent hour we rode along, listening

WHERE THE VILLA CHASE HALTED

The heavy black line indicates the route of the punitive expedition in its hunt for the bandit. At Parral a detachment of the Thirteenth Cavalry was attacked by a mob and then by a regular force of Carranza troops. It retreated eight miles to the northeast, and the Americans were north and west of the city when The Independent went to press. It was at Cusihuirachic that Villa is said to have died

now and then for sounds from the other commands.

Suddenly we came in view of a bright fire gleaming on a hilltop, supposedly a Villista signal, while below it lay the village, a light gleaming here and there among the adobes. As we reached the village we found the other details already in the town. The house to house search revealed nothing new except the quaint lie that the signal fire on the hill was that of a lone sentry guarding a Villista cache of treasure.

Finally the command withdrew, only to take up a ten-mile trot across country to another village, where the same scene was reënacted, with the same empty return.

The Parral Fight   A significant incident, which may have important, perhaps serious, results, occurred on the twelfth, at the mining town of Parral. Major Tompkins with two troops of the Thirteenth Cavalry entered Parral, with the cordial acquiescence of the Mexican commander. They were cordially received by the high civic and military officials. General Pershing, in his report, describes what then happened:

"In the outskirts of the town groups of native troops and civilians, following, jeered, threw stones and fired on column. Major Tompkins took definite position north of railroad that was soon flanked by native troops and forced to retire further. About three hundred Carranza-troops joined in pursuit, and Major Tompkins continued to withdraw to avoid further complications until he reached Santa Cruz, eight miles from Parral. Fighting ceased about fifteen miles from town. Major Frank Tompkins deserves great praise for his forbearance. General Lozano attempted to control his men when he first began, but failed. Colonel Brown, with Major Charles Young, and a squadron of the Tenth Cavalry, was eight miles away when notified, and joined Major Frank Tompkins, 7 p. m. (Sentence deleted at this point.) Reported privately forty Mexicans killed, all soldiers, including one major. One civilian wounded. Americans killed, two; wounded, six; missing, one. Major Tompkins slightly wounded in foot (?) by spent bullet."

This attack upon American forces by Carranzista troops naturally raises the question whether the activities of the

American forces in Mexico are long to be free from obstruction and active defiance by the people in general. It also suggests the possibility that not all of the Carranzista officers and troops are coöperating in good faith with the American expedition.

It was announced officially last week that 12,000 soldiers were already in Mexico, and 18,000 engaged in guard duty on the border. This leaves, according to the War Department's announcement, only 4000 regular troops in all the United States.

It becomes obvious that if larger forces become necessary for the completion of our task in Mexico, the militia of the several states must be called upon or the enlistment of a volunteer army resorted to.

Not the Body, but the Soul   Mr. Roosevelt continues to set forth the articles of his political creed with vigor and directness. In so doing he disagrees with certain leaders of the Republican party as to the principal issue on which the campaign against the Administration must be waged. Last week Senator Harding, of Ohio, who has been selected to act as temporary chairman of the Republican National Convention, declared that the tariff was the paramount issue. In commenting on this point of view, Mr. Roosevelt said:

From time to time it has recently been announced that the fight against Mr. Wilson is to be waged only, or almost only, on the tariff. Such an appeal would be an appeal to the belly and not to the soul of the American nation. By all means provide the things of the body, but only on condition that we treat the body as the servant of the soul.

I believe heartily in a protective tariff. Unless we return to a protective tariff, preferably administered thru a commission of experts, we shall face widespread economic disaster at the end of this war.

But this is not the great issue on which the fight is to be made if the highest service is to be rendered the American people. The issue is that the American people must find its own soul. National honor is a spiritual thing that cannot be haggled over in terms of dollars. We must stand not only for America first, but for America first and last and all the time, and without any second.

Weed in Philadelphia Public Ledger
A STUDY IN EXPRESSIONS

Harding in Brooklyn Eagle
WAR PAINT

Kirby in New York World
THE WELL'S GOING DRY

Our loyalty must be to the whole United States. The East must stand for the safeguarding of the Pacific Coast against every foe. The West must stand for the safeguarding of the Atlantic Coast against every foe. East and West and North and South alike must hold the life of every man and the honor of every woman on the most remote ranch on the Mexican border as a sacred trust to be guaranteed by the might of our united nation.

We can be true to mankind at large only if we are true to ourselves. If we are false to ourselves we shall be false to every one else. We have a lofty ideal to serve, a great mission to accomplish for the cause of freedom and of genuine democracy and of justice and fair dealing thruout the world.

If we are weak and slothful and absorbed in mere money getting and rapid excitement we can neither serve these causes nor any others. We must stand for national conscience, for national discipline and for preparedness—military, social and industrial—in order to help the soul of this nation.

We stand for peace, but only for the peace that comes as a right to the just man armed, and not for the peace which the coward purchases by abject submission to wrong. The peace of cowardice leads in the end to war, after a record of shame.

Mr. Roosevelt sees but one issue and states that issue over and over again with characteristic forcefulness.

Germany Appeals to The Hague   The German note of April 10 reports an investigation by the Admiralty of the recent cases of submarine attacks. In regard to the British steamers "Berwindvale," "Englishman" and "Eagle Point," it is claimed that these were given fair warning and ample time for the crews to take to boats. In regard to the French steamer "Sussex" the commander of the submarine reports that he sank a vessel at about that time and place, but he believed it to be a British mine-layer and his sketch of it does not correspond exactly with the picture of the "Sussex" as published in the London illustrated papers. The German note concludes:

No other attack whatever by German submarines occurred at the time in question for the "Sussex" upon the route between Folkstone and Dieppe. The German Government must therefore assume that the injury to the "Sussex" is attributable to another cause than an attack by a German submarine.

For an explanation of the case the fact may perhaps be serviceable that no less than twenty-six English mines were exploded by shots by German naval forces in the channel on the 1st and 2d of April alone. The entire sea in that vicinity is, in fact, endangered by floating mines and by torpedoes that have not sunk. Off the English coast it is further endangered in an increasing degree thru German mines which have been laid against enemy naval forces.

Should the American Government have at its disposal further material for a conclusion upon the case of the "Sussex," the German Government would ask that it be communicated, in order to subject this material also to an investigation.

In the event that differences of opinion should develop hereby between the two governments, the German Government now declares itself ready to have the facts of the case established thru mixed commissions of investigation, in accordance with the third title of The Hague agreement for the peaceful settlement of international conflicts, November 18, 1907.

A German Ship Plot Discovered   Thru the efforts of the New York police force a splendid beginning has been made at uncovering the activities of a group of German sympathizers in this country who have been engaged in putting inflammable bombs into the cargoes of ships sailing for ports of the allied powers. Last week eight arrests were made, seven of them of men connected with the Hamburg-American Line, the eighth of a man connected with a German chemical firm in Hoboken.

The prisoners are Captain Otto Wolpert, commander of the "Friedrich der Grosse," of the Hamburg-American Line; Captain Enno Bode, pier superintendent for the Atlas Line, a subsidiary company of the Hamburg-American; Captain Charles Von Kleist, superintendent of the New Jersey Agricultural and Chemical Company, and Ernest Becker, Carl Schmidt, Frederick Praidel, Wilhelm Paradies and Frederick Garbade, all connected with the engineering staff of the "Friedrich der Grosse."

The story as told by the police is that the bombs were made on board the steamer and sent to the chemical company's works to be filled. The bombs were then turned over to German officers to be secreted in the cargoes of allied merchant ships, and to be shipped to other ports for similar purposes.

The bombs were steel tubes about six inches long and three-quarters of an inch in diameter. Into the top of the tube was screwed an aluminum tube, shaped like a rocket. This inner tube was filled with a liquid chemical which

© *Underwood & Underwood*
SCOUTING IN MEXICO

Lieut. Gorrell and Lieut. Dargue scouting somewhere south of field headquarters at Casas Grandes, Mexico. The aviators have not yet been able to locate their quarry, but they are conducting service both as couriers and in reconnoitering over country that makes flying, especially in these antiquated low-power machines, exceedingly perilous. Eight new machines are expected in a fortnight

© *Underwood & Underwood*

WHAT ARE THEY MARCHING INTO?

The Thirteenth Cavalry, with their backs to the United States and their faces toward Mexico City. The clashes between Mexicans and American soldiers at Parral suggest ugly possibilities in the path of the punitive expedition

would eat its way thru the wall of the tube in a certain calculated time, depending upon the thickness of the aluminum shell. When this liquid had penetrated the shell it came into contact with another chemical substance in the main tube, generating such extreme heat as to burst and destroy the outer steel tube and set fire to anything surrounding it.

The first hint of the plot was obtained when the steamer "Kirk Oswald" was being unloaded at Marseilles on June 8 last. A bag of sugar broke open and nine metal objects rolled out. An investigation by the French police showed that these objects were fire bombs. One of them was subsequently sent to the American State Department and turned over to the New York police. From this single clue the city's detectives, after ten months of work, built up the case against the men who have now been arrested.

It is reported that two, at least, of the prisoners have already confest their share in the manufacture of the bombs. It is believed that evidence will be forthcoming connecting Captain von Papen, the recalled German Military Attaché, and Captain Boy-Ed, the recalled German Naval Attaché, with the plots; and that other Germans of prominence, still in this country, will also be implicated in responsibility for them.

Losses to Merchant Shipping   According to a statement given out by Admiral Sir Cyprian Bridge the total losses to merchant shipping from the beginning of the war to March 23 amount to 980 vessels all told. The British losses amount to six per cent of their total tonnage, the French to seven, the Russian to five and the Italian to four and a half per cent of their total tonnage. On the other hand, ship building in Great Britain has been so rapid that British shipping has gained 344,000 tons since the war began. The distribution of losses is as follows:

Losses to Belligerents

Steamers

Nationality.	Number.	Tonnage.
British	379	1,320,000
French	41	140,000
Belgian	10	30,000
Russian	27	42,000
Italian	21	70,000
Japanese	3	19,000
Totals	481	1,621,000

13⁹

Sailing Vessels

Nationality.	Number.	Tonnage.
British	31	19,000
French	12	18,000
Russian	8	7,000
Italian	6	3,000
Totals	57	47,000

Trawlers: British, 237; French, 7; Belgian, 2.

Losses to Neutrals

Steamers

Nationality.	Number.	Tonnage.
Norway	50	96,000
Denmark	18	33,000
Holland	22	74,000
Sweden	33	42,000
United States	6	16,000
Greece	11	22,000
Spain	4	9,000
Persia	1	750
Portugal	1	625
Totals	146	263,375

Sailing Vessels

Nationality.	Number.	Tonnage.
Norway	22	20,000
Denmark	10	1,600
Sweden	7	2,000
Holland	2	225
United States	1	176
Totals	42	24,001

Trawlers: Denmark, 1; Holland, 7.

Recruiting the British Army   The efforts of the government to raise the army to four million are meeting with increasing difficulty. There were 1,400,-000 more men needed at the beginning of the year, and it was hoped that they might be obtained by Lord Derby's

THE GREAT WAR

April 10—Germany expresses willingness to refer "Sussex" case to The Hague. British take crater at St. Eloi.

April 11—80,000 Germans attack Avocourt front at Verdun. Ten vessels, three of them neutrals, sunk.

April 12—Rumania signs commercial agreement with Germany. British repulsed by Turks on the Tigris.

April 13—Fighting continues on Dead Man's Hill. British Government agrees to pay American packers $15,000,000 for meat cargoes seized.

April 14—Austrians take Italian position near Görz. Russians advance a hundred miles west of Erzerum.

April 15—Russians attacking German lines at Dvinsk. British aeroplanes drop bombs on Constantinople.

April 16—French attack south of Doumont. Russians defeat Turks at Bitlis, Armenia.

scheme of personal solicitation of every eligible man. But this did not bring out enough volunteers, so the government has begun to apply the draft to the unmarried men over eighteen. On April 7 all the married men who have registered as volunteers were ordered to report at the recruiting offices. As three months is regarded as the minimum period of training before sending men to the front, it will be hard to get the field forces up to full strength in time for a vigorous offensive before fall.

On account of the dissatisfaction of the married men at being called out so soon the government is making every effort to reduce the number of men who are ineligible for enlistment by reason of being needed in the manufacture of munitions and other essential industries. This has been done chiefly by the greater employment of women. In commercial, clerical and transport work 275,000 women have found employment and 14,000 in farm work, thus releasing about as many men for military duty.

The conviction is spreading that it will soon be necessary to resort to universal conscription, and it is argued that this would be much more fair and equable than the present semi-volunteer system which places a premium upon dishonesty and cowardice. A faction of both the Unionist and the Liberal parties favor conscription and the Cabinet is similarly divided. Lloyd-George, the Minister of Munitions, is said to favor it, but Mr. Asquith has declared that conscription shall never be adopted so long as he is Prime Minister. It is quite likely, therefore, that the present coalition ministry may be reorganized before very long.

No attempt has been made to extend any of these measures to Ireland, where there is heated and organized opposition even to volunteer recruiting. John Redmond, T. P. O'Connor and most of the Nationalist leaders favor recruiting, but the radical faction known as the Sinn Fein is bitterly anti-English. There are a dozen newspapers openly denouncing the enlistment of Irish in the British army and the efforts of the government to suppress them have been ineffectual

Rumania's Attitude   One of the important events of the week is the announcement from Bucharest that Rumania has concluded a commercial agreement with Germany, according to which each country is free to export to the other all goods for home consumption. This means primarily that Germany can get the surplus of grain crop from Rumania, which amounts to more than 100,000,000 bushels. With the Bulgarian, Rumanian and Turkish grain fields to draw upon, it would seem that Germany is relieved of any danger of being starved out by the British blockade.

The probable action of Rumania has been a puzzle from the start. The Rumanians, claiming, as their name implies, to belong to the Latin race, were by blood and culture in sympathy with the French rather than the Germans and their national ambition was to take from Hungary the territory on the other side of the Transylvanian Alps inhabited by their own people. In the first winter of the war, when the Russians had occupied Galicia and Bukovina and seemed about to invade Hungary, Rumania was expected to enter the war. Indeed it has been asserted that a treaty to that effect had been signed and sealed.

But then the tide turned. The Russians were swept out of Austrian territory. The British, who, it was said, had an option on the Rumanian wheat, failed to open the Dardanelles, so Rumania could get no market except the Central Powers, for Russia, her neighbor on the east, is also an exporter of grain.

It looks as if Rumania had watched to see how the spring campaign opened before deciding which side to take, and now, finding that the Russians were not accomplishing anything and that the Germans were vigorously taking the offensive at Verdun, had made up her mind that the Allies stood little chance of winning. The diplomacy of the Allies in the Balkans has been exceedingly unfortunate. At the start Rumania and Greece were decidedly pro-Ally and almost pledged to enter the war on that side, while Bulgaria was on the fence. Now Bulgaria is actively hostile, Rumania is feeding the enemy and Greece is sullenly submitting to the occupation of her territory by the Allied forces. Serbia and Montenegro are wiped out and Albania is practically lost to the Allies. Of the five Balkan states the Allies have not got one to show for the money they have expended and the armies they have sent to Gallipoli and Salonica.

The Chinese Revolution   The revolt against the rule of Yuan Shih-kai continues to spread and his renouncement of his intention to assume the throne has not allayed it. Nine out of the eighteen provinces of China have now declared their independence or are under the control of the revolutionists.

The revolt originated last December in Yun-nan, the most distant of all the provinces from Peking. Thence it spread to Si-chuan (Sze-chuen), the next province on the north, and gradually advanced eastward until it reached the coast, thus pursuing much the same course as the revolution of 1911 which overthrew the Manchu dynasty and the unsuccessful rebellion of 1913 against Yuan Shih-kai. Canton, the chief port of southern China, has declared its sympathy with the movement. In some cases the governors of provinces and cities have spontaneously renounced their allegiance to the Peking government and thousands of government troops have joined the republican army. The five warships at Canton also have gone over to the revolutionists. From Peking have come frequent reports of battles in which the rebels were crushed, but apparently there has not been much real fighting.

The leaders of the insurrection assured the American Minister, Paul S. Reinsch, that they would protect the lives and property of foreigners in the territory they took over, and so far there have been no complaints by the missionaries and foreign residents.

The national assembly of 1912 elected Yuan Shih-kai President for five years, but last September it was announced that the office was to be made permanent and hereditary. At New Year's, Yuan Shih-kai became Emperor and the coronation was to follow as soon as a propitious date was determined and the necessary preparations made. Later—as the insurrection spread—it was announced that the coronation was postponed, and recently Yuan Shih-kai resumed the title of President and acknowledged that he had misinterpreted the will of the people. But the republicans of the south, who have always been suspicious of him, have now altogether lost confidence in him and his latest change of position fails to conciliate them.

Two contradictory theories as to the origin of the rebellion are current among the supporters of the imperial régime, some laying it to Japanese and others to German intrigue. The republicans, however, indignantly deny that they are under any outside influence. For the German theory there is no apparent evidence. On the contrary, Yuan Shih-kai is supposed to have the support of Germany. But Japan is at least disposed to sympathize with the revolutionary party. The Japanese Government opposed Yuan's plan of becoming Emperor and tried to get the other Powers to unite in thwarting it. The attempted revolution of 1913 received the support of the Japanese interests in the Yang-tse valley and when it failed the leader of it, Dr. Sun Yat-sen, sought refuge in Japan, from which he appears to be directing this new rising. The Chinese in the United States, especially the students, are actively supporting the revolution.

THE SPREAD OF THE CHINESE REVOLUTION

As the shaded area on the map shows the republicans who are fighting Yuan Shih-kai have now control over the southern half of the Chinese empire. If they are not able to overthrow the Peking Government they are likely to convert the southern provinces into an independent republic with Canton as the capital

FROM STATE TO STATE

ALABAMA: Never before in the history of Alabama has so much been done for the removal of illiteracy from the state as in the last year. Hundreds of communities in which a year ago there were no schools of any kind, some in which there was no person who could read or write, now have well appointed school houses and a competent corps of teachers. Now that the people are theroly aroused, much is being done by state and county authorities, but the greater part of the work is still carried on by private enterprise.

DELAWARE: For several years the public schools of Wilmington have suffered because of differences between the City Council and the Board of Education. The law requires the board to conduct the schools effectively, but forbids it to create floating debts. The City Council is required by law to appropriate annually such sums as the Board of Education may deem actually necessary, but it is said the council in recent years has made its school appropriations without consulting the board and that the sums have been insufficient. The board therefore claims it has had to create floating debts or close the schools, while the council claims that if the schools had been managed economically the appropriations would have been ample. Now the board has not enough money to keep the schools open any longer and has determined to appeal to the courts unless the council makes an immediate appropriation.

DISTRICT OF COLUMBIA: An organization to be known as the District of Columbia Referendum Association has been effected by a large number of leading residents of Washington. In the absence of suffrage or any other organized means for the citizens of the District to express their needs or desires, it is the purpose of the association to petition Congress "to enact legislation providing machinery that will take jurisdiction by referendum on all matters affecting the general welfare of the citizens of the District of Columbia, and after said referendums are executed that they shall be presented to the Congress of the United States."

FLORIDA: The Legislature last year provided for the organization of a state roads department, but made no direct appropriation for its maintenance. It was supposed that fifteen per cent of the money received by the several counties for automobile licenses would provide a sufficient fund, the remaining eighty-five per cent to be used as road funds by the counties collecting it. But the county authorities have been so lax in the collection of these license fees since the department was organized in October that the commissioner has been practically without money. It is said that motor tourists, who make the most use of the roads, are the worst offenders in escaping payment, the the law requires only a small fee in one county for use of the roads anywhere in the state during the year.

ILLINOIS: The University of Chicago has determined upon a site for the chapel which John D. Rockefeller, the university's founder, desires shall be the central and dominant feature of the university group. In a letter setting forth his ideas concerning this structure Mr. Rockefeller said: "It is my desire that at least $1,500,000 be used for the erection and furnishing of a university chapel. . . . The chapel may appropriately embody those architectural ideals from which the other buildings, now so beautifully harmonious, have taken their spirit, so that all the other buildings on the campus will seem to have caught their inspiration from the chapel and in turn will seem to be contributing of their worthiness to the chapel."

KANSAS: Topeka calls upon the world to look at what she has done in the matter of city-owned lighting and water plants. Twenty-five years ago she established her lighting plant. Up to the present time she has invested $103,515.03 in it. She lights with arc lamps 94.52 miles of streets and with tungsten lamps 34.5 miles. Counting all costs of operation and allowing for depreciation of plant, she is able to supply electricity at the switchboard at a cost of a little more than one and a half cents per kilowatt hour. Consumers buying from a private concern pay at the rate of seven cents. Ten years ago the city bought the water works from a private company for $620,000. Since then the plant has been more than doubled, the rates to consumers reduced four times, yet a sinking fund of $143,249.50 has been accumulated, and $341,618.08 has been spent on improvements and extensions.

KENTUCKY: In the week recently devoted by the citizens of Louisville to raising money for an auditorium, $252,445 was contributed. Never before in the history of the city had so many people contributed to a public improvement. It had been said that $250,000 must be the minimum sum for putting the project thru, and many had predicted that this amount could not be raised, but in the week it was exceeded, and the people had determined to have a $300,000 auditorium.

MARYLAND: A unique situation has arisen in Maryland out of the battle for statewide prohibition, which has been raging for a long time in the General Assembly. The "dry" counties of the state have been forcing the fight for months, but by means of the McIntosh amendment, which the House has adopted by a vote of fifty-three to forty-seven, the question whether the "wet" counties and cities are to remain "wet", is to be left to them alone. The amendment provides for a compulsory vote on prohibition in those counties and cities which are now "wet," but calls for no vote in other places.

MICHIGAN: At a recent meeting of the Michigan State Tax Association a movement was inaugurated for the investigation of the state government with a view to ascertaining where all the tax money goes and what the people are getting for it. The per capita taxes in Michigan, for all branches of state and local government, have increased 130 per cent in the last ten years. The investigation is to be made first in the state departments, all of which, with a single exception, have increased their expenditures by percentages ranging from 21 to 27.73 in the last ten years.

MONTANA: The army cutworm, which caused serious loss of winter wheat in this state last year, has made its appearance again this spring in even larger numbers. The State Entomologist has issued a special bulletin requesting farmers to examine their fields carefully at once and to communicate with him as soon as they discover evidence of the worm's presence. He says he could have saved a great deal of grain last year if he had received earlier reports.

NEBRASKA: Of the 386,000 children of school age in this state about 350,000 attend rural schools. Yet until less than a year ago only the elementary grades were taught in most of these schools. Since last spring, however, 191 new high schools have been put into operation, and the way is now open for at least 10,000 rural children to reach the college and university without having to go to the larger cities for their preparation. A large number of villages and small towns have also increased the number of their high school grades.

OHIO: At the recent executive meeting of the trustees of the Ohio Anti-Saloon League it was decided to make a campaign for $350,000, which, it is estimated, will be required for "organization and educational purposes" and for carrying out the statewide survey of the liquor traffic which has been decided upon. This survey is for the purpose of gathering all possible information regarding the amount of money spent for liquor in the state and of determining the relation of drinking to crime and pauperism. Also its aim will be to learn the attitude of all employers and employees in the state toward prohibition as related to efficiency.

TENNESSEE: At the suggestion of Mayor Littleton, of Chattanooga, a call has been issued by mayors of leading cities in fourteen states for a representative convention in Chattanooga on June 2, the purpose being to discuss freely all matters pertaining to national defense. The plan is to have each mayor appoint not less than ten representative residents of his city and each county judge appoint a similar number of other citizens of his county to attend the conference. It is hoped thus to gain accurate knowledge of the prevailing sentiment of each section represented and to bring together for discussion many various views of preparedness.

UTAH: One of the most elaborate organization campaigns ever attempted in this country by a highway association had its beginning at Grand Junction in this state a few years ago, when a committee left for the National Midland Trail to Washington, D. C. On the way thru Colorado, Kansas, Missouri, Illinois, Indiana, Kentucky, West Virginia and Virginia the committee will seek to stir up enthusiasm for highway construction and organize local branches of the association in all cities, towns and villages. At the end of the journey a report will be made by the highway engineer on the condition and needs of every section of the road. This will be published with the general report and widely distributed.

WASHINGTON: An aerial passenger and freight line between Seattle and Tacoma, which was authorized by the Legislature recently, promises to begin a regular schedule of trips on June 1. The hydroaeroplane with which the company will begin operations measures 100 feet in wingspread. Below the plane is a car which will carry ten passengers and two pilots, and beneath this are two pontoons, each designed for carrying an aeroplane gun in time of war, but which may be used at other times for carrying certain light freight or baggage. The machine is driven by two 120-horsepower engines.

WISCONSIN: People of this state and Michigan, especially those of the port cities, are theroly aroused over the proposed granting of permission by the Federal War Department for the diversion of additional volumes of water from Lake Michigan into the drainage canal at Chicago for the purpose of making the canal navigable to the Illinois River. They say it would so lower the level of the Great Lakes and tributary rivers as to impose heavy additional expense upon lake cities for maintenance of harbor and channel depths. It is believed that when this fact is realized every city on the entire chain of lakes will join in the protest.

WYOMING: A remarkable change of opinion concerning the settlement of the public domain has taken place in this state in the last few years. What is known as the 640-acre homestead bill in Congress is now receiving the support not only of the general public, but also of the large ranchmen, who have heretofore vigorously opposed all such propositions, but who are now among the most active leaders in favor of the bill. Practically all the newspapers in the state are also supporting it.

132

HOW MUCH PREPAREDNESS?

BY CHAMP CLARK

SPEAKER OF THE HOUSE OF REPRESENTATIVES

TODAY we are facing two important national problems, each awaiting Congressional solution, and these problems are popularly known as preparedness and revenues. Both are of the utmost importance, and in writing of them I do so with a thoro and solemn sense of responsibility.

I believe that the average American is in favor of reasonable and adequate preparation by land and sea, not for the purpose of attacking any nation on earth, but to repel the attack of any and every nation under the sun, should any nation be so unwise as to assail us. While he is not eager to pay taxes, he is willing to foot the bills for reasonable and adequate preparedness.

A great many people—I am not talking about foreigners now, but about our own citizens—sadly misjudge our national character. We are constantly told that this is the most peaceable nation beneath the stars; but that is only half the truth. The whole truth is that, while we are the most peaceable nation in the world, we are at the same time the most martial. The proof of that seeming paradox is that in April, 1861, there were not 20,000 soldiers in America, while four years later the continent trembled beneath the tramp of 2,000,000 of the finest soldiers the sun ever looked down upon, some in blue and some in gray.

Notwithstanding the senseless and malicious abuse heaped upon the Congress, what Congress invariably does, when it can ascertain with a reasonable degree of assurance what the will of the people is, is to transmute this will into law. That is exactly what Congress is trying to do at the present time, and those impatient folks who have been criticizing the Senate and the House for going too slow have no conception whatever of the toil, thought and investigation which their members have expended on important measures, especially the measure of preparedness. Now, what is the will of the people on this?

SINCE the agitation for and against what is popularly known as preparedness became acute I have spoken and lectured in thirty-one states, and have tried to find out public opinion by reading magazines and newspapers, by experiments in my speeches and lectures on many audiences, and by interrogating every sort of citizen; section bosses, firemen, engineers, conductors, farmers, merchants, lawyers, laborers, preachers, statesmen, soldiers and teachers.

There are certain fundamental propositions on which the vast majority of the American people are agreed. They want peace, but not peace at any price; they want peace with honor. While peace is the normal condition of Americans, and while they love it most fondly and pray for it most devoutly, they believe thoroly that there are things worth fighting for. They do not intend to see this country turned into an armed camp, and are unalterably opposed, always have been, and forever will be, to a large standing army. They are not willing to bankrupt the country in military and naval preparations. They are, however, willing to spend all that is necessary for the public defense. They are almost to a man against conscription in times of peace, but they are for it should it become necessary in times of war. For in war, as in other undertakings, having put their hand to the plow, they do not look back. While proud of the record of our small army in all our wars, they have always depended upon our volunteers to do most of our fighting, and they glory in the valor of our volunteers on hundreds of historic fields. And last, they have no desire or ambition to have our country pose as a great military power, and they have no intention of seeing it as helpless as China. They know beyond a peradventure that a great, rich country without the means of defense is a constant temptation to the cupidity of mankind.

THESE hard-headed Americans believe profoundly in the philosophy that an ounce of prevention is worth a pound of cure. They are against a war of aggression, but they will fly to arms any day in a war for defense. They know that the navy constitutes the first line of defense and that it has proved a very present help in every time of trouble. They know that coast fortifications constitute the second line of defense and that observation of the stupendous war across the sea proves that battleships cannot batter down well-constructed land defenses. They know that regulars, with such other troops as we can put into the field, constitute our third and last line of defense.

In view of all these facts, beliefs, observations and desires, the average American is, I repeat, in favor of reasonable and adequate preparation by land and sea.

FROM time to time something is said about our revenues, and how to meet the bills that will be accumulated by an enlarged preparedness program. Personally, I can see no reason at present for considering a revision of the Underwood tariff, either in general or in regard to special schedules of the law. The bill seems to be doing what was expected of it, and for the present, at least, it should be left alone.

I cannot favor the imposition of further stamp taxes or burdensome excise taxes to meet the needs of the Treasury now or in the near future. Stamp taxes are onerous at best and should be resorted to only as emergency measures. I believe the present war-tax law should be revised and many of the stamp taxes which it contains should be eliminated.

Under the recent decision of the Supreme Court of the United States the income tax law becomes available as a means of raising additional revenue without making its provisions especially burdensome to any one class of citizens. Thru the income tax we can raise a large part of the money we need for various purposes. An increase in the income tax rates and a general rearrangement of the classification of incomes under the income tax law would produce a large amount of revenue and would not unduly burden any one.

Then I believe the proposal to levy a tax on the manufacturers of war munitions, who are shipping vast quantities of their products abroad, should be favorably considered. These munition manufacturers are making vast profits out of the present increased trade in their product. They are probably the most prosperous class in the country today. I am convinced that they should bear their share of any increased taxation. I believe that a fair and equitable scheme of raising revenue thru this tax can very easily be evolved.

Of course, we are not in a position to settle upon a definite detailed revenue program until we have some definite idea of what the expenditures of the government for the fiscal year 1917 will be. This we cannot have until the various appropriation bills have taken form and we know what expenditures are proposed for increased national defense.

Washington, D. C.

THE ONLY SON LEFT

A SOLDIER TELLING HIS OLD MOTHER HOW
HIS THREE BROTHERS FOUGHT AND
DIED FOR FRANCE

THE NEW SHAW

RECENT PHASES IN THE DEVELOPMENT OF G. B. S.

BY EDWIN E. SLOSSON

AUGUST 4, 1914, cuts time in two like a knife. We are already beginning to look back upon the antebellum days as a closed period, and those who were conspicuous in it are being seen in an historical perspective such as the lapse of a generation of ordinary times is needed to produce. Some reputations are shrinking, others are rising, as mountains seem from a departing train to rearrange themselves according to their true hight. The true prophets are becoming distinguishable from the false.

Among those who have stood the test and stand higher than before, is George Bernard Shaw. Whether he will write better plays than before remains to be seen. Perhaps he will write no more of any kind. But those he has written will be regarded with more respect because we can see their essential truth, whereas before we feared lest we might be merely fascinated by their glitter. Warnings which the world took for jokes because of their fantastic guise now turn out too terribly real, and advice which the world ignored would better have been heeded.

Few writers have as little to take back on account of the war as Shaw, altho few have exprest such decided opinions in such extreme language on so many topics. For instance, Kipling's "The Bear That Walks Like a Man" makes queer reading now that England is fighting to give Russia what then she was ready to fight to prevent her getting. But the full significance of Shaw's fable farce of "Androcles and the Lion" is now for the first time being realized. The philosophy of this, his most frivolous and serious play, is summed up by Ferrovius, a converted giant of the Ursus type, who finds it impossible to keep to his Christian principle of non-resistance when brought into the arena. The natural man rises in him and he slays six gladiators single-handed. This delights the emperor, who thereupon offers him a post in the Pretorian Guards which he had formerly refused. The fallen and victorious Ferrovius accepts, saying:

In my youth I worshiped Mars, the god of war. I turned from him to serve the Christian God; but today the Christian God forsook me; and Mars overcame me and took back his own. The Christian God is not yet. He will come when Mars and I are dust; but meanwhile I must serve the gods that are, not the God that will be. Until then I accept service in the Guard, Caesar.

In speaking of "the new Shaw" I mean merely that he looks new. The

This is the ninth article of a series entitled "Twelve Major Prophets of Today." The first six, dealing with Maurice Maeterlinck, Henri Bergson, Henri Poincaré, Elie Metchnikoff, Wilhelm Ostwald and Ernst Haeckel, have been published in book form by Little, Brown & Co., Boston. In the second group of studies, the sketch of Rudolf Eucken appeared in The Independent of February 17, 1915, and that on H. G. Wells in the issue of November 20, 1913. Articles on G. K. Chesterton, F. C. S. Schiller and John Dewey will complete the series.—THE EDITOR.

great cataclysm does not seem to have changed his opinions one iota, but all England is changed, and so he appears in a different light. More of his countrymen agree with what he used to preach to them than ever before, yet he was never so disliked as he is today—which is saying a great deal. The British press has boycotted him. His letters once so sought after by the most dignified journals now no longer appear except in *The New Statesman*. His speeches, be they never so witty and timely, are not reported or even announced.

Consequently those who wish to hear him have to resort to the advertising expedients of the era before printing. A friend of mine just back from London tells me that he saw chalked on the sidewalk a notice of a meeting to be address by Shaw in some out-of-the-way hall. Going there he found it packed with an enthusiastic crowd gathered to hear Shaw discuss the questions of the day. It will be interesting to see how long he can be kept out of print. We cannot help thinking of the time when certain New York papers took a similar vow in regard to another man famous enough to be known by initials. But when T. R. ran for President and got shot at he could no longer be kept off the front page.

But Shaw thrives on unpopularity or at least on public disapproval, which is not quite the same thing. It is not only that Shaw would rather be right than Prime Minister; he would rather be leader of the Opposition than Prime Minister. He would be "in the right with two or three"; in fact, if his followers increased much beyond the poet's minimum he would begin to feel uneasy and suspect that he was wrong.

Shaw's brain secretes automatically the particular antitoxin need-

ed to counteract whatever disease may be epidemic in the community at the time. This injected with some vigor into the veins of thought may not effect a cure, but always excites a feverish state in the organism. It is his habit of seeing that there is another side to a question and calling attention to it at inconvenient times that makes him so irritating to the public. At present he is interned in Coventry as a pro-German on account of his pamphlet, "Common Sense About the War." But this is almost the only thing produced in England during the first weeks of the war that reads well now. Compare it with its numerous replies and see which seems absurd. Doubtless it was not tactful, it might have been called treasonable, but it certainly was sensible. Shaw kept his head level when others lost theirs. That was because he had thought out things in advance and so did not have to make up his mind in a hurry with the great probability of making it up wrong. In that pamphlet he presented the case for the Allies in a way much more convincing to the American mind than many that came to us in the early days of the war, and his arguments have been strengthened by the course of events while others advanced at that time were weakened.

As for the charge of pro-Germanism, that may best be met by quoting from a letter written by him to a friend in Vienna early in 1915:

As regards myself, I am not what is called a Pan-German. The Germans would not respect me, were I at such a time as this, when all thoughts of culture have vanished, not to stand by my people. But also, I am not an anti-German. The war brings us all on to the same plane of savagery. Every London coster can stick his bayonet deeper into the stomach of Richard Strauss than Richard Strauss would care to do to him.

Militarism has just now compelled me to pay a thousand pounds war taxation in order that some "brave little Serbian" may be facilitated in cutting your throat or, that a Russian Moudjik may cleave your skull in twain, altho I would gladly pay twice that sum to save your life, or to buy some beautiful picture in Vienna for our National Gallery.

Shaw has always condemned militarism because of the type of mind it engenders in officers and men. But he has never been opposed to preparedness or to the use of force. In the London *Daily News* of January 1, 1914,—note the date—he said:

I like courage (like most constitutionally timid civilians) and the active

135

use of strength for the salvation of the world. It is good to have giants in strength and it is not at all tyrannous to use it like a giant provided you are a decent sort of giant. What on earth is strength for but to be used and will any reasonable man tell me that we are using our strength now to any purpose?

Let us get the value of our money in strength and influence instead of casting every new cannon in an ecstasy of terror and then being afraid to aim it at anybody.

At that time, seven months before the storm burst, he not only anticipated the war, but said that it might be averted.

By politely announcing that war between France and Germany would be so inconvenient to England that the latter country is prepared to pledge herself to defend either country if attacked by the other.

If we are asked how we are to decide which nation is really the aggressor we can reply that we shall take our choice, or when the problem is unsolvable we shall toss up, but that we will take a hand in the war anyhow. International warfare is an unmitigated nuisance. Have as much character building civil war as you like, but there must be no sowing of dragon's teeth like the Franco-Prussian war. England can put a stop to such a crime single handed easily enough if she can keep her knees from knocking together in her present militarist fashion.

Of course Shaw may have been wrong in supposing that an open announcement of Great Britain's determination to enter the war would have deterred Germany, but as we now know from the White Paper this same opinion was held by the governments of both France and Russia. On July 30 the President of France said to the British Ambassador at Paris that

If His Majesty's Government announced that England would come to the aid of France in the event of a conflict between France and Germany as a result of the present differences between Austria and Servia, there would be no war, for Germany would at once modify her attitude.

And on July 25 M. Sazonof, the Russian Foreign Minister, said to the British Ambassador at Petrograd that

He did not believe that Germany really wanted war, but her attitude was decided by ours. If we took our stand firmly with France and Russia there would be no war. If we failed her now, rivers of blood would flow and we would in the end be dragged into war.

SHAW now gives the same advice to the United States that he gave to his own country before the war, that is, to increase its armament and not be afraid to use it. In a recent letter to the American *Intercollegiate Socialist* he said:

I should strenuously recommend the United States to build thirty-two new dreadnoughts instead of sixteen, and

SHAW AND SHAKESPEARE
From a cartoon by E. T. Reed in *Punch*. This and the cartoon on the opposite page reproduced by courtesy of Stewart & Kidd, publishers of Henderson's *George Bernard Shaw*

to spend two billion dollars on its armament program instead of one. This would cost only a fraction of the money you are wasting every year in demoralizing luxury, a good deal of it having been in the past scattered over the continental countries which are now using what they saved out of it to slaughter one another.

If the United States wishes to stop war as an institution, that is, to undertake the policing of the world, it will need a very big clubhouse for the purpose.

If I were an American statesman I should tell the country flatly that it should maintain a Pacific navy capable of resisting an attack from Japan and an Atlantic navy capable of resisting an attack from England, with Zeppelins on the same scale, a proportionate land equipment of siege guns, and so forth. And until the nations see the suicidal folly of staking everything in the last instance on the ordeal of battle no other advice will be honest advice.

In "Major Barbara" Cusins abandons the teaching of Greek to take up the manufacture of munitions because he has the courage "to make war on war." It is in this play, which has recently been running in New York, that is expounded the theory on which President Wilson is now acting. Lady Britomart tells Cusins: "You must simply sell cannons and weapons to people whose cause is right and just, and refuse them to foreigners and criminals." But Undershaft, the munition-maker replies: "No; none of that. You must keep the true faith of an Armorer, or you don't come in here." And when Cusins asks: "What on earth is the true faith of an Armorer?" he answers:

To give arms to all men who offer an honest price for them, without respect of persons or principles; to aristocrat and republican, to Nihilist and Tsar, to burglar and policeman, to black man, white man and yellow man,

to all sorts and conditions, all nationalities, all faiths, all follies, all causes and all crimes. . . . I will take an order from a good man as cheerfully as from a bad one. If you good people prefer preaching and shirking to buying my weapons and fighting the rascals, don't blame me. I can make cannons; I cannot make courage and conviction.

In this same conversation Shaw also gives a hint of his theology, when Cusins says to Undershaft: "You have no power. You do not drive this place; it drives you. And what drives this place?" Undershaft answers, enigmatically, "A will of which I am a part." This doctrine of an immanent God working thru nature and man to higher things was developed more definitely in a debate which Mr. Shaw held some years ago with the Rev. R. J. Campbell, then of the City Temple. Here he argued that God created human beings to be "his helpers and servers, not his sycophants and apologists." Shaw continues:

If my actions are God's nobody can fairly hold me responsible for them; my conscience is mere lunacy. . . . But if I am a part of God, if my eyes are God's eyes, my hands God's hands, and my conscience God's conscience, then also I share his responsibility for the world; and so is me if the world goes wrong!

This position enables him to explain evil on evolutionary principles as "the Method of Trial and Error." When Blake asks of the tiger, "Did he who made the lamb make thee?" Shaw conceives the Life-Force as replying:

Yes, it was the best I could devise at the time; but now that I have evolved something better, part of the work of that something better, Man, to wit, is to kill out my earlier attempt. And in due time I hope to evolve Superman, who will in his turn kill out and supersede Man, whose abominable cruelties, stupidities and follies have utterly disappointed me.

IN the unactable third act of his "Man and Superman" is to be found one of the most eloquent arraignments of war in all literature. It is, remember, the Devil who is speaking:

The plague, the famine, the earthquake, the tempest were too spasmodic in their action; the tiger and the crocodile were too easily satiated and not cruel enough; something more constantly, more ruthlessly, more ingeniously destructive was needed; and that something was Man, the inventor of the rack, the stake, the gallows and the executioner; of the sword and gun; above all, of justice, duty, patriotism, and all the other isms by which even those clever enough to be humanely disposed are persuaded to become the most destructive of all destroyers.

Three years before the war Shaw wrote a little satirical skit, "Press Cuttings," which was deemed so dangerous to both Britain and Germany that the censors of both countries agreed in prohibiting its production on the stage. Since the British censor seemed to fear that the principal characters, "Balsquith" and "Mitchener," might be taken by the public as referring to certain well-known statesmen, Shaw offered to change the names to "Bones" and "Johnson." But even that concession would not satisfy the censor's scruples, so the play was never put on the stage, tho, since there was then no censorship of literature, it was published as a book. Here is a bit of the dialog:

Balsquith—The Germans have laid down four more Dreadnoughts.
Mitchener—Then you must lay down twelve.
Balsquith—Oh, yes; its easy to say that; but think of what they'll cost.
Mitchener—Think of what it would cost to be invaded by Germany and forced to pay an indemnity of five hundred millions. . . . .
Balsquith—After all, why should the Germans invade us?
Mitchener— Why shouldnt they? What else have their army to do? What else are they building a navy for?
Balsquith—Well, we never think of invading Germany.
Mitchener— Yes, we do. I have thought of nothing else for the last ten years. Say what you will, Balsquith, the Germans have never recognized, and until they get a stern lesson, they never *will* recognize, the plain fact that the interests of the British Empire are paramount, and that the command of the sea belongs by nature to England.
Balsquith—But if they wont recognize it, what can I do?
Mitchener—Shoot them down.
Balsquith—I cant shoot them down.
Mitchener—Yes, you can. You dont realize it; but if you fire a rifle into a German he drops just as surely as a rabbit does.
Balsquith—But dash it all, man, a rabbit hasnt got a rifle and a German has. Suppose he shoots you down.
Mitchener—Excuse me, Balsquith; but that consideration is what we call cowardice in the army. A soldier always assumes that he is going to shoot, not to be shot.

The play ends with the establishment of universal military training and equal suffrage, thus doing away with a militarism that was both timorous and tyrannical, snobbish and inefficient, and at the same time making the nation truly democratic. It is characteristic of Shaw that recently when the papers were discussing what sort of a monument should commemorate Edith Cavell, he interjected the unwelcome suggestion that the country could honor her best by enfranchising her sex.

SHAW has two defects which militate against his popularity; first, he is too conventional and, second, his convenations are peculiarly his own. "There is," says his Undershaft, "only one true morality for every man, but not every man has the same morality," Shaw is easily shocked, but never by the same things that shock other people.

There is no doubting Shaw's intent to undeceive the world or his willingness to undeceive himself. "My way of joking is to tell the truth," says his Father Keegan.

But when he strains his eyes to see something clearly he sees only that one thing. By following consistently one line of logic—instead of several as he should—he gets tangled up in illogicalities. His mode of reasoning is often the *reductio ad absurdum* of his own theories, and this is not a persuasive way of argumentation.

By temperament Shaw is a mystic, but his conscience compels him to assume the method of cold intellectualism. He is an artist in the disguise of a scientist, an uncommon thing to see in this so-called age of science.

Probably Shaw is not more inconsistent than any man of agile mind who is capable of seeing in succession different sides of a thing, but he is franker in expressing the point of view he holds at the time. Consequently he has many admirers but

SHAW IN ACTION
From a cartoon by Max Beerbohm in *Vanity Fair* (London)

few followers. They can't keep up. The only possible Shavian is Shaw.

PERHAPS the reader will think that I am rather too presumptuous in professing to know just what Shaw means and believes, when most people are puzzled by him. So I should explain that I have the advantage of a personal acquaintance with Shaw. I may say without boasting—or at least without lying—that at one period of his life I was nearer to him than any other human being. The distance between us was in fact the diameter of one of those round tables in the A. B. C. restaurants, and the period was confined to the time it took to consume a penny bun and a cup of tea, both being paid for by him. I resorted to thoro Fletcherizing for the purpose of prolonging the interview, and I wished that either he or I had been a smoker. But altho a vegetarian he eschews the weed, and smoking did not seem to be in accordance with Fabian tactics.

The occasion was a recess in a Fabian Society conference. I did not suppose that anything could shut off Socialists in the midst of debate. The theme of discussion was the House of Lords, which the Fabians unanimously agreed ought to be abolished, tho no two of them agreed on the substitute. But while they were iconoclasts as to one British institution, they rendered homage to another by stopping to take tea in the midst of a lovely scrap.

The Fabian Society is the fruit of one of the seeds which Thomas Davidson scattered in many lands. You can track this peripatetic philosopher thru life, as you can Johnny Appleseed, by the societies that sprung up along his pathway. In the Adirondacks he found the Glenmore School of Philosophy. In the Jewish quarter of New York City another of his schools still thrives and is enthused with something of his zeal for learning. In England he started the Society for Psychical Research and the Fellowship of the New Life, of which the Fabian Society was an offshoot. Yet Davidson himself was neither a spiritualist nor a Socialist.

AT the Fabian Society one sees Shaw in his element. Every creature, says Browning, like the moon, Boasts two soul-sides, one to face the world with,
One to show a woman when he loves her. The Fabian Society is Shaw's own true love, and to her he turns a different face than to the outside world. As I watched him during the afternoon —preceding and following the brief

period of personal contact of which I have been boasting—I was struck by the tact and kindliness which he showed in the course of the discussion. There was in his occasional remarks no trace of the caustic and dogmatic tone which one gets from his writings. He is not merely the "shining light" or "presiding genius" of the society, but one of the "wheel horses," and devotes himself diligently to the detailed and inconspicuous work of the organization.

The question under discussion at the conference was that of the reconstruction of the House of Lords. This was shortly before the war, when such questions were regarded as important. Various plans were proposed in order to secure the election of the fittest, when Shaw took the floor in defense of genuine democracy. His argument ran something like this:

Our idea is that any 670 people is as good as any other for governing, just as any twelve chosen by chance on the jury have our lives and property in their hands.

Now if I and Mr. Sydney Webb were sent to the House of Commons it should be with unlimited opportunity to talk but not to vote. To give us a vote would be to permit the violation of the fundamental principle of democracy that people should never be governed better than they want to be. If you had a government of saints and philosophers the people would be miserable. For instance, I would want to stop all smoking and meat-eating and liquor drinking, but like all superior persons now I have to convince other people because I cannot compel them.

These remarks, delivered in a musical and sympathetic voice with frequent flashes of a broad row of white teeth, sounded very different from the way they read in cold type. I do hope the phonograph will be perfected before Shaw dies or his voice goes cracked so posterity can have a vocal version of his plays and prefaces. Otherwise his personality stands little chance of being understood.

Shaw is tall and uses his eyeglasses for gesticulating as an orchestra leader uses a baton. His hair was once a fiery red, but is now tempered into gray. Between his brows there are three perpendicular wrinkles, but not of the cross and fretful type. His face is long and pointed, but he looks not in the least Mephistophelian as the caricaturists represent him. In short, Shaw is not so black as he is painted by himself and others.

If I were to sum up Shaw in two words it would be that his distinguishing characteristics are courage and kind-heartedness. The sight of suffering and injustice drives him mad, and then he runs amuck, slashing right and left, without much regard to whom he hits and no regard at all to who hits him. He is, like Swift, a cruel satirist thru excess of sympathy. If Ibsen is right, that "the strongest man in the world is he who stands most alone," then George Bernard Shaw is not to be ignored.

A SONG FOR FRANCE EMBATTLED

BY ROBERT UNDERWOOD JOHNSON

Across the sea that once was free now
    let the message leap
That France has won our Western
    hearts, and waked our souls from
    sleep!
Proud land! No more shall we mistake
    the shallows for the deep.

They knew her not who lightly thought
    her frivolously gay—
She who first taught our grimmer world
    the sanity of play;
They saw the birds that fly the nest
    but not the brood that stay.

And we who knew and loved her true
    and shared her welcome kind—
The welcome of her heart, and more,
    the welcome of her mind—
How could we know these newer bonds
    that evermore shall bind!—

That she, the Queen of Peace serene,
    who sought the sword no more—
That she, the Queen of Art, who keeps
    the key of Beauty's door,
More royal than her royal lines, should
    be the Queen of War!—

For, tho the years have drowned in
    tears her thrones and quarterings,
She, kingless, has not lost the proud
    residuum of kings:
Noblesse oblige is written fair on every
    flag she flings.

Let others plead a brutal need and
    compromise with faith,
And soil the robe of honor, and make
    of joy a wraith,
No taint of lie shall linger in any word
    she saith.

They reckoned ill who thought her will
    was sunk in sloth or pride,
Who held as weak her patience and on
    her feuds relied.
No power can lock the scabbards where
    thinking swords abide.

Oh, there is calm of Sabbath psalm and
    there is calm of wo,
And calm of slaves who never the calm
    of freemen know,
When, tho the storm may tear the
    wave, the sea is calm below.

Upon the air no martial blare proclaimed the fateful call;
No drum need make the summons the
    spirit makes to all;
Not softlier to the solemn earth the
    autumn leaflets fall.

With gaze that saw far things of awe
    she stood as in a trance,
But faltered not before the shock of
    War's long-dreaded chance,
And every soul was born again—an
    effigy of France!

Oh, eyes that weep in lonely sleep but
    show no waking tear,
Oh, lips with their brave silences and
    lingering words of cheer:
What memories of parting have made
    the danger dear!

And when the breath of icy Death
    sweeps like a winter rain,
And like a scythe the iron hail cuts
    down the human grain,
How bleed we with her wounded and
    sorrow for her slain!

And when beside the Marne's red tide—
    a lioness at bay—
She gave September unto Mars to make
    him holiday,
She saved with hers our kindred soil
    three thousand miles away.

How we acclaim Man's sacred name, as
    second unto God,
And deem our bond a brotherhood divine of cloud and clod!
Where are men fellows but in France,
    save underneath the sod?

Her heart a cup of joy filled up to greet
    the dancing day,
How willingly she spilled the wine and
    threw the cup away
That deserts yet unpeopled may live in
    peace for aye!

The triple watchword of her faith shall
    spread to every land,
Till free and equal comrades th' ennobled nations stand,
And all shall take the sacrament from
    her devoted hand.

And when Hate's last far crop is past,
    sown broadcast by the blind,
The memory of her chivalry shall stir
    in humankind
A love akin to bridal love—the passion
    of the mind.

ENVOI, TO THE REPUBLIC

When Peace and Toil shall guard thy
    soil in all its ancient right,
And Freedom, by thy fortitude, has
    found a newer birth,
We still shall cry, "My France, our
    France, the France of all the
    Earth!"

HOW WINIFRED LEARNS

BY WINIFRED SACKVILLE STONER

WHEN my big little g i r l, Winifred Sackville Stoner, Jr., was twelve years old, Dr. M. V. O'Shea, of the University of Wisconsin, said: "This child knows more and can do more than the average college graduate."

Now, Winifred and I are passing thru the most trying time of life together. I refer to the adolescent period when my daughter is neither a child nor a woman. I say that *we* are passing thru this period together because I am Winifred's co-worker in all things.

WINIFRED

Every day I receive letters from parents asking me what my little girl is doing since "she knows everything." Such statements make us both laugh, for we know that no one can be thoroly educated. Education began when the first man performed a conscious act by taking a deep breath and wriggling his finger, and education will continue as long as there is life. By *natural education* I mean practical education thru play to a purpose from the cradle to the grave—and it is just this sort of education which we are both gaining.

When Winifred was a baby I talked to her as if she were an intelligent being. I got my reward as she soon responded and could express her thoughts in intelligent forms of speech long before the age at which most children learn to talk. I have continued this plan of making my baby my chum.

Believing that work is for an end, but play is the very end itself, I have used all sorts of games to teach different lessons. For tools I have employed those which have been familiar in the nursery from time immemorial. I have, however, banished all toys which lead to the destructive idea, such as toy swords and pistols, and I have used only constructive toys.

In the belief that children should learn foreign languages before the twelfth year I taught Winifred to speak some eight languages by the time that she was eight years of age. She learned them in the Simian fashion of mimicry and knew nothing of rules of grammar.

As I believe that the foundation

Because of her remarkably rapid development both physically and mentally, Winifred Stoner, Jr., has attracted the attention of prominent educators and envious mothers all over the country. When she was five years old she knew the first book of the Æneid by heart. At eight she spoke eight languages easily, and she has written several books for children.— THE EDITOR.

THE LETTERS

Of consonants there are a-plenty,
Altogether there are twenty.
In numbers vowels don't go so high,
A, E, I, O, U and Y.

FROM THE BONY SONG

Eight and twenty bones, 'tis said,
Are located in my head.
In my trunk are fifty-four
That I add to my bone store;
While my limbs have plenty more—
Full one hundred twenty-four.

Eight carpals help to form my
*   wrists,*
Five metacarpals in my fist,
While all my fingers have but
*   three*
Phalanges that are strong but
*   wee;*
But my poor thumbs can only boast
Of two phalanges at the most.

—From *Facts in Jingles,* by Winifred Sackville Stoner. Published by Bobbs, Merrill Co.

of a practical education should be laid before the thirteenth year and that children should not be forced in the adolescent period, I am not giving Winifred any set tasks at the present time. This does not mean that she is idle. She has been given a taste for knowledge and she will not discontinue her search for it. Each day she writes original jingles, short stories or descriptions of places she has seen or people she has met. The typewriter, next to the children's encyclopedia, is our best helper. Winifred can write long stories with only a fraction of the fatigue she would get from the use of a pen. Typed stories show more plainly the construction and thus help her in composition. The typewriter also helps her in memorizing. At five she had made a thousand gems from the classics her own.

Music should be instilled into the child's being from the very first moments of his life. When Winifred was but a few days old she heard good music, and I have attempted to give her opportunities for musical development in all of her thirteen years. Each day we play together on the violin and piano, mandolin and

MRS. STONER

piano or other musical instruments. When possible we go to hear good music and at other times we listen to the best "canned" music.

Jingles are a great help in our home and in my natural education schools. We grown-ups often fall back upon the rime "Thirty Days Hath September." Thru jingles Winifred has salted down important facts in all of the sciences, in history and art. She has used this jingle memorizer even in learning facts about her body and a jingle which she calls *Bony Song* has become very popular among medical students, who say that they never forget the names of their bones after having learned Winifred's jingle. The little girl has written perhaps 500 jingles and several hundred of these rimes have been published in a book called *Facts in Jingles.* This book, as Winifred says in the introduction, was written to help make the pathway to knowledge a joy for other children.

Judging from the number of jingles which Winifred has written some people may imagine that the child spends her time writing rimes. Not so! She rides her bicycle, plays tennis, rows, swims, boxes, fences, takes long walks, drives or rides.

And now I hear some mothers ask: "And how about discipline?" We mothers who are leading our children thru the transition adolescent period all have occasion to think of discipline. So far there has been none in our home.

I have taught Winifred that there are but two objects in life—to learn self-control and the joy of service. Self-control can be taught only thru example. I have striven not to lose control of my feelings before my little daughter. She has been taught to bear pain with fortitude and to "laugh at the world." We mothers cannot expect to have happy sweettempered children if we show them anger, tears, grief and fears.

The only true joy comes from doing something for some one else; that has been the mainspring of Winifred's training. She has been taught that in order to give service, which means joy to self, she must be an all-around well-developed person—a jack-of-all-trades and master of one. Both of us strive to learn everything within our reach and we find that we can gain knowledge from all whom we meet. We learn how to use our hands as well as our heads and our hearts. We have no genius-qualities, but thru occupation, which is the secret of happiness, and thru striving to "do a good turn each day before we go to bed," we are healthy, happy and—let us hope —intelligent, normal beings.

Wilmington, North Carolina

WHAT WILL ROOSEVELT DO?

BY GUTZON BORGLUM

R ECENTLY, while on a Northwestern train from St. Paul to Chicago, I heard the following conversation between two Western lawyers—lawyers, I say, for one addrest the other as "Judge" and they referred to pending cases.

Both had been Roosevelt men; both were amazed at Wilson's flop from "too proud to fight" to "Johnny, get your gun" speeches. Both were for universal training and limited universal service.

The "Judge," who, I afterwards learned, was one of the best known federal judges of the Northwest, but whose name I may not give, was portly. He drest the part of the Middle West politician.

"What do you think of Roosevelt now?" the judge said after they had finished with Wilson's Chicago speech. The judge looked wistful.

"Oh, watching for another chance to break the slate," snapped the other.

The judge's eyes were almost shut, avoiding the smoke curling about his shrewd face, but he turned toward his friend in surprize for an instant; then said slowly: "You are wrong, Bob; the Colonel will not be a candidate next June, and that is how he will score again over your dog-in-the-manger Republicans, who are wasting all this precious time barricading yourselves against troubles you will not have, at least would avoid if you were preparing the country and public opinion for your confidence."

"Then you still believe in him, Judge?" the other said, wearily.

"Yes, he is, in some ways, the greatest force among us, but the worst advised. His Cabinet was the strongest that has governed America since the Civil War. Since his Presidency his advisers have been largely the unsuccessful men, or men unfortunate in their success. Yes, I believe in him still. I believe he will weather this final Waterloo you chaps are planning for him in June. I believe he will come out of it vindicated and gloriously successful."

"You mean he will be our next President?"

"Oh, no! If my estimate of the Colonel is right, you won't be able to even push him into the chair, and

Mr. Borglum is a sculptor who has not shut himself up in a studio. He is always heard from when the public is threatened with civic ugliness, and is strong for preparedness. Here he plays reporter for an interesting conversation.—THE EDITOR.

that is how he will win. The Colonel really wants America to believe in him, and he wants more than anything in this world to expunge from his life all responsibility for the past three years of American history. No man can do so much as the Colonel to right whatever wrong is there. It means sacrifice—in fact, it can be accomplished in no other way—and I believe the Colonel is prepared for any sacrifice necessary, and that is where he'll beat you fellows. You don't appear to have noticed the Colonel is about the only man in the country who has been really worrying about the ignoble position our nation has put itself into. No, you can gamble on it, the Colonel is not and will not permit himself to be a candidate."

"Who do you think will be the nominee of the reunited Republican party? You admit they will be reunited, don't you, Judge?"

The judge laughed, but was earnest: "Certainly they will unite, and God help the man on either side who plays Iago next June. The candidate disturbs me a great deal, and lately, discussing this very subject with Mr. Hill, I remarked what a raw, unordered civilization we have and how much that is really bad lies between our most efficient men and their ability to serve mankind!"

"Don't you think we have good Presidents, Judge?"

"I would shock you if I told you how few I think we have had since we became a nation. I regret I can't see a clear way nor a big available man. La Follette of Wisconsin, Cummings of Iowa, Hadley of Missouri, Borah of Idaho, Johnson of California, Estabrook of Nebraska, then Sherman of Illinois and Mann of Illinois, Fairbanks of Indiana, Burton of Ohio—Herrick is out of it, he wants the senatorship—then Knox of Pennsylvania and Whit-

man and Root, McCall of Massachusetts, Weeks also—that is not a list of experienced administrators. And then there is Colonel Goethals, who is being kept in a dark stall to be sprung at the last moment—none of these men measure up to the needs of the services they must render."

"You have missed Wood and Hughes, Judge."

"No, I did not mention Wood, because politicians avoid ability; they never turn to men they cannot control, unless in absolute necessity. But this country never more needed a man with the known and tried administrative ability and long experience Wood possesses. For the services required, compare his equipment with any of the names in the long list pressing before the convention, and what becomes of them? And as for Hughes—Hughes's main qualification is his incorruptibility. That being true, it will protect him and it will protect his colleagues."

"You object to going to the Supreme Court bench then for a candidate?"

"Certainly not, but I object to letting the Supreme Court find it out. You have no idea how subtle and corrupting preferment is."

The judge paused, looked concerned and continued: "Do you know, if the Supreme bench should ever become a reserved group of Presidential possibilities there would cease to be a Supreme Court in the United States, and no decision of national importance would be safe after, or wholly free from suspicion.

"Justice Hughes knows that to consent to the use of a Supreme Court justice's name in a political convention would irreparably injure the whole bench—the one branch of the government that must remain sacred and out of politics. No, my friend, Justice Hughes has his opportunity, and that is, to place the Supreme Court above the Presidency, where it is if it is what it boasts being."

"And if he fails?"

"He will not fail. Justice Hughes knows as well as any man living that the Supreme Court is more important to America than his candidacy."

New York City

THE CO-EE COMPANY MARCHING TO THE SEA
Thirty volunteers from a backwoods town in Australia set out to walk to Sydney, 320 miles away, to enlist. As they past thru the country giving the Co-ee call hundreds of men left their farms and flocks to join the company

AUSTRALIANS TO THE RESCUE

THE youngest of the British colonies set an example in preparedness which the Mother Country was slow to follow. It was not until a year and a half after the war began that Parliament could be brought to sanction the least degree of conscription and no premier has yet dared to propose universal military training. But four years before the war Australia and New Zealand had started to train all of their young men for the war, which was then clearly foreseen. In a recent speech in London the commissioner from New Zealand told how the Prime Minister of Great Britain at the Imperial Conference of 1909 had asked the Prime Ministers of the Oversea Dominions to prepare to fight Germany.

The Labor party was then in power in the Australian Commonwealth and Andrew Fisher, a Scotch coal miner, was Prime Minister. He at once called to his aid the same man whom England called upon at the outbreak of the war, Kitchener of Khartum, who went to Australia and drew up a plan for compulsory service which Mr. Fisher promptly put into effect. This provides for military training from the age of twelve to the age of twenty-six. At first it is part of the regular school work. The junior cadets get not less than fifteen minutes for 120 days a year, devoted to drilling, athletic exercizes and shooting. The senior cadets, fourteen to eighteen years old, are put into uniform and have company drills of from one to four hours. At eighteen they are classed as citizen soldiers and for the next eight years must have from 16 to 25 training days a year, part of it in camp.

Those who fear that the enfranchisement of women will effeminate the race should note that the only parts of the British empire where universal military training and compulsory service have been established are the two dominions where equal suffrage prevails. In the British Isles, where the women have been scornfully denied the vote, general military training is unknown and the mere idea of compulsory service meets with violent opposition.

Under this system Australia with a population less than five million will have 270,000 boys and men under training all of the time. These are not required to serve outside of Australia, but at the outbreak of the war most of the citizen soldiery as well as many civilians volunteered for the imperial service. The Australasian troops were mostly employed on the Gallipoli peninsula, where, owing, as is now admitted, to the blunders of the British generals, many of them found graves in the Anzac zone.

This is not the first time that Australia has contributed to the defense of the empire, for she sent a large contingent to fight the Boers.

THE LAUNCHING OF THE "BRISBANE"
The protected cruiser "Brisbane" of the new Australian navy was nearly completed when the war broke out

141

A SUFFRAGE OASIS

ANOTHER PRIZE ARTICLE IN THE BEST THING IN YOUR TOWN CONTEST

BY WILLIAM O. STEVENS

THE word "best" is not only superlative, but comparative. The best thing in a thousand square miles of sand, for example, is a little Oasis, and to appreciate it one must see the desert first.

Our town, as a biennial legislature makes us realize all too keenly, is the capital of our state. It has but ten or eleven thousand inhabitants, counting white, black, and intermediary tints. In the eighteenth century, however, it was one of the most important cities in the country. Here Washington resigned his commission in the presence of the Continental Congress, here met the assembly of notables which issued the call for the Constitutional Convention, here occurred many other historic events, which every member of the Peggy Stewart Chapter, D. A. R., has at her tongue's end. Our Town contains many beautiful colonial mansions, rather down at the heel now, perhaps, but still gratifying evidence that there was once a time in American history when wealth and taste went together.

To put the matter kindly, Our Town is like a dear old lady nodding over her knitting by the fire and dreaming of the days when she was the toast of the town. To put it less sentimentally, the "Ancient City," as it loves to be called, has been so long satisfied with its historic fame that it is content to fuddle along without a particle of enterprise, glorying in the superstitions of sixty years ago. Politically it lies flat beneath the wheels of a Democratic machine, whose boss can always scare off any independent spirit by waving the time-worn negro bogy.

The aridity of business and politics, however, is not the driest feature of this desert. For the genuine Sahara one must turn to the intellectual life of Our Town. Long ago it sank to the position of an outlying fringe, or limbo, for the great naval school in its borders. Accordingly, such thought as escaped the limits set by our First Families has run thru the narrow channels of Navy Yard life. The intellectual activities of the naval officer are concerned with the problems of his profession. Bound as he is to serve any administration, he is likely to take small interest in political or economic issues. His wife, rejoicing in his shore leave, naturally tries to make up for the lean and lonely years of sea duty by getting as much fun as she can out of social activities. Navy Yard life, therefore, becomes a round of calls, teas, hops,

card-parties; and conversation seldom rises above the level of shop and personalities. Since the naval influence is predominant, the "nice people" of Our Town are content to color their lives and thoughts after the Navy Yard style. This combination of naval influence with hoary tradition forms a kind of stopper that hermetically seals the mental life of Our Town. Music, drama, art, literature, science, social progress—all put together do not weigh against an invitation to the Officers' Hops.

So much for the desert.

The Oasis is a small group of women organized in the interests of woman's suffrage. No one in naval society has yet "taken up" suffrage, and the very idea of Lovely Woman soiling her Purity at the polls is anathema to the "chivalry" of our First Families. Hence that little organization means a defiance of the laws of the social Medes and Persians. Its president is one of our best citizens, and the woman editor of our one local paper gives loyal support, but as it is extremely unfashionable to be a suffragist in Our Town the organization has no flowery road to travel.

Moreover, these women are not content to hold meetings and read

APRIL MUSIC

BY CLINTON SCOLLARD

The lyric sound of laughter
Fills all the April hills,—
The joy-song of the crocus,
The mirth of daffodils.

They ring their golden changes
Thru all the azure vales;
The sunny cowlips answer
Athwart the reedy swales.

Far down the woodland aisleways
The trillium's voice is heard;
The little wavering wind-flowers
Join in with jocund word.

The white cry of the dogwood
Mounts up against the sky;
The breath of violet music
Upon the breeze goes by.

Give me to hear, O April,
These choristers of thine
Calling across the distance
Serene and hyaline.

To clear my clouded vision
Bedimmed and dulled so long,
And heal my aching spirit
With fragrance that is song!

reports. When the cry went up last fall for Belgian relief, the leader of navy society declined to help for fear of being unneutral. The reason was quite intelligible in her case on account of her husband's official position. But the effect of the refusal was that scarcely any other woman in Navy Yard or Town would touch the project, and Belgian relief, as far as Our Town was concerned, would have died had not the suffrage president responded energetically to the appeal and opened the suffrage rooms as headquarters for receiving contributions and making garments.

On another occasion, when our Boss attempted to reward a faithful henchman by making him postmaster, the only protest came from the suffragists, and they finally carried the day for a worthier candidate. It is an eloquent fact that a representative of the Boss was seen handing over a fistful of banknotes to an "anti" speaker when she visited Our Town. Moreover, these women who want the vote insist on digging up embarrassing facts about the government of Our Town and the county. While the male voters are content to be pulled about by the nose and "let well enough alone," these suffragists raise questions about school funds, sanitation, the almshouse, child labor in canning factories and silk mills, and they are the only people in Our Town doing anything of the kind.

There are no women of "means" among these suffragists, and they have some difficulty in raising the money they need, but they manage to spare a little now and then for a good book for a little library in their rooms. There is no public library in Our Town, and our local reading taste is satisfied with the confections of Harold Bell Wright and others of the Marshmallow School of American Literature. The only place in Our Town where a person may obtain a political discussion like "The New Freedom," a novel like "Angela's Business," or an exposition of feminism like "What Women Want," is the book-shelf in the suffrage rooms.

This, then, is the oasis in our desert, a handful of women with their faces set toward enlightenment and progress, and making a sturdy fight against the overwhelming odds of indifference, ridicule, and active opposition on the part of town and society. For this reason the suffrage organization is the best thing in Our Town.

Annapolis, Maryland

A SHORT CUT THAT COST TWELVE MILLION DOLLARS AND SAVES TWENTY MINUTES

The viaduct across the Tunkhannock Valley which was built by the Lackawanna Railroad to reduce a circuitous, hilly route of thirty-nine miles to a straight, level road of three and a half, and to save twenty minutes' time for passenger trains and an hour for freight between New York and Buffalo. It is the largest concrete structure in the world, containing more than 500,000 cubic yards of material. Its dimensions are approximately those of Brooklyn Bridge, except that it is a hundred feet higher

THE MAIL-ORDER SUFFRAGIST

Seven miles from the nearest post-office, ten miles from a railroad, tied down by a multiplicity of housekeeping duties, and hampered by the difficulties of transportation—how is a woman going to find out why and how to be a suffragist?

It is a country-wide problem, and strange to say it is from the city of subways and mass-meetings that the answer to the country woman's question comes. For the New York State Woman Suffrage Party is the first organization to propose a really satisfactory solution of the problem.

Under the direction of the New York state president, Mrs. Raymond Brown; the chairman of the Educational Section, Mrs. Howard Mansfield; and the lecturer on suffrage history and argument at the New York Suffrage Training School, Miss Louise Grant a correspondence course in suffrage has been prepared—a twelve-lesson presentation of the history of the vote, and the bedrock reasons for extending it to women.

The course was started about two months ago as an extension department of the Suffrage Training School in New York City, which gives a series of about fifty lectures on suffrage history, public speaking, parliamentary law, civil government, and suffrage organization.

These lectures are attended principally by suffrage workers. Mrs. Beatrice Forbes-Robertson Hale, whose reputation as a lecturer and as a feminist is already well established, gives the course in public speaking. Mrs. James Lees Laidlaw, one of the leaders in the recent New York state campaign, talks on suffrage organization. Of course it takes a man to explain a man-made government, and the suffragists have borrowed Mr. Arthur Macmahon, a Columbia University instructor, to tell them just how the machinery of government works. When I visited the school was showing a gallery of charts to indicate how state laws are made, with red and green and blue lines to mark their various maneuvers, tho he confest that the actual passage of a bill would have to be drawn with invisible ink in convoluted spirals.

A similar course is to be held two or three evenings a week thru the spring for suffragists who cannot attend the lectures during business hours.

As soon as other women began to hear about these lectures there was a demand for an extension of the field. Suffragists "upstate" wanted the same sort of training and they had no way of getting it.

So the correspondence school, an entirely unexpected development of the original plan, was organized—and already it has grown to ten times the enrollment of its parent institution.

The lessons are mailed at intervals of a week, with test questions every month. A six months' magazine subscription is the *magna cum laude* reward, to be given at the end of the course to the twenty women whose answers rank highest.

The success of the correspondence school has practically forced the New York suffragists to become missionaries to the whole country. From most of the non-suffrage states (and even from Nova Scotia) requests have already come for permission to take the course. Twenty-five cents, to cover the cost of postage, is the tuition fee. And every applicant is welcome.

SENTINELS OF THE DESERT

Travel in the Painted Desert would be a dangerous matter were it not for the silent sentinels erected by the Navajo Indians to direct the stranger traveling thru this country, where once there was water in plenty, but where now there are only the dry beds of rivers.

If you have never experienced the pangs of thirst, you cannot conceive of the terrible agony it may bring to a prospector lost in the desert. Half-crazed with delirium, he loses all sense of direction. His swollen tongue protrudes from his mouth. His lips are raw and cracked by the action of the fine alkali dust which rises from every movement of his leaden feet. He strives to reach the fantom lake so clearly seen in the quivering heat waves of 'the mirage'—only to have it fade before his blood-shot eyes, just as he stoops eagerly to drink of the unreal waters.

It is to avoid just such occurrences, that the Navajo Indians have placed their stone sentinels to point the way to water in the desert.

These sentinels are piles of rock as high as a man, located on the higher ground, where they may be readily seen. In the body of the monument is placed a projecting rock, which is arranged to point the direction to the nearest spring or water-hole. If you follow the direction indicated, tho you may have to travel considerable distance, the precious water will always be found.

Frequently it is only a very weak seep, supplying no more than a few cups an hour. Or it may be a pool located deep in the recesses of a rocky ledge and collected from the melted snows of the past winter. Sometimes it may be situated in an out-of-the-way place and in that case there may be two, or even three, smaller monuments erected along the route designated.

Along the way there may be arrows cut in the rocks, or crooked grooves symbolizing the windings of a brook, or signs of various kinds which will attract attention. These directions all help to make the way plainer and reduce the chances that the traveler will become confused.

IN A THIRSTY LAND
One of the cairns put up by Navajo Indians to guide the traveler in the desert to water

143

UNUSUAL VERSE

Hotly rebelling against the illness that sentenced her to exile at Saranac Lake, longing passionately for the normal opportunities of work and self-expression, Adelaide Crapsey found in verse her means of making life worth while. Seventy poems, published just after her death in a slim, unobtrusive gray volume which somehow suggests her own personal appearance, had been chosen by her to embody, as she exprest it, her "immortal residue." Into them she put all her longing for the beauty of life—the outcry of a spirit unreconciled to its fate—and thru them she gave expression to

Infinite passion, and the pain
Of finite hearts that yearn.

Most of the *Verse* is somber, some of it tragic—it could not be otherwise and be true.

To her genuine poetic ability Miss Crapsey added a considerable technical knowledge of metrics. She was for several years Instructor in Poetics at Smith College. In the verse form which she invented and called the cinquain she has done some of her best work—clear cut ideas sharply focused, single impressions etched in a few significant lines. Thus she writes of Night Winds:

The old,
Old winds that blew
When chaos was—what do
They tell the clattered trees, that I
Should weep?

The Triad shows another interesting use of the cinquain:

These be
Three silent things:
The falling snow—the hour
Before the dawn—the mouth of one
Just dead.

Verse, by Adelaide Crapsey. Rochester: The Manas Press. $1.

INDUSTRIAL PROBLEMS

The eight million women engaged in "gainful occupations" are gradually awakening to the realization that they hold a permanent place in the industrial world. From being content with casual work and casual conditions, they are becoming organized for their own education and for the education of the public as to their rightful place in modern society. *The Trade Union Woman*, by Alice Henry, formerly editor of *Life and Labor*, gives an account of the union movement, its current methods and aims, as well as its history. It is difficult to separate woman's development in industry from her social and political aspirations; the chapters in this book treat the various aspects of the movement as rather distinct problems, altho there is a unity of attitude and ideals running thru the whole story. The emphasis on the larger life of all workers and on the immanence of human dignity in the labor movement commands for this book the serious attention of thoughtful readers.

Among the special studies made for the Federal Commission on Industrial Relations was one on *Scientific Management and Labor*, by Professor Hoxie of the University of Chicago. This is now published in book form. With the coöperation of a representative of the employers and of a trade-unionist, Mr. Hoxie investigated the labor claims of the late Frederick W. Taylor, and of Harrington Emerson and H. L. Gantt, the leaders of the sci-

entific management movement. The studies were made in a number of establishments selected by the efficiency engineers, and a few other factories selected for purposes of comparison. The formulated objections of labor representatives were also checked off, and the final statement received the unqualified approval of the two partizan members of the investigating committee. Many of the suspicions and fears of the workers appear to be groundless; but many of the more serious objections urged by them against the employers' efficiency methods are abundantly sustained.

The most serious aspects of the controversy deal with the ultimate status of the worker as a human being; and this status is not protected by scientific management. The tremendous economic gains made possible by the application of science to the organization of industry certainly appear to have given some measurable advantage to the unskilled workers; but this leveling upward is more than compensated by the relative degradation of the skilled workers. The only protection that the workers have had against the mechanical search for increased productiveness has been their own organization.

The Trade Union Woman, by Alice Henry. Appleton. $1.50. *Scientific Management and Labor*, by Robert Franklin Hoxie. Appleton. $1.50.

THE COST OF WAR

The shock given the moral world by the engulfing European war is not greater than that to the financial world. The first estimates of expense were astonishing, the figures have finally become appalling, and now, while adequate indemnities and liquidation of war debts are usually thought possible, many begin to look on them as verging to improbability and impossibility.

W. R. Lawson, a financial authority, in *British War Finance*, foresees a great reduction in Great Britain's bloated civil and municipal lists and in her army and navy. He compares the present cost to Great Britain of £2,000,000,000 (December 31, 1915) with the twelve million sterling debt left by William the Third's campaigns and the debt of but twice that left by Marlborough and Eugene. "War in those days was dirt cheap compared with what it is now," he laconically and picturesquely observes: How vague the figures are after all, for the experts vary from seven to ten shillings per day as to the average cost per soldier; and there is some uncertainty as to the number of soldiers! But Mr. Lawson himself cannot be called vague. He writes from a large knowledge of international relations and the resources of nations and of bond issues, exchange, scrip schemes and silver bullets. He describes the great difficulties met by the financiers, and critically reviews the means by which the whole almost superhuman task has been and is being in a way accomplished.

Thus far the war has produced few books that for profound interest surpass this vividly written but unfortunately drily entitled volume.

British War Finance, 1914–16, by W. R. Lawson. Van Nostrand. $2.

MYSTERY A LA MODE

Gertrude Atherton's *Mrs. Balfame* is a perfectly conventional murder mystery story, well constructed and ably written. It has, however, an unconventional beginning. "Mrs. Balfame had made up her mind to commit murder." By the time you have found out whether she did or not, you will have been well entertained.

Stokes. $1.35.

AN AMERICAN SALON

Memories and Anecdotes, Kate Sanborn's entertaining chat concerning folk of note in American letters during the latter half of the last century, has many good stories but none more interesting than that of Mrs. Botta's famous and delightful Saturday Evenings, at which gathered all that was finest in literary New York.

Putnam. $1.75.

A FIRST VOLUME

Apparently a first volume, *Laurentian Lyrics and Other Poems,* by Arthur S. Bourinot, is marred by most of the sins of first volumes. Occasional slip-shod riming and mediocrity mark the little collection. But Summer is a pretty picture, and To the Memory of Rupert Brooke a convincing poem.

Toronto: The Copp Clark Co. 50 cents.

THE FRINGES OF THE FLEET

When Kipling writes of the sea and the men who go down to it in fighting ships, the thing has been done once for all. The romance, the self-denial, the bravery, the endurance, the patriotism—all are there in *The Fringes of the Fleet,* set forth by the master hand. But Kipling is no pacifist —and the other side of the shield is kept resolutely turned away.

Doubleday, Page. 50 cents.

"X"

A second series of communications to Elsa Barker supposed to come from the late Judge Hatch is *War Letters from a Living Dead Man.* Striking as are such descriptions as that of the Kaiser's will, raised into a separate being and become his particular devil, yet the letters would seem a not unnatural result of subconscious mental activity or thought transference and remind one of the powerful "Letters from Hell" introduced to us years ago by George MacDonald.

Kennerley. $1.25.

ENJOYING SHAKESPEARE

Lovers of Shakespeare will find the second edition of Dr. Stalker's *How to Read Shakespeare* a delightful volume that points out much that is best in Shakespeare's work. The young reader will find the book a happy introduction to Shakespeare's plays,—clear, free from scholastic details and dry-as-dust material, interesting, and leading at once to points of modern interest. The advice to begin with the English histories,—King John, for example—is undoubtedly wise.

Doran. $1.50.

WOMANKIND

The first paper in Miss Tarbell's *Ways of Woman* is firmly rooted in the thirteenth United States Census, and shows that the business of the overwhelming majority of women is still that of the mother and home-maker. For the rest, this volume pleads for systematic training of girls for motherhood and in domestic science; makes an ingenious and plausible apology for the talkativeness of the sex; laughs at ill-directed feminine efforts in the quest of culture; protests against the notion that low wages are directly responsible for the lapses of working-girls.

Macmillan. $1.

Partial Interior View of One of the Hundreds of Big Storage Warehouses in which the Choicest Burley Leaf is Aged in Wood Three to Five Years for Tuxedo Tobacco. The Large Central Inset Shows a Hogshead Opened.

All Smoking Tobaccos Are Aged

Have to be to make them smokable. Tobacco in its natural state is raw and harsh. Ageing makes it mellower, milder.

The leaf for some tobacco is aged for only one or two years.

That for Tuxedo is aged in wooden hogsheads for *three to five years*—until it is as nearly perfect as nature can make it.

Most manufacturers simply age the leaf and *let it go at that.* But—

Tuxedo Is *More* Than Aged

After nature has done all it can to mellow the leaf, then the *original* "Tuxedo Process" is applied.

This famous process—a doctor's discovery—takes out all the bite left by nature. Prevents irritation of mouth and throat. Makes Tuxedo the mildest, most comfortable smoke possible to produce. Enables men to enjoy

a pipe who formerly could not do so.

The "Tuxedo Process" has many imitators. Millions of dollars have been spent trying to invent a "just as good" process. But it still remains the great *original* method for making tobacco absolutely biteless and non-irritating.

Tuxedo

The Perfect Tobacco for Pipe and Cigarette

Get a tin of Tuxedo. Try it for a week. Note how sweet and fragrant it is and how mild! You can smoke it all day and have a sound tongue and a perfectly comfortable throat all the time. A week's trial is bound to make you a permanent smoker of Tuxedo.

YOU CAN BUY TUXEDO EVERYWHERE

Convenient, glassine-wrapped, moisture-proof pouch **5c**

Famous green tin with gold lettering, curved to fit pocket **10c**

In Tin Humidors, 40c and 80c   In Glass Humidors, 50c and 90c

PATTERSON'S
Tuxedo
TOBACCO

SPECIALLY PREPARED
FOR PIPE & CIGARETTE

THE AMERICAN TOBACCO COMPANY

PEBBLES

Villa may have taken the grin out of gringo, but he left the go.—*Columbia State.*

We don't want the hyphen in America, but a dash in Mexico is just about right.—*Philadelphia North American.*

About the only objection that could be urged against LaFollette is that he has his photograph taken reading a book.—*Atlanta Journal.*

Customer—"I want a pound of coffee in the bean, please."
Clerk—"You'll have to go upstairs, madam. This is the ground floor."—*Judge.*

Mr. Pessimist (cheering up, as he reads paper)—"British Mesopotamian success."
Mrs. Pessimist—That's the worst of it. They mess up all their successes.—*Punch.*

The Republican position on the Philippine question is now clear. The administration of the islands by the Democrats has been so bad that it proves the natives incapable of self-government.—*The Masses.*

Commercial candor in the *Mexico* (New York) *Standard:* "For Sale—Eight room house, two barns, hen house, two acres of land. Fine place for a cow. Enquire of Walter Smith, Pulaski street."—*New York Tribune.*

Speaking of Mr. Theodore Roosevelt's style, may one say that the secret of its strength lies in the fact that he uses verbs in the active voice and vindictive mood? And the Masculine Number?—*New York Tribune.*

An anonymous check for five hundred dollars was received for one seat from some one who merely signed himself Mr. Winter's great admirer.—*New York Telegraph.*
No wonder paying-tellers say their job is hard.—*New York Tribune.*

"I proposed to four different girls," said a newlywed of not more than twenty-five. He even told their names—Clara and Jane and Margaret and Sue.
"What is your wife's name?" I asked.
"Geraldine," he answered.—*Pittsburgh Press.*

"When Jones bought his new house it was with the express understanding that he should have a room all of his own—a den or study."
"Yes, I know what you mean. Did he get it?"
"Yes, and his wife furnished it."
"How?"
"With a sewing machine, a cutting table, two dressers, dummies, three sewing chairs and a full-length mirror."—*Tit-Bits.*

The Scotch version of Tipperary, which reaches us from Glasgow, deserves a wider publicity. It is given with the caution that it cannot be lightly attempted save by a Scotsman:

It's a lang wye tae Auchtermuchty,
It's a lang wye tae Perth,
It's a lang wye tae get tae onywhere
Frae anywhere else on airth.

Guid-bye tae Ballachulish,
Farewell but an' ben;
It's a lang, lang wye tae Auchtermuchty,
But I'll gang back again.
—*Christian Science Monitor.*

A Chinaman was brought before a magistrate in Salt Lake City and received a fine for a slight misdemeanor. But the judge could not make him understand.
"Look here, man," he said, disgustedly, "you pay one dollar or go to jail, see?" There was no gleam of intelligence from the Oriental and the judge repeated his explanation, but without results.
Finally the officer who had arrested the man came up. "Say, you dish-face," he called, "can't you hear anything? You've got to pay a five dollar fine."
"You're a liar," yelled the Chinaman. "It's only one dollar."—*New Thought.*

MR. PURINTON'S EFFICIENCY QUESTION BOX

239. Mrs. B. F. J., Michigan. "I belong to a club of middle-aged people, several of whom are deeply interested in the study of longevity, and the prevention of those weaknesses and disorders which commonly afflict persons from forty to sixty years of age. Will you please name a few books for personal study likely to prove beneficial?"

Every home should have a library shelf of books of this kind. We gladly suggest a few: "Prevention and Cure of Old Age," by Sanford Bennett; "The Nature Cure," by Dr. H. Lindlahr; "Autology," by Dr. E. R. Moras; "How to Live," by Prof. Irving Fisher and Dr. E. L. Fisk. These books may be all obtained thru Efficiency Publishing Company, Woolworth Building, New York City.

240. Prof. T. W. A., Minnesota. "As a school principal, I am especially interested in efficient teaching and school administration. Will you give me some clue as to the best literature in this field?"

In general, books on all phases of personal or professional efficiency may be secured thru Efficiency Publishing Company, Woolworth Building, New York. You might also write the National Educational Service Corporation, 230 Fifth avenue; Librarian of Teachers' College, 525 West 120th street; editor of *American Educational Review*, 154 Nassau street; and such large booksellers as Putnam's, Brentano's, or Baker & Taylor; all of New York City.

241. Mr. E. E. B., Florida. "I figured my grade on your Personal Efficiency Test as about 50 per cent. The answers to questions Nos. 4 and 13 were zero. I am most concerned about answering these properly. Can you advise me?"

For detailed information on No. 4, consult authorities in character analysis and vocational guidance, mentioned in these columns since your letter was received. For more knowledge regarding No. 13, get book catalogs from the publishers of *Good Health*, Battle Creek, Michigan; *Health Culture*, Passaic, New Jersey; *Physical Culture*, Flatiron Building, New York City; *Herald of Health*, 110 East Forty-first street, New York City; *Nautilus*, Holyoke, Massachusetts.

242. Mrs. J. S. L., Michigan. "To succeed in literary work has been my ambition. I have plunged wholeheartedly into the work I love. Unprejudiced critics admit my stories and verses give evidence of merit; yet almost everything I submit to magazine editors is promptly returned; often, I have reason to believe, unread. I am told this is because my name is not well enough known. Can you advise me how to proceed?"

Get a stock of unlimited patience—you will need it. Work so many hours a day, whether you sell anything or not. Write of the people and events you *know*. Criticise your output continually and relentlessly—never mind about its "merit." Ask your friends not to eulogize it, but tear it to pieces. Master a mail course in short-story writing, and another in advertising or business English. Look up author's agents, generally advertised in such periodicals as *The Dial. The Black Cat*, the weekly Book Supplement of the *New York Times*. Submit your copy to editors right—get a book like *Preparing Manuscript for the Printer*, Funk and Wagnalls, 354 Fourth avenue, New York. Contribute to your local newspapers, and if your work is good enough, it will command a larger field. Get rid of the impression that editors do not read the manuscripts submitted to them, or are unduly influenced by well-

Partial Interior View of One of the Hundreds of Big Storage Warehouses in which the Choicest Burley Leaf is Aged in Wood Three to Five Years for Tuxedo Tobacco. The Large Central Inset Shows a Hogshead Opened.

All Smoking Tobaccos Are Aged

Have to be to make them smokable. Tobacco in its natural state is raw and harsh. Ageing makes it mellower, milder.

The leaf for some tobacco is aged for only one or two years. But—

That for Tuxedo is aged in wooden hogsheads for *three to five* years—until it is as nearly perfect as nature can make it.

Most manufacturers simply age the leaf and *let it go at that.*

Tuxedo Is *More* Than Aged

After nature has done all it can to mellow the leaf, then the *original* "Tuxedo Process" is applied.

This famous process—a doctor's discovery—takes out all the bite left by nature. Prevents irritation of mouth and throat. Makes Tuxedo the mildest, most comfortable smoke possible to produce. Enables men to enjoy

a pipe who formerly could not do so.

The "Tuxedo Process" has many imitators. Millions of dollars have been spent trying to invent a "just as good" process. But it still remains the great *original* method for making tobacco absolutely biteless and non-irritating.

The Perfect Tobacco for Pipe and Cigarette

Get a tin of Tuxedo. Try it for a week. Note how sweet and fragrant it is and how mild! You can smoke it all day and have a sound tongue and a perfectly comfortable throat at the end. A week's trial is bound to make you a permanent smoker of Tuxedo.

YOU CAN BUY TUXEDO EVERYWHERE

Convenient, glassine-wrapped, moisture-proof pouch **5c**

Famous green tin, with gold lettering, curved to fit pocket **10c**

In Tin Humidors, 40c and 80c In Glass Humidors, 50c and 90c

PATTERSON'S Tuxedo TOBACCO
SPECIALLY PREPARED FOR PIPE & CIGARETTE

THE AMERICAN TOBACCO COMPANY

F. A. Ringler Co.

DESIGNING
PHOTO - ENGRAVING
AND ELECTROTYPING

21 and 23 Barclay Street to
26 and 28 Park Place
NEW YORK

Romeike's Press Clippings

are used nowadays by every modern up-to-date business man; they bring you in constant touch with all public and private wants, and supply you with news bearing upon any line of business. We read for our subscribers all the important papers published in the United States and abroad. If you have never used press clippings, drop us a postal and we will show how they can be of advantage to you. Write for booklet and terms.

ROMEIKE, INC.　106-110 Seventh Ave., New York City

PEBBLES

Villa may have taken the grin out of gringo, but he left the go.—*Columbia State.*

We don't want the hyphen in America, but a dash in Mexico is just about right.—*Philadelphia North American.*

About the only objection that could be urged against LaFollette is that he has his photograph taken reading a book.—*Atlanta Journal.*

Customer—"I want a pound of coffee in the bean, please."
Clerk—"You'll have to go upstairs, madam. This is the ground floor."—*Judge.*

Mr. Pessimist (cheering up, as he reads paper)—"British Mesopotamian success."
Mrs. Pessimist—That's the worst of it. They mess up all their successes.—*Punch.*

The Republican position on the Philippine question is now clear. The administration of the Islands by the Democrats has been so bad that it proves the natives incapable of self-government.—*The Masses.*

Commercial candor in the *Mexico* (New York) *Standard*: "For Sale—Eight room house, two barns, hen house, two acres of land. Fine place for a cow. Enquire of Walter Smith, Pulaski street."—*New York Tribune.*

Speaking of Mr. Theodore Roosevelt's style, may one say that the secret of its strength lies in the fact that he uses verbs in the active voice and vindictive mood? And the Masculine Number?—*New York Tribune.*

An anonymous check for five hundred dollars was received for one seat from some one who merely signed himself Mr. Winter's great admirer.—*New York Telegraph.*
No wonder paying-tellers say their job is hard—*New York Tribune.*

"I proposed to four different girls," said a newlywed of not more than twenty-five. He even told their names—Clara and Jane and Margaret and Sue.
"What is your wife's name?" I asked.
"Geraldine," he answered.—*Pittsburg Press.*

"When Jones bought his new house it was with the express understanding that he should have a room all of his own—a den or study."
"Yes, I know what you mean. Did he get it?"
"Yes, and his wife furnished it."
"How?"
"With a sewing machine, a cutting table, two dressers, dummies, three sewing chairs and a full-length mirror."—*Tit-Bits.*

The Scotch version of Tipperary, which reaches us from Glasgow, deserves a wider publicity. It is given with the caution that it cannot be lightly attempted save by a Scotsman:

It's a lang wye tae Auchtermuchty.
It's a lang wye tae Perth.
It's a lang wye tae get tae onywhere
Frae anywhere else on airth.
Guid-bye tae Ballachulish.
Farewell but an' ben;
It's a lang, lang wye tae Auchtermuchty.
But I'll gang back again.
　　—*Christian Science Monitor.*

A Chinaman was brought before a magistrate in Salt Lake City and received a fine for a slight misdemeanor. But the judge could not make him understand.
"Look here, man," he said, disgustedly, "you pay one dollar or go to jail, see?" There was no gleam of intelligence from the Oriental and the judge repeated his explanation, but without results.
Finally the officer who had arrested the man came up. "Say, you dish-face," he called, "can't you hear anything? You've got to pay a five dollar fine."
"You're a liar," yelled the Chinaman. "It's only one dollar."—*New Thought.*

MR. PURINTON'S EFFICIENCY QUESTION BOX

239. Mrs. B. F. J., Michigan. "I belong to a club of middle-aged people, several of whom are deeply interested in the study of longevity, and the prevention of those weaknesses and disorders which commonly afflict persons from forty to sixty years of age. Will you please name a few books for personal study likely to prove beneficial?"

Every home should have a library shelf of books of this kind. We gladly suggest a few: "Prevention and Cure of Old Age," by Sanford Bennett; "The Nature Cure," by Dr. H. Lindlahr; "Autology," by Dr. E. R. Moras; "How to Live," by Prof. Irving Fisher and Dr. E. L. Fisk. These books may be all obtained thru Efficiency Publishing Company, Woolworth Building, New York City.

240. Prof. T. W. A., Minnesota. "As a school principal, I am especially interested in efficient teaching and school administration. Will you give me some clue as to the best literature in this field?"

In general, books on all phases of personal or professional efficiency may be secured thru Efficiency Publishing Company, Woolworth Building, New York. You might also write the National Educational Service Corporation, 230 Fifth avenue; Librarian of Teachers' College, 525 West 120th street; editor of American Educational Review, 154 Nassau street; and such large booksellers as Putnam's, Brentano's, or Baker & Taylor; all of New York City.

241. Mr. E. E. B., Florida. "I figured my grade on your Personal Efficiency Test as about 60 per cent. The answers to questions Nos. 4 and 13 were zero. I am most concerned about answering these properly. Can you advise me?"

For detailed information on No. 4, consult authorities in character analysis and vocational guidance, mentioned in these columns since your letter was received.

For more knowledge regarding No. 13, get book catalogs from the publishers of Good Health, Battle Creek, Michigan; Health Culture, Passaic, New Jersey; Physical Culture, Flatiron Building, New York City; Herald of Health, 110 East Forty-first street, New York City; Nautilus, Holyoke, Massachusetts.

242. Mrs. J. S. I., Michigan. "To succeed in literary work has been my ambition. I have plunged wholeheartedly into the work I love. Unprejudiced critics admit my stories and verses give evidence of merit; yet almost everything I submit to magazine editors is promptly returned; often, I have reason to believe, unread. I am told this is because my name is not well enough known. Can you advise me how to proceed?"

Get a stock of unlimited patience—you will need it. Work so many hours a day, whether you sell anything or not. Write off the people and events you know. Criticize your output continually and relentlessly—never mind about its "merit," ask your friends not to eulogize it, but tear it to pieces. Master a mail course in short-story writing, and another in advertising or business English. Look up author's agents, generally advertised in such periodicals as The Dial, The Black Cat, the weekly Book Supplement of the New York Times. Submit your copy to editors right—get a book like Preparing Manuscript for the Printer, Funk and Wagnalls, 354 Fourth avenue, New York. Contribute to your local newspapers, and if your work is good enough, it will command a larger field. Get rid of the impression that editors do not read the manuscripts submitted to them, or are unduly influenced by well-

Safe, Easy and Sure

Mother knows that Foster Friction Plug won't let her slip.

No matter what your age, you can have the child-step, the safety, surety and buoyancy of youth.

Walking is a pleasure on

CAT'S PAW
CUSHION
RUBBER HEELS

There are no holes in Cats' Paw Rubber Heels to track mud and dirt, and they make all slippery roads and pavements safe.

Because the Foster Friction Plug won't let you slip—makes the heels wear longer, too—therefore most economical.

They cost no more than the ordinary kind—they are easy to find—all dealers sell them—50 cents attached—Black or Tan. Walk easy, safe and sure. Get a pair today.

THE FOSTER RUBBER CO.
105 Federal Street · · · · Boston, Mass.

Originators and Patentees of the Foster Friction Plug, which prevents slipping.

known names attached to articles submitted. The editor who is abreast of his
job is more anxious to discover a new
writer of real merit than to accept a manuscript from a writer whose reputation is
already made.

243. A Western Educator. "I have been unexpectedly appointed to the deanship of a college, without having grown into the position at
all, as a dean normally should do. I am conscious of serious shortcomings, in the general
routine of the position, in natural temperament;
especially in the ability to keep in close and
sympathetic touch with the heart and thought
of the student body."

We gladly refer you to several possible
sources of help, as follows : The book on
College Administration by President
Charles F. Thwing, of Western Reserve
University, Cleveland, Ohio ; the Association of College Deans, whose next convention occurs at Columbus, Ohio (we are informed), particulars of which may doubtless be had from the President or the Registrar of Ohio State University ; the work
of the Educational Magazine Publishing
Company, 31 East Twenty-seventh street,
New York ; that of the Educational Publishing Company, 18 East Seventeenth
street, New York ; the publications of the
Teachers' College, 525 West 120th street,
New York ; the literature of the University
Extension Society, 105 East Seventeenth
street, New York ; of the University Forum
of America, 550 West 118th street, New
York.

The president of your state university
should know of conferences and bulletins
by college executives. The Librarian of the
University of Chicago will probably cite
books of value. A student cabinet, for student problems, is worth considering.

244. Mrs. M., Pennsylvania. "Will you please
suggest what seems to you a wise budgeting of
an income of $1600 a year, for a family of
two, who desire to save now while they are
young and healthy ? Are the following groupings correct ? What amount should go to each ?
(a) Savings account, insurance, etc. (b) Household expenses—food, laundry, help, up-keep. (c)
Outside expenses—rent, water, fuel. (d) Personal expenses for wife—clothes, dentistry, tithe,
gifts, postage, etc. (e) Personal expenses for
husband—similar to above. (f) Recreation, books,
travel, concerts, etc."

The groupings are approximately correct
—tho we should transpose the order somewhat, as food, rent and clothing precede
the items of savings and insurance. Local
prices and conditions, also the professional
and social responsibilities of the husband
and wife, cause variations in any financial
budget. We hardly ever assume to give
exact figures, where the personal equation
is unknown. However, we should fix the
amounts roughly as follows : (a) $300 a
year, (b) $480, (c) $340, (d) $220, (e)
$190, (f) $70. If the wife is an expert
cook, buyer and seamstress, probably she
can reduce (a) and (d). If the husband
has no professional appearance to maintain, he can reduce (e).

245. Mr. C. J. H., Pennsylvania. "Am nineteen, have had three years' practical railroad
work ; would like to take a good traffic course.
(a) Do you think such a course would pay ?
(b) Would Spanish in connection be an advantage ? (c) Is there a demand for an expert
manager of traffic ? (d) Please refer me to a
few good authorities or institutions. (e) Where
can I obtain your 'Triumph of the Man Who
Acts ?' "

(a) Yes. (b) Decidedly—our affiliations
with South American countries will make
Spanish a larger asset in many trade lines ;
get particulars of the new association for
United States industrial expansion founded
by President Frank A. Vanderlip, of the
National City Bank, New York. (c) There
is always a demand for an expert anybody.
(d) Write the Traffic Club, 291 Broadway ; the *Railroad Men's Magazine*, 8
West Fortieth street ; the Traffic Service
Bureau, 143 Liberty street ; *Railway Engineering*, 50 Church street ; *Railway Review*, 30 Church street ; all of New York
City. (e) This was reprinted in The Independent of January 17, 1916.

Independent Opinions

Mr. Purinton's article in our issue of March 20 on "The Efficient Housewife" brought in many counter-criticisms. We quote from the letter of one who signs herself modestly—or defiantly—"The Inefficient Housewife," but who nevertheless seems to know her business or businesses.

It is economy to buy leg of lamb rather than chops. Yes, especially for a small family, for neither ice, nor paraffin paper, nor disguise will keep the meat from growing dry and flavorless as the days go by, and before it disappears you will find the family leaning strongly toward vegetarianism. I, the inefficient, never serve a roast when my family, small meat eaters all, numbers less than five.

Pound for pound fish costs less than meat, but that scientific table of food values which "should be the constant guide of the housekeeper," gives it only half the food value. The Boston Cooking School Cook Book says it is cheaper only when compared with the choice cuts of meat.

Likewise, brown sugar, cheaper by the pound than granulated, is not so pure and does not "spend" so well. Several years ago a friend of mine gave it a careful trial for a period of weeks. She reported that her sugar bill was not diminished in the least. I tried it long enough to convince myself that if there were any saving it was not enough to pay the room rent of a second sugar bucket.

Fruit is cheaper at wholesale than at retail. But would the amount saved on a winter's supply pay the rent of a cold storage room? For the most of us the fruit and vegetable cellar belongs to the days of our grandfathers.

I wish I knew where Mr. Purinton buys his grapes and cornmeal. I cannot make grape juice at 8 cents a pint; even tho I leave out of account bottles, fuel and labor. I can remember buying cornmeal for 3 cents a pound, but that was in the dim and distant past. My last cost me 8 cents. Even at that five ounces is cheaper than ten eggs. But how did Mr. Purinton happen to think of substituting for the expensive egg the cheap cornmeal? Did he wish to make that change in his own dietary? He certainly did not find the suggestion in that scientific table of food values which he recommends to inefficient women, for that shows that cornmeal, rich in energy-producing carbohydrates but poor in tissue-building proteids and fats, is in no way an equivalent for the egg with its high nutritive value. I believe that cornmeal is the staple article of food in certain sections whose inhabitants, ill-nourished and poorly developed, are subject to the dread pellagra.

And then there is the labor-saving machinery. Much of this is impractical in a small family, where the time and energy it saves will not keep it clean and in running order. Much of it, too, saves energy, but not time, as, for instance, the vacuum cleaner and the sewing machine motor. For the average woman to say that her kitchen is "fully supplied and equipped with labor-saving devices" is to confess to the hight—or depth—of "inefficiency." The work in the average family of today is on too small a scale and too diversified to warrant the outlay. A man might as profitably equip his kitchen garden with all the tools and machines of the big farms, or use a motor truck to transport a wheelbarrow load ten rods.

Wherever there is a discussion of woman's work and labor-saving there appears also our old friend, "What is a hen's time worth anyhow?" A hen's time

To the man who would stay young

PONCE DE LEON failed in his search—just as has everyone else who believed that the secret of youth lay in other than simply the conservation of the youth that Nature herself gives.

The secret of youth lies in making good, promptly and thoroughly, the many drains and overdraughts that modern ways of living impose upon the bodycells—for the cells are the brick and mortar of the body structure. It lies in guarding and husbanding the finer strength of the nervous system, which overwork, worry and stress undermine.

It is in this work of conservation that Sanatogen has proven itself of such distinct merit. In rebuilding

wasted tissues, revitalizing starved cells, enriching blood and thus storing up health and energy against the passage of time, Sanatogen has been preeminently successful.

As Sir Gilbert Parker, the statesman-novelist, has written:

"Sanatogen is to my mind a true food-tonic, feeding the nerves, increasing the energy, and giving fresh vigor to the overworked body and mind."

And when you realize that more than 21,000 physicians have written—as they have—their approval of the use of Sanatogen, you can see for yourself that its reputation is founded not on theory but on actual results.

Let Sanatogen be the guardian of your youth!

Sanatogen is sold by good druggists, everywhere, in sizes from $1.00 up.

Grand Prize, International Congress of Medicine, London, 1913

Sanatogen

ENDORSED BY OVER 21,000 PHYSICIANS

Send for "The Art of Living," a charming booklet by Richard Le Gallienne, the popular poet-author, touching on Sanatogen's kindly help, and giving other interesting aids in the quest for contentment and better health. The book is free. Tear this off as a reminder to write THE BAUER CHEMICAL COMPANY, 26R Irving Place, New York City.

THE INDEPENDENT EDUCATION SERVICE

A directory of Schools and Colleges which are advertising in The Independent. By using the coupon below, parents will secure prompt and complete information to aid them in selecting the right education for son or daughter. This list will increase in number as the School Advertising season approaches.

COLORADO
1 University of Colorado...........Boulder

CONNECTICUT
2 Hartford Theological Seminary...Hartford
3 The Ely School...............Greenwich
4 Wheeler School........North Stonington
5 Hillside.....................Norwalk
6 The Sanford School.......Redding Ridge
7 Ridgefield School for Boys....Ridgefield

ILLINOIS
8 American School of Home Economics, Chicago
9 The University of Chicago.......Chicago
10 Northwestern University......Evanston
11 Todd Seminary..............Woodstock

MARYLAND
1 National Park Seminary......Forest Glen

MASSACHUSETTS
13 Abbot Academy ....Andover
14 Boston University ....Boston
15 Emerson College of Oratory....Boston
16 Miss McClintock's School for Girls..Boston
17 School of Expression...........Boston
18 Bradford Academy ....Bradford
19 Sea Pines ....Brewster
20 New Church Theological School..Cambridge
21 Sargent School ....Cambridge
22 Powder Point School for Boys...Duxbury
23 Williston Seminary ....Easthampton
24 Dean Academy ....Franklin

25 Walnut Hill School..............Natick
26 The Brookfield School....North Brookfield
27 Wheaton College for Women.......Norton
28 Miss Hall's School...........Pittsfield
29 Worcester Academy ....Worcester

NEW YORK
30 The Holbrook School...........Ossining
31 St. John's School.............Ossining
32 Crane Normal Institute of Music..Potsdam
33 Peate & Beattie...........Spencerport
34 Onondaga Seminary ....Syracuse
35 Russell Sage College of Practical Arts, Troy

PENNSYLVANIA
36 Yeates School ....Lancaster
37 Mercersburg Academy ....Mercersburg
38 The Latshaw School of Psychoculture, Philadelphia
39 Kiskiminetas Springs School for Boys, Saltsburg

RHODE ISLAND
40 Moses Brown School..........Providence

TENNESSEE
41 Martin College ....Pulaski

VIRGINIA
42 Randolph-Macon Woman's College, Lynchburg
43 Mary Baldwin Seminary.......Staunton
44 Stuart Hall ....Staunton

TEAR COUPON HERE

THE INDEPENDENT EDUCATION SERVICE, 119 West 40th Street, New York.

Send me information about the following schools and colleges listed on this page.

Numbers...

Send Information to..

Address...

---

is worth so much that if you are hatching eggs by the hundred you cannot afford to use hens. If you aim to hatch only a dozen you cannot afford to use an incubator. But can you afford to hatch a paltry dozen of eggs? That is another question. The fact is, the whole scheme of our domestic life today is a relic of the time when each family was a community complete in itself. Brought over into the present it is an anachronism and an economic waste. Women know this now; some day men will see it and consent to a change. Let me here say to Mrs. Bruère, Amen, and Amen, and Amen.

But Mr. Purinton's efficient housewife would be dubbed most inefficient by her neighbors, like the restaurateur who, by cutting out the frills and fancies, reduced his expenses to a minimum—and lost his patrons. No, the truly efficient housewife must, with her minimum expenditure of money, time and labor, produce the maximum of comfort, happiness and content for her family. She cannot do this by serving the correct proportion of proteid, fat and carbohydrates at the least possible cost, or by labor-saving machinery or by system.

THE INEFFICIENT HOUSEWIFE
Worcester, Mass.

Referring to your editorial "Where Public Buildings Are Needed" in your number of March 13th:

Keep on telling the country about how much of Uncle Sam is living in lodgings here in his own home town, and we may live to see him respectably housed on his own premises. It is generally understood here that the Government lately signed a ten-year lease for an office building erected by private capital at a rental that will more than pay the cost of the building in that time!

That is not the worst. When the Navy Department decided to evacuate the Mills Building at the end of the term of its lease on account of the extortionate rent, the Department of Labor promptly filled the void and moved in one door as fast as the naval contingent moved out of the other. It would take more than a C. P. A. to figure out the gain that justified that upheaval in two of our departments. Since we must needs remain in the Rental Age a while longer, let us have a Manager of Government Leases, that spectacles like this shall not cause us to pray for a Teutonic injection into the veins of our body politic.

TENCH T. MARTE
Washington, D. C.

Of the many editorials which have been written upon the Hubert Eaves case, discussed in our editorial pages on March 27, one of the most sensible is that of the negro weekly, *The New York Age*. After discussing the first reason alleged by the boy for his action, that the flag "doesn't have God in it," the *Age* says:

Hubert, in his second reason for not saluting the flag, says: "I haven't any country. It all belongs to the white man." This statement would be more rational than the first, if it were true. But is it true? It is not. Three hundred years of labor and loyalty makes this country belong to the negroes as much as it belongs to anybody else; and a good deal more than it belongs to many who are living under its flag. Of course, we have been wronged, we are still being wronged, many of our rights are still denied us, but the American negro is not going to renounce his rights because some people in the country are opposed to his having them. No, he is going to work and fight until his every right is recognized and accorded. If he should lie down and say, "I haven't any country, it all belongs to the white man," he would not deserve a country.

Hubert seems to feel that the country is all wrong; that God is nowhere in it; Hubert is mistaken. Altho many, sometimes a majority of the people in this country are wrong, yet that abstract thing we call the Country is right, and is always making for the right.

I wish to commend your editorial, "A Negro Nonconformist," in The Independent for March 27. Hubert Eaves has been sentenced to the state reformatory and the sentence has been suspended on the agreement of his parents to educate him in a private school. If it should seem probable that such action would increase respect for the flag the boy refuses to salute, then severity might be commendable. But it is difficult to see how just the reverse will not be true. It is a very one-sided contest when the commonwealth of Iowa is pitted against a little negro boy and his parents. In such an unequal struggle the sympathy of the onlooker is likely to be with the under dog. Depriving him of the rights enjoyed by others in his class will seem to many lovers of justice much like persecution. He is thus elevated to the position of a martyr, and achieves a publicity he could not otherwise easily have attained.

Now the general effect of all this cannot be good. It may, as you say, thru that enforce a hypocritical compliance with custom. It may bring about a result very different: it may encourage in some who desire notoriety a nonconformity as hypocritical as is enforced conformity. It is not easy to believe it will add to the affection for the flag on the part of those who already love it.

If, on the contrary, no attempt had been made to compel a show of reverence the heart does not feel, the case of Hubert Eaves would never have been heard of outside of his school, or at any rate outside of Des Moines. He would have been tolerated as any other eccentric person is tolerated. His act would have acquired none of the glamour it attains the moment he is arrayed in a matter of conscience against a power able to do with him what it will. Because no punishment followed his nonconformity no sympathy would have been felt for him, and thru him for his act. The whole tendency under such circumstances would have been to discredit, not necessarily him, but unquestionably his act.

And this brings us back to where we began. For certainly the only aim here is to increase respect for the emblem of our national life and devotion to the ideals it represents. Therefore it is good that you speak out on the matter with no delusion that the punishment of Hubert Eaves will attain the object at which it aims.

           A. STARBUCK

Iowa State College of Agriculture

I cannot resist resenting the letter of the Rev. Mr. R. S. Lindsay in your issue of March 27th. "A few adventurers have been killed." Personally acquainted with the men who were slaughtered at Santa Isabel I resent such terms, and wish to criticize the ignorance, in lieu of other words for such attitude, which rushes into print.

At least three of the Santa Isabel victims were university men, and all of them were high grade men far from being "adventurers." It is rather a benighted intellect that considers its vocation as the only one in life, and its sinuous lines of least resistance the broad way. These men were mining engineers, found where sent in pursuit of their vocation.

The slaughtered at Columbus were reputable American citizens, as well as Federal soldiers, engaged in their pursuits in their own country, tho it was a border town. Villa came near to getting a Congregational minister who was in Columbus that night. Was he an "adventurer?"

I might inquire whether Mr. Lindsay considers the Congregational missionaries at Chihuahua, Guadalajara and elsewhere in Mexico "adventurers?" One of these missionaries, to my knowledge, retired only two weeks ago.

           F. C. GREEN

Phoenix, Arizona

The Market Place

STEEL RAILS GO UP

As foreshadowed last week, the Steel Corporation has announced that the price of steel rails is to be advanced. The advance will be $5 a ton, making the price $33 a ton for Bessemer rails and $35 a ton for open hearth rails. This is the first increase in the price of rails in fifteen years. It is intimated that it is the intention of the manufacturers not to make this a merely temporary advance during the time of the war, but to establish the new price as a standard base figure, to be maintained permanently. The controlling factors in the increased prices are said to be the higher cost of labor and of the raw materials entering into the manufacture of rails.

It is an interesting fact that the price of rails has been maintained at the same level ever since the formation of the Steel Corporation in 1901, in spite of the fact that the semi-finished steel which enters into the manufacture of rails has at times been quoted above the price of rails. During the present period of industrial prosperity the discrepancy between the price of the semi-finished steel and the completed rails has been wider than ever before. For example, Bessemer and open hearth billets are quoted at $45 a ton, as compared with prices of $20 a ton a year ago. Steel bars are quoted at double the prices at which rails have been selling. Under these conditions, an advance in the price of rails was inevitable.

THE PAN-AMERICAN HIGH COMMISSION

The International High Commission, composed of the Secretary of the Treasury or Finance Minister of each of the nine American Republics, has completed its organization at Buenos Ayres. Secretary McAdoo has been elected president, John Bassett Moore vice-president, and L. S. Rowe, of the University of Pennsylvania, secretary general. The headquarters of the commission are to be at Washington.

The commission made a number of important recommendations, including the following: Completion of an intercontinental railway system; improvement of telegraph and cable facilities between the American republics; absolute government control of all wireless communication; uniformity of law regarding bills of exchange; clarifying international conventions on trade marks and copyrights; reduction of postal rates.

The commission adopted resolutions declaring the creation of an American merchant marine to be of paramount importance. Strong sentiment developed at the meeting in favor of coöperation between the leading South American governments and the United States to secure results. Speakers at the meeting declared that Latin America looked to the United States to meet the situation, and the belief was exprest that full development of inter-American relations was impossible without an adequate American merchant marine.

SKYROCKETTING OCEAN FREIGHTS

In the last two years the freight rates on grain between New York and Liverpool have increased 900 per cent. The rates on flour have been multiplied six times, and the rates on provisions five times. In ordinary times grain is carried at especially low rates because of its desirability as ballast and because of the comparative ease with which it is loaded and discharged. This explains the more rapid rise of rates on grain.

The rates on cotton, both from New York and New Orleans, have also been increased tenfold. But it is still cheaper, in spite of the congestion at the Northern port, to ship cotton from New York than from New Orleans.

The facts in regard to this phenomenal increase of rates of ocean freight are contained in a letter addrest to the chairman of the House Committee on the Merchant Marine and Fisheries by the chief of the Bureau of Foreign and Domestic Commerce in the Department of Commerce.

The shortage of ships that has led to the remarkable increases in shipping rates is attributed to the following causes: (1) The elimination of the merchant ships of Germany and Austria-Hungary; (2) the withdrawal of merchant ships for military and naval purposes, and (3) the loss of ships thru submarine and mining operations.

EARNINGS OF INDUSTRIALS

While many of our industrial corporations have not yet given to the public their reports for the year 1915, the figures submitted by fifty of them show that their average earnings on stock were 31.4 per cent, against 10 per cent in 1914. In some instances there were deficits in that year, which have been succeeded in 1915 by considerable profits. Among those companies whose reports are not yet available there are several—oil corporations and manufacturers of arms or explosives—whose very large earnings would increase the average.

In the first two months of the present year 72 American mines and similar undertakings paid $14,539,000 in dividends, against $6,701,000 in the corresponding months of 1915, and the dividends of fifteen copper companies rose from $1,833,000 to $8,879,000.

The following dividends are announced: Westinghouse Electric and Manufacturing Company, common, 1¼ per cent, payable April 29. Pacific Gas and Electric Company, full paid first preferred and original preferred, quarterly, $1.50 per share, payable May 15.

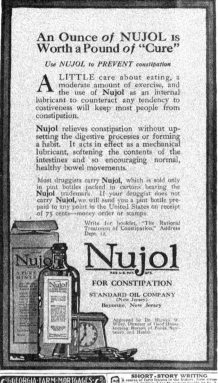

An Ounce *of* NUJOL is Worth a Pound *of* "Cure"

Use NUJOL to PREVENT constipation

A LITTLE care about eating, a moderate amount of exercise, and the use of **Nujol** as an internal lubricant to counteract any tendency to costiveness will keep most people from constipation.

Nujol relieves constipation without upsetting the digestive processes or forming a habit. It acts in effect as a mechanical lubricant, softening the contents of the intestines and so encouraging normal, healthy bowel movements.

Most druggists carry **Nujol**, which is sold only in pint bottles packed in cartons bearing the **Nujol** trademark. If your druggist does not carry **Nujol**, we will send you a pint bottle prepaid to any point in the United States on receipt of 75 cents—money order or stamps.

Write for booklet, "The Rational Treatment of Constipation." Address Dept. 12.

Nujol

REG. U.S. PAT. OFF.

FOR CONSTIPATION

STANDARD OIL COMPANY
(New Jersey)
Bayonne, New Jersey

Approved by Dr. Harvey W. Wiley, Director of Good Housekeeping Bureau of Foods, Sanitation and Health

Insurance
Conducted by
W. E. UNDERWOOD

RECKLESS RAPACITY

For forty-one years, from 1867 to 1908, the Union Central Life Insurance Company of Cincinnati, Ohio, did business on a capital of $100,000. At the end of that period its assets aggregated $62,242,454; it had a clear surplus of $2,410,620 and its total insurance in force amounted to $256,082,462. Keeping in mind the amount of assets and net surplus, a practical business man will readily conclude how utterly insignificant as a security to policyholders was the paltry $100,000 owned by the stockholders. The only effect its retirement could have had on their interests would have been the saving of $10,000 a year which the company was paying stockholders on their original investment.

In 1904, John M. Pattison, then president of the company, interrogated on the subject by the actuary of the Ohio Insurance Department, asserted that with the exception of this stockholders' dividend, all the earnings of the company belonged to the participating policyholders. The company had written some non-participating business, the profits from which under the articles of incorporation belonged to the stockholders; but Mr. Pattison said that no separate account had been kept of the two kinds of policies and he intimated that they had yielded no profit. Whether or not there had been, no one in the company knew, and, as Mr. Pattison stated, it was understood by all the stockholders that their interests were limited to the semi-annual dividend of five per cent on the invested capital. That is all they had ever received, such surplus as was earned over that being credited every year to the policyholders.

Mr. Pattison died in 1906 and was succeeded in the presidency by Jesse R. Clark. In 1908 the claim was set up by the new management that $779,000 of the accumulated surplus had been earned by non-participating policies, and they thereupon declared a stock dividend of $400,000, raising the capital from $100,000 to $500,000, thus quintupling the value of the stock holdings and increasing their annual dividends by $40,000. This action was taken in the face of the fact that the company did not need even a dollar's worth of capital.

And now the management come forward with a plan again increasing the capital to $2,500,000, paying it up out of an alleged non-participating surplus of more than that amount, of which they propose to distribute to the stockholders at once the sum of $1,500,000 in stock, leaving $500,000 in the company's treasury, presumably for future distribution. But they have, magnanimously, reduced the annual dividend rate to stockholders from ten per cent to six per cent. Under this arrangement the stockholders will now receive $120,000 a year on an original investment of $100,000, in addition to which the latter is multiplied twentyfold.

We shall now have to wait and see what the courts of Ohio will do in connection with this attempt to saddle this tax on the policyholders of a company for the use of money earned by the company itself and which, up to 1908 and for more than forty years prior thereto, was regarded as surplus belonging to and distributable among the policyholders.

E. S., Wenatchee, Wash.—The New Amsterdam Casualty Company is thoroly reliable and the policy it is offering is a good one. As you have no one dependent on you, such a policy would be advisable.

D. D. D., Weiser, Idaho.—If you will consult The Independent of March 13, 1916, you will find an article devoted to the Continental Life of Salt Lake City. Write to the Insurance Commissioner of Utah, Salt Lake City, for a copy of the report of an examination made by his department in conjunction with those of Colorado and Wyoming.

S. P., Aurora, Ill.—As the Guarantee Fund Life Association does not make provision in calculating its rates for a proper mathematical reserve, I am compelled to conclude that it cannot furnish insurance at a level rate during the term of life. The best managed old line life insurance companies are providing life insurance at the lowest cost consistent with security and no assessment scheme claiming to do it lower can deliver the goods.

M. C. P., Cleveland, Ohio.—The Royal Union Mutual of Des Moines and the Home Life of New York are both good companies. Life insurance work offers substantial rewards to women who have the ability and the desire to do it. It requires courage, stedfastness of purpose and a quality of persistence that defies failure. If you are made of that sort of stuff and will study life insurance when you are not seeking applications and will seek applications when you are not studying, you will win.

W. W. H., Sewickley, Pa.—If you have no dependents to protect against the results of your death, I would advise you to take a twenty-year endowment in one of the thoroly established companies which has a good dividend record. If you have dependents, take as much ordinary life insurance in such a company as you can afford to keep up. Without discussing the merits or demerits of any particular company, that is the sum of my advice. It would be difficult for me to advise you as between life insurance and accident and health insurance; your circumstances should decide the question.

J. G., Bucyrus, O.—On January 1, the assets of the Bankers' Life of Lincoln, Nebraska, were $9,439,832; its gross surplus, $2,753,328. Of this gross surplus, however, the sum of $2,664,139 is carried as a liability, being the accumulated dividends due under its deferred dividend policies. The net surplus, therefore, is $89,189. The bulk of this company's business is written on deferred dividend plans, a scheme which involves the forfeiture of valuable equities by policyholders who die or lapse. So opposed to good public policy is that plan of insurance that, after thoroly investigating it in 1905, a committee of the New York Legislature reported against it, and a law was enacted in 1906 forbidding traffic in such policies by companies transacting business in the State of New York.

THE SAGE OF POTATO HILL
Ed. Howe's Thoughts on Men, Women & the World

EDWARD EARLE PURINTON, a writer in The Independent, says he has never known a half dozen efficient housekeepers. Where has the man lived? I have known thousands of them. The most wonderful thing in the world to me is the patience and efficiency of good women; and first of all a very large majority of these are good housekeepers. Another writer in The Independent (Martha Bensley Bruère, a graduate of Vassar, an active worker for women suffrage and socialism) says "it is a mistaken notion that we need more and better housekeepers"; and she proceeds to tell us why girls should not be taught housework. And this in the face of Mr. Purinton's declaration that he "has not met a dozen housewives who really knew their business." I am old-fashioned; please consider me as screaming in protest because of these startling examples of New Thought and Progress.

A notable and worthy class of men are country bankers. I have lately visited several big towns, and met many bankers. "Where did he come from?" I have often asked, on being introduced to a banker. And in nine cases out of ten I learned that the bigger came from a country bank. The big cities are full of prominent bankers who came from the country. Governor Bailey, my neighbor, lately called on me in the evening; his wife was giving a party, and he ran away from it. Governor Bailey was a country banker and farmer before he became a governor, and manager of the largest bank in my town. He is now, also, a member of the Federal Reserve Board, and knows many noted bankers. He talked about them, and I inquired into their history. All of the men began as country bankers. . . . I was once a passenger on a ship which stopped at Mombassa, on the east coast of Africa. A quiet man came aboard there who attracted little attention at first; but one evening, when I was taking a constitutional around the decks after dinner, he fell in with my step, and asked: "Which way are you going home?" Then I knew he was a Yankee. I spent many hours with him, and discovered a remarkable man: A. Barton Hepburn, Comptroller of the Currency under Harrison; now of the Chase National Bank, of New York. His titles in Who's Who in America fill nearly a page. But he began as a country banker. . . . The same thing is true of other callings: our big men began in the country; in villages and on farms, far away from the Bright Lights. And these men are as steady now as they were as country bankers; they are rarely the men who make champagne-drinking records or supply the big city social scandals. Frequently you hear of them in

connection with Organized Robbery—not the small, disreputable kind, such as porch climbing or pocket picking—but in connection with developing steel mills, railroad and steamship lines, and other forms of what we know as Commercialized Greed.

A girl friend of mine, who had been notoriously spoilt by her parents, lately married. Her husband came of an old-fashioned family, and refused to have a spoilt wife. So he insisted upon certain things, and his wife carried them out; but she did nothing that a wife should not have done—indeed, she became an object lesson to shiftless young married women in my town, since she was useful, sensible, and a good wife and home maker. But I wish you could have heard the fuss the neighbors made! They said the husband was a "slave driver" and a brute, altho he did nothing he should not have done; and his wife confest to me only lately that she loves her husband, and is happy. The bride's own mother says her daughter was spoilt, and that her husband has made a woman of her. But the neighbors are not satisfied, altho most of them are losing some of their resentment. . . . I know a little girl of fourteen who is useful to her mother; who is brought up as a child should be, and she has gained something because of her years at school. But the neighbors talk about the sensible mother as they talk about the sensible husband: real family efficiency is becoming almost discreditable among us shiftless Americans.

A popular dog lately is the Airedale. These dogs are actually nothing except idealized curs. Everyone knows that cur dogs are wonderfully smart, so some man mixt a number of particularly smart and ugly cur dogs, and called the result the Airedale. . . . We Americans have in our veins the blood of all the best nations, and we are as famous the world over as the Airedales. I saw a statement the other day that of 4000 of our wealthy men taken at random, all except seventeen began as poor boys. The author of the statement is Dr. Russell H. Conwell, and he adds that all of the 4000, except a pitiful forty, have been of the greatest use to their several communities. . . . So it seems that our great prizes are in the air, free to poor boys willing to be industrious, polite, fair, and to accumulate such common sense as they can beg or borrow.

I do not hope to print in The Independent a story that is new, since its readers see the almanacs as soon as I do. I relate this one to illustrate a point: In Germany there is a section known as Schwabland, and those living there are said to be particularly dull. A

Schwab mayor was once presented with a gold-headed cane by his admiring constituency, and, finding it too long, cut off the gold head. "Why didn't you cut it off at the bottom?" he was asked. "Well, it was all right down there," the mayor replied. . . . We Americans are guilty of many Schwab tricks. When anything goes wrong, we say the trouble is at the top; never at the bottom. When there is an accident, we say the trouble was at the head; that everything was all right down below. At East Youngstown, Ohio, 4000 strikers engaged in rioting, and burned and looted ten blocks of buildings. What did we do? We indicted the employers, who had nothing whatever to do with the rioting.

The Proletariat are usually mean, lazy and unreliable; yet in all public references to them, have you ever heard these facts stated except in the dictionary? On the contrary, are they not always referred to as the opprest? Are not industrious and successful people being abused forever because of their failure to do more for the Proletariat? Did you ever before see in print a declaration that the Proletarians might help themselves, as others are compelled to do?

Every day or two I meet a man who is mad at everybody because of his own faults.

The world is finally considering the problem of over-education. In the West we hear it frequently said of a certain noted place of learning that it never turned out a graduate who was not a cad; its pupils are over-educated, and finally become social politicians.

Liberty is the one thing we Americans want to give everyone plenty of. The average voter is an amiable chump who can't quite decide about anything, except that he is always willing to listen to those who say they have been deprived of Liberty or Justice.

The man who has only Belief should not be classed with those who have Knowledge.

Much goes on in public life that causes me regret; not as a crank or critic, but as a citizen.

One of the tragic and amusing things of life is a love affair between a couple who go together a long time, and finally the woman becomes afraid to marry the man, and the man becomes afraid to marry the woman; so they drift apart.

When you see a woman running, there is something doing. She may not be able to do it, but she is hurrying to try.

The Independent

FOR SIXTY-SEVEN YEARS THE
FORWARD-LOOKING WEEKLY OF AMERICA

THE   CHAUTAUQUAN
Merged with The Independent June 1, 1914

MAY 1, 1916

OWNED AND PUBLISHED BY
THE INDEPENDENT CORPORATION, AT
119 WEST FORTIETH STREET, NEW YORK
WILLIAM B. HOWLAND
FREDERIC E. DICKINSON, TREASURER

WILLIAM HAYES WARD
HONORARY EDITOR

EDITOR: HAMILTON HOLT
ASSOCIATE EDITOR: HAROLD J. HOWLAND
LITERARY EDITOR: EDWIN E. SLOSSON

PUBLISHER: KARL V. S. HOWLAND

ONE YEAR, THREE DOLLARS

SINGLE COPIES, TEN CENTS

Postage to foreign countries in Universal Postal
Union, $1.76 a year extra; to Canada, $1 extra.
Instructions for renewal, discontinuance or
change of address should be sent two weeks
before the date they are to go into effect. Both
the old and the new address must be given.

We welcome contributions, but writers who
wish their articles returned, if not accepted,
should send a stamped and addrest envelope. No responsibility is assumed by The
Independent for the loss or non-return of
manuscripts, tho all due care will be exercised.

Entered at New York Post Office as Second
Class Matter

Copyright, 1916, by The Independent

Address all Communications to
THE INDEPENDENT
119 West Fortieth Street, New York

CONTENTS

THE MENTAL INVENTORY

In our issue of March 27 we published a list of a hundred questions used
in the Friends' Schools of Baltimore
and Germantown to test the range of
general information possest by the pupils. The percentage of correct answers
usually ranges from about fifteen per
cent for pupils twelve years old to about
sixty per cent for those eighteen years
old; the boys almost always averaging
better than the girls. Not many grown
people can score 100 per cent.

For the benefit of those who have
tried this information test on themselves or others we give below the answers. Of course, in some cases an alternative answer or different wording
is allowable. The answers are often
amusing. Mardi Gras was defined by
one person as "the gas which the Germans are using in the war" and by another as "a goose liver pie." The sublime Porte was variously defined as "a
good wine" and also as "heaven." W. J.
Bryan was given as "the Great Commoner" and also as "Old Scratch."
Adam's Ale is, according to one boy, "a
drink given early in human history"
and by another as "the lump in a man's
neck." White Wings were thought to be
"members of the Anti-Saloon League"
and "lovers of peace." A hyphenated
American is, we are surprized to learn,
"an American who talks in short sentences." There seems to be a very general impression that Alaska is southwest of the North Pole.

1. Woodrow Wilson. 2. Robert Lansing.
3. Champ Clark. 4. Josephus Daniels. 5.
Local. 6. Local. 7. Cærranza. 8. Mary E.
Wiley. 9. Nicholas Murray Butler. 10.
William Pitt. 11. The Duke of Wellington. 12. The devil. 13. Thomas Edison. 14. Norway, Sweden, Denmark, Holland, Switzerland, Spain, Rumania, Greece.
15. England and the United States. 16.

James Whitcomb Riley. 17. Dr. Theodore
Richards. 18. Enrico Caruso. 19. Guiana
(British, Dutch or French). 20. Local. 21.
Exodus, or Deuteronomy. 22. Canada (or
Great Britain) and the United States. 23.
St. Louis. 24. Chicago. 25. Texas. 26. In
southwestern Germany. 27. Between Ver-
mont and New Hampshire. 28. "Do unto
others," etc. (or Matt. vii; 12). 29. The
sign of the Italian Secret Society (the
Mafia). 30. Title of novel by Nathaniel
Hawthorne. 31. Sensational newspaper
writing. 32. The W. C. T. U. emblem. 33.
"Derisive name for a literary woman." 34.
Wireless call for help. 35. Society for Pre-
vention of Cruelty to Animals. 36. Baltimore & Ohio Railroad. 37. Compare. 38.
In the year of our Lord. 39. Bachelor of
Science. 40. Seed. 41. Root. 42. Fleshy
stem or tuber. 43. Bark. 44. Flower bud.
45. Christ. 46. Edward Everett Hale. 47.
William Shakespeare. 48. Charles Dickens.
49. Mahomet. 50. Rudyard Kipling. 51. J.
M. Barrie. 52. Psalms of David 103; 1, 63.
Benjamin Franklin. 54. Omar Khayyam,
translated by Edward Fitzgerald. 55.
Henry Ford. 56. United States. 57. Belgium. 58. Holland. 59. England. 60. Feminist: one who believes in women's rights;
effeminate: having feminine qualities, unmanly. 61. Direct taxation: on individual
property; indirect taxation: on exports and
imports. 62. Custom-house: the place where
duties on imported merchandise are paid
and vessels cleared; clearing house: the
place where checks are exchanged and bal-
ances adjusted. 63. Indulging in personalities: making disparaging remarks about a
person; having personality: possessing individual mental and spiritual characteristics. 64. Diadem: a crown; diaphragm: an
important muscle used in breathing. 65.
Shrove Tuesday, carnival time. 66. Government of Turkey. 67. New York street
cleaners. 68. A geyser in Yellowstone Park.
69. Water. 70. Americans of foreign ancestry and proclivities. 71. Late president
of Tuskegee Institute. 72. Ex-president of
National American Woman Suffrage Association. 73. Founder of Quakerism. 74. Author of "Alice in Wonderland." 75. Famous
Austrian violinist. 76. British Secretary of
State for Foreign Affairs. 77. A Philadelphia artist. 78. French actress. 79. Former
Premier of Greece. 80. Prison reformer,
former warden of Sing Sing. 81. Great
evangelist. Y. M. C. A. worker. 82. American novelist. 83. Justice of Supreme Court,
former governor of New York. 84. Commander of the English troops in France.
85. Sea of Marmora and Ægean Sea. 86.
Unterseeboot. 87. Monument erected on
boundary to commemorate peace between
Chile and Argentina. 88. To insure workmen and their families against loss of
health or life. 89. Damascus. 90. "Dr.
Jekyll and Mr. Hyde." 91. Philadelphia.
92. "Be prepared." 93. League to Enforce
Peace. 94. Madame Curie. 95. Japan. 96.
Haiti. 97. David Lloyd-George. 98. A compulsory enrolment of men for military or
naval service. 99. Fall. 100. South.

REMARKABLE REMARKS

GEN. EMILIO ZAPATA—We will drive
the Americans clear beyond Texas.

BILLY SUNDAY—I'll fight hell and the
devil till I go so fast they can't see my
dust.

PROF. ASHLEY V. THORNDIKE—In Shakespeare's time the regular drama had a popularity like that of the movies today.

LUKE McLUKE—When we used to take
them out in buggies, you could let the girl
drive while you hugged her. But au automobile isn't a buggy.

THE PRINCE OF MONACO—The only
chance for the survival and future civilization of Europe is the infusion of American
blood into European peoples.

PORK PACKER EDWARD MORRIS, JR.—
Hardly a day passes that some prominent
man does not break into print with a "set
of rules for success."

THOMAS A. EDISON—My rule is when
you build something the first time you
ought to run it to destruction in order to
discover any possible defect.

The Independent

VOLUME 86   MAY 1, 1916   NUMBER 3517

NOW LET GERMANY CHOOSE

THE final turn which the relations between the United States and Germany shall take is to be determined solely by the Imperial German Government. If Berlin prefers its lawless methods of submarine warfare to the friendship of the United States, it will cause the breaking off of diplomatic relations. There is nothing the United States can now do to prevent such a rupture.

The latest note of President Wilson to Germany is not technically an ultimatum. But in its essence there is no difference. The United States has now said to Germany in unmistakable language, "Unless the Imperial Government should now immediately declare and effect an abandonment of its present methods of submarine warfare against passenger and freight-carrying vessels, the Government of the United States can have no choice but to sever diplomatic relations with the German Empire altogether."

The United States has been long-suffering. It has given Germany the benefit of every possible doubt. It has taken every assurance of the Imperial Government at its face value. But the acts of the German navy have repeatedly given the lie to the declarations of the German Government. The torpedoing of the "Sussex"—of which Washington has given Berlin complete proof—is the last straw. We can parley no longer.

The President in the note to Germany sets forth in vigorous phrase the case against the German methods of warfare on merchant shipping:

Great liners like the "Lusitania" and "Arabic" and mere passenger boats like the "Sussex" have been attacked without a moment's warning, often before they have even become aware that they were in the presence of an armed ship of the enemy, and the lives of non-combatants, passengers and crew have been destroyed wholesale and in a manner which the Government of the United States cannot but regard as wanton and without the slightest color of justification. No limit of any kind has in fact been set to their indiscriminate pursuit and destruction of merchantmen of all kinds and nationalities within the waters which the Imperial Government has chosen to designate as lying within the seat of war. The roll of Americans who have lost their lives upon ships thus attacked and destroyed has grown month by month, until the ominous toll has mounted into the hundreds.

For fourteen months German submarines have carried on warfare in plain violation of indisputable rules of international law. They have attacked merchantmen without warning—and international law forbids it.

They have sunk merchant ships without affording opportunity for the non-combatants on them to seek safety—and international law forbids it. They have killed unresisting men, women and children—and international law, to say nothing of every dictate of civilization and humanity, forbids it. They have wantonly refused to follow the immemorial rule of visit and search, the only procedure recognized by the law of nations for the lawful apprehension by belligerent ships of merchant vessels.

They have done these things for just two reasons: because the British navy has kept the German navy bottled up in harbor, so that only its submarines dared take the open sea; and because the submarine, being an especially vulnerable type of vessel, does not dare to approach openly near enough to its intended victim to carry out the stipulated program of visit and search. Neither of these reasons is one that the rest of the world can admit as valid. The United States has never recognized their validity. It cannot do so now.

It is now for Germany to choose. Its choice will be made known not by its words, but by its deeds. In the words of President Wilson, it must not only "declare," it must "effect," an abandonment of its present methods of submarine warfare against passenger and freight-carrying vessels. Not only must the Imperial Government promise; the Imperial navy's submarines must perform.

If a German submarine should now sink or attack illegally a merchant ship with an American citizen on board, the severance of diplomatic relations will follow inevitably, Count von Bernstorff will go home, and Mr. Gerard will be recalled. Then once more the next step will be for Germany to take. There will be no war between Germany and the United States unless and until Germany wills it.

If Germany should will it, our national conscience will be clear. We shall enter upon the fateful undertaking serene in the conviction that no honorable word or act has been omitted by which we might have striven to avert it. We shall know that we are fighting for the cause not only of our own national sovereignty and honor, but of humanity and the sacred rights of neutral nations.

TWO MISUSED CONCEPTIONS

IN the current discussions of preparedness the terms "police" and "insurance" have been frequently handled in incomplete and misleading ways. Altho these words have come to symbolize in common parlance fairly well defined modern conceptions, they are often used in total disregard of all their accumulated social significance when applied to the state as a unit. It is only fair that these symbols of social solidarity and effectiveness should be used in their full meaning when we are demanding the extension of their systems and safeguards to international affairs.

Our police system has been created to protect the rights of the group and its component parts against the encroachments of any of the rebellious or delinquent individuals who go to make it up. Policing, in this modern acceptation of the term, is wholly unthinkable without organization. Nor would it be allowed for a moment that one group could rightfully use its police power to intimidate, or coerce, or impose its will upon another group not bound to it by governmental ties. Moreover, all the members of a community supporting the police system must, by virtue of their participation in its benefits, submit to the police regulations. In other words, our whole modern notion of police is out of harmony with individual arming for private defense, and has no application whatever to relationships unsecured by governmental agreement and organization.

Slowly we have come to realize that individual or private police is not only an insufficient protection, but is a menace to society as a whole. Now, it is easy to see that the creation of a great fleet and army for the protection of a single nation is, not in line with the present social conception of policing, but rather the application of an ancient outworn method, wherein the police represented not the whole municipality or community, but some specially strong class or individual attempting to secure protection in a disorganized or anarchic condition of society. In spite of the fact that the old idea has been revived again and again in our country in the Pinkertons and other detective agencies, the conscience of society condemns all such methods as undemocratic, inefficient, and an ever ready means of injustice, cruelty and oppression. If we are to have a police system in our international relationships, let us go the whole length of our modern conceptions and moral ideals. Let us enter into an organization with other nations. Let us do our share toward the support of a true international police directed by representatives of the larger grouping, and let us show our willingness to submit to whatever policing may be demanded.

The same reasoning applies to the questions of insurance, a term which still bears a double meaning. There has always been thruout the history of mankind one kind of insurance, the insurance that exists in accumulations made to meet losses of a more or less uncertain character. Individuals have ever sought to prepare against the accidents of fortune by holding in reserve enough to insure them against complete downfall in the day of possible calamity. But such insurance the experience of mankind has come to discount in many spheres because of its expensiveness, ineffectiveness and useless risks. In fact, when we speak of insurance today we give the term a social significance and appraise its value in accordance with its socially acquired power to reduce the necessary reserves, transfer the risk from the individual to the group, and give greater security that possible or accidental loss will not entail utter destruction.

Economic development has long since taught us that "self-insurance," while not a failure, is at the same time not sufficient to meet the needs of modern society. Up-to-date insurance presupposes a number of individuals or units banded together to secure at the minimum cost the maximum of protection and to share as a group those unforeseen and perhaps unavoidable losses that otherwise would light upon the few with crushing weight. There is no good reason why we should not in this modern way insure against national calamity, against accident, against unseen foes; but it ought to be the real insurance of international obligation, agreement, alliance, federation, and it ought to be supported by legal regulations, courts and police power.

It is true, of course, that the conceptions which we have set forth of police and insurance did not come into being until mankind had developed at least some semblance of organized society. Before a community police was possible, it was necessary for each man to protect his own rights and those of his own household. Before coöperative insurance was evolved each individual did well to protect his own future by "self-insurance.' So in the international community national self-protection must obtain until international organization shall make possible the protection of the rights of the individual nation by the power of the whole group of nations united to maintain justice. National "self-insurance" continues to be a national duty until such time as coöperative insurance can be substituted for it.

But even in our present imperfect stage of international development, we should be looking steadfastly forward to the larger conception of the police function and the broader interpretation of national insurance. To present these ideas, in their narrow and incomplete significance, as final solutions of the problems of national safety and international justice is to ignore the teachings of history and social evolution.

RUSSIA TO THE RESCUE

THIS is "Russia Week" in the history of the Great War. While one body of Russian troops was crossing the Black Sea to occupy the ancient stronghold of Trebizond, another was crossing the Mediterranean Sea to land at Marseilles. In both fields their advent will be heartily welcomed, for the British are hard prest in the Asian field and the French in the European.

The British expedition which started up the Tigris toward Bagdad in November, 1914, is still held back at Kut-el-Amara, a hundred miles down stream. The Russians coming down from the Caspian are probably nearer to Bagdad than the British and may be able to reach the besieged force before the British relief expedition can fight its way thru the Turkish lines. The Turks have not been able, and seem not to have tried, to make a stand against the Russians since the Grand Duke Nicholas took command of the Caucasian army. Let us hope that the Russian occupation of Armenia comes not too late to save the remnant of the race from massacre.

The arrival of the Russians in France is a retarded realization of an early rumor of the war. A myth, according to the latest psychology, is the offspring of a supprest longing and we may account in this way for the illusion of the French and British soldiers in their retreat from Mons that angels from heaven or Russians from Archangel were coming to their rescue. The latter legend, it is said, arose from a telegram which leaked out in London. "Forty thousand Russians sent via Archangel," was the way it was sent from Petrograd, and it was meant to convey to the commission merchant who received it that the usual shipment of forty thousand Russian eggs had been sent by way of Archangel on account of the closing of the Baltic. Nevertheless there were many who swore to seeing the Russian soldiers as they came down from Scotland by train in the night, and one Englishman said he knew they were Russians because "they wore cossacks." Not long after the dispatches from France told us of the arrival of Japanese on the scene, but these were equally mythical.

This time we cannot doubt that Russian troops have really reached France, tho how many they are and how they came is yet hidden from us. But, however few they may be, their presence will do much to reassure the French and restore confidence in the good faith of their Slavic ally. The transfer of Russian soldiers to the Western front leaves one to surmise that they are not expected to do much in their own country this summer. The German line in Russia is thinly held, yet the Russians have not been able to break it or to push it back perceptibly for more than a year. Of men Russia has no lack. Her population is probably a million more than it was when the war began. But in leaders and munitions she is wofully wanting, while in France the Russian soldiers can be put under able commanders and competently equipt.

THE DIVORCE EVIL

SEVERAL hundred editorials are written every year under this heading. Yet it seems to us that there is still need for a little clear thinking and plain speaking on the subject. In the first place, the divorce evil is not the divorce. Neither is the divorce the remedy for the divorce evil. The divorce evil is the evil, whatever it may be, which leads to divorce. Consequently the divorce never removes the evil. The divorce only alleviates—or aggravates—the unfortunate situation arising in some particular case from a previously existing evil.

A uniform divorce law is therefore no remedy for the divorce evil. A uniform divorce law is simply imposing upon the whole United States the ethical standards of one community. South Carolina permits no divorce for any cause. Oregon permits divorce for "indignities rendering life burdensome." Shall South Carolina be brought under the law of Oregon or Oregon under the law of South Carolina? Or shall both be brought under a law that neither desires? Uniformity of legal phraseology and of court procedure are desirable, so also are restrictions on interstate migration for divorce purposes. To go further than this would do little to lessen the number of divorces and nothing to lessen the divorce evil.

The alleged causes for divorce are rarely the real reasons. Unless the plaintiff is vindictive the grounds brought forward are the least serious and disgraceful that the law allows. On the other hand, those who are determined on divorce will not shrink from the ostensible commission of a statutory crime.

Neither can we infer anything as to which is the guilty party from the court records as to which brought the proceedings. People get married because they want to. People get divorced because they don't want to. The state refuses to marry a couple unless both express a desire to be married. The state refuses to divorce a couple if both express a desire to be divorced. Yet probably most divorced couples do actually separate by mutual consent and would much prefer not to bring disgraceful charges against one another unless the law obliged them to.

The American rate of one divorce for twelve marriages is deplored and denounced on all sides. Yet when one knows intimately the causes which impel any particular couple to separate he usually comes to the conclusion that it would be a wrong to themselves and to the community for them to continue living together.

Whether one argues for greater or less freedom of divorce or for no divorce at all, these plain facts should be taken into consideration.

BROTHERHOOD OR BIGOTRY

IT is deeply discouraging to find in a paper like *The Sunday School Times*, intensely devoted to the study of the documents on which Christianity is founded, the declaration that "perhaps the worst fact in the fallacy and modern fetish of the brotherhood of man is not merely that it is foolish and futile, but that it has failed —it contains a deadly poison." If ever buffeted and suffering humanity needed the proclamation of this great principle of the gospel, it is now. To regard the assertion of universal brotherhood as a denial of essential Christian doctrine and as "blasphemy," to maintain that "we cannot be brothers to the unsaved," is to seek to drag the church and the faith into obscurity and contempt.

If any spiritual power is able to save civilization from being turned backward at this juncture and inspire men to go forward in the achievements of righteousness and peace, it must be a larger consciousness of the brotherhood of all men and the eternal justice of God. If the church is so bound by bigotry, narrowness and the fetters of medieval dogmatism that it cannot sound this clear note for humanity's guidance in the hour of direst peril, it will miss the greatest opportunity of all the ages for asserting the supremacy and worth of the gospel, and the leadership in moral and spiritual progress will pass into more worthy hands. The church, and even Christianity itself, now stands at the cross roads. Large vision and courageous leadership are essential to future power.

SIMPLIFIED SPELLING IN COLLEGES

IT is natural that the movement for a more rational orthography should be taken up by the colleges and normal schools, for education tends to free one from the popular superstitions in regard to English spelling. The student of literature soon learns that spelling is not a fixity, but that it has changed a great deal in the history of the language. He learns that spelling does not automatically adjust itself to the progress of the language, but that any improvements have to be made by individual initiative and coöperative effort. He learns that the current spelling of English came into use accidentally and has been perpetuated by the conservatism of the printer and the authority of the schoolmaster. He learns that the spelling in many cases represents neither the sound nor the derivation of the word. He learns that spelling reform is not an impossibility but has actually been achieved to a considerable extent by official action in languages such as German and Spanish, where the need of it was less than in English.

Every teacher knows that the present unscientific and unnatural fashion of spelling can only be imposed upon each succeeding generation by strenuous and continuous exertion, for every pupil has a tendency to adopt forms that are more regular and phonetic. This tendency, altho annoying to those hired to suppress it, is obviously a wholesome sign of intelligence and needs only to be guided into proper channels to effect a reform of the written language. The Simplified Spelling Board of New York was organized for the purpose of guiding it in such a way as to lead to gradual and progressive improvement in so far as this can be done with the existing alphabet. The Board in a recent circular urges college faculties to take action of two kinds: first, to give their students a chance to choose the better of two authorized spellings and, second, to set them a good example. For the first it is sufficient to allow the students in their written work to use any forms found in the vocabulary of such dictionaries as the Standard, Webster's or Century, such as *center, color, rime*, and *surprize* instead of *centre, colour, rhyme* and *surprise*. For the second it is recommended that the institution adopt in its official publications and correspondence the twelve words adopted by the National Educational Association, *program, catalog, decalog, prolog, tho, altho, thorofare, thru, thruout*. This very moderate program of reform has been adopted by 138 universities, colleges and normal schools comprising about 120,000 students. The movement is also making encouraging progress in the press. There are now in the United States 92 dailies and 58 periodicals with a combined circulation of 12,000,000 which have followed the example of The Independent in using simplified spellings. A large part of the public is thus becoming used to the new forms and the only real objection to them, that is, their strangeness, is being gradually removed.

JUSTICE ?

JOHN GALSWORTHY'S plays move with the fatalistic force of the ancient Greek drama. Given the characters and the conditions, the action and the end are inevitable. For instance in "Justice," familiar to readers all over the country in book form and now drawing packed houses every night in New York, Galsworthy makes us feel in turn the point of view of each of the participants. We can understand, and therefore we cannot altogether condemn, the weak hero, or rather victim, driven to crime by sympathy and ruined by his imprisonment; his upright but inexorable employer; the mechanical but humane clerk, in which rôle we recognize our old friend Androcles, of Shaw's play ; the wronged wife; the advocates of both sides; even the ridiculous judge—all of them are real, none of them is a caricature.

The scene is laid in England, but the lesson is one for America as well. The three evils which Galsworthy attacks, antiquated court procedure, stringent divorce laws and cruel prison methods, are indeed worse there than here, but any newspaper affords proof that the shoe fits us as well and pinches us at the same points. All Galsworthy's plays end with a question mark, and none more demands an answer than "Justice."

A FUTILE PASSION

THE Presbytery of Cincinnati has taken the extraordinary action, by a vote of 42 to 29, of overturing the General Assembly at its meeting in May to remove the Presbytery of New York from membership in the General Assembly. The reason given is that the Presbytery of New York, in its support of Union Theological Seminary, and in its licensing of heretical students of that seminary, has flouted the instructions of the General Assembly and has proved itself unfaithful to the Standards of the Presbyterian Church.

This looks serious, but is not so serious as it looks. Cincinnati is the most conservative of presbyteries, but it is a century too late for it to rule the General Assembly. In the thirties of the last century the General Assembly had trouble with Auburn Seminary and Dr. Albert Barnes over the question of general and particular atonement. Some held that Christ's sufferings were sufficient to atone for all the sins of the world, while others held that they were only enough to atone for the sins of the elect, and the liberals were driven out to organize the New School Presbyterian Church. They remained apart for forty years and then they came together again on the same old Standards, neither party yielding, but practically putting the Standards on the shelf and adopting an explanatory statement. Since then new theological questions have arisen relating to inspiration of the Bible, but there is no sign that it will split the Church; the only secessions have been the transfer of Professor Briggs to the Episcopalians and that of Professor McGiffert and Professor H. P. Smith to the Congregationalists. The Presbytery of New York is not in danger, nor Union Seminary, although the new wine may burst a few bottles. One is reminded by this outburst of John Milton's discourteous retort to Salmasius: "Si non lubeat rumpatur," and at the futile anger, on a certain occasion, of one who

> Wroth to see his kingdom fail
> Swindges the scaly horror of his folded tail.

THE PUNISHMENT FITS THE CRIME

FOR the enlightenment of the one-half of one per cent of our readers who do not know the difference between a niblick and a stymie, be it known that Francis Ouimet is the wizard who startled the world not so very long ago by defeating Harry Vardon and Edward Ray for the National Open Golf Championship of the United States.

But alas and alack! He can never again play with these admirable gentlemen of the leisure class known as "pure amateurs." For the executive committee of the United States Golf Association has handed down the golden decision that hereafter he is ineligible for any amateur match.

And why, pray, must he thus be hurled into this irrevocable gloom of outer darkness? Because, forsooth, he has gone into the sporting goods business. This is his offense in all its abandoned heinousness and depravity!

Poor Ouimet—and, likewise, *poor United States Golf Association!*

THE AMERICAN ULTIMATUM TO GERMANY

THE Government of the United States has been very patient. . . . It has accepted the successive explanations and assurances of the Imperial Government as of course given in entire sincerity and good faith, and has hoped, even against hope, that it would prove to be possible for the Imperial Government so to order and control the acts of its naval commanders as to square its policy with the recognized principles of humanity as embodied in the law of nations. It has made every allowance for unprecedented conditions and has been willing to wait until the facts became unmistakable and were susceptible of only one interpretation.

It now owes it to a just regard for its own rights to say to the Imperial Government that that time has come. It has become painfully evident to it that the position which it took at the very outset is inevitable, namely, the use of submarines for the destruction of an enemy's commerce is of necessity, because of the very character of the vessels employed and the very methods of attack which their employment of course involves, utterly incompatible with the principles of humanity, the long-established and incontrovertible rights of neutrals, and the sacred immunities of non-combatants.

If it is still the purpose of the Imperial Government to prosecute relentless and indiscriminate warfare against vessels of commerce by the use of submarines, without regard to what the Government of the United States must consider the sacred and indisputable rules of international law and the universally recognized dictates of humanity, the Government of the United States is at last forced to the conclusion that there is but one course it can pursue.

Unless the Imperial Government should now immediately declare and effect an abandonment of its present methods of submarine warfare against passenger and freight-carrying vessels, the Government of the United States can have no choice but to sever diplomatic relations with the German Empire altogether. This action the Government of the United States contemplates with the greatest reluctance, but feels constrained to take in behalf of humanity and the rights of neutral nations.

The full text of the note will be found on page 192

The Crisis With Germany — A final note on the submarine question was sent to Berlin on Tuesday of last week, by the President; and on Wednesday Mr. Wilson appeared before Congress and addrest the two houses on the same critical subject. His address was practically a repetition of the note. It was received by the members of the Congress and the audience that completely filled the galleries in intense silence followed by applause, whose moderateness seemed to suggest the strain under which all the President's hearers were laboring.

In other parts of this issue we print in full the note to Germany, and an article, from one who was present at the joint session of Congress, descriptive of the scene. We also comment editorially upon the crisis in the relations of the United States and Germany.

The note to Berlin was accompanied by a very complete statement of the evidence in the possession of the State Department showing that the explosion on the "Sussex" was actually caused by a German torpedo. This evidence included the testimony of many eye witnesses, and the results of the examination by officers of the United States Army and Navy of the fragments of the instrument whose explosion damaged the "Sussex." These fragments have positively been identified, by their characteristic shape and structure, and by marking upon them, as pieces of a German torpedo. The evidence is overwhelming. It is substantiated, as we pointed out editorially last week, by the statements in the German Government's note on the case.

The American note demanded an immediate reply; but it has been explained by Ambassador von Bernstorff that the interposition of the Easter holidays will make it impossible for an answer to be forthcoming for at least ten days.

German Plot Developments — Further developments occurred last week in the uncovering of German plots in this country. Indictments were handed down by a Federal grand jury in New York against five men, charging them with a conspiracy in the early days of the war to destroy the Welland Canal, the Canadian

© *International Film Service*

COUNT VON BERNSTORFF
Who will be sent home—if relations are broken—after a long-continued endeavor to reconcile Germany and America

American Press Association

JAMES W. GERARD
American ambassador at Berlin, who has made many friends in the German capital and whose departure would be regretted

waterway connecting Lake Erie and Lake Ontario. The most prominent of the indicted men is Captain Franz von Papen, the recalled Military Attaché of the German Embassy. His indictment is an unusual incident; for diplomatic representatives of a foreign government are privileged characters not subject to the normal legal processes of the country to which they are accredited. Obviously, also, there is no expectation that Captain von Papen will be brought to trial, as he is now in Germany, where he will doubtless remain. The indictment was doubtless secured merely for the sake of the record, and justified on the ground that he is no longer a diplomatic representative accredited to this country.

The other persons indicted are Captain Hans Tauscher, the husband of Mme. Johanna Gadski, the opera singer, and agent in Jamaica of the Krupps; Alfred A. Fritzen, and Constantine Covani. None of the men indicted has been arrested. One other name was included in the indictment, but it was kept secret for several days. It then became public, however, thru the arrest by the Federal authorities of Wolf von Igel, secretary of Captain von Papen while he was in this country. Von Igel was arrested at his office in Wall Street after a hand to hand struggle with several Secret Service officials. With him were taken a great quantity of official records and secret correspondence of German officials and agents of the German Government. Von Igel was immediately released upon $20,000 bail.

Promptly upon the arrest and the seizure of the papers, strenuous protests were made by the German Ambassador on the ground that Captain von Igel is a recognized member of the force of the German Embassy, and his person and the documents in his office therefore inviolable.

The contention of the Federal Government in the case of the man was that the crime for which he was indicted was committed before he was given a place on the Embassy staff and therefore while he was still a private

citizen. The protests against his arrest were accordingly ignored. The Embassy, however, seemed much more concerned over the loss of the papers which had been taken, and rapid fire demands for their return intact were made. Meanwhile the Federal authorities went quietly on collating, cataloging and photographing them, persistently turning a deaf ear to Count von Bernstorff's protests.

The Army Bills — The Chamberlain Army Reorganization bill passed the Senate last week without a roll-call. Scarcely a dozen Senators opposed its passage. In its final form the bill differed largely from the Hay bill, dealing with the same subject, as passed by the House.

It provides for a regular army of 250,000 men; for a federal volunteer army, something like the Continental Army plan of Secretary Garrison, of 261,000 volunteers; for military instruction in schools and colleges; for making the term of enlistment in the five years, two years with the colors and three years in the reserve.

The most significant provisions were added to the bill at the last moment apparently under the spur of the news that the President was to address the Congress on the submarine controversy with Germany. They deal with the increase of the army to a quarter of a million men, and with the training of schoolboys for military service.

The bill as it passed the Senate provided for a possible regular army as large as has been proposed by Colonel Roosevelt—250,000 men. This figure is to be compared with our present army of 100,000; with the proposal of the House of Representatives for an increase to 140,000; and with the number suggested by the Senate Committee on Military Affairs, 180,000. The amendment was adopted by a vote of 43 to 37; an amendment to make the number 150,000 having previously been rejected by a vote of 66 to 17.

The school training amendment was adopted by a vote of 56 to 24. It provided for the assignment for service

as instructor in military tactics of one or more commissioned officers of the army to any college or school having 100 or more boys fifteen years of age or older, provided the school authorities make the request, and enough boys agree to take the training and to become a part, during their school or college course, of the reserve forces of the United States. The Government is to provide equipment, arms and ammunition for such reserve forces. In case of war or threatened war, the President is empowered to call into active service the members of reserve forces so created who have reached the age of eighteen years.

It is significant that practically the whole of the debate upon this amendment was in the affirmative, the only differences of opinion being upon points of detail. Not only in this debate, but in the whole consideration of the Army bill, the division was not at all upon party lines.

The Chamberlain bill and the Hay bill now go to a conference between the two houses. The wide differences between the two measures will doubtless result in sharp disagreement; and out of the inevitable compromise resulting will come a measure whose nature no one can predict.

Paying for Preparedness — While the Army Reorganization bills are being considered in Congress, the House of Representatives is proceeding to consider the Navy bill, and to work out plans for raising the additional revenue needed to pay for the enlarged preparedness program.

The Navy bill, as it comes from the House Committee on Naval Affairs, will probably provide for two battle cruisers, to cost $21,000,000 each, two dreadnoughts, to cost $18,000,000 or $19,000,000 each, and fifty submarines. An effort will be made, it is believed, to increase the number of battle cruisers to four. The Navy bill is expected to provide for an expenditure of about $230,000,000, which is about $80,000,000 more than was carried by the last Naval Appropriations Act.

Harding in Brooklyn Eagle
THE END OF THE PATH

Pease in Newark Evening News
"HIS HAND TO THE PLOW——"

Cesare in New York Sun
THIS CARTOON NEEDS NO CAPTION

It is intimated that Chairman Kitchin, of the House Ways and Means Committee, and Chairman Simmons, of the Senate Finance Committee, have agreed that the additional revenue needed for preparedness shall be secured by taxing incomes, inheritances and the manufacture of munitions of war. It is proposed to retain a portion of the taxes levied under the present .emergency tax law, furnishing between forty and fifty millions·of the needed ·money; while the income tax will be readjusted to yield seventy-five millions, an inheritance tax will provide fifty-five millions, and the tax on munitions forty-five millions.

These, of course, are merely the tentative proposals, which have yet to run the gauntlet of both Houses of Congress and be subjected to the test of public opinion.

In Mexico During the past week the punitive expedition into Mexico has been at a standstill. The report of Villa's death and burial has apparently been proved false; but where the bandit has gone is a black mystery.

After the unprovoked attack by Carranzista soldiers upon the force of American cavalrymen that entered Parral, the advance guard of the expedition retired several miles to the north and entrenched itself. All along the line of communication, it was reported, trenches were being dug by our troops ostensibly for practise. The problem of the next move in the campaign was complicated by the possibility of further armed interference by Carranza forces; by the fact that the American line of advance had been stretched about to the limit of safety with the forces available; by the reported concentration of Carranza troops in the regions thru which runs the American line of communication; and by the growing signs of hostility on the part of the population in general.

General Scott, chief of the general staff, went last week to San Antonio for conference with General Funston. Pending his report and recommendations no decision was made as to the next move in the Mexican campaign.

Peace and Prohibition in Nebraska The Nebraska primaries produced some interesting results. In the Republican Presidential primary Henry Ford polled a very large vote, being beaten on the final count by Senator Cummins of Iowa by·a narrow margin. Mr. Ford has emphatically declared that he is not a candidate for the Presidency; but this large vote for him in Nebraska following his heading the poll in Minnesota a week before seems significant of the strength of pacifist sentiment in the Middle West. The success of Mr. Cummins looks in the same direction, for his activities in Congress have been decidedly on the side of subordinating the rights of Americans to the endeavor to keep out of war.

On the other hand, the results in the Democratic primaries seem to indicate quite the reverse. For William Jennings Bryan was defeated as delegate-at-large to the National Convention. With him the whole ticket which he had endorsed, including his brother as candidate for the Democratic nomination for Governor, went down to defeat. But the Bryan campaign was really made on the prohibition issue. So that Nebraska may be assumed, on the face of the primary returns, to be for peace and against prohibition.

New York Solves a Hard Problem For years New York City has been struggling with the problem of disposing of the freight tracks of the New York Central Railroad which run down the greater part of the western side of Manhattan Island. The presence of these tracks has been a constant nuisance to many citizens living along the line, a serious blemish upon the city's fine park system along the river, and a dangerous menace to life and limb where the tracks run thru the open streets. The number of casualties, especially to children, has earned for Eleventh Avenue, thru which the tracks run for several miles, the sobriquet of "Death Avenue."

A committee of the city's Board of Estimate and Apportionment has at last worked out in coöperation with officials of the New York Central a plan for removing the tracks entirely from the surface. They will be run either in subways or on an elevated structure, depending on the conditions at the various points along the line.

In the residence and park sections, the tracks will be put beneath the ground; in the commercial districts they will run on an elevated structure, not along the streets, but thru the backyards between the blocks.

The improvements are to cost something like $50,000,000, of which the city is not asked to provide a penny. The city, however, is to contribute, thru the exchange of real estate rights and easements, values amounting to a little over $6,000,000. But when the increased safety of life and the great improvements in park facilities and in dock accommodations that will be made possible are considered, the city will be seen to be acquiring a vast benefit at a phenomenally low cost.

Prohibition in Canada Canada is rapidly going dry. Ontario has recently adopted temporary prohibition—to cover the duration of the war—and Alberta, Saskatchewan, Manitoba and Nova Scotia had previously closed their bars.

The Ontario law, the essential clauses of which have been passed, altho details are still to be adjusted, makes the sale of liquor illegal for about three years, probably until June, 1919. There is to be no referendum on this measure, and the date of its termination was fixed with a view to allowing the returned soldiers to vote on the question of prohibition. This is not to be taken at its face value, however, as an official estimate of the length of the war, as it takes several months to get names entered on the voting lists in rural Ontario, and it was thought wise to provide an ample margin to make

Harding in Brooklyn Eagle

DON'T LAUGH

© *McCutcheon, in Pittsburgh Gazette Times*

ALAS, POOR VILLA! DEAD AGAIN

Harding in Brooklyn Eagle

POSITIVELY IDENTIFIED

HALTED

This, of course, is only a temporary halt, where a wagon train has made camp. The expedition as a whole, however, has reached the end of its rope

sure that all the soldiers might be counted. The bill goes into effect on September 16, 1916.

Since there is no prohibition on the importation of liquor or its possession in any quantity for personal use, the net effect of the law will be to close the bars of the province. The present plan is to allow druggists to dispense small quantities upon prescription. The bill was a Liberal measure, fathered by N. W. Rowell, leader of the opposition, but it was adopted by the Conservative government and passed its second reading without a division.

Manitoba's prohibition act is similar in its terms, tho it remains in force until repealed, and was carried by a two to one vote at a popular election in the middle of March. In Saskatchewan there is a government dispensary system.

This wave of prohibition legislation is to be taken as chiefly a phenomenon of the Great War. The Prince Albert *Herald* said in commenting on the Manitoba vote:

In the western provinces it is very much the outcome of cold business judgment that revolts at the squandering of millions of dollars in a commodity that lessens the efficiency of the people at a time when physical, mental and material resources are called upon to bear an unprecedented strain.

Russians Arrive in France — French hopes have been revived and French enthusiasm aroused to the highest pitch by the arrival at Marseilles of a flotilla of transports bearing a contingent of Russian troops for service on the western front. As the huge ships approached the quays at noon on April 30 they passed between the vessels of the French fleet whose yard arms were manned by the sailors and whose bands were playing the Russian national hymn. The Russian commander, General Lochwescy, was greeted by General Menassier, Governor of Marseilles, and General Guerin, representing General Joffre, and the Russian soldiers were cheered by the French troops on the quay and the populace on the streets.

The Russians were seen to be picked men, many of them wearing medals of honor and all equipped with new uniforms and accouterments. Two days later they were sent north, presumably to reinforce the line at Verdun.

Nothing is said about their number

or where they came from. It has been thought possible that Russia could send 40,000 men a month for the next five months, since there are more men in the Russian army than can be armed and equipped.

Dead Man's Hill — For another week the terrible conflict has raged about the hill named, in sinister anticipation of its future rôle in history, Le Mort Homme. Both sides have claimed this hight for some time, but so far as one can judge from the dispatches the Germans have gained the eastern slope and minor crests on this side while the French hold the summit. The withdrawal of the French from Bethincourt two weeks ago has made Le Mort Homme and Hill 304, just west of it, the main points on the line defending Verdun on this side. Against these hills and the woods between the German troops have been hurled with slight gains. On the whole the Germans gained less than in any week since the battle of Verdun began.

Besides the fighting in the vicinity of Dead Man's Hill on the west of the Meuse, the Germans have renewed their attacks upon the French positions east of that river. In the section about forts Douaumont and Vaux 75,000 troops were employed in the German operations and some ground was gained by them but lost again, it appears, in the French counter attacks. The Germans, however, claim to have captured here 1700 unwounded prisoners.

The French estimate the German losses before Verdun at 200,000. On the other hand, the Germans declare this a gross exaggeration and make the counter claim that the French have lost 150,000. The French having denied the German statements of their captures, the Germans propose to publish in the *Gazette des Ardennes* the names of 711 officers and 38,155 men whom they have taken since the battle of Verdun began, February 21, 1916. In the same journal they are publishing the names of French and Belgian civilians who have suffered from the French, British and Belgian air raids and long range bombardments. Up to February this list of non-combatant victims amounted to 793, including 131 women killed and 208 wounded and 75 children killed and 108 wounded.

The Capture of Trebizond — The Russians have won a great victory in the taking of Trebizond, the chief port on this part of the Black Sea coast and the point from which trade routes run into the interior of Armenia. After the fall of Erzerum it was realized that the Turks could hardly hope to save Trebizond, for it was open to attack by land from Erzerum and also by water, since the Russian navy commands the Black Sea. But it was commonly expected that the Turkish garrison of 50,000 or more would hold out for some time, since it had been reported that the ancient defenses of the city had been modernized by German engineers and big guns, brought by sea from Constantinople on the "Sultan Selim," formerly the German "Goeben," had been installed. In the old days of its glory Trebizond stood many a famous siege against Turks and Tatars and Greeks and Genoese, for its citadel stood upon a precipitous rock, the "trapezium" from which the city got its name, and was protected in the rear by mountains seven thousand feet high.

After taking Erzerum the Russians attempted to send a force from this point over the mountains to reach Trebizond from the rear, but the Turks have been able to hold this force in check at the Choruk River. On the other hand, the Russian force which was sent westward from the Caucasus along the shore of the Black Sea has made continuous progress, for it had the support of the fleet on its right flank. When it had fought its way to within a few miles of Trebizond on the east, the Russians suddenly landed another force about five miles west of the city. This seems to have surprised and so disconcerted the Turks that they gave up all idea of resistance, if such had been their intention, and hastily evacuated the city and retired into the mountains. Whether their retreat was cut off by the Russians on the Choruk or whether the Russians from the coast were able to pursue and overtake them in their flight is not yet known.

Ever since the fall of Erzerum the Russians from the Caucasus have been in pursuit of the Turkish army which evacuated that city. They have almost reached Erzingan, a hundred miles beyond Erzerum on the road to Sivas, when the Turks turned upon them and took the offensive. New forces have evi-

166

THE GREAT WAR

April 17—Germans attack north of Verdun. British defeated by Turks on right bank of Tigris.

April 18—Russians take Trebizond. Germans attack at Les Esparges, southeast of Verdun.

April 19—Germans take British trenches near Ypres. President Wilson protests against German submarine warfare.

April 20—Russian troops arrive at Marseilles. Field Marshal von der Goltz dies at Bagdad.

April 21—Responsible cabinet installed in China. British gaining in German East Africa.

April 22—Germans attack Le Mort Homme. Italians take trenches on the Carso.

April 23—German attacks in Dvinsk region. Russians checked south of Bitlis.

dently been brought from Constantinople by way of the German Bagdad railroad and have made their presence felt both by the British in Mesopotamia and the Russians in Armenia.

The capture of Trebizond is a great gratification to the Russians, for they have been trying to secure the city for the last hundred years, but hitherto they have been kept out, less by the valor of the Turks than the opposition of the English.

The Commercial War   The Allied Powers are already planning for a united opposition to Germany after the war is over. An Interparliamentary Economic Conference was opened at the Luxembourg Palace on April 27 to devise methods by which Germany may be prevented from assuming her former commercial dominance. Eight nations are represented by members of parliament, ministers and other statesmen. Great Britain has a delegation of forty-two, France of forty-four, Italy of forty-three, Serbia of twenty-two, and Portugal of ten. Russia, Japan and Belgium also have delegations. The countries represented possess more than half the population of the world and much more than half its wealth and form together a trade combination of unprecedented power.

It is, of course, uncertain what sort of an agreement will be reached. The interests of the various countries will be difficult to reconcile, and besides there is a difference of opinion inside each country as to how far such a movement should be carried. In Great Britain, for instance, some are advocating a boycott of all German-made goods, either perpetually or for a term of years. Australia has already taken action to that effect without waiting upon the mother country. On the other hand other Englishmen argue that it is not desirable or possible to crush German industry permanently and that trade between the two countries will be mutually beneficial. It seems likely that some sort of a customs union will be formed among the Allied Powers with preferential rates among themselves

and a tariff wall against Germany and the rest of the world.

Great Britain has adopted a more friendly policy toward the United States of late and has somewhat relaxed her restrictions upon American commerce. She has granted permission for the importation of a single shipment of anilin dyes from Germany amounting to 15,000 tons. Germany has also consented to allow the exportation of the dyestuffs on guarantee that none of them are resold to her enemies. This supply will be enough for American consumption for about six months and greatly relieve the distress of our textile industries.

The British Government has agreed to pay a sum of $15,000,000 to $17,000,000 for the thirty-four shiploads of meat products which had been seized by British cruisers on their way to neutral ports in vessels of the neutral powers. In consideration of this settlement the American packers agree to allow the British Government to supervise and regulate their future shipments even to neutral countries.

On the other hand the American Red Cross has been unable to secure from the British Government permission to send its hospital supplies to Germany by any route even by American ships. The Red Cross warehouses in Brooklyn are overcrowded with medicines, surgical appliances and foods for the sick, but since these cannot be shipped a request has been issued that no further contributions for Germany and Austria can be received.

A thousand bags of parcel mail were taken off the Scandinavian-American liner "United States" by the British authorities at Kirkwall. Fifty thousand boxes of California fruit, bound for Copenhagen, were also seized.

On April 15 the British Government abolished completely the distinction made by international law between

conditional and absolute contraband. Henceforth merchandise, whether absolute or conditional contraband, will be subject to capture by the mere fact of its enemy destination, whether it is sent by direct or indirect manifest or is concealed. Further, no ship or cargo will be exempt from capture for violation of the blockade simply because that at the time it was examined it was apparently on its way to an unblockaded port.

China's New Cabinet   Yuan Shih-kai, alarmed at the rapid progress of the insurrection, is trying to make such concessions as may win back the six provinces which have turned against him. He has now announced that a responsible cabinet will be established with the same powers over the administration and the army as is possest in European governments. At the head of it is placed Tuan Chi-jui, a staunch republican, and since he will, as Minister of War, have the army in his control, he may be able to prevent any further efforts to overthrow the republic even on the part of the President. The Ministry of the Interior has been given to Wang Shih-lang, who was educated in the United States and is the general secretary of the Y. M. C. A. of China. Most of the new ministers were in the first cabinet of the republic, which Yuan dismist when he assumed autocratic powers.

It remains to be seen whether these concessions will satisfy the insurgents. The republicans of the south distrust Yuan on account of his repeated changes of party and part of them at least will insist upon his entire elimination. Yet it is questionable if they have a man of equal ability to put into his place. Dr. Sun Yat-sen, tho a devoted republican, is not supposed to be the equal of President Yuan in statesmanship.

THE RUSSIAN INVASION OF TURKEY AND PERSIA

The Russian armies from the Caucasus are now in possession of northwestern Persia and northeastern Turkey. The chief Ottoman strongholds in this region, Erzerum and Trebizond, were evacuated as soon as attacked and the Turks have retreated beyond Bitlis and Erzingan. On the other hand the British expedition which went up the Tigris to take Bagdad was defeated last December and driven back to Kut-el-Amara where it has ever since been besieged. The relief expedition is held up some twenty miles below. The shaded area shows territory held by the Russians and British

ARIZONA: Statewide controversy, rather more spirited than the subject seems to warrant, has been stirred up by the action of the State Board of Trade in adopting a copper emblem for the new battleship "Arizona" instead of the conventional silver service. The claim of the protesters is that the naval people do not want the copper emblem because it is something new and would prove a "jinx" to the superstitions sailors. They say it would also expose the state to ridicule for flying in the face of established custom. The more earnestly the protestants protest, the more earnestly the defenders of the new departure defend, while still a third party stands between, declaring that the controversy itself is the thing most likely to bring ridicule upon the state.

ARKANSAS: Work is soon to begin on the large irrigation ditch to the rice fields in the Grand Prairie section of this state. This improvement, which will be of great benefit to the many farmers in the region, has been contemplated for several years. It is not probable that the work will be completed in time for the 1916 crop, but it is hoped that a considerable portion of the vast prairie will be watered this season.

CALIFORNIA: The decision of the United States District Court enjoining the order of the Interstate Commerce Commission which made the cities of Sacramento, San José, Stockton and Santa Clara non-terminal rate points is cited by Californians as a striking illustration of the superiority of their own state railroad regulation law over the Federal Interstate commerce law. The court, without denying the justice of the commission's order, simply held that under the Federal law the commission had no power to consider anything but the specific complaint before it. On the contrary, the California law empowers the state commission to consider all phases of every case before it.

GEORGIA: Because the new prohibition laws go into effect May 1, after which no beverage containing as much as one-half of one per cent of alcohol can be lawfully sold in Georgia, many saloons, locker clubs and "near-beer" resorts are already going out of business, while breweries are being converted into ice factories and other manufacturing establishments.

IOWA: First steps are being taken in a statewide movement for the naming and marking of all roads and the numbering of all houses in the rural sections as well as in the cities. The start has been made at Iowa Falls and other points on the Hawkeye Highway, which runs from Dubuque across the state to Sioux City. Permanent metal signs are to mark every turn of the road and numbers will be assigned to all houses along the way. Organizations for similar work are forming in other parts of the state, the ultimate purpose being to make

it as easy for a farmer as for a city man to give his address and for travelers on the country roads to know just where they are.

MAINE: In common with other New England states whose governors recently met in Boston for the purpose of considering methods of making this section the summer playground of the nation, Maine is preparing for a vigorous campaign of publicity and for a general cleaning up and beautifying of its natural vacation spots. In addition this state has started an independent "See New England First" movement, to be carried out by a post card campaign. As a part of the plan for bringing summer visitors to the state the Maine Historical Society has begun work on a celebration in June of the two hundredth anniversary of the founding of Portland.

MASSACHUSETTS: So many amendments to the state constitution were proposed to the Legislature this year that the body finally decided not to submit any of them to the people, but to refer instead a proposition for a constitutional convention. Prominent among the problems which it is hoped such a convention may work out on more equitable and permanent lines are those of taxation and assessment, which long have been subject to the fluctuating devices of successive legislatures. No constitutional convention has been held in Massachusetts since 1853.

MINNESOTA: More than one hundred residents on the 65,000 acres of land within the Minnetonka game refuge are to raise mallard ducks, pheasants and quail this season. Eggs in large numbers are to be distributed, and if the usual ratio of young birds holds true the refuge will be heavily stocked this fall, while outside of it by 1917 there should be more of these birds as marks for hunters than there are now under protection. Frank D. Blair, field superintendent of the Minnesota Game and Fish Protective League, says that by fall next year wild ducks, pheasants and quail should be as numerous and as cheap in the markets as chickens, turkeys and geese are now.

MISSOURI: The making of good roads is receiving more attention in Missouri now than was ever before given to any public improvement in the state. There is hardly a county that does not intend to increase its work on roads this year. St. Louis County, with 1165 miles of roads, 565 of which are of rock and gravel, recently decided by a vote of 12,796 to 2190 in favor of a $3,000,000 bond issue, no part of which can be sold except to pay for a road the contract for which has been let to the lowest bidder and on which work is ready to begin. Besides the plans for local roads in every county, work is well along on one north-and-south and two east-and-west cross-state links of national highways.

NEVADA: The women of this state, under the leadership of the Women Citizens' League of Reno, are making an effort to have the Pittman land bill, which grants 7,000,000 acres in Nevada for schools, so granted by Congress that the lands will be sold to actual settlers instead of to large holders and speculators. Past experiences are said to show that Nevada legislatures cannot always be depended on to protect the interests of the schools and of the state against ranchmen and influential speculators; that funds have been unlawfully diverted from the schools, and that under loose legislative methods the expense of selling school lands has been, in many cases, equal to the amounts received from the sales.

NEW HAMPSHIRE: The recently inaugurated movement for a revival of agriculture in New Hampshire is meeting with more success than its most sanguine friends expected. Eight of the ten counties in the state have already formally adopted the county agent plan. Sullivan County has set an example, which others are expected to follow, by employing two agents—a man and a woman—in order that woman's work on the farm may be made as efficient as man's. Under the county agent plan funds are available from the Federal Government and the New Hampshire College of Agriculture and the Mechanic Arts to afford the county organizations such assistance as they may require during the current year.

NEW YORK: For several weeks the New York City Commission on Building Districts and Restrictions has been holding hearings at which residents and property owners in different sections of the city have given their views concerning city planning as against haphazard building. The instability of real estate values caused by the location of unsightly factories, tenements, etc., in fine residence sections and by the invasion of retail districts by small manufacturers has created much dissatisfaction with present methods. Hence the effort of the commission to assemble all the suggestions possible in the hope that from them a plan may be evolved for future building operations which shall encourage the aesthetic and sanitary as well as the commercial advancement of the city.

NORTH CAROLINA: It is the announced purpose of the association which has the National Music Festival of America in charge to make Black Mountain, in this state, "the greatest musical center in the world." The festival this year will include a presentation of "The Creation" and "Elijah" by the New York Symphony Orchestra of 100 pieces and a chorus of 1000 trained voices under the leadership of Walter Damrosch, and next season's program, already in course of preparation, is to be much more elaborate.

NORTH DAKOTA: After extensive and convincing experiments made last year, Bottineau County early this spring began a systematic campaign for the complete extermination of gophers, which, it is estimated, destroy more than $1,500,000 worth of grain in North Dakota every year. Under the direction of the county board and Department of Agriculture every acre in the county is to be treated with a strychnine solution known to be safe and effective. Each township is supplied with enough oats and strychnine to treat all lands within its boundaries, the cost, which is from 2 to 4 cents an acre, being assessed against the township, whose board is to see that every acre is treated. If the results are satisfactory a state-wide campaign will be instituted.

OKLAHOMA: The entire state is aroused over what is known as the Oklahoma City third degree case. It seems that Loren Wilson, a boy of eighteen, never before arrested, was charged with having stolen a suit of clothes by the unsupported statement of another boy who had been first arrested for the theft. Wilson denied the charge, but it is said the police beat him so unmercifully that, after three days of this brutality, fearing for his life, he made a false "confession." For many days afterward doctors said he was in a precarious condition. When arraigned in court he withdrew his statement to the police and the judge said there was no evidence against him. State Commissioner of Charities and Corrections Matthews has notified the Oklahoma City Board of Commissioners, in substance, that if they do not prosecute the police he will.

PENNSYLVANIA: It is reported that the University of Pittsburgh is preparing to establish a course in aviation in honor of Prof. Samuel P. Langley, whose pioneer experiments, so cruelly ridiculed thirty years ago, are held to be responsible for the successful heavier-than-air flying machines of today, since his failures were due solely to want of a proper engine, which was not then available. In addition to being a fitting, tho belated, tribute, a course in aviation is declared to be one of the prime needs of preparation for our national defense.

WEST VIRGINIA: Judge H. C. Hervey of the Circuit Court, sitting in Wheeling, has set a precedent which, it is said, will be followed in all cases of injunction granted to restrain owners from permitting their property to be used for the illegal sale or storing of liquor. In granting a permanent injunction Judge Hervey declared the property a public nuisance and assessed not only the ordinary costs against the owners, but added $100 as a fee for the attorney who prosecuted for the state. As several similar cases are on the dockets of the state, it is expected that this ruling will be contested in the higher courts.

HOW WASHINGTON HEARD THE PRESIDENT'S MESSAGE

BY ONE WHO LISTENED

WHEN Washington waked up on the morning of the 19th of April, it read the morning paper as usual. Then the telephone bells began to ring, and every member of the House of Representatives, every senator, every judge, every head of department, every ambassador, and everybody else who could be supposed to have influence, was called from his breakfast or his morning mail to say that it was impossible to supply the tickets asked for to admit those at the other end of the wire to the House of Representatives at one o'clock to hear the message of the President.

There were 600 tickets, and to say that 6000 people wanted them, and believed they were really entitled to them, is to speak with studied moderation. My own case was certainly not exceptional. I had sent my luggage to the station before I saw the morning papers, counting on the eight o'clock train for New York. I decided, of course, to stay and hear the President's speech. Three friends joined me—each with wide and influential acquaintance. Each began to use the telephone, calling up congressmen, cabinet officers, journalists, senators, ambassadors, friends. The replies were perfectly friendly, even solicitous, but perfectly uniform: "To grant the request is impossible." From the Speaker's office came word that only eight persons could occupy eight chairs. From the press gallery the statement that 250 at least wished to be provided for in space crowded with one-fifth the number. From one of the great embassies the statement that only a single ticket was available for the whole staff. Every Congressman consulted had already assigned his one ticket, and could neither beg, borrow nor steal another.

But at one o'clock I stood within the chamber, and heard the applause as the President followed the members of the Senate up the aisle, shook hands with the big Missouri Speaker, whom the whole country likes to call affectionately Champ Clark, and erect and grave, faced the men comprising the national Congress,

and the galleries brilliant with color and having no empty chair.

Fifteen minutes later the Speaker's gavel fell, and the joint session was declared adjourned.

In those fifteen minutes the President of the United States had reviewed the history of the submarine warfare waged by the Imperial German Government during the past fifteen months, and uttered the fateful words that, unless that government should "now immediately declare and effect an abandonment of its present methods of warfare against passenger and freight-carrying vessels, this government can have no choice but to sever diplomatic relations with the Government of the German Empire altogether."

As the clear-cut sentences of the compact message fell upon the ears of those who listened, there was no demonstration of approval or dissent—every man and woman was tense and eager, keenly conscious of the vital import of the words, and the profound gravity of what might follow as their consequences developed.

The message itself all have read. There was no request for action by Congress—no opening for discussion, then or later. It was made clear that the final decision had been made, the ultimate word spoken: "We owe it to a due regard for our own rights as a nation, to our sense of duty as a representative of the rights of neutrals the world over, and to a just conception of the rights of mankind, to take this stand now with the utmost solemnity and firmness."

When the President said, with

deepened emphasis, "I have taken it, and taken it in the confidence that it will meet with your approval and support," the audience obviously felt the thrill, but was still silent and intent, as the closing hope was uttered that "the Imperial German Government, which has in other circumstances stood as the champion of all that we are now contending for in the interest of humanity, may recognize the justice of our demands and meet them in the spirit in which they are made."

As the last word was spoken the Congress rose, and hearty but moderate applause, beginning with the adherents of the Administration, extending to the opposition, and then to the galleries, exprest or seemed to express a general approval of the spirit of the address, while it left on one mind at least a sense of reserving final judgment as to the complete effectiveness of the message.

Following the applause, the President, tall, stately, and stern, left the chamber; the House was called to order; and the further consideration of the agricultural bill, which was interrupted to give way for the joint session, was resumed in the usual prosaic fashion.

I fell in with a member of the Administration on my way to the street, and he exprest some disappointment that the ultimatum had not been a shade more definite and "ringing," as he exprest it. A foreign journalist of high ability said it was "all right," and in line with his own recent predictions. The people on the street car with whom I rode back to the city were mostly talking about something else. Washington had enjoyed the surprise which the President had given it, appreciated its dramatic quality, and was ready to turn to other things.

The man in the White House, who must use the first person singular and say "I have taken it," goes back to his desk, and waits for the answer that the man in Berlin will make to the demand which, in the name of a hundred millions of people, was in that fifteen minutes made upon the German Empire.

OUR CROWN OF PRAISE

BY KATHARINE LEE BATES

A praise beyond all other praise of ours
This nation holds in jealous trust for him
Who may approve himself, even in these dim,
Swift days of destiny, the soul that towers
Above the turmoil of contending powers,
A beacon firm, while seas of fury brim
The world's long-labored fields and vineyards trim,
Remembering forests and unconscious flowers.
Our nation longs for such a living light,
Kindred to stars and their eternal dreams,
A stedfast glow whatever breakers roll,
Cleaving confusions of the stormy night
With gracious lustres and revealing gleams,—
Longs for the shining of a Lincoln soul.

THE AMERICAN FLYING SQUADRONS

BY HAROLD HOWLAND

THE uniform was not unbecoming. Or so my sense of the fitness of things—the entirely commendable masculine substitute for the deplorable feminine vice of vanity—assured me as soon as I had it on. The big khaki overcoat made me feel military and official. The little khaki fatigue cap—a Glengarry bonnet without the ribbons—made me feel jaunty. The yellow puttees—*real* puttees made of endless strips of cloth wound round and round the legs in neat and graceful spirals—satisfied an ancient longing bred of an earnest perusal of attractive pictures and enticing advertisements in English sporting periodicals. The starred and striped bronze shield on the cap and the gold AA on the collar of the overcoat infused me with a warm glow of patriotic altruism.

Here I was, for the moment a perfectly good member of the transportation squad of the American Ambulance.

In the late afternoon a couple of dozen of us were loitering in the courtyard of the American Ambulance—we should call it a hospital at home—at Neuilly, just outside the walls of Paris. Some of the drivers were looking over the motors of their ambulances, filling petrol tanks and radiators, pumping up tires, making connections and adjustments. We orderlies were chatting, smoking or playing with Margot, the guardian magpie of the Ambulance, picturesque in his brave coat of white and purple and green and blue and bronze. We were waiting for the call to action.

L'ambulance Americain is a splendid institution. It occupies, by grace of the intelligent coöperation of the French Government, a fine group of buildings in the suburb of Neuilly, just outside the Maillot gate of Paris. The buildings are perfectly new; they were built to house a school, the Lycée Pasteur. When the war broke out they were all but completed, and the government p r o m p t l y requisitioned them and turned them over to the group of American volunteers who offered to create a modern hospital equipment for the care of the French wounded.

The Ambulance has two different aspects—hospital and flying squadrons. To describe the former would be a little commonplace; for a hospital is, after all, only a hospital—even when it is thoroly modern, generously equipped and ably managed. It is true there is something unusual about this hospital, a spirit, an atmosphere, a quality. It is an organization of amateurs, in the real sense of that hardly used word. They are in it not for gain, nor for fame, nor for any worldly advantage; not even for patriotism; but for the love of it. They work without pay, without publicity or popular applause for the individual, with only the sense of a good job well done for brother men as intangible reward.

THIS spirit of service, keyed up to concert pitch in some cases perhaps by a touch of the spirit of adventure, has produced some interesting phenomena. The wife of one of the leading men in the Ambulance organization is a lady of so-

WAITING FOR THE TRAIN

WHERE THE WOUNDED COME INTO PARIS
The red, blue and green barracks are on the right, the operating room on the left

cial prominence in the American colony in Paris. In the course of her daily activities—for she, too, is a worker among these volunteers—she found that she was getting coöperation of a high order of intelligence and fidelity from one of the orderlies. His appearance seemed somehow tantalizingly familiar to her, but not quite familiar enough. So one day she put the question squarely:

"Have I not known you somewhere?"

"Not exactly," was the reply. "But I have often waited on you at dinner. I was the second footman at Lady ——'s."

The service of humanity is a great leveler.

Another orderly was a gilded American youth of quite unnecessary wealth. He was a splendid orderly, quite as good as the second footman—but, by the same token, not a bit better. Which should afford comfort alike to the believer in aristocracy and to the devotee of democracy.

Consider the case, now, of Mr. X. He was the Paris representative of a great American drug house. When the war broke out his job vanished into thin air. He straightway volunteered for service at the Ambulance, and h i s special knowledge and training fitted him into an appropriate corner as pharmacist. He soon became indispensable. But before many months had passed word came from the home office of his concern that a splendid position was waiting for him if he would return at once. The choice was a hard one. One of his Ambulance chiefs wrote to his employers, w i t h o u t h i s knowledge, telling of the important work he was doing for the Ambulance and asking if the position at home could not be held open for him. But the time when he must sail for America or lose the opportunity came and no reply had been received. He had to decide—and he did not sail. He chose to sacrifice his opportunity rather than the inconspicuous service. Then the letter came; and it contained a whole hearted recognition by his employers of his unselfish desire and a promise that the chance at home would be kept open until he came back.

In one obscure corner of the Ambulance may be found at any hour of any day an American woman who has lived in Paris a decade or so as a portrait painter. Her official job is that of supervising the supplies of linen bandages, and such like hospital supplies. But she has developed, by the application of sheer feminine wit and Yankee ingenuity, an astounding ability as an inventor of mechanical appliances for the treatment of surgical cases. Modern shrapnel and shell fragments and bomb splinters have a devilish inventiveness in producing new problems in reconstructive surgery. But their ingenuity is nothing to hers. Let us imagine a scene:

The little cubby hole where the mistress of the linen chest presides. Enter a surgeon.

Surgeon—"Here's a new one for you, Miss Y. This *poilu* has a smashed up arm. We've set the bones, but the nerve centers are affected so that he can't bear the slightest pressure on any part of the arm. We must suspend the arm to relieve every bit of pressure, and at the same time it must be possible to have motion in the elbow joint to prevent its stiffening and becoming useless. We don't know of any appliance that will do the business. Please make us one."

Miss Y. (with such a look in her eyes as an artist might have when trying to pierce thru the flesh and blood semblance of his sitter to the portrait behind) — "Um—yes. Yes—I see. Give me till tomorrow."

When tomorrow comes the appliance is ready, made perhaps out of a couple of splints, a wire or two, a piece of string, and—one is inclined to suspect—a hairpin. But it works, and the surgeons marvel once more, and before long surgeons from other hospitals drop in and go away with some new ideas in their heads that it took a simple American woman—with an artistic temperament—to discover for them.

Then there's—but the boys of the flying squadron are waiting in the courtyard, and the call to action has just come. The adjutant has come to the door of the Ambulance and announced, "Everybody down to La Chapelle. Three trains coming in tonight."

LA CHAPELLE is a huge barn of a freight station—in the piping times of peace. Now it is a well organized receiving station for the wounded from the front. It lies well out toward the city walls on the northeast, where the enemy's trenches are still less than fifty miles from Paris. As our bunch of a dozen ambulances filters into the station yard, there are already scores of other cars there and more arriving every minute. They are military ambulances, cars from other hospitals, and those provided by the splendid organization of the women of France which has done the finest kind of service for their wounded countrymen. We line up our cars, take out the *brancards*, the little four legged stretchers that have already borne thousands of smashed up soldier bodies, and set ourselves to wait. Trains from the front do not come in on time. The railroads from over there are very busy things; and more often than not the wounded have to make way for troop trains and food supplies and ammunition stores. So we wait.

FEEDING THE WOUNDED JUST LANDED FROM THE TRAIN

THE KITCHEN AT LA CHAPELLE

As we wait, we grumble. For that is the inalienable prerogative of the man of action when he has nothing to do. We grumble at the military authorities—we *know* how easy it would be for them to get their trains in on time if they only wanted to. We grumble at our own officers—*they* might have let us stay comfortably at the Ambulance until the trains were really coming, if they only cared anything for our well being. We grumble at the whole thing. We recount the hours that we have spent in useless waiting, we bewail the sleep that we have lost because some one has been stupid. We declare roundly that we are *thru*, that we shall refuse to come down the next time the call comes, that we shall quit the Ambulance. We are a bunch of two dozen assorted grouches.

Then, when five hours of waiting and grumbling have pounded us into mutinous misery, there is a stir of life thru the station, the atmosphere becomes electric with expectation, a train slides in. Where are the grouches now, where the grumblers, where the mutiny? Where are the snows of yesteryear? You only see a group of fellows in khaki, eager, cheerful, tense like terriers at a rathole or football players ready for the referee's whistle. Youth does not like to wait, but youth does like to do.

There is admirable system in this station; lost motion is conspicuously absent. Let us keep the train standing for a minute while we look about. The wounded, poor devils, have nothing to do but wait.

Next one wall of this huge oblong barn lies the train, a score of ordinary freight cars, with here and there a special hospital car donated by some good friend of France—or of humanity. Beside the train are four barracks like portable houses, painted severally red, blue, green and yellow. They are empty now. Three other similar houses provide offices and sleeping quarters for the administrative force, and an emergency operating room. Open spaces at either end of the station hold benches around great braziers filled with glowing charcoal. A kitchen, spotless and fragrant, occupies one corner. Around one brazier are nurses in

Sister of Mercy garb; around the other lounge a half company of infantry men, of the middle aged reserve type, without arms. Army officers, surgeons, gendarmes, ambulance drivers and orderlies fill the intervening spaces in shifting groups.

Now the car doors are opened. The infantrymen, *brancardiers* now, pick up their stretchers, two men to a *brancard*, and enter the cars. They lift their wounded comrades on to the stretchers and carry them into the barrack, the red, the blue, the yellow, the green. There come the Sisters with hot soup and great baskets of bread to feed and comfort the uncomplaining sufferers. Once one hears a scream of pain as a shattered body is lifted to a stretcher; but it only serves to emphasize the general rule of stoical endurance. Your mercurial Frenchman knows how to suffer with his tongue between his teeth.

AS each barrack fills, clerks go down the line of stretchers and copy down on cards—four names to a card—the particulars of each case as shown upon the slip pinned to each man's clothing. They try, so far as possible, to put like cases together. Each card is marked with the color of the barrack in which the group lies. In the office these facts are entered in record books; then the officer in charge assigns each group to some one of the hospitals in the city. The cases are now ready for transportation—and here we come in.

I have been standing with the driver of the car to which I have been assigned, watching the *brancards* go by. He is a British-American, chauffeur to a Philadelphia captain of industry. When the war broke out he wanted to enlist in Kitchener's army; but his family already had six boys at the front or in training and his parents did not want him to go too. So he got a leave of absence from his employer and joined the American Ambulance, to "do his bit" in one way if not in another.

Out comes our senior officer and hands Harry a card. He takes a look at it and assigns me my job:

"Get eight *brancardiers* and come to the red barrack."

It is a totally inexperienced but entirely willing orderly that approaches the non-commissioned officer by the brazier and ventures in his best French—of Stratford-atte-Bowe:

"*Huit brancardiers, s'il vous plait.*"

Almost to my surprize, I get them, and stride off to the little red house, swelling a little with the pride of my first military command. Harry has meanwhile hunted up our charges in the red barrack. My *brancardiers* pick up the four stretchers, lug them out to our car, and under my confident direction slip them into place in the ambulance body. Harry cranks up, we mount to the front seat, and roll off thru the dusky, deserted streets of Paris to the appointed hospital. This time it is the improvised government hospital in the Palais des Beaux Arts, on the Champs Elysées. It might have been any one of hundreds of other hospitals in and about Paris. There are all kinds, from the great military hospital of Val de Grace to little private ones of the type characterized as possessing "only a license and a clinical thermometer." Our second trip takes us out to the American Ambulance with a quartet of surgical cases; the Ambulance is noted for its excellent surgical work, and the authorities are glad to turn the hardest kind of cases over to the volunteers from over the water. They know from experience what splendid results are achieved by the Yankee surgeons out there, and what fine care and nursing the *poilu*—the French Tommy Atkins—gets from the Yankee girls. The *poilus* know it, too; it is good for American eyes to see the contented

A SECTION AT THE FRONT

THE AMBULANCE AT NEUILLY

smile with which the poor fellows take the news that they are going to *l'ambulance Americain*. It has a reputation, that Ambulance, all thru the army.

Which reminds me that I heard only two criticisms of the Ambulance during all my stay. One was that it was equipped and managed too extravagantly. Not, mind you, that money was wasted; there was no suggestion of that. But that the work could have been carried on with something less than the finest and most elaborate equipment; and that those responsible for the direction of the work had refused to be satisfied with anything less than the best. Well, that's good American doctrine. There's just one way to take any possible sting out of that particular criticism. Let the folks at home go on supporting the Ambulance in such generous measure that it can always afford the best.

The other criticism is that the Americans spoil the French boys that fall into their hands. Which again is hardly a criticism to be vigorously resented.

Our second load safely delivered at the Ambulance, we slip off to bed for a few hours, for the third train is not due now till eight o'clock in the morning. In the long dormitory we drop off without sleeping potions; grumbling mutineers no longer, but healthily tired young men, satisfied with our job and looking forward already to more of it next day. Bright and early we are at it again. This time the train brings in, quite on time, a load of convalescents and *malades*, the victims not of German shells, but of exposure and disease germs.

Harry and I this morning draw a consignment of "birds"—just whence came this not unfriendly epithet as applied to all kinds of *blessés* and *malades* I do not know; I only know its universality in the Ambulance vocabulary—to go to a sanitarium, run by a sisterhood thirty miles from Paris. It is a delightful trip under a warm September sky thru a smiling bit of the pleasant land of France. We lunch royally at a quiet inn, the only possible suggestions of war about us a single biplane that goes booming across the sky and the uncanny dearth of men in the village and on the roads, for a fine Sunday morning. Then back to Neuilly, ready for the next night's work.

So goes the life in one of the flying squadrons. But this has been easy compared to a week ago. The G. O. G.—the grand g e n e r a l offensive—had just begun then, and the w o u n d e d poured into Paris as thru a broken dike. One night, they said, there were two trains standing alongside the La Chapelle station and one inside, and eight more waiting in the yards outside the city to come in. Wounded men were taken from the train on the very *brancards* on which they had been picked up where they fell. The mud of the trenches was thick on stretchers and uniforms. The dressings on shattered arms and legs, on mutilated heads and faces—so many of the wounds in these days of trench fighting are about the head—were the blood-soaked emergency bandages of the dressing stations just behind the firing line. These grimly patient *poilus* were hot off the fire—the hellish hot fire of a modern battlefield. They came in a running flood like a mountain stream under a torrential rain.

The flying squadron was ready for them. While the flood persisted, those quondam grumblers, who in their hours of idleness were all resolved to "quit," took neither sleep nor rest. For three full days, making no difference of night and day, snatching

"SOMEWHERE IN FRANCE"
Down on that plain an American Ambulance section has lived and worked for months under fire and been rewarded with the Croix de Guerre

random bits of food at curious hours, they drove their cars, lugged stretchers, cheered their broken charges with cigarettes and genial chaff, and "stayed on the job." You see, it isn't doing his job that such a man dislikes, it's waiting for the next job that's to be done. Men are like that; at least these ambulance fellows are. It makes one glad to be American.

THIS is one flying squadron. I tell about it, for all of this I saw, and a tiny part of it I for a moment was. But there are other flying squadrons, "somewhere in France," doing the same faithful, unremitting, merciful work. Those others, tho, lead a more thrilling life. Close behind the battle line they live, and work—and grumble when they have to wait.

They live under fire all the while; t h e y drive their cars blithely over roads pitted by bursting shells; they play at hide and seek with hissing shrapnel and earthquaking "Jack Johnsons"; they lead breathless lives —and they bear charmed lives. There is nothing they do not dare, when the wounded *poilus* need them—and daring, "get away with."

The *poilus* love them, the people of France bless t h e i r careless, selfless, chivalrous devotion, the military authorities bestow upon them their most coveted honors. A score of them already have won the Croix de Guerre, the Victoria Cross of France. Last July one of the ambulance sections was cited in the divisional order of the day in these hearty words:

"Composed of volunteers friendly to our country, it has never ceased to draw attention to itself by the dash, the courage and the zeal of all its members, who, careless of danger, have employed themselves without respite in assisting our wounded, and have thus acquired their gratitude and friendship."

This is the way the people of France appreciate the splendid service that the men of the American flying squadrons are rendering in their time of national suffering. Here is one aspect of the great war in which the American people need feel nothing but pride.

WHAT YOU CAN DO FOR THE FLYING SQUADRONS

THERE is no work being done by Americans for alleviating the suffering caused by the Great War that should make a stronger appeal to the support of the people of the United States than this—of the American Ambulance in Paris. The entire expense of the work of the Ambulance is borne by Americans thru individual contributions. The expense is considerably more than $1000 a day. In the sixteen months ending with the first of February, 3760 patients had been treated at the Ambulance, most of them serious cases, for the high quality of the Ambulance's equipment and treatment causes the French authorities to send there chiefly the grands blessés, the dangerously wounded. The transportation service of the Ambulance both at the front and in Paris has in the same time carried 105,000 wounded. To carry on this great work and maintain it on its present high plane of effectiveness, new and increased contributions are continually needed.

$1.25 will pay the salary of a trained nurse for one day.

$1.65 will keep a patient for one day. (This includes medical attendance, drugs and foods.)

$37.50 pays the salary of a trained nurse for one month.

$400 pays the traveling expenses of a nurse and her salary for six months.

$600 will support a bed for a year. This bed will be marked in the name of the donor and the nurse in charge will send reports about the work. You or your society or church can be represented in this way.

$1500 will buy, equip and maintain for six months an ambulance which will be marked in the name of the donor. The volunteer driver will report to the donor regarding the work the ambulance is doing.

Cities, societies or communities can arrange for the support of wards to bear commemorative names.

It is a noteworthy fact in relation to the financing of this work that the contributions are sent to the Ambulance without the deduction of a single cent for expenses of administration, office rent, secretary or clerk hire, printing, postage or advertising, so that every cent of every dollar goes directly and entirely to the purpose for which it is contributed.

The wounded get it all.

Give your subscription to your own bank, which will forward it to Messrs. J. P. Morgan & Co., the financial agents in New York of the American Ambulance Hospital in Paris.

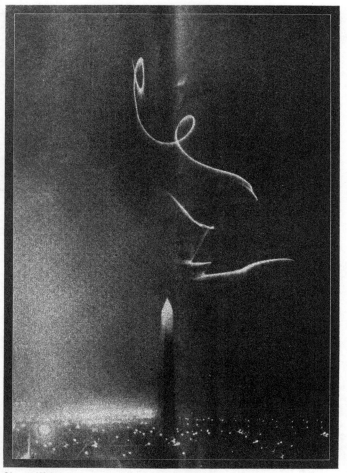

A PROPAGANDIST BOMBARDMENT

DE LLOYD THOMPSON FLYING OVER WASHINGTON ON APRIL 15 AND DROPPING FIRECRACKER "BOMBS" TO SHOW HOW EASILY HOSTILE
AIRMEN COULD ATTACK THE CAPITAL. A FEW DAYS LATER HE TREATED NEW YORK TO A SIMILAR OBJECT LESSON.
THE TRAIL OF SMOKE LEFT BY HIS MACHINE SHOWS HIS DEVIOUS COURSE

THE VANISHING GENTLEMAN

BY LOUISE COLLIER WILLCOX

AUTHOR OF "THE HUMAN WAY," "THE ROAD TO JOY"

HE passed very quietly and quickly. One might almost assert that it was accomplished in one generation. The fathers still held a tradition of which the sons were unaware. There was no pomp and circumstance about the end; there was very little lamentation.

Mrs. Comer proclaimed loudly and eagerly the vanishing lady. She raised a pean of praise to the housed, headachy, hampered mid-Victorian type and she saw no good in the candid, athletic, open air, open minded creature who replaced her. But has anyone spoken of the vanishing gentleman? It is said that the bustle and hurry of modern life is the cause of his passing and one must admit that it is in the mart, in the centers of commercialism that one meets his successor. I have conversed with him in his office with his hat on and a cigar in his mouth. I have met him and lunched with him, when he was a representative in Congress, and winked across the table at a confrère when anything amused him. He is short and incisive of speech and definitely prefers bad grammar. In certain localities and grievous to state, from one university, he is capable of sitting in the presence of ladies, with his feet higher than his head. Yes, he even spits! He is the apotheosis of the lowbrow in manners. His speech is wrecked on a false ideal of freedom and ease; his traditions are huddled up under aggression and haste; his manners are sacrificed to a false democracy.

Since the days of Confucius, men have been outlining and defining the gentleman. We have been told that it takes three generations at least to make one. But I have seen two generations of perfect gentlemen produce the up-to-date hoodlum.

There are varying theories as to where a gentleman begins. It used to be the theory that if the heart was right, the manners followed. If I read William James aright, he says that we begin to cry and then are sorry and I know the New-thought prophets say that if you will but persistently smile, you will become happy; ergo, perhaps if you make the manners, the heart will grow right.

There are certain schools, one, at least, in this country and two in England who still lay stress upon all their graduates being gentlemen. Winchester 'has carven all over it "Manners maketh man." And of a certain school, in our land, it is said that you can always recognize a representative by the way he apologizes for a mistake or an inadvertency.

Some one asked a Southern gentleman to define the difference between a Northern and a Southern gentleman, "Well," he said, "the difference is this, one is born in the North and in a different environment, with different traditions, but whatever his thinking and his trappings, the gentleman part of him is just the same as the Southerner's." For after all being a gentleman is having a trained heart, just as being a scholar is having a trained mind. There is a hero of fiction whose life maxim was *tristem neminem fecit*. This type of gentleman may be found in every walk of life. He may load coal or collect pictures for a profession and live in an attic or a palace, but he is trained not to sadden or insult his fellow-sojourner. He may be a college professor or a butler, but at heart he is courtly and self-restrained. He may be a gentleman because he owes it to other people, or because he feels that he owes it to himself, but he has learned somehow to "go softly." He is thoughtful because thoughtlessness may do injuries; he is gentle because he knows that he is not alone in the world and that each person in it has a claim to consideration. He has been trained to believe that the world must be kept lovely as well as vigorous. Lafcadio Hearn speaks somewhere of someone who "never did anything which is not—I will not say right, that is commonplace—but beautiful." This then is the aim of manners, to make life beautiful.

When one unexpectedly runs across a gentleman in an unexpected spot, it comes over one with a rush of pleasure, that a gentleman was after all nearly as wonderful a thing as a lady. Life is more fluid, more colored, freer in his presence. He is not listening for an inadvertence; he is taking his hearer on trust and for granted and he sets him at ease. He wants no advantage and he refrains from bullying or browbeating.

Oddly enough, this definition of a gentleman is some two thousand years old.

"A gentleman has nine aims: to see clearly; to understand what he hears; to be gentle in manner; dignified in bearing; faithful in speech; painstaking at work; to ask when in doubt; in anger to remember difficulties; in sight of gain to remember right. His modesty escapes insult; his truth gains trust; his earnestness brings success; his kindness is a key to open men's hearts."

Tho the species is vanishing, there are still gentlemen in the world, and if the ideal were held aloft and waved there would still be many who would enroll themselves in the order of those who believe in the value of fine manners.

Paul Elmer More has recently made an eloquent plea that there should be a conscious solidarity at the core of the aristocratical class; that class which is capable of finer discriminations into grades of taste and character than exist in untutored nature. Tho he speaks for scholarship and moral and political standards, the result would include the manners also of the Vanishing Gentleman.

Norfolk, Virginia

ELECTRIC COACHING

A novel electrical device for keeping a crew in perfect time with the stroke is being tried out this spring on the rowing machines at Cornell University. Its purpose is to synchronize the movements of the eight oarsmen who make up the crew, so as to produce a single smooth pull from their eight separate efforts.

The apparatus is a very simple one, described in *The Cornell Daily Sun* as "a series of tiny electric bulbs, a red and a white one in front of each oarsman, with a set of eight together, one representing each rower, in front of the entire combination.

"Pulling the stroke oar of the combination, number 8, lights all of the white lights down the row and the one representing stroke in the group in front. Then as each of the other oars is pulled the individual red lights, together with the given one in the front group, flash on. Exact correspondence of action between the red and white lights in front of any oarsman shows that he is in time with the stroke. Exact correspondence of the eight lights of the group shows that the entire crew is rowing in perfect regularity."

The mechanism has the double advantage of making a complete and accurate record and of freeing the overworked coach from much of his routine observation and so enabling him to devote his attention to perfecting the oarsmen individually in necessary points of form and style.

The chief point of interest in the invention is the peculiar design of the switch, which is so arranged as to complete the circuit on the forward stroke of the oar and to break it instantly on the beginning of the return. The inventor of the apparatus is W. F. Beachey, a 1917 Cornell man.

JOHN KENDRICK BANGS
Presents THE GENIAL PHILOSOPHER

THIS Preparedness talk," said the Cynical Sciolist, with an angry glance at his newspaper, "makes me everlastingly tired."

"Me, too," said the Genial Philosopher, nodding his head approvingly. "More than that, it gives me a positive pain in my spiritual innards; and the worst of it all is that there doesn't seem to be any kind of concoction known to the *materia medica* that can relieve it."

"I am glad to hear you say that," said the Cynical Sciolist. "I don't know how, but somehow or other I'd got the notion in my head that you were for Preparedness."

"O I am," said the Genial Philosopher. "I am for Preparedness to the last turn of the wheel. That's why I suffer so acutely from all the *talk* about it. Talk is a first-class weapon of Offense, but for Defense it is a rimless zero, and we are wasting more good, bad, and indifferent English on the subject than would be needed to supply an ordinarily loquacious world with gab for a thousand years; and it's all so futile!"

"Still," said the Cynical Sciolist, "I had supposed that an ordinarily sane man like yourself would be against War—War, the most heinous, hideous, hateful crime in the whole category of the Divvle's offenses against God and Man, combining as it does all the others, murder, arson, theft, rapine, false-witness, blasphemy, covetousness——"

"That'll do—I know," interrupted the Genial Philosopher. "You don't have to give us the whole bill-of-fare. I'm as familiar with the list as any of us. I read a snappy little article once entitled *The Decalogue* that told all about 'em. It was divided up into Ten Chapters, very short, and called *Commandments*. They gave us a fairly comprehensive idea of the things we'd better not do if we wished to lead a comfortable, happy, and moderately healthy life. You ought to read them over some time, Mr. Simnick. I fancy you can get them at most any bookstore if you'll ask the clerk for——"

"O Tut!" retorted the Cynical Sciolist. "You needn't think you are the only man in the world who has ever read the Ten Commandments."

"Well, then, if you have read 'em, old man," smiled the Genial Philosopher, "perhaps you will recall one very concise little Chapter that has always seemed to me to be a complete résumé of all the others. It ran something like this: *Honor thy Father and thy Mother that thy days may be long upon the land which the Lord, thy God, giveth*

thee. Remember that? Wasn't that a first-class plank for any kind of a human being to stand on? Eh? What?"

"None better," said the Cynical Sciolist, "but I fail to see what it has to do with what we were talking about. We started in on the subject of *Preparedness*."

"I'm afraid that is the trouble with many of us," sighed the Genial Philosopher. "We fail to see what that little injunction has to do with many things. We think we are honoring our Father and our Mother when we sit down and tell their grandchildren what corking good people they were, when as a matter of fact we are not honoring them at all. We are only gassing about them. If we really honored those dear old people we'd take stock of all the fine creations of their genius which have become our heritage—our splendid institutions, not their pies—our wonderful country made habitable and fructiferous by their toil and self-sacrifice; and we'd demonstrate the honor in which we held them by resolutely resolving that no conceivable combination of earthly circumstances, no conspiracy of hostile forces either inside or outside of our borders, should ever invade or destroy, or take from us and squander on others, the splendid fabric in which their very life's blood was interwoven.

"What is it, Sir, but the persistent Preparedness of our forebears that has made of you and me the most perfect specimens of human horticulture known to the ages? From the dawn of that great day back in 1620 when they first landed on Plymouth Rock, with that marvelous cargo of Highboys, Four-Poster Bedsteads, and Fiddle-Back Kitchen Chairs, that has propagated even faster than the guinea-pig, the rabbit, or the common-garden housefly, it has been old *Semper Paratus* that has ruled the roost. Life was, and has ever since remained, just one endless sequence of Preparations. It was the man who was Unprepared with a good husky wood-pile who either curled up and expired in winter, or accumulated an internal surplusage of frigidity, traces of which are even today to be discerned in the manners of the most exclusive social circles of the Hub.

"Later on it was nothing but the Spiritual Preparedness in the hearts and souls of Washington, Jefferson, Hamilton, Franklin, and the rest of those gallant old ancestral heroes of ours, that preserved our Liberties for us in the free air of America rather than in alcohol in a bottle in the British Museum. And what's more it was the lack of Preparedness that enabled those same cousins of ours once removed to come again to pay us a party call and make a pretty little bonfire of our Capitol Building at Washington.

"And so it has gone from the begin-

ning. The solid, substantial growth of this Republic of ours has not been the result of mere chance, but of foresight and preparedness. The reasonably well-made thing they have handed on to us, not for our own selfish enjoyment, but to hand on to our children that they in turn may pass it on to theirs. We may not care much for our country ourselves. Some of us may have grown weary of it—but that doesn't alter our duty. *It isn't our exclusive possession. It is entailed, and we are acting today merely as Trustees for Posterity! We MUST protect the Trust!*"

"O Posterity nothing," sniffed the Cynical Sciolist. "Posterity! What on earth has posterity ever done for us?"

"An old question, my friend," said the Genial Philosopher, "and one of the easiest to answer. *Posterity has done pretty nearly everything for us*. Those poor infants of the future have built our railroads for us. They are up to their chins in debt for our postoffice buildings and our water supply. They owe millions—some three hundred of 'em—for our Panama Canal. The unconstructed cradles made of unplanted trees, and to be occupied by millions of unborn children ten generations hence will be taxed for all these splendors that you and I enjoy today. If you don't believe it foot up the totals of the Bonds floating about the market today, payable in 1947, 1999, 2028 and 2135. *What has posterity done for us?* Why man, we of this generation have been playing the middle against both ends for a quarter of a century. We have accepted the glorious gifts of a watchful ancestry, and mortgaged the prospects of a helpless series of generations yet to be born; and the least we can do in return is to honor our Fathers and Mothers by preserving intact, and defending to the last gasp, the goodly structure they have built up; and to vow by all that we hold most sacred that when it finally does pass into the hands of posterity, there will be not less than seven cents' worth of equity left in the property after the mortgages have been paid."

"Ha! Hum!" said the Cynical Sciolist. "There is something in that. I hadn't thought of it in just that way. And you think this nation needs—what? Just what to make it right?"

"A stiff dose of spiritual ginger," said the Genial Philosopher.

"And a little knowledge?" suggested the Cynical Sciolist.

"No," said the Genial Philosopher. "A little knowledge is a dangerous thing. We already have too much *little knowledge*. What we really need is a good deal of knowledge—knowledge of the kind that will teach us that while *hindsight* is very revealing, *foresight* is the only safe insurance for a house that is not fireproof, and built in a world red with the flames of war."

176

DEMOCRATIZING THE MOTOR CAR

BY ALBERT L. CLOUGH

EVERY important invention that conduces to human comfort or efficiency has, when first introduced, been appropriated almost exclusively by the rich. It could not be otherwise, for the apparatus embodying it is developed at great experimental cost, is at first produced very expensively in very small quantities; and is very costly to operate and maintain because of its crudity and inefficiency. Gradually, however, the experimental stage passes; it is produced more economically in larger quantities, is perfected so as to give more economical service, and can thus be bought and used more cheaply. Little by little a larger class can afford to buy and use it, and its employment is gradually popularized, this wider use being reflected in lower prices due to quantity production, so that in time its benefits accrue to all classes of society.

Electric lights, the telephone, cameras, and even watches, are a few among countless available examples of this economic phenomenon, but no better illustration could be chosen than the automobile.

Motor car history, condensed as it is within the last fifteen years, is familiar to all, but it may be worth while to note certain of the influences which have transformed the automobile from the exclusive vehicle of the wealthy to the accepted conveyance of all but the least financially favored classes. The fact that this process is even now going on at an ever-quickening rate gives it especial interest. It may safely be taken for granted that the desire for automobiles is and has long been practically universal, and that the sole impediment to its gratification has been the pecuniary one. Thus, the discussion of the democratization of the motor car narrows down to a consideration of how the cost of acquiring and of running one has been and is being reduced.

Sweeping reductions in prices of cars have certainly been the principal factor in realizing the "motor age" which is now being entered upon, and a few of the causes contributing to lower prices for cars will here be mentioned. These may mostly be summed up under the head of economies in cost of production and the reduction of the manufacturer's profit upon the individual car.

By all means the most important condition acting to reduce the productive cost of the finished vehicle as delivered to the user is the enormous increase which has been made in the scale upon which cars are now built. There is a cumulative action here, for the more cars there are built, the cheaper they can be produced, and the greater is the resulting demand, which can be met only by more cars built at a still lower factory cost.

Mainly thru the influence of a few concerns which equipt themselves to build more cars in enormous numbers, automobile prices have been forced down to the point at which the general public can purchase, and at present a small number of such manufacturers are producing a large proportion of all the cars being turned out, while the tendency is strongly toward a further concentration of production.

What are some of the advantages enjoyed by the manufacturer of 100,-000 cars annually over the manufacturer of 1000 cars annually, in point of low cost of the individual finished car delivered to the user?

In order to keep its name prominently before the public the big plant need spend little more on advertising than the small one, and the advertising cost per car is much lower in the case of the former. The very largely used car advertises itself; the other gets little of this kind of publicity.

The maintenance of local selling branches to dispose of 100,000 cars calls for an outlay in no way proportionate to that required for distributing 1000 cars and the vending cost chargeable to each car is much lower in the case of the larger manufacturer. And the agent of the large manufacturer disposes of so many more cars annually than the small manufacturer's agent that he can afford to accept a lower commission.

Manufacturing upon a stupendous scale implies the buying of raw materials in colossal quantities, and therefore at prices lower than the smaller manufacturer can secure. The largest scale operators, moreover, can secure materials conforming to their own specifications as to quality and form and thus more economical to use, while the smaller operator may have to be content with stock materials.

Not only raw materials but finished component car parts, such as axles, radiators, transmissions, and the like, can be bought much cheaper in immense quantities, and the big manufacturer, again, can secure parts built to his specifications, while the small one may have to accept standard parts.

Obviously, it costs little or nothing more to design a model of which 100,000 cars are to be manufactured than one of which 1,000 are to be produced, and thus the engineering, drafting and pattern making costs per car are much lower in the case of the big concern.

In order to minimize labor costs, extremely expensive special dies and machine tools are required, and sometimes the special apparatus for economically producing a single part costs tens of thousands of dollars. The cost of such apparatus is necessarily divided among the parts which it is used to produce, and the larger this number is, the smaller is the charge per part for such equipment.

The division of labor, with its great economic advantages, can be carried much further in the immense establishment than in the smaller plant.

And finally, the immense concern can operate profitably on a smaller profit per car than can the small one.

Leaving the effect of stupendous scale production upon the reduction of productive costs and selling prices, there are certain other factors that have made possible the low-priced car.

No longer is there any considerable experimentation required in bringing out a car of ordinary model, for practise is so thoroly standardized that the expectations of the drafting room are very nearly realized on the road. Manufacturing operations have been greatly reduced in number, complexity and time, and special automatic tools have immensely curtailed the human labor required. The development of the automobile parts industry, a gigantic recently organized business, which is as highly developed as the automobile industry itself, has cut down costs greatly. Motor car manufacturers can now buy from their specialized producers very many component parts at lower prices and of better quality than they themselves can make them.

The result? For from $600 to $700 one can now buy a better four-cylinder touring car than was obtainable at any price six or seven years ago, or for twice this sum five years ago. Six-cylinder, five or seven passenger touring cars, not long ago the exclusive possession of the wealthy, can now be bought around $1100. or less than good "fours" sold for five years ago. Closed cars, until lately a most exclusive type, are now sold as low as $650, and sedan or other closed bodies for touring cars for $200 or so.

All attempts by certain manufacturers to bring out exclusive "inno-

177

vations" in motor cars have failed; for example, the eight-cylinder car was originally marketed at about $2000, but cars with this type of motor are now marketed at below $1000, while twelve-cylinder cars at first introduced at almost $3000, are now obtainable at $1000. Knight motored cars, introduced at $4000, are now to be had at $1000. In short, when a desirable innovation has been introduced at a high price, it has soon been popularized by sweeping price reductions.

Leaving now the democratization of the automobile thru reductions in its first cost, a few reasons why it may now be more economically operated will be mentioned. The repair bill, formerly the strongest deterrent against owning a car, has been shorn of its terrors, as all car parts are now of such materials and proportions as to be proof against breakage and premature wears, assuming that intelligent care is given them. A modern car should serve several years and cover at least 25,000 miles without any important repairs. People generally have now learned to use and care for automobiles, destructive driving speeds are no longer "good form" and roads have been so improved as to reduce wear and tear.

Until recently most manufacturers sold touring cars weighing nearly or quite 4000 pounds; necessarily such cars consumed tires and fuel at an excessive rate. It is to the credit of the general public that it never believed in these heavy cars. Praise for initiating the modern movement toward light cars must be accorded to the manufacturer of America's most popular light car, the name of which has become a household word. The employment of improved materials, such as alloy steels, and of designs which place every bit of properly formed metal just where it is needed for strength, have brought about much of the weight reduction which is responsible for light four-cylinder cars of from 1400 to 2400 pounds and for sixes well below 3000 pounds, but the introduction of the small-bore, high-speed motor has also been an important factor.

The faster a motor is run the more explosions it makes in a given time, and the greater horsepower can be obtained from a certain number of cylinders of a given capacity. By lightening the pistons and connecting rods, by enlarging the valve openings and improving the lubrication, American designers, following the lead of European engineers, have more than doubled the speeds at which their motors can safely be

"Not the name of a thing, but the mark of a service"

No lamps can ever be marked MAZDA unless they embody MAZDA Service standards of excellence

The Meaning of MAZDA

MAZDA is the trademark of a world-wide service to certain lamp manufacturers. Its purpose is to collect and select scientific and practical information concerning progress and development in the art of incandescent lamp manufacturing and to distribute this information to the companies entitled to receive this Service. MAZDA Service is centered in the Research Laboratories of the General Electric Company at Schenectady.

The mark MAZDA can appear only on lamps which meet the standards of MAZDA Service. It is thus an assurance of quality. This trademark is the property of the General Electric Company.

RESEARCH LABORATORIES OF GENERAL ELECTRIC COMPANY

operated and have nearly doubled the horsepower obtainable from a certain number of cylinders of a certain size. Thus the weight of a motor capable of developing a certain horsepower has been greatly reduced and the total car weight has been reduced more than accordingly. Increasing motor speed proportionately reduces the mechanical stresses acting on shafts and other transmission parts, and permits their elements being made of lighter weight.

The development of lighter cars has greatly reduced that "bugbear" of motoring, the tire bill, and the introduction of better designed springs, the more rational distribution of car weight, the reduction in tire prices, the passing of the "speed mania," and the more general understanding of how to care for tires, have all contributed to this result.

Fortunately for the user, the modern high speed motor is not only lighter but is more economical of fuel, horsepower for horsepower. Not only so, but in recently designed cars no effort has been spared to secure high gasoline economy. Carburetors and fuel-feed systems have been improved and great pains have been taken to heat the fuel charge properly as it enters the cylinders, with the result that these modern light cars, even the sixes, run much further on each gallon of fuel than the cars of a few years ago. Economy of lubricating oil is also marked in the modern small-bore motor, with its tight pistons and oil-proof crank case and the prices of lubricants are lower than formerly.

With all these factors reducing the purchase prices of cars and the cost of running them it is not strange that the number of automobiles has increased so that there is now one car owned in the United States for each fifty persons, and that the purchase of cars has increased rapidly even thru the recent period of hard times.

This process of democratization of the automobile bids fair to continue until a car is owned by every family in the land, which possesses any appreciable margin of income over actual living expenses.

Manchester, New Hampshire

Judge—You let the burglar go to arrest an automobilist?
Policeman—Yes. The autoist pays a fine and adds to the resources of the state; the burglar goes to prison, and the state has to pay for his keep.—*Life.*

Our esteemed contemporary says that in reciting "Sheridan's Ride" at the Methodist Church festival last week we looked and acted like a jackass. We could retort in a way that would embitter the man's whole future, but we have learned to pass such things by. Suffice it to say that he is an infernal liar and a crawling scoundrel!—*Leesville (Col.) Light.*

The New Books

BUSINESS AND GOVERNMENT

That government is primarily a matter of economic systems and relations was but a few years ago a dogma of a small political party; today the proposition is the center of earnest and heated controversy, and the fundamental issue in approaching political contests. Professor Samuel P. Orth, of Cornell University, has gathered some of the most important studies and essays on various aspects of *The Relation of Government to Property and Industry*, in a volume that should be of value to the lay student of practical administration of a modern democracy, as well as to the college students for whom the "readings" are primarily intended. The material is classified roughly into seven divisions, dealing respectively with the changing conception of property and of government, response of legislatures and courts to new demands, the police power, corporations, commissions and boards as instruments of regulation, labor laws, and the tendency toward federal control of commerce and industry.

The Relation of Government to Property and Industry, by Samuel P. Orth. Ginn. $2.25.

TRAINING FOR WORK

It is a promising sign when those who address the public on matters of public concern take the pains to explain what it's all for. If we always insisted upon a definition of aims we should save ourselves the trouble of attending to a deal of talk and writing. In *Learning to Earn*, J. A. Lapp and C. H. Mote have undertaken to discuss education in terms of the kind of life people want to live. In addition they have discussed the problems not merely on the basis of opinions and pious wishes, but on that of expert knowledge. The method, equipment and spirit of these authors are commended to all who sit down to write for other people to read. The authors point out that "democracy" requires a certain distribution of the advantages of civilization, and show the relation between traditional educational methods and the life that was common when these were established, and the maladjustment between these educational elements and the life of today.

After this survey attention is directed to the need for a continuation of education for those who "go to work." The methods of the various grades of schools, in their relation to the modern needs, are explained briefly—and adequately. The types of specialized education, their advantages and disadvantages are presented in terms of human beings living and adjusting themselves to further living. There is an excellent

chapter on the opportunities for the library to meet the vocational needs of today and tomorrow. There are chapters on vocational guidance, the training of teachers, work and culture, training for citizenship, meeting the cost, and "the ideal school."

The outlook of the authors is comprehensive, and sympathetic. They see the social advantages of increasing the workers' efficiency, but also the danger of exploiting this efficiency for the benefit of the employer too exclusively. They are not deluded by the frequent association of unemployment with lack of training and they see in vocational efficiency something more than increased wages.

Not too technical for ordinary folk, every parent should make an effort to read this book, while for educators there are few books on this subject likely to be of so much value.

Learning to Earn, by John A. Lapp and Carl H. Mote. Bobbs-Merrill. $1.50.

AT HOME AND ABROAD

SICILY

The story of *Taormina* is ancient tho little known history. Little remains to the town save its beauty, but that still lures travelers, and to these Raley Husted Bell's account, with its attractive pictures, will be of interest.

Hinds, Noble & Eldridge. $1.25.

THE LAND OF THE NILE

W. Laurence Ball has prepared an excellent, well illustrated handbook, *Egypt of the Egyptians,* which includes a history, a study of the present conditions and the influence of the foreigner, data for the tourist and a bibliography.

Scribner. $1.25.

ON LAKE MICHIGAN

Among the many attractive drawings with which Earl H. Reed illustrates his records of *The Dune Country,* the sandy lands of the eastern and southern shores of Lake Michigan, are several etchings which deserve warm mention for the delightful sense of space and motion.

Lane. $2.

PORTUGAL

Some space in *Portugal of the Portuguese* is taken by such vital facts as the population of districts and per cent of wooded areas, but A. F. G. Bell tells also of the picturesque life of the peasants and enlivens his guidebook by amusing scenes from the sixteenth century but still living pages of Gil Vicente.

Scribner. $1.25.

BIG GAME

Moose, grizzlies, caribou and white Dale sheep are the animals Harry A. Auer hunted in the far north, and tells of in his *Camp Fires in the Yukon.* The appendix contains notes on the appearance and habits of these animals, and the illustrations, from pictures taken on the trip, are singularly clear.

Cincinnati: Stewart, Kidd. $1.75.

PICTURESQUE AMERICA

John Martin Hammond's *Quaint and Historic Forts of North America* is something new in travel in America. Till one turns the attractive pages one does not realize how many military mementoes, outside the region of the Civil War, there are upon these shores. Mostly Spanish, French and Dutch, very picturesque and full of interest they are, as the many and really beautiful illustrations show.

Philadelphia: Lippincott. $5.

SPORT AND ARCHEOLOGY

Mr. Roosevelt's recent essays, gathered under the title, *A Booklover's Holiday in the Open,* range from the Andes to Canada, and from California to Zambesi. To him hunting includes a study of any and every animal he sees, including the personality of the guide. The future of the Indian shares interest with the future of our wild birds. This hunter finds this world so full of a number of things that he is never uninterested nor uninteresting.　Scribner. $2.

THE SHAKESPEARE TERCENTENARY

FOR THE TERCENTENARY?

The two books in which "Brander," as his Columbia students call that facile essayist, Professor Matthews, has made his greatest contribution to literary scholarship, *Shakspere as a Playwright* and *Molière*, have just been reissued in handsome dress—each with a fine frontispiece, in a "University Edition."　Scribner. $2 each.

THE SHAKESPEARE MASQUE

The article on the Shakespeare Tercentenary by Percy Mackaye, published in The Independent for April 10, contained several extracts from *Caliban*, the masque that is to be given late in May at the Stadium in New York. The entire text with illustrations and descriptions of the scenery and action, is now on sale.

Doubleday, Page. paper 50 cents, cloth $1.

WHEN BURBAGE PLAYED

The intelligent reader who wants to learn in considerable detail what scholars have found out about *Shakespeare's Theater* will do well to read this book by Professor A. H. Thorndike of Columbia. He will particularly enjoy the commonsense handling of controverted questions and the rather lively picture of the Elizabethan public. Some repetition mars a well-rounded presentation of a large body of fact.　Macmillan. $2.50.

IN SHAKESPEARE'S HONOR

Louise Ayers Garnett has written a delightful play, *Master Will of Stratford*. The prolog and epilog are pictures of the boy Shakespeare in his home, the play itself his dream in which mingle Sir Thomas Lucy, Queen Bess and the Fairy folk, destined to be immortalized later in "A Midsummer Night's Dream." The play takes in so many characters that it will be especially useful for a club or school wishing to include a large number in a tercentenary celebration.

Macmillan. 50 cents.

HALF A DOZEN STORIES

MEXICO

Chained Lightning, by Ralph Graham Taber, is the story of two youths, telegraph operators in Mexico. It is a well told account of adventures among the mining camps and Indians, and in the more civilized parts of the country.

Macmill. . $1.25.

ARABS

Masoud the Bedowin, by Alfred Post Carhart, is a volume of vivid, dramatic pictures of desert life. A few deal with the missionary in relation to the native, but most of them are tales of modern Bedouin life and excellent stories.

N. Y. Missionary Education Movement. $1.

IN FAERYLAND FORLORN

With an excellent foreword John Galsworthy introduces us to the whimsical beauty, strange simplicity and natural romance of W. H. Hudson's *Green Mansions*. We have here the tale of an elusive passion in a tropical forest, a passion that is thwarted but immortal, the true love of a spiritual ideal.

Knopf. $1.50.

THE ETERNAL BATTLEGROUND

The Mastering of Mexico by Kate Stephens, tho a tale thrice told, is also a

Insure Yourself Against Loss

$2.00

Invested now in this wonderful invention may tomorrow save you Hundreds of Dollars.

Actual Size

The SAFETY Check Protector

is the last word in efficient check protecting. No matter where you have to draw a check—at your business desk, in another man's office, in your home, on the train or boat, in your hotel or club, the SAFETY is always ready. It goes in your vest pocket—in a neat leather case. As simple as a toy, this substantial business device is revolutionary. Weighs just one ounce. Made to last. It does everything that machines costing ten times as much will do. It works quickly and surely. Sharp points pierce holes in the check for any amount you desire—inking the holes with an acid and water-proof ink. All characters are visible—no danger of erasure or spoiling check. Made in German Silver heavily gold plated. Cannot rust or change color. SEND COUPON TODAY. Money back if not satisfied.

WACHUSETT SPECIALTY CO.   Box 794, Worcester, Mass.

Name..

Address...

wishes to receive one heavily gold plated German Silver SAFETY Check Protector in leather case (with money-back privilege), $2.00 here enclosed.

VULCAN INK-PENCIL

Dependable for a life time. Made right to write right. Long or Short—Red or Black

$1.00 COMPLETE POSTAGE PREPAID

J. D. ULLRICH & CO., 27 Thames St., New York

$99.00 Make Your Own Electric LIGHT

GRAY MOTOR CO., 519 Gray Motor Bldg., Detroit, Mich.

LE PAGE'S GLUE 10c

FIXES RICKETY FURNITURE

THE LIVERPOOL AND LONDON AND GLOBE

INSURANCE COMPANY, Limited
NEW YORK OFFICE, No. 80 WILLIAM STREET.

NATIONAL DEFENSE MONROE DOCTRINE

and 25 equally vital topics sharply debated by Roosevelt, Garrison, Bryan, Taft, and other leaders of thought, in Debaters Handbook Series. Cloth, $1 each postpaid.

Send for complete list.

H. W. Wilson Co., Box R, White Plains, N. Y.

CHANGE OF ADDRESS

If you are going away for the summer you will want The Independent to follow you. Let us know your new address, if possible, three weeks ahead. Be sure to give us your old address also.

THE INDEPENDENT

Faultless

Preparedness for restful slumber

Since 1881   Pajamas   Night Shirts

E. Rosenthal & Co. Baltimore and New York

tale told rather differently from its predecessors. We have here a narrative of the exploration and conquest of Mexico based on the artless story of a sixteenth century adventurer, that is interesting at a time when Mexico is once more remodeling her destinies.

Macmillan. $1.50.

A NEW ENDING

In *The Spinster*, Sarah N. Cleghorn has developed a character to a logical climax. The incidents of Ellen Graham's life in a Vermont village, her girlish talks at Radcliffe, the experiences which go to the forming of her social consciousness, are well described. Thru struggles, amusing, pathetic, fine and very real, she finds a solution, not matrimony, of the problem of what to do with her life.

Holt. $1.35.

A GENTLE TALE

In his dedication "to Pity and Faith" James Lane Allen strikes the keynote of his latest story, *The Cathedral Singer*, a pseudo-sermon disguised as fiction. Sentimentality is its chief characteristic, and a multiplicity of words effectually conceals most of its meager action. The Cathedral of St. John the Divine in New York City, which "flings across the land its spiritual shaft of light," is taken as the text.

Century. $1.

ON SUNDAYS

SUNDAY SCHOOL LESSONS

The Monday Club publishes yearly a volume of *Sermons on the Sunday School Lessons*. These are for the International Series. They are by well known preachers and often deal with the subjects from a standpoint quite different from the usual lesson helps. They should be suggestive to teachers of older classes.

Boston. Pilgrim Press. $1.

LIGHT BEARERS IN MANY LANDS

One of the most inspiring books published by the Missionary Education Movement is Miss Margaret E. Burton's *Comrades in Service*. There are eleven sketches of the life and work of noted servants of enlightenment and progress in many lands. Jacob Riis, Dwight L. Moody, Grace Dodge, Chundra Lela, of India, and Kaji Yajima, of Japan, will indicate their character and range.

Missionary Education Movement. 60 cents.

WHY I BELIEVE

Dr. George Williamson Smith, formerly president of Trinity College, Hartford, writes *A Short Apology for Being a Christian in the Twentieth Century* in the form of a reply to a letter received from a friend who announced that he had been led to repudiate Christianity by the claims of science and historical criticism. One by one the attacks are met and a belief in the Bible, the atonement, the resurrection and the supernatural justified.

Longmans, Green. 80 cents.

SACRED HISTORY IN COLOR AND LINE

Too much praise cannot be given to the *Atlas of the Historical Geography of the Holy Land*, designed and edited by Principal George Adam Smith, and prepared under the direction of the well-known bartographer, J. G. Bartholomew. The best historical scholarship has been united with the finest facilities for map making in the production of these sixty clear and beautifully colored maps and plans and the notes, explanations, chronological tables and bibliographies.

Doran. $7.50.

CHURCH EFFICIENCY GUIDE

The new conception of the church as the servant of the community is calling for new methods. To make the organization effective in these new ways it is necessary to know the needs, the environment, as well as the resources of the church. How to secure this knowledge and make it available in church work is concretely set forth in Rev. Charles E. Carroll's *Community Survey in Relation to Church Efficiency*, a splendid guide for workers in city, town and country parishes, and profusely illustrated with charts, diagrams and photographs.

Abingdon Press. $1.

HANDY BOOKS

PIGEONHOLES FOR IDEAS

In the *Universal Plot Catalogue*, H. A. Phillips advises those who have taken the short story as their job as to the collection of plot suggestions and their filing in a plot file warranted to keep ten thousand items handy enough for even the most unsystematic genius.

Larchmont, N. Y.: Stanhope-Dodge. $1.20.

WHAT THE WORLD DID IN 1915

In combining comprehensiveness, convenience, compactness, promptness and accuracy the *American Yearbook* is unique among the annuals. Merely as an index to important articles it is worth the money. Its surveys of recent progress in arts, science, literature, religion, government and business are useful to any one who wants to keep up with the procession.

Appleton. $3.

A UNIVERSAL WHO'S WHO

Of course we have marked "keep in the office" on A. M. Hyamson's *Dictionary of Universal Biography of All Ages and All Peoples*. Each notable has a line, with his dates and nationality. Giving only the data needful for further research, this has many times the number of entries to be found in other biographical works and is invaluable for ready reference.

Dutton. $7.50.

REAL CRITICISM

The *Brief Bibliography* of books relating to Latin-America prepared by Peter H. Goldsmith, Director of the Pan-American Division of the American Association for International Conciliation, differs from most bibliographies in that the author tells just what he thinks about each book in frank and often very uncomplimentary language. But nowhere is such drastic criticism needed more than in the voluminous and in large part worthless literature of Latin-America.

Macmillan. 50 cents.

ESSAYS: GRAVE AND GAY

A NOVEL ESSAY

Dr. Frank Crane has written a charming and philosophical book entitled *Adventures in Common Sense*. In it he has explained why he exchanged a certainty for an uncertainty, and has given other biographical details. His exploitation of a new note in literature provokes attention. Dr. Crane has deftly snatched the essay away from supernaturalism, and by his enthusiasm and skill, has given it virility. It will pay any one to read this little volume.

Lane. $1.

THE ROMANCE OF A LIFE

In his book of memoirs called *My Harvest*, Richard Whiteing carries us lightly over 300 odd pages of excellent reading. He tells of his life discursively, with a keen humor, much historical knowledge and a convincing sense of values. The introduction of celebrities is liberal, but not overwhelming, the theme of self so unusually unobtrusive that we close the book regretfully feeling that we have just failed to become intimate with a charming personality.

Dodd, Mead. $2.50.

"THIRD LEADERS"

Short discussions of all sorts of nonpolitical topics, from the Victorian Age to Horse Chestnut Burrs and Learners and Teachers, are to be found in *Modern Essays*, a collection of sometimes wise, sometimes witty and always pleasant pa-

pers from the editorial columns of the London *Times*.

Longmans, Green. $1.40.

JOURNEYS TO BAGDAD

Charles S. Brooks plays gracefully with the English of Lamb, even of Sir Thomas Browne, and the leisurely whimsical essays of *Journeys to Bagdad* are charming even tho today's journalist may call them "precious." But why this recent fashion in pictures, when wood-engraving may be so beautiful, of harking back to the style of Webster's Spelling Book?

Yale Univ. Press. $1.50.

A LIVELY SHILLALAH

Nothing save Japanese tea is quite right to the eyes of Marian Cox, as she sets forth her views in the vivacious essays of *Ventures in Worlds*. One would sometimes agree with her did she leave out the reasons for her beliefs, but her scientific proofs lead to an extraordinary universe, and it is hard, for instance, to lay the entire problem of domestic service to our unintelligent interest in music.

Kennerly. $1.25.

JAPANESE FLOWER ART

The Japanese idea of flower arrangement is that one perfect individual flower, together with leaves and stem, is more beautiful than masses of them bunched together.

In the Flowery Kingdom they work wonders with their flowers. They make calendars of them. They tell stories with them. They symbolize aeroplanes, dainty women and everything else by means of floral units, which we in America would use merely for a bouquet. The folklore and mythology of Japan are often vividly exprest in flower arrangement.

In arranging flowers, the Japanese try to place them in the same position that they would naturally take. An American would put a bunch of cherry blossoms into a vase, upright; a Japanese would place the branch in a horizontal position, such as they occupy in growing.

By using special containers and supports, the Japanese make flowers last twice as long as we do. In arranging flowers in a receptacle they trim the leaves from the stalks below the water, and for a short distance above. This gives the flower the appearance of growing. By taking a piece of bamboo, the Japanese will conventionally place flowers in it in such a way as to reproduce a ship in a calm or in a storm.

The Japanese do not like the rose and the lily. Flowers that have thorns are cruel and those whose petals drop off symbolize inconstancy. The cherry, wistaria, magnolia, azalea, peony, camellia, peach, plum, maple, pine, chrysanthemum, iris, lotus and morning glory all find more popular favor.

The foregoing reflections were suggested by a visit to the Yamanaka exhibition of Japanese flower arrangement recently held in New York, and the tea ceremony at which lectures and demonstrations were given by Miss Mary Averill, of Boston, Massachusetts, the author of "Japanese Flower Arrangement" and "The Flower Art of Japan." The exhibition was a particularly realistic presentation of the Oriental ideas of flower arrangement. It is to be hoped that it will be repeated next year.

PEBBLES

Our controversy with Germany appears to be a contest of might vs. write.—*Brooklyn Daily Eagle.*

Sing Sing has a prohibition club. They naturally want to get rid of the bars.—*Columbia State.*

There's one thing to be said in behalf of Villa: he's not in the habit of making disavowals.—*New York Sun.*

"He who gives quickly gives twice."
"Yes, mainly because he's always called upon to give again later."—*Judge.*

Teuton scientists seem to have found a substitute for everything but war.—*Wall Street Journal.*

It is a comforting reflection that the United States army is full of undiscovered Dodds.—*Boston Transcript.*

I hear that they buried the janitor last week.
Yes, they had to; he died.—*Lehigh Burr.*

"Harold! You mustn't strike your father when he's asleep."
"But, mother, I'm a submarine."—*Life.*

"Is this Somerville 227?"
"No."
"Then why did you answer?"—*Harvard Lampoon.*

"How did you cure yourself of walking in your sleep?"
"Took car-fare to bed with me."—*Yale Record.*

The "peace" hat is hailed out West as the latest note in feminine headgear. Meaning, apparently, that it must be had at any price.—*New York Herald.*

Every now and then this reporter concludes that about the only special privilege a married woman has is that of talking and the men complain about that one.—*Atchison Globe.*

"I see' that Charlie Chaplin gets $10,000 a week just to make people laugh. Why, that is almost as much as a state senator gets in a year."
"Just to make people laugh, too."—*Life.*

"Old Millyuns says that since he made his pile of money he feels like a neutral nation."
"Why is that?"
"Because he has so many diplomatic relations."—*Judge.*

"Why can't I come to see you tomorrow night?"
"Don't blame me," said the beautiful girl. "Our cook has the use of the parlor under the new domestic relation law."—*Louisville Courier-Journal.*

Friend—Any innovations in your 'Uncle Tom's Cabin' show this season?
Showman—Oh, yes! Instead of having Eliza escape by crossing the river on the floating ice-cakes, we have her escape by crossing Broadway at Forty-third street.—*Judge.*

Willis—Then you don't think there is any danger of us New Yorkers ever being prisoners of a foreign foe?
Gillis—Absolutely none. How could the enemy get in? The trains don't run in the winter, the roads are too muddy in the fall, and the streets are all torn up in the spring, and if they did get in during the summer they'd find everybody away.—*Life.*

All this talk of hyphenated citizenship has evidently had its effect upon a San Francisco youngster, American-born, who recently rebelled fiercely when his Italian father punished him.
"But, Tommaso, your father has a right to whip you when you are bad," some one of the family said.
Tommaso's eyes flashed. "I am a citizen of the United States," he declared. "Do you think I am going to let any foreigner lick me?"—*Argonaut.*

Now it's

GLACIER NATIONAL PARK

Established as America's Vacation Paradise

Discovered by thousands of American tourists, who, deprived of the Old World, found a still greater wonderland at home. They came last year to Glacier National Park, Uncle Sam's greatest playground, twenty thousand strong. Many of them were second- and third-timers—answering again the call irresistible of the "land of shining mountains."

YOU step into a new world at Glacier Park. You measure Nature with a newer, bigger vision. Above you rise the towering Rockies—the far-stretching Continental Divide—cloud-piercing peaks and glistening glaciers; skyland lakes of turquoise and emerald.

Tour by auto-stage or go by saddle-horse, or over wide, safe trails afoot. Stop at splendid modern hotels or Swiss chalets, or live in a tepee, cook your own meals.

Vacations, $1 to $5 per day.

Great Northern through trains of supreme comfort daily reach this Vacation country. Low round trip summer tourist fares via Great Northern, from June 1 to September 30.

Handsomely illustrated Glacier Park booklets giving exact expense figures—mailed free. Send for copy now. Write for information concerning Pacific Coast and Alaskan tours.

C. E. STONE, Passenger Traffic Manager, St. Paul, Minn.
C. W. PITTS, Asst. Gen. Pass. Agt.   S. LOUNSBERY, Gen. Agt. Pass. Dept.
210 S. Clark St., Chicago   1184 Broadway, New York

The train palaces of the Pacific, S.S. "Great Northern," S.S. "Northern Pacific," three times weekly between Portland, Astoria and San Francisco. Folder on request

CHIEF "THREE BEARS"

—His Mark
Meet me at Glacier National Park this Summer

See America First
GREAT NORTHERN RAILWAY
Glacier National Park

C. E. STONE, Pass. Traf. Mgr., Great Northern Ry., Dept. 112, St. Paul, Minn.
Please send me Walking Tours Book, Aeroplane Folder and other descriptive literature on Glacier National Park, free.

NAME .... ADDRESS ....

CITY .... STATE ....

Pine Tree Camp for Girls On beautiful Naomi ... in nine-laden air of Pocono Mountains. Four hours from New York and Philadelphia. Bungalows and tents on sunny hill. Experienced councilors. Hockey, basketball, canoeing—all outdoor sports. Tutoring if desired. Endorsed by parents and girls. Penn., Philadelphia, 805 S. 47th St., Miss Blanche D. Price.

SHORT-STORY WRITING A course of forty lessons in the history, form structure, and writing of the Short-Story taught by Dr. J. Berg Esenwein, Editor Lippincott's Magazine. 250-page catalogue free. Please address THE HOME CORRESPONDENCE SCHOOL Dept. 305, Springfield, Mass.

Here Is the Camp for Your Boy

where he can spend his summer in real boy fashion; where he has every facility and the right men to teach him how to manage a canoe, play ball, swing a tennis racket and make things with tools. When your boy returns from a summer or part of a summer at **CAMP YUKON**, you will be astonished and pleased to see how he has improved in health, physique, stamina, and all-round manhood. No more beautiful location for a camp could be imagined than on Lake Cobbosseecontee in the magnificent hard wood grove, sixty miles from Portland, Maine. A readable booklet, full of pictures, will tell you all about **CAMP YUKON**. Write personally to Frank D. Smith, Director, 200 West 96th Street, New York, and you will receive by return mail something that will be to your advantage and that of your boy.

THE MARKET PLACE
A REVIEW OF FINANCE AND TRADE

MUNICIPAL BONDS FOR INVESTMENT

IN periods of drastic reorganization in the world of finance, the careful investor finds himself in possession of securities upon which principal and interest are paid when due. Foremost among investments of this class are bonds of American municipalities—more properly towns, cities and counties, but now generally regarded as including states as well.

No class of investment security has a better record in the last quarter of a century or so for safety of principal and interest than bonds which are the direct obligations of our states or their political subdivisions. Defaults have only occurred, with minor exceptions, during the reconstruction period after the War of the Rebellion; so the statement is quite appropriately made that no American municipality of any importance has defaulted in recent years in the principal or interest of any of its obligations.

The good faith of the inhabitants of a municipality is pledged for the payment of the principal and interest, and sinking fund where one exists, of such bonds. The fact that American municipal bonds of the highest grade are selling at equal or better prices than the best railroad bonds is an infallible indication of their high standing as investments. There are sold yearly to investors hundreds of millions of dollars of such securities and the demand for municipal bonds from postal savings depositories, federal reserve banks, savings banks, institutions, trust companies and private investors is so steady that the investment basis upon which such bonds are sold is about the best gauge of a municipality's credit that can be found. It is quite obvious that a city that can sell its 4 per cent bonds at par is not so highly rated as one that can get 102.

Municipalities issue bonds for varied purposes, such as construction of water plants, school buildings, hospitals, and libraries, also other public buildings, parks, playgrounds, docks, roads, etc., some of which are self supporting or produce revenue while others are not. Water plants are built by municipalities to provide a steady water supply to the city for domestic and manufacturing purposes, and such plants entail the expenditure of a considerable initial amount which cannot be, and should not be, readily obtained by ordinary yearly taxation.

Funds are borrowed for a term of years thru the issuance of bonds and taxes are levied to meet the annual interest and other charges on the bonds. Often a certain percentage of the bonds is retired each year thru the operation of a sinking fund. The most approved and modern plan of financing for municipalities is to issue bonds which mature yearly in series during the life of the improvement for which they were issued. In this manner future generations need not be taxed unjustly for an improvement which will have become depreciated and which the coming generation will not, therefore, have an opportunity to enjoy.

For example, a road which cost $1,-000,000 may last for ten years or twenty, depending upon construction, amount of traffic passing over it and annual maintenance charges. In ten years, a small expenditure may place it in a condition to last a decade more without the necessity for extraordinary expenses. Nevertheless, the time does come when an extraordinary expenditure must be incurred to place the road in usable condition. If the road bonds are issued to mature in twenty equal annual instalments, the debt is retired during the probable life of the road and future generations can be justly taxed for any further improvements or additions to the road.

The serial method is not only used for road financing, but in case of bonds issued for construction of public buildings, schools, parks, docks, etc. The serial bond issue is of great advantage to the issuing municipality, as it provides a "pay-as-you go" policy which is very commendable and more economical in the long run. While this form of bond is becoming quite generally adopted by progressive municipalities, and, in time, will replace the long term bond, the latter is to all intents and purposes a perfectly safe investment so far as the investor is concerned.

Interest and serial payments are met by taxation of property located in the boundaries of the municipality issuing the securities.

When a municipality has need of funds for a public improvement, the proper legal resolutions are passed by a governing board and the controller is instructed to advertise for bids for a new bond issue. The advertisement will set forth the amount of bonds to be issued, rate, maturity, purpose of issue, legality, etc., and banking houses, institutions, banks and private investors submit their bids for the bonds accompanied by a check for a nominal amount as a proof of good faith. At a specified time the bids are opened and the bonds awarded to the person, firm or corporation offering the highest figure.

As a matter of course, the municipality furnishes the successful bidder with copies of all resolutions and other papers in connection with the issue of bonds, together with the opinion of counsel competent to pass on the legality of securities of the class, certifying that the bonds are legally issued. For this reason, circulars on municipal bonds issued by banking firms will contain the phrase "Legality approved by Messrs. Blank & Blank, Attorneys, New York." Investment houses furnish to the investors copies of legal opinions on the issuance of the bonds.

As a matter of precaution municipalities are guided by law as to how many bonds they may issue. The law limits a city's right to borrow, spend money and levy taxes; so the borrowing of funds is not a haphazard proposition. Municipal bonds are usually legal investments for trustees in the states where the municipality is located, and the savings bank laws of the various states provide that bonds of cities in other states which have complied with certain requirements are legal investments.

Municipal bonds are safe because ordinarily nobody can own tangible property and escape taxation. Vacant land, buildings, public service corporations, bonds, mortgages and corporate property are taxed in order to pay interest and principal on the bonded debt of a municipality and the tax is levied every year without fail. A booklet recently issued by a municipal bond house very pertinently says: "Taxes are a first lien upon any property; a mortgage can only be a lien second thereto."

In many states bonds of municipalities are exempt from taxation when held in the state where issued, but all municipal bonds are exempt from the Federal Income Tax, both normal and super-tax, and no mention of the income received from such bonds is required on the income tax return. This is a distinct advantage to the small as well as the large investor. To the small investor it obviates the necessity for ownership certificates to accompany the coupons, while the large investor does not have to pay a super-tax on his income from municipal bonds.

Bonds of the United States Government, states and municipalities are the only class acceptable by the Post Office Department as security for postal savings deposits, and banks which receive the privilege to carry such deposits for the government are required to turn over a specific amount of eligible bonds in exchange for the government funds so deposited.

Municipal bonds have stood the test for many years, but, as is natural, along with safety one must accept low yield. The best grades of municipal bonds are now selling on from a 3.75 per cent basis to a 4.25 per cent basis, when a year ago they were .25 higher. Along with the many railroad receiverships came the demand for bonds which were not likely to be affected by business conditions, and with the great demand for bonds that followed the tremendous activity in commercial lines, there was experienced a steady rise in the prices of municipal bonds and high grade railroad bonds.

It does not necessarily follow that an investor must content himself with 4 per cent, for while bonds of large cities sell on about a 4 per cent basis, that is because of some special feature, such as legality for savings banks, or exemption from local taxes, and not because of any relatively better security. There are many bonds of small cities that are obtainable on from a 4½ per cent to a 5 per cent basis which are as sound as bonds can be and form desirable holdings for the small or large investor.

The following dividend is announced: Federal Sugar Refining Company, preferred, quarterly, 1¾ per cent, payable May 1.

Insurance
Conducted by
W. E. UNDERWOOD

THE COINSURANCE CLAUSE

A correspondent asks for an explanation of coinsurance as practised in fire insurance. As this is a subject that is either not understood at all, or misunderstood, by many people, it will be given special treatment here.

The principle of coinsurance rests on the theory that the whole value of any given risk should contribute to the payment of any loss by fire incurred by it. The owner of uninsured property bears the whole of any loss sustained. He is his own insurer.

Suppose the value of the property is $10,000. If he insures it for its full value, then the whole risk contributes to any fire loss suffered. But if he insures it for $5000, thus saving one-half the premium, virtually carrying the remaining $5000 himself, unless there is a coinsurance provision in the company's policy, his half will not contribute to the payment of any partial loss. This would work no inequity to the insurance company if the property were totally destroyed, for in that case the owner would actually bear his full share of the loss. But experience shows that the greater number of the losses incurred are partial losses.

To meet this inequity the coinsurance clause is employed—generally, the eighty per cent clause. In substance, this clause provides that the owner of the property shall keep it insured for an amount not less than eighty per cent of its value, failing in which, in the event of loss, he shall become liable, as a coinsurer with the company, for such proportion of any loss or damage as the amount insured by the company shall bear to eighty per cent of the property's value.

Reverting to the illustration, under the eighty per cent coinsurance clause, the owner must have at least $8000 insurance on the property. He is carrying but $5000. This makes him a coinsurer for $3000. In the event of loss the company's liability would be five-eighths of it; the owner's, three-eighths. If the loss is total, the company would have to pay $5000, because five-eighths of $10,000 more than uses up its policy. But suppose the whole loss is $5000 only. The company's contribution to it would be five-eighths of $5000, or $3125; the owner's contribution would be three-eighths of $5000, or $1875. The use of the clause also prevents discrimination in insurance service between insured persons. To illustrate: A and B each own property valued at $10,000, the insurance rate on each piece being 1 per cent. A insures for $5000, paying $50 premium, and B insures for $8000, paying $80. Each has

a $5000 loss. Without the clause A gets as much protection for $50 as B gets for $80. With the clause in both policies, A would have received five-eighths of $5000 ($3125) and B, five-eighths of $8000 ($5000).

H. G. C., Sioux City, Iowa.—The Mutual Benefit Health and Accident Association of Omaha is an assessment organization, the financial standing of which does not appear in any of the insurance handbooks to which I have access. Read the article, "Low-Priced Accident Policies" in The Independent of February 21, 1916. The Mystic Workers of the World is a fraternal assessment order, accumulating an insufficient fund to meet future increases in mortality, therefore I cannot recommend it as an institution furnishing permanent security.

C. A. B., Cassopolis, Mich.—The Ancient Order of Gleaners is a fraternal assessment life insurance order which is not making adequate provision for increasing mortality due to the advancing age of its membership. It has $56,000,000 outstanding insurance, supported by about $525,000 of net assets. Contrast these figures with an established old-line company of approximate insurance liabilities, say the Michigan Mutual. That company's outstanding insurance aggregates $54,000,000, behind which there is a necessary cash reserve of about $11,000,000. I cannot recommend the Gleaners as an insurer.

G. A. N., Washington, D. C.—You are probably inquiring about the Puritan Life of Providence, R. I. There is no company in Pittsburg bearing that title. This company was organized in 1907; its assets are $472,879; surplus, $171,946, which includes $151,000 of capital. It is a slow-growing, sound old line company. Its expenses for new business are a little heavier than normal and its mortality rate is a trifle high. It writes participating and non-participating insurance. In my judgment a life company should not be permitted to transact both kinds. The Puritan has about $2,500,000 insurance in force.

L. C. H., Dandridge, Tenn.—You say that your policy will be fully paid up in September and that its surrender and loan value is $412.63. You also say you can get eight per cent for money in your locality. Now, the loan from the company will cost you five per cent. Wouldn't it be better to borrow at five per cent and loan the money at eight per cent, thus keeping the insurance in force, plus the annual dividend you will get, than to surrender and cancel the insurance? I think so. Another thought: Would you not do better in the long future by leaving the money where it is and having all future dividends converted into additions payable with the policy at death? All your ventures with money might turn out unfortunately. Old age is a risk to be insured against. You can always get the full cash value of your policy. It is wise to leave it until needed.

C. R. P., Anaheim, Cal.—I am quite sure that no insurance institution can maintain thru life a level premium rate of $9 per $1,000 at ages 21-30. Therefore, I am constrained to assert that the Western Mutual Life of Los Angeles is mistaken. The actual mathematical reserve, calculating at 3 per cent, at age 25, is $8 at the end of the first year; the tabular mortality is $8.07. That is $16.07. The mortality increases every year and, unless the premium contains enough money in addition to that each year for investment, higher or additional assessments will be necessary. In the tenth year the accumulated reserve is $98.94, greater than at the end of the ninth year by $11.27; the mortality in the ninth year is $8.83. These figures prove that it has been necessary for the policyholder to pay during the ninth year the sum of $11.27 plus $8.83, which equals $20.10. And so it runs upward thru the years.

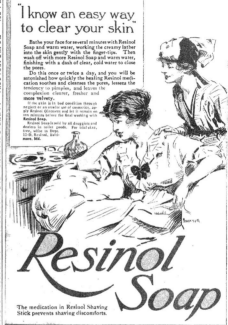

"I know an easy way to clear your skin"

Bathe your face for several minutes with Resinol Soap and warm water, working the creamy lather into the skin gently with the finger-tips. Then wash off with more Resinol Soap and warm water, finishing with a dash of clear, cold water to close the pores.

Do this once or twice a day, and you will be astonished how quickly the healing Resinol medication soothes and cleanses the pores, lessens the tendency to pimples, and leaves the complexion cleaner, fresher and more velvety.

If the skin is in bad condition thru neglect or an unwise use of cosmetics, apply Resinol Ointment and let it remain on ten minutes before the final washing with Resinol Soap.

Resinol Soap is sold by all druggists and dealers in toilet goods. For trial size, free, write to Dept. 11-D, Resinol, Baltimore, Md.

Resinol Soap

The medication in Resinol Shaving Stick prevents shaving discomforts.

THE PRESIDENT'S LAST WORD TO GERMANY

THE NOTE DATED ON THE ANNIVERSARY OF CONCORD AND LEXINGTON

INFORMATION now in the possession of the Government of the United States fully establishes the facts in the case of the "Sussex," and the inferences which my Government has drawn from that information it regards as confirmed by the circumstances set forth in Your Excellency's note of the 10th instant. On the 24th of March, 1916, at about 2:50 o'clock in the afternoon, the unarmed steamer "Sussex," with 325 or more passengers on board, among whom were a number of American citizens, was torpedoed while crossing from Folkestone to Dieppe. The "Sussex" had never been armed; was a vessel known to be habitually used only for the conveyance of passengers across the English Channel, and was not following the route taken by troopships or supply ships. About eighty of her passengers, non-combatants of all ages and sexes, including citizens of the United States, were killed or injured.

A careful, detailed and scrupulously impartial investigation by naval and military officers of the United States has conclusively established the fact that the "Sussex" was torpedoed without warning or summons to surrender, and that the torpedo by which she was struck, was of German manufacture. In the view of the Government of the United States these facts from the first made the conclusion that the torpedo was fired by a German submarine unavoidable. It now considers that conclusion substantiated by the statements of Your Excellency's note. A full statement of the facts upon which the Government of the United States has based its conclusion is inclosed.

The Government of the United States, after having given careful consideration to the note of the Imperial Government of the 10th of April, regrets to state that the impression made upon it by the statements and proposals contained in that note is that the Imperial Government has failed to appreciate the gravity of the situation which has resulted not alone from the attack on the "Sussex," but from the whole method and character of submarine warfare as disclosed by the unrestrained practise of the commanders of German undersea craft during the past twelvemonth and more in the indiscriminate destruction of merchant vessels of all sorts, nationalities and destinations.

If the sinking of the "Sussex" had been an isolated case the Government of the United States might find it possible to hope that the officer who was responsible for that act had wilfully violated his orders or had been criminally negligent in taking none of the precautions they prescribed, and that the ends of justice might be satisfied by imposing upon him an adequate punishment, coupled with a formal disavowal of the act and payment of a suitable indemnity by the Imperial Government.

But, tho the attack upon the "Sussex" was manifestly indefensible and caused a loss of life so tragical as to make it stand forth as one of the most terrible examples of the inhumanity of submarine warfare as the commanders of German vessels are conducting it, it unhappily does not stand alone.

On the contrary, the Government of the United States is forced by recent events to conclude that it is only one instance, even the one of the most extreme and most distressing instances, of the deliberate method and spirit of indiscriminate destruction of merchant vessels of all sorts, nationalities and destinations which have become more and more unmistakable as the activity of German undersea vessels of war has in recent months been quickened and extended.

The Imperial Government will recall that when, in February, 1915, it announced its intention of treating the waters surrounding Great Britain and Ireland as embraced within the seat of war and of destroying all merchant ships owned by its enemies that might be found within that zone of danger, and warned all vessels, neutral as well as belligerent, to keep out of the waters thus proscribed or to enter them at their peril, the Government of the United States earnestly protested. It took the position that such a policy could not be pursued without constant gross and palpable violations of the accepted law of nations, particularly if submarine craft were to be employed as its instruments, inasmuch as the rules prescribed by that law, rules founded on the principles of humanity and established for the protection of the lives of non-combatants at sea, could not in the nature of the case be observed by such vessels. It based its protest on the ground that persons of neutral nationality and vessels of neutral ownership would be exposed to extreme and intolerable risks; and that no right to close any part of the high seas could lawfully be asserted by the Imperial Government in the circumstances then existing.

The law of nations in these matters, upon which the Government of the United States based that protest, is not of recent origin or founded upon merely arbitrary principles set up by convention. It is based, on the contrary, upon manifest principles of humanity and has long been established with the approval and by the express assent of all civilized nations.

The Imperial Government, notwithstanding, persisted in carrying out the policy announced, expressing the hope that the dangers involved, at any rate to neutral vessels, would be reduced to a minimum by the instructions which it had issued to the commanders of its submarines and assuring the Government of the United States that it would take every possible precaution both to respect the rights of neutrals and to safeguard the lives of non-combatants.

In pursuance of this policy of submarine warfare against the commerce of its adversaries, thus announced and thus entered upon in despite of the solemn protest of the Government of the United States, the commanders of the Imperial Government's undersea vessels have carried on practises of such ruthless destruction which have made it more and more evident as the months have gone by that the Imperial Government has found it impracticable to put any such restraint upon them as it had hoped and promised to put. Again and again the Imperial Government has given its solemn assurances to the Government of the United States that at least passenger ships would not be thus dealt with, and yet it has repeatedly permitted its undersea commanders to disregard those assurances with entire impunity. As recently as February last it gave notice that it would regard all armed merchantmen owned by its enemies as part of the armed naval forces of its adversaries and deal with them as with men-of-war, thus, at least by implication, pledging itself to give warning to vessels which were not armed and to accord security of life to their passengers and crews; but even this limitation their submarine commanders have recklessly ignored.

Vessels of neutral ownership, even vessels of neutral ownership bound from neutral port to neutral port, have been destroyed, along with vessels of belligerent ownership, if constantly increasing numbers. Sometimes the merchantmen attacked have been warned and summoned to surrender before being fired on or torpedoed; sometimes their passengers and crews have been vouchsafed the poor security of being allowed to take to the ship's boats before the ship was sent to the bottom. But again and again no warning has been given, no escape even to the ship's boats allowed to those on board.

Great liners like the "Lusitania" and "Arabic" and mere passenger boats like the "Sussex" have been attacked without a moment's warning, often before they have even become aware that they were in the presence of an armed ship of the enemy, and the lives of non-combatants, passengers and crew have been destroyed wholesale and in a manner which the Government of the United States cannot but regard as wanton and without the slightest color of justification. No limit of any kind has in fact been set to their indiscriminate pursuit and destruction of merchantmen of all kinds and nationalities within the waters which the Imperial Government has chosen to designate as lying within the seat of war. The roll of Americans who have lost their lives upon ships thus attacked and destroyed has grown month by month, until the ominous toll has mounted into the hundreds.

The Government of the United States has been very patient. At every stage of this distressing experience of tragedy after tragedy it has sought to be governed by the most thoughtful consideration of the extraordinary circumstances of an unprecedented war and to be guided by sentiments of very genuine friendship for the people and government of Germany. It has accepted the successive explanations and assurances of the Imperial Government, as of course given in entire sincerity and good faith, and has hoped, even against hope, that it would prove to be possible for the Imperial Government so to order and control the acts of its naval commanders as to square its policy with the recognized principles of humanity as embodied in the law of nations. It has made every allowance for unprecedented conditions and has been willing to wait until the facts became unmistakable and were susceptible of only one interpretation.

It now owes it to a just regard for its own rights to say to the Imperial Government that that time has come. It has become painfully evident to it that the position which it took at the very outset is inevitable, namely, the use of submarines for the destruction of an enemy's commerce is of necessity, because of the very character of the vessels employed and the very methods of attack which their employment of course involves, utterly incompatible with the principles of humanity, the longestablished and incontrovertible rights of neutrals, and the sacred immunities of non-combatants.

If it is still the purpose of the Imperial Government to prosecute relentless and indiscriminate warfare against vessels of commerce by the use of submarines, without regard to what the Government of the United States must consider the sacred and indisputable rules of international law and the universally recognized dictates of humanity, the Government of the United States is at last forced to the conclusion that there is but one course it can pursue.

Unless the Imperial Government should now immediately declare and effect an abandonment of its present methods of submarine warfare against passenger and freight-carrying vessels, the Government of the United States can have no choice but to sever diplomatic relations with the German Empire altogether. This action the Government of the United States contemplates with the greatest reluctance, but feels constrained to take in behalf of humanity and the rights of neutral nations. LANSING

The Independent

FOR SIXTY-SEVEN YEARS THE
FORWARD-LOOKING WEEKLY OF AMERICA

THE CHAUTAUQUAN
Merged with The Independent June 1, 1914

MAY 8, 1916

OWNED AND PUBLISHED BY
THE INDEPENDENT CORPORATION, AT
119 WEST FORTIETH STREET, NEW YORK
WILLIAM B. HOWLAND, PRESIDENT
FREDERIC E. DICKINSON, TREASURER

WILLIAM HAYES WARD
HONORARY EDITOR

EDITOR: HAMILTON HOLT
ASSOCIATE EDITOR: HAROLD J. HOWLAND
LITERARY EDITOR: EDWIN E. SLOSSON

PUBLISHER: KARL V. S. HOWLAND

ONE YEAR, THREE DOLLARS
SINGLE COPIES, TEN CENTS

Postage to foreign countries in Universal Postal
Union, $1.75 a year extra; to Canada, $1 extra.
Instructions for renewal, discontinuance or
change of address should be sent two weeks
before the date they are to go into effect. Both
the old and the new address must be given.

We welcome contributions, but writers who
wish their articles returned, if not accepted,
should send a stamped and address envelope. No responsibility is assumed by The
Independent for the loss or non-return of
manuscripts, tho all due care will be exercised.

Entered at New York Post Office as Second
Class Matter

Copyright, 1916, by The Independent

Address all Communications to
THE INDEPENDENT
119 West Fortieth Street, New York

CONTENTS

BERCEUSE

The justly famous orb of day
    Had sought the celebrated West
To tide—(and who would say it nay?)—
    In its inimitable way
        A needed rest.

The moon—whose light is hardly less
    Esteemed than is Apollo's own—
Came up and shone with that success
Which not to know is to confess
        Oneself unknown.

'Twas night—But I need hardly speak
    Of ev'ning's charms altho they are
So beneficially unique
And, with the rather younger clique,
        So popular.

And some of us—please don't infer
    We were in any way alarmed
By nightfall—*au contraire sans peur*
We laid us down to sleep and were
        Quite pleased and charmed.
                —*T. N. Metcalf, in New York Evening
                Post Magazine.*

POTENT PREPAREDNESS

Perhaps you have heard the story
about the Kaiser's visit a year or two
before the war. He exprest his desire
to go to Switzerland, and was cordially
invited to come at the time of the
maneuvers. He was taken about and
given every chance to see and admire
the fitness of the men and their accurate marksmanship and skill.

The story goes that he stopped before
one of the soldiers and said: "Yes, you
are splendid fellows, but only four hundred thousand of you at the most. What
would you do if I should bring my
army of a million men thru here?"

"Why, sire," as proudly responded
the Swiss, "it's very simple. Each one
of us would shoot twice; that's all."

There is a sequel to this tale: It is
said that in the council called to decide
as to which road Germany should take
into France—Switzerland or Belgium
—Switzerland was saved by two votes,
and those opposed to molesting it were
the staff of military officials who had
accompanied the Kaiser upon his visit
to the maneuvers.—*The Ladies' Home
Journal.*

REMARKABLE REMARKS

DORIS BLAKE—Flirting is ill bred.

WINIFRED STONER, JR.—How far can a
cat spit?

MARY PICKFORD—It is all my own natural hair.

ED. HOWE—Most men prefer to eat fast
like a dog.

REV. J. HOWARD MELISH—Love alone
can save the world.

W. H. TAFT—The nerve center of this
country is Chicago.

AMY LOWELL—Chicago is the greatest
center of the new school of poetry.

REGINALD KAUFMAN—The backbone of
knowledge is wfeeness.

WOODROW WILSON—It is a pity that
this is a campaign year.

GENERAL EMILIO ZAPATA—I am fighting for the common people.

SPEAKER CLARK—You Republicans
haven't got the world by the tail.

WILLIAM BARNES, JR.—Mr. Roosevelt is
an enemy of the American Republic.

PROF. BRANDER MATTHEWS—The greatest enemy of the theater is the high-brow.

LUKE McCLURE—Quick now, who was
Vice-President when Taft was President?

JOHN MASEFIELD—I suppose Vachel
Lindsay is your best writer of verses today.

PROF. H. H. TURNER—Life has a terrible way of getting more and more difficult.

POLICE INSPECTOR FAUROT—Not one-
tenth of the loot in precious stones is ever
returned.

PUBLISHER GEO. P. BRETT—The best
slang of today becomes the language of tomorrow.

COMMISSIONER OF MARKETS DILLON—
There is not an average of one bad egg in
a thousand.

JESS WILLARD—Of the several methods
of defense ducking is perhaps the most
dangerous.

SENATOR POMERENE—If necessary, I
would have the troops follow Villa to
Patagonia.

COL. EDWARD F. GLENN—The American
army is the most pathetic thing that ever
came along in history.

WILLIAM BRADY, M.D.—Every six
months every adult should undergo a complete physical examination.

CONGRESSMAN HEFLIN—If we can prosecute bulls for putting up the price, we can
prosecute bears for putting down the price.

ATTORNEY GENERAL GREGORY—Woodrow Wilson would not be willing to be
President unless he felt in his heart that
he was right.

H. G. WELLS—The western nations
have taken a peculiar pride in having a
free press; that is to say, a press that can
be bought by any one.

SENATOR SMITH—When Woodrow Wilson took the oath of office, one man in
every four in this country had a bank account, where are they now?

EVERETT P. WHEELER—Politics are exciting and engrossing, and once women are
drawn into the vortex they are more excited and engrossed than men are.

BILLY SUNDAY—I could preach sermons
that would make the gum-chewing, face-
painted manicured, highball-guzzling, card-
playing, marcel-waved society women say
"Oh, isn't Mr. Sunday a nice man."

MARJORIE DORMAN—The worst thing
which could happen to the wage-earning
woman would be for the law to place her
on an equality with men. She needs equality plus.

ARNOLD BENNETT—Those hogsheads of
blood, lacerated limbs, smashed bones,
glaring eyes, screams of pain, are exactly
what we all in every country asked for
when we voted supplies.

TO RIDE IN THE CADILLAC
IS TO REVISE YOUR IDEAS
OF WHAT CONSTITUTES
LUXURIOUS MOTORING

BETWEEN two cars, even of excellent riding qualities, you may be able to observe certain slight or indifferent distinctions.

But you will recognize that the difference between the smoothest, steadiest car you have ever known, and the eight-cylinder Cadillac, is not merely slight or indefinite.

It is impressively brought home to you that you must reject your previous ideals and that you must adopt new standards of what constitutes real motoring luxury.

Before you have ridden a mile in the Cadillac, you find that the qualities which you have most desired in a motor car have been developed to a point that is absolutely new to you.

You discover—immediately the car glides into motion—that the quality of quietness has been given a new significance.

You find that neither the engine nor any other part of the marvelously efficient mechanism intrudes itself upon you.

You relax into forgetfulness of the means by which you are carried forward.

You find that you are traveling more continuously on direct drive than you had thought possible in any car.

Pick-up, from a snail's pace to express train speed, is accomplished with so little effort that it is scarcely apparent.

Hills which, before, had compelled a car to strain and labor, seem almost to subside into a level roadway—so easily, so quietly and with so little exertion does the Cadillac surmount them.

Fatigue and exhaustion, which may have characterized your journeys in the past, are replaced by a sense of intense exhilaration and keen enjoyment.

The most enthusiastic Cadillac admirers are those whose motor car experience has been most extended.

There have been no exceptions to the astonishment and delight of those who have ridden in this unusual car.

The handling and control are so easy; the springs and the deep, soft upholstery are so yielding; the smoothness, the quietness, the activity and the flexibility are so delightfully soothing; there is such a sense of velvet softness in every movement of the car, that you cannot resist its supreme charm.

And so your experience with the Cadillac, resolves itself into something even broader than complete satisfaction.

It carries with it the gratifying sense of owning something different and something superior—a car which surpasses ordinary standards and deepens and intensifies the enjoyment of every phase of motoring.

The Independent

| VOL. 86. | MAY 8, 1916 | No. 3518 |

THE INDEPENDENT HAS ACQUIRED HARPER'S WEEKLY

[This memorandum was given to the daily press on Friday, April 28]

"HARPER'S WEEKLY" has been acquired by the Independent Corporation, and, after fifty-nine years of existence, it is to be incorporated in The Independent. This brings together two of the oldest and best known of American weekly periodicals.

The Independent is sixty-eight years old, "Harper's Weekly" fifty-nine. The older periodical has during all its history been associated with a single family. The present editor, Hamilton Holt, is the grandson of the founder, Henry C. Bowen. Two and a half years ago Mr. Holt was joined in the ownership and management of The Independent by William B. Howland, for twenty-three years publisher of "The Outlook," and his two sons, Karl V. S. Howland and Harold J. Howland, who had also been associated with "The Outlook" in the advertising and editorial fields.

"Harper's Weekly" was for fifty-six years one of the well-known group of periodicals published by the famous house of Harper and Brothers. Prior to and during the last presidential campaign it was edited by Colonel George Harvey, who was the first publicist to propose and urge the nomination and election of Woodrow Wilson as President.

For the past three years "Harper's Weekly" has been owned by an independent corporation, and has been edited by Norman Hapgood, the former editor of "Collier's Weekly."

The incorporation of "Harper's Weekly" in The Independent is a logical event. The purpose and spirit of the two periodicals have been similar from the beginning. Both have had for their prime functions the treatment and interpretation of the current history of the world, and the cultivation of sound opinion on the questions of the day. Both periodicals have not feared to be radical and to utter vigorous editorial views even when they were most unpopular. If at any time in the last sixty years a librarian or well-informed reader had been asked to name the leading American periodicals, he would certainly have mentioned among the foremost The Independent and "Harper's Weekly." These two, as friendly rivals, have always stood for the best in American life, for purity in politics, for social reform, for national progress, for high ideals in literature and art. The eighty-six volumes of The Independent and the sixty-two volumes of "Harper's Weekly" form a contemporary history of the United States and of the world of extraordinary value, a treasury of information of current events and opinions such as few libraries are fortunate to possess.

To "Harper's Weekly" belongs the honor of publishing the essays of George William Curtis, the cartoons of Thomas Nast, and the farces of William Dean Howells, while The Independent has credit for publishing the editorials of Horace Greeley, the sermons of Henry Ward Beecher, and the poetry of Tennyson, Lowell, Whittier, Browning and Kipling.

MORE BLOOD SPILT ON IRISH SOIL

© Brown & Dawson

A HUMANITARIAN TRAITOR

Sir Roger Casement, captured off the coast of Ireland while attempting to land arms from a German auxiliary. He had previously been known chiefly for his activities as British consul, in behalf of mistreated natives in the Putumayo rubber fields of South America

N. Y. Herald Service

TO CRUSH THE IRISH REBELLION

Major-General Sir John Maxwell, recently commander of the British forces in Egypt, has been put in charge of the Irish situation. Martial law was proclaimed in the city and county of Dublin and soon extended to the whole of Ireland

Paul Thompson

LIBERTY HALL IN DUBLIN, NOW RIDDLED BY BRITISH SHELLS

The headquarters of the Sinn Fein, demolished on April 29, has been a labor center for a long time. In 1913 Jim Larkin's striking transport workers gathered here, and the photograph shows some of his "citizen soldiery" on guard during one of his revolutionary enterprises

HOW GERMANY'S REPLY WILL COME

GERMANY has not replied to the American note on the submarine situation. Ambassador Gerard is busily conferring with the Foreign Office and has even journeyed to the German General Headquarters "somewhere in France" to consult face to face with the Kaiser. Many rumors, reports and conjectures are going about as to what the German answer will be and there is much debate as to whether it will be "satisfactory."

It will be interesting, of course, to read the German note when it comes. If it should contain a hearty and unqualified acceptance of the American point of view, it would be very gratifying.

But the main point should not be overlooked. Germany's real answer is not to be made thru diplomatic channels. It will be made on the high seas. If Germany from this time forward does actually cease to use its submarines in violation of the accepted principles of international law, the American people will go on living in amicable and harmonious relations with the German people. But if a German submarine should attack a merchant vessel with an American citizen on board, that act of itself would cause the severance of diplomatic relations.

There is no need for Germany to argue the case longer.

The latest note of the United States is this nation's final word—or it is nothing.

Not German words, but German acts, will determine the future.

THE IRONY OF IRELAND

TWO years ago the Irishmen of Ulster were getting guns from Germany to fight the King's troops. Last week the Irishmen of Dublin were getting guns from Germany to fight the King's troops. Sir Edward Carson, who was two years ago conspiring against the government, was only a few months ago made a member of that government. Sir Roger Casement, who is now under arrest for conspiring against the government, was the man who made out the government's case against Belgium in 1903.

The Blue Book on the "Belgian atrocities," prepared by Mr. Casement thirteen years ago, was, if we remember aright, about the size and shape of the Blue Book on the "Belgian atrocities" prepared last year by Lord Bryce, but the contents were different. The former told how the Belgians cut off the hands of children in the Congo; the latter told how the Germans cut off the hands of children in Belgium. On July 9, 1903—that is, before the report of the Casement investigations had come out—The Independent published a photograph of one of these maimed children in an article by the Rev. Dr. Morrison, telling how a missionary had seen eighty-one human hands drying over a fire to be turned in to the state officer as proof of a successful raid. It was also shown that the Belgians were monopolizing trade and permitting slavery.

The British public was so shocked by these revelations of cruelty and oppression in the administration of a state founded for the purpose of protecting the natives and opening up the territory to free trade that the British Government interposed a veto to the proposed acquisition of the "Congo Free State" by Belgium. It was in fact not until 1914 that Great Britain consented to the Belgian annexation of the territory. The United States, altho it took part in the international conference which founded the Congo Free State and declared its perpetual neutrality, made no protest when it was taken over by Belgium.

But England, which did oppose with all its power the acquisition of the Congo by Belgium, is now, curiously enough, fighting that Belgium may retain the Congo. For it has been more than once intimated that Germany would be willing to stop the war at once and evacuate Belgium if Belgian Congo be ceded to her. But such a transfer would not be to the advantage of the natives if we may judge by Germany's cruel treatment of the Hereros.

So it happens that Sir Roger Casement, knighted for his exposure of the iniquities of "red rubber," lies now in the Tower of London, caught in the act of rebellion and liable, according to existing English law, to be beheaded for high treason. He is more likely, however, to be made Attorney General like Sir Edward Carson, who organized the Ulster rebellion, or made Premier, like General Botha, who led the Boer armies against Kitchener, or set at liberty, like General De Wet, who was a few months ago convicted of high treason, or elected to Parliament like Arthur Lynch, the Irish colonel in the Boer army. Such is the British way of treating malcontents; illogical, ironical, absurd, it may be called, yet it works, and no better way has been discovered of turning foes into friends. Most of the Irish have been won over by the conciliatory policy which the British Government has in recent years adopted toward Ireland. The reform of the land laws has in large part removed the economic grievance, and the passage of home rule promises to remove in large part the political grievance. But the evil effects of the old injuries still trouble the world. It is quite probable that the Kaiser would have hesitated to make war if he had not relied upon Irish discontent. This effect was anticipated in an article written for The Independent of January 30, 1902, by Arthur Lynch, then under sentence of death for treason, who said:

> The South African war has shown the weakness of England and has aroused the hopes and rekindled the hatred of her Continental foes. The attitude of Ireland, so pronouncedly hostile to England in this undertaking, has been a source of weakness not only in its direct moral effect and by the influence on public opinion in America, but also in the most material way by the limitation of the recruiting ground of England for her soldiers and sailors.

Every point in this paragraph is verified by the news of the day. The recruiting ground of England has been limited, for the British Government has not dared to extend its enlistment acts to Ireland. The Democratic party, which in its platform denounced England for the destruction of the Boer republics, is now in power at Washington. The Dublin insurgents have received encouragement if not more substantial aid from Irish in America. The hopes and the hatreds of England's continental foes have precipitated the Great War.

MORE BLOOD SPILT ON IRISH SOIL

© Brown & Dawson

A HUMANITARIAN TRAITOR

Sir Roger Casement, captured off the coast of Ireland while attempting to land arms from a German auxiliary. He had previously been known chiefly for his activities as British consul, in behalf of mistreated natives in the Putumayo rubber fields of South America

A. P. Donald

TO CRUSH THE IRISH REBELLION

Major-General Sir John Maxwell, recently commander of the British forces on Egyptian front, sent to avenge all the Irish situation. Martial law was declared in the city and county of Dublin and placed at once in the county of Ireland

Paul Thompson

LIBERTY HALL IN DUBLIN, NOW BOMBED BY BRITISH SHELLS

The headquarters of the Sinn Fein, demolished on April 26, has been a mute spot to which the workers gathered here, and the photograph shows some of his "citizen army"

HOW GERMANY'S REPLY WILL COME

GERMANY has not replii to the American note on the submarine situat n. Ambassador Gerard is busily conferring wit the Foreign Office and has even journeyed t the German General Headquarters "somewhere in Fince" to consult face to face with the Kaiser. Many rumrs, reports and conjectures are going about as to wi t the German answer will be and there is much deba as to whether it will be "satisfactory."

It will be interesting, of cc ue, to read the German note when it comes. If it shoul contain a hearty and unqualified acceptance of the Amrican point of view, it would be very gratifying.

But the main point should rt be overlooked. Germany's real answer is not to b made thru diplomatic channels. It will be made on the high seas. If Germany from this time forward does actually cease to use its submarines in violation of the accepted principles of international law, the American people will go on living in amicable and harmonious relations with the German people. But if a German submarine should attack a merchant vessel with an American citizen on board, that act of itself would cause the severance of diplomatic relations.

There is no need for Germany to argue the case longer.

The latest note of the United States is this exact final word—or it is nothing.

Not German words, but German acts, will determine the future.

THE IRONY OF IRELAND

TWO years ago the Irishmenf Ulster were getting guns from Germany to fighthe King's troops. Last week the Irishmen of Dublin wre getting guns from Germany to fight the King's trods. Sir Edward Carson, who was two years ago conspirig against the government, was only a few months agonade a member of that government. Sir Roger Casemen who is now under arrest for conspiring against the grernment, was the man who made out the government'scase against Belgium in 1903.

The Blue Book on the "Belgia atrocities," prepared by Mr. Casement thirteen years go, was, if we remember aright, about the size and shee of the Blue Book on the "Belgian atrocities" prepari last year by Lord Bryce, but the contents were diffrent. The former told how the Belgians cut off the hds of children in the Congo; the latter told how the Genans cut off the hands of children in Belgium. On July 1 1903—that is, before the report of the Casement invegations had come out —The Independent published a hotograph of one of these maimed children in an artic by the Rev. Dr. Morrison, telling how a missionary d seen eighty-one human hands drying over a fire to turned in to the state officer as proof of a successful rd. It was also shown that the Belgians were monopeing trade and permitting slavery.

The British public was so shked by these revelations of cruelty and oppression i he administration of a state founded for the purpose f protecting the natives and opening up the territo o free trade that the British Government interposed veto to the proposed acquisition of the "Congo Fre ate" by Belgium. It was in fact not until 1914 that reat Britain consented to the Belgian annexation the territory. The United States, altho it took part i he international conference which founded the Cong Free State and declared its perpetual neutrality, me no protest when it was taken over by Belgium.

But England, which did oppose ith all its power t acquisition of the Congo by Belg m, is now, curiou enough, fighting that Belgium y retain the Co For it has been more than once i mated that Bel would be willing to stop the war t once and re Belgium if Belgian Congo be ce l to her. But transfer would not be to the adva age of th we may judge by Germany's cruel treatmen Hereros.

So it happens that Sir Roger Case his exposure of the iniquities of "red in the Tower of London, caught in th and liable, according to existing Eng headed for high treason. He is more to be made Attorney General like S who organized the Ulster rebellion, like General Botha, who led the Kitchener, or set at liberty, like G was a few months ago convict elected to Parliament like Art colonel in the Boer army. Such treating malcontents; illogical be called, yet it works, and covered of turning foes into f have been won over by the British Government has in r Ireland. The reform of the removed the economic gri home rule promises to re cal grievance. But the evi trouble the world. It is would have hesitate upon Irish discontent. article written for The son, who said:

The Sou land an her Con edly hes source e by the most me of Eng

Eve of the

rinciple of the American omen from the ballot are ons. It shoul no pre r how "so to de within its hall be

the Unite uld not he United ny state

But now, when Ireland's hopes are highest, they are blasted by her own act. Never in the last three hundred years has an Irish rebellion had less justification and less chance of success. The factionalism which has always been the curse of the country has again brought ruin to its cause in the hour of its triumph. The same paper that tells of the Irish attack on the English at Dublin tells also how the Irish fought for the English at Loos.

═══

CAST OUT FROM EDEN

THE capture by the Turks of General Townshend's army on the Tigris is a severe blow to British prestige. Three-quarters of the second year of the Great War have now gone. Great Britain has raised an army of four million and they have been fighting on eight distinct fields in three continents, yet nowhere have they achieved a distinct victory. Twice they have suffered distinct defeats, and—what is most humiliating—by the Turks. The Turks! who for more than a century have been regarded as incapable of carrying on an aggressive campaign against any of the great powers of Christendom. At Gallipoli the British thought themselves lucky to get their troops away. At Kut-el-Amara they were not so lucky.

To be sure, the numerical loss is small, 2970 British and 6000 Indians. The Germans reported on the same day the capture of 5600 Russians and little attention is paid to it. The Germans have lost as many in a single charge at Verdun. But the surrender of the army of the Tigris means more than these. It means the definite failure of the British attempt to take Bagdad, and Bagdad is a sort of symbol of the prize for which Germany and Great Britain have been contending. The two powers came into conflict thru the desire of each to gain possession of Mesopotamia, the land between the rivers where tradition locates the Garden of Eden, and where the great empires of the ancient world flourished for thousands of years. With this region again brought under irrigation as it was in those days it may become rich and populous as of old. At Bagdad the ambitions of the rival powers clashed. Before the war the Germans were getting to Bagdad from the west by rail and the British were strengthening their hold on the water approach from the east. When the war broke out both sides pushed forward on the same lines, the Germans building their Bagdad railroad with feverish haste thru the Taurus Mountains and over the Anatolian desert, the British taking possession of the Persian Gulf and sending expeditions up the Tigris and Euphrates Rivers.

But ten miles from Bagdad the British were turned back and the expeditionary force, caught in the bend of the river at Kut-el-Amara, has been besieged for 143 days. The world has watched with amazement General Townshend's plucky stand, for it was not expected that he could hold out long without relief. Realizing, tho faintly, what he must be enduring in the midst of a desert, surrounded by Turks and Arabs, cut off from supplies of food, medicines and ammunition, we have felt the courage which dictated the facetious messages he has sent out by wireless, his requests for new needles for his phonograph, for his dress suit, and for flower seeds to plant in the spring.

According to a government statement in Parliament, General Townshend's force consisted of "considerably more than a division," which must mean at least 25,000 men. The number surrendered, according to the same authority, was less than 9000. A simple subtraction tells us a little of what has happened during those terrible five months on the Tigris.

The blame for this foolhardy expedition rests not upon General Townshend, but upon Sir John Nixon, who was removed from command of the Mesopotamian campaign some time ago. The blunders disclosed were numerous. There was lack of light draft river boats. There was scandalous lack of medical supplies for the wounded and sick. There was lamentable lack of information about the strength of the enemy. If the statement is true that Field Marshal von der Goltz died of spotted fever the other day at Bagdad, then the Turks were commanded in person by one of the ablest strategists of the generation, whose text-books on the art of war are used at West Point. What is still less excusable is the lack of knowledge of their own men, shown by the British Government of India, the expectation that Mohammedan soldiers would willingly follow a Christian leader in the capture of one of their own sacred cities. It is said that the expedition started out with Mohammedan troops who had to be withdrawn and replaced by Hindus, because of their reluctance to attack Bagdad.

So the Tigris campaign must be added to the list of the fatal mistakes of the British command, to the Antwerp expedition, the Gallipoli expedition, the Salonica expedition, the battle of Loos and the battle of Neuve Chapelle. All these are blunders that have been publicly recognized and frankly admitted. The British soldier has everywhere fought bravely. The British fleet is supreme on the seas. The British people have cheerfully borne unprecedented taxation and raised an unprecedented volunteer army. What has kept that army comparatively inactive and unsuccessful must be mostly a matter of surmise for the present. It has held from thirty to fifty miles of the line in France and Flanders and that is about all. So far the British army has not retrieved the reputation that it lost in the Boer War.

═══

VON DER GOLTZ

VON DER GOLTZ is dead.

Von der Goltz was assassinated in Constantinople when news was received of the fall of Trebizond. No; seeing that his army was driven back by the Russians and that twenty years of labor was lost, he made a rush upon the enemy, with his staff, and was killed. No; he died from the rigors of retreat on horseback when pushed by the enemy. No; he died from spotted fever contracted at Bagdad. No? We don't know what he did die of, but it is agreed that he is dead, and his labors of twenty years in building up the Turkish army have resulted in ruin for Turkey.

His work was for war, for the glory of war, for the glory of Germany, to create a strong ally in war likely to come. His work was not quite all a failure. He drove back the British at Gallipoli, captured the army at Kut-el-Amara, and with great success he starved and slaughtered some hundreds of thousands of Armenians. He had the power and might have prevented it. Because he dared not prevent it, he assented. The curse rests on his name, for he ruled the Turkish army.

Some years before Von der Goltz went to Constantinople, a number of American missionaries and teachers went to Turkey from America with no prestige behind them, backed by no Kaiser or President, all unarmed, to preach love and knowledge. They carried books, and opened schools and colleges. They used no force, no violence, but they taught the ignorant and they healed the sick. It is in their way and not with cannon that Turkey is being regenerated, and therefore it is that in the ages to come monuments will be built and pilgrimages be made to the shrine of the soldiers of peace, and the names of Cyrus Hamlin and George Washburn and the Blisses, father and son, and a hundred other good men and women, will be held in everlasting remembrance when the name of Von der Goltz shall rot.

CHAIN CHARITY

NOT long ago the Editor received the following letter:

No. 34.

DEAR SIR—I have been asked by a friend of mine to help this party along. I am doing the necessary with one dime and trust that you will be able to do the same, and pass the letter along until it has reached No. 50.

This chain is started for the purpose of raising a fund to assist an old railroad man, Mr. W. D. Westbury, who is down and out on account of a long siege of illness. He can never get well, and having only one arm, a widowed mother, and no means of support, we will assist him in this way, and if all will respond (under the circumstances they surely will) a sufficient fund will be raised to make "Billy" comfortable while he is with us.

Please make five copies of this letter, as I have done, only changing the date and put the next highest number and date of each letter the same, sign your name and mail the five copies to your friends, whom you feel will do likewise.

This chain will end with No. 50. The party receiving No. 50 will please return the letter with ten cents and make no copies at the end of the chain.

Please do not break the chain, and I earnestly appeal to you to give it prompt attention and assist a worthy railroad boy, who has devoted his life to the cause.

Mail this letter with ten cents to Mr. W. Y. Proctor, general agent, C., M. & St. P., 309 Marquette Building, Chicago, Illinois. Mr. Proctor will see that the funds are promptly delivered.

Now, we do not begrudge ten cents to a poor railroad man. Nor the other ten cents necessary to dispatch the five letters. But before asking our friends to contribute to the worthy cause we thought it best to figure up how much the chain was bringing in, and we were pleased to find that we need not bother our friends, for the recipient of this charity was already rich beyond the dreams of avarice. This letter is Number 34, and if the other branches of the chain have gone as far as this, Mr. Proctor has turned over to Mr. Westbury the tidy sum of

$11,641,532,182,693,481,445,312.50.

This seems to us sufficient "to make Billy comfortable while he is with us," even tho he should live to the age of Methusaleh.

We appreciate the thoughtfulness of the originator of the scheme in limiting the number to fifty. Otherwise all the money in the world—or at least all the money in the pockets of the charitable—would in the course of time have flowed into the pocket of the one-armed railroad boy, and caused more ruin than the war. Even with fifty as the limit, he would have received, if our figures are right (tho they are not really our figures, but those of the expert accountant of our business office, for the Editor never had occasion to calculate such large amounts of money), the sum of

$11,102,230,246,251,565,444,236,285,680,231,712.50.

The fine thing about this is that the United States will have received two-fifths of that sum for postage on the letters. This ought to be enough to remove the deficit of the Post Office Department, and no other method has ever been able to accomplish this.

If Little Marjorie, instead of sending her ten-cent piece to Secretary Daniels to start a new battleship, had only started a multiple chain with it, the government might now be in a condition to carry out the President's desire for the biggest navy in the world.

A few months ago a New York nurse, discovering that there was a shortage of anesthetics in the hospitals of the Allies, was inspired to send out a similar chain letter asking for twenty-five cents to buy chloroform. Since nobody wants to feel that he is responsible for some poor wounded soldier suffering "untold agony," she is now receiving quarters by the bushel, and if the receipts keep on increasing in geometrical progression she will soon have enough chloroform to put all the Allied armies to sleep—or all the Germans, if the Allies used it in their asphyxiating bombs. The Post Office Department has been asked to put an end to it, but there seems to be no way of stopping a snowball when it once gets going.

It would, therefore, be well for one who contemplates sending an unlimited draft upon the charity of the world to figure out in advance just how much he is asking for and not leave it to chance or hardheartedness to prevent him from precipitating a financial crisis.

WOMAN SUFFRAGE AND THE CONSTITUTION

MR. ROOSEVELT has announced his endorsement of the movement for an amendment to the Federal Constitution extending the suffrage to women. He states the grounds for his belief thus:

I believe the time has come for a greater and truer nationalism in this country. I believe in the nationalization of the issues which affect not only men, but women also. The great problems of our country are national. In the matter of the railroads, for example, forty-six different sets of laws for their regulation merely check and handicap their development and management. A universal Federal law is essential for railroads. In the same way, the question of enfranchisement of women has become national and demands Federal action.

Mr. Roosevelt's championship of the cause of a federal suffrage amendment, if he should by any chance be nominated for the presidency, would bring this issue squarely before the country. President Wilson has repeatedly declared that in his judgment woman suffrage is a matter that should be left to the states.

Mr. Wilson is wrong and Mr. Roosevelt right. The fundamental conditions of suffrage should be the same everywhere regardless of state lines. If it is right that women should vote—and its rightness is beyond question—all women should vote, whether they live in Colorado or in New York.

Democracy, the foundation principle of the American nation, and the exclusion of women from the ballot are mutually destructive conceptions. It should be no prerogative of a state, no matter how "sovereign," to determine whether democracy within its borders shall be partial or complete.

The right of citizens of the United States should not be denied or abridged by the United States or any state on account of sex.

THE STORY OF THE WEEK

Conferring Over the Mexican Expedition The American expedition into Mexico passed last week into a quasi-diplomatic stage. The question of the future status of the expedition in relation to the de facto government of Mexico is under discussion between representatives of the War Department and of the Carranza administration. Meanwhile, the American troops mark time. Where Villa is nobody knows. He may be dead, he may be recovering from his wounds, he may be merely hiding from his pursuers, he may be planning some new offensive. Only one thing is certain. He has not yet been captured, either by his American pursuers or by his Mexican enemies.

Last week General Hugh Scott, Chief of the General Staff of the United States Army, accompanied by General Funston, went into conference at El Paso with General Obregon, Señor Carranza's Minister of War, and other Carranzista officers. No official reports of the first meeting were given out, but it was intimated with some show of authoritativeness that the two sides presented widely differing proposals.

General Obregon communicated a practical demand that the American troops withdraw from Mexico forthwith. There is no reason to believe that such a demand was entertained for a moment by General Scott, or will receive the slightest favorable consideration from the American Government. Indeed it is asserted that

General Scott informed the Mexican representatives that he was not authorized to discuss this question.

General Scott presented, it is said, the proposal that the Carranza Government cooperate with the American force in Mexico in an energetic pursuit of the Villista bandits. Up to the present time there has been little such cooperation, which ought to have been forthcoming if General Carranza had desired in good faith the success of the American purpose of punishing Villa and the bandit raiders of Columbus.

It is reported that the general conditions upon which the American representatives at the conference will insist are about as follows:

Open and effective coöperation of the Carranza forces with the Americans.

Extension of the American lines into Mexico at least as far south as Casas Grandes and probably further.

Relegation to the American military of the duty of policing "a northern zone," consisting of the territory directly south of the international boundary.

Policing of the remainder of the territory—a "southern zone"—by Carranza forces.

Coöperation in the handling of supplies for the American troops.

Granting of use of the Mexican railways to the expeditionary force.

The acceptance of these conditions would secure from the American Government an agreement that the American forces would not go farther south than an agreed upon line, and would retire just as soon as it was made evident that the Villa bands had been eliminated.

In Congress The Army Reorganization bill makes no progress in conference. There appears to be an insoluble difference of opinion between the conferees of the Senate and the majority of those of the House on three points: The size of the regular army, the proposals for a volunteer reserve army, and the establishment of a government nitrate plant. The Senate conferees are determined in their insistence upon a regular army of 250,000 men. One of the House conferees, Congressman Kahn, agrees with them, but the other two, Representatives Hay and Dent, are equally insistent upon the House provision for only 140,000. It seems probable that the conference will continue to disagree, and a complete deadlock result. In that case the House and the Senate will be asked to consider the bills again in the light of their conflicting desires.

Last week there was serious dissension in the House Democratic caucus over the Philippine bill. An attempt was made to commit the party members to the passage of the bill just as it came over from the Senate. The attempt was reinforced by a letter from President Wilson, but twenty-eight Democrats refused to pledge themselves to vote for the measure with all the Senate amendments included.

The main point of dissent is, of course, the Clarke amendment decreeing absolute independence for the Philippines in from two to four years. This amendment was one of the two points

© *Underwood & Underwood*

A PACK TRAIN CAMPING AT LAS CRUCES AFTER A THIRTY-TWO-MILE MOUNTAIN DRIVE

COLORED TROOPERS OF THE TENTH CAVALRY ON THE MARCH IN MEXICO. THEY ARE MORE POPULAR WITH THE MEXICANS THAN THE WHITES AND HAVE DONE GOOD SERVICE

that led to the break between Secretary Garrison and the President. President Wilson has apparently changed his mind on the Clarke amendment since the Secretary of War's resignation, for at that time he declared in a letter to Mr. Garrison that he believed such action was "unwise at this time," whereas now he urges the Democrats in the House to accept the bill as it stands, including this provision. In view, however, of the defection of the twenty-eight Democrats, it seems probable that the definite promise of the Clarke amendment will be at least modified, if it is retained at all.

No Strike in the Anthracite Fields The joint conference of anthracite operators and representatives of the United Mine Workers of America, which has been meeting daily behind closed doors at the Union League Club since March 9 in an effort to negotiate a new wage agreement for 176,000 miners, has resulted in an unexpected agreement. If the proposed terms are accepted by the Miners' Convention, which was to have been held at Pottsville, Pennsylvania, on May 2, there will be no strike in the hard coal fields.

At the sessions of the conference the miners presented demands which had been drawn up at the anthracite convention in Wilkesbarre, last September and endorsed at the Indianapolis convention of the United Mine Workers in January last. The miners were represented by a sub-committee consisting of John P. White, president of the union, and the heads of the three anthracite district boards. S. D. Warriner, president of the Lehigh Coal and Navigation Company, headed the operators.

The principal demands of the miners, which numbered eleven, were for an eight-hour day, a twenty per cent. increase in wages, and recognition of their union. About five weeks were consumed in a discussion of the demands in detail, and just when it seemed probable that no agreement would be possible, the operators accepted the bulk of the miners' demands. The new wage scale agreement drawn up by the conference provides for recognition of the union, for an eight-hour day instead of a nine-hour day, for specific increase in wages ranging from three per cent for day workers to seven per cent for contract miners (it being estimated that the shortening of the working day is equivalent to a general increase of twelve

and a half per cent in wages), for the establishment of a price scale for mining by machine, for an arrangement for speedier adjustment of grievances, for the readjustment of the selling of mining supplies to the individual miners by the operators, so that no more than a fair profit will be charged.

This outcome of the conference is intensely gratifying, both because it was hardly expected by those who have followed the negotiations and because it is one more victory for the cause of the peaceful settlement of industrial disputes.

A New Ambassador to Turkey Henry Morgenthau has offered his resignation as Ambassador to Turkey and it is to be accepted by the President. Mr. Morgenthau is now in this country and will take up immediately important organization work for the Democratic party in the coming campaign. The retiring Ambassador has made an admirable record in his three years at Constantinople, and the President has been reluctant to acquiesce in his retirement from the post.

Besides the important American interests in Turkey, Mr. Morgenthau has had to take under his protection the nationals of most of the allied powers. When the Turkish Government proposed to utilize Constantinople College for Girls as army barracks he put a stop to it by saying that he would move the American Embassy into the building. His vigorous protest prevented the Turks from putting British and French civilians of prominence in the towns of Gallipoli, to protect them from British bombardment. He did all that could be done to rescue the Armenians and Greeks from massacre and alleviate their sufferings.

The nomination of his successor is to go to the Senate as soon as the formal inquiries as to his acceptability have been responded to by the Turkish Government. He is Abram I. Elkus, a prominent lawyer of New York. There are few men in New York City who have such an unusual record in promoting legislation for the correction of industrial abuses and the furtherance of commercial welfare as Mr. Elkus. He was the counsel for the New York State Factory Investigation Commission, whose recent report is recognized as a model of thoroness and impartiality. The set of laws which he drew up to safeguard the lives and health of workers was subsequently

passed by the New York Legislature. He has been counsel for the Merchants' Protective Association of New York City, and has long been active in stamping out fraud in mercantile life, particularly in bankruptcy cases. He was nominated for judge of the Court of Appeals of New York on the Democratic ticket in 1913, and is now an active worker in many benevolent and civic organizations.

The Defense of the Allied Blockade The British Government has addrest to the American Government a long and elaborate explanation and defense of the blockade which the British navy has been maintaining about Germany. The note indicates no intention to relax the stringency of the blockade; but it does express a desire to make the exercise of what the Allies "conceive to be their belligerent rights as little burdensome to neutrals as possible." The note is concurred in by the French Government.

The United States has protested against the methods which have been adopted to interrupt American trade with Germany on several grounds. It has declared that these methods do not constitute a lawful blockade on several grounds:

1. Because the blockade is not, as required by international law, effective, or impartial as between neutral nations, since the British fleet cannot blockade the Baltic and thus cut off shipments to Germany from Scandinavian countries;

2. Because it involves the capture of goods destined for neutral countries, on the supposition that their actual ultimate destination is Germany;

3. Because the blockade, as administered, works unnecessary hardship to innocent shippers, since vessels are taken into British ports for examination of their cargoes, and subjected to long and costly delay before their cases are finally decided.

To these contentions the British Government makes the following rejoinders:

1. The blockade is effective, since "it is doubtful whether there ever has been a blockade where the ships which slipped thru bore so small a proportion to those which were intercepted. The passage of commerce to a blockaded area across a land frontier or across an inland sea never has been held to interfere with the effectiveness of a blockade.

2. The blockade of Southern ports by

201

the United States in the Civil War established the doctrine of continuous voyage to cover all cases where there was an intention to thwart or evade the blockade by "whatever means, direct or indirect." Much evidence is available to show that goods in great quantities ostensibly intended for neutral countries were actually destined for use in belligerent countries. For instance, the total import of lard into Sweden during 1915 from the United States was 9,029 tons, while the average annual import from all countries for the preceding three years was 888 tons. "It is difficult to believe that the requirements of Sweden in respect of lard even when every allowance is made for possible diversions of trade due to the war, could suddenly have increased more than tenfold in 1915. The inference indeed is irresistible that the greater part of these imports must have had another and an enemy destination." When the Allies found it necessary to intercept shipments of cotton to Sweden, it transpired that tho the quays and warehouses of Gothenburg were congested with cotton, none was available for the use of the spinners of Sweden. Contracts falling into British hands proved that goods were not intended for consumption of neutrals to whom they were consigned, but were in reality bound for Germany.

3. It is often necessary to bring suspected vessels into port for examination of their cargoes, because of the difficulties of making searches at sea, imposed by weather conditions, the size of modern steamships, the manner in which contraband can be concealed, and the possibility of submarine attack while the search is in progress. Vessels are also brought into port because of the necessity for close examination of all suspected persons made necessary by "the German practise of misusing United States passports to procure a safe conduct for military persons and agents." On this point the British note says further: "The difference between the British and the German procedure is that we have acted in the way which causes the least discomfort to neutrals. Instead of sinking neutral ships engaged in trade with the enemy, as the Germans have done in so many cases, in direct contravention of their own prize regulations . . . we examine them, giving as little inconvenience as modern naval conditions will allow, sending them into port only where this becomes necessary."

The note announces that an "impartial and influential" commission has been appointed to find ways to minimize delays, and pledges the Allies to makes their restraints on trade as little burdensome to neutrals as possible.

It closes with the following interesting statement:

"In every theatre and in each phase of the war has been visible the same shocking disregard by the enemy of the rights of innocent persons and neutral peoples. His Majesty's Government would welcome any combination of neutral nations, under the lead of the United States, which would exert an effective influence to prevent the violation of neutral rights, and they cannot believe that they or their allies have much to fear from any combination for the protection of those rights which takes an impartial and comprehensive view of the conduct of this war and judges it by a reasonable interpretation of the generally accepted provisions of international law. . . ."

The Irish Revolt For some months it has been noticed that the anti-British movement in the south of Ireland was growing and assuming a dangerous form. Seditious literature was printed and circulated in spite of the extraordinary powers conferred upon the government by the Defense of the Realm Act. Recruiting posters were torn town or defaced or satiric posters pasted up beside them. At the outbreak of the war civil strife seemed imminent in Ireland, for the Ulster Volunteers were openly armed and drilled to oppose Home Rule when it should pass Parliament, while in the south of Ireland the Nationalist Volunteers had been organized to fight them. But in August, 1914, the leaders of the antagonistic factions, Sir Edward Carson and John Redmond, both declared their support of the British Government and a large proportion of the Ulsterites and many of the Nationalists enlisted in the regular army. Mr. Redmond took an active part in the recruiting campaign at first, but his request to have distinct Irish brigades formed under their own officers was refused by the government. Of late recruiting has languished in Ireland and the government has not dared to apply any of the semi-compulsory measures which have been adopted for Great Britain. In spite of the promise of Home Rule after the war and of the reform measures which Parliament has passed in recent years there remained a faction of irreconcilables who would be satisfied with nothing less than complete separation. "England's extremity is Ireland's opportunity" has been their motto, and the continued failure of British armies seemed to give them their chance. The organization of this extreme wing of the Nationalist party is the Sinn Fein (Gaelic for "Ourselves Alone"), a society for the promotion of Celtic language and literature and the revival of the race spirit.

The young Irishmen who were unwilling to serve in the British army tried to escape to America, but the authorities refused to allow them to embark on any of the steamers. Many of these thereupon joined the militant organization, which daily became stronger and began openly to display revolutionary aims. The Sinn Fein Volunteers paraded publicly in arms and even practised sham battles and the tactics of street fighting in the city of Dublin. A few months ago a band of them rehearsed an attack on Dublin castle, which was theoretically captured at midnight. These various manifestations of disaffection were

Carter in Washington Herald

"WHOA!"—HAS IT COME TO THIS?

Weed in Philadelphia Public Ledger
THE TIGHT LITTLE ISLE!

called to the attention of the government, but neither Baron Wimbourne, Lord Lieutenant of Ireland, nor Augustine Birrell, Chief Secretary for Ireland, took any efficient measures to suppress them, probably for fear of making the matter worse by a display of force.

The Landing of Casement

How much help or encouragement the militant movement in Ireland received from Germany is not known. It is said, however, that some of the guns found on the insurgents are marked "made in Germany" and it is certain that an attempt was made last week to land a cargo of some 15,000 rifles on some part of the west coast of Ireland. The arms were on board a German vessel so skilfully disguised as a Dutch merchantman that she passed the inspection of the two British patrols on her way out of the North Sea. She was under convoy of a German submarine, but was captured before the arms could be put ashore. Sir Roger Casement, who had put off from the vessel in a small boat, was taken prisoner and is now confined in the Tower of London on the charge of high treason. Sir Roger Casement is well known thru his exposures of the cruelties practised in the collection of rubber, first, by the Belgians in the Congo River basin and later by the British and Peruvian companies in Putumayo on the headwaters of the Amazon. His report in the Congo case was confirmed by American missionaries and in the Peruvian case by a commissioner of the American Government.

On the outbreak of the war he fled to Sweden, where, according to his own account, the British consul tried to entrap him and offered a bribe to his servant to betray him. Since then he has been in Germany trying to enlist the support of the German Government for the Irish insurgents. He is of an erratic and irresponsible disposition and his enemies call him insane.

The Outbreak in Dublin

About the same time that Sir Roger Casement was caught at gun-running the insurgent movement came to a head in the Irish capital. Taking advantage of the absence of many of the officials at the races on Easter Monday, April 24, the Sinn Feiners gathered in the heart of the city and at noon seized the post office on Sackville Street. This and the Imperial Hotel opposite were put in a state of defense with sand bags and then the insurgents crost the Liffey River and took possession of St. Stephen's Green, a park square not far from the bridge. Here they entrenched themselves in military fashion and erected barricades on all sides by overturning tramcars, busses and automobiles. The streets were closed

A NEW SEAT OF WAR
The anti-British feeling in the south of Ireland culminated in open revolt at Dublin and elsewhere. Local disturbances are reported from the counties shaded in the above map

© *Brown & Dawson*
A PRICE ON HIS HEAD

Harding in Brooklyn Daily Eagle
"MADE IN GERMANY!"

by barbed wire entanglements. The gas works were seized and a biscuit factory and a distillery converted into fortresses. The insurgents only took such provisions and supplies as they needed, but the shops on the fashionable streets were looted by men and women.

A wireless sent out from the post office announced the establishment of an independent Irish republic and the flag of the republic, white, green and orange with a harp, was flown over Liberty Hall, the headquarters of the insurgents, and over the captured buildings. Peter Pearse, headmaster of St. Enda's School and editor of a Gaelic journal, was named as president, and James Connolly, a labor leader and the author of "Labor in Irish History," assumed the rank of "Commandant General of the Irish Republican Army."

The insurgents were many of them in dark blue uniforms, with slouch hat and black shoulder straps. The number of those actively engaged at Dublin is estimated at 1500. Their arms were various; some were modern rifles, others old guns with balls of lead slugs or iron nuts, and in some cases shotguns. They seemed to have an abundance of ammunition for they frequently fired recklessly and uselessly. But from the roofs and from the corner houses the snipers covered the streets in the center of town and picked off any uniformed soldier who showed himself. The insurgents were inspired by the presence of the Countess Markiewicz, in a neat green uniform. She is the wife of a Polish nobleman, sister of Sir Josslyn Booth, and cousin of the Marquis of Zetland. She supported the strikers of Jim Larkin in 1913 and last January, when her house was raided, revolutionary and pro-German literature was found there.

The telegraph and telephone lines leading out of Dublin were mostly cut but the one leading to Curragh Camp was overlooked and thru this the troops were summoned to the city. With their machine guns they were more than a match for the insurgents, but they made slow progress and at the end of the week the insurgents still held the center of the city. Liberty Hall was demolished by shells from a gunboat in the river. Most of the other buildings held by the Sinn Feiners were set on fire by the artillery. Trinity College, where most of the students belong to the Officers' Training Corps, was converted by them into a regular fortress, from the loopholes and windows of which the students kept up a hot fire upon any Sinn Feiners in sight. Finally, after both Pearse and Connolly were wounded or killed the remnant of the insurgents surrendered.

In the six days of street fighting the non-combatant population suffered severely. Over a hundred deaths have been reported, including women and children. Arrangements had been made for two simultaneous risings in various parts of Ireland, and in a half dozen counties these took place but none of them except Dublin seems to have been serious. The commandant of the home forces is Sir John French, recently recalled from France, and the subjection of the rebellion has been placed in the hands of General Sir John Maxwell.

The Irish Republic

The seven men who styled themselves the "Provisional Government of the Irish Republic" issued from Liberty Hall, Dublin, the following proclamation:

Irishmen and Irishwomen, in the name of God and of the dead generations from which you received the old traditions of nationhood, Ireland, thru us, summons her children to her flag and strikes for her freedom, having organized and trained her manhood thru her secret revolutionary organization, the Irish Republican Brotherhood, and thru her open military organization, the Irish Volunteers, and the Irish citizen army.

Having patiently perfected their discipline and resolutely waited for the right moment to reveal itself, she now seizes that moment, and, supported by her exiled children in America, and by her gallant allies in Europe, by relying on her own strength, she strikes, in full confidence of victory.

We declare the right of the people of Ireland to the ownership of Ireland and to the unfettered control of Irish destinies to be sovereign and indefeasible. Long usurpation of that right by a foreign people and government has not extinguished that right, nor can it ever be extinguished except by the destruction of the Irish people.

In every generation the Irish people have asserted their right to national freedom and sovereignty. Six times during the past 300 years they have asserted it in arms. Standing on that fundamental right and again asserting it in arms in the face of the world, we hereby proclaim the Irish Republic as a sovereign, independent state, and we pledge our lives and the lives of our comrades in arms to the cause of its freedom, its welfare and its exaltation among nations.

The Irish Republic is entitled to, and hereby claims, the allegiance of every Irish man and Irish woman. The republic guarantees religious and civil liberty, equal rights and equal opportunities to all its citizens, and declares its resolve to pursue the happiness and prosperity of the whole nation, and of all its parts, cherishing all the children of the nation equally, and oblivious of the differences, carefully fostered by an alien government, which have divided the minority from the majority in the past.

THE GREAT WAR

April 24—Sir Roger Casement caught while trying to land guns from German vessel on Irish coast. Irish insurgents seize heart of Dublin.

April 25—Liberty Hall, Dublin, shelled by British gunboat. Premier Asquith notifies Parliament in secret session that conscription will have to be adopted unless 50,000 have volunteered by May 27.

April 26—Second contingent of Russian troops landed at Marseilles. Zeppelins raid English coast for the third consecutive night.

April 27—All Ireland under martial law. Germans attack British lines in France and Flanders.

April 28—Germans take 5600 Russian prisoners at Narocz Lake. British battleship "Russell" sunk by mine in Mediterranean, with loss of 125 lives.

April 29—British troops clear St. Stephen's Green, Dublin. British army at Kut-el-Amara surrenders to Turks.

April 30—Dublin insurgents surrender. Russians repulse Turks near Diarbekr.

Until our arms have brought the opportune moment for the establishment of a permanent national government, representative of the whole people of Ireland and elected by the suffrage of all her men and women, the provisional government hereby constituted will administer the civil and military affairs of the republic, in trust for the people. . . .

The unfortunate British expedition in Mesopotamia has come to an end. The force under General Townshend, which was defeated at Ctesiphon near Bagdad four months ago, was overtaken by the Turks in its retreat down the Tigris, and has ever since been beleaguered in the bend of the river at Kut-el-Amara.

The expedition which was sent up the Tigris to the relief of General Townshend has not yet been able to get nearer than twenty miles of Kut-el-Amara. Here the Turks occupy a

strongly fortified position on high ground with the right resting on the river and the left protected by swamps of Suwekie, two miles to the north. The Turks also hold the southern bank of the Tigris just opposite.

The river, swollen by the spring freshets, has overflowed its banks and both sides, making it difficult for the British to advance. General Gorringe is in charge of the force on the left or northern bank and General Keary on the right. A frontal attack by General Gorringe on April 5 broke thru the Turkish lines at Umm el Henna, altho there were successive rows of entrenchments for a distance of 2500 yards stretching between the swamp and the river and the front trenches were nine feet deep.

But in trying a week later to force the next Turkish position at Felahie, five miles beyond, General Gorringe, it appears, met with a severe setback. The report from Constantinople states loss of more than three thousand men in the battle of Felahie, but according to the London report the British loss is by no means as this. Another attack on Felahie was made by a force of some ten thousand men on April 22-23, but this also was repulsed with losses to the British of some two thousand.

On the night of the 17th the Turks attacked on the right or southern side of the Tigris with ten thousand men and succeeded in driving back the British half a mile. But, according to the British report, the Turks suffered a loss of more than three thousand men, while the British losses were considerably less. In front of one of the British brigades 1200 to 1500 Turkish corpses were counted.

After holding out for 143 days against overwhelming odds General Townshend surrendered the army at Kut, numbering 2970 British and some 6000 Indian troops and their followers. He destroyed his guns and munitions before capitulating.

THE COLLAPSE OF THE BRITISH MESOPOTAMIAN CAMPAIGN

The British expedition under General Townshend, which has for nearly five months been besieged at Kut-el-Amara, has at last surrendered unconditionally to the Turks. The force which was sent up the Tigris to his relief was defeated with heavy losses twenty miles below. The shaded area represents territory acquired by the Russians and British. On another page of this issue will be found an article on the literary and historical interest attaching to this region

FROM STATE TO STATE

ALABAMA: The increasing scarcity of materials from which paper can be made has caused a revival of effort in this state to establish a large plant for the manufacture of paper, alcohol and other things from cotton stalks. For many years this subject has been discussed, but never before with so good prospect of action upon it. It is estimated that the South pays $75,000,000 a year to have its cotton stalks gathered and destroyed, whereas for $2 a ton they might be gathered, baled, shipped to central points and converted into pulp for making many useful materials.

COLORADO: Vast preparations are being made in this state for the entertainment of a large number of expected summer visitors. As a result of the war in Europe and of the two great expositions in California last year thousands of Americans who had habitually spent their summers abroad paid their first visit to the Rocky Mountain states. Many of those who passed thru Colorado were so delighted with the scenery and climate that they planned to come back for longer stays this summer. Local capitalists are therefore putting large sums of money into making the many resorts of the state more attractive. Also the United States forest officers announce that they will be glad to make surveys for summer home sites in the national forests of Colorado or to lease "special use" cabins, 279 of which have been built.

DELAWARE: After years of discussion of many various plans for improving the city's water front the people of Wilmington have generally concluded that the suggestion of Mr. Joseph S. Wilson, of the Wilson Line, is the best that has been made. He says: "Let the Chamber of Commerce consider ways and means of raising funds to employ a first-class authority on harbor improvement to come to Wilmington, study our conditions and needs and make recommendations." This course will probably be adopted.

FLORIDA: The completion of a forty-foot dipping vat at the Union Stockyards at Jacksonville marks the beginning of the end of the tick in this state. The fight against this destructive pest has been a long and a hard one, and there is still much to do before Florida takes her place among the tick-free states, but with a convenient vat large enough for the safe-dipping of horned cattle, horses and mules, and the segregating pens that go with it, the infested sections must rapidly become fewer and smaller.

IDAHO: The first jury composed entirely of women to serve in one of the higher courts of this state recently decided an appealed case in the District Court of Ada County at Boise. The case was brought in two causes involving an intricate transaction in a sale of sheep with the question of commissions to be decided. The jury allowed the commission in one cause and denied it in the other, which was precisely what the lower court had done, the the women were not permitted to know this until after their decision had been rendered. Of the venire of twenty-four women, only one asked to be excused, her reason being that her young children needed her.

INDIANA: An entertaining and instructive procession of more than 1000 employes of the City of Indianapolis recently paraded the streets of that city for the purpose of showing to the taxpayers where and how their money goes. Each department of the city government was accompanied by its machines or implements or by floats or pictures which showed the nature of its work and what it is accomplishing. Such of the more important activities as could not be thus illustrated were briefly outlined by printed banners which were easily read by the thousands of citizens who lined the streets.

KANSAS: For three years the club women of this state have been making a determined fight for a "clean Kansas." During two of these years they had little help or encouragement, but this year they have the aid of a state law and many local ordinances as well as organizations of school boys and girls thruout the state. In every community that supports a street department officials must set the machinery of the law at work on every bad spot reported by any of the women's inspectors. It is said the streets and yards are cleaner than ever before.

MISSISSIPPI: Gubernatorial abuse of the pardoning power has been for many years a subject of popular complaint in Mississippi. Now, under a new law, Governor Bilbo has appointed five citizens as a board of pardons. Those familiar with the situation, while admitting that division of authority and responsibility may do some good, say that the real trouble arises from the common practise of signing petitions for pardon without looking into the merits of the cases. It is said that in several instances in the past influential citizens have signed such petitions with so little thought that they have afterward publicly censured the governors who acted favorably on them.

NEW JERSEY: The referendum proposition, passed by the Legislature and approved by Governor Fielder, to bond this state for $7,000,000 for the construction of a state highway system provides for the payment of principal and interest from the motor vehicle department receipts, but adds that if these receipts are insufficient the payments shall be made from the state fund. Opponents of the proposition say that this contingency is not to be mentioned on the ballot for the voters. They also assert that, since no provision is made for the maintenance of roads from the motor vehicle department's funds, money for this purpose will have to be raised by taxation or by largely increased automobile license fees.

NEW MEXICO: A proclamation just signed by President Wilson changes the boundaries of the Alamo national forest in New Mexico and, among other things, provides for the restoration of 28,810 acres of the public domain. This area will be subject to settlement June 5 to July 2, and thereafter to entry and disposition under any applicable public land law. The excluded land, most of which is in rough hills, lies in the southeastern part of the state.

OHIO: The Garden Club of Cincinnati, comprising a large number of prominent women, is not confining its efforts to the beautifying of the city, but is adorning the country highways for many miles in several directions. For example, thousands of rosebushes have been planted along Wooster pike and other main roads leading into the city. As an indication of the interest this club has awakened, it is said that the 6000 rambler rosebushes which it had provided for a recent public sale were all disposed of in a single day.

OREGON: A mammoth shipbuilding plant to construct wooden vessels for river service and transoceanic trade is to be located at Portland; work upon it to begin at once. Portland, Seattle, Spokane and Eastern capital is behind the enterprise. The plant itself is to be built largely of wood, one of the objects of the project being the stimulation of the lumber industry of Oregon.

RHODE ISLAND: The commission appointed a year ago to make a detailed study of the farm situation in Rhode Island and to suggest how the state may promote a back-to-the-land movement has made its preliminary report to Governor Beeckman. It finds that farm lands are now at a minimum use, there being only 5292 farms in the state, twenty-six per cent of which are under twenty acres in extent. Among the commission's suggestions is a plan for the state to buy lands and colonize upon them. Another suggestion is that mill corporations in towns where there is much unused land buy large tracts and build next homes on five or ten acre lots, to be sold on amortization payments to their employees.

SOUTH CAROLINA: The farmers of South Carolina are said to be organizing to defeat the proposition for state fire insurance, which some of the political leaders regard as the only answer to the forced companies which have withdrawn from the state rather than submit to its new insurance laws. The farmers are calling attention to the fact that they pay taxes on about one-third of the property assessed for taxation by the state and buy only one-tenth of the fire insurance sold in the state. They also argue that, since most of the heavy losses by fire are sustained in cities, the risking of the state's money would amount to extreme discrimination against the rural taxpayers.

SOUTH DAKOTA: The commercial clubs of several counties have taken up the matter of putting the roads of this state in good condition. Each of them invites everybody who knows of a bad piece of road in its vicinity to report it. The entire influence of the club is then brought to bear, if necessary, on the officer whose duty it is to repair that road. Some of the clubs are arranging to hire men to patrol the roads of their counties regularly, as trackmen patrol railroads. As a result of the club's activities, it is said, road officials are giving more attention to their duties than ever before and the highways of the state are in better condition.

TEXAS: The State Pure Food and Drug Department, having made independent experiments which proved beyond doubt that flies carry disease germs, has begun an active campaign for the screening of all foodstuffs in the state. Inspectors have been sent out with strict orders to compel all storekeepers, hucksters and others who offer anything edible for sale to keep it covered in such a manner that flies cannot get to it. In most of the cities the women's clubs are giving active aid to the inspectors and promising to withdraw their trade from merchants who persist in violating this law.

VERMONT: Under the leadership of several large woolen manufacturers, aided by State Commissioner of Agriculture Brigham, another attempt is to be made to enact legislation favorable to a revival of sheep raising in Vermont. The first step to be taken is toward the education of the public to the necessity of restraining dogs. For many years it has seemed that dog lovers have exerted more influence over legislation than the sheep-raising interests. But now that short supplies of meats have sent prices so high, it is believed that the financial advantage of having large flocks of sheep grazing on the thousands of untillable acres in this state will be influential.

VIRGINIA: The Supreme Court of Appeals of this state has decided that Superintendent Hodges of the Alexandria County public schools must pay back $970 which he unlawfully received in the last three years as increased salary. the court holding that salaries of public officers cannot be increased during their terms of office. For many years it has been a common practise of Virginia state and county legislative bodies to alter salaries during such terms. It is believed thousands of past and present public officials will come under this ruling; and since very few salaries have been decreased, it is expected that a large sum of money will have to be paid back to the public treasuries.

© *Underwood & Underwood*

PREPAREDNESS IN PROCESS
THE NAVAL GUN WORKS AT WASHINGTON WHERE
BIG GUNS FOR THE NEW BATTLESHIPS
ARE BEING TURNED OUT

THE COMING FLOOD OF IMMIGRATION

BY ISAAC DON LEVINE

THERE has been a great deal of discussion in this country since the war began about the volume of immigration to the United States after the restoration of peace in Europe. There are those who argue that conditions in the Old World will be such after the war is over that there will hardly be any increase in the present rate of immigration, which is negligible. But the overwhelming number of authorities on immigration, among whom are the numerous representatives of immigrant aid societies as well as most of the United States Immigration officials, are of the opinion that immigration to this country after the war will assume unprecedented proportions.

It may be safely said now that this latter view has come to be generally recognized as the right one. Those who believe that for years to come this country will know no immigration problem disregard economic conditions. They hope for an era of marvelous recuperation and reconstruction in Europe, an attractive hope, but hardly justified by reason.

HOWEVER, to settle all doubts as to the proportions of the immigration following after and resulting from the European War there is one convincing source of information that has been overlooked so far, and that is to ask the immigrants who are in this country themselves about it. The millions of immigrants in the United States are linked with as many more of their relatives and friends across the ocean so closely that to them the sentiments of the people of the Old World are a certainty, and *vice versa*. And these sentiments cannot be mistaken. Whatever the foreign press in this country is saying about American neutrality and whatever the American jingo press is saying about hyphenism, the fact remains that the vast body of immigrants in America are immensely appreciative of the haven they have found here. If one considers the number of subjects of Russia, Italy, Austria-Hungary and Great Britain (the four leading contributors to American immigration) that have actually responded to the call to the colors from home in comparison with those who have not, one will discover what the immigrant thinks of America and how he feels about the peace he has found here. And whatever he thinks and feels about it, his brother or father or cousin or friend abroad is sure to think and feel.

Mr. Levine is a young Russian Jew who has been in this country several years. He worked on the staff of the Kansas City Star and has more recently been doing various journalistic work in New York. His own appreciation of the haven of America may be judged from the fact that out of his savings he has brought over, one by one, all the eight members of his family, whom at first he left behind in Russia.—THE EDITOR.

A canvass of the rank and file of the immigrant body in this country would speedily reveal the fact that with the conclusion of peace in Europe a colossal increase in immigration to America will occur. The fact that the country has proved impregnable in perhaps the greatest catastrophe in history is a recommendation that will appeal more strongly than ever to the war-tortured, tax-burdened Slav, Teuton and Saxon as well as Jew, Hungarian and Italian. If up to the present time America has attracted millions mainly because it was to them the symbol of Light, Liberty and Prosperity, how many more will she entice from now on, when it will also become the emblem of Peace, Safety and Protection?

In face of the expected vast stream of immigration, this already important and complicated problem looms up before us in all its new magnitude and demands our immediate attention. As a problem of the near future, as one that vitally concerns all parts of the country and all classes of the population, it has no equal in urgency and importance. But it is evident that the country has not yet come to realize its full import, for what preparations is she making to meet the rushing current of immigrants? Has the government taken any steps in the direction of such preparation? Has she devised any means and methods to cope with extraordinary conditions? The answers to these questions are all negative. Our government has not so far demonstrated any real disposition to deviate from the narrow course to which its immigration activities are confined, activities limited to the admitting and barring of the immigrants.

Perhaps it is in the latter that the government hopes to find a solution of all the difficulties that may arise from a heavy post-bellum immigration. Truly, an easy way of getting rid of the immigrant is simply not to admit him. But what about the

Constitution? What about the profest mission of this nation to serve humanity? What about the large foreign population's attitude toward such a means of settling the immigrant problem? How could the government turn away healthy, enterprising people who come to this haven of peace to build their homes under the protection of the Stars and Stripes? And, then, if the government prefers to deal with the immigration problem at the time it reaches its most critical stage, does she forget that at the same time she would most probably have her hands full with the financial and industrial crisis that is certain to come in this country upon the conclusion of peace? Or, is it in order to avoid this latter crisis by keeping the ammunition factories busy that the government has evolved its program of Preparedness at a time when half the world is in ruins and all the great nations are nearly exhausted physically and economically?

TO be sure, we are just at present in need of preparedness, but not with the capital "P." We must finally rise to the demands of civilization, of history, upon us, and be prepared to meet adequately the multitudes of newcomers to our shores. If this country has a mission to perform in the world in this crucial day, that is its mission. I cannot refrain from quoting a remark made by a fellow-immigrant: "If this country were to spend the hundreds of millions of dollars intended for military purposes on the immigrant, what glorious results she could achieve, what an immense amount of good and strength she would derive from it! Nothing can be more wonderful than actually building up a nation!"

Of course there are very few people in this country to whom it ever occurred that such large sums could be profitably spent on the immigrant, for there are very few Americans who are aware of the vast latent possibilities contained in the material furnished us by the immigrant. It is time, however, to drive it home to every American that it is not Tariff nor is it Preparedness that is on the *Tagesordnung* of our national life, but Immigration or Preparedness for Immigration. Immigration is the paramount question of the day, and the sooner the government and the people of these United States realize it the better for the country.

There is one good thing at least that the Preparedness movement has begotten, and that is the idea of the

Naval Advisory Board. This idea should be utilized by the government in another field, and should take there the bodily shape of an Immigration Advisory Board. The foremost naturalized citizens of this country plus a group of eminent representatives of all the classes of the country's population should coöperate with the government in an endeavor systematically to help the immigrant do what he is unable to do himself and what the country expects him to do. This board should make it its chief aim to help the immigrant become a permanent member of the nation as soon as possible, to take care of him in all the phases of Americanization, to bring out and make full use of all the potentialities of the immigrant so as to aid in the material upbuilding and spiritual uplifting of this nation.

Such a board would have at its command for its initial activities the Immigrant Head-Tax Fund amounting to about $10,000,000 and constantly growing. Many suggestions have been made for the use of this fund. Perhaps none of them deserves more attention than that proposing its employment in a colonization scheme. Immigration has so much to do with unemployment, and unemployment is to a great extent the result of the urban life of a country. To relieve the pressure upon the cities of this country by a formidable "Back to the Soil" movement would certainly serve a double purpose. It would be beneficial to the country's old citizens as well as to the new. That such a movement, backed by the government's financial support, launched among the immigrant population, would prove very successful no one who knows the immigrant will doubt. There is no one so eager as the immigrant to have his permanent home built upon the soil of this "land of the free." The large majority of the immigrants in this country have the elementary agricultural experience that should soon make of them a healthy and productive part of population, if properly supported.

There is nothing visionary or impracticable in such a suggestion. The Baron de Hirsh Fund, a private corporation, has been engaged in similar work for years. It has bought large tracts of land in Argentina, Canada and the United States, distributed it among members of the Jewish nationality, and lent them money to start as independent farmers. Thousands of prosperous colonists scattered thruout this hemisphere are a good proof of the success accomplished with the help of that fund. And when one remembers that the Jews, having been away from the soil for eighteen centuries, are not easily transformed into agriculturists, while the material at the disposal of the United States Government was originally largely rural; that the Baron de Hirsh Fund as a foreign corporation had to *buy* land and was hampered by all kinds of federal and state laws in its activities, while the United States *owns* extensive tracts of land and commands numerous facilities both as a state and as a business institution, one will be inclined to believe that the idea of immigrant colonization on a vast scale promoted by the government merits the highest consideration of the entire nation, and in itself constitutes a problem that warrants the creation of an Immigration Advisory Board.

Now is the time to tackle the immigration situation as it will be forced upon this country after the war. Now is the time to become prepared. The government should inaugurate immediately a strong organization which should make the country ready for emergencies. In the court of civilization this government will be condemned should a flood of immigration make this nation hysterical and cause it to commit grave errors. The country needs preparedness for immigration, and the government should realize that at present this is the *real* preparedness that we need.

New York City

GERMANY
BY MORRIS GILBERT

Germany?—Why that's the land
That children seem to understand.
They know about the sunny hills
Crowned with chattery bustling mills,
Where a Miller's Son may seize his staff
And swing his pack up with a laugh,
And gayly go 'mid blessings hurled
To seek his fortune in the world. . . .

And children know just how the way
Winds onward all the livelong day,
Until at last the Miller's Son
(The last, the third and youngest one)
Gets himself lost, at night, alone,
Within a forest overgrown.
But there he'll find without a doubt
Some friend to seek adventure out—
Perhaps a fiddler debonnaire
A-prancing with a dancing bear,
Perhaps a soldier old and gray
Back from the wars and out of pay,
Perhaps a talking wolf or owl,
Perhaps a giant on a prowl,
Or dwarf, or tailor's 'prentice wise
With whom a youth could fraternize.

And probably towards break of day
They'll discover far away
A tiny spark of light—and then
They'll see it is a robber's den!
And so will plot and plan to go
(The children—ah, the children know!)
And scare that robber from the spot,
And eat his meal and make his cot
Their own to use like honest men—
(The robber won't come back again) . . .

Next day the dauntless Miller's Son
Will start once more when breakfast's done
To roam the wide world up and down—
Perhaps to win a royal crown,
Perhaps to help his brothers when
They are attacked by evil men—
Always happy and fine and free
And shrewd as Miller's Sons must be,
Kindly and quick and penniless
And glad to share his merriness,
And not a bit surprised to find
A princess in a pumpkin-rind—

And that's what little children see
In Germany . . . .
                              Ah, Germany!

REFORMING THE GROCER'S BOY

ONE MORE PRIZE ARTICLE ON "THE BEST THING IN YOUR TOWN"

BY E. W. BEIMFOHR

THE best thing in our town must be locally well known and generally approved; it must contribute in no uncertain sense to the economic and moral welfare of the majority of the citizens of our community; it must exemplify the principle of "the greatest good to the greatest number." I am convinced that our Merchants' Coöperative Delivery Company best fulfils these requirements.

This company was incorporated about a year ago. Its purpose was to systematize the delivery of goods by the retail stores, especially the grocery stores, and to eliminate the waste of time, energy and money incident to individual deliveries.

The delivery equipment owned by each merchant was turned over to the company and stock was issued for its appraised value. While only fifteen merchants were original subscribers to the stock, twenty-six more added their names after the company began demonstrating its ability to handle the business. Now there remain but few merchants in the city making deliveries who are not having this work done thru the company. The manager and the delivery men were also allowed an allotment of the stock, so the company is coöperative in every feature.

Everett has a population of approximately thirty-five thousand. Both its business and residence districts are widely scattered. It was necessary, therefore, to have a central station where goods from all coöperating stores could be collected and routed for distribution. This central station serves a purpose not unlike that of the post office in receiving mail and arranging its delivery thru carriers assigned to different routes. The city was then divided into definite delivery districts. These were numbered and a map showing the boundaries of each district was posted in a place where it could be conveniently referred to.

Information regarding the proposed operations of the company was given thru a letter and time card mailed to the customers of each store coöperating. The time card showed the hours at which deliveries were scheduled to leave the stores and the hours of arrival at the homes of the customers.

The company supplied each merchant with sanitary boxes built specially for delivery purposes, and instructed the merchants and their clerks to place the order of only one customer in a box, to prevent mixing and needless handling of the goods.

On the morning the company began making deliveries, drivers called at all stores coöperating, loaded the outgoing goods and brought them to the central station for the 8 o'clock delivery. When all goods had been sorted, each driver loaded his vehicle in the order in which the goods were to be distributed in his district, made the deliveries and returned to the stores to pick up the goods for the 10 o'clock delivery. These trips were repeated at 2 and at 4 o'clock in the afternoon. This schedule has been maintained daily, except Saturdays, when three afternoon deliveries are made: at 1:30, 3:30 and 5:30 o'clock.

Each driver delivers the goods from all coöperating stores billed to addresses in his district. This eliminates entirely overlapping of territory and reduces to a minimum expense of delivery. Fifteen vehicles, eleven horse-drawn and four motor-driven, make all the deliveries for forty-one stores and are taking the place of forty-five vehicles formerly in service.

This outlines in brief the purpose, organization and operation of our Merchants' Coöperative Delivery Company. Let us now consider its effect upon the community.

Let us first consider the merchants. It has brought them together in a common cause. This closer associa-

tion developed an acquaintance which has ripened into a spirit of friendly coöperation seldom seen among competitors. It has systematized, simplified, improved and cheapened an annoying and costly item of their business. It has shifted the entire burden of deliveries upon a responsible company organized and equipped for this purpose, and has given the merchants more time for other details of their business. It has also developed greater efficiency in the service of the clerks. Orders are now put up more promptly to meet the scheduled deliveries.

The effect upon the delivery men has been entirely wholesome. They work with more spirit, knowing that when the last scheduled delivery has been made they will not be asked to make another trip on account of a few belated orders. And with a financial interest in the company, they feel a sense of ownership and responsibility which assures better service and also avoids strained relations between them and their employers.

The effect of the company has been to make the customers more thoughtful and systematic in time and method of giving their orders. These are now placed at regular hours and are more complete because given more thoughtful consideration. A careful record kept by the company shows a steady decrease in the number and a marked decrease in the size of orders given. With a time card at hand, the customers know when to place their orders and when to expect deliveries, and so the systematic service of the company is reflected in greater system in the homes.

Surely, it would seem as if a company which thus daily affects the majority of our citizens, which teaches and exemplifies system, coöperation, economy and efficiency, deserves the distinction of being considered "the best thing in our town."

Everett, Washington

THE MERCHANTS OF EVERETT ARE PREPARED TO DELIVER THE GOODS

THE PEOPLE vs. ALCOHOL

SOME WITNESSES FOR THE PROSECUTION

BY LEIGH MITCHELL HODGES

ONE summer evening five years ago the editor of one of the best-known American newspapers and a member of his staff who just had finished a 20,000-mile tour of the country were talking about the liquor situation.

"Within twenty-five years we'll have nation-wide prohibition," said the editor.

"Impossible!" exclaimed his associate. "If it ever comes, your children and mine will be dust before the day of its arrival."

That was only five years ago.

And within the past year the man who was foolish enough to use the word "impossible" has been looking into the situation thru the eyes of assorted observers.

The resultant scrap-book is so eloquent in a certain direction that even a few of its pastings may serve to strengthen the case of the People vs. Alcohol.

Because of his well-known aversion to sensationalism, Dr. Charles W. Eliot, president emeritus of Harvard, cannot be accused of anything worse than an interest in humanity when he says:

The German investigations on the mental effects of very limited doses of alcohol, doses which most people have always supposed to be completely innocuous, . . . seemed to me to prove that even twenty-four hours after taking a small dose of alcohol the time-reaction in the human being is unfavorably affected. Now the quickness of the time-reaction is important to every mechanic and to every artisan.

By way of contrast, the next whack is selected from the New York Clipper, a periodical devoted to theatrical and circus interests.

Showfolk, has John Barleycorn and his numerous offshoots been draining your bankroll? Did they eat up the better part of your earnings last season? Have you a bank account upon which to rely when the dark days come? Did booze ever do you any good?

No! We are not preaching. We are just giving you some food for thought.

Boys! There's nothing to it. Let's all get together and give old John Barleycorn and his piratical crew such a wallop that he never can come back.

The fact that this nation spent more than $2,000,000,000 on drink last year—the total cost of our public schools for the same period was less than half that sum—lends interest to the following editorial quotation from The Umpire, a paper published by and for the convicts in the Eastern State Penitentiary of Pennsylvania:

When the bill for abolishing the death penalty in New Jersey was be-

fore the State Legislature, one of the members, a former prosecuting attorney of Camden, stated that of forty capital punishment cases he had been connected with, every man who committed a murder was actuated either directly or indirectly by liquor.

Governor Goldsborough, of Maryland, recently stated that in his investigations of the many applications for pardons that have come to him since he has been the state's chief executive, he has found that in a least ninety per cent of the cases, the crimes committed by the persons seeking pardons were either directly or indirectly the result of their indulgence in intoxicating liquor. . . .

According to the report of the State Superintendent of Prisons in New York for the year ending September 30, 1914, there were received 1403 prisoners at Sing Sing of whom 860 acknowledged the use of liquor; a total of sixty-two per cent.

During the same year, 702 prisoners were received at Clinton, of whom 506 drank liquor; a total of seventy-two per cent.

At Joliet, Illinois, there were 1618 prisoners committed during the past two years, of whom only 328 were abstainers, leaving eighty per cent as drinkers of liquor.

For Exhibit Number Four I choose a dialog recently quoted in the Kansas City Star, in which a man who for years had owned saloons in that city is addressing an attorney who has filed with the police commissioners many remonstrances against the renewal of licenses:

"I want you to do me a favor," he said. "I want you to put in a protest against a license for me."

"Why, what's the matter?" asked the lawyer, astonished, as he remembered the many times the saloon owner had been before the board to urge a new location for his own saloon.

"I'll tell you something mighty serious is the matter. A fellow has filed for a license in the block where I live. Why, he wants to put a saloon just two doors from my children and I've got a daughter just growing up. I don't want her put up against a saloon two doors away."

"Why don't you file the protest yourself?" asked the lawyer.

"Say, I would be a fine person to file a protest against a saloon because it is near my home after the times I have asked for saloons in residence districts, wouldn't I?"

And following this aroused father, in my drink book, comes a man whose name is pretty generally known thruout the world—Professor Irving Fisher of Yale—who says:

In studying the conditions of health and efficiency during the last ten years, the conditions which enable an athlete, for instance, to be at his best, I have had occasion to examine the conflicting popular ideas concerning alcohol. I began the study quite willing to be convinced that alcoholic beverages had some virtues. But I have ended in

the conviction that they have none, and I have found that this conclusion is almost universally reached by those who have examined the facts.

These facts demonstrate that a man who takes alcohol, in even moderate degree, is harming himself physically, mentally, morally and economically.

Some folks have a special hankering for "government" figures. So let me insert here a note from a Government official, John H. Snodgrass, consul general at Moscow. He says that, according to statistics gathered by a reputable newspaper, the consumption of vodka during the months of July, August, September and October, 1914, was only a little more than one-tenth what it was during the same months in 1913—before the Czar's ukase against intoxicants—and adds:

It is observed in the manufacturing concerns that labor has become much more productive than before. Formerly at the Moscow mills many workmen would not appear on Monday, and a number of those who did were unfit for duty in consequence of their Sunday excesses. This is no longer the case; both the quality and quantity of labor performed have improved.

As a companion piece to this war-flavored note, it is quite in place to quote the following statement made by Colonel Maus, recently retired as surgeon-general of the Eastern Department of the United States after forty-one years of service, during which he organized the health service in the Philippines:

Practically all of the crime committed in the army, directly or indirectly, can be traced to the effects of alcohol.

And when the next edition of that ponderous and official tome, the U. S. Pharmacopeia, comes out, for the first time in its long and useful history it will contain no mention of either whiskey or brandy as drugs.

A majority of the members of the national committee in charge of the revision think alcohol should not be classed as a medicine.

Of course, there's an economic strain running thru all the quotations here given—for whatever affects health, morality or conduct is of economic importance.

But just to give the right finish, it is well to quote an official of the Du Pont Powder Company who, when issuing an order prohibiting use of intoxicating liquors by the company's workmen at Penn's Grove, New Jersey, took occasion to remark that "A man with a bottle of whiskey in his possession is as dangerous around a powder plant as a bomb thrower."

Doylestown, Pennsylvania

210

RODIN'S GIFTS TO TWO NATIONS

THE sculptor whom some critics choose to name in the same breath with Phidias and Michelangelo, and who leaves with others chiefly "an impression of the sordidness and ugliness of life," Auguste Rodin, has made a lasting expression of his devotion both to France and to her ally across the Channel. Early in the war, when the threat to Paris made it wise for the sculptor—then seventy-five years old—to seek safety in London, he presented to the British nation "as a token of his admiration for the British soldiers who have been fighting side by side with my compatriots," eighteen of his statues which were then on exhibition at the Victoria and Albert Museum. Among them were a replica of the exquisitely modeled "Age of Brass," the figure of a young man in whom the impulses of civilization have just begun to dawn, and a study for the brusque portrait of Balzac which aroused such commotion.

Medem Photo Service
AUGUSTE RODIN

Even before making this gift to Great Britain he had offered to the French nation the complete collection of his works housed in his studio in Paris, the Hôtel Biron. But there was opposition, led by Calmette, the editor of *Le Figaro*, whom Mme. Caillaux murdered, and the offer was refused. Recently, however, the good sense of the French Government has reasserted itself and the gift has been accepted, to be maintained perpetually as a museum.

"Auguste Rodin is in person a man of middle hight," wrote Camille Mauclaire in 1905, "with an enormous head upon a massive head upon a massive torso. At first sight one sees nothing of him but this leonine bust, the head, with its strong nose, flowing gray beard, and small, keen, light-colored eyes."

After "The Thinker," "The Hand of God" is perhaps the Rodin statue best known to Americans. The Metropolitan Museum in New York has a marble original. Bernard Shaw declares the hand is a reproduction of his own, and critics have pointed out how its modelling suggests the artist's hand, the creative hand. "The Wounded Lion," the photograph of which we reproduce by courtesy of the owner, Mr. Samuel P. Colt, and of *Vanity Fair*, is a recent work. It was made since the war by Rodin and is now at Bristol, Rhode Island.

Courtesy of Metropolitan Museum of Art
THE HAND OF GOD

De Witt C. Ward
WOUNDED LION

WHO GOES TO SCHOOL?

Of the 20,792,879 students enrolled in the educational institutions of this country in 1913, about 19,000,000 were in elementary schools, about 1,367,000 in high schools, academies and preparatory schools, and about 361,000 in higher institutions. These students were graded as follows:

Grade.	Enrollment. Estimated
First grade	4,480,225
Second grade	2,819,682
Third grade	2,651,912
Fourth grade	2,531,804
Fifth grade	2,150,508
Sixth grade	1,763,493
Seventh grade	1,454,643
Eighth grade	1,212,520
Total elementary	19,064,787
First year high school	560,397
Second year high school	369,752
Third year high school	252,962
Fourth year high school	183,838
Total high school	1,366,822
Higher institutions	361,270
Grand total	20,792,879

Of those above high school grade about 200,000 were in universities and colleges, about 66,000 in professional schools, and the remainder in normal schools.

The very large enrollment in the first grade of the grammar schools is due to the fact that kindergarten scholars, beginners and repeaters or retarded pupils are all included in this number. It is a somewhat remarkable fact that only about two-fifths of the students who enter high school complete the course. Out of every 1000 pupils entering the first grade of the grammar schools in 1904, only 109 will graduate from the high school in 1916. Nearly nine-tenths have fallen by the wayside for one cause or another. In 1920 the number of students completing a four-year college course will amount to about 27,000. This means that of every 1000 scholars who entered the first grade of the grammar school in 1904 fourteen will obtain a college degree. If we assume that the average length of the professional school is three years, it is probable that not more than two-thirds of the number of college graduates will obtain an additional degree. The cost of the public elementary schools in this country is $450,000,000 a year or $26 per student. The high schools cost $64,000,000 or $56 per student. The universities, colleges

THE EDUCATION OF THE VIRGIN
A sixteenth century French statue now in the Metropolitan Museum in New York

and professional schools spend $90,000,000 each year or $335 per student.

It is estimated that the following proportion of the population distributed by age groups is enrolled in schools.

Age.	Enrollment Per Cent.
Five years	18.6
Six to nine years	80.4
Ten to fourteen years	96.4
Fifteen to seventeen years	55.9
Eighteen to twenty years	16.6
Twenty-one to twenty-four years	4.8

From ten to fourteen years all but 3.6 per cent of the children are at school. After the seventeenth year the proportion falls rapidly. The Bureau of Education has estimated that in 1870 the number of years of 200 days schooling for the average individual before leaving the public school was 2.9 years. This has gradually increased until, in 1913, the average was 5.5 years.

Figures of this kind make us wonder whether grammar schools should aim primarily to enable their students to enter the high school, and whether the high school should focus attention upon college entrance examinations. Should the grammar schools have in mind the one scholar out of a hundred who graduates from college, or the ninety and nine who never get so far?

SAINT ANNA

Even in its best days, some three centuries ago, it was of a dingy color, this statue of the wise Anna and her little daughter, the Virgin Mary. Mottled and stained by time it is but one of the lesser treasures in the wonderful Hoentschel collection of Gothic art, long a loan, now recently given by Mr. Morgan to the Metropolitan Museum in New York. One would never dream of a dish of gossip with the stately gods and goddesses of the Greek sculptors, but the men and women beloved of Gothic artists are fellow-saints and sinners. They are lovable or hateful, beautiful or homely, glad or sorrowful, like our neighbors, and there is no better illustration of the intimacy and realism of Gothic art than this unpretentious brown carving by some long forgotten French sculptor. Its rough stone recalls the weather worn images of wayside shrines, but the lines are still sharp, and the figures are full of life. The Virgin's lesson is from a bound book such as Palestine never saw.

A docile little figure is the small maiden with her childish face, her long frock, her flowing hair and her gay little chaplet of flowers. Her eagerness to turn the pages to another lesson is altogether human. But the mother, with her grave, strong features shadowed by her veil, her beautiful, straight draperies, her patient hands, is so simple, so sincere, so real that one wishes one might know the name of the unknown master carver whose own mother, or grandmother, one fancies, still stands before us.

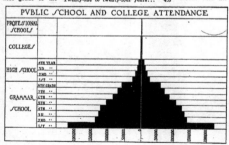

PVBLIC SCHOOL AND COLLEGE ATTENDANCE

PROFESSIONAL SCHOOLS		
COLLEGES		
HIGH SCHOOL	4TH YEAR	
	3D "	
	2ND "	
	1ST "	
GRAMMAR SCHOOL	8TH GRADE	
	7TH "	
	6TH "	
	5TH "	
	4TH "	
	3D "	
	2ND "	
	1ST "	

COLLEGE VS. WORK
The black pyramid represents the diminishing enrollment in school, college and professional school. But the large white spaces on each side are representative of the much larger number of pupils who "left school to go to work"

A LITERARY WAR MAP OF ASIA

BY EDWIN E. SLOSSON

IN The Independent of November 16 and December 21, 1914, I referred to the wealth of poetry and romance which is associated with the European battlefields. But my survey stopped with the Caucasus and the Danube and since then the war has swept over mountain and river into lands yet richer in history and legend than western Europe. In fact the latest war news comes now from countries whose wars first found record in literature, Egypt, Persia, Mesopotamia, Byzantium, Greece and Italy.

The other night a great crowd gathered in the station at Budapest to watch the first Balkan Express pull in, but their triumph was marred by the fact that the train was twenty-three minutes late, an unpardonable sin in Teuton eyes, but which Americans would be disposed to overlook, considering that the train on its way from Constantinople had to pass thru Serbian territory, where a few weeks before tracks and bridges had been destroyed.

Now if in imagination we take this Balkan Express on its return trip we arrive at Constantinople and, ferrying across the Bosphorus, we find another German railroad, the famous *Bagdad-bahn*, leading, with how many and how wide gaps none but Turks and Teutons know, to the Tigris at Mosul. This road, we may presume, is not yet open to tourist traffic. When it is we shall expect the Cook—or Koch—guide to go thru the train announcing to his party that they will here change to the river steamers, but will have plenty of time, twenty minutes, for lunching, inspecting the ruins of Nineveh on the opposite bank and listening to a lecture on the history of Assyria from B. C. 2000 to the present. Doubtless the personal conductor will conclude his peripatetic lecture at the gangplank with Rossetti's poem to the Bull-God in the British Museum:

So may he stand again, till now,
In ships of unknown soil and prow,
Some tribe of the Australian plow
Bear him afar,—a relic now
    Of London, not of Nineveh.

Curious this feeling on the part of British authors that the antipodal branch of their race will take the lead in civilization when the mother country has sunk into decay like the empires of Assyria and Rome. In Macaulay's vision of the future it was a New Zealander who sat on the broken arch of London bridge sketching the ruins of St. Paul's. Well, old England is most emphatically still in the ring, but the Australasians have given her valiant aid on the Nile, the Dardanelles, the Tigris and Euphrates.

How the hearts of our literary pilgrims will throb as the excursion steamer bears them down the Tigris to Bagdad. Those who have a good memory or a good guide book will be quoting from Tennyson:

A goodly place, a goodly time,
For it was in the golden prime
    Of good Haroun Alraschid.

Or from Southey:

Thou, too, art fallen, Bagdad! City of
        Peace,
    Thou, too, hast had thy day;
And loathesome Ignorance and brute
        Servitude
    Pollute thy dwellings now.

    . . . .

Then Pomp and Pleasure dwelt within
        thy walls,
The merchants of the East and the West
    Met in her arched bazaars;
        All day the active poor
Showered a cool comfort o'er her
        thronging streets;
        Labor was busy at her looms,
    Thru all her open gates
Long troops of laden camels lined the
        roads,
And Tigris bore upon her tameless
        stream
Armenian harvests to her multitudes.

But more will turn to the tale which was told by that wideawake lady, Shahrazad, on the Five Hundred and Thirty-Sixth Night of her marriage with the jealous Sultan of Persia:

There lived in the city of Bagdad, during the reign of the Commander of the Faithful, Harun al-Rashid, a man named Sindbad, the porter, one in poor case who bore burdens on his head for hire. It happened to him one day of great heat that . . . . . when he set his load upon the bench to take rest and smell the air, there came out upon him from the court-door a pleasant breeze and a delicious fragrance, . . . the melodious sound of lutes and other stringed instruments and mirth-exciting voices, singing and reciting, together with the song of birds warbling and glorifying Almighty Allah in various tones and tongues, whereat he marveled to himself and was moved to mighty joy and solace. . . . .

Now we have a right to include Bagdad in our literary war map because General Townshend's soldiers got within sight of its minarets when they were defeated by Turks and driven back down the Tigris to Kut-el-Amara, where they were besieged. But the fighting mostly took place at Ctesiphon. Here, under the shadow of the great palace of Chosroes, General Townshend was checked and turned back, as was the Emperor Julian sixteen centuries and a half ago. The Apostate Emperor retreated up the Tigris to Samara, the present terminus of the German railroad from Bagdad. Here he was struck down by a Persian javelin and died with the words upon his lips—or, if tradition be uncredited, at least the feeling in his heart,—of "Thou hast conquered, Galilean!" The life of Julian the Apostate has so often figured in literature that I may only mention Merejkowski's novel *The Death of the Gods*, Ibsen's drama *Emperor and Galilean* and Swinburne's poem.

Just across the Tigris River from the Parthian city of Ctesiphon was the Greek colony of Seleucia, founded by Alexander the Great, and here also the British met with defeat and were driven back into that region from which our first parents were with equal reluctance driven out. Poor Tommy Atkins, I fear, will come back skeptical, for in his opinion the Garden of Eden is "not what it was cracked up to be," to which, however, the orthodox will reply: "But you should have seen it before the fall."

The other British column under General Brookings is at Nasirjeh on the Euphrates, better known to some of us as "Ur of the Chaldees," where Abraham was born. General Townshend's expedition, which has surrendered at Kut-el-Amara, was some sixty miles from Babylon, so we need not yet consider its ten thousand years of history and legend, but will hasten on eastward to Persia, where the British from Shuster and the Russians from Hamadan are trying to get together. It is an ancient and well-worn highway, this from Ctesiphon to Susa, and we will use the vehicle of verse provided by Nicholas Michell since he goes our way, tho at a stage coach gait:

Two cities molder here—and can it be,
Seleucia ! Ctesiphon! we gaze on ye?
Boast of the Greek and pride of Parthia's kings,
How has your glory flown on eagle wings!

Far south of Ctesiphon, where Ulai flows,
That heard of old the song of Israel's woes,
Ye meet a shapeless building, low and rude,
Wild as the scene, where all is solitude.

    . . . .

Towers near a mighty mound—'tis all ye see
Of Persia's boast, of Susa's majesty.

Susa! that held the wealth of Persia's kings,
Gold, silver, gems and luxury's sweetest things;
Susa! the pleasant city of delight,
With groves so shady and with streams so bright,
Where sang the bulbul to his flashing rose,

Half matched by Beauty's lyre at evening's close.

Yet interest haloes still fair Susa's name,
And hearts unborn shall treasure up her fame,
Shall thrill sweet Esther's varied tale to hear,
And for the wrongs of Vashti ask a tear.

Shuster, the center of the oil fields which the British Government bought up shortly before the war to supply their navy, was not, as we might suppose, named after our young American financier who tried in vain to rescue Persia from bankruptcy. It is derived instead from the old Persian capital of Susa or Shushan, whose ruins are near. Here reigned Ahasuerus over an empire extending from Ethiopia to India and here hung Haman on a gallows fifty cubits high. The Jews to this day celebrate by their Feast of Purim their narrow escape from massacre. What a pity they had no Esther in the court of the Czar to save them from the horrors of Kishinef. At Susa the tourist will be shown the tomb of Daniel, and he may believe it or not as he please. He may exercise a similar option of credence or incredulity as to the legend that from Susa came Memnon whom Achilles slew upon the plains of Troy, not far from where the French landed in their recent attempt to take the Dardanelles.

The Russians moving down from the north to join the British at Shuster have passed Hamadan and reached Kermanshah, where the rugs come from or are supposed to. Here are to be seen the monuments of Sapor III of the Rawlinson's Seventh Great Monarchy, the Sassanian or Later Persian empire.

Hamadan is the ancient Ecbatana, with its seven walls each of a different color, the outermost white, the next black, then scarlet, blue, orange, silver and finally gold. It must have looked like a Bakst stage setting. Within the golden citadel dwelt Cyrus the Great and his successors, ruling his wide realm by laws which differed in durability from ours. Chained to the palace door in the time of Darius might have been seen the last of the Median kings, his nose, ears and tongue cut off. Here Alexander put to death his last safe councillor, Parmenio, and here are still to be seen, or at least to be shown, the tombs of Esther and Mordecai.

But to get the best stories of those times and places you must hunt up your grandfather's big Bible. Somehow there have been drop't out from our modern Bibles two sections which used to lie between the Old

Testament and the New, and which used to interest me when a child quite as much as any other parts. One section contained the records of births, deaths and marriages of the family, and the other contained some good stories and very sensible advice. The child of today knows Judith thru Griffith's movies, tho he gets the impression that the scenery about Bethulia looks remarkably like that about Los Angeles. The story of Judith begins by telling us that the walls of Ecbatana (alias Hamadan) were 105 feet high and 75 feet wide. Then the scene shifts to Nineveh (alias Mosul), where King Nebuchadnezzar and his army celebrated their victory by a banquet that lasted a hundred and twenty days. This, I guess, beats the Broadway record on banquets both for numbers and duration. Starting from the Tigris at Mosul his chief captain, Holofernes, marched eastward by the German Bagdad railroad route, then south along the line of the Aleppo and Jerusalem Railroad, which the Germans will take if they go to Suez. The rest of the story is familiar to the movie fan.

But let me direct his attention to the book that lies next to Judith in the Apocrypha and is called Tobit, because this, so far as I know, has not yet been used in motion pictures, altho it would make a fine scenario. In it he will find the same towns named, for Tobias journed from Nineveh-Mosul to Ecbatana-Hamadan accompanied by his man-servant and his dog. At Ecbatana he found his cousin Sara, who had become unpopular among the eligible young men of the city because her seven bridegrooms had been strangled in succession by the demon Asmodeus, who was in love with her himself. But his man-servant, who turned out to be Raphael, one of the seven holy angels, showed him how to get rid of the demon and marry the girl in safety. It was a simple expedient but effective, just throwing some fish liver on the coals. But anybody who has smelt burnt fish will know why the demon Asmodeus flew away to the Sudan and never came back.

The line of march which the Russians are taking from Erzerum by Lake Van to Bagdad is familiar to all the older college graduates. They know what a hard road to travel it is, for they have painfully plodded over it, day by day, parasang by parasang. But Xenophon took it in the reverse direction from the Russians, marching up from near Bagdad to the mountains overlooking Trebizond, where the shout of "Thalassa! the sea!" burst fom the lips of the Greeks.

May Sale
at McCutcheon's

THE time for our May Sale has come 'round once more and finds us wholly prepared for it.

Table Linens, Bed Linens, Towels, etc. Our stocks have never been more abundant notwithstanding the constantly limiting supplies in the hands of manufacturers, and the difficulties of transportation. While prices are not quite so low as a year ago, we are able to offer Housekeeping Linens at this time at prices which are for the most part much below present market values.

Ladies' Suits, Dresses, etc.—The styles and models are so attractive this season that this Department has won a great many new friends and has caused much favorable and congratulatory comment on the variety, values and styles exhibited.

French Lingerie—We considered last year's display remarkable, especially under war conditions, but this year's display is larger and better. Happily the war has not noticeably changed the prices.

Our assortment of American-made Lingerie is equally complete and attractive.

Booklet describing goods offered at May Sale, free on request

Mail Orders receive our prompt attention

James McCutcheon & Co.
Fifth Ave., 34th and 33d Sts., N. Y.

Reg. Trade Mark

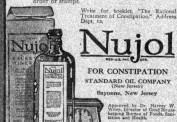
Trebizond, which the Russians have just captured, has a strange and romantic history of more than twenty-five centuries. It was originally a Greek colony, which, of course, was why the Ten Thousand Greek mercenaries under Xenophon fled there for refuge. After the fall of Byzantium in the Fourth Crusade, A. D. 1204, a young man of twenty-two, Alexius Comnenus, propelled by an ambitious mother, set himself up as "Emperor of the Romans" at Trebizond. This upstart empire lasted, until 1461, when Sultan Mohammed II captured Trebizond. After that it remained Turkish until it was taken by the Grand Duke Nicholas of Russia on April 18, 1916.

So far as I am aware, no poet, novelist or dramatist in English has used the Empire of Trebizond as a *mise en scène*, which seems strange considering its wealth of picturesque material. It was at that time the richest and most luxurious city in the world, renowned alike for the beauty of its scenery and its inhabitants. But enervated by ritualism, athleticism and similar vices, the splendid city was easily conquered by the vigorous young republic of Genoa. It happened that a Genoese merchant was struck by a page, the favorite of the Emperor, in a quarrel over a game of chess. The Genoese came back with two armed galleys, took the palace, and cut off the ears and noses of everybody in it—except the page; he was kicked downstairs.

In their march inland to the Tigris the Greeks under Xenophon took much the same route as is now being used in sending the Turkish and German troops from Aleppo to Mesopotamia; that is, the line of the projected Bagdad railroad. This is the old "Royal Road," the ancient and the modern channel of communication between Occident and Orient, followed by Alexander, the Greek, when he conquered Persia, followed by Xerxes, the Persian, when he set out to conquer Greece.

From Ecbatana departing
Or Susa or the Kissian fortress,
Forth they sped upon their journey.

So says Aeschylus in *The Persians*. And now the British are departing from Susa and the Russians from Ecbatana for the same destination, and along the same route as Xerxes took nearly 2400 years ago, when, with 2,000,000 men, he crossed the Dardanelles into Gallipoli over a pontoon bridge strewn with myrtle boughs, and perfumed with incense. Here we must leave him for the present, for to follow him would carry us into a region too rich in literature and legend to be here considered.

The New Books

SOULS ON FIFTH

Granville Barker calls Fifth avenue "a relentless street." In a weird, arresting story he finds it just before dawn swept by a swirl of souls, drifting before the wind, aimlessly and endlessly. A spiritual gravitation holds them to the spot which was their highest ambition while they were alive. "We can achieve no new desires here," he is told by a restless, dissatisfied Soul, unhappy in its eternal drifting. The story of the soul of a former popular pastor, the Rev. Evan Thomas, is most interesting in its delineation of the gradual hardening of an eager spirit of helpfulness into a contented worldliness; and he explains, in part, why the souls are there: They had taken Heaven so much for granted that it had become the vaguest of ideas to them, and had entirely ceased to believe in Hell. "Now people cannot possibly go to places they don't understand or believe in—'a man died and went to his own place.'" The description of the sermons he had found palatable to his fashionable flock is full of veiled but biting sarcasm. The story ends on a less tragic note in the finding of the Little Soul of a finer quality than the rest. *Souls on Fifth* is a modern "morality," provoking the query: What is the highest ideal of the average New Yorker?

Souls on Fifth, by Granville Barker. Boston: Little, Brown. $1.

WAR BOOKS AT RANDOM

Occasionally a narrative comes to hand which for its unaffected simplicity, its total lack of striving for effect, produces in the reader an equal liking for the book and its author. In this not easily won class we place William J. Robinson's *My Fourteen Months at the Front*. At the outbreak of war, this young American found himself in London with business connections severed. Stirred by the onsweeping enthusiasm around him, he enlisted as a trooper in the Fifth Dragoon Guards. He faithfully tells of the beginning of a soldier's career, which had barely proceeded beyond a drastic initiation when at his own request he was ordered to the front in Flanders.

Of those fourteen months of almost daily peril, dread periods when the "fear of God" was truly upon him, he writes in straightforward fashion. He frankly confesses to terror, but out of it wins respect by sticking to his task as a staff motor car driver, a task that led him along the Ypres road to one of the most calmly heroic and horrible incidents thus far recorded. He came to know the British soldier as a comrade, and he was "proud to belong to such an

The Story of the Fact-Hunters

T O every intelligent man or woman the march of world events that came to so shocking a climax in August 1914, is of course common knowledge."

Jamieson read this aloud to his wife from an editorial in his favorite magazine.

"Such momentous affairs as the Ems telegram," continued the editorial, "Fashoda, the Kiel Canal, the Helgoland bargain—such names as Boulanger, Algeciras, Marchand, Delcasse, Lord Lansdowne, Zola, von Buelow, Draga, Kirk Kilisseh, Jaures, Bagdad, Erzerum, Verdun, Salonika, Dardanelles—all of these and many more must of necessity be readily familiar to any one who would so much as attempt an intelligent discussion of the war.

"And likewise such matters as the influence of the war on fine arts, science, political science, economics, engineering, politics, government, law, literature, etc."

Jamieson put down the magazine and stared blankly at his wife, who stared blankly back.

"Whe-ew!" said Jamieson, finally.

"Gracious!" exclaimed Mrs. Jamieson. "Why, I hardly know any of those things."

"And I've been airing my opinions about this war pretty thoroughly for about two years now," said Jamieson, gloomily.

"Well, it's high time we began to collect facts," said Mrs. Jamieson, briskly. "Where can you and I find out about those things?"

* * * *

The Jamiesons' hunt for facts took them to many places—to their book store, where the amount of reading necessary to get any comprehensive survey of what they sought frightened them away; to their newspapers, where they found only tantalising hints of the big, vital things they were after; to the library, where books and magazines seemed strangely antiquated; and finally to their librarian, Mr. White, who said: "My dear friends, what you want is an Encyclopædia. Only an Encyclopædia can answer these questions; everyone who wishes to read intelligently should have an Encyclopædia at hand. Every subject in the editorials to which you refer is covered by a first-class Encyclopædia, provided, of course, that it is late. It must be late, remember. An Encyclopædia five or ten years old will not be satisfactory. And it must be easily consulted—no confusing index to direct you to different places where you get only smatterings of information which you must patch together to obtain the facts you want. Each subject should have its own article and the subjects arranged alphabetically like the words in a dictionary."

"Well, Mr. White, where can we get such an Encyclopædia—is such a work published?"

"Oh, yes. Dodd, Mead & Co., Inc. are now publishing a thorough, complete revision of the New International Encyclopædia. It is late, just now coming from the press. It is authentic, prepared by the best men whom money can interest; it is easily consulted, every subject has its own article; no index is necessary; a schoolboy can understand it; its language is not technical."

Full information regarding this work, how it can be obtained, etc., will be given anyone sending us the attached coupon. Better mail this today.

army." He praises the British officers under whom he served, and he reveals the peculiar characteristics of the British soldier better than has any other war writer.

Arthur Ruhl is an extremely rapid literary traveler. In his *Antwerp to Gallipoli* you have no sooner thrillingly escaped with him from Antwerp to Paris and from the aftermath of the Marne, than he whisks you off to Bordeaux. You are just beginning to settle down comfortably there with the French Government in secure semi-exile, when you turn a page and—presto! —you find yourself in the middle of Berlin. Then you begin to learn things not hitherto imagined. You gather that "nobody had ever heard of Bernhardi," "Treitschke—who was he?" Prussian militarism is a foreign invention, and the Ruhleben British prisoners' camp has quite a cheerful atmosphere. You are eager to know more about all this, but no, this tireless spirit is off again to dandified Rumania, stately little Bulgaria, the amiable Turks at Gallipoli, charming Austria, and the dust of a Russian retreat. You have been going at a terrible pace with Mr. Ruhl, but nevertheless grasped the impression that the Teutonic Allies treated him very well indeed. England ought straightway to catch this traveler and entertain him at a Lord Mayor's banquet, to beat the Germans in the social field, otherwise he will likely accept an Iron Cross—"of the second class worn inside." As it is, his graphic and entertaining book will please those of German sympathies.

It has been forecast that none of the countries involved in the war will present the same national and social aspects as heretofore. To us in the United States the outlook for our close kin to the north must appear as a bright, and progressive future. It is with this attitude we read *Canada in Flanders*, by Sir Max Aitken. What can we add to this record of a young people rising spontaneously to the summons of what they believe to be manifest duty, passing in splendid manner thru their national baptism of fire, to stand in the breach and hurl back the foe where an empire tottered? Ypres, Festubert, Givenchy; is it too much to venture the prediction that after the war these names will be found to have given historic birth to a nation—no longer a dependent colony, but taking equal part and responsibility with Great Britain herself, Australia, New Zealand and South Africa in the affairs of empire?

If politics are said to make strange bedfellows, war would seem to make extraordinary ones. Otherwise there is no accounting for *The War Lords*, by A. G. Gardiner. Even so it takes mental ingenuity to group President Wilson and Karl Liebknecht with Von Bernhardi, the German Crown Prince, and Ferdinand of Bulgaria, the "old fox of the Balkans." The author has courage even to the point of rashness. As to Herr Dernberg, he is "stupid," while Mr. Bryan impresses him as "a quiet, still man, who does not live with his ear to the ground and his eye on the weather-cock, who refuses to buy popularity with infinite handshaking and robustious speech." One feels inclined to make a note of "robustious speech" for future use. About the rest of his war lords Mr. Gardiner writes in a robustious (that word simply will not keep off the paper), sure-about-everything style. If he had applied the art of shading his characters a trifle—not presenting them for the most part as either white or black—and adopted a less toplofty method of expression, he would have saved himself in places from being regarded as amusing when he apparently intended to speak with almost desperate earnestness.

In presenting the case for Italy, W. O. Pitt in *Italy and Her Unkoly Alliance* lucidly and logically argues that no other course was open to her but to break with the Teutonic Alliance and cast in her fortunes with the Entente Powers. The long struggle for Italian national unity was jeopardized by an old peril from the north, commercial as well as military, carried on with every device toward the subjugation of her bitterly won liberties. It was the voice of the Italian people which would not down, and the king was heartily in accord with his subjects. There may be, of course, another view, but this is a strong defense of Italy's action. While his sequence of historical and political data will need an able controversial pen to outweigh him, Mr. Pitt is also personally well equipped for his task by a sympathetic grasp of Italy's economic and other problems. It is a book to be read by everyone wishing to know why Italy entered the war.

My Fourteen Months at the Front, by William J. Robinson. Boston: Little, Brown. $1. *Antwerp to Gallipoli,* by Arthur Ruhl. Scribner. $1.50. *Canada in Flanders,* by Sir Max Aitken. Doran. 60 cents. *The War Lords,* by A. G. Gardiner. Dutton. 40 cents. *Italy and the Unholy Alliance,* by W. O. Pitt. Dutton. $1.

THE BUSINESS WORLD

TRUST CASES

Some four hundred pages of new matter is included in the revised edition of W. Z. Ripley's *Trusts, Pools and Corporations.* This book deals with the topic by applying the principles of economics to discussions of recent notable cases in point.

Ginn. $2.75.

WORLD COMMERCE

Professor Russell Smith's *Commerce and Industry* is designed as a textbook, but is such good reading, so admirably illustrated by diagrams, maps and pictures, that anyone will find it interesting and will gain from it in a brief time a comprehensive view of natural resources and their modern utilization.

Holt. $1.40.

HOW TO BECOME AN ENGINEER

The vocational guidance movement creates a demand for definite information regarding various occupations. In *Engineering as a Career,* F. H. Newell and C. E. Drayer have added a volume of papers by prominent engineers. Amid the many platitudes about advice and application, industry and honor, are scattered a number of valuable suggestions as to the requirements in various branches of engineering service, and as to opportunities.

Van Nostrand. 75 cents.

COMMERCIAL OPENINGS

From the Cleveland Educational Survey may be obtained *Boys and Girls in Com.*

mercial Work, by B. M. Stevens, a report (one of a series of twenty-two forthcoming monographs) on the work, wages and training, opportunities for promotion, etc., of those entering the various commercial offices of that city. While the study is based on local statistics, still the appeal raised in behalf of the potential wage-earner who will have to shoulder business responsibility, however limited, is one that should be recognized by schools and ruling powers.

Cleveland, Ohio: Cleveland Foundation. 25 cents.

ADVENTURES

IN THE ROCKIES
If you like exciting stories, stories full of hard riding and gun play, stories where the hero would have died seven times before the happy ending, if he had not been the hero, then read *Nan of Music Mountain*, by Frank H. Spearman. It is a well written story of what happened when Henry de Spain, manager of the Thief River State Line, fell in love with Nan, one of a family of outlaws.

Scribner. $1.35.

A ROMANCE OF ENGINEERING
The Cyrus Townsend Bradys have taken two magnificently dramatic romances of engineering and diluted them with a very bad love story. *Web of Steel*, so long as it deals with engineers in the wilderness is interesting. The fall of a great bridge and the heroic struggle to save a dam are well told. The men in these scenes are real, but we could dispense with the other characters without a tear.

Revell. $1.35.

A GOOD WHALING STORY
The Real Story of the Whaler, by A. Hyatt Verrill, is the history of the rise and progress, decline and fall of the whaling industry. Its romance and adventure, the hardihood, the daring, the courage required in the day's work, are clearly pictured. Here are interesting data, concerning whaling ship logs, and their quaint, symbolic illustrations, whaling chanteys, "gamming," and the whaler's scrimshaw work.

Appleton. $2.

IN THE ADIRONDACKS
In *The Shepherd of the North*, Richard Aumerle Maher has minded a rather forceful plea for the Catholic Church with a plot involving thrilling adventure in a forest fire, a fight with an unprincipled railroad company and a murder trial. The hero, a Catholic bishop, of New England extraction, with a diocese on the Canadian border, is fairly well done, but the other characters are uninteresting.

Macmillan. $1.35.

AN IDYL OF CRIME
F. Berkeley Smith has written a picturesque tale of provincial France, Montmartre and the underworld of crime. Theft is treated as an interesting game, the of course it is better to live honestly if you can afford it. The hero is a dashing gentlemanly rogue, and the heroine, *Babette*, a peasant girl for whose sweet sake he reforms and becomes a detective. *Babette's* father, keeper of the dungeon at La Fourche, is a person worth meeting.

Doubleday, Page. $1.25.

LAST STORIES
A long short story, *Somewhere in France*, gives the title to the book published just before Richard Harding Davis' sudden death. The principal character is Marie Gessler, a German adventuress, useful to the German Intelligence Department, who in ordered to remain in an old chateau at Neufchelles after the German retreat, to aid in relaying messages to their general staff. Five tales on other themes make up the book, written with all this author's skill, strong characterization and polished style.

Scribner. $1.

MR. PURINTON'S EFFICIENCY QUESTION BOX

246. *Mrs. A. M. L., Ohio.* "I should greatly appreciate a list of publications to which I may submit an article on health conservation."

Health magazines pay little or nothing for general articles. Their contributors are mostly people who have a hobby to ride or pet theory to lead around in public, or who strenuously desire to see their name in print. Only writers with an established reputation, or experimenters who have done something novel and useful, may reasonably hope for adequate pay from health journals.

A few representative magazines are as follows: *Health Culture, Passaic, New Jersey; Physical Culture,* Flatiron Building, New York; *Herald of Health,* 110 East Forty-first street, New York; *Health,* Eureka Springs, Arkansas; *Brain and Brawn,* Los Angeles, California; *Good Health,* Battle Creek, Michigan; *Your Health,* Burke, Sonoma County, California; *Nautilus,* Holyoke, Massachusetts.

247. *Rev. S. C. S., Nebraska.* "I am a Baptist minister, with two small children. Have just returned from four years of missionary service in Burmah, India. Have had full academy and seminary training, but no college education. I feel I could do more efficient work if I could take a college course; but I have no money for this purpose, and a family to maintain. What do you advise?"

Get over the notion that a college course is fundamental to efficiency and usefulness. It is not. For a man who has done pioneer service in India to go back and herd with college striplings would be like sending a master road-builder to a kindergarten. You probably know more about life than the average college professor—why pay him to teach you?

There are special studies that you could take to advantage by correspondence. Make a list of these from a good college catalog. Then apply to your State University, to the University of Chicago, and to the University of North Dakota, for particulars of all extension courses given by mail. Try to take a summer term at the University of Chicago.

248. *Miss I. G., Minnesota.* "I am a teacher of languages, like the work, and think I have a talent for translating. I could do plays or scientific articles, but prefer the fiction of Keller, Storm, Heyse and men of that school. Is there a field for such translating?"

A limited field, already somewhat crowded. You would have a much better chance if you first became an authority, made a name for yourself, in some branch of English literature. Unknown translators have a harder time even than unknown authors. Ask the Professor of German in several colleges near you for names of publishers of German books and periodicals—then write the publishers. Consult also the secretary of the Deutscher Akademischer Bund, 225 Fifth avenue; of the German Historical Society, 1650 Second avenue; of the German Press Club, 21 City Hall place; of the German Publication Society, 507 Fifth avenue; all of New York City.

249. *Dr. L. M. D., Connecticut.* "Should a man past thirty change his profession for work more congenial? I am a physician of thirty-five, with a good practise; but I realize now, from a study of vocational science, that my talents lie in the realm of business. Should I stay in medicine and be always discontented—or give it up and waste all the years of medical training?"

Neither. A wise man does not "choose between the lesser of two evils." He learns to find, and to blend, the good in both "evils." Your age is immaterial—a man is never old while he has something to learn and to love. But your previous training should not be lost, and need not be.

The Kingdom of the Subscriber

In the development of the telephone system, the subscriber is the dominant factor. His ever-growing requirements inspire invention, lead to endless scientific research, and make necessary vast improvements and extensions.

Neither brains nor money are spared to build up the telephone plant, to amplify the subscriber's power to the limit.

In the Bell System you have the most complete mechanism in the world for communication. It is animated by the broadest spirit of service, and you dominate and control it in the double capacity of the caller and the called. The telephone cannot think and talk for you, but it carries your thought where you will. It is yours to use.

Without the co-operation of the subscriber, all that has been done to perfect the system is useless and proper service cannot be given. For example, even though tens of millions were spent to build the Transcontinental Line, it is silent if the man at the other end fails to answer.

The telephone is essentially democratic; it carries the voice of the child and the grown-up with equal speed and directness. And because each subscriber is a dominant factor in the Bell System, Bell Service is the most democratic that could be provided for the American people.

It is not only the implement of the individual, but it fulfills the needs of all the people.

AMERICAN TELEPHONE AND TELEGRAPH COMPANY
AND ASSOCIATED COMPANIES

One Policy　　One System　　Universal Service

"Don't tell me you never had a chance!"

"Four years ago you and I worked at the same bench. I realized that to get ahead I needed special training, and decided to let the International Correspondence Schools help me. I wanted you to do the same, but you said, 'Aw, forget it!' You had the same chance I had, but you turned it down. No, Jim, you can't expect more money until you've trained yourself to handle bigger work."

There are lots of "Jims" in the world—in stores, factories, offices, everywhere. Are you one of them? Wake up! Every time you see an I. C. S. coupon your chance is staring you in the face. Don't turn it down.

Right now over one hundred thousand men are preparing themselves for bigger jobs and better pay through I. C. S. courses.

You can join them and get in line for promotion. Mark and mail this coupon, and find out how.

I. C. S., Box 4508, Scranton, Pa.

FACTS, arguments, briefs for debates. Outlines, literary, historical, scientific and other material for club papers, orations, speeches and lectures. BUREAU OF RESEARCH, 316 E. 5th Street, New Albany, Ind.

EVANSTON ACADEMY
of NORTHWESTERN UNIVERSITY

A preparatory school emphasizing high scholastical standards, wholesome and carefully directed athletics, literary and social activities, and attention to individual needs and interests.
All the advantages of Northwestern University gymnasium, libraries, lectures and debating societies. Write for "Student Life."
E. W. Marcelius.   Box 50, Evanston, Ill.

The large corporations, foundations, and civic associations now employ physicians on their staff, to conduct health research, offer health advice, prepare health publications. Get literature of Safety First Society, 6 East Thirty-ninth street; Life Extension Institute, 25 West Forty-fifth street; United States Steel Corporation Safety Exhibit, 71 Broadway; The Rockefeller Foundation, 61 Broadway; then plan how to remain a physician, but enlarge your field of action.

250. Mrs. A. T. K., New Jersey. "I have grown up in the habit of speaking very slowly, drawing out the syllables in a monotonous way, tho I am seldom conscious of it. My friends say it is a strain on their nerves to hear it. Would you kindly suggest some kind of exercise that would help me to overcome the habit?"

The best one we can think of is a college yell. Or, a "rag-time" selection in six-eight or two-four times, sung twice as fast as the tempo indicates, would be almost as effective. Consult Grenville Kleiser, care Funk and Wagnalls, 354 Fourth avenue, New York; or the Emerson College of Oratory, Huntington Chambers, Boston; or the Department of Elocution and Public Speaking of your State University. Get a big sheet of cardboard, print on it in large letters "TALK FASTER," hang it over your table, where you will see it the first thing every morning.

251. Miss L. S. R., Pennsylvania. "How can I discover a nurses' training school that will teach one how to care for both mind and body?"

Ask the editor of American Medicine, 20 East Forty-first street; editor of Trained Nurse and Hospital Review, 28 West Thirty-second street; Superintendent of New York Medical College and Hospital for Women, 19 West 102d street; all of New York City.

252. Miss B. P. H., Tennessee. "Please advise me how I may best dispose of photoplays. Also please tell me if little verses or rimes suitable for occasions are ever in demand, and by whom."

First make sure that your plot is in acceptable form. Have you read a standard book, or taken a correspondence course, on photoplay writing? Do you study regularly one of the best motion picture magazines, for suggestions and cautions? A few leading companies are these: American Vitagraph Company, 116 Nassau street; Pathé Frères, 115 East Twenty-third street; Reliance Motion Picture Corporation, 20 Union Square; Colonial Motion Picture Corporation, 18 East Forty-first street; Imperial Motion Picture Company, 1476 Broadway; Thanhouser Syndicate Corporation, 71 West Twenty-third street; all of New York. Ask these companies if they will consider your productions.

You might compose verses for a local advertising agency on goods to be advertised; for a city newspaper on current events or topical themes; for a publisher of Christmas or birthday cards—ask your bookseller or stationer for addresses of such publishers.

253. A Woman Reader from Georgia. "I was a successful teacher till seven years ago, when a great family sorrow broke something in me so that I have lost my power of decision. I went into mission work, to try to forget my trouble; but am now secretary of a college for well-to-do girls. A position is offered me in the far West, to teach delinquent girls—wards of the Juvenile Courts. This is my problem: Can I do more good by staying here and helping to build up this school, or by serving and advising the other 'down-and-out' little sisters? I have debated the question too long to see it straight."

While it is hardly within the province of an efficiency counsel to offer suggestions in so personal a matter, we shall say your finest work would be for the "down and out" little sisters. Your own sorrow will put you in touch with those who have suffered; and enable you to fill their needs. Unfortunately, the girls of modern well-to-do families have not had sufficient pain or privation to render them susceptible to your kindness and sympathy. To reclaim, guide and develop the wayward girls who never had a fair chance seems to us a nobler, and also more fascinating, life work than to become a cog in the wheel of a classical institution.

PEBBLES

Portugal is having by far the nicest war of all.—*Syracuse Post-Standard.*

Anyway, Villa's invasion of the United States has been changed to evasion.—*Brooklyn Daily Eagle.*

Lucky for Bryan that he reserved a seat at the press table for the St. Louis convention.—*Philadelphia North American.*

Anzac Lieutenant—The Turks are as thick as peas. What shall we do?
Anzac Captain—Shell them, you idiot, shell them !—*Tit-Bits.*

A member of the first Canadian contingent, writing home, says: "I guess the first seven years of this war are going to be the worst."—*Canadian American.*

Fe, fi, fo, fum,
Pancho Villa is keeping mum.
Whether alive or whether dead,
Or where he's buried, he hasn't said.
—*Brooklyn Eagle.*

Tom—When you proposed to her I suppose she said, "This is so sudden !"
Dick—No; she was honest and said, "This suspense has been terrible."—*Boston Transcript.*

Why the Transcript Proofreader Wears a Hunted Look—Mr. Scudder and his bride are to live at 9 Park Vale Avenue, Allston, where they will welcome their funds after June 1.—*Boston Transcript.*

"Wait a moment, lady, until the car stops." "Will you please not address me as lady, sir?" she said sharply. "I beg your pardon, madam," said the conductor. "The best of us are apt to make mistakes."—*Buffalo Courier.*

According to *Les Annales*, a *poilu* writes home as follows :
"You ask me if I need socks. I am still wearing the pair you sent me last July. I have not seen them since, but I presume they are in bad shape."

First Married Man—What are you cutting out of the paper?
Second Married Man—An item about a California man's securing a divorce because his wife went thru his pockets.
First Married Man—What are you going to do with it?
Second Married Man—Put it in my pocket.—*Yale Record.*

If they keep on deciding that Shakespeare didn't write his own plays it may yet make a revival of them profitable. What is needed is a boisterous discussion of the subject to arouse true public interest.—*New York Evening Sun.*

A New Yorker tells of a married couple he observed at a county fair in Ohio. They found themselves in the center of quite a crowd near one of the amusement booths and the husband addressed his wife in this wise:
"I say, dearie, I think you'd better give me the lunch-basket. Don't you see we are apt to lose each other in this crowd."—*Harper's.*

Dear Sir: Will you kindly publish directions for tying a bow-tie?
ROGER COOT.

Well, Roger, you hold the tie in your left hand and your collar in the other. Slip your neck in the collar, and cross the left-hand end of the tie over the right with the left hand, steadying the right end with the other hand. Then drop both hands, catching the left with the right and the other with the other. Reverse hands, and pick up the loose ends with the nearest hands. Pull this end thru the loop with your unengaged hand, and squeeze. You will find the knot all tied and all you have to do is to untangle your hands.—*Dartmouth Jack-o'-Lantern.*

Teaching People How to Eat
for
Health, Strength and Efficiency

By ARTHUR TRUE BUSWELL, M. D.

IF YOU have ever lived on a farm you have heard of "balanced rations" and what remarkable results they have accomplished when fed to cattle and other animals. The United States Government has a department devoted to teaching farmers how to feed their stock so as to develop it to the highest point of health and efficiency.

Yet until recently I have never heard of "balanced rations" for humans or, in fact, of any serious attempt made to teach people what to eat and what not to eat. I was therefore greatly interested in the work of the Corrective Eating Society of Maywood, New Jersey, founded by Eugene Christian, the eminent food scientist. It seems that this Society is dedicated to teaching people how to combine and proportion food for greater health and efficiency and their work is meeting with success so great that it almost seems too good to be true.

Twenty years ago Eugene Christian was at death's door. For years he had suffered the agonies of acute stomach and intestinal trouble. His doctors—among them the most noted specialists in this country—gave him up to die. He was educated for a doctor, but got no relief from his brother physicians, so as a last resort he commenced to study the food question, especially its relation to the human system, and as a result of what he learned he succeeded in *literally eating his way back* to perfect health without drugs or medicines of any kind —and in a remarkably short space of time.

Today Eugene Christian is a man 55 years young. He has more ginger, more vitality, and physical endurance than most youngsters in their 'teens. He literally radiates energy and power.

So remarkable was his recovery that Christian knew he had discovered a great truth which fully developed would result in a new science—the science of Correct Eating.

From that day to this he has devoted his life to telling others of the power of Correct Eating. From his research work he became convinced that 90 per cent of the ills of mankind originate in the stomach and intestines. He found that these ills responded to corrective eating. Since then he has told 23,000 people how to eat, what to eat and what not to eat with the result that almost invariably they were brought back to a type of health that they never dreamed they could reach.

Very often good foods, when eaten in combination with other good foods, create a chemical action in the digestive tract and are converted into dangerous toxic poisons, which are responsible for nearly all sickness. In other words, good foods wrongly combined will cause acidity, fermentation, gas, constipation and numerous sympathetic ills leading to most serious consequences.

These truths have been strongly brought out by Professor Metchnikoff in his treatise on the "Prolongation of Life" and by many other modern scientists. But most efforts in the past have been designed solely to remove the effect, by cleansing out the system and removing the poisons *after* they had formed, wholly disregarding the cause.

The Corrective Eating Society, however, has gone a step further. Instead of waiting until the poisons accumulate, they tell you how to prevent them. They have shown that just as some combinations of food produce slow consuming poisons that wreck the system, other combinations of food taken in the right proportions become the greatest tonics for health, efficiency and long life ever discovered. And a wonderful feature of their method is that results come practically with the very first meal.

As Christian explains, in no case are patented or proprietary foods prescribed. All of the foods may be obtained from your garden, at your local stores or in any restaurant. It is not necessary to upset your table to follow his remarkably simple suggestions.

In order to help as many people as possible, not only those who are ailing but those who want to maintain their health, The Corrective Eating Society has prepared a book based upon Eugene Christian's 20 years' experience. This book, Corrective Eating in 24 Lessons, is being offered for free examination to those who are interested. This work was written expressly for the layman. Technical terms have been avoided and every point is explained so that there can be no possible misunderstanding.

But the lessons do not merely tell you why you should eat correctly and what the results will be, they also give actual menus for breakfast, luncheon and dinner, curative as well as corrective, covering every condition of health and sickness for all ages from infancy to old age and covering all occupations, climates and seasons.

Christian says that every thinking man or woman—young or old—well or sick—should know the science of correct eating. That most people dig their graves with their teeth is as true as gospel, in his estimation. Food is the fuel of the human system. And just as certain fuels will produce definite results when consumed in a furnace, so will certain foods produce the desired results when put into the human furnace.

Yet not one person in a thousand has any knowledge of food as fuel. Some of the combinations we eat every day are as inefficient and dangerous as soggy wood, wet leaves, mud, sawdust and a little coal would be for a furnace. No wonder most of us are only 50 per cent efficient.

The relationship of health to material success is so close that the result of the Society's teaching is a form of personal efficiency which puts people head and shoulders above their fortunate brothers. Everyone knows that the best ideas, plans and methods are worked out when you are brimful of vitality —when you feel full of 'ginger.'" The better you feel—the better work you can do. I understand that The Corrective Eating Society's lessons have times without number been the means of bringing great material prosperity to its students by endowing them with health so perfect that work seems like play.

If you would like to see the Book of 24 Lessons in Corrective Eating written by Eugene Christian out of his vast experience, merely write and ask the Society at the address given below to send the lessons for five days' free examination with the understanding that you will either return the lessons within that time or remit $3, the small fee asked.

If the more than 300 pages contained in the course yield but one single suggestion that will bring greater health, you will get many times the cost of the course back in personal benefit—yet hundreds write the Society that they find vital health on every page.

I suggest that you clip out and mail the following form instead of writing a letter, as this is a copy of the official blank used and will be honored at once.

CORRECTIVE EATING SOCIETY, INC., 45 Hunter Ave., Maywood, N. J.

Gentlemen :—You may send me prepaid a copy of Corrective Eating in 24 Lessons. I will either remail these to you in five days or send you $3.

Name .... Address ....

The Market Place

STEEL PROGRESS

Interesting news in relation to the
business and affairs of the United
States Steel Corporation continues to
be forthcoming.

The unfilled orders on the corporation's books at the end of the first
quarter of the year amounted to
$9,331,000. This is an increase of near-
ly nine per cent over the figures of the
preceding month and of practically 120
per cent over the condition on the same
date a year ago.

The distribution of finished products in the quarter just ended was also
a high record. The shipments of rolled
steel products in the first three months
of this year were only a little less than
4,000,000 tons. In the same period last
year they were a trifle over 2,000,000
tons.

Another increase of wages, amounting to ten per cent, goes into effect in
the plants of the Steel Corporation on
May 1. This follows a similar advance
made in February.

Most of the other steel companies
are following the lead of the Steel
Corporation in thus advancing wages,
and it may be estimated that 500,000
workers will be benefited by the unprecedented increase in activity in the
steel industry. Comparing the present
payroll of the Steel Corporation with
its payroll a year ago, it appears that
if the new wage scale continues thru
the year, it will involve an added expenditure of $26,000,000 over the
same period of last year.

The stock books of the Steel Corporation show that in the past two
years more than half of the Steel Common owned abroad has been returned
to this country. On March 31, 1914,
European investors owned 1,285,636
shares of Steel Common, constituting
about one-quarter of the common stock
of the corporation. On March 31, 1916,
Europe's holdings had shrunk to 639,-
469 shares. This affords an interesting
measure of the liquidation by foreign
investors of their American investments. It is such liquidation as this
that was feared when the war broke
out, and that led to the closing of the
New York Stock Exchange. The fact
was that when, after the reopening of
the Exchange, the selling of European
holdings did actually come and continue in such volume as these figures
suggest, the American market was able
to absorb the offerings and thrive on
the diet.

It should be noted, however, that the

European holdings of the preferred stock of the Steel Corporation have not shrunk in anything like the same proportion. Two years ago 312,832 shares of preferred were held in Europe, while today the holdings are still 262,-091 shares. European investors evidently realize, in these days of financial upheavals, the value of high-class American securities as investments.

THE PHILADELPHIA IDEA

A joint committee, composed of representatives of ten leading trade and business organizations of Philadelphia, has begun a nationwide campaign for a simpler and more centralized system of railroad regulation. The basic principle of the committee's recommendations is the removal of the railroads from the jurisdiction of state commissions and their exclusive regulation by the Federal Government.

The committee has completed a nine months' study of the problem which has convinced them that the present dual regulation by the Federal Government and state governments is one of the most apparent evils of the present situation, impairing the efficiency of the roads and handicapping shippers. Accordingly, while the preliminary investigation is made the basis for a detailed study, the findings of the committee are to be laid before between 700 and 800 trade associations for their consideration and action. The committee has endorsed the proposed Congressional joint commission to investigate railway transportation and legislation, and, if the commission is created, it will be asked to consider the findings of the Philadelphia committee.

The campaign booklet, which the committee is sending out, contains the report of the preliminary study and the recommendation for unqualified federal regulation. While the joint committee as a whole merely suggests to other organizations the consideration of a number of solutions, the Philadelphia Bourse, in an appendix, urges the following:

1. Legislation providing for the federal incorporation of companies engaged in interstate transportation of persons or goods.

2. All companies engaged in such business under charters granted by any state or territory or the District of Columbia to be privileged to accept federal charters without surrender of their state charters, and without impairment of the rights of the several states with regard to taxation of property value of corporations within their borders.

3. All corporations accepting federal charters to be subject to regulation by the Federal Government alone thru the Interstate Commerce Commission.

4. The Interstate Commerce Commission to be reformed into district courts, one for each freight traffic district, as now organized in the form of territorial freight traffic districts.

5. Each court to have a president judge, a jurist and six association justices, three being business men and three expert railroad men. The district courts to have full power to regulate the corporations operating under federal charters within their districts without appeal except as to questions of principle.

6. The president judges to form a supreme interstate commerce court, sitting in Washington, to determine questions of principle of country-wide application.

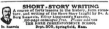

7. The district courts to sit at some central point in their respective districts and to hold court for six weeks out of each three months of each year. The supreme court to hold court for one month twice a year. All decisions to be rendered within sixty days of final argument.

8. Definite limits to be placed upon the powers of the commission along the lines of regulations of rates, corrections of inequalities and abuses and arbitration of labor disputes, with such other features as a closer study of the subject may suggest.

GERMAN DYES TO COME OVER, PERHAPS

One of the most serious effects of the war upon American industries results from the shortage of dyestuffs. The vast majority of the dyes used by the world are "made in Germany," for German scientific ingenuity and industrial efficiency have largely put an end to the production of natural vegetable dyes by the introduction of the manufactured coal tar colors.

Recent action of the German Government will afford the manufacturers of the United States an ample supply of dyestuffs for the next half year—provided two other conditions can be effectively met. Berlin will permit the export of 15,000 tons of dyes to this country, if definite assurance will be given that none of them will be re-exported to Germany's enemies.

The two problems that remain to be solved are getting past the British blockade and securing the ships to bring the cargoes over. Licenses have already been issued by the British Government permitting the bringing out of the port of Rotterdam of $5,000,-000 of German dyes which await shipment there. An attempt is to be made at once to secure from London additional licenses covering the rest of the 15,000 tons which Germany will now permit to be exported. The success of this attempt is of course problematical. The shipping question is no less perplexing. The British licenses already granted expire on June 1; and it is likely to prove a hard task to get the necessary tonnage for their shipment before that date. If the amount to be brought over should be something like trebled, the difficulty will be increased manifold.

But we need the dyes, unless we are all to take to wearing white; and great needs often produce effective remedies.

It is reported that the rapid recovery of the stock market last week from the depressing effect of the diplomatic crisis with Germany was largely due to ,the odd lot buying of the general public. Thousands of small speculators, who formerly patronized bucket shops and other brokerage concerns having no Stock Exchange connections have transferred their trading to Stock Exchange houses and those having Stock Exchange connections.

They have been forced to do so, or not trade at all. For the bucket shops have been driven out of business. The Stock Exchange, by long and painstaking effort, has made it impossible for the bucket shops—those institutions that pretend to be bona fide brokerage houses, but that in reality are purely gambling houses, where no stocks are actually bought and sold—to continue their business. The effect upon the actual, legitimate trading in stocks upon the Stock Exchange is already marked.

Insurance
Conducted by
W. E. UNDERWOOD

LIFE INSURANCE AND ENDOWMENT

A correspondent at Rutherfordton, N. C., gently disagrees with a piece of advice I recently gave a young man respecting the advantages of the endowment form of life insurance. My Southern friend regards the life forms (continuous or twenty payment), the difference in annual premiums considered, the more serviceable. "He could," observes my correspondent, referring to my inquirer, "almost buy $1000 ordinary and $1000 twenty-year life for price of $1000 endowment."

True; but the young man's chances of outliving the twenty-year period are so many times greater than those of dying within it, and the cash fund at the end is so much greater under $1000 of endowment than the combined values of $1000 ordinary and $1000 twenty-payment life, that I lean to the endowment. Of course, if protection against death is of paramount importance to a young man, the life plans should be used. Each individual's circumstances must govern in these matters. As observed here on several occasions, all the regular forms of life insurance are endowments at some age.

My correspondent errs in believing that companies and agents stimulate the sale of endowments for selfish purposes. In fact, there are many leading companies which either discourage the writing of endowments by their representatives, or fail to encourage them in securing applications on that form. As evidence tending to show that the life forms are easy leaders, I quote from the New York Insurance Department's report on the business for the year ending December 31, 1914, the latest statistics available, the distribution of the total insurance in force on that day in the thirty-five life companies reporting to that department:

Total insurance in force $14,933,-150,899, under 7,849,680 policies. The total insurance under life forms was $9,795,393,878, the number of policies being 4,896,234. There were 2,297,816 endowment policies, carrying $3,305,-860,013 insurance. Of all other forms there were 655,630 policies for $1,720,-902,468 insurance. In other words, there were more than twice as many policies, and nearly three times as much insurance under the life forms as under the endowments.

═══

W. L. C., Joplin, Mo.—The Mutual Benefit and Northwestern Mutual rank as two of the best managed life companies in the country. My solution of your problem would be that you divide the business between them.

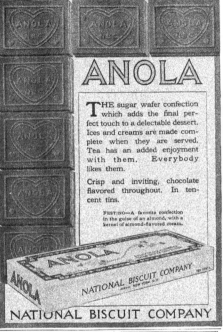

ANOLA

THE sugar wafer confection which adds the final perfect touch to a delectable dessert. Ices and creams are made complete when they are served. Tea has an added enjoyment with them. Everybody likes them.

Crisp and inviting, chocolate flavored throughout. In ten-cent tins.

FESTINO—A favorite confection in the guise of an almond, with a kernel of almond-flavored cream.

NATIONAL BISCUIT COMPANY

BOTH SIDES   A DEBATE

SHOULD THE UNITED STATES FIGHT?

RESOLVED: That the United States should now enter the Great War on the side of the Entente Allies.

THE President of the United States has threatened to put an end to all diplomatic relations with Germany and her allies if these powers do not at once abandon their present submarine warfare against merchantmen or so modify it that the lives of American citizens may not be endangered by it. This decision of the President may eventuate in war. Many critics of the administration maintain that the United States should long ago have entered the Great War on the side of the entente allies. Others oppose any abandonment of the traditional policy of the United States which enjoins neutrality and non-intervention in all extra-American wars. This debate was prepared by Preston William Slosson.

ARGUMENT FOR THE AFFIRMATIVE

I. American interests demand that we should participate in the Great War.
  A. Diplomatic isolation is impossible for any power under modern conditions.
    1. All the other powers have their allies and all the smaller nations their protectors, and to this they owe whatever security they enjoy.
    2. When we adopted our policy of non-intervention in European affairs we were a small, weak nation without colonial obligations; today we have extensive commercial and financial interests all over the world and aspire to play the part of a great power in international politics.
    3. By taking part in the conferences at The Hague we have but ourselves on record as concerned in the upbuilding of international law throuout the world.
  B. The United States cannot if it would remain neutral in this war.
    1. By permitting loans and the sale of munitions of war our government is effectively assisting the entente allies; by forbidding the sale of munitions or participation in war loans it would greatly assist the central powers.
    2. Neutral rights are not respected by any warring nation. As a neutral, we are disliked and disregarded by both opposing groups.
  C. Participation in the Great War would give this country representation at the coming peace conference.
    1. This would give the United States an opportunity to see that American rights were not menaced by political or commercial treaties and agreements after the war.
    2. Our moral influence would be potent to make a satisfactory world peace, since we would be the most disinterested of all the nations at the conference.
II. American interests demand that we give aid to the entente allies.
  A. The central powers have given us just cause for war.
    1. On repeated occasions American lives have been lost by the submarine warfare on merchant ships conducted by the central powers.
    2. In spite of numerous warnings and protests these injuries have continued and there is no evidence of their ceasing in the future.
  B. The victory of the central powers would endanger our future security.

1. Germany, Austria-Hungary and Turkey are all autocratic and bureaucratic in government and militaristic in policy. Their victory would put an end to democracy and liberty wherever they conquered and would force all other countries, including the United States, to adopt burdensome armament in self-defense.
  2. Germany is desirous of colonial expansion, and is therefore opposed to the Monroe Doctrine.
  3. Germany would find cause for quarrel with the United States in the aid and sympathy given by the people of this country to her foes.
  C. The United States would profit by joining the entente allies.
    1. Our commercial prosperity and our political security alike depend upon an understanding with the greatest naval power—Great Britain.
    2. An alliance with the numerous powers already leagued together might form the nucleus of a league to guarantee world-peace after the war.
III Our intervention would be effective.
  A. Our navy is usually reckoned the third most powerful in the world.
  B. Altho our standing army is small, we could raise a volunteer army in a few months that would make the outcome of the war absolutely certain.
  C. Our financial and industrial resources for carrying on the war are of illimitable importance.
  D. The entry of the United States into the war would induce the central powers to sue for an early peace.

ARGUMENT FOR THE NEGATIVE

I. American interests demand that we remain neutral during the Great War.
  A. The cost of intervention in life, in wealth, in social development would be incalculable. We would be impoverished and militarized as the nations of Europe have been. Our country would be divided against itself by conflicting sympathies.
  B. The fundamental foreign policy of the United States has always been to avoid entangling alliances and participation in European wars.
  C. We have duties that lie nearer home. It would be folly to leave the Mexican question unsettled to intervene in a war beyond the Atlantic.
  D. By intervention we would lose our chance to act as impartial mediator between the warring powers.
  E. By our participation in the war the neutral nations would lose the only champion of their interests.
  F. The philanthropic work which our government has performed in Belgium, in Poland and elsewhere would end upon our entrance into the war.
II. American interests do not demand that we give military aid to the entente allies.
  A. The policy of submarine warfare pursued by the central powers need not involve us in the war.
    1. The exact nature of maritime law upon the points at issue is open to discussion.
    2. It is still possible that a working agreement upon these controverted matters may be reached by further negotiations.
    3. The entente allies have inflicted more serious injuries upon our trade than the central powers and have been equally defiant of international maritime law.
  B. American interests do not at all correspond with the policies of the entente allies.

    1. The British maritime policy of seizing private property at sea if destined for the enemy is widely different from that which the United States has always supported.
    2. Japanese expansion in China is contrary to the American "open door" policy.
    3. The United States has no interest in the territorial ambitions of Russia, France and Italy in continental Europe.
  C. America could gain nothing from participation in the war.
    1. The United States expects neither territory nor indemnity from a victory in the war.
    2. All that could be obtained for this country would be a pledge on the part of the defeated powers that they would observe maritime law more strictly in future wars; but this pledge would be unenforceable.
    3. Upon the actual entrance of the United States into the war the central powers would be free to wage their submarine war against merchantmen without restraint, so the security of American citizens would be lessened.
III. Our intervention would be futile.
  A. The entente allies already enjoy complete command of the sea, so the American navy could accomplish little.
  B. Our army is wholly inadequate to undertake a foreign war.
    1. It would take years to reorganize the army on the European scale.
    2. A large force must be retained in the Philippines and on the Mexican border.
    3. We lack officers and equipment for a large volunteer army.
  C. If we should enter the war. we could not afford to ship munitions to Europe; they would be needed to equip our own forces.
  D. The aid we could render the entente allies by military intervention would be so slight that it would give us very little influence in the peace conference at the end of the war.

REFERENCES

Clapp, E. J. *Economic Aspects of War.* Yale University Press. Shepherd, W. R. *Protection of Neutral Rights at Sea.* Sturgis & Walton. Bingham, *ar., European War II.* Wilson, White Plains, N. Y. *New Republic,* 6:303-5, April 22, 1916. *Current Opinion,* 58:375-85, 394-6, June, 1915. *Everybody's,* 19*:2-21, January, 1916. *Congressional Record,* vol. 53:4196-4223, March 7, 1916.

Affirmative

Usher, Roland G. *The Challenge of the Future.* Houghton, Mifflin. Roosevelt, Theodore, *Fear God and Take Your Own Part.* Doran. Wister, Owen, *The Pentecost of Calamity.* Macmillan. Root, Elihu, Address. Dutton. *Independent,* 86:102,3, April 17, 1916. *Outlook,* 112:848, March 22, 1916; 111:893, December 15, 1916.

Negative

Angell, Norman, *The World's Highway.* Doran. Bryce, Vincent, *Neutral Nations and the War.* Macmillan. Higgins, A. P. *Non-Combatants and the War.* Oxford Press. New York, Contemporary Review, 107:602-7, May, 1915. *Independent,* 85:81-2, January 17, 1916. *Literary Digest,* 50: 587, March 13, 1916.

Further information may be obtained by inquiry from the numerous propagandist organizations interested in the war, such as, The American Rights Committee (pro-Ally), 45 Cedar street, New York City; the American Truth Society (pro-German), 210 Fifth avenue, New York City; The National Security League, 31 Pine street, New York City; The Woman's Peace Party, 70 Fifth avenue, New York City; The Anti-Preparedness Committee, Munsey Building, Washington, D. G.; Association to Abolish War, 12 Hazelwood street, Roxbury, Mass.

228

The Independent

FOR SIXTY-SEVEN YEARS THE
FORWARD-LOOKING WEEKLY OF AMERICA

THE CHAUTAUQUAN
Merged with The Independent June 1, 1914

M A Y   1 5 ,   1 9 1 6

OWNED AND PUBLISHED BY
THE INDEPENDENT CORPORATION, AT
119 WEST FORTIETH STREET, NEW YORK
WILLIAM B. HOWLAND, PRESIDENT
FREDERIC E. DICKINSON, TREASURER

W I L L I A M   H A Y E S   W A R D
HONORARY EDITOR

EDITOR: HAMILTON HOLT
ASSOCIATE EDITOR: HAROLD J. HOWLAND
LITERARY EDITOR: EDWIN E. SLOSSON

PUBLISHER: KARL V. S. HOWLAND

ONE YEAR, THREE DOLLARS
SINGLE COPIES, TEN CENTS

Postage to foreign countries in Universal Postal
Union, $1.75 a year extra; to Canada, $1 extra.
Instructions for renewal, discontinuance or
change of address should be sent two weeks
before the date they are to go into effect. Both
the old and the new address must be given.

We welcome contributions, but writers who
wish their articles returned, if not accepted,
should send a stamped and addrest envelope. No responsibility is assumed by The
Independent for the loss or non-return of
manuscripts, tho all due care will be exercised.

Entered at New York Post Office as Second
Class Matter

Copyright, 1916, by The Independent

Address all Communications to
T H E   I N D E P E N D E N T
119 West Fortieth Street, New York

C O N T E N T S

ST. THOMAS AGAIN

Frequent conversations between Secretary Lansing and the Danish Minister
have led to renewed talk of the sale of
the Danish West Indies to the United
States.

The visit of Colonel Roosevelt to the
Danish Islands was, as he was careful
to explain, purely recreational and unofficial. Nevertheless the people, remembering his efforts as President to buy
the islands from Denmark, did not fail
to find in this visit an encouragement
of their hopes for annexation. He refused to grant interviews to the newspaper men, but one eagle-eyed editor
detected a symbolic significance in his
attitude as he landed, for it was noted
that he kept a tight grip on "his Panama" with one hand while the other
was outstretched toward the people
who thronged to meet him.

In the *St. Thomas Tidende* appeared
the following greeting and advice:

TO COLONEL THEODORE ROOSEVELT

Welcome to our shores, dear Colonel,
　Right welcome to old St. Croix;
May you have a pleasant time, Colonel,
　Ere from us "ye gang awa."

And when you leave our shores, dear
　Colonel,
　To visit the southern isles,
May you find them so charming, Colonel,
　That you'll be wreathed in smiles.

When you get to Panama, Colonel,
　May you find the ditch O. K.;
May your deal prove a success, Colonel,
　And earn Uncle Sam big pay.

When you return at home, dear Colonel,
　May our isles engage a thought;
Whisper a "square deal" to him, Colonel,
　"Unk, these islands should be bought."

"Seward got scared and left them, Uncle,
　In the earthquake of sixty-seven.
He never went back, dear old Uncle,
　To see if they had gone to h-eaven.

"Thirty-five years after, good old Uncle,
　Strenuous efforts again were sought;
But 'in the neck' we got it, Uncle,
　The answer was 'they could not be
　bought.'

"Let's try the move again, kind Uncle,
　St. Thos would be our all in all;
Her geo. po. is splendid, Uncle,
　For she holds the key to the Canal."
　　　　　　　　　　　　　—R.

*Frederiksted, St. Croix, Danish West
Indies, 16th February, 1916.*

From a literary point of view this
poem is hard to classify on account of
its originality in rime and cadence. But
it shows good sense if not poetic genius,
and we should not think of finding fault
with its form any more than with the
peroration of the Jamaican preacher:
"God bless the American eagle and
hasten the time when Jamaica shall
come under the shadow of the wings of
that great bird of prey."

A MOVIE OF THE NEWS

These heads, from successive editions
of a journal especially fertile in headline variations, suggest the dramatic
way in which the latest German note
became public. The early sections, defiant and ironical, caused resentment
and apprehension, which were somewhat lessened as, after long delay, the
rest of the note, with its more or less
definite concessions, came over the sea
by wireless and filtered out to the public thru the news agencies and newspaper composing rooms.

The Evening Telegram

BERLIN DEFIES U. S. IN SUBMARINE WAR

The Evening Telegram

BERLIN YIELDS ONLY IF BLOCKADE CEASES

The Evening Telegram

REPLY RAISES DOUBT
BREAK SURE, IS ONE VIEW; DEMAND MET, OTHERS SAY

The Evening Telegram

REPLY ACCEPTABLE IF BERLIN KEEPS PLEDGE, IS CABINET ATTITUDE

The Evening Telegram

KAISER GIVES PLEDGES
IF VERIFIED, NEW U-BOAT ORDERS MAY AVERT BREAK

The Evening Telegram

U. S. ACCEPTS NOTE; NO BREAK IF BERLIN FULFILS PROMISES

THE PRESIDENT'S ANSWER TO GERMANY

After this issue of The Independent had gone to press the following note, dated May 8, was given to the public. Comment in the editorial pages is, of course, based on the situation prior to the publication of this brief and altogether admirable reply to the German note (which is reprinted in full on page 235).

The note of the Imperial German Government under date of May 4, 1916, has received careful consideration by the Government of the United States. It is especially noted, as indicating the purpose of the Imperial Government as to the future, that it "is prepared to do its utmost to confine the operation of the war for the rest of its duration to the fighting forces of the belligerents," and that it is determined to impose upon all its commanders at sea the limitations of the recognized rules of international law upon which the Government of the United States has insisted.

Thruout the months which have elapsed since the Imperial Government announced on February 4, 1915, its submarine policy, now happily abandoned, the Government of the United States has been constantly guided and restrained by motives of friendship in its patient efforts to bring to an amicable settlement the critical questions arising from that policy. Accepting the Imperial Government's declaration of its abandonment of the policy which has so seriously menaced the good relations between the two countries, the Government of the United States will rely upon a scrupulous execution henceforth of the now altered policy of the Imperial Government such as will remove the principal danger to an interruption of the good relations existing between the United States and Germany.

The Government of the United States feels it necessary to state that it takes it for granted that the Imperial German Government does not intend to imply that the maintenance of its newly announced policy is in any way contingent upon the course or result of diplomatic negotiations between the Government of the United States and any other belligerent government, notwithstanding the fact that certain passages in the Imperial Government's note of the 4th inst. might appear to be susceptible of that construction.

In order, however, to avoid any possible misunderstanding the Government of the United States notifies the Imperial Government that it cannot for a moment entertain, much less discuss, a suggestion that respect by German naval authorities for the rights of citizens of the United States upon the high seas should in any way or in the slightest degree be made contingent upon the conduct of any other government affecting the rights of neutrals and noncombatants. Responsibility in such matters is single, not joint; absolute, not relative.

The Independent

| VOLUME 86 | MAY 15, 1916 | NUMBER 3519 |

THE IRREDUCIBLE MINIMUM

THE German reply to the "Sussex" note is an adroit mixture. It gives so much with one hand that the United States would not be justified in breaking off diplomatic relations forthwith. But it withholds so much with the other hand that the situation remains full of difficulty and potential danger. The note may be condensed to two significant passages. The first is this:

German naval forces have received the following order: "In accordance with the general principles of visit and search and the destruction of merchant vessels recognized by international law, such vessels, both within and without the area declared a naval war zone, shall not be sunk without warning and without saving human lives, unless the ship attempt to escape or offer resistance."

This is eminently satisfactory. It is what the Government of the United States has contended for from the first. It is the irreducible minimum. With nothing less will the American people be content.

So long as the German navy carries on its operations against merchant shipping in accordance with the letter and the spirit of this order, there will be no cause for rupture between the two nations.

But the other passage in the note lays down an unacceptable condition, and makes a scarcely veiled threat. It reads thus:

But neutrals cannot expect that Germany, forced to fight for existence, shall for the sake of neutral interests restrict the use of an effective weapon if the enemy is permitted to apply at will methods of warfare violating rules of international law. . . .
Accordingly, the German Government is confident that in consequence of the new orders issued to the naval forces, the Government of the United States . . . will now demand and insist that the British Government shall

forthwith observe the rules of international law universally recognized before the war. . . . .
Should steps taken by the Government of the United States not attain the object it desires, to have the laws of humanity followed by all belligerent nations, the German Government would then be facing a new situation in which it must reserve to itself complete liberty of decision.

This can mean nothing but that, unless the United States can and will compel England to bring to an end its blockade of Germany as at present enforced, the German Government will feel free to return to the methods of submarine warfare which it has been carrying on for more than a year.

Such a proposal we cannot consider. It involves an intolerable threat. The sufficient answer to it was made in the American note of July 21, 1915:

The Imperial German Government will readily understand that the Government of the United States cannot discuss the policy of the Government of Great Britain with regard to neutral trade except with that Government itself, and that it must regard the conduct of other belligerent governments as irrelevant to any discussion with the Imperial German Government of what this government regards as grave and unjustifiable violations of the rights of American citizens by German naval commanders.

On this position we must stand.

Our duty is clear. We should inform the German Government without delay that the pledge implied in the order to the German submarine commanders is satisfactory, but the condition sought to be imposed is not.

We shall continue to act toward each nation as our honor and our conscience demand, regardless of any attempt by any other nation to dictate our course. Meanwhile, we should make it unmistakably plain to Germany that any single violation of its pledge will automatically break off diplomatic relations.

ROOSEVELT, HUGHES OR——?

WHOM will the Republicans nominate for President?

The Democratic nominee is certain. No opposition worth a minute's thought has arisen to Mr. Wilson. By his achievements as President and as the leader of the Democratic party he has made himself the logical candidate.

But the outcome at Chicago is shrouded in uncertainty. There are plenty of avowed aspirants for the Republican nomination. Many state delegations will propose favorite sons. Nevertheless, there are just two personalities that stand out with the distinctness of probability.

Theodore Roosevelt or Charles Evans Hughes? That is the question.

In considering the answer there are several categories to be considered: character, ability, temperament, ex-

perience, convictions, political availability. The balance sheet of the two should contain all these items.

Two of these categories may be dismissed with a word. Both Mr. Roosevelt and Justice Hughes are men of proved ability and high character. They cannot, however, be said to be equal in ability, for their abilities are of different kinds.

Mr. Hughes is primarily a thinker. Mr. Roosevelt is first of all a man of action. With Mr. Hughes the thought is the thing; the action which may follow is of subordinate interest. With Mr. Roosevelt action is the one consuming passion; thought finds its important function in directing and controlling the action.

Any difference that there might seem to some—on one side or the other—in point of character is in reality a difference of temperament. Their characters manifest themselves thru different mediums. Mr. Roosevelt is a very difficult personality to analyze. He is something of a paradox. It is almost impossible to make any generalization about him that is strictly true. Mr. Hughes, however, is more easy to define. You may like him or not, but every one agrees on what manner of man he is.

On the point of experience it is a matter of degree. No man in the country has had more experience to fit him for the presidency than Mr. Roosevelt—for no man living has already been President so long as he. But Mr. Hughes was for three years Governor of New York State and for six years he has been a justice of the United States Supreme Court. His previous activity as counsel for the legislative commissions investigating the gas and insurance situations in New York City brought him into intimate touch with important questions of American public life. His contribution to the solution of the underlying problems in those cases has been as permanent as it was brilliant.

The most important item on the balance sheet must, of necessity, be that of convictions. What do these two men profoundly believe about the fundamentals of government, business, industry, human rights, national duties, and international responsibilities? What views do they hold as to the problems of immediate and insistent importance which confront the American people today?

Fundamentally the two men are not far apart. They are both true democrats; they both believe in the people and would have the rule of the people a real and living thing. They both believe in social justice, in the right of the men and the women who work with their hands to the largest possible measure of consideration and fair dealing in the working out of our industrial conditions. To them both human rights mean more than the mere privilege of existence subject to all the vagaries of fortune and the oppressions of unrestricted natural forces and unregulated human passions. They both believe in government, not merely as a necessary evil—"that government is best which governs least"—but as an effective instrument to be used for the protection of the general warfare against individual greed and self interest, and for the constructive development of the conditions of living of the whole people. Both hate the political boss, the corrupt alliance of predatory interests and greedy politicians, the exploitation of humanity for private gain.

So much for fundamentals of government. What of the more immediate issues of this present troubled time?

Here the comparison is not easy. What Mr. Roosevelt believes no man in the United States can have any excuse for not knowing. For a year and a half he has been giving utterance to his convictions with definiteness, particularity, and vigor. Mr. Roosevelt sees two great issues before the American people today: our national duty and responsibility in the field of international relations, and adequate preparedness for national defense and for the assumption of that national responsibility.

His views on the first point—and one aspect of the second—are well set forth in an address at Williams College eleven years ago:

I demand that the nation do its duty and accept the responsibility that must go with greatness.

I ask that the nation dare to be great, and that in daring to be great it show that it knows how to do justice to the weak no less than to exact justice from the strong.

In order to take such a position of being a great nation the one thing that we must not do is to bluff.

The unpardonable thing is to say that we will act as a big nation and then decline to take the necessary steps to make the words good.

Keep on building and maintaining at the highest point of efficiency the United States navy or quit trying to be a big nation. Do one or the other.

In order that we may be prepared for defense Mr. Roosevelt would have us create and maintain the second navy in the world, provide a regular army of 250,000 men and establish a system of universal military training on the general lines of the Swiss and Australian systems. In his book, "Fear God and Take Your Own Part," he wrote:

A democracy should not be willing to hire somebody else to do its fighting. The man who claims the right to vote should be a man able and willing to fight at need for the country which gives him the vote. I believe in democracy in time of peace; and I believe in it in time of war. I believe in universal service. Universal service represents the true democratic ideal.

These Mr. Roosevelt declares to be the great issues that confront the people of the United States today. He is convinced that the demand of events for the settlement of these issues is peremptory. He would have us subordinate for the moment the consideration of the other great problems which we must ultimately solve in order to safeguard our national future and continue to make our national contribution to the progress of mankind. Whether these will continue to be the issues of the campaign with a man other than Mr. Roosevelt running against Mr. Wilson is by no means certain. Even with Mr. Roosevelt as nominee, the Democrats may be able to shift the issue so that he will be on the defense rather than the offense. They did that during the last campaign. It must also be remembered that the next President, whosoever he may be, can hardly put into effect any military policy for two years unless we go to war, for the new Congress will not assemble till next March, and it will take months to agree on a policy and months more to execute it.

With Mr. Hughes the matter is not so easy. For six years his voice has been heard only in the judicial utterances of the bench. What at this moment are his views on our national relations to the rest of the world and on our duty in the matter of preparations for national defense must be largely a matter of conjecture. On these points he has not spoken; he may not speak while he remains within the judicial borders.

As far as the single issue of preparedness is concerned, however, he did give expression in a general way, to his views on these questions eight years ago, when he said:

We are devoted to the interests of peace and we cherish no policy of aggression. The maintenance of our ideals is our surest protection. It is our constant aim to live in friendship with all nations and to realize the aims of a free government, secure from the interruptions of strife and the wastes of war. It is entirely consistent with these aims and it is our duty to make adequate provision for our defense and to maintain the efficiency of our army and navy. And this I favor.

This, of course, might have been said by Mr. Wilson or any other less extreme man than Mr. Roosevelt. It is entirely conceivable that if Mr. Hughes were to speak out today fully and frankly he would be found to be much nearer to the President than to the President's most ardent critic. The party does not know, and under present conditions cannot know, exactly where Mr. Hughes is to be found.

The question of political availability is an important

one. It is the business of a political party to select as candidate for President not only a man who would make a good President, but a man who will have a good chance of being elected. How lies the balance of political availability between Mr. Roosevelt and Mr. Hughes?

Both are popular men. Both have multitudes of admirers. But Mr. Roosevelt has many more enemies than Mr. Hughes—both the fact that he has been President and the special characteristics of his personality make that inevitable. It is probable that more regular Republicans would "bolt" Mr. Roosevelt than Mr. Hughes, but which would draw the greater proportion of independent votes is a puzzling question.

But suppose neither Mr. Roosevelt nor Mr. Hughes is to be the man? What then? It all depends upon what the Republican party wants.

An indefatigable advocate of preparedness? There is Leonard Wood, a soldier, with two great achievements of administration to his credit, in Cuba and the Philippines, a hard-headed, high-minded, solid man.

An uncompromising advocate of anti-militarism? Henry Ford has already received astonishing support in several states in the Middle West. He is a tyro in politics. But he is a man of vision, in business as in more spiritual concerns; a great constructive genius, as the article we publish elsewhere in this issue attests.

A man of distinctly progressive tendencies, tho not a last-ditch Progressive? There is Herbert S. Hadley, of Missouri, enemy of bosses and machines, liberal minded, believer in preparedness.

A conservative? There is Senator Root, the "best Secretary of State the country has ever had," brilliant and profound intellectually, stern critic of the Wilson administration. But no such man could secure the hearty support of the confirmed Progressives. The nomination of such a conservative would mean disunion and a possible third ticket.

After these, the field, full of the shadowy forms of the proverbial "dark horses." Which shall it be? It all depends upon what the Republican party wants.

COINCIDENCE OR CONSEQUENCE?

WOMEN have voted in New Zealand for twenty years. The lowest death rate for babies in the world is in New Zealand.

Women also vote in Norway, Australia, Sweden, Denmark and Finland. The next lowest death rates for babies in the world are in these countries.

ONE WOMAN

NOTHING has done more to align the sentiments of humanity against the Central Powers than their mistreatment of women, especially the execution of Edith Cavell.

The latest case is that of Alice Mazaryk, a devoted and beautiful Bohemian girl now in a Vienna prison awaiting trial for her life on a charge of high treason.

The case is one to appeal to the American people. Her mother is an American. Her father, a professor at the University of Prague, is perhaps the greatest living Bohemian champion of democracy and the rights of small nations. As a member of the Austrian Parliament he was often outspoken for Serbia and Bosnia. At the beginning of the war he refused to take up arms against Serbia. When his newspaper, Cas, was supprest he and his daughter were both arrested. He was only saved from execution by the activity of his compatriots at home and in the United States. The daughter is still in peril of death.

Miss Mazaryk has many friends in the United States. Some years ago she spent a year at the University Settlement in Chicago writing a history of the Bohemians. We rejoice that a large body of American women are interesting themselves in her behalf. May success crown their efforts. Amidst the frightful taking of life in this sad war, surely such a gentle and rare spirit can be spared.

THE CLOAK AND SUIT MAKERS' LOCKOUT

IN the conflict now in progress in the cloak and suit industry in New York City we have a new and unusual alignment on a matter of principle. The manufacturers have declared a lockout in order that they may fight out their differences with their employees. The union is standing for the opposite principle. It wishes to arbitrate.

Up to 1900 the employers and employees fought out all their differences by means of strikes and lockouts, and the public was put thereby to great expense and inconvenience. But in 1900 they established the famous "Peace Protocol," with its board of arbitration and the preferential shop as a compromise between the closed shop and the open shop, and for five years there was peace in the industry. In the spring of 1915, however, there began to be rumblings of discontent, and finally the protocol was abrogated. In order to avert the conflict toward which both sides were drifting Mayor Mitchel appointed a Council of Conciliation. This succeeded the board of arbitration. In July, 1915, the council rendered a decision adverse to the union in the matter of the preferential shop—and the union accepted it. In March, 1916, it rendered a decision adverse to the manufacturers—and the manufacturers repudiated it.

In a further effort to avert trouble, however, the mayor requested representatives of the Manufacturers' Association and of the union to meet the Council of Conciliation and a group of public spirited citizens in his office. The representatives of the union came, but the manufacturers took the position that their conduct of their business is none of the public's affairs and declined to come.

Upon this point Mr. Oscar S. Straus, chairman of the New York Public Service Commission, said at the conference:

The public is deeply interested in the matter. I maintain that no two groups of men have a right to make trouble in a great city; that a great city should not be dependent upon two groups of men for the peace of that city, and that the manufacturers have assumed a mighty responsibility in refusing to come before the mayor and to conciliate their differences.

But in spite of all the efforts of the public, on April 28 the manufacturers declared a lockout, throwing 30,000 employees out of work, and this was followed last week by a strike of some 30,000 more union workers who were employed in shops technically independent of the Manufacturers' Association, but which were largely engaged on sub-contracts from them.

At the present time about 60,000 cloak and suit makers are out of work, and between 200,000 and 300,000 people are without income. The workers are still anxious to arbitrate their differences, but the manufacturers still refuse to do so. The obligation of both sides to show a decent respect for the public and public opinion has come to be the leading issue in this industrial war. And just as in our political life no party or group of men would be justified in breaking off relations with the government because an election or a court decision had gone against them, so neither side to an industrial agreement is justified in breaking off relations because of the adverse decision of a board of arbitration on which both sides as well as the public are represented. The time has long since passed when the public can be either ignored or defied. Its verdict will in the end prevail.

A POLL OF THE JURY ON THE GERMAN NOTE

A HASTY reading of the German reply leads me to think that it should be accepted as satisfactory. Germany has now ordered the conduct of her submarine warfare in strict conformity with the rules of international law. The United States must accept that order as an accomplished fact. The issuance of these orders by the German Government constitutes apparently and in all sincerity a compliance with the demands of the President.

GEORGE E. CHAMBERLAIN
Chairman of the Senate Committee on Military Affairs

I SHOULD say that Germany has measurably met the first demand made by the United States, which was for a revised public policy of submarine warfare. This has been granted. The second demand was that Germany make effective this revised policy. It is to be assumed from the temper of the note that the new order will be made effective. The suggestions regarding Great Britain's blockade, to my mind, do not qualify Germany's action in the least.

THOMAS J. WALSH
Senator from Montana, expert on international law

THE whole problem remains unsolved. Much depends on the practise under the new order of modified submarine warfare. But there is the important paragraph which recognizes the contention of the United States respecting international law. That official admission is a sufficient basis—or ought to be—upon which to plant the hope of continued friendly relations. Time will tell just how far Germany has yielded to American demands—or whether she has yielded not at all.

WARREN G. HARDING
Senator from Ohio and Temporary Chairman of the Republican National Committee

THE new German note leaves ground for much discussion. To my mind the note leaves us just where we were after the "Lusitania" note was forwarded to the German Government eleven months ago. The paragraph about other nations obeying international law neutralizes the paragraph just preceding about Germany's good intentions. She still leaves herself to act as she pleases.

MILES POINDEXTER
Senator from Washington and Chairman of the Committee on Expenditures in the War Department

GERMANY seems to have yielded substantially what our government asked for.

BENJAMIN IDE WHEELER
President of the University of California

IT is not clear that the note warrants a diplomatic rupture. Some captious sentences are probably meant for home consumption, but the concessions are considerable and the demands not unreasonable. The "Sussex" contention is practically yielded. On the whole, it sounds as if Germany means to keep the peace.

WASHINGTON GLADDEN
Pastor Emeritus of the First Congregational Church, Columbus, Ohio

THE German note is a compliance with the American demand, but contingent upon our obtaining concessions from the Entente Powers. It is discourteously phrased. Whether it is a real concession depends upon (1) the exact terms of the new order to U-boats, (2) the future interpretation of the conditions, (3) German good faith, in government and submarine officers alike.

THEODORE S. WOOLSEY
Recently Professor of International Law at Yale University

THE manner of the German note might have been happier; its matter marks a triumph for our government. A victory has been won without the rattling of sabers. It is due to the unassailable justness of the American stand for law and humanity. President Wilson's leadership may prove to be prophetic of a new method of international adjustment.

STEPHEN S. WISE
Rabbi of the Free Synagogue, New York City

WHILE the German reply to the American note is not a gracious concession, it is nevertheless a concession. In its form it is bad, but in its substance it is for the present at least sufficient and would not justify a diplomatic break with Germany. If the renewed or reiterated and apparently more emphatic instructions which she has given to the commanders of her undersea boats should be faithfully carried out, that, it seems to me, would meet the main contentions of our government, and no steps toward severing the relations between the two nations should be taken unless or until those instructions should be disregarded.

DAVID HUMMELL GREER
Bishop of New York Protestant Episcopal Church

GERMANY'S concessions have caused general feeling of relief, and the country will rejoice at the President's reported decision to accept them. War to avenge injury to travelers who have no regard for their country would be inconceivable, and I regard its avoidance a dictate of patriotic statesmanship.

RICHARD BARTHOLDT
President of the American Section of the Interparliamentary Union

GERMANY'S reply concedes more than history will hold justice demanded, while her severe arraignment of our course is unfortunately deserved. We may smart under it, but ought to remember what we should have written ourselves if our women were threatened with starvation and we were haunted by the hunger cry of babies.

EDMUND VON MACH
Author and Lecturer

CANADIANS are suffering the pains and losses of actual war, but not the intrigues of Bernstorff and the insolence of Berlin notes. We hope Americans will be spared actual war, but the humiliation and shame of North American civilization are too high a price even for neutrality.

Break diplomatic relations and redeem democracy from the insulting scorn of Prussian despotism. We need your military arm less than your conscience and companionship in the struggle for the world's freedom.

JOHN A. MACDONALD
Lately Editor of the Toronto Globe

THE GERMAN NOTE OF MAY 4, 1916

THE German Government handed over to the proper naval authorities for early investigation the evidence concerning the "Sussex," as communicated by the Government of the United States. Judging by the results that the investigation has hitherto yielded, the German Government is alive to the possibility that the ship mentioned in the note of April 10 as having been torpedoed by a German submarine is actually identical with the "Sussex."

The German Government begs to reserve further communication on the matter until certain points are ascertained which are of decisive importance for establishing the facts of the case. Should it turn out that the commander was wrong in assuming the vessel to be a man-of-war, the German Government will not fail to draw the consequence resulting therefrom.

In connection with the case of the "Sussex" the Government of the United States made a series of statements the gist of which is the assertion that the incident is to be considered but one instance of a deliberate method of indiscriminate destruction of vessels of all sorts, nationalities, and destinations by German submarine commanders.

The German Government must emphatically repudiate, the assertion. The German Government, however, thinks it of little avail to enter into details in the present stage of affairs, more particularly as the Government of the United States omitted to substantiate the assertion by reference to concrete facts.

The German Government will only state that it has imposed far-reaching restraints upon the use of the submarine weapon, solely in consideration of neutrals' interests, in spite of the fact that these restrictions are necessarily of advantage to Germany's enemies. No such consideration has ever been shown neutrals by Great Britain and her allies.

The German submarine forces have had, in fact, orders to conduct the submarine warfare in accordance with the general principles of visit and search and the destruction of merchant vessels recognized by international law, the sole exception being the conduct of warfare against enemy trade carried on enemy freight ships encountered in the war zone surrounding Great Britain. With regard to these, no assurances have ever been given to the Government of the United States. No such assurances are contained in the declaration of February 8, 1916.

The German Government cannot admit any doubt that these orders were given or are executed in good faith. Errors actually occurred. They can in no kind of warfare be avoided altogether. Allowances must be made in the conduct of naval warfare against an enemy resorting to all kinds of ruses, whether permissible or illicit.

But apart from the possibility of errors, naval warfare, just like warfare on land, implies unavoidable dangers for neutral persons and goods entering the fighting zone. Even in cases where the naval action is confined to ordinary forms of cruiser warfare, neutral persons and goods repeatedly come to grief.

The German Government has repeatedly and explicitly pointed out the dangers from mines that have led to the loss of numerous ships.

The German Government has made several proposals to the Government of the United States in order to reduce to a minimum for American travelers and goods the inherent dangers of naval warfare. Unfortunately the Government of the United States decided not to accept the proposals. Had it succeeded, the Government of the United States would have been instrumental in preventing the greater part of the accidents that American citizens have met with in the meantime.

The German Government still stands by its offer to come to an agreement along these lines.

As the German Government repeatedly declared, it cannot dispense with the use of the submarine weapon in the conduct of warfare against enemy trade. The German Government, however, has now decided to make a further concession, adapting methods of submarine war to the interests of neutrals. In reaching its decision the German Government is actuated by considerations which are above the level of the disputed question.

The German Government attaches no less importance to the sacred principles of humanity than the Government of the United States. It again fully takes into account that both governments for many years coöperated in developing international law in conformity with these principles, the ultimate object of which has always been to confine warfare on sea and land to armed forces of belligerents and safeguard as far as possible noncombatants against the horrors of war.

But although these considerations are of great weight, they alone would not under present circumstances have determined the attitude of the German Government. For in answer to the appeal by the Government of the United States on behalf of the sacred principles of humanity and international law, the German Government must repeat once more, with all emphasis, that it was not the German, but the British Government which ignored all accepted rules of international law and extended this terrible war to the lives and property of noncombatants, having no regard whatever for the interests and rights of neutrals and noncombatants that thru this method of warfare have been severely injured.

In self-defense against the illegal conduct of British warfare, while fighting a bitter struggle for national existence, Germany had to resort to the hard but effective weapon of submarine warfare.

As matters stand, the German Government cannot but reiterate regret that the sentiments of humanity, which the Government of the United States extends with such fervor to the unhappy victims of submarine warfare, are not extended with the same warmth of feeling to many millions of women and children who, according to the avowed intention of the British Government, shall be starved, and who by sufferings shall force the victorious armies of the Central Powers into ignominious capitulation.

The German Government, in agreement with the German people, fails to understand this discrimination, all the more as it has repeatedly and explicitly declared itself ready to use the submarine weapon in strict conformity with the rules of international law as recognized before the outbreak of the war, if Great Britain likewise was ready to adapt the conduct of warfare to these rules.

Several attempts made by the Government of the United States to prevail upon the British Government to act accordingly failed because of flat refusal on the part of the British Government. Moreover, Great Britain again and again has violated international law, surpassing all bounds in outraging neutral rights. The latest measure adopted by Great Britain, declaring German bunker coal contraband and establishing conditions under which English bunker coal alone is supplied to neutrals, is nothing but an unheard-of attempt by way of exaction to force neutral tonnage into the service of British trade war.

The German people knows that the Government of the United States has the power to confine the war to armed forces of the belligerent countries, in the interest of humanity and maintenance of international law. The Government of the United States would have been certain of attaining this end had it been determined to insist, against Great Britain, on the incontrovertible rights to freedom of the seas. But, as matters stand, the German people is under the impression that the Government of the United States, while demanding that Germany, struggling for existence, shall restrain the use of an effective weapon and while making complication with these demands a condition for maintenance of relations with Germany, confines itself to protests against illegal methods adopted by Germany's enemies. Moreover, the German people knows to what considerable extent its enemies are supplied with all kinds of war material from the United States.

It will, therefore, be understood that the appeal made by the Government of the United States to sentiments of humanity and principles of international law cannot, under the circumstances, meet the same hearty response from the German people which such an appeal otherwise always is certain to find here. If the German Government, nevertheless, is resolved to go to the utmost limit of concessions, it has been guided not alone by the friendship connecting the two great nations for over 100 years, but also by the thought of the great doom which threatens the entire civilized world should the cruel and sanguinary war be extended and prolonged.

The German Government, conscious of Germany's strength, twice within the last few months announced before the world its readiness to make peace on a basis safeguarding Germany's vital interests, thus indicating that it is not Germany's fault if peace is still withheld from the nations of Europe. The German Government feels all the more justified in declaring that responsibility could not be borne before the forum of mankind and in history if after twenty-one months of the war's duration the submarine question, under discussion between the German Government and the Government of the United States, were to take a turn seriously threatening maintenance of peace between the two nations.

As far as lies with the German Government, it wishes to prevent things from taking such a course. The German Government, moreover, is prepared to do its utmost to confine operations of the war for the rest of its duration to the fighting forces of the belligerents, thereby also insuring the freedom of the seas, a principle upon which the German Government believes, now as before, that it is in agreement with the Government of the United States.

The German Government, guided by this idea, notifies the Government of the United States that German naval forces have received the following order:

In accordance with the general principles of visit and search and the destruction of merchant vessels, recognized by international law, such vessels, both within and without the area declared a naval war zone, shall not be sunk without warning and without saving human lives unless the ship attempt to escape or offer resistance.

But neutrals cannot expect that Germany, forced to fight for existence, shall, for the sake of neutral interests, restrict the use of an effective weapon, if the enemy is permitted to continue to apply at will methods of warfare violating rules of international law. Such a demand would be incompatible with the character of neutrality, and the German Government is convinced that the Government of the United States does not think of making such a demand, knowing that the Government of the United States repeatedly declares that it is determined to restore the principle of freedom of the seas, from whatever quarter it has been violated.

Accordingly, the German Government is confident that in consequence of the new orders issued to the naval forces the Government of the United States will also now consider all impediments removed which may have been in the way of a mutual coöperation toward restoration of the freedom of the seas during the war, as suggested in the note of July 23, 1915, and *it does not doubt that the Government of the United States will now demand and insist that the British Government shall forthwith observe the rules of international law universally recognized before the war, as are laid down in the notes presented by the Government of the United States to the British Government December 28, 1914, and November 5, 1915.*

Should steps taken by the Government of the United States not attain the object it desires, to have the laws of humanity followed by all belligerent nations, the German Government would then be facing a new situation in which it must reserve to itself complete liberty of decision.

VON JAGOW

THE STORY OF THE WEEK

Another Mexican Raid — Just as the agreement between the United States Government and the de facto Mexican Government on the future status of the punitive expedition into Mexico was on the point of being consummated, another outrage by Mexicans was committed on American soil. A band of 200 armed Mexicans, rumored to be disaffected Carranza soldiers, crost the Rio Grande at a point 150 miles southeast of El Paso and attacked a guard of American soldiers. The guard, composed of nine men of the Fourteenth Cavalry, was stationed near Glen Springs in the Big Bend region of Texas. At eleven o'clock on Friday evening they were attacked in their little adobe hut by the Mexican raiders. For three hours they stood off their attackers. It was only when the roof of the hut was set on fire that they had to make a rush for safety. By that time three of the troopers were dead and two badly wounded. In spite of the danger Sergeant Smith and the three other survivors succeeded in carrying away not only their wounded but their dead comrades. The wounded and the bodies were sent off on a motor truck driven by one of the troopers. This left only the sergeant and two privates to continue the fighting against the bandits. They were reinforced, however, by American ranchmen, attracted by the sound of the firing and by four in the morning the Mexicans were driven off.

The bandits rode east to Glen Springs, where they looted a store and killed a ten year old boy. They then sacked two other towns, Boquillas and Deemers, and returned across the Rio Grande, taking with them two American civilians.

A punitive expedition was promptly got under way, and the pursuit will be prest with vigor.

This repetition of the Columbus incident will almost certainly put a quite different aspect on the negotiations between Señor Carranza and the American Government. It makes it clear that our task in Mexico is nowhere near its end. It raises at once the question whether the available troops of our regular army are sufficient in number to complete the task before us.

No "Scuttling" of the Philippines — Congress makes slow progress. Last week the attempt to set a definite time for granting independence to the Philippines was given its deathblow in the house. The Clark amendment, adopted by the Senate, which would have decreed the withdrawal of the United States from the islands before four years had passed, was defeated in the House by a vote of 213 to 165. Thirty Democrats, as foreshadowed in the Democratic caucus the week before, joined the solid Republican minority in voting against the amendment. Two attempts to retain in modified form the provision making a definite promise of independence were also defeated. The first set the time at from two to six years; the second set it at a minimum of four years and a maximum of eight years. The House then voted to substitute for the measure as it came from the Senate the Jones bill, which merely declares in its preamble that it has always been the intention of the United States to grant the Philippines their freedom. The bill was sent to conference and the House conferees were instructed to agree to no declaration in the bill setting a definite time for giving the islands their freedom. There is apparently no reason to believe that the movement for the fixing of the end of the American régime can be revived during the present Congress. This is a defeat for the President, who had recommended to Congress the acceptance of the Senate bill with the amendment.

Slow Progress in Congress — The conferees on the Army Reorganization bill have agreed on two of the disputed points, but are as wide apart as ever on two others. A compromise has been reached on the size of the regular army. One hundred and eighty thousand is the number of men agreed upon in conference, thus splitting the difference, though not at the half-way point, between the House figure of 140,000 and the Senate figure of 250,000. A scheme of elastic organization adopted by the Senate, which would permit the expansion of the army in time of threatened war to 220,000, was also concurred in. The conferees came to an agreement as well on the reorganization plan of the House bill for the National Guard, which would expand this reserve force to 400,000 men and "federalize" it.

The conference could not concur, however, on the provisions of the Senate bill for a federal volunteer reserve army and for a government owned nitrate plant. The conference adjourned pending further instructions from the House.

The next great measure to engage the attention of the House will be the Rural Credits bill, which is now being debated in the Senate. This will be followed by the Administration's Ship Purchase bill. This measure is still under consideration by the House Merchant Marine and Fisheries Committee, and will probably be reported out before the end of the present week. It is considered doubtful whether the ship purchase measure can be pushed thru the House without resort to a Democratic caucus.

Other bills which it is hoped can be disposed of before the national conventions in June are that granting a greater measure of self government to Porto Rico and the Fortifications Appropriation bill.

The annual supply bills are so far behind that it seems probable that the session of Congress will run far into the summer.

If We Want a Greater Navy — The advocates of naval preparedness want the United States to have the second navy in the world. That is the place we occupied until Germany passed us. It is an important question how rapidly we could build up our navy with that end in view, if we decide that that is the policy to adopt.

The Secretary of the Navy has transmitted to Representative Butler of Pennsylvania, ranking Republican member of the House Naval Committee, a report of the General Board of the Navy bearing on this point. The report shows that we cannot tell what would be needed to bring us back to second place, because we cannot tell what European nations have been doing since

Starrett in New York Tribune
CHASING VILLA

Stanley in Arkansas Democrat
"I'LL WATCH YOU DO IT, GENERAL"

THE NEW PHASE OF THE MEXICAN EXPEDITION

the war began. It declares, however, that the country is now equipped to begin building simultaneously within six months five dreadnoughts, five battle cruisers, nine scout cruisers, twenty-two destroyers and an unlimited number of submarines. If Congress should direct that private ship builders abandon all private work, it adds, a great increase in this capacity would be possible.

Also, if the government were willing to pay for the employment of three shifts of labor, the time of construction would be cut in half in all probability at an estimated increased cost of 40 per cent. The report points out, however, that the available supply of skilled labor, now undetermined, would control in a large measure any attempt to speed up a great building program.

Apparently, then, we can have naval preparedness if we want it and are willing to pay for it.

Labor and Capital Fall Out Here and There

May Day is, by common consent of workingmen, Strike Day. This year was no exception to the rule. The first of the month this year found serious labor troubles under way in the cloak and skirt industry in New York City, among the marine engineers operating tugs and tow-boats in New York Harbor, and in steel and electric manufacturing plants in the Pittsburgh district. There were two bright spots, however, on the industrial horizon. The agreement between the operators and the miners in the hard coal field, arranged at the end of the long conference between their representatives, was ratified by the Miners' Convention at Pottsville, Pennsylvania. There was some opposition to the ratification of the new wage scale because the agreement did not go to the full length of providing for the closed shop. But John P. White, president of the United Mine Workers of America, told the miners that the new contract was the best agreement ever negotiated by the mine workers, and that in obtaining the eight-hour day the dreams of the last forty-eight years in the anthracite regions had been realized. The agreement was finally ratified by a vote of 581 to 206.

A strike was also averted in the men's clothing trade in New York thru the efforts of Charles W. Bernheimer, chairman of the arbitration committee of the New York Chamber of Commerce. The employers and the workers finally consented to submit their differences to a board of arbitration composed of Mr. Bernheimer, Dr. Henry L. Moskowitz and the Rev. Dr. J. L. Magnes. Both sides in the controversy agreed to accept the decision of the board.

In the cloak and skirt industry efforts at conciliation were not so successful. Mayor Mitchel of New York and Mr. Jacob Schiff each made proposals for bringing the employers and workers together thru arbitration. But the manufacturers were obdurate and not only refused to treat with their employees, but declared a lockout which involved 30,000 workers. A strike was immediately declared in retaliation and twice as many workers are now idle. Many of the employers belong to the Manufacturers' Protective Association, and it is this association which is chiefly responsible for the troubles reaching an acute stage. Toward the end of last week it was reported that many of the independent manufacturers were coming to terms with their workers.

The difficulties in the Pittsburgh region were in the Westinghouse Electric and Manufacturing Company's works, the Carnegie Steel Company's plant, the mines of the Pittsburgh Coal Company, and about thirty smaller manufacturing plants. They involve 100,000 men. The chief demand is for an eight-hour day. In this region the strikes were marked by violence and the Pennsylvania State Constabulary and numerous deputy sheriffs have been kept busy guarding property and keeping the peace.

The strike in New York Harbor has badly crippled the shipping business at the country's principal port. The de-

Carter in New York Evening Sun

A STRANGE BIRD

mand of the engineers is for higher pay. An effort was being made at the end of last week by representatives of the Federal Department of Labor to bring about a settlement of the strike by means of conciliation, but the progress made was inconsiderable.

All these labor disputes are a not unnatural outcome of the wave of prosperity that the war has caused to sweep over the country. Labor quite logically wants its share of the mounting profits. But capital has its eyes on the time to come after the war when normal conditions will return. It is seldom easy to put wages back which have once gone up, even if the time of prosperity that sent them up comes to an end.

The War in the Air

Raids upon Great Britain by German aircraft have been frequent of late, sometimes every night. The most extensive, tho not the most serious, took place on the night of May 2 when five or six Zeppelins visited the east coast going as far north as Rattray Head, Scotland. About a hundred

THE MOBILIZED MULES OF THE SIXTH ARTILLERY ADVANCING WITH SUPPLIES IN MEXICO

bombs were dropt, but little damage was done except at one point where twelve explosive and four incendiary bombs were used, causing the death of six men and three women, and the wounding of nineteen men and eight women. Among the victims were five soldiers, which would indicate that this time at least some military buildings were hit. The Germans claim that blast furnaces, factories, warships and batteries were attacked.

On their return one of the Zeppelins, the L-20, ran short of gasoline, so was not able to keep up with the squadron, but was driven by the wind to the Norwegian shore near Stavanger. Most of the crew jumped into the water, but three remained on to destroy the machinery so the secret of its construction should not be discovered. The dirigible finally blew up against a mountain on the side of a fjord and was wrecked. All of the crew, sixteen in number, were rescued, altho several had broken limbs. The Zeppelin was burned.

Two British cruisers, the "Galatea" and the "Phaeton," fired upon a Zeppelin scouting in the North Sea and brought her down.

Another Zeppelin passing over the harbor of Salonica was hit by the artillery of the French and fell in flames at the mouth of the Vardar River, killing all the crew.

Reports are received of many aerial combats between the Italians and Austrians. On May 4 an Austro-Hungarian naval air squadron dropt bombs on the barracks and sulfur factory in Ra-

venna and on the following day it bombarded the Italian port of Brindisi and the Albanian port of Avlona on the other side of the Adriatic.

Collapse of the Irish Revolt　The Sinn Fein insurrection which broke out on Easter Monday was practically quelled at the end of a week, altho snipers were still being rounded up during the following week. Several hundred persons were killed and the property loss by shell and fire is estimated at $9,000,000 in Dublin alone.

The government troops took a thousand prisoners, who are being transferred to London. The leaders were taken to the Tower, where they were tried by court-martial and eight of them shot. Thirty-three others were sentenced to death, but their sentences were commuted to imprisonment. Those executed are Peter H. Pearse, "President of the Irish Republic," dramatist, headmaster of St. Enda's School and editor of *The Morn of Light;* William Pearse, his brother, a sculptor and teacher; Joseph Plunket, the eighth member of his family to be executed for treason; Michael O'Hanrahan, a leader in the movement for the revival of the Gaelic language and literature; Edward Daly, whose father and uncle were prominent in the Fenian movement; Thomas J. Clarke, who served fourteen years in prison for Fenian conspiracies; Major John McBride, a Boer officer, and Thomas MacDonagh, poet and schoolmaster. James Connolly, the socialist who served as "Commandant General of the Irish Republican Army," is too badly wounded to stand trial. James M. Sullivan, former American Minister to Santo Domingo, has been arrested for participation in the rebellion.

The chief center of insurgency outside of Dublin was at Enniscorthy, sixty miles south in County Wexford. Here the rebels on Thursday, April 27, took possession of the Athenæum and hoisted the flag of the Irish republic. They then cut the telegraph and telephone wires and tore up the railroad tracks. Enniscorthy Castle and most of the important buildings were seized and food and arms commandeered. But the food supply ran short and on Sunday, as the insurgents were leaving the church after

mass, they learned that the Dublin rising had failed. A delegation of Enniscorthy clergy was sent to Dublin to verify the report and on their return with its confirmation Monday the Sinn Feiners surrendered to the regiment sent out to overcome them.

At Galway, on the west coast, the insurrection seemed likely to prove formidable, but the 1200 rebels who were marching on that city were driven back by shell fire from a naval vessel just off the coast.

In County Meath, north of Dublin, the insurgents fired from ambush upon a detachment of the constabulary, killing ten, wounding eighteen and capturing forty. The insurgents, who numbered four hundred, gave up when they heard of the failure at Dublin.

The completeness with which the rebellion had been planned is shown by the discovery of a stock of the postage stamps of the "Irish Republic," printed in green, white and orange with pictures of the three martyrs, Larkin, O'Brien and Allen.

Augustine Birrell, who as Chief Secretary for Ireland is held responsible for this unexpected rebellion, has resigned his position.

The Surrender of Kut　The surrender of the British army on the Tigris River is acknowledged to be a severe blow to British prestige in the East. It is now clear that for a few thousand men to attempt to penetrate four hundred miles into the enemy's country with no support on either flank and with only a shallow and uncertain river to connect with the base of supplies was a very reckless undertaking. Nevertheless it seemed near to success and last November London was rejoicing in anticipation of the speedy capture of Bagdad, for the British expedition was at Ctesiphon, only eighteen miles away. But the battle of Ctesiphon, which in the London *Times'* "Diary of the War" is recorded as a great British victory, was the turning point of the Mesopotamian campaign. General Townshend could not retreat fast enough to rejoin the reinforcements down the river, but was overtaken by the Turks at Kut-el-Amara, a hundred miles below Bagdad.

But as at Balaclava bravery of the action in part redeemed the folly of the undertaking. "Some one had blundered" undoubtedly in sending General Townshend up the Tigris with insufficient forces and supplies, but the story of his twenty months' siege will—whenever it comes to be told—form a thrilling chapter in the British annals of war. The beleaguered garrison on a bluff in the bend of the river soon ran short of provisions and medicine. They were weakened by disease and incessantly beset by superior numbers of Turks and Arabs under German officers. The narrow circumference of their camp afforded no landing place for aeroplanes and when these attempted to soar low enough in passing over to drop bags of flour they were apt to be brought down by the fire of their foes.

When General Townshend found he could no longer hold out he offered to

A PREPAREDNESS PRESIDENT?
General Leonard Wood is attracting increasing attention as a possible nominee of the Republican Convention for President. He is a clean-cut American, with a strong sense of the immediate duty of preparedness, an administrator of very high achievement in Cuba and the Philippines and a popular and effective speaker

THE GREAT WAR

May 1—Dublin insurgents surrender. French bring down seven German aeroplanes.

May 2—Five Zeppelins raid British coast. Enniscorthy rebels surrender.

May 3—Birrell resigns Irish Secretaryship. French extend positions on Le Mort Homme.

May 4—Conscription bill passes Commons on second reading by 328 to 36. Austrian aeroplanes bombard Ravenna.

May 5—Germans take trenches on Hill 304. Zeppelin brought down at Salonica.

May 6—Heavy German bombardment of Dvina River, east of Riga. Russians nearing Diabekir and Erzingan.

May 7—Germans make further gains at Verdun. Berlin reports Russian transport sunk near Corfu.

surrender his artillery and his money, over $5,000,000, on condition that his troops be allowed to retire down the river with military honors. The Turkish commander, Halil Pasha, refused, whereupon General Townshend surrendered unconditionally. He was allowed by Halil Pasha to retain his sword. The prisoners, according to Constantinople, included four generals, 240 British officers and 270 Indian officers with some 9000 men. If we may credit the Turkish estimates on this point, the British casualties on the Tigris amounted to 20,000 during March and April. Most of these losses were suffered by the forces under General Gorringe and General Keary in their last desperate attempts to rescue the Townshend expedition, only twenty miles away.

After the surrender a truce was declared for the purpose of burying the dead on both sides and arrangements were made for the exchange of wounded prisoners.

The surrender of Kut releases, in large part at least, the Turkish army which has been defending Bagdad from a British advance up the Tigris. Now it can be turned to the defense of Bagdad from the Russians who are approaching it from the north thru Armenia and Persia. The Russian army moving westward from Erzerum is reported to have reached Erzingan and

that moving south to have reached Diabekir.

Draft Act in England — The extraordinary maneuvers of the British Government during the last fortnight are quite inexplicable from what has been disclosed to the public. In the latter part of April it was understood that the Cabinet was divided on the question of compulsory military service; that the Minister of Munitions, David Lloyd George, who has long been convinced of the necessity of conscription, was trying to force the Cabinet to adopt it; that Premier Asquith was unalterably opposed to it; and that the Labor men would fight it to the bitter end.

Later it was announced that the ministers, realizing that the fall of the Coalition Cabinet would be disastrous at this crisis, had agreed upon a compromise by which conscription would be adopted in case volunteers failed to come forward at the rate of 50,000 a month.

Then the Labor members requested the Premier to hold secret sessions of Parliament at which he might frankly explain the situation and its requirements. It is almost unprecedented for Parliament to meet in secret session since the days of Cromwell, altho the public has only been admitted within the last hundred years. This plan was adopted and Parliament met in secret session on April 25 after an Order in Council had been issued making it a criminal offense to disclose any of the proceedings.

The official report of the session states that the Premier explained fully the measures which had been taken to expand the army to its present strength and how many more troops were necessary. He discussed the finances of the war and told how much money had been advanced by Great Britain to her Allies. The recruiting measures so far adopted had proved insufficient, so the government proposed several minor measures. These were that the service of men whose time had expired be prolonged to the end of the war; that the territorials be transferred to any units where they were needed, and that youths arriving at the age of eighteen be brought into service unless they volunteered within one month.

But the bill introduced by the government differed decidedly from these proposals. It provided for the conscription of every unmarried man between the ages of 18 and 45. It was thought that the consent of the Commons had been secured in the secret session, but that proved erroneous, for in the open session the opposition was so strong that the Premier withdrew it. The Labor party, the Nationalists represented by John Redmond and the Ulsterites represented by Sir Edward Carson, threatened to withdraw their support of the government if this bill was insisted upon.

Then came two calamities, the loss of the British army in Mesopotamia and the rebellion in Ireland. This effected a violent change of opinion. Immediately a much more sweeping

bill than any previously proposed was introduced and the opposition to it practically vanished. The new bill will force into the army all males from 18 to 41, whether married or single, except such as are necessary for carrying on the essential industries. Even these will be under military discipline. The bill passed its second reading by a vote of 328 to 36. There is even talk of extending it to Ireland, which has hitherto been excluded from all the recruiting bills.

The Mystery of Verdun — When the battle of Verdun began on February 21, we said that it was hard to understand why the Germans chose this point of attack since it was the strongest fortress and the most remote from Paris. Now, more than ten weeks later, the mystery remains. If the German army had captured the city within a week or two it would undoubtedly have given them great prestige and possibly dis-heartened the French, tho it would not have materially weakened their powers of defense. But as it is German prestige has rather suffered than gained, for if with the employment of half a million troops and enormous expenditures of ammunition they have not made any substantial inroads into the French lines it is decidedly encouraging to the defense. The Germans, of course, may take Verdun yet, but if they do it will not be accounted a great victory, as it would have been earlier.

So far the battle of Verdun might be called a drawn game. The Germans have gained some ground almost every week, but on the other hand the main fortifications of the French are still intact. Which is to be regarded as the winning side up to the present depends

Starrett in New York Tribune

HOW LONG WILL IT STAY?

© *Medem Photo Service*

THE MAN-HIGH SHELL

The new French 40-centimeter—ft rival for the famous 42-centimeter guns with which Germany startled the world. The French have begun to change their artillery theories in view of the German successes with siege guns, tho heretofore they have relied chiefly on their famous "75's"

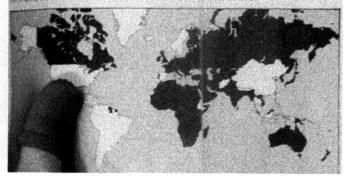

THOSE HENRY FORD VOTES

BY ELLIS O. JONES

SUPPOSE you had been asked, before the recent primary vote in Michigan, how many votes Henry Ford would get. Our first impulse would have been to treat the matter as one of those far-famed Ford "jokes."

But suppose some Ford enthusiast had prest you to take it seriously and spend a moment canvassing the probabilities. You could then have pointed out with ease that it was impossible for him to get any votes. First, considering that it was only a primary, you could have shown that only faithful party Republicans would vote and, as the party organization was against him, these faithful party workers would be against him also.

Then you could have shown that Mr. Ford would not appeal to the people because he had never given any evidence of knowing anything about practical politics. He had never made a speech or written an article or even been to college. You could have recalled Mr. Ford's recent confession that he has voted only twice in the last twenty years. What chance would such a man have in a political primary against such a seasoned campaigner as Senator William Alden Smith with the Republican organization solidly behind him? No chance in the world. What Ford carried Michigan? Rock-ribbed Republican Michigan? Impossible.

Then the impossible happened. Ford did carry Michigan in a most miraculous manner. The Republicans voted for Ford, who was not a candidate, and refused to vote for Senator Smith who was a very active candidate.

Now suppose you had been asked to prognosticate the result of the primary in Nebraska. You would have been nearly as positive as before that Mr. Ford's chances were slim. You would have said, "Oh, well, he might be able to get a big 'complimentary' vote in his own home state, but what chance has he got in a state like Nebraska?"

Again the organization was against him and again he was opposed by a seasoned campaigner, Senator Cummins. But again the impossible happened. Mr. Ford came within such a small margin of defeating Senator

Mr. Jones is a humorist with a serious purpose—an effective social satirist. But he takes Mr. Ford seriously—just as the voters of Michigan and Nebraska did, and as students of present-day political tendencies must do. The Ford vote is to date the most unexpected element in a topsy-turvy Presidential campaign, and we are glad to present this analysis of its meaning in the midst of our articles on the many phases of this exciting political year—after Mr. Bryan and the Views, and before Senator Harding, the Republican keynote man, John LaFollette, who speaks for four million women voters, and others to be announced. Mr. Jones was on the Peace Ship and knows Ford at first hand.—THE EDITOR.

Cummins as to leave not a single boast in the victory.

Taken together, these two votes constituted a political event of great interest. It brought the politicians up standing. The burden of explaining the phenomenon was a tremendous one to the wiseacres. Here was an unknown quantity, a dark horse. What about him? How did it happen? The people had never acted so foolishly before. What had got into them? What undiscovered

law of mob psychology caused these voters in great numbers to walk up to the polls and scratch in the name of this man whom they did not know, who had never been discussed and analyzed by the sage and solemn editors and who had not been vouched for by the political leaders?

The explanations came, but they did not explain. As there was a tendency before the vote to minimize his chances, now, strangely enough, there is a tendency to minimize what has happened, to ascribe it to a public whim upon a question of "peace" or "militarism" or perhaps of "wages." But we must remember that others are in favor of peace and against militarism, but the people do not flock to the polls and vote for them for President. Others have instituted profit-sharing systems, but the people do not flock to the polls and vote for them for President. Others have been successful in business to a high degree, but the more successful they are, the less inclination is there usually to flock to the polls and vote for them for President.

The true explanation lies deeper than any one or two of these reasons. It must embrace them all and more. In a word, Henry Ford, thru a series of acts and utterances, has taken a powerful hold of the popular imagination. He imprest his personality and his democratic philosophy upon the public mind in an emphatic manner.

No one who sees Mr. Ford can fail to be drawn to him irresistibly. This stood out clearly on the Ford Peace Ship. On that famous voyage the passengers ... disagreed, ... such an extent ... reports of dis... was perhaps ... so many ... viduals gathered ... quickly and ... closely. But there ... point upon which ... agreed and that ... gard to the mag... amiable personality ... Ford himself—at ... quiet, friendly and ... proachable; always ... positive in his op... but with never the sl... effort to force his opinions upon others. He ... stopped to develop a thought... in conversation, but was content to announce a conclusion that he had already pondered over and to announce

THE MOST LAUGHED-AT SERIOUS MAN IN AMERICA

Harding in Brooklyn Eagle
THE BLUNDERBUSS

Starrett in New York Tribune
STILL GROPING

Kirby in New York World
PINCHED

upon which has suffered the greater loss of men and munitions relatively to its total strength, and this is something that cannot be told.

If the Germans expected to carry Verdun by storm it is evident that they vastly overrated their own ability or were grievously deceived as to the natural strength of the fortress and the French power of resistance. But another theory suggests itself, that is, that the French designed to make Verdun their starting point for their spring offensive, and that the Germans, finding this out, forestalled them by attacking first. Verdun lying at the apex of the French salient pointing directly toward Metz would be the natural base for such a movement if the French intended to carry the war into the enemy's country. But whatever may have been the plans of the Allies for a spring offensive the German attack on Verdun evidently spoiled them. So far the Allies have been kept busy on the defensive and there are no signs of any change in this respect. On the contrary, their concern seems to be to determine where the Germans will strike next. The fact that the Germans recently closed the Swiss frontier and refused to allow either mails or passengers to cross the line is taken to indicate that troops are being sent along the border to attack the French line south of Verdun. On the other hand, it is reported that German troops are being massed near the Belgian frontier for an attack upon the British lines.

The fighting about Verdun is of the same monotonous character as it has been of late. The Germans have continued their attacks upon Hill 304 and Le Mort Homme, west of the Meuse, and upon Pepper Ridge and Douaumont on the east. The French extended their holdings on Le Mort Homme in the first half of the week, but on May 4 the Germans began the assault of Hill 304 with a vigor equal to any of their earlier efforts. The French trenches and underground shelters were completely shattered by their large shells and then carried by the aid of clouds of suffocating gas.

The arrival of further contingents of Russian troops at Marseilles is announced by the French War Office. The rumor from Berlin that a transport bearing Russian troops struck a mine near Corfu and six hundred lives were lost tends to confirm the surmise that the troops sent to Marseilles are in part or in whole Serbian soldiers from Corfu instead of Russians from Archangel.

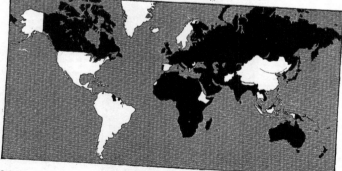

THE WORLD-WIDE WAR

Gradually the shadow of the war has spread until now it covers the greater part of the habitable globe. The twenty-one American republics are exempt, thanks to the Monroe doctrine. In Europe Spain, Scandinavia, Switzerland, Holland and Rumania are not yet involved. Greece and China, tho ostensibly non-combatants, have been made the battleground of the belligerents. And if a person in pursuit of peace should seek refuge in the apparent oases of Afghanistan, Abyssinia or Borneo he would find that he had exchanged the frying pan for the fire

THOSE HENRY FORD VOTES

BY ELLIS O. JONES

SUPPOSE you had been asked, before the recent primary vote in Michigan, how many votes Henry Ford would get. Your first impulse would have been to treat the matter as one of those far-famed Ford "jokes."

But suppose some Ford enthusiast had prest you to take it seriously and spend a moment analyzing the probabilities. You could then have pointed out with ease that it was impossible for him to get many votes. First, considering that it was only a primary, you could have shown that only faithful party Republicans would vote and, as the party organization was against him, these faithful party workers would be against him also.

Then you could have shown that Mr. Ford would not appeal to the people because he had never given any evidence of knowing anything about practical politics. He had never made a speech or written an article or even been to college. You could have recalled Mr. Ford's recent confession that he has voted only twice in the last twenty years. What chance would such a man have in a political primary against such a seasoned campaigner as Senator William Alden Smith with the Republican organization solidly behind him? No chance in the world. What! Ford carried Michigan? Rock-ribbed Republican Michigan? Impossible.

Then the impossible happened. Ford did carry Michigan in a most miraculous manner. The Republicans voted for Ford, who was not a candidate, and refused to vote for Senator Smith who was a very active candidate.

Now suppose you had been asked to prognosticate the result of the primary in Nebraska. You would have been nearly as positive as before that Mr. Ford's chances were slim. You would have said, "Oh, well, he might be able to get a big 'complimentary' vote in his own home state, but what chance has he got in a state like Nebraska?"

Again the organization was against him and again he was opposed by a seasoned campaigner, Senator Cummins. But again the impossible happened. Mr. Ford came within such a small margin of defeating Senator

Mr. Jones is a humorist with a serious purpose—an effective social satirist. But he takes Mr. Ford seriously—just as the voters of Michigan and Nebraska did, and as students of present-day political tendencies must do. The Ford vote is to date the most unexpected element in a touch-and-go Presidential campaign, and we are glad to present this analysis of its meaning in the midst of our articles on the many phases of this exciting political year—after Mr. Bryan and the Young Business Man Who Wants Teddy, and before Senator Harding, the Republican keynote man, Fola LaFollette, who speaks for four million women voters, and others to be announced. Mr. Jones was on the Peace Ship and knows Ford at first hand.—THE EDITOR.

Cummins as to leave not a single boast in the victory.

Taken together, these two votes constituted a political event of great interest. It brought the politicians up standing. The burden of explaining the phenomenon was a tremendous one to the wiseacres. Here was an unknown quantity, a dark horse. What about him? How did it happen? The people had never acted so foolishly before. What had got into them? What undiscovered

Paul Thompson

THE MOST LAUGHED-AT SERIOUS MAN IN AMERICA

law of mob psychology caused these voters in great numbers to walk up to the polls and scratch in the name of this man whom they did not know, who had never been discussed and analyzed by the sage and solemn editors and who had not been vouched for by the political leaders?

The explanations came, but they did not explain. As there was a tendency before the vote to minimize his chances, now, strangely enough, there is a tendency to minimize what has happened, to ascribe it to a public whim upon a question of "peace" or "militarism" or perhaps of "wages." But we must remember that others are in favor of peace and against militarism, but the people do not flock to the polls and vote for them for President. Others have instituted profit-sharing systems, but the people do not flock to the polls and vote for them for President. Others have been successful in business to a high degree, but the more successful they are, the less inclination is there usually to flock to the polls and vote for them for President.

The true explanation lies deeper than any one or two of these reasons. It must embrace them all and more. In a word, Henry Ford, thru a series of acts and utterances, has taken a powerful hold of the popular imagination. He imprest his personality and his democratic philosophy upon the public mind in an emphatic manner.

No one who sees Mr. Ford can fail to be drawn to him irresistibly. This stood out clearly on the Ford Peace Ship. On that famous voyage the passengers often disagreed, occasionally to such an extent as to warrant reports of dissension. This was perhaps inevitable with so many strong-minded individuals gathered together so quickly and packed in so closely. But there was one point upon which all were agreed and that was in regard to the magnetic and amiable personality of Mr. Ford himself—at all times quiet, friendly and easily approachable; always clear and positive in his opinions, but with never the slightest effort to force his opinions upon others. He rarely stopped to develop a thought in conversation, but was content to announce a conclusion that he had already pondered over and to announce

241

Next Week

NORMAN HAPGOOD

"The Spirit of the Administration"

In an Early Number

SENATOR HARDING

"Reënter Republicanism"

it in a terse epigrammatic fashion that carried conviction. On the other hand, he was a splendid listener, so that in his talks with the newspaper men he was usually less interviewed than interviewing.

Long before the "Oscar II" reached the bleak shores of Norway, it was the unanimous belief that the personality of Mr. Ford was the expedition's chief asset, that his mere appearance at receptions and public meetings could not fail at once to win the hearts and confidence of the people of the European neutral nations, and consequently there was universal regret when he was forced, on account of illness, to turn back at Christiania.

But what has all this to do with the votes in Michigana and Nebraska? These voters have not had the privilege of meeting Mr. Ford personally and looking him in the eye.

True enough. He has not met them personally. Nevertheless he has met them in spirit. He has made himself known to them by his deeds and they are willing to trust him. They believe that his spirit is essentially democratic, that he always thinks in terms of the people as a whole and not exclusively of any one class.

This will appear more clearly by briefly running over the prominent events in his career. First, he has risen from the ranks. Second, his wonderful success in the automobile business was not due to "trust" methods, to his controlling some great necessity of life at its source. It is due to his taking what was looked upon as a luxury but a few years ago and making it a necessity. He put the "mob" in automobile. This was a great democratic accomplishment.

Furthermore, he built solidly. His was not an ephemeral success. The steadily increasing growth of his business in this highly competitive industry, extending over a number of years, proves that Ford buyers and Ford owners feel they are getting their money's worth and it is natural for them to be grateful to the man who gave it to them. This is a large class, to which should be added many more who are grateful for the news which has gone abroad of Mr. Ford's low-priced farm tractor, which promises to revolutionize farming.

But notwithstanding Mr. Ford was selling a high grade product at a low price, he paid the very highest wages. While others talked about "profit-sharing," he introduced the most liberal profit-sharing plan that was ever known on a large scale in this or any other country. Without the slightest coercion on the part of labor unions, he fixed his schedules so that no man or boy in his huge factory would receive less than five dollars a day. This was something absolutely unheard of. The news was carried to every nook and cranny of the land and was the sensation of the hour.

His next prominent move in behalf of the people was in favor of peace and against militarism. Many months before the Ford Peace Expedition, he made it clear that he was on the democratic side in this war. It was always uppermost in his mind that it was the common people who had to support with their toil the tremendous tax burdens of militarism in time of peace and who had to do all the dying in time of war. The Peace Ship made the big dramatic moment in this campaign.

What did the Expedition accomplish? It did not stop the war or "take the boys out of the trenches," but it did, to use Mr. Ford's own epigram, "advertise peace" as peace had never before been advertised. Its appeal to the popular imagination was most profound. It did not stop the war, but it was easily the most noteworthy move toward that end and its influence will long be felt in many subtle and intangible ways.

The peace question has two sides: the European side and the American side. Mr. Ford is not one of those who has fought militarism abroad, while supporting it at home. He has viewed with the greatest alarm the recent encroachments of the military spirit in this country. He has looked upon it as a dangerous reversal of the proud traditions of peace upon which our country has been built. He has lent his time and his money to combat every effort to "Europeanize" the United States.

Those in brief are the outstanding events which have attracted the public to Mr. Ford. On the other hand, there has been nothing in his record to repel them. Altho a dreamer and idealist, nobody can accuse him of being impractical. Altho one of the richest men in the United States, nobody can accuse him of being monopolistic or grasping. He shows an unequivocal desire to take "the greatest good of the greatest number" at all times into consideration, but without upsetting any of our cherished institutions. He attracts employees without repelling employers. He goes ahead simply and sincerely, seeing clearly with a democratic vision, but without relating himself to any particular fads, isms or formulæ which have grown unpopular thru over-emphasis by intolerant devotees. He evinces a marvellous sense of values and a four-track mind which can accommodate all kinds of antagonistic mental traffic without collision.

Suppose someone should ask you how many votes Mr. Ford will get if he runs as a third candidate in the coming campaign. Don't treat the matter too lightly. You might be fooled as you were in Michigan and Nebraska. Think it over. It is dangerous to measure the present chaotic political situation by former standards. There are millions of citizens in this wide country who are tired of threshing over old straw and are eagerly watching for any opening that leads in a more profitable direction.

New York City

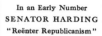

Carter in N. Y. Evening Sun

KEB, SIR! STRAIGHT TO THE WHITE HOUSE!.

THE WHIPS OF LIFE

BY HARRY KEMP

Life had me by the throat when I was young:
This way and that her pitiless lashes swung
Striving to strike me calm, yet she beheld
Twenty rebellions rise where one was quelled;
I felt the sky, itself, too closely bent . . .
My days were infinite with discontent.
I often longed for times when peace would pour,
Like sunlight on a solitary moor,
Her quiets over me.
⠀⠀⠀⠀⠀⠀⠀⠀⠀⠀But now *that's* come,
And youth's sweet voice of madness, long struck dumb,
Gives way to measured music learned by rote—
Oh, that life once more had me by the throat!

IRELAND'S HOLY DEAD

BY SEUMAS MacMANUS

GOD rest our holy dead! For them, Irishmen, dispersed the world round, mourn and rejoice.

Mourn for a moment. Rejoice forever.

Our Masters' lead, seeking to give them miserable death, has given them glorious life. They shall live as long as Ireland lives; as long as Freedom lives.

Thru the endless ages of Ireland's bloody travail England has unceasingly taken toll of our noblest. Always our noblest.

But never at one sweep did she gather to herself a nobler three.

Tom Clark, the undaunted, whose frame had grown frail in English prisons, but the fire of whose eye dungeons could not dim, and the fiber of whose soul shackles could not soften.

Tomás MacDonough, the eager, the ardent, the boy, bubbling with enthusiasms—the playful teacher, the merry piper, the joyous Gael.

Search America, which fosters a multitude of noble men, and you might find many as noble, but few more noble, than these.

And in your great America you would find a few as noble as, but no single soul more noble than, the third who fell to the English executioner's bullet—he the gentle and the earnest—Pádraic Pearse—he, with the heart of a child at its most childlike, and the spirit of a man at its most manlike—he, with the vision of a poet, the brain of a thinker, the hand of a doer, the soul of a patriot.

With such a man as Pádraic Pearse it is rarely God blesses a nation. For him, the rare educationist, the sub-

The author of "Yourself and the Neighbors" and a dozen other books has long been familiar to our readers and the American public as an interpreter of Irish life and Irish thought in both prose and verse. He is one of the prominent ones in the Young Ireland movement, and this threnody written on the execution of Tom Clark, Tomás MacDonough and Pádraic Pearse in the Tower of London expresses the spirit of militant Ireland.— THE EDITOR.

lime idealist, the wonderful achiever, not Ireland alone, but the world, may well mourn. For the lofty ideals to which he had been giving concrete form in the land of his soul's love would have uplifted mankind.

In other lands the vanquished soldier, reverenced and respected, but forfeits his liberty for a little while. Thru seven hundred years of unceasing war in Ireland the Irish soldier who has 'fought the unequal brave fight for his country's freeing has always been branded criminal, and for his crime paid forfeit with his life, or his lifetime's liberty. Till the English prison cell has, to us, become holy as a saint's cloister — and the gibbet, hallowed by the last steps of our bravest, an emblem only less sacred than the Cross.

No Irishman should idly sorrow. No Irishman should raise complaint. They whose bodies were shot thru by the Tyrant's bullets would rather die a thousand deaths than live by the unctuous grace of their country's conqueror.

And sorrow is not now for Ireland —but work. The three who lie in

English earth today, with England's lead in their hearts, did *their* work. They struck one brave, bold blow for Freedom, which, in the valleys of our unconquered and unconquerable land shall reverberate adown the centuries—insistently urging all workmen to the work.

That the crowd will call them foolish visionaries and failures matters not. A rabble that clattered down Calvary's Hill, one morning, prated contemptuously, too, of visionaries and failures. O short-sighted mobs!

And short-sighted was the Executioner, who, that gloomy morn, tying bandages on the eyes of these three men, thought to blind them— whereas he was only blinding the eyes of his own nation—while the bandaged eyes of the three Failures looked far down the future, seeing something that made them smile in their sleeve.

Short-sighted, too, when, believing that he put out these men's lives, he gave them earthly immortality

Tom Clark, Tomás MacDonough, Pádraic Pearse, for loved Ireland's sake, fearlessly faced their Executioner. And the trickling hearts' blood of these three brave fellows, dying, has done more to hasten Erin's harvest than could the gleaming blades of thirty thousand living.

They ARE thirty thousand—tho they were but three.

And they are not dead, but live.

Whoso dies for Ireland lives forever.

And from the myriad misty valleys of our ancient land I hear the clamant voices of a hundred thousand young men, crying, "Let US live! Let US live!"

243

War Cartoons from Seven Nations

"WE cartoonists are merely reporters with a drawing pen or brush instead of a pencil," said W. A. Rogers, one of the foremost of American cartoonists.

Cartoons are the most direct expression of what the people are actually thinking.

In Europe now the cartoons are of course all of war. English cartoons deal chiefly with social conditions at home and with the duty of enlisting. The dangers and the suffering of war are minimized or denied, and even

Drawn by Roubet

PETITS FRANCAIS IN WARTIME
A sketch in colors as delicate as those of the Italian cartoon, below, are violent

Drawn by Walter Klem

THE PEOPLE'S SACRIFICE—GERMANY

Courtesy of Punch, London

JOHN BULL FINDS ZEPPELINS HIS "BEST RECRUITER"

Courtesy of L'Asino

THE WAR OF LIBERATION FOR ITALY

the Zeppelin raids are turned inside out to show their silver lining.

France, on the other hand, considers more fundamental questions, and strikes a note of pity and of high idealism. The accompanying sketch of "Petits Français" was drawn just after the war began and it represents France as taking care of "another little brother—a little Belgium." The artist is Roulbot, a French cartoonist of recognized ability, whose work has artistic merit as well as popular appeal.

In Italy, where there is less fighting, there is a more vindictive attitude. For the most part Italian cartoons are scathing in their attacks on the enemy—sometimes savagely personal but usually symbolic rather than realistic. A characteristic example is the one entitled "The War of Liberation" — a soldier shooting at the heart of the double-headed eagle, which crushes un-

Courtesy of The Masses TO THE U. S.: "DID YOU CALL?"

windmills. Holland's cartoons have been among the most forceful in their grim realism. Jan Wiegman in his silhouettes of war such as the accompanying cartoon of "The Battlefield" gives a striking presentation of the misery of war.

In this country there is a less unified response in war cartoons. There is the same feeling of horror and of sympathy which is felt by all the neutrals, but considerations of preparedness outweigh the more objective emotions and throw the emphasis on our own application of the lessons of the war, as in the vigorous cartoon from *The Masses* voicing Death's question to the United States, "Did you call?"

Copyright by S. S. von Loor THE BATTLEFIELD—AS HOLLAND SEES IT

der its feet the Irredenta provinces of Trieste and Trent.

But the fiercest of war cartoons come from Germany, leeringly scornful or grimly suggestive of frightfulness. German war art deals oftenest with the battlefield, as it is depicted in The People's Sacrifice, by Walter Klem—an emotional study of what war may mean. Sometimes, however, the German cartoonists go to the other extreme and picture the follies of war with good-humored ridicule.

The spirit of the warring nations, as we see it in their art, is seldom war-glory, but rather pity, horror, and a patriotic sense of duty.

The neutral nations see the horror of war, too, and they frequently express a longing for peace. Spain is warned of the futility of her getting into the war by cartoons such as the one by Rubio on this page, in which Don Quixote tilts against 42 centimeter guns instead of

Courtesy of Nuevo Mundo SPAIN REVISES DON QUIXOTE

THE EFFICIENT HOME

BY EDWARD EARLE PURINTON

DIRECTOR OF THE INDEPENDENT EFFICIENCY SERVICE

HOME is the half-way house between earth and heaven. As such it needs the practical, and the ideal, both combined, more than any other human institution. The earth side of a home must be absolutely practical, and the heaven side must be absolutely ideal, if the home is to be a home.

There is more need for science in the home than for science anywhere else. Not because science is the most important thing in the home, but because the most neglected thing is always the most important. The average home is a conglomeration of guess-work, patch-work, and over-work. The guess-work is the fault of the man, the overwork of the woman, the patch-work of them both. A little science in advance would prevent most of the trouble.

As the one place where all human interests gather, center and radiate, the home should be given first consideration in a real efficiency program for a man, a city, or a nation. School efficiency, business efficiency, church efficiency, community efficiency, all depend to a large extent on home efficiency.

Because of lack of space, we must here confine ourselves largely to the home as a house. But we would first emphasize the supreme value of the home as an institution. Many a good woman—good but stupid—thinks so much of her home as a house that she forgets to be anything but a housekeeper. But the house is merely a shell for the home.

If you cannot have your home a model house and a model institution at the same time—never mind about the model house. A little dust in the corner of your parlor is better than a layer of dust on your mind.

Furthermore, a dollar with your best thought and feeling in it can do as much to make your home attractive as ten dollars spent rashly, thoughtlessly, flippantly.

THE HOME AS AN INSTITUTION

THE efficient home, as a modern institution, covers ten cardinal points, namely—*health, economy, beauty, productivity, hospitality, education, devotion, ambition, coöperation, character*. These points are universal in application. They have nothing to do with the size, cost or location of your house. You do not need to have a house, you may live in a $10-a-month flat, and still observe these ten cardinal points. We will consider them briefly.

1. *Health.* Half the disease in the United States could be prevented by the universal adoption of a home health system, including health instructions, health foods, baths, exercizes, garments, habits of life and methods of work. Many physicians claim that epidemics such as typhoid, grippe and scarlet fever would be impossible in a civilization where the home science of prevention of disease were understood and applied.

2. *Economy.* Every home should have installed a modern scheme of cost-finding, cost-keeping and cost-reducing, personal expenses on a scientific budget basis. Mother doubtless wastes a little, but father is apt to waste more, and the children are sure to waste most. Why reform mother exclusively?

3. *Beauty.* Home discord is largely the result of discordant surroundings. The sensory nerves must be soothed in the home. They are more often irritated.

4. *Productivity.* The home is fundamentally a social unit. The business of it, therefore, is to enable each member of the family to do more and better work in the community. For this purpose, physiological, psychological and industrial principles should be taught and embodied in the household. Are you improving the quantity and quality of your vocational output by at least ten per cent every year? If not, something is wrong with your home.

5. *Hospitality.* By this word I do not mean card parties, pink teas or pay-your-debts functions of any sort. I mean just a handclasp with some heart in it, an open home door. A test for your hospitality is that the fellow you invite never thinks what or how much you are going to give him to eat.

6. *Education.* The despair of conscientious teachers is the lack of and indifference to sound educational methods in the home. Careless thought and speech, unbridled emotions, superficial judgments, artificial standards—these home defects can never be redeemed by any curriculum of high school or college.

7. *Devotion.* This should be mutual, and reciprocal. Too often one member of the family—most often the mother, least often the son—expresses devotion for the entire group. The fires of destiny are kindled in the crucible of devotion. Back of the great man has always been some one's home prayer, faith, sacrifice.

8. *Ambition.* The purpose in our habitation is our evolution. Accordingly, every home must be outgrown, every blood tie broken, every association of mere kinship finally put off and away, as the locust drops his skin. Can you forget that your brother is your brother, your son is your son, your wife is your wife, and want for each only the highest good of each, whether *you* reap joy or sorrow from it? Do you know what the great ambition of each member of your family really is, and are you helping him or her to achieve it?

9. *Coöperation.* Every home should provide for a systematic study of coöperative method, as shown in the modern factory, mill or department store. The scientific grouping and control of individual tasks and relations in the family is almost unknown. Therefore, a burden of unnatural and unnecessary weight falls on some one member of the family—the most unselfish, and usually the least endowed with physical strength.

10. *Character.* The great need of the American home today is for a Spartan courage. With few exceptions, the backbones of our children are mush. We deny them the supreme strength which grows only from doing the hardest thing. The very multiplicity of conveniences and luxuries robs this generation of self-resource and self-reliance. Clearly and strongly as I urge the use of labor-saving devices in the home, I would beg of you to forget them all unless at the same time you teach the boys and girls how to *work*—hard and long and well, and painfully if need be. Nothing can ever take the place of old-fashioned hardship in the home production of character.

THE HOME AS A HOUSE

NOW for the home as a house. My friend, the architect, says there are five principal reasons why ninety-five per cent of the home owners are dissatisfied with their own work. These reasons may be summarized thus: (a) Failure to plan all details ahead; or even to know what the necessary details are; (b) failure to secure in advance all the available information; (c) failure to employ the best architect, builder and other helpers; (d) failure to sign a comprehensive, minute, iron-clad contract; (e) failure to keep the entire job under personal supervision. The aim of this article is to mark out lines of thought for the prevention of these mistakes.

The first suggestion is to begin home planning early in life. Every young man or woman over eighteen should be regularly saving for a

246

home. If you can save only $10 a year, this much will buy books and periodicals that should prevent a waste of hundreds, or even thousands of dollars, when you build later. Whatever your age, if you have not a home of your own, resolve now to have one—then start your plan. Real estate, properly chosen, bought and managed, is the universally good investment.

Build for yourself. Don't buy a second-hand house; it won't fit you any better than a second-hand suit of clothes. Your individual home tastes, needs and preferences must be learned before you build—not after. When they are clear to you, no house on earth but the house you make will satisfy you.

Be your own designer. The business of the architect you hire is to embody your ideas. If you haven't any, his work will fail, no mattter how good an architect he is.

Devote a year to learning home science. Take a mail course if possible, in advance of building. Purchase a small library of new and trustworthy books. Answer advertisements in popular and technical magazines; you can obtain a large assortment of booklets on all phases of home building, furnishing and decorating, merely by asking for these publications from various manufacturers, who will mail them without charge or on receipt of postage. Study these booklets. If you have a sweetheart, study them together.

Draw a rough plan of your home, lawn and garden, on a big sheet of bristol board or "art paper," allowing, say, half an inch on the draw-

ing for each foot of ground. This preliminary sketch will have to be altered considerably, first by yourself to grow with your ideas, then by the architect to be made practical. But get the whole thing on paper as early as possible, and exact in every detail.

Choose your architect—don't hire one because he lives near you or a friend of yours knows him. Be sure (1) that he is a specialist in your kind of home—whether a bungalow, a Queen Anne cottage or a Colonial manse; (2) that he can refer you to a number of satisfied clients; (3) that he belongs to national associations of architects, with high professional standing; (4) that he will guarantee the final cost of your home not to exceed the initial appropriation. There are some fifty trades and professions involved in the making of a home, from start to finish. These are mostly uncorrelated; hence delays, mistakes, and numerous "extras" in the bill are very likely, unless a blanket contract fully protects you against loss.

BUYING THE LAND

CONSIDER many things before you buy your land. Regard this purchase as an investment, apart from household features. Weigh its value by the possibility of resale at a good price—what you paid, or more. Ask a number of good business men their opinion of 125 feet front and 150 to 200 feet in depth; a front less than seventy-five feet, in a populous section, crowds one too close to his neighbors, while a front longer than 125 feet means too much lawn

mowing and general upkeep. Location should be high and dry, with house on highest part—a damp cellar breeds disease fast. Air and light must be plentiful on all sides (before you build study plans of the air-light health cottages now so popular in Europe). Neighborhood should be quiet, no street car within five or six blocks, and no garage, theater or other place of pandemonium nearby. Stores, schools and churches should be in reach of comfortable travel, with the place of work of each member of the family kept in view, as to daily loss of time in transit.

Always buy, however, just ahead of the crowd, where new transportation lines are sure to come, but have not yet come. The same rule holds in the country, where the "good roads" movement will increase the value of land. Have your title guaranteed by a title guarantee company or a firm of responsible lawyers. Before signing the contract, go and visit the property some winter day, with a blizzard howling above and a snow-drift rising beneath, and no suave, summery land agent breathing soft nothings in your ear. The time to look at real estate is when the real estate man isn't looking.

Buy your land on instalments if necessary, paying the same as rent, after you negotiate with a building and loan company to advance money for the house. But pay cash for all the contents of the house. Furnish one room at a time, or buy one chair or picture—only pay cash. Comforts on credit are discomforts.

Place your house at least fifty feet back from the street if possible, for

---

EFFICIENT HOME TEST

FOR SELF-APPLICATION BY ANY MAN OR WOMAN DESIRING TO IMPROVE HOME CONDITIONS AND OPPORTUNITIES

DIRECTIONS. Where answer is Yes, write numeral 5 in blank space opposite. Where answer is No, leave space blank. Where answer is partially affirmative, write numeral between 1 and 5 expressing degree of assurance. Add column of numerals for total grade in per cent. This Test is not complete, merely indicative. Queries on the subject will be gladly answered by Mr. Purinton, so far as practicable; address your letter in care of The Independent Efficiency Service, 119 West Fortieth Street, New York.

1. Is your home free of debt, and insured fully—both house and contents? ....
2. Could you sell the property today for at least 20 per cent more than it cost you? ....
3. Is your outdoor and indoor color scheme artistic, restful, individual? ....
4. Are your pictures, tapestries and other ornaments very few but very good? ....
5. Have you electric light and automatic ventilation for every room? ....
6. Before installing your heating system, did you study at least four other systems? ....
7. Are kitchen, pantry, laundry arranged according to the plans of experts? ....
8. Could you keep house comfortably without a maid? ....
9. Have you a home gymnasium and playroom? ....
10. Has everybody in the family given the sleeping-porch a fair trial? ....
11. Have you plenty of flowers, a prize lawn, and a profitable garden? ....
12. Does the whole family enjoy together at least one evening a week? ....
13. Do you entertain the rich and the poor equally well, and equally often? ....
14. Have the home duties and responsibilities been fairly apportioned among the occupants? ....
15. Is the right home regimen helping you to do more and better work each year? ....
16. Are you saving a little money regularly, for home developments and improvements? ....
17. Does each member follow the budget system of personal finances? ....
18. Do you take at least two home science magazines, have you read at least two home science books? ....
19. Have you joined a civic or domestic improvement association? ....
20. Do you consider moral backbone the finest home product, and are you making it? ....

Copyright, 1916, by
Edward Earle Purinton

Total equals your approximate grade in conception and creation of an efficient home

seclusion and symmetry, and at or near the center of your plot, thus leaving space in front for flower beds, at sides for shrubbery, in rear for vegetable garden and perhaps fruit trees or berries.

BUY THE BEST

PRACTISE real economy by having the best where only the best will serve. Thus, after wide investigation and comparison, choose the best in grass, seed, in flower and vegetable seeds, in building and roofing material, in house paint, in heating, lighting and ventilating systems, in plumbing and fireproofing, in wall finish and interior decoration, in bedroom, bathroom and kitchen furnishings, in hygienic factors thruout. Among building materials are wood, stone, tile, concrete, face brick, tapestry brick, tile-and-brick, tile - and - stucco, frame-and-stucco, patent compounds of different kinds. Among roofing materials are shingle, tin, slate, galvanized iron, tile, asphalt, and special chemical fabrics. Don't build without learning what your best material is for house and roof.

Study with extra care the problems of heat, light and ventilation. Most heating boilers burn only about sixty per cent of their fuel; they become enthusiastic in hot weather and apathetic in cold. Get a *good* boiler, gentle, pliable, and considerate of your purse, time and temper. The heating plant may be steam, hot water or hot air. Each claims advantages over the others. Whichever you order, be sure there is supplied at least thirty cubic feet of fresh air per minute for each occupant of every room. Some plants change the air completely every half hour. National heating companies will often study your house plan, and make specific recommendations, without charge. As for illumination, a modern electric plant may now be installed for less than the price of a good piano. Or, acetylene may be used, or a self-generating gas now on the market.

Ponder long your color scheme. Before you paint your house, get a wide assortment of "color cards" from the leading paint companies, and make your house harmonious, or leave it unpainted.

Fix the size, location and arrangement of your rooms only after reading several books on home building, or consulting a domestic engineer. Otherwise, you are almost sure to neglect some vital pont, learned only by experience. A wise procedure would be to visit one of the "practise cottages" in home economics now maintained by the more progressive schools, particularly agricultural colleges and state universities.

Ask your friends and neighbors what mistakes and omissions were found in the construction of their homes, and avoid these. Among things commonly overlooked are these: A cellar for storing fruits and vegetables, made of concrete, and thus rat-proof; a ten or twelve foot porch around two sides of the house —on the least exposed side an arrangement for outdoor sleeping; a laundry extension to the rear of the house, with space for modern machines and equipment; a flight of back stairs, for surreptitious use when "company" is in the parlor and you haven't your company clothes on; a numerous and generous array of closets—closets being to a woman's comfort what pockets are to a man's; a playroom and gymnasium, where all the family can be children together; a lavatory on each floor; a speaking tube or interphone system of communication between floors; a grouping and spacing of kitchen, pantry and dining room according to the principles of scientific management; a sound-proof, detached study or library; a conservatory and solarium, where potted plants and also human flowers may take sun baths for their health.

BE MODERN

PLAN to make your home thoroly modern; in this respect do not take any house of a neighbor for a pattern, since new methods and utilities unknown even a few months ago are now available. Some of the typical modern improvements are these: Patent wall linings, fire-resisting, sound-deadening and moisture-proof; liquid wall finish, artistic, washable and durable, to take the place of wall-paper; colorfast, reversible moth-proof rugs, made to harmonize with color scheme of room; china and porcelain bathroom fixtures; new material, heat, acid and rust proof, for kitchen cabinets, ranges and refrigerators; non-rusting, non-corroding, wrought iron sanitary piping; weather - proof screening for windows and doors; hygienic ventilators, keeping out drafts, dust and storms; combination cellar window and coal-chute, to protect house and lawn from both coalman and burglar; milk bottle and package receiver, weather-proof and burglar-proof; underground garbage receiver, always closed, fly and rat proof; house revolving fan, run by alcohol; smokeless oil heater, for speedy warmth on winter mofnings; lawn mower that stays sharp but fails to cut up the lawn, confining itself to the grass; outdoor living room for lawn or garden use; old-fashioned fireplace and hearth in new dress; bird houses and bird baths; hand fire extinguishers, to quench a blaze quickly and decisively; hammerless safety revolver, for protection against intruders; complete sectional furniture, made in a factory to your order, and shipped ready to frame; complete sectional houses, built and bought in a similar way, at prices from $300 to $10,000.

This article must be incomplete; space forbids proper mention of interior decoration; furnishings and equipment; music, books and pictures; games, tool-kit, emergency chest; landscape gardening; flower and vegetable culture; care of birds and other household pets; consideration of personal factors in housing and developing each member of the family. But these things may be learned thru books, magazines, mail courses and special institutions.

An important question, however, must be answered—a question that many of our readers will ask. "How can a dreary, skimpy and faulty house, built in the last generation, be transformed into a model home—comfortable, hygienic and artistic?" We affirm, as always: *Anything can be done that should be done.* At least two-thirds of the suggestions offered here may be *adapted* to any home, anywhere, by means of sufficient thought, work, ingenuity and persistence. Whoever can remodel his mind can remodel his home. The mind problem is the real one. Cases are on record where an old, ramshackle farmhouse in the last stages of decrepitude was rebuilt, refurnished, made wholesome, attractive and profitable at slight comparative cost.

Furthermore, it does not matter now where you live—whether in city, town or country; as you can order anything by mail, from the nameplate on your door to the house itself. Indeed, the best home is neither a country home nor a city home—it is a country home in the city or a city home in the country. The city home has conveniences, refinements and improvements that the country home needs; the country home has health, quiet and freedom that the city home needs; wherever you live, put them together and enjoy the advantages of both.

Every home, with the right combination of heart, head and hands, may become a storehouse of health, a model of thrift, a palace of comfort, a dream of beauty, and a mount of peace. To make a home like this will be a crucial test, and a supreme triumph of wisdom, affection, skill, devotion, character.

THE FRIENDSHIP OF FOUR NEUTRALS

THE WORK OF THE AMERICAN-SCANDINAVIAN FOUNDATION IN IMPROVING OUR ACQUAINTANCE WITH THE NORTHERN KINGDOMS

FREDERICK LYNCH

The President of the Trustees of The American-Scandinavian Foundation since its establishment, who was originally consulted by Mr. Poulson in formulating his great international ideals. Dr. Lynch is Secretary of the Church Peace Union and is prominently identified with many other organizations working either for world peace or for internationalism. He is a graduate of Yale and a Congregational minister, but resigned his pastorate in 1910 to devote himself entirely to his work as a writer and lecturer. He is the editor of *Christian Work and Evangelist*

JOHN ALLYNE GADE

The Vice-President of the Foundation. His father was a Norwegian, for many years honorary Consul of the United States in Christiania. Mr. Gade was graduated from the Harvard School of Architecture and has followed for many years his profession of architect in New York. Largely by his assistance Roald Amundsen was enabled to make his dash for the South Pole. Mr. Gade has been the promoter and benefactor of numerous Scandinavian undertakings in the United States, and performed a notable service in bringing to this country the Scandinavian Art Exhibition, in 1912-13

WITHOUT ignorance, no war. It has often been maintained that if nations understood each other thoroly, appreciated the alien habits of thought of their neighbors, there would be no incitement to strife. While most of Europe is busily tearing down the civilization constructed with pains thru the centuries, while in America many factors are contributing either directly or indirectly to war, other agencies are quietly and steadily establishing friendship and understanding between nations. Such a force is The American-Scandinavian Foundation, which is building on a solid basis an intellectual bridge between our great neutral democracy and three small democratic kingdoms, neutral likewise, of Northern Europe. This Foundation is not a peace society, but its international propaganda contributes actually to the cause of peace.

The American-Scandinavian Foundation was established in 1911 by the late Niels Poulson, president of the Hecla Iron Works of Brooklyn. Mr. Poulson was a native of Denmark and came a poor mechanic to America. Here he amassed a fortune and, fortunately, put it to the service of a great ideal—the elimination of ignorance, especially concerning the relations past and present of Scandinavia and the United States. To a self-perpetuating board of fifteen trustees, whom he himself named, he entrusted property valued at half a million dollars. The act of incorporation of this board, approved by Mr. Poulson, directed that the interest from his endowment, and other funds which the board might receive, should be expended "for the purpose of maintaining an exchange of students and teachers, and for supporting all other forms of educational intercourse between the United States of America, Denmark, Norway, and Sweden." The following year the three Scandinavian kings became patrons of the Foundation and appointed committees in each country to coöperate with the trustees.

What form should their endeavor take? The constitution gave the trustees much freedom. They were directed to use the income in any way that might seem to them most likely to promote intellectual relations between the four countries. The easiest process would have been to turn the whole income into stipends for Scandinavian stu-

HENRY GODDARD LEACH

As Secretary of the Foundation and the executive director of its activities, Dr. Leach has done much to spread a better knowledge of Scandinavian life and institutions. He lived two years in Sweden, Denmark, and Norway, and is the author of "Scandinavia of the Scandinavians." He was graduated from Princeton in 1903. He was an instructor at Harvard in English and Old Norse until called to New York in 1912 to devote his whole time to The American-Scandinavian Foundation

OSCAR MONTELIUS

The Chairman of the Swedish Committee of eleven named by King Gustav V., in each of the three Scandinavian countries. The monarchs, who are Patrons of the Foundation, appoint advisory committees, who in their turn select two Fellows annually to study in America. Professor Montelius is a member of the Swedish Academy, and the author of several works on archeology. It is said that he knows Sweden in the stone age better than any living man knows his country today

249

dents wishing to study in America. They were unwilling, however, thus to minimize their responsibility. They conceived of the Foundation as a broad international opportunity. They answered the call for public service by creating an educational bureau for information and publicity, and for lending moral support to all forms of intellectual intercourse. Without salary or other compensation, the fifteen trustees have given unstintingly of their time and energy.

They entrust the executive routine of the Foundation to a secretary, formerly instructor in Harvard University, who is aided by a small salaried staff. With an income as yet less than twenty thousand dollars, due to the untiring efficiency of this small staff and the disinterested coöperation of the trustees, a work of public service has developed which probably equals that of some endowments which are many times greater.

The educational program of the Foundation aims to interpret the literature, art, science, and social life of Scandinavia to the American people. One of the first acts of the Foundation was to vote a subvention to the Scandinavian Art Exhibit of 1912-13, organized by Mr. John A. Gade, which in Chicago alone, was visited by 69,094 persons. In 1913 the trustees voted to form an international affiliation of associates, inviting all who were interested in the work of the Foundation to become enrolled.

The number of associates now exceeds four thousand, including teachers, bankers, authors, statesmen, and in large measure, representative Americans of Scandinavian descent. The associate organizations embrace the American Society of Denmark, formed in 1914, among whose members are directors of many business houses having trade relations with the United States.

Over and above the performance of routine duties, the staff of the Foundation have been able to assist in the progress of Scandinavian studies in schools and colleges, to give lectures, ·to advise women's and social service clubs in arranging their programs, to encourage concerts of Northern music and dramatic performances, to make connections for Scandinavian students and lecturers visiting this country, to advise authors in disposing of their manuscripts, to aid publishers in putting on the market books translated from the Scandinavian languages, to send out bulletins to the press, to answer requests

NIELS POULSON
Who endowed The American-Scandinavian Foundation, was born of poor parents in Horsens, Denmark, in 1843, and died in Brooklyn in 1911. He came to America as a young journeyman builder. Mr. Poulson was one of the first to realize the possibilities of iron construction in a modern city and, with his friend, Michael Eger, started the Hecla Iron Works in Brooklyn, which brought him his fortune

for expert information; in short, to perform all the functions of a public-spirited bureau of education.

Niels Poulson had much at heart the dissemination of correct information about the Scandinavian countries by means of an illustrated periodical, and in making his first bequest to the cause he specified as one purpose "educating public opinion concerning these nations thru platform and press." Such a periodical, *The American-Scandinavian Review*, was established by the Foundation, beginning in January, 1913, and has since appeared bi-monthly, being sent to all associates of the Foundation and other subscribers. Its literary editor is Miss Hanna Astrup Larsen, an American essay-writer of distinguished Norwegian ancestry.

In 1914 the trustees established two series of books, also published by the Foundation, under the supervision of a Committee on Publications. The chairman of the committee is William Henry Schofield, Professor of Comparative Literature at Harvard University, and the other members, Professor Arthur Hubbell Palmer, of Yale University, and Dr. Leach, Secretary of the Foundation.

In one series, the *Scandinavian Classics*, four translations have already been printed: *Comedies* by Holberg, *Poems* by Tegnér, *Poems and Songs* by Björnstjerne Björnson, and *Master Olof*, Strindberg's great historical drama. In the other

series, the *Scandinavian Monographs*, two books have appeared: *The Voyages of the Norsemen to America*, by Professor William Hovgaard, of the Massachusetts Institute of Technology, and *Ballad Criticism in Scandinavia and Great Britain During the Eighteenth Century*, by Dr. Sigurd Bernhard Hustvedt, of the University of Illinois.

In spite of the expenses of maintaining an educational bureau and these various publications, so well have the resources of the Foundation been husbanded that about one-third of the annual income can be devoted to scholarships· for traveling students. In Sweden, Denmark, and Norway each year the Advisory Committees appointed by the kings select two Fellows of the Foundation who come· to American universities and corresponding institutions for research.

About ·half of their number have been engineers, but practically all branches of study are open for the applicants. At present one Fellow is studying road building at Columbia University, another industrial organization at the College of the City of New York, a third library methods at the New York Public Library School. The fourth is a lawyer investigating our inheritance laws at the Harvard Law School; a fifth is a naval engineer, studying at the naval tank at the University of Michigan; and the sixth·is an agricultural specialist investigating animal breeding problems at the University of Illinois. Two years ago one Fellow of the Foundation was a former student of Madame Curie, Miss Ellen Gleditsch, lecturer at the University of Christiania, who carried on important investigations in radium at Yale and was awarded the honorary degree of Doctor of Science at Smith College. Similarly, American students are sent by the Foundation to universities in Denmark, Norway, and Sweden, where they are at present studying literature, languages, history, and bacteriology.

The propaganda conducted by The American-Scandinavian Foundation in the United States is consistent at every point with loyal Americanism. Even when exhorting descendants of Scandinavians to keep alive in English dress their inherited traditions of art and literature, this Foundation is not encouraging the perpetuation of alien groups within our midst, but rather is aiding these children of Northern stock to assimilate and to support with their high idealism the principles of American liberty.

THE CHAUTAUQUA IDEA

THE MOST AMERICAN THING IN AMERICA

IF I were a cartoonist I should symbolize Chautauqua by a tall Greek goddess, a s y l v a n goddess with leaves in her h a i r — not vine leaves, oak leaves — tearing o p e n the bars of a cage wherein has been confined a bird, say, an owl, labeled "Learning." For that is what Chautauqua has done for the world, it has let learning loose.

Once upon a time—and it was not so long ago but what some of us can remember it, tho most of us have forgotten it—education was thought to be a thing which could be imparted to one sex at one place within one particular period of life; it was confined to those young men, more rarely young women, who had been trained in a rigidly prescribed course and who could afford to spend four years studying certain designated subjects in a rigidly prescribed way. No allowance was made for differences of age, creed, sex, race or previous condition of intellectual servitude.

Nowadays all that is changed. All except the most conservative universities now make some provision for the education of those of different sex and ages and take into consideration differences of past training and future plans. Many of them recognize "absent treatment" as a legitimate branch of mental therapeutics, and aim to meet the demand by some sort of correspondence or local center work. Most of them recognize the right of adults and non-professional students to receive instruction by means of lectures and evening classes.

In this revolution Chautauqua has been one of the most efficient factors. It did not start out to supplant the colleges, but to supplement them. It has never diverted from the colleges any who could go to them. On the contrary, it has fed the colleges—and opened their eyes. It has demonstrated the practicability of various new forms of education which previously had been ignored or inadequately provided for, but now are undertaken by all sorts of agencies, public and private. Chief among the innovations for which we are largely indebted to Chautauqua I should name the following four:

Self-Education. This is, after all, the only possible kind of education, tho there is a spurious imitation of education which consists of forcible feeding, like that practised upon geese at Strassburg and elsewhere. But cramming in coops results in nothing more than fatty degeneration of the assimilative organs, for real development of the muscles can only come from their exercise.

An old schoolmate of mine, who was recently called to a professorship of a great eastern university was telling me

of his experiences. He noticed that a young man, obviously a member of the rich and leisure class, who had registered for his course, had not appeared since the opening day. Meeting the student one day as he was hurrying across the campus to some extra-curricular activity, my friend asked why he was not attending class. "Oh, that's all right, professor," answered the youth, "I send my secretary instead. He takes down your complete lectures in shorthand every day, while if I was there I could not get half of it."

Now the person who pegs away by himself, hour after hour, day after day, month after month, on a Chautauqua course of study, or a Five-foot Bookshelf or a correspondence school course or any other scheme of systematic reading is getting a sort of self-education which is worth something, even tho it may not give him the right to wear a square cap with a tassel on it.

Home Education. To gather people together where the books are was the old form of education. To scatter the books among the people is the new way; not equal to the old in many respects, but having certain advantages of its own. Not every student devours his weight of books in the course of a college year and when he does not it is cheaper to move the books than to move the man. The invention of printing and photography, as well as the motion picture and the phonograph, has mobilized information, and so far as mere learning is concerned one can usually find out whatever is to be known without leaving his own home. Nor need he be altogether without the stimulus of personal contact with great thinkers, for Chautauqua has discovered that men are movable as well as books. The number of speakers who are really worth listening to is comparatively small, and even they cannot talk continually to the same audience without running out of things worth saying, so it is better

policy to send them around the country than to keep them in one place. Now it is something of a privilege to be able to talk face to face with a million people, and the men who wished to influence their contemporaries soon found that they could do it most effectively thru the Chautauqua assemblies and various lecture centers which sprang up in imitation of them thruout the country.

Spare-time Education. The utilization of idle minutes in systematic study is another Chautauqua scheme which has spread amazingly. This is due to the discovery that it is possible to learn something worth while even tho one cannot devote his whole time and attention to study. Even boys who are sent to college for the purpose do not, as is well known, devote their whole time and attention to study. We speak about "getting an education" as if it were some single thing to be got at a particular time and place like buying an overcoat. As well might we talk of "getting an exercise" to last thru life by paying a visit to a gymnasium. Education, true education, is a form of mental growth, like developing and maintaining a sound muscular system. It requires time and the gain does not depend altogether upon the number of hours a day which can be devoted to study. The college student who dilutes his learning with play is wise, tho often the dilution is excessive. The non-collegian who dilutes his work with learning is wise, and his progress is often greater than seems possible from the time spent in study.

Lifelong Education. This follows from the former. The educative process is not to be confined within four years any more than within four walls. Adults need it as well as youths, tho of a different kind. "Call no man educated until he is dead" might have been said by Solon. A diploma should not be granted till the death certificate is filed, otherwise the world and the holder of the degree is likely to be deceived into thinking that he has been educated. Chautauqua has done a double service in teaching people who thought they had been educated that they were not, and people who thought they could be educating themselves. It has set men and women all over the country collectively to listening, singly to thinking, and coöperatively to reading along certain well planned lines of study.

EDWIN E. SLOSSON.

Americanization Week at Chautauqua will be July 17-21, when authorities on the problems of the immigrant in America are to discuss various questions—admission tests, naturalization plans and state and national policies of assimilation. Professor Edward A. Steiner, author of "The Immigrant Tide," will give the principal address.

THE NEW BOOKS

WAR—AND RUMORS OF WAR

Those who go to training camps and may later become citizen soldiers will find Captain Andrews' *Fundamentals of Military Science* useful in leading them to a comprehensive knowledge of the soldier's life in its routine. It is a serious manual on camp work, army organization, guard duty, sanitation, in short, on all the manifold duties of the citizen soldier. It is popular, not over-technical, and ought to be a great aid to true preparedness. It is a real work.

A plea for the recognition of our individual and national responsibilities is made in *Wake Up, America*, a little book by William R. Castle, Jr. He calls for national and patriotic thought and coöperation, which he thinks better than the panaceas of minimum wage, woman suffrage, government control and socialism; his political philosophy is that in return for its protection all should equally serve or be ready to serve the country by undergoing a system of athletic and military drill akin to the Swiss. None of our prominent leaders come to his standard, tho Roosevelt approaches it. The book should have been longer in training camp.

Cleveland Moffett's "Great Romance of the Invasion of the United States in 1921," *The Conquest of America*, is as full of thrills as the most excitable and fearful patriot need ask. His scientific aptitude gives plausibility to the narrative of the German invasion and conquest of America by striking at New York and New England, and then New Jersey and then the office of the *Saturday Evening Post*. The Panama Canal is dynamited. Our available navy, just gone to the Pacific to be looked at by Japan, has to chase around thru the Straits to meet the huge German fleet and finally succumb to it in the Caribbean—a thrilling spectacle as seen from Vincent Astor's aeroboat. Really we have here a sort of elite directory of "the military heart of America," and if all the prominent Americans named in the tale, as hostages or otherwise, get about the business of preparedness, this invasion will never be.

Fundamentals of Military Science, by Capt. L. C. Andrews. Philadelphia: Lippincott. $1.50.
Wake Up, America, by William R. Castle, Jr. Dodd, Mead. 50 cents. *The Conquest of America*, by Cleveland Moffett, Doran. $1.50.

THE ROMANY RYE AGAIN

Certain tributes to friends contributed from time to time in *The Athenæum* by Theodore Watts-Dunton have now been collected and published under the title, *Old Familiar Faces*. Tho most of the papers are slight, written shortly after the death of one or another of the old circle that had been wont to gather at "The Pines," the home of Watts-Dunton and Swinburne one finds in the least of them keen character analysis, wide sympathy and apt criticism. In the sketches of Borrow, of Groome and of Hake we come upon

252

the Romany interests out of which grew years ago "Alwyn" and "The Coming of Love." The papers on the Rossettis and Morris leave singularly lively impressions of these households. The most complete study is that of Tennyson, which includes a review of the life by his son and much worth while reflection on this matter of biography. It is a pity that so acute and thoughtful an observer and so gentle a judge has left us but a novel, a few poems and a handful of essays.

Old Familiar Faces, by Theodore Watts-Dunton. Dutton. $1.75.

A CARICATURE OF YOUTH

"The real thing—the real thing at last," William Sylvanus Baxter, aged seventeen, nodded solemnly to himself as he meditated on his first momentous discovery of the One and Only Girl.

And thus unintentionally William also achieved the rare distinction of reviewing his own book, *Seventeen*—that delightful "tale of youth and summertime and the Baxter family—especially William," in which Booth Tarkington has gaily vivisected Youth, not as the poets fancy it, but Youth "as is."

The hero—or rather the victim—is of course William. His ludicrous failures to make others see him as he sees himself furnish a whole summer of laughter-provoking situations, ingeniously complicated by a dress-suit, a small sister, a wash-boiler, a picnic, and a host of bewildered and unfeeling relatives and friends—as well as by The Girl, known to the privacy of William's day-dreams as "My baby-talk lady."

In their meeting Mr. Tarkington finds occasion for one of his best bits of analytical description, beginning with William's manly indifference to the whole tribe of girls—"I never saw one in my life I'd care whether she lived or died. They could all die. I wouldn't notice" —and his scornful exit from the enthusiastic discussion of May Parcher's new visitor, "a reg'lar ringdinger."

He walked in his own manner, using his shoulders to emphasize an effect of carelessness which he wished to produce upon observers. For his consciousness of observers was abnormal, . . . and it had reached a crucial stage whenever he perceived persons of his own age, but of opposite sex, approaching.

Soon he saw coming toward him a person of that opposite sex—no other than the recently despised "ringdinger" and his future divinity.

William began to suffer from breathlessness and pressure on the diaphragm, while his complexion altered—he broke out in fiery patches. They would presently meet and she would look at him, a thing for which he endeavored to prepare himself by a strange, weaving motion of his neck against the friction of his collar—for thus instinctively he strove to obtain greater ease and some decent appearance of manly indifference. But he felt his efforts to be such a failure that, deprest and panic-stricken, he seized upon an inspiration that flashed upon him just in time:

He opened his mouth somewhat and

as her eyes met his, full and startlingly, he placed three fingers across the orifice and also offered a slight vocal proof that she had surprised him in the midst of a yawn.

That was William's only attempt to conceal his devotion. For the rest of the entrancing summer—singularly blest with moonlight—he shared the honors of Miss Pratt's fickle favor with Flopit, most fortunate of 'lap-dogs.

But tho Miss Pratt sometimes smiled on William, fate was unvaryingly cruel —always waiting just around the corner to trip him up and shatter his young dignity. Even the author cannot help feeling a bit sorry for the tragedies he has provided. "Seventeen," he says, "cannot always manage the little boy yet alive under all the coverings." So he promises William better luck next time—that promise, by the way, is one of the jolliest twists of the whole ingenious plot—and leaves the reader still convinced of his discovery of "the real thing at last."

For whether you choose to read *Seventeen* as a clever caricature, a "rattling good story," a "gay analysis of calf-love," a remarkable picture of small-town American life, or a serious study in adolescent psychology, you will find what you are looking for—and enjoy yourself hugely into the bargain.

Seventeen, by Booth Tarkington. Harper. $1.35.

A GREAT EDITOR

In 1908 Arthur I. Dasent compiled what may be described as the authoritative biography of Delane. Now comes *Delane of the Times*, as the first volume in a series of biographies entitled Makers of the Nineteenth Century. Full as Mr. Dasent's biography is as regards Delane's part in politics and his social relations, it conveys no adequate impression of the actual working life of the editor of a daily newspaper, or of the methods of work and organization that made the *Times* the greatest newspaper of the Victorian period. The distinctive features of Sir Edward Cook's biography are that it shows Delane at work; it fits him into the political life of England from 1841 to 1877; it describes the position of the *Times* during its best period in English political and social life; and analyzes the great influence which Delane exercised on English politics and on the newspaper world of England.

Sir Edward Cook was active in journalism for thirty-five years. He enjoyed Fleet street, else he could not have written the graphic descriptions of Delane at work, and of the internal and external organization of the *Times* which give this book its distinctive value. There is much in its pages concerning the newer world of London journalism and the conditions that have developed since the position of the *Times* and its contemporaries of the period of Delane were adversely affected by the extension of the parliamentary franchise in 1885 and the incoming of the half-penny morning journals in 1896. There is, for instance, much that is true of English journalism today in the enlightening chapter discussing the influence of Delane, and the exceptionally favorable conditions that made his great influence possible. "Comparatively little of his time and thought," Sir Edward Cook writes, "was occupied in what sometimes imposes a heavy disability upon an editor—namely, dissension with the proprietor of the paper." From all such anxieties, Delane was happily free. *The Times* thruout his editorship was financially prosperous. Sir Edward Cook's volume abundantly makes good his claim that the *Times* of Delane was a national institution, and that Delane of the *Times* deserves a place among the notable Englishmen of the Victorian era.

Delane of the Times, by Sir Edward Cook. Holt. $1.75.

THREE OXFORD MEN

The lectures by Dr. Cadman on *The Three Religious Leaders of Oxford and Their Movements* may be compared with the historical addresses delivered a generation ago by Dr. Storrs, and with the yet earlier "Beacon Lights of History," by Dr. John Lord. The three religious teachers of Oxford are Wycliffe, the morning star of the Reformation, and Wesley and Newman, diverse prophets of a later great religious movement. While Wesley and Newman possest the same religious fervor, they moved in opposite directions out of the Church of England. Dr. Cadman brings out very clearly the story of the conflict, the growth of the Oxford movement and the reaction in the development of the Broad Church. Newman is a most lovable character, but his spirit is not the spirit which controls the Church to which he went, while John Wesley's influence animates the whole Protestant world.

The Three Religious Leaders of Oxford and Their Movements, by S. Parkes Cadman. Macmillan. $2.50.

THE CAMPAIGN

According to former representative Fowler of New Jersey, the *National Issues of 1916* will include the tariff, the American banking system and our merchant marine. His book reproduces three addresses which contain mostly truisms and pompous phrases. For example, Lincoln and Nationality—about one hundred pages—contains possibly a score of lines on Lincoln, including a few brief quotations of well known passages, the remainder being a broadside against the Wilson administration. Incidentally it may be noticed that he makes free use of such words as "idiot," "idiotic," etc., in reference to Wilson's policies. The remaining 300 pages of the book are given to a campaign treatment of An American Banking System and An American Merchant Marine. They contain a good, tho diffuse, statement of what has been said on these topics during the past few years. In order to build up a merchant marine the United States should return to the law of 1794, which

GENERAL WOOD

On Preparedness

to *Prevent* War

Our Military History

Its Facts and Fallacies

By Leonard Wood
Major General, U. S. A.

The first metropolitan newspaper review said:

"Because of General Wood's long and efficient service in the present diminutive American army, what he has written is probably the most authoritative work on this country's military needs ever so placed before the public."

General Wood points out the defects of our past military policy—costly in money, time, men and results—the perils of its continuation; and presents a practical plan to meet our present and future needs.

Ready now. $1.00 Net

Imperiled America

By John Callan O'Laughlin

A discussion of the complications forced upon the United States through the World War. The author was Assistant Secretary of State under President Roosevelt and is now in active newspaper work. Writing from behind the scenes with full knowledge of the happenings on both sides of the curtain, his conclusions are sometimes startling. A work of present importance and permanent value. *Ready now. $1.50 net.*

The Reilly & Britton Co., Chicago

imposed a duty of 10 per cent on all goods imported in foreign bottoms. This would bring in a large revenue, which could be spent in part in a preparedness · program, it being fit that foreigners should furnish the money to provide for our defense, since it is a defense against their aggression. He replaces the Federal Reserve system by an extended clearing-house system with forty-five or fifty commercial zones, the whole bound together with one central reserve. This would give the United States the simplest and best system in the world.

The National Issues of 1916. by C. N. Fowler. Harper. $1.50.

ISLAM AND THE TURK

A notable and authoritative work is *Modern Movements Among the Moslems,* by Samuel Graham Wilson. In personal support of an exhaustive treatment of his subject Dr. Wilson brings over thirty years of residence in the Orient. Commencing with the accepted hypothesis of several scholarly writers that Islam is impervious to outside influence and therefore incapable of change, the author demonstrates that the currents of modern thought are breaking thru the barriers of Mohammedan dogmatic absolutism. To that end he reviews the principal advance movements of Suffism, Bahaism and the Ahmadiyas; he proves the slow but certain betterment in social conditions—pointedly that of Mohammedan women—and the persistent demand for political liberty as separate from, if not contrary to the rule of the Koran. But the whole is swept by 'cross purposes the resultant of contrary religious and intellectual forces . . . energetic, aggressive, determined and anti-Christian." Apart from his direct objective, in the main successfully accomplished, Dr. Wilson illumines social conditions in various parts of the Mohammedan world. But in passing comment it is perhaps singular that when he was gathering supporting testimony, he did not summon to his aid that philosophic dreamer, just law maker, and broadly tolerant religious reformer Akbar—truly—the Great Mohammedan Mogul Emperor. Unhappily, from the works of many competent judges of the Turkish character, there is no reason to doubt any part of Dr. Gibbons' sweeping indictment of the Turks in their monstrous slaughter of the Armenians, *The Blackest Page of Modern History.* Concealed somewhere both in the apparently benevolent Turkish gentleman and the mild peasant is a ferocity—blind and unreasoning—when kindled by fanaticism. Authorities hold it is not entirely of religious incentive, for the Turk has been equally ruthless toward other races of his own faith. Among Mohammedan peoples he comes nearest to the term barbarian, for in him is neither the saving chivalry of the Arab nor the culture of the Persian. While conceding that Dr. Gibbons makes his case, it may be stated that to the Oriental mind as a whole cruelty is not the crime against humanity it stands with us. Whether it be the Oriental's fatalistic spirit, or that he possesses less physical sensitiveness—possibly both combined—it is a fact that neither the perpetrator of cruelty nor his victim regard imposed human suffering with the indignation, pain and horror of the Occidental.

Unquestionably *The Foundation of the Ottoman Empire* by the same author is a work of deep scholarly learning, yet written in such a manner as to be easily grasped by the average reader of history. It follows as an appropriate complement to the previous little volume showing how the Osmanli Turks have come to their present state of decadence from a beginning of considerable culture and tolerance. At this period when the fate of the Turk hangs in the balance—when his existence as an independent nation would seem to be at the eleventh hour—this book by Dr. Gibbons should be given wide and serious attention. It possesses a further value as a reference volume for its excellent chronological tables and copious authoritative notes. Personally Dr. Gibbons writes from the vantage ground of a resident professor of history at Roberts College, Constantinople.

Modern Movements Among the Moslems, by Samuel Graham Wilson. Revell. $1.50. *The Blackest Page of Modern History*, by Herbert Adams Gibbons. Putnam. 75 cents. *The Foundation of the Ottoman Empire*, by Herbert Adams Gibbons. Century. $3.

PEBBLES

You may have noticed how "preparedness brings on war" in Holland.—*Philadelphia North American.*

In addition to the German denial, President Wilson has a lot of other evidence that the "Sussex" was torpedoed by a German submarine.—*Chicago Herald.*

She—Which do you like the best, Williams or Colgate?
He—What are you talking about: colleges or shaving soap?—*Cornell Widow.*

The Lady—Didn't I hear you quote Omar Khayyam just now?
The Broker—I think not. In fact, I don't think I ever heard of the stock.—*Boston Transcript.*

Musical Student—That piece you just played is by Mozart, isn't it?
Hurdy-Gurdy Man—No, by Handel.—*Quincy H. S. Golden Rod.*

You have heard perhaps of the Englishman in the South Station, Boston, who read over a door "Inside Baggage," and chuckled with glee: "You Americans are so droll! Now we should say 'Refreshment Room.'"—*The Living Church.*

"How did you contrive to convince your wife you could not afford to own an automobile?"
"Pure luck on my part. She wanted to have an old dress cleaned, and bought a gallon of gasoline."—*Richmond Times-Dispatch.*

Already we see signs of German hatred. At a reception the other night in a neutral city, the guest of honor said to a man who had just been presented to her:
"You are a foreigner, are you not? Where do you come from?"
"From Berlin, ma'am," he answered.
The lady stared at him thru her lorgnette.
"Dear me!" she said. "Couldn't you go back and come from somewhere else?"—*London Opinion.*

ALL ABOARD FOR BUENOS AIRES

Secretary McAdoo has returned from Buenos Aires, where he has been attending the meeting of the Pan-American High Commission, of which he is the first president. On his return he made an interesting statement in the course of which he said:

Everywhere I found an earnest desire to strengthen commercial, financial and political relations with the United States, and everywhere we went there was a genuinely friendly attitude and a complete absence of that suspicion and distrust of the United States which has, until recently, existed to a more or less degree in some, at least, of the Central and South American countries.

Every leading statesman in South America with whom I talked emphasized the paramount importance of a merchant marine under the flag of the United States, or under the flags of the different American nations.

Many prominent men told me that the surest foundation of better relations was the establishment of ample means of communication, so that the products of the different countries could be quickly moved in mutually profitable trade.

Another question of great importance is the completion of the intercontinental railway connecting North and South America through the Isthmus of Panama. The total distance between New York and Buenos Aires by rail is 10,300 miles, of which approximately 7400 miles have been built and are now in operation, leaving approximately 2900 miles to be constructed. The principal gaps in the intercontinental railway are in the countries of Central America and in Colombia, Ecuador and Peru in South America, and the estimated cost of construction is, roughly speaking, $150,000,000.

With these links completed, it would require only a relatively small amount of additional construction to connect the main trunk line with Santiago, Chile, and Rio de Janeiro, Brazil, and then practically all the principal capitals of Central and South America will be connected with each other and with all the cities of the United States. "All aboard for Buenos Aires," when shouted in the railroad stations of New York City, will be a thrilling announcement some day, and in the not remote future this announcement will be heard.

The net revenues of the railroads of the country, according to the preliminary estimates of the Interstate Commerce Commission, reached high figures in March. The net revenue of the leading ninety-four roads of the country was $425 per mile of line operated, in comparison with $301 per mile during March, 1915. The net revenue of the Eastern roads was estimated to be $623 per mile, an increase of $227 per mile. The net revenue of the Southern roads was $386, an increase of $115 per mile, and the net revenue of the Western roads was $352, an increase of $82 per mile. The net revenue of these same ninety-four roads during the nine months ending with March totaled $3828 per mile of road operated, an increase of $1034 in comparison with the same nine months of last year. The net revenue of the Eastern roads during this nine months' period was $6076, an increase of $2054 per mile of line operated.

The revenues of the Eastern roads averaged $2138 per mile of line operated during March, an increase of $481. The revenues of these same lines during the nine months ended with March totaled $18,703 per mile, an increase of $3120.

WHAT THE WAR HAS DONE TO SHIPPING

Twenty-one months of war have destroyed 1216 merchant vessels. They aggregated nearly two and a half million gross tons. The following tables show how the different shipping nations of the world have suffered in this respect:

Allied Shipping Destroyed

Nation—	Gross Tons.
Great Britain	1,571,293
France	180,283
Italy	71,443
Russia	42,258
Belgium	25,858
Japan	16,015
Total gross tons	1,917,161

Neutral Shipping Destroyed

Nation—	Gross Tons.
Norway	147,580
Holland	82,629
Denmark	40,653
Sweden	37,896
Greece	15,017
Spain	14,550
United States	10,377
Total gross tons	348,702

Teutonic Shipping Destroyed

Nation—	Gross Tons.
Germany	165,006
Turkey	18,150
Austria-Hungary	13,240
Total gross tons	196,396

England has lost the most ships, 727; Norway the next largest number, 107; France next, 72; Germany next, 68; Denmark, Holland, Italy, Russia and Sweden are not far apart in their losses, which range from 31 to 40. The United States, Japan and Spain stand at the bottom of the list, with six, three and seven respectively.

The British losses are naturally the greatest. For Great Britain has the most ships on the sea; and the German submarine warfare has been directed primarily against England. The German losses are naturally light, for since the first few months of the war German shipping has been tightly locked up in home and neutral harbors.

Last week Earl Curzon announced in the House of Lords that a total of 450 enemy ships had been detained, seized or captured by the Allies in all parts of the world since the war began.

He added that it was an encouraging fact and a curious coincidence that the British merchant ships lost thru war operations were exactly balanced in number and tonnage by the new ships added to the register during the war.

The following dividends are announced:
Pacific Gas and Electric Company, first preferred and original preferred, quarterly, $1.50 per share, payable May 15.
Liggett & Myers Tobacco Company, common, quarterly, 3 per cent, payable June 1.
International Silver Company, Coupons No. 35 of First Mortgage Bonds, payable on and after June 1.

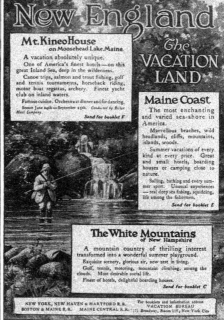

New England

The VACATION LAND

Mt. Kineo House
on Moosehead Lake, Maine

A vacation absolutely unique.
One of America's finest hotels—on this great Inland Sea, deep in the wilderness.
Canoe trips, salmon and trout fishing, golf and tennis tournaments, horseback riding, motor boat regattas, archery. Finest yacht club on inland waters.
Famous cuisine. Orchestra at dinner and for dancing.
Season June 24th—September 24th. *Conducted by Ricker Hotel Company.*

Send for booklet F

Maine Coast

The most enchanting and varied sea-shore in America.
Marvellous beaches, wild headlands, cliffs, mountains, islands, woods.
Summer vacations of every kind at every price. Great and small hotels, boarding houses or camping close to nature.
Sailing, bathing and every summer sport. Unusual experiences—real deep sea fishing, squidding, life among the fishermen.

Send for booklet E

The White Mountains
of New Hampshire

A mountain country of thrilling interest transformed into a wonderful summer playground.
Exquisite scenery, glorious air, new zest in living.
Golf, tennis, motoring, mountain climbing, among the clouds. Most desirable social life.
Finest of hotels, delightful boarding houses.

Send for booklet C

NEW YORK, NEW HAVEN & HARTFORD R.R.
BOSTON & MAINE R.R. MAINE CENTRAL R.R.
For booklets and information address
VACATION BUREAU
775 Broadway, Room 115, New York City

DIVIDENDS

Office of International Silver Company
Meriden, Conn., May 15, 1916.
Coupons No. 35 of the First Mortgage Bonds of this Company, due June 1, 1916, will be paid on and after that date on presentation at the American Exchange National Bank, 128 Broadway, New York City.
FRARAY HALE, Treasurer.

The Board of Directors of The American Cotton Oil Company, on May 3, 1916, declared a semi-annual dividend of three per cent. upon the Preferred Stock, and a quarterly dividend of one per cent. upon the Common Stock of the Company, both payable June 1, 1916, at the Banking House of Winslow, Lanier & Co., 59 Cedar Street, New York City, to holders of record of such stock at the close of business on May 15, 1916.
The Stock Transfer Books of the Company will not be closed. JUSTUS E. RALPH, Secretary.

NILES-BEMENT-POND COMPANY.
New York, May 3, 1916.
The Board of Directors of NILES-BEMENT-POND COMPANY has this day declared the regular quarterly dividend of ONE AND ONE-HALF PER CENT. upon the PREFERRED STOCK of the Company, payable May 15, 1916.
The transfer books will close at 3 o'clock in the afternoon of May 4, 1916, and will re-open at 10 o'clock in the forenoon of May 16, 1916.
JOHN R. CORNELL, Treasurer.

NILES-BEMENT-POND COMPANY.
New York, May 3, 1916.
The Board of Directors of NILES-BEMENT-POND COMPANY has this day declared a dividend of ONE AND ONE-HALF PER CENT. upon the COMMON STOCK of the Company, payable June 20, 1916.
The transfer books will close at 3 o'clock in the afternoon of June 3, 1916, and will re-open at 10 o'clock in the forenoon of June 21, 1916.
JOHN R. CORNELL, Treasurer.

GENERAL DEVELOPMENT COMPANY
61 Broadway, New York
May 1st, 1916.
At a meeting of the Board of Directors of the General Development Company held this day, a dividend of One dollar and fifty cents ($1.50) per share on the capital stock of the Company was declared, payable June 1st, 1916, to stockholders of record at the close of business on May 19th, 1916. Books will not close.
SAM A. LEWISOHN, Treasurer.

Insurance
Conducted by
W. E. UNDERWOOD

HOW A LIFE RATE IS MADE

From two correspondents come requests for information which, simple in the asking, are difficult to answer in a limited space. One wants me to demonstrate the accuracy of an assertion I occasionally make to the effect that life insurance is an expense; the other desires an explanation of the manner in which the premium rate on an old life policy is calculated. If I can successfully impart the information called for under the second request, both questions will be answered.

As it is a matter of mathematics, the difficulty lies in making the explanation chiefly in words. But I will try; it being understood, of course, that such mathematical results as I employ are accepted as authoritative, for I have not sufficient room here to include the detailed figures.

Let us suppose that we want the annual premium rate for an Ordinary Life policy of $1000 at age 43, the assumed interest rate for money being 5 per cent., the highest standard now in use. We must have an authoritative mortality table on which to base our calculations, and we will choose that known as the American Experience Table of Mortality. We will also assume that our calculation includes 20,000 lives. Keep in mind the essential fact that the contract known as the Ordinary Life policy runs for the whole of life and that it cannot be canceled by the company. It must provide $1000 on the death of the last man as well as on the death of the first. We don't know when any of the 20,000 will die, but we know that all will be dead by the time age 96 is reached.

That being true, we must have an itemized bill of mortality for each of 53 years, charging up, at $1000 apiece, the deaths occurring each year. According to the Mortality Table we are using, 210 persons will die the first year; 214 the second year; 219 the third year; 276 the tenth year; 452 the twentieth year; 479 the fortieth year, and so on thru the whole period of 53 years, until all are dead. If this money were paid as each man died, the whole sum would amount to $20,-000,000. But premiums are paid in advance, therefore the sums required are discounted at 3 per cent. Instead of collecting $210,000 for the 210 deaths of the first year, only $203,-383.54 is required, which, at 3 per cent., is worth just $210,000 at the end of the year. This discounting process continues thruout the entire period, and we find at the end that it amounts to a total of $9,716,976.72.

It now becomes necessary for us to

find each insured person's just proportion of that sum, or rather each survivor's. To do that in the simplest way let us see how much of it would be yielded by a contribution of one dollar from each survivor. In the first year, all being alive, we would get $20,000. That year 210 will die, leaving 19,790 to contribute a dollar apiece, or $19,790; that year 214 die, leaving 19,576, yielding $19,576. This process is also carried year by year thru the 53 years and the total at the end is $353,050.51. We see, of course, that $353,050.51, or one dollar apiece, will not pay the mortality bill of $9,716,976.72; but if we divide the last figure by the first, we will have the exact answer: $27.52. This is the Net Premium. It represents nothing but death losses. No provision has been made for the company's expenses.

When the net premium has been ascertained in the manner described, another sum, called the Loading, is added for expenses, in this case $9.18, making the Gross Premium of $36.70 for $1000 participating Ordinary Life insurance on a 3 per cent basis.

The company's selection of risks will result in an actual mortality experience less than that assumed in the Table; its actual expenses will be less than the loading assumed; and the rate of interest actually earned will be higher than 3 per cent. All the gains from these sources will be returned to policyholders at the end of each year as dividends, so-called.

This is an explanation of an old line legal reserve level premium rate, and yet nothing has been said about an accumulated reserve. All the money yielded by the Net Premiums seems to be used for paying death claims. That is an essential office of the reserve—it is really a fund in liquidation of future mortality. At $27.52 each, 20,000 persons would pay the first year a total of $550,400. At 3 per cent, by the end of the year, this sum would be increased $16,512, interest bringing it up to $566,912. Deduct the death losses that year, $1000 to each of 210 persons, or $210,000, and we have remaining $356,912, which is called reserve. If we wish to know what share of this reserve belongs to each outstanding policy, we divide it by the number of survivors, 19,790, and we have $18.03.

The second year we start with a fund of $356,912 reserve, to which is added the premiums paid by survivors the second year (19,790×$27.52), $544,620.80, or a total of $901,532.80. Add 3 per cent interest, $27,046, making the sum $928,578.80. There are 214 deaths, at $1000 each, in the second year, $214,000, which, deducted from the amount on hand, $928,578.80, leaves $714,578.80, the reserve at the end of the second year. If we divide this sum by the number of survivors, 19,576, we get $36.52 each.

At the beginning of the 53d year there will remain but one person alive at age 95. He will pay his premium of $27.52 which, added to what is left in the reserve fund, and both improved

at 3 per cent interest, will exactly equal $1000 by the end of that year.

Those who surrender their policies receive such a proportion of the reserve held against them as the policy contracts or the rules of the companies governing withdrawals provide. Now, to demonstrate the claim that life insurance is an expense, let us suppose that one of these insured persons surrenders his policy for its cash value at the end of twenty years. We will not consider the interest increment on the premiums he paid, nor on the dividends he received; but we will assume that the amount of the dividends aggregated 20 per cent of the premiums. In twenty years, at $36.70 a year, the policyholder paid the company a total of $734. His dividends amounted to $146.80. His share of the reserve is $418. The two last figures, added, total $564.80. The difference between what he paid and received is $179.20. These figures only demonstrate the fact. To calculate it exactly, we should add to the premiums and dividends the interest value of the money.

The explanation of the process followed in ascertaining an adequate level premium rate amply proves the fallacy of such systems of assessment life insurance as make no provision for a sufficient reserve.

W. S. H., White Plains, N. Y.—The Bankers Mutual Casualty is an assessment organization, a system which has not proven practicable in any branch of insurance. Security is the prime requisite. The stock accident and casualty companies of repute furnish that.

C. B., Coshocton, Ohio.—The Security Life Insurance Company of America is a corporation organized (1902) under the laws of Virginia, with its principal office at Chicago. On January 1, this year, its assets were $2,583,479; its liabilities, $2,146,053; its surplus (including $220,000 capital), $437,426. Last year it wrote $3,823,385 new insurance and had on January 1, $17,000,000 in force. The company now writes non-participating insurance only. Its methods are sound and its financial condition satisfactory. Comparing it with the best policyholders' companies, it is commonplace.

N. R. W., Wichita, Kan.—A young man of twenty who has arrived at the conclusion that a part of his earnings should be devoted to life insurance possesses exceptional wisdom. He should secure all that he can conveniently pay for, because the premium rate at that age is the lowest offered by any of the companies; and for that reason also, he should not permit that insurance to lapse. Perhaps, in the course of nine or ten years there will be dependents to protect; later on, the hardships of one's old age are to be guarded against. Now, what kind of policy is what sort of company should be selected? If some ready cash capital is desired at forty or forty-five, a part of the insurance should consist of a twenty or twenty-five year endowment; the remainder of ordinary life. If protection is important, make it an ordinary life; the ultimate cash surrender values are smaller, proportioned to premiums paid, but they are substantial in time, when service rendered is considered. At age twenty, $2000 of ordinary life will cost about the same as $1000 twenty-five year endowment; and the cash surrender values would be, in twenty-five years, about $550 on the $2000 ordinary life and $1000 on the endowment. These are participating policies and, of course, the annual dividends will materially reduce the cost. As to the company, the contract is to be a long one, perhaps a lifetime; choose an old, thoroly established, well managed institution.

HOMEMAKER OR HOUSEKEEPER?

MRS. BRUÈRE TALKS IT OVER WITH HER INDEPENDENT CRITICS

THE letters received concerning the articles on "The Habits of Women under Domestication," published between March 20 and April 17, contain some very valuable suggestions and give the sense of a great body of both men and women breaking the crust of merely domestic life in all sorts of unexpected places and becoming consciously a part of the larger social group. Some are, however, still making the mistake of thinking that housekeeping and homemaking are necessarily the same thing. From Missouri comes the question:

If housework is obsolescent, who, then, is going to be the homemaker for the future generations? . . . It is the mother, the housekeeper and the homemaker [Pardon me, madam, the *homemaker* undoubtedly but not necessarily the *housekeeper*, who may be quite a different person], who molds the plastic mind, who guides the little feet and, taking the trusting hands in hers, leads them on day by day and year by year, training and fitting them for a useful life.

It is indeed important that the mother should be able to do all this but it is not a part of housekeeping.

One domestic science teacher insists that a housekeeper should "regard her work as a profession requiring her best thought and skill." Another says

The aim of household economics in the high school is to show girls the dignity of housework, to show them that there are problems here which are worthy of their best mental powers.

Says a woman from the East:

If our girls are made to think that home service is beneath them, we are doing that which is dangerous to the foundation of good citizenship.

An adequate answer to these domestic science teachers comes from a member of their own profession in California:

Homemaking is a profession where a woman may use all her skill and originality. To do her best work she cannot shut herself up with her problems, but must remember that she is a citizen of the world and must save time from her labors to keep in touch with the great outside world.

She does not make this broad claim for *housekeeping* but for *homemaking*, which is in its essence quite a different thing. As a Montana woman says:

To be a housekeeper is infinitely easier than to be a homekeeper, for the one deals with inanimate objects and the other with souls. . . . Why can we not make a profession of our homekeeping rather than looking elsewhere for professions? Why can we not put into it our educational advantages and the added time which the easier running of the household routine permits? Why can we not put the stamp of individuality into the training of our children instead of turning them over to professional caretakers?

But this is not the solution of the problem either! The beautiful and poetic idea that women, being freed from housework, are at liberty to concentrate on homemaking is—fortunately for the race—not true. Even a near-democracy like ours is beginning to demand as a service, at the same time that it grants as a privilege, a life time of productive industry from every adult human being, male or fe-

260

male. See what a little Western girl in the eleventh grade writes:

I do not think any woman or mother would give up a happy home, her regular line of cooking and sewing, the comfort and pleasure of working for her children and seeing that they are brought up with the right kind of training, and the framing of a household, merely to factorize her household duties.

Bless the child—as tho cooking food and bringing up a child were the same thing! And what a good bluff mother must put up when she sits down with the darning bag after the day's work is over, when she coaxes the dried egg off the edges of the plates, when she turns the twenty-pound mattresses, when she "does up" little daughter's best white dress, when she performs the hundred other pleasant and comforting things we all know so well! Not that one does not appreciate the mitigating circumstances and honor the sacrifice whenever it is necessary—but it is ceasing to be necessary.

But to go back to the suggestion of the Montana woman that the time saved from drudgery be devoted to the training of children—what better profession can men or women take up if they happen to have that exceptionally high order of ability, than that of training their own children — and other people's, too?

A gentleman from Connecticut explains the type of people who are engaged in domestic service by asking:

May it not be that because the more esthetic and enlightened modern woman is shirking her duties [in housework] that the profession has fallen into the hands of the pauper and criminal classes?

Possibly it is. Certainly it is because the more enlightened and esthetic modern men have devoted themselves to other work than digging ditches, passing coal, being justices of the peace, dog-catchers and grave diggers, that these necessary and meritorious occupations have fallen into the hands of ignorant and unskilled men. It is, however, when we come to some heirloom of the sentiment which man wraps around woman, that we find the greatest confusion of values. A physician from the State of Washington writes:

Come with me to the "mountain cabin" or the Jewish homes on Sixth and Seventh Avenues and we will see women to whom we can have our heads in reverence—real women who are "doing things," not merely "keeping busy"—women that we would feel proud to call "Mother"—women who achieve—not parasites, living an artificial life.

Such women are to be found increasingly everywhere. Many of them do housework, but it is not housework that makes them noble. As an Ohio woman says:

I believe that most of us will admit that when we advocate more and better housekeepers we have in mind that type of "uncrowned queen" of the home who "looketh well to the ways of her household," not alone because it is her job, but because it is her joy. . . . But is it not true that we have estimated the services of the uncrowned queen from an almost entirely sentimental point of view?

Her worth and her services to her household cannot be estimated in dollars and cents—and they very seldom are. . . . Yet, suppose the need should arise in the life of the homemaker for commercializing some ability which she possesses. In this exigency the woman who can do nothing but housework is in hard lines . . . the girl who has a knowledge of chemistry and physics can very soon learn to cook. Or even if a girl is a *good* office woman, saleswoman, or what not, she can make herself a capable houseworker a thousand times more surely than can the houseworker train herself for other lines of activity.

There seems also to be a general feeling that the only thing that can be done with housework if the housewife does not do it is to shift it to a servant. An Illinois physician declares:

We will not develop the home in a democracy by depending on a scientific servant class. . . . It [the family] is the basis of a democracy in which every one does his necessary part. A paid servant class is no part of it.

If more of our citizens believed that a class of personal servants whether paid or unpaid has no place in a democracy and took stringent measures to eliminate it, we might be much nearer a nation of happy homes than we are now. But we all have—and all of us ought to be—community servants; and that not in any sentimental sense, but as our every day way of earning a living. The girl who irons collars in a laundry is a community servant as the woman who stands over your private and particular wash tub is not.

But no one takes very kindly to the statement that we need more and better community servants instead of more and better housekeepers. An Ohio woman sums it up forcefully:

Who said we did not need more and better housekeepers?

Not the army of consumptives whose wasted bodies testify to poorly cooked food and worse sanitation.

Not the thousands of epileptics who must be housed and fed by the state.

Not the school children whose nerves break down before the grades are complete.

Not the rows of baby graves.

Not the number of bankruptcy cases among small business men.

Not the divorce courts.

And how would any of these things be changed did all the women of all the spheres housekeep unceasingly? It is not housekeeping, but the readjustment of industry, the broadening of education and the enforcement of law that can help us to stay tuberculosis. Wherever the infant mortality rate is going down, it is being reduced thru such social measures as control of the milk supply, the education of mothers before and after childbirth, the enforcement of sanitary regulations and the extension of district nursing—not by any increase in housekeeping. It is in order that women should have time to be better homemakers, better wives when they choose to marry, better mothers when they are fortunate enough to have children, and above all better citizens, that the time and strength now wasted in needless housework ought to be saved.

New York City

The Independent
Founded 1848

HARPER'S WEEKLY
Founded 1857
Incorporated with The Independent May 22, 1916

THE CHAUTAUQUAN
Incorporated with The Independent June 1, 1914

The Independent is owned and published by the Independent Corporation, at 119 West Fortieth Street, New York, New York. B. Howland, president; Frederic E. Dickinson, treasurer; Hamilton Holt, editor; Harold J. Howland, associate editor; Edwin E. Slosson, literary editor; William Hayes Ward, honorary editor; Karl V. S. Howland, publisher. The price of The Independent is Ten Cents a copy; Four Dollars for one year. Postage to foreign countries in the Postal Union, $1.75 extra; to Canada, $1 extra. Writers who wish their articles returned should send stamped and addrest envelopes. No responsibility is assumed for the loss or non-return of manuscripts. Entered at the New York Post Office as Second Class matter. Copyright, 1916, by The Independent. Address all communications to The Independent, 119 West Fortieth Street, New York

VOLUME 86 NUMBER 3520

CONTENTS FOR MAY 22, 1916

IF YOU HAVE A CAMERA

Harper's Weekly, when it sent Thomas Nast into the field to draw Civil War sketches that appeared later as huge woodcuts, was obeying the journalistic law that telling and hearing some new thing is not enough: folks want to see it, too. And The Independent, in adding to its already liberal picture service the News-Pictorial that begins this week, is carrying on the same tradition in a new way and with tremendously increased mechanical advantages.

For years The Independent has been drawing on those wonderfully organized agencies that photograph the new things at the end of the earth and do everything short of actually telegraphing them (even that has been done in Europe) to place them in the hands of American readers in minimum time.

But no agency can cover all the square miles of this country alone, nor the infinite range of interests of Independent readers, and to supplement this service we shall adopt a coöperative plan. We want news-pictures from our readers. For the best in any single issue of the News-Pictorial (not counting those we receive from the commercial agencies) we shall pay Ten Dollars. For all others so submitted that we find good enough to print we shall pay Two Dollars each.

When a nose for news and an eye for the picturesque are associated in the same physiognomy the owner thereof has the essential qualifications for making news-pictures. The camera is secondary, but, in order to give it and us a fair chance, use black-and-white glossy paper. In order to give yourself a fair chance, put your name and address and a *full* caption on the back of every print. "t. f."

JUST A WORD

When Winter lingers in the lap of Spring as persistently and nonchalantly as he has done this year, we worry lest we may be unable to keep winter sports out of the Vacation Number, which long-established Independent custom fixes in the first week in June. But we have a valiantly summery cover—a splendid piece of color work, and a breezy article on canoeing, in which we promise to say nothing about ice-boating, no matter what the thermometer may do. As usual, we will have a group of "Little Travels"—brief, usable itineraries of summer holiday trips to eight different American pleasure-points, which will be of material help in making vacation plans. As to pictures—wait and see!

A little later comes the annual Chautauqua Number, dated June 26. This will not lack that larger interest in popular education that appeals to readers both inside and outside the immediate circle of Chautauqua. The leading feature will be an article by President Vincent of the University of Minnesota, Chancellor of Chautauqua Institution, on "The Future of National Education." This will carry the series of prophecies of the next generation in American life one step farther. There will also be brief articles by other Chautauqua authorities on the new developments of the Chautauqua plan and of Chautauqua itself, with perhaps a bit of antiquarian information about the richly historic territory which the parent of all the Chautauquas occupies. Pictures, of course.

REMARKABLE REMARKS

MARY PICKFORD—I cry real tears.

LILLIAN RUSSELL—Use your mirror.

GENERAL PETAIN—We will get them.

WILLIAM BARNES, JR.—Stop hero worship.

W. H. TAFT—I claim to be a progressive.

"BUGS" BAER—Very few piano drummers carry samples.

EMPEROR WILLIAM—The present war must end at Verdun.

IRVING S. COBB—I just naturally hate to say "No" to anybody.

GEORGE W. PERKINS—Colonel Roosevelt will be the next President.

GEN. EMILIO ZAPATA—Mexico can produce everything she needs.

REV. J. H. JOWETT—Everything is being read today but the Bible.

REPUBLICAN LEADER MANN—The President never has been neutral.

FORMER NATIONAL CHAIRMAN McCOMBS—Wilson is invincible.

"NICK" LONGWORTH—When the call for volunteers comes I will be there.

GEORGE BERNARD SHAW—It was perfectly correct to shoot Miss Cavell.

BILLY SUNDAY—Come on, you ball players; try stealing home to God.

DAVID LLOYD GEORGE—We have means. The Central Powers have methods.

WOODROW WILSON—There are some humbugs that have been at large a long time.

LUKE McLUKE—Save your old champagne corks; they are worth $3 a thousand.

REV. F. N. McMULLAN—I want to see more church people going to the baseball games.

JOHN B. WALKER—Of all words of human invention the most frightful is "conscription."

NORMAN HAPGOOD—It is not the wicked who are most cruel. It is the good who "crucify."

SENATOR HARDING—If I were in authority I would tell Carranza to go jump off the mountain top.

GOV. FERGUSON OF TEXAS—It is now the solemn duty of the United States to enter Mexico and assume control of that unfortunate country.

EVANGELIST HALL—I had rather being in God than go into a dark room and get a message from my grandmother thru some Indian squaw.

PROF. THOMAS J. McCORMACK—The public school should be primarily the temple of Minerva, and not of Vulcan, or of his wife, Venus.

PROF. ALBERT BUSHNELL HART—Within five years the so called Republic of Mexico will be under the benevolent superintendence of the U. S.

JOSEPH PENNELL—If Broadway were a street in a European city, centuries old, Americans would flock there by hundreds of thousands to visit it.

DR. SALMON—At Ellis Island, where I spent three years as a physician, doctors spent as much time in examining the mental condition of an immigrant as is spent by the gateman at a railroad station in examining your ticket.

G-E Electric Fans

The Independent

WITH WHICH IS INCORPORATED
HARPER'S WEEKLY
A Journal of Civilization

TO HARPER'S WEEKLY READERS

IT is not forms that matter, so much as tendencies. If Harper's Weekly had been incorporated with a publication representing the opposite side in the great strife between privilege and liberty, it would have been a disaster. When, however, two circulations are combined that stand for the same political, economic and moral tendencies, it is easily conceivable that more may be accomplished than when they were separate. In stepping out of journalism myself, whether it be temporarily or permanently, I can recommend to those who have been reading Harper's Weekly, more enthusiastically than I could have done had it been merged in any other publication whatsoever, that they follow it in its new embodiment.

The management of The Independent, as I understand it, mean to preserve to a considerable degree the identity of Harper's Weekly in those special features that seem to have had most to do with its individuality. What interests me most, however, in any publication is its soul—the thing it is undertaking to accomplish in the far-reaching struggles of the day. How few the magazines are today that have been able to remain anything except reflections of money standards. That deplorable tendency is now plain to everybody. It has become a by-word. The Independent stands out as representing moral freedom, disinterested thought, genuine enthusiasm for progress and for principles. All luck to it! May those who have read Harper's Weekly under my editorship find themselves permanent and loyal readers of that admirable publication into which the Weekly has been absorbed.

NORMAN HAPGOOD

TO OUR NEW READERS

THE INDEPENDENT welcomes its new readers. It desires their approval and continued support. It has known and valued Harper's Weekly under its successive line of distinguished and brilliant editors. Shoulder to shoulder for three generations the two weeklies have fought the good fight for national progress and human rights.

For the benefit of our new readers as well as the old we may say that the merged magazine will continue to support the great issues that each has always championed. In general, our editorial policy will be liberal rather than radical or conservative. The country and the world are moving forward, knowing more, doing better, and The Independent has never been content to be dragged along behind, but has persisted in pulling from the front. The Independent will continue to look forward, not backward.

Among our contributed articles, however, will be found many that go to the extreme of radicalism or conservatism. We have always taken pride in printing both sides of the great controverted questions of the day. All we ask is that our contributors keep within the bounds of sanity, decency and fair play. It is our aim to provide instruction more than entertainment. The purpose of The Independent is serious; the tone not always so. In our various departments and in our special features, whether text or pictures, The Independent purposes to be in full advance of new thought and knowledge. It avoids no question that interests the people. It gathers articles from all sources. It has been said that "The Independent prints more articles from distinguished writers than any other periodical in America." But The Independent has ever been quick to recognize young and unknown writers. Many of the first articles and poems of our most famous authors were published in The Independent.

Thus we give our warmest welcome to our new readers, assuring them that we will do what we can for their pleasure and profit and trusting that whatever they miss will be more than made up. We thank Mr. Hapgood, late Editor of Harper's Weekly, for his kind introduction of The Independent to his readers, and we accept with confidence our new responsibility to our new friends.

HAMILTON HOLT

THREE PRESIDENTS ON THE LEAGUE TO ENFORCE PEACE

A NATION which by the standards of other nations, however mistaken those standards may be, is regarded as helpless, is apt in general counsel to be regarded as negligible; and when you go into a conference to establish foundations for the peace of the world, you must go in on a basis intelligible to the people you are conferring with. . . . In the last analysis the peace of society is obtained by force, and when action comes,—it comes by opinion, but back of the opinion is the ultimate application of force. The greater body of opinion says to the lesser body of opinion, "We may be wrong, but you have to live under our direction for the time being, until you are more numerous than we are."

Now, let us suppose that we have formed a family of nations and that family of nations says, "The world is not going to have any more wars of this sort without at least first going through certain processes to show whether there is anything in its case or not." If you say, "We shall not have any war," you have got to have the force to make that "shall" bite. And the rest of the world, if America takes part in this thing, will have the right to expect from her that she contribute her element of force to the general understanding. Surely, that is not a militaristic ideal. That is a very practical ideal. . . . I believe that if the world ever comes to combine its force for the purpose of maintaining peace, the individual contributions of each nation will be much less, necessarily, than they would be in other circumstances; and that all they will have to do will be to contribute moderately and not indefinitely.

—President Wilson Interviewed at the White House, May 8, 1916

WHAT should be the fundamental plan of the League?

It seems to me that it ought to contain four provisions. In the first place, it ought to provide for the formation of a court, which would be given jurisdiction by the consent of all the members of the League to consider and decide justiciable questions between them.

Second: A Commission of Conciliation for the consideration and recommendation of a solution of all non-justiciable questions that may arise between the members of the League should be created, and this commission should have power to hear evidence, investigate the causes of differences, and mediate between the parties and then make its recommendation for a settlement.

Third: Conferences should be held from time to time to agree upon principles of international law, not already established, as their necessity shall suggest themselves. When the conclusions of the commission shall have been submitted to the various parties to the League for a reasonable time, say a year, without calling forth objection, it shall be deemed that they acquiesce in the principles thus declared.

Fourth: The members of the League shall agree that if any member of the League shall begin war against any other member of the League, without first having submitted the question if found justiciable to the arbitral court provided in the fundamental compact, or without having submitted the question if found non-justiciable to the Commission of Conciliation for its examination, consideration and recommendation, then the remaining members . . . agree to join in the forcible defense of the member thus prematurely attacked.

—William Howard Taft, in The Independent, June 14, 1915

ALL the civilized powers which are able and willing to furnish and to use force, when force is required to back up righteousness . . . should join to create an international tribunal and to provide rules in accordance with which that tribunal should act. These rules would have to accept the status quo at some given period; for the endeavor to redress all historical wrongs would throw us back into chaos. They would lay down the rule that the territorial integrity of each nation was inviolate; that it was to be guaranteed absolutely its sovereign rights . . . in matters affecting its honor and vital interest. . . . All other matters that could arise between these nations should be settled by the international court. . . . Then, and most important, the nations should severally guarantee to use their entire military force, if necessary, against any nation which defied the decrees of the tribunal or which violated any of the rights which in the rules it was expressly stipulated should be reserved to the several nations, the rights to their territorial integrity and the like. . . .

In addition to the contracting powers, a certain number of outside nations should be named as entitled to the benefits of the court. These nations should be chosen from those which were as civilized and well behaved as the great contracting nations, but which, for some reason or other, were unwilling or unable to guarantee to help execute the decrees of the court by force. . . .

No power should be admitted into the first circle, that of the contracting powers, unless it was civilized, well behaved and able to do its part in enforcing the decrees of the court.

—Theodore Roosevelt, in The Independent, January 4, 1915

THE TIME HAS COME

PRESIDENT WILSON, in his response to a delegation from the American Union Against Militarism which interviewed him at the White House last week, made a statement of his hopes for the permanent establishment of peace which shows that he is in accordance with ex-President Taft and ex-President Roosevelt on the fundamental principle of the League to Enforce Peace. A comparison of the three declarations printed above will show the unanimity in aim and method of the three men now living who have stood at the head of the American Government.

The two paramount questions now before the world are: first, how can the Great War be stopped, and, second, how can all future war be prevented.

The second of these questions may prove to be more easily solved than the first. The League to Enforce Peace has already drawn up a program which seems to offer a practical and constructive plan for the establishment of a durable peace.

It is quite within the bounds of possibility, however, that the League to Enforce Peace may prove to be the solution not only of the second, but also of the first question. For if the nations can be brought to an agreement as to the basis of a durable peace, then all immediate issues become relatively insignificant and peace terms ought readily to be arranged. The declaration of Sir Edward Grey, cabled here last week, suggests that at least one of the great combatants is ready to consider the principle of such a League as the basis for the peace that is to come.

Long before this war Sir Edward suggested a League of Nations that would say to the nations that came forward with grievances and claims:

Put them before an impartial tribunal; subject your claims to the test of law or the judgment of impartial men. If you can win at this bar you will get what you want; if you cannot you shall not have what you want; and if you start war we shall adjudge you the common enemy of humanity and treat you accordingly. As footpads, burglars and incendiaries are supprest in a community, so those who would commit these crimes and incalculably more than these crimes will be supprest among the nations.

The Editor of The Independent has just received the following cablegram from The Hague:

'S GRAVENHAGE, THE NETHERLANDS, MAY 10, 1916.
The "Dutch Anti-War Council" Committee considers the fact that the German Government says in its recent note to America that it has twice publicly declared its willingness

to make peace, a new cause for mediative action on the part of neutral nations. The Swedish Second Chamber has officially expressed the wish to coöperate with neutrals in such mediation. The Anti-War Council urged the same upon the Dutch Government. Switzerland is also strong for similar action. The recent speeches between the German Chancellor, Dr. von Bethmann-Hollweg, and the English Premier, Mr. Asquith, have opened the possibility of conciliation. The Dutch Committee hopes that you will deem it possible to secure the coöperation of the American peace organizations and eventually the Mohonk Conference in urging President Wilson to promote a Conference of Neutrals to offer mediation for a durable peace, and the arrangement of an international system which will secure the principle of equal rights for all civilized states in the future which Premier Asquith described as the purpose of the Allies.

H. C. DRESSELHUIS, LL.D.,
President
B. DE JONG VAN BEEN EN DONK, LL.D.,
Honorary Secretary

This cablegram comes from the president and secretary of the Dutch Anti-War Council, under whose auspices was formed over a year ago "The Central Organization for a Durable Peace," the most influential and representative peace body now actively working in Europe. It has branches in the belligerent as well as the neutral countries, and its various national committees are now engaged in the study of its "minimum program" for a permanent peace after the war ends and in bringing the idea before their respective nations. The editor of The Independent is chairman of the American branch.

This is a highly important message, and indicates that the time may at last have come for President Wilson to renew his offer of mediation. He has waited long and patiently. He may fail now. But he is the only man on earth who has a chance to succeed.

It is intimated from Washington that the President will not offer mediation again until he receives assurances from both sides that his good offices will be welcome. In other words, the initiative must come from the belligerents.

That is not the best statesmanship. The Hague Conferences expressly stipulated that

It is expedient and desirable that one or more powers strangers to the dispute should on their own initiative and as far as circumstances may allow, offer their good offices in mediation to the states at variance.

Powers strangers to the dispute have the right to offer good offices of mediation even during the course of hostilities. The exercise of this right can never be regarded by either of the parties in dispute as an unfriendly act.

It is therefore evident that Woodrow Wilson has everything to gain and nothing to lose by renewing his offer of mediation.

AN UNAMERICAN INNOVATION

THE war has accustomed us to censorship as an institution, but it has not made it any less abhorrent to the American mind. It may be a military necessity, but it always involves a dangerous infringement of personal liberty. We have purer plays and purer periodicals than European countries which have a censorship of the theater and the press.

The imposition of a censorship upon an infant art like that of the motion picture is especially objectionable. What would have been the effect if a censorship had been established over still photography fifty years ago? Instead of photography being, as it now is, one of the commonest and most profitable of pastimes, it would mean that the art would be confined to a few rich and powerful organizations, for every one who took a picture

would have to have it inspected and stamped at the cost, say, of a dollar, by his local censor; then, before it could be sent into another state or published in a periodical, it would have to be passed upon by the national censors at Washington.

Now the motion picture camera will soon be made cheap enough so that almost any one can afford one. If not interfered with by censorial laws it will in a few years be the common custom to take motion pictures of home and street scenes, to exhibit these in school, church and theater within a few hours after taking, and to mail them cheaply to any part of the country for exhibition in the family circle or in public. But this very desirable democratizing of the art will be impossible under a national or state censorship where one has to pay a fee of some ten dollars for every new film or two dollars for every duplicate, and have them shown to the censors before being exhibited in public.

But the motion picture is more than a means of amusement and more than a method of education. It is one of the most powerful forms of propaganda yet discovered. Some day there will, we hope, be films attacking the entrenched wrongs of modern society, as "Uncle Tom's Cabin" attacked slavery, for which it was not allowed to circulate in the South, or as "The Servant in the House" attacked phariseeism, for which it was prohibited by the censor in England, or as Tolstoy's "Resurrection" attacked autocracy, for which it was prohibited by the censor in Russia. Does any one suppose that our political appointees would in like emergencies stand for the freedom of the film against the pressure of vested interests and popular prejudice? No, we should have again what Shakespeare calls "art made tongue-tied by authority," and the old battle which has been won by the press would have to be fought over again for the screen.

COMPULSORY VOLUNTEERING

THE British Parliament has passed a law to the effect that youths reaching the age of eighteen would be allowed one month's grace in which to enlist voluntarily. If they do not volunteer then they will be conscripted. We now for the first time believe the old story of the Mexican governor who wrote his chief: "In accordance with your request, I am sending you twenty volunteers. Please return the rope."

THE BRANDEIS HERESY TRIAL

FOR nearly four months now the Senate has had under consideration the Brandeis case. And a most discreditable proceeding it has been! Here was a man appointed by the President of the United States to perhaps the most august political office on earth. According to the United States Constitution, the appointment has to be confirmed by the Senate. Two proper courses were open. The Senate could have investigated his fitness quietly, as a committee on admissions of a club would have done, or else they could have called him before them and publicly let him meet his accusers face to face. The Senate adopted neither course. It has instead held open hearings in which various and sundry individuals have appeared before it, bringing all sorts of charges founded in large measure on hearsay and innuendo. If Mr. Brandeis is now rejected his reputation will be smirched, if not ruined, for life, and yet he has had no opportunity to confute his calumniators. The man has been charged with serious violations of the ethics of his profession without the legal safeguard of an ordinary trial.

We especially deplore the methods of the attorney retained to handle the case for the opposition. This attorney, Mr. Austen G. Fox, of New York, besides examining and cross-examining witnesses, prepared a brief against the confirmation of Mr. Brandeis, which was submitted, we believe, not only to the Senate committee and the whole Senate, but was allowed to become public. The sub-committee rendered its report on May 5, after Mr. Fox's brief had been in their hands. The majority of the sub-committee found all the charges in the brief groundless; the minority agreed that a number of them were groundless. The charges in which the minority reports did not find against Mr. Brandeis included the Warren, Gillette, Kirby, Illinois Central, New Haven Merger, Old Dominion and Consolidated Gas cases. And yet as late as April 20 letters were sent out signed by Mr. Fox, requesting communications, based on his brief, to be sent to senators to influence their final vote on Mr. Brandeis' nomination. In other words, Mr. Fox asked individuals thruout the country to write to their senators, basing their letters on a brief which was repudiated in whole or in part by every member of the Senate sub-committee.

The whole affair has simmered down to a heresy trial. Mr. Brandeis holds views unacceptable to great and powerful interests, and they are determined to "break" him. But we venture to predict that, if they succeed, they will have done more to injure the Supreme Court than Mr. Brandeis' election to it could have done if the charges made against him were true. When the American people once come to believe that the Supreme Court is the last refuge of stand-patism and political obscurantism, and that privilege at all costs will endeavor to keep men who espouse popular rights off the bench, then the popular distrust of the Supreme Court will become intensified and serious. Mr. Brandeis is needed on the Supreme bench.

A SOCIAL DANGER

A LEADING Berlin daily paper, described as semi-official, has introduced the proposition to revolutionize the institution of marriage. "Sister M." calls attention to the alarming decrease in the birth rate, which is natural enough because of the war, and she suggests, as a relief, that all births shall be made equally legitimate, and that no special advantage in law or sentiment should be given to children born in honorable wedlock. The editor says that the correspondence he has received from Prussia overwhelmingly approves the proposition. In France the situation is equally serious.

We have been anticipating something of this sort. It has been reported that during the Thirty Years' War a social license prevailed, but the present movement, we believe, does not mean free love or promiscuity. It means rather that the community would take radical measures for its own advantage controlling prospective motherhood and fatherhood, for what is thought to be the advantage of the race. Germany is not going to leave things to accident, but if she acts will act intelligently and purposively.

War has in many generations and in many countries killed off the men, and the result has sometimes been polygamy and concubinage. But we have passed that stage. In this country the abolition of slavery made concubinage no longer legal. An attempt now in Germany or in any other country devastated by war to overthrow the institution of monogamous marriage might be very disastrous while it lasted, but it would be temporary. In nature the births of males and females are about equal, and civilized nature requires monogamy. We have had in this country one extraordinary example in the Oneida Community of doing what it is proposed to do in Germany. There the leaders of this Socialist community organized what they called plural marriage, and they decided who should have children, and when. The experiment continued for a generation, but after a while the victims of it would have none of it. It would not be at all surprizing if in the uprush and confusion of wild revolutionary theories following the war the sanctities of marriage should be attacked, and it would seem as if the foundations of society were being overthrown, but the basis of public order stands firm in the constitution of human nature.

GASOLINE FOUNTAINS

THE trouble with our sculptors and architects is that they are always behind the times. They persist in making grand staircases when we are using elevators. They construct elegant fireplaces for our steam-heated flats. They carve candlesticks for our electric lights. But, what is most annoying of all, they insist upon encumbering our streets and parks with monumental fountains while leaving our hydrants and taps in naked ugliness.

What is more absurd than to see beside the Speedway a gigantic confection in marble and bronze professing to supply water to man and beast? Neptune and the nymphs are dry and dusty now. The turtles and dolphins are gasping instead of spouting. Their usefulness has departed and of course their beauty has vanished with it. The pedestrians no longer dare to drink at the public fountain, but hasten on to where they can get water or other beverages bottled, boiled or filtered. Horses are few and far between. The vehicles that stream past are run by motors that take water but rarely, tho often athirst for liquid of another sort.

Now, what our artists should do, if they were alive to their opportunities as were the artists of old Greece and Italy, is to erect fountains to supply gasoline. Doubtless it could not be furnished free. None of our philanthropic millionaires could afford this except Mr. Rockefeller. But some sort of a quarter-in-a-slot machine could be constructed whereby the exhausted engine could quench its thirst.

And think of the opportunities a gasoline fountain would afford to the sculptor. Instead of Neptunes and nixies, sea-horses prancing and dryads with invert vases, of which the artists must be almost as tired as the public, we should see gnomes and kobolds, the elves of the mines and all the fairies of the fire, with statues of the dancing Loki, of Prometheus stealing fire from heaven for the service of mankind, a ring of Vestals guarding the sacred flame, or the stately figure of Zoroaster, the high priest of petroleum.

Of course, the artists will make us such fountains in time—but that time will be when the oil wells are emptied and the carriages are run by electricity.

THE BIGGEST PARADE SINCE '65

LAST SATURDAY, MAY 13, 125,000 MEN AND WOMEN, MORE AMERICANS THAN HAVE MARCHED BEHIND ONE LEADER
SINCE THE GRAND REVIEW OF THE G. A. R., MARCHED UP BROADWAY AND FIFTH AVENUE
IN NEW YORK TO ADVERTISE THEIR BELIEF IN NATIONAL PREPAREDNESS

No Progress in Mexico The conference between General Scott and General Funston, representing the United State Government, and General Obregon, representing the de facto President of Mexico, has come to nothing. A tentative agreement had been drawn up and had received the approval of President Wilson. But General Carranza, after apparently trustworthy reports had been forthcoming that he was satisfied with the agreement, suddenly rejected it. General Scott has returned to Washington. The status of the American troops in Mexico is still unfixed by any agreement between the two governments.

The one point of disagreement between the American Government and Señor Carranza appears to be one that is hard to get over. Carranza wants the American soldiers brought back from Mexico. If that were to be done, there would be no need of any agreement at all. Fortunately, the Administration has shown no inclination to give up the purpose which led it to send the troops across the border in the first instance. It must be admitted, however, that that purpose is not being pursued with appreciable vigor.

Almost all the available soldiers in the United States are now in Mexico or on the border. It has even been judged necessary to withdraw a number of coast artillery companies from their posts and send them to Texas. General Funston now has 50,000 men at his command. The President has also called out the militia of three border states, Texas, Arizona and New Mexico. They will presumably take the place of some of the regular troops along the border and release them for duty nearer the front.

Meanwhile Villa, the bandit, is as mysteriously invisible as ever. He has not been captured; he is not even being pursued.

At Polaris, a border mining camp near Lochiel, Arizona, and at Glen Springs, Bouquillas, and Deemers, Texas, there have been minor repetitions of the raid on Columbus that precipitated the punitive expedition.

Doubling the Regular Army Out of the deadlock between the House of Representatives and the Senate on the size of the army to be provided by the Army Reorganization bill has come sudden agreement. The conference reports the bill to the two houses this week and prompt ratification should be the outcome.

Under the present law a maximum size is provided for the army, but no minimum. Under the Army bill, as now amended, there will be a minimum of 160,000 men, and it will be the duty of the War Department to see that the forces do not fall below that number. The maximum size of the army in time of peace may be 175,000, if the President so decides, and in event of a national emergency the President may increase the number to 218,750 men, without further action by Congress.

In addition to these numbers, which include only the fighting regulars, there will be in time of peace in round numbers 5000 Philippine scouts, 6000 of the Quartermaster corps, 7000 of the Medical corps, 3000 of the Signal corps, and nearly 9000 unassigned enlisted men. So that in case of threatened war the President could create, without Congressional action, an army of 254,000 men. This is more than double the size of the present regular army.

There will be added to the existing organization 35 regiments of infantry, 10 regiments of cavalry, 15 regiments of field artillery, 30,000 men in the coast artillery, five regiments of engineers. The largest increases come in the field artillery and engineering branches, where the need for technical skill and special training makes sudden increases most difficult.

Other Provisions of the Army Bill The enlistment term is fixed in the Army bill at seven years, three years with the colors and four years in the reserve. There is a further provision that men whose rating is "excellent" may be transferred to the reserves at the end of one year. This system, when it has come into complete operation, will provide a maximum peace army of 175,000, and a trained reserve with from one to three years' experience with the colors behind it of 233,000. The distance which the House conferrees have come in the direction of a larger army is shown by the fact that the maximum figure set in the Hay bill originally passed by the House was 140,000.

The Senate conferrees, on their side, have given up the provision for a volunteer reserve army, and accepted the House provision for a "federalized" state militia of 425,000 men. The size of the National Guard in each state is determined by the ratio of 800 men to each Senator and Congressman. It is decreed that members of the National Guard shall take a double oath of allegiance, to the state and to the nation.

Further provision is made for carrying out the idea set forth by the President of a "citizenry trained to arms," by encouraging the establishment all over the country of training camps on the Plattsburg plan. While it is decided not to provide pay for the men training under this system, all the necessary expenses of transportation, uniforms, subsistence and medical attendance are to be borne by the Government.

The House proposal for the government ownership and operation of nitrate

THE AFFAIRS OF STATE

Washington Evening Star
THE INTERRUPTED CONFERENCE

Wood in Philadelphia Public Ledger
JUST ANOTHER "PUNITIVE EXPEDITION"
WHO IS BEING PUNISHED?

Copyright Brinkerhoff in Boston Journal
THE TACK IN THE ROAD

plants for providing materials for the making of explosives is retained in the bill. These plants in time of peace are to produce nitrates which may be sold for fertilizing purposes. The selection of the sites for nitrate plants is left to the President, and $20,000,000 is set as the limit of cost for the establishments.

Authority is given to the President to seize and operate in time of threatened war private plants for manufacturing munitions of war. He is empowered to create a board of five, composed of three civilians and two army officers, to study the advisability of the government's entering upon such manufacture of munitions.

The probable passage of the Army bill in the form worked out by the conferees indicates what increase there has been in the country in the past year in sentiment for military preparedness. Two elements have done much to establish this conviction that we need to be better prepared than we have been: the fact that practically the entire available forces of the regular army are in service in Mexico and along the border, and that it has been found necessary to call upon militia as well, while the end is not yet in sight; and the continuing tension over the submarine activities of the German navy, only partially relaxed by the repeated assurances of the German Government.

The Great Preparedness Demonstration

A most impressive demonstration of the strength of the preparedness sentiment, at least in the East, was afforded by the gigantic parade in New York City last Saturday. For eleven hours a body of citizens larger than the United States army moved steadily over a route along Broadway and Fifth Avenue from the City Hall to Central Park. They were followed by several thousand women marchers and by 8000 of the New York National Guard. The count made by the New York *Times* set the number of march-

ers at 125,683. Other estimates put the figure from ten to twenty thousand higher, but the lowest figure is quite impressive enough.

No parade of equal size has been seen in this country since the Grand Review of the Federal Army in Washington at the close of the Civil War. It was probably the greatest procession of civilians that the world has ever seen.

The marchers were reviewed at Twenty-fourth Street by Major General Leonard Wood, Commander of the Department of the East; Rear Admiral Usher, Commandant of the Brooklyn Navy Yard, and Mayor John Purroy Mitchel, of New York City. The list of professions, trades, businesses, organizations and groups represented in the line suggests the universality of the preparedness sentiment in the country's greatest city:

MEN
New York City Employees
Rubber Trade
Dry Goods Trade
Knit Goods and Worsted Trades
Woolen Trade
Theater and Allied Arts

Printing and Printing Inks
Electrical
Furs
Candy
Silks
Lace and Embroidery Importers
Engineers
Men's Hat Trade
Corsets
Mail Order Houses
Publishers
Pianos
Haberdashers
Upholsterers
Carpets
Pottery and Glass
Garment Salesmen
Needle Trades
Lighting Trades
Architects
Clergymen's Association
Wholesale Millinery Trade
Clothing
Boot and Shoe Trades
Paper Trade
Hardware Trade
Wholesale Grocery Trade
Brooklyn Business Men
Lumber Trade
Sporting Goods
Hide and Leather Trades
Coal Association
Oil Association
Exporters' Association
Certified Accountants' Association
Insurance Association
Drug Association

THE HARASSED BORDER COUNTRY
While almost the whole mobile army of the United States is in Mexico with the announced purpose of catching Villa—a purpose at present abandoned, however—American towns along the international line are suffering fresh raids. The militia of Texas, New Mexico and Arizona has been mobilized for guard duty and General Funston has planned a rearrangement of his troops to secure an effective patrol

Shipping Association
Grinding Wheels, Glue and Sandpaper
    Association
Steam, Water and Gas Supplies Asso-
    ciation
Wine and Spirits Association
Financial Association
Produce Exchange Association
Cotton Exchange Association
Transportation Association
Lower Wall Street Association
Lawyers' Association
Jewelers' Association
Real Estate Association
Saddlery and Harness Association
Physicians and Surgeons' Association
Furniture Association
Automobile Trade
Tailors
Columbia University Battalion
Public Schools' Athletic League

WOMEN

New York City Employees
Teachers
American Women's League for Self-
    Defense
Self-Supporting Women's Battalion
Stenographic Division
Young Women's Battalion
Art Students' League
Insurance Women
Oil Industries Women
Brooklyn Women
College Women
Silk Trades
Wall Street Women
Department Stores
Women's Preparedness Battalion
Lighting Trades Women
Women Doctors, Nurses and Auxiliaries
Independent Patriotic Women's Division

The marching thruout the parade
was done in admirable style and good
order. Never less than 13,000 marchers passed the reviewing stand in an
hour, and at times the number rose to
20,000. General Wood described it as
the best citizen marching he had ever
seen, and Joseph H. Choate said of the
parade as a whole, "I am deeply im-

prest with the splendid physical appearance, and apparent intelligence of
the men. They would make good soldiers. They have an earnest and brave
bearing and show that they do not take
their marching as play. They are in
deadly earnest. The parade is bound to
have a great influence on the country."

It was estimated that a million people watched the parade as it passed.

The British   The French troops on
Front   the western part of the
             line have been with-
drawn, doubtless for the defense of
Verdun, and the British have taken
their places. The British lines now extend from the sea—except for the
short distance held by the Belgians—
to Frise, beyond Peronne. The
"Anzac" troops, that is the Australian
and New Zealand Army Corps, who
were employed at Gallipoli, have been
in part transferred to France. As soon
as they took their places at the front
the Germans in the opposing trenches
hoisted a banner inscribed "Welcome,
Australians."

The Germans seem to be determined
here as elsewhere to keep the offensive
in their own hands, so without waiting
for Kitchener's army to begin its over-
due "spring drive" they have begun
with attacks at various points in
Flanders and France. At the old
Hohenzollern redoubt near Hulluch
they succeeded in capturing some of
the British trenches. In Ploegsteert
wood, north of Armentières, the Germans sapped and blew up the front
trenches.

It is rumored that the Germans are

THE BRITISH LINE OF BATTLE
The Germans are reported to be massing great
bodies of troops, including Turkish and Bulgarian contingents, on the western front in
France and Flanders. The line here has scarcely
been shifted at all for more than a year and is
now held by British, Canadian and Australasian
troops. The shaded side represents territory held
by the Germans. The arrows show the points
where the British have recently made counter-
thrusts. The Germans last week delivered heavy
blows at St. Eloi, Armentières, Hulluch and
Givenchy, but it is not yet apparent where they
intend to direct their main offensive

making great preparations for a desperate attempt to break thru the British lines and reach Calais, and that
among the troops collected for this
purpose are Turks and Bulgars. This
report, whether true or not, may be
intended to offset the effect of the announcement by the French that they
have been receiving reinforcements of
Russians from Port Arthur on the
Pacific. Nothing is said on either side
about the numbers of the Russians or
Turks who have gone to France.

On the   The efforts of the Ger-
Meuse Hills mans to gain a substan-
           tial success at Verdun
have been renewed with more energy
than ever. Their attack was directed as
before against the sector between Forts
Vaux and Douaumont, east of the
Meuse, and against Le Mort Homme
and the adjacent hills, Nos. 304 and 287,
west of the Meuse. Their only success

Copyright Underwood

MOBILIZING MUSIC
This collection of real musical instruments—and harmonicas—is to be sent to the soldiers in the
trenches who have proved their eagerness for concerts by banging "Tipperary" on tin-pans

was achieved in the western field. Here after a terrific bombardment four infantry charges were made in two days which gave the Germans possession of the French entrenchments at several points, notably those on the crest of Hill 304. The Germans claim the capture in these operations of fifty-three officers and 1515 men. The French regained some of their lost positions in counter attacks later in the week.

General Petain, who has had charge of the defense of Verdun from the beginning of the battle, has been appointed to the chief command of the entire right wing of the French army. He is succeeded at Verdun by General Robert G. Nivelle, who was at the beginning of the war merely a colonel in the Fifth Artillery. He is sixty years old.

The Seven Who Were Shot

All seven of the men who constituted the provisional government of the short-lived "Irish Republic" and signed its manifesto have been shot by order of the court-martial. Besides these seven more have suffered the same penalty. Others who had also been condemned to death have had the sentence reduced to imprisonment for life or a limited period. Among these is the Countess Georgina Markiewicz, who has been condemned to penal servitude for life. Joseph Plunkett, just before his death, was married to Grace Gifford, daughter of a prominent solicitor of Dublin. When she heard that he was to be shot she bought an expensive wedding ring, put on widow's weeds, and went to the barracks, where the ceremony was performed. Her sister, Muriel, was the wife of Thomas MacDonagh, who was shot the day before.

These summary executions have aroused considerable resentment even in England, and among those who had no sympathy with the rebellion. In one case at least it seems that a comparatively innocent man was unwarrantably put to death. This was F. Sheehy Skeffington, editor of the *Irish Citizen*, who was a pacifist and had taken no part in the rebellion, tho he had previously been active in the anti-enlistment movement.

In the House of Commons John Redmond urged clemency and John Dillon denounced the government in furious terms such as these:

If Ireland were governed by men out of Bedlam, they could not pursue a more insane policy. You are letting loose a river of blood between two races, which, after 300 years of hatred, we had nearly succeeded in bringing together. You are washing out our whole life work in a sea of blood.

If your program is to be enforced in Ireland you had better get ready 100,000 men to garrison the country. And then what sort of appearance will you make as the champions of small nationalities?

It would be a good thing if your soldiers were able to put up as good a fight—3000 against 20,000 with machine guns and artillery.

I am proud of their courage, and if the English people were not so dense they would have these people fighting for them.

Premier Asquith, in replying, said Mr. Dillon had forgotten the elementary rules of justice. Since he had spoken of a "sea of blood," it would be well to recall the actual facts. The total casualties of the military were 124 killed and 397 wounded, and of civilians 180 killed and 614 wounded.

Mr. Asquith later went to Dublin to investigate the situation in person.

Germany Sank the "Sussex"

In the note of May 4 the German Government professes doubt that the French steamer "Sussex," which was sunk in the Channel on March 24, was the victim of a German submarine. The commander of the submarine reported sinking a vessel at about that time and place, but he believed it to be a troop transport and his sketch of the vessel had two masts, while the photograph of the "Sussex" published in the London *Graphic* showed only one. But a photograph of the "Sussex" taken after the explosion shows two masts. Besides this a fragment of bronze found in the wreck and sent to Washington by the British Government was found by our naval officers to be identical with the metal used in the German torpedoes. Consequently, the German Government frankly acknowledges its mistake and in accordance with its previous promise assumes full responsibility. In the note of May 8 Foreign Minister von Jagow says:

In view of the general impression of all the facts at hand the German Government considers it beyond doubt that the commander of the submarine acted in the *bona fide* belief that he was facing an enemy warship. On the other hand, it cannot be denied that, misled by the appearance of the vessel, under the pressure of the circumstances, he formed his judgment too hurriedly in establishing her character and did not, therefore, act fully in accordance with the strict instruction which called upon him to exercise particular care.

In view of these circumstances the German Government frankly admits that the assurance given to the American Government, in accordance with which passenger vessels were not to be attacked without warning, has not been adhered to in the present case. As was intimated by the undersigned in the note of the 4th instant, the German Government does not hesitate to draw from this resultant consequences. It therefore expresses to the American Government its sincere regret regarding the deplorable incident and declares its readiness to pay an adequate indemnity to the injured American citizens. It also disapproved of the conduct of the commander, who has been appropriately punished.

The Capture of Kut

From details which have been disclosed since the surrender it is evident that General Townshend held out to the last extremity. It was November 21 when he encountered a force of 13,000 Turks entrenched at Ctesiphon with

CLEARING THE STREETS OF DUBLIN

British troopers with machine guns and rifles sheltered behind a movable barricade from which they shot down the snipers. As each section of street was cleared the barricade was shoved forward and the process repeated

Copyright International Film

DUBLIN IN FLAMES

Looking down Sackville street at the hight of the insurrection. The McConnell Monument in the foreground, silhouetted in the background the Trafalgar Column, opposite which, on the right, was the Post Office Building, captured by the rebels and held for days against the British troops

thirty-eight cannon. He penetrated the first and second lines and took eight of the guns, but the Turks received reinforcements on the following day and he was driven down the Tigris to Kut-el-Amara. This town he held until April 29, when he sent out his last wireless to the relief expedition down the river announcing that he was out of food and had hoisted the white flag. For the last two weeks the troops had nothing to eat but four ounces of flour a day and the flesh of the horses that they had slaughtered. Their only source of supply was the food brought by aeroplanes, which dropt the bags as they flew over the town, since there was no place for them to land. In this way 18,800 pounds of food had been brought from the supply stations down the river.

But the British had also to provide not only for their troops but for the native population of Kut as well, and these numbered six thousand. They tried to expel the civilians, but the Turks threatened to shoot any who were sent out. Besides these dependents there were over a thousand sick and wounded in the garrison. These have been sent down the river to General Suke in exchange for disabled Turks.

According to the official Ottoman report, the force captured at Kut consisted of one-fourth English and three-fourths Hindus. The number of officers taken was 550, half of them Hindus. On the day of the surrender, General Townshend ordered the arms and munitions to be destroyed or thrown into the Tigris, but the Turks claim to have recovered forty cannon, twenty machine guns and five thousand rifles in a condition so they can be repaired.

The Russians approaching from the northwest have now got within a hundred miles of Bagdad, as near as the British were at Kut. They recently defeated a Turkish force at Kasr-i-Shirin, near the Persian frontier, capturing a camel supply train

and three guns. From the north the Russians have reached Rowanduz, only two miles from Mosul on the Tigris above Bagdad.

The Turco-Russian War

The surrender of General Townshend's army at Kut-el-Amara has eliminated the British from the Asiatic field, at least for the time, and left the Russians and the Turks to fight it out between them. Two famous commanders who last year met in the swamps of Poland are now confronting one another in the mountains of Armenia. The Grand Duke Nicholas, who vainly attempted to defend the Russian frontier against the Germans in the first part of the war was, after having lost Poland, Courland and Galicia, sent to the Caucasus. There was much speculation at the time as to whether this transfer was to be interpreted as punishment for his failure in Europe or as an opportunity for a new campaign in Asia. Perhaps it was both. The Czar, who nominally superseded the Grand Duke

THE GREAT WAR

May 8—Russians defeated by Turks west of Mush, Armenia. Germans gain crest of Hill 304 west of Verdun.

May 9—Russians reach Persian frontier, 100 miles from Bagdad. Four more Irish rebels executed.

May 10—Official British estimate of German casualty lists makes the total for the war to the end of April 2,822,978, of whom 604,552 are dead.

May 11—Germans take British trenches at Hulluch. Germans attack British in East Africa.

May 12—Food riots in Germany. Premier Asquith goes to Dublin.

May 13—Heavy artillery firing on Trentino and Isonzo fronts.

May 14—Belgians invade German East Africa.

as commander-in-chief of the Russian armies in Europe, has done nothing except to hold the line of defense. But the offensive of Grand Duke Nicholas has cleared the Turks from a great semicircular belt, over a hundred miles wide to the south and west of the Caucasus. Within this zone of conquered territory are the two great lakes of Van and Urumia, and such important cities as Trebizond, Erzerum, Mush and Bitlis. If the Grand Duke can hold these gains he will have the honor of being the only one of the Allied generals to effect an important conquest.

But now comes the tug of war. General von Mackensen, who drove the Russian armies back from the German frontier and then conquered Serbia, has been sent to take command of the Caucasus and to check the Russian advance from the Caucasus. So far he seems to be doing it. The Russians who were advancing from Erzerum to Erzingan and from Mush to Diarbekr have met with stout resistance and some setbacks. In the mountains west of Mush an all day battle was fought in a snowstorm which, according to the Constantinople report, resulted in the rout of the Russians and the capture by the Turks of six officers, three hundred men and four machine guns.

The Turkish armies defending Erzerum and Trebizond were not captured with these towns but mostly retreated to the west where they have now presumably been reorganized under the direction of General von Mackensen and other German officers. Nothing, however, is known to the public about the size and condition of these Turkish troops or how they compare with their Russian opponents in these respects. With the clearing away of the snow from these Armenian highlands the campaign, which has been dragging along here for a year and a half, is likely to be brought to a speedy and decisive issue.

NO PIGTAIL FOR UNCLE SAM

BY THEODORE ROOSEVELT

THE editors and publishers of The Independent have asked me for a word of greeting on the occasion of its acquisition of Harper's Weekly and for an expression of my views on the present critical situation in our national life.

I am heartily glad to congratulate them upon what they have just accomplished. I have been intimately associated with the president of the Independent Corporation, the publisher and the associate editor of The Independent in journalistic work in recent years, and they and their associates have my very best wishes for their continued success.

Harper's Weekly is a historic American publication. At one time it was as strong a force in American weekly journalism as our country contained. Under George William Curtis and Thomas Nast it played a commanding part as a "Journal of Civilization," in the decade succeeding the Civil War.

MY views upon the vital questions of this crucial time in the history of the United States have been repeatedly set forth during the last twenty-one months. I am glad to give again to the readers of The Independent and of Harper's Weekly, now a single group, my conception of the primary duty of America at this crisis, in the words I recently used at Chicago

"A year and three-quarters have passed since the opening of the great war. War has been waged on a more colossal scale than ever before in the world's history; and cynical indifference to international morality and willingness to trample on inoffensive, peace-loving peoples who are also helpless or timid have been shown on a greater scale than since the close of the Napoleonic wars over a century ago. Alone of the great powers, we have not been drawn into this struggle. A twofold duty was imposed upon us by the fact of our prosperity and by the fact of our momentary immunity from danger.

"This duty was, first, to make our voice felt for the weak who had been wronged by the strong and for international humanity and honor and for peace on terms of justice for all concerned; and, second, immediately and in thorogoing fashion, to prepare ourselves so that there might not befall us on an even greater scale such a disaster as befell Belgium.

"We have failed in both duties. Incredible to relate, we are not in any substantial respect stronger at this moment in soldiers or rifles, in seamen or ships, because of any governmental action taken in consequence of this war; and, moreover, we have seen every device and provision designed by humanitarians to protect international right against international wrongdoing torn into shreds and have not so much as ventured to speak effectively one word of protest. The result is that every nation in the world now realizes our weakness and that no nation in the world believes in either our disinterestedness or our manliness.

"There are persons in this country who openly advocate our taking the position that China holds, the position from which the best and wisest Chinamen are now painfully trying to raise their land. Nothing that I can say will influence the men and women who take this view. The holding of such a view is entirely incompatible with the right to exercize the privileges of self-government in a democracy, for self-government can-

not exist amongst people incapable of self-defense.

"But I believe that the great majority of my fellow countrymen, when they finally take the trouble to think on the problem at all, will refuse to consent to or acquiesce in the Chinafication of this country. I believe that they will refuse to follow those who would make right helpless before might, who would put a pigtail on Uncle Sam and turn the Goddess of Liberty into a pacificist female huckster, clutching a bag of dollars which she has not the courage to guard against aggression.

"I SPEAK of the United States as a whole. Surely it ought to be unnecessary to say that it spells as absolute ruin to permit divisions among our people along the lines of creed or of national origin as it does to permit division by geographical section. We must not stand merely for America first. We must stand for America first and last; and for no other nation second—except as we stand for fair play for all nations. There can be no divided loyalty in America. There is no room in this country for German-Americans or English-Americans, Irish-Americans, or French-Americans; just as there is no room in this country for a political party based on fealty or opposition to any particular creed, whether Protestant, Catholic or Jew. There is just one way to be a good citizen of the United States, and that is to be an American and nothing else. This is not a question of birthplace or national origin or creed. Any big group of loyal and patriotic Americans will include men of many creeds and many different race strains and birthplaces. But they will not be loyal and patriotic Americans at all unless they are Americans and nothing else. The first step in preparedness is dependent upon our common and exclusive American nationality.

"Preparedness must be both of the soul and of the body. It must be not only military, but industrial and social. There can be no efficient preparedness against war unless there is in time of peace economic and spiritual preparedness in the things of peace. Well-meaning men continually forget this interdependence. Well-meaning men continually

COLONEL ROOSEVELT AND GENERAL WOOD
Two preachers of Preparedness at the Plattsburgh Camp, encouraging the practice of Preparedness. "I speak for military preparedness. I speak for the performance of international duty"

speak as if efficient military preparedness could be achieved out of industrial and social chaos, whereas such military preparedness would represent merely a muscular arm on a withered body. Other well-meaning people speak as if industrial preparedness, social preparedness, would by itself solve the problem. This is worse folly than the first. Let these men look at Belgium and compare her fate with that of Switzerland. Belgium was one of the countries in Europe in which the greatest advance had been made in industrial efficiency, and as regards social justice she was at least well ahead of us. But there had been no corresponding military preparedness. The result is that both materialist and the humanitarian have been ground into the dust together, simply because the men so successful in peace had not in peace trained themselves so as to be able to defend themselves in war, and to make other nations realize in advance that they were able to do so.

"I SPEAK for military preparedness. I speak for industrial preparedness. I speak for the performance of international duty, which can only come when we fit ourselves to do our duty to ourselves, and when we have made up our minds never to make a promise to any other nation which cannot be kept, which ought not to be kept and which will not be kept. I speak of all this in the interests of national unity and manhood, of international peace, and of the service of our country and of the world at large.

"I appeal to Americans everywhere to stand against the crass materialism which can show itself just as much in peace as in war. I appeal to our people to prepare in advance so that there shall be no hideous emergency which renders it necessary to submit to inordinate profit-making by the few simply because, when the emergency comes, we must improvise at whatever cost the things that for our sins we have failed to provide beforehand. We cannot afford to leave this democracy of ours inefficient.

"Our national character is in the balance. Americanism is on trial. If we produce merely the self-seeking, ease-loving, duty-shirking man, whether he be a mere materialist or a mere silly sentimentalist; if we produce only the Americanism of the grafter and the mollycoddle and the safety-first, get-rich-quick, peace-at-any-price man, we will have produced an America faithful only to the spirit of the Tories of 1776 and the Copperheads of 1861, and fit only to vanish from the earth."

Oyster Bay, Long Island

THE PORT OF THE MIDNIGHT SUN

RUSSIA, foiled in her efforts to acquire an ice-free port to the south, has turned toward the north instead, and there, upon the Arctic Ocean, has opened a new harbor for Petrograd. The war, by closing the Baltic, has forced Russian trade to seek its ancient outlet thru Archangel. Before the time of Peter the Great, England used to receive from Archangel exports amounting to more than a million dollars a year. But when Peter opened his "window upon Europe," named after himself or his patron saint, he ruthlessly closed the north window, opening upon the Arctic. In recent years it has been regaining something of its former importance, and since the war began it has been the sole channel thru which England and France could supply their needy ally unless they sent arms around the world and into Russia by way of Vladivostok. Consequently the single track narrow gage four-hundred-mile railroad running to Archangel has been congested with traffic and thousands of tons of munitions and supplies needed at the front have been piled up on the shores of the White Sea.

What is worse, the channel leading to Archangel is blocked with ice for six months of the year. So the Russian determined to open the port still further to the north, but on the open sea, and kept ice-free by the expiring efforts of the Gulf Stream. A naval base had been started in 1895 at Kola Bay or Alexandrovsk, but the new port of Ekaterina is established beyond this on the Murman or Norman coast and only sixty-six miles east of the Norwegian boundary.

It is not probable that Ekaterina or Catherine Bay will ever become a popular place of residence, since it is mostly dark for half the year and the region round about consists chiefly of barren rocks, fir forests and dismal swamps. But it is some six hundred miles nearer the Atlantic and it is always accessible.

To construct a double track railroad 700 miles long thru this almost

RUSSIA'S NEW SEAPORT

uninhabited and very inaccessible country was no easy task in wartime, yet we are told it has been accomplished at the rate of a hundred miles a month and is now open to traffic. It seems, however, that the stretch along the shore of the White Sea is not yet finished, so goods have to be transported by boat from Kandelax to Kem. The rolling stock of the new railroad is mostly American-made. A large part of the roadbed had to be built upon piles over the marshes and lakes.

Where the new railroad from Petrograd first strikes the White Sea, just below Kem, a new commercial port of Soroka has been opened for traffic, or will be as soon as the Sea is free from ice. Soroka is much nearer to Petrograd than the old port of Archangel or the new port of Ekaterina, so it will probably be used by merchantmen during the open season of summer. At the present time there are nearly a hundred vessels waiting in the White Sea for the ice to melt so they can discharge their cargoes.

The port and railroad of Archangel are henceforth to be reserved by the government for military purposes exclusively. It is possibly from Archangel that the Russian troops are being dispatched to Marseilles for service in France.

The opening of these new ports is of considerable importance to America because all signs point to a great increase of commerce between Russia and the United States, part of which will find an entrance thru the Arctic Ocean.

WHEN ANOTHER REPUBLICAN NOMINATION WAS IN DOUBT

Among these "prominent candidates for the Republican nomination" pictured in Harper's Weekly for May 12, 1860, the man who was to dominate half a century of American history has as inconspicuous a place as, perhaps, the next President holds now in the public thought. These three illustrations reproduced by courtesy of Harper and Brothers

PEACE INSECURE—AFRAID FOR HER LIFE   PEACE SECURE—SAFE AND PROTECTED

A PAIR OF NAST CARTOONS FORTY YEARS OLD THAT SMACK OF THE PRESENT

In Harper's Weekly for February 13, 1875, these twin cartoons by the most famous of American cartoonists were published apropos of a message from President Grant urging an appropriation for coast defenses

PEOPLE AND THE PARK

BY HELEN HOYT.

ON THE CAR TO WORK

Doors and doors and doors go past:
  Hardly a tree: only bricks to be seen. . . .
Three more blocks,—two more—one—at last
  The park! Filling all the view with green.

Now quickly I look, quickly take,
  Thru branches low, branches high,
Blue snatches of the far lake;
  Quick, far snatches of the blue in the sky.

Whirling, twinkling jets of spray
  Drench the lawns from the thirst of the sun;
They spread out their silver and shift and sway,
  And the wetness sparkles where they run.

I can feel thru the peopled car
  How fresh and pleasant is that air;
Thru the clangor and jar
  The delicacy of the shadows there;

And feel the cool paths under my feet. . . .
  But now, good-bye, park! Until to-night!
I am a prisoner here in my seat. . . .
  O, my prison is hurrying me out of sight.

THE JEALOUS PARK

I went into the park to think,
To ponder over difficult things;
But the park would not let me think.
The grass would always be saying
"Lay your fingers in my softness,"
And the water was saying
"Listen, listen, listen,"
And "Follow" said the paths,
Leading away before me
With invitations.
But most of all the trees called to my thoughts,
Reaching out their branches to me;
Drowning my thoughts in a green flood.

FROM A HIGH WINDOW

Roof after roof,
Gables and turrets and chimneys,—
Dingy,
Angular,—
Yet softened now by the twilight
These lofty places
Quiet and unencumbered and apart,
Are full of shadows
And shadowy restfulness.

O darkening sky,
Is it like this our city looks to you
Uncrowded and dim?
And you never guess the turmoil
Under this calm of roofs.

BEAUTY

How strange it is to remember
That the turning red of the leaves in autumn
Is chemistry
As much as when litmus changes its color
Over the acid fumes of the test-tube:

Is chemistry, and physics and botany
As much as any that professors teach
Out of books in classrooms;
Follows the same ancient laws as litmus;
Follows them as blindly as litmus;
And knows nothing at all
Of that which we have named "beauty"!

FLIRTATION

He whistled soft whistlings I knew were for me,
Teasing, endearing.
Won't you look? was what they said,
But I did not turn my head.
(Only a little I turned my hearing.)

My feet took me by;
Straight and evenly they went:
As if they had not dreamed what he meant:
As if such a curiosity
Never were known since the world began
As woman wanting man!

My heart led me past and took me away;
And yet it was my heart that wanted to stay.

THE SPIRIT OF THE ADMINISTRATION

BY NORMAN HAPGOOD

DURING the thirteen years that I have been more or less connected with public affairs, I have been occasionally accused of enthusiasm. It was so when Roosevelt was President, when Hughes was Governor, as it is now that Wilson is President, that Mitchel is mayor. The charge is not disturbing. Critical faculty is not shown by an evenly distributed censoriousness. It is shown by choice of standards and perception of whether they are being attained. In my opinion, the world is better because Wilson has been President and will be further benefited by his continued leadership.

He is a statesman, not merely a crusader. In the head of Mr. Bryan or Mr. Ford, a mere idea may take lodgment and remain there regardless of the facts at present existing in the universe. Such men are useful, but we do not make executives of them. For a national executive we seek a man who is in politics what Mr. Ford is in his own business, progressive but also exact. The usual defect of the tory is that he lacks spir-

Those who read The Independent this week know Mr. Hapgood well, some thru the pages of Harper's Weekly, the others thru his wide reputation as a constructive liberal. We are glad to have him set forth here, for both groups in the enlarged family of Independent readers, his reasons for believing that President Wilson's Administration has made good.—THE EDITOR.

itual inspiration; that of the radical that he lacks proportion. An American Tolstoy would make a troublesome President. If John D. Rockefeller, on the other hand, were President, he would lack the apostolic element. Woodrow Wilson's mind dwells on upward principles, and at the same time he connects them successfully with the facts of 1916. Lincoln said he ran the machine as he found it. He had fanatics to combat, and Wilson likewise has pacifists, militarists, socialists, prohibitionists and single-taxers who think him blind. But Lincoln, while balanced, was in-

tellectually and morally progressive, and so is Wilson.

Roosevelt had a valuable message. He brilliantly pounded it into the heads of the masses, and when Taft tried to recede he found himself in trouble. Wilson, taking political liberty where Roosevelt dropt it, carried it further, to the great disgust of the former President, among whose many virtues the habit of admiring rivals is not discernible. Wilson could not have done the simple pioneering as audibly as Roosevelt did, for more than twenty years, but on the other hand Roosevelt's work ended itself. He could not have passed the Currency Act, removed privilege from the tariff, and completely destroyed the lobby. It is to be doubted whether he would have secured a rural credits bill and an income tax. In foreign affairs he would have continued successful, but his success would have been different. It would not have been so profound in principle. It would have been, altho with American breeze, *Welt Politik*, in the established sense. The success would have been external. It would be taking an isthmus if he desired it; or stopping a war before one of the belligerents was ready; or, if we can believe his own fulminations, the forcing on Mexico of order at the cost of evolution.

All these things are the opposite of Mr. Wilson's foreign policy. In the Colombian treaty, the Panama tolls repeal, the disapproval of the six power loan, the Pan-American doctrine, the sympathetic leniency toward the Mexican revolution, he has proceeded on the theory that he is not a lawyer retained by the United States to wrest from others every point, right or wrong; but an official whose vast power is lodged there to be used with complete fairness. Entire fairness is extraordinarily hard to put in practise in domestic affairs, and still more in foreign, and it is the practical success of ideal principles that gives to Mr. Wilson his distinction. The public, when it put him in office, talked as if that was what it desired. The next election may show whether it really had such a desire, or merely dreamed it had.

I say "may," for of course a dozen things may obscure the true and underlying issue. But those of us who are interested in the development, power and originality of American life will do what is possible to keep this question to the front.

THIS is not an administration gifted in advertising. Seldom is so much accomplishment accompanied by so little celebration. The work of the departments is a notable illustration. Mr. Houston's work, combined with the rural credits act, has done so much for the farmer that it might well have been the talk of the nation. It has also included the first great steps toward decrease in the waste of agricultural distribution—a monumental contribution—toward lessening the cost of living; yet of that record not one man in a thousand has ever heard. Mr. McAdoo's resourcefulness carried the country easily thru dangerous financial crises, but he reaped little for it save abuse.

The one member of the cabinet whose every move was applauded was one whose methods made his continuance impossible, and Mr. Garrison's popularity with newspapers, society and business was due to qualities the very opposite of those which mark the nature of this administration. Whether in water-power legislation, in relation to powerful individuals, or in the general nature of his thought, he is an attractive expression of the status quo. There is in him nothing to disturb the man of satisfied commonplace. It is interesting and even significant that praise should have been almost unmixt for him, with so little praise and so much censure for those who truly lead. If the President is reëlected, as I think he will be, it will be because of what he has done, not because of any of the arts of dramatization or conciliation. I like to think often of a conversation he had on the morning of March 5, his first day in office. He was speaking of Jefferson, specifically of his finished work as architect and builder at the University of Virginia, but generally of the number of big ways in which he had found expression. The President declared that it was much harder to be true to the best in one's self in these complex days; harder to disentangle one's self from manifold detail and do the large things well; but that he was for his part determined so to do; determined to give to the public not a frittered attention, but a concentration on essentials. Those who complain that he shakes fewer hands, holds fewer conversations than most Presidents, should at least read the fact in the light of its meaning to the President himself. He likes to be alone with his thought, which is what we used to call being alone with God. And it might be well to reread Jefferson's epitaph, written by himself, and see what to that philosopher were the essentials of a lifetime. He did not mention, you remember, that he had been Secretary of State, Vice-President, or twice President of the United States. Those positions might be accidental. He mentioned only that he had written the Declaration of Independence and the Virginia Bill of Rights, and that he had founded the University of Virginia. It was not externals, in other words, that he thought worthy of recording, but contributions to liberty and to human thought.

In foreign affairs, the President has had to steer an untried course in a mighty storm. The nerves of the passengers have frequently been shaky. They have mistaken their brain-storms for firmness. If the ship has changed its direction to fit current, wind and coastline, some of the more vocal among them have been convinced that the captain has changed his mind. In truth, the captain's mind is peculiarly stedfast. It watches developments; it admits new information; but it knows always its direction, the principles of its conduct. I do not mean that it never slips. That would be absurd. But I do mean that the slips are slight, unimportant, and temporary, and that they affect the general portrait not at all. They come usually when he tries for a moment to comply, instead of thinking for himself. If partizanship ever stops at the water's edge, it certainly hasn't done so in the nearly two years of ordeal since August, 1914. Rocking the boat and screaming has been a popular pastime. Mr. Hearst and Mr. Roosevelt must be recognized as the leaders in the attempt to turn foreign policy to partizan advantage, but Mr. Root and other notable Americans have joined in. Some German-Americans have been obstreperous, and a society of allied sympathizers was formed to bring us into the war against Germany on general principles. The small extent to which a President in this country can count on fair play from the opposition was shown in Mr. Roosevelt's extraordinary about-face in the Belgium matter, in which he found it expedient to excoriate Mr. Wilson for a procedure that was exactly what he himself had recommended. His proved mis-statements about his own course in Mexico form another illustration, and his attempt to stir up the Catholics forms another.

AGAINST all types of opposition, the President has maintained a policy in the war that has been humane and sound, patient but firm. He has held that peace was what we are to seek, confidence in reason and in love, and that in upholding principle no nervous tantrums by others should stampede his judgment. But he has held also that, in the world we actually live in, certain ultimate duties do fall on the most powerful neutral, notably the duty to prevent murder on the world's highway. Again, he has stood half way between those who rely on an anti-force theory to the extent of unlimited pacifism, on the one hand, and, on the other, those who think they are brave or elevated because they are hostile, impatient, or rash.

To sum up: The Administration has done a good job. It has been done under difficulties, with power, unconventionality, and understanding of a complex situation. It has been done at the same time with purity and with practical sagacity. There is little real point of view in American politics. The Wilson administration has had point of view. The list of accomplishments, unequaled since the Civil War, are visible as parts of a single, undivided whole. They represent enlightened liberalism, which is the desire to extend moral ideas and to equalize the opportunities for living well. The President has been able to make himself the master-liberal of his country, holding the forces together, keeping them headed toward the sun, and making them work.

New York City

The Independent-Harper's Weekly
NEWS~PICTORIAL

Underwood

Mt. Cavell, an 11,000-foot peak in the Canadian Rockies, formerly Mt. Geikie, rechristened in honor of Edith Cavell. * * * Elsie Ferguson makes her Shakespearean debut as Portia in Sir Herbert Tree's "Merchant of Venice"; Tree plays Shylock

White Studio

Antoinette B. Hervey

The Cathedral of St. John the Divine, crowning Morningside Heights in New York City. Ground was broken on May 8, with a brilliant ceremony, for the huge nave, which is to be finished in five years if the necessary three millions are subscribed

Copyright Underwood

United States soldiers in Mexico starting on a long march at sunrise, near San Antonio, where the expedition is halted

Medem
The censor. Doesn't he look the part? Gautier is hated by French journalists. The French censorship is exceedingly rigid and hence efficient. In letters objectionable passages are not merely blacked out, as by the English, but erased by acid

London Sphere, Copyright N. Y. H
The schoolboy of Rheims, with shining morning face very sadly disguised to protect his lungs against the deadly greenish fumes of poison gas that he may encounter as he walks thru the ruin-littered streets. The folk of Rheims have little to learn about Purgatory

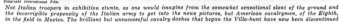

Copyright International Film
Not Italian troopers in exhibition stunts, as one would imagine from the somewhat sensational slant of the ground and the incorrigible propensity of the Italian army to get into the news pictures, but American cavalrymen, of the Eighth, in the field in Mexico. The brilliant but unsuccessful cavalry dashes that began the Villa-hunt have now been discontinued

G. V. Buck

While Major General Hugh L. Scott was negotiating with General Obregon at El Paso, his wife, in this trim khaki uniform, was drilling at Chevy Chase with the women and girls who have made a feminine Plattsburg out of this national encampment near Washington

Copyright Medem

He gave his eyes for France. Now, home from the wars, he has a fascinating story for the children, who gather around him just as children here will cluster about Grandfather next week to hear again how he got the empty sleeve at Gettysburg

Copyright Underwood

May Day means strikes, and red-flag parades, and wildflower hunts and country festivities, and, in the city, a determined attempt to recapture some of the out-of-doors gaiety that belongs to the season. Here are little New Yorkers dancing around their maypoles in Central Park, bringing folk-customs of many nations to this piece of Americanization thru play

In all South America there is no finer monument than this in Buenos Aires. Tho given by Spanish residents, it marks the centennial of Argentine independence from Spain, May 25, 1910. It has recently been completed by the addition of the bronze groups about the base

Copyright Brown-Dawson-Neuman

Copyright Underwood

Copyright Underwood

"The British Empire ought to be an organized empire; organized for trade, for industry, for economic justice, for national defense, for the preservation of the world's peace, for the protection of the weak against the strong." With such a revolutionary idea this man, William Morris Hughes, the Labor Prime Minister of the Australian Commonwealth, appeared unexpectedly in England and upset the politics of the mother country

At the other end of the Presidential receiving line from Henry Ford, peace man, is T. Coleman Du Pont, powder man. He has been president of the Du Pont de Nemours Powder Company, the largest concern of the kind in the country, has large coal and iron properties, and owns a controlling interest in the Equitable Life. If we only had two consuls instead of one president, what a well-balanced ticket the peace man and powder man would make!

Copyright Medem

Saved from the sea—to die on land? Russian troops near Marseilles offering a prayer of thanksgiving for their safe arrival in France. The soil of France drips with the blood of fighting men gathered from more nations than have ever been seen in war together since the day of the Roman eagles, and from distances vastly greater than the Romans knew

ROBERT FROST, A POET OF SPEECH

BY GEORGE H. BROWNE

A YEAR ago, Robert Frost was an unfamiliar name in this country. Within a year, however, seven editions of "North of Boston" have been printed! Why? Not because he was "discovered in England" [as a matter of fact, he was "discovered" by The Independent in 1894] but because American readers have discovered that they can understand and enjoy poetry which deals veraciously with the life and the people they know—poetry which is written in a language they can understand and enjoy, because it is the language they speak, vibrant with the feeling and force and form of the familiar spoken sentence. In Frost's poetry, as in all effective writing and in any animated conversation, the sentence does double duty: not only conveys the necessary information, but also records, in an unmistakable tho unwritten notation, the natural tones and inflections which alone give emotional and imaginative vitality to the expression of live thought.

Most people misconceive the real reason why verse of this kind gets its message over so quickly and so effectively. In language, most of us are not used to observing closely (either physically or imaginatively) the really most significant technical elements, namely, the audible tones in which the thought of the sentence-unit is conceived and is to be uttered. The domination of the newspaper, the magazine, and the expository essay—of reading by eye without hearing anything, so that, as a result, our untrained ears cannot even understand most oral reading without seeing the text—has made us content, in poetry as well as in prose, with the dead level of a flat, emotionless, mere algebraic informatory tone. Too much of our so-called poetry is only words fitted to metres—no true tone values, no emotional realities—plenty of melodious rhythm, perhaps, but none of the live tones that infuse with expressiveness even our most ordinary and uninspired conversation. Now, the spoken language is alive with characterizing tones, as nature and the human face are alive with characterizing colors. These tones may be, but seldom caught by ear, reimagined, and fixed on the page, so that the reader will hear and reproduce them exactly.

Verse like Robert Frost's gets its message over, therefore, because in form as well as in substance it is true to life; and no popular verse "gets 'over' to stay except when it is thus true. Frost is as simple in his diction and imagination as Wordsworth and even more sympathetic with his subjects, whether people or nature. He gets more music and pathos and force out of homely Saxon monosyllables than any other writer, not excepting Lincoln; and he acquired his mastery in quite the same way that Lincoln did: never letting pass any but the best attainable expression of his thought. Frost has more than once brought a letter back from the country post-office and rewritten it, because one sentence in it was not as good as he thought he could make it. "I recall distinctly the joy with

MY BUTTERFLY

BY ROBERT LEE FROST

Thine emulous, fond flowers are dead,
  too,
  And the daft sun-assaulter, he
That frighted thee so oft, is fled or
  dead;
  Save only me
  (Nor is it sad to thee),
  Save only me
There is none left to mourn thee in
  the fields.
  The gray grass is scarce dappled
    with the snow;
  Its two banks have not shut upon the
    river;
    But it is long ago,
It seems forever,
Since first I saw thee glance,
With all the dazzling other ones,
  in airy dalliance,
Precipitate in love,
Tossed, tangled, whirled and whirled
  above,
  Like a limp rose-wreath in a fairy
    dance.
When that was, the soft mist
  Of my two tears hung not on all the
    fields,
  And I was glad for thee,
And glad for me, I wist.

And didst thou think, who tottered
  wandering on high,
Fate had not made thee for the pleasure of the wind,
  With those great, careless wings?
'Twas happier to die
And let the days blow by.
  These were the unlearned things.
It seemed God let thee flutter from his
    gentle clasp,
  Then, fearful he had let thee win
  Too far beyond him to be gathered
    in,
  Snatched thee, o'er-eager, with ungentle grasp,
  Jealous of immortality.

Ah, I remember me
How once conspiracy was rife
Against my life
  (The languor of it!) and
Surging, the grasses dizzied me of
    thought,
  The breeze three odors brought,
  And a gem flower waved in a wand.
Then, when I was distraught
  And could not speak,
  Sidelong, full on my cheek,
What should that reckless zephyr fling
But the wild touch of your dye-dusty
    wing!

I found that wing withered to-day;
  For you are dead, I said,
And the strange birds say.
  I found it with the withered leaves
  Under the eaves.

which I had the first satisfaction of getting an adequate expression for my thought," he has said; "it was the second stanza of the little poem on the 'Butterfly,' written in my eighteenth year." That was twenty-five years ago! Thus, tho Frost is a recent candidate for popular American favor, and to that extent is new, he is no novice; few American poets have had a longer or more fruitful training, either in technique or in experience.

Born in San Francisco (1874), he came back in his twelfth year with his widowed Scotch mother to live in Salem, New Hampshire, not far from his father's people in Lawrence, Massachusetts. Up to the time of graduation from the Lawrence High School, young Robert was a docile pupil; but then he declared his intellectual independence, and never again took much interest in tasks not self imposed. He spent a few months at Dartmouth (1892), "acting like an Indian in a college founded for Indians." He left abruptly (but voluntarily), took his mother's school, worked in the mill, engaged in newspaper work, married at twenty-one; and after another futile attempt to conform to the "academics," this time at Harvard, retired again to school-teaching and farming in Derry, New Hampshire (1899). For the next seven years he farmed, thought, and wrote—among shorter lyrics the first of his longer poems in the newer characteristic style: "The Death of the Hired Man," "The Housekeeper," and "The Black Cottage," subsequently incorporated into "North of Boston." In 1906 he began to teach English in the Pinkerton Academy at Derry. His success was so marked that he was invited to the Plymouth Normal School (1911) to teach psychology; but the restrictions of even freer teaching there again became irksome; and only two weeks before he sailed (August, 1912), with wife and four children, he decided upon England as a freer field for poetical composition and the realization of his literary ideals.

The Frosts had neither letters nor letters of introduction. Like migratory birds they flitted into solitary independence at Beaconsfield, about twenty miles from London—almost by accident. The publication in London (1913) of his first book of poems, which he carried over with him, was almost accidental; his first meeting with literary friends was most accidental; but the success of his book and the intensity of concentration in the composition of his second book,

"North of Boston" (1914), were far from accidental. It was fortunate for him (and perhaps for us) that his work received immediate and hearty recognition in England; but it is a pity that the force and originality of the New England idylls, written in home-sickness over there, should have diverted attention at home from the merits of the first book, written in rustic isolation over here; for tho more traditional in form, it is hardly less original and forcible. As its name implies, "A Boy's Will" is the lyrical record of a young man's thoughts — "and the thoughts of youth are long, long thoughts." This, on his art, from "Pan with Us":

Pan came out of the woods one day—
His skin and his hair and his eyes were
  gray; . . .
He tossed his pipes, too hard to teach
A new-world song, far out of reach; . . .
Times were changed from what they
  were;
Such pipes kept less of power to stir; . . .
They were pipes of pagan mirth,
*And the world had found new terms of
  worth.*
He laid him down on the sun-burned
  earth,
And ravelled a flower and looked
  away—
Play? Play?—What should he play?

No longer, was the answer, only beautiful lyrics, in a variety of traditional meters, lyrics which will maintain an enviable position in any anthology of American verse; but, in a new and original rapid measure,

gripping, dramatic pictures of the places and the people he was brought up among—interpretations of New England life and character, displaying a psychological insight, spiritual veracity, and artistic simplicity, power and originality, such as no other contributor to American literature has displayed since Emerson and Whitman.

Frost finds his metrical freedom, not in *vers libre* like Whitman, but in decasyllabic, unrimed verses, no two of which are alike, because of the tones of living speech in them—the stressed pauses, the little hurries of extra-syllabled feet, the preponderance of light and weak endings to the run-on lines, and fresh metrical inflections, which reproduce in verse the actual shape of the colloquial sentence. It is a new kind of blank verse, strange at first sight, from its very colloquialism; but its strangeness disapears if it is read out loud.

"When I began to teach, and long after I began to write," he told the boys in our school, "I didn't know what the matter was with me and my writing, and with other people's writing. . . . I found the basis of all effective linguistic expression to be the sound in the mouths of men—not merely words or phrases, but sentences—living expressions flying around—the only vital 'parts of speech.'" And his poems are to be read most appreciatively, out loud, in

the natural tones of this live speech. The first poem, "Mending Wall," the author likes best in "North of Boston," because the verses best catch the sentence sounds. Can't you see and hear the old farmer shaking his head, challenging, threatening, playing and mistrusting his neighbor across the old wall in the spring?

Mr. Frost is not a vers librist, or imagist, or even realist, except that he agrees with Carlyle that a poet has not far to seek for his subject. "It all depends upon what you call 'beauty,'" says Frost. "Terror is beautiful. A mob raging down the street may be made beautiful if you catch the right tones and rouse the right emotional reaction by the poetic expression of it. You can catch the tones only with the imagination." Mr. Frost, if he is a realist, is an imaginative realist.

Mr. Frost is not a Socialist nor a profound moralist, but he is sane and simple and moral. He is a philosopher, even if he doesn't preach and interpret. He is above all a dramatist, for all poetry is to him dramatic. Fortunately for us he is still in the prime of his creative activity. Much of his recently written work, which he has been reading in public this winter, surpasses the best of his published verse; and he will soon be giving us still better.

Browne and Nichols School, Cambridge, Massachusetts

Photograph by Huntington, Boston Post
THE POET OF NEW ENGLAND AT WORK IN HIS NEW HAMPSHIRE HOME

THE SAGE OF POTATO HILL

Ed. Howe's Thoughts on Men, Women & the World

WHEN I see a disagreeable person approaching, I walk away; I don't wait until he gets started. The most disagreeable people, when they approach, say a few agreeable things to begin with; then is the time for disappearing. It's no use to argue with disagreeable people: if they could help it, no doubt they would. Possibly they regard the annoying things they say as Criticism; every one likes to think of himself as a Critic. The only complete answer to a disagreeable person is flight, or a fight; and no one cares to be mussed up constantly by fighting.

The Jews are not always agreeable people, but they are certainly a great people. And their greatness consists mainly in looking out for themselves: every one should have. A favorite story "on" the Jews represents a Jew as saying: "I'd like to, but can't afford it." There is an important Moral in that joke; you can use that moral to advantage a hundred times a day.

In olden times much was said, and justly, of social injustice. But in course of time public wrongs have been righted: in the United States today we suffer none of the wrongs formerly complained of by our forefathers across the sea, and who still have some cause for unrest. But we of the United States have every right that can be given us by law; we enjoy the fruits of every revolution of the past: we have as much as the old reformers claimed we should have. We have as many rights as can be accomplished by revolution or legislation. The people are in control; we must now remedy the faults of the family, the neighborhood, the individual. The wrongs we have now are the fault of the majority; of what we know as the People, and we have no higher court of resort. We have much impoliteness, idleness and intemperance, but both the rulers and the laws beg us to improve in all these respects.

Formerly Arthur Brisbane attracted wide attention because of the size of his salary. Newspapers and public speakers took delight in referring to the big figures attached to Mr. Brisbane's name; his salary was an inspiration to young men, they said, and we all loved to hear about it. But suddenly Charley Chaplin appeared with a salary of $650,000 per annum. And now we never hear of the Brisbane figures. Will the Brisbane press agent get busy, or will he submit to ignominious defeat?

If you are pursuing a wrong course, you can't afford it, since you are being damaged. But your competitor can afford it: he is being benefited by your folly. When you talk wrong, or act wrong, remember that you are not only damaging yourself, but helping the person you think least of: the Opposition.

Keep out of Court; you may have justice on your side, but at any time you are liable to run into a judge like that one in Chicago who decided lately that Bacon wrote the plays attributed to Shakespeare.

It is an affront for an agent to call on me. He has decided that he is smarter than I am, and can argue me into giving up some of my hard-earned money for his benefit. There is some question about the desirability of my giving up the dollar he covets; if there were not a question about it, the agent would not call on me, in an attempt to out-talk me, or deceive me in some way. . . . I need certain things, and know it; I am willing to give a dollar for them. It is not necessary for an agent to call on me: I voluntarily go after the supplies, and cheerfully pay my money, and carry the supplies home. But certain other things I do not need, and it is an agent's business to fool me into thinking I do. Therefore I do not like an agent. Possibly the reason I dislike him is that he is so clever that he nearly always sells me when I do not actually want to buy.

I wish more things were like the English sparrow. How it thrives, altho every man's hand is against it! But we must spray fruit, and use a serum on meat animals, and doctor the soil which produces the cereals. It always pleases me to visit a patch of wild plums; they get along without bothering any one. What a fight man is compelled to make for the apple, and what a free gift the wild plum is! I lately rode thru the country in an automobile, and the road was lined with wild crab apple trees. The crab apple trees were in full bloom, and very beautiful; but no one had sprayed them, or trimmed them: they were a free gift of nature. Are the English sparrows, the wild plums and the wild crab apples so healthy because they have never been reformed?

I have never been afraid of the Devil; but it frightens me to think of having a tooth pulled.

The greatest inequality of the sexes I know anything about is that many of the best women are unknown outside of their immediate neighborhoods, whereas a man who is fair, capable, polite and industrious rarely fails to come to the top in some sort of fashion. One of the most useful and capable women I ever knew is not known a half dozen miles from home, whereas her husband, who doesn't equal her, is a member of the legislature, and quite a prominent man. No really capable, modest and useful man can be buried alive, but most women of that description are.

I know a very bright man, and one day complimented him to his sister. "I suppose he is smart enough," she said, "but I become very tired hearing him repeat. . . ." We all do that; next time you are talking around the family fireside, ask yourself if you are not repeating.

I sometimes suspect that there is no such wise and beneficent legislation as the shiftless of all countries have talked about for centuries.

When we get all we are entitled to, more results in harm somewhere. Liberty can accomplish so much, and no more. Food is a human necessity, but too much of it results in harm. The Germans are an affront to shiftless Americans; they have less liberty and a poorer government than we have, but in time of peace they have more prosperity, better institutions, better scholars, better philosophers, better musicians, better mechanics, and better farmers. In the United States sentimental nonsense has become a crime; we talk of White Man Slavery when we actually have more liberty than we should have.

The world is so crowded with amiable hypocrites that it can not get a fair start toward simple common sense and truth.

If we have injustice that the best human society cannot get rid of, then we should go over the argument again. Possibly what we call injustice is really justice asserting itself, and taking its terrible toll.

"My wife don't go much," a Potato Hill man said lately. "When I ask her to go anywhere with me, she begins to remember the great number of things she has to do, and I can't budge her."

If the people of this country do not pay more attention to little problems, and less to the big ones, they'll finally get into serious trouble; in the opinion of a little man combating some of the opinions of the big ones.

Women have as great a variety of notions in serving company meals as they have in selecting the hats they wear.

What wonderful things you hear of! And how few you see!

WOMAN IN THE MARKET PLACE

BY MARGARET DELAND

The author of "Old Chester Tales," "The Iron Woman" and "The Awakening of Helena Richie" has studied the woman question for many years, and she writes of it from wide observation and with kindly insight.—THE EDITOR.

T HAT Woman is in the Market Place will probably be admitted without discussion. That some of us don't like to see her there does not alter the fact: *She is there!*

And she is going to stay there.

The voices that say that her "place is in the home" are growing a little less assured, because it is dawning—even upon those most anxious to "put her in her place"—that frequently she has no home to which to go. Or that if she has, it is because she has gone into the Market Place to get it.

Another thing is being reluctantly conceded by those who object to Woman in the Market Place—namely, that she is not there necessarily because she likes to be. It has been hard for the advocates of the home to admit this; some still refuse to admit it! To such persons the girl out in the world of industry, jostling up against men, competing with them, fending for herself, getting the bloom rubbed off her mind, and her eyes opened to certain facts in our civilization which men (for her innocence and their own comfort) have found it convenient to hide from her —that sort of girl is, to this almost obsolete type of mind, wilful and conceited and undutiful. But this type of mind is so rapidly becoming extinct that it need not be considered. Most people grant that the girl who has gone out of the Home into the Market Place has done so under the pressure of economic necessity. She has to earn—or die.

THE PASSING OF THE HOME

F OR the startling thing that has happened is that the Home, as a center of self-support, has practically ceased to exist. . . . It was built up as a physical fact, when humanity lived in caves, and the women hung skins on the damp walls, shaped clay pots in which to cook, and sewed what clothing they had with a bone needle and deer sinews. Humanity went on making the Home still as a physical fact, but little by little as a spiritual idea, when the men began to build shelters, and thatch roofs. When they did this, the women still hung things on the walls according to their ideas of "decoration"; still cooked, still sewed;—but by and by the pots grew into spits, or what not

286

(they are timbale irons today!) ; the bone needles became steel—and what those needles accomplish now we had better not try to state! But in the beginning, both needles and spits were used inside the four walls of the shelter. It was there that women spun and wove, cured meats, cared for their sick, literally "earned their living." So, naturally enough, the phrase "Woman's place is in the Home," became, as we got further away from the cave, a shibboleth for women. "Home" meant duty and decency and dignity; it meant love and service and self-sacrifice. Yet as far back as when men discovered the principles of mechanics—the lever, the inclined plane, the wheel—there was preparing a movement of women away from the Home.

WOMAN IS IN THE MARKET PLACE

T HEN, suddenly, with a rush, mechanics captured civilization, and domestic industries ended. Now, practically everything needed by the household is made outside of it—in the Market Place. Woman, instead of spinning and weaving her own cloth, buys it, spun and woven in factories —largely by women. Instead of molding candles, she touches a button and gets her light from metal filaments (manufactured by the hands of women). Instead of kneading bread, she speaks into a telephone transmitter, and the operator—a woman—connects her with the baker, and bread is left at her door. Woman, stopping short in the ages-old routine of toil *in* the Home, is toiling now outside of it!

This change has come with a suddenness which has jarred the whole fabric of society, and as a result we are today in the midst of an adjustment of Nature to environment, of which, at present, we cannot see the outcome. We can only admit that it is woman, almost as much as man, who sustains the family by labor in the Market Place. If she should say, "*My place is in the Home,*" and flock back from the factories and shops and offices, to sit down in the old Shelter and let her men support her, the peo-

ple who are so sure about her "place" would have some very uncomfortable moments! They would be more uncomfortable than some of the Market Place women themselves, in whom, indeed, the instincts of the cave woman decorating her walls, the spinning woman listening to the whirr of her wheel, the housekeeper standing, red-faced, over her revolving spit, still linger. I remember hearing one very efficient, very weary business woman say, wistfully, "I wish *I* had time to hem pillow cases!" Which only goes to show, as I said in the beginning, that the woman in the Market Place is not there necessarily because she likes it. She is there because she has to be.

HOW SHE ADJUSTS HERSELF THERE

B UT what is going to be the effect of the Market Place upon her? The effect of any pressure of necessity is either adjustment to conditions or extinction. That is a biological fact. It is that which makes—not the narrow people, vociferating about "woman's place"—but thoughtful human beings, look on this extraordinary change in civilization with apprehension as well as with hope. The hope inherent in the economic independence of women is so obvious that it scarcely needs comment. Indeed, the dignity and self-reliance and intelligence of the Woman in the Market Place bring into somewhat dismaying contrast the foolishness and selfishness of some of the women who, because their men toil for them, are deprived of the old wholesome obligations of duties and services. Happily, this parasitic class is small. Many of the women who are served by the brains of their living men (or of their dead men!) have wakened to a sense of civic and social responsibility, and *are* working—not in the Market Place, to be sure, but in human existence!

As for the toiling Woman, machinery has given her respite from certain personal services of love and duty, but the spirit of service—without which a Home is nothing but a House!—is just as consecrated in the Market Place where she supports a home in which she herself dwells only when her working hours are over, as it ever was in the days when Adam delved and Eve span. So no one can deny the hope in the new state of things. Indeed, it is so splendid that the dazzle of it blinds some of us to the dangers that have come with

MARGARET DELAND

AUTHOR OF "OLD CHESTER TALES," "THE AWAKENING
OF HELENA RICHIE," "THE IRON WOMAN,"
"AROUND OLD CHESTER"

it. Yet, for the fulfilment of the hope, it is well to recognize the dangers.

What are they? Not those to which the fearful folk who talk about the "Home" direct our attention. Not neglected children, nor unfaithful wives, nor ill-kept houses, nor "unwomanly women." These fears are too foolish for discussion! Look at the wise and tender mothers —in the Market Place when, no doubt, they would prefer to be in their nurseries. Look at the working women who are their husbands' good comrades. Look at their well-kept houses, or flats, or single rooms—their "Homes," in fact! The right kind of a wife can carry "Home" about in a suit case, if, for any reason, she and her husband are wanderers! No; the dangers of the Market Place are too real to spend our time in vaporing over the threat to the Home because Woman works *for* it and not *in* it. The real dangers fall into two classes:

The danger—physical;
The danger—spiritual.

The physical menace of the Market Place is perfectly apparent:

Fatigue, leading to bodily deterioration.

We have but to consider the conditions under which many women work and their bodily limitations. That Industry gives no thought to those limitations goes without saying. The girl who stands on her feet all day behind a counter; the pregnant woman who works up to the last moment; the mother who goes back to the factory when the baby is hardly ten days old;—such women must suffer structural and emotional changes which may ultimately tell upon the race.

The spiritual danger is more subtle:

Arrogance, leading to sex isolation.

With our first excited consciousness that we are economically independent of men, that we can buy and sell and get gain quite as successfully as they can, there has come to some women the idea that we are biologically independent of men. They even—some of these economically independent women—dare to speak of human passion with contempt! With this has come a suspicion of men as men. Such women fear masculine comradeship, lest the comrade may have ulterior purposes—he has had them ever since the world began! The arrogance of such self-sufficiency is very foolish, but no one can read feminist literature and deny many women are arrogant. We see feminine conceit, like a spot of decay, in the very flower of efficiency! We see it, with real alarm,

This is the fifth article in The Independent's series on THE NEXT GENERATION IN AMERICAN LIFE, in which William Allen White has written on Government, Liberty H. Bailey on Country Living, Elbert H. Gary on Business, and Shailer Matthews on Religion. In the Chautauqua Number, which will be the issue of June 26, President George E. Vincent of the University of Minnesota will forecast THE EXPANSION OF POPULAR EDUCATION.—The Editor.

in that new and noble sense of social responsibility which has been developed in women in the last two decades. Woman is going to reform the world over night! She is going to solve the old puzzles of humanity, cure the old sores that men have allowed to fester in the body politic—run the universe! Sometimes it seems as if she was leaving God out, for "male *and* female created He them."

Of course, the occasionally violent talk of the new woman is no more an arraignment of economic independence than a single case of measles is an arraignment of the public health. But suppose it is only the poisonous blossom of a rooted belief that women are "better" than men? That there is such a belief is not to be denied. It is one of the reasons some women give for a universal and unqualified suffrage for their sex: "Yes," they say; "universal man suffrage is still in the experimental stage, and it is a pity men vote so foolishly—and wickedly. But it will be different when women have the vote; *because women are wiser than men, and better!*" "Woman," said another advocate of unlimited suffrage, "will save civilization, because Women have consciences!" The inference that men have not would be irritating if it were not so silly.

HOW WOMEN WILL SAVE THEMSELVES

BUT here, it seems to me, are the two dangers of the Market Place —the menace to the body, Fatigue; and the menace to the soul, Arrogance. How are we going to meet them? Not by sending Woman back to the Home. We couldn't do that if we wanted to—*and we don't want to!* So the first thing for us to do is to teach women to recognize their physical limitations and disabilities; and educate them in matters of health. A slow process, and relatively uninteresting; but of lasting importance. In doing this we shall gradually create a public opinion which shall demand that conditions of the Market Place

shall improve. The Consumers' League is demanding this; and various state legislatures have been quietly and steadily pushed into improving by Law the conditions under which women work. We may even, by an aroused public conscience, reach the point of having, as Germany has, a maternity insurance. But legislation alone can't accomplish much. Laws, to be enforced, must be recognized as reasonable—so we come back to the only thing that can demand and enforce improvement in physical conditions—*Education*.

And for the arrogance? How shall we meet that? Economic independence is so new to women—what wonder that some of us have lost our sense of proportion? What wonder that some of us dare to say that the mother who is supported by her husband is (of all things in the world!) a *parasite!* If there is one human being who is not parasitical, one human being who "earns her living," it is the woman who bears and rears children! What wonder, intoxicated with self-sufficiency, that some of us say to the men, "We can do without you —and good riddance!" Men have never said that of women. Men know they can't do without women.

SHOULDER TO SHOULDER WITH MAN

MY own opinion is that this conceit, which just now is expressing itself in so many foolish and dangerous and unlovely ways, is a phase of growth. We have got to be patient with it. Of course, it is ridiculous and rather irritating;—but it is pitiful, too, just as a child's effort to walk is somehow a little pitiful. But one of these days the child will run! It will stop stumbling and tumbling, and making itself ridiculous, and perhaps injuring itself. Even now the tide of feminine self-sufficiency seems to be ebbing a little. The excitement of the new sense of ability, which we have treated rather like a new toy, is sobering into the realization that economic independence brings great spiritual responsibility, and that it involves the acceptance of the two master words of human nature: Love and Service.

Once let Woman in the Market Place or out of it, accept these two words, and she will march—not ahead of man, still less behind him—but shoulder to shoulder, in the home, in business, and in the world of ideals! And those of us who are a little fearful, a little discouraged, who are (we might as well admit it!) rather on the shelf—we shall look at this Woman in the Market Place with love, and admiration, and confidence, and envy!

Boston.

Teach children to get a receipt

IT is often necessary to send children to the store. It is irritating when they bring back the wrong change. Usually it means a trip to the store for father or mother to straighten it out.

Have you had this experience only to find that the clerk couldn't remember the transaction? Or that he insisted it was not his error? Either you got the missing change with an apology, or the proprietor gave it back reluctantly, or he wouldn't give it back at all.

If the clerk feels he is right, he may suspect the child.

If the proprietor is convinced you are right, the clerk is open to censure.

In either case an unpleasant impression is left, and confidence destroyed.

Merchants who equip their stores with the up-to-date National Cash Register render their customers a more than ordinary service.

They protect the buyer, child or grown-up, against disputes. They protect their clerks against errors. They protect themselves against loss.

This machine furnishes every customer with a receipt or sales slip.

It prints on this the amount paid or charged.

On this is also printed the date of sale and who made it.

It forces a duplicate, printed record for the merchant.

It pays to trade in stores equipped with the up-to-date National Cash Register.

The National Cash Register Company, Dayton, Ohio

LOOK FOR THIS SIGN IN THE WINDOW

MR. MERCHANT:

One by one we have discovered new ways to protect merchants' profits.

We have now ready for delivery many new models of the National Cash Register.

These 1916 models are the very last word in protection to you, your clerks and the public. The added improvements are worth your investigation.

Write for full information. Address Dept. AC

Independent Opinions

On January 24, in congratulating the *Congregationalist and Christian World* on its one hundredth birthday, we casually alluded to it as "the first religious weekly in this or any other country." This got us into a peck of trouble, for it seems that to say one religious paper is younger than another is as offensive as to say that one lady is older than another. First, we hear from the *Christian Observer*, which was started as early as September 4, 1813, under the name of *The Religious Remembrancer*. Then comes a *fac-simile* copy of the *Herald of Gospel Liberty*, Vol. I, No. 1, bearing date of September 1, 1808, and we are informed that The Independent "thrashed out this question a good many years ago and declared that the evidence was beyond all question in favor of the *Herald of Gospel Liberty*." Since an appeal to such an authority is unimpeachable—by us—we must revert to our prior opinion and hereby declare—not that the *Herald of Gospel Liberty* is the oldest religious weekly, no, that would be rash again,—but that it is the oldest we have seen.

Another instance of the danger of superlatives is our remark of March 20 that "The oldest Bible Society in the world apart from the Christian Church is the British and Foreign Bible Society, organized in 1804." But the Rev. Frank C. Oberly, of the Lutheran Church of Butler, Pennsylvania, calls our attention to the statement of the Schaff-Herzog Encyclopedia that "The first society formed for the exclusive purpose of publishing the Bible at a low price seems to have been the Canstein Bible Institute, established in 1710, at Halle, in Germany, by Baron Canstein."

We are prepared now to second the motion of the famous litterateur and logician who declared that all superlatives should be banished from the language as never necessary and often incorrect.

On page 22 of your issue of April 3, reference is made to the University of Michigan as the "oldest of our state universities." May I ask your authority for so classifying it? Undoubtedly, Michigan is one of the foremost, and has long been one of the leading state universities.

But in point of age, she is quite young, compared to some others. Georgia, established in 1785, is the oldest in that sense, tho it was not originally called the state university, but Franklin College. Vermont, dating from 1791; North Carolina, 1793; Tennessee, 1794;—all precede Michigan, which was established, so far as my knowledge goes, in 1837. The University of Virginia, founded by Jefferson in 1819 and opened in 1825, was the one to establish the principle of a state university as the apex of the public school system. This was eighteen years before Michigan's foundation, so I am puzzled to know in what respect she is called the oldest. The report of the Commissioner of Education for 1913, 11,220, gives 1841 as the "date of open-

New York Life Insurance Company

Darwin P. Kingsley, President

The New York Life is a Purely Mutual Company, now in its seventy-second business year.

On January 1, 1916, its outstanding business was 1,175,321 Policies, insuring the sum of $2,403,800,878.

The number of policyholders insured is over one million, eighty per cent. of whom reside in the United States and Canada.

The other 200,000 are scattered over the civilized world, chiefly in Europe, including both the belligerent and the neutral countries.

The Company's program being one of International Peace and Prosperity, it has been able to observe a strict neutrality, and to relieve suffering humanity to a degree scarcely equaled by any other human institution.

The New York Life is a Republic of Man in which the "war-drum throbs no longer and the battle-flags are furled," because its program is founded upon equal and exact justice to all, and there is no room for international hatred or greed.

It holds in trust over Eight Hundred and Fifty Millions of Dollars: the largest amount of funds ever gathered by a single corporation for beneficent purposes.

Its income for 1915 was over One Hundred and Thirty-one Millions; its disbursements to beneficiaries and additions to book value of assets were over One Hundred and Fourteen Millions.

The Company's death-losses in 1915 were only 73 per cent. of the amount provided in the premiums for the mortality of the year, including what may be called war losses.

No security issued by or in any country engaged in the present war and held by the New York Life is in default of either principal or interest.

The policies now offered by the New York Life receive annual dividends at the end of the second year, and those written since 1906 have received extra dividends at the end of the fifth and tenth years.

The Company's Policies contain guarantees of valuable benefits not required by the laws of any State or country, including insurance against total and permanent disability. The disability benefits include a waiver of premium payments and the annual payment of one-tenth of the face of the Policy until the disability ceases or the full amount of the Policy has been paid. The annual cost of this additional safeguard at age 35 is 54 cents per $1,000 insured.

Policies are payable either in one sum, in annual instalments during a selected period, or during the life of the beneficiary. Or, the proceeds of the policy may be left with the Company at interest, and drawn out as needed in sums of $100 or more at any one time. This $100 will be furnished in five checks of $20 each. You may insure not only against the contingency of premature death, but also against the danger of loss to the beneficiary through bad investments. A Monthly Income Policy furnishes ideal protection to a growing family.

The Annual Report showing business of 1915 and the condition of the Company at the close of that year will be sent on request to any Branch Office or to

NEW YORK LIFE INSURANCE COMPANY

346 & 348 BROADWAY, NEW YORK

The Craving for Excitement

That Same Healthful Instinct
Inspires the Love for Oats

What has placed the oat—think you?—in the king place among foods.

Was it flavor? That has helped, no doubt.

But was it not, above all else, that desire to "feel one's oats"?

Oat-fed animals, like horses, first proved their spirit-giving power. And the ages have confirmed it in mankind.

The oat is the vim-food supreme.

The joy of living suggests it—the universal love for vigor and vivacity.

This is not a mere luxury dish. Everyone knows it is surcharged with life-force.

The desire for snap and sparkle—for stamina, reserve force—is back of the love for oats.

Quaker Oats

The Fascinating Vim-Flakes

But we argue that oat-food should also be made delightful to the taste.

To that end, we make Quaker Oats out of queen grains only. We get but ten pounds from a bushel.

10c and 25c per package

Flavor and aroma abound in those big, plump grains, while small grains are insipid.

Asking for Quaker Oats will bring you this doubly-delicious grade. And without any extra price. It will pay to remember that.

Except in Far West and South

A $2.50 ALUMINUM COOKER

Made to our order, extra large and heavy, to cook Quaker Oats in the ideal way. Send us five trademarks—the picture of the Quaker—cut from the fronts of five Quaker Oats packages. Send $1 with them, and this double cooker will be sent by parcel post. This offer applies to the United States and Canada.

The Quaker Oats Company, Chicago

---

ing" of Michigan. The same volume, page 210, *et seq.*, gives the following additional dates of opening earlier than Michigan, all of state universities, please note: Alabama, 1831; Delaware, 1834; Indiana, 1824; South Carolina, 1805.

MILLEDGE L. BONHAM, JR.,
Professor of History and Political Science, Louisiana State University

This, like other questions of priority, is mostly a matter of definition. Michigan is commonly called "the mother of state universities" because it was the first to assume the form of that peculiar educational institution now known as the state university. The earlier state universities and the many Eastern colleges have been more or less remodeled to conform to its type. Georgia received its charter in 1784 and the University of the State of New York the same year. Both these institutions, however, are quite different in constitution from the ordinary state university. If we define a state institution as one in part supported by the state or in part governed by state officials, then Harvard and Yale would in their early days be so classed. If we regard the connection with the public school system as the deciding factor, then the University of Virginia is entitled to priority.

While the hills are still reverberating with the echo of your sarcastic comment on "the brave Los Angeles Chamber of Commerce," that body of hysterical men who had the temerity to say the West coast should have one-tenth of the total military strength suggested, let your memory get busy.

Who was it that became hysterical when the Spanish fleet was lost and our fleet hunting it? . . . Have you forgotten the chills that rattled New York's shuddering bones when she feared Cervera was steering for Hell Gate? If you have, I have not. . . .

And now we have a camp of soldiers, backed by artillery and three battleships, just below the line at Turtle Bay. Suppose you had a hostile camp of like character at Cape Fear? Would you think of it with some foreboding or would you laugh it off? I am one of 1000 reserve fighters in this city, backers of the local police, and my rifle stands beside my desk. I am not a minute man, I am a ten second man, with my rifle and shells, my revolver and its shells, all ready for *instant* use, and my start will require only what time it takes to buckle my belt, pick up my rifle and hat. And don't you believe I can't use my weapons. That is one thing I can do well. Twenty-twenty years in the woods taught me.

When the training camp opens at Monterey on July 10, there will be a gray head there that is ready to go against any enemy of our land, and I am hoping my appeal of two years ago to Secretary Garrison will find its answer in the organization of the Gray Headed Brigade.

D. E. HARRISON
Los Angeles, California.

No, we have not forgotten that foolish fear of the Spanish fleet which excited Boston and New York as much as the equally fictitious rumor of a Japanese invasion alarms the Pacific coast. The Independent at that time used much the same language about the Spanish war scare as it is now using about the Japanese war scare. But so long as California has "Ten Seconds Men" of the type of our veteran correspondent we believe that the West-coast can be held safe until some of us from the East—not so handy with the rifle doubtless but not altogether unprepared—can come to their aid.

PHONE 192 REGENT

J. E. Jewell.   *163ᵃ & 164, Piccadilly*

London, 6th January 191 6
W.

To the Managing Director,
CADILLAC MOTOR CAR MANUFACTURING CO.
Detroit. Mich. U. S. A.

Dear Sir:

       Having in May last decided to purchase a new car, I was in the usual
position of uncertainty that most would-be purchasers are in as to the car one
can get as the best value for money.

       I happened to see in the "Saturday Evening Post" one of your very
clearly - and to my mind - very fairly worded advertisements, and immediately
went to see your polite and courteous Manager, Mr. Bennett , with the idea of
looking over the chassis of one of your new 7 seater 8 cylinder cars - I think
you call it type 51.

       I took my engineer with me (in whose ability I place very great con-
fidence) and we had a thorough examination of the chassis and loose parts, and
both came to the conclusion that apparently a better constructed and more carefully thought out engine, etc. would be practically impossible to find. As a
matter of fact I placed an order with Messrs.Bennett for one of your cars.

       I may add that I have been a very keen motorist since the year 1903,
and have possessed several cars of British and French make, and have at the present time two other English-made cars as well as your 8 cylinder.

       It may interest you to know that we took delivery of your car early in
August last, and at time of writing she has done between 5 and 6 thousand miles,
and up to the present we have never had occasion to lift up the bonnet, unless it
has been to show an interested motorist the details of your engine. What I wish
to say more particularly is, that in the whole of my motoring experience I have
never struck a car that has given such complete and general satisfaction as the
"Cadillac" has done, and I feel quite entitled by my experience to give an opinion. I do not know whether it is your firm, or another firm in America that
makes use of the phrase : "One has not enjoyed the pleasures of motoring until he
has ridden in a"... but if it is your firm, I have the greatest pleasure in thoroughly endorsing your statement: if it is not your firm that makes use of the a-
bove phrase in its advertisements, you are, in my opinion, thoroughly entitled to
do so. Comparisons are always odious, but my experience of the "Cadillac" is
that it is value for money in every sense of the word, which, I regret to say, I
have never yet found in the purchase of any other car. It gives one a certain
amount of pleasure to be able to write about an article that one finds all right;
my previous experience of motor-cars was like taking a dip in the lucky tub - you
paid your money and you either got a decent or a bad car ; but from what I know
of several people this side who are the happy possessors of a "Cadillac" I may
say in all fairness to yourself , that I have never heard one that had anything
detrimental to say about your car.

       You may possibly think it strange that I take the trouble to dictate
this letter to you : you do not know me, and I do not know you ; but I think it
only fair to yourself to let you know that you have at least got one very ardent
admirer and happy owner of a "Cadillac".

       I hope to be in New York the first week in February on my way to Pasa-
dena, Calif. and if possible would like to have an opportunity of looking over
your works in Detroit. Am not sure yet whether I shall have time enough to go to
Detroit to do so, neither do I know whether you allow strangers to go over your
works, but if you do, I should be very pleased indeed to do so if possible.   A
letter will find me if addressed to the Waldorf Hotel, 5th Avenue, New York.

                 Faithfully yours,

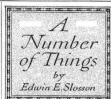

A Number of Things
by
Edwin E. Slosson

When a couple become engaged it is the custom—or anyhow it used to be—for them to look over the family album together. Seated side by side so that the leaves lie on both their laps, they proceed to get acquainted with each other's relatives and former selves. What delights them most at such times is to strike a baby picture—"So that's the way you looked when you were a kid! What a sweet thing you were *then.*" (Here should follow the "archly" punctuation mark, only the printers haven't provided one.)

Led by the same natural impulse, as soon as I heard that *Harper's Weekly* was engaged to be married to The Independent, I went at once to the periodical room of the School of Journalism and dug out Vol. 1, No. 1, of our *fiancée*. It was not the first time I had seen it, for more than one home I used to haunt as a boy boasted the possession of "Harper complete, with all the war numbers intact, sir," and naturally I reveled in them. Not a bad way of learning American history. "I've learned the little that I know by this."

Yes, the heading was familiar, the torch—enlightening, not incendiary—passing from hand to hand, and beneath the arts and sciences quite clearly indicated by a palette, a bust, a harp and an inkwell on the left, and a telescope, a book, a pair of compasses and a globe on the other.

The first lines announce the result of the Presidential election:

Buchanan	1,850,766
Fremont	1,336,815
Fillmore	870,146

I have an ancestral memory of that campaign, for my father used to tell me of how he had cast his first vote for "Free Soil, Free Speech, Free Labor, Free Men and Fremont." He was twenty-one the day before and on the day after he left for Kansas with a "Beecher Bible" on his shoulder to make that territory "Free Soil."

The figures are significant, for if there had not been a third party in the field—Fillmore ran on the "Know-Nothing," or as we should say the "Anti-Hyphenate" party — Fremont might have been elected and the Civil War averted.

Harper's interpreted the election as meaning "Compromise and Union," but was doubtful about the possibility of preserving the Union by Compromise or any other way.

It is already threatened by that intense love of gain, which is the peculiar vice of our age—

(It is the peculiar privilege of every age to boast of this vice.)

which has sapped the source of our public virtue, and has lowered the character of our public men; it is threatened by the local jealousies of communities, by the local ambitions of individuals, by the violent and reckless exponents of extreme opinions in all parts of the country. . . .

This sounds much like Roosevelt, or Cato, or Demosthenes, or Jeremiah, or whoever preceded them in Egypt and Assyria.

When we turn to an old periodical like this we expect to find something new. I skip over to the foreign events page and what do I find there? That the King of Prussia complains that his patience has been abused by his enemies. That the rebels in China are making progress in the south, but that the Peking government is soon going to send an army to crush them. That Russia is concentrating troops on the Persian and Bessarabian frontiers. That Mexico is in turmoil and the insurgent bands are gaining strength. That England and the United States have just concluded a treaty that disposes of the Nicaragua question. That Colombia [only it is called New Granada] is protesting against American interference in Panama. That Washington has decided that the shipment of arms to a belligerent is not a violation of neutrality. I rub my eyes and look back at the date. Am I reading the *first* number of Harper's Weekly or the last? But there it is, "January 3, 1859," not May 13, 1916. History repeats itself. What's the use?

I turn to the editorials. The leader is devoted to the denunciation of feminine extravagance. It appears that the women of those days spent more on their clothes than their menfolks thought they should. The author reaches the novel conclusion that it is because women dress to suit other women instead of following the chaster taste of men.

If women drest to please their male admirers, they might lessen their ambitious rivalry and diminish their bills at Stewart's and Diedea's, for it is the universal sentiment of mankind that "beauty unadorned is adorned the most," and that even homeliness gains nothing by being richly set.

There is nothing so charming to a cultivated man as the exhibition on a woman's dress of a refined taste, exercised in the simplest materials. A plain calico neatly made and cunningly trimmed, with nice proprieties of a pure white collar, a hand well gloved and a foot bien chaussée, is the drapery the most provocative of admiration the male observer is conscious of.

I infer from the wording of the last sentence that George William Curtis had not yet taken charge of Harper's. For, as the grammarians say: "One should never use a preposition to end a sentence with."

But it seems that the editor had reason for complaint if as he says the women of his day were in the habit of paying $1000 for a Cashmere shawl when a $20 French shawl would do as well. He figures out that a fashionable lady's toilet costs no less than $17,850.

Lace, furs and shawls are the most expensive items in the list. Furs have come back. So has lace. Shawls are said to be on their way and due to arrive soon. Is there no way of heading them off? I could write an editorial commending calico and pure white collars, but somehow it seems to do little.

But perhaps all prices were higher then. I turn to the market report. "Eggs, 28 cents a dozen." I am paying 50. "Fowls, 8½ cents a pound." My grocer charges four times that. "Butter, 20 cents"; now twice that. "Bear meat, 17¾ cents a pound." Bear meat is out of sight. It is twenty-five years since I have eaten a bear steak.

The Literary Editor complains that too many books are published nowadays. Funny how Literary Editors are always making a fuss about this. You never hear a doctor complaining that there are too many sick people or a lawyer that people are too litigious. "Thousands of people are now writing books in this country." They are at it still. Among the books reviewed are Robertson's "Charles V" with the addenda by Prescott, "The Thucydides of Modern History," a book of poems by Stoddard and a volume of essays by Mrs. Sigourney.

Martin F. Tupper, whom no modern poet can equal for popularity, contributes to this number "A Rhyme for the Atlantic Telegraph" which I forbear to quote. Let the Paradoxical Philosopher rest on his laurels.

A literary letter from Florence signed "Cicerone" is filled with personal gossip of Macaulay, Gladstone, Ruskin, Thackeray, Bulwer-Lytton, the Brownings and the Trollopes. Think of it! A Florentine tea party in 1857 must have seemed like living in an encyclopedia of literary biography. Ah, there were giants on the earth in those days.

The Brownings, it seems, exprest to our correspondent their gratification at the liberal check sent them for their advance sheets by Tichnor, Fields & Co. [I hope that the advertising department did not fail to send a clipping to T., F. & Co.] Mr. Browning was engaged in expanding and simplifying his "Sordello." [Where is this simplified version to be found?] As for Mrs. Browning, "an English clergyman of note says of her recent poem, 'Aurora Leigh,' it is quite unfit for lady readers." Whereupon our Cicerone comments, "To the nasty all things are nasty." Which strikes me as quite a nasty thing to say about an English clergyman of note. I have heard critics say that "Aurora Leigh" was quite unfit for any readers, but not for the same reason.

Mrs. Trollope, then in her seventy-ninth year, was just finishing her 120th volume. The reason why her output was so scanty was because she did not begin to write until she was forty-five and wouldn't then except she needed the money badly. She had cleared $100,000 on her books, but spent it all on her large and extravagant family, so says the all-wise Cicerone. But it is no use

Spreading Advertising News Nationally, in Record Time

THE news of the world is brought to readers of The Independent from one to five weeks earlier than by other periodicals.

The news one really needs to know is here condensed, verified, clarified and interpreted for the benefit of the alert reader who wants his information clear, compact and exact, and who wants it on the minute.

This news record and editorial presentment is illuminated by timely photographs of events and new things, by cartoons, views, maps and portraits.

It is supplemented by striking articles and vivid messages from the field, written for The Independent while the events are white hot, by those who speak with authority and exact knowledge, by those actively engaged in the events described, by those who are living close to great events, by those who themselves are making history.

The Independent's list of contributors from the day it was founded is an unmatched roll call of famous names in literature and public life.

From the first shot of the Great War, The Independent has m a r c h e d squarely abreast with its stupendous events, every number throbbing with live news, flashing out the swift changing drama of current history and ringing with messages of the hour.

At least a week in advance of other periodicals with its account, discussion and picture treatment of outstanding events of the European conflict, The Independent is recognized as having fair claim to the now familiar appellation, "the most satisfactory war journal in America."

Just as The Independent supplies the swiftest periodical news and picture service in America, so also does it provide the swiftest national Advertising Service.

Within two short days the last news forms close, presses start, mailing begins, and first copies begin to reach the readers.

Consider what this means to the fast growing group of merchants and manufacturers who perceive the value of the *news* element in advertising and the stimulus of news interest on the reader.

When Barney Oldfield makes his wonderful no-stop record with a Maxwell, when the New York Central wins the Harriman medal, when the Cadillac makes its world's record from Los Angeles to San Francisco, when Borden's Milk wins the Grand Prize, when any advertiser achieves new marks of distinction which the public ought to know about *quickly*, it pays to remember the speed of The Independent, which handles current events, business news, war news, advertising news, everything live people must know about to be well posted, from one to five weeks ahead of other periodicals.

Almost the speed of the daily newspaper, and yet with the fine printing, national distribution, influence and prestige which only such a weekly journal can give.

Note this contrast. Some months ago a leading weekly published the advertisement of a prominent motor car company which began thus:

"This advertisement is written five weeks before its appearance, so we cannot quote the latest sales figures."

As it happened, the latest sales figures showed that the model advertised was oversold more than a week before the company's advertisement saw the light of day!

What if the copy for this advertisement could have been written five *days* (instead of five weeks) before its appearance—as it *can* be for The Independent?

Is there any question as to its comparative effectiveness and value? Is there any question as to the value of *Speed*, as well as character and prestige, in national publicity?

News published five weeks late is *not* news. Remember that The Independent, a high-power vehicle to people's minds, carries the advertiser's news message to the cream of the public, nationally, in *record time*.

> The incorporation with The Independent this w e e k of Harper's Weekly, America's distinguished pictorial review for more than half a century, is a logical and important step in The Independent's broad editorial plan for perfecting and expanding its weekly news and picture service, already the swiftest among American periodicals.

The Independent

WITH WHICH IS INCORPORATED

HARPER'S WEEKLY

talking about Mrs. Trollope to Americans. She queered herself when she
criticized our *Domestic Manners.*

Humor is not lacking in the old *Harper.* There is a column headed "Things
Wise and Otherwise," corresponding
somewhat to our "Remarkable Remarks," I quote two, leaving it to the
reader to decide whether they are wise
or otherwise. The first is a conundrum:

'What did Adam and Eve do when they
were turned out of Paradise?
They raised Cain!

The second is a suppositicious advertisement:

A young gentleman on the point of getting married is desirous of meeting a man
of experience who will dissuade him from
such a step.

Harper's Weekly in later years was
distinguished by its numerous illustrations, but in this first number there are
only two small woodcuts, apparently
imported, with the attached jokes:

Lady of the House—We are sadly short
of Gentlemen, Captain Fitzdrawle. Pray,
let me introduce you for the next Galop."
Able-Bodied Swell—Aw, tha-a-a-anks,
no—aw—fact is—aw—I've given up Gymnastics—they—aw—diaswange one's Dwess
so!

Police Constable (to Boy playing Hoop)
—Now, then, off with that Hoop, or I'll
precious soon Help you!
Lady (who imagines the observation is
addressed to her)—What a Monster!

If fashions continue in the direction
they are now tending perhaps we can
use these old jokes again, as well as the
news items.

But I must not leave the impression
that there is nothing new in this old
paper. I see that "the celebrated African traveler," Dr. Livingston, has just
returned to England after seventeen
years in the Dark Continent and that
he had almost forgotten how to talk
English. The good doctor could hardly
have imagined that Germans, Belgians
and British, with the aid of their native
converts on opposing sides, would sixty
years later be fighting for the country
he explored.

A big meeting, it appears, was held
at the Broadway Tabernacle, not to
protest against preparedness, such as
we should now expect, but quite the
contrary, to express sympathy and give
aid to an illegal invasion of one of our
southern neighbors, Walker's filibustering expedition. Three American generals and the Nicaraguan minister addrest the meeting in behalf of Walker
and a collection of $1307 was raised to
support the movement. A few days
later a ship was sent to Walker loaded
with munitions and provisions and carrying 300 volunteers. Uncle Sam shut
his eyes.

Walker's rebellion is now almost forgotten, but an epoch-making event is
recorded in an inconspicuous item on
the same page, that an American frig-
ate has landed Consul General Harris
in Japan against the strenuous opposition of the Japanese Government. From
this dates the real "opening of Japan"
to American influences and today both
countries revere the memory of the man
who was left in the deserted Buddhist
temple of a Japanese fishing village.

The New Books

A DOUBLE LENS ON FEMINISM

Mr. and Mrs. John Martin have written a book on the Woman's Movement which is a curious compound of sane judgment and willful misapprehension of their subject. With many of the authors' contentions every fair-minded feminist must agree. That motherhood is the supreme duty and delight of a normal woman; that the home is the best place in which to rear the children; that the education of girls should heedfully concern itself with their preparation for home-making and trained motherhood; that it is better to pay a father enough to support his family in modest comfort than to half-pay him and his wife for sharing outside work —with these and a few other postulates, equally sensible, most people will agree. But that any of these desirable things will be jeopardized by granting political equality to women and men is manifestly absurd. So simple a partnership in the affairs of the Larger Home of the city or state cannot and does not, when tried, militate against the well-being of the household.

"Feminism" is cleverly contrasted by Mr. Martin with "Humanism," altho it is surely one-half of Humanism, not necessarily the better half, but worthy respect. We have no criticism to offer upon many of these incisive and suggestive pages. There is much hard sense in them. The reader may be trusted to sift the wheat from the chaff, and, so bright and witty and self-possest are Mr. and Mrs. Martin even at their absurdest moments, he will find it a most enjoyable task. Indeed, the irrational chapters of the book seem to have wandered in by accident and to have little to do with the main thread of the argument. The chapter which Mrs. Martin devotes to woman suffrage, for example, does not contend that voting would ruin women or that women would injure government, but rather that politics are so dull, trifling and sordid that any one, man or woman, who can escape it is to be congratulated on his or her good luck. "Somebody has got to vote because, unfortunately, we have to have a government, just as, in our climate, we have to burn fires and, therefore, have to order fuel. But there is nothing joyous, nothing exhilarating, nothing elevating about either act, nothing that confers an atom of weight or a spark of glory upon those who perform it." The reader will probably agree with us that this is a most morbid and unwholesome attitude to take in regard to the great tasks of statesmanship which confront the citizens of the world; that it is just this contemptuous indifference to public affairs which has led on the one hand to boss rule and on the other to labor riots, lynchings and other outbreaks of lawlessness. But, right or wrong, this lack of civic idealism has obviously nothing to do with Feminism.

Feminism, by Mr. and Mrs. John Martin. Dodd, Mead. $1.50.

GENERAL JACKSON

The Life of Andrew Jackson, by J. S. Bassett, first published in 1910, has already secured a permanent place. The new edition, tho practically the same as the first, is, in a few points, a revision, and it is likely to remain the most popular work on the subject for some time, being briefer and much more judicious than Parton's work and more ambitious than Sumner's. It is sympathetic, but also critical. Particularly clear and illuminating is the picture of conditions on the Western frontier during the early part of the last century and of the campaigns against the Indians of Florida and Alabama during and immediately following the Anglo-American War. The book contains the best brief account of Jackson's struggle for the Presidency and its significance in our history, as well as the fight for the recharter of the Second National Bank.

Life of Andrew Jackson, by J. S. Bassett. Macmillan. $2.50.

DR. GLADDEN ON THE WAR

The thousand-dollar prize offered by the Church Peace Union for the best essay on Peace and War was won by Dr. Washington Gladden. *The Forks of the Road* is a wise and noble essay which will arrest the thought of those who, from their comfortable 1913 belief that war is practically of the past, have swung to the more intelligent but more dangerous 1916 opinion that war is an inevitable fact in human life. The failure of the church in this matter has been its complete lack of understanding or of admission that universal brotherhood is the center of all Christ's teaching and that this is a practical, and the only practical law of life. The law of love, he writes,

is sentimental in just the same sense as the law of hydrostatics . . . , it is an induction from the facts of life; and its sanctions no more depend on any positive injunction than does the law of dietetics. If you eat poisonous or indigestible food, the retribution is not deferred until after death and the judgment, nor is there any scheme of substitution by which you may evade the penalty; it follows the transgression instantly and inevitably. Not less swift and certain are the consequences of every violation of the moral law. . . . Every violation of the law of love sets up irritations, resentments, suspicions, jealousies, which disturb all human relationships, which tend to break out in quarrels and collusions of will, and to make helpful relationships difficult or impossible. The enmities and fightings which keep human society in turmoil are therefore thus perfectly explicable; there is nothing occult or mysterious about them; if they should cease we should know exactly how to go to work to reproduce them; if we should decide that they are undesirable, we should know how to get rid of them.

It is the scandal of the centuries that this has not been learned, and now the price is being paid today in Europe. This is the past. Now for the future. It is inconceivable that after this unspeakable retribution the nations shall

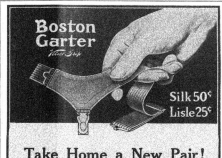

consent to go on as before. With the close of the war comes the great opportunity for an alliance to safeguard peace. Our influence will be great in bringing about "what seems our only hope of deliverance from a hell on earth, a League of Peace with an international police force." That we may not be hampered in this task soon before us Dr. Gladden argues earnestly against any present increase of our naval and military forces, since such a movement now cannot but cause propositions from us to be regarded with distrust by the other powers.

The Forks of the Road, by Washington Gladden. Macmillan. 50 cents.

OUR NEXT-DOOR NEIGHBORS

JAPAN AND THE WEST

A handbook on the recent causes for disagreement between this country and Japan is a fair description of *The Japanese Crisis,* by James A. B. Sherer. After a discussion of the Japanese character and desires and aims, the appendix gives the text of the last treaty, the California land law and other data needful to a clear understanding of this grave problem.

Stokes. $1.

SCHOOLS IN JAPAN

In the midst of the crowd of volumes that explain and do not explain Japan, it is pleasant to open so serene an essay as that on *Pre-Meiji Education in Japan,* by F. A. Lombard, of Doshisha University. Here teachers, feminists and lovers of Japan will all find matter of interest, and in a book, moreover, that is a delight to hand and eye.

Methodist Publishing House, Tokio, Japan.

JAPAN WITH CLOVEN HOOF

Carl Crow in his new book on the East, *Japan and America,* interprets Japanese action, almost from the beginning of our intercourse, as unfriendly to the United States. Three chapters deal with the recent moves in China and give the Japanese ultimatum as presented to China and as published abroad, two quite different papers. The book will set the western reader on guard before news from Japan, but would be more convincing if it allowed one least virtue to the Japanese.

McBride. $1.50.

AN ORIENTAL MONROE DOCTRINE

James Francis Abbott, sometime instructor in the Imperial Japanese Naval Academy, has written a careful, dispassionate study of *Japanese Expansion and American Policies.* While regarding seriously the causes of discord that may one day bring about a contest between the two nations, he looks on this as suicidal for Japan and as avoidable by regard on our part to the ambitions of Japan in the Orient. He does not discuss the theoretic right or morality of Japan's plans and methods, but their practicability and their effects.

Macmillan. $1.50.

FIVE SORTS OF STORIES

THE ASHES OF SUCCESS

The Least Resistance, by Kate L. McLaurin, an actress of experience, is said to be a true transcript of the life of the stage, ranging from vaudeville to legitimate drama—a life so hard, so exacting and exhausting, so uncertain, and so treacherous, in spite of its tinsel attraction, that we wonder any one could choose it. None but adventurous spirits could endure its precarious shifts. The heroine takes "the easiest way," which, of course, is the hardest way in the end.

Doran. $1.25.

GOOD DETECTIVE STORIES

If you like mystery stories you will enjoy Percy James Brebner's *The Master Detective, Being Some Further Investigations of Christopher Quarles.* An old professor of philosophy, in conjunction with a young detective, who is engaged to this professor's granddaughter, solves numerous complex riddles of crime and brings to justice a vast number of clever thieves, gangsters and murderers.

Dutton. $1.35.

A POET-SOLDIER

Beulah Marie Dix has written a book which, tho marred by certain affections of diction, is vastly superior to her usual pleasant, sentimental tales. *The Battle Months of George Deurella* is the story of a young lieutenant in the early part of the war. He has a poetic temperament and a military training. His reaction to battle, captivity, horror, kindness and love, is described with sympathy and insight.

Duffield. $1.25.

A SOCIETY NOVEL

Justus Miles Forman went down with the "Lusitania." This, his last story, *The Twin Sisters*, is a cosmopolitan romance built round the fact that kinship does not necessarily mean likeness. He sets off the character of his strong-minded and attractive heroine against that of her weak and shifty sister in their dealings with each other, society and the other sex. The simple story, with its somewhat obvious *dénouement* is told in an attractive way that is sure to appeal to many.

Harper. $1.35.

JACK LONDON AT HIS WORST

In *The Little Lady of the Big House* there is the eternal triangle composed of two supermen and a superwoman. They are so thoroly incredible that they are interesting, but they solve their problem in a manner not to be recommended for general use. Much space is occupied by a detailed account of a colossal stock farm, described with such relish that one wonders if this book be not an embodiment of Mr. London's pet daydream.

Macmillan. $1.50.

PULPIT AND PEW

THE MORMON SIDE

We doubt if *The Real Mormonism*, by Robert C. Webb, will make any converts to that cult, but it is well to read it in order to see what the Mormons have to say for their creed and customs. To form one's opinion of any institution exclusively from enemies and outsiders is not a safe thing, and this bulky volume presents the Mormon case in good temper, if not convincingly or very interestingly.

Sturgis & Walton. $2.

TALKING WITH THE UNSEEN

A little volume of unusual power and insight has been written by Dr. Charles L. Slattery, rector of Grace Church in New York, in answer to the question, *Why Men Pray.* The meaning of prayer, its value and results in life and character are very practically and helpfully explained. It is written especially for lay readers, but may properly be recommended to the clergy.

Macmillan. 75 cents.

A METHODIST ST. FRANCIS

A century has passed since the death of *Francis Asbury, the Prophet of the Road.* Dr. Tipple's book is rather a study in the great leader's personality than another life or an account of the beginnings of Methodism in America. The extracts from the journal recall the notes of that other unworldly wandering preacher, John Woolman.

Methodist Book Concern. $1.50.

"WASTED"

WASTED light and flaking paint! Do you realize how much *wasted money* it means? Three thousand of the biggest plants in the country realize it, and they now treat their ceilings and walls with a finish *that increases daylight 19% to 36% and is permanent.* By using this finish, they help their workmen do more and better work; they decrease accidents; they save as much as three-quarters of an hour electric lighting every day; and they all save scaling and recoating of cold water mixtures, and flaking of paint into the machinery. In addition, they have ceilings and walls that can be washed like a dinner-plate, and are thus kept wonderfully clean and sanitary. The finish they use is Rice's Gloss MillWhite, an oil paint, made by a special process, discovered and owned exclusively by the makers. Repeated tests have shown, without a single exception, that Rice's remains white longer than any other gloss paint. *By the Rice Method*, it can be applied over old cold-water paint. It does not flake or scale with the jar of machinery, it does not yellow like ordinary oil paints, and saves big money on painting, because it does not need renewing *for years.*

Write for our interesting book "More Light"—and sample board.

ON CONCRETE SURFACES. On inside concrete Rice's Granolith makes the best possible primer for a second coat of Rice's Gloss Mill White—giving a glossy tile-like finish at no more expense than lead and oil paint. Rice's Granolith.

WHAT A FEW USERS SAY

Sanitary conditions in our plant have improved wonderfully. We should judge we are getting 40% more light than before.—**Kellogg's Toasted Corn Flakes Co.**, Battle Creek, Mich.

We are indeed astonished to note the vast amount of daylight created by this paint—especially where we were formerly forced to use electric lights all day. Now find it entirely unnecessary. Agreeably surprised to observe how easy it is to keep clean.—**Kno-tair Hosiery Co.**, Philadelphia, Pa.

Out of six comparative tests, Rice's Mill White leads.—**Killingly Mfg. Co.**, Killingly, Conn.

RICE'S
GLOSS
MILL WHITE

Awarded Gold Medal at the San Francisco Exposition

(Reg. U. S. Pat. Off.)

U. S. Gutta Percha Paint Co.
30 Dudley St., Providence, R. I.

Barreled Sunlight

THE INDEPENDENT EDUCATION SERVICE

A directory of Schools and Colleges which are advertising in The Independent. By using the coupon below, parents will secure prompt and complete information to aid them in selecting the right education for son or daughter.

COLORADO

1 University of Colorado.............Boulder

CONNECTICUT

2 Hartford Theological Seminary...Hartford
3 The Ely School................Greenwich
4 Wheeler School........North Stonington
5 Hillside ....Norwalk
6 The Sanford School......Redding Ridge
7 Ridgefield School for Boys.......Ridgefield

ILLINOIS

8 American School of Home Economics, Chicago
9 The University of Chicago.......Chicago
10 Northwestern University........Evanston
11 Todd Seminary................Woodstock

INDIANA

12 Interlaken School..........Rolling Prairie

MARYLAND

13 National Park Seminary......Forest Glen

MASSACHUSETTS

14 Abbot Academy................Andover
15 Boston University.............Boston
16 Emerson College of Oratory........Boston
17 Miss McClintock's School for Girls, Boston
18 School of Expression...........Boston
19 Bradford Academy............Bradford
20 Sea Pines..................Brewster
21 New Church Theological School, Cambridge
22 Sargent School.............Cambridge
23 Powder Point School for Boys....Duxbury
24 Williston Seminary..........Easthampton
25 Dean Academy................Franklin
26 Monson Academy for Boys.........Monson
27 Walnut Hill School...........Natick
28 The Brookfield School....North Brookfield

29 Wheaton College for Women........Norton
30 Miss Hall's School.............Pittsfield
31 Worcester Academy.............Worcester

NEW YORK

32 Manor School for Girls........Larchmont
33 Craven School...............Mattituck
34 Columbia Grammar School.......New York
35 Scudder School for Girls.......New York
36 The Holbrook School...........Ossining
37 St. John's School............Ossining
38 Crane Normal Institute of Music, Potsdam
39 St. Faith's School......Saratoga Springs
40 Foute & Beattie............Spencerport
41 Syracuse University..........Syracuse
42 Russell Sage College of Practical Arts, Troy

OHIO

43 Oberlin School for Girls..........Oberlin

PENNSYLVANIA

44 Yeates School ....Lancaster
45 Mercersburg Academy ....Mercersburg
46 The Latshaw School of Psychoculture, Philadelphia
47 Pennsylvania College for Women, Pittsburgh
48 Kiskiminetas Springs School for Boys, Saltsburg
49 Lehigh University ....So. Bethlehem

RHODE ISLAND

50 Moses Brown School...........Providence

TENNESSEE

51 Martin College ....Pulaski

VIRGINIA

52 Randolph-Macon Woman's College, Lynchburg
53 Mary Baldwin Seminary........Staunton
54 Stuart Hall ....Staunton

TEAR COUPON HERE

THE INDEPENDENT EDUCATION SERVICE, 119 West 40th Street, New York.

Send me information about the following schools and colleges listed on this page.

Numbers...

Send Information to...

Address..

VIRGINIA

Randolph-Macon Woman's College, Lynchburg, Va.

One of the leading colleges for women in the United States, offering courses for A.B. and A.M.; also Music and Art. Four laboratories, library, astronomical observatory, modern residence halls. Scientific course in physical development. $20,000 gymnasium with swimming pool, large athletic field. Fifty acres in college grounds. Healthful climate free from extremes of temperature. Endowment, recently increased by $250,000. Expenses moderate. Officers and instructors, 60; students, 624, from 40 states and foreign countries. For catalogue and book of views illustrating student life, address   WILLIAM A. WEBB, President, Box A.

AGENCIES

PEBBLES

Never throw away an old sink strainer. It can be used as a frame for a chiffon hat.—*Cincinnati Post.*

Urban—What do you miss most since moving to the country?
Rural—Trains.—*Princeton Tiger.*

"My voice is for war."
"But are you willing to offer the rest of yourself?"—*Boston Transcript.*

Ford's selection in the Michigan presidential preference primary will doubtless be regarded as a victory for the Ford machine.—*Chicago Herald.*

"Money doesn't always bring happiness." "That may be true enough; but it's one of the things we all prefer to learn by personal experience."—*Boston Transcript.*

I doff my hat
To my friend Brewster,
Whose auto killed
My neighbor's rooster.
—*Cincinnati Enquirer.*

"Yes," said the old grad. "I guess that the thing that surprizes the college man most when he gets out in the world is to find out how much uneducated people know."—*The Cornell Widow.*

"That's the Goddess of Liberty," explained the New Yorker. "Fine attitude, eh?"
"Yes, and typically American," replied the Western visitor. "Hanging to a strap."—*Everybody's.*

"Where, did you find this wonderful follow-up system? It would get money out of anybody?"
"I simply compiled and adapted the letters my son sent me from college."—*Kansas City Journal.*

"Give us our place in the sun!" they cried;
"A place that matches our worth."
"Take all the sun," mankind replied,
"But please get off the earth."
—*Life.*

The *New Haven Evening Register,* like the rest of us, printed the German Note. But the linotyper had his own ideas about not following copy and he made the Note speak to "the seared principles of humanity."—*New York Tribune.*

A Jersey boy came home the other day to communicate unusual news.
"And so your teacher is dead?" asked the mother, horrified at the lad's announcement.
"Yes," said the boy. But, after a moment's reflection, he added. "After all, what's the good of that while the school is still there?"—*Harper's.*

LET US EXCUSE POOR VILLA

Perhaps he had been studying the European war and thought it was the only really proper way to treat a neutral nation—or perhaps he had been reading our newspaper editorials and decided that if we were in the condition we said we were he could easily lick us—or perhaps he thought the United States would warn all Americans to keep out of New Mexico, Arizona and Texas—or perhaps he thought we would write him a note.—*Life.*

"Now, children," said the teacher, "I have been talking to you about the duty of cultivating a kindly disposition, and I will tell you a little story of two dogs. Henry had a nice dog, gentle as a lamb. He would not bark at the passers-by or at strange dogs, and would never bite. William's dog, on the contrary, was always fighting other dogs or flying at the hens and cats in the neighborhood; and several times he seized a cow by the nostrils and threw her. He barked at strangers, and was always making trouble. Now, boys, which dog would you like to own—Henry's or William's?"
The answer came instantly, in one eager shout:
"William's!"—*Everybody's.*

MR. PURINTON'S EFFICIENCY QUESTION BOX

I knew I should get into trouble when I started to advise ladies. It can't be done. However, a principal object of the article on "The Efficient Housewife" has been realized—to challenge thought and evoke discussion. I beg to offer a few supplementary statements, on reading the letter from our kind friend, "The Inefficient Housewife," in The Independent of April 24.

Wholesale prices may be had by a small family on the new plan of coöperative buying, where two or more neighboring families unite in ordering a quantity. Thus a leg of lamb, or a crate of Florida fruit, may be economically bought, and eaten while fresh, with no "fruit and vegetable cellar" required.

Fish, cheaper than meat, is also better *because* it contains less protein. Experiments by Kellogg, Chittenden, and others go to prove that the American dietary is too rich in protein, therefore conducive to kidney troubles, rheumatism, arteriosclerosis, and other serious ailments. Here the old fashioned cook books are misleading, with their excess of red meat menus.

In our own family we put up grape-juice for eight cents a pint, therefore I assume it can be done. All figures I quote are based on demonstrated facts.

Reference in our friend's letter was made to pellagra—and cornmeal. The cause of pellagra, while unproven, is held to be *spoilt maize*—not good cornmeal; aggravated by a lack of essential mineral salts, which, of course, the best corn does not supply. Readers of The Independent may partake of corn bread without fear of pellagra.

The objection to a superfluity of labor-saving devices in a small kitchen is reasonable and perhaps timely. But for one kitchen over-equipped, there are nine kitchens under-equipped. The over-trained housewife is as rare as the over-trained athlete. Our work is for the great majority—we would not presume to write for the expert few.

Neighbor Ed. Howe says he has known "thousands of efficient housekeepers." Then he explains "the most wonderful thing in the world is the patience and efficiency of good women." His first statement is as untrustworthy as the second is true. He reasons loosely. Modern efficiency is a science, and to judge accurately the efficiency of any professional worker demands a thoro training in the science. I am not reflecting on the *character of womankind*—efficient fathers are much more scarce than efficient housewives.

All the criticisms I have read, such as those of Neighbor Howe and "The Inefficient Housewife," are based on faulty generalization in the mind of the critic.

SCHOOLS AND COLLEGES

MASSACHUSETTS

PENNSYLVANIA

TENNESSEE

NEW YORK

CONNECTICUT

OHIO

Copyright U.S.A. 1916, by The B.V.D. Company

May we not ask all our readers to judge the truth of our exact statements, no more and no less, and to be on their guard against premature conclusions and illogical inferences? We desire honest criticism. But honest criticism must be honest mentally as well as morally. And the first essential of honest criticism is to be sure you know the *meaning* of the man you criticize.

254. Mr. A. F., New York. "I am a lad of eighteen, weighing 180 pounds, with a deep bass voice. What would you advise me to speak in a high school prize contest—a sad or humorous piece? What pieces would you recommend?"

Avoid "sad" pieces as you would the plague. And hesitate long before attempting a "humorous" piece—your audience will be more likely to laugh at you than with you. A selection of a martial, heroic or energetic tone would probably suit you best. You are physically big—choose a theme mentally or morally big, and you have a good chance to win the prize. Get something new if possible. If you prefer a standard piece, you might select one of the stirring poems of Kipling, or some classic patriotic oration.

255. Mr. H. K. P., District of Columbia. "I recently purchased your set of Five Efficiency Booklets. These partially answer a number of questions in my mind, but I desire more extended knowledge. (a) What books would you recommend dealing with health, diet, baths, clothing, exercise, etc.? (b) Kindly suggest some reliable organization or institution engaged in efficiency promotion. (c) Can you name a few good magazines on self-improvement in general? (d) What are some of the tests of vocational guidance mentioned in your fifth article in The Independent? (e) Can you recommend some good books on mind-culture, dealing with memory, concentration, will-power, energy, economy, faith, optimism?"

We would recommend no book, magazine, person or institution. We merely put you in touch—then leave you to form your own judgments.

(a) Get book catalogs from the respective publishers of the following magazines: *Good Health*, Battle Creek, Michigan; *Health Culture*, Passaic, New Jersey; *Physical Culture*, Flatiron Building, New York; *Herald of Health*, 110 East Forty-first street, New York; *Nautilus*, Holyoke, Massachusetts.

(b) Efficiency Society, 41 Park Row; National Association of Corporation Schools, Irving Place and Fifteenth street; Emerson Institute, 30 Irving Place; all of New York City.

(c) Obtain copies of magazines listed under (a).

(d) This has been answered repeatedly, as in January 31, 1916, No. 197; April 3, 1916, No. 239 (b); and elsewhere.

(e) Apply to Efficiency Press Syndicate, Woolworth Building, New York City.

256. Mr. R. S. D., New York. "Am very much interested in your Personal Efficiency Test. Will you kindly explain how a man may find his supreme talent—and thus determine the answer to Question 8 of the test?"

Since the receipt of your letter, names of vocational experts and character analysts have been cited repeatedly in these columns; doubtless you have made investigations. Watch The Independent for a full discussion later in the year—a forthcoming article entitled "Choosing a Life Work."

257. Miss H. H., Montana. "I desire information concerning schools for stuttering and stammering children, also information as to any authoritative literature on the matter of defective speech."

This trouble is usually of psychic and nervous origin, but an examination by a good throat specialist might well be required. Often a home course in physical culture, aided by suggestive therapeutics, brings relief or cure. A device to prevent stammering is offered by Peate & Beattie, Box 85, Spencerport, New York.

A school for nervous children, such as the Florence Nightingale Sanatorium School, 238th Street and Riverdale Avenue,

New York City, might be effectual; or a school of elocution, such as the Emerson College of Oratory, Huntington Chambers, Boston, might afford helpful suggestions. The Boston Stammerers' Institute, Boston, would be worth investigating.

We do not know of any "authoritative" literature—all the books we have seen exploit some special theory, system or device.

258. Mr. D. W. M., Ohio. "We contemplate installing a machine which will manufacture ozone in the office room of our bank. The claim of the maker is that ozone will purify the air and so make our ventilation better. We have wondered if the ozone could be in any way harmful if used all the time. Would the benefit justify buying the machine?"

No. If Nature had meant us to breathe more ozone than the air contains, she would have put the ozone in the air—not waited 50,000,000 years for a patent machine to help her out. You don't need it. What you need is a modern automatic system of perfect *ventilation*, that gives you more pure air.

259. Mr. W. M. D., Rhode Island. "I am a high school student of seventeen. It takes me from 50 to 75 per cent longer to learn a lesson than it takes the average pupil—and then I seldom learn it well. My mind is quick and receptive; but I jump at conclusions, and seem unable to think slowly and clearly, or to concentrate. How may I learn concentration?"

Study my article entitled "Concentrate!" in April 17, 1916, Independent. Get Haddock's book, "Power of Will." Investigate systems of memory training—Loisette, Berol, Dickson, Atkinson. Learn to like your studies more, and put them to some practical use—a *theory* is seldom worth studying, and you may be more scientific than the young folks whose minds are only automatic memory-machines.

· 260. A Reader from Pennsylvania. "I am an employee of a large company, whose chief plans to publish a bulletin describing and advertising certain products of our business. This new publication may be turned over to me, and I want to be prepared to handle it. How can I obtain knowledge of the best ways to do this?"

Get George Frederick Wilson's book, "The House Organ," from Washington Park Publishing Company, Thirty-fourth Street, Milwaukee, Wisconsin; also the book, "Type Data," from A. R. Arkin & Co., Federal Street, Chicago. Study the advertisements for ideas, in *System Magazine*, Wabash and Madison, Chicago; *Advertising* and *Selling Magazine*, 95 Madison Avenue, New York. Answer advertisements of all concerns like yours in your trade journal, and analyze their literature. Buy a few standard books on salesmanship and the mail-order business. Take a mail course in advertising from International Correspondence Schools or some other good institutions.

261. Miss 'E. G., California. "I am a girl of fourteen, a freshman in high school. I have just won a debate from the Juniors, and now I am challenged by the whole school on the question: *Resolved, That the republics of North and South America should be united under a system similar to that of the United States.* I do not know where to get material on this question, and other topics of the day, and shall feel very grateful for your advice on debating in general."

You may obtain material for debates and other literary productions from one of these concerns: Bureau of Research, 318 East Fifth Street, New Albany, Indiana; Research Bureau, 500 Fifth Avenue, New York City; Wilson Package Library, Box R, White Plains, New York. Items of current news and opinion may be had from one of the clipping bureaus mentioned in previous Question Box.

Prepare first an outline of your speech by headings and numerals for logical sequence. Base all argument on facts—not feelings or supposings. Avoid flowery language. Quote authorities. Use local analogies and illustration. Bring in maps, charts or blackboard diagrams if possible. Open your speech with a few short, crisp statements that will challenge attention; close with a straight heart appeal, blended, of course, with good, sound sense.

Am sorry we have no space here to answer other question.

A CRATER OF DEATH

Mined areas played an important part in breaking the great German offensive against Verdun, and they cost many thousand lives. In one such battle the German dead lay on the battlefield so thickly that in the faint light of early morning the French took them for a new army advancing, and opened artillery fire on them. The shells made wide gaps in the enemy lines, but the Germans stood firm and not until daylight did the French realize that they were firing on a pile of dead bodies.

A French sapper, who has been fighting since 1914, tells of the last German attempt against the Cote du Poivre.

"We were in the first line, on the flank of the Cote du Poivre, and expected an attack in the evening. The intensity of the German cannonade showed that they intended something extraordinary, but our trenches, our barbed wire, mines, antitrailleuse and our spirit gave us confidence.

The debauch of shells became fantastic, and our aviators reported the Germans massing behind the village of Louvemont, where their numbers were so great it was impossible for them to conceal themselves, and they seemed to spread over the field like a huge drove of cattle on one of those fabulous ranches of western America.

Soon after midday the captain said to me: 'You are designated for the post that controls the mine field. It is delicate work. Good luck!'

I had to go to a little shelter hidden in the open field, where there was a button to which came wires from all the mines laid under the ground for a hundred yards yet further on, and there wait the charge of the Germans. My route was by a tunnel so small that in some places I wriggled thru on my belly. The shelter, when reached, was like a tomb of wood and earth and mud. A narrow slit in the front was the sole contact with the living world.

The sun settled to the horizon and the heavens flew a yellow flag, warning of death at hand, but the Germans gave no heed. I could see them swarming up the road from Beaumont to Vacherauville, like a wide gray band which polished the snow.

Shells fell unceasingly on their printed helmets and the smoke from the bursting shrapnel was like a low hanging cloud over their heads. Day changed to night, and the Germans advanced with the advancing darkness. They believed our trenches had failed under the storm of shell and that they could seize the Cote du Poivre.

Our trenches and our shelters were in ruins; it is true, but our soldiers held firm. We were all at our posts with rifles loaded and ready. The enemy were within 200 yards of my post and the German cannon stopped.

At the same time an immense roar came from behind me. It was the mighty chorus of rifles and mitrailleuse of my comrades. The disappear German advance of our first line, coming, threw themselves on the ground. My breath came quick.

Would they stop there? I had my hand on the electric button, waiting patiently for them to reach the mine field. Hoarse shouts came to me, and then the deep roll of the "Wacht am Rhine," and the German horde again sprang forward furiously to the assault, running, gesticulating, singing, but mostly falling in a bloody heap on the white snow.

And now they reached the mine field. My heart leaped. My hand trembled. I waited until they crowded by hundreds on the fatal strip of earth, and then—a slight pressure of my index finger.

In that majestic tempest of smoke and steel and fire, was it really human being that I saw? Yes, I assure you I have seen it. I saw a sneering face hurtling aloft. I saw men entire spewed up from that diabolical crater. The wave of the enemy was broken. Only dead bodies remained in the smoking hole, and, scattered around it, twisted corpses half buried in the snow.—*New York Tribune.*

The Market Place

SILVER GOES UP

Silver has reached the highest price
the commodity has commanded in over
twenty years. The price has gone over
77 cents an ounce.

The present advance is unusual in its
causes. Silver generally goes up because of increased demand from the
East; but neither China nor India has
increased its purchases to any appreciable extent.

An important factor in the rise is
the unprecedented demand for silver by
European mints. The English mint has
been a heavy buyer, and large quantities have been taken by France and
Russia. The silver coinage now being
put out in Europe is on an unprecedented scale. The exigencies of the war
have practically eliminated gold from
circulation abroad. Some coin was
needed to meet the requirements of the
people largely accustomed to a metallic
currency, and in addition to this a great
amount has been used in paying the
soldiers of the different nations. A
further potent cause of the recent
strength of the market is the fact that
the Egyptian Government has given the
silver rupee a legal tender status, with
the result that large amounts of coin
have been taken to Egypt from India.
This has necessitated considerable purchases of silver in London for account
of the Indian Government. The practical elimination of the large output of
silver that would come from Mexico if
normal conditions prevailed there constitutes another factor in the situation.

WAR BUSINESS AND PREPAREDNESS FOR PEACE

The Secretary of Commerce does not
believe that we need to be unduly worried over what will happen when war
is suddenly followed by peace. Mr. William F. Malburn, Assistant Secretary
of the Treasury, had written Mr. Redfield suggesting that the American people are in danger of overlooking preparedness for peace. To this Mr. Redfield replied declaring that while the
necessary readjustments after the war
will be important and perhaps serious,
the relative importance of war business
generally is overestimated. The Secretary said further:

So far as we can learn, it does not exceed
one-quarter of our exports, and possibly is
not quite that much. Even without them
our exports would be much larger than before the war. Our shipments to South
America, for example, have doubled or
more.

It does not seem to be quite proportional

A CRATER OF DEATH

Mined areas played an important part in breaking the great German offensive against Verdun, and they cost many thousand lives. In one such battle the German dead lay on the battlefield so thickly that in the faint light of early morning the French took them for a new army advancing, and opened artillery fire on them. The shells made wide gaps in the enemy lines, but the Germans stood firm and not until daylight did the French realize that they were firing on a pile of dead bodies.

A French sapper, who has been fighting since 1914, tells of the last German attempt against the Cote du Poivre:

We were in the first line, on the flank of the Cote de Poivre, and expected an attack in the evening. The intensity of the German cannonade showed that they intended something extraordinary, but our trenches, our barbed wire, mines, mitrailleuse and our spirit gave us confidence. The debacle of shells became fantastic, and our aviators reported the Germans massing behind the village of Louvemont, where their numbers were so great it was impossible for them to conceal themselves, and they seemed to spread over the field like a huge drove of cattle on one of those fabulous ranches of western America.

Soon after midday the captain said to me: "You are designated for the post that controls the mine field. It is delicate work. Good luck."

I had to go to a little shelter hidden in the open field, where there was a button to which some wires from all the mines led under the ground for a hundred yards yet farther on, and there wait the charge of the Germans. My route was by a tunnel so small that in some places I wriggled thru on my belly. The shelter, when reached, was like a tomb of wood and earth and mud. A narrow slit in the front was the sole contact with the living world.

The sun settled to the horizon and the heavens flew a yellow flag, warning of death at hand, but the Germans gave no heed. I could see them swarming on the road from Beaumont to Vacherauville, like a wide gray band which polluted the snow.

Shells fell unceasingly on their pointed helmets and the smoke from the bursting shrapnel was like a low hanging cloud over their heads. Day changed to night, and the Germans advanced with the advancing darkness. They believed our trenches had faded under the storm of shell and that they could seize the Cote du Poivre.

One trenches and our shelters were in ruins, it is true, but our soldiers held firm. We were all at our posts with rifles loaded and ready. The enemy were within 200 yards of my post and the German cannon stopped.

At the same time an immense roar came from behind me. It was the mighty chorus of rifles and mitrailleuse of my comrades. The surprized Germans of the first line, cursing, threw themselves on the ground. My breath came quick.

Would they stop there? I had my hand on the electric button, waiting patiently for them to reach the mine field. Hoarse shouts came to me, and then the deep roll of the "Watch on the Rhine," and the German horde again sprang forward furiously to the assault, running, gesticulating, singing, but mostly falling in a bloody heap on the white snow.

And now they reached the mine field. My heart leaped. My hand trembled. I waited until they crowded up hundreds on the fatal strip of earth, and then—a slight pressure of my index finger.

In that majestic tempest of smoke and steel and fire, was it really human being that I saw? Yes, I assure you I have seen it, I saw a sneering face hurtling aloft. I saw men entire spewed up from that diabolical crater. The wave of the enemy was broken. Only dead bodies remained on the smoking hole and, scattered around it, twisted corpses half buried in the snow.—*New York Tribune.*

The Market Place

SILVER GOES UP

Silver has reached the highest price the commodity has commanded in over twenty years. The price has gone over 77 cents an ounce.

The present advance is unusual in its causes. Silver generally goes up because of increased demand from the East; but neither China nor India has increased its purchases to any appreciable extent.

An important factor in the rise is the unprecedented demand for silver by European mints. The English mint has been a heavy buyer, and large quantities have been taken by France and Russia. The silver coinage now being put out in Europe is on an unprecedented scale. The exigencies of the war have practically eliminated gold from circulation abroad. Some coin was needed to meet the requirements of the people largely accustomed to a metallic currency, and in addition to this a great amount has been used in paying the soldiers of the different nations. A further potent cause of the recent strength of the market is the fact that the Egyptian Government has given the silver rupee a legal tender status, with the result that large amounts of coin have been taken to Egypt from India. This has necessitated considerable purchases of silver in London for account of the Indian Government. The practical elimination of the large output of silver that would come from Mexico if normal conditions prevailed there constitutes another factor in the situation.

WAR BUSINESS AND PREPAREDNESS FOR PEACE

The Secretary of Commerce does not believe that we need to be unduly worried over what will happen when war is suddenly followed by peace. Mr. William F. Malburn, Assistant Secretary of the Treasury, had written Mr. Redfield suggesting that the American people are in danger of overlooking preparedness for peace. To this Mr. Redfield replied declaring that while the necessary readjustments after the war will be important and perhaps serious, the relative importance of war business generally is overestimated. The Secretary said further:

So far as we can learn, it does not exceed one-quarter of our exports, and possibly is not quite that much. Even without them our exports would be much larger than before the war. Our shipments to South America, for example, have doubled or more.

It does not seem to be quite proportional

A CRATER OF DEATH

Mined areas played an important part in breaking the great German offensive against Verdun, and they cost many thousand lives. In one such battle the German dead lay on the battlefield so thickly that in the faint light of early morning the French took them for a new army advancing, and opened artillery fire on them. The shells made wide gaps in the enemy lines, but the Germans stood firm and not until daylight did the French realize that they were firing on a pile of dead bodies.

A French sapper, who has been fighting since 1914, tells of the last German attempt against the Cote du Poivre:

We were in the first line, on the flank of the Cote du Poivre, and expected an attack in the evening. The intensity of the German cannonade showed that they intended something extraordinary, but our trenches, our barbed wire mines, rat-traffiléries and our spirit gave us confidence. The debacle of shells became fantastic, and our aviators reported the Germans massing behind the village of Louvemont, where their numbers were so great it was impossible for them to conceal themselves, and they seemed to spread over the field like a huge drove of cattle on one of those fabulous ranches of western America.

Soon after midday the captain said to me: "You are designated for the post that controls the mine field. It is delicate work. Good luck!"

I had to go to a little shelter hidden in the open field, where there was a button to which came wires from all the mines laid under the ground for a hundred yards yet further on, and there was the charge of the Germans. My route was by a tunnel so small that in some places I wriggled thru on my belly. The shelter, when reached, was like a tomb of wood and earth and mud. A narrow slit in the front was the sole contact with the living world.

The sun settled to the horizon and the heavens flew a yellow flag, warning of death at hand, but the Germans gave no heed. I could see them swarming on the road from Beaumont to Vacherauville, like a wide gray band which polluted the snow.

Shells fell increasingly on their pointed helmets and the smoke from the bursting shrapnel was like a low hanging cloud over their heads. Day changed to night, and the Germans advanced with the advancing darkness. They believed our trenches had failed under the storm of shell and that they could seize the Cote du Poivre.

Our trenches and our shelters were in ruins, it is true, but our soldiers held firm. We were all at our posts with rifles loaded and ready. The enemy were within 300 yards of my post and the German cannon stopped.

At the same time an immense roar came from behind me. It was the mighty chorus of rifles and mitrailleuse of my comrades. The surprized Germans of the first line, cursing, threw themselves on the ground. My breath came quick.

Would they stop there? I had my hand on the electric button, waiting patiently for them to reach the mine field. Hoarse shouts came to me, and then the deep roll of the "Watch on the Rhine," and the German horde again swung forward furiously to the assault, running, gesticulating, singing, but mostly falling in a bloody heap on the white snow.

And now they reached the mine field. My heart leaped. My hand trembled. I waited until they crowded by hundreds on the fatal strip of earth, and then—a slight pressure of my index finger.

In that majestic tempest of smoke and steel and fire, was it really human being that I saw? Yes, I assure you I have seen it. I saw a quivering face hurtling aloft. I saw an entire spewed up from that diabolical crater. The wave of the enemy was broken. Only dead bodies remained in the smoking hole; and, scattered around it, twisted corpses half buried in the snow.—*New York Tribune.*

The Market Place

SILVER GOES UP

Silver has reached the highest price the commodity has commanded in over twenty years. The price has gone over 77 cents an ounce.

The present advance is unusual in its causes. Silver generally goes up because of increased demand from the East; but neither China nor India has increased its purchases to any appreciable extent.

An important factor in the rise is the unprecedented demand for silver by European mints. The English mint has been a heavy buyer, and large quantities have been taken by France and Russia. The silver coinage now being put out in Europe is on an unprecedented scale. The exigencies of the war have practically eliminated gold from circulation abroad. Some coin was needed to meet the requirements of the people largely accustomed to a metallic currency, and in addition to this a great amount has been used in paying the soldiers of the different nations. A further potent cause of the recent strength of the market is the fact that the Egyptian Government has given the silver rupee a legal tender status, with the result that large amounts of coin have been taken to Egypt from India. This has necessitated considerable purchases of silver in London for account of the Indian Government. The practical elimination of the large output of silver that would come from Mexico if normal conditions prevailed there constitutes another factor in the situation.

WAR BUSINESS AND PREPAREDNESS FOR PEACE

The Secretary of Commerce does not believe that we need to be unduly worried over what will happen when war is suddenly followed by peace. Mr. William F. Malburn, Assistant Secretary of the Treasury, had written Mr. Redfield suggesting that the American people are in danger of overlooking preparedness for peace. To this Mr. Redfield replied declaring that while the necessary readjustments after the war will be important and perhaps serious, the relative importance of war business generally is overestimated. The Secretary said further:

So far as we can learn, it does not exceed one-quarter of our exports, and possibly is not quite that much. Even without them our exports would be much larger than before the war. Our shipments to South America, for example, have doubled or more.

It does not seem to be quite proportional

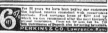

to the facts to suggest that we may "find ourselves at the close of the war with a vast organization suitable to the production of goods needed in war times, which organization will be useless." In the first place, the extent of the new organization of this kind is not great compared to all our industries. There are a few cases of large additions of the kind, but in their comparative bulk they are not great. Neither is it, I venture to think, quite the fact that they would be useless in time of peace. Plants of this kind are not limited to one particular product, or even one group of products, but are available for many forms of manufacture, and the new organization and equipment will be a great asset in maintaining our export trade when the war is over.

I doubt if there is any such extent of war business as to involve such consequences as having many plants lying idle and railroads suffering from lack of goods to carry. Of the total industrial and commercial business of the country, I think it is probably safe to say that the so-called war business does not exceed five per cent.

THE MOUNTING BALANCE OF TRADE

March was the greatest month for foreign trade that the United States has ever seen. Not only the value of our exports, but the value of our imports as well, was the largest in the country's history.

The imports for March amounted to $214,000,000; in the same month last year they were $158,040,216. The exports for March were $410,000,000; in the same month last year they were $299,009,563.

For the nine months of the fiscal year ending April 1, the imports amounted to $1,505,000,000; for the same period of the last fiscal year they were $1,213,671,843. This is an increase of twenty-four per cent. The exports for the nine months, however, jumped fifty per cent over last year's figures. Last year they were $1,933,475,580; this year they are $2,996,000,000. Because of the greater pace at which the exports have climbed, the favorable balance of trade—the excess of exports over imports—has gone up like a rocket. In the first nine months of the last fiscal year it was $719,803,737; in the corresponding period this year it is $1,491,000,000. This shows the phenomenal increase of 107 per cent. The favorable balance is not only twice that of last year, but over three times that of the next preceding year.

Are there to be any limits to our prosperity?

BRITAIN PAYS FOR COTTON

During March and April of last year the British Government seized the cargoes of about thirty steamers carrying cotton from the United States to neutral European ports. By the terms of the so-called Cotton Arrangement, entered into between representatives of the British Government in this country and leading cotton exporters, the seized cotton was to be paid for at the contract price which the shipper would have received if the cotton had been allowed to proceed to destination in ordinary course.

Over 200,000 bales were seized, valued at something like $12,000,000. Practically all of this cotton has now been paid for by the British Government, at the full price with interest at 5 per cent from the date of seizure added.

There was no difficulty in arranging the rate of payment in the case of cotton definitely sold on contract. In that case the contract price plus the 5 per cent made up the amount paid. But much of the seized cotton had been sent forward by American shippers on consignment. The question in these cases was as to the price basis on which the payment should be computed.

The British authorities acted in the matter in a thoroly fair and reasonable spirit and found no serious difficulty in meeting the shippers half way. It was finally agreed to pay on the consigned cotton the market price at the port of shipment on the date of seizure, such market price to be ascertained by reference to all the usual sources, particularly official quotations at American exchanges; and also to pay all charges incurred by the shippers, including freight, marine and war risk insurance premiums and interest at the rate of 5 per cent per annum from the date of maturity of the draft drawn against the cotton or from date of shipment where no drafts were drawn, plus also a profit of 50 cents per bale.

Practically all of the American shippers of consigned cotton have accepted payment on this basis and the matter has been satisfactorily adjusted.

AFTER THE WAR

In a recent address before the American Cotton Manufacturers' Association, Beverly D. Harris, vice-president of the National City Bank, of New York, made some interesting comments on the question, What will happen to us in our foreign trade relations after the war:

By reason of its wealth and strong position, the United States has been projected into the position of the world's banker for the time being. Altho not entirely out of debt to Europe, the indebtedness is fast being wiped out and is negligible compared to the present resources of the country. When the war is over and normal conditions return, there will not be the burden of interest on American securities to be paid to Europe in exports, as heretofore. This will have a tendency to curtail European imports from this country, for the crippled nations of Europe cannot afford to import more goods from us than are absolutely necessary for their rehabilitation and actual needs. The necessity will be forced on them to build up and protect their gold supplies, and as those nations are creditor nations, and other countries—principally the Latin-American republics—are heavily indebted to Europe, very strong considerations will obtain for making their purchases of raw materials and supplies, as far as possible from South America and other debtor countries—owing them—the more so as those countries produce and export similar raw materials to ourselves. The needs of Europe normally are essentially for raw materials, and her exports essentially manufactured products. South America's exports of raw materials are to a considerable extent of the same character as ours. It is to be expected that as normal conditions are restored, Europe will put forth every ounce of available energy to create a balance of trade against this country, to drain our gold supply, to restore her manufacturing industries, reestablish her foreign trade, and give us the hardest possible competition in all respects.

Insurance
Conducted by
W. E. UNDERWOOD

TEACHERS' CASUALTY UNDERWRITERS

Lately there have come to this department from various sections of the Middle West requests for information respecting the financial condition and management of the Teachers' Casualty Underwriters of Lincoln, Nebraska, an organization which, on its literature, proclaims itself "The National Organization of Teachers." Search thru all the available handbooks of insurance failed to reveal the existence of an insurance company or association of this name located anywhere in the United States. Finally aid was sought of the Insurance Commissioner of Nebraska, whose information is that the Teachers' Casualty Underwriters is operated by the Pioneer Insurance Company of Lincoln.

From this I presume that the Teachers' Casualty Underwriters may be regarded as an agency for the procurement and management of casualty risks for the Pioneer Insurance Company. Such advertising literature as I have seen prompts the conclusion that the Teachers' Casualty Underwriters is offering two restricted accident and health policies: one at a premium of $15, the other at $19.80 a year. The premiums seem adequate to the benefits granted, by which I mean that the company is not offering something for nothing. To put it in another way, it seems to be safe undertaking.

The figures of the Pioneer Insurance Company for the year ending December 31, 1915, are not available; but I find that at the end of the previous year the assets were $33,104; total liabilities, including $10,000 capital stock, $32,890; net surplus, $214. During 1915 the total premium receipts were $99,642 and the total losses $30,358.

Such reports as are accessible indicate that the Pioneer Insurance Company is owned and operated by reputable and capable men. One report is to the effect that the company operates only in Nebraska. My correspondents are in other states, from which I conclude that the company is endeavoring to transact business outside Nebraska, probably without complying with the insurance regulations and laws of such outside states. If so, that is a point against it. Nor is it easy to understand why it should canvass for business under any title other than its own. We are not to conclude, either, that there is anything in the claim that it is "The National Organization of Teachers."

This information is furnished for the benefit of a number of persons who

have made special inquiry, as well as others who may be solicited to make application for insurance.

MUTUALIZING THE HOME LIFE

Policyholders of the Home Life Insurance Company of New York have before them for consideration a proposition made by the directors to retire the capital stock and transform the organization into a mutual institution.

The Home was incorporated and began business in 1860 with a paid-up capital of $125,000, dividends to stockholders being authorized at the rate of six per cent semi-annually. As compared with a few other companies of its age and possibilities, its progress may be described as moderate, due undoubtedly to the conservatism of its management. It has never striven for volume of insurance written or premium income. But its affairs have been very carefully administered and the treatment accorded policyholders has been exemplary.

On January 1 last the company's total admitted assets were $32,029,440; its surplus, $2,263,455; and the whole amount of insurance in force aggregated $125,660,173.

It now proposes to sell its stock interests to the policyholders at $450 per $100 share, plus accrued dividends at date of closing the transaction, the funds for the purchase to be appropriated out of the surplus. A meeting of the stockholders has been held and the proposal approved by them. The policyholders are to vote on the question May 25.

According to my way of thinking, they should regard it as an opportunity to improve their interests and the interests of all other persons who in the long future are to become policyholders in that company. The price to be paid for the stock is a substantial one, but not high in view of the manifold future advantages to be derived by the change.

But, in my judgment, that is not the feature which causes me to regard the price as a reasonable one. The value of the purchase to the policyholder lies in the passing of the control of a $30,-000,000 company from the possession of the owners of $125,000 capital to the owners of the $30,000,000 insured. The control is everything. The policyholders will make a mistake if they do not approve the proposition and forever insure themselves against any attempt by future holders of the stock to exploit the assets in their own interests.

A. M. S., Meadville, Pa.—The Reliance Life is thoroly sound financially and is well managed. It commenced writing annual dividend policies in 1913 and has not had time to make a dividend record. However, I do not think it will soon succeed in excelling or equalling the Connecticut Mutual in that respect, one of the best dividend payers in the country. I regard a premium of $2 a year for $2000 accident insurance with $10 a week indemnity as very low; $11 annual premium for $10 a week unlimited sickness benefits is reasonable. Nearly all the life companies now include the disability clause in their policies. I can not say, but I think the Metropolitan, Equitable of New York, Postal, Union, Central and Germania provide for periodical examinations of policyholders. There may be a few others which do.

NATIONAL INSTITUTE OF EFFICIENCY

The second meeting of the Board of Governors of the National Institute of Efficiency was held on Friday, May 12, at the Lawyers' Club, 115 Broadway, New York, when the publication of the first four issues of the series of Monographs of Efficiency was authorized. Number 1 embraces Edward Earle Purinton's "The Triumph of the Man Who Acts" and "Efficiency and Life," with the widely-known chart which Mr. Purinton devised for calculating individual efficiency, and a brief introduction by Mr. Melvil Dewey, president of the Efficiency Society. Not less than four of the series are to be issued to Institute members each year, three additional forthcoming monographs being announced, as follows: "Personal Efficiency and National Defense," by Major-General Leonard Wood, one of the governors of the Institute; "The Efficiency Factor in the Expansion of American Industry," by Dr. Edwin E. Slosson, and "Personal Efficiency as Applied to Home Economy," by Mrs. Flora McDonald Thompson, president of the Housekeepers' Alliance.

The Hon. Theodore Roosevelt has accepted election as an honorary patron of the Institute, which, during the first month of its existence, has added members from the states of Pennsylvania, New York, New Jersey, Rhode Island, Connecticut, Massachusetts, Utah, South Carolina, Washington, Florida, Missouri, Alabama and the District of Columbia.

Hon. J. C. Pritchard, of Asheville, North Carolina, who has accepted appointment as State Counselor for North Carolina, has made a number of nominations for membership in the Institute. Readers of The Independent—the official organ of the Institute—desirous of recommending candidates for membership are offered an opportunity of doing so on page 304 in this issue.

IN TOUCH WITH HEADQUARTERS

There was something almost dramatic in the demonstration of preparedness which the recent mobilization of the telephone and telegraph services afforded. Most people are vaguely aware that, in the event of war, national claims would be made upon all facilities of national significance, from automobiles and highways to wireless stations and railroads. Few were prepared, however, for the suddenness with which Washington was linked, at a given signal, with every point of importance affecting the whole country: with the Great Lakes and the Gulf of Mexico, with the Naval Stations on either coast, and so on, in thousand mile spans, until Uncle Sam's sentinels at their farthest outposts were in touch with headquarters. A secret process or method is said to be at the command of the navy in this connection. Be that as it may, the results are themselves sufficient proof of the efficiency that exists in one of the nation's most vital services.

EFFICIENCY WEEK AT CHAUTAUQUA

The Board of Governors of the National Institute of Efficiency has accepted an invitation of Chautauqua Institution to hold an Efficiency Week at Chautauqua, beginning Monday, June 26, and it has also been decided to have the first annual summer conference and semi-annual dinner of the National Institute during the Efficiency Week. Addresses on various aspects of Efficiency, by men of distinction who are identified with the National Institute of Efficiency, have already been provisionally arranged, among these speakers being General Leonard Wood, Mr. Henry A. Wise Wood, Mr. Gutzon Borglum, Mr. Melvil Dewey, Mr. Edward Earle Purinton, Dr. Henry S. Drinker, and Rev. Percy S. Grant, while steps are being taken to secure equally representative men and women as speakers upon other phases of the subject in which they have specialized. A program of remarkable interest is assured, and the Efficiency Week promises to be a unique contribution to the development of the movement.

THE SMOKE NUISANCE

Indianapolis would like to be a cleaner city, and Smoke Inspector Silva P. Leach is organizing a conference under the auspices of the Chamber of Commerce in which many civic bodies and women's clubs will assist in finding a remedy for the too heavy soot fall. The proposals which the conference will discuss are eminently practical, and include a scheme for financial aid to operators of power plants, thru the municipality, in any attempts they make to reduce their smoke output by improved methods or better fuel. The idea is also to arrange lectures and supply instructive booklets to engineers, firemen and others concerned with the operation of power plants.

MOSQUITOES AND THE MOVIES

Official Spring, beside opening the golf season, saw the recommencement of the Interstate Anti-Mosquito Committee's campaign against the pest whose existence is proof of widespread carelessness and inefficiency. In part, the mosquito comes from neglected marshy areas and salt meadows, and adequate draining—a matter to be undertaken by the community thru legislation—is the accepted solution of this side of the problem. The cleanliness and fore-

thought that will prevent the breeding of the house variety is a personal factor, however, and in connection with the Interstate Committee two of the best known motion picture companies are preparing a film that will offer to the general public, in striking form, the facts as to the domestic mosquito's origin and instructions as to how to swat him before he has a chance, so to speak, to take wing. This is but one medium thru which the committee, which was organized by Health Commissioner Emerson, of New York, and represents also New Jersey, Long Island and Connecticut, will popularize anti-mosquito hygiene. Live mosquito larvæ are being supplied to school teachers for demonstration purposes, for experience has shown that children are enthusiastic workers in the No Mosquitoes Campaign, once they are put in possession of the facts.

A STEP TO PREPAREDNESS

An invention of extraordinary potentialities is shortly to be tried out at Fort Hancock. Described as an entirely new type of gun, it has already answered stringent tests under the supervision of Government officials at the Sandy Hook proving grounds, and the discoverer—reported to be an American citizen, but as yet not publicly named—is confident that his gun will do everything expected of it. Among the remarkable features of the gun are that no explosive is used; that it has no barrel; that it can be constructed in any machine-shop at comparatively trifling cost, and that its accuracy is demonstrably greater than that of present types of artillery. A model so small that it could be contained in a three-foot cubic box threw missles in recent tests with record-breaking accuracy at a range of seven miles. The best non-technical explanation of the principle of the new weapon is that it "harnesses centrifugal force"; motor power takes the place of the usual propulsive agent, and the missile obtains its maximum velocity before leaving the machine. The invention is being sponsored by a woman—Mrs. Kathryn M. Stanton, of Whitestone, Long Island—who personally superintended every detail connected with the setting up of the models.

ROOM FOR THE BIG IDEA

Efficiency experts are troubled, says *Collier's Weekly*, in the issue of April 22, because in all the Bible they find no mention of efficiency nor scientific management. They object to the description of Creation as given in the first chapter of Genesis, maintaining that if Frederick Winslow Taylor and St. Elmo Lewis and Edward Earle Purinton had been consulted, the job that took six days could have been done in three. But probably these efficiency fellows would have objected to the job in the first place on the ground that the overhead would prove prohibitive.

The Independent

Founded 1848

HARPER'S WEEKLY
Founded 1857
Incorporated with The Independent May 22, 1916

THE CHAUTAUQUAN
Incorporated with The Independent June 1, 1914

The Independent is owned and published by the Independent Corporation, at 119 West Fortieth Street, New York. William B. Howland, president; Frederic E. Dickinson, treasurer; William Hayes Ward, honorary-editor; Hamilton Holt, editor; Harold J. Howland, associate editor; Edwin E. Slosson, literary editor; Karl V. S. Howland, publisher. The price of The Independent is Ten Cents a copy; Four Dollars per year. Postage to foreign countries in the Postal Union, $1.75 extra; to Canada, $1 extra. Writers who wish their articles returned should send stamped and address envelopes. No responsibility is assumed for the loss or non-return of manuscripts. Entered at the New York Post Office as Second Class matter. Copyright, 1916, by The Independent. Address all communications to The Independent, 119 West Fortieth Street, New York

CONTENTS FOR MAY 29, 1916
Volume 86 Number 3521

HELP THE WAR SUFFERERS

America, getting rich in spite of the war and in some cases because of the war, has not done as much proportionally for the relief of the innocent victims of the war as have the belligerent nations themselves. In every country there are thousands of destitute women and children and helpless men who need your help. Do not wait for an accidental appeal. Decide where the need is greatest and send your money without delay to the American committee representing that country. The Relief Committees recommended by the Federal Council of Churches are given below with the names of the treasurers. The address is New York City in all cases except the Red Cross.

WAR RELIEF COMMITTEES

Commission for Relief in Belgium.—Alexander J. Hemphill, 120 Broadway.

American Committee for Armenian and Syrian Relief.—Charles R. Crane, 70 Fifth avenue.

Serbian Relief Committee.—Murray H. Coggeshall, 70 Fifth avenue.

War Relief Clearing House for France and Her Allies.—Thomas W. Lamont, 40 Wall street.

East Prussian Relief Fund.—Hubert Cillis, 17 Battery place.

Relief Committee for War Sufferers (German).—Charles Froeb, 531 Broadway.

Polish Victims' Relief Fund.—Frank A. Vanderlip, Aeolian Building.

American National Red Cross.—John Skelton Williams, 1624 H street, Washington, D. C.

British-American War Relief Fund.—Henry J. Whitehouse, 681 Fifth avenue.

American Jewish Relief Committee for Sufferers from the War.—Felix M. Warburg, 174 Second avenue.

American Relief Committee in Berlin for Widows and Orphans.—John D. Crimmins, 30 East Forty-second street.

Union Nationale des Eglises Reformées Evangeliques de France, Emergency Relief Fund.—Alfred R. Kimball, 105 East Twenty-second street.

American Huguenot Committee.—Edmond E. Robert, 105 East Twenty-second street.

Fund for Starving Children.—Frederick Lynch, 70 Fifth avenue.

A PREPAREDNESS PLAN

From Arthur Sherburne Hardy, the novelist, comes this succinct statement of a plan for military training to which we are glad to give publicity. Mr. Hardy was graduated from West Point in '69 and as American Minister to Switzerland had special opportunities to study the Swiss military system. He has also been accredited to the governments of Spain, Persia, Greece, Rumania and Serbia.

To the Editor of The Independent:

In the May number of the *Review of Reviews* Admiral Caspar F. Goodrich has an article, entitled "What Can We Do for Our Boys?" It is really a plan for national preparedness. Admirable as are many of the projects and efforts in this direction, they are spasmodic, local and temporary in character. Admiral Goodrich's plan is radical, general and goes to the root of the matter.

Briefly, he would call to the colors every American boy reaching the age of eighteen for one year's military training.

At the age of eighteen because, generally speaking, he has at that time finished his high school course, has not entered college, nor begun a professional or business career and therefore can at that age be spared with the least personal loss and with the least disturbance to the economic life of the country; for one year, because this is the minimum time adequate for an effective military training, and because at that age he is passing out of the stage when habits and ideals are formed.

The advantages of this system gained by the boy would be these:

He would learn how to take care of himself and his kit.

He would be taught respect for law and authority, obedience to his superiors, and, if an elementary course in American history were added, a knowledge of the great men and events of his country.

In short, it would be for him a school of patriotism as well as of military training and discipline—a school of character.

The gain to the country would be approximately a body of 600,000 men passing back every year into civil life with one year of military training, improved manhood and conceptions of duty, liable for service in an emergency, and at a minimum expense to the Treasury. The instruction to be furnished by the regular army and the navy in camps and on naval vessels selected and administered by the Army and Navy Departments.

As purely defensive and educational in its character, no patriotic pacifist could take alarm at this plan. The Swiss system, admirable for a small republic, is not practical for one of 100 millions. Preparedness in camps, school drills and other efforts in the direction of military training are inadequate. Preparedness in the German sense is neither possible nor desirable in a democracy. Has any better plan than the above been proposed?

Admiral Goodrich asks whether the average American boy is well set up, has he respect for law, authority, his elders? No one will give an enthusiastic affirmative answer. What would be the effect of infusing into the national life every year 600,000 who had acquired these indispensable elements of good citizenship, acquired under the leveling influences of such a national school?

To the objection that there would be a year's loss in vocational preparation, the answer is: there is no service without some sacrifice. Could a year be better spent, on the whole, for the individual and collective good?

Because of some verbal suggestions, Admiral Goodrich asked me to sign with him his article. Not every one reads the *Review of Reviews*. I bespeak for his plan the widest possible publicity and discussion.   ARTHUR S. HARDY

THE PRESIDENTIAL-SPHINX

The Independent

WITH WHICH IS INCORPORATED

HARPER'S WEEKLY

CONTEMPTIBLE COURTESY

"SENATORIAL courtesy" sounds like a fine old phrase. It suggests the picture of a dignified band of courtly elder statesmen debating in a fine spirit of mutual consideration the weighty problems of a nation's governance. It is an inspiring picture—but it has nothing to do with the facts.

What is the reality?

Months ago President Wilson sent to the Senate for confirmation the appointment of George Rublee, of New Hampshire, as a member of the newly created Federal Trade Commission.

It is conceivable that there may be in the United States a man better fitted for this post than Mr. Rublee —but we do not know who he is. He had made an elaborate and painstaking study of the functions that the Trade Commission would be called upon to perform. He is precisely the man that any executive called upon to select the members of such a body ought to be overjoyed to find.

President Wilson appointed him, and the Senate, after months of delay, refused to confirm the appointment. On what conceivable ground?

Because, forsooth, he is "personally obnoxious" to Senator Gallinger, of New Hampshire. No one contends that he is an unfit person for such an important position; no one suggests that he would not make an admirable trade commissioner.

Simply and brutally, Senator Gallinger does not like Mr. Rublee because he opposed the Senator's reëlection to the Senate. "Senatorial courtesy" does the rest. A majority of the Senate have upheld Senator Gallinger's right to punish thus a political opponent. The President of the United States must have an appointment flung back in his face, the people of the United States must be deprived of the services of the best qualified man for the place, in order to feed fat a single Senator's ancient grudge.

This is mere puny spitefulness on the part of the senior Senator from New Hampshire. It displays "senatorial courtesy" as a contemptible system.

THE MOHONK CONFERENCE AND THE ENFORCEMENT OF PEACE

THE purpose of the Lake Mohonk Conference on International Arbitration—which held its twenty-second annual meeting last week under the characteristically delightful auspices of Mr. and Mrs. Daniel Smiley at the picturesque resort from which the Conference takes its name—is not pacifist in any extreme sense. For two decades the Conference has been held consistently to the single object of attempting to find a better way than war for securing international justice. It is not a peace conference; it is an arbitration conference.

It was not inappropriate, therefore, that the Conference this year should display more interest in the League to Enforce Peace than in any other subject. It was also intensely gratifying to those who, like The Independent, find in the plan of the League the sanest proposals yet made for the elimination of war.

The central idea of the League and its specific proposals were discussed from many points of view. It was evident that the thought of bringing the sanction of force to the support of the quest for international justice and peace appeals strongly to many different minds and diverging temperaments.

The most notable advocate of the League at Mohonk was ex-President Taft, the League's chief officer. Its most prominent critic was William Jennings Bryan.

Mr. Bryan drew an indictment against the League on four counts:

1. It would mean a departure from the national American policy enunciated by George Washington in the famous adjuration to "avoid entangling alliances."

2. It would commit the United States to the necessity of making war—not on the decision of the American Congress, as the Constitution provides—but at the dictation of a council of European powers.

3. It would imply the abandonment of the Monroe Doctrine, since, if we are to intrude into the quarrels of Europe, we cannot object longer to European intervention in affairs in this hemisphere.

4. It would mean a step downward, and not upward. "I would have the United States a moral force, not a policeman." ·

Mr. Bryan's criticisms resolve themselves into two: Peace should not be sought by force; and the business of the United States is with the United States, let the rest of the world manage its own affairs.

From both of these dicta—considered as absolute dicta —we cordially dissent.

The quest of the world should be for international justice and international peace. We must look forward to the day when justice and peace will rule thruout the world thru the power of man's moral nature—or we must despair of the world.

But the day has not yet come when justice and peace prevail between individual man and individual man without the overshadowing sanction of the force of the community. It is idle to expect that in the community of nations—a community of vastly more complex organisms than the community of men and women—the day of peace and justice unsanctioned by the potentiality of force will come more quickly. The state has always needed police to keep the peace between man and man'; the world state will need police to keep the peace between nation and nation for indefinite years to come.

On the question of foreign entanglements it should be remembered, as Mr. Bryan seems not to remember, that the world is a very different place from what it was in Washington's time. The world is becoming, not a group of unrelated and isolated communities, but more and more a single vast community. The brotherhood of man connotes a brotherhood of nations. The brotherhood of man will never be realized so long as each individual feels free to shut himself up within the walls of his own selfish interests and to let his neighbors severely alone. The brotherhood of the world will never be realized so long as each people on the earth feels free to circumscribe its duties and its responsibilities within its own national confines and to let the world go hang.

Justice and peace, like charity, begin at home; but if they stop there they are very poor sticks of virtues indeed.

THE GREAT FORUM

IF the citizen and loyal population of the United States becomes of one mind upon our foreign relations it will be a more momentous thing than the amount of our preparedness in the ways and means of defense. Unity of mind will be the power and substance of defense.

We say of one mind, not merely one emotion or one sentiment. We mean one intellectual conclusion, one judgment, one understanding. Throwing out of consideration the foreign-born residents whose allegiance is to other governments, the disloyal men who profess to be Americans but are not, and the contingent of eccentric folk, numerous in all great modern nations and mischievous in times of crisis, there remains the great majority of citizen Americans who may be of many opinions or may be of one thought upon the questions of public policy. It is certain that these citizens were not like-minded upon the duty of Americans to observe a neutrality of thought and speech toward the European conflict when President Wilson admonished them to do so. It is certain that they have not been like-minded upon preparedness. Not less certain it is that today they are more nearly of one mind upon these matters than they were a year ago, or even six months ago.

The process by which unity of mind is reached in America is complicated, and, by comparison with the rapidity with which emotional unity may be created, it is slow. The press has a part in it, but not the important part. Man to man discussion is essential, and the Forum contributes more than the deliberative assembly.

In the Roman Senate fateful decisions were made with an eye to the behavior of the Roman people. It was in the Forum that patrician senators and tribunes of the people clashed, and that the intellectual reaction of the people was determined. The English House of Commons has been and is yet a great deliberative body; but it is necessary to remember that it became great with the rise of the platform, when free public meeting became a popular right and opportunity. The public opinion of England is shaped by the House of Commons and the hustings, reacting upon each other.

In the United States the mechanism and the methods of molding the collective mind are in various important details unlike those found elsewhere. For a brief period in our history debate in the House of Representatives, and still more in the Senate, influenced popular thinking. There was a time before and after the Civil War when a relation of action and reaction existed between Congress and the popular lyceum or debating club that was not unlike that between the House of Commons and the hustings. There is no such relation now. Instead of it we have developed the American "convention," the relatively new Forums, so called, especially the labor Forums, and such programs of discussion as those which are from year to year brilliantly carried out under the auspices of the Academies of Political and Social Science that meet in New York City and at Philadelphia.

The essential quality of discussion in these bodies is sincerity. Parliamentary deliberations, whether in a board of education, a board of aldermen, a state legislature, or the Congress of the United States, are never entirely frank, never quite genuine. Every speaker has his own reservations, and, as a member of a faction or a party, he is observing the rules of a game. In the conventions of societies and trade organizations, and in the discussions of such bodies as the American Academy of Political and Social Science, men commonly say what they think. It is therefore of no little significance that these discussions bring together the intellectuals, the politicians, and the leaders of business enterprise. More often than not they strike fire, as they did the other day at Philadelphia, when the questions of militarism, pacificism, and preparedness were being threshed out.

We doubt if a better mechanism has ever existed than these characteristically American inventions are for the creation of a true intellectual unification of the public mind. It is our opinion that today the American mind is being pulled together upon supremely important matters on a scale and with a strength of cohesion that will prove to be one of the most fateful facts in history.

IF NOT OUT OF ORDER

THERE is much talk in the English papers of a reorganization of the British Cabinet so as to get new blood in the Government. If they are in earnest about this we beg leave to suggest the following nominations:

For Prime Minister,
WILLIAM MORRIS HUGHES, OF AUSTRALIA
For Foreign Secretary,
SIR ROBERT BORDEN, OF CANADA
For Secretary of State for War,
LOUIS BOTHA, OF AFRICA

Premier Hughes in his recent speeches in England has shown a grasp of Imperial problems quite beyond the capacity of the untraveled Asquith. Premier Borden living outside London fogs would view the war with other eyes than Sir Edward Grey. Premier Botha as the only British general who has a conquest to his credit might well replace his ancient adversary, Earl Kitchener of Khartum.

But perhaps the English do not really want new blood in the government.

UNIVERSITY OF COLORADO VINDICATED

IN discussing "University Management" in our issue of April 24 we called attention to the fair-minded attitude taken by the American Association of University Professors in regard to the question of academic freedom. Another evidence of their intent to be judicial in their investigation of alleged cases of administrative tyranny is afforded by their report on the cases of Colorado and Wesleyan.

In the former case Professor Brewster charged the authorities of the University of Colorado with having dropped him from the law faculty because he had acted as counsel for the Miners' Union before a congressional committee and had testified before the Industrial Relations Commission on the Colorado strike. The evidence in the case is conflicting. There is direct contradiction of testimony as to certain conversations. But the investigating committee of five professors from different universities came to the conclusion that Professor Brewster was dropt not because of his action in the labor troubles but because of a reorganization of the department. It appears that Governor Ammons urged his dismissal on the ground of his public activities in the labor cause, but that President Farrand resisted this official pressure and asserted "the principle that the conscientious utterances of a university professor in the performance of duties imposed on him as a citizen" should not be called in question.

The other case was the forced resignation of Professor Fisher after twenty years of service in Wesleyan University, on the ostensible ground of some rash remarks on church-going and Sunday observance which he made before a men's club. The Association does not go into details on this case, but it condemns the action of the authorities.

A NATIONAL PARK SERVICE

THE United States has fourteen national parks. They have an area of five million acres. They include some of the finest tracts of wild scenery on the earth's surface.

The Yosemite and the Yellowstone are too well known to need description. Glacier National Park, in Montana, contains in its 900,000 acres two hundred and fifty lakes and eighty glaciers. Sequoia National Park, in California, includes within its boundaries a wonderful forest of the giant redwood trees. Casa Grande Reservation and Mesa Verde National Park enclose prehistoric ruins of great picturesqueness and high educational value.

The nation has also thirty-one national monuments, including the Grand Canyon of the Colorado, the Petrified Forest in Arizona, the Muir Woods in California, the Natural Bridges in Arizona, the Devil's Tower in Wyoming, and the Lewis and Clark Cavern in Montana.

These national possessions afford unexampled opportunities for the enjoyment of outdoor life, exploration and popular recreation. Their preservation from abuse and reckless exploitation is guaranteed by national laws. But the provisions for their enjoyment by the people are inadequate and ineffective. In only a single case —that of the Yellowstone Park—has anything like satisfactory preparation been made for their public use.

One of the bills now before Congress, which is likely to attract liberal interest because it is non-political and uncontroversial, provides for the establishment of a National Park Service. The bill has been prepared by the American Civic Association, which has done splendid work in the preservation from destructive exploitation of Niagara Falls. To this Service, to be created in the Department of the Interior, would be entrusted the task of administering these splendid national possessions. It is an admirable measure, for it would unify administrative functions which are now scattered, unrelated and utterly lacking in coördination. It would insure a uniform and far-sighted policy of administration for the national parks and monuments, and make possible the increasing use by the people of these great national playgrounds. Canada, thru its national park bureau, has so thoroly and wisely exploited its several park areas that during the season of 1915, when the war conditions in Europe naturally turned a large volume of travel toward the interior of our own country, the Canadian parks attracted more visitors than the corresponding parks of the United States.

We have done well to set aside these areas of natural beauty and recreative opportunities for popular use. What remains to be done is so to coördinate and develop their administration that their use by the people may be facilitated and encouraged.

HERESY HUNTERS

IT is a most gratifying sign that some journals and presbyteries of the Presbyterian Church are protesting strongly against the heresy charges bandied about by some mischief makers of that denomination and their followers. It is high time that those who seem determined to put our growing, expanding Christianity into an intellectual strait jacket should be called to account before the bar of enlightened Christian opinion. The attempt to force upon men of vision and conviction prescribed religious views has always been attended by grave disaster to the Christian Church and to the progress of the Gospel. It is really suicidal to pursue such a course at this juncture, when all the resources of every denomination and section of the Christian world are needed, as never before, to stay the war-making forces of the world, and bring about peace, established on the basis of brotherhood and internationalism. So long as the Church itself resorts to outward compulsion, fear, force and suspicion in order to maintain its own strength and integrity, it is difficult to see how its leaders can achieve success in counseling international good will and the replacing of force by law and reason. The Christian conscience is deeply concerned over this inner antagonism of traditional method and the present high call to sacrificial service for the good of humanity.

The solution of the difficulty is bound to come. There are indeed many indications that this destructive crisis in Western civilization is bringing into clearer view the essence of the Christian religion, and focusing the minds of Christian leaders upon the common aid and tasks before them rather than on their differences of creed and historical organization. It will be fortunate if, in the great upheaval and realignment that are in progress, the Church should be able to free itself forever from the divisive spirit of heresy hunting and become imbued with the unifying spirit of coöperation with all who serve the interests of the ideal kingdom.

GOD SAVE THE UNITED STATES

JAPAN has a population of 60,000,000 souls. The United States has over 100,000,000.

Japan is about the size of California. Her arable land is a trifle larger than Maryland.

Japan is still an agricultural country. Her manufacturers are a generation behind ours.

The annual value of Japan's farm products is one-twelfth that of the United States, her mineral products one-fortieth, her forestry products one-twentieth and her exports of raw materials and manufactures one-eighth.

The value of Japan's farm lands is one-twentieth that of the United States, and the value of her bank deposits is one-one-hundred-and-fortieth.

Tho the Japanese army is somewhat larger than ours, our navy is a third larger than Japan's.

Before the war broke out Japan was the most heavily taxed nation on earth. As a result of the Russo-Japanese War out of every hundred dollars of wealth produced thirty dollars is said to have gone to the government directly or indirectly in the form of taxes. The general poverty of Japan is very great.

It will be evident, therefore, to our preparedness-at-any-cost friends that Japan is amply able to embark on a great war of aggression against us with every expectation of success. To arms, Americans! To arms!

ANOTHER POETICAL PERIODICAL

THAT the long foretold revival of verse is upon us seems to be evidenced by the number of new magazines devoted to it. The latest is *The Poetry Review of America*, published at Cambridge, Massachusetts. The first number is true to its name; half poetry and half review. It leads off with a two-page contribution, "No. 3 on the Docket," by Miss Amy Lowell, high priestess of *vers libre*, but the editors admit rimed verse without prejudice.

MARRIAGE VOWS

THE Methodist General Conference, in eliminating the words "With all my worldly goods I thee endow" from the wedding ritual, has taken an advance step, tho a timid one, in the direction of verbal honesty. But this action, because it is obviously merely a verbal change, shows how meaningless the ceremony has become. What a commotion would have been created if a clause of equal prominence had been dropt out of a deed, a contract or a legislative act! We frequently hear references to "the sanctity of the marriage vows," but as a matter of fact they are not expected to be kept and have no standing before the courts. Jove laughs at lovers' vows, they say, and the law laughs at marriage vows.

"With all my worldly goods I thee endow" means too often that when a wife wants a dollar for a matinee or a missionary she has to wheedle it out of her husband with smiles or tears. If the wife appeals to the court for the endowment promised her, the judge shakes his head and tells her, possibly, that she may get the income on a third of her husband's property after he is dead. If a husband appeals to the court to compel the wife to obey him as she promised to, the judge shakes his head and smiles. English law allows, or did until recently allow, the husband to use "a stick no thicker than his thumb" in the enforcement of wifely obedience, but American law or custom has snatched even this inadequate weapon from the husband's hand and left him powerless. In certain churches brides may still promise to obey, but they don't mean to and they don't.

Altho it makes no difference what the man and woman say when they stand before the minister or the magistrate, yet on the other hand the law holds them strictly to a lot of marital obligations to which they have never pledged themselves. The simplified service of the embarrassed justice of the peace, "Have her? Have him? Hitched!" commits the contracting parties to just the same duties and responsibilities as the most elaborate ritual and the most impressive promises. We do not advocate reducing the wedding ceremony to this simple form, but it does seem to us that a little more truthfulness would be in order on such an occasion.

INVOLUNTARY ARCHEOLOGISTS

MANY people have deplored the labor wasted in the war and wished that the millions of men who have spent the last year and a half digging trenches for shelter had dug them for drainage and irrigation instead. There seems no prospect for diverting their labors in this direction, but incidentally some benefit of an unexpected sort has come from the activity of the human gophers. Archeologists have long realized that the neighborhood of Salonica offered a rich field for excavation, but they never could get their governments to pay for the excavation. Suddenly and without the urging of archeologists, the British and French Governments have sent some three hundred thousand men to Greece and set them to digging over the whole territory from the Aegean to the Serbian frontier regardless of expense. They have turned up enough objects of art and inscriptions to establish a museum and now the antiquarians flock after the soldiers like crows after the plowmen. As a result of this unprecedented excavation the world is likely to learn a great deal of the life of the ancient Greek city of Thessalonica, which was named by the founder after his wife, the sister of Alexander the Great, and which was a thriving city when Paul was called into Macedonia.

Such archeological by-products of war are no new thing. When Napoleon took a party of savants and incidentally some soldiers into Egypt one of them—one of the soldiers, not one of the savants—discovered in the Rosetta mouth of the Nile the stone which gave the clue to the interpretation of the hieroglyphics.

The morning paper tells us that the Russians are soon to attack the Turks at Mosul on the Tigris River. If this field is dug over like Verdun it ought to turn out some rich finds, for Mosul is near the site of Nineveh, that great city which Jonah once converted, probably for the only time in the five thousand years of its wicked history.

THE STORY OF THE WEEK

Preparedness in Congress — The Army Reorganization bill, as agreed to by the conference committee of the two houses of Congress, is ready for the President's signature. The conference report was adopted in the Senate without a roll-call. In the House the vote adopting it was 349 to 25.

The bill as it goes to the President provides for a regular army whose maximum peace strength is variously estimated, depending upon the interpretation put by the War Department upon certain provisions, at from 206,-000 to 211,000; and for a Federalized National Guard of 457,000. It further provides for a government nitrate manufacturing plant to cost not more than $20,000,000; for the establishment of a system of military training camps for civilians paid for out of the Federal Treasury; for a board to investigate the advisability of establishing a government munitions plant; and for vocational education in the army. Federalization of the National Guard would be accomplished thru Federal pay and thru a requirement making the militiamen subject to the orders of the President.

The next step in the preparedness activities of Congress has to do with the Naval bill. The majority of the House Committee on Naval Affairs has prepared a report which ignores the recommendation of the Secretary of the Navy for the adoption of a five year building program, and cuts down as well his proposals for the coming year. The Daniels program for 1917 called for two dreadnoughts, two battle cruisers, three scout cruisers, fifteen destroyers, five fleet submarines, twenty-five coast submarines, two gunboats and one hospital ship. The Naval Committee's proposals are for five battle cruisers, four scout cruisers, ten destroyers, three fleet submarines, seventeen coast submarines, one hospital ship, one fuel ship and one ammunition ship. The Daniels program for the next five years would provide for ten dreadnoughts, six battle cruisers, ten scout cruisers, fifty destroyers, fifteen fleet submarines, eighty-five coast submarines, four gunboats, two fuel ships, one ammunition ship and one repair ship. This aspect of the naval situation, involving the element of planning for a period of years to come, is ignored by the Democratic majority of the Naval Committee.

The Republican minority is to recommend a program for building six battle cruisers, two dreadnoughts, six scout cruisers, twenty-eight destroyers, fifty submarines and several auxiliary ships.

The calm disregard by the majority of the committee of the Navy Department's recommendations, approved by the President in his annual message to Congress, and its revolutionary proposal to build no dreadnoughts what-ever next year, is sure to cause a pretty fight in Congress. The final program will doubtless be quite different from anything now suggested.

The House Does Some Legislating — The Rural Credits bill, which was adopted in the Senate with but five dissenting votes, passed the House last week with only ten voting in the negative. Two hundred and ninety-five Representatives voted for the bill. The two bills passed by the Senate and the House are not identical, tho the differences between them are ones of detail rather than of principle. In conference the measure will be worked out into more practical shape, and the ultimate passage of the composite bill will, of course, be merely a matter of time.

The House has also passed the Administration's shipping bill by almost a purely party vote. The 211 affirmative votes included those of a dozen minority members and the 161 negative votes those of two Democrats. The purpose of the bill is twofold: to permit the Federal Government to create a merchant marine by building, purchasing, leasing or chartering vessels to be used for commercial purposes, as naval auxiliaries and army transports, such vessels to be operated by a corporation organized by the government in case private capital would not avail itself of the opportunity to lease government-owned vessels and operate them; and to create a shipping board with power to regulate the rates and practises of ocean carriers.

Before the bill could be passed it was found necessary to adopt an amendment limiting the government operation of steamship lines to a period of five years after the close of the Great War. It is hoped, and indeed expected, that it will be friendly in tone and will not insist upon the request for the withdrawal of the American troops.

A bill providing appropriations of $45,000,000 to be expended for the general improvement of the Mississippi and Sacramento rivers for the purpose of controlling floods was passed last week in the House and now goes to the Senate.

In Mexico — The status of the American expeditionary forces in Mexico is no more definite than it has been from the start. A new note from General Carranza on the situation is expected in Washington at any time. It is hoped, and indeed expected, that it will be friendly in tone and will not insist upon the request for the withdrawal of the American troops.

Meanwhile a little flying squadron of the Eighth Cavalry has come up with some of the raiders upon Glen Springs and rescued the two Americans who were captured in that raid. Five of the bandits were killed by the pursuing cavalry and two captured.

General Funston is going steadily ahead with the work of organizing the border patrol for the purpose of policing the danger zone across the line.

There is no news of Villa.

The Roosevelt Platform — It is characteristic of Mr. Roosevelt, when he wants to attack a policy, to go to the place where that policy is, so to speak, at home. So last week he went to Detroit and set forth at length his views on those issues before the country, the opposition to which has been personified by Henry Ford. In his speech Mr. Roosevelt made no personal attack upon Mr. Ford or anyone else, for that matter, but contented himself with a long, elaborate and particularly temperate statement of his beliefs. He prefaced his discussion of the issues with a brief appreciation of the man whose views he was to combat, in which he said:

For Mr. Ford personally, I feel not merely friendliness, but in many respects a very genuine admiration. There is much in the methods and very much in the purposes with which he has conducted his business, notably in his relations to his working people, that commands my hearty sympathy and respect. Moreover, there is always something attractive to an American in the career of a man who has raised himself from the industrial ranks until he is one of the captains of industry.

As Mr. Roosevelt sees it, and there is a great deal of evidence that many other Americans see eye to eye with

BRANDEIS OR ————?
The portrait of Mr. Brandeis on a recent cover of The Independent was altered by a student at the College of Wooster to bring out the striking resemblance between the "People's Attorney" and Abraham Lincoln

323

THE LADY OR THE JINGO—BOTH SIDES OF THE PREPAREDNESS QUESTION

The Committee on Industrial Preparedness recently mobilised a number of illustrators and cartoonists at a dinner in New York to enlist them in the campaign for adequate national defenses. James Montgomery Flagg brought the drawing, "Armless," which heads the preparedness poster parade. In New York the Woman's Peace Party is holding an exhibition designed to drive home the anti-preparation case, and Uncle Sam, prepared, is a leading exhibit

him in this matter, "there are at this time two great issues before us, both inseparably bound together. They are the issues of Americanism and preparedness." In facing these issues he declares that there can be no compromise.

If there is to be no compromise, then we must have real and not sham preparedness. The issue is, says Mr. Roosevelt,

Are we prepared with a sane and lofty idealism to fit ourselves to render great service to mankind by rendering ourselves fit for our own service, or are we content then we are prepared by preparing to tread the path that China has trodden? . . . There is no use in saying that we will fit ourselves to defend ourselves a little, but not much. Such a position is equivalent to announcing that, if necessary, we shall hit, but that we shall only hit soft. The only right principle is to prepare thoroly or not at all. The only right principle is to avoid hitting if it is possible to do so, but never under any circumstances to hit soft. To go to war a little, but not much, is the one absolutely certain way to insure disaster. To prepare a little, but not much, stands on a par with a city developing a fire department which, after a fire occurs, can put it out a little, but not much.

The object of preparedness, in the view of Mr. Roosevelt, is not war but the prevention of war. As he put it, "I am advocating preparedness so as to avoid war, and I am advocating preparedness in the work of peace as in military matters."

The measure of the preparedness which he desires in military and naval matters is this:

I believe in a thoroly efficient navy, the second in size in the world. I believe in a small but thoroly efficient regular army, an army of 250,000 men, with a proper reserve. This would give us a mobile army of 125,000 men. But back of the regular army and navy must stand the strength of the people themselves, and this strength must be prepared in advance or it will be utterly useless in time of trial.

To the end that the people may be themselves prepared to stand behind the army and the navy in the time of

national danger, Mr. Roosevelt believes in "universal service based on universal training."

I think it would be not only of incalculable benefit to the nation in the event of war, but of inculculable benefit to the individuals undergoing it, and, therefore, to the nation, as regards the work of peace. I believe that the dog-tent would prove a most effective agent for democratizing and nationalizing our life; quite as much so as the public school, and far more so than the American factory and the American city as they are today.

But Mr. Roosevelt does not believe "that preparedness for national power lies wholly in guns and ships and armed men." In order that we may have the other essentials of preparedness, he declares:

There must be a deliberate purpose to see that health and well-being of the workers, their standard of wages and of living and the education of their children are held up to the level that will insure the greatest national efficiency, not only for the present, but for the future. . . .

We must abolish pork-barrel methods in the army—as regards army posts, navy yards, as regards everything else. . . .

Pork-barrel graft is a crime against the nation when the army and navy are involved. But honesty and efficiency in managing the army and navy only represent the beginning of military preparedness.

We can have no effective army unless business is mobilized and especially unless our transportation system is nationalized. The railroads, whose business is directly or indirectly interstate, must, in all their relations, be regulated by the national government and not by forty-eight conflicting state governments.

The merchant marine must be developed not only for our own purposes of peace, but as a basis for the navy. It must be proportionate to the transportation needs and to the navy of this country. Our merchant fleet must build up a naval reserve. We must safeguard the rights of our sailors, but we can only do so if we upbuild the lines of ships on which they are to serve.

It was a forceful and effective speech. No better statement could be made of the position of those who hold the view that preparedness in full measure is the one great national duty that confronts us at this time.

The President's Problems   In an address before the Press Club in Washington last week President Wilson set forth some of the most perplexing difficulties under which the Chief Executive labors in critical times like these. In the course of his address he said:

You can imagine the strain upon the feeling of any man who is trying to interpret the spirit of his country when he feels that that spirit cannot have its own way beyond a certain point. And one of the greatest points of strain upon me, if I may be permitted to point it out, was this:

There are two reasons why the chief wish of America is for peace. One is that they love peace and have nothing to do with the present quarrel, and the other is that they believe the present quarrel has carried those engaged in it so far that they cannot be held to ordinary standards of responsibility, and that, therefore, as some men have exprest it to me, since the rest of the world is mad, why should we not simply refuse to have anything to do with the rest of the world in the ordinary channels of action? Why not let the storm pass, and then, when it is all over, have the reckonings?

Knowing that from both these two points of view the passion of America was for peace, I was, nevertheless, aware that America is one of the nations of the world not only, but one of the chief nations of the world—a nation that grows more and more powerful almost in spite of herself; that grows morally more and more influential even when she is not aware of it, and that if she is to play the part which she most covets it is necessary that she should act more or less from the point of view of the rest of the world.

If I cannot retain my moral influence over a man except by occasionally knocking him down; it that is the only basis upon which he will respect me, then for the sake of his soul I have got occasionally to knock him down.

So I say that I have been aware that, to do the very thing that we are proudest of the ability to do, there might come a time when we would have to do it in a way that we would prefer not to do it; and the great burden on my spirits, gentlemen, has been that it has been up to me to choose when that time came.

Can you imagine a thing more calculated to keep a man awake at nights than that? Because, just because, I did not feel that I was the whole thing and was aware that my duty was a duty of interpretation, how could I be sure that I had the right elements of information by which to interpret truly?

What we are now talking about is largely spiritual. You say, "All the people out my way think so and so." Now, I know perfectly well that you have not talked with all the people out your way, I find that out again and again, and so you are taken by surprise. The people of the United States are not asking anybody's leave to do their own thinking, and are not asking anybody to tip them off what they ought to think. They are thinking for themselves, every man for himself; and you do not know, and the worst of it is, since the responsibility is mine, I do not know what they are thinking about.

I have the most imperfect means of finding out, and yet I have got to act as if I knew. That is the burden of it, and I tell you, gentlemen, it is a pretty serious burden, particularly if you look upon the office as I do—that I am not put here to do what I please. If I were, it would have been very much more interesting than it has been. I am put here to register, to suggest, and, more than that, and much greater than that, to be suggested to.

Truly, there is no bigger job, no harder task than being President, and it does not take the man who has the fortune to be selected for the job very long to find it out.

The End of Sing Sing in Sight

The session of the New York Legislature which came to a close a month ago left some trying problems for Governor Whitman to solve. For instance, in the matter of a new prison to take the place of Sing Sing, the legislators avoided responsibility by the clumsy expedient of passing two bills with different provisions. It was obvious that both bills could not become law; the Governor must veto one or both of them. Fortunately Mr. Whitman rose to the opportunity presented by the cowardice of the legislators, and vetoed the bad bill of the pair, and signed the good one.

Sing Sing Prison has long been a pestilential disgrace to civilization. Not only is it old, unsanitary and inadequate, but the plan upon which it is built—the Bastile cell block plan—is a relic of the Dark Ages.

The need for radical improvement in the State's chief prison, long voiced by advocates of prison reform, was brought vividly into public notice by the appointment as warden of Thomas Mott Osborne. Mr. Osborne is still suffering under the persecution waged against him under the guise of law for ulterior motives. The criminal case brought against him is being smashed just as fast as the deliberate machinery of the law can move its ponderous wheels; but it may be several months yet before the process is complete.

Meanwhile Mr. Osborne has the satisfaction of knowing that the medieval cell block of Sing Sing is to give way to a new institution built in accordance with the ideas of modern enlightenment as to the treatment of those who have broken the State's laws. The house of horrors that is Sing Sing, the propagating and distributing station for disease and vice, is to go. A farm and industrial prison on a better site is to take its place.

Other Vetoes by Governor Whitman

Another courageous veto by Governor Whitman of a vicious legacy of the departed legislature dealt with the conditions of labor of women and minors in the canning industry. Each year an attack is made in the New York Legislature upon the laws which protect these workers from exploitation. Each year legislators are found ready to serve the selfish ends of greedy manufacturers at the expense of humanity. The bill passed this year by the Legislature would have made it possible for women to be worked twelve hours a day, seven days a week, during the rush season from June 15 to October 15.

Governor Whitman also refused his approval to the bill establishing a board of censorship over moving picture films and imposing a tax upon each film presented. The tax provision, it was estimated, would return an annual income to the state of more than a million dollars. It would, said Mr. Whitman, impose an unnecessary hardship upon the motion picture industry. "The moving picture theater," said the Governor, "because of the nominal admission fee of from five to ten cents, has become the principal form of entertainment which can generally be enjoyed by persons of limited means. . . . I believe it to be a fact that the burden imposed by this bill in respect to the tax on the producers and lessors of these films would be so great as to close many of these places of exhibition." He further declared that he had found such fundamental objections to the procedure under the censorship provision of the bill that it was not necessary or possible to consider the fundamental question of the desirability of such censorship.

The Independent recently exprest editorially its views on the unsoundness of any governmental censorship whatever over dramatic productions, even when the screen takes the place of the stage. Governor Whitman's veto is in the line of sound public policy.

A Terrible Crime in Texas

In the town of Waco, Texas, last week a crowd of 15,000 persons watched a human being burned to death. It was no accident, but deliberate intent. A negro boy of eighteen had criminally assaulted and killed a white woman seven days before. He had been arrested, indicted, tried, convicted, and sentenced to death in astonishingly brief space of time.

Then the mob seized him and burned him to death in the public square, while men, women and children looked on. It was a peculiarly atrocious case of lynch law. It had none of the usual circumstances that are offered in palliation. The offender had been convicted and would have been put to death legally in due course. There could be no contention that justice might be cheated. His lynching was simply an orgy of mob brutality and savage lust.

The young negro's crime was a horrible one. The crime of the people of Waco was more horrible and a deeper stain upon the fair name of Texas.

Beyond the Alps Lies Italy

On Monday, May 15, almost exactly a year from the date when Italy declared war upon Austria, the Austrian troops in the Trentino began an advance movement which in a few days carried them over the Italian frontier. During all this time the Austrians have kept to the defensive and been content to hold the lines that had been fortified a few miles within the boundary. The Italian troops, tho outnumbering their opponents some four to one, have been unable to break thru these lines at any point or to capture any important stronghold. The Italian soldiers appear to have fought bravely and they seem to have been abundantly supplied with munitions, but the utmost they have been able to accomplish is to push their lines from three to five miles into Austrian territory in several sectors and at one point near the coast about ten miles.

Even more humiliating to Italian pride was the course of events on the other side of the Adriatic. Here Italy has long claimed special interests, for the Queen of Italy, and the Albanian coast has been regarded as eventually coming within the domain of Greater Italy. Yet the Italian troops that had been shipped across the Adriatic offered no resistance when the Austrians swept over Montenegro and Albania. Only one point on the eastern shore of the Adriatic, the city of Avlona, has been held by the Italians and this is now threatened by Austrian attack from sea and land. A hundred and fifty vessels are said to have been assembled at Fiume, the Hungarian port on the Adriatic, in order to convey an Austrian army to Durazzo, the capital of Albania. From this point they can march down the coast to Avlona.

Copyright *Underwood*

WHERE OUR OWN WAR NEWS COMES FROM

General Pershing giving an interview to the newspaper correspondents at Field Headquarters near Namiquipa, Mexico

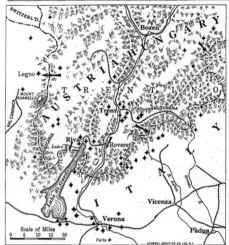

THE AUSTRIAN INVASION OF ITALY
The Austrians have taken the offensive by massing troops in the Trentino tongue and attacking the frontier at various points in the direction of Verona and Vicenza

Italy's Part in the War The Allies naturally expected that the accession of Italy with some three million potential troops would make a great difference in the course of the war, and they have not been able wholly to conceal their disappointment at the failure of the Italians to deliver any effective blows or even to divert any considerable proportion of the Austrian army from the Russian and Serbian fields to the Italian frontier. None of the Allied armies, with the exception of the British, has made so little progress as the Italian. Since Italy did not enter the war until nine months after its outbreak she had ample opportunity for preparation, and she was supplied with all the necessary funds for this purpose by Great Britain and France.

But by bringing Italy into the war the Allies alienated Greece, and as it has turned out Greece might have been more use to them, for it was thru the inactivity of Greece and the accession of Bulgaria that the Central Powers were enabled to conquer Serbia and connect with Constantinople. From this followed the defeat of the British on the Dardanelles and the Tigris. Meanwhile Greece has seized the opportunity to occupy the Epirote provinces of southern Albania, back of Avlona,

which Italy has coveted. The representatives of this district are now admitted to the Greek Parliament.

Italy has never declared war upon Germany, so the old treaty which binds these nations in a defensive alliance is still nominally in force. Nor have the German ships in Italian ports yet been seized by the Italian Government, altho, curiously enough, the German ships seized by the Portuguese Government have been sent to Italy to aid in the campaign against the Austrians.

A year ago, when Italy was hesitating whether to engage in the war, Austria offered her the Trentino and a strip along the Isonzo frontier if she would maintain her neutrality, but this was rejected as insufficient to satisfy the aspirations of the Italian Irredentists. The territory gained by the Italians during the past year at a cost of several hundred thousand men is not nearly so large as that offered Italy to remain at peace.

But the entrance of Italy in the war has been of great advantage to the Allies in many ways, especially in closing the ring around the Central Powers and shutting the last door thru which they could get supplies from the outside world. The lack of success of the Italian troops in the field does not appear so surprising when we consider

that the Austrian frontier fortifications, which they were attacking, were not improvised entrenchments in the open plain like those held by the French, British and Germans in France and Belgium, but a carefully constructed system of defenses located upon the hights overlooking the Italian plains. When Austria surrendered the province of Venetia to Italy in 1866 she insisted upon drawing the boundary line upon the edge of the mountains, so as to give her the strategic advantage that she is now utilizing.

The Trentino Campaign The southern point of Austrian Tyrol, known from its chief city as the Trentino, juts down into Italy like an Alpine peninsula. At its tip it is split by the Lago di Garda, most of which is Italian waters, but dominated by the hills on either side which were held and fortified by the Austrians. Verona and Vicenza are both within twenty-five miles of the Austrian frontier and an advance of another twenty-five miles beyond Vicenza would bring the Austrians to Venice and cut off the province of Venetia from the rest of Italy. Venetia was gained by Italy fifty years ago thru Prussian prowess rather than her own efforts, for the Italian generals and admirals made a muddle of the 1866 campaign against Austria. Austria has never ceased to look with longing upon her lost Venetia, altho the province is altogether Italian in population and sympathies.

But the reconquest of Venetia seems too ambitious a project for the Austrians to undertake at this stage of the war—and it may be that the invasion of Italy from the Trentino is intended, like the German attack upon Verdun, to forestall an offensive on the part of the Italians in another quarter. We may surmise that the recent visit of Premier Asquith to Rome for the purpose of stimulating the Italians to greater activity and it was rumored that they were massing troops for a vigorous attack upon the eastern front along the Isonzo River.

At any rate General Cadorna has been forced to transfer his headquarters

THE GREAT WAR

May 15—Austrians advance in Trentino. Trial of Sir Roger Casement for high treason begins.

May 16—Austrians gain on Adige and Astico. Russians cross Persian border toward Mosul.

May 17—Three German ships sunk by British submarines in the Baltic. French and German aviators fight 35 battles in the air.

May 18—Germans take trenches on Hill 304, El Arish, near Egyptian frontier, bombarded by British warships and aeroplanes.

May 19—Austrians take Col Santo, south of Rovereto. Dunkirk bombarded by German aeroplanes.

May 20—Italians take Col di Lana, in Venetian Alps. Germans repulsed on Dead Man Hill.

May 21—Cossacks join British on Tigris. French regain Haudromont quarries, east of Meuse.

from the Isonzo frontier to the Trentino, where the Austrians are pouring down the valleys leading into Italy. Three of these leading southeast from Trent seem to be the avenues chosen for the Austrian invasion. The first is the Lagarina valley thru which flows the Adige River, a gorge so wild that it was taken by Dante for one of the scenes of his "Inferno." The Adige runs down just east of Lake Garda to Verona. Further to the east is the Astico River, which flows thru Vicenza to Venice. Beyond this is the Brenta River, which forms the Sugana valley.

The Italian troops during the past year have been trying to push their way up these three valleys to the cities of Rovereto and Trent, but had not succeeded in penetrating more than five miles at the most, and much of this ground was recovered by the Austrians within four days after their advance movement began. The Italians who held the passes and peaks seem to have been taken by surprize and lost heavily. According to the Vienna report, the Austrians took in four days 257 officers, 12,900 men, 107 guns, 12 28-centimeter howitzers and 68 machine guns. On the other hand, the Italians claim that the Austrians lost 35,000 men in the four days' offensive.

Dead Man Hill   The Germans have by no means given up hope of capturing Verdun. On the contrary they have, during the week, renewed their efforts to take the hills west of the Meuse River, and their latest attack was pushed with as much vigor as their first two months ago. A night assault gave them possession of part, at least, of the top of Hill 304, and later they gained some of the outer trenches on Dead Man Hill, which stands next to it. But at the second line of entrenchments the French curtain of fire was so fierce that the German wave was stopped and turned back. The Germans have during the week straightened their line in this sector and are now able to attack Dead Man Hill from the west, south and north simultaneously.

At other points along the line in France and Belgium the Germans have been active. In the Argonne forest, west of Verdun, and in the Champagne

Copyright Medem

THE RUSSIANS IN FRANCE MUST LEARN TO FIGHT A LA FRANCAIS

region beyond, they attacked the French lines and near Loos and Armentières the British. A squadron of German aeroplanes flying over Dunkirk and Bergues killed a dozen persons including women and children.

Russians Advance on Mosul   Mosul on the Tigris is likely soon to see a bigger fight than in the days when its name was Nineveh and it was the leading city of the world. Now its importance is derived from the fact that the overland caravan route from Aleppo along which the German Bagdad railroad was to come here reaches the Tigris River. The capture of this junction by the

Russians from the Caucasus would cut Turkey in two and leave Persia to be divided between the British and Russians.

The news from this field is too fragmentary and unreliable to enable us to place the armies with exactitude or even to tell which way the tide is going. But it appears that since Field Marshal von Mackensen has taken charge of the Turkish forces in Armenia the westward advance of the Russians from Erzerum upon Erzingan has been checked and that the Russians who are moving south toward Mosul are meeting with increasing resistance as they approach the Tigris River. Besides this army from the north there are said to be two other armies approaching from the Persian frontier to the northeast, one headed toward Mosul and the other toward Bagdad, 220 miles down stream. But the Turkish troops which have been engaged against the British on the Tigris are now released, thru the capture of General Townshend's army, and may be turned against the advancing Russians.

General Sir Percy Lake, who now has charge of the British forces in Mesopotamia, reports that "a force of Russian cavalry has joined General Gorringe after a bold and adventurous ride." These Cossacks probably came down thru the mountains from the Russian army which has marched from the Caspian Sea thru Hamadan and Kermanshah and crost the border into Turkey.

Paul Thompson

TRAINING CIVILIANS FOR WAR DUTY IN THE SHOPS

England not only calls women and some men into her munition plants, but she gives them special training for effective work there. This is a class conducted by the London County Council and, as the blackboard shows, the teaching gives the workers an intelligent appreciation of their tasks

CONNECTICUT: According to the latest report of State Labor Commissioner Hyde, the employment agencies conducted by his department in Hartford, New Haven, Bridgeport, Waterbury and Norwich procured employment for 1623 persons out of 2750 who applied to them in March of this year. Of these applicants 1956 were men and 794 women. About fifty-five per cent of the men and seventy per cent of the women were placed in employment. On the other hand, there were more than 2000 applications for help in the month, and about eighty per cent of these demands were supplied. This was the largest volume of business ever done in a month by these agencies.

DISTRICT OF COLUMBIA: Congress finally has passed the bill, so many times rejected, incorporating the American Academy of Arts and Letters in the District of Columbia. Among the incorporators are some of the best known authors and artists of the East and one, James Whitcomb Riley, from west of the Alleghenies. The bill limits the membership of the academy to fifty. The stated purpose of incorporation is "to enable the organization to receive and expend any fund which, for the purpose of advancing literature and the arts, may be entrusted to its good faith, its experience and its knowledge of the best use to which such fund may be put." As vacancies occur members of the academy are to be chosen from the membership of the National Institute of Arts and Letters, by which the academy was established in 1905.

ILLINOIS: The formal opening of Chicago's municipal pier will be celebrated on Memorial Day. It is said to be the largest and best equipped city pier in the world. Located at the mouth of the Chicago River, it extends 3000 feet into the lake and is 300 feet wide, with large recreation facilities at its end. It is intended to relieve congestion in the river by taking care of most of the freight and passenger service outside. It has cost about $4,600,000, but engineers say its rentals and concessions will cover the cost of maintenance of all its buildings, amortize the original cost and pay four per cent on the investment.

KENTUCKY: The passage of the so-called Hutcheraft bill by the Legislature is said to have been followed by the "dryest" Sundays Kentucky has ever known. One provision of this bill requires the revocation of a liquor license as soon as a violation of the law has been proved, and a year must elapse before another license can be issued to the same person or to any other person at the same location. The Sunday closing law has long been a dead letter in most of the cities and towns of the state, but it is said that this new provision has changed the situation. In Louisville on the Sunday following the passage of the law not a drunken man was seen and not an arrest was made for any cause at the central police station between 7 a. m. and 11 p. m.

MARYLAND: A new law, said to be unlike any other ever enacted by a legislature in this country, has been signed by Governor Harrington and is to go into effect on June 1. It is one of the results of that condition exposed last year by the Goldsborough Vice Commission, which learned that thousands of new-born infants had been disposed of to private institutions, in which a large percentage of them had died. The new law provides that no illegitimate child under six months of age may be separated from its mother to be placed in any foster home, except under duly attested necessity for the physical good of the mother or child. Opponents of the measure fear it will lead to many cases of deliberate infanticide.

MICHIGAN: The tuberculosis survey of this state, begun last October by the Michigan Board of Health, has proved surprisingly popular, and the board has found it impossible to keep up with the demands made by people who wish to be examined. In the six months thirteen of the eighty-three counties in the state have been visited and more than 5000 persons examined. 2242 cases with either positive evidences or suspicious indications of tuberculosis were found. Nurses visit the homes of these persons and give instructions for the improvement of living conditions and information on how to prevent contagion.

MISSOURI: The United States Supreme Court has dismissed the appeal of the St. Louis street railway lines from the decision of the Missouri courts, which upheld the ordinance by which the City of St. Louis places a tax of one mill on each street railway passenger. As a result of this dismissal the city will receive about $3,000,000 in back taxes.

MONTANA: Yellowstone County, of which Billings is the chief city, has voted $175,000 in bonds for the construction of the first extensive permanent roads in the state to be built in this way. These roads are to extend for a distance of thirty-five miles along the line of the Yellowstone trail, a popular automobile route for tourists to the Yellowstone and Glacier national parks. The Billings Chamber of Commerce prepared the plans and conducted the campaign for the bond issue.

NEBRASKA: After long negotiation the Missouri River navigation committee of the Omaha Commercial Club has secured a steamboat of 150 tons cargo capacity to run regularly between Omaha and Kansas City. This last link in the chain makes possible river traffic from St. Louis to Sioux City, as there is already established between St. Louis and Kansas City and another between Omaha and Sioux City.

NEVADA: The discovery of rich deposits of tungsten in Humboldt County has created as much excitement thruout the state as that incidental to the free-gold strike in the Willard district a few years ago. The hills, valleys and gulches in the vicinity of Lovelock are alive with prospectors, and the towns are doing a booming business in outfits and supplies. As a result of the furious search many deposits have been found, and money and properties are changing hands in rapid succession. One mill is said to be turning out more than $100,000 worth of concentrates a month.

NEW HAMPSHIRE: Among the many new fields into which the New Hampshire state college at Durham has sent its influence and assistance is that of community development. The college has just called its first community conference, the announced purpose being "to offer men and women interested in the social problems of community life in this state an opportunity to consider and discuss common problems and opportunities." An extensive three-day program has been arranged, with addresses by well-known men and women on a wide range of pertinent subjects.

OKLAHOMA: Last year, under a new law, the collection of the Oklahoma income tax was taken out of the hands of the county assessors and turned over to the State Auditor. Under the old law the assessors had found only 157 persons subject to the tax and had collected only $2900. In the first year under the new law State Auditor Howard succeeded in collecting more than $200,000, believing he had not yet found more than half of what was due, he recently went to Washington to get the names of 2300 Oklahomans who are understood to have paid income tax to the Federal Government. Access to the records there was denied him, and he took the matter to Senator Gore and the Oklahoma congressmen, with the result that they are seeking to change the federal law so as to provide for the interchange of such information between the federal tax authorities and those of states having income tax laws.

TENNESSEE: This state has what is called an "ouster" law. The Chattanooga Times describes it as "a law to enforce a law that was passed to enforce another law for which the people apparently had no respect." Under this three-ply law Squire Barrett was ousted from the Bradley County Court, whereupon he went to the people of his district upon the proposition that the ouster law was an instrument of persecution of the "ins" by the "outs," and not wanted on the statute books; and the people stood by him. Now the whole state is taking sides, and it looks as if nothing short of a referendum could settle the matter.

WASHINGTON: By a vote of six judges to three, the Supreme Court of this state has decided that the $1,500,000 capitol bond issue is unconstitutional. This issue was authorized by the Legislature last year for the purpose of paying back into the general fund moneys borrowed by the Capitol Commission and of completing the Temple of Justice. The Legislature guaranteed interest payments on the bonds by providing a tax levy to tide over until the sale of capitol grant lands would cover this expense and repay to the general fund the amounts paid by direct taxation on the capitol bonds. The court holds this to be contrary to the constitutional provision which restricts the imposition of taxes without authorization by vote of the people.

WEST VIRGINIA: For two years Philip J. Walsh, general superintendent of road construction in Kanawha County, has been in charge of convicts from the state to that county at 75 cents for a day of nine hours of road work. The state feeds, clothes and guards the prisoners, who work entirely under the honor system and are treated as paid laborers, the guards being unarmed. In a recent report, Mr. Walsh said: "I would rather work with a crew of prisoners from the state penitentiary, because I can secure better results than with any gang of free labor I ever saw. This is the way to build your highways. It gives the poor unfortunates a leg up in life; it's a man-to-a-man's job, and it gives you a dollar's worth of road for every dollar spent."

WISCONSIN: In 1893 the state Legislature authorized Milwaukee to establish a municipal lighting plant. Five times since then the people of the city have voted strongly in favor of issuing bonds for this purpose, the amount to be spent increasing each time. Four times nothing came of it; At the recent city election they voted three to one for a bond issue of $750,000 to establish a distribution system, the city to provide the entire equipment, but to buy current from a private company. Now the Council has passed the necessary ordinance and the new mayor has signed it. But it has cost the people five elections and twenty-three years of waiting.

WYOMING: An article on "Resources of the Arid Land States," by I. S. Bartlett, of Cheyenne, was recently read into the United States Senate journal by Senator Shafroth of Colorado as an argument in favor of the proposed 640-acre homestead law. Among other things, it contained a statement of the value of just a few of Wyoming's undeveloped resources as tabulated from United States geological surveys, state geological reports and official investigations. Included in a total of $61,305,000,000 are such items as 424,000,000,000 tons of coal at ten cents a ton, and 20,000,000 acres of oil deposits at $500 an acre. Yet Wyoming has a population of only 150,000, the its area equals that of Maine, New Hampshire, Massachusetts, Rhode Island, Connecticut and Pennsylvania combined, where there are 15,000,000 inhabitants.

328

HUGHES—WHY?

BY JACOB GOULD SCHURMAN

The man whom we have asked to interpret the Hughes "boom" for us is a staunch Republican. As President of Cornell University he was associated with Justice Hughes when he taught there, and he has seen service in the diplomatic corps and as a Philippine commissioner.—THE EDITOR.

PERHAPS the most remarkable thing in the life of Charles E. Hughes is that in whatever position he has been placed he fixed his eyes upon the need of the situation, used all his energy and devotion in meeting it, and accomplished his task with extraordinary success.

There was no better student at Madison or Brown, no better young lawyer at the New York bar, no better professor at Cornell University, no better public investigator in all the body of insurance experts. When he was summoned to the office of Chief Executive of the State of New York he gave us an administration and a leadership which ranked him among the greatest Governors we have had in the entire history of the state. And, tho a layman may hesitate to pronounce any verdict upon judges, I am confident that public opinion does not rate Mr. Justice Hughes second to any judge who to-day sits upon the bench of the Supreme Court of the United States.

But whether sitting in the high and sheltered places of justice, or administering in the full blaze of party criticism the multifarious and weighty affairs of the Empire State, or engaged in the private practise of a stirring and keenly competitive profession, the thing that arouses wonder and admiration is the adequacy, the ample and apparently easy adequacy, which Mr. Hughes brings to every task. His whole public life has been a succession of great and surprizing achievements. If any man is equal to the Presidency he is, for he has been equal to every other great office. And there is no better training school for the Presidency, and no better testing-place for a Presidential candidate, than the Governorship of the State of New York.

WHAT a leader Hughes would make for the Republican party! His personality, character and public record would reinspire and intensify popular confidence in "the party of moral ideals." For, strong and capacious as his intellect is, it was not primarily by his intellect, but by his honesty, sincerity, courage, independence, inflexible principle, and resolute devotion to the public good, uncolored by the shadow of personal or party advantage, that he rallied to his standard the voters of New York State and established thruout the Republic the reputation of a great statesman and high-minded party leader.

And what a campaigner he would

be! In the presidential campaign of 1908 he so far surpassed every other Republican speaker that he had scarcely a second. His great speech at Youngstown was like a broadside from a whole battalion of orators. His luminous exposition and fiery eloquence pierced even to the dividing asunder of the joints and narrow of all the progeny of Mr. Bryan's rhetoric. And not only Mr. Bryan, but President Wilson, at once the most finished and the most effective speaker of the Democratic party, will be in the campaign of 1916. It will be no easy thing to overcome him, for the President besides being an able man and a trained orator, is also a shrewd politician with a thoro knowledge of recent politics. What other Republican is so well qualified to be our protagonist in this combat as Charles E. Hughes?

The instinct of the people, as is always the case, is wiser than the plans and devices of the political managers. The people have made up their minds that Hughes is to be the next President of the United States. They are demanding in no uncertain tones his nomination by the Republican Convention in Chicago. A man must be blind indeed who does not recognize the strength, the pervasiveness, the insistency, and the constant growth of the "Hughes sentiment." And the amazing thing is that it is absolutely and entirely spontaneous. There are no Hughes agents, no Hughes organization, no Hughes money, no Hughes press—nothing, as Colonel Harvey has so well said, *but the people.* The time, however, has arrived in America when the people have their way, and no political Canute dare attempt in Chicago to sweep back this irresistible tide of popular Hughes sentiment.

Who else is there that the Republicans can assuredly elect? With any other nominee the prospect of election is at best a hope; with Hughes it is a certainty. President Wilson is going to be a much stronger candidate than our Republican managers and spokesmen imagine. We need an opposing candidate who can unite the

Republican party, inspire it with heroic leadership, and evoke all its latent strength. Hughes, who was on the Supreme Court bench two years before the party disruption of 1912, is the man capable of accomplishing these results. Conservatives and progressives, organization men and independents, will alike support the man they came to know, admire, and trust while Governor of New York. It would almost seem as if, in the interval, he had been specially set apart and preserved for the present emergency in the life of our nation and of mankind.

But may not some "dark horse" emerge at Chicago? The day of "dark horses" is gone. A "dark horse" presupposes a party organization capable of delivering the party vote. But the people are today too independent to suffer this delivery of their votes.

THE strength of Hughes is the people's desire for him. He himself has not been and will not be a candidate for the presidential nomination. There is, in my opinion, only one way in which the Republican party can secure him. If they want him they must draft him for the service. Such a call he could not decline. Read the words he addrest to the New York Republican Club on October 18, 1907:

"To me public office means a burden of responsibility—a burden of incessant toil at times almost intolerable—which under honorable conditions and at the command of the people it may be a duty and even a pleasure to assume, but is far from being an object of ambition."

Mr. Justice Hughes is today stopped from saying a word on politics. But fortunately his acts and speeches while Governor of New York give ample information as to his attitude, not only on state, but on national policies.

President Wilson has been successful in establishing himself as leader of his party, but the price paid has been especially marked in the impairment of the nation's administrative service. Now Governor Hughes held that "the administration of office is at least three-fourths of political life," and he devoted his supreme energies to the maintenance of the highest administrative standards. He held that a perfect administration of every office would dispel almost all the problems which now perplex us.

This conception determined the kind of men he appointed to office.

329

CONNECTICUT: According to the latest report of State Labor Commissioner Hyde, the employment agencies conducted by his department in Hartford, New Haven, Bridgeport, Waterbury and Norwich procured employment for 1623 persons out of 2750 who applied to them in March of this year. Of these applicants 1956 were men and 794 women. About fifty-five per cent of the men and seventy per cent of the women were placed in employment. On the other hand, there were more than 2000 applications for help in the month, and about eighty per cent of these demands were supplied. This was the largest volume of business ever done in a month by these agencies.

DISTRICT OF COLUMBIA: Congress finally has passed the bill, so many times rejected, incorporating the American Academy of Arts and Letters in the District of Columbia. Among the incorporators are some of the best known authors and artists of the East and one, James Whitcomb Riley, from west of the Alleghenies. The bill limits the membership of the academy to fifty. The stated purpose of incorporation is "to enable the organization to receive and expend any fund which, for the purpose of advancing literature and the arts, may be entrusted to its good faith, its experience and its knowledge of the best use to which such fund may be put." As vacancies occur members of the academy are to be chosen from the membership of the National Institute of Arts and Letters, by which the academy was established in 1905.

ILLINOIS: The formal opening of Chicago's municipal pier will be celebrated on Memorial Day. It is said to be the largest and best equipped city pier in the world. Located at the mouth of the Chicago River, it extends 3000 feet into the lake and is 300 feet wide, with large recreation facilities at its end. It is intended to relieve congestion in the river by taking care of most of the freight and passenger service outside. It has cost about $4,600,000, but engineers say its rentals and concessions will cover the cost of maintenance of all its buildings, amortize the original cost and pay four per cent on the investment.

KENTUCKY: The passage of the so-called Hutcheraft bill by the Legislature is said to have been followed by the "dryest" Sundays Kentucky has ever known. One provision of this bill requires the revocation of a liquor license as soon as a violation of the law has been proved, and a year must elapse before another license can be issued to the same person or to any other person at the same location. The Sunday closing law has long been a dead letter in most of the cities and towns of the state, but it is said that this new provision has changed the situation. In Louisville on the Sunday following the passage of the law not a drunken man was seen and not an arrest was made for any cause at the central police station between 7 a. m. and 11 p. m.

MARYLAND: A new law, said to be unlike any other ever enacted by a legislature in this country, has been signed by Governor Harrington and is to go into effect on June 1. It is one of the results of that condition exposed last year by the Goldsborough Vice Commission, which learned that thousands of new-born infants had been disposed of to private institutions, in which a large percentage of them had died. The new law provides that no illegitimate child under six months of age may be separated from its mother to be placed in any foster home, except under duly attested necessity for the physical good of the mother or child. Opponents of the measure feel it will lead to many cases of deliberate infanticide.

MICHIGAN: The tuberculosis survey of this state begun last October by the Michigan Board of Health, has proved surprisingly popular, and the board has found it impossible to keep up with the demands made by people who wish to be examined. In the six months thirteen of the eighty-three counties in the state have been visited and more than 5000 persons examined, 2242 cases with either positive evidences or suspicious indications of tuberculosis were found. Nurses visit the homes of these persons and give instructions for the improvement of living conditions and information on how to prevent contagion.

MISSOURI: The United States Supreme Court has dismissed the appeal of the St. Louis street railway lines from the decision of the Missouri courts, which upheld the ordinance by which the City of St. Louis places a tax of one mill on each street railway passenger. As a result of this dismissal the city will receive about $3,000,000 in back taxes.

MONTANA: Yellowstone County, of which Billings is the chief city, has voted $175,000 for the construction of the first extensive permanent roads in the state to be built in this way. These roads are to extend for a distance of thirty-five miles along the line of the Yellowstone trail, a popular automobile route for tourists to the Yellowstone and Glacier national parks. The Billings Chamber of Commerce prepared the plans and conducted the campaign for the bond issue.

NEBRASKA: After long negotiation the Missouri River navigation committee of the Omaha Commercial Club has secured a steamboat of 150 tons cargo capacity to run regularly between Omaha and Kansas City. This last link in the chain makes possible river traffic from St. Louis to Sioux City. A line is already established between St. Louis and Kansas City and another between Omaha and Sioux City.

NEVADA: The discovery of rich deposits of tungsten in Humboldt County has created as much excitement throughout the state as that incidental to the free-gold strike in the Willard district a few years ago. The hills, valleys and gulches in the vicinity of Lovelock are alive with prospectors, and the towns are doing a booming business in outfits and supplies. As a result of the furious search many deposits have been found, and money and properties are changing hands in rapid succession. One mill is said to be turning out more than $100,000 worth of concentrates a month.

NEW HAMPSHIRE: Among the many new fields into which the New Hampshire state college at Durham has sent its influence and assistance is that of community development. The college has just called its first community conference, the announced purpose being "to offer men and women interested in the social problems of community life in this state an opportunity to consider and discuss common problems and opportunities." An extensive three-day program has been arranged, with addresses by well-known men and women on a wide range of pertinent subjects.

OKLAHOMA: Last year, under a new law, the collection of the Oklahoma income tax was taken out of the hands of the county assessors and turned over to the State Auditor. Under the old law the assessors had found only 157 persons subject to the tax and had collected only $2990. In the first year under the new law State Auditor Howard succeeded in collecting more than $200,000. Believing he had not yet found more than half of what was due, he recently went to Washington to get the names of 2300 Oklahomans who are understood to have paid income tax to the Federal Government. Access to the records there was denied him, and he took the matter to Senator Gore and the Oklahoma congressmen, with the result that they are seeking to change the federal law so as to provide for the interchange of such information between the federal tax authorities and those of states having income tax laws.

TENNESSEE: This state has what is called an "ouster" law. The Chattanooga Times describes it as "a law to enforce a law that was passed to enforce another law for which the people apparently had no respect." Under this three-ply law Squire Barrett was ousted from the Bradley County Court, whereupon he went to the people of his district upon the proposition that the ouster law was an instrument of persecution of the "ins" by the "outs," and not wanted on the statute books; and the people stood by him. Now the whole state is taking sides, and it looks as if nothing short of a referendum could settle the matter.

WASHINGTON: By a vote of six judges to three, the Supreme Court of this state has decided that the $1,500,000 capitol bond issue is unconstitutional. This issue was authorized by the Legislature last year for the purpose of paying back into the general fund moneys borrowed by the Capitol Commission and of completing the Temple of Justice. The Legislature guaranteed interest payments on the bonds by providing a tax levy to tide over until the sale of capitol grant lands would cover this expense and repay to the general fund the amounts paid by direct taxation on the capitol bonds. The court holds this to be contrary to the constitutional provision which restricts the imposition of taxes without authorization by vote of the people.

WEST VIRGINIA: For two years Philip J. Walsh, general superintendent of road construction in Kanawha County, has been in charge of camps of prisoners furnished by the state to that county at 75 cents for a day of nine hours of road work. The state feeds, clothes and guards the prisoners, who work entirely under the honor system and are treated as paid laborers, the guards being unarmed. In a recent report, Mr. Walsh said: "I would rather work with a crew of prisoners from the state penitentiary, because I can secure better results than with any gang of free labor I ever saw. This is the way to build your highways. It gives the poor unfortunates a leg up in life; it's a man-to-a-man's job, and it gives you a dollar's worth of road for every dollar spent."

WISCONSIN: In 1893 the state Legislature authorized Milwaukee to establish a municipal lighting plant. Five times since then the people of the city have voted strongly in favor of issuing bonds for this purpose, the amount to be spent increasing each time. Four times nothing came of it. At the recent city election they voted three to one for a bond issue of $750,000 to establish a distribution system, the city to provide the entire equipment, but to buy current from a private company. Now the Council has passed the necessary ordinance and the new mayor has signed it. But it has cost the people five elections and twenty-three years of waiting.

WYOMING: An article on "Resources of the Arid Land States," by I. S. Bartlett, of Cheyenne, was recently read into the United States Senate journal by Senator Shafroth of Colorado as an argument in favor of the proposed 640-acre homestead law. Among other things, it contained a statement of the value of just a few of Wyoming's undeveloped resources as tabulated from United States geological surveys, state geological reports and official investigations. Included in a total of $61,305,-000,000 are such items as 424,-000,000,000 tons of coal at ten cents a ton, and 20,000,000 acres of oil deposits at $500 an acre. Yet Wyoming has a population of only 150,000, tho its area equals that of Maine, New Hampshire, Massachusetts, Rhode Island, Connecticut and Pennsylvania combined, where there are 15,000,000 inhabitants.

HUGHES—WHY?

BY JACOB GOULD SCHURMAN

The man whom we have asked to interpret the Hughes "boom" for us is a staunch Republican. As President of Cornell University he was associated with Justice Hughes when he taught there, and he has seen service in the diplomatic corps and as a Philippine commissioner.—THE EDITOR.

PERHAPS the most remarkable thing in the life of Charles E. Hughes is that in whatever position he has been placed he fixed his eyes upon the need of the situation, used all his energy and devotion in meeting it, and accomplished his task with extraordinary success.

There was no better student at Madison or Brown, no better young lawyer at the New York bar, no better professor at Cornell University, no better public investigator in all the body of insurance experts. When he was summoned to the office of Chief Executive of the State of New York he gave us an administration and a leadership which ranked him among the greatest Governors we have had in the entire history of the state. And, for a layman may hesitate to pronounce any verdict upon judges, I am confident that public opinion does not rate Mr. Justice Hughes second to any judge who today sits upon the bench of the Supreme Court of the United States.

But whether sitting in the high and sheltered places of justice, or administering in the full blaze of party criticism the multifarious and weighty affairs of the Empire State, or engaged in the private practise of a stirring and keenly competitive profession, the thing that arouses wonder and admiration is the adequacy, the ample and apparently easy adequacy, which Mr. Hughes brings to every task. His whole public life has been a succession of great and surprising achievements. If any man is equal to the Presidency he is, for he has been equal to every other great office. And there is no better training school for the Presidency, and no better testing-place for a Presidential candidate, than the Governorship of the State of New York.

WHAT a leader Hughes would make for the Republican party! His personality, character and public record would reinspire and intensify popular confidence in "the party of moral ideals." For, strong and capacious as his intellect is, it was not primarily by his intellect, but by his honesty, sincerity, courage, independence, inflexible principle, and resolute devotion to the public good, uncolored by the shadow of personal or party advantage, that he rallied to his standard the voters of New York State and established thruout the Republic the reputation of a great statesman and high-minded party leader.

And what a campaigner he would

be! In the presidential campaign of 1908 he so far surpassed every other Republican speaker that he had scarcely a second. His great speech at Youngstown was like a broadside from a whole battalion of orators. His luminous exposition and fiery eloquence pierced even to the dividing asunder of the joints and marrow of all the progeny of Mr. Bryan's rhetoric. And not only Mr. Bryan, but President Wilson, at once the most finished and the most effective speaker of the Democratic party, will be in the campaign of 1916. It will be no easy thing to overcome him, for the President besides being an able man and a trained orator, is also a shrewd politician with a thoro knowledge of recent politics. What other Republican is so well qualified to be our protagonist in this combat as Charles E. Hughes?

The instinct of the people, as is always the case, is wiser than the plans and devices of the political managers. The people have made up their minds that Hughes is to be the next President of the United States. They are demanding in no uncertain tones his nomination by the Republican Convention in Chicago. A man must be blind indeed who does not recognize the strength, the pervasiveness, the insistency, and the constant growth of the "Hughes sentiment." And the amazing thing is that it is absolutely and entirely spontaneous. There are no Hughes agents, no Hughes organization, no Hughes money, no Hughes press—nothing, as Colonel Harvey has so well said, *but the people.* The time, however, has arrived in America when the people have their way, and no political Canute dare attempt in Chicago to sweep back this irresistible tide of popular Hughes sentiment.

Who else is there that the Republicans can assuredly elect? With any other nominee the prospect of election is at best a hope; with Hughes it is a certainty. President Wilson is going to be a much stronger candidate than our Republican managers and spokesmen imagine. We need an opposing candidate who can unite the

Republican party, inspire it with heroic leadership, and evoke all its latent strength. Hughes, who was on the Supreme Court bench two years before the party disruption of 1912, is the man capable of accomplishing these results. Conservatives and progressives, organization men and independents, will alike support the man they came to know, admire, and trust while Governor of New York. It would almost seem as if, in the interval, he had been specially set apart and preserved for the present emergency in the life of our nation and of mankind.

But may not some "dark horse" emerge at Chicago? The day of "dark horses" is gone. A "dark horse" presupposes a party organization capable of delivering the party vote. But the people are today too independent to suffer this delivery of their votes.

THE strength of Hughes is the people's desire for him. He himself has not been and will not be a candidate for the presidential nomination. There is, in my opinion, only one way in which the Republican party can secure him. If they want him they must draft him for the service. Such a call he could not decline. Read the words he addrest to the New York Republican Club on October 18, 1907:

"To me public office means a burden of responsibility—a burden of incessant toil at times almost intolerable—which under honorable conditions and at the command of the people it may be a duty and even a pleasure to assume, but is far from being an object of ambition."

Mr. Justice Hughes is today stopped from saying a word on politics. But fortunately his acts and speeches while Governor of New York give ample information as to his attitude, not only on state, but on national policies.

President Wilson has been successful in establishing himself as leader of his party, but the price paid has been especially marked in the impairment of the nation's administrative service. Now Governor Hughes held that "the administration of office is at least three-fourths of political life," and he devoted his supreme energies to the maintenance of the highest administrative standards. He held that a perfect administration of every office would dispel almost all the problems which now perplex us.

This conception determined the kind of men he appointed to office.

329

Appreciating political activity and party service, he would nevertheless not use public office to reward party workers. An honorable political experience might indeed be a supplementary advantage in an official, but what Governor Hughes demanded primarily and fundamentally was "men adapted to the office with the character and the capacity which will enable them to discharge its duties."

THE issue of the hour is preparedness. But as far back as January 31, 1908, Governor Hughes, while asserting that American ideals were those of peace and opposition to aggression, which he regarded as "our surest protection," made also this memorable declaration:

"It is entirely consistent with these aims, and it is our duty, to make adequate provision for our defense and to maintain the efficiency of our Army and Navy. And this I favor."

In the same speech Governor Hughes declared that he believed in a protective tariff. It was essential, he said, to the maintenance of the American scale of wages and the American standard of living. But he was opposed to a tariff which authorized exorbitant rates or special privileges, and he recommended the appointment of an expert tariff commission to ascertain just and reasonable rates in harmony with the protective principle.

As to the Philippines Governor Hughes held that "in the meantime" we must omit no effort to prepare the Filipinos for self-government. And looking to the future, he added:

"When they are able to govern themselves and are in a position to maintain their independence, the American people will not deny them the boon which we ourselves have so highly prized."

Governor Hughes's attitude toward property on the one hand and to special privilege on the other was finely illustrated in his campaign for the regulation of our public service corporations which finally issued in the enactment of a memorable statute establishing the New York Public Service Commissions. He insisted that the Legislature should no longer harry the railways with adverse legislation, but leave it to those Commissions after patient investigation of the facts to do justice in each individual case.

Governor Hughes was always deeply interested in every effort to improve the conditions of the wage-earners. He favored employers' liability legislation and approved the laws with regard to safety appliances and hours of labor in railroad service; and he laid down the principle that

"wherever the Government comes into direct relation to labor, proper conditions with regard to hours, wages, safety, and compensation for accidents should be provided."

The extension of the functions of the National Government in consequence of the operation of powerful forces in the world of business which ignore state lines was as obvious to Governor Hughes as to other thoughtful men who had given attention to the matter. The recognition of this potent factor in the economic life of the nation will involve legislation in the future. And when the world-war is over, and international relations readjusted, perhaps there will be no graver or more difficult question to come before the American people. Governor Hughes summarized his views on the subject in 1908 in the following sentences:

"It cannot be regarded as a policy of unwise centralization that, wherever there is a serious evil demanding governmental correction which afflicts interstate commerce and hence is beyond the control of the states, the power of Congress should unhesitatingly be exercised."

At any rate the questions of today will not be the questions of the next four years, which, of course, no one can foretell. The American people are called on this year to elect to the Presidency a man brave, wise, honest, independent, and strong enough to grapple successfully with whatever issues may arise. For this office both his own public record and the general voice of the people have designated Charles Evans Hughes.

Ithaca, New York

WILL THE MOUNTAIN COME TO MAHOMET?

IN THE TRENCHES

FROM THE GERMAN OF BRUNO FRANK

TRANSLATED BY MUNROE SMITH

Dort, wo der Tod am nächsten droht,
  Dort ist nicht Hohn und ist nicht Hass,
  Bereitschaft herrscht ohn' Unterlass
Und Schweigen vor dem Tod.

Ein Schicksal tötet, nicht der Feind;
  Und einmal muss die Sense ruhn;
  Und die sich schuldlos Arges tun,
Sie werden doch vereint.

Where men stand closest to their fate,
  Prepared for every sudden chance,
  And fronting death with level glance,
There is no scorn nor hate.

Not hate but destiny demands
  The death-toll; and the men who slay
  Each other blamelessly today
Tomorrow may clasp hands.

KILLING THE WOUNDED

BY WILLIAM J. ROBINSON

I WAS with the troops who were acting as supports to the Canadians in a certain engagement in the spring of 1915. The French Algerian troops who were holding a part of the line on our left were surprised by a heavy gas attack, and with their eyes streaming, their lungs torn by the knife-like stabs which accompanied every effort to breathe, they retired. They left the British flank unprotected, for the Germans advanced two miles before they stopped. The men on the staff, about 1500 in all, were rushed up to try and hold the Germans until more troops arrived.

The troops sent for were the Canadians, who were just out from England, never having been in action as yet. Dawn was beginning to break when they arrived. Their advance was not preceded by a bombardment. They did not even stop for breath. They fixed bayonets and went straight over us at the Germans.

The suddenness of their advance surprised the Germans, and they gave ground with very little resistance at first. Trench after trench the Canadians took, and we acted as their supports all the way. It was not until we had advanced nearly half a mile that the enemy got their machine guns into action. After that it was harder, and our losses were heavy. The men were carried away with their enthusiasm, however, and nothing could stop them. Trench after trench, trench after trench they took. If there were any Germans left in them they died quickly, for Canada was showing her fighting spirit, and it was a case of hack, stab, shoot, club, anyway to get the "Huns" back where they belonged.

When we had regained about half the ground the Algerians had lost,

Mr. Robinson is a young Bostonian who enlisted in the British army in August, 1914, for a term of one year, or until the war should end. He was in active service in Belgium and in France, was made a Sergeant-Major and voluntarily resumed the rank of private because the unpromoted Tommies under him "made things so mighty unpleasant." He was wounded once. After "Fourteen Months at the Front," graphically described in his book of that title, he came back to America convinced that "the worst imaginings of war are totally inadequate before its reality." His story is neither theory nor generalities, but the straightforward record of actual experience. — THE EDITOR.

the enemy brought up reinforcements and made a final attempt to break up our counter attack. Swarms of them appeared as if from the bowels of the earth, and they rolled upon us like a great tidal wave. They forced us back and back until it looked as tho we would soon be back where we started from. But the cost to the Germans was tremendous.

Soon our boys rallied and again we went at them. Their fearful losses seemed to have taken the heart out of them, for this time it was even easier than before. On and on we went, and soon some of our men were cheering, because we had recovered the four pieces of artillery which had been lost.

Bear in mind the fact that the Germans had driven us back after our counter attack was well started. When we retreated we left many killed and wounded on the ground we gave over. When we advanced again we found the wounded we had left had all been killed. They had either been finished with the bayonet or had

had their skulls crushed in by a blow from the butt of a rifle. This, of course, drove the men mad, but there was yet worse to be found.

A sergeant was found crucified to a barn door.

There were several bayonets thru his body, and when he was found by his comrades *he was still alive!* Picture, if you can, the horror of it!

The men had been under a terrible strain anyway. It was their first time in action, and is it any wonder that this ghastly deed should turn them into raving savages? Under circumstances such as these are there any of the pacifists who can truthfully say that they should have "turned the other cheek"? God forbid!

I saw this poor man about two hours after he had been taken down. He was dead then, but I saw the holes in his body; the jagged blood-soaked rents in his uniform, and the sight of it drove me as near mad as anything ever has done.

If there was a German left alive on the ground recovered from the "Huns" it was truly because the devil cares for his own.

There is, to my knowledge, no official report of the incident to corroborate what I say, but any soldier who was in the vicinity of Ypres during the spring of 1915 will vouch for the truth of this statement.

This was the beginning of the awful practise, rumors of which have even reached the neutral countries. It has been, and still is carried on even to the present time, and so bad has it become that I am safe in saying that a very large per cent of the soldiers of the allied armies shoot themselves rather than be taken prisoner when wounded. Reports have been circulated that neither side is taking prisoners, and that they are killing wounded rather than make them prisoners. That the Allies have ceased to take prisoners is absolutely untrue. Prisoners are taken just as they were before the engagement I am describing.

Many say, "Oh, well, this might have happened once, but it probably stopped there." The pity of it is that it did not stop there. It has gone on and on, and will go on to the end of the war. I will not cite cases I have heard about. I am only telling what I have seen.

After a sharp engagement near Hooge last summer I saw it happen again. It was just coming daylight, and the affair lasted only a short time. When it was over there were many dead and wounded left on the ground which separated our trenches from the Germans. As the sun came up and it commenced to get hot many of the poor fellows tried to drag themselves back to our trenches.

The German sharpshooters made it their business to shoot every man who moved, and many a poor devil, who would have made our trenches and been cared for, was foully murdered because he tried to save himself for his loved ones at home.

Would it be natural for men to stand all day and see this happen to their comrades without retaliating? Our fellows did the same thing, *and they did right!* A few of our boys lived thru the broiling hot day with sun pouring down on them, heaps of dead around them, the stink of decaying flesh in their nostrils and their throats parched with thirst. Yes, a few of them lived, but, oh, it was a pitiful few!

In the afternoon I saw one poor fellow who had been worming his way in inch by inch. He probably went mad, for he suddenly staggered to his feet, faced the German trenches and started shrieking curses at the top of his voice. The words died in his throat and he went down riddled with bullets. During the day many of them managed to get a weapon in their hands and did the deed themselves.

I think of all this when people tell me about the "good feeling" that exists between the English "Tommy" and the German "Fritz." I saw another incident later which will show how "good" the feeling is. A party of prisoners was being escorted to the rear by a squad of men who had

watched their own wounded die in the way I have described. A sergeant, in charge of the party, swung along in front, a pipe in his mouth and his rifle slung on his shoulder. He was a very short man and was probably sensitive about it. Directly behind him was a great big hulking German about six feet four. As the party passed us we smiled at the contrast. The German saw us, and he grinned and made a gesture as much as to say: "Look at the little sawed-off!" I don't know how this sergeant saw him, but he rapped out the order: "Party, halt!" He calmly put his pipe in his pocket, clubbed his rifle, and smashed in the head of the big German before he knew what was happening. He looked at the body and snarled: "Now laugh, you ———!" Then he lit his pipe and the party moved on. That is typical of the "good feeling."

Who began the practise of doing away with the wounded? *The Germans began it.* I could go on and on and tell many more such cases, but it is unnecessary. I have told what I have *seen*. This is war as it is today.

New York City

RELATIVES AND FRIENDS

IN THE FAMILY

UNCLE HENRY married my father's cousin. They lived alone in a great house which had the most dismal library in the whole wide world. It was all black walnut, lined with books with dull leather backs and uninteresting titles. Over the shelves, against a border of black velvet, were rows of marble statuettes that came from Europe.

There were two invalid chairs with big wheels, altho neither Uncle Henry nor Aunt Ella were really invalids, and in one corner of the room was a Swiss music box that played lugubrious airs, and in another a basket where a very old mangy-haired dog lay dying. Finally he did die, and then Uncle Henry died, and then Aunt Ella, and all the property had to be divided.

Aunt Ella had always worn a large black cameo likeness of Uncle Henry, which had been cut in Rome. It was set as a brooch and was surrounded with rather large sized diamonds, and was an ob-

ject of most sacred veneration to us all. We felt that it should go—as the greatest treasure of all—to the niece with Uncle Henry's name. Can you imagine our perplexity when she had it made into a belt buckle?

TARTY

SHE is eighty-five years old, a little dumpy, apple-cheeked person, wrinkled and double chinned. Her thin hair held tight in one small knot

on the top of her head is gray only on the temples. She is Irish and of good blood. When a girl of sixteen she inherited a fortune of fifty thousand pounds—an enormous sum in that land and in those times. She had danced with King Edward when he was the Prince of Wales, in those golden days, and this was the only reference she ever made to that part of her life. She had never married, and when still young she had adopted a little cousin, a baby boy. After he grew up he squandered her last penny and left her alone in London without even a good-bye. From that time she had lived entirely on the bounty of the friends she had made by her indomitable courage, her intense interest in life and her cheerful spirit. Today she awaits death as bravely as she has lived. "Don't blame Willie," she says. "If he had left me enough to live on, I should never have really known the world, how good it is, how kind. I've had a very happy life and I've nothing to regret."

The Independent-Harper's Weekly
NEWS-PICTORIAL

Adolph Treidler's prize poster for Newark's festival.

Newark, New Jersey, has come out from under New York's shadow to celebrate her 250th anniversary with five months of festivities under the direction of a citizen Committee of One Hundred. This is Henry W. Mack, "executive adviser," ready to present "Paints and Colors" in the historical pageant on May 30 and 31.

A musician from the Germanic episode in "Caliban, by the Yellow Sands." Dramatic art in medieval Germany, France, Spain, and Italy is presented in symbolic ritual in one of the interludes of Percy Mackaye's Shakespeare Memorial Masque, which is being given as a community festival in the Stadium of New York City College.

CALIBAN

The "damned witch Sycorax," as Robert E. Jones sees her.

As wicked dew as e'er my mother brush'd with raven's feather from unwholesome fen drop on you!

An apprentice to the devil, on duty in the Shakespeare Masque.

killing wounded rather than make them prisoners. That the Allies have ceased to take prisoners is absolutely untrue. Prisoners are taken just as they were before the engagement I am describing.

Many say, "Oh, well, this might have happened once, but it probably stopped there." The pity of it is that it did not stop there. It has gone on and on, and will go on to the end of the war. I will not cite cases I have heard about. I am only telling what I have *seen*.

After a sharp engagement near Hooge last summer I saw it happen again. It was just coming daylight, and the affair lasted only a short time. When it was over there were many dead and wounded left on the ground which separated our trenches from the Germans. As the sun came up and it commenced to get hot many of the poor fellows tried to drag themselves back to our trenches.

The German sharpshooters made it their business to shoot every man who moved, and many a poor devil, who would have made our trenches and been cared for, was foully murdered because he tried to save himself for his loved ones at home.

Would it be natural for men to stand all day and see this happen to their comrades without retaliating? Our fellows did the same thing, *and they did right!* A few of our boys lived thru the broiling hot day with sun pouring down on them, heaps of dead around them, the stink of decaying flesh in their nostrils and their throats parched with thirst. Yes, a few of them lived, but, oh, it was a pitiful few!

In the afternoon I saw one poor fellow who had been worming his way in inch by inch. He probably went mad, for he suddenly staggered to his feet, faced the German trenches and started shrieking curses at the top of his voice. The words died in his throat and he went down riddled with bullets. During the day many of them managed to get a weapon in their hands and did the deed themselves.

I think of all this when people tell me about the "good feeling" that exists between the English "Tommy" and the German "Fritz." I saw another incident later which will show how "good" the feeling is. A party of prisoners was being escorted to the rear by a squad of men who had

watched their own wounded die in the way I have described. A sergeant, in charge of the party, swung along in front, a pipe in his mouth and his rifle slung on his shoulder. He was a very short man and was probably sensitive about it. Directly behind him was a great big hulking German about six feet four. As the party passed us we smiled at the contrast. The German saw us, and he grinned and made a gesture as much as to say: "Look at the little sawed-off!" I don't know how this sergeant saw him, but he rapped out the order: "Party, halt!" He calmly put his pipe in his pocket, clubbed his rifle, and smashed in the head of the big German before he knew what was happening. He looked at the body and snarled: "Now laugh, you ———!" Then he lit his pipe and the party moved on. That is typical of the "good feeling."

Who began the practise of doing away with the wounded? *The Germans began it.* I could go on and on and tell many more such cases, but it is unnecessary. I have told what I have *seen*. This is war as it is today.

New York City

RELATIVES AND FRIENDS

IN THE FAMILY

UNCLE HENRY married my father's cousin. They lived alone in a great house which had the most dismal library in the whole wide world. It was all black walnut, lined with books with dull leather backs and uninteresting titles. Over the shelves, against a border of black velvet, were rows of marble statuettes that came from Europe.

There were two invalid chairs with big wheels, altho neither Uncle Henry nor Aunt Ella were really invalids, and in one corner of the room was a Swiss music box that played lugubrious airs, and in another a basket where a very old mangy-haired dog lay dying. Finally he did die, and then Uncle Henry died, and then Aunt Ella, and all the property had to be divided.

Aunt Ella had always worn a large black cameo likeness of Uncle Henry, which had been cut in Rome. It was set as a brooch and was surrounded with rather large sized diamonds, and was an ob-

ject of most sacred veneration to us all. We felt that it should go—as the greatest treasure of all—to the niece with Uncle Henry's name. Can you imagine our feelings when she had it made into a belt buckle?

TARTY

SHE is eighty-five years old, a little dumpy, apple-cheeked person, wrinkled and double chinned. Her thin hair held tight in one small knot

WHAT HAVE YOU FOR THE NEWS-PICTORIAL?

The Independent-Harper's Weekly News-Pictorial is two weeks old this week. Before it is three weeks old we shall have made a selection from the first samples of The Independent Readers' Picture Service, Unlimited—for which every reader is invited to become a field agent at once. For the pictures which we accept from this new agency we pay Two Dollars each, except for the one which we consider the best of the lot in any single issue, for which we pay Ten Dollars. Remember that a news-picture is something new, something picturesque, and something that may be expected to interest readers everywhere. The rules of the News-Pictorial Contest are simple: 1. Use black-and-white glossy paper. 2. Put your name, address and a full caption on the back of every print. 3. Send stamps if you want the prints back.

on the top of her head is gray only on the temples. She is Irish and of good blood. When a girl of sixteen she inherited a fortune of fifty thousand pounds—an enormous sum in that land and in those times. She had danced with King Edward when he was the Prince of Wales, in those golden days, and this was the only reference she ever made to that part of her life. She had never married, and when still young she had adopted a rising cousin, a baby boy. After he grew up he squandered her last penny and left her alone in London without even a good-bye. From that time she had lived entirely on the bounty of the friends she had made by her indomitable courage, her intense interest in life and her cheerful spirit. Today she awaits death as bravely as she has lived. "Don't blame Willie," she says. "If he had left me enough to live on, I should never have really known the world, how good it is, how kind. I've had a very happy life and I've nothing to regret."

The Independent~Harper's Weekly
NEWS~PICTORIAL

Adolph Treidler's prize poster for Newark's festival.

Newark, New Jersey, has come out from under New York's shadow to celebrate her 250th anniversary with five months of festivities under the direction of a citizen Committee of One Hundred. This is Henry W. Mack, "executive adviser," ready to present "Paints and Colors" in the historical pageant on May 30 and 31.

A musician from the Germanic episode in "Caliban, by the Yellow Sands." Dramatic art in medieval Germany, France, Spain, and Italy is presented in symbolic ritual in one of the interludes of Percy Mackaye's Shakespeare Memorial Masque, which is being given as a community festival in the Stadium of New York City College.

CALIBAN

The "damned witch Sycorax," as Robert E. Jones sees her.

As wicked dew as e'er my mother brush'd with raven's feather from unwholesome fen drop on you!

An apprentice to the devil, on duty in the Shakespeare Masque.

Underwood

Here the defenders of the Irish Republic made their stand—the interior of the Dublin Post Office, one of the first buildings captured by the rebels. It was completely wrecked in the fight between the Sinn Feiners and the British troops. The question of compensation to Dublin for the damage done has not yet been decided, but out of the disorder a new adjustment of the Irish problem seems to be coming.

Copyright Underwood

Five million, eight hundred and seventy-three thousand, five hundred and twenty-seven surgical dressings have been sent to the war hospitals of the Allies since the war began by the Surgical Dressings Committee, a volunteer organization of which this woman, Mrs. Mary Hatch Willard, is international chairman. Twenty-one states are organized to collect old and new materials and enlist workers.

London Sphere, Copyright N. Y. H.

Far behind the lines at Verdun and in the Champagne these thousands of shells are being constantly shaped, filled, packed and shipped. Rumor has it that the Germans at Verdun are now fighting chiefly to deplete the French supply of munitions.

Copyright International Film

After a thirty-eight day tour of all the Western states where women vote, envoys of the Women's Congressional Union wound up their campaign with demonstrations, speeches and a parade and swarmed up the steps of the Capitol.

They mean to convince Congress that American women will work together at the next election for woman suffrage by a national amendment and will use their four million votes to elect the Presidential candidate who stands on that plank.

Medem

"Wounded for France"—that is the meaning of the device this "poilu" wears on the sleeve of his uniform.

J. Campbell White, LL.D., was inaugurated on May 12 as president of the College of Wooster, Wooster, Ohio. Dr. White is a graduate of this Presbyterian college, which celebrates its semicentennial in 1918, and has been a leader in American and foreign Y. M. C. A. activities and the Laymen's Missionary Movement, of which he was general secretary when he was called to Wooster.

Paul Thompson

Learning "fine laundry" in the domestic science courses which are given at the House of Industry in New York.

BELASCO: STAGE REALIST

BY MONTROSE J. MOSES

AUTHOR OF "THE AMERICAN DRAMATIST," "FAMOUS ACTOR FAMILIES OF AMERICA"

DAVID BELASCO'S chief claim to distinction lies, not in the particular emphasis which can be placed on his position as a dramatist, but in his value as an all-round force in the theater, as a maker of actors, and as a creator of productions. The theater of ideas is a secondary consideration to him, inasmuch as his problem is always how to "get it across," to use his own words, into the hearts of his audience.

The fact of the matter is that Mr. Belasco is much more interested in the organic response of the heart than he is in the quickening of the spirit. In his acting methods he usually asks, "What is the quickest way I can, by external means, produce a given emotional mood in my audience? How may I best grip the heart?" And instead of going to the fundamental value of his play, he superimposes upon his dialog those small details which are so persistently criticized by the critics, but which, in general, satisfy his need and the public's curiosity.

Note that his question is, "What are the small details I can make use of?" rather than, "What are the most typical details suggestive of the mood I have in hand?" His process is one of an accumulation in the choice of stage accessories, rather than of elimination, and that is probably his greatest limitation as a producer. His chief claim to distinction is his genius for small stage business—a genius which would rather risk much on the scenic possibilities of a poor play, like Roland Molineux's "The Man Inside," than on the austere scenic possibilities of a great play, like Galsworthy's "Justice."

Whatever Mr. Belasco has touched since the days of his apprenticeship in San Francisco, he has succeeded in imposing upon it what is now popularly known as "the Belasco atmosphere." He has resorted to all the tricks of his trade; and it is legitimate in the theater to have tricks. The present-day theater-goer probably first heard of Mr. Belasco when Mrs. Leslie Carter made a sensational swing across stage, holding to the clapper of a bell in "The Heart of Maryland." They next began to identify Mr. Belasco with stage effect

DAVID BELASCO

when, as a producer of "The Darling of the Gods" and "Du Barry," he literally threw away the possibilities of commercial profit by his exuberant use of detail for atmospheric effects.

Out of that period of spectacular drama, which further imprest upon the public mind the fact that a Belasco play meant a play in which Belasco atmosphere was uppermost, there came two distinctive pieces, which still hold the stage today, one the exquisitely poignant "Madame Butterfly" and the other "The Girl of the Golden West"—both of which were selected by Puccini as librettos for his now two famous operas. In Belasco Signor Puccini discovered the only American playwright who could furnish that stage color which opera demands.

For some time after the production of these large pieces—which afforded him likewise the opportunity of training some of his "stars" in a particularly picturesque and over-emotional style of acting—Mr. Belasco looked here and there for new material of the same character. He was satisfying his love for experiment.

All his career has been spent in converting the fortune made on one play in his new production for the next season. He came from an age when most of his stage illusive effects

were obtained thru the use of a locomotive headlight. He advanced into the age of "Edisonian incandescence," and with the effective eye of the alert manager, he has since that time made use of the switchboard in his theater as a performer would make use of some mechanical invention attached to the piano. In Mr. Belasco's hands a switchboard is nothing more than a measure of emotional effect.

Within recent years he has dropt from the ways of the spectacular. He has entered the realm of realism. He is impatient whenever a manager tries to answer reality thru the medium of the imagination, "What do they expect?" I have often heard him say, "How on earth could one suggest a broken pitcher without showing it?" This was apropos of the new symbolism, examples of which had recently been brought to this country by Reinhardt and Mr. Granville Barker.

For some time Mr. Belasco has been interested in two topics—spiritism and dual personality. Like all progressive managers, he is a man of intense energy. He has attacked these psychological problems with the same energy that he attacked the over-colored emotionalism in the days of "Du Barry" and "Adria." In "Peter Grimm," however, one detected a conflict between Mr. Belasco's taste as a realist and his interest in psychological drama. It seems inconsistent that spiritism should knock against reality so persistently as it sometimes does on Mr. Belasco's stage. After Peter died and returned, one was speculating quite as much over whether he would hit against the Belasco furniture as whether one would feel that he was a spirit rather than of the flesh. Yet, curiously, thru legitimate trickery, Mr. Belasco produced in us the effect he most desired.

Talk with Mr. Belasco on his method, and in his quiet, enigmatic manner he will look at you and smile. He has given plays without footlights, he has produced dramas with apron stages, he has, as a creator of actors, done much to bring to the theater a special method of acting. He has contributed more to the actual working stage in New York than anyone since the time of Augustin

336

Daly and Wallack. But one has to consider Mr. Belasco from the point of view he has chosen to take. A play of intellect *per se* has no appeal for him. A play whose mysticism is misty and unconvertible into tangible effect does not interest him. It is the play of the large emotion, the play of the large canvas, the play of the brilliant color, the play of the fine "property" detail, and the small trick, that instantly catches his fancy; and when it catches his fancy he is restless until he gains the picture value conjured up in his mind.

Is there room for an external drama, which gains its emotional ends thru physical effects, as well as for an internal drama which gains its effects thru suggestion and repression? I think there is, and that is Mr. Belasco's rightful claim to value in the theater today.

New York City

THE FARM HORSE DOESN'T PAY

BY JULIAN A. DIMOCK

MORE than one-fifth of the cultivated land of this country is required to feed the horses on the farm. These horses work on the average only three hours a day.

It costs $250 a year to keep a team of horses. One-third of the farmers in Tompkins County, New York, made less than $200 for their time during 1907, while the average labor income in 1911 in three typical counties in Indiana, Illinois and Iowa, prosperous communities with a capital investment of $30,000 per farm, was only $408. A team of horses costs more to keep than the average farmer of the country makes for his year of labor.

In order to get from him one hour of work, the farm horse is fed for seven hours of idleness.

Furthermore, the horse is not a satisfactory worker for the conditions existing on the farm. He cannot adequately respond to the pressure of work at certain seasons. His hours of work are limited, however urgent the demand. The farmer does not plough properly because he has not enough power on the place to do it. His harrowing and cultivating are skimped because he lacks the labor to do a better job. He does not do as much farming as he might because the chores, including the care of the horses, use up so much of his time.

The farmer is not efficiently employed unless he is directing the power of many horses. It takes the time of one man to cultivate cotton with a mule; it requires a man's work to direct the team of horses which ploughs a New England hillside, but one man can hold the reins over the backs of six powerful animals hitched

to a gang plough, or one man can sit at the wheel of a tractor which draws sixteen ten-inch ploughs, three six-foot harrows and a seeder. Such an outfit will plough, harrow and seed

HOW LONG WILL HE STAND FOR IT?

seventy-five acres in a day; and, furthermore, a tractor does not consume when it is not at work. It consumes in proportion to the work done. A thirty horse-power motor does not use fuel for the development of thirty horse-power when it is only producing fifteen horse-power. The cost of the unused power is simply that of interest on the investment and the depreciation. The tractor is thus adapted to the needs of the farm. It does not eat its head off when not in use and it can be used

to full capacity for as long a period as necessary.

With headlights, the tractor could plough day and night, for any necessary part of a season. It could plough thru the day and haul on the road at night, or with the end of the season of work, it could be put away and kept until springtime with only the cost of idle money.

After the day's work, the farm family can be taken to town for the grange meeting, to a neighbor's for a social time, or thirty miles away to attend a dance. The motor, having worked in the field all day, does not need to stand idle in a stall resting for the morrow's work.

Quick transportation widens the farmer's market. He can reach out for local consumers by ensuring prompt delivery and can take advantage of special conditions creating temporary prices by getting his goods on the spot without delay.

It is interesting to note that already a system by which a small tractor will plough and cultivate a field of several acres without human supervision has been evolved. A guiding line runs from the steering device to a small drum on a pole planted in the center of a circular field. As the tractor moves around the circumference of the circle the line wraps around the drum and each revolution is a little nearer the center.

The horse crosses off from the list of states that might provide food for man Kentucky, Tennessee, Alabama, Mississippi, Louisiana, Texas, Oklahoma and Arkansas!

How long can we pay his price?

Boston

W. H. Belton

THE TRACTOR WORKS IN GERMANY

This "Big 4" engine can plow, harrow and level a field, or haul three machines at once. It is a highly developed type of the tractor which in one form or another is likely to drive out the farm-horse

BETTER TOWNS

Frederic C. Howe Tells How We Are to Get Them
Independent Readers Tell How We Are Getting Them

WE might as well face the fact that more and more people are going to live in the cities, and that fewer and fewer people will live on the farm. The "Back to the Land" movement receives little encouragement even in those countries that do the most for agriculture. The city is the center of civilization today; of comfort, convenience, and a larger happiness than is possible in the country districts. That is the reason people want to live in the city.

That being true, our efforts should be directed to making the town a better place to live in. We should recognize the city as a permanent thing, and build it, plan it and control it much as we would a private house, our homes, for that is what the city is. It is the home in which we live.

If we think of the town in these terms, what are the things that should be done to make it better; better not for a few, but for every one. Some of the things to be done are outlined here.

The machinery for governing the town ought to be as simple as possible, so that every one can understand it and every one can participate in it. The commission form of government or manager plan seems to be the best device yet suggested for the honest, efficient and democratic administration of the town. The commission plan is like the board of directors of a corporation; the mayor or manager is like the president or executive official. He carries out the orders of the commission, or the people behind the commission direct. And with the initiative, referendum and recall, we have a means by which public opinion can express itself at all times in improving the town, just as the stockholders of a corporation meet together annually for expressing their will.

The town should be planned so that it will grow in an orderly and beautiful way. The suburbs should be laid out with broad streets; with playgrounds, parks and lots of open space. The hight of the buildings should be regulated; business should be excluded from the residence districts; the streets should be lined with trees; and provision made for the growth of the town for a genera-

Among the leaders of the new city movement that has done so much to strengthen American democracy at its weakest point stands Frederic C. Howe, now Commissioner of Education at the Port of New York. "The City, the Hope of Democracy" and "European Cities at Work" are especially familiar titles among his numerous contributions to the literature of city and community progress.—THE EDITOR.

tion in advance of its present size. That is the way the German, French and English cities are now being planned. They all improve the health, comfort and happiness of the people by building their towns like a private estate, or as a rich individual plans his home.

The town should own its plumbing. When we build a home we put in the plumbing. And we own it ourselves. The street railroads, gas, electric light and telephones are the plumbing of the city. They are its circulating system. They control the health, size of the town, industry and the comfort of the people in hundreds of ways. And just as the owner of the house owns his own plumbing, so the owners of the town should own and operate their own circulating system for the benefit of everybody. These industries should be operated at cost, and any one who will take the trouble to compare the publicly owned water system of the city with the privately owned street railroads or electric lighting system will see how much easier it is to own and operate than it is to regulate; will see how much cheaper the water is than the services rendered by private companies; how much less corruption there is when the city operates a thing directly than when it leaves these valuable monopoly rights in private hands. European cities are a unit in their agreement that it is not possible to build a city properly or to care for the people unless these agencies are owned by the city and are made a part of its life.

The city should provide generously for recreation and leisure. One-third of our life is given to work, one-third to sleep, and one-third to leisure. We make provision for work and for sleep; but we make little pro-

vision for leisure. And this is the time when the life of the people is most influenced for good or bad. Experience has shown that the community itself must provide for its leisure, if it is to be wholesome, clean and adequate.

The two great agencies for a wholesome leisure life are parks and playgrounds adequate for everyone. The second and more important new device is the building of schools and the use of schools for a great variety of purposes. The public school should be the temple of democracy; it should be big, spacious and generous. It should have provision for a great auditorium with a stage for musicals, dramas and other community gatherings. There should be playrooms, gymnasiums, public baths. Provision should be made for all kinds of meetings in this temple of democracy, for political meetings, for conferences with the mayor and aldermen, and for the discussion of public and even private affairs. The Gary system of Gary, Indiana, indicates the use that may be made of the public school and the possibility of uniting education with recreation for all ages and all classes.

Women should participate in the housekeeping of the city as well as men. They should have the right to vote. For the city is their home just as it is the home of men; and in many ways it affects them more vitally than it affects men. Health, food, recreation, the schools, the places the boys and girls go in the evening, these are matters of vital concern to the women of the community; and they can only control the community's life and make it what they will by the ballot.

The town must spend money. We are coming to realize in America that we get more out of taxes than we do out of any other money that we spend. And we will have to spend generously for a better city, a more wholesome city, a city that serves us. The great cities of America and of the world are those that spend generously; that have a big debt; that own things and do things; and care for the people rather than leave them to private exploitation. The German cities have the largest indebtedness of any cities in the world, and in

338

many ways they spend more generously than do even our own cities. We cannot have a city unless we are willing to pay for it, and we get bigger dividends from this expenditure than from any other.

Who will pay the bills for this city of tomorrow? From what sources will we get our revenues? Providentially nature has provided a treasure house that we need only to tap to secure all the revenues needed for every public use. That treasure house is the increasing land values of the city; values that are created by the growth of population. Every person that comes to a city adds from $600 to $1000 to the value of its land. They create an unearned increment which is appropriated by the land owner. This land value yields a ground rent which in the city of New York is es-

timated at nearly $250,000,000 a year. It is from $40 to $50 per capita. And this value was created by all the people, not by any individual. It is a speculative value, due to the growth of the city, which we permit private individuals to appropriate. German cities, Australian cities, Canadian cities are taking the taxes off houses, buildings, improvements, and placing them all on the land alone. They are appropriating the wealth which was created by the community and which belongs to the community, for running the city. They are doing just what a private individual would do with anything belonging to him. They are doing this by taxing the increasing value of the land which the city itself creates. And this revenue is adequate for all possible uses. It increases from year to year with the growth of the

population. It is never exhausted. It is more than sufficient for all of the needs of the city of tomorrow, and by taxing it we compel those who own land to either use it or sell their land to someone who will. That is the great advantage of taxing land, of the single tax. It prevents land speculation and compels those who own land to build houses or otherwise to improve their property, rather than sit idle while the community goes on enriching them by its growth.

These are some of the things that should be done if we would have better towns to live in; these are the things that progressive cities all over the world are doing in their recognition of the fact that the city is a permanent thing and must be regulated and controlled for the benefit of all.

New York City

THE BEST THING IN OUR TOWN

WHEN in our issue of October 4 last we asked our readers to write us what they regarded as the most interesting feature of the place in which they lived, we had no idea that we should get so many responses, so many readable responses, that it would be five months before we printed the last of them. But the display of civic pride that we had solicited took such a variety of forms and proved so interesting as a revelation of the ideals of the American people that we have from week to week published more of them and even now cannot discard the rest without picking out a few paragraphs from some of those that we are not able to print entire. For those we have still upon our desk are many of them as well worth reading as those that have already appeared.

Viewing the contributions as a whole what strikes one most is their diversity. We had no idea that people could find so many different reasons for liking their home town. The first prize of $100 went to D. R. Piper, of La Grange, Missouri, for a eulogy of his home paper, the La Grange *Indicator*, which we published February 28. Other prize winners for which we paid $25 each were "Hopedale's Glorified Mill-Pond," by James Church Alvord (April 3); "A Suffrage Oasis," by William O. Stevens (April 24); "Reforming the Grocer's Boy," by E. W. Beimfohr (May 8).

In order to give some idea of the civic attractions specified we have attempted a rough classification of some nine hundred of the letters.

As we should expect the schools are the chief pride of American towns. Next to these we are glad to see made prominent something that cannot be photographed, or, indeed, described, but which is, after all, the most important thing for a town to possess, for when it has this all other things may be added unto it, that is what may be called "the community spirit," the esprit de corps:

Subject	Number
Schools	113
Spirit of unity, coöperation, etc.	86
Industries	76
Water supply	57
Scenery, climate	54
Personalities	53
Clubs	49
Parks	45
Churches	38
General description	35
History	31
Civic organization and institutions	30
Libraries	26
Progress	25

Buildings and monuments	23
People	21
Hospitals, sanitariums, and "Homes"	13
Amusements	13
Health, cleanliness and sanitation	12
Homes	11
Music	10
No saloons	8
Children	8
Trees	7
Good roads	7
Newspapers	6
City planning	6
Museums	6
Y. M. C. A.	5
Railroads	4
Suffrage for women	3

If we can judge by number of contributions received, Ohio and Pennsylvania have the best towns in the country, or, at least, those who live in them think so, for these two states tied on 70 competitors each. Iowa came next with 63; then follow New York (52), Colorado (44), California (44), Michigan (43), Illinois (42), Kansas (33), and Wisconsin (31). We are surprised at Wisconsin. We thought she thought better of herself than that. Almost all the states are represented, and besides these Porto Rico sends five contributions and Hawaii, Panama, Canada and Brazil come to be counted in.

Kenmare has a park with a plum tree. Nothing to brag about, you think? But that is because you do not know what a rare delight it is to see grass and trees and spouting water in the bleak prairie plain.

The Park occupies the central block in town and is surrounded by a beautiful hedge. It has been set out to trees and shrubbery and seeded to lawn grasses which grow luxuriantly. In the center is a large fountain which sends up its sparkling waters continuously. Not an employer or employee but every day must see for a few minutes this thing of beauty. Many times I have

SILVERTON, COLORADO, A MODEL TOWN IN THE MOUNTAINS
Its civic spirit is comparable only to its altitude, says L. M. Grimes

seen people pause on the steps of a business house and exclaim, "How beautiful the park is!"; then, with an unconscious straightening of weary shoulders, go on their way. Many weary farmers' wives rest for a few minutes on the park benches and I am sure they carried with them to their bare prairie homes, perhaps to a half discouraged husband, renewed enthusiasm and fresh courage; and also, a firmer belief that these prairies can be made to blossom like the rose. We have boys in our town—no better, no worse, than boys everywhere—yet in the heart of our little village, in this park, a plum tree blossomed and bore fruit to maturity and was not molested.

ADA B. CLEMONS
Kenmare, North Dakota

Another of the time honored home industries has taken flight to the factory. Coöperative effort in Chatfield has transferred the burden of Blue Monday from the back of the farmer's wife to the broader shoulders of a gasoline engine.

One day, some years ago, the buttermaker in the coöperative creamery attached a washing machine to his machinery to use in washing his towels, and that is where he found his idea. Why not have a coöperative laundry in connection with the coöperative creamery, let the farmers carry their clothes when they do their cream, and charge their laundry bills to their cream accounts? The creamery company built an addition to its building to house the new institution, stock was sold to the amount of about $3000 to use in purchasing the machinery, and a practical laundryman was put in charge.

From the start the patronage was large. At least twice a week every farmer takes his turn "going to town" with the cream. One day he takes in a basket of soiled clothes, another day he brings them back clean. The prices are low, five cents a pound for washing and what ironing the mangler can do. The cost of collection is nothing.   GEORGE A. HAVEN.
Chatfield, Minnesota

Many towns tell of community centers, but that of Grandview, Alabama, is aquatic and the splash party is the center of civic solidarity:

Splash!
"It's fine!"
"Look out! I'm coming in!"
"Come on!"

No, this isn't "th' old swimmin' hole." It is the big concrete swimming pool owned by the community at Grandview, Alabama, with a "splash party" going on inside.

For about a hundred dollars the pool was constructed forty feet or more long, ten or fifteen wide and four deep. When the water was allowed to run in—10,000 gallons of it, pure and sparkling—everything was ready for the first plunge.

It became necessary before long to prevent the boys from going in more than twice a day, tho the privilege of three times was earnestly besought. The girls and women learned to be expert swimmers. The business men, on returning from the city in the afternoon, stopped for a swim before going home. But it was perhaps the younger children who got most pleasure from the new institution. The swimming pool quickly became a place to romp and play. If there ever was an effective community center, it is that Grandview swimming pool.   WYATT RUSHTON

The following comes from an R. F. D. subscriber who nevertheless

THE TOTEM POLE
R. Hamilton says Seattle, Washington, is proud of it

has been given a place in town life thru that admirable institution the Rest Room:

Suppose you were a country woman with a family of young children and no auto nor street car, and that you and the little ones rode to town on a load of potatoes which the man of the family had for sale. The potatoes were not engaged. And suppose the load failed to sell and they had to be peddled over town while, after shopping was done, mother and children waited all day in a store till sunset before she could return home. Would you not be tired? This is a real true story of real true people in our town before the P. E. O. society found a way to establish a Woman's Free Rest Room.

Out-of-town shoppers, both from the nearby country and those who come by rail from nearby towns, find this a desirable place to eat lunches, leave packages, put babies to sleep or procure a free cab to wheel them over town, wash up, brush up, rest up and be comfortable while waiting, instead of hanging around a store a wearisome time. EMILY BIRD McDUFF
Atchison, Kansas

The jitney which New York is not allowed to have lest it interfere with the profits of the taxis is reported as the "best thing" in many Western towns:

There are about ten jitneys to one trolley car. They come along frequently. The drivers are anxious to pick up passengers because they own their own cars, and are not indifferent, like the motormen. They make every effort to accommodate people who wish to ride. The busses run easily, safely, almost noiselessly, and are much more comfortable generally than are the street cars. There is no jarring, or grinding of brakes, or dust, and everybody gets a seat—which is quite an item, from a woman's standpoint.

These jitneys busses which run thru our town have installed and carry two signs to which we attach great importance. One reads: "Any where; any time." The jitney is working a revolution in passenger street traffic, and it is a great convenience to thousands of our townspeople, many of whom believe that the jitney is but the forerunner of a universal bus service without rails or trolley wires and poles, and that it will be but a few years before there will be no cars running through our streets with their attendant noise, dust and general discomfort.

IRENE M. MASON
Santa Monica, California

The following from Florida was written—you would know it anyway—by a real estate man. No other profession commands so poetic a pen:

A city to dream of is this, as it lies on its hills by the sea, its winter roses and violets a-bloom, the palms and camphor trees of its parked streets stirred by the soft southern winds. The oleander, the jessamine, the azalea, the crape myrtle, the scarlet hibiscus, the kum-

quat bushes laden with their little golden fruit, and the red dahlias glowing against the green and gold of the orange trees, all help to make the varying seasons one round of beauty, fragrance and delight.

Surrounding are forests of long-leaf pine, thru which wind roads carpeted brown with the fallen pine needles. There are gray ghosts of trees, festooned with Spanish moss. There are yopon trees, vivid with their emerald evergreen leaves and scarlet berries. There is hill and hollow, limpid creek and placid river.

C. E. DOBSON
Pensacola, Florida

Many towns boast of their waterworks, but the capital of Idaho is the only one to claim credit for keeping its people in hot water all the time:

Boise is the only city in the whole world that uses artesian water for the heating of homes, business blocks and public buildings. All that is necessary in these buildings is to turn a button and permit the *natural hot water* to run thru the pipes. No chimneys are needed. There is no smoke, no ashes, no dust, no work.

M. F. CUNNINGHAM
Boise, Idaho

Ogden is a city where the women vote, and as a natural consequence, where the saloons close at 9 o'clock and do not open Sunday, where there is no red light district, where there is a day nursery for working mothers, where—but just go there and see for yourself:

Can you imagine a jitney bus driver reading Laura Jean Libbey while he waits for passengers? An old man in peg-top trousers, sport shirt and top hat? A young man playing checkers while his wife holds a clinic? Can you imagine that? That, then, is Ogden, Utah.   C. S. WALLACE
Ogden, Utah

From Romulus, Michigan, comes a story of Harmony Grange and a photograph of its new hall on the site of a former saloon. We do not publish the picture because the hall is not beautiful, but the work done there is:

Harmony Grange has done more than keep the peace among its members; it has well-nigh transformed life both in the village and the countryside.

It was organized ten years ago, and now enrolls between two and three hundred members—farmer folk and business folk and teacher folk, with a doctor and a minister thrown in for Scripture measure, all playing and planning and working together for the uplift of the community. It is a kind of high tension power-house, with some two hundred sixty odd wires radiating to every corner of the surrounding country. Think of a society which allows no segregation either of sex or age, and which brings together more than twenty-five times each year children, parents and grandparents in one close-knit social group! ESTELLE DOWNING
Romulus, Michigan

Plain City must be a pleasant place to live in, which is more than you can say of many cities of more than its 1500 inhabitants. Mrs. Robinson finds 1500 words too scant to tell of all the things they do together and for each other.

IN THE FOREST OF ARDEN
From Edwin S. Potter, of Arden, Delaware, we have an account of the craft gild of that interesting community. It is too long to print and too good to cut; so we simply steal a picture from it showing the pageant of the free performances which the Actors' Gild gives every Saturday night in an outdoor theater

THE PARK WHICH MAKES KENMARE, NORTH DAKOTA, A PLEASANTER PLACE TO LIVE IN IN SPITE OF THE PRAIRIE

Plain City is a simple, friendly place where folks like to do things together. This spirit of comradeship is her greatest charm. We have no rich folk to spoil our simplicity, nor very many poor folk to make us uncomfortable. About the only hard feelings we ever have is when the Presbyterians try to steal some of the Methodist poor, to give presents to, at Christmas time.

Years ago we built a plant that furnishes electric light and water to the town so reasonably that practically every man uses both in his home. . . . Of course, our school is the best, the very best for a town of our size, in Ohio . . . Didn't we raise the first grade teacher? Isn't she wonderful? . . . In August we take up the serious matter of cultivating our minds; and for ten days work hard at a Chautauqua. Not a circuit Chautauqua, oh, mercy, no. We run it ourselves; and we have a better "program," with less cost, than the "talent" our neighbors who are in a circuit have sent to them. About 200 of us go out and live in the woods. We get a lot of sociability out of it, and make up our minds, incidentally, about a few national affairs. ELIZABETH LANE ROBINSON
Plain City, Ohio

Our modesty forbids us to give the prize to Mr. Campton, whatever may be our private opinion of his suggestion:

Permit me to say that the most interesting feature that I know of in our town is The Independent. If you think there is anything more interesting, you will not send me a prize. W. J. CAMPTON
New York City

Calgary, Canada, was hard hit by the war, for the city had overgrown itself—from 12,000 to 75,000 in ten years—and was convalescing from its real estate boom. But with true Western energy it turned its unsold lots to account:

The Vacant Lots Garden Club is one of the big factors which is helping to bring about a more prosperous and equitable condition, as well as to beautify the city. A membership fee of $1 entitles the holder to receive one or more twenty-five-foot lots. An extra charge of the same amount for plowing each lot may be overcome by the gardener's digging the land himself. He receives "seeds, plants and garden tools at special discount, the produce of his lots, free expert supervision, and bulletins on gardening." In return, he is expected to clear his land for plowing, cultivate it, and keep it weeded. The report of the committee for the first year far exceeded expectations, 254 lots being taken up by 170 members. The second year the amount of ground was almost quadrupled, for 1000 lots were cultivated by 450 members. Those who have held a lot one season have first claim on it the following year. The vacant lots movement has tried to encourage the growth of excellent vegetables and flowers by prize competitions for potatoes and other vegetables grown on club lots only.
JULIA C. STOCKETT
Calgary, Alberta

The city of Madison several times a year ropes off one of its streets for half a block and gives a community ball on its waxed pavement:

Municipal Dance.
Thursday, September 30, 1915
8:30 p. m.
Liberty Street, between Jefferson and Madison Avenues.
Music by Spencer's Band.
HARRIETTE M. WHEATON
Madison, Wisconsin

When we opened the envelope from Miss Kysor and a picture of a police van fell out we thought "what a queer thing to take pride in." But on reading we found that it was as creditable as it was queer:

The finest thing in our town is the police patrol. "Carrying 'drunks'?" you ask? No, carrying crippled children to school and home. I stood on the corner this morning. They went by, the lucky two on the driver's seat looking as happy as if they had good legs and straight backs instead of pitiful crooked substitutes. They backed up to a curb. Standing on the porch was a boy on crutches, and the big officer who sits by the steps of the "wagon" gathered him up, crutches and all, into his strong arms, carried him gently down, and put him in with the rest of this group with such old-young faces. They have milk and wafers at ten o'clock, a warm meal at noon, lunch at three, then ride home. Blankets and windproof curtains keep them warm on the way. The quarters for the school for crippled children are especially adapted and furnished for their needs. DANIA KYSOR
Detroit, Michigan

Emporia, regardless of grammar, has two best things and who can deny it?

The two best things that Emporia, Kansas, has are William Allen White and Walt Mason. Where is there a town the size of Emporia (12,000 population) that can beat this combination? The former being the editor of our local paper, the *Emporia Gazette*, one of the most quoted papers in America, and dear old "Uncle Walt" Mason, whose wholesome homely philosophy is now read every day wherever any English-printed metropolitan daily newspaper is published. We all love them.
J. E. E.
Emporia, Kansas

We have no space for further quotations, but we must mention a few more of the distinctive features to which our correspondents call attention. Oshkosh, according to Miss Lucia B. Clow, a student of the Normal School, finds distinction in its name, which is known all over the country and keeps the place from being confused with the common run of American towns. "Oshkosh," she concludes, "could never be an Athens, but on the other hand Athens could never have been an Oshkosh." Both cities are to be congratulated on the fact.

Albion, Michigan, has a "Boosters and Knockers Club," which lunches every Tuesday in the interests of a "better Albion."

The civic center and index of prosperity in Lisbon, Ohio, is "The Hitching Rail," of which Willis R. Hale sends us a graphic description.

Grandma Lincoln, of East Lake Shore, Canandaigua, who has read The Independent for more than fifty years, writes of a rural Sunday School.

Salt Lake City, says Mrs. Guy Montgomery, has a monthly magazine, *The Utah Survey*, devoted to community interests.

The Young Men's Booster Club, of Guthrie, Oklahoma, 200 strong, sends us the article on "Our Mineral Waters," by E. C. Ralston, that took first prize in their local contest.

Towns used to boast of the number of churches they possest, but Miss Lee McCrae, of Claremont, California, writes: "In the twenty years of its existence this town has had but one church and the people fervently hope that it will never have any other." This sounds wicked, but when we read of all the things this church does we agree that Claremont is better off than if it had six.

Edward R. Fickenscher, of the Land Office, thinks that the ingenious system of numbering streets so that the stranger can find his way by looking at the signs imprinted in the cement walks is the best thing about Great Falls, Montana.

Our Brazilian contributor, George T. Coleman, writes of the excellent sanitary service of Sao Paulo, and as a contrast encloses a photograph of one of the "pest-ships" on which crews having yellow fever were formerly left to die.

Little things, you say? Yes, but every one is a symptom of American progress toward better towns.

341

TALES OF THE PAST

There was a beautiful simplicity in life a thousand years ago. If you hated a man you cut his head off; daily papers did not exist, and women had no desire for economic independence. It is refreshing to read of such uncomplicated days in Maurice Hewlett's *Frey and His Wife* and Francis o'Sullivan tighe's *The Portion of a Champion*. The first is a tale of Norway. It is a good story, told with vividness, an exhilarating freshness and a touch of sweetness. The great god Frey is a most interesting person, so is Frey's wife, and so is the hero, Gunnar.

The scene of the other book is fifth century Ireland and Gaul. It lacks the directness and vigor of *Frey and His Wife*, but is filled with exciting adventures and interesting pictures of the ancient manners and customs of Eirinn. There is plenty of hard fighting, with a little love making to flavor it.

Frey and His Wife, by Maurice Hewlett. McBride. $1. *The Portion of a Champion*, by Francis o'Sullivan tighe. Scribner. $1.35.

HEREDITY

In recent years the chemist and the physicist and the mathematician have contributed quite as much to the advance in biology, thru their stains and microscopes and statistics, as have the taxonomist, field explorer and breeder. A critical examination of the philosophical assumptions underlying the methods used in the study of the most aggressive and the most interesting department of biological research—the field of genetics—suggests the interdependence of our sciences in a striking way. Mr. Raymond Pearl, who has himself made important studies in the heredity of egg-production in poultry, leaves the "practical" animal breeders' convention long enough to ask some pertinent questions about methods and value of research. In his little book there is a careful analysis of the problems of heredity, and of the various methods used in the attempt to solve them. Mr. Pearl looks forward to the development of biochemistry as furnishing a promising field for the study of genetic problems. The notes on the nature of statistical knowledge are of general interest and significance. We are all exposed to the arguments from statistics but we are not all forearmed as to the limitations inherent in the statistical method of proof. There is a rather technical chapter on the mathematical aspects of genetics in relation to practical breeding. The advantages he considers real and measurable, if not altogether revolutionary.

The best account of the principles of heredity and of their practical application to human problems is, from the point of view of the general reader, Professor Guyer's *Being Well Born*. When it is added that the book is quite authoritative and reliable as well as

342

interesting and readable, and that its price puts it within the reach of all who really care, it is intended to intimate that there should hereafter be no excuse whatever for the "superficiality and the superstition" that surrounds this subject in the minds of most people, even among the "educated" classes.

Modes of Research in Genetics, by Raymond Pearl. Macmillan. $1.25. *Being Well Born*, by Michael F. Guyer. Bobbs-Merrill. $1.

LABOR LAWS

Professor Commons and Dr. Andrews, in their *Principles of Labor Legislation*, have rendered the public a real service in bringing together a summary of what has been accomplished in the various states and in foreign countries in the way of readjusting labor conditions and labor relations thru legislation. In addition to the historical material, there is a discussion of the economic basis, the operation and the results of various types of laws, such as those affecting hours of labor, minimum wages, safety and health, unemployment and social insurance. The constitutional aspect of the legislation is closely followed, and there are citations of important court decisions. There's a good general index, a special index of cases referred to, and a selected and classified bibliography of the most helpful sources.

Principles of Labor Legislation, by John R. Commons and John B. Andrews. Harper. $2.

A CURE FOR WAR

Peace, like war, has its battles, its victories, its defeats; it has its call to heroism in action; and its call to courage of another kind in the fight against social injustice, political corruption, and industrial enslavement. But battles of words and pens and printer's ink somehow fail to stir the heart as does the martial trumpet. And why?

In *A Substitute for War*, Percy Mackaye answers the question somewhat to this effect. War knows how to throw over its brutal realities the glamor of imagination, embodying itself in splendid symbols and dramatic displays—flags, uniforms, and banners; color and music; ordered evolutions and the rhythm of marching feet. Peace has no pageantry, and for symbols only the pale dove and the olive branch. Give peace a splendid dramatic investiture, and its activities will assume an enthusiasm such as war has hitherto enlisted. This dramatic investiture should take the form of masques and pageants celebrating peaceful labors and triumphs. As evidence of the beneficent effects to be expected from such dramatic displays, Mr. Mackaye cites the great masque he and others managed at St. Louis, with the coöperation of 7500 citizens and a chorus of 600. Direct results of this civic drama, we are told, were a progressive charter, a municipal bridge, and a choral society. Perhaps he is a

little sanguine about his "substitute," but whether he is or not, his suggestions can do only good, and the more they are realized, the better. This plan is sympathetically introduced by Professor Fisher of Yale, Viscount Bryce, and Norman Angell.

A Substitute for War, by Percy Mackaye. Macmillan. 50 cents.

TO READ ALOUD

Dallas Lore Sharp lives in *The Hills of Hingham* as a compromise between Boston and the Forest of Arden. He loves hills and bees and open fires. He has a sense of humor and a sense of the infinite. He writes with charm and sincerity of the little things of life, and of the big things. You will read *The Hills of Hingham* twice, or even three times.

Houghton, Mifflin. $1.25.

FOR AMERICAN FISHERMEN

Louis Rhead, artist and fisherman, has discovered that European flies are not the best lures for American fishing. "America for Americans" applies forcibly to our fish. They prefer native insects, the varieties of which vary month by month. Mr. Rhead's pioneer book on *American Trout Stream Insects* is a valuable contribution to the literature of American fishing, and the artificial entomology described is full of interest to fly fishers.

Stokes. $2.50.

A UNIQUE LOITERING-SPOT

The San Diego Garden Fair, which has outlived its showier neighbor, is discussed by Eugen Neuhaus in much the same way as was the San Francisco Exposition in the California professor's earlier books. There is a bit of history and some illuminating criticism of architecture, but one wishes for even more of the finely reproduced photographs, particularly more pictures of the lavishly beautiful gardens.

San Francisco: Elder. $1.50.

A MAN BUILDS HIS HOUSE

A married Thoreau with a family to shelter is a piquant contrast to the celibate lover of the Walden woods. In *Child and Country* Will Levington Comfort, in his hermitage by Lake Erie, talks of Life and Nature to several fascinating little people. Some of the essays written by the "Little Girl" have a charm as engaging as that of Pet Marjorie. The book is breathed thru with love for the out-of-doors and the sincerities and inspirations of country life at its best.

Doran. $1.25.

FOR AMATEUR PLAYERS

Master Skylark, Joan Bennett's fine tale of a boy and girl in Shakespeare's time and town, has been dramatized very simply by A. M. Littlenhaus in *Plays for School Children*, and now comes a fuller dramatization by E. W. Burrill, who has made such a delightful drama of the delightful story that it is used as the commencement play by Wellesley this June.

Century. $1.25 and $1.

ANOTHER SCHOOL SHAKESPEARE

In the Globe Theater edition of Shakespeare's plays arranged for school by D. H. Rich, much unexpected and some naïve information is packed into small compass. Each play has introduction and glossary, and being planned for class use, this concisely and clearly given data on the drama of the Elizabethan stage. Shakespeare's life and the advice as to methods of study are printed with each play.

Harper. 35 cents each.

THE COAST OF MAINE

Instead of the Thorn, by Clara Louise Burnham, is the story of a Chicago girl, charming, spoiled and wealthy. The financial ruin and death of her father, under circumstances which seem to involve her lover, transfer her for a time to a little town on the Maine coast. There she "finds herself." The morality is a trifle obvious, the story a trifle dull.

Houghton, Mifflin. $1.25.

STEALING FOR PLEASURE

An Amiable Charlatan is a typical piece of E. Philips Oppenheim fiction. There is a conventional young Englishman, a lovely American girl, and her father, an eccentric but agreeable gentleman who has read too many detective stories. Their extraordinary adventures, sprinkled with Scotland Yard detectives, gambling dens, much valuable jewelry and many, many restaurants and taxis, are entertainingly told.

Boston: Little, Brown. $1.30.

IN THE USUAL WAY

When an author as deservedly popular as William J. Locke fails to the pot-boiler plane, not even a "girl cover" can save him. For *Viviette*—his latest story—makes no attempt to redeem by novel situation or skillful characterization its trite triangle of two men and a flirt, who go thru all the usual motions in an exceedingly usual English country house, embellished by butlers and duels and ancestors and tea and all the rest.

Lane, $1.

PIONEERS OF AUSTRALIA

The reviewer usually looks askance at a "prize novel," and his distrust is, in many cases, justified by the perfunctory character of the book. But *The Pioneers*, a $5000 prize story of Australian life, by Katherine Susanna Prichard, is exceptionally interesting. It goes back to the earliest days of settlement; of convict camps; of privation, hard work and well won success for the settlers. Their children reap the harvest, and we feel that the struggle was worth while.

Doran. $1.25.

A CALIFORNIA FOREST PLAY

Jack London has entered upon a new field, the drama. *The Acorn-Planter* is a pageant play "to be sung by efficient singers accompanied by a capable orchestra." Allegorical in form, its theme is the conflict between the warrior and the planter or life-maker. The characters are Indians and pioneers, which affords opportunity for picturesque stage effects, costuming and dancing. Plus appropriate music, it would make an effective production. It is good reading, too.

Macmillan. 75 cents.

ETHICS AND THEOLOGY

THE ROOTS OF CIVILIZATION

Our knowledge of the history of the Tigris-Euphrates valley has been of late so enlarged and modified by new discoveries that books of so recent a date as 1900 have become antiquated. Professor Rogers has almost completely rewritten his *History of Babylonia and Assyria*, and the volumes now give the story of the modern excavations and interpret according to this new knowledge the historical materials that reveal the course of human development in one of the three ancient centers in which are found the roots of western civilization.

Abingdon Press. $10.

WHEN MISSIONS COME OF AGE

In the *Devolution of Missionary Administration* Dr. Fleming discusses the conducting of Christian missions in foreign lands. Dr. Fleming gives the history of this devolution in connection with five American missions in India, and shows the difficulties that appear in such transfer,

The Dish That Belongs to June

Puffed Wheat and Rice—the bubble grains—seem to belong to summer. They are light and airy, dainty and inviting.

Summer brings flower-decked breakfast tables, and Puffed Grains seem to fit there. Summer brings berries, and Puffed Grains mixed with them make them doubly delightful.

Summer brings dairy suppers. And these airy tit-bits, flaky, toasted and crisp, are the morsels to float in milk.

Playtime Bonbons
Mealtime Foods

These are both foods and confections. Keep a package of them salted, or doused with melted butter, for the children to carry at play.

Use them in place of nut meats, in candy making, on a frosted cake, or as garnish for ice cream.

Almost every hour of the day, from breakfast to bedtime, brings some use for Puffed Grains. People consume, at this time of the year, a million packages weekly.

Puffed Wheat	Except in	**12c**
Puffed Rice	Far West	**15c**

Corn Puffs—Bubbles of Corn Hearts—15c

Consider Puffed Grains, above all else, as scientific foods. They are Prof. Anderson's invention. Every food cell is exploded. Every granule is made digestible. Every atom feeds.

They are not mere tit-bits—not mere palate-pleasers. They are made to make whole grains wholly digestible. They are made to avoid any tax on the stomach.

Why serve these grains in a lesser form when everyone prefers them puffed? And why serve only one of them when there are three of these perfect dainties?

The Quaker Oats Company

Sole Makers

(1319)

JUNE 26

The Independent

WITH WHICH IS INCORPORATED

HARPER'S WEEKLY

The Man Prepared

Mr. Purinton's greatest article since "The Triumph of the Man Who Acts" will be a leading feature of The Independent's Chautauqua and Efficiency Number of June 26.

The Future of National Education

will be another great feature of that number. In this article, by President George E. Vincent, of the University of Minnesota, and Chancellor of Chautauqua Institution, will sound the keynote of "The Most American Thing in America," the Chautauqua idea of popular education with special reference to the future of this gigantic national movement. Other articles by Chautauqua authorities will deal with new and live phases of the Chautauqua plan. This number will also be The Independent's

Quarterly Financial and Insurance Review

an institution unique among periodicals of general circulation.

The Independent

---

and yet the great advantage which comes thereby to the churches.

Revell. $1.50.

WORSHIP

Two suggestive books for Sunday school leaders are *The Manual for Training in Worship* and *The Book of Worship for the Church Schools*, by Hugh Hartshorne, of the Union Theological Seminary. The first discusses the need for more care in planning the devotional part of the children's services, and the second provides excellent material.

Scribner. 51 and 55 cents.

SCIENTIFIC STUDY OF ST. JAMES

A noteworthy addition to the International Critical Commentary is Professor Ropes's *St. James*, a minute exegetical study for specialists. The wealth of illustration from Greek and Rabbinic literature make the work invaluable to those who love to deal with parallelisms of thought and expression. The epistle is ascribed to an anonymous writer of the second century.

Scribner. $3.

SEMITIC LIFE

The Social Legislation of the Primitive Semites is a careful resumé of what is known of the primitive customs and laws of the Hebrews, Babylonians and Arabians. In each of fourteen chapters covering such subjects as Matriarchy, Next of Kin, Slavery, Inheritance, Sabbatical Year, and Taxation, Dr. Henry Schaeffer gathers all the indications which the Old Testament offers of the early Hebrew practice, compares it with the pre-Mohammedan practice of Arabia and then adds the data from the cuneiform inscriptions.

Yale University Press. $2.35.

FOR CITIZENS

AXIOMATIC SUFFRAGE

"Let us no longer speak of woman's rights, or of man's rights, but consider human rights," says Nathaniel C. Fowler, Jr., in his concise and careful summary of the A B C reasons justifying votes for women. As a source book for suffrage orators *The Principle of Suffrage* ought to prove valuable, but as an argument it fails to convince because of the very multiplicity of its propositions.

Sully & Kleintelch. 25 cents.

CHARACTER AND CONDUCT

An excellent manual for moral instruction is found in *An Introduction to Ethics for Training Colleges*, by G. A. Johnston, of the University of Glasgow. The author first traces the development of character and defines the various elements which constitute it. On this basis he examines in a clear and concise way the relation of character and life to different spheres of conduct and activity.

Macmillan. $1.

THE MEN OF THE HARBOR

In a study of *The Longshoremen* made by Charles B. Barnes the economic problems connected with the six thousand men handling freight at the New York docks receive most attention, but the author never loses his human sympathy. A group of men that have the reputation of being shiftless and disposed toward drink and idleness, but who refuse to work with drunkards, presents interesting problems in group psychology.

Survey Associates. $2.

SAFEGUARDS FOR HEALTH

In *The New Public Health*, Dr. H. W. Hill explains significant changes that research has brought about in the course of the last fifteen years. The prevention of infection now means the eradication of germ-carriers, chiefly the sick persons, the prevention of contacts, and the elimination of flies. Fumigation after disease is being discontinued; garbage is no longer judged a source of danger; "sewer gas" and "dust" have lost their terrors. But protection of the water, food and milk supplies comes to be an important part of the public administration.

RELIGION

in the Assembly Program and Summer Schools

AT CHAUTAUQUA

Director of Religious Work, Dr. Shailer Mathews

(President Federal Council of Churches, President Northern Baptist Convention, Dean Divinity School, University of Chicago)

WEEKLY CHAPLAINS

Daily Devotional Studies, Lectures and Conferences

Dean Charles R. Brown, (Congregational), Yale Divinity School.
Bishop William F. McDowell (Methodist Episcopal), Chicago, Ill.
Dr. Herbert L. Willett (Disciples of Christ), Memorial Church of Christ, Chicago.
Dr. James I. Vance (Presbyterian) First Presbyterian Church, Nashville, Tenn.
Bishop William F. Oldham (Methodist Episcopal) New York City.
Dr. C. L. Goodell (Methodist Episcopal), St. Paul's M. E. Church, New York City.
Dean Shailer Mathews (Baptist), The University of Chicago.
Dr. James A. Francis (Baptist), First Baptist Church, Los Angeles, Calif.
Pres. J. Ross Stevenson (Presbyterian) Princeton Theological Seminary.

SCHOOL OF RELIGION

Daily Class Work, June 29-August 27. The Life of Christ. The Life of Paul. Moral Leaders of Israel. Religious Education in the Family. Geography of Palestine. The Sunday School. The Telling of Bible Stores.

Faculty:

Dean Shailer Mathews,
    University of Chicago

Dr. Milton S. Littlefield
    Congregational Sunday School and
    Publishing Society

Miss Georgia L. Chamberlin,
    American Institute of Sacred Literature

Prof. Herbert L. Willett, Chicago

Dr. Jesse L. Hurlbut, Newark N. J.

Dr. Henry F. Cope,
    Gen. Secy. Religious Education Assn.

Dr. William E. Gardner,
    Secy. Prot. Episc. Bd. Religious Education

THE CHURCH REMAKING THE WORLD

(Minister's and Christian Worker's Institute)

General Assembly Program for entire week August 20-25 devoted to the Church in its relation to world progress. Leaders: Pres. J. Ross Stevenson, Rev. James A. Francis, Dean Shailer Mathews, Mr. Raymond Robins. Important speakers representing several great nations.

HOME MISSIONS INSTITUTE	FOREIGN MISSIONS INSTITUTE
Directed by Women's Council for Home Missions	Directed by Women's Council for Foreign Missions
August 12-18	August 20-25

WORK FOR CHILDREN AND YOUNG PEOPLE

Study Hour on Sunday with graded work, The Junior Congregation, Daily Bible Study, under expert leadership, all in co-operation with well organized clubs which direct the life of the young people.

Chautauqua is an ideal place for the study and practice of a normal, progressive, healthy life, for mind and body, of which religion is one of the essential elements.

For full circulars, programs, rates, and all information, address

CHAUTAUQUA INSTITUTION, Chautauqua, N. Y.

THE PUBLIC SCHOOLS

Measuring the Work of the Public Schools, compiled by Charles H. Judd for the Cleveland Survey, contains conclusions that would probably apply to half the city school systems in the country. Study of non-promotions shows need for courses of study better adapted to the character of the population. Class room observations show too little adaptation of material to current needs. The kindergartens need better correlation and supervision; the upper grades and high schools richer courses of study, and more symmetrical development of the system.
Cleveland Foundation. 50 cents.

PEACE AND WAR

PERMANENT PEACE

Ways to Lasting Peace is a collection of sixty-five of the most significant constructive programs, proposals and manifestoes issued by responsible organizations and individuals thruout the world for ending the war and establishing thereafter a durable peace. There is an admirable running comment by Dr. David Starr Jordan.
Bobbs-Merrill. $1.

WAR AS RELAXATION

Sustained attention is the distinction of civilized man. The resulting tension, says G. T. W. Patrick in his *Psychology of Relaxation*, requires relief found normally in such activities as play, sport and laughter. Profanity and slang have a like effect. Alcohol and the deeper debauch of war used for this end cannot be banished "by summary means nor direct suppressions." They will require substitutes which meet fundamental, virile needs.
Houghton, Mifflin. $1.25.

HOW THE SUBMARINE WORKS

The dream of flying is almost as old as the race. That of boating under water began about 1620. Modern science' has realized both dreams and thereby revolutionized warfare and made it yet more horrible. Washington hoped for submarines. The Confederates had one—a gallant tale. Farnham Bishop's *Story of the Submarine* is a timely book, telling in simple style of the evolution, the mechanism, the power of this new engine of destruction.
Century. $1.

"OUR GLORY IS TO SAVE"

Amid the needful but none the less deplorable talk of preparedness comes in a new edition the story of the army that marches the world over under *The Red Cross Flag*. Miss Boardman tells well humorous incidents of its beginnings and splendid tales of its work in great disasters and gives four chapters to its work in this war. The book's fault seems to the outsider to lie in needlessly scant credit to the first chief.
Philadelphia: Lippincott. $1.50.

ANATOLE FRANCE ON THE WAR

The Path of Glory, which appears in a translation combined with the original text, is a collection of sketches and letters relating to the French side of the Great War. Anatole France, the Patriot, retains his vivid and graceful style, but while it is unthinkable that anyone else in the world could have written a line of the works of Anatole France, the Skeptic, any clever patriotic French author might have written this volume.
Lane. $1.50.

WHEN WAR IS RIGHT

War and Religion is a booklet of 87 pages by the French scholar, Alfred Loisy, translated by Arthur Galton. The writer's point is that the religion of Jesus is rejected by those who have perpetrated the present war; yet he believes that the spirit and essence of religion is in the heart of those who defend their country, for self-sacrifice is religion. He gives great honor to Cardinal Mercier, but holds the position of the Pope of Rome to be indefensible.
Longmans, Green. 50 cents.

PEBBLES

Do It Now. Today Will Be Yesterday Tomorrow.—*Cincinnati Enquirer.*

Wilson Lauds Lincoln.—*Head-line.* The campaign is on at last.—*Philadelphia North American.*

Abe—Did you get the opera score? Pandora—Yeah; they were tied in the last minute of the play.—*Stanford Chaparral.*

"Preparedness" is in the air. Frinstance, the Indianapolis telephone directory carries a line: "In case of fire call fire department."—*Boston Herald.*

The European belligerents who are turning the clock one hour ahead are probably wishing they could turn it back about two years.—*Brooklyn Daily Eagle.*

The common folks live in the hope
That they will hear the calliope;
But people in society
Must list to the calliope.
    —*Cincinnati Enquirer.*

All the mechanics and laborers are receiving the highest pay kuown in their history, but they are demanding more.—*Pittsburg Dispatch.* How different from capital is labor. Capital, it is well known, invariably is content with just enough.—*Puck.*

IT PAYS TO KNOW YOUR OWN MIND

It is rumored that the cause of the death of W. J. Evans, who died here last fall, will be investigated. Mr. Evans was thought to have killed himself at the time, but was later undecided.—*Little River News.*

The door opened suddenly and a lady rushed in. "Oh, doctor," she cried, "the baby has swallowed some ink and now he's looking blue. What shall I do?"

"Give him a dose of blotter," said the doctor. "This is certainly an absorbing case."—*Cornell Widow.*

"How did you come out?" asked his friend. "Will she have you?"

"Her answer," replied the diplomatic attache, "is partially satisfactory. Enough so to continue negotiations. She says if she ever does marry it will be a man of good looks, courage, and ability."—*Judge.*

Having stood for the steam roller process as long as could be expected, the worm backfired and our East made a clean sweep.—*Bozeman Bulger,* in the *Evening World.* When a good pilot is at the throttle nothing can stop the early bird in its drive up the ladder.—*New York Tribune.*

"Can you tell me," said the Court, addressing Enrico Ufuzzi, under examination at Union Hill, New Jersey, as to his qualifications for citizenship, "the difference between the powers and prerogatives of the King of England and those of the President of the United States?"

"Yezzir," spoke up Ufuzzi promptly. "King, he got steady job."—*New York Morning Telegraph.*

If, However and But one night
Sailed in a German note.
Sailed on a river of phrases bright
That the Foreign Office wrote.
Sailed on the cable across the sea
Snuggled away in a special plea.
And they're always there, are the little words three,
If, However and But.
    Brooklyn Daily Eagle.

A Long Island teacher was recounting the story of Red Riding Hood. After describing the woods and the wild animals that flourished therein, she added:

"Suddenly Red Riding Hood heard a great noise. She turned about, and what do you suppose she saw stabbing there, gazing at her and showing all its sharp, white teeth?"

"Teddy Roosevelt!" volunteered one of the boys.—*New York Times.*

RICHARD HENRY LITTLE
At the front in the Spanish-American, Russian-Japanese and the greatest European wars. Mr. Little says:
"I have found Tuxedo a faithful companion in the field and in the camp. In all my campaigns I have regarded a few good pipes and a plentiful supply of Tuxedo tobacco as the most important part of my impedimenta."
    Richard Henry Little

WM. PHILIP SIMMS
Manager Paris Bureau United Press and the first American correspondent permitted to visit the French front. Mr. Simms says:
"Tuxedo gives me more real pleasure than any other tobacco I ever smoked. It always tastes good, outdoors or indoors, morning, noon or night."
    Wm. Philip Simms

WALTER NIEBUHR
With the German army during the drive on Warsaw, for the United Press. Mr. Niebuhr says:
"Tuxedo is remarkably mild and delightfully fragrant. I find that I can smoke it all day and enjoy the last pipeful just as much as the first."
    Walter Niebuhr

Famous War Correspondents Smoke Tuxedo!

Among the most brilliant men in the world today are those who give us in vivid pen pictures the stirring story of the greatest of all wars.

Here, famous reporters of the gigantic conflict tell why the modern war correspondent smokes Tuxedo.

That wholesome taste of "Tux" keeps his mind vigorous—and it's so wonderfully mild he can smoke it any time, every time and all the time and never know he has nerves!

Tuxedo
The Perfect Tobacco for Pipe and Cigarette

Tuxedo is made of ripe old Burley leaf, aged **3** to **5** years—*and*—it's "Tuxedo Processed!"

That's the big, overshadowing reason why Tuxedo is in a class by itself.

After the aged leaf has been "Tuxedo Processed," every particle of bite is absolutely removed — the tobacco becomes supremely mild — and you can smoke Tuxedo all you please—the sweet, fragrant, pleasant smoke that makes your pipe your best friend.

Tuxedo has plenty of imitators—but you insist on getting Tuxedo and avoid disappointment.

YOU CAN BUY TUXEDO EVERYWHERE

Convenient, glassine wrapped, moisture-proof pouch . . . **5c**

Famous green tin, with gold lettering, curved to fit pocket **10c**

In Tin Humidors, 40c and 80c   *In Glass Humidors, 50c and 90c*

THE AMERICAN TOBACCO COMPANY

A Number of Things
by Edwin E. Slosson

I know one man who will be pleased at Judge Tuthill's decision that Bacon wrote Shakespeare. He lives, or did live some thirty years ago, in Kansas and had then upon his library shelves a dozen volumes handsomely rebound in morocco and lettered in gold on the backs, "Dramatic Works of Francis Bacon."

Another Kansas admirer of that elusive author was lured by an unscrupulous agent into buying a set which he understood to be "Lord Bacon's Lights of History," but which when he got them turned out to be "Lord's Beacon Lights of History," a deservedly popular work for the parlor what-not.

Now that this controversy has been settled—for I suppose it would be contempt of court to question the decision of the Chicago judge—it seems appropriate to quote Arthur St. John Adcock's lines from the *Anthology of Humorous Verse*:

As Shakespeare couldn't write his plays
   (If Mrs. Gallup's not mistaken),
I think how wise in many ways
   He was to have them done by Bacon;
They might have moldered on the shelf,
   Mere minor dramas (and he knew it!),
If he had written them himself
   Instead of letting Bacon do it.

And if it's true, as Brown and Smith
   In many learned tomes have stated,
That Homer was an idle myth,
   He ought to be congratulated.
Since thus, evading birth, he rose
   For men to worship at a distance:
He might have penned inferior prose,
   Had be achieved a real existence.

To him and Shakespeare mere
   In making very nice allusions;
But no one thinks of praising me,
   For I compose my own effusions;
As others wrote *their* works divine
   And they immortal thus today are,
Perhaps had some one written mine
   I might have been as great as they are.

Whether *vers libre* is beautiful or not is still a matter of dispute, but that does not matter now since it is turning out to be useful. It seems to be just the thing for newspaper controversy. In the New York *Evening Post* — what would its erstwhile editor, William Cullen Bryant, have thought about it?—a debate on Dr. Flexner's modern school has been carried on in the new medium. The plan for a school, in which most of the studies should be vocational and scientific, without the classics and abstract mathematics, was published in pamphlet form by the General Education Board "with a request for criticism." Professor Erskine, of the depart-

ment of English in Columbia, was accommodating enough to comply with the request, which he did in this fashion:

ODE TO DR. A—— F——

Just after the Board had brought the
   schools up to date,
To prepare you for your Life Work
Without teaching one superfluous thing,
Jim Reilly presented himself to be edu-
   cated.
He wanted to be a bricklayer.
So they taught him to be a perfect brick-
   layer
And nothing more.
He knew so much about bricklaying that
   the contractor made him a foreman.
But he knew nothing about being a fore-
   man.
So he spoke to the School Board about it,
And they put in a night course for him,
On how to be a foreman
And nothing more.
He became so excellent a foreman that the
   contractor made him a partner.
But he knew nothing about figuring costs,
Nor about bookkeeping,
Nor about real estate,
And he was too proud to go back to night
   school.
So he hired a tutor, who taught him these
   things.
Prospering at last, and meeting other men
   as wealthy as he,
Whenever the conversation started, he'd
   say to himself:
"I'll lie low till it comes my way—
Then I'll show 'em !"
But they never mentioned bricklaying,
Nor the art of being a foreman,
Nor the whole duty of being a contractor,
Nor figuring costs,
Nor real estate ;
So Jim never said anything.
But he sent his son to college.

              JOHN ERSKINE.

Whereupon another odist whom we may surmise to be Professor Robinson, of the history department of Columbia, retorts as follows:

ODE TO PROFESSOR J—— E——

(In allusion to his Ode to A—— F——.)

Jim Reilly's son Tom didn't know what
   he wanted to do.
So he took Latin and Mathematics and
   hoped they'd discipline his mind,
And prepare him for sharing in polite
   intercourse.
After three years he knew that two
   straight lines perpendicular to the
   same plane
Are parallel to each other.
For a short time he could say what were
   both *sine* and *cosecant;*
But a month after the examination he un-
   happily forgot which was which.
He had learned a list of diminutives; only
   culum and *bulum* remained to
   him—
So sweet was their euphony.
He knew the mute with l or r played a
   mystic rôle in the higher life,
Which in moments of depression he felt
   he didn't grasp.
An old book by an old man for the old
Tightened the reins of his youthful spirit.
When he reached the two gates of slum-
   ber at the end of Lib. VI
They gave him ready exit, and he never
   began Lib. VII.
But he had the elements of a liberal edu-
   cation, and,
Like his philistine father before him,
Whenever the conversation started he'd
   say to himself:
"I'll lie low till it comes my way—
Then I'll show 'em."
But they never mentioned the cæsural
   pause,
And rarely the first Archilochian strophe,
Nor Vercingetorix, nor the mute with l
   or r.
He had never got far enough to meet a
   reflection of Horace's
About those on whose cradles Melpomene
   smiles.
But he knew he couldn't play an Isth-
   mian game as well as T. R.

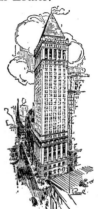

National Defense and International Peace

★ ★ ★ ★ ★ ★ ★ ★ ★ ★ ★

What the Engineers are Doing

THIRTY thousand American engineers are making a card index survey of American industry so that it may be prepared for its vital part in defending the Country, if need comes. The past eighteen months have taught us here in America what lack of industrial preparedness has meant to some of the countries now at war. These nations had the ships and they had the men; but when the hour struck, their factories were not able to furnish the colors with arms and shells and powder. Their factories were not prepared. And our factories are not prepared.

But it is not enough to draw a moral. In the United States five great Engineering Societies — Civil, Mining, Mechanical, Electrical and Chemical — have pledged their services to the Government of the United States, and are already working hand in hand with the Government to prepare industry for the national defense. They receive no pay and will accept no pay. All they seek is opportunity to serve their country, that she may have her industries mobilized and prepared as the basic line of defense.

All elements of the nation's life — the manufacturers, the business men, and the workingmen — should support this patriotic and democratic work of the engineers, and assist them cheerfully when asked. *There can be no better national insurance against war.*

The Associated Advertising Clubs of the World, representing all advertising interests have offered their free and hearty service to the President of the United States, in close co-operation with these five Engineering Societies, to the end that the Country may know what the engineers are doing. The President has accepted the offer. The engineers have welcomed the co-operation.

This advertisement, published without cost to the United States, is the first in a nation-wide series to call the country to the duty of co-operating promptly and fully with the Engineers to prepare industry for

NATIONAL DEFENSE AND INTERNATIONAL PEACE

Father Jim took him into the office.
He did not seem the worse for disciplining his mind.
He could make a deal *untoe securus*, however disadvantageous to the buyer,
And knew the difference betwixt a Martini and a Bronx,
And appreciated the roundness of a maiden's arms,
Without the help of Horace.
          J. H. R.

I need not quote the controversy further since it is evident that the two lines of arguments, like lines perpendicular to the same plane, will never meet however far they may be produced.

The astronomer has his own peculiar way of looking at things. According to Camille Flammarion the history of the world is a rectilinear movement thru space in the direction of the Zeta of Hercules.

If so, the main object of our endeavors is so to act that the inhabitants of Zeta won't be ashamed of us when we get there. Judging by the present condition of terrestrial affairs we'll have to hurry.

It is proposed in Parliament to put a tax of $5 on every cat in the kingdom. But cats are comparatively harmless creatures; even useful. How much better it would be to tax mice instead.

I have always heard that Valparaiso University was an up-to-date institution, but I was not aware that the students there were reading Caesar's *Commentary* on the Mexican War. Such, however, seems to be the case if I may judge from the following paragraph in the University *Torch*. Will it be as *Wilsonus cunctator* that our President goes down in history?

Apud Mexicanos longe dirtissimus et orneryissimus est Villa. Is F. Carranza et C. Obregona consulibus regni, cupiditate inductus coniunctionem banditi fecit et eis persuasit ut de finibus suis cum omnibus copiis exirent; perfacile esse, cum omnibus praestarent,—et quod forte copiae Americani, quamquam premoniti erant, dormitabant in castra Columbi. Id hoc facilius eis persuasit, quod undique loci natura Mexicani continentur; una ex parte flumine Rio Grando, latissimo atque altissimo, qui agrum Mexicanatum a Americanis dividit; altera ex parte monte Sierra altisimo, qui est inter copias Villae et exercitum Americanum; qua ex parte homines bellandi cupidi, in medio nocte, Columbum oppugnaverant. Qua de causa Woodrocus Wilsonus cunctator, conspicatus honorem Americani populi violatem decimam legionem in Mexicano, misit.
        ALMA V. JONES

In the Middle Ages scholars spent their time speculating how many angels could stand on the point of a needle. Nowadays scholars spend their time determining how many microbes can stand on the point of a needle.

The world is so full of a number of things
It's strange we're not all as unhappy as kings.
       —*New York Evening Post.*

Do the best you can until you can do better.

Insurance
Conducted by
W. E. UNDERWOOD

SWAPPING POLICIES

Perhaps as often as a dozen times a year I receive letters from readers advising me of offers made them by life insurance agents involving the surrender of policies for the purpose of replacing them by other policies to be secured by the agents. The enterprising agents in each case always prove by figures the advantages to be derived thru the exchange. Sometimes the insurance sought to be thus terminated is of long standing—I recall one case in which the policy was eleven years old.

Now, it must be admitted that some people have a poor lot of life insurance, and they would only be benefited by abandoning it for something reliable, the sooner the better, for time is an important factor. But these are exceptional cases. The man who owns a policy in a good average company and has paid premiums on it for five or ten years or longer makes a mistake in surrendering it for the purpose of taking another policy in another company. He loses the advantages accruing to him thru the lower rate at the younger age; he probably sacrifices a portion of the reserve by withdrawing; and he loses at the other end of the transaction the years during which he has paid premiums by postponing maturity to that extent.

The agent who endeavors to make an exchange of this character is called a "twister"; the practise is sternly prohibited by all reputable companies; and in many of the states it is forbidden by law. The only person who profits by such a trade is the "twisting" agent, who gets for himself out of the surrender value of the retired policy a good round commission as his pay for selling the new policy.

A proposition of that kind from an insurance agent—and there are some agents who can write new business for their companies in no other way—should put the recipient of the proposal on guard against him, particularly if the existing policy is of some years' standing. If in any case it can be thoroly established that the policyholder's interests warrant the discontinuance of an existing policy, the proceeding is legitimate. Many persons who are carrying coöperative insurance that is unsupported by an adequate mathematical reserve, to illustrate, are losing time by keeping it; for as the years pass the cost increases until in old days it becomes prohibitive.

P. B. H., Marion, S. C.—The North American Accident is entirely sound financially, is well managed, has the reputation of settling its claims justly and promptly.

JOHN KENDRICK BANGS
Presents THE GENIAL PHILOSOPHER

THE Genial Philosopher had been gazing out of the window for a considerable period, apparently too deeply absorbed in thought for words. The Cynical Sciolist, becoming restive under the unwonted silence, finally broke it.

"You seem to be doing a pile of thinking this morning, old man," he said. "What's on your mind?"

"I've been wondering about that very thing myself for the past hour and a half," replied the Genial Philosopher, arousing himself from his obsession with difficulty. "One minute it's one thing, and another minute it's another. Ten minutes ago I was trying to figure out just who is going to ride the Republican Elephant to victory or defeat and I hadn't more than got the Convention itself definitely pictured in my mind when a June-Bug, butting its head upon the window-pane, reminded me that these were bully days to go a-fishing; and just as I was endeavoring to decide whether I'd rather fish for trout in the Berkshires, for salmon on the Columbia River, for whales off the coast of Labrador, or Hudson River shad at Delsherrico's, the possibility of war with Japan popped into my mental machinery and discombobulated the whole mechanism. At the moment you spoke my mental processes were proceeding from an effort to concentrate upon the real causes of the latter-day degeneration of the buckwheat cake from a dainty edible into an unregenerate porous plaster to the undesirability of June marriages viewed from a strictly commercial standpoint, owing to the prevalence of bargain-sales in all our shops, and the consequent cheapness of desirable wedding presents."

"I should say that you were suffering from a bad case of intellectual scatter," said the Cynical Sciolist.

"Who's going to be the Republican nominee, speaking of the price of clams in the Philippines?"

"As to that there is only one sure thing to be said at this time," said the Genial Philosopher, using both hands to push his temples closer together in his effort to concentrate. "You may announce to a waiting world as coming from me that *Theodore Roosevelt will positively NOT accept the nomination for the Vice-Presidency.* He will not accept it if it is offered to him, and if elected he will not serve. Otherwise the thing is still open. As a prophet I believe that a policy of Watchful Waiting will prove more prophetable.

"Well, I guess you are right," said the Cynical Sciolist, "I don't see much sense in worrying about who's to be our next President anyhow. We may have a Kaiser by that time."

"Or a Mikado," said the Genial Philosopher, with a sly wink at the hydrant across the street. "And that gives me a real idea, Brother Sinnick. With the Atlantic Coast in hysterics over an impending Kaiser, and the Pacific Coast smashing all the seismographs in creation with its tremblings over an overhanging Mikado, why wouldn't it be a good thing for us instead of dwelling upon gruesome thoughts of war and gore to set about a subtler way of meeting our problem. Why not lure both Germany and Japan into our midst; let the Germans land in New York, and the Japanese in San Francisco without firing a shot. Greet them with Committees of Welcome, who will escort them to their respective City Halls, and there with due ceremonial present them with the freedom of the country. Say to them, 'Gentlemen, our fat and teeming land is yours—GO TO IT!' A brief period of German Efficiency in the New York City Hall would work wonders for the great metropolis, and similarly San Francisco's municipal government under the astute management of the thrifty Japs would solve a good many of the problems with which the children of the Sierras are now impotently wrestling. *Institute a new and subtler kind of warfare based upon smiling courtesy, and a killing kindness.* Give the invaders public banquets, and while secretly undermining their digestions, lull them into a state of fancied security with the honeyed words of our most mellifluous after-dinner orators. Gas them not with noxious vapors, but with honeyed vaporings. Call upon Brother Bryan with his most fetching smile to address them over flowing bowls of liquid grape, and extending the glad hand of welcome to the Kaiser, speak not as two enemies, but as one Bill to another. And to the Mikado, just arrived at the Golden Gate, let Uncle Hiram Johnson in exalted periods say similarly, 'O Son of the Sun, Cousin of the Moon, and Father-in-Law of the Milky Way, today have Fujiyama and Shasta, like Righteousness and Peace, osculated in one glorious osculation. In the name of our fructiferous State of California I welcome you to our shores, and present to you at the unanimous request of my constituents all our State and Municipal Bonds, our Country, Shire, and Ward Deferred Debenture Certificates; indeed, Sire, with all the obligations past, present, and future, which our splendid Commonwealth has set apart as its gift to posterity.' And so on.

"What would be the result? Destruction? Not a bit of it. Murder, pillage, arson and rapine? Not in the least. The Kaiser completely disarmed would settle down at the Ritz, the Mikado at the St. Francis, and then, my friend, *one of two things would happen.* They would either succumb, as have we, to the allurements of their new environment, and grow soft and flabby, or they would become profoundly jealous of each other. Probably the latter, after the fashion of potentates. The Mikado hearing of the enormous fortunes made in War Brides by the Eastern invaders on Wall Street, would be stirred to envy. The Kaiser, receiving reports thru his secret agents of the romantic times the Mikado was having, sleeping on delicious soft-cushions stuffed with thornless cactus, raising freckles on the highly manicured freckle ranches of Pasadena and Santa Barbara, feasting on toke-point oysters, fresh grape-fruit, luscious crab-meat, and green asparagus all the year round, with the climate of heaven itself bathing him from morn to dewy eve in its soft silkiness, would become a perfect Fafner of green-eyed jealousy. Ultimatums, Penultimatums, and Superdreadultimatums would be exchanged, and then WAR. Wilhelm would start for San Francisco, with an overwhelming force; the Mikado would start East for New York with another overwhelming force. They'd meet somewhere on the plains this side of the Rockies, and then would follow the titanic contest of the ages. We Americans would stand to one side and let them fight it out, manufacturing munitions for both sides, and then——"

The Genial Philosopher slapped his knee with a resounding thwack.

"Then, Brother Sinnick," said he, his voice trembling with emotion, "when these two overwhelming forces had fought themselves to a stand-still, and each was but the shadow of a frazzle, THEN would be Uncle Sam's opportunity. *He could summon the police and arrest what was left of 'em both for disorderly conduct, resume possession of his reorganized country, and fulfil his manifest Destiny.*"

"It sounds good," said the Cynical Sciolist, "but after all it won't work. Both parties would make us pay all the expenses of the war, and we'd be ruined economically anyhow."

"Not in the end," said the Genial Philosopher, "for, don't you see, my dear Sinnick, that after having captured both the Kaiser and the Mikado we could put 'em in a cage and send them out upon the Vaudeville Circuit, and let the public look at 'em at ten cents a head. Why, my dear man, as a drawing card they would have Charlie Chaplin beaten to a frazzle, and as long as they lived Uncle Sam would never have to levy another tax!"

The Independent

Founded 1848

HARPER'S WEEKLY
Founded 1857

Incorporated with The Independent May 22, 1916

THE CHAUTAUQUAN
Incorporated with The Independent June 1, 1914

The Independent is owned and published by the Independent Corporation, at 119 West Fortieth Street, New York. William B. Howland, president; Frederic E. Dickinson, treasurer; William Hayes Ward, honorary editor; Hamilton Holt, editor; Harold J. Howland, associate editor; Edwin E. Slosson, literary editor; Karl V. S. Howland, publisher. The price of The Independent is Ten Cents a copy; Four Dollars for one year. Postage to foreign countries in the Postal Union, $1.75 extra; to Canada, $1 extra. Writers who wish their articles returned should send stamped and addrast envelopes. No responsibility is assumed for the loss or non-return of manuscripts. Entered at the New York Post Office as Second Class matter. Copyright, 1916, by The Independent. Address all communications to The Independent, 119 West Fortieth Street, New York

THE NEW PLAYS

A realistic, the highly colored picture of United States army life on the Mexican border is Augustus Thomas' timely melodrama, *Rio Grande*. (Empire.)

A Lady's Name is an amusing English comedy that affords Marie Tempest an opportunity for one of her inimitable characterizations. (Maxine Elliott.)

Beau Brummel, a revival of Clyde Fitch's masterpiece with Arnold Daly in the title rôle, made famous by Mansfield. Good, but not "darn" good. (Cort.)

Justice, by John Galsworthy, is probably the finest play in New York, and also convincing propaganda for prison reform. John Barrymore and O. P. Heggie do some excellent acting. (Candler.)

A Woman of No Importance. One of Oscar Wilde's brilliant, superficial and artificial high society dramas, with Margaret Anglin and Holbrook Blinn as stars. Nothing better of its kind. (Fulton.)

The beautiful scenic effects in the Washington Square Players' production of *The Sea-Gull,* by Tchekoff, redeem their rather unfinished acting. The play is an interesting contrast to American drama. (Bandbox.)

The Tempest, under Drama Society auspices, lacks poetry, but presents an uncut text and an interesting compromise between Elizabethan and modern staging. (Century.)

Shakespeare's Sophomore show, *Merry Wives of Windsor,* is played by Sir Herbert Tree's company with a roisterous, almost undergraduate, good humor. (New Amsterdam.)

The colored people of New York City, practically excluded from most of the theaters, have established their own stage and the Wright Dramatic Company is now playing *Othello* in a way superior to many a white stock company. (Lafayette.)

Caliban by the Yellow Sands, by Percy Mackaye, is a remarkable achievement—elaborate pageantry, colorful scenery, music, recitation and pantomime, all blended into a community festival in honor of Shakespeare. (New York City College Stadium.)

REMARKABLE REMARKS

THEDA BARA—I loathe hot milk.

RICHARD LE GALLIENNE—Be jocund thou.

WOODROW WILSON—This war was brought on by rulers.

DR. CHARLES H. PARKHURST—Poverty is nothing but a habit.

BISHOP J. F. BERRY—Everything is money, money, money.

JAMES J. HILL—Capital may be a shy bird for some time to come.

SENATOR CHAMBERLAIN—Everything we do in life is a compromise.

ED. HOWE—I know plenty of men who have been ruined by the church.

THEODORE ROOSEVELT—I am straight United States and nothing else.

DR. WOODS HUTCHINSON—The real risks of war are not bullets but bugs.

HERBERT KAUFMAN—The "meant" in postponement won't help matters.

GEORGE BERNARD SHAW—We are the champion mendicants of the world.

MARY PICKFORD—But it's awful skeery man attending strictly to his own job.

J. PIERPONT MORGAN—I believe in every man attending strictly to his own job.

BARON D'ESTOURNELLES DE CONSTANT—The English people get up too late.

"DIAMOND JIM" BRADY—Broadway is New York and New York is Broadway.

CHRYSTAL EASTMAN BENEDICT—Alimony is not thought of by a real feminist.

HOWARD S. HADLEY—Roosevelt will be the next Republican Senator from New York.

ALICE G. KIRK—Underneath the dining room table should always be found a small hassock.

K. K. KAWAKAMI—Japan does not want Peking to become the Constantinople of the Far East.

ARTHUR BRISBANE—The moving picture in history will equal the discovery of the printing press.

GEORGE JEFFERSON—If I were the Pope I should order every combatant to lay down his arms instantly on pain of excommunication.

SIR ROGER CASEMENT—If London suffered what London has caused Brussels, Louvain, Liège to suffer—there would be no war in Europe.

THE DUKE OF MANCHESTER—I don't believe there is a single member of the British aristocracy who is not working for the government in some capacity.

PROF. STANLEY LANE-POOLE—The English ideal of imperialism is a state composed of nations. The German ideal of imperialism is a nation composed of states.

REV. CHARLES E. JEFFERSON—Every girl in her twenties who has found a man that has won her heart has the right to marry him in spite of the opposition of her parents.

ELIHU ROOT—Whether it will be necessary for the United States to act in defense of the Monroe Doctrine or abandon it, may well be determined by the issues of the present war.

SCHOOL PHYSICAL DIRECTOR OCKER—Military training in schools fosters a bombastic spirit of tin soldierism and false sense of patriotism which does not appreciate the seriousness of war or the glories of peace.

THE SALMON—At Ellis Island, where I spent three years as a physician, doctors spent as much time in examining the mental condition of an immigrant as is spent by the gateman at a railroad station in examining your ticket.

THE BISHOP OF LIMERICK—If any one thinks that the millions of workingmen trained in arms in Europe will settle down peaceably after the war to starvation in order to help reamass fortunes for their "betters" he may have a rude awakening.

The Independent

WITH WHICH IS INCORPORATED

HARPER'S WEEKLY

A GATEWAY TO THE OUTDOORS

Photograph by Ella M. Boult

The Independent

WITH WHICH IS INCORPORATED

HARPER'S WEEKLY
A Journal of Civilization

A GATEWAY TO THE OUTDOORS

Photograph by Ella M. Boult

America Ready to Join a League to Enforce Peace, Declares President Wilson

An Address Delivered Before the League to Enforce Peace, May 27, 1916, at Washington

WHEN the invitation to be here tonight came to me, I was glad to accept it, not because it offered me an opportunity to discuss the program of the league (that you will, I am sure, not expect of us), but because the desire of the whole world now turns eagerly, more and more eagerly, toward the hope of peace, and there is just reason why we should take our part in counsel upon this great theme. It is right that I, as spokesman of our government, should attempt to give expression to what I believe to be the thought and purpose of the people of the United States in this vital matter.

This great war that broke so suddenly upon the world two years ago, and which has swept within its flame so great a part of the civilized world, has affected us very profoundly, and we are not only at liberty, it is perhaps our duty, to speak very frankly of it and of the great interests of civilization which it affects.

With its causes and its objects we are not concerned. The obscure fountains from which its stupendous flood has burst forth we are not interested to search for or explore. But so great a flood, spread far and wide to every quarter of the globe, has of necessity engulfed many a fair province, of right that lies very near to us. Our own rights as a nation, the liberties, the privileges, and the property of our people have been profoundly affected. We are not more disconnected lookers-on. The longer the war lasts the more deeply do we become concerned that it should be brought to an end and the world be permitted to resume its normal life and course again. And when it does come to an end, we shall be as much concerned as the nations at war to see peace assume an aspect of permanence, give promise of days from which the anxiety of uncertainty shall be lifted, bring some assurance that peace and war shall always hereafter be reckoned part of the common interest of mankind.

We are participants, whether we would or not, in the life of the world. The interests of all nations are our own also. We are partners with the rest. What affects mankind is inevitably our affair as well as the affair of the nations of Europe and of Asia.

One observation on the causes of the present war we are at liberty to make, and to make it may throw some light forward upon the future, as well as backward upon the past. It is plain that this war could have come only as it did, suddenly and out of secret counsels, without warning to the world, without discussion, without any of the deliberate movements of counsel with which it would seem natural to approach so stupendous a contest. It is probable that it had been foreseen just what would happen, just what alliances would be formed, just what forces arrayed against one another, those who brought the great contest on would have been glad to substitute conference for force.

If we ourselves had been afforded some opportunity to apprise the belligerents of the attitude which it would be our duty to take, of the policies and practises against which we would feel bound to use all our moral and economic strength, and in certain circumstances even our physical strength also, our own contribution to the counsel, which might have averted the struggle, would have been considered worth weighing and regarding.

And the lesson, which the shock of being taken by surprise in a matter so deeply vital to all the nations of the world has made poignantly clear, is that the peace of the world must henceforth depend upon a new and more wholesome diplomacy. Only when the great nations of the world have reached some sort of agreement as to what they hold to be fundamental to their common interest, and as to some feasible method of acting in concert when any nation or group of nations seeks to disturb those fundamental things, can we feel that civilization is at last in a way of justifying its existence and claiming to be finally established. It is clear that nations must in the future be governed by the same high code of honor that we demand of individuals.

We must, indeed, in the very same breath with which we avow this conviction admit that we have ourselves upon occasion in the past been offenders against the law of diplomacy, which we thus forecast; but our conviction is not the less clear, but rather the more clear, on that account.

If this war has accomplished nothing else for the benefit of the world, it has at least disclosed a great moral necessity and set forward the thinking of the statesmen of the world by a whole age. Repeated utterances of the leading statesmen of most of the great nations now engaged in war have made it plain that their thought has come to this: That the principle of public right must henceforth take precedence over the individual interests of particular nations and that the nations of the world must in some way band themselves together to see that that right prevails as against any sort of selfish aggression; that henceforth alliance must not be set up against alliance, understanding against understanding, but that there must be a common agreement for a common object, and that at the heart of that common object must lie the inviolable rights of peoples and of mankind.

The nations of the world have become each other's neighbors. It is to their interest that they should understand each other. In order that they may understand each other it is imperative that they should agree to coöperate in a common cause and that they should so act that the guiding principle of that common cause shall be even-handed and impartial justice.

This is undoubtedly the thought of America. This is what we ourselves will say when there comes proper occasion to say it. In the dealings of nations with one another arbitrary force must be rejected and we must move forward to the thought of the modern world, the thought of which peace is the very atmosphere. That thought constitutes a chief part of the passionate conviction of America.

We believe these fundamental things:

First, that every people has a right to choose the sovereignty under which they shall live. Like other nations, we have ourselves no doubt once and again offended against that principle when for a little while controlled by selfish passion, as our franker historians have been honorable enough to admit; but it has become more and more our rule of life and action.

Second, that the small states of the world have a right to enjoy the same respect for their sovereignty and for their territorial integrity that great and powerful nations expect and insist upon.

And, third, that the world has a right to be free from every disturbance of its peace that has its origin in aggression and disregard of the rights of peoples and nations.

So sincerely do we believe in these things that I am sure that I speak the mind and wish of the people of America when I say that the United States is willing to become a partner in any feasible association of nations formed in order to realize these objects and make them secure against violation.

There is nothing that the United States wants for itself that any other nation has. We are willing, on the contrary, to limit ourselves along with them to a prescribed course of duty and respect for the rights of others, which will check any selfish passion of our own, as it will check any aggressive impulse of theirs.

If it should ever be our privilege to suggest or initiate a movement for peace among the nations now at war, I am sure that the people of the United States would wish their government to move along these lines:

First—Such a settlement with regard to their own immediate interests as the belligerents may agree upon. We have nothing material of any kind to ask for ourselves, and are quite aware that we are in no sense or degree parties to the present quarrel. Our interest is only in peace and its future guarantees.

Second—A universal association of the nations to maintain the inviolate security of the highway of the seas for the common and unhindered use of all the nations of the world, and to prevent any war, begun either contrary to treaty covenants or without warning and full submission of the causes to the opinion of the world—virtual guarantee of territorial integrity and political independence.

But I did not come here, let me repeat, to discuss a program. I came only to avow a creed and give expression to the confidence I feel that the world is even now upon the eve of a great consummation, when some common force will be brought into existence which shall safeguard right as the first and most fundamental interest of all peoples and all governments, when coercion shall be summoned not to the service of political ambition or selfish hostility, but to the service of a common order, a common justice, and a common peace. God grant that the dawn of that day of frank dealing and of settled peace, concord, and coöperation may be near at hand!

THE PRESIDENT ON THE ENFORCEMENT OF PEACE

THE address of President Wilson at the first annual banquet of the League to Enforce Peace will afford intense gratification to every one who believes that the world has come to the point where the united force of the nations must be made available to compel the settlement of international disputes by peaceful means. For the President of the United States is more than an individual; he is the spokesman of a great nation. As such he was attempting to give expression to what he believed to be "the thought and purpose of the people of the United States in this vital matter" of the hope of peace.

At the outset of his address the President entered a disclaimer; he was not discussing the program of the League. But what he had to say thereafter was quite as satisfactory as if he had taken up that program point by point. For it is not, after all, the program of the League that profoundly matters. It is its central idea, its basic principle. Of this principle Mr. Wilson's utterances were in thoro recognition and support.

The President's thought focussed itself in two passages of his address. In the first he declared the belief of the American people in these fundamental things:

First, that every people has a right to choose the sovereignty under which it shall live;

Second, that the small states of the world have a right to enjoy the same respect for their sovereignty and for their territorial integrity that great and powerful nations expect and insist upon;

Third, that the world has a right to be free from every disturbance of its peace that has its origin in aggression and disregard of the rights of peoples and nations.

So sincere is the belief of the people of the United States in these principles, Mr. Wilson continued, "that the United States is willing to become a partner in any feasible association of nations formed in order to realize these objects and make them secure against violation."

In the second passage the President referred to the contingency that it might some time be our privilege to suggest or initiate a movement for peace among the nations now at war. In the event of such a possibility we ought to move along the line of "a universal association of the nations to maintain the inviolate security of the seas for the common and unhindered use of all the nations of the world, and to prevent any war, begun either contrary to treaty covenants, or w i t h o u t warning and full submission of the causes to the opinion of the world—a virtual guarantee of territorial integrity and political independence."

Finally, the President gave expression to his confidence "that the world is even now upon the eve of a great consummation, when some common force will be brought into existence which shall safeguard right as the first and most fundamental interest of all peoples and all governments, when coercion shall be summoned not to the service of political ambition or selfish hostility, but to the service of a common order, a common justice and a common peace."

These are admirable statements of the basic principles on which the platform of the League to Enforce Peace is builded. The only difference between the two expressions—the President's and the League's—is one of method of approach. Mr. Wilson philosophizes on the truths which must be recognized in seeking international justice and world peace; the League outlines the course of action which the nations must take in the quest of these great ends. Mr. Wilson lays down principles; the League proposes ways and means.

Other difference there is none. When the President speaks of an association of nations to prevent any war begun without full submission of the causes to the opinion of the world he describes accurately the organization which the League proposes to establish. When he speaks of coercion summoned to the service of a common order, a common justice and a common peace, he sets forth the idea which distinguishes the League to Enforce Peace from every other peace movement.

With this high endorsement—this almost official endorsement—of its principles and its purposes, the League to Enforce Peace takes a commanding position a m o n g organized plans for the securing of international peace. An almost indispensable element in the success of the proposals of the League is the initiation of the plan among the nations of the world by the Government of the United States. The taking of such an initiatory step at the appropriate time is foreshadowed by the President's address.

In thus endorsing its principles Mr. Wilson has given a lead to the people of the United States. The League in its first year of existence has achieved notable popular support. This popular adherence to its program ought to wax and multiply in ever increasing measure until it has accomplished its work for the world's welfare.

A DECLARATION OF INTERDEPENDENCE

I T is hardly possible to exaggerate the importance of the President's speech last Saturday evening at the dinner of the League to Enforce Peace.

Here for the first time in history the responsible head of a great world power publicly proposes to translate the highest ideal of the greatest minds of all ages into an act of statesmanship substituting among the nations of the earth the reign of law for the reign of war.

It is a proposal that if accepted may change the course of history.

But more than that: Once let the warring nations be convinced of the wisdom of entering a League for the maintenance of a durable peace, and all the issues for which they are now fighting fade into insignificance. The President's high statesmanship may not only furnish the basis of permanent peace, but may also be the means of bringing the Great War to an end.

Woodrow Wilson has added to the Declaration of Independence a Declaration of Interdependence.

THE LEAGUE TO ENFORCE PEACE

EVER since the calling of the First Hague Conference, The Independent and its editor have been urging a League to Enforce Peace as the next great step in the political evolution of the world.

Tho the idea of world federation has been the dream of the poets, prophets and philosophers down the ages it is only in recent times that it has been put forward here and there as a practical possibility.

In 1905 at the Thirteenth Interparliamentary Conference at Brussels Richard Bartholdt, member of Congress from Missouri and president of the American delegation, presented a plan for consideration that would furnish the basis of world federation.

In the same year Andrew Carnegie in his rectorial address at St. Andrew's University in Scotland developed the same idea.

In 1907, at the Second Hague Conference, Señor Ordoney, ex-President of Uruguay, in behalf of that republic, officially introduced a detailed proposal for a League of Peace to go into effect when adopted by "ten nations, of whom half shall have at least 25,000,000 inhabitants each."

In 1910, in his Nobel Peace address, delivered at Christiania, Norway, Theodore Roosevelt proposed a league of nations to guarantee national territory and sovereignty, to arbitrate all other questions, and to limit armaments by international agreement.

In 1911, at Baltimore, Maryland, the editor of The Independent, as president of the Third American Peace Congress, devoted his entire opening address to the exposition and elaboration of the principles of a league of nations.

When the Great War broke out, The Independent was the first paper in this country—possibly in the world—to urge editorially the formation of a League to Enforce Peace as the one sure way to maintain a lasting peace. This editorial, which appeared in our issue of September 28, 1914, under the title of "The Way to Disarm: A Practical Proposal," was reprinted by various organizations and widely distributed. It received much comment both in the United States and Europe.

It was this editorial, more than anything else, that led to a meeting of a small group of publicists and political scientists in New York City, who, after a series of conferences, formed themselves into a preliminary committee, drafted proposals for a League to Enforce Peace, and launched the idea on the 17th of last June, at a public meeting at Independence Hall, Philadelphia, the very spot where the United States of America was born.

The Independence Hall meeting organized a permanent committee, with ex-President Taft at its head, President Lowell, of Harvard University, as the chairman of its executive committee, and a thousand other of America's most distinguished citizens coöperating.

This American branch of the League to Enforce Peace has now, within less than a year, increased its membership and prestige until it is organized in almost every state and congressional district in the Union.

It has not only extended itself in the United States, but the idea has taken strong hold abroad; the group in England, for instance, being so close to the British Government that we can almost assume that Great Britain is officially behind it.

And now, at its first annual meeting at Washington last week, delegates foregathered from every state in the Union to hear the principles of the League expounded and to devise ways and means to carry out its program. Nearly $400,000 was subscribed to its treasury, and, to cap the climax, the President of the United States endorsed the League and put himself, as spokesman of the United States Government, at the head of this movement to enthrone reason instead of force as the final arbiter of the destinies of nations.

BRAWN

WE learn from the *Yale Alumni Weekly* that of the forty-five fortunates from the Junior Class who were "tapped" on May 18 for Yale's three famous secret senior societies, thirty-five, or seven-ninths, have athletic records.

As the greatest honor that can come to a Yale undergraduate is considered to be an election to "Bones," "Keys" or "Wolf's Head," it follows that the athletic ideal is still paramount at New Haven.

And yet the common sense of mankind never has rated and probably never will rate mere athletic aptitude very high compared with other human values.

GOOD WILL TO ALL MEN

THE American people, realizing that the Great War, like an earthquake, is a calamity bringing ruin alike upon innocent and guilty, have distributed their charities to the war victims of all nations. The sufferings of the Armenian and Syrian Christians have appealed especially to us because thousands of Americans have been for years contributing to the mission schools and churches of this region, and American indignation has been rightfully aroused against the Turkish Government for the cruel deportations and wholesale massacres which have been perpetrated under its authority. An effort is now being made to raise in America the large sum of money necessary to rescue the Armenians and Syrians from their present distress, and collections will be taken up in churches and Sunday schools all over the land. Yet the philanthropists who are heading the subscription list have just telegraphed the sum of $60,000 to Constantinople for the relief of the Turkish people who are in little less need than their Christian compatriots. The Jews have set a good example to the Christians in this. The Jewish Relief Committee has ordered that the funds it has collected from the Hebrews in this country be divided between the Hebrews and Moslems of Turkey.

So, too, the American people, in spite of their justifiable indignation against the German Government, have contributed liberally for the Red Cross in Germany. Unfortunately their benevolent intentions in this direction have been frustrated by the action of the British Government, which prohibited the sending of hospital supplies to the German Red Cross even when sent from America by American ships to neutral European ports. Consequently the medicines and surgical appliances intended for the sick and wounded of Germany remain piled up on the docks at New York, while those for the Allies go forward regularly. The American Red Cross has accordingly been compelled to notify the public that no more contributions for the Central Powers can be received until England raises its embargo. Ex-President Taft has written to our State Department, protesting against this outrageous violation of Article 16 of the Geneva Convention, which prohibits making Red Cross supplies contraband of war. It is to be hoped that President Wilson may induce the British Government to modify its blockade rules so that this one limitation on the universality of American charity may be removed.

WHICH?

THE Republicans at Chicago have three choices.

They can nominate Justice Hughes if they are willing to take him with his convictions on present issues veiled in impenetrable mystery.

They can nominate Mr. Roosevelt if they are willing to take him with his unequivocally exprest and forcefully definite convictions on present issues.

They can—but there is no other sane choice.

WHAT THE MIDDLE WEST THINKS

NOWHERE else in the world is there an area so large, wealthy and homogeneous as the stretch of states between Pittsburgh and Lincoln, and Duluth and Louisville. What it thinks today is likely to be the opinion of the dominant party tomorrow and what it will not stand for today is probably already lost. Ever since the Republican party emerged from it unexpectedly and completely in 1854 it has set the tune for American life. Its adherence to its own special leader, Lincoln, made possible the preservation of the Union; its peculiar financial troubles brought the United States face to face, first, with greenback inflation and then with silver inflation—and it was its own sober second thought rather than the campaign funds of Mark Hanna or the frenzied opposition of the East that stopped both of these cheap money movements short of disaster. In our own day its readiness to try remedies for political ailments has made it the stamping ground of reform and the hunting ground of reformers. What it thinks today will be the determining factor in the election next fall and in the foreign problem.

The public opinion of the Middle West is created by a comfortable middle class. When times are hard every one is discouraged; when times are good pessimism drops off and is forgotten. The over-rich are not feared, but they are suspected. Few are over-poor.

The Middle West is national-minded and idealistic. It is proud of the United States as such, and has felt that pride ever since it drove the reluctant East into the War of 1812. It likes to think of American intellectual leadership. It has caught the idea that Mr. Wilson has been teaching so patiently since the war began, and has glimpsed the notion of the United States as defending law for the sake of justice. It will fight for this relentlessly if it has to, but it will enter no fight for the sake of the fight itself, for the abstraction known as honor, or for conquest. Even the seductive appeal of its greatest newspaper, the *Chicago Tribune* (that does not disguise its lust for a second rape of Mexico), cannot stir it.

Ready to defend what it conceives to be a higher law of nations, the limitations of the Middle West have kept it from seeing all that such defense implies, and its inherited attitude toward great wealth has deflected its view. It has never consciously prepared itself for anything, and its political or social policies have been cor-

rective rather than constructive. It has not been accustomed to think of preparation, and few of its leaders have themselves felt the need of leading in this direction. In the present situation it might be more willing to undertake military preparedness did it not feel that much of the cry for preparedness comes from a tainted source. The great corporations that make, and make much out of, munitions have been disliked and mistrusted for so many years that the Middle West cannot now believe in their disinterested patriotism. Senator Cummins led an attack upon the trusts and the protective tariff in Iowa long ago; Senator LaFollette has ever preached suspicion against big business; Mr. Roosevelt's utterances against malefactors of great wealth have not yet cooled off. And with such an education Middle Westerners distrust a movement so obviously led by persons who may be selfish.

The Middle West will fight to defend an idea if it must, but no leader has yet explained preparedness on the right grounds, and until such an explanation has been imprest on the Middle Western mind the Western delegations in Congress will continue to wobble and shift. The support of Mr. Wilson is lukewarm because the Middle West is, on the whole, Republican. Mr. Roosevelt has not aroused the old thrills that used to be stirred up by his leadership because his allies are subject to suspicion and because he is charged with wanting a war. Mr. Bryan is weakening because he wants a peace. But the essential sympathy of the Middle West with the knight errant notion of an international law that the United States may have to defend is lying ready to be turned into political support for any leader whose connections are clear and who understands the homogeneous West.

P. P. C. OF SHAKESPEARE

MANY years ago a young man fresh from Johns Hopkins was called upon suddenly to take charge of a class in Shakespeare at a western university. The professor whom he succeeded was a veteran of the "scientific" school of literary research, one who would spend an hour discussing the age of Anne Hathaway or whether a punctuation mark on the thirty-third page of the First Folio was a period or a flyspeck. The newcomer faced a class expecting something of the same sort, only more so. But his first question was a surprize: "How many of you have come provided with Shakespeare? None of you? Well, every one in the class must have Shakespeare complete by tomorrow. That's all for today."

The next morning the campus saw a curious sight, a procession of students toiling up the hill loaded down with the Immortal Bard in all shapes and bindings. Some had their pockets stuffed out with handy volumes. Some bore old tomes as big as a dictionary or a family Bible. Some had a cheap padded leather volume with microscopic print. Some carried on alternate arms a twelve-volume set in a morocco leather case which had been locked up in the parlor bookcase since the day it had been received as a wedding present by their parents.

The new professor surveyed the class and their picturesque burdens with grim satisfaction. "Have you all got Shakespeare now? Well, read him. After that I shall have something to say to you. Class is dismissed."

The young man who started on his career in this unconventional style is now at the head of one of the English departments in one of our largest universities. He still insists that his students read the books they are talking about.

We are reminded of this incident in considering the attitude of some people toward the Shakespeare Tercentenary. They appear to have deposited their P. P. C. cards on Shakespeare's tomb and gone on their way rejoicing that they would not have to think of him again for the next hundred years.

Now, the Shakespeare celebration was really intended more as an introduction than as a leave-taking. All of the various pageants, speeches and contests, including our own contest, were designed, as we may now confess, to trick people into reading an author, who, it seemed to us, deserved more reading than he got. So far as our own share in the movement is concerned, it seems to have accomplished its purpose even better than we anticipated. Some ten thousand students from all parts of the country competed for The Independent Shakespeare Medal. This involved not merely reading the eight articles on Shakespeare's life and works by Dr. Frederick Houk Law in The Independent, but also considerable study of the plays themselves, in order to write the required essays. In about four hundred schools and colleges there were a sufficient number of contestants to secure one of the medals awarded by The Independent.

Now, of these ten thousand young people who have been induced to read Shakespeare by this device, and the hundred thousand or more who have been indirectly concerned in the contests, and the millions who have been interested thru the medium of the various Tercentenary festivities, there will be some who will continue to read Shakespeare, not for a prize, not because it is an anniversary, not because people are talking about him, but because they find him interesting and profitable. That's what all this fuss is for.

MOTORS AND MOVIES

THE 128th General Assembly of the Presbyterian Church in session at Atlantic City last week devoted time to denouncing the evil effects of the automobile and the moving picture. One speaker referred to the "movie" theater as "The modern Diana of the Ephesians." Another declared that the automobile was "carrying away from the Church the magnificent army of Christ."

Let not the brethren forget, however, that the automobile and the moving picture are the greatest educators of the age. The automobile carries you everywhere. The moving picture carries everywhere to you.

CONSCRIPTION

HAS the state of New York gone stark crazy? Her legislature has passed and Governor Charles S. Whitman has signed five bills that require, among other things, all men between eighteen and forty-five to be enrolled as members of the Militia Reserve beginning August 1, and all schoolboys between sixteen and nineteen to drill not more than three hours each week and go to summer military camps under the direction of the officers of the National Guard, and all school children over eight—girls as well as boys—to "receive as part of the prescribed course of instruction such physical training as the regents, after conference with the military training commission, may determine during periods which shall average at least twenty minutes in each school day."

These laws mean conscription in time of peace. They should be forthwith repealed. The American people believe in preparedness—sane preparedness—but this goes to the very brink of the precipice of militarism.

THE AMERICAN INVASION OF EUROPE

THERE is much difference of opinion as to whether there will be a large volume of immigration from Europe to this country after the war or not, but it is quite evident that there will be a host of people from America flocking over to Europe by the first steamers that cross after the treaty of peace is signed. Some of these will be immigrants or the sons of immigrants looking up their relatives or their property, but most will be tourists visiting the battlefields of the greatest war in history. Already we learn that all the rooms in the leading hotels of London and Paris have been engaged in advance by Americans who are going when the war is over.

In former times American tourists have spent something like $150,000,000 a year in Europe, and the shutting off of this revenue for two years has caused great hardship, especially in Italy and Switzerland. The return of the tourist will revive their prosperity and his ready cash will do much to repair the ravages of war. Americans have a passion for ruins and thousands of travelers who have never cared to see the townhall of Ypres or the cathedral of Rheims in the hight of their beauty will now be drawn to them for their historic interest. It is quite likely that the expenditures of visitors to Louvain will in the course of a few years be sufficient to rebuild the burnt quarter of that city. At any rate, tourism will contribute considerably toward the reconstruction of Belgian towns on a more wholesome and habitable scale according to plans which had been made before the war. The slums which had been the despair of the Belgian reformers then have in many cases been swept away by the tide of battles along with the irreplaceable treasures of antiquity and the city planner will have what he rarely gets in the old world, a *tabula rasa* for his model dwellings.

The long serpentine line of battle stretching from the sea to Switzerland and coiling about Ypres and Verdun will be a path of pilgrimage for all future time. It is historic ground sacred to the memory of the millions of young men who have here given their lives for their country. It should never be touched by the plow or allowed to lapse to mercenary use, like common soil, but should be preserved for a memorial of those who held the line against the invader. If one of those fine roads that the French know how to make were laid along the neutral strip between the battle lines, automobiles and buses could carry tourists all the way from Nieuport to Pont-a-Mousson. If the trenches on each side are kept intact and as nearly as possible as they look now they would prove as interesting as the Hotel des Invalides and far more worthy of reverence than the tomb of Napoleon. Such shrines we have in our own country at Gettysburg and Bunker Hill, silently teaching their lessons of patriotism to young and old, generation after generation. The battlefields of the Great War should likewise be dedicated to the perpetual service of calling to mind the awfulness of war and the glory of self-sacrifice. "It is altogether fitting and proper that we should do this."

THE STORY OF THE WEEK

The State Department has address to the governments of Great Britain and France a vigorous protest against their interference with United States mails moving between this country and Europe. In principle there would seem to be no difference between the allied powers and ourselves on this point. For the American Government agrees that merchandise, whether carried by parcel post or in sealed letter mail, stocks, bonds and securities, money orders, checks, drafts, notes and other negotiable instruments, which may pass as the equivalent of money, are all subject to the same treatment of capture and confiscation as merchandise shipped in any other manner. Obviously it would not be fair to permit a belligerent or a neutral to beat the devil around the stump by sending contraband by post and claiming that it was to be treated otherwise than if it had been shipped as freight or as express matter. On the other hand, the allied governments admit that under international law and practise genuine correspondence is inviolable, and may not be seized or unduly detained.

The method of applying these principles in practise, says Secretary Lansing in the note, is the chief cause of difference. The allied governments, while declaring that they will not seize genuine correspondence on the high seas, seek to get around the assurance that they have thus given by seizing and confiscating mail from vessels in port instead of at sea. They compel neutral ships to enter their own ports or induce shipping lines, by some form of duress, to send their mail ships via British ports. They thus acquire by force or unjustifiable means an illegal jurisdiction.

The note further sets forth the nature of the illegal procedure adopted by the allied governments:

Acting upon this enforced jurisdiction, the authorities remove all mail, genuine correspondence as well as post parcels, take them to London, where every piece, even tho of neutral origin and destination, is opened and critically examined to determine the "sincerity of their character." In accordance with the interpretation given that undefined phrase by the British and French censors. Finally the expurgated remainder is forwarded, frequently after irreparable delay, to its destination. Ships are detained en route to or from the United States, or to or from other neutral countries, and mails are held and delayed for several days and, in some cases, for weeks and even months, even tho not routed to ports of north Europe via British ports.

The note further sets forth the injuries to neutral business caused by this improper and vexatious proceeding:

The arbitrary methods employed by the British and French governments have resulted most disastrously to citizens of the United States. Important papers which can never be duplicated, or can be duplicated only with great difficulty, such as United States patents for inventions, rare documents, legal papers relating to the settlement of estates, powers of attorney, fire insurance claims, income tax returns, and similar matters have been lost.

Delays in receiving shipping documents have caused great loss and inconvenience by preventing prompt delivery of goods. In the case of the MacNiff Horticultural Company, of New York, large shipments of plants and bulbs from Holland were, I am informed, frozen on the wharves because possession could not be obtained in the absence of documents relating to them which had been removed from the "Nieuw Amsterdam," "Oosterdyk" and "Rotterdam."

Business opportunities are lost by failure to transmit promptly bids, specifications and contracts. The Standard Underground Cable Company, of Pittsburgh, for example, sent by mail a tender and specifications for certain proposed electrical works to be constructed in Christiania. After several weeks of waiting, the papers having failed to arrive, the American company was told that the bids could not be longer held open and the contract was awarded to a British competitor. Checks, drafts, money orders, securities and similar property are lost or detained for weeks and months. Business correspondence relating to legitimate and bona fide trade between neutral countries, correspondence of a personal nature, and also certain official correspondence, such as money order lists and other matter forwarded by government departments are detained, lost or possibly destroyed.

For instance, the Postmaster General informs me that certain international money order lists from the United States to Germany, Greece and other countries, and from Germany to the United States, sent thru the mails, have not reached their destination, tho dispatched several months ago.

Because of these injurious practises the Government of the United States expects the present practise of the British and French governments in relation to mails from and to the United States to be altered forthwith. "Only a radical change in the British and French policy," says Mr. Lansing in closing, "restoring to the United States its full rights as a neutral power, will satisfy this Government."

The appointment of George Rublee to the Federal Trade Commission has been finally rejected in the Senate by a the vote of 38 to 33. We commented editorially last week upon this disgraceful application of the system of so-called "Senatorial courtesy." Since then the vote has been reconsidered and once more the motion to confirm the appointment defeated by a very close vote.

It is probable that the appointment of Louis D. Brandeis to the Supreme Court will be confirmed. The Senate Committee on the Judiciary has voted, by the close margin of 9 to 8, in favor of confirmation. It is not likely that the opposition of conservatism and prejudice will be able to accomplish in the Senate—even in executive session —what it has failed to accomplish in the committee room.

Congress continues to avoid the issue of woman suffrage. By a parliamentary trick—most of the members of the House being at a ball game—Minority Leader Mann secured the adoption of an amendment to the bill to reorganize the government of Porto Rico providing for woman suffrage there. The next day the question was reopened and the amendment rejected. Care was taken, however, to avoid putting any Congressman on record by means of a roll-call.

The House Judiciary Committee, which has before it the proposed constitutional amendment extending the suffrage to women, avoids the necessity of acting upon it by the simple expedient of not meeting. For this cowardly procedure the Democratic majority of the committee has been called to account by Congressman Mondell, who said:

To dodge the suffrage issue, or prevent the development of a majority favorable to the suffrage resolution, the chairman and the majority of the committee not only neglect the suffrage question, but all of the other important matters, responsibility for which has been placed on the committee by the Congress.

Whatever one may think of the suffrage amendment, whatever one's attitude may be toward it, there can be no difference of opinion as to the dodging and evasive tactics of the majority of the committee in attempting the avoidance of this issue, and in so doing, neglecting all of the important and responsible duties of the committee.

Honest opposition to the suffrage amendment on the part of the majority of the committee might be forgiven, at least by those who are not favorable to suffrage; but the policy of cowardly dodging and of neglect of duty will not be justified by anyone.

All is quiet along the border. Carranza is to address a new note to the American Government. Whether it will reiterate the demand for the withdrawal of the American troops no one knows. The regular troops on the border are being reinforced by militia from the border states. But 116 national guardsmen of Texas have refused to respond to the call to mobilize, and are to be tried by court martial. It is continually being reported that the Carranza forces are about to take some decisive action against the bandits who have made the attacks upon United States territory.

Meanwhile Villa is—nowhere.

The lockout and strike of 60,000 garment workers in New York City goes doggedly on. The fact which makes this industrial conflict unusually deplorable is that it disrupted perhaps the most promising plan ever invented for the avoidance of such disputes between employers and workers. In such a conflict it is always a difficult matter to fix the responsibility for its beginning. In the present case, however, there is now available the deliberate judgment of a group of independent

361

conventional style is now at the head of one of the English departments in one of our largest universities. He still insists that his students read the books they are talking about.

We are reminded of this incident in considering the attitude of some people toward the Shakespeare Tercentenary. They appear to have deposited their P. P. C. cards on Shakespeare's tomb and gone on their way rejoicing that they would not have to think of him again for the next hundred years.

Now, the Shakespeare celebration was really intended more as an introduction than as a leave-taking. All of the various pageants, speeches and contests, including our own contest, were designed, as we may now confess, to trick people into reading an author, who, it seemed to us, deserved more reading than he got. So far as our own share in the movement is concerned, it seems to have accomplished its purpose even better than we anticipated. Some ten thousand young students from all parts of the country competed for The Independent Shakespeare Medal. This involved not merely reading the eight articles on Shakespeare's life and works by Dr. Frederick Houk Law in The Independent, but also considerable study of the plays themselves, in order to write the required essays. In about four hundred schools and colleges there were a sufficient number of contestants to secure one of the medals awarded by The Independent.

Now, of these ten thousand young people who have been induced to read Shakespeare by this device, and the hundred thousand or more who have been indirectly concerned in the contests, and the millions who have been interested thru the medium of the various Tercentenary festivities, there will be some who will continue to read Shakespeare, not for a prize, not because it is an anniversary, not because people are talking about him, but because they find him interesting and profitable. That's what all this fuss is for.

MOTORS AND MOVIES

THE 128th General Assembly of the Presbyterian Church in session at Atlantic City last week devoted time to denouncing the evil effects of the automobile and the moving picture. One speaker referred to the "movie" theater as "The modern Diana of the Ephesians." Another declared that the automobile was "carrying away from the Church the magnificent army of Christ."

Let not the brethren forget, however, that the automobile and the moving picture are the greatest educators of the age. The automobile carries you everywhere. The moving picture carries everywhere to you.

CONSCRIPTION

HAS the state of New York gone stark crazy? Her legislature has passed and Governor Charles S. Whitman has signed five bills that require, among other things, all men between eighteen and forty-five to be enrolled as members of the Militia Reserve beginning August 1, and all schoolboys between sixteen and nineteen to drill not more than three hours each week and go to summer military camps under the direction of the officers of the National Guard, and all school children over eight—girls as well as boys—to "receive as part of the prescribed course of instruction such physical training as the regents, after conference with the military training commission, may determine during periods which shall average at least twenty minutes in each school day."

These laws mean conscription in time of peace. They should be forthwith repealed. The American people believe in preparedness—sane preparedness—but this goes to the very brink of the precipice of militarism.

THE AMERICAN INVASION OF EUROPE

THERE is much difference of opinion as to whether there will be a large volume of immigration from Europe to this country after the war or not, but it is quite evident that there will be a host of people from America flocking over to Europe by the first steamers that cross after the treaty of peace is signed. Some of these will be immigrants or the sons of immigrants looking up their relatives or their property, but most will be tourists visiting the battlefields of the greatest war in history. Already we learn that all the rooms in the leading hotels of London and Paris have been engaged in advance by Americans who are going when the war is over.

In former times American tourists have spent something like $150,000,000 a year in Europe, and the shutting off of this revenue for two years has caused great hardship, especially in Italy and Switzerland. The return of the tourist will revive their prosperity and his ready cash will do much to repair the ravages of war. Americans have a passion for ruins and thousands of travelers who have never cared to see the townhall of Ypres or the cathedral of Rheims in the hight of their beauty will now be drawn to them for their historic interest. It is quite likely that the expenditures of visitors to Louvain will in the course of a few years be sufficient to rebuild the burnt quarter of that city. At any rate, tourism will contribute considerably toward the reconstruction of Belgian towns on a more wholesome and habitable scale according to plans which had been made before the war. The slums which had been the despair of the Belgian reformers then have in many cases been swept away by the tide of battles along with the irreplaceable treasures of antiquity and the city planner will have the rarely gets in the old world, a *tabula rasa* for his model dwellings.

The long serpentine line of battle stretching from the sea to Switzerland and coiling about Ypres and Verdun will be a path of pilgrimage for all future time. It is historic ground sacred to the memory of the millions of young men who have here given their lives for their country. It should never be touched by the plow or allowed to lapse to mercenary use, like common soil, but should be preserved for a memorial of those who held the line against the invader. If one of those fine roads that the French know how to make were laid along the neutral strip between the battle lines, automobiles and buses could carry tourists all the way from Nieuport to Pont-a-Mousson. If the trenches on each side are kept intact and as nearly as possible as they look now they would prove as interesting as the Hotel des Invalides and far more worthy of reverence than the tomb of Napoleon. Such shrines we have in our own country at Gettysburg and Bunker Hill, silently teaching their lessons of patriotism to young and old, generation after generation. The battlefields of the Great War should likewise be dedicated to the perpetual service of calling to mind the awfulness of war and the glory of self-sacrifice. "It is altogether fitting and proper that we should do this."

Allied Interference With United States Mails The State Department has addrest to the governments of Great Britain and France a vigorous protest against their interference with United States mails moving between this country and Europe. In principle there would seem to be no difference between the allied powers and ourselves on this point. For the American Government agrees that merchandise, whether carried by parcel post or in sealed letter mail, stocks, bonds and securities, money orders, checks, drafts, notes and other negotiable instruments, which may pass as the equivalent of money, are all subject to the same treatment of capture and confiscation as merchandise shipped in any other manner. Obviously it would not be fair to permit a belligerent or a neutral to beat the devil around the stump by sending contraband by post and claiming that it was to be treated otherwise than if it had been shipped as freight or as express matter. On the other hand, the allied governments admit that under international law and practise genuine correspondence is inviolable, and may not be seized or unduly detained.

The method of applying these principles in practise, says Secretary Lansing in the note, is the chief cause of difference. The allied governments, while declaring that they will not seize genuine correspondence on the high seas, seek to get around the assurance that they have thus given by seizing and confiscating mail from vessels in port instead of at sea. They compel neutral ships to enter their own ports or induce shipping lines, by some form of duress, to send their mail ships via British ports. They thus acquire by force or unjustifiable means an illegal jurisdiction.

The note proceeds to describe the nature of the illegal procedure adopted by the allied governments:

Acting upon this enforced jurisdiction, the authorities remove all mail, genuine correspondence as well as post parcels, take them to London, where every piece, even tho of neutral origin and destination, is opened and critically examined to determine the "sincerity of their character," in accordance with the interpretation given that undefined phrase by the British and French censors. Finally the expurgated remainder is forwarded, frequently after irreparable delay, to its destination. Ships are detained en route to or from the United States, or to or from other neutral countries, and mails are held and delayed for several days and, in some cases, for weeks and even months, even tho not routed to ports of north Europe via British ports.

The note further sets forth the injuries to neutral business caused by this improper and vexatious proceeding:

The arbitrary methods employed by the British and French governments have resulted most disastrously to citizens of the United States. Important papers which can never be duplicated, or can be duplicated only with great difficulty, such as United States patents for inventions, rare documents, legal papers relating to the settlement of estates, powers of attorney, fire insurance claims, income tax returns, and similar matters have been lost.

Delays in receiving shipping documents have caused great loss and inconvenience by preventing prompt delivery of goods. In the case of the MacNiff Horticultural Company, of New York, large shipments of plants and bulbs from Holland were, I am informed, frozen on the wharves because possession could not be obtained in the absence of documents relating to them which had been removed from the "Nieuw Amsterdam," "Oosterdyk" and "Rotterdam."

Business opportunities are lost by failure to transmit promptly bids, specifications and contracts. The Standard Underground Cable Company, of Pittsburgh, for example, sent by mail a tender and specifications for certain proposed electrical works to be constructed in Christiania. After several weeks of waiting, the papers having failed to arrive, the American company was told that the bids could not be longer held open and the contract was awarded to a British competitor. Checks, drafts, money orders, securities and similar property are lost or detained for weeks and months. Business correspondence relating to legitimate and bona fide trade between neutral countries, correspondence of a personal nature, and also certain official correspondence, such as money order lists and other matter forwarded by government departments are detained, lost or possibly destroyed.

For instance, the Postmaster General informs me that certain international money order lists from the United States to Germany, Greece and other countries, and from Germany to the United States, sent thru the mails, have not reached their destination, tho dispatched several months ago.

Because of these injurious practises the Government of the United States expects the present practise of the British and French governments in relation to mails from and to the United States to be altered forthwith. "Only a radical change in the British and French policy," says Mr. Lansing in closing, "restoring to the United States its full rights as a neutral power, will satisfy this Government."

In Congress The appointment of George Rublee to the Federal Trade Commission has been finally rejected in the Senate by a tie vote of 38 to 38. We commented editorially last week upon this disgraceful application of the system of so-called "Senatorial courtesy." Since then the vote has been reconsidered and once more the motion to confirm the appointment defeated by a very close vote.

It is probable that the appointment of Louis D. Brandeis to the Supreme Court will be confirmed. The Senate Committee on the Judiciary has voted, by the close margin of 9 to 8, in favor of confirmation. It is not likely that the opposition of conservatism and prejudice will be able to accomplish in the Senate—even in executive session —what it has failed to accomplish in the committee room.

Congress continues to avoid the issue of woman suffrage. By a parliamentary trick—most of the members of the House being at a ball game—Minority Leader Mann secured the adoption of an amendment to the bill to reorganize the government of Porto Rico providing for woman suffrage there. The next day the question was reopened and the amendment rejected. Care was taken, however, to avoid putting any Congressman on record by means of a roll-call.

The House Judiciary Committee, which has before it the proposed constitutional amendment extending the suffrage to women, avoids the necessity of acting upon it by the simple expedient of not meeting. For this cowardly procedure the Democratic majority of the committee has been called to account by Congressman Mondell, who said:

To dodge the suffrage issue, or prevent the development of a majority favorable to the suffrage resolution, the chairman and the majority of the committee not only neglect the suffrage question, but all of the other important matters, responsibility for which has been placed on the committee by the Congress.

Whatever one may think of the suffrage amendment, whatever one's attitude may be toward it, there can be no difference of opinion as to the dodging and evasive tactics of the majority of the committee in attempting the avoidance of this issue, and in so doing, neglecting all of the important and responsible duties of the committee.

Honest opposition to the suffrage amendment on the part of the majority of the committee might be forgiven, at least by those who are not favorable to suffrage; but the policy of cowardly dodging and of neglect of duty will not be justified by anyone.

In Mexico All is quiet along the border. Carranza is to address a new note to the American Government. Whether it will reiterate the demand for the withdrawal of the American troops no one knows. The regular troops on the border are being reinforced by militia from the border states. But 116 national guardsmen of Texas have refused to respond to the call to mobilize, and are to be tried by court martial. It is continually being reported that the Carranza forces are about to take some decisive action against the bandits who have made the attacks upon United States territory.

Meanwhile Villa is—nowhere.

Who Is to Blame? The lockout and strike of 60,000 garment workers in New York City goes doggedly on. The fact which makes this industrial conflict unusually deplorable is that it disrupted perhaps the most promising plan ever invented for the avoidance of such disputes between employers and workers. In such a conflict it is always a difficult matter to fix the responsibility for its beginning. In the present case, however, there is now available the deliberate judgment of a group of independent

Morris in Puck

WILL THE JUDGE SAVE THE LADY?

THE ADVENTURES OF AN ELEPHANT——

Weed in Philadelphia Public Ledger

TEASING THE ELEPHANT

observers, who do not hesitate to put the blame squarely on one side.

Twenty-four professors in Columbia University have signed a statement of the results of their study of this lockout in the needle trades. It is so unequivocal in its conclusions and so convincing in the reasons it gives for those conclusions that we print it entire:

The trade agreement between employers and employees in the cloak, suit and skirt industry in this city maintained for five years a relation of peaceful coöperation and brought about great betterment in the industry. The breakdown of this voluntary plan, which has attracted the attention of the entire country, cannot be a matter of indifference to students and teachers of economics and political science.

After a careful examination of statements of the Manufacturers' Protective Association we prepared what we believed to be a fair statement of the facts, drawn almost entirely from the written statements and explanations submitted to us by the Manufacturers' Protective Association, with the request that they correct or amplify it in any regard in which it might seem to them inaccurate or incomplete.

To this request, the officers of the Manufacturers' Protective Association have replied that our statement of the facts is substantially correct. Our conclusion, after careful consideration, is that the Manufacturers' Protective Association broke its two-year agreement—which still had more than a year to run—without other justification than the fear that the agreement might thereafter be broken by the union, at a time less favorable to the manufacturers' interests.

The basis for this fear that the union was planning to strike at a favorable time is hard to discover. It seems to us that the real reason for the action of the Manufacturers' Protective Association is that its officers were unwilling to accept the consequences of their agreement, and, as their president has stated, they wished to return to the conditions existing prior to 1910. We regard this as little less than a public calamity, and earnestly urge that every effort be made to restore the agreement.

In our opinion, a just interpretation of the admitted facts warrants fixing the burden of the responsibility for the present crisis directly upon the shoulders of the executive committee of the Manufacturers' Protective Association. The breaking of this important trade agreement involves a responsibility which we feel the rank and file of the employers in this industry cannot afford to assume.

We, therefore, sincerely hope that the action taken may in some way be subjected to revision after more deliberate consideration on the part of the entire membership of the Manufacturers' Protective Association.

Among the names signed to this statement are those of such men as John Dewey, professor of philosophy; Charles A. Beard, professor of politics; Samuel McCune Lindsay, professor of social economy; Franklin H. Giddings, professor of sociology; Edwin R. A. Seligman, professor of political economy.

Such a statement made by such men demands more than the general denial entered by the representatives of the manufacturers. Unless weighty evidence can be produced against its conclusions, it will have a great influence on the public opinion, which is the real court of final jurisdiction in such controversies.

An Exciting Week at Verdun Following upon several weeks in which the news from Verdun contained nothing except the uncertain loss and gain of a few hundred yards of trenches we hear of important operations on both sides of the Meuse. The French executed offensive movements with unexpected vigor, but on the whole the advantage at the end of the week seems to lie with the Germans.

The French began on Monday with an assault of Fort Douaumont. This was the first important point taken by the Germans when they began their attack upon Verdun last February, and in fact is the only one of the older

Copyright Underwood

TWO WHO FLEW TO WASHINGTON

Alan R. Hawley, president of the Aero Club of America, and Victor Carlstrom, the pilot, with the 190-horse power Curtiss machine which carried them from New York to Washington, 237 miles, in 187 minutes—a speed of 78 miles an hour. The aeroplane, the J. N. 8, is the gift of the Aero Club to the National Guard of New Mexico and the flight to Washington was the first stage of transportation to the border. A heavy packet of newspapers was carried to prove that an aerial mail service is feasible

Harding in Brooklyn Eagle
"WAITIN' FER AN ANSWER"

Brinkerhoff in New York Evening Mail (Copyright)
ANIMAL INTELLIGENCE

Kirby in New York World
TRYING TO STAMPEDE HIM

——IN SEARCH OF A MASTER

forts about Verdun that they have yet captured. It stands upon a ridge five miles northeast of Verdun and commands a view of that city. From this hight the German guns have been brought to bear upon Verdun and have demolished most of the buildings with the exception of the Cathedral. This historic edifice has been hit by only one shell and this was doubtless an accident since it towers above the rest of the town.

Except for its use as an artillery station, however, the possession of Douaumont was not of much value to the Germans, for they could not advance along the plateau toward Verdun because this is covered by the guns on Dead Man Hill on the other side of the Meuse. Accordingly the Germans have ever since the capture of Douaumont been devoting their efforts to getting possession of the hills west of the river.

After two months of the hardest kind of fighting the Germans seemed likely to gain Le Mort Homme and Hill 304, the chief hights west of the Meuse when General Nivelle turned tables upon them by delivering an assault upon Fort Douaumont on the eastern side of the river. He brought his heavy artillery to bear upon the fort and after a bombardment that began on Sunday and continued till Monday afternoon he ordered a charge. The infantry advanced singing the "Marseillaise" and carried everything before them until they reached the fort. This also they captured with the exception of the northeast corner to which the Germans clung tenaciously. But the French were not able to keep the foothold they had gained at Douaumont. During the next two days the Germans drove them out of the fort and out of the trenches to the south of it. In the fighting at Douaumont the Germans claim to have taken prisoner 48 officers and 1943 men.

West of Douaumont are the quarries of Haudromont, which have been converted into a labyrinth of underground passages. The quarries were captured by a charge of Saxon troops on April 16 but the French regained them at the same time that they took Douaumont tho here again they were not able to hold their gains against the German counterattack.

On the west side of the Meuse a body of Thuringians carried by storm the village of Cumières, taking more than three hundred prisoners. A few days later the French regained part of it. Cumières stands on comparatively low ground near the river two miles east of Le Mort Homme. Its sole importance lies in the fact that thru it the Germans can get access to Le Mort Homme from the east as they already have access to it from the west and north. One of the two summits of Le Mort Homme is now held by the Germans and they have possession of part if not all of Hill 304, which stands next to it on the southwest. Sixty thousand fresh German troops have just been brought up against these hills, so it is evident that the Germans are determined to persist in their attack on Verdun. On page 396, under the title "Half a Million Madmen," we quote from an eye witness of the fighting at Verdun.

The Austrian Plan

The Italians admit that the Austrian drive in the Tirol took them by surprize, and the general in command of that sector of the frontier has been removed for negligence. The attention of General Count Cadorna, commander-in-chief of the Italian forces, was fixed upon the eastern frontier, where he was delivering heavy blows on the defenses of Görz, when it was suddenly distracted by a powerful Austrian of-

VERDUN AFTER THREE MONTHS

During the past week the French have made a strong but not altogether successful effort to regain Fort Douaumont and Haudromont on the eastern side of the Meuse, while the Germans on the western side have taken the village of Cumières and gained some ground on Le Mort Homme and Hill 304. The shaded area is that held by the Germans. That within the lighter dotted line shows their latest gains

fensive from the Trentino in his rear. It seems strange that the Italians should not have been forewarned if not forearmed against attack from this quarter, for the Trentino, where the preparations were being made, is chiefly inhabited by Italians who would be only too glad to give information to their brethren over the border. The concentration of troops in the Trentino, as the southern part of Austrian Tirol is called, began early in the spring, and if we can accept the Italian estimates, the Austrians massed in these mountains some 600,000 troops, with over 3000 cannon. Many of these troops have been brought from Serbia and Galicia, showing that the Austrians have little fear of a serious offensive either by the Russians on the Galician front or by the French and British at Salonica. Further evidence of the lessened importance attached to the Balkans is found in the Italian report that Bulgars have been brought to the Isonzo front.

Such an offensive as the Austrians have now undertaken was feared a year ago when Italy entered the war, and pessimistic prophets were heard to say that the Austrians would be in Venice within three weeks. It appears that troops were actually massed in the Trentino with this object, but they were transferred instead to Galicia, where the Russians were threatening to cross the Hungarian frontier.

The inner meaning of the Austrian invasion of Italy is as difficult to divine as of the German attack upon Verdun. It may be merely a demonstration of strength to forestall an Italian offensive and to relieve the pressure on the Isonzo front. On the other hand, it may be an attempt to disable or dismember Italy and so compel her to withdraw from the war. An advance of thirty-five miles by the Austrians in the direction they are now headed would put them in possession of Padua and deliver the whole province of Venetia into their hands. This would serve as valuable "trading stock" when it came to making terms of peace, but it is hardly likely that Austria would attempt to annex Venetia again, even if she could, for this would be a permanent source of danger to Europe and insure the implacable enmity of Italy.

The Descent from the Tirol   Some clue to the Austrian intentions may be inferred from the instructions found on the Austrian prisoners. From these it appears that the movement is called "the offensive in Po Valley." The soldiers on entering the enemy's territory were told that they must not show themselves weak, but that they must avoid all brutality. They were promised for the summer baths in the Adriatic at the Lido, the fashionable bathing beach on the reef outside Venice.

The Austrians therefore intend, or

desire to be understood as intending, to advance down the Po River to the Adriatic. But so far their advance has been to the north of this; that is, they are striking east from Trent toward Vicenza, not south from Rovereto toward Verona. At least the movement southward down the Adige River toward Verona seems not to be pushed with much vigor and the Italians claim to have brought it to a halt. Verona forms the northeast angle of the famous Italian Quadrilateral, the smashing of which gave Napoleon his reputation as a military genius. The other angles are Peschiera at the foot of Lake Garda and Mantua and Legnago, forming the southern side of this Quadrilateral of fortresses.

But the Austrians by striking east instead of south will avoid the Quadrilateral. They are pressing forward on a twenty-mile front between the Astico and the Brenta Rivers. This leads them to the frontier towns of Schio, Arsiero and Asiago, from which railroads lead down to Vicenza. The 38-centimeter guns of the Austrians have already been brought to bear upon the defenses of these towns and the inhabitants have fled into the interior. The Italians seem to have given up hope of holding back the Austrians in the mountains and are withdrawing from the valleys of the Brenta and the Astico. The Austrians claim to have taken some thirty thousand prisoners and numerous guns.

But the Italians in falling back are

London Sphere, Copyright N. Y. H.

THE AUSTRIAN INVASION OF ITALY

The Austrians from the Trentino are moving out of the mountain passes into the valleys leading toward Venice. Their guns are already thundering at the forts of Arsiero and Asiago, in their effort to reach Vicenza and push on to the Adriatic. In this sketch map the dark portion represents Italian territory. The boundary line was drawn in 1866 along the edge of the mountains so as to give the Austrians the advantage which they are using in this war

Cesare in New York Sun
GERMANY OFFERS PEACE

Kirby in New York World
NO PLACE TO LIGHT

Starrett in New York Tribune
NOT PEACE BUT VICTORY

IS EUROPE READY FOR PEACE?

getting upon a terrain more favorable to their forces, while the difficulties of the Austrians will increase with their advance. If they succeed in taking Arsiero and Asiago and entering the plateau beyond they will be subject to attack from both sides. Here the Italians will have the advantage of railroads, while the Austrians will have no means of communication with their base in the Trentino except by the mountain passes thru which they have entered Italy. The Italians should be able to put into the field a force from three to five times as great as any the Austrians could muster and in the open country numbers will count for more than in the mountains.

Let George Do It   The recent outbreak in Ireland has shown the necessity of a radical and immediate reorganization of the Irish Government. As soon as the disorder had been supprest Premier Asquith went to Dublin for a personal investigation. He was sworn in as a member of the Irish Privy Council and held conversations with all parties, including some of the captured rebels. On his return he announced that the cabinet had selected David Lloyd George to negotiate a settlement of the Irish question and requested that in the meantime all criticism be avoided.

Mr. Lloyd George seems to be regarded as the handy man of the cabinet to be sent to settle difficult disputes because of his unusual ability in conciliating warring factions. In his new post of Minister of Munitions he has induced both employers and employees to suspend their most cherished rights and to submit to unprecedented burdens and restrictions. He stands well with both Sir Edward Carson, leader of the Ulster party, and John Redmond, leader of the Nationalists, and may be expected to effect a possible compromise on the home rule question.

It is assumed that some sort of local government for Ireland will be established, but under the authority of Parliament, and that both the Ulster and Nationalist volunteers will be brought into the army. An attempt to disarm

either of these bodies would precipitate trouble. The government did not dare attempt it before the war and it would be still more ticklish to do it now. Premier Asquith has publicly recognized the fact that the execution of the rebel leaders has caused an unfortunate impression in America. This is evidenced by the very unusual action of 28 members of the House of Representatives who petitioned the Speaker to have reported from the Committee on Foreign Affairs the Dyer resolution expressing "the horror of the American people" at the execution.

A Food Dictator   No sausages to be had. The weekly butter allowance cut down from four ounces to three. Potatoes limited to less than a pound a day. Meat reduced to half a pound a week. Not enough milk for the babies. The beer supply running short as summer begins. Riots in the market place. Such are the reports from Berlin.

That the situation is alarming is proved by the extraordinary measures taken to alleviate it. The Kaiser came suddenly back to Berlin and reorganized the department of the interior.

THE GREAT WAR

May 22—Turks withdraw on Tigris south of Kut-el-Amara. French enter Fort Douaumont.

May 23—Germans take Cumières. Italians retiring from Sugana Valley.

May 24—British expenses for two years of war $11,900,000,000. Lloyd George takes charge of Irish situation.

May 25—German Government takes over all food supplies. Germans regain Douaumont.

May 26—Rockefeller Foundation appropriates a million dollars for Polish and Balkan relief. Austrians attack fortifications of Arsiero.

May 27—General Gallieni, defender of Paris, dies. French regain part of Cumières.

May 28—Bulgars occupy Demirhissar in Greek territory. Germans attack British front near Loos.

Dr. Clemens Delbrück, Vice Chancellor and Minister of the Interior, was graciously permitted to resign on the ground of ill health and overwork. Dr. Karl Helfferich, the brilliant young Minister of Finance, is likely to succeed him. A Department of Food Supplies has been created and at the head of it has been placed Tortilowitz von Batocki, who has distinguished himself by the ability he has displayed in the administration of East Prussia during the war. The Bundesrat or Federal Council has empowered this new officer to seize and dispose of all the foodstuffs and fodder of the empire and to regulate sales, prices, transportation, importation, exportation and consumption. His power is not limited to Prussia but overrides the administration of the several States. He even has the right in cases of emergency to overrule the regulations of the Federal Council itself, tho he must submit his acts to the approval of the Council immediately afterward. In short Herr von Batocki is a food dictator with practically unlimited power over all matters of food except in the army.

The adoption of bread tickets and the use of potatoes in bread were sufficient to carry the population thru the first year of the war, but the harvest of 1915 was short by nine million tons in wheat, rye, barley and oats. Cattle and pigs had to be killed because it was not possible to import fodder for them as had been done in former years. Thanks to these precautions the grain supply held out and there will be more than enough bread to last till the harvest. But meats and fats of all kinds are running low and the people of Germany will have to go upon a vegetarian diet in part at least. It is believed, however, that season may be tided over by taking stock of all the food supplies of the empire and so regulating their distribution that all classes shall share in them. Bavaria and the other southern states are better off than Prussia in the matter of food. The conquered territory of Belgium, France, Lithuania, Poland and Courland is being put in crops by the government.

Drawn by W. C. Morris

THE NATIONAL DEFENSE THERMOMETER.

RE-ENTER REPUBLICANISM

BY W. G. HARDING

THE people of the United States are ready and eager to acclaim the Republican party returned to the nation's service. The tide is swelling and irresistible, altho the political situation is unmatched in all our history. There is as marked a desire for a Republican restoration for our industrial sake as when the American people turned hopefully to William McKinley in 1896, and there is an anxiety for our nationality not unlike that which sought out Abraham Lincoln in 1860.

A good many people thought they saw the end of the Republican party in 1912, but when the effects of defeat were measured in the country's misfortune, we saw we had wasted perfectly good Republican energy in smashing a precedent which might have been flung aside with one sweep of a sober hand, and concord was shattered in the smashing. But it is useless to talk of 1912. I prefer to regret the unhappiness and its attending defeats, and turn and invite all who believe in Republican principles to touch elbows again and move on to the triumphant national return which has already been hailed so gladly in many states.

The Republican party has applied the best of thought and honest intent to the solution of all problems which attend exceptional growth, and means to go on—without stopping the growth—deliberately, orderly, conscientiously, neither yielding nor appealing to prejudice or passion, but strengthening the weak in the supremacy of law, always seeking the ideal over safe and proven paths.

This is not always easy in popular government. The Republican party became so absorbed in national perils that it ignored party weakness. That was our undoing. A party could become so concerned about its own affairs and its appeal for popular approval that it might ignore a national peril. There are always extremes to be avoided, and there is no loftier statesmanship than that which finds the righteous mean. There must be some safe attitude, for example, between being "too proud to fight" and magnifying the chip on the shoulder which calls for a scrap.

It seems characteristic of our American life that we must have periodical Democratic disaster to bring us to appreciation of the healthful glow of Republican activity. There would be worse depression in the land today than there was between 1893 and 1897 if the European war had not saved us from the blight of Wilsonian Democracy. We have

the burden of a war emergency tax when imports exceed those of the corresponding months of peace, and our exports far surpass all previous figures because of our enormous war shipments to Europe. Not only has the European war *not* destroyed our business, but it has given us the *only* business we have. It has given us a fictitious, sectional prosperity, but it does not blind us to the depression

Copyright International Film

SENATOR HARDING

likely to follow, nor to the industrial reconstruction which must be worked out, nor to the industrial and commercial menace of desperate Europe struggling, after peace is restored, for its own rehabilitation.

All that the Wilson Administration has said concerning its economic policy is disproved by facts, and is challenged by its change of attitude on sugar and the tariff commission. A party committed to a tariff for revenue only has again proven a party deficient in revenue always. The tariff commission plan is a professed conversion, not to magnify the series of succeeding changes, but to hide the tariff blunder of 1913. On the other hand, while nobody pretends that any Republican tariff has been perfect, we know that none has ever been destructive.

Democracy reduced the capacity to live and left the cost mounting higher. It has been talking a hundred years about the interests of the American consumer, and never a thought for the American producer. In saying "producer" I mean the toiler. It is not what the consumer pays that counts so much; the big thing is the consumer's ability to buy. It is the prospering producer that makes a capable consumer. It is not the consumer who made the higher American standard, but the producer with coin in his pocket and attending ability to buy.

Our protective policy is certain to be the great issue of the coming campaign. There will be more spectacular issues, there will be the patriotic appeal for preparedness, with Republican committal to an adequate program for national defense. And it will be no new declaration for the Republican party. But the protective policy is inseparable from any preparedness discussion. Aside from the self-dependence in production, which is a nation's first reliance, it affords the means of providing an army and navy without the burden of direct and odious taxation. I like the thought of making our foreign competitor pay this cost of guarding us against his possible trespass of our national rights.

One cannot recall a yawning Federal Treasury under Republican administration, but the pathetic spectacle of the present attempt at preparedness by the present Administration is due to threatened bankruptcy of the Treasury amid the demands of ordinary expense and the utter inadequacy of income notwithstanding the emergency war tax and the new Federal levies. The Democracy that

367

"would have burned the custom houses" is in the saddle, and the inadequacy of revenue is the invariable effect of a Democratic cause.

I do not mean to dilate upon the weakness of the Democratic party or detail its blunders, or to proclaim the weakness of the Democratic policy or the wobbling of the Wilson Administration. I do not object to a president changing his mind, but I do not think that it ought to be made a specialty. I would rather proclaim the strength of the Republican party and its capacity to promote the common weal and the nation's good.

, One is reluctant to criticize the Administration in its foreign policies, at a time of anxiety like the passing days. I should prefer to present a united front to the world, even at the sacrifice of some notions of my own, than to convey the impression of a divided people. I want to stand by the President, but I want him to stand by my country. It is good to keep out of war, but not at the sacrifice of all American rights. It is possible to speak for justice and be unneutral, but we may assert an American right with partiality to America and neutrality to the world.

We want a real and righteous Americanism abroad, and we need a newly-consecrated Americanism at

G. O. P. EPIGRAMS

It is useless to talk of 1912.
The war has given us a fictitious, sectional prosperity.
I do not object to a president changing his mind, but I do not think that it ought to be made a specialty.
We should make America prosper first.
The Republican party is too big to trail any man.

home. We want the spirit truly American and all-pervading, and we want an outward manifestation. We must be a people with one great ideal, one all-encompassing aspiration, one guiding hope, one common interest, one people and one flag. That's why I am Republican. I do not mean to say that our party has a monopoly on American patriotism. But we must have a slogan of prosperity and we should *make America prosper first.* That is the Republican doctrine. It is our doctrine to proclaim the same preparedness in Illinois that we proclaim in Massachusetts. We must exalt the same Americanism. in Iowa that we exalt in Texas. We must urge the same tax on incomes in Louisiana that we urge in New York, and give

one the same authority in spending that tax as the other. We must urge the same economic policy for North Dakota as we do for Connecticut or Pennsylvania, and the same social justice in Oregon as we do in South Carolina. This is the course of political righteousness, and the blend of Americanism which bespeaks the great nation.

The editor of The Independent wishes to know my views about Colonel Roosevelt. There is no reason why Theodore Roosevelt should not be consulted *if* he is back in the Republican party, but *the party is too big to trail any man.* The principles of the party stand ahead of any candidate or all the candidates together. I am distinctly a party man. We are a popular government, thru the agency of political parties, and principles come first. The nominee should best represent our platform.

The salvation of the country rests with the Republican party. I think we all feel that. I think Colonel Roosevelt himself feels it as deeply as any of us. If Colonel Roosevelt wishes to be a member of the Republican party we welcome him, and want him, his advice and coöperation, but the Republican party, as I have said, will not trail any man.

Washington, D. C.

A WOMAN OF PARIS

(SEPTEMBER 10, 1914)

BY EDNA DEAN PROCTOR

For more than half a century Miss Edna Dean Proctor has been writing poems, articles of American and European travel and stories for The Independent. Now, nearly ninety years old, she writes with the same interest and vigor of events today.—THE EDITOR

Retreating towards the Marne, his regiment
  Would pass at morn a neighboring suburb
    thru;
And thither walked his glad young wife,
  intent
    To see her soldier, strong and brave and
      true;
And in her arms, or pattering with light feet
  Beside her steps, she held her baby boy—
O the proud moment when his eyes should
    greet
    Their little Victor brimming o'er with joy!

Upon the curb she stood as past they filed,
  When something barred the way and, unawares,
      awares,
The line a moment stayed; then wife and
    child
    A corporal saw—the father's friend and
      theirs—

And springing from the ranks he seized her
    arm:
  "Courage, courage, Madame! Your husband
    fell
Yesterday, by my side, at Maux." . . . Ah well. . .
  Ah well . . . her eyelids closed, her heart
    stood still. . . .
What joy henceforth can wile, what grief can
    harm! . . .
  Then swift above her head, with deathless
    will
She raised her boy, presenting him, and cried,
  For all her anguish, "Vive la France!"
    A thrill
Ran thru the throng, and with the line's advance
    vance
  Cheers filled the morning sky for her and
    France
As if no soldier in his place had died!—
  For. France, secure, invincible, immortal,
  While women such as she are at its portal!

THREE OF US WITHOUT A CARE

BY HAROLD HOWLAND

FOR the perfect holiday three things are essential: one canoe, one chosen companion, and all outdoors. The canoe should be light—Grey Brother weighs but fifty-five pounds; seaworthy—Grey Brother rides rough water like a gull; stanch—Grey Brother carries eight times his own weight without a stagger; faithful and friendly—if you have ever known a canoe like Grey Brother intimately, you know what I mean.

The chosen companion should have all those qualities of sportsmanship, understanding, cheerfulness, patience, and grit that you pray for yourself in your secret moments with the Red Gods. Such companions are rare, but those same gods sometimes grant us companionship not after our deserts but according to their own great-heartedness.

The outdoors should be as nearly pure wilderness as may be; the works of man can do nothing but mar the perfect holiday.

There lie before me two diaries of such a great adventure, of a splendid two weeks wherein Milady Joconda and the Tortoise—to say nothing of the good Grey Brother—went "to dance before the Trues."

Let us turn over the pages of these journals, and see what simple doings spell contentment when the feverish ways of men are left behind. The story opens with sundry lists. This sounds prosaic, but if you are of the vagabond fellowship yourself, you know that one of the sure manifestations of the return of the wander longing when the crows begin to caw again in the spring is an explosive, "Let's make a list!" It matters not how far away the trip itself may be, to "make a list" is the one sure way to clap a mortgage on the future.

The story proceeds antiphonally, now Joconda speaking, now the Tortoise. The scene is in the Canadian wilds, where one steps from the train, launches Grey Brother and slips into solitude.

Sunday, September 24—Left Joe Lake Station at 10:50 a. m. Paddled thru Joe Lake, Little Joe and an endless, tortuous creek, lifting over beaver dams, tracking here and there, and carrying around falls. Stopped for lunch at head of carry into Island Lake: hardtack, cheese, one piece Peter's and three dates apiece. Decided to camp there. Dinner: corn-bread, broiled ham, stewed apricots.

Weather cloudy and overcast, with occasional showers. Saw downy woodpecker, flicker, loon with chicks, blue jay, Canada jay, sandpiper, kingfisher, chickadee, great blue heron, and some other unidentified birds; also a mink and four deer. Heard continually the voice of the white throat. To bed at 7:15.

Three of us without a care
In the red September

Making merry with the rain,
With the fellow winds a-fare
Where the winds remember.

JOCONDA AND GREY BROTHER MAKE A PORTAGE

Solitude? Not exactly the right word, you think? A much peopled solitude, indeed, with all these woods folk about. But they are not man; and it is only man that produces crowds and noise and bustle and fretfulness. In another sense, too, it is the reality of solitude. The chiefest of vagabonds, R. L. S., said it once for all, "There is a fellowship more quiet even than solitude, and which, rightly understood, is solitude made perfect. And to live out of doors with the woman a man loves is of all lives the most complete and free."

Monday, September 25—Passed a very good night for the first out of doors. Rained at intervals. During the night a deer, presumably annoyed at finding something with a strange and disagreeable odor on one of his favorite stamping grounds, made a great fuss. He whistled "whi-i-s-s-s-h, whi-i-i-s-s-s-h," and went off stamping his feet and blowing as if to clear his nostrils of the hateful man scent. Lay in bed till late. Misty, with rain from time to time, so no good reason for hurrying to get up. Breakfast about nine, in tent, off cold corn-bread, cheese, nuts and raisins. Spent morning chiefly in extended toilets. Dull gray all day,

only sometimes darker gray than others. Lunch: bacon, rice, apple sauce.

Walked across portage to take an observation, came back and carried Grey Brother across. Paddled up to end of pond, where found another portage half the length of the first, leading to another body of water. Can this be Island Lake? The morrow will tell. Certainly the maps won't!

Great inspiration—packed up three food bags, leaving out only what we wanted for supper, breakfast and lunch. Packed them across the portage with tump line to leave them with Grey Brother, thus saving labor tomorrow. Second great inspiration—if we leave the grub there unprotected, bears or porcupines may get it. Too great risk —so packed them back again.

Supper: Mock turtle soup, hot biscuits, stewed prunes. Mem. If you turn the biscuits over in the reflecting baker when they are nicely brown on the bottom, they will brown nicely also on the top—now the bottom—rare discovery. To bed at seven.

What odd hours one keeps in the woods, to be sure. "Lay in bed till late" and breakfasted—at nine. What slothfulness! "To bed at seven." What sleepy-heads! But that is what Mother Nature teaches when you sit at her feet and give yourself up to learn. In her school a day is a day—each divided from the other as the light was divided from the darkness in the first days. You are ready for bed when the sun seeks his—for you have had plenty of good hard work to tire your body and relax your nerves; and ready to begin again when he comes round once more—for refreshing sleep is one of the open's freest gifts.

Tuesday, September 26 — Morning dawned white and misty, but with promise of a beautiful day. Rose at seven, made breakfast (bacon, cold biscuits and prunes) and put up lunch of fried ham and biscuit sandwiches. Broke camp and portaged into pond seen the day before. Made portage in two trips, tho it was really too hard for the Tortoise. (Umph!—T.) Paddled across pond and made short portage into Island Lake. Three trips each, including Grey Brother. Sun shining, tho occasionally obscured by great flying masses of cloud. A glorious day! Paddled thru the strait and part way up Island Lake. Stopped on a point to eat sandwiches. Then paddled on and delightedly watched a bunch of six ducks and the antics of three foolish loons. Made camp on point of island—which must give the lake its name—about two o'clock. Camp of the loons.

Dinky little stone fire-place of Tortoise's construction about two yards in front of tent door, which is now raised, making little piazza roof.

Made camp and explored island a little. Supper: delicious cocoa, apple sauce and toasted biscuits. Work all done by six o'clock; sat before fire till eight. "Wonderful clear night of stars." Heard what we thought to be barking of a fox on eastern shore—later consideration suggested bob-cat more probable. Loons were very diverting again;

369

practised flying exercises for our benefit. Evidently very curious; they laughed and wailed till late. T. slept well, J. badly first half, well second half. Thought pine needles falling on White Cap were rain; had fire drill in consequence, madly dashing out and collecting all damageables inside of tent. Fooled again—but it is good practice.

The simple life! Just paddling, tramping, cooking, eating, sleeping, working, loafing, contemplating, observing, musing—in fact, just living. "The world is so full of a number of things—"

Wednesday, September 27—. . . Toward evening the nor'wester which has been steadily blowing up mounts to half a gale. It drives smoke-black clouds fearsomely over the sky. An awe-inspiring evening. We do not like the fury with which the wind tears at White Cap, and beats its sides. Joconda suggests that White Cap be dropt where he stands and that we make our bed under him, with our heads at the doorway. Done as suggested. We go to bed without supper—lunch had been a great feast—and spend an excellent, warm night, assisted by the hot-water bottle (it was a wise woodsman who declared that device worth many pounds of extra blankets), in spite of wind and cold.

Thursday, September 28—Real ice in the water bucket when we get up and frost on everything. Brilliant sunshine but considerable northwest wind with lots of snap in it. Rice cakes, werry delectable, bacon and apple sauce for breakfast Paddled across Windy Bay, which lived pretty well up to the name we proceeded to give it, to Otter Slide portage and walked across to Little Otter Slide Lake. Killed a partridge with the Browning pistol (see any foreign or English detective story) after sadly ineffectual attempts at two others. A rifle and a pistol with a five inch barrel are two things. Said killing a heinous violation of the law; but we want chicken for dinner, and quiet our consciences with weighty reflections on the difference between *malum prohibitum* and *malum in se*, and the absence of moral turpitude. Anyhow we had chicken for dinner.

Back to camp with our treasure trove of one partridge, a dozen potatoes from a sack hanging in the deserted shelter hut, a can of Dutch cleanser, and two boards for the 'satiable fire. Partridge broiled in the baker, fried potatoes and onions (a 'most galumpshious mess), hard-tack and butter, nuts and raisins for dessert. As Kim used to say, rubbing his tummy softly the while, "It was a great feast."

After the feast made a balsam bed and a windbreak to the nor'west of White Cap. Windbreak made of great pine branches from an old tree which had been cut down, presumably for just such a purpose, by other campers. It was a shame to sacrifice so noble a tree, but being sacrificed, it would have been a shame not to make use of his offerings. Windbreak made, the wind went down; but it made camp so cosy that we regretted the labor not at all. No supper except a bowl of bouillon for the Tortoise. To bed betimes on a fragrant couch of new pulled balsam.

There is a great deal of food in this chronicle, is there not? There are several reasons for it. The vivid woods hunger makes meal time a real event; one never comes reluctant to table. Then the gentle labor of preparing meals is part of the fun of it all. Cooking over an open fire, in whatever weather may be going at the moment, with simple implements, and the elementary ingredients that one is able to carry in canoe and on back from trip's end to trip's end—this is not drudgery, it is an absorbing interest. It is a fascinating game to see what variations you — she, rather—can play upon that simple scale of staple food-stuffs. Finally, it tastes so good withal—wood smoke and an occasional cinder give a rare flavor.

While we are on the subject of what the boys of the family call "eats," let me give some gratuitous hints. You will find in our food list a number of "fads and frills"—nuts and raisins, dates, milk chocolate, dried fruits, cheese, maple sugar. But these are not sheer frivolity. They have their real uses.

The Indian and the hardened woodsman may find it easy to live on salt pork, flapjacks and beans. But the sophisticated appetite of the town-dweller soon demands more variety and a greater proportion of what may be called "interesting" victuals. We have tried it both ways; believe us, the "frills" will save your digestion and your disposition. But do not neglect the staples. For a day's paddling and portaging you need something that will "stick to the ribs."

Friday, September 29—In the morning it still rained and we still slept. (Note—White Cap no longer leaked.) At ten we sat up in bed and ate hardtack and butter, cheese and maple sugar. Then we slept. At five we woke. The Tortoise cooked some ham (it no longer rained but was still misty), which with hard-tack topped off with dates was consumed. Then we slept. Woke maybe once in the night to discover that it had cleared; but then we slept—and dreamed—and both were good.

What a sleep! Such lack of energy, such laziness! What waste of time! Not so at all. What better way to recreate oneself than giving up in perfect relaxation to "the season of all natures, sleep." The sleep that you get in the woods, lulled by the fragrance of balsam and pine, harmonized by the wind whispering in the trees, the tiny waves lapping on the shore, the quiet under-chatter of a little rapid in the stream, the steady diapason of a tireless water-fall—that is one of the best medicines for fretted mind and jaded nerves.

At home weather is either largely a matter of course when it is good, or emphatically a nuisance when it is bad. In the woods there is no bad weather, if you are worthy of the woods life. If the sun shines and the skies smile you expand your soul and glory in it; if it rains and blows and glooms, you go about your business just the same—and glory in it.

Sunday, October 1—A fine night of sleep. About six a wonderful display of red, pink and opal tints in the east. In half an hour it had passed, leaving only the familiar dull uniform gray. "Morning red" to complete the prophecy, and the wind in the south. Before breakfast—late—is ready the rain is here, mild but steady. Corned beef hash with onions and corn bread—best yet—for breakfast, eaten in tent. Then to vegetate under the blankets; a little "Don Quixote" and "Wild Wales," a few poems, some sleep and a couple of repair jobs, to say nothing of several pipes. About three the rain stopped, tho the sky remained overcast. We bestirred ourselves, prepared and disposed of another great feast of ham, spaghetti with cheese, cocoa, nuts and raisins. Night came on with the wind shifted a little toward the northeast, but with little promise for the morrow. To bed at seven.

Do not forget the books. Cervantes and Borrow, Kipling ("Five Nations"), and "The Open Road," an anthology of outdoor verse—these made up our library, and fitted royally our vagabond mood. There are plenty of others; we shall choose another list next time. But, oh, leave behind all "summer novels" and such like trash. If they have any proper place in the world's cosmogony, it is not the woods.

Tuesday, October 3—Morning dawned unwontedly propitious, so we struck camp and turned our faces—and Grey Brother's nose—southward. The loons bade us farewell; and with many backward glances at our dear island home we sought new scenes and adventures. The Tortoise soon wearied of paddling in the stern, so Joconda joyously took his place and had a fine fierce struggle against wind and wave across Island Lake. Lunch of hard-tack, cheese and nuts and raisins at beginning of first portage, which then accomplished the two portages and the intervening pond with considerable ease and the minimum of fatigue. Paddled down the stream to the falls and there made a very comfortable "lodging for the night."

Wednesday, October 4 — Morning broke almost fair after rain in the night. Took up our way again. Very bad going thru the stream. Water low and beaver dams frequent as well as fallen logs. Lifted and carried and sloshed around in the mud and water. As we progressed a great wind sprang up which waxed and raged and beat with fury upon the tree tops. These bent and sometimes broke with a report like a rifle. They came hurtling down, now to fall among the trees on the bank, now to drop into the stream itself. Our advance become thrilling—almost perilous. The black fir tops tossing and rocking against the flying gray clouds made a splendid picture. Our little craft working his way down the winding stream seemed very frail and quite at the mercy of the great elements.

After a considerable struggle we came out into the open water of Little

(Concluded on page 406)

The Independent - Harper's Weekly
NEWS~PICTORIAL

Copyright Medem

Will they hammer out a victory? French soldier-blacksmiths at the forge in a wrecked smithy in the village of Verdun

Perhaps it's water sport for you. Here is a star-class race off Seagate, next door to Coney Island.

But if you want speed, here is a "sea-sled" that tears thru the billows at 35 or 40 miles per hour.

Is tennis your game? Here is Miss Molla Bjurstedt, from Norway, who won just about everything a woman could win here last year. She likes tennis, for she "always had a desire to run about and hit something."

Photographs by Levick

But the golfer will have none of your makeshift sports when he can drive like this at Wykagyl. And we have no room here for the "national game," nor fishing nor flying, nor a score of other variations in the one universal summer pastime of young and old America—getting outdoors and staying there till white faces are brown and even blue blood runs red.

"Thruout the night the big guns of the enemy pealed the fall of a great nation." A striking "still" from the film "The Fall of a Nation," which Thomas Dixon and Victor Herbert have created as a preparedness sermon and movie thriller.

Copyright International Film

A submarine turned merchantman? According to rumor, this 450-foot Unterseeboot is to break the British blockade and ply between Germany and the United States this summer, carrying mail, supplies and perhaps a few passengers.

Copyright Medem

A canal that goes under the mountains—from Marseilles to the Rhone. Begun in 1910, this project was not allowed to lapse during the war, and has now been completed. Four and a half miles are cut thru the Rove Mountains.

Copyright Underwood

Eastern delegates wanted Mrs. Samuel B. Sneath, of Ohio—first vice-president now—for their next president.

Paul Thompson

Mrs. Percy V. Pennybacker is president of the federation of two and half million club women in the United States.

Copyright Underwood

But California spoke for the West in urging the election of Mrs. Josiah Cowles, a pacifist and a Republican.

Paul Thompson

The second vice-president of the Federation—she hopes to be first—is Miss Georgie A. Bacon of Worcester, Massachusetts, a city not too far from Boston.

E. F. Foley

As president of the Local Biennial Board Mrs. William Grant Brown is officially the hostess of 20,000 women delegates now convening in New York.

Paul Thompson

Sorosis, founded in New York in 1868, was the first of all the woman's clubs. Mrs. Benjamin Prince is now president of this pioneer organization.

BY YOUR LONE

BY O. W. SMITH

NOT everybody can endure the silent places without human companionship, but for those who can, their ministry is very real and very satisfying.

I am an outfit crank, and have evolved one weighing only a few pounds and costing more than a few dollars. From silk shelter tent to folding cooking kit I think it about the lightest, most compact and serviceable equipment for the man who desires to make his way alone into the wilderness. That outfit is the result of years of experience. But right now I desire to select an outfit within the reach of Mr. Everyman.

"A square of sheeting," five feet by nine, will make a satisfactory tent. Simply rub into the fiber of the cloth hot linseed oil, first having sewed in a braided clothes-line around the edges with loops every two feet. Such a sheet can be used for a multitude of purposes, from a shelter tent to a sleeping sheet, one end under, the other over, and it is waterproof. A hand ax, a sheet iron fry-pan, a three-quart pail with a two-quart to fit inside, both provided with sacks, granite iron cup and plate, knife, fork, and spoon, and there you are. Of course you will purchase a good blanket like the U. S. army, or better, the Hudson Bay. Do not economize in the matter of a blanket. For a pack-sack use a common grain sack, tying a small potato in one corner of the bottom about which you can knot a scarf, fastening the other end to the puckered throat.

Perhaps I should pause right here to discuss the matter of food, tho to do so adequately in a few words is exceedingly difficult. Much will depend upon the character of the country into which you are going. If there are farms contained within reach, you can call upon them for supplies whenever your stock runs out; but if you plan to penetrate an uninhabited wilderness the problem is somewhat complicated. I am writing of short trips, tho my wife and I have gone into the wilderness for three weeks and suffered no great inconvenience. Let us suppose then that you will be within the reach of a farm house once in every two or three days. You need not bother with flour unless you wish to putter with bread making. Buy your loaf; you will get better bread. Carry a little screw-top jar for butter and another for bacon. Sugar can be kept in an oiled sack such as can be secured of any supply house, or in a screw-top can. Keep each article in a separate sack plainly

Independent readers will recognize Outdoors W. Smith—otherwise the Rev. O. Warren Smith—as one who has often gossiped with them about the woods, waters and fishing, especially fishing. — THE EDITOR.

marked on the outside. Confine yourself largely to the "solids," like rice, beans, etc. Plan to live off the country as much as possible. Unless in harvest time I carry a little dried fruit, not much, but enough to add variety to the bill of fare. You will crave sweets, and even dried apples help out wonderfully. Do not forget the necessary things, like salt, pepper, tea, coffee, and the like. Carry a few spare matches in a well corked bottle, not many, but enough for an emergency should the contents of your pockets become soaked. You will be surprised to discover how simple is the matter of food provision.

I have said nothing of personal equipment, as that is a matter for the individual to settle for himself. I carry a change of underclothing, stockings and sweater only, a good serviceable old suit, with well-worn

THE AUTHOR BY HIS LONE

but sturdy shoes. Do not load up with a lot of non-essentials. If you are a fisherman you probably will invest in one of those little "Sunday rods," than which nothing is better for your purpose, tho you can carry a few flies and a line, cutting your rod from Nature's supply. You will find yourself turning to the primitive with joy. Your pockets will contain a good knife, waterproof match box, compass and whatever you consider absolutely essential to happiness. But do not overload. Essentials are few.

"But," some one is saying, "suppose it should rain, suppose it should be unusually cold, suppose——" Stop. Suppose it should do any of a hundred and one things. Let it. If it rains, remain under your shelter. You have all the time there is. If it is cold, build a large fire with a backlog that will reflect the heat into your shelter. Take what the gods send with a grin. Bless you, a week of pack-sack sauntering in the wilderness near home will teach you more than a hundred and one sermons.

In packing, wrap your blanket up in the oiled sheet and put it in the bottom of the sack with the other articles on top. I would not so arrange them if I were carrying supplies for a couple of weeks, but you are not, and you desire the edibles get-at-able and you will not want to disturb the tent and bed until camp-making time. Always bear in mind what you are going to want next when you pack the sack, and so save a deal of trouble and rummaging.

So there is a vacation within the reach of any one with a scrap of courage and modicum of imagination. I can not begin to tell you how much good even a week-end will do a frayed business man. You can find wilderness enough out where the street car line ends, a wilderness as quiet, recreative, restful, and as near the great heart of mother Nature as can be found in the North Woods.

As I said at the beginning, not every man can go alone, for it takes something of a man to stand his own society; then select a companion, but as you hope to forget the work-a-day world, select a fellow saunterer with all the care you would exercise in choosing a life companion. Personally, I believe in the go-alone theory as an antidote for present day difficulties, mental, physical and spiritual, yes, spiritual. What we need is not better spiritual advisers, but opportunity for Moses' God to make bushes burn.

Dare you go alone? Prove it.

Washburn, Wisconsin

STORM

Photograph by John Rabel

JUNE BRIDES

BY CORRA HARRIS

AUTHOR OF "A CIRCUIT RIDER'S WIFE," "THE RECORDING ANGEL," "THE CO-CITIZENS"

APRIL is a child, ever divided, like a child, between smiles and tears. May is a maiden, pale and sweet, twisting blossoms in her hair like any other maiden. But June wears a wedding veil, and every flower in the fields, every rose in her gardens, is a bridesmaid to witness every nuptial morning, and every blissful night nature's marriage vows.

And here they come, the other brides in June, a long procession, from everywhere. They are moving down cathedral aisles. They are standing before dingy altars in village churches. They are joining hands with their bridegrooms in the humblest mountain cabins, and at the foot of grand staircases in the grandest mansions. They are flying along green country roads to face 'squires and magistrates, passionate little outlaws of prudence and reason, hurrying to swear into life-long obedience to love.

So many flowers are blooming in June, so many girls are marrying in June. What a month of wisdom it is. When youth casts aside all other wisdom, and chooses love for its faith with the courage of youth and love! And they are justified in this love —locked like a treasure, kissed with peace, filled with every hope and promise.

There is no reasonable danger to their happiness. They have only to labor for love, and to be faithful to love, forsaking all others for the sake of this one man and this one woman each has chosen. It is a simple ritual which has survived all other rituals and every other form of government, because it is founded upon the one everlasting thing in the heart of nature—love. June is no time to appoint a receiver for bankrupt marriages in a divorce court. It is the season to send for the priest and found your estate in hopes and start your dividend in happiness.

And all this is so because this is June in a country where peace is a principle, and love is a heritage which no man has dared to destroy. But what shall we say of those other lands where hate is the ruling principle, and death is the heritage of love? It is June in France and Belgium and Germany, too. But what a June! All her roses and blossoms trampled beneath the feet of armed men, and her wedding veil a shroud. Her brides are the widows of love. Her bridegrooms lie in a million graves, slain by the sword. They are falling day by day before Verdun, and behind Verdun, along all the battle lines in Belgium, in the trenches in Argonne, all the best and strongest young men of many nations. And somewhere in the shades of sorrow never lifted by the brightness of June days stand the maidens, one for every lover slain, pale and tear-stricken while they watch the smoking ruins of churches where they might have been married—in June.

When this war is over, it will not be finished, when every field in France is a cemetery, and the streets of the cities are filled with the lame and blind beggars which the long fight has turned into so many victims, the makers of war will face a terrific reckoning. There will be debts to pay, widows and orphans to pension, fighting men to teach peace, and a thousand noisy demands for a justice which has been slain and cannot be resurrected. And behind all importunate multitudes, ever retreating into the deeper obscurity of the fruitless years will be the brides of the dead, who never can know the hopes and happiness of love, who cannot voice their sacred grief, nor even dare to mourn the lover whom they might have married in June.

The Valley, Georgia

FOUR MILES HIGH

BY FANNY BULLOCK WORKMAN, F. R. G. S.

THE most difficult mountain I have ascended in the high Himalayas is the Hispar Watershed peak, lying above the source of the Hispar Glacier and overlooking both the Hispar and Biafo glaciers. It is a very sharp pyramid, as the picture shows. From the Hispar Glacier it looks unclimbable on all sides. It lies some four miles north of the Hispar Pass, and these four miles of rising, snowy upland are broken by ice falls of gigantic ice pinnacles and slants riven by wide, bridgeless chasms, so that it was well-nigh impossible to arrive at its base to see if any side of it could be scaled.

As the view from its summit would be incomparably grand and of geographical importance, showing all

Mrs. Workman is well known to the older readers of The Independent, for whom she has several times written of her twenty-five years of exploration among the world's highest mountains. She was made Officier de l'Instruction Publique, France, for her brilliant scientific achievements. — THE EDITOR.

the upper area of two great Karakoram glaciers, I was determined to reach its apex if a way could be found. Only the guide, Savoye, and three Italian porters accompanied us that season, so we had to depend on Nagar coolies to carry loads. Unlike the Suru men, they "would rather cut their throats" than climb a mountain.

However, after endless difficulties

and by dint of much parleying we succeeded in bringing nineteen of them from the upper Hispar Glacier camp to a hollow on the flank of the peak at over 19,000 feet, where small shelter tents were pitched. I have always wondered how Savoye and the porters got the grumbling coolies over the intricate and dangerous snow surface that had to be covered. In fact, ten of them threw down their loads some 300 feet below camp and left them to the porters to bring up. Late in the afternoon Savoye and a porter went out to examine the difficult arêtes of the peak, which rose like perpendicular needles above camp, to see which could be attempted the next day.

At dusk he returned to tell us that there was only one shoulder, that fac-

ATOP OF HISPAR, 21,350 FEET HIGH. THE TINY DOTS AT THE TOP ARE MRS. WORKMAN AND HER PARTY, TELEPHOTOGRAPHED BY DR. WORKMAN FROM ANOTHER PEAK THREE MILES AWAY

ing the Hispar Pass, which offered any chance of access to the summit. This appeared to be a narrow ice precipice of over 2000 feet, but the other arêtes, while less steep, were fluted with snow cornices which would probably give way if trod upon.

We were just at the end of a period of fine weather. When, at dawn, we were ready to start, the sky had a filmy look which we knew would bring storm within ten hours. I therefore left with Savoye and two porters for this peak, while Dr. Workman and the third porter started for another one east, which had also to be climbed for geographical observation. It was necessary to get the two peaks in that day, for to be storm-bound in the present camp would most probably prove fatal to the whole party.

After a twenty minutes' crossing of some snow slopes the ascent of the arête was begun. Seen from below this great shoulder shot skyward like an appalling blue pillar of verglas. The sun had not yet touched it and each step had to be cut in the ice covering, which slow process caused us to feel the near-zero temperature greatly.

We continued straight up for one and a half hours. Had I been in the least inclined to vertigo I should have turned back at the outset, for the

arête we were on was at most a foot and a half wide and the precipices on either side the most awful I recall on any ascent. They fell sheer 3000 feet into a dark intangible depth. It is much less nerve-trying when a precipice is only on one side, for a wall or broad snow slope on the other offers a certain moral support. At last a small ice shelf broke the upward monotony, and here we halted five minutes for taking photos and a bit of breakfast. The sky looked uncertain, so we hastened to attack an ice wall which now rose in our way. This was a nasty bit of about twenty feet; the sun had melted the snow and steps had to be hacked in the blue ice, and these filled with water as soon as cut. We moved sideways, each foot only half in a step. Below, exposed to view, lay half the mountain, a tortuous mass courting instant death to him who made a false step.

The wall overcome, we arrived again on the shoulder, which rose sharper than ever and was doubly arduous in the now softened snow. Still, by plodding on, we came in sight of the top at last, and crossing an easier slant we arrived at the apex, a small cone, which was really a snow cornice upon which only one person at a time could stand in safety.

Looking across a great void we saw the other party on their summit.

Our mountain was still clear of cloud and Dr. Workman succeeded in taking a telephotograph of my party just as it approached the top. In view of the mist soon to envelop all, we were very lucky to secure this souvenir.

The scene spread before us from this peak was, as I had expected, most remarkable for grandeur and topographical interest. Before my dazzled eyes lay one of the most magnificent of the world's mountainscapes; two of Asia's largest glaciers ran thirty miles east and west, made more splendid by their beautiful tributary glaciers and bordered by hundreds of wild and picturesque snow and rock peaks, varying from twenty to twenty-five thousand feet in hight.

I had barely finished noting my instruments when a wreath of cloud encircled our peak below where we stood, and before we had time to realize it, more than half the surrounding mountain world was lost in fluffy cloud vapor. But I had seen and learned much of the topography of the region in the short time I stood on the Hispar Watershed peak at 21,350 feet above sea level, and fully satisfied with my day's work, began the dangerous descent of the great arête. Slowly we moved amid mist and snow flurries, which rendered great caution necessary at every downward, slippery step. Still,

Packard
TWIN-SIX

IN PLAIN SPEECH, that car is best which will start quickest, control easiest, ride smoothest and run longest. To obtain this result, the PACKARD MOTOR CAR COMPANY a year ago created the *twelve-cylinder engine*, and provided in the *PACKARD TWIN-SIX* greater safety, smoother action, longer wear—with the elegance of a really fine carriage. By its performance in the hands of more than 6000 owners, this latest Packard has made the twelve-cylinder car the world's standard of automobile sufficiency and value.

Thirteen styles of open and enclosed bodies. Prices, with any open body, f. o. b. Detroit — The 1-35, $3150.00; the 1-25, $2750.00

ASK THE MAN WHO OWNS ONE

we passed safely thru the shifting fog, down the long inclines, past the deep precipices now filled with cloud and finally arrived at camp.

Altho we had had quite enough with the severe day's climb it was deemed unsafe to remain that night at the high camp, so packing up as quickly as possible we pushed down about 1500 feet over the broken snow area before mentioned to a fairly safe snow plateau, where by the time tents were pitched a storm destined to last forty-eight hours burst in all its fury.

One of our most delightful first ascents was of Mt. Bullock-Workman, the first time we had climbed to over 19,000 feet. The mountain is in the region of the Baltoro glacier, Western Karakoram, and the guide with us that season was the famous Swiss exploring guide, M. Zurbriggen. The camp made before the ascent was on moraine strewn glacier at 17,400 feet and we christened it Haunted Camp. It was just safe from rock avalanches, which fell with reverberating thunder all night from some tall needles which towered 4000 feet above. Evidently the glacier spirits wished to warn us from further invasion of their habitat, for at intervals thru the night we experienced distinct writhing movements of our beds, similar to the sensation noticed during earthquake shocks.

During pauses in the avalanche cannonade, my already overwrought nerves were treated to another sensation, that of the approaching quick tread of booted feet as on a polished floor. It came on steadily, growing louder as it neared the tent, then ceased a bit and began over again. No pabooshod coolie nor European booted mountaineer could walk thus regularly and daintily over moraine blocks in inky darkness, so I prefer to credit the glacier sprites with the mysterious noises.

My companions insisted on naming the new peak Mt. Bullock-Workman, after me. I have wished since that I had not allowed this, as I don't approve of personal names for new peaks and glaciers which one may discover, and have avoided their use on subsequent expeditions.

My highest climb was made in the Nun Kun group situated in the Punjab Himalaya. It is a vast massif of lofty mountains, the highest of which is 23,450 feet, and from it flow large and intricate glaciers. Besides exploring these glaciers, from which several high peaks were ascended, we made the first circuit of the group, covering in doing this a distance of ninety miles, mostly on snow and ice.

As we wished to make a study of rarefied air on the human body by camping at great hights for several days, we took with us, besides the guide, Savoye, six Courmayeur porters, who were to replace the coolies when they should give out and refuse to go higher. Our base camp on the Shafat Glacier, in the heart of the range, was at 15,000 feet. Here we remained two weeks getting acclimated and making minor ascents of eighteen or nineteen thousand feet. From here, as weather

A man is born with relations; he picks out his friends for himself.

So with tires—the tires that are on a new car the car manufacturer selects.

When a car owner buys tires he selects them himself.

Nearly every Kelly-Springfield tire used is selected by the car owner.

Kelly–Springfield
Automobile Tires – Hand Made

THERE is an important fundamental principle involved in this tire selection. You ought to understand it.

Few users buy Kelly-Springfield tires until after they have had experience with other tires. And fewer, having once used Kelly-Springfield tires, voluntarily discontinue their use. There is a reason for both conditions.

The reason few users try Kelly-Springfield tires first is that the initial selection of their tires is made by the manufacturer who equips the cars which they buy. And Kelly-Springfield tires cost more.

The manufacturer must put tires on the car he sells, but need not put on tires which give excess mileage. He is only obliged to equip with tires which yield the mileage most tire manufacturers guarantee. That is all the car buyer expects.

If the car manufacturer equips with a tire which gives a greater mileage than this, he has to pay the additional cost out of his own pocket —and why should he?

Considering proper manufacturing economies, he equips with tires which cost him least and yet give reasonable satisfaction. He equips his car with higher priced tires only when he buys advertising value for his car, as well as tires.

Now we cannot meet the manufacturer's price requirements. Hand-made tires cost more to make and yield excess mileage. We cannot compete on price when the excess mileage doesn't count. So we rarely sell tires to car manufacturers.

Kelly-Springfield tires are sold almost exclusively to car owners who pay higher initial prices because they know they receive excess value. At present the demand is far in excess of our production.

The demand has been so great that owners order tires before they need them to get them when they need them.

It is important to you to know these conditions and to know true tire economy.

Kelly-Springfield Tire Co.
Factories in Akron and Wooster, Ohio
Executive Offices: B'way & 57th St., New York
Send 12c. for the new game, "Going to Market"

allowed, the guides and porters made reconnaissances of the highest snow peaks lying above us, to plan out a route to the one I wished to attempt.

When all was ready a start upward was begun, with as little kit as possible, consisting of five or six small flannel-lined tents, the necessary warm clothes, bedding and tinned food for eight days. The first snow camp was at 17,660 and the second at 19,900 feet. The third day's climb was short but very trying, being at first up an ice wall which brought us to a snow covered ice-slant with a convex surface inclined at sixty degrees which overhung a 3000-foot precipice. We Europeans were roped by a light silk rope tested to a strain of 2500 pounds, but I must say that when a porter stumbled once, altho he was quickly hauled up by the guide, my whole spine shivered. The natives were attached to a second rope led by two Italian porters and no one was loaded to over thirty-five pounds.

At over 20,000 feet halts to breathe were so frequent that progress at these precarious places was exasperatingly slow, as we trod silently the white ladder of approach to the mysterious unknown. The mental strain of a prolonged dizzy climb at such a hight is intense. Finally this scarp ended in a snow crest which on measurement proved to be at 21,000 feet; here we just saw the tops of the highest Nun Kun peaks.

In this never-before-trodden snow vale, at an altitude of 7000 feet higher than the Matterhorn, we were destined to pass three nights. A descent of 400 feet now had to be made into the basin where, as clouds were rushing in bringing snow flurries, and the snow under foot became too soft and deep for further progress, tents were pitched at 20,600 feet.

The coolies flung down their loads and then began a series of deep salaams toward the summits peering thru the clouds. Having finished these exercises, they begged to be allowed to descend, showing no fear of facing such a descent alone in uncertain weather. A coolie will never find his way up a mountain alone, but is usually expert enough when bent on going down.

There were still three miles to the actual base of the peak. After a descent to the center of the plateau, the ascent at about thirty degrees was continuous over an undulating surface, for this elevated basin was by no means an easy flat snow meadow as might be imagined from its designation. Near the base of the peak a spot safe from avalanches was chosen and two tents pitched. Mist coming in so softened the snow that it was doubtful if the guides could return to us with their kit as planned, so it was agreed with Savoye that they should all go down to the last night's camp and return by night if snow conditions allowed; if not, they would sleep at the lower camp and rejoin us at daybreak. We unpacked kit and instruments and set to work at our observations, but the idea of passing the night alone, as we should probably have to do, at such an altitude, was

Chautauqua Institution Summer Schools

Fourteen Departments
1916

July 10 to August 18

Chautauqua New York

I. English.
II. Modern Languages.
III. Classical Languages.
IV. Mathematics.

V. Science.
VI. Education.
VII. Social Science and History.

VIII. Library Training.
IX. Home Economics.
X. Music.

XI. Arts and Crafts.
XII. Expression.
XIII. Physical Education.
XIV. Practical Arts.

RAILROADS:

Chautauqua, N. Y., is midway between New York and Chicago, 12 hours from either. Reached by New York Central, Erie, Pennsylvania, and Nickle Plate railroads. Through tickets and direct connections. Special rates. Stop-over privileges on all roads.

ASK FOR:

Catalog of Schools, Physical Education Circular, Music Announcements, Illustrated Faculty Religious Announcements, Public Assembly Program, Travel Information, Handbook of Accommodations, Map of Chautauqua. Address Chautauqua Institution, Chautauqua, N. Y.

rather uncanny. We named this Camp America and its hight proved to be 21,-300 feet. Altho the sun shone sickly thru the mist, the afternoon heat was intense, the solar thermometer registering 102° Fahr. at 2 p. m. At sunset the temperature fell to freezing and an hour after to 10°, reaching a minimum of 4° below zero before morning.

The night seemed the longest and coldest we ever passed in camp and little sleep came to break the dragging hours. One can breathe better in the erect position than when lying down. As soon as we began to doze, and the respiratory movements diminished in force and frequency, the tissues did not get enough oxygen, and we would start up gasping for breath, so that our night rest was worth little. We suffered also greatly from thirst, the water in the flasks having, of course, become solid ice. At last the gray dawn penetrated the tent canvas and soon the welcome footsteps of Savoye and two porters were heard on the hard snow without.

Those who start out from a warm hotel in the Alps to make a winter ascent often think they are enduring hardships, but that is really mere play compared to getting up in an unwarmed tent on snow, with the glass below zero, collecting one's things, trying to boil coffee over a stove so affected by diminished atmosphere that it won't light and, above all, to my mind, the wrestle with frozen boots! However, we got off in time.

I will not describe in detail the ascent of the sharp peak broken by dangerous ice falls and gashed by yawning crevasses. Happily the day was clear to begin with and the sun when it came warmed us a bit, for movement was of necessity slow at 22,000 feet. The latter part of the ascent of 300 feet was mostly over rock, which is much harder to negotiate than snow at a great hight. The gradients were from 60 to 65 degrees. The view from the summit was a bird's-eye one, for we overlooked most of the wide galaxy of mountains, tortuous glaciers and ribbon-like valleys stretching on all sides.

The rarity of the air was severely felt on the least exertion with camera or instruments. An icy wind and want of time soon drove us down to join the others, where, after a light meal, the descent to camp was completed. I named the peak Pinnacle. It was a glorious climb, but like others of similar nature, enjoyed more in retrospect than at the time. A second uncomfortable night was passed at Camp America, where none of us had a wink of sleep. The temperature fell to 6° below zero.

The following morning we descended to 19,900 feet, where our fifth night on snow at high altitudes was spent, and the day after reached base camp, very well satisfied with our high journey. It was arduous, but it had resulted in the first ascent of a high peak, which gave me the world altitude record for women, and in the acquisition of interesting information on climatology and the effects of rarefied air.

Paris

the new Encyclopaedia Britannica

["HANDY VOLUME" ISSUE]

will advance in price—$11 *on the*

cheapest binding; $19 *on the highest-priced* [other bindings proportionally]

THIS advance is due to circumstances over which we have no control. The war has forced up the cost of all raw materials for making these books. *Paper* costs very much more than it did before the war. Some *leathers* cost 75 per cent more, and others cannot be imported —they are under embargo.

It will soon be impossible for us to supply sets in the most expensive leathers at any price because of the British embargo on fine leathers.

The Britannica is *a work that you need.* The greatest of all reference works, in this new edition, it is made up of 29 volumes, more than 30,000 pages, 44,000,000 words, 41,000 articles, written by 1500 experts chosen for their supreme fitness. There are 15,000 pictures and maps. An index of 500,000 entries makes all this wealth of information easily available.

All yours now at a great price saving—in any binding, shipped complete for a first payment of only $1. Satisfaction guaranteed or your money back.

If your order is to be accepted at the present low prices it must be postmarked *before* 7.33 p. m., June 17th. *Don't wait* until the last minute. *Order to-day.*

We take all the risk. You are protected by our guarantee. There will never be such a chance again.

Sears, Roebuck and Co.

Sole Distributors

Chicago

LITTLE TRAVELS

MORE AND MORE THE CALL OF THE AMERICAN PLAYGROUNDS IS BEING HEARD BY AMERICANS WHO MAKE HOLIDAY IN THE SUMMER MONTHS. FROM THE MAINE COAST TO THE HARBOR OF THE SUN, FROM THE RUGGED ROCKIES TO THE WELL-GROOMED WHITE MOUNTAINS, FROM THE WILDERNESS TO THE HISTORIC ST. LAWRENCE, THERE IS A WIDE RANGE OF SUMMER PLEASURES TO BE FOUND ON OUR OWN CONTINENT WHICH BECKON TO THE ADVENTURER—DOUBLY SO IN THIS SECOND YEAR OF THE EUROPEAN EMBARGO ON TOURISTS. HERE ARE EIGHT TRIPS CONVENIENTLY PLANNED, WIDELY DIFFERENT IN COST, TIME AND CHARACTER, ADAPTED TO DIFFERENT TASTES AND PURSES, BUT ALL RICH IN POTENTIAL ENJOYMENT

NIAGARA FALLS, TORONTO, THOUSAND ISLANDS	GLACIER NATIONAL PARK
ADIRONDACKS, MONTREAL, QUEBEC	WESTERN NORTH CAROLINA
MAINE COAST, WHITE MOUNTAINS	NEW JERSEY SHORE RESORTS
NOVA SCOTIA	GRAND CANYON, CALIFORNIA, YELLOWSTONE PARK

ADIRONDACKS — MONTREAL — QUEBEC

Time—Two or Three Weeks

First Day. Leave *NEW YORK* in the morning. Leave *OLD FORGE* in the afternoon. Arrive *RACQUETTE LAKE* in the evening. Hotels and camps $2.50 up per day, American plan. This is one of the prettiest of the many lakes in the section. One day must be given for the trip to Blue Mountain and Lake and return. The steamer crosses Racquette Lake and then winds its way thru the narrow Marion River. Change to train is made over a short carry and another steamer awaits to take you to your destination. After luncheon at one of the many hotels or camps, you start on the journey back. You will find it a unique and interesting trip.

Third Day. Leave *RACQUETTE LAKE* in the morning and by boat and auto arrive *LONG LAKE* about noon. Hotels and Camps $2.50 up per day, American plan. Spend the afternoon and night here and in the morning leave by stage for Long Lake West and there meet train.

Fifth Day. Arrive *LAKE PLACID* in the afternoon. Hotels and Boarding Houses $2 up per day, American plan. A boat trip around Lake Placid with its thickly wooded shores, drives to Wilmington Notch, Saranac Lake, Keene Valley in the heart of the mountains, climbing and horseback riding will make the days go quickly here.

Tenth Day. Leave *LAKE PLACID* in the afternoon. Arrive *MONTREAL* in the evening. Hotels $1 up per day, European plan. Spend the first day in seeing the many points of interest in the city. Sightseeing cars will give you a good general idea. A sightseeing car also makes a trip around the mountain and the Incline Railway will take you to the top of Mt. Royal, where you can get a magnificent view of the city.

Thirteenth Day. Leave *MONTREAL* by steamer or rail.

Fourteenth Day. Arrive *QUEBEC* by steamer or within five hours by rail. Hotels from $2.50 up per day, American plan. This quaint town has unlimited attractions. Old landmarks, picturesque streets, convents and cathedrals must all be visited. One day should be given for the trip to St. Anne de Beaupres via electric cars. On the way you will get a fine view of the falls of Montmorency. You will stop off there on the return trip and take the elevator which rises 274 feet and lands you near the Kent House, built in 1778. Refreshments can be had here. A side trip may be made to the Saguenay. The steamers leave at night, returning the third evening.

Twentieth Day. Leave *QUEBEC* in the morning. Arrive *MONTREAL* in time to connect with train for Plattsburg. Arrive *PLATTSBURG* in the evening, board steamer for trip thru Lake Champlain and Lake George.

Twenty-first Day. Leave *PLATTSBURG* in the morning. Arrive *LAKE GEORGE* in the evening. Hotels $3 up, European plan. Small houses $2.50 up, American plan. Boat and trolley trips may be had here.

Twenty-third Day. Leave *LAKE GEORGE* in the morning. Arrive *SARATOGA* in about an hour. Hotels $2.50 up per day, American plan. This Spa now ranks favorably with those of Europe. The drives are many and varied and Saratoga Lake is attractive.

Twenty-fifth Day. Leave *SARATOGA* in the morning. Arrive *NEW YORK* in the evening.

Approximate cost of trip from New York and return $48.55

NIAGARA FALLS — TORONTO — THOUSAND ISLANDS

Time—About Ten Days

First Day. Leave *NEW YORK* in the morning. Arrive *NIAGARA FALLS* in the evening. Hotels $2 up per day, American plan. Three days at least must be spent here to appreciate the majesty and beauty of the Falls and to enjoy the walks and drives along the main avenues and in the by-ways. There are also many interesting trolley trips.

Fourth Day. Leave *NIAGARA FALLS* in the morning. Arrive *TORONTO* at noon. Hotels from $1.50 up per day, European plan. Spend one day here driving about the city and visiting the points of interest.

Fifth Day. Leave *TORONTO* in the afternoon by steamer.

Sixth Day. Arrive *ALEXANDRIA BAY* in the morning. This attractive resort is a good central point from which to take delightful excursions among the wondrously beautiful islands, rich in natural attractions. One day must be spent in taking the trips via steamer among the islands and one day in fishing with a competent guide, who will cook the fish you catch. A trip to the quaint city of Kingston is also enjoyable.

Tenth Day. Leave *ALEXANDRIA BAY* in the morning. Arrive *NEW YORK* in the evening.

Approximate cost of trip from New York and return $24.05

GLACIER NATIONAL PARK

(Season—June 15-October 1)
Time—About Two Weeks

First Day. Leave *NEW YORK* in the evening.

Second Day. Leave *CHICAGO* in the evening.

Fourth Day. Arrive *GLACIER PARK* in the evening. Glacier Park Hotel $4 up day, American plan. This is the gateway to the second largest of our national playgrounds. During the day spent here you will decide on the various points you may want to take. Some of those already planned are: One day tour, by auto stage, from Glacier Park Hotel to Two Medicine Chalet and return; cost $8. One day tour, by auto stage, from the Hotel to St. Mary's Chalet, thence by launch to Going-to-the-Sun Chalet and return; cost $8. Two day tour, by auto stage, from Hotel to Many Glacier Hotel; spend the afternoon and evening here and after breakfast the following morning leave by auto stage for St. Mary's Chalet, then by launch to Going-to-the-Sun Chalet on one of the most beautiful of the Glacier Park lakes; cost

$13.50. Three day tour, by auto stage, to Many Glacier Hotel; the next morning a horseback ride to Iceberg Lake and return, and the third day return to Glacier Park Hotel via St. Mary's Chalet and Going-to-the-Sun Chalet; cost $17. Four day tour, daily, July 1st to Sept. 1st. First day, by auto stage to Many Glacier Hotel. Second day, by saddle horse over Swiftcurrent Pass to Granite Park Chalets. Third day, by saddle horse to Many Glacier Hotel. Fourth day, by auto stage back to Glacier Park Hotel, including side trip by launch from St. Mary's Chalet (passed en route) to Going-to-the-Sun Chalet; cost $21.50. Five day tour, from July 1st to Sept. 1st. This tour is similar to the four day tour, but in addition you take a horseback trip to Iceberg Lake; cost of this trip $25. These tours are laid out for you and tickets are sold covering the entire trip. If you prefer you can wander about the Park at will. The two hotels, one at the entrance to the Park and the other in the heart of it, make rates of $4 up day, American plan. The Chalets, which are most attractive, have a uniform rate of $3 per day, American plan, and the Tepee Camps charge fifty cents per bed per night. These are located near the Chalets, where food may be purchased at reasonable prices. Use of utensils and range in the camps is allowed.

Eleventh Day. Leave *GLACIER PARK* in the evening.

Thirteenth Day. Arrive *CHICAGO* in the evening.

Fourteenth Day. Arrive *NEW YORK* in the evening.

Round trip rate from New York to to Glacier Park via New York Central or Pennsylvania R. R....	$86.70
Via other lines....................	82.20
Round trip rate from Chicago to Glacier Park	48.00
Pullman berth from New York, one way.........................	14.00
Pullman berth from Chicago, one way.........................	9.00

NOVA SCOTIA

Time—About Three Weeks

First Day. Leave *NEW YORK* in the evening by boat.

Second Day. Arrive *BOSTON* in the morning. You will have the morning to get a glimpse of Boston by taking one of the sight-seeing tours, returning to the dock in time to leave. Leave *BOSTON* at one p. m. by steamer.

Third Day. Arrive *YARMOUTH* in the morning. Hotel $3 up per day, American plan. Yarmouth has charm of scenery and environment. The climate is good and immune from hay fever. All these points make it popular with the summer visitor. You will find a good hotel here which adds much to the comfort of the traveler. A couple of days will give you an opportunity to take some of the popular drives, the most interesting being to the bathing beach at Port Maitland, twelve miles distant. You will also get fine boating and fishing.

Fifth Day. Leave *YARMOUTH* in the morning. Arrive *DIGBY* in about two hours. Hotels $2.50 up per day. Digby is located on Annapolis Basin. Its back ground of hills makes an attractive setting. Sail-

Prepared by Bertha Ruffner

ing, boating, bathing and driving are among its many diversions. It is in the center of a number of summer resorts which can easily be reached and are objective points of the more important drives. Take one day for a trip to St. John, New Brunswick. This will show you the beauties of the Basin and the narrow strait which separates it from the Bay of Fundy. You will have several hours to spend in St. John.

Ninth Day. Leave *DIGBY* at noon. Arrive *ANNAPOLIS* in about one hour. Hotels $2 up per day, American plan. This town is one of the oldest on the American Continent and was settled by the French in 1604. It is a delightful spot and typically Nova Scotia.

Tenth Day. Leave *ANNAPOLIS* in the early afternoon. Arrive *KENTVILLE* in about three hours. Hotels $2.50 up per day; American plan. A stop is made here for the purpose of visiting Cape Blomidon, the highest point of land in the province. Connection is also made for Parrsboro by train and boat. This will give you an opportunity to see Minas Basin, where the famous Nova Scotia tides reach a hight of from fifty to sixty feet.

Twelfth Day. Leave *KENTVILLE* at noon. Arrive *WOLFVILLE* in an hour. Hotels $2.50 up per day, American plan. This is the University and Academy town of Nova Scotia, and many fine and delightful drives may be taken. This is the very heart of the "Land of Evangeline." Be sure and drive to the old church at Grand Pré and en route from one of the high points near Wolfvile get the view of lovely and peaceful Gasperau Valley, one of the most charming pictures in all Nova Scotia.

Fifteenth Day. Leave *WOLFVILLE* about noon. Arrive *HALIFAX* in the evening. Hotels $3 up per day, American plan. This is the capital of the Province and a picturesque garrison city. Its public buildings and its parks and public gardens are of much interest. Spend one day in a trip to Chester, which is considered one of the most delightful shore resorts in Nova Scotia. While here take a side trip to Charlottetown, Prince Edward's Island and also to Cape Bretton, thru the Bras d'or Lakes.

Nineteenth Day. Leave *HALIFAX* in the evening (Tuesday).

Twenty-first Day. Arrive *BOSTON* in the morning. Arrive *NEW YORK* in the evening.

Approximate cost of trip, New York
to Nova Scotia and return......$26.00

GRAND CANYON, CALIFORNIA AND YELLOWSTONE PARK

Time—About a Month

First Day. Leave *NEW YORK* in the morning.

Second Day. Arrive *CHICAGO* in the afternoon. Leave *CHICAGO* in the evening.

Fifth Day. Arrive *GRAND CANYON.* Hotel El Tovar $4 up per day, American plan. Bright Angel Cottages $1 up per day, European plan. This tremendous chasm in the northwest corner of Arizona is 6000 feet deep and thirteen miles wide. There is nothing in the world so stupendous; its grandeur cannot be described. Visit Hopi House opposite the hotel, a reproduction of the dwelling of the Hopi Indians. Here live a small band of Hopis—men and women—weaving, making pottery or hand silver ornaments. In the evening they entertain you with their weird songs and queer dances. There are many drives, among them to Mt. Hopi and return, leaving morning and afternoon; cost $1.50. Mohave Point and return, leaving 9 a. m. and 2 p. m.; cost $2. Hermit Rim Road and return, leaving morning and afternoon; cost $3. All of them give fine views of the Canyon. If you prefer you may take the many horseback rides or longer motor trips.

Seventh Day. Leave *GRAND CANYON* in the evening.

Eighth Day. Arrive *SAN DIEGO,* Cal., in the afternoon. Hotels $1 up per day,

WHERE ONCE THEIR FATHERS FOUGHT AND NOW THE WHITE MAN P[...]
THAT IS NOW A PART OF GLACIER NA[...]

INDIANS, ANCIENT OWNERS OF THE FINE MOUNTAIN COUNTRY
KING TOWARD ROMNEY GLACIER

WHERE ONCE THEIR FATHERS FOUGHT AND NOW THE WHITE MAN P...
THAT IS NOW A PART OF GLACIER NA...

THE FINE MOUNTAIN COUNTRY

R

up per day. European plan. A sightsee
trolley leaves the hotel about 10 a. m.
going about the city as far as Fort Douglas. This will give you a good idea of
Salt Lake City and also of the surrounding country. On the return the car stops
at the Mormon Tabernacle in time for
the noon concert. After this is over, visit
the various buildings in Temple Square
open to the public. A guide is usually
sent around and the trip is most interesting, as well as instructive; cost $1. In
the afternoon go by train to Saltair
Beach on Great Salt Lake. The fare is $1
at Saltair is the bathing. Cost from 25c
and return on train is 25 cents.

Twenty-sixth Day. Leave SALT LAKE
CITY in the evening.

Twenty-seventh Day. Arrive YELLOWSTONE STATION in the morning. (I five
days in the Park.) You leave the Park
entrance in the morning, after an early
breakfast at the Station dining room, follow the road which winds along the Madison River to where it joins the Gibbon,
the two forming the Firehole. Fountain
Hotel is reached by eleven o'clock and you
stop there for luncheon. Time is given to
walk about and see some of the geysers
and the Paint Pots. Arrive Old Faithful In
about 4 p. m. The evening is spent here
as there are many interesting geysers near
about, such as the Grotto, Giant, Oblong
and others. Old Faithful, the most note
of all, adjoins the hotel and it plays with
scarcely a variation every sixty-five minutes. It rises to a height of from 125 to
150 feet and one never tires watching it
both at sunset and at night, when the
searchlight illuminates it. The next morning the stage leaves for the second day's
trip, and between the Upper Geyser Basin
and Yellowstone Lake the tourist twice
crosses the Great Continental Divide.
Thumb Station is reached next and then
you stop for luncheon. At this point
choice of routes is given the traveler. You
can continue by stage over the mountain
or go by boat up Yellowstone to the next
night stop at Lake Hotel. This is a delightful resting place, where you may enjoy fishing excursions or boating about
the lake. The third day the stage road
leads along the Yellowstone River thru
the lovely Hayden Valley, Cañon Hotel is
reached soon and you spend the afternoon
and night here. There is plenty of time to
visit the canyon. Other canyons may be
larger, but none can compare with this in
beauty of coloring. The lower falls of the
Yellowstone, 308 feet in hight, are near
by and may be reached by good roads
and trails. The fourth morning you
go thru pine forests and along the Gibbon
River to Norris Geyser Basin, where a
stop is made at Norris Hotel for luncheon.
There are many boiling springs all about
covering a large tract no safe for walking
except on the boardwalks which cross it.
Here may be seen the Black Growler, the
Hurricane, the Constant and other important geysers. Stages leave after luncheon and arrive at Mammoth Hot Springs
Hotel about 4 p. m.

Thirty-first Day. Leave MAMMOUT
HOT SPRINGS in the morning. Arrive
YELLOWSTONE STATION in the afternoon in time to connect with night
train.

Thirty-second Day. Arrive SALT LAKE
CITY in the morning.

Thirty-second Day. Leave SALT LAKE
CITY in the morning.

Thirty-third Day. Arrive GLENWOOD
SPRINGS in the evening. Hotel Colorado $5 up per day, American plan. A most
Glenwood Springs makes an interesting break in the journey. It is in the heart
of the Rockies and is noted for its fine
caves, its natural hot vapor baths and
open air swimming pool (near the hotel),
which is 600 feet long and 110 feet

Thirty-fourth Day. Leave GLENWOOD
SPRINGS in the morning.

Thirty-fifth Day. Arrive COLORADO
SPRINGS in the afternoon. Hotel $1.50 up
day, European plan. Colorado Springs is

Spend Your Vacation
at the
Seashore

The ideal summer resort.

Enjoy the cool sea breezes; surf bathing;
sailing on bay and ocean, boating,
fishing, crabbing and many other amusements and recreations.

You may golf also at the leading resorts.
And there are delightful automobile trips.

The New Jersey Coast offers such attractive and
famous resorts as Atlantic City, Cape May,
Wildwood, Ocean City, Sea Isle City, Beach
Haven, Seaside Park, Spring Lake, Asbury
Park, Ocean Grove, Long Branch and over
thirty others.

Write Geo. W. Boyd, Passenger Traffic Manager, Broad Street
Station, Philadelphia, Pa., for a copy of the

"40 Beaches of New Jersey"

Pennsylvania Railroad
The Standard Railroad of the World

European plan. San Diego is old in history and is favored in location, mountains, climate. Coronado, should you prefer to stay there, is reached via trolley and ferry. Two days must be given to the Exposition—the grounds, the buildings, the wonderful open air organ on which daily concerts are given, and the exhibits. Spend a day in taking various trips, among them the one to the Old Mission.

Eleventh Day. Leave *SAN DIEGO* in the morning. Arrive *LOS ANGELES* in the afternoon. Hotels $1 up per day, European plan. There are many delightful trips to be taken here. Around the beaches by trolley; cost $1. Old Mission trolley trip; cost $1. Balloon Route Trip; cost $1. Mount Lowe, considered the greatest mountain scenic trip is America; cost $2. Spend one day in visiting Catalina Island; cost $2.75; and take a one day trip to Riverside and Redlands, going by train and trolley, cost $3.

Fifteenth Day. Leave *LOS ANGELES* in the morning. Arrive *SANTA BARBARA* at noon. Hotels $3 up per day. American plan. One day must be given to this charming city which in location resembles Mentone, in France. Take the mountain drive in the afternoon—get the fine views of the ocean and islands and return via Miramar.

Sixteenth Day. In the morning visit the Mission, the most interesting and best preserved of any in the state.

Sixteenth Day. Leave *SANTA BARBARA* at noon. Arrive *DEL MONTE* in the evening. Hotel Del Monte $4 to $6 per day, American plan. "The Riviera of America" is the name given to the peninsula on which Del Monte is located. This delightful resort is situated in a park of 126 acres, the beauty of which is worth the trip across the continent. Take the famous seventeen-mile drive. You will be interested in the grove of ancient cypress. Visit Monterey, from 1770 to 1840 the capital of California. It has many landmarks—old adobe buildings and early missions. Then drive three miles to the Carmel Mission, where lies the body of Father Junipero Serra. There are many other drives here if time permits. A fine golf course of eighteen holes, tennis courts in perfect condition, a bowling green and archery provide for sports

Nineteenth Day. Leave *DEL MONTE* in the morning. Arrive *SAN FRANCISCO* in the early afternoon. Hotels from $1 up per day, European plan. You get a good idea of the city by taking the sightseeing car, leaving Ferry Loop at 10 a. m.; cost 75 cents. A three hour ride, with stop at the Cliff House to see the beach, the Seal Rocks and Golden Gate. Take one day for the trip to Mt. Tamalpais, including Muir Woods on the return journey; cost $2. Take Sausalito Ferry from Ferry Building and at Sausalito change to electric railway nestled in a canyon. Transfer here for the trip to the summit (2592 feet), which is made over the "crookedest railroad in the world." The views are impressive. Stop here long enough to take the walk around the peak and then have luncheon at the tavern. At 2 p. m. the train leaves for Muir Woods. A stop of two hours is made here, giving you an opportunity to walk thru the valley and see many "big trees." San Francisco is reached at 5 p. m. Another day visit Berkeley and Oakland. This is over the Key Trolley Route and the boat leaves Ferry Building at 10 a. m. It covers sixty-eight miles and the cost is $1. In Berkeley you see the University of California campus and recent buildings, the Greek Theatre. Campanile and new library. The grounds are very beautiful. The trip to Oakland takes in the public buildings. Lake Merritt and Oakland Museum. There are sightseeing cars, as well as autos, which take you about the city, showing you all the points of interest.

Twenty-fourth Day. Leave *SAN FRANCISCO* in the morning.

Twenty-fifth Day. Arrive *SALT LAKE CITY* in the afternoon. Hotels from $1

---

up per day, European plan. A sightseeing trolley leaves the hotel about 10 a. m., going about the city as far as Fort Douglas. This will give you a good idea of Salt Lake City and also of the surrounding country. On the return the car stops at the Mormon Tabernacle in time for the noon concert. After this is over, visit the various buildings in Temple Square open to the public. A guide is usually sent around and the trip is most interesting, as well as instructive; cost $1. In the afternoon go by train to Saltair Beach on Great Salt Lake. The feature at Saltair is the bathing. Cost from city and return on train is 25 cents.

Twenty-sixth Day. Leave *SALT LAKE CITY* in the evening.

Twenty-seventh Day. Arrive *YELLOWSTONE STATION* in the morning. (Five days in the Park.) You leave the Park entrance in the morning, after excellent breakfast at the Station dining room, follow the road which winds along the Madison River to where it joins the Gibbon, the two forming the Firehole. Fountain Hotel is reached by eleven o'clock and you stop there for luncheon. Time is given to walk about and see some of the geysers and the Paint Pots. Arrive Old Faithful Inn about 4 p. m. The evening is spent here, as there are many interesting geysers all about, such as the Grotto, Giant, Oblong and others. Old Faithful, the most noted of all, adjoins the hotel and it plays with scarcely a variation every sixty-five minutes. It rises to a height of from 125 to 150 feet and one never tires watching it, both at sunset and at night, when the searchlight illuminates it. The next morning the stage leaves for the second day's trip, and between the Upper Geyser Basin and Yellowstone Lake the tourist twice crosses the Great Continental Divide. Thumb Station is reached next and there you stop for luncheon. At this point a choice of routes is given the traveler. You can continue by stage over the mountains or go by boat up Yellowstone to the next night stop at Lake Hotel. This is a delightful resting place, where you may enjoy fishing excursions or boating about the lake. The third day the stage road leads along the Yellowstone River thru the lovely Hayden Valley. Cañon Hotel is reached soon and you spend the afternoon and night here. There is plenty of time to visit the canyon. Other canyons may be larger, but none can compare with this in beauty of coloring. The lower falls of the Yellowstone, 508 feet in hight, are near by and may be reached by good roads and trails. The fourth morning you go thru pine forests and along the Gibbon River to Norris Geyser Basin, where a stop is made at Norris Hotel for luncheon. There are many boiling springs all about, covering a large tract unsafe for walking except on the boardwalks which cross it. Here may be seen the Black Growler, the Hurricane, the Constant and other important geysers. Stages leave after luncheon and arrive at Monmouth Hot Springs Hotel about 4 p. m.

Thirty-first Day. Leave *MONMOUTH HOT SPRINGS* in the morning. Arrive *YELLOWSTONE STATION* in the late afternoon in time to connect with night train.

Thirty-second Day. Arrive *SALT LAKE CITY* in the morning.

Thirty-second Day. Leave *SALT LAKE CITY* in the morning.

Thirty-third Day. Arrive *GLENWOOD SPRINGS* in the morning. Hotel Colorado $5 up per day, American plan. A stop at Glenwood Springs makes an interesting break in the journey. It is in the heart of the Rockies and is noted for its fine drives, its natural hot vapor baths and its open air swimming pool (near the hotel), which is 600 feet long and 110 feet wide.

Thirty-fourth Day. Leave *GLENWOOD SPRINGS* in the morning.

Thirty-fifth Day. Arrive *COLORADO SPRINGS* in the afternoon. Hotel $1.50 up per day, European plan. Colorado Springs

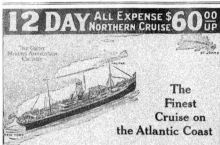

is well worth a couple of days' stay. A trip to Manitou and Pike's Peak will take one day. The sightseeing automobiles make the trip to the Garden of the Gods and to South Cheyenne Canyon. The thirty mile auto trip to Crystal Park must not be omitted, as it takes you into the heart of the Rockies.

Thirty-eighth Day. Leave *COLORADO SPRINGS* in the afternoon. Arrive *DENVER* in about three hours. Hotels $1.50 up per day, European plan. Visit the public buildings and take a trip on the sightseeing cars. There are also many outings via trolley and autos to the nearby mountain peaks. Among them Mt. McClellan, Lookout Mountain, "Moffat Road," etc. There are also trips to Boulder, New Rocky Mountain National Park and Estes Park.

Forty-third Day. Leave *DENVER* in the evening.

Forty-fifth Day. Arrive *NEW YORK* in the evening.

Cost of ticket from New York back to New York, not including Canyon or Yellowstone Park	$115.20
Additional cost for trip to Canyon	7.50
Additional cost for trip through Yellowstone Park, including stage fare and hotel accommodations..	53.50
	$176.20

Lower berth to the coast, $19.

WESTERN NORTH CAROLINA

Time—Two Weeks

First Day. Leave *NEW YORK* in the afternoon.

Second Day. Arrive *ASHEVILLE* in the afternoon. Asheville, the center from which many delightful resorts can be easily reached, is a city of charming hotels and attractive boarding houses. Ten days may be well spent here visiting the various points of interest.

Third Day. Drive thru the Biltmore estate, over fine roads and thru beautiful scenery, stopping to visit the model dairy with its hundred head of registered cows and incidentally indulge in a dish of ice cream made of pure cream.

Fourth Day. Drive to Mountain Meadows Inn for luncheon. The views of mountains and valleys on the way are glorious.

Fifth Day. Go via train in the morning to Lake Toxaway, which you will reach in time for luncheon at Toxaway Inn, situated on the shore of the lake near the station. The lake is 3000 feet above sea level, fifteen miles in circumference, a beautiful sheet of water with rugged Mt. Toxaway at one end of it. Trains leave in the late afternoon and you are back in time for dinner at your hotel in Asheville.

Sixth Day. Climb or drive to Sunset Mountain, from which you get a fine view of Asheville and the far off majestic Blue Ridge, of which Pisgah, 6940 feet high, forms the center.

Seventh Day. Trip to Mt. Mitchell at an altitude of 6711 feet, the highest point east of the Rockies. Train leaves Asheville at 8:30 a. m. and arrives at Mitchell Ridge at 1 p. m. This is a part of the great National Forest owned by the United States. Three hours are given to luncheon about, have luncheon and revel in the wonderful panorama of mountains and valleys for scores of miles on every side. At 4 p. m. you leave and 8 p. m. finds you back in Asheville.

Eighth Day. Leave some time during the day by rail or auto for a trip to Hendersonville and Flat Rock. The former is one of the most delightful and progressive cities of western North Carolina. Here you will find good hotels and see many attractive homes and parks. Historic Flat Rock is a short distance to the south. This spot was settled by Charleston people in 1820. Highland Lake has an attractive hotel where there are opportunities for golf, tennis, boating and bathing.

Ninth Day. Spend the day in a trip to Bat Cave Section, Hickory Nut Gap. The drive is delightful because of the variety of scenery it presents. You cross the plateau on which Asheville is located, skirt the mountains and then climb up and across the range into the Gap. A roaring stream follows the road and on either side tower the mountains, one of the most interesting being Chimney Rock, 6000 feet high. If you are wise you will bring your luncheon and find a cosy spot near the stream and spend a couple of hours in the glorious out-of-doors before beginning the return journey.

Tenth Day. The clearest and brightest day of your visit must be given to a trip by auto to Mt. Pisgah, the most beautiful of all these mountains. The road up the mountain, seventeen miles long, was built by the late George Vanderbilt. It winds about the face of the mountain till the Lodge is reached at an elevation of about 5800 feet. Luncheon under the trees with the wonderful panorama of valleys and mountains stretching on every side is an experience out of the ordinary.

Thirteenth Day. Leave ASHEVILLE in the afternoon.

Fourteenth Day. Arrive NEW YORK at noon.

Cost of round trip, New York to Asheville and return	$31.50
Cost of Pullman berth	4.25
Cost of round trip Chicago to Asheville and return	27.90
St. Louis to Asheville	23.40

THE MAINE COAST AND THE WHITE MOUNTAINS

Time—About Two Weeks

First Day. Leave NEW YORK in the afternoon by boat.

Second Day. Arrive PORTLAND in the afternoon, or

First Day. Leave NEW YORK in the evening by train.

Second Day. Arrive PORTLAND in the morning. Hotels $3 up per day. Boarding houses $2 up per day. Portland combines the attractions of city life and the pleasures of a shore resort and, being famous for its beautiful natural scenery, is well worth several days' visit.

Third Day. Spend the day wandering about the city by trolley, visiting the Eastern Promenade with its view of the Harbor and then the Western Promenade with its view of forests, rolling farm land and distant mountain peaks.

Fourth Day. If the day is fine take the sail among the islands of Casco Bay, stopping for luncheon (shore dinner) at one of the islands. Cost of trip 75 cents.

Fifth Day. Go to the celebrated Poland Springs. Autos may be hired at reasonable prices, or you can go by train to Danville station and motor to the springs. Cost $3.50. The mammoth hotel, the spring, the library and art gallery, the beautiful grounds and the view are all well worth seeing.

Sixth Day. Leave PORTLAND at 9 a. m. by rail for a trip thru the Songo River. Change to steamer at Sebago Lake Station. The sail is varied and full of interest. You sail up a river called the "crookedest" of all Maine rivers, go thru a lock and after crossing the Bay of Naples enter narrow Long Lake. The last landing is made at 1:15 p. m. and shortly after that you start on the return journey. Portland is reached at 5:30 p. m. Cost of trip $2.50.

Seventh Day. Take a trip by trolley to Old Orchard, one of the finest beaches on the Atlantic Seaboard and one of Maine's leading shore resorts.

Eighth Day. Leave PORTLAND in the morning. Arrive INTERVALE about noon. Hotels $3 up per day. American plan. This is one of the interesting resorts at the gateway to the White Mountains, noted for its many hotels and boarding houses to suit all purses. The climate is dry and there are fine groves and pine trees. Take a drive by auto to Mt. Surprise and on to Jackson, returning thru Conway.

An Envious Vacation

Ever envy the lucky fellow who strikes a place for his vacation among active people—people who are in for every sport—bathing, fishing, golfing, tennis, etc.? That's what constitutes the *ideal vacation*—good people, good times, good climate—nothing out of the ordinary but simply a regular vacation on

Long Island

You have the same opportunity as the fellow you envied last year. All the tackle you need to land such a place is the book of actual pictures and condensed reading matter of Long Island, entitled "Long Island & Real Life." It contains a list of the best hotels and boarding cottages, their rates, etc. Mailed upon receipt of ten cents postage by the General Passenger Agent, Long Island Railroad, Pennsylvania Station, New York.

Ninth Day. Leave *INTERVALE* in the afternoon. Arrive *BRETTON WOODS* in about two hours. Hotels $4 up per day, American plan. This is the radiating point for many trips and while you are here go via train or auto to Jefferson with its fine hotel and wonderful views of the White Mountain range; to Crawford House for a trip up Mt. Webster by foot or on stage; to Bethlehem, whose unique Main Street, extending about one mile, is lined on either side with summer hotels, large and small. Take one day for the trip to the summit of Mt. Washington, reached either by carriage road or inclined railway.

Twelfth Day. Leave *BRETTON WOODS* in the morning. Arrive *PROFILE* in about an hour. Hotel $5 up per day, American plan. This is the place in the White Mountains where the Great Stone Face is to be seen. The Profile, called the "Old Man of the Mountain," is renowned as the most wonderful rock formation in the world. While here, drive to Franconia for the mountain views there.

Fourteenth Day. Leave *PROFILE* in the morning by stage for North Woodstock, where connection is made by train for New York. Arrive *NEW YORK* in the evening.

Approximate cost of trip, New York boat to Portland, rail to New York $21.00

NEW JERSEY SHORE RESORTS
Time—One Week to Ten Days

First Day. Leave *NEW YORK* in the morning by train or boat. Arrive *ASBURY PARK* in about two hours. Hotels $3 up per day. Boarding houses $2 up per day. Asbury Park is a miniature Atlantic City, with superb bathing beach, boardwalk, casino, fishing piers and fine hotels. Take time to visit Ocean Grove, which you will find a contrast to its gay neighbor. It is a popular Methodist Camp Meeting Ground. Its great auditorium seats 10,000 persons and has a fine organ.

Third Day. Leave *ASBURY PARK* by train or trolley. Arrive *SPRING LAKE* in fifteen minutes. Hotels $3 up per day, American plan. This place is noted for having some of the most beautiful hotels in the country. The walks and drives are attractive. Bathing, fishing, golf and tennis are all popular. Take a part of a day for a trip by trolley to Sea Girt, one and a half miles distant. It is the summer headquarters of the National Guard of New Jersey. You may continue the trip to Point Pleasant, which extends from the ocean to the Manasquan River.

Fifth Day. Leave *SPRING LAKE* in the morning. Arrive *BEACH HAVEN* in a few hours. Hotels $2.50 up per day, American plan. This resort is located on a narrow island twenty miles long, and is noted for its wonderful beach. The bathing is ideal, the beach being level, hard and clean. The bay is one of the finest for sailing; a large fleet of comfortable boats are here and may be hired by the day or season. Fishing and hunting are both good. It is an ideal resort for people suffering from hay fever.

Seventh Day. Leave *BEACH HAVEN* in the morning. Arrive *ATLANTIC CITY* in the afternoon. Hotels $2.50 up per day, American plan. The "Playground of the World," is one of the most attractive cities of America. Its boardwalk, sixty feet wide, is five miles in length. There are four great steel piers crowded with features of interest, and along the opposite side of the walk are shops, theaters and hotels in almost unbroken succession. Here you may spend your time yachting, boating, fishing and crabbing. The chief pleasure is bathing. Golf can be had at the Country Club, and many of the hotels have tennis courts nearby. Trips by trolley may be taken both on the island and the main land.

Tenth Day. Leave *ATLANTIC CITY* in the afternoon. Arrive *NEW YORK* in about three hours.

Cost of trip, New York to Atlantic City and return $8.93

AN EXTRAORDINARY CONCESSION BY JAPAN
By Rev. J. Ingram Bryan

The Expatriation bill recently passed by the Imperial Japanese Diet will prove one of the most significant international measures in the country's history. One of the chief difficulties of the immigration problem has been the refusal of the Japanese Government to acquiesce in the naturalization of Japanese subjects abroad. The attitude was not a mere whim or conceit of narrow nationalism, but the logical and necessary outcome of Japan's theory of citizenship and patriotism, which holds the Imperial House to be divine and expatriation to be treason.

What Japan had in mind was that altho Orientals are not conceded rights of naturalization in America, yet anyone born in the United States may be regarded as an American citizen. Not to be liberal beyond the barest necessity, the new expatriation law enacted by the Imperial Diet in Tokyo allows only those Japanese subjects who have been born abroad to seek naturalization in foreign countries. A Japanese born at home and going abroad temporarily or permanently is not allowed foreign naturalization. Even those born abroad and desiring to become citizens of a foreign country must first obtain the permission of the Minister of Home Affairs in Tokyo.

That the question was brought forward just at the present juncture is probably due to the problem created by the Germans in the United States. Since many German subjects in America have proved a source of menace to American neutrality during the war, Japan began to feel that the natural uneasiness thus likely to be aroused concerning the status and behavior of aliens in the United States would possibly work against the interests of Japanese there, as most of them were without the privileges of American citizenship. This consideration, taken together with the fact that the Webb law militated against Japanese interests chiefly because she Japanese were supposed ineligible to citizenship, forced the legislators of Japan to take some action. Japan maintained that the Webb law was aimed directly at the Japanese, tho the measure singled out no race or nation. In fact, the one and only reason why the law worked against the interests of Japanese nationals was because of their inability to acquire citizenship, which, as a matter of fact, most of them did not wish to obtain, since it would be to them something like what loss of salvation would mean to a Christian.

None but those familiar with the peculiar genius of Japanese civilization realize how radical is the move involved in this new expatriation law. To suggest that a Japanese born abroad might be allowed to exchange allegiance to the Emperor for allegiance to an alien sovereign or potentate, was like suggesting to the Christian that if his chil-

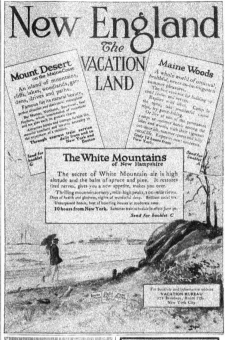

New England
The VACATION LAND

Mount Desert
on the Maine Coast
An island of mountains, cliffs, lakes, woodlands, gardens, drives and paths.
Famous for its natural beauty, perfect situation and ideal atmosphere.
Bar Harbor, Northeast, Southwest, Seal Harbor, whose combination of commercial attractions vie each in greatest charm and are unsurpast in this land eternity to the enjoyment hotels and famous serenity to the enjoyment of a remedial...
Through express train service daily from and to New York and Boston

Send for booklet G

Maine Woods
A whole world of unusual healthful, never-to-be-forgotten summer pleasure.
The best vacation for building up tired, jaded and nervous. Camp in the open, lake and forest.
Explore wild scenes. Come tramps, game hiking.
Or try game hiking...
Camp at side of the permanent lakes and worthy hotels amide the out-door life, summer sports and jolly social life. Expenses most moderate.
Only 12 hours from New York.

Send for Booklet A

The White Mountains of New Hampshire

The secret of White Mountain air is high altitude and the balm of spruce and pine. It restores tired nerves, gives you a new appetite, makes you over.
Thrilling mountain scenery, mile-high peaks, 100-mile views. Days of health and gladness, nights of wonderful sleep. Brilliant social life. Unsurpassed hotels, best of boarding houses at moderate rates.

10 hours from New York. Summer train schedule in effect June 30.

Send for booklet C

For booklets and information address
VACATION BUREAU
173 Broadway, Room 115,
New York City

F. A. Ringler Co.

DESIGNING
PHOTO - ENGRAVING
AND ELECTROTYPING

21 and 23 Barclay Street to
26 and 28 Park Place
NEW YORK

LET US PLAN YOUR
Vacation Tours to

Colorado and Utah
California
Yellowstone Park
Puget Sound Country
Alaska and the Black Hills

LOW ROUND TRIP FARES affording a wide choice of routes, numerous side trips, liberal return limits.

Seven fast splendidly equipped through trains leave the new Chicago Terminal at convenient hours daily.

We will be pleased to submit an attractive itinerary, furnish illustrated booklets and full information regarding rates, schedules, etc.

CHICAGO &
NORTH WESTERN RY.
A. C. Johnson, P. T. M.
C. A. Cairns, G. P. & T. A.
Chicago, Ill.

dren were born in India they should become Brahmins or Buddhists. To Japan patriotism is religion. Worship is devotion to the Emperor and the imperial ancestors; and the ancestral spirits are the gods of the nation. How the House of Peers, which represents the old aristocracy of Japan, and the House of Assembly, which stands for the masses, could agree to so revolutionary a measure is something that astonishes those who know Japan.

As the law stands it will effect the relief of about 15,000 Japanese born in American territory, speaking in round numbers; but doubtless they will, if granted citizenship by the American authorities, be able to take advantage of sufficient privilege to accommodate all the remaining hundred or more thousand Japanese in America and Hawaii. The only question now is whether the American Government is prepared to grant citizenship to all Japanese born in the United States. At present much indignation is expresit in Japan that her nationals are refused citizenship, while the favor is granted negroes and Filipinos; America excludes Orientals from citizenship; Japanese are Orientals, but Filipinos are not. Or, as the Japanese vernacular papers allege, the Japanese, in American eyes, are yellow, and the Filipinos white. All of which to the Japanese mind savors of insincerity and effrontery.

Tokyo, Japan

HALF A MILLION MADMEN

When the Verdun deadlock changed to the most terrific pitched battle in history, fully half a million men were engaged in the slaughter. Whole regiments melted in a few minutes, but others took their place, only to perish in the same way.

A staff captain who left the fortress on a special mission to Paris tells this story of "the battle of madmen in the midst of a volcano eruption":

Between Saturday morning and noon Tuesday we reckon the Germans "used up" 100,000 men on the west Meuse front alone. That is the price they paid for the recapture of our recent gains and the seizure of our outlying positions. The valley separating Le Mort Homme from Hill 287 is choked with bodies. A full brigade was mowed down in a quarter hour's holocaust by our machine guns. Le Mort Homme itself passed from our possession, but the crescent Bourru position to the south prevents the enemy from utilizing it.

The scene there is appalling, but is dwarfed in comparison with fighting around Douaumont. West of the Meuse, at least, one dies in the open air, but at Douaumont is the horror of darkness, where the men fight in tunnels, screaming with the lust of butchery, deafened by shells and grenades, stifled by smoke.

Even the wounded refuse to abandon the struggle. As the possest by devils, they fight on until they fall senseless from loss of blood. A surgeon in a front line post told me that in a redoubt at the south part of the fort of 200 French dead fully half had more than two wounds. Those he was able to treat seemed utterly insane. They kept shouting war cries and their eyes blazed, and, strangest of all, they appeared indifferent to pain. At one moment anæsthetics ran out owing to the impossibility of bringing forward fresh supplies thru the bombardment. Arms even legs, were amputated without a groan, and even afterward the men seemed not to have felt the shock. They asked for a cigarette or inquired how the battle was going.

Never have attacks been pushed home so continuously. The fight for Cemetery Hill at Gettysburg was no child's play, nor for Hougoumont at Waterloo, but here men have been flung 5000 at a time at brief intervals for the last forty-eight hours. Practically the whole sector has been covered by a cannonade, compared to which Gettysburg was a hailstorm and Waterloo mere fireworks. Some shell holes were thirty feet across, the explosion killing fifty men simultaneously.

Before our lines the German dead lie heaped in long rows. I am told one observer calculated there were 7000 in a distance of 700 yards. Besides, they cannot succor their wounded, whereas of ours one at least in three is removed safely to the rear. Despite the bombardment supplies keep coming. Even the chloroform I spoke of arrived after an hour's delay when two sets of bearers had been killed.

The dogged tenacity needed to continue the resistance far surpasses the furious élan of the attack. We know, too, the Germans cannot long maintain their present sacrifices. Since Saturday the enemy has lost two, if not three, for each one of us. Every bombardment withstood, every rush checked brings nearer the moment of inevitable exhaustion. Then will come our recompense for these days of horror.

In the twilight preceding the dawn the French sentinels announced that the enemy were advancing in streams along parallel communication boyaux until their trenches were filled. The 75s immediately concentrated on the hostile trench line, including the new saps mentioned by the sentinels, as they were pushed forward during the night. The enemy suffered heavily, but persevered, and soon dense columns appeared amid the shell-torn brushwood on the southern fringe of Corbeaux Wood, pouring down into the valley separating them from the former French position on the hillside.

Thinking the French still held the latter they deployed with the most recent trench-storming device in the form of liquid fire containers, which special groups of four installed, two then working the pump and two directing the fire-jet. The grayness of the dawn was illumined by sheets of green and red flame, and black oily clouds rolled along the valley toward the river like smoke from a burning "gusher."

Suddenly the air was filled with shrill whistling as shells of the 75s were hurled against the attackers. Thanks to the devoted sentinels dying at their posts in the sea of fire, the range was exact, and the exploding melinite shattered the charging columns. An appalling scene followed. The shells had burst or overthrown the fire containers, and the Germans were seen running wildly amid the flames, which overwhelmed hundreds of wounded and disabled.

In this confusion the French charged with the bayonet, despite the furnace heat and fumes produced by the red-hot containers lying in all directions. The enemy offered little resistance. It was like a slaughter of frenzied beasts.

Vainly the officers tried to maintain order. The demoralized mass broke again in a rush for shelter to the nearest shell holes. Hundreds fought in a terror-stricken mob to hide in a hole that might have sheltered a score. Those beneath were stifled. Those above threw themselves screaming into the air as the bullets pierced them, or fell dead in a dash toward a safer refuge. Flushed with success the French charged again, right to the entrance of the wood, and the slaughter recommenced.

Of a brigade 5000 strong that began the attack it is estimated that under 500 reached their own trenches in safety. In shell holes and boyaux the French captured some hundreds, and a similar number of wounded were removed by our stretcher bearers, but nearly 3000 grayclad corpses covered the slopes and valley, the majority charred out of human semblance.—*New York Times.*

Why It's GLACIER NATIONAL PARK

GLACIER PARK is established as America's Vacation Paradise—*for reasons.* It surpasses the Old World's most famous Nature-pictures in mountain splendor, the azure beauty of its 250 sky-land lakes.

Here, at the Continental Divide, the Rocky Mountains reach their supreme glory. Go on horseback over wide trails, through sky-reaching passes, join a hiking party or drink the Park's cool breezes in luxurious automobile or launch. Fine modern hotels and Swiss chalet groups. Tepee camps. Vacations, $1 to $5 per day.

Glacier Park is on the main transcontinental line of the Great Northern en route to Spokane and its vacation places—Seattle, Tacoma and Puget Sound resorts—Portland, Astoria, with the new Columbia River Highway and Clatsop Beach resorts—Vancouver, Victoria and Alaska.

Round trip fares to Glacier National Park in effect June 1 to Sept. 30; to the Pacific Northwest, Puget Sound and Alaska May 1 to Sept. 30.

The twin Palaces of the Pacific—S. S. "Great Northern" and S. S. "Northern Pacific"—three times weekly between Portland, Astoria and San Francisco. Folder on request.

Write for folder "Western Trips for Eastern People" and illustrated Glacier National Park literature.

C. E. STONE, Pass. Traffic Mgr., St. Paul, Minn;
C. W. Pitts, Asst. Gen. Pass. Agt., 210 S. Clark St., Chicago;
S. Lounsbery, Gen. Agt., Pass. Dept., 1184 Broadway, N. Y.

REAL ESTATE

SUMMER CAMPS

THE NEW BOOKS

OLD LANDS AND NEW

Pathetically few this year are the volumes that treat of travel abroad. Among the handful published is an attractive little book, *Rambles in the Vaudois Alps*, by F. S. Salisbury. It has nothing to do with adventurous mountain climbing nor does it touch on the characteristics of the Swiss people, but any lover of Alpine flowers and Alpine scenery will enjoy it. It is a pleasure, too, to mention the third edition of P. H. Ditchfield's *Cathedrals of Great Britain*, which includes the five recently added, and with those of Wales and Scotland, brings the number above fifty. The accounts are shorter than in Mrs. Van Rensselaer's handbook that Americans have for a generation been tucking in their satchels, but this is the guide to take on a trip that is to include the lesser sees. The host of illustrations are delightful drawings by Symonds and other English artists.

When—long ago—there were plans for the celebration of a century of peace, Sulgrave Manor, the home of Washington's forebears, came into frequent notice. Anne Hollingsworth Wharton of course visited that among the other *English Ancestral Homes of Noted Americans*, but she found out also many less known spots, as the two lovely dwellings of William Penn, and Ecton, the home of the Franklin family of sturdy blacksmiths. Even in London she leads to some little trodden corners, as that of the Church of St. Ethelburga, where Washington and his men took communion before setting sail on their first voyage.

This year, however, such books as these serve only as reminders or as prophecies. For practical purposes we read of this side the water. Here the distance be not limited, variety is, and after the rush of books occasioned last year by the two Panama fairs, the presses are rather quiet. The latter half of Thoreau's delightful journal, "In the Maine Woods," is just published in an illustrated edition, entitled *Canoeing in the Wilderness*, and tho the Maine Woods and ways of camping have changed a bit since 1857, Thoreau, the forerunner and the master of all our prophets of the woods and hills, never loses his charm.

As far as may be from his simplicity, indifference to conveniences and absorption in nature is the sophisticated guide *By Motor to the Golden Gate*. The journey as described consists mainly of runs from one hotel to the next, and the book has practical value in that it tells precisely what you are to expect in each place; adds daily expense records; maps of each day's run, for the Lincoln Highway is still "like the equator"; and sound advice as to the car to use and what to put in it. But one fancies that the folk who have done this trip less

luxuriously, camping out most of the nights instead of one, made up in fun and interest what they lacked in creature comforts.

Mary R. Rinehart's *Through Glacier Park* is yet another sort of a story. On horseback for days among the fastnesses of the Great Divide, with early mornings starts and evenings around the camp fire; with paths along precipices and fishing in mountain streams; this is a real holiday, and a bit of life that the old world can never give us. If everyone who reads this lively little book follows his certain impulse and writes to reserve a place in one of the long single file processions that follow Howard Eaton where the motor can never go, there will surely be another clerk needed at the Glacier Park Post Office.

Rambles in the Vaudois Alps, by F. S. Salisbury. Dutton. $1. *English Ancestral Homes of Noted Americans*, by A. H. Wharton. Philadelphia. Lippincott. $2. *The Cathedrals of Great Britain*, by P. H. Ditchfield. Dutton. $1.75. *Canoeing in the Wilderness*, by H. D. Thoreau. Houghton, Mifflin. $1. *By Motor to the Golden Gate*, by Emily Post. Appleton. $2. *Through Glacier Park*, by Mary R. Rinehart. Houghton, Mifflin. 75 cents.

CAVE MEN

The history of the prehistoric is nowhere more interestingly or more broadly painted than in the *Men of the Old Stone Age*, by Professor Osborn. During a three weeks' tour of the regions containing the best preserved relics of the Stone Age in France and Spain, he was impressed by the continuity of the record of man's residence and activities for a period of some 100,000 years. In addition to giving the chronological sequence of the cave men's development, the climatic changes, the character of the environment and the animal life of each period are described.

The author acknowledges his indebtedness to the artists of the stone age, for he has drawn upon the engravings, sculptures and paintings of the caves and grottos for much of his illustrative material, and this adds incalculably to the interest. One is impressed by the keen observation and the skilful strokes of the ancient artists, quite as much as by the inventiveness of the artizan. The many restorations from human remains include the work of American as well as European scientists. The restorations of Professor McGregor impress one at first as being somewhat glorified, in view of the antiquity of the people they are supposed to represent; but Professor Osborn's theory that these ancient worthies were rapidly developing a high degree of intelligence justifies the upward look and alertness exprest in the faces. The importance of the Stone Age in the evolution of the human race is summarized as follows:

During this age the rudiments of all the modern economic powers of man were developed; the guidance of the hand by the mind, manifested in his creative industry; his inventive faculty; the currency or spread of his inventions; the adaptation of means to ends in utensils, in weapons and in clothing. The same is true of the esthetic powers, of close observation, of the sense of form, of proportion, of symmetry, the appreciation of beauty of animal form and the beauty of line, color, and form in modelling and sculpture. Finally, the schematic representation and notation of ideas so far as we can perceive was alphabetic rather than pictographic. Of the musical sense we have at present no evidence. The religious sense, the appreciation of some power or powers behind the great phenomena of nature, is evidenced in the reverence for the dead, in burials apparently related to notions of a future existence of the dead, and especially in the mysteries of the art of the caverns.

Our 200 illustrations with maps and diagrams add to the interest and value of a book that has already twice outrun its printing.

Men of the Old Stone Age, by Henry Fairfield Osborn. Scribner. $5.

HERE AND THERE IN EUROPE

A manifest change is taking place in the tenor of war books. With actual military operations for the most part barred against correspondents, they now proceed to describe conditions in the countries involved. This is what chiefly interests in *With the French in France and Salonika* by Richard Harding Davis. His is the attitude of a man who has seen much of the world and become broadly tolerant. Thus he refers to former troubles at the French front in an entertaining vein, and consorts with Levantines of endless guile determined to preserve a humorous outlook. But he is clearly serious when he comments upon the adverse sentiment in Europe directed upon his own country. He lays responsibility upon several home causes, not the least being overeagerness on the part of some Americans to profit financially from the war, together with indifference toward the acute distress of nations for whom he felt a deep sympathy. This, while the French are fully appreciative of the help rendered by other Americans. As an able war correspondent, a writer possessing the rare gift of strength and charm combined, it is with regret we turn the cover upon his active and useful career.

Doubtless the publishers of Stanley Washburn's *Victory in Defeat* have in their safe the warrant, *ukase,* or whatever document is necessary for permission to emblazon the Russian Imperial Arms on the cover. It is very artistically done, but Grand Chamberlains and Grand Marshals of the Court are chary of their privileges. Even in democratic England you get into serious trouble for using the royal arms without a license. However, as the publishers announce on the wrapper that the author is a friend of the Czar, Grand Duke Nicholas, Foreign Minister Sozonov, General Alexieff and all other Russians in high war authority—quite a social circle to keep up with—probably no international difficulty would result had the aforementioned rescript been overlooked.

Now the book "by the one American who can say 'I saw'" the ravishing of

Yosemite Waterfalls
brim full from Sierra Snows

June is the month to see them

Heaviest snowfalls in Sierras for years means abundant water in Yosemite • • • Other attractions in California this summer such as the Panama California International Exposition, open all of 1916. Bigger, better, more beautiful • • • California summer weather is cool by the sea and in the mountains • • • The cool way to go is on the Santa Fe; like a mountain top through Colorado, New Mexico & Arizona. Enroute visit the Grand Canyon of Arizona •

Four daily California trains
Ask for California Outings Yosemite and San Diego folders

Low Excursion Fares

Santa Fe

Belgium. Thus introduced to Arthur Gleason's *Golden Lads*, with the further indorsement of Theodore Roosevelt, we have read the evidence produced with impartial care. From this we gather that Mr. Gleason saw twenty-six peasant houses burning at Melle, a babbling old man *threatened* by a German sentry with a bayonet, three bodies carried out of the houses, a dead farmer in a yard, and himself with others destined for a screen of German troops marching on Ghent. But the latter was merely a surmise, for nothing of the kind transpired. He saw the wreck of the convent school at Melle, but learned none of the sisters had been harmed. At Witteren Mr. Gleason visited a hospital and witnessed eleven peasants suffering from bayonet wounds. The statements of these people are credible in so far as no testimony from the other side was obtainable. But contributory to it is Mr. Sweetser's report in "Roadside Glimpses of the Great War" of a German surgeon's horrified recollection at Valenciennes of Belgian peasant atrocities committed upon captured German soldiers.

Mr. Gleason also saw the ruins of bombarded Belgian cities. Otherwise his evidence is at second or third hand mainly. While granting all this makes no creditable German reading, yet it is far from convicting the whole German army of deliberate barbarity as distinct from what some persons insist upon terming *civilized* warfare. More convincing is the author's chapter on the spy. Unquestionably Germany prepared thoroly, and was a painstaking news-gatherer. Especially noteworthy is Mrs. Gleason's contribution: How War Seems to a Woman. It is such an entirely modern feminine view, yet ethically so ancient that the writer offers a subject likely to produce discussion. Briefly, as Mrs. Gleason puts it, let a woman but share a man's danger and she occupies her natural place. What that natural place is, the reader must be left to discover.

It is but reasonable that an artist should feel personally wounded before the destruction of beautiful monuments, and naturally Walter Hale dwells with feeling on this form of atrocity in *By Motor to the Firing Line*. Presently, however, the mind flits to the statue of Oliver Cromwell in London, and wonder takes us that an English sculptor of the first rank could have been found to fashion in bronze a representation of him who was as impeachable a Hun in this respect as anyone. The answer may be that in human dramas of such appalling magnitude architectural and all other material treasures sink into insignificance. It is the American news-gatherer — traveling hither and yon in rapid passage — who grasps a stray gleam of promise, not, as we read, the imaginative or artistic observer who seems to halt dumb-founded and bewildered as he confronts the grim facts swept into the foreground in the tornado of strife. There is no charm in war, no picturesqueness anywhere. But, as Mrs. Gleason says in *Golden Lads*, "What is in the man comes out

under the supreme test." If out of him should happily come an awakened conscience of justice, truth and right the world over, our loss in precious monuments will not have been in vain. Mr. Hale has written a very readable book illustrated with several sketches of distinct merit.

It would be impossible in less than a chapter to do justice to the wealth of vividly contrasting material gathered by John Reed in *The War in Eastern Europe*. In Salonika, onward thru Serbia, a military prisoner at Cholm, into Russia, back to Constantinople and the Bulgarian Declaration of War, the author presents a succession of swiftly moving pictures, from which strange character sketches of all manner of strange people hang in the reader's mind.

For example, at the station of typhus stricken Gieviegli "a stout man in a dirty collar, spotted clothing, etc.," revealed a financial scheme for selling Serbia outright to America "for a music" and "make money big." Mr. Reed's experiences in Russia hardly present that country as on the verge of a new enlightenment. He saw political prisoners on the way to Siberia, was warned not to ask too many questions, was trailed by detectives and found bribery everywhere unblushingly practised. With frankness the Jew was excluded from benefit in any future political reform. As Mr. Reed, however, entered Russia under suspicion of being a German secret agent, it is possible he was unable to reach channels of broader public opinion. Wayfarers in Russia appear to be extremely chary of suspicious traveling companions, and tell them perchance what is considered best for German consumption. The illustrations are by Boardman Robinson in the new art style, which makes the book a bit risky to leave near a child with a pair of scissors.

With the French in France and Salonika, by Richard Harding Davis. Scribner. $1. *Victory in Defeat*, by Stanley Washburn. Doubleday, Page. $1. *Golden Lads*, by Arthur Gleason. Century. $1.50. *By Motor to the Firing Line*, by Walter Hale. Century. $1.50. *The War in Eastern Europe*, by John Reed. Scribner. $2.

DEMOCRATIC EDUCATION

Professor John Dewey in *Democracy and Education* presents for the first time in a unified form the philosophic foundation of his educational theory.

Growth, "the characteristic of life," is one with education. The possibility of growth means the power to learn from experience, or the capacity of adaptation and the forming of dispositions which give "control over environment, and power to use it for human purposes. Education or growth so defined is an end in itself and can look to nothing further except more growth. The native impulses, however, must be set toward the aims of the group, which can be achieved by creating an "identity of interest." The subject matter of education will, therefore, be that which has meaning with reference to these aims. Only that which has meaning can be operative in the development of a fruitful experience.

Education is on this view a social process. For a democratic society the criteria of valuation of any "form of social life" are "the extent in which the interests of a group are shared by all its members and the fullness and freedom with which it interacts with other groups."

The aims of education, like all aims, are but conscious projections into the future of the results of our natural activities. It is the task of philosophy to criticize the various possible results and propose methods of harmonizing the various interests. Professor Dewey's book is itself a most brilliant example of the function of philosophy, for he gives us a transvaluation of educational ideals and methods in the light of a theory of knowledge of which he has been the chief originator.

Democracy and Education, by John Dewey. Macmillan. $1.40.

"OUR" GERALDINE FARRAR

Pleasant and exhilarating reading is this brief little autobiographic sketch of a great American prima donna. From it one might almost think that a great *artiste's* life was a succession of dazzling triumphs easily won. Almost, yet not quite, for there are disquieting allusions to the long, toilsome years of preparation, the ceaseless grinding labor, the nervous strain of holding huge audiences, and the cruel fatigues that follow thereupon. For all these allusions to the laborious and troubled side of such a life, this autobiography throws no such realistic light upon the difficulties that beset the path of actress or opera singer as is thrown by Sarah Bernhardt's larger, and discreet yet illuminating, account of her early and painful struggles and subsequent successes. Americans, however, be the shortcomings of this book what they may, cannot fail to read with pride and pleasure this sprightly account of the world-wide triumphs of their compatriot, who began life humbly in a little New England town; and who, after successes in Berlin, Paris and elsewhere, was proudest when she returned to her own country, and won by her great gifts, her art and her irresistible beauty and charm her high place in the hearts of her own people.

Geraldine Farrar: The Story of an American Singer, by Herself. Houghton, Mifflin. $2.

FOREST AND HILLS

Let Us Go Afield is a group of essays on out of door topics. Emerson Hough betrays himself as by birth an angler, but one wishes every bird hunter might read *Wealth on Wings*, and his discussion of being a sportsman versus paying to see other men play is worth notice. (Appleton, $1.25.)

Chronicles of the White Mountains, by Frederick W. Kilbourne, is accurately named. In it one finds almost nothing of the geology, the plant and animal life, the scenery, but one does find the legend and the history of man's connection with those loveliest highlands of the East. (Houghton, Mifflin, $2.)

To the lover of the hills, *The Mountains*, by John C. Van Dyke, with its mingling of science, philosophy and esthetic appreciation, will be a welcome little essay, and the knowledge it imparts by the way, of how the mountains came to be and what they are and what they do, is all interesting and worth while. (Scribner, $1.25.)

The Latch String is the attractive title of Walter Emerson's discursive but enthusiastic description of the attractive land of Maine. (Houghton, Mifflin, $2.)

In *Along New England Roads*, W. C. Prime writes of the delights of travel, with horse and carriage. Scenery, sunshine, birds, flowers and whatever might be seen in such now novel wandering, he makes mighty interesting reading. His chapter on epitaphs and names culls the rare and unusual out of the commonplace. (Harper $1.)

WHEN SCHOOL CLOSES

In *Marooned in a Forest*, A. Hyatt Verrill adapts the Robinson Crusoe plot as a thread to string all sorts of woodcraft lore. It is an impossible tale, but it gives an amount of miscellaneous information most attractive to any boy or girl who loves adventure and the woods. (Harper, $1.25.)

A much more reliable work by Mr. Verrill is *The Ocean*, a good book to take to the seashore, where it will answer many questions for grown-ups as well as youngsters. (Duffield, $1.25.)

For *Commencement Days* Dr. Gladden truly did, as he says one must, bring his best. These papers ranging from personal counsel to national needs, are broad minded and inspiring. Do not be deceived by the sentimental blue cover! (Macmillan, $1.25.)

Thompson Seton may not teach science, but he is a master in inspiring sympathy with our furry kin and in writing healthful and charming romance. *Wild Animal Ways* has a dog story, a horse story, one of a bat, one of a bad monkey, and best of all, one of a razor back hog. (Doubleday, Page, $1.50.)

On the shelf of popular handbooks of growing things there was one real gap which Elizabeth Marie Dunham's *How to Know the Mosses* fills. This introduces them without the aid of microscope, and will find warm welcome by those who cannot be scientists but who still love moss. (Houghton, Mifflin, $1.25.)

An uncommonly beautiful and useful book is *A Year with the Birds*, by Allce E. Ball. Under the headings Winter, Early Spring, Later Spring, the 56 color plates, by W. H. Horsfall, of the Museum of Natural History, and the accompanying verses, which children will love, will teach any child to notice bird life and know our commoner birds. (Gibbs & Van Vleck, $3.)

BOTH WORK AND PLAY

A Living from Eggs and Poultry, by H. W. Brown, a city man who has succeeded in a country business, is not a scientific treatise, but a handbook of practical directions for beginners. It goes into details often taken for granted in larger works. (Judd, 75 cents.)

The Vegetable Garden, by R. A. Watts, the director of the Pennsylvania experiment station, is a good guide for novices. It contains careful directions for soil preparation, and then directions for the special culture needed for each kind of vegetable. (Outing Pub. Co., 75 cents.)

In *Low Cost Suburban Homes*, edited by Richardson Wright, the would-be builder will find a discussion of the initial cost and upkeep of buildings of various materials, with their relative cost in various parts of the country. The plans are attractive and range in price from about $4000 to $10,000. (McBride, $1.25.)

Tennis for Women is by Molla Bjurstedt, the Norwegian player, who won our championship in last year's tournaments.

It is a clear, practical and modest discussion of training of the different strokes and of the play desirable for women. She makes a vital difference between the men's game and the women's. (Doubleday, Page, $1.25.)

Dominoes, by F. W. Lewis, will cause you to take the dust covered set from the top shelf, for the simple old game the children played of rainy days is but a small part of the amusement to be drawn from the black and white counters. There are the French and Spanish games, and Threes and Fives, and Sebastopol, and more. (Dutton, 50 cents.)

A valuable primer of general information on mechanics and the psychology of handling a car is A. H. Verrill's *A B C of Automobile Driving*. The chapter on Getting Out of Difficulties is packed with ingenious first-aid suggestions, and the introductory talk on Safety First ought to be "required reading" for every licensed operator. (Harper, 50 cents.)

PRESENT DAY TOPICS

A timely and interesting book is *Presidential Nominations and Elections*, by J. D. Bishop. These chapters do not present idealistic pictures from our history, but give none the less needful to our understanding of present and past political situations. (Scribner, $1.50.)

There is now issued in book form the *Address* delivered by Elihu Root last February before the New York Republican Convention, in which he scored the present administration on many counts, but especially its policy in regard to the European war. (Dutton, 50 cents.)

Woodrow Wilson, by H. J. Ford, is a "mid career appreciation." It is made up largely of extracts from speeches and writings, and the one must wait for a critical analysis or a really human picture of the President, since these cannot be made *en route*, this will prove very useful for setting forth the obvious features of his life. (Appleton, $1.50.)

In the Social Service Series are three small books for the general reader on present day topics; *Government Finance*, by C. C. Plehn, an argument for business in place of hit or miss methods; *Trusts and Competition*, by J. F. Crowell, on "big business": *The American City*, by H. C. Wright, dealing with the kinds and the duties of city government. (Chicago: McClurg, 50 cents each.)

Arthur Lynch, M. P., attempts in *Ireland's Vital Hour* to explain to England and the world Ireland's present position in respect to internal problems, economic, political, and social. In fact the author, a voluminous writer on a variety of subjects, pretends, and not without considerable success, to be an authoritative interpreter of Ireland. In politics the author is an Irish Nationalist and apparently thoroly loyal to the British Government; the book is valuable for an understanding of present-day Ireland. (Philadelphia: Winston, $2.50.)

CELEBRATED DAYS

Mother in Prose and Verse, one of the Shauffler and Rice anthologies, gathers within reach some real poetry, as well as sincere verse and prose. (Moffat, Yard, $1.50.)

Easter is the latest volume in the handy books of verse and prose for holidays compiled by S. T. Rice and edited by R. H. Shauffler. One wishes more of the quaint early and medieval hymns had been included in the small carol section, but the collection covers a wide range. (Moffat, Yard, $1.)

Our Mothers, compiled by M. A. Ayers, is less successful, tho in it will be found many popular favorites. As one looks over

these collections, called forth by Mother's Day, however, one wonders if feeling for one's own mother or even for motherhood be not an emotion rather personal for public celebration. (Boston: Lothrop, Lee & Shepard, cloth, $1; leather, $2.)

SUMMER AFTERNOONS

The Sign of Freedom, by Arthur Goodrich. To write a Civil War story today seems a rather thankless task, but an exciting plot, a complicated duel love affair and a good deal of wholesome patriotism makes this attempt not unsuccessful. (Appleton, $1.35.)

The Light That Lies, by George Barr McCutcheon. The story of a young man who thought that he did not want to do any duty. A very slight but comparatively entertaining bit of fiction, with a clever climax which is somewhat slow in coming. (Dodd, Mead, $1.)

Susan Clegg and Her Love Affairs, by Anne Warner. Probably you have met Susan Clegg before. Her amusing monologic conversations make the sort of easy, entertaining reading which is highly to be recommended to convalescents. (Boston: Little, Brown, $1.30.)

Hearts and Faces, by John Murray Gibbon, is a distinctly interesting description of artist life in Scotland, London and Paris. The much of the material is unpleasant. It is namely and simply treated. The plot is weak, but the characters are extremely well done. (Lane, $1.35.)

The Desire of the Moth, by Eugene Manlove Rhodes, has a good, unhackneyed plot. It would make an excellent film drama of western life, thru its transferring it to the screen, the eccentric and entertaining conversation of its hero, John Wesley Pringle, would unfortunately be lost. (Holt, $1.)

Seven Miles to Arden, by Ruth Sawyer, contains a dozen or more impossible situations from which the hero and heroine are extricated by a whole Pantheon of *dei ex machina*. Patricia O'Connell, late of the National Players, and the Tinker are entertaining tho highly incredible people. (Harper, $1.25.)

Under the Country Sky, by Grace S. Richmond, is a pretty little love story, quite free from "problems," complex characters, "thrills" and similar incumbrances. It is sure to appeal to any one who, in this day and generation, is fortunate enough to have time for such gentle reading. (Doubleday, Page, $1.25.)

My Lady of the Moor, by John Oxenham. A curious tale of the regeneration of two men by the love of a woman who had great faith. It is a strange book, compelling attention tho not altogether convincing. There are excellent descriptions of Dartmoor, the scene of the story. (Longmans, Green, $1.35.)

People Like That, by Kate Langley Bosher. A society girl goes to live among "people like that" to learn what they are really like and the responsibilities of her sort of people toward them. A love affair mingles with the interesting problems which she meets and the solutions she suggests. (Harper, $1.25.)

The Proof of the Pudding, by Meredith Nicholson, is a pleasant story of the Middle West. Every town must have a country club in these days. Better, it is granting the fashion to have a boys' club and a gymnasium. The lesson of this wholesome story lies in the heroes idea of life; "just helping, just being kind." (Houghton, Mifflin, $1.35.)

Old Judge Priest, by Irvin S. Cobb, Judge Priest and his friends the old soldiers, politicians and other citizens of a sleepy southern town, form the material for some very good stories, dramatic pathetic, but chiefly humorous. Taken in large doses, however, Mr. Cobb's easy journalistic style does grow wearisome. (Doran, $1.25.)

THREE OF US WITHOUT A CARE

(Continued from page 370)

Joe Lake. We were met by a furious head wind which contested every foot of the crossing with us. But eventually we prevailed and slipped into the comparatively quiet waters of the creek. It soon became apparent that we must promptly make camp, for the wind continued to blow with unabated fury, making the crossing of the larger lake a difficult if not a hazardous undertaking. To add to our troubles bursts of rain descended upon us every few minutes.

Camp sites there were none. Everywhere the shores were encumbered with fallen dead stuff and the banks behind were choked and slashed to a tremendously uncomfortable degree. At last we fought our way thru and up to a comparatively clear bit of woodland and sat us down on a log to consume hard-tack, cheese and figs. Hunting in vain for a good camp site, we were constrained to pitch White Cap in a kind of trail that afforded barely room for his eight-foot spread. Despite the interminable rain we contrived to make a dry camp with a fairly good balsam bed, to which we presently retired with our books. Later we sat up in bed and ate hard-tack and raw onions (the result of the Tortoise's reading about the gustatory habits of Sancho Panza).

Two toilsome days. But what splendid, purple days! To pit your so finite strength against the mighty power of the elements is royal sport. You defy the waves with Grey Brother's fragile shell, you push his quivering length forward foot by foot against the vicious thrust of a blustering head wind, your two slender paddles springing and bending under the strain. You bend and sway instinctively like rope walkers as the waves shoulder Grey Brother about. It is slow, muscle-cracking business, this paddling into the teeth of a fine young gale. But every inch you gain is a new count to your credit in the rude game you play with Nature. When at last you have won, and the farther shore is yours, you have done something well worth the doing. You have added by a hair's breadth to your moral stature.

When you have made camp where camp site there is none, have drawn in the dripping, freezing wilderness a little circle of warmth and dryness and comfort, have made a home to you, another victory is yours. The Red Gods nod approval of your hardihood, endurance, courage, resourcefulness, as the rough elements growl vanquished at your feet.

Too high a note this is? Just try it once. Match yourself bare-handed against wild Nature's forces, and win —you will not think it so, if red blood flows in you.

Friday, October 6—Still gray and cold. Made good breakfast of ham, cold biscuit and cocoa. N. B.—Cocoa very good; take two cans next time and more evaporated cream. After washing up sat before the fire and ruminated. Began to rain, donned rubber fishing shirts and continued to sit. Then it snowed and eventually we filled the hot water bag and retired to the blankets where we now are. We intend to have dinner of spaghetti and tomato sauce. It is snowing hard and very cold. . . .

And so home. With vivid, glowing memories to be with us and keep us all alive and brightly happy until we come this way—or another way, so we three be together and alone—once more.

GOOD·BOOKS

THE ABINGDON PRESS

*The Abingdon Press is the trade imprint of
the oldest publishing house in the United States*

THIS HOUSE OF GOOD BOOKS has been actuated by the ideal of distinctive service ever since it was established in 1789. It has always aimed to give disinterested help to readers and authors alike, and realizing this parents have freely consulted it with regard to their own reading and the mental food of their children.

The spirit of THE ABINGDON PRESS is expressed in one way by a special book service. If you want the best book on a certain topic, ask THE ABINGDON PRESS for its name.

Should there be any question among the staff as to which book should be recommended, the matter will be referred to a specialist in that particular line. This service is without cost other than the regular charge if the book is furnished.

The better shops everywhere carry the ABINGDON PRESS publications. Catalog on request. Below are given two of the latest issues:

SIX FOOLS

By ROLLO F. HURLBURT

A series of ethical essays designed to show the folly of certain courses of living. Suggestive chapter headings are: "The Companion Fool," "The Woman Fool," "The No-God Fool," with many illustrations from the Bible.

Price, net, $1.00

FARES, PLEASE!

And Other Essays on Practical Themes

By HALFORD E. LUCCOCK

The reader of these essays is bound to receive mental quickening. There is about them a uniqueness of conception and an originality of style at once refreshing and stimulating. It will be impossible to get drowsy over these pages.

Price, net, 75 cents

THE ABINGDON PRESS
NEW YORK   CINCINNATI

CHICAGO   BOSTON   PITTSBURGH
DETROIT   KANSAS CITY   SAN FRANCISCO

have your name printed upon the checks in your personal check book free of charge? Have you supplied yourself with such a personal check book? Do you believe that personal checks add dignity and authority to your profession or housewife?

9. Do you preserve receipted bills and other business communications in letter files?

10. Have you adopted a cost-keeping system which is a complete record of every day's expenditures? Are you able to state clearly, at the end of each month or year, exactly how much money you have spent and for what?

11. Is your house planned thruout for your own specific use on sanitary, economic principles?

12. Are the heating and ventilating systems adequate and hygienic?

13. Is the light, both natural and artificial, up to the maximum of quality and quantity, but down to the minimum cost?

14. Have you accurate knowledge of every labor-saving device applicable to your household? Have you supplied those which you approve and can afford?

15. Have you taken all possible fire protection and precaution? Have you a complete inventory of all your household belongings?

16. Have you a practical knowledge of the intelligent planning of the work of a household, so that labor may be justly divided and each employee given a reasonable time of rest?

17. Do you tell each worker exactly what to do, how to do it, and then hold him or her responsible for results?

18. Have you a practical knowledge of cooking? Of economical buying? Of the balanced ration?

19. Have you a complete personal grocery list, stating the brands or varieties which you have assured yourself, to the best of your ability, to be unadulterated and healthful? Do you take stock of the groceries in your house at the beginning of each week or month? Do you buy in quantities and as economically as possible? Do you think that this plan saves time, money, and the nervous strain of the daily ordering of supplies?

20. Have you compared all your methods of housekeeping, in detail, with those of at least a dozen other women whose similar incomes might make their experiences of value to you? Are you willing to be told that your methods might be improved, by such practical housekeepers, by an employee, by an expert?

Copyright, 1916: Doubleday, Page.

E. F. Foley   MRS. FRANKS

THE "SQUEEZE-PLAY" AT THE CAPITAL

BY W. J. GHENT

THIS is not a tale of the daring and ingenious device practised in our favorite national game by which a runner secures an unearned base. It has to do wholly with the various minor grafts, pinches, "squeezes," hypothecations and excises by which our national lawmakers convert to their own use money or service, which, according to law, does not belong to them. The major grafts—pork barrels, river-and-harbor, "good-roads" and building appropriations, retainer fees, outright bribes and other considerable sources of revenue—have from time to time been treated by others. This time only the minor grafts will be considered—grafts which, though often petty enough individuality, make up a staggering collective total.

Curiously enough, the real facts are never presented in print. Often an attempt is made to treat one small phase of the subject—for instance, the mileage graft. Sometimes will appear a sensational article regarding the penknives, manicure sets and chatelaine bags obtained by Senators and Representatives from the official stationery rooms. The implications made in such an article, however, are always absurdly misleading. On the one hand, none of these commodities can be had by anybody without purchase; and, on the other hand, they can be bought by anybody about the Capitol—the elevator boy or the doorkeeper being quite as privileged a purchaser as the Congressman. And as a wide assortment of excellent stock is kept, and as prices are only a little above manufacturers' rates, there is no wonder that our statesmen and their women folk, as well as others, buy liberally. These stationery sales do not in themselves furnish a case of graft, tho there is, perhaps, a question of graft in the whole stationery allowance. And yet it is only a trifling matter when compared with the other grafts by which our statesmen piece out their earnings. These various "squeezes" constitute a system of pilfering which goes on uninterruptedly.

A Congressman's perquisites are many, and the average Congressman makes full use of all of them. Sent to the Capital to make laws for the government of all of us and to safeguard the public treasury, he first sees to it that nothing tangible to which, under the shadow of the law, he can lay claim escapes him. Some of the lawmakers, of course, are there for any kind of graft, legal or illegal, customary or unusual; but even the legislator who prides himself on being above bribery will unblushingly practise forms of graft that are despicable in their meanness.

There is, for instance, the mileage graft—in which all draw in it. It is an old "squeeze," dating back to the early days of the Republic. Before the close of the Civil War the rate was 40 cents a mile. By the Salary Act of 1866 the Congressmen lifted their net recompense from $3000 to $5000, but they

cut the mileage to 20 cents. In 1873 they pushed their salaries another notch forward, to $7500, but the protest that went up from every part of the nation persuaded them, during the following year, to repeal the raise. In 1907, however, they restored the $7500 figure. In all this salary legislation they left the mileage rate untouched, and it has thus remained constant since 1866. Technically, it has no basis in law, since it was not mentioned in the law of 1907; it is, however, included in the appropriations every year.

THE MILEAGE GRAFT

MILEAGE works both ways—that is, going and coming. Also, it works whether the Congressman takes a train or an auto. Or if one session runs close to another, the Congressman may remain right in Washington, and still draw his mileage for two round trips. When Representative Tawney, of Minnesota, acting as chairman of the Committee of the Whole in the House, on January 29, 1904, made his decision in the matter of the special session which ended on the fifth of the previous December, and the regular session which began two days later, a settled precedent was established which gives the lawmaker his double mileage even though he doesn't return home.

Now, mileage isn't much of a matter to the Congressman who lives in Maryland or Virginia. To the Kansan or Missourian, however, it is an agreeable bonus, and to the Californian it is a juicy "melon." And nobody in high place these days is rejecting melons. Yet somehow, among the people, there has grown to be a fairly widespread objection to this particular form of graft, and consequently the echoes of this feeling are often heard on the floor of the House of Representatives. The Senate, heretofore indirectly elected, has not usually bothered itself with such an undignified subject; but among the direct representatives of the people at the other end of the Capitol a discussion has often arisen which has prompted shudders of apprehension.

Every year, in the discussion of either the general appropriation bill or an urgent deficiency bill, up comes the mileage question. The procedure is almost always the same. A new member, fresh from the people, moves that the rate be reduced to 10 cents a mile. Another, not to be outdone, amends to make it 5 cents. Still another moves a substitute to reduce the allowance to the actual expenses of travel. Then there is a discussion and a cross-fire of parliamentary motions. The subject is

soon lost in a fog; there is an adjournment, and the next day the old rate is re-enacted without argument.

Or perhaps it transpires that one of the movers is really in earnest and that an alarming number of Representatives show a disposition to vote for a reduction. Thereupon one of the old-timers, from a district where the people never revolt at anything, rushes into the breach with a plea which allays all objections. Mileage, he contends, has nothing to do with the transportation rate on railways. It is an addition, a bonus, to the regular salary, which a grateful people decrees to its representatives. Time and precedent, he argues, are on its side. That the rate happens to be very much in excess of the average railway rate for transporting passengers is a point at once irrelevant and incompetent. The people should not be insulted by the supposition that they entertain any picayunish ideas about the recompense of their representatives, and anyhow the old rate should stand. Of course his grateful auditors agree with him; there is a synchronous sigh of relief from all present as they realize the averting of a threatened disaster; and the old rate stands.

Every year, and sometimes twice a year, this farce is repeated. The fact that at a recent conflict over the matter in the House the present rate was sustained by a majority of only ten carries small significance of a change. Usually it is known beforehand, by a counting of noses, just about how the vote will stand. Those members, therefore, who want the rate continued, but who stand in a wholesome fear of a critical constituency, are enabled to have their votes recorded in favor of a reduction, in the blissful confidence that everything is safe. Nor is the fact that at a still more recent consideration of the matter the reduction was actually carried in the House, indicative of a change. The amendment was, of course, defeated in conference. The Senate—even the directly-elected-by-the-people Senate—is confidently expected to act its historic role as a check on popular caprice, and there is nothing to fear.

THE FRANKING GRAFT

THE franking privilege is a rational one so long as it is not abused. No Senator or Representative who performs his duties and attends to the correspondence of his constituents could afford to pay first-class postage for all his letters or other class postage for his documents and seeds. But every one about the Capitol and the two big office buildings knows that this privilege is not honestly observed. Of course there are none of the outrageous abuses of several years ago. Too much publicity spoiled that graft. No Congressman would now frank his weekly laundry home to be washed and ironed by his colored washwoman and franked back again. No one would now frank his typewriting machine for a transcontinental trip.

But the two big boxes—and one of them is cedar, so that it may repel moths from clothing—to which each Congressman is entitled, make their way back and forth between sessions at Uncle Sam's expense. Millions of franked speeches—many of them of no earthly interest to any one—clog the mails. Carloads of seeds, 85 per cent of which have been purchased from private growers, and 50 per cent of which go to seed stores, are freely distributed. Letters—hundreds of thousands of them—and telegrams, too, which have nothing whatever to do with public business, journey post free or wire free. It is no part of Uncle Sam's contract to pay the campaign expenses of his Congressmen. Yet much of this correspondence—perhaps most of it—is personal; it concerns itself with politics, with conditions in the home district or State, with promises of rewards or with mollifying explanations of unfulfilled pledges. It is the Congressman's own business and not the public's. And yet the public pays for it.

There are some Congressmen who, along with their secretaries, scrupulously observe the distinction between private and public matter and who pay postage where postage is due. But even a limited experience with official life in the legislative buildings will convince an observer that the franking privilege is grossly abused by a large number, if not a majority, of the members of both Houses.

THE STATIONERY GRAFT

The stationery allowance of $125 may also, for present purposes, be admitted to be a reasonable one. Technically, it is a yearly allowance; but as a matter of practise it is made for every session. An industrious Congressman, or any kind of Congressman with an industrious secretary, may well use up $125 worth of stationery during a busy session. One of the first things a Congressman learns, however, is that this allowance may be demanded in cash. The thing he usually learns second is that he can get absolutely free from any of the committees of which he is a member all the printed letter heads and envelopes that he can use. He will still have to pay for ink, pencils, pens, paste and similar articles. But it happens that a large number of Congressmen have only the most incidental and infrequent use for stationery. They therefore draw their stationery allowance in cash at the beginning of the session. If they need stationery, they run up a bill for it; oftener they do without. A soft picking of $125 is not to be ignored.

It is very likely that this allowance was not intended, when first made, as a cash addition to a Congressman's salary. The public, in the main, is not acquainted with the fact that it is so regarded by the Congressmen themselves. In so far as public opinion sanctions it, the grant is merely a maximum allowance for needed supplies. The general practise of grafting, however, has transformed it into a cash perquisite. A good many Congressmen graft it in

THE BAFFLING of BOGGS

"Congratulations, Tommy"

THE dinner-table talk went casually about such topics as the latest play, the new dance, servants and sermons, until the great voice of Boggs suddenly boomed the lighter talk into stunned silence.

Boggs roared his views of the international situation, raked the Administration over verbal coals, shot off into Mexico, and made a side trip into our National Parks and the conservation problem—all between the roast and the salad. Only the need for food ended this tremendous onslaught.

And then as the revived Boggs opened his mouth to begin again, Tom Ainsworth, noted for his modesty and reserve, surprised everyone by saying:

"So far, Mr. Boggs, you have misstated nearly every fact."

Boggs glared. Round eyes turned on Thomas. But for once he didn't seem to mind. Coldly and patiently as an analytic chemist in his laboratory, he took every one of Boggs' statements, held them up for a moment in a mental test-tube, let all the diners see their fallacy, and then proceeded to demolish them with a bewildering explosion of fact piled upon fact. When it was over, Boggs' face was a study in chagrin.

Later on, when the women and Boggs had gone, the host rose solemnly and took Ainsworth by the hand.

"It was cruel, Tom, cruel, but absolutely necessary. Now tell me, confidentially; where did you get that dope?"

"Can you keep a secret?" asked Tom. "Well, a short time back I invested in a set of the latest encyclopædia. The one I had been using was five or six years old, and I found I didn't dare trust to it for the late information everybody needs just now. By the merest chance, I happened to have read up on just those subjects that Boggs was manhandling. I tell you what, a man ought to have some real facts if he wants to back up his opinions in this new, truth-seeking time we're living in, and I don't know any more agreeable way of getting facts than is offered by this new, up-to-date encyclopædia."

* * * *

Thomas Ainsworth is right. Ignorance of facts that are bound to affect your very existence and the future of your country is inexcusable.

You'll be surprised to find with what absorbing interest subjects you've always intended to read up are treated in the Second Edition of the New International Encyclopædia.

This edition is a thorough, complete revision of the preceding work. Every article has been rewritten, every page reset and the whole work printed from new type. It is the latest, most authoritative and most accurate encyclopædia published today. Its information is easily gotten at—the subjects are arranged alphabetically, like the words in a dictionary. Anyone can understand it.

You can now buy this encyclopædia at a special introductory price and pay for it in small monthly amounts while you are using it.

Write your name and address in the blank space below, tear off and mail today. We'll send you full particulars of our offer, a free 80-page book of information about the work, or a volume of the encyclopædia for examination and comparison. Of course, you do not obligate yourself in any way.

a lump as soon as they reach Washington. Of course there are others—the busy and industrious ones—who exhaust it entirely, and expend a good deal more besides, for supplies. But there is probably not a single Congressman in either House who does not, on figuring up his purchases from the stationery room and finding a balance in his favor, draw the amount in ready money.

CURBING THE PRINTING GRAFT

There would be a huge printing graft if it were not for the ceaseless watchfulness of the Congressional Record Clerk at the Capitol. A Congressman likes to see his name in print. Also he likes to have his constituents see it. If he writes a speech and delivers it, he wants them to see that also. If his secretary writes it for him, or if he buys it ready-made from one of the numerous literary bureaus about town, he is perhaps even more eager that it shall meet the eyes of his constituents. In such a case it is likely to be a greatly superior production to the Congressman's own effort. So whenever he delivers anything on the floor of the House to which he belongs, he is tempted to have the matter separately printed and distributed back home. Sometimes this temptation lures him into great expense. Printing costs money, and tho the Government Printing Office does the work as cheaply as it can be done anywhere, the cost of a few large editions of several speeches may mount up into the heavy hundreds. The impulse to print more than one can pay for is strong with some Congressmen, and the determination to stave off payment as long as possible is strong with many others. Here is where the Congressional Record Clerk finds a large part of his duty. His business is to see that the delinquent gets no more printing till he pays for the former lot, and to harry him more or less gently until payment is made. Sometimes this official must appeal to the sergeant-at-arms, who pays the salaries. Sometimes, in spite of all precautions, the Congressman finishes his term a debtor to Uncle Sam. That the case is infrequent is due not so much to the scruples of Uncle Sam's lawmakers, as to the alertness of the Record Clerk.

THE CLERK HIRE GRAFT

But the meanest and most detestable of all the Congressional grafts is the outright theft of money due the Congressmen's employees, or in the case of those Congressmen who do not employ a secretary, due the government. Every Representative and Senator is by law entitled to a secretary, with a salary of $1500. This appropriation is known as "clerk hire." It was presumably not intended as an added compensation to Congressmen, but as an allowance for a supposedly needed assistant. Formerly the pay was $1200. But when the Congressmen, in 1907, raised their own wages by $2500 each, they very generously added $300 a year to the compensation of their secretaries. This money is paid, however, not to the employee, but to the Congressman.

As a consequence, only a part of it may get beyond the Congressman's pockets.

In the winter of 1911-12 an attempt was made to organize a social club of Congressional secretaries. A thoro canvass of the House Office Building and the Capitol brought forth the report that there were only 185 bona fide male secretaries to be found. Of course there were some women secretaries, and of course some of the men secretaries may have been temporarily absent from the city. A general discussion of the matter resulted in the optimistic estimate that the total of actual secretaries might be as high as 225 or even 250. But the membership of the House at the time was 394. It would thus appear that from 144 to 169 of Uncle Sam's lawmakers converted either a part or the whole of their clerk hire to their own pockets. This is not all; for it happens that a good many bona fide secretaries do not receive the full wage the government allots them. It is therefore probable that more than 200 Representatives, or more than half of the total, were at this time swindling the government or their help out of money voted for a specific purpose. It is unlikely that the number has declined.

HOW THEY WORK THE GRAFT

There is a class of Congressmen who are elected, the Lord only knows how or why, who do no work, who pay little or no attention to the demands of their constituents, who write few or no letters, who distribute few documents or seeds, and incur no expenses other than living expenses. Such men, of course, employ no secretary, not even an underpaid stenographer and typewriter. They merely put the government money into their own pockets. There is another class, who are thrifty, who perform only a limited service to their constituents, and who share the expenses of a stenographer, usually underpaid, with one or two of their fellow-members. In such cases the Congressman pockets the major part of the salary. And finally, there is another class of Congressmen who employ a man or woman under the designation of secretary, but compel this person to work for less than the statutory wage. In such cases the theft is of only a minor part of the salary designated.

The members who engage in this despicable swindling and cheating are not merely the obscure or unknown. They are not usually the reactionary or the corrupt members. Often they are men who make a great ado about their devotion to democracy, ethics, justice, the rights of labor and the eternal verities. One of the Representatives in the 61st and 62nd Congress, who made a practise of withholding nearly 40 per cent of his secretary's salary, was particularly hailed as a representative of organized labor. One of the Senators who is doing the same thing today is applauded in the progressive press as the champion of popular rights.

Congressmen continue to practise this graft in spite of the fact that its

consequences are sometimes serious. Several Representatives have been retired from public life by reason of an issue having been made of the matter in their home districts. It could be made an issue in half of the districts and half of the States of the Union. Yet such is the desperate determination to hold on to this contemptible form of robbery that the average Congressman will risk his career rather than let go.

For many years the secretaries and their defenders sought to get upon the statutes a law compelling the payment of this salary direct. In the winter of 1912-13 a partial recognition of this demand was made in the enactment of the law that every secretary should be formally registered. But no change was made in the practise of paying the Congressman instead of the secretary. As a consequence, there has been not the slightest change for the better. At least half of the statesmen who are biennially selected from among the people to make laws, to decide ethical questions, to safeguard the treasury and to protect the rights of the weaker, constantly practise this swindling upon their hard-working employees, or else filch the money in a lump sum from the government. The theft is odious enough when practised in the House; it is more odious yet when practised in the Senate. That highly distinguished body divides itself up into enough committees to give almost three-fourths of its members chairmanships. To each of these chairmen goes a committee clerk, who in most cases is hardly to be distinguished, by the nature of his services, from a private secretary. Thus the Senate lays an extra heavy tax on Uncle Sam for clerk hire, and the individual Senators—a number of them—convert a part of this money to their own uses.

When this money is filched outright —that is, when no part of it is paid out for clerical services—the sum is apparently taken only from the public treasury. That impersonal thing, the government, is the sufferer, and nobody seems to care. In reality, however, it is taken from some unemployed person whose labor has been designated, and whose recompense has been provided, by Uncle Sam. Somebody somewhere has been cheated out of a job. When only the major part of it is pocketed, and a miserable wage paid to an overworked typewriter, there is both exploitation of an employee and faithlessness to the Congressman's obligation to have actual secretarial duties performed. The government pays for the work, not presumably for the mere convenience of the Congressman, but for the extension of public service. And when, finally, a part of this compensation is squeezed from a person who does real secretarial service, the meanness of the theft is such that it cannot be fittingly characterized.

For to many of these Congressmen the secretary's coöperation is of the utmost helpfulness. Many of them would cut but a sorry figure indeed if it were not for their subordinates' alertness and industry. Upon the efficient secretary falls all the necessary routine labors of the office and a good many extra-routine duties. On the care and intelligence with whi h he performs these duties a good deal of the Congressman's reputation and efficiency depend. Yet there are Congressmen in plenty who have accepted the fullest measure of such faithful service from their secretaries and have meanly pocketed a portion of the governmentally designated wage.

The men who practise all these grafts are the nation's lawmakers. They draft statutes which define embezzlement, misfeasance in office, malversation of funds and violation of trust, and they penalize offenses by fine and imprisonment. But do they ordain punishment for other men who pilfer, they are themselves pilfering from the government and from their hard-working employees.

Los Angeles, California

ODDLY STATISTICAL

The retail business center of New York City is moving uptown at the rate of an inch an hour.

Compressed paper with a thin leather covering is being used in Germany as a substitute for leather shoe soles.

During the last year 2,658,717 people used the books and magazines in the central building of the New York Public Library.

The average floating population that goes thru New York City every day is about 200,000. During last winter it increased to 250,000.

United States investors have put $645,-000,000 into railroads in Mexico; $250,-000,000 more of American money have gone into Mexican mines.

In the 1916 edition of the *Almanach de Gotha*, a French year book, appears the curious information that the German Crown Prince is colonel of a regiment of British hussars.

The most valuable fruit tree in the world is said to be an alligator pear in Whittier, Los Angeles County, California. It is insured by Lloyd's of London for $30,000. Last year the tree earned $3000.

Greece has made enormous profits from her merchant marine since the war began. Freight rates are so high that the proceeds of a single voyage are sometimes more than the entire value of the ship making it.

Recently a Paris newspaper asked French women to answer the question, "Do you believe in woman suffrage?" It hoped to obtain about 200,000 answers in all, but it got a million replies in the affirmative.

When the immigration officers recently threatened to deport Delia Burke, for fear she might become a public charge, 600 anxious housewives, looking for a servant girl, were on hand with promises of a situation for her at good wages.

The safety record for railroads is held by the Hudson Tunnels. Since they were opened, eight years ago, 400,000,000 passengers have been carried under the river without loss of a single life attributable to train operation. Eighteen hundred trains are sent thru each day, with only ninety seconds headway during rush hours.

The largest contribution ever made to the government "conscience fund" was $30,000, just received from some one in Philadelphia. The sender explained that it was the last installment on a payment of $80,000, which he had made to the United States Government in order to return fourfold the money he had stolen years ago. The "conscience fund" now contains over $500,000.

Independent Opinions

We can remember the time when the youthful aspirant to oratorical honors made choice between the speeches of Spartacus, Regulus and Patrick Henry or, if he wanted something ultra-modern, Wendell Philips' "Toussaint L'Ouverture." But now it takes a question of current interest to win the award of the judges. We are flattered to find that The Independent has been employed for this purpose in the schools where it is used and that our editorials, properly voiced and furnished with gestures other than those we used while composing them, have brought laurels to the contestants. We had not thought of aspiring to compete with Demosthenes and Cicero on their own ground, but hereafter we will read our editorials aloud in order to see if the sentences swing right. The clatter of the typewriters should serve as well as the noise of the surf.

We find that the editorials make excellent orations, of the type that is most appealing to the modern audience. In one of the preliminary oratorical contests, one of the boys in the Junior class won a place in the June finals on the editorial on the Mexican situation in a February issue. A Sophomore girl won honorable mention by reciting some weeks ago a portion of an article by Mr. Purinton on "Concentrate." Other pupils have selected parts of editorials and given them with marked effect. Our Friday lessons on current topics have been most interesting since we have used The Independent. The Senior class in their study of argumentation find the occasional briefs in the magazine helpful to them in preparing their own briefs, and in arranging for their debates. In short, The Independent is the ideal magazine for the teacher of English looking for help.

ALICE M. DUNBAR
Wilmington, Delaware

Has it ever been explained—
—Why the English quietly permit the Germans to do all the air-raiding? Is the trip so far as the Kiel Canal, where the latter's navy is supposed to be, too much for the nerve of the English aviators? Or is there other reason for doing nothing?
—What the force is of the complaint of outrageous "inhumanity" in trying to "starve the innocent women and children." and other noncombatants, of a nation, by shutting off their food supply? Except in the scale of it, is it anywise different from the "siege" which has always been regarded as a legitimate method of reducing a city to surrender?
—Why, if England may prevent intercourse with the Central Powers by more or less successful "blockade," the same thing is not permissible to Germany by the establishment of a "war zone"? No tolerance, of course, for contemptibly sneaking modes of enforcing such blockade, or whatever it may be called, by any combatant.
R. H. YOUNG
Haines City, Florida

1. In regard to the backwardness of the English in air-raiding, you must remember that they have no Zeppelins or other dirigibles of equal size. They have, however, made a number of aeroplane raids over towns in Germany and

the German territory in France and Belgium. In these they claim to have done considerable military damage, altho the Germans deny this, and refer instead to the number of innocent civilians killed.

2. There is no apparent difference between besieging a city and besieging a country. No doubt the Germans would have completely isolated the British Isles and starved out the population if it had been possible.

3. Either country has a right to blockade the other if it can, but as a matter of fact neither side has declared a formal blockade, because it could not enforce it. Our protests to Great Britain have been because they have stopped neutral ships and confiscated non-contraband goods by Orders in Council when there is no blockade, and our protests to Germany have been because of the sinking of merchantment without warning.

Those who read MacManus's rhapsody on "Ireland's Holy Dead" in your issue of May 15 should read also as a wholesome commentary thereon "Story of the Week," on page 258 of same issue, especially the paragraph referring to the ambushing of the constables in Meath, killing ten of them and wounding eighteen, and the story of the snipers who kept up their work *some amore* for some days after the organized revolt was over. I think that Mr. MacManus himself, if he should read and realize all that happened, might not have so much to say about the holiness of the dead on the one side only. It is still true as of old that as a man sows, so shall he reap, and that they who take the sword, shall perish by the sword. It is not only true, but it is right.　　　J. W. MILLER, JR.

Philadelphia, Pennsylvania

Mr. Miller has acquired the art of reading The Independent. To see things in their proper perspective two eyes are necessary and the farther apart they are the better the object can be seen. That is why we publish opinions and facts on both sides of a question, altho we thereby offend those readers who want to look on the world thru one eye.

The number for April 17 is better than usual, but I beg to disagree with the editorial, "Illiterate Humbuggery." The crowds of unemployed, the fact that the great mines and foundries prefer foreign workers and so pay only low wages, show the foreigners do have a bad influence on wages. Further, if immigration is going to be toward Europe, what does our law restricting something that does not exist matter? The Efficiency paper was the best yet.
　　　　　　　　　　　　　　THADDEUS LAW

Amsterdam, Missouri

On the question now being debated all over the country, is Ford a joke or not, and if so is he a good joke or a bad joke, the Professor of Law in the University of Michigan makes an interesting communication:

To citizens of Michigan few things have been more amusing than the way in which the outside world has taken the vote for Ford at the Presidential primary. The writer, for some time an Independent subscriber, regrets to see the Independent no more discriminating than the rest. In your editorial note heading the article by one Ellis O. Jones in your issue of May 15 you say: "But he takes Mr. Ford seriously—just as the voters of Michigan and Nebraska did." I know nothing about the Nebraska vote, but I do know something

After the Walk

Your first and best thought is

Coca-Cola

Oftenest thought of for its deliciousness—
highest thought of for its wholesomeness.
Refreshing and thirst-quenching.

Demand the genuine by full name—
nicknames encourage substitution.

THE COCA-COLA CO.　　ATLANTA, GA.

*Send for free booklet,
"The Romance of Coca-Cola."*

about the Michigan vote. The point of it all is that Mr. Ford's win over Senator Smith was due to the votes of thousands who did *not* take Mr. Ford, as a Presidential candidate, seriously, however he may be taken as a maker of automobiles. When any one man knows of dozens of voters who voted for Mr. Ford for reasons other than a belief in his fitness to be President of the United States, the conclusion is forced upon one that the vote should not be taken seriously.

Curiously, Mr. Jones, in his article, stumbled unwittingly upon the real reason for the Ford vote. He says: "The Republicans voted for Ford, who was not a candidate, *and refused to vote for* Senator Smith, who was a very active candidate." There, in the italicized words, you have it all. On the ballot were the names of Smith, Ford and Simpson—at least as I write that is the name I recall. Could you beat it? Very few voters really thought that any one of the three was fit to be President, or had a chance to be. The result was that thousands of voters looked upon the whole matter as a joke, and Ford jokes are popular. There was involved also a desire on the part of many to repudiate Smith, a presumptuous politician.

The Independent might well take the Michigan vote as the basis of an editorial on the worth of Presidential primaries. You could argue to either conclusion, for look at the rebuke to Smith.

RALPH W. AIGLER
University of Michigan

In "Story of the Week," issue of The Independent of May 1, you state: "So Nebraska may be assumed, on the face of the primary returns, to be for peace and against prohibition."

On the face of the complete official returns Nebraska seems to be for peace all right enough; but certainly *not* against prohibition. Here are the figures for the candidates for Governor as officially reported:

Republican		Democratic	
Sutton (Dry)	30,902	C. Bryan (Dry)	33,022
McKelvie (Dry)	30,097	Neville (Wet)	46,662
Madget (Dry)	5,039		
George (Dry)	8,426		
Miles (Wet)	20,020		

Total Dry vote:		Total Wet vote:	
Republican	74,464	Republican	20,020
Democratic	33,022	Democratic	46,662
Total	107,486	Total	66,682
Dry majority			40,804

M. BRUGGER
Columbia, Nebraska

Some time ago you stated in an article that General French of the English Army had been in the habit of going to Belgium every summer for several years prior to the war to look over his future battlefields. Upon your authority I made this statement and have been asked to prove it. Will you kindly let me have any information which will prove this?

FRED D. GOLDSTONE
Milwaukee, Wisconsin

There is no secret now about the preparations made by the French, British and Belgians to meet the anticipated German invasion. The following paragraphs from the *London Times History of the War,* of June 15, 1915, will show what part Sir John French took in them:

As Lord Haldane publicly testified in a speech delivered on March 20, 1915, Sir John French had been studying the possibilities of a conflict for five years or more. The Lord Chancellor admitted that Sir John's interest had been that he might have to command the Expeditionary Force, and with this in mind he had given the closest study to the possibilities of the future. Particularly did he familiarize himself with Belgium, where he knew that the inevitable struggle would be contested, just as Marshal von Hindenburg spent years of his life in studying the bare plains and lonely swamps of Poland, with which his name will forever be attached. Always a believer in following out on the ground the lessons taught in the military text and history books, Sir John had made annual pilgrimages to Belgium for a number of years in succession, accompanied by one or two of his staff, visiting the battlefields of Marlborough's and Napoleon's campaigns, but always studying the ground with an eye to a possibility which he knew could not long be delayed. Among the Field Marshal's friends the name of "The Traveling Party" was given to him and his companions on these tours.

Our monthly briefs on current questions are intended primarily for the use of debaters, but they are also proving useful to readers who want a concise and impartial summary of the arguments on "both sides" and references for further reading. Mr. F. L. Faurote of the Lesan Advertising Agency, New York, writes us that "'Both Sides' is one of the greatest things that has been done in tabloid journalism for some time."

In view of the complaints by the British that the British prisoners have been ill-treated in Germany, and the counter complaints of the Germans that the German prisoners have been ill-treated in France, the suggestion made by the Rev. Dr. McNeill of Westminster Hall, Vancouver, has a special timeliness. Certainly the Germans, since they suffer more than any of the other belligerents from shortage of food, would be willing to agree to it.

Are neutral nations doing all they can for the relief of suffering among prisoners of war? As the economic situation in a belligerent nation becomes acute there is an inevitable temptation to reduce the rations of prisoners. To languish in slow starvation is a fate surely worse than death on the field of battle. And in view of past events now familiar to all there is cause for grave anxiety over the lot of prisoners in Germany during the last stages of that nation's losing struggle.

Why not have all prisoners interned in neutral nations, and fed and maintained at the expense of their own governments? The increased cost (if anything at all) would be inconsiderable; the humane advantages would be incalculable. It could hardly make any difference in the outcome of the war; and it is difficult to see any insurmountable obstacle to the adoption of such a proposal if it were agreed upon by leading neutrals and urged upon belligerents in a friendly way. Only from neutrals could such a measure originate. Why not at least give the warring nations this humane proposal to consider?

JOHN T. McNEILL.
Vancouver, British Columbia

I wish to express my gratification for the courageous, strong editorials in The Independent touching on the race problem. I have known many brave, patriotic men who would charge in the very mouth of a cannon in the defense of their country, but when it came to speaking boldly in defense of justice and humanity to a weaker race they would either say nothing or dodge the issue.

Your strong, practical editorial on Haiti, the editorial on the St. Louis segregation ordinance, and "The Negro Nonconformist" have the ring of the true patriot of the Garrison-Sumner-Phillips type, who still has in his bosom the spirit of freedom and justice to humanity, the foundation upon which the Republic was built.

We all go up or down together. Reason and common sense demand that all forces work together for the development and elevation of the entire citizenship.

SAMUEL D. HOOKER.
Muskogee, Oklahoma

Here Are the Facts About
Nujol
POR US PAT OFF

OUR booklet, "The Rational Treatment of Constipation," summarizes briefly some of the facts which doctors have learned about constipation—what causes it, and why the use of Nujol as an internal lubricant is an effective method of treatment.

Casual dosing with laxatives and cathartics is an extremely unwise way of dealing with a disorder which is so full of potential dangers as is constipation.

If you are interested in learning the facts about a far saner and safer treatment, you should have this booklet. Clip and mail the attached coupon.

Most druggists carry Nujol, which is sold only in pint bottles packed in cartons bearing the Nujol trademark. If your druggist does not carry Nujol, we will send you a pint bottle prepaid to any point in the United States on receipt of 75 cents—money order or stamps.

STANDARD OIL COMPANY
(New Jersey)
BAYONNE　　　　　NEW JERSEY

Approved by Dr. Harvey W. Wiley, Director of Good Housekeeping Bureau of Foods, Sanitation and Health.

Standard Oil Company (New Jersey) Bayonne, New Jersey Dept. 12

Please send me your booklet, "The Rational Treatment of Constipation."

Name ....
Street and No. ....
Town and State ....

Romeike's Press Clippings

are used nowadays by every modern up-to-date business man; they bring you in constant touch with all public and private wants, and supply you with news bearing upon any line of business. We read for our subscribers all the important papers published in the United States and abroad. If you have never used press clippings, drop us a postal and we will show how they can be of advantage to you. Write for booklet and terms.

ROMEIKE, INC.　106-110 Seventh Ave., New York City

THE MARKET PLACE

A REVIEW OF FINANCE AND TRADE

THE INVESTOR'S SERVICE

The Independent is now offering a Service for Investors in which personal attention will be given to the desires of its subscribers for information in regard to investments of all kinds. We cannot of course decide for our readers where they should put their savings and will not undertake the responsibility of recommending specific securities to any individual. But we ask our readers to write to us frankly and this Department will give them by letter or thru the columns of The Independent such impartial information as may assist them in making a wise decision for themselves.

RAILROAD STOCKS FOR INVESTMENT

THE small investor has been continually told to steer clear of stocks; the argument was in favor of being a bondholder rather than a stockholder. Yet there are good corporations and bad ones, as there are good stocks and poor bonds, and the small investor should place himself in a position to discriminate between them. Since this article was planned, railroad stocks have had somewhat of a rise, but may still be purchased at a price where the return on the investment is quite respectable. A man who purchased five years ago the stocks of such railroads as the Atchison, Union Pacific, Southern Pacific, Great Northern, Northern Pacific, Pennsylvania, New York Central or Norfolk & Western is still receiving dividends and the stocks are all selling at about par or much over. On the other hand, the bonds of many railroad systems that were developed at an extravagant rate and fell into the hands of receivers have been selling at foreclosure prices, as low as ten cents on the dollar, whereas at one time they sold in the nineties.

There is no argument against all stocks and in favor of all bonds without any qualifications. It all depends upon the character of stocks and what percentage of one's entire holdings such stocks will form.

The question of investment in either stocks or bonds resolves itself into a matter of earnings record, value of property, territory served, management and other factors rather than whether we have to deal with bonds or stocks. As a rule stocks are not desirable as sole investments for a woman because they are speculative, but they may form a small part of a woman's investment holdings if selected with care. A business man having investments amounting to say ten thousand dollars in high grade bonds yielding around 4.50 per cent might very well afford to place say five thousand dollars additional in such stocks as Pennsylvania Railroad or Atchison unless he was buying at a time when prices were the highest in years.

The man or woman who can set aside ten, twenty or fifty dollars a month to apply to the purchase of good stocks is better off in the long run than if that sum were placed in the savings bank at 3½ per cent or 4 per cent. But the person without a "rainy day" fund in the savings bank should not think of placing his savings in stocks. By a "rainy day" fund is meant a sum equivalent to several months' salary to be used only in case of illness or unemployment.

At the same time it should not be forgotten that sound stocks have a value as collateral for loans and many stocks listed on the New York Stock Exchange have an immediate and close market and better value as collateral than some comparatively inactive and unknown bonds. So, in the absence of funds, the holder of conservative stocks can always pledge his certificates for a loan, either at his bank or at his broker's office.

Dividends on stocks are paid by check either quarterly or semi-annually, without any deduction for the normal Federal income tax. The wise investor will place his dividend checks in the savings bank to accumulate until they have reached an amount sufficient to purchase an even share of the same stock, which may be added to the investment.

If a fond parent wishes to provide a fund for his son's college expenses, there is no better form of saving than the systematic purchase of high grade stocks. A man having a son of seven years whom he expects to send to college at seventeen has ten years in which to accumulate a fund. Twenty-five dollars a month for ten years will produce $3,000, exclusive of accrued interest, and that amount should be sufficient to send a normal boy thru one of our best universities.

To the investor who has his eye on some "war bride" which is reputed to be earning 30 per cent, or 100 per cent, and not yet paying dividends, this article will not appeal because the most that can be offered is 5 to 6 per cent. The war stocks have sold far above normal, due to exaggerated reports of earnings, and have tumbled in a heap when the truth has come out. Many a man has seen his savings of years fade away because he wanted 20 to 30 per cent.

Railroad stocks may still be purchased at prices which will admit of some enhancement and where the return is ample. Unless stocks can be bought to yield at least 5 per cent, there is no object in buying them as there are many bonds which can be had on that basis. The small investor should buy stocks not so much with the view of future enhancement as for steady income, though he is a wise man who buys good stocks when they are low.

There are so many "tips" going around these days that a word regarding them may not be amiss. The lambs had best be wary of such advice. While money has been made on "tips," the money-maker is usually on the ground in Wall Street and knows when the so-called insiders are unloading their accumulations at high prices. The man in Great Falls or Oshkosh may be dreaming of melons while his stock has dropped twenty or thirty points. There is a time to buy on a tip and also a time to sell. So the small man who is not in direct touch with Wall Street had better keep strictly away from tipsters and be satisfied to purchase conservative railroad stocks.

It is well to mention that stocks may be purchased on the partial payment plan, on the same basis as outlined in the case of "Baby Bonds" in our February 7 issue. However, investors are warned not to buy more than they are sure they can pay for. It is preferable to take on one share at a time for cash and obtain the certificate than to buy ten and have a misfortune occur which may prevent one from continuing his payments. There is no embarrassment to be felt in going to a banker or broker with an order to purchase one share of stock. The buyer of one share today may buy a thousand in the future.

CONSERVATIVE RAILROAD STOCKS

	*Current Earnings	Per cent Div.	Range of Prices 1916	Range of Prices 1915	Present Price	Yield
Atchison	11.00	6	108½-100¼	111¼- 92½	105½	5.70
Balt. & Ohio	9.00	5	96 - 82⅞	96 - 63¾	91⅞	5.50
Chic. & Northwest.	10.30	7	134⅞-124⅞	135½-118½	131½	5.40
Chic., Mil. & St. Paul	7.80	5	102½- 91	101⅛- 77¾	98⅜	5.10
Delaware & Hudson	13.20	9	155 -149⅛	154½-138¼	155	5.80
Great Northern	9.50	7	127½-118	128⅜-112¾	121¼	5.80
Illinois Central	7.20	5	109½- 99¾	113 - 99	103½	4.90
Lehigh Valley ($50 par)	14.80	10	83 - 74½	83½- 64⅝	79	6.35
Norfolk & Western	14.30	7	126⅜-114	122⅝- 99½	126⅜	5.60
Northern Pacific	10.30	7	118⅞-109¾	118⅜- 99½	113⅞	6.20
Pennsylvania ($50 par)	9.30	6	59¾- 55¼	61½- 51¼	57⅞	5.25
Southern Pacific	10.30	6	104⅛- 94¼	104½- 81¼	100⅜	6.00
Union Pacific	14.00	8	140¼-129¾	141½-115¾	140	5.70

*Estimate of *Wall Street Journal*.

PEBBLES

Germany finds it easier to set the clock than to set the table.—*Brooklyn Daily Eagle.*

Carranza seems to be much stronger for the recall than the initiative.—*Columbia State.*

At the present rate, there isn't going to be much left of the earth for the meek to inherit.—*Columbia State.*

At least Villa and the Crown Prince have proved that dying is not nearly so fatal as it once was.—*Chicago Daily News.*

Villa may derive some consolation from the thought that the whipping he's getting hurts us more than it does him.—*Washington Post.*

Flossie Flirt—Jack, that man in the box hasn't taken his eyes off me for an hour. Her Escort—How do you know?—*Punch Bowl.*

'G. M. Sickles, M.D., has leased from Mrs. Arnold the vacant lot adjoining his residence and will begin operations in the spring.'—*From the Watkins Review.*

Lawyer—Don't worry. I'll see that you get justice. Client—I ain't hiring you for justice; I'm hiring you to win the suit!—*Puck.*

A little boy only six years old was boasting that he worked in a blacksmith shop. "What do you do there?" he was asked. "Do you shoe horses?" "No, sir!" he answered promptly. "I shoo flies."—*Our Dumb Animals.*

"Why must you always go out every time one of my women friends calls?" "Well, my dear," responded her husband, "I am glad to meet your friends. But you must remember that I have heard the story of your Atlantic City trip about seventeen times now."—*Indianapolis Star.*

"Won't you be very, very happy when your sentence is over?" cheerfully asked a woman of a convict in prison. "I dunno, ma'am, I dunno," gloomily answered the man. "You don't know?" asked the woman amazed. "Why not?" "I'm in for life."—*The Christian Herald.*

Berlin, April—There is no question that terrible damage was caused in London by the latest "Zeppelin L-10" raid. The commander of the "Zeppelin L-10" has brought back with him to Germany a sketch which he made while he was flying over the British metropolis. It clearly shows the houses of Parliament in flames and Sir Edward Grey running along Piccadilly with his coattails afire. The sketch has been warmly commended by art and military critics.—*New York Times.*

One of the diminutive flower maidens at a school fête attended by the Queen Mother was both pretty and plump, and when Her Majesty stopped for an instant to smile down upon her, what did she do but put up her wee mouth for a kiss, which she received.

"Molly!" gasped her astounded mother, after the distinguished visitor had passed on. "How could you?"

Molly gave good reason. "I fought." said she, "it 'ud be interestin' to tell my gran'children."—*The Christian Herald.*

Here is a story which if it is not true ought to be. The soldier in the train was dilating on his changed life.

"They took me from my home," he said, "and put me in barracks; they took away my clothes and put me in khaki; they took away my name and made me 'No. 575'; they took me to church, where I'd never been before, and they made me listen to a sermon for forty minutes. Then the parson said, 'No. 575, art thou weary, art thou languid?' and I got seven days' C.B. for giving him a civil answer."—*Manchester Guardian.*

Insurance
Conducted by
W. E. UNDERWOOD

A SEMI-CENTENNIAL

This year the National Board of Fire Underwriters completes the first fifty years of its existence. The event is to be fittingly celebrated by the fire insurance people. In addition to the regular annual meeting held in May, the program of which is unusually elaborate, there is to be a banquet at the Waldorf-Astoria at which United States Senator Sherman of Illinois, Hon. Thomas U. Sisson, member of Congress from Mississippi; Hon. Burton Mansfield, Insurance Commissioner of Connecticut; other citizens of national and state representatives and prominent fire underwriters will speak. Commemorative of the event, the Board has ready for distribution an historical volume, "Fifty Years of a Civilizing Force," written by Harry Chase Brearley.

There are many fire underwriters' organizations of national and sectional scope, but the National Board of Fire Underwriters is the great representative body of that important business and may fairly be regarded as the parent of all others, the special object of which, thru the lessening of fire hazards, is to reduce the tremendous destruction of values which occurs in this country every year. As an organization, the National Board ranks in point of service in its sphere with the American Bankers' Association, the National Association of Manufacturers and the National Association of Credit Men in their lines. Devoting itself to the big general problems of building construction, scientific investigation and analysis of hazards, legislation and the relations of fire insurance to the community, the Board assumes no jurisdiction over rate-making nor any of the lesser functions and details involved in the administration of the fire insurance business. It is a purely deliberative body.

Contrary to popular belief, fire insurance associations do not exist primarily for the purpose of imposing, thru combination, the will of the companies on the premium-paying public. Their object is a more comprehensive one, as any impartial investigator will conclude if he will take the trouble. Compared with other nations, we are an extravagant, careless and improvident people. As the result of these characteristics, we permit the destruction by fire every year of from $200,000,000 to $250,000,000 of the national wealth, seventy-five per cent of which is due to preventable causes. In working for the enactment of proper building codes, fire marshal laws, standard fire prevention measures and fire-fighting facilities, efficient fire departments and adequate water supplies, in maintaining laboratories for analyzing building materials, sustaining, unsupported, *propaganda* of education in fire prevention, these associations are rendering a valuable public service. All these efforts are aimed at reducing the waste by fire and cheapening the cost of insurance protection. In work of this kind the National Board has been an aggressive leader and it truly embodies the title chosen by Mr. Brearley for his book. Its contribution to the civilizing forces of the past fifty years is a substantial one.

W. C. N., Martinsville, N. J.—Presbyterian Ministers' Fund is an excellent institution. Records of associations named will be looked up and reported on in a later issue.

W. C. J., Waitsburg, Wash.—The Western States Life is of good repute. It writes non-participating policies only. On January 1 its assets were $2,067,624; its surplus, $1,070,023. This surplus includes the capital of $1,000,000.

H. W. W., Roulette, Pa.—The assets of the Standard Life of Pittsburgh on January 1 were $1,162,760; its surplus (including capital of $347,225) was $416,076. It writes non-participating insurance only. The management expenses are rather high. Claims are paid promptly.

O. M. S., Mason City, Iowa.—In my judgment you would make a mistake to surrender an ordinary life policy taken at age 23 after carrying it eight years. I recognize the argument made to induce you to surrender and take another kind of policy in another company; but it is plausible only, and misleading. Such advantages as you now see are transitory. Keep your policy.

A. W. B., Newark, N. J.—If you read the explanation of how life insurance rates are calculated, which appeared in this department of May 15, you must conclude that the assessment charges of nearly all the fraternal orders are inadequate. The Teachers' Protective Union of Lancaster, Pa., which is not even listed in the directories or handbooks especially devoted to coöperative life associations, seems to be a small affair with $8000 to $10,000 total assets, with no liabilities in the form of reserves. Figures of 1915 are unavailable yet, but I find that in 1914 the total income was $31,161; claims paid, $15,494; expenses, $10,332; total disbursements, $25,827. It is clear that it is accumulating no reserve, in which case, if its contracts include life insurance, I cannot recommend it.

C. D., West Somerville, Mass.—You have raised a question that is often discussed on the inside of life insurance. The custom of charging interest on deferred premiums is an old one. The annual premium, as calculated, requires that it be wholly paid by the policyholder in advance, so that the company may invest it at the rate assumed in the calculation. When only one-fourth of it is paid once every three months, unless interest is added, the calculation goes awry. The general rule is to add 4 per cent to the annual premium and divide by two to ascertain the semi-annual rate, and to add 6 per cent and divide by four for quarterly premiums. That some amount of interest should be added, is plain; the real question revolves around the rate: Are 4 and 6 per cent too high? Many think so. You have indicated a remedy when you propose to divide the amount of insurance by two or four and securing annual rates under as many policies dated six months or three months apart. In that case, however, the applicant would be compelled to undergo a physical examination each time. I am of the opinion that the companies will eventually reduce the interest rates on deferred premiums.

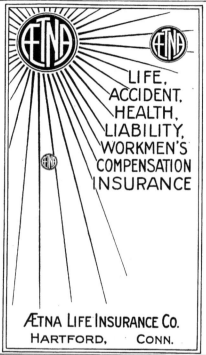

LIFE,
ACCIDENT,
HEALTH,
LIABILITY,
WORKMEN'S
COMPENSATION
INSURANCE

ÆTNA LIFE INSURANCE Co.
HARTFORD, · CONN.

The Independent

Founded 1848

HARPER'S WEEKLY
Founded 1857
Incorporated with The Independent May 22, 1916

THE CHAUTAUQUAN
Incorporated with The Independent June 1, 1914

The Independent is owned and published by the Independent Corporation, at 119 West Fortieth Street, New York. William B. Howard, president; Frederic E. Dickinson, treasurer; William Hayes Ward, honorary editor; Hamilton Holt, editor; Harold J. Howland, associate editor; Edwin E. Slosson, literary editor; Karl V. S. Howland, publisher. The price of The Independent is Ten Cents a copy. Four Dollars for one year. Postage to foreign countries in the Postal Union, $1.75 extra; to Canada, $1 extra. Writers who wish their articles returned should send stamped and addrest envelopes. No responsibility is assumed for the loss or non-return of manuscripts. Entered at the New York Post Office as Second Class matter. Copyright, 1916, by The Independent. Address all communications to The Independent, 119 West Fortieth Street, New York

CONTENTS FOR JUNE 12, 1916

Volume 86 Number 3523

YOUR PICTURES, PLEASE

The Independent-Harper's Weekly News Pictorial has begun publishing pictures from our readers' news-photograph service. There is a page of them this week. We want to print more pages —and better ones—from this time forward. Remember that we buy pictures from everywhere and everybody, if they are, first, good news, and second, good pictures. News, in our way of thinking, is something too fresh to be passed by without notice and too big to be interesting just in your street or your town or your state. Ten Dollars for the best one in any single week, Two Dollars for each of the others—those are the prices we pay. We want you to be watching all the time for the picture-opportunity that may bring a fresh increment of interest to us and a check for ten dollars to you.

REMARKABLE REMARKS

HENRY FORD—I am likely to do most anything.

THEODORE ROOSEVELT—Whatever defects I have, I do not pussyfoot.

M. SANTOS DUMONT—The modern flying machine can brave any gale.

HAVELOCK ELLIS—The English have always been great amateurs.

WOODROW WILSON—I would gladly assent to a disentangling alliance.

EMILIO ZAPATA—I am the man who should be President of Mexico.

JAMES HUNEKER—My country 'tis of thee, oh land of pork and preparedness.

ROSE PASTOR STOKES—Capitalistic society has not succeeded in making me bitter.

HAMLIN GARLAND—Today the great magazines are edited largely for the advertisers.

FRANK P. WALSH—No man should be permitted to work more than eight hours a day.

LAURA JEAN LIBBEY—The average widow is unsuspicious regarding matrimony.

ELLIS O. JONES—Why should Britannia rule the waves. Let the waves rule themselves?

MARY PICKFORD—Children are always so unhappy when they witness the death of flowers.

DR. W. LEE HOWARD—She who motors with open mouth will never have sweet lips to kiss.

OSCAR L. STRAUS—We need a man of the majestic mental stature of Theodore Roosevelt.

H. G. WELLS—The educated and leisure classes have been rotten with individualism for a century.

PROF. R. L. GARNER—I should say that there are not now more than 2000 gorillas in the world.

J. PIERPONT MORGAN—It isn't my job to deal with the international affairs of the United States.

CHARLES S. MELLEN—I'm not so sure that transportation isn't at the bottom of all preparedness.

PRES. WILLIAM DEWITT HYDE—Selecting a professor is almost as solemn an act as taking a wife.

E. LOWES DICKINSON—One of the attractions of war is that it affords an opportunity for the gratifications of passions represt in normal life.

CARDINAL FARLEY—The Papacy stands alone today as the world power for peace and righteousness.

SENATOR SHAFROTH—I do not believe that the right to vote should be dependent on the right to kill.

BISHOP J. F. BERRY—I am absolutely opposed to this highly organized tabernacle form of evangelism.

CONSUL GENERAL CITTADONI—Argentina and the United States are now enjoying their honeymoon.

SENATOR ASHURST—I would like to see the color of the hair of the man who can imprison my thoughts.

SENATOR LA FONTAINE—Your great cities are crushing all neighborliness out of your community life.

DR. MAX BAFF—The runaway germ which impels girls to leave their homes is due to high blood pressure.

THEDA BARA—I have known girls with rosebud mouths and limpid violet eyes—and the hearts of criminals.

PROF. G. F. PEABODY—Not one of the historical creeds of the church pledges a disciple to a consistent Christian life.

MRS. AMELIA E. BARR—For girls to play golf, tennis and other games that rightfully are men's sports is outrageous.

W. J. BRYAN—Those who have nothing but the Eastern metropolitan press to rely upon are fortunate if they get any truth.

SULTAN HUSSEIN KEMAL OF EGYPT—One of the greatest results of the war to the Orient will be the complete emancipation of women.

E. H. SOTHERN—My parting wish is that we may soon see the plays of Shakespeare being presented to the plain people at a nominal price.

JOHN D. ROCKEFELLER, JR.—Some think life is like a layer cake, a layer of ability, some jelly, then a layer of character, then a layer of religion.

G. K. CHESTERTON—The Germans heave up a lumbering wooden doll drest in tintacks to tell us that their culture has found expression at last.

JUST A WORD

We reproduce on the cover this week the spirited statue by Barye, by courtesy of Dr. George Frederick Kunz, of Tiffany & Co.

We are mostly concerned nowadays with the woman of tomorrow and with prophecies, both bright and gloomy, of the place she is to take in the world's work. But Corra Harris, who, as much as any writer of today, has helped to answer the "Woman question" in the light of common sense, finds that the chief importance should be given to The Woman of Yesterday. In an article soon to be published in The Independent she supports convincingly her belief that "The woman of yesterday was the most truly and wisely progressive woman this country has yet produced."

Are you ready? As a nation, as a community, as an individual are you looking to the future and planning how best to meet it? For the secret of achievement is preparedness and "the test and sum of our preparedness is to prepare for life, to fight for opportunity," says Edward Earle Purinton in a stirring appeal for The Man Prepared, the next article in his efficiency series for The Independent.

The Independent

WITH WHICH IS INCORPORATED
HARPER'S WEEKLY

ARMAGEDDON ON THE SEA

OUR eyes have been for so long earthbound and myopic, watching daily gains and losses measured by the yard as on a football field, that we had almost forgotten the possibility of a sudden and decisive combat on the sea. But the thunder of the guns off Skagerak reminds us that the Great War, which seems likely to drag on painfully for another year, might be brought to an end in a single day if the fleets met and fought to a finish in the North Sea. Should it chance that the British fleet was destroyed Germany would easily win the war, for the British Isles, blockaded on all sides, would be soon starved out, and the continental Allies, deprived of British money and munitions, could not hold out long. If, on the other hand, the German fleet should be destroyed, the victory of the Allies would be equally sure, altho perhaps not so easy. It is not certain that the Central Powers could be starved out, altho completely isolated, and Gallipoli has shown that it is practically impossible to break thru a defended coast line even with full command of the sea. If this were possible a British army would long ago have been landed at Zeebrugge on the Belgian coast and so have taken the German army in the rear. But once the German fleet were out of the way the British and Russians would have command of the Baltic as well as the North Sea and the Kiel Canal connecting them. Germany would then have a new frontier to guard, and she has not men enough to do it.

It is this thought that has hitherto kept the German navy safely hid away behind Heligoland, while it was left to the submarines and a few sea rovers to do what they could to harry British commerce. Winston Churchill's threat that if the German warships did not come out of the Kiel Canal soon the British would "dig them out of their holes like rats" did not induce Admiral von Tirpitz to alter his opinion that discretion was, under the circumstances, the better part of valor. Another famous phrase of Churchill's proved his finish, that the British at Gallipoli were "within a few miles of victory," a perfectly true tho misleading statement. After this Mr. Churchill was removed from the position of First Lord of the Admiralty to one better suited to his talents, that of critic of the First Lord of the Admiralty.

But while it was obviously wise for the Kaiser not to risk his precious fleet in a fight that might prove to be fatal, it was equally wise for the British to let it alone so long as it remained bottled up at Kiel. The conse-

quence was that Great Britain has had so far almost as complete freedom of action as tho there had not been a German fleet in being. Her total losses hitherto have probably been less than the new ships built during the war, and in all parts of the world except in European waters her commerce has been practically uninterrupted. English writers discussing strategic problems before the war generally exprest the fear that the German warships would make communication with France difficult if not impossible, and a tunnel was talked of for that reason. They could not have imagined that a British army of two million would be transported to France and kept in supplies by a Channel ferriage more frequent and almost as safe as in times of peace.

SO the North Sea, which the Germans for some reason or perhaps purely by preference call the German Ocean, has remained under British control in spite of the Germans, while the Baltic Sea has remained under German control in spite of the Russians. Traffic between Sweden and Germany across the Baltic has been as free as between England and France across the Channel. No British warships except an occasional submarine have tried to pass thru the narrow and tortuous channels connecting the two seas, the Skagerak and Cattegat, but the Kiel Canal has enabled the German fleet to play hide and seek behind Denmark and appear in either sea as needed. For the last twenty years the Kiel Canal has controlled the peace of Europe. When it was completed in 1895 it doubled the power of the German navy, for it enabled one fleet to patrol both seas. But in 1906 England regained her supremacy on the sea by introducing a new and more formidable fighting machine, the "Dreadnought," that doomed to the scrap-heap all existing battleships. Germany could not outbuild the "Dreadnought" because the Kiel Canal was not deep enough. So the possibility of war was postponed until the canal could be doubled in width and deepened from 29½ feet to 36. This task was undertaken the very next year and on June 24, 1914, the enlarged canal was opened. Five days later the Austrian Crown Prince was shot at Sarajevo and the Great War had virtually begun.

In the ten years since the first "Dreadnought" was launched hundreds of millions of dollars have been put into this new type of battleship, which was tried out for the first time last week between the Skagerak and Kiel. Here, on the last day of May, the greatest naval battle in all history was fought, but whether it will prove to be one of the decisive battles of the world remains to be seen. The vantage lies with the Germans, but the victory is questionable. It appears that the British loss in total tonnage is at least twice that of the German, but the British claim the victory on the ground that the German fleet withdrew from the North Sea.

The British navy was at the beginning of the war twice as strong as the German, according to the estimate of the British Admiralty. In the twenty-two months since both countries have of course been building as rapidly as possible, but nobody knows how they now stand. Great Britain was accustomed to build more ships in a year than all the rest of the world put together, and with the outside world to draw upon and a smaller proportion of her workmen at the front she has probably been able at least to keep her lead. For some years before the war the British Government had allowed its building rate to drop from twice to 1.6 times the rate of German construction, but this was not so much from inability to keep up with the German program as from a belief that a larger navy was not necessary.

But even tho the British supremacy of the sea remains unshaken, it is undeniable that British prestige has received a hard blow. Not since 1667, when a Dutch fleet sailed up the Thames, has the British navy suffered such a shock. The battle-cruisers that were sunk on Wednesday were the pride of the fleet. In the "Times History of the War" of a year ago a naval officer speaks of them in the following fashion. He is describing as an eyewitness the battle of August 28, 1914, when, to use William Watson's infelicitous phrase, "We bit them in the Bight, the Bight of Heligoland":

There straight ahead of us in lordly procession, like elephants walking thru a pack of pi-dogs, came the "Lion," "Queen Mary," "Invincible" and "New Zealand," our battle-cruisers. Great, grim and uncouth as some antediluvian monster, how solid they looked, how utterly earth-quaking!

But now two of these elephants, the "Queen Mary" and the "Invincible," walking thru this pack of pi-dogs, were brought down and four others with them. Altogether since the war began the British have lost twenty-three dreadnoughts and cruisers of over 7000 tons, while the Germans have lost seven, or, according to British belief, nine, of such major warships.

The loss of life in the North Sea battle, some eight thousand, counting both sides, is not more than may fall in a single day at Verdun, yet the sea fight may prove to be more important than the capture of Verdun would be. There is an appalling element of chance in a naval engagement. If the battleship fleet had arrived on the scene an hour earlier, or if the weather had been clearer, the German fleet, we are told, might have been wiped out. On the other hand, if twenty shells of the thousands that the Germans fired had happened to hit a vital spot in the largest British vessels, or if twenty German torpedoes had been true to their aim, the British sea power might have been destroyed. The calculus of probabilities is against such a happening, but one cannot banish the thought of it. Granting that the British are twice as strong as the Germans on the sea, there is, a greater chance that an fleet may beat another twice its strength than that an army should beat another twice its strength. What could not be settled by two years of steady fighting at Ypres and Verdun may possibly be determined any summer afternoon on the

North Sea. Perhaps despite the prophets Armageddon may be fought, not on the land, but on the sea and in the air.

THE MAN IN THE STREET

IF you stopped the first ten men you met on the street and asked them whom they would choose for President, what would they say?

We were curious to find out, so we tried it right in front of The Independent's office, not a hundred paces from Broadway. No straw vote, tho it run into the thousands, is conclusive; we give this one for what it is worth. The answers surprized us; perhaps they will surprize you.

1. *Business man in a hurry, about thirty:* "Wilson for me," with enthusiasm. "I'd vote for him three times if I had the chance."

2. *Young man with Panama and pink carnation. What people from Oshkosh call "typical New York," which means typical Broadway:* "Oh, I don't know. I'm disgusted with the whole thing, and I haven't read the papers. The way sentiment is turning, it looks like Roosevelt. But the public is very fickle; you never can tell."

3. *Prosperous, portly citizen, middle age:* "Wilson, decidedly. He's had experience in extraordinary times, and it doesn't do to swap for an unknown horse."

4. *Ruddy, stocky Teuton, bristly brown mustache:* "Dot iss my bussiness." Enter the hyphen.

5. *Chauffeur, about thirty:* "Wilson. He may not be perfect, but he's as good a man as we can get. He knows the ins and outs better than anybody else."

6. *Hebrew, young man; after much urging:* "I'd vote for a Republican. Yes, Roosevelt if he gets nominated. Wilson? No. No."

7. *Middle-aged business man:* "I'm not voting for Wilson. Roosevelt? No, anybody but that. Republican? Yes, possibly. Any Republican but Teddy."

8. *Elderly business man, white mustache:* "I voted for Wilson last time, but never again. It's Roosevelt for me this time, if I get the chance."

9. *Porter, moving furniture:* "I'm for Wilson. He ain't looking for trouble, and there's plenty of it 'round."

10. *Young fellow, also rather "New York":* "I voted Democratic last year, but this time I've got a leaning toward Teddy. Oh, there's no doubt about his getting nominated. He's got 'em buffaloed. They'll have to take him whether they want him or not, and the country's in something the same position."

That is the poll. The safe and sane Wilson man comes out on top, with plenty of evidence of the spell of the Preëminent Personality. But who's for Hughes?

THE CANADIAN MENACE

THE "Japanese Menace" and the "German Menace" we have been hearing about so long that we have got quite used to them. The "Mexican Menace" has materialized, so we need no longer shiver at it. But the idea that we must prepare without delay to repel an invasion from the north brings a new terror into our peaceful life. It has been a hundred years since we tried to conquer Canada and we had not expected that Canada would try to conquer us for at least a hundred more to come. In fact we had hoped that the mutual invasion of each other's territory by unarmed armies that is going on all the time would prevent any armed aggression for all time.

But it appears not. According to the "preparedness" people we have got to get some guns right away and point them at our Canadian cousins. The Patriot Film Corporation is presenting at the Lyceum Theater, New York, "an object lesson in preparedness to the United States" in which the fortifying of the Canadian frontier as well as other frontiers is urged as essential to our safety. In a very striking motion map the northern border is shown bristling with cannon all the way from Quebec to Vancouver, 42-centimeter caliber or bigger, and enough of them to blow every Canuck to the North Pole or beyond. Of course, thus to erect defenses on our northern border would convert the Anglo-American agreement of 1817 into "a scrap of paper," but what do the "preparedness" people care about that?

What is worse, this plea for the violation of our pledged word to England by fortifying our northern boundary is backed up by a series of films showing that Great Britain has now "a vast and efficient army" of five million. These pictures showing "How Britain Prepared" were, it is stated, "photographed by authority of Hon. Arthur J. Balfour, First Lord of the Admiralty; Earl Kitchener, Minister of War, and the Hon. Lloyd George, Minister of Munitions." If so, to use these really fine films as an argument for arming America against England seems to us a bit discourteous, besides being very foolish and wicked. This exhibition is represented as having the approval of Secretary of War Baker and Assistant Secretary of the Navy Roosevelt, but we venture to doubt whether they realized fully what sort of an argument they were putting their names to.

MR. JUSTICE BRANDEIS

THE confirmation last week by the Senate of Louis D. Brandeis as an Associate Justice of the Supreme Court of the United States, tho belated, is most gratifying. The Republicans, however, by making it a party issue and voting solidly in opposition have committed a serious political blunder. The Democrats will not be slow to make the most of it during the coming campaign. In fact, Mr. Wilson can ask nothing better than to have the Brandeis issue brought before the voters between now and November 4.

But all's well that ends well. Mr. Brandeis, we feel confident, will add luster to the Court and his nomination will tend to strengthen the confidence of the people in its impartiality and freedom from reactionary bias.

NATURAL ALLIES

JOHN BARLEYCORN and the Captain of the Men of Death are an extraordinarily fit team. French physicians have the saying: Consumption is contracted *sur le zinc*—that is, across the bar. Also that alcoholism *fait le lit*, that is, makes the bed, of consumption. The physician Lancereaux computes that more than half the cases of tuberculosis among men have been chronic alcoholics. And any interne working in the male wards of any large charity hospital will express the same half and half proportion. Physicians declare that consumption is more frequent in heavy drinkers than in people of moderate habits in the proportion of three to one.

So much for the idea a good many people have that whisky cures, or helps in the cure of, consumption. Pulmonary tuberculosis is almost invariably found in persons who have died in the course of chronic alcoholism; abdominal tuberculosis is pretty sure to accompany hobnail liver. Acute ("galloping") consumption is all the more "hasty" in alcoholics, who must inevitably succumb. The English physician Kellynack has found eighty per cent of consumption in patients that

have died of alcoholic neuritis; and Osler's proportion in such cases is eight in eleven.

By no means all men whose alcoholism has led to consumption have been ill-intentioned. Many workmen, of a cold winter's morning, will take their dram before going to work, not to satisfy a vicious appetite, but in the hope of tiding their below par constitutions over another day. And the stuff they do take down!—fusel oil, wood alcohol whisky—"the kind of stuff you put on old doors to scrape off the paint with." One must remember, too, the concomitants of whiskey in these circumstances—insanitary habits, poverty, sunlessness, ill-ventilated living rooms, lack of nutrition, bad food, wifely ignorance of how to cook—and the lack of a living wage. Also there is the baneful property of stimulants when taken into an empty stomach—to give a transient sense of sufficiency and to destroy the appetite for food.

CONGRESSIONAL POETRY

CONGRESSMEN haven't time to give sufficient consideration to the river and harbor bill, the preparedness bill, the immigration bill, the Philippine bill and other measures of this kind. One reason why they haven't time is because they waste it. Recently Mr. Moore of Pennsylvania moved to strike out the last word of the agricultural bill in order that the Clerk of the House should read the following unoriginal poem which he regarded as applicable to the question of the appropriation for the eradication of the bugs infesting cotton, tobacco and sugar cane:

> Eat a plate of fine pigs' knuckles
> And the headstone cutter chuckles,
> 　While the gravedigger makes a note upon his cuff.
> Eat that lovely red bologna
> And you'll wear a wooden kimono,
> 　As your relatives start scrapping 'bout your stuff.
>
> Some little bug is going to find you some day,
> Some little bug will creep behind you some day;
> 　Eating juicy sliced pineapple
> 　Makes the sexton dust the chapel;
> Some little bug is going to find you some day.

The *Congressional Record* devotes nearly a column to this stuff at the expense of the taxpayer for time lost and printing. And the men who are responsible for this sort of thing are the same who propose to establish a censorship over the motion pictures of the United States! What the country needs more is a board of censors for Congress, one to censor their poetry, one to censor their science and one to give them some notion of efficiency.

THE HONORABLE HYPHEN

THAT the hyphen may weld—and not separate—two nationalities is a possibility which we seem to find little reason for remembering these days. We are scathing in our criticism of the immigrant who fails to become a true American, but we pay little attention to the means by which his transformation must be accomplished. We forget that the hyphenated American should be simply the American in the making.

Fortunately the immigrants do not wait for us to Americanize them, but go ahead finding their own opportunities and creating their own agencies for assimilation. Among these perhaps the most important are the 1500 foreign language newspapers published in the United States, which reach daily an audience of nine million people, most of whom have no other way of learning about American ideals and institutions. Naturally their editorial influence is enormous and their responsibility proportionate.

Recently some of these papers have proved their keen realization of this responsibility by publishing the following announcement of their aim:

> To help preserve the ideals and sacred traditions of this, our adopted country, the United States of America. To revere its laws and inspire others to respect and obey them. To strive unceasingly to quicken the public's sense of civic duty. In all ways to aid in making this country greater and better than we found it.

This is a statement of which every American may well be proud. It shows intelligent purpose as well as stedfast loyalty. And, best of all, these foreign language papers seem to be practising what they preach. Many of them publish daily lessons in English, civics, history and the methods of acquiring citizenship in the United States. They are now even proposing to hold a conference of the foreign language editors of America for the purpose of uniting on a definite program of Americanization. That program may well be worthy of our earnest consideration—whether we are owners of an actual hyphen or merely of a framed facsimile from the Society of Genealogical Research.

FIAT TIME

THE Kaiser has decreed that noon shall be called one o'clock from May 1 to October 1: France, Denmark and other European countries followed the example of Germany. England, where the scheme was first proposed, was the last of the Powers to adopt it, but on May 21 the British clocks were by act of Parliament set ahead one hour. Luxemburg and Ireland, as we should expect, decline to concur with the rest of Europe.

The change was made as a war measure for the purpose of economizing on light and heat and it remains to be seen whether it will prove to have sufficient advantages to compensate for its manifest inconveniences. It has been talked about for ten years. Now we shall see it tried.

As a war measure it may be justified like fiat money and bread tickets. Nobody knows how much a mark is worth, tho it is suspected to be worth considerably less than twenty-four cents. If setting the clock wrong will make the English go to bed earlier it will doubtless reduce the danger from Zeppelins and perhaps have a good influence on health and morals.

But it appears doubtful whether a permanent change in habits can be effected by such a simple trick. Many people have tried to speed themselves by keeping their watches five minutes fast or setting their alarm clock half an hour ahead of the time when they must get up. But such self-deception does not last long with persons of intelligence. They soon get to allowing for it as they do for a banquet that is announced for "7:30 sharp" and really begins at 8.

So we question whether setting the alarm clocks of a nation one hour too fast by law will make people get up earlier or go to bed earlier in the long run. If they really wanted to get up earlier they could do it now, most of them, without any legislation. The early morning hours are highly spoken of by poets who nevertheless are apt, like the rest of us, to spend them in bed.

The fact of the matter is that people prefer darkness to daylight for their hours of recreation, and whenever they get money and leisure enough they shift their working day to later hours. It is the object of all social climbers to get to a stage where they can stop breakfasting by lamplight and take to dining by lamplight. As the days get longer the dinners get later. When the theaters give a performance in the daytime they exclude the light. The amusement parks are very dull places until the electricity is turned on. The lights of the Great White Way are mostly used for decoration, not illumination.

The advocates of the change call it a "daylight-saving" measure and present figures to show what a great economy would be effected by setting the clock ahead. But we question if people want to save daylight and we are skeptical of the economy. The basis of the argument is that sunlight is always cheaper and better than artificial light, but this is not necessarily the case. In a great city sunlight is expensive. One can rent a dark room and provide it with electric light cheaper than he can rent a sunlit room. Writers and students, who can arrange their hours to suit themselves and have tried both plans, often come to the conclusion that they can work better at night than in the daytime. Much of the prejudice against artificial light has been carried over from the days when the faint and flickering candle or the foul smelling kerosene was the only means of illumination. So, too, some of the calculations of daylight-saving that appear in American papers are borrowed from the British without allowing for the fact that England is in the latitude of Labrador and that north of Edinburgh it is twilight all night in the summer time. We even hear it said that there are more hours of daylight before noon than after noon in summer and so the clocks should be set ahead!

The maximum amount of daylight work is obtained at all seasons of the year when noon comes in the middle of the working day. Shifting it earlier would allow some of the workers to go to bed soon after dark—if they want to—but it would compel others to get up before dark. To make milkmen, newsboys, market men, domestic servants and factory operatives and their wives lose their summer privilege of lying abed till daybreak in order that a few employers may have time to play golf in the afternoon is not fair play. So the tradesunionists of Germany view the change with disfavor.

Farmers go by the sun anyway, so a change in nominal time would not affect them. Most factories and business houses could, if they wished, set their hours ahead in the summer time and if there was any great demand on the part of patrons or employees for such a change they would do so. But so long as there seems no disposition to make such a change on the part of those who are now at liberty to arrange their hours to suit themselves it would be bad policy to trick them into it by monkeying with the clock. The Kaiser's decree sounds too much like Jack Cade's reform proposals: "There shall be in England seven half-penny loaves sold for a penny; the three hooped pot shall have ten hoops." Since time and tide wait for no man it would be better for man to adjust himself to them rather than pretend to alter them. As to the working of the plan in England all we hear so far is that the clocks have all joined in the forward movement, but the sundials have unanimously adopted a policy of passive resistance.

HARD CHOOSING

CAN'T YOU TALK?

CAN'T YOU STOP TALKING?

Roosevelt or Hughes? The Old Guard will reluctantly accept Hughes in order to beat Roosevelt. The Old Guard will reluctantly coöperate with Roosevelt in order to beat Hughes. The Old Guard will negotiate with the Progressives thru conference committees and nominate a candidate who will command Roosevelt's support. The Old Guard is at sea and has lost its grip of the convention.

These rumors were characteristic of the last few days before the Republican and Progressive National Conventions opened at Chicago on June 7, and one could take his pick. The one thing clear was that these two candidates, active and passive (or neuter?) dominated the thought of the delegates, and that while the definite refusal of the Progressives to accept a still silent Hughes, together with the definite refusal of the Republicans to take Roosevelt, might lead to a compromise candidate, the choice was most likely to lie between the two men.

Colonel Roosevelt finished a Middle Western tour on June 1, with a speech at Newark, New Jersey. He was heard with great enthusiasm at Kansas City and St. Louis. Justice Hughes said nothing during the week, not even "No." His secretary denied that Frank H. Hitchcock, former chairman of the Republican National Committee, who has been heading the Hughes workers, was acting on the authority of the Justice, but as Mr. Hitchcock had already repudiated any such claim, the announcement was not of material importance. More significant was the visit of three German-American editors and publishers to Chairman Hilles of the Republican National Committee to announce that the German-American voters would never accept either Roosevelt or Root, but would support Hughes.

Tho Root, Fairbanks and Burton somewhat emerged from the swarm of favorite sons, the principal activity on behalf of that aspiring company was a series of dickers for the Vice-Presidency. The respective managers of the less conspicuous candidates, however, claimed first-ballot votes as follows: Weeks, 200; Burton, 112; Cummins, 106; Fairbanks, 93; Root, 75; Sherman, 65; Knox, 56; Brumbaugh, 41; Ford, 30; LaFollette, 26; General Wood, 15; DuPont, 14; Borah, 5.

Mr. Justice Brandeis After more than four months' delay, the nomination of Louis D. Brandeis to be an associate justice of the Supreme Court was confirmed by the Senate on June 1. The vote was 47 to 22, one Democrat, Newlands of Nevada, voting against confirmation on the ground that Mr. Brandeis was lacking in the judicial temperament, and three Republicans voting with the Democratic majority.

THE CONVENTIONS

Republican National Convention at Chicago June 7.

Progressive National Convention at Chicago June 7.

Democratic National Convention at St. Louis June 14.

Harold J. Howland, associate editor of The Independent, will report the three conventions. His first article, summarizing and analyzing the action of the Chicago conventions, will be published, with convention photographs, in The Independent for next week, dated June 19, 1916.

House Passes Navy Bill While the news of the Battle of Jutland reached the House of Representatives too late to affect details of the Naval Appropriation Bill, which was passed on June 2, the destruction of the British battle-cruisers is likely to influence the action of the Senate, which now takes up the bill. The House appropriated a total of about $270,000,000, with a building program of no dreadnoughts, five battle-cruisers, four scout cruisers, ten destroyers, fifty submarines, and one fuel ship. Probably the result of the sea fight will lead to the addition of two dreadnoughts to this program, perhaps at the expense of the battle-cruisers. The Republican minority in the House fought for these dreadnoughts, as well as for additional vessels in all classes, and a motion whose effect would have been to adopt this minority plan was lost by the close vote of 189 to 183.

Important amendments made last week increased the number of submarines from twenty to fifty, and the appropriation from $2,000,000 to $3,500,000 (both at the initiative of the Republican minority); provided for a government armor-plate plant at a cost of eleven millions; and appropriated six millions for equipment in the navy yards to make possible the building of capital ships at Philadelphia, Puget Sound, Norfolk and Boston, and construction work at other yards in case private contractors should not offer satisfactory terms. A curious addition to the bill authorizes the President to initiate an international court of arbitration. Since the Senate has already passed a bill providing for a government armor-plate plant that provision now needs only the President's approval.

Los Angeles, Long Beach, San Diego, Duluth and Superior will divide over a million and a half dollars of Rivers and Harbors money if the additions made by the Senate to the House bill are accepted in conference. The total appropriation as the bill was passed by the Senate came to about $44,000,000. The Republicans, charg-

---

ing that the bill was a grossly extravagant pork-barrel measure, and aided by several Democrats, had been filibustering against it for more than a month, and the majority in its favor was only three votes.

Carranza Charges Bad Faith The Mexican situation is still muddled. After delay and general denials that such action was contemplated, the Mexican Ambassador-designate at Washington presented, on May 31, a garrulous and offensive note from Carranza. It charged that the United States was acting in a way to justify the suspicion that it expected to fight Mexico, and demanded a precise statement of American intentions and an immediate withdrawal of American troops in Mexico.

Meanwhile, however, General Obregon continued to dispose his troops so as to coöperate with the American forces in policing Chihuahua, and General Gavira, Carranza's local commander, conferred amicably with General Pershing as to details of this program. No immediate answer was made to the note, and the Administration was inclined to minimize its importance, and by no means to withdraw the expeditionary force until Carranza's ability to keep order was proved.

The note may be summarized as follows: General Pershing's force was sent into Mexico, "thru error or haste," before the conclusion of any protocol permitting such action. No agreement having been reached at the El Paso conference, and General Scott, according to the Mexican version, having admitted there that Villa's band was dispersed, there was no longer either legality or apparent justification for the military presence in Mexico of American troops. The subsequent pursuit of the Glen Springs raiders by Major Langhorne, in violation of General Scott's alleged promise that no more soldiers would enter Mexico, tended "to convince the Mexican Government that something more than a mere error is involved."

The Mexican Government, after having made clear its unwillingness to permit the crossing of new American troops into Mexican territory, will have to consider the latter as an act of invasion of its territory, and therefore it will be forced to defend itself against any group of American troops which may be found within it.

Tho the President had emphatically declared that the action of the United States was wholly disinterested, there was evidence of warlike intentions on the part of the military forces, for the troops had not been withdrawn when their work was done, the United States declined to limit operations to a border zone, Mexican rebels were equipt and armed on American soil, and shipments of arms and machinery to the Carranza government were held up in the United States.

. . . There has been a great discrepancy between the protests of sincere friendly coöperation on the part of the American authorities and the actual attitude of the expedition, which, on account of its distrust, its secrecy regarding its movements and the arms at its disposal, clearly indicated that it was a hostile expedition and a real invasion of our territory.

The note was well received in Mexico City and may have been intended chiefly, in the new diplomatic phrase, "for home consumption." Several of its premises are contradicted by the facts as American officials hold them.

Actors in the A. F. of L. The Actors' Equity Association, which has 3,000 members among "legitimate" actors, voted on May 29 to affiliate with the American Federation of Labor. Its president, Francis Wilson, explains that the step was taken to secure

the wonderful psychological effect such a power has on the minds of our opponents. They feel then that for the first time in our existence we have the power, whether we exert it or not—and, mark you, it is generally not exerted—that we have the power to call a strike, the power to call into operation a boycott under the guidance of past masters in the art. It is the logical offset to the present blacklist.

At present the association is confining its efforts to securing for its members what it calls an equitable contract, which adjusts transportation allowances, limits the period of free rehearsals, requires two weeks' notice—thus assuring that much salary to the cast of a play that fails, provides extra pay for extra performances, and requires full pay for the week before Christmas and Holy Week, when half salaries are usually paid.

This contract has been for some time in use by Daniel Frohman, and it has been adopted in whole or in part by other managers. David Belasco and others object to the union as "undignified." As the musicians and stage mechanics are now unionized, and vaudeville performers are organized as the "White Rats," the coercive power of those employed in the theaters will be considerable if the new union can maintain its solidarity.

Three Labor Disputes The cloak, suit and skirt lockout in New York, which has kept 30,000 garment workers idle for six weeks, became a strike on June 1, when the 409 shops of the Cloak, Suit and Skirt Manufacturers' Protective Association opened their doors and invited their employees to return to work, for practically none of the union workers went back to their machines. Another 30,000 are striking against the members of the Mutual Cloak and Suit Manufacturers' Association, composed of manufacturers who were nominally independent, but have now formally allied themselves with the other group in fighting the union. The strikers stand for the abolition of sweatshops, a 48-hour week, an arbitration agreement, a guarantee of the preferential union shop, and a wage increase. The manufacturers, who forfeited public support by repudiating the award of

the Mayor's Council of Conciliation, refuse to concede or to arbitrate what they declare to be the vital issues: the right of discharge and the closed shop. In a statement they explain that they declared the lockout to forestall a threatened strike in July, which is the busy season, and state their conclusion, after six years of experiment with arbitration and conciliation, that "adjustments by such methods do not result in substantial justice."

The Manufacturers' Association looked for a gradual return of several thousand workers to their places. Union leaders, however, expected to be able to hold out until July, when the strike would be most embarrassing to the employers.

The Commercial Telegraphers' Union, with 30,000 members, threatened a strike on the eve of the Republican National Convention. Their principal grievance is that the Western Union admittedly makes a practice of discharging men who are found to belong to the union, but they also want an eight-hour day and a ten per cent wage increase. Secretary Wilson sent Roland B. Mahany, of the Bureau of Mediation of the Department of Labor, to treat with the union at its convention in New York last week, and owing largely to his efforts immediate action was postponed, pending an investigation ordered by the Massachusetts Legislature into the discharge of union telegraphers in Boston.

A big piece of collective bargaining was begun on June 1, when representatives of 235 railway systems, with 250,000 miles of tracks, met the delegates of the four great railway brotherhoods, with a total of 350,000 members, to ne-

gotiate the demands of the workers and counterdemands of the railroads. The unions ask, in freight, yard and hostling service (a railroad hostler cares for a locomotive between runs and takes it in and out of the roundhouse), an eight-hour day, with time and a half for overtime. It is the overtime charges that make up a large part of the $100,000,000 increase in running expenses which the railroads say they will have to assume if the demands are granted, and which will put a stop to all expenditures for improvements. But the men declare that since 65 per cent of all freight trains make more than ten miles per hour it will be possible to do a day's run, 100 miles, in eight hours, and overtime pay will normally not be necessary. The union delegates have no power to call a strike or to accept arbitration, but are instructed simply to negotiate for these concessions. The hearings are public and both sides have taken steps to enlist public sympathy.

A Week of Pageantry The outdoor dramatic spectacle has gripped American fancy so completely that one hears of scores of pageants, masques and plays at a time, and the commencement season is filling many campuses with revels, Shakespearean and otherwise, but mostly Shakespearean this year.

The great spectacles of the month have been seen in New York City and Newark, New Jersey. The Shakespeare Masque in New York, "Caliban by the Yellow Sands," was presented ten times in the stadium of the College of the City of New York, from May 24 to June 5, to audiences ranging from

THE FROST OF THE PROPHETS
Every year the men and women of the Art Students' League in New York hold a burlesque exhibit of their own. Ordinarily it satirizes the Academy of Design exhibit. But this year the art students have gone further afield for their victims

THE GREAT SEA FIGHT OF THE GREAT WAR

The German fleet, coming probably out of the Kiel Canal, but perhaps out of the Skagerak, was met in the afternoon of May 31 by Admiral Beatty's fleet of swift cruisers and a twelve hour battle ensued. Toward night the British superdreadnoughts, presumably from Firth of Forth, arrived on the scene and the Germans retired to the shelter of their mine fields behind Helgoland.

See, in addition to the account on this page, the article on page 439

17,000 to 21,000. It was the climax of the Tercentenary Celebration in New York, and was the result chiefly of the initiative and energy of Miss Mary Porter Beegle, chairman of the Festival Committee of the New York branch of the Drama League. Percy MacKaye wrote the masque; Arthur Farwell composed the music; Joseph Urban, Robert E. Jones (who designed the setting for Barker's production of "The Man Who Married a Dumb Wife") and Mrs. John W. Alexander were responsible for the setting and the costumes; Joseph Ordynski was director.

As Mr. MacKaye explained in The Independent for April 10, 1916, the theme of the masque was the civilizing influence of the theater on brute man—Caliban, who in the person of Lionel Braham was a huge and dominating figure. Ten fragments from Shakespeare's plays were presented on a superbly designed inner stage, and there were many dance interludes, of which the most spirited was an Elizabethan May-day presented by the English Folk Dance Society. The various historical interludes were given in part by national groups—the Germanic epoch by the German University League, for instance—and the assembling of the 1500 performers was a notable piece of coöperation. A number of distinguished actors, among them John Drew

as William Shakespeare and Edith Wynne Matthison as Miranda, were volunteer participants. A permanent organization in the interest of community drama is being formed as the outgrowth of this successful experiment.

In Newark, at a natural amphitheater in Weequahic Park, a pageant and masque were given from May 30 to June 2 to audiences of 40,000 and over. The two hundred and fifty years of the city's history were summarized in a pageant created by Thomas Wood Stevens, author of the St. Louis Pageant of 1914. It began, after a prolog devoted to the Lenni Lenape, who held New Jersey when the white man came, with the settlement of the city in 1666 by Robert Treat and his Puritans from Connecticut and carried the narrative thru four episodes.

The pageant ended with a masque in which the city's future was symbolized, Strife, Greed and Ignorance yielding to Religion, Education and Law, and representatives of all nations taking their place in Newark's life.

Under the direction of Mr. Stevens and H. Wellington Wack, executive adviser, the performance was carefully planned and executed, even to the addition of three barrels of bluing to the artificial lagoon in front of the natural stage for the sake of precise decorative harmony.

The Greatest of Naval Battles The event that has been anxiously expected for twenty-two months has at last come to pass. For the first time in history two modern fleets have come in conflict. The superdreadnought has been put to the ordeal of battle.

The details of the battle are obscure, but from the various accounts the general course of events is tolerably clear. The engagement began with battle-cruisers on both sides, but later they were joined by German and British battleships. The battle-cruiser is a new type of vessel that aims to combine the highest possible speed with the greatest possible gun power. Naturally something has to be sacrificed, and in this case it is defensive armor. For instance, the battleship "Warspite" has a belt of 13½-inch armor, while the battle-cruiser "Queen Mary," almost as large, has only 9-inch. Battle-cruisers usually carry eight guns, of 12-inch caliber on the "Invincible," of 13½-inch on the "Queen Mary." They can make 26 or more knots an hour, but they are not able to stand punishment like the regular battleship. For safety the battle-cruiser depends mostly upon its speed, which enables it to keep its distance and pound the enemy at long range.

A cruiser squadron under Vice-Admiral Sir David Beatty while patroling the North Sea on the afternoon of May 31 encountered a similar squadron about 150 miles west of the Danish coast and 125 south of the Norwegian. The British flagship was the "Lion," and with her were the "Queen Mary," "Tiger," "Princess Royal" and "Indefatigable," besides lighter cruisers and minor craft.

The German advance squadron under the command of Rear-Admiral Hipper was inferior to the British, but this was soon reinforced by the most powerful of the German battleships, which had at first been kept in the background and concealed by the mists along the Jutland coast. Vice-Admiral Reinhard Scheer was in command. The battle joined about four in the afternoon and kept up until it was too dark to fire, but the torpedo boats and destroyers of both sides continued their activity all thru the night.

The battle-cruisers opened fire at a distance of fifteen miles, but soon closed in to ten, and finally to five. A second British squadron, composed of the "Invincible," "Indomitable" and "Inflexible," under Rear-Admiral Horace Wood, came to the aid of Admiral Beatty, and shortly before dark the largest vessels of the British navy, the superdreadnoughts completed since the war began, the "Warspite," "Barham," "Valiant" and "Malaya," with Admiral Sir John Jellicoe in command, appeared on the scene, but too late to take an active part in the fight.

The Germans had one decided advantage over the British. They had eyes in the air. Their Zeppelin warned them of the approach of the main British fleet and they retired under cover of the night to their base at the en-

LOSSES IN NORTH SEA BATTLE

British

Name	Tonnage
Queen Mary (battle-cruiser)	27,000
Indefatigable (battle-cruiser)	18,750
Invincible (battle-cruiser)	17,250
Defense (armored cruiser)	14,600
Warrior (armored cruiser)	13,550
Black Prince (armored cruiser)	13,550
Tipperary (destroyer)	1,850
Turbulent (destroyer)	1,850
Shark (destroyer)	950
Sparrowhawk (destroyer)	950
Ardent (destroyer)	950
Fortune (destroyer)	950
Nomad (destroyer)	950
Nestor (destroyer)	950
Total (fourteen ships)	**114,100**

German

Name	Tonnage
Pommern (battleship)	13,200
Wiesbaden (cruiser)	5,600
Frauenlob (cruiser)	2,715
Elbing (cruiser)	5,000
Six destroyers (reported)	6,000
Total (ten ships)	**32,515**

[Reported by British, but not admitted by Germany]

Westfalen (dreadnought)	18,600
Derfflinger (battle-cruiser)	26,200
Another battle-cruiser	26,200
A light cruiser	4,870
One submarine	1,000
Three destroyers	2,000

trance to the Kiel Canal. Here the British could not pursue them because of the mine fields which are laid all about Heligoland.

The losses, so far as they are known, are given in the accompanying table. On the British side the chief loss is the "Queen Mary," a battle-cruiser of the largest size and armament, completed the year before the war. She had on board about a thousand officers and men, and of these only eight are known to have been saved. The Germans at first claimed to have sunk the "Warspite," a still more important vessel, but this was apparently a mistake for the "Invincible," which the Germans did not include in their list of British losses. The "Invincible" took to the bottom with her all on board, some 780, including Admiral Hood. More than five thousand men must have perished on the British side and at least half as many on the German.

The German Admiralty report mentioned no losses except the "Pommern," a battleship of the predreadnought type, and three small cruisers, the "Wiesbaden," "Frauenlob" and "Ebling."

But the British Admiralty asserts that the official statement of the German losses is certainly false:

We cannot yet be sure of the exact truth, but from such evidence as has come to our knowledge, the Admiralty entertains no doubt that the German losses were heavier than the British, not merely relative to the strength of the two fleets, but absolutely.

Bulgars Enter Greece　It has been repeatedly rumored that the Allied troops at Salonica were preparing for an invasion of Bulgaria or Serbia as soon as the season was far enough advanced. The French and British troops stationed here during the winter are supposed to number two or three hundred thousand and they were reinforced in April by the Serbian soldiers, who after being driven out of their own country were conveyed to the Greek island of Corfu and there recuperated and reorganized.

The opposing lines are held by some three hundred thousand Bulgars and such Austrian and German troops as still remain on the Balkan front. But it has been reported that Bulgarian soldiers are in the Austrian army in Italy and in the German army in France, and some of the Serbs are said to have been transported to France, so it is impossible to make any true estimate of the number of troops on either side.

Hitherto the Bulgars have scrupulously refrained from violating Greek territory, notwithstanding the fact that it had been occupied by the armies of the Allies. Now, however, they seem to have determined to take the initiative and they have crost the boundary to the northeast of Salonica. Here the Bulgo-Greek frontier is formed by an almost impassable range of mountains, thru which runs the Struma River by the Rupel Defile. A body of 25,000 troops have come thru this pass from the Bulgarian side and occupied Demir-hissar, ten miles within the Greek line. The Greek garrison evacuated under protest, but without resistance, as they did when the Allies occupied their fortifications on the Serbian frontier. The Bulgarian, German and Austrian officers signed a promise to restore the forts as soon as the military necessity for holding them had ceased and to indemnify Greece for any damage done by the occupation.

This move gives the Bulgars command of the railroad running east from Salonica to Constantinople and affords them an opportunity to attack the Allies on the right flank if they advance north into Serbia.

The Austrian Offensive　In the third week of their advance from the Trentino the Austrians seem to have made less progress than at first. Whether this apparent slackening is due to the diversion of Austrian troops to Verdun, as the French report, or whether it is merely that it takes time to bring up ammunition thru the mountain passes and to establish the 38-centimeter howitzers in new positions cannot yet be ascertained.

During the first fortnight of their offensive, according to the Vienna account, the Austrians captured 30,388

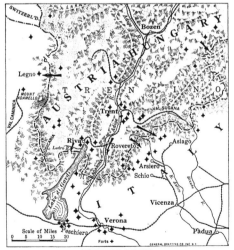

THE TRENTINO CAMPAIGN

The Austrians are attempting to invade Italy from the Tirolean Alps by way of the Adige, the Astico and the Brenta rivers. On the first and third of these valleys, the Val Lagarina and the Val Sugana, they are making little progress, but between these, they have advanced down the Astico River and crossed the frontier, where they are now threatening Schio, Arsiero and Asiago. If they break thru the Italian defenses here they may keep on to Vicenza and perhaps even to Padua and Venice. The shaded area is Austrian territory before the war. The arrows indicate their advance

Italian prisoners, including 694 officers, and took 298 cannon. The valleys of the Astico and Brenta rivers were sufficiently cleared to enable the Austrians to cross the frontier and come within reach of the Italian towns on the southeastern slopes of the Tirolean Alps. Three of these towns stand in a row about ten miles inside the Italian boundary, Schio, Arsiero and Asiago, barring the way to Vicenza, with which they are connected by a single line of railroad. The hills in front of them were fortified long before the war for the purpose of meeting just such an Austrian attack as they now must support, but it remains to be seen how long they can endure the shock of modern artillery. All three towns have been evacuated by their civilian population. Arsiero, as the foremost and midmost of the three, has to stand the brunt of the attack. The Austrian troops, debouching from the mountains, have crost the Porsina torrent, which runs just south of Arsiero into the Astico River, and are now in a position to take this town or to strike at Schio on their right or Asiago on their left. On account of his failure to fortify the passes thru which the Austrians are now invading Italy, General Brusati, hitherto commander-in-chief of the Italian armies in the Trentino, has been relieved of his command.

Attack on Ft. Vaux   The hundredth day of the battle of Verdun saw the Germans within two miles and a half of their goal. Fresh troops have been brought up from the other fields and the attacks renewed with redoubled vigor. The French say that they have never had to face such furious artillery fire or to withstand such fierce assaults as during the past week, German troops recently stationed in Russia, Serbia and Belgium have appeared at Verdun and, according to the French account, 50,000 or more Austrian troops have also been brought here. We might expect that the withdrawal of troops from these fronts would have so weakened the lines that the Russians, Italians or British might assume the offensive with some chance of success, but there is as yet no evidence of such activity on their part.

The Germans have followed their custom of attacking alternately on the western and the eastern side of the Meuse, and made gains on both. The situation in the two sectors is curiously the same, that is, the French line projects in a loop about a hill and the Germans are trying to cut it off by capturing the woods behind. On the west the hill is La Mort Homme, of which the French still hold some of the slopes. Behind it is the forest of Caurettes, which the Germans are striving to penetrate from the village of Cumières, a railroad station on the bank of the Meuse, as well as from Hill 304 on the other side. But even if they succeed, as they seem likely to, in cutting off the French salient and bringing their own line down to Chattancourt, they will still have before them what is supposed to be the hardest part of

their task, that is, the capture of the permanent fortifications that cover the hights between Chattancourt and Verdun.

On the other side of the Meuse the French have not been able to hold Fort

Underwood
THE MOST SUCCESSFUL AUSTRIAN
Field Marshal Conrad von Hoetzendorff, chief of the Austrian General Staff, is in charge, with Archduke Frederick, of the important offensive which has once more put the Austrian army on the map—the map of Italy

Douaumont, which they recovered a fortnight ago by an unexpected offensive. By a succession of mass attacks the Germans drove the French out of the fort and of the trenches beyond. Then they carried Caillette Wood that lies behind, taking there 2000 prisoners. This brings them also in the rear of Fort Vaux, which they are also attacking from Damloup on the other side. The capture of these points would give the Germans possession of the plateau lying northwest of Verdun and within two miles of that city.

While increasing their efforts at Verdun, the Germans are also keeping up their attacks upon the British front in Belgium. Southeast of Ypres, where the Canadians hold the ridges between Zillebeke and the famous Hill 60, the fighting has been incessant. Here the Germans took the front line on the evening of June 2, and during the fol-

lowing night they carried by storm the trenches beyond to a depth of 700 yards. Much of this ground was recovered by repeated charges of the Canadians on the next morning. Both sides lost heavily in these operations. The Germans report the capture of 15 officers and 350 unwounded men. Two generals of the Third Canadian Division, General Mercer and General Williams, who were inspecting the front trenches, were lost.

A Disastrous Antarctic Expedition   Sir Ernest Shackleton, who started out in August, 1914, to cross the Antarctic continent, has returned without having even been able to reach that continent. The relief expedition which was sent out to meet him on the other side of the Pole likewise had to return unsuccessful. Both expeditions had to leave parties behind whom it is hardly possible to rescue.

This is Shackleton's third attempt to reach the South Pole. As a lieutenant in the Royal Navy he accompanied Scott in his dash for the Pole in 1901, but broke down on the way back to the coast. In 1908 he returned with an expedition of his own and got within ninety-seven miles of the Pole, when he was obliged to turn back on account of a shortage in provisions. For this achievement he was knighted, but the Norwegian explorer, Amundsen, reached the Pole December 16, 1911, about a month ahead of Scott.

Shackleton's present expedition, fitted out by the gift of an unknown friend at a cost of $375,000, was the best equipt of any that have attacked the Antarctic. It was his intention to enter the continent south of Cape Horn, penetrate to the Pole and come out on the side opposite New Zealand. The "Endurance" left the island of South Georgia in December, 1914, but as it approached the Antarctic coast it was caught among the ice floes, from which it never escaped. In July the ice had piled about the ship in ridges forty feet high. By fall the pressure had become so terrific as to throw the ship up upon the ice. When the ice broke up the "Endurance" was so strained and leaky that she was abandoned on October 27 and sank a month later.

The party rescued such supplies as they could and camped all winter on the ice, which was drifting toward the north. In April they came within reach of Elephant Island, one of the South Shetland group. Here Shackleton left most of his party and with five men set out in a small boat for South Georgia Island. This he reached two weeks later and walked across the island over the glaciers to Stromness, where there is a Norwegian whaling station. South Georgia Island had been visited by German scientists, but no one had ever ventured to cross it before. With a boat and crew provided by the Norwegians, Shackleton tried to rescue the party left on Elephant Island, but could not reach it, so he went to the Falkland Islands for help.

THE GREAT WAR
May 29—Austrians attacking defenses of Arsiero, Italy.
May 30—Germans take Caurette woods from Cumières, northwest of Meuse River.
May 31—Great battle on the North Sea between British and German fleets.
June 1—Germans take Caillette woods behind Vaux, northeast of Verdun.
June 2—Germans take British trenches at Zillebeke.
June 3—Austrians take 5000 Italian prisoners near Asiago.
June 4—British Admiralty claim that eighteen German ships were sunk in Wednesday's fight.

CALIFORNIA: In 1909 President Taft withdrew from settlement certain lands in the Mariposa district of this state on which there were no settlers and on which no discovery of oil had been made. Subsequently, several oil companies entered that field and took millions of dollars' worth of oil from it. Ever since that time the government has been trying to oust those companies and get an accounting of the oil taken. Now the United States District Court, sitting at Fresno, has rendered a decision authorizing prosecution of six suits against more than 100 defendants for such accounting. It is said this decision means more than $5,000,000 to the United States; and there are twenty other similar suits pending.

COLORADO: Under the leadership of the women of the Civic League, "Plant Day" is celebrated each year by practically the entire population of Colorado Springs. On that day the league receives contributions of plants and seeds, which it distributes among householders who promise to plant and care for them. This spring it made a new departure by converting a portion of the grounds of one of the public schools into a flower garden, which the pupils have promised to care for thruout the year. The league's plan is to provide a similar garden for one additional school each year. As another part of the general scheme of beautifying the city, the County Agriculturist is organizing boys' and girls' clubs for converting vacant lots from weed patches and making dumping grounds into vegetable gardens.

DELAWARE: The Wilmington Board of Health is being severely criticized for the manner in which it handled the recent smallpox flurry in that city. It is generally admitted that the first steps were taken with commendable promptness and energy. All houses in which the disease was found to have existed were at once quarantined, and schools, churches, theaters, saloons and other places where people were likely to congregate were ordered closed. Almost immediately, however, the order closing the saloons was rescinded, while those against the other places were left in force. The charge is freely made that even in so important a matter the board could not resist the temptation to play politics.

FLORIDA: Thru the efforts of the Children's Homes Society of Florida, a bill was passed by the last legislature providing for a commission to investigate and report on the need of a law to pension indigent mothers by the state. This commission has now been organized and sufficient work has been done by it to warrant the belief that its report to the next session of the legislature will recommend the enactment of such a law. In this work the Florida Sunday School Association has given notable aid. In its recent state-wide observance of Mothers' Day the subject of these pensions was made a prominent feature.

IDAHO: Work has been begun on a new irrigation system and a parallel electric railroad leading from Boise into the new territory, which is locally known as the Bruneau country. The system, installed under the Carey Act, will reclaim about 75,000 acres of land. One of the provisions of the contract is that no land is to be sold by the promoting company until water is running in the canals. The railroad which will connect this section with Boise will pass thru the Grandview project also, and will cut the Oregon Short Line railroad at Orchard.

INDIANA: As one of the monuments to be erected in this her centennial year, Indiana proposes to establish a number of state parks for the preservation of her most impressive scenic tracts and historic spots. Richard Lieber, a member of the Indiana Historical Commission, is credited with having done most of the preliminary work, even to the writing of the proclamation which Governor Ralston recently issued, calling upon the people of the state to contribute the money needed for the purchase of the sites. Civic bodies and public spirited individuals are soliciting these funds and they hope to establish many parks this year.

IOWA: This state now puts its seal on butter manufactured here under the rules of the Dairy and Food Commission. One plant has complied with the conditions required by the state law and eleven others are trying to meet them. The law provides that creameries which put out a butter rating above 93 per cent may use the Iowa stamp, a guarantee that the state stands behind the product.

KANSAS: Thru a news bureau, to the maintenance of which the state contributes $10,000 conditioned upon the contribution of a similar amount by the newspaper proprietors, this state is furnishing Eastern manufacturers with information as to the needs of Kansas people; so that the manufacturers will give more advertising to the Kansas newspapers and help to increase the business of the local merchants.

MAINE: A delegation of state congressmen, with Richard B. Dorr, of Mt. Desert, recently called on President Wilson to offer informally to the United States 5000 acres of forest land on Mt. Desert island to be used as a national reserve. It was suggested that the President accept it under the Roosevelt act without consulting Congress. Representative Guernsey of Maine already has a bill in the House to authorize the Secretary of Agriculture to select lands in the region of Mt. Katahdin for a national park, one of the provisions of which is that no lands shall be taken without the consent of the Maine State Legislature.

MINNESOTA: The first meeting of the All-Minnesota Development Association has been called. This organization was effected by a combination of the Northern Minnesota, the Southern Minnesota and the West Central Minnesota development associations, in accordance with a wish expressed by the late Governor Hammond only a short time before his death. He pointed out that the three associations were to a considerable extent neutralizing each other's work, whereas if they would all pull together they might accomplish much for the state as a whole. River control will be one of the first matters taken up by the new organization, with special view to better drainage of the extensive swamp lands of northern Minnesota.

MISSISSIPPI: A law which has just gone into effect makes it illegal to circulate, post or print any kind of liquor advertisement in this state. This means that no publication, wheresoever printed, containing such an advertisement may be circulated in Mississippi. The same law prohibits the making of any mailing list of residents of this state for the purpose of furnishing it to liquor dealers anywhere. The statute relating to shipments of liquor into the state permits each adult citizen to import two quarts of whisky or twelve quarts of beer every four weeks.

NEW JERSEY: Newark's celebration of her 250 years of community life is realizing all that was expected of it, which is saying much. The program, which includes five months of activities, was successfully begun on May 1 with elaborate parades, soon followed by the opening of an attractive industrial exposition, to be continued for a month. Other special features of the program are a local historical pageant, an interdenominational meeting to unite the church interests in the celebration, summer athletic contests and a large number of national conventions which are bringing multitudes of visitors.

NEW MEXICO: It has been the common practice of New Mexican cattle and sheep raisers to send their stock out of the state for "finishing"—that is, for final feeding and fattening for market. Even those farmers who raised alfalfa and other feed frequently have sold it outside the state and then sent their cattle and sheep away to be fattened upon it. Last year Mr. Frank A. Hubbell, who had recognized this practice as an economic waste, undertook to demonstrate it to the stock men. His experiments have shown them how to make stock-raising much more profitable.

NORTH DAKOTA: At the college of mining engineering of the University of North Dakota at Grand Forks and at the mining substation at Hebron extended work is being done on a variety of new and practical methods of using lignite. Special attention is paid to the production of gas for heating, lighting and power purposes and the manufacture of briquets. Lignite deposits in this state cover approximately 32,000 square miles, many of them from ten to fifteen feet thick and capable of producing several hundred billions of tons of lignite. Since the Federal Government controls great tracts of this land, the

United States Bureau of Mines is aiding in the experiments, which promise wonderful results in the production of cheap fuels.

OHIO: The recently closed season of entertainments for children given by the juvenile motion picture committee of Columbus ran for ten weeks and was so successful that plans are being made for a larger series next year. The entertainments were given at a local theater on Saturday mornings, the proceeds being used for charitable purposes. Students from the Ohio State University acted as ushers.

OREGON: The people of this state have just celebrated the dedication, on June 7, of the Columbia River Highway, which has been declared by experts in road engineering to be one of the greatest highways ever built to meet the conditions of modern traffic. The scenic attractions along this road are said to be unsurpassed by those of any highway in the world.

PENNSYLVANIA: The exhibit for which the Pennsylvania Board of Health received the grand prize at the Panama-Pacific International Exposition last year was placed on view recently in Philadelphia to show the public what its state board is doing in the way of preventing disease, and to teach individuals how to make their surroundings healthful. Models of homes, schools, factories, under both proper and improper conditions, and a large number of educative maps and diagrams, are intended to create a stronger popular sentiment behind the board in its fight for better health conditions.

RHODE ISLAND: Under the auspices of a local committee, the membership of which includes leading men and women from all the important civic and social bodies of the state, Mr. John Ihlder, secretary of the Ellen Wilson Homes in Washington, has begun a systematic study of the housing conditions of Providence. He expects to be able some time this summer to report fully on the real housing conditions, including density of settlement, numbers in households, accommodations provided for them, and matters pertaining to cleanliness and sanitary conditions. He will then make recommendations as to what the city should do to improve the situation.

TEXAS: The farmers and fruit growers of Texas are rapidly learning the lesson of coöperation. A coöperative poultry association at Friendswood has been of so much advantage to its members that it has extended its activities beyond the marketing of products and now buys all supplies at a great saving to its members. It has also undertaken the management of a creamery and a coöperative loan company. The success of coöperative organizations in the state has induced the large number of Satsuma orange growers to come into the South Texas Citrus Exchange, which has increased the profits of its members without adding to the prices paid by consumers.

THE DEATH OF AN AIRMAN

THIS REMARKABLE PHOTOGRAPH OF THE DESTRUCTION OF THE AEROPLANE IN WHICH FLIGHT LIEUTENANT R. C.
FERRICK OF THE BRITISH AVIATION CORPS WAS MAKING OBSERVATIONS WAS TAKEN FROM THE
GERMAN TRENCHES AFTER THE MACHINE HAD BEEN STRUCK BY A SHELL FROM A GERMAN
ANTI-AIRCRAFT GUN AND HAD CAUGHT FIRE AS IT FELL

THE BATTLE OF JUTLAND

BY REAR-ADMIRAL CASPAR F. GOODRICH, U. S. N. (RETIRED)

SINCE the launching in 1907 of the first battle-cruisers, the three British invincibles, their general value, and especially their employment in engagements, have provided topics for endless discussions, not only among naval officers but among civilians as well. Few persons, if any, wholly condemn this new type; many there be, chiefly outside of naval circles, who advocate it as a complete and satisfactory substitute for the battleship proper. Until last Wednesday, when facts took the place of theory, this controversy, always piquant and at times heated, has been purely academic, but recent events have supplied fresh and hitherto unavailable data to help in solving a vexed question.

Since this is written with the information available Sunday morning it is entirely possible that subsequent news may impeach the soundness of our conclusions. The meager official reports from Berlin and London, together with private dispatches from abroad, furnish a very slender basis upon which to construct the story of the battle between the German "High Sea Fleet" and a detachment of Great Britain's "Grand Fleet." Some facts, however, are well known. They relate to the place, the time, and in a certain extent to the results admitted by both sides.

The place—About eighty nautical miles north of Heligoland and in the North Sea lies a shoal called Horns Reef, some ten miles off the Danish shore. Between this reef and the shore, the northern extremity of Denmark, the opposing forces met, probably not far from Ring Koping, approximately twenty - five miles north of Horns Reef. This inference is drawn from the fact that windows were broken in that Danish town by the shock of heavy gun fire. What courses the opposing ships followed thereafter is still in doubt. The British Admiralty states that the engagement began at 3.15 p. m., Wednesday, May 31, and continued during the night, altho the big ship fighting was over by fifteen minutes past nine o'clock of that evening; after that the work was done by destroyers and submarines.

The forces employed—Here we enter upon debatable ground. According to the British Admiralty the ships present at the opening were "the battle-cruiser fleet, some cruisers and light cruisers, supported by four fast battleships." The numbers are not given. They were under the command of Vice-Admiral Sir David Beatty. Opposed to him were five

large modern dreadnoughts, "hardly exact as to type," eight cruisers and twenty destroyers, as counted by a Danish steamer which witnessed this part of the fight. The British official report gives to this van of the German fleet five battleships and three battle-cruisers without mentioning other vessels. Reinforcements of battleships, the Germans first, arrived later on the scene. How many is nowhere mentioned. Berlin dispatches state that the full German High Sea Fleet was engaged—a remark corroborated by the British Admiralty's announcement that "we met and defeated the entire German battle fleet." As Admiral Jellicoe, in command of the Grand Fleet, is reported not to have been in the action, it is apparent that the whole British fleet was not engaged. Doubtless it was unable to reach the scene in time.

Incidents of the battle—While the Danish steamer above-mentioned was being boarded by two British destroyers the German fleet came in sight and opened fire. This approach to within range was due to the hazy weather which prevailed that day. It is these destroyers, presumably, which went to the westward pursued by the German fleet. Evidently this movement brought the German battleships in contact with the British battle-cruisers, upon which the brunt of the action fell. The Admiralty divides the battle into four phases. The first opened at a quarter past three o'clock, when the British battle-cruisers, at a range of six miles, joined action with German battlecruisers. Shortly after, the second phase began with the arrival on both sides of battleships, the Germans arriving first. The third phase was the engagement of battleships, which was never more than partial; this phase included a running fight as the German dreadnoughts fled toward their base. Then came one of the most weird features of the battle, as German destroyers made attack after attack like infantry following artillery preparation, on the British big ships, but their onslaughts were singularly futile, not a single torpedo launched by them getting home. With the morning these attacks ended and the scene of battle was swept by Admiral Jellicoe's fleet; not a single enemy vessel remained in sight. It is much to be regretted that we have not a similar account from German official sources to give the other side of this story.

General results as claimed—Germany contends that they are highly satisfactory, not only in respect of

the comparative losses of the two fleets, but in the fact that the Germans maintained the field after the battle. Great Britain contends that she met and defeated the entire German fleet and compelled them to return to port. It is not for a neutral to award the palm of victor in this instance, but it may be remarked that seldom if ever in history have the results of such a great fight been so gratifying to both of the contestants. The German sortie cannot be regarded a parade of bravado; it must have had some serious purpose. If we knew what that purpose was we could better judge the success or failure which followed.

Lessons taught—It would seem from what we are told that overconfidence in the battle-cruisers led to their taking an undue share of hard knocks and that it would have been more prudent to let them draw the German battleships to within range of the British battleships fast coming to their relief. Apparently with two Zeppelins, if not more, the Germans were better informed than the British of the state of affairs beyond the visible horizon. The need of an abundance of air scouts should not be lost sight of by us. There can be no doubt that the German gun fire was exceedingly accurate; how much of this accuracy may be credited to observations from Zeppelins and aeroplanes can only be guessed. In the opinion of many experts this use of aircraft is their best rôle in naval warfare. Altho the battle continued until after nine o'clock that evening it must be remembered that the sun did not set on the scene that day before eight o'clock, and that in so high a latitude, 55° 56′, the twilight is of long duration.

It will be instructive to learn how much damage was done respectively by gun fire, mines, Zeppelins, destroyers and submarines. Such information would be invaluable in shaping our own naval policy. If the gun was actually the most efficient weapon we may call attention to the fact that the Germans had none above eleven inches in caliber, while the British battle-cruisers mounted twelve, or even, in the case of the "Queen Mary," 13.5. From the technical standpoint this great contest is particularly illuminating as to the vext question of the right tactical use of the battle-cruiser; furthermore, it is likely to strengthen the belief, general among naval officers, that the battleship remains, as before, the arbiter of fights on the sea.

Pomfret, Connecticut

WILL THE WOMEN VOTE TOGETHER?

BY FOLA LA FOLLETTE

FOR the first time in the history of this country "Votes for Women" promises to be a national political issue. According to the estimate based on the United States census of 1910, in the twelve states where women now vote, there will be over four million women eligible to cast their ballots for President in November, 1916, and by the time this article reaches its readers Iowa will have voted on woman suffrage and may have increased the number of women voters to almost five million. The power of these women voters to aid in securing the vote for their disfranchised Eastern sisters depends solely on how effectively they can be mobilized for united action. Since this is the first national election at which an organized appeal has been made to voting women to put the enfranchisement of all women of the United States before other political issues in casting their ballots, the election returns will be regarded by many as an acid test of the sex solidarity of American women. The degree of unity these women voters will achieve is difficult to predict, as there is no previous national record from which deductions can be made. At minor elections, however, a sufficient number of Congressmen have already been penalized for their party's lethargy toward the federal enfranchisement of women to warn party leaders that these Western women may have dangerous potentialities of national solidarity hitherto unsuspected. Therefore it is not suffragists alone, but astute politicians as well, who are anxiously asking in what degree these four million women voters of the West will respond to the appeal of the disfranchised Eastern women.

The difficulty in predicting the policy and power of this new political factor lies not only in its being an unknown quantity, but also in the fact that the suffragists themselves are divided as to the way in which the Western women's vote should be organized and directed against political candidates. There are at present two distinct organizations of women —the Congressional Union and the Congressional Committee of the National American Woman Suffrage Association —working along entirely different lines to secure the passage of the Susan

One of the women who can speak with most authority on the significance of the 4,000,000 votes which will be cast by women in the next presidential election is Fola La Follette, a prominent suffragist in New York City. Since her graduation from the University of Wisconsin she has been in touch with the public as an actress, an author, a political speaker, and a suffrage campaigner. We are glad to present the case for the woman vote, as we have already done for the Roosevelt vote, the Hughes vote, the Ford vote, and the "straight" party votes of the Republicans and the Democrats.—THE EDITOR.

B. Anthony suffrage amendment, which reads as follows:

Resolved by the Senate and House of Representatives of the United States of America in Congress assembled (two-thirds of each house concurring therein), That the following article be proposed to the legislatures of the several states as an amendment to the Constitution of the United States, which, when ratified by three-fourths of the said legislatures, shall be valid as part of said Constitution, namely:

"Article —, Section 1. The right of citizens of the United States to vote shall not be denied or abridged by the United States or by any State on account of sex.

"Section 2. Congress shall have power, by appropriate legislation, to enforce the provisions of this article."

Both these organizations are appealing to the power of the women voters to force congressional action on this amendment. But they are asking Western women to direct their votes along entirely different lines of attack.

The Congressional Committee, for example, as a branch of the National American Woman Suffrage Association, believes in working simultaneously for federal and state enfranchisement of women. The officers of the Congressional Committee and their followers consider it still both necessary and expedient to gain more equal suffrage states in order to secure the passage of the Susan B. Anthony amendment. Therefore, the Congressional Committee, not wishing to complicate state suffrage campaigns, follows the traditional nonpartisan policy of the National American Woman Suffrage Association. It is a negative policy in that it supports neither individual candidates nor parties. Its action is based on the theory of the individual legislator's responsibility for failure to pass legislation. It concentrates all its efforts on defeating candidates who are individually opposed to suffrage regardless of their party affiliations.

The Congressional Union, on the other hand, confines its work entirely to passing the Susan B. Anthony amendment because it considers this the simplest and quickest method of securing political freedom for all the women of the United States. The Congressional Union has no interest in the enfranchisement of women by state action, for it regards this method as a wasteful, slow process no longer necessary. It believes that thru the political power women already possess Congress can be forced to pass the federal suffrage amendment. Since it holds the need for state enfranchisement obsolete, the Congressional Union quite logically bases its policy entirely on the idea of party responsibility. It attacks the party in power, whatever that party may be, so long as it refuses to pass the federal suffrage amendment. It holds the party in power responsible for the activity or lethargy of its Congress, just as men hold the dominant party responsible for its foreign policy in "hard times" occurring during its administration. On this basis the Congressional Union endeavors to align the women voters against the candidates of any party in power which has failed to pass the Susan B. Anthony amendment, regardless of the individual conviction or vote of those candidates on suffrage legislation. At present the Congressional Union is making every effort to mobilize the women's vote in the equal

A TEMPTING MORSEL

suffrage states to secure the passage of the federal amendment during the present Congress. If the present Congress fails to pass the amendment, then this mobilized force will be directed against the Democratic party at the presidential election in 1916, just as it was at the minor elections in 1914.

There is a further corollary to this attack: namely, that every effort will be made to have this mobilized force throw its votes wherever they will prove most helpful to the enfranchisement of women by federal amendment. Should the present Congress, for example, pass the federal amendment, the Democratic party would undoubtedly secure the cordial support of these mobilized voters. If, however, Congress fails to pass the amendment and the Republican party should nominate a presidential candidate who openly declared himself for the federal amendment, or if it should even go further and put a pledge in its platform for the federal amendment, one may reasonably assume that the Republican party would secure the votes of a majority of the Congressional Union followers.

The Democratic presidential candidate, who will undoubtedly be Wilson, will, of course, be opposed by the Congressional Union forces, unless the present Congress passes the federal suffrage amendment. The Congressional Committee of the National Suffrage Association will, however, not oppose him, as he has personally declared himself for suffrage. It is not possible to predict the Republican candidate so definitely as yet. But should it be Roosevelt, he will, of course, not be opposed by the Congressional Committee, as he is a suffragist. And, if nominated, his recent declaration in favor of the Susan B. Anthony amendment will undoubtedly assure him the votes of the Congressional Union forces that are deflected from Wilson.

If, however, the Republican party should nominate Root, or any other candidate who is an avowed anti-suffragist, he would probably not secure any votes from either the Congressional Union or the Congressional Committee forces. Furthermore, there would be a considerable number of both men and women who might not have felt intensely enough the finer distinctions of states' rights versus federal enfranchisement, or party responsibility versus individual responsibility, to ally themselves with either the Congressional Union or the Congressional Committee. Yet many of these women, and men, too, would be sufficiently devoted to the principle of equal suffrage to make that the

Copyright *Underwood*

PERSONALITY PLUS
Miss La Follette takes up some weighty arguments for woman suffrage in New York

deciding factor in scratching the name of an avowed anti-suffrage presidential nominee. It is also entirely conceivable that if the Republicans nominated Root or any declared "anti," an organized opposition might develop, not only in the Western equal franchise states, but also in the man suffrage states of the East and Middle West. The suffragists are organized thruout the country, and have developed able speakers with varied experience in political campaigning. They would undoubtedly conduct a concerted attack on such a candidate, not alone along the line of his suffrage opposition, but also on all the weak points in his political record. The results of a well organized country-wide campaign of this sort, conducted even by disfranchised women, might develop into a serious menace.

It may be argued that if the suffragists campaigned against an anti-suffrage presidential candidate the organized anti-suffragists would support him. This is also conceivable.

But the active and open support of the organized anti-suffragists would prove a dangerous boomerang to any national candidate they might support. For a clean-cut contest between Eastern suffrage and anti-suffrage forces regarding a presidential candidate would arouse women voters to a greater degree of solidarity of intention and activity than could be achieved in any other way. This increased activity of Western women resulting from Eastern "anti" opposition might easily focus the political fight within their states on this particular issue, and force many local political leaders into the arena against an "anti" candidate, either on principle or to save their official necks. As one-fifth of the votes for President come from the equal suffrage states, such a potentiality would scarcely be offset by the contribution of even well organized anti-suffrage indirect influence.

It would seem, therefore, that for the first time in the history of this country no wise political leaders of any party would dare nominate as candidate for President any individual openly opposed to suffrage, however desirable his other vote-getting qualities might be. This is in itself an interesting touchstone of the tremendous advance Votes for Women has made in this country.

So far the sex solidarity of American women has never been really tested. What the efforts of the organizations now mobilizing the women's vote will accomplish not even the most astute politician can foretell with certainty. It is an unknown quantity which may prove far less powerful than suffragists hope; on the other hand, it may prove far more dangerous than politicians yet realize. It is a well known fact that Presidents who have had a popular majority have failed of election because they did not secure a majority of the presidential electors. Women vote for ninety-one electors; that is, over one-sixth of the electoral college. If Iowa goes for suffrage this week this total will be increased to one hundred and four. Altho women are in a minority in the equal suffrage states, when one recalls that California went Progressive by only five hundred votes, it becomes apparent that in a close election their votes might prove the deciding factor in electing a President.

Perhaps the time has come when the passage of the federal suffrage amendment by the Democratic party or a Republican plank pledging national enfranchisement to women may be good politics.

Croton-on-Hudson, New York

UNNUMBERED WORLDS

BY HARRY KEMP

Unnumbered worlds flash round unnumbered suns:
  World-generations battle, labor, cease,
  And millions go down to the final peace
Thru all the starry Vast, while on there runs
Fierce generation still, and little ones
  Clap tiny palms on million mothers' knees—
  Themselves to toil and strive till death's release
And from their loins pour newer millions.
From time to time all Space doth halt and cry
  On Thee, or Life,—for they would gladly know
Whence they have come and whither they must go—
Then a star falls, and Silence gives reply . . .
  No answer else!—and Nature trudges on
  With death, and life, and sunset, night and dawn.

READING AFTER THIRTY

BY ROBERT C. HOLLIDAY

SOMEWHERE in the mass of that splendid, highly personal journalism of his, William Hazlitt declares that he was never able to read a book thru after thirty. That penetrating man, Samuel Butler, reflecting in his "Note-Books" on "What Audience to Write For," says: "People between the ages of twenty and thirty read a good deal, after thirty their reading drops off and by forty is confined to each person's special subject, newspapers and magazines." Thirty again, you see.

We all have friends who have been omnivorous readers, persons who, to our admiration and despair, seem to have read everything in "literature." It may have struck us, however, as a curious thing that, except possibly in rare instances, such persons appear not to read much now, beyond newspapers and magazines. The upshot of what they are able to say, when you ask them why this is true, is that one simply reaches a time of life when one "quits reading," as one ceases to dance, or cools in interest toward the latest fashions in overcoats.

But, undoubtedly there are persons who continue to read, apparently with unabated industry and zest, no matter how old they may become. Dr. Johnson, of course, was a constant reader all his life, and would cheerfully read anything whether it was readable or not. Tho did not he somewhere confess to himself that he did not read things thru? Mr. Huneker, who is well on the other side of thirty, would seem to read everything printed about five minutes after it has left the press, and before anybody else has had a chance to see it. There are so many capital letters on the pages of his own books

that it makes one dizzy to look at them. Whether or not he reads thru all the books he mentions is of course (as he is a reviewer) a question. And, then, both Mr. Huneker and the Doctor belong to the trade, so to say. Another startlingly prodigious reader is Theodore Roosevelt, hilariously past thirty, and not exclusively identified with literary "shop." He is continually discovering and vigorously recommending new poets and short-story writers whom professional critics have not yet had time to get around to. It does not appear that a fundamental or organic change in the composition of the human brain which inhibits reading occurs more or less suddenly at thirty.

Why then do so many reading animals cease at about that time to read? Butler does not say. Arnold Bennett (was it not?) has asked what's the use of his reading more, he knows enough. Hazlitt, in his own case, surmised that the keener interest of writing rather asphyxiated the impulse to read. And, doubtless, that generally is about the size of it. As in the cure of the drink habit, a new and more intense interest will drive out the old. The reader, of course, is a spectator, not an active participant in the world's doings. After thirty, desirable citizens of ordinary energy have little opportunity for the rôle of noncombatant, and the taste of action and of success, like the taste of war, makes them impatient with quieter things. Failures read more than successful men. Bachelors no doubt read much more than husbands. And fathers seldom are great readers. This last fact may explain the observation that even college professors do not

read fanatically. When they are "off" awhile they "play with" their children (children are great enemies everywhere to reading), who are much more real to them than study.

In one of his later books George Moore chronicles his resolve to cultivate the habit of reading, to learn to read again. And he sucks much naïve pleasure from the contemplation of this prospective enterprise; but he finds it very difficult to persevere in it, and drifts away instead into reveries of what he has read. There is a thought here, however, to be hearkened to: the idea of learning to read again.

What is it that happens to one in consequence of his ceasing to read? He suffers a hardening of the intellectual arteries. There are quaint old codgers one knows here and there who declare that in fiction there has "been nothing since Dickens." They are delightful, of course; but one would rather see than be one. We all know many persons whose intellectual clock stopped some time ago, and there are people whose minds apparently froze at about the time when they should have begun to ripen, and which are like blocks of ice with a fish (or a volume of Huxley) inside. Nothing now can get in.

At those times of earnest introspection, when one would "swear-off" this or that, would reduce one's smoking, would adopt the principle of "do it now," and so on—at those times an excellent New Year's resolution, or birthday resolution, or first day of the month resolution, would be to re-learn to read, to keep, as Dr. Johnson said of his friendships, one's reading continually "in good repair."

New York City

Copyright Underwood

The angel of Newark—who actually "flew"—on a rope and tackle—over Broad street to symbolize the spirit of the city. This was part of the 250th anniversary celebration which is giving New Jersey's metropolis more publicity than it has ever had before.

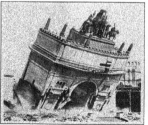

Underwood

The fall of Asia. On top of this "Arch of the Nations" at the San Francisco Exposition—now fallen before the wreckers like most of its fellow-structures in that splendid array of courts and palaces—is the fine group representing the Nations of the East that we reproduced in The Independent over a year ago.

Copyright International Film

Major Langhorne, remarking "I am clear of red tape and know no Rio Grande," chased the Glen Springs raiders till he caught up with them, killed five, captured two, and rescued their captives.

Copyright International Film

Gubernatorial inspiration for Pennsylvania road-makers. Governor Brumbaugh driving a split-log drag on Good Roads Day, when 150,000 Pennsylvanians worked to get better highways.

The last log raft on the upper Mississippi. The pine woods of northern Minnesota and Wisconsin have been denuded till lumber is too costly to risk in the river, and the dam at Keokuk bars the way to the South. Rafting down the river was once a picturesque occupation of the sort that Mark Twain made famous. From Mrs. J. Wecrevel, Fort Madison, Iowa.

Not all Mexicans hate all Americans—here are tars from the U. S. S. Machias, now at Tampico, who have made friends with Mexican youngsters and their mothers. From B. M. Fairbanks, Yeoman First Class, U. S. Navy.

Practicing at coast defense—a big shell, ready to be loaded on a truck, carried to the mortar in which it is used, rammed home and sent on a five-mile flight, at Fort Barrancas, Florida. From William Reed, 22d Coast Artillery.

Union workers thruout the country gave the money for this monument, in Wheeling, West Virginia, to Augustus Pollack, a stogie manufacturer who was known as a fair employer. From C. C. Kline, Wheeling, Ten Dollar picture.

Ruins of men—blind poilus learning again to walk—in the dark.   *Ruins of homes—a village near the horror of Verdun.*

On Saturday, June 3, this great parade of 130,000 persons proclaimed Chicago's belief in national preparedness. The marchers are passing north on Michigan avenue. Eight other cities from Connecticut to Utah had similar parades that day.

A WORLD PLAN FOR DURABLE PEACE

BY FANNY FERN ANDREWS

SECRETARY OF THE AMERICAN BRANCH OF THE CENTRAL ORGANIZATION FOR A DURABLE PEACE

OF all the efforts designed to place the nations on a permanent basis of international order, the Central Organization for a Durable Peace occupies a unique position. This was formed by the International Confidential Meeting at The Hague in April, 1915, when thirty international jurists, statesmen, economists and publicists from Germany, Belgium, England, Austria, Hungary, Italy, Holland, Norway, Sweden, Denmark, Switzerland and the United States came together to discuss the basis of a durable peace.

This remarkable group, representing belligerents and neutrals, stipulated that their deliberations should not be concerned with the present war, and further determined that the names of the members should be held confidential and that the sessions should not be open to the press. It was only under these conditions, in fact, that the belligerent members were willing to take part in a conference while their respective nations were at war. The wisdom of these rules is apparent. The confidential character of the meeting rendered discussion free and unembarrassed by fear of unwise publicity. It was only after the close of the meeting that the eager press learned the conclusions which were summed up in what was called the Minimum Program. The names of the participants were still held confidential. As the Minimum Program, however, began to influence the minds of thinkers beyond the countries represented in the confidential meeting, and national groups of the Central Organization for a Durable Peace became established, the International Executive Committee voted to publish the names of that committee and also the names of those who are actively engaged in promoting the plans of the Central Organization. The program of this unique organization is now given to the public with a plea for united support.

The Central Organization for a Durable Peace is inspired by the conviction that the fundamental basis of a new world order which must come after the present war must be laid to-day, and it offers the Minimum Program "as a foundation for common action." The nine points of this program were drawn up with the view of meeting the practical situation after the war.

The establishment of a durable peace involves two steps: (1) The settlement of immediate questions, those touching the political, financial and territorial situation; and (2)

the reëstablishment and the strengthening of international law.

In the congress that will assemble to draw up the terms of peace there will probably be a limited number of states, for it is natural that the people who have carried the heavy burden of the war will reserve to themselves the right to regulate the settlement of immediate questions. In order that this settlement, however, may not result in a mere armistice, having in it the seeds of future war, it must adhere to certain principles. The Minimum Program points out two safeguards. It calls attention, first, to the principle of nationality. The Central Organization for a Durable Peace recognizes that the political frontiers in Europe, coinciding only rarely with the limits of nationalities, are a constant cause of war. It does not attempt to regulate these con-

---

THE MINIMUM PROGRAM

1. No annexation or transfer of territory shall be made contrary to the interests and wishes of the population concerned. Where possible their consent shall be obtained by plebiscite or otherwise.

2. The states shall guarantee to the various nationalities, included in their boundaries, equality before the law, religious liberty and the free use of their native languages.

3. The states shall agree to introduce in their colonies, protectorates and spheres of influence, liberty of commerce, or at least equal treatment for all nations.

4. The work of the Hague Conferences with a view to the peaceful organization of the Society of Nations shall be developed. The Hague Conference shall be given a permanent organization and meet at regular intervals.

5. The states shall agree to submit all their disputes to peaceful settlement. For this purpose there shall be created, in addition to the existent Hague Court of Arbitration, (a) a permanent Court of International Justice, (b) a permanent International Council of Investigation and Conciliation.

6. The states shall bind themselves to take concerted action, diplomatic, economic or military, in case any state should resort to military measures instead of submitting the dispute to judicial decision or to the mediation of the Council of Investigation and Conciliation.

7. The states shall agree to reduce their armaments.

8. In order to facilitate the reduction of naval armaments, the right of capture shall be abolished and the freedom of the seas assured.

9. Foreign policy shall be under the effective control of the parliaments of the respective nations.

Secret treaties shall be void.

---

ditions, which are the result of an historical evolution, but it urges that whatever may be the issue of the war, the number of such cases may not be augmented by the next treaty of peace. The second safeguard is the insistence that states shall introduce in their colonies, protectorates and spheres of influence, liberty of commerce, or at least equal treatment for all nations. In this domain, we find a fruitful source of conflict, and it is incumbent upon any congress which bases its settlement on the principles of a durable peace to deal with this branch of economic rivalry because of its potency in creating dangerous oppositions and thereby provoking wars.

The program anticipates the calling of two assemblies, a comparatively small body to draw up the terms of peace as just described, and a large body representative of all civilized states to deal with the reëstablishment and strengthening of international law. It is evident that the matters mentioned above concern the whole body of civilized states, since there can be no permanent settlement of some of the questions which immediately concern the belligents until many world questions of international law are satisfactorily dealt with. In this connection, the problem of armaments and the freedom of the sea are especially urged for present consideration.

It is necessary to organize peace if it is to be durable. The program proposes, in addition to the Hague Court of Arbitration, a Court of Justice, a Council of Investigation and Conciliation, and the permanent organization of the Hague Conference. Thus no entirely new institution is included in the plan. The Hague Court of Arbitration presents a successful record of fifteen cases since its organization in 1902. The Second Hague Conference voted by a large majority for the project of an International Court of Justice, altho, as is well known, it failed of realization on account of the difficulties incident to the problem of its composition. The idea of a Council of Investigation and Conciliation for dealing with non-justiciable questions, those indeed which are most likely to lead to war, has developed from the Commission of Inquiry established by the First Hague Conference. Finally, to look forward to the development of the Hague Conference into an international assembly, meeting periodically to formulate and codify rules of international law, coincides with the spirit of the Second Hague

Conference in providing for the calling of the third.

Besides urging the consideration of those principles of durable peace which should govern the peace settlement congress and the plan for international organization, the Central Organization for a Durable Peace believes that the stability of peace will never be maintained wholly thru measures of international order. In speaking of the limitations of international law, Mr. Root said: "Law can not control national policy, and it is thru the working of long continued and persistent national policies that the present war has come. Against such policies all attempts at conciliation and good understanding and good will among the nations of Europe have been powerless." The program mentions two measures in this domain which are especially indispensable: (1) The guarantee to the national minorities of civil equality, religious liberty and the free use of their native languages; (2) the parliamentary control of foreign politics with interdiction of all secret treaties.

The most striking part of the Minimum Program, and that which offers a great departure from present international procedure, is the provision for an international treaty, binding states to refer their disputes to an arbitral or judicial tribunal or to the Council of Investigation and Conciliation, and further to use concerted diplomatic, economic and military pressure against any state that breaks the treaty. According to this plan, we find developed a world League of Peace, which, if supported by a strong public opinion, can come into existence thru the action of the world congress to convene after the war.

The Central Organization for a Durable Peace has already formed national groups in almost all countries to make a technical study of the proposals laid down in the Minimum Program. Nine Research Committees have been organized, representing the nine points of the Minimum Program. Some thirty-five research studies, including nine prepared by members of the American Committee, have already been published. These are now used by the various national groups as a basis of technical study and discussion, and after final editing, they are to be sent to the governments of the world.

Thru these study groups, which now represent twenty-six nations, this organization is building up a united support of the underlying principles of equitable law, and is thereby destined to become a world factor in influencing the great settlement. The effort demands the support of the world. The people of one nation alone, or of a group of nations, cannot effect a new world order; it is a task for the civilized world. The work of the Central Organization for a Durable Peace may be described as a simultaneous world study to prepare for action at the supreme moment of the world's history which we shall witness after the war.

Boston, Massachusetts

For the King

The Dish of the Palaces
Nearly All the World Over

"I was taken," he writes, "through the Emperor's kitchen, and what do you suppose? Why, there was Quaker Oats."

But in his own kitchen it wasn't.

It's a curious fact. We Americans import Scotch and Irish oats to sell at fancy prices. But in the British Isles, where these oats grow, Quaker is the dominant brand.

And some of us take any oats that are offered, thinking oat flakes much alike.

But the connoisseurs of a hundred nations send here for their favorite oats.

Here is one American product—one of the few—which has won the whole world's admiration. Don't you know that such a product must deserve supremacy?

Quaker Oats
The Supreme Morning Dainty

Oats, to have the finest flavor, must be Northern grown.

But we go further. We take the choicest Northern oats and pick out the choicest third. That is, we discard two-thirds of the oats because they are underfed.

From the big, plump grains—just the cream of the oats—we make these luscious flakes. That's why this flavor has won the world.

Remember that. Without extra price—without extra effort—you can get Quaker Oats when you order. You can breakfast the same as kings. After that, a lesser oat dainty will hardly be served on your table.

10c and 25c per package
Except in Far West and South

A $2.50 Aluminum Cooker

Made to our order, extra large and heavy, to cook Quaker Oats in the ideal way. Send us five trademarks—the picture of the Quaker—cut from the fronts of five Quaker Oats packages. Send $1 with them, and this double cooker will be sent by parcel post. This offer applies to the United States and Canada.

Address **The Quaker Oats Company, 1708 Railway Exchange, Chicago**

What Good Was Your Schooling?

A Composite Educational Autobiography of Independent Readers

WITH a view of getting some light upon the much discussed question of the merits and defects of the school system, we called upon our readers in the issue of January 10 to answer these two questions:

1. Of all you were taught at school what has proved most useful to you in after life?

2. What have you had to learn since leaving school which you might have been taught there?

Those who responded represented all kinds and degrees of education and of practical life, so we have in the letters an experience meeting of the widest scope on what knowledge is of most worth.

The first lesson we learn from them is the impracticability of prescribing any single course of study as suited to all minds and future careers. Almost every conceivable study is mentioned among those which have proved most useful, and some inconceivable studies are mentioned among those most missed. Many, it is true, specify the same study, but do not agree as to what they got out of it. It is therefore impossible to classify and tabulate the answers, and we can only give in a general way their trend.

English in its double sense of composition and literature is most often mentioned. Perhaps then we should begin our quotations with a teacher of English in the Horace Mann School of Columbia University.

Question I. English! Hence, expression, communication—a broad highway, easily traveled, between mine and the world's life. Hence, also, acquaintance with the treasuries—and treasurers—of literature—of "the best that mankind has thought and said and done."

Question II.—Perhaps a course in *how to teach* administered to most college and university professors. Students are developed into cisterns, not dynamos! A course, in any subject, which puts a premium on power and original, creative effort on the part of students, would be the most useful course I did not get.
F. H. BAIR
New York City

I. Of all that I learned at school, the English language has been most useful to me both in its technique and its literature.

II. I wish I felt equally safe and firm in planning meals, home-sewing, house decoration, and kindergarten amusements. In less than a year of such courses in school I could have arrived definitely at information toward which I now travel a fitful and worried march.
MRS. HENRY A. DANFORTH
Charleston, Missouri

I. Language, commencing with McGuffey's spelling book—learned by heart, every word—McGuffey's readers, Kidd's elocution, Harvey's grammars, Harkness' Latin grammars and Cæsar's Commentaries.

II. Proper consideration for others. Everything that helped one to cultivate the love of the beautiful.
FANNIE A. CALDWELL
Piqua, Ohio

I believe what I value most has been my love of good literature, which we all imbibed from McGuffey's old fifth and sixth readers. We had daily drills in pars-

ing and sentence construction. but we were *never once* told to speak correctly.

The old fashioned reader with its "gems of choice literature," nowadays so sneered at, is regarded with gratitude by those who were drilled in it. Many of our correspondents specify the bits of poetry and prose they had to memorize as "the most useful" of all they learned at school.

The reading and learning by heart of classic bits of English prose and poetry, starting a real love for the best in literature, Next to this, a grounding in Latin that helped much in the use of English and in the understanding and study of Romance languages.
E. H. SMITH
Philadelphia

A love of reading, a training in thought getting, in concentration—the memorizing of poems of Shakespeare, Scott, Cowper, Tennyson and others, while very young, were the best things I got at school. The seeds from which my ideals grew many years after were these stored-up thoughts of the masters.
ETHEL SPRIGGS
Sarahsville, Ohio

The classicists turned out strong in this questionnaire. They are evidently not afraid to put their favorite study to the pragmatic test implied by the wording of the question. We will first call upon a chemist to testify:

I believe Latin and Greek were my most useful studies. They were the key that unlocked some of the world's best literature, and the logical background for subsequent modern language study. The close application demanded to master these subjects, and the student habits thereby acquired, have proved of permanent value. The professors were men of strong personality, real teachers, and not a little of the benefit came from associations with them.
NICHOLAS KNIGHT
Cornell College, Mount Vernon, Iowa

The most useful thing that I learned at school was an interest in Latin literature gained while listening to older pupils translate Virgil. This led to my own later study of Latin after leaving school and to my wider knowledge of language forms. Whatever of later professional success I have had is by a house-that-Jack-built process referable to this and to my home training.
E. I. HARRIS
Washington State Normal School, Ellensburg, Washington

I am particularly glad that my language work was studying Latin and Greek, not the inanities in English that are sometimes taught at the present day; that I had *real* metaphysics.

"Down mid the tangled roots of things
That coil about the central fire,"
not experiments in the behavior of chickens, and that I had Dio Lewis' "Light Gymnastics" instead of the terrible athletics that are breaking down the bones of our children and youth today.
SAMANTHA WHIPPLE SHOUP
Indianapolis, Indiana

1. "Small Latin and less Greek" learned in two years in the Boston Latin School opening up a new world to me; but being poor I had to stop and go to work.
B. L. S., 1865
Boston

Mental arithmetic—the very name of which is a refection on other kinds of arithmetic—is mentioned by several as a most valuable exercise.

In the early '50's, in a "Little Red School House" in Maine, I had a drill in

Colburn's Mental Arithmetic, conducted by the schoolmistress of that period. I believe it was the most important event of my early schooling. The inevitable result of such a mental gymnastic was to induce a habit of brain activity, sometimes brain agility.
S. E. GEDDES
New York City

Fifteen minutes of arduous mental gymnastics started the educational ball rolling every morning of my school days. Important practical drill in remembering telephone numbers and messages, shopping lists, etc., were judiciously mixed in with the memorizing of really good prose and verse. Then there were always a few minutes of stiff mental arithmetic that ended the "memory" period like a snap of the whip, and the whole idea was one of the most productive in the curriculum.
ELEANOR WOODS BURR
New York City

If we count the votes, then the three R's have it by a large plurality. More than half our correspondents specify "reading, 'riting and 'rithmetic" in some form, as their "most useful study."

But many mention less tangible kinds of education:

I. I drove down from "Muskrat Medder," where I was the head of a mouse and attended school in the city, where I immediately became the nineteenth odd hair on the tail of a lion. This consciousness that there are so many people in the world smarter than I am was the most valuable thing I gained from my schooling.

II. I should have been taught: To endorse a check correctly; to put the "Dr." of a bill in the right place; to pound the nail and not my thumb; to read "sermons in stones, books in the running brooks"; to love Jesus; to tend a garden; to write legible words instead of hen-scratches; to spell most words of six letters and a few words with ten; to stop when I've said enough.
RALPH C. JENKINS
Manchester, Vermont

The most useful thing I learned in college was reverence for and belief in authority.

The greatest lesson I have had to learn since is reverence for and belief in myself.

This is not a paradox. These lessons are not contradictory; they are supplementary. "Faith without works is dead."
LEE W. COOKE
Walla Walla, Washington

The most useful thing that I was taught at school: know thyself and not everything.

Have had-to learn since leaving school: to be alert, prompt, systematic, considerate, and last but not least: cultivate sunshine on life's journey.
FRANK JOHNSON
Pomeroy, Iowa

Much criticism and ridicule has been directed against the college student for his propensity to choose by professors instead of by subjects in his electives. But this course is not so irrational as it may appear, to judge by the many correspondents who refer to the influence of some teacher rather than the learning of a certain study. For instance, the principal of the Mars High School:

Outside of the three R's I learned nothing while in school. Of. course. I passed the examinations. Either a well trained dog or boy-can do this—if subjected long enough to the beating in methods of our public schools. But one thing I did assimilate, namely, the spirit of a teacher. It haunted me in after years like a ghost.

448

Not history outlines, not dates, not names she used to make us learn, but the spirit of her face went home. It led me into pastures of thought where I finally learned to live.

In answer to the second question I might say that I have had to learn how to react against an iron-faced world without beating my brains out. My classroom experiences as a student made me too conscious of the unreality of life. Bread and butter, sin and suffering, selfishness and love, justice and injustice—the approximate meaning of these things as I would have to find them was not brought home to me. My teachers were strong on the past but weak on the present. Get stronger teachers in the school room, especially men that can and will think courageously and then we shall have men and women going forth from our schools eager to sacrifice for the redemption of our social life, political, religious, economic.   A. H. FORMAN
Mars, Pennsylvania

Many of our women correspondents complain that their schools and colleges failed to provide for the expanding opportunities of feminine life. We surmise that the next generation will have the same complaint to make of some present-day schools.

Since leaving school I have learned that every human being has some one power by which he may reach happiness and usefulness, and that every life should be planned for the use of the special gift with which the individual may be endowed. In common with most girls' schools my Alma Mater was diligent in season and out of season to keep us "womanly." As individuals we were to be all that was pure and lovely, but no ideals of active life were held out to us. It was generally understood that we would have a year or two of young ladyhood and drift into matrimony. In the case of a majority of women this kind of training may be fraught with no evil consequences, but thru dependence and mental misery a sorrowful minority realize that they and the world would have been better off if they had been taught as individuals and not as a sex whose work in life was predestined to lie in only one field of usefulness. Some men who are square pegs get into round holes, but thousands of round female pegs are forced into square holes with utter unconsciousness of the lifelong tragedy involved.   MRS. L. H. HILL
Bastrop, Texas

The women of the Library Club of Glen Elder, Kansas, took The Independent questions as the topic of a meeting and got a very frank and interesting discussion out of them. We quote a few of their experiences:

I wish I had learned that fooling the teacher was really harming myself.

Learned truthfulness is advisable even with little children.

I wish I had not been taught to count on my fingers. It seems impossible to break the habit.

I learned to mind at school. I always had my way at home.

My drill in accurate spelling has made me the dictionary of the family.

The most useful thing was the Golden Rule.

I wish I had been allowed more chance for self-expression—not forced to express the teacher's ideas.

Our second question, concerning the sins of omission of the schools and colleges, called out, as might be expected, more various replies than the first, but they fall readily into two general classes; one calls for more practical, especially vocational, instruction; the other complains of the lack of training in character-building, personal efficiency and the art of getting along with other people.

We will consider the practical demands first, as they are easier met. Among the "long felt wants" mentioned are knowledge of applied science, especially mechanics; manual training (the kind that really trains), domestic science, business methods, law, hygiene and agriculture. We give a few specimen replies:

What I have had to learn in the years since leaving school that I might have learned while there is largely a practical acquaintance with what might be called the mechanics of everyday life. I think it possible to instruct all children in simple everyday mechanical operations, such as would be suggested by locks and hinges, a bicycle or a sewing machine.

FLORA WARREN SMITH SEYMOUR
Chicago

All of my life I have felt the lack of general and specific physical and manual training—the practical application of principles of mathematics, chemistry, physiology, psychology, etc., to the actual work of everyday life. So I say, not mildly but from passionate conviction, that courses in practical business, domestic science, kindergartening, carpentering, etc., should accompany mental training. Much of the time in school was wasted, because many of us could have done twice the work in the time if we had not been limited to the grade schedule. This unused time and certain hours of the long summer vacation days could well have been devoted to "play" in the form of vocational work.

MARY WHITE SLATER
Ironton, Ohio

I think that my school should have taught me some handicraft and that its failure to do so was its most obvious failure. It is true that for a year or so I was kept sawing and planing at little bits of wood for a few hours a week, but I cannot say that I even learned to drive a nail without an even chance of hitting my thumb. The classes were too large, the work stereotyped and formal, the teachers undertrained, overdriven and probably underpaid. Other students were far more skillful than I and received better marks, but none of them seemed to find in this inadequate routine shopwork either pleasure or enhanced ability to do.

P. W. S.
New York City

No man or woman in these days can afford to be ignorant of the working and construction of an automobile. It ought to be part of everybody's education.

FREDERICK A. BINNEY
San Diego, California

In the secondary schools I ought to have received:

1. Training of the fingers by means of sewing.
2. Training of the eye by means of drawing.
3 Training of the ear by means of singing.
4. Training of the whole body by means of physical exercises so that instead of being flat-chested and stoop-shouldered I might now be supple and strong.

In college I should have been taught dietetics and chemistry applied to food and cleanliness.

I did receive the ability to enjoy good music, and as I am a near-monotone I greatly appreciate it.

MRS. A. J. ERICKSON
Franksville, Wisconsin

The most serious lack in my training was the absence of any course of instruction which could give me even a meager knowledge of my present profession of home-making and child culture.

A. E. BAKER
Baltimore, Maryland

Chemistry would have prevented me from committing many gastronomical crimes and taught me how to live to be a hundred years old and be useful to my fellow-man.

C. BIERCE
Memphis, Tennessee

1875
The First Telephone

1916
The Country-wide System

Forty-one Years of Telephone Progress

The faint musical sound of a plucked spring was electrically carried from one room to another and recognized on June 2, 1875. That sound was the birthcry of the telephone.

The original instrument—the very first telephone in the world—is shown in the picture above.

From this now-historic instrument has been developed an art of profound importance in the world's civilization.

At this anniversary time, the Bell System looks back on forty-one years of scientific achievement and economic progress, and gives this account of its stewardship:

It has provided a system of communication adequate to public needs and sufficiently in advance of existing conditions to meet all private demands or national emergencies.

It has made the telephone the most economical servant of the people for social and commercial intercourse.

It has organized an operating staff loyal to public interests and ideals; and by its policy of service it has won the appreciation and good will of the people.

With these things in mind, the Bell System looks forward with confidence to a future of greater opportunity and greater achievement.

Mr. Bierce, like many of our other correspondents, is perhaps asking more than the schools in their present imperfect state can be expected to teach. Chevreul is the only chemist we remember to have lived more than a hundred years.

Cooking and sewing. My mother did not have time to teach them to me at home, and I could learn neither till after I was married, and had to learn them from neighbors' books, by experiment, or any way I could. With three babies, coming right along, one after the other, my lack of knowledge on these subjects has been deplorable.

ANNA GILLESPIE McCLELLAN
Greeley, Colorado

I might have been given:
1. A short, simplified course in banking and trade operations *acted* out.
2. Some concrete examples of business organization.
3. A few lessons on the uses and handling of tools, wood finishes and building materials.
4. Some definite knowledge of the different lines of work that make up our industries, of the opportunities that exist in each line, and of the qualities and qualifications that each line calls for, to the end that I might intelligently have chosen a vocation for which I was by nature fitted.

NORMAN P. LAWSON
Corfu, Washington

II. There is no subject that I have had occasion to study since leaving school that I believe should have been taught there unless I may regard as such the art of handwriting; the formation of a neat and thoroly practical hand is a matter of importance but too lightly esteemed and its successful teaching in the United States seems to be almost an unknown art.

BREWSTER PHILLIPS
Biltmore, North Carolina

A course in agriculture would have been a blessing to me. I studied about the earth, but it was of a far-away earth instead of the world at home. I could describe the course of the Yang-tse-Kiang river and a hundred other streams that drained strange lands, but I was not taught the value of drainage for my own home fields.

L. DILLON
Bedford, Virginia

But more often than the demand for the applied physical sciences comes the expression of a need of what might be called applied psychology and sociology, that is, of some form of education that shall enable one to develop his faculties and to deal with fellow-men. Our correspondents are not very definite about how these things can be taught, if at all, in the schools, but they evidently feel the lack of something very essential in their training. Apparently it is more a matter of discipline, experience and moral culture than any formal instruction. But a few samples of answers to our second question will define the need better than a definition.

I failed to get a clear conception of the demands and responsibility of society and thereby neglected the social side of life which enables one to be a good mixer.

S. F. GOLLEHON
Tazewell, Virginia

A knowledge of human nature in real life. Few things could be of greater or more lasting value than a careful study of the nature and effects of the motives and ideas which mold the character and govern the conduct of our fellow-men.

CHARLES RICHARDSON
(age 75)
Philadelphia, Pennsylvania

What I think I lacked most was the ability to meet people fairly and openly in the affairs of everyday life. Particularly to meet those of opposing views without giving unnecessary offense and yet stand firmly for what I consider to be right.

A. H. COUCH
Haviland, Kansas

Practice in oral and written expression, a *synthetic* use of the school subjects, some knowledge of the underlying impulses, incentives and mental methods of ordinary men. ALFRED GUILLON
Berkeley, California

Born a poor farmer's boy I was never taught in school independent thinking or any standard of true values, so that I might live a full life without wealth or fame. God forgive my well intentioned teachers; from them I learned chiefly what *not* to teach others.

W. J. MEREDITH,
Vice Principal, Montezuma Mountain Ranch School for Boys
Los Gatos, California

What I was not taught and learned later, and painfully, was the ability to discriminate between capital and income, not in the general but the individual sense, and with reference to health as well as wealth. A. B. JACKSON
North Adams, Massachusetts

Self-reliance. The school system of today tends to place all responsibility on the teacher. This is wrong. Unless a scholar is made to feel that it is *he* himself who is responsible for his own welfare he will never attain success.

W. L. BIDDLE
Philadelphia.

Typewriting. Also more efficient methods of work, conserving energy and increasing output. Perhaps this cannot be learned in any school as well as one learns it by experience and intellectual alertness, but a beginning along these lines might well be made in school or college.

R. S. BOARDMAN
Bloomfield, New Jersey

I. Chiefly that I was not different from other boys and that all human beings have many points of similarity.

II. Everything in essentials and all of the little that I really know. It was outside of school that I learned how to learn and by association with other and older people to see what they saw.

PRINCE TANNATT WOODS, M. D.
Silver Lake, Massachusetts

We conclude with a few replies not easy to classify, but too interesting to omit.

I. Psychology, in my junior college year, brought me up with a start. It taught me keen observation and introspection.

II. I have had to learn thoroness. My teachers did not seem able to make things appeal to me. Moreover, they were easily satisfied and accepted work that was so poorly done that I actually formed habits of incompetence. Why not give the curriculum a rest and agitate for thoroly trained, well educated teachers? Is not the teacher the curriculum after all?

R. W. LEWIS
Pacific College, Newberg, Oregon

I believe that of all I learned at school the habit of "looking it up" in an authority instead of asking my neighbor has helped me most to keep up to date and correct in my various professions of wife, mother and housekeeper.

The subject of efficiency, personal and occupational, has seemed, since I began to study it, to have been the most essential subject omitted from the curriculum of my schools and one perfectly possible to teach there. MRS. F. C. JACCARD
Anaconda, Montana

I. A constructively critical attitude on life—without faultfinding—I believe to be the most useful thing gained from my university training. No one course or person was responsible. The spirit of the University of Michigan, some professors, notably Smalley and Taylor in economics, a tradition of friendly criticism in my fraternity—all helped. C. B. TAYLOR
Des Moines, Iowa

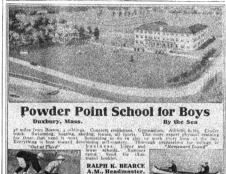

I. Music is the most useful thing I learned at school. In prosperity a pleasure to myself and friends; in adversity, a means of livelihood.

II. I have had to learn method, organization, and, greater than all, a *fixed, definite object*. This is the greatest lack of our schools. We find ourselves too late.
MRS. JAMES BACON
Winthrop, New York

I. The most useful thing I learned at school was that the sum of the three angles of a triangle is equal to two right angles; in other words, that there are things in the universe that are beyond debate. (REV.) ALBERT DONNELL
Burlington, Massachusetts

1. To observe.
2. To observe better.
NATHANIEL BOWDITCH POTTER
New York City
School introduced me to habits of mental concentration. Beyond that little.

It should also have taught self-control, health principles, love of work, thrift, value of time, use of leisure, helpful fatherhood, the service of society, Nation, and God; also knowledge and appreciation of trees, flowers, birds, constellations, pictures, sculpture, architecture, music, biography, history, literature; also interest in uplift, and familiarity with child psychology, world classics in translation and the literary and spiritual values of the Bible. I needed bread; I received stones.
THEODORE C. BLAISDELL
Dean of the School of Liberal Arts Pennsylvania State College

PEBBLES

"Carranza," says an exchange, "dearly loves a joke." Egotist!—*Columbia State.*

"See America first" also applies to international relations.—*Chicago Daily News.*

If there is no change in the Mexican situation, it at least has nothing on the Mexican Treasury.—*Washington Post.*

The Plumber—Take it from me, Joe, them that doesn't believe in preparedness ain't no good on earth. By the way, ye'll have to go back to the shop for a monkey wrench and the soldering outfit.—*Judge.*

A society for disseminating religious literature once sent a bundle of tracts to a railway manager for placing in the waiting room, with the title: "A Route to New Jerusalem." He returned them with the message:
"We cannot place the tracts, as New Jerusalem is not on our system."—*New York American.*

I met a politician,
Of greetings he was chary;
He passed me by with frosty eye—
This was in January.
I met a politician,
The same, on one hot noon:
He bade me stand and wrung my hand—
For this, you see, was June.
—*Columbia State.*

An aged negro was crossing-tender at a spot where an express-train made quick work of a buggy and its occupants. Naturally, he was the chief witness, and the entire case hinged upon the energy with which he had displayed his warning signal.

A grueling cross-examination left Rastus unshaken in this story: The night was dark, and he had waved his lantern frantically, but the driver of the carriage paid no attention to it.

Later the division superintendent called the flagman to his office to compliment him on the steadfastness with which he stuck to his story.

"You did wonderfully, Rastus," he said. "I was afraid at first you might waver in your testimony."

"Nossir, nossir," Rastus exclaimed, "but I done feared ev'ry minute that 'ere durn lawyer was agwine to ask me if mah lantern was lit."—*Puck.*

The New Books

HALF TRUTHS

To call a book *Essays and Literary Studies* and expect it to sell is a flattering tribute to the reputation of the author, and fortunately one which Stephen Leacock's popularity warrants. But the admirers of "Moonbeams from the Larger Lunacy" may be surprized and the seekers for deep philosophy in "Behind the Beyond" will be interested to find a book by Mr. Leacock serious as well as clever, thoughtful and humorous at the same time.

Of the several essays included, two betray Mr. Leacock's classroom point of view—rarely acknowledged in his writings. The Lot of a Schoolmaster sugarcoats numerous educational theories and suggestions, full of valuable information, which by no means prevents them from being entertaining. And because he can show us one professorial mind which is not "seriously damaged by education and by perpetual contact with students" Mr. Leacock makes convincingly The Apology of a Professor.

Then he turns to a consideration of American Humor—not yet boiled down to wit—and sidesteps The Woman Question by remarking that "Perhaps in the modern age it is not the increased freedom of women that is needed, but increased recognition of their dependence. Let the reader remain agonized over that till I write something else."

But meanwhile he pays sincere tribute to The Amazing Genius of O. Henry; attempts The Rehabilitation of Charles II, whom he succeeds in making out a first class hero; and incidentally tells us how to read his books, in which "Most of the statements are at best only half truths. But the half truth is to me a kind of mellow moonlight in which I love to dwell. One sees better in it."

Essays and Literary Studies, by Stephen Leacock. Lane. $1.25.

WHY THEY FIGHT

With a reminder of General Sherman's definition of war we pass from the introductory pages of explosive wrath at the Germans for their superior efficiency and scientific weapons, in Frederic Harrison's *The German Peril,* to the substance of his book. Herein he shows comprehensive grasp of the trend of events and remarkable foresight. From papers of his printed from as far back as 1870 until two weeks previous to the Great War he demonstrates that again and again he endeavored to rouse his money-seeking, sport-loving fellow countrymen to the sense of a threatened human cataclysm.

He maintained that neither the German people, as such, nor their Emperor, peace abiding from policy, wield-

---

What's Keeping Me Back?

You've wondered why you don't get ahead. Why your pay isn't increased. Why you don't get promoted. You've blamed everything and everybody, when the real drawback is *yourself*.

You're standing still because you lack *training*. Because you have not *prepared* yourself to do some one thing better than others. If you really want to get ahead, the way is open to you.

For 25 years the International Correspondence Schools have been helping men to climb into good paying positions. Nearly 5000 reported last year that I. C. S. training had won them advancement. *You* can get I. C. S. training in your spare time in your own home without losing a day or a dollar from your present employment.

Position, power, good money, independence, are within your reach. The I. C. S. are ready to help you be the man you want to be. Let them show you how. Mark and mail this coupon.

I. C. S., Box 4512, Scranton, Pa.

ed the destiny of the German nation. It was the German Junker caste—the only flourishing survivor in Europe of medieval feudalism, hundreds of thousands strong, who ruled Germany absolutely and were determined to dispute, if not destroy England's commercial rivalry and power. Concomitant was the political situation developing in Europe since 1870, particularly that in the Balkans. Dr. Harrison held that "given the circumstances *as they are*, and apart from any question of responsibility for those circumstances, the warning of Germany that 'Who attacks Austria, attacks me,' seems such as the average German patriot, *with the ideas now dominant*, could hardly refuse to back." He goes further and admits sympathy with the German who "finds his redundant population shut out from all the most desirable possessions of the planet," while "England . . . neither seeks to humiliate nor weaken the German Empire, yet she confronts Germany with a maritime power which is not only paramount, but claims that it always must remain predominant." Herein he foresaw diametrically opposed forces leading inevitably toward war, joined by other national currents surging in the same direction.

Finally he looks into the future, when German Junkerdom with its backbone of Prussian Militarism is swept away. It is not a hopeful outlook, and hardly gratifying to the United States to feel that we are to be the financial and commercial residuary legatees of all this ruin, desolation and slaughter. This most illuminating volume is emphatically worthy of Dr. Harrison's long-established reputation as an able and discerning writer on public affairs.

Dr. Thomas F. A. Smith's *What Germany Thinks* is disappointing in that it is not a personal review of a supremely momentous subject, of which he, as late English Lecturer at the University of Erlangen, should be a well qualified exponent, but is, for the most part, a partisan treatise compiled from printed and verbal expressions of the German attitude toward the war. While everything republished or reported in Dr. Smith's book may be authentic, still there doubtless are contrary revelations of German thought not quoted which would "relieve Germany, as a people, somewhat from the deliberate wickedness Dr. Smith sets forth to prove out of her own mouth. He finds himself called upon, here and there, to shift his ground a little. He yields the inefficiency, the lack of common knowledge possest by the British diplomatic and consular services in Germany, together with the "dry rot" in England.

Herewith another book which goes deeper into the origin of the war than a Alsace-Lorraine, the Serbian pistol shot, or the German invasion of Belgium. In *Germany vs. Civilization* William Roscoe Thayer treats it as a world embracing conflict of ideals as between despotism and democracy, barbarism and all we have striven to attain in betterment of the human race, of long growth and of desperate future portent.

He recalls a Germany which, for its solid plodding qualities, won his admiration; but which is now engulfed in the terrible pagan forcefulness of the ruling caste of Junkerdom. Again appears the question how far the Emperor has been a free agent in directing German policy. A German view of him revealed in private discussion may throw light on this subject. According to this the German Emperor was never the Junker ideal, nor was he popular with the German masses. Somewhat curiously this was chiefly owing to his physical defects. His stature, infirmity and general build were not of the approved German pattern for a Kaiser, in nowise resembling the heroic mold of "Unser Fritz." Besides he was the Englishwoman's son! He soon grew to comprehend this unfavorable attitude toward him, and made almost desperate efforts to prove his sturdy Germanism in spite of it. Hence his grandiloquent utterances, his impulsive actions, and his anti-English sentiments. How far these would seem to have imprest his subjects is doubtful, since they brought down upon him the sobriquet of The Gadabout—as nearly as the term can be translated. Mr. Thayer does not seem to have lit upon this view, the other pro-Ally writers hint the German Emperor's position was not entirely secure in the councils of Junkerdom.

The German propaganda in the United States is reviewed and we are warned not "to be lulled into inaction by the belief that this titanic struggle does not and cannot concern us," for the "Germans make no secret of their calculation that, when they have destroyed the British Empire, only Russia and the United States will stand between them and world dominion in a final triumph of despotism over democracy."

The German Peril, by Frederic Harrison. London: Unwin. $1.25. What Germany Thinks, by Thomas F. A. Smith. Doran. $1.25. Germany vs. Civilization, by William Roscoe Thayer. Houghton, Mifflin. $1.

PSYCHOLOGY AND ECONOMICS

All economic theory is more or less related to prevailing psychological beliefs, but it is seldom that the economist takes the trouble to check his theories against the more advanced teachings of contemporary psychologists. Professor Taussig's Brown University sesquicentennial celebration lectures therefore have a certain refreshing quality that other economists may do well to study. In *Inventors and Moneymakers* the author may be said to cashier the traditional "economic man" and to deal with the more familiar organism that obeys his impulses with very little thought of material gain. People have the "instinct" to contrive, and they will continue to invent, just as they will continue to write verses and make graven images, whether we have patent laws or not, whether we can capitalize inventions or not, whether we need the money or not. The classic arguments for privation and economic conflict as the sole sources of "incentive" to effort are shown to be untenable for the class of people whose distinctive economic contributions are most significant. And the prevailing antagonisms in industry are shown to be economically wasteful as well as socially injurious in that they force so many workers to bridle their constructive instincts.

As for the money-makers, they follow the constructive as well as the accumulative instinct, altruistic motives no less than emulative ones. The directors of corporations have frequently shown themselves imbued with a sense of responsibility, and a captain of industry may conceivably conduct his economic functions in the spirit of a patriotic and devoted statesman. The discussion again brings forward the question whether industrial leadership can be reconciled with industrial democracy.

A radically different application of modern psychology to economics is *The Executive and His Control of Men*, by Enoch Burton Gowin, of New York University. This essay postulates the increase of executive ability as the great economic and social need of our times, and proceeds to analyze the sources of the executive's power. It embraces the principles of scientific management applied to the increase of power, and to the control of others—"motivating the group." In spite of the distinctly commercial attitude of the author, the book contains a mass of valuable material.

Inventors and Money-makers, by F. W. Taussig. Macmillan. $1. *The Executive and His Control of Men*, by Enoch Burton Gowin. Macmillan. $1.50.

JEWS IN GREECE AND ROME

In the present volume Max Radin, a young scholar of much promise, has made a needed study of the relation of the Jewish people to the Greek and Roman civilization about them during the period from the return from the Captivity to the Conquest by Christianity in the Roman Empire. For the material of this study the author has depended upon the Old Testament and its Apocryphal writings, the works of Josephus, and particularly the collection of classical references to the Jews made by M. T. Reinach. The New Testament sources are scarcely referred to, the author appearing to regard them as comparatively late and untrustworthy. While his reading has covered a wide field, he has given the result in broad outline, not confined by any means to what is directly Jewish. Thus chapters are given to the discussion of Greek and Roman religious ideas and to the constitution of city governments and, particularly, Alexandria. We observe that the author does not seem to regard the Persian period as critical for Jewish religion, nor does he explain the belief in magic and in good and evil spirits. He has taken pains, at considerable length, to defend the Jews against absurd charges, such as their worship of the golden head of an ass. While the apologetic purpose is not concealed, the book will be of value to other than Jewish scholars.

The Jews Among the Greeks and Romans, by Max Radin. Philadelphia: Jewish Publication Society. $1.50.

DIVIDENDS

LIGGETT & MYERS TOBACCO COMPANY.
St. Louis, Mo.,   May 25th, 1916.
A dividend of One and Three-quarters per cent (1¾%) has been declared upon the Preferred stock, of Liggett & Myers Tobacco Company, payable on July 1st, 1916, to stockholders of record at the close of business June 15th, 1916. Checks will be mailed.
T. T. ANDERSON, Treasurer.

AMERICAN CAR AND FOUNDRY COMPANY.
New York, June 1, 1916.
PREFERRED CAPITAL STOCK
DIVIDEND No. 68.
A dividend of one and three-quarters per cent (1¾%) on the Preferred Stock of this Company has this day been declared, payable Saturday, July 1, 1916, to stockholders of record at the close of business Saturday, June 10, 1916. Checks will be mailed by the Guaranty Trust Company of New York.
WM. M. HAGER, Secretary.
S. S. DELANO, Treasurer.

AMERICAN CAR AND FOUNDRY COMPANY.
New York, June 1, 1916.
COMMON CAPITAL STOCK
DIVIDEND No. 85.
A dividend of one-half per cent (½%) on the Common Stock of this Company has this day been declared, payable Saturday, July 1, 1916, to stockholders of record at the close of business Saturday, June 10, 1916.
Checks will be mailed by the Guaranty Trust Company of New York.
WM. M. HAGER, Secretary.
S. S. DELANO, Treasurer.

MEETING NOTICE

AMERICAN CAR AND FOUNDRY COMPANY
STOCKHOLDERS MEETING
The stockholders of the American Car and Foundry Company are hereby notified that the regular Annual Meeting of the stockholders of said Company will be held at its offices No. 243 Washington Street, Jersey City, New Jersey, June 29, 1916, at 12 o'clock noon for the purpose of electing a Board of Directors and transacting such other business as may be properly brought before the meeting.
WM. M. HAGER, Secretary.

Insurance
Conducted by
W. E. UNDERWOOD

A STRIKING COMPARISON

Occasionally I am in receipt of requests from readers seeking information about the Royal Arcanum, a fraternal life insurance order organized in 1877, which has a present membership of about 240,000 persons, assets of more than $12,000,000 and an aggregate outstanding insurance of about $450,000,000.

The order has unlimited power of assessing members for the purpose of raising funds with which to meet its liabilities. To that extent it can be regarded as solvent. But measured by the tests to which a regular life insurance company must conform, its so-called reserves, or surplus funds, are greatly inadequate. As a means of illustrating the difference between its methods and those practised by an old line company I reproduce, in my own way for the sake of brevity, a comparison I saw between a Royal Arcanum contract and one of the Mutual Benefit, each for $3000, at age thirty-five, both issued in 1878. Time is the supreme test in such a case. In 1878 this insurance cost $11.76 in the Royal Arcanum and $78 in the Mutual Benefit. During the subsequent years the cost in the Royal Arcanum fluctuated, but steadily increased. In 1885 it was $20.16; in 1895, $25.20; in 1905, $66.51; in 1915, $160.20. The Mutual Benefit's premium remained at $78 a year thruout the period, except as it was reduced by annual dividends.

At the end of 1915 the net cost in the Royal Arcanum was $2,937.23. The rate had risen from $11.76 to $160.20 a year; the policyholder was sixty-three years old and, of course, had accumulated no values. In that respect, he was just where he started thirty-eight years before.

In the Mutual Benefit the gross cost (38 × $78) was $2,964. The dividends paid, $864.22, reduced this to $2,099.78. The cash surrender value of the policy is $1,899.24. If the holder of this policy wishes to quit, and takes his cash value, his protection in the company during thirty-eight years will have cost him $110.54, net.

For the benefit of those who are investing their money and their years in reserveless life insurance, I present this experience as something invaluable because it is actual.

R. J. N., Marion, N. C.—If you can conveniently do so, leave your annual dividends with the company as purchase money for additional insurance payable at death. These additions have equivalent cash values, if at any time you wish to convert them or to apply them in shortening the term during which premiums are payable for the original amount.

NEW YORK   LOS ANGELES

Across the Continent from Monday to Monday

Cadillac in thrilling dash from Pacific to Atlantic
shows incomparable stability and sustained speed

Los Angeles to New York in 7 days, 11 hours, 52 minutes

THE quickest way to appreciate the wonder of this triumphant trans-continental Cadillac trip, is to close your eyes and call up two pictures—one of the start, and the other of the finish.

Transport yourself first, to beautiful Los Angeles, and imagine a Cadillac leaving the city one minute after midnight on a Monday morning, the second week in May.

Then, blot out the picture of Los Angeles and substitute New York, and try to conceive *the same car with the same driver swinging blithely up Broadway the Monday following.*

No effort of your imagination, no words of ours, and nothing less graphic than a motion picture record can portray the heroic character of the work done by this Cadillac in the interim—between these two Mondays in May.

But the start and the finish, the distance covered, the remarkable time made, the great reduction made from the previous record—all these spell the superlative character of the performance so plainly that no motorist can fail to grasp its meaning.

The Cadillac which 'conquered the continent' was just such a Cadillac as you might buy and drive yourself.

It was equipped as your Cadillac would be equipped, with no special preparations other than those which would ordinarily be made for a long distance tour.

The trans-continental Cadillac was not a specially built car 'stripped for action'—but a fully equipped standard Roadster; and, granting that you possessed the stamina of its single driver, the journey was one which you yourself might take if you were so inclined.

But, because of the terrific speed almost continually sustained, it involved, of course, hardships to man and car of an unprecedented character.

What it proves of Cadillac stability and endurance is aptly illustrated by a comparison between the Cadillac cross-continent record and the railroad schedule between the two cities.

The distance by rail is 3240 miles—the distance covered by the one Cadillac was 3371 miles.

In the regular railroad schedule between Los Angeles and New York, in spite of smooth tracks, solid road-bed and clear right-of-way, a relay of twenty-two locomotives is called into action.

Consider, now, the almost miraculous endurance of the car, handicapped a hundred times over in the matter of road-bed, yet it traveled its distance without so much attention to its motor as the cleaning of a spark plug.

Its rate of travel ranged from only 5 miles per hour, plowing through hub-deep mud, to 68 miles per hour on smooth stretches.

The railroad schedule is 90 hours—and the Cadillac *cut 91 hours and 23 minutes off the previous motor car record* made by the same driver in another make of car.

The Cadillac left Los Angeles at 12:01 A.M. Monday, May 8th, and arrived in New York City at 2:53 P.M. Monday, May 15th, with intervals for food and sleep.

In that eventful period of a little more than a week, it was put through a more terrific trial of stamina than the majority of cars encounter in ten years of travel.

Over mountain ranges, along precipitous passes, through desert wastes, fording unbridged streams, and through roads almost impassable at their best but made worse by this spring's copious rains, the Cadillac hurtled heroically on—not merely defying destruction, but unruffled, undisturbed and undaunted.

The wonder of the thing, is not that the trip was made without disaster.

The real wonder of it is not in the limited time that elapsed.

No, the real wonder, and the really valuable lesson, is that this wonderful thing was done with such unprecedented ease.

That this trans-continental Cadillac broke the previous record by nearly four days is incidental to the real achievement.

The real achievement rests in the fact that it emerged from the fray virtually as good a Cadillac as when it began.

It is still a Cadillac with many thousands of miles of service ahead of it.

All that the Cadillac has demonstrated before is now demonstrated anew in another way.

We all know, now, beyond doubt, that there is not in this nation a set of road conditions which can successfully challenge Cadillac construction.

We all know that the Cadillac has again proven itself to be

The World's Greatest Road Car.

Cadillac

Standard
of the World

The Independent
Founded 1848

HARPER'S WEEKLY
Founded 1857
Incorporated with The Independent May 22, 1916

THE CHAUTAUQUAN
Incorporated with The Independent June 1, 1914

The Independent is owned and published by the Independent Corporation, at 119 West Fortieth Street, New York. William B. Howland, president; Frederic E. Dickinson, treasurer; William Hayes Ward, honorary editor; Hamilton Holt, editor; Harold J. Howland, associate editor; Edwin E. Slosson, literary editor; Karl V. S. Howland, publisher. The price of The Independent is Ten Cents a copy; Four Dollars for one year. Postage to foreign countries in the Postal Union, $1.75 extra; to Canada, $1 extra. Writers who wish their articles returned should send stamped and address envelopes. No responsibility is assumed for the loss or non-return of manuscripts. Entered at the New York Post Office as Second Class matter. Copyright, 1916, by The Independent. Address all communications to The Independent, 119 West Fortieth Street, New York

CONTENTS FOR JUNE 19, 1916
Volume 86   Number 3524

UNCONVENTIONAL CONVENTION NEWS

The tumult and the shouting, such as they were, have died. The captains and kings and the delegates and Mr. Brown and the reporters and the favorite-son fat ladies have departed. They were a fickle lot, those favorite-son fat ladies. All wore Hughes badges today.

Big Mike has the floor now. His power is as great as that of Penrose, Murray Crane and Barnes put together. He has only to say "Sweep," and every man in the building will obey him.

It's a hard task that Big Mike and his delegates have before them. History in the making is a messy thing. Ask Mike, and he will tell you that there's never a world crisis but leaves its egg shells, its broken ham sandwiches and its lemon soda bottles behind it.—*New York Tribune.*

[APPLAUSE]

Whose name, resounding thru the hall,
Provokes a chorus far from small—
Inspires applause from one and all?
    Most anybody's.

Whose name, upon the waiting ear
Descending loud and strong and clear,
Will cause the long and hearty cheer?
    Whose won't?

Who will, 'mid waving hats and coats.
And cheers from thrice three thousand throats.
Poll a majority of votes?
    Read the front page.
      —*New York Tribune.*

Under the green and white trimmings on the ceiling of the Coliseum the giant amphitheater looks not unlike the bottom of a swimming tank. The resemblance was hightened by the fact that all day long myriads of bubbles were rising.

Governor Willis, of Ohio, stayed under water longest. He nominated Theodore Burton and surprised everybody when he named his candidate. During the time he was quoting from the Gettysburg address and the second inaugural, it looked very much like Lincoln, but later he seemed about to throw his strength to Blaine. Maine cheered him wildly.

At the end of the first half hour Willis was still going strongly, using the breast stroke for the most part. Willis is a man of great strength and lung power. One of the achievements which brought him the Governorship was the fact that he ate ten chicken pies at a county fair. This was duly chronicled in the Ohio papers, and cartoonists of that state are fond of drawing the doughty Governor with a lunch basket strapped about his waist.

It is possible that Burton's sponsor would still be speaking but for a delegate from Ohio who sat in the front row, not ten feet from the Governor. While the speaker was in the middle of one of his most eloquent flights the delegate seized a ham sandwich in both hands and held tight for fear of being stampeded.

Seeing the sandwich, Willis quickly got down to personalities and named his man. Burton, it seems, "is common without being commonplace." His manner was described as "cordial without being effusive," something after the demeanor of John J. McGraw toward a new umpire.

Senator Fall did not take long in nominating Roosevelt. As soon as he said "the one colossal figure of American manhood" the galleries began to cheer.

William R. Wood, who nominated Fairbanks, broke all the rules. He named his candidate three times before he finished. This lessened the dramatic element in his appeal somewhat, because when he got down to the "who was it?" everybody knew the answer in advance. The inspiring slogan which Wood pinned on his candidate was "he has never given offense to anybody."—*New York Tribune.*

Up in the gallery above the speaker's platform a short, plump young woman arose and turned loose the "rebel yell." It threw the first touch of life into the convention. The Root men cheered her and laughed, and one of them gave her a flag. She arose again, and this time she let out that famous screech four times. This time another man gave her a flag. From that time she led the Root demonstration.

The "rebel yell" is a noise like no other; it goes screaming across a hall or a field like the shriek of a shell; it seems to possess the power of motion. Beside it, hurrahs are whispers, and a scream is a whine. This young woman knew exactly how to produce that horrific sound; it is safe to say that if she let it off on top of the Singer Building she would make the babies cry in Central Park.

In the row in front of her there was a nice old gentleman with white whiskers, with a nice old lady beside him, and every time Mrs. Blanche Root, of Washington—the young woman under consideration—turned on that shattering yell they would both shudder and put their fingers in their ears. Presently the whole convention was watching the old gentleman and the old lady and howling with laughter. Every time it laughed it would shout, and this helped along the Root demonstration mightily. The nice old couple, still shuddering and stopping their ears with clocklike regularity, were totally ignorant of the large part they were playing in creating sentiment favorable to the nomination of Root, were oblivious, in fact, of everything except the distressing noise produced by the young woman behind; and this added greatly to the convention's contentment with the whole proceeding. . . . By this time Job Hedges had become interested. He mounted a chair and signaled to Mrs. Root, far up in the gallery, from his place on the floor. Mrs. Root arose and looked at him expectantly. Mr. Hedges wagged his finger at her and opened his mouth, producing therefrom no sound, but going thru the motions of a "rebel yell."

Mrs. Root obliged—obliged with joy. The nice old couple stuck their fingers in their ears and shuddered, and the Root demonstration was on again. Thereafter Mr. Hedges conducted her. Yes, he conducted her, like an orchestra leader. Using his forefinger as a baton, he beat time, and she followed him closely and with a touching confidence. A man from Tennessee, the home of the "rebel yell," got jealous and gave the "rebel yell" himself, but it was a feeble thing to Mrs. Root's. Hedges looked scornfully at him and he wilted; and then Hedges turned toward the gallery again and Mrs. Root the pitch, and she rose to it with a "rebel yell" that made all her previous efforts seem like a whisper.—*New York Times.*

"MR." HUGHES ON THE FIRST DAY OF HIS MISTER-HOOD

THIS PHOTOGRAPH WAS TAKEN AS THE FORMER JUSTICE WAS ON HIS WAY TO CHURCH LAST SUNDAY, THE DAY
AFTER HIS NOMINATION. BESIDES THIS DAUGHTER, CATHERINE, MR. HUGHES
HAS TWO DAUGHTERS AND ONE SON

T

T

The Independent

WITH WHICH IS INCORPORATED

HARPER'S WEEKLY

WHAT WAS DEMONSTRATED AT CHICAGO

THE conventions at Chicago have demonstrated two facts. One is the irresistible power of public opinion. There were but two serious candidates at Chicago. The politicians wanted neither of them. They had to take one of them or they would have had to take the other. The politician is impotent when public opinion sufficiently bestirs itself. The nomination of Mr Hughes, like that of Mr. Wilson four years ago, was made in spite of the politicians, tho in the case of Mr. Hughes those gentlemen capitulated more gracefully. The presence of two such candidates in the field during the coming campaign presents a new hope for the rising power of the people over their self-appointed managers.

Mr. Hughes is a man whom everybody respects and who will command support outside the limits of his own party. His record is honorable, his ability is proved and his character is irreproachable. He had no part in the factional fight of 1912, and is the one man to reunite the divided party.

The conventions demonstrated as well the bigness of Theodore Roosevelt. In the face of a demand of unparalleled vigor and insistence from the party which he created that he bear their standard once more he has not yielded. He has taken the broader view. He will support Mr. Hughes, and it will not be easy. For it will mean going back to the party which he left because he believed it had committed a crime of which he was the victim. It will mean supporting a man with whom he is not sympathetic by temperament and from whom he believes he has not received fair treatment in the past. Whatever the merits of this belief, the fact that he holds it makes the path hard. His refusal to accept the Progressive nomination is a stunning blow to most of the Progressives who followed the exodus four years ago, burned their political bridges behind them and staked their all on his leadership. But the Progressive party is disintegrating and if Mr. Roosevelt galvanized it into life for another campaign all hope of his coöperating with the Republicans would be gone, doubtless, forever.

Now his declaration cannot fail to exalt him in the estimation of his countrymen. Indeed it is not inconceivable that if he throws himself wholeheartedly into the fight for Hughes he may yet be the dominant personality of the campaign.

KITCHENER OF KHARTUM

THE introduction of scientific method into warfare has not impaired the power of personality. The bigger the machine the greater must be the man to manage it. In the peaceful days of 1914 an effort was made by the government to have Earl Kitchener shelved by a sinecure. But when the storm broke he was nominated by acclamation for War Minister. He alone saw what must be done. He alone had the power to do it. England had at that time as little appreciation of the magnitude of the task before her as the United States had when Lincoln called for 75,000 men for three months to put down the rebellion. People said that the war would be over by Christmas. Kitchener said it would begin in May. People said that England would have done her duty when she fulfilled her promise of 1911 to send 160,000 men to France. Kitchener said millions of men would be needed and for three years.

And he got them. "Kitchener wants you" proved a more effective recruiting advertisement than "Your King needs you." Never before in the history of the world has a man raised and equipt a volunteer army of five million men. Probably no one will ever have to do it again, so both pacifists and militarists hope, tho with different reasons in mind. The country called him and he called the country. Both responded nobly. What was at first sneered at as "Kitchener's mob" is now respected as "Kitchener's army." That this army has not yet gained a victory cannot rightfully be called his fault. Troops can be extemporized. Generals have to be trained. Lord Kitchener has been criticized—and justly—for failing to provide the quantity and kind of ammunition needed by modern warfare and for neglecting to organize in the factory as well as in the field. But this came from attempting to do too much by himself and cannot detract from his great achievements. He had been relieved of part of his multifarious duties and it was expected that the responsibility of his office would before many months have been divided or devolved upon another. But death came to him, as doubtless he would have wished to have it come, in the path of duty and in the hight of his power and reputation. England's loss is irreparable, but Kitchener's life came to a noble and appropriate close. His grave is deeper than any dug by man and, like some ancient king, two hundred of his warriors are buried in his tomb. No coffin could be found for him more fitting than a British cruiser, for the enumeration of his manly qualities reads like the catalog of ships. "Indefatigable," "Indomitable," "Inflexible," "Implacable," "Invincible"; these are the adjectives his biographers use in describing his character.

He was of the hero type, whom women adore and men follow. In O. Henry's best story, the "Unfinished Story," it was Kitchener's portrait on the bureau that saved the shop-girl in her hour of temptation. While still living he became a legend and figured in many a story and poem. Conan Doyle's "Bimbashi Joyce" and Kipling's "Kitchener's School" will come to mind. Khartum, which stood for England's disgrace, for it meant the sacrifice of Gordon and defeat by the Mahdi, became to him a title of honor. He fought the desert with a railroad and he conquered the Sudanese twice, first by force and second by fair dealing. He foiled the French in their attempt to acquire the Nile valley, yet they will mourn his death as much as the English. Colonel Marchand, whom he met and checkmated at Fashoda on the Nile in 1898, he met again a few months ago in France, this time not as foe and rival but as friend and ally. Now both are dead.

When Kitchener was twenty he went on a holiday to his father's home in Dinan, France. The Germans invaded the country and young Kitchener promptly enlisted in the French army as a private. His father had him discharged and sent him back to Woolwich Military Academy. But early ambitions are not so easily quenched and Kitchener ends his career at sixty-five as he began it, fighting to free France from the Germans.

IN A DOZEN WORDS

NOBODY wanted Hughes but the people. The office, therefore, sought the man.

A FORTUNATE DEATH

THE death of Yuan Shih-kai from stomach trouble, whether natural or artificially induced by himself or others, removes the greatest obstacle to the security of the Chinese republic. Yuan might have been revered by future generations as the Washington of his country, but instead he will be regarded as its Benedict Arnold. When he was chosen in February, 1912, as the first president of the whole of China, he commanded the confidence or at least the support of all factions, conservatives and radicals, Manchus and Chinese. But instead of devoting his great administrative powers to establishing the new republic, he declared himself emperor and aspired to become a god. The proofs of his conspiracy to overthrow the constitution that he had sworn to protect have now been placed before the world in a pamphlet recently issued by the republican leaders in revolt against his authority. This pamphlet, which bears upon its cover our good old American motto: "Rebellion to tyrants is obedience to God," contains in Chinese and English the code telegrams sent out from Peking to the provincial authorities instructing them to force the election and forge the returns in order to make it appear that the people favored the restoration of the monarchy. We quote a few significant sentences from these secret instructions, proving that for ways that are dark and tricks that are vain Yuan Shih-kai was peculiar.

It was never intended that the citizens should have any choice between a republic and a monarchy. For this reason at the time of voting all the representatives must be made unanimously to advocate a change of the republic into a monarchy.

In order to clothe the proceedings with an appearance of regularity the representatives of the districts, tho they are really appointed by the highest military and civil officials of the province, should still be nominally elected by the districts. The necessary documents . . . should be properly antedated.

The Superintendent of Elections should then under cover of inviting them to a social gathering or dinner party, request their presence at his official residence and improve the occasion . . . by making known to them the names of those who are to be elected. As these documents concern the very foundation of the state, they will, in case they become known, leave a dark spot on the political history of our country. Upon their secrecy depends our national honor and prestige in the eyes of both our own people and foreigners. . . . The Central Government has concluded that it would be better to sort out and burn the documents so as to remove all unnecessary records and prevent regrettable consequences.

But some of these documents escaped the fire and abundantly justify the Yun-nan province in starting last January the revolt against Yuan Shih-kai in which most of the southern provinces have joined. The Chinese republicans blame President Goodnow of Johns Hopkins for the civil war that has involved the country during the last six months, for his opinion as constitutional adviser was put forward at Peking as the justification of Yuan's assumption of the throne. Dr. Goodnow is reported to have said in his memorandum on the best form of government for China:

It is of course not susceptible of doubt that a monarchy is better suited than a republic to China. China's history and traditions, her social and economic conditions, her relations with foreign powers, all make it probable that the country would develop that constitutional government which it must develop if it is to preserve its independence as a state more easily as a monarchy than as a republic.

With Professor Frank Goodnow giving such advice as this; with Professor Jeremiah Jenks sending out circulars eulogizing Yuan even when he expelled his opponents from parliament, "and by so doing silenced and terrified the others"; with the American Government delaying the recognition of the Chinese republic as long as possible and withdrawing from the "six-power loan" necessary for the defense and development of the country, it is no wonder that the Chinese republicans felt themselves betrayed in the house of their friends. They had a right to expect from America sympathy and aid if not official support in their noble endeavors to gain political freedom, but instead they received indifference and distrust. Now that Yuan Shih-kai is out of the way and Li Yuan-hung, a real republican, is in the presidential chair, we earnestly hope that the Chinese people will have an opportunity to prove that Dr. Goodnow is wrong in believing that the Chinese are unfit for a republican form of government.

THIRD PARTIES

THE brief history of the Progressive party proves that it is easier to start something than to keep it going.

OUT OF THE MOUTHS OF THE FACULTY

CERTAIN professors of the political sciences at Columbia took a significant step recently, when they decided to investigate, on their own initiative, the controversy which has kept 50,000 garment workers in New York idle for more than six weeks.

They invited representatives of the Manufacturers'

Association and the unions to meet them and present their respective pleas. The unions accepted the invitation; the manufacturers declined, but did send a considerable amount of documentary material. This the investigators studied carefully, together with the evidence offered by the union spokesmen. After submitting their digest of the facts to the Manufacturers' Association for verification, they issued a public statement, from which The Independent quoted on June 5, expressing their belief that the rights of the dispute lay with the workers, and giving their reasons.

The method of the study was unimpeachable; its motive and effect seem to us admirable. A disinterested group of experts, like the instructors of a strong university, can serve the community well in clarifying public issues on which the individual citizen has little or no critical information except that furnished by a hasty and none too impartial daily press. At Columbia, of course, one would expect the liberal view to prevail, tho that view unfortunately is not always characteristic of academic persons. But in the great universities, both east and west, the faculty has so often and so heartily taken its part in public service of one sort and another that the taint of the cloister has become purely imaginary and there is small reason to suspect bias.

It is reasonable to believe that in the long run faculty judgment will be worthy of thoughtful acceptance by the man who will not judge without knowledge and has neither time nor aptitude for getting that knowledge by himself. The university ought to help mold public opinion more directly than thru the classroom, and in doing so it is serving the state in a way for which it is peculiarly fitted.

FAIR AND SQUARE

THE country is to be congratulated that the issues of the campaign will be measures, not personalities. It is the habit of neither Charles Evans Hughes nor of Woodrow Wilson to descend to abuse.

The fight will be fair, square and vigorous, and whichever wins, the country will not go to the dogs.

VIA PANAMA

IT was particularly unfortunate for us that the opening of the Panama Canal should have been followed so quickly by its closing, at a time when its chief rival, the Suez Canal, had been put out of business by the war. But now that the Panama Canal is again open and, according to Colonel Goethals, "for keeps," its advantages are becoming realized. In the first month after its reopening 137 ocean ships past thru its locks, which is more than the monthly average before the slides closed it. The New Zealand Shipping Company, which runs a line of Royal Mail steamers from England to New Zealand, has announced that its steamers will hereafter go by way of Panama instead of around the Cape of Good Hope as hitherto.

Besides being safer from submarines the Panama route is 2380 miles shorter than the Cape route from London to Wellington. The chief objection to the Panama route has been that it involved a longer voyage in the tropics and this required a greater consumption of coal, since coal is used for cooling the refrigerated steamers that bring meats to Great Britain. Just now, however, the price of coal at the Cape turns the scale in favor of Panama. It is evident that the future of Panama depends upon how cheaply coal and oil can be furnished at Balboa.

MEASURED BY CONVENTIONAL APPLAUSE

THEODORE ROOSEVELT ....93 minutes
  Charles E. Hughes ....16 minutes
John M. Parker ....213 seconds
Charles W. Fairbanks ....26 seconds

FRENCH LEAVE

IN the tedious, long distance and entrenched warfare of our day it is the newest fighting-man, the aviator, who retains most of the old romantic spirit of individual heroism. When Navarre, the French champion, brought down his seventeenth German in single combat, his officers were at a loss how to honor him, since for previous achievements he had won all the badges and ribbons at their disposal. So they called in the victorious airman and asked him to name his own reward. "Fortyeight hours in Paris," answered Navarre.

There spoke the true Frenchman. So spake Hervé Riel, two centuries before, when Admiral Damfreville offered him any reward he chose for saving the French fleet from the British:

"Since 't is ask and have, I may—
  Since the others go ashore—
Come! A good whole holiday!
  Leave to go and see my wife, whom I call the Belle
    Aurore!"
That he asked and that he got,—nothing more.

Whether M. Navarre has a wife whom he calls the Belle Aurore we do not know, but the holiday he asked, ending with a banquet at a restaurant on the Champs Elysées, that he got and nothing more.

THE DICKENS YOU SAY

A LETTER by Charles Dickens, recently sold at auction in New York, contains the following passage:

I fear the North to be utterly mad and war to be unavoidable. I do not doubt that England could shell the City of New York off the face of the earth in two days.

Yet it was Dickens who by his jibes and sneers at our hypocritical pretense of freedom spurred the American people to get rid of slavery at any cost.

His letter is dated December 1, 1861, and obviously refers to the "Trent" case, where we took two Confederate emissaries from a British ship. Yet when a British cruiser searched an American ship, the "China," and took from her all the Germans and Austrians, did any of our leading novelists, say Owen Wister, demand that London be shelled off the face of the earth? Not so that you could hear them.

We apologized for our blunder in the "Trent" case and gave up Mason and Slidell. England is expected to apologize for her blunder in the "China" case and give up the thirty-eight Germans and Austrians. This is a better way of settling our differences than shelling each other's cities off the face of the earth.

MEN AND MEASURES

THE Republican Platform and the Progressive Platform are practically identical.

It was men, not measures, that separated the two conventions.

CONVENTIONAL HISTORY

THE Republican Convention—Anybody but Roosevelt.
The Progressive Convention—Nobody but Roosevelt.

TO THE GRADUATES OF 1916

I WAS graduated from Amherst College sixty years ago and had hoped to be able to meet the few of my class who continue after so many years, but physical weakness prevents, and I venture to say a few words out of my own experience to those who are beginning their life where mine own ends.

The trustees of the college have been good enough to add my portrait to those belonging to the college, and I am not sorry that the accessories are such as to suggest my interest in Oriental archeology, because it is one of the subjects to which, for a number of years, I gave special study, altho by no means my life work. Forty years ago, on the fiftieth anniversary of the founding of Amherst College I presented a translation of the cuneiform inscriptions in the college cabinet.

At that time I believe I was the only man in the country who had begun the study of Assyriology, and I was ambitious to pursue the subject, but I soon discovered that the field was so broad that it required more than all one's time to cover it, time which I could not give. Meanwhile the universities, led by Johns Hopkins, established such a department, and I was content to give my spare hours to a field in archeology not covered by others.

I do not pretend that archeology is an important study. It is not especially practical. It is like astronomy, which is the queen of all the physical sciences and the most useless of them all, and one which has added almost nothing to human wealth and comfort since the days when Ulysses boasted that as a pirate guided by the stars he had harried the Mediterranean coasts. No more can one's studies in archeology add wealth to the world. It will not improve our ancestors to learn what was their ignorance or what gods they worshipped, but such ancestral history is as fascinating as the study of astronomy, and it is a worthy ambition to add something to human knowledge, even if no material advantage appears to follow. It is the dessert after the meal, the spice of recreation that gives savor to the loaf and roast of service. Life is service, but life is not all service. There must be relaxation and play, and the desire to add something to human knowledge is one of the keenest of delights. Of course one must serve, that is what he lives for, to make the world happier and better, freer, to extend the rule of liberty and justice everywhere; but if one can also have the consciousness that he is adding a little something to the sum total of human knowledge he may feel he has not lived quite in vain. But the great mass of one's human life and endeavor should be given to service, while the spare hours of lamplight can be allowed for the excitement of less useful study.

I have a young business friend who once surprized us at a prayer meeting by saying "I know well enough that Jesus Christ was the great model for us all, but I always like Gunga Din." Kipling tells us of that black, barefoot Hindu heathen, with his water bag on his back, carrying drink for the weary and wounded soldiers, bullied and insulted, but always patient, faithful and fearless in his humble duties, and it is not strange that the poem ends:

By the living Gawd that made you
You're a better man than I am, Gunga Din.

It is the willingness of service, whether great or small, which brings satisfaction. When Milton lost his eyesight "overplied in liberty's defense," he took pride in the sacrifice.

This thought would bear me through the world's vain masque

Content, though blind, had I no better guide.

And I may venture to say that in no other service of my life do I take so much satisfaction as in the remembrance that I initiated and pushed to conclusion the work of organizing the federation of our American churches, and that I wrote the invitation to the denominations which met to organize the Federal Council of Churches, and no other disappointment has been so keen as that which followed my failure once, and twice, and a third time, to unite two or more denominations in corporate union. Where I failed wiser and more fortunate ecclesiastical statesmanship will yet succeed.

In another of his poems, perhaps the finest, Kipling gives honor to those supra-human heroes who have created our civilization:

Such as fought and sailed and ruled and loved and made our world,
and whose spirits rest in felicity, as it were, above the pole of the heavens, yet ready to do God's service.

Tis theirs to sweep through the ringing deep where Azrael's outposts are,
And buffet a path through the pit's red wrath when God goes forth to war.

To this company of the world's mightiest victors came the spirit of Kipling's brother-in-law, but a very different man was he.

He scarce had need to doff his pride or slough the dross of earth.
E'en as he trod that day to God so walked he from his birth,
In simpleness and gentleness and honor and clean mirth.

"Simpleness," "gentleness," these were not their virtues. Their biographers, from Alexander and Julius Cæsar down to Cecil Rhodes, have forgotten to extol their simple and gentle nature, but that's a quality that any one of us can reach. And

So "cup to lip" in fellowship they gave him welcome high,
And made him place at their banquet board, the strong men ranged thereby,
Who had done his work and held his peace, and had no fear to die."

"He had done his work" in fearless patience, but that is what Gunga Din did. It is what any one of us can do and so

Beyond the loom of the last lone star through open darkness hurled;
Further than rebel comet dared or hiving star-swarm swirled,
Sits he with those who praise our God for that they served His world.

"They served God's world." That is feasible for any of us, and I would have the youth who now go forth from these halls pledge a solemn oath by the living God that made them that when sixty years from now, in the year 1976, their feeble, trembling relics shall return to lead this academic procession, it shall be recorded of the noble clan of 1916 that they served God's world. That is all, and that is enough.

WILLIAM HAYES WARD

WHAT HUGHES THINKS

In 1908, when Charles E. Hughes was Governor of New York State and was being talked of for the Presidency, there was then as now a great desire on the part of the public to know his views on the great problems of American politics. To meet this need The Independent, with the cordial coöperation of Mr. Hughes, compiled a volume of his most important public utterances. This volume, issued under the imprint of G. P. Putnam's Sons of New York, consisted of 289 pages containing fifteen addresses and papers. It was provided with an introduction by President Jacob Gould Schurman of Cornell University (who wrote on Hughes in our issue of May 29, 1916) and a preface by Hamilton Holt. From this book, which is the only volume of Justice Hughes's writings, we select the following quotations, which have not only a close bearing upon the issues of the campaign but also serve as an index to the character and caliber of the man.—THE EDITOR.

WE are devoted to the interests of peace and we cherish no policy of aggression. The maintenance of our ideals is our surest protection. It is our constant aim to live in friendship with all nations and to realize the aims of a free government secure from the interruptions of strife and the wastes of war. It is entirely consistent with these aims, and it is our duty, to make adequate provision for our defense and to maintain the efficiency of our Army and Navy. And this I favor.

By his vigorous administration, his virility, his broad humanity, and his determined opposition to notorious abuses, our fellow citizen, the distinguished President of the Republic, Theodore Roosevelt, has won the hearts of the people. We have not only his example, but we know that he is and has been in cordial sympathy with every effort for efficient administration, for the correction of evil and for the improvement of our laws.

I have been a Republican from the time I came of age. There is no political organization in this country which at this time has such an opportunity of serving the people by efficient administration and by wise constructive effort in the correction of known evils. The party has its future in its own keeping, and if it will measure up to its traditions and meet its opportunities it will for many years be invincible.

It has been stated that I have not paid sufficient attention to those who are politically active and who bear the burden and heat of the day in political campaigns. It has been said that I regard political activity as a disqualification for public office. Now no cause can be advanced without hard work and it must be the object of zealous devotion. I esteem those who in an honorable manner work for the party.

In education, in journalism, in the professions of medicine and law, in trade and commerce, in every department of activity, and every sphere of philanthropy, our citizens of German birth or descent furnish constant examples of notable effort and of the highest achievement. We can not write any chapter of the history of American endeavor without doing them honor.

Making all allowance for the extremes of avarice and artifice, for the unwholesome spectacles of exploitation and infidelity to trust, without blinking any evil or glossing over any wrong, the fact remains that the business men of the country are for the most part honest men.

I promise all members of the party fair treatment and just consideration. No individual, but no group of individuals, and no private interest will be permitted to dictate my policy. I shall decide and act according to my conscience and as I believe the public interest requires.

To me public office means a burden of responsibility—a burden of incessant toil at times almost intolerable—which, under honorable conditions and at the command of the people, it may be a duty and even a pleasure to assume, but it is far from being an object of ambition.

A sullen and defiant attitude toward public opinion ill becomes an American citizen. Both unprincipled attempts to corrupt it and despotic efforts to defy it must, in this land of sound common-sense, inevitably fail.

With regard to the Filipinos, we are placed under the most sacred obligations. In justice to them and in justice to ourselves, we must omit no effort to prepare them for self-government.

Political activity, by virtue of the experience and knowledge of affairs gained in it, so far from being a disqualification, may be a most important qualification for office.

I am deeply interested in all efforts to better the condition of our working men. Every practical measure for the real benefit of labor will have my cordial support.

We shall never attain the full measure of our opportunity in this country until the meaning of trusteeship sinks deep into the American consciousness.

I make no request for personal support. So far as I am personally concerned, my interests lie in a profession to which I would be glad to devote myself.

No man is a friend of the Republican party who asks me or any one in authority to appoint a man or to retain a man who is not equal to his job.

We make our appeal to the common-sense of the American people, which has never failed to express itself decisively in a great crisis.

I reckon him one of the worst enemies of the community who will talk lightly of the dignity of the bench.

I have stedfastly refrained from becoming associated in any manner with factional controversies.

The great purpose to be achieved is the prevention of war, and not its regulation.

Federal regulation is not a substitute for state regulation.

I believe in a protective tariff. It is an established policy.

I have asked no man for favors.

I do not aim to be a party boss.

THE MAN WHO MADE A SACRIFICE HIT

The Two Conventions The story of the Chicago conventions is told at length elsewhere in this issue of The Independent. A brief summary of their action will be made here.

Wednesday.—Both conventions open, organize and hear keynote speeches, by Senator Harding, of Ohio, for the Republicans, Raymond Robins, of Illinois, for the Progressives.

Thursday.—Progressives hear platform, table it, and invite Republicans to conference. Republicans accept. Conference committee named; meets late Thursday night and reaches no decision.

Friday.—Republicans make nominations and take two ballots, on which Hughes leads but fails to get necessary vote; they adjourn to permit further harmony conferences. Progressives do nothing. Conference committee meets again at night without tangible result.

Saturday.—At 5 a. m. Roosevelt suggests compromise on Lodge. Conference

HOW THE CONVENTION VOTED

Candidate	Ballot		
	1st	2d	3d
Hughes	253½	328½	949½
Weeks	105	79	3
Root	103	98½	
Cummins	85	85	
Burton	77½	76½	
Fairbanks	74½	88½	
Sherman	66	65	
Roosevelt	65	81	18½
Knox	36	36	
Ford	32		
Brumbaugh	29		
La Follette	25	25	3
Taft	14		
Du Pont	12	13	5
Willis	4	1	
Borah	2		
McCall	1	1	
Wanamaker		5	
Harding		1	
Wood		1	
Lodge			7
Necessary to a choice			494

committee decides to suggest Hughes to Progressives. Neither suggestion gets any attention. Progressives nominate Roosevelt at 12:31; Republicans nominate Hughes two minutes later. Fair-

banks, Indiana, Republican candidate for vice-president; Parker, Louisana, Progressive. Hughes accepts; Roosevelt declines. Republicans adjourn without waiting for Hughes' statement, which is printed in full below.

The Platforms The Republican and Progressive platforms differ rather in emphasis and precision than in substance. Both declare for the enforcement of American neutral rights and duties, for adequate preparedness, for a firm policy in Mexico, for a protective tariff and a tariff commission, for the upbuilding of an American merchant marine, for woman suffrage, for a budget system of national appropriations, and for Federal child labor and workmen's compensation laws.

The platforms, needless to say, are widely different in tone. The Republican is business-like, matter-of-fact, conventional. The Progressive is eloquent, persuasive, literary. It is cast in the form of an essay and follows close-

HUGHES' PLATFORM AS TELEGRAPHED TO THE CONVENTION

I HAVE not desired the nomination. I have wished to remain on the bench. But in this critical period in our national history, I recognize that it is your right to summon and that it is my paramount duty to respond. You speak at a time of our national exigency, transcending merely partisan considerations. You voice the demand for a dominant, thorogoing Americanism with firm protective upbuilding policies, essential to our peace and security; and to that call, in this crisis, I cannot fail to answer with the pledge of all that is in me to the service of our country. Therefore I accept the nomination.

I stand for the firm and unflinching maintenance of all the rights of American citizens on land and sea. I neither impugn motives nor underestimate difficulties. But it is most regrettably true that in our foreign relations we have suffered incalculably from the weak and vacillating course which has been taken with regard to Mexico—a course lamentably wrong with regard to both our rights and our duties. We interfered without consistency; and while seeking to dictate when we were not concerned, we utterly failed to appreciate and discharge our plain duty to our own citizens.

At the outset of the Administration the high responsibilities of our diplomatic intercourse with foreign nations were subordinated to a conception of partisan requirements, and we presented to the world a humiliating spectacle of ineptitude. Belated efforts have not availed to recover the influence and prestige so unfortunately sacrificed; and brave words have been stripped of their force by indecision.

I desire to see our diplomacy restored to its best standards and to have these advanced; to have no sacrifices of national interest to partisan expediencies; to have the first ability of the country always at its command

here and abroad in diplomatic intercourse; to maintain firmly our rights under international law; insisting stedfastly upon all our rights as neutrals, and fully performing our international obligations; and by the clear correctness and justness of our position and our manifest ability and disposition to sustain them to dignify our place among the nations.

I stand for an Americanism that knows no ulterior purpose; for a patriotism that is single and complete. Whether native or naturalized, of whatever race or creed, we have but one country, and we do not for an instant tolerate any division of allegiance.

I believe in making prompt provision to assure absolutely our national security. I believe in preparedness, not only entirely adequate for our defense with respect to numbers and equipment in both army and navy, but with all thoroness to the end that in each branch of the service there may be the utmost efficiency under the most competent administrative heads. We are devoted to the ideals of honorable peace. We wish to promote all wise and practicable measures for the just settlement of international disputes.

In view of our abiding ideals, there is no danger of militarism in this country. We have no policy of aggression; no lust for territory, no zeal for strife. It is in this spirit that we demand adequate provision for national defense, and we condemn the inexcusable neglect that has been shown in this matter of first national importance. We must have the strength which self-respect demands, the strength of an efficient nation ready for every emergency.

Our preparation must be industrial and economic as well as military. Our severest tests will come after the war. We must make a fair and wise readjustment of the tariff, in accordance with sound protective prin-

ciple, to insure our economic independence and to maintain American standards of living. We must conserve the just interests of labor, realizing that in democracy patriotism and national strength must be rooted in evenhanded justice. In preventing, as we must, unjust discriminations and monopolistic practises, we must still be zealous to assure the foundations of honest business. Particularly should we seek the expansion of foreign trade. We must not throttle American enterprise here or abroad, but rather promote it and take pride in honorable achievements.

We must take up the serious problems of transportation, of interstate and foreign commerce, in a sensible and candid manner, and provide an enduring basis for prosperity by the intelligent use of the constitutional powers of Congress, so as adequately to protect the public on the one hand, and, on the other, to conserve the essential instrumentalities of progress.

I stand for the principles of our civil service laws. In every department of government the highest efficiency must be insisted upon. For all laws and programs are vain without efficient and impartial administration.

I cannot within the limits of this statement speak upon all the subjects that will require attention. I can only say that I fully indorse the platform you have adopted.

I deeply appreciate the responsibility you impose. I should have been glad to have that responsibility placed upon another. But I shall undertake to meet it, grateful for the confidence you express. I sincerely trust that all former differences may be forgotten and that we may have united effort in a patriotic realization of our national need and opportunity.

I have resigned my judicial office and I am ready to devote myself unreservedly to the campaign.

CHARLES E. HUGHES

ly the familiar comments of Colonel Roosevelt on what he defines as the vital issues.

On preparedness the Progressive platform has the advantage in stress and precision. It calls for "a navy restored to at least second rank in battle efficiency; a regular army of 250,000 men" and universal military training in time of peace. The Republicans call in more general terms for

a sufficient and effective regular army and a provision for ample reserves, already drilled and disciplined, who can be called at once to the colors when the hour of danger comes.

We must have a navy so strong and so well proportioned and equipped, so thoroly ready and prepared that no enemy can gain command of the sea and effect a landing in force on either our Western or our Eastern Coast.

The Republicans declare for the performance of all our duties and an insistence on all our rights as a neutral, and "believe in the pacific settlement of international disputes and favor the establishment of a world court for that purpose." The Progressives discuss our international obligations at great length and assert that our duty has three phases:

To secure the rights and equal treatment of our citizens, native or naturalized, on land and sea, without regard to race, creed or nativity.

To guard the honor and uphold the just influence of our nation.

To maintain the integrity of international law.

These are the corner-stones of civilization. We must be strong to defend them.

While the Progressives call vaguely for the "re-establishment of our merchant marine," the Republicans come out explicitly for mail subsidies and against government-owned shipping.

Neither party commits itself definitely, as the Congressional Union urged, to the enfranchisement of women by amending the Federal Constitution. The Progressives declare that women should be given "the full political right of suffrage either by state or Federal action," and the Republicans distinctly recognize "the right of each state to settle this question for itself."

A minority report was presented from the Republican Resolutions Committee, embodying in a general way the pro-German position, declaring for a tax on munitions, against the export of munitions, and in favor of government ownership of all munition works. It was overwhelmingly defeated.

The two platforms differ chiefly, however, in their treatment of the whole preparedness - international obligations issue. With the Progressives, as was inevitable, the burden of the whole document is "Americanism and pre-

paredness." The Republicans, while making a firm stand for united loyalty and adequate preparation, treat these issues as important but not exclusively important elements in their established party policy.

Riots in Mexico Anti-American demonstrations in northern Mexico indicate a growing restlessness over the continued presence of American troops. On Tuesday and Wednesday of last week a mob attacked the American consulate, the Foreign Club and American residences in Chihuahua City, and American killed three mob leaders in defense of his house. The disorders followed a mass meeting called by General Jacinto Trevino to consider the defense of the city, as he said. At Durango City the American consulate was burned, and thruout the border states there has been much public talk denouncing the United States.

Meanwhile the punitive force holds its line, which now stretches about 250 miles from Columbus to a point thirty miles south of San Antonio, Chihuahua, and does nothing more. Roads are being repaired in preparation for the rains, and the American troops are scrupulously refraining from contact with Carranza forces.

A PARADE THAT KNEW NO WEATHER

The Woman Suffrage cohorts attended strictly to business in their Chicago parade on June 7. The damp chill of an unseasonable shower did not deter them from their determined demonstration on Michigan Boulevard, to which they confined themselves because there were gathered the Convention delegates whom they were out to convert

T. R.: "THIS HURTS ME WORSE THAN IT DOES YOU"

In Mexico City railroad and general strikes have been put down by the Carranza troops, street cars being run with two soldiers to every motorman, but concessions have been made to the workers in the way of substituting new paper for old in the payment of wages. The Government's efforts to maintain a modest value for its paper money have not been successful. A new issue of 500,000,000 pesos is being put gradually into circulation to retire about 700,000,-000 of old paper that is now worthless, and on the basis of a gold reserve fund, which the Government is endeavoring to build up, the value of the new notes is to be fixed at 20 cents national gold (the normal value being about 49 cents American money). But large amounts of the new notes have already been issued and are worth much less than their official valuation.

No answer has been made to Carranza's peremptory demand that our troops leave Mexico. It was said that President Wilson was considering the plan of submitting all differences between the two countries, including large claims for damages, to an international commission of conciliation, provided for in our treaty of 1848 with Mexico.

Cloakmakers and Railroad Men The garment workers in New York are still striking, and the employers who belong to the Cloak, Suit and Skirt Manufacturers' Association are still refusing to arbitrate the issues. The manufacturers claim that 125 of their 409 shops are running, but the strikers have organized a huge picket force—15,000, they claim—and at the most only a few workers have gone to their machines. It is also claimed that the employers have opened shops outside New York City where their work is going forward, but such experiments heretofore have not been successful and this maneuver will not seriously affect the strikers' strength. Only one case of disorder has been reported so far.

A number of New York clergymen, including some of the most prominent ministers in the city, have signed a statement condemning the manufacturers for their refusal to arbitrate.

The employers of about 20,000 workers voted last week to ask Mayor Mitchel to arrange for mediation. They are not members of the Protective Association, but are organized as the Mutual Cloak and Suit Manufacturers' Association, and the Independent Cloak and Suit Manufacturers. They did not participate in the lockout, but their employees struck because if these shops were kept open the work of the Protective Association could be done there on subcontract. The union is suspicious of the motives of these manufacturers in thus accepting the principle of mediation, but will probably not refuse to enter into negotiations.

The conference between representatives of the railroads of the United States and the four railroad workers' unions continued during the week without reaching any decisive point. The proposals of the unions have been thoroughly explained, and the union representatives have asked numerous questions as to the application of the proposed schedules and as to the significance of the railroads' counter proposals. If the railroads refuse to accept the union demands, as seems likely, and insist on a compromize schedule, the conference will come to an end and the four Brotherhoods will vote on the question of giving their representatives power to call a strike. Further negotiations will be based on the results of that referendum.

Dominican Disorders Two thousand marines of the United States Navy are now in Santo Domingo for the purpose of maintaining order and protecting foreigners in one of the little republic's sporadic revolutions, and an additional thousand have been ordered there.

Juan I. Jiminez, the sixth president since the assassination of Caceres in 1911, was recently deposed after it had been charged that his entire family had their hands in the national treasury, and Francisco Henriquez Carajal was chosen to succeed him. Two leaders, General Arias and General Desiderio, are now busy with revolutionary enterprises.

At Puerto Plata, on the north coast, the American consulate was robbed during the last week of May, and marines were sent from Santo Domingo City to occupy that town and Monte Cristi, near the Haytian frontier. They landed on June 1. At Puerto Plata Captain H. J. Hirshinger was shot as the

KITCHENER OF KHARTUM
Whose loss on the cruiser "Hampshire" was a spectacular sequel to the disastrous naval "victory" in the North Sea

International Film

TO SUCCEED KITCHENER?
Lieutenant-General Sir William Robert Robertson, chief of the Imperial Staff, who may become War Minister

party landed, and the rebels held the fort for two hours. At Monte Cristi there was no resistance to the landing, but a force of rebels attacked the outposts of the marine camp a few days later and were driven off with no American casualties.

Rear Admiral Caperton, who has been in charge of the marines in Hayti, is in command of these forces. Tho we have had a Receiver General of Customs in Santo Domingo since 1907, in charge of the national finances, there is no explicit treaty provision for the maintenance of order there, as there is now in the case of Hayti. W. W. Vick, Receiver General in 1913-14, who received the notorious "deserving Democrats" letter from Bryan, has made a statement in which he asserts that graft runs riot in the Dominican Government and the only solution of the problem is for the United States to assume complete control for from five to ten years.

Revolutionists from Guatemala have been crossing repeatedly into British Honduras and have fought an engagement with a force of British colonials. They killed an American physician, Dr. Le Moise Lafleur, who was making explorations in the Honduras jungle.

Lord Kitchener Drowned

The cruiser "Hampshire" went down on Monday night about eight o'clock off the western shore of the Orkney Islands. All on board, some two or three hundred, were lost except twelve of the men. Among the victims were Earl Kitchener, Secretary of State for War, and his staff, who were going to Archangel in order to confer with the Russian General Staff at Petrograd, presumably in regard to the supply of munitions for the Russian offensive just started in Volhynia. The party included two of the chief ordinance experts of England, as well as the former counselor of the British Embassy at Petrograd. Mr. Lloyd George, Minister of Munitions, had intended to go to Russia on the same boat, but was detained because the settlement of the Irish question had been put into his hands.

The cause of the disaster is not known. If it was done consciously by a German submarine the German system of espionage must be more complete than has been imagined, for Lord Kitchener's mission and time of departure were known to only a few of the inner circle. He left the train at a small station in Scotland, was taken to the shore in an automobile and conveyed to the waiting cruiser in a destroyer. It is hardly likely that a German submarine should have happened to be lurking in such close vicinity to one of the chief British naval stations. Probably the ship was blown up by a British mine, for the coast here is protected by mine fields and one of them may have been wrenched loose from its moorings by the prevailing storm.

Four boats are said to have got off from the cruiser, which sank in twenty minutes, but none of them reached the shore, altho this was only two miles off. One warrant officer and eleven men were washed ashore on a raft alive and some eighty bodies have been recovered. Several of these had torn off their finger and toe nails trying to climb up the steep cliffs that fence the Orkneys on their western side.

The loss of Lord Kitchener was a greater shock to the British public than almost any other news of the war, for there was no one in whose ability and energy so much confidence was felt. It is expected that he will be succeeded as Secretary for War by General Sir William Robertson, chief of the British General Staff, as soon as a seat in Parliament can be found for him. He is fifty-six years of age and is one of the very few British generals who have worked their way up from the ranks.

Yuan Shih-kai Dies

The President of the Chinese Republic died at Peking on June 6. He had for several days been ill from a disorder of the stomach and nervous breakdown. There are rumors of poisoning, either as suicide or assassination, but these are officially denied. Upon his deathbed President Yuan exprest repentance for his error in attempting to become emperor and explained that he had been misled by his advisers. He asked for protection to his wives and children and authorized a mandate calling upon all military and civil officials to recognize the authority of the Vice-president, Li Yuan-hung. His eldest son committed suicide on the following day.

Vice-president Li assumed office without opposition and received the recognition of all factions. He is not generally regarded as so able a man as Yuan, but is believed to be a stancher republican. He was, in fact, one of

YUAN SHIH-KAI
First President, almost emperor, of China, hated and feared, at once the strength and the weakness of the Republic, probably poisoned

LI YUAN-HUNG
Vice-president of China, who became president on the death of Yuan. He had already been acclaimed as president by some of the rebels

the leaders of the revolution which started at Wu-chang in 1911, and overthrew the Manchu dynasty. He was educated in Japan and served on a Chinese cruiser during the war with Japan. He is fifty-two years old, that is, five years younger than the late President.

The death of Yuan has had a favorable effect upon the country. The provinces of Sze-chuen, Hu-nan, Chekiang and Shen-si, which had declared their independence of the Peking government, have returned to their allegiance, and all the other rebellious provinces are expected also to give their support to the new president. In fact, these provinces had some time before asserted their intention of establishing a southern republic with Li Yuan-hung as president, so they certainly ought to be satisfied with the peaceful accession of their candidate.

Fort Vaux Captured   After a week of ferocious fighting the Germans have succeeded in gaining complete possession of Fort Vaux, northeast of Verdun. The recapture of Fort Douaumont and of the Caillette woods south of it last week brought the Germans in behind Fort Vaux and made its ultimate fall inevitable, but Major Raynal, a young officer who had previously distinguished himself by his courage and had been several times wounded, was left in the fort with little more than a thousand men under orders to hold out as long as possible. On the 2nd the Germans stormed the fort and secured a lodgement, but the garrison defended the armored casements for five days longer altho they were cut off from communication with Verdun except for an occasional courier who managed to creep thru the lines. But not one in five of those who attempted it were able to get thru the German cordon. The German charges up the hill were met with a fatal fire from the French machine guns, and when the Germans tried to force their way thru the underground passages of the fort, the French beat them back with clubbed rifles and knives, even using their steel helmets swung by the strap as maces. The bravery of the garrison won the respect of the Germans and when Major Raynal finally surrendered, with the

THE GREAT WAR

June 5—Cruiser "Hampshire" sunk with Kitchener on board. Russian drive in Volhynia begins.

June 6—President Yuan Shih-kai of China dies. Germans take Fort Vaux.

June 7—Russians take fortress of Lutsk. Austrians have taken 12,400 Italian prisoners since June 1.

June 8—Germans take Hooge from British. Allies compel Greece to demobilize part of troops.

June 9—Russians take Buczacz. Austrians advance upon Asiago, Italy.

June 10—Russians claim 108,000 Austrians taken during the week. Germans south of Vaux take 500 prisoners and twenty-two machine guns.

June 11—Salandra Ministry in Italy resigns on account of Trentino defeat. Russians take fortress of Dubno.

seven hundred men left alive and unwounded, he received the honors of war and was permitted to keep his sword.

The capture of Vaux makes a wide breach in the ring of forts surrounding Verdun at a distance of about five miles. The first of the forts on the northeast side, Douaumont, was taken by the Germans at the beginning of their offensive last February, but their efforts to capture Fort Vaux, which stands next to Fort Douaumont and about two miles away, were unsuccessful altho it was once erroneously claimed to have been carried by storm. The Germans are now beginning the bombardment of Fort Tavannes, the third fort in this sector of the ring. (See the map on the following page.)

Between the present German position and their goal, Verdun, there is Fort Souville, which stands upon Hill 388, near the village of Fleury. Fort Vaux is lower, only 349 meters, while Douaumont stands on the other end of the same ridge as Souville and has the same altitude, that is, 388 meters. The hills on the western side of the Meuse are lower; Hill 304 and Le Mort Homme (295 meters), which the Germans are still trying to gain, are among the highest on this side of the river.

On the British front in Belgium and France the Germans keep up their attacks, inflicting very heavy losses on the Canadians stationed there. A charge of the Württemberg and Silesian troops carried the British trenches at Hooge, southeast of Ypres. The British casualties now amount to about a thousand a day.

TIGHTENING THE LINES ABOUT VERDUN

The capture of Fort Vaux this week together with Fort Douaumont, captured last February, gives the Germans possession of the ridge commanding Verdun on the northeastern side. The corresponding dominant positions on the western side of the Meuse river are 304-Meter Hill and Le Mort Homme, which the Germans are now striving to gain. The lower line shows the extent of the German advance and the arrows their present attack

Great Russian Drive

One of the most brilliant feats of the war is the Russian offensive against the Austrian front begun last week. Catching the Austrians unawares or at least unprepared, the Russians have broken thru their fortified lines for a hundred miles and at one point made a gain of thirty-two miles. By this swift advance the Russians have taken a large number of prisoners and immense quantities of the ammunition that had been collected behind the Austrian trenches. The week's booty comprizes 124 cannon, 180 machine guns and 58 bomb mortars. The number of prisoners reported by the Russian War Office is 1649 officers and 106,000 men. Among them are 2,000 Germans.

This part of the line has been supposed to be defended by forty Austrian and two German divisions, probably not more than 700,000 altogether. Austrian troops have been recently removed from this front to be used for the attack on Italy from the Trentino, and evidently the line was left too weak to resist the Russian thrust. The Austrians have never been able to hold their own against the Russians except with the aid and guidance of the Germans, who have now concentrated all their energies upon the western front.

The Russian offensive is in charge of General A. A. Brussiloff, one of the ablest and most energetic of the Russian officers. His troops are fresh and thoroly equipt with artillery. By means of a lavish expenditure of ammunition he battered down the first line defenses in a single day, and then leaving his big guns behind pushed on as rapidly as possible with field pieces alone. The Austrians had been established on

THE RUSSIANS SWEEP WESTWARD

By a sudden and vigorous offensive the Russians have driven the Austrians back twenty-five miles and crossed the Styr and Strypa rivers. All three of the triangle of Volhynian fortresses, Lutsk, Dubno and Rovno, are now in Russian hands and both Lemberg and Czernovitz are threatened. The Germans hold the northern end of the line in the Pripet swamps. The southern end rests upon the Pruth river. The shaded area is that now in Russian possession

this front ever since September and had, as they supposed, made their trenches impregnable. At some points, there were as many as twenty lines of barbed wire entanglements.

The region involved in the fighting is the Russian province of Volhynia and the Austrian province of Galicia. When the Austro-German advance came to a halt last fall their forces held a line extending from the Pripet River on the north to the Dniester River on the south and following in a general way the course of the tributaries of these rivers, the Styr running north and the Strypa running south. The northern end of this line at Pinsk is buried in the midst of the Pripet swamps. The southern end is protected by the Dniester and the Pruth rivers. Previous attempts of the Russians to force either of these flanks have proved fruitless, so now they have hit the line in the middle. Here the Russian frontier had long before the war been protected against Austrian invasion by a triangle of fortresses, Lutsk, Dubno and Rovno. Two of these strongholds the Austrians took, but Rovno they never reached. Now the Russians have regained both Lutsk and Dubno. Lutsk was first taken by the Austrians September 1, 1915, but they lost it three weeks later. The Russians, however, were only able to hold it a few days, and it has been in Austrian hands ever since.

The Russian advance in Galicia is following the same course as their first drive in the fall of 1914, and if it is not checked they will soon get possession of Lemberg, the capital of Galicia, for the second time. They also seem likely to regain Czernovitz, the capital of Bukovina.

474

THE CONVENTIONS AT CHICAGO

BY HAROLD HOWLAND

IT is half-past nine on Friday night. The hungry, disheveled, exhausted crowd in the great Coliseum is going home. On the platform a little group of harassed officials is trying to find out from the restless mass of a thousand delegates on the floor below whether it is also their sovereign will to adjourn. It probably is—but the crowd does not care. It is going home anyway.

It has been a glorious day. For ten and a half hours 14,000 people sat and listened to thunders of oratory that must have echoed across the Stygian shores and shot a pang into the heart of many a togaed shade. They had heard the comforting assurances accumulate that there were just one short of a dozen men, each one of whom was the very man to reunite the Republican party, to send the Democratic administration down to defeat in November, to save the state, to restore the Republic to its former grandeur—sullied now by the crimes of Democratic ineptitude, to bring peace to a warring world, and to set the millennium several notches farther along its road. Every time such a warming assurance had come to them concerning the favorite son of some sovereign state a little cohesive group of delegates, another solid little band of alternates, and scattered patches of citizens along the side lines and in the galleries had erupted and "demonstrated." They yelled and shrieked and whistled and clapped, waved flags and hats and umbrellas and things. They wore themselves out, tortured their vocal chords into husky mutiny, gradually collapsed into rebellious pantomime, took a look at their watches—and burst forth again. For in a convention "demonstration" time is of the essence of the matter. The favoriteness of your favorite son is measured by the number of minutes of shrieking and howling that can be evoked from some portions of the crowd at the mention of his name.

The day had been a grand old test of endurance. The waves of oratory had surged and beat upon the gradually numbing brains of the assembled people, the skyrockets and pinwheels and torpedoes and giant crackers of the demonstrations had paralyzed their optic nerves and harassed their ear-drums. When all the enthusiasm had been poured out, which had been painstakingly prepared, fermented, bottled up and brought here from half a score of states for this ebullient day, the convention settled down to business. The balloting began—and the fact which had been becoming steadily clearer as the hours passed sprang into sharp relief. The convention did not know whom it wanted. It had no candidate for the presidency which it was ready and eager to nominate. So the delegates spread themselves all over the shop. A few delegations went solidly for favorite sons. A smaller few voted solidly, as they had been directed by the voters at the presidential primary, but New York had two more or less favorite sons. So had Pennsylvania. Aside from these predestined votes, there were hundreds and hundreds that were cast, it seemed, not from strong conviction, but because they had to be cast for some one. Most of the delegates, it appeared, were waiting for a lead—and did not like the only leads in sight. The Texas delegation was a case in point. Its twenty-six votes were cast like this—Burton 1, Cummins 1, du Pont 1, Fairbanks 1, Hughes 1, Roosevelt 1, Root 1, Sherman 1, Weeks 1, Borah 1, McCall 1, Willis 1. and Taft 14.

Now Mr. Taft was not a candidate

FAIRBANKS
The gentleman from Indiana, who never offended anybody, runs again for the Vice-Presidency

for the nomination. So one suspects a humorous intent all round on the part of Texas. Just one-quarter of the states voted solidly for a single candidate and in just one-quarter of those states the vote was for a favorite son, Indiana for Fairbanks, Iowa for Cummins, Ohio for Burton, Illinois too, had a favorite son, but Senator Sherman missed the solid endorsement of his state delegation by just two votes.

The one outstanding fact in the voting, aside from the intricate and artistic pattern in which the shots were spattered all over the target, was the concentration on Mr. Justice Hughes.

Two hundred and fifty-three and one-half votes fell to his lot, and only thirteen states passed him by. Four hundred and ninety-four were needed for a nomination, so that his first vote was just two hundred and forty and a half short of the mark. As the result of the first ballot was announced and the chairman was proceeding to call for a second, a plaintive challenge on a question of personal privilege came from the floor. "We've passed lunch," shrilled the tragic voice, "we've passed dinner. Are you going to make us pass supper too?" But a burst of laughter swallowed up the objection and the balloting began again; there was little change in the result. Just as the roll-call was beginning Governor Brumbaugh of Pennsylvania withdrew his name and asked, "Why don't we nominate the man that fits the platform we've adopted, Theodore Roosevelt?" But his advocacy only availed to add fifteen votes to the Roosevelt total of 65, while the Hughes vote went up seventy-five. There the matter rested, as the delegates went out to that belated supper and to overnight thoughts on the state of the union and other important matters.

For three days now the Republican National Convention had proceeded steadily and stolidly upon its appointed course. Everything had been done in the stereotyped way on the stereotyped time table in the stereotyped language. No impropriety or infelicity had been permitted to mar the smooth texture of its surface. The temporary chairman in his keynote speech had been as mildly oratorical, as diffusely patriotic and nobly sentimental as any Fourth of July orator of a bygone day. The whole tone of the convention had been subdued and decorous, with the

475

decorum of incertitude and timidity. That convention did not know what it wanted. It only knew that there was one thing it did not want, and was afraid of, and another thing it would rather not have and was afraid it would have to take. It was an old-fashioned convention of the hand-picked variety. It smacked of the former days when the direct primary had not yet introduced the disturbing thought that the voters ought to select their candidates and not the office holders and party leaders.

It was a docile, submissive convention, not because it was ruled by a strong group of men, who knew what they wanted and proposed to compel their followers to give it to them, but because it was composed of politicians great and small to whom party regularity was the breath of their nostrils. They were ready to do the regular thing; but the only two things in sight were confoundedly irregular.

The mien of that convention suggested strongly the plight of the man in the fable who announced on a Saturday night, "I'm going downtown to get drunk; and gosh! how I do dread it."

Two drafts were ready for their drinking and they dreaded both. They could nominate one of two men,

International Film

JOHNSON

The Governor of California was a persistent fire-eater at the Progressive Convention—but he won't head a third ticket

and to nominate either of them was to fling open the gates of the citadel of party regularity and conformity and let the enemy in. Roosevelt or Hughes. Roosevelt they would not have. Hughes they would give their eye teeth not to take. No wonder they were subdued and inarticulate. No wonder they suffered and were unhappy. So they droned along thru their stereotyped routine, hoping dully against fate.

Meanwhile a mile away quite other scenes were being enacted. In another place another convention as different from the first as champagne from ditch water boiled and sparkled and effervesced. Its thousand members were possessed of one idea. Its forty-eight delegations rendered spontaneous and untrammeled fealty to a single man. Unbossed, uncontrolled, insurgent, they were cemented into a solid phalanx of purpose by a single overmastering desire.

They knew precisely what they wanted; they proposed to have it or know the reason why. And behind the shadowy curtains of the future their fate lay heavy upon them. For they were destined not to have it. The Progressive party in national convention assembled wanted Theodore Roosevelt once more for their leader. They were ready to put themselves behind him again and fight another bitter, heart-breaking fight on behalf of the thing he represents and the things they all believe in.

On this point they were united to a man. The only point of difference was as to the tactics to be adopted in preparing for the fight. The hotheads, the irreconcilables, were all for going right ahead, nominating Mr. Roosevelt out of hand, adopting a platform in a jiffy, and going home. They were ready to consign the convention in the other hall a mile away to whatever form of perdition it might choose for itself and to act as tho there were nothing of smallest desirability in the thought of a reunion of Republicans and Progressives. But there were cooler heads among the Progressives. They realized the importance of union between the two parties, whose fundamental principles, no matter how much they might have been degraded by wrong-headed leaders on one side or how much embroidered by scatterbrained reformers on the other, were essentially the same. They believed that failure to get together would mean renewed defeat for both.

So they counseled moderation and deliberation; and proposed that overtures be made to the Republican convention with a view to agreement between the two bodies. The counsel was not taken without vigorous protest and clamorous dissent. But taken it was, and an invitation sent to the Republican convention for the appointment of joint committees of the two bodies for conference. The invitation was promptly accepted by the Republican convention. Forthwith Butler, of Columbia; Senator Crane, of Massachusetts; Senator Borah, of Idaho, and A. R. Johnson, of Ohio, on the one side, and George W. Perkins, of New York; Governor Johnson, of California; Horace B. Wilkinson, of New York; John M. Parker, of Louisiana, and Charles J. Bonaparte, of Maryland, on the other, went into conference.

Meanwhile the Progressive caldron seethed on. At intervals it threatened to boil over.

But the cool wisdom of its leaders, reinforced by the knowledge that the attempt at reconciliation had the earnest sanction of the leader at Oyster Bay, kept the fires banked.

The convention in the Auditorium, like the one at the Coliseum, went steadily ahead with its business.

Its Resolutions Committee presented the draft of a platform and it was discussed plank by plank. In the course of this discussion a significant incident occurred, which was without precedent in the history of political conventions. A plank was

Copyright Underwood

HITCHCOCK

The man who managed Taft's first campaign spent two sleepless nights at Chicago—and got Hughes nominated

proposed declaring in favor of national prohibition. Now, political parties, time out of mind, have been afraid of the liquor problem. It is too full of dynamite to make even its open discussion in a political convention an attractive undertaking. But here the Progressive convention set itself to debate the question right out in meeting. After both sides had been presented with vigor and freedom, the matter went to a vote and the plank was rejected. It was rejected not on the merits of the liquor question itself, but on the proposition that the inclusion of such a plank at this time would distract the attention of the country from the real issues of the campaign and substitute for them the single issue of prohibition. Then came an unconventional and startling thing. The chairman invited every delegate who believed in prohibition to stand up, and a great majority of them arose to their feet.

In the Republican convention there was no debate upon the platform. Henry Cabot Lodge, chairman of the Committee on Resolutions, read the committee's draft to the accompaniment of moderate applause for Americanism, preparedness and protection. Then a fiery young man from Wisconsin presented a minority report signed by himself alone in

MRS. ABBIE KREBS
She was one of three women delegates to the Republican Convention—two from California and one from Montana

which numerous radical planks were made to carry pronouncements on pacifism and kindred subjects obviously intended for consumption in German-American sections. The convention refused to take him seriously. Then the platform was adopted without appreciable dissent. One humorous incident enlivened the solemnity of the proceedings over the platform—tho the humor was rather sardonic. The last plank in the platform was read by Senator Lodge thus: "The Republican party, reaffirming its faith in government of the people by the people, for the people, as a measure of justice to one-half the adult people of this country, favors the extension of the suffrage to women"—the pause at this point affording opportunity for a pleasant demonstration by the friends of woman suffrage thruout the galleries. The moment had been anxiously awaited. On Monday evening a new political party had been born in Chicago, to be known as the Woman's Party. It is composed of the women voters of the twelve suffrage states and its one purpose is to use the votes of women in the coming presidential election on behalf of the party or candidate promising most for the passage of the Federal Constitutional amendment extending the suffrage to women. It was an enthusiastic convention and the new party gave some promise of political significance. Its birth had been followed on the next day by a parade in which over five thousand women tramped thru a thin, steady, soaking rain with persistency and cheerfulness. They bore placards and banners whose inscriptions belied the traditional feminine lack of humor.

"Get your ribs back, here they are." "We want to be citizens, do we look desirable?" "Why can't I speak for myself, John?" "Women, the devoted mothers of our country." "We can vote for President, watch your step." It was a splendid demonstration of feminine spirit and determination.

As Senator Lodge paused and the cheers broke out it looked as if it had had its effect. But soon the shouting died down and Mr. Lodge resumed in a louder tone and with a kind of biting emphasis on 'he words, "But recognizes the right of each state to settle this question for itself."

Then the jeers broke out from all over the body of delegates while Senator Lodge stood and smiled. It was a big disappointment, but the half loaf of a general declaration in favor of the principle was probably quite all one had any right to expect from such a politicians' convention.

While platforms were being made and adopted, the conference committee was busy talking things over. The first report to the Republican convention announced a gratifying good-will among the conferees and a sincere desire on both sides to get together. It declared further that the Progressive representatives were firm in their conviction that Mr. Roosevelt was the one man on whom the two parties could unite logically and with hope of success. The convention took no notice of the report and the conferees went at it again.

So we come again to Friday night and the end of that weary session of oratorical efflorescence. There was no one in sight but Hughes, tho he had a long way to go to a majority. But the situation was ripe for a rush to the band wagon. The rumor that Illinois would swing from favorite son Sherman to Hughes on the next ballot looked like the beginning of a speedy end. So came Saturday morning. The Progressive convention met first and soon received a report from the conference committee. The Republican members had proposed for the first time with unanimity Mr. Hughes as the nominee of both conventions. But it was apparent that the Progressive delegates would have none of it. They were there to nomi-

PERKINS
Of all the Progressives at Convention he worked hardest for harmony, but he didn't get it—in the way it was expected

THE MOST INTERESTING REPUBLICAN CONVENTION EN

RY, IN SESSION AT THE COLISEUM IN CHICAGO

PENROSE
He threw away all Pennsylvania's votes on Knox till he caught the drift of things

nate their own beloved leader and they intended to do it whether or no. A telegram was received from Oyster Bay proposing Senator Lodge as the compromise candidate, and the restive delegates in the Auditorium could with the greatest difficulty be held back until the telegram could be received and read at the Coliseum. A direct telephone wire from the Coliseum to a receiver on the stage of the Auditorium kept the Progressive body in instant touch with events in the other convention. In the Auditorium the atmosphere was electric. The delegates bubbled with excitement. They wanted to nominate Roosevelt and be done with it. The fear that the other convention would steal a march on them and make their nomination first set them crazy with impatience. The hall rumbled and sputtered and fizzed and detonated. The floor looked like a giant corn popper with the corn jumping and exploding like mad.

The delegates wanted action; the leaders wanted to be sure that they had kept faith with Mr. Roosevelt and with the general situation by giving the Republican delegates a

chance to hear his last proposal. Bainbridge Colby, of New York, put Mr. Roosevelt in nomination with brevity and vigor; Governor Johnson seconded the nomination with his accustomed fire. Then, as the word came over the wire that balloting had been resumed in the Coliseum, the question was put at thirty-one minutes past twelve, and every delegate and alternate in the convention leaped to his feet with upstretched arm and shouted "Aye."

Doubtless more thrilling moments may come to some men some time somewhere, but you will hardly find a delegate of that Progressive convention to believe it. Then the convention adjourned, to meet again at three to hear what the man they had nominated would say.

At almost the same moment, in the Republican' convention, the floodgates were opened and the votes began to pour thru for Mr. Justice Hughes. The name of candidate after candidate was withdrawn, and as the third roll-call ended the nomination was all but unanimous. Then the Republicans nominated Charles W. Fairbanks for Vice-President again, and went away. They had done the thing they did not want to do, and their only consolation was that the one thing they dreaded more had not been forced upon them.

When the Progressives met again they knew that Mr. Hughes had resigned from the Supreme Court and had accepted the nomination. What Mr. Roosevelt would do they could only surmise—and hope. They filled in the time of waiting for his message, which they were assured was on the way, with nominating John M. Parker of Louisiana for Vice-President, with pledging a goodly sum for campaign expenses, with performing certain routine business, and with listening to fighting speeches. As the hand of the clock moved on to five, the hour at which the chairman had promised adjournment, Mr. Robins rose and read the message from the man they had called to lead them again. It fell like lead upon their exuberant spirits. It was not the unqualified acceptance they had dared in their exaltation to hope for. It read thus:

I am very grateful for the honor you confer upon me by nominating me as President. I cannot accept it at this time. I do not know the attitude of the candidate of the Republican Party toward the vital questions of the day. Therefore, if you desire an immediate decision, I must decline the nomination.

But if you prefer to, I suggest that my conditional refusal to run be placed in the hands of the Progressive National Committee. If Mr. Hughes's statements, when he makes them, shall satisfy the committee that it is for the interest of the country that he be

SMOOT
The old guardsman from Utah served on the Republican Conference Committee

elected, they can act accordingly and treat my refusal as definitely accepted.
If they are not satisfied, they can so notify the Progressive Party, and at the same time they can confer with me, and then determine on whatever action we may severally deem appropriate to meet the needs of the country.

THEODORE ROOSEVELT

Puzzled, disheartened, overwhelmed, they went away. They could not then see how wise, how farsighted, how inevitable it was. Some of them will never see it. Probably few of them as they went out of those doors realized that they had taken part in the last act of the romantic and tragic drama of the National Progressive Party. But such must be the fact. For the march of events was too much for it. Fate, not its enemies, brought it to an end. And in its death it has performed a sterling service. Without its presence at Chicago Mr. Justice Hughes would never have been nominated for the presidency. That politician-hyphenmade convention of politicians would have selected some one of their own kind and sent him blindly out to meet his fate.

Chicago

WEEKS
The favorite sons soon began to look anxious, Weeks was the only one of importance whose boom broke on the second ballot, however

CRANE
The thought that the Progressives were negotiating with Crane and Smoot—rock-ribbed Republican regulars—was galling to men like Johnson

HUGHES—MAN AND STATESMAN

BY GEORGE W. WICKERSHAM

FORMER ATTORNEY-GENERAL OF THE UNITED STATES

IN the long and varied history of American politics, the career of Charles Evans Hughes affords one of the few and most striking examples of the application of the true republican principle that the office should seek the man, not the man the office. Mr. Hughes has been Governor of the state of New York, Associate Justice of the Supreme Court of the United States, and is now become the candidate of the Republican party for the presidency, without in any instance lifting his hand or raising his voice to obtain any of those positions. He affords a demonstration of the real value lying behind that much-abused word, "preparedness." His whole life has been a course of preparation for the work which successive public demands have laid upon him.

He comes of rugged Welsh stock. His father was a Baptist minister, born and reared in Wales, the exponent of a strong, independent, individualistic faith. Charles was born at Glens Falls, New York, in 1862, and was brought up amid simple surroundings. He never knew that "chill penury" which represses "noble warmth." But he enjoyed the advantage of an early life of self-denial and the need of earning by his own efforts everything but the bare necessities of life.

Hughes was graduated at Brown University in 1881; taught Greek and mathematics for a time in a school at Delhi, New York; then studied law at the Columbia University Law School and was admitted to the New York bar in 1888, the year of his marriage to the daughter of Walter S. Carter, the head of the firm of lawyers who employed him.

After three years' experience in a law office, he accepted a professorship in the law school of Cornell University, where he taught the law of contracts and international law for two years. In 1893, he returned to New York and became junior partner in his father-in-law's firm. During the next seven years, despite the exactions of a growing practise, he was a regular lecturer at the New York Law School. This work not only required him to continue the systematic study of the law, as few successful practitioners in our large cities are able to do, but it gave him a training in the art of exposition which contributed much toward making him a convincing advocate, a forceful debater, and a powerful campaign orator.

His practise developed in the field of commercial law and litigation. He soon became recognized by his fellows at the bar as a formidable antagonist. His professional work was characterized by thoroness of preparation. Thus his cases were won before they came into court. His presentation of facts was lucid and convincing, and his clear statement of applicable rules of law won for him the confidence of the bench.

His successes at the bar never were won by mere cleverness or chicanery. They were attained by the exercise of that genius which Daniel Webster declared was the only kind he ever knew—the genius for hard work. They soon brought public recognition. In 1905, there was a legislative investigation into the gas companies of New York. It was carried on under the chairmanship of State Senator Frederick W. Stevens, who retained Hughes as counsel to the committee. The work was done quietly and effectively. It required a knowledge of complicated and intricate accounting, and in that field Hughes had no superior. The report, which he drafted, was considered a model by all those who had occasion to examine it. It was made the basis of valuable constructive legislation. It was followed by the creation of a commission to regulate the operations of gas and electric companies, and the fixing of an eighty-cent rate for gas.

His work with that committee led to his retention as counsel in the following year to the committee appointed by the Senate of New York to investigate the great life insurance companies, of which Senator Armstrong was chairman and Senator Stevens a member. The demands for this investigation and the problems presented by it required treatment very different from that which had sufficed with the gas companies. There was a widespread impression that the great wealth and vast power of the large life-insurance companies had been used to influence legislation, control elections and affect official action, both state and national. It was also charged that officers and directors of these companies had abused their powers, and thru underwritings, and otherwise, enhanced their personal fortunes, sometimes at the expense of their companies.

The series of questions prepared by Mr. Hughes and sent to the executive officers of the various companies as the first step in the investigation, was

so searching in character, so intelligently framed to develop the ultimate facts by which the management of these companies must be judged, that a perusal of them brought a sudden realization of the meaning of the phrase "pitiless publicity." The public examinations of witnesses which followed, turned a calcium light on to the inmost recesses of the administration of the life insurance companies. Many abuses were revealed, and officials responsible for them driven from office. But the inherent financial soundness of these great and useful organizations was demonstrated and with the correction of abuses and changes in the personnel of their management public confidence was restored. The work of Mr. Hughes was not merely destructive. On the contrary, he had the satisfaction of demonstrating the inherently healthy character of the American life insurance business, and its reliability as a means of securing the families of many thousand persons of small means against want or dependence. The public was convinced that the needed surgical work had been performed by an unflinching hand, the diseased parts cut out and a sound healthy body left.

A widespread demand arose among all classes of the people that the man who had so ably and fearlessly performed that work should be placed at the head of the State government. His nomination for the governorship on the Republican ticket in the autumn of 1906 was in compliance with this demand. While, officially, the Republican nominee, then, as ten years later, Mr. Hughes was not the choice of the leaders of the political organization. He was the choice of the people. At the ensuing election he was the only candidate elected on the Republican State ticket.

When he assumed the office of Governor on January 1, 1907, he knew that he was put there to represent the people of the State, and he interpreted the people's will as no political manager at that time was able to do, and as few elected officials of government ever have done. He was a militant temperature, swift to divine the public thought, inflexible in his determination to have placed on the statute book laws which he knew the people rightly demanded, implacable in dealing with every form of abuse of public trust.

His greatest constructive work was the Public Service Law, which

481

he drew and caused to be enacted and which has served as a model for almost every other state in the Union. He was no corporation baiter. He believed in the fundamental duty of government to protect the legitimate rights of private property. But he fully realized the just concern of the public in all corporations engaged in operations under franchises granted by the people.

When, shortly after the enactment of the Public Service Law and the appointment of the commissions in conformity with it, the legislature passed an act fixing a uniform passenger rate of two cents per mile over all the railways of the state, he vetoed the measure, pointing out that one of the very purposes of the creation of the public service commissions was that these bodies, clothed with appropriate powers and administrative machinery, should investigate questions of that character, and, upon ascertaining all the facts involved, determine whether or not particular rates were unduly high or unjustly discriminatory, and in the public interest should be changed.

With similar vigor and unswerving determination, Governor Hughes compelled the repeal of the act of the legislature under which gambling on horse races was carried on in defiance of the express provisions of the State Constitution. On the other hand, when inflammatory attacks were made in the "yellow" press upon the New York Stock Exchange, accompanied by demands for drastic measures to control its operations, Governor Hughes, before acting, appointed a commission of bankers and lawyers of recognized integrity and disinterestedness to examine into the complaints and recommend what legislation, if any, was necessary for the public protection. He was ever swift to attack abuses. But in public life, as in private, he always insisted upon ascertaining the facts of any given case before determining upon his course of action.

While he had been always a member of the Republican party, thruout his term of office, Mr. Hughes sought support and political strength from the people directly rather than from any political organization. He developed in an extraordinary degree the faculty of talking to crowds in the language they understood. He appealed to "the man in the street"—to employ a phrase of his coinage. He trusted in the common sense and inherent sanity of what Mr. Lincoln called "the plain people." In return, they understood and trusted him. His renomination and reëlection as Governor in 1908 became as irresistible as the progress of a live glacier. During the presidential campaign of that year, Mr. Hughes made his first appearance on the stage of national politics. His speech on the national issues delivered at Columbus, Ohio, September 1, 1908, was regarded at the time by men of all political creeds as one of the most lucid and convincing presentations of political issues in the annals of American oratory. Sober judgment has since confirmed that opinion.

Mr. Hughes's style of speaking is simple and devoid of rhetorical embellishment. His method consists in marshaling his facts and presenting them in language so simple that the ordinary mind easily can understand their meaning and significance. He has the magical power of coining phrases which touch the imagination and linger in the memory.

While the judicial quality of patiently investigating the facts and hearing both sides of a case has been carefully cultivated by Mr. Hughes, he is far from being neutral in his feelings. It is impossible for those who know him to believe that he was indifferent to the German occupation of Belgium or the destruction of the "Lusitania."

It is said that recently, in discussing with some friends the possible effects of the European war, he pointed out that one of its most serious results to us would be that when it ended the American people would be the only "soft" nation in the world. All the others would have been hardened by strife.

No institution over which Mr. Hughes has any control will long remain "soft." Under his determined will, directed by his clear, vigorous intelligence, the national impulse towards "preparedness" will receive a practical and intelligent direction which will fit this nation to take its proper place in the councils of the world and to protect the rights and interests of its citizens at home and abroad.

When Mr. Hughes, six years ago, accepted President Taft's offer of an associate justiceship of the Supreme Court, he turned his back upon political life and deliberately dedicated himself to the arduous duties and secluded existence of the judiciary. Doubtless he believed that ample opportunity would be afforded for the exercise of his best thought and labor, and nothing in his opinions from the bench affords any reason to doubt the continued vigor of his thought or expression.

But his seclusion was to be of short duration. The people literally have beaten a path thru the wilderness to his door, and called him forth to the field of political strife.

Cincinnatus was not summoned from his plow by a more imperious public demand than has Hughes been called by the people of his political faith to exchange comfort, certainty of position and the life which was his highest ambition, for the toil and vexation of a political campaign having as its highest reward the incumbency of the most exacting office ever created by man. But Charles Evans Hughes is by nature a fighter. His opponents forgot this fact when, during the long and trying period just passed, he remained silent, true to the proprieties of his judicial office, refusing to lift hand or voice for a position he did not seek, or to repudiate the accusation of timidity which was unknown to him, and the imputation of opinions which he held in abhorrence.

The reputation for austerity and coldness acquired by Mr. Hughes during his struggles with adverse forces in Albany was speedily dissipated by the congenial atmosphere he found in Washington, both in his official and his social life. No one is a more popular dinner companion than he. His broad culture, wide reading, quick wit and easy manner have made him a welcome guest wherever people of intelligence and refinement are assembled. The life of a member of an appellate court compels a toleration of the opinion of one's associates, and requires patient attention to views however divergent from one's own. For a man of strong self-confident nature, no training could be more valuable than that which first requires attention to arguments presented by opposing counsel, then discussion with other judges, gradual modification of views and opinions, and finally concurrence in a general conclusion. A president with such a training would certainly avoid the reproach so commonly expressed concerning Woodrow Wilson, of unwillingness to confer with others or even to listen to facts or opinions which he had reason to think might be at variance with his a priori assumptions.

Mr. Hughes is possest of those qualities of sobriety, self-command, perfect soundness of judgment and perfect rectitude of intention, which Lord Macaulay ascribed to John Hampton. These qualities, added to an intuitive knowledge of the people, and a rare understanding of popular thought, afford reason to those who know him to believe that no better qualified candidate for the presidential office ever has been presented to the people of these United States.

New York City

UNCLE SAM—"I'M PROUD OF YOU BOTH—NOW FOR A GOOD SQUARE FIGHT!"

THE WOMAN OF YESTERDAY

BY CORRA HARRIS

AUTHOR OF "A CIRCUIT RIDER'S WIFE," "THE RECORDING ANGEL," "THE CO-CITIZENS"

THE one woman whom we really know, and concerning whose future there can be no reasonable doubt, is the Woman of Yesterday.

She is the fanciful heroine of ballads and romance because only one-half the history of this country has been written. If her services and sacrifices had been recorded they would have been different, but they would not have been less important than the best deeds of her bravest men, and we should discover in her more than a figure of speech in poetry and fiction. She accomplished some of the best and sternest scriptures of American life. She was intelligent. She had the courage of a pioneer, and the patience of a saint, and she was no less progressive than the woman of today. She started further back in time and had further to go. This is the only difference. She was a pioneer who faced a wilderness and wrought with faith and infinite labor to establish the ideals of liberty and righteousness upon which this civilization was founded. If the women of today run with the same courage the race that is set before them, if they preserve these ideals with the same fortitude, they will do well, but not better than she has done.

She was a gentlewoman who practised her virtues delicately and in secret as if these were the ritual of her faith.

SHE was a domestic economist who never wrote a paper nor addrest a club on this subject. But she literally practised these arts of the home about which we agitate more than we achieve. She was that woman of the proverbs who "looketh well to the ways of her household and eateth not the bread of idleness." She made the things which we buy, and she knew better how to save than we know how to spend. All the doors of industrial and professional life were closed to her. Nevertheless she was, strictly speaking, a producer, not a consumer. She founded the best and most stable American home that has ever existed, and she maintained it with a dignity and diligence which the woman of today cannot surpass. She produced great men, not great issues, and she did not produce herself at all. She was only the blessed medium through which all life flowed, receiving from her a certain fineness, a color of the spirit, a vague and gentle effulgence. She was not the epochal woman. She was the

mother and patient prophet of that woman.

They who fail to comprehend that the woman of today is the product as well as the descendant of the women of yesterday do not know her history. She led no movements, but she herself moved ever forward in the sweeter grace of silence.

SHE was the most truly and wisely progressive woman this country has yet produced. She failed of recognition deliberately. She had not advanced so far as organizations and attendant publicity. But she deserves no less praise for that which she accomplished. There is not a single righteous issue advocated by the women of today which cannot be traced back to this silent, diligent, thoughtful woman of yesterday. It was Frances E. Willard, a woman of yesterday, who first advocated the cause of temperance. The idea of suffrage for women is older than Susan B. Anthony. Frau Cower was the Grand Old Woman of Germany. She gave sixty of her eighty-six years to those reforms which have resulted in wider opportunities for German women. She was working for this long before there was a single women's organization in Germany. Mademoiselle Minot did the same thing in France many years ago. When the manhood of the British Empire was concerned with wars and bloodshed, it was Florence Nightingale, a woman of yesterday, who founded the Red Cross and financed it from her own fortune when the government failed to support her. Have the women of today with their colossal organization and their wealth accomplished any better work than this? It was a woman of yesterday, the mother of a large family, who did the work of her home and wrote "Uncle Tom's Cabin." I am from the South, and I

do not think the facts justified the passionate ardor of that story, but has any woman of today written a book which has had so much influence upon American life? It was a New England woman of yesterday who accomplished humane reforms in the treatment of the insane. There is the statue of a woman with a sunbonnet on her head in New Orleans, raised to the memory of an old Irish woman of yesterday who loved and gave her life for the poor in that city without straining her fortune through a charitable organization. It was a Georgia woman of yesterday who worked single handed with the Legislature of that state until she accomplished reforms in the treatment of women prisoners.

AND the spirit of the pioneer persisted in these women to the last. Until recently a very old woman of yesterday lived on a farm near my home in the Valley. When the Civil War closed, her husband returned to her a helpless invalid. She ploughed her fields, cut her wheat with an old-fashioned hand cradle, bound and shucked her sheaves, and harvested all her crops. She never bought anything. She literally made a living for her family out of the ground, and they lived well. She spun and wove their clothes, she kept an immaculate house. She was the mother of ten children. She brought them up in the faith and gave each of them a college education. They are the best people in the community. Not one of them failed her. She was never twenty miles from the place where she was born in her life. Are there many women of today who can give a better account of themselves? We are so much taken up with our "preparedness" plans for living that we do not realize that this woman of yesterday did prepare and that she is still far ahead in actual service.

There is no standard of morals however high, no culture, no ideal of justice for which we merely contend, that she did not practise with modesty and patience. She left us to reap the harvest of her labors with the same spirit of willing sacrifice which marks her history from the beginning.

The women of today hold in trust the heritage of the women of yesterday for the women of tomorrow, and it is our most sacred duty that they may receive it from us with interest, not squandered by idleness nor damaged by decadent theories.

The Valley, Georgia

WHY WE HONOR HER

She was a gentlewoman.
She was a domestic economist.
She wrought to establish the ideals of liberty and righteousness.
She had the courage of a pioneer and the patience of a saint.
She founded the best and most stable American home.
She was the most truly and wisely progressive woman this country has yet produced.
There is no standard of morals however high, no culture, no ideal of justice for which we merely contend, that she did not practise with modesty and patience.

CARTY

CARTY'S HALL

BY JOHN FINLEY

For the first time in the history of the world, so far as known, a meeting was conducted by telephone, as if the participants were in the same city and hall, the some of them were three thousand miles away. It was a meeting of the American Institute of Electrical Engineers, and several sections met in the cities named, motions being put in one, seconded in another, and voted for in all. Dr. J. J. Carty, who presided, received next night the Franklin Medal in recognition of his achievements in telephony.

Carty? You've never heard of Carty? Well,
That's no reflection, as it seems to me,
On Carty,—Carty who's been farther heard
Than any other man that ever lived,
Excepting Vail who from his New York tower
Called Carty up in Honolulu once
And conversation held without a wire.
"What hath God wrought!" were man's first words
Transmitted o'er Atlantic's wire-strung shores;
But o'er Pacific's waves the first to fly
Were simply "Hello, Carty! Are you there?"

Well, Carty hired a hall, as big it was
As all outdoors. One wall was firmly set
On Plymouth Rock, where freedom-loving waves
Still beat upon a "stern and rock-bound coast";
The western looked upon the placid sea,
Which from a lonely peak in Darien
Balboa saw, and had a Golden Gate
Which oped upon the jewelled Orient.
The other walls to North and South were hung
With tapestries diaphanous and dim,
Woven of straight imaginary lines
Of latitude, and filmy argent threads
Spun on gray waters and the desert plains.
And o'er these walls there spread a ceiling such,
By night, as that which ever hangs above
The hurrying migrants to and from New York
In its vast terminal, yet vaster far,
And sprent with stars, millions of miles away,
With which such as Pupin have often talked
In spectroscopic tongue and learned what things
Are burning in their hearts beyond our ken,—
Such was the wondrous hall which Carty hired,

Almost as large as all the ancient world
Of Ptolemy, from Ethiopia
To Thule, and from Sera to the sea.

You think this but a wild Arabian tale?
But let me tell you more: Last night did I
Attend a meeting in this spacious "Carty Hall,"
And Carty was presiding genius there.
A black-haired, wiry, Celtic man he was,
Of gentle, clear-voiced, speech and wireless ways,
Without a gavel, such as chairmen use,
To order he commanded all the host.
Wide-scattered as the flocks on Grampian Hills;
And many thousands hearing made response,
From far Atlanta to the farther sea.
Chicago, Philadelphia, Boston,—all
Cried "here," New York and San Francisco, too;
They listened all to speeches and to songs,
They stood as one and cheered the Stars and Stripes,
Tho mountains, lakes and prairies lay between—
For "Carty's Hall" was The United States.

'Tis prophesied that all the quick and dead,
From Boston to Bombay and back again,
Shall at one moment hear the selfsame sound,
The stirring sound of Gabriel's final trump:
But long before that day shall come, perchance,
A Carty, or his scientific heir,
Will make the universe his "Carty Hall"
Wherein each earth-encircling day shall be
A Pentecost of speech, and men shall hear,
Each in his dearest tongue, his neighbor's voice
Tho separate by half the globe.

THE NEW BOOKS

THE AMERICAN SHORT STORY

Of the twenty-two hundred most promising short stories by American writers, which were published in 1915, Edward J. O'Brien has selected the twenty "best"—a collection of such wide range and diverse style as to represent almost every type of deservedly popular magazine story. In a foreword Mr. O'Brien analyzes the entire short story product of the year, which, he says, impresses him "more than ever with the leadership maintained by American artists in this literary form." He lists and grades these authors in four groups: A Roll of Honor, the ones who fall just short of excellence, the merely good, and the negligible.

But it is as an explorer rather than as a judge that Mr. O'Brien makes his work most valuable. Discovering new authors and comparatively unknown magazines is his specialty. Perhaps his zeal in that direction influenced his choice of Zelig by Benjamin Rosenblatt as the best short story of the year. It appeared in "The Bellman," a weekly magazine which Mr. O'Brien puts at the head of its class among fiction periodicals. Probably most of its readers will disagree as to the first of the collection —In Berlin, by Mary O'Reilly. The Water-Hole, by Maxwell Burt; The Bounty-Jumper, by Mary Synon; and T. B., by Fanny Hurst may all be ranked as better than the "best." But at any rate it seems to me to determine the worth of the collection as a whole—good tales, varied, well-told, new, are sure of popular approval.

For They of the High Trails, romances of life in the Rockies, we are not so optimistic. Hamlin Garland writes of the outdoors understandingly; he makes us feel the vastness and the solitude of the mountains, and their power in shaping the lives of men. But when he sets people to influencing people his insight is less true. He falls back on the accepted formulas of magazine fiction, and the men and women in his stories fail to live up to the possibilities of their setting.

Rex Beach gives us the other extreme in The Crimson Gardenia and Other Tales of Adventure. Each plot is shaped by a tyrannical ruling passion, and from Alaska's icy mountains to the tropics' coral strand the masculine emotions predominate.

It is a relief to turn from these crude colors to the delicately shaded sketches of Stamboul Nights, photographic in their realism, yet subtly interpretative of the Oriental people. H. G. Dwight has done more than record his experiences—he has sensed their dramatic values and put into words all their atmosphere as well as action. The Leopard of the Sea is a vivid tale of a ship's last voyage—altogether different, of course —yet comparable to Kipling's The Ship That Found Herself.

Two other collections of short stories

interpreting a people have recently been published. God's Remnants is a series of pictures of the Jewish race, in Austria, Galicia; Poland, Russia, London, New York—wherever the Chosen People gather to uphold their traditions. Samuel Gordon has drawn the significant characteristics of the Jewish temperament with a sympathetic presentation of their racial point of view, too frequently misunderstood. Beggars on Horseback deals more definitely with individuals and suggests rather than explains their characteristics as a people. These are uncanny, Poe-like tales of Cornish peasant women, who live their philosophy of life unhampered by convention. F. Tennyson Jesse sketches them with clear-cut, forceful skill, directed by a remarkable imaginative power.

Thru all these various collections of stories there runs a trace of the exaggerated American demand for novelty, a fault induced perhaps by our insatiable appetite for fiction. Fortunately, however, our best writers are wise enough to disregard this demand of the public—and the public likes them for it. William Allen White has long been famous for his studies of plain Middle Western folk, the people who live "in Our Town." His latest book, God's Pup-

DAILY PAPERS

"Well," said Father Payne, "a great deal of the news most worth telling can be told best in pictures. I believe very much in illustrated papers. They really do help the imagination. That's the worst of words—a dozen scratches on a bit of paper do more to make one realize a scene than columns of description. I would do a lot with pictures, and a bit of print below to tell people what to notice. Then we must have a number of bare facts and notices—weather, business, trade, law—the sort of thing that people concerned must read. But I would make a clean sweep of fashion and all sensational intelligences—murders, accidents, sudden deaths. I would have much more biography of living people as well as dead, and a few of the big speeches. Then I would have really good articles with pictures about foreign countries—we ought to know what the world looks like, and how the other people live. And then I would have one or two really fine little essays every day by the very best people I could get, amusing, serious, beautiful articles about nature and art and books and ideas and qualities—some real, good, plain, wise; fine, simple thinking. You want to get people in touch with the best minds!"

From Father Payne, Putnam, $1.50.

pets, includes four long short stories, humanly interesting and squarely true to life. We know the characters they portray as real people, but he makes us know them better than we usually succeed in knowing real people.

Perhaps we need not worry about this exaggerated demand for novelty, after all, for the final verdict of popularity seems to go to the genuinely worthwhile. People have enjoyed for more than twenty years the Stories of H. C. Bunner, now collected in two volumes. All the old-time favorites are included —Love in Old Cloathes, The Midge, The Zadoc Pine Labor Union, Our Aromatic Uncle, and enough others to provide good reading for many summer afternoons.

The Best Short Stories of 1915, ed. by Edward J. O'Brien. Small, Maynard. $1.50. They of the High Trails, by Hamlin Garland. Harper. $1.35. The Crimson Gardenia and Other Tales of Adventure, by Rex Beach. Harper. $1.30. Stamboul Nights, by H. G. Dwight. Doubleday, Page. $1.35. God's Remnants, by Samuel Gordon. Dutton. $1.35. Beggars on Horseback, by F. Tennyson Jesse. Doran. $1.25. God's Puppets, by William Allen White. Macmillan. $1.25. The Stories of H. C. Bunner. Scribner. 2 vols. $1.25 each.

PRESENT DAY SCRIPTURES

President William DeWitt Hyde pursued a novel course in delivering the Lyman Beecher Lectures on Preaching at Yale this year. Instead of dwelling upon the technical devices or philosophy of preaching, he sets forth the Gospel which is to be preached and practised. He finds The Gospel of Good Will not only in the historic documents and creedal statements of Christianity, but "revealed in contemporary scriptures," which, at their best, interpret the religious life of our time.

He takes a text and lesson from some recent well known writing and from it draws his Gospel message. In Jerome's "The Passing of the Third Floor Back" he finds the real essence of the gospel of good will, Christ's expectation of men. From Masefield's "The Everlasting Mercy" and "The Widow in the Bye Street" he draws lively portrayals to show the meanness of sin; and—in—Brook's biography of William H. Baldwin, Jr., "An American Citizen," he sees the religion of good will exprest in the social service and trusteeship of a great business and industrial leader. In like manner he treats Sarolea's "How Belgium Saved Europe" as a true embodiment of Christian sacrifice; and Riis's "The Making of an American" and "The Battle with the Slum" as depicting the typical, practical reformer moved by Christian idealism.

Thomas Mott Osborne, Charles Rann Kennedy and Winston Churchill also furnish materials for separate phases of the subject. A lucid style, a sympathetic treatment of present tendencies, and a high ideal of Christian service make this a fascinating volume.

The Gospel of Good Will, by William DeWitt Hyde. Macmillan. $1.50.

Copyright 1916 by
The B.V.D. Company

Night or Day, at Work or Play
B.V.D. Conserves Your Comfort

NOTHING is so typical of the American "level head," as the nation-wide popularity of B.V.D. It is the Summer Underwear of Efficiency—of the man who conserves his comfort at work or at play, just as he conserves his health—as an asset.

Loose fitting, light woven B.V.D. Underwear starts with the best possible fabrics (specially woven and tested), continues with the best possible workmanship (carefully inspected and re-inspected), and ends with complete comfort (fullness of cut, balance of drape, correctness of fit, durability in wash and wear).

If it *isn't* This Red Woven Label

MADE FOR THE
B.V.D.
BEST RETAIL TRADE

It *isn't* B.V.D. Underwear

(Trade Mark Reg. U.S. Pat. Off. and Foreign Countries)

B.V.D. Closed Crotch Union Suits (Pat. U.S.A.) $1.00 and upward the Suit. B.V.D. Coat Cut Undershirts and Knee Length Drawers, 50c. and upward the Garment.

The B.V.D. Company, New York.

CHANGE OF ADDRESS

If you contemplate changing your address, either permanently or temporarily, you should notify us at least three weeks in advance, giving us both the old and new address, so as to insure copies reaching you without interruption.

THE INDEPENDENT

NEW YORK

The GLEN SPRINGS
WATKINS, N. Y. ON SENECA LAKE
Wm. E. Leffingwell, Pres.
OPEN ALL THE YEAR

A Mineral Springs HEALTH RESORT and HOTEL, known as THE AMERICAN NAUHEIM
In Private Park with miles of accurately graded walks for Oertel hill climbing, ranging in altitude from 750 to 1100 feet. Midway between the Great Lakes and the Hudson on the Southern Tier Highway, all macadam. Attractive and well-kept Golf Course, Miniature Golf, Clock Golf, Tennis, Motoring.

THE BATHS
are directly connected with the Hotel and are complete in all appointments for **Hydrotherapy, Electrotherapy and Mechanotherapy.**

The Bathing Springs are similar to the waters of Bad Nauheim, in the proportions of Calcium Chloride and Sodium Chloride, but are about five times as strong. The Radium Emanation from Brine Spring No. 1 averages 68 Mache Units per liter of water and is due to Radium Salts in solution.

For the treatment of Heart, Circulatory, Kidney, Nutritional and Nervous Disorders; Rheumatism, Gout and Obesity we offer advantages unsurpassed in this country or in Europe.

Our Illustrated Booklets and Latest Reports on our Mineral Springs will be Mailed on Request

---

Red Swan Inn
Warwick, New York
Open May 28th to October 1st.

Modern hotel, electric lights; ELEVATOR; steam heat; beautifully located in the mountains of Orange County, 63 miles from New York City; rooms en suite, with or without bath; excellent cuisine; vegetables from own garden; gold mines on hotel grounds; tennis courts; orchestra; concerts daily; dancing every evening; golf room; fine roads for motoring; fireproof garage, livery; illustrated booklet.
BERKELEY S. DAVIS.

CEDAR CLIFF INN
MONROE,   Orange County,   NEW YORK
A delightful resort among the hills and lakes; suites with bath, 800 ft. elevation, 49 miles from city; own garden, golf, tennis, boating, bathing, fishing, music, garage. Booklet. M. E. HAIGHT.

GOLF
DUTCHER HOUSE
PAWLING, N. Y.
Always open.   Leland W. Blankinship, Lessee

THE SPA SANATORIUM
A. J. THAYER, M.D., Ballston Spa, N. Y., near Saratoga Springs. Refined, homelike, well equipped. New bath house, swimming pool. Electro and Nauheim baths. Booklets.

Ross Health Resort and Arborea Inn Annex
IN THE PINES OF LONG ISLAND. Valuable for those needing quiet and rest in the country. Resident nurses and physician. Write for booklet. Telephone 55 Brentwood. Address Ross Health Resort, Brentwood, L. I.

MAINE

THE HOMESTEAD
Bailey Island, Maine
Will reopen June 15. Illustrated booklet on application to T. E. HAZELL, Summit, N. J.

NEW YORK CITY

The St. Hubert
120 West 57th St.
Modern, fireproof, located in the residential section of the city.
Two blocks from Central Park.
Apartments, furnished or unfurnished, of one room to as many as desired.
PEABODY & BABCOCK, Props.

DOUGLAS INN and COTTAGES
DOUGLAS HILL, MAINE
Attractive Mountain Resort now open.
Send for Booklet and rates

MR. PURINTON'S EFFICIENCY QUESTION BOX

262. Mr. C. T., Arkansas. "Please inform me concerning a good diet for a person preparing to run a long race."

Natural wheat, oats, corn, rye, barley; figs, dates, prunes, raisins, fresh milk and eggs; limited portion of nuts; occasional fish, fowl or game; plenty of fruit and vegetables; a little pure candy, especially chocolate. No red meat, pork, salt or canned meat; no tea or coffee; no spices, greases, condiments; no pastry; no stimulants, carbonated beverages or ice-water; no denaturized fare such as white flour bread or patent breakfast foods. Investigate the remarkable endurance tests made on special diet by Chittenden and others at Yale—you might get particulars from Prof. Irving Fisher, New Haven, Connecticut.

263. Professor A., New Hampshire. "Am thirty-four years of age, have had theological training, been in school work in America and mission work in Burma, want to enter business or the consular service. My present plan is to apply for a position as teacher in the Philippines, then study a mail course with the American Law and Consular College in Washington, D. C., and learn Spanish also. (a) Is the plan a good one? (b) Is the institution mentioned the best for my purpose? (c) How should I apply for a teaching position in the Philippines?"

(a) We think so. (b) It is hardly safe to declare any school the "best"; we do not, however, know of a better one for your purpose, unless you can find a local institution more convenient in the Islands. (c) Apply for information to the United States Commissioner of Education, Washington, D. C. The man to give you most excellent advice, if he will do so, is Right Rev. Charles H. Brent, bishop of the Philippine Islands, Zamboanga, Philippine Islands.

264. Miss E. U., California. "I graduate from high school this June, and it is necessary that I immediately earn my living. Is there any work I could do in which I could use my knowledge of history and debating? I have had four years of history, and short terms of civics and economics."

You might obtain a position in a literary research bureau; a public library; a woman suffrage campaign organization; the office of your state historian or the woman's department of a national association like the National Civic Federation. Apply also to your State Federation of Women's Clubs. Get copies of the largest newspapers in Los Angeles and San Francisco; then try to discover how your special knowledge could be made to serve the newspaper, and ask for a job accordingly. Typewrite all your letters—your penmanship is poor. If you knew typewriting, bookkeeping or office filing, you would have three times as good a chance for a desirable position.

265. Mr. C. F. B., New York. "I am a public accountant, and have heard much lately in regard to personal efficiency. I greatly need the benefit of an understanding of this subject. Will you kindly indicate how I may best pursue the study?"

Obtain as many as possible of the efficiency articles and Question Box answers in back files of The Independent. Read my book, "Efficient Living," grade yourself on the different tests, and ask us how to increase your lowest percentages. Apply to Efficiency Publishing Company, Woolworth Building, New York, for a list of modern books on the subject. See announcement on page 445 of The Independent for March 27, 1916, and keep in touch with the work of the Institute, chronicled in these pages.

266. Mr. C. H. R., New Jersey. "(a) Can you advise me where to obtain instruction in commercial art? (b) Can such study be done after business hours? (c) Is the profession overcrowded? (d) How is the work best disposed of?"

(a) We infer your wish to study by correspondence. Write these schools for data: Fine Arts Institute, Omaha, Nebraska; Federal School of Commercial Designing, Warner Building, Minneapolis, Minnesota; W. L. Evans School of Cartooning, Leader Building, Cleveland, Ohio; Rosing School of Lettering and Design, Union Building, Cleveland; De Beck and Carter Feature Service, First National Bank Building, Pittsburgh. Also get a copy of the *Students' Art Magazine*, Lockwood Publishing Company, Kalamazoo, Michigan. (b) Yes—while you are learning the technique. (c) With amateurs, but not with artists of talent and skill. (d) Ask the schools mentioned above, prior to enrolling.

267. Mr. L. T., Nebraska. "I am a high school senior, nineteen years old. (a) I would like your advice as to a profitable means of making some of my college expenses during the summer months. (b) I am told that Chautauqua systems employ young fellows to set up tents, look after the grounds, etc. Will you please give me the address of some such companies?"

(a) You might sell books, life insurance, office appliances or household utensils; work in hay fields; buy a candy machine and follow the outdoor amusement companies, or obtain a concession at a summer resort; wait on table in a summer hotel or boarding house; act as agent for weekly and monthly periodicals. Apply for a summer job to the new Federal Employment Bureau—ask your local postmaster for details.

(b) Chautauqua Institution, Chautauqua, New York; Community Chautauqua, Incorporated, Equitable Building, New York City.

268. Mr. S. Y., New York. "What system of saving should one take, to save $500 in five years, by monthly payments?"

The Postal Savings system would probably serve as well as any; inquire at your post office. Write also The American Bankers' Association, 5 Nassau Street, New York, for their literature on cultivation of thrift. A series of booklets on savings may be had from John Muir & Co., 61 Broadway, New York.

269. Miss H. W., Maine. "I want information regarding the Gary System of Education. I would be very glad to 'Learn to do by doing' if I could make expenses. I have a seminary education and have taught rural schools. (a) Could I get a chance as assistant in any of the Gary Schools? If not, could I take a correspondence course?"

(a) Apply to the Commissioner of Education, Washington, D. C., for a list of schools conducted on the Gary plan; write the principals of the schools you prefer, as to obtaining a position.

(b) No correspondence courses are offered, to our knowledge. The Gary plan is more for the utilization of school buildings and the practicalization of teachers and scholars than for the adoption of a new scheme of education proper. It cannot be used, except inferentially, by teachers apart from a Gary School. Read "Schools of Tomorrow," by John and Evelyn Dewey, published by Dutton at $1.50, for general information.

270. Mr. L. H. O., Argentina. "I want more energy, more vitality. I feel too much like a half-empty bag, instead of an overflowing one. I believe I am weak in both mind and body—perhaps more exercise would improve matters. I work ten hours as cashier and bookkeeper, and with two for travel and one for lunch have little time each day for exercise. Please make suggestions."

You can do tensing and breathing exercises while traveling. You can omit lunch—or make it liquid—and take a brisk walk at the noon hour. You can systematize your work so as to cut an hour off each afternoon, and spend the hour in the open air. You can sleep outdoors, in a sleeping porch on a window-tent.

Secure magazines listed in Question Box answer No. 241, issue of April 24, 1916. Study the advertisements and investigate. Meanwhile reduce your breakfast a third or a half, and watch yourself brace up.

MR. PURINTON'S EFFICIENCY QUESTION BOX

262. Mr. C. T., Arkansas. "Please inform me concerning a good diet for a person preparing to run a long race."

Natural wheat, oats, corn, rye, barley; figs, dates, prunes, raisins, fresh milk and eggs; limited portion of nuts; occasional fish, fowl or game; plenty of fruit and vegetables; a little pure candy, especially chocolate. No red meat, pork, salt or canned meat; no tea or coffee; no spices, greases, condiments; no pastry; no stimulants, carbonated beverages or ice-water; no denaturized fare such as white flour bread or patent breakfast foods. Investigate the remarkable endurance tests made on special diet by Chittenden and others at Yale—you might get particulars from Prof. Irving Fisher, New Haven, Connecticut.

263. Professor A., New Hampshire. "Am thirty-four years of age, have had theological training, been in school work in America and mission work in Burma, want to enter business or the consular service. My present plan is to apply for a position as teacher in the Philippines, then study a mail course with the American Law and Consular College in Washington, D. C., and learn Spanish also. (a) Is the plan a good one? (b) Is the institution mentioned the best for my purpose? (c) How should I apply for a teaching position in the Philippines?"

(a) We think so. (b) It is hardly safe to declare any school the "best"; we do not, however, know of a better one for your purpose, unless you can find a local institution more convenient in the Islands. (c) Apply for information to the United States Commissioner of Education, Washington, D. C. The man to give you most excellent advice, if he will do so, is Right Rev. Charles H. Brent, bishop of the Philippine Islands, Zamboanga, Philippine Islands.

264. Miss E. U., California. "I graduate from high school this June, and it is necessary that I immediately earn my living. Is there any work I could do in which I could use my knowledge of history and debating? I have had four years of history, and short terms of civics and economics."

You might obtain a position in a literary research bureau; a public library; a woman suffrage campaign organization; the office of your state historian or the woman's department of a national association like the National Civic Federation. Apply also to your State Federation of Women's Clubs. Get copies of the largest newspapers in Los Angeles and San Francisco; then try to discover how your special knowledge could be made to serve the newspaper, and ask for a job accordingly. Typewrite all your letters—your penmanship is poor. If you knew typewriting, bookkeeping or office filing, you would have three times as good a chance for a desirable position.

265. Mr. C. F. B., New York. "I am a public accountant, and have heard much lately in regard to personal efficiency. I greatly need the benefit of an understanding of this subject. Will you kindly indicate how I may best pursue the study?"

Obtain as many as possible of the efficiency articles and Question Box answers in back files of The Independent. Read my book, "Efficient Living," grade yourself on the different tests, and ask us how to increase your lowest percentages. Apply to Efficiency Publishing Company, Woolworth Building, New York, for a list of modern books on the subject. See announcement on page 445 of The Independent for March 27, 1916, and keep in touch with the work of the Institute, chronicled in these pages.

266. Mr. C. H. R., New Jersey. "(a) Can you advise me where to obtain instruction in commercial art? (b) Can such study be done after business hours? (c) Is the profession overcrowded? (d) How is the work best disposed of?"

(a) We infer your wish to study by correspondence. Write these schools for data: Fine Arts Institute, Omaha, Nebraska; Federal School of Commercial Designing, Warner Building, Minneapolis, Minnesota; W. L. Evans School of Cartooning, Leader Building, Cleveland, Ohio; Rosing School of Lettering and Design, Union Building, Cleveland; De Beck and Carter Feature Service, First National Bank Building, Pittsburgh. Also get a copy of the *Students' Art Magazine*, Lockwood Publishing Company, Kalamazoo, Michigan. (b) Yes—while you are learning the technique. (c) With amateurs, but not with artists of talent and skill. (d) Ask the schools mentioned above, prior to enrolling.

---

267. Mr. L. T., Nebraska. "I am a high school senior, nineteen years old. (a) I would like your advice as to a profitable means of making some of my college expenses during the summer months. (b) I am told that Chautauqua systems employ young fellows to set up tents, look after the grounds, etc. Will you please give me the address of some such companies?"

(a) You might sell books, life insurance, office appliances or household utensils; work in hay fields; buy a candy machine and follow the outdoor amusement companies, or obtain a concession at a summer resort; wait on table in a summer hotel or boarding house; act as agent for weekly and monthly periodicals. Apply for a summer job to the new Federal Employment Bureau—ask your local postmaster for details.

(b) Chautauqua Institution, Chautauqua, New York; Community Chautauqua, Incorporated, Equitable Building, New York City.

---

268. Mr. S. Y., New York. "What system of saving should one take, to save $500 in five years, by monthly payments?"

The Postal Savings system would probably serve as well as any; inquire at your post office. Write also The American Bankers' Association, 5 Nassau Street, New York, for their literature on cultivation of thrift. A series of booklets on savings may be had from John Muir & Co., 61 Broadway, New York.

---

269. Miss H. W., Maine. "I want information regarding the Gary System of Education. I would be very glad to 'Learn to do by doing' if I could make expenses. I have a seminary education and have taught rural schools. (a) Could I get a chance as assistant in any of the Gary Schools? (b) If not, could I take a correspondence course?"

(a) Apply to the Commissioner of Education, Washington, D. C., for a list of schools conducted on the Gary plan; write the principals of the schools you prefer, as to obtaining a position.

(b) No correspondence courses are offered, to our knowledge. The Gary plan is more for the utilization of school buildings and the practicalization of teachers and scholars than for the adoption of a new scheme of education proper. It cannot be used, except inferentially, by teachers apart from a Gary School. Read "Schools of Tomorrow," by John and Evelyn Dewey, published by Dutton at $1.50, for general information.

---

270. Mr. L. H. O., Argentina. "I want more energy, more vitality. I feel too much like a half-empty bag, instead of an overflowing one. I believe I am weak in both mind and body—perhaps more exercise would improve matters. I work ten hours as cashier and bookkeeper, and with two for travel and one for lunch have little time each day for exercise. Please make suggestions."

You can do tensing and breathing exercises while traveling. You can omit lunch —or make it liquid—and take a brisk walk at the noon hour. You can systematize your work so as to cut an hour off each afternoon, and spend the hour in the open air. You can sleep outdoors, in a sleeping porch or a window.

Secure magazines listed in Question Box answer No. 241, issue of April 24, 1916. Study the advertisements and investigate. Meanwhile reduce your breakfast a third or a half, and watch yourself brace up.

WHAT THE TOMMIES THOUGHT OF KITCHENER

BY WILLIAM J. ROBINSON

These personal impressions of Lord Kitchener are written by an American who fought as a British Tommy. His graphic description of "Killing the Wounded" was published in The Independent of May 29.—THE EDITOR.

LORD KITCHENER was not a sentimental man. He was generous in his reward of the right, and he was terrible in his punishment of the wrong. Yet he was loved. "Tommy" is not given to sentiment as a rule, and he doesn't care much for any one who is. He loves a strong man; and Kitchener was his ideal.

Lord Kitchener, like his men, despised a fop. I saw "K. of K." but twice during my time of service, and it was the second time I saw him that the following incident happened. He was to review a new brigade at a point "somewhere in France," and I took two of our officers down to the railroad to meet his train. These officers were to serve with the guard of honor which was to meet him. There were officers from practically all of the units then in France there at the station, and they lined up according to rank while waiting for the train.

Contrary to the popular idea in this country the monocle is not common among army men. I think I am safe in saying that not one in a hundred officers would be bothered with one. The few who do use them are generally the fops, and they are ridiculed for their silliness. As I sat at "attention" at the wheel of my car I noticed one officer, a subaltern by the way, who had a monocle screwed in his eye, and he bore other marks which placed him in the "asses" class.

Finally the train pulled in, every one sprang to "attention" and Lord Kitchener stepped from the train. He returned the general salute, and shook hands with some of the senior officers. Then he walked down the line of officers on the platform. As he came to the "gay dog" with the monocle he stopped. "Is there anything the matter with your eyesight?" he asked. "No, sir," replied the subaltern.

"Then take that thing out!" growled "K. of K," and I noticed that his order was not long in being obeyed. Needless to say the story flew like wildfire.

I have talked with men who have served under him in South Africa, Egypt, and India, and I can truthfully say that I have never heard a man say a word of anything but admiration for him. The grief felt by the civilian population in England will be great, but I know the sorrow felt by the men of the British Expeditionary Force will be the deepest, for he was the leader, the man who never failed them, and the man they would go thru ten thousand hells to serve.

THE HORROR OF THE FIRST-LINE TRENCHES

"I fought at Ypres. I fought at St. Julien. I fought at Lacouture and Festubert. I fought at Cuinchy. I fought at Givenchy and La Bassée, and in the first-line trenches at Messines. And before all these I fought in the first line at Richebourg and Laventie, and I live, one of sixteen alive out of 500."

That is the remarkable record of Romeo Houle, a Massachusetts boy who enlisted as private in a French Canadian regiment when the war broke out. In the spring of 1916 the American Government procured his discharge, since he had enlisted when he was under age, and he came back to this country, "the one I'd best die for, if die I must for any." He tells graphically the story of what war means to the men in the trenches:

The true story of the trenches has never been told. I know, because for many months I have lived in trenches. I have slept daily in dread of bullet, shrapnel, mine, and deadly gas—and the man-eating rats of mine and gas—and the man-eating rats.

I am one of the few soldiers living who entered the front trenches at the opening of the war and who lived to fight the Germans in the front trenches in February, 1916. And returning unexpectedly, snatched by the American Government out of the very jaws of death, I discovered how much American people have been talking of the trenches and how little, after all, they really know.

Who has seen hell? Who has experienced the horrors of Milton's terrible vision or the slow tortures of Dante's inferno? God! If Dante's dream madness were truth, and those seven circles were seven encircling battle lines in northern France or the torn fringe of brave little Belgium, I could stand up and say there is no agony of body or mind which I have not seen, which I have not experienced. I thank God and give Him the glory that I still am sane.

Gas? What do you know of it, you people who never heard earth and heaven rock with the frantic turmoil of the ceaseless bombardment? A crawling yellow cloud that pours in upon you, that gets you by the throat and shakes you as a huge mastiff might shake a kitten, and leaves you burning in every nerve and vein of your body with pain unthinkable; your eyes starting from their sockets; your face turned yellow-green.

Rats? What did you ever read of the rats in the trenches? Next to gas, they still slide on their fat bellies thru my dreams. Poe could have got new inspiration from their dirty hordes. Rats, rats, rats—I see them still, slinking from new meals on corpses, from Belgium to the Swiss Alps. Rats, rats, rats, tens of thousands of rats, crunching between battle lines while the rapid-firing guns mow the trench edge—crunching their hellish feasts. Full fed, slipping and sliding down into the wet trenches they swarm at night—and more than one poor wretch has had his face eaten off by them while he slept.

Stench? Did you ever breathe air foul with the gases arising from a thousand rotting corpses? Dirt? Have you ever fought half madly thru days and nights and weeks unwashed, with feverish rests between long hours of agony, while the guns boom their awful symphony of death, and the bullets zip-zip-zip ceaselessly along the trench edge that is your skyline—and your deathline, too, if you stretch and stand upright?

Yes. I. Romeo Houle, know the trench. I longed for big adventures, you see, and now, ah, God! I am sick of adventure, for the adventures I have had will plague my sleep until I die.—*New York Times.*

What's Keeping Me Back?

You've wondered why you don't get ahead. Why your pay isn't increased. Why you don't get promoted. You've blamed everything and everybody, when the real drawback is *yourself.*

You're standing still because you lack *training.* Because you have not *prepared* yourself to do some one thing better than others. If you really want to get ahead, the way is open to you.

For 25 years the International Correspondence Schools have been helping men to climb into good paying positions. Nearly 5000 reported last year that I. C. S. training had won them advancement. *You* can get I. C. S. training in your spare time in your own home without losing a day or a dollar from your present employment.

Position, power, good money, independence, are within your reach. The I. C. S. are ready to help you be the man you want to be. Let them show you how. Mark and mail this coupon.

The Market Place

FOR MORE REVENUE

Owing mainly to the projected increase in the army and enlargement of the navy, Congress must provide for additional revenue by new taxes. Some thought that an increase of $225,000,000 would be needed, but Secretary McAdoo has said to the House committee on Ways and Means that $150,000,000 will be sufficient. Estimates unofficially made some time ago have recently been reduced by unforeseen yields of revenue from existing laws. For example, the Treasury Department expects that the income taxes for the fiscal year ending with this month will amount to at least $110,000,000, altho only $80,000,000 was collected last year, and the Department's estimate, in December last, of the receipts for the current year was only $85,000,000. Prosperity accounts for the addition. And it is predicted that internal revenue collections will show a new high record. There are additions of $5,500,000 for tobacco and $10,000,000 for distilled spirits. These changes are ascribed by the Treasury Department to prosperity, increases of wages, and a more effective enforcement of the laws against those who seek by fraud or otherwise to avoid payment.

The bill for new taxes must originate, of course, in the House, where the Democratic members of the Ways and Means committee are now at work upon it. They have reached an agreement as to inheritance taxes and the proposed additions to the taxes on income, but have found some difficulty in framing a list of taxes to be imposed upon munitions and other war supplies. It is reported that the inheritance tax will not be applied to any estate which does not exceed $100,000, and that the committee will not ask for a reduction of the present income tax exemption limits of $3000 and $4000. But taxes on all incomes exceeding $10,000 will be heavily increased.

In the same bill provision will be made for a Tariff Commission of six members (not more than three from one and the same political party), which will be empowered to make investigations at the request of the President or of the committees in Congress which have charge of tariff legislation. It is now expected that the bill will also impose duties—which may be temporary—for the encouragement and protection of manufacturers of dyestuffs in this country. For dyestuffs we have been dependent upon Germany.

Chairman Kitchin says that the committee's bill will make it possible for manufacturers here within the next five years to produce at least sixty-five per cent of the quantity required for domestic consumption. Probably the new Tariff Commission and the Federal Trade Commission will be authorized to defend our manufacturers against a possible "dumping" of foreign goods here at low prices after the war. The stamp taxes of the present law will be repealed. After the national political conventions the bill will be reported to the House.

RAIL AND MOTOR STOCKS

In May the average advance for railroad stocks on the New York Exchange was about 3 points. For the shares of industrials the gain was slight, and 2 points measured the average addition for combined representative groups of both kinds of securities. That month saw the beginning of a new speculative movement in the stock of motor companies, due to reports about mergers and consolidations, in which well known and notably successful corporations were involved. This movement was subjected to some restraint when the rate for call loans rose, on the 6th inst., to 4 per cent for the first time since the Exchange was reopened in December, 1914, but it continues to be the most interesting feature of the market. The advance of the call interest rate was due in part to the demand for large sums to be used in the motor merger operations.

Many who know how railroad earnings, both gross and net, have been growing do not see why the market value of railroad shares has not moved upward in accord with these gains. In April several prominent roads made new high records. The New York Central's increase was 52 per cent; the Pennsylvania's was 55. A statement published by the Interstate Commerce Commission shows that the net per mile for all the roads in the ten months ending with April was increased by 36 per cent. But it must be borne in mind that there has been continuous selling here of stocks owned abroad, and that there has been no settlement of the wages controversy between all the companies and their employees. This dispute is now the subject of conferences in New York. If the demands of the men should be granted the cost of operating the roads would be increased by about $100,000,000 a year. A strike would cause great loss; a compromise must largely reduce net earnings.

By a new tax of 10 per cent on income, added to 25 per cent now paid, the British Government promotes the sale of American railroad stocks owned in Great Britain. This tax is imposed if the securities be not sold to or deposited with the government in accordance with the mobilization plan. One estimate is that $400,000,000 of securities held abroad have been absorbed by our market since January 1, in addition to $1,500,000,000 taken before that date. Continuous liquidation on

foreign account, and the possible or probable effect of the labor dispute, tend to prevent any considerable upward movement in railroad shares.

A long list of increased or extra dividends has tended to support the market, although such advances as might have been expected do not yet appear. Increased rates or extra payments have been announced by five copper companies, two companies that produce zinc, one cotton mill in Fall River, and a powder company, whose special payment of 23½ per cent makes 79 per cent in one year on a capital of $120,000,000. Oil companies continue to distribute great profits in cash or stock. With good reason, there is cheerful activity in the industrials on the Exchange and elsewhere.

THE YEAR'S GRAIN CROPS

In the Government's crop report for June we have for the first time an official estimate of the new crop of wheat. Another billion crop—last year's was 1,011,505,000 bushels—could not reasonably have been expected, for the enormous yield in 1915 exceeded the greatest of preceding crops by 120,000,000 bushels, and the average for eight years by 300,000,000. But it is disappointing to learn that only 715,000,000 are promised this year. There is, and will be for some time to come, an exceptionally good market for all the wheat that we can spare.

There are only 469,000,000 bushels in winter sown wheat in sight, altho 655,000,000 were harvested last year, and the estimate of spring-sown (not included in preceding reports), is 246,000,000, against a yield of 356,000,000 in 1915. A large reduction of acreage is noticeable. This was due mainly to unfavorable weather at seeding time and to large supplies still on hand. And the condition of the growing plants has been far below normal and the ten years' average. Since the May report the winter estimate has been reduced by 30,000,000 bushels. Condition is only 77¾, against 88 one year ago, and a ten years' average of 86. Still, the new crop promises to exceed the annual average to which we were accustomed for a series of years preceding 1914. Demand for export shows no decline, and reports from other parts of the world indicate that it must continue.

Last year we had a record breaking crop of oats. Now, on about an equal acreage, poor condition permits a promise of 1,255,000,000 bushels, against last year's 1,540,362,000, but there have been only two larger yields. On a reduced area the barley crop will be cut down from 237,000,000 to 189,000,000 bushels. All of the June estimates may be improved in the harvest totals. Such changes have sometimes taken place in past years.

The following dividends are announced: Liggett & Myers Tobacco Company, preferred, 1¾ per cent, payable July 1.

American Car and Foundry Company, preferred, 1¾ per cent; common, ½ per cent; both payable July 1.

American Can Company, preferred, quarterly, 1¾ per cent, payable July 1.

Insurance

Conducted by

W. E. UNDERWOOD

ON CHOOSING A PLAN

One of the most difficult of the tasks set me by correspondents of this department involves the selection, with supporting reasons, of one out of two or more plans of life insurance proposed by the writer. It is made difficult by the fact that I am generally without any but the most meager information about the seeker of advice, sometimes not even his age being furnished.

Circumstances govern this matter. Chief among these are: income, occupation, the source of income, present and future; number of dependents and probable duration of dependency; approximate amount of premium which may be spared annually, and of prime importance, age at nearest birthday.

Just as in whist, one in doubt is admonished to lead trumps; so in this matter, if in doubt take the Ordinary Life or a long term Endowment. Persons up to 45 will find the latter affording numerous advantages; those beyond that age would better choose the former for general, all-round service.

In addition to wife and children, men should remember several other facts in building up a line of life insurance. Among these, their own old age, the misfortunes of which are to be guarded against, a mortgage on the family home, which should be neutralized by a special policy for the same amount; and the business ability, or lack of it, of their beneficiaries. The improvident inclination of beneficiaries demands, for the conservation of the life insurance money, that most of the fund be payable in monthly or quarterly instalments. This is achieved under the Income Policy.

C. C. S., Carlsbad, N. M.—The accident and casualty companies write so many different policies it would be difficult and impracticable to select one fitted to the needs and circumstances of any individual. The North American Accident Insurance Company is thoroly sound and reliable. Write to the Chicago office, state what you need and they will serve you properly.

B. O. G., Eveleth, Minn.—The National Life Insurance Company of the U. S. A. has assets of $13,407,828 and a surplus of $1,011,330. As you see, it is financially satisfactory. You do not state what kind of policy you have; at present, only non-participating insurance is written. The management is of average ability. If your policy has any age, keep it.

I. C. P., Monmouth, Ore.—Efforts have been made to secure a statement from the Bankers' Life of Lincoln, Nebraska, itemizing the sources from which it pays its deferred dividends on matured policies. but the company refuses to make one. I am of the opinion that a very respectable proportion of them come from the heavy charges it makes against reserves on surrendered policies.

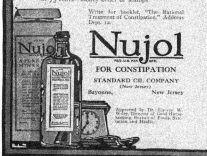

RED LIGHTS AND RED TAPE

Where would you put red light "exit" signs on a Chautauqua tent which is open all the way around? This is the fine legal question which the State Superintendent of Police of Connecticut had to decide when the Chautauqua Association opened up in Stamford, and Stamford did not have motion pictures because the Chautauqua representative and the State Superintendent of Police could not agree on where the legal "exit" to a wide open tent should be.

The association, in order to keep within the law, sent its representative, H. E. Wells, to Hartford to interview the Superintendent of Police as to the requirements.

"Motion pictures in a tent!" exclaimed the Superintendent of Police. "No such request has ever been made in Connecticut. We've never had motion pictures except in buildings. We haven't any laws on our statute books to cover any such case."

When the representative explained that motion pictures are a part of the program and had been given in the neighboring states, the Superintendent of Police said that he sometimes made concessions. Connecticut towns had no authority in the matter, since concessions lay within the power of the state official only. After much discussion he conceded the privilege for Chautauqua to run motion pictures, provided it marked the exits to the tent with red lights and fastened the chairs down.

"These are excellent rules for a building," replied Representative Wells, "but how can I fasten seats to the ground."

The Connecticut Superintendent of Police shook his head thoughtfully, then added, "You'll have to tie them together with ropes."

"And where," inquired Mr. Wells, "shall I put the red exit lights on a wide open tent?"

That seemed to be a poser for Connecticut. But shades of the blue laws, the state Police Superintendent handed down the decision that the exit lights should be placed at the right and left of the platform.

This was too much for the Stamford Chautauqua. The management concluded that in case of accident roped together chairs would be dangerous. Secondly, it seemed as if red light exits anywhere on an entirely wide open Chautauqua tent would look ridiculous anyhow. But, thirdly, red lights hung on the dressing rooms for program talent, located at the right and left of the platform, could but mislead a panicky audience to the only obstructions in the tent. So that, finally, the law-abiding Stamford Chautauqua had no motion pictures at all.

Shakespeare celebrations go on apace these days. But the Vincent Chautauqua Circle in Des Moines, Iowa, has the lead in tercentenary preparedness. Twenty-three years ago it inaugurated Shakespeare parties and has held them annually ever since.

The Independent

Founded 1848

HARPER'S WEEKLY
Founded 1857
Incorporated with The Independent May 22, 1916

THE CHAUTAUQUAN
Incorporated with The Independent June 1, 1914

The Independent is owned and published by the Independent Corporation, at 119 West Fortieth Street, New York. William B. Howland, president; Frederic E. Dickinson, treasurer; William Hayes Ward, honorary editor; Hamilton Holt, editor; Harold J. Howland, associate editor; Edwin E. Slosson, literary editor; Karl V. S. Howland, publisher. The price of The Independent is Ten Cents a copy; Four Dollars for one year. Postage to foreign countries in the Postal Union, $1.75 extra; to Canada, $1 extra. Writers who wish their articles returned should send stamped and addrest envelope. No responsibility is assumed for the loss or non-return of manuscripts. Entered at the New York Post Office as Second Class matter. Copyright, 1916, by The Independent. Address all communications to The Independent, 119 West Fortieth Street, New York

CONTENTS FOR JUNE 26, 1916
Volume 86　Number 3525

JUST A WORD

The next issue of The Independent, dated the day before Independence Day, will have a striking cover devoted to a portrait of Major-General Leonard Wood, whose timely article on the subject of universal military training will be the leading feature.

Two and a half pages of this issue are devoted to comments on the union of Harper's Weekly with The Independent. It is doubtful whether any other equal space contains matter that will be read with greater interest. Of course it was and is impossible to find space for printing all the friendly and complimentary messages that have come to us concerning this historic event. We appreciate them all, and hereby thank every one who has taken the trouble to put on paper the congratulatory words which seem to be in the minds of practically all the readers of Harper's Weekly, as well as of The Independent.

The Independent has been doing some rather lively pictorial work of late, in honor of its union with Harper's Weekly—the most distinguished illustrated journal in the history of America. The photograph of Mr. Hughes and his daughter which was reproduced last week as a frontispiece was made in Washington on Sunday, and forty-eight hours later completed copies of The Independent containing it were in the hands of readers—together with a complete story of the two Chicago conventions, a cover portrait of the Republican candidate, a late and striking picture of Colonel Roosevelt, and a double-page picture of the convention in session at the Coliseum.

This is the third annual Chautauqua Number of The Independent—and the cover design will be, we feel sure, an interesting suggestion to all true Chautauquas of the Round Table conferences which represent so much of the Chautauqua spirit. How many readers of The Independent, we wonder, know that "King Arthur's Round Table" is a real piece of furniture? It was a dozen years ago that the writer saw it, quite by accident, hanging on the wall in the Great

Hall of the Castle at Winchester, England, built by William the Conqueror. Tennyson's poems had long been familiar, but there was in mind no more expectation of seeing a Round Table of real English oak than of seeing the father of Hamlet at Elsinore. It is worth while to add that the table is something like seventeen feet in diameter, and that its appearance is accurately given in this reproduction of a rare engraving bought in Winchester.

OUR RECORD ON HUGHES

From The Independent—Jan. 30, 1908.

Governor Hughes richly deserves the support which his party in New York will give him. He has been faithful not only to his party, but to all the people of his State. An earnest Republican, he laid aside his party affiliations when he assumed the duties of his high executive office. Representing all the people who desired good government, he believed that if he should do his duty he could rely upon them to hold up his hands. They will never forget either his firm confidence in them or his devotion to their interests.

From Harper's Weekly—May 23, 1908.

The record of Governor Hughes is written in existing and working laws, not in interviews nor in fruitless agitation.

From The Independent—Aug. 6, 1908.

There should be no question about it. In the interest of clean politics and good government Governor Hughes should be chosen by acclamation. Thruout his term his service has been an admirable example of devotion to the interests of the people. When menaced by defeat he has always called upon the people for their support and they have given it to him.

From Harper's Weekly—Oct. 24, 1908.

How then should an independent minded citizen of New York vote this year? As we have observed before, there seems to be no valid reason why a Republican should refuse to support Governor Hughes. His administration has been notable for integrity, efficiency and resistance of influence by party leaders. . . . How any member of his party pledged to the maintenance of the Republican theory of government of people for their own good can consistently vote against Hughes passes our comprehension. He is the most exact embodiment of that theory now living, surpassing by far in strict interpretation and rigid determination the variable Roosevelt and of course to a yet greater degree the tolerant and broad-minded Taft.

From Harper's Weekly—Nov. 7, 1908.

Governor Hughes pulled thru and on the whole we are not sorry. . . . It would have been a pity to defeat the most notable representative of the best type of public servant the country has developed in recent years. . . . Moreover, aside from his deserts as a public official Governor Hughes fairly won his election personally. By sheer force of ability he became the most notable figure in the campaign.

What Every Voter Should Know About the National Issues of 1916

A Message to The Independent-Harper's Weekly Readers

I SHOULD not be willing to authorize this advertisement, if the financial consideration were not entirely secondary to my earnest desire to contribute in so far as I may to a clearer understanding of the vital political issues of 1916 on the part of the great army of intelligent voters who read The Independent. I look upon this as a real national service.

I shall here confine myself almost entirely to what others have said about my new book, "The National Issues of 1916," in the hope that many of you will be sufficiently interested to let me send you, without placing you under any obligation, a copy of this 455-page book, handsomely bound in cloth, for examination.

Just mail the coupon. No immediate remittance is necessary—unless you prefer. If you find that the book is what you want send me $1.50. If you do not care to keep it return it at my expense and you will then owe nothing.

The five divisions of "The National Issues of 1916" take up in turn The Flag and the Nation, Lincoln and Nationality, A Tariff Commission, An American Banking System, and An American Merchant Marine.

And now, let others describe the scope and value of this work as they see it:

President Nicholas Murray Butler of Columbia University says: "It deals, with clearness and conviction, with those questions which now most fully engage the attention of the American people. Our fellow-citizens will be assisted in voting intelligently by reading it."

United States Senator Knute Nelson says: "Your book will prove a 'Bible' and a veritable reservoir from which to draw facts and arguments in the coming political campaign. Every Republican speaker who intends to discuss the issues of the campaign ought to have this book at his side, for there is no better store-house from which to obtain arguments and facts."

Senator W. E. Borah of Idaho says: "It is a splendid, thorough, comprehensive discussion of some of the most vital issues of the day."

Senator W. L. Jones of Washington says: "You are entitled to a vote of thanks from the country for the forceful and comprehensive treatment of the issues of vital interest to the people of this country. The book is a mine of information upon all the issues discussed, and your discussion of the facts is most interesting and illuminating. This work will really be a handbook in connection with the coming campaign."

Mr. Robert L. McCabe of Ohio says: "Your book should be made the leading textbook on Americanism and placed in the hands of every voter. Not only that but if our public men would read and master the clearly stated principles of this book

they would be infinitely better informed and better prepared to legislate for the nation."

President Alba B. Johnson of the Baldwin Locomotive Works says: "The book contains a vast amount of useful information and many interesting discussions of present-day political and economic problems. It is well worth being read by every American citizen."

Professor John W. Wetzel of Yale University says: "Your first chapter, 'The Flag and the Nation,' is a veritable 'New Testament' for the inspiration and upbuilding of this Republic. It should be scattered broadcast over this country, from the Atlantic to the Pacific, by the million. In fact it should be made a part of the regular curriculum in our public schools and colleges, and the girls, as well as the boys, of the country should be required to commit it to memory."

The New York Sun says: "For all those who would look further ahead than next election day, for whom all the issues of the campaign are not crowded into a partisan phrase—Anything to beat Wilson-or—Anything to re-elect Wilson, who would know what the U. S. must do to make the most of the opportunities that are open to them, this is a book worth while."

Philadelphia North American says: "This is no mere campaign document—on the contrary, much of the contents of Mr. Fowler's book relates the patriotic concerns that are far removed from partisanship. It is a notable contribution."

The Financial Age says: "He has no personal facts or fancies to saddle upon the public, but from study and reflection simply writes down his observation of the natural evolution of banking caused by the practices of the people, and points out in a convincing manner the sound economic

principles upon which an independent banking system capable of serving all the established banks in the country should be founded."

The Financier says: "Mr. Fowler has not only written the American textbook of the future, but he has outlined what undoubtedly will be, sooner or later, the real system of American banking. His views on this question are based on premises as sound and certain as the law of gravitation, and his conclusions hold equally true. No man can say that he understands the theory of banking until he has read Mr. Fowler's book."

The Albany Times-Union says: "This book is a plain, common-sense interpretation of national problems, written for the voter. He is admirably qualified to analyze our national needs."

The Iola Register of Kansas says: "His discussion of the merchant marine, the tariff, and other great questions which are to be conspicuous in the coming campaign, is so informing and convincing, it certainly is true that every Republican who expects to participate in the coming campaign, either as a writer or a speaker, should have the book, for he will find a mine of material from which to draw, both for facts and for arguments, with no danger that his facts ever will be questioned, and little fear that his arguments ever will be refuted."

The Commercial and Financial Chronicle says: "We have never seen the principles underlying a bank note currency, and its functions, presented with greater lucidity and with more convincing and compelling logic. Nor have we ever seen an argument on the subject fortified with such a wealth of illustrations derived from history and experience."

The Philadelphia Inquirer says: "An especially lucid, vigorous, comprehensive, authoritative and convincing review of the political situation which ought to be in the hands of every voter and particularly of every young voter, throughout the land."

The Marine Journal says: "To those who are seeking for the reason why our shipping has disappeared from the sea and why it seems so herculean a task to restore it, Congressman Fowler's book will be a revelation."

The Bankers' Magazine says: "Not since the days of Alexander Hamilton and Albert Gallatin has there been anything presented in the banking and financial literature of America,—so sound, comprehensive and so absolutely overwhelmingly convincing as the truths which Mr. Fowler clearly and logically sets forth."

The privilege of offering to Independent-Harper's Weekly readers for free examination my handbook for voters and students of present day issues is one that I count very highly. As a member of the United States House of Representatives for sixteen years and Chairman of the Banking Currency Committee for eight years I enjoyed a rare opportunity to form the ground-work for this book and to store up material from actual experience, first hand study and intimate acquaintance with the great National problems which I have endeavored to clarify and illuminate in "The National Issues of 1916."

CHARLES N. FOWLER

The Independent

WITH WHICH IS INCORPORATED

HARPER'S WEEKLY

Copyright Underwood

THE CHOICE OF A UNITED PARTY

THE MARCHING SOLDIERS

FOR the first time in the history of the nation the President of the United States has called out the entire National Guard to secure our country's border against invasion.

In every one of the forty-eight states—and from almost every town—are marching to the appointed rendezvous our sons, brothers, husbands and fathers.

They go with devotion to the flag, and all that the flag stands for. They go to protect American life and American honor. They go with enthusiasm, because it is their duty to go, and it is for this purpose that they became soldiers and swore allegiance to their country. They go with serious recognition of the horrors of war—more keenly alive in the consciousness of the world than ever before in the history of mankind.

That their going may help to check the international tragedy that today seems so nearly inevitable is the hope and prayer of all.

That the men will do their duty, will honor their country, will fight if fighting comes, with the courage and vigor of their fathers, we all believe and know.

THE CAMPAIGN IS ON

THE Democratic convention at St. Louis disclosed a perfectly united party. There was not even a rumble of discontent at any point of the proceedings. Mr. Bryan, who had been looked upon as a severe critic of Mr. Wilson on the score of his advocacy of preparedness, came out whole-heartedly as a supporter of the President. The elements which had been most hostile to Mr. Wilson at Baltimore four years ago, Tammany in New York and the Roger Sullivan machine in Illinois, uttered not a syllable of protest at St. Louis.

In renominating Mr. Wilson the Democratic party not only did the inevitable thing, it did the one thing that it could have done that holds most promise for the nation's future well being. It is a splendid prospect that the voters of the United States have before them next November—the opportunity to choose between two men of such high character as Mr. Wilson and Mr. Hughes, and particularly between two men both of whom are products not of machine politics and blind conformity to party traditions, but of the reaction against these sinister tendencies in our political life. There are differences between the two men, but they are not divergencies in fundamental purpose, in honesty of conviction, or in personal character. They are rather differences in temperament, in type of mind, in method of approach to the problems of political life, in intellectual power, and in the qualities of leadership.

No member of either party need feel called upon to forsake his party standard because it is not worthily borne. No independent voter need be swayed to either side in the present contest by any considerations other than those of intellectual agreement with the program proposed by either leader or preference for the type of leadership offered in their respective persons. In casting his ballot in November the independent voter—and it is largely the independent voter that decides such elections as that of this year—will find it a close thing between Mr. Wilson and Mr. Hughes.

In the campaign now beginning The Independent will carry out its important function of presenting with fairness and impartiality both sides in the contest. Its performance of this function will not be impaired by the fact that it favors the election of Mr. Hughes. Beginning next week The Independent will set forth, in a series of editorials on the parties, the platforms and the personalities of the candidates, the reasons for such advocacy.

OUR DUTY IN MEXICO

OUR relations with Mexico were never more critical. Whether we shall have war with that distressful country depends on whether some Mexicans want it or not. It lies apparently in the hands of General Carranza to will war or to decree peace.

It is not a question of American intervention in Mexico. It is not the time now to consider what we may ultimately be forced to do there for the sake of ourselves, of the Mexican people and of civilization and good order in the Western Hemisphere. Our problem now is more circumscribed.

We have sent American troops into Mexico and massed American forces along the border with a single purpose. We propose to protect American territory from invasion, to punish those lawless men who have made predatory attacks across the border and to insure our immunity from attack by cleaning up the parts of Mexico contiguous to our boundary. We intend to use whatever force is necessary to accomplish this purpose effectively.

The President has already made use of all the forces of the regular army that are available for active service. He has now found it necessary to add to those forces the National Guard of the United States. He has done this not because our purpose has broadened or our intention become magnified. He has done it because the de facto President of Mexico threatens to oppose us in our lawful and righteous purpose.

We would execute our purpose in friendly coöperation with General Carranza if he will. But if he will not, no bluster, or threat or act of his shall deter us from the prosecution of our duty. The work we have set out to do shall be done, come what may.

This is not intervention. The United States wants neither intervention nor war. It will do everything that a nation can honorably do to avert these catastrophies. It will meet Carranza and the Mexican people more than half way in conference and deliberation and council. The American mind is set not upon conquest or even aggression, but upon its plain duty.

THE ROUND TABLE

AS the symbol of Chautauqua we print upon our cover in its original colors the Round Table preserved in the castle that William the Conqueror built at Winchester. Whether it was painted in the days of Arthur or Stephen or Henry VIII does not matter to anybody but the antiquarian. The rest of us take such relics at their real value, that is to say, their legendary value, what they mean. Now the Round Table differs from other tables in that it is round. It is, to use the language of science, acephalous. Here a MacGregor may assert that where he sits is the head of the table, but anybody else has an equal right to claim the same. According to Layamon's Brut the Knights of Arthur's court got into a fight one Yuletide over which should sit at the head of the table and several of them were slain. As a rebuke for such table manners King Arthur killed the men-folk of the family of the knight who started the row and cut off the noses of his women-folk. Then in order to prevent similar disputes over precedence in the future—for incidents like this are quite out of place at a Christmas feast and cause unpleasant feelings—King Arthur had a table constructed at which there should be no head.

So Arthur sat henceforth an equal in the circle of his knights, *primus inter pares*, all vowed to high emprize and chivalrous devoir;

> In that fair Order of the Table Round
> A glorious company, the flower of men,
> To serve as models for the mighty world,
> And be the fair beginning of a time.

So ever since the Round Table has stood for democratic comradeship in aspiration for the highest conceivable ideal. It was not by chance that it was chosen as the symbol of the Chautauqua Literary and Scientific Circle. For more than a generation the Chautauqua Round Table has met in the Hall in the Grove and in other halls and other groves thruout the country. Admission to the League of the Round Table is the reward of those who follow for five years a persistent course of study. The monthly *Round Table* bulletin serves as a telephone central to keep in touch those who sit around its vast circumference.

A circle has neither top nor bottom, beginning nor end. It is the emblem of equality and eternity. The Chautauqua Circle is a school without a teacher. Some stints; they kept their own study hours; they maintain ers. In Chautauqua all are learners. They set their own stints; they keep their own study hours; they maintain their own discipline; they pursue their own paths toward their common goal. Like a knight-errant each sallies forth into the land of the unknown in search of adventure, pledged to a lifelong quest of the Holy Grail of Eternal Truth, that is never to be found but ever to be sought.

EVERYBODY FOR SUFFRAGE BUT THE ANTIS

THE two great political parties in convention assembled have declared for woman suffrage. The month of June in the year 1916 will stand as one of the most important milestones on the road to full democracy. With the political parties for it, who that counts politically can be against it?

Of course it is not all over yet. We shall not have universal suffrage tomorrow or next month or even next year. For, alas, the gap between the political platform and the statute book is often dishearteningly broad. Then, too, each party accompanied its declaration of belief in woman suffrage with a weasel phrase that sucked a lot of the life blood out of it. Both parties would leave the matter to each state to decide for itself. Well, a quarter of the states have already achieved full democracy by that road. With the declaration of the two parties in favor of the principle to help along, the coming of suffrage, even state by state, should be speeded up.

What can any good party politician say to the question, "Do you or do you not accept the declaration of your national party platform in favor of woman suffrage?"

Democracy does march.

JAMES J. HILL: MASTER OF EFFICIENCY

WHEN a great man dies, people forthwith begin to look for the secret of his greatness. Sometimes they find it; often they overlook it because they are blind and call it luck.

James J. Hill was a great American. His legacy to his heirs is in money a certain number of millions of dollars. His legacy to the country in which he lived is a vast new territory, peopled and made productive; thousands of miles of railway projected, built and made profitable; the commerce and agriculture of a region the size of an old world empire developed and made prosperous; an example of enlightened, unselfish citizenship; an influence spanning the continent and widening the vision of the train man and the office boy as well as the captain of industry and the master of commerce.

Hundreds of thousands of men and women are more prosperous and more happy because he came. America is a greater nation because he saw and conquered.

What is the secret of it all? Not luck. The really great are not great because they are lucky, they are lucky because they are great.

James J. Hill was a master of efficiency.

Not efficiency in any narrow and niggling sense of stop-watch time studies and leak-plugging economies, and minute-saving improvements in method. All these are good, but they are not good enough.

Efficiency has been well summed up in an epigram: Doing the right thing at the right time in the right way. The first requisite to this right doing is vision. If there was any one thing that characterized James J. Hill in surpassing degree it was this elusive quality. His imagination projected itself into the future and laid hold on realities that were to be. He dreamed dreams and the dreams came true.

As a youth in Canada a vision came to him. A traveler stopping at the Hill homestead tossed the young man as he left an American newspaper and called out, "Go there, young man. That country needs youngsters of your spirit." The next morning young Hill chopped his last tree on the old homestead—the stump still bears the rudely cut legend, "The last tree chopped by James J. Hill"—and set out for the land of opportunity across the border.

Twelve years later he landed from a Mississippi River packet at St. Paul and began to look about—and always ahead. After twenty years of successful business career, the vision broke upon him with compelling force of the great territory in the Northwest that needed only transportation facilities to become an empire of agricultural richness. Like most prophets, he was laughed at for his dreams. But he was more than prophet, and "Hill's Folly," as his Great Northern railway enterprise was called, soon became a great and powerful reality. It opened up a new land to settlement and development. Through the genius of its creator it turned that unpeopled wilderness into a land of fruitful farms and thriving towns.

He had not only the vision to see, but the will to do. When his imagination showed him the way to an inspiring goal, he set out upon it with vigorous energy and kept to it with grim persistence. He foresaw not what was going to happen anyway, but what ought to happen—and then went out and made it happen.

When no one else could see that there was room for a fourth railroad system to the Pacific Coast, he saw it. When no one believed that a new road could compete with the established lines founded on government land grants and aided by government subsidies, he believed it, and made his own unconquerable energy and his own grim determination take the place of those artificial advantages.

He added to the faith of a clear vision and the energy of an indomitable will the knowledge and the intelligence of a master mind. He saw what was to be done, he determined that it should be done, and he knew how it must be done.

There is the triple secret of his success: vision, knowledge, will power. There is the triple secret of all efficiency: to see, to know, to do.

The monument to his greatness is a vast territory taken from forbidding wilderness and transformed into smiling affluence. The inscription upon the monument, for those who have eyes to read, is James J. Hill, Master of Efficiency.

OSBORNE VINDICATED

THE whole American people will rejoice that, under its decision last week, the Appellate Division of the Supreme Court of New York has left very little of the indictment against Thomas Mott Osborne, former warden of Sing Sing Prison. It has reduced it to the simple charge of neglect of duty, whatever that may mean. Thus the whole legal campaign against the greatest prison reformer of modern times collapses.

Governor Whitman should forthwith restore Mr. Osborne to his post. This is the very least a grateful state can do for the man who has demonstrated that the law of love still operates on earth—even among the outcasts and sinners.

THE PARAMOUNT ISSUE

NOW that the conventions have concluded their work we can see just where the difference between the parties lies. It is "Americanism versus Americanism." With two great parties struggling to stand on the same platform the campaign promises to be a hot one.

THE DEATH OF FREE TRADE

ONE of the economic results of the war which we must recognize whether we like it or not is that free trade has been killed or at least postponed to a future too far to be foreseen. The trade conference of the Allied Powers held this month in Paris for the purpose of shutting German products out of their markets after the war means that some sort of a tariff union will be established between them. Since England is the leader in this movement for protection, the Paris conference marks the definite abandonment of free trade by the power that originated the doctrine and has clung to it longest.

Reginald McKenna, Chancellor of the Exchequer, and Bonar Law, Colonial Secretary, speaking respectively for the Liberal and Unionist members of the Cabinet, have announced that the British Government will join its Allies in such a movement. The self-governing dominions of the British Empire have long ago repudiated the free trade policy of the mother country, and have erected tariff walls even against English goods. India threatens revolution unless she is allowed to do the same.

The frankest confession of this change of mind and the clearest expression of the reasons for it comes from Premier Hughes of Australia, who took part in the Paris conference. In an address to the British Imperial Chamber of Commerce he said:

I certainly approach the matter without bias against what is called free trade. When fiscalism was a live question in Australia I was a free trader of free traders. The "Wealth of Nations" was my Bible; Adam Smith was my prophet. But it was always disconcerting me to see how blind the world has been to the great virtues of free trade. Tried by this standard, it would appear that Britain was the only country in the world that was in step!

But if it were a question of trade only affecting our pockets, the fiscal question might fairly be left to settle itself. But it reaches down into the very roots of our lives. You cannot proceed upon the assumption that the economic policy of a nation has no relation to its national welfare. The relations between the two are inseparable, intimate, and complex. This fact is fundamental; to ignore it is not only to invite but to ensure national destruction. For a time the trade of a nation that treats trade as if it had no connection with national safety may make great strides, as did ours, but there comes a day of reckoning to such nations, as it has come to us.

I am no more concerned to deny that a case can be made out in favor of allowing trade to flow along what are termed its "natural channels" than I am to deny the virtues of the Spartan method of producing a virile nation by exposing its weaklings to certain death. Much might be said for both, but modern sentiment is definitely against the one and the inexorable circumstances of the modern world are against the other.

The present and prospective abandonment by Great Britain of the policy on which its commercial dominance has been built up leaves Holland as the only free trade nation in the world. Holland is quite a country when the tide is out, but in comparison with others it constitutes hardly more of an exception than the Freibezirk or free port district of Hamburg.

Up to 1860 it seemed likely that free trade would sweep over the world. But the tide has been ebbing ever since. In 1861 the Morrill tariff bill was passed as a war measure and protection was more firmly entrenched by the McKinley bill of 1890 and the Dingley bill of 1897. The Wilson bill of 1894 and the Underwood bill of 1913 made some reduction in the duties, but left the principle of protection essentially unshaken. France had been tending toward free trade up to the Franco-Prussian war, but after that turned in the other direction and the tariff laws of 1881 and 1892 were planned deliberately as protective rather than revenue measures. Italy, Austria, Belgium, Switzerland and Spain changed their policy during the same period in the same direction. The Prussian policy has always been protection, so much so that one is tempted to translate Hohenzollern as "high tariff." The German empire grew out of a customs union, the Zollverein of 1831, and it must be admitted that it has prospered as much commercially under protection as its great rival, England, has under the opposite policy.

The war, by increasing the fiscal burdens and by intensifying the national spirit, will drive in the same direction, and we cannot expect any country to stand out against it. Free trade is undeniably dead, and whether we may hope for a resurrection depends upon the strength of our faith in the coming of the Great Day when all artificial barriers between the nations shall be removed.

A FRIENDLY MEXICAN STATE

ONE encouraging feature of the Mexican situation is the evidence that Lower California does not share the enmity against the United States manifested generally in Mexico, but especially in the southern part. Colonel Esteban Cantu, Military Governor of the territory of Lower California, has declared that in the event of war between the United States and Mexico, Lower California will remain neutral. He made the same announcement when the American troops were landed at Vera Cruz. If this neutrality is maintained the city of San Diego and the Imperial Valley will be free from the danger of an invasion from the peninsula. We trust that in the final settlement our government will see to it that Lower California does not suffer from its friendly action in this crisis.

CONSTANTINE OF CONSTANTINOPLE

THE Athenians who assembled in mass-meeting last week to express their sympathy for the President of the United States as a victim like themselves of the tyranny of Great Britain alluded to their sovereign as Constantine XII. This harks back to 1453, when the eleventh and supposedly the last of the Constantines was struck down by a Turkish sword and cried in vain for a Christian to cut off his head. The Turks who that day battered down the walls of Byzantium with their new weapon, the cannon, have held the city ever since, but now there are many aspirants for it, the Czar of the Russias, the Czar of the Bulgars, and the King of the Hellenes among them. The last mentioned, half Dane and half Russian and married to a German, has no claim to the succession by right of Byzantine descent. The imperial line ran out with Ferdinando Paleologus, who found a humble grave in St. John's churchyard, Barbados.

The people who now live in Greece have perhaps as little of the old Greek blood as they show of the old Greek spirit, but because they speak Greek and because they have named their king Constantine they claim to be heirs of the ancient glory of the Greek Empire on the Bosporus. That is why they refuse to join with the Allies in giving Constantinople to the Czar. Better the Turk than the Russian, they think, because the Turk's hand is weakening, but the Russian bear never lets go what he gets his claws on.

THE VERDICT OF HISTORY

FIVE hundred representative American citizens have given their signatures positively and definitively supporting France, Great Britain, Russia and Italy against Germany, Austria, Turkey and Bulgaria. Herein they express, we believe, beyond question, the almost unanimous judgment of the American people.

Have they a right thus to express themselves? Who are these five hundred men? Are they qualified to speak the judgment of the people?

Three-fourths of them are college and university professors. Of all classes of Americans, they are students. It is their business to know the conditions of public his-

tory. They have the time for study. They have the documents and the libraries. If there is any class in the community that has the right to form and express a sound judgment it is these teachers of economics, ethics and history. They represent all our leading colleges and universities in all our states. What they say in sharp condemnation of the Teutonic Allies in beginning and conducting this war is what nine-tenths of their associates would say. Thru them intelligent America has spoken to the world. They have given their full sympathy to the one side and their condemnation of the other.

And they are not prejudiced. A multitude of them, hundreds perhaps, have studied in German universities, many more than have attended lectures in Great Britain or France. They loved Germany—they have dear memories of its universities. Some are of German birth or parentage, but they all agree, and with them the country agrees, that the course of Germany in this war is indefensible. But one criticism has been raised against their utterance. One or two congressmen and some others have complained to the President that these men have violated his instructions to the people urging them to maintain strict neutrality. Many of these signers are instructors in state universities supported by the public funds, and it is implied that they have no right to take sides or express a judgment on matters of public concern. Then who does have this right? They are qualified, and it is their business to teach. Not simply to teach the youth, but also to teach the nation. The liberty of speech is not forbidden to college teachers. We are not willing to understand that the President has undertaken to forbid the expression of public or private judgment, and if he had been so foolish as to define neutrality as silence there would have been every reason to protest against his prohibition.

The judgment of these five hundred leading men is a decision of American intelligence, and the decision of the world. They have anticipated the verdict of history.

WHAT WE DID FOR CANADA

IF all Americans were as frank in recognizing international debts and as judicious in making international comparisons as the editor of the *Edmonton Journal*, we and our Canadian neighbors would be spared a good deal of the bumptious talk that spread-eagle "statesmen" sometimes indulge in. He says:

A peace-at-any-price speaker in Madison Square Garden, New York, the other night told the crowd that Canada was politically as well off as the United States and that therefore the American Revolution was an unnecessary war. Canadians think they are better off politically than the people of the United States, but, if they are, it is largely because of the armed fight for the principle of self-government which the fathers of the republic made. If it had not been for the recognition, which that struggle enforced, of the folly of such a policy as George III's, the British Empire, such as we know it today, would not have come into existence.

John A. Macdonald, the Canadian publicist who is as stanchly Liberal as the *Edmonton Journal* is conservative, says that the development of the colonies—Canada or Australia—into a nation without a war, and the deliberate establishment and maintenance of self-government by the United States, are the outstanding phenomena of modern history. The fathers of our nation were pretty deeply involved, directly or indirectly, in both these tremendous achievements.

THE STORY OF THE WEEK

National Guard Called Out

To protect the American border from Mexican raids, the President has called out practically the entire state militia. The National Guard of Arizona, New Mexico and Texas had already been summoned; the new order calls troops from the remaining forty-four states (Nevada has no organized militia). The total paper strength of the militia in these states is 125,606; about 100,000 troops are called, leaving the rest for emergency and recruiting service.

The official summons to the governors of the states based the call upon "the possibility of further aggression upon the territory of the United States, and the necessity for the proper protection of that frontier." These forces will be used for border patrol duty only, for the present, as until the new law providing for the "Federalization" of the militia goes into effect, on July 1, they cannot be sent out of the country except by authority of Congress and after they have themselves volunteered. But their presence will release for General Pershing's use the regular troops, supposed to be about 40,000, who are now patrolling the border.

Seven destroyers and nine other small war vessels have been ordered to Mexican waters, seven to the east coast, probably to Vera Cruz and Tampico, and the rest to the west coast. This brings the total of American war vessels on Mexican duty to twenty-five, the battleship "Nebraska," at Vera Cruz, being the largest.

The Mexican Crisis

War with Mexico seemed nearer when this call was issued than at any time since the Vera Cruz expedition. The threatening situation had two phases: Carranza's peremptory declaration, made thru General Jacinto Trevino, that any movement of General Pershing's troops from their present position, except to retire from Mexico, would be resisted by force; and a series

of raids in the Laredo and Brownsville regions, resulting in the crossing of the Rio Grande by a third and a fourth American force in direct defiance of Carranza and by his local commander.

As we reported two weeks ago, General Gavira, of the Constitutionalist army, conferred with General Pershing and agreed to place his troops in such a way as to avoid clashes between the American and Mexican forces. General Trevino, who commands the Carranzista Army of the North, first notified General Pershing that Gavira had no authority to enter into such an agreement, and then transmitted Carranza's order to the American general to stay where he was or leave Mexico. General Gavira was recalled to Mexico City, where, according to unconfirmed rumors, he was executed.

General Pershing holds a line of 250 miles with his force of about 10,000 men. It stretches from Columbus, New Mexico, to Namiquipa, with field bases at El Valle and Colonia Dublan, and is dependent on motor truck trains, moving over miserable roads, for its supplies. Large stores of food and munitions have been stored at the field headquarters, Namiquipa, and the field bases.

The Carranza manifesto, if literally applied, would prevent the occasional excursions which American troops have been making to run down bandits. For instance, Pedro Lujan, a Villa lieutenant who was one of the Columbus raiders, was captured on the 13th at a point thirty-five miles east of Namiquipa. But General Pershing replied to General Trevino that he could not recognize the Mexican general's authority to control the movements of the American force, and it is expected that the order will be ignored. The Carranza forces have been so disposed as to enclose the American line roughly in a long "V" stretching south from the American border to a point below Namiquipa, and Trevino is said to have

25,000 or 30,000 troops under his command. The American forces hold a compact line, however, and a considerable amount of entrenchment has been done.

Raiding Southern Texas

The storm center on the Rio Grande has been moving steadily to the southeast. The Villa raid, which precipitated the sending of the punitive force, was made at Columbus, New Mexico; a second raid harried several towns in the "Big Bend" region of Texas, then raids were reported from the vicinity of Laredo, one a repetition of the Columbus incident; and the latest disorders have roused the country about Brownsville, almost at the mouth of the river.

The horse-stealing expedition, near Laredo, mentioned last week, proved to be of some importance, tho no horses were taken over the border, because one of the three bandits who were shot down by a sheriff's posse was identified as a lieutenant-colonel in the Constitutionalist army, named Villareal. After this additional troops were ordered to the border to reinforce General Funston's patrol, 600 from the Engineer Corps, from the city of Washington, and 1000 from the Coast Artillery, mostly from the northern Atlantic fortifications.

More serious forays followed. At two o'clock in the morning of June 15 a band of about a hundred Mexicans attacked the camp of the Fourteenth Cavalry at San Ignacio, near Laredo, and killed three privates and wounded six before they were driven off. Major Alonzo Gray crost the river in pursuit, but failed to find the bandits' trail and soon returned to the American side. Nine Mexicans were killed in the fight. General Alfredo Ricaut sent 1000 troops from Matamoras to chase the bandits. American troops are patrolling the border at Laredo and the international bridge has been closed.

New York Amer-n

THE HARRIED BORDER

A, The scene of the latest raids and the fourth crossing of American troops; B, The "Big Bend" country recently raided; C, The Carranza armies which threaten Pershing

504

IF THEY WILL ONLY STAY ON TILL NOVEMBER

Cesare in New York Sun

HE'S STEALING MY ISSUE

Rehse in New York World

THE BLAZED TRAIL

Brinkerhoff in New York Evening Mail (Copyright)

ONCE THERE WERE THREE PARTIES, NOW THERE ARE TWO ON ONE PLATFORM

On June 16 a detachment of the Twenty-sixth Infantry was fired on from the brush by a band of twenty-five or thirty Mexican bandits near San Benito, west of Brownsville. General James Parker promptly sent a troop of cavalry across the river on the trail of this band, and additional troops followed. About 400 cavalrymen encountered a force of Mexicans near the border and fought a stiff skirmish in the dense brush, apparently without casualties.

General Ricaut responded with an ultimatum announcing that he would attack this force if it was not withdrawn. This was in harmony with Carranza's declaration in his note of May 22 that the sending of any additional troops would be considered an act of invasion and would be resisted. Railroad tracks on the bridge between Brownsville and Matamoras were torn up and the population of Matamoras was armed.

The American detachment, the third squadron of the Third Cavalry, under Major Edward Anderson, went two miles into Mexico, camped and sent out scouting parties. The band of bandits having apparently been dispersed, and no further traces of them being found, the force returned to the United States when General Ricaut had promised that he would capture and punish the raiders. As they were returning, a few mounted Mexicans, led by an officer partly in Carranzista uniform, attacked them, and were put to flight with two killed.

The tension in northern Mexico increases. At Juarez, opposite El Paso, volunteers have been called for and are training for a possible break with the United States. City officers have been fired on in El Paso. American consuls from Matamoros, Monterey and Saltillo, and Piedras Negras have left their posts. Mass-meetings and newspaper attacks on America continue.

The reply to Carranza's note was delayed in order to include references to the fresh outrages, but it was understood that it would contain a flat refusal to withdraw the American troops from Mexico, and would accept Carranza's alternative and make a clear statement of the American position that the troops must stay until Carranza proved that he could patrol the border effectively.

The Democratic Convention　The Democratic National Convention at St. Louis was a model of unity and harmony. It bubbled with enthusiasm and sparkled with hope and confidence. The only task that it found at all difficult was to stretch out its proceedings over a long enough time to enable the city of St. Louis to make as much money out of the delegates and guests as a convention city is by common consent entitled to. But thru the Fabian tactics of the chairman of the Resolutions Committee, this desirable end was accomplished and the hotelkeepers and other entertainers of the city received their full due.

One other problem was a little perplexing—that of so arranging the program that the candidate for the Presidency should not be nominated on Friday. It required a little juggling, but the matter was finally arranged, and the nomination was made at five minutes before midnight on Thursday night.

Among the interesting features of the convention were the spontaneous and genuine enthusiasm for Mr. Bryan, the impressive silence of Tammany Hall and all other normally recalcitrant elements, and the fact that one delegate spoiled the unanimity of things by voting against the candidate of the convention.

Incidentally, Woodrow Wilson, of New Jersey, President of the United States, was nominated to succeed himself; and Thomas R. Marshall, of Indiana, Vice-President of the United States, was nominated to succeed himself.

The Democratic Platform　The platform adopted at St. Louis naturally indorses the administration of Woodrow Wilson, and challenged comparison of the party's record, its keeping of pledges and its constructive legislation with "those of any party at any time." It

Underwood

McCORMICK
The young Pennsylvanian whom Wilson has chosen to manage his campaign, in defiance of the party leaders

Copyright Buck

MARSHALL
Thomas Riley Marshall, Vice-President, renominated for the same office, with Thomas Marshall Sutherland, a namesake

ARMORED TRUCKS TO FEED OUR TROOPS IN MEXICO
Nearly all the trucks which serve as connecting links between all parts of the 250-mile line in
Mexico and the base at Columbus carry machine guns for protection

points with pride to the achievements of the past three years in reforming the tariff, rescuing "our archaic banking and currency system" by means of the Federal Reserve Act, creating a Federal Trade Commission, thru which "fair competition in business is now assured," lifting "human labor from the category of commodities" and securing "to the workingman the right of voluntary association for his protection and welfare," improving the postal service, and placing it upon a self-supporting basis.

The platform emphasizes the note of Americanism and uses strong words of criticism of all those whose activities are antagonistic to it. It says:

Whoever, actuated by the purpose to promote the interest of a foreign power, in disregard to our own country's welfare, or to injure this government in its foreign relations, or cripple or destroy its industries at home, and whoever by arousing prejudices of a racial, religious or other nature, creates discord and strife among our people so as to obstruct the wholesome process of unification, is faithless to the trust which the privileges of citizenship repose in him and is disloyal to his country.

We, therefore, condemn as subversive of this nation's unity and integrity, and as destructive of its welfare, the activities and designs of every group or organization, political or otherwise, that has for its object the advancement of the interest of a foreign power, whether such object is promoted by intimidating the government, a political party, or representatives of the people, or which is calculated and tends to divide our people into antagonistic groups, and thus to destroy that complete agreement and solidarity of the people and that unity of sentiment and national purpose so essential to the perpetuity of the nation and its free institutions.

The platform commits the party on the subject of preparedness without being specific as to the measure of preparedness that is necessary. It says:

We, therefore, favor the maintenance of an army fully adequate to the requirements of order, of safety, and of the protection of the nation's rights, the fullest development of modern methods of seacoast defense and the maintenance of an adequate

reserve of citizens trained to arms and prepared to safeguard the people and territory of the United States against any danger of hostile action which may unexpectedly arise; and a fixed policy for the continuous development of a navy worthy to support the great naval traditions of the United States, and fully equal to the international tasks which the United States hopes and expects to take a part in performing.

The platform repeats, in practically identical language, what President Wilson said at the annual meeting of the League to Enforce Peace in Washington the other day:

We believe that every people has the right to choose the sovereignty under which it shall live; that the small states of the world have a right to enjoy from other nations the same respect for their sovereignty and for their territorial integrity that great and powerful nations expect and insist upon, and that the world has a right to be free from every disturbance of its peace that has its origin in aggression or disregard of the rights of peoples and nations; and we believe that the time has come when it is the duty of the United States to join with the other nations of the world in any feasible association that will effectively serve these principles, to maintain inviolate the complete security of the highway of the seas for the common and unhindered use of all nations.

It reasserts the Monroe doctrine; declares that our troops must stay in Mexico until the repetition of incursions into the United States by Mexican bandits is improbable; indorses the shipping bill now before Congress; declares for improved legislation governing labor conditions in Federal employ; favors the enactment of a Federal child labor law; indorses the "purpose of ultimate independence for the Philippine Islands" expressed in the preamble of the Philippine bill; and recommends the extension of suffrage to women by the several states.

Returning to the subjects arising from the Great War, the platform makes this utterance:

We again declare the policy that the sacred rights of American citizenship must

be preserved at home and abroad, and that no treaty with any other government shall receive the sanction of our government which does not expressly recognize the absolute equality of all our citizens, irrespective of race, creed or previous nationality, and which does not recognize the right of expatriation.

The American Government should protect American citizens in their rights, not only at home but abroad, and any country having a government should be held to strict accountability for any wrongs done them, either to person or property.

At the earliest practical opportunity our country should strive earnestly for peace among the warring nations of Europe and seek to bring about the adoption of the fundamental principle of justice and humanity, that all men shall enjoy equality of right and freedom from discrimination in the lands wherein they dwell.

Railway Men to Vote on Strike The possibility of a nation-wide railway strike was brought one step nearer last week, when the conference of railway men and union representatives in New York broke up after two weeks' fruitless effort to adjust the demands of the men and the counterproposals of the railways. A referendum will now be taken by each of the four unions on the question whether their representatives shall be given the right to call a strike in case the railways hold their present position. This would not immediately result in a strike, but would put the union officials in a better tactical position when negotiations with the railroads are reopened. The vote will probably take about five weeks to poll, and a two-thirds vote is necessary before a strike can be called.

The railroad managers, calling attention to the threefold interest of the employees, the railroad owners, and the public, suggested to the unions that the matter be referred for adjustment either to the Interstate Commerce Commission, which should be specially empowered by Congress to fix wages if its present authority proved inadequate, or to a board of arbitration to be created under the Newlands Act. The union men deny the right of the Commission to fix wages, and refuse to consider arbitration until they have used the threat to strike as a weapon. Union sentiment among railway men is strongly against arbitration, for they regard the arbiters as being incapable of making a technical award so clear and definite that it cannot be misconstrued, in application.

Consequently they insisted on their own terms, an eight-hour day and time and a half for overtime, in exactly the form in which they were submitted. The railroads, declaring that they must be allowed a voice in the adjustment of these terms to existing wage schedules, stood pat for several detail provisions, of which the most important was that double compensation should not be paid for the same service or time.

The Pennsylvania Railroad has taken the first step to fight the proposed strike by calling on all "loyal" employees for volunteers to take the places of striking engineers, firemen, conductors and brakemen should a strike be begun.

Four Months at Verdun Since the Germans began their attack upon the French fortress of Verdun on February 21 the fighting has been incessant in that sector and the end of it is not yet in sight, for the Germans have not yet slackened their efforts nor the French their resistance. From its length, the number of men and guns engaged, the fierceness of the fighting and the expenditure of ammunition, Verdun would have to be called the greatest battle in the world's history but not necessarily one of the "decisive battles," for it is hard to see what effect its outcome may have upon the war except as it exhausts the strength of one or both the combatants. If the French continue to hold out the situation will remain the same as it was at the beginning. If the Germans persist until they take Verdun their victory will be an empty one, giving them little prestige except that of conquering an apparently insurmountable obstacle at a frightful cost. For the French would then withdraw to the western side of the Meuse, taking a new position on a shortened line, less strong perhaps than the Verdun hills but still not untenable if they have the men to hold it.

Indeed, it is said that the French General Staff favored withdrawing to the western side of the river when the German attack began, but the government overruled them because of the political effect that the abandonment of this famous fortress would have upon the French people and the outside world. This rumor of a proposed withdrawal has been confidently affirmed and authoritatively denied and the controversy over it has led to a demand for a frank discussion of the situation between the government and the Chamber of Deputies. Accordingly a secret session of the Chamber has been held, the first since 1871, when the Assembly at Versailles held a secret session to consider the communist rising in Paris.

Altho the loss of Verdun three or four months ago would have been a severe blow to French prestige, it would not be so regarded now, for the defense has been conducted with consummate courage and skill. General Pétain has contested every foot of ground as stubbornly as possible, yet he has not wasted men in attempting either to hold on to untenable positions or to recover them when lost. When it is decided that a certain fort or line of trenches must ultimately be captured all troops are withdrawn except enough to man the guns.

The small number of prisoners is one of the most amazing features of the battle. A hill that required months of bombardment and the sacrifice of thousands of men to capture may yield only two or three hundred prisoners. Fort Vaux is an instance of this. For three months the Germans, according to the French official estimate, fired 8,000 projectiles a day at this fort, yet when it was taken last week the garrison found in it numbered six or seven hundred.

This week the Germans have followed up their success at Vaux by attacking and gaining some foothold upon Hill 321, which is the next hill to Douaumont in the direction of Verdun. On the other side of the Meuse river the Germans have admittedly lost some trenches on Hill 304 and La Mort Homme.

The British Front There has been much speculation as to why the British Army on the Continent has been inactive at a time when the French and the Italians were so hard prest and the Russians were creating a diversion on the eastern front. Last year the British twice undertook an offensive, at Neuve Chapelle in March and at Loos, September, 1915, but in both cases they were checked before they had made any considerable advance. These failures were said to be due in part to the incompetency of the officers and in part to the deficiency of forces and shells. The latter defects at least have now been remedied, for Great Britain has raised and armed five million men and a large part of these are in France

and Belgium. The Germans opposite the British front are estimated to number from 600,000 to 800,000. The troops of which the German order of battle is supposed to be composed is given in the accompanying map. This, of course, is not official, and since the information on which it is based is obtained from spies, aeroplanes and prisoners, and since the various divisions are being shifted about, the map cannot be taken as accurate. But Winston Churchill, former First Lord of the Admiralty, who has been serving on this front, stated in Parliament that he had every reason to believe that the map was substantially correct.

Colonel Churchill criticized the government because of the large proportion of inactive men kept in England or back of the trenches in France. There were, for instance, 200,000 officers, each of whom had to have a servant. He further said in the House of Commons:

What is the proportion of rifle to ration strength? Half the total ration strength of the British Army is at home and half abroad. Of the half abroad, one-half fights and one-half does not fight. Of the half that

WHAT THE BRITISH ARE FACING

This remarkable map, prepared by the London Times, is the first case where an attempt has been made by a British expert to give the disposition of the German forces on the battle line. The British now hold the line between Ypres and the River Somme. Between Ypres and the sea the line is mostly held by the Belgians

fights about three-quarters, perhaps rather less, fight as infantry in the trenches and in the assaults, and nearly all the losses fall on them. The other quarter of the half consists of artillery and other services who come under fire, who render most effective service against the enemy, and do not suffer anything like the same proportion of casualties. On this calculation, which is a very liberal one and one very much on the safe side, for every six men who were taken from the nation at the one end one effective infantry rifle was produced over the parapet at the other end. There are two conclusions to be drawn. First that the number and proportion of those who actually fight ought to be greatly raised; and could be greatly raised by a comparatively small addition of the total aggregate. Secondly, that so far as possible able-bodied men, and especially young men employed on all the other parts of the organization, ought to take their turn at the front, and not leave it to the same lot to go on continuously, and go back wounded, time after time, until they were finally knocked out. It happened to my own battalion to receive a draft of thirty-five men of whom twenty-six had been previously wounded, some of them very severely. And this at a time when there are probably over 2,000,000 of men in the army who have never heard the whistle of a bullet.

The Allied armies are now under the command of one joint council, so we may assume that it is with the full approval of General Joffre that the British have not attempted to relieve the pressure upon Verdun by an attack upon the other end of the German line. The British forces are probably ready for action, but are being held until the time appointed for them to strike. There are many things to indicate that that time will soon come.

The Russian Steam Roller   This appellation, which the press gave to the Russian advance into East Prussia at the beginning of the war, is much more appropriate to the present Russian drive, for it is crushing everything before it. Along a front of three hundred miles the Russian line has moved westward and in the center of this sector the gain amounts to forty miles within two weeks. Two fortresses, Lutsk and Dubno, have been regained by the Russians and they have for the fourth time taken Czernovitz, the capital of Bukovina. The amount of booty captured is enormous; 163 cannon, 266 machine guns, 139 bomb throwers and 32 mine throwers. Most astonishing, however, is the number of Austrian prisoners. Over 150,000 are reported captured, including one general, three commanders and 2467 other officers.

The capture of so many prisoners is said to be due to the way the Russian artillery is employed. First the fire is directed upon the front trenches until these become untenable; then the guns are elevated so that an impassable curtain of fire is thrown behind the positions about to be evacuated and the Austrians thus caught between two fires have no option but surrender. The efficiency of the Russian artillery is ascribed to the American and Japanese ammunition which all thru the winter has been shipped over the Siberian railroad from the Pacific ports of Vladivostok and Dalny. The rapid pursuit of the retreating Austrians was car-

ried out in part by young Belgians in armored motor cars.

The Austrian line thru which the Russians have broken was strongly entrenched, altho weakly manned, for troops had been withdrawn for service in the Serbian and Italian campaigns. The foremost line of entrenchments consisted usually of a deep ditch, boarded over and protected in places by iron roofs. In front of this were some twenty lines of barbed wire entanglements. The shelters or dugouts in which the men lived were fifteen feet underground and were in some cases handsomely fitted up with upholstered furniture, musical instruments and pictures. Deep and crooked communication trenches led to the listening pits in front and to the second and third lines of trenches behind. The second line was put a mile and a half behind the first, and in the rear of this the Austrian soldiers had put in flower and vegetable gardens where the Russians found potatoes, radishes, lettuce and onions growing. The guns were placed in casements of reinforced concrete. Light field railroads connected the entrenchments with the supply bases behind, and the advance of the Russians was so swift that much of the rolling stock fell into their hands.

The rapid advance of the Russians north of the Pruth river cut off the Austrians in Bukovina from those in

Galicia and on the evening of June 17 the bridgehead on the northern bank of the river opposite Czernovitz was carried by storm and 1000 prisoners taken. This gave the city of Czernovitz into their hands, but the bulk of the Austrian garrison appear to have withdrawn into the Carpathians to the west.

Italian Ministry Out   Premier Salandra, when called to account before the Italian Chamber of Deputies, was obliged to confess that his optimistic assurances of the safety of the country had proved unfounded and that the Trentino frontier had not been adequately protected or properly defended against the Austrian invasion. As a consequence, he found himself without a majority in the parliament. The King has asked Paolo Boselli, former Minister of Finance, to form a new cabinet out of the best men in all parties. Baron Sonnino, veteran Minister of Foreign Affairs, and General Morrone, Minister of War, will be continued in the cabinet, which includes also two Socialists and one Republican. Probably there will be no decided change in policy, as only thirty-seven votes, those of the orthodox Socialists, out of 508 members, were cast against continuing the war.

General Brusati, whose incompetency is blamed for the Italian defeat, is said to have owed his position to his having been the brother of the King's side-decamp. He has now been removed and the Italian defense strengthened, so the Austrians have made little progress in the past week, tho they report some gains south of Arsiero and Asiago. The need of men on the Galician frontier to meet the Russian drive will probably relieve the pressure on the Italian side, but according to reports from Rome no Austrian troops have yet been withdrawn from this sector.

In Defense of Bagdad   The Turks seem to be offering a successful resistance to the Russian and British advance upon Bagdad. After the Russians had taken Trebizond and Erzerum it was commonly assumed that the Turkish power in Asia Minor had collapsed and it was even prophesied that the Grand Duke Nicholas would soon reach the Bagdad railroad and the Tigris river or even Constantinople. But since then the Russian armies in Armenia and Persia have made little progress. Their advance westward from Erzerum has met with what Constantinople calls a decisive defeat in the mountains before Erzingan. The column that was moving south from Erzerum toward Bagdad has been checked. The column that crost the Persian border at Khanikin, also headed toward Bagdad, has been driven back over the border with the loss of 800 men.

The British also, if we may accept the Constantinople reports, have met with reverses upon both the Tigris and the Euphrates rivers, which, it appears, they have been attempting to reascend toward Bagdad. A force from

THE RUSSIAN DRIVE

During the winter the Austrians and Germans occupied the line marked on the map but since the first of June the Russians have advanced over the shaded area beyond and captured the fortresses of Lutsk and Dubno and city of Czernovitz

Kurna where the two rivers join was sent up the Euphrates in boats, but on trying to land on the northern bank was attacked and routed by the Turks, leaving 180 dead behind. Some of the British boats on the river were sunk by the Turkish guns.

The Turkish Minister of the Interior, Talaat Bey, in reporting the results of the investigation of Armenian troubles, states that it was necessary to deport the Armenians from certain localities because it was found that they were conspiring to assist the Russians in conquering the country, and in fact had actually taken up arms against the Ottoman government in some places. He admits that in the process of deportation some abuses unfortunately occurred, but the perpetrators are being tried and punished. Fifty-one Turkish soldiers convicted of mistreating Armenians have been shot.

This very mild statement of the case bears little resemblance to the reports received from eye-witnesses of the massacres. According to the American Board of Commissioners for Foreign Missions the 20,000 Armenians in Erzerum were all killed with the exception of two hundred of whom thirty were saved in the house of the American missionary, Mr. Stapleton. The Moslems came several times and demanded that the Armenian girls be given over to them, but Mr. Stapleton answered, "You must kill me before you can touch them." The Russians entered the city just in time to prevent their house from being blown up and looted like the others.

Allies Blockade Greece   The grip of the Allies upon Greece has been strengthened so that the Greek government has been practically displaced in Macedonia by British and French administration. The Allies have declared martial law in Salonica and taken possession of the Greek railway, postal, telegraph and customs systems. A French naval officer has taken the place of the Greek commander of the port. The national banks of Greece proposed to issue an additional $6,000,000 in paper currency to supply the pressing needs of the Greek government, but the Allies have refused to allow this under threat of withdrawing all financial assistance in the future.

The Greek army, which was mobilized last September, has been for the most part kept under arms ever since, but now the Allies have insisted upon its being disbanded. King Constantine insisted that the army was necessary for the defense of the country and tried to compromise by demobilizing half of it. But the Allies are trying to force him to issue an order for complete demobilization by blockading the Greek coast.

The Greek ships in British and French ports were held and no coal or food was permitted to enter Greece except for use of the Allied troops. Since Greece is dependent upon its commerce

Starrett in New York Tribune

ARE WE STILL WINNING, WILHELM?

and there was only food enough in the country to last ten days, the people are threatened with starvation unless they give in.

These violent measures have aroused great indignation in Athens and mass meetings were held denouncing the conduct of the Allies toward neutral nations and "especially toward the President of the United States." A mob of several hundred made demonstrations before the British and French legations and the offices of the Venizelos newspapers. Ex-Premier Venizelos is hated because when in power he tried to bring Greece into the war on the side of the Allies. Skoloudis, the present premier, is striving to preserve neutrality, in spite of the pressure of the Allies.

Altho Greece is by treaty of the powers a free and independent state the British and French have been using Greek territory as tho it were their own ever since the war began. The Gallipoli campaign was conducted from the Greek islands in the Aegean and the island of Corfu has been utilized for the rehabilitation of the Serbian army, which has now been transported to Salonica, where several hundred thousand British and French troops are now assembled for an attack upon Bulgaria.

The Bulgars, claiming the same rights of occupation of Greek soil as the Allies, have advanced down the Struma river and taken possession of the Greek forts at Rupel and Demir-hissar, to the east of Salonica. The Allies interpreted this concession to the Bulgars as indicating an intention on the part of the King of the Greeks to take the side of the Central Powers, so they are determined to have the Greek troops sent to their homes.

The Battle of Skagerak   Both the Germans and the British claim as a victory the naval engagement in the North Sea on the last day of May. The Kaiser declares that the British supremacy of the seas has at last been overthrown and he has promoted Vice-Admiral Scheer to Admiral because of his defeat of a British fleet greatly outnumbering his own. On the other hand, A. J. Balfour, First Lord of the Admiralty, asserts that "Great Britain not merely obtained the honors of battle, but also its substantial fruits."

The number of ships lost on either side is not yet certainly known. The German Admiralty has admitted the loss of battle-cruiser "Lützow" and the cruiser "Rostock" as claimed by the British, but formerly denied by the German Admiralty "for military reasons." The loss of the new and largest of the German battle-cruisers, the "Hindenburg," is still denied at Berlin.

On the other hand, the Germans assert that the British superdreadnought "Warspite" was sunk. The captain of the "Warspite," however, gives out an interview in which he tells how he brought her safe back to port, altho even some of the British observers thought her lost when her steering gear was shattered and she drifted into the midst of the German fleet. She was shelled by six German ships, but managed to escape under cover of the smoke and spray.

Leaving out the "Warspite" and the "Hindenburg," the Germans figure that their losses were 60,720 tons against 117,750 tons on the part of the British. They further claim that the British navy has lost 130 ships of all sorts since the war began, with an aggregate tonnage of more than 600,000. So far as reported, the British loss of life is 343 officers and 6,104 men; the German is 173 officers and 2,414 men. The Germans saved 177 of the officers and men on the lost British warships.

According to the British Admiralty, the "Hampshire" went down from striking a mine, not from the torpedo of a German submarine. Lord Kitchener when last seen was on the quarter deck about to enter a boat, but the night was so stormy that no boat could keep afloat.

It is reported that on the same day of the battle of Skagerak fourteen German merchant-steamers being convoyed across the Baltic were attacked by Russian destroyers, which sank two of them and a small auxiliary cruiser.

"HE KEPT US OUT OF WAR"

SOUNDING THE KEYNOTE AT ST. LOUIS

BY HAROLD HOWLAND

"WITHOUT orphaning a single American child, without widowing a single American mother, without firing a single gun, without the shedding of a single drop of blood, Woodrow Wilson wrung from the most militant spirit that ever brooded over a battlefield an acknowledgment of American rights and an agreement to American demands."

Crash! Bang! The explosion had come. The Coliseum at St. Louis was in cheerful, jubilant, orderly tumult. The permanent chairman of the Democratic Convention, Ollie James, the genial giant from Kentucky, "with the shoulders of a buffalo," as I heard him described by his introducer on a similar occasion eight years ago in Denver, had just put into thunderous words the thought which the Democrats hope to drive home to the people of the United States in the next five months. Delegates and spectators clapped and shouted for a while and then eager voices began to chant, "Say it again! Say it again!" So he said it again, with a little more fire and a little more punch. Then the crowd went mad, and with the aid of the band kept up its delighted frenzy for a quarter of an hour or so.

On this second day of the con-

THE DEMOCRATIC DOVEKEY

vention the good old Democratic party was enjoying itself hugely. It had had a pretty good time the day before when former Governor Glynn of New York had first blown the keynote on the pitch pipe of the temporary chairmanship. Mr. Glynn is Irish, with plenty of Celtic fire and flow of words. The crowd had made him, too, "say it again," when he declared that though the policy of neutrality of President Wilson might not satisfy the fire-eater or the swashbuckler, it does satisfy the mothers of the land at whose hearth and fireside no jingoistic war has placed an empty chair. It does satisfy the daughters of this land from whom bluster and brag have sent no loving brother to the dissolution of the grave. It does satisfy the fathers of this land who will fight for our flag, and die for our flag when Reason primes the rifle, when Honor draws the sword, when Justice breathes a blessing on the standards they uphold.

The floor and the galleries enjoyed and approved that thoroly, and promptly set the expectant welkin echoing with their endorsement of it. But they did not get thoroly aroused to the spirit of the occasion until the second day, when the booming voice of Ollie James said it all over again.

By that time every one had realized that the convention had just one real function to perform. The candidate had already been selected by the logic of events and the momentum of public opinion. The ratification of the nomination even was hardly necessary. The platform would be the natural product of three things, the party record, the pronouncements of the Republicans at Chicago, and the wishes of the President. All the convention had to do was to aid by its presence and its enthusiasm in sending ringing thru the land the keynote of the campaign.

Well, the task was well done. There is no uncertainty about the keynote. It took shape in a dozen

THE WALKLESS PARADE—A SOLID LINE OF WOMEN WHO ONLY STOOD AND WAITED FOR SUFFRAGE AT ST. LOUIS

different ways in the words of orator after orator, but translated from oratory into colloquialism it runs, "He kept us out of war."

It received its final seal of approval just before the nomination of the Presidential candidate on Thursday night. For two days the crowd had been spoiling for a speech from Bryan. He was not a delegate to the convention—his party associates in Nebraska had not wanted him to be—but, as he had done at the two conventions in Chicago, he occupied a prominent seat in the press gallery. Every time he came in the delegates and spectators cheered him. Then when Ollie James had shot his bolt of oratory, a roar of "Bryan—Bryan—Bryan" began to beat in waves of sound upon the chairman's devoted head from all over the Coliseum. Ollie James struggled manfully with gavel and waving hand for a chance to say something, but the roaring crowd would have none of him. At last it had to take breath for a moment, and the chairman was able to interpolate the information that Mr. Bryan had slipped out to make a speech somewhere else, and that the chance to hear him must come later.

In the evening the moment came, and the former Secretary of State

> ### THE SCHOOL MASTER
> #### BY HARRY KEMP
>
> *School Master—yes. School Master of the World,*
> *No hasty demagog who would have hurled*
> *His Country into war! A Man whose pride*
> *Stands clear of leaning unto either side*
> *Of hate and murder, see him tower supreme*
> *Above the blinded sneers, with his great dream*
> *Of peace for all the world. He would not bring*
> *Upon our souls that dreadful old-world Thing*
> *That drags asunder on its rock of hate*
> *The Life of Europe. Good and wise and great,*
> *Lofty in vision, humble in his pride,*
> *He has THE GREATEST TEACHER on his side!*

in the Wilson Cabinet made an upstanding, riproaring, fighting speech in praise and endorsement of his quondam chief. The climax of his eulogy came when he thundered out, "I have differed with the President as to some of his methods, but I join with the American people in thanking God that we have a President who does not want us to take part in this war." The now familiar keynote met the now stereotyped response—if the adjective is not out of place in describing anything so spontaneous and genuine and hearty.

It is a good keynote. It is a popular one. And already it has performed one valuable service. It has removed the single possibility of dissension in the Democratic ranks—at the moment when the reunion of Progressives and Republicans makes unanimity the one indispensable condition for the Democracy. It has brought Mr. Bryan back from outside the breastworks. The atmosphere of that convention showed all too plainly that Mr. Bryan—off the ticket—is still a substantial political asset.

Conventions are different. The Progressive convention seethed; the Republican convention sulked; the Democratic convention smirked. The Bull Moose could not help seething; it is (was, must we say now?) made that way. The Elephant could not be blamed for sulking; it was not only led to bitter water, it was made to drink. The Donkey is entitled to smirk; it has a splendid rider with a splendid record behind him.

The convention smirked and preened its feathers and grew complacent whenever it got its mind off the keynote and took thought for the party record. It was the first time in twenty years, as Ollie James pointed out, that the Democratic party had had a record. He said:

During the three years of its national control, Democracy has enacted into law more progressive remedial legislation than the nation has ever had written

upon its statute books since its birth. In former national contests in the last two decades, our party came as a prophet. Today we come with deeds, not words; with performance—greater than our promise. The Democratic party has kept its word with the American people. We have made good.

He then proceeded to point out two amendments to the Federal Constitution, one to tax the wealth of the country thru the income tax, the other to "free the Senate of the United States from the control of the great interests by making it elective by the people at the polls." He held up also the Underwood tariff, the Federal Reserve Board, and the rural credit law as shining examples of Democratic constructive legislation.

Mr. Bryan, when his turn came, drove home the same record of constructive achievement with those triple-barreled detonations of hand on hand with which he characteristically punctuates his most earnest statements.

The Democracy smirked, and nominated Wilson and Marshall—at five minutes of twelve on Thursday night, because Friday is an unlucky day—and adopted a platform, and went home, contented, happy, hopeful, confident. For why should it not be?

And it will be a very pretty fight.

SENATOR STONE
The chairman of the Senate Foreign Relations Committee had a difficult position as chairman of the Resolutions Committee at the convention

JUDGE WESTCOTT
Twice he has nominated Woodrow Wilson for the Presidency. Once his man won the nomination and the election; the second time—

EDUCATION IN THE NEXT GENERATION

BY GEORGE E. VINCENT

PRESIDENT OF THE UNIVERSITY OF MINNESOTA

HE American people from now on will be forced more and more to consider their lives and activities from a national standpoint. Whether or not the country should be ready for war, it must be prepared for a peace which will bring challenges and tests. World markets are not to be mastered by "manifest destiny," nor is moral power to be exerted by mere assertion. The days of drift, of self-indulgence, of slip-shod methods, of complacency, of isolation are numbered. Will Americans have the intelligence and character to train, discipline, organize, unify themselves, or must they undergo an ordeal imposed from without?

The tasks to be undertaken are heavy and exacting. The efficiency of underlying industries, notably agriculture, must be greatly increased; the problems of marketing must be more satisfactorily solved; an alert and resourceful commercial organization both governmental and private must be set up in foreign countries; conduct of public affairs, taxation, municipal, state and Federal administration must be of a better, more modern kind; public health must be safeguarded, child welfare promoted; housing, industrial insurance, relations of employers and workmen must receive careful attention; differences of race, language, and traditions, of economic and social status, must be reconciled; moral standards must be sturdily maintained; a sense of national purpose and ideals, of loyalty and devotion must be deepened.

EDUCATION FOR NATIONAL SERVICE

EVERY one of these tasks, and countless others, make demands upon the educational system of the country. Education, therefore, may no longer be looked at individually or locally; it must be considered nationally. Attention shifts from the personal career of the pupil to the needs of the country. For Emerson America spelled in capital letters "opportunity"; tomorrow "national service" will appear in larger type. The ideals of West Point and Annapolis will translate themselves into the standards of technical and professional training of all kinds. The same spirit

512

Few educators are so well acquainted with the broad field of university and popular education as President Vincent of the University of Minnesota. He is the son of Bishop Vincent, who founded Chautauqua, and himself served as editor of the Chautauqua Press, vice-principal, principal and president of the Chautauqua Institution before his recent election to the office of chancellor. His teaching was done mostly at the University of Chicago, where he became dean of the faculties of art, literature and science in 1907; he has held his present office at Minnesota since 1911. He is the author of "Social Mind and Education."—THE EDITOR.

may be expected slowly to permeate the entire educational system.

Long before the war brought Americans face to face with a new national situation, there were many signs of discontent with the organization, methods, ideals and results of education in the United States. Nowhere more than in schools, colleges and universities did the tendency to follow tradition, to drift, to "muddle thru" seem more pronounced. Business men, parents, teachers, pupils, college professors and students have been finding fault.

Here are some of the things they have been saying: Training for occupations has been neglected; children leave school because they are bored; they drift into "blind alley" occupations; the studies of the elementary school are too formal and meaningless to hold the interest of the pupils; school children learn nothing thoroly and well, but have a vague smattering of many things; the rural schools are backward and country children are slighted; the great mass of teachers are ill-trained, inexperienced, underpaid, ephemeral, "a mob of mobile maidens meditating matrimony"; the school is not connected closely with the life of the community which it is supposed to serve; colleges are loafing places for young barbarians without mental interests; even the graduate work of universities is too much a kind of formal and pretentious erudition; professional schools for all their efficiency are sending out lawyers, doctors, engineers, dentists, bent upon personal success and regarding the public as a mine to be worked rather than a community to be served.

These indictments as a whole are too sweeping, undiscriminating, unfair. They vary widely in their validity and value. As a symptom they are significant and encouraging. An enlarging group of educational leaders, specialists in education, college professors, school superintendents, principals and teachers is alive to the situation.

While these people naturally resent such criticisms as seem to be an outcome of ignorance, self-interest, or class feeling, they welcome all suggestions, and are always experimenting fruitfully with new ideas and methods. The chief hope for the gradual development of an educational system fitted to serve the national purposes lies in this company of open-minded men and women.

Educational experiments now being carried on suggest possibilities for the future. University practice schools, public school systems, private institutions, and individuals are testing new theories and methods in elementary education. In the vocational field, bureaus of guidance, trade schools, continuation classes, part time shop and class schools are in operation. Pre-vocational subjects, manual training, shopwork, domestic science, commercial branches, and agriculture are being taught in hundreds of high schools. College curricula are being gradually modified to give more room to the natural and the social sciences. There is a tendency also to introduce courses in business, journalism, and other pursuits which have a vocational or professional character. The scope of popular education is being extended by means of University Extension, short courses, correspondence teaching, reading courses like that of the Chautauqua Circle, and in many other ways. Industrial and educational surveys such as those recently undertaken in Richmond, Minneapolis, and Cleveland are significant and promising evidences of scientific interest.

THE MACHINERY OF EDUCATION

THE present situation, then, reveals an encouraging spirit of educational pioneering and many things already accomplished. The main lines of development in the creation of a system which shall be in the best sense national begin to emerge. Attention may first be turn-

GEORGE E. VINCENT
PRESIDENT OF THE UNIVERSITY OF MINNESOTA
CHANCELLOR OF CHAUTAUQUA INSTITUTION

ed to organization, the machinery of administration, supervision, public support, standards.

The deadly effect of mere mechanism is well-known. Bureaucracy is always a potential blight. But no system can get on without organization. So far American education has suffered more from unorganized localism. The rural district, the village and town unit have asserted their right to manage their own affairs independently. Politically elected county superintendents—many of them excellent individuals—as a class must give more time to their political fences than to their pedagogical flocks. Many states distribute school funds from the state treasury. But too generally these forms of state aid serve to lower rather than to supplement local tax rates. Even when the subsidy is conditioned upon an equal local contribution, the plan results in rewarding the strong rather than in helping the weak.

EDUCATING ALL CHILDREN

THE general policy which seems likely slowly to be adopted in the different states will assert the state's equal interest in all the children of the commonwealth, and will explicitly demand an equal educational opportunity for all children, poor or well to do, rural or urban. This policy will involve several lines of development; consolidation of one-room schools into central, graded schools 'to which pupils are transported in large vehicles; supervision by appointed superintendents and assistants with professional training; administrative units, based on the county, or socially homogeneous, with boards sharing local responsibility with a state board of education; a state school fund carefully apportioned so as to stimulate local activity and to maintain standards; provision for turning over to the State Board the administration of backward, sparsely settled, or negligent districts which fail to maintain satisfactory schools; more severe requirements for teachers' certificates with correspondingly increased salaries, provisions for promotion, premiums on permanency, pension systems; and in the rural regions especially, school manses which will provide for teachers comfortab'e and dignified living quarters. High school opportunities will be brought within the reach of every ambitious country boy or girl, either at the nearest consolidated school · or at the town high school, where the rural pupil will be maintained at the expense of the district.

The state system will also include vocational and cultural continuation classes, "short courses," correspondence teaching, social center activities for adults. In this way localism will yield to a unified, well-administered state system concerned with providing opportunities of an appropriate and equivalent kind for all the people of the state. Local responsibility will not be wholly surrendered; it will be shared with the state authority whose leadership will be recognized. This central organization will probably consist of a state board of education, a board-appointed state superintendent of recognized professional standing, and a staff of competent supervisors and specialists. State funds will be apportioned by this board.

Just as each state will attempt to equalize educational opportunities within its own borders, so the Federal Government will be compelled to coöperate with the states in bringing about something like democracy in education thruout the nation. "States' rights" will not be overridden; the subtle influence of subsidy will accomplish in this larger field what it is already doing within the individual states. For years state agricultural colleges have been supported in part by grants from the Federal treasury. From the same source state extension work in agriculture and home economics is receiving a progressive appropriation. A bill is now before Congress to stimulate by a similar subsidy the teaching of industrial subjects thruout the Union. The policy of national subsidy for education is under way and gaining momentum; the national aspect of education is clearly recognized.

One may be in heartiest sympathy with this general policy, and yet foresee serious dangers if the policy is not well considered and wisely administered. There is very real peril from a pedagogical pork-barrel. It is easy to imagine the perfervid eloquence with which a congressman would denounce any attempt to oppose an educational bill carrying a large appropriation for his district when he might hesitate to urge a new post office or the improvement of an unnavigable creek.

NATIONAL DEPARTMENT OF EDUCATION

CONGRESS ought to provide an adequate educational administration before the subsidy policy goes much further. The status of the United States Commissioner of Education is eloquent of the value which the people place upon education as a national function. A subordinate of the Department of the Interior, poorly paid, with pitifully meager appropriations and a wholly inadequate staff, destitute of real authority, the United State Commissioner of Education at a given time commands respect by reason of his personal qualities, almost in spite of his humiliating position.

The new responsibilities which face the country will compel a recognition of the importance of education as a national task. There should be a Federal department of education with a secretary. A national board should be created, an adequate staff of supervisors and experts provided. All legislation concerning education should be either initiated by the board or submitted to it for advice; all Federal subsidies should be distributed under its authority. Such a national department would coördinate, complete, and give Federal leadership to a national system of education.

WHAT ENDS SHALL WE SEEK?

WHAT aims will the national and state administrations set up as they work out a more conscious, purposeful system of education? They will have to keep in mind: first, training for occupational efficiency; second, the encouragement of spontaneity and initiative, and, third, the fostering of capacity for civic life. The nation will depend for highest success upon the ability of its citizens to do their work expertly and economically, to discover new and useful ways of thought and action, and to live together on terms of mutual confidence and good will as they work for common ends.

Plato's philosophers in the *Republic*, endowed with almost supernatural insight, assigned the children to the social status and occupations for which they were by nature fitted. This was true vocational guidance. No time and effort were wasted. Each child was predestined and prepared. There were no blind alleys. In America there are people who would have the children of the obviously humble quickly set upon the paths to shop, mill, department store, field, mine or railway. There is an insistent demand for "practical" training with no "frills" or "fads." Manual dexterity, minds early automatic in a certain routine, docility and "contentment" are requirements. The men who half unconsciously are seeking employees see the first function of national education, but they are in danger of ignoring the other two. They do not realize that there are no philosophers to assign American children at the outset to their places in the social order, nor that in a way these children are later to form a part of that control which democracy substitutes for the all-wise philosophers of Plato's "Aristocracy of Intellect."

In the elementary school, the basis of the national system, will begin the guided growth which will contribute to all three of the educational aims, occupational skill, initiative, civic consciousness. It is certain that the elementary school of the future will be far less formal. Arithmetic, reading, grammar and nature study will emerge much later as conscious tasks. Even then they will be taught in a quite different way. Doing, seeing, handling things; excursions in the country; observation and recording of weather conditions; study of rocks and soils of plants, trees and animals; visits to stores, post office, fire-engine houses, to farms, creameries, elevators, following up vivid interests; making houses and furniture; finding out about familiar things, like food, clothing and shelter; using weights and measures, figuring because one wants to know results; listening to stories, retelling them, learning to read them, playing and working with one's mates; learning the need for rules and respect for others' rights—these are the materials and methods which in the earlier years will almost wholly take the place of books. Bodies and minds will grow; dexterities and concrete, vivid experiences will accumulate ready for the reflective, more formal training to follow.

IS "MENTAL DISCIPLINE" NEEDED?

GOOD people are shocked by the idea of this "royal road," this "primrose path." What of discipline and duty, and the moral power which comes from doing disagreeable things? The answer is that enough children have already been subjected to this demoralizing theory and practise to give some notion of results. It is fairly well established that boys and girls who under this system postpone formal studies make progress so rapidly that on entrance to high school they are quite able to hold their own in reading, spelling, and arithmetic, while in freshness of interest, wide range of practical knowledge and experience, and ability to reason independently they are noticeably superior to the graduates of the conventional school.

By the eleventh or twelfth year, tested by the varied experiences of the earlier grades, children begin to display special aptitudes and interests. These will influence the activities and studies suggested to the pupils. The persons assigned to the work of vocational guidance will begin to discuss with boys and girls their future plans. Courses will be adapted to individual needs. Out of

This is the sixth article in The Independent's series on THE NEXT GENERATION IN AMERICAN LIFE. "Government of the People, for the People and by the People" has been discussed by William Allen White, "Country Living in the Next Generation," by Liberty H. Bailey, "Business Tomorrow," by Elbert H. Gary; "A Religion for Democracy," by Shailer Mathews, and "Woman in the Market Place," by Margaret Deland.

the elementary school pupils will be guided according to aptitudes, ambitions and circumstances to schools of different types which give special training in mechanical pursuits, commercial subjects, fine and industrial arts, agriculture and rural life, general education, preparation for technical and professional schools or colleges. Many pupils will be directed to special occupational courses which they will pursue until they are of legal age to enter upon wage earning.

Even when students have begun to work they will not sever their connection with the educational system. In part time or continuation classes they will learn to connect theory and practise and will follow pursuits of a cultural or recreative character. Thru evening classes, social centers, extension activities, debating clubs, public libraries, reading courses, civic associations, public concerts and recitals, popular lectures, exhibitions of industrial arts, social museums, etc., the whole adult population will realize that national education is a continuous growth from childhood to the end of life.

The system sketched above offers an opportunity for self-development, spontaneity and personal initiative. The pupil is not cowed by coercion. He has been allowed to express himself in many ways, by work, talk, drawing, singing, playing. He is not forced to learn meaningless symbols, to accept a great number of statements on the authority of book or teacher. His knowledge is personal and first hand. He has the habit of dealing with concrete realities, of finding out things for himself, of inventing ways of solving problems—in short he has been learning to think. This is so valuable a national asset that it would be a calamity if the demand for premature ability to read, write, cipher and work docilely were to regiment American children into methodical, lock-step, disciplined automata for common industrial and commercial uses. Quite apart from the rights of these children to enjoy a period of free, spontaneous, happy growth, the short cut to efficiency

theory would do untold harm to national welfare and the democratic idea of life.

In secondary and higher education problem solving and tests of thinking power rather than information will be the rule. Even now the imaginative teachers of law, economics, political science, and the natural sciences do not ask for definitions but set problems for the student to discuss in the light of all his knowledge of the situation. This is true education because it is so much like life. In a democratic society the conventionalizing forces, imitation, fashion, social rivalry, tyranny of the majority, are so strong that the duty of education to promote individuality and independent thinking is imperative.

CREATING A SENSE OF THE NATION

IN seeking the third end, the fostering of civic loyalty and idealism, national education will aim to cultivate in young and old the historical and social imagination. History, the social sciences, literature and philosophy as the expression of human culture will constitute the "New Humanities." From the earliest years of the elementary school thru the university and all the agencies of popular education, effort will be made to develop in every mind some sense of the vast, ongoing collective life men call the nation, a panorama of the past with its great figures, its story and song, its struggles and victories, its mistakes and failures. And this will be done with the hope of projecting into the future a vision of purpose and responsibility which will give meaning to each individual life. A national education would be a failure which did not transcend material efficiency and touch this with idealistic aims and loyalties.

Yet it would be a narrow conception of true culture which did not place the nation in its relation to general civilization, and inspire a patriotism which seeks to make one's country strong and true not only to its own interests but to those of all mankind. National education should produce not Chauvinism but chivalry.

This national system will not be all under national and state control. Privately endowed universities, colleges and schools will continue to be experimental laboratories for educational progress. Uniformity in educational methods would be unfortunate. The very principle of spontaneity and initiative calls for a variety of institutions free to try new things, but proud to declare themselves a part of the national system and ready to serve the common country.

Minneapolis, Minnesota

CHAUTAUQUA

THE BODY OF CHAUTAUQUA
BY E. H. BLICHFELDT

HISTORIC CHAUTAUQUA
BY IDA B. COLE

SUMMER SCHOOLING
BY PERCY H. BOYNTON

THE BODY OF CHAUTAUQUA

BY E. H. BLICHFELDT

"WHO steals my purse steals trash." An article about building and machinery at Chautauqua is a treatise of non-essentials, not that physical properties could be dispensed with altogether but that they are accessory; something before them determined their evolution. When a disastrous fire had visited Chautauqua in 1909, the Institution sent out to its friends the confident message, which was quoted from Boston to San Francisco, "You can't burn down an idea."

It may have been half-counterfeit satisfaction, to be sure, with which the early Chautauquans declared that when they grew tired on the flat amphitheater benches, they "leaned back upon the salubrious atmosphere." Mark Hopkins on one end of a log and a boy on the other might, provisionally, have constituted a university; but if they had done so, the log would naturally and inevitably have become, in course of time, paraphernalia *emeritus*. Housing, environment, and access are demanded and commanded by the educational genius, though not by the recluse. So the Chautauquans of the early 70's, while rejoicing in things as they were, started a program of material growth.

Yet the order is important. Chautauqua did not begin with an aggregation of material, into which life must somehow be pumped. It began with an idea, and the contagious enthusiasm of a group of people for that idea, as they saw it incarnate in one man. This genius, which soon became social rather than personal, diffuse rather than particular, gradually lifted roofs over the heads of its devotees, gave dignity and solidity to their gathering places, provided facilities for their community life, and adapted their surroundings to their growing needs from year to year.

To infer that Chautauqua has become rich and can order costly structures and roadways at will would be beside the mark. On the contrary Chautauqua still lives from hand to mouth, as an educational institution ought. With what justification could it grow rich? President Frost of Berea College worthily put this thought, when he declared, "Berea can never be rich as long as anybody in these mountains is poor." Chautauqua is poor in the sense that recognized needs or opportunities every year must be disregarded for lack of means. When a need becomes vital enough and articulate enough,

however, means and disposition to provide for it somehow come forth.

It is as a sign of "inward grace" that Chautauquans recognize in external growth a cause of rejoicing. Brick paved high-ways, double-track interurban car lines, entrances of brick and concrete in good architectural design, landscape treatment on a broad scale, educational buildings in comprehensive groups, hotel rooms with steam heat and other like conveniences, private residences costing a fortune to build do not grow up around an enterprise of fleeting character; yet all these things are taking shape of late at Chautauqua. The fact is that the parent institution of the Chautauqua movement, on Chautauqua Lake, in western New York, has within a decade passed into a wholly new phase, the "city of tents" giving way very fast to a city that "has foundations." Electric light and power plants, gas mains, water supply and sewerage, paved sidewalks, year-round office buildings of fire-proof or slow burning construction are among the things that one by one have supplanted the earlier makeshifts. Over a quarter of a million dollars is being expended this year to present the assembly to 1916 visitors in its

A NEW PORTAL FOR CHAUTAUQUA—THE INTERURBAN ELECTRIC RAILWAY STATION

CHAUTAUQUA BEFORE CHAUTAUQUA WAS

BY IDA M. COLE

NO spot in America has been the scene of more spectacular pilgrimages than the shores of Chautauqua Lake. The tall trees could relate wonderful tales of days long before the French occupancy, when this beautiful region knew only the moccasined tread of the "red ruler of the shade"; of the days when the Eries fought heroically for their native land and were exterminated by the hostile Senecas.

As you see the evening lights streaming from the windows of hundreds of houses on the Chautauqua Assembly grounds, you think of that night, years and years ago, when, the historian tells us, the Senecas took horrible revenge on the Eries and all along the lake region there burned a "thousand fires," each fire an Erie burning at the stake. That was fifteen years before La Salle came over the portage and sailed down the lake

THE NEW BOAT LANDING AT CHAUTAUQUA

GATHERED ABOUT THE HALL OF PHILOSOPHY UNDER THE TREES AT CHAUTA...

and he must have seen on either bank the old Erie villages overgrown with vines and crumbling in decay.

Standing at the foot of Miller Tower, on the grounds of the Chautauqua Institution, and looking toward the head of the lake, one can visualize the appearance of that intrepid band led by the famous explorer La Salle, who after traversing the portage from Lake Erie dropt their canoes into Chautauqua Lake. What a motley crew it was which followed La Salle that day—French soldiers, Canadian settlers and Indians—on their mission to establish the claim of France to the newly discovered territory.

But La Salle was not the first white man to find this region. In 1615, five years before the Pilgrims landed on the Massachusetts coast, the youthful Etienne Brulé, accompanied by twelve friendly Hurons, sailed on Lake Chautauqua. On his journey from Canada he came over the old portage to the present village of Mayville, and there embarked on Chautauqua Lake, passed into the Chadakoin, and thence to the Allegheny. He is said to have been the first white man to visit Chautauqua county. A few years after, Brulé's journey, La Salle came and still later this lake was the scene of the picturesque expedition under de Celeron.

Another band which probably came this way, seeking not territorial conquest but a haven of peace, was the group of Acadian pilgrims on their way to the "Beautiful River" which carried them "into the golden stream of the broad and swift Mississippi."

518

While Longfellow in "Evangeline" does not state the way of journeying, yet of all the conjectural routes this is the most plausible. For it is known that for centuries the Indians followed this route from gulf to gulf, a distance of some four thousand miles, from Barcelona on Lake Erie, over the portage to Chautauqua Lake, a distance of some eight miles, then over the waters of Chautauqua to the Chadakoin and to the Allegheny.

It is said that a barn some five miles from Chautauqua Institution drains one side into the Gulf of St. Lawrence and the other into the Gulf of Mexico. It is certain that the divide between the two great systems—that of the Great Lakes and that of the Mississippi—is situated where the barn stands.

Chautauqua Lake is only a few miles from Lake Erie and several hundred feet higher, so that at first thought the visitor takes it for granted that it drains into the Great Lakes and is surprised to find that such is not the case.

In 1749 still another voyage, as picturesque as it was momentous, was made by Capt. Bienville de Celoron. In July of that year he landed at Barcelona and started over the old portage for Chautauqua Lake. In his company were men who had explored the primeval forests of Canada, soldiers, sailors, pioneers, a Jesuit priest and Indians. Some of these men afterward became famous for their valorous deeds in the French and Indian war.

Celoron had in his possession several leaden plates, duly inscribed, which he was to bury at certain

points as tokens of French occupancy. One of these plates bore the name Tchadakoin, the first time the name was used by civilized man. The manuscripts kept by Celoron on this voyage and the diary and maps of de Bonnecamps, a member of the expedition, have been preserved, the former by the French Government and the latter in the possession of the Jesuit College at Quebec. The name Tchadakoin appears on de Bonnecamps's maps. This is supposed to be the French rendition of the name "Ja-da-quah"—Chautauqua.

A spectacular expedition and one of far-reaching importance, since it was one in the chain of events which finally led up to the Seven Years' War in Europe, was the landing at Barcelona of the French forces who transformed the old portage into a military built road. In the spring of 1753 Govenor Duquesne of Canada sent an expedition to build a string of forts in the Allegheny Valley and make a route southward which they thought would be better than the one followed by Celoron and La Salle. A detachment of this force was sent by the governor to cut a wagon road from Barcelona to Lake Chautauqua. Traces of this old French road still remain and now the automobile whizzes over parts of that old portage over which the Indian once carried his canoe and the French explorers and gallant soldiers trod with certain step as they declared the claim of their native land against the English.

Barcelona is now a little fishing village with its quaint lighthouse and other reminiscences of "days of old when knights were bold." The dense forest has been cleared to make way for prosperous villages. The fierce and beautiful wildcat, for which this region was once noted and which gave the Eries the name of "Nation of the Cat," has gone the way of the buffalo. The shores which were thick with tall trees when Etienne Brulé passed them are now lined with attractive residences, and the name on the leaden plate borne by Celoron has since become synonymous with Christian culture. Many reasons have been given for the name, Chautauqua, but that generally accepted by historians is the tale of the party of Seneca Indians who, on one occasion, as they were journeying up the trail, caught a muscallonge in Lake Chautauqua, threw it into the bottom of the canoe, where it lay during the trip over the portage. On reaching Lake Erie they found the fish still alive and threw it into that lake.

Previous to this time no muscallonge had been found in Lake Erie and the subsequent abundance was attributed to this finny ancestor taken from the lake at the other end of the portage, which was accordingly named by the Senecas "Ga-jah" (fish) and "Gadah-guah" (taken out). In time the prefixes of both words were dropt, leaving "Jah-dah-guah" (the place where the fish was taken out).

Chautauqua, New York

SUMMER SCHOOLING

BY PERCY H. BOYNTON

DEAN IN THE JUNIOR COLLEGES, UNIVERSITY OF CHICAGO; PRINCIPAL OF SUMMER SCHOOLS, CHAUTAUQUA INSTITUTION

THE summer school movement of this last generation has been one of several agencies to bring American education closer to the life of the people, a development in which education as a whole has been moving parallel to science, religion, and philosophy. Plant breeding, the layman's movement, and pragmatism are all floated on the same current with vocational training and vacational schools. Forty years ago American philosophy was still absorbed in the contemplation of Kant and Hegel, religion was expressed in sectarian theology, and science was a noble but a remote pursuit. Naturally the colleges and universities in which these subjects were studied were places where, as Lowell fairly said, "nothing useful was taught."

With the founding in 1874 of what is now Chautauqua Institution there was ostensibly started "a system of popular education" which was supposed to stand in contrast with the college system of education maintained for the cultured and professional classes. The contrast, however, has always been more apparent than real. In the early years the main issue was a question of opinion as to whether the summer could be turned to academic account, especially in a six-week session. Half the first set of courses at Chautauqua were in the nature of regular college work in ancient and modern languages. The remainder were normal school studies in pedagogy. From the outset came people who gained in these weeks their first view of the "college outlook," or who returned for further vistas in which they could not possibly indulge themselves during the school year.

In these later days Chautauqua has continued to be popular in a legitimate sense—has even become much more so than at first—but most of the universities and many of the colleges are now unwilling to be outdone. The regular college menus are displayed—cafeteria fashion—with a seductive array of pedagogical side-dishes, and the people swarm to them. In 1915 at the summer sessions of the leading twenty-three universities there were 35,642 students. Yet in the face of European war and California expositions, Chautauqua lost—for the first time in six years—only a small percentage of its more than 3000 students. In both college and Chautauqua camps there has been a skilful attack in the double problem of finding out what the public wanted, and of teaching the public to want what it ought to.

What has taken place at Chautauqua in the way of natural growth in the forty-two years since its founding can be stated in a formula which is almost too neat to be credible. The saving fact about it is that the for-

519

Barony

MRS. MADISON CAWEIN
Gertrude McKelvey Cawein, widow of the poet, is to read poetry at Chautauqua in August. Her programs include an afternoon of her husband's work and also readings from Masefield, John Luther Long and the Irish playwrights

Harris & Ewing

MRS. HARRIET CHALMERS ADAMS
The woman who has explored nearly every corner of Central and South America, who has followed Columbus's trail and who has studied the Philippines, will lecture at Chautauqua on July 4 and 6

mula states only the broadest aspects of a story which is humanly full of inconsistent and contradictory and—still worse—irrelevant details. They are inconsistent, like the decline of interest in Anglo-Saxon and the persistence of enthusiasm for Hebrew; contradictory, like the right-handed introduction of pageants and "moral interludes" and the left-handed opposition to the theater; or irrelevant, like the rise and fall of "pyrography," "mothercraft" and other ill-fated subjects of the moment.

Yet, largely speaking, the first stage in the Chautauqua summer schools was the oldest fashioned stage of study-for-knowledge courses. The founders started with a School of Languages, and a Teachers' Retreat, which was a school of pedagogy. When they introduced the first lectures on science, the lecturers did all the talking and experimenting and the students listened and watched; and for ten years they stuck to books and abstractions and had a pleasantly exciting time pursuing knowledge as it appeared on the printed page and was heard in the fluent period of the instructor and public lecturer.

The second stage marked the addition of various activity courses. The first three on the records happened to be an alliterative trio, music, microscopy, and mineralogy. It would have amounted to the same thing if they had been birds, botany, and bookbinding; the significance lay in the fact that two new kinds of work were being offered, science courses involving observation, and process courses demanding proficiency in technique. It was an important

step, tho merely in keeping with the progress of the times, for it led eventually to the present modest group of scientific subjects which can be well presented with the simple laboratory equipment available at Chautauqua and the rich natural resources of the region; and it led further to the present departments of Library Training, Home Economics, Music, Arts and Crafts, Expression, Physical Education, and Practical (business) Arts which were useful in 1915 to more than 1400 students.

The third aspect of Summer Schools —and all other educational work—is only now developing, and at Chautauqua is developing rather slowly. This is the direct attempt to promote a sense of social responsibility. One reason, perhaps, why this has been hitherto neglected in formal class room study at Chautauqua is that the aroma of social service is generally permeative there. It is the twentieth century equivalent for the old time "odor of sanctity." It suffuses the headquarters of the Department of Religious Work, it is wafted from the public platform in scores of sermons and addresses, and it is perceptible in the whole atmosphere of the city, in the woods, which is itself a vastly interesting social laboratory. Yet in the last two seasons courses have been introduced or re-established in history and social science, and this year the problems of internationalism at peace and at war will be discussed in class and conference as well as in lecture halls.

Thus the Summer School idea, undertaken very early at Chautauqua, has been adopted as widely in the colleges as the Summer Assembly

Olman

JOHN ERSKINE
Professor of English at Columbia. The author of "The Moral Obligation to be Intelligent," ought surely to sympathize with the Chautauqua idea. He will lecture on American poets, nineteenth century verse, the romantic poets and Ibsen at Chautauqua this summer

idea—which has converted Chautauqua to a common noun—has been adopted by the local uplifters and the enterprising bureau managers. And the evident reason is that both ideas are fundamentally sensible. The colleges recognize now that there are other adults than their own graduates who can get some good out of college courses, that if there is any virtue in the use of the margin, the first of all to be used is the wide expanse of summer, that the teacher in particular can gain more literal recreation by spending some of the vacation in the class room than by dedicating it all to the front porch.

Furthermore the Summer School idea is so practical and sound that nothing but its wide adoption has saved Chautauqua from being utterly overwhelmed by over-patronage. Rapid as have been the establishment of new schools and the growth of the old ones, Chautauqua has grown along with them. Permanent plants, libraries, and laboratories have given the colleges certain advantages that Chautauqua has always recognized; but as their superior equipment has logically confined certain kinds of advanced work to them, Chautauqua's superior flexibility has led to the experiments in new fields which have more than once led to further extension of college enterprize. There is little rivalry; only coöperation and parallel endeavor; and to any one with a bit of experience and some imagination it is perfectly clear that there are more things for the Summer Schools in the next generation than are yet dreamed of in the philosophy of 1916.

Chautauqua, New York

The Independent-Harper's Weekly
NEWS-PICTORIAL

What the Balkans were to the peace of Europe—when there was peace in Europe—the railroads are to the economic prosperity of the country. Representatives of 235 systems on the one hand and 350,000 employees on the other have broken off their conference over the demands made by the Brotherhoods of Locomotive Engineers, Locomotive Firemen and Enginemen, and Railroad Trainmen, and the Order of Railway Conductors. A strike vote will now be taken. Elisha Lee, of the Pennsylvania Railroad, on the right, was chairman at the conference for the railroads; Warren S. Stone, on the left, Grand Chief Engineer of the Brotherhood of Locomotive Engineers, headed the union conferees.

Juley

"The Freight Yards," by Gifford Beal, from this year's New York "Academy." Freight service is the bone of contention.

Copyright International Film

The ablution squad—the first day at Plattsburg. There are 1316 men under canvas for the first of the military camps. The "Old Man," Charles E. Courtney, who has coached Cornell crews for years, is retiring on account of ill health. Cornell's record of victories in his term is unmatched in college rowing.
Copyright Underwood

The new fashion in commencement celebrations—the seniors of the Fort Hays, Kansas, Normal School unveiling a Custer memorial at Custer's Island, where Custer camped in '69, made in concrete by the class. From L. D. Wooster, Hays, Kansas.

Underwood

Ten thousand trained men—a fragment of Canada's volunteer half-million army, reviewed at Toronto on the King's Birthday.

Another American borrowed by Canada—A. D. Little, of Boston, a distinguished chemist, who heads the Canadian Pacific's bureau for studying Canada's huge mineral resources.

Copyright Medem

From the oldest even unto the youngest—here are old, old women, long past threescore and ten, who serve France by putting the finishing work on large caliber shells, while boys are going into the trenches and girls into the hospitals.

Copyright Medem

Two French youngsters, whose father has been killed in the trenches, are telling one of father's comrades all about it.

HAVE you read the story of Pétain the Prepared?

Here it is. Read it, heed it, rouse your friends with it, save it for your children's children. Over the blackness and earthiness of the Great War it shines like a star in the night.

Only yesterday, as time goes, Pétain the Prepared was a common French soldier. Today Pétain the Prepared is the world-famed hero of Verdun, the idol of the French Army, the savior of the French people. Pétain did the impossible; not because he was Pétain, but because he was Pétain the Prepared.

He spent forty years getting ready for the crisis at Verdun. When the man was ready, the crisis called the man. Suppose he *was* sixty years old before his chance came—what of that? His job was to get ready—not go hunting chances. *You* may be thirty or forty or fifty, and your chance hasn't come. What of that? Your job is to get strong enough and big enough to handle your chance when it does come.

At the beginning of the siege of Verdun, a rabble of high-strutting military dolts had seats of honor over Pétain. That didn't worry him—he was too busy outgrowing the small place given him. They botched the defense, used the wrong tactics, lost men and ground. Pétain said nothing, he only worked harder getting ready. Thousands of good men, conscientious in their business or profession, lose the chance of promotion because they childishly criticize their superior officer, instead of learning silently from his mistakes and resolving to make *their* work error-proof.

HOW PÉTAIN WINS

PÉTAIN is a wonderful athlete—he holds the record for holding his tongue. He never talks of what he is going to do, he merely does it. And he never lets others talk of what he has done—he is already planning something so much bigger that his former achievement looks now like a boy playing marbles. In our schools, stores, factories, offices and armies may be seen hundreds of thousands of young men who move their tongues but nothing else. The more you are heard, the less you will be heard of. And fame? Oh, fame is all the things you didn't say about yourself.

In the stretch of his sixty years Pétain never had time to polish up the brass buttons of his uniform, wax his mustache, and visit the photographer with a smug self-conscious look of high elation. Pétain hates photographers. He muzzles reporters. He looks thru politicians. He regards fashion-mongers as he would ants. He sweeps away the artificial with one good swing of his fencing-foil, and his mind is always fencing. The man born to conquer does not let you think of his clothes. Fate never pinned a medal on the breast of a fashion model.

Another thing Pétain forgets. He forgets to count how many times he tries to do a thing—he just keeps on trying till he does it. In this respect he is like Edison, Vanderlip, Burbank, Hammond, Eliot, Gary, Peary and others of our own great men. In advance of the crisis at Verdun *he* had charted on the map of his mind more than 500 strategic positions and martial encounters. For every move the efficient Germans made, or any move they could make, Pétain had a counter-move ready. We are all under fire, at the hands of Fate. Can we meet with the calmness, power and skill of Pétain each and any emergency that could arise in our business, our home, our financial, social and personal life? Have we figured out these emergencies ahead—five hundred or one hundred or twenty or even ten—and overcome them by forethought, imagination, diagrammatic detail?

Pétain is confessedly a dreamer. Not only that, but he proclaims it the duty of a soldier to think and dream battles! Are you ever tempted to ridicule a dreamer? Don't. He may some day command a situation that you, spiritually blind, could not even see.

One of the special delights of this remarkable warrior is a habit of doing hard jobs for others, after the specified others had failed to do them and said they could not be done. When the corps of a stupid general was in wild retreat, Pétain took charge, gave the men a spine, showed the men a man, led the men to victory. When the Germans fortified a key situation and called it impregnable, Pétain was summoned and was given

three days in which to break down the German defense. Pétain was thru the lines in three hours. What about that extra hard problem in your business or profession? Have you made it a habit to overcome in three hours any difficulty that your superior officer would take three days to solve? When your associates leave a task unfinished how long do you let it lie there a failure? Would you rather see it done than get your dinner on time?

Pétain has a number of watchwords—the slogans of his leadership and of his life. Among these are: Patience, confidence, independence, persistence, energy, tact, speed, concentration. He everlastingly drills these principles into his men. But first he made himself live them. Precisely what physical powers, mental traits and moral qualities are needed in you to make you a man the size of Pétain —equal to your chance when it comes? How are you developing these guarantees of greatness? Influence doesn't happen; it is a confluence of hidden forces in yourself. Men follow the man who follows a light. Your light, what is it? How hard are you following it? Would you die following it? If not, you could not serve as cup-bearer for Pétain. No man lives until he would gladly die for something greater than life. We are nothing to the world until our work is everything to us. Whether we have chosen to lead an army, or teach a school, or serve a parish, or build homes, or write poems, or cobble shoes, does not really matter. All that matters is how we lose ourselves in our work.

And two hundred thousand of the Kaiser's picked men lie rotting at Verdun. And two hundred thousand tons of the Kaiser's steel and copper have been aimed at Verdun—only to spend and bury themselves in the earth. Pétain the Prepared was stationed on the breastworks at Verdun. Calmly and surely, in his curtain of fire, he rolled back the world's greatest army. Not then was he Pétain. He was just The Prepared—an impersonal, overmastering force. The man prepared is a match for the world. To him the world must yield, before him the world must bow, of him the world must learn, in the end.

Health

This is to certify that the
is fully insured against the
ment of impure and low gra
and cake such as baking pow
ces. Royal is made from who
which is derived from grap
food. Roy
from Phosp
harmful a
mineral in

NO ALUM

ROY
Baking Po
Is Absolutely

Policy

...ser of Royal Baking Powder
...s that arise from the employ-
...e ingredients in making biscuits
...rs made from mineral substan-
...esome Cream of Tartar
... – a natural, healthful
... is free from Alum,
...ate, and from all
... unhealthful
...redients

...AL
...wder
...Pure

"Royal
is the Best
Policy"

ROYAL

ROYAL
BAKING POWDER

BAKING POWDER

We are amazed and thrilled by the superb sight of one man holding at bay the mightiest army in the world's history. But when we look around, right here at home, we are shocked and appalled by facts as ugly as the feat of General Pétain was glorious.

WE ARE UNPREPARED

WE are the nation of the unprepared. It took nothing more than a cheap Mexican bandit like Villa to show how fearfully we were unprepared for war. But, for peace, and everyday life, and a safe and happy future we are as little ready. We are, in fact, the June-bug among nations. We start to buzz and bat around only when our day of opportunity is closing and the light in some other nation's house—the glare of war just lately—reveals the darkness in our own house. Look at these facts recently compiled by an expert.

Tho our national wealth is $187,-000,000,000 — three times that of France and twice that of Great Britain or Germany—about 12,-000,000 of our citizens are in actual want, and one person in every ten dying in a large city is buried in a pauper's grave.

Every year we spend $90,000,000 for candy, soda water and moving-picture shows; while to ethical and industrial education in foreign lands we give only $20,000,000. Yet the stabilizing force of America's future is the religious extension work of to-day. We think more of our palate than we do of our posterity.

Our annual income of $35,000,000,-000 is the largest proportionate increase of any nation; yet we rank fifteenth in relative number of savings-bank accounts; and of the 20,-000,000 homes we occupy, more than 14,000,000 are encumbered by mortgage, rent or otherwise.

Nearly 2,000,000 children from ten to fifteen years of age are working—and growing prematurely old and sick, when they ought to be in school. Of our 18,000,000 adult wage-earners, 15,000,000 are inadequately trained or temperamentally unfit for the work they are trying to do; hence they can never succeed as they should. Every year 35,000 workers in American industries are killed, and 1,590,000 injured by shop machinery and railroads. This army of cripples, if saved and prepared, could effectively guard our entire coast from invasion by any foreign power.

The need for industrial, financial, educational and social preparedness is here, all about us, all the time. Must Fate plunge us in war to cleanse us of our national sins and follies? Or have we the courage and wisdom to redeem ourselves?

Now the individual is the nation. *The man who has formed the preparedness habit* is the man to save his country, his community, his family and himself. The technical details of national preparedness must be founded on the broad base of PERSONAL PREPAREDNESS. To be ready for whatever comes—physically, mentally and morally ready; here is the test for a soldier and a man!

To be prepared for life is to be ready in two ways—against calamity and for opportunity. Calamity is really opportunity hiding in a shadow. Our worst foe is usually our best friend in disguise. Not then hating our foes, how may we discover them, attack them, outwit them, surpass them, learn from them without being injured by them?

How did Pétain hold Verdun? By learning who and what his foes were, their wonderful efficiency, and how and when and where they would probably attack—then massing all his forces behind his weakest point! Mental shrewdness we must have to locate our enemies, but also moral braveness to mend our own weak spots! The strength of a *man* lies in his wrath at his weakness.

What do you fear? Why? Fear is the guaranteed seed of failure. And everything we call misfortune is the fruit of some failure in ourselves. Do you fear pain, poverty, loneliness, grief, loss, unpopularity, abuse, drudgery, fatigue, responsibility, failure, disease, old age, death? Is there anything or anybody that could make you lose heart, or presence of mind? If there is, prepare! Be sure that whatever can test you most will some day come to you. Don't wait and have to run like a rat to its hole. Study your moves and martial your forces while yet there is time.

The common tragedy of life is to be unequal to the unexpected. The crown of every conqueror is moulded from a crisis; and in lifting or lowering men the agency of Fate is an emergency.

Make a friend of Misfortune; you will have a friend you can always count on. Ask yourself what the worst affliction could be, and prepare to meet it. Should it come, you might falter in the depths of sorrow, as all

Went to School Again

THIS is an inspiring story of a big-minded business man. Some men regret that their training in business is not *complete*. Some men never even realize it. This man realized it, but he did no regretting. Despite his wide experience, despite his huge income he left his business for a year and enrolled for a university course in business with men young enough to be his sons, while he *learned the fundamental principles* that were back of his income and back of his experience, so he could *control* them. The problems he had to solve in his business were far more complicated than those listed here. If any man cannot answer them, however, he should let the story of this business genius sink in.

MANY BIG MEN DOING THE SAME

We men who are struggling along, earning $1,000, $2,000, $3,000 and $5,000 a year—worrying day and night to increase this a paltry few hundred—should beware not to consider this inspiring man exceptional. If we do, we may miss the lesson of him.

That Fatal Mistake!

We may make the mistake of thinking that we know enough about business; that this openminded man was but a crank; that he, too, knew enough, but just wasn't satisfied. The fact is, he is far from exceptional. The *brainiest men in America today are doing what he did, for exactly the same reason he did it.* The only difference is that they do not have to leave their business as this man did. Instead, the Alexander Hamilton Institute now brings this business training right to their desks or their home reading table.

Alfred I. DuPont, executive head of the Du-Pont Powder Companies, capitalized at $120,000,-000; Melville W. Mix, President of the Dodge Mfg. Co., a $1,500,000 corporation; Geo. M. Verity, President of the American Rolling Mills, a $5,000,000 corporation; N. A. Hawkins, General Sales Manager of the Ford Motor Car Co., Wm. Ingersoll, Marketing Manager of the biggest watch company in the world; and scores of other men, of like calibre.

The motives that prompted these men to this action; how they are profiting by it—and how you can profit are explained in the book "Forging Ahead in Business," which will be sent you free on request. To get it, clip the coupon below.

Already 40,000 Men Enrolled

One can hardly name a nationally-known business in this country, in which many of the coming young men, and often the leading executives, are not enrolled in the Alexander Hamilton Institute. In the United States Steel Corporation, no less than 450 young young men are enrolled. In the Standard Oil Company, there are 215; in the Ford Motor Car Co. 181; in the Westinghouse Mfg. Co., #235; in the General Electric Co., 240; in the great National City Bank, 83; in the Pennsylvania Railroad, 76; in the National Cash Register Co., 187; in the Goodyear Tire and Rubber Co., 164;—and so on, down the list of the biggest firms in America.

Altogether, up to date, 40,000 live-wire men in business have enrolled in this great course of business training. Surely you should read the free book that explains the idea back of such a movement.

HOW MEN MAKE GOOD

What the Alexander Hamilton Institute has done for its subscribers will probably never be known in its entirety. But daily there filter into the headquarters in New York many intensely human stories showing how it helps men make good.

One day you hear of a brilliant lad of twenty-two, in a big New York bank, rising to a $9,500 job and giving credit to the Institute for his success.

The next day a factory manager writes that the course has just helped him save his firm $7,000 a year, and that "a fair slice" of this went to increase his salary.

The next day a man in a Western concern tells how he saved the firm $37,000 a year by *one suggestion*, and what happened then to *his* salary.

A "copy writer" rises to be advertising and sales manager. A billing clerk wins a position as head accountant with his concern. A general manager saves his firm from impending bankruptcy.

These are only typical cases.

There are literally hundreds of them—many of them really amazing cases—of men grasping big opportunities, and succeeding in enterprises they dared never even attempt before. And it's all explained in a most interesting way in the free book "Forging Ahead in Business." To get a copy fill out and send in the attached coupon.

Based on the Actual Experience of the Most Successful Business Men

The Institute collects, classifies and transmits to you through the Modern Business Course and Service the best thought and practice in modern business. It will give you a thorough and sound training in the fundamental principles underlying all departments of business—it will give you a knowledge that could be otherwise obtained *only* by years of bitter experience—if at all.

Advisory Council

Business and educational authority of the highest standing is represented in the Advisory Council of the Alexander Hamilton Institute. This advisory council includes Frank A. Vanderlip, President of the National City Bank; Judge E. H. Gary, head of the U. S. Steel Corporation; John Hays Hammond, the famous engineer; Joseph French Johnson, Dean of the New York University School of Commerce, and Jeremiah W. Jenks, statistician and economist.

"Forging Ahead in Business"

A careful reading of his 128-page book, "Forging Ahead in Business," which we will send you free, will repay you many times over. It will help measure what you know—what you don't know, and what you should know—to make success *sure*. Every business man should read this book—whether he wishes to climb to bigger, surer success, or a career to guide to bigger, surer success, should read this book. You need send no money for it—simply the coupon below.

ALEXANDER HAMILTON INSTITUTE

351 Astor Place   New York City

Send me "Forging Ahead in Business" FREE

Name . . . .

Business
Address . . . .

Business
Position . . . .

must falter when human hearts break; but men should in the end pursue the plan laid out, and go on with their work. How would *you* meet *your* keenest hardship, rise to your most painful test, bear your supreme loss? Prepare for the hardest thing, and all things grow easier.

FOES YOU MUST MEET

DIVIDE your campaign of personal preparedness into lines of defense and offense, with your foes and your allies properly balanced. First, as to defense. Among the assailants for whom one should prepare are these: Failure, Sorrow, Disease, Age, Death. Why let these foes rush upon us and ride over us—us with our armor off, guns spiked, swords dull and flags in the dust? We can, we can, forestall them; by summoning as our allies Faith, Courage, Knowledge, Forethought, System, Science, Work.

Prepare to meet Failure. And not once, but often. I know a man who had twenty battles with Failure, one after another, and each fight seemed lost. His war with Failure lasted thirty years. At the close he had so everlastingly routed Failure that the world crowned him the most successful man in his field who ever lived. Few of us fail enough. Envy the man who makes a big mistake, he's going somewhere—but pity him if he makes it twice, he's crawling back. When Failure attacks you, mark the weak spot aimed for and strengthen it. Do this well enough, and Failure stops.

Prepare to meet Sorrow. If your best friends should all die or desert you, could you face the world with a smile? If you lost all your money, would you feel just as rich? If you lost your reputation, would you have as much character left?

Prepare to meet Disease. If you want to endear yourself to your wife, learn to endure pain as sweetly as she can. There is nothing to fear in disease—except the fear. But almost every man has a constitutional weakness that he must guard against. What is *your* weak spot—heart, stomach, liver, lungs, kidneys, nerves, eyes? Are your daily habits ordered with a view to correcting that and keeping your health defense high?

Prepare to meet Age. What are you going to do when you're seventy or eighty? Loaf on your family and friends? Depend on their charity—moral or financial? Mumble of the past and hobble in your mind as in your muscles? Die in heart and brain before you die in body? Or grow younger, stronger, wiser, braver, happier and better as the little years go by? Will you be financially independent at sixty? Are you absorbed in a fine work that you can still be doing, no matter how old the world calls you? A man should be in his mental prime at sixty. Whoever is not, died in his youth.

Prepare to meet Death. Not only in a religious sense, but in a psychological and biological sense. Do you know what Death is for, why necessary, how welcomed—and yet postponed? Have you studied the conclusions of the world's thinkers, scientists and philosophers regarding the final transition? Are you so thoroly convinced of the truth of immortality that you rely on it merely as an intelligent man, quite apart from the faith of your church? All that dies when we die is our fear of Death. When we overcome that we can die as calmly, bravely and superbly as the millions of soldiers whose hearts remained whole as their bodies bled away on the battlefields of Europe.

PREPARE FOR THE BIGGEST THING

BUT the test and sum of our preparedness is to prepare for life—to wage an offensive warfare as fiery as our defensive is firm. The great thing to fight for is opportunity. Gain this, hold it, utilize it, and you have won the world.

The president of the largest corporation of its kind in the world states that he always has a number of $10,000 positions waiting, unfilled and unasked for. He can't find the men to hold them. A $10,000 man is sure of a job, while a $500 man goes begging. Are you a $10,000 man, or more? If not, why not? If you don't expect some day to be earning five times what you earn now you should be ashamed of yourself. You are mentally asleep. Of course, a man can be a moral giant—and financially poor; but if he knows his job, works his job, and has a job worth having, he won't stay poor.

Your big chance, has it come? Are you sitting around waiting for it? Then you will die Expecting. Pull yourself together, prepare for your chance, get up and go out and hunt it. You can no more get a chance without a focus than you can get a picture without a camera. Put your mind in shape to record and develop your chance when it looms ahead.

Prepare by *action*. Things turn up for the man who digs. Doing big things means trying new things. A man, like a tree, is fruitful only after he branches out.

Prepare by *thrift*. The chance of a lifetime may be lost because you haven't a few thousand dollars, or even a few hundred, in cash for immediate use. Never let a pay-day go by without putting something in the

Barreled Sunlight

A "Tungsten" for Sunlight

Reg. U. S. P. Off.

What Tungsten Filament did for electricity, Rice's Gloss Mill White (Barreled Sunlight) does for daylight. Treating ceilings and walls of factory buildings with it increases daylight 19% to 36%—saves half to three quarters of an hour of time you would burn artificial lights.

RICE'S GLOSS MILL WHITE is an oil paint made by a special process discovered and owned exclusively by the makers. It is the only oil paint giving a glossy tile-like finish at no more expense than lead and oil paint. It is as clean as it is bright—can be washed like a piece of white china. Sanitary.

By the Rice Method, it can be applied over old cold-water paint. Over 3,000 plants have proved Rice's the most efficient finish for ceilings and walls. Repeated tests have shown without a single exception that Rice's remains white longer than any others. Users are protected by the Rice Guarantee.

Write for our Booklet-"More Light"

U. S. GUTTA PERCHA PAINT CO.
30 Dudley Street, Providence, R. I.

On Concrete Surfaces
On inside concrete, Rice's Granolith makes the best possible primer for a second coat of Rice's Gloss Mill White.

RICE'S GRANOLITH

bank. Learn the fascination in watching money grow. Study the science of investment. Plan what you will do with the money you have saved. Ask a rich man, or a bank president, how to save most wisely. Get a book on thrift, and read it in the family, then start together to economize.

Prepare by *work*. More work, better work, faster work—follow these steps and nothing on earth can keep you down. The time to go to work is an hour before you have to. Make believe you like work as much as play. Do your work so well you are proud of it—then you will like it. Failure sits on the doorstep of the man who hates what he has to do. You say you aren't appreciated and you aren't paid enough? Do you need a pat on the head and a sugar-plum for doing what you ought to do? In the end, work wins. The hardship of the present means nothing when the hope of the future means everything.

Prepare by *study*. Carry a book in your pocket as an efficiency habit. Learn self-improvement in your spare time. Locate and investigate the correspondence schools that may teach you self-advancement. Join some national organization of leaders in your profession; and equal, then surpass, the leaders. Know all the magazines and books of technical worth in your line. Study your men, materials, methods with the zeal you would put into a game of chess or baseball. Study yourself constantly, humbly, critically, ruthlessly; and make yourself over as you will have to, to make yourself overcome the world.

Prepare by *service*. Only what we do for others makes us immortal. This life is so short we cannot afford to waste it in self-seeking. And the big chance comes to him who is ready to advance the welfare of the world. The great misfortune is to worship fortune. Every man who earns a huge salary, from the President of the United States down, made his place by exalting the service rendered above the money received.

Personal preparedness, the need of the hour, will be the watchword of the man out to win.

Here's to the brightness of your armor, the keenness of your sword, the steadiness of your march, the pulse of your fighting blood!

Every full-size man has to fight; the man who is wrong has to fight himself, and the man who is right has to fight the world. Hail to you, conqueror, in both battles! Some have bled more than you are bleeding, yet have lived to wear the laurel-wreath. And the real reward of any triumph is to *know you can!*

HON. WOODROW WILSON, President of the United States: The combination of The Independent with Harper's Weekly seems to me a particularly happy thing. The two journals have grown thru very much the same period of our national life, each has maintained high editorial standards, and both have acquired a permanent hold upon the interest of thoughtful people throut the country. I congratulate you upon the happy combination.

HON. THEODORE ROOSEVELT, ex-President of the United States: I am heartily glad to congratulate you upon what you have just accomplished. I have been intimately associated with the president of the Independent Corporation, the publisher and the associate editor of The Independent in journalistic work in recent years, and they and their associates have my very best wishes for their continued success.

HON. WILLIAM H. TAFT, ex-President of the United States: I am very glad that The Independent has taken over Harper's Weekly. I am sure that this union of two of the oldest and best known periodicals under the single management of The Independent will be for the public good.

HON. CHARLES W. FAIRBANKS, ex-Vice-President of the United States: I thank you dor copy of The Independent, with which Harper's Weekly has been incorporated. I heartily congratulate you upon this forward step of The Independent. The Independent and Harper's Weekly have for many years been upon our regular list of family magazines. They have each exercised a widespread and wholesome influence. The consolidation, I venture to believe, will greatly strengthen their power for good throut the entire country. Accept my best wishes in your new undertaking.

HON. CHARLES S. WHITMAN, Governor of the State of New York: I want to congratulate both parties to the union. I am sure that I express the sentiment of all who like myself have read the two periodicals for many years when I wish for the new weekly long life. May it render as real and genuine public service in the years to come as have the two journals out of which it has grown each rendered in the years that are gone.

MAJOR-GENERAL LEONARD WOOD: I congratulate your company on the taking over of Harper's Weekly, and trust that under your direction this well known weekly will resume the place it so long held as one of our very influential publications. Its coming under the control of the Independent Corporation places two of the oldest and best known periodicals in America under a common management.

HON. R. C. STEARNES, State Superintendent of Public Instruction, Virginia: The merger of The Independent and Harper's Weekly means the combination of two good things whose long recognized usefulness will be quadrupled in the future. In the past I have read both periodicals with pleasure and profit. In the days to come I expect to derive even greater satisfaction and more substantial benefits from the combined magazine.

HON. A. O. THOMAS, State Superintendent of Public Instruction, Nebraska: If this union produces a magazine in keeping with the strength of the two contracting parties, I am sure it will be a very valuable contribution to the reading public.

HON. E. J. TAYLOR, Superintendent State Department of Education, North Dakota: The new journal, if it may be so called, is one which will surely meet with great popular favor.

HON. JOHN D. SHOOP, State Superintendent of Schools, Illinois: The blending of these two great publications with their wealth of history and influence contributes to the literary world a noteworthy example of progress. Each rich in history and prestige will supplement the other in the larger field of influence on which they are now entering.

HON. JOHN PURROY MITCHEL, Mayor of New York City: Let me congratulate you on the first issue of The Independent since its absorption of Harper's Weekly. It is highly attractive in its new form. It is as true in journalism, as in most other public and semi-public enterprises, that money standards exercise entirely too much influence, and that we have not enough independent and unobtruded forces devoted solely to the pursuit of ideals and principles. The Independent has always stood for moral freedom, for official honesty and for the advancement of the true interests of America. It is fortunate that it inherits in Harper's Weekly a splendid spirit and tradition of the same kind from the régime of Mr. Hapgood. I wish you increased prosperity and usefulness.

HON. ALTON B. PARKER, Former Chief Justice of the Court of Appeals of New York: It is a rare union that brings together two publications each having so many years of character building to its credit as The Independent and Harper's Weekly. May the absorption of the latter prove as satisfactory to the owners of The Independent as I know it will to the readers of Harper's.

HON. JOB E. HEDGES: With real interest I note the taking over of Harper's Weekly by The Independent. With the historic context of each of these periodicals there should be added momentum and influence given to The Independent. That periodical occupies a unique field in presenting its weekly summary of local and world events. It seems to me that The Independent is particularly fortunate in its policy. While taking its own stand on all questions to which it draws attention and giving its reasons, it had never appeared to me to do it in such a dogmatic manner that it leaves the reader to two alternatives, of either accepting its views or placing himself beyond the purview of The Independent's approval. It performs a real service in provoking thought on the part of its readers and furnishing them enough data to come to their own conclusions.

SIR EDMUND WALKER, of the Canadian Bank of Commerce, Toronto: I am sure you are to be complimented upon the incorporation in The Independent of a journal such as Harper's Weekly, the memory of which carries one back so far in the history of the United States. That in this way its life should be continued must be a gratification to countless individuals in America.

MR. GEORGE W. PERKINS: I wish you success in your new enterprise. It is full of attractive possibilities and I am sure they will be worked out to the best advantage of the community as a whole.

MR. OSWALD GARRISON VILLARD: The steady growth and development of The Independent is a profound source of satisfaction to all people who believe in clean, responsible and conscientious journalism in America. May it long enjoy the prosperity it deserves.

PRESIDENT J. G. SCHURMAN, Cornell University: You deserve congratulations for your success in uniting these two of the oldest, most distinguished and most progressive and enlightening periodicals in America. As a journal of civilization I wish it the fullest measure of success.

HON. EDWARD HYATT, State Superintendent of Public Instruction, California: I have just seen the first issue of The Independent as combined with Harper's Weekly. Concerning this union of two of the best known periodicals in America, what God hath put together let no man put asunder. I am sure the union will bear good fruit, and I hope to be able to dance at the golden wedding.

HON. JACOB H. SCHIFF: My congratulations upon the consolidation of two of the oldest and most serious weeklies, both of which have retained—notwithstanding the length of their existence—youthful vigor in the treatment of the great issues and problems of the day. I can only hope, as I believe, that this union is destined to bring forth the best and most advantageous results to your increasing circle of readers.

MISS JANE ADDAMS: By rather a curious coincidence I find that the two periodicals I remember from my earliest childhood are The Independent and Harper's Weekly. I suppose my father had other periodicals on his table but those are the two which seem to have remained in my mind, and thru the half century since I have always read them fairly steadily. I am, of course, enormously interested in the incorporation. If the spirit of each can be preserved it will be a wonderful undertaking and I congratulate you upon being at the head of such an interesting experiment in "reconstructing the world in which we live."

MR. DARWIN P. KINGSLEY, President New York Life Insurance Company: I was delighted when the last Independent came to notice, in familiar form, and as a part of the title the words Harper's Weekly. To us older chaps who knew the Weekly when Thomas Nast made his tremendous appeal to the American conscience, the entire disappearance of the publication seemed almost a tragedy. I am glad that you have preserved the name and I have no doubt you will give place, in the new and greater Independent, to the spirit that made the Weekly such a power in the sixties.

HON. CLINTON ROGERS WOODRUFF: The merger of The Independent and Harper's Weekly is a significant event in weekly journalism and will, I think, go far to demonstrate that two and two sometimes make more than four, especially when the units added represent so much in the way of progressive thought and activity. I anticipate that the enlarged Independent will surpass all of its former most creditable records.

MR. HENRY A. WISE WOOD, President American Society of Aeronautic Engineers: I think it a great good fortune that the readers of Harper's Weekly should have had that publication fall into your hands. What you are doing for the columns of The Independent by way of illuminating our national problems and making them easier of solution makes of your publication a public service institution of the highest value. The readers of Harper's are most fortunate in thus having been given the opportunity by you of joining The Independent family.

MR. ROBERT UNDERWOOD JOHNSON: The public is to be congratulated that Harper's Weekly has fallen into such good hands as those of the conductors of The Independent, since its readers will find there the best traditions of the good old type of literary weekly which was so vital and so popular in the period after the Civil War.

HON. CHARLES M. DOW, President National Chautauqua County Bank and former President of the Commissioners of the State Reservation at Niagara: I am always interested in each step in progress of The Independent, which I have read since boyhood. You are to be congratulated on combining with your constituency that of so well known and highly respected a publication as Harper's Weekly. It cannot be regarded as other than a noteworthy event in publishing circles. From the days of George William Curtis, editor, and Thomas Nast, cartoonist, Harper's Weekly has exerted a wide influence on public sentiment in this country. Its former readers will find in The Independent under its present management no loss in vigor nor independence of thought, and plenty of broad mindedness and liberality.

HON. ALBERT J. BEVERIDGE, ex-Senator from Indiana: Accept my hearty congratulation on having acquired Harper's Weekly. The combination of these two famous journals, The Independent and Harper's Weekly, under your able management, is a notable event in the American literary world. I am delighted with the number of The Independent which you were so kind as to send me. It is admirable from every point of view. I am sure that the union of these two historic periodicals will receive that support from the American public as merited by the benefit which this splendid publication gives to its readers.

MR. RICHARD B. WATROUS, Secretary American Civic Association: The marriage of The Independent and Harper's Weekly is a happy one, and the admiring friends of both periodicals are sure to watch with keen interest and profit the successful progress of the united magazines. It would be hard to imagine a better Independent that it has been for the past two years, but this union opens the way for still greater achievements.

HON. PHILIP H. GADSDEN, President Charleston Consolidated Railway and Lighting Company: It was with a great deal of satisfaction that I learned of the incorporation of Harper's Weekly with The Independent. These two periodicals have so long represented the very best thought in our country's life that it is great satisfaction to their readers to know that they have now been brought together under the same management, which is a guarantee that the ideals and principles which they have both so strongly supported and advocated will be preserved for the future, and that their usefulness in guiding and moulding the public thought of America will be enhanced as the years go by.

MR. J. HORACE McFARLAND, President American Civic Association: The Independent has always been just that, if one thinks of independence as upward and forward looking. For Harper's Weekly I have the affection based upon just about fifty years of acquaintance, with the further feeling that its summit of usefulness is yet to be reached in the combination thus just happily effected. If the management of the ideals and principles which be such as to cause me to think of Harper's Weekly when I see The Independent, and to favorably note The Independent when a Harper's Weekly feature sticks out, then the marriage cannot possibly have other than a wholly favorable outcome.

MR. WILLIAM F. DIX, Secretary Mutual Life Insurance Company: Here are two historic American weeklies which have never lost their dignity through all the changes of magazine fashion nor their hold on the respect and interest of the better class of the reading public nor their close touch with life, joined together to work henceforth as one. The union is a happy one, the subscribers of each are to be congratulated, and you, my dear Mr. Howland, and your associates, are abundantly able to carry forward the high ideals of these two great American periodicals. May a greater success than ever be yours.

MR. MARSHALL BALLARD, Managing Editor *New Orleans Item:* It has been my impression for some time that The Independent has been "coming." Let me express the hope that the two ancient yoke fellows shall derive a new access of youth and vigor from their union.

MR. JOHN A. STEWART, Chairman Executive Committee American Peace Centenary Association: Harper's Weekly and The Independent are bound to the memory of my youth by an indissoluble tie. Such a conjunction of reputation, character, stability and high-minded but human usefulness is one that must appeal to the American people and bring success to the venture so auspiciously and characteristically launched.

DR. CHARLES F. THWING, President Western Reserve University: The union of The Independent and Harper's Weekly is to me a rather personal matter. It takes on the relation of a marriage. For decades I have been a contributor to each. But what I have given to the papers is as nothing to that which they have given to me in opportunity and in enrichment.

DR. GEORGE F. KUNZ, Vice-President Tiffany & Company: I hope that, under the able administration of your splendid corporation, Harper's Weekly will again acquire the place it occupied for so many years—I read it from earliest boyhood until recently—and I have every reason to believe that with your joint abilities and energy, you will make this one of the great periodicals of the country. I wish you every success.

DR. JOHN H. FINLEY, Commissioner of Education of New York State: As one who had to do, for a little time long ago, with that journal of civilization, Harper's Weekly, whose torch is still to be kept burning in the hands of The Independent, I send my good wishes and pray that the flame may leap to greater brightness.

MR. RAYMOND B. PRICE, Vice-President United States Rubber Company: In these times when the unselfish thought and action of every intelligent American citizen are necessary to overcome the abnormal difficulties with which American Democracy is now threatened, it must be a rare satisfaction to be connected with a great publicity organization with its almost unlimited power for helpfulness. The fine traditions surrounding Harper's Weekly, and the worthy ambitions of The Independent combine to present a most unusual opportunity for usefulness to this country, and I wish you the fullest measure of success in your great undertaking.

HON. CONRAD H. SYME, Corporation Counsel of the City of Washington: The date, May 22, 1916, marks the confluence of two of the most powerful, truth-seeking and right-thinking forces which have manifested themselves in American journalism. Since 1848, The Independent has sought to truly teach the American people to look forward along righteous lines of political, economic, and ethical progression. It has taught the fundamental principles upon which moral, intellectual, political and economic freedom must be attained; its teachings have been untouched by personal interest and untarnished by unworthy motive, and Harper's Weekly has pursued a similar course of principle. Neither has ever been tongue-tied by authority, shackled by material money standards, or "hog-tied" by self-interest. The combination of the moral and ethical forces of these two publications into united effort along the familiar paths by each so long separately pursued, can result in nothing but great good to our country.

MR. HENRY H. HUNT, Conneaut, Ohio: I want to take off my hat to you on this great achievement. Your publication stands at the head of weekly papers in America, if not in the world.

HON. THOMAS W. MEACHEM, President New Process Gear Corporation: The union of two such influential and elevating publications as The Independent and Harper's Weekly is a truly eugenic marriage, promising a plentiful progeny of vigorous and lofty ideas and entitling the matchmaker to the thanks and hearty congratulations of the reading public. May the two who are now one live and prosper.

HON. ELIHU ROOT: I was brought up on The Independent *inter alia*, and I am rather glad that in the combination it has had the lion's and the Weekly has had the lamb's part.

MR. HENRY WOODHOUSE, Governor of the Aero Club of America: Both The Independent and Harper's Weekly have performed a great public service during the past half century as educative forces, and I am sure the amalgamation

will result in the continuance and acceleration of the excellent work these two journals have to their credit.

PROF. A. T. ROBERTSON, Southern Baptist Theological Seminary: I wish you great success in your tremendous opportunity for service represented by the combination of Harper's Weekly and The Independent.

HON. HERBERT W. RICE, President U. S. Gutta Percha Paint Company: I am very much pleased to see that The Independent has taken over the famous periodical Harper's Weekly, thus combining two of the oldest and best known periodicals in America. I do not see how the Harper's Weekly could have fallen into better hands.

DR. HENRY STURGIS DRINKER, President Lehigh University: May I, as a member of the National Institute of Efficiency, of which The Independent is the official organ, express my congratulations at the incorporation of Harper's Weekly with The Independent? This joinder of two of the oldest and best known periodicals in America should certainly result in great benefit to the reading public.

HON. PAUL A. SCHOELLKOPF, Commissioner of the State Reservation at Niagara: I have before me The Independent of May 22, which is an earnest that the high standards maintained by that journal for nearly seventy years, and by Harper's Weekly for nearly sixty years, will be continued in the unified publication whose life of well doing will be, I trust, at least one hundred and thirty years. Every page is full of interest and "punch."

HON. A. T. CLEARWATER, President New York State Bar Association: I have no doubt but that the combined publication will prove to be a benignant and beneficent factor in the progress of civilization, always in the lead of the advance, but never destructive of that which is good. That you will deal fairly with those great questions regarding the solution of which men inevitably differ, and ever will lean to the protection of the rights of the individual as against the oppression of the mass and the powerful is taken for granted by all of us who long have been numbered among your admirers.

MR. PAUL U. KELLOGG, Editor *The Survey:* The uprising of The Independent has been one of the big, encouraging things in journalism in the last ten years. Here's to the next ten. In the days of its adversity and short commons, the two factors which, to my mind, enabled it to come thru were its hospitality to thinkers whose causes were as yet unwon, and the grit of its editor in holding to the full human significance of the magazine's name. With those two factors to hold to, the new and combined magazine need not fear even prosperity.

HON, GEORGE J. MEYER, Commissioner of the State Reservation at Niagara: It affords me great pleasure to learn that the Independent Corporation has acquired Harper's Weekly. This will certainly enhance the value materially of your already famous and widely read periodical, and the two papers incorporated as one will undoubtedly become one of the most desirable periodicals issued and have a tendency to largely increase in circulation.

MR. FRANK KNOX, Editor *Manchester Union:* I congratulate you upon this consolidation and wish for the consolidated magazine a most prosperous and useful career.

MR. GEORGE BATTEN, of the George Batten Advertising Company: I haven't a doubt that The Independent-Harper's under the new conditions will attain an important place in American journalism and secure the circulation and advertising patronage that it deserves.

MR. G. R. CHADBOURNE, Editor *Daily Kennebec Journal:* The combination "looks good" to us. A journal of independent thought and a journal of civilization,

AGAINST INVESTMENT LOSS

there is but one protection—alert application of sound business principles.

As a prudent person, you would not think of lending money to an individual until you were satisfied not only of the value of the security offered, but also of the character of the person soliciting the loan.

Now, it should not be so, but the same attitude of mind is not always preserved by the person who becomes a partner in a corporation through the purchase of its stocks, or who becomes its creditor through the purchase of its bonds. The cases are identical.

Yet it is an indisputable fact that men who are careful, intelligent and successful in their ordinary lines of business often exercise so little judgment in the selection of securities that they lose all or the greater part of the money invested.

But how, you ask, can the investor obtain the same detailed knowledge before investing as he would require in ordinary business transactions?

There are card reports—the daily revised Standard Corporation Card Reports—which embody all known facts.

It would be a mistake to represent that Standard Corporation Card Reports can supply information which a corporation refuses to furnish stockholders regarding its own affairs. But Standard Corporation Card Reports do assemble, classify and analyze all available information in a way to make it comprehensible to the user.

No opinions are given, but by remarkable analyses the strength or weakness of a corporation is accurately outlined. With Standard Corporation Card Reports it is entirely possible to tell if a corporation is going forward or backward, if its growth has been healthy or unsound and if it promises well for the future.

Standard Corporation Card Reports are available at 50 cents each.

You would insist on getting detailed reports of any business you were about to engage in. Is it, then, any more than ordinary business caution for you to fortify yourself with reports covering your investments?"

List the corporations on which you would like to have the latest reports. Enclose check, money order or stamps, and the latest Standard Corporation Card Reports will be forwarded you at once, postage prepaid. Your inquiry will be treated as confidential, and your money will be cheerfully refunded upon request.

STANDARD STATISTICS CO., Inc.
47-49 West Street, New York

*Standard Corporation Card Reports have been used for 10 years by the leading banks and investment houses who have them on file for their own and their clients' convenience.

PLEASANT COMMENT
(Concluded)

each standing for human rights and national progress for generations, are joined; the issue should be a triumph for eugenics. The Independent was all that could be asked by the lover of moral freedom and the student of "both sides," but the merger is more.

PROF. W. W. JOHNSTON, Michigan Agricultural College: Congratulations to the management of The Independent! Each of the two magazines now combined has had a long and honorable history, and each has today a well established reputation for independent, courageous, and progressive leadership.

MR. J. WALTER THOMPSON, of the J. Walter Thompson Advertising Agency: I note that you have incorporated the famous periodical, Harper's Weekly, with The Independent. This seems fitting in every way. The putting together of two famous journals ought to make one that will be par excellence of its kind. Both of these publications date back in my own recollection at least fifty years, and with their united clientele and interest should become more than ever a factor in the publishing world.

MR. HOLLINGTON K. TONG: I learn with great pride of the incorporation of Harper's Weekly with The Independent. I am sure that under your able and efficient management the merged Independent will achieve even greater success in the field of magazines.

MR. ARTHUR M. WOLFSON, Principal Julia Richman High School, New York: I have always liked the clean, fresh, forceful point of view of The Independent. Harper's Weekly has expressed my idea of leadership. I am sure that the combination will double the value of the paper.

MR. WILBUR D. NESBIT, Chicago: I note with pleasure that Harper's Weekly has been combined with The Independent. I know that is going to be a good thing for Harper's Weekly, and I certainly hope it will be a mighty good thing for The Independent. You are getting out a splendid periodical. Everywhere I go, I find it on the table of the really live people.

MR. FRANK A. ARNOLD, Editor The Countryside: The famous "War Weekly" is no more, but in The Independent, with its broad, forward outlook, the loyal supporters of Harper's Weekly will find reflected the type of constructive editorial treatment to which they are accustomed, and which will result in permanently transferring to The Independent this large clientele of new and eminently desirable readers.

GRACE RAYMOND HEBARD, Librarian University of Wyoming: It was with sincere regret that I took a wet sponge and a sharp knife to remove the label which for twenty-five years of my librarianship in this university had marked the place in the periodical racks for Harper's Weekly. I feel as tho a friend has gone away, but leaving behind him a most pleasant remembrance. There is one compensation in the disappearance of Harper's Weekly, which has appeared to us fifty-two times a year and given to us so many pages each week of desired information, that it is to be wedded to The Independent, which is also one of the household idols.

HON. CHARLES H. LUGG, Superintendent State Department of Public Instruction, South Dakota: What the American people need and what they can appreciate just now is a publication that will give them the facts of the world's news without coloring and without distortion to promote the interests of any particular propaganda. The Independent has been a standard publication for impartial information; Harper's Weekly has been particularly noted for its happy hits in cartoons and illustrations. The combination will find a large field of usefulness and an appreciative army of readers.

NAPOLEON'S disastrous Russian Campaign marks the beginning of his downfall. This map herewith shows his line of march from Berlin to Moscow, a distance of 1250 miles. This march by Napoleon at the head of over 600,000 trained soldiers was made in less than four months. Moscow was captured, but the Russians burned their famous capital and all supplies, forcing Napoleon to retreat in mid-winter. He reached Paris with less than 100,000 men, over half a million of his trained soldiers having fallen along the line of that disastrous retreat.

Once again the thunder of invading armies has awakened Russia from her lethargy. Will the rigors of the Russian climate again prove the salvation of that nation and the turning point in the present tremendous European War? At the causes of the present conflict—the deep racial antipathies, the commercial rivalries, the sting of past defeats, the vaulting ambition for world empire—may be discerned from the pages of history, and the one great history of every empire, kingdom, principality and power, from the beginning of civilization to the present, is the world famed publication,

Ridpath's History of the World

Dr. Ridpath is universally recognized as America's greatest historian. Other men have written histories of one nation or period; Gibbon of Rome, Macaulay of England, Guizot of France, but it remained for Dr. Ridpath to write a history of the entire World from the earliest civilization down to the present. We offer the remaining sets of the last edition

At a Great Sacrifice in Price

We will name our special low price and easy terms of payment only in direct letters. A coupon for your convenience is printed on the lower corner of this advertisement. Tear off the coupon, write your name and address plainly and mail now. Our plan of sale enables us to ship direct from factory to customer on approval and guarantee satisfaction. We employ no agents, nor do we sell through book stores, so there is no agent's commission to pay. Mail the coupon now.

Rise and Fall of Nations

Here you discern the causes which have led to the extortions of monarchies and kingdoms. Peoples and races, and it History has proven any fact it is that the rich and defenseless nation must sooner or later fall beneath the heel of the more warlike and aggressive power. If you would know the fate of the rich and defenseless nation then read the story of ancient Assyria or Chaldea or Persia or Babylon whose glory now is but a memory most inadequate preparation for self defense against the aggression of warlike powers. Dr. Ridpath gives the complete history of every race, every nation, every time and holds you spellbound by his wonderful eloquence. Nothing more interesting, absorbing and inspiring has ever been written.

Western Newspaper Asso.
Chicago

FREE COUPON

Western Newspaper Association

H. E. Severn, Pres.
140 S. Dearborn St.
CHICAGO, ILL.

Picture mail 46 free sample pages of Ridpath's History of the World, containing photogravure of Napoleon, Caesar and a hundred other subjects. Map of European War Zone and a colored map of the world. It is a book of 100 pages of our special offer to Independent readers.

Name ....

Address ....

MAIL THIS COUPON

DEBATING SOCIETIES

The Single Six-Year Term for President.
The Death Penalty.
Price Maintenance.
Minimum Wage Legislation.
Mothers' Pensions.
Who Is Responsible for the War?
Government Owned Merchant Marine.
Shall We Enlarge the Army?
Convict Labor in the United States.
The Problem of the Trusts.
The Monroe Doctrine.
Military Training for College Students.
An Embargo on Arms.
Mexico and the United States.

Both sides of all these fourteen debates will be furnished for only 25 cents.

THE INDEPENDENT
119 West 40th Street   New York

Independent Opinions

We have received several criticisms of the article by J. O. Dimock on "The Farm Horse Doesn't Pay" in our issue of May 29. Of these replies we pick out the following letters for publication as they seem to be based upon experience and careful counting of the relative cost of horse and tractor:

I have farmed all my life, have raised horses, bought and sold horses and have used horses for my farm power. I have also used a tractor and have one at the present time.

I believe the tractor is practical for a large farm of 200 acres or more where the fields are level, the soil is firm, and the fields are square or rectangular, and providing the tractor has a good engineer. I do not, however, believe Mr. Dimock's statement, "that the tractor is of no expense so long as it is not running." For example, say we pay $1000 for a tractor and borrow the money, paying interest at 8 per cent or $80 per year. I figure it takes about 2½ gallons of gasoline to plow one acre with any tractor, making a cost of $110 for plowing 200 acres; just for plowing alone, remember. The average life of a tractor is from five to eight or maybe ten years at the most. The depreciation in ten years would cost $100 per year. Oil and grease we'll figure at $5 per year. It is hard to estimate the cost of repairs, for one tractor might run five years with very little repair cost while another might cost a new one in that length of time. Castings and parts are very expensive after the manufacturer's guarantee runs out. Let's figure the repair cost at an average of $35 per year, which is, I think, reasonable.

Now if every farmer was an experienced and expert engineer it would add favor to the tractor a little, but I believe that unless the farmer is a good mechanic it will pay him big to hire a good engineer. An engineer would cost more than an ordinary farm hand: Let's figure his wages at $60 per month. A $1000 tractor and outfit ought to plow ten acres a day, taking twenty days to plow the 200 acres (providing everything goes well). Engineer hire $40. We would have to pay $150 for a special plow. Interest on this $12. The annual expenses would figure up as follows:

Interest on investment	$92
Depreciation of tractor and plow per year	110
Gasoline, 200 acres plowing	110
Repairs	35
Engineer	40
Cyl. oil and trans. grease	5
Total	**$392**

Now I would like to know where Mr. Dimock got his information that the horse is not a satisfactory worker for the conditions existing on a farm. If he is writing from experience he must have kept horses such as were represented in the cartoon.

The modern farmer keeps nothing in the line of horses except good brood mares. It is an established fact that a good mare will raise a good colt every year. This colt will bring enough to pay for the mare's feed the whole year. There is always and always will be a demand for good horses. The man holding the reins over the backs of six powerful brood mares hitched to a gang plow need not envy his neighbor who drives a tractor, unless as previously stated he has a large level farm. In my mind I doubt very much if Mr. Dimock ever had experience with farming or that he ever

had the experience of paying for the expense of the tractor.

If a man runs a tractor for a ten hour day, he won't feel like putting on headlights and running all night. If he runs two shifts he must have another engineer. What's more, he won't feel like taking his family to a dance thirty miles away at night. He had better spend his spare time looking over his tractor, tightening up nuts, etc.

The brood mare should pay for her keep, so I cannot see any reason why the average farmer should worry his head about a tractor.   RAY W. HODGSON

St. Cloud, Minnesota

From an experience of some ten years in North Dakota, where we have ample room to try horses, tractors or whatever power we wish, I venture to disagree flatly with some of Mr. Dimock's arguments.

The first argument against the horse is. that he works on the average only three hours a day. No doubt Mr. Dimock has good authority for this statement. Still, consider a minute. It is a well known fact, that we work about as little, here in the North, as in any farming community. We cannot seed, hay, harvest, thresh and plow for the next crop in less than six months—from April 15 to October 15. More commonly we spend seven or more months. We work from ten to fourteen hours a day during that season. We have to, in order to finish. If we worked only ten hours a day, for only six months of the year, our horses would work five out of every twenty-four of the hours in a year.

The next point is well taken. The tractor more adequately responds to the rush season. This spring our season is at least two weeks late. Every farmer is in a mad rush to get his crop in. Every hour counts. Across the road is a two section farm, on which six fine horse teams strain from six-thirty to six-thirty, six days in the week. Behind the machine shed stands a $2000 tractor, used only for grinding feed. Why? Because the land is so wet the engine buries itself in the field. But even if it could run, the farmer would not use it. He ran it one day this spring and decided that the wear and tear on the gears, the danger of wiring and the cost of buying fuel, and yet keeping his horses idle, was. prohibitive. We need speed this year if we ever did. Yet, within a radius of three miles, there are six tractors lying idle, while the horses till the fields. Experience has proved, to the satisfaction of the hardheaded business farmer, that horses *do* the work, *when* it should be done, at a less average expense than the tractor.

Third, it is claimed that to be efficient a farmer must direct the work of many horses. Occasionally, perhaps, but sometimes more than sometimes, I have never seen the tractor that will efficiently manipulate a corn cultivator. Have you? I have never seen a tractor advertised to plow a 45° hillside of New England. Have you? And yet it is considered necessary to plow corn and potatoes and do many of those inefficient, but useful jobs. Our next neighbor rented a big bunch of virgin prairie land. He broke, pressed and drilled in fifty acres a day for forty even days. It was only possible, of course, because the land was level as a floor—stoneless, swampless, and in one big piece. That was in 1910. In 1911 he seeded back 1500 acres. In 1912 he couldn't borrow any more money for gasoline and seed so he sold his bonanza outfit and went back to farming. We do not need a machine that will plow fifty acres a day sometimes, in some places. We do need, and must have, power to plow ten, or even five acres, every day, on most any kind of a field.   A. R. JAQUA

Leal, North Dakota

Mr. Dimock, to whom we submitted some of these letters, writes us as follows:

The article on the farm tractor was meant to be suggestive and prophetic rather than a statement of facts as they are today. Yet since the article was published I have read that the headlight has actually been used for night plowing because of the rush of work consequent upon continued rains.

My suggestion of the road traveling tractor was based on Henry Ford's statement to an engineering friend of mine. He expects to produce a tractor that will do the work on the average small farm, and then make a speed of twenty miles on the road. A prophecy by Mr. Ford in regard to motor problems is entitled to the best respect of the country.

The critic quoted above has raised an economic objection by figuring the first cost of the tractor at $1000, and the interest on this cost at eight per cent and the depreciation at ten per cent. Possibly these figures are correct for today, but I venture the prophecy that they will not be correct five years hence, for Mr. Ford's tractor is promised at from $250 to $300. Moreover, this same critic in figuring costs between horse plowing and tractor plowing does not take into account the value of the man's time.

Mr. Hodgson bases his figures on conditions existing in Minnesota today in regard to costs and interest charges. He is perfectly correct in suggesting the big farm as the proper field for the tractor. I will go him one better and suggest that the big farm is the only proper field for the farmer's activities. A very little study in the subject of farm management will tell him that the small farmer hasn't the ghost of a show to make a good living. Between the lines, I must here state that "size" is not simply a matter of acres. The florist with his greenhouses may be carrying on a large business with mighty little ground.

In these northeastern states, with their uncertain weather, the item of insurance is a good sized factor. During this wet spring many farmers have been unable to get their crops into the ground because the rains have delayed them beyond any calculations. A little added cost, making possible the planting of crops, would save enough in a single year to make up a small discrepancy.　　　　JULIAN A. DIMOCK

East Corinth, Vermont

An Illinois correspondent says that to "print both sides" according to our custom is not sufficient in the case of the presidential election because there is a third side, the anti-preparedness, which is not likely to be represented in either of the party platforms:

For the first time in the history of this country millions of her citizens will be disfranchised next November. Never before have the issues been more clearly defined, but without a candidate and an organization the citizens holding to certain definite and well-defined principles will remain silent rather than cast his vote for a condition that his conscience, business and family interests rebel against.

The old parties are committed to Preparedness, and next November it will simply be a choice between the size of their guns and their number. Are we to have a million or half a million men taken from their homes, school houses and industrial life and made ready for the trenches? The voter will be called upon to decide this issue, but he will not be informed that it is the first step to Militarism, that regardless of either party we have turned away our form of government and propose to adopt methods employed by the monarchs of Europe that have kept their broods on the throne for ages, and enslaved their subjects except those that have fled to America to escape military duty.

Is it reasonable to suppose that those two or three millions of foreigners but naturalized American citizens will vote for the same form of government they have already escaped from? To a man, these industrious, frugal and useful citizens will vote against militarism; increased taxation, conscription and the disgusting army

aristocracy and flunkyism. A tremendous "vest pocket" vote is ready to come from the taxpayers who see a burden about to be placed on them and their descendants for future ages and generations. These men will not talk but they will vote to protect themselves against such burdens of taxation as their foreign brethren are breaking under; the mother that secretly yearns for her boy will either vote or use her influence to secure votes to keep her boy "out of the trenches." The laborer, the farmer, the Christian and all genuine Americans that are naturally opposed to royalty and their forms of preparedness, will quietly cast their vote for freedom against militarism, financial oppression and conscription. Let a call be issued for a national convention stating the issues involved and let the representative members of the citizens above mentioned meet and form a "National Party" or the American Party, nominate a candidate to represent them from these plain people; an Abraham Lincoln, the man of the hour will be discovered.   ADDISON C. THOMAS

Winnetka, Illinois

Have just read your editorial of May 1 on "The Divorce Evil." The churches of this country could stop the divorce business if they took a firm stand, as the Roman Catholic Church does. I am a Protestant, but I admire the consistency of the Roman Catholic Church on this question.

Barring action by the churches, a most effectual halt in the divorce business could be made if the press would turn its attention to the repeal of our alimony laws. There is no doubt at all that alimony figures large in the minds of many would-be divorcees, who wrap their clouded name in a cloak of alimony, except for the biblical cause of divorce. No woman who deliberately forswears herself by breaking the solemn marriage vow should be supported by the man she despises. Repeal the alimony laws and the "free life" will lose its attractiveness to very many.   M. D. BROWN

Bellevue, Pennsylvania

Our correspondent may be right in preferring the attitude of the Catholic Church on the divorce question, but he does injustice to the Protestant position when he alludes to it as inconsistent. Both churches are consistent with their historic principles, but they proceed upon different theories of marriage. The theory of the Catholic, Roman and Anglican, is that marriage is an ecclesiastical sacrament and therefore indissoluble. The theory of the Protestants is that marriage is a civil contract, and therefore dissoluble for sufficient cause. The Reformers repudiated the Catholic theory of the sacrament of marriage just as they did the Catholic theory of the sacrament of the Eucharist. Luther and Milton took very advanced ground on the divorce question. The Pilgrim Fathers established civil marriage and civil divorce in New England, and were careful to prevent the clergy from getting control of it. Marrying was entrusted to the magistrate rather than to the minister. The United States as a whole has adopted in its legislation the Puritan system of civil marriage and the Census report showed that divorce is more frequent in those states and parts of states settled from New England than in the Southern States that had been colonized under Roman or Anglican influences. Whether this indicates a higher or a lower state of morals depends upon the point of view.

PEBBLES

COLLEGE

First I became
A copy of a book.

Then I became
A copy of a man
Who was also
A copy of a book.

Now
I would not know
What I am

Except that I have
On my wall
A framed paper
Which explains it fully.

—MARY CAROLYN DAVIES in *The Masses*.

Poor China—her last President was poisoned and her new President is Hung.

Mr. Hughes to meet Mr. Wiskersham here! (Headline). Or, as the convention reports explained, "Hughes badges were much in evidence."

Old Bob Whiting has a —— watch and a —— car, and he says he thinks the parts ought to be interchangeable.—*New York Tribune*.

Rookie Hughes Digs in Silence. (Headline.) An interesting family trait somewhat strongly developed.—*Philadelphia Public Ledger*.

Good morning. Have you used Pear's soap.
No. I'm not rooming with Pear any more.—*Cornell Widow*.

If either of the belligerents in this war knew the depressing facts about themselves that their opponents know, they would surrender at once.—*Chicago Daily News*.

The official announcements of Washington's preparedness demonstration read:
"The only uniforms allowed in the parade will be an American flag and a parasol."

OUR COUNTRY, 'TIS OF THEE
"'America First' is the plank for me,"
Declared the Republican nominee.

"Americanism, I'm for that,"
Asserted the foremost Democrat.

"All hyphenism is what I hate,"
Said the Socialist candidate.

"I stand as America's special pleader,"
Exclaimed the Prohibition leader.

So, whatever happens, this best of lands
Will be in safe and protecting hands.
　　　　　—*New York Tribune*.

One of the Scottish golf clubs gives a dinner each year to the youngsters it employs as caddies. At the feast last year one of the boys disdained to use any of the forks he found at his place, and loaded his food into himself with his knife. When the ice-cream course was reached and he still used his knife, a boy who sat opposite to him, and who could stand it no longer, shouted:

"Great Scot! Look at Skinney, usin' his iron all the way round!"—*Tit-Bits*.

"Say, Reed," said Higgins, as he met a friend, "do you know why you are like a donkey?"

"Like a donkey!" echoed Reed thoughtfully. "No. I don't."

"Because your better half is stubbornness itself," said Higgins.

"That's not bad," said Reed. "I'll have to try that on my wife when I get home tonight."

Accordingly, when they were at dinner, Reed asked:

"Annie, do you know why I am so much like a donkey?"

He waited a moment, expecting Mrs. Reed would give it up. But, on the contrary, she gazed at him somewhat commiseratingly as she replied:

"I suppose because you were born so."—*New York Times*.

Ten Lessons Free
Wonderful New Offer

Yes—ten lessons in New Way Typewriting *Free*—if you write *at once*. Every stenographer, every typewriter user, experienced or beginner, should get this wonderful new offer! Now, in your own home, you can quickly and easily learn to typewrite 80 to 100 words a minute, without errors, without fatigue, and as a result, increase your salary to $25, $30 and even $40 weekly. The New Way has completely revolutionized the typewriting situation. Thousands who formerly wrote 30 to 40 words a minute are now writing 80 to 100, and their salaries have been doubled and trebled as a result!

THE NEW WAY IN TYPEWRITING
SPEED　ACCURACY
INCREASED SALARY

Salary Increased $15 Per Week
"The Course proved very profitable to me, as at the time I took it up I was making but $18.00 per week, and it brought my salary as a stenographer up to $25."—Mr. Oscar R. Huster, 2931 H St., N.W., Washington, D. C.

From $900 a Year to $1800
"From a speed of 30 words per minute, I studied without difficulty a rate of 89 words a minute. I was earning $900 a year at the time I began the Course, and am now receiving $1800 in the Isthmian Canal Commission."—Richard Clarke, Cafe Isthmian Commission, Culebra, C. Z. Panama.

80 to 90 Words a Minute
"Inasmuch as the first seven lessons of the Tulloss System brought my speed up from 48 to between 88 and 90 words per minute, I could not do other than praise the instruction highly."—E. C. Hendershott, c/o Arizona Copper Co., Clifton, Ariz.

Worth 10 Times Cost
"The Special Exercises for Finger Training are simply amazing in their results. Beginning the study of the Tulloss Course in a mediocre typist, writing but over thirty words per minute, I was within a few months, enabled to use all my fingers with perfect ease, and reach an average of almost 100 words per minute in doing my regular work. It has been worth to me ten times the money I invested."—Miss Tillie Lalime, St. Hyacinthe, Que., Can.

Over 80 Words a Minute
"As a result of my study of the Tulloss Course, I am now able to stroke any letter or character blindfolded and without the slightest hesitation. I do all my work by the New Way system, and my speed has been brought up to over 80 words per minute. I do not think too much praise can be given to the Tulloss School."—C. H. Estrink, Adrian Furnace Co., Du Bois, Pa.

80 to 100 Words a Minute Guaranteed!

Don't confuse this new way in typewriting with any system of the past. There has never been anything like it before. Special *Gymnastic* Finger Training Exercises bring results in *days* that ordinary methods, or "touch" system, will not produce in months if ever. It is without question the greatest advance in typewriting since the typewriter itself was invented—already its success has become world-wide.

So overwhelming has been the success of this easy new way in typewriting that we are now offering the entire Course on *trial*, 10 lessons are FREE to every student. The balance of the Course can be paid for a little at a time so you hardly notice the cost. You get an absolute guarantee which provides that, unless you are thoroughly satisfied with the results, the entire course will cost you not one cent.

48 Page Book Free

We have prepared a book which tells all about the New Way in Typewriting. It is a big 48-page book, brimful of eye-opening ideas and valuable information. It explains how this unique new method will quickly make your fingers *strong* and *dextrous*, bring them under perfect control, make them *extremely rapid* in their movement—how in a few short weeks you can transform your typewriting and make it *easy, accurate* and *amazingly speedy*—how the results of the New Way have doubled and trebled the salaries of thousands of others. Let us tell you about our "Ten Lessons Free" offer as well as our special price and easy terms to new students in each locality, which is made for limited time only. Write at once. Tear off the coupon now, before you turn the page, or write a postal or letter.

THE MARKET PLACE

A REVIEW OF FINANCE AND TRADE

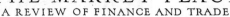

INDUSTRIALS OR WAR ORDER STOCKS

	Low in 1914	1915 High	1915 Net Change	Opening 1910	Net Change in 1916 to March 15	Net Change in 1916 to June 14
Am. Can	19¼	68½	+ 36½	60½	+ 2	— 2¼
Allis-Chalmers	6	49⅛	+ 23⅞	31	+ 1⅜	— 4⅜
Am. Car & Foundry	42¼	98	+ 33¾	77	— 4½	—17
Am. Locomotive	20¼	74¼	+ 46⅞	68½	+12⅞	+ 4½
Am. Smelting	50¼	101⅛	+ 51⅞	106⅝	— 4½	— 9⅜
Anaconda	24¾	91⅝	+ 40½	90	— 2⅜	— 2⅜
Baldwin Locomotive	38½	154½	+ 77⅜	115½	— 4⅞	—25¾
Beth. Steel	29½	600	+425½	450	+67½	— 6
Gen. Electric	137½	185½	+ 34¾	174½	— 4	— 4½
Gen. Motors	37⅝	535	+443	495	—20	+65
Maxwell	14½	92	+ 58⅝	75	—12⅞	— 7⅜
Nat. Lead	40	70⅜	+ 18¾	66	+ 1½	+ 2½
N. Y. Air Brake	58	164¼	+ 75	139½	+ 9¾	+ ½
Pressed Steel Car	26¼	78¼	+ 29⅞	64	— 6½	—15½
Studebaker	20	195	+128⅞	163½	—17	—22
Indus. Alcohol	15	129¾	+101	127	+28¼	+32⅝
Willys Overland	..	268	+146	233	+ 3	+55¼
U. S. Steel	48	88⅜	+ 37⅛	87⅛	— 1⅝	— 1¾

THE COURSE OF FINANCE AND TRADE

A REVIEW OF THE SECOND QUARTER OF 1916

BY FRANK D. ROOT

AT the beginning of the present year industrial and financial conditions in the United States were distinctly favorable. Some of the most notable features of industrial growth in 1915 were mentioned in a brief review published in The Independent three months ago. Attention was also directed to abundant proof that in prevailing conditions there had been no change to our disadvantage during the new year's first quarter.

In the year's second quarter there has been no backward movement. At the furnaces we are now making pig iron at the rate of 40,000,000 tons a year, and a new high record for output was shown in May. The product of our steel mills is limited only by their capacity. Railroad earnings continue to be very large, and three companies have recently increased their dividend rates. Our exports have for the first time exceeded $400,000,000 in a month, and our imports have risen to a value never before reported. At the same time the excess of exports over imports—that excess which is sometimes called a favorable balance of trade—is at the rate of nearly $2,300,000,000 a year. Commercial failures for five months have shown liabilities of only $99,000,000, against $170,000,000 in the corresponding months of 1915. Clearings for five months exceed by 43 per cent. those of last year's first five months. In the building projects of four months there is a gain of 18 per cent. The resources of our national banks, $14,-195,000,000,000, exceed by $356,000,000 those reported at any time in the past. We read every day of new extra dividends in cash or stock. More than $50,-000,000 of gold has come to us since the second week of May, and we are making new loans to the belligerents.

IRON AND STEEL

It has been said that we are now making pig iron at the rate of 40,000,-000 tons a year. The output in May was 3,351,768 tons. A total of 40,000,-000 may be compared with the largest quantity produced in any preceding year—30,724,581 tons, in 1913. The condition of the steel mills is fairly represented by the reports of the great Steel Corporation, whose net earnings have grown from only $12,500,000 in the first quarter of 1915 to $60,713,-000 in the first quarter of this year. In that earlier quarter there was not enough set aside to pay the dividend on the preferred shares, but in the later one the payment of that dividend and of the resumed dividend on the common stock left $32,000,000 to be used in other ways. The company increased the wages of its employees by 10 per cent on February 1, and added 10 per cent on May 1, at a cost of $33,000,-000 a year. It has on hand unfilled orders for 9,331,000 tons of its products. The prices of steel products are now, on an average, about 125 per cent higher than they were one year ago, but only $5 has been added to the old price, $28, of railway rails. The price of copper is about 29½ cents a pound. In 1915 it rose from 13 to 20 cents.

THE RAILROADS

There is plenty of evidence that railroad earnings, both gross and net, are not declining. We see official reports of an increase of New York Central's net of 52 per cent in April, and an increase for the Pennsylvania of 55 per cent in the same month. These two companies had in the four months ending with April a gross increase of $60,-

COURSE OF RAILROAD STOCKS

The gains made in the last quarter of 1915, due to improvement which began to be seen in September, have not been retained since the opening of the present year, altho the losses of the first two and one-half months have, as a rule, been reduced. Advances warranted by earnings have been prevented by continuous selling of American stocks owned abroad, and by the menace of a great labor controversy.

	Net Change in 1914	Net Change in 1915	Opening 1916	Net Change in 1916 to March 15	Net Change in 1916 to June 14
Atchison	— ½	+15¼	108	— 4¼	— 1¾
B. & Ohio	—24⅛	+17⅛	95	— 5¾	— 3⅝
Can. Pac.	—53	+29	182	—14½	— 5½
St. Paul	—13	+14⅛	101	— 5¼	—
Northwestern	— 5½	+13	134½	— 7½	— 4½
Del. & Hud.	— 9¾	+12¼	153½	— 1	— ⅞
Gt. Northern	—13¼	+14⅛	126¼	— 3¾	— 4⅜
Lehigh	—19½	+17⅛	81½	— 2¼	+ 1
M., K. & Tex.	—10½	— 1⅝	6½	— 2¼	— 2⅜
Mo. Pac.	—17	— 3¼	4½	+ ¾	+ 2¼
N. Y. Central	— 8⅛	+26	109½	— 3¼	— 2¼
North Pac.	— 9⅜	+18¼	118	— 3⅝	— 2⅝
Pennsylvania	— 5	+ 6⅞	59	— 1⅛	— ¼
Reading	—24⅞	+12¼	83	+ 5	+22¼
So. Pac.	— 6¾	+21⅞	102½	— 2⅞	— 3¼
Un. Pac.	—39⅛	+23⅝	138	— 3⅝	+ ¾

FOREIGN TRADE

Since the beginning of the year new high records have been made in exports, imports, and the excess of exports over imports, exports having risen in March to nearly $410,000,000, and the excess in the short month of February to $209,000,000.

1915	Exports	Imports	Excess of Exports
January	$207,879,313	$122,148,317	$145,730,996
February	299,805,869	125,123,391	174,682,478
March	296,611,852	157,982,016	138,629,836
April	294,745,913	160,576,106	134,169,807
May	274,218,142	142,284,851	132,933,291
June	268,547,416	157,695,140	110,852,276
July	268,974,610	143,244,737	125,729,873
August	261,025,230	141,804,202	119,221,028
September	300,676,822	151,236,026	149,440,796
October	328,018,300	149,172,729	178,845,671
November	327,670,413	155,496,675	172,173,738
December	359,306,492	171,832,505	187,473,987
Total, 12 mos.	$3,547,480,372	$1,778,596,695	$1,768,883,677
1916			
January	$335,535,303	$184,192,299	$151,343,004
February	402,911,118	193,935,117	209,056,011
March	409,850,425	213,589,785	196,260,640
April	404,300,000	217,800,000	186,500,000

000,000 and a net increase of $35,000,000. Union Pacific's increase of net in ten months was 31 per cent. The Interstate Commerce Commission shows that for all the roads the net rose, in the ten months ending with April, from $3053 to $4173 per mile, or about 37 per cent. Improvement began to be seen in the first weeks of last September. It should be borne in mind that the prices of the things a railroad must buy have been rising. What appears to be a trustworthy list, prepared by a railroad officer, shows an average increase of 53 per cent in the cost of supplies. The increase of earnings and of surpluses, however, has warranted an advance of share prices in the stock market. Tables printed herewith show that the gains made in the latter part of 1915 have not been retained.

The explanation is that price advances in harmony with the notable growth of traffic and earnings have been prevented mainly by the continuous selling here of American railroad securities owned abroad, especially in England; by the menace of the entire railway system's wage controversy with its employees, and by the attitude of some investors who say that the prosperity is only temporary because in large measure it depends upon the war. This quiet selling of securities from week to week by foreign owners or a foreign government tends to restrain, if not to depress. There is evidence that such sales of Steel Corporation shares in the first quarter of this year amounted to $7,465,000. The number of Steel shares held in Europe before the war, about 1,500,000, has been reduced by more than one-half. There is no available record showing the amount of other sales made here since the beginning of the war. One estimate is that $400,000,000 is the measure of sales since January 1, and that previous sales were in the neighborhood of $1,500,000,000. Sir Robert Fleming, a British financier, says we have taken back $1,000,000,000 worth. Professor Folwell's guess is that we have absorbed $1,750,000,000 in American securities, the majority of them from Great Britain. The selling is not ended. It has been promoted by the new British tax of 10 per cent on the income of such securities, in addition to 25 per cent already imposed.

It is asserted by the railroad companies that their operating expenses would be increased by $100,000,000 a year if the demands of the four brotherhoods or unions should be granted. If there should be a strike the railroads would suffer, and if a settlement is reached by compromise there will be an increase of operating expenses and a decrease of net earnings.

FOREIGN TRADE

Six years ago our annual exports had not risen to $2,000,000,000, but now our products are going abroad at the rate of nearly $5,000,000,000, surpassing Great Britain's highest record, which was a little more than $3,000,000,000. Not until this year have the shipments in any month amounted to $400,000,000, and before last Septem-

OUTPUT OF PIG IRON, TONS

The condition of the iron and steel industry has been called a barometer indicating the condition of trade and manufactures. Pig iron output grew steadily in 1915. In May of this year all records were broken, and production now is at the rate of more than 40,000,000 tons a year.

1908	15,936,018
1909	25,795,471
1910	27,298,545
1911	23,649,547
1912	29,727,137
1913	30,724,581
1914	23,049,792

1915

January	1,001,241
February	1,074,771
March	2,063,854
April	2,116,494
May	2,263,470
June	2,380,827
July	2,563,420
August	2,779,647
September	2,852,561
October	3,125,491
November	3,037,398
December	3,203,322

1916

	20,682,506
January	3,185,121
February	3,087,212
March	3,337,691
April	3,227,691
May	3,351,708

ber the $300,000,000 mark had not been reached. It was for the short month of February that $400,000,000 (nearly $403,000,000) was first reported. March and April followed with larger amounts. The figures for May are not yet before the public. A new high record of the excess to our credit, $209,000,000, was made in the short month of February. Thereafter the excess was reduced—not on account of reduced exports, for these were growing—but because the imports were making a new record for themselves and for the first time had crost the $200,000,000 line. It should be noted that in April's total of $217,000,000 crude materials for manufacturers stand for $95,000,000, while such imports a year ago were only $65,000,000.

WAR ORDERS AND LOANS

Meanwhile the new war orders have not been of a kind that attracts public attention. Old orders will keep many manufacturers busy for a long time to come. The British Government has recently bought 400,000 tons of shell forgings and $2,800,000 worth of sugar. France has taken 23,400,000 pounds of tobacco, has ordered 100,000 tons of rails, and is negotiating for a large number of railroad ties. Russia seeks 200,000 tons of barbed wire, 5000 freight cars, 100 locomotives and 100,000 tons of rails. Of 8000 cars made in May 4500 went to fill foreign orders.

Negotiations for a loan to Russia have been in progress for several months, and at last the plan has been completed. A credit of $50,000,000 is granted by a banking group which includes the National City Bank, the Guaranty Trust Company and J. P. Morgan & Co. Russia pays 6½ per cent. Foreign trade reports show how Russia's indebtedness to us has grown. In the ten months ending with April our exports to that country were $229,-000,000, against only $35,000,000 in the preceding year. The Canadian Province of Ontario is borrowing $4,000,-000 here at 5 per cent. The $50,000,-000 credit arranged for Great Britain at 4½ per cent and based upon deposits of British bonds in the Bank of England expired on June 20 and has been extended for one year at 5 per cent. It is expected that a loan to France, or a credit, of $100,000,000 will be announced in a few weeks.

CROPS

The government's reports indicate that we shall have this year a wheat crop of only 715,000,000 bushels (which may be compared with last year's extraordinary yield of 1,011,-505,000); also, that we must be content with nearly 300,000,000 bushels less of oats than were harvested in 1915, and with a barley crop reduced from 237,000,000 to 189,000,000 bushels. In the face of these reports the price of wheat at Chicago has declined from $1.17 in April to about $1.02, owing mainly to large stocks on hand and slack demands from abroad. But what we can spare of the new crop will probably be needed there, as the yield in Europe will fall below last year's.

THE STOCK MARKET

The course of the market for stocks has been comparatively uneventful, except in a recent movement affecting motor shares. At times there have been signs of weakness, due to rumors of impending peace in Europe, and market values were affected temporarily during the controversy with Germany concerning submarine warfare. A majority of the railroad shares, while they have been firmly held, are still below the prices of January 1. In the industrial or war order group there have been wide fluctuations. There has been a pany, which has declared extra dividends, in cash or stock. In this list are seven copper companies, two companies that make zinc, a sugar company, and a cotton goods company in Fall River. One powder company has paid 79 per cent in the past year on a capital of $120,000,000. The E. W. Bliss Company, which has declared extra dividends, earned 434 per cent. on its capital last year, against 72 per cent. in 1914. Large dividends in cash or stock have been paid by the oil companies. The former constituent or subsidiary corporations of the Standard Oil of New Jersey have recently distributed $29,300,000 in stock and $29,731,000 in cash.

A wild movement in the shares of automobile companies was caused by an attempt to combine the Willys Overland, Hudson, Chalmers, Chevrolet and possibly other corporations in a new company that was to be capitalized at $220,000,000. It was estimated that the annual output of the proposed company would be 480,000 cars. Motor shares went up, because of one company showing a gain of 87 points in a week. But the project was given up on June 14, "on account of complications," the organizers said.

INSURANCE
CONDUCTED BY W. E. UNDERWOOD

LIFE INSURANCE

A special feature of recent life insurance history during the preceding three months was the unexpected action taken by the owners of the Union Central Life Insurance Company of Cincinnati in raising the amount of that company's capital from $500,000 to $2,500,000, following an increase in June, 1908, from $100,000 to $500,000. This additional (and wholly superfluous) capital of $2,400,000 was not paid up out of the pockets of the stockholders; it was voted out of the company's funds as profits made on non-participating policies, earnings which, under by-laws provisions that were a dead letter from 1867 to 1908, belong to the stockholders.

The life insurance world was amazed in March at an announcement from the president of the Union Central that a further sum of $2,000,000 non-participating profits had been capitalized as of March 1. It was a bold move. No going life insurance company needs any capital. In 1908, reversing the precedents of forty years, pleading the necessities imposed by the laws of several states, the management of this company increased the capital fivefold. Its right to do it was challenged by six insurance commissioners in the courts of Ohio. The stockholders won.

No such alleged necessity existed this year. But there was an accumulated sum of $2,027,000 surplus claimed to have been earned on non-participating surplus since 1908. No half-way measures were indulged in this time—$2,000,-000 of it was voted out as a stock dividend. In order to carry out the plan to transform this money into an investment for stockholders, the company's charter had to be amended; and this was accomplished without attracting attention by filing in the Secretary of State's office at Columbus a document called "Increase of Capital Stock Certificate."

A committee of state insurance commissioners has been appointed to investigate the matter. They are expected to report to the National Convention of Insurance Commissioners at their mid-year meeting in September. That report will be narrowly watched for by the managements of other life insurance companies.

Critics of the Union Central management are skeptical as to the claim that the non-participating business has earned $2,400,000 and they expect the state investigators either to confirm or to refute that claim. If it is found that the money has actually been earned, they cannot see why the stockholders should not be compelled to withdraw it in cash, instead of leaving it there in the shape of a burden on participating policyholders. Under the provisions of the company's by-laws the stockholders receive an annual dividend of 10 per cent. Here is a possible $250,000 a year to be paid by policyholders for an entirely useless service. The management claims it is leaving the money in the company in the shape of capital for the security of policyholders. This is a piece of insincerity, as everybody who knows anything of life insurance finance is aware. The company has a clear net surplus of $3,647,724 and is increasing that with every premium collected.

Leaving this subject, it appears from announcements made by the agency departments of a number of the leading life companies that this year promises to break all previous records in the matter of new business transacted. Up to date there has been an unusual expansion in the volume of life insurance transactions, indicating a high state of commercial prosperity.

THE FIRE INSURANCE FIELD

Estimating the underwriting results of the fire insurance business thus far this year by a comparison of the tabulated fire waste in the United States and Canada for the first five months of 1916, 1915 and 1914, we would be warranted in concluding that the balance is against the companies taken as a whole. Guiding ourselves by the underwriting profit and loss computations for the companies operating in Connecticut as found in the annual reports of the Insurance Department of that state for the last two years indicated, we find that the aggregated net gain in surplus for those companies was $3,936,413, the recorded fire waste for the first five months being $81,497,050. In 1914, the fire waste was estimated at $103,670,-250 for the first five months and the aggregate net loss in surplus found by the Connecticut Department for the companies reporting there was $8,796,-709. It now appears that the estimated fire waste for the period January 1, 1916, to May 31, 1916, greatly exceeds that of the same period of 1914, the figures being $113,528,920.

These two separate sets of figures, it must be understood, are from different sources and are not related to each other, those for the fire waste being gathered by the *Journal of Commerce* by its correspondents in this country and Canada day by day and compiled monthly, serving only as a close estimate of the burning rate; while the Connecticut figures represent actual results experienced by the companies annually. The two sets have been brought together here merely to indicate probable profit or loss results. They may, when thus thrown into juxtaposition, be regarded as serving that purpose. To illustrate: it is more than probable that as the fire waste during the first five months of 1916 is more than $10,-000,000 higher than for the like period of 1914 when the whole of the latter year showed a loss in surplus, that the results thus far in 1916 are at least as unfavorable to the companies as they were up to June 1, 1914. We cannot, however, conclude that the whole of the year 1916 will prove to be unprofitable, if it is really so to date, for the remaining seven months may change what seems to be the present tendency. If, happily, this should turn out to be the case, we are likely to find it indicated in the figures representing the estimated fire waste. Just now, the outlook is for a net underwriting loss on the fire insurance business of the year 1916.

Since our last review, the most important single event in fire insurance involved the withdrawal of all the outside fire companies from the State of South Carolina because of their inability to continue business there under a new and most drastic law which went into force in April. The companies had endeavored to convince the legislators that they could not with safety to their own interests comply with the proposed provisions and gave warning that if the bill was passed they would retire from the state. But they did not succeed in impressing the politicians in charge with their sincerity, the latter regarding their attitude as a "bluff." The bill became law and the companies promptly retired. Since that time innumerable efforts have been made to effect a compromise, but without avail.

Always serious, the fire insurance situation in Texas has recently culminated in a specific demand made by the companies on its Insurance Commission that rates be advanced 33 1-3 per cent. Hearings for and against were commenced about a month ago and are now in progress. The expense involved in doing the business there is the matter chiefly under investigation, the companies' adversaries presumably contending that the cost is subject to material reduction. As a substantial fact, however, the fire loss in that state is and is quite possible that unless an increase in rates to meet them is permitted, Texas will add itself to the territory from which fire insurance companies absent themselves.

This department of The Independent will undertake to furnish on the request of readers any information respecting the business of insurance and the companies transacting it which we have or can procure. We cannot, however, pass upon the debatable comparative differences between companies that conform to the requisite legal standards set up for all, except in so far as the claims made by any of them seem to be inconsistent with the principles of sound underwriting. Address all communications on insurance subjects to the editor of the Insurance Department.

THE NEW BOOKS

MIRRORS TO RUSSIA

As strangers see family resemblances of which members of the family are unconscious, so English readers see or fancy they see a certain likeness of method, if not of something deeper, pervading all Russian literature. Leonard A. Magnus, in his translation of *Russian Folk Tales*, speaks of this as "factualism," not realism, since that connotes anti-romanticism, but a certain direct simplicity of outlook and of treatment. This does not strike the foreign reader so noticeably in the folk tales, for the reason that these characteristics belong to the legends of all lands. Russian fairy stories, however, differ essentially from the Celtic in the absence of the whimsical and from the German in the lack of homely, intimate touches. The Russian superhumans are saints, witches, wizards, and good fortune comes not from cleverness or integrity, but from pure luck or from kindness. Kindness is the great virtue. On such tales as on facts were all Russian children fed till within the half century. In *Years of Childhood*, the remarkable recollections of Serge Aksakoff, he speaks of the influence of these nursery stories and reprints the favorite of his childhood, The Scarlet Flower. In *Oblomov*, too, Goncharov's masterly study of the indecisive, indolent landed class, the fairy tales of the hero's childhood influence his whole life.

The *Years of Childhood*, now first printed in English, is the account of a boy's life in Eastern Russia at the close of the eighteenth century. Written with amazing simplicity, it sets the reader in the midst of living men and women in whose small daily affairs one finds one's self taking an intense interest. As a study in child psychology it is, all unconsciously, a valuable document.

In *Oblomov*, translated by C. J. Hogarth, is another picture of a Russian childhood. The book has also what one finds in Goncharov more than in most Russian writers, most lovely descriptions of scenery. Painting a failure tho it does, the story yet leaves one with a sense of the essential worth of human nature. Comic in their bovine content, tragic in their utter stupidity, pathetic in their gentle virtues, the Oblomovs are yet loveable, while the soldiers who figure in *The Duel*, by Kuprin—also an analysis of an indecisive character—are of the untidy sort distastefully frequent in Russian novels. The publishers describe the sentimental, wobbly hero as of the "Hamlet type," which shows a lack of knowledge of either Hamlet or Romanshov. The work has a mission, however. If widely read in Russia it should threaten any military system that fosters such an outrageous, brutal life as that of the army post described. No bet-

ter anti-militarist tract could be found than extracts from these grimy pages.

We have always supposed that Russians must read something besides problem novels and the translations now coming from the presses bring us several cheerful volumes, among them *Makar's Dream*, four short stories by Korolenko. There is romance, affection, humor in these tales, albeit written by a man reared in extreme poverty and, like most of the able youth of his generation, serving his time in Siberia. But he came forth from his six years triumphant, an artist not the wielder of a scalpel.

The same sort of experience acting on a less healthy nature, albeit a more powerful genius, brought forth *Dostoievsky*. The sympathetic but critical study by Soloviev of this tragic figure is another example of that clear cut, bare, forceful writing which seems the inheritance of the Russian, however far in subject matter he journey from the lived-happy-ever-after folk tales of his childhood.

Russian Folk Tales, tr. by L. A. Magnus. Dutton. $2. *Years of Childhood*, by S. Aksakoff. Longmans, Green. $2. *Oblomov*, by Ivan Gonchárov. Macmillan. $1.50. *The Duel*, by Kuprin. Macmillan. $1.50. *Makar's Dream*, by V. Korolenko. Duffield. $1.50. *Dostoievsky*, by E. Soloviev. Macmillan. $1.75.

PAST, PRESENT AND FUTURE

Authors are generally agreed that life aboard ship is not conducive to satisfactory work. There are several reasons, the chief of which is that so much depends on whether the ship keeps an even keel or plunges unhappily thru tempestuous waters. Mr. Patterson does not inform us regarding weather conditions on his "Cymbric" Atlantic crossing, but he assuredly presents us in *The Notebook of a Neutral* with a green-portfolio-steward-and-beef-tea view of the world, both present and future. No matter if the Entente Allies do win, German *kultur* must triumph. In fact, Great Britain and France are now *kulturing* themselves as their only possible salvation. Since he does not believe the United States can be induced to adopt *kultur*—the "Cymbric" perhaps gave a dreadful lurch here—we are in for a frightful beating by Germany or Japan —5,000,000 Japanese and Chinese settled on our Pacific Coast. (Eight bells and a stormy night, mates!) In our rich, soft and helpless condition our single hope lies in a threat to stop supplying Great Britain with munitions unless she promises to protect us from Germany or Japan, possibly Germany, Japan and Russia combined. It must be done now, because if we wait until after the war, Great Britain will leave us to our mercenary fate. We hope at this dismal conclusion the steward induced Mr. Patterson to crawl up on deck.

Nine contributions by as many au-

THE NEW BOOKS

MIRRORS TO RUSSIA

As strangers see family resemblances of which members of the family are unconscious, so English readers see or fancy they see a certain likeness of method, if not of something deeper, pervading all Russian literature. Leonard A. Magnus, in his translation of *Russian Folk Tales*, speaks of this as "factualism," not realism, since that connotes anti-romanticism, but a certain direct simplicity of outlook and of treatment. This does not strike the foreign reader so noticeably in the folk tales, for the reason that these characteristics belong to the legends of all lands. Russian fairy stories, however, differ essentially from the Celtic in the absence of the whimsical and from the German in the lack of homely, intimate touches. The Russian superhumans are saints, witches, wizards, and good fortune comes not from cleverness or integrity, but from pure luck or from kindness. Kindness is the great virtue. On such tales as on facts were all Russian children fed till within the half century. In *Years of Childhood*, the remarkable recollections of Serge Aksakoff, he speaks of the influence of these nursery stories and reprints the favorite of his childhood, *The Scarlet Flower*. In *Oblomov*, too, Gancharov's masterly study of the indecisive, indolent landed class, the fairy tales of the hero's childhood influence his whole life.

The *Years of Childhood*, now first printed in English, is the account of a boy's life in Eastern Russia at the close of the eighteenth century. Written with amazing simplicity, it sets the reader in the midst of living men and women in whose small daily affairs one finds one's self taking an intense interest. As a study in child psychology it is, all unconsciously, a valuable document.

In *Oblomov*, translated by C. J. Hogarth, is another picture of a Russian childhood. The book has also what one finds in Gancharov more than in most Russian writers, most lovely descriptions of scenery. Painting a failure tho it does, the story yet leaves one with a sense of the essential worth of human nature. Comic in their utter stupidity, pathetic in their gentle virtues, the Oblomovs are yet loveable, while the soldiers who figure in *The Duel*, by Kuprin—also an analysis of an indecisive character—are of the untidy sort distastefully frequent in Russian novels. The publishers describe the sentimental, wobbly hero as of the "Hamlet type," which shows a lack of knowledge of either Hamlet or Romanshov. The work has a mission, however. If widely read in Russia it should threaten any military system that fosters such an outrageous, brutal life as that of the army post described. No bet-

ter anti-militarist tract could be found than extracts from these grimey pages.

We have always supposed that Russians must read something besides problem novels and the translations now coming from the presses bring us several cheerful volumes, among them *Makar's Dream*, four short stories by Korolenko. There is romance, affection, humor in these tales, albeit written by a man reared in extreme poverty and, like most of the able youth of his generation, serving his time in Siberia. But he came forth from his six years triumphant, an artist not the wielder of a scalpel.

The same sort of experience acting on a less healthy nature, albeit a more powerful genius, brought forth *Dostoievsky*. The sympathetic but critical study by Soloviev of this tragic figure is another example of that clear cut, bare, forceful writing which seems the inheritance of the Russian, however far in subject matter he journey from the lived-happy-ever-after folk tales of his childhood.

Russian Folk Tales, tr. by L. A. Magnus. Dutton. $2. *Years of Childhood*, by S. Aksakoff. Longmans, Green. $3. *Oblomov*, by Ivan Gancharov. Macmillan. $1.50. *The Duel*, by Kuprin. Macmillan. $1.50. *Makar's Dream*, by V. Korolenke. Duffield. $1.50. *Dostoievsky*, by E. Soloviev. Macmillan. $1.75.

PAST, PRESENT AND FUTURE

Authors are generally agreed that life aboard ship is not conducive to satisfactory work. There are several reasons, the chief of which is that so much depends on whether the ship keeps an even keel or plunges unhappily thru tempestuous waters. Mr. Patterson does not inform us regarding weather conditions on his "Cymbric" Atlantic crossing, but he assuredly presents us in *The Notebook of a Neutral* with a green-porthole-steward-and-beef-tea view of the world, both present and future. No matter if the Entente Allies do win, German *kultur* must triumph. In fact, Great Britain and France are now *kulturing* themselves as their only possible salvation. Since he does not believe the United States can be induced to adopt *kultur*—the "Cymbric" perhaps gave a dreadful lurch here—we are in for a frightful beating by Germany or Japan—5,000,000 Japanese and Chinese settled on our Pacific Coast. (Eight bells and a stormy night, mates!) In our rich, soft and helpless condition our single hope lies in a threat to stop supplying Great Britain with munitions unless she promises to protect us from Germany or Japan, possibly Germany, Japan and Russia combined. It must be done now, because if we wait until after the war, Great Britain will leave us to our mercenary fate. We hope at this dismal conclusion the steward induced Mr. Patterson to crawl up on deck.

Nine contributions by as many au-

thors make up the volume, *Towards a Lasting Settlement*, edited by Charles Roden Buxton. When such widely debatable subjects as The Basis of Permanent Peace, The Freedom of the Seas, and The Democratic Principle and International Relations are condensed within a few pages, it is impossible to expect full treatment of the various themes. Generally the trend of the papers is toward the conclusion, that the solution of the problem lies in the voluntary willingness of humanity at large to abide by a lasting peace. This would seem to be more logical reasoning than that of those who would force peace upon humanity, for the hand of suppression may fall in oppression, thereby rousing the very evil to be abolished.

Is there any end to the causes of the war? No sooner has one publicist demonstrated his hypothesis, than along comes another to brush aside the former view with never-before-thought-of evidence. Who, for example, would imagine that the French Foreign Legion, beloved of the swash-buckling fictioneer, was one of the offenses Pan-Germanism grasped to demand the subjugation of France. Yet Paul Vergnet proves it out of the Pan-German mouth. Aside from this new origin of the war, the author of *France in Danger* discloses the machinations of the Pan-German League in Alsace-Lorraine and elsewhere.

One element in the German view of the causes of the war should appeal to the jurist. That is blunt frankness in admitting certain responsibilities. Thus, as it were, "I tore up that scrap of paper, invaded Belgium, and would have captured Paris if I could. Necessity compelled me to do these things." Here we have at least tangible ground to stand upon. *Germany Misjudged* is the display of a case for German defense, tho Roland Hugins, while inviting "American Tories" of Entente sympathy to hasten in shiploads for the trenches, fails to condemn equally the German propaganda in this country. Complementary to the above is *Belgium and Germany*, a Dutch view, by J. H. Labberton. As emphatically and heroically as she could Belgium has repudiated this specious plea for German invasion of her territory,—tho dubiously granting "Prussia is the ethically sound kernel of Europe, from which in the end is to spring the ethical regeneration of our desperately ailing world."

Two little volumes in vivid yellow wrappers, *France and the War* and *War Letters from France*, are the one by Professor James Mark Baldwin, and the other edited by Lapradelle and Coudert. Professor Baldwin discloses hardly anything new from his subject, tho he announces such is his purpose: "French participation having remained under certain obscurities." A concise recapitulation of all this in a single volume, touched with the author's evident sincerity, is the book's chief recommendation. *War Letters from France* is a collection of admirably selected extracts from the letters of French soldiers. Nothing has hitherto come to hand which so impressively reveals the patriotic, liberty-loving spirit of the French citizen soldier, in marked contrast to the forceful regime of the German army. There is no need to compel discipline in the French army, it is willingly even gaily borne for the sake of "beautiful France."

The Notebook of a Neutral, by Joseph Medill Patterson. Duffield. $0 cents, Towards a Lasting Settlement, ed. by Charles Roden Buxton, Macmillan. $1. France in Danger, by Paul Vergnet. Dutton. $1. Germany Misjudged, by Roland Hugins. Belgium and Germany, by J. H. Labberton. Open Court Pub. Co. $1 each. France and the War, by James Mark Baldwin. War Letters from France, ed. by Lapradelle and Coudert. Appleton. 50 cents each.

WHAT SCHOOLS ARE FOR

In his *Education and Social Progress* Principal Alexander Morgan very simply and directly traces certain social defects to organic and environmental factors, from which he separates the systematic educational forces. His first desire is to "catch the children young," for he sees no hope in attempting to reform adults with fixed habits and prejudices. In addition to reorganizing the schools to take more definite cognizance of the nature of the developing child on the one hand, and of our complex society and economic system on the other, Dr. Morgan would have teachers selected and trained for conscious coöperation with the social purpose of the times. The school, in addition to providing training for the child, "is also one of the main instruments of society for securing its upward progress."

Education and Social Progress, by Alexander Morgan. Longmans, Green. $1.20.

HUMAN PERSONALITY

Very serious and important subjects are those which Dr. Smyth has treated in a series of volumes on theology, Christian philosophy and ethics, and none more serious than his present volume, *The Meaning of Personal Life.* The purpose of the first part of the book is an argument against materialism. Even in physical nature the author sees hints of spiritual forces which become clearer as life appears, so that "the pursuit of the course of organic neural differentiation and animal psychology puts us upon the scent of some non-physical form of energy, which introspective psychology shall seek, if possible, to overtake."

By a careful course of study, depending upon the later investigations of psychology, Dr. Smyth shows that the several powers of the mind, whether in instinct, or reason, or feeling, are utterly incommensurable with the forces seen in physical law, which latter have to do with space and dimension, and he reaches the sound conclusion that mind is distinct from matter and that mind uses the brain as an organ of the free-willing soul.

A discussion follows of the growth of personality in the soul, allowing for access of power in ways perhaps mysterious, until he finds in Jesus Christ a new development of personality previously unknown and from which a similar spiritual growth has come to the Christian world. The miracles of healing performed by Jesus he assigns to

natural law, but under laws not yet fully understood, for he seems to assert that a miracle that would contradict natural law is impossible. He finds it reasonable and natural that the church should have developed a doctrine of the Virgin Birth, but he does not hold it essential to faith.

The Meaning of Personal Life, by Newman Smyth. Scribner. $2.

MUSIC AND DRAMA

Pazon's Dramatic Index is an invaluable annual for all needing information on stage affairs. It contains references to magazine articles, biographic notes, lists of books on the drama, and also what has been difficult to come at, a record of the prominent moving picture plays. (Boston Book Company, $4.)

In spite of the index, with familiar composers aplenty, Geraldine Farrar's *My Favorite Songs* will be something of an unexplored country to the average student. These unworn songs of some of the best of ancient and modern music are a welcome relief and are well worth some effort to become acquainted with them. (Ditson, $1.)

Collections of music for elementary work are discouragingly prone to be stereotyped and commonplace, but the two volumes *Something to Play* and *Something to Sing* are fairly free from the expected triteness and the critical notes on the songs in the latter are suggestive. Sprinkled throuout are some really good things. (Ditson, 75c. each.)

The workmanship of Theodore Dreiser's *Plays of the Natural and the Supernatural* is excellent. But what is the author trying to get at? The reader's impression is somewhat like the remarks of the "Power of Physics": "Deep below deep! High above high! No beginning, no end! No end—no beginning!" But that is not nonsense. (Lane, $1.25.)

One of the most interesting of the Tercentenary publications is *A Book for Shakespeare Plays and Pageants*, by O. L. Hatcher. This describes customs, scenes, dress, furniture, contemporary pageants, and is lavishly illustrated. Aside from its immediate use, it is a delightful and valuable collection of all sorts of Shakespearean miscellany. (Dutton, $2.)

THE MINISTER'S SHELF

A booklet by Richard T. Stevenson, of Ohio Wesleyan University, entitled *Missions versus Militarism*, argues eloquently the thesis that Christianity is the cure of war, and urges the missionary campaign. (Abingdon Press, 50 cents.)

The Afflictions of the Righteous, by W. B. MacLeod, is made up of sermons on the Book of Job. Learning, vigorous reasoning, and enthusiasm characterize these interpretations wrought out in the light of Christian truth. (Doran, $1.50.)

In *Jerusalem to Rome*, Professor Charles F. Sitterly gives a new translation of the Acts of the Apostles in the language and style of present day English. The result is an attractive and self-explanatory translation of the book. (Abingdon Press, $1.50.)

It is difficult to trace *The Dawn of Religion in the Mind of the Child*, but Edith E. Read Mumford gives us valuable aid. The author is a student of child psychology, and a sympathetic interpreter of children's actions, impulses and questionings. (Longmans, Green, 90 cents.)

The Work and Teachings of the Apostles, by Charles F. Kent, is the latest addition to the valuable Historical Bible series of textbooks for Bible study. It has the same

excellent qualities of arrangement, translation, and historical interpretation as the preceding volumes. (Scribner, $1.25.)

The Great Revival in the West, 1797-1805, by Catharine C. Cleveland, gives a careful historical survey of the religious conditions in the West prior to 1800, and a full account of the leaders, extent, phenomena, and results of this great religious awakening. (Univ. of Chicago Press, $1.)

The Apostles' Creed, by Dr. David J. Burrell, comprises a series of addresses or essays of a dogmatic and homiletic character based on the various words and phrases of this great symbol of the Christian faith. The exposition is strictly orthodox and uncompromising. (American Tract Society, $1.)

The Law of Human Life, by Elijah V. Brookshire, in an octavo volume of 471 pages and is composed of a series of predictions on biblical characters whose history is treated as symbolical of religious life and experience. This will be approved by adepts in biblical exegesis after the manner of the Swedish Seer. (Putnam, $2.50.)

The New Home Missions, Dr. Harlan Paul Douglass regards as a group of church activities having for their end the Christianization of the United States. Thus conceived, the social problems of country and city, racial developments and immigration become the central features of the mission program. (Missionary Education Movement, 60 cents.)

The Centennial History of the American Bible Society, by H. O. Dwight, tells of the greatest auxiliary force there is in all Protestant religious work the world over. This enterprise began with printing 6000 Bibles in one language, and issued in its hundredth year over 6,000,000 Bibles and portions of the Bible, in 164 tongues. (Macmillan, 2 vols., $2.)

SOME GOOD VERSE

Among the sincere little lyrics that make up Muriel Strode's *Rainbow Gold,* is a lullaby, Bide a Wee, which is charming and a bit out of the ordinary in conception. (Badger, $1.)

In *Wild Apples* Jeanne Robert Foster is no imagist and she clings still to form. She is best in objective verse, and of this, one chooses first the lines on the "William P. Frye" that well speak the feeling of those who know the sailing vessels of our "down east." (Boston: Sherman, French, $1.)

Five Men and Pompey, Sertorius, Lucullus, Crasus, Cicero and Caesar, are live, interesting figures in Stephen Vincent Benét's blank verse, and more picturesque and dramatic, we venture, than if he had used the *vers libre* he likes so well. They are new Lays of Ancient Rome in soberer meter. (Boston: Four Seas Company, 60 cents.)

The Path of Dreams recalls the writings of Whittier's early companions. But George M. McClellan, when he writes of his own people, does more than make a beginning in poetry. The strength of feeling and yet the restraint with which he writes of the negro in such poems as The Feet of Judas and Decoration Day makes for noble verse. (Louisville, Ky.: Morton, $1.50.)

Profiles, by Arthur Ketchum, has a group of those naive free line impressions that stand to poems as sketch book drawings do to pictures. But these are as finished in form as they are unfinished in thought, and there are other poems to which one returns gladly. (Badger, $1.)

We are glad to welcome the new editions of Vachel Lindsay's prose and poetry—say, rather, all poetry, whatever the form—*General William Booth Enters into Heaven* and *Adventures While Preaching the Gospel of Genius.* He understands our prairie people as few writers do. (Macmillan, $1.25 and $1.)

PRACTICAL SCHOLARSHIP

The choice of Mr. Ernest Martin Hopkins to succeed President Ernest Fox Nichols as the head of Dartmouth College is recognition of the growing importance of social organization and of one who has achieved remarkable distinction in this field, notwithstanding he is less than forty years of age. In deciding upon their new president, the trustees declared their belief that "the function of the modern college president is even more to coördinate the work of scholarly men to the end of preparing young people for life than himself to set an example in research and discovery." The new president, however, is likely to do both. While he was an undergraduate at Dartmouth, President William J. Tucker recognized his promise of conspicuous ability and appointed him secretary to the president.

In 1910 Mr. Hopkins resigned his secretaryship to become a student and practitioner of applied economics, and the practical results he has obtained during the past six years have brought him into the front rank of interpreters of the problems involved in the relation of employment and employees, viewed from the standpoint of management. For the Western Electric Company, of Chicago; the Filene Department Store, Boston; the American Felt Company, Boston; the Curtis Publishing Company, of Philadelphia, and later the New England Telephone Company, of Boston, he has done remarkable things as an "expert on human relations," and he has sounded the same practical note in his new capacity. "Dartmouth's progress," he says, "has always been most marked during the periods demanding intelligent service, and the immediate needs of a distraught world must be accepted as the compelling opportunity of the college."

HOW TO BUY ADVERTISING

Advertising is no longer a haphazard matter of guess work, and rule of thumb. It has developed into an art—it would hardly be too much to say a science. The wise national advertiser seeking publicity no longer maps out his course guided by his own personal whims or dazzled by sparkling generalities or wild claims as to circulations. The modern advertiser demands accurate, specific information as to what each periodical has to offer in extent of circulation and in kind of readers. He wants to know what his money is buying. One of the most effective agencies at the service of the advertiser today in his quest for effective publicity is the Audit Bureau of Circulations. This independent, impartial organization with a membership composed of advertisers and periodical publishers, examines the circulation books of the periodicals that belong to it, at irregular and unexpected intervals in the same way that Federal bank examiners descend upon national banks. Thru the bureau's work the advertiser knows the truth, the whole truth, and nothing but the truth about the circulation of each periodical availing itself of the bureau's service. Such service as the Audit Bureau provides is an exceedingly interesting example of the application in modern business of efficiency methods. The annual meeting of the bureau has just been held in Chicago, and the former officers and board of directors—with a single exception—were reëlected. The officers of the bureau are: Louis Bruch, American Radiator Company, president; Curtis P. Brady, *Woman's World*, first vice-president; A. W. Erickson, The Erickson Company, Inc., second vice-president; M. F. Harris, Armour & Co., secretary; Hopewell L. Rogers, Chicago *Daily News*, treasurer; Russell R. Whitman, managing director. The board of directors includes: Frank E. Long, *Farmer's Review*; W. B. Cherry, Merrell-Soule Company; Stanley Clague, Taylor-Critchfield-Clague Company; F. R. Davis, General Electric Company; F. C. Grandin, Postum Cereal Company; O. C. Harn, National Lead Company; Frank C. Hoyt, *The Outlook*; Charles F. Jenkins, *Farm Journal*; Emery Mapes, Cream of Wheat Company; L. B. Jones, Eastman Kodak Company; S. C. Dobbs, Coca-Cola Company; M. C. Robbins, *Iron Age*; E. R. Shaw, *Practical Engineer*; F. H. Squier, Pabst Brewing Company; William Wrigley, Jr., William Wrigley, Jr., Company; Lafayette Young, *Des Moines Capital.*

REPRESENTING UNCLE SAM

Striking tribute to the value of an efficient consular service was given at a recent meeting of the Associated Chambers of Commerce of the United Kingdom, held in London for the purpose of finding means of stimulating the foreign trade of the empire. During an outspoken discussion of the relative merits of the various consular services two delegates stated that they had failed altogether to get certain information concerning their business from British representatives, who they naturally assumed could supply it. The sequel was that the delegates ultimately applied to the American consuls, and in each case were willingly and promptly supplied with the desired information. In view of the much higher salaries which Great Britain pays her consular representatives, as compared with the United States, the British business men did some hard thinking.

EYES IN THE AIR

"Eyes in the air," which are claimed to have given the German fleet its advantage in the North Sea battle, have other than military uses. Walter Niles, an American aviator who recently returned from Japan, was flying over Mineola, Long Island, when, from a hight of over a thousand feet, he saw flames bursting from the roof of a house. Trees concealed the fire from people who were working in a field less than a block away. Dropping within shouting distance, the airman warned them of the fire, and having seen an alarm duly turned in, circled off into the air again. Niles was trying out a new high-power battleplane.

TEACHING THE YOUNG IDEA

Commenting editorially on the formation of the National Institute of Efficiency, the *St. Louis Watchman* says: "By all means let us have efficiency; but let us bear in mind that it is not something we are going to come by in merely mastering the instrumentalities of work. The human will is the controlling element and has to be rightly schooled and directed . . . or there is a primal wastage that no perfection of system can overcome." "Seven little girls of one family up in Saskatchewan, Canada, made up their minds," the writer concludes, "to do without candy and also to do their mother's washing, so that each might be able to defray the expenses of a child that is preparing for baptism over in Africa—$5 in each case. Here was initiative, zest and work, and here the sesame to genuine efficiency."

PRESIDENT HOPKINS OF DARTMOUTH